south america
on a shoestring

Danny Palmerlee, Kate Armstrong, Sandra Bao, Sara Benson, Celeste Brash, Molly Green, Michael Kohn, Carolyn McCarthy, Jens Porup, Regis St Louis, Lucas Vidgen

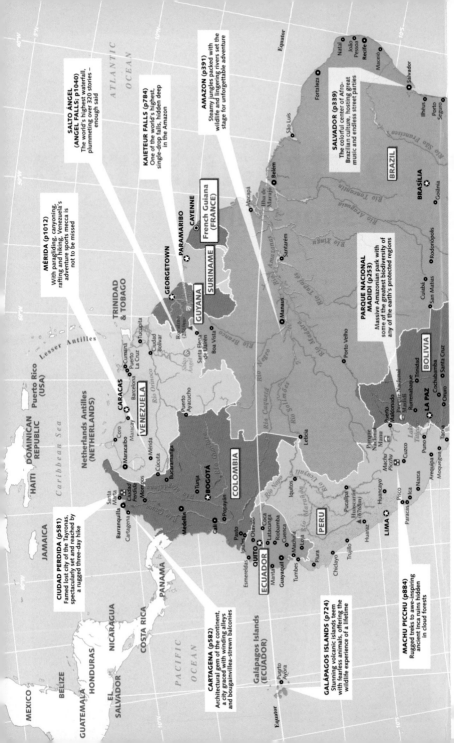

SALTO ANGEL (ANGEL FALLS; p1040)
The world's highest waterfall, plummeting over 320 stories – enough said

KAIETEUR FALLS (p784)
One of the world's highest, single-drop falls, hidden deep in the Amazon

AMAZON (p391)
Steamy jungles packed with wildlife and lingering rivers set the stage for unforgettable adventure

SALVADOR (p339)
The colorful center of Afro-Brazilian culture, hosting great music and endless street parties

MÉRIDA (p1012)
With paragliding, canyoning, rafting and hiking, Venezuela's adventure sports mecca is not to be missed

PARQUE NACIONAL MADIDI (p253)
Massive Amazonian park with some of the greatest biodiversity of any of the earth's protected regions

CIUDAD PERDIDA (p581)
Famed lost city of the Tayronas, spectacularly set and reached by a rugged three-day hike

CARTAGENA (p582)
Architectural gem of the continent, a city graced with winding alleys and bougainvillea-strewn balconies

GALÁPAGOS ISLANDS (p724)
Stunning volcanic islands teem with fearless animals, offering the wildlife experience of a lifetime

MACHU PICCHU (p884)
Rugged treks to awe-inspiring ancient Inca ruins hidden in cloud forests

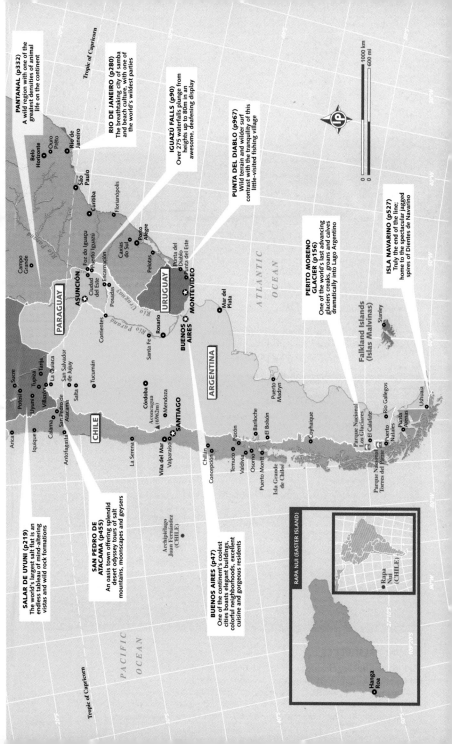

PANTANAL (p332)
A wild region with one of the greatest densities of animal life on the continent

RIO DE JANEIRO (p280)
The breathtaking city of samba and beach culture, with one of the world's wildest parties

IGUAZÚ FALLS (p90)
Over 275 waterfalls plunge from heights up to 80m in an awesome, deafening display

PUNTA DEL DIABLO (p967)
Wild terrain and wilder surf contrast with the tranquility of this little-visited fishing village

PERITO MORENO GLACIER (p156)
One of the world's last advancing glaciers creaks, groans and calves dramatically into Lago Argentino

ISLA NAVARINO (p527)
Truly the end of the line; home to the spectacular jagged spires of Dientes de Navarino

SALAR DE UYUNI (p219)
The world's largest salt flat is an endless tableau of mind-altering vistas and wild rock formations

SAN PEDRO DE ATACAMA (p455)
An oasis town offering splendid desert odyssey tours of salt mountains, moonscapes and geysers

BUENOS AIRES (p47)
One of the continent's coolest cities boasts elegant buildings, colorful neighborhoods, excellent cuisine and gorgeous residents

Responsible Travel

One of *the* joys of travel is leaving responsibilities behind, so who really wants to think about responsible travel? But responsibility clings to us like a good backpack, and no matter how, we still have an impact on the communities and natural habitats we visit. The question is how to make that impact a positive one.

Throughout this book we recommend ecotourism operations (business that help preserve natural environments and their communities through tourism) and community tourist projects (projects created and controlled – at least significantly – by the communities people visit, rather than outside entrepreneurs). Community-managed tourism is especially important when visiting indigenous communities, which are often exploited by businesses that channel little money back into the community.

See also p22 for listings of general social etiquette tips for your travels.

TIPS TO KEEP IN MIND

- **Ask before taking someone's photo** This is especially true when photographing indigenous people, who may not like to be photographed.

- **Don't litter** Sure, many locals do it, but many also frown upon it.

- **Don't shell out cash for coral** Avoid buying souvenirs or products made from endangered species.

- **Have shower willpower** Don't take hot showers if water is heated by wood fire, especially in rural areas where wood gathering damages local ecosystems.

- **Hire responsible guides** When you hire a guide, make sure they have a good reputation and will respect the environment and communities you'll visit.

- **Learn the lingo** Take a Spanish or Portuguese (or Quechua/Quichua) class before or during your travels. Knowing the language shows respect.

- **Pay your porter, tip your guide** Porters, guides and cooks are despicably underpaid. Tip as much as you can.

- **Respect local traditions** Dress appropriately when visiting churches and shrines and consider the effect of your presence.

- **Spend at the source** Try to buy crafts directly from artisans themselves.

- **Support community** Seek out community-based services that keep dollars local. Ask where your operator is based and where the money ends up.

INTERNET RESOURCES

www.ecotourism.org Links to businesses devoted to ecotourism.
www.peruweb.org/porters/index.html Info on hiring porters.
www.planeta.com Ron Mader's outstanding ecotourism website.
www.tourismconcern.org.uk UK-based organization dedicated to promoting ethical tourism.
www.transitionsabroad.com Focuses on immersion and responsible travel.

Contents

The Authors

DANNY PALMERLEE
Coordinating Author, Ecuador

Danny is a freelance travel writer and photographer who has spent most of the past decade traveling in and writing about Latin America. His work has appeared in the *Los Angeles Times, Miami Herald, Dallas Morning News, San Francisco Chronicle, Houston Chronicle* and other publications. His most recent stint was a year in Buenos Aires, broken only by a three-month dash through the Ecuadorian Andes while researching part of that chapter for this book.

Along with other Lonely Planet titles, Danny is the coordinating author of *Ecuador, Argentina* and *Best of Buenos Aires*.

KATE ARMSTRONG
Bolivia, Paraguay

Kate first wandered to Bolivia during a year-long trip through South America. Captivated by the country's flavors, she holed up in Sucre to learn Spanish, and inadvertently joined a folkloric dance troupe, after two ungraceful *cueca* lessons in her hiking boots. Thanks to a subsequent two-year stint in Mozambique, she also speaks Portuguese. When not floating her way up an Amazonian tributary in a rickety canoe, Kate is a freelance writer in Australia. She has contributed to Lonely Planet's *Greece, Greek Islands, South Africa, Lesotho & Swaziland* and associated Africa titles.

SANDRA BAO
Argentina

Sandra has traveled extensively, but she thinks South America is the best continent. She was born in Buenos Aires – making her a little biased – and enjoyed *bife de chorizo* and *dulce de leche* often until she was nine, when her family moved to the US.

Sandra gained a degree in psychology from UC Santa Cruz, which of course meant a career in guidebook writing.

She's the author of Lonely Planet's *Buenos Aires* city guide and has contributed to *Argentina, Mexico* and several other titles.

SARA BENSON
Peru

Sara's first baby steps in South America were along the Inca Trail to Machu Picchu. There she fell in love with the land of the Incas. Detours off the Gringo Trail have since led her to forgotten towns that still groove to Afro-Peruvian beats and on rickety boats across Lake Titicaca to Bolivia. When she's not off backpacking around Asia, Oceania and the Americas, Sara calls the San Francisco Bay area home. Already the author of more than 20 travel and nonfiction books, she also helped write Lonely Planet's *Peru* guide.

CELESTE BRASH
The Guianas

Celeste admired the *moai* of Easter Island, danced at a beach bonfire in Chile, lounged on the beaches of Rio and crossed the equator in Macapá, Brazil to reach the Guianas from her home in Tahiti. Ultimately, the mission across South America was the voyage of a lifetime and the Guianas were the highlight. Back home in the South Pacific she is a freelance travel writer and a part-time black pearl farmer but one day she might pack it all up to become a cowgirl in Guyana's Rupununi Savannas.

MOLLY GREEN
Brazil

During a 12-year obsession with Brazil, Molly has become an accomplished samba dancer and Portuguese speaker, a Latin American literature graduate, a *capoeira* initiate, familiar with 21 Brazilian states, and smitten with a Paulista (São Paulo native). While researching this edition, she gave a three-meter crocodile a backrub. Molly has surfed in Mexico, eaten chicken foot soup in Guatemala, studied and lived in Venezuela and Argentina, fainted from altitude in Peru, hiked in Patagonia, lived out of a van in Australia and been robbed by monkeys in Indonesia. She's from Santa Cruz, California.

MICHAEL KOHN
Colombia

Michael's first forays into Latin America came in 1994 when he traveled by ship from the Bahamas to Venezuela and Brazil. Sultry nights in Salvador and a helicopter ride over the Iguazú Falls had him yearning for more, and later Michael made trips to Mexico, Puerto Rico and the eastern Caribbean. In 2005 he returned to South America to write the 4th edition Lonely Planet guide to Colombia, and followed up in 2006 with a second trip. You can follow his route through Colombia by searching for his author blog at www .lonelyplanet.com.

CAROLYN MCCARTHY
Chile

Carolyn lives in the south of Chile, where she came to guide trekking trips and study the pioneer culture of rural Patagonia. This oasis of would-be poets, crystalline rivers, mate and volcanoes has been her home base for over three years. Prior to that she lived in Boston, Buenos Aires and Boulder, Colorado. A freelancer and former Fulbright fellow, she co-authored *Ecuador & the Galapagos* and has published in the Lonely Planet anthology *The Middle of Nowhere*, *South American Explorer*, *The Boston Globe* and Spanish-language titles.

JENS PORUP
Venezuela

Jens Porup is a playwright, essayist and travel writer living in Cali, Colombia. He previously covered Venezuela for Lonely Planet's *Venezuela* guidebook and is now hard at work on a novel that takes place in Colombia. You can read more about Jens on his website, www.jensporup.com.

REGIS ST LOUIS
Brazil

Like many other travelers, sailors and a king or two, Regis has fallen hard for Brazil. Following his first trip to the tropics many years back, he realized Brazil is a lifetime taste, and he's returned often to sail the Amazon, trek through the Pantanal and wander the streets of Rio de Janeiro. Regis speaks both Portuguese and Spanish, and he has written many articles on Brazil and the tropics. Regis is also the author of Lonely Planet's *Brazil* and *Rio de Janeiro* guides. He lives in New York City.

LUCAS VIDGEN
Argentina, Uruguay

Geographically confused from the outset, Lucas was blessed with an Italian first name, a Dutch surname and grew up in Heidelberg, an Australian suburb named after a German town. He soon realized that his place was elsewhere. He's been roaming the planet ever since, dropping in to Argentina and Uruguay every so often to make sure that the quality of the wine and beef remains high. In his 'spare time,' Lucas lives in Guatemala where he publishes *XelaWho*, the country's leading culture and nightlife magazine.

CONTRIBUTING AUTHORS

Lara Dunston contributed the boxed text on South American film, in the Snapshot chapter. Lara's first foreign adventures were backpacking trips to Mexico and Cuba. Once she had her film degree and feature-length movie under her *cinturón*, Lara completed a Masters in International Studies in Latin America and Spanish. For her year of in-country research on Latin American cinema, Lara watched hundreds of films at festivals across the continent, interviewed filmmakers and taught video in shantytowns in Brazil and Peru. Now travel writing full-time, she's ensured her PhD topic (on film and travel) is broad enough to give her an excuse to return to South America!

David Goldberg MD wrote the Health chapter. David completed his training in internal medicine and infectious diseases at Columbia-Presbyterian Medical Center in New York City, where he has also served as voluntary faculty. At present, he is an infectious diseases specialist in Scarsdale, New York, and the editor-in-chief of the website MDTravel Health.com.

LONELY PLANET AUTHORS

Why is our travel information the best in the world? It's simple: our authors are independent, dedicated travelers. They don't research using just the internet or phone, and they don't take freebies in exchange for positive coverage. They travel widely, to all the popular spots and off the beaten track. They personally visit thousands of hotels, restaurants, cafés, bars, galleries, palaces, museums and more – and they take pride in getting all the details right, and telling it how it is. For more, see the authors section on www.lonelyplanet.com.

Destination South America

Machu Picchu (p884) overlooking the Río Urubamba valley, Peru

Real travelers love South America. It's as if the continent was built for travel; it's the sort of place that presents you with challenges every step of the way and rewards you with euphorias you've never imagined. Sweat yourself dizzy during an Amazon canoe ride and be rewarded with a cool evening of caiman-watching on a black-water lagoon. Brave a white-knuckle bus ride and be astounded by endless Andean vistas. Face the chaos of a massive metropolis like Buenos Aires or Salvador and feel the elation of comprehension when the city suddenly makes sense. Endure Patagonia's wind-driven rain and finally stumble out of your tent beneath an astonishing sunset. The real reward, however, is the South American spirit. It seems like the entire continent approaches life like a good road trip: with the windows rolled down and the music up loud. It's a subtle approach to uncertainty that will surely infect you. And as for the music – it's the one thing that never leaves your side. With every adventure there's a soundtrack. Samba spices up the sandy streets of Brazilian beach towns, panpipes liven Andean markets, Argentine *folklórica* (folk music) trickles out of a truck radio in the pampas, and the jolting rhythm of cumbia makes those Andean bus rides even more absurd. In the end, don't think of South America as a place. Rather, it's something you turn yourself onto, that engulfs you and changes you – your state of mind, your outlook on life. As soon as you step foot on South American soil, the transformation begins.

Marine iguana, Galápagos Islands (p724), Ecuador

HIGHLIGHTS

BEST ADRENALINE RUSHES

Flying in Pedra Bonita and Iquique ▪ hang-glide over Rio from Pedra Bonita (p287) or paraglide over surf and dunes in Iquique, Chile (p459)

Surfing in Peru ▪ surf the epic lefts on Peru's northern coast (p899), a paradise of lonely breaks and coastal desert scenery

Climbing in Central Argentina ▪ feel the rush of accomplishment when you reach the summit of Cerro Aconcagua (p127), the western hemisphere's highest peak

Skiing and snowboarding in Portillo and Las Leñas ▪ carve the powdery slopes of Portillo, Chile (p432) and Las Leñas, Argentina (p129)…in July!

Rafting in Futaleufú, Tena and Cuzco ▪ raft Río Futaleufú (p512), Río Misahuallí (p702) and Río Apurímac (p875) – so good we had to name them all

BEST PARKS & NATURAL ATTRACTIONS

Iguazú Falls ▪ boggle your mind beneath the thundering roar of the world's most magnificent waterfalls (Argentina, p90; Brazil, p326)

Parque Nacional Los Glaciares ▪ stand awestruck by Argentina's advancing Perito Moreno Glacier (p156) and hike beneath the Fitz Roy Range (p152)

The Pantanal ▪ experience the continent's best wildlife-viewing in this vast Brazilian wetland (p332), the largest in the world

Galápagos Islands ▪ stare down iguanas and snorkel with penguins on Ecuador's unique archipelago famous for its fearless wildlife (p724)

Parque Nacional Canaima ▪ experience two of South America's most breathtaking natural attractions – Salto Ángel (Angel Falls; p1040) and Roraima (p1042) – in Venezuela

Woman dancing in a Carnaval parade (p290), Rio de Janeiro

BEST FESTIVALS & EVENTS

Carnaval ▪ go wild at the Bacchanalian frenzy in Brazil (Rio, p290 or Salvador, p341) or experience Bolivia's La Diablada in Oruro (p213)

Diablos Danzantes ▪ watch dancing devils shimmy and whirl down the streets of San Francisco de Yare in Venezuela (p999)

Buenos Aires Tango ▪ catch Buenos Aires' weeklong tango festival, featuring milongas, shows, and street performances throughout the city (p168)

Bumba Meu Boi ▪ bounce with bull puppets through the streets of São Luís, Brazil during this festival of music, dance and theatre (p375)

New Year's Eve in Valparaíso ▪ watch fireworks from a fishing boat or join the frolic on the streets of Chile's most beautiful city (p437)

BEST BEACHES

Parque Nacional Tayrona ▪ hit the jungle-covered coast and explore some of Colombia's finest beaches within this coastal national park (p580)

Praia do Gunga ▪ bliss out on the fine white sand of this little-visited slice of Brazilian paradise (p357)

Archipiélago Los Roques ▪ snorkel, camp, hike and otherwise find nirvana on the heavenly white beaches of this Caribbean archipelago (p1000)

Ilha Grande ▪ sail over to this remote Brazilian island of tropical beaches, Atlantic rainforest and long, quiet walks (p302)

Punta del Diablo ▪ leave the crowds, grab your board and venture off to this forgotten fishing village on a stunning beach (p967)

Traditional *moai* (massive anthropomorphic statue) carved from soft volcanic rock, Rapa Nui (Easter Island; p530)

BEST CITIES

Buenos Aires ▣ wander leafy Palermo Viejo, explore historic San Telmo, down steaks and fine wine and dance all night (p47)

Paramaribo ▣ let Suriname's capital suck you into a fascinating world of colonial Dutch architecture and Latin culture (p765)

Rio de Janeiro ▣ fall in love with the world's most beautifully set city and the *cariocas* (people from Rio) themselves (p280)

Valparaíso ▣ walk the cobblestone streets of Chile's cultural capital, stunningly perched on steep hillsides above the Pacific (p433)

Mérida ▣ party the night away after a day of outdoor fun in this totally unpretentious university town in Venezuela (p1012)

BEST HISTORICAL SITES

Machu Picchu ▣ mystify your mind at South America's most famous and spectacular archaeological site (p884)

Ciudad Perdida ▣ trek through jungle to the 'Lost City' of the Tayronas, one of the America's largest pre-Columbian cities (p581)

Rapa Nui (Easter Island) ▣ marvel at the colossal stone *moai* (massive anthropomorphic statues) on this remote Chilean island (p530)

The Nazca Lines ▣ fly over these ancient and mysterious line-drawings in Peru, visible only from the sky (p851)

Potosí ▣ tour the stunningly hellish cooperative mines that bankrolled Spanish colonialism (p237)

ITINERARIES

THE BIG LOOP

How long?
The Big Loop:
4–8 months;
short version:
6–8 weeks

When to go?
Year-round; consider
Carnaval in Feb/Mar;
if you add Patagonia,
Dec–Mar is best

Budget?
Daily average if you
scrimp: US$20–25

This is it – the loop of loops, the mother of all treks, the time-is-not-an-issue journey of a lifetime (plus an alternate for folks with less time).

Ease into Latin American culture in **Buenos Aires** (p47). If you want to see Patagonia, travel south to **Bariloche** (p136) and follow the Austral Projection itinerary back to BA. Then head to **Iguazú Falls** (p90). Cross into Brazil and hit **Campo Grande** (p336) for a wildlife tour of the **Pantanal** (p332). Cut west to **Corumbá** (p337) and cross into **Bolivia** (p174). If you don't have time for the entire circuit, explore Bolivia then head into **Northwest Argentina** (p92) and continue down the Andes to **Mendoza** (p122). Fly out of BA or **Santiago** (p418), Chile.

For the big loop, continue through Bolivia into **Peru** (p820) via **Lake Titicaca** (p864). Cross into **Ecuador** (p637) and follow the Andean Mountain High itinerary. Continue into Colombia to see the spectacular **Zona Cafetera** (p601). Then go to **Cartagena** (p582) to chill out on the Caribbean. See **Parque Nacional Tayrona** (p580) and **Ciudad Perdida** (p581) before bussing from **Santa Marta** (p577), Colombia to **Maracaibo** (p1008), Venezuela. Then head to **Mérida** (p1012), and hang out for awhile before heading to **Salto Ángel** (p1040) and **Roraima** (p1042). Cross into Brazil at **Santa Elena de Uairén** (p1043). Travel to **Manaus** (p388) and boat down the Amazon River to **Belém** (p377). Then hit **Parque Nacional dos Lençóis Maranhenses** (p377), **Jericoacoara** (p371), **Olinda** (p362) and **Salvador** (p339). Finish in style in **Rio de Janeiro** (p280).

From the Argentine
pampas to the chilly
Andean *páramo*,
from the Caribbean
to the Amazon,
the Big Loop winds
through seven
South American
countries, giving
the unbound
wanderer heaps to
write home about.
To see Patagonia,
combine this
with the Austral
Projection itinerary.

ANDEAN MOUNTAIN HIGH

For rugged adventure, unparalleled alpine vistas, rich indigenous cultures, fabulous crafts and some of the best, most colorful markets on the continent, journey down the Andes from Ecuador to Argentina.

Fly into **Quito** (p647), shack up in the recently restored colonial **Old Town** (p652), and put a few Spanish lessons under your belt before heading south through the volcano-studded Andes. Do the **Quilotoa Loop** (p679), hit the hot baths in **Baños** (p680) and visit colonial **Cuenca** (p688). Cross into Peru and pause at **Huaraz** (p913) for Peru's best trekking and climbing. Peru's big must is **Machu Picchu** (p884), but skip the overrun Inca Trail and try an alternative **trek** (p888). From there head south across shimmering **Lake Titicaca** (p864) into Bolivia for more hiking, trekking and mountaineering in the **Cordillera Real & Yungas** (p201). Then head south to the hallucinogenic landscapes around **Salar de Uyuni** (p219) before continuing to Argentina by way of **La Quiaca** (p112) and the spectacular **Quebrada de Humahuaca** (p110). Travel through the majestic Argentine Andes until you hit **Mendoza** (p122), near massive **Cerro Aconcagua** (p127), the western hemisphere's highest peak.

Mix this itinerary up by starting in **Cuzco** (p870), Peru, a fabulous place to study Spanish (many prefer it to Quito). Or, to make the entire journey longer, start in **Caracas** (p984) and travel south through **Colombia** (p542), one of the continent's hottest new destinations.

Opportunities for detours abound: the most obvious is a flight from Ecuador to the **Galápagos Islands** (p724). To depart the trodden trail, wander off to some of the world's most remote natural areas, including **Parque Nacional Manu** (p929) in Peru, or **Parque Nacionale Madidi** (p253) and **Parque Nacionale Noel Kempff Mercado** (p248) in Bolivia.

How long?
Partial route: 1 month; full route: 2 months

When to go?
Year-round

Budget?
Per day US$10-25 day (Galápagos trip extra)

Not including side trips, the Andean Mountain High route winds through the more than 4000km of rugged Andean highlands, passing snowcapped volcanoes, windswept páramo, indigenous villages, incredible vistas and some of the western hemisphere's highest peaks. Primary transport? The bus, a South American highlight in itself!

AUSTRAL PROJECTION

Mysterious, windswept, glacier-riddled Patagonia is one of South America's most magical destinations. For tent-toters, outdoor nuts, climbers, and hikers, it's a dream. Patagonia – and the archipelago of Tierra del Fuego – is best visited November through March, and you can see more for cheaper if you camp. Remember, the going can be *slo-o-o-w*.

Start in busy **Bariloche, Argentina** (p136), in the Argentine Lake District. The Andes here are magnificently forested and studded with azure lakes. Don't miss **Parque Nacional Nahuel Huapi** (p139) or **Parque Nacional Lanín** (p133). Head to **Puerto Montt** (p501), Chile, and down to the serene archipelago of **Chiloé** (p505). After exploring the islands (and eating the seafood!), take the ferry to **Chaitén** (p510) and travel east to the Andean hamlet of **Futaleufú** (p512) for some of the continent's best rafting. Cross into Argentina, stop in **Esquel** (p142), and bounce down the desolate RN 40 to **El Chaltén** (p152), in spectacular **Parque Nacional Los Glaciares** (p156). Hike and climb your brains out before having them warped by the **Perito Moreno Glacier** (p156) near **El Calafate** (p153). Hike beneath the famous granite spires of Chile's **Torres del Paine** (p524) and rest up in **Puerto Natales** (p521). Head to **Punta Arenas** (p518) before traveling south into **Tierra del Fuego** (p158) and bottoming out at **Ushuaia, Argentina** (p159). After severe southern exposure, work north along the Atlantic, stopping for penguins in **Reserva Provincial Punto Tombo** (p150) and whales in **Reserva Faunística Península Valdés** (p148). By this point you'll be achin' for civilization, so beeline to **Buenos Aires** (p47).

An alternate, though pricey, route south is aboard Chile's world-famous **Navimag ferry** (p418), which sails through majestic fjords to Puerto Natales.

How long?
3 weeks is pushin' it;
2 months is lovin' it

When to go?
mid-November–
mid-April

Budget?
Argentina per day
US$15-20;
Chile per day about
US$40 (cheaper if
you camp)

By the end of this epic adventure, you'll have traveled over 5000km and seen the very best of Patagonia. Bus and hitching are the cheapest modes of travel, but lake crossings are possible and flights make things faster. Argentina's RN 40 is covered by private minivan.

AMAZON & ON & ON...

Few rivers fire the imagination like the Amazon. Ever dreamt of going down it? You can. But there's a reason everything west of **Manaus** (p388), Brazil is off the beaten track: boat travel on the Amazon can be bleak, boring, sightless, uncomfortable, hot and dirty. Truthfully, it's *hardcore*.

Just to make the journey as long as possible, set off from **Yurimaguas, Peru** (p931). Start with a 10-hour warm-up float to Lagunas and check out the **Reserva Nacional Pacaya-Samiria** (p932) before heading on to **Iquitos** (p932), on the Río Marañón (which becomes the Amazon). From Iquitos (inaccessible by road), get a three-day boat to the tri-border region of Peru, Colombia and Brazil, and take a break – and a jungle excursion – in **Leticia, Colombia** (p620). From Leticia, it's three more arduous days to Manaus, but breaking the trip at the amazing **Reserva de Desenvolvimento Sustentável Mamirauá** (p393) makes it all worthwhile. Once you do hit Manaus, you're getting into well-traveled territory. But, having come this far, the journey is only over when you hit majestic **Belém** (p377), 3½ days away on the Atlantic. Break the journey in **Santarém** (p386) to visit beautiful **Alter do Chão** (p387).

For those who really want a challenge, an interesting alternative would be starting this journey in the Ecuadorian oil town of **Coca** (p699) on the Río Napo. From here it's a 12- to 15-hour journey to **Nuevo Rocafuerte** (p701) on the Peruvian border. You can spend the night (or a few weeks if you don't time the cargo-boat departure right) before undertaking the six-day boat ride to Iquitos, Peru. In Iquitos, pick up the first part of the itinerary.

How long?
Two weeks if you time it right and never stop (nuts). One month with breaks.

When to go?
Year-round

Budget?
Per day US$25-40

By the time you finish this maniacal journey, you'll have motored over 4000km, slapped hundreds of mosquitoes, eaten loads of lousy food, met some true characters and seen a *lot* of water. Most importantly, you'll have floated the Amazon from its Peruvian headwaters to the Atlantic.

GOING GUIANAS

How long?
3 weeks: doable;
5 weeks: plenty of
time to get stuck
in the mud

When to go?
Year-round;
ideally Jul-Dec

Budget?
French Guiana
per day US$60;
Suriname
per day US$25;
Guyana
per day US$30

They're expensive, they're hard to reach, they're largely unpopulated, and they can be very, very captivating. And they're *definitely* off the beaten path. Where you start depends on where you're coming from: Guyana via New York, Cayenne via Paris (it's a French domestic flight!) or Paramaribo via Amsterdam. For the sake of a route, let's say you're traveling overland from Brazil.

From **Oiapoque, Brazil** (p385), hire a dugout canoe (unless the bridge is complete) across the Oyapok River into **French Guiana** (p744). You're now officially off the beaten track. Make your way by bus across the verdant, forgotten landscape (complete with burned-out cars along the roadside) to **Cacao** (p753). From here, embark upon the two-day hike along **Sentier Molokoï de Cacao** (p753) for some wildlife-spotting fun. Then make your way up to **Kourou** (p754) and take a ferry (or a more comfy catamaran) across shark-infested waters to the **Îles du Salut** (p755), a former island prison where you can sling up a hammock in the old prison dormitories! Back on the mainland, head up the coast and watch the turtles nesting at **Awala-Yalimapo** (April to July only; p758) before crossing into **Suriname** (p762). Hang out for a few days in weirdly wonderful **Paramaribo** (p765), and set up a tour into the majestic **Central Suriname Nature Reserve** (p770). From Paramaribo, continue west to **Nieuw Nickerie** (p770), where you cross into **Guyana** (p774). Head up to **Georgetown** (p778), and make a detour by boat up to isolated **Shell Beach** (p783) or to see the spectacular **Kaieteur Falls** (p783). Back in Georgetown, get a bus south across the majestic Rupununi Savannahs, stopping in **Annai** and **Lethem** (p784) to savor the vast isolation.

Exploring the
Guianas means
leaving the beaten
path behind and
journeying some
2500km, as the
crow flies. You'll
see tropical jungle,
fascinating capital
cities, real cowboy
country and a
couple of the
continent's most
pristine beaches.

SURREAL SOUTH AMERICA

Travel becomes magical when the real turns surreal, which happens a lot in South America. Some places are especially strange and well worth a detour. In Venezuela, journey to Lago Maracaibo and witness the **Catatumbo lightning** (p1010). Rest your travelin' bones in **Vilcabamba, Ecuador** (p697), where people live to be over 100, mountains resemble faces, and local cacti do funny things to people's brains. In Peru, fly over the **Nazca Lines** (p851) and catch the kaleidoscopic sunrises near **Tres Cruces** (p891). Journey to Bolivia and marvel at the surreal landscapes of **Salar de Uyuni** (p219). In Argentina, the **Difunta Correa shrine** (p128) is one of the strangest sights you'll ever see.

For a truly bizarre experience, sling up a hammock inside the abandoned island prison on **Îles du Salut** (p755). Ghost towns are marvelous places to bend the brain, so stop in **Humberstone** (p462), Chile, a spookily abandoned town. The only thing approaching the surreal, moonlike quality of Argentina's **Parque Provincial Ischigualasto** (p128) are the sand dunes and crystalline pools of Brazil's dreamlike **Parque Nacional dos Lençóis Maranhenses** (p377). When you've seen it all, spend a luxurious night in São Paulo's **Hotel Unique** (p308), for architectural unreality at its best.

NOCTURNAL WILDLIFE TOUR

Sometimes you just need to let loose. And, hey, since partying is often the best way to meet the locals, just consider it…blending in.

A university vibe and all-night music scene make **Mérida** (p1012) the best place to tear up Venezuela. The Guyanese will tell you that Georgetown's **Sheriff Street** (p782) is the hottest party on the Caribbean. Of course, a night out in beautiful **Cartagena** (p582), Colombia, might convince you otherwise. But, for the real thing, head to **Cali** (p604). For small-town beach scene, hit **Montañita** (p716), Ecuador. In Peru, spend a night crawling Lima's **Barranco neighborhood** (p842). Later, treat new friends to drinks in the sand-dune oasis of **Huacachina** (p850).

Whatever you do, don't miss a night in **Buenos Aires** (p47), which starts after midnight with mandatory bar-hopping in Palermo Viejo. Time things right and you'll catch the summerlong party at swanky **Punta del Este, Uruguay** (p964). Of course, you can't say you've partied in South America until you do Brazil: hit **Salvador** (p339) for the music, and then the epicenter of saturnalia itself, **Ipanema** (p285), in Rio de Janeiro. Come down slowly in **Arraial d'Ajuda** (p354) or **Jericoacoara** (p371) on Brazil's northern coast.

Getting Started

Psyching yourself up for the trip (some call it planning) is half the fun. This section is intended to help you decide when to go and predict what kind of cash you'll drop, plus offer a glimpse into what you might experience while bouncing around South America. Also browse the South America Directory (p1057), which covers subjects ranging from activities to volunteering.

WHEN TO GO

See under Climate in the Directory section of each country chapter for country-specific information.

South America spans from the tropics – where sweltering lowlands can lie only hours from chilly Andean highlands – nearly to Antarctica, so when to go depends on where you go.

Climbing and trekking in the Andes of Ecuador, Peru and Bolivia is best in the drier months from May to September but possible year-round. Travel in the Amazon is also possible year-round, though regional rainy seasons throughout the Amazon make river travel easier. Ski season in Argentina and Chile is June to September. Patagonia is best visited during the region's summer months of December to April, but hotels and campgrounds book solid and prices are highest during the peak months of January and February.

The continent's wild array of colorful festivals (see p1066) is also a consideration; Carnaval, the most famous celebration of all, is in late February/early March.

South Americans love to travel during the two- to three-week period around Semana Santa (Holy Week/Easter) and during the Christmas–New Year holidays. Both foreign and national tourists are out in droves in July and August. During these tourist high seasons prices peak, hotels fill up and public transportation gets slammed. The flip side is a celebratory, holiday atmosphere that can be wonderfully contagious.

COSTS & MONEY

Brazil, Chile, Venezuela, Uruguay and the Guianas are the most expensive countries, while the cheapest are Bolivia, Ecuador, Colombia and – as travelers worldwide now know – Argentina.

Generally, it will cost less per person if you travel in twos or threes, spend little time in big cities and travel slowly. Costs rack up as you tag on comforts like air-conditioning and a private bathroom, expensive tours to places such as the Galápagos Islands, or activities like skiing or clubbing.

WHAT TO TAKE?

Remember this: you can buy just about anything you'll need in South America. Certain items, however, can be hard to find. For more on what to bring, flip through the South America Directory (p1057). And don't forget the following:

- alarm clock
- big map of South America
- duct tape
- earplugs
- first-aid kit
- flashlight or head lamp

- insect repellent
- photocopies of important documents
- pocket USB-type flash drive for digital storage
- Swiss Army knife or multitool (with corkscrew)
- universal sink plug

WHAT YOU'LL PAY

To give a very rough idea of relative costs, let's assume you're traveling with another person, mostly by bus, staying in cheap but clean hotels, eating in local restaurants and food stalls, with the occasional splurge on sightseeing or a night out dancing. Not including juicy side trips and/or tours into interior regions, you could expect the following as a minimum per person/ per day budget:

- Argentina – US$20 to US$25
- Bolivia – US$15 to US$25
- Brazil – US$35 to US$45
- Chile – US$35 to US$40
- Colombia – US$15 to US$25
- Ecuador – US$15 to US$20
  (substantially more with a Galápagos trip)
- French Guiana – US$50 to US$60
- Guyana – US$25 to US$30
- Paraguay – US$20 to US$30
- Peru – US$15 to US$25
- Suriname – US$25 to US$30
- Uruguay – US$25 to US$35
- Venezuela – US$20 to US$50

Traveler's checks (best if in US dollars) are the safest way to carry money, but hardly the most convenient. They usually entail waiting in lines during standard bank hours, which makes an ATM card much more appealing. ATMs are available in most cities and large towns. Many ATMs accept personal identification numbers (PINs) of only four digits; find out whether this applies to your destinations before heading off.

Also see Money in the country chapter directories and in the South America Directory at the back of this book (p1057).

LIFE ON THE ROAD

Whether you're thumbing a ride in Chilean Patagonia, waiting curbside for a milk truck in the Ecuadorian Andes or listening to the airbrakes hiss on a hair-raising ride through the Bolivian *altiplano,* South America kicks out unforgettable experiences on the road. In fact, some argue the road *is* the experience.

And then there's *life* on the road. In South America, it's never short on challenge. But that's what makes it South America. Travel here is about

---

TEN TIPS TO STAY ON A BUDGET

There's no need to bargain locals out of every last peso when other tried-and-true techniques will actually save you more. Try the following:

- Camp whenever you can, especially in Patagonia and in hostel backyards.
- Wash your clothes in hotel sinks.
- Form a group for tours; your bargaining power increases the more people you have.
- Skip the taxi during daylight hours and walk or take local buses.
- Instead of eating at restaurants, buy food at open-air markets and eat outdoors.
- Always ask about the *almuerzo* or *menú* (set lunch).
- Take overnight buses in countries such as Argentina and Brazil to save a night's hotel costs.
- Take 2nd-class buses.
- Travel slowly.
- Visit museums on free days.

struggling awake for a dawn departure after being kept up all night by a blaring soccer game. It's about sucking dust on a long bus ride while manically trying to guess which of the towns you keep passing through is the one you intended to visit. It means peaceful relief when you finally arrive and find your pack still on the roof. It's the sight of begging children, the arduous haul to the hotel, a screaming bladder and the excitement of a new town all catapulting your mind from one emotional extreme to another.

The hotel manager says the showers are hot, but the water hitting the skin is as cold as a Patagonian glacier. There's no seat on the toilet. (At least the bowels are behaving.) You call that a fan? It sounds like a helicopter! OK – food. Leave the pack in the corner, get out the map, locate the market, grab the passport (or leave it behind?) and go. The sun feels great. Then you get lost, your mood turns sour as your blood sugar crashes, you find the market, you smell the mangos, and you try to haggle but have no clue what the fruit seller is saying. You finally hand over the cash – did you just get ripped off? – and walk out to find a good place to eat. And when you do, it's sheer and incomparable bliss.

CONDUCT
Introductions
In general, South Americans are gregarious, not easily offended, and will want to exchange pleasantries before starting a conversation; skipping this part of any social interaction is considered unrefined and tactless. Public behavior can be very formal, especially among government officials, who expect respect and deference. Casual introductions, on the other hand, are relaxed and friendly. In countries like Argentina, Chile and French Guiana men and women kiss other women on the cheek, rather than shaking hands. Men usually shake hands with other men, unless they're real pals, in which case they kiss each other on the cheek. In countries like Ecuador and Guyana the handshake is the norm in business and casual introductions alike. If in doubt, wait to see what the other person does and then respond.

Indigenous People
The word *indígenas* refers to indigenous men and women, who are especially present in the Andes and in the Amazon Basin. You may hear the term *indio/a* batted around among *mestizos* (people of mixed indigenous and European descent) but it is considered very derogatory.

Access to many remote Amazon Basin areas where people retain the most traditional ways of living is heavily restricted, and it is essential to respect these restrictions. Such regulations help to deflect unwanted interference and protect the communities from diseases to which they have little immunity.

Other indigenous groups or subgroups have opened their doors to travelers who want to learn about their culture. Community tourism is one

---

DOS & DON'TS

- Do tip 10% if *servicio* (service) isn't included in the bill.
- Do be respectful when haggling for anything.
- Do approach eating with an adventurous attitude.

- Don't take pictures of people without permission.
- Don't feel uncomfortable when people stare in the Andean countries.
- Don't hesitate to deny food from strangers.

of the highlights of South America, but remember to take ceremonies and rituals seriously, despite the fact that they may be organized for your sake. Ayahuasca and other psychoactive drugs play an important part of religious life for some rainforest communities; it is illegal for foreigners to take these drugs, although you may be offered a trip down shaman lane by certain opportunists. Do your research.

Dress
Casual dress has become more acceptable recently, but most South Americans still take considerable pride in their personal appearance, especially in the evening. Foreign visitors should, at the very least, be clean and neatly dressed if they wish to conform to local standards and be treated with respect by officials, businesspeople and professionals. When going out at night, you'll stand out in typical travelers' attire in all but the most gringo-haunted hangouts.

To people of modest means, even shoestring travelers possess considerable wealth. Flaunting items such as expensive cameras, watches and jewelry is likely to attract thieves. Police and military officials are often poorly paid and may resent affluent visitors who do not behave appropriately. (Read: bribery attempts could be coming your way.)

TOP TENS

Our Favorite Albums

- *África Brasil* by Jorge Ben (Brazil, 1976)
- *Arepa 3000: A Venezuelan Journey into Space* by Los Amigos Invisibles (Venezuela, 2000)
- *La Argentinidad al Palo 1 & 2* by Bersuit Vergarabat (Argentina, 2004)
- *The Nada* by Kevin Johansen + the Nada (Argentina/USA, 2001)
- *Jolgorio* by Peru Negro (Peru, 2004)
- *Os Mutantes* by Os Mutantes (Brazil, 1968)
- *Salsa Explosiva!* by Fruko y sus Tesos (Colombia, US release, 2004)
- *Samba Esporte Fino* by Seu Jorge (Brazil, 1999)
- *Tribalistas* by Tribalistas (Brazil, 2003)
- *Tropicalia: Ou Panis Et Circenses* by Various Artists (Brazil, 1967)

Must-Read Books

- *Dona Flor and her Two Husbands* by Jorge Amado (Brazil, 1978)
- *Ficciones* by Jorge Luis Borges (Argentina, 1944)
- *Hopscotch* by Julio Cortázar (Argentina, 1963)
- *House of Spirits* by Isabel Allende (Chile, 1982)
- *In Patagonia* by Bruce Chatwin (England, 1977)
- *Marching Powder* by Rusty Young (Australia, 2002)
- *One Hundred Years of Solitude* by Gabriel García Márquez (Colombia, 1967)
- *Open Veins of Latin America* by Eduardo Galeano (Uruguay, 1971)
- *Papillón* by Henri Charrière (France & French Guiana, 1970)
- *The Story Teller* by Mario Vargas Llosa (Peru, 1987)

Sex

Sexual contact between locals and visitors, male and female, straight and gay, is quite common, and some areas could be described as sex-tourism destinations. Prostitution exists, but is most common in Brazil, where the distinction between prostitution and promiscuity can be hazy. Child prostitution is not common but, sadly, exists. There are harsh penalties for those convicted of soliciting children and real risks of entrapment. AIDS is widespread among gay and straight people alike, so always protect yourself.

Taking Photographs

Don't photograph individuals without obtaining their permission first, especially indigenous people. If someone is giving a public performance, such as a street musician or a dancer at Carnaval, or is incidental to a photograph, in a broad cityscape for example, it's usually not necessary to request permission – but if in doubt, ask or refrain. Also see p1070.

Snapshots

CURRENT EVENTS

You'd have to be holed up in an underground bunker in the Paraguayan Chaco to miss the trend sweeping South America today: the continent is leaning to the left – big time. In voting booths across the continent, South Americans have firmly expressed their frustration with government corruption and the International Monetary Fund (IMF), World Bank and US policies that have fed it. The message: we're doing things *our* way.

When you line up the list of South American leaders today, it's no wonder the White House and international lenders are worried. The zealously anti-US and self-proclaimed socialist-revolutionary Hugo Chávez heads Venezuela and considers Fidel Castro one of his closest allies. Left-winger and former shoeshine boy Luiz Inacio 'Lula' da Silva leads Brazil. In 2005 Uruguayans elected Tabare Vazquez, who immediately restored ties with Cuba, signed an energy plan with Venezuela, and announced sweeping welfare packages for poor Uruguayans. In December 2005 Bolivians elected Evo Morales, the nation's first indigenous president and a former coca farmer who deemed himself 'Washington's nightmare.' In 2006 Morales boldly nationalized the country's natural-gas supplies and moved forward with plans for land reform.

Chilean voters, in 2006, chose South America's second democratically elected female president, Michelle Bachelet. The 54-year-old pediatrician is agnostic, a socialist, a long-time human rights activist and a single mother of three – hardly minor issues in a predominantly Catholic country that legalized divorce only two years prior to her election. Even Argentina's center-left president, Nestor Kirchner, took a serious stand against the powers that be: in 2005, he paid off Argentina's entire debt to the IMF to avoid the institution's free-market policy demands.

But it's not *all* politics *all* the time. The hot news on travelers' tongues is Colombia – not that the international coffee icon Juan Valdez hung up his actor's hat in 2006 (which he did), but that the country has become increasingly safe for travelers. Colombia saw a 21% increase in foreign visitors between 2004 and 2005. In other news, the country became one of the handful of South American nations to take steps – small steps, but steps nonetheless – toward legalizing abortion. It's somewhat surprising, considering the 2006 re-election of Alvaro Uribe solidified Colombia as one of the last bastions of conservatism on the continent.

Argentina still holds the title of hippest hot spot, and travel there remains cheap, despite the fact that the economy continues on its upswing – good news for travelers and locals alike. In 2006 a German explorer convinced the Peruvian government to map, measure and announce to the world the presence of the planet's third-highest waterfalls, Gocta Falls in the Amazon Basin. Local inhabitants (who feared the curse of a mermaid should they disclose the falls' location) had kept the waterfalls secret until 2002. In May, 2006 a wave of violence struck Sao Paulo, Brazil, when protesting prison gangs orchestrated the killing of 41 police officers. Police responded by killing 107 people in what human-rights organizations have deemed a throwback to Brazil's dictatorial days.

All news, however, seemed to pale in comparison to South America's most beloved event – the World Cup. Unfortunately, no South American team made it to the final, despite the initial show of strength by hopefuls Brazil and, especially, Argentina. Both teams were knocked out during the

Visit Global Exchange (www.globalexchange .org) to read why South American countries blocked the US-backed Free Trade Agreement of the Americas (FTAA; ALCA in Spanish) at the 2005 Americas Summit in Mar del Plata.

When Evo Morales became Bolivia's first indigenous president, he kept his casual style of dress and his signature striped wool sweaters. Soon, stores everywhere were selling striped sweaters and one Bolivian designer even launched a new line, called 'Evo Fashion.'

quarter-finals, by France and Germany, respectively. The big surprise was the Ecuadorian team, which, in only its second World Cup appearance, reached round 16 before losing to England. Just wait until next time.

HISTORY
The First South Americans

Back in the salad days (sometime between 12,500 and 70,000 years ago), humans migrated from Asia to Alaska over a land bridge across the Bering Strait and slowly hunted and gathered their way south. Settled agriculture developed in South America between 5000 BC and 2500 BC in and around present-day Peru, and the emerging societies ultimately developed into major civilizations, of which the Inca empire was the most sophisticated.

In October 2005, Venezuelan president Hugo Chávez urged families to shun Halloween, calling it a 'game of terror' and part of the US culture of creating fear.

Enter the Spanish

At the time of the Spanish invasion in the early 16th century, the Inca empire had reached the zenith of its power, ruling over millions of people from northern Ecuador to central Chile and northern Argentina, where native peoples of the Araucanian language groups fiercely resisted incursions from the north.

The Spanish first arrived in Latin America in 1492, when Christopher Columbus, who was bankrolled by Queen Isabella of Spain to find a new route to Asia's spice islands, accidentally bumped into the Caribbean islands. Meanwhile, the Portuguese navigator Vasco da Gama founded the new sea route to Asia. These spectacular discoveries raised the stakes in the brewing rivalry between Spain and Portugal, and to sort out claims of their newly discovered lands, they decided it was treaty time.

At its peak, the Inca empire governed at least 12 million people from 100 separate cultures and 20 language groups. Its highways traversed more than 8000km of the Andes.

Dividing & Conquering

Spanish and Portuguese representatives met in 1494 to draw a nice little line at about 48° west of Greenwich, giving Africa and Asia to Portugal and all of the New World to Spain. Significantly, however, the treaty placed the coast of Brazil (not discovered until six years later) on the Portuguese side of the line, giving Portugal access to the new continent.

Between 1496 and 1526, Spanish exploration from Panama intensified. Rumors surfaced of a golden kingdom south of Panama, prompting Francisco Pizarro to convince Spanish authorities to finance an expedition of 200 men.

When Pizarro encountered the Inca, the empire was wracked by dissension and civil war and proved vulnerable to this invasion by a very small force of Spaniards. Pizarro's well-armed soldiers terrorized the population, but his deadliest weapon was infectious disease, to which indigenous people lacked any immunity. The Inca ruler Huayna Capac died, probably of smallpox, in about 1525.

Lima, founded in 1535 as the capital of the new viceroyalty of Peru, was the base for most of the ensuing exploration and conquest, and became the seat of all power in Spanish South America. By 1572 the Spanish had defeated

TIMELINE

| 1524–26: Spanish navigator Francisco Pizarro begins preliminary explorations down South America's Pacific coast | 1816–30: Spanish colonies, beginning with Argentina and Venezuela, win independence from Spain | 1935: First official samba parade performed at Rio's Carnaval |

| 1400 | 1500 | 1600 | 1700 | 1800 | 1850 | 1900 | 1910 | 1920 | 1930 |

1430–40: Inca victory over the Chankas marks beginning of rapid expansion of Inca empire

1535: Lima founded as the capital of the new viceroyalty of Peru

1930: First World Cup held in Montevideo, Uruguay

and killed two successive Inca rulers – Manco Inca and Tupac Amaru – and solidified Spain's dominance over much of the continent.

Silver, Slavery & Separation

Following the conquest, the Spaniards, who above all else wanted gold and silver, worked the indigenous populations mercilessly in the mines and the fields. Native American populations declined rapidly, however, due to introduced diseases. In several parts of the continent, African slaves were introduced to make up for the lack of indigenous labor, notably in the plantations of Brazil and the mines of Bolivia.

The movement for independence by the Spanish colonies began around the end of the 18th century, when Spain, devoting its energy and troops to the war against France, began to lose control of the colonies. By the end of the war in 1814, Venezuela and Argentina had effectively declared independence from Spain, and over the next seven years, the other Spanish colonies followed suit. Brazil became autonomous in 1807 and declared independence in 1822.

Published in 1552, Bartolomé de las Casas' impassioned *Short Account of the Destruction of the Indies* is one of the only accounts written during the Spanish conquest that is sympathetic to indigenous Americans.

Independence & Dependence

After independence, conservative rural landowners, known as caudillos, filled the power vacuum left by the departed colonial regime. Strong dictatorships, periods of instability and the gross inequality between powerful elites and the disfranchised masses have since characterized most South American countries.

After WWII, which marked the beginning of industrialization throughout South America, most countries turned to foreign loans and investment to make up for their lack of capital. This set the stage for the massive debt crises of the 1970s and 1980s, as South American governments accelerated their borrowing, and profits from industry and agriculture made their way into Western banks and the pockets of corrupt South American officials. Dictatorships provided a semblance of stability, but oppression, poverty and corruption bred violent guerrilla movements in many countries, most notably (and most recently) in Peru and Colombia (see those chapters for details). Many of the problems facing South America today are a direct result of foreign debt and the systems of corruption and inequality that date back to colonial and post-independence years. The recent upsurge of populist and nationalist leaders (see Current Events, p25) is largely a democratic response to unpopular austerity measures forced upon South American countries by the IMF and World Bank.

THE CULTURE
Indigenous Culture

When foreigners imagine indigenous South Americans, odds are they imagine either the colorfully dressed *indígenas* (indigenous people) of the Andean highlands or the people of the Amazon rainforests. The Quechua and other

1963: Antonio Carlos Jobim writes bossa nova hit *Girl From Ipanema*

1973: General Augusto Pinochet ousts Chilean President Allende, beginning brutal 17-year dictatorship

2001–02: December: Argentine economy crashes; January 1: Eduardo Duhalde becomes fifth president in two weeks

Present Day

| 1940 | 1950 | 1960 | 1970 | 1980 | 1990 | 2000 | 2001 | 2006 |

1952: Future revolutionary Che Guevara journeys around South America by motorcycle

1967: Gabriel García Márquez' *One Hundred Years of Solitude* is published and receives world acclaim

1976: On March 24, military coup in Argentina begins 'Dirty War'; estimated 30,000 people disappear by 1983

2006: Bolivia's Evo Morales nationalizes the country's natural-gas industry

SOUTH AMERICAN CINEMA   *Lara Dunston*

Films first traveled to South America when the French Lumière brothers – the inventors of the first movie camera – sent teams around the world to demonstrate (and sell) their new inventions. In 1896 their first camera and projection crews headed off to Buenos Aires and Rio de Janeiro (stopping also in Mexico City and Havana). Interestingly, Argentina and Brazil today have the most well-developed film industries and produce the most cinematically sophisticated movies on the continent.

The Lumière teams were soon followed by American Biograph company camera crews hired to shoot exotic footage from the continent. As a result, the first images of South America to be seen by the rest of the world were shot by foreigners – the forerunners to the kind of programs we now watch on the Travel Channel. These films showed the rest of the globe what South American cities looked like – their splendid architecture and bustling streets, their traditional rituals and colorful festivities, the political pomp and ceremony – along with picturesque vistas of ancient ruins, wonderful countryside, lush jungles and forests, and arid landscapes. No doubt they inspired many travelers, adventurers and opportunists to journey to 'the end of the earth.'

In South America itself, people who lived in towns along railway lines were the first to experience the thrill of watching flicks, until the entrepreneurial mobile moving-picture men *(comicos de la legua)* arrived in town with horse-drawn projection houses to set up temporary cinemas. Now there are movie theaters in most towns, from state-of-the-art multiplexes in slick shopping malls to atmospheric art-house cinemas showing challenging films that are difficult to see outside South America. Make an effort to seek these and you'll be rewarded.

Like the continent's overall industrial development, film industries in countries such as Bolivia, Chile, Colombia, Peru and Venezuela developed slowly and unevenly. Some countries experienced sporadic flurries of activity during the 20th century, while in small countries such as Ecuador, Paraguay and Uruguay there was very little film production until recently. Although production costs are comparatively low in South America, it still takes a lot of money to finance a movie. As a result, filmmaking has often been artisanal in nature, using only small crews, basic equipment and natural light. On the other hand, the more industrialized countries of Argentina and Brazil have had solid histories of fairly continuous Hollywood-style studio production, with strong local audiences and markets for their films all over the continent and overseas in Spain and Portugal.

Although Hollywood has always saturated the continent's market with Spanish-language versions of its movies, many distinctly South American genres have emerged. The Brazilian *chanchada* is a comic, carnival-like musical, while Argentina's *tangueras* are centered on the tango. There are several versions of the Western cowboy genre, including Argentine *gaucho* films, often based on epic novels, and Brazil's *cangaçeiro*. Melodrama has always been popular throughout South America, providing vehicles for stars like Brazilian Carmen Miranda, and Argentine singer Carlos Gardel, whose appeal spread across the continent and, later, to Hollywood. You'll see these classic films sold at corner newsstands in most cities and large towns in South America.

South American films have long had a sociopolitical focus, from the genre pics of the 1940s and '50s to the more explicitly political films of the 1960s and '70s and the innovative dramas of the 1980s and '90s. These films highlighted the struggles of the poor, the disadvantaged or the dispossessed, with plots centered, for example, on the rural classes' oppression of indigenous workers, a servant girl's rape by her master and subsequent vengeance, a political prisoner's difficult life behind bars, or an old woman's search for her orphaned grandchild stolen during the military dictatorship.

See Luis Puenzo's *La historia oficial* (The Official Story, 1984) about Argentina's 'dirty little war' and victims of that military junta (the *desaparecidos*) and you'll better understand why the Mothers of the Plaza de Mayo marched in front of Buenos Aires' presidential palace for 25 years. Chilean Gonzalo Justiniano's *Amnesia* (1994) is about one man's inability to forget the atrocities committed by soldiers during dictator Augusto Pinochet's reign of terror.

The films of the 1960s and '70s were the most politically radical and were part of an idealistic continent-wide movement known as the New Latin American Cinema *(el nuevo cine latinoamericano)*. Inspired by the gritty postwar Italian neorealism movement, many South American filmmakers went to study film in Rome in the 1950s. They returned to shoot stories that depicted the realities of contemporary South American life with the aim of motivating people to act to change society. Often documentary-like, these films highlighted (rather than disguised) their low budget to create a unique visual style that was raw yet rich, stark and sometimes surreal. Their impoverished aesthetics were rooted in the philosophies of the filmmakers; Argentines Fernando Solanas and Octavio Getino sought to develop a 'third (world) cinema,' while Brazilian Glauber Rocha aimed to depict the 'aesthetics of hunger.'

Solanas and Getino are best-known for their innovative collagelike, four-hour-long leftist documentary *La Hora de los Hornos* (The Hour of the Furnaces, 1968). Made and shown in secret, this extraordinarily powerful film was intended to politically incite viewers to rally in support of Perón and against social injustice – and it proved very successful. Twenty years later, Solanas received the Best Director award at Cannes for his mesmerizing feature film *Sur* (South), and in 2005, critical acclaim for his documentary *La Dignidad de los Nadies* (The Dignity of the Nobodies), about Argentina's recent political and economic crises and its impact on everyday life. Rocha's epic 1964 film *Deus e o Diabo na Terra do Sol* (Black God, White Devil), about the struggles of the country's poverty-stricken northeastern population, is considered by many to be Brazil's greatest film, closely followed by his 1968 film *Antonio das Mortes,* about a paid assassin, which also earned him a Best Director award at Cannes.

The 1980s and '90s saw a uniquely South American form of magical realism appear in films from all corners of the continent. The magical realist form in cinema was an extension of a style that had existed in literature since the previous century and was made popular in the writings of authors such as Gabriel García Márquez and Isabelle Allende. Argentine director Eliseo Subiela's film *Hombre Mirando al Sureste* (Man Facing Southeast) was an early example. These decades also saw a return to melodrama, with these 'women's films' now being made by feminist women such as Argentine María Luisa Bemberg. Bemberg didn't begin her career until she was in her 50s and a divorced grandmother. Outside of Argentina, she's best known for *Miss Mary* (1986), a drama about society's repression of women starring Julie Christie as a governess working for a wealthy Argentine family. Her bizarre romantic comedy *De Eso No Se Habla* (I Don't Want To Talk About It, 1994) was considerably lighter in tone and starred Marcello Mastroianni as a suave older bachelor who falls for a dwarfed village girl and leads a happy life until the circus comes to town.

The 21st century has seen a new wave of South American films succeeding at the box office at home and abroad like never before. Brazilian Walter Salles, who first attracted attention with *Central do Brasil* (Central Station, 1998), has been one of South America's most prolific filmmakers, telling simple yet life-changing stories set in splendid environments. Fernando Meirelles won raves for *Cidade de Deus* (City of God, 2002), his brutal but life-filled portrait of a Rio *favela* (shanty town). In Argentina, Lucrecia Martel, director of *La Cienaga* (The Swamp, 2001) and *La Nina Santa* (The Holy Girl, 2004), both set in Salta, has offered extraordinary insights into the intricate complexities of family relationships.

The one constant in South American cinema is its sense of place. Stunning landscapes have always played a major role, from the escapist rural utopias of the 1940s and '50s to the more realistic portraits of indigenous land struggles of the 1960s and '70s. The land continues to inspire contemporary moviemakers. These striking images of the continent are in themselves deeply political and personal, telling a larger story about South America's exploitation and development, its struggles and survival, and its more recent flourishing, skillfully woven into the fabric of its films.

Best Film Festivals

▪ Mar Del Plata Film Festival (www.mardelplatafilmfest.com), Mar Del Plata, Argentina, March – a gorgeous seaside location and lots of glamorous stars at one of the most respected festivals on the continent.

▪ Mostra International Film Festival (www.mostra.org), São Paulo, Brazil, October to November – this excellent festival hosts an enormous number of independent films from Latin America and around the globe at a number of São Paulo cinemas.

▪ Festival Internacional de Cine (www.festicinecartagena.com), Cartagena, Colombia, March – one of the oldest film festivals in South America with film screenings held around the city, and workshops and seminars at universities making it a great place to meet young filmmakers and students.

▪ Uruguay International Film Festival (www.cinemateca.org.uy), Montevideo, Uruguay, April – this laidback festival of Latin American cinema will give you the opportunity to mix it with a cool young crowd in charming Montevideo.

Must-See Movies

▪ *Diarios de Motocicleta* (The Motorcycle Diaries) Dir: Walter Salles, Brazil, 2004 – Che Guevara's life-changing motorcycle road trip across South America in the '50s.

▪ *Cidade de Deus* (City of God) Dir: Fernando Meirelles, Brazil, 2002 – a rare insight into life in Rio de Janeiro's *favelas* (shanty towns).

▪ *Central do Brasil* (Central Station) Dir: Walter Salles, Brazil, 1998 – a hard old woman and orphaned boy's sentimental journey to the sertão in search of his family.

▪ *Historias Minimas* (Minimal Stories) Dir: Carlos Sorín, Argentina, 2002 – a complex portrait of seemingly simple lives, set in stunning Patagonian landscapes.

▪ *Nueve Reinas* (Nine Queens) Dir: Fabián Bielinsky, Argentina, 2000 – an unpredictable, edge-of-your-seat tour of the Buenos Aires of scam artists and swindlers.

▪ *La Ciénaga* (The Swamp) Dir: Lucrecia Martel, Argentina, 2001 – a tense, often edge-of-your seat, claustrophobic family drama set one sultry summer in the small town of Salta.

▪ *Play* Dir: Alicia Scherson, Chile, 2005 – an engaging, puzzling film about two young people who stroll the city streets in search of love, set against the lonely backdrop of contemporary Santiago.

▪ *En la Puta Vida* (Tricky Life) Dir: Beatriz Flores Silva, Uruguay, 2001 – an extraordinary comedy tracing the rapid life-changing events that leads a young woman from hairdressing in Montevideo to prostitution in Barcelona.

▪ *La Sombra del Caminante* (The Wandering Shadows) Dir: Ciro Guerra, Colombia, 2004 – this award-winning film tells a moving tale of two very different, but equally troubled, men who meet in downtown Bogota.

▪ *1809–1810 Mientra Llega el Dia* (1809–1810 Before Dawn) Dir: Camilo Luzuriaga, Ecuador, 2004 – a portrait of a tempestuous love affair between an academic and his student in Ecuador on the eve of the 1810 revolution.

Also worth checking out:

▪ *Orfeu Negro* (Black Orpheus) Dir: Marcel Camus, Brazil, 1959

▪ *Machuca* Dir: Andrés Wood, Chile, 2004

▪ *Hombre mirando al sudeste* (Man Facing Southeast) Dir: Eliseo Subiela, Argentina, 1986

▪ *La historia oficial* (The Official Story) Dir: Luis Puenzo, Argentina, 1985

▪ *Ratas, ratones, rateros* (Rodents) Dir: Sebastian Coredero, Ecuador, 1999

▪ *El Perro* (The Dog) Dir: Carlos Sorín, Argentina, 2004

linguistic groups of the Bolivian, Ecuadorian and Peruvian highlands have coexisted with the *mestizo* (people of mixed indigenous and European descent) majority – although not without conflict – for centuries. Their cultures are strong, autonomous and reticent to change and have influenced their country's culture (through music, food, language and so on) to its core. For travelers, experiencing these highland cultures firsthand can be as simple as getting on a bus, shopping in a market or hanging around a village. Many indigenous people are friendly with foreigners; but many are wary of them, as outsiders have brutally oppressed their people for centuries.

The lives of rainforest peoples are usually vastly different from what the tourist brochures floating the world suggest. Except under unique circumstances, travelers generally will not encounter indigenous people of the rainforest traditionally dressed, unless they're doing so specifically for the sake of tourism – not an inherently negative situation, but one to approach with awareness. Most rainforest communities have only recently been hit with the Western world. Many are facing the complete upheaval – if not annihilation – of their cultures and lives, and the culture one encounters as a visitor is one in the throes of dramatic change.

Bolivia, Peru and Ecuador have the highest percentages of indigenous people, most of whom live in the highlands. Other important groups include the Tikuna, Yanomami and Guaraní of Brazil, the Mapuche of northern Patagonia, the Aymara of Bolivia, and the Atacameños and Aymara of Chile's *altiplano* (Andean high plain).

Music

How do you spell 'life' in South America? M-u-s-i-c. Turn it off, and the continent would simply grind to a halt. South America's musical landscape is incredibly varied, and its more popular styles – samba, lambada and bossa nova from Brazil, the Argentine tango, Colombian salsa and Andean *música folklórica* (traditional Andean music) – are known internationally. But there are countless regional styles that will likely be new to foreign ears, including *vallenato* in Colombia, Afro-Peruvian music, *joropo* in Venezuela, *chamamé* and *cumbia villera* in Argentina and *forró* and *carimbo* in Brazil. For those who happen to have more Western pop sensibilities, there's a rich history of *rock en español* (Spanish-language rock) and Nueva Canción (political folk music) in Argentina and Chile. South American musical influences are equally diverse, with Eastern European polkas, African rhythms and North American jazz and rock all factoring into the equation.

Online music links, you request? Visit the Humanities section on the Latin American Network Information Center (Lanic; www.lanic .utexas.edu); the Music page will link you up to just about everything having to do with South American music online.

Population & People

Over three-quarters of all South Americans live in cities, while large areas such as the Amazon Basin and Atacama Desert are relatively uninhabited. Population growth and internal migration have led to the emergence of supercities, such as São Paulo (population 11 million; 20 million including greater São Paulo), Buenos Aires (13.5 million counting greater Buenos Aires), Rio de Janeiro (11 to 12 million in the entire metropolitan area), Lima (7.6 million) and Bogotá (7.5 million). These megalopolises concentrate some of the most severe social and environmental problems on the continent.

Infant mortality rates are shockingly high in some countries, most notably Bolivia, Brazil and Peru. South America has a high proportion of people younger than 15 years old (30%), but some of the countries (in particular Bolivia, Brazil, Columbia, Ecuador, Peru and Venezuela) have even more youthful populations, with nearly 40% of the people younger than 15. It's likely that populations will continue to burgeon as these individuals reach childbearing ages, and it's doubtful that local economies will be able to provide employment for so many in such a short period of time.

Although the majority of South Americans are *mestizos*, a large percentage of the Peruvian, Ecuadorian and Bolivian populations are self-identified indigenous. Many Brazilians claim African heritage, and the Guianas are a mosaic of East Indians, Indonesians, Africans, Creoles, Chinese and their descendants. Even in the most racially homogeneous countries (eg Argentina, Chile and Paraguay), Syrians, Chinese, Japanese and other immigrants and their descendants are represented in the population.

For news on the Americas' and the world's indigenous struggles, see the News section at Survival International (www.survival-international.org).

Religion

About 90% of South Americans are at least nominally Roman Catholic. Virtually every city, town and village has a central church or cathedral and a calendar loaded with Catholic holidays and celebrations. Spreading the faith was a major objective of colonization.

Among indigenous peoples, allegiance to Catholicism was often a clever veneer adopted to disguise traditional beliefs ostensibly forbidden by the church. Similarly, black slaves in Brazil gave Christian names and forms to their African gods, whose worship was discouraged or forbidden. Syncretic beliefs and practices such as Candomblé in Brazil have proliferated to this day, but they do not exclude Christianity. There is no conflict between attending mass one day and seeking guidance from a *brujo* (witch) the next.

In recent decades, various Protestant sects have made inroads among the traditionally Catholic population. There is also a small number of Jews and Muslims sprinkled throughout the continent.

Sports

Baseball, bullfighting, cockfighting and the rodeo are important in some South American countries, but nothing unites most South Americans like football (in the soccer sense, that is). It's the national passion in every South American country. Brazil won its fifth World Cup final in 2002, snatching the world record for most titles taken. Argentina's Boca Juniors are one of the world's most famous teams. If you want to get anyone blabbing, just bring up former Boca Junior star Diego Maradona's infamous 'Hand of God' goal that knocked England out of the 1986 World Cup. He scored with his hand. The passion can reach extremes: in 1994, after Colombian defender Andreas Escobar scored an own-goal in a World Cup game against the US, he was shot 10 times outside a Medellín nightclub. According to police, the gunman shouted *'Gol!'* after each shot. To say the least, football is serious. The annual South American championship is the Copa Libertadores. The Copa América is a continent-wide championship played in odd-number years, and non-South American teams are invited.

Stay up to date on all South American soccer games and tournaments played throughout the continent and the world at www.latinamericanfootball.com.

Volleyball has become extremely popular throughout South America, especially in Brazil. There, people also play a variation called *futvolei*, in which players use their feet instead of their hands.

Rallies (dirt- and off-road auto races) are big in Chile, Argentina, Bolivia and Brazil. Argentina is famous for polo, Buenos Aires being the best place to see a match.

ENVIRONMENT
The Land

The Cordillera de los Andes, the longest continuous mountain system on earth, forms the western margin of the continent, snaking nearly 8000km from Venezuela to southern Patagonia. Riddled with volcanoes, the Andes are part of the volcanic 'Ring of Fire' running from Asia to Alaska to Tierra del Fuego. East of the Andes, the Amazon Basin – the largest river basin in the world – covers parts of Bolivia, Venezuela, Colombia, Peru, Ecuador, the Guianas and Brazil. In the center of the continent (in parts of Brazil, Bolivia and Paraguay), the vast Pantanal is the largest inland wetland on earth. Yep, this place is *big*.

On the geographical side-stage, other physical features include the Orinoco River Basin, which drains the *llanos* (plains) of Venezuela; the barren Chaco of southern Bolivia, northwestern Paraguay and the northern tip of Argentina; the extensive Paraná–Paraguay river system; the fertile pampas of Argentina and Uruguay; and arid, mystical Patagonia, in the far south.

'Glaciers on the equator – whoa, this place is weird.'
Traveler reflecting on her whereabouts.

Wildlife
Plant and animal life are generally unique to their habitats. There are numerous habitats throughout South America, but the following are the most important.

AMAZON BASIN RAINFORESTS
Tropical rainforest is the earth's most complex ecosystem. Check out the Amazon: it contains an estimated 50,000 species of higher plants, one-fifth of the world's total. In some of its two-hectare plots, it's possible to find more than 500 tree species; a comparable plot in a midlatitude forest might have three or four. One study found 3000 species of beetle in five small plots and estimated that each tree species supported more than 400 unique animal species. The rainforest canopy is so dense, however, that little to no sunlight penetrates to the forest floor, and nearly all life is found in the trees.

More than 75 monkey species reside in the Amazon, and they're wonderful to spot. Other Amazonian animals include sloths, anteaters, armadillos, tapirs, caiman, pink and grey dolphins, the Amazon manatee and the western hemisphere's greatest feline, the jaguar. Needless to say, the bird-watching is amazing.

The Amazon River, from its inconspicuous source in the Peruvian highlands to its mouth near Belém, Brazil, measures more than 6200km. Its flow is 12 times that of the Mississippi, it carries one-fifth of the world's freshwater and its discharge into the Atlantic every 24 hours equals that of the Thames in a full year.

TROPICAL CLOUD FORESTS
In remote valleys at higher elevations, tropical cloud forests retain clouds that engulf the forest in a fine mist, allowing wonderfully delicate forms of plant life to survive. Cloud-forest trees have low, gnarled growth, dense, small-leafed canopy, and moss-covered branches supporting orchids, ferns and a host of other epiphytes (plants that gather moisture and nutrients without ground roots). Such forests are the homes of rare species such as the woolly tapir, the Andean spectacled bear and the puma. Some cloud forest areas host over 400 species of birds.

HIGH-ALTITUDE GRASSLANDS
Even higher than the cloud forest, the *páramo* is the natural sponge of the Andes and is characterized by a harsh climate, high levels of ultraviolet light and wet, peaty soils. It's an enormously specialized habitat unique to tropical America and is found only from the highlands of Costa Rica to the highlands of northern Peru. Flora of the *páramo* is dominated by hard grasses, cushion plants and small herbaceous plants, and features dense thickets of the *queñoa* tree, which, along with Himalayan pines, share the world-altitude record for trees. Animals of the *páramo* include Andean foxes, deer and *vicuña,* a wild, golden-colored relative of the llama.

CENTRAL ANDEAN REGION
Another unique ecosystem exists between the coast and the *cordillera,* from northern Chile to northern Peru. The coastal Atacama Desert, the

Believe it or not, there are still uncontacted tribes in the Amazon. One of the most notable is the Tageiri, a band of the Ecuadorian Huaorani, which has refused all attempts at contact by the outside world, sometimes with violence.

world's driest, is almost utterly barren in the rain shadow of the Andes. The cold Peru current (also called the Humboldt current) moderates the temperature at this tropical latitude and produces convective fogs (*garúa* or *camanchaca*) that support hillside vegetation (*lomas*) in the coastal ranges.

SAVANNAS

Savannas are vast, low-altitude, primarily treeless tropical and semitropical grasslands. Because of their openness, they can be the best places to observe wildlife in South America. The most famous example is Brazil's Pantanal, which spills over into Bolivia. Other savannas include the Venezuelan *llanos* and, to a lesser extent, the pampas of southern Brazil and Argentina.

TROPICAL DRY FORESTS

Hot areas with well-defined wet and dry seasons support the growth of dry forests. In South America these climatic conditions are mostly found near the coast in the northern part of the continent. Because many of these coastal regions have a dense and growing population, tropical dry forest is a fast-disappearing habitat – only about 1% remains undisturbed. The majestic bottle-trunk *Ceiba* (or kapok) tree is the forest's most definitive species. It has a massively bulging trunk and seasonal white flowers that dangle like lightbulbs from otherwise bare tree branches. Parrots, parrotlets, monkeys and a variety of reptiles inhabit these forests.

MANGROVES

Found in coastal areas of Brazil, Colombia, Ecuador, the Guianas and Venezuela, mangroves are trees with a remarkable ability to grow in salt water. They have a broadly spreading system of intertwining stilt roots to support the tree in unstable sandy or silty soils. Mangrove forests trap sediments and build up a rich organic soil, which in turn supports other plants. Mangrove roots provide a protected habitat for many types of fish, mollusks and crustaceans, while the branches provide nesting areas for sea birds.

National Parks

There are over 200 national parks in South America and a staggering number of provincial parks and private reserves. They are undeniably one of the continent's highlights, covering every terrain imaginable, from tropical rainforest and cloud forest to Andean *páramo* to tropical and temperate coastal regions. The most popular parks have well-developed tourist infrastructures and high-season crowds and are fairly easy to reach. Some parks have only faint trails, basic camping facilities or refuges and, if you're lucky, a park ranger to answer questions. Others are impossible to reach without 4WD transport or a private boat. Maps are generally tough to come by, so if you plan to do any trekking, research the park first and check larger cities for topographical map sources. See Maps in both the South America Directory (p1068) and in individual country directories for information on where to obtain maps.

Environmental Issues

Deforestation – of the Amazon rainforest, the temperate forests of Chile and Argentina, the coastal mangroves and cloud forests of Ecuador, and the Chocó bioregion of pacific Panama, Colombia and Ecuador – is perhaps the single greatest environmental problem facing South America. Oil exploration has opened pristine tracts of Amazon rainforest to colonization and has lead to large-scale toxic spills and the poisoning of rivers and streams. Conservation of Brazil's Pantanal, the largest wetland in the world, may soon take backseat to more profitable industrial projects such as the Bolivia–Brazil natural-gas pipeline, hydroelectric projects, a thermal electric plant, mills and mining. The list goes on, and the best way to help is to study up and get involved. The following websites are great starting points:

Amazon Watch (www.amazonwatch.org)
Ancient Forests International (www.ancientforests.org)
Conservation International (CI; www.conservation.org)
Rainforest Action Network (RAN; www.ran.org)

Argentina

HIGHLIGHTS

- **Buenos Aires** – take in the capital's glorious European buildings, distinctive neighborhoods, fine restaurants, sensual tango culture and throbbing nightlife (p47)
- **El Chaltén** – hike, climb and camp among the Fitz Roy range, home to some of the world's most dramatic mountains (p152)
- **Northwest deserts** – witness the Andean northwest's cactus-dotted deserts, highlighted with painted mountainsides and the lofty Tren a las Nubes (p105)
- **Iguazú Falls** – oooh and aaah at these unbelievable, thundering cascades, which stretch almost 3km long and 70m high (p90)
- **Off the beaten track** – the Valles Calchaquíes, running from Cafayate to Cachi, are some of Argentina's most stunning valleys, boasting striking scenery and picturesque villages (p104)
- **Best journey** – follow in Che Guevara's motorcycle ruts along desolate Ruta 40, the legendary road that winds along the Andean ridge and covers almost the whole of Argentina (p156)

FAST FACTS

- **Area:** 2.8 million sq km (roughly the size of India)
- **Best bargain:** who can beat a large, US$5 grass-fed steak?
- **Best street snack:** *empanadas* (meat, vegetable or cheese turnovers)
- **Budget:** US$25 a day
- **Capital:** Buenos Aires
- **Costs:** hostel US$7, pasta dinner US$3.50, 5hr bus ride US$13
- **Country code:** ☎ 54
- **Famous for:** *gauchos* (cowboys), tango, steak and Maradona
- **Languages:** Spanish; Quechua in the Andean northwest
- **Money:** US$1 = 3 pesos
- **Phrases:** *genial, bárbaro* (cool), *asqueroso* (disgusting), *fiesta/pachanga* (party)
- **Population:** 39 million
- **Time:** GMT minus 3hr
- **Tipping:** 10% in restaurants; leftover change in taxis
- **Visas:** not needed by North American and most European citizens

TRAVEL HINTS

Pack light but for Patagonia bring layers and foul-weather gear. Family photos help chat up the locals.

OVERLAND ROUTES

Argentina has three border crossings each with Bolivia, Paraguay, Brazil and Uruguay. There are many, many border crossings with Chile.

The secret is out: with its gorgeous landscapes, cosmopolitan cities, lively culture and amazingly affordable economy, Argentina is a traveler's paradise. It stretches almost 3500km from Bolivia to the tip of South America, encompassing a wide array of geography and climates, and almost reaches the size of India. Nature-lovers can traverse the Patagonian steppe, climb South America's highest peak, walk among thousands of penguins, and lie on trendy beaches. You'll love the lush Lake District with its glorious lakes and verdant mountains, and revel in Patagonia's glacier-carved landscapes and painted Andean deserts. City slickers will adore fabulous Buenos Aires, full of opportunities to learn Spanish, watch *fútbol* (soccer) games, dance the sexy tango and interact with dynamic *porteños* (people from Buenos Aires). You'll be out shopping for designer clothes at bargain prices and eating the world's best steaks every day while dancing at nightclubs all night long.

Argentina is safe, friendly and wonderfully affordable. And the time to come is now, so get your spirit in gear and prepare to have an unforgettable adventure!

CURRENT EVENTS

The big news is that the economy has been growing at a healthy pace since Argentina's financial meltdown in 2001. The country has paid off its $10 billion debt to the International Monetary Fund (IMF), agriculture exports are rising and unemployment is falling.

Argentina is also coming to terms with its ugly past by finally prosecuting ex-military officers from its dictatorship years for human rights abuses. In 2006, March 24 – the day the Dirty War officially started – was declared a national holiday.

In other news, skeletons of some of the biggest dinosaurs that ever lived have been unearthed in Neuquén province. Huge meat-eaters in Argentina? But of course.

HISTORY
The Good Old Days

Before the Spanish hit the scene, nomadic hunter-gatherers roamed the wilds of ancient Argentina. The Yámana (or Yahgan) gathered shellfish in Patagonia, while on the pampas the Querandí used *boleadoras* (weights on cords) to snag rhea (ostrichlike birds) and guanaco (the llama's cousin). Up in the subtropical northeast, the Guaraní settled down long enough to cultivate maize, while in the arid northwest the Diaguita developed an irrigation system for crops.

In 1536 the Querandí were unfortunate enough to meet pushy Spaniards in search of silver. Like most reasonable people they refused to be treated like doormats, and eventually drove the explorers away to more welcoming Paraguay. (Left behind were cattle and horses, which multiplied and gave rise to the legendary *gaucho* – cowboy). The Spanish were persistent, however, and in 1580 they returned and

managed to establish Buenos Aires, though trade restrictions from Spain limited the new settlement's growth. The northern colonies of Tucumán, Córdoba and Salta, however, thrived by providing mules, cloth and foodstuffs for the booming silver mines of Bolivia. Meanwhile, Spaniards from Chile moved into the Andean Cuyo region, which produced wine and grain.

Cutting the Purse Strings

In 1776 Spain designated the bootlegger township of Buenos Aires as 'capital of the new viceroyalty of the Río de la Plata,' a nod to its strategic port location. A rogue British force, hoping to snag a piece of the trade pie, invaded in 1806 but was given the boot soon after by the rallied settlers. With newfound power, the confident colonists revolted against Spain, which they held a grudge against for the trade restrictions. Complete independence was their reward six years later in 1816.

Despite the unity hatched by independence, the provinces resisted Buenos Aires' authority. Argentina split allegiances between the inhabitants of Buenos Aires (Unitarists) and the country folk (Federalists). A civil war ensued, and the two parties' bloody, vindictive conflicts nearly exhausted the country.

In 1829 Juan Manuel de Rosas came into power as a Federalist, but applied his own brand of Unitarist principles to centralize control in Buenos Aires. He built a large army, created the *mazorca* (a ruthless secret police), institutionalized torture and forced overseas trade through the port city. Finally, in 1852, Justo José de Urquiza (once Rosas' supporter) led a Unitarist army that forced the dictator from power. Urquiza drew up a constitution – still in force today – and became Argentina's first president.

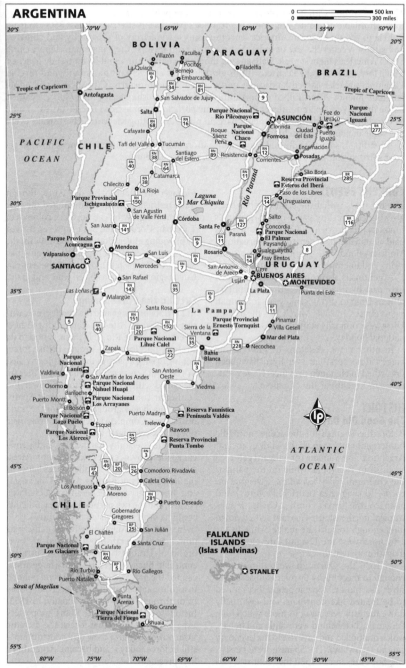

ARGENTINA

The Fleeting Golden Age

Argentina's new laws opened up the country to foreign investment, trade and immigration. In the following decades, sheep, cattle and cereal products were freely exported while Spanish, Italian, French and other European immigrants came in search of a better life. Prosperity arrived at last, and Argentina became one of the richest countries in the world, although much of that wealth belonged to relatively few landowners and urban elite.

This was a tenuous opulence, as global economic fluctuations brought about new foreign trade restrictions that mostly benefited rich producers of wheat, wine and sugar. After the 1880s poor immigrants continued to flood in to work in the port, and nearly doubled Buenos Aires' population to one million residents. The city's face changed: old colonial buildings were torn down, major streets were widened and urban services improved. The industrial sector couldn't absorb all the immigrants and their needs, however, and the gap between rich and poor widened. In 1929 the military took power from an ineffectual civilian government, but an obscure colonel – Juan Domingo Perón – was the first leader to really confront the looming social crisis.

The Peróns – Love 'em or Hate 'em

Today the Peróns have become Argentina's most revered – as well as most despised – political figures. Many people believe that Argentina has never recovered, either economically or spiritually, since Perón's first presidency.

From a minor post in the labor ministry, and with the help of his charismatic soon-to-be wife, Eva Duarte (Evita), Juan Perón won the presidency in 1946. His social welfare and new economic order programs helped the working class, who benefited from improved wages, job security and working conditions.

His heavy control over the country, however, was tinged with fascism: he abused his presidential powers by using excessive intimidation and squelching free press. Dynamic Evita, meanwhile, had her own sometimes vindictive political ends, though she was mostly championed for her charitable work and women's rights campaigns.

Rising inflation and economic difficulties (due especially to a shortage of capital from war-torn Europe) undermined Perón's second presidency in 1952; Evita's death the same year was another blow. After a coup against him in 1955, Perón retreated to Spain to plot his return. The opportunity came almost two decades later when Héctor Cámpora resigned the presidency in 1973. Perón won the elections easily, but his death in mid-1974 sucked the country back into the governmental coups and chaos that had plagued it since his exile. In 1976 military rule prevailed once again, and Argentina entered its darkest hour.

Dirty War (1976–83)

In the late 1960s, when antigovernment sentiment was rife, a left-wing, highly organized Perónist guerrilla group called the Montoneros was formed. The mostly educated, middle-class youths bombed foreign businesses, kidnapped executives for ransom and robbed banks to finance their armed struggle and to spread their social messages. On March 24, 1976, a military bloodless coup led by General Jorge Videla took control of the Argentine government and ushered in a period of terror and brutality. Euphemistically called the Process of National Reorganization (aka El Proceso), this movement became an orgy of state-sponsored violence and anarchy, and their primary target was the Montoneros.

Some estimate that up to 30,000 people died in the infamous Guerra Sucia (Dirty War).

Zero tolerance was the theme: the dictatorship did not distinguish between the revolutionary guerrillas or those who simply expressed reservations about the dictatorship's indiscriminate brutality. To 'disappear' meant to be detained, tortured and probably killed, without legal process. Ironically, the Dirty War ended only when the Argentine military attempted a real military operation, the repossession of the Islas Malvinas (Falkland Islands).

(Today, Argentina has slowly come to grips with its past by finally putting military figures from the dictatorship on trial. To remember the tragedy and prevent its repetition, the date March 24 was made into a state holiday in 2006, and given a theme: 'Nunca Mas' – Never Again. This is exactly 30 years after the Dirty War started, but better late than never.)

Falklands War

Argentina's economy continued to decline during military rule and eventually collapsed into chaos. El Proceso was coming undone.

In late 1981 General Leopoldo Galtieri took the presidential hot seat. To stay in power amid a faltering economy, a desperate Galtieri played the nationalist card and launched an invasion in April 1982 to dislodge the British from the Islas Malvinas (Falkland Islands).

The brief occupation of the Malvinas, claimed by Argentina for 150 years, unleashed a wave of nationalist euphoria that lasted about a week. Then the Argentines realized that iron-clad British prime minister Margaret

Thatcher was not a wallflower, especially when she had political troubles of her own. Britain fought back, sending a naval contingent to set things straight, and Argentina's mostly teenaged, ill-trained and poorly motivated forces surrendered after 74 days. The military, stripped of its reputation, finally withdrew from government. In 1983 Argentina handed Raúl Alfonsín the presidency.

Argentina Today

Alfonsín brought democracy back to Argentina and solved some territorial disputes with Chile. He also managed to curb inflation a bit, but couldn't pull the long-struggling country back onto its feet again.

Carlos Menem, president from 1989 to 1999, brought brief prosperity to Argentina by selling off many private industries and borrowing heavily. He also practically stopped inflation in its tracks by pegging the peso with the US dollar, but this was only a quick fix. After a few years the peso became so overvalued that Argentine goods weren't competitive on the global market. Toward the end of Menem's rule unemployment spiraled steadily upwards.

In 1999 Fernando de la Rúa was sworn into office. He inherited an almost bankrupt government which witnessed yet another economic downturn, even higher unemployment and a widespread lack of public confidence. By 2001 the economy teetered on the brink of collapse, and in December de la Rúa resigned. The country went through three more

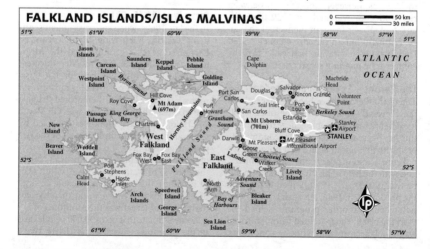

FALKLAND ISLANDS/ISLAS MALVINAS

presidents within two weeks before finally putting Eduardo Duhalde in charge. Duhalde devalued the peso in January 2002, defaulting on US$140 billion in debt.

Since then, with the peso hovering at around three to the US dollar, things have settled down, and there's even a positive mood. Argentine exports are up and some of the country's debts have been paid off. In May 2003 the left-leaning Néstor Kirchner was handed the presidential reins and has managed to keep the economy growing over the past few years. For Argentines, the standard of living is still one of Latin America's highest, and while times are still tough there's definitely optimism in the air.

ISLAS MALVINAS (FALKLAND ISLANDS)
☎ 500 / pop 2500

The sheep boom in Tierra del Fuego and Patagonia owes its origins to the Islas Malvinas (to the Argentines) or Falkland Islands (to the British). Very little transpired on these islands until the mid-19th-century wool boom in Europe, when the Falkland Islands Company (FIC) became the islands' largest landholder. The population, mostly stranded mariners and *gauchos* (cowboys), grew rapidly with the arrival of English and Scottish immigrants.

Argentina has laid claim to the islands since 1833, but it wasn't until 1982 that Argentine president Leopoldo Galtieri decided that reclaiming the islands would unite his country behind him. However, English Prime Minister Margaret Thatcher (who was also suffering in the polls) didn't hesitate in striking back, thoroughly humiliating Argentina. The Falkland Islands War succeeded in severing all diplomatic ties between the two nations – and today, despite a few amends, relations remain chilly.

What is there about the Falklands that might intrigue the intrepid traveler? Bays, inlets, estuaries and beaches create a tortuous, attractive coastline that is home to abundant wildlife. Striated and crested caracaras, cormorants, oystercatchers, snowy sheathbills, sheldgeese and a plethora of penguins – Magellanic, rockhopper, macaroni, gentoo and king – share top billing with elephant seals, sea lions, fur seals, killer whales and some five species of dolphins.

Stanley, the capital, is an assemblage of brightly painted metal-clad houses and is a good place to throw down a few pints and listen to island lore. 'Camp' – as the rest of the island is known – is home to settlements that began as company towns (hamlets where coastal shipping could collect wool) and now provide lodging and a chance to experience pristine nature and wildlife.

The best time to visit is from October to March, when migratory birds and mammals return to beaches and headlands. For more information in England, contact **Falkland House** (☎ 020-7222-2542; www.falklandislands.com; 14 Broadway, Westminster, London SW1H 0BH). For general information see Lonely Planet's *Falkland Islands* guidebook.

Information

Everyone entering the Falkland Islands needs an onward ticket, proof of sufficient funds (credit cards are fine) and prearranged accommodations for the first few nights. Stanley's **Visitors Centre** (☎ 22215; www.tourism.org.fk) is at the public jetty on Ross Rd.

Pounds sterling and US dollars in cash or traveler's checks are readily accepted, but the exchange rate for US currency is low. Visa and MasterCard are widely accepted. The only bank is Standard Chartered Bank in Stanley; ATMs do not exist. In peak season, expect to spend US$70 to US$90 per day.

Getting There & Around

Unless you're on a cruise ship, you'll arrive by air.

LANChile heads to Mt Pleasant (near Stanley) once weekly from Santiago, Chile, via Puerto Montt and Punta Arenas. Chilean airline **Aerovías DAP** (www.dap.cl) offers charter flights. There are also regular flights from RAF Brize Norton, in Oxfordshire, England.

Several tour operators run day trips to East Falkland settlements; check with the tourist office in Stanley.

ARGENTINA

THE CULTURE
The National Psyche
Argentines have a worldwide reputation for being spoiled, stuck-up and egotistical. They think they're better than anyone else, and that they belong in Europe rather than at the tail end of a third-world continent like South America. They undergo more cosmetic surgery and psychoanalysis than anyone else in the world. It's no wonder people make fun of them.

Frankly, most Argentines just don't fit this profile. And this stereotype usually refers to *porteños*. While a huge number of people do live in the capital and its suburbs, a full two-thirds live in the rest of Argentina, where attitudes and egos are more modest. In fact, many folks outside the capital don't even *like porteños*. And, not all *porteños* are sniffy aristocratic wannabes – quite a few, as you'll find out, are friendly, helpful and curious about where you come from.

It's not hard to see how Argentines got their reputation. They live in a fabulous country with vast natural resources, a gorgeous capital and rich culture. Yet they've seen their country – one that was once one of the richest in the world – collapse into almost third-world status asking for financial handouts. Even today, with a recovering economy, Argentines are cautiously optimistic about the future – and if they can maintain their proud spirit, more power to them.

Lifestyle
Despite a recent economic uplift, almost 50% of Argentines are still considered to be living in poverty. To save resources and maintain family ties, several generations often live under one roof.

Families are pretty close, and Sundays are often reserved for the family *asado* (barbecue). Friends are also highly valued and Argentines love to go out in large groups. They'll give each other cheek kisses every time they meet – even introduced strangers, men and women alike, will get a kiss.

Argentines like to stay out *late;* dinner is often at 10pm, and finishing dessert around midnight on a weekend is the norm. Bars and discos often stay open until 6am or so, even in smaller cities.

The important culture of mate is very visible in Argentina; you'll see folks sipping this bitter herb drink at home, work and play. They carry their gourds and hot-water thermoses while traveling and on picnics. Consider yourself honored if you're invited to partake in a mate-drinking ritual.

Population
About 90% of the country's population lives in urban areas. Argentina's literacy rate is over 97%.

Nineteenth-century immigration created a large population with feisty Italian or Spanish blood, though many other European nationalities are represented. Fresh mixes include Japanese, Koreans and Chinese (rarer outside the capital), and other South American nationalities such as Peruvians, Bolivians, Paraguayans and Uruguayans.

The major indigenous groups (thought to make up less than 2% of Argentina's population) are the Quechua of the northwest and the Mapuche of Patagonia, and smaller groups of Guaraní, Matacos, Tobas and Wichi inhabit other northern pockets. Around 15% of the country's population is *mestizo* (of mixed indigenous and European ancestry); most *mestizo* reside up north.

SPORTS
Rugby, tennis, basketball, polo, golf, motor racing, skiing and cycling are popular sports, but soccer is an obsession. The national team has twice won the World Cup, once in 1978 and again in 1986, when Diego Maradona (Argentina's bad-boy, rags-to-riches soccer star) surreptitiously punched in a goal to beat England in the quarterfinals. If you get a chance to see a *fútbol* game, take it. The game between River Plate and Boca Juniors is a classic match not to be missed, as the rivalry between the two teams is intense (see p68).

RELIGION
Over 90% of Argentina's population is Roman Catholic, but there are other popular beliefs. Spiritualism and veneration of the dead, for instance, are widespread: visitors to Recoleta and Chacarita cemeteries will see endless processions of pilgrims communing with icons like Juan and Evita Perón, Carlos Gardel and psychic Madre María. Cult beliefs like the Difunta Correa of San Juan province attract hundreds of thousands of fans; evangelical Protestantism is growing; and what is probably South America's largest Islamic mosque was built in Palermo. Buenos Aires is also home to one of the largest Jewish populations outside Israel.

ARTS
Literature
Argentina's biggest literary name is Jorge Luis Borges, famous for his short stories and poetry. Borges created alternative-reality worlds and elaborate time circles with vivid and imaginative style; check out his surreal compendiums *Labyrinths* or *Ficciones*. Internationally acclaimed Julio Cortázar wrote about seemingly normal people, while using strange metaphors and whimsical descriptions of peoples' unseen realities. His big novel is *Hopscotch*, which requires more than one reading.

Ernesto Sábato is known for his intellectual novels and essays, many of which explore the chasm between good and evil. Sábato's notable works include *On Heroes and Tombs*, popular with Argentine youth in the '60s, and the startling essay *Nunca Más,* which describes Dirty War atrocities. Other famous Argentine writers include Manuel Puig *(Kiss of the Spider Woman)*, Adolfo Bioy Casares *(The Invention of Morel)*, Osvaldo Soriano *(Shadows)* and Silvina Ocampo (poetry and children's stories).

Juan José Saer penned poetry, short stories and books, including complex crime novels. Novelist and journalist Rodrigo Frésan wrote the best-selling *The History of Argentina* and the psychedelic *Kensington Gardens.*

Cinema
In the past, Argentine cinema has achieved international stature through such directors as Luis Puenzo (*The Official Story*, 1984) and Héctor Babenco *(Kiss of the Spider Woman,* 1985*)*.

More recent notable works by Argentine directors include Fabián Bielinsky's witty and entertaining *Nueve reinas* (Nine Queens; 2000), Lucrecia Martel's dysfunctional-families *La Ciénaga* (The Swamp; 2001) and Pablo Trapero's gritty *El bonaerense* (2002). Carlos Sorín's *Historias mínimas* (Minimal Stories; 2002) is a rich yet minimalist character study.

Juan José Campanella's *El hijo de la novia* (The Son of the Bride) was Oscar nominated for best foreign-language film in 2002, while Martel's *La niña santa* (The Holy Girl; 2004) won acclaim for its take on sexual awakening. Solín's *Bonbón, el perro* (Bonbón, the Dog; 2004) is a captivating tale of man's best friend and changing fortunes. And in 2005 Juan Diego Solanas won top prize at the Stockholm Film Festival for his well-executed and mature *Nordeste* (Northeast), which tackles difficult social issues like child trafficking.

Music
Legendary figures like Carlos Gardel and Astor Piazzolla popularized tango music, and contemporaries such as Susana Rinaldi, Adriana Varela and Osvaldo Pugliese carry on the tradition. Recent tango 'fusion' groups include Gotan Project and BajoFondo Tango Club.

Folk musicians Mercedes Sosa, Leon Gieco, Atahualpa Yupanqui and Los Chalchaleros are popular performers.

Rock star Charly García is Argentina's best-known musician, but past popular groups have included Fito Páez, Los Piojos Babasónicos, Divididos and Los Fabulosos Cadillacs (who in 1998 won a Grammy for best alternative Latin rock group).

Contemporary Argentine musical artists include wacky Bersuit Vergarabat, alternative Catupecu Machu, experimental Los Natas, versatile Gazpacho and the multitalented Kevin Johansen.

Theater & Dance
Buenos Aires' monumental Teatro Colón is one of the world's finest acoustic facilities, offering classical music and ballet, among other things. The capital also has a vibrant theater community, and there's live theater in the provinces as well.

Tango is Argentina's sultry dance, thought to have started in Buenos Aires' bordellos in the 1880s. It wasn't mainstream until it was filtered through Europe, finally hitting high popularity in Argentina around 1913. Carlos Gardel is tango's most famous songbird.

Visual Arts
Well-known painters include Xul Solar, who did busy, Klee-inspired dreamscapes; Guillermo Kuitca, who experimented with cartographic illustrations; and Víctor Hugo Quiroga, who concentrated on provincial topics. Benito Quinquela Martín depicted the hard-working laborers on docks of Buenos Aires' La Boca neighborhood. Painter, poet, songwriter and '60s icon, the multifaceted Jorge de la Vega dabbled in mixed media and geometric abstracts.

Famous sculptors include Graciela Sacco, who worked in audio, video and with life's common objects; Rogelio Yrurtia, whose art chronicles the struggles of the working people; and Alberto Heredia, who enjoyed ridiculing solemn official public art.

Buenos Aires' Galerías Pacífico, on Av Florida, has restored ceiling murals by Antonio Berni and Lino Spilimbergo, two European-influenced artists who also dealt with political themes. For street art keep an eye out for creative stencils (www.bsasstencil.com.ar) and graffiti (www.bagraff.com).

ENVIRONMENT
The Land

Argentina is huge – it's the world's eighth-largest country, after India. It stretches almost 3500km north to south and encompasses a wide range of environments and terrain.

The glorious Andes line the edge of northwest Argentina, where only hardy cactus and scrubby vegetation survive. Here, soaring peaks and salt lakes give way to the more subtropical lowland provinces of Salta and Santiago del Estero. To the south, the hot and scenic Tucumán, Catamarca and La Rioja provinces harbor agriculture and viticulture.

Drier thornlands of the western Andean foothills give way to the forked river valleys and hot lowlands of Formosa and Chaco provinces. Rainfall is heaviest to the northeast, where swampy forests and subtropical savannas thrive. Densely forested Misiones province contains the awe-inspiring Iguazú Falls. Rivers streaming off these immense cataracts lead to the alluvial grasslands of Corrientes and Entre Ríos provinces. Summers here are very hot and humid.

The west-central Cuyo region (Mendoza, San Juan and San Luis provinces) pumps out most of Argentina's world-class wine vintages. Central Argentina has the mountainous Córdoba and richly agricultural Santa Fe provinces. The Pampas is a flat, rich plain full of agriculture and livestock. Along the Atlantic Coast are many popular and attractive beaches.

Patagonia spans the lower third of Argentina. Most of this region is flat and arid, but toward the Andes rainfall is abundant and supports the lush Lake District. The southern Andes boasts huge glaciers, while down on the flats cool steppes pasture large flocks of sheep.

The Tierra del Fuego archipelago mostly belongs to Chile. Its northern half resembles the Patagonian steppe, while dense forests and glaciers cover the mountainous southern half. The climate can be relatively mild, even in winter (though temperatures can also drop below freezing). The weather in this region is very changeable year round.

Wildlife

The famous Pampas is mostly sprawling grasslands and home to many birds of prey and introduced plant species; most of the region's remaining native vegetation survives up north along the Río Paraná. Also in the northern swamplands live the odd-looking capybara (the world's largest rodent), swamp deer, the alligator-like caiman and many large migratory birds.

The main forested areas of Argentina are in subtropical Misiones province and on the eastward-sloping Andes from Neuquén province south, where southern beech species and coniferous woodlands predominate; look for the strange monkey-puzzle tree (Araucaria araucana or pehuén) around the Lake District. In the higher altitudes of the Andes and in much of Patagonia, pasture grasses are sparse. Northern Andean saline lakes harbor pink flamingos, and on the Patagonian steppe you're likely to see guanacos, rheas, Patagonian hares, armadillos, crested caracaras and gray foxes. Pumas and condors live in southern Andean foothills, but sightings are rare.

Coastal Patagonia, especially around Península Valdés, supports dense and viewable concentrations of marine fauna, including southern right whales, sea lions, southern elephant seals, orcas and Magellanic penguins.

National Parks

Argentina's national parks protect over three and a half million hectares (about 1.25% of the country's land) and have incredibly varied environments. Many outdoor-oriented cities have their own national park information office, and in Buenos Aires you can visit **Administración de Parques Nacionales** (☎ 4312-0783; www.parquesnacionales.gov.ar; Av Santa Fe 690).

Some of Argentina's best national parks:

Parque Nacional Iguazú (p90) World-renowned for its waterfalls.

Parque Nacional Los Alerces (p143) Site of ancient *alerce* (false larch) forests.

Parque Nacional Los Glaciares (p156) Awesome for its glaciers and alpine towers.

Parque Nacional Nahuel Huapi (p139) Offers vivid alpine scenery.
Parque Nacional Tierra del Fuego (p165) Exceptional beech forests and fauna.
Parque Provincial Aconcagua (p127) Boasts the continent's highest peak.
Reserva Faunística Península Valdés (p148) Famous for coastal fauna.
Reserva Provincial Esteros del Iberá (p82) Home to swamp-dwelling wildlife.

Environmental Issues

Argentina doesn't have a huge rainforest to destroy, but does claim some environmental problems. Rapid growth in some cities (El Calafate comes to mind), related to the country's tourist boom, is seldom thought out well enough. Air and noise pollution is always a problem in Buenos Aires and other large cities. Some rural areas suffer soil erosion from improper land use or flood control, as well as river pollution from pesticide or fertilizer runoff.

Argentina has lost about two-thirds of its forests in the last century. Practically all of the pampas is now cattle grazing land, and the Patagonian steppe region suffers from overgrazing and desertification. Some celebrities, such as Kristine McDivitt Tompkins (ex-CEO of clothing company Patagonia) and Ted Turner, have bought huge tracts in Patagonia with the idea of protecting much of the land. For more information check www.vidasilvestre.org.ar and www.patagonialandtrust.com.

In 2006 folks in Gualeguaychú protested against two paper mills being built on the Uruguay River, worried about possible area contamination. Another recent environmental issue is the proposed Pascua Lama gold mine along the Chilean border; though most of the mining would be in Chile, the waste dump would be in Argentina.

TRANSPORTATION

GETTING THERE & AWAY
Air

Cosmopolitan Buenos Aires is linked to most of the capitals in South America.

Argentina's main international airport is Buenos Aires' Aeropuerto Internacional Ministro Pistarini (known as Ezeiza). Aeroparque Jorge Newbery (known simply as Aeroparque)

> **DEPARTURE TAX**
>
> International passengers leaving from Ezeiza are required to pay a US$18 departure tax in either pesos or US dollars. Other airports such as El Calafate and Ushuaia also charge departure taxes.

is the capital's domestic airport. For information on getting into town from the airports, see p48. A few other Argentine cities have 'international' airports, but they mostly serve domestic destinations.

Boat

Ferries link Buenos Aires to several points in Uruguay. For more information, see p69.

Bus

It's possible to cross into Argentina from Bolivia, Paraguay, Brazil, Uruguay and Chile. See (p36) for border cities.

GETTING AROUND
Air

The airline situation in Argentina is in constant flux; minor airlines go in and out of business regularly. Ticket prices are unpredictable, though they are always highest during holiday times (late December–February and July). Certain flights in extensive Patagonia are comparable to bus fares when you consider time saved.

Some airlines have adopted a two-tier system where foreigners pay a much higher fare than Argentine residents. Unless you're legally living in Argentina and can prove it, you'll probably pay a higher price.

The major airlines are **Aerolíneas Argentinas** (AR; www.aerolinasargentinas.com), **Austral** (www.austral.com.ar), AR's domestic partner, and **LADE** (www.lade.com.ar), the air force's passenger service, which serves mostly Patagonian destinations with cheap but infrequent flights. There's a list of principal airline offices, both international and domestic, in the Buenos Aires section (see p69), and addresses of regional offices appear in each city entry.

There may be special air-pass deals available when you plan to travel. It's best to check with a travel agency specializing in Latin America, since deals come and go regularly. One theme with these passes is that they need to be purchased outside Argentina (sometimes

ARGENTINA

FLIGHT WARNING

Be aware that domestic flights in Argentina can often arrive late, and in high season many flights (especially to Patagonia) book up early. The occasional strike can dampen your travel plans, so if it's important you arrive on time (like to Ushuaia, for an Antarctic cruise) plan on getting to your destination a day earlier.

---

in conjunction with an international ticket), you need to be a foreign resident to use them, and they're often limited to travel within a certain time period.

For more information, see p1081.

Bicycle

Cycling around the country has become popular among travelers. Beautiful routes in the north include the highway from Tucumán to Tafí del Valle, the direct road from Salta to San Salvador de Jujuy, and the Quebrada de Cafayate. The Lake District also has scenic roads, like the Siete Lagos route. Drawbacks include the wind (which can slow progress to a crawl in Patagonia) and reckless motorists. Less-traveled secondary roads carrying little traffic are good alternatives. Rental bikes are common in tourist areas and a great way to get around.

For information on biking around South America see p1082.

Bus

Long-distance buses are modern, fast, comfortable and usually the best budget way to get around Argentina. Journeys over six hours or so will either have pit stops for refreshments or serve drinks, sweet snacks and sometimes simple meals. All have bathrooms, though they're often grungy (bring toilet paper). The most luxurious companies offer more expensive *coche cama* recliners (overnight trips save hotel costs), but regular buses are usually fine, even on long trips.

Bus terminals usually have kiosks, restrooms, cheap eats and luggage storage. In small towns you'll want to be aware of the timetable of your next bus out (and possibly buy a ticket), since some routes run infrequently. During holiday periods like January, February or July, buy advance tickets.

Car

Renting a car in Argentina is not cheap, but can get you away from the beaten path and start you on some adventures. Figure US$50 per day average for the cheapest model with some free mileage (consider partnering up with others to share the costs). The minimum driving age in Argentina is 18, but car rental offices require drivers to be at least 21.

Forget driving in Buenos Aires; traffic is unforgivable and parking is a headache, while public transport is great. See Legal Matters (p170) for dealing with police.

The Automobile Club Argentina (ACA) has offices, service stations and garages in major cities. If you're a member of an overseas affiliate (like AAA in the United States) you may be able to obtain vehicular services and discounts on maps (bring your card). ACA's main headquarters is in **Buenos Aires** (☎ 4802-6061; www.aca.org.ar; Av del Libertador 1850, Palermo).

Hitchhiking

Good places for a pickup are gas stations on the outskirts of large cities, where truckers refuel their vehicles. In Patagonia, distances are great and vehicles few, so expect long waits and carry snack foods and warm, windproof clothing. Carry extra water as well, especially in the desert north. Realize that many cars are full with families.

Haciendo dedo is fairly safe for women in Argentina; however, don't do it alone, don't get in a car with two men and don't do it at night. There is also nothing especially unsafe

---

GETTING TO CHILE

For most travelers, crossing the border from Argentina into Chile is a relatively quick, easy procedure. Usually the same bus takes you right through and there are no fees. Border outposts are open daylight hours; Dorotea (near Puerto Natales) is open 24 hours in summer. Just have your papers in order, don't take anything illegal (including fresh food) and you should be golden. And try to get your ticket as soon as possible, as Chile-bound buses often fill up quickly. Note that you do have to get off and on the bus for passport checks on both sides. For information on crossing the border *from* Chile, see p417.

---

about hitchhiking in rural Argentina, but don't hitchhike in Buenos Aires.

Having a sign will improve your chances for a pickup, especially if it says something like *visitando Argentina de Canada* (visiting Argentina from Canada), rather than just a destination.

For good information see www.autostop argentina.com.ar (in Spanish).

Local Transportation

Even small towns have good bus systems. A few cities use magnetic fare cards, which are usually bought at kiosks. Pay attention to placards indicating an ultimate destination, since identically numbered buses may cover slightly different routes.

Taxis have digital-readout meters that start at about US$0.75. Tipping isn't expected, but you can leave extra change. *Remises* are taxis that you book over the phone, or regular cars without meters; any hotel or restaurant should be able to call one for you. They're considered more secure than taxis since an established company sends them out. Ask the fare in advance.

Buenos Aires is the only city with a subway system, known as Subte.

Train

The British-built train system in Argentina is not as widespread as it once was, and currently bus travel is faster, more flexible and more reliable. There are long-distance services from Buenos Aires to Rosario and the Atlantic beach resorts, and from Viedma to Bariloche. Buenos Aires and Rosario have commuter routes to their suburbs.

The very scenic, famous and expensive *Tren a las Nubes* chugs from Salta, in the north, toward Chile. In Patagonia there are a couple of short touristy train rides (both narrow-gauge) such as *La Trochita,* which originates in Esquel or El Maitén, and *El Tren del Fin del Mundo,* in Ushuaia.

BUENOS AIRES

☎ 011 / pop 13 million (greater BA)

Believe everything you've heard – Buenos Aires is one of South America's most electrifying cities, graced with European architecture, atmospheric neighborhoods and bustling nightlife. It has the sophistication of a fine-cut diamond, the charm of an unshaved Casanova, the mind of a frenzied lunatic and the attitude of a celebrity supermodel. And BA's passionate residents are prideful and haughty, but once you get to know them they'll bend over backwards to help.

Since Argentina's economic collapse in 2002, BA has quelled doubters by bouncing back and creating a renaissance that's keeping the city aglow. Argentines now find the 'outside' world prohibitively expensive, and have turned their energy inwards – with impressive results. Loads of new restaurants, boutiques and businesses have popped up in the last few years, not only to deal with the locals and their pesos, but also to cater to the influx of foreign tourists bringing hard currency and taking advantage of incredible bargains.

Yet to every great metropolis is a poor side. Cracked sidewalks, ubiquitous graffiti and rough edges – even in the wealthiest neighborhoods – speak volumes about this city. Poverty and beggars exist, and at night the *cartoneros* (garbage recyclers) appear. There's a deep melancholy here – an acknowledgement of Argentina's riches coupled with the despair of not realizing its potential. The undeniable reality is that BA comes with a third-world twist.

So throw yourself into this heady mix and hold on tight, 'cause you're going for a wild, fun ride. And don't be surprised if you fall in love with this amazing and sexy place – you won't be the first, or the last.

ORIENTATION

Buenos Aires is a very large city, but most sights are within the compact downtown area. Interesting surrounding *barrios* (neighborhoods) are easily accessed via public transport. The major thoroughfare is broad Av 9 de Julio; all north–south streets (except for Av 9 de Julio) change names at Av Rivadavia.

DON'T MISS...

- strolling busy Av Florida
- savoring a steak dinner
- enjoying a tango show
- exploring Recoleta cemetery
- experiencing a *fútbol* game
- shopping at San Telmo's antiques fair

GETTING INTO TOWN

If you fly into Buenos Aires from outside Argentina, you'll probably land at **Ezeiza Airport** (☎ 5480-6111; www.aa2000.com.ar), about 35km south of the city center. Ezeiza is clean and modern and has food services, shops, (expensive) internet access and luggage storage.

The best way into town is to take the frequent, comfortable shuttle service by **Manuel Tienda León** (MTL; US$8, 40 minutes); its booth is just outside customs. For taxis avoid MTL's hiked-up prices and head behind it to the city taxi booth, which charges around US$18 (including tolls). *Do not* go with just any taxi driver; make sure you find the booth and pay up front. Hard-core penny-pinchers can take bus 86 (US$0.75, 1½ hours) from outside the Aerolíneas Argentinas (domestic) terminal, which is a short walk away.

If you need to change money, avoid the *cambios* (exchange houses) as their rates are bad. Instead, head to the nearby Banco de la Nación, which has fair rates and should be open 24 hours.

Most domestic flights land at **Aeroparque Jorge Newbery** (Map p49; ☎ 5480-6111; www.aa2000.com.ar), only a few kilometers north of the city center. Manuel Tienda León shuttles to the city center cost US$3 (15 minutes). Buses to the center include the 33 and 45; take them going south (to the right as you leave the airport; US$0.30). Taxis cost about US$5.

Shuttle transfers from Ezeiza to Aeroparque cost US$8.50.

Retiro bus station (Map pp52–3) is about 1km north of the city center. Hundreds of BA's local bus lines converge here; outside, it's a seething mass and not to be figured out after a 14-hour bus ride. You can take the Subte (subway) if your destination is near a Subte stop, or seek out the 24-hour information kiosk (at the south end of the station) for help with bus lines. Taxis are cheap; try to get one marked 'radio taxi' on the doors. The tourist information office (look for it under bus counter 105) is only open 7:30am to 1pm Monday to Saturday.

The *microcentro* (city center; north of Av de Mayo and east of Av 9 de Julio) is the heart of BA's downtown bustle. To the north are chic Recoleta, Barrio Norte and Palermo, while to the south lie the working-class neighborhoods of San Telmo and La Boca. The waterside *barrio* Puerto Madero, with its modernized brick warehouses and promenades, lies east of downtown.

For help getting around check out Lonely Planet's *Buenos Aires* map.

INFORMATION
Bookstores

ABC (Map pp52-3; Maipú 866) English and German books, including Lonely Planet guides, are available here.

El Ateneo (Map pp52-3; cnr Av Florida 340) Has some books in English. There's another branch at Av Santa Fe 1860.

Walrus Books (Map pp52-3; Estados Unidos 617; ☽ closed Mon) Used books in English; run by an American. Buys books in excellent condition.

Cultural Centers

Biblioteca Lincoln (Map pp52-3; ☎ 5382-1528; www.bcl.edu.ar; Maipú 672) English-language books, newspapers and magazines; to check out materials must join up (US$23 per year).

Centro Cultural Borges (Map pp52-3; ☎ 5008-8011; www.ccborges.org.ar; San Martín cnr Via-monte) Dance classes and art exhibits of all kinds, plus plenty more.

Centro Cultural Recoleta (Map pp52-3; ☎ 4803-1040; www.centroculturalrecoleta.org; Junín 1930) Inexpensive exhibitions, theater, classes etc.

Centro Cultural Ricardo Rojas (Map pp52-3; ☎ 4954-5521; www.rojas.uba.ar in Spanish; Av Corrientes 2038) Zillions of inexpensive, art-oriented classes.

Centro Cultural San Martín (Map pp52-3; ☎ 4374-1251; www.ccgsm.gov.ar; Sarmiento 1551) Inexpensive galleries, theater, lectures, films and workshops.

Emergency

Ambulance ☎ 107
Fire ☎ 107
Police ☎ 101
Rape Crisis Line ☎ 4981-6882, 4958-4291
Tourist Police (Map pp52-3; ☎ 4346-5748, 0800-999-5000; Av Corrientes 436; ☽ 24hr) Provides interpreters and helps crime victims.

Immigration Offices

Immigration (Map pp52-3; ☎ 4317-0200; www.migraciones.gov.ar; Av Antártida Argentina 1355; ☽ 8am-1pm Mon-Fri)

Internet Access

Internet access is everywhere and connections are relatively fast. Charges run about US50¢ per hour.

Medical Services

Most of BA's hospitals have English-speaking staff; call for appointments.

British Hospital (www.hospitalbritanico.org.ar) Perdriel (Map pp52-3; ☎ 4304-1081; Perdriel 74); Marcello T de Alvear (Map pp52-3 ☎ 4812-0040; Marcello T de Alvear 1573)

Hospital Municipal Juan Fernández (Map pp56-7; ☎ 4808-2650; Cerviño 3356)

Money

The 2001 peso crash stimulated a gray market for US dollars. You may hear people on pedes-trian Av Florida call out '*cambio, cambio,*' but it's wiser to change money at a bank or *cambio* (exchange house) – scams and counterfeit bills do exist.

Some banks won't change less than US$100 and may require ID. *Cambios* have slightly poorer exchange rates, but are usually much quicker and have fewer limitations. US dollars are accepted at many retail establishments at a pretty fair rate.

Traveler's checks are very hard to cash (try exchange houses rather than banks) and incur bad exchange rates; one exception is **American Express** (Map pp52-3; Arenales 707). ATMs are commonplace. Visa and MasterCard holders might be able to get cash advances, but ask your bank before traveling.

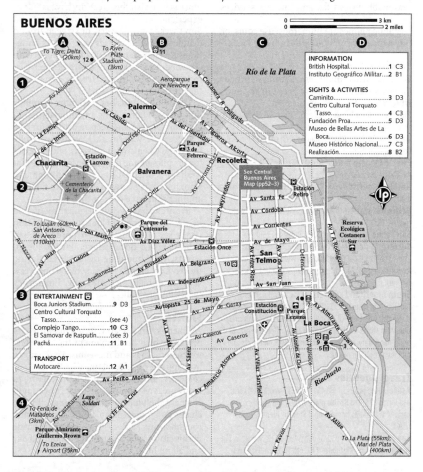

BUENOS AIRES

INFORMATION
British Hospital.......................**1** C3
Instituto Geográfico Militar....**2** B1

SIGHTS & ACTIVITIES
Caminito...............................**3** D3
Centro Cultural Torquato
Tasso.................................**4** C3
Fundación Proa......................**5** D3
Museo de Bellas Artes de La
Boca...................................**6** D3
Museo Histórico Nacional......**7** C3
Realización...........................**8** B2

ENTERTAINMENT
Boca Juniors Stadium...........**9** D3
Centro Cultural Torquato
Tasso..............................(see 4)
Complejo Tango..................**10** C3
El Samovar de Rasputin........(see 3)
Pachá..................................**11** B1

TRANSPORT
Motocare.............................**12** A1

ARGENTINA

Post

Correo Postal Internacional (Map pp52-3; ☎ 4891-9191; www.correoargentino.com.ar; Av Antártida Argentina) Near Retiro bus station. For international parcels 2kg to 20kg; website has prices. Bring open box, contents must be checked; boxes sold here.

FedEx (Map pp52-3; ☎ 0810-333-3339; www.fedex.com; Maipú 753) Several branches.

Main post office (Map pp52-3; ☎ 4316-3000; Sarmiento 151) Many branches; parcels under 2kg accepted.

Telephone

The easiest way to make a call is from a *locutorio* (telephone office), where you enter a booth and make calls in a safe, quiet environment. Costs are comparable to street telephones and you don't need change. Most *locutorios* offer reasonably priced fax and internet services as well.

Public phones are numerous; use coins, or buy a magnetic phone card from any kiosk.

Tourist Information

Buenos Aires' many small tourist offices (www.bue.gov.ar) are spread out in key tourist locations throughout the city.

Florida tourist kiosk (Map pp52-3; cnr Avs Florida & Diagonal Roque Sáenz Peña)

Galerías Pacífico kiosk (Map pp52-3; cnr Avs Florida & Córdoba, 2nd fl)

Puerto Madero tourist kiosk (Map pp52-3; Av Alicia Moreau de Justo, dique 4)

Recoleta tourist kiosk (Map pp52-3; cnr Av Quintana & RM Ortiz)

Retiro bus station (Map pp52-3; suite L83, under bus counter 105)

San Telmo kiosk (Map pp52-3; Defensa 1250)

Secretaría de Turismo de la Nación (Map pp52-3; ☎ 4312-2232, 0800-555-0016; www.turismo.gov.ar; Av Santa Fe 883) Mostly info on Argentina but helps with BA.

South American Explorers (www.saexplorers.org) Membership costs US$50 (US$80 for couples; 20% student discount). Great source of South American travel information. Also stores luggage, receives mail, offers internet and wi-fi, has library with book exchange, puts on events and maintains bulletin board.

Travel Agencies

Asatej (Map pp52-3; ☎ 4114-7566; www.asatej.com; Av Florida 835, 3rd fl) This place is busy but cheap; come early or wait. Sells International Student Identity Cards (ISIC).

Say Hueque (Map pp52-3; ☎ 5199-2517; www.sayhueque.com; Viamonte 749, 6th fl) Friendly, excellent service. This place mostly books adventure trips for backpackers around Argentina, but also books BA activities like tango shows.

Tangol (Map pp52-3; ☎ 4312-7276; www.tangol.com; Av Florida 971, suite 31) Organizes adventurous activities such as skydiving, *estancia* (ranch) visits, helicopter flights and night tours of BA. Also takes travelers to *fútbol* games.

DANGERS & ANNOYANCES

Petty crime certainly exists in Buenos Aires, as it does in any big metropolis. In general, however, BA is pretty safe. You can comfortably walk around at all hours of the night in many places, even as a lone woman (people stay out very late, and there's often other pedestrians on the streets). Truth be told, most tourists who visit this great city have fabulous experiences – but they're travel smart and don't wear fancy jewelry, or stagger around drunk with their purses and wallets hanging out. They're cautious of pickpockets in crowded places. They're aware of their surroundings and at least *pretend* to know where they're going.

If anything, BA is besieged more by minor nuisances. When buying anything, try not to get shortchanged and keep an eye out for fake bills (see the watermark?). Watch carefully for traffic when crossing streets, and look out for the piles of dog crap underfoot. Note that fresh air is often lacking – air pollution and smoking are big issues. Dealing with taxis are another thing; see p71 for tips.

Every city has its edgy neighborhoods, and in BA these include Constitución Estación (train station), the eastern border of San Telmo and La Boca (where, outside tourist streets, you should be careful even during the day). Av Florida is best avoided only very, very late at night. See p48 under Emergency for the tourist police.

SIGHTS

At Buenos Aires' heart is its *microcentro* (city center), which holds many of the city's historical buildings and museums. To the north lies upper-crust Recoleta, with its famous cemetery, and park-filled Palermo, home to many great restaurants and bars. Down south is where the blue-collar class hangs: this includes tango-mecca San Telmo and colorful, roughhousing La Boca. There's enough bustle in this city to keep you trotting around all day and all night.

City Center

Buenos Aires' *microcentro* holds many 19th-century European buildings, which surprises many travelers expecting a more Latin American feel. The liveliest street here is pedestrian **Av Florida**, packed with masses of harried businesspeople, curious tourists and angling leather salespeople. Make sure to stop at **Galerías Pacífico** (Map pp52–3), one of BA's most gorgeous shopping malls; peek at the ceiling paintings inside. South of Av Florida is busy Av Corrientes, and if you head west on this thoroughfare you'll cross superbroad Av 9 de Julio (run!). It's decisively punctuated by the famously phallic **Obelisco** (Map pp52–3) a major symbol of Buenos Aires. Just beyond is the city's traditional theater district, also full of many cheap bookstores.

The remodeled 18th-century **Museo del Cabildo** (Map pp52–3; admission US$0.35, Fridays free; 10:30am-5pm Tue-Fri, 11:30am-6pm Sun) is all that's left of the colonial arches that once surrounded Plaza de Mayo. Nearby, the neoclassical **Catedral Metropolitana** (Map pp52–3; finished in 1827) contains the tomb of liberator José de San Martín, Argentina's most venerated historical figure. A block east you'll see the pink presidential palace, **Casa Rosada** (Map pp52–3) and the famous balcony where vibrant Evita energized adoring crowds during her heyday in the 1940s. Around the southern side of the building is **Museo de la Casa Rosada** (Map pp52–3; admission US$0.35; 10am-6pm Mon-Fri, 2-6pm Sun), the most interesting feature of which is the catacombs of the Fuerte Viejo, an 18th-century colonial ruin. Free English tours of the Casa Rosada are given at 5pm Friday; reserve in person a few hours beforehand and take identification.

A block south of Plaza de Mayo is **Manzana de las Luces** (Block of Enlightenment; Map pp52–3), a solid square of 18th-century buildings that includes **Iglesia San Ignacio**, Buenos Aires' oldest church, and **Colegio Nacional**, an elite secondary school. Underground are old defensive military tunnels.

Over to the west, at the other end of Av de Mayo, is the green-domed **Palacio del Congreso** (Map pp52–3; modeled on Washington, DC's Capitol Building). It was completed in 1906 and faces pigeon-filled Plaza del Congreso and its **Monumento a los Dos Congresos**, the granite steps of which symbolize the Andes.

Since its opening in 1908, visitors have marveled at magnificent **Teatro Colón** (Map pp52–3; 4378-7133; www.teatrocolon.org.ar), further north at Tucumán 1171. The luxurious seven-story building seats 2500 spectators on plush red-velvet chairs and surrounds them with tiers of gilded balconies; it's a world-class facility for opera, ballet and classical music. Several daily tours in English and Spanish are given (US$4, reserve one day in advance).

East of the city center is BA's newest barrio, **Puerto Madero** (Map pp52–3). This renovated docklands area is lined with pleasant pedestrian walkways, expensive lofts, trendy restaurants and bars and some of the city's priciest hotels. Further east is the completely different world of **Reserva Ecológica Costanera Sur** (Map p49; 8am-7pm Nov-March, to 6pm Apr-Oct), a large marshy ecological reserve with dirt paths and natural landscapes. The entrance is east of San Telmo, via the street R Vera Peñaloza.

San Telmo

Six blocks south of Plaza de Mayo, San Telmo – home of BA's main tango culture – is full of cobbled streets and aging mansions. Historically its low rents have attracted artists, but prices are up and these days you'll see more boutiques than studios. The neighborhood was a fashionable place until 1870, when a series of epidemics over 20 years drove the rich elite northwards; many houses were then subdivided and turned into cramped immigrant shelters.

On Sundays, **Plaza Dorrego** (Map pp52–3) buzzes with its famous **antiques fair**: hordes of tourists clash elbows for rusty pocket watches, vintage dresses, ancient crystal- and metalware, delicate china and old coins. Good tango street shows add excitement and photo ops, but don't forget to drop some change into the hat. Surrounding the plaza are pleasant cafés where you can sip anything from cognacs to *cortados* (coffee with milk) while lazily people-watching. Afterwards, stroll the atmospheric streets to window-shop for that perfect *victrola* (gramophone) – you just may find it. At night check out the clubs that put on those famous tango shows.

Four blocks south at Defensa and Brasil is leafy **Parque Lezama** (Map p49), the presumptive site of Buenos Aires' foundations; mix with the locals playing chess, or visit the large and well-presented **Museo Histórico Nacional** (Map p49; admission US75¢; 11am-6pm Tue-Sun, closed Jan).

CENTRAL BUENOS AIRES

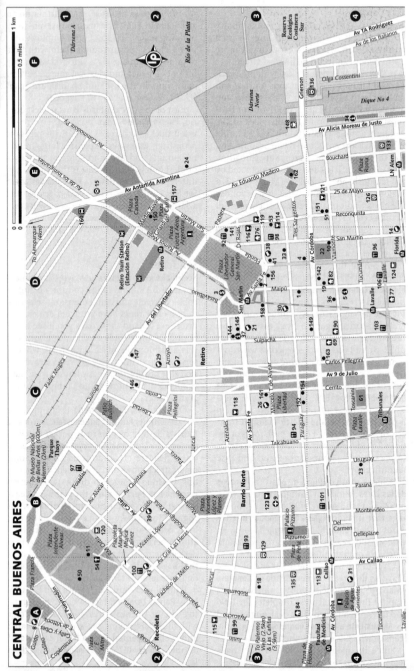

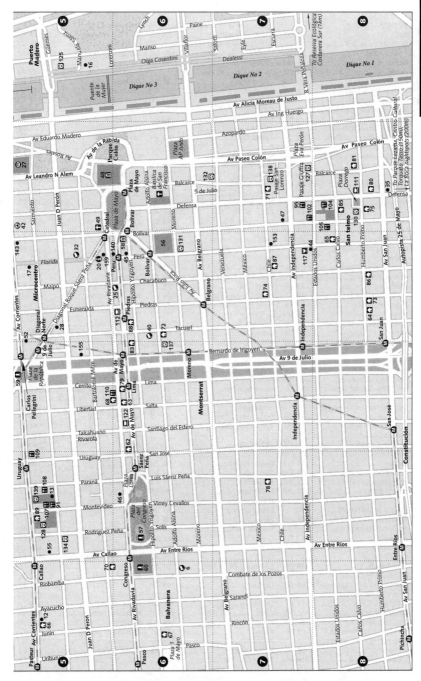

La Boca

Vivid, working-class La Boca, situated along the old port and at the *boca* (mouth) of the Río Riachuelo, was built by Italian immigrants from Genoa. Its main attraction is colorful **Caminito** (Map p49), a short pedestrian walk lined with corrugated-metal buildings. Local artists display their brightly colored paintings, adding to the vibrant ambience. The neighborhood is also home to the Boca Juniors soccer team (see p68 for more information).

Boca's standing as an artists' enclave is the legacy of painter Benito Quinquela Martín; his old home and studio is **Museo de Bellas Artes de La Boca** (Map p49; Pedro de Mendoza 1835; donation US35¢; 10am-5:30pm Mon-Fri, 11am-5:30pm Sat & Sun). Also, don't miss the excellent **Fundación Proa** (Map p49; www.proa.org; Pedro de Mendoza 1929; admission US$1; 11am-7pm Tue-Sun), which exhibits cutting-edge contemporary art; there's a wonderful view from its rooftop.

Be aware that this is one of the poorer *barrios* of Buenos Aires and, whether day or night, you shouldn't wander from the beaten path of tourist hangouts. Buses 29, 130 and 152 run to La Boca.

Recoleta

One of Buenos Aires' prime tourist attractions, **Cementerio de la Recoleta** (Map pp52-3; 7am-6pm) sits in the plushest of neighborhoods, ritzy Recoleta. High walls surround this necropolis where, in death as in life, generations of Argentina's elite rest in ornate splendor. It's fascinating to wander around and explore this extensive minicity of lofty statues, detailed marble façades and earthy-smelling sarcophagi. Follow the crowds and you'll find Evita's grave.

Next to the cemetery is the 1732 **Iglesia de Nuestra Señora de Pilar** (Map pp52-3) and Centro Cultural Recoleta (p48), which hosts cultural events. A weekend hippie fair takes place on the surrounding paths, attracting lively performers and crowds of tourists. Sit at a café and take in the nearby attractive greenery of **Plaza Intendente Alvear**; note the giant *ombú* trees. If you're lucky you'll spot a *paseaperros* (professional dog-walker) strolling with 15 or so leashed canines of all shapes and tails.

The **Museo Nacional de Bellas Artes** (Av del Libertador 1473; admission free; 12:30-7:30pm Tue-Fri, 9:30am-7:30pm Sat & Sun) houses works by famous French impressionists and Argentine artists; it's well worth a visit.

Palermo

Full of green parks, imposing statues, elegant embassies and large sporting complexes, Palermo on a sunny weekend afternoon is a *porteño* yuppie magnet. **Jardín Botánico Carlos Thays** (botanical gardens; Map pp56-7) is good for a stroll, while the **Jardín Zoológico** (zoo; Map pp56-7; 4806-7411; cnr Avs Las Heras & Sarmiento; admission US$2-3.50; 10-6pm Jan & Feb, 10-5pm Tue-Sun Mar-Dec) has mostly humane animal enclosures and some attractive classic structures to boot. There's also the pleasant **Jardín Japonés** (Japanese Gardens; Map pp56-7; 4804-4922; cnr Avs Casares & Berro; admission Mon-Fri US$1, Sat & Sun US$1.35; 10am-6pm). The **Rosedal** (rose garden; Map pp56-7) is OK during the day, but be warned – at night it's a transvestite hangout. On weekends, rent bikes and cruise the lakes of **Parque 3 de Febrero** (Map pp56-7).

Not too far from these green spots is the cutting-edge **Museo de Arte Latinoamericano de Buenos Aires** (Malba; Map pp56-7; www.malba.org.ar; Av Presidente Figuero Alcorta 3415; admission US$3.25, Wed free; noon-8pm Mon, Thu-Fri, noon-9pm Wed, 10am-8pm Sat & Sun), which has exhibitions by Latin American artists. Another interesting place is **Museo Evita** (Map pp56-7; Lafinur 2988; admission US75¢; 3-8pm Tue-Sun), chronicling this legendary and effervescent woman's life and work. Palermo also contains the **Campo de Polo** (polo grounds; Map pp56-7), **Hipódromo** (racetrack; Map pp56-7) and **Planetario** (observatory; 4771-9393; cnr Avs Sarmiento & Belisario Roldán; admission free, astronomy shows US$1.50; 9am-5pm Mon-Fri, 1-7.30pm Sat & Sun).

Make sure to stroll through the subneighborhood of **Palermo Viejo** (Map pp56-7), just south of the parks; it's further divided into Palermo Soho and Palermo Hollywood. Here you'll find BA's hippest restaurants and trendiest boutiques, along with some lively nightlife. Its beautiful old buildings make for some great wanderings, and many expats have planted roots here.

ACTIVITIES

Porteños' main activities are probably walking, shopping and dancing tango. Those searching for greener pastures, however, head to Palermo's parks, where joggers run past strolling families and *fútbol* scrimmages (join in only if you're very, very confident of your skills).

Safe cycling is possible in this city, but only in specific places. Good places to pedal are

ARGENTINA

PALERMO & AROUND

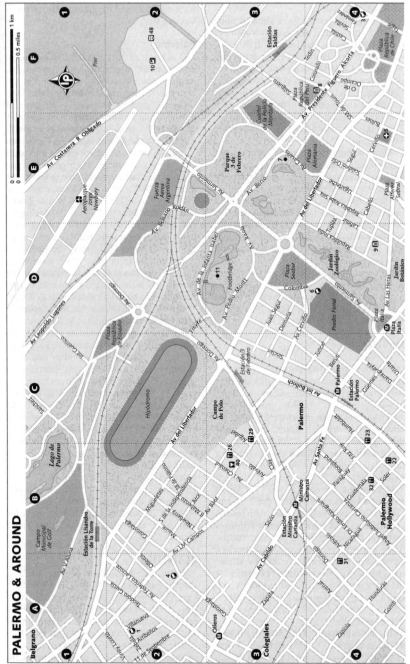

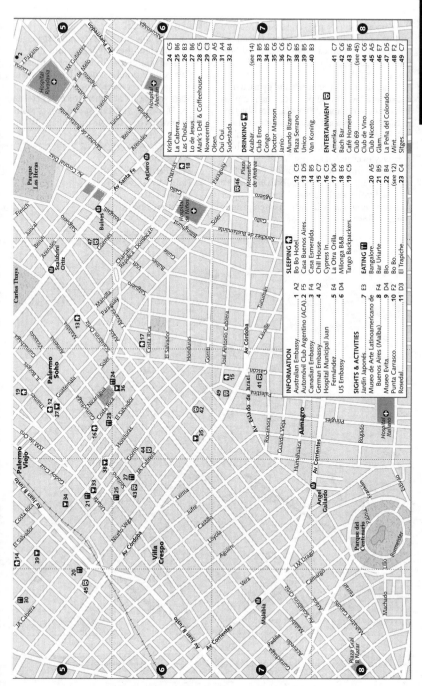

Krishna.................................24 C5
La Cabrera............................25 B6
Las Cholas............................26 B3
Lo de Jesús..........................27 B6
Mark's Deli & Coffeehouse...28 C5
Novecento.............................29 C3
Olsen....................................30 A5
Oui Oui.................................31 A4
Sudestada............................32 B4

DRINKING
Acabar.............................(see 14)
Club Eros.............................33 B5
Congo..................................34 B5
Doctor Manson....................35 C6
Janio....................................36 C6
Mundo Bizarro.....................37 C5
Plaza Serrano.......................38 B5
Unico...................................39 B5
Van Koning..........................40 B3

ENTERTAINMENT
Amerika................................41 C7
Bach Bar..............................42 C6
Café Homero........................43 B6
Club 69...........................(see 45)
Club de Vino........................44 C6
Club Niceto..........................45 A5
Glam....................................46 E7
La Peña del Colorado...........47 D5
Mint.....................................48 F2
Sitges..................................49 C7

INFORMATION
Australian Embassy...................1 A2
Automóvil Club Argentino (ACA)...2 F5
Canadian Embassy....................3 F4
German Embassy.......................4 A2
Hospital Municipal Juan
   Fernández...............................5 E4
US Embassy..............................6 D4

SIGHTS & ACTIVITIES
Jardín Japonés..........................7 E3
Museo de Arte Latinoamericano de
   Buenos Aires (Malba)...............8 F4
Museo Evita..............................9 D4
Punta Carrasco........................10 F2
Rosedal..................................11 D3

SLEEPING
Bo Bo Hotel.............................12 C5
Casa Buenos Aires...................13 D5
Casa Esmeralda.......................14 B5
Chill House.............................15 C7
Cypress In...............................16 C5
La Otra Orilla..........................17 D6
Milonga B&B...........................18 E6
Tango Backpackers...................19 C5

EATING
Bangalore...............................20 A5
Bar Uriarte.............................21 B5
Bio..22 B4
Bo Bo................................(see 12)
El Trapiche.............................23 C4

Palermo's parks (see p55) and Puerto Madero and its nearby Reserva Ecológica Costanera Sur (see p51). You can rent bikes from bike tour companies, who also do guided tours (see opposite).

Other than at major hotels and gyms, tennis courts and swimming pools can be found in Palermo's parks and at **Punta Carrasco** (Map pp56-7; ☎ 4807-1010; www.puntacarrasco.com.ar; cnr Costanera Norte & Sarmiento). Climbers can head to **Realización** (Map p49; ☎ 4854-6009; Aráoz 129), a climbing gym way over in Villa Crespo.

Some companies like **Tangol** (Map pp52-3; ☎ 4312-7276; www.tangol.com; Av Florida 971, suite 31) offer activities such as skydiving, helicopter tours and *estancia* visits, which often include horse-riding.

WALKING TOUR

Recoleta is Buenos Aires' wealthiest neighborhood. Here the privileged elite shop in expensive boutiques, sip tea at elegant cafés and walk their purebred dogs. It's also where they're put to rest when they die.

Start your walk at **Cementerio de la Recoleta** (**1**; p55), where you can spend hours visiting hundreds of elaborate sarcophagi. When

> **WALK FACTS**
> **Start** Recoleta Cemetery
> **Finish** Alvear Palace Hotel
> **Distance** 3km
> **Duration** 3 hours

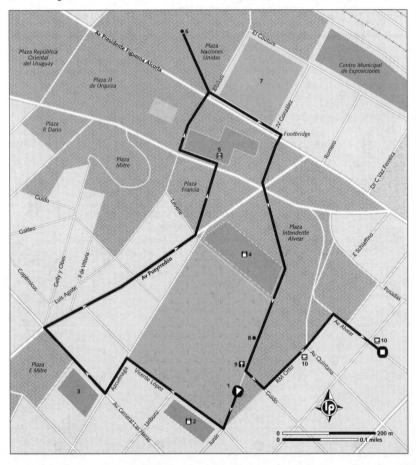

you're ready for the living again, come out and head south. Stroll by shopping mall **Village Recoleta (2)**, then turn left at Azcuénaga and go a block. At the intersection you'll see the **Facultad de Ingenieria (3)**, an engineering school and wonderfully Gothic statement. Follow Av General Las Heras a couple blocks, then turn right at Av Pueyrredón. Go north past the home-oriented mall **Buenos Aires Design (4)**; it's worth a look if you like home furnishings. Cut across Plaza Francia and head to the **Museo Nacional de Bellas Artes (5**; p55), with its grand collection of classical art. Head behind the museum and carefully cross Av Presidente Figueroa Alcorta. Enter Plaza Naciones Unidas, where you'll see the giant metal flower sculpture **Floralis Generica (6)**; at night the petals close like a real flower. Walk by the mammoth **Facultad de Derecho (7**; law school), cross the footbridge and make your way back to Plaza Intendente Alvear; if it's a weekend you'll have a huge crafts market to explore (weekdays it's smaller). See what's up at the **Centro Cultural Recoleta (8**; p48) and glance inside the pretty **Iglesia de Nuestra Señora de Pilar (9)**.

If it's a sunny warm day, grab an outdoor table at **La Biela café (10**; p65); if it's cloudy, walk a couple blocks to the sumptuous **Alvear Palace Hotel (11)**, where a luxurious afternoon tea awaits.

COURSES
Language
It's official: BA is a hot destination for Spanish learners. There are plenty of schools and even more private teachers, so ask around for recommendations. All offer social excursions and can help with accommodation.

Prices for institutions listed here range from US$110 to US$190 per week for group lessons (four hours perday); private classes average US$12 per hour. Check websites for specifics; also try www.123teachme.com, where students rate language schools.

Academia Buenos Aires (Map pp52-3; ☎ 4345-5954; www.academiabuenosaires.com; Hipólito Yrigoyen 571, 4th fl)

BA Spanish (Map pp52-3; ☎ 4381-2076; www.baspanish.com; Av Rivadavia 1559 2C)

Centro de Estudio del Español (Cedic; Map pp52-3; ☎ 4312-1016; www.cedic.com.ar; Reconquista 715, 11E)

Estudio Buenos Aires (EBA; Map pp52-3; ☎ 4312-8936; www.ebatrust.com; Reconquista 962, 3rd fl)

Íbero Spanish Argentina (Map pp52-3; www.iberospanish.com; ☎ 5218-0240; Uruguay 150)

Instituto de Lengua Española para Extranjeros (ILEE; Map pp52-3; ☎ /fax 4782-7173; www.argentinailee.com; Av Callao 339, 3rd fl)

International Bureau of Language (IBL; Map pp52-3; ☎ 4331-4250; www.ibl.com.ar; Av Florida 165, 8th fl)

Tango
Tango classes are available everywhere – your own hostel may offer them. All *milongas* (dance halls) offer inexpensive classes. They can also put you in touch with private teachers, some of whom speak English. Cultural centers (see p48) often have affordable classes as well. Check tango magazines like *La Tanguata* or *BA Tango*, available at tourist offices, for more options; a good website is www.tangodata.com.ar.

Academia Nacional del Tango (Map pp52-3; ☎ 4345-6967; www.anacdeltango.org.ar; Av de Mayo 833) Cheap tango classes (US$2) from 6pm to 8pm Monday to Friday.

Centro Cultural Torquato Tasso (Map p49; ☎ 4307-6506; Defensa 1575) Great San Telmo venue with US$5 classes, free Sunday night *milongas*, and excellent shows (US$6.50, Wednesday to Saturday).

Confitería Ideal (Map pp52-3; ☎ 4601-8234; Suipacha 384) One of BA's main tango meccas, with continuous classes (US$5), frequent *milongas* (US$3.25) and nightly shows (US$5).

TOURS
If you have little time and want to take a tour, that's OK. Just avoid those big buses full of languid sightseers – much more creative tours exist.

Baires Bikes (Map pp52-3; ☎ 4300-5068; www.bairesbikes.com; Bolivar 762) Daily three-hour tours (US$21) cover the city's major *barrios*. English-speaking guides; also rents bikes (per day US$12).

Cicerones (☎ 4330-0800; www.cicerones.org.ar) Nonprofit organization that relies on volunteers to show visitors key parts of Buenos Aires. Tours go on foot or public transport.

Eternautas (☎ 4384-7874; www.eternautas.com) Economical weekend walking tours (US$2); also tours with a political, artistic, social or historical bent (US$25 and up). Guides speak various languages and are certified historians; custom tours available.

Gobierno de la Ciudad de Buenos Aires (☎ 4114-5791; www.bue.gov.ar/recorridos) Free guided tours of the city, including some with historical-figure themes (Evita, Gardel, Borges). Ask if English-speaking guides are available.

Urban Biking (☎ 4568-4321; www.urbanbiking.com) Offers similar services to Baires Bikes.

ARGENTINA

FESTIVALS & EVENTS

Buenos Aires' biggest celebrations:

Tango festival (www.festivaldetango.com.ar) Late February to early March.

Book fair (www.el-libro.com.ar) First three weeks of April.

Independent film festival (www.bafilmfest.com) Mid to late April.

Art festival (www.arteba.com) Mid-May.

Livestock fair (www.ruralarg.org.ar) July to August.

SLEEPING

Buenos Aires' *microcentro* is central and close to many sights and services, though it's busy and noisy during the day. San Telmo is about 15 minutes' walk south and good for those seeking old colonial atmosphere, cozy cobbled streets, proximity to many tango venues and a blue-collar flavor around the edges. Palermo Viejo is northwest of center and about a 10-minute taxi ride. It's a pretty area full of wonderful old buildings and dotted with the city's best ethnic restaurants, trendiest boutiques and liveliest bars.

Note that private rooms (and even dorm beds) in some hostels can cost more than rooms in a cheap hotel. All hostels listed here include kitchen access and light breakfast; most have free internet (some even wi-fi) and lockers (bring your own lock). The bigger ones offer many services and activities. Most hostels (especially smaller ones) don't take credit cards. To obtain a Hostelling International card (US$14) head to BA's **Hostelling International office** (Map pp52-3; ☎ 451-8712; www.hostels.org.ar; Av Florida 835, 3rd fl, suite 319).

BA has some decent budget hotel choices. Most offer a simple breakfast and cable TV; a few take credit cards, which might incur a fee of up to 10% (be sure to ask).

City Center

Lime House (Map pp52-3; ☎ 4383-4561; www.limehouseargentina.com; Lima 11; dm US$6-7, d US$23, with shared bathroom US$22; 🖳) Funkier than most, this hostel offers busy atmosphere (music plays inside and 9 de Julio roars outside), rustic surroundings (could use a lick of paint), grungy kitchen and a pool room. Dorms range from four to 12 beds.

Milhouse (Map pp52-3; ☎ 4345-9604; www.milhousehostel.com; Hipólito Yrigoyen 959; dm with/without HI card US$7.50/8.50, d with/without HI card US$26/29; 🗶 🖳) Large, central and BA's premier 'party hostel.' Dorms are 4-8 beds (most with inside bath), doubles are beautiful, there are Monday night

DJ parties and plenty of activities are available. About 150 beds, with a nearby annex being built.

V&S Hostel Club (Map pp52-3; ☎ 4322-0994; www.argentinahostels.com; Viamonte 887; dm US$8.50, s US$26, d US$29; 🗶 🖳) One of BA's best, this central hostel has a great atmosphere, good sex-segregated dorms (though some get large with triple bunks) and decent services. There's a small outdoor patio and tiny kitchen. The beautiful private rooms all have baths; reserve in advance.

Maípu (Map pp52-3; ☎ 4322-5142; Maípu 735; s/d US$16/20, with shared bathroom US$13/16) Grand old place with original tile work, high ceilings and dim lighting. Rooms are large, simple and reasonably kept up. Good central choice but don't expect any modern conveniences.

Hotel El Cabildo (Map pp52-3; ☎ 4322-6745; Lavalle 748; s/d US$16/20) An unbeatable deal for its location, right on pedestrian Lavalle. Rooms are carpeted and good, and some are large. No breakfast.

Gran Hotel Oriental (Map pp52-3; ☎ 4951-6427; ghoriental@hotmail.com; Bartolomé Mitre 1840; s/d US$16/20) Popular for its very pleasant, well-priced and modern rooms. They're remodeling, so prices may fluctuate. Reserve ahead.

Hotel Central Córdoba (Map pp52-3; ☎ 4311-1175; www.hotelcentralcordoba.com.ar; San Martín 1021; s/d US$23/26; 🗶) Good-value rooms are on tap at this downtown hotel, located within swilling distance of BA's two most popular bars. If you want to pass out on the satin bed sheets make sure you reserve ahead.

Goya Hotel (Map pp52-3; ☎ 4322-9269; www.goyahotel.com.ar; Suipacha 748; s/d from US$29/39; 🗶) A good, friendly choice with central location. Forty modern, comfortable and carpeted rooms; they're remodeling, so prices might increase. The 'presidential' suite (US$58) comes with jets in the tub.

Also recommended:

Downtown Mate (Map pp52-3; ☎ 4381-0647; www.downtownmate.com.ar; Av Rivadavia 1181; dm US$6-8, d US$16; 🖳) Nothing fancy, but cheap for its central location.

Alkimista (Map pp52-3; ☎ 4383-2267; www.alkimistahostel.com; Av de Mayo 1385, 2nd fl C; dm US$6.50, s/d US$11/16; 🖳) In a high-rise building. Cramped rooms, but tall ceilings and some charm.

Hostel Clan (Map pp52-3; ☎ 4334-3401; www.hostelclan.com.ar; Addfoh Alsina 912; dm US$7, d US$18; 🖳) Grungy, casual and loose sorta place, with a very social atmosphere.

Milonga (Map pp52-3; ☎ 4815-1827; www.milonga hostel.com.ar; Ayacucho 921; dm US$7-8.50, s/d US$13/20; 🖥) Old house with decent rooms facing outdoor hallways and patios; good common spaces. See also their annex, Milonga B&B.

BA Stop (Map pp52-3; ☎ 4382-7406; www.bastop .com; Av Rivadavia 1194; dm US$7.50, s/d US$12/15) Small, popular place with excellent location, comfortable common areas and good breakfast.

Portal del Sur (Map pp52-3; ☎ 4342-8788; www .portaldelsurba.com.ar; Hipólito Yrigoyen 855; dm US$9-10, s/d US$23-30; 📶 🖥) Clean, beautiful, gorgeous doubles and luxurious rooftop terrace. Good dorms.

San Telmo

Carlos Gardel (Map pp52-3; ☎ 4307-2606; www.hos telcarlosgardel.com.ar; Carlos Calvo 579; dm US$6-7, d US$16-23; 🖥) Reception is beautiful, with antiques and tango-theme decor. Rooms don't follow suit, but are decent; avoid the 10-bed dorm. There's a pleasant mezzanine dining area and tiny rooftop terrace. One small single available (US$10).

Nomade (Map pp52-3; ☎ 4300-7641; www.hostel nomade.com; Carlos Calvo 430; dm US$6.50, d with shared bathroom US$16; 🖥) One block from Plaza Dorrego. Boasts large sunny terrace, pleasant patios, two basic doubles and cramped six-bed dorms. Its annex nearby has six doubles and a couple of dark, eight-bed dorms under a covered patio.

Hostal de Granados (Map pp52-3; ☎ 4362-5600; www.hostaldegranados.com.ar; Chile 374; dm US$6.50-13, d US$28-31, with shared bathroom US$24; 📶 🖥) On a café-filled street is this tall hostel (think stairs) with outdoor halls, large high-ceilinged rooms, dim kitchen and slick downstairs restaurant. Most rooms have a fridge; there's a small rooftop terrace. Lacks a cozy common room.

Hostel-Inn Tango City (Map pp52-3; ☎ 4300-5764; www.hostel-inn.com; Piedras 680; dm with/without HI card US$7/8, d with/without HI card US$22/27; 📶 🖥) A large hostel in a tall, almost claustrophobic building with six floors (there's an elevator). Cramped rooms come with or without bath. The barlike area downstairs, complete with pool table and small kitchen, is good for chatting up fellow travelers.

Hostel-Inn Buenos Aires (Map pp52-3; ☎ 4300-7992; www.hostel-inn.com; Humberto Primo 820; dm with/without HI card US$7/8, d with/without HI card US$18/22; 📶 🖥) Much cozier than its big brother four blocks north is this colorful hostel, also offering plenty of services. Small dorms have four to six beds, doubles all share bathrooms and there's a pleasant sunny rooftop.

Hotel Carly (Map pp52-3; ☎ 4361-7710; www.hotelcarly .com.ar; Humberto Primo 466; s/d US$7/11, with shared bathroom US$6.50/9; 🖥) This old standby continues to offer outstanding location and cheap but good basic rooms with high ceilings, open hallways and tiled patios. Ancient charm and funky kitchen.

Ostinatto (Map pp52-3; ☎ 4362-9639; www.ostin atto.com.ar; Chile 680; dm US$8-9, d US$25, with shared bathroom US$22, penthouse US$39; 🖥) Gorgeous new hostel with its own bar on the ground floor, Z-shaped dining room table and slick penthouse off the rooftop terrace. Free tango classes.

Brisas del Mar (Map pp52-3; ☎ 4300-0040; Humberto Primo 826; d US$10-15) A variety of well-tended rooms, some with shared bathroom and/or carpet, are on offer at this quiet, family-run hotel. Also has tiled outdoor hallways and tiny limited-use kitchen.

Palermo Viejo

Tango Backpackers (Map pp56-7; ☎ 4776-6871; www .tangobp.com; Thames 2212; dm with/without HI card US$6/7, d with/without HI card US$16/19.50; 🖥) Decent small HI hostel in a converted old house with grungy kitchen and sunny rooftop patio. Three blocks to Plaza Italia (metro and bus lines).

Casa Buenos Aires (Map pp56-7; ☎ 6341-9893; www .casabuenosaires.com.ar; Charcas 3912; dm/s US$6.50/13, d US$20-26; 🖥) A plain, quiet and safe place that's best for long-term tenants. Not a party place at all and only offers 20 beds; its nearby annex is much more modern and attractive. Free bike rental; reservations required.

SPLURGE!

Bo Bo Hotel (Map pp56-7; ☎ 4774-0505; www .bobohotel.com; Guatemala 4882; r US$70-130; 📶 📶 🖥) One of the slickest boutique hotels in BA, offering up seven gorgeous rooms with minimalist lines, contemporary textures and rich color schemes. For something extra special shoot for the 'Minimalist' or 'Argentinean' (Jacuzzi!) rooms, both with their own private terrace. 'Rationalista' is wheelchair accessible. The restaurant downstairs offers some of Palermo Soho's finest fare, while other pluses include security box, room service and wi-fi. Wear your best threads to fit in, and remember to reserve at least one month in advance.

LONG-TERM STAYS

Heaps of long-term guesthouses and apartments have popped up in recent years to meet the demand from travelers and expats wanting to spend weeks or months (or years) in BA. Prices are higher than locals pay but these come furnished and often have an English-speaking manager. Also, there's no need to pay the 'guarantee' deposit that locals have to ante up when renting an apartment. Reserve in advance for any place listed here.

La Casa de Etty (Map pp52-3; ☎ 4384-6378; www.angelfire.com/pq/coret; Luis Sáenz Peña 617; r per person per month US$80-225) Señora Esther Corcias offers three basic double-occupancy rooms in her house, all with shared bathroom and kitchen access. She also places tenants in other apartments and guesthouses; check website for more information.

Segura Homestay (Map pp52-3; ☎ 5139-0476; www.homestay-buenos-aires.com; Av Corrientes 1642, 4th fl, suite 87; s/d per week from US$91/147, per month from US$265/397) Just five simple but spacious rooms are on offer at this no-nonsense apartment, which is in a large building on bustling Av Corrientes. All rooms share bathrooms and there's a large bleak patio. Popular with Spanish students.

Casa de Plata (Map pp52-3; ☎ 4953-3950; www.casadeplata.com.ar; Av Corrientes 2092, 4th fl; s per week/month US$110/330, d per person per week/month US$85/250) Just five comfortable, carpeted rooms in an old house are available here; all share bathrooms and come with balcony. The decor is a bit eclectic, but overall atmosphere is good. Shared quadruple room also available (per person per week/month US$60/180).

Casa Los Angelitos (Map pp52-3; ☎ 4954-4079; www.casalosangelitos.com; Hipólito Yrigoyen 2178; s/d per month from US$270/400; 🖳) Located in a charming old house, with seven large comfortable rooms (two with private bathroom) and beautiful terraces. One room has kitchenette; one week minimum stay.

M&M Homestay (Map pp52-3; ☎ 4362-0356; magdalena@argentina.com; Balcarce 1094; s/d per day US$16/33) Just two good rooms in a well-maintained, gorgeous old house in San Telmo (reserve well in advance!), but an annex will hold four more rooms. Tiny kitchen and rooftop terrace; friendly dog on premises.

These are a few of the many apartment websites available:

Apartmentsba.com (www.apartmentsba.com)

Craigslist (www.craigslist.com)

Friendly Apartments (www.friendlyapartments.com/apart.htm) Gay friendly.

My Space BA (www.myspaceba.com)

Piso Compartido (www.pisocompartido.com.ar)

Reynolds Propiedades (www.argentinahomes.com)

Roomargentina (www.roomargentina.com)

StayinBuenosAires (www.stayinbuenosaires.com)

Tu Casa Argentina (www.tucasargentina.com)

Your Home in Argentina (www.yourhomeinargentina.com.ar)

Chill House (Map pp56-7; ☎ 4861-0863; www.chillhouse.com.ar; José Antonio Cabrera 4056; dm US$8, s/d with shared bathroom US$18/22; 🖳) Laid-back hostel on the southern fringe of Palermo Viejo. Good for those who don't need luxury or many services, and who care more about party action. Music is always playing and French is spoken (the owners are international and into BA's nightlife). One double comes with private bathroom.

Casa Esmeralda (Map pp56-7; ☎ 4772-2446; www.casaesmeralda.com.ar; Honduras 5765; dm US$8, d US$21-25; 🖳) Peaceful spot with homey common spaces, pleasant garden, rooftop patio and friendly dog. Good location in Palermo Hollywood (a subneighborhood of Palermo Viejo).

Milonga B&B (Map pp56-7; ☎ 4825-7217; www.milongabnb.com; Agüero 1389; dm US$9/32, s/d with shared bathroom US$19/27; 🖳) A good, intimate choice in a less 'trendy' part of Palermo Viejo. Has just nine rooms, mostly private ones, all in a pretty, remodeled old house. See website for monthly rates.

La Otra Orilla (Map pp56-7; ☎ 4867-4070; www.otraorilla.com.ar; J Alvarez 1779; r US$30-85; 🖳) A gorgeous place located off the beaten path in Palermo Viejo. Just seven luxurious and romantic rooms are available in a beautiful old house. There's a cute garden patio, and the service is friendly.

Cypress In (Map pp56-7; ☎ 4833-5834; www.cypressin .com; Costa Rica 4828; r US$54-96; ✕ ▦) Just eight small but comfortable and aesthetically pleasing rooms are available at this excellent guesthouse in Palermo Viejo. Common spaces are colorful and contemporary, with minimalist styling. Other pluses are pleasant patio, meeting rooms and range of professional services.

EATING

Buenos Aires is chock full of excellent food, and you'll dine very well whether you eat meat or not. Most restaurants serve a standard fare of *parrillada* (grilled meats), pastas and/or *minutas* (short orders), but in recent years a large number of more international and ethnic eateries have popped up in Palermo Viejo and nearby Las Cañitas. Another food-oriented neighborhood is Puerto Madero, but 90% of the restaurants here are very fancy, relatively expensive and lean more toward steaks than stir-fries.

Vegetarians rejoice: unlike the rest of Argentina, there is a good range of meat-free restaurants in BA – you just have to know where to look. Most restaurants will offer a few pastas, salads and pizzas – but not much else that's meat-free.

City Center

Pizzería Güerrín (Map pp52-3; Av Corrientes 1368; slices US75¢) Great for good, cheap pizza slices; eat standing up, like the penny-pinching locals, or sit down for a rest.

El Cuartito (Map pp52-3; Talcahuano 937; slices US75¢-US$1.25) Another excellent, inexpensive stand-up pizzeria, and a BA institution. Great old sports posters.

Cocina Patora (Map pp52-3; San Martín 1141; mains under US$3.50) Wonderfully cheap northern Argentine treats like *locro* (spicy meat stew), tamales, empanadas and *cazuelas* (meat or vegetable pot stews). Good modern atmosphere and a little paradise from busy San Martín.

La Esquina de las Flores (Map pp52-3; Av Córdoba 1587; meals under US$4; ✕ 8:30am-8:30pm Mon-Fri, to 3pm Sat) BA's veggie haven, with dishes changing daily. Takeout available, plus a small store selling wheat breads, soy flour and organic mate.

Lotos (Map pp52-3; Av Córdoba 1577; meals under US$4; ✕ 11:30am-6pm Mon-Fri) Next door to La Esquina, this vegetarian cafeteria also serves fresh and healthy meals. Its store downstairs sells seitan, brown rice and lentils.

Cumaná (Map pp52-3; Rodríguez Peña 1149; mains under US$4) Insanely popular for its low-priced pizzas, empanadas and *cazuelas*. Great rustic atmosphere – just get here early (you've been warned).

Parrilla al Carbón (Map pp52-3; Lavalle 663; mains under US$4) For fast, cheap and tasty grilled meats in the city center you won't do much better than this small joint. Order a set meal (steak, fries and cola) for US$4.25 or grab a *choripan* (sausage sandwich) for a ridiculous US75¢.

Filo (Map pp52-3; San Martín 975; mains US$4-8) Wonderful hip and contemporary surroundings; there's an art gallery in the basement. Wide selection of salads, pizzas, pastas and desserts – all of it good.

Chiquilín (Map pp52-3; Montevideo 310; mains US$4-9.50) A good choice for upscale pasta and *parrillada*. Dine under hanging hams and international flags; this place bustles even after midnight.

Also recommended:

Pippo (Map pp52-3; Paraná 356; mains US$2.25-6) Cheap, casual and open late. There's another branch at Montevideo 341.

La Huerta (Map pp52-3; Lavalle 895; set menu US$3.25; ✕ lunch Mon-Fri, dinner Fri & Sat) Vegetarian cafeteria.

Puerto Leyenda (Map pp52-3; Av Rivadavia 1119; set menu under US$3.50) All you can eat.

El Patio (Map pp52-3; Av Florida btwn Lavalle & Tucumán; meals under US$4; ✕ lunch Mon-Fri) Food court.

Galerías Pacífico (Map pp52-3; cnr Avs Florida & Córdoba; meals under US$4) Food court downstairs.

Grant's (Map pp52-3; Junín 1155; set menu US$4.25-6) All you can eat. There's another branch at Ave General Las Heras 1925.

El Sanjuanino (Map pp52-3; Posadas 1515; meals under US$5) Cheap Recoleta eats – *locro*, tamales and empanadas.

Granix (Map pp52-3; Av Florida 165; meals US$5.25; ✕ lunch Mon-Fri) Fancy veg cafétería; on first floor in Galería Güemes.

San Telmo

La Vieja Rotissería (Map pp52-3; Defensa 963; mains US$2.25-4) Hopelessly stuffed on Sunday afternoons, this cheap *parrilla* offers classic atmosphere, tango tunes and excellent meats.

El Desnivel (Map pp52-3; Defensa 855; mains US$2.75-6.50) Popularity has driven prices up some, but it's still worth a visit. The *vacío* (flank steak) is nice and tender – ask for it *bien jugoso* (rare) if you dare.

ARGENTINA

Las Marías (Map pp52-3; Bolívar 949; mains US$3.25-6.50) Good old standby, with traditional surroundings, tasty *parrillada* and homemade pastas. Unpretentious.

La Farmacia (Map pp52-3; Bolívar 898; mains US$5-7 ☽ closed Mon-Fri lunch) Great wall art accompanies creative cuisine at this fun eatery. Sit on the rooftop terrace if it's warm, or inside the old house for a more cozy atmosphere.

Palermo Viejo

Oui Oui (Map pp56-7; Nicaragua 6068; sandwiches under US$3) Cute as a bug, this small French bistro comes pretty close to authenticity. It serves delicious pastries, gourmet salads and outstanding sandwiches. Weekend brunch is awesome, but come early – it's popular.

Mark's Deli & Coffeehouse (Map pp56-7; El Salvador 4701; mains US$3-4) This is a modern eatery that cooks up excellent soups, salads and sandwiches. Cool modern decor, pleasant outside seating and a guaranteed wait on sunny weekends.

Bangalore (Map pp56-7; ☎ 4779-2621; Humboldt 1416; mains US$3.25-7) Mainly a pub, but upstairs there's a small space with just a few tables. Indian food is the name of the game: choose the pumpkin curry, beef vindaloo, chicken Madras or Saag Aloo.

Krishna (Map pp56-7; Malabia 1833; mains under US$4; ☽ lunch & dinner Wed-Sun, lunch Tue) A tiny place full of Indian drapes and colorful mosaic tables. Wash down your *thalis*, tofu and seitan with a lassi and chai tea.

Lo de Jesus (Map pp56-7; ☎ 4831-1961; Gurruchaga 1406; mains US$4-7) Wonderful corner restaurant with white tablecloth-covered tables (including on the sidewalk) and suited-up wait staff. Grills up outstanding *parrillada* (try the *ojo de bife* – that's ribeye) and pastas.

El Trapiche (Map pp56-7; Paraguay 5099; mains US$5-9) A bit more traditional than most Palermo Viejo eateries, this large modern restaurant serves an exceptional range of pastas, salads and – most importantly for meat-lovers – awesome *parrillada*. Try the house specialty, the *lomo* (tenderloin).

Bo Bo (Map pp56-7; Guatemala 4882; mains US$6-8) This snazzy minimalist restaurant offers gorgeously presented international cuisine. Try the squash and goat cheese *sorrentinos* (large raviolis) in artichoke pesto, or the stuffed rabbit in port sauce with sautéed mushrooms.

Bar Uriarte (Map pp56-7; ☎ 4834-6004; Uriarte 1572; mains US$7-9) This is yet another slick modern

---

SPLURGE!

La Cabrera (Map pp56-7; ☎ 4831-7002; JA Cabrera 5099; mains US$6.50-9) If you eat at only one steakhouse in BA, make it this one. Some of the city's best meats are professionally grilled up and presented to you on wood boards and in huge portions, along with a few dainty condiments (olives, sun-dried tomatoes, goat's cheese) on the side. The ambience is less sniffy than most other Palermo Viejo eateries, yet still elegant. It's very popular, but there's a nearby annex to ease your wait.

---

eatery serving excellent food. The emphasis at Bar Uriarte is on a limited menu graced with Mediterranean-influenced dishes, but there's also an adobe oven in back for pizza. Try the US$4.50 lunch deal.

Also recommended:

Club Eros (Map pp56-7; Uriarte 1609; mains under US$3) Dirt cheap local club that's stuffed with diners.

Bio (Map pp56-7; Humboldt 2199; mains under US$5; ☽ closed Sun & Mon nights) Small corner joint serving tasty and original veg fare.

Las Cholas (Map pp56-7; ☎ 4899-0094; Arce 306; mains under US$5) Cheap northern Argentine food in hip Las Cañitas. Upscale rustic and very popular.

Novecento (Map pp56-7; ☎ 4778-1900; Av Báez 199; mains US$5.25-10) Gourmet pastas, meats, fish and salads. Fancy corner bistro in Las Cañitas.

Sudestada (Map pp56-7; ☎ 4776-3777; Guatemala 5602; mains US$7-10) Magnificent Southeast Asian dishes; make reservations and try the duck.

Olsen (Map pp56-7; ☎ 4776-7677; Gorriti 5870; mains US$8.50-13) Gorgeous spaces, luscious food, high prices.

DRINKING

BA is all about the night, and there are plenty of cafés, bars and live-music venues in which to drink the night away. Cafés have very long hours: they're often open morning to late night. Bars and live-music venues open late and stay open even later; on weekends they'll often be hopping until 6am the next day.

Cafés

Buenos Aires has a heavy café culture, which is obvious once you notice the number of cafés in the city. Some are famous institutions, full of elegant old atmosphere and rich history. *Porteños* will spend hours solving the world's problems over a few *medialunas* (croissants) and a *cortado*. Many offer full menus too.

Bar Plaza Dorrego (Map pp52-3; Defensa 1098) One of San Telmo's most atmospheric cafés, smack on Plaza Dorrego. The dark wood surroundings (check out the graffiti) and old-world ambience can't be beaten, and on weekends this place buzzes to the hilt.

Café Tortoni (Map pp52-3; Av de Mayo 829) The Cadillac of BA's cafés, the well-known Tortoni takes you back in time with charming old atmosphere – though its self-promoting souvenir counter is a sign of recent times. Nightly tango shows (US$8; see p68).

Richmond (Map pp52-3; Av Florida 468) Take a java break from Av Florida's hustle and bustle at this elegant café. Plenty of coffees, snacks, meals and cocktails grace the menu. The Richmond was a popular meeting point for BA's famous writers, including Borges.

La Biela (Map pp52-3; Av Quintana 600) The uppercrust elite dawdle for hours at this classy joint in Recoleta. Prices are relatively expensive, and the outside seating menu costs even more – but it's simply irresistible on a warm sunny day, especially on weekends.

Clasica y Moderna (Map pp52-3; Av Callao 892) Classic, cozy café with heavy bohemian vibe. These brick walls have seen famous poets, philosophers, singers and musicians come and go. Artsy bookstore inside, otherwise there's usually a newspaper or two.

Los 36 Billares (Map pp52-3; Av de Mayo 1265) Another long-running spot on Av de Mayo, with wood details and classic surroundings. It's popular as a billiards hall, with plenty of tables and occasional competitions. Tango, folkloric music and even belly-dancing shows take place in the evenings.

Bars

Palermo Viejo has BA's highest concentration of trendy and popular bars, though there are a few good ones downtown and in San Telmo as well. *Porteños* aren't big drinkers and getting smashed is generally frowned upon. For cheap thrills, buy some bottles of brew and hang out with the masses in Plaza Serrano (Palermo Viejo) on a weekend night.

Gibraltar (Map pp52-3; Perú 895) One of BA's most popular expat pubs that also attracts heady mix of backpackers and locals. Good, unpretentious atmosphere; serves tasty international foods like beef and ale pie, green Thai curry and Caesar salad. Plenty of whiskeys.

Milión (Map pp52-3; Paraná 1048) Bar-restaurant located in a richly renovated old mansion. The drinking happens on the 2nd and 3rd floors, in the small rooms with high ceilings. Loud, smoky and very popular. Nice terrace overlooking leafy garden.

Gran Bar Danzón (Map pp52-3; Libertad 1161) Trendy and upscale restaurant-wine bar with good selection of wines by the glass. Asian-inspired dinner selections. Very popular, so come early for happy hour and snag a good seat on the sofas. Live jazz Thursday and Friday.

Acabar (Map pp56-7; Honduras 5733) Among BA's most eclectic bar-restaurants. Flowery and colorful 'anything goes' decor, board games for everyone and good music keeps this large place packed with fun-seekers. Calmer on weeknights.

Congo (Map pp56-7; Honduras 5329) A great Palermo Viejo drinking den. Mellow yet superhip, and playing some of the best music in town. Check out the sultry back garden and sip an exotic cocktail or two – they're really good.

Mundo Bizarro (Map pp56-7; Guatemala 4802) Cool Palermo Soho watering hole, complete with retro booths, rockabilly music and potent potions. Food ranges from sushi to Tex-Mex; come early if you want a good seat.

Unico (Map pp56-7; Honduras 5604) Crazy popular, this Palermo Hollywood corner bar has a shortage of tables even on weekday nights (come early). Good music, airy sidewalk tables, heady drinks and cozy atmosphere help, plus it's a great place to be seen.

Janio (Map pp56-7; Malabia 1805) Snazzy corner bar-restaurant in Palermo Soho. Several floors high, with covered terrace at the top. The catwalks inside are interesting but the sidewalk tables are the highlight on a balmy summer night. Music gets progressively louder as the night wears on.

Kilkenny (Map pp52-3; Marcelo T de Alvear 399) BA's most famous Irish pub. Fashionable with businesspeople on weekdays after work, and crammed full of everyone else on weekend nights. Good dark, smoky atmosphere, but too popular for its own good.

Druid In (Map pp52-3; Reconquista 1040) Half a block from Kilkenny and much cozier. Offers classic Irish pub fare (steak and kidney pie, Irish stew) and live Celtic music on Fridays and Saturdays.

Le Cigale (Map pp52-3; 25 de Mayo 722) Hip and moody downtown lounge with retro atmosphere and good cocktails; especially popular for its Tuesday night DJ spins. Good party crowds on weeknights, when tables are supremely hard to find.

Deep Blue (Map pp52-3; Ayacucho 1240) This is by far the best place for slick billiards action. Corrugated-steel ceilings, a dozen blue-felted pool tables and DJ house music Thursday to Saturday. Plus, get a personal beer tap at your table. Smaller branch at Reconquista 920 (Map pp52–3).

Doctor Mason (Map pp56-7; Aráoz 1199) Fancy corner joint that pours on the microbrews, including some of Argentina's best. Also bottled Guinness, Isenbeck and Duvel. Good creative cuisine, and check out the pool tables downstairs.

Van Koning (Map pp56-7; Av Báez 325) Best pub to quench your thirst in trendy Las Cañitas. Comes with fun, medieval, nautical Dutch-themed details. Three bars lurk among the dark, cozy spaces and multilevels; popular with expats.

ENTERTAINMENT

Buenos Aires never sleeps, so you'll find something to do every night of the week. There are continuous theater and musical performances, and tango shows are everywhere. On weekends (and even some weeknights) the nightclubs shift into high gear.

Every modern shopping center has its multiscreen cinema complex; most movies are shown in their original language, with subtitles. Check the *Buenos Aires Herald* for screening times.

Discount ticket vendors (for select theater, tango and movie performances) include **Cartelera Vea Más** (Map pp52-3; ☎ 6320-5319; Av Corrientes 1660, suite 2) and **Cartelera Baires** (Map pp52-3; ☎ 4372-5058, Av Corrientes 1382). **Ticketek** (☎ 5237-7200; www.ticketek.com.ar) has outlets throughout the city and sells tickets for large venues.

Classical Music & Performing Arts

Av Corrientes, between 9 de Julio and Av Callao, is Buenos Aires' answer to Broadway.

Teatro Colón (Map pp52-3; ☎ 4378-7133; www .teatrocolon.org.ar; cnr Tucumán & Cerrito) The capital's most prestigious performing-arts venue is richly opulent and an excellent place to see opera, ballet, theatre and classical music. Some events are surprisingly affordable, though foreigners pay double for higher end tickets.

Teatro General San Martín (Map pp52-3; ☎ 0800-333-5254; www.teatrosanmartin.com.ar; Av Corrientes 1530)

Inexpensive shows and events (half-price on Wednesdays) are on offer here, but practically all are in Spanish. Several auditoriums and galleries.

Luna Park (Map pp52-3; ☎ 4311-5100; www.luna park.com.ar; cnr Av Corrientes & Bouchard) Takes up a whole city block and serves as a venue for operas, dances, rock concerts, sporting gigs or any other large event. Check their website for schedules.

Nightclubs

Buenos Aires is all about the night, and clubbing is no exception. The action doesn't even start until after 2am, and the later the better. Those in the know take a nap before dinner, then stay up 'til the early morning light – or even until noon the next day!

In December 2004 a fire at the República Cromañón club claimed 194 lives. New regulations were swiftly slapped into place, closing some places down for good. Others have since reopened, but are presently prohibited from allowing dancing or live music. As clubs adapt changes will keep occurring, so ask where the hottest nightspots are during your stay.

Asia de Cuba (Map pp52-3; ☎ 4894-1328; Dealessi 750; ☯ Wed-Sat) By day it's a restaurant, but at night Asia de Cuba becomes one of BA's slickest clubs. The location is pretty darn romantic, and the exotic dockside lounges don't hurt. Dress well and look important. Best on Wednesdays.

Bahrein (Map pp52-3; ☎ 44315-2403; Lavalle 345; ☯ Tue, Wed, Fri & Sat) On Tuesdays this popular downtown spot offers up the best drum'n'bass in town, but weekends rock just as good. Multifloors, chill-out spaces and eclectic decor add to the cool-vibe mix. The beats get faster as the night wears on.

Club Niceto (Map pp56-7; ☎ 4779-9396; Niceto Vega 5510) One of BA's biggest crowd pullers. Best on Thursday nights, when theater company Club 69 takes over and puts on a raucous transvestite show that's popular with both the straight and the gay. Plenty of blue spotlights and dry ice add atmosphere.

Maluco Beleza (Map pp52-3; ☎ 4372-1737; Sarmiento 1728; ☯ Wed, Fri-Sun) Located in an old mansion, this Brazilian magnet draws in long lines of hip-wigglers. Latin beats and lithe stage dancers stir up excitement, but you can always head upstairs for more intimate spaces. Especially good on Sundays.

Mint (Map pp56-7; ☎ 4806-8002; cnr Costanera Norte & Sarmiento; ⊗ Wed-Sat) A huge, popular club out by the Costanera Norte. Known for its techno on Fridays, when big-name DJs bring in the crowds of sniffy twenty-somethings. Other nights see a mix of house and hip-hop. Great riverside lounges.

Opera Bay (Map pp52-3; ☎ 4315-8666; Grierson 225; ⊗ Wed-Sat) Beautiful by day or night, this huge waterside club looks like a flattened Sydney Opera House. Plenty of bars and terraces make getting a drink and fresh air easy – great for those more interested in smooching than dancing. Come on Fridays.

Pachá (Map pp56-7; ☎ 4788-4280; Av Costanera Norte; ⊗ Fri & Sat) Famous international guest DJs spin tunes for spruced-up and sniffy clientele at this huge, riverside mecca. It's a younger crowd on Fridays, and on Saturdays techno beats take over. Lines outside are long, so try to get a VIP invite. It's near Av La Pampa.

Live Music
Some bars have live music, though recent fire regulations may have affected schedules. For classical music and tango shows, see opposite and p68.

Notorious (Map pp52-3; ☎ 4815-8473; www.notorious.com.ar; Av Callao 966) Small place with great intimate feel, and one of BA's premier venues for live jazz music (almost nightly; Saturdays it's bossa nova). Dinner available; up front is a CD shop where you can listen before buying.

Club de Vino (Map pp56-7; ☎ 4833-0049; Cabrera 4737) Classy Palermo Viejo complex boasting a romantic restaurant, fancy bar, 180-seat music hall, wine shop and even small wine museum. Excellent for fine jazz, folklore and tango performances. Good wines (of course) and cheese platters too.

La Trastienda (Map pp52-3; ☎ 4342-7650; www.latrastienda.com; Balcarce 460) International acts specializing in salsa, merengue, blues, Latin pop

---

GAY & LESBIAN BUENOS AIRES

Buenos Aires is now South America's top gay destination, and offers a vibrant range of gay bars, cafés and clubs. You'll have to know where to look, however; despite general tolerance for homosexuality, this ain't SF or Sydney yet. BA's lesbian scene also definitely exists, though it's not nearly as overt as the boys'.

Look up current sweetheart spots in free booklets such as *La Otra Guía*, *The Ronda* and *Queer*, available at gay destinations. Magazines such as *NX* and *Imperio G* can be bought at newsstands. A lively nighttime cruising area is around Avs Santa Fe and Pueyrredón, where discount admission coupons are handed out on street corners.

Good websites are www.thegayguide.com.ar and gaybuenosaires.blogspot.com. For travel details there's **Pride Travel** (Map pp52-3; ☎ 5218-6556; www.pride-travel.com; Paraguay 523, 2E). The website www.friendlyapartments.ar specializes in renting to gay visitors, or try the San Telmo B&B **Lugar Gay** (☎ 4300-4747; www.lugargay.org; Defensa 1120; s US$35-45, d US$45-65).

In November there's a gay and lesbian **cinefest** (www.diversafilms.com.ar) as well as a **gay pride parade** (Marcha del Orgullo Gay; www.marchadelorgullo.org.ar). Looks like gay pride has arrived in Buenos Aires, and is here to stay.

Popular gay nightspots:

Amerika (Map pp56-7; ☎ 4865-4416; Gascón 1040; ⊗ Fri-Sun) All-you-can-drink madness; large crowds, dark corners and thumping music.

Bach Bar (Map pp56-7; JA Cabrera 4390; ⊗ Tue-Sun) Rowdy fun, especially for lesbians. Intimate and packed, with occasional stripper shows. Best Fridays and Saturdays.

Contramano (Map pp52-3; Rodríguez Peña 1082; ⊗ Wed-Sun) One of BA's oldest gay venues, catering to older gay men. Trannie shows and raffle on Sundays.

Glam (Map pp56-7; JA Cabrera 3046; ⊗ Thu-Sat) A fun gay club in a big old mansion. Plenty of lounges, bars and pretty boys. Come on Thursday and Saturday.

Sitges (Map pp56-7; ☎ 4861-3763; Av Córdoba 4119; ⊗ Fri-Sun) A big checkout scene for both girls and boys, with karaoke on Sunday. Loud but good.

Palacio Alsina (Map pp52-3; ☎ 4331-1277; Adolfo Alsina 934; ⊗ Thu-Sun) Palatial like a fairy tale, with hot dancers and packed floor. Friday and Sunday are mostly gay, while Thursday and Saturday are mixed.

For Club 69 see Club Niceto (opposite).

ARGENTINA

and tango play at this large venue (400 seats plus 1000 standing room), but rock rules the roost. Big names like Pericos, Café Tacuba and Yo La Tengo have jammed here; check website for schedules.

La Peña del Colorado (Map pp56-7; ☎ 4822-1038; Güemes 3657) Wonderfully local music venue, complete with guitar-strumming clientele, nightly folk shows and plenty of smoky air. Plus northern Argentine food specialties like spicy empanadas, *locro* and *humitas de Chala* (like tamales).

El Samovar de Rasputín (Map p49; ☎ 4302-3190; Del Valle Iberlucea 1251) Supremely funky blues joint at the heart of touristy La Boca. Run by eccentric, ex-hippie Napo, who's met the likes of Mick Jagger, Taj Mahal and Eric Clapton (not to mention Pavarotti). Live weekend blues.

Sports

If you're lucky enough to witness a *fútbol* match, you'll encounter a passion unrivaled in any other sport. The most popular teams are **Boca Juniors** (Map p49; ☎ 4362-2260; www.bocajuniors.com.ar; Brandsen 805) in La Boca and **River Plate** (☎ 4788-1200; www.carp.org.ar; Alcorta 7597) in Belgrano, northwest of Aeroparque Jorge Newberry.

Ticket prices ultimately depend on the teams playing and the demand. In general, however, *entradas populares* (bleachers) are the cheapest seats (US$6.50 to US$8) and attract the more emotional fans of the game; don't show any signs of wealth in this section, including watches, necklaces or fancy cameras. *Plateas* (fixed seats) cost US$10 to US$30.

If you don't want to go by yourself, join a tour with **Tangol** (Map pp52-3; ☎ 4312-7276; www.tangol.com; Av Florida 971, suite 31), which charges US$36 for a ticket, hotel transfers and tour guide. For more information on *fútbol* in Argentina see www.afa.org.ar.

Polo is most popular from October through December at Campo de Polo in Palermo. Rugby, horseracing and *pato* (a traditional Argentine game played on horseback) are also spectating possibilities.

Tango Shows

Most travelers will want to take in a tango show in BA, as they should. It's a bit futile to look for 'nontouristy' shows, however, since basically all tango shows are geared toward tourists in one way or another. If you want less sensationalism, then look for cheaper shows; they'll tend to be more traditional. *Milongas*

(dance halls, or the dances themselves) are where *tanguistas* strut their stuff, but spectators don't really belong there.

There are 'free' (donation) street tango shows on Sunday at San Telmo's antiques fair (p51). Some restaurants in BA (especially in San Telmo and La Boca) offer free tango shows, but you have to eat or drink something there.

Café Homero (Map pp56-7; ☎ 4701-7357; JA Cabrera 4946; shows US$5) In Palermo Hollywood, this perfectly sized venue has good inexpensive shows – but you'll need to consume something. Call for reservations.

Café Tortoni (Map pp52-3; ☎ 4342-4328; www.cafetortoni.com.ar; Av de Mayo 825; shows US$8) Good, inexpensive tango in the back of an old café. Shows run twice nightly; also see p65.

Centro Cultural Torquato Tasso (Map p49; ☎ 4307-6506; www.tangotasso.com; Defensa 1575; shows US$6.50) Excellent San Telmo venue with good shows (Wednesday to Saturday). See also p59.

Club de Vino (Map pp56-7; ☎ 4833-8330; JA Cabrera 4737; shows US$7-12) Upscale Palermo Hollywood venue with live tango music and singers only (no dancers). Friday and Saturday nights; call for reservations.

Confitería Ideal (Map pp52-3; ☎ Suipacha 384; shows US$5) A Buenos Aires institution that offers cheap nightly shows. See also p59.

El Balcón (Map pp52-3; ☎ 4362-2354; Humberto Primo 461) Free tango shows from Friday to Sunday at 9pm, but you have to eat here.

Mitos Argentinos (Map pp52-3; ☎ 4362-7810; www.mitosargentinos.com.ar; Humberto Primo 489) Live rock music on Friday and Saturday nights, but on Sundays offers tango classes and shows all afternoon.

These touristy, sensational dinner-tango shows (BA is full of them) are oriented at wealthy tourists. Many have a Las Vegas–like feel, and often involve costume changes, dry ice and plenty of high kicks. Reservations are crucial.

Bar Sur (Map pp52-3; ☎ 4362-6086; Estados Unidos 299; dinner show US$44, show only US$31) Intimate venue, just a dozen small tables.

Complejo Tango (Map p49; ☎ 4308-3242; www.complejotango.com.ar; Av Belgrano 2608; dinner show US$58, show only US$42) Includes a group tango class.

El Querandí (Map pp52-3; ☎ 5199-1770; www.querandi.com.ar; Perú 302; dinner show US$63, show only US$47) Also a restaurant.

Taconeando (Map pp52-3; ☎ 4307-6696; www.taconeando.com; Balcarce 725; dinner show US$36, show only US$26) About 130 seats.

SHOPPING

If you earn hard currency, Buenos Aires is a good place to spend money. The city is full of modern shopping malls, along with long, flashy store-lined streets like Avs Florida and Santa Fe. You'll find decent-quality clothes, leather, accessories, electronics, music and homewares, but anything imported (like electronics) will be very expensive.

Palermo Viejo is the best neighborhood for boutiques and creative fashions. Av Alvear, toward the Recoleta cemetery, means Gucci and Armani. Defensa in San Telmo is full of pricey antique shops. There are several weekend crafts markets such as the hippy *feria artesanal* in front of Recoleta's cemetery (p55). The famous San Telmo antiques fair (p51) takes place on Sunday (on Saturdays there's an artsy fair). For cheap third-world imports head to Av Pueyrredón near Once train station (Estación Once; Map pp52–3); you can find just about anything there.

Feria de Mataderos (www.feriademataderos.com.ar; cnr Av de los Corrales & Lisandro de la Torre) Way out west in the Mataderos *barrio* is this exceptional street market. People flock here for the cheap *asado*, good craft market, traditional folk dances and *gauchos* on horseback. Open Saturdays (6pm to midnight) from January to March, and Sundays (11am to 8pm) the rest of the year; call for exact dates. Buses 180 and 155 get you there in about an hour.

GETTING THERE & AWAY
Air

Most international flights leave from **Ezeiza** (Map p49; ☎ 5480-6111; www.aa2000.com.ar). **Manuel Tienda León** (MTL; Map pp52-3; ☎ 4314-3636; www.tiendaleon.com; cnr Av Eduardo Madero & San Martín) runs frequent shuttles to/from Ezeiza (US$8, 40 minutes). Penny-pinchers can take bus 86 (US75¢, 1½ hours). Taxis cost around US$18, including tolls.

MTL charges US$3 for the 15-minute ride to Aeroparque. Or take city bus 45 from Plaza San Martín (US30¢). Taxis cost around US$5.

Argentina's departure tax is US$18, payable in US dollars or pesos. The following is a list of airline offices:

Aerolíneas Argentinas/Austral (Map pp52-3; ☎ 0810-222-86527; www.aerolineasargentinas.com; Av Leandro N Alem 1134) Another branch at Perú 2.
Air Canada (Map pp52-3; ☎ 4393-9090; www.aircanada.com; Av Córdoba 656)

Air France (Map pp52-3; ☎ 4317-4700; www.airfrance.com; San Martín 344, 23rd fl)
Alitalia (Map pp52-3; ☎ 4310-9999; www.alitalia.com; Av Santa Fe 887)
American Airlines (Map pp52-3; ☎ 4318-1111; www.aa.com; Av Santa Fe 881)
British Airways (Map pp52-3; ☎ 0800-666-1459; www.britishairways.com; Av del Libertador 498, 13th fl)
Delta (Map pp52-3; ☎ 0800-666-0133; www.delta.com; Av Santa Fe 887)
KLM (Map pp52-3; ☎ 4317-4700; San Martín 344, 23rd fl)
LADE (Map pp52-3; ☎ 0810-810-5233; Perú 714)
Lan (Map pp52-3; ☎ 0800-999-9526; Cerrito 866)
Lloyd Aéreo Boliviano (Map pp52-3; ☎ 4323-1900; www.labairlines.com.bo; Carlos Pellegrini 141)
Lufthansa (Map pp52-3; ☎ 4319-0600; Marcelo T de Alvear 590, 6th fl)
Pluna (Map pp52-3; ☎ 4120-0530; Av Florida 1)
Swissair (Map pp52-3; ☎ 4319-0000; Av Santa Fe 846, 1st fl)
Transportes Aéreos de Mercosur (TAM; Map pp52-3; ☎ 0800-333-3333; www.tam.com.ar; Cerrito 1026)
United Airlines (Map pp52-3; ☎ 0-810-777-864833; Av Eduardo Madero 9000)
Varig (Map pp52-3; ☎ 4329-9211; Av Córdoba 972, 3rd fl)

Boat

Buquebus (Ferrylineas; Map pp52-3; ☎ 4316-6500; www.buquebus.com; cnr Avs Antártida Argentina & Córdoba) offers several daily ferries to Colonia via a fast boat (US$18, one hour) or slow boat (US$31, three hours). It also goes to Montevideo (US$53, three hours) and has seasonally available boat–bus services to Punta del Este, Uruguay's top beach resort. Buquebus has other offices at Av Córdoba 879 (Map pp52–3) and in Recoleta's Patio Bullrich mall. More services and higher prices exist in the summer season,

---

GETTING TO URUGUAY

Traveling from Buenos Aires into Uruguay is fairly straightforward, and you can see charming Colonia Del Sacramento (p955) in a day (Montevideo, the capital, takes longer). Nationals of Western Europe, the USA, Canada, Australia and New Zealand don't need a visa, though it's wise to check the current situation during your tenure.

Uruguay's unit of currency is the peso, but US dollars and Argentine pesos are widely accepted for tourist services.

ARGENTINA

when it's a good idea to buy your ticket an hour or two in advance. Some nationalities may need visas to enter Uruguay.

Bus

Retiro (Map pp52-3; ☎ 4310-0700; cnr Avs Antártida Argentina & Ramos Mejía) is a huge three-story bus station with slots for 75 buses. Inside are cafeterias, shops, bathrooms, luggage storage, telephone offices with internet and a 24-hour information kiosk. There's also a **tourist information office** (suite L83; ☺ 7:30am-1pm Mon-Sat); look for it under bus counter 105.

The following list is a small sample of very extensive services. Prices will vary widely depending on the season, the company and the economy. During holidays prices rise; buy your ticket in advance.

Domestic destinations:

Destination	Duration (hr)	Cost (US$)
Bahía Blanca	9	18
Bariloche	22	33
Comodoro Rivadavia	26	57
Córdoba	10	18
Gualeguaychú	4	8
Mar del Plata	6	13
Mendoza	15	31
Neuquén	18	24
Puerto Iguazú	17	39
Puerto Madryn	28	42
Resistencia	13	25
Rosario	4	8
Salta	21	44
San Martín de los Andes	20	40
Santa Rosa	9	15
Tucumán	16	34

International destinations:

Destination	Duration (hr)	Cost (US$)
Asunción, Paraguay	18	26
Foz do Iguazú, Brazil	19	43
Lima, Peru	3 days	135
Montevideo, Uruguay	8	26
Punta del Este, Uruguay	10	33
Rio de Janeiro, Brazil	44	97
Santiago, Chile	20	50
São Paulo, Brazil	34	76

Train

With very few exceptions, rail travel in Argentina is limited to Buenos Aires' suburbs and

provincial cities. It's cheaper but not nearly as fast, frequent or comfortable as hopping on a bus.

Each of BA's train stations has its own Subte stop.

Estación Constitución (Map p49; ☎ 4018-0719, 4305-5577) Services to La Plata, Bahía Blanca, Atlantic beach towns.

Estación Once (Map p49; ☎ 4861-0043, 4317-4400) Services to Luján, Bahía Blanca, Atlantic beach towns.

Estación Retiro (Map pp52-3; ☎ 4317-4400) Services to Tigre, Rosario.

GETTING AROUND
Bicycle

Buenos Aires has several companies that offer guided bike tours to select destinations (see p59). They also rent out bikes, but be aware that downtown motor vehicles in this city consider bikes a pest – and very low on the traffic totem pole. If you must, ride bikes in safer neighborhoods like San Telmo and Palermo (both with some cobbled streets) or Puerto Madero and the nearby Reserva Ecológica Costanera Sur. And if you want to live another day to eat another steak, ride defensively!

Bus

Sold at many kiosks, the Guia T (pocket version US75¢) details some 200 bus routes. Fares depend on the distance, but most rides are US30¢; say 'ochenta' to the driver, then place coins in the machine behind him (change given). Offer front seats to elderly passengers.

Car & Motorcycle

We don't recommend you rent a car to drive around Buenos Aires. Porteño drivers turn crazy behind the wheel and you shouldn't compete with them. Also, public transport is excellent. Cars are good to explore the countryside, however. Try **Avis** (Map pp52-3; ☎ 4326-5542; www.avis.com; Cerrito 1527), **New Way** (Map pp52-3; ☎ 4515-0331; www.new-wayrentacar.com.ar; Marcello T de Alvear 773) or **Hertz** (Map pp52-3; ☎ 4816-8001; www.hertz.com.ar; Paraguay 1138).

For motorcycle rentals see **Motocare** (Map p49; ☎ 4782-1500; www.motocare.com.ar/rental; Av del Libertador 6588).

Subway

Buenos Aires' Subte (www.metrovias.com.ar) is fast, efficient and costs only US25¢ per ride. Four of the five lines (Líneas A, B, D and E) run from the *microcentro* to the capital's western and northern outskirts, while Línea C links Estación Retiro and Constitución. A new H line is due to open in 2007, eventually connecting Estación Once with Retiro.

Trains operate from approximately 5am to 10:30pm except Sunday and holidays (when hours are 8am to 10pm); they run frequently on weekdays, less so on weekends.

Taxi & Remise

Black-and-yellow cabs are very common and reasonably priced. Meters start at around US75¢; tips are unnecessary, but leaving extra change is appreciated. If you're taking a taxi into town from Ezeiza airport, head to the city taxi counter, just behind the first row of transport booths. Don't just go with any driver.

Many people might warn you it's not safe to take street taxis in Buenos Aires, because of robbery – and it's true, some people have been robbed in taxis. It's all a matter of luck, and usually it's OK to take a taxi off the street (even as a lone woman). In fact, some taxi drivers are better at ripping you off than robbing you. Just make sure the driver uses the meter (and have an idea of where you're going), know your money (fake bills don't have watermarks) and try to pay with low-denomination bills (some drivers deftly replace high bills with low ones). And try to remember that most *taxistas* are honest men making a hard living.

If you want to play it safer, however, call a *remise*. They're considered safer than street taxis, since an established company sends them out. Any business should be able to phone a *remise* for you.

AROUND BUENOS AIRES

TIGRE

North of BA about an hour is this favorite *porteño* weekend destination. You can check out the popular riverfront, take a relaxing boat ride in the Delta del Paraná and shop at **Mercado de Frutos** (a daily crafts market that's best on weekends).

Tigre's **tourist office** (☎ 011-4512-4497; www .tigre.gov.ar; Mitre 305; ☺ 9am-5pm) is next door to McDonald's. Nearby are ticket counters for commuter boats that cruise the waterways; the tourist office is good and can recommend a destination.

The quickest, cheapest way to get to Tigre is by taking the Mitre line from Retiro train station (US35¢, 50 minutes, frequent).

SAN ANTONIO DE ARECO
☎ 02326 / pop 21,300

Dating from the early 18th century, this serene village northwest of Buenos Aires is the symbolic center of Argentina's diminishing *gaucho* culture. It's also host to the country's biggest *gaucho* celebration, **Día de la Tradición**, in November.

The **tourist office** (☎ 453-165; ☺ 8am-8pm) is at the northern end of Arellano.

Narrow tree-lined streets make this low-rise, stoplight-free town pleasant to stroll, so walk a few blocks beyond the old bridge to **Museo Gauchesco Ricardo Güiraldes** (☎ 454-780; admission US75¢; ☺ 11am-5pm Wed-Mon), a ranch sheltering the *gaucho* collection of a famous Argentine author.

Plaza Ruiz de Arellano is beautifully landscaped and sports a parochial church, while local artisans are known for producing mate paraphernalia, *rastras* (silver-studded belts) and *facones* (long-bladed knives).

Buses run from BA's Retiro bus terminal (US$4, two hours); Chevallier has departures every 1½ hours.

LA PLATA
☎ 0221 / pop 970,000

On Plaza Moreno is La Plata's beautiful neo-Gothic **cathedral**; it took 115 years to finish and was finally completed in 2000. North of town, the extensive 60-hectare **Paseo del Bosque** is home to the ancient but excellent **Museo de La Plata** (☎ 425-7744; admission US$4; ☺ 10am-6pm Tue-Sun). On display are heaps of interesting exhibits such as dried insects, musty mummies and dinosaur skeletons. Nearby is the **Jardín Zoológico** (☎ 427-3925; admission US75¢; ☺ 9am-6pm Tue-Sun).

To get to La Plata, take bus 129 (US$2, one hour). It departs frequently from the short street Martín Zuviría, across from Retiro train station. La Plata's bus terminal is at Calles 4 and 42, while its train station (corner Av 1 and Calle 44) has half-hourly services to Constitución (US75¢, 1¼ hours).

URUGUAY

Day trips to small, charming, cobbled **Colonia** are popular, and it's also possible to travel to nearby **Montevideo** (Uruguay's capital) for a couple of days. A good summer destination is the beach resort of **Punta del Este**, only a few hours away from Buenos Aires. For transport links to Uruguay see p69. For more information on these destinations, see the Uruguay chapter, p944.

NORTHEAST ARGENTINA

From the spectacular natural wilderness of Iguazú Falls in the north to the chic sophistication of Rosario in the south, the northeast is one of Argentina's most diverse regions. Wedged between the Paraná and Uruguay Rivers (thus earning it the nickname 'Mesopotamia'), the region relies heavily on those rivers for fun and its livelihood, while next door, the Chaco is sparsely populated, and often called Argentina's 'empty quarter.'

HISTORY

This was Guaraní country first. They were semisedentary agriculturalists, raising sweet potatoes, maize, manioc and beans and eating river fish until the Spanish arrived in 1570, pushing their way south from Paraguay. Santa Fe was founded in 1573, Corrientes a few years later. The Jesuits came soon after, herding the Guaraní into 30 *reducciónes* (settlements) in the upper Paraná in the hope of converting them by way of prayer and labor. The *reducciónes* were doing a roaring trade in yerba mate (herb mate) production until Carlos III, busy with nation-building back in Spain, decided that the Jesuit's growing power base was too much of a distraction, and booted them all off the Americas in 1767.

Some Guaraní were still out there, though, in the steamy thorn forests of Chaco and Formosa, resisting the newcomers. They lasted until 1850 when the woodcutters from Corrientes came through, looking for the *quebracho* (axe-breaker) tree to satisfy their tannin lust. After the land had been cleared (in more ways than one), the Guaraní who were left were kept busy picking the newly planted cotton and raising cattle.

The War of the Triple Alliance (1865–70) put an end to Brazil and Paraguay's claims on the territory and for a few years Entre Ríos was an independent republic, before joining the Buenos Aires–based Unitarist coalition under Rosas. Local *caudillo* (chief) Justo José Urquiza brought about Rosas' defeat and the eventual adoption of Argentina's modern constitution.

By the late 19th century, Rosario had become the regional superstar (it even vied for capital status for a while there) as its port did a roaring trade and thousands of rural-dwellers poured in from the countryside in search of a better life.

ROSARIO
☎ 0341 / pop 909,000
So, you dig the vibe of the capital, but the sheer size of it is sending you a little loco in the coco? Rosario may be the place for you.

Located just a few hours north, this is in many ways Argentina's second city. Not in terms of population, but culturally, financially and aesthetically. The city never had much of a backpacker scene, but the huge university and corresponding population of students, artists and musicians means it's all ready to go.

Nighttime the streets come alive and the bars and clubs pack out. In the day, once everybody wakes up, they shuffle down to the river beaches for more music, drinks and a bit of a lie down.

It's not all fun and games, though. Culture vultures won't be disappointed by the wealth of museums and galleries in this historic city, and Che Guevara fans will want to check out his birthplace.

Orientation & Information
The long-distance **bus terminal** (☎ 437-2384; Cafferata 702) is 4km west of center. Many local buses (marked 'Centro' or 'Plaza Sarmiento') go to the center; buy US70¢ magnetic cards at kiosks beforehand. Bus 138 leaves from the train station.

The informative **tourist office** (☎ 480-2230; Av del Huerto) is on the waterfront.

Cambios along San Martín and Córdoba change traveler's checks; there are many banks and ATMs on Santa Fe between Mitre and Entre Ríos.

Sights
Prices, dates and hours change throughout the year. Check with the tourist office to be sure.

The colossal **Monumento Nacional a la Bandera** (Monument to the Flag; ☒ 9am-7pm), located

NORTHEAST ARGENTINA

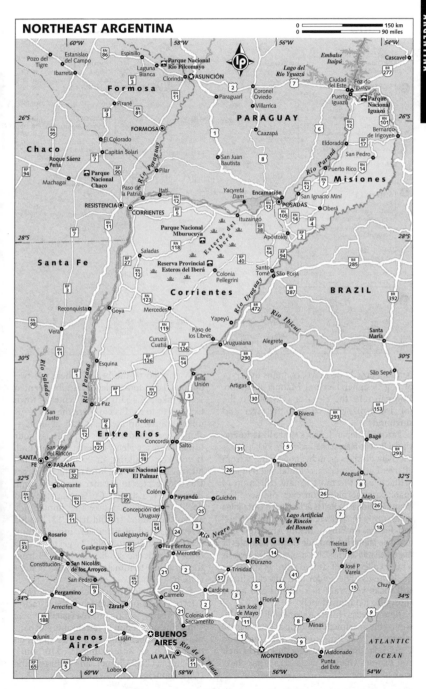

0 — 150 km
0 — 90 miles

ROSARIO

INFORMATION	
Tourist Office.....................1 D2	

SIGHTS & ACTIVITIES	
Crafts Fair.........................2 D2	
Entre Ríos 480, Ernesto 'Che'	
Guevara's First Home......3 C2	
Monumento Nacional a la	
Bandera..........................4 D2	
Museo Histórico Provincial Dr	
Julio Marc.......................5 A3	
Museo Municipal de Bellas Artes	
Juan B Castagnino...........6 A3	
Museo Provincial de Ciencias	
Naturales Dr Ángel	
Gallardo.........................7 B2	

SLEEPING	
Hotel Britania...................8 C2	
Hotel Plaza del Sol............9 C3	
La Casona de Don Jaime...10 B2	
Rosario Inn......................11 C2	
Savoy Hotel.....................12 C2	

EATING	
La Casa de Nicolas............13 C3	
La Delfina........................14 C3	
Roots Café.....................(see 10)	
Tyzio..............................15 C1	

DRINKING	
Gothika...........................16 C3	
Louis............................(see 19)	
Mel at Rivers..................(see 19)	
Peña la Amistad...............17 C3	
Taura............................(see 19)	

TRANSPORT	
Aerolíneas Argentinas........18 C2	
Austral..........................(see 18)	
Estación Fluvial.................19 D2	
Local Bus Terminal.............20 C2	

behind Plaza 25 de Mayo, contains the crypt of flag designer General Manuel Belgrano. You can take the elevator (US30¢) to the top for a dizzying view of the river and surrounds.

Parque Independencia's **Museo Histórico Provincial Dr Julio Marc** (admission free; ⏰ 9am-5pm) has excellent displays on indigenous cultures from all over Latin America, colonial and religious artifacts and the most ornate collection of mate paraphernalia you ever did see. The **Museo Municipal de Bellas Artes Juan B Castagnino** (cnr Av Carlos Pellegrini & Blvd Oroño; admission US30¢; ⏰ 2-8pm) focuses on European and Argentine fine art. The **Museo Provincial de Ciencias Naturales Dr Ángel Gallardo** (Moreno 750; admission free; ⏰ 3-6pm) is a huge collection of stuffed animals and other grisly items. The spider and insect exhibits will make you want to rush out and buy a mosquito net immediately.

Renowned architect Alejandro Bustillo designed the apartment building at **Entre Ríos 480** where, in 1928, Ernesto Guevara Lynch and Celia de la Serna resided after the birth of their son Ernesto Guevara de la Serna, popularly known as Che.

Wanna go to the beach? There are two options. For a more relaxed, family-oriented scene, take bus 153 from the center of town 6km north to Av Puccio (here the bus turns inland). Stroll up the boardwalk along Catalunya beach and look for a spot to lay your towel. There are plenty of restaurants around. If you keep walking, in 20 minutes you'll hit private beach Av Florida, which charges US$1 for access to a wider stretch of sand. Beyond it is Estación Costa Alta (the boat dock), where you can take a 15-minute ride across the Paraná (round trip US$1) to **Isla Invernada**, land of woodsier, more natural beaches (camping possible). To get to the boat dock without the stroll, take bus 103 from the local bus terminal on San Luis; it stops close by.

For a younger, noisier experience, catch a ferry (US$2 one way) from the Estación Fluvial (Ferry Station) to **Isla Espinillo** where you'll find a selection of restaurants and bars, music, hammock space and water sports on offer, such as waterskiing (US$10/hour), jetskiing (US$23/hour) and windsurfing (US$7/hour).

Out at the airfield, **Paracaidismo Rosario** (☎ 456-6585; www.paracaidismorosario.com.ar in Spanish) offers one-off tandem skydives and longer certification courses.

Back in town, there's a weekend **crafts fair** on Av Belgrano, south of the tourist office.

Festivals & Events

Weekends in January and February, Rosario hosts an excellent open-air **arts and cinema festival** in plazas and parks around the city. Accommodation can get tight during this time. For program details, check with the tourist office or munisur@rosario.gov.ar.

Sleeping

Rosario Inn (☎ 421-0358; Sargento Cabal 54; dm/d US$5/10) A sweeping marble staircase welcomes you into this classic converted Rosario house. The wooden floorboards, *parrilla* in the patio, spacious kitchen and balconies with river views all make this an excellent, comfortable option.

La Casona de Don Jaime (☎ 527-9964; www.youth hostelrosario.com.ar; Roca 1051; dm US$6/7 with/without HI card, d US$13/20 with/without HI card) Rosario's first (and best) hostel is pretty much everything a hostel should be: laid back and run by young travelers. There are comfy sitting areas and a bar attached. There's also a small, clean kitchen, lockers and a variety of activities around town on offer.

Savoy Hotel (☎ 448-0071; San Lorenzo 1022; s/d US$10/15) The jury's still out on this one: half say it's like a creepy old haunted mansion, others claim it's a grand old place that's fallen on hard times. Regardless, all rooms have high ceilings and ornate fittings and most have balconies.

Hotel Britania (☎ 440-6036; San Martín 364; s/d US$10/15) The owners are slowly doing this place up, one room at a time, so it's worth asking to see a few. Rooms in the older, front section have way more character.

Hotel Plaza del Sol (☎ 421-9899; www.hotelesplaza .com; San Juan 1055; r US$40; P ⊠ ⌨ ⊜) This four-star property offers excellent-value doubles. The breakfast buffet is huge and the swimming pool and sundeck on the 11th floor have great city views.

The most natural campsites are on **Isla Invernada** (per person US$1) – see opposite – for details on how to get there. On the mainland, **Camping Municipal** (☎ 471-4381; campsites per person US$1) is 9km north of the city; take bus 35 from the center to Barra 9.

Eating

Rosario is a big city and it doesn't have an obvious center when it comes to restaurants – they're scattered all over the place – but thankfully there's a *confitería* (café/snack bar) on just about every street corner.

La Casa de Nicolas (Mendoza 937; per kilo US$3) You might get a tan sitting under the strip lighting, and maybe food-by-the-kilo doesn't strike you as the classiest concept, but there's some good vegetarian food on offer at this Asian-themed place, including nori rolls and braised shitake mushrooms.

Roots Café (Roca 1051; mains US$3-4) 'Ethnic' food is a relatively new concept in Rosario, but Roots takes a pretty good stab at it, with rotating weekly specials from different countries like Peru, China and Mexico.

La Delfina (cnr 3 de Febrero & Mitre; mains US$4) La Delfina edges away from the pizza, pasta, *parrillada* grind (but not too far) with a good, varied menu and some excellent *picadas* (hors d'oeuvres).

Tyzio (cnr Salta & Paraguay; pizza US$4-10, mains US$5) Finally, somebody cottoned onto the fact that pizzas can have more than one ingredient. The folks at Tyzio do it in style, too, with toppings like artichoke hearts, rocket, brie cheese and char-grilled capsicum.

Drinking

For the latest on the nightlife scene, check out the free magazine *Fuera de Hora*, available in tourist offices and hostels around town.

Gothika (Mitre 1539; admission US$2-4; ☯ 24hr Thu-Sat) Rosario's hottest club (this week, anyway) is set up in a renovated church. Music varies, but concentrates on drum'n'bass and breakbeat. The crowd is young and there doesn't seem to be a dress code (unless it says something about having to wear brown leather slip-ons with shorts).

Peña la Amistad (Maipú 1111; ☯ 10pm-late Fri & Sat) *Peñas* (clubs/bars that host informal folk music gatherings) have been enjoying a resurgence of popularity among young Argentines of late, and if you haven't checked one out, this is one of Rosario's oldest and best respected, and a fine place to start. Things get pretty rowdy later on once the vino starts flowing, with lots of clapping, stomping and singing along.

The biggest buzz in town is about the converted ferry station, the **Estación Fluvial** which has been turned into a complex of upmarket bars and nightclubs. Among your options are the following:

Louis (admission US$3-5; ☺ 9pm-late Thu-Sat) Louis is hip and laid-back, a lounge-style club/bar with plenty of different rooms to check out and a DJ spinning cool tunes.

Mel at Rivers (☺ 1pm-late) If you just want to hang out by the water's edge, or have a few drinks before hitting the clubs, this stylish little open-air bar with balconies overlooking the water is the place to be.

Taura (admission US$3-5; ☺ 9pm-late Thu-Sat) Attracting a slightly older crowd and playing mostly mainstream house and pop remixes, Taura is gorgeously decked out, and you'd better be too, if you want to get in.

Getting There & Away
Aerolíneas Argentinas & Austral (☎ 420-8138; www.aerolineasargentinas.com; Santa Fe 1412) have several daily flights to Buenos Aires (US$45).

Bus fares from Rosario include Buenos Aires (US$10, four hours), Córdoba (US$11, six hours), Santa Fe (US$5, 2½ hours), Mendoza (US$18, 12 hours) and Montevideo, Uruguay (US$38, nine hours).

The **train station** (☎ 430-7272; Av del Valle 2700), 3km northwest of the center of town, has services to Buenos Aires (US$4, five hours), leaving at 6am Sundays. Due to the poor condition of tracks and carriages and frequent delays, the train isn't such a great option.

SANTA FE
☎ 0342 / pop 369,600
Santa Fe would be a fairly dull town if not for the university population. Thanks to this, there's a healthy bar and club scene, and plenty of fun to be had during the day.

Relocated during the mid-17th century because of hostile indigenous groups, floods and isolation, the city duplicates the original plan of Santa Fe La Vieja (Old Santa Fe), but a 19th-century neo-Parisian building boom and more recent construction have left only isolated colonial buildings, mostly near Plaza 25 de Mayo.

Orientation
Av San Martín, north of the plaza, is the main commercial artery. The airport is 15km south of town. The bus marked 'A (aeropuerto)' goes past San Luis and Hipólito Yrigoyen (US$50¢, 45 minutes). From the bus terminal, ask at Tata Rapido or Rio Coronda for their

express airport bus service (US$50¢). A taxi should cost about US$5.

Information
Municipal tourist office (☎ 457-4123; www.santafe-turistica.com.ar; Belgrano 2910) In the bus terminal.
Tourfe (Av San Martín 2500) Collects 3% commission on traveler's checks; there are several ATMs along the San Martín *peatonal* (pedestrian mall).
Post office (Av 27 de Febrero 2331).

Sights & Activities
Some colonial buildings are museums, but the churches still serve their ecclesiastical functions, like the mid-17th-century **Templo de Santo Domingo** (cnr 3 de Febrero & 9 de Julio). The exterior simplicity of the 1696 Jesuit **Iglesia de la Compañía** (Plaza 25 de Mayo) masks an ornate interior. The restored, two-story **Casa de los Aldao** (Buenos Aires 2861) dates from the early 18th century.

Built in 1680, the **Convento y Museo de San Francisco** (Amenábar 2257; ☺ 8am-noon & 3:30-7pm Mon-Fri, 3:30-5pm Sat & Sun), south of Plaza 25 de Mayo, is Santa Fe's most important landmark. Its meter-thick walls support a roof of Paraguayan cedar and hardwood beams fitted with wooden spikes rather than nails. The doors are hand-worked originals, while the baroque pulpit is laminated in gold. Its museum covers secular and religious topics from colonial and republican eras.

The **Museo Etnográfico y Colonial Juan de Garay** (25 de Mayo 1470; admission free, donations encouraged; ☺ 8:30am-noon & 4-7pm Mon-Fri, 4:30-7pm Sat & Sun) has a scale model of Santa Fe La Vieja, but the real show-stopper is the *gaucho* 'campchair' – made entirely of cow bones and leather. Gruesome – but comfortable! There are also colonial artifacts, indigenous basketry, Spanish ceramics and a stuffed horse.

Santa Fe has its own **brewery** (☎ 450-2234; www.cervezaschneider.com; Calchines 1401) and brand of beer (called, uh, Santa Fe). Free guided tours of the ultramodern facility are available and culminate in a tasting session, which consists of only one glass per person, regardless of wheedling. Reservations for tours are necessary and you must wear long pants and closed shoes.

The little **skate park** on the shores of Lago de Sur has a half-pipe, ramps and rails. If you've got the moves, you can probably borrow a deck and impress the locals. If not, you can still borrow one and give them something to laugh at. Your call.

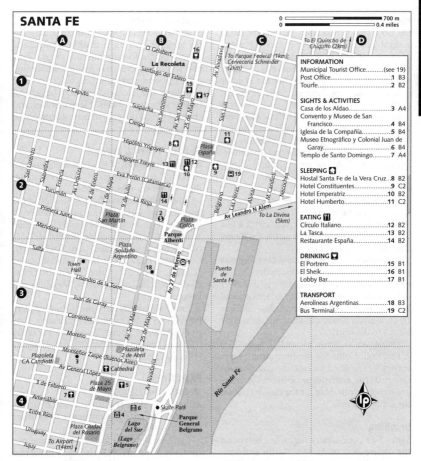

SANTA FE

INFORMATION	
Municipal Tourist Office..........(see 19)	
Post Office....................................1 B3	
Tourfe..2 B2	

SIGHTS & ACTIVITIES	
Casa de los Aldao.......................3 A4	
Convento y Museo de San	
Francisco.................................4 B4	
Iglesia de la Compañía................5 B4	
Museo Etnográfico y Colonial Juan de	
Garay.....................................6 B4	
Templo de Santo Domingo..........7 A4	

SLEEPING	
Hostal Santa Fe de la Vera Cruz..8 B2	
Hotel Constituentes....................9 C2	
Hotel Emperatriz.......................10 B2	
Hotel Humberto........................11 C2	

EATING	
Círculo Italiano.........................12 B2	
La Tasca...................................13 B2	
Restaurante España...................14 B2	

DRINKING	
El Portrero................................15 B1	
El Sheik...................................16 B1	
Lobby Bar................................17 B1	

TRANSPORT	
Aerolíneas Argentinas................18 B3	
Bus Terminal............................19 C2	

Festivals & Events

Santa Fe's **beer festival** (Parque Federal; admission US$2) takes place on the last weekend in January and first weekend in February. Festivities include plenty of live music and a certain carbonated alcoholic beverage.

Sleeping

The surprisingly seedy area around the bus terminal is the budget hotel zone. It's not dangerous – just the town center for various unsavory transactions.

Hotel Humberto (☎ 455-0409; Crespo 2222; s/d US$8/12) Rooms in this mom-and-pop-run hotel are clean and reasonable, with some inlaid brick walls giving the place a very Brady Bunch feel. Some cheaper, smaller singles are available.

Hotel Emperatriz (☎ 453-0061; emperatrizhotelsf@hotmail.com; Irigoyen Freyre 2440; s/d US$9/13; P ☒) The best of the budget picks, this place is set in a beautifully remodeled old house. The lobby is a lot more impressive than the rooms, but they're still light and spacious.

Hotel Constituentes (☎ 452-1586; San Luis 2862; s/d US$10/15) A block from the bus terminal, this hotel has large carpeted rooms with TV. Get one at the back to avoid street noise.

Hostal Santa Fe de la Vera Cruz (☎ 455-1740; hostal_santafe@ciudad.com.ar; Av San Martín 2954; s/d standard US$25/33; P ☒) The standard rooms here are just fine, but for an extra US$10, you can go for the Superior, which are some of the best rooms in town.

ARGENTINA

Eating

On Belgrano, across from the bus terminal, several good, inexpensive places serve Argentine staples like empanadas, pizza and *parrillada*. Midnight munchers will be happy to know that the bus terminal sports a 24-hour snack bar, serving huge portions of decent grub.

La Tasca (Av San Martín 2846; breakfast US$1.50, lunch & dinner US$3-4) Nothing mind-blowing on the menu here, but it's got a great old-time feel with tiled walls and hardwood furniture. Breakfast and snacks are good and cheap, and there are occasional exhibitions featuring local artists.

Restaurante España (Av San Martín 2644; meals US$3-5) A huge menu covers the range of seafood, steaks, pasta, chicken and crepes, with a few Spanish dishes thrown in to justify the name. The wine list is a winner, too.

El Quincho de Chiquito (cnr Brown & Obispo Vieytes; all you can eat US$5-7) Tourists and locals flock to this riverside eatery for outstanding grilled river fish, such as *boga* and *sábalo,* and exceptional hors d'oeuvres, like fish empanadas. Take bus 16 on Gálvez, which parallels Suipacha four blocks to the north.

Círculo Italiano (Hipólito Yrigoyen 2457; mains US$3-5) A real find. Come for the ritzy atmosphere, the waiters in linen jackets, the complimentary paté, the extensive wine list or the inexpensive set meals. Stay for the classic rock on the sound system.

Drinking

Santa Fe's rock-steady nightlife centers on the intersection of Av San Martín and Santiago del Estero, an area known as La Recoleta. Bars come and go in this area; it's worth going for a wander and seeing where the crowds are. Here are a few to get you started:

El Portrero (25 de Mayo 3455; 6pm-late Wed-Sat) A supersmooth option to start your night, with big-screen TVs, board games and plenty of polished wood and black steel tubing to set the mood.

El Sheik (25 de Mayo 3452; 7pm-1am Tue-Sat) Laid-back without being tranquil, this place attracts a young crowd with its cheap drinks and good music.

Lobby Bar (25 de Mayo 3228; 6pm-late Thu-Sat) The hottest 'predance' in town is this retro-themed bar. The action starts to heat up after 11pm.

Entertainment

La Divina (Costanera Este s/n; 1pm-late Tue-Sat; admission free-US$5) This huge tentlike structure is the city's definitive summertime disco. Come and you'll hear everything from *cumbia* (big on horns and percussion, a cousin to salsa, merengue and lambada) and *marcha español* (aggressive drum beats, bleepy noises and chanted lyrics) through to mainstream house and techno.

Getting There & Around

Aerolíneas Argentinas (452-5959; www.aerolineasargentinas.com; 25 de Mayo 2287) has 45 weekly nonstop flights to Buenos Aires (US$41).

The **bus information office** (457-4124) at the bus terminal posts fares for all destinations.

Buses leave hourly for Paraná (US$1, one hour). Other fares include Rosario (US$5, two hours), Buenos Aires (US$15, six hours), Corrientes (US$20, 10 hours) and Posadas (US$23, 12 hours). Other destinations include Córdoba and its sierras, Mendoza and Patagonia.

International services go to Porto Alegre (US$47, 16 hours) and Rio de Janeiro, Brazil (US$100, 36 hours); Asunción, Paraguay (US$40, 13 hours); and Montevideo, Uruguay (US$35, 11 hours).

PARANÁ

0343 / pop 238,000

Although less famous than its sister city across the river, Paraná is in many ways a much more attractive place.

Built on the hilly banks of its namesake river, the historical center is largely intact and the city boasts a couple of majestic plazas. As is the rule in this part of the world, funseekers hit the riverbanks at night to choose from an array of restaurants, clubs and bars.

Orientation

The city's irregular plan has several diagonals, curving boulevards and complex intersections. From Plaza Primero de Mayo, the town center, Calle San Martín is a *peatonal* for six blocks. Bus 1 goes from the bus terminal past the center to the riverside.

Information

There are several ATMs along the San Martín *peatonal*.

Municipal tourist office (420-1837; Oficina Parque, cnr Bajada San Martín & Laurencena) Paraná's municipal tourist office has branches at the bus terminal and at the Oficina Parque on the riverfront. The freecall number (☎ 0800-555-9575) is handy if you find yourself in need of on-the-spot, low-cost tourist information.

Post office (cnr 25 de Mayo & Monte Caseros)
Provincial tourist office (☎ 422-3384; Laprida 5)

Sights & Activities

Plaza Primero de Mayo has had an **Iglesia Catedral** since 1730, but the current building dates from 1885. When Paraná was capital of the confederation, the Senate deliberated at the **Colegio del Huerto**, at the corner of 9 de Julio and 25 de Mayo.

A block west, at the corner of Corrientes and Urquiza, are the **Palacio Municipal** (1889) and the **Escuela Normal Paraná**, a school founded by noted educator (later President) DF Sarmiento. Across San Martín is the **Teatro Municipal Tres de Febrero** (25 de Mayo 60), dating from 1908. At the west end of the San Martín *peatonal*, on Plaza Alvear, the **Museo Histórico de Entre Ríos Martín Leguizamón** (☯ 7:30am-12:30pm & 3-7:30pm Tue-Fri, 9am-noon & 4-7pm Sat, 9am-noon Sun) flaunts provincial pride, as knowledgeable guides go to rhetorical extremes extolling the role of local *caudillos* in Argentine history. The adjacent subterranean **Museo de Bellas Artes Pedro E Martínez** (☯ 9am-noon & 4-9pm Mon-Fri, 10:30am-12:30pm & 5:30-8pm Sat, 10:30am-12:30pm Sun) displays works by provincial artists. Both museums welcome the US30¢ voluntary contribution.

The modern **Museo de la Ciudad** (Parque Urquiza; admission free; ☯ 8am-noon Tue-Fri, 4-8pm Tue-Sun, 9am-noon Sat) focuses on Paraná's urban past and surroundings. Winter opening hours are slightly shorter.

From the Puerto Nuevo at the corner of Av Laurencia and Vélez Sársfield, the **Paraná Rowing Club** (☎ 431-6518) conducts hour-long **river excursions** (tickets US$3; ☯ Fri-Sun) at 3:30pm and 5pm.

Baqueanos del Rio (☎ 15-543-5337; tours per hr from US$7) organizes fascinating tours of the river and islands, with special attention paid to wildlife and the traditional lifestyle of the islands' inhabitants. Departs from riverfront tourist office.

Sleeping

Camping Balneario Thompson (☎ 420-1583; campsites per person US$3) The most convenient campground. Buses 1 and 6 ('Thompson') link it to downtown.

Hotel Bristol (☎ 431-3961; Alsina 221; s/d US$10/17, with shared bathroom US$6/10) Spitting distance from the bus terminal (although you might want to go up on the roof to get a clean shot), rooms here are tastefully if sparsely decorated and the beds are superfirm.

Hotel Latino (☎ 431-1036; San Juan 158; s/d US$10/17) The best of the budget picks in the center, with a maze of small but comfortable rooms, patio areas and a lounge/living area for guest use.

Hotel City (☎ 431-0086; Racedo 231; s/d with TV US$13/18) Halfway between the bus terminal and the center (and therefore nowhere near the river), the City has a surprising amount of class for the price, with touches like wooden floorboards, original tilework and leafy patio areas.

Hotel Mayorazgo (☎ 423-0333; www.mayorazgohotel.com; Etchevehere, Parque Urquiza; s/d US$30/50; P ⌧ ⌨) Every room in this expansive five-star hotel faces the river; only those on the 1st floor, however, have huge balconies. A casino, pool, travel agency and tanning booths are a few of the amenities available. It's near Blvd Moreno.

Eating & Drinking

A good place to stock up on food is the **Mercado Central** (cnr Pellegrini & Bavio).

Parrilla Brava (Costanera s/n; mains US$4-6) This is a great place for a sunset beer on the balcony overlooking the river (it's opposite the rowing club). Fish and *parrillada* are on the menu.

Bugatti (☎ 15-504-0770; Portside; mains US$4-5) No surprises on the menu here – meat, chicken, pasta and fish – but the elegance of the dining room in this renovated post office is worth making the trip for. Even if you're not hungry, the balcony bar is a great place for a few drinks as the sun goes down.

El Viejo Marino II (Av Laurencina 341; mains US$7) Spend five minutes in this town and people will be telling you that you have to try the fish. Stay another couple of minutes and they'll be telling you to check this place out. They're right, too – the atmosphere is loud and fun, the servings huge, and the specials, like *surubí milanesa* (river fish fried in breadcrumbs, US$6), keep the locals coming back.

Entertainment

Tequila (Costanera s/n; ☯ midnight-dawn Thu-Sat) This Tex-Mex-flavored dance club on the river plays the usual mix of mainstream *marcha*, house and salsa.

Getting There & Around

Aerolíneas Argentinas (☎ 423-2425; www.aerolineas argentinas.com; Corrientes 563) has offices in town; flights leave from Santa Fe's airport (see p78).

The **bus terminal** (☎ 422-1282) is on Ramírez between Posadas and Moreno. Buses leave hourly for Santa Fe (US$1, one hour). Other services and fares closely resemble those to and from Santa Fe.

GUALEGUAYCHÚ

☎ 03446 / pop 76,200

Gualeguaychú is a summertime river resort for families. As such, you're likely to see several men who have taken their tops off who really shouldn't have. You have been warned.

It's also a popular gateway for Uruguay and the site for some of the country's most outrageous *Carnaval* celebrations in February, featuring young people who have taken their tops off and should do so more often.

Orientation & Information

Plaza San Martín marks the city center. The **tourist office** (☎ 422-900) is on the Plazoleta de los Artesanos. Several banks have ATMs.

Sights & Activities

The colonial **Casa de Andrade** (cnr Andrade & Borques) once belonged to 19th-century poet, journalist, diplomat and politician Olegario Andrade.

At the former Estación Ferrocarril Urquiza, at the south end of Maipú, the **Museo Ferroviario** has a free open-air exhibit of locomotives, dining cars and a steam engine. Alongside the station, the **Corsódromo** (Blvd Irazusta) is the main site for Gualeguaychú's lively Carnaval.

Ahonike Turismo (430-706; 25 de Mayo 581) arranges two-hour city bike tours for US$5 on weekends.

Felipe Tommasi (425-194) offers two-hour sailboat cruises on the river for US$8 per person and all inclusive two-day return trips to Fray Bentos (Uruguay) for US$50 per person.

Sleeping & Eating

Camping Costa Azul (☎ 423-984; campsites per person US$4) Good facilities overlooking the Río Gualeguaychú, 200m north of Puente Méndez Casariego.

Hotel Tykuá (☎ 422-625; www.tykuahotel.com.ar; Luis N Palma 150; s/d US$12/23) Bright and modern rooms in this new building surround a very

Zen-like courtyard. Beds are good and firm and all rooms have cable TV.

Hotel Amalfi (☎ 426-818; 25 de Mayo 571; s/d US$13/20) The best budget deal in town. Rooms have high ceilings, balconies and are extensively carpeted (they even did the bed bases).

Dacal (☎ 427-602; cnr San Lorenzo & Andrade; mains US$4-5, parrillada for 2 US$7) One of the better places to eat in town, Ducal looks right across the *costanera* (riverside road) to the river and serves good fish, pasta and meat. This place fills up quickly in summer, so it's worth making a reservation.

Punta Obeliscos (cnr Costanera & Bolivar; mains from US$4) A great place for fish dishes or a few drinks as the sun goes down. The raised outdoor deck is the place to be on a balmy night.

Getting There & Away

The sparkling **bus terminal** (☎ 440-688; cnr Blvd Jurado & Gral Artigas) is 1km southwest of downtown. Departures include Buenos Aires (US$8, three hours), Paraná (US$5, five hours), Corrientes (US$14, 10 hours) and Fray Bentos, Uruguay (US$2.50, one hour).

PARQUE NACIONAL EL PALMAR

☎ 03447

The yatay palm *(Syagrus yatay)* covered much of the littoral until 19th-century agriculture, ranching and forestry destroyed palm savannas and inhibited their reproduction. On the west bank of the Río Uruguay, 360km north of Buenos Aires, surviving yatays of 8500-hectare El Palmar have again begun to thrive, under protection from fire and grazing. Reaching 18m in height, they punctuate a soothing subtropical landscape.

To see wildlife, walk along the watercourses or through the palm savannas early in the morning or just before sunset. The most conspicuous bird is the *ñandú* (rhea), but look for parakeets, cormorants, egrets, herons, storks, caracaras, woodpeckers and kingfishers too. The *carpincho* (capybara), a semiaquatic rodent weighing up to 60kg, and the vizcacha are among the most conspicuous mammals.

At night, squeaking vizcachas infest the campground at Arroyo Los Loros and gigantic toads invade the showers and toilets, but both are harmless. The *yarará* is a highly poisonous pit viper. Bites are unusual, but watch your step and wear high boots and long trousers when hiking.

Sights

The park's **Centro de Interpretación** (☎ 493-031), across from the campground, offers evening slide shows and contains a small **reptile house**. At the Arroyo Los Loros campground, rental canoes are available for exploring the placid river. A short hike from the campground, **Arroyo Los Loros** is a good place to observe the **wildlife**.

Five kilometers from the campground, **Arroyo El Palmar** is a pleasant stream with a beautiful **swimming hole**, and a good site for **bird-watching**. Crossing the ruined bridge, you can walk several kilometers along a palm-lined road being reclaimed by savanna grasses.

Sleeping & Eating

Camping Arroyo Los Loros (☎ 493-031; campsites per person US$2) Good sites, hot showers, a shop and a *confitería*. There's an additional one-off US$2 charge per tent.

Getting There & Away

Northbound buses from Buenos Aires to Concordia can drop you at the entrance to **Parque Nacional El Palmar** (admission US$4). No public transport serves the Centro de Interpretación and campground, but hitching is feasible.

PASO DE LOS LIBRES

☎ 03772 / pop 43,800

Aside from getting to Brazil, there is absolutely no reason to be in Paso de los Libres, which lies directly across the Río Uruguay from Uruguaiana. The bus terminal is a half-hour walk from the center through a series of very dodgy neighborhoods – the US60¢ bus fare is a good investment. **Libres Cambio** (Colón 901) will change cash.

Across the dirt lot from the bus terminal, the **Hotel Capri** (☎ 421-260; M Llanes s/n; s/d US$10/13) is the place to be if you need a lie down and an early breakfast between bus treks.

GETTING TO BRAZIL

The bridge that connects Paso de los Libres with Uruguaiana is about 10 blocks southwest of central Plaza Independencia. Taxis charge about US$4 to get you to immigration, but cannot cross. The border is open 24 hours. The nearest town covered in the Brazil chapter is Porto Alegre (p324).

A new(ish) hotel, **Hotel Las Vegas** (☎ 423-490; Sarmiento 554; s/d US$15/25; 🖃) maintains a very '70s motel feel. Still, it's comfortable and reasonably central.

La Giralda (Colón 887; breakfast US$1; mains US$3-5) is a popular breakfast spot in a town that will never be known for its culinary achievements. It also serves pizza, *lomitos* (steak sandwiches), pastas, burgers and beer.

From the **bus terminal** (☎ 425-600; cnr San Martín & Santiago del Estero), there are services to Corrientes (US$8, five hours), Santo Tomé (US$5, 1½ hours), Paraná (US$13, 5½ hours) and Santa Fe (US$13, seven hours).

Expreso Singer and Crucero del Norte buses pass near Paso de los Libres regularly en route between Buenos Aires and Posadas and can drop you at the Esso station on RN 14, 16km from town. A taxi into town will cost around US$8.

YAPEYÚ

☎ 03772 / pop 2100

Mellow little Yapeyú lies 72km north of Paso de los Libres and has exactly two attractions: the birthplace of national hero General José de San Martín and some remnants from its Jesuit mission past. It once had a population of 8000 Guaraní, who tended up to 80,000 cattle. After the Jesuits' expulsion, the Guaraní dispersed and the mission fell into ruins. Tiny Yapeyú is trying its hardest. What few sights exist are well signposted in Spanish, English, Portuguese and Guaraní.

The **Museo de Cultura Jesuítica**, consisting of several modern kiosks on the foundations of mission buildings, has a sundial, a few other mission relics and interesting photographs.

It's a measure of the esteem that Argentines hold for the Liberator that they have built **Casa de San Martín**, a building to protect the house where he was born, even though it's mostly been eroded to its foundations.

Near the river, **Camping Paraíso** (Maipo s/n; campsites per person US$3.50) has good hot showers. Insects can be abundant, and low-lying sites can flood in heavy rain. **Hotel San Martín** (☎ 493-120; Sargento Cabral 712; s/d US$10/13) has cheerful rooms that face an inner courtyard.

Comedor El Paraíso (Gregoria Matorras s/n; mains US$4-6) serves passable meals and has good river views. It's next to the Casa de San Martín.

Buses stop three times daily at the small **bus terminal** (cnr Av del Libertador & Chacabuco), en route between Paso de los Libres and Posadas.

ARGENTINA

RESERVA PROVINCIAL ESTEROS DEL IBERÁ

Esteros del Iberá is a wildlife cornucopia comparable to Brazil's Pantanal do Mato Grosso. Aquatic plants and grasses, including 'floating islands,' dominate this wetlands wilderness covering 13,000 sq km. Trees are relatively few. The most notable wildlife species are reptiles like the caiman and anaconda, mammals like the maned wolf, howler monkey, neotropical otter, capybara, pampas- and swamp-deer and more than 350 bird species.

Bird-watchers and nature nuts from all over the world converge on the village of Colonia Pellegrini, 120km northeast of Mercedes, to take advantage of the ease of access to the park (Colonia Pellegrini lies within the park's boundaries). It's a charming enough place in its own right: dirt roads, no traffic and plenty of trees. There is a **visitor center** across the causeway from Colonia Pellegrini, with information on the reserve. One-hour **launch tours** (US$8) are outstanding value.

Camping is possible at Colonia Pellegrini and costs about US$2 per person.

A number of *hospedajes* (family homes) offer rooms with private bathroom for around US$7 per person, the best of which is probably **Hospedaje los Amigos** (☎ 15-49375), which also has a decent *comedor* (basic caféteria) out front serving meals for US$2 to US$4.

The peaceful, rustic and comfortable **Hosteria Ñandé Retá** (☎ 03773-499411; www.nandereta.com; s/d with full board US$30/42) in Colonia Pellegrini is a good deal for the price. It also arranges transport from Mercedes and offer tours of the wetlands.

Buses run from Corrientes and Paso de los Libres to Mercedes, where Itatí buses to Colonia Pellegrini (US$5, four hours) leave at 8am and noon, returning to Mercedes at 5am Monday to Friday, and 11am Saturday.

CORRIENTES

☎ 03783 / pop 323,000

Capital of its namesake province, Corrientes is a big, serious city with a couple of decent museums and a reputation for being very budget-unfriendly. Once the sun starts setting, a walk along the riverfront might make you feel a bit happier about being here.

It's one of Argentina's oldest cities and the early-20th-century balconied buildings rising up from the muddy waters of the Río Paraná were the setting for Graham Greene's novel *The Honorary Consul.* The once-moribund **Carnaval Correntino** (www.carnavalescorrentinos.com) has experienced a revival and now attracts crowds of up to 80,000.

Perhaps as a reply to nearby Resistencia's claim as the City of Sculpture, Corrientes is setting itself up as the City of Murals, and there are indeed quite a few to be seen as you wander the streets. The tourist offices have maps detailing their locations.

Orientation

Plaza 25 de Mayo is the center of Corrientes' extremely regular grid plan. The commercial center is the Junín *peatonal,* between Salta and Catamarca, but the most attractive areas are Parque Mitre and the shady riverside along Av Costanera General San Martín. Bus No 106 runs between San Lorenzo downtown and the bus terminal.

Information

There are several banks with ATMs around 9 de Julio.

Cambio El Dorado (9 de Julio 1341) changes cash and traveler's checks

Municipal tourist office (☎ 428-845; Plaza JB Cabral) More central than the provincial tourist office, but hopelessly disorganized.

Provincial tourist office (☎ 427200; 25 de Mayo) The best in town.

Post office (cnr San Juan & San Martín)

Sights

The east side of San Juan, between Plácido Martínez and Quintana, is a shady, attractive area. The **Monumento a la Gloria** there honors the Italian community; a series of striking **murals** chronicles local history since colonial times.

The **Museo de Bellas Artes Dr Juan Ramón Vidal** (San Juan 634; admission free; ☼ 9am-noon & 6-9pm Tue-Sat) is as interesting for the house it occupies as for the jumble of works found within. It emphasizes sculpture and oil paintings from local artists, as well as hosting the occasional international exhibition.

The **Museo Histórico de Corrientes** (9 de Julio 1044; admission free; ☼ 8am-noon & 4-8pm Mon-Fri) features exhibits of weapons, coins and antique furniture, and displays on religious and civil history.

Visit the **Santuario de la Cruz del Milagro**, on Belgrano between Buenos Aires and Salta. According to local legend, the 16th-century cross here defied indigenous efforts to burn it.

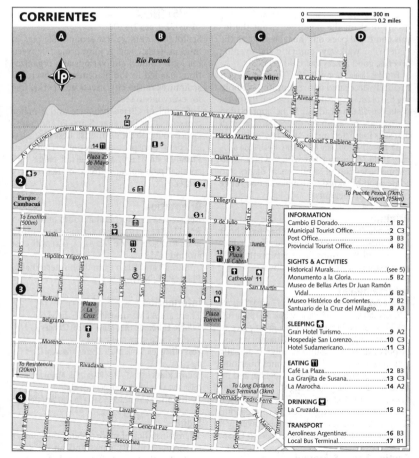

CORRIENTES

INFORMATION	
Cambio El Dorado...................................1	B2
Municipal Tourist Office........................2	C3
Post Office...3	B3
Provincial Tourist Office.......................4	B2

SIGHTS & ACTIVITIES	
Historical Murals............................(see 5)	
Monumento a la Gloria........................5	B2
Museo de Bellas Artes Dr Juan Ramón	
Vidal..6	B2
Museo Histórico de Corrientes.............7	B2
Santuario de la Cruz del Milagro.........8	A3

SLEEPING	
Gran Hotel Turismo...............................9	A2
Hospedaje San Lorenzo.......................10	C3
Hotel Sudamericano............................11	C3

EATING	
Café La Plaza.......................................12	B3
La Granjita de Susana.........................13	C3
La Marocha...14	A2

DRINKING	
La Cruzada..15	B2

TRANSPORT	
Aerolíneas Argentinas.........................16	B3
Local Bus Terminal.............................17	B1

Sleeping

Corrientes bites off the big one in terms of budget accommodation: what there is isn't cheap, and what's relatively cheap isn't very good. In fact, fuck Corrientes – it's not even that interesting *and* they want us to pay top dollar to stay here? If you really want to check out the city, nearby Resistencia (p84) is just down the road and much more wallet-friendly. During Carnaval, the tourist office maintains a list of *casas de familia* (accommodations in a family home) ranging from US$8 to US$16 per person.

Hospedaje San Lorenzo (☎ 421-740; San Lorenzo 1136; d US$13) Small, badly ventilated, some say overrun by cockroaches, but still one of the only true budget options in the center.

Hotel Sudamericano (☎ 469-058; Hipólito Yrigoyen 1676; d from US$13; ❄) Probably nice once, though it's looking a bit tired these days. About as good as it gets in this price range.

Gran Hotel Turismo (☎ 433-174; Entre Ríos 650; s/d US$20/27; ❄ ❄ ❄) Built in 1948, this stately old hotel has an attractive restaurant, a large pool, a bar and an excellent riverside location. The rooms are slightly worn, but it's a charming old place, and a lot more atmospheric than other hotels in town.

Eating

La Granjita de Susana (cnr San Lorenzo & Hipólito Yrigoyen; mains US$2-5) A good budget option, serving empanadas, burgers and steaks at sidewalk tables across from Plaza JB Cabral.

Café La Plaza (Junín 1076; mains US$4) Nothing exceptional on the menu here, but the locals come and pack out the tables out on the pedestrian walkway, enjoying the evening breezes, good pizzas and cold beer.

Enófilos (Junín 172; mains US$5-8) This modern yet rustically decorated bar-restaurant overlooking the plaza is a great place to get off the pizza, pasta, *parrillada* treadmill. Wine-appreciation courses are occasionally offered and a small deli sells imported meats and cheeses.

La Marocha (cnr Salta & Quintana; meals US$4-6) A cute little restaurant-bar with a wider-than-normal selection of salads, meat dishes and some good breakfasts. Also has a good range of wines and cocktails.

Drinking

La Cruzada (Junín 941) This tiny bar has about four times as many tables outside than it does inside, and the atmosphere gets pretty lively as the sun (and the beers) go down.

Entertainment

Puente Pexoa (☎ 451-687; RN 12 at La Rotonda Virgen de Itatí roundabout; ☽ from 8:30pm,1st band at 11:30pm Fri & Sat) This relaxed restaurant is a great place to check out *chamamé*, a sort of Guaraní version of polka dancing. Sound deadly? It actually gets very rowdy and is sometimes hilarious. People show up in full *gaucho* regalia, and up to four bands play each night. From downtown, take bus 102 marked '17 de Agosto' 7km out of town to the Virgen de Itatí roundabout. It's just off the roundabout; the driver will point it out. A taxi back costs US$4 to US$6.

Getting There & Around

Aerolíneas Argentinas (☎ 423-918; www.aerolineas argentinas.com; Junín 1301) flies daily to Buenos Aires (from US$80). Local bus 105 (US$40¢) goes to the **airport** (☎ 458-358), about 15km east of town on RN 12. A *remise* should cost around US$4.

Frequent buses to Resistencia (US$50¢) leave from the **local bus terminal** (cnr Av Costanera General San Martín & La Rioja). From the **bus terminal** (☎ 458-322; Av Maipú), southeast of town, Ciudad de Posadas goes to Paso de los Libres (US$8, five hours) via Mercedes for access to Esteros del Iberá. Other destinations include Posadas (US$11, four hours), Formosa (US$4, 3½ hours), Puerto Iguazú (US$15, nine hours), Buenos Aires (US$25, 11 hours) and Asunción, Paraguay (US$9, five hours).

RESISTENCIA
☎ 03722 / pop 276,000

Sculpture-lovers wallow around like pigs in mud in Resistencia. A joint project between the local council and various arts organizations has led to the placement of over 300 sculptures in the city streets and parks, free for everyone to see.

Capital of Chaco province and a major crossroads for Paraguay, Santa Fe and trans-Chaco routes to the northwest, Resistencia has excellent transport connections. Delightful Plaza 25 de Mayo, a riot of tall palms and comical *palo borracho* trees, marks the city center.

Orientation

Resistencia's airport is 6km south of town on RN 11; Bus 3 (marked 'aeropuerto/centro') goes to Plaza 25 de Mayo. A taxi will cost around US$2.

Buses 3 and 10 go from the bus terminal to Plaza 25 de Mayo.

Information

There are ATMs near Plaza 25 de Mayo.

Cambio El Dorado (Jose María Paz 36) Changes traveler's checks at reasonable rates.

Post office (cnr Sarmiento & Hipólito Yrigoyen) Faces the plaza.

Tourist kiosk (☎ 458-289; Plaza 25 de Mayo) About 450m away from the tourist office. Handy.

Tourist office (☎ 423-547; Santa Fe 178) Well stocked.

Sights

There's insufficient space to detail the number of **sculptures** in city parks and on the sidewalks, but the tourist office distributes a map with their locations that makes a good introduction to the city. The best starting point is the open-air **Parque de las Esculturas Aldo y Efraín Boglietti** (cnr Avs Laprida & Sarmiento), a 2500 sq meter area alongside the old French railroad station (1907). The station is now the **Museo de Ciencias Naturales** (admission US30¢; ☽ 8:30am-12:30pm Mon-Fri, 5-8:30pm Sat).

El Fogón de los Arrieros (Brown 350; admission US$1; ☽ 8am-noon, 4-8pm & 9-11pm Mon-Sat) is the driving force behind the city's progressive displays of public art and is famous for its eclectic assemblage of art objects from around the Chaco province, Argentina and the world.

The **Museo del Hombre Chaqueño** (Museum of Chaco Man; Arturo Illía 655; admission US30¢; ☽ 9am-noon Mon-Sat) focuses on the colonization of the

Chaco and has exhibits and information on the Guaraní, Mocoví, Komlek and Mataco provincial indigenous cultures.

The **Museo Policial** (Roca 223; admission US$1; 8am-noon & 5-9pm Mon-Fri summer, 8am-noon & 4-8pm Mon-Fri winter) is better than one might expect, partially redeeming its trite drug-war rhetoric with absorbing accounts of *cuatrerismo* (cattle-rustling, still widespread in the province) and social banditry.

Sleeping

Camping Parque 2 de Febrero (Avalos 1100; campsites US$3) Has excellent facilities.

El Hotelito (☎ 1564-5008; el_hotelito@yahoo.com .ar; Alberdi 311; s/d with shared bathroom US$6/9) Airy, whitewashed rooms. The bathrooms are huge and spotless and the owners speak some English.

Residencial Bariloche (☎ 421-412; Obligado 239; s/d US$10/13) The Bariloche's rooms are an excellent deal: spacious, clean and quiet with cable TV. You can pay an extra US$3 for air-con or just get blown away by their industrial-sized room fans.

Hotel Colón (☎ 422-861; hotelcolon@gigared.com .ar; Santa María de Oro 143; s/d US$17/25; P 🍴 🖳) An older hotel with some lovely touches, such as dark wood paneling and multiple light wells. Rooms are neat, but unrenovated and showing their age a bit.

Eating & Drinking

Several attractive *confiterías* and ice creameries have rejuvenated the area north and northwest of Plaza 25 de Mayo; you should try, for instance, the bohemian **Café de la Ciudad** (Pellegrini 109; mains US$4-7), formerly a sleazy bar, for slightly pricey sandwiches, burgers and beer.

Fenix Bar (Don Bosco 133; meals US$3-5) The wooden floorboards and muted lighting give this little place a great atmosphere. The menu runs the usual gamut of pizza, meats and pastas, but the food is well presented and the wine selection excellent.

La Bianca (Colón 102; mains US$3-5) The exposed brick walls lined with good art make La Bianca one of the more charming options in town. Pasta and steak feature heavily on the menu, but there are some delicious fish dishes as well.

Charly (Güemes 213; meals around US$4) You know times are tough when the snobbiest restaurant in town can only bring itself to charge US$4

for a meal. Carefully prepared meat and fish dishes are the winners here, but there's also a wide range of salads and almost too many wine choices. Budget fiends can eat the same dishes in a more humble environment in the restaurant's *rotisería* around the corner at Brown 71.

Har Bar (cnr Donovan & Perón; 24hr) Pool is a popular pastime in Resistencia, and many people get together for a few games before going out. The center is dotted with pool halls, all icily air-conditioned and with full bars. The Har Bar is as good a place as any to rack 'em up.

Zingara (Güemes; 6pm-late Wed-Sat). This hip, minimally decorated bar wouldn't be out of place in fashion capitals like Milan or Paris. Cocktails feature heavily on the drinks menu and light snacks are served.

Getting There & Away

Aerolíneas Argentinas (☎ 445-550; www.aerolineas argentinas.com; JB Justo 184) has daily flights to Buenos Aires (from US$80).

The **bus terminal** (☎ 461-098; cnr MacLean & Islas Malvinas) has an urban service (marked 'Chaco-Corrientes') between Resistencia and Corrientes for US30¢. You can catch it in front of the post office on Plaza 25 de Mayo.

La Estrella goes to Capitán Solari, near Parque Nacional Chaco, four times daily (US$2, 2½ hours). Godoy goes to Laguna Naick-Neck and Laguna Blanca, near the Parque Nacional Río Pilcomayo (US$5, 5½ hours).

Other destinations include Buenos Aires (US$27, 13 hours), Santa Fe (US$22, 9½ hours), Rosario (US$24, 9½ hours), Córdoba (US$22, 12 hours), Salta (US$25, 14 hours), Posadas (US$12, five hours), Puerto Iguazú (US$17, 10½ hours) and Asunción, Paraguay (US$9, five hours).

PARQUE NACIONAL CHACO
☎ 03725

This little-visited park, 115km northwest of Resistencia, preserves 15,000 hectares of marshes, grasslands, palm savannas, scrub and dense forests in the humid eastern Chaco. Mammals are few, but birds include rheas, jabiru storks, roseate spoonbills, cormorants and caracaras. The most abundant species is the mosquito, so visit in the relatively dry, cool winter (June to August) and bring insect repellent.

Some swampy areas are accessible only on horseback; inquire in Capitán Solari (5km east of park entrance) for horses and guides.

The **Administración** (☎ 496-166; park entrance free) is located at the park entrance. Rangers are extremely hospitable and will accompany visitors if their duties permit.

The shaded **camping area** (free) has clean toilets and showers. There is no food available so bring supplies from Resistencia, although you can buy basics in Capitán Solari.

La Estrella runs four buses daily from Resistencia to Capitán Solari (US$2, 2½ hours); from there you must walk or catch a lift to the park entrance (5km). You could also try inquiring at **Remis Satur** (☎ 421-004; Alberdi 770) about a share *remise* (US$3 per person).

FORMOSA
☎ 03717 / pop 198,000

Way out here on the Río Paraguay, this town has a much more Paraguayan feel than others in the region. The riverfront has been tastefully restored and makes for an excellent place to go for a wander once the sun starts going down. In November, the weeklong **Fiesta del Río** features an impressive nocturnal religious procession in which 150 boats from Corrientes sail up the Río Paraguay.

Hotel San Martín (☎ 426-769; 25 de Mayo 380; s/d US$12/21; 🏊) Good for the price, but otherwise uninteresting, the San Martín is surprisingly quiet for its central location. Some rooms are definitely better than others, so have a look around if you can.

Mercobus (☎ 431-469; Lelong 899) has regular buses to Clorinda, Laguna Naick-Neck and Laguna Blanca (Parque Nacional Río Pilcomayo), departing daily at 6:30am, 9:30am, 12:30pm and 4pm.

PARQUE NACIONAL RÍO PILCOMAYO

West of Clorinda, the wildlife-rich wetlands of 60,000-hectare Parque Nacional Río Pilcomayo hug the Paraguayan border. The outstanding feature is the shimmering **Laguna Blanca** where, at sunset, *yacarés* (alligators) lurk on the surface. Other wildlife, except for birds, is more likely to be heard than seen among the dense aquatic vegetation.

Parque Nacional Río Pilcomayo's free camping facilities are basic. Just outside the park entrance, a small shop sells basic food and cold drinks. There is a bus service from Formosa and Clorinda along RN 86 to Laguna Naick-Neck and the park entrance at Laguna Blanca ranger station (US$4, 2½ hours).

POSADAS
☎ 03752 / pop 255,000

If you're heading north, now's about the time that things start to feel very tropical, and the jungle begins to creep into the edges of the picture. Posadas is mainly interesting as an access point, both to Paraguay and the Jesuit mission sites north of here. But it's a cool little city in its own right, with some sweet plazas and a well-developed eating/drinking/partying scene down on the waterfront.

Orientation

Plaza 9 de Julio is the center of Posadas' standard grid. Streets were renumbered several years ago, but local preference for the old system occasionally creates confusion.

Buses 8, 15, 21 and 24 go downtown from the bus terminal.

Information

There are several downtown ATMs.
Cambios Mazza (Bolívar btwn San Lorenzo & Colón) Changes traveler's checks.
Post office (cnr Bolívar & Ayacucho)
Provincial tourist office (☎ 555-0297; turismo@misiones.gov.ar; Colón 1985) Has a wealth of printed material.

Sights & Activities

The natural-history section of the **Museo de Ciencias Naturales e Historia** (San Luis 384; admission free) focuses on fauna and the geology and mineralogy of the province. The museum also has an excellent serpentarium (with demonstrations of venom extraction), an aviary and an aquarium. Its historical section stresses prehistory, the Jesuit missions and modern colonization.

In the cool of the afternoon, the **costanera** (riverside promenade) comes alive. It's a favorite spot for joggers, cyclists, dog walkers, mate sippers, hotdog vendors and young couples staring wistfully at the lights of Paraguay across the water.

Sleeping

Residencial Misiones (☎ 430-133; Av Azara btwn La Rioja & Córdoba; s/d US$8/12) It's casual, clean and quiet here, and a well-equipped kitchen and clothes-washing facilities are at guests' disposal. Rooms (and beds) vary in quality, so have a look at a few.

Hotel City (☎ 439-401; Colón 7854; r from US$10; ❄) The drab exterior masks the fact that the City has some of the best budget rooms in town: spacious, with firm beds and good clean bathrooms. Some have air-con and plaza views.

Posadas Hotel (☎ 440-888; www.hotelposadas.com .ar; Bolívar 1949; s/d US$30/40; P ❄) With by far the best-looking interiors of any hotel in town, the Posadas has that somber ambience missing from many modern hotels. Rooms are spacious, comfortable and well decorated.

Eating & Drinking

Ipanema (Av Azara 1629; breakfast US$1-2, lunch & dinner US$3-5) Set in an arcade a few steps from the plaza, the Ipanema has good-value breakfasts and plenty of outdoor seating. A full bar and *minutas* (short orders) are also on offer.

De la Costa (Costanera 1536; mains US$3-5) This is the best of the riverside budget eateries. There aren't any surprises on the menu – pizzas, burgers, steaks – but the drinks are cheap and the views unbeatable.

Café Vitrage (cnr Bolivar & Colón; mains US$5) With its brass fittings and dark wood features, the Vitrage oozes style. Mostly a bar/café, it can also whip up a juicy steak any time of the day or night.

La Querencia (Bolívar 322; mains US$3-7) This is Posadas' spiffiest *parrilla*, on the south side of Plaza 9 de Julio. It has a wide menu, a good wine list and a battery of overhead fans that keep the place from getting stuffy.

Shopping

There's something for everyone at the indoor **Mercado La Placita** (cnr Sarmiento & Av Roque Sáenz Peña), from counterfeit sneakers to Paraguayan handicrafts and homemade cigars.

Getting There & Around

Aerolíneas Argentinas (☎ 422-036; www.aerolineas argentinas.com; cnr Ayacucho & San Martín) flies 13 times weekly to Buenos Aires (US$85).

Bus 8 from San Lorenzo between La Rioja and Entre Ríos goes to the airport, 12km southwest of town and Aerolíneas Argentinas runs its own shuttle service. A *remise* costs about US$4.

International departures from the **bus terminal** (☎ 4526106; cnr Ruta 12 & Santa Catalina) include

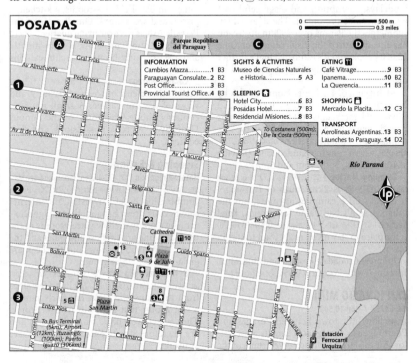

POSADAS

0 — 500 m
0 — 0.3 miles

Río Paraná

INFORMATION		SIGHTS & ACTIVITIES		EATING	
Cambios Mazza	1 B3	Museo de Ciencias Naturales		Café Vitrage	9 B3
Paraguayan Consulate	2 B2	e Historia	5 A3	Ipanema	10 B2
Post Office	3 B3			La Querencia	11 B3
Provincial Tourist Office	4 B3	SLEEPING			
		Hotel City	6 B3	SHOPPING	
		Posadas Hotel	7 B3	Mercado la Placita	12 C3
		Residencial Misiones	8 B3		
				TRANSPORT	
				Aerolíneas Argentinas	13 B3
				Launches to Paraguay	14 D2

To Costanera (500m);
De la Costa (500m)

Parque República del Paraguay

Ivanowski
Gral Frías
Av Almafuerte
Pedernera
Moritán
Coronel Álvarez
Av II de Urquiza
Alvear
Belgrano
Santa Fe
Sarmiento
San Martín
Cathedral
Bolivar
Guido Spano
Plaza 9 de Julio
Córdoba
La Rioja
Entre Ríos
Plaza San Martín

Av Cobernador Roca
N Casto
E Ramírez
R García
A Acuña
BR González
JB Alberdi
L Torav
De Artechea
Coronel Reguera
Lezcano
F Pérez

Av Guacurarí
Av Polonia
San Luis
Junín
Ayacucho
San Lorenzo
Colón
Av Azara
Buenos Aires
Rivadavia
3 de Febrero
25 de Mayo
Gral Paz
Av Roque Sáenz Peña
Av Madariaga
Triquihuela

To Bus Terminal (5km); Airport (12km); Ituzaingó (100km); Puerto Iguazú (306km)

Catamarca

Estación Ferrocarril Urquiza

GETTING TO PARAGUAY

Launches across the Paraná to Encarnación (US$1) continue to operate despite the bridge. They leave from the dock at the east end of Av Guacurarí but because there are no immigration procedures on this route, you're best off crossing by the bridge.

Buses to Encarnación (US$1) leave every 20 minutes from the corner of Mitre and Junín, passing through downtown before crossing the bridge (get off for immigration procedures and hang on to your ticket; you'll be able to catch another bus continuing in the same direction).

Buses also go from Puerto Iguazú to Ciudad del Este (US$1).

Both borders are open 24 hours. Most non-EU citizens require a visa to enter Paraguay. For info on entering Argentina from Paraguay, see p808.

Asunción, Paraguay (US$8, six hours) and São Paulo, Brazil (US$50, 24 hours).

Domestic fares include Corrientes (US$11, four hours), Resistencia (US$12, five hours), Puerto Iguazú (US$12, 5½ hours), Buenos Aires (US$17, 13 hours; US$22 in *coche cama*) and Salta (US$32, 15 hours). Buses to San Ignacio Miní (US$1.50, one hour) leave frequently.

YACYRETÁ DAM

A vivid lesson in foreign debt, this gigantic hydroelectric project has been plagued by delays, corruption and disgraceful cost overruns since the outset. The dam, which submerges the Paraná over 200km upstream, has already caused the displacement of some 12,000 people and it's estimated that a further 50,000 people, mostly Paraguayans, will be displaced.

At Ituzaingó, 1½ hours from Posadas by bus, the Argentine–Paraguayan Entidad Binacional Yacyretá is still trying to put this boondoggle in the best possible light, the task falling to their public relations **office** (☎ 03786-420-050), which runs free guided tours (leaving at 10am, 11am, 3pm, 4pm and 5pm).

Camping Mattes (☎ 03786-421-272; 4-6 person cabañas US$15-20) is 2km south of Ituzaingó. It doesn't offer camping anymore, but the cabañas aren't bad value for groups. **Hotel Géminis** (☎ 03786-420-324; Corrientes 9430; s/d US$10/20) is the place to stay if you really want to stay in town.

Empresa Ciudad de Posadas and Singer link Ituzaingó with Posadas (US$4, one hour).

SAN IGNACIO MINÍ

☎ 03752 / pop 10,500

A mellow little town between Posadas and Puerto Iguazú, San Ignacio attracts most visitors for the large, well-preserved ruins of the Jesuit mission that gives the town its name. If you're staying here and have some time to kill, it's well worth checking out the Casa de Quiroga, too.

Sights

At its peak, in 1733, the **mission of San Ignacio Miní** (admission US$4; ☼ 7am-7pm) had an indigenous population of nearly 4500. The enormous red-sandstone church, embellished with bas-relief sculptures, was designed in 'Guaraní baroque' style. Adjacent to the tile-roofed church were the cemetery and cloisters; the same complex held classrooms, a kitchen, a prison and workshops. On all sides of the Plaza de Armas were the living quarters. There is a sound and light show at 7pm nightly and a set of fairly bizarre museum exhibits as you enter.

Casa de Quiroga (Quiroga s/n; admission US$1) is at the southern end of town, offering grand views of the Río Paraná. A small museum contains photos and some of the famous Uruguayan writer's possessions and first editions.

Sleeping & Eating

Hotel San Ignacio (☎ 470-422; cnr Sarmiento & San Martín; s/d US$10/13, cabañas for 4 people US$23; ☒) For a combination hotel/bar/restaurant/internet café/pool hall/teen hangout the San Ignacio's actually a pretty mellow place. Rooms in the main building are spotless and quiet and the funky A-frame bungalows out the back are great value for larger groups.

Residencial Doka (☎ 470-131; residoka@yahoo.com.ar; Alberdi 518; s/d US$13/17; P ☒) Just a few steps from the ruins, the Doka has fairly nondescript rooms that sleep up to five people. They're set well back from the road and are therefore quiet. Kitchen facilities are available.

La Aldea (Los Jesuitas s/n; mains US$3-7; set meals US$2.50) Five hundred meters from the entrance to the ruins, this barn of a place has tables at the front, inside and on the rear deck. They serve excellent pizzas and *minutas* and are one of the only eating options open late at night.

La Carpa Azul (Rivadavia 1295; mains US$4-7;) Much more of a feed-trough for hungry tour groups than an actual restaurant, the big bonus here is that you can use the swimming pool out the back once you've finished chowing down.

Getting There & Away

The **bus terminal** (Av Sarmiento) is at the west end of town. Services are frequent between Posadas (US$1.50, one hour) and Puerto Iguazú (US$7, 4½ hours).

PUERTO IGUAZÚ

☎ 03757 / pop 32,000

With a world-class attraction just down the road, Puerto Iguazú should feel overrun by tourists, but it somehow manages to retain its relaxed, small-town atmosphere. The falls are definitely the drawcard here: you'll meet plenty of people who have come straight from Buenos Aires, and are heading straight back afterwards. There's a steady backpacker population and a correspondingly lively hostel and restaurant scene.

Orientation

Puerto Iguazú's very irregular street plan is compact enough for relatively easy orientation. The main drag is the diagonal Av Victoria Aguirre.

Information

Banco de Misiones ATM (Av Victoria Aguirre 330)
Post office (Av San Martín 780)
Tourist office (☎ 420-800; Av Victoria Aguirre 311) This is the main office. There's also a tourist kiosk at the bus terminal.

No visa is required for entry into Paraguay, but pretty much everybody entering Brazil (even on a day trip) will need one. The **Brazilian Consulate** (☎ 421-348; Av Córdoba 264) here arranges visas within a half hour, much better than the week that it takes their Buenos Aires counterparts to do the same job.

PUERTO IGUAZÚ

INFORMATION	
Banco de Misiones (ATM)	1 C2
Brazilian Consulate	2 D2
Post Office	3 C2
Tourist Kiosk	(see 13)
Tourist Office	4 C2

SLEEPING	
Che Roga	5 D2
Hostería San Fernando	6 D2
Hotel Esturión	7 A2

EATING	
El Andariago	8 C2
El Charo	9 D2
Lautaro	10 C2

DRINKING	
Cuba Libre	11 C2

TRANSPORT	
Aerolíneas Argentinas	12 C2
Bus Terminal	13 D2
Caracol	14 C2

Sleeping

Camping El Pindo (☎ 421-795; per tent US$3.50 plus per person US$3.50) At km 3.5 of RN 12 on the edge of town.

Hostel Inn (☎ 421-823; www.hostel-inn.com; RN 12, km 5; dm with/without HI card US$7/9, d with/without HI card US$23/40; P ⊠ ☐ ☑) Set on three hectares of land, this ex-casino is one of the best hostels in the country. Offering free internet, wi-fi access, a bar, restaurant and a huge pool, it's a great place to stay, relax and meet people. It also offers jungle treks and canoe tours around lesser-known parts of Missiones province.

Hostería San Fernando (☎ 421-2429; cnr Avs Córdoba & Guaraní; s/d US$18/25) Just across from the bus terminal, the San Fernando is leafy and quiet. The reasonable rooms are smallish, but well ventilated.

Che Roga (☎ 422-931; cnr Bompland & Feliz de Azara; cabins from US$27; ⊠ ☑) If you're traveling in a group of four or more, the cabins at Che Roga are an excellent deal: spacious and well-appointed with kitchenette.

Hotel Esturión (☎ 420-100; www.hotelesturion.com; Av Tres Fronteras 650; s/d US$35/40; P ⊠ ☐ ☑) If you're planning on splashing out on accommodation while you're in Puerto Iguazú, the Esturión's the place to do it. A Zen-like lobby, beautifully sculptured grounds, tennis courts, restaurant, an excellent pool area and some great views – this place has it all.

Eating & Drinking

El Andariego (P Moreno 229; mains US$2-4) This no-frills neighborhood *parrilla* has plenty of tables on the street (heck, even the *parrilla* is on the street!) and does good, cheap meat and pasta dishes.

Lautaro (Av Brasil 7; mains US$3-6) Great pizzas and well-presented meals are on offer at this ultramodern café/restaurant/bar. There's live music some nights, and breezy sidewalk seating for people-watching.

El Charo (Av Córdoba 106; set meals US$5) A great place to sit and watch the world go by, El Charo has the usual range of *parrillada* offerings, with outdoor seating and some good-value set meals.

Cuba Libre (cnr Av Brasil & Paraguay; ☒ Wed-Sat) Going out in Puerto Iguazú is so much fun that *Brazilians* come here to dance. Imagine that. For now, this place is an atmospheric little pub with a reasonable-sized dance floor, but the owner has big plans and by the time

you come through, it may just be a mega-disco with a capacity for 3000 people.

Getting There & Around

AIR

Aerolíneas Argentinas (☎ 420-168; www.aerolineasargentinas.com; Av Victoria Aguirre 295) flies daily to Buenos Aires (US$100).

Caracol (☎ 420-064; Av Victoria Aguirre 563) charges US$2 to the airport and makes hotel pickups; phone for reservations. *Remises* run about US$9.

BUS

The **bus terminal** (☎ 423-006; cnr Avs Córdoba & Misiones) has departures for Posadas (US$12, 5½ hours), Buenos Aires (US$40, 20 hours) and intermediate points. Frequent buses leave for Parque Nacional Iguazú (US$1, 30 minutes), and there are international buses to Foz do Iguaçu, Brazil (US$1, 35 minutes) and Ciudad del Este, Paraguay (US$1, one hour).

TAXI

For groups of three or more hoping to see both sides of the falls as well as Ciudad del Este and the Itaipú hydroelectric project, a shared cab or *remise* can be a good idea; figure about US$55 for a full day's sightseeing, but make sure you account for the cost of your visa if going to the Brazilian side. Contact the **Asociación de Trabajadores de Taxis** (☎ 420-282), or simply approach a driver.

PARQUE NACIONAL IGUAZÚ

People who doubt the theory that 'negative ions generated by waterfalls make people happier' might have to reconsider after visiting the **Iguazú Falls**. Moods just seem to improve the closer you get, until eventually people degenerate into giggling, shrieking messes. And this is grown men we're talking about.

But getting happy isn't the only reason to come here. The power, size and sheer noise of the falls have to be experienced to be believed. You could try coming early, but you're unlikely ever to have the place to yourself. The **park** (☎ 03757-491-445; admission US$10; ☒ 9am-6pm) quickly fills with Argentines, backpackers, families and tour groups, but who cares? Get up close to the Garganta del Diablo (Devil's Throat) and the whole world seems to drop away.

Guaraní legend says that Iguazú Falls originated when a jealous forest god, enraged by a warrior escaping downriver by canoe with a young girl, caused the riverbed to collapse in front of the lovers, producing precipitous falls over which the girl fell and, at their base, turned into a rock. The warrior survived as a tree overlooking his fallen lover.

The geological origins of the falls are more prosaic. In southern Brazil, the Río Iguazú passes over a basalt plateau that ends just above its confluence with the Paraná. Before reaching the edge, the river divides into many channels to form several distinctive *cataratas* (cataracts).

The most awesome is the semicircular Garganta del Diablo, a deafening and dampening part of the experience, approached by launch and via a system of *pasarelas* (catwalks). There's no doubt that it's spectacular – there's only one question: where's the bungee jump?

Despite development pressures, the 55,000-hectare park is a natural wonderland of subtropical rainforest, with over 2000 identified plant species, countless insects, 400 bird species and many mammals and reptiles.

If you've got the time (and the money – see p407), it's worth checking out the Brazilian side of the falls, too, for a few different angles, plus the grand overview. For more information, see p326.

Information

Buses from Puerto Iguazú drop passengers at the Centro de Informes, where there's a small natural-history museum. There's also a photo-developing lab, gift shop, bar and many other services, including restaurants and snack bars.

Dangers & Annoyances

The Río Iguazú's currents are strong and swift; more than one tourist has been swept downriver and drowned near Isla San Martín.

The wildlife is potentially dangerous: in 1997, a jaguar killed a park ranger's infant son. Visitors should respect the big cats and, if you should encounter one, do not panic. Speak calmly but loudly, do not run or turn your back, and try to appear bigger than you are by waving your arms or clothing.

Sights

Before seeing Iguazú Falls themselves, grab a map, look around the museum, and (if it has reopened) climb the nearby tower for

GETTING TO BRAZIL

Buses to Foz do Iguaçu (US$1) leave regularly from Puerto Iguazú's bus terminal. The bus will wait as you complete immigration procedures. The border is open 24 hours, but buses only run in daylight hours. For info on entering Argentina from Brazil, see p329.

Frequent buses leave from Puerto Iguazú's bus terminal for Ciudad del Este, Paraguay (US$1, one hour) and wait at the border as you complete customs formalities.

a good overall view. Plan hikes before the mid-morning tour-bus invasion. Descending from the visitor center, you can cross by free launch to **Isla Grande San Martín**, which offers unique views and a refuge from the masses on the mainland.

Several *pasarelas* give good views of smaller falls, and, in the distance, the **Garganta del Diablo**. A train from the visitor center operates regularly to shuttle visitors from site to site. At the last stop, follow the trail to the lookout perched right on the edge of the mighty falls.

Activities

Best in the early morning, the Sendero Macuco nature trail leads through dense forest, where a steep sidetrack goes to the base of a hidden waterfall. Another trail goes to the *bañado,* a marsh abounding in birdlife. Allow about 2½ hours round trip (6km) for the entire Sendero Macuco trail.

To get elsewhere in the forest, hitch or hire a car to take you out along RN 101 toward the village of Bernardo de Irigoyen, and it is still nearly pristine forest. **Iguazú Jungle Explorer** (☎ 03757-421-696), at the visitor center, can arrange 4WD excursions on the Yacaratía trail to Puerto Macuco as well as thrilling speedboat trips below the falls (US$15).

Moonlight walks (☎ 03757-491-469; www.iguazu argentina.com; guided walks with/without dinner US$27/17) to the falls are offered at 8:30pm and 10:45pm on the five nights around the full moon. Call to reserve a place.

Getting There & Away

For information on getting here by bus, see opposite.

NORTHWEST ARGENTINA

With a very tangible sense of history, the northwest is Argentina's most 'indigenous' region, and the sights and people here show much closer links with the country's Andean neighbors than the European image of its urban centers.

HISTORY

The Central Andean population spread never got much further than what is now northwest Argentina. Before the Spanish arrived, the place was crawling with indigenous tribes: the Lule south and west of modern Salta, the Tonocote of Santiago del Estero, and the Diaguita, doing the roaming nomad thing. Even today, Quechuan communities reach as far south as Santiago del Estero.

Diego de Almagro's expedition came through Jujuy and Salta on the way from Cuzco to Chile in 1535, but it wasn't until 1553 that the first city of the region, Santiago del Estero, was established. Local resistance meant slow going for the conquistadors in these parts, but eventually San Miguel de Tucumán (1565), Córdoba (1573), Salta (1582), La Rioja (1591) and San Salvador de Jujuy (1593) were founded. It took Catamarca another 100 years to find its feet.

As the double horns of disease and exploitation decimated indigenous populations and the *encomiendas* (grant of land and native inhabitants given to settlers) lost their economic value, the region's focus shifted. Tucumán provided mules, cotton and textiles for the mines of Potosí, and Córdoba became a center for education and arts. The opening of the Atlantic to shipping in late colonial times diminished Jujuy's and Salta's importance as trade posts, but Tucumán grew in stature as the local sugar industry boomed.

The region's continued reliance on sugar and tobacco farming meant that it was hard hit during recession times, and even today Jujuy province is one of the poorest in the country. There's an air of optimism, though, as the booming tourist industry brings much-needed income to the area.

CÓRDOBA

☎ 0351 / pop 1,272,000

In 2006 Córdoba was named Cultural Capital of the Americas (hefty title, huh?), which gives you a fair idea of what to expect here – music, theater, film: whatever you want, you can be pretty sure it's going on somewhere in town. The city also rocks out with seven (count 'em) universities, so the streets, bars and clubs are always hopping and the city has a buzz that some say is unmatched in the whole country.

Orientation

On the south bank of the Río Primero (or Sequoia), 400m above sea level at the foot of the Sierra Chica, the city sprawls north of the river and into the countryside. Its attractive downtown comprises a labyrinth of plazas and colonial architecture.

Plaza San Martín is the nucleus for Córdoba's one million inhabitants, but the commercial center is northwest of the plaza, where the 25 de Mayo and Rivera Indarte pedestrian malls intersect. Local buses don't serve the bus terminal, but it's an easy eight-block walk to the center; just keep moving toward the big steeple. A taxi should cost US$1.

Information

There are ATMs near Plaza San Martín.

Cambio Barujel (cnr Buenos Aires & 25 de Mayo) For changing traveler's checks.

Municipal tourist office (☎ 428-5600; www.visite cordobaciudad.com.ar; Rosario de Santa Fe 39)

Municipal tourist office satellite office (☎ 433-1980) At the bus terminal.

Post office (Av Gral Paz 201)

Provincial tourist office (☎ 428-5856) In the historic *cabildo* (colonial town council) on Plaza San Martín.

Sights

To see Córdoba's colonial buildings and monuments, start at the **cabildo**, on Plaza San Martín. At the plaza's southwest corner, crowned by a Romanesque dome, the **Iglesia Catedral** (begun in 1577) mixes a variety of styles.

The 1645 Jesuit **Iglesia de la Compañía de Jesús** (cnr Obispo Trejo & Caseros) has a modest exterior, but its unique interior is a masterpiece featuring a timber ceiling shaped like an inverted ship's hull.

The **Iglesia de Santa Teresa** and its **convent** have a museum of religious art, the **Museo de Arte Religioso Juan de Tejeda** (Independenciá 122; admission US50¢; ⊙ 9:30am-12:30pm Wed-Sat).

The huge, stark and modern space of the **Museo Provincial de Bellas Artes Emilio Caraffa** (Av Hipólito Yrigoyen 651; admission free; ⊙ 11am-7pm Tue-Sun)

NORTHWEST ARGENTINA

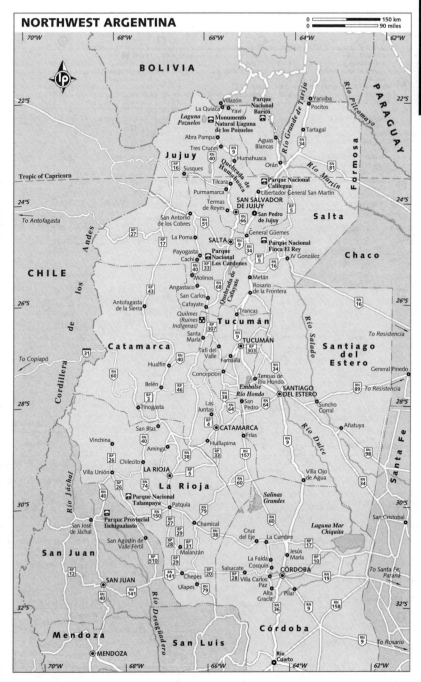

ARGENTINA

CÓRDOBA

0 ————————— 500 m
0 ————————— 0.3 miles

INFORMATION
Cambio Barujel.......................1 C3
Latitud Sur Travel Agency..........(see 17)
Municipal Tourist Office...............2 C4
Municipal Tourist Satellite Office..(see 28)
Post Office.............................3 B3
Provincial Tourist Office..............(see 5)

SIGHTS & ACTIVITIES
Bayaderos.............................4 D4
Cabildo................................5 B4
Cine Teatro Córdoba...................6 B4
Iglesia Catedral.......................7 B4
Iglesia de la Compañía de Jesús....8 B4
Iglesia de Santa Teresa y Convento de
  Carmelitas Descalzas de San José.9 B4
Museo de Arte Religioso Juan de
  Tejeda..............................10 B4
Museo Histórico Provincial Marqués de
  Sobremonte.........................11 C4

Museo Provincial de Bellas Artes Emilio
  Caraffa.............................12 B6
Spanish Central.......................13 C3

SLEEPING
Córdoba Backpackers.................14 B3
Ducal Suites..........................15 C4
Hotel Claridge........................16 C3
Tango Hostel..........................17 B5

EATING
La Candela............................18 B4
La Parrilla de Raul....................19 B3
La Vieja Esquina......................20 B4
La Zete...............................21 C5
Las Tinajas...........................22 B4
Sol y Luna............................23 B3

DRINKING
Casa Babylon..........................24 C1
Good Bar.............................25 B6
Ojo Bizaro...........................26 C2

TRANSPORT
Aerolíneas Argentinas...27 A3
Austral....................(see 27)
Bus Terminal..............28 D5
Mercado Sud Minibus
  Terminal................29 B5
Varig.....................30 B3

To Santiago
del Estero
(439km)

Río Primero

Parque
Las Heras

To Chateau
Carreras (5.5km);
Eros Hotel (6km);
Airport (15.5km)

To Municipal
Campground
(13km)

Hospital de
Urgencias

Centro

Paseo
Sobremonte

To Coimed
(25m)

To Alamo Car
Rental (1.5km)

Güemes

Universidad
Nacional
de Córdoba

Iglesia
San Roque

Estación
Ferrocarril
Mitre (not
functioning)

Nueva
Córdoba

Plaza de
los Niños

To Villa
Carlos Paz
(36km)

To Buenos Aires
(710km)

Plaza
España

Parque
Sarmiento

provides contrast to the excellent contemporary art on display. Exhibits are arranged thematically and always have a few wild cards thrown in.

The **Museo Histórico Provincial Marqués de Sobremonte** (Rosario de Santa Fe 218; admission US$1; ☯ 9am-1pm Tue-Sat) is set in one of Córdoba's oldest surviving houses (1752).

Córdoba has many good cinemas; one of the oldest is the **Cine Teatro Córdoba** (27 de Abril 275), which features art-house films.

Activities

There's plenty of stuff to do in and around Córdoba: paragliding, skydiving, trekking, rafting, rock-climbing, horse-riding and mountain biking to name a few options. Latitud Sur Travel Agency (in Tango Hostel; below) offers all of this and more, and has been recommended for its good service and willingness to give advice on how to do things independently.

Courses

Bayaderos (☎ 422-5572; Santiago del Estero 14) Offers private (US$7 per hour) and group (US$3 per hour) dance classes for styles including salsa, tango, contemporary and Arabic.

Spanish Central (☎ 526-1158; www.spanishcordoba .com.ar; Rivadavia 85) Offers individual Spanish classes from US$8 per hour, with discounts for more hours per week or group classes.

Sleeping

Municipal campground (☎ 433-8012; per person US$1.50) Spacious but basic, in the Parque General San Martín, 13km west of downtown. Bus 1 from Plaza San Martín goes to the Complejo Ferial, an exhibition and entertainment complex about 1km from the park.

Cordoba Backpackers (☎ 422-0593; www.cordobaback packers.com.ar; Deán Funes 285; dm/d US$6/14; 🖳) Good sized four- to six-bed dorms, a supercentral location, excellent rooftop area and grassy backyard combine to make this a fine option.

Tango Hostel (☎ 425-6023; www.latitudsurtrek.com .ar; Fructuoso Rivera 70; dm/d US$6/14) Run by young travelers who know their stuff about the whole of Latin America, the Tango features a welcoming atmosphere and good social spaces. It's a great place for meeting up with people and just generally hanging out. Also here is Latitud Sur Travel Agency.

Hotel Claridge (☎ 421-5741; 25 de Mayo 218; s/d US$11/14) If the staff on the front desk were a little more cheerful, this would be a pretty good budget hotel. Pretend you don't speak Spanish, and head upstairs for clean, aging rooms with balconies overlooking the pedestrian street below.

Ducal Suites (☎ 570-8888; www.hotelducal.com.ar; Corrientes 207; s/d US$40/50; P 🎏 🖳) One of the most comfortable hotels in the center, the rooms here have kitchenettes, spacious bathrooms and (some) excellent views out over the city. In summer months the rooftop pool is a bonus.

Eating

There are many cheap bars and pizzerias in the student haunts around Plaza Vélez Sársfield.

La Candela (Corrientes; mains US$2-5) A rustic student hangout featuring empanadas and *locro*. It's near Obispo Trejo.

Sol y Luna (Av Gral Paz 278; set meals US$3.50) Don't let the size of this little vegetarian place fool you – the menu selection is wide and changes every day, featuring South American– and Japanese-influenced dishes.

La Vieja Esquina (cnr Belgrano & Caseros; mains US$2-3) This tiny, atmospheric restaurant features a minimenu of four items (*locro, humitas, empanadas* and *tortas*) but all are definitely worth checking out.

La Parrilla de Raul (Jujuy 278; mains US$2.50-3.50) Founded in 1906, this is the most atmospheric *parrilla* in town. It's small and dimly lit, and the walls are stacked with Argentine wines. *Parrillada* for two costs only US$3.50 to US$5.

La Zete (Corrientes 455; mains US$4-6) The smells that hit you as you walk into this authentic Middle Eastern eatery are guaranteed to get your mouth watering, and the kebabs, empanadas and salads won't disappoint.

Las Tinajas (Blvd San Juan 32; lunch Mon-Fri US$4, Sat & Sun US$5, dinner US$6) The country's largest *tenedor libre* (all-you-can-eat restaurant) is big in every sense, from the selection of Asian food, seafood, salads and pastas to the artificial waterfall and river running through the middle of it.

Drinking

Córdoba's drink of choice is Fernet (a strong, medicinal tasting, herbed liquor from Italy), almost always mixed with Coke. If you don't mind a rough morning, start in on the Fernet con Coke. There are basically two areas to go out in Córdoba: Nuevo Córdoba, where all the bright young things go to be fashionable, and the area to the north of town known as Abasto, where things are kept much more real. Most venues charge US$3 admission, which entitles you to a free drink.

Ojo Bizaro (Igualdad 176; 11pm-late Wed-Sat) One of Córdoba's truly bohemian hangouts, the Ojo is split into various rooms with plenty of low-slung vinyl sofas, eclectic decorations and two DJs, one out front spinning pop, the other in the back doing electronica.

Casa Babylon (Las Heras 48) Córdoba's definitive ska and reggae club is small, but about 90% dance floor, so you should find the skanking relatively easy. Things get irie around 1am and stay that way 'til sunup.

Good Bar (cnr Buenos Aires & Larrañaga) You'll recognize it by the surfboard stuck on the front of the building and the crowd inside warming up after midnight.

Entertainment
On Friday nights, the city hosts the Patio del Tango (admission US$1, with dance lessons US$2) on the outdoor Patio Mayor of the historic *cabildo* (weather permitting), kicking off with two-hour tango lessons.

Getting There & Around
AIR
Aerolíneas Argentinas & Austral (482-1025; www .aerolineasargentinas.com; Av Colón 520) fly regularly to Buenos Aires (from US$50).

Varig (425-6262; 9 de Julio 40, 7th fl) flies to Porto Alegre, Florianópolis and São Paulo, Brazil, but all flights go via Buenos Aires, so you're better off going there first and getting a cheaper flight.

Internet-based **Gol** (www.voegol.com.br) flies to Brazil, Paraguay and Buenos Aires. Check their website for specials.

The **airport** (465-0392) is about 15km north of town. Bus A5 (marked 'Aeropuerto') leaves from Plaza San Martín. Buy a US30¢ *cospel* (token) from a kiosk before traveling. Taxis to the airport cost about US$4.

BUS
Córdoba's **bus terminal** (433-1988; Blvd Perón 380) has departures for Tucumán (US$12, eight hours), Buenos Aires (US$24, 10 hours), Mendoza (US$16, 10 hours), Posadas (US$25, 18 hours) and Salta (US$24, 13 hours). There are also international services to Florianópolis, Brazil (US$66, 32 hours); Montevideo, Uru-

guay (US$43, 15 hours) and Santiago, Chile (US$32, 16 hours).

AROUND CÓRDOBA
Frequent minibuses leave from the **Mercado Sud Minibus Terminal** (Blvd Illia), near Buenos Aires, for all of the following destinations.

Cosquín
03541 / pop 19,000
Cosquín will always be famous for its nine-day **Festival Nacional del Folklore** (held every January for more than 30 years), the best place to spot hot new Argentine talent. It *used* to be famous for the totally balls-out Cosquín Rock Festival, but then the suits got involved, 'administrative problems' arose and the festival moved elsewhere. Typical. If you want to stay here for the folk festival, book months in advance. Otherwise it's an easy day trip from Córdoba.

Cerro Pan de Azúcar, east of town, offers good views of the sierras and the city of Córdoba. Hitch or walk (buses are few, but a taxi costs US$6 return) 7km to a saddle, where an *aerosilla* (chairlift; US$3) climbs to the top, or take a steep 25-minute walk to the 1260m summit. Also at the saddle is a *confitería*, the owner of which, a devotee of Carlos Gardel, has decorated the grounds with Gardel memorabilia.

There's nothing special going on at **Hospedaje Remanso** (452-681; Gral Paz 38; s/d US$9/13), but the rooms are quiet and the place is clean and well run.

Warning: the woman who runs **Hospedaje Siempreverde** (450-093; Santa Fe 525; d US$18) is so charming you'll probably end up feeling guilty if you don't stay here. The hotel's a charmer, too: lovingly decorated spacious rooms around a shady garden area.

The tiny **Mi Rancho** (San Martín 478; mains US$3-4) expands somewhat with sidewalk seating, and does excellent empanadas, *locro* and pizza.

There's nothing small or intimate about **Parrilla Posta Maiten** (Perón 587; mains US$4-6), but it gets warm recommendations from all over town.

Frequent buses run to Córdoba (US$2, 1½ hours) and La Falda (US$1, 45 minutes).

La Falda
03548 / pop 15,000
Obviously a resort town (and if anybody knows why, feel free to write in), La Falda's hotels outnumber all other businesses combined.

There's hiking in them there hills; trails leave from the miniature train museum (see following) where there are also swimming pools and lookouts over town. More swimming can be had at **7 Cascadas** (entry with transport from tourist office US$1), which counts on three pools and a variety of swimming holes under waterfalls that were created when the local dam was built. The **tourist office** (☎ 423-007; España 50) opens erratically, but it's very helpful.

The **Museo de Trenes en Miniatura** (Miniature Train Museum; admission US$3; ☼ 9am-8pm) warrants a quick visit.

Hostería Marína (☎ 422-640; Güemes 134; r per person incl breakfast US$4) is La Falda's best value lodging. **Hospedaje San Remo** (☎ 424-875; Argentina 108; r per person incl breakfast US$5) is another good bet.

There are many *parrillas* and pizzerias along Av Edén.

Real budget-watchers should check out **Tentaciónes** (Diagonal San Martín 74; mains US$1-5). Mostly takeout, but with a few tables, the offerings here are basic but filling burgers, sandwiches and pizza.

Way up the hill, past 15 very tempting options, **La Parrilla de Raúl** (Edén 1000; all you can eat US$5.50) is worth the wait: a huge selection of meats and salads and live music on weekends.

Buses run to and from Córdoba (US$2, two hours).

Jesús María
☎ 03525 / pop 27,000

After losing their operating funds to pirates off the coast of Brazil, the Jesuits produced and sold wine from Jesús María to support their university in colonial Córdoba. These days the town, 51km north of Córdoba via RN 9, hosts the annual **Fiesta Nacional de Doma y Folklore** (www.festivaljesusmaria.com), a celebration of *gaucho* horsemanship and customs, during early January.

If you're only planning on seeing one Jesuit Mission, **Museo Jesuítico Nacional de Jesús María** (admission US$1) should probably be it. Easily accessed, but in a peaceful rural setting, it's been wonderfully preserved and restored and is crammed full of artifacts. For some reason there's a contemporary art exhibition on the top floor. Go around the back to check out the antique wine-making gear.

Buses run between Córdoba and Jesús María (US$1.50, one hour).

Alta Gracia
☎ 03547 / pop 43,000

Only 35km southwest of Córdoba, the colonial mountain town of Alta Gracia is steeped in history. Its illustrious residents have ranged from Jesuit pioneers to Viceroy Santiago Liniers, Spanish composer Manuel de Falla and revolutionary Ernesto 'Che' Guevara. The tourist office is located in the clocktower opposite the museum Virrey Liniers and has a good town map.

From 1643 to 1762, Jesuit fathers built the **Iglesia Parroquial Nuestra Señora de la Merced**, on the west side of the central Plaza Manuel Solares; the nearby Jesuit workshops of **El Obraje** (1643) are now a public school. Liniers, one of the last officials to occupy the post of Viceroy of the Río de la Plata, resided in what is now the **Museo Histórico Nacional del Virrey Liniers** (admission US$1; 9am-8pm Tue-Fri, 9:30am-12:30pm & 5-8pm Sat, Sun & holidays), alongside the church.

Though the Guevaras lived in several houses in the 1930s, their primary residence was **Villa Beatriz**, which has now been converted into the **Museo Casa Ernest 'Che' Guevara** (Avellaneda 501). The museum focuses heavily on the legend's early life, and, judging by the photographs, Che was a pretty intense guy by the time he was 16, and definitely had his cool look down by his early 20s.

The charming, simple rooms at **Hostería Asturias** (☎ 423-668; Vélez Sársfield 127; s/d US$8/15) are often booked out.

The long, narrow rooms at **Hostal Hispania** (☎ 426-555; Vélez Sársfield 57; s/d US$15/25; ☒) are supermodern and set around a lovely garden area featuring a beautifully tiled swimming pool. Many of the rooms have balconies.

Edgards (Vierra 225; mains US$2-3) has excellent Middle Eastern food, including doner kebabs (US$2), plus a range of *lomitos*, empanadas and pizzas.

Hispania (Urquiza 90; mains US$3-5) is another good choice, specializing in large portions.

From the **bus terminal** (cnr Perón & Butori), buses run every 15 minutes to and from Córdoba (US$1, one hour).

Villa Carlos Paz
☎ 03541 / pop 56,000

Let's be honest. You're either going to love it here or hate it. A little slice of Vegas in the Sierras, Carlos Paz has everything you could hope for, and many things you probably didn't realize you were hoping for: hotels done out like Egyptian pyramids and the Kremlin, miniature trains zipping around doing day tours, fun parks galore and – the city's pride and joy – a two-story cuckoo clock (*reloj cucu* for the Spanish speakers among us). The **tourist office** (☎ 436-430; San Martín-Hipólito Yrigoyen intersection) is behind the bus terminal.

The excellent **Carlos Paz Backpackers** (☎ 433-0593; cnr Sarmiento & Edison; s/d US$5/8), a 10-minute walk from 'the clock', has spacious four- to six-bed dorms and a sitting area with great views. It organizes canoeing, canopy, rafting, trekking and rappelling trips in the nearby mountains from US$15 per day.

Smack in the center (some rooms even have views of the *cu-cu*!), the big pink **Terrazas del Redantor** (☎ 434-430; www.acarlospaz.com/terrazas delredentor.html; Ameghino 48; s/d US$13/26; 🖳) has modern, spacious rooms and a comfortable, if somewhat stark, garden area.

Locals insist **Parrilla Saint Jean** (San Martín 200; mains US$2.50-7) is the best *parrilla* in town.

There are frequent buses from here to Córdoba (US$1.50, one hour) and Cosquin (US$1, 45 minutes).

LA RIOJA

☎ 03822 / pop 146,000

This is siesta country, folks. Between noon and 5pm *everything* shuts down (except, for some reason, bookstores). Once the sun starts dipping behind the surrounding mountains, people emerge from their houses, and the city and its three gorgeous central plazas take on a lively, refreshed feel.

In 1591 Juan Ramírez de Velasco founded Todos los Santos de la Nueva Rioja, at the base of the Sierra del Velasco, 154km south of Catamarca. The 1894 earthquake destroyed many buildings, but the restored commercial center, near Plaza 25 de Mayo, replicates colonial style.

Information

La Rioja's **tourist office** (☎ 426-345; Pelagio Luna 345) has a decent city map and many kilos worth of brochures covering other provincial destinations.

La Rioja has no *cambios*, but several banks have ATMs. The **post office** is at Perón 764.

Sights

The following two museums were closed 'for renovations' at the time of research, and have been for some time. If they ever open, no doubt they'll welcome the US$1 voluntary contribution.

The **Museo Folklórico** (Pelagio Luna 811) is set in a wonderful 19th-century house, displaying ceramic reproductions of mythological figures from local folklore as well as *gaucho* paraphernalia and colorful weavings.

The **Museo Inca Huasi** (Alberdi 650) exhibits over 12,000 pieces, from tools and artifacts to Diaguita ceramics and weavings.

The **Convento de San Francisco** (cnr 25 de Mayo & Bazán y Bustos) houses the Niño Alcalde, a Christ-child icon symbolically recognized as the city's mayor. The **Iglesia Catedral** (cnr San Nicolás & 25 de Mayo) contains the image of patron saint Nicolás de Bari, another devotional object.

Festivals & Events

The December 31 ceremony **El Tinkunako** re-enacts San Francisco Solano's mediation between the Diaguitas and the Spaniards in 1593. When accepting peace, the Diaguitas imposed two conditions: resignation of the Spanish mayor and his replacement by the Niño Alcalde.

Sleeping

Country Las Vegas (campsites per person US$2) The campground is at km 8 on RN 75 west of town; to get there, catch city bus 1 southbound on Perón.

Pensión 9 de Julio (☎ 426-955; cnr Copiapó & Vélez Sársfield; s/d incl breakfast US$7/10) Large rooms with private bath and a lovely shaded courtyard overlooking Plaza 9 de Julio.

Hotel Imperial (☎ 422-478; Mariano Moreno 345; s/d US$13/20; P 🖳) If you're at all tile-ophobic, you'll want to give this one a miss – they're everywhere. Otherwise, it's an excellent deal: big, airy rooms with cable TV and modern bathrooms a 10-minute walk from the center.

Hotel Plaza (☎ 425-215; www.plazahotel-larioja.com.ar; cnr 9 de Julio & San Nicolás de Bari; s/d US$30/35; P 🖳 🖳) Some rooms here overlook the plaza, making them a good deal. Others open onto internal lightwells (not so attractive, but still good for ventilation). The place has a pleasant old-time feel in the lobby and restaurant that vaguely follows through to the rooms.

Eating

Hollywood (cnr Rivadavia & San Martín; meals US$3-4) This could well be the perfect restaurant. Outdoor or air-con seating, tasty Middle Eastern–styled tapas, a wide range of Argentine standards on the menu, and it's open 'til the wee, wee hours for postmidnight munching.

Café del Paseo (Pelagio Luna & 25 de Mayo; mains US$3-5) An appealing *confitería*, with tables around a shaded courtyard.

La Aldea de la Virgen de Lujan (Rivadavia 756; mains US$3-5) This place serves excellent homemade pasta and, very occasionally, regional specialties. Either way, the servings are big and the food is wholesome.

Stanzza (Dorrego 160; mains US$4-6) One of the best places to eat in town, this friendly neighborhood restaurant serves up imaginative seafood and Italian dishes in an intimate environment.

Entertainment

New Milenium (San Martín 150; ☽ Wed-Sat) If you're in the mood for a mega-disco (and aren't we all, always?) this is a central option for shaking that thing.

Getting There & Away

Aerolíneas Argentinas (☎ 426-307; www.aerolineas argentinas.com; Belgrano 63) flies Monday to Saturday to Buenos Aires (US$90).

La Rioja's **bus terminal** (☎ 425-453; cnr Artigas & España) has departures to Chilecito (US$3, three hours), Catamarca (US$7, two hours), Tucumán (US$12, five hours), Córdoba (US$12, 5½ hours), San Luis (US$11, eight hours), San Juan (US$8, six hours), Mendoza (US$17, eight hours), Salta (US$17, 10 hours) and Buenos Aires (US$33, 16 hours).

CATAMARCA

☎ 03833 / pop 141,000

Surrounded by mountains and centered around shady Plaza 25 de Mayo, Catamarca is an attractive place. The only problem is that it lacks anything of any real substance to do. Once a year, the town gets mobbed by hard-core religious types, groupies of the Virgen del Valle. After that things quieten down pretty quickly.

Orientation

The bus terminal is five blocks south of the center: as you walk out of the terminal turn right, walk along Güemes until you get to Plaza 25 de Agosto, then hang a right up Hipólito Yrigoyen until you bump into Plaza 25 de Mayo.

Information

Several downtown banks have ATMs.

Banco Catamarca (Plaza 25 de Mayo) Can change traveler's checks in 24 hours.

Municipal tourist office (☎ 437-743; turismocata marca@cedeconet.com.ar; República 446) Has a wealth of material on the town and surrounds. Staff are usually very helpful.

Post office (San Martín 753)

Sights

The neocolonial **Iglesia y Convento de San Francisco** (cnr Esquiú & Rivadavia) contains the cell of Fray Mamerto Esquiú, famous for his vocal defense of the 1853 constitution. After being stolen and left on the roof years ago, a crystal box containing his heart (perched on a velvet cushion) is on display in the church.

Enough with these thematically organized, artistically lit 'cultural installations' curated by spiky haired, facially pierced Curatorial Engineers. **Museo Arqueológico Adán Quiroga** (Sarmiento btwn Esquiú & Prado; admission US$1; ☽ 7am-1pm & 2:30-8:30pm Mon-Fri, 10am-7pm Sat & Sun) is how a museum should be – crammed so full of precolonial pottery, mummies, skulls, metalwork, and colonial and religious artifacts that you practically have to get down on your hands and knees to rummage through it all, and curated by an old guy in a grey dustcoat with ear hair who doesn't want to know about you, but once he warms up, he rambles on for hours.

Festivals & Events

Fiesta de Nuestra Señora del Valle On the Sunday after Easter thousands of pilgrims from across Argentina honor the Virgen del Valle. On December 8, a colorful procession carries the Virgin through the town.

Fiesta del Poncho A more provincial event, held during two weeks in July.

Sleeping

Autocamping Municipal (campsites per tent/person US$2/1) This place gets heavy use on weekends and holidays, and has some ferocious mosquitoes. It's about 4km from downtown. To get there take bus 10 (marked 'camping') from Convento de San Francisco, on Esquiú.

Residencial Avenida (☎ 422-139; Güemes 754; s/d US$5/9) The Avenida offers good-value (for the price) rooms *really* close to the bus terminal. Singles have shared bathrooms, doubles huge private ones. The central courtyard is a good place to soak up the sun.

Sol Hotel (☎ 430-803; solhotel@hotmail.com; Salta 1142; s/d US$13/18) The Sol's bright, cheery rooms are the best value out of the cheapies near the terminal. Some are much better than others; ask to see a few.

Hotel Casino Catamarca (☎ 432928; César Carman s/n; s/d US$15/23; 🖳 🖳) With the most character of all of Catamarca's hotels, this one is a real bargain. Rooms are spacious, with terracotta tilework and brass fittings. Rear rooms overlook a well-kept garden area with a huge pool. The place can get noisy on weekends when it hosts parties.

Eating & Drinking

Richmond Bar (República 540; mains US$2-7) Right on the plaza, this classy restaurant/bar is a great place to stop in for a coffee or snack any time of day or night.

Sociedad Española (Virgen del Valle 725; mains US$3-7) The Spanish Society is always worth hunting down for traditional Spanish dishes, including seafood. It's a grand old place, and well worth the trek for some fine dining.

Los Troncos (M Botello 25; mains US$3-7) Judging by what pretty much every taxi driver says (and these guys know their stuff), this is the best *parrilla* in town. It also does good fish and pasta dishes.

Bars and discos can be found on Av Galindez (the western extension of Prado), reasonably close to the center; a taxi out here should cost about US$1.

Getting There & Away

Aerolíneas Argentinas (☎ 424-460; www.aerolineasargentinas.com; Sarmiento 589, 8th fl) flies to Buenos Aires (US$100) from Monday to Saturday.

Catamarca's **bus terminal** (☎ 423-415; Güemes 850) has departures to La Rioja (US$7, two hours), Tucumán (US$6, three hours), Santiago del Estero (US$6, five hours), Córdoba (US$9, 5½ hours), Salta (US$10, eight hours), San Juan (US$16, seven hours), Mendoza (US$17, 10 hours) and Buenos Aires (US$43, 16 hours).

SANTIAGO DEL ESTERO
☎ 0385 / pop 231,000

Due to its central location, Santiago is a major transport hub: you can catch a bus from here to just about anywhere in the country. Unfortunately for 'modern' Argentina's oldest city, its list of charms pretty much ends there. The Museo Wagner is worth a look in if you've got a couple of hours to kill between buses,

but after that even the tourist office is kinda stumped about why you would be here.

The provincial **tourist office** (☎ 421-3253; Libertad 417) sometimes shows work by provincial artists. Several banks in the downtown area have ATMs but it is difficult to change traveler's checks. The post office is at the corner of Buenos Aires and Urquiza.

The **Museo Wagner de Ciencias Antropológicas y Naturales** (Avellaneda 355; ☺ 7:30am-1:30pm & 2-8pm Mon-Fri, 10am-noon Sat & Sun) offers free guided tours of its well-presented collection of fossils, funerary urns, Chaco ethnography and dinosaur findings.

Sleeping & Eating

Campamento Las Casuarinas (Parque Aguirre; campsites per person US$1.50) Offers shady campsites less than a kilometer from Plaza Libertad.

Residencial Emaus (☎ 421-5893; Moreno Sur 673; s/d US$10/13) Somebody's been doing weird stuff to the walls in the rooms here, but apart from that they're all spotless.

Hotel Savoy (☎ 421-1234; www.savoysantiago.com.ar; Tucumán 39; s/d US$15/25; 🅿 🖳) The eye-popping grandeur of the facade and lobby here make up for the fairly ordinary rooms. Excellent value, smack in the middle of town.

Mercado Armonía (Tucumán btwn Pellegrini & Salta) Cheap, but less appealing than some Argentine markets.

Jockey Club (Independencia 68; mains US$3-5) For fine dining right on the square, check this place out. You don't even have to be short or talk funny to eat here. There's a fairly standard range of dishes, but the set meals (US$4) are a bargain.

Getting There & Around

Aerolíneas Argentinas (☎ 422-4335; www.aerolineasargentinas.com; 24 de Septiembre 547) flies daily to Buenos Aires (US$100).

The **bus terminal** (☎ 421-3746; cnr Pedro León Gallo & Saavedra) is eight blocks south of Plaza Libertad. A *remise* from the airport costs around US$2.

There are frequent departures to Tucumán (US$3, two hours), Catamarca (US$5, five hours) and Buenos Aires (US$16, 13 hours).

TUCUMÁN
☎ 0381 / pop 528,000

A big city with a small-town feel, Tucumán is definitely improving in terms of the backpacking scene. There are some good hostels, a pumping nightlife and some excellent

TUCUMÁN

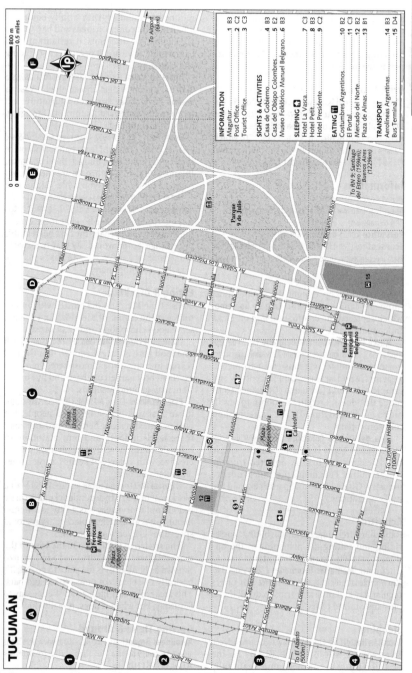

INFORMATION	
Maguitur	1 B3
Post Office	2 C2
Tourist Office	3 C3

SIGHTS & ACTIVITIES	
Casa de Gobierno	4 B3
Casa del Obispo Colombres	5 E2
Museo Folklórico Manuel Belgrano	6 B3

SLEEPING	
Hotel La Vasca	7 C3
Hotel Petit	8 B3
Hotel Presidente	9 C2

EATING	
Costumbres Argentinos	10 B2
El Portal	11 C3
Mercado del Norte	12 B2
Plaza de Almas	13 B1

TRANSPORT	
Aerolíneas Argentinas	14 B3
Bus Terminal	15 D4

0   800 m
0   0.5 miles

To Airport
(6km)

Parque
9 de Julio

To RN 9; Santiago
del Estero (159km);
Buenos Aires
(1229km)

Estación
Ferrocarril
Belgrano

Estación
Ferrocarril
Mitre

Plaza
Alberdi

Plaza
Urquiza

Plaza
Independencia

Cathedral

To Tucuman Hostel
(100m)

To El Abasto
(500m)

adventures to be had in the surrounding hills. Independence Day (July 9) celebrations are especially vigorous in Tucumán, which hosted the congress that declared Argentine independence in 1816.

Orientation

The bus terminal is a few blocks from the center, an easy walk if you don't want to fork out the US$1 cab fare. Tucumán's **airport** (☎ 426-5072) is 8km east of downtown. Catch bus 120, which passes the center on the way to the bus terminal (US$1). A taxi there will cost US$4.

Information

ATMs are numerous.

Maguitur (San Martín 765) Cashes traveler's checks (2% commission).

Post office (cnr 25 de Mayo & Córdoba)

Tourist office (☎ 430-3644; Av 24 de Septiembre 484) On Plaza Independencia. There's also a booth at the bus terminal.

Sights

Spectacularly lit up at night, Tucumán's most imposing landmark is the **Casa de Gobierno**, which replaced the colonial *cabildo* on Plaza Independencia in 1912.

Museo Folklórico Manuel Belgrano (Av 24 de Septiembre 565; admission free; �},9am-12:30pm) displays horse gear, indigenous musical instruments, weavings, woodcarvings, Quilmes pottery and samples of *randa* (a Puerto Rican lace technique that doesn't require a bobbin to sew it, only a needle and thread). The museum shop sells some items.

Casa del Obispo Colombres (Parque 9 de Julio; �},8am-noon & 4-8pm) is an 18th-century house that preserves the first ox-powered *trapiche* (sugar mill) of Tucumán's postindependence industry. Guided tours in Spanish explain the mill's operations.

Activities

Rappelling, trekking, mountain biking, horseriding and rafting are just some of the options for stuff to do in the mountains around Tucumán. **Montañas Tucumanas** (☎ 1560-93336; http://montanastucumanas.com; Catamarca 375) offers regular day and multiday trips to do all these, plus customized tours.

Sleeping

Tucumán Hostel (☎ 420-1584; www.tucumanhostel.com; Buenos Aires 669; dm/d US$6/13; P ⬛) By far the best of Tucumán's hostels, in a beautifully redone old building with a fully equipped kitchen, good common areas and bar. Guests are eligible for discounts at restaurants and bars around town and it organizes paragliding and canoeing trips.

Hotel La Vasca (☎ 421-1288; Mendoza 289; s/d US$8/11) A good budget choice, the La Vasca's rooms have classy hardwood furniture and face a pretty courtyard. Bathrooms are aging, but well maintained.

Hotel Petit (☎ 421-3902; Crisóstomo Álvarez 765; s/d US$9/16) With a maze of leafy patios, this place is definitely the best budget hotel in town. Rooms with shared bathroom are cheaper, but paying a bit more gets you cable TV, too.

Hotel Presidente (☎ 431-1414; www.tucuman.com/hotelpresidente; Monteguado 249; s/d US$27/34; P ⊠ ⬛) A modern, comfortable hotel near the center, the Presidente is perhaps the best hotel in this price range. Some would say that two swimming pools are excessive, but that's just the way they do things here.

Eating & Drinking

Stalls at the Mercado del Norte, with an entrance at the corner of Mendoza and Maipú, serve good cheap food and great pizza.

Custumbres Argentinos (San Jaun 666; mains US$1-4) The food here is decent enough, but the real reason to come is the atmosphere: there's an excellent beer garden out back and live music Thursday to Sunday nights.

Plaza de Almas (Maipú 791; mains US$3-5) Although it can seat well over a hundred people, the well-designed spaces here, spread out over three levels indoors and out, maintain an intimate atmosphere. The menu is simple but creative, with a range of kebabs, meat dishes and salads on offer.

El Portal (Av 24 de Septiembre; mains US$3-10) Half a block east of Plaza Independencia, this rustic indoor/outdoor eatery has a tiny (six items) menu, but is an excellent place to try regional specialties like *locro* and *humitas*.

The stretch of Calle Lillo to the west of the market between La Madrid and San Lorenzo (known as El Abasto) is the place to go out; it's basically five blocks of pubs, discos and bars. This area really only kicks from Wednesday to Saturday, but when it does, it really does.

Getting There & Around

Aerolíneas Argentinas (☎ 431-1030; www.aerolineasargentinas.com; 9 de Julio 110) flies daily to Buenos Aires (US$110).

Tucumán's **bus terminal** (☎ 422-2221; Brígido Terán 350) has a post office, *locutorios*, a supermarket, bars and restaurants, all blissfully air-conditioned.

Aconquija goes to Tafí del Valle (US$4, 2½ hours), and to Cafayate (US$9, seven hours).

Long-distance destinations include Santiago del Estero (US$4, two hours), Córdoba (US$13, eight hours), Salta (US$8, 4½ hours), Corrientes (US$20, 12 hours), La Rioja (US$10, five hours) and Buenos Aires (US$35, 16 hours).

TAFÍ DEL VALLE
☎ 03867 / pop 4000

Set in a pretty valley overlooking a lake, Tafí is where folks from Tucumán come to escape the heat in summer months. Off-season it's much mellower (which isn't to imply that there's any sort of frenzy here in summertime), but still gorgeous and makes a good base for exploring the surrounding countryside and nearby ruins at Quilmes (p104).

Information
The helpful **Casa del Turista** (☎ 421-084) is in Tafí's central plaza. **Banco Tucumán** (Miguel Critto) has an ATM.

Sights & Activities
At 2000m, a temperate island in a subtropical sea, Tafí produces some exceedingly good handmade cheese and the **cheese festival** held during the second week in February is well worth a look (and, possibly, a nibble). At **Parque Los Menhires**, at the south end of La Angostura reservoir, stand more than 80 indigenous granite monuments collected from nearby archaeological sites. Some say they resemble the standing stones of the Scottish Hebrides.

Sleeping & Eating
Autocamping del Sauce (☎ 421-084; campsites/cabañas per person US$2/3) The tiny cabañas with bunks would be very cramped at their maximum capacity of four people.

Hostel la Cumbre (☎ 421-768; Perón 120; www.lacumbretafidelvalle.com; dm/d US$7/14) These basic rooms set around a cheery courtyard are the pick of Tafí's budget options. The owner has loads of information on tours and hikes in the area (as well as a good little tour company) and there's a cozy TV room.

Hostería Huayra Puca (☎ 421-190; www.huayrapuca .com.ar; Menhires 71; s/d US$20/27; 🖳) Set in a light and airy building of interesting design, this place offers comfortable, good-sized rooms. Multilingual staff, loads of local information and transfers to and from Tucumán are other bonuses.

Don Pepino (Juan de Perón; mains US$3-5) The coziest of the *parrilla* options, usually featuring live entertainment at mealtimes. If you've been hanging out to try *chivo a la parrilla* (barbecued goat), this is probably the place to do it.

Getting Around
Mountain bikes can be rented from the elegant **Hotel Rosada** (Belgrano 322) for US$1 an hour.

CAFAYATE
☎ 03868 / pop 11,800

Set at the entrance to the Quebrada de Cafayate, 1600m above sea level and surrounded by some of the country's best vineyards, Cafayate provides the opportunity to indulge in two of life's great pleasures: drinking wine and exploring nature. If you're pressed for time, you can combine the two and take a bottle out into the Quebrada with you, in which case we would recommend a local *torrontés*, provided you can keep it chilled.

February's **La Serenata** music festival draws big crowds.

Information
The tourist information kiosk is at the northeast corner of Plaza San Martín.

Sights
The **Museo de Vitivinicultura** (Güemes; admission US50¢; ⏰ 10am-1pm & 5-8pm Mon-Fri), near Colón, details the history of local wines. Three central **bodegas** (wine cellars) and three nearby vineyards offer tours and tasting; try the fruity white *torrontés*. From 25 de Mayo, a 5km walk southwest leads you to the Río Colorado. Follow the river upstream for about two hours to get to a 10m **waterfall**, where you can swim. Look out for hidden rock paintings on the way (for a small tip, local children will guide you).

Sleeping & Eating
Camping Lorahuasi (☎ 421-051; per car, person & tent US$1) Has hot showers, a swimming pool and a grocery.

ARGENTINA

Hostel El Balcon (☎ 421-739; Pasaje 20 de Febrero 110; dm/d US$5/15) This wonderful hostel does indeed have a good balcony, and also light, airy common rooms, a well-stocked kitchen and an excellent rooftop patio. It also organizes some of the best tours of the Quebrada and local sights, as well as having a wealth of do-it-yourself options to keep you entertained.

Hostal Killa (☎ 422-254; hostalkillacafayate@hotmail .com; Colón 47; s/d US$24/29) One of the most comfortable options in town are the sunny and spacious rooms in this converted colonial house. The whole place has been beautifully restored and there's a stylishly rustic breakfast/sitting area out back.

Cheap eats can be found at the various *comedores* inside the **Mercado Central** (San Martín & 11 de Noviembre). Restaurants around the plaza do good regional dishes at reasonable prices.

Rincon de los Amigos (San Martín 25; mains US$3-7) The shady sidewalk tables looking out over the plaza here are a good place to try regional dishes like grilled goat (US$4) and *locro* (US$2).

Baco (Güemes & Rivadavia; meals US$4-7) Crammed full of rustic decorations, this is the most frequently recommended restaurant in town. It serves up interesting variations on Argentine standards and a good selection of local wines for around US$6 per bottle.

Heladería Miranda (Güemes btwn Córdoba & Almagro; per scoop from US$45¢) This place sells imaginative wine-flavored ice cream with a considerable alcoholic kick.

Getting There & Around

El Indio (Belgrano btwn Güemes & Salta) has buses to Salta (US$7, 3½ hours), San Carlos (US$1, 40 minutes), up the Vallee Calchaquíes, and Angastaco (US$2.50, two hours).

Take one of the daily buses to Santa María to visit the ruins at Quilmes (right), in Tucumán province. **El Aconquija** (cnr Güemes & Alvarado) has departures to Tucumán (US$9, seven hours), passing through Tafí del Valle.

Bike rental from **Hostel El Balcon** (☎ 421-739; Pasaje 20 de Febrero 110) costs US$3 a day.

AROUND CAFAYATE
Quebrada de Cafayate

From Cafayate, RN 68 slices through the Martian-like landscape of the Quebrada de Cafayate on its way to Salta. About 50km north of Cafayate, the eastern Sierra de Carahuasi is the backdrop for distinctive sandstone landforms like the Garganta del Diablo (Devil's Throat), El Anfiteatro (Amphitheater), El Sapo (Toad), El Fraile (Friar), El Obelisco (Obelisk) and Los Castillos (Castles).

Other than car rental or organized tours, the best way to see the Quebrada is by bike or on foot. Bring plenty of water and go in the morning, as unpleasant, strong winds kick up in the afternoon. At Cafayate, cyclists can load their bikes onto any El Indio bus heading to Salta and disembark at the impressive box canyon of Garganta del Diablo. From here, the 50-odd kilometers back to Cafayate can be biked in about four hours, but it's too far on foot. When they've had enough, walkers should simply hail down another El Indio bus on its way back to Cafayate.

Valles Calchaquíes

In this valley north and south of Cafayate, once a principal route across the Andes, the Calchaquí people resisted Spanish attempts to impose forced labor obligations. Tired of having to protect their pack trains, the Spaniards relocated many Calchaquí to Buenos Aires, and the land fell to Spaniards, who formed large rural estates.

CACHI
☎ 03868 / pop 5200

Cachi is a spectacularly beautiful town and by far the most visually impressive of those along the Valles Calchaquíes. There's not a whole lot to do here, but that's all part of the charm.

For accommodations, check out the **municipal campground & hostel** (campsites/dm US$2/4) or **Hotel Nevado de Cachi** (☎ 491-004; r per person US$3), a modest, good-value hotel. The best hotel in town is the **Hostería Cachi** (☎ 491-105; www .soldelvalle.com.ar; s/d US$30/40; P 🖳 🐾), with an excellent hilltop location and stylish modern rooms. Cheap restaurants surround the plaza.

You can only reach Cachi from Cafayate if you have your own transport or are prepared to hitchhike a stretch of RN 40 between Angastaco and Molinos. It's easier to take a bus from Salta (US$7, four hours), via the scenic Cuesta del Obispo route past Parque Nacional Los Cardones.

QUILMES

This pre-Hispanic **pucará** (indigenous Andean fortress; admission US$1), in Tucumán province, 50km south of Cafayate, is Argentina's most extensive preserved ruin. Dating from about AD 1000, this complex urban settlement covered about 30 hectares, housing perhaps 5000 people. The Quilmes people abided contact with the Incas but could not outlast the Spaniards, who, in 1667, deported the last 2000 to Buenos Aires.

Quilmes' thick walls underscore its defensive functions, but evidence of dense occupation sprawls north and south of the nucleus. **Parador Ruinas de Quilmes** (☎ 03892-421-075; s/d US$30/40) also has a restaurant.

Buses from Cafayate to Santa María pass the Quilmes junction, but from there, it's 5km to the ruins by foot or thumb.

SALTA

☎ 0387 / pop 465,000

Salta has experienced a huge surge in popularity as a backpacking destination over the last few years, and rightly so – the setting's gorgeous, the hostels are attractive, the nightlife pumps and there's plenty to do in and around town.

Orientation

Salta's commercial center is southwest of the central Plaza 9 de Julio. Alberdi and Florida are pedestrian malls between Caseros and Av San Martín. Bus 5 connects the train station, downtown and bus terminal.

Information

There are ATMs downtown.

Administración de Parques Nacionales (APN; ☎ 431-2686; España 366, 3rd fl) Has information on the province's national parks.

Cambio Dinar (Mitre 101) Changes cash and traveler's checks.

Municipal tourist office (☎ 437-3341; cnr Av San Martín & Buenos Aires) Runs an information kiosk in the bus terminal in high season.

Post office (Deán Funes 140)

Provincial tourist office (☎ 431-0950; Buenos Aires 93) Very central.

Sights

CERRO SAN BERNARDO

For spectacular views of Salta and the Lerma valley, take the **teleférico** (gondola; round trip US$3) from Parque San Martín, or climb the winding staircase trail that starts behind the Güemes monument.

MUSEUMS

The **Museo de Arqueología de Alta Montaña** (Mitre 77; admission US$3; ☼ 9am-1pm & 3-8pm) documents the amazing discovery of three mummies found at an altitude of 6700m on the Llullaillaco volcano. The climate kept the bodies and a collection of textiles and sacred objects almost perfectly preserved.

The **Museo de Artes Contemporaneo** (Zuviría 90; admission US30¢; ☼ 9am-1pm & 4:30-8:30pm) exhibits the work of contemporary artists from the city, as well as Argentine and international artists. The space itself is world-class, well lit and expertly curated. Exhibits change rapidly, so it's always worthwhile popping in to see what's on offer.

CHURCHES

The 19th-century **Iglesia Catedral** (España 596) guards the ashes of General Martín Miguel de Güemes, a hero of the wars of independence. So ornate it's almost gaudy, the **Iglesia San Francisco** (cnr Caseros & Córdoba) is a Salta landmark. Only Carmelite nuns can enter the 16th-century adobe **Convento de San Bernardo** (cnr Caseros & Santa Fe) but anyone can admire its carved *algarrobo* (carob tree wood) door or peek inside the chapel during Mass, held at 8am daily.

EL TREN A LAS NUBES

From Salta, the Tren a las Nubes (Train to the Clouds) makes countless switchbacks and spirals to ascend the Quebrada del Toro and reach the high *puna* (Andean plateau). The La Polvorilla viaduct, crossing a broad desert canyon, is a magnificent engineering achievement at 4220m above sea level.

Turismo Tren a las Nubes (☎ 401-2000; Buenos Aires 44) operates full-day excursions as far as La Polvorilla; most trips take place on Saturday only from April to November, but can be more frequent during July holidays. The US$70 fare does not include meals, which cost around US$7.

Activities

White-water rafting outside of town is available with **Salta Rafting** (☎ 401-0301; www .saltarafting.com; Buenos Aires 88 loc 13) from US$32 for a half-day or US$50 with a canopy tour included. **Extreme Games** (☎ 422-2394; www.ex tremegame.todowebsalta.com.ar; Buenos Aires 68 loc 1) can take care of all your bungee-jumping (US$28), jetski (US$12), horse-riding (from US$21), paragliding (US$50) and kite-buggy (US$60) requirements. If that all sounds a bit full-on for you, paddleboats are available on the

ARGENTINA

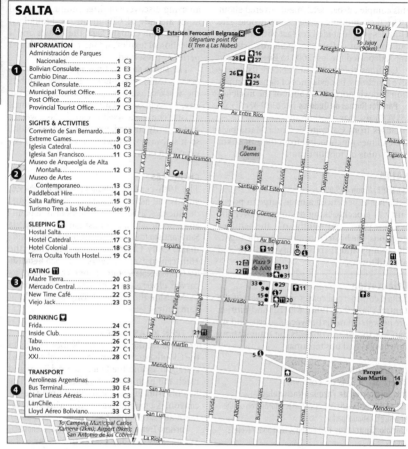

lake in Parque San Martín for US$2 for 20 minutes.

Sleeping

Camping Municipal Carlos Xamena (☎ 423-1341; Libano; campsites per person/tent US$1/1;) Features a gigantic swimming pool. Take bus 3B from the corner of Mendoza and Lerma near the bus terminal.

Hostal Salta (☎ 431-7191; Balcarce 980; dm/r US$6/15;) Smack in the middle of Salta's *zona viva*, and offering discounts and 'excursions' to local pubs and clubs, this one's definitely the party animal's choice. Rooms are surprisingly quiet, although they lack decent ventilation.

Terra Oculta Youth Hostel (☎ 421-8769; Córdoba 361; dm/d US$7/15;) A real 'backpacker's' vibe.

Dorms are spacious; there's a Ping-Pong table, cheap internet access and two kitchens. A sunny roof terrace with bar and BBQ are further bonuses.

Hostel Catedral (☎ 422-7843; Alvarado 532; s/d US$17/20) The staff may well be distant relations of the Addams family, but the rooms are good, the bathrooms clean and the central location here is a winner.

Hotel Colonial (☎ 431-0805; www.hotelcolonial salta.com.ar; Zuviría 6; s/d US$20/27) This classic building on the plaza is aging, but loaded with character. The furniture has obviously been there since day one (check the sponge factor on your mattress, for that matter), but the balconies have plaza views, there's a delightfully bright and cheery breakfast

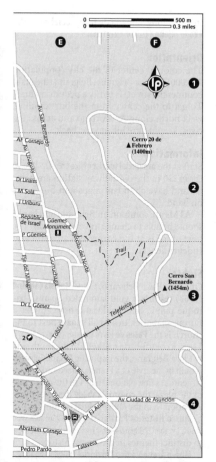

San Bernardo and cathedral, a leafy plaza across the way…they also serve coffee and food.

Viejo Jack (Av Virrey Toledo 139; mains US$4-6) Warmly recommended by just about every local that you talk to for its *parrillada* and pasta dishes.

Frida (Balcarce 935; meals US$5-7) A good selection of red and white meats (try the rabbit in mustard sauce – yum!), eclectic decor and a good wine list make this place one of the finer dining options in the area.

Balcarce south of the train station is Salta's very happening *zona viva* – four blocks stacked with restaurants, bars and clubs.

Smaller bars include **Uno** (Balcarce 996) and **Tabu** (Balcarce 869).

Entertainment

For the mega-disco experience, check out **XXJ** (Balcarce 915) and **Inside Club** (Balcarce 836).

Getting There & Around

AIR

Aerolíneas Argentinas (☎ 431-1331; www.aerolineas argentinas.com; Caseros 475) flies daily to Buenos Aires (US$120).

Dinar Líneas Aéreas (☎ 431-0500; Caseros 492) also flies daily to Buenos Aires (US$120).

Lloyd Aéreo Boliviano (LAB; ☎ 431-0320; Caseros 529) flies Tuesday, Thursday and Sunday to Santa Cruz (Bolivia). **LanChile** (☎ 421-7330; Buenos Aires 88) has seasonal flights over the Andes.

Transport to Salta's **airport** (☎ 423-1648), 9km southwest of town on RP 51, leaves from airline offices about 1½ hours before the flight (US$2).

BUS

Salta's **bus terminal** (☎ 401-1143; Hipólito Yrigoyen) is southeast of downtown.

Géminis services the Chilean destinations of San Pedro de Atacama (US$45, 12½ hours) and Calama, Chile (US$45, 14 hours) on Tuesday and Friday mornings, connecting to Antofagasta, Iquique and Arica.

There are daily departures to Cafayate (US$5, 3½ hours). El Quebradeño leaves for San Antonio de los Cobres at 3pm daily (US$5, five hours).

Empresa Marcos Rueda serves Cachi daily (US$7, four hours); it also goes to Molinos daily except Tuesday and Thursday (US$10, seven hours).

Long-distance services include Tucumán (US$8, 4½ hours), La Quiaca (US$10, seven

area and even a saloon/piano bar (with piano).

Eating & Drinking

The west side of Plaza 9 de Julio is lined with café/bars with tables out on the plaza; great spots for coffee, snacks or a few drinks.

Mercado Central (Av Florida & San Martín) At this large, lively market you can supplement inexpensive pizza, empanadas and *humitas* with fresh fruit and vegetables.

Madre Tierra (Alvarado 508; mains US$3-4) Seriously good vegetarian food, with options along the lines of brown rice, tofu and seaweed.

New Time Café (cnr Mitre & Caseros; breakfast US$1-2, snacks US$2-4) The ultimate in plazaside cafés: shady tables, great views of the *cabildo*, Cerro hours), Resistencia (US$30, 14 hours), Rosario (US$35, 16 hours), Mendoza (US$30, 18 hours) and Buenos Aires (US$42, 21 hours).

SAN ANTONIO DE LOS COBRES
☎ 0387 / pop 5400

This is a long way from BA in every sense: geographically, culturally and visually. The dominant color here is brown: the dirt roads, adobe houses, surrounding landscape. It's not a pretty place, but for travelers on the colonial pack trains to Peru crossing the Puna de Atacama to the Pacific on this route, San Antonio (3700m) must have seemed an oasis. Well into the 20th century, it was a stopover for drovers moving stock to Chile's nitrate mines, but railways and roads have now supplanted mules.

El Palenque (☎ 490-9019; Belgrano s/n; r per person with shared bathroom US$5) is the most comfortable of the very basic budget accommodations here. Make sure you stock up on blankets, as nights can get very chilly.

With 12 rooms with private bathrooms, double-glazed windows, and a total of 30 beds, **Hostería de las Nubes** (☎ 490-9059; Caseros 441; s/d US$18/25) is the only hotel worthy of the name in San Antonio. It also has a restaurant, central heating and a TV lounge.

One of the few actual restaurants in town, **Huari Huasi** (Belgrano s/n; meals US$2.50-4) is pretty good. It offers filling meals in a cozy, simple environment.

Daily El Quebradeño buses make the trip from Salta to San Antonio (US$5, five hours); the bus leaves San Antonio for Salta at 9am. It's probably easier (and faster) to catch a taxi in San Antonio for the return trip to Salta (US$9 per person, based on at least four people sharing).

SAN SALVADOR DE JUJUY
☎ 0388 / pop 234,000

If you're heading north, Jujuy is the where you start to feel the proximity to Bolivia; you see it in people's faces, the chaotic street scenes, the markets that spill out onto sidewalks and restaurant menus, which offer *locro, humitas* and *sopa de mani* (spicy peanut soup) as a matter of course, rather than as 'regional specialties.'

Originally a key stopover for colonial mule-traders en route to Potosí, Jujuy played an important part in the wars of independence when General Manuel Belgrano directed the evacuation of the entire city to avoid royalist capture; every August Jujuy's biggest event,

the weeklong Semana de Jujuy, celebrates the **éxodo jujeño** (Jujuy exodus).

Orientation
The colonial center of the city (population 200,000) is Plaza Belgrano. Belgrano (the main commercial street) is partly a pedestrian mall. To get to the center from the bus terminal, walk north along Av Dorrego and across the river, keeping the hill at your back.

Information
Staff at the **provincial tourist office** (☎ 422-1326; Av Urquiza 354) in the old railway station are helpful and have abundant maps and brochures on hand.

ATMs are common on Belgrano and banks should be able to change traveler's checks. The post office is at the corner of Lamadrid and Independencia.

Sights
Opposite Plaza Belgrano, Jujuy's **Iglesia Catedral** (1763) features a gold-laminated Spanish baroque pulpit, built by local artisans under a European master. In a small square next to the church is the **Paseo de los Artesanos** (9am-12:30pm & 3-6pm), a colorful arts market. On the south side of Plaza Belgrano, the imposing **Casa de Gobierno** is built in the style of a French palace and houses Argentina's first national flag. On the north side of the plaza, the colonial **cabildo** deserves more attention than the **Museo Policial** within.

Museo Histórico Provincial (Lavalle 256; admission US50¢; 8am-12:30pm & 4-8pm) has rooms dedicated to distinct themes in provincial history.

Museo Arqueológico Provincial (Lavalle 434; admission free; 8am-1pm & 2-9pm) If you have even a basic grasp of Spanish, this museum is well worth your while: the guided tour is excellent and the strong emphasis on shamanism in the area fascinating. If not, the poorly labeled exhibits will probably leave you a bit cold.

Don't leave Jujuy without wallowing in the **thermal baths** (admission US$1; 9am-7pm) at **Hostería Termas de Reyes**, 20km northwest of downtown, overlooking the scenic canyon of the Río Reyes. Look for the bus leaving the north side of the bus terminal with 'Termas de Reyes' on the placard. Bring food, since the *hostería's* restaurant is expensive.

Sleeping
Camping El Refugio (☎ 490-9344; per tent US$1 & per person US$1) About 3km west of downtown.

SAN SALVADOR DE JUJUY

0 ————— 300 m
0 ————— 0.2 miles

INFORMATION
Bolivian Consulate..............1 B2
Post Office.......................2 C2
Provincial Tourist Office.....3 D1

SIGHTS & ACTIVITIES
Cabildo...............................4 D2
Casa de Gobierno................5 D2
Iglesia Catedral....................6 D2
Mercado del Sur..................7 C3
Museo Arqueológico
    Provincial........................8 C1
Museo Histórico Provincial..9 C2
Museo Policial................(see 4)
Paseo de los Artesanos......10 D2

SLEEPING
Casa de Barro....................11 D2
Hotel Jujuy Palace.............12 B2
Residencial Chung King.......13 C1

EATING
Chung King.................(see 13)
Los Dos Chinos................14 C1

Madre Tierra.....................15 C2
Mercado Municipal.....16 C1
Sociedad Española......17 B2
Zorba.............................18 C2

DRINKING
Carena...........................19 C2
Savoy.............................20 D1

TRANSPORT
Aerolíneas Argentinas...21 B2
Bus Terminal.................22 C3

Bus 9 goes there from downtown or the bus terminal.

Residencial Chung King (☎ 422-8142; Alvear 627; s/d US$8/10) Good rooms, but make sure you're at the back away from the noisy restaurant downstairs. This is the best budget option near the city center; it's a poky little place and some rooms are better than others. Have a look at a few.

Casa de Barro (☎ 422-9578; www.casadebarro.com.ar; Otero 294; r per person with shared bathroom US$8) Beautifully decorated with indigenous motif stencils on the walls and rustic room fittings, this place adds a touch of class to Jujuy's otherwise workaday hotel scene.

Hotel Jujuy Palace (☎ 423-0433; jpalace@imagine .com.ar; Belgrano 1060; s/d US$38/48; P 🅿 🍴 🖥) If you've got a bit extra to spend, it's well worth getting a room at the Palace. The large rooms are spacious and modern, tastefully decorated with terrific views and the bathrooms feature good-sized tubs.

Eating & Drinking

Mercado Municipal (cnr Alvear & Balcarce) Upstairs, several eateries serve inexpensive regional specialties that are generally spicier than elsewhere in Argentina; try chicharrón con mote (stir-fried pork with boiled maize).

Los Dos Chinos (Alvear 735; mains US$2-5) The excellent, old-man pool hall atmosphere at this neighborhood confitería is added to by the existence of pool tables out the back. Minutas, cheap breakfasts and good coffee are on the menu.

Chung King (Alvear 627; mains US$3-7) An extensive Argentine menu and fine service. Its rotisería and pizzeria next door are good budget options.

Madre Tierra (Belgrano 619; 4-course lunch US$3.50) An Argentine standout. The vegetarian food is excellent and the salads, crepes and soups can be washed down with either carrot or apple juice. It's an earthy place where the simple, wholesome, home-cooked food makes a welcome change to the standard Argentine fare.

Zorba (cnr Necochea & Belgrano; mains US$5-8) Seriously good Greek food (yes, you read that right) in the middle of Jujuy! It's all here: the salads, the dolmades, the koftas (balls of ground vegetables). Fans of the big breakfast will want to check out the Americano – it has one of pretty much everything you could hope for to start the day.

As far as drinking in Jujuy goes, you have two options: ultrahip and minimalist at **Carena** (cnr Balcarce & Belgrano; ☯ lunch & dinner Tue-Sat) or down-home and rowdy at the *peña* **Savoy** (cnr Alvear & Gorriti; ☯ Thu-Sat), where live folkloric music goes into the wee hours.

Getting There & Around
AIR
Aerolíneas Argentinas (☎ 422-2575; www.aerolineas argentinas.com; Belgrano 1056), flies to Buenos Aires (US$120) Tuesday to Friday.

Jujuy's **airport** (☎ 491-1103) is 32km southeast of town. The airline provides transport to the airport.

BUS
Jujuy's scruffy **bus terminal** (☎ 422-1375; cnr Av Dorrego & Iguazú), blends in with the Mercado del Sur. It has provincial and long-distance services, but Salta has more alternatives.

Chile-bound buses from Salta to Calama (US$33 to US$40; prices depend on whether you're traveling on a day or night bus) stop in Jujuy Tuesdays and Fridays. Make reservations in advance at the Géminis office at the terminal.

El Quiaqueño goes to La Quiaca (US$7, five hours), Humahuaca (US$3.50, two hours) and Tilcara (US$3, two hours). Cota Norte goes daily to Libertador General San Martín (US$3, two hours), for access to Parque Nacional Calilegua.

Long-distance fares include Salta (US$3, 2½ hours), Tucumán (US$10, five hours), Córdoba (US$25, 13½ hours), Mendoza (US$32, 14 hours), Resistencia (US$26, 14 hours) and Buenos Aires (US$40, 20 hours).

QUEBRADA DE HUMAHUACA
North of Jujuy, RN 9 snakes its way through the Quebrada de Humahuaca, a painter's palette of color on barren hillsides, dwarfing hamlets where Quechua peasants scratch a living from growing maize and raising scrawny livestock. On this colonial post-route to Potosí, the architecture and other cultural features mirror Peru and Bolivia.

Earthquakes leveled many of the adobe churches, but they were often rebuilt in the 17th and 18th centuries with solid walls, simple bell towers, and striking doors and wood paneling from the *cardón* cactus.

Tilcara
☎ 0388 / pop 5600
The most comfortable of the Quebrada towns, Tilcara is also one of the prettiest, and hosts a number of fine eating and sleeping options.

Tilcara's hilltop *pucará*, a pre-Hispanic fortress with unobstructed views, is its most conspicuous attraction, but the village's museums and its reputation as an artists colony help make it an appealing stopover. The tourist office in the municipal offices distributes a useful map. Banco Macro, on the plaza, has an ATM.

SIGHTS
The well-organized **Museo Arqueológico Dr Eduardo Casanova** (Belgrano 445; admission US$1, Tue free; ☯ 9am-12:30pm & 2-6pm), run by the Universidad de Buenos Aires, features some artifacts from the site of the *pucará*. The room dedicated to ceremonial masks and their manufacture is particularly impressive. The museum is located in a striking colonial house on the south side of Plaza Prado. Admission is also good for El Pucará.

The **Museo José Antonio Terry** (Rivadavia 459; admission US$2, Thu free; ☯ closed Mon) features the work of a Buenos Aires–born painter whose themes were largely rural and indigenous; his oils depict native weavers, market and street scenes, and portraits. Also featured is work from local artists, and the occasional traveling exhibition of contemporary art.

Rising above the sediments of the Río Grande valley, an isolated hill is the site of **El Pucará** (admission US$1), 1km south of central Tilcara. There are fantastic views of the valley from the top of the fort, which has been brilliantly reconstructed in parts. The admission fee includes entry to the Museo Arqueológico Dr Eduardo Casanova.

Only a few kilometers south of Tilcara, the hillside cemetery of **Maimará** is a can't-miss photo opportunity.

SLEEPING & EATING
Autocamping El Jardín (☎ 495-5128; campsites per person US$2) At the west end of Belgrano near the river, with hot showers and attractive vegetable and flower gardens.

Albergue Malka (☎ 495-5197; tilcara@hostels.org.ar; dm US$8) Excellent hilltop accommodations on lovingly landscaped grounds four blocks from Plaza Prado at the east end of San Martín. It's about a 10-minute walk from the center.

CHILDREN OF THE CARNIVAL

In early 2006 the Argentine government initiated a ground-breaking sex-education and condom-distribution program in the towns of the northwest. This was in response to the fact that, nine months after Carnaval is celebrated in these towns (a time when alcohol consumption goes up and inhibitions go down), an unusually high number of babies are born to single, teenage mothers. The people in these towns have long known about this phenomenon, of course, and they have a special name for babies born in late November/early December – *los hijos del carnaval* (children of the carnival).

Discounts are available for HI cardholders. The owners can arrange trekking and vehicle tours of the Quebrada.

Posada de Luz (☎ 495-5017; www.posadadeluz.com.ar; Ambrosetti & Alverro; r US$30-40; P ⊠) With a nouveau-rustic charm, this little place is spectacular. More expensive rooms have sitting areas, but all feature pot-bellied stoves and individual terraces with great views out over the valley. A fantastic place to unwind for a few days.

El Cafecito (cnr Belgrano & Rivadavia) This little place is a very agreeable spot for coffee and croissants, and the homemade cakes (US$1) are worth keeping an eye out for.

La Chacana (Paseo Tierra Azul; mains US$3-5) With indoor and outdoor seating (in a very Zen patio), La Chacana has the most interesting menu in town, featuring quinoa, wild mushrooms and local herbs.

ENTERTAINMENT

La Peñalta (Rivadavia s/n) A folkloric *peña* (folk club) with live music on the north side of Plaza Prado.

GETTING THERE & AROUND

Both northbound and southbound buses leave from the bus terminal on Exodo, three blocks west of Plaza Prado. Sample destinations include Jujuy (US$3, two hours), Humahuaca (US$1.50, 40 minutes) and La Quiaca (US$5, four hours).

Bike rental can be arranged opposite Autocamping El Jardín for US$1/7 per hour/day. The bike-rental place also provides good area maps for day-trip options.

Humahuaca

☎ 03887 / pop 11,400

A popular stopover on the Salta–Bolivia route, Humahuaca is a mostly Quechuan village of narrow cobbled streets lined with adobe houses. There's plenty to do in the surrounding countryside and the town provides some great photo opportunities.

INFORMATION

The **tourist office** (cnr Tucumán & Jujuy) in the *cabildo* is rarely open, but Federico Briones, who runs El Portillo (p112), is a good source of local information, can organize trekking in the Quebrada and speaks English. The post office is across from the plaza.

SIGHTS

From the clock tower in the **cabildo**, a life-size figure of San Francisco Solano emerges daily at noon. Make sure you arrive early, because the clock is erratic and the figure appears only very briefly.

Humahuaca's patron saint resides in the colonial **Iglesia de la Candelaria**, which contains 18th-century oil paintings by Cuzco painter Marcos Sapaca. Overlooking the town is Tilcara sculptor Ernesto Soto Avendaño's **Monumento a la Independencia**.

Museo Folklórico Regional (Buenos Aires 435/447; admission US$3.50) is run by local writer Sixto Vázquez Zuleta (who prefers his Quechua name 'Toqo'). It's open for formal tours only.

Ten kilometers north of Humahuaca by a dirt road on the east side of the bridge over the Río Grande, northwestern Argentina's most extensive pre-Columbian **ruins** cover 40 hectares at **Coctaca**. Many appear to be broad agricultural terraces on an alluvial fan, but there are also obvious outlines of clusters of buildings.

FESTIVALS & EVENTS

Carnaval celebrations are particularly boisterous here, and on February 2, the village holds a **festival** in honor of the town's patron saint, the Virgen de la Candelaria.

TOURS

Turismo Hasta las Manos (☎ 421-075; www.hlmexpeditions.com.ar; Barrio Milagrosa) is a young tour company specializing in unconventional tour options in the region, including sandboarding and trekking to remote locations. It also hires bikes for US$2/10 per hour/day.

SLEEPING & EATING

Posada del Sol (☎ 421-466; Barrio Milagrosa s/n; dm/d US$7/17) Just 400m across the bridge, Posada del Sol is a funky adobe place with beautifully designed rooms, all with shared bathroom. There is a well-stocked kitchen, and you can call to get them to pick you up from the bus terminal.

Residencial Humahuaca (☎ 421-141; Córdoba 401; s/d US$13/20) There's nothing too exciting about this place, but it's clean, and comfortable and close to the plaza and bus terminal.

El Portillo (Tucumán 69; mains US$3-5) A simple but good menu in rustic surrounds. If you've got a hankering for llama stew, this is probably the place to try it. Live music is on offer nightly from 8pm.

There's an acceptable confitería at the bus terminal, but on Belgrano, very close to the bus terminal, is El Rancho Confitería, a better alternative for coffee and a light meal.

GETTING THERE & AWAY

From the **bus terminal** (cnr Belgrano & Entre Ríos) there are several departures to Salta (US$6, five hours) and Jujuy (US$3.50, two hours), and northbound buses to La Quiaca (US$4, three hours).

LA QUIACA

☎ 03885 / pop 15,000

There really is no reason to be here unless you're headed for Bolivia. That said, if you arrive late at night, it's best to stay here as

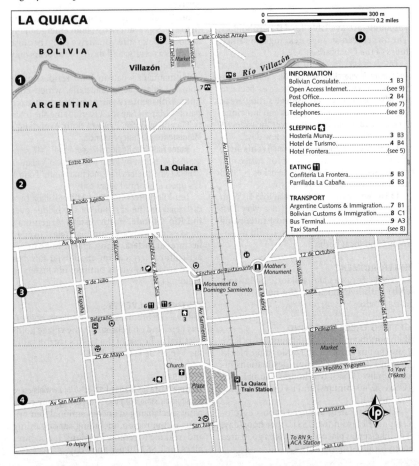

LA QUIACA

0 — 300 m
0 — 0.2 miles

INFORMATION
Bolivian Consulate..............................1 B3
Open Access Internet.....................(see 9)
Post Office...2 B4
Telephones.....................................(see 7)
Telephones.....................................(see 8)

SLEEPING
Hostería Munay...................................3 B3
Hotel de Turismo.................................4 B4
Hotel Frontera................................(see 5)

EATING
Confitería La Frontera.........................5 B3
Parrillada La Cabaña...........................6 B3

TRANSPORT
Argentine Customs & Immigration......7 B1
Bolivian Customs & Immigration........8 C1
Bus Terminal.......................................9 A3
Taxi Stand..(see 8)

the services are much better than across the border in Villazón (see p226).

La Quiaca has no tourist office, but the ACA station on RN 9 has maps. If Banco de la Nación will not cash traveler's checks, try Universo Tours in Villazón. The post office is at the corner of Av Sarmiento and San Juan.

If you're here in mid-October, you might luck onto the **Manca Fiesta** when *campesinos* (rural dwellers) pour in from the surrounding countryside to barter goods and dance.

Sleeping & Eating

Hotel Frontera (☎ 422-269; cnr Belgrano & República de Árabe Siria; s/d with shared bathroom US$4/6) You can tell from the prices that there's nothing fancy going on here, but it's OK for a night and the restaurant out front is good, cheap and popular.

Hostería Munay (☎ 423-924; www.munayhotel.jujuy .com in Spanish; Belgrano 51-61; d per person US$5) Not as good value as it used to be, but quiet and central in La Quiaca. Rooms with bathroom, TV and breakfast also available ($13).

Hotel de Turismo (☎ 422-243; cnr Av San Martín & República de Árabe Siria; s/d US$13/22) The best place to stay in town has parquetry floors, a plant-filled lobby and good spacious rooms with TV, telephone and reading lights.

Parrillada La Cabaña (España 550) The best thing about this place is that it's open all day for snacks and light meals. The set lunch (US$2.50) is an absolute bargain.

Confitería La Frontera (Belgrano & República de Árabe Siria; everything under US$2) An old-school diner where four-course set meals fetch US$2.

Getting There & Away

From the **bus terminal** (cnr Belgrano & Av España), there are frequent connections to Jujuy (US$7, five hours), Salta (US$10, seven hours) and intermediate points, plus long-distance services.

AROUND LA QUIACA

At the village of **Yavi**, 16km east of La Quiaca, the 17th-century **Iglesia de San Francisco** is renowned for its altar, paintings, carved statues and gold leaf–covered pulpit. The nearby **Casa del Marqués Campero** belonged to a nobleman whose marriage to the holder of the original *encomienda* created a family that dominated the region's economy in the 18th century.

Friendly **Hostal de Yavi** (☎ 03887-490-508; hostal deyavi@hotmail.com; Güemes 222; dm/s/d US$5/15/23) has clean facilities in a cozy building.

Regular buses go from La Quiaca to Yavi (US$5, 1½ hours), but shared cabs (US$5 round trip, including waiting time) are another alternative. Every half hour or so, there's a pickup truck (US$1) that runs from La Quiaca's Mercado Municipal on Hipólito Yrigoyen.

ATLANTIC COAST

The beaches along the Atlantic coast form Buenos Aires' backyard, and summer sees millions of *porteños* pouring into towns like Mar del Plata and Pinamar for sun and fun. The rest of the year, and in smaller towns, the pace of life rarely approaches anything resembling hectic.

MAR DEL PLATA

☎ 0223 / pop 512,000

On summer weekends, the beach in Mardel (as it's commonly known) gets really, seriously comically crowded. We're talking people standing shoulder to shoulder, knee-deep in water. During the week, and in the non-summer months, the crowds disperse, hotel prices drop and the place takes on a much more relaxed feel.

Founded in 1874, this most popular of Argentine beach destinations is 400km south of Buenos Aires. First a commercial and industrial center, then a resort for upper-class *porteño* families, Mardel now caters mostly to middle-class vacationers.

Filled with skyscrapers built without much planning, this city also has charming older buildings and neighborhoods left over from its elite days. The wide and attractive beach bustles with activity during summer, there are some interesting museums in town, and nightlife can be just as kick-ass as Buenos Aires.

Orientation

South of town, the salty port offers close-up viewing of a sea lion colony (you'll smell 'em before you see 'em). The airport is 9km northwest of town (take bus 542); taxis there cost US$5, more in summer. To get from the bus terminal to the center, take the 511 bus, a taxi (US$2) or walk 20 minutes.

Information

The **tourist office** (☎ 495-1777; Blvd Marítimo 2240) is near Plaza Colón. Most *cambios,* banks and

---

GETTING TO BOLIVIA

The border is a 1km walk from the bus terminal. There is no public transport, but if there's a taxi around, they should be able to take you for US$1. The border is open 6am to 8pm daily. For info on entering Argentina from Bolivia, see p227.

ATMs are near the intersections of San Martín/Córdoba and Avs Independencia/Luro.

Sights

Now the Italian consulate, 1919 **Villa Normandy** (Viamonte 2216) is one of few surviving examples of the French style that was *en vogue* in the 1950s. A block away near the top of the hill, **Iglesia Stella Maris** has an impressive marble altar; its virgin is the patron saint of local fishermen. On the summit, **Torre Tanque** offers outstanding views.

Museo del Mar (admission US$2; �9am-2am Dec-Mar, 8am-9pm Mon-Thu, 8am-midnight Fri & Sat, 9am-9pm Sun Apr-Nov), opposite Villa Normandy, is probably the most extensive seashell museum you'll ever see. Based around central cafés on two floors are a small tide pool and an aquarium. It's a good place to rest and have tea.

Activities

Oceania Expediciones (☎ 480-0323; Yacht Club, Puerto) hosts scuba-diving trips from US$33 per dive, including equipment.

Paracaidismo Mar del Plata (☎ 464-2151) offers tandem parachute jumps for US$93 and videotapes the experience for US$30.

Catamaran Regina Australe (☎ 486-4879; www .reginaaustrale.com.ar; Playa Grande) offers 1½-hour cruises around the bay for US$8 and dinner cruises on weekends for US$20. Call for free pickup from the center.

Sleeping

Prices are about 30% higher in January and February, when it's worth making reservations.

Rates at Mardel's crowded campgrounds, mostly south of town, are around US$2 per person; the tourist office prints out information about their facilities.

Hotel Pergamino (☎ 495-7927; hotelpergamino@ ciudad.com.ar; Tucumán 2728; dm/s/d US$6/12/18) The best thing about this hotel is the range of rooms on offer: dorms, cheap tiny singles, all the way up to very comfortable doubles.

Casa Grande (☎ 476-0805; www.casagrandealbergue .com.ar; Jujuy 947; dm/d US$7/20; ☐) Truly a big house, this is part of the welcome 'new wave' of hostels in Mardel – run by travelers, with plenty of activity options including tango and salsa classes and yoga sessions.

Casa Santiago (☎ 491-9759; Santiago del Estero 1342; dm/s/d US$7/10/20; ☐) This intimate hostel (capacity 17) has a great garden area and well-equipped kitchen. Book well ahead if you're coming in summer.

Eating

There are many *tenedor libres* in the center of town for US$4 to US$5, not including drinks. They're a great deal if you're a big eater.

Moringa (Alsina 2561; mains US$4-5) This upscale Middle Eastern restaurant serves an excellent assortment of authentic dishes including falafel, kebbe and shish kebabs. Saturday nights feature dinner and belly dancers for US$9.

Centro Vasco Denak Bat (Moreno 3440; mains US$5-8) If there's one thing the Basques know how to do, that would be cook great seafood dishes. If there's another thing, it would be to decorate their restaurants in an atmospheric, rustic dining saloon kind of way. If the prices downstairs seem hefty, try sneaking into the members' *comedor* upstairs, where the food's the same, only cheaper.

Piedra Buena (Centro Comercial Puerto; meals US$7-11) Of the bunch of seafood restaurants down at the port, this is reputedly the best, and is certainly the most atmospheric. There's a huge range of seafood on offer, a good atmosphere and a seafood bisque (US$8) that comes highly recommended.

Drinking

La Bodeguita del Medio (Castelli 1252) This bar takes a fair stab at the whole Cuban thing: there's plenty of graffiti and photos on the walls, two for one *mojitos* every day from 7pm to 9pm and a range of Cuban dishes like *ropa vieja* (shredded beef, tomatoes and onions), *moros y cristianos* (white rice with black beans) and roast pork.

Antares (Córdoba 3025) This microbrewery serves up seven of its own brews (including the punch-packing Barley Beer, weighing in at a hefty 10% alcohol content) and a range of German-influenced dishes and meat-and-beer stews. There's live music on Mondays and Thursdays.

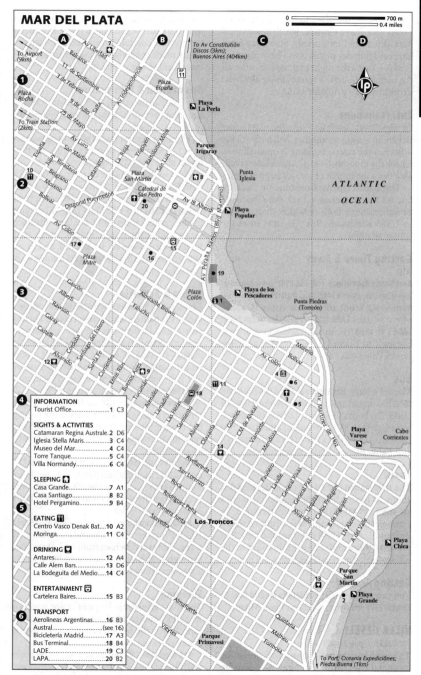

MAR DEL PLATA

0 — 700 m
0 — 0.4 miles

To Av Constitutión
Discos (3km);
Buenos Aires (404km)

ATLANTIC OCEAN

ARGENTINA

Weekends, the place to be is Calle Alem, down near Playa Grande, which is a strip of bars, discos and restaurants. Stay away from here on Thursday nights if you have plans for Friday – that's the night that the bars offer all the beer and Gancia (a vermouthlike alcoholic drink) you can drink for US$3.

Entertainment
Cartelera Baires (Santa Fe 1844) Sells discount theater tickets in summer; another *boletería* (ticket office) in the casino building is open all year. Check the monthly *Guía de Actividades* (available from the tourist office) for happenings.

The discos on Av Constitución heat up late on the weekends. Check out Chocolate or Sobremonte, both of which charge US$6 to US$8 admission. Bus 551 runs from the center all night.

Getting There & Away
AIR
Aerolíneas Argentinas (☎ 496-0101; www.aerolineas argentinas.com; Moreno 2442) and **Austral** (☎ 496-0101; Moreno 2442) scoot to Buenos Aires (US$65) often, as does **LAPA** (☎ 495-9694; San Martín 2648). **LADE** (☎ 493-8211), in the casino building, is cheapest to Buenos Aires (US$45) and also serves Patagonia.

BUS
Mardel's busy **bus terminal** (☎ 475-6076; Alberti 1602) has departures to Buenos Aires (US$7 to US$9, 5½ hours), Pinamar (US$3, 2¼ hours), Villa Gesell (US$9, two hours) and Necochea (US$3, two hours), La Plata (US$9, five hours), and Bahía Blanca (US$7, seven hours).

TRAIN
The **train station** (☎ 475-6076; cnr Av Luro & Italia) is about 20 blocks from the beach, but there's an **office** (☎ 451-2501) at the bus terminal. In summer there are trains seven times daily to Buenos Aires for US$8 in *turista* and US$16 in *primera* (those under 25 get a discount in the off-season). The trip takes about 5½ hours.

Getting Around
You can rent bikes at **Bicicletería Madrid** (Hipólito Yrigoyen 2249; per hour/day US$2/6) on Plaza Mitre.

VILLA GESELL
☎ 02255 / pop 24,000
This laid-back dune community sleeps for most of the year, but in summer it's a favorite

for young vacationing *porteños*, who stream in to party the warm nights away. It's one of the prettiest coastal towns: small, with windy, sandy roads sporting charming summer cottages (and grander retreats).

Orientation & Information
The lively main street, Av 3 sees most of the action; a section of it becomes a pedestrian mall in summer.

There's a central **tourist office** (www.gesell.gov.ar; Av 3 ☉ summer only), near Paseo 108; another **tourist office** (☎ 458596; Buenos Aires), about a 20-minute walk northwest of town, is open all year. Banks and their ATMs are on Av 3. The main **bus terminal** (cnr Av 3 & Paseo 140) is south of town; bus 504 or a US$2 taxi ride will get you to the center. Short- and medium-distance buses stop at the mini terminal, which is at Blvd Gesell (known as 'Boulevard'), and Paseo 100 (at Buenos Aires), about a 20-minute walk from the center.

Sights & Activities
Gesell's long **beach** and boardwalk draw swimmers, sunbathers and horse riders. There's year-round **fishing** from the pier, and surfers can rent boards from **Windy** (Paseo 104; per 2hr/day US$10/20; ☉ 9am-6pm) on the beachfront. Bikes rent at **Casa Macca** (cnr Buenos Aires & Paseo 204; per hr/day US$1/5; ☉ 9am-6pm). There's a nightly summer **crafts fair** on the corner of Av 3 and Paseo 112.

Turismo Adventura (☎ 463-118; cnr Av 3 & Paseo 111) offers four-hour 4WD tours to the nearby lighthouse that are a combination of hair-raising dune-bashing and excellent photo opportunities.

MotoFox (☎ 454-646; cnr Buenos Aires & Alameda 212) rents 4WD motorbikes from US$20 per hour for use on the dunes and beach around town. It's cheaper (from US$35) to take a two-hour excursion with them.

Feria Artesanal (Regional y Artística; Av 3 btwn Paseos 112 & 113) is an excellent arts and crafts fair that takes place every evening from mid-December through mid-March. The rest of the year it's a weekend-only event.

Sleeping
The most affordable *hospedajes* are north of Av 3. It's important to book ahead in summer, especially in the second half of January, when prices rise even more.

Los Medanos (☎ 463-205; Av 5, No 549; per person US$8) One of the better budget options in town, with decent-sized rooms and modern bathrooms. Try to get a room upstairs for better light and ventilation.

Residencial Viya (☎ 462-757; residencialviya@gesell.com.ar; Av 5, No 582, btwn Paseos 105 & 106; s/d US$8/16) Rooms are smallish, but pleasant, and open onto a small patio at this friendly, owner-operated *residencial* on a quiet street.

Hotel Walkirias (☎ 468-862; Paseo 102 btwn Av 2 & Buenos Aires; s/d US$20/40) Rampantly ugly from the outside, the Walkirias has a good cozy feel to it on the inside, with exposed beams and spacious modern bathrooms. There's a pool table and an excellent *quincho* (covered patio area) for all your BBQing requirements.

Gesell's campgrounds charge US$3 to US$36 per person. Most close off-season, but **Casablanca** (☎ 470-771), **Mar Dorado** (☎ 470-963) and **Monte Bubi** (☎ 470-732), clustered at the south end of town on Av 3, are open all year.

Eating & Drinking

Sutton 212 (cnr Av 2 & Paseo 105; mains US$2-5) With its fabric-covered ceilings, Rajasthani lampshades and Zen rock garden, this is one of the hippest places along the coast. Surprisingly, the food, imported beers and cocktails are all reasonably priced.

El Estribo (cnr Av 3 & Paseo 109; mains US$2-5) You won't get far in this town without somebody recommending that you eat at El Estribo. A *bife de chorizo* (thick sirloin) will set you back US$4 and the *parrillada* for two (with enough meat for three) costs US$8.

Rias Baixes (Paseo 105, no 335; meals US$3-13) With its strip lighting and plastic chairs, this local *marisquería* (seafood restaurant) isn't about to win any interior-design prizes, but it definitely serves some of the freshest, best-value seafood in town.

The beachside restaurants are great places to have a few drinks and a snack at sunset, or a meal if your wallet is up to the challenge. The sidestreets off Av 3 between Paseo 103 and 107 are packed with small bars that fire up on weekends.

Entertainment

Anfiteatro del Pinar (☎ 467-123; cnr Av 10 & Paseo 102) Performances in January, February and Semana Santa. Gesell's Encuentros Corales take place annually in this lovely amphitheater.

Cine Teatro Atlas (☎ 462-969; Paseo 108 btwn Avs 3 & 4) Such rock-and-roll greats as Charly García and Los Pericos have played this small theater,

which doubles as a cinema during off-season months.

Pueblo Límite (☎ 452845; www.pueblolimite.com; Buenos Aires 2600; admission incl drink US$7) A small-town megadisco, this complex, across from the Secretaría de Turismo, has three dance clubs, two bars and a restaurant in summer. Off season, it's just two discos, one for Latin pop, the other electronica.

Getting There & Away

Sample bus destinations include Buenos Aires (US$12, six hours), Mar del Plata (US$9, two hours) and Pinamar (US$1, 40 minutes).

PINAMAR

☎ 02254 / pop 21,000

Rivaling Uruguay's Punta del Este in the fashion stakes, Pinamar is where wealthy Argentine families come to play in summertime.

Orientation & Information

Libertador, roughly paralleling the beach, and perpendicular Bunge are the main drags; streets on each side of Bunge form large fans. The **tourist office** (☎ 491-680; Bunge 654) has a good map. The **bus terminal** (cnr Shaw & Del Pejerrey) is 12 blocks from the beach and seven from the center. The train station is a couple of kilometers north of town, near Bunge.

Sights & Activities

Many places are only open on weekends and in summer, but at other times you can stroll peacefully in bordering pine forests and along the wide, attractive **beach** without being trampled by holidaymakers.

Sandboarding trips are available with **Sand Wave** (www.sandwave.com.ar). Bike hire is available from **Macca Bikes** (Bunge 1089; per hr/day US$2/5; ☉ 9am-6pm). Surfboards hire for US$3/hour from the pier in summertime.

Sleeping

Several campgrounds, charging US$5 for two, line the coast between Ostende and Pinamar.

Albergue Bruno Valente (☎ 482-908; cnr Mitre & Nuestras Malvinas, Ostende; dm US$7) The painstakingly slow renovations at this former hotel won't be done any time soon, so for now this remains a good, cheap option in summer and a cold and dreary one in winter. It's close to the beach, far from the center and some of the front rooms have balconies with sea views.

Hotel La Gaviota (☎ 482-079; Del Cangrejo 1332; s/d US$13/20) Has my grandmother been moonlighting as an interior designer? Spotless, smallish rooms that go a bit over the top on decoration (sorry, granny) and a comfortable patio area out back. About a 10-minute walk from the beach.

Hotel Cedro Azul (☎ 407-227; Jasón 497; www.cedro azulpinamar.com.ar; s/d US$27/34) An excellent, central location and rooms with plenty of cedar finishings make this good value for money. The big buffet breakfast is a bonus, too.

Eating & Drinking

During summer, after midnight, the restaurants along the beachfront turn into bars and discos and generally go until the break of dawn. The rest of the year, and earlier, there are a couple of central bars worth checking out.

Jalisco (Bunge 478; mains US$4-6) You'd think that throwing 'Argentine' into the Tex-Mex mix might bring some unholy results, but not so – and besides, where else are you going to get a shrimp burrito in this town?

Con Estilo Criollo (cnr Bunge & Marco Polo; mains US$5-8) Don't be fooled by the 'international cuisine' sign out front: this is straight-down-the-line old-school *parrillada* stuff – but it's well done, and the US$10 set meal is a bargain.

Cantina Tulumei (Bunge 64; mains US$6-13) The seafood here isn't outrageously priced, and the atmosphere is better than most in town. Sunny days and warm nights, the tables out front are the place to be.

Antiek Bar (Libertador 27) With an old-time feel, and plenty of beer on tap, this is a good place to start the night. There's live music on weekends and a healthy cocktail list.

La Luna (Bunge 1429; ⏰ 8pm-late Fri & Sat) Pinamar's hippest bar is heavy on the cocktails, crossover electronica, blacklighting and facial piercings.

Getting There & Away

Bus schedules resemble those from Villa Gesell. Trains run in summer to Buenos Aires. Purchase tickets at the bus terminal.

NECOCHEA

☎ 02262 / pop 89,000

Another family-oriented beach resort, Necochea is a lot more humble than Pinamar and is just barely saved from high-rise ugliness by the adjacent Parque Miguel Lillo, a huge green space along the beach whose dense pine woods are good for cycling.

Orientation & Information

The **bus terminal** (☎ 422-470; cnr Av 58 & Ruta 86) is 4km from the beach. Bus 502 winds its way to the coast via the town center (itself 2km from the beach). The **tourist office** (☎ 430-158; Av 2 & Calle 79) is on the beach.

Activities

The Río Quequén, rich in trout and mackerel, allows for adventurous canoeing and rafting. Contact **Necochea Rafting** (☎ 1547-3541; necochea_rafting@hotmail.com) to get picked up from the tourist office.

Rent bikes at **Stop Bicicletas** (cnr Av 79 & Calle 10; per day US$5; ⏰ 9am-12:30pm & 3-6pm).

Azul Profundo (Av 79, No 293) offers diving and boat trips.

Sleeping

Camping Americano (☎ 435-832; cnr Av 2 & Calle 101; campsites per person US$3) In Parque Miguel Lillo.

Hotel Neptuno (☎ 422-653; Calle 81, No 212; s/d US$10/13) One step out of this excellent little budget hotel and you can see waves crashing. Rooms are small but have good bathrooms and cable TV.

Hotel Flamingo (☎ 420-049; hotflamingo@mixmail .com; Calle 83, No 333; s/d US$10/15) Simple, decent-sized rooms. Ask to see a few; some are much bigger and come with bonuses like minifridges.

Hostería del Bosque (☎ 420002; jfrigerio@telpin .com.ar; Calle 89, No 350; s/d US$23/27; P) Once home to a Russian princess, this is by far the most atmospheric place to stay in town. Rooms are quaint and comfortable, bathrooms modern and the beautiful Parque Lillo is right outside the front door.

Eating & Drinking

There are plenty of reasonably priced *parrillas* and *confiterías* along the beachfront and around the plaza.

Las Terrazas (beachside; mains US$3-5) Most of the beachfront *balnearios* (private bathing resorts) serve food; this one also has an excellent deck area looking out over the waves.

Taberna Española (Calle 89, No 360; mains US$4-8) For the Spanish take on the whole seafood thing, this is the place to come, and come hungry. The *picada de mariscos* (series of small seafood dishes; US$7) is a gut buster – delicious fishy dishes just keep on coming.

La Frontera (beachside) The mix of rustic driftwood and marine ropes and ultramodern interiors with electronica and Latin pop music somehow works at this beachfront disco/bar. Weekends, the whole party spills out onto the beach and goes 'til the wee, wee hours. It's at the end of Av 75.

Getting There & Away
Bus destinations include Mar del Plata (US$4, two hours), Bahía Blanca (US$12, 5½ hours) and Buenos Aires (US$18, seven hours).

BAHÍA BLANCA
☎ 0291 / pop 285,000
Mostly just a stopover point for people headed elsewhere, Bahía Blanca is surprisingly cosmopolitan for its size, and boasts Argentina's worst-signposted museum. For the lowdown on music, art and theater happenings around town, pick up a copy of the *Agenda Cultural,* available in the tourist office, restaurants and bars.

Information
Tourist office (☎ 459-4007; Alsina 45) Almost overwhelmingly helpful.
Post office (Moreno 34)
Pullman Cambio (San Martín 171) Changes traveler's checks.

Sights
The most worthwhile sight is **Museo del Puerto** (Guillermo Torres 4180, Puerto Ingeniero White; ☒ 8am-11am Mon-Fri), a 'community museum' that's a whimsical tribute to the immigrant population of Bahía Blanca. From downtown, buses 500 and 501 drop passengers a few blocks away – ask for plenty of directions. Looming above the trees behind the museum are the battlements of the castlelike thermoelelctric plant, which is in the process of being turned into a railway museum and should be worth a look-in for the building it houses if nothing else. On weekends there's a **feria artesanal** (crafts fair) on Plaza Rivadavia.

Sleeping
Balneario Maldonado (☎ 452-9511; campsites per person US$2) The campground is 4km southwest of downtown. Bus 514 gets you there.
Hotel Victoria (☎ 452-0522; Gral Paz 84; s/d US$17/25) A range of pleasant rooms (including some cheaper ones with shared bathroom) in a nicely maintained older mansion with a courtyard.

Hotel Los Vascos (☎ 452-0977; Cerri 747; d US$13, s/d with shared bathroom US$7/10) Across from the train station, Los Vascos is without doubt the best of the budget bunch in the area. Rooms are pleasant and basic, and the wooden floors and spotless shared bathrooms add to the appeal, as does the friendly family who run the place.

Eating & Drinking
Piazza (cnr O'Higgins & Chiclana; mains US$3-5) A popular lunch spot right on the plaza, with an imaginative menu and a fully stocked bar. Chocoholics should not miss the chocolate mousse (US$1.50).

Your best bet for a few midweek drinks is the strip of bars on Alsina between Mitre and Alvarado. Weekends, the place to go is **Fuerte Argentina**, a cluster of bars, restaurants and discos at the north end of Salta. It's walkable, but a taxi from the center should cost about US$1.50.

Getting There & Around
The airport is located 15km east of town. **Austral** (☎ 456-0561; San Martín 298) hops to Buenos Aires (US$75). **LADE** (☎ 452-1063; Darregueira 21) flies cheaply but slowly to Patagonian destinations.

The bus terminal is about 2km east of Plaza Rivadavia; there are many local buses into town (fare is US30¢; buy magnetic cards from kiosks). Destinations include Sierra de la Ventana (US$4, two hours), Buenos Aires (US$22, 10 hours), Santa Rosa (US$12, 4½ hours), Mar del Plata (US$12, seven hours), Neuquén (US$14, seven hours) and Río Gallegos (US$50, 30 hours).

The **train station** (☎ 452-9196; Cerri 750) has nightly service to Buenos Aires. Fares are US$5/15 in *turista/cama* class.

SIERRA DE LA VENTANA
☎ 0291 / pop 3100
Sierra de la Ventana is where *porteños* come to escape the summer heat, hike around a bit and cool off in nearby swimming holes. The nearby mountain range of the same name in Parque Provincial Ernesto Tornquist attracts hikers and climbers to its jagged peaks, which rise over 1300m.

Near the train station is the **tourist office** (☎ 491-5303; Roca 15).

For a nice walk, go to the end of Calle Tornquist and cross the small dam (which makes a local **swimming hole**). On the other side you'll see **Cerro del Amor**; hike to the top for good views of town and pampas.

Sleeping & Eating

There are several free campsites along the river, with bathroom facilities nearby at the pleasant and grassy municipal swimming pool (US$1).

Camping El Paraíso (☎ 491-5299; Diego Meyer; per person US$2) For organized campgrounds.

Hospedaje La Perlita (☎ 491-5020; Morón; s/d US$7/9) Clean and simple rooms face a peaceful, relaxing garden. The huge dog is overly friendly; the surly owner less so. It's near Islas Malvinas.

Hotel Atero (☎ 491-5002; cnr San Martín & Güemes; s/d US$13/20) By far the most comfortable option in town, the Atero comes with all the conveniences, except for the swimming pool, but with the creek just down the road, this isn't such a drama.

Sol y Luna (San Martín 393; mains US$4-7) The standard menu in this cute little restaurant is spiced up by some local trout dishes and imaginative vegetarian options.

Sher (Güemes s/n; mains US$5-7) Of the various *parrilla* joints around town, this one has the best atmosphere and service.

Getting There & Away

From in front of the *locutorio* on San Martín near Islas Malvinas, La Estrella has nightly buses to Buenos Aires (US$19, eight hours), plus an 8am service to La Plata (US$15, 12 hours). Expreso Cabildo goes to Bahía Blanca twice daily (US$4, two hours).

The train station is near the tourist office. There's nightly train service from here or nearby Tornquist to Plaza Constitución in Buenos Aires for US$5/6 in *turista/cama* class (11 hours).

AROUND SIERRA DE LA VENTANA

Popular for ranger-guided walks and independent hiking, 6700-hectare **Parque Provincial Ernesto Tornquist** (entry US$1.50) is the starting point for the 1136m summit of **Cerro de la Ventana**. It's about two hours' routine hiking for anyone except the wheezing *porteño* tobacco addicts who struggle to the crest of what is probably the country's most climbed peak. Leave early: you can't climb after 11am in winter, noon in summer.

Friendly **Campamento Base** (☎ 0291-491-0067; RP 76, km 224; campsites per person US$2) has shady campsites, clean bathrooms and excellent hot showers.

Buses traveling between Bahía Blanca and Sierra de la Ventana can drop you at the entrance, and there are also buses directly to the park from the village (US$1, one hour).

CENTRAL ARGENTINA

Containing the wine-producing centers of Mendoza, San Luis and San Juan (which themselves comprise an area known as Cuyo), there's no doubt what Central Argentina's main attraction is. Once you've polished off a few bottles, you won't be left twiddling your thumbs, though – this is also Argentina's adventure playground, and the opportunities for rafting, trekking, skiing and climbing are almost endless.

HISTORY

In the 16th century, Spaniards crossed from the Pacific over Uspallata Pass toward Mendoza to manage *encomiendas* among the indigenous Huarpe. Though politically and economically tied to the northern viceregal capital in Lima, Cuyo's isolation fostered a strong independence and political initiative which later provided the basis for present-day Cuyo's defined regional identity.

Irrigated vineyards became important during later colonial periods, but Cuyo's continued isolation limited the region's prosperity. It wasn't until the arrival of the railway in 1884 that prosperity arrived; improved irrigation systems also allowed for expansion of grape and olive cultivation, plus alfalfa for livestock. Vineyard cultivation grew from 6400 hectares in 1890 to 240,000 in the 1970s, and many vineyards remain relatively small, owner-operated enterprises to this day.

SAN LUIS

☎ 02652 / pop 153,000

San Luis is coming up as a backpacking destination, but still has a long way to go. Most people come here to visit the nearby Parque Nacional Sierra de las Quijadas. The commercial center is along the parallel streets of San Martín and Rivadavia, between Plaza Pringles in the north and Plaza Independencia to the south.

The **tourist office** (☎ 423-957; www.turismoensanluis .gov.ar; intersection of Junín, San Martín & Arturo Illia) has an

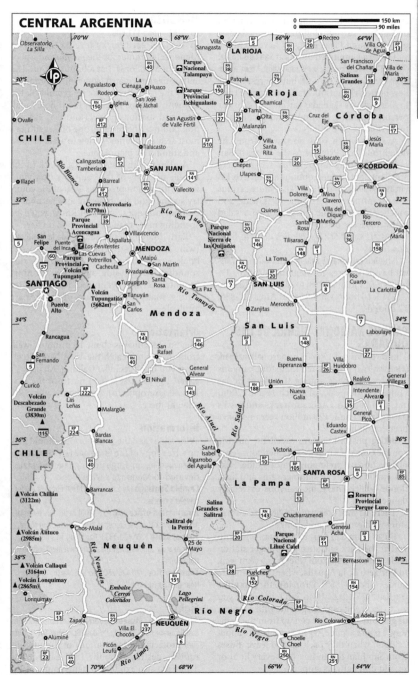

CENTRAL ARGENTINA

ARGENTINA

almost overwhelming amount of information on San Luis' surrounding areas. Several banks, mostly around Plaza Pringles, have ATMs.

The large, multibed dorms at **San Luis Hostel** (☎ 424-188; Falucho 646; www.sanluishostel.com.ar; dm US$6) are a bit of a turnoff, but the rest of this new hostel is beautiful. Staff can arrange trips to Sierra de las Quijadas (around US$20 per person including transport and guide) and tours of local gold mines.

Av Illia, which runs northwest from the delightful Plaza Pringles, is the center of San Luis' moderately hopping bar scene. There are plenty of fast-food options along here. **Las Pircas** (Pringles 1417; mains US$3-7) is a more serious restaurant/*parrilla*. The menu is wide and touches like balsamic vinegar for your salad really make the place.

Austral (☎ 452-671; Illia 472) flies daily to Buenos Aires.

The **bus terminal** (España btwn San Martín & Rivadavia) has departures to Mendoza (US$10, 3½ hours), San Juan (US$8, four hours), Rosario (US$13, 10 hours) and Buenos Aires (US$30, 12 hours).

PARQUE NACIONAL SIERRA DE LAS QUIJADAS

This rarely visited 150,000 hectare **national park** (admission US$2) protects red sandstone canyons and dry lake beds among the Sierra de las Quijadas, the peaks of which reach 1200m at Cerro Portillo. Dinosaur tracks and fossils dating from about 120 million years ago have been found here.

Hiking possibilities are excellent, but the complex canyons require a tremendous sense of direction or, preferably, a local guide. Hikers should beware of summer rains and flash floods, which make the canyons extremely dangerous.

There's a shady **campground** (free) and a small store with groceries and drinks.

Buses from San Luis to San Juan will drop you at the park entrance and ranger station (US$3, 1½ hours), from where it's a 6km walk to Portrero de la Aguada, where you can hire guides (about US$5). Drop into the **park office** (San Martín 874, local 2, 1st fl) in San Luis before you go, to see if you can't snag a ride with a ranger, or get someone to pick you up from the highway. To hire a guide, try to arrive before about 2:30pm, when they pack up and leave. Buses from San Juan to San Luis pass every hour or so, but don't always stop.

MENDOZA
☎ 0261 / pop 111,000

In 1861 an earthquake leveled the city of Mendoza. Bummer for the *mendocinos* (people from Mendoza), but a bonus for us. The authorities anticipated (somewhat pessimistically) the *next* earthquake by rebuilding the city with wide avenues (for the rubble to fall into) and spacious plazas (to use as evacuation points). The result is one of Argentina's most seductive cities – a joy to walk around and stunningly picturesque.

Add to this the fact that it's smack in the middle of many of the country's best vineyards (the region produces 70% of the country's wine) and the base for any number of outdoor activities, and you know you'll be spending more than a couple of days here.

Early March's **Fiesta Nacional de la Vendimia** (wine harvest festival) attracts big crowds; book accommodation well ahead. The surrounding countryside offers wine tasting, mountaineering, cycling and white-water rafting. Many different tours of the area are available.

Orientation

The bus terminal is about 15 minutes' walk from the center; catch the Villa Nueva trolley if you don't feel like walking. Mendoza's **airport** (☎ 448-7128) is 6km north of the city. Bus 60 (Aeropuerto) goes from Calle Salta straight there.

Information

Wine snobs and the wine-curious should pick up a free copy of the **Grapevine** (www.thegrapevine -argentina.com), an English-language magazine devoted to Mendoza's wine scene.

Cambio Santiago (Av San Martín 1199) Charges 2% for traveler's checks.

Information office (☎ 431-5000) In the bus terminal. Another kiosk is at the corner of Avs Las Heras and Mitre.

Tourist kiosk (☎ 420-1333; Garibaldi) This helpful kiosk near Av San Martín is the most convenient information source.

Tourist office (☎ 420-2800; Av San Martín 1143) Near the tourist kiosk.

Sights

The spacious **Museo Fundacional** (cnr Alberdi & Videla Castillo; admission US$1.50; ⏰ 8am-8pm Mon-Sat, 3-10pm Sun) protects the foundations of the original *cabildo*, destroyed by the 1861 earthquake. There are also exhibits of items found at the site and scale models of old and new Mendoza. Check out the 1893 painting depicting the social hierarchy – with the Spanish at the top, and the 'Mulattos and Indios' at the bottom – it'd be nice to think of it as a relic from the past.

The Virgen de Cuyo in the **Iglesia, Convento y Basílica de San Francisco** (Necochea 201) was the patron of San Martín's Army of the Andes. Unique **Museo Popular Callejero**, along the sidewalk at the corner of Av Las Heras and 25 de Mayo, consists of encased dioramas depicting the history of one of Mendoza's major avenues.

Parque General San Martín is a forested 420-hectare green space containing **Cerro de la Gloria** (nice views), several museums and a lake, among other things. Bus 110 gets you here from Plaza Independencia.

Plaza Independencia has a **crafts fair** Thursday through Sunday night, while Plaza Pellegrini holds its own weekend **antique market** with music and dancing. Also check out the beautiful tile work in Plaza España.

WINERIES

Argentina's wines are constantly improving, and consequently attracting international attention. Wine tasting is a popular activity at the many wineries in the area. Bus 170 leaves from Rioja between Garibaldi and Catamarca to get to both of the following. Call first to confirm opening hours.

About 17km southeast of downtown in Maipú is **Bodega Viña El Cerno** (☎ 481-1567; Moreno 631, Coquimbito, Maipú; ☺ tours 9am-5pm Mon-Fri, or with reservations Sat & Sun), built in 1864, a romantically small winery surrounded by vineyards.

Also in Maipú is **La Rural** (Museo del Vino; ☎ 497-2013; Montecaseros 2625, Coquimbito, Maipú; ☺ 9:30am-5:30pm Mon-Fri, 10am-1pm Sat & Sun). Its museum displays wine-making tools used by 19th-century pioneers, as well as colonial religious sculptures from the Cuyo region. Tours run every half hour on weekdays, hourly on weekends.

Cyclists can consider biking a 40km circuit that would cover these wineries and more. Tourist information in Mendoza has an area map.

Activities

Scaling nearby Aconcagua (see p127) is one of the most popular activities here, but there are also plenty of operators offering rafting,

climbing, mountain biking, trekking etc. All the hostels listed in the Sleeping section can organize these.

Inka Expediciones (☎ 425-0871; www.inka.com.ar; Juan B Justo 345) offers fully serviced guided treks to the summit of Aconcagua as well as logistical support for independent climbers.

Altos Andes (☎ 429-7024; www.altosandes.com.ar; Rivadavia 122, office 13) does half-hour light-plane scenic flights over Mendoza for US$60; longer flights around the Aconcagua summit are US$190.

Bethancourt Rafting (☎ 429-9965; www.betan court.com.ar; Lavalle 35, Local 8) offers rafting from US$12, mountain biking (US$20), rappelling and mountain climbing (US$20).

Snow Sky (Av Las Heras 555) has ski equipment and mountain-bike rental: skis, poles and boots US$17 per day, snowboards US$20.

Courses

IAIM Instituto Intercultural (☎ 429-0269; www.span ishcourses.com.ar; cnr San Juan & Rondeau) offers group/individual Spanish classes for US$120/300 for a 20-hour week and homestays with local families for US$150 per week.

Sleeping

Note that hotel prices rise from January to March, most notably during the wine festival in early March.

Parque Suizo (☎ 444-1991; campsites for 2 US$4) About 6km northwest of town, in El Challao, this woody campground has hot showers, laundry facilities and a grocery. Get here on Bus 110, which leaves from LN Alem just east of Av San Martín and from Av Sarmiento.

Hostel Independencia (☎ 423-1806; www.hostel independencia.com.ar; Av Mitre 1237; dm/d US$8/19; ⌨) This excellent 60-bed hostel occupies a historic mansion with an ornate interior of wainscoting, hardwood floors, and an excellent common area. There's a huge back patio and spacious rooms with four to 10 beds in each. The showers are a bit of a hike from the dorms.

Itaka House (☎ 423-9793; Villanueva 480; dm/d US$8/27; ⌨ ☻) Set in a beautiful big house in the middle of the bar strip, the Itaka has decent four- to six-bed dorms, a good outdoor bar downstairs and a lovely terrace overlooking the street. It's west of the center.

Break Point (☎ 423-9514; www.breakpointhostel.com .ar; Villanueva 241; dm US$9; ⌨ ☻) Hostels in Argentina have come a long way, and this place west of the center is an excellent example. It

MENDOZA

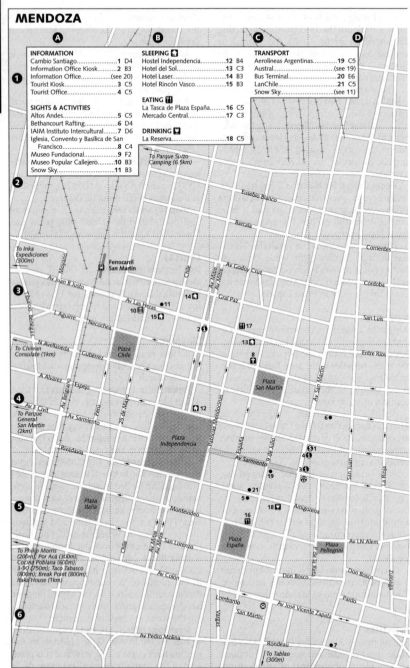

INFORMATION
Cambio Santiago.....................**1** D4
Information Office Kiosk...........**2** B3
Information Office................(see 20)
Tourist Kiosk...........................**3** C5
Tourist Office..........................**4** C5

SIGHTS & ACTIVITIES
Altos Andes............................**5** C5
Bethancourt Rafting.................**6** D4
IAIM Instituto Intercultural.......**7** D6
Iglesia, Convento y Basílica de San
   Francisco...........................**8** C4
Museo Fundacional..................**9** F2
Museo Popular Callejero.........**10** B3
Snow Sky..............................**11** B3

SLEEPING
Hostel Independencia.............**12** B4
Hotel del Sol.........................**13** C3
Hotel Laser............................**14** B3
Hotel Rincón Vasco................**15** B3

EATING
La Tasca de Plaza España........**16** C5
Mercado Central.....................**17** C3

DRINKING
La Reserva.............................**18** C5

TRANSPORT
Aerolíneas Argentinas.............**19** C5
Austral..................................(see 19)
Bus Terminal..........................**20** E6
LanChile...............................**21** C5
Snow Sky.............................(see 11)

To Parque Suizo
Camping (6.5km)

Eusebio Blanco

Barcala

To Inka
Expediciones
(300m)

Corrientes

Moyano

Ferrocarril
San Martín

Chile

Av Mitre
Av Mitre

Av Godoy Cruz

Córdoba

Av Juan B Justo

Av Las Heras

Gral Paz

San Luis

L Aguirre

Necochea

To Chilean
Consulate (1km)

N Avellaneda

Gutiérrez

Plaza
Chile

Entre Ríos

Paso de los Andes

A Álvarez

A Álvarez

Espejo

Belgrano

Perú

25 de Mayo

Plaza
San Martín

Av San Martín

To Parque
General
San Martín
(2km)

Av E Civil

Av Sarmiento

Plaza
Independencia

Patricias Mendocinas

España

9 de Julio

Rivadavia

Av Sarmiento

San Juan Sur

La Rioja

Plaza
Italia

Montevideo

Av Mitre
Av Mitre

San Lorenzo

Plaza
España

Amigorena

To Philip Morris
(200m); Por Aca (300m);
Cocina Poblana (600m);
3-90 (750m); Taco Tabasco
(800m); Break Point (800m);
Itaka House (1km)

Chile

Av Colón

Plaza
Pellegrini

Av LN Alem

P de la Reta

Don Bosco

Don Bosco

Zolova

Lombardo

Vargas

San Martín

Av José Vicente Zapata

Pardo

Av Pedro Molina

Rondeau

To Tablao
(300m)

To Tablao

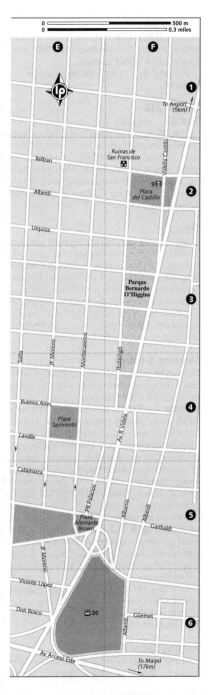

has spacious, comfortable sitting areas, an excellent garden and pool area and a well-appointed kitchen. First class.

Hotel Laser (☎ 438-0218; Gral Paz 360; s/d US$8/12) Budget hotels aren't exactly jumping out at you in Mendoza, but this is a pretty good one: central and no-frills, but comfortable enough; this section of Gral Paz and Av Godoy Cruz has many similarly priced small hotels and *hospedajes*.

Hotel Rincón Vasco (☎ 423-3033; Av Las Heras 590; s/d US$15/23; P ✷) In a good location on the busy, restaurant-strewn Av Las Heras, this slightly worn hotel is good value, especially if you get a balcony (and don't mind street noise).

Hotel del Sol (☎ 438-0218; hoteles@ciudad.com.ar; Av Las Heras 212; s/d US$20/28; P) On busy Av Las Heras in a well-preserved old building, offering fair-sized rooms with ample bathrooms and small, stark lounge areas on each floor.

Eating

Sidewalk restaurants on pedestrian Av Sarmiento are fine places to people-watch. The restaurants along Avs Las Heras and San Martín offer good-value set meals; see signboards for details.

Mercado Central (cnr Av Las Heras & Patricias Mendocinas) The best budget choice; its various stalls offer pizza, empanadas and sandwiches.

Cocina Poblana (Villanueva 217; mains US$3-4) The very tasty, inexpensive Middle Eastern food comes as a welcome break from all that steak. This is the current hot favorite in this part of town – come early or drop in to reserve a table, otherwise you may be in for a wait.

Tablao (San Juan 165; mains US$3.50) If you're a *lomito* (steak sandwich) fan, don't miss this place. If you're not, get with the program. For a place whose seats are sponsored by the local beer company, Tablao manages to scrape together a bit of style, but the real reason to come here is the *lomitos* – delicious, fresh and served on homemade bread.

3-90 (Villanueva 463; mains around US$4) Now *this* is a pasta restaurant: 20 types of sauce, 30 types of pasta, all for under US$4, served on sidewalk tables with a decent wine list.

La Tasca de Plaza España (Montevideo 117; meals US$4-6) With excellent Mediterranean and Spanish tapas (mostly seafood), great wines, intimate atmosphere, good art and friendly service, La Tasca is one of Mendoza's best.

Taco Tabasco (Villanueva 334; meals US$4-6) We've all suffered Mexican Restaurant Letdown in the past, but this place does alright – it's definitely more Tex than Mex, but the portions are big and the food is tasty.

Drinking

Av Villanueva, west of the center, is ground zero in terms of Mendoza's happening bar scene. Going for a wander is your best bet, but here are a few to get you started.

Philip Morris (Villanueva s/n) A classic Argentine bar story – the owners couldn't come up with a name, so people started calling it by the cigarette billboard above the door. The name stuck, as did the laid-back ambience and varied music selection.

Por Acá (Villanueva 557) Purple and yellow outside and polka-dotted upstairs, this bar-cum-lounge gets packed after 2am, and by the end of the night, dancing on the tables is not uncommon. Good retro dance music.

La Reserva (Rivadavia 34; admission free–US$3) This small, nominally gay bar packs in a mixed crowd and has outrageous drag shows at midnight every night, with hard-core techno later.

Getting There & Away

AIR

Aerolíneas Argentinas & Austral (☎ 420-4185; www.aerolineasargentinas.com; Av Sarmiento 82) has daily flights to Buenos Aires for US$97 to US$107.

LanChile (☎ 425-7900; Rivadavia 135) flies twice daily to Santiago de Chile (US$100 to US$190).

BUS

The **bus terminal** (☎ 431-1299) is about 10 blocks east of the town center.

Destination	Duration (hrs)	Cost (US$)
Aconcagua	3½	6
Buenos Aires	14	38
Córdoba	10	17
Las Leñas	7	10
Los Penitentes	4	5
Malargüe	6	10
Neuquén	12	24
San Juan	2	5
San Luis	3¼	9
San Rafael	3¼	5
Tucumán	14	26
Uspallata	2	5
Valparaíso	8	17

Getting Around

Mendoza buses take magnetic fare cards, sold at kiosks in multiple values of the US60¢ fare. Trolleys cost US60¢ in coins.

For bike rentals, try **Snow Sky** (Av Las Heras 555; per day US$5).

USPALLATA

☎ 02624 / pop 3500

In an exceptionally beautiful valley surrounded by polychrome mountains, 105km west of Mendoza at an altitude of 1751m, this crossroads village along RN 7 is a good base for exploring the surrounding area, which served as a location for the Brad Pitt epic *Seven Years in Tibet*.

Sights

One kilometer north of the highway junction toward Villavicencio, a signed side road leads to ruins and a museum at the **Bóvedas Históricas Uspallata**, a metallurgical site since pre-Columbian times. About 4km north of Uspallata, in a volcanic outcrop near a small monument to San Ceferino Namuncurá, is a faded but still visible set of **petroglyphs**. Tourist information is available opposite the bus terminal.

Sleeping & Eating

Camping Municipal (campsites US$2; P 🐕) Uspallata's poplar-shaded campground is 500m north of the Villavicencio junction.

Hostel Uspallata (in Mendoza ☎ 429-3220; www .hosteluspallata.com.ar; RN 7 s/n; dm/d US$8/28) A plain but comfortable lodge in a beautiful setting 5km out of town. Horse-riding, trekking and trout fishing are available from the hostel. It also arranges rafting and climbing trips. From Mendoza, tell the bus driver you're getting off here. Otherwise it's a US$2 *remise* ride from town.

Hostería Los Cóndores (☎ 420-002; Las Heras s/n; s/d US$23/32; 🖳 🐕) Close to the junction, this hotel has spacious, carpeted rooms with huge bathrooms and an on-site restaurant. A sign warns that no mate drinking is allowed in the swimming pool.

Café Tibet (RN7 & Las Heras; mains US$2-5) Tibetan artifacts (leftover props from the movie) clash slightly with the gangsta rap on the sound system. Food on offer is your standard café fare.

Getting There & Away

Expreso Uspallata runs a few buses daily between Mendoza (US$5, two hours) and

Uspallata. Santiago-bound buses will carry passengers to and across the border but are often full; in winter, the pass can close to all traffic for weeks at a time.

AROUND USPALLATA

Los Penitentes

Both the terrain and snow cover can be excellent for downhill and Nordic skiing at Los Penitentes (☎ 02624-420-229; www.lospenitentes.com), two hours southwest of Uspallata at an altitude of 2580m. Lifts and accommodations are very modern; the maximum vertical drop on its 21 runs exceeds 700m. A day ski pass costs around US$32. The season runs June to September.

The cozy converted cabin of **Hostel Los Penitentes** (in Mendoza ☎ 0261-429-0707; www.penitentes.com.ar; dm US$6) accommodates 20 in extremely close quarters, and has a kitchen, wood-burning stove and three shared bathrooms. Meals are available for US$3. The hostel offers Nordic- and downhill-skiing trips and snowshoeing expeditions in winter and Aconcagua treks and expeditions in summer.

From Mendoza, several buses pass daily through Uspallata to Los Penitentes (US$5, four hours).

Puente del Inca

About 8km west of Los Penitentes, on the way to the Chilean border and near the turnoff to Aconcagua, is one of Argentina's most striking wonders. Situated 2720m above sea level, Puente del Inca is a natural stone bridge spanning the Río Mendoza. Underneath it, rock walls and the ruins of an old spa are stained yellow by warm, sulfurous thermal springs. You can hike into Parque Provincial Aconcagua from here.

The little, no-frills hostel of **La Vieja Estación** (in Mendoza ☎ 0261-452-110; www.viejaestacion.com; campsites per person US$2, dm US$7) offers mountain climbing, glacier trekking, snowshoeing and has plans to introduce dogsledding. A cheap restaurant and bar are also on the premises.

Cozy, wood-paneled rooms and a big dining hall give **Hostería Puente del Inca** (☎ 02624-420-222; s/d US$33/37) a real ski-lodge feel.

Daily buses from Mendoza take about four hours (US$6).

PARQUE PROVINCIAL ACONCAGUA

On the Chilean border, Parque Provincial Aconcagua protects 71,000 hectares of high country surrounding the western hemisphere's highest summit, 6960m Cerro Aconcagua. There are trekking possibilities to base camps and refuges beneath the permanent snow line.

Reaching Aconcagua's summit requires at least 13 to 15 days, including some time for acclimatization. Potential climbers should get RJ Secor's climbing guide, *Aconcagua*, and check www.aconcagua.com.ar for more information.

Mid-November to mid-March, permits are mandatory for trekking and climbing; these permits vary from US$20 to US$40 for trekkers and US$100 to US$300 for climbers, depending on the date. Mid-December to late January is high season. Purchase permits in Mendoza in the main **tourist office** (☎ 0261-420-2800; www.aconcagua.mendoza.com.ar; Av San Martín 1143).

Many adventure-travel agencies in and around Mendoza arrange excursions into the high mountains. See the Mendoza Activities section (p123) for details.

SAN JUAN

☎ **0264 / pop 113,000**

Smelling kerosene? Don't panic – that's just the proud folks of San Jaun *polishing their sidewalks*. Uh-huh. An attractive enough place, San Juan's big claim to fame are the nearby wineries and access to Parque Provincial Ischigualasto, though the adventure tourism scene is definitely growing here.

The **tourist office** (☎ 422-2431; www.turismo.sanjuan.gov.ar; Sarmiento 24 Sur) also has a smaller office at the bus terminal. Cambio Santiago is at Gral Acha 52 Sur, and there are several ATMs. The post office is on Roza near Tucumán.

Sights

The **Museo de Ciencias Naturales** (admission free; 🕑 9am-1pm), now in the old train station at the corner of España and Maipú, has exhibits of Triassic dinosaur skeletons found in the area, and you can see the preparation labs.

Museo de Vino Santiago Graffigna (Colón 1342 Norte; admission free; 🕑 9am-1pm Tue-Fri, 10am-8pm Sun, wine bar 9am-2am Fri & Sat) is a new wine museum well worth a visit. It also has a wine bar where you can taste many of San Juan's best wines.

Sleeping & Eating

Camping El Pinar (campsites per person US60¢, per tent US$1) Buses go to this woodsy municipal site on Benavídez Oeste, located about 6km west of downtown.

Zonda Hostel (☎ 420-1009; www.zondahostel.com
.ar; Laprida 572 Oeste; dm US$6; **P**) A new hostel in a
lovingly converted house with a big backyard,
Ping-Pong table, 16 beds and friendly young
owners. Trekking, horse-riding, winery tours
and rafting trips are on offer.

Triasico Hostel (☎ 421-9528; www.triasicohostel
.com.ar; P Echagüe 520 E; dm US$6; 💺 💺) A sweet
little hostel about 15 minutes' walk from the
terminal, the Triasico has slightly cramped
rooms, good common areas and a well-
stocked kitchen. They offer Spanish classes,
waterskiing, windsailing, rafting and trekking
in the Valle de la Luna.

Hotel Nuevo San Francisco (☎ 427-2821; www
.nuevo-sanfrancisco.com.ar; España 284 Sur; s/d US$15/20;
P 💺) One of the best in town, this welcoming, immaculate hotel has good-sized rooms
with massive bathrooms.

Soychú (Roza 223 Oeste; tenedor libre US$2.50) Most
vegetarian buffets just whack out a few salads
and let you fend for yourself, but this little
place goes all out. Arrive early for the best
selection. Fresh juices too.

Club Sirio Libanés (Entre Ríos 33 Sur; mains US$3-5)
This classy old-school establishment serves
dishes with a Middle Eastern flare. The *pollo
deshuesado en salsa de ajillo* (boned chicken
in garlic sauce) is especially good.

Getting There & Away

Aerolíneas Argentinas/Austral (☎ 421-4158; San
Martín 215 Oeste) fly daily to Buenos Aires for
US$100.

The **bus terminal** (☎ 422-1604; Estados Unidos 492
Sur) has buses to Mendoza (US$4, two hours),
Córdoba (US$13, eight hours), San Agustín
de Valle Fértil (US$5, four hours), La Rioja
(US$11, six hours), Tucumán (US$22, 11
hours) and Buenos Aires (US$26, 15 hours).

AROUND SAN JUAN
Vallecito

According to legend, Deolinda Correa trailed
her conscript husband on foot through the
desert during the civil wars of the 1840s before
dying of thirst, hunger and exhaustion, but
passing muleteers found her infant son alive
at her breast. Vallecito, 60km southeast of San
Juan, is believed to be the site of her death.

Since the 1940s, the once simple and now
offbeat **Difunta Correa Shrine** has become a small
town. Truck drivers are especially devoted
believers: all around the country, roadside
shrines display her image surrounded by candles, small banknotes, and bottles of water left
to quench her thirst.

Vallecito has an inexpensive *hostería* and
a decent restaurant, but it's a better day trip
than an overnighter. Empresa Vallecito buses
arrive regularly from San Juan (US$3, 1½
hours), but any other eastbound bus will drop
you at the site.

San Agustín de Valle Fértil

This relaxed, green little village is 250km
northeast of San Juan and set amid colorful
hills and rivers. It relies on farming, animal
husbandry, mining and tourism. Visitors to
Parques Ischigualasto and Talampaya use San
Agustín as a base, and there are nearby **petroglyphs** and the Río Seco to explore.

The tourist office, on the plaza, can help set
you up with tours of the area. There's camping and several cheap accommodations, and
a couple of good *parrillas*. Change money
before you get here.

Buses roll daily to and from San Juan (US$5,
four hours).

Parque Provincial Ischigualasto

At every meander in the canyon of Parque
Provincial Ischigualasto, a desert valley between sedimentary mountain ranges, the
intermittent waters of the Río Ischigualasto
have exposed a wealth of Triassic fossils and
dinosaur bones – up to 180 million years old –
and carved distinctive shapes in the mono-
chrome clays, red sandstone and volcanic ash.
The desert flora of *algarrobo* trees, shrubs and
cacti complement the eerie moonscape, and
common fauna include guanacos, condors,
Patagonian hares and foxes.

Camping is (unofficially) permitted at the
visitors center near the entrance, which also
has a *confitería* with simple meals and cold
drinks. There are toilets and showers, but
water shortages are frequent and there's no
shade.

Ischigualasto is about 80km north of San
Agustín. Given its size and isolation, the only
practical way to visit the park is by vehicle.
After you pay the US$5 entrance fee, a ranger
will accompany your vehicle on a two- or
three-hour circuit over the park's unpaved
roads, which may be impassable after rain.

If you have no transport, ask the tourist office in San Agustín about tours or hiring a car
and driver, or contact the **park** (☎ 0264-491-100).
Ischigualasto Tour (☎ 0264-427-5060; Entre Ríos 203 Sur,

San Juan), has tours for about US$25 per person (English-speaking guides may cost more). Some tours can be combined with **Parque Nacional Talampaya**, almost 100km northeast of Ischigualasto.

Empresa Vallecito buses from San Juan to San Agustín and La Rioja stop at the Los Baldecitos checkpoint, about 5km from the park's entrance.

MALARGÜE

☎ 02627 / pop 23,000

From precolonial times, the Pehuenche people hunted and gathered in the valley of Malargüe, but the advance of European agricultural colonists dispossessed the original inhabitants. Today petroleum is a principal industry, but Malargüe, 400km south of Mendoza, is also a year-round outdoor activity center: Las Leñas (right) offers Argentina's best **skiing**, and there are archeological sites and fauna reserves nearby, as well as organized **caving** possibilities. Hotel prices go up in ski season. The hotels listed here offer guests a 50% discount on ski tickets at Las Leñas. Ask at the desk before checking in.

The **tourist office** (☎ 471-659; www.malargue.gov.ar; RN40, Parque del Ayer) is at the north end of town, directly on the highway. They sometimes give out free pens.

Open all year, **Camping Municipal Malargüe** (☎ 470691; Alfonso Capdevila; campsites US$2) is at the north end of town.

Located five blocks east of the clock tower, **Corre Caminos** (☎ 471-534; Telles Meneses 897; dm/d US$7/20; 🖳) has six- to 12-bed dorms, one double, discount ski hire and a cozy atmosphere.

Hostel Nord Patagonia (☎ 472-276; Fray Inalican 52 este; dm/d US$7/14; 🖳) is a friendly hostel in a small converted house with fireplace. Summer activities include volcano treks, rafting and horse-riding. In winter it offers transfers to Las Leñas for US$7 per person.

Hotel Turismo (☎ 471-042; San Martín 224; s/d US$20/27) has plain but comfortable rooms (the upstairs ones are best) with TV and phone. The downstairs restaurant has a real ski-lodge feel.

In the land of thick and juicy steaks, **La Posta** (Roca 374; mains US$3-5) serves up some seriously thick and juicy steaks. There's also a good pasta selection and a fine wine list.

The **bus terminal** (cnr Roca & Aldao) has regular services to Mendoza (US$10, six hours) and Las Leñas (US$5, 1½ hrs). There's a weekly summer service across the 2500m Paso Pehuenche and down the awesome canyon of the Río Maule to Talca, Chile.

LAS LEÑAS

Wealthy Argentines and foreigners alike come to Las Leñas, the country's most prestigious ski resort, to look dazzling zooming down the slopes and then spend nights partying until the sun peeks over the snowy mountains. Summer activities include hiking, horseriding and mountain biking. Despite the fancy glitter, it's not completely out of reach for budget travelers.

Open approximately July to October, Las Leñas is only 70km from Malargüe. Its 33 runs reach a peak of 3430m, with a maximum drop of 1230m. Lift tickets run about US$30 to US$41 (depending on the season) for a full day of skiing. The **ticket office** (☎ 02627-471-100; www.laslenas.com; ☺ mid-Jun–late Sep) can provide more information.

Budget travelers will find regular transport from Malargüe, where accommodations are cheaper. Buses from Mendoza (US$10) take seven hours.

SANTA ROSA

☎ 02954 / pop 95,000

One of the only towns of any size out on the Pampas, Santa Rosa doesn't have a whole lot to offer the average traveler, except for being a staging point for nearby Parque Nacional Lihué Calel, an isolated but pretty park that's home to a surprising assortment of vegetation and wildlife.

Information

You'll find several ATMs near Plaza San Martín.

Tourist information center (☺ 24hr) At the bus terminal.

Tourist office (☎ 424-404; www.turismolapampa.gov .ar; cnr Luro & San Martín) Near the bus terminal.

Post office (Hilario Lagos 258)

Sights

The **Museo de Bellas Artes** (cnr 9 de Julio & Villegas; admission free; ☺ 7am-1:30pm & 2-8pm Tue-Fri, 6:30-9:30pm Sat & Sun) is an unexpectedly modern gallery containing work by local and national artists. There are five rooms of rotating exhibitions with a strong emphasis on contemporary/ abstract art, and a little sculpture garden out the back.

Laguna Don Tomás is the place where locals boat, swim, play sports or just stroll.

Sleeping & Eating

Centro Recreativo Municipal Don Tomás (☎ 455-358; campsites per person US$1) Provides decent campsites at the west end of Av Uruguay. From the bus terminal, take the El Indio bus.

Hostería Santa Rosa (☎ 423-868; Hipólito Yrigoyen 696; s/d US$7/10) This great little cheapie near the bus terminal offers fine rooms and a homey atmosphere.

Hotel Calfucurá (☎ 433-303; calfuar@cpenet.com.ar; San Martín 695; s/d US$38/44; P ❄ ☎) The Calfucurá's sedate atmosphere and handy location around the corner from the bus terminal make it a winner. This is the best hotel in town by far, and rooms are comfy, if nothing special.

Club Español (Hilario Lagos 237; meals US$3-8) There's good Argentine and Spanish food here, as well as outstanding service, and the Spanish tiled courtyard (replete with tinkling fountain) is as good a place as any to while away a few hours.

Getting There & Away

Austral (☎ 433-076; cnr Lagos & Moreno) flies to Buenos Aires. Taxis to the airport, which is 3km from town, cost about US$2.

The **bus terminal** (☎ 422-952; Luro 365) has services to Bahía Blanca (US$9, five hours), Puerto Madryn (US$22, 10 hours), Buenos Aires (US$15, nine hours), Mendoza (US$18, 12 hours), Neuquén (US$16, 15 hours) and Bariloche (US$19, 21 hours).

PARQUE NACIONAL LIHUÉ CALEL

This park's small, remote mountain ranges, 226km southwest of Santa Rosa, were a stronghold of Araucanian resistance during General Roca's Conquista del Desierto (Conquest of the Desert). Its salmon-colored granites, reaching 600m, offer a variety of subtle environments that change with the season and even with the day.

Sudden storms can bring flash floods to this 10,000-hectare desert and create spectacular, temporary waterfalls. Even when there's no rain, subterranean streams nourish the *monte*, a scrub forest of surprising botanical variety.

The most common mammals are gray foxes, guanacos, *maras* (Patagonian hares) and vizcachas (cute relatives of the chinchilla). Birds include *ñandú* (rhea) and the carancho (crested caracara).

From the park campground, a signed trail leads through a dense *caldén* thorn forest to a site with **petroglyphs**, unfortunately vandalized. From here, another trail reaches the 589m summit of **Cerro de la Sociedad Científica Argentina**, with outstanding views of the sierra, surrounding marshes and *salares* (salt lakes). Look for flowering cacti between the boulders.

Sleeping & Eating

The free campground near the visitor center has shade, picnic tables, firepits, cold showers and many birds. Bring food; the nearest supplies are at the town of Puelches, 35km south.

ACA Hostería (02952-436-101; s/d US$7/10) If you don't want to camp, you have one choice: this basic but functional place on the highway. There is a restaurant (which is nothing to get excited about) and the park entrance is a short walk away.

Getting There & Away

Buses leave from Santa Rosa for the park daily (US$5, four hours).

THE LAKE DISTRICT

Extending from Neuquén down through Esquel, Argentina's Lake District is an exceptional place. There are glorious mountains to climb and ski down, rushing rivers to raft, clear lakes to boat or fish and beautiful national parks to explore. From big-city Bariloche to hippie El Bolsón, the Lake District's towns and cities each have their own distinct geography, architecture and cultural offerings. The region offers something to do in every season and beautiful scenery at every turn, and both vacationing Argentines and foreign backpackers have discovered this wealth of lush landscapes and outdoor activities – so don't you miss it.

The Lake District's original inhabitants were the Puelches and Pehuenches, so named for their dependence on pine nuts from the *pehuén,* or monkey-puzzle tree (which you'll no doubt investigate curiously when you visit). Though Spaniards explored the area in the late 16th century, it was the Mapuche who dominated the region until the 19th century, when European settlers arrived. Today you can still see Mapuche living around here, especially on national park lands.

NEUQUÉN

☎ 0299 / pop 247,000

Palindromic Neuquén is a provincial capital nestled in the crook of where the Limay and Neuquén Rivers meet. It's the gateway to Patagonia and the Andean Lake District, and an important regional commercial and agricultural center. Neuquén isn't a major tourist magnet, but it isn't unpleasant either. There are worse places to pause on your way to somewhere else.

Information

There are several banks with ATMs.

Cambio Pullman (Ministro Alcorta 144) Changes travelers checks.

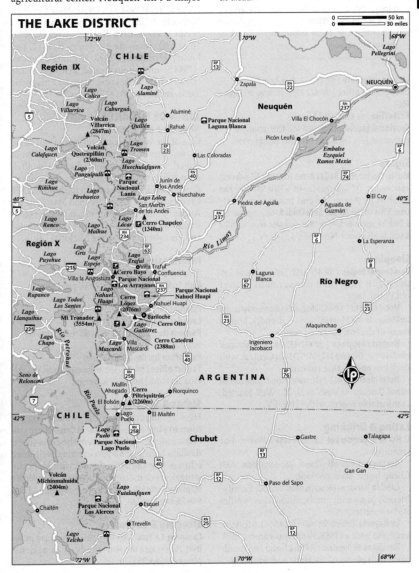

THE LAKE DISTRICT

ARGENTINA

THROW AWAY YOUR GUIDEBOOK!

Neuquén province has one of the world's richest concentrations of dinosaur bones. A few hints: Plaza Huincul, Villa El Chocón, Centro Paleontológico Lago Barreales – all within a few hours' drive. The greater region also boasts lakes, hot springs, a few *bodegas* (vineyards), a notable bird sanctuary and some world-class fishing.

Interested in more information? Get it yourself, and go!!

Chilean consulate (☎ 442-2727; La Rioja 241).
Immigration office (☎ 422-2061; Santiago del Estero 466)
Post office (cnr Rivadavia & Santa Fe)
Provincial tourist office (☎ 442-4089; www.neu quen.gov.ar; Félix San Martín 182) Sells fishing licenses.

Sights

Museo Nacional de Bellas Artes (cnr Mitre & Santa Cruz; admission free; ✛ 10am-9pm Tue-Fri, 6-10pm Sat & Sun) has exhibits by Argentine and international artists. The small **Museo de la Cuidad** (cnr Independencia & Córdoba; admission free; ✛ 8am-9pm Mon-Fri, 6-10pm Sat & Sun) is all about Neuquén's history.

Sleeping

Residencial Inglés (☎ 442-2252; Félix San Martín 534; s/d US$12/18) Tidy, good rooms run by a sweet old Polish lady.

Hotel Alcorta (☎ 442-2652; alcortahotel@infovia.com.ar; Ministro Alcorta 84; s/d US$13/23) A friendly, homey maze of decent, carpeted rooms.

Hostería Belgrano (☎ 442-4311; hosteriabelgrano@infovia.com.ar; Rivadavia 283; s/d US$13/23) Central, with dark but good-value rooms.

Hotel Ideal (☎ 442-2431; www.interpatagonia.com/ho telideal; Olascoaga 243; s/d US$16/25; 🖭) Well-located, comfortable rooms with cable TV.

Eating & Drinking

El Norte supermarket (cnr Olascoaga & Moreno) For takeout.

Restaurant Alberdi (Alberdi 176; mains under US$3) Cheap home-style cooking.

Cabildo (Rivadavia 68; mains under US$3.50) Family-friendly place with pizzas, sandwiches, waffles and omelettes.

La Rayuela (Alberdi 59; mains US$4.50-7) Modern, large and with a US$5.50 all-you-can-eat deal.

Meridiano 69 (Rivadavia 69) Dark, loud and trendy place with plenty of cocktails and whiskeys.

Getting There & Around

The airport is 6km away (bus US40¢, taxi US$4). **Aerolíneas Argentinas** (☎ 442-2409; www.aerolineasargentinas.com; Santa Fe 52) and **LADE** (☎ 443-1153; Brown 163) have services.

Neuquén's large, new bus terminal is 4km west of the center; to get downtown take either a 'Pehueche' bus (US35¢; buy ticket at Puerta D) or a taxi (US$2.75). Destinations include Bariloche (US$15, six hours), Bahía Blanca (US$13, 7½ hours), Buenos Aires (US$22, 16 hours), Junín de los Andes (US$12, five hours), Mendoza (US$23, 12 hours), Viedma (US$15, nine hours) and Temuco, Chile (US$23, 10 hours). Local buses take magnetic cards, easily bought at any kiosk.

JUNÍN DE LOS ANDES

☎ 02972 / pop 12,000

One of the lake district's most pleasant small towns, Junín proclaims itself Argentina's 'trout capital' – and there are indeed some beautiful, trout-filled rivers in the area. It's a tranquil and slow-paced hamlet located on the beautiful Río Chimehuín, 42km north of San Martín de los Andes. There's nothing much to do except wander around, explore the river or mountains and visit gorgeous Parque Nacional Lanín.

Information

There's a bank (ATM) on the plaza.
Club Andino (☎ 491-207) For hiking info; near the tourist office.
Internet (Suárez 445)
Laundry (Ponte 330)
Parques Nacionales (☎ 491-160) Next door to the tourist office.
Post office (cnr Don Bosco & Suárez)
Tourist office (☎ 491-160; turismo@jdeandes.com.ar; Plaza San Martín) Issues fishing permits.

Sights & Activities

Hike 15 minutes from the western edge of town to pine-dotted **Cerro de la Cruz**, where you can wander the 21 stations of the cross (open daylight hours). It's a very creative, well-done effort fusing Christian themes with Mapuche struggles. For indigenous artifacts, visit **Museo Mapuche** (Ponte 540; admission free; ✛ 9am-noon & 3-8pm Mon-Fri, 9am-noon Sat).

Sleeping & Eating

Camping La Isla (☎ 492-029; campsites per person US$2.25; ✛ open Dec-Mar) Shady sites and RV plugs (US$3.25).

Laura Vicuña (☎ 491-149; majandes@smandes.com.ar; campsites per person US$2.75, cabañas from US$16) Pleasant and open all year, with sunny riverside sites. Cabañas also available (US$16 to US$29).

Residencial Marisa (☎ 491-175; residencialmarisa@ deandes.com.ar; Rosas 360; s/d US$10/13) Good-value rooms; upstairs is brighter. On the highway but relatively peaceful, and a block from the bus terminal.

El Cedro (☎ 02944-15-601-952; elcedro2004@yahoo.com .ar; La Madrid 409; s/d US$16/20) Simple, small budget rooms with cable TV; just off the plaza.

Posada Pehuén (☎ 491-569; www.camarajuninandes .com.ar/posadapehuen; Suárez 560; s/d US$18/28) Ten comfortable rooms, all with bathroom and good breakfast, in a family home. Pretty garden in back.

Hostería Chimehuín (☎ 491-132; www.interpatago nia.com/hosteriachimehuin; cnr Suárez & 25 de Mayo; s/d US$23/33) Grassy grounds, pleasant location and decent rooms; the best have balconies over the gorgeous river. Big with fishing aficionados; apartments available.

Posada Pehuén (Suárez 560; meals from US$8) Delicious homemade meals in a living-room setting; also wine/cheese nights and weekend tea. Reserve one to two days in advance.

Ruca Hueney (on the plaza; mains US$4-6) Classy and popular, serving meats, pastas and trout. Takeout counter next door.

Roble Pub (Ginés Ponte 331) A wonderfully rustic and intimate place; after dinner it becomes a bar.

Getting There & Away
The airport is 19km south, toward San Martín de los Andes.

The bus station is three blocks west of the plaza. Destinations include San Martín de los Andes (US$1.75, 45 minutes), Bariloche (US$7, three hours) and Neuquén (US$12, six hours). Chilean destinations include Pucón (US$15, four hours), Temuco (US$15, seven hours) and Valdivia (US$15, eight hours).

PARQUE NACIONAL LANÍN
At 3776m, snowcapped Volcán Lanín is the dominating centerpiece of tranquil Parque Nacional Lanín, where extensive stands of *lenga* (southern beech) and the curious monkey-puzzle tree flourish. Pleistocene glaciers left behind blue finger-shaped lakes, excellent for fishing and camping. There was no entry fee at the time of writing, but this could change. For detailed information and maps,

contact the Parques Nacionales office in Junín or San Martín.

In summer **Lago Huechulafquen** is easily accessible from Junín; there are outstanding views of Volcán Lanín and several excellent hikes. Mapuche-run campgrounds include Raquithue, Piedra Mala and Bahía Cañicul; charges per person are US$1.75 to US$2.25. Free campsites also available. Purchase supplies in Junín de los Andes. The forested **Lago Tromen** area also offers good hiking and camping.

From San Martín you can boat west on **Lago Lácar** to Paso Hua Hum and cross by road to Puerto Pirehueico (Chile); there's also bus service. Hua Hum has camping and hiking trails. Fifteen kilometers north of San Martín, serene **Lago Lolog** has good camping and fishing.

Summer 'Traficc' vans from Junín's bus station go all along Lago Huechulafquen to Puerto Canoas (US$5, twice daily in summer). Buses to Chile over the Hua Hum and Tromen passes can also stop at intermediate points, but are often crowded.

SAN MARTÍN DE LOS ANDES
☎ 02972 / pop 27,000
Argentina's elite *love* San Martín, rowdily crowding the streets of this small fashionable town during their vacations. Nestled between two verdant mountains on the shores of Lago Lácar, San Martín boasts many wood and stone chalet-style buildings, most of which seem to be chocolate shops, ice-cream stores and souvenir boutiques. But behind the touristy streets lie pleasant residential neighborhoods with pretty rose-filled gardens, and the surrounding area has wonderful forested trails perfect for hiking and biking.

Information
There are several ATMs.

Andina Internacional (Capitán Drury 876) Changes traveler's checks.

Parques Nacionales (☎ 427-233; Frey 479) Near the tourist office. Sells fishing licenses.

Post office (cnr Pérez & Roca)

Tourist office (☎ 427-347; www.sanmartindelosandes .gov.ar; San Martín) Near the plaza.

Sights
The 2.5km steep, dusty hike to **Mirador Bandurrias** (US35¢; fee in summer only) ends with awesome views of Lago Lácar; be sure to take

a snack or lunch. Tough cyclists can rent bikes at **Rodados** (San Martín 1061; per hr US$2; 9am-12.30pm & 4-8.30pm Mon-Fri, 9am-1pm Sat), and reach the *mirador* (viewing point) in about an hour via dirt roads.

Walk, bike or hitch to **Playa Catrite**, 5km away down RN 234 (there's public transport in summer). Popular with families and young folk, this protected rocky beach has a laid-back restaurant with nice deck; there's camping nearby. Cerro Chapelco, a ski center 20km away, has a downtown **information office** (☎ 427-845; cnr San Martín & Elordi).

From the pier you can take daily boat tours to Paso Hua Hum (round trip US$26) to access walks and a waterfall, and to Quila Quina (round trip US$8) for beaches and water sports.

Numerous area tours include trips to nearby *miradores* and beaches, Volcán Lanín, Lagos Huechulafquen and Traful, Siete Lagos and Cerro Chapelco.

Sleeping

Reserve ahead in high seasons (January to March and July to August).

La Grieta Hostel (☎ 429-669; www.lagrietasma.com.ar; Ramayón 767; dm/d US$7/18) Intimate hostel in a cozy house, with small rooms (one double) sharing bathroom.

Albergue Rukalhue (☎ 427-431; www.rukalhue.com.ar; Juez del Valle 682; dm/s/d US$7/23/29) Bleak halls, large dining room, industrial feel and simple rooms; doubles have bathroom and TV.

Puma Youth Hostel (☎ 422-443; www.pumahostel.com.ar; Fosbery 535; dm with/without HI card US$7.50/8.50, d US$23/24; 🖳) Good, clean HI hostel with great kitchen and spacious dorms. Three doubles with bathroom available.

Hostería Cumelen (☎ 427-304; Elordi 931; s/d US$20/26) A good central choice, with very pleasant rooms sporting cable TV.

Las Lucarnas Hostería (☎ 427-085; hosterialasluc rnas@hotmail.com; Pérez 632; s/d US$26/29) Beautiful, comfortable rooms with beamed ceilings. Good value.

Casa Alta (☎ 427-456; casaalta@sma.com.ar; Obeid 659; d/tr US$33/42) Pleasant, with only three simple rooms and a beautiful garden. English, German, Italian and French spoken. Only open December to March.

On the eastern outskirts is spacious **Camping ACA** (☎ 429-430; campsites per person US$4). There's also good camping at **Playa Catrite** (campsites per person US$3), 5km south of town.

Eating & Drinking

El Bodegón (Mascardi 892; mains under US$3.50) Cheap, generous portions of home-cooked food. Simple, very basic menu. Friendly.

Pura Vida (Villegas 745; mains under US$4) Excellent, mostly vegetarian place serving spinach crepes, vegetable tarts and stuffed squash.

Pulgarcito (San Martín 461; mains US$4-5.25) Intimate restaurant serving up meat and trout, but best for pasta: ravioli, *ñoqui* and lasagna. Thirty different sauces.

Avataras (☎ 427-104; Ramayón 765; mains US$4-9) Sophisticated ethnic dishes such as trout in orange sauce, chicken in red curry and crab ravioli. Cozy bar in back.

Ku (San Martín 1053; mains US$4-10) Elegant, pricey *parrilla* and regional cuisine. Excellent, but with spotty service.

Downtown Matias (cnr Coronel DíArizona & Calderon) Spacious and lofty yuppie magnet, with pool tables, rock music and pricey drinks. Short, steep hike uphill.

Avataras Pub (Ramayón 765) Intimate fancy pub with booths, bar stools and sofas. Plenty of drinks, upscale grub and Marley on the speakers.

Getting There & Away

The **airport** is 23km north of town (taxi US$12). Airlines include **Aerolíneas Argentinas** (☎ 427-003; www.aerolineasargentinas.com; Capitán Drury 876) and **LADE** (☎ 427-672), at the bus station.

The bus station is five blocks west of Plaza San Martín. Destinations include Junín de los Andes (US$1.75, 45 minutes), Villa La Angostura (US$6.25, 2½ hours) and Bariloche (US$8, four hours). Chilean destinations include Puerto Pirehueico (US$15, 2½ hours), Panguipulli (US$15, seven hours) and Temuco (US$15, eight hours).

VILLA LA ANGOSTURA

☎ 02944 / pop 10,000

Tiny Villa la Angostura is a darling chocolate-box town that takes its name from the *angosta* (narrow) 91m neck of land connecting it to the striking Península Quetrihué. There's no doubt that Villa is touristy, but it is so in a charming way: regional wood-and-stone alpine buildings line the three-block-long main street, and dusty back streets come off the main drag. There's skiing at nearby Cerro Bayo in winter.

El Cruce is the main part of town and contains the bus terminal and most hotels and businesses; the main street is Av Arrayanes. Woodsy La Villa, with a few restaurants, hotels and a nice beach, is 3km southwest and on the shores of Lago Nahuel Huapi.

Information

Andina (Av Arrayanes 256) Changes traveler's checks.
National park office (☎ 494152; La Villa)
Post office (Av Arrayanes 282l, ste 17)
Tourist office (☎ 494124) Across from the bus station.

Sights & Activities

The cinnamon-barked *arrayán*, a myrtle relative, is protected in the small but beautiful **Parque Nacional Los Arrayanes** on the Península Quetrihué (the peninsula itself is located within another much larger national park, Nahuel Huapi). The main *bosque* (forest) of *arrayanes* is situated at the southern tip of the peninsula; it's reachable by a 35-minute boat ride (one-way/round-trip US$6.50/12) or a relatively easy 12km trail from La Villa. There's a US$4 entry fee.

Experienced riders should rent a bike to reach the *arrayán* forest. The first section is very steep, but the trail more or less evens out. It's possible to boat either there or back, hiking or biking half the way (buy your return boat ticket in advance). Take food and water; there's an ideal picnic spot next to a lake near the end of the trail.

At the start of the Arrayanes trail, near the beach, a steep 30-minute hike climbs to panoramic viewpoints over Lago Nahuel Huapi.

From the El Cruce part of town, a 3km walk north takes you to **Mirador Belvedere**; 1km further on is **Cascada Inayacal**, a 50m waterfall (you'll need to backtrack and take another path).

Sleeping

The following are all in El Cruce. Prices are for the January–February high season, when you should reserve in advance.

Osa Mayor (☎ 494-304; www.campingosamayor.com.ar; Calle Osa Mayor 230; campsites per person US$3.25) About 1km from town toward Bariloche. Pleasant grassy sites and common spaces. Also large dorms (US$5) and bungalows (from US$39).

Camping Unquehué (☎ 494-922; unquehue@cuidad .com.ar; campsites per person US$3.50) On the highway across from the YPF station and 600m west of the terminal. Good grassy, shady sites; also rents tents and sleeping pads. Gets crowded in summer.

Italian Hostel (☎ 494-376; www.italianhostel.com .ar; Los Marquis 233; dm US$6.50, d US$20-23) Dorms are very large (six to 12 beds) and loud, so go for an upstairs double. Nice garden with berry bushes. Owners know about biking in the area.

Hostel El Hongo (☎ 495-043; www.hostelelhongo .com.ar; Pehuenches 872; dm US$7) Ten blocks from center is this small place with just 19 beds (no doubles). It's worn around the edges, but has cute carpeted dorms.

Hostal Bajo Cero (☎ 495-454; www.bajocerohostel .com; dm/d US$8/20) On Av 7 Lagos (1200m from the bus terminal) is this beautiful HI-affiliated hostel with wonderful rooms. Stone and wood accents, bright and airy.

Hostel La Angostura (☎ 494-834; www.hostella angostura.com.ar; Barbagelata 157; dm/d US$8/26; 🖳) Large but excellent and well-run hostel with comfy lodgelike spaces and clean, modern rooms. Pool table and Saturday BBQs.

Residencial Río Bonito (☎ 494-110; riobonito@ciudad .com.ar; Topa Topa 260; d/apt US$25/48) Just five good, simple, comfortable rooms with bathroom in this home.

Las Cumbres (☎ 494-945; www.hosterialascumbres .com; Confluencia 944; s/d US$36/39) One kilometer from town and just off the highway (look for hiker statue). Eight wonderful, cozy rooms; the bright, relaxing common room has great wood trunk details and deck.

Eating & Drinking

Las Varas (Arrayanes 235; mains US$3-6.50) Attractive high-beamed place with great *parrillada*, pastas and plenty of salads. Inside small shopping mall.

La Buena Vida (Arrayanes 167; mains US$4.50-10) Choose foods like risotto, soufflé or Hungarian goulash. Also pastas, salads, fish and crepes. Nice front terrace.

Nativa Café (cnr Arrayanes & Inacayal; mains under US$5) Airy, popular tourist hangout with sports on TV and wood deck to catch the street action.

Tinto Bistro (☎ 494-924; Nahuel Huapi 34; mains US$6-12) Wonderful, well-prepared food, great cocktails and extensive wine list. Owned by the Dutch princess' Argentine brother; reserve ahead.

La Camorra (☎ 495-554; Cerro Bayo 65; mains US$6-14) This place has a small but excellent menu of Spanish- and Italian-influenced dishes like paella, risotto, pastas and lamb. Also has regional specialties.

Getting There & Around

From the **bus station** (cnr Avs Siete Lagos & Arrayanes) buses depart for Bariloche (US$3, 1¼ hours) and San Martín de los Andes (US$6.25, 2½ hours). If heading into Chile, reserve ahead for buses passing through.

There are buses to La Villa (where the boat docks and park entrance are located) every two hours. Bike rentals are available at **Instintos Deportivos** (La Fucsias 365; per day US$6) or at **Pegaso** (Cerro Inacayal 44; per day US$8).

BARILOCHE

☎ 02944 / pop 97,000

A magnet for visitors in both summer and winter, San Carlos de Bariloche is the Argentine Lake District's largest city. It sits on the shores of beautiful Lago Nahuel Huapi and is ringed by lofty mountain peaks. The city center bustles with touristy streets full of chocolate shops, souvenir stores and trendy boutiques. Bariloche's real attractions, however, are outside the city: Parque Nacional Nahuel Huapi offers spectacular hiking, and there's also camping, trekking, rafting, fishing and skiing in the area. Despite the heavy touristy feel, Bariloche is a good place to stop, hang out, get errands done and, of course, have some fun.

Information

As in practically every Argentine town and city, the internet is everywhere (and cheap). Banks with ATMs are common.

Cambio Sudamérica (Av Bartolomé Mitre 63) Changes travelers checks.

Chilean consulate (☎ 527-468; Av Juan Manuel de Rosas 180).

Club Andino (☎ 527-966; 20 de Febrero 30) Sells topo maps but does *not* offer hiking information; try Patagonia Andina hostel.

Hospital Privado Regional (☎ 525-000; cnr 24 de Septiembre & 20 de Febrero)

Immigration office (☎ 423-043; Libertad 191)

Information kiosk (☎ 422-623; cnr Perito Moreno & Villegas)

Intendencia del Parques Nacionales (☎ 423-188; San Martín 24) Has information on Parque Nacional Nahuel Huapi.

Librería Cultura (Elfein 78) For Lonely Planet guides.

Municipal tourist office (☎ 429-850; www.bariloche patagonia.info; Centro Cívico)

Post office (Perito Moreno 175)

Provincial tourist office (☎ 423-178; cnr Av 12 de Octubre & Emilio Frey)

Sights & Activities

The heart of town is the Centro Cívico, a group of well-kept public buildings built of log and stone (architect Ezequiel Bustillo originally adapted Middle European styles into this form of architecture, now associated with the Lake District area). Here you'll find the diverse **Museo de la Patagonia** (admission US$1; ☉ 10am-12:30pm & 2-7pm Tue-Fri, 10am-5pm Sat), offering good displays of stuffed critters and archaeological artifacts along with an explanation (in Spanish) of Mapuche resistance toward the European conquest.

Rafting and kayaking trips on the Río Limay (easy class II) or Río Manso (class III to IV) have become popular. They're generally 20km day trips and include all gear and transfers. Other popular activities include biking, paragliding, horse-riding and skiing (in winter only, of course).

There are many agencies in town offering area tours. One backpacker-oriented agency is **Overland Patagonia** (☎ 437-654; www.overlandpat agonia.com); it's located at Periko's hostel.

Courses

La Montaña (☎ 524-212; www.lamontana.com; Elflein 251) is a good Spanish school. Group classes cost US$44 per week; private classes cost US$11 per hour. Family stays can be arranged; volunteering opportunities available (see website).

Sleeping

All rates are for January, February and holidays, when you should make reservations. If you need to rent camping gear there's **La Bolsa** (☎ 433-431; Diagonal Capraro 1081).

IN BARILOCHE

Arko (☎ 423-109; Güemes 691; campsites per person US$4.25, r per person US$16-20) Just three rooms available (one with private bathroom) at this cute, homey place with lovely garden. English spoken and small kitchen available.

Hostel 1004 (☎ 432-228; www.lamoradahostel.com; San Martín 127, 10th fl, ste 1004; dm/d US$7/20) Simply unbeatable views, both from the rooms and awe-inspiring terrace. Good common areas, friendly service and good atmosphere.

Hostel 41 Below (☎ 436-433; www.hostel41below .com; Juramento 94; dm US$7, d with shared bathroom US$21) Intimate hostel with clean dorms, fine doubles (with view) and mellow vibe. Great common room playing good music; run by a laid-back Kiwi.

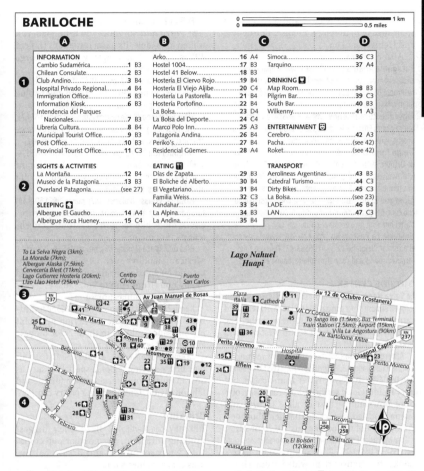

BARILOCHE

0 ———— 1 km
0 ———— 0.5 miles

To La Selva Negra (3km);
La Morada (7km);
Albergue Alaska (7.5km);
Cervecería Blest (11km);
Lago Gutierrez Hostería (20km);
Llao Llao Hotel (25km)

Lago Nahuel Huapi

Centro Cívico

Puerto San Carlos

Av Juan Manuel de Rosas

Plaza Italia   Cathedral

Av 12 de Octubre (Costanera)

VA O'Connor

To Tango Inn (1.5km); Bus Terminal;
Train Station (2.5km); Airport (15km);
Villa La Angostura (90km)

Av Bartolomé Mitre

Perito Moreno

Hospital Zonal

Elflein

To El Bolsón
(120km)

Marco Polo Inn (☎ 400-105; www.marcopoloinn.com.ar; Salta 422; dm with/without HI card US$7/8, d with/without HI card US$23/26; 💻) Large, modern hostel with all the services, including a bar-restaurant room with pool table. Excellent large doubles with bathrooms and dorms with loft.

La Bolsa del Deporte (☎ 423-529; www.labolsadelde porte.com.ar; Palacios 405; dm US$7.50, d US$16-20; 💻) Awesome hostel with artistic wood details, good dorms, cozy common areas and great hangout garden with boulder wall.

Periko's (☎ 522-326; www.perikos.com; Morales 555; dm/d US$8/23; 💻) Beautiful, well-run hostel with pleasant atmosphere, grassy yard and wonderful kitchen. Great dorms and four exceptional doubles with private bathroom. Travel agency next door.

Hostería Portofino (☎ 422-795; Morales 435; s/d US$16/26) This central, intimate and comfortable place offers great value. Eight small but warm rooms; good breakfast and friendly.

Residencial Güemes (☎ 424-785; fax 435-616; Güemes 715; d US$25; 🅿) A hike up the hill for plain, comfortable rooms, but the relaxing living room has a fireplace and fabulous views. Owner Cholo knows the area well.

Hostería El Viejo Aljibe (☎ 423-316; nsegat@infovia.com.ar; Emilio Frey 571; d/tr US$29/39) Friendly, homey place with a pretty garden and simple, small and tidy rooms. Five- and six-bed apartments available for US$58.

Hostería El Ciervo Rojo (☎ 435-241; www.elciervorojo.com.ar; Elfein 115; s/d US$33/39) Central, attractive place with simple but comfortable rooms (some with partial views) and a cozy living room area with fireplace. English, Portuguese and Hebrew spoken.

Also recommended:

Patagonia Andina (☎ 421-861; www.elpatagonia andina.com.ar; Morales 564; dm US$6-7, s/d with shared bathroom US$9/18) Basic, crowded dorms in old house. Good trekking information.

Albergue Ruca Hueney (☎ 433-986; www.ruca hueney.com; Elflein 396; dm US$6-7, d US$21) Casual and decent, with airy kitchen and OK dorms.

Tango Inn (☎ 430-707; www.tangoinn.com.ar; Av 12 de Octubre 1915; dm with/without HI card US$6.50/8, d with/without HI card US$23/26; ☐) Located 500m from bus terminal and 1.5km from center; so-so atmosphere.

Albergue El Guacho (☎ 522-464; www.hostelelgau cho.com; Belgrano 209; dm/d US$6.50/20; ☐) Plain hostel but with nice entrance patio.

Hostería La Pastorella (☎ 424-656; www.lapastor ella.com.ar; Belgrano 127; s/d US$33/47) Thirteen fine, carpeted rooms and cozy atmosphere. Sauna available.

OUTSIDE CENTER

La Selva Negra (☎ 441-013; campingselvanegra@infovia .com.ar; campsites per person US$4) Pleasant, terraced camping sites under trees, some with shelters, though all side by side. It's 3km west of town; take buses 10, 20 or 21.

Albergue Alaska (☎ /fax 461-564; www.visitbariloche .com/alaska; Lilinquen 328; dm US$6.50-7, d US$13-14, bunga- lows US$16-42; ℗ ☐) Large A-frame cabin, but cozy inside. Good services, bike rentals, group bungalows and – best of all – Jacuzzi and sauna. Located in a residential neighborhood 7.5km west of town; take bus 10, 20 or 21.

La Morada (☎ 442-349; www.lamoradahostel.com; dm US$8, d US$22-25; ☐) Far up Cerro Otto's flanks, but transport provided from Hostel 1004 (see earlier). Best for those who want peace: it's relaxing, cozy and the views are incomparable.

Lago Gutierrez Hostería (☎ 467-570; www.lagogu tierrezhotel.com; Ruta 82, km 16; d US$39-64; ☐) About 20km southwest of Bariloche, on Lago Gutier- rez, is this modern lodge with 16 spacious and very comfortable rooms. Grassy garden and the breakfast is hearty.

Eating

Regional specialties include *jabalí* (wild boar), *ciervo* (venison), and *trucha* (trout).

Simoca (Palacios 264; mains under US$3.50) Excel- lent, cheap eatery serving northern Argentine cuisine like empanadas, *locro, humitas* and tamales.

El Boliche de Alberto (Villegas 347; mains US$3.25- 5.25) *Parrillada* so good you'll be glad you waited for a table. Its pasta restaurant (Elflein 49) is excellent and equally popular. Large portions all around.

La Andina (Quaglia 95; pizzas US$3.25-8) Small, no- nonsense corner joint baking up good-value pizzas. Also pastas and empanadas.

El Vegetariano (20 de Febrero 730; mains under US$4.25; ☺ closed Sunday) Simple homemade pastas, veg- etarian plates, salads, fish and fresh juices.

Tarquino (cnr 24 de Septiembre & Saavedra; mains US$4- 8) Hobbit-like (but gorgeously so) restaurant serving meats and pastas, with panna cotta and brownies for dessert.

Familia Weiss (Palacios 167; mains US$4.50-8.50) Large family restaurant specializing in re- gional foods like venison and trout. Conven- ient picture menu.

Días de Zapata (Morales 362; mains US$5.50-7) Serves Mexican standbys such as quesadillas, faji- tas and enchiladas. Festive atmosphere (and happy hour from 7pm to 9pm) makes it easy to down that tequila sunrise.

Kandahar (20 de Febrero 698; mains US$6.50-9) Inti- mate gourmet restaurant offering up rabbit in wine sauce, salmon in three-color mousse and raviolis with mushroom sauce.

La Alpina (Perito Moreno 98; mains US$6.50-13) Cute al- pine house serving regional specialties such as boar in mushroom sauce, venison fondue and salmon ravioli. Great-looking pastry case.

Drinking

Wilkenny (San Martín 435) Bariloche's biggest drinking attraction, this popular pub comes with wraparound bar and occasional live music. Serves meals too.

Pilgrim Bar (Palacios 167) Another popular yup- pie hangout with old photos, good music and Pilgrim beer. Live music and sidewalk tables.

South Bar (cnr Juramento & 20 de Febrero) Intimate, laid-back bar with Celtic theme, dim light- ing and dartboard. Great music and talkative bartender named Pablo.

Cervecería Blest (☎ 461-026; Bustillo km 11; ☺ noon- 1am) Touristy brewery/restaurant, but with a nice atmosphere. Try pilsner, lager, bock and even raspberry beers. West of city 11km; take a taxi (US$4.50) or bus 20.

Map Room (Urquiza 248) Pleasant pub-restaurant decorated with maps from all around the world. Excellent food, including a real Ameri- can breakfast (run by US-Argentine couple).

Entertainment

The most popular discos – Roket, Cerebro and Pacha – are clustered together by the lake on Av Juan Manuel de Rosas, west of center.

Getting There & Around

AIR

The **airport** (☎ 426-162) is 15km east of town (bus US$1; taxi US$10). **Aerolíneas Argentinas** (☎ 422-425; www.aerolineasargentinas.com; Av Bartolomé Mitre 185), **LAN** (☎ 431-077; Av Bartolomé Mitre 500) and **LADE** (☎ 452-124; Villegas 480) provide services.

BICYCLE

Rent bicycles at **La Bolsa** (☎ 433-431; Diagonal Capraro 1081) or **Dirty Bikes** (☎ 425-616; VA O'Connor 681). Rates run US$6.50/10 per half/full day.

BUS

The bus terminal is 2.5km east of center (bus US35¢; taxi US$3).

Catedral Turismo (☎ 425-444; www.crucedelagos.cl; Palacios 263) arranges the beautiful 12-hour bus–boat combination tour over the Andes to Puerto Varas (US$160).

Destination	Duration (hr)	Cost (US$)
Buenos Aires	20	36
Comodoro Rivadavia	15	30
El Bolsón	2	4.50
Esquel	5	10
Puerto Madryn	13	31
San Martín de los Andes	4	8
Trelew	12	38
Viedma	14	20
Villa La Angostura	1-1½	3
Osorno (Chile)	5	16
Puerto Montt (Chile)	7	16

CAR

There are plenty of car rental agencies in town. Car-rental rates run from US$50 (with 200km); ask for weekly discounts.

TRAIN

The **train station** (☎ 423-172) is next to the bus terminal. There's train service to Viedma (US$10/23 in *turista*/Pullman class, 17 hours) twice weekly.

PARQUE NACIONAL NAHUEL HUAPI

Lago Nahuel Huapi, a glacial relic over 100km long, is the centerpiece of this gorgeous national park. To the west, 3554m Monte Tronador marks the Andean crest and Chilean border. Humid Valdivian forest covers its lower slopes, while summer wildflowers blanket alpine meadows.

The 60km **Circuito Chico** is probably Parque Nacional Nahuel Huapi's most popular excursion. Every 20–30 minutes, bus 20 (from San Martín and Morales) does half the circuit along Lago Nahuel Huapi to end at Puerto Pañuelos, where boat trips leave a few times daily for beautiful **Puerto Blest**, touristy **Isla Victoria** and pretty **Península Quetrihué** (see p135). Bus 10 goes the other way, inland via **Colonia Suiza** (a small woodsy Swiss community), and ends at Bahía López, where you can hike a short way to the tip of the peninsula Brazo de la Tristeza. In summer, bus 11 does the whole Circuito, connecting Puerto Pañuelos with Bahía López, but in winter you can walk the 6km stretch along the nonbusy highway, with much of that being on a wonderfully woodsy nature trail. There's a beautiful two-hour side hike to Villa Tacul, on the shores of Lago Nahuel Huapi. It's best to walk from Bahía López to Puerto Pañuelos rather than the other way around, since many more buses head back to Bariloche from Pañuelos. Get an area map at Bariloche's tourist office.

Skiing is a popular winter activity from mid-June to October. **Cerro Catedral** (☎ 02944-423-776; www.catedralaltapatagonia.com), some 20km west of town, is one of the biggest ski centers in South America. It boasts more than 50 runs, 40 lifts, a cable car, gondola and plenty of services (including rentals). The best part, however, is the views: peaks surrounding the lakes are gloriously visible.

Hard-core cyclists can bike the whole paved circuit. See left for bike rentals.

Hikers can climb Cerros Otto (two to three hours), Catedral (four hours), López (three hours) and Campanario (30 minutes), as well as Monte Tronador (six hours from Pampa Linda). If trekking, check with Club Andino (p136) or Patagonia Andina (opposite) for trail conditions; snow can block trails even in summer. If camping, get an area map (detailing campsites) at Bariloche's tourist office.

EL BOLSÓN

☎ 02944 / pop 22,000

Hippies rejoice – there's a must-see destination for you in Argentina, and it's called El Bolsón. Within its liberal and artsy borders live alternate-lifestyle folks from all over the country who've made their town a 'non-nuclear zone' and 'ecological municipality.' Located about 120km south of Bariloche, El Bolsón is peaceful, plain and unpretentious, surrounded by dramatically jagged mountain peaks that host activities for nature-lovers. Its economic prosperity, however, comes from a warm microclimate and fertile soil, both of which support a cadre of organic farms devoted to hops, cheese, soft fruits such as raspberries, and orchards. This, and El Bolsón's true personality, can be seen at its famous **feria artesanal** (craft market), where creative crafts and healthy food are sold; catch it on Plaza Pagano on Tuesdays, Thursdays and weekends (best on Saturdays).

The **tourist office** (☎ 492-604; www.elbolson.gov.ar) is next to Plaza Pagano. Get trail information at **Club Andino** (☎ 492-600; Av Sarmiento), near Roca. There are two ATMs in town. The post office is opposite the tourist office.

For area activities like rafting on Río Azul, paragliding and horse-riding, contact **Grado 42** (☎ 493-124; Av Belgrano 406) or **Patagonia Aventura** (☎ 492-513; Pablo Hube 418).

Sleeping

All rates listed are for summer, when you should book ahead. Surrounding mountains offer plenty of camping opportunities (other than the ones here), including at *refugios* (US$1.50 to US$2; also bunks for US$3.25 to US$5.25).

Camping & Hostel Refugio Patagonia (☎ 15-411061 for camping, ☎ 15-635-463 for dm; www.refugio patagonico.com.ar; Islas Malvinas s/n; campsites per person US$3, dm US$6.50; ▢) Premier camping, with both sunny and shady sites, mountain views and expansive fields. Also has beautiful dorms with great kitchen and dining room area. One queen-bed double available (US$16).

Camping La Chacra (☎ 492-111; lachacra@elbolson .com; Av Belgrano; campsites per person US$3.25, cabañas US$33) This well-tended campground has pleasant, grassy and shady sites in a fruit orchard. There's a small dining room (food available).

Albergue El Pueblito (☎ 493-560; www.hostels.org .ar; dm with/without HI card US$4.50/5.25; d US$13-20) Cozy and tranquil countryside hostel with creaky-floor dorms (bring ear plugs). Great hangout area; bike rentals and cabaña (US$33) available. Take a bus (it's 4km north of town) or *remise* (US$1.75).

Albergue Sol de Valle (☎ 492-087; albahube@hotmail .com; 25 de Mayo 2345; dm/s/d US$5/8/13) Impersonal and lacking interesting decor, this 55-bed *albergue* (youth hostel) has tiled halls, small rooms and kitchen access.

La Casa del Viajero (☎ 492-092; aporro@elbolson.com; near Libertad and Las Flores, Barrio Usina; dm US$6.50) Seeking a friendly, laid-back vibe with few amenities? Head to artist Augustin Porro's rustic plot of land – it's all 'natural' and homemade. Located 20m north of the pedestrian bridge (look for a sign over the bushy entrance).

Hospedaje Salinas (☎ 492-396; Roca 641; r per person US$6.50) Five no-frills older rooms (all with shared bathroom), tiny cooking facilities and nice garden patio in which to hang and meet other travelers.

Steiner (☎ 492-224; Av San Martín 670; s/d US$10/20; ▣) South of town about 2km (*remise* US$1.25) is this peaceful hotel on grassy grounds. Rooms are simple and unmemorable, but there's a pool. Meals available.

Residencial Los Helechos (☎ 492-262; Av San Martín 3248; s US$16, d US$23-29, apt US$39) Has eight wonderfully spotless, modern rooms, a flowery garden and kitchen access. Some doubles have kitchenette. Look for the 'Kioscón' sign.

La Posada de Hamelin (☎ 492-030; www.posadade hamelin.com.ar; Granollers 2179; s/d US$20/26) Wonderfully cozy rooms in this sweet, friendly and vine-covered family home. Excellent breakfast (US$2.25).

Cabañas Bungalow Montes (☎ 455-227; www.montes .bolsonweb.com.ar; Azcuénaga 155; apt US$26-33, cabañas US$45-58) Three cute and well-tended A-frame cabañas available (six to eight beds). Also two apartments (two to four beds). All have kitchen.

Eating

Food at the *feria artesanal* is not only great value; it's also tasty and healthy.

La Anónima supermarket (cnr Av San Martín & Dorrego) Cheap takeout.

La Vertiante (cnr Güemes & Rivadavia; US$3-6) Traditional menu, with well-priced homemade pastas and trout dishes. Excellent.

Patio Venzano (cnr Av Sarmiento & Pablo Hube; US$3.25-6.50) Great cozy wood atmosphere and nice patio add to the tasty *parrillada* and pasta offerings here.

Calabaza (Av San Martín 2518; mains US$3.25-6.50) Mixed reviews, but still draws them in with regional dishes and vegetarian offerings like squash *milanesas*. Cozy, with sidewalk tables.

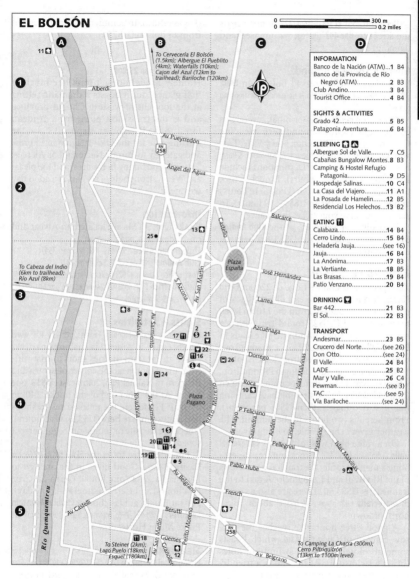

EL BOLSÓN

0 — 300 m
0 — 0.2 miles

INFORMATION
Banco de la Nación (ATM)...**1** B4
Banco de la Provincia de Río
  Negro (ATM).................**2** B3
Club Andino....................**3** B4
Tourist Office...................**4** B4

SIGHTS & ACTIVITIES
Grado 42...........................**5** B5
Patagonia Aventura............**6** B4

SLEEPING
Albergue Sol de Valle.........**7** C5
Cabañas Bungalow Montes.**8** B3
Camping & Hostel Refugio
  Patagonia......................**9** D5
Hospedaje Salinas............**10** C4
La Casa del Viajero...........**11** A1
La Posada de Hamelin.......**12** B5
Residencial Los Helechos...**13** B2

EATING
Calabaza..........................**14** B4
Cerro Lindo......................**15** B4
Heladería Jauja..............(see 16)
Jauja...............................**16** B4
La Anónima......................**17** B3
La Vertiente.....................**18** B5
Las Brasas.......................**19** B4
Patio Venzano..................**20** B4

DRINKING
Bar 442...........................**21** B3
El Sol..............................**22** B3

TRANSPORT
Andesmar........................**23** B5
Crucero del Norte...........(see 26)
Don Otto.......................(see 24)
El Valle...........................**24** B4
LADE..............................**25** B2
Mar y Valle......................**26** C4
Pewman........................(see 3)
TAC...............................(see 5)
Vía Bariloche.................(see 24)

To Cervecería El Bolsón
(1.5km); Albergue El Pueblito
(4km); Waterfalls (10km);
Cajon del Azul (12km to
trailhead); Bariloche (120km)

Alberdi

Av Pueyrredón

RN 258

Ángel del Agua

Castello

Balcarce

Plaza
España

José Hernández

To Cabeza del Indio
(6km to trailhead);
Río Azul (8km)

S Azcona

Av San Martín

Larrea

Azcuénaga

Rivadavia

Av Sarmiento

Dorrego

Roca

Islas Malvinas

Plaza
Pagano

Perito Moreno

P Feliciano

25 de Mayo

Saavedra

Anden

Liniers

Pablo Hube

Pastorino

Islas Malvinas

Av Castelli

Rivadavia

Av Sarmiento

Pellegrini

French

Río Quemquemtreu

Berutti

RN 258

To Steiner (2km);
Lago Puelo (18km);
Esquel (180km)

Güemes

Av San Martín

Perito Moreno

Crahólier

Av Belgrano

To Camping La Chacra (300m);
Cerro Piltriquitrón
(13km to 1100m level)

Av Belgrano

Cerro Lindo (Av San Martín 2524; mains US$3.25-10)
Next door to Calabaza and serving meat,
pastas and local specialties.

Las Brasas (cnr Av Sarmiento & Pablo Hube; US$3.25-8)
Long-standing *parrilla*; not the best nor the
worst, but the most consistent in town.

Jauja (Av San Martín 2867; US$3.50-9) Modern, bus-
tling place with highly varied menu. Next

door, Heladería Jauja is definitely worth the
long wait. Wi-fi zone.

Drinking
El Bolsón is too small to be big on nightlife.

Cervecería El Bolsón (☎ 492-595; Ruta 258) This
relaxing place brews about a dozen beers and
serves food. It's 2 km north of town.

Peek into bar **El Sol** (Dorrego 423) or hop across the street to **Bar 442** (Dorrego 442) for weekend dancing.

Getting There & Around

It's unlikely you'll fly to El Bolsón on **LADE** (☎ 492-206; cnr Av Sarmiento & Hernandez, in shopping center).

There's no central bus terminal; several bus companies are spread around town inlcuding Crucero del Norte, Don Otto, Mar y Valle, TAC and Via Barilcohe. **El Valle** (cnr Av Sarmiento & Roca) has the most departures. Destinations include Bariloche (US$5, two hours), Esquel (US$5, two hours), Puerto Madryn (US$36, 12 hours) and Buenos Aires (from US$37, 19 hours). In summer, reserve your ticket in advance.

Rent bikes at Pewman, at the **Club Andino** (☎ 492-600; Av Sarmiento), for US$5/8 a half/full day (summer only).

AROUND EL BOLSÓN

The spectacular granite ridge of 2260m **Cerro Piltriquitrón** looms to the east like the back of some prehistoric beast. From the 1100m level, reached by taxi (US$25 round-trip with 1½ hour wait), a further 30-minute hike leads to **Bosque Tallado** (admission US$1.25), a shady grove of about 30 figures carved from logs. Another 15-minute walk uphill is Refugio Piltriquitrón, where you can have a drink or even sack down (bunk US$3.25, bring sleeping bag; camping free first two nights, then US$1 per night). From here it's two hours to the summit. The weather is very changeable, so bring layers.

On a ridge 6km west of town is **Cabeza del Indio** (admission US$0.35), a rock outcrop resembling a man's profile; the trail has great views of the Río Azul and Lago Puelo. A taxi to the trailhead is US$3.50. There are also a couple of **waterfalls** (admission each US35¢) about 10km north of town.

A good three-hour hike reaches the narrow canyon of **Cajón del Azul**, which boasts some absolutely glorious swimming holes (bring a swimsuit!). At the end is a friendly *refugio* where you can eat or stay for the night (bunks US$5.25, camping US$1.35). Town buses drop you a 15-minute steep, dusty walk from the Cajón del Azul trailhead (US$1), or take a *remise* (US$5.25).

About 18km south of El Bolsón is windy **Parque Nacional Lago Puelo** (☎ 499-064; admission US$2). You can camp, stay at a *refugio*, take a boat tour or a ferry to the Chilean border

(US$8 return). In summer, regular buses run from El Bolsón (US75¢).

ESQUEL

☎ 02945 / pop 25,000

Homely Esquel doesn't look like much at first glance, but it boasts a dramatic setting at the foothills of western Chubut province and is the transition point from Andean forest to the Patagonian steppe. It's also the starting gate for the Old Patagonian Express and gateway to Parque Nacional Los Alerces. There's good hiking in the area, and the pleasant Welsh stronghold, Trevelin, is a good day trip away.

Information

Banks with ATMs are located on Alvear and on 25 de Mayo near Alvear.

Chilean consulate (☎ 451-189; Molinari 754)
Club Andino (☎ 453-248; Pellegrini 787)
Post office (Alvear 1192) Next to the tourist office.
Tourist office (☎ 451-927; www.esquel.gov.ar; cnr Alvear & Sarmiento)

Sights & Activities

La Trochita (Old Patagonian Express; ☎ 451-403; www .latrochita.org.ar) is Argentina's famous narrow-gauge steam train. It does short tourist runs from the station near the corner of Brown and Roggero to Nahuel Pan, 20km east (US$8, one hour). At the other end of the tracks, 140km away, is El Maitén; the railroad's workshops and a museum are here (US$26, nine hours). Check the website or tourist office for current schedules.

For adventure tours try **EPA** (☎ 454-366; cnr Rivadavia & Roca). Good hikes in the area go to Laguna La Zeta (one hour), Cerro La Cruz (1½ hours) and Cerro Nahuel Pan (one day). For mountain guides contact **Cholila Mountain Explorers** (☎ 456-296; www.cholilaexplorers.com) at Piuke Mapu Hostel.

Sleeping

El Hogar del Mochilero (☎ 452-166; Roca 1028; campsites per person US$2.25, dm US$3.25) A shady well-run camping paradise; kitchen available. Also huge 31-bed dorm; bring sleeping bag. If Carlos isn't around, check the house across the street.

Casa del Pueblo (El Batxoky; ☎ 450-581; www.epa adventure.com.ar; San Martín 661; dm US$6-8, d US$18) A bit mazelike and worn, but a decent hostel with cozy common areas. Good kitchen and grassy garden. Bike rentals available.

Piuke Mapu Hostel (☎ 456-296; www.piukemapu .com; Urquiza 929; dm US$6.50) Small hostel that's a bit rough around the edges, but friendly and intimate. Good mountain-climbing information available.

Casa de Familia Rowlands (☎ 452-578; Rivadavia 330; r per person US$6.50) Friendly with three homey, basic rooms (two share bathrooms). About seven blocks from center.

Residencial El Cisne (☎ 452-256; Chacabuco 778; s/d US$8/15) Nine comfortable and quiet rooms in two buildings (ring at No 777 if no answer at No 778). Limited dining facilities.

Hotel Argentino (☎ 452-237; 25 de Mayo 862; s/d US$8/16) Atmospheric old digs with personality, filled with antiques. Odd but cool place, with eclectic bar atmosphere (see following section).

Parador Lago Verde (☎ 452-251; Volta 1081; s/d US$10/20) Six tiny and dark rooms, but there's a peaceful grassy garden. About six blocks from center.

Eating & Drinking

La Anónima supermarket (cnr Roca & 9 de Julio) Cheap takeout.

María Castaña (cnr 25 de Mayo & Rivadavia; mains US$3-5) Busy café with sidewalk tables and plenty of menu choices. Great overstuffed chairs in back.

La Española (Rivadavia 740; mains US$3.25-6.50) Locally recommended place for good *parrillada* using choice meats.

Dionisio (Fontana 656; mains US$3.25-8) Tranquil, artsy restaurant that's big on crepes, both savory and sweet. Also open at 6pm for tea.

Mirasoles (Pellegrini 643; mains US$3.50-8) Small and intimate upscale spot with natural foods such as stuffed squash and soy *milanesas*. In residential neighborhood.

Hotel Argentino (25 de Mayo 862) Old-time Wild West saloon bar and pool tables. There's a disco in back. Funky.

Morena (San Martín & Roca; ☯ closed Mon) More like a yuppie watering hole, with brick atmosphere and old wood tables. Food available.

Getting There & Around

The airport is 20km east of town (taxis US$8). **Aerolíneas Argentinas** (☯ 45-3614; Fontana 408) and **LADE** (☎ 452-124; Alvear 1085) provide services.

The bus terminal is six blocks north of center, at the corner of Alvear and Brun. Destinations include Parque Nacional Los Alerces (US$2.75, 1½ hours), El Bolsón (US$5.25, two hours), Bariloche (US$9, four hours), Puerto Madryn (US$29, nine hours) and Comodoro Rivadavia (US$18, nine hours). Buses go to Trevelin (US$75¢, 30 minutes) from the terminal, stopping along Av Alvear on their way south.

Bike rentals are available at **Casa del Pueblo** (El Batxoky; ☎ 450-581; www.epaadventure.com.ar; San Martín 661).

TREVELIN

☎ 02945 / pop 6000

Historic Trevelin is a calm, sunny and laidback community only 24km south of Esquel. The **tourist office** (☎ 480-120) is located on Plaza Fontana.

Landmarks include the historical **Museo Regional** (admission US75¢; ☯ 9am-9pm), in a restored brick mill, and **Capilla Bethel**, a Welsh chapel from 1910. **Tumba de Malacara** (admission US$1.75; ☯ 10am-12:30pm & 2-8pm), two blocks northeast of the plaza, is a monument to the horse that saved John Evans, Trevelin's founder.

For camping find **Policial** (campsites per person US$2; ☯ closed winter), with fine grassy, shady sites (they're building cabañas). From Av San Martín 600 block, walk two blocks west on Coronel Holdich and turn left down the gravel road (the Esquel bus goes beyond the plaza and stops at the intersection).

The best budget accommodation in town is friendly and serene **Hostel Casaverde** (☎ 480-091; www.casaverdehostel.com.ar; Los Alerces s/n; dm with/without HI card US$6.50/7, d US$20/23, cabaña US$48-65), at the top of a small hill. The rooms, kitchen, atmosphere and views are so welcoming you'll be tempted to extend your stay.

You can have afternoon tea (4pm to 7pm) and conquer a platter of pastries at **Nain Maggie** (☎ 480-232; Perito Moreno 179) and **Las Mutisias** (☎ 480-165; San Martín 170), while keeping your ears pricked for locals speaking Welsh.

Hourly buses run from Esquel to Trevelin (US75¢).

PARQUE NACIONAL LOS ALERCES

West of Esquel, the spacious Andean **Parque Nacional Los Alerces** (admission US$4) protects extensive stands of *alerce (Fitzroya cupressoides)*, a large and long-lived conifer of humid Valdivian forests. Other common trees include cypress, incense cedar, southern beeches and *arrayán*. The *colihue* (a bamboolike plant) undergrowth is almost impenetrable.

The receding glaciers of Los Alerces' peaks, which barely reach 2300m, have left nearly

ARGENTINA

THROW AWAY YOUR GUIDEBOOK!

Follow in the footsteps of Butch Cassidy and the Sundance Kid and head to Cholila, which looks to open up as a tourist attraction in the years to come. Right now there's not much for the traveler except a teahouse and the outlaws' decrepit log cabin, but the region is growing and a hostel may be built at some point (check with the guys at Piuke Mapu Hostel in Esquel). For general information there's Cholila's **Casa de Informes** (☎ 498-040; RP 15 at RP 71).

---

pristine lakes and streams with charming vistas and excellent fishing. Westerly storms drop nearly 3000mm of rain annually, but summers are mild and the park's eastern zone is much drier. An **interpretative center** (☎ 02945-471-015) provides information.

The most popular day-long tour sails from Puerto Limonao (on Lago Futalaufquen) up the Río Arrayanes to Lago Verde (US$36). Launches from Puerto Chucao (on Lago Menéndez) cover the second segment of the trip to **El Alerzal**, an accessible stand of rare *alerces* (US$23). A two-hour stopover permits a hike around a loop trail that passes Lago Cisne and an attractive waterfall to end up at **El Abuelo** (Grandfather), a 57m tall, 2600-year-old *alerce*. You can buy boat tickets in Esquel.

There are organized **campgrounds** (campsites per person US$3-6.50) at Los Maitenes, Lago Futalaufquen, Bahía Rosales, Lago Verde and Lago Rivadavia. Free sites exist near some of these locations. Lago Krüger, reached by foot (12 hours) or taxi boat from Villa Futalaufquen, has a campground, restaurant and expensive *hostería*. See Esquel's tourist office for a complete list of accommodation options.

For getting there and away information, see Getting There & Around under Esquel.

PATAGONIA

Few places in the world inspire the imagination like mystical Patagonia – and each year more and more travelers are experiencing awesome adventures down here. You can cruise bleak RN 40 (South America's Route 66), watch an active glacier calving house-sized icebergs and hike among some of the

most fantastic mountain scenery in the world. The sky is wide, the clouds are airbrushed and the late sunsets can tingle your spirit. Patagonia's other highlights include Welsh teahouses, petrified forests, quirky outpost towns, rich oilfields, penguin colonies, huge sheep *estancias* and some of the world's largest trout.

Patagonia was thought to be named after the Tehuelche people's moccasins, which made their feet appear huge – in Spanish, *pata* means foot. Geographically, the region is mostly a windy, barren expanse of flat nothingness that offers rich wildlife only on its eastern coast, and rises into the spectacular Andes way into its western edge. It's attracted an interesting range of famous personalities, however, from Charles Darwin to Ted Turner to Bruce Chatwin to Butch Cassidy and the Sundance Kid. But despite the big names, Patagonia maintains one of the lowest population densities in the world.

VIEDMA

☎ 02920 / pop 49,500

Patagonia's eastern gateway is this unremarkable provincial capital. Viedma is the finish line for January's **La Regata del Río Negro**, the world's longest kayak race, which starts 500km away in Neuquén. Other attractions include a couple of museums and a scenic riverside walk. Nearby Carmen de Patagones (p146) takes most of the family charm.

The **tourist office** (☎ 427-171; cnr Costanera & Colón) is by the river. There's a **post office** (cnr 25 de Mayo & San Martín), ATMs and plenty of internet access.

Sights & Activities

The history of local indigenous cultures can be seen at **Museo Gobernador Eugenio Tello** (San Martín 263; admission free; ◷ 9am-1pm & 5:30-8:30pm Mon-Fri, 10am-noon & 5:30-8:30pm Sat Dec-Mar). **Museo Cardenal Cagliero** (Rivadavia 34; admission free; 8am-noon Mon, 8am-noon & 7-9pm Tue-Thu) has some amazing ceiling paintings and a neat fish-vertebrae cane.

Summer activities include **kayaking** (walk north along the shore and look for rentals) and weekend **catamaran rides** (US$3.25).

The Atlantic shoreline, Patagonia's oldest lighthouse and the town of **Balneario El Cóndor** lie 30km southeast of Viedma; daily buses go from Plaza Alsina (US$1). A further 30km south is **Punta Bermeja**, a sea-lion colony. In summer only, buses from Viedma drop you 3km from the colony (US$1.75).

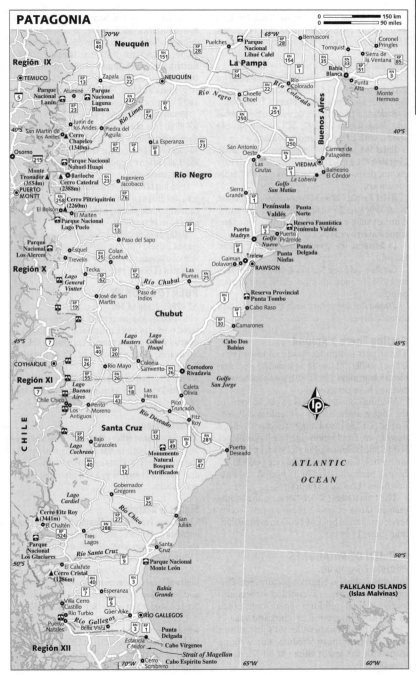

ARGENTINA

Triton Turismo (☎ 431-131; Namuncurá 78) does tours of the area; it also rents cars for about US$30 per day (with 100km).

Sleeping & Eating

Camping Municipal (☎ 15-608-403; campsites per person US$1.50) Northwest of center about 1km; riverside with bleak gravel sites (taxis US$1.75).

Residencial Tosca (☎ 428-508; residencialtosca@hotmail .com; Alsina 349; s/d US$15/21; 🖳) Small, simple rooms with cable TV and breakfast.

Hotel Spa (☎ 430-459; spaiturburu@rnonline.com.ar; 25 de Mayo 174; d US$23) Mazelike place with tiny rooms; despite 'spa' services (extra) it's hardly luxurious.

Hotel Austral (☎ 422-615; www.hoteles-austral.com .ar; cnr 25 de Mayo & Villarino; s/d US$36/41) For more comfort snag a carpeted, no-frills room here; some have river views.

La Anónima (cnr Alberdi & Rivadavia) For cheap takeout.

Camila's Café (cnr Saavedra & Buenos Aires; snacks under US$3.25) Good for sandwiches and drinks; popular.

Dragon (366 Buenos Aires; meals under US$4) Good *tenedor libre*.

Getting There & Around

The airport is 4km southwest of town (taxis US$4). **LADE** (☎ 424-420; Saavedra 576) and **Aerolíneas Argentinas** (☎ 422-018; www.aerolineasargen tinas.com) have services.

Viedma's bus terminal is 13 blocks south of the center, at the corner of Guido and Perón. Buses (US25¢) and taxis (US$1.50) head downtown. Destinations include Bahía Blanca (US$6.50, 3½ hours), Puerto Madryn (US$15, six hours), Comodoro Rivadavia (US$30, 12 hours), Bariloche (US$20, 14 hours) and Buenos Aires (US$25, 13 hours).

The **train station** (☎ 422-130) is on the southeast outskirts of town; there's twice-weekly service to Bariloche (US$10/23 in *turista*/Pullman class, 15 hours).

CARMEN DE PATAGONES
☎ 02920 / pop 18,500

Just across the Río Negro is picturesque 'Patagones,' with historic cobbled streets and lovely colonial buildings. There's not much to do other than stroll around and take in the relaxing atmosphere, and it's just a short boat ride from busy Viedma. For walking maps visit the **tourist office** (☎ 461-777, ext 296; Bynon 186).

Across from the boat dock is the good **Museo Histórico** (admission free; ☎ 9:30am-12:30pm & 7-9pm Mon-Sat); check out the cane with hidden stabber. Salesians built the **Iglesia Parroquial Nuestra Señora del Carmen** (1883); its image of the Virgin, dating from 1780, is southern Argentina's oldest. Note flags captured in the 1827 victory over the Brazilians.

Residencial Reggiani (☎ 461-065; Bynon 422; s/d US$10/16) has small, decent rooms (upstairs they're brighter). Better is **Hotel Percaz** (☎ 464-104; hotel@hotelpercaz.com.ar; Comodoro Rivadavia 384; s/d US$13/20), offering good budget rooms, though carpets are worn.

The **bus terminal** (cnr Barbieri & Méjico) has services to Buenos Aires and Puerto Madryn (among other places) but long-distance buses are more frequent from Viedma.

Patagones is connected to Viedma by frequent buses, but the *balsa* (passenger boat) is more scenic. It crosses the river every few minutes (US30¢, two minutes).

PUERTO MADRYN
☎ 02965 / pop 66,000

Founded by Welsh settlers in 1886, this sheltered port city owes much of its popularity to nearby wildlife sanctuary Península Valdés. It holds its own as a modest beach destination, however, and boasts a lively tourist street scene and popular boardwalk. From June to mid-December visiting right whales take center stage.

Information

There's a **tourist office** (☎ 453-504; www.madryn.gov .ar; Av Roca 223) both in the center and at the bus station. There are many banks with ATMs, and **Cambio Thaler** (Av Roca 493) changes travelers' checks.

Sights & Activities

The **Museo Provincial de Ciencias Naturales y Oceanográfico** (cnr Domecq García & Menéndez) was being remodeled at research time, but should be worth a visit. Well-done **EcoCentro** (☎ 457-470; Julio Verne 3784; admission US$5; 🕔 5-9pm) offers excellent exhibits of local sea life, complete with touch-pool and lofty glass tower. Take the Linea 2 bus to the last stop, then walk 1km (taxis US$3).

Other area activities include kayaking, windsurfing and horse-riding. Scuba diving is also possible; dives start at US$40 (try Scuba Duba at Blvd Brown 893 or Lobo Larsen at Hipólito Yrigoyen 144). You can pedal 17km southeast to **Punta Loma** (admission US$3.25), a sea-lion rookery, or 19km northwest to **Playa El Doradillo**, which offers close-up whale-watching in season. See p148 for bike rentals.

Tours

Countless agencies sell tours to Península Valdés (p148) and Punta Tombo (p150). All charge a set rate of US$37. Most hotels and hostels will also offer tours; in choosing, it's always best to get recommendations from fellow travelers. Ask how large the bus was, if it came with an English-speaking guide, where they ate and what they saw where – different tour companies often visit different locations. And remember to take water, as it's a long drive to both reserves.

Sleeping

Prices listed are for the high season, approximately October to March. In January it's a good idea to reserve ahead.

ACA Camping (☎ 452-952; campsites for 2/4 US$7.50/10, d US$18; ✕ Sep-Apr) Shady sandy sites; food service available. South of center 4km; take Linea 2 bus to last stop, then walk 800m (taxis US$2.75).

La Tosca (☎ 456-133; www.latoscahostel.com; Sarmiento 437; dm US$6.50, d US$20-23; ✕ closed May) Small hostel with good common area and simple, neat rooms lining a nice grassy yard. Free pickup from bus station.

El Gualicho (☎ 454-163; www.elgualicho.com.ar; Marcos A Zar 480; dm with/without HI card US$7/8, d with/without HI card US$26/28; 🖳) Great place with clean dorms,

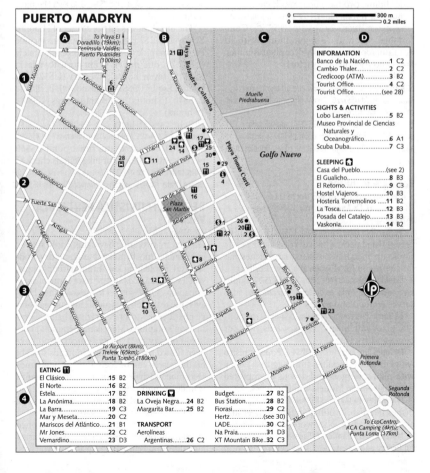

PUERTO MADRYN

0	300 m
0	0.2 miles

To Playa El Doradillo (19km); Península Valdés; Puerto Pirámides (100km)

Muelle Piedrabuena

Golfo Nuevo

Plaza San Martín

To Airport (8km); Trelew (65km); Punta Tombo (180km)

Primera Rotonda

Segunda Rotonda

To EcoCentro; ACA Camping (4km); Punta Loma (17km)

INFORMATION
Banco de la Nación.....................**1** C2
Cambio Thaler.............................**2** C2
Credicoop (ATM)..........................**3** B2
Tourist Office..............................**4** C2
Tourist Office..............................(see 28)

SIGHTS & ACTIVITIES
Lobo Larsen................................**5** B2
Museo Provincial de Ciencias
  Naturales y
  Oceanográfico..........................**6** A1
Scuba Duba.................................**7** C3

SLEEPING 🏠
Casa del Pueblo............................(see 2)
El Gualicho..................................**8** B3
El Retorno....................................**9** C3
Hostel Viajeros............................**10** B3
Hostería Torremolinos..................**11** B2
La Tosca......................................**12** B3
Posada del Catalejo......................**13** B3
Vaskonia......................................**14** B2

EATING 🍴
El Clásico.....................................**15** B2
El Norte.......................................**16** B2
Estela..**17** B2
La Anónima..................................**18** B2
La Barra.......................................**19** C3
Mar y Meseta...............................**20** C2
Mariscos del Atlántico...................**21** B1
Mr Jones......................................**22** C2
Vernardino...................................**23** D3

DRINKING 🍷
La Oveja Negra............................**24** B2
Margarita Bar...............................**25** B2

TRANSPORT
Aerolíneas
  Argentinas.................................**26** C2
Budget...**27** B2
Bus Station...................................**28** B2
Fiorasi...**29** C2
Hertz...(see 30)
LADE...**30** C2
Na Praia......................................**31** D3
XT Mountain Bike..........................**32** C3

good-vibe living room, spacious kitchen and grassy garden. Bike rentals and free pickup from bus station.

Hostel Viajeros (☎ 456-457; www.hostelviajeros.com; Gobernador Maíz 545; dm/d US$8/25; ▣) Long strip of no-nonsense rooms (all with bath) facing a grassy lawn. Large *quincha* (cabaña) with dining area and BBQ. Doubles are small; free pickup from bus terminal.

Vaskonia (☎ 472-581; buce23@infovia.com.ar; 25 de Mayo 43; s/d US$20/23) Long-running but remodeled standby with tight, tidy rooms around a small plant area. Good location just three blocks from bus station.

Casa del Pueblo (☎ 472-500; www.madryncasadepue blo.com.ar; Av Roca 475; s/d US$26/33) Just five simple and homey rooms available at this remodeled older home; two have boardwalk views.

Hostería Torremolinos (☎ 453-215; patagoniator remolinos.com; Marcos A Zar 64; s/d US$49/55; Ⓟ) Comfortable, cozy and clean guesthouse with six beautiful rooms, tastefully decorated common areas and friendly proprietors.

Also recommended:

El Retorno (☎ 456-044; www.elretornohostel.com.ar; Mitre 798; dm/d US$7/26) Decent digs with tiled halls and small common spaces.

Posada del Catalejo (☎ 475-224; info@posada delcatalejo.com.ar; Mitre 446; dm/d US$8/23) Small and unmemorable; rough around the edges. Doubles share baths.

Eating & Drinking

Supermarkets include **El Norte** (28 de Julio), near Mitre, and **La Anónima** (cnr Hipólito Yrigoyen & 25 de Mayo).

Vernardino (Blvd Brown; mains US$3-8) Best for its breezy wood deck, which overlooks the beach. Cooks up breakfast, pizza and sandwiches; has fancier menu for dinner. It's near Perlotti.

Estela (Roque Sáenz Peña 27; mains US$3.25-11) Popular, intimate and excellent *parrillada;* also serves seafood and pastas.

La Barra (Blvd Brown 779; mains US$4-8) Large popular place with meats, pastas, salads, outdoor tables and sea views.

Mr Jones (9 de Julio 116; mains US$4-8) Popular bistro with European specialties (think goulash) along with pizzas, burgers and dozens of imported beers like Negro Modela and Guinness.

Mar y Meseta (Av Roca 485; mains US$4.25-13) Tasty dishes like fish in honey, rabbit in beer and lamb shish kebab. Nice wood deck in front.

Mariscos del Atlántico (Av Rawson 288; mains US$4.50-10) Pretty good seafood dishes, with great local

ambience. Hard to find: behind Club Nautico, past arches 20m and up the stairs.

El Clásico (cnr 28 de Julio & 25 de Mayo; mains US$5.25-8.50) Old-fashioned corner joint serving lamb with herbs, crab ravioli and fish in prawn sauce.

Margarita Bar (cnr Av Roca & Roque Sáenz Peña) Hip bar with brick walls, international cocktails and simple food menu. Live jazz on Wednesdays.

La Oveja Negra (Hipólito Yrigoyen 144) Live music, pub grub and plenty of drinks at this intimate venue.

Getting There & Around

Madryn has an airport (shuttles US$1.50, taxis US$5), but most flights arrive 65km south at Trelew (shuttles US$5, taxis US$23). **Aerolíneas Argentinas** (☎ 451-998; www.aerolineasargentinas.com; Av Roca 427) and **LADE** (☎ 451-256; Av Roca 119) have services.

The bus station is on the corner of Hipólito Yrigoyen and San Martín. Destinations include Puerto Pirámide (US$3.25, 1½ hours), Trelew (US$2.25, one hour), Comodoro Rivadavia (US$15, seven hours), Viedma (US$20, six hours), Esquel (US$28, nine hours), Bariloche (US$40, 15 hours) and Buenos Aires (US$50, 19 hours).

Rent cars at **Hertz** (☎ 474-287; Av Roca 115), **Budget** (☎ 451-491; Av Roca 27) and **Fiorasi** (☎ 456300; Av Roca 165). Cheapest rates run around US$60 per day with 400km. For bike rentals check **XT Mountain Bike** (☎ 472-232; Av Roca 742; per day US$6.50) or **Na Praia** ☎ 455-633; Blvd Brown 860; per day US$8).

RESERVA FAUNÍSTICA PENÍNSULA VALDÉS

☎ 02965

Gouged by two large bays, this oddly shaped peninsula is mostly a flat, bleak and dry landscape of unrelenting low shrubs. Driving along, you'll spot guanacos and perhaps some rheas or armadillos. Once you get to the coastlines, however, the real celebrity wildlife awaits: sea lions, elephant seals, southern right whales, Commerson's dolphins, Magellanic penguins and – if you're very, very lucky – orcas (who have been filmed here snatching pinnipeds straight off the beach) can be seen. June through mid-December is whale-watching season, penguins waddle around from October to March, and elephant seals and sea lions lounge around all year. Commerson's dolphins are best September to November, while dusky dolphins are spotted all year. The orca phenomenon happens during high tide from February to April – and you have about a 3% chance of witnessing it, so don't get your hopes up too high.

As you enter the **Reserva Faunística Península Valdés** (admission US$12) you'll pass the thin 5km neck of the peninsula. If you're on a tour bus, it will stop at a good interpretation center and lookout. Squint northwards for a glimpse of **Isla de los Pájaros**. This small island inspired Antoine de Saint-Exupéry's description of a hat, or 'boa swallowing an elephant,' in his book *The Little Prince* (from 1929 to 1931 Saint-Exupéry flew as a postal manager in the area). Also, keep an eye out for Argentina's lowest spots, salt flats **Salina Grande** and **Salina Chico** (42m below sea level).

Caleta Valdés is a bay sheltered by a long gravel spit and favored by elephant seals. Just north of here lives a substantial colony of burrowing Magellanic penguins. At **Punta Norte** a mixed group of sea lions and elephant seals snoozes, with the occasional orca pod keeping an eye out offshore. Watch for armadillos in the parking lot here.

Puerto Pirámide – a sunny, sandy, shrubby, one-street kinda town – is home to 300 souls. You can stay here, the peninsula's only sizable settlement, to enjoy a calmer spot and be closer to wildlife attractions. Services, however, are very limited compared to Puerto Madryn (there's one ATM that may or may not work). Scuba diving and area tours are definitely available though. Boat rides (US$20) outside whale-watching season aren't really worth it unless you adore shorebirds and sea lions, though there's a chance of seeing dolphins.

Buses from Puerto Madryn leave for Puerto Pirámide twice daily in summer (US$3.25, 1½ hours). Schedules are less frequent in the off-season.

Sleeping & Eating
In summer, call ahead to reserve any of these places. All are located near the main road.

Camping Puerto Pirámides (☎ 495-084; campsites per person US$1.75) Gravel sites sheltered by shrubs and dunes; beach access available, showers US35¢ extra.

Hostel Bahía Ballenas (☎ 495-050; dm US$10) The only hostel in town, with huge 18-bed, sex-segregated dorm (no doubles). New, with good kitchen and common area. Bike rentals and tours available.

Casa de la Tia Alicia (☎ 495-046; per person US$10) Just three basic but comfortable rooms, all with shared outside bathrooms. Rustic.

La Posta (☎ 495-036; www.postapiramides.com.ar; d US$23) Great for families or groups, with three cute apartments with kitchen. One four-bed apartment costs US$80; dorms are coming.

Estancia del Sol (☎ 495-007; d US$31) Good midrange place with comfy rooms and large breakfast area.

Refugio de Luna (☎ 495-083; dm/d US$16/33) Small place with only 10 beds total; two-level suite available for US$58. Artsy, natural and relaxing place with beautiful common room.

Among food options, La Estación, across from the YPF gas station, has a nice deck and atmosphere. There are many restaurants by the water, down the first street to the right as you enter town; La Posta, with wood deck out front, is a good inexpensive choice.

TRELEW
☎ 02965 / pop 95,000
Trelew is not an exciting city, but does have a pleasant bustling center with leafy plaza and some historical buildings. There's an excellent dinosaur-oriented museum, and it's a convenient base for exploring the nearby Welsh villages of Gaiman and Dolavon, along with the noisy Punta Tombo penguin reserve. Trelew's major cultural event is late October's **Eisteddfod de Chubut**, celebrating Welsh traditions.

Information
There's a **tourist office** (☎ 420-139; cnr San Martín & Mitre) on the plaza, where many banks with ATMs can be found, along with the **post office** (cnr Av 25 de Mayo & Mitre).

Sights
In the former railway station, the nicely presented **Museo Regional** (cnr Fontana & 9 de Julio; admission US$0.75; ☻ 8am-8pm Mon-Fri, 2-8pm Sun) has good Welsh artifacts; check out the glass 'breast' bottle and the hat iron. Nearby is the excellent **Museo Paleontológico Egidio Feruglio** (admission US$5; ☻ 9am-8pm Mon-Fri, 10am-8pm Sat & Sun) with realistic dinosaur exhibits. Don't miss the 1.7m ammonite.

Tours
Travel agencies organizing tours to Península Valdés (opposite) and Punta Tombo (p150) include **Alcamar Travel** (☎ 421-213; San Martín 146) and **Nievemar** (☎ 434-114; Italia 20). Tours are similarly priced to those from Puerto Madryn. There are also tours to see black-and-white Commerson's dolphins (US$20, best viewed

September to November). Request English-speaking guides beforehand.

Sleeping

Camping Patagonia (☎ 154-06907; campsites per person US$2.25) Seven kilometers outside town, off Ruta 7 on the way to Rawson. Green and clean, with shady sites near river.

Residencial Argentino (☎ 436-134; Moreno 93; s/d US$10/15) Full of funky murals, kitschy decor and plain rooms, the best overlooking the plaza. Near the bus terminal; TV costs US$1.75 extra.

Residencial Rivadavia (☎ 434-472; hotel_riv@infovia .com.ar; Rivadavia 55; s/d from US$11/15) The best and priciest rooms are upstairs, where it's brighter; downstairs is the old wing, with bearable rooms.

Hotel Touring Club (☎ 425-790; htouring@speedy .com.ar; Fontana 240; s/d US$16/26) Has classic old feel, with marble touches and decent small rooms (though inside ones are depressing) with cable TV. Breakfast is served in the atmospheric café downstairs.

Hotel Galicia (☎ 433-802; www.hotelgalicia.com.ar; 9 de Julio 214; s/d from US$16/29) Decent doubles with carpet and cable TV, but some singles are claustrophobically tiny and windowless.

Eating & Drinking

El Norte supermarket (cnr 9 de Julio & Rivadavia) For cheap takeout.

La Bodeguita (Belgrano 374; mains US$3.25-10) Modern, popular place big on pizzas, but also does meats, pasta and seafood. Attentive service and family atmosphere.

Confitería Touring Club (Fontana 240; mains US$4-6.50) Excellent for its old-time atmosphere. Breakfast, sandwiches and alcoholic drinks available.

El Quijote (Belgrano 361; mains 4-7) One word: *parrilla*.

El Viejo Molino (Gales 250; mains US$5-10) Beautifully renovated old mill, with lofty and artsy interior. Look for the BBQ window grill; also pastas, fancy salads and tango on weekends.

San Javier (San Martín 57) Café, ice-cream parlor and sidewalk tables up front, but bar serving cans of Guinness and Kilkenny in back. Fancy, modern atmosphere.

Getting There & Around

The airport (☎ 433-433) is 6km north of town (taxis US$3). **Aerolíneas Argentinas** (☎ 420-170; www .aerolineasargentinas.com; 25 de Mayo 33) and **LADE** (☎ 435-740), at the bus station, provide services.

Trelew's bus station is six blocks northeast of downtown. Destinations include Puerto Madryn (US$2.25, one hour), Gaiman (US75¢, 30 minutes), Comodoro Rivadavia (US$13, five hours), Viedma (US$17, seven hours), Bariloche (US$35, 14 hours) and Buenos Aires (US$45, 20 hours).

Car-rental stands are at the airport and in town; cheapest rentals run about US$50 with 200km.

AROUND TRELEW
Gaiman
☎ 02965 / pop 5500

For a taste of Wales in Patagonia, head 17km west of Trelew to Gaiman. The streets are calm and wide and the buildings nondescript and low; on hot days the local boys swim in the nearby river. The real reason travelers visit Gaiman, however, is to down pastries at one of several good **Welsh teahouses**. Most open around 3pm and offer unlimited tea and homemade sweets for US$6.50 (eat a very light lunch). To get oriented visit the **tourist office** (☎ 491-014; www.gaiman.gov.ar; cnr Rivadavia & Belgrano).

The small **Museo Histórico Regional Gales** (admission US35¢; ☻ 3-7pm Tue-Sun) details Welsh colonization with old pioneer photographs and household items. Support Joaquín Alonso's eccentricity at **Parque El Desafío** (admission US$2.25; ☻ dawn-dusk), a garden–forest area methodically strewn with bottles, cans, and even old TV sets.

Gaiman is an easy day trip from Trelew, but if you want to stay try homey **Dyffryn Gwirdd** (☎ 491-777; www.dwhosteria.com.ar; Tello 103; s/d US$15/21; ℗), with seven simple but good rooms and pleasant atmosphere, or clean and comfortable **Hostería Gwesty Tywi B&B** (☎ 491-292; www.advance.com.ar/usuarios/gwestywi; MD Jones 342; s/d US$15/23). There's also camping outside the town center (ask at the tourist office).

Frequent buses arrive from Trelew (US75¢, 30 minutes).

Reserva Provincial Punta Tombo

From September to April, over a half-million Magellanic penguins breed at Punta Tombo, 115km south of Trelew (1½ hours by road). It's the largest penguin colony outside Antarctica. Other area birds include rheas, cormorants, giant petrels, kelp gulls and oystercatchers. You may also spy some land critters such as armadillos, foxes and guanacos on the way there.

You can get very close to the birds for photos, but don't try to touch them – they'll nip. To get there, arrange a tour in Trelew or Puerto Madryn (from US$29 plus US$6.50 admission) or hire a taxi (US$59). Car rentals are also a possibility. For more information, see the Puerto Madryn and Trelew sections.

COMODORO RIVADAVIA
☎ 0297 / pop 142,000

Comodoro Rivadavia is popular only as a convenient pit stop along Argentina's long eastern coastline. It's a homely city with busy streets and the ugliest cathedral you'll likely ever see. Founded in 1901, Comodoro boomed a few years later when well-diggers made the country's first major petroleum strike. The state soon dominated the sector through now-privatized YPF (Argentina is self-sufficient in petroleum, with over one-third of it coming from this area). For a neat view hike 212m to the *mirador* atop Cerro Chenque.

Information

Comodoro's other services include banks with ATMs (along San Martín).

Cambio Thaler (Mitre 943)

Chilean consulate (☎ 446-2414; Brown 456, 1st fl).

Information counter At the bus station.

Post office (cnr San Martín & Moreno)

Tourist office (☎ 446-2376; www.comodoro.gov.ar; Rivadavia 430)

Sights

Die-hard petroleum fans head to **Museo del Petróleo** (☎ 455-9558; admission US$1.75; ☷ 8am-1pm & 3-8pm Tue-Fri, 3-8pm Sat & Sun), which covers the social and historical aspects of petroleum development. Tours available; call ahead. From San Martín, take the 7 Laprida or 8 Palazzo bus (US40¢, 10 minutes); get off at La Anónima supermarket.

Sleeping

Comodoro is a transport hub, and hotels can get full later in the day.

Hostería Rua Marina (☎ 446-8777; Belgrano 738; s/d from US$12/23) The rooms are fine, if small, but are dark and face the indoor hallway. Best are rooms 18, 19 and 20, with outside windows.

Cari-Hue (☎ 447-2946; Belgrano 563; s/d US$15/28) Seven clean and tidy budget rooms, all with

shared bathroom. The indoor patio is strewn with plants and garden gnomes.

Hotel Victoria (☎ 446-0725; Belgrano 585; s/d US$25/31; P) Larger midrange place with good modern rooms with cable TV.

Also recommended:

Hotel El Español (☎ 446-0116; 9 de Julio 950; s/d US$8/15) Very simple; upstairs rooms brighter.

25 de Mayo (☎ 447-2350; 25 de Mayo 989; d US$15) Very basic, with outdoor hall and kitchen access.

Belgrano (☎ 447-8439; Belgrano 546; d US$29, s/d with shared bathroom US$12/20) Nice halls and simple homey rooms.

Eating & Drinking

El Norte supermarket (cnr Rivadavia & Pellegrini) Cheap takeout.

Patio de Comidas (cnr Güemes & San Martín; meals under US$3) Good and cheap.

La Barra (San Martín 686; mains US$1.75-7.50) Popular café serving pastas, salads and meats, along with plenty of cocktails.

Café del Sol (San Martín 502; snacks US$2-4) Hip and softly lit café which doubles as a late-night bar. Serves breakfast.

Molly Malone (San Martín 292; mains US$3-5) Small and funky bar/restaurant with tea, snacks, meals and alcoholic drinks.

La Rastra (Rivadavia 348; mains US$3.50-9) One of the better *parrillas* in town, and also serves pasta and seafood.

Los Tres Chinos (Rivadavia 341) Modern, large *tenedor libre* for US$5.25.

Getting There & Around

The **airport** (☎ 454-8093) is 8km east of center (bus US40¢). **Aerolíneas Argentinas** (☎ 444-0050; www.aerolineasargentinas.com; 9 de Julio 870) and **LADE** (☎ 447-0585; Rivadavia 360) provide services.

The bus terminal is in the center of town. Destinations include Trelew (US$13, 5½ hours), Los Antiguos (US$15, six hours), Esquel (US$20, nine hours), Bariloche (US$30, 14 hours), Río Gallegos (US$22, 11 hours) and Buenos Aires (US$56, 24 hours). Buses to El Calafate all go through Río Gallegos. Chilean destination include Coyhaique, Chile (US$23, nine hours, twice weekly) and Puerto Montt (US$43, 22 hours, three times weekly).

LOS ANTIGUOS
☎ 02963 / pop 2400

Situated on the shores of Lago Buenos Aires, Los Antiguos is a little oasis with rows of poplar trees sheltering *chacras* (farms) of cherries, strawberries, apples, apricots and peaches. Travelers come to cross the border into Chile, but getting here via RN 40 can be an adventure in itself.

Los Antiguos' **Fiesta de la Cereza** (cherry festival) occurs the first or second weekend in January, and the nearby countryside has good **hiking** and **fishing**. The **tourist office** (☎ 491-261; www.losantiguos.gov.ar; 11 de Julio 446) has transport information. There's one bank with ATM.

Two kilometers east of center lies cypress-sheltered **Camping Municipal** (☎ 491-265; campsites per person US75¢, tent US$1). Windowless, six-bunk log cabins also available (per person US$6.50). **Hospedaje Padillo** (☎ 491-140; San Martín 44 Sur; dm US$10) is a friendly, family-run place right where Chaltén Travel buses stop; it has good dorms, one double with bathroom (US$23) and a nice cooking area. For more comfort try **Hotel Argentino** (☎ 491-132; s/d US$16/26), which offers decent modern rooms. **Agua Grande** (☎ 491-165; 11 de Julio 871) is the best restaurant in town.

Buses cross the border to Chile Chico (p517) three times daily. From November through March, **Chaltén Travel** (www.chaltentravel .com) goes to El Chaltén on even-numbered days (US$42, 13 hours). Other destinations include Perito Moreno (US$3.25, one hour), Río Gallegos (US$33, 16 hours) and Comodoro Rivadavia (US$15, seven hours). There are weekly Tacsa buses to both Esquel (US$45, 10 hours) and El Chaltén (US$42, 14 hours) though they may be unreliable. The gradual paving of RN 40 and subsequent future services will keep transport options in a flux, so get current information.

EL CHALTÉN
☎ 02962 / pop winter 500, summer 1800

One of Patagonia's premier traveler magnets, this small and homely but fast-growing village is set in a pretty river valley. The reason travelers come are the extraordinary snowcapped towers of the **Fitz Roy range**, offering plenty of world-class hiking and camping along with some of the most stunning mountain scenery you'll ever witness. Climbers from around the world are drawn here for their chance to summit **Cerro Fitz Roy** (3441m), as well as other peaks. Pack for wind, rain and cold temperatures even in summer, when views of the peaks can be obscured. If the sun is out, however, El Chaltén is paradise on earth – but come and see it soon, as the road to El

Calafate is being paved and changes are sure to come.

All water sources in the area are potable, so help keep them clean. Note that El Chaltén is within national park boundaries, and rules regarding fires and cleaning distances from rivers must be followed (park headquarters has details). El Chaltén mostly shuts down from April to October. For more information see www.elchalten.com.

Information
On the left just before the bridge into town, **park headquarters** (☎ 493-004) has maps and hiking information; day buses automatically stop here. You need to register for anything longer than a day hike. To find the **tourist office** (☎ 493011) look for the satellite dish and picket fence after crossing the bridge into town.

Bring enough Argentine pesos for your stay in El Chaltén. There are no banks, ATMs or exchange houses, and the few places that take traveler's checks, credit cards or US dollars offer poor exchange rates. Many travelers have left sooner than they wanted to because they ran out of money.

Locutorios and limited internet access are available; **Rancho Grande Hostel** (☎ 493-005; www .hostelspatagonia.com; San Martín 724) has the best internet connection, but it's not cheap. A decent selection of camping food and supplies is readily available at the small supermarkets in town. Gear like stoves, fuel, sleeping bags, tents and warm clothes can be bought or rented from Camping Center, Eolia and Viento Oeste, all on San Martín (the main drag).

If you need a mountain/climbing/ice-trekking guide, visit **Casa de Guias** (Costanera Sur s/n; www.casadeguias.com.ar); they speak English and also offer rock-climbing classes.

Activities
One popular hike goes to **Laguna Torre** and the base camp for skilled technical climbers attempting the spire of **Cerro Torre** (3128m); it's three hours one way. Another climbs from Camping Madsen to a signed junction, where a side trail leads to backcountry campsites at Laguna Capri. The main trail continues gently to Río Blanco, base camp for the Cerro Fitz Roy climb, and then very steeply to **Laguna de los Tres** (four hours one way). The hike to Laguna Toro is seven hours one way, so most folks camp overnight (register at park

headquarters). You can rent horses in town for some of these hikes.

Sleeping

Prices following are for January and February, when you should arrive with reservations.

Rancho Grande Hostel (☎ 493-005; www.hostelspat agonia.com; San Martín 724; dm/d US$10/42) El Chaltén's largest hostel, with spacious, modern dorms and common areas. Good services and busy atmosphere. Great doubles, all with bathroom. Takes credit cards and travelers checks; HI discount.

Albergue Patagonia (☎ 493-019; patagoniahostel@ yahoo.com; San Martín 493; dm US$10) Cozy areas, an intimate homey feel and small dorms make for a very friendly stay. Bathrooms can get cramped, however. Bike rentals available; HI discount.

Condor de los Andes (☎ 493-101; www.condorde losandes.com; cnr Río de las Vueltas & Halvorsen; dm/d US$10/45) Small hostel with good common spaces and backpacker feel. Each dorm (four to six beds) has its own bathroom. HI discount.

Hospedaje La Base (☎ 493-031; cnr Lago del Desierto & Hensen; dm US$10) Good spacious rooms with bath, all facing outside and with kitchen access. Rooms 5 and 6 share an inside kitchen with dining area; great for large groups. Video loft in reception area.

Albergue Hem Herhu (☎ 493-224; hugoacostacastilla@ hotmail.com; Las Loicas s/n; dm US$10) Unkempt front yard at this small grungy place, but laid-back with spacious dorms. Just 16 beds; two- and four-bed cabañas also available (US$54/65).

Albergue Los Nires (☎ 493-009; www.elchalten.com /losnires; Lago del Desierto s/n; dm/d US$10/42) Rather impersonal hotel with cold tiled halls. There are 30 good-sized rooms, some with carpet.

Albergue del Lago (☎ 493-245; eduardomonacochalten@ yahoo.com.ar; Lago del Desierto 135; dm US$10, campsites per person from US$3.25) Not the best atmosphere, with rather bare dining area and small dorm. Rooms in back are better.

Nothofagus B&B (☎ 493-087; www.elchalten.com/no thofagus; Hensen s/n; s/d from US$25/26) Seven carpeted, warm and cozy rooms in this charming guesthouse. Friendly, helpful, spotless and family-run; four rooms share two bathrooms. No smoking.

There are two free campsites. Confluencia is smaller and right at the entrance to town. Camping Madsen, at the other end of town, is larger and a bit more private; it's also near the start of the Fitz Roy hike. Both have an outhouse and potable river water nearby. Campfires are not allowed; do all washing at least 100 steps from the river. El Refugio offers US$1.30 showers.

Eating & Drinking

Lunchboxes are available at most hostels/ hotels and at some restaurants for about US$5.

Patagonicus (cnr Güemes & Madsen; pizzas US$3.25-8) Popular pizzería baking 20 kinds of pie.

El Bodegón Cervecería (San Martín s/n; mains US$3.25-10) Wonderfully cozy pub with creative driftwood decor, good homemade brews and feisty female beer-master. Pizza, pastas and *locro* available.

Fuegia Bistro (San Martín 493; mains US$4.50-8; ☯ dinner Mon-Sat) Upscale and serving some of the best food in town: lamb in ginger sauce, trout with sage butter and vegetarian crepes.

Ruca Mahuida (Terrey 104; mains US$5.50-12) Excellent restaurant serving dishes like squash soufflé, salmon ravioli and venison in berry sauce.

Estepa (cnr Cerro Solo & Antonio Rojo; mains US$6.50-11) Well-prepared and tasty dishes like lamb with Calafate sauce, trout ravioli, spinach crepes and eggplant lasagna. Plenty of pizzas and it also makes lunch boxes.

Getting There & Away

The following schedules are for January and February; during other months services are less frequent or nonexistent. After paving work is done, the travel time to El Calafate will be much shorter.

There are several daily buses to El Calafate (US$16; 4½ hours). **Chalten Travel** (www .chaltentravel.com) goes to Los Antiguos from mid-November to mid-April, but only on odd-numbered days (US$54, 13 hours). It also provides transport to Lago del Desierto (US$12 round-trip, one hour), where it's possible to hike and take a boat into Chile.

EL CALAFATE
☎ 02902 / pop 8000

Fast-growing El Calafate has become a gungho Patagonian destination, but despite its touristy facade makes a pleasant-enough pit stop for a few days. Its prime location between El Chaltén and Torres del Paine (Chile) also means that most travelers pass through here at some point or another, and fortunately for them there is one incredible, unmissable

ARGENTINA

attraction: the dynamic Perito Moreno Glacier, located 80km away in Parque Nacional Los Glaciares (p156).

Information

There are several banks with ATMs in town. Many tour agencies line Av Libertador.

Cambio Thaler (9 de Julio 57) Changes traveler's checks.

La Cueva (☎ 492-417; Moyano 839; ☼ Sep-May) Is a basic mountaineers *refugio* that organizes area treks.

Parques Nacionales (☎ 491-545; Av Libertador 1302) Issues trekking permits, fishing licenses and hiking information.

Post office (Av Libertador 1133)

Tourist office (☎ 491-090; www.elcalafate.gov.ar) At the bus terminal.

Sights & Activities

Within town there's not much to do besides souvenir shopping and people-watching, but a few distractions exist. **Centro de Interpretación Histórica** (☎ 492-799; cnr Brown & Bonarelli; admission US$4; ☼ 10am-9pm) explains the history of Patagonia via photos, diagrams and a video. It's just north of the center. **Laguna Nimez** (admission US75¢; ☼ 9am-9pm Oct-Mar) is a wetlands sanctuary 15 minutes' walk from town. Walk north on Alem, go over the small white bridge and at the *cervecería* (brewery restaurant) jog right, then left. There's also good horse-riding in the area.

Sleeping

In January and February reservations are crucial.

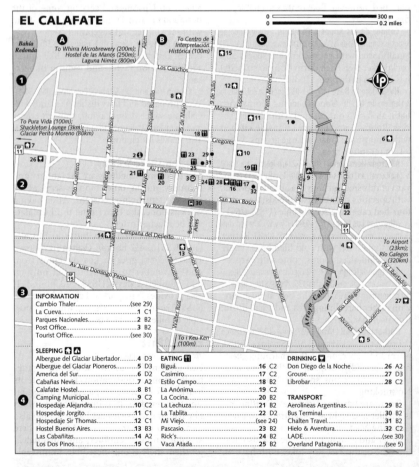

EL CALAFATE

Camping Municipal (☎ 492-622; José Pantín s/n) Woodsy creekside sites with firepits. Being renovated at research time so contact for prices.

Hospedaje Jorgito (☎ 491-323; hjor2@latinmail.com; Moyano 943; campsites per person US$3.25, r US$26, with shared bathroom US$20) Twelve bright, warm and old-fashioned rooms, all in a large family house with kitchen. Pleasant orchard sites.

Los Dos Pinos (☎ 491-271; www.losglaciares.com /losdospinos; 9 de Julio 358; campsites per person US$3.50, dm/d US$6.50/42, cabañas US$80-97) A veritable compound of lodging, hardly personal but there is something for everyone. There is a large kitchen/dining area in separate building. Decent campsites.

Hostel de las Manos (☎ 492-996; www.hosteldelas manos.com.ar; Feruglio 59; dm US$8) Small hostel with intimate and bright common area, but tiny dorms with outside lockers. Breakfast extra (US$1.75). North of center; free pickup from bus station.

Albergue del Glaciar Pioneros (☎ 491-243; www .glaciar.com; Los Pioneros 255; dm US$8.50, d US$29-44) Pleasant and modern hostel with small, clean dorms and spacious common areas. Small restaurant on premises. Superior doubles are excellent; HI discount.

Calafate Hostel (☎ 492-450; www.calafatehostels .com; Moyano 1226; dm US$8-9, d US$36-42) Huge, beautiful log cabin hostel surrounded by balconies inside and out. A bit impersonal and almost hotel-like (good for large groups). Many services including restaurant; HI discount.

America del Sur (☎ 493-525; www.americahostel .com.ar; Puerto Deseado 151; dm/d US$10/50) One of Calafate's best lodgings, with wonderfully airy common spaces (and views), spacious modern dorms (each with its own bath) and exceptional service. Clean and tidy, with floor heating.

Hospedaje Sir Thomas (☎ 492-220; www.cotecal.com .ar/hospedajesirthomas; Espora 257; s/d US$34/39) Fourteen beautiful and tidy rooms with bath. Well-run, friendly and intimate.

Las Cabañitas (☎ 491-118; lascabanitas@cotecal.com .ar; Valentín Feilberg 218; cabañas US$39-53) Just five small and dark but very cute cabañas, along with one room, are available at this friendly place.

Cabañas Nevis (☎ 493-180; www.cabanasnevis.com .ar; Av Libertador 1696; cabañas US$80-104) Fourteen cute, two-story A-frame cabins with four to eight beds, kitchen and cable TV, all on a grassy lot. Just outside center; English spoken.

Also recommended:

i Keu Ken (☎ 495-175; www.patagoniaikeuken.com .ar; Pontoriero 171; dm US$10, d US$33) Up a hill; cool common areas and good clean dorms. Free pickup.

Albergue del Glaciar Libertador (☎ 491-792; www .glaciar.com; Av Libertador 587; dm/d US$10/44) Modern large hostel, with all rooms facing a dark, tall inside courtyard. HI discount.

Hospedaje Alejandra (☎ 491-328; Espora 60; d US$20) Seven small, homey rooms with shared bathrooms in family house.

Hostel Buenos Aires (☎ 491-147; buenosaires@ cotecal.com.ar; Buenos Aires 296; dm US$8, d US$26-33) Small, dark and mazelike, with tiny kitchen.

Eating

In January and February make reservations at higher-end places.

La Anónima (cnr Av Libertador & Perito Moreno) Cheap takeout.

La Tablita (☎ 491-065; Colonel Rosales 28; mains US$4.25-6.50; ☯ closed Wed lunch) Very popular for its great *parrillada*, with lots of sides and dessert. Reserve ahead.

Casimiro (☎ 492-590; Libertador 963; mains US$5-14) Very fancy place with well-prepared dishes of homemade pastas, risotto, lamb stew and grilled trout. Upscale rustic atmosphere and extensive wine list. Also try nearby sister restaurant Biguá.

La Lechuza (Av Libertador 1301; pizzas US$6.50-10) Large variety of excellent pizzas, along with inexpensive sandwiches, salads and empanadas. Warm brick atmosphere; popular.

Pura Vida (Av Libertador 1876; mains US$6.50-10; ☯ dinner Thu-Tue) Awesome healthy food and huge portions. Try the gnocchi with saffron rice, rabbit with cream or Patagonian lamb stew. Ten minutes' walk west of center.

Pascasio (☎ 492055; 25 de Mayo 52; mains US$7-14) One of Calafate's best, serving exotic dishes like hare in wild mushroom sauce, venison loin wrapped in bacon and ñandú with leek pudding.

Also recommended:

La Cocina (Av Libertador 1245; mains US$3-8; ☯ closed Tue) Intimate, popular place serving excellent pastas.

Rick's (Av Libertador 1091; mains US$5-10) *Parrillada libre* for US$9.50, but try the huge à la carte *bife de chorizo* (salad bar included). Mi Viejo, next door, has similar menu but better service.

Vaca Atada (Av Libertador 1176; mains US$5.25-8; ☯ closed Wed) Small and upscale, with good dishes of fish, pastas and grilled lamb.

Estilo Campo (cnr Gregores & 9 de Julio; lunch US$6, dinner US$6.50) All-you-can-eat place with a good range of dishes. Drinks extra.

Drinking

Librobar (Av Libertador 1015) Pocket-sized café-bar with great views over Libertador. Small, friendly and sports a wall of books. Snacks available.

Shackleton Lounge (Av Libertador 3287) Three kilometers from center, but worth it for the good music, strong daiquiris and Shackleton theme. Two levels, with artsy laid-back lounge on top.

Grouse (Av Libertador 351) Celtic pub with cozy ambience, glass ceiling, dart board and Guinness. Occasional live music.

Whirra Microbrewery (Brown 1391; ⊙ closed Tue) On the way to Laguna Nimez is this small place serving snacks and local microbrews.

Don Diego de la Noche (Av Libertador 1603) Cozy, long-running place offering live music like tango, guitar and folklore. Also serves dinner, and the bar is open 'til 5am.

Getting There & Around

Book your flight into and out of El Calafate as soon as possible; flights have been booked solid all summer in the past.

The **airport** (☎ 492-230) is 23km east of town; the departure tax is US$6. **TransPatagonia** (☎ 493-766) has shuttle services for US$4; taxis cost US$9. **Aerolíneas Argentinas** (☎ 0870-222-86527; www.aerolineasargentinas.com; 9 de Julio 57) and **LADE** (☎ 491-262), at bus terminal, provide services.

Bus destinations include Río Gallegos (US$11, five hours), El Chaltén (US$16, 4½ hours) and Puerto Natales, Chile (US$16, five hours).

In summer, **Chalten Travel** (www.chaltentravel.com; Av Libertador 1174) and **Overland Patagonia** (www.overlandpatagonia; Los Pioneros 255) go from El Calafate to Bariloche via adventurous Ruta 40. Prices range from US$120 to US$180.

Car rentals in El Calafate will cost you around US$52 per day with 200km.

PARQUE NACIONAL LOS GLACIARES

Few glaciers on earth can match the activity and excitement of the blue-hued **Perito Moreno Glacier**. Its 60m jagged ice-peaks sheer off and crash-land with huge splashes and thunderous rifle-cracks, birthing small tidal waves and large bobbing icebergs – while your neck hairs rise a-tingling. It's the highlight of **Parque Nacional Los Glaciares** (admission US$10) and measures 30km long, 5km wide and 60m high. What makes this glacier exceptional is that it's constantly advancing – up to 2m per day – while constantly calving icebergs from its face. While most of the world's glaciers are receding, the Perito Moreno Glacier is considered 'stable.' Every once in a while, however, part of its façade advances far enough to reach the Península de Magallanes and dam the Brazo Rico arm of Lago Argentino. This causes tremendous pressure to build up, and after a few years a river cuts through the dam and eventually collapses it – with spectacular results. The last time this happened was in March 2006.

The Perito Moreno Glacier was born to be a tourist attraction. The ideally located Península de Magallanes is close enough to the glacier to provide glorious panoramas, but far enough away to be safe. A long series of catwalks and platforms give everyone a great view. Hanging around for a few hours, just looking at the glacier and awaiting the next great calving, can be an existential experience.

Most tours cost US$29 for transport, guide and a few hours at the glacier; some 'alternative' tours include a short hike or boat ride for a few more pesos. Practically all hostels and hotels offer tours to their guests. If you don't want a tour, head to El Calafate's bus station; round-trip transport only costs US$20. Buses leave at 9am and 3pm and return at 4pm and 8pm. Groups can hire a *remise* for about US$60 (negotiate rates, times and what is included); this gives more flexibility and the option to visit nearby *estancias*. Consider seeing the glacier later in the day, when many of the crowds have gone (afternoon tours are also available).

There are several other kinds of tours, including an all-day boat ride to different glaciers (US$65) and a fun 'Minitrekking' excursion, which has you in crampons hiking on the glacier (US$80). **Hielo & Aventura** (☎ 492-205; www.hieloyaventura.com; Av Libertador 935) is a recommended tour agency.

RÍO GALLEGOS

☎ 02966 / pop 88,000

Río Gallegos is certainly not the world cup of tourist destinations. Optimists, however, can point out the city's lively downtown and improving facade: modern buildings are going up and the boardwalk is being made over. There are some amazingly low tides here (they dip down 14m) and some of the continent's best fly-fishing is nearby. You can even take a tour to see penguins. Still, most travelers stop in this coal-shipping, oil-refining and wool-raising port city just long enough to catch the next bus to El Calafate, Puerto Natales or Ushuaia.

Information

Most banks with ATMs are on or near Av Roca.

Chilean consulate (☎ 422-364; Mariano Moreno 136).
Immigration office (☎ 420-205; Urqiuza 144)
Municipal tourist office (☎ 436-920; www.riogal legos.gov.ar; cnr Av Roca & Córdoba)

Post office (cnr Avs Roca & San Martín)
Provincial tourist office (☎ 438-725; Av Roca 863)
Thaler Cambio (cnr Av San Martín & Alcorta)
Tourist office (☎ 442-159) Bus terminal's tourist office.

Sights & Activities

The **Museo Padre Molina** (Ramón y Cajal; admission free; ☺ 10am-7pm Mon-Fri, 11am-7pm Sat & Sun) is an odd combination of dinosaur dioramas and strange modern art. In an 1890s house typical of southern Patagonia nestles the small and scanty **Museo de los Pioneros** (cnr El Cano & Alberdi; admission free; ☺ 10am-7:30pm). Note Saint-Exupéry's photo in the stairway. Get inside a local's head as to why the Malvinas are Argentine at **Museo Malvinas Argentinas** (Pasteur 74; admission free; ☺ 1:30-7pm Mon-Fri).

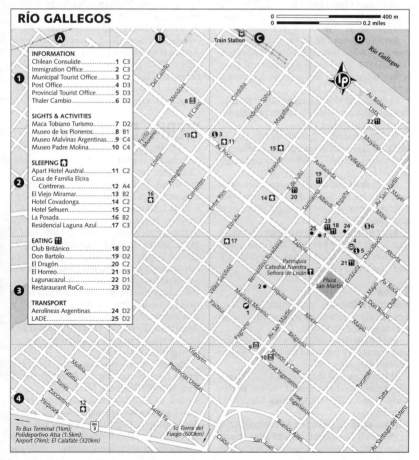

RÍO GALLEGOS

Tours

Cabo Vírgenes, 140km southeast of Río Gallegos, hosts a large penguin rookery from October to March; **Maca Tobiano Turismo** (☎ 422-466; Roca 998) offers eight-hour excursions for US$29 (plus US$2.25 park admission).

Sleeping

Book ahead in summer.

Polideportivo Atsa (☎ 442-310; cnr Asturias & Yugoslavia; campsites per person US$1.75, tent US$1.75) Camping sites about 500m southwest of bus terminal.

Casa de Familia Elcira Contreras (☎ 429-856; Zuccarino 431; dm US$7) Clean and homey dorms have kitchen access. One double available (US$16). It's far from the center but a 10-minute walk from the bus terminal (taxi US$1.75).

Residencial Laguna Azul (☎ 422-165; Estrada 298; s/d US$13/18) Cramped rooms, some with bunks and tiled floors. Ask for bigger rooms.

Hotel Covadonga (☎ 420-190; hotelcovadongargl@ hotmail.com; Av Roca 1244; s/d US$16/25, with shared bathroom US$11/18; **P**) This is a central old place with a bit of charm and good budget rooms with cable TV.

La Posada (☎ 436445; Ameghino 331; s/d US$23/26) Good rooms surrounding an internal garden in an attractive older place.

El Viejo Miramar (☎ 430401; Av Roca 1630; s/d US$23/29) Ten wonderful rooms: clean, carpeted and with cable TV. Friendly and excellent value.

Hotel Sehuen (☎ 425683; www.hotelsehuen.unlugar .com; Rawson 160; s/d US$23/30; **P**) Serene hotel with a bright lobby and lovely rooms with carpet and cable TV.

Apart Hotel Austral (☎ 434314; www.apartaustral .com; Av Roca 1505; s/d from US$26/39) Good small, modern and carpeted rooms with cable TV and many with kitchenette.

Eating

Restaurant RoCo (Av Roca 1157; mains US$3.25-8) Clean, upscale place with good service, cooking up meats, seafood and pasta.

Don Bartolo (Sarmiento 125; mains US$3.25-10) Meat and pizzas. Try the *vacio portion* – it's good enough for two.

El Horreo (Av Roca 862; mains US$4-7.50) Has it all: crepes, omelettes, paella, meats, pastas, seafood and regional specialties. Classic old standby.

Lagunacazul (cnr Lista & Sarmiento; mains US$4.25-8; ☾ closed Mon) Fresh creations and artsy atmosphere make this Río Gallegos' best restaurant.

Club Británico (Av Roca 935; mains US$5.25-8) Dark and stuffy, but classic atmosphere for lamb and pastas. Bring your ascot.

El Dragón (9 de Julio 39; buffet US$6) When you just want to eat it all.

Getting There & Away

Río Gallegos' airport (☎ 442-340) is 7km from center (taxis US$4). **Aerolíneas Argentinas** (☎ 422-020; www.aerolineasargentinas.com; Av San Martín 545) and **LADE** (☎ 422-316; Fagnano 53) provide services.

The bus terminal is about 2km from the center, on RN 3 (bus 'B' US50¢, taxis US$1.75). Destinations include El Calafate (US$11, four hours), Ushuaia (US$29, 12 hours), Comodoro Rivadavia (US$22, 11 hours), Puerto Madryn (US$37, 19 hours), Río Grande (US$21, eight hours), Río Turbio (US$10, five hours) and Buenos Aires (US$79, 36 hours). Chilean destinations include Punta Arenas (US$10, five hours) and Puerto Natales (US$13, six hours). In high season buy tickets to Punta Arenas one to two days in advance. If buses to Puerto Natales are full, try going via Río Turbio.

TIERRA DEL FUEGO

Reluctantly shared by both Argentina and Chile, this 'land of fire' really is the end of the world. Its faraway location has drawn explorers since the days of Magellan and Darwin, and this tradition continues with today's travelers. A triangular archipelago surrounded by the stormy South Atlantic and the Strait of Magellan, Tierra del Fuego offers plenty of natural beauty: scenic glaciers, lush forests, astounding mountains, clear waterways and a dramatic sea coast. The region's largest city, Ushuaia, is also the 'southernmost city in the world' – a major draw for list-tickers – but has also become the main gateway to wondrous Antarctica. Tierra del Fuego is isolated and hard to reach, but for true adventure-seekers in Argentina it's a must.

Passing ships gave Tierra del Fuego its name: they spotted distant shoreline campfires that the Yámana (or Yahgan) people tended. In 1520 Magellan paid a visit, but it wasn't land he was seeking – it was passage to the Asian spice islands. So as ships sailed by, the indigenous Ona (or Selknam) and Haush continued hunting land animals, while the

Yámana and Alacalufe ('Canoe Indians') lived on seafood and marine mammals. Spain's withdrawal from the continent in the early 1800s, however, brought on European settlement – and the demise of these indigenous peoples.

RÍO GRANDE
☎ 02964 / pop 63,000

Unless you're an avid fisherman, there's no reason to stop for long in Río Grande. With an economy based on sheep and oil, this bleak and windy town has only a couple of decent museums for the traveler. The surrounding countryside, however, offers large sheep *estancias* and some truly fine trout fishing.

Information

There are banks with ATMs at the corner of San Martín & 9 de Julio.

Post office (Rivadavia 968)

Thaler Cambio (Rosales 259)

Tourist office (☎ 431-324; www.riogrande.gov.ar) In the main plaza.

Sights

The **Museo Municipal de la Ciudad** (cnr Alberdi & Belgrano; admission free; �9am-5pm Mon-Fri, 3-7pm Sat) explains the area's colonization and has surprisingly good exhibits on fauna, indigenous history and local pilots (including Antoine de St Exupéry). The **Museo Salesiano** (☎ 421-642; admission US75¢; �9:30am-noon & 3-7pm Tue-Sun), 10km north of town, has exhibits on geology, natural history and ethnography. Take Bus B from San Martín.

Sleeping

Albergue Hotel Argentino (☎ 422-546; hostelargentino@yahoo.com.ar; San Martín 64; campsites per person US$3.25, dm/d US$10/65) The closest thing to a hostel in town. In an old house, with simple dorms, homey kitchen and living room.

Hospedaje Noal (☎ 427-516; Rafael Obligado 557; d US$23, s/d with shared bathroom US$10-20) One block from Tecni-Austral is this basic, small, warm place with 10 rooms.

Residencial Rawson (☎ 430-352; Estrada 756; s/d from US$12/20) Rough around the edges but friendly; offers small OK rooms with TV.

Patagonia Feugo B&B (☎ 433-232; patagoniafuego bb@hotmail.com; Moyano 788; s/d US$16/23) Just four rooms (all with shared bathroom) in this plain but clean place with a few homey touches. Kitchen available.

Eating & Drinking

La Nueva Piamontesa (Belgrano 402; � 24hr; mains US$2-6) Best for takeout, with decent sandwiches, pasta, pizza and *parrillada*. Lots of deli items and its restaurant is next door.

Epa!!! Bar-café (Rosales 445; mains US$2-6) The hippest spot in town, with colorful booths, futuristic tables and standard dishes.

Café Sonora (Moreno 705; mains US$3.25-6) Modern and bright corner joint with sandwiches and 30 kinds of pizza.

Galway Irish Bar (Moreno 645) As close to Ireland as you'll get in Río Grande.

Also recommended for cheap takeout:

El Norte supermarket (cnr Belgrano & San Martín)

La Anónima (cnr Belgrano & San Martín)

Getting There & Away

Río Grande's airport (☎ 431-340) is 4km west of town (taxis US$3). **Aerolíneas Argentinas** (☎ 424-467; www.aerolineasargentinas.com; San Martín 607) and **LADE** (☎ 422-968; Lasserre 445) provide air services.

Río Grande does not have a bus terminal. **Lider** (☎ 420-003; Moreno 635), **Montiel** (☎ 420-997; 25 de Mayo 712) and **Tecni-Austral** (☎ 426-953; Moyano 516) go to Ushuaia daily (US$10, 3½ hours). Tecni-Austral also has connections to Punta Arenas, Río Gallegos and Comodoro Rivadavia.

USHUAIA
☎ 02901 / pop 61,000

Many different kinds of travelers end up in Ushuaia. There are the independent backpackers, the cruisers, the Antarctica-bound and those who finally end their South American biking, motorcycling or driving journeys here – at the southernmost city in the world. And while the main attraction is indeed simply *being* at the edge of the world, Ushuaia is a pleasant enough destination in itself. Its main street is prime-time touristy, yes, but the city's surrounding landscapes are quite stunning: Ushuaia lies nestled beside the attractive Canal de Beagle (Beagle Channel) and boasts a world-class backdrop of spectacular 1500m Fuegan Andes peaks. There's spectacular hiking, trekking, skiing and boat trips in the area, as well as the chance to go as far south as highways go: RN 3 ends at Bahía Lapataia, in Parque Nacional Tierra del Fuego.

This fast-growing city was originally established as a notorious penal colony. Ushuaia became a key naval base in 1950, and gold,

TIERRA DEL FUEGO

lumber, wool and fishing brought in revenue over the years. Tourism now drives the city's economy, however, and flights and hotels are full in January and February, when cruise ships arrive almost daily. Even the shoulder months of December and March see crowds and good (though changeable) weather, and with Antarctica becoming hotter every year (both climatically and as a tourist destination), Ushuaia's popularity won't be waning anytime soon.

Information

The internet is everywhere. Several banks in town have ATMs.

Boutique del Libro (25 de Mayo 62) Carries Lonely Planet guides and area maps.

Cambio Thaler (Av San Martín 788) Changes traveler's checks.

Chilean consulate (☎ 430-909; Jainén 50)

Club Andino (☎ 422-335; Juana Fadul 50) Does *not* give out hiking information, but does offer a monthly guided walk and trekking registration (as does the tourist office).

Immigration office (☎ 422-334; Beauvoir 1536)

Municipal tourist office (☎ 424-550; Av San Martín 674) Is informative; it has a branch at the base of the pier.

National Parks Administration (☎ 421-315; Av San Martín 1395).

Sights & Activities

The small but good **Museo del Fin del Mundo** (Av Maipú 179; admission US$3.25; ☉ 9am-8pm summer) explains Ushuaia's indigenous and natural histories; check out the bone harpoons,

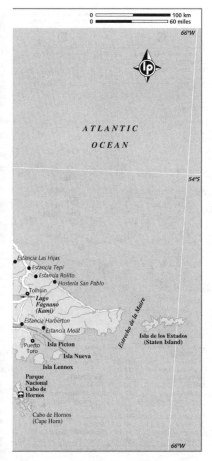

of town; from here it's about two hours up to the glacier (shorter if you take the chairlift, US$5 round-trip).

Hop on a **boat tour** to *estancias*, a lighthouse, Puerto Williams, bird island and sea-lion or penguin colonies (penguins waddle October through March). Ask about the size of the boat (small boats mean small groups that get closer to wildlife), whether there are bilingual guides and if there are any landings. Tours range from US$25 to US$50; buy tickets at the pier or from your hotel.

Hiking and trekking opportunities aren't limited to the national park: the entire mountain range behind Ushuaia, with its lakes and rivers, is an outdoor person's wonderland. Many trails are poorly marked, however, so hire a guide from **Compañía de Guías** (☎ 437-753; www.companiadeguias.com.ar; Campos 795) – which has guides for mountaineering, ice/rock climbing, kayaking, sailing and fishing (it also organizes expeditions) – or ask for details at the tourist office.

Plenty of ski resorts dot the nearby mountains, with both downhill and cross-country options. The largest resort is **Cerro Castor** (☎ 499-301; www.cerrocastor.com), 27km from Ushuaia, with almost 20 slopes. Another large area is Altos del Valle, 19km from town, known for breeding Siberian Huskies – you can get pulled in dog sleds here. Ski-rental equipment is available at each resort, and shuttles run several times daily from town. Ski season runs June to October.

Tours

Many travel agencies sell tours around the region; you can go horse-riding, visit Lagos Escondido and Fagnano, spy on birds and beavers, and even get pulled by husky-dog sleds (winter only). Award-winning tour agency **Canal** (☎ 437-395; www.canalfun.com; Rivadavia 82) organizes adventure tours, but it's not cheap.

Courses

Learn Spanish at **Finis Terrae Spanish School** (☎ 433-871; www.spanishpatagonia.com; cnr Triunvirato & Magallanes). One- to six-week courses available, along with private classes; see website for prices. Also helps with accommodation.

Sleeping

Again, if you're coming in summer – reserve ahead!

elephant-seal skulls and a surprised stuffed beaver in the gift shop. The excellent **Museos Marítimo & Presidio** (cnr Yaganes & Gobernador Paz; admission for both US$8; ⏰ 9am-8pm) are both in the same building, which held up to 700 inmates in 380 small jail cells. There are also various exhibits, including ones on expeditions to Antarctica. A daily English tour is given at 10am. Tiny **Museo Yámana** (Rivadavia 56; admission US$2.75; ⏰ 10am-9pm summer) has some history on the area's original folk.

After seeing the Perito Moreno Glacier in El Calafate, the **Glaciar Martial** here will seem like an overgrown ice-cube – but at least it's located in a beautiful valley with great views of Ushuaia and the Beagle Channel. Walk or taxi (US$3.25) to a short chairlift 7km northwest

ARGENTINA

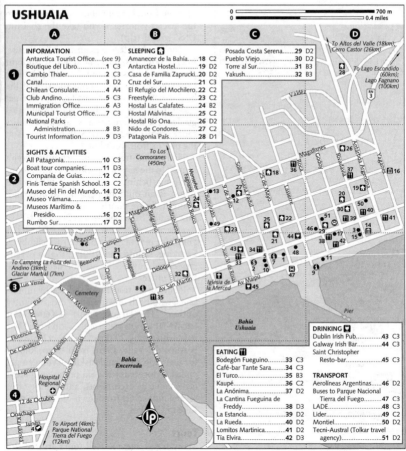

USHUAIA

0 — 700 m
0 — 0.4 miles

INFORMATION	
Antarctica Tourist Office	(see 9)
Boutique del Libro	1 C3
Cambio Thaler	2 C3
Canal	3 D2
Chilean Consulate	4 A4
Club Andino	5 C3
Immigration Office	6 A3
Municipal Tourist Office	7 C3
National Parks Administration	8 B3
Tourist Information	9 D3

SIGHTS & ACTIVITIES	
All Patagonia	10 C3
Boat tour companies	11 D3
Compañía de Guías	12 C2
Finis Terrae Spanish School	13 C2
Museo del Fin del Mundo	14 D2
Museo Yámana	15 D3
Museos Marítimo & Presidio	16 D2
Rumbo Sur	17 D3

SLEEPING	
Amanecer de la Bahía	18 C2
Antarctica Hostel	19 D2
Casa de Familia Zaprucki	20 D2
Cruz del Sur	21 C3
El Refugio del Mochilero	22 C2
Freestyle	23 C2
Hostal Las Calafates	24 B2
Hostal Malvinas	25 C2
Hostal Río Ona	26 D2
Nido de Condores	27 C2
Patagonia País	28 D1

Posada Costa Serena	29 D2
Pueblo Viejo	30 D2
Torre al Sur	31 B3
Yakush	32 B3

To Altos del Valle (18km);
Cerro Castor (26km)

To Lago Escondido
(60km);
Lago Fagnano
(100km)

To Los
Cormoranes
(450m)

To Camping La Pista del
Andino (3km);
Glaciar Martial (7km)

*Bahía
Ushuaia*

*Bahía
Encerrada*

Pier

DRINKING	
Dublin Irish Pub	43 C3
Galway Irish Bar	44 C3
Saint Christopher Resto-bar	45 C3

EATING	
Bodegón Fueguino	33 C3
Café-bar Tante Sara	34 C3
El Turco	35 B3
Kaupé	36 C2
La Anónima	37 D2
La Cantina Fueguina de Freddy	38 D3
La Estancia	39 D2
La Rueda	40 D2
Lomitos Martinica	41 D2
Tía Elvira	42 D3

TRANSPORT	
Aerolíneas Argentinas	46 D2
Buses to Parque Nacional Tierra del Fuego	47 C3
LADE	48 C3
Lider	49 C2
Montiel	50 D2
Tecni-Austral (Tolkar travel agency)	51 D2

To Airport (4km);
Parque Nacional
Tierra del Fuego
(12km)

Camping La Pista del Andino (☎ 435-890; www.la pistadelandino.com.ar; Alem 2873; camping/RV sites per person US$3; ☼ Oct-Apr) Some 3km from the center, this pleasant camping spot offers grassy or forest sites with views. There are cooking facilities, good common areas and bikes for rent. Call for free pickup (taxis to the center US$2).

Torre al Sur (☎ 430-745; www.torrealsur.com.ar; Gobernador Paz 1437; dm with/without HI card US$6.50/7.50, d US$15) Friendly hostel with intimate spaces, mazelike halls and rickety, small dorm rooms which can get noisy. Some rooms have great views; doubles have bunks.

Los Cormoranes (☎ 423-459; www.loscormoranes.com; Kamshen 788; dm with/without HI card US$6.50/8, d US$29/36; ☐) Ten minutes' uphill walk, this good hostel has good six- and eight-bed dorms facing

outdoor plank hallways. The best double is room 10; free pickup from airport.

Amanecer de la Bahía (☎ 424-405; www.ushuaiahos tel.com.ar; Magallanes 594; dm/d US$7.50/26; ℗) A bit of a walk uphill lies this decent, friendly hostel, complete with homey eating area and small but good dorms. All doubles share bathroom; resident basset hound.

Cruz del Sur (☎ 434-099; www.xdelsur.com.ar; Deloquí 636; dm/d US$8/16; ☐) Casual, laid-back hostel with small four- to eight-bed dorms (some with partial view). Lots of photos and post-cards on the walls; pleasant library room. One double.

Antarctica Hostel (☎ 435-774; www.antarcticahostel .com; Antártida Argentina 270; dm/d US$8/29; ☐) Good, popular hostel with relaxing front lounge, grassy backyard, loft dining area, underfloor heating and *buena onda* (good vibes). Doubles share bathroom.

Freestyle (☎ 432-874; www.ushuaiafreestyle.com; Gobernador Paz 866; dm/d/apt US$10/45/58; ☐) Ushuaia's slick five-star hostel, boasting fine spacious dorms (all with view) and beautiful doubles with bathroom and kitchenette. The top-floor lounge comes with banks of windows on both sides (awesome mountain and water views), faux-leather sofas and pool table.

Hostal Los Calafates (☎ 435-515; loscalafates@hotmail .com; Fagnano 456; s/d/t US$23/29/36) Just seven homey and warm rooms (all with private bathroom) at this clean, friendly, family-run guesthouse.

Posada Costa Serena (☎ 437-212; www.posadacosta serena.com.ar; Roca 129; s/d US$36/42, with shared bathroom US$26/31; ☐) Very central, this friendly and homey guesthouse comes with eight warm rooms, spotless bathrooms and free pastries all day. There's a great kitchen and some rooms have views. Apartment available downstairs.

Casa de Familia Zaprucki (☎ 421-316; Deloquí 271; apt US$39-98) This little Eden is run by an elderly couple and has four clean, just-like-home apartments (three with kitchen) that hold up to six; one comes with three bedrooms. Pretty garden, cable TV and very comfortable and private.

Also recommended:

El Refugio del Mochilero (☎ 436-129; www.refugio delmochilero.netfirms.com; 25 de Mayo 231; dm/d US$8/29; ☐) Small, dark dorms; get one upstairs. Dining area being remodeled.

Patagonia Pais (☎ 431886; www.hostelpatagoniapais .com.ar; Alem 152; dm US$8; ☐) A walk from center, with mostly good dorms (24 beds total).

Yakush (☎ 435-807; www.hostelyakush.com.ar; Piedrabuena 118; dm/d US$9/33) Colorful hostel with large, good dorms, awesome upstairs lounging room and attractive kitchen/dining area.

Pueblo Viejo (☎ 432-098; www.puebloviejo.info; Deloquí 242; s/d US$26/33; ☐) Small, clean and tidy rooms, all of which share bathrooms. But it's friendly, and a good, intimate choice.

Hostal Río Ona (☎ 421-327; www.rioona.com.ar; Magallanes 196; s/d US$29/36) Ten comfortable rooms, all with private bathroom and most with kitchenette.

Hostal Malvinas (☎ 422-626; www.hostalmalvinas .net; Deloquí 615; s/d/tr US$47/57/66) Sixteen well-decorated, comfortable rooms, all with private bathroom, fridge, cable TV. Tea/coffee all day.

Eating

La Anónima (cnr Gobernador Paz & Rivadavia) For cheap takeout.

Lomitos Martinica (Av San Martín 68; mains under US$4.25) Excellent, cheap *parrillada*, huge sandwiches and no-nonsense service.

Café-bar Tante Sara (Av San Martín 701; mains US$3-5.50) Popular corner bistro with some classic atmosphere. Has it all: breakfast, burgers, sandwiches, salads, snacks and tapas.

El Turco (Av San Martín 1040; mains US$3.50-6.50; ⊙ closed Sun lunch) Not very central, but popular for its cheap meats, pizza and pasta.

Bodegón Fueguino (Av San Martín 859; mains US$4-8; ⊙ closed Mon) Locally recommended eatery with homemade pastas, 12 kinds of *cordero* (lamb) and *calafate* berry ice cream. In cute yellow house.

La Cantina Fueguina de Freddy (Av San Martín 326; mains US$6.50-12) Good food including pizza, pastas, stews and seafood. Check out the crab tank.

Tía Elvira (Av Maipú 349; mains US$6.50-20) Pricey but excellent seafood joint, with plenty of meat and fine wine choices.

Kaupé (☎ 422-704; Roca 470; mains US$7.50-12; ⊙ closed Sun lunch) Ushuaia's high cuisine, with exceptional international dishes such as chicken Bengali and parchment-baked sea bass. Romantic, with great views; reservations are recommended.

La Rueda (Av San Martín 193; dinner buffet US$9) Good *tenedor libre* with tasty *parrillada* cooked up at the huge grill in the window.

Nearby **La Estancia** (Av San Martín 253) is similar.

Drinking

Note that the southernmost bar in the world isn't in Ushuaia, but on a Ukrainian research station in Antarctica. Sorry.

Galway Irish Bar (Lasserre 108) Large drinking hole with semiauthentic pub decor, dart board and Beagle beer (Ushuaia's beer) on tap. Wide variety of music, with some DJ nights.

Dublin Irish Pub (9 de Julio 168) Intimate, smoky place with good atmosphere and dim lighting. Popular with foreigners, who down bottles of Guinness.

Saint Christopher Resto-bar (Av Maipú 822) This boat-shaped restaurant, complete with nautical theme, serves food during the day but becomes more of a drinking spot at night. Note the rusty hulking shipwreck just offshore.

Getting There & Around

In January and February it's a good idea to book your passage into and out of Ushuaia as early as possible or you might end up waiting

ARGENTINA

days for a seat – this counts for both buses and airplanes.

Ushuaia's airport is 4km south of center (taxis US$3); the departure tax is US$6.50. **Aerolíneas Argentinas** (☎ 0810-222-86527; www.aero lineasargentinas.com; Roca 116), **LADE** (☎ 421-123; Av San Martín 542) and (Chilean) **Aerovías DAP** (www.dap .d) provide services.

Ushuaia does not have a bus terminal. **Tecni-Austral** (☎ 431-412; Roca 157) has almost-daily service to Río Grande (US$10, 3½ hours), Río Gallegos (US$31, 13 hours) and Comodoro Rivadavia (US$49, 24 hours), and heads to Punta Arenas three times per week (US$29, 13 hours). It's based out of the Tolkar travel agency. **Lider** (☎ 436-421; Gobernador Paz 921) and **Montiel** (☎ 421-366; Deloqui 110) go to Río Grande up to eight times daily (US$10, 3½ hours).

Taxis around town are cheap. Many bus companies go to Lagos Escondido/Fagnano

---

BEYOND THE EDGE OF THE WORLD – ANTARCTICA

A trip to awe-inspiring Antarctica is a once-in-a-lifetime adventure. It's expensive but worth every penny, and is so much more than just a continent to tick off your list. The land and ice shelves pile up hundreds of meters thick with kilometers of undulating, untouched snow, while countless glaciers flow down mountainsides. Icebergs get as big as tall buildings and come in shapes you didn't think were possible, from triangles to dragon-silhouettes to graceful sculptures with circular arches. The wildlife is magnificent; you'll see thousands of curious penguins and a wide variety of flying birds, seals and whales. Antarctica is an astounding place, and its tourism industry is growing fast as more and more people visit. We can only hope that careful management will assure that this glorious continent remains beautiful.

For the average person, cruising is the easiest and best way visit the White Continent. The season runs from mid-November to mid-March; peak voyages often get sold out. Last-minute tickets might be available later in the season, but will still cost around US$3000. Regular tickets run from around US$4000 on up, depending on the company. Ask how many days you will actually spend in Antarctica, as crossing the Southern Ocean takes up to two days each way. And how many landings will there be? The smaller the ship, the more landings per passenger (always depending on the weather, of course).

Because of its relatively close location to the Antarctic peninsula, most cruises leave from Ushuaia. Travel agencies such as **Rumbo Sur** (☎ 422-275; www.rumbosur.com.ar; Av San Martín 350), **All Patagonia** (☎ 433-622; www.allpatagonia.com; Juana Fadul 60) and **Canal** (☎ 437-395; www.canalfun .com; Rivadavia 82) offer packages, though there are many more. **Alicia Petiet** (aliciapetiet@hotmail .com) is a tour consultant who helps travelers with Antarctic cruises.

Check that your company is a member of **IAATO** (www.iaato.org), whose members must abide by strict guidelines for responsible travel to Antarctica. Following are just a few companies that go to Antarctica.

Adventure Associates (www.adventureassociates.com) Australia's first tour company to Antarctica, with many ships and destinations.

Clipper Cruise Line (www.clippercruise.com) Longer voyages on a 122-passenger ship that include the Falklands and South Georgia Islands.

Gap Adventures (www.gap.ca) Highly recommended new company with affordable trips, excellent service and ecological bent.

Heritage Expeditions (www.heritage-expeditions.com) Award-winning New Zealand company that also goes to Ross Sea/East Antarctica regions.

Peregrine Adventures (www.peregrineadventures.com) Offers unique trips that include visiting the Antarctic Circle, with kayaking and camping options.

Quark Expeditions (www.quarkexpeditions.com) Three kinds of ships, from an icebreaker to a 48-passenger small ship for close-knit groups.

WildWings Travel (www.wildwings.co.uk) UK-based company that focuses on birds and wildlife in Antarctica.

For more information see Lonely Planet's *Antarctica* guidebook. In Ushuaia there's an **Antarctica tourist office** (☎ 421-423; antartida@tierradelfuego.org.ar) at Ushuaia's pier. And one last thing: bring more film and/or extra memory cards than you think you'll need. You'll thank us later.

for US$20 return. For transport to Parque Nacional Tierra del Fuego, see the following section.

PARQUE NACIONAL TIERRA DEL FUEGO

West of Ushuaia by 12km lies the beautiful **Parque Nacional Tierra del Fuego** (admission US$6.50), which extends from the Beagle Channel in the south to beyond Lago Fagnano in the north; only a small part of the park is accessible to the public, however. Despite a tiny system of short, easy trails more suited to day-trippers than backpacking trekkers, the views along the bays, rivers and forests are wonderfully scenic. Southern beeches like the evergreen *coihue* and deciduous *lenga* thrive on heavy coastal rainfall, and in autumn the hillsides of deciduous *ñire* burst out in red.

Plenty of bird life graces the coasts here. Keep your eyes peeled for *cauquén* (upland geese), cormorants, oystercatchers, grebes, steamer ducks and even rare condors or albatross. The most common land critters you'll see are the European rabbit and North American beaver, introduced species that have wreaked havoc on the ecosystem. Foxes and the occasional guanaco may also be seen, and marine mammals are most common on offshore islands.

One good, moderate hike runs 6.5km along the north shores of Ensenada Zaratiegui and Bahía Lapataia; it starts at the boat pier. For a longer hike, you can continue along the road, past the Lago Roca campground, to the start of the Lago Roca trail, which goes for 5km to the Chilean border (best not to cross it). About 1.5km into this trail a side trail to the right leads to steep Cerro Guanaco, with decent views (side trail 3km). Taking the bus all the way to the end of RN 3 gives you access to some short scenic walks. For the complete picture, get a map of the area from the tourist office or National Parks Administration in Ushuaia.

Park admission is collected between 8am and 8pm daily October through April. Weather can be very changeable, even in summer, so come prepared.

Sleeping

The only organized campground is **Lago Roca** (☎ 2901-433313; ☼ Oct–Apr). Pitch a tent for US$2.75 to US$4 per person; a *confitería* and tiny grocery are nearby. Free campsites in the park include Las Bandurrias, Laguna Verde and Los Cauquenes, Ensenada and Río Pipo.

Getting There & Away

Minibuses to the park charge US$3.25 to US$5 (depending on destination). They leave about every half-hour from 8am to 8pm daily, from the corner of Av Maipú and 25 de Mayo. For a complete list of bus companies, see the tourist office.

If you've got money to burn, take **El Tren del Fin del Mundo** (☎ 2901-431600; www.trendelfindelmundo .com.ar) to the park. The one-hour, scenic, narrow-gauge train ride comes with historical explanations in English and Spanish (US$18 return, not including park admission). The station is 8km from Ushuaia (taxis US$5 one way; bus US$5 return) and there are several departures daily in summer. Reserve in January and February, when cruise-ship tours take over.

ARGENTINA DIRECTORY

ACCOMMODATIONS

There's an excellent range of affordable hostels throughout Argentina, including those affiliated with Hostelling International (HI). Most are friendly and offer tours and services. All include kitchen access and sheets; most have towel rental, internet access, luggage storage, light breakfast and double rooms (book these ahead). Typical prices for dorm rooms range from US$6.50 to US$9, while doubles can be up to US$25. For information on two excellent hostel organizations see www.hostels.org .ar (HI) or www.argentinahostels.com (Argentina Hostel Club). You can obtain an HI card in Buenos Aires (see p60).

Residenciales are small hotels, while *hospedajes* are usually family homes with extra bedrooms and shared bathrooms. Hotels can range from one to five stars, and usually come with private bathroom and a light breakfast (coffee, tea and bread or croissants with jam). Some hotels in Buenos Aires and other tourist destinations operate on a two-tier system, charging foreigners more than residents. As far as we know, the accommodations we've listed here don't use this system.

Camping is cheap (around US$3 per person) and popular in Argentina, though sites aren't always near the center of town. National parks usually have organized sites, and some offer distant *refugios* (basic shelters for trekkers).

Peak tourist months in Buenos Aires are July, August and November to January, when accommodation prices are at their highest. Patagonia is busiest during the summer (November to February) though ski resort towns fill up fast in July and August. Northern destinations and the Atlantic beach towns attract the most travelers in December and January (the latter are practically ghost towns the rest of the year). In peak season it's important to make reservations ahead of time.

We've listed general high-season rates here, but not ultrapeak rates (Easter week or Christmas). In low season, or if you're staying for more than a few days, you can always try asking for a discount.

ACTIVITIES

Argentina has plenty for the adventure-seeking traveler. A multitude of beautiful national parks offer awesome summer hiking and trekking, especially around Bariloche (p136) and Patagonia's Fitz Roy range (p152). For the highest peak outside Asia there's lofty Aconcagua, at 6960m (p127).

Skiing is world-class, with major resorts at Cerro Catedral (Bariloche, p139), Las Leñas (Malargüe, p129), Los Penitentes (p127) and Chapelco (San Martín de los Andes, p133). The ski season runs about mid-June to mid-October. In summer, these mountains turn into activity centers for mountain biking.

Cycling is a popular activity in Mendoza, the Andean northwest, the Lake District and Patagonia (where winds are fierce!). Mountain bikes are best for pedaling the sometimes remote and bad roads, many of which are gravel. Many tourist cities have bike rentals, though quality is not up to Western standards.

The Lake District and Patagonia have some of the world's best fly-fishing, with introduced trout and landlocked Atlantic salmon reaching epic proportions. The season in these areas runs from November to mid-April; it's almost always catch-and-release.

White-water rafting can be enjoyed near Mendoza (as well as in the Lake District) and horse-riding and paragliding are popular in many tourist areas.

BOOKS

Lonely Planet's *Argentina* guidebook, *Buenos Aires* city guide and *Best of Buenos Aires* are *número uno* for exploring Argentina in greater depth.

Travelogues on the country include *The Voyage of the Beagle* (Darwin on *gaucho* life), *The Uttermost Part of the Earth* (Lucas Bridges on Tierra del Fuego's indigenous folk), *In Patagonia* (Bruce Chatwin's classic) and *The Motorcycle Diaries: A Journey Around South America* (Che Guevara on adventurous travel with a dilapidated motorcycle).

WH Hudson's *Idle Days in Patagonia* tells of the naturalist's adventures in search of the region's fauna; see also his *Tales of the Pampas,* a compendium of short stories. Mountaineers should check out Gregory Crouch's *Enduring Patagonia,* a detailed account of his Cerro Torre climb. Richard W Slatta's *Gauchos and the Vanishing Frontier* depicts the engaging frontier life of Argentina's favorite icon.

Ronald Dworkin's *Nunca Mas: The Report of the Argentine National Commission on the Disappeared* details queasy personal accounts of victims in Argentina's Dirty War (beware – holds back no punches). *The Argentina Reader,* edited by Gabriella Nouzeilles and Graciela R Montaldo, is a gripping collection of readings from historical figures to minority groups to modern culture.

For the capital there's Jason Wilson's quirky *Buenos Aires: A Cultural and Literary Companion.* For something fun pick up a copy of Miranda Frances' timeless *Bad Times in Buenos Aires,* or Marina Palmer's sexy *Kiss and Tango.*

BUSINESS HOURS

Traditionally, businesses open by 9am, break at 1pm for lunch and then reopen at 4pm until 8pm or 9pm. This pattern is still common in the provinces, but government offices and many businesses in Buenos Aires have adopted the 9am to 6pm schedule.

Restaurants generally open noon to 3pm for lunch and 8pm to midnight for dinner. On weekends hours can be longer. Cafés are open all day long; most bars tend to open late, around 9 or 10pm. For tourist office hours see p172.

Opening hours aren't listed in reviews unless they vary widely from these standards.

CLIMATE

January and February are oppressively hot and humid in the subtropical north (including Iguazú Falls) and Buenos Aires. These are the best months, however, to visit the high Andes and southern Patagonia – and you'll still need warm clothes. Buenos Aires is best in spring or fall. Skiers enjoy the Andes during the winter months, June to September. For more information and climate charts see p1062.

DANGERS & ANNOYANCES

Don't let anyone tell you otherwise: despite the public's constant dissatisfaction with its government and a lumbering economy that gives rise to occasional crime waves, Argentina remains one of the safest countries in Latin America. Most tourists who visit Buenos Aires leave happy and unscathed. Outside the big cities, serious crime is rare.

In general, the biggest dangers in Argentina are speeding cars and buses: be careful crossing streets, and *never* assume you have the right of way as a pedestrian. If you're sensitive to cigarette smoke, be aware that Argentines are truly addicted to nicotine: they'll light up in banks, post offices, restaurants, cafés and everywhere else. Other small concerns include air pollution (in big cities), cracked sidewalks, ubiquitous dog piles and the occasional hole in the ground. Stray dogs are common, but usually don't bite.

For big-city advice, see Buenos Aires (p50). For general advice on traveling safely, see the South America Directory (above).

DRIVER'S LICENSE

To rent a car in Argentina you must be 21 years old and have a valid driver's license and an International Driving Permit. Most rental agencies require a credit card as well. If driving an Argentine car you must carry a *tarjeta verde* (green card); make sure you get one if renting. Foreign vehicles can use their customs permission instead.

ELECTRICITY

Argentina's electric current operates on 220V, 50Hz. Most plugs are either two rounded prongs (as in Europe) or three angled flat prongs (as in Australia).

EMBASSIES & CONSULATES

For visa information see Visas, p172.

Embassies & Consulates in Argentina

The following is not a complete list. For locations of these and other consulates see individual city maps.

Australia (Map pp56-7; ☎ 011-4777-6580; Villanueva 1400, Buenos Aires)

Bolivia Buenos Aires (Map pp52-3; ☎ 011-4381-0539; Adolfo Alsina 1886; La Quiaca (☎ 03885-42-2283; cnr San Juan & Árabe Siria); Salta (Map pp106-7; ☎ 0387-421-1040; Mariano Boedo 34); San Salvador de Jujuy (Map p109; ☎ 0388-424-0501; Independencia 1098)

Brazil Buenos Aires (Map pp52-3; ☎ 011-4515-6500; Carlos Pellegrini 1363, 5th fl); Paso de Los Libres (☎ 03772-425-444; Mitre 842); Puerto Iguazú (Map p89; ☎ 03757-421348; Av Guaraní 70)

Canada (Map pp56-7; ☎ 011-4808-1000; Tagle 2828, Buenos Aires)

Chile Bariloche (Map p137; ☎ 02944-422-842; Av Juan Manuel de Rosas 180); Buenos Aires (Map pp52-3; ☎ 011-4327-1762; San Martín 439, 9th fl); Comodoro Rivadavia (☎ 0297-446-2414; Brown 456, 1st fl); Mendoza (Map pp124-5; ☎ 0261-425-4844; Paso de los Andes 1147); Neuquén (☎ 0299-442-2727; La Rioja 241); Río Gallegos (Map p157; ☎ 02966-422-364; Mariano Moreno 136); Salta (Map pp106-7; ☎ 0387-431-1857; Santiago del Estero 965); Ushuaia (Map p162; ☎ 02901-430-909; Jainén 50)

France (Map pp52-3; ☎ 011-4312-2409; Av Santa Fe 846, 4th fl, Buenos Aires)

Germany (Map pp56-7; ☎ 011-4778-2500; Villanueva 1055, Buenos Aires)

Israel (Map pp52-3; ☎ 011-4338-2500; Av de Mayo 701, 10th fl, Buenos Aires)

Italy (Map pp52-3; ☎ 011-4816-6132; Marcelo T de Alvear 1149, Buenos Aires)

Netherlands (Map pp52-3; ☎ 011-4338-0050; Olga Cossetini 831, 3rd fl, Buenos Aires)

New Zealand (Map pp52-3; ☎ 011-4328-0634; Carlos Pellegrini 1427, 5th fl, Buenos Aires)

Norway (Map pp52-3; ☎ 011-4312-2204; Esmeralda 909, 3rd fl B, Buenos Aires)

Paraguay Buenos Aires (Map pp52-3; ☎ 011-4814-4803; Viamonte 1851); Posadas (Map p87; ☎ 03752-423-858; San Lorenzo 179)

Peru (Map pp52-3; ☎ 011-4334-0970; Av Florida 165, Buenos Aires)

South Africa (Map pp52-3; ☎ 011-4317-2900; Marcelo T de Alvear 590, 7th fl, Buenos Aires)

Spain (Map pp52-3; ☎ 011-4811-0070; Guido 1760, Buenos Aires)

Sweden (Map pp52-3; ☎ 011-4342-1422; Tacuari 147, Buenos Aires)

Switzerland (Map pp52-3; ☎ 011-4311-6491; Av Santa Fe 846, 10th fl, Buenos Aires)

UK (Map pp52-3; ☎ 011-4803-7070; Dr Luis Agote 2412, Buenos Aires)

Uruguay Buenos Aires (Map pp52-3; ☎ 011-4807-3040; Av Gral Las Heras 1915); Gualeguaychú (☎ 03446-426-168; Rivadavia 510)

USA (Map pp56-7; ☎ 011-5777-4533; Colombia 4300, Buenos Aires)

Argentine Embassies & Consulates Abroad

Argentina probably has an embassy or consulate in your country; this is only a partial list.

Australia (☎ 02-6273-9111; www.argentina.org.au /index.htm; Level 2, 7 National Cct, Barton, Canberra, ACT 2600)

Canada (☎ 613-236-2351; www.consargenmtl.com; Suite 700, 81 Metcalfe St, Ottawa, Ontario K1P 6K7)

France (☎ 01-45-53-33-00; 6 rue Cimarosa, Paris 75116)

Germany (☎ 0228-249-62-88; Robert-Koch-Str. 104, Venusberg, 53127 Bonn)

New Zealand (☎ 04-472-8330; www.arg.org.nz/em bassy/default.htm; Level 14, 142 Lambton Quay, Wellington)

UK (☎ 020-7318-1300; www.argentine-embassy-uk.org in Spanish; 65 Brook St, London W1K 4AH)

USA (☎ 202-238-6401; www.embajadaargentinaeeuu .org; 1600 New Hampshire Ave NW, Washington, DC 20009)

FESTIVALS & EVENTS

This is just a brief list; check city listings for more. For Argentine holidays see opposite.

February/March

Carnaval Late February/early March. Especially rowdy in Gualeguaychú and Corrientes.

Buenos Aires Tango Late February/early March. Argentina kicks up its high heels (www.tangodata.com.ar).

May

Día de la Virgen de Luján May 8. The Virgin Mary is tops in Luján.

November

Día de la Tradición Mid-November. *Gaucho* celebrations, especially in San Antonio de Areco.

FOOD & DRINK
Argentine Cuisine

As a whole, Argentina does not have widely varied cuisine – most folks here seem to survive on meat, pasta and pizza – but the country's famous beef is sublime. At a *parrilla* (steakhouse) or *asado* (private barbecue) try *bife de chorizo* (thick sirloin), *bife de lomo* (tenderloin) or a *parrillada* (a mixed grill of cheaper beef cuts and organ meats). Ask for *chimichurri*, a spicy sauce of garlic, parsley and olive oil. If you want your steak rare say *jugoso*; medium is *a punto*, but you're on your own with well-done.

The Italian influence is apparent in dishes like pizza, spaghetti, ravioli and chewy ño-quis (gnocchi). Vegetarian fare is available in Buenos Aires and other large cities. *Tenedor libres* (all-you-can-eat buffets) are popular everywhere and often great value. Middle Eastern food is common in the north, while the northwest has spicy dishes like those of Bolivia or Peru. In Patagonia lamb is king, while specialties such as trout, boar and venison are served around the Lake District.

Confiterías usually grill sandwiches like *lomito* (steak), *milanesa* (a thin breaded steak) and hamburgers. *Restaurantes* have larger menus and professional waiters. Cafés are important social places for everything from marriage proposals to revolutions, and many also serve alcohol and simple meals.

Large supermarkets often have a counter with good, cheap takeout. Western fast-food chains exist in larger cities.

Breakfast is a simple affair of coffee, tea or mate with *tostadas* (toast), *manteca* (butter) and *mermelada* (jam). *Medialunas* (croissants) come either sweet or plain. Lunch is around 1pm, teatime around 5pm and dinner usually after 8pm (few restaurants open before this hour).

Empanadas are baked or fried turnovers with vegetables, beef, cheese or other fillings. *Sandwichitos de miga* (thin, crust-free sandwiches layered with ham and cheese) are great at teatime. Commonly sold at kiosks, *alfajores* are cookie sandwiches filled with *dulce de leche* (a thin milky caramel) or *mermelada* and covered in chocolate.

Postres (desserts) include *ensalada de fruta* (fruit salad), pies and cakes, *facturas* (pastries) and flan, which can be topped with *crema* (whipped cream) or *dulce de leche*. Argentina's Italian-derived *helados* (ice cream) are South America's best.

The usual *propina* (tip) at restaurants is 10%, provided a service charge hasn't already been included in the bill.

Drinks
ALCOHOLIC DRINKS

Argentines like to drink (but not to excess), and you'll find long lists of beer, wine, cognac, whiskey and gin at many places. Both Quilmes and Isenbeck are popular beers; in bars or cafés, ask for *chopp* (draft or lager). Microbrews are widely available in the Lake District.

Some Argentine wines are world-class; both reds *(tintos)* and whites *(blancos)* are excellent, but Malbecs are especially well known. The major wine-producing areas are near Mendoza, San Juan, La Rioja and Salta.

NONALCOHOLIC DRINKS

Soft drinks are everywhere. For water, there's *con gas* (carbonated) or *sin gas* (noncarbonated) mineral water. Or ask for Argentina's usually drinkable *agua de canilla* (tap water). For fresh-squeezed orange juice, ask for *jugo de naranja exprimido*. *Licuados* are water- or milk-blended fruit drinks.

Even in the smallest town, coffee will be espresso. *Café chico* is thick, dark coffee in a very small cup (try a *ristretto,* with even less water). *Café cortado* is a small coffee with a touch of milk; *cortado doble* is a larger portion. *Café con leche* (a latte) is served for breakfast only; after lunch or dinner, request a *cortado*.

Tea is commonplace. You shouldn't decline an invitation for grasslike mate, although it's definitely an acquired taste.

GAY & LESBIAN TRAVELERS

Argentina is a strongly Catholic country, but enclaves of tolerance toward gays and lesbians do exist (especially in Buenos Aires, which is now South America's top gay tourist destination). In fact Argentina has become Latin America's first country to accept civil unions between same-sex couples.

Argentine men are more physically demonstrative than you may be used to, so behaviors such as cheek kisses or a vigorous embrace are commonplace. Lesbians walking hand in hand should attract little attention, as heterosexual Argentine women often do, but this would be suspicious behavior for males. In general, do your thing – but be discreet.

For more information in Buenos Aires see the boxed text, p67.

HEALTH

Argentina requires no vaccinations. Malaria is a minor concern in the more rural, lowland border sections of Salta, Jujuy, Corrientes and Misiones provinces. In the high Andes, watch for signs of altitude sickness and use more sunscreen. For more (conservative) information see www.cdc.gov/travel/temsam.htm.

Urban water supplies are usually potable, making salads and ice safe to consume. Many prescription drugs are available over the counter. Seek out an embassy recommendation if you need serious Western-type medical services. For more information, see the Health chapter (p1090).

HOLIDAYS

Government offices and businesses close on most national holidays, which are often moved to the nearest Monday or Friday to extend weekends. Provincial holidays are not listed here.

Año Nuevo (New Year's Day) January 1
Semana Santa (Easter) March/April; dates vary
Día de la Memoria (Anniversary of 1976's military coup) March 24
Día de las Malvinas (Malvinas Day) April 2
Día del Trabajador (Labor Day) May 1
Revolución de Mayo (May Revolution of 1810) May 25
Día de la Bandera (Flag Day) June 20
Día de la Independencia (Independence Day) July 9
Día de San Martín (Anniversary of San Martín's death) August 17
Día de la Raza (Columbus Day) October 12
Día de la Concepción Inmaculada (Immaculate Conception Day) December 8
Navidad (Christmas Day) December 25

INTERNET ACCESS

Argentina is online: every city and town in the country, no matter how small, has internet cafés. In downtown Buenos Aires they're on practically every corner. Most *locutorios* (telephone offices) also offer internet access. Costs are very affordable, from around US50¢ per hour, depending on the city. Unless they're exceptional, we don't mention internet cafés in our city listings.

To type the @ *(arroba)* symbol, hold down the Alt-key while typing 64 on the keypad.

INTERNET RESOURCES

Argentina Turistica (www.argentinaturistica.com) Good all around info on Argentina.
Buenos Aires Expatriates Group (www.baexpats .com) Also good for travelers.
Buenos Aires Herald (www.buenosairesherald.com) BA's excellent English newspaper.
Lanic (www.lanic.utexas.edu/la/argentina) A massive list of Argentine websites.
Lonely Planet (www.lonelyplanet.com) The internet's best, with awesome forum.
Sectur (www.sectur.gov.ar) The official tourism site.

LANGUAGE

Besides flamboyance, the unique pronunciation of *castellano* – Argentina's Italian-accented version of the Spanish language – readily identifies an Argentine elsewhere in Latin America or abroad. If you're in Buenos Aires you'll also hear *lunfardo,* the capital's colorful slang.

Some immigrants retain their language as a badge of identity. Quechua speakers, numerous in the northwest, tend to be bilingual in Spanish. Many Mapuche speakers live in the southern Andes, while most Guaraní speakers live in northeastern Argentina. English is understood by many Argentines, especially in Buenos Aires.

See the Language chapter for more information. And pick up a copy of Lonely Planet's *Latin American Spanish Phrasebook* to avoid cluelessness.

LEGAL MATTERS

Argentina's police have a reputation for corruption and abuse of power, so do your best to obey the law. Marijuana and many other substances that are illegal in the US and most European countries are also illegal here. Though constitutionally a person is innocent until proven guilty, people are regularly held for years without a trial. If arrested, you have the constitutional right to a lawyer, a telephone call and to remain silent.

If you behave, it's unlikely you'll run into trouble with the police. Mention contacting your consulate if you do have a run-in. In all events, it's a good idea to carry identification (or copies in a pinch) and always be courteous and cooperative when dealing with police or government officials.

MAPS

If you plan to hang around the capital, grab a copy of Lonely Planet's *Buenos Aires* laminated map.

All tourist offices will have decent maps for general sightseeing. In many cities, newspaper kiosks and bookstores stock good maps. For detailed hiking maps check with the local Club Andino or any National Parks office, which have outlets in outdoors-oriented cities.

Argentina's legal age for:

■ Drinking: 18

■ Voting: 18

■ Driving: 18

■ Sex (heterosexual or homosexual): 16

The **Automóvil Club Argentino** (ACA; www.aca .org.ar), the main branch of which is in **Palermo** (☎ 011-4802-6061; Av del Libertador 1850), publishes some excellent city and provincial maps; members of ACA's overseas affiliates get discounts with their card. True map nerds can visit the **Instituto Geográfico Militar** (☎ 011-4576-5576; Cabildo 381) in Buenos Aires.

MEDIA

The English-language daily *Buenos Aires Herald* (www.buenosairesherald.com) covers the world from an international perspective. The most important Spanish dailies are upper class *La Nación* and the fun tabloid *Clarín*. *Página 12* provides a refreshing leftist perspective and often breaks important stories. *Ámbito Financiero* is the voice of the business sector, but it also provides good cultural coverage.

Argentina has dozens of channels on cable TV, with plenty of radio stations across the country as well.

MONEY

Carrying a combination of US dollars, Argentine pesos and at least one ATM card is best. Since devaluation in 2002 the peso has stabilized at about three to one US dollar, though in a volatile country like Argentina this could quickly change.

ATMs

Cajeros automáticos (ATMs) are the best way to go in Argentina, whether you're in a big city or small town. Practically every bank has one, transactions are straightforward and exchange rates are reasonable. Most ATMs have English instructions. Savvy travelers bring more than one card, just in case.

When getting cash out consider withdrawing an odd number like 390 pesos, instead of 400. This will guarantee you some small bills; just *try* breaking a 100 peso note for a 10 peso sale – you'll get groans for sure.

Bargaining

Bargaining is possible in the northwest and in craft fairs countrywide. If you stay several days at a hotel, you can often negotiate a better rate. Many higher-range hotels will give discounts for cash payments.

Cash

Bills come in denominations of two, five, 10, 20, 50 and 100 pesos. One peso equals

---

TWO-TIER COSTS IN ARGENTINA

Don't be surprised if, as a traveling foreigner, you're charged more than Argentine residents on occasion. Since the devaluation of the peso in 2002, some hotels, many museums, most national parks and one major airline have adopted a two-tier price system. Rates for foreigners can be close to double the locals' price. While it's somewhat useless to complain to service personnel at government-run entities about this discrepancy, you can at least choose to stay at hotels that don't discriminate. Simply ask them if they charge more for foreigners than residents, and if you don't like it go to a hotel that charges everyone the same.

To our knowledge, no accommodation listed in this Argentina chapter has adopted this two-tier system.

---

100 centavos. Coins come in five, 10, 25 and 50 centavos and one peso. Always carry change.

Although all prices in this book are quoted in US dollars, and many businesses in Argentina will accept US dollars, not all places will take them. Carry local currency for small purchases, patriotic merchants and government offices.

In Buenos Aires especially be aware of fake bills. For photos of authentic coins and bills see www.easybuenosairescity.com/currency.htm.

Credit Cards

The larger a hotel is, the greater the chance it will accept credit cards. Ditto for stores and other services. Some businesses add a *recargo* (surcharge) of up to 10% to credit card purchases; always ask before charging. Note that restaurant tips can't be added to the bill and must be paid in cash.

MasterCard and Visa are the main honchos, but American Express is also commonly accepted. Cash advances are possible but discuss the terms with your credit card company beforehand. Also, let your company know you'll be using your card(s) abroad.

Exchanging Money

US dollars and certain other currencies can be converted to Argentine pesos at most banks or *cambios* (exchange houses). Some banks will only exchange a minimum amount (say, US$100) so check before lining up. *Cambios* offer slightly poorer rates, but usually have fewer restrictions.

Since the major currency devaluation in January 2002, Buenos Aires' Av Florida has seen a proliferation of shady figures offering '*cambio, cambio, cambio*' to passing pedestrians. Using these unofficial street changers is not recommended; there are quite a few fake bills floating about.

Traveler's checks are very difficult to cash (even at banks) and suffer poor exchange rates. They're not recommended as your main source of traveling money.

Exchange rates at press time included the following:

Country	Unit		Arg$ (peso)
Australia	A$1	=	2.32
Canada	C$1	=	2.74
euro zone	€1	=	3.90
Japan	¥100	=	2.60
New Zealand	NZ$1	=	2.04
UK	UK£1	=	5.76
United States	US$1	=	3.09

POST

Letters and postcards (up to 20g) to the US, Europe and Australia cost around US$1.50. You can send packages under 2kg from any post office, but anything heavier needs to go through *aduana* (a customs office).

Correo Argentino (www.correoargentino.com.ar) – the privatized postal service – has become more dependable over the years, but send essential mail *certificado* (registered). Private couriers, such as OCA and FedEx, are available in some larger cities – but are much more expensive.

RESPONSIBLE TRAVEL

Unlike Bolivia or Peru, modern Argentina doesn't have huge numbers of indigenous peoples with delicate cultures. Most responsible travel here includes how you behave in the country's more pristine areas, such as the village of El Chaltén (which is located inside a national park!). Common sense rules: keep water sources potable by washing 100 steps away from rivers and lakes, don't litter (this includes cigarette butts) and avoid walking off-trail.

STUDYING

Since the devaluation of the peso, Argentina has become a hot (and cheap) destination in which to learn Spanish. For a partial list of Spanish schools in Buenos Aires, see p59. Other large cities, such as Bariloche, Mendoza and Córdoba, also have Spanish schools.

TELEPHONE

Telecom and Telefónica are the major Argentine phone companies. *Locutorios* (small telephone offices) are very common in any city; you enter private booths, make calls, then pay at the front counter. These may cost more than street phones but are better for privacy and quiet, and you won't run out of coins.

Calling the US, Europe and Australia from *locutorios* is expensive, but rates are discounted evenings and on weekends (and remain cheaper than collect or credit card calls). Least expensive is buying credit phone cards at kiosks or making calls over the internet using Skype or some other system.

To call a cell phone you must first dial ☎ 15, unless you are calling from another cell. When calling out of your area code dial ☎ 0 first. Toll-free numbers in Argentina start with ☎ 0800.

To call someone in Argentina from outside Argentina, you'll need to dial your country's international access code, then Argentina's country code (☎ 54), then the city's area code (leaving out the first 0), then the number itself. (When dialing an Argentine cell phone from outside Argentina, dial your country's international access code, then ☎ 54, then ☎ 9, then the area code and number, leaving out the ☎ 15).

Argentina's main cell phone systems are CDMA and TDMA. It's also possible to use tri-band GSM world cell phones. This is a fast-changing field so check websites like www .kropla.com. For cell phone rental in BA or Córdoba see www.phonerental.com.

TOILETS

Argentina's public toilets are better than most other South American countries, but not quite as good as those in the West. Head to restaurants, fast-food outlets, shopping malls and even large hotels to scout out a seat. Carry toilet paper and don't expect hot water, soap or paper towels to be available.

TOURIST INFORMATION

All tourist-oriented cities in Argentina have a conveniently located tourist office, and many of them have English-speaking staff. Opening hours run from around 8am until around 10pm in the summer months of November to February. Off-season hours are a bit shorter. There are many local variations, of course.

In Buenos Aires, each Argentine province has a tourist office. Also in BA is the excellent **Secretaría de Turismo de la Nación** (Map pp52-3; ☎ 011-4312-2232; 0800-555-0016; www.turismo.gov.ar; Av Santa Fe 883), which dispenses information on all of Argentina.

TRAVELERS WITH DISABILITIES

Mobility-impaired folks will have a tough time in Argentina, where sidewalks are often busy, narrow and cracked. Ramps don't exist at every corner and in smaller towns the side streets are gravel. Higher-end hotels tend to have the best wheelchair access; with restaurants and tourist sights it's best to call ahead.

There are some kneeling buses in Buenos Aires (forget the Subte), but taxis are so common and cheap that it's definitely best to use them. Even small towns have *remises*. In Buenos Aires **Movidisc** (Map pp52-3; ☎ 011-4328-6921, 15-5247-6571; www.movidisc-web.com.ar; Diagonal Roque Sáenz Peña 868, 3rd fl) provides transportation, while **Casa Escalada** (☎ 011-4683-6478; www .casaescalada.com.ar; Rivadavia 9649) offers wheelchair rental.

These websites have no Argentina info but are good for general travel tips: www.access -able.com and www.sath.org.

VISAS

Residents of Canada, the US, Australia, and many western European countries do not need visas to enter Argentina; they receive an automatic 90-day stamp on arrival. It's smart to double-check this information with your embassy before you leave, as changes often occur.

For visa extensions (90 days), visit *migraciones* (immigration offices) in the provincial capitals. There's also an immigration office in Buenos Aires (see p48). For a list of embassies and consulates, see p167. For information on obtaining Argentine residency, see www .argentinaresidency.com.

VOLUNTEERING

Volunteer opportunities in Argentina include the following:

Buenos Aires Volunteer (www.bavolunteer.org.ar) Work in social organizations while taking Spanish classes and participating in cultural activities.

Help Argentina (www.helpargentina.org) Positions from distributing food to graphic design to fundraising to event organizing. Also offers internships.

Interrupción (www.interrupcion.net) Instigators of social responsibility and change, with volunteer and internship jobs. Offers organizational platforms for social project developments.

La Montaña (www.lamontana.com) This Spanish school in Bariloche runs social, educational and environmental volunteer programs, but you don't have to be a student to participate.

Parque Nacional Los Glaciares (in El Chatén ☎ 02962-430-004; seccionallagoviedma@apn.gov.ar) Summer work with park rangers in El Chaltén. College degree required; outdoor experience and Spanish language skills preferred.

Patagonia Volunteer (www.patagoniavolunteer.org) Skills needed in medicine, teaching, construction, agriculture etc. Works for indigenous people's rights. Also contact Dario Calfunao at Piuke Mapu Hostel in Esquel.

South American Explorers (www.saexplorers.org) Contact its Buenos Aires clubhouse (where volunteers can also work) for more information.

WOMEN TRAVELERS

Being a woman traveler in Argentina is not difficult, even if you're alone. In some ways Argentina is a safer place for a woman than Europe, the USA and most other Latin American countries. Argentina is a *machismo* culture, however, and some men will feel the need to comment on a woman's attractiveness. They'll try to get your attention by hissing, whistling, or making *piropos* (flirtatious comments). Much as you may want to kick them where it counts, the best thing to do is completely ignore them – like Argentine women do. After all, most men don't mean to be rude, and many local women even consider *piropos* to be compliments.

On the plus side of *machismo*, expect men to hold a door open for you and let you enter first, including getting on buses; this gives you a better chance at grabbing an empty seat, so get in there quick.

WORKING

Despite a recovering economy, many Argentines are still unemployed or underemployed. Don't expect to find a quick job here and get rich – it just won't happen.

There are some English-teaching jobs in Buenos Aires and other major cities, but most teachers make just enough to get by, maybe US$5 per hour. Having a TESOL or TESL certificate will be an advantage in acquiring work.

Many teachers work 'illegally' on tourist visas, which they must renew every three months (in BA this usually means hopping to Uruguay a few times per year). Work schedules drop off during the holiday months of January and February, when those who can afford to take English classes can afford to travel around the country.

For job postings, check out the classifieds in the **Herald** (www.buenosairesherald.com), or contact expat organizations like **Buenos Aires Expatriates Group** (www.baexpats.com/article13/html).

BOLIVIA

Bolivia

HIGHLIGHTS

- **Lake Titicaca** – hop between islands on the sapphire-blue waters of the world's highest major lake (p205)
- **Amazon Basin trips** – penetrate deep into the lush pampas and rainforest of the Amazon lowlands on a riverboat (p248)
- **Carnaval** – join the revelrous crowds in Oruro and devour *la Diablada* and other dancing delights (p211)
- **Salar de Uyuni** – cruise through the eerie hallucinogenic salt deserts, and marvel at spurting geysers and colored lagoons (p219)
- **Off the beaten track** – stay in an ecolodge in Parque Nacionale Madidi and marvel at the magical isolation and wildlife (p253)
- **Best journey** – trot, cycle and walk your way through the stunning quebradas around Tupiza on horse, bike and foot (p219)

FAST FACTS

- **Area:** 1,098,580 sq km (France & Spain combined)
- **Best bargain:** *almuerzos* (set lunches)
- **Best street snack:** *salteña* (delicious meat and vegetable pasties)
- **Budget:** US$15-25 a day
- **Capitals:** Sucre (constitutional), La Paz (de facto)
- **Costs:** La Paz bed US$3-5, 1L bottle of domestic beer US$1, 4hr bus ride US$2.50
- **Country code:** ☎ 591
- **Famous for:** world's highest everything, being landlocked, *peñas* (folk-music shows), coca
- **Languages:** Spanish, Quechua, Aymara, Guaraní
- **Money:** US$1 = $8.03 bolivianos
- **Phrases:** *genial* (cool), *la bomba* (party), *mugre* (disgusting)
- **Population:** 8.8 million (2003 UN estimate)
- **Time:** GMT minus 4hr
- **Tipping:** 10% in better restaurants, small change elsewhere; don't tip taxis
- **Visas:** most North & South American & Western European citizens get a free 30-day tourist card upon arrival, although US travelers need a visa.

TRAVEL HINTS

Take it easy at altitude. Visit a toilet before boarding buses. Request the *yapa* (the 'extra bit'; see p260).

OVERLAND ROUTES

Bolivia's border crossings include Guajará-Mirim (Brazil), San Pedro Atacama (Chile), Desaguadero (Peru) and Fortín Infante Rivarola (Paraguay).

Simply superlative – this is Bolivia. It's the hemisphere's highest, most isolated and most rugged nation. It's one of earth's coldest, warmest, windiest and steamiest places. It boasts among the driest, saltiest and swampiest natural landscapes in the world. Although the poorest country in South America, it's one of the richest in terms of natural resources. It's also South America's most indigenous country: over 60% of the population of 8.8 million claim indigenous heritage. Bolivia has it all…except, that is, for beaches.

This landlocked country boasts soaring peaks and hallucinogenic salt flats, steamy jungles and wildlife-rich grasslands. Unparalleled beauty is also reflected in its vibrant indigenous cultures, colonial cities, and whispers of ancient civilizations.

In recent years, it's hit the travelers' radar; opportunities for activities and off-the-beaten-path exploration have exploded.

Bolivia's social and political fronts are frequently shaky, thanks to an impotent economy, and a populace worn ragged by poverty, unemployment and disfranchisement. Protests, marches and demonstrations (mostly peaceful) are a perpetual part of the country's mind-boggling landscape. Put on your high-altitude goggles, take a deep breath (or three) and live superlatively.

BOLIVIA

CURRENT EVENTS

With the election of the country's first indigenous president, Evo Morales, a Constitutional Assembly sat for the first time in August 2006 to review the country's Constitution. They will meet for one year, after which a public referendum will be held. Bolivians wait with bated breath to see what changes will be made. Morales, a former coca grower and left-wing antiprivatization activist, quickly made his mark by nationalizing the country's gas reserves in April 2006. Protests and marches, a favorite pastime of Bolivians, are more common than ever, as people stress their demands to their new president. Bolivia remains landlocked, despite ongoing public disgruntlement and discussions with Chile about access to the ocean.

HISTORY
Pre-Gringo Times

Sometime around 1500 BC, Aymara people, possibly from the mountains of modern central Peru, swept across the Bolivian Andes to occupy the *altiplano* (high plain of Peru, Bolivia, Chile and Argentina). The years between AD 500 and AD 900 were distinguished by imperial expansion and increasing power and influence of the Tiahuanaco (or Tiwanaku) culture. The society's ceremonial center near Lake Titicaca rapidly became the highland's religious and political center. In the 9th century AD, however, Tiahuanaco's power waned. Ongoing submarine excavations in Lake Titicaca are attempting to identify the cause of Tiahuanaco's downfall.

Before the Spanish Conquest, the Bolivian *altiplano* had been incorporated into the Inca empire as the southern province of Kollasuyo. Modern Quechua speakers around Lake Titicaca are descended from immigrants who arrived under an Inca policy of populating newly conquered colonies with Quechua-speaking tribes.

There's considerable speculation that ruins on the scale of Macchu Picchu, possibly the lost Inca city of Paititi, may be buried in the Bolivian rainforest.

Conquistadores

By the late 1520s, internecine rivalries began cleaving the Inca empire. However, it took the arrival of the Spaniards – initially thought to be emissaries of the Inca sun god – to seal the deal. The Inca emperor Atahualpa was captured in 1532, and by 1537 the Spanish had consolidated their forces in Peru and securely held Cuzco.

After the demise of the Inca empire, Alto Perú, as the Spaniards called Bolivia, fell briefly into the hands of the conquistador Diego de Almagro. Before long, Francisco Pizarro dispatched his brother Gonzalo to subdue the rogue, silver-rich southern province. In 1538 Pedro de Anzures founded the township of La Plata (later renamed Chuquisaca and then Sucre), which became the political center of Spain's eastern territories.

In 1545 tremendous deposits of high-quality silver were discovered in Potosí. The settlement grew into one of the world's richest (and highest) cities on the backs of forced labor: appalling conditions in the mines led

BOLIVIA

| 0 | 200 km |
| 0 | 120 miles |

National Parks & Reserves
Parque Nacional Amboró.............1 B3
Parque Nacional Apolobamba.....2 A2
Parque Nacional Cotapata.........3 A3
Parque Nacional Madidi...........4 A2
Parque Nacional Noel Kempff
  Mercado.....................5 C2
Parque Nacional Sajama..........6 A3
Parque Nacional Torotoro........7 B3
Parque Nacional Tunari..........8 B3
Reserva Biosféra Pilon-Lajas....9 B2
Reserva Nacional de Fauna Andina
  Eduardo Avaroa...............10 B4

to the deaths of perhaps eight million African and Indian slaves. In 1548 Alonso de Mendoza founded La Paz as a staging post on the main silver route to the Pacific coast.

In 1574 the Spaniards founded the granaries of Cochabamba and Tarija, which served to contain the uncooperative Chiriguano people. Then colonialism and Jesuit missionary efforts established settlement patterns that defined the course of Bolivian society.

Coups de Grâce

In 1781 a futile attempt was made to oust the Spaniards and reestablish the Inca empire. Three decades later a local government was established in the independence movement

stronghold of Chuquisaca (Sucre). Chuquisaca's liberal political doctrines soon radiated throughout Spanish America.

In 1824, after 15 years of bloodshed, Peru was finally liberated from Spanish domination. However, in Alto Perú, the royalist general Pedro Antonio de Olañeta held out against the liberating forces. In 1825, when offers of negotiation failed, Simón Bolívar dispatched an expeditionary force to Alto Perú under General Antonio José de Sucre. On August 6, 1825, independence was proclaimed, Alto Perú became the Republic of Bolivia, and Bolívar and Sucre became the new republic's first and second presidents.

In 1828 *mestizo* (a person of mixed Indian and Spanish descent) Andrés de Santa Cruz took power and formed a confederacy with Peru. This triggered protests by Chile, whose army defeated Santa Cruz in 1839, breaking the confederation and throwing Bolivia into political chaos. The confusion peaked in 1841, when three different governments claimed power simultaneously.

Such spontaneous and unsanctioned changes of government continued through the 1980s in a series of coups and military interventions. At the time of writing, Bolivia had endured nearly 200 changes of government in its 181 years as a republic.

Chronic Territorial Losses

By the mid-19th century, the discovery of rich guano and nitrate deposits in the Atacama Desert transformed the desolate region into an economically strategic area. Since Bolivia lacked the resources to exploit the Atacama, it contracted Chilean companies. In 1879, when the Bolivian government proposed taxing the minerals, Chile occupied Bolivia's Litoral department, prompting Bolivia and Peru to declare war on Chile.

During the War of the Pacific (1879–83), Chile annexed 350km of coastline, leaving Bolivia landlocked. Though Chile offered to compensate Bolivia with a railway from Antofagasta to Oruro and duty-free export facilities, Bolivians refused to accept their *enclaustramiento* (landlocked status). The Bolivian government still lodges coastal claims; diplomatic relations with Santiago appear to be improving: the country's first indigenous leader, President Morales first met with Chile's leader in 2006.

Bolivia's losses continued. In 1903 Brazil annexed a huge chunk of the rubber-rich Acre region, which stretched from Bolivia's present Amazonian border to halfway up Peru's eastern border.

Between 1932 and 1935, Bolivia lost a third – and particularly brutal – war to Paraguay for control of the Chaco region (a total of 80,000 lives lost). Foreign oil companies began (mistakenly) speculating about potential Chaco petrol deposits. A quarrel was sparked, with Standard Oil backing Bolivia and Shell siding with Paraguay. Bolivia had more firepower, but the Chaco's hellacious fighting conditions favored the Paraguayans. A 1938 peace settlement granted 225,000 sq km of the Chaco to Paraguay.

Revolution & Counterrevolution

Following the Chaco War, friction between disenfranchised miners and their absentee bosses escalated. Radicals, especially in Oruro, gathered beneath the banner of the Movimiento Nacional Revolucionario (MNR). The turbulent 1951 presidential elections brought victory to the MNR's Victor Paz Estenssoro, but a military coup prevented him from taking power. The bloody revolution of 1952 forced the military to capitulate and Paz Estenssoro finally took the helm.

The new government spearheaded reforms aimed at ensuring the participation of all social sectors. Mining properties were nationalized and the sole right to export mineral products was vested in the state. The government introduced universal suffrage and an unprecedented policy of agrarian and educational reform, including a redistribution of estates among *campesinos* (farmers) and universal elementary education. For the first time since the Spanish Conquest, indigenous people felt that they had a voice in the government.

The MNR government lasted an unprecedented 12 years but had trouble raising the standard of living. Paz Estenssoro became increasingly autocratic as dissension in his own ranks percolated. Shortly after his second reelection in 1964, he was overthrown by his vice president, General René Barrientos, reviving Bolivia's political instability.

A series of repressive military governments ensued, starting with that of the right-wing general Hugo Banzer Suárez (1971–78). In 1982 a civilian government returned under Hernán Siles Zuazo and his left-wing Movimiento de la Izquierda Revolucionaria (MIR), but the country suffered from labor disputes, monetary devaluation and staggering inflation.

Under the Bolivian constitution, a candidate must earn 50% of the popular vote to become president in a direct election. When no candidate emerges with a clear majority, congress makes the decision, usually via a backroom deal between the major candidates. In 1989 the right-wing Acción Democrática Nacionalista (ADN) made a deal with the MIR, and the MIR's leader Jaime Paz Zamora was appointed president. In 1993 MNR leader Gonzalo Sánchez de Lozada ('Goni'; the Gringo) garnered the most votes, but had to ally with a *campesino* party to secure the presidency. He embarked on an ambitious privatization program, notable because much of the proceeds were invested in a public pension program. The new economic policies were met with protests and strikes, while antidrug programs sparked more unrest.

In the 1997 elections, comeback king Hugo Banzer Suárez and his rightist ADN party won just 23% of the vote. Due to pressure from the International Monetary Fund (IMF), neoliberal economic reforms were instituted, the currency was stabilized and many major industries were privatized. In August 2001 Banzer resigned due to cancer and handed over the reins to his vice president Jorge Quiroga Ramirez. With strong US backing, Sánchez de Lozada returned to power in the 2002 elections, only to face a popular uprising in February 2003 over the privatization of the gas industry ('The Bitter Gas War'), which forced him from office and into exile in the US. His deputy and successor Carlos Mesa held a referendum to permit Bolivia to export gas through Chile, but the questions were deemed complicated and the results uncertain. With this crisis and unrest on his hands, Mesa tried unsuccessfully to resign but Congress did not accept his offer. However, street demonstrations and unrest escalated, and as thousands marched into La Paz in June 2005, his resignation was accepted.

Former leader Eduardo Rodríguez was appointed as interim president until the elections in December 2005. In these elections, Evo Morales won in a landslide, having promised to change the traditional political class and empower the country's poor majority. Indeed, he was quick to act, nationalizing the country's gas reserves in April 2006 (see p175). At the time of print, Morales was talking about ceasing the US coca-crop eradication, integral to the US War on Drugs program.

Although the GDP grew steadily in the 1990s, Bolivia remains the continent's poorest nation. In 2005 the G8 announced a debt-forgiveness plan to the tune of US$2 billion over the next few decades to help reduce fiscal pressures. Infrastructure shortcomings and high unemployment rates continue to plague the country.

Coca Quandary

Coca has always been part of Bolivian culture: the Inca love goddess was represented holding coca leaves. Chewing the bitter leaf increases alertness and reduces hunger, cold and pain (see boxed text, below). It's believed that the Spanish conquistadores reaped the rewards

---

THE COCA CRAFT

Chewing coca leaves into an *akullico* – a soggy wad of golf-ball proportions – is an important ritual in Andean culture and is said to reduce fatigue, hunger and cold, as well as the effects of altitude. Most travelers try it, at least once. The following is a novice's guide to a good chew:

■ Buy a good-quality leaf *(elegida* or *seleccionada)*. 'Prime' leaves are moist, green and healthy.

■ De-vein the leaves one by one and insert them into the side of your mouth, between your cheek and choppers. Start macerating – not chewing! – the leaves. (The Bolivians say *pijchar*.) Sufficient maceration can take up to 45 minutes or more.

■ Resist the urge (or not) to spit out the bitter-tasting mass!

■ When the leaves are sufficiently soggy and the mass resembles a 'ball,' add a pinch of the alkaline substance *llipta* (also called *lejía;* these are plant ashes, normally from *quinua)* or sodium bicarbonate (baking soda). The easiest way is to crush the *llipta* into a powder and add it to a leaf before putting it in your mouth. This alkaline substance helps release the leaves' alkaloids.

■ Sense (or not) a strong tingling and numbing sensation in your cheek. (Resist the temptation to slap your face and declare 'I can't feel anything!' – like any anesthetic it wears off.)

■ Enjoy a mild sensation of alertness, reduction of appetite and resistance to temperature fluctuations. (Coca leaves do not produce a rush or a 'high'.)

■ Spit out when sated or before your mouth is the color of the Incredible Hulk. If imbibing is more to your taste, opt for a coca leaves tea.

of coca's lucrative regional trade. The world's (in)famous cola company incorporated derivatives into its 'secret' recipe, and some 19th-century patent medicines were based on coca. The raw leaf is neither harmful nor addictive and is said to be high in calcium, iron and vitamins.

But when its derivative – cocaine – became the recreational drug of choice (particularly in the USA), demand for Bolivian coca leaves rocketed. Since 1988, Bolivian law has permitted 12,000 hectares (30,000 acres) of coca to be cultivated for local (legitimate) use, but in reality, experts say that actual cultivation exceeds this limit.

In the '80s, in a desperate bid to curb Bolivia's status as primary producer of coca, the US sent its Drug Enforcement Agency (DEA) squadrons into the primary coca-growing regions of Chapare and Beni to 'assist' in coca eradication. It also injected millions of 'development aid' into the regions to develop alternative agricultural industries. This program largely failed: the alternative crops grow slowly, profits were negligible and, as poverty increased among *cocaleros* (growers), they shifted their cultivation to other areas. There were reports of brutality and human-rights abuses initiated by the DEA against the *cocaleros*.

In Chapare, it was Evo Morales – a former coca grower and by then a union organizer – who lead the resistance against the eradication policies. Soon after his recent election as president, Morales was quick to reinforce the slogan: '*coca sí, cocaína no*' ('coca yes, cocaine no'), an emphasis on solving the cocaine problem – at the consumer, not the *campesino*, end. He has also suspended eradication programs and wishes to increase cultivation, while seeking export opportunities for alternative coca-based products. In trying to appease both his constituents and the US, however, Morales could be playing with fire. At stake is the Bolivia–US trade agreement, crucial to the Bolivian textile producers, interestingly named the Andean Trade Promotion and Drug Eradication Act.

THE CULTURE
The National Psyche
Bolivian attitude varies widely depending on climate and altitude. *Kollas* (highlanders) and *cambas* (lowlanders) enjoy expounding on what makes themselves 'better' than the other. Lowlanders are said to be warmer, more casual

and more generous to strangers; highlanders are supposedly harder working but less open-minded. The reality is that seemingly every *camba* has a kind *kolla* relative living in La Paz and the jesting is good-natured.

Bolivians are all very keen on greetings and pleasantries. Every exchange is kicked off with the usual *buen(os) día(s)* (hello/good day), but also with a *¿Cómo está?* or *¿Qué tal?* (How are you?). Bolivian Spanish is also liberally sprinkled with endearing diminutives such as *sopita* (a little soup) and *pesitos* (little pesos, as in 'it only costs 10 little pesos').

Lifestyle
Day-to-day life varies from Bolivian to Bolivian, depending on whether they live in the country or city, their class and cultural background. Many *campesinos* live a largely traditional lifestyle in small villages, often without running water, heat or electricity, while those in the cities enjoy the comforts and modern conveniences and follow more Western practices. Clothing customs vary dramatically, from the women (Cholitas) of the *altiplano* in their pleated skirts and hats, to those who opt for the latest in designer wear.

Nevertheless, from ritual offerings to Pachamama (Mother Earth) to the habitual chewing of coca, Bolivia is long and strong in traditional culture. An entire canon of gods and spirits are responsible for bountiful harvests, safe travels and matchmaking. One especially unique tradition is the *tinku*, a ritual fistfight that establishes a pecking order, practiced during festivals in the northern Potosí department. The bloody, drunken battles (some fatal) go on for days, may feature rocks or other weapons and don't exempt women.

Population
Thanks to its amazing geographic diversity, Bolivia is anything but homogenous. Around 60% of the population claims indigenous identity. Many *campesinos* continue to speak Quechua or Aymara as a first language and some still live by a traditional lunar calendar. Miraculously, the frigid *altiplano* region supports nearly 70% of the populace.

Most Bolivians' standard of living is alarmingly low, marked by substandard housing, nutrition, education, sanitation and hygiene. The country has a high infant mortality rate (52 deaths per 1000 births); a birth rate of 2.85 per woman and a literacy rate of 87.2%.

Bolivia's economic landscape is bleak, but not completely dire, thanks to a thriving informal economy. The largest slice of the economic pie comes from coca exports, which exceed all legal agricultural exports combined.

SPORTS

Like in most of Latin America, the national sport is *futból* (soccer) and the national side typically fares quite well in *futsal* or *futból de salon* (five-versus-five minisoccer) world championships. Professional matches happen every weekend in big cities and it's easy to pick up impromptu street games. On the *altiplano*, liberated women have been playing more and more in recent years – in full skirts. Bolívar and Canada Strongest (both from La Paz) usually represent (albeit weakly) in the Copa Libertadores. Wrestling is becoming popular among a small but growing group of hardy *altiplano* females. Racquetball, billiards, chess and *cacho* (dice) are also huge. The unofficial national sport, however, has to be festing and feting – competition between dancers and drinkers knows no bounds.

RELIGION

Roughly 95% of Bolivia's population is Roman Catholic, with varying degrees of commitment. Particularly in rural regions, locals mix their Inca and traditional belief systems with Christianity, resulting in syncretism, an amalgamation of doctrines and superstitions.

Natural gods and spirits form the beliefs of these indigenous religions, with Pachamama, the earth mother, central to sacrificial offerings. The Aymara believe in mountain gods: *achachilas* are spirits of high mountains.

Talismans are also popular to guard against evil or bring good luck, as is Ekeko, a little elf-like figure and the Aymara household god of abundance, and the *cha'lla* (ritual blessing) of vehicles at the cathedral in Copacabana.

ARTS
Architecture

Tiahuanaco's ruined structures and a handful of Inca remains are about all that's left of pre-Columbian architecture in Bolivia. The classic Inca polygonal-cut stones that distinguish many Peruvian sites are rare in Bolivia, found only on Isla del Sol and Isla de la Luna (Lake Titicaca).

Some colonial-era houses and street facades survive, notably in Potosí, Sucre and La Paz.

Many existing colonial buildings are religious and their styles overlap several periods.

Renaissance (1550–1650) churches were constructed primarily of adobe, with courtyards and massive buttresses, such as that in Tiahuanaco. Renaissance churches with Moorish Mudejar influences include San Miguel (Sucre), and Copacabana (on the shores of Lake Titicaca).

Baroque (1630–1770) churches were constructed in the form of a cross, with an elaborate dome, such as the Compañía in Oruro, San Agustín in Potosí and Santa Bárbara in Sucre.

Mestizo style (1690–1790) is defined by whimsical decorative carvings including tropical flora and fauna, Inca deities and gargoyles. See the wild results at San Francisco (La Paz); San Lorenzo, Santa Teresa and the Compañía (Potosí).

In the mid-18th century, the Jesuits in the Beni and Santa Cruz lowlands went off on neoclassical tangents, designing churches with Bavarian rococo and Gothic elements. Their most unusual effort was the mission church at San José de Chiquitos.

Since the 1950s many modern city high-rises have been constructed. There are some gems: look for triangular pediments on the rooflines, new versions of the Spanish balcony and hardwoods of differing hues. In La Paz, chalet-type, wooden houses are all the rage and the more recent cathedral in Riberalta sings the contemporary gospel of brick and cedar.

Dance

Traditional *altiplano* dances celebrate war, fertility, hunting prowess, marriage and work. The Spaniards' European dances blended with those of the African slaves to evolve into the hybrid dances of Bolivian contemporary celebrations.

Bolivia's de facto national dance is the *cueca,* derived from the Chilean original and danced by handkerchief-waving couples, primarily during fiestas. The most colorful dances are performed at *altiplano* festivals, particularly during Carnaval: Oruro's *la Diablada* (Dance of the Devils) fiesta draws huge international crowds. The festival's *la morenada* reenacts the dance of African slaves brought to the courts of Viceroy Felipe III; dancers don hooped skirts, shoulder mantles and devilish, plumed masks.

Music

Despite motley, myriad influences, each of Bolivia's regions has developed its own musical styles and instruments. Andean music, from the cold, bleak *altiplano*, is suitably haunting and mournful, while music from the warmer lowland areas like Tarija has more vibrant, colorful tones.

Under the military regimes, *peñas* (folk-music shows) were a venue for protest; today, cities host *peñas*. Major artists to look for include *charango* masters Celestino Campos, Ernesto Cavour and Mauro Núñez (the recording is *Charangos Famosos*). Also sound out Altiplano, Savia Andina, Chullpa Ñan, K'Ala Marka, Rumillajta, Los Quipus, Wara, Los Masis and Yanapakuna.

The ukulelelike *charango* originally featured five pairs of llama-gut strings and a *quirquincho* (armadillo carapace) sound box that produced the pentatonic scale. Modern *charangos* are now usually made of wood. Tarija's stringed instrument, the *violín chapaco*, is a variation on the European violin.

Before the *charango*, melody lines were 'aired' exclusively by woodwind instruments. Traditional musical ensembles use the *quena* (reed flute) and the *zampoña* (pan flute). The *bajón*, an enormous pan flute with separate mouthpieces in each reed, accompanies festivities in the Moxos communities of the Beni lowlands.

Percussion sets the tone in most folkloric performances. Instruments include the *huankara*, a drum of the highlands, and Tarija's *caja*, a tambourinelike drum played with one hand.

Bolivia has its share of pop groups. Those in the mix include long-time Azul Azul, Octavia and Los Kjarkas. The last are best known for their recording of 'Llorando se Fue' which was lifted and reshaped (without permission) into the blockbuster hit *Lambada*. Inevitably, rap music has hit the scene, with some of the youngsters in El Alto catching on to its beat.

Weaving

Weaving methods have changed little in Bolivia for centuries. In rural areas, young girls learn to weave and women spend their spare time with a drop spindle or weaving on heddle looms. Before colonization, weavers used llama and alpaca wool, but today, sheep's wool and synthetic fibers are the cheaper options.

Bolivian textiles have wonderfully diverse patterns. The most common pieces include the *manta* or *aguayo*, a square shawl made of two handwoven strips, the *chuspa* (coca pouch), the *falda* (skirt) with patterned weaving on one edge and woven belts.

Each region boasts a different weaving style, motif and use. Zoomorphic patterns feature in weavings from Charazani country (near Lake Titicaca) and in several *altiplano* areas outside La Paz (Lique and Calamarka). Potolo, near Sucre, is renowned for its distinctive red-and-black designs. Finer weavings originate in Sica Sica, a dusty and nondescript village between La Paz and Oruro, while the expert spinning in Calcha, southeast of Potosí, produces an extremely tight weave and some of Bolivia's finest textiles.

ENVIRONMENT
The Land

Despite the loss of huge chunks of territory in wars and concessions, landlocked Bolivia is South America's fifth-largest country. Two Andean mountain chains define the west, with many peaks above 6000m. The western Cordillera Occidental stands between Bolivia and the Pacific coast. The eastern Cordillera Real runs southeast past Lake Titicaca, then turns south across central Bolivia, joining with the other chain to form the southern Cordillera Central.

The haunting *altiplano*, which ranges from 3500m to 4000m, is boxed in by these two great *cordilleras*. It is an immense, nearly treeless plain punctuated by mountains and solitary volcanic peaks. At the north end of the *altiplano*, straddling the Peruvian border, Lake Titicaca is one of the world's highest navigable lakes. In the bottom left corner, the land is drier and less populated. Here are the remnants of two ancient lakes, the Salar de Uyuni and the Salar de Coipasa, which form an ethereal expanse of blindingly white desert plains when dry, and hallucinogenic mirror images when under water.

East of the Cordillera Central are the Central Highlands, a region of scrubby hills, valleys and fertile basins. Cultivated in this Mediterranean-like climate are olives, nuts, wheat, maize and grapes.

North of the Cordillera Real, where the Andes abut the Amazon Basin, the Yungas form a transition zone between arid highlands and humid lowlands. More than half of

BOLIVIA

Bolivia's total area is in the Amazon Basin. The northern and eastern lowlands are sparsely populated and flat, with swamps, savannas, scrub and rainforest.

In the country's southeastern corner lies the flat, nearly impenetrable scrubland of the Gran Chaco, which extends into northern Paraguay.

Wildlife

National parks and reserves comprise 35% of Bolivia's territory and harbor myriad animal and bird species. Several national parks and protected areas (Parque Nacional Amboró, for example) boast among the world's greatest densities of species concentration. The *altiplano* is home to camelids, flamingos and condors. The harsh Chaco hides jaguar, tapir and *javeli* (peccary). The Amazon Basin boasts an amazing variety of lizards, parrots, snakes, insects, fish and monkeys (the most recently discovered species of *titi* monkey is worth its weight in gold; it was named after an online Canadian casino – *Callicebus averi palatti;* Golden Palace – after the casino won an auction to raise money for environmental foundations). Bolivia has several rare and endangered species including giant anteaters and spectacled bears.

River travelers might spot *capybaras* (large rodents), turtles, caimans and pink dolphins. Anacondas exist in the Beni, as do armadillos, sloths, rheas and *jochis* (agoutis).

National Parks

Bolivia has 22 officially declared parks, reserves and nature areas under the National Park Service, Sernap. Areas that are accessible to visitors – albeit often with some difficulty – include the following:

Amboró (p248) Near Santa Cruz, home to rare spectacled bears, jaguars and an astonishing variety of birdlife.

Apolobamba Excellent hiking in this remote park abutting the Peruvian border beneath the Cordillera Apolobamba.

Cotapata Most of the Choro trek passes through here, midway between La Paz and Coroico in the Yungas.

Madidi (p253) Protects a wide range of wildlife habitats; home to more than 1100 bird species.

Noel Kempff Mercado (p248) Remote park on the Brazilian border; contains a variety of wildlife and some of Bolivia's most inspiring scenery.

Pilón Lajas Biosphere Reserve A continuation of Madidi Park offering stunning landscape and living cultures.

Reserva Nacional de Fauna Andina Eduardo Avaroa A highlight of the Southwest Circuit tour, including wildlife-rich lagoons.

Sajama Adjoining Chile's magnificent Parque Nacional Lauca; contains Volcán Sajama (6542m), Bolivia's highest peak.

Torotoro Enormous rock formations with dinosaur tracks from the Cretaceous period, plus caves and ancient ruins.

Tunari Within hiking distance of Cochabamba; features the Lagunas de Huarahuara and lovely mountain scenery.

Environmental Issues

The 1990s saw an enormous surge in international and domestic interest in Amazonian ecological issues. Though environmental organizations have crafted innovative ways to preserve selected spots (including external funding), in other areas intensive development continues, often – in the past at least – with governmental encouragement. The jury is still out on how the Morales government will help the environmental cause. Contact the following nonprofit groups for information on countrywide environmental conservation efforts:

Armonía (☎ /fax 03-356-8808; www.birdbolivia.com; Lomas de Arena 400, Santa Cruz) Everything you need to know about Bolivian birding and bird conservation.

Conservación Internacional (CI; ☎ 02-279-7700; www.conservation.org.bo in Spanish; Calacoto Calle 13, No 8008, La Paz) Promotes community-based biodiversity conservation and ecotourism.

Fundación Amigos de la Naturaleza (FAN; ☎ 03-355-6800; www.fan-bo.org) Branches in Santa Cruz and Samaipata. Working in Parques Nacionales Amboró and Noel Kempff Mercado.

Proteción del Medioambiente del Tarija (Prometa; ☎ 04-664-5865; www.prometa.org; Carpio E-659, Tarija) Working in Sama and Tariquía reserves, Parque Nacional Serranía Aguaragüe and El Corbalán and Alarachi Private Reserves.

Servicio Nacional de Areas Protegidas (Sernap; ☎ 231-7742/47; www.sernap.gov.bo in Spanish; Edificio Full Office, btwn Camcho & Mariscal Santa Cruz) Bolivia's national park service manages all reserves and protected areas. Its website has a clear overview of each national park.

TRANSPORTATION

GETTING THERE & AWAY
Air

Only a few airlines are brave enough to offer direct services to La Paz' Aeropuerto El Alto (LPB), thus fares are as high as the altitude; flights to and from Chile and Peru are the cheapest. Many travelers land in Lima (Peru)

DEPARTURE TAX

A departure tax is charged for all domestic flights (US$2) and all international flights (US$25), payable after check-in. There is a 16% tax on all international airfares purchased in Bolivia.

or Santiago (Chile) and travel overland to enter Bolivia. Santa Cruz' Viru Viru International (VVI) is an increasingly popular entry point from western European hubs and for regional destinations not linked to La Paz.

Direct flights serve Arica (Chile), Asunción (Paraguay), Bogotá (Colombia), Buenos Aires (Argentina), Caracas (Venezuela), Cordoba (Argentina), Cuzco (Peru), Iquique (Chile), Lima (Peru), Manaus (Brazil), Río de Janeiro (Brazil), Salta (Argentina), Santiago (Chile) and São Paulo (Brazil).

Boat

The Brazilian and Peruvian Amazon frontiers are accessible via irregular riverboats. A more popular crossing is across the Río Mamoré by frequent ferry from Guajará-Mirim (Brazil) to Guayaramerín (see p255). From there, you can travel overland to Riberalta and on to Cobija or Rurrenabaque and La Paz.

Bus & Camión

Daily *flotas* (long-distance buses) link La Paz with Buenos Aires (Argentina) via Bermejo or Yacuiba; Salta (Argentina) via Tupiza/Villazón; Corumbá (Brazil) via Quijarro; and Arica and Iquique (Chile) via Tambo Quemado. Increasingly popular is the crossing to San Pedro de Atacama (Chile) as a detour from Salar de Uyuni tours (see p216). The most popular overland route to and from Puno and Cuzco (Peru) is via Copacabana (see boxed text, p209), but traveling via Desaguadero is quicker. Villamontes is the gateway for hearty souls attempting the Trans Chaco 'Highway', which now hits Paraguay at Fortín Infante Rivola (with customs at Mariscal Estagarribia in Paraguay) and rambles all the way to Asunción. Note: for those travelers going by car, the two Bolivian border posts are at Boyuibe or Ibibobo. Cheaper *camiones* (open-bed trucks) carry more contraband than passengers across borders, but they are useful for reaching obscure border crossings where there is little regularly scheduled public transport,

but check where you must get your entry and exit stamps on departure and arrival.

Car & Motorcycle

While most travelers enter Bolivia from adjoining lands by bus, train and/or boat, a few thrill seekers pilot their own vehicles. Motoring in Bolivia is certain to try your patience (and mechanical skills!), but will be a trip of a lifetime. Most rental agencies accept national driver's licenses, but if you plan on doing a lot of motoring bring an international license. For motorcycle and moped rentals, a passport is all that is normally required. See also p1085.

Train

Bolivia's only remaining international railway route detours west from the Villazón–Oruro line at Uyuni. It passes through the Andes to the Chilean frontier at Avaroa/Ollagüe then descends precipitously to Calama, Chile (see p218). Other adventurous routes dead end at the Argentine frontier at Villazón/La Quiaca (see the boxed text, p227) and Yacuiba/Pocitos and in the Brazilian Pantanal at Quijarro/Corumbá.

GETTING AROUND

You can get anywhere cheaply via bus, hitchhiking or camion. The most common (and locally popular) option is buses, which come in all shapes and sizes (as do their wheels) – and in all states of luxury or disrepair. Think twice about booking the cheapest ticket – a 24-hour-plus torture trip into the jungle at the end of rainy season (many stop operating during the rainy season). Boats, planes and trains are a much better choice when river crossings are high and unpaved roads have turned to mud. Trains are always the best option in the far south and in the north, moto-taxis will zip you around cheaply in every Beni town. Whatever your mode of transport, always take as a travel companion a stash of snacks, warm clothes, water and toilet paper.

Air

The national carrier **Lloyd Aéreo Bolviano** (LAB; reservations ☎ 800-10-3001, info ☎ 800-10-4321; www.labairlines.com in Spanish) and the private **AeroSur** (www.aerosur.com) are two long-standing airlines. At the time of research, AeroSur was a safer bet as LAB was experiencing cruising problems due to major debt issues.

BOLIVIA

BOLIVIA

A couple of no-frills domestic air services have hit the runways in recent years. They charge around the same fares and have a wide network with frequent flights and services to virtually everywhere you might wish to go. **Amaszonas** (www.amaszonas.com in Spanish) wings it from La Paz to Rurrenabaque twice daily. Note: services to Rurrenabaque are frequently delayed or cancelled. This is not (as many believe) always due to unreliable service, but to adverse weather conditions. The dirt runways turn to mud after heavy rains, so the planes will take off or land only when it is safe to do so. Always allow a couple of days to arrive or return at destinations such as Rurrenabaque.

The rough-and-ready military airline **Transportes Aéreos Militares** (TAM; ☎ in La Paz 02-212-1582/1585; tam@entelnet.bo) is a good alternative for Rurrenabaque and hard-to-reach places. Fares are cheap but seats are unreserved and flights are often late or canceled. AeroSur and LAB both offer four-flight, 45-day air passes (around US$250) between any of the main cities. (LAB also offers a similar Vibol Pass; it can only be bought *outside* Bolivia; three to five flights US$155 to US$250. See www.labairlines.com.bo for conditions.) The only catch with all the passes is that you can't pass through the same city twice, except to make connections.

Boat

Half of Bolivia's territory lies in the Amazon Basin, where rivers are the main (and during the rainy season often the only) transport arteries. The region's main waterways are the Beni, Guaporé (Iténez), Madre de Dios and Mamoré Rivers, all Amazon tributaries. Most cargo boats offer simple accommodations (cheap hammocks and mosquito nets are available in all ports) and carry everything from livestock to vehicles. Patience and plenty of spare time are key to enjoying these off-the-beaten-path journeys.

Bus, Camión & Hitchhiking

Thankfully, the Bolivian road network is improving as more kilometers are paved. Unpaved roads range from good-grade dirt to mud, sand, gravel and 'only at own risk.' Modern coaches use the best roads, while older vehicles ply minor secondary routes.

Long-distance bus lines are called *flotas*. Large buses are called *buses* and small ones are called *micros*. A bus terminal is a *terminal terrestre*.

To be safe, reserve bus tickets at least several hours in advance; for the lowest fare, purchase immediately after the driver starts up the engine. Many buses depart in the afternoon or evening, to arrive at their destination in the wee hours of the morning. On most major routes there are also daytime departures.

An alternative on many routes is a *camión*, which normally costs around 50% of the bus fare. This is how *campesinos* travel, and it can be excruciatingly slow and rough, depending on the cargo and number of passengers. *Camiónes* offer the best views of the countryside. Each town has places where *camiónes* gather to wait for passengers; some even have scheduled departures. Otherwise, the best places to hitch a lift will be the *tranca*, the police checkpoint at every town exit.

On any bus or *camión* trip in the highlands, day or night, layer well for the freezing nights (on and off the *altiplano*) and take food and water. Expect much longer travel times (or canceled services) in the rainy season when roads are challenging or impassable.

Taxi & Moto-taxi

Taxis are cheap but none are metered. Confirm the fare before departure or you're likely to be overcharged. Cross-town rides in large cities rarely exceed a couple of dollars (except to and from the airport which costs around US$6) and short hops in smaller towns are less than US$1. Fares are sometimes higher late at night, with excessive luggage (bargain hard!) and are always more for uphill runs. Full-day taxi hire is often cheaper than renting a car. Hourly moto-taxi rentals are common in balmy Beni towns.

Train

Since privatization, passenger rail services have been cut way back. The western network runs from Oruro to Uyuni and Villazón (on the Argentine border); a branch line runs southwest from Uyuni to Avaroa, on the Chilean border. Between Oruro, Tupiza and Uyuni, the comfortable *Expreso del Sur* trains run twice weekly. The cheaper *Wara Wara del Sur* also runs twice weekly between Oruro and Villazón. See www.fca.com.bo.

In the east, there's a line from Santa Cruz to the frontier at Quijarro, where you cross to the Pantanal in Corumbá, Brazil. An infrequently used service goes south from Santa Cruz to Yacuiba on the Argentine border a couple of times a week.

Rail travel in Bolivia requires patience and determination. Most stations now have printed timetables, but they still can't be entirely trusted. In older stations, departure times may be scrawled on a blackboard. When buying tickets, take your passport. For most trains, tickets are available only on the day of departure, but you can usually reserve seats on better trains through a local travel agent for a small commission.

LA PAZ

☎ 02 / pop 1.5 million (including El Alto)

La Paz is dizzying in every respect, not only for its well-publicized altitude (3660m), but for its quirky beauty. All travelers enter the city via the flat sparse plains of the sprawling El Alto, an approach which hides sensational surprises of the valley below; the first glimpse of La Paz will, literally, take your breath away. The city's buildings cling to the sides of the canyon and spill spectacularly downwards. On a clear day, the imposing, showy, snowy Mt Illamani (6402m) looms in the background.

The posher suburbs, with skyscrapers, colonial houses and modern glass constructions, occupy the city's more tranquil lower regions, but most of the daily action takes place further up the incline where a mass of irregular-shaped steep streets and alleys wind their way skywards. Here, locals embrace their frenetic daily life. Women, sporting long black plaits, bowler hats and vivid *mantas,* attend to steaming pots or sell everything from dried llama fetuses to designer shoes while men, negotiating the heavy traffic and its fumes, push overladen trolleys.

La Paz must be savored over time, not only to acclimatize to the altitude, but to experience the city's many faces. Wander at leisure through the alleys and markets, marvel at the many interesting museums, chat to the locals in a *comedor* (basic cafeteria or dining room in a hotel), or relax over a coffee and newspaper at many trendy cafés. There is a happening night scene and outside of the city there are interesting day trips.

La Paz was founded by Alonso de Mendoza in 1548, following the discovery of gold in the Río Choqueyapu. Although gold fever

fizzled, the town's location on the main silver route from Potosí to the Pacific assured stable progress. By the mid-20th century, La Paz had grown rapidly as thousands of *campesinos* migrated from the countryside. Today it is the country's governmental capital (Sucre remains the judicial capital).

The sky-high altitude means that warm clothing, sunscreen and sunglasses are essential. In the summer (November to April), the harsh climate assures afternoon rainfalls and the steep streets are awash with water torrents. In winter (May to October), days are invigoratingly crisp. While the sun shines, temperatures may reach the high teens, but at night it often dips below freezing; see p1095 for advice on dealing with altitude sickness.

ORIENTATION

You are more likely to get winded than lost in La Paz. There's only one major thoroughfare, which follows the canyon of the Río Choqueyapu. Often referred to as the Prado, it changes names several times from top to bottom: Autopista El Alto, Av Ismael Montes, Av Mariscal Santa Cruz, Av 16 de Julio (the Prado) and Av Villazón. At the lower end, it splits into Av 6 de Agosto and Av Aniceto Arce. If you become disoriented and want to return to this main street, just head downhill. Away from this thoroughfare, streets climb steeply uphill, and many are cobbled or unpaved.

The city has a number of districts, including the Zona Central (the blocks around and down from Plaza Pedro D Murillo), Sopocachi (the upmarket commercial and residential zone around Av 6 de Agosto), Miraflores (climbing the slope east of Zona Central) and Zona Sur (the most expensive residential area, further down the valley). A handful of Zona Sur suburbs, including Obrajes, Calacoto and Cotacota, have clinics, government offices and other services of interest to travelers.

A free map of La Paz is available from any one of the information kiosks (Map pp186–7).

Instituto Geográfico Militar (IGM; Map pp190-1; ☎ 254-5090; Pasaje Juan XXII 100) publishes Bolivia's best topographical maps. The most popular maps are often only available as photocopies (US$5 to US$13 per map). It's located off Rodríguez between México/Murillo and Linares.

BOLIVIA

LA PAZ

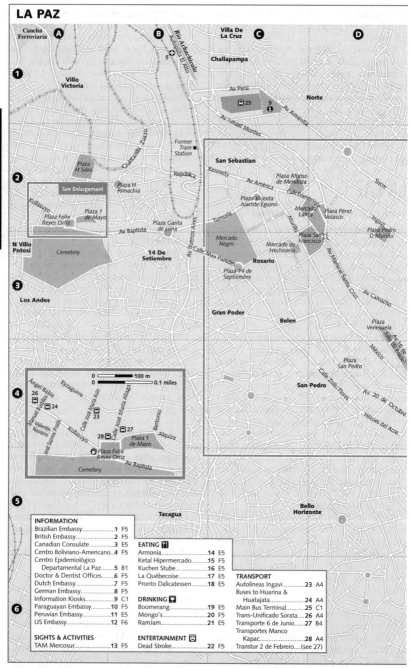

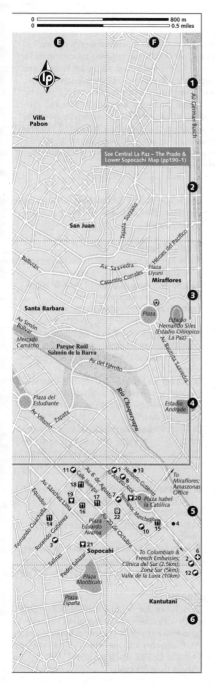

See Central La Paz – The Prado &
Lower Sopocachi Map (pp190-1)

INFORMATION
Bookstores

Bookshops include the following:

Gisbert & Co (Map pp190-1; Calle Comercio 1270) Good
stock of maps and Spanish-language literature.

Los Amigos del Libro (Map pp190-1; Mercado 1315)
Widest selection of foreign-language novels and periodi-
cals, plus a good selection of travel guides.

La Paz is the place for book exchanges with
good English titles. If you don't have luck in
some of the cheap hotels near Sagárnaga, then
the following offer good selections:

Gravity Assisted Mountain Biking (Map pp190-1;
Av 16 de Julio 1490, Edificio Av, No 10)

Oliver's Travels (Map pp190-1; Murillo 1014)

Sol y Luna Cafe Bar (Map pp190-1; cnr Murillo &
Cochabamba)

Cultural Centers

Centro Boliviano-Americano (Map pp186-7;
☎ 234-2582; www.cba.com.bo in Spanish; Parque
Zenón Iturralde 121) Language classes and current US
periodical library.

Goethe Institut (Map pp190-1; ☎ 244-2453; www
.goethe.de; Av 6 de Agosto 2118) Films, language classes
and good German-language library.

Emergency

Tourist police (Policía Turistica; Map pp190-1;
☎ 222-5016; Plaza del Estadio, Puerta 22, next to Disco
Love City, Miraflores) To report a crime or file a *denuncia*
(police report), contact the English-speaking tourist
police.

Numbers for emergency services are the same
in cities throughout the country:

Ambulance (☎ 118)

Fire department (☎ 119)

Police (Radio Patrol; ☎ 110)

Immigration Offices

For information on embassies and consulates
in La Paz, see p258.

Immigration (Migración; Map pp190-1; ☎ 211-0960;
Av Camacho 1478; ☷ 8:30am-4pm Mon-Fri) Extensions to
length of stay granted here.

Internet Access

La Paz has nearly as many cybercafés as shoeshine boys. Charges are from US40¢ to US75¢
an hour.

Internet Alley (Pasaje Irrturalde; Map pp190-1) Just off
Av Villazón near Plaza del Estudiante. Fastest, cheapest
connections in town.

BOLIVIA

BOLIVIA

GETTING INTO TOWN

The main bus terminal is 1km uphill from the center. *Micros* (US25¢) and minibuses (US30¢) marked 'Prado' and 'Av Arce' pass the main tourist areas but are usually too crowded to accommodate swollen backpacks. If walking, snake your way down to the main drag, Av Ismael Montes, and keep descending for 15 minutes past several plazas and street markets until you see San Francisco Church on your right, where Sagárnaga, the main tourist street, heads uphill.

Heading into town from El Alto Airport (10km outside the center) between 7:30am and 7pm, catch *micro* 212 (US50¢) directly outside the terminal, which will drop you anywhere along the Prado. A proper taxi from the rank to the center should cost no more than US$5 to US$6.50 for up to four people. If arriving by bus in Villa Fatima or the cemetery district, take particular care. At night, it's best to take a cab (US$1), but approach an official driver and *never* share with other strangers. By day, frequent *micros* run to the center from both locations.

Tolomeo's (Map pp190-1; cnr Loayza & Calle Comercio; per hr US30¢; ⊗ 8:30am-10:30pm Mon-Sat, 10:30am-6:30pm Sun) Warm and nonsmoking. Good machines; scanners and CD burning available.

Internet Resources
La Paz municipal (www.ci-lapaz.gov.bo in Spanish) Flash site with good culture and tourism sections.

Laundry
Lavanderías are the cheapest and most efficient way of ensuring clean (and dry) clothes in La Paz.

Illampu, at the top of Sagárnaga, is lined with laundries. Most *residenciales* (budget accommodations) offer cheap hand-washing services. For quick, reliable same-day machine wash-and-dry service (US$1 per kilo), try the following:
Limpieza Laverap (Map pp190-1; Illampu 704; ⊗ 8am-8pm Mon-Sat) Delivery to hotels with prepaid service.
Lavandería Maya (Map pp190-1; Sagárnaga 339) At Hostal Maya.

Left Luggage
Most recommended places to stay offer inexpensive or free left-luggage storage, especially if you make a return reservation. Think twice about leaving anything valuable in deposit – on a short- or long-term basis – as there have been numerous reports of items, including cash, going missing. Always put a lock on your luggage items if possible.

Media
La Razon (www.la-razon.com in Spanish), **El Diario** (www.eldiario.net in Spanish) and **La Prensa** (www.laprensa.com.bo in Spanish) are the major daily newspapers in La Paz. National media chains **ATB** (www.bolivia.com in Spanish) and **Groupo Fides** (www.fidesbolivia.com in Spanish) host websites with the most up-to-date news.

Medical Services
After-hours farmacias de turno (pharmacies) are listed in daily newspapers.
24-hour pharmacy (Map pp190-1; Av 16 de Julio at Bueno) A good pharmacy on the Prado.
Centro Epidemiológico Departamental La Paz (Centro Pilote; Map pp186-7; ☎ 245-0166; Vásquez 122 at Peru; ⊗ 8:30-11:30am Mon-Fri) Off upper Av Ismael Montes near the brewery. Anyone heading for the lowlands can pick up cheap antimalarials, and rabies and yellow-fever vaccinations.
Clínica del Sur (☎ 278-4001; Siles 3539, Obrajes) Frequently recommended by readers and embassies as friendly, knowledgeable and efficient. It's around 3km southeast of the center.
Dr Elbert Orellana Jordan (Unidad Medica Preventiva; ☎ 242-2342, 706-59743; asistmedbolivia@hotmail.com; cnr Freyre & Mujia) Gregarious English-speaking doctor makes emergency house calls around the clock at reasonable rates.
Dr Fernando Patiño (Map pp186-7; ☎ 243-0697, 772-25625; fpatino@entelnet.bo; Av Aniceto Arce 1701, Edificio Illimani, 2nd fl) Opposite the US embassy. American-educated, English-speaking high-altitude medicine expert.
Dr Jorge Jaime Aguirre (Map pp186-7; ☎ 243-0496; Av Aniceto Arce 1701, Edificio Illimani, 1st fl) Frequently recommended dentist, from routine cleaning to root canals.

Money
Watch out for counterfeit US dollars, especially with *cambistas* (street money changers), who loiter around the intersections of Colón, Av Camacho and Av Mariscal Santa Cruz. Outside La Paz you'll get 3% to 10% less for checks than for cash.

Casas de cambio (authorized foreign currency exchange houses) in the city center are quicker and more convenient than banks. Most places open from 8:30am to noon and 2pm to 6pm weekdays and on Saturday mornings. Outside these times, try the following:

Hotel Gloria (Map pp190-1; Potosí 909)
Hotel Rosario (Map pp190-1; Illampu 704)

The following places change traveler's checks for minimal commission:

Cambios América (Map pp190-1; Av Camacho 1223)
Casa de Cambio Sudamer (Map pp190-1; cnr Colón & Av Camacho) Sells currency from neighboring countries.

Cash withdrawals of US dollars and bolivianos are also possible at ATMs at major intersections around the city. For Visa and MasterCard cash advances (bolivianos only) with no commission and little hassle, try the following:

Banco Mercantil (Map pp190-1; cnr Mercado & Ayacucho) Has an ATM.
DHL/Western Union (Map pp190-1; ☎ 233-5567; Calle Juan Jose Perez 268) For urgent international money transfers. Outlets are scattered all around town.
Magri Turismo (Map pp190-1; ☎ 244-2727; www.magri-amexpress.com.bo; Capítan Ravelo 2101) This helpful representative does everything (including holding client mail) but doesn't change traveler's checks.

Photography

AGFA (Map pp190-1; ☎ 240-7030; Av Mariscal Santa Cruz 901) Perfect for passport photos in a flash.
Casa Kavlin (Map pp190-1; ☎ 240-6046; Potosí 1130) Good for one-hour slide or print processing.
Tecnología Fotográfia (☎ 242-7402; www.tecnologiafotografica.com; 20 de Octubre 2255) For camera problems, Rolando's your man.

Post

Ángelo Colonial (Map pp190-1; Linares 922; ☒ 9am-7pm) Convenient, gringo-friendly branch with an outgoing-only service.
Central post office (Ecobol; Map pp190-1; Av Mariscal Santa Cruz & Oruro; ☒ 8am-8pm Mon-Fri, 8am-6pm Sat, 9am-noon Sun) A tranquil oasis off the bustling Prado. Holds *lista de correos* (poste restante) mail for three months.

Telephone

You'll find convenient Punto Entels scattered throughout the city. Competitive communications companies include Cotel and Viva. Street kiosks on nearly every corner offer brief local calls for B$1. Hawkers with mobiles on a leash offer cellular calls for B$1 per minute.
Internet Call Centers (Map pp190-1; cnr Sagárnaga & Murillo, Galería Doryan; ☒ 8am-8pm) Cheap worldwide internet-based phone calls.
Main Entel office (Map pp190-1; Ayacucho 267; ☒ 7am-10pm) Best place to receive incoming calls and faxes.

Tourist Information

Ángelo Colonial (Map pp190-1; Linares 922) Privately run tourist information office with a book exchange and notice board.
Information kiosk (Map pp186-7) Outside the main bus terminal.
Mirador Laikakota (Map pp190-1)
Tourism information office (Map pp190-1; ☎ 237-1044; ☒ 8:30am-6:30pm Mon-Fri, 9am-1:30pm Sat & Sun) A map of the city is about as good as you'll get from here – but ask the helpful staff about the monthly calendar of events. It's on the north side of Plaza del Estudiante.

Travel Agencies

America Tours (Map pp190-1; ☎ 237-4204; www.america-ecotours.com; Av 16 de Julio, Edificio Av 1490, ground fl, No 9) Highly recommended English-speaking agency for help organizing trips to anywhere in the country. The environmentalist owners are especially good on new routes and community-based ecotourism projects.
Valmar Tours (Map pp190-1; ☎ 220-1499/1519; www.valmartour.com in Spanish) Sells International Student Identity Cards and has a few discounts for students. Best to talk to the English-speaking manager. Can also arrange some volunteering opportunities.

DANGERS & ANNOYANCES

While living the high life in La Paz is fun, it's important to take it easy, no matter how well you think you are feeling at nearly 4km above sea level. To avoid *soroche* (altitude sickness), take local advice '*camina lentito, come poquito…y duerme solito*' ('walk slowly, eat only a little bit…and sleep by your poor little self'), especially on the first day or two. More annoying than dangerous, ski mask–clad *lustrabotes* (shoeshine boys) hound everyone who wears footwear, but for US30¢ you can support their cause.

Scams

Sadly, La Paz seems to have caught on to South America's common ruses. Fake police officers and bogus tourist officials are on the rise. Note: authentic police officers will always be uniformed (undercover police are under

CENTRAL LA PAZ – THE PRADO & LOWER SOPOCACHI

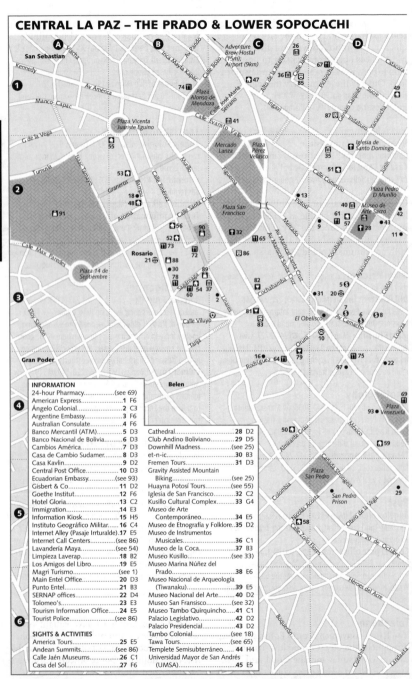

BOLIVIA

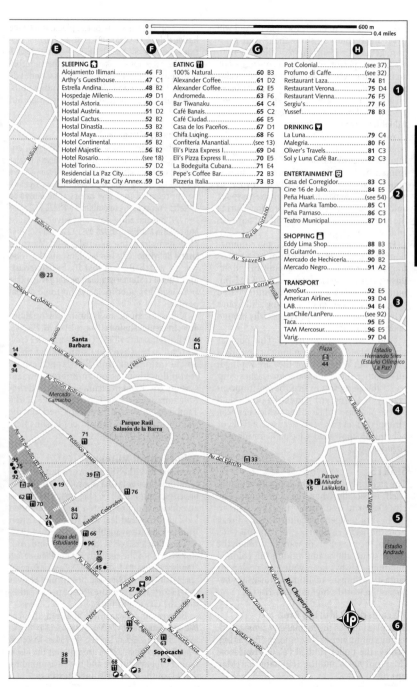

SLEEPING 🏠
Alojamiento Illimani................**46** F3
Arthy's Guesthouse................**47** C1
Estrella Andina.......................**48** B2
Hospedaje Milenio.................**49** D1
Hostal Astoria........................**50** C4
Hostal Austria........................**51** D2
Hostal Cactus........................**52** B2
Hostal Dinastía......................**53** B2
Hostal Maya...........................**54** B3
Hotel Continental...................**55** B2
Hotel Majestic........................**56** B2
Hotel Rosario.....................(see 18)
Hotel Torino...........................**57** D2
Residencial La Paz City...........**58** C5
Residencial La Paz City Annex..**59** D4

EATING 🍴
100% Natural.........................**60** B3
Alexander Coffee....................**61** D2
Alexander Coffee....................**62** E5
Andromeda............................**63** F6
Bar Tiwanaku.........................**64** C4
Café Banáis............................**65** C2
Café Ciudad...........................**66** E5
Casa de los Paceños...............**67** D1
Chifa Luqing..........................**68** F6
Confitería Manantial...........(see 13)
Eli's Pizza Express I................**69** D4
Eli's Pizza Express II...............**70** E5
La Bodeguita Cubana.............**71** E4
Pepe's Coffee Bar...................**72** B3
Pizzeria Italia.........................**73** B3

Pot Colonial......................(see 37)
Profumo di Caffe...............(see 32)
Restaurant Laza.....................**74** B1
Restaurant Verona..................**75** D4
Restaurant Vienna..................**76** F5
Sergiu's.................................**77** F6
Yussef....................................**78** B3

DRINKING 🍸
La Luna..................................**79** C4
Malegria.................................**80** F6
Oliver's Travels.......................**81** C3
Sol y Luna Café Bar................**82** C3

ENTERTAINMENT 🎭
Casa del Corregidor...............**83** C3
Cine 16 de Julio.....................**84** E5
Peña Huari.........................(see 54)
Peña Marka Tambo.................**85** C1
Peña Parnaso.........................**86** B3
Teatro Municipal....................**87** D1

SHOPPING 🛍
Eddy Lima Shop......................**88** B3
El Guitarrón...........................**89** B3
Mercado de Hechicería............**90** B2
Mercado Negro.......................**91** A2

TRANSPORT
AeroSur..................................**92** E5
American Airlines....................**93** D4
LAB.......................................**94** E4
LanChile/LanPeru..............(see 92)
Taca......................................**95** E5
TAM Mercosur........................**96** E5
Varig.....................................**97** D4

strict orders not to hassle foreigners) and will never insist that you show them your passport, get in a taxi with them or allow them to search your person in public. If confronted by an imposter, refuse to show them your valuables (wallet, passport, money etc), or insist on going to the nearest police station on foot. Of course, if physically threatened, hand over valuables immediately!

Another popular Bolivian bother is the bogus South American tourist who, on engaging you in conversation in English, is confronted by the aforementioned fake tourist police. The 'tourist' abides by an 'order' to show the policeman his bag/papers/passport, and 'translates' for you to do the same. During the search, the cohorts strip you of your cash and/or belongings.

Fake 'taxi drivers' are working in conjunction with gangs who steal from or – as has tragically been the case – assault or kidnap unsuspecting travelers (to extort ATM pin numbers). Beware of hopping into shared cabs with strangers or of accepting a lift from a driver who approaches you (especially around dodgy bus areas).

And finally, psst my friend! This popular scam involves a shyster spilling or spitting a phlegm ball. While you or they are wiping it off, another lifts your wallet or slashes your pack; the perpetrator may be an innocent granny or young girl. Similarly, don't bend over to pick up a valuable item which has been 'dropped.' You risk being accused of theft, or of being pickpocketed. (See p258 for more *en vogue* scams.)

SIGHTS

The steep city is a breathtaking attraction in itself, especially when the sun shines. The city's colorful and rowdy markets swirl to the beat of indigenous cultures. For a break from the hectic rhythm of everyday street life, head to the museums or wander through the cobblestone alleys and among the colonial buildings. Always keep your eyes peeled for fantastic glimpses of Illimani towering between the world's highest high-rises.

Plaza Pedro D Murillo Area

This plaza marks the formal city center, with various monuments, the imposing **Palacio Legislativo**, the bullet-riddled **Palacio Presidencial** (Map pp190–1) and the 1835 **cathedral** (Map pp190–1).

Just off the west side of the plaza, the **Museo Nacional del Arte** (Map pp190-1; ☎ 240-8600; cnr Comercio & Socabaya; admission US$1.25; 🕒 9am-12:30pm & 3-7pm Tue-Sat, 9:30am-12:30pm Sun) is in the superbly restored pink granite Palacio de los Condes de Arana (1775). The collection of indigenous, colonial and contemporary arts is small but rewarding.

Calle Jaén Museums

Five blocks northwest of Plaza Murillo, colonial Calle Jaén has four small **museums** (Map pp190-1; combined admission US50¢; 🕒 9:30am-12:30pm & 3-7pm Tue-Fri, 9am-1pm Sat & Sun) that can easily be appreciated in a few hours. The **Museo de Metales Preciosos Precolombinos** (☎ 228-0329; Calle Jaén 777) has dazzling gold and silver artifacts; **Museo Casa Murillo** (☎ 228-0553; Calle Jaén 790) displays items from the colonial period; **Museo del Litoral Boliviano** (Calle Jaén 789) laments the 1884 war in which Bolivia lost its Pacific coast; and **Museo Costumbrista Juan de Vargas** (cnr Calle Jaén & Sucre) has good displays on the colonial period.

A must for musicians is the impressive **Museo de Instrumentos Musicales** (Map pp190-1; ☎ 233-1075; Calle Jaén 711; admission US65¢; 🕒 9:30am-1pm & 2-6pm), with an exhaustive hands-on collection of unique instruments from Bolivia and beyond. If you don't happen on an impromptu jam session, check out museum founder and *charango* master Ernesto Cavour's Peña Marka Tambo (p198) across the street. Check out the *charango* and wind-instrument lessons here for around US$5 per hour.

Other Central Museums

Travelers love the slightly worn but very interesting **Museo de la Coca** (Map pp190-1; ☎ 231-1998; Linares 906; admission US$1; 🕒 10am-7pm), which gives an educational, provocative and evenhanded look at the sacred leaf and its uses. Written translations are available.

The cloisters, cells, the garden and roof (for views!) of the recently opened **Museo San Francisco** (Map pp190-1; ☎ 231-8472; Plaza San Francisco; admission US$2.50; 🕒 9am-6pm) beautifully revives the history and art of the 460-year-old cathedral, the city's landmark.

Between the plaza and Calle Jaén, the free **Museo de Etnografía y Folklore** (Map pp190-1; ☎ 240-6692; cnr Ingavi & Genaro Sanjinés; 🕒 9:30am-12:30pm & 3-7pm Tue-Sat, 9:30am-12:30pm Sun) explores the fascinating Chipaya culture and has an astounding exhibit of the country's finest textiles.

Adjacent is the **Museo Tambo Quirquincho** (Map pp190-1; ☎ 239-0969; admission US15¢; ◯ 9:30am-12:30pm & 3-7pm Mon-Fri, 9:30am-noon Sat & Sun) is a former tambo (wayside market and inn) displaying old-fashioned dresses, silverware, photos, artwork and Carnaval masks. It's off Calle Evaristo Valle at Plaza Alonzo de Mendoza.

Near Plaza del Estudiante, the **Museo Nacional de Arqueología** (Map pp190-1; Tiwanaku 93; ☎ 231-1621; admission with guide US$1.25; ◯ 9am-12:30pm & 3-7pm Mon-Fri, 10am-12:30pm & 3-6:30pm Sat, 10am-1pm Sun) holds an interesting collection of Tiahuanaco (Tiwanaku) pottery, sculptures, textiles and other artifacts.

Miraflores features the **Templete Semisubterráneo** (Map pp190-1; Museo al Aire Libre, cnr Ilimani & Bautista Saavedra), a free, open-air reproduction of part of the Tiahuanaco archaeological site. Only merits a thought if you can't make it to the site itself (see p200).

The works of Bolivia's most renowned sculptor are housed in her former (stunning) mansion, **Museo Marina Núñez del Prado** (Map pp190-1; ☎ 232-4906; Ecuador 2034; admission US65¢; ◯ 9:30am-1pm & 3-7pm Tue-Fri, 9:30am-1pm Sat & Sun), in Sopocachi. Opening hours can be unreliable.

The private **Museo de Arte Contemporáneo** (Map pp190-1; ☎ 233-5905; Av 16 de Julio 1698; admission US$1.25; ◯ 9am-9pm) is more notable for its 19th-century mansion designed by Gustave Eiffel, with glass roof and stained-glass panels, than for its Bolivian art collection.

Parque Laikakota Mirador & Kusillo Cultural Complex

For great cityscape views, head to the **mirador** (lookout; Map pp190-1; admission US15¢; ◯ 9am-5:30pm) in a tranquil park setting overlooking La Paz. The nearby **Museo Kusillo** (Map pp190-1; ☎ 222-6187; Av del Ejército; admission Tue-Fri US75¢, adult/child Sat & Sun US$1.50/1.25; ◯ 10:30am-6:30pm Tue-Sun), is a hands-on interactive play space for kids.

To get there, walk 20 minutes east of the Prado along Av Zapata; this turns into Av del Ejército.

ACTIVITIES
Mountain Biking

For an adrenaline rush at altitude, head off on wheels with **Gravity Assisted Mountain Biking** (Map pp190-1; ☎ 313-849; www.gravitybolivia.com; Av 16 de Julio 1490, Edificio Av, No 10). Two of the most popular full-day options (there are many others) are to zoom down from Chacaltaya to La Paz or from La Cumbre down the 'World's Most Dangerous Road' to Coroico. Many other outfits on Sagárnaga offer the La Cumbre to Coroico trip for a few bucks less but consider what corners are being cut before you go plunging downhill. Also, think twice before going with any of the agencies who offer these trips during the rainy season (January/February). Also see the boxed text, below. **Downhill Madness** (Map pp190-1; ☎ 239-1810; www.downhill-madness.com; Sagarnaga 339) is also recommended for the trip to Coroico.

Trekking & Climbing

Club Andino Boliviano (Map pp190-1; ☎ 231-2875; fecab@bolivia.com; México 1638) has a small lodge with café (per person US$5), where you can stay the night. The Club organizes several day trips, including skiing outings (although this is seasonal – unfortunately, the glacier has retreated and skiing is no longer a year-round activity).

Many La Paz tour agencies offer daily hiking tours to Chacaltaya (US$15), a fun and

---

DEADLY TREADLIES

Many agencies offering the La Cumbra to Coroico mountainbike plunge give travelers T-shirts plastered with: 'I've survived the World's Most Dangerous Road.' Keep in mind, the gravel road is just that: it's narrow (just over 3.2m wide) and has precipitous cliffs up to 600m…and there's traffic. At the time of research, eight people (higher figures sometimes quoted) have died doing the 64km trip (with a 3600m vertical drop) and readers have reported close encounters and nasty accidents. Most of these are due to little or no instruction and preparation, and poor quality mountain bikes (beware bogus rebranded bikes). In short, many agencies are less than ideal. Be aware of outfits which deflate prices – cost cutting can mean dodgy brakes, poor-quality parts and literally, a deadly treadly. Multilingual guides are necessary for coaching and control. Ask agencies for proof of rescue equipment (rope rescue, harnesses, belays, oxygen), and a predeparture briefing. Ensure a quality company on this spectacular route before you freewheel your life away.

easy way to bag a high peak. For rock climbing, mountaineering, paragliding and other extreme adventure possibilities, contact the Oruro-based **Club de Montañismo Halcones** (www .geocities.com/yosemite/gorge/1177), which has pioneered many routes around La Paz.

WALKING TOUR

A good starting point is **Iglesia de San Francisco (1)**, on the plaza of the same name. This imposing church was started in 1549 but went unfinished until the mid-18th century. Its architecture reflects the mestizo style, emphasizing natural forms. Watch for colorful wedding processions on weekend mornings.

From **Plaza San Francisco (2)**, huff up Sagárnaga, the main tourist strip, lined with weavings (ponchos, *mantas* and coca pouches), musical instruments, antiques, and 'original' Tiahuanaco artifacts. Turn right at Linares and poke around the uncanny **Mercado de Hechicería** (3; Mercado de los Brujos or Witches Market; p198).

Heading up Calle Santa Cruz to **Plaza 14 de Septiembre (4)** and Calle Max Paredes, you'll find the **Mercado Negro (5**; p198).

> **WALK FACTS**
> **Start** Iglesia de San Fransisco
> **Finish** Plaza Pedro D Murillo
> **Distance** 2½ to 3km
> **Duration** two to three hours

From here, wander downhill, (along Graneros and left onto Figueroa), north and east of the markets, through streets choked with people and *micros* to **Plaza Alonso de Mendoza (6)** – stay alert here. Visit the adjacent **Museo Tambo Quirquincho (7**; p193).

Continue past the bustling **Mercado Lanza (8**; p197) along pedestrian-only **Calle Comercio (9)** to end at **Plaza Pedro D Murillo (10**; p192).

COURSES

Spanish classes are offered by the Centro Boliviano-Americano (p187) and private teachers who charge around US$5 per hour. **Isabel Daza Vivado** (☎ 231-1471; maria_daza@hotmail .com; Murillo 1046, 3rd fl) is frequently recommended for her professionalism.

For Bolivian-style guitar or *charango* lessons, stop by the Museo de Instrumentos Musicales (p192).

Casa del Sol (Map pp190-1; ☎ 244-0928; Goitia 127; class US$3.20) offers yoga, tai chi and meditation classes. Monthly memberships (US$30) and student discounts are available.

TOURS

There are many tour operators in La Paz, especially around Sagárnaga; others are based at the larger hotels and cater to individuals or tour groups. With four to six people, a half-day city tour costs around US$10 per person and a day trip to Chacaltaya and Valle de la Luna or Tiahuanaco costs around US$15 to US$20, including entrance fees. Most companies offer much the same on the

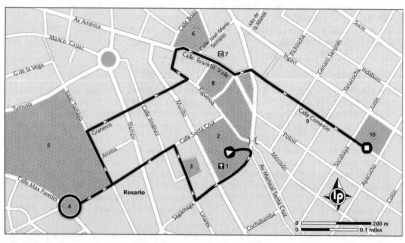

more standard trips. Speak to travelers for recommendations.

FESTIVALS & EVENTS

Of the major festivals and holidays during the year, Alasitas (January 24), the festival of abundance, and El Gran Poder (late May to early June) are the most interesting to visitors. The Fiestas Universitarias take place during the first week in December, accompanied by riotous merrymaking and enough water-balloon bombs to sink the Chilean navy.

SLEEPING

Most backpackers beeline for Central La Paz to find a crash pad. The area west of the Prado between Plazas Mendoza and Murillo is chock full of cheap, popular places and all the services you'll need.

Also near here is the Witches Market (between Calle Santa Cruz and Sagárnaga), the true traveler's ghetto. Here you'll find scores of dives, hostels and some plusher digs all cheek by jowl with adventure-tour operators, gringo cafés and touristy *peñas*. If you want to stay closer to a wider array of restaurants and bars, consider staying further south in the Lower Prado, around Plaza San Pedro where there are a few choice cheapies. The area around the bus terminal boasts some excellent new additions.

In the cheapest accommodations, expect communal bathrooms, cold showers, no heat and lots of partying, although some impose a curfew. Spend a bit more if you need your sleep.

West of the Prado

Hostal Cactus (Map pp190-1; ☎ 245-1421; Calle Jiménez 818; r per person US$3.15) This joint could do with a mild cleaning spell or two, but its location, smack in the middle of the Witches Market, makes up for the shabby student-style digs. The communal kitchen and rooftop 'terrace' appeal to those on a budget.

Hostal Maya (Map pp190-1; ☎ 231-1970; mayahostal@hotmail.com; Sagárnaga 339; r per person US$6.90, with bathroom US$8.20; ☐) Some rooms are as smoky and windowless as a witch's den; others, such as those with a front balcony, are more appealing, if a little noisy. A *charango*'s strum stumble away from Peña Huari. Breakfast included.

Hotel Majestic (Map pp190-1; ☎ 245-1628; Calle Santa Cruz 359; s/d/tr incl breakfast US$10.50/12.35/15) Its pink

bathrooms and smart parquetry floors provide some distraction from its nondescript, yet clean surrounds in the heart of things. Excellent value.

Estrella Andina (Map pp190-1; ☎ 245-6421; Illampu 716; s/d US$18/28) If you're suffering from altitude sickness, amuse yourself at this clean and well-run place. Each room has its own mural (or three) and cable TV. Good value for this price range.

East of the Prado

Alojamiento Illimani (Map pp190-1; ☎ 220-2346; Illimani 1817; s/d US$3.15/6.30) The religious pictures on the walls of these stark rooms are the most blessed things in this out-of-the-way abode… except for the kitchen, which the friendly owner will let you use for a small fee.

Hostal Austria (Map pp190-1; ☎ 240-8540; Yanacocha 531; r per person US$3.15-4.40) This shabbily rambling number gets trotted out time and time again. Despite its 11pm curfew, short beds (some in windowless cells) and dicey shared bathrooms, this old place is a good place to meet and team up with people. Hot showers and cooking facilities available.

Hotel Torino (Map pp190-1; ☎ 240-6003; Socabaya 457; s/d/tr US$6.30/10/19, without bathroom US$3.80/5/7.50) 'Dark, cold and draughty' is one traveler's view of this modernized (in the '50s) rambling, colonial building. It's more popular for its services – restaurant, book exchange, luggage storage – than its comforts.

Hostal Dinastía (Map pp190-1; ☎ 245-1076; hostel dinastia@yahoo.com; Illampu 684; r per person US$4, with bathroom & cable TV US$7) Shabby with slightly soiled semicarpeted rooms, but you're right in the middle of the action. Some rooms have cable TV.

Hotel Continental (Map pp190-1; ☎ 245-1176; hotelcontinental626@hotmail.com; Illampu 626; r per person US$5, s/d with cable TV US$10/14) This older, two-star HI-affiliate is clean, well located and popular among thrifty tour groups. It's hard to meet people due to its unsociable hotel-style design.

Lower Prado

Residencial La Paz City Annex (Map pp190-1; ☎ 236-8380; México 1539; r per person US$3.80) Affiliated to Los Balcones Blancos, Residencial La Paz City Annex is also shabby, but has some OK rooms with balconies.

Los Balcones Blancos (Map pp190-1; ☎ 248-9471; Nicolás La Costa 477; r per person US$5-7.55) A friendly and faded digs. Ask for the nicer rooms in the newer extension.

Residencial Sucre (Map pp190-1; ☎ 249-2038; Colombia 340; r per person US$7.50/10, s/d with bathroom & cable TV US$10/15) The management is helpful and the rooms are around a secure and pleasant courtyard (good for cycle storage). It's handy to Plaza San Pedro.

Hostal Astoria (Map pp190-1; ☎ 215-4081; Almirante Grau 348; s/d US$12/18) To avoid the traveler's ghetto, head to this underrated, excellent-value hotel-style choice with spotless rooms. It is located on a quiet and pleasant plaza, and is a beer's breath away from the bars of Sopocachi.

Near the Main Bus Terminal

Some of the city's best choices are handy to the main bus terminal.

Hospedaje Milenio (Map pp190-1; ☎ 228-1263; Yanacocha 860; s/d US$3/5.35) As yellow and mellow as you'll get. It is run by friendly staff and includes kitchen use, hot water and is close to the bus terminal. The best rooms, including the single room in the tower, are upstairs and outward facing. It also has a travel agency and laundry service.

Adventure Brew Hostel (Map pp190-1; ☎ 246-1614; Av Montes 533; www.theadventurebrewhostel.com; dm/r US$5/8) The name says it all. This brand-new abode on the block offers designer-style rooms, funky communal spaces, pancake breakfasts, as well as fun on tap. Yes, there's an authentic microbrewery on site. Owner Alistair is of Gravity Assisted Biking fame.

Arthy's Guesthouse (Map pp190-1; ☎ 228-1439; arthyshouse@gmail.com; Av Montes 693; r per person US$5) This clean and cozy place, hidden behind a bright-orange door, deservedly receives rave reviews as a 'tranquil oasis,' despite its location on one of La Paz' busiest roads. Chill in the living room over a choice of DVDs. The friendly English-speaking owners will do all they can do to help you. Kitchen facilities available.

EATING

'Love food? Will eat.' La Paz enjoys an abundance of inexpensive eateries offering everything from local treats to more Western-style dishes. For local fare, your cheapest bets are the *almuerzos* (set lunches) in the countless hole-in-the-wall restaurants; look for the chalkboard menus out front. Common dishes include *lomo* (tenderloin), *churrasco* (steak),

milanesa (breaded and fried beef or chicken cutlets) and *silpancho* (beef schnitzel). Street stalls offer tasty morsels and there are vegetarian restaurants around.

West of the Prado
CAFÉS & QUICK EATS
Tambo Colonial (Map pp190-1; Hotel Rosario, Illampu 704; breakfast US$2.50; ⏲ 7-10:30am & 7-10:30pm) Offers an excellent fruity breakfast buffet and great salads and soups in the evening.

100% Natural (Map pp190-1; Sagárnaga 345) A satisfying snack place with big breakfasts and tremendous, sanitary salads.

Pepe's Coffee Bar (Map pp190-1; Calle Jiménez 894) Take a spell from the Witches Market and linger over a coffee or fruit salad.

Profumo di Caffe (Map pp190-1; Plaza San Fransisco) Guilt-free coffee in a new and stylish café attached to the Cathedral's museum.

Café Banaís (Map pp190-1; Sagárnaga) Great salads, vego meals and breakfasts in the heart of things. It's below Hotel Naira.

RESTAURANTS
Angelo Colonial (Map pp190-1; Calle Linares 922; mains US$2.50-5) This quirky, darkened colonial-style restaurant sports more than a ramshackle collection of antiquities – pistols, swords and antique portraits – but it has excellent soups, salads and a luscious lasagna for vegetarians (US$3). A pleasant place to spend a rainy afternoon.

Pot Colonial (Map pp190-1; Linares; mains US$3-5) This relaxing place serves reliable meat dishes at armadillo pace. It's next to Coca Museum.

Pizzeria Italia (Map pp190-1; Illampu 809; ⏲ 7am-11pm) Pastas, pizzas and vegetarian options with a daily happy hour.

Yussef (Map pp190-1; Sagárnaga) Cheap, cheerful and Middle Eastern. Hummus, kebabs and the like are purchased by portion.

Restaurant Laza (Map pp190-1; Calle Bozo 244, Plaza Alonso de Mendoza) This lunchtime hole-in-the-wall is a winner.

Bar Tiwanaku (Map pp190-1; cnr Oruro & México; lunch US75¢) Has a good set lunch and hosts live music some weekends.

East of the Prado
Alexander Coffee (Av 16 de Julio (Map pp190-1; Av 16 de Julio 1832); Potosí (Map pp190-1; Potosí 1091) Fashionable café chain serving all manner of java drinks, pastries and sandwiches. The best place for a frothy cappuccino.

Eli's Pizza Express I & II (Map pp190-1; Av 16 de Julio 1491 & 1800) A local favorite where you can choose between pizza, pasta, pastries and ice cream.

Confitería Manantial (Map pp190-1; Potosí 909) This place in Hotel Gloria has a popular veggie lunch and dinner buffet.

Restaurant Verona (Map pp190-1; Colón; mains US$1-2) Open daily for sandwiches, pizzas and *almuerzos*. It's near Av Mariscal Santa Cruz.

Confitería Club de La Paz (Map pp190-1; ☎ 719-26265; Camacho & Av Mariscal Santa Cruz; mains US$1.50-4.50) For a quick coffee or *empanada*, hit this literary café and haunt of politicians known for its strong espresso and cakes.

Lower Prado
CAFÉS & QUICK EATS
Café Ciudad (Map pp190-1; Plaza del Estudiante; ⏲ 24hr) Average food, but the full menu is available around the clock and they don't mind travelers lingering over coffee.

Kuchen Stube (Map pp186-7; Rosendo Gutiérrez 461; ⏲ 8am-9pm) Espresso coffee, German pastries and other decadent homemade goodies.

Sergiu's (Map pp190-1; Av 6 de Agosto; ⏲ evenings only) The best by-the-slice pizza in town. The hot dogs and chili are also winners. It's near Aspiazu steps.

Andromeda (Map pp190-1; Av Aniceto Arce; lunch US$1.75) Located at the bottom of Aspiazu steps, this is recommended for *almuerzos*.

RESTAURANTS
Chifa Luqing (Map pp186-7; Av 20 de Octubre 2090; almuerzo US$2; ⏲ 11am-11pm) One of the most deceptive places around. The nondescript outer hides bright Asian flavors.

Armonía (Map pp186-7; Ecuador 2286; ⏲ noon-2:30pm Mon-Sat) La Paz' best all-you-can-eat vegetarian lunch is found above Liberia Armonia in Sopocachi.

Restaurant Vienna (Map pp190-1; ☎ 239-1660; Federico Zuazo 1905; mains US$4-7) Worth the splurge: this place is classy and arguably La Paz' best international restaurant.

The area's other recommended eateries serving international food include the following:
La Bodeguita Cubana (Map pp190-1; Federico Zuazo 1653; mains US$3-6) An appealing hole-in-the-wall with meaty offerings, Cuban tunes and strong *mojitos* (rum-and-lime-juice cocktails).

Pronto Ristorante (Map pp186-7; Jáuregui 2248; mains US$4-7) This is a pricey but '*dali*-ciously' surreal experience. Chocolate lovers will scream for the 'Paranoia

of textures and tastes of Daliano chocolate' (B$25). It's between Av 6 de Agosto and Av 20 de Octubre.
La Québecoise (Map pp186-7; ☎ 212-1682; Av 20 de Octubre 2387; mains US$5-10; ⏲ Mon-Sat) Lauded for its romantic atmosphere and excellent French-Canadian cuisine.

Markets & Street Food
For cheap, filling eats hit the markets. Cheap DIY meals can easily be cobbled together from the abundance of fruit, produce and bread sold there.

Mercado Camacho (Map pp190-1; cnr Av Simon Bolivar & Bueno) Stands sell *empanadas* (deep-fried pillows of cheese-lined dough), and chicken sandwiches, while *comedores* serve up daily fare. A set feast of soup, a meat dish, rice and *oca* (edible Andean tuber resembling a potato) or potato comes in under US$1.

At Mercado Lanza (Map pp190-1), in the streets surrounding Calle Evaristo Valle and Figueroa, is a mass of stalls selling anything and everything. While hygiene in the *comedor* is questionable, don't miss the rank of fruit drink stalls at the Figueroa entrance.

For excellent *empanadas*, go to the first landing on the steps between the Prado and Calle México. For around US40¢, you'll get an enormous beef or chicken *empanada* served with your choice of sauces – hot, hotter and hottest.

Self-Catering
Ketal Hipermercado (Map pp186-7; Av Aniceto Arce, Sopocachi) Picnic-basket goods – from olives to cheese, crackers and beer – are available here, just beyond Plaza Isabel la Católica.

DRINKING
There are scores of cheap local drinking dens around the city, especially near the Prado. Drunken marathons often typify Bolivian partying so single women should be aware of the type of establishments they're immersing themselves into.

There are a few great bars with a mixed traveler/Bolivian scene.

RamJam (Map pp186-7; Presbitero Medina 2421) If La Paz had a Paris Hilton, she'd be here. This new, trendy (but welcoming) hot spot has the lot: great food and drinks, mood lighting, live music, English breakfasts, microbrewed beer. You can breathe easy on the bar's 1st floor in Ozone, the most novel oxygen bar in the world (oxygen mask US$10 for five minutes).

BOLIVIA

BOLIVIA

Oliver's Travels (Map pp190-1; Murillo 1014) The best (or worst) cultural experience in La Paz is to be had at this in-your-face unashamed English-style drinking hole. As the promo literature proclaims, it aims 'to offer nothing original – just beer, football, curry, typical English food, cheeky banter and lots of music you've heard before.' And luckily for owner Olly himself, crowds of revelers swallow this stuff.

Sol y Luna Cafe Bar (Map pp190-1; cnr Murillo 999 & Cochabamba) A relaxed Dutch-owned joint where cocktails, coffee, occasional live music and games are on the menu. For those too tight to buy their own guidebooks, there's a good reference collection here.

Boomerang (☎ 242-3700; Pasaje Gustavo Medinacelli, 2282) A new and appealing bar-cum-pizzeria in a bright and open atrium, which has little to do with an Australian icon. That is, unless the slightly soggy but tasty pizzas, Entel cellular phone chargers and Spanish newspapers keep you comin' back.

Mongo's (Map pp186-7; Hermanos Manchego 2444; ☺ 6:30pm until late) La Paz' long-standing hip, hot (it gets crowded) and happening spot. Open (as the promo literature says) till the last head hits the table.

Malegria (Map pp190-1; Goitia 155) A good place to mingle with students. It features Afroboliviano drumming and dancing on Thursday and live bands on weekends.

The local gilded youth mingle with up-market expats at trendy bars and clubs along 20 de Octubre in Sopocachi and lower down in Zona Sur, where US-style bars and discos spread along Av Ballivián and Calle 21. You'll need more than a backpacker's clothes (and budget) to fit in here.

ENTERTAINMENT

The municipal tourist office can tell you what's on, but promo matter is limited.

Teatro Municipal (Map pp190-1; cnr Genaro Sanjinés & Indaburo) Offers a program of folk-music concerts and foreign theatrical presentations.

Dead Stroke (Map pp186-7; Av 6 de Agosto 2460; ☺ nightly) Rack up a few wins at this popular billiards place.

Peñas

Typical of La Paz are folk-music venues called *peñas*. Most present traditional Andean music, but they often include lavish guitar and song recitals. The cover charge for the places listed here is US$4 to US$5. The most touristy are **Peña Huari** (Map pp190-1; Sagárnaga 339) and **Peña Parnaso** (Map pp190-1; Sagárnaga 189), which both serve dinner and advertise nightly shows but often only go off when tour groups are in town. **Casa del Corregidor** (Map pp190-1; Murillo 1040) and **Peña Marka Tambo** (Map pp190-1; Calle Jaén 710) attract local music fans as well.

Cinemas

Cinemateca Boliviana (Map pp190-1; ☎ 244-4090; www.cinematecaboliviana.org; cnr Zuazo & Rosando Gutiérrez; tickets US$1.50) For classics and arty flicks in a wonderful art and cultural space try this place which, at the time of research, was being constructed.

Modern cinemas on the Prado – including **Cine 16 de Julio** (Map pp190-1; admission US$2.50), near Plaza del Estudiante – show recent international releases, usually in the original language with Spanish subtitles.

SHOPPING

Street stalls are the cheapest place to buy everything from batteries and film to bootleg CDs.

Tight travelers can grab a bargain or three at the Mercado Negro (Map pp190–1); mere mortals, however, might enjoy the bulk bargains galore. It's a clogged maze of makeshift stalls that sprawls over several blocks. The name means 'black market,' but it's mostly above board and is a good place for cheap clothing and household goods. It is, however, notorious for pickpockets and recently, a few 'spitters' have been reported here (see p189).

Calle Sagárnaga is the street for tasteful and kitsch souvenirs and the nearby Witches Market (Mercado de Hechicería; Map pp190–1) is the place for oddities. It's asses-to-elbows with herbs, magical potions and shriveled llama fetuses, which locals bury under the porches of their new homes for luck and good fortune. If you're lucky, you might convince a *yatiri* (Aymara healer) to toss the coca leaves and tell your fortune, but they usually refuse gringo customers. Taking photographs here may be met with unpleasantness – unless you are a customer and first ask politely.

There are plenty of CD shops along Sagárnaga. Music and musical instruments can also be sourced around Calle Max Paredes. Other good places for musical instruments include the following:

Eddy Lima Shop (Map pp190-1; Illampu 827)
El Guitarrón (Map pp190-1; Sagárnaga 303)

GETTING THERE & AWAY
Air
Call **Aeropuerto El Alto** (☎ 281-0240) for flight information. Airline offices in La Paz:

AeroSur (Map pp190-1; ☎ 231-2244; Av 16 de Julio 1616)

Amaszonas (☎ 222-0848; Saavedra 1649, Miraflores)

American Airlines (Map pp190-1; ☎ 235-5384; www
.aa.com; Plaza Venezuela 1440, Edificio Herrmann Busch)

LAB (Map pp190-1; ☎ 237-1020/1024, 800-10-4321, 800-10-3001; Av Camacho 1460)

LanChile/LanPeru (Map pp190-1; ☎ 235-8377; www
.lanchile.com, www.lanperu.com; Av 16 de Julio 1566, Edificio Ayacucho, Suite 104)

Taca (Map pp190-1; ☎ 274-4400; El Prado, Edificio Petrolero PB)

Transportes Aéreos Militares (TAM; ☎ 212-1582/1585, TAM airport 284-1884; Av Montes 738)

TAM Mercosur (Map pp190-1; ☎ 244-3442; www
.tam.com.py in Spanish; Heriberto Gutiérrez 2323)

Domestic flight prices vary little between airlines, except for TAM, which is sometimes cheaper. Most travel agents sell tickets for internal flights for the same price as the airlines. The following schedule and price information is subject to change. Prices quoted are one way. Many domestic flights are not direct and often involve a stopover or more to pick up passengers, with legs usually lasting less than an hour. Be aware that some flights cannot go during wet season, especially to the Beni region.

Cobija US$119, three flights weekly with AeroSur or TAM.

Cochabamba US$49, three flights daily with AeroSur and three weekly with LAB/TAM.

Guayaramerín US$142, one daily flight with Amaszonas/TAM.

Puerto Suarez US$171, three flights weekly via Santa Cruz with AeroSur/TAM.

Riberalta US$142, two to three flights weekly with Amaszonas/TAM.

Rurrenabaque US$60, daily flights with Amaszonas and TAM.

San Borja US$53, two daily flights with Amaszonas.

Santa Cruz US$108, two to three flights daily with AeroSur and LAB/TAM.

Sucre US$106/70, daily flights with AeroSur (direct) and LAB (via Cochabamba or Santa Cruz), one to two flights weekly with TAM.

Tarija US$108, daily flights with AeroSur (direct or via Santa Cruz), LAB (via Cochabamba or Santa Cruz) and TAM.

Trinidad US$70, daily flights with Amaszonas (via San Borja) and LAB (via Cochabamba or Santa Cruz).

Yacuiba US$94, weekly flight (via Sucre and Tarija) with TAM.

Bus
There are three *flota* departure points in La Paz: the main terminal, the cemetery district and Villa Fátima. Fares are relatively uniform between companies, but competition keeps prices low. Allow for longer travel times (often double) in the rainy season.

MAIN TERMINAL
Buses to all places south of La Paz leave from the main **terminal** (Map pp186-7; ☎ 228-0551). A few companies have ticket offices in the terminal, but their buses usually leave from the cemetery; sometimes you'll pay more if you buy your passage here. There's a secure **left-luggage facility** (☾ 5am-10pm) and a B$2 terminal fee.

Approximate one-way fares and journey times from the main terminal are shown in the following table. Buses provide connections between major cities several times daily, and more expensive *bus cama* (sleeper) services are available on long overnight runs.

Destination	Duration (hr)	Cost (US$)
Arica, Chile	8	10-13
Cochabamba	7	3-5
Cuzco, Peru	12-17	15-20
Iquique, Chile	11-13	12-17
Oruro	3	2
Potosí	11	5-7
Puno, Peru	8	6-8
Santa Cruz	18	12-15
Sucre	14	10-12
Tarija	24	10-15
Trinidad	40	20
Uyuni	13	6-10
Villazón	23	7-12

CEMETERY AREA
Micros and minibuses run to the *cementerio* (cemetery) constantly from the center: catch them on Av Mariscal Santa Cruz or grab *micro* 2 along Av Yanacocha. Heading into the city from the cemetery by day you can catch *micros* along Av Baptista. At night always take a taxi.

Transportes Manco Kapac (Map pp186-7; Plaza Felix Reyes Ortiz) and Transtur 2 de Febrero run to Copacabana (US$2.50, three hours) all day from Calle José María Aliaga. Transporte 6 de Junio also goes to Copacabana between 5am and 6pm. Or for US$4 to US$5 try the more comfy tourist buses that do hotel pickups. From Copacabana, lots of *micros* and minibuses sprint to Puno (US$3 to US$4, three to four hours).

BOLIVIA

Between 5am and 6pm, **Autolíneas Ingavi** (Map pp186-7; Calle José María Asín) has departures every 30 minutes to Desaguadero (US$1.50, three hours). Nearby is **Trans-Unificado Sorata** (Map pp186-7; cnr Ángel Babia & Manuel Bustillos), which operates five or so daily buses to Sorata (US$1.50, 4½ to five hours). Seats are in short supply, so turn up one hour before; sit on the left for views of Sorata. Buses to Huarina and Huatajata also leave from this area.

VILLA FÁTIMA

You can reach Villa Fátima by *micro* or minibus from the Prado or Av Camacho. Turbus Totai and Flota Yungueña minibuses to Coroico (US$2, four hours) leave from the *ex-surtidor*, a former gas station. Flota Yungueña also has daily departures to Rurrenabaque (US$7, 22 hours) at noon.

From here, there are hourly departures to Chulumani (US$2.50, four hours) – a heinous trip in the rainy season; a bus to Guanay (US$8, eight hours) at 9:30am daily; and another to Rurrenabaque (US$11, 16 hours) at 11:30am daily.

GETTING AROUND

La Paz is well serviced by public transportation. There are full-size buses and *micros* (medium-size buses), which charge US20¢ for trips around the city center. *Kombi* minibuses charge slightly less around town and US25¢ to the Zona Sur. Buses, *micros* and minibuses announce their route with signs on the windshield; barkers shout out destinations on minibuses ad nauseam. *Trufis* are shared taxis that follow a fixed route and charge US25¢ per person around the center. Any of these vehicles can be waved down anywhere, except in areas cordoned off by the police.

Radio taxis, which you can phone or flag down, charge US75¢ around the center and US$1 to the cemetery district, slightly more at night, slightly less coming downhill. Charges are for up to four passengers and include pickup, if necessary.

AROUND LA PAZ

VALLE DE LA LUNA

The **Valley of the Moon** (admission US65¢) makes a pleasant half-day break from La Paz' bustle. It's not a valley but a bizarrely eroded maze of canyons and pinnacles technically known as badlands, 10km down the canyon of the Río Choqueyapu from the city center.

To get here, catch any *micro* marked 'Mallasa' or 'Zoológico' from Plaza del Estudiante. Get off after the Cactario at the junction for Malasilla Golf Course and walk for a few minutes toward Mallasa village. When you see a green house on your right, you're at the top of the *valle*. Be careful walking here in the rainy season – the route is eroded and can be slippery.

From the top of Valle de la Luna, catch another *micro* headed down the valley or continue a couple of kilometers on foot.

TIAHUANACO (TIWANAKU)

Tiahuanaco is Bolivia's most significant archaeological site, 72km west of La Paz on the road toward the Peruvian frontier at Desaguadero.

Little is known of the people who constructed this great ceremonial center on Lake Titicaca's southern shore. Archaeologists generally agree that the civilization that spawned Tiahuanaco rose in about 600 BC. The site was under construction around AD 700, but after AD 1200 the group faded into obscurity. However, evidence of its influence has been found throughout the area of the later Inca empire.

There are a number of megaliths (up to 175 tons in weight) strewn around the site, including a ruined pyramid and the remains of a ritual platform. Much has been restored, not always with total authenticity, and travelers fresh from Peru may be disappointed. Across the railway line from Tiahuanaco is a **site museum** (admission US$3.50; 9am-5pm) and the ongoing excavation of **Puma Punku** (Gateway of the Puma). For a greater appreciation of Tiahuanaco's history, hire a guide (a reasonable one costs up to US$10).

You can stop at Tiahuanaco en route between La Paz and Puno, Peru (via Desaguadero), but most travelers prefer to travel from La Paz to Puno via Lake Titicaca (p205) and visit Tiahuanaco as a day trip from La Paz. Autolíneas Ingavi *micros* depart every half hour for Tiahuanaco (US$1, 1½ hours) from Calle José María Asín near the cemetery; some continue to Desaguadero. To return to La Paz, flag down a bus (expect to stand), or walk 1km west into Tiahuanaco village and catch one from the plaza.

Several La Paz agencies (p189) offer guided tours to Tiahuanaco for US$15 to US$20.

CORDILLERA REAL & THE YUNGAS

Northeast of La Paz, the dramatic Cordillera Real rises before giving way to the Yungas, beautiful subtropical valleys where steep forested mountainsides fall away into humid, cloud-filled gorges. The Yungas, which contain several Afrobolivian settlements, form a natural barrier between the *altiplano* and the Amazonian rainforests. Heading northeast from La Paz, the road winds up to La Cumbre (4600m), then descends 4340m to the Beni lowlands. Tropical fruits, coffee and coca all grow here. The climate is moderate with misty rain possible at any time of year.

COROICO

☎ 02 / pop 3500

Perched on the shoulder of Cerro Uchumachi (2548m) at an elevation of 1500m to 1750m, Coroico is a Bolivian Eden. It serves as a lowland retreat for middle-class *paceños* (citizens of La Paz), an enclave for a few European immigrants and a popular base for short treks into the countryside. As many expats can attest, it's so laid-back that it's hard to break away.

Orientation & Information

Coroico is 7km uphill from the transport junction of Yolosa. There's a 'tourist office' on the plaza which has hotel information only. The Parque Nacional Cotapata office is on the plaza; check here for permission to camp at the park's biological research station off the Choro trail.

Entel is on the western side of the plaza. MCM, near the bus offices, and Internet La Casa, one block east of the plaza, offer internet access for US$2 an hour.

Banco Unión offers cash advances and may change cash. **Hotel Esmeralda** (☎ 213-6017; www .hotelesmeralda.com) changes traveler's checks at 5% commission.

Sights & Activities

For pretty views, trek an easy 20 minutes up to **El Calvario**, where the stations of the cross lead to a grassy knoll and **chapel**. To get there, head uphill toward Hotel Esmeralda. There are two good trailheads from El Calvario. The one to the left leads to the **cascadas**, a trio of waterfalls

6km (two hours) beyond the chapel. The trail to the right leads up to **Cerro Uchumachi** (a five-hour round trip), which affords terrific views of the valley. Don't set off on these routes on your own.

You can rent horses from **El Relincho** (☎ 719-13675), 100m past Hotel Esmeralda, for US$6.20 an hour or US$44 per day or US$100 for a two-day camping trip, all including guide. Hotel Bella Vista rents bicycles.

Siria Leon (☎ 719-55431; siria_leon@yahoo.com; JZ Cuenca 062) is recommended for Spanish lessons (US$4 an hour).

Sleeping

Rates rise as much as 20% on weekends and holidays; bargain midweek and for longer stays. There are many more places to sleep than those listed here and most have restaurants as well.

Residencial Coroico (r per person US$1.75) One block north of the plaza, these are the dustiest, cheapest digs in town; rooftop rooms are best.

Hostal Sol y Luna (☎ 715-61626, in La Paz 02-236-2099; www.solyluna-bolivia.com; camping per person US$1.85, s/d with shared bathroom US$5/7.50, cabanas with bathroom US$20-30; 🏊) This splendid German-run gringo-friendly retreat is well worth the 20-minute walk east of town. It has scenic campsites, self-contained cabins and comfortable rooms, with shared bathroom, near the pool. Bonuses include restaurant with veggie options, book exchange, shiatsu massage (US$18 an hour) and a sublime slate hot tub (US$6.20 per person).

Hostal Cafetal (☎ 719-33979; Rancho Beni; Miranda s/n; r per person weekdays/weekends US$3.35/4.50; 🏊) A superlative option with stunning views, reputedly the best eats in Bolivia and a pool in a lush garden setting. Follow your nose (and the signs) from the plaza.

Hostal Kory (☎ in La Paz 243-1311; s US$6, s/d with bathroom US$11/20) Southwest of the plaza, the most 'solid' and plain of the budget options, with great views.

Hotel Bella Vista (☎ 221-36059; r per person US$10, without bathroom US$5) Bounce on in to this spotless place with racquetball courts and a small rooftop patio with expansive views.

Hotel Esmeralda (☎ 213-6017; www.hotelesmeralda .com; s/d/tr from US$12/15/18; 🏊) Everyone (including most tour groups) seems to end up at Hotel Esmeralda, for the pool, sunny patio, restaurant and killer views. The complex

BOLIVIA

BOLIVIA

THE MOST DANGEROUS ROAD IN THE WORLD

Flanked by epic scenery and punctuated with waterfalls during the rainy season, the La Paz–Coroico road plunges over 3000m in 80km. It's called the 'World's Most Dangerous Road' because it sees the most fatalities annually (over 100 on average), but the road itself is not that treacherous. True, it's extremely narrow and can be muddy, slippery and deeply rutted, but Andean veterans will recall much worse routes in Peru and Ecuador. What makes the road so dangerous is the drivers: a combination of weekend warriors, macho bus drivers on sleep-deprived benders and tenderfooted tourists. To minimize the danger, avoid traveling on public holidays when the locals head down for big weekends.

---

range of prices depends on views and bathrooms. The cheapest have neither, and are dank and rather overpriced. It's located about 400m uphill east of the plaza; phone for free pickup. Ensure that your belongings are secure at all times.

Eating & Drinking

Coroico has a good choice of eateries; you'll sometimes wonder which country you're in. Back-Stube Konditorei is good for breakfast, Yungas coffee and homemade German desserts. It's near Hostal Kory.

Restaurante Cafetal (☎ 719-33979; mains US$3.50-5; ☺ breakfast, lunch & dinner) Bolivia's culinary gold medal goes to this French-run restaurant. It's worth every step of the 15-minute walk east of town for its phenomenal salads, crêpes, and breezy atmosphere.

La Casa (Ayacucho s/n; ☺ Tue-Sun) Fine European cuisine; book ahead for fondue or raclette.

La Bella Vista (plaza) Little Italy comes to Coroico – the best pizza in town.

Comedor popular (meals under US$1) Typical Bolivian meals all day. It's northwest of the plaza.

For nightlife try **Bamboo's** (Iturralde) with live music on the weekend, cocktails and Mexican food, or Taurus, with a similar vibe.

Getting There & Away

Buses and minibuses leave hourly (between 7am and 4pm) from next to the *ex-surtidor*

(former gas station) in La Paz' Villa Fátima neighborhood. A Flota Yungueña or Trans Totai minibus (US$2, 3½ hours) is the best way to go. In Coroico, buses leave from the two main offices on the plaza and Calle Sagárnaga (the main road). There are hourly departures from Coroico to La Paz from around 6am (book in advance on Sundays), and daily buses to Rurrenabaque (US$7.25, 15 hours) which leave from Yolosa if and when the buses have made it down the 'World's Most Dangerous Road' (see left). Those with stamina can risk the rough Coroico–Chulumani road (via Coripata) by *camión*; departures from the market.

CHULUMANI

☎ 02 / pop 4500

This placid town is the terminus of the Yunga Cruz trek (see opposite) and a great detour off the gringo circuit. It's also the capital of Sur Yungas province and is in a main coca-growing region.

Banco Unión, on the plaza, changes cash and traveler's checks (5% commission) and an Entel office is on the plaza.

For great views, head to the **mirador** two blocks south of the plaza. The gregarious owner of the Country Guesthouse (see following) is full of ideas for hiking, biking, river tubing and camping outside the town. **Ramiro Portugal** (☎ in La Paz 02-213-6016, 02-279-0381) takes groups on day trips (US$25 for up to five people) to **Bosque Apa Apa**, a cloud forest rich in birds and flora. Camping, including tents, is US$10 plus US$1 per person per night.

Sleeping & Eating

Alojamiento Daniel (r per person US$2.50, with bathroom US$3.50) Half a block uphill from the plaza, this place has clean rooms with shared showers. Next door is the similarly priced Alojamiento Chulumani.

Country Guesthouse (camping per person US$2.65, r with bathroom & breakfast US$6.65; ☒) The nicest place to stay is Xavier Sarabia's rustic guesthouse, a 10-minute walk southwest of the plaza. There's a pool, homey bar and good meals on request.

Hotel Panorama (☎ 213-6109; Murillo at Andrade; s/d US$6.50/9; ☒) You pay for the views here. Moving up a notch in comfort, this friendly hotel has reasonable rooms.

For chow, try the restaurant at the Country Guesthouse or one of the basic *comedores* at the *tranca*. The clean market also has good cheap meals.

El Mesón (plaza) dishes up cheap *almuerzos*. Across the plaza, Restaurant Chulumani has an upstairs dining terrace.

Getting There & Away

From Villa Fátima in La Paz, Turbus Totai buses go to and from Chulumani (US$2.50, four hours) when full from 8am to 4pm. From Chulumani, Trans San Bartolomé departs for La Paz at 5:30am and noon daily. Trans Chulumani and 24 de Agosto minibuses leave regularly from the *tranca*. The Chulumani–Unduavi road (where the paved bit begins) is hazardous in the rainy season. Bring lots of snacks and water and expect delays.

It's possible to go to Coroico via Coripata: take a La Paz–bound bus and get off at the crossroads just after Puente Villa at Km 93. Here, wait for a bus or *camión* to Coripata and then change again for a lift to Coroico (for a lo-o-o-ng, dusty trip).

TREKKING IN THE CORDILLERA REAL

Several worthwhile treks run between the *altiplano* and the Yungas, all of which cross the Cordillera Real on relatively low passes. Most popular are the **Choro** (La Cumbre to Coroico, 70km), **Taquesi** (Takesi; 40km) and **Yunga Cruz** (114km). These two- to four-day treks all begin with a brief ascent, then head down from spectacular high-mountain landscapes into the riotous vegetation of the Yungas.

Trekking the Choro independently is only tricky at the trailhead: take any bus from La Paz to Coroico and alight at **La Cumbre**, the highest point on the road. The path begins on the left and is distinct for the first kilometer, but then gets harder to discern. Stay to your right and pass between two ponds (one often dry) before heading uphill. From here it's clear sailing to Coroico. Security is a concern as nasty incidents have been reported. Many tour agencies offer this as a three-day trip for around US$100 to US$150, all-inclusive (see p264). Serious trekkers should consult Lonely Planet's *Trekking in the Central Andes,* which includes maps and detailed descriptions of these treks, as well as other routes.

GUANAY

Isolated Guanay is a detour from the Coroico–Rurrenabaque road, and it's at the end of the Camino del Oro trek from Sorata. It makes a good base for visits to the gold-mining operations along the Ríos Mapiri and Tipuani. If you can overlook the devastation of the landscape wrought by gold fever, a visit with the miners is interesting. Access to the mining areas is by jeep along the Llipi road, or by motorized dugout canoes up the Río Mapiri.

Dollars can sometimes be changed with gold dealers or at the farmacias (pharmacies). Caranavi's Banco Unión does cash advances and changes traveler's checks.

Sleeping & Eating

Hotel Pahuichi (r per person US$2.50) A block downhill from the plaza, this is the best value in town and has a reasonable restaurant.

Hospedaje Los Pinos (d US$4.50) This friendly spot near the dock has clean doubles with private bathroom and fan.

Several other basic but friendly places within a block of the plaza all charge around US$2 per person.

There are many restaurants on the main strip and around the plaza.

Getting There & Away

Four companies offer daily runs to and from La Paz via Caranavi and Yolosa (US$5, 10 hours). For Coroico, get off at Yolosa, 7km west of Coroico, and catch a lift up the hill. If you're heading to Rurrenabaque (US$7.50, 14 hours), get off in Caranavi and connect with a northbound bus.

Boats to Mapiri leave daily at 9am (three to four hours) from Puerto Mapiri. When the river is too low (August to September) departures are by jeep (US$5, five hours).

Charter boats take travelers to Rurrenabaque, but these are pricey (US$300 for a 10- to 15-person boat, eight to 10 hours when high water levels). Bear in mind the boat owners face a three-day return trip with no income and a hefty fuel bill. Stock up on equipment and food.

Gung-ho travelers can hire a guide (around US$30 per day), build a balsa raft and float to Rurrenabaque. The journey takes five to seven days; you need to be self-sufficient and provide for the guide, too.

SORATA

☎ 02 / pop 2200

Sorata is the kind of place in which the hardiest soccer thug would consider taking up yoga. Surrounded by green mountains, and at the confluence of the Ríos San Cristobal and Challa Suya, its calm beauty attracts tourists needing relaxation, as well as mountaineers and trekkers seeking adventure in the surrounding snowcapped peaks of Illampu (6362m) and Ancohuma (6427m). On Sunday, jeeps and buses ferry flocks of locals to the local market. On Monday many places are closed.

Activities

WALKING

More fun for the walk than the site is the 12km trek to the **Gruta de San Pedro** (San Pedro Cave; admission US$1; 8am-5pm), a six-hour round trip from Sorata (a one-way taxi costs around US$2.50). Bring water and snacks – or, better yet, stop by Café Illampu en route.

TREKKING

Peak hiking season is April to September. Ambitious adventurers can do the six-day **Camino del Oro trek**, an ancient trading route between the *altiplano* and the Río Tipuani goldfields. Alternatively, there's the steep climb up to **Laguna Challata**, a long day trek with multiple trails (it's best to take a guide; you can't see the lake until you get there); **Comunidad Lakathiya**, another long day trek; **Laguna Glacial**, a two- to three-day trek; the arduous six- to seven-day **Mapiri Trail** (note: this is disappearing due to landslides); or the seven-day **Illampu circuit**. Although this is one of the best trails, there have been ongoing incidents and it should not be attempted without well-informed guides.

The **Sorata Guides & Porters Association** (guia sorata@hotmail.com; Sucre 302) can help organize many different treks. Budget on US$12 to US$20 per day for a group plus food, depending on the group size.

MOUNTAIN BIKING

Andean Biking (712-76685; www.andeanbiking.com; plaza) runs a series of awesome rides around Sorata for beginners to hard-core riders. Where else in the world can you cycle on pre-Inca paths, jump at 6000m and plunge thousands of meters downwards? A minimum of four people is required for most rides; prices are from US$50 to US$70 per ride. The main gig is a bike-boat extravaganza: a four- to five-day trip, with two days riding, two to three in a motorized dugout canoe, ending at Rurrenabaque (US$250, all inclusive). Mountain-bike

guru and owner Travis has been building a downhill track for more experienced riders – 2000m of downhill thrills.

Sleeping

Camping Altai Oasis (715-19856; resaltai@hotmail.com; camping per person US$1.25, s/d US$2.65/6, r with bathroom from US$10, cabins US$45-60) Come for a day, stay for a week. Travelers describe this place – set around greenery and river – as 'gold' and '*el paraiso*' (paradise). There's a good bar-café, a book exchange, laundry service, hot showers and a communal kitchen. Thirty-minutes walk from the plaza, 1km down a winding detour off the road to San Pedro caves.

Residencial Sorata (213-6672; resorata@entelnet .bo; r per person US$1.85-5) Friendly ghosts loom in this large, rambling quirky colonial mansion on the northeast corner of the plaza. Unkempt antiques (including the beds!) reflect a former glory. Louis is great on the trekking information.

Hostal Las Piedras (719-16341; laspiedras2002@ yahoo.de; r per person US$2.50, s/d with bathroom US$5/7.50) Hard to beat. English-speaking German owner Petra is as *simpático* as her spotless artistically decorated rooms. Basic 'kitchen.' Head to the soccer field, a 10-minute walk from the plaza, down Calle Ascarrunz (a rough track).

Paraiso Hotel (213-6671; Villavicencio s/n; r per person US$4.40, without bathroom US$3) Paradise it ain't, but the sunny terrace makes up for the musty rooms.

Hotel Santa Lucia (213-6686; r without bathroom US$3.80) An intimate hotel with delightful house-proud owner. Ten minutes from the plaza, down Calle Ascarrunz.

An obligatory stop on the way to San Pedro is the atmospheric Swiss-run Café Illampu (opposite), which has rental tents, grassy camping and terrific views.

Also recommended:

Hostal El Mirador (289-5008; Muñecas 400; s/d US$1.90/3.80) The terrace has a more sunny disposition than this HI-affiliate's owner.

Hostal Italia (289 5009; r per person US$2.50) In the main plaza above the pizzeria.

Eating & Drinking

Small, inexpensive restaurants around the market and the plaza sell cheap and filling *almuerzos*; Restaurant Sorata has veggie options.

For a quick B$1 burger piled high with weenies and fries, hit the hamburger stands on the northwest corner of the plaza.

The main square should be renamed Plaza Italia, such are the number of (identical) pizzerias (oh! plus a Mexican). There are other international options.

Pete's Place (Hostal Don Julio, 1st fl, off the plaza; ☽ noon-10pm) For the latest trekking news and great food, this is the place. A yummy selection of veggie and international dishes will cure what ails you. Look for the signs on the plaza.

Café Illampu (☽ Thu-Mon) On the road to San Pedro, this café, run by the jovial Stephan the Swiss pastry chef, is where you'll find killer coffee and cakes, plus fresh berry *licuados* (fruit shakes).

Camping Altai-Oasis (☎ 715-19856) The café here offers coffee, drinks and its trademark steaks, veggie treats and great muesli (US$2.20). See opposite for directions.

Getting There & Away

Sorata is far removed from the other Yungas towns and there are no direct connections to Coroico.

From La Paz, Trans Unificado Sorata departs the cemetery district 10 times daily (US$1.70, 4½ hours). From Sorata, La Paz-bound buses depart from the plaza hourly from 4am to 4pm (5pm on weekends).

For Copacabana you must get off at the junction town of Huarina and wait for another bus.

LAKE TITICACA

Lake Titicaca is deservedly awash with gushing clichés. Although it is often wrongly described as the highest navigable lake in the world (both Peru and Chile have higher navigable bodies of water), this incongruous splash of sapphire amid the stark plains of the *altiplano* is rightly described as one of the most beautiful sights in the region.

At an elevation of 3820m, and more than 230km long and 97km wide, the lake straddles both Peru and Bolivia, and is a remnant of Lago Ballivián, an ancient inland sea. The lake's traditional Aymaran villages along the shore, ancient legends, and snow-topped peaks of the Cordillera Real in the background, provide a magical landscape and experience.

COPACABANA

☎ 02

Nestled between two hills and perched on the southern shore of Lake Titicaca, Copacabana (Copa) is a small, bright and enchanting town. It was for centuries the site of religious pilgrimages, and today the pilgrims flock to fiestas – the locals love a party.

Although it can appear a little tourist-ready, the town is a pleasant place to wander around, with excellent cafés, and walks along the lake and beyond. It is the launching pad for visiting Isla del Sol, and makes a pleasant stopover between La Paz and Puno or Cuzco (Peru). At 3800m, the days are pleasant and sunny (with rain in December and January) but nights are chilly throughout the rest of the year.

Information

The best book exchange is at La Cúpula (p208).

Alf@Net (cnr 6 de Agosto & Av 16 de Julio) A popular hangout with speedy internet access for US$1.80 an hour. There are a couple more internet places on 6 de Agosto heading toward the lake.

Casa de Cambio Copacabana (6 de Agosto s/n) There's no ATM in town but this place, at Hotel Playa Azul, changes cash and traveler's checks (5% commission).

Pacha (cnr 6 de Agosto & Bolívar) For laundry; two-hour service for US$1.25.

Prodem Near Casa de Cambio Copacabana. Is meant to do Visa cash advances (5% commission), but strangely often can't.

Tourist office (northeast cnr of plaza) If open, this office has some informative brochures.

Sights & Activities

The sparkling Moorish-style **cathedral**, built between 1605 and 1820, dominates town. The famous wooden **Virgen de Copacabana statue** is housed upstairs in the **Camarín de la Virgen** (admission by donation; ☽ 9am-noon & 2:30-6pm). Don't miss the **Capilla de Velas** (Candle Chapel), around the side of the cathedral, where thousands of candles illuminate an arched sepulchre and wax graffiti cakes the walls. The colorful **Bendiciones de Movilidades** (*cha'lla;* blessing of automobiles) occurs daily at 10am and 2:30pm in front of the cathedral.

The hill north of town is **Cerro Calvario** (3966m), which can be reached in 30 minutes and is well worth the climb, particularly at sunset. Many pilgrims make this climb, placing stones at the stations of the cross as they ascend. Less impressive are the minor Inca

BOLIVIA

sites around town: **Horca del Inca** on the hill Niño Calvario; the **Tribunal del Inca** (🕙 Tue-Sun 9:30am-6pm), near the cemetery; and **Baño del Inca** and **museum** (🕙 9am-6pm), 2km north of town. They are often closed despite their advertised opening hours.

Head to the lakeshore to rent **bicycles**, **motorcycles**, **paddleboats** or **sailboats**.

Festivals & Events

A Bolivian tradition is the blessing of miniature objects, like cars or houses, at the **Alasitas festival** (January 24), as a prayer that the real thing will be obtained in the coming year. These miniatures are sold in stalls around the plaza and at the top of Cerro Calvario.

Following Alasitas, the **Fiesta de la Virgen de Candelaria** is celebrated on the first two days of February. Dervishes from Peru and Bolivia perform traditional Aymara dances amid much music, drinking and feasting. On **Good Friday**, the town fills with pilgrims, who join a solemn candlelit procession at dusk. The biggest fiesta lasts for a week around **Independence Day** (around the first week in August),

WARNING

Particular care should be taken during festivals, particularly those for Semana Santa (Easter Week) and Independence Day week. Petty theft is common, and there have been more serious reports of tourists being tackled around the neck – these maneuvers cause you to faint, whereupon you are relieved of your goods.

featuring parades, brass bands, fireworks and lots of alcohol.

Sleeping

There is an incredible variety of cheap places to snooze. During fiestas, however, everything fills up and prices can jump threefold. Most places will store backpacks for free while you overnight at Isla del Sol and beyond. Wild camping is possible on the summits of Niño Calvario and Cerro Sancollani. Following are the cheapest acceptable options, asking US$1.25 to US$4.50 per person for rooms without bathroom.

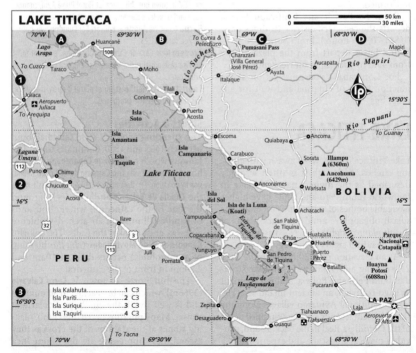

LAKE TITICACA

Isla Kalahuta	1	C3
Isla Pariti	2	C3
Isla Suriqui	3	C3
Isla Taquiri	4	C3

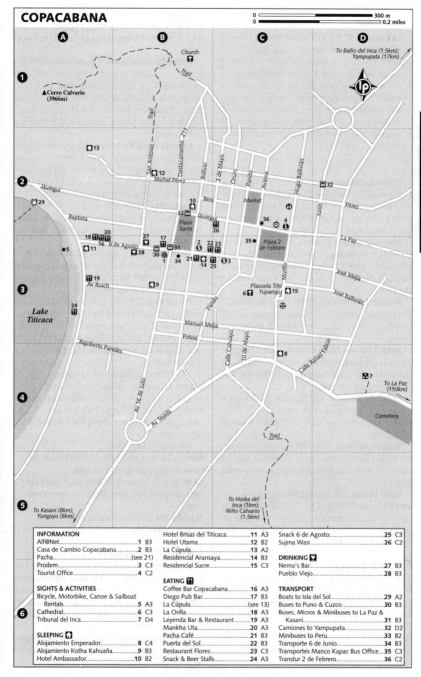

COPACABANA

BOLIVIA

BOLIVIA

> **SPLURGE!**
>
> **La Cúpula** (☎ 862-2029; Michel Peréz 1-3; r from US$US12) No doubt Bolivia's best. With the individuality of a boutique hotel and the range of facilities of a resort, this German-run great-value place has the lot: excellent food (see right), hammocks, gardens, books and a relaxing vibe. Every room is uniquely decked out – you can even hole up in the 'cúpula.' The new artistic cabins are a treat (US$32).

Alojamiento Emperador (☎ 862-2083; Murillo 235) Upbeat and colorful with a delightful señora who loves travelers. Use of small kitchen, firm beds and a sunny mezzanine. A new section has rooms with private bathrooms.

Alojamiento Kotha Kahuaña (☎ 862-2022; Av Busch 15) A mini Tiahuanaco awaits you at this clean (if pebbly) abode, which offers good upstairs rooms with lake views and hot water around the clock.

Residencial Aransaya (☎ 862-2229; 6 de Agosto 121) Very smart rooms with private bathroom, an inviting, sunny patio and a good restaurant below.

Hotel Brisas del Titicaca (☎ 862-2178; 6 de Agosto) This HI-affiliate overlooks the lake. Pity about the rude and disinterested staff that we encountered on our visit.

Hotel Ambassador (☎ 862-2216; cnr Jáuregui & Bolívar; r with bathroom & TV per person US$5) A frilly no-frills experience with a cheerful rooftop restaurant.

Residencial Sucre (Murillo 228, r per person incl breakfast US$5) Classy hotel-style entrance with a large courtyard and room choice of varying quality.

Hotel Utama (☎ 862-2013; Michel Peréz; r per person incl breakfast US$7-10) This friendly midrange option has comfortable rooms with private bathroom (it often gets the overflow from the nearby La Cúpula).

Eating & Drinking

The local specialty is farmed Lake Titicaca *trucha criolla,* one of the world's largest trout. As usual, the cheapest meals are in the market. In the morning, head there to smell the fish and sate your sweet tooth with *api morado* (purple *api*; a syrupy beverage made of maize, lemon, cinnamon and sugar) and syrupy *buñuelos* (doughnuts).

La Cúpula (☎ 862-2029; Michel Peréz 1-3; ❍ from 7:30am) Great selection with veggie (and scenic) delights. No breakfast or lunch on Tuesdays.

Coffee Bar Copacabana (6 de Agostso s/n; almuerzos US$1.25) Laid-back in more ways than one – eat quickly before the delicious food slides off your plate (thanks to the slanting concrete floor). Extensive list of teas and gourmet coffees, breakfasts, pastas, nachos and everything in between.

Leyenda Bar & Restaurant (cnr Costañera & Busch; mains US$3-6; ❍ breakfast, lunch & dinner) You can hardly go wrong at this atmospheric lakefront spot, where delicious juices, pizzas and trout are served to the strains of Bob Marley.

Sujma Wasi (Jáuregui 127; mains US$4-6) An interesting choice with delightful courtyard tables and a varied menu including many Bolivian specialties.

Pacha Cafe (cnr 6 de Agosto & Bolívar; mains US$8-12) Try the superlative hot chocolate and excellent pizza here (US$1.90 to US$3.15), and listen to occasional live entertainment.

Pueblo Viejo (6 de Agosto 684) Readers love this rustic, cozy and chilled bar-café, run by some 'cool dudes' who are proud of their ethnic decor, quirky lighting (check out the fire light) and laid-back atmosphere. Live music is a regular feature.

There are a number of cheap, typical places. On the main drag, Snack 6 de Agosto is good value, or give Restaurant Flores, Puerta del Sol or Diego Pub Bar a shot. The snack and beer stalls along the lakeshore are other options.

Also recommended:

Nemo's Bar (6 de Agosto 684) A British/Bolivian-run warm and cozy place perfect for a tipple.

La Orilla (6 de Agosto s/n) With full bar, fireplace and huge portions of pasta pesto, stuffed trout and coconut curry.

Mankha Uta (6 de Agosto s/n; set meals US$1.50) Features veggie options.

Getting There & Away

Transportes Manco Kapac and Transturs 2 de Febrero both have several daily connections from La Paz (near the cemetery) via Tiquina Straits to Copacabana (US$2, 3½ hours), with extra weekend departures. Faster (but packed) Transporte 6 de Junio minibuses depart frequently from 4am to 5pm. Note: buses depart Copacabana from Plaza Sucre, but often arrive at Plaza 2 de Febrero.

Comfortable nonstop tour buses from La Paz to Copacabana cost US$4 to US$5. You can arrange to break the journey in Copacabana and then continue into Puno (Peru) with the same agency. You can do just the Copacobana–Puno leg (US$3 to US$4, three to four hours) or go all the way to Cuzco (US$10, 15 hours); book ahead.

COPACABANA TO YAMPUPATA TREK

The 17km walk from Copacabana to Yampupata (just across the strait from Isla del Sol) takes three to four hours. The scenery along the trek rocks, and you can take a boat across to Isla del Sol for a few more days of hiking, and then hop on a boat back to Copacabana – it makes a phenomenal trip.

From Copacabana, head northeast along the road across the flat plain. At the 3km mark you'll see the village of Kusijata; a 10-minute detour will take you to the Baño del Inca. Another 5km on you will notice the **Gruta de Lourdes** (Virgin in a Cave) on a hillside, well visible from the main road to Yampupata. Continue up the steep hill up the main road (for an alternative shortcut, turn right immediately after the small bridge. Follow the **Inca road** until it peters out at which point head straight up the hill until you hit the main dirt road). At the junction, take the road to the left, which leads down to the village of **Titicachi**.

At **Sicuani**, the next village 2km further on, **Hostal Yampu** (basic accommodations per person around US$2) has meals. Further up the road on the right, ask for Hilario Paye, a colorful character, who will happily take you on a ride on his puma-headed reed boat, or for a trip in his motorboat to the peninsular and beyond. It's another hour to the piers at Yampupata, where you can hire a boat to Yumani on Isla del Sol (US$8 to US$10 per boat). It is not easy to return to Copacabana by car, but you can try your luck with *movilidad* (anything that moves)!

ISLA DEL SOL & ISLA DE LA LUNA

The Island of the Sun is the legendary Inca creation site and is the birthplace of the sun in Inca mythology. It was here that the bearded white god Viracocha and the first Incas, Manco Capac and his sister-wife Mama Huaca (or Mama Ocllo), made their mystical appearances. Isla de la Luna (Koati; Island of the Moon), the site of a deteriorating convent housing the virgins of the sun, is smaller and less touristed; a small admission fee may be charged.

With a population of around 5000, Isla del Sol is dotted with several villages, of which **Yumani** and **Cha'llapampa** are the largest. The island's Inca ruins include **Pilko Kaina** (admission US60¢) at the southern end and the **Chincana** complex in the north, which is the site of the sacred rock where the Inca creation legend began. At Cha'llapampa, there's a **museum** with artifacts from the underwater excavations near Isla Koa, north of Isla del Sol. The museum entry ticket (US$1.25) is also valid for the northern ruins and the now further abandoned **Museo Templo de Sol** at Cha'lla, which features a collection of dusty pots; its opening hours are erratic.

Networks of **walking tracks** make exploration easy, but the sunshine and altitude can take their toll. You can see the island's main archaeological sites in one long day, but it's best to stay overnight. Bring food, water and sunscreen. On a day tour, the boat arrives at Cha'llapampa near the northern end of the island at about 10am. A Spanish-speaking guide shows groups around the museum and accompanies them to Chincana. From there it's a moderately strenuous three- to four-hour walk along the ridgeline to Yumani, where food and accommodations are available. The **Escalera del Inca** (Inca Stairway) goes down to the jetty at **Fuente del Inca**, from where tour boats leave at 4pm for the return journey. Most

GETTING TO PERU

There are two options to enter Peru: the first via Copacabana and Yunguyo (Kasani–Yunguyo border crossing open 8am to 6pm), and the faster but less interesting route via Tapena/Desaguadero (open 9am to 9pm). If leaving direct from La Paz, the easiest way is to catch an agency bus to Puno (Peru); the bus breaks in Copacabana and again for immigration formalities in Yunguyo. Similar buses go direct to Cuzco. A cheaper way from Copacabana is via minibus from Plaza Sucre to the Kasani–Yunguyo border (US50¢, 30 minutes); there's onward transport to Puno, changing buses in Yunguyo. For information on travel from Peru to Bolivia, see p868. Note: Peruvian time is one hour behind Bolivian time.

BOLIVIA

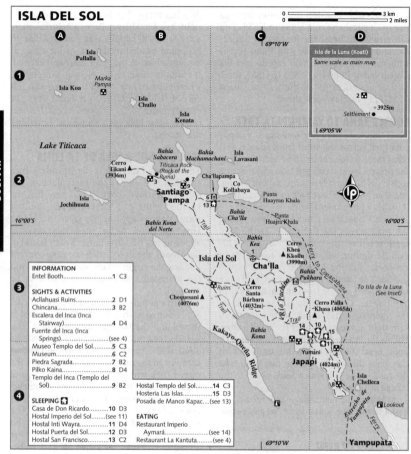

ISLA DEL SOL

0 — 3 km
0 — 2 miles

Isla Pallalla
Isla Koa
Marka Pampa
Isla Chullo
Isla Kenata

Isla de la Luna (Koati)
Same scale as main map
2
+3925m
Settlement

Lake Titicaca

Cerro Tikani (3936m)
Bahía Sabacera
Titicaca Rock (Rock of the Puma)
Bahía Machamachani
Isla Lavasani
Cha'llapampa
Co Kollabaya
Isla Jochihuata
Santiago Pampa
Punta Huayran Khala
Bahía Cha'lla
Punta Huajra Khala
Bahía Kona del Norte
Bahía Kea
Cerro Khea Kkollu (3990m)
Isla del Sol
Cha'lla
Bahía Pukhara
To Isla de la Luna (See Inset)
Cerro Chequesani (4076m)
Cerro Santa Bárbara (4032m)
Río Pachini
Cerro Palla Khasa (4065m)
Bahía Kona
Yumani
Japapi (4024m)
Isla Chelleca
Lookout
Kakayo-Queña Ridge
Yampupata

BOLIVIA

16°00'S

69°10'W
69°05'W
69°10'W

tour boats stop to visit the Pilko Kaina ruins on the way back, finishing at Copacabana at around 6pm.

Most tour tickets theoretically let you return on a later day, so you can stay on the island to explore. But hooking up with your original company for the return isn't always easy. Half-day tours (US$2) only give a glimpse of either end of the island and are hardly worthwhile. The easiest solution is to purchase two separate one-way tickets, which allows flexibility and works out at around US$3.25.

Sleeping & Eating

Isla del Sol's infrastructure has exploded in recent years, with more restaurants and ac-commodation options than sun rays. Note though that shops for self-catering are still rather scarce. You can camp just about any-where away from the village and cultivated land.

There are a growing number of *alojamientos* on the hilltop in Yumani. There's little to distinguish them: they all charge US$3 to US$5 per person with shared cold (and some hot) showers, rooms with peach-colored walls and wooden floors, and lots of frilly bedcovers. Meals under US$3 are sometimes available. Most *alojamientos* enjoy spectacular views.

At the north end of the island, you'll find lodging and meals in houses around Cha'llapampa and the beach behind. Lucio, owner of Posada de Manco Kapac (☎ 712-88443; room per person US$2.50), knows his stuff about the island. Hostal San Fransisco (room per person US$3) is a clean, helpful option.

Restaurant Imperio Aymará, on the hilltop, and Restaurant La Kantuta, at the top of the Escalera del Inca, are the best bets for simple meals.

Hosteria Las Islas (☎ 719-39047) Smack in the middle of the village, this is the pick for new, clean rooms, large terrace and a view you could eat from the outdoor café. You may have to book – it's a travel group hangout.

Hostal Inti Wayra (☎ 719-42015, in La Paz 02-246-1765) This large, two-story, ever-expanding white house offers some bright rooms in a familial atmosphere.

Hostal Imperial del Sol (☎ 719-42015) A perfectly peachy place – clean enough to eat an *empanada* off the floor. A deal pricier with own bathroom (US$25).

Other options:

Hostal Templo del Sol (☎ 712-27616; s/d US$2.50) Run-down but with spectacular views of Peru.

Hostal Puerta del Sol (☎ 719-55181; s/d US$3/5) A cheery white house.

Casa de Don Ricardo (☎ 719-34427; birdy zehnder@hotmail.com; d incl breakfast US$20) Pricier and very friendly place halfway up the hill from Fuente del Inca. Meals on request and spectacular sunny views, although unfortunately, Ricardo is not always there.

Getting There & Away

Day tours by boat from Copacabana to Isla del Sol and back cost from US$2 to US$4 per person, plus admission charges; buy tickets at the kiosks on the beach or at agencies in town. Tours cost the same if you walk from Cha'llapampa to Yumani. You will pay similar for a round-trip passage to the Pilko Kaina ruins but will end up spending more time on the water than on land. Boats leave Copacabana for Isla del Sol at 8:15am and 1:30pm, returning around 11am and 5pm. You can hop on a Copacabana-bound boat at the foot of the Escalera del Inca and have it drop you at Cha'llapampa in the north for US$1.50.

If you have the time and energy, it's more interesting to walk from Copacabana to Yampupata and then cross to Isla del Sol by boat (see p209).

THE SOUTHWEST

Nowhere tantalizes the senses as much as Bolivia's southwest. Picture windswept basins, white-capped volcanic peaks and blinding white salt deserts. Feel indeterminable distances. Taste red dust. Further east, enjoy silence as the *altiplano* drops into ethereal and spectacular rainbow-rock surrounds. And as you head lower again, breathe in the scent of the region's magical orchards and vineyards.

ORURO

☎ 02 / pop 216,000

Set at 3700m around a range of mineral-rich hills, and set on the dusty and dry plains of the *altiplano*, this distinct city has a flavor all of its own.

Accommodations and transportation are in high demand during festivals and events, so advance booking is essential and inflated prices are the norm.

The city is three hours south of La Paz on a decent paved road, and is the northern limit of Bolivia's limited rail network. It's fiercely cold and windy year-round, so come prepared.

Information

There are a couple of Enlace ATMs on the plaza. Watch your cash stash – local pickpockets and bag-slashers are quite competent, especially during drunken festivals.

Banco Boliviano Americano (cnr Calle Bolívar & Soria Galvarro) Changes cash and traveler's checks (5% commission).

Banco de Santa Cruz (Calle Bolívar 460) Also changes cash and traveler's checks (same commission).

Hotel Sucre (cnr Calle Sucre & 6 de Octubre) Charges US$1.90 per dozen items for hand-wash-and-dry laundry service.

Immigration (☎ 527-0239; Ayacucho 322, 2nd fl) Extend your stay here (see p264).

Mundo Internet (Calle Bolívar 573; per hr US65¢; 9am-midnight) The best of several internet places.

Municipal tourist office (☎ 525-0144; Plaza 10 de Febrero) On the west side of the plaza and has more printed literature than anywhere else in the country.

Tourist police (525-1923; Plaza 10 de Febrero) Only seem to be out in force during Carnaval.

Sights & Activities

Museo Patiño (☎ 525-4015; Soria Galvarro 5755; admission US$1; 9am-noon & 2-6pm Mon-Fri) is a former

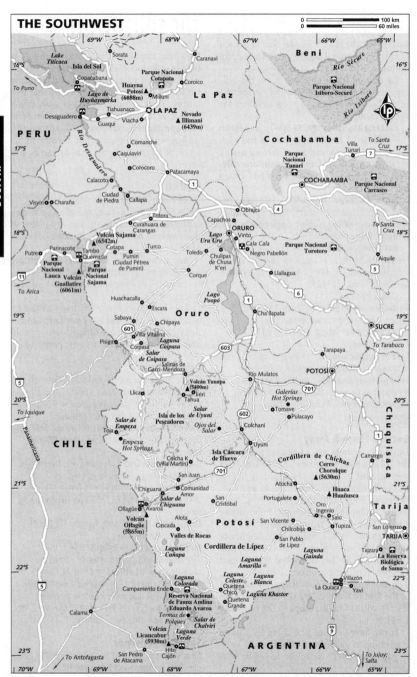

THE SOUTHWEST

BOLIVIA

residence of tin baron Simon Patiño. Exhibits include period furnishings, paintings, photographs and some fine toys.

Adjacent to the **Santuario de la Virgen del Socavón** is the **Museo Sacro, Folklórico, Arqueológico y Minero** (☎ 525-0616; Plaza del Folklore; admission US80¢; ⏳ 9am-noon & 3-6pm Mon-Fri), some of which is in a defunct mine, with displays on mines, miners and the all-important, devilish miners' god, El Tío.

At the south end of town, the **Museo Antropológico Eduardo López Rivas** (admission US$1; ⏳ 9am-noon & 2-6pm) has artifacts from the early Chipaya and Uru tribes. Take *micro* C marked 'Sud' from the plaza's northwest corner or opposite the railway station and get off just beyond the tin foundry.

The **Museo Mineralógico y Geológico** (☎ 526-1250; admission US$1; ⏳ 9am-2pm & 3-7pm Mon-Fri, 9am-noon Sat), on the university campus south of the center, has exhibits of minerals, precious stones, fossils and crystals. From the center, take *micro* A, also marked 'Sud.'

The **Obrajes hot springs** (admission US$1.25), 25km northeast of town, are the best of several nearby soaking options. From the corner of Caro and Av 6 de Agosto, catch an 'Obrajes' *micro* (US60¢, 45 minutes), which departs from 7:30am to 5pm daily; it also passes by the less appealing **Capachos hot springs**, 10km northeast of town. On weekends, local rock climbers flock to the area called **Rumi Campana**, 2km northwest of town; contact the **Club de Montañismo Halcones** (www.geocities.com/yosemite/gorge/1177).

Festivals & Events

During the spectacular **Carnaval**, from the Saturday before Ash Wednesday, the city turns into a parade of party animals, and it's a devilish time. Revelers – including proud locals, 90% of whom call themselves *quirquinchos* (armadillos) – pitch water at each other (which, frankly, can be downright tiresome). Several parade days (including the **Entrada** and **la Diablada**) feature dancers in intricately garish masks and costumes.

Sleeping

Near the train station on Velasco Galvarro there are quite a few handy, if not classy, *alojamientos*.

Alojamiento Copacabana (☎ 525-4184; Velasco Galvarro No 6352; r per person US$2, with bathroom US$2.50) Clean and secure (the backpacker-friendly owner sleeps by the door at night) – the best on this strip.

Residencial San Salvador (☎ 527-6771; Velasco Galvarro No 6325; r per person US$2.50) If you don't mind doggy smells, surly service and dark receptions, then it's OK.

Alojamiento San Juan de Dios (☎ 527-7083; Velasco Galvarro No 6346; r per person US$2.50) A short step up from the bottom of the barrel.

Hotel Bernal (☎ 527-9468; Av Brasil 701; s/d US$7.50/11.30) Opposite the bus terminal. What it lacks in personality, it makes up for in orderliness.

Other solid options include the following:
Residencial Gloria (☎ 727-6250; Potosí 1569; r per person US$2.50, with bathroom US$3.15) Spacious and secure in colonial building. Midnight curfew and bathrooms not its strong point.
Residencial San Miguel (☎ 527-2132; Calle Sucre 331; r per person US$3.15, with bathroom US$5)
Hostal Hidalgo (☎ 525-7516; 6 de Octubre 1616; s/d US$10/17) A modernish central option with clean rooms.
Hotel Samay Wasí (☎ 527-6737; samaywasioruro@hotmail.com; Av Brasil 392; s/d incl breakfast US$13/20) This modern, high-rise HI-affiliate near the bus terminal has gas showers around the clock, cable TV and phones.

Eating

Life doesn't really get going here until 11am, so Mercado Campero is your best bet for an early breakfast. Stalls serve mostly *api* and pastries in the morning, but look out for *falso conejo* ('false rabbit,' a rubbery meat-based concoction), mutton soup, and beef and potatoes smothered with hot *llajhua* (spicy tomato-based sauce). For bargain lunch specials, check out the small eateries around the train station.

Salteñería La Casona (Av Presidente Montes 5969) The best *salteñas* are found here, just off Plaza 10 de Febrero; it also has sandwiches and pizza and pasta.

SPLURGE!

Restaurant Nayjama (☎ 527-7699; cnr Aldana 1880 & Pagador; mains US$4-7) Cordon bleu cuisine on the *altiplano*? *Si señor*. The elegant, nonsmoking Restaurant Nayjama is run by celeb chef Don Roberto. He has catered to jet-setters the world over – invite him for a glass of wine to find out who. The house specialties are novel, international interpretations of classic Bolivian dishes and vegetarian options are available on request.

BOLIVIA

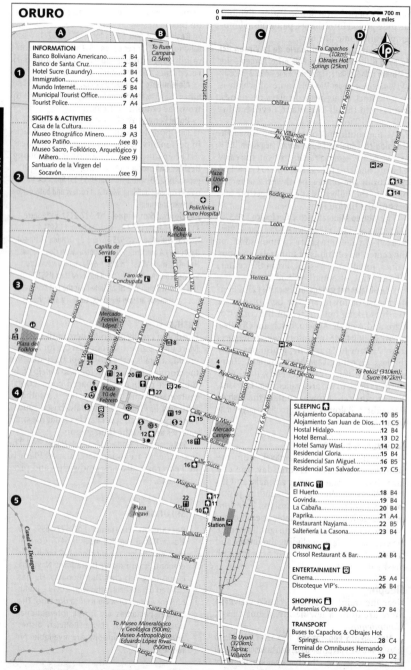

ORURO

0 — 700 m
0 — 0.4 miles

INFORMATION
Banco Boliviano Americano..........1 B4
Banco de Santa Cruz................2 B4
Hotel Sucre (Laundry)..............3 B4
Immigration........................4 C4
Mundo Internet.....................5 B4
Municipal Tourist Office...........6 A4
Tourist Police.....................7 A4

SIGHTS & ACTIVITIES
Casa de la Cultura.................8 B4
Museo Etnográfico Minero...........9 A3
Museo Patiño....................(see 8)
Museo Sacro, Folklórico, Arquelógico y
  Mihero........................(see 9)
Santuario de la Virgen del
  Socavón.......................(see 9)

SLEEPING
Alojamiento Copacabana............10 B5
Alojamiento San Juan de Dios.....11 C5
Hostal Hidalgo....................12 B4
Hotel Bernal......................13 D2
Hotel Samay Wasi..................14 D2
Residencial Gloria................15 B4
Residencial San Miguel............16 B5
Residencial San Salvador..........17 C5

EATING
El Huerto.........................18 B4
Govinda...........................19 B4
La Cabaña.........................20 B4
Paprika...........................21 A4
Restaurant Nayjama................22 B5
Salteñería La Casona..............23 B4

DRINKING
Crissol Restaurant & Bar..........24 B4

ENTERTAINMENT
Cinema............................25 A4
Discoteque VIP's..................26 B4

SHOPPING
Artesenías Oruro ARAO.............27 B4

TRANSPORT
Buses to Capachos & Obrajes Hot
  Springs.........................28 C4
Terminal de Omnibuses Hernando
  Siles...........................29 D2

Govinda (6 de Octubre 6089; mains US$1-2) For Hare veggie fare, try this godlike place.

Paprika (Calle Junín 821) Join the locals for some lively banter. Where else can you be served a US$1.25 lunch by bow-tied waiters?

El Huerto (Calle Bolívar) Lunch for around US$1.35. It's near Pagador.

La Cabaña (Calle Junín 609; mains US$1-4) Serves juicy steaks and typical Bolivian dishes in a pleasant setting.

Drinking

Crissol Restaurant & Bar (☎ 525-3449; cnr Adolfo Mier & La Plata) Is that really a car suspended from the roof? Rev into the *altiplano*'s classiest place for a game of pool. Live music and dancing on weekends, full menu and sports TV lounge. Lunchtime salad buffet served upstairs for US$1.25.

Entertainment

In the evenings you can hit the right note at one of many karaoke bars around town or at the sleazy **Discoteque VIP's** (cnr Calle Junín & 6 de Octubre). The **cinema** (Calle Bolívar; admission US$1), on the west side of the plaza, screens relatively recent releases.

Shopping

Go on, be a devil! The design and production of artful Diablada masks and costumes is a booming cottage industry. Drop by the workshops on Av La Paz, between León and Villarroel.

Artesanías Oruro ARAO (☎ 525-0331; cnr Soria Galvarro & Calle Adolfo Mier) Opposite the cathedral, this place stocks a diverse selection of fine fair-trade Bolivian handicrafts.

Getting There & Away

BUS

All buses arrive and depart from **Terminal de Omnibuses Hernando Siles** (☎ 527-9535; Av Villarroel), a flat 15-minute walk northeast of the center. Buses to La Paz (US$1.90 to US$2, three to four hours) run every 30 minutes. There are daily services to Cochabamba (US$1.75, 4½ hours), Potosí (normal/*cama* US$2/9, five hours) with connections to Tupiza and Villazón, and several nighttime services to Uyuni (US$3 to US$4, eight hours), but the train is the ticket on this rough route.

Basic services to Sucre (US$5, eight to 10 hours) go via either Cochabamba or Potosí, or there's four overnight direct buses. Flota Bolivar goes direct to Santa Cruz (US$12, 18 to 20 hours), or you can make connections in Cochabamba.

There are daily departures for Arica, Chile (US$11, nine hours) via Tambo Quemado (passing through Parque Nacional Sajama) with connections to Iquique. Most travelers, however, prefer to enter Chile further south at San Pedro Atacama via Uyuni and a *salares* (salt plains) tour.

TRAIN

Oruro became a railroading center thanks to its mines, but the only surviving passenger connection is with Uyuni and points south. You must take your passport to the **ticket window** (☎ 527-4605; ⏰ 8am-noon & 2:30-6pm Sun-Fri); arrive early and purchase your ticket a day ahead to avoid long lines.

A taxi between the train station and the center costs US50¢ per person.

The privatized service is run by the Chilean **Empresa Ferroviaria Andina** (FCA; www.fca.com.bo in Spanish) and offers two services. The top-notch *Expreso del Sur* has two classes: the quite serviceable salon and top-of-the-line executive premier, which includes meals, videos and a dining car. It departs Oruro at 3:30pm on Tuesday and Friday for Uyuni (salon/executive US$6.50/13, 6½ hours), Tupiza (US$11.50/25.50, 11¾ hours) and Villazón (US$13.70/30, 15 hours). It's a thoroughly enjoyable trip with beautiful scenery as far as Uyuni, but unfortunately the stretch to Tupiza is after dark.

The *Wara Wara del Sur* is the 2nd-class train, departing Oruro at 7pm Wednesday and Sunday, stopping at numerous stations en route to Uyuni (salon/executive US$5/11, seven hours), Tupiza (US$9/20, 13 hours) and Villazón (US$11/23, 16¾ hours). The slightly cheaper 3rd class is called *popular*: prime your wrestling persona before joining the fray. There's no dining car, but snacks are peddled at every stop.

UYUNI

☎ 02 / pop 14,000

This 'climatically challenged,' otherworldly and isolated community (elevation 3675m) today seems to exist only for the tourist hoards who venture out to the extraordinary *salares*. The town itself has two notable sights: the archaeology museum and the rubbish-strewn Cementerio de Trenes (a graveyard of rusting locomotives 3km south of town).

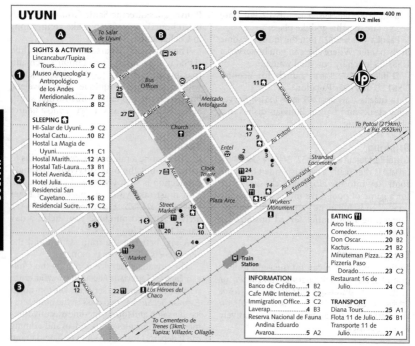

SIGHTS & ACTIVITIES	
Lincancabur/Tupiza Tours	6 C2
Museo Arqueología y Antropológico de los Andes Meridionales	7 B2
Rankings	8 B2

SLEEPING	
HI-Salar de Uyuni	9 C2
Hostal Cactu	10 B2
Hostal La Magia de Uyuni	11 C1
Hostal Marith	12 A3
Hostal Tati-Laura	13 B1
Hotel Avenida	14 C2
Hotel Julia	15 C2
Residencial San Cayetano	16 B2
Residencial Sucre	17 C2

EATING	
Arco Iris	18 C2
Comedor	19 A3
Don Oscar	20 B2
Kactus	21 B2
Minuteman Pizza	22 A3
Pizzería Paso Dorado	23 C2
Restaurant 16 de Julio	24 C2

INFORMATION	
Banco de Crédito	1 B2
Cafe M@c Internet	2 C2
Immigration Office	3 C2
Laverap	4 B3
Reserva Nacional de Fauna Andina Eduardo Avaroa	5 A2

TRANSPORT	
Diana Tours	25 A1
Flota 11 de Julio	26 B1
Transporte 11 de Julio	27 A1

Information

At the time of research, the tourist information office, normally housed in the clock tower, was closed.

Banco de Crédito (Av Potosí) Near Av Arce. Break big boliviano notes and change cash here. Otherwise, try the streetchangers near the bank, bigger tour companies or popular restaurants; several places on Potosí buy Chilean and Argentine pesos.

Cafe M@c Internet (Av Potosí) Opposite the plaza.

Immigration office (cnr Sucre & Av Potosí) If you're traveling to Chile, you're best off picking up a Bolivian exit stamp (officially US$2) at this Las Vegasesque office, since the hours of the Bolivian border post at Hito Cajón (just beyond Laguna Verde) are about as reliable as *altiplano* transport.

Laverap (Av Ferroviaria) Does laundry for US$1 per kilo. Some hostals and hotels offer the same service.

Reserva National de Fauna Andina Eduardo Avaroa office (REA; ☎ 293-2225; Avaroa) Sernap's friendly office is more user-friendly than the park's name.

Sights

The trippy **Museo Arqueología y Antropológico de los Andes Meridionales** (cnr Av Arce & Colón; adult/student US65¢/30¢; ⊙ 8:30am-noon & 2-6pm Tue-Fri, 9am-1pm Sat & Sun) features mummies, loads of skulls and Spanish-language descriptions of the practices of mummification and deformation.

Tours

A drive across the Salar and surrounds is a surreal and must-do experience: salt plains, hot springs, geysers, colored lagoons, volcanoes and flamingos are the tour trademarks. In the wet season, some areas cannot be reached.

THREE- OR FOUR-DAY TRIPS

The most popular tour is a jeep trip: a four-day circuit visiting the Salar de Uyuni (p219), Laguna Colorada, Sol de Mañana and Laguna Verde. If you want to head into Chile, you can do three days of the tour, hop off at Laguna Verde and connect there with transport to San Pedro de Atacama (often the price is the same; check whether transfer is included in fee). Before leaving Uyuni, get a Bolivian exit stamp; better tour agencies can often arrange stamps outside office hours. (There is a border outpost at Laguna Verde but it's best to get the stamps in Uyuni.)

CUSTOM TRIPS

Shorter trips traverse the northern crescent of the Salar de Uyuni, stopping overnight at the friendly village of Jirira, with a climb on Volcán Tunupa. Depending on the season, you can arrange longer custom trips visiting Llica, the Salar de Coipasa or Laguna Celeste via the world's highest motorable road near the Argentine border.

Sleeping

Uyuni's tourism boom means the best hotels fill up fast; advance booking is advisable in high season. In a pinch, crash out for free in the railway station's waiting room; it's toasty with all the bodies in there and quite safe.

Cheap places near the station come in handy (although can be noisy) since most trains arrive and depart at ungodly hours. Most places are associated with one tour operator or another.

Hostal Marith (☎ 693-2174; Av Potosí 61; r per person US$2.50, with bathroom US$5) Clean and painted rooms off the main drag. Extras include laundry sinks and a social patio.

Hostal Cactu (Plaza Arce; r per person US$3.15) A typical but OK cheapie, which seems to be forever renovating. It's on the southwest side of the plaza.

HI-Salar de Uyuni (☎ /fax 693-2228; www.hostellingbolivia.org; cnr Av Potosí & Sucre; dm US$3.15, d per person US$7.55; 🖳) A veritable labyrinth of rooms and a bit on the dark side, but clean.

Hotel Avenida (☎ 693-2078; Av Ferroviaria 11; r per person US$5-6, without bathroom US$2-3) A popular and clean option for pre-departure and return trips. Good laundry sinks and hot showers between 7am to 9pm.

Hotel Julia (☎ 693-2134; Av Ferroviaria/Aniceto Arce; s/d US$7.55/14.40) More 'grown up' than the cheapies, and good for a comfortable posttrip sleep.

Hostal La Magia de Uyuni (☎ 693-2541; magia_uyuni@yahoo.es; Colón 432; s/d incl breakfast US$15/20) A bit twee, but the homey rooms are arranged around a indoor courtyard. It's popular among small tour groups.

Other options:

Residencial San Cayetano (Plaza Arce; r per person US$2) On the north side of the plaza. Serviceable. Rise early to use the one decent shower (US50¢).

Hostal Tati – Laura (☎ 742-21226; Cabrera 334; r US$2.50) This new concrete block is nicer on the inside than the out.

Residencial Sucre (☎ 693-2047; Sucre 132; r per person US$2.50) Marginal, saggy mattresses and cold water only.

BOLIVIA

CHOOSING AN OPERATOR

There are more than 60 travel agencies offering trips to the Salar de Uyuni. Most offer Spanish-speaking drivers and the identical four-day trip. On the positive side, more competition means more choice; the brackish side is it has lowered quality as many dodgy and fly-by-night operators try to make a fast buck. It is your right to negotiate, but remember that cost-cutting leads to operators cutting corners – at the expense of your safety and the environment. At least 16 people, including 13 tourists, have been killed in jeep accidents on the Salar de Uyuni salt plains since May 2008.

There have been alarming reports of ill-equipped vehicles, speeding tour operators and a lack of emergency equipment. Common exploits include trying to cram an extra body into the jeep (six is comfortable), or joining forces with other agencies to make up the numbers. 'Grainy' experiences include ill-maintained jeeps, breakdowns, drunk drivers, poor food and service, and disregard for the Salar's once-pristine environment (eg chasing flamingos for good photos, leaving garbage behind – including toilet paper – or using the facilities of the salt hotel, an illegal structure).

The best operators provide written itineraries outlining meals (vegetarians can be catered for), accommodations and trip details. The average costs are between US$60 and US$100; plan on the higher figure during peak season (July to September). In most cases, price reflects quality. Booking and professional operators outside Uyuni cost extra, but may be worth it.

If touring from Uyuni, you could visit the Rankings (Av Potosi 9, 1st fl) office. More like a dating agency than an official ranking service, it helps match up travelers with operators according to their requirements: food, accommodations and other preferences (although many operators promote a high 'ranking' on posters – a misrepresentation). Your best bet is to talk to travelers to get the latest scoop.

Eating

Minuteman Pizza (☎ 693-2094; Av Ferroviaria 60, at Hotel Toñito; pizzas US$3.80-6.30; ⏰ from 8am) When the owner built a purpose-built pizza kitchen, he meant business. And he got it. Uyuni's best all-round eating choice offers the most gourmet of gourmet pizzas, Budweiser, wines, and a huge range of breakfasts. Ideal for the pretrip carbo loading or the return trip binge (by the way, 'large' means *large*).

Comedor (cnr Av Potosí & Avaroa) If you've got a strong stomach, cheap meals are on offer at the market *comedor* and nearby street food stalls. For a piquant dose of *altiplano* culture, look for *charque kan* (mashed hominy peppered with bits of dried llama meat), often found inside tamales.

Arco Iris (Plaza Arce) The best spot to cobble together a tour group. It's a warm place with good pizzas, cold beer and occasional live music.

Pizzeria Paso Dorado (Plaza Arce 49; pizzas US$4-10) Serves nonround choices on the plaza.

Don Oscar (cnr Av Potosí & Bolívar) This friendly spot does decent dinners.

The more upmarket **Restaurant 16 de Julio** (Plaza Arce 35; mains US$2-4; ⏰ from 7am) and nearby **Kactus** dish out tasty pasta, international dishes and Bolivian fare.

Getting There & Away

Arrive from Tupiza via the badlands to avoid the crowds. In high season, it can be tricky to get out of isolated Uyuni. Buy your bus ticket the day before or ask a tour agency how much they charge to purchase train tickets; lines are long and *quien es mas macho* (literally 'who is the most macho') shoving matches can break out for the limited seats.

BUS & JEEP

All buses leave from the west end of Av Arce behind the church.

Todo Turismo (☎ 211-9418; Antofagasta Sq 504 near the bus station; one way US$25) in La Paz has introduced a new (and more comfortable) direct bus service. This can be booked direct or through tour agencies for the same price. If you opt to go the cheaper option, Transporte 11 de Julio buses blast off at 10am and 7pm daily for Potosí (US$3 to US$4, seven hours) and Sucre (US$6 to US$7, nine to 11 hours). Diana Tours runs the same service at 10am and 7pm daily. Flota 11 de Julio goes to Tupiza (US$5 to US$6, 10 to 12 hours) at

9am on Wednesday and Sunday, and Calama in Chile, via Avoroa (US$10, 12 to 15 hours), at 4am Monday and Thursday. Oruro (US$3.80 to US$6.30, eight to 10 hours) depart at 7:45pm daily. Daily services go to La Paz (US$8, 11 to 14 hours).

Daily *rapiditos* (4WD Jeep services) shuttle between Uyuni and Tupiza (US$6.50, six to seven hours) departing at around 5:30am. Several companies depart around 5am after they've stuffed in as many as 10 passengers.

TRAIN

Uyuni has a modern, well-organized **train station** (☎ 693-2153); confirm hours on the noticeboard inside as the train can be delayed, then queue at least two hours before departure (in the high season only). Comfortable but crowded *Expreso del Sur* trains ramble to Oruro (salon/executive US$6.50/12.70, seven hours) on Thursday and Sunday at 12:05am (that's Wednesday and Saturday night folks!). Departures south to Tupiza (US$3.60/5.15, five hours) and Villazón (US$5.40/8, 9½ hours) are at 10:40pm on Tuesday and Friday. If tickets sell out, you could take a bus 111km south to Atocha, where the train stops at 12:45am.

Chronically late *Wara Wara del Sur* trains are supposed to chug out of the station for Oruro (3rd/2nd/1st class US$3.90/5/11, 7½ hours) at 1:45am on Tuesday and Friday and at 2:50am on Monday and Thursday for Tupiza (US$4.50/6/12.45, 5½ hours) and Villazón (US$4.50/6/12, nine hours).

At 3:30am on Tuesday, a train trundles west for the town of Avaroa on the Chilean border, where you cross to Ollagüe and have to wait several hours to clear Chilean customs. Another train continues the journey to Calama (US$14). The whole trip takes 20 to 40 hours and is strictly for masochistic rail junkies. Note: these train timetables are subject to change so double check before you wait up 'til the wee hours.

WARNING

In the past couple of years, pre-departure robberies have been increasing, where farewelling 'friends' enter the train and relieve others of their goods. Don't store your belongings in the overhead compartments.

SOUTHWEST CIRCUIT

Different times of year offer different experiences: from April to September, the *salares* are dry and blindingly white. In the rainy season, they're under water, projecting a perfect mirror image of clouds, sky and land to the horizon. At this time, roads may be quagmires, making passage difficult, and hail and snow are always a possibility.

Salar de Uyuni

The world's largest salt flat sits at a lofty 3653m and blankets an amazing 12,000 sq km. It was part of a prehistoric salt lake, Lago Minchín, which covered most of southwest Bolivia. When it dried up, it left a couple of seasonal puddles and several salt pans, including the **Salar de Uyuni** and **Salar de Coipasa**.

Towns of note include **Colchani** on the eastern shore and **Llica** on the west, where there are basic accommodations. A maze of tracks crisscrosses the *salar* and connects nearby settlements and several islands that pepper this blindingly-white desert. **Isla de los Pescadores** bears amazing stands of giant cactus and a marooned colony of vizcachas (long-tailed rodents related to chinchillas). Please stay away from **Isla Cáscara de Huevo**; flamingos breed here.

At the time of research, the salar's famous salt hotels, Hotel Playa Blanca and the Palacio de Sal, were being deconstructed and moved block by block to the edge of salar near Colchani due to environmental concerns. One remains as a 'museum' (read 'illegal structure') and continues to be included as a stopover in many tours.

Far Southwest

Several startlingly beautiful sights are hidden away in this remote corner. The surreal landscape is nearly treeless, punctuated by gentle hills and volcanoes near the Chilean border. Wildlife in the area includes three types of flamingos (most notably the rare James species), plus plenty of llamas, vicuñas, emus and owls.

The following sites comprise the major stops on most tours. **Laguna Colorada** is a bright adobe-red lake fringed with cakey-white minerals, 25km east of the Chilean border. On its western shore is Campamento Ende and beside it the meteorological station, where those with marginal tour companies find shelter and visitors without tents can crash overnight.

The thin, clear air is bitterly cold and between June and September, the temperature at night drops below -20°C (-4°F). The air is perfumed by *llareta*, a rock-hard, mosslike shrub that is broken apart to be burned for fuel.

Most independent transport to Laguna Colorada will be supplying or servicing mining and military camps or the on-hold geothermal project 50km south at **Sol de Mañana**. The main interest here is the 4950m-high **geyser basin**, with its boiling mud pots and sulfurous fumaroles. Tread carefully when approaching the site; any damp or cracked earth is potentially dangerous. The nearby **Termas de Polques** hot springs spout comfortable 30°C (86°F) sulfurous water and provide a relaxing morning dip at 4200m.

Laguna Verde, a splendid aquamarine lake, is tucked into Bolivia's southwestern corner at 5000m. Behind the lake rises the dramatic 5930m cone of **Volcán Licancabur**.

GETTING THERE & AROUND

The easiest way to visit the far southwest is with a group from Uyuni (see p216). Some agencies in both La Paz and Potosí arrange tours, but charge more because of their commission. Alternatively, you can set out from Tupiza (see p221) and end up in Uyuni, a very worthwhile option.

The sparsely populated far southwest region is even more remote than the *salares,* but there are several mining and military camps and weather stations that may provide a place to crash in an emergency. The determined can do it independently, but you'll need a compass, maps, camping gear, warm clothing, food, water, patience, fortitude, a loose screw and people skills (for when you get stuck).

TUPIZA

☎ 02 / pop 22,300

If ever there's a place where you want to throw your leg over a horse, brandish spurs and say, 'ride 'em cowboy,' this is it. Reminiscent of the American Wild West, but more spectacular, this tranquil settlement is set at 2950m and ringed by an amazing landscape of rainbow-colored rocks, hills, mountains and canyons of the Cordillera de Chicas. It was the apt setting for the demise of Butch Cassidy and the Sundance Kid: after robbing an Aramayo payroll at Huaca Huañusca, some 40km north of Tupiza, the pair reputedly met their makers in the mining village of San Vicente in 1908.

BOLIVIA

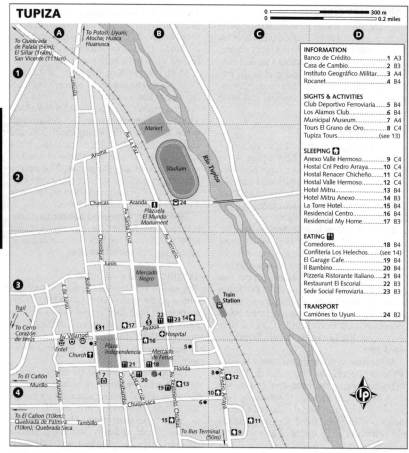

TUPIZA

INFORMATION	
Banco de Crédito.................................1	A3
Casa de Cambio...............................2	B3
Instituto Geográfico Militar.....3	A4
Rocanet...4	B4

SIGHTS & ACTIVITIES	
Club Deportivo Ferroviaria......5	B4
Los Alamos Club..............................6	B4
Municipal Museum.......................7	A4
Tours El Grano de Oro...................8	C4
Tupiza Tours.............................(see 13)	

SLEEPING	
Anexo Valle Hermoso..................9	C4
Hostal Cnl Pedro Arraya..........10	C4
Hostal Renacer Chicheño.........11	C4
Hostal Valle Hermoso...............12	C4
Hotel Mitru.......................................13	B4
Hotel Mitru Anexo......................14	B3
La Torre Hotel................................15	B4
Residencial Centro.....................16	B4
Residencial My Home...............17	B3

EATING	
Comedores.......................................18	B4
Confitería Los Helechos.......(see 14)	
El Garage Cafe...............................19	B4
Il Bambino..20	B4
Pizzeria Ristorante Italiano.....21	B4
Restaurant El Escorial.................22	B3
Sede Social Ferroviaria.............23	B3

TRANSPORT	
Camiónes to Uyuni.....................24	B2

Hiking, biking and horse-riding opportunities abound and the variety of bizarre geologic formations, deep gorges and cactus forests are dramatic backdrops. Unsurprisingly, it's finally been discovered by travelers, and is well and truly on the gringo trail. Many people who visit for a day end up staying for a week to enjoy a tranquil and friendly experience.

Information

Several internet places on the plaza have decent connections for US40¢ an hour. The quiet, nonsmoking **Rocanet** (Florida) has the best connections.

Most hotels offer same-day laundry service for around US$1 per kilo.

For maps, try the Instituto Geográfico Militar, upstairs inside the Municipalidad on the plaza. A map of the town costs US60¢.

Tupiza Tours (☎ /fax 694-3513; www.tupizatours.com; Av Regimento Chichas 187, at Hotel Mitru) is a wealth of information, has a book exchange and gives cash advances for around 3% commission. To change cash, try the *casa de cambio* inside the *librería* (stationery store) on Avaroa or Banco de Crédito on the plaza's north side, which also gives Visa and MasterCard advances (US$5 per transaction).

There's no tourist office.

Sights & Activities

Tupiza's main attraction is the stunning surrounding countryside, best seen on foot or horseback. Recommended destinations include the following canyons and rock formations: **Quebrada de Palala** (10km round trip), **Quebrada de Palmira** (10km), **El Cañon** (10km), **Quebrada Seca** (10km to 20km) and **El Sillar** (32km).

A short trek up **Cerro Corazón de Jesús**, west of town, reveals lovely views over the town, especially at sunset. Lively **street markets** convene on Thursday and Saturday morning near the train station. You can steam in a sauna (US65¢) at **Los Alamos Club** (Chuquisaca) or play a set of tennis (US$1.35) on the clay courts at **Club Deportivo Ferroviaría** (set back from Av Serrano, about a block from the train station). Hotel Mitru enthusiastically promotes its pool (all day use US$1.25) to the public, although it doesn't always have water in it! There's a dusty **municipal museum** (admission free; ☽ 3-6pm Mon, Wed & Fri) off the plaza.

Tours
Tour companies are being trotted out at a pace in Tupiza. Ask other travelers for recommendations. Most operators offer day trips exploring Tupiza's rugged *quebradas* (ravines) for around US$20 per person. Several now offer the triathlon, where you visit Tupiza's best places in a full-day circuit by bicycle, horse and in a jeep (from US$20 per person for group of six).

The best operators have safety equipment for the triathlon (helmets and jackets for bike trips, and hard hats for horse-riding), but most do the same or similar circuits.

Tours El Grano de Oro (☎ 6944-4763; elgranodeoro tours@hotmail.com; Av Pedro Arraya 492) A new company worth checking out (if only for the owners' local knowledge and ecofriendly attitude). Trips to the Salar de Uyuni (US$100 per person for six people), two-day horse and camping trips (US$12.50 to US$17 depending on sleeping arrangements; they have their own 'hacienda') and tailor-made triathlons.

Tupiza Tours (☎ /fax 694-3513; www.tupizatours .com; Av Regimento Chichas, at Hotel Mitru) A reliable company. As well as the jeep or triathlon trips, Tupiza Tours offers fanatics the more arduous Butch and Sundance trail to Huaca Huañusca and the lonely mining village of San Vicente where the outlaws' careers abruptly ended (per person US$140). It also arranges horseback trips for US$2.50/15 per hour/day or you can embark on a recommended four-day, three-night tour from Tupiza to the Salar de Uyuni (see p219) for around US$115 per person (with six people, showers US60¢ extra).

Sleeping
The cheapest options are several basic *residenciales* opposite the train station.

Hostal Cnl Pedro Arrayo (☎ 694-2734; hostal arraya@hotmail.com; Av Pedro Arraya 494; per person US$2.50, per person with bathroom US$4.50) This brand-new sparkling place is arranged in stablelike fashion around a clean courtyard. Riders of the bike variety will love it; secure storage guaranteed. A tour company is attached to the hostal.

Residencial Centro (☎ 694-2705; Av Santa Cruz 287; r per person US$2.50, with bathroom US$4) This central option has well-kept and clean rooms with perennially hot showers.

Hostal Valle Hermoso (☎ 694-2370; www.bolivia .freehosting.net; Av Pedro Arraya 478; r per person US$2.50, with bathroom US$4.40) An HI hostel with a book exchange, optional breakfast and laundry service. Boards advertise group tours. The same family has recently opened the bright, new Anexo Valle Hermoso up the road, near the bus station, for similar prices.

Residencial My Home (☎ 694-2947; Avaroa 288; r per person US$3.15, with bathroom US$4.40) A local doctor and his nurse wife have recently taken over this and are in the throes of operating. Hospital beds to match, in freshly painted, bright and airy rooms. Prognosis is looking great.

Hotel Mitru Anexo (☎ 694-3002; Avaroa at Serrano; s/d US$6.30/11.30, without bathroom US$3.15/6.30) Affiliated with the Mitru and located near the train station, this hotel is also excellent value. Guests can use the kitchen, as well as the Hotel Mitru pool (if it has water in it).

Hotel Mitru (☎ 694-3001; Av Regimento Chichas 187; s US$4-8, d US$15-20, ste US$35-40; ☒) The prices have been extended as much as the hotel over the last couple of years, but it's bright and airy and still good value.

La Torre Hotel (☎ 694-2633; Av Regimento Chicas 220; s/d US$5/9) Readers recommend this hotel's clean rooms with reasonable beds, TV and telephone. The owners have just opened up a tour company in the same location.

Eating
Affordable street meals are also served outside the train station and at the *comedores* around the market.

Restaurant El Escorial (☎ 694-2010; cnr Av Chichas & Abaroa; almuerzos US$1) Large mirrors, ornaments and the ubiquitous TV set contrast with the plastic chairs of this signless eatery. Excellent *almuerzos* (US$1.25 on Sunday).

BOLIVIA

BOLIVIA

El Garage Cafe (Av Regimento Chichas; snacks US$1-2.25) A café in a garage or vice versa? This quirky place (and equally eccentric owner, perhaps) have had their share of fumes. Now, it boasts formica tables, vinyl records, cacti and a Che Guevara shrine. A fun place to idle. It's opposite Hotel Mitru.

Il Bambino (cnr Florida & Santa Cruz; almuerzos US$1.25) Try the southern *altiplano*'s best *salteñas* at this friendly place which also has massive *almuerzos*.

Pizzeria Ristorante Italiano (Florida s/n; pizzas US$2-6.30) You name it, it's got it, from breakfasts to pasta and dishes à la Chinese (despite the name). Not the cheapest in town but a popular gringo hangout just off the plaza.

Confitería Los Helechos (Avaroa; mains US$2.50-3.15) This place in Hotel Mitru Anexo reliably serves three meals a day. Breakfasts with real coffee are especially nice. Later in the day, there's a salad bar, good chicken, burgers, *licuados* and cocktails.

Locals (mainly males) head to the **Sede Social Ferroviaria** (cnr Avaroa & Av Regimento Chichas).

Getting There & Away

BUS, JEEP & CAMIÓN

Buses depart from the **terminal** (Av Pedro Arraya) at the southern end of the *avenida*. Fares for Oruro-bound routes north double a month before Carnaval. Several companies have 10am and evening departures to Potosí (US$5, at least eight hours), with Sucre connections. Several services depart for Tarija (US$4, eight hours) at 8pm, with connections to Yacuiba. Many companies serve Villazón (US$1.25, three hours) at 4am and 2pm daily; sit on the right for views. There are daily departures to La Paz (US$8 to US$12, 16 hours) via Potosí at 10am and 3:30pm. O'Globo leaves for Cochabamba at 10am and 8:30pm daily.

Flota Boquerón leaves on Monday and Thursday for Uyuni (US$6.30, 10 to 12 hours) but the train is much less nerve-racking. 4WD Jeep services to Uyuni (US$6.75, seven to eight hours) depart around 10:30am when there is enough demand. Irregular *camiones* to Uyuni (check about times) leave from just east off Plazuela El Mundo, a traffic circle around an enormous globe.

TRAIN

The **ticket office** (☎ 694-2527; ☽ 8am-noon & 3-6pm), sells tickets for the *Expreso del Sur* and *Wara Wara del Sur*, or if you don't want to queue, have Tupiza Tours buy your ticket for a small surcharge. The scenery is brilliant, so travel by day if possible. The *Expreso del Sur* trundles north to Uyuni (salon/executive US$5/12, five hours) and Oruro (US$12/26, 11¾ hours) at 6:25pm on Wednesday and Saturday. At 4:10am on Wednesday and Saturday (having left Oruro on Tuesday and Friday the previous evening) the *Expreso del Sur* speeds south to Villazón ($US2/6, three hours).

The cheaper *Wara Wara del Sur,* which are always late and crowded, leave at 7:05pm on Monday and Thursday for Uyuni (salon/executive US$2.75/5.75, six hours) and Oruro (US$8.80/20, 13¾ hours), and at 8:35am on Monday and Thursday for Villazón (US$1/2, three hours), having left Oruro the previous days.

TARIJA

☎ 04 / pop 392,000

Befitting of a viticultural city, Tarija is like an aging red wine: it's modest, displays positive attributes, and consistently improves over time. The city is almost Mediterranean in nature and design: stately date palms line the beautiful plaza, colonial houses abound, and a central market pulsates with life and flavors. The city's numerous cafés, plazas and museums provide a pleasant place to relax. A significant student population adds action to the ambience.

The surrounding region has many sights and activities, bottled for the traveler. Vineyards, Inca trails and fossilized regions occupy a diverse range of habitats, from lush fertile valleys to desert-type plains (the start of the Chaco). With planning, these areas are accessible by hiking, or with the growing number of tour operators. The valley's springlike climate is idyllic. *Chapacos* (as *tarijeños* refer to themselves) are in many ways more Spanish or Argentine than Bolivian. They are proud of their fiestas, unique musical instruments and local foods, including the fortified wine *singani*. But, although rich in so many ways, over half the population of the region is said to live in poverty.

Orientation

Street numbers are preceded by an O (*oeste*) for those addresses west of Colón and an E (*este*) for those east of Colón; addresses north of Av Las Américas (Av Victor Paz Estenssoro) take an N.

TARIJA

BOLIVIA

BOLIVIA

Information

Several internet places around Plaza Sucre and in Calle Ingavi (between Sucre and Campos) charge less than US50¢ an hour and are open until midnight. ATMs are numerous around the plazas.

Banco Bisa On the main plaza. Changes traveler's checks (up to US$1000 for US$6 fee).

Casas de cambio (Bolívar btwn Sucre & Daniel Campos) Changes US dollars and Argentine pesos.

Departmental tourist office (☎ 663-1000; ⏲ 8am-noon & 2.30-6.30pm Mon-Fri) On the main plaza, this helpful office has maps and trees worth of information.

Entel A block southeast of the plaza on Virginio Lema.

Esmeralda Lavandería (☎ 664-2043; La Madrid 0-157) Offers quick machine wash-and-dry service for US$1 per kilo.

Immigration (☎ 664-3450; cnr Bolívar & Ballivían) Is very friendly and worth visiting about border crossings or to extend your visa.

Municipal tourist office (☎ 663-3581; cnr Bolívar & Sucre; ⏲ 8am-noon & 2:30-6:30pm Mon-Fri, 8am-noon Sat) Staff very friendly but don't always know their stuff.

Post office (cnr Sucre & Virginio Lema)

Sights & Activities

It's worth a stroll around the center to see what remains of the colonial atmosphere. For fossil frolickers, the university-run **Museo de Arqueología y Paleontología** (Virginio Lema; admission US60¢; ⏲ 8am-noon & 3-6pm Mon-Fri, 9am-noon & 3-6pm Sat & Sun) houses a good overview of the region's geology and prehistoric creatures. It's near Gral Bernando Trigo.

Wealthy 19th-century merchant Moisés Navajas left behind the partially restored **Casa Dorada** (cnr Ingavi & Gral Bernando Trigo) – now the **Casa de la Cultura** – which houses a quirky extravaganza of European furniture, imported by a Spanish couple in 1903. Open for guided tours (US50¢).

A popular weekend retreat is **San Lorenzo**, 15km northwest; you can pop into the former home of the *chapaco* hero Moto Méndez. San Lorenzo *micros* leave from the corner of Domingo Paz and JM Saracho. Another getaway is **Tomatitas**, 5km northwest. Have a dip in the natural swimming hole or trek to the 50m-high **Coimata Falls**. Tomatitas *micros* leave frequently from the west end of Av Domingo Paz. For Coimata Falls, walk or hitch 5km to Coimata; the falls are a 40-minute walk upstream.

As the region's viticulture center producing both wine and *singani*, Tarija caters to those who love a good drop. Brands include La Concepción/Rujero, Santa Ana de Casa Real and Kohlberg (see p260). Note: many of these *bodegas* (wineries) have offices in town where you can buy the wine at lower prices than the shops. Brands include La Concepción/Rujer, Santa Ana de Casa Real, Campos de Solana and Kohlberg. **Viva Tours** (☎ 663-8325; www.vivatour@cosett.com.bo; Calle 15 de Abril 0-509) can sate your appetite with excellent and reasonably priced half-day winery tours (US$15 per person for three, less if more people). Full-day trips incorporate surrounding areas, including the stunning **La Reserva Biológica de Sama**, Inca trail, colonial villages of the *campiña* (countryside) and the varied Gran Chaco hinterlands.

Recommended companies offering similar routes include the following:

Gaviota Travel (☎ 664-7180; gaviota@cosett.com.bo; Sucre 681)

Paula Tours (☎ 665-8156; toursbo@hotmail.com; Plaza Luis de Fuentes y Vargas)

VTB (☎ 664-4341; vtb@entelnet.bo; Hostal Cermen, Ingavi 0-0784)

Sleeping

Alojamiento El Hogar (☎ 664-3964; cnr Paz Estenssoro & La Paz; r per person US$2) The best of several dodgy options near the bus terminal is basic but friendly and family-run.

Hostería España (☎ 664-1790; Corrado 0-546; r per person US$3.15, with bathroom US$5) A helpful place offering all-round value with kitchen, hot showers and patio. It has many long-term university student residents.

Residencial El Rosario (☎ 664-2942; Ingavi 0-777; r per person US$3.15, with bathroom US$5.60) The owner is as aged and thorny as the unkempt rose bushes (in a caring kind of way), and runs a tight ship. Good gas showers, laundry sinks and cable TV room.

Residencial Zeballos (☎ 664-2068; Sucre N-966; r per person US$3.35, with bathroom & cable TV US$6.35) Leafy with bright, comfortable rooms, laundry service and a sunny courtyard. Rates include breakfast.

Hostal Bolívar (☎ 664-2741; Bolívar E-256; s US$5.50-9.50, d US$11.30-16) Sunny geranium-filled courtyards and funky tiles are the main features of this spotless place. The more expensive rooms are larger and nicer and have street-facing windows.

Hostal Libertador (☎ 664-4231; Bolívar O-649; s/d with bathroom US$9/15) Welcoming, family-run place with phone, cable TV and good optional breakfast (US60¢).

Also recommended:

Hostal Miraflores (☎ 664-3355; Sucre N-920; r per person US$3.15, s/d with bathroom US$7.50/12.50) The position near the market, and the rambling courtyard, makes up for the dingy and dark budget rooms. Rooms upstairs are better.

Gran Buenos Aires Hostal (☎ 663-6802; hostalbaires@mail.com; Daniel Campos N-448; s/d with bathroom US$8.80/15) A comfortable option with pleasant open eating areas. Can arrange tours.

Eating

At the northeast corner of the Mercado Central, at the intersection of Sucre and Domingo Paz, vendors sell local pastries and snacks, including delicious crêpelike *panqueques*. Breakfast is served at the back of the market, other cheap meals are available upstairs and fresh juices can be found in the produce section. Don't miss the huge bakery and sweets section off Bolívar.

Heladería Napoli (Campero N-630) The ice-cream cones are simply divine.

Cafe Mokka (Plaza Sucre; snacks US60¢-$1.20, pizza US$3-4) You'll spend as much time looking at the creative table tops as you will at the menu, a selection of sandwiches to pastas that fills the guts of many a gringo.

Club Social Tarija (Plaza Luis de Fuentes y Vargas; almuerzos US$1) Get a whiff of past grandeur in this wonderful old dining room.

Taverna Gattopardo (☎ 663-0656; Plaza La Madrid; mains US$1.25-6.30) Deservedly popular for its snacks, including fondue. It has a wine-tasting bar where you can sample the region's best vintages between bites of local Serrano ham. It's on the north side of the plaza.

Cabaña Don Pepe (☎ 664-2426; cnr Daniel Campos & Av Victor Paz; lunch US$1.90) A culinary must in Tarija. Formal and floral with smart service, and the best kebabs this side of the Argentinean border. Specialty Sunday lunches – 14 varieties of meat '*a la brasa*' (hot coals).

Chifa New Hong Kong (Sucre N-235; almuerzos US$2.25) Cheap cocktails and big Asian *almuerzos*.

Chingo's (Plaza Sucre) Get fried at this local hangout, which serves popular greasies.

Drinking

Bagdad Café (Plaza Sucre) Has a full bar and light dinner menu.

Entertainment

Earplug alert: karaoke runs rampant around Plaza Sucre. For more tone-deafness try the hip **Karaoke Discoteca Amor** (Sucre at La Madrid) or **Karaoke Lujos** (Campero), near the corner of Alejandro del Carpio.

Cine Gran Rex (La Madrid at Colón) This cinema screens double-feature first-run flicks for a couple of bucks.

Coliseo Deportivo (Campero) Entertaining basketball, *futsal* and volleyball games are played here.

Asociación Tarijeña de Ajedrez (Campero) After 6pm, chess heads can find a game next door to Coliseo Deportivo where you can play for free if you respect club rules: no smoking and quiet, please.

Getting There & Around
AIR

The airport (off Av Victor Paz Esstenssoro) is 3km east of town. **LAB** (☎ 664-2195; Gral Bernando Trigo N-329) has regular service to Cochabamba and a couple of flights a week to Santa Cruz and La Paz. **TAM** (☎ 664-2734; La Madrid O-470) has Tuesday flights to Santa Cruz and Wednesday flights to La Paz via Sucre. (Note: schedules change regularly.) **AeroSur** (☎ 663-0893; Calle 15 de Abril 143) flies twice a week to La Paz and Santa Cruz.

Taxis into town (US$2.50) cost twice as much from the terminal as from the road 100m outside. *Micro* A (US20¢) will drop you two blocks from the airport and returns to the Mercado Central.

BUS

The **bus terminal** (☎ 663-6508) is at the eastern end of town, a 20-minute walk from the center. Cross the street from the bus stop to catch *micro* A (US20¢) to the center.

Several buses travel daily to Potosí (US$6 to US$9, 12 to 15 hours), Oruro (US$12, 16 hours), Cochabamba (US$12.50 to US$15, 18 hours) and Sucre (US$11.50, 18 hours). For Tupiza (US$5.50, nine to 10 hours), there are daily evening departures. Daily buses to Villazón (US$4 to US$5, eight to nine hours) follow a spectacular unpaved route. Daily buses for La Paz (US$12.50 to US$15, 24 hours) leave at 7am and 5pm, and to Santa Cruz at 7:30am and 6:30pm (US$12 to US$15, 24 hours). There's one daily departure for the rough ride to Uyuni (US$8, 20 hours) at 3:30pm.

BOLIVIA

International connections to Argentina, via Bermejo or Yacuiba, involve long hauls through beautiful scenery.

VILLAZÓN

☎ 04 / pop 28,000

The main Argentine–Bolivian border town is the dusty, haphazard conglomeration of Villazón. Most focused travelers are arriving or leaving Bolivia or Argentina and don't have any need to stay. Sights and attractions aren't big on the town's priorities, but the busy market is a fun place to visit. Surprisingly, despite its frontier status, the busy town doesn't feel overly sinister. The locals appear too busy dealing in contraband items to smuggle your backpack, but that said, you should still be on your guard, especially as you walk down the 'gadget thoroughfare': petty theft, scams and counterfeit US banknotes are not unheard of here. Bolivian time lags one hour behind Argentine time.

Information

There are decent internet places (US$1 per hour) opposite the bus station and several others north of the plaza along Av Independencia. Public phones are plentiful near the frontier.

Numerous *casas de cambio* along Av República Argentina offer rates for dollars, Argentine pesos, and bolivianos. **Casa de Cambio Beto** (Av República Argentina s/n) changes traveler's checks at similar rates, minus 5% commission. **Banco de Crédito** (Oruro 111) changes cash but lacks an ATM.

Sleeping

Several passable *residenciales* along the main drag between the bus and train stations cater to locals. Accommodations on the Argentine side can be better value, if a tad more expensive. For sleeping options in neighboring La Quiaca, Argentina, see p113.

Residencial Martínez (☎ 596-3353; 25 de Mayo 13; r per person US$2) The gas showers (no electric death-trap heater!) of this red faux-brick place are appealing; only one of the rooms has private bathroom. It's opposite the bus terminal.

Residencial El Cortijo (☎ 596-2093; 20 de Mayo 338; d US$2.50, with bathroom & cable TV US$10) The empty

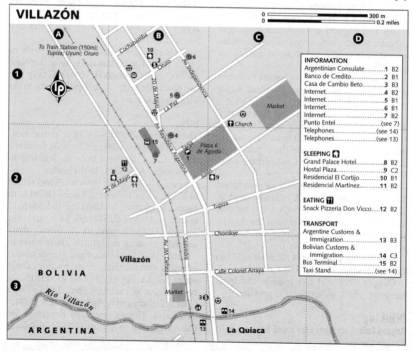

VILLAZÓN

To Train Station (150m);
Tupiza; Uyuni; Oruro

Market

Church

Plaza 6
de Agosto

Villazón

BOLIVIA

Río Villazón

Market

ARGENTINA   La Quiaca

pool looks a bit sad in the middle, but the rooms have been well maintained, with a clean, waxy odor. Two blocks north of the bus terminal. Hot showers cost an extra US65¢ for rooms without bathroom.

Grand Palace Hotel (☎ 596-5333; 25 de Mayo 52; r per person US$4.50-5, without bathroom US$2.65) More like a boarding house dorm, with long corridors, pink walls and a selection of '60s-style furniture, but the rooms (some windowless) meet the grade of a school matron.

Hostal Plaza (☎ 596-3535; Plaza 6 de Agosto 138; s/d US$4.65/6.65, with bathroom US$6.30/12.50) Sunny, light, hotel-style rooms overlooking the plaza. The nicest place in town.

Eating

Villazón's food choices are limited. Try the market *comedores,* or hop over to La Quiaca (p113) for a better selection of cheap eateries. There are a few places opposite the bus terminal on Av República Argentina. Or try **Snack Pizzeria Don Vicco** (Av República Argentina s/n).

Getting There & Around
Bus

All northbound buses depart from Villazón's central terminal (US25¢ terminal fee). Daily buses head for Tupiza (US$1.25, two to three hours) at 7am, 8am, 3pm and 5pm. Many continue or make connections to Potosí (US$6.30 to US$11.30, 10 to 12 hours) with further connections to Sucre, Oruro, Cochabamba and La Paz. There are daily services along the rough but amazing route to Tarija (US$3.15, seven hours). Agencies across from the terminal sell tickets to most major Argentine destinations, including Buenos Aires.

Train

Villazón's train station is 600m north of the border crossing; a taxi costs US$2.50. The

---

GETTING TO ARGENTINA

Exit stamps are obtained from **Bolivian immigration** (☯ 24hr), at the Villazón bridge/border post; there is no official charge for these services. Formalities are minimal, but you may be held up south of the border by exhaustive customs searches (mainly for locals and their contraband goods). For information on La Quiaca, Argentina and travel to Bolivia, see p112.

Expreso del Sur departs Wednesday and Saturday at 3:30pm for Tupiza (salon/executive US$2.15/4.50, 2¾ hours), Uyuni (US$7/17, eight hours) and Oruro (US$13.70/30, 15 hours). This is an enjoyable trip with superb scenery for the first few hours. The more crowded and basic *Wara Wara del Sur* departs Monday and Thursday at 3:30pm for Tupiza (US$2/4, three hours), Uyuni (US$6/12.20, 9½ hours) and Oruro (US$11/23, seven hours). It's a good option as far as Tupiza, but after dark it turns tedious.

COCHABAMBA
☎ 04 / pop 517,000

With a massive statue of Christ looming over the metropolis, Cochabamba has not been blessed as the most exciting city in Bolivia, albeit an economically successful one. The old center features beautiful colonial houses, balconies, overhanging eaves and large courtyards, while the more modern area to the north is home to a standard strip of high-rises and glitzy cafés.

A definite plus is the weather – warm, dry and sunny (with the odd downpour) – a welcome relief after the chilly *altiplano.* There's a generous tree-lined plaza and vibrant markets, and some interesting museums. The town's congenial nightlife is thanks to the university population. Don't leave without sampling some *chicha cochabambina,* a traditional fermented corn brew quaffed throughout the region.

The city was founded in 1574, and soon blossomed into the country's primary granary, thanks to its fertile soil and mild climate.

Orientation

Addresses north of Av de las Heroínas take an N, those below take an S. Addresses east of Av Ayacucho take an E and those west an O. The number immediately following the letter tells you how many blocks away from these division streets the address falls. Good maps are available at kiosks on the west side of the plaza or at the well-stocked Amigos del Libro (see following), which also carries guidebooks.

Information

Internet places are as common as *empanadas.* Banks and *casas de cambio* will change traveler's checks and there are ATMs located all around town. The unnamed *casa de cambio* on

BOLIVIA

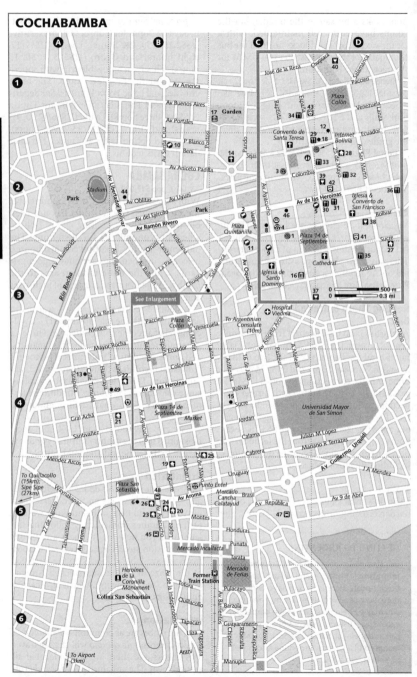

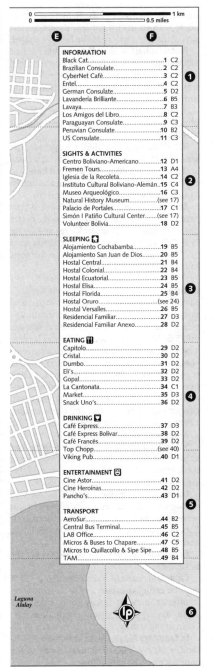

B O L I V I A

the southwest side of the plaza gives OK rates (3% commission). You'll find street money changers on Av Heroínas and around the **Entel** (Gral Achá) office.

Black Cat (cnr Bolívar & Aguirre)

Bolivian immigration (☎ 422-5553; cnr Junin & Arce) Can extend your length of stay. See p258 for details on consular representation in Cochabamba.

CyberNet Café (cnr Colombia & Baptista)

Lavandería Brilliante (Av Aroma H118) For laundry.

Lavaya (cnr Salamanca & Antezana) For laundry.

Los Amigos del Libro (☎ 450-4150; Av Ayacucho 156) The best-stocked bookshop with the company's knowledgeable and company founder at the helm.

Dangers & Annoyances

Avoid the areas around Mercados Cancha Calatayud and Mercado de Ferias (near the former train station) and west from here to Av de la Independencia (bus station); locals say it's dangerous. Do not climb the hill Colina San Sebastián as assaults have been reported.

Festivals & Events

The **Fiesta de la Virgen de Urcupiña** (around August 15 to 18) is huge, with pilgrims converging on the village of Quillacollo, 13km west of Cochabamba.

Sights & Activities

Museo Arqueológico (cnr Jordán & Baptista; admission US$1.90; 8am-6pm Mon-Fri, to noon Sat) has a fine collection of Bolivian mummies and artifacts in three sections: paleontology, fossils and archaeology. Exhibits date from as early as 12,000 BC.

Tin baron Simón Patiño never actually lived in the pretentious **Palacio de Portales** (☎ 224-3137; admission with guide US$1.35; gardens 2:30-6:30pm Mon-Fri, 10:30am-12:30pm Sat & Sun), a French-style mansion in the *barrio* of Queru Queru, north of the center. It was built between 1915 and 1925 and everything, except perhaps the bricks, was imported from Europe. Now the Simón I Patiño Cultural Center, it's used for music recitals and art exhibitions. Entrance is by guided tour only. Tours in Spanish/English start at 5pm/5:30pm from Monday to Friday, and 11am/11:30am on Saturday; call ahead to verify tour times. Don't miss the **Natural History Museum** next door. Take *micro* 'E' north from Av San Martín.

The **Cristo de la Concordia** statue, which towers over the city's east side, can be reached by taxi

BOLIVIA

(US$4.50 round-trip from the center). There's a **teleférico** (cable car; round-trip US80¢; ☺ 10am-8pm Tue-Sun) that climbs the 2900m to the top.

Courses

Cochabamba is a good spot for studying Spanish, Quechua or Aymara. Private teachers charge around US$5 per hour, but not all are experienced. Ask for recommendations at the following places:

Centro Boliviano-Americano (CBA; ☎ 222-1288/2518; www.cbacoch.org in Spanish; 25 de Mayo N-365)

Instituto Cultural Boliviano-Alemán (ICBA; ☎ 645-2091; www.icba-sucre.edu.bo; Avaroa 326)

Volunteer Bolivia (☎ 04-452-6028; www.volunteer bolivia.org; 342 Ecuador btwn 25 de Mayo & España)

Tours

To visit nearby national parks and reserves, contact **Fremen Tours** (☎ 225-9392; www.andes-ama zonia.com; Calle Tumusla N-245).

Sleeping

There are a few thrifty places around town, but quality isn't always their virtue.

Alojamiento Cochabamba (☎ 222-5067; Aguirre S-591; r per person US$2) You won't be caught short at this basic flophouse – there are chamber pots under each bed. But watch out for the wobbly veranda...

Alojamiento San Juan de Dios (López S-871; r per person US$2) Recommended only for the price.

Hostal Oruro (☎ 424-1047; López S-864; r per person US$3.15) If Hostal Elisa is full, head next door to this passable place. The shared bathrooms have solar-heated showers.

Hostal Versalles (☎ 422-1096; Av Ayacucho S-714; r per person US$3.25, with bathroom US$4.50) The best choice nearest the bus terminal is a clean, friendly HI-affiliate where breakfast is included. More expensive rooms have cable TV.

Hostal Florida (☎ /fax 225-7911; floridahostal@latinmail .com; 25 de Mayo S-583; r per person US$3.80, with bathroom, phone & cable TV US$6.30) An OK choice with quirky outdoor furniture in a central courtyard.

Hostal Elisa (☎ /fax 423-5102; López S-834; s/d per person US$3.80/6.30, with bathroom US$7.50/12.50) The top pick: an oasis in an otherwise unattractive location in a dodgy part of town. Behind the door there's friendly management, gas-heated showers and a sunny, flowery courtyard. Convenient to the bus station.

Hostal Colonial (☎ 222-1791; Junín N-134; s/d US$5/8.80) If you can overlook the saggy mat-

tresses, the rooms are pleasant. Mellow atmosphere with courtyard garden. Expunge your sins of the night before in the hostel's chapel.

Hostal Central (☎ 222-3622; General Achá O-235; s/d with bathroom US$6.30/11.30) Starts promisingly, but soon disintegrates. The overgrown central courtyard, missing curtain hooks and unfriendly management detracts from what was formerly an excellent choice. TV is a plus, however, and prices are less without this luxury.

Hostal Ecuatorial (☎ 455-6370; Av Ayachucho; r per person US$7.55) The place of paradox: it's clean and modern in a dodgy district, but handy to the bus station if travel schedules are untimely. Watch your stuff on the way to and fro.

Residencial Familiar (☎ 222-7988; Sucre E-554; r per person US$3.25, d with bathroom US$10) and the better but worn **Residencial Familiar Anexo** (☎ 222-7986; 25 de Mayo N-234; r per person US$3.25, d with bathroom US$10) have poor beds and are a bit on the nose, but are popular with travelers.

Eating

Markets are cheap for simple but varied and tasty meals; don't miss the huge, mouthwatering fruit salads. The most central market, on 25 de Mayo, is between Sucre and Jordán. There are plenty of tantalizing *salteñerias* about town. Av Heroínas is fast-food row and is good for pizza, chicken and burgers. Av Ballivián (known as El Prado) is packed with up-market bars and restaurants and is also worth checking out for *almuerzos* and classy coffees. Economical *almuerzos* are everywhere.

More central options:

Snack Uno's (cnr Avs de las Heroínas & Lanza Lanza; set lunch US$1.25) Cochabamba's best vegetarian food. Pizza and pasta dishes are also available and there's a good *salteñería* next door.

Dumbo (Av de las Heroinas; mains US$1.30-4.40) May mouse around with Mickey's copyright but serves good light meals and fancy ice creams. Packed on weekend afternoons for a social tea and ice cream.

Eli's (Colombia & 25 de Mayo N-254) Pizzas are the ticket here.

Capitolo (cnr España & Ecuador; mains US$2.50-4.50) A popular eating, drinking and socializing spot. It offers somewhat pricey soup, salad and pasta, among other more imaginative fare. Open at night only.

La Cantonata (España & Mayor Rocha; mains US$5-10) One of the city's best restaurants, one of the country's best Italian splurges.

Also recommended:

Restaurant Marvi (Cabrera at 25 de Mayo; lunch US$1.50) A nice, family-run place. At dinner you'll pay a bit more for hearty helpings of *comida típica*.

Cristal (Av de las Heroínas E-352) Try this place for a big breakfast, great juice, eggs, coffee, pancakes and *salteñas*.

Gopal (España N-250) Vegetarian lunch or dinner with an Indian take.

Drinking

CAFÉS

Café Express ('Clac'; Aguirre S-443; ⏰ 8am-1pm & 2-9pm Mon-Fri) Pours Cochabamba's best espresso drinks (starting price US$1.50). Other good coffee spots include **Café Francés** (España N-140) and **Café Express Bolívar** (Bolívar E-485).

BARS

The liveliest nightlife is found up España and 25 de Mayo, which feature restaurants, bars, discos and revelers. The Prado (Av Ballivián) has a range of nightclubs. There's more drinking and less eating at **Top Chopp** (Av Ballivián), a Bolivian beer barn, and the **Viking Pub** (Av Ballivián), which showcases loud music. Or, sing and boogie at any of the strip's discos and karaoke bars.

Entertainment

Pancho's (España N-460; cover US$2) The hard-rocking scene jams on Saturday nights here, when live bands cover Kiss, Metallica and Deep Purple.

Big, bright **Cine Heroínas** (Av de las Heroínas E-347) and **Cine Astor** (cnr Sucre & 25 de Mayo) both screen first-run movies.

Getting There & Around

AIR

To reach Aeropuerto Jorge Wilsterman (CBB) take *micro* B from the main plaza or a taxi (around US$3 per person). The airport is served regularly by **AeroSur** (☎ 440-0911; Villarroel 105) and **LAB** (☎ 425-0750; office at airport). LAB flies daily to La Paz, Santa Cruz and Sucre, and several times a week to Tarija and Trinidad. **TAM** (☎ 458-1552; Hamiraya N-122) lifts off from the military airport twice weekly to La Paz.

BUS & CAMIÓN

Cochabamba's **central bus terminal** (☎ 155; Av Ayacucho) is just south of Av Aroma. There's a US25¢ terminal fee and comfortable *bus cama* service is available on the main routes for roughly double the regular price. There's frequent service to La Paz (US$2 to US$3, seven hours) and Oruro (US$2.50, four hours). Most buses to Santa Cruz (US$3.15 to US$6, 10 to 13 hours) leave before 9am or after 5pm. Several daily buses depart for Sucre (US$8, 10 to 11 hours) and Potosí (US$8, 10 to 11 hours).

Micros and buses to Villa Tunari (US$2.50, three to four hours) and Puerto Villarroel (US$3, seven hours) in the Chapare region leave every hour or so from the corner of Avs 9 de Abril and Oquendo.

AROUND COCHABAMBA

Two to three hours' walk from the village of **Sipe Sipe**, 27km southwest of Cochabamba, are the ruins of **Inca-Rakay**. It makes a good side trip for the scenery, rather than any archaeological grandeur, but there have been several serious reports of campers being assaulted here.

Sunday is market day. Sipe Sipe is accessible by *micro* from **Quillacollo**, which is reached by *micro* from Cochabamba.

About 160km northeast of Cochabamba is the steamy, relaxed Chapare town of **Villa Tunari** and **Inti Wara Yassi** (Parque Machía; www.intiwarayassi.org), a wildlife refuge and mellow place to chill out and warm up after the *altiplano*. Volunteers are welcome (15-day minimum) and you can camp for US$2. In town, there are numerous places to stay and eat, though there is no bank.

SUCRE

☎ 04 / pop 215,000

Dazzling whitewashed buildings. Decorative archways. Rooftop views of terracotta. The stunning city of Sucre has a rich colonial heritage, evident in its buildings, streetscapes and numerous churches. In 1991 Unesco declared it a Cultural Heritage site. Although the city has expanded rapidly over recent years, the center maintains a cozy, convivial atmosphere, with colorful indigenous markets, upmarket shops and diverse eateries. The flowery plazas, the city's social and focal points, truly reflect the diverse colors of the city and its people, many of whom are indigenous.

Sureños are proud people, and maintain that the heart of Bolivia beats in their city, despite the fact that La Paz usurped Sucre's capital status to become the governmental capital. But Sucre remains as the judicial capital; the supreme court still convenes here.

BOLIVIA

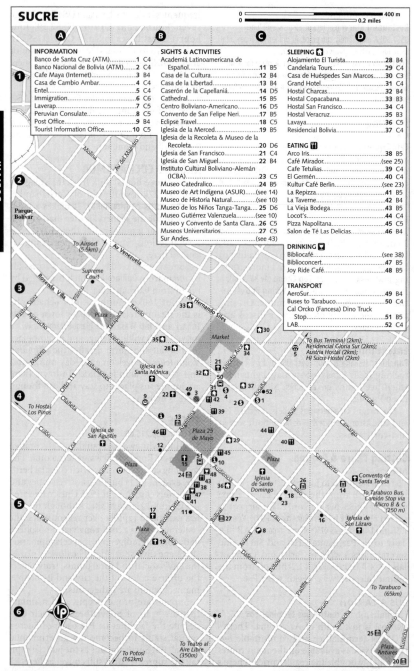

SUCRE

0 ━━━━━━━━━ 400 m
0 ━━━━━━━━━ 0.2 miles

INFORMATION
Banco de Santa Cruz (ATM)...............**1** C4
Banco Nacional de Bolivia (ATM)........**2** C4
Cafe Maya (Internet)........................**3** B4
Casa de Cambio Ambar......................**4** C4
Entel..**5** C4
Immigration.....................................**6** C6
Laverap..**7** C5
Peruvian Consulate...........................**8** C5
Post Office......................................**9** B4
Tourist Information Office...............**10** C5

SIGHTS & ACTIVITIES
Academiá Latinoamericana de
   Español.....................................**11** B5
Casa de la Cultura...........................**12** B4
Casa de la Libertad..........................**13** B4
Caserón de la Capellaniá...................**14** D5
Cathedral.......................................**15** B5
Centro Boliviano-Americano...............**16** D5
Convento de San Felipe Neri..............**17** B5
Eclipse Travel..................................**18** C5
Iglesia de la Merced.........................**19** B5
Iglesia de la Recoleta & Museo de la
   Recoleta...................................**20** D6
Iglesia de San Francisco....................**21** C4
Iglesia de San Miguel.......................**22** B4
Instituto Cultural Boliviano-Alemán
   (ICBA).......................................**23** C4
Museo Catedralico............................**24** B5
Museo de Art Indígena (ASUR)......(see 14)
Museo de Historia Natural...........(see 10)
Museo de los Niños Tanga-Tanga....**25** D6
Museo Gutiérrez Valenzuela...........(see 10)
Museo y Convento de Santa Clara...**26** C5
Museos Universitarios......................**27** C5
Sur Andes..................................(see 43)

SLEEPING
Alojamiento El Turista......................**28** B4
Candelaria Tours..............................**29** C4
Casa de Huéspedes San Marcos.........**30** C3
Grand Hotel....................................**31** B4
Hostal Charcas................................**32** B4
Hostal Copacabana..........................**33** B3
Hostal San Francisco........................**34** C4
Hostal Veracruz...............................**35** B3
Lavaya..**36** C5
Residencial Bolivia...........................**37** C4

EATING
Arco Iris..**38** B5
Café Mirador..............................(see 25)
Cafe Tetulias..................................**39** C4
El Germén.......................................**40** C4
Kultur Café Berlin.......................(see 23)
La Repizza.......................................**41** B5
La Taverne.......................................**42** B4
La Vieja Bodega...............................**43** C5
Locot's..**44** C5
Pizza Napolitana..............................**45** C5
Salon de Té Las Delicias....................**46** B4

DRINKING
Bibliocafé...................................(see 38)
Biblioconcert...................................**47** B5
Joy Ride Café..................................**48** B5

TRANSPORT
AeroSur...**49** B4
Buses to Tarabuco............................**50** C4
Cal Orcko (Fancesa) Dino Truck
   Stop...**51** B5
LAB..**52** C4

Parque
Bolivar

To Airport
(5.5km)

Molina

Av del Maestro

Av Venezuela

Supreme
Court

Rosenda Villa

Av Hernando Siles

Ravelo

Pastor Sainz

Pilinco

Junin

Ayacucho

Plaza

Arenales

Moreno

Market

Junacato Arce

Estudiantes

Iglesia de
Santa Mónica

Otto 111

Olañeta

To Hostal
Los Pinos

Colón

Loa

Argentina

Junín

Iglesia de
San Agustín

Plaza 25
de Mayo

Iglesia de
San Agustín

Plaza

Bustillos

Nicolás Ortiz

Audiencia

Plaza

Iglesia de
Santo Domingo

Calvo

Convento de
Santa Teresa

To Tarabuco Bus,
Camión Stop via
Micro B & C
(250 m)

San Alberto

Camargo

Urcullo

Iglesia de
San Lázaro

Iglesia de
San Agustín

La Paz

Plaza

Azurduy

Pérez

Nicolás Ortiz

Bolívar

Grau

Dalence

To Tarabuco
(65km)

Padilla

Potosí

Onuro

Supacha

Rolando

Plaza
Anzures

To Teatro al
Aire Libre
(350m)

To Potosí
(162km)

To Bus Terminal (2km);
Residencial Gloria Sur (2km);
Austria Hostal (2km);
HJ Sucre Hostel (2km)

Sucre was founded in 1538 (under the name La Plata) as the Spanish capital of the Charcas. In 1776, when new territorial divisions were created by the Spaniards, the city's name was changed to Chuquisaca. During this time, it was the most important center in the eastern Spanish territories and heavily influenced Bolivia's history. Independence was declared here on August 6, 1825, and the new republic was created here and named after its liberator, Simón Bolívar. Several years later, the name of the city was changed again to Sucre in honor of the general who promoted the independence movement, but you could be forgiven for thinking that it means 'sugar,' for it is a sweet treat.

Information

EMERGENCY
Tourist police (☎ 648-0467)

IMMIGRATION OFFICES
Immigration (Argandoña 4; ☽ 8:30am-4:30pm) Can extend your stays.
Peruvian consulate (☎ 645-5592; Avaroa 462; ☽ 9:30am-2:30pm Mon-Fri) Issues visas.

INTERNET ACCESS
Sucre has many internet places.
Cafe Maya (Arenales) A reliable internet café but watch your bags!

LAUNDRY
Both of these are reliable and efficient laundries, charging about US$1 to US$1.20 per kilo.
Lavaya (Audiencia 81)
Laverap (Bolívar 617)

MONEY
Casas de cambio are around the main market. Street money changers operate along Hernando Siles, behind the main market.
Banco de Santa Cruz (cnr España & San Alberto) Has an ATM and also does cash advances.
Banco Nacional de Bolivia (cnr Espana & Ravelo) Changes traveler's checks (3% commission); there is an ATM here.
Casa de Cambio Ambar (San Alberto) Changes traveler's checks at good rates.

POST
Post office (cnr Junín & Estudiantes) Also has internet access.

TELEPHONE
Entel (cnr España & Urcullo) Also has internet access.

TOURIST INFORMATION
Casa de la Cultura (Argentina s/n) You may be able to extract some tourist information from the friendly English-speaking staff here.
Tourist information office (Estudiantes 49) The university's Tourism Faculty runs this office, which is sometimes staffed by enthusiastic English speakers; ask here about guided city tours.

Sights
Ride the Dino Truck to Fancesa's cement quarry, **Cal Orcko** (☎ 645-1863; admission US$3.80), a sort of Grauman's Chinese Theater for large and scaly types with hundreds of dinosaur tracks measuring up to 80cm in diameter. It departs from the plaza at 9:30am, noon and 2:30pm Monday to Saturday.

For a dose of Bolivian history, visit the **Casa de la Libertad** (☎ 645-4200; Plaza 25 de Mayo 11; admission US$1.25; ☽ 9-11.45am & 2:30-6:30pm Tue-Sun), an ornate house-cum-museum where the Bolivian declaration of independence was signed in 1825; it displays the era's artifacts.

The excellent **Museo de Arte Indígena** (ASUR; ☎ 645-3841; museo@asur.org.bo; San Alberto 413; admission US$2; ☽ 8:30am-noon & 2:30-6pm Mon-Fri, 9:30am-noon Sat) displays fine Candelaria, Potolo and Tarabuco weavings; ask for English translations of the labels. It's part of a successful project to revitalize handwoven crafts. You can see weavers in action and browse the superb works for sale.

The **Museos Universitarios** (☎ 645-3285; Bolívar 698; admission US$1.25; ☽ 8:30am-noon & 2:30-6pm Mon-Fri, 8:30am-noon Sat) are three separate rooms housing colonial relics, anthropological artifacts and modern art. The university also operates the **Museo Gutiérrez Valenzuela** and **Museo de Historia Natural** (☎ 645-3828; Plaza 25 de Mayo; admission US$1.35; ☽ 8:30am-noon & 2-6pm Mon-Fri, 8:30am-noon Sat) in the southeast corner of the plaza; the former is an old aristocrat's house with decorative 19th-century decor. The **Museo de los Niños Tanga-Tanga** (☎ 644-0299; Plaza La Recoleta; adult/child US$1/65¢; ☽ 9am-noon & 2:30-6pm Tue-Sun) hosts cultural and environmental programs for kids, including theater performances and ceramic classes. The museum's Café Mirador is open from 9am to 7pm. The museum is in the northwest corner of the plaza.

The wonderful **Casa de la Cultura** (Argentina 65) has regular art exhibitions, music and dance recitals, and a library.

Sucre boasts several lovely colonial churches but opening hours are unpredictable. The

BOLIVIA

cathedral (entrance at Nicolas Ortiz 61; ☽ mornings only) dates from the 16th century, though major additions were made in the early 17th century. Just down the block is the **Museo Catedralico** (admission US$1.25; ☽ 10am-noon & 3-5pm Mon-Fri, 10am-noon Sat), which holds an interesting collection of religious relics.

Iglesia La Merced (Pérez 512; admission US80¢; ☽ 10am-noon & 3-5pm Mon-Fri) has the finest interior of any Sucre church, but it's rarely open. Both **Iglesia de San Miguel** (Arenales 10; ☽ 6am-noon & 3-5pm Mon-Fri, Mass on weekends) and **Iglesia de San Francisco** (Ravelo 1; ☽ 6am-noon & 3-8pm) reflect Mudejar influences, particularly in their ceiling designs. The beautiful **Convento de San Felipe Neri** (Nicolas Ortiz 165; admission US$1.25; ☽ 3-6pm Mon-Fri, Sat during high season) has good rooftop views. If you're interested in sacred art or antique musical instruments, the 1639 **Museo y Convento de Santa Clara** (Calvo 212; admission US$1.25; ☽ 9am-noon & 3-6pm Mon-Fri, 9am-noon Sat) has a renowned collection.

For spectacular city views, trek up to the **Iglesia de la Recoleta & Museo de la Recoleta** (Plaza Anzures; admission US$1.25; ☽ 9:30-11:30am & 2:30-4:30pm Mon-Fri, 3-5pm Sat), which houses many religious paintings and sculptures.

Activities

Sucre's surrounding valleys offer the perfect venues for action-packed adventure, from hiking, mountain biking, tubing and horse-riding. Paragliding is the latest thrill on the adventure menu. Popular destinations include the Crater of Maragua via the pre-Hispanic Chataquila (Inca) trail, rock paintings, waterfalls, and villages of Yotala, Ñucchu, and Q'atalla.

There are as many prices as there are trip combos. Based on a group of four people, (shorter) hiking trips start at about US$6, mountain-bike trips US$14 per person, and horse-riding US$17 upwards.

Recommended operators:
Joy Ride (☎ 642-5544; www.joyridebol.com; Nicolas Ortiz)
Locot's (☎ 691-5958; www.locotsbolivia.com; Bolivia 465)
Eclipse Travel (☎ /fax 644-3960; eclipse@mara.scr.en telnet.bo; Avaroa 310).

See also operators listed on p236.

Courses

The number of language courses available here has exploded over recent years. There are several reliable options.

Academía Latinoamericana de Español (☎ 646-0537; www.latinoschools.com/bolivia; Dalence 109) Has a comprehensive program that features language, dance and cooking lessons, homestay options and volunteer opportunities.
Centro Boliviano-Americano (CBA; ☎ 644-1608; www.cba.com.bo in Spanish; Calvo 301) Gives referrals to private teachers.
Instituto Cultural Boliviano-Alemán (ICBA; ☎ /fax 645-2091; www.icba-sucre.edu.bo in Spanish; Calle Avaroa 326) Offers excellent Spanish, Quechua and even dance lessons. Homestay options are available.

Recommended Spanish teachers:
Aida Rojas (☎ 728-66966; aida_1122@hotmail.com)
Sofía Sauma (☎ 645-1687; fsauma@hotmail.com; Loa 779)

Festivals & Events

Sucre loves an excuse for a party or parade and it's worth checking out the list at the tourist office for the many religious festivals. **Festival de la Cultura** attracts many artists and intellectuals who give theatre, music, dance, literature and folkloric performances.

Sleeping

Sucre has plenty of budget accommodations around the market and along Ravelo and San Alberto, but it's also a good place to splurge on something a bit more stylish. The *casas de huéspedes* (guesthouses) offer a more distinctive, homey feel.

Alojamiento El Turista (☎ 645-3172; Ravelo 118; s/d US$2.50/3.70) If budget's your aim, you might be game. (But don't poke your nose into the toilet and shower first up.)

La Plata (☎ 645-2102; Ravelo 32; s/d US$3/5) This older central option offers surly service and basic, but adequate – if a little noisy – rooms.

Casa de Huéspedes San Marcos (☎ 646-2087; Aniceto Arce 233; r per person US$4, with bathroom US$4.30) The deceptive entrance hides tranquil surroundings: clean, quiet rooms with kitchen and laundry access for guests. Travelers report motley mattresses.

Hostal Veracruz (☎ 645-1560; Ravelo 158; s/d incl breakfast US$3.70/7) A modern, popular tour-group choice with a variety of rooms.

Residencial Bolivia (☎ 645-4346; res_bol@cotes .net.bo; San Alberto 42; s/d/tr US$3.70/7/9.50, with bathroom s/d/tr US$6.20/10.50/15) A traveler's treat. It's slightly worn, but its two garden-filled courtyards, central position, and spacious (if empty) rooms make it a favorite. Breakfast is included and it has an excellent travel information board.

HI Sucre Hostel (☎ 644-0471; www.hostellingbolivia .org; Loayza 119; dm US$4.30, s/d US$12.50/23; ☐) By far Bolivia's swankest hostel: full-service hostel with Rococco-style dining rooms to boot. It's not the most central, but handy to the bus station (follow the signs). Some private rooms have cable TV.

Hostal Charcas (☎ 645-3972; hostalcharcas@yahoo .com; Ravelo 62; s/d/tr US$5/8/11, with bathroom US$8/ 12.50/19) The rooftop views of this clean and central spot are reminiscent of Florence. The owner runs an efficient, clean and friendly place and ensures it's one of Sucre's best-value spots.

Hostal San Francisco (☎ 645-2117; hostalsf@cotes.net .bo; Aniceto Arce 191; r with bathroom per person US$6) The rooms don't quite live up to the light, bright and sunny exterior, with its fancy balustrades, but it's a safe option. Breakfast extra (US$1).

Hostal Copacabana (☎ 644-1790; Av Hernando Siles; s/d US$8/12.30) If you want 'colonial' avoid this place – the series of Louvre-like glass pyramids are 'cutting edge' for Sucre. But with modernity comes good clean rooms, cable TV and operational plumbing.

Hostal Los Pinos (☎ 645-5639; Colón 502; s/d US$8.70/ 12.50) More like a house than a hotel, this place has eight clean rooms in a less touristy part of town. House rules apply: you pay for kitchen use and there's an 11:30pm curfew.

Grand Hotel (☎ 645-2104/2461; grandhot@mara.scr .entelnet.bo; Aniceto Arce 61; s/d US$12.50/16) This glowingly recommended, refurbished old building houses comfortable rooms in a great location. Unventilated bathrooms can create bronchial bothers, however.

Reasonable places across from the bus terminal include the following:

Residencial Gloria Sur (☎ 645-2847; r per person US$2.50) Clean and modernish.

Austria Hostal (☎ 645-4202; r per person US$4.30/ 5.60) With a range of comfy rooms.

For homestay options (usually on a longer term basis), see Lizbeth Rojas at **Candelaria Tours** (☎ 646-1661; www.candelariatours.com; Audiencia 1).

Eating

With many quality restaurants and relaxing cafés catering to the town's students, locals and tourists, Sucre is ideal for lounging around and lingering about.

Upstairs in the market, you'll find delicious *api* and *pasteles* (pastries) while downstairs there's fruit salads and juices, mixed to your taste.

Head downhill from the plaza along Nicolas Ortiz for an interesting selection of bars and eateries.

Café Mirador (Plaza La Recoleta, in Museo de los Niños Tanga-Tanga; ☺ from 9am) The place for a suntan. Great garden, better views, and the food's not bad either.

Cafe Tetulias (Plaza 25 de Mayo; mains US$1.50-6; ☺ 6pm-late) An artsy place offering tasty light meals, coffee and snacks. It's on the north side of the plaza.

La Taverne (Aniceto Arce 35; mains US$3) Francophiles will enjoy this pleasant and refined place, run by Alliance Française, and serving international gourmet dishes (but with French *panache*). Films (mostly French) are screened several times a week.

Locot's (☎ 691-5958; Bolivar 465; mains US$2-5; ☺ 8am-late) A friendly Dutch-Bolivian team runs this new laid-back place with super outdoor dining and a fun bar. Occasional live music.

El Germén (San Alberto 231) Serves vegetarian food and has great *almuerzos* and German pastries.

Pizza Napolitana (Plaza 25 de Mayo) Has cheap set lunch, reasonably priced standard pizza and pasta, excellent ice cream and a good mix of locals and visitors. It's on the east side of the plaza.

Kultur Café Berlin (Avaroa 326; mains US$4.30-5.60) A German coffee shop and restaurant with tasty pastries and light meals; try the *papas rellenas* (stuffed potatoes).

La Vieja Bodega (Nicolas Ortiz) For US$7.50 for two, you can fiddle with a fondue, or have a lasagna prepared.

Arco Iris (Restaurant Suizo; Nicolas Ortiz) For delights such as *roeschti* (Swiss hash browns), fondue and chocolate mousse. Vegetarian meals are available and there's occasional live music.

La Repizza (cnr Dalence & Nicolas Ortiz) Serves pizza and cocktails and hosts live music on Friday and Saturday nights.

Salon de Té Las Delicias (Estudiantes 50; snacks US40¢-$1.20) For an authentic Bolivian experience, join the locals here in the late afternoon for tea and cakes or *empanadas*.

For back-to-basics Bolivian, check the chicken-and-chips shops on Av Hernando Siles, between Tarapaca and Junín.

BOLIVIA

BOLIVIA

Drinking

Some of the bars and restaurants on and near the plaza have live music and *peña* nights.

Joy Ride Café (☎ 642-5544; www.joyridebol.com; Nicolas Ortiz; ✆ from 7:30am Mon-Fri, from 9am Sat & Sun) It may be 'gringofied' but it's also the current 'it' place among Sucre's gilded youth. This Dutch-run enterprise – bar, restaurant (mains US$2 to US$5) and cultural space – features three popular and vibey 'spaces' depending on your mood: a bar, a patio-come-café, and a laid-back beanbag hangout for watching the big screen. For the homesick there's imported beers and deli fixes. The Joy Ride salad is a must (US$2.50).

Bibliocafé (Nicolas Ortiz; ✆ 10am-11pm) Head here for a warm, chilled and publike atmosphere. It also serves good pastas (mains US$2 to US$2.50) and snacks. Open on Sundays.

The neighboring Biblioconcert hosts live music on Friday and Saturday nights.

Entertainment

For discos and karaoke, check Calle España just up from the plaza. The Teatro al Aire Libro, southeast of the center, is a wonderful outdoor venue for music and other performances. There are several cinemas around town.

Getting There & Away
AIR
The airport is 6km northwest of the city center. **AeroSur** (☎ 645-4895; Arenales 31) and **LAB** (☎ 691-3181; España) have flights to most major cities.

BUS & SHARED TAXI
The bus terminal, located 2km northeast of the city center, is accessed by *micro* A or 3 or 4 from the center (you can flag it down anywhere along Hernando Siles near the market), but the *micros* are too tiny to accommodate lots of luggage. There are numerous daily buses to Cochabamba (US$5 to US$8, 12 hours), leaving around 6pm or 7pm. Direct buses to Santa Cruz (ie not via Cochabamba) run daily (US$7 to US$10, 15 hours). Numerous companies leave daily for Potosí (US$2 to US$2.50, three hours) throughout the day; some continue to Tarija (US$10, 15 hours), Oruro, Villazón and Uyuni. Alternatively, most hotels can arrange shared taxis to Potosí (US$4 per person with four people). There is frequent *bus cama* service to La Paz (US$7 to US$10, 14 to 16 hours).

Getting Around

Local *micros* (US30¢) take circuitous routes around Sucre's one-way streets. Most eventually converge on the stop on Hernando Siles, north of the market, but they can be waved down virtually anywhere. You can reach the airport on *micro* F or 1 (allow an hour) or by taxi (US$3.50).

AROUND SUCRE
Tarabuco
This small, predominantly indigenous village, 65km southeast of Sucre, is known for its beautiful weavings and colorful, sprawling Sunday market, and is famous for the festival of Phujllay. This is the most photogenic of places, but be aware of the locals' reactions to the long lenses. It's best to request a shot beforehand. Take care of your things. The spitting scam is, unfortunately, becoming more common (see p189).

Plenty touristy, the **market** is overflowing with amazing woven ponchos, bags and belts as well as *charangos* (buy only wooden ones – have mercy on endangered armadillos). However, much of the work for sale is not local but acquired by traders, so don't expect many bargains.

Phujllay (meaning 'to play' in Quechua) takes place on the third Sunday of March. The town becomes the gathering place for hundreds of indigenous people from the surrounding countryside, beginning with a Mass, followed by a procession around the main plaza, the selection of the *ñusta* and the ritual of the *pucara*, a magical spiritual symbol.

You can visit Tarabuco with a tour (US$3) or take a *micro* from Sucre (on Ravelo in front of the market) at 8am on Sunday (US$1, one to two hours). **Trans Real** (☎ 644-3119; 73 San Alberto St) buses depart on Sundays at 8am from their office. Buses and *camiones* returning to Sucre leave from the main plaza in Tarabuco between 1pm and 3pm. A taxi charges around US$22.

Cordillera de los Frailes
This range runs through much of western Chuquisaca and northern Potosí departments and offers scenic trekking opportunities. Sites in the Sucre area worth visiting include **Capilla de Chataquila**, the 6km **Camino del Inca**, the rock paintings of **Pumamachay**, the weaving village of **Potolo**, pastoral **Chaunaca**, dramatic **Maragua Crater** and the **Talula hot springs**.

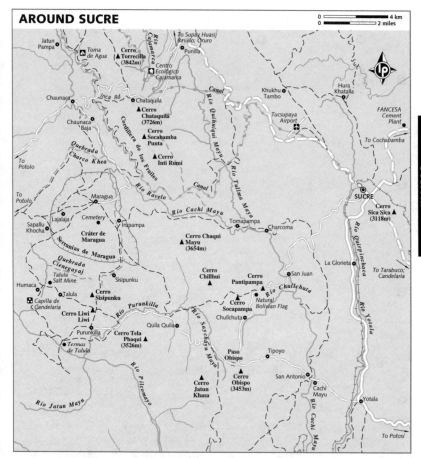

AROUND SUCRE

BOLIVIA

There are plenty of **trekking routes**, but they traverse little-visited areas; to minimize cultural impact and avoid getting hopelessly lost, hire a registered guide. Several Sucre travel agencies also arrange excursions. See those operators listed under Activities (p234) or try **Sur Andes** (☎ /fax 645-2632; Nicolas Ortíz 6) or **Candelaria Tours** (☎ 646-1661; www.candelariatours.com; Audiencia 1). The latter is more upmarket, but backpacker rates can be arranged.

POTOSÍ
☎ 02 / pop 146,000

Potosí shocks. A visit to the world's highest city (4060m), a Unesco World Heritage site, reveals a former and current splendor and past and present horror, tied to its one precious metal – silver. Potosí is set against the backdrop of a rainbow-colored mountain, the Cerro Rico. The city was founded in 1545 following the discovery of ore deposits in the mountain, and Potosí veins proved the world's most lucrative. By the end of the 18th century the streets were 'paved' with silver; it grew into the largest and wealthiest city in Latin America, underwriting the Spanish economy for over two centuries.

Millions of indigenous people and imported African slaves laborers were conscripted to work in the mines in appalling conditions, and millions of deaths occurred. Today thousands continue to work in the mines: although the silver has been depleted, they continue to work in spine-chilling conditions to extract

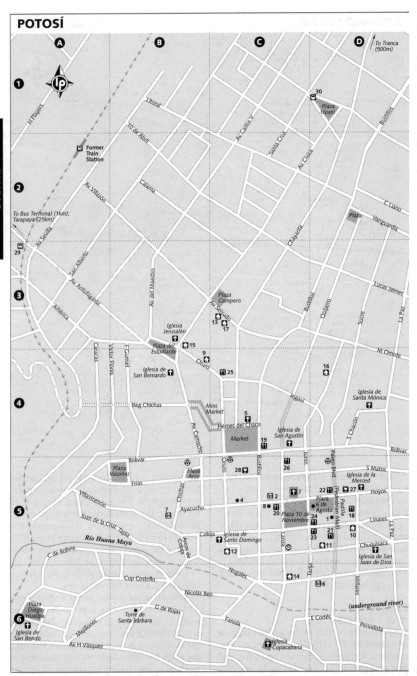

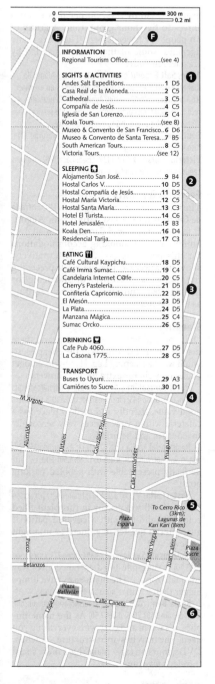

```
0          300 m
0          0.2 mi
```

INFORMATION
Regional Tourism Office...................(see 4)

SIGHTS & ACTIVITIES
Andes Salt Expeditions......................**1** D5
Casa Real de la Moneda...................**2** C5
Cathedral...**3** C5
Compañía de Jesús............................**4** C5
Iglesia de San Lorenzo......................**5** C4
Koala Tours.....................................(see 8)
Museo & Convento de San Francisco...**6** D6
Museo & Convento de Santa Teresa...**7** B5
South American Tours........................**8** C5
Victoria Tours..................................(see 12)

SLEEPING
Alojamento San José..........................**9** B4
Hostal Carlos V.................................**10** D5
Hostal Compañía de Jesús...............**11** D5
Hostal María Victoria.......................**12** C5
Hostal Santa María............................**13** C3
Hotel El Turista.................................**14** C6
Hotel Jerusalén.................................**15** B3
Koala Den..**16** D4
Residencial Tarija..............................**17** C3

EATING
Café Cultural Kaypichu.....................**18** D5
Café Imma Sumac.............................**19** C4
Candelaria Internet C@fe.................**20** D5
Cherry's Pasteleria............................**21** D5
Confitería Capricornio......................**22** D5
El Mesón...**23** D5
La Plata...**24** D5
Manzana Mágica...............................**25** C4
Sumac Orcko......................................**26** C5

DRINKING
Cafe Pub 4060...................................**27** D5
La Casona 1775.................................**28** C5

TRANSPORT
Buses to Uyuni..................................**29** A3
Camiónes to Sucre............................**30** D1

minerals. To protect them in their hell below, they worship their devil, known as *Tío*. Above ground, echoes of the once-grand colonial city reverberate through the narrow streets, bouncing from the formal balconied mansions and ornate churches. This city is not to be missed, but go slowly, be prepared for the harsh climate, and brace yourself for a jolt.

Information

Internet access is available for US50¢ per hour at several places along the pedestrian mall.

Lots of businesses along Bolívar, Sucre and in the market change US dollars at reasonable rates. ATMs are common in the center.

There is a **tourist information center** (☎ 262-2643; cnr Ayacucho & Bustillos) in the Compañía de Jesús.

Sights

Potosí's central area contains a wealth of colonial architecture. At the time of research, the **cathedral** was closed for long-term restoration, but you can see the **Iglesia de San Lorenzo** (Heroes del Chaco), famous for its classic mestizo facade.

The **Casa Real de la Moneda** (Royal Mint; Ayacucho; admission for mandatory 2hr guided tour US$2.50; 🕑 9am-noon & 2.30-6.30pm Tue-Sat, 9am-noon Sun, last tour 4.30pm) is worth its weight in silver; it's one of Bolivia's finest museums. Constructed between 1753 and 1773 to control the minting of colonial coins, the restored building now houses religious art, Tiahuanaco artifacts, ancient coins, wooden minting machines and the country's first locomotive.

The highlight of the **Museo & Convento de San Francisco** (Nogales; admission US$1.85; 🕑 9-11am & 2:30-5pm Mon-Fri, 9-11am Sat) is the view from the roof. The **Museo & Convento de Santa Teresa** (Villavicenzio; admission US$2.60; 🕑 9am-12:30 & 3-6:30pm) is a must for flagellation fans, but tours are in Spanish only.

The **Compañía de Jesús on Ayacucho** (🕑 8:30am-noon & 2-6pm) affords great views of the terracotta rooftops and beyond.

Activities
COOPERATIVE MINE TOURS

A visit to the cooperative mines is demanding, shocking and memorable. Tours typically involve scrambling and crawling in low, narrow, dirty shafts and climbing rickety ladders – wear your gnarliest clothes. Working practices are medieval, safety provisions nearly nonexistent and most shafts are unventilated; chewing coca helps. Work is done by hand with basic tools, and underground temperatures vary from belo w freezing to a stifling 45°C (113°F). Miners, exposed to myriad noxious chemicals, often die of silicosis pneumonia within 10 years of entering the mines. They work the mine as a cooperative venture, with each miner milking his own claim and selling his ore to a smelter through the cooperative. (Look out for the multi-award-winning US-made film *The Devil's Miner*; 2005.)

Most tours start at the **miners' street market** where you buy gifts for the miners: coca leaves, alcohol and cigarettes to start; dynamite and fuses if you're after an explosive experience. You may also visit a **mineral refinery.** Then you're driven up to **Cerro Rico** where guides often give a **demonstration blast**. After donning a jacket and helmet, the scramble begins. You can converse with the miners, take photos (with flash) and share gifts as a tip.

All guides work through tour agencies, and all must be licensed. Most guides speak Spanish – ask around the agencies if you need an English speaker – and some are former miners themselves. Expect to pay

around US$6 to US$7.50 per person for a three- to five-hour group tour. A group of 10 people or fewer is best. There are many agencies; some of those recommended by travelers include:

Andes Salt Expeditions (☎ 622-5175; 3 Alonso de Ibañez) Recommended by readers and run by an ex-miner.
Koala Tours (☎ 622-4708; Ayacucho 7) Repeatedly recommended for its professional, personable service. Worth every bit of the US$10 per person price.
South American Tours (☎ 622-28919; Ayacucho 11) Also has tours to the *lagunas*.
Victoria Tours (☎ 622-2132; Chuquisaca 148) Also runs Lagunas de Kari Kari and hot-springs trips.

Festivals & Events

The most popular annual party is the **Entrada de Chu'tillos** on the last Saturday in August. It features traditional dancing from all over South America. Booking accommodations for this period is essential. Alternatively, show up a week early; the week preceding the festival is given over to practicing for the big event and can be nearly as exciting as the real thing.

Sleeping

Only top-end hotels have heating, and there may be blanket shortages in the cheapies, so you'll want a sleeping bag. Hard-core budget places may charge extra for hot showers.

Hotel Jerusalém (☎ 622-4633; hoteljer@cedro.pts .entelnet.bo; Oruro 143; r incl breakfast US$2.30-3.50) This good-value, friendly and mellow place has a cafeteria with a view. Prices vary seasonally so 'confirm and be firm.'

Residencial Tarija (☎ 622-2711; Av Serrudo 252; per person without/with bathroom US$2.60/6.50) Plain, but perfectly presentable with pebbled parking point.

Hostal Carlos V (☎ 622-5121; Linares 42; r per person US$3.25) You'll feel peachy in this plant-filled colonial building with a covered patio. It guarantees a quieter stay (there's a midnight curfew).

Alojamiento San José (622-4394; Oruro 171; r per person US$3.70) A shag-pile-filled entrance gives way adequate rooms. The mattresses have lumps bigger than a miner's coca-filled cheek.

Koala Den (☎ 622-6467; ktourspotosi@hotmail.com; Junín 56; dm US$3.70-5, d US$7.50) As the name implies, it's warm and cozy with everything you need. The travelers' infrastructure – kitchen, DVDs, tours on tap – make this a more social traveler's favorite.

WARNING!

The cooperatives are not museums, but working mines and fairly nightmarish places. Anyone undertaking a tour needs to realize that there are risks involved. Anyone with doubts or medical problems – especially claustrophobes, asthmatics and others with respiratory conditions – should avoid these tours. While medical experts including the NHS note that limited exposure from a few hours' tour is extremely unlikely to cause any lasting health impacts, if you have any concerns whatsoever about exposure to asbestos or silica dust, you should not enter the mines. Accidents also happen – explosions, falling rocks, runaway trolleys, etc. For these reasons, all tour companies make visitors sign a disclaimer absolving them completely from any responsibility for injury, illness or death – if your tour operator does not, choose another. Visiting the mines is a serious decision. If you're undeterred, you'll have an eye-opening and unforgettable experience.

Hostal María Victoria (☎ 622-2144; Chuquisaca 148; s US$4-6, d US$9) A beautiful colonial mansion with clean rooms facing onto a courtyard; worth staying for views from an underutilized roof terrace.

Hostal Compañía de Jesús (☎ 622-3173; Chuquisaca 445; r per person US$5, with bathroom & breakfast US$6) With its lovely historical entrance, this place is better on the outside (by day) than the cold inside (by night). A passable – but not the best – option.

Hostal Santa María (☎ 622-3255; Av Serrudo 244; s/d US$10/12.35) An overlooked excellent option, in a lovely colonial home, lined with geranium pots and squeaky hospital-style corridors. You might be praying for warmth, however.

Hotel El Turista (☎ 622-2492; Lanza 19; s/d US$10/16.50) The owner takes his job very seriously: a clean spacious place, but no smiling please.

Eating & Drinking

The market *comedor* offers inexpensive breakfasts, and a couple of small bakeries along the pedestrian stretch of Padilla do continental breakfasts.

La Plata (Plaza 10 de Noviembre; snacks US$1.50-2.20) A favorite, hip and comfortable gringo hangout, with great hot chocolates (US80¢) and games to fill in the colder hours.

Sumac Orcko (Quijarro 46; lunch US$1.50, mains US$3) One of the best-value places in town, it offers filling, four-course *almuerzos* and evening meals.

Café Cultural Kaypichu (Millares 24; mains US$1.70-2.20; ☯ 7am-2pm & 5-9pm Tue-Sun) Overlooked by the café's religious icon, this is for pure veggie vultures.

Confitería Capricornio (Padilla at Hoyos) Notable for its affordable meals and snacks.

Cherry's Pasteleria (Padilla) The spot for apple strudel, chocolate cake and lemon meringue pie; the coffee is mediocre.

Candelaria Internet C@fe (Ayacucho 5; lunches & dinners US$2.70; ☯ 7.30am-9pm) Ethnic-style café and internet.

El Mesón (cnr Linares & Junín; mains US$3-5) For a more formal treat, try this tablecloth ed place, where US$3.70 gets you spicy meat dishes ('to warm you up' says the waiter).

Manzana Mágica (cnr Oruro & Ingavi; breakfasts B$7-15; ☯ 7:30am-10pm) A vegetarian café serving muesli and yogurt for breakfast, as well as dinners and snacks.

Café Imma Sumac (Bustillos 987) For great *salteñas*, hit this spot.

Cafe Pub 4060 (Hoyos 1) '*Quatro mil seisenta*' is the altitude of Potosí, and this new funky bar in town reaches the heights in quality. Excellent snacks available. Evenings only.

The best place for cocktails is **La Casona 1775** (Frias 41).

Getting There & Around

The bus terminal is 1km northwest of town (30 minutes' walk downhill from the center), reached by frequent *micros* (US15¢) from the west side of the cathedral or by taxi (US50¢ per person). Several companies serve La Paz (US$5 to US$10, 11 hours) daily. There are morning and evening buses to Oruro (US$4, eight hours), with connections to Cochabamba.

Most buses to Sucre (US$2, three hours) leave daily at 6:30am and 7am. There are shared taxis to Sucre (US$5 per person, two hours) if you're rushed, and slow *camiones* and *micros* that leave from Plaza Uyuni if you're not.

Heading south, buses leave for Tupiza (US$6, eight hours) daily around 7:30pm and several continuing to Villazón at 7am, 8am, 6:30pm, 7pm and 8pm (US$6, 10 to 12 hours). A few daily services go to Tarija (US$6, 14 hours) and there are daily departures for Camargo, Yacuiba and Bermejo. For Santa Cruz, it's best to go to Sucre or Cochabamba.

Buses to Uyuni (US$2 to US$3.50, six to seven hours) depart between 11am and 6pm – a scenic and popular route. Emporador buses go from the terminal at noon and 2pm, the others from Av Universitario.

THE SOUTHEAST

The vast lowlands of the Bolivian Oriente are rich and varied, and home to much of the country's natural resources. Numerous cultural highlights include stunning Jesuit missions and natural wonders like Parque Nacional Amboró and the more remote Parque Nacional Noel Kempff Mercado. Che Guevara fans can follow his footsteps, while stalwart travelers can venture into Paraguay through the wild Chaco. Brazil is a hop, skip and a train ride away.

SANTA CRUZ

☎ 03 / pop 1.3 million

Santa Cruz de la Sierra (elevation 415m) prides itself on being more Brazilian than Bolivian. Indeed, thanks to the warm and tropical ambience, the *cambas*, as the locals

BOLIVIA

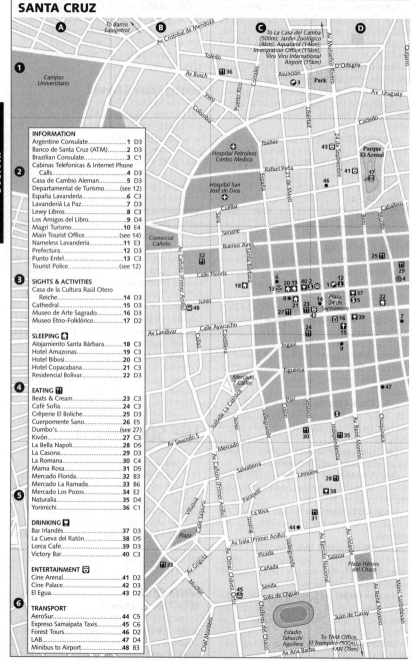

SANTA CRUZ

INFORMATION
Argentine Consulate	1 D3
Banco de Santa Cruz (ATM)	2 D3
Brazilian Consulate	3 C1
Cabinas Telefonicas & Internet Phone Calls	4 D3
Casa de Cambio Aleman	5 D3
Departamental de Turismo	(see 12)
España Lavandería	6 C3
Lavanderiá La Paz	7 D3
Lewy Libros	8 C3
Los Amigos del Libro	9 D4
Magri Turismo	10 E4
Main Tourist Office	(see 14)
Nameless Lavandería	11 E3
Prefectura	12 C3
Punto Entel	13 C3
Tourist Police	(see 12)

SIGHTS & ACTIVITIES
Casa de la Cultura Raúl Otero Reiche	14 D3
Cathedral	15 D3
Museo de Arte Sagrado	16 D3
Museo Etno-Folklórico	17 D2

SLEEPING
Alojamiento Santa Bárbara	18 C3
Hotel Amazonas	19 C3
Hotel Bibosi	20 C3
Hotel Copacabana	21 C3
Residencial Bolívar	22 D3

EATING
Beats & Cream	23 C3
Café Sofia	24 C3
Crêperie El Boliche	25 D3
Cuerpomente Sano	26 E5
Dumbo's	(see 27)
Kivón	27 C3
La Bella Napoli	28 D5
La Casona	29 C3
La Romana	30 C4
Mama Rosa	31 D5
Mercado Florida	32 B3
Mercado La Ramada	33 B6
Mercado Los Pozos	34 E2
Naturalia	35 D4
Yorimichi	36 C1

DRINKING
Bar Irlandés	37 D3
La Cueva del Ratón	38 D5
Lorca Cafe	39 D3
Victory Bar	40 C3

ENTERTAINMENT
Cine Arenal	41 D2
Cine Palace	42 D3
El Egua	43 D2

TRANSPORT
AeroSur	44 C5
Expreso Samaipata Taxis	45 C6
Forest Tours	46 D2
LAB	47 D4
Minibus to Airport	48 B3

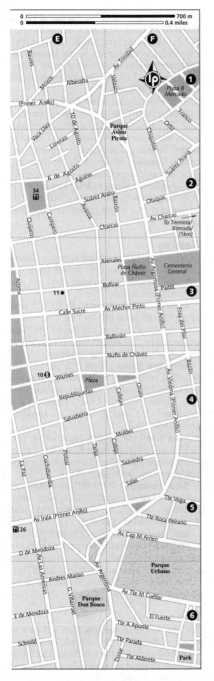

call themselves, seem more laid-back than their *kolla* (Andean) countrymen.

The city was founded in 1561 by Spaniard Ñuflo de Chaves, 220km east of its current location. It proved vulnerable to indigenous attack and was moved to its present position, near the Cordillera Oriental foothills. Santa Cruz mushroomed from a backwater town to Bolivia's largest city. Renowned as one of the main centers of the cocaine trade, today it is more in the news as the center of the controversial energy sector.

The modern area to the north, with its stylish shops and smart cafés, has not monopolized the city's colonial center; the terra-cotta-tiled and balconied buildings maintain a delightful colonial ambience, particularly around the tree-lined plaza. (If you're lucky you might see a sloth. Despite their relocation, the odd one makes an appearance.)

Santa Cruz is an excellent base for exploring still-pristine rainforests, the Che Guevara trail, and 18th-century Jesuit missions.

Orientation

The city center is laid out in a straightforward grid. Ten numbered *anillos* (ring roads) form concentric circles around the compact city center, indicating separate suburbs or regions. *Radiales* (spokes) connect the rings. The city's cheaper options are in the centre, within the first *anillo;* the smarter restaurants and hotels are on Av San Martin to the north.

Information
BOOKSTORES
Lewy Libros (Junín 229) Stocks travel guides and has a selection of maps and used English- and German-language paperbacks.
Los Amigos del Libro (Ingavi 114) Slim pickings.

EMERGENCY
Tourist police (☎ 322-5016; Plaza 24 de Septiembre) Inside the Palacio Prefectural, on the north side of the plaza.

IMMIGRATION OFFICES
The main immigration office is north of the center, opposite the zoo's entrance. If you're arriving overland from Paraguay, pick up a length-of-stay stamp here. There's a more convenient office at the **train station** (✆ 10am-noon & 1:30-7pm) but the station is plagued by phony officials; use as a last-ditch resort. The most reliable office is at the airport. For

BOLIVIA

those braving the Death Train (see p246), exit stamps are reportedly only available at the Brazilian frontier; ask around before departing.

For information on consulates in Santa Cruz, see p258.

INTERNET ACCESS

Internet places are dotted all over the city center, with several options at Entel offices.

LAUNDRY

España Lavandería (España 160) Same-day service (drop off before noon) costs around US$1 per kilo.
Lavandería La Paz (La Paz 42) Central, efficient wash 'n' dry.
Nameless lavandería (Bolívar 490) Efficient wash 'n' dry (US$1 per kilo); ring the bell.

MONEY

Banco de Santa Cruz (Junín) Cash advances and ATM. Less efficient but may have slightly better rates for changing traveler's checks.
Casa de cambio Aleman (Plaza 24 de Septiembre) Changes cash or traveler's checks (2% to 3% commission).
Magri Turismo (☎ 334-5663; cnr Warnes & Potosí) American Express agent; doesn't cash traveler's checks.

TELEPHONE

There are telecom stores along Bolívar for making cheap international internet calls.
Punto Entel (Junín 284) Near the plaza; has land lines.

TOURIST INFORMATION

Departamental de Turismo (☎ 336-8901; Plaza 24 de Septiembre) Inside the Palacio Prefectural, on the north side of the plaza.
Fundación Amigos de la Naturaleza (FAN; ☎ 355-6800; www.fan-bo.org; Km7, Carretera a Samaipata) Dispenses information on Amboró and Noel Kempff Mercado national parks. West of town (*micro* 44) off the old Cochabamba road.
Main tourist office (☎ 336-9595; Plaza 24 de Septiembre). On the ground floor of the Casa de la Cultura, west side of the plaza.

Sights

There are few attractions in Santa Cruz proper, but the shady **Plaza 24 de Septiembre** with its **cathedral** is an attractive place to relax by day or night. On the plaza's west side, the **Casa de la Cultura Raúl Otero Reiche** (☺ 8am–noon & 3-5:30pm Mon-Fri) hosts free music and contemporary art exhibitions in addition to theater performances.

Locals relax around the lagoon at **Parque El Arenal**, north of the center, where there's a handicrafts market and paddle boats for rent. Overlooking the lagoon is the **Museo Etno-Folklórico** (admission US75¢), with a small collection of regional anthropological finds. Don't dawdle here at night.

The underfunded **Jardín Zoológico** (☎ 342-9939; adult/child US75¢/50¢; ☺ 9am-6pm) is worth a visit. The collection includes South American birds, mammals and reptiles – don't miss the sloths. Take any 'Zoologico' *micro* from the center. Discover the wonder of sequins, big hats and gold rope trim at the cathedral's air-conditioned **Museo de Arte Sagrado** (Plaza 24 de Septiembre; admission US60¢), with a dazzling collection of gowns, jewels and spooky paintings upstairs.

Sleeping

In a bind, there are several cheap, indistinguishable places to crash across from the terminal bimodal. Otherwise, there are few reasonable cheapies.

Alojamiento Santa Bárbara (☎ 332-1817; Santa Bárbara 151; r per person US$3.70) You'll be blown away by the industrial-sized fans (but less impressed by the beds) at this very basic, but friendly place, with sunny courtyard.

Residencial Bolívar (☎ 334-2500; Calle Sucre 131; dm US$5.50, s/d/tr US$9/15/19) The two pet toucans add to the color of this highly recommended place. Inviting courtyard with hammocks and excellent communal showers. Call ahead or arrive early.

Hotel Bibosi (☎ 334-8548; bibosi@scbbs-bo.com; Junín 218; s/d US$10/12.35) Hotel Bibosi has a great rooftop view and clean, spacious rooms with fan, phone and bathroom.

Hotel Amazonas (☎ 333-4583; leanch@bibosi.scz .entelnet.bo; Junín 214; s/d US$10/12.35) Next door to Bibosi, with plants, clean corridors and 'brown-tiley' kind of rooms.

Hotel Copacabana (☎ 332-9924; Junín 217; s US$12.35-18, d US$19-23) Lots of red lacework and red plants add color to the small, '70s disco rooms with ceiling fans. A pleasant, if unremarkable, stay. Some rooms with air-con. Avoid the noisy ground-floor rooms.

Eating

For simple, cheap eats, try Mercado La Ramada or the mall-like Mercado Los Pozos with food stalls on the top floor. The latter is especially good for unusual tropical fruits.

Mercado Florida is wall-to-wall blender stalls serving exquisite juices and fruit salads for US50¢.

Cuerpomente Sano (Av Irala 437; per kg US$4) Healthy-mind-healthy-body type place – full on and fabulous vegetarian buffet.

Beats & Cream (Av Ayacucho & 21 de Mayo) Come here for the finest of fine ice creams. Locals rave.

La Casa del Camba (Av Cristobel de Mendoza 1355, 2nd anillo; buffet US$3, mains US$2.50-3.70) All sorts of *cambas* (and visitors) come here for Bolivian specialties and Argentinean meat. Nightly traditional music, plus dance performances on Fridays and Saturdays.

La Casona (☎ 337-8495; Arenales 222; mains US$5-7; ☺ Mon-Sat) Can't look at another *empanada*? Lash out on international gourmet numbers at this tasteful and relaxed German-run eatery.

La Bella Napoli (Independencia 683; pizza & mains US$6-8) A pleasant vine-covered terrace and fine pasta dishes deliver the flavors of Italy.

Yorimichi (☎ 334-7717; Av Busch 548; mains around US$10) You should give this place a try if you're craving sashimi or udon. It's not cheap, but it's sushi. It's near the Campus Universitario.

Crêperie El Boliche (☎ 333-9053; Arenales 135) A splash-out option serving dinner only.

Naturalia (Independencia 452) Organic grocery store with a wide selection of healthy goodies.

Also recommended:

Café Sofia (Velasco 40) Very simple, but with cooked-on-the-premises pastries.

La Romana (Velasco 47A) Bakes stunning breads, croissants and addictive sweet buns.

Mama Rosa (Velasco) Serves feisty pizzas, chicken and big *almuerzos*. It's near Av Irala.

Similar in menu and style are **Dumbo's** (Ayacucho 247) and **Kivón** (Ayacucho 267), both a block west of the plaza.

Drinking

Victory Bar (cnr Junín & 21 de Mayo) Upstairs and a block from the plaza, this is one of several central sociable watering holes.

Bar Irlandés (cnr Junín & 24 de Septiembre) There's a hopping gringo scene and good plaza views from the balcony bar.

La Cueva del Ratón (La Riva 173) Barnlike bar with big-screen music videos.

Lorca Cafe (Ave René Moreno 20) Bar-café cultural space with regular program of live music and other cultural performances.

Entertainment

Many *boliches* (nightclubs) are spread out along Av San Martin in Barrio Equipetrol, northwest of the city, between the second and third *anillos*. You'll need to take a taxi (around US$2). Cover charges start at US$2 and drinks are expensive.

El Egua (24 de Septiembre 651; ☺ Thu-Sun) One of the most popular Cuban salsa clubs in town.

Cine Palace (Plaza 24 de Septiembre; admission US$2.50) First-run flicks are shown nightly at this cinema on the plaza's west side.

Cine Arenal (Beni 555; admission US$2.50) Older releases play at this cinema facing Parque El Arenal.

Aqualand (☎ 385-2500; www.aqualand.com.bo in Spanish; half-day US$5-8, full-day US$7.50-10; ☺ 10:30am-5:30pm Thu-Sun) For a real splash, dive into this water park near the airport.

Getting There & Around

AIR

The modern **Viru Viru International Airport** (VVI; ☎ 181), 15km north of the center, handles domestic and international flights.

AeroSur (☎ 385-2151; Av Irala at Colón) and **LAB** (☎ 800-10-3001; Chuquisaca 126) both have flights on most days to Cochabamba, La Paz and Sucre, with connections to other Bolivian cities. **TAM** (☎ 353-2639) flies direct to La Paz on Monday morning as well as a couple more times a week from El Trompillo, the military airport south of the center. Aerosur, AeroCon, Amaszonas and Aeroest all operate from there to the Egni and Pando districts, and Puerto Suarez. More expensive air taxis are also available in El Trompillo to any part of the country.

Taxis to the airport charge a standard US$6.20; a *micro* costs US60¢.

BUS

The full-service **Terminal Bimodal** (☎ 348-8382; terminal fee US30¢), a combo long-distance bus and train station, is 1.5km east of the center, just before the 3rd *anillo* at the end of Av Brasil. *Micro* 4 heads straight to the center.

There are regular services to Cochabamba (US$4 to US$6, 10 to 12 hours), with connections to La Paz, Oruro, Sucre, Potosí and Tarija. Direct overnight buses to Sucre (ie not via Cochabamba) depart between 5pm and 6pm (US$6 to US$12, 14 to 17 hours) and to La Paz (US$10 for *bus cama*, 16 hours) between 5pm and 7:30pm.

BOLIVIA

There are also afternoon and night buses south to Yacuiba and Bermejo, with connections to Salta. Buses leave daily (during the dry season) at 6:30am for the grueling trip through the Chaco to Asunción (around US$50, 30 hours minimum), Paraguay. There are morning and evening buses to Vallegrande. At least four companies have nightly buses for Concepción (US$4, six hours) and San Ignacio de Velasco on the Mission Circuit; 31 del Este has additional daytime departures.

To Trinidad and beyond, several buses leave between 5pm and 7pm nightly (US$4 to US$10, at least 12 hours).

TRAIN

There are three opportunities to travel to the Brazilian border: the efficient and upmarket *Ferrobus*, the *Expreso Oriental* (the infamous Death Train; see below), and the *Regional* (or *mixto*), predominantly a cargo train with a few passenger seats.

The most comfortable and efficient option is the *Ferrobus*, which departs on Tuesday, Thursday and Sunday at 7:30pm (*semicama/cama* US$28/33) and returns Monday, Wednesday and Friday. (Note: these schedules change.)

The *Expreso Oriental* runs to Quijarro, on the Brazilian border, on Monday, Wednesday and Friday at 5pm (Pullman/1st class US$6.50/15.50, 15½ hours), returning on Tuesday, Thursday and Sunday at 4:30pm. Tickets can be scarce and carriages are often so jammed with people and contraband that there's nowhere to sit. Ticket windows (supposedly) open at 8am, and you can only buy your ticket on the day of departure, when lines reach Cuban proportions. An adventurous alternative is to stake out a place in the *bodegas*

(boxcars) of a *treno mixto* (mixed train) and purchase a 2nd-class ticket on board (for 20% of the ticket-window price).

The upmarket option is to buy a 1st-class ticket through a Santa Cruz travel agent. You must pay a small national/international departure tax (US50¢) after purchasing your ticket.

Tickets can be purchased from the English-speaking **Forest Tours** (☎ 337-2042; www.forestbolivia .com; Cuéllar 22), which also offers excellent tours around the region.

A *mixto* train also runs to Yacuiba (on the Argentine border; Pullman/1st-class US$10.50/4.70, 18 hours) departing at 3:30pm on Monday and Wednesday.

AROUND SANTA CRUZ
Samaipata
☎ 03 / pop 3000

The beautiful village of Samaipata (1650m) is set amid the stunning wilderness surrounds of the Cordillera Oriental. It's a popular weekend destination (especially for partying visitors from Santa Cruz) and the perfect base to chill, hike or explore the numerous sights. Get in early – it's set to become one of *the* places to visit in Bolivia.

INFORMATION

See the town's promotional website, www .samaipata.info.

Sernap has a new office 1km outside of town on the road to Santa Cruz.

Note: there is no ATM in town.

SIGHTS & ACTIVITIES

Samaipata is a good launching point for **Parque Nacional Amboró**. Highlights include the **Pajcha waterfalls**, giant ferns and the **Cueva Mataral**

THE DEATH TRAIN

El 'tren de la muerte,' or the Death Train, travels from Santa Cruz to Quijarro, on the Brazilian border. Numerous theories abound as to how it – the *Expreso Oriental* or the *Regional (mixto)* – derived this dark name. The most obvious is that it sums up the trip itself: a bone-jarring, back-breaking journey as the train chugs through soy plantations and scrub to the steamy Pantanal on the Brazilian border. After several hours – despite the magnificent scenery – you'll want to throw yourself onto the rails. Then there are the long delays in swampy areas – bring plenty of food, water and mosquito repellant, and dress warmly in winter season. The more likely interpretation of the name relates to former accidents (especially in the '80s). Locals stored large quantities of contraband goods inside the carriages; they themselves preferred to sit on the roof of the train. Occasionally, an unfortunate soul or three toppled over the edge, especially when the overladen train derailed, which it did with regularity.

BOLIVIA

GETTING TO BRAZIL

From Quijarro, taxis shuttle passengers to the Brazilian border town of Corumbá, 2km away. You can change dollars or bolivianos into *reais* (pronounced *hay*-ice) on the Bolivian side, but the boliviano rate is poor. Note that there's no Brazilian consulate in Quijarro, so if you need a visa, get it in Santa Cruz. Bolivian officials may demand a bribe for an exit stamp at Quijarro. From Corumbá there are good bus connections into southern Brazil, but no passenger trains.

Coming from the border the bus runs to Rua Frei Mariano and the local bus terminal on Rua 13 do Junho.

You won't be allowed to enter Brazil without a yellow-fever vaccination certificate: there's a medical van at the border.

For information on travel from Brazil to Bolivia, see p337.

---

cave paintings. Forays to the site of **Ché's last stand** near Vallegrande are also possible. Many rare bird species are in the area and there is a **condor sanctuary** nearby.

The pre-Inca site of **El Fuerte** (admission US$4; 8:30-noon & 2-6pm Mon-Sat, 8:30am-4pm Sun), is on a hilltop 10km southeast of town. Hitching from the village is easiest on weekends, but it also makes a fine day-long walk. Taxis for the round-trip, including a one-, two-, or three-hour stop at the ruins, cost around US$6/7.40/8.65 for up to four people. The ticket for the ruins is also valid for admission to the small **archaeological museum** (8:30am-12:30pm & 2-6pm) in town.

The following agencies organize trips in the area, including El Fuerte, Amboro National Park, cave paintings, the waterfalls and the condor and Ché Guevara routes (US$10 to US$50 per person per day). The highly recommended biologist **Michael Blendinger** (/fax 944-6227; www.discoveringbolivia.com; Bolívar s/n, in front of museum) also does birding tours (in English and German) and specialises in tours to the southern Amboro. Others include the friendly German- and English-speaking Frank and Olaf at **Roadrunners** (03-944-6294; theroadrunners@hotmail .com); **Bolviajes** (at La Víspera; www.lavispera.org); and **Amboro Tours** (03-944-6293; erickamboro@yahoo.com) which also rents bikes Spanish-speaking Samaipata native **Don Gilberto** (03-944-6050) lived inside what is now the national park for many years. For further information see the town's promotional website, www.samaipata.info.

The **FAN office** (www.fan-bo.org; cnr Sucre & Murillo) can arrange trips to the community of La Yunga at the edge of the park.

SLEEPING

Mama Pasquala's (campsites per person by donation; entrance US15¢) The basic camping at this secluded spot, 500m upstream from the river ford en route to El Fuerte, is a deal.

Residencial Chelo (944-6014; Sucre s/n; r per person from US$2.50) A basic but adequate place just off the plaza.

Residencial Kim (944-6161; r per person US$3, with bathroom s/d US$3.70/6) A quiet, clean and sunny place (with a penchant for eighties music) just north of the plaza.

Hotel Paola (944-6903; southwest cnr of plaza; r per person US$3) The lovely terrace overlooking the plaza makes up for the shortcomings of this messy family-run place. The rooms are OK, and there's a shared kitchen.

Finca La Víspera (/fax 944-6082; www.lavispera.org; camping per person with own tent US$4, without tent US$5, guesthouse per person US$10-18) Fifteen minutes on foot southwest of the plaza is this lovely organic oasis: there's grassy camping, firm beds in the 'backpacker's house,' and charming self-contained guesthouses. The owners rent horses and organize Amboró treks.

Palacio del Ajedrez (Chess Club; 944-6196; paulin -chess@cotas.com.bo; Bolívar s/n; r per person US$5, s/d with bathroom US$8/13) Rooms with good beds and it's a great place to pick up a game of chess with Bolivian junior champions. Next to the archaeology museum.

Land-haus (944-6033; cabin per person US$10;) After a morning's hike, relax by the pool in this beautiful garden. Lovely cabins and rooming options.

At Km 100, Las Cuevas is another recommended camping spot with good swimming.

EATING

La Vaca Loca (snacks US60¢-$3.20) 'Mad cow' is possibly not the best choice of name; anyway, this handy place serves better cakes than it does meaty mains. It's on the south side of the plaza.

Latina Café (mains US$2-3.70) A cozy place to hang out. Good selection and even better views.

Landhaus (mains US$2.70-6; Y dinner Thu-Sun) For gourmet (slightly pricier) fare, try this place near the northern end of town.

Descanso en las Alturas (mains US$2.50-6.50) Roll from the Mosquito Bar (also a must) onto the massive terrace of this eatery to indulge in pizzas and meats.

La Chakana (Southern Cross) This European-owned place on the west side of the plaza is the main gringo hangout. It has vegetarian options, omelets and pancakes.

GETTING THERE & AWAY

Four-passenger Expreso Samaipata Taxis (US$3.20 per person, 2½ hours) leave Santa Cruz for Samaipata when full from the corner of Av Omar Chávez Ortiz and Solis de Olguin. Alternatively, a small bus departs from Av Grigotá at the third *anillo* at 4pm daily (US$2, three hours). From Samaipata, **shared taxis** (☎ 944-6133/6016) depart for Santa Cruz from the gas station on the highway (US$12 per cab). *Micros* leave from the plaza daily around 4:30am and between noon and 3pm on Sunday.

Parque Nacional Amboró

This extraordinary park crosses two 'divides': the warmer northern Amazonian-type section, and the southern Yungas-type section, with cooler temperatures (and fewer mosquitoes!). The village of Buena Vista, two hours (100km) northwest of Santa Cruz, is a staging point for trips into the spectacular forested northern lowland section of Parque Nacional Amboró. For a park entry permit and cabin reservations visit Buena Vista's **Sernap office** (☎ 932-2054), two blocks south of the plaza. See p246 for recommended tour companies that visit the park.

There are several places to sleep and eat, and camping is also possible in the park. Try the basic **Residencial Nadia** (☎ 932-2049), where the owner is a good source of park information. For food, Los Franceses has a savory menu and a jovial *très*-French owner.

Jesuit Mission Circuit

From the late 17th century, Jesuits established settlements called *reducciones* in Bolivia's eastern lowlands, building churches, establishing farms and instructing the Indians in religion, agriculture, music and crafts in return for conversion and manual labor. A circuit north and east of Santa Cruz takes in some mission sites, with buildings in various stages of reconstruction or decay. (Get in now before mass tourism takes over!) Santa Cruz and Samaipata agencies organize tours, or you can do it on your own (allow time). Basic food and lodging are available in most of the towns. Heading clockwise from Santa Cruz are the following:

San Ramón Noteworthy only as a transport junction.
San Javier The oldest mission (1692), recently and sympathetically restored.
Concepción An attractive town with a gaudy restored 1756 church.
San Ignacio de Velasco Much less attractive but still worth a stop, with an elaborate mission and church (1748) demolished in 1948.
San Miguel A sleepy town with a beautiful church (1721) that has been painstakingly restored.
Santa Ana A tiny village with a rustic 1755 church.
San Rafael The 1740s church is noted for its fine interior.
San José de Chiquitos Has an impressive 1748 stone church situated in a complex of mission buildings.

You can take the Santa Cruz–Quijarro train to San José first and then proceed counterclockwise. You can also take buses to San Ignacio, visit the villages south of there as an excursion, skip San José and return by bus from San Ignacio or continue to Brazil. Renting a car in Santa Cruz is another option, affordable between a few people.

Parque Nacional Noel Kempff Mercado

The remote Parque Nacional Noel Kempff Mercado lies in the northernmost reaches of Santa Cruz department. Not only is it one of South America's most spectacular parks, but it also takes in a range of dwindling habitats of world-class ecological significance. Its 1.5 million hectares encompas rivers, waterfalls, rainforests, plateaus and rugged 500m escarpments. On top of this, there's an awe-inspiring variety of Amazonian flora and fauna.

THE AMAZON BASIN

Bolivia's slice of the magical Amazon Basin encompasses over half of the country's entire territory and is a prime place to experience pristine rainforest and savanna lands. The Amazon includes some of the best-known national parks and reserves, including the incred-

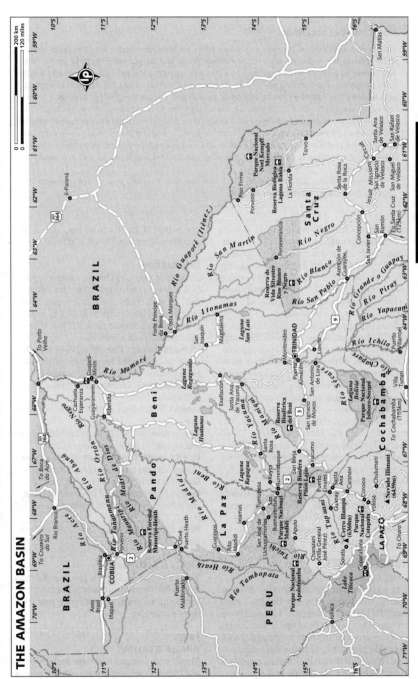

THE AMAZON BASIN

DON'T PAT THE PIRAÑAS!

'Ecofriendly' operators of pampas and jungle tours are increasing faster than mosquito larvae. Unfortunately, many of these undercut the official prices and, despite claiming to be ecofriendly, don't seem to practice what they preach, especially regarding the removal of inorganic waste from campsites, and handling of animals. As much as it's great to see the Amazonian animals, bear in mind that spotting caiman, anaconda, pirañas and the like is a privilege and not a 'right.' Operators and guides should not promise animal sightings (this encourages their unethical capture), are not supposed go looking for wildlife and should under no circumstances feed or handle any animals. Unfortunately, this is not always the case. One reader states: 'ecofriendly-wise, our operator was pretty awful – grabbing hold of anacondas when they found them and capturing baby caimans to show us. We heard of one adult caiman that was captured and in a panic, bit off its own tail.'

Your demands can put the 'friendly' back into the 'eco.' In short, your choice is vital to the ongoing protection of this wilderness area.

---

ible Parque Nacional Madidi (p253). But the Amazonian paradise is not without its problems: much of the area is heavily populated and degraded through logging and mining. There has been an influx of highland settlers and an upsurge in slash-and-burn agriculture. In the lowland areas, around Trinidad, cattle ranching exists on a large scale.

Boat trips provide a wonderful chance to view life from the water. Be aware that cargo vessels that ply the northern rivers lack scheduled services or passenger comforts – monotonous menus, river water and no cabins are de rigueur. Throw in a hammock or a sleeping bag. Other necessities are snacks, a water container, water-purification tablets, antimalarials and mosquito protection. The most popular river routes are Puerto Villarroel to Trinidad on the Río Ichilo and Trinidad to Guayaramerín on the Río Mamoré. Tour agencies offer comfortable river trips focused on wildlife-watching.

Towns with air services include Cobija, Guayaramerín, Reyes, Riberalta, Rurrenabaque, San Borja and Trinidad, but flights are often delayed or canceled, especially during the rainy season.

RURRENABAQUE

☎ 03 / pop 13,000

The bustling and friendly frontier town of 'Rurre' (elevation 105m) is Bolivia's most beautiful lowland settlement. The town thrives on tourism: travelers head up the Río Beni to visit the surrounding lush jungle and the savannalike grasslands, or to the stunningly precious Madidi National Park and its ecolodges. Hammocks are a way of life and relaxing in

one is part of an otherwise hot, humid (and occasionally mosquito-infested) visit.

Information

Some tour agencies change traveler's checks (4% to 5% commission). Tours can usually be paid for with credit cards, and *simpático* bars, agencies and hotels may be willing to facilitate cash advances. Podem Bank will give Visa and MasterCard cash advances.

PN Madidi/Sernap Office (☎ 892-2540) Across the river at San Buenaventura. Has information on the park; independent visitors must pay a US$10 entrance fee.

Cactri (Santa Cruz) Cash dollars can be changed here, next to Bala Tours.

Camila's (Santa Cruz s/n; per hr US$2.20) Pricey internet service.

Immigration (☎ 892-2241; Plaza 2 de Febrero) Extend your stay here. It's on the plaza's northeast corner.

Laundry Service Rurrenabaque (Vaca Diez) Recommended. Same-day laundry service (US$1.20 per kg).

Municipal tourist office (cnr Vaca Diez & Avaroa)

Number One (Avaroa) Around the corner from Laundry Service Rurrenabaque. Same-day laundry service (US$1.20 per kg).

Punto Entel (cnr Santa Cruz & Comercio) For telephone calls.

Sights & Activities

You can relax in Rurre's glorious **Balenario El Ambaibo** (swimming pool; Santa Cruz; admission US$2). Just south of town, a short uphill trek away, there's a **mirador.**

Tours

JUNGLE & PAMPAS

Jungle and pampas tours are Rurre's bread and butter. Operators are as common as mosquitoes. To choose an operator, the best bet is to speak to other travelers who've returned from trips – some operators are less than impressive. There are two main types of tours: jungle and pampas.

Jungle tours typically include a motorized canoe trip up the Beni and Tuichi rivers, with camping and rainforest treks along the way. Basic huts or shelters (with mosquito nets) are the main form of accommodation. (Note: rain, mud and insects can make the wet season – especially January to March – unpleasant for some jungle tours.)

If you're more interested in watching wildlife, opt for a pampas tour, which visits the wetland savannas northeast of town. They include rewarding guided walks and daytime and evening animal-viewing boat trips.

Jungle and pampas tours officially cost US$30 per person per day, including transport, guides and food. These are great trips, but the guides' (often poor) treatment of the wildlife depends upon travelers' demands. In short, animals should not be fed, disturbed or handled. Stock up on bottled water and insect repellant. Ask to see the guide's *autorización* (license). The best guides can provide insight on the fauna, flora, indigenous people and forest lore without pushing the boundaries. Most agencies have offices on Avaroa. Recommended agencies:

Fluvial Tours/Amazonia Adventures (☎ 892-2372; Avaroa s/n) At Hotel Tuichi. The longest-running agency.

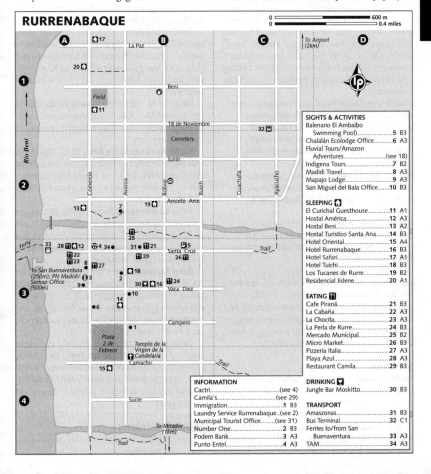

RURRENABAQUE

0   600 m
0   0.4 miles

To Airport (2km)

La Paz

Beni

Field

18 de Noviembre

Cemetery

Junín

Río Beni

Comercio   Avaroa   Bolívar   Busch   Guachalla   Ayacucho

Aniceto Arce

Santa Cruz

Trail

Ferry

To San Buenaventura (250m); PN Madidi/ Sernap Office (500m)

Vaca Díez

Campero

Plaza 2 de Febrero

Templo de la Virgen de la Candelaria

Camacho

Trail

Sucre

To Mirador (1km)

Trail

SIGHTS & ACTIVITIES	
Balenario El Ambaibo Swimming Pool)	5 B3
Chalalán Ecolodge Office	6 A3
Fluvial Tours/Amazon Adventures	(see 18)
Indigena Tours	7 B2
Madidi Travel	8 A3
Mapajo Lodge	9 A3
San Miguel del Bala Office	10 B3

SLEEPING	
El Curichal Guesthouse	11 A1
Hostal América	12 A3
Hostal Beni	13 A2
Hostal Turístico Santa Ana	14 B3
Hotel Oriental	15 A4
Hotel Rurrenabaque	16 B3
Hotel Safari	17 A1
Hotel Tuichi	18 B3
Los Tucanes de Rurre	19 B2
Residencial Jislene	20 A1

EATING	
Cafe Piraná	21 B3
La Cabaña	22 A3
La Chocita	23 A3
La Perla de Rurre	24 B3
Mercado Municipal	25 B2
Micro Market	26 B3
Pizzería Italia	27 A3
Playa Azul	28 A3
Restaurant Camila	29 B3

DRINKING	
Jungle Bar Moskitto	30 B3

TRANSPORT	
Amazonas	31 B3
Bus Terminal	32 C1
Ferries to/from San Buenaventura	33 A3
TAM	34 A3

INFORMATION	
Cactri	(see 4)
Camila's	(see 29)
Immigration	1 B3
Laundry Service Rurrenabaque	(see 2)
Municipal Tourist Office	(see 31)
Number One	2 B3
Podem Bank	3 A3
Punto Entel	4 A3

BOLIVIA

BOLIVIA

SPLURGE!

The Bolivian Amazonia's most notable community-based ecotourism project is Chalalán Ecolodge, fronting a wildlife-rich lake five hours up the Río Tuichi from Rurre. Since 1995 it has provided employment for the Tacana villagers of San José de Uchupiamonas and is often cited as a model for sustainable tourism, with the profits going directly back into the community. It's an awesome place, with an extensive trail system, excellent meals and night hikes. An all-inclusive three-day, two-night stay costs around US$280 per person, minimum four people. For details, visit the office in **Rurrenabaque** (☎ 892-2419; www.chalalan.com in Spanish; Comercio btwn Vaca Diez & Campero) or contact America Tours (p189) in La Paz.

Indigena Tours (☎ 892-2091; indigenaecologico6@ hotmail.com; Avaroa s/n)

COMMUNITY-BASED ECOTOURISM

Other outstanding alternatives are the community-run and community-based ethno-ecotourism projects. Most are based several hours upriver and offer all-inclusive (comfy individual cabañas, *simpático* guides, food) overnight visits to the local communities, and activities such as bow-and-arrow fishing and rainforest trekking. Projects include the following:

Madidi Travel (www.madidi-travel.com; per person per day US$40-60) La Paz ☎ 02-245-0069; Jimenez 806); Rurrenabaque (☎ 892-2153; Comercial btwn Santa Cruz & Vaca Diez) Working within the private protected area of Serere. Volunteering opportunities available.

Mapajo Lodge (☎ 892-2317; www.mapajo.com; Santa Cruz btwn Avaroa & Comercio; per person per day US$65) Overnight visits to the Mosetén Chimán communities.

San Miguel del Bala (☎ 892-2394; www.san migueldelbala.com; Av Comercio; per person per day US$50-60) Opened at the end of 2005 and project of the Tacana community.

Inquire at the tourist office about day-long **Day for the Community tours** (tours US$25), which visit four *altiplano* immigrant colonies and highlight alternative sustainable development efforts, including agroforestry, organic foods and *artesanía* (handicrafts) projects.

Sleeping

Hostal América (☎ 892-2413; Santa Cruz; r per person US$2) This basic *hostal* is worthwhile only for its top-floor rooms, which afford a superb view of the river and the hills.

El Curichal Guesthouse (☎ 892-2647; elcurichal@ hotmail.com; 1490 Comerico; r per person US$2.50, with bathroom US$4.30) It's worth the effort to swing by

this brand-new, spotless place, located behind the owner's house. And yes, swingin' hammocks, too.

Hotel Oriental (☎ 892-2401; Plaza 2 de Febrero; r per person US$2.50, with bathroom US$10) Another sedate, good-value place with garden hammocks. It's on the south side of the plaza.

Residencial Jislene (☎ 892-2552; Comercio; r per person from US$2.50, with bathroom US$3.70) The Caldera family's riverside 'retreat': a bit rough around the edges, but makes up what it lacks in creature comforts with hospitality. It's located near Beni.

Hotel Tuichi (☎ 892-2372; Avaroa s/n; dm US$2.50, r per person US$4-5) Classic, party-hearty backpackers haunt with plain, decent rooms in an unkempt yard.

Hostal Touristico Santa Ana (☎ 892-2399; Avaroa btwn Diez & Campero; r per person US$3, s/d with bathroom US$6/8.65) You'll be hard pushed to clamber out of the hammocks in this peaceful, leafy and clean place.

Hotel los Tucanes de Rurre (☎ 892-2039; tucanes derurre@hotmail.com; cnr Bolivar & Aniceto Arce; r US$5, with shared bathroom US$3) The eccentric Anna runs a neat ship, complete with the ubiquitous hammocks. Breakfast included.

Hotel Rurrenabaque (☎ 892-2481, in La Paz 02-279-5917; Vaca Diez; s/d incl breakfast US$8/13.35, without bathroom US$4.65/9) Friendly and far from the maddening late-night disco crowd. It has basic but clean rooms with fan and hammocks on a breezy balcony.

Other midrange places include the clean and recommended **Hostal Beni** (☎ 892-2408; Comercio at Arce; s/d US$3/6.20, d with bathroom & TV US$9; 🖭), near the river; and **Hotel Safari** (☎ /fax 892-2210; s/d US$25/34; 🖭), in a pretty setting right on the river.

Eating & Drinking

The Mercado Municipal is full of good *come-dores* and juice bars.

Several fish restaurants occupy shelters along the riverfront – they're all pretty good; try Playa Azul or La Chocita or La Cabaña.

Cafe Piraña (Santa Cruz; ☺ 7am-2pm) Relaxed joint with great vegetarian options. It's next to the Amazonas office.

Restaurant Camila (Santa Cruz s/n) A travelers hotspot with a full menu and massive jungle mural.

Pizzería Italia (Commercio s/n) Good you-know-what in a social indoor-outdoor setting.

Club Social (Commercio s/n; lunch US$1.25, mains US$3-5) A pleasant place to enjoy à la carte lunch or dinner, and cocktails from outdoor tables overlooking the river.

La Perla de Rurre (Bolivar s/n; fish dinners US$3) Join the schools of fish-lovers at this raved-about place. Tasty fish dinners.

Jungle Bar Moskkito (Vaca Diez) Rurre doesn't see a lot of action, but this is an undisputed travelers' favorite. Happy hour runs 7pm to 9pm, and there are pool tables and good music. Great spot to form tour groups.

Getting There & Around

AIR

The number of flights to Rurre is increasing all the time, but they are often sold out. Note, too, they're often delayed or canceled in the rainy season for safety reasons: the planes cannot land or take off from muddy air strips. Have your tour agency purchase your return ticket in advance.

In theory, **TAM** (☎ 892-2398; Santa Cruz) has flights between La Paz and Rurre (US$60) to changing schedules. **Amazonas** (☎ 892-2472; www.amazonas .com; Santa Cruz) attempts to fly to and from La Paz (US$60) three to four times daily. The humble airport is a grassy landing strip a few kilometers north of town. Airport transport costs US$4.30, whether by bus (which drops you in the center), packed taxi or, if you're traveling light, on the back of a motorcycle.

BOAT

Thanks to the new Guayaramerín road, there's little cargo transport down the Río Beni to Riberalta. Taxi ferries across to San Buenaventura (US15¢) sail frequently all day.

BUS

When the roads are dry, buses run daily between Rurrenabaque and La Paz (US$6.20, 16 hours), but it's best to break the journey at Coroico, which is 'only' 14 hours from

Rurre; actually, you get off at Yolosa, 7km west of Coroico, where there's an *alojamiento* if you get stranded. Caranavi, with a couple of basic places to sleep and eat, is a less desirable stopover option and the transfer point for minibuses to Guanay (US$2, 2½ hours).

Daily buses to Trinidad (US$15, *bus cama* US$17, 18 hours) go via Yucumo, San Borja and San Ignacio de Moxos when the road is clear. There are also daily buses to Riberalta (US$15, 20 hours) and one to Guayaramerín (US$17, 20 hours to three days!).

AROUND RURRENABAQUE
Parque Nacional Madidi

The remarkable Río Madidi watershed features the greatest biodiversity of the earth's protected regions. The most ecologically sound section is protected by Parque Nacional Madidi (US$10 entry), which encompasses a huge range of wildlife habitats, from torrid rainforests to Andean glaciers at 6000m. Researchers have observed over 1000 bird species – 10% of the world's known species.

The park's populated sections along the Río Tuichi remain *territorio comunitario original*, which allows indigenous people to continue with their traditional practices: hunting, fishing and utilizing other forest resources. So far, the Quechua, Araona and Tacana communities are coexisting successfully with the park.

Logging activity along the Tuichi and at the northern end of the park, however, is a major threat, with rogue timbermen still felling mahogany, cedar and other valuable trees. A proposed dam project has been slated for the Bala Gorge area for years, just upstream from Rurre, which would flood vast tracts of rainforest, destroy settlements and obliterate native flora and fauna. The kibosh appears to have been put on the dam, but a more pressing threat is the proposed road from Apolo to Ixiamas, which would bisect the park.

GETTING THERE & AWAY

The most accessible and popular access point is Rurre. The easiest way to visit the park is a trip to Chalalán Ecolodge (see opposite) or one of the ecotourism projects (see opposite). Those erring on the side of adventure can visit the park's fringes independently, but must register with the Sernap office (see p250) in San Buenaventura and must be accompanied by an authorized guide. Penetrating deeper into Madidi will depend on luck, patience and

BOLIVIA

the generosity of your hosts. Ixiamas-bound trucks, *micros* and buses depart daily from San Buenaventura for Tumupasa, 50km north of Rurre. From Tumupasa, it's a 30km trek through the forest to San José de Uchupiamonas. Travelers making this trip should be entirely self- sufficient. For a taste of just how wrong things can go, read *Return from Tuichi* (also published as *Heart of the Amazon*) by Yossi Ghinsberg.

TRINIDAD

☎ 03 / pop 80,000

There's more than meets the eye to 'Trini' (elevation 235m), Beni's capital. Founded on June 13, 1686, by Padre Cipriano Barace as La Santísima Trinidad (the Most Holy Trinity), it was southern Beni's second Jesuit mission. The town's open drains don't help its reputation as a backwater, but it's an enjoyably lazy town, and with a bit of effort there is plenty to do: from the mission route to the prehispanic route, featuring the unique system of water channels attributed to the *Moxeñas*.

There's a new Spanish-funded **ethno-archaeological museum** (admission US60¢; ☺ 8am-noon & 3-6pm) at the university, 1.5km out of town. Motorbikes are not merely transport, but a pastime: for US$1.20 per hour you can rent a bike and join the youth in their mechanical flirtations.

The lovely Ignaciano Indian village of **San Ignacio de Moxos** is 89km west of Trinidad. The annual **Fiesta del Santo Patrono de Moxos** (July 31) attracts revelers from around the country. Boat passages can be arranged at Puerto Almacén.

Information

The **tourist office** (☎ 462-4831) has lifted its game and has good brochures on surrounding sights and a town map. Enter through the Prefectura building. ATMs are near the main plaza.

Tours

Agencies arrange horse-riding trips, fishing and river outings, trekking, visits to local communities and bird-watching. Try **Moxos Turismo** (☎ 462-1141; turmoxos@sauce.entelnet.bo; 6 de Agosto 114) or **Paraíso Travel** (☎ 462-0692; paraiso@sauce .ben.entelnet.bo; 6 de Agosto 138).

Sleeping

Hostal Palmas (☎ 462-0182; La Paz 365; per person US$3.70, with bathroom US$6.50) Ask for a room up-

stairs; those downstairs don't have external windows.

Hotel Paulista (☎ 462-0018; cnr 6 de Agosto & Suárez; r per person US$3.70) This basic but adequate hotel comes with its own shrine and US$1 lunches.

Hostal Sirari (☎ 462-4472; Santa Cruz 538; s/d US$8.65/15) Run by a house-proud mother-and-daughter team, this indoor-outdoor living space is the best-value option around. Ask the resident toucan.

Hotel Copacabana (☎ 462-2811; Villavicencio 627; s with air con US$10-19, d with air-con US$17-23) A friendly, good-value hotel with a range of prices. No-frills rooms US$5.

Eating & Drinking

Trinidad is cattle country, so beef is bountiful. If budget is the priority, hit the Mercado Municipal, where for a pittance you can try the local specialty, *arroz con queso* (rice with cheese), plus shish kebabs, *yuca* (cassava), plantain and salad. There are several decent places around the plaza. Extravaganza and Palo Diablo are the places to party. Live music on weekends.

La Casona (east side of plaza) This welcoming place has sidewalk tables, good pizza and inexpensive *almuerzos*.

Restaurant Brasileiro (18 de Noviembre s/n) A help-yourself tasty extravaganza by the kilo (US$4.30 per kilogram).

Club Social (plaza; almuerzos US$1.20) These generous *almuerzos* are more than you can eat in the heat.

El Moro (Bolívar & Velasco) Feeling fishy? Drop anchor here.

Getting There & Around

AIR

The airport is northwest of town, a feasible half-hour walk from the center. Taxis charge around US$2 per person, but if you don't have much luggage, a motorcycle taxi is only US90¢. **AeroCon** (☎ 462-4442; Vacadiez, cnr 18 de Noviembre) and **Amazonas** (☎ 852-3933; 18 de Noviembre 267) fly daily to Santa Cruz, Riberalta and Guayaramerín. **LAB** (☎ 462-1277; La Paz 322) flies to Cochabamba, and **TAM** (☎ 462-2363; Bolívar at Santa Cruz) less frequent flights to all these destinations, plus La Paz.

BOAT

The closest ports are Puerto Almacén, on the Ibare, 8km southwest of town, and Puerto Barador, on the Río Mamoré 13km in the

---

GETTING TO BRAZIL

Frequent motorboats (around US90¢) link the two ports of Guayaramerín and Guajará-Mirim (Brazil). There are no restrictions entering Guajará-Mirim for a quick visit, but if you intend to travel further into Brazil, you must pick up an entry/exit stamp. A yellow-fever vaccination certificate is officially required to enter Brazil; have it handy in case of a 'spot (the tourist) check'.

For departure stamps from Bolivia head to the Policía Federal in **Bolivian immigration** (⏰ 8am-8pm) by the dock. For information on travel from Brazil to Bolivia, see p397.

---

same direction. (Note: at the time of research, the Río Mamoré was a lagoon due to drought conditions so boats were not departing from Puerto Barador.) Trucks charge around US$1 to Puerto Almacén and US$2 to Puerto Barador.

For boats heading north to Guayaramerín or south to Puerto Villarroel, inquire at *La Capitania*, the port office in Puerto Almacén. Speak to the captain for the boat schedule and ask around in the village for Lidia Flores Dorado, the Sub-Alcaldeza, who will confirm the boat captain's reliable reputation. The Guayaramerín run takes up to a week (larger boats do it in three to four days) and costs around US$30 to US$35, including food. To Puerto Villarroel, smaller boats take eight to 10 days.

BUS

The rambling bus terminal is on Rómulo Mendoza. *Flotas* depart nightly for Santa Cruz (normal/*cama* US$3.70/7.40, 10 hours) and road conditions permitting, several companies head daily to Rurrenabaque (12 to 24 hours) via San Borja. In the dry season the daily Flota Copacabana beelines direct to La Paz (US$24 *bus cama*, 30 hours). Frequent *micros* and *camionetas* run to San Ignacio de Moxos (US$3.70, three to five hours) from the corner of Mamoré and 18 de Noviembre. There are also daily dry-season departures to Riberalta and Guayaramerín.

RIBERALTA

☎ 03 / pop 76,000

You may not go nutty over Riberalta (elevation 115m), despite it being one of the major Brazil nut processors. As Bolivia's major northern frontier settlement, located on the Brazilian river border, the town's importance as a Río Beni port has faded since the opening of the La Paz road.

Riberalta is cursed with open drains, but otherwise it's a laid-back place. It's hammock heaven – in the paralyzing heat of the

day, both strenuous activity (and you) are suspended. Chilling in the Club Náutico's sparkling riverside pool (two blocks north of the plaza) is highly touted. On fine evenings backlit by Technicolor sunsets, the plaza buzzes with cruising motorcycles, while the anomalous cathedral stands watch.

There are a of couple banks (but no ATM) and a reasonable internet place on the plaza.

Sleeping

Palace Hotel (☎ 852-2680; Molina 79; r per person US$2) The eccentric *señorita*, her knick-knacks and cabaña create the atmosphere. Basic but fun.

Residencial Los Reyes (☎ 852-2615; General Sucre 393; r per person US$2.50, with bathroom US$3.70) Spotless, near the airport, good hammocks but no fans.

Residencial Las Palmeras (☎ 852-2353; r-laspalmeras@hotmail.com; Nicolás Suarez 391; s/d US$12.50/16.50, with air-con US$23/25) the nearest thing to a B&B: a 'pretty and pink,' neat and clean, family-run suburban home.

Hotel Colonial (☎ 852-3018; s/d US$19-22.50/21-25, ste s/d/tr US$30/33/35; 🖳) The town's upmarket option is this stunningly renovated colonial home, complete with antique furniture, delightful garden, and what else, hammocks. Near the plaza.

Eating

The market is the best place to cobble together a classic breakfast of *api*, juice and *empanadas*. There are several ice-cream places on the plaza.

Club Social (Dr Martinez; set lunches US$1.20) Serves inexpensive set lunches.

Horno Camba (mains US$1.30-2) Popular for lunch and dinner on the plaza near the cathedral.

La Parilla (Dr Martinez; mains US$2.20) Meaty portions in every BBQ's meaty shape and form. Highly recommended by the locals.

La Cabaña de Tío Tom (Sucre; mains US$2.20-2.70) A small veranda on the street is a pleasant setting for pleasant meals.

BOLIVIA

Getting There & Away

AIR

The airport is 15 minutes from the main plaza. **Amaszonas** (☎ 852-3933; Chuquisaca s/n), **TAM** (☎ 852-3924; Chuquisaca) and **AeroCon** (☎ 852-2870; Plaza Principal Acera Norte 469) have several flights a week to Trinidad. The companies connect to either La Paz, Santa Cruz or Cochabamba, plus a few per week to Cobija. TAM's 20-minute, four-times-a-week Riberalta to Guayara flight (US$15) is surely one of Bolivia's cheapest thrills.

BOAT

Boats up the Río Beni to Rurrenabaque are rarer than jaguar, but sometimes run when the road becomes impassable in the wet season. If you do find something, budget on US$100 per day (three people) for the five- to eight-day trip in an '*expreso*.' For details, visit the port captain's office.

BUS & CAMIÓN

Several *flotas* run daily between Riberalta and Guayaramerín (US$2.50, three hours), or you can wait at the *camión* stop on Av Héroes del Chaco. Daily *flotas* from Guayaramerín to Cobija, Rurrenabaque and La Paz stop at Riberalta en route. *Flotas* to Trinidad (US$25) leave Monday to Thursday with two different companies.

GUAYARAMERÍN

☎ 03 / pop 40,444

The cheerful little town of Guayaramerín (elevation 130m) is Bolivia's back door to Brazil. It lies on the banks of the Río Mamoré. This frontier settlement thrives on legal and illegal trade with the Brazilian town of Guajará-Mirim, just across the river. A road links Guayaramerín to Riberalta, connecting south to Rurrenabaque and La Paz, and west to Cobija.

Information

Exchange US dollars at the Banco Mercantil, Hotel San Carlos (also does traveler's checks) or the *casa de cambio* on the plaza. There is internet on the plaza.

Sleeping & Eating

Hotel Litoral (☎ 855-3895; 25 de Mayo; r per person US$3.20, without bathroom US$2, tr with bathroom US$6.20) Mellow and pleasant with a homely flavor.

Hotel Santa Ana (☎ 855-3900, 25 de Mayo 611; r per person US$3.50, without bathroom US$2.65) This quiet, shady hotel is an attractive choice.

Hotel San Carlos (☎ 855-3555; 6 de Agosto; r per person US$20) This clean and modern option resembles a '70s-style tile factory, such are the range of decorative ceramics. It even has a pool with a '70s slide...if there's water.

On the plaza, both Snack Antonella and Restaurant Los Bibosis serve yummy juices and snacks. Restaurant Brasileiro off the plaza has a US$2 all you can eat.

Getting There & Away

AIR

Amaszonas (☎ 855-3731; Frederico Román) and **AeroCon** (☎ 855-3882; Oruro s/n) both have daily flights from/to Guayaramerín–Riberalta–Trinidad–Santa Cruz (US$134). **AeroSur** (☎ 855-3731) serves Cobija a couple times a week. **TAM** (☎ 855-3924) flies twice a week from La Paz to Riberalta and Guayaramerín, twice a week to Trinidad and once a week to Cochabamba and Santa Cruz.

BOAT

Boats up the Río Mamoré to Trinidad leave almost daily (around US$25 with food). Speak to the port captain. Fishing trips may be possible.

BUS & TAXI

The bus terminal is at the western end of town, beyond the market. Buses go to Riberalta (US$2.50, three hours) several times daily. Shared taxis to Riberalta (US$3.70, two hours) leave from the terminal when they have four passengers. In the dry season, several foolhardy *flotas* head out daily for Rurrenabaque (US$18, 14 to 36 hours) and La Paz (US$23, 30 to 60 hours). There are five buses weekly to Cobija (US$13, 13 hours) and seven to Trinidad (US$23, 24 hours).

BOLIVIA DIRECTORY

ACCOMMODATIONS

Bolivian accommodations are among South America's cheapest, though price and value are hardly uniform. Prices in this chapter reflect standard, high-season rates; rates can double during fiestas. Negotiate during slow times; a three-night stay may net you a deal. Room availability is only a problem during fiestas (especially Carnaval in Oruro) and at popular weekend getaway destinations (eg Coroico).

The Bolivian hotel-rating system divides accommodations into *posadas*, *alojamientos*, residenciales, casas de huéspedes, hostales and hoteles. This rating system reflects the price scale and, to some extent, the quality.

Posadas are the cheapest roof and bed available. They're frequented mainly by campesinos visiting the city, cost between US$1 and US$2 per person and provide minimal cleanliness and comfort. Shared bathrooms are stinky, some have no showers and hot water is unknown.

A step up are alojamientos, which are marginally better and cost slightly more, but are still pretty basic. Bathing facilities are almost always communal, but you may find a hot shower. Some are clean and tidy, while others are disgustingly seedy. Prices range from US$1.25 to US$5 per person.

Quality varies at residenciales, casas de huéspedes and hostales. Most are acceptable, and you'll often have a choice between shared or private bathroom. Plan on US$5 to US$20 for a double with a private bathroom, about 30% less without. Bolivia also has plenty of midrange places and five-star luxury resorts when you're ready for a splurge.

In this chapter, we assume that residenciales and casas de huéspedes (and some hostales, depending on the city) have shared bathroom facilities, while hotel rooms come with separate bathroom.

Hostelling International (HI; www.hostellingbolivia .org) is affiliated with eight or so accommodations around the country. Atypical of 'hostelling' networks in other countries, members range from two-star hotels to camping grounds, but few offer traditional dorm beds or amenities like shared kitchens. HI membership cards may be for sale at HI Sucre Hostel, the flagship hostel in Sucre, or at Valmar Tours in La Paz.

Bolivia offers excellent camping, especially along trekking routes and in remote mountain areas. Gear can be rented in La Paz and popular trekking towns like Sorata. There are few organized campsites, but you can pitch a tent almost anywhere outside populated centers. Remember, however, that highland nights are often freezing. Theft from campers is reported in some areas; inquire locally about security.

ACTIVITIES

Hiking, trekking and mountaineering (see p264) in and around the Andes top the to-do list; opt for camping or fishing if you're feeling lazy. The most popular treks (see p203) begin near La Paz, traverse the Cordillera Real along ancient Inca routes and end in the Yungas. Jungle treks (see p250) are all the rage around Rurrenabaque.

An increasing number of La Paz agencies organize technical climbs and expeditions into the Cordillera Real and to Volcán Sajama (6542m), Bolivia's highest peak.

Mountain biking (p193) options around La Paz are endless. Kayaking and white-water rafting are gaining popularity near Coroico and in the Chapare (in the lowlands around Cochabamba).

Countrywide, Bolivians are loco for karaoke, racquetball, billiards, chess, cacho and fútbol.

BOOKS

For in-depth coverage, pick up a copy of Lonely Planet's Bolivia.

If walking is on your itinerary, add LP's Trekking in the Central Andes, or Trekking in Bolivia, by Yossi Brain, to your kit. Bolivian Andes, by Alain Mesili, is a must for madcap mountaineers.

For a good synopsis of Bolivian history, politics and culture, check out Bolivia in Focus, by Paul van Lindert. If you'll be in-country for the long haul, pick up Culture Shock! Bolivia, by Mark Cramer. Another fascinating read is Marching Powder, by Rusty Young, an account of life in La Paz' San Pedro Prison. The Fat Man from La Paz: Contemporary Fiction from Bolivia, a collection of 20 short stories edited by Rosario Santos, makes great roadside reading.

English-, German- and French-language publications are available at Los Amigos del Libro in La Paz, Cochabamba and Santa Cruz. The books are pricey. There's an ample selection of popular novels, Latin American literature, dictionaries and coffee-table books.

Bibliophiles rejoice: used-book outlets and dog-eared book exchanges are now commonplace along the Bolivian part of the gringo trail.

BUSINESS HOURS

Few businesses open before 9am, though markets stir awake as early as 6am. Cities virtually shut down between noon and 2pm, except markets and restaurants serving lunch-hour crowds. Most businesses remain open until 8pm or 9pm. If you have urgent business to attend to, don't wait until the weekend as most offices will be closed.

CLIMATE

Bolivia has a wide range of altitude-affected climatic patterns. Within its frontiers, every climatic zone can be found, from stifling rainforest heat to arctic cold.

Adventurers will likely encounter just about every climatic zone, no matter when they visit. Summer (November to April) is the rainy season. The most popular, and arguably most comfortable, time to visit is during the dry winter season (May to October).

The high season is from June to September, and the low season runs from October to May.

The rainy season lasts from November to March or April (summer). Of the major cities, only Potosí receives regular snowfall (between February and April), though flakes are possible in Oruro and La Paz toward the end of the rainy season. On the *altiplano* and in the highlands, subzero nighttime temperatures are frequent.

Winter in Cochabamba, Sucre and Tarija is a time of clear skies and optimum temperatures. The Amazon Basin is always hot and wet, with the drier period falling between May and October. The Yungas region is cooler but fairly damp year-round.

For more information and climate charts, see p1062.

DANGERS & ANNOYANCES

Sadly, Bolivia no longer lives up to its reputation as one of the safest South American countries for travelers. Crime against tourists is on the increase, especially in La Paz and, to a lesser extent, Cochabamba, Copacabana and Oruro (especially during festival times). Scams are commonplace and fake police, false tourist police and 'helpful' tourists are on the rise. Be aware, too, of circulating counterfeit banknotes. (See p189 for a detailed rundown of *en vogue* cons.)

There is a strong tradition of social protest: demonstrations are a weekly occurrence and this can affect travelers. These are usually peaceful, but police occasionally use force and tear gas to disperse crowds. *Bloqueos* (roadblocks) and strikes by transportation workers often lead to long delays.

The rainy season means flooding, landslides and road washouts, which means more delays. Getting stuck overnight behind a slide can

happen: you'll be a happier camper with ample food, drink and warm clothes on hand.

Emergencies

Emergency service numbers in major cities:
Ambulance (☎ 118)
Fire department (☎ 119)
Police (RadioPatrol; ☎ 110)
Tourist Police (☎ 02-222-5016)

DRIVER'S LICENSE

Most car-rental agencies will accept a home driver's license, but it's wise to back it up with an International Driver's License. (The more official papers in this official-paper-loving country, the better!)

ELECTRICITY

Electricity operates on 220V at 50Hz. US-type plugs are used throughout Bolivia.

EMBASSIES & CONSULATES

See relevant city and town maps for the position of embassies and consulates.

Embassies & Consulates in Bolivia

Argentina Cochabamba (☎ 04-422-9347; Blanco 0-929); La Paz (Map pp190-1; ☎ 02-241-7737; Aspiazu 497); Santa Cruz (Map pp242-3; ☎ 03-334-7133; Junín 22); Tarija (Map p223; Ballivián N-699; ☑ 8:30am-12:30pm Mon-Fri); Villazón (Map p226; Saavedra 311; ☑ 9am-1pm Mon-Fri) The Santa Cruz branch is above Banco de la Nación Argentina facing Plaza 24 de Septiembre. The Tarija branch Issues visas and entry stamps.
Australia (Map pp186-7; ☎ 02-243 3241; Aspiazu 416, La Paz)
Brazil Cochabamba (Map pp228-9; ☎ 04-425-5860; Edificio Los Tiempos II, 9th fl); Guayaramerín (☎ /fax 03-855-3766; cnr Beni & 24 de Septiembre; ☑ 9am-1pm & 3-5pm Mon-Fri); La Paz (Map pp186-7; ☎ 02-244-0202; embajadabrasil@acelerate.com; cnr Av Ancieto Arce & Gutierrez, Edificio Multicentro); Santa Cruz (Map pp242-3; ☎ 03-334-4400; Av Busch 330)
Canada (Map pp186-7; ☎ 02-241-5021; lapaz@ international.gc.ca; Sanjinéz 2678, Edificio Barcelona, 2nd fl, La Paz)
Chile La Paz (☎ 02-279-7331; Calle 14, Calacoto); Santa Cruz (☎ 03-343-4272; 5 Oeste 224, Barrio Equipetrol) Northwest of the city center.
Colombia (☎ 02-278-6841; 9 No 7835, Calacoto, La Paz)
Ecuador (Map pp190-1; ☎ 02-231-9739; Av 16 de Julio s/n, Edificio Herrmann, 14th fl, La Paz)
France La Paz (☎ 02-278-6114; cnr Siles 5390 & Calle 8, Obrajes); Santa Cruz (☎ 03-343-3434; 3rd Anillo btwn San Martin & Radial, 23)

Germany Cochabamba (☎ 04-425-4024; Edificio La Promontora, 6th fl); La Paz (Map pp186-7; ☎ 02-244-0066, 1133/66; www.embajada-alemana-bolivia.org; Av Ancieto Arce 2395); Santa Cruz (☎ 03-336-7585; Nuflo de Chavez 241); Tarija (Map p223; ☎ 04-664-2062; Campero 321)

Italy La Paz (☎ 02-243-4955; 6 de Agosto 2575 btwn P Salazar & Pinilla); Santa Cruz (☎ 03-353-1796; El Trompillo, Edificio Honnen, 1st fl)

Netherlands La Paz (Map pp186-7; ☎ 02-244-4040; Av 6 de Agosto 2455, Edificio Hilda, 7th fl); Santa Cruz (☎ 03-358-1866; Aguilera 300, 3rd Anillo); Cochabamba (☎ 04-525-7362; Av Oquendo 654)

Paraguay Cochabamba (☎ 04-458-1081; Edificio America, Av Ayacucho, btwn Santiváñez & General Acha); La Paz (Map pp186-7; ☎ 02-243-3176; cnr Av 6 de Agosto & P Salazar, Edificio Illimani)

Peru Cochabamba (☎ 04-4486-556; Edificio Continental, Av Santa Cruz); La Paz (Map pp186-7; ☎ 02-244-0631; Av 6 de Agosto 2455, Edificio Hilda); Santa Cruz (☎ 03-336-8979; Edificio Oriente, 2nd fl)

Spain (☎ 02-243-0118; Av 6 de Agosto 2827, La Paz)

UK (Map pp186-7; ☎ 02-243-3424; www.embassyof bolivia.co.uk; Av Ancieto Arce 2732, La Paz)

USA Cochabamba (Map pp228-9; ☎ 04-425-6714; Oquendo E-654, Torres Sofer, Rm 601); La Paz (Map p186-7; ☎ 02-216-8216; lapaz.usembassy.gov; Av Ancieto Arce 2780)

Bolivian Embassies & Consulates Abroad

Bolivia has diplomatic representation in most South American countries and also in the following countries:

Australia (☎ 02-9247 4235; Suite 305, 4 Bridge St, Sydney)

Canada (☎ 613-236-5730; www.boliviaembassy.ca; 130 Albert St, Suite 416, Ottawa, Ontario K1P 5G4)

France (☎ 01 42 24 93 44; embolivia.paris@wanadoo.fr; 12 Ave du President Kennedy, F-75016 Paris)

Germany (☎ 030 2639 150; www.bolivia.de; Wichmannstr 6, PLZ-10787 Berlin)

UK (☎ 020-7235 4248/2257; www.embassyofbolivia .co.uk; 106 Eaton Sq, London SW1W 9AD)

USA (☎ 202-483-4410, 202-328-3712; 3014 Massachusetts Ave NW, Washington DC, 20008)

FESTIVALS & EVENTS

Bolivian fiestas are invariably of religious or political origin and typically include lots of music, drinking, eating, dancing, processions, rituals and general unrestrained behavior. Water balloons (gringos are sought-after targets!) and fireworks (all too often at eye-level) figure prominently.

Alasitas (Festival of Abundance) January 24. Best in La Paz and Copacabana.

Fiesta de la Virgen de Candelaria (Feast of the Virgin of Candelaria) First week in February. Best in Copacabana.

Carnaval Held in February/March; dates vary. All hell breaks loose in Oruro during la Diablada.

Semana Santa (Easter Week) March/April; dates vary.

Fiesta de la Cruz (Festival of the Cross) May 3. May or may not have anything to do with the cross Jesus hung on.

Corpus Christi May; dates vary.

Fiesta de la Virgen de Urcupiña (Festival of the Virgen of Urcupiña) August 15 to 18. Best in Quillacollo.

FOOD & DRINK
Bolivian Cuisine

Generally, Bolivian food is palatable, filling and ho-hum. Figuring prominently, potatoes come in dozens of varieties, most of them small and colorful. *Chuño* or *tunta* (freeze-dried potatoes) often accompany meals and are gnarled looking and tasting, though some people love them. In the lowlands, the potato is replaced by *yuca* (cassava).

Beef, chicken and fish are the most common proteins. Campesinos eat *cordero* (mutton), *cabrito* (goat), llama and, on special occasions, *carne de chancho* (pork). The most common *altiplano* fish is *trucha* (trout), which is farmed in Lake Titicaca. The lowlands have a great variety of freshwater fish, including *sábalo*, *dorado* and the delicious *surubí* (catfish). Pizza, fried chicken, hamburgers and *chifas* (Chinese restaurants) provide some variety.

The tastiest Bolivian snack is the *salteña*. These delicious meat and vegetable pasties originated in Salta, Argentina, but achieved perfection in Bolivia. They come stuffed with beef or chicken, olives, egg, potato, onion, peas, carrots and other surprises – watch the squirting juice. *Empanadas*, pillows of dough lined with cheese and deep fried, are toothsome early morning market treats.

Standard meals are *desayuno* (breakfast), *almuerzo* (lunch; the word normally refers to a set meal served at midday) and *cena* (dinner). For *almuerzo*, restaurants – from backstreet cubbyholes to classy establishments – offer bargain set meals consisting of soup, a main course and coffee or tea. In some places, a salad and simple dessert are included. *Almuerzos* cost roughly half the price of à la carte dishes: less than US$1 to US$5, depending

BOLIVIA

on the class of restaurant. Reliable market *comedores* (basic eateries) and street stalls are always the cheapest option.

Some popular Bolivian set-meal standbys include the following:

Chairo Lamb or mutton stew with potatoes, *chuño* and other vegetables.
Fricasé Stew of various meats with ground corn.
Milanesa Breaded and fried beef or chicken cutlets.
Pacumutu Grilled beef (or sometimes fried chicken) chunks.
Pique a lo macho Heap of chopped beef, hot dogs and French fries topped with onions, tomatoes and whatever else.
Saice Spicy meat broth.
Sajta Chicken served in hot pepper sauce.
Silpancho Thinly pounded beef schnitzel.

Drinks
ALCOHOLIC DRINKS
Bolivia's wine region is centered around Tarija. The best label is La Concepción's Cepas de Altura (from the world's highest vineyards). The same winery also produces *singani*, a powerful spirit obtained by distilling grape skins and other by-products. The most popular cocktail is *chuflay*, a refreshing blend of *singani*, 7-Up (or ginger ale), ice and lemon.

Bolivian beers aren't bad either; popular brands include Huari, Paceña, Sureña and Potosina. Beer is ridiculously fizzy at the higher altitudes, where it can be difficult to get the brew from under the foam.

The favorite alcoholic drink of the masses is *chicha cochabambina*, a fermented corn brew. It is made all over Bolivia, especially in the Cochabamba region. Other versions of *chicha*, often nonalcoholic, are made from sweet potato, peanuts, cassava and other fruits and vegetables.

NONALCOHOLIC DRINKS
Beyond the usual coffee, tea and hot chocolate, *mate de coca* (coca leaf tea) is the most common boiled drink. *Api*, a supersweet, hot drink made of maize, lemon and cinnamon, is served in markets; look for *mezclado*, mixed yellow and purple *api*. Major cola brands are available and popular. Don't miss *licuados*, addictive fruit shakes blended with milk or water. Be sure to request the *yapa* or *aumento*: the second serving remaining in the blender. *Zumos* are pure fruit and vegetable juices. *Mocachinchi* is a ubiquitous market drink made from dried fruit and more sugar than water.

GAY & LESBIAN TRAVELERS
Naturally, homosexuality exists in Bolivia. In short, discretion is still in order – even in cities, people are conservative.

Although homosexuality is legal (though the constitution does prohibit same-sex marriages), the overwhelmingly Catholic society in Bolivia tends to both deny and suppress it. To be openly gay can limit social opportunities. Gay bars and venues are limited to the larger cities. Sharing a room in a hotel is no problem as long as you don't request a double bed.

Gay rights lobby groups are active in La Paz (MGLP Libertad), Cochabamba (Dignidad) and most visibly in progressive Santa Cruz. In June 2003 Santa Cruz organization La Comunidad Gay, Lésbica, Bisexual y Travestí (GLBT) replaced their fourth annual Marcha de Colores on Día del Orgullo Gay (Gay Pride Day, June 26) with a health fair called Ciudadanía Sexual in an effort to gain wider public acceptance. In La Paz, watch for flyers advertising drag performances by La Familia Galan, the capital's most fabulous group of cross-dressing queens.

HEALTH
Sanitation and hygiene are not Bolivia's strong suits, so pay attention to what you eat. Most tap water isn't safe to drink; stick to bottled water if your budget allows (your bowels will thank you). Carry iodine if you'll be trekking.

The *altiplano* lies between 3000m and 4000m, and many visitors to La Paz, Copacabana and Potosí will have problems with altitude sickness. Complications like cerebral edema have been the cause of death in otherwise fit, healthy travelers. Diabetics should note that only the Touch II blood glucose meter gives accurate readings at altitudes over 2000m.

Bolivia is officially in a yellow-fever zone, so a vaccination is recommended; it may be obligatory for onward travel (such as Brazil, which requires the certificate). Anyone coming from a yellow-fever infected area needs a vaccination certificate to enter Bolivia. Take precautions against malaria in the lowlands.

While medical facilities might not be exactly what you're used to back home, there are decent hospitals in the biggest cities and passable clinics in most towns (but *not* in remote parts of the country). For more information on altitude sickness and other critical matters, see the Health chapter (p1090).

HOLIDAYS

On major holidays, banks, offices and other services are closed and public transport is often bursting at the seams; book ahead if possible.

Año Nuevo (New Year's Day) January 1.
Día del Trabajador (Labor Day) May 1; watch out for dynamite in plazas.
Días de la Independencia (Independence Days) August 5 to 7.
Día de la Raza (Columbus Day) October 12.
Día de Todos los Santos (All Souls' Day) November 2.
Navidad (Christmas Day) December 25.

Not about to be outdone by their neighbors, each department has its own holiday: February 22 in Oruro, April 1 in Potosí, April 15 in Tarija, May 25 in Chuquisaca, July 16 in La Paz, September 14 in Cochabamba, September 24 in Santa Cruz and Pando, and November 18 in Beni.

INTERNET ACCESS

Nearly every corner of Bolivia has a cybercafé. Rates run from US30¢ to US$1.25 per hour. In smaller towns, check the local Entel office for access.

INTERNET RESOURCES

Bolivia Web (www.boliviaweb.com) Makes a good starting point, with good cultural and artistic links.
Bolivia.com (www.bolivia.com in Spanish) Current news and cultural information.
Enlaces Bolivia (www.enlacesbolivia.net) Reasonable collection of up-to-date links.

LEGAL MATTERS

Regardless of its reputation as the major coca provider, drugs – including cocaine – are highly illegal in Bolivia, and possession and use brings a gaol sentence. Foreign embassies are normally powerless to help (or won't want to know!). In short, don't even think about it.

MAPS

Government topographical and specialty maps are available from the Instituto Geográfico Militar (IGM; see p185 for details). For Cordillera Real and Sajama trekking maps, the contour maps produced by Walter Guzmán are good. Good climbing maps

are published by the Deutscher Alpenverein and distributed internationally. The excellent *New Map of the Cordillera Real,* published by O'Brien Cartographics, is available at various travelers' hangouts. O'Brien also publishes the *Travel Map of Bolivia,* which is about the best country map. South American Explorers distribute the O'Brien maps, plus maps of major cities.

MEDIA
Newspapers & Magazines

Major international English-language news magazines are sold at Amigos del Libro outlets. Bolivian towns with daily newspapers include Cochabamba, La Paz, Potosí and Sucre.

Radio

Bolivia has countless radio stations broadcasting in Spanish, Quechua and Aymara. Recommended listening in La Paz includes noncommercial FM96.5 for folk tunes and FM100.5 if you're after a good English-Spanish-language pop mix. In Cochabamba, Radio Latina at FM97.3 spins a lively mix of Andean folk, salsa and rock. For a good selection of recorded typical music, try **Bolivia Web Radio** (www.boliviaweb.com/radio).

TV

There are two government-run and several private TV stations. Cable (with CNN, ESPN and BBC) is available in most midrange and upmarket hotels.

MONEY

Bolivia's unit of currency is the boliviano (B$), which is divided into 100 centavos. Bolivianos come in 10, 20, 50, 100 and 200 denomination notes; the coins are worth 10, 20 and 50 centavos. Often called pesos (the currency was changed from pesos to bolivianos in 1987), bolivianos are extremely difficult to unload once you're outside the country. See also p20.

ATMs

Just about every sizable town has a *cajero automatico* (ATM). ATMs dispense bolivianos in 50 and 100 notes (sometimes US dollars as well) on Visa, Plus and Cirrus cards. Be aware that some British and European travelers have reported access problems with this system outside of larger cities.

BOLIVIA

Cash

Finding change for bills larger than US$10 is a national pastime as change for larger notes seems to be scarce countrywide. When you're exchanging money or making big purchases, make sure you request small denominations. If you can stand waiting in the lines, most banks will break large bills.

Credit Cards

Brand-name credit cards, such as Visa, MasterCard and (less often) American Express, may be used in larger cities at better hotels, restaurants and tour agencies. Cash advances of up to US$1000 per day are available on Visa (and less often MasterCard) with no commission from Banco de Santa Cruz, Banco Mercantil and Banco Nacional de Bolivia. Travel agencies in towns without ATMs will often provide cash advances for clients for 3% to 5% commission.

Exchanging Money

Visitors generally fare best with US dollars. Currency may be exchanged at *casas de cambio* and at some banks in larger cities. You can often change money in travel agencies. *Cambistas* (street money changers) operate in most cities but only change cash dollars, paying roughly the same as *casas de cambio.* They're convenient after hours, but guard against counterfeits. The rate for cash doesn't vary much from place to place and there is no black-market rate. Currencies of neighboring countries may be exchanged in border areas and at *casas de cambio* in La Paz. Beware of mangled notes; unless both halves of a repaired banknote bear identical serial numbers, the note is worthless.

Exchange rates at press time included the following:

Country	Unit		B$ (boliviano)
Australia	A$1	=	5.98
Canada	C$1	=	7.09
euro zone	€1	=	10.07
Japan	¥100	=	6.71
New Zealand	NZ$1	=	5.30
UK	UK£1	=	14.90
United States	US$1	=	8.03

International Transfers

The fastest way to have money transferred from abroad is with Western Union. It has offices in all major cities but charges hefty fees. Your bank can also wire money to a cooperating Bolivian bank for a smaller fee, but it may take a couple of business days.

Traveler's Checks

The rate for traveler's checks (1% to 3% commission) is best in La Paz, where it nearly equals the rate for cash; in other large cities it's 3% to 5% lower, and in smaller towns it's sometimes impossible to change checks at all. American Express is the most widely accepted.

POST

Even small towns have post offices; some are signposted Ecobol (Empresa Correos de Bolivia). The post is generally reliable from major towns, but when posting anything important, pay the additional US20¢ to have it certified.

Reliable free *lista de correos* (poste restante) is available in larger cities. Mail should be addressed to you c/o Poste Restante, Correo Central, La Paz (or whatever the city), Bolivia. Using only a first initial and capitalizing your entire last name will help to avoid any confusion. Mail is often sorted into foreign and Bolivian stacks, so those with Latin surnames should check the local stack.

A postcard costs from US45¢ to US$1.15 depending on where you are sending it. A 2kg parcel will cost about US$50 to the USA or US$80 by air; to airmail it to Australia costs US$150. Posting by sea is s-l-o-w but considerably cheaper.

RESPONSIBLE TRAVEL

Traveling responsibly in Bolivia is a constant struggle. Trash cans (and recycling bins) are few and far between and ecological sensitivity is a relatively new – but growing – concept. Nearly every tour operator in the country claims to practice 'ecotourism,' but don't take their word for it. The best thing to do is grill agencies about their practices and talk to returning travelers to see if their experiences match the propaganda.

On the level of personal behavior, there are several things you can do to leave minimal impact (or maximize your positive impact) on the country. If you're taking a jungle or pampas tour around Rurrenabaque, request that your guide does not catch or feed wildlife for the benefit of photo opportunities. Before visiting an indigenous community, ask if the guide is from the community or make sure that the agency has permission to visit. On the Salar de Uyuni, encourage drivers to carry garbage and to follow existing tire tracks to minimize damage to the fragile salt flats. In the Beni, don't eat fish out of season and resist the urge to purchase handicrafts made from endangered rain-forest species.

When it comes to dealing with begging, think twice about indiscriminately handing out sweets, cigarettes or money. Instead, teach a game, share a photograph of family or friends, or make a donation (basic medical supplies, pens or notebooks) to an organization working to improve health, sanitation or education. If invited to someone's home for a meal, take something that won't undermine the local culture, such as a handful of coca leaves or fruit.

SHOPPING

Compact discs and cassettes of *peñas,* folk and pop music make good souvenirs. Cassettes, however, may be low-quality bootlegs; higher-quality CDs cost around US$10. Selection is best in La Paz.

Traditional instruments (eg *charangos, zampoñas*) are sold widely throughout the country but avoid buying ones made from endangered armadillos.

Bolivian woven ware is also a good buy. Touristy places such as Calle Sagárnaga (La Paz) and Tarabuco (near Sucre) have the greatest selection, but may be more expensive than buying direct from a craftsperson. Prices vary widely with the age, quality, color and extent of the weaving: a new and simple *manta* might cost US$20, while the finest antique examples will cost several hundred. Another good buy is alpaca goods, either finished or raw wool.

STUDYING

Sucre, Cochabamba and La Paz are all loaded with Spanish schools. Private lessons are starting to catch on in smaller retreats like Sorata and Samaipata. In bigger cities, it's also possible to find one-on-one music, weaving and other arts lessons. Instruction averages around US$5 an hour.

TELEPHONE

Entel, the Empresea Nacional de Telecomunicaciones, has telephone offices in nearly every town (as increasingly does Cotel, Viva and other competing companies), usually open 7am to late. Local calls cost just a few bo-

livianos from these offices. *Puntos* are small, privately-run outposts offering similar services. Street kiosks are often equipped with telephones that charge B$1 for brief local calls.

One-digit area codes change by province: ☎ 2 for La Paz, Oruro and Potosí; ☎ 3 for Santa Cruz, Beni and Pando; and ☎ 4 for Cochabamba, Sucre and Tarija. When making a long distance call from a public telephone, you must dial a '0' before the codes. In this chapter, a 0 has already been added to the codes and these are presented – as two digits – at the start of each town section. Drop the initial code if you're calling within a province. If you're calling from abroad, drop the 0 from the code. If you're ringing a local mobile phone, dial the 8-digit number; if the mobile is from another city, you must first dial a three-digit carrier number. These range from 010 to 021.

Bolivia's country code is ☎ 591. The international direct-dialing access code is 00. Some Entel offices accept reverse-charge (collect) calls; others will give you the office's number and let you be called back. For reverse-charge calls from a private line, ring an international operator (beware that these calls are bank breakers):

Canada (☎ Teleglobe 800-10-0101)
UK (☎ BT 800-10-0044)
USA (☎ AT&T toll-free 800-10-1111, MCI 800-10-2222)

Calls from Entel offices are getting cheaper all the time to the USA (US60¢ per minute), more expensive to Europe (US$1 per minute), Asia, Australia and Oceania (US$1.50 per minute). Reduced rates take effect at night and on weekends. Much cheaper Net2Phone internet call centers, charging US15¢ a minute to the USA and less than US$1 a minute to anywhere else in the world, are springing up in major cities.

TOILETS

Take your 'toilet humor' – stinky *baños publicos* (public toilets) abound. Learn to live with the fact that toilet facilities don't exist in many buses. Carry toilet paper with you wherever you go at all times! That, and learn to hold your breath.

TOURIST INFORMATION

The national tourist authority, the Vice-Ministerio de Turismo, has its head office in La Paz. It assists municipal and departmental

BOLIVIA

tourist offices. These are merely functional and, when open, distribute varying amounts of printed information.

TOURS

Tours are a convenient way to visit a site when you're short on time or motivation, and are frequently the easiest way to visit remote areas. They're also relatively cheap but the cost will depend on the number of people in your group. Popular organized tours include Tiahuanaco, Valle de la Luna, Uyuni, and excursions to remote attractions such as the Cordillera Apolobamba. Arrange organized tours in La Paz or the town closest to the attraction you wish to visit.

There are scores of outfits offering trekking, mountain-climbing and rain-forest adventure packages. For climbing in the Cordilleras, operators offer customized expeditions, including guides, transport, porters, cooks and equipment. Some also rent trekking equipment. Recommended La Paz–based agencies include the following:

America Tours (Map pp190-1; ☎ 02-237-4204; www.america-ecotours.com; Av 16 de Julio 1490, Edificio Av, No 9) Highly recommended English-speaking agency specializing in community-based ecotourism: PN Madidi, PN Sajama, Rurrenabaque and the Salar de Uyuni.

Andean Summits (Map pp190-1; ☎ 02-242-2106; www.andeansummits.com; Aranzaes 2974, Sopocachi) Mountaineering and trekking all over Bolivia, plus adventure tours and archaeology trips.

Colibri (Map pp190-1; ☎ 242-3246; Calle Manuel Caseres 1891; cnr Alberto Ostria) Offers comprehensive trekking, mountaineering, mountain biking, jungle trips and 4WD tours, and also rents gear. French and English spoken.

et-n-ic (Map pp190-1; ☎ 02-246-3782; www.visita bolivia.com; Illampu 863) Recently opened Swiss-run agency. Offers good-quality rental equipment, plus adventure trips to just about anywhere.

Fremen Tours (☎ 02-240-7995; www.andes -amazonia.com; Santa Cruz & Socabaya, Galeria Handal, No 13) Upmarket agency specializing in the Amazon and Chapare; there is also an office in Cochabamba (Map pp228-9; ☎ 04-425-9392; Tumusla 0245).

Gravity Assisted Mountain Biking (Map pp190-1; ☎ 02-231-3849; www.gravitybolivia.com; Av 16 de Julio 1490, Edificio Av, No 10) Downhill mania on two wheels, from the 'World's Most Dangerous Road' to stylin' singletrack. Ask about exploratory adventures. Best to book ahead on the 'net.

Tawa Tours (☎ 02-232-5796; tawa@ceibo.entelnet .bo; Sagárnaga 161) French-speaking company with a wide selection of adventure options including mountaineering, jungle trips, trekking, horse-riding and mountain biking.

Zig-Zag (☎ 245-7814, 715-22822; www.zigzagbolivia .com; Illampu 867) Delightful and knowledgeable English-speaking owner offers trips to Choro and Takesi and is happy to help with custom-made trips. Also rents gear – tents, sleeping bags and boots.

TRAVELERS WITH DISABILITIES

The sad fact is that Bolivia's infrastructure is ill-equipped for disabled travelers. You will, however, see locals overcoming all manner of challenges and obstacles while making their daily rounds. If you encounter difficulties yourself, you're likely to find locals willing to go out of their way to lend a hand.

VISAS

Passports must be valid for one year beyond the date of entry. Entry or exit stamps are free. Attempts at charging should be met with polite refusal; ask for a receipt if the issue is pressed. Always carry a photocopy of your passport (and visa), and if possible, store your valuables safely elsewhere when not in transit.

Bolivian visa requirements can be arbitrarily interpreted. Each Bolivian consulate and border crossing may have its own entry requirements, procedures and idiosyncrasies.

Citizens of most South American and western European countries can get a tourist card on entry for stays up to 90 days. Citizens of the USA, Canada, Australia, New Zealand, Japan, Israel and many other countries are usually granted 30 days; if you want to stay longer, ask at the point of entry for 90 days and officials will likely oblige. Otherwise, you have to extend your tourist card (easily accomplished at the immigration office in any major city; some nationalities pay for extensions) or apply for a visa. Visas are issued by Bolivian consular representatives, including those in neighboring South American countries. Costs vary according to the consulate and the nationality of the applicant: up to US$50 for a one-year multiple-entry visa.

Overstayers can be fined US$2 per day and may face ribbons of red tape at the border or airport when leaving the country. See the website of the **Ministerio de Relaciones Exteriores y Culto** (www.rree.gov.bo) for a complete list (in

Spanish) of overseas representatives and current regulations.

VOLUNTEERING

Volunteer organizations in Bolivia include the following:

Comunidad Inti Wara Yassi (www.intiwarayassi.org; Parque Machía, Villa Tunari, Chapare) Volunteer-run wild-animal refuge. The minimum commitment is 15 days and no previous experience working with animals is required.

Volunteer Bolivia (Map pp228-9; ☎ 04-452-6028; www.volunteerbolivia.org; 342 Ecuador btwn 25 de Mayo & España, Cochabamba) Runs Cafe La Republika cultural center and arranges short- and long-term volunteer work, study and homestay programs throughout Bolivia.

WOMEN TRAVELERS

Women's rights in Bolivia are nearing modern standards. That said, avoid testing the system alone in a bar in a miniskirt. Conservative dress and confidence without arrogance are a must for foreign women. Men are generally more forward and flirtatious in the lowlands than in the *altiplano*.

WORKING

There are many voluntary and nongovernmental organizations working in Bolivia, but travelers looking for paid work shouldn't hold their breath. Qualified English teachers can try the professionally run Centro Boliviano-Americano (see p187) in La Paz; there are also offices in other cities. New, and as yet unqualified, teachers must forfeit two months' salary in return for their training. Better paying are private-school positions teaching math, science or social studies. Accredited teachers can expect to earn up to US$500 per month for a full-time position.

BOLIVIA

Brazil

HIGHLIGHTS

- **Rio de Janeiro** – watch the people-parade on lovely Ipanema beach, explore bohemian Santa Teresa and find your groove at wild samba clubs in Lapa (p280)
- **Salvador** – spend your days strolling colorful Pelourinho and your nights dancing to seriously addictive beats in the steamy capital of Afro-Brazilian culture (p339)
- **Ouro Prêto** – wander the cobblestone streets in search of haunted churches and rare *cachaças* (sugarcane rums) in one of South America's most beautiful colonial towns (p310)
- **Pantanal** – get a taste of the wildlife, from monkeys and macaws to caiman and capybaras, in this incredibly biodiverse region (p332)
- **Off the beaten track** – visit the white-sand beaches of Caribbean-esque Alter do Chão, deep in the heart of the Amazon (p387)
- **Best journey** – roll past sand dunes and splash through creeks, ducking palms as the untouched landscape unfolds around you, on the epic 4WD journey from Tutóia to Parque Nacional dos Lençóis Maranhenses (p373)

FAST FACTS

- **Area:** 8,456,510 sq km (about the size of the continental United States)
- **Best bargain:** people-watching on the beach (never a cover charge, always fun)
- **Best street snack:** *agua de coco* (coconut water)
- **Budget:** US$35-45 a day
- **Capital:** Brasília
- **Costs:** double room in a comfy *pousada* (hotel) US$30, bus ride from Rio to Ouro Prêto US$13
- **Country code:** ☎ 55
- **Famous for:** Carnaval, the Amazon, music, soccer, beaches
- **Languages:** Portuguese and 180 indigenous languages
- **Money:** US$1 = 2.2 reais
- **Phrases:** *legal, bacana* (cool), *repugnante* (disgusting), *festa* (party)
- **Population:** 188 million
- **Time:** GMT minus 3hr to minus 5hr, depending on the region

- **Tipping:** 10% in restaurants, often included
- **Visas:** many nationalities require visas (US$40-100), which must be arranged in advance (p407)

TRAVEL HINTS

Eat well (and cheaply) at Brazil's many per-kilo restaurants. School yourself in the varieties of Brazilian buses (p279).

OVERLAND ROUTES

Brazil's many border crossings include Oiapoque (French Guiana); Bonfim (Guyana); Boa Vista (Venezuela); Tabatinga (Colombia and Peru); Brasiléia, Guajará-Mirim, Cáceres and Corumbá (Bolivia); Ponta Porã (Paraguay); Foz do Iguaçu (Paraguay and Argentina); Chuí (Uruguay).

Sprawling across half of South America, Brazil has captivated travelers for at least 500 years. Powdery white-sand beaches, lined with palm trees and fronting a deep blue Atlantic, stretch for more than 7000km. Dotting this coastline are tropical islands, music-filled metropolises and enchanting colonial towns. Inland, Brazil offers dazzling sights of a different flavor: majestic waterfalls, red-rock canyons, and crystal-clear rivers – all just a small part of the natural beauty. Its larger and more famous attractions are the Amazon and the Pantanal, the pair hosting some of the greatest biodiversity on the planet. Wildlife-watching is simply astounding here, as is the opportunity for adventure – though you needn't go to the jungle to find it. Kayaking, rafting, trekking, snorkeling and surfing are just a few ways to spend a sun-drenched afternoon in nearly any region in Brazil.

Some of the world's most exciting cities lie inside of Brazil's borders, and travelers need not come to Carnaval to experience the music, dance and revelry that pack so many calendar nights. Given the country's innumerable charms, the only drawback to traveling in Brazil is a logistical (and financial) one: you simply won't want to leave.

CURRENT EVENTS

As Brazil welcomed the world to the 2007 Pan-American Games in Rio de Janeiro, the country had much to celebrate. Its economy, the world's eighth largest, was booming. In fact, before 2006 Brazil paid off its debts to the UN, the IMF and the Paris Club *ahead* of schedule. Brazil, the buzzword of foreign investors, seemed more stable than ever, and in trade talks with both the US and other developing nations, the country was clearly carving a new place for itself in the world. In terms of energy, Brazil produces enough oil to meet over 90% of its needs, and as gasoline prices reach staggering heights, many Brazilian motorists run their cars on the less-polluting lower-cost alternative of plant-derived alcohol.

Despite its successes, Brazil has serious problems, with a long list of woes. Millions of Brazilians still live in abject poverty. Meanwhile, crime continues to flare throughout the country, even as the divide between rich and poor remains absurd: 1% of citizens own half the land. Whether the government can address these seemingly relentless problems will play no small role in Brazil's future in years to come.

HISTORY
The Tribal Peoples

Little is known of Brazil's first inhabitants, but from the few fragments left behind (mostly pottery, trash mounds and skeletons), archeologists estimate that the first humans may have arrived 50,000 years ago, predating any other estimates in the whole American continent.

The population at the time of the Portuguese landing in 1500 is also a mystery, and estimates range from two to six million. There were likely over 1000 tribes living as nomadic hunter-gatherers or in more settled, agricultural societies. Life was punctuated by frequent tribal warfare and at times, captured enemies were ceremonially killed and eaten after battle.

When the Portuguese first arrived, they had little interest in the natives, who were viewed as a Stone-Age people; and the heavily forested land offered nothing for the European market. All that changed when Portuguese merchants expressed interest in the red dye from brazilwood (which later gave the colony its name), and slowly colonists arrived to harvest the land.

The natural choice for the work, of course, was the Indians. Initially the natives welcomed the strange, smelly foreigners and offered them their labor, their food and their women in exchange for the awe-inspiring metal tools and the fascinating Portuguese liquor. But soon the newcomers abused the Indians' customs, took their best land, and ultimately enslaved them.

The Indians fought back and won many battles, but the tides were against them. When colonists discovered that sugarcane grew well in the colony, the Indians' labor was more valuable than ever and soon the sale of Indian slaves became Brazil's second-largest commercial enterprise. It was an industry dominated by *bandeirantes*, brutal men who hunted the Indians in the interior and captured or killed them. Their exploits, more than any treaty, secured the huge interior of South America for Portuguese Brazil.

Jesuit priests went to great lengths to protect the Indians, a few even arming them and

BRAZIL

BRAZIL

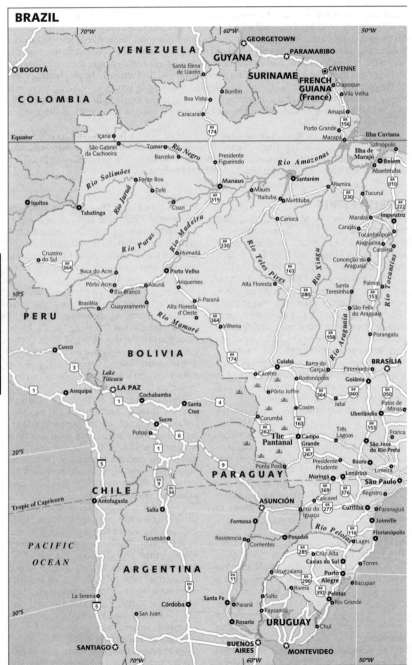

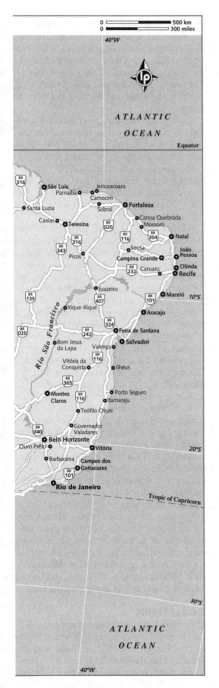

fighting alongside them against *bandeirante* incursions. But they were too weak to stymie the attacks (and the Jesuits were later expelled from Brazil in 1759). Indians who didn't die at the hands of the colonists often died from introduced European diseases.

The Africans

During the 17th century African slaves replaced Indian prisoners on the plantations. From 1550 until 1888 about 3.5 million slaves were shipped to Brazil – almost 40% of the total that came to the New World. The Africans were considered better workers and were less vulnerable to European diseases, but they resisted slavery strongly. *Quilombos*, communities of runaway slaves, formed throughout the colonial period. They ranged from *mocambos*, small groups hidden in the forests, to the great republic of Palmares, which survived much of the 17th century. Led by the African king Zumbí, Palmares had 20,000 residents at its height.

More than 700 villages that formed as *quilombos* remain in Brazil today, their growth only stopped by abolition itself, in 1888.

Those who survived life on the plantation sought solace in their African religion and culture through song and dance. The slaves were given perfunctory instruction in Catholicism and a syncretic religion rapidly emerged (see Religion p272). Spiritual elements from many African tribes, such as the Yorubá, were preserved and made palatable to slave masters by adopting a facade of Catholic saints. Such were the roots of modern Candomblé and Macumba, prohibited by law until recently.

Life on the plantations was miserable, but an even worse fate awaited many slaves. In the 1690s gold was discovered in present day Minas Gerais, and soon the rush was on. Wild boomtowns like Vila Rica de Ouro Prêto (Rich Town of Black Gold) sprang up in the mountain valleys. Immigrants flooded the territory, and countless slaves were brought from Africa to dig and die in Minas.

The Portuguese

For years, the ruling powers of Portugal viewed the colony of Brazil as little more than a moneymaking enterprise. That attitude changed, however, when Napoleon marched on Lisbon in 1807. The prince regent (later known as Dom João VI) immediately transferred his court to Brazil. He stayed on even after Napoleon's Waterloo in 1815, and when he became king in 1816 he declared Rio de Janeiro the capital of a united kingdom of Brazil and Portugal, making Brazil the only New World colony to serve as the seat of a European monarch. In 1821, Dom João finally returned to Portugal, leaving his son Pedro in Brazil as regent.

The following year the Portuguese parliament attempted to return Brazil to colonial status. According to legend Pedro responded by pulling out his sword and shouting out 'Independência ou morte!' (Independence or death), crowning himself Emperor Dom Pedro I. Portugal was too weak to fight its favorite colony, so Brazil attained independence without bloodshed.

Dom Pedro I ruled for nine years. He scandalized the country by siring a string of illegitimate children, and was finally forced to abdicate in favor of his five-year-old son, Dom Pedro II. Until the future emperor reached adolescence, Brazil suffered a period of civil war. In 1840 Dom Pedro II ascended the throne with overwhelming public support. During his 50-year reign he nurtured an increasingly powerful parliamentary system, went to war with Paraguay, meddled in Argentine and Uruguayan affairs, encouraged mass immigration, abolished slavery and ultimately forged a state that would do away with the monarchy forever.

The Brazilians
During the 19th century coffee replaced sugar as Brazil's primary export, at one time supplying three-quarters of world demand. With mechanization and the building of Brazil's first railroads, profits soared and the coffee barons gained enormous influence.

In 1889 a coffee-backed military coup toppled the antiquated empire, sending the emperor into exile. The new Brazilian Republic adopted a constitution modeled on the USA's, and for nearly 40 years Brazil was governed by a series of military and civilian presidents through which the armed forces effectively ruled the country.

One of the first challenges to the new republic came from a small religious community in the northeast. An itinerant holy man named Antônio Conselheiro had wandered for years through poverty-stricken backlands, prophesying the appearance of the Antichrist and the end of the world. He railed against the new government and in 1893 gathered his followers in the settlement of Canudos. Suspecting a plot to return Brazil to the Portuguese monarchy, the government attempted to subdue the rebels. It succeeded only on the fourth try, in the end killing every man, woman and child and burning the town to the ground.

Coffee remained king until the market collapsed during the global economic crisis of 1929. The weakened planters of São Paulo, who controlled the government, and an opposition alliance formed with the support of nationalist military officers. When their presidential candidate, Getúlio Vargas, lost the 1930 elections, the military seized power and handed him the reins.

Vargas proved a gifted maneuverer, and dominated the political scene for 20 years. At times his regime was inspired by the Italian and Portuguese fascist states of Mussolini and Salazar: he banned political parties, imprisoned opponents and censored the press. He remained in and out of the political scene until 1954, when the military called for him to step down. Vargas responded by writing a letter to the people of Brazil, then shooting himself in the heart.

Juscelino Kubitschek, the first of Brazil's big spenders, was elected president in 1956. His motto was '50 years' progress in five.' His critics responded with '40 years of inflation in four.' The critics were closer to the mark, owing to the huge debt Kubitschek incurred during the construction of Brasília. By the early 1960s, inflation gripped the Brazilian economy, and Castro's victory in Cuba had spread fears of communism. Brazil's fragile democracy was crushed in 1964 when the military overthrew the government.

Brazil remained under the repressive military regime for almost 20 years. Throughout much of this time the economy grew substantially, at times borrowing heavily from international banks. But it exacted a heavy toll on the country. Ignored social problems grew dire. Millions came to the cities, and *favelas* (shantytowns) spread at exponential rates.

Recent Events
November 1989 saw the first presidential election by popular vote in nearly 30 years. Voters elected Fernando Collor de Mello over the socialist Luíz da Silva ('Lula'). Collor promised to fight corruption and reduce inflation,

but in 1992 he was removed from office on charges of corruption – accused of heading a group that siphoned more than US$1 billion from the economy.

Itamar Franco replaced Collor and introduced a new currency, the *real*, which sparked an economic boom. Franco's finance minister, Fernando Henrique Cardoso, later won a landslide presidential victory riding the *real's* success.

Cardoso presided through the mid-1990s over a growing economy and record foreign investment, and small efforts were made toward education, land reform and antipoverty measures. But by the end of Cardoso's office, the problems facing the country were considerable.

Corruption and violent crime was rife. In the late 1990s murders were running at 700 a month in greater São Paulo, making it (along with Rio de Janeiro) among the most violent cities on earth. Fifty million Brazilians lived in serious poverty.

Given the numbers, it's not surprising that sooner or later a presidential candidate would campaign solely on a platform of social reform. In 2002 Lula, running for the fourth time, won the presidency. From a humble working-class background, Lula rose to become a trade unionist and a strike leader in the early 1980s. He later founded the Workers Party (PT), a magnet for his many followers seeking social reform.

His accession initially alarmed investors, who had envisioned a left-leaning renegade running the economy amok. In fact, he surprised friends and foes alike with one of the most financially prudent administrations in years, while still addressing Brazil's egregious social problems. Lula's antipoverty program of Fome Zero (Zero Hunger) collapsed under poor management, though its successor Bolsa Familia (Family Purse) did bring hardship relief to more than eight million people. Lula has made employment a top priority, and an estimated three million jobs were added under his watch. Lula also raised the minimum wage by 25%, which had an immediate impact on many working families.

Unfortunately, Lula's administration had some setbacks, including a wide-reaching corruption scandal. The most serious allegation (with one official caught on videotape): monthly bribes (of up to US$12,000) were paid to lawmakers by PT (Lula's party) so that they would vote in line with PT initiatives. A huge shake-up in the government followed, with a number of PT members resigning in disgrace. The scandal never quite touched Lula, who apologized to the country and repeatedly claimed his innocence. Lula remains popular despite the scandal, and he continues to champion an optimistic future for Brazil.

THE CULTURE
The National Psyche

Despite the country's social and economic woes, Brazilians take much pride in their country. The gorgeous landscape is a favorite topic, and although every Brazilian has a different notion of where to find paradise on earth, it will almost certainly be located within the country's borders. Soccer is another source of pride – less the national pastime than a countrywide narcotic to which every Brazilian seems to be addicted.

Famed for their Carnaval, Brazilians love to celebrate, and parties happen year-round. But it isn't all samba and beaches in the land of the tropics. At times, Brazilians suffer from *saudade*, a nostalgic, often deeply melancholic longing for something. The idea appears in many works by Jobim, Moraes and other great songwriters, and it manifests itself in many forms – from the dull ache of homesickness to the deep regret over past mistakes.

When Brazilians aren't dancing the samba or drowning in sorrow, they're often helping each other out. Kindness is both commonplace and expected, and even a casual introduction can lead to deeper friendships. This altruism comes in handy in a country noted for its bureaucracy and long lines. There's the official way of doing things, then there's the *jeitinho*, or the little way around it, and a little kindness – and a few friends – can go a long way. One need only have patience, something Brazilians seem to have no shortage of.

Lifestyle

Although Brazil has the world's eighth-largest economy, with abundant resources and developed infrastructure, the living standard varies wildly. Brazil has one of the world's widest income gaps between rich and poor.

Since the mass urban migration in the mid-19th century, the poorest have lived in *favelas* that surround every city. Many dwellings consist of little more than a few boards pounded together, and access to clean water, sewage and healthcare are luxuries few *favelas* enjoy. Drug lords rule the streets, and crime is rampant.

The rich often live just a stone's throw away, sometimes separated by nothing more than a highway. Many live in modern fortresses, with security walls and armed guards, enjoying a lifestyle not unlike the upper classes in Europe and America.

Carnaval brings the two together – albeit in different ways. The *favelas* take center stage, parading through the streets, while the rich enjoy the spectacle; and everyone racks up a few sins before Lent brings it all to a close.

Population

In Brazil the diversity of the landscape matches that of the people inhabiting it. Officially 55% of the population is white, 6% black, 38% mixed and 1% other, but the numbers little represent the many shades and types of Brazil's rich melting pot. Indians, Portuguese, Africans (brought to Brazil as slaves) and their mixed-blood offspring made up the population until the late 19th century. Since then there have been waves of immigration by Italians, Spaniards, Germans, Japanese, Russians, Lebanese and others.

Immigration is only part of the picture when considering Brazil's diversity. Brazilians are more prone to mention regional types when speaking of the racial collage. *Caboclos*, who are descendants of the Indians, live along the rivers in the Amazon region and keep alive the traditions and stories of their ancestors. *Gaúchos* (herdsmen) populate Rio Grande do Sul, speak a Spanish-inflected Portuguese and can't quite shake the reputation for being rough-edged cowboys. By contrast, *baianos*, descendants of the first Africans in Brazil, are stereotyped for being the most extroverted and celebratory of Brazilians. And let's not forget *cariocas* (residents of Rio), *paulistanos* (who inhabit Rio's rival city, São Paolo), *mineiros* (who come from the colonial towns of Minas Gerais), and *sertanejos* (denizens of the drought-stricken *sertão*). These groups represent but a handful of the many types that make up the Brazilian soul.

SPORTS

Futebol (soccer) is a national passion. Most people acknowledge that Brazilians play the world's most creative, artistic and thrilling style of football, and Brazil is the only country

to have won five World Cups (1958, 1962, 1970, 1994 and 2002). Games are an intense spectacle – one of the most colorful pageants you're likely to see. Tickets typically cost between US$3 and US$10. The season goes on nearly all year, with the national championship running from late July to mid-December. Local newspapers as well as the daily *Jornal dos Sports* and the website www.netgol.com list upcoming games. Major clubs include Botafogo, Flamengo, Fluminense and Vasco da Gama (all of Rio de Janeiro); Corinthians, Palmeiras and São Paulo (all of São Paulo); and Bahia (of Salvador), Sport (of Recife) and Cruzeiro (of Belo Horizonte).

RELIGION

Brazil is officially a Catholic country, but embraces diversity and syncretism. Without much difficulty you can find churchgoing Catholics who attend spiritualist gatherings or appeal for help at a *terreiro* (the house of an Afro-Brazilian religious group).

Brazil's principal religious roots comprise the animism of the indigenous people, Catholicism and African religions introduced by slaves. The latest arrival is evangelical Christianity, which is spreading all over Brazil, especially in poorer areas.

The Afro-Brazilian religions emerged when the colonists prohibited slaves from practicing their native religions. Not so easily deterred, the slaves simply gave Catholic names to their African gods and continued to worship them. The most orthodox of the religions is Candomblé. Rituals take place in the Yoruba language in a *casa de santo or terreiro*, directed by a *pai de santo* or *mãe de santo* (literally, 'a saint's father or mother' – the Candomblé priests).

Candomblé gods are known as *orixás* and each person is believed to be protected by one of them. In Bahia and Rio, followers of Afro-Brazilian cults turn out in huge numbers to attend festivals at the year's end – especially those held during the night of 31 December and on New Year's Day. Millions of Brazilians go to the beach at this time to pay homage to *Iemanjá*, the sea goddess, whose alter ego is the Virgin Mary.

ARTS

Brazilian culture has been shaped by the Portuguese, who gave the country its language and religion, and also by the indigenous population, immigrants and Africans.

The influence of the latter is particularly strong, especially in the northeast where African religion, music and cuisine have all profoundly influenced Brazilian identity.

Architecture

Brazil's most impressive colonial architecture dazzles visitors in cities like Salvador, Olinda, São Luís, Ouro Prêto, Diamantina and Tiradentes. Over the centuries, the names of two architects stand out: Aleijadinho, the genius of 18th-century baroque in Minas Gerais mining towns (he was also a master sculptor; see p313) and Oscar Niemeyer, the 20th-century modernist-functionalist who was chief architect for the new capital, Brasília, in the 1950s and designed many other striking buildings around the country.

Visual Arts

The photographer Sebastião Salgado is Brazil's best-known contemporary artist outside the country. Noted for his masterful use of light, Salgado has earned international acclaim for his highly evocative black-and-white photographs of migrant workers and others on the margins of society.

The best-known Brazilian painter is Cândido Portinari (1903–62) who early in his career made a decision to paint only Brazil and its people. He was strongly influenced by Mexican muralists like Diego Rivera.

Cinema

Brazil's large film industry has produced a number of good films over the years. One of the most recent hits is the 2005 *Dois Filhos do Francisco* (*The Two Sons of Francisco*), based on the true story of two brothers who rise from poverty to become successful country musicians.

For a trip back to 1930s Rio, check out *Madame Satã* (2002). Rio's gritty red-light district at the time is the setting for the true story of Madame Satã (aka João Francisco dos Santos), the troubled but good-hearted transvestite, singer, *capoeira* master and symbol of Lapa's midcentury bohemianism.

One of Brazil's top directors, Fernando Meirelles, earned his credibility with *Cidade de Deus* (*City of God*), which showed the brutality of a Rio *favela*. Following his success with *Cidade de Deus*, Meirelles went Hollywood with *Constant Gardener* (2004), an intriguing conspiracy film shot in Africa.

Eu, Tu, Eles (*Me, You, Them*, 2000), Andrucha Waddington's social comedy about a Northeasterner with three husbands, has beautiful cinematography and a score by Gilberto Gil.

Walter Salles, one of Brazil's best-known directors, won much acclaim (and an Oscar) for *Central do Brasil* (*Central Station*; 1998), the story of a lonely woman accompanying a young homeless boy in search of his father.

Salles' latest foray is his bio-epic *Diarios de Motocicleta* (The Motorcycle Diaries, 2004), portraying the historic journey of Che Guevara and Alberto Granada across South America.

For a taste of the dictatorship days see Bruno Barreto's *O Que É Isso Companheiro* (released as *Four Days in September* in the US, 1998), based on the 1969 kidnapping of the US ambassador to Brazil by leftist guerrillas.

Another milestone in Brazilian cinema is the visceral film *Pixote* (1981), which shows life through the eyes of a street kid in Rio. When it was released, it was a damning indictment of Brazilian society.

Carlos Diegues' *Bye Bye Brasil* (1980) chronicles the adventures of a theater troupe as they tour the entire country. It charts the profound changes in Brazilian society of the second half of the 20th century.

One of the old classics is *Orfeu Negro* (*Black Orpheus*), Marcel Camus' 1959 film. Set during Carnaval, it opened the world's ears to bossa nova by way of the Jobim and Bonfá soundtrack.

Literature

Joaquim Maria Machado de Assis (1839–1908), the son of a freed slave, is one of Brazil's early great writers. Assis had a great sense of humor and an insightful – though cynical – take on human affairs. His major novels were *Quincas Borba, The Posthumous Memoirs of Bras Cubas* and *Dom Casmurro*.

Jorge Amado (1912–2001), Brazil's most celebrated contemporary writer, wrote brilliantly clever portraits of the people and places of Bahia, notably *Gabriela, Clove and Cinnamon* and *Dona Flor and her Two Husbands*.

Paulo Coelho is Latin America's second-most-read novelist (after Gabriel García Márquez). His new-age fables *The Alchemist* and *The Pilgrimage* launched his career in the mid-1990s.

Chico Buarque, better known for songwriting, has written several books. *Budapest*, his best and most recent novel, is an imaginative portrait of both his hometown of Rio de Janeiro and Budapest.

Music & Dance

Music is as integral to Brazilians as sleeping and eating.

Samba, a Brazilian institution, has strong African influences and is intimately linked to Carnaval. The most popular form of samba today is *pagode*, a relaxed, informal genre whose leading exponents include singers Beth Carvalho, Jorge Aragão and Zeca Pagodinho.

Bossa nova, another Brazilian trademark, arose in the 1950s, and gained the world's attention in the classic *The Girl from Ipanema*, composed by Antônio Carlos Jobim, and Vinícius de Moraes. Bossa nova's founding father, guitarist João Gilberto, still performs, as does his daughter Bebel Gilberto who has sparked renewed interest in the genre, combining smooth bossa sounds with electronic grooves.

Tropicalismo, which burst onto the scene in the late 1960s, mixed varied Brazilian musical styles with North American rock and pop. Leading figures such as Gilberto Gil and Caetano Veloso are still very much around. Gil, in fact, is Brazil's Minister of Culture. Another brilliant songwriter not to overlook is Chico Buarque, recently nominated Brazil's musician of the century by the weekly journal *Isto É*.

The nebulous term Música Popular Brasileira (MPB) covers a range of styles from original bossa nova–influenced works to some sickly pop. MPB first emerged in the 1970s under talented musicians like Edu Lobo, Milton Nascimento, Elis Regina, Djavan and dozens of others.

Jorge Benjor is another singer whose early career in the 1960s has survived up to the present. Known for writing addictive rhythms, Benjor uses African beats and elements of funk, samba and blues in his eclectic songs.

The list of emerging talents gets longer each day, but Brazilian hip-hop is reaching its stride with talented musicians like Marcelo D2 (formerly of Planet Hemp) impressing audiences with albums like *A Procura da Batida Perfeita* (2005). Seu Jorge, who starred in Cidade de Deus, has also earned accolades for the release of *Cru* (2005), an inventive hip-hop album with politically charged beats.

Brazilian rock (pronounced 'hock') is also popular. Groups and artists such as Zeca Baleiro, Kid Abelha, Ed Motta, the punk-driven Legião Urbana and the reggae-based Skank are worth a listen.

Wherever you go in Brazil you'll also hear regional musical styles. The most widely known is *forró* (foh-*hoh*), a lively, syncopated northeastern music, which mixes *zabumba* (an African drum) beats with accordion sounds. Stars of this style include Luiz Gonzaga, Jackson do Pandeiro and São Paulo *forró* group Falamansa. *Axé* is a label for the samba-pop-rock-reggae-funk-Caribbean fusion music that emerged from Salvador in the 1990s, popularized especially by the flamboyant Daniela Mercury. In the Amazon, you'll encounter the rhythms of *carimbó*, along with the sensual dance that accompanies it.

ENVIRONMENT
The Land

The world's fifth-largest country after Russia, Canada, China and the USA, Brazil borders every other South American country except Chile and Ecuador. Its 8.5 million sq km area covers almost half the continent.

Brazil has four primary geographic regions: the coastal band, the Planalto Brasileiro, the Amazon Basin and the Paraná-Paraguai Basin.

The narrow, 7400km-long coastal band lies between the Atlantic Ocean and the coastal mountain ranges. From the border with Uruguay to Bahia state, steep mountains often come right down to the coast. North of Bahia, the coastal lands are flatter.

The Planalto Brasileiro (Brazilian Plateau) extends over most of Brazil's interior south of the Amazon Basin. It's sliced by several large rivers and punctuated by mountain ranges reaching no more than 3000m.

The thinly populated Amazon Basin, composing 42% of Brazil, is fed by waters from the Planalto Brasileiro to its south, the Andes to the west and the Guyana shield to the north. In the west the basin is 1300km wide; in the east, between the Guyana shield and the *planalto*, it narrows to 100km. More than half the 6275km of the Rio Amazonas lies in Peru, where its source is found. The Amazon and its 1100 tributaries contain an estimated 20% of the world's freshwater. Pico da Neblina (3014m) on the Venezuelan border is the highest peak in Brazil.

The Paraná-Paraguai Basin, in the south of Brazil, extends into neighboring Paraguay and Argentina and includes the large wetland area known as the Pantanal.

Wildlife

Brazil has more known species of plants (55,000), freshwater fish (3000) and mammals (520 plus) than any other country in the world. It ranks third for birds (1622) and fifth for reptiles (468). Many species live in the Amazon rainforest, which occupies 3.6 million sq km in Brazil and 2.4 million sq km in neighboring countries. It's the world's largest tropical forest and most biologically diverse ecosystem, with 20% of the world's bird and plant species and 10% of its mammals.

Other Brazilian species are widely distributed around the country. For example the biggest Brazilian cat, the jaguar, is found in Amazon and Atlantic rainforests, the *cerrado* (savanna) and the Pantanal.

Many other Brazilian mammals are found over a broad range of habitats, including five other big cats (puma, ocelot, margay, oncilla and jaguarundi); the giant anteater; several varieties of sloths (best seen in Amazonia) and armadillos; 75 primate species, including several types of howler and capuchin monkey, the squirrel monkey (Amazonia's most common primate) and around 20 small species of marmosets and tamarin; the furry, long-nosed coati (a type of raccoon); the giant river otter; the maned wolf; the tapir; peccaries (like wild boar); marsh and pampas deer; the capybara (the world's largest rodent at 1m in length); the pink dolphin, often glimpsed in the Amazon and its tributaries; and the Amazon manatee, an even larger river dweller.

Birds form a major proportion of the wildlife you'll see. The biggest is the flightless, 1.4m-high rhea, found in the *cerrado* and Pantanal. The brilliantly colored parrots, macaws, toucans and trogons come in dozens of species. In Amazonia or the Pantanal you may well see scarlet macaws and, if you're lucky, blue-and-yellow ones. Unfortunately, the macaws' beautiful plumage makes them a major target for poachers.

In Amazonia or the Pantanal you can't miss the alligators. One of Brazil's five species, the black caiman, grows up to 6m long. Other aquatic life in the Amazon includes the *pirarucú*, which grows 3m long. Its red and silvery-brown scale patterns are reminiscent of Chinese paintings. The infamous piranha comes in about 50 species, found in the basins of Amazon, Orinoco, Paraguai or São Francisco rivers or rivers of the Guianas. Only a handful of species pose a risk, and confirmed accounts of human fatalities caused by piranhas are *extremely* rare.

National Parks

Over 350 areas are protected as national parks, state parks or extractive reserves. Good parks for observing fauna, flora and/or dramatic landscapes:

Parque Nacional da Chapada Diamantina (p347) Rivers, waterfalls, caves and swimming holes make for excellent trekking in this mountainous region in the northeast.

Parque Nacional da Chapada dos Guimarães (p336) On a rocky plateau northeast of Cuiabá, this canyon park features breathtaking views and impressive rock formations.

Parque Nacional da Chapada dos Veadeiros (p332) 200km north of Brasília, among waterfalls and natural swimming holes, this hilly national park features an array of rare flora and fauna.

Parque Nacional da Serra dos Órgãos (p298) Set in the mountainous terrain in the southeast, this park is a mecca for rock climbers and mountaineers.

Parque Nacional de Aparados da Serra (p323) Famous for its narrow canyon with 700m escarpments, this park in the southeast features hiking trails with excellent overlooks.

Parque Nacional dos Lençóis Maranhenses (p377) Spectacular beaches, mangroves, dunes and lagoons comprise the landscape of this park in the northeast.

Reserva de Desenvolvimento Sustentável Mamirauá (p393) Deep in Amazonia, the wildlife viewing is spectacular at this tropical rainforest reserve north of Manaus.

Environmental Issues

Sadly, Brazil is as renowned for its forests as it is for destroying them. At last count more than one-fifth of the Brazilian Amazon rainforest had been completely destroyed. All its major ecosystems are threatened and more than 70 mammals are endangered.

Although deforestation has slowed in recent years, the forest is still on a fast track to oblivion (*only* 9000 sq km of forest was chopped down in 2005 compared to 18,000 sq km the year before). In 2005, the Amazon also suffered its worst drought in 100 years. River levels dropped dramatically, killing off fish and stranding boats and whole villages. The drought also caused major forest fires, destroyed crops and wreaked economic havoc.

BRAZIL

Some scientists attribute this catastrophic drought to global warming and suggest dire environmental problems like these will occur more frequently as surface and sea-level temperatures around the world continue to rise.

Brazil first began chopping down the forest on a grand scale in the 1970s when the government cleared roads through the jungle in order to give drought-stricken northeasterners a chance to better their lives on newly created cropland of Amazonia. Along with the new arrivals came loggers and cattle ranchers, both of whom further cleared the forests. The few settlers that remained (most gave up and moved to the *favelas* of Amazonia's growing cities) widely employed slash-and-burn agriculture with devastating consequences.

The government continues development projects in the Amazon, although the protests have become more vocal in recent years. In 2005 a Roman Catholic Bishop went on a hunger strike to protest the government's US$2 billion plan to divert water from the São Francisco River to help big agricultural businesses. President Lula declared a temporary halt to the project and agreed to open dialogue about the controversial project.

Deforestation has led to some unexpected consequences. Dozens of people have died from rabid vampire bats in the Amazon, with thousands more treated for rabies. Some experts blame these attacks on the forest's destruction. As the bats' natural habitat is destroyed, the bats are forced into more populated areas.

TRANSPORTATION

GETTING THERE & AWAY

Brazil has several gateway airports and shares a border with every country in South America except Chile and Ecuador.

Air

The busiest international airports are Aeroporto Galeão (formally known as Aeroporto Internacional António Carlos Jobim) in Rio de Janeiro (p280) and São Paulo's Aeroporto Guarulhos (p304). Brazil's bankrupt main carrier, **Varig** (www.varig.com), was still operating at the time of research, though it was continuing to cancel flights, sometimes with little advance notice. Varig flies into Brazil from 11 South American cities. Better deals, however, are usually found on Gol Airlines

(www.voegol.com.br), which flies to six other South American cities.

For student fares, try the **Student Travel Bureau** (STB; Map p286; ☎ 0xx21-2512-8577; www.stb.com.br; Rua Visconde de Pirajá 550, Ipanema, Rio), which has some 30 branches around the country. **Andes Sol** (☎ 0xx21-2275-4370; Av NS de Copacabana 209, Rio) arranges economical itineraries.

A Brazilian website to search for cheap flights is www.viajo.com.br.

ARGENTINA
Round-trip flights from Buenos Aires to Rio or São Paulo are available on Varig, Gol or Aerolíneas Argentinas. Other flights from Buenos Aires go to Porto Alegre, Curitiba, Florianópolis and Puerto Iguazú in Argentina, a short cross-border hop from Foz do Iguaçu.

BOLIVIA
Gol flies from Santa Cruz to Campo Grande (and onto São Paulo). Varig, TAM and Lloyd Aéreo Boliviano (LAB) fly from Santa Cruz to São Paulo. LAB also flies from Santa Cruz and Cochabamba to Manaus.

Inside Bolivia, Aerosur and Aerocon fly from other Bolivian cities to Cobija, Guayaramerin and Puerto Suárez, across the border from the Brazilian towns of Brasiléia, Guajará-Mirim and Corumbá respectively.

CHILE
Varig, TAM and LanChile fly from Santiago to Rio and São Paulo.

COLOMBIA
AeroRepública flies from Bogotá to Leticia, from where you can walk, taxi or take a *combi* (minibus) across the border into Tabatinga, Brazil. A Rio–Bogotá round-trip flight on Varig or Avianca is costly.

ECUADOR
Flights from Quito or Guayaquil to São Paulo are pricey, and none are direct.

DEPARTURE TAX

The international departure tax from Brazil is a hefty US$36, which is usually included in the price of your ticket. If not, you must pay it in cash (either in US dollars or reais) at the airport before departure – so remember to keep that amount in reserve.

THE GUIANAS

Meta, a Brazilian regional airline, flies from Georgetown (Guyana), Paramaribo (Suriname) and Cayenne (French Guiana) to Belém and Boa Vista. French Guiana carrier Air Caraïbes also flies between Belém and Cayenne. Puma, a Brazilian carrier, flies from Macapá to Oiapoque, just across the border from St Georges, French Guiana.

PARAGUAY

Varig flies between Asunción and Rio or São Paulo. Gol flies from Asunción to Curitiba. You can also fly from Asunción to Ciudad del Este, a short cross-border hop from Foz do Iguaçu, Brazil.

PERU

Varig flies from Lima to Rio or São Paulo. From Iquitos, Peru, Peruvian airliner Aviaselva flies to Leticia, Colombia on the Brazil–Peru–Colombia triple frontier.

URUGUAY

Varig and Pluna fly from Montevideo to Rio and São Paulo. Gol flies from Montevideo to Porto Alegre.

VENEZUELA

A Varig round-trip flight from Caracas to Rio de Janeiro or São Paulo is costly.

Boat

From Trinidad in Bolivia, boats take about five days to sail down the Río Mamoré to Guayaramerín (Bolivia), opposite Guajará-Mirim (Brazil).

From Peru fast passenger boats make the 400km trip along the Rio Amazonas between Iquitos (Peru) and Tabatinga (Brazil) in eight to 10 hours. From Tabatinga you can continue to Manaus and Belém.

Bus

ARGENTINA

The main crossing used by travelers is Puerto Iguazú-Foz do Iguaçu, a 20-hour bus ride from Buenos Aires. Further south, you can cross from between Uruguaiana (Brazil) and Paso de los Libres (Argentina), which is also served by Buenos Aires buses. Other crossings are at San Javier-Porto Xavier and Santo Tomé–São Borja on the Rio Uruguai.

Direct buses run between Buenos Aires and Porto Alegre (US$64, 20 hours) and Rio

de Janeiro (US$141, 42 hours). Other destinations include Florianópolis, Curitiba and São Paulo.

BOLIVIA

Brazil's longest border runs through remote wetlands and forests, and is much used by smugglers.

The busiest crossing is between Quijarro (Bolivia) and Corumbá (Brazil), which is a good access point for the Pantanal. Quijarro has a daily train link with Santa Cruz, Bolivia. Corumbá has bus connections with Bonito, Campo Grande, São Paulo, Rio de Janeiro and southern Brazil.

Cáceres, in Mato Grosso (Brazil) has a daily bus link with Santa Cruz (Bolivia) via the Bolivian border town of San Matías.

Guajará-Mirim (Brazil) is a short river crossing from Guayaramerín (Bolivia). Both towns have bus links into their respective countries, but from late December to late February rains can make the northern Bolivian roads very difficult.

Brasiléia (Brazil), a 4½-hour bus ride from Rio Branco, stands opposite Cobija (Bolivia), which has bus connections into Bolivia. This route is less direct than the Guayaramerín–Guajará–Mirim option, and Bolivian buses confront the same wet-season difficulties.

CHILE

Although there is no border with Chile, direct buses run between Santiago and Brazilian cities, such as Porto Alegre (US$116, 36 hours), Curitiba, São Paulo and Rio de Janeiro (US$130, 62 hours).

COLOMBIA

Leticia, on the Rio Amazonas in far southeast Colombia, is contiguous with Tabatinga (Brazil). You can cross the border on foot, *combi* or taxi, but river and air are the only ways out of either town.

FRENCH GUIANA

The Brazilian town of Oiapoque, a rugged 560km bus ride (or a quick flight) from Macapá, stands across the Rio Oiapoque from St Georges (French Guiana). A newly opened road connects St Georges to the French Guiana capital, Cayenne, with minibuses shuttling between the two. (Get there early in the morning to catch one.) Another option is to fly directly from Belém to Cayenne, which if booked early

BRAZIL

enough can often be cheaper than ground transportation (see p276).

GUYANA
Lethem (southwest Guyana) is a short boat ride from Bonfim (Roraima, Brazil), a two-hour bus ride from Boa Vista.

PARAGUAY
The two major border crossings are Ciudad del Este–Foz do Iguaçu and Pedro Juan Caballero–Ponta Porã. The latter gives access to the Pantanal. Direct buses run between Asunción and Brazilian cities such as Curitiba (US$40, 18 hours), São Paulo and Rio de Janeiro (US$69, 28 hours).

PERU
The only land access to Peru is via Iñapari, a five-hour minibus or truck ride north of Puerto Maldonado (Peru). This route is only open during the dry season. You wade across the Rio Acre between Iñapari and the small Brazilian town of Assis Brasil, a three- to four-hour bus or 4WD trip from Brasiléia.

SURINAME
Overland travel between Suriname and Brazil involves first passing through either French Guiana or Guyana.

URUGUAY
The crossing most used by travelers is at Chuy (Uruguay)–Chuí (Brazil). Other crossings are Río Branco–Jaguarão, Isidoro Noblia–Aceguá, Rivera–Santana do Livramento, Artigas–Quaraí and Bella Unión–Barra do Quaraí. Buses run between Montevideo and Brazilian cities such as Porto Alegre (US$58, 12 hours), Florianópolis, Curitiba, São Paulo and Rio de Janeiro (US$130, 39 hours).

VENEZUELA
Paved roads run from northern Venezuela to Boa Vista and Manaus, crossing the border at Santa Elena de Uairén–Pacaraíma. Buses run to Manaus from as far away as Puerto La Cruz on Venezuela's coast (US$80, 33 hours).

GETTING AROUND
Air
DOMESTIC AIR SERVICES
Brazil's major national carriers are Varig, TAM and Gol. At least one of these serves every major city.

A host of other airlines serves Brazil, including Fly, Trip, Penta, TAVAJ, Rico and Meta.

In general, Gol is the cheapest of the airlines, though smaller regional carriers sometimes offer good deals. Airline tickets can be purchased at any travel agent. Travelers with American Express cards can also buy Gol tickets online – otherwise you'll have to pay in cash at a travel agency.

Overall Brazilian airlines operate efficiently, but schedules can change and it's wise to reconfirm your flights. Most airlines have national telephone numbers for reservations and confirmations:

Fly (☎ 0300-313-1323; www.voefly.com.br)
Gol (☎ 0300-789-2121; www.voegol.com.br)
TAM (☎ 0800-570-5700; www.tam.com.br)
Trip (☎ 0300-789-8747; www.airtrip.com.br)
Varig (☎ 0800-701-2670; www.varig.com.br)

In order to secure a seat, book as far ahead as possible during busy seasons (Christmas to Carnaval, Holy Week and Easter, July and August). At other times, you can buy tickets for same-day flights, with no added cost.

Embarkation tax on domestic flights ranges from US$3 at minor airports to US$8 at major ones. If it isn't already included in the price of your ticket, you have to pay it in cash (reais only) at check-in.

AIR PASSES
If you're combining travels in Brazil with other countries in southern South America, it's worth looking into the Mercosur Airpass (see above).

For flights solely within Brazil, Varig and TAM both offer a Brazil Airpass, which gives you four flights anywhere within the country starting at US$499. Up to four further flights can usually be added for US$120 each. All flights must be completed within 21 days. Given the astronomical prices of flights, the Airpass can be an excellent investment.

A few provisos: the Brazil Airpass must be purchased outside Brazil and to do so you need an international round-trip ticket to Brazil. You have to book your airpass itinerary at the time you buy it, and there are usually penalties for changing reservations. You're not allowed to visit the same city twice.

Varig Airpasses cost more (US$692 for up to five flights) if you don't fly to Brazil on Varig or another Star Alliance airline (see www.staralliance.com). With TAM Airpasses, you must fly into Brazil on TAM, or else the Airpass costs US$572 (four flights).

Boat

The Amazon region is one of the last great bastions of river travel in the world. The Rio Negro, the Rio Solomões and the Rio Madeira are the highways of Amazonia, and you can travel thousands of kilometers along these waterways (which combine to form the mighty Rio Amazonas), exploring the vast Amazon Basin traveling to or from Peru or Bolivia. Travel may be slow and dull along the river (with distances measured in days rather than kilometers), but it is cheap.

For more information, see the boxed text, p379.

Bus

Buses are the backbone of long-distance transportation in Brazil, and are generally reliable and frequent. Unfortunately, bus ticket prices in Brazil are among the highest in South America, with *comun* (economy class) fares averaging US$4 per hour.

Road quality varies from well-paved roads in the south to decent highways along the coast to ravaged, pockmarked terrain in the northeast interior.

There are three main classes of long-distance buses. The cheapest, *comum*, is fairly comfortable with reclining seats and usually a toilet. The *executivo* provides roomier seats, costs about 25% more and makes fewer stops. The more luxurious *Leitos* can cost twice as much as *comum* and have spacious, fully reclining seats with pillows, air-conditioning and sometimes an attendant serving sandwiches and drinks. Overnight buses, regardless of the class, often make fewer stops.

Most cities have one central bus terminal (*rodoviária*, pronounced 'hoe-doe-vee-ah-rhee-ya'), often located on the outskirts of town. Usually you can simply show up at the station and buy a ticket for the next bus out, but on weekends and holidays (particularly from December to February) it's a good idea to book ahead.

Car

Brazilian roads can be dangerous, especially busy highways such as the Rio to São Paulo corridor. There are tens of thousands of motor-vehicle fatalities every year. Driving at night is particularly hazardous because other drivers are more likely to be drunk and road hazards are less visible. Another peril is the police, who rarely lack reasons to impose fines.

All that said, driving can be a convenient if somewhat expensive way to get around Brazil. A small four-seat rental car costs around US$35 to US$60 a day with unlimited kilometers (US$60 to US$80 with air-con) and basic insurance. Ordinary gasoline costs around US$1.20 a liter. Familiar multinationals dominate the car-rental business and getting a car is safe and easy if you have a driver's license, credit card and passport and are over the minimum age (25 with most firms, 21 with others). You should also carry an international driver's license.

Hitching

Hitchhiking in Brazil, with the possible exception of the Pantanal and other areas where it's commonplace among locals, is difficult. The best way to hitch is to ask drivers when they're not in their vehicles – for example, by waiting at a gas station or a truck stop. But even this can be difficult. The Portuguese for 'lift' is *carona*.

Local Transport

BUS

Local bus services are frequent and cheap, with extensive routes. Many buses list their destinations in bold letters on the front, making it easier to identify the one you need. Drivers don't usually stop unless someone flags them.

Typically, you enter the bus at the front and exit from the rear. The price is displayed near the money collector, who sits at a turnstile and provides change for the fare (usually about US$1). You'll have difficulty getting a bulky backpack through the narrow turnstile. Avoid riding the bus after 11pm and at peak (read packed) times: noon to 2pm and 4pm to 6pm in most areas, and keep a watchful eye for pickpockets and thieves.

TAXI

City taxis aren't cheap, though they are quite useful for avoiding potentially dangerous walks and late-night bus rides, or if your baggage is too bulky for public transport. Most meters start around US$2 and rise by US$1 or so per kilometer (prices increase at night

BRAZIL

and on Sunday). Make sure the driver turns on the meter when you get in. Sometimes the fare is fixed – typically on trips between the airport and the city center.

If possible, orient yourself before taking a taxi, and keep a map handy in case you find yourself being taken on a wild detour. As elsewhere in the world, don't get into a taxi with more than one person.

The worst place to get a cab is where the tourists are. Don't get one near one of the expensive hotels.

TRAIN

There are very few passenger trains in service. One remaining line well worth riding runs from Curitiba to Paranaguá, descending the coastal mountain range (p318).

RIO DE JANEIRO

☎ 0xx21 / pop 6.2 million

Known as the *cidade maravilhosa* (marvelous city), Rio occupies one of the most spectacular settings on the planet. Gorgeous mountains, white-sand beaches and verdant rainforests fronting deep blue sea have enchanted visitors for centuries, and there are dozens of ways to fall in love – aside from simply people-watching in Ipanema. You can surf great breaks off Prainha, hike through Tijuca's rainforests, sail across Guanabára or rock-climb the face of Pão de Açúcar. By nightfall samba, that incredibly seductive sound, fills the streets and *cariocas* follow the beat to the dance halls, bars, and open-air cafés proliferating Rio.

While Rio has its share of serious problems, there are plenty of residents – expats included – who wouldn't dream of living anywhere else. Keep that in mind when booking your return flight.

HISTORY

The city earned its name from early Portuguese explorers, who entered the huge bay (Baía de Guanabara) in January 1502, and believing it a river, named it Rio de Janeiro (January River). The French were actually the first settlers along the bay, establishing the colony of Antarctic France in 1555. The Portuguese, fearing that the French would take over, gave them the boot in 1567 and remained from then on. Thanks to sugar plantations and the slave trade their new colony

developed into an important settlement, and grew substantially during the Minas Gerais gold rush of the 18th century. In 1763, with a population of 50,000, Rio replaced Salvador as the colonial capital. By 1900, after a coffee boom, heavy immigration from Europe and internal migration by ex-slaves, Rio had 800,000 inhabitants.

The 1920s to 1950s were Rio's golden age, when it became an exotic destination for international high society. Unfortunately the days of wine and roses didn't last. By the time the capital was moved to Brasília in 1960, Rio was already grappling with problems that would continue for the next half-century. Immigrants poured into *favelas* from poverty-stricken areas of the country, swelling the number of urban poor. The 'Cidade Maravilhosa' by the 1990s was better known as the '*cidade partida*' (the divided city), a term reflecting the widening chasm between rich and poor.

Despite its problems the city has had its share of successes, hosting the Pan Am games in 2007. Rio was also the launchpad for the Favela-Bairro project, which has brought to the *favelas* better access to sanitation, health clinics and public transportation. Meanwhile, urban renewal and gentrification continues in Centro, Lapa, Santa Teresa and parts of the Zona Sul.

ORIENTATION

The city can be divided into two zones: the *zona norte* (north zone), consisting of industrial, working-class neighborhoods, and the *zona sul* (south zone), full of middle- and upper-class neighborhoods and well-known beaches. Centro, Rio's business district and the site of its first settlement, marks the boundary between the two, and a number of the important museums and colonial buildings are there.

The parts of Rio you are most likely to explore stretch along the shore of the Baía de Guanabara and the Atlantic Ocean. South from Centro are the neighborhoods of Lapa, Glória, Catete, Flamengo, Botafogo and Urca dominated by the peak of Pão de Açúcar (Sugar Loaf). Further south are Copacabana, Ipanema and Leblon.

Other areas of interest include the colonial hilltop neighborhood of Santa Teresa overlooking Centro, and the looming statue of Cristo Redentor (Christ the Redeemer), atop Corcovado.

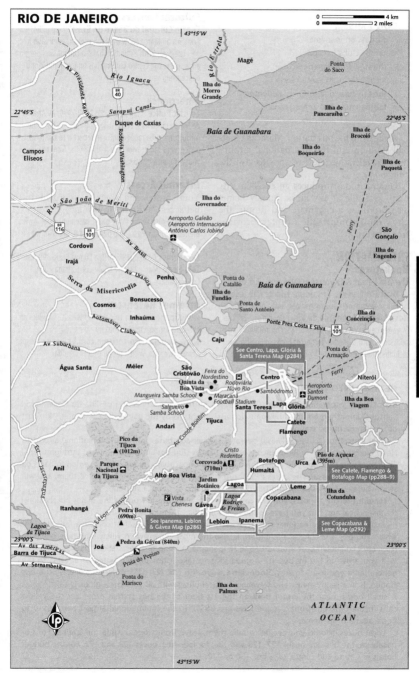

RIO DE JANEIRO

0 ——— 4 km
0 ——— 2 miles

43°15'W

Magé

Ponta do Saco

Rio Estrela

Rio Iguacu

BR 40

Ilha do Morro Grande

Av Presidente Kennedy

Sarapui Canal

22°45'S

Duque de Caxias

Rodovia Washington

Baía de Guanabara

Ilha de Pancaraíba

Ilha de Brocoió

22°45'S

Campos Elíseos

Ilha do Boqueirão

Ilha de Paquetá

Rio São João de Meriti

BR 116

BR 101

Cordovil

Av Brasil

Ilha do Governador

Aeroporto Galeão (Aeroporto Internacional António Carlos Jobim)

São Gonçalo

Ilha do Engenho

Ferry

Irajá

Serra da Misericordia

Av Uranos

Penha

Ponta do Catalão

Ilha do Fundão

Baía de Guanabara

Bonsucesso

Cosmos

Inhaúma

Automóvel Clube

Ponta de Santo António

Ponte Pres Costa E Silva

Ilha da Conceição

BR 101

BRAZIL

Av Suburbana

Caju

Ponta de Armação

Água Santa

Méier

São Cristóvão

Feira do Nordestino

Rodoviária Novo Rio

See Centro, Lapa, Glória & Santa Teresa Map (p284)

Centro

Ferry

Niterói

Quinta da Boa Vista

Aeroporto Santos Dumont

Sambódromo

Mangueira Samba School

Maracanã Football Stadium

Santa Teresa

Lapa

Glória

Ilha da Boa Viagem

Salgueiro Samba School

Andari

Av Conde Bonfim

Tijuca

Catete

Flamengo

Pico da Tijuca (1012m)

Cristo Redentor

Corcovado (710m)

Botafogo

Urca

Pão de Açúcar (395m)

Parque Nacional da Tijuca

Alto Boa Vista

Humaitá

See Catete, Flamengo & Botafogo Map (pp288–9)

Anil

Est de Jacarepaguá

Jardim Botânico

Lagoa

Leme

Ilha da Cotunduba

Itanhangá

Vista Chenesa

Lagoa Rodrigo de Freitas

Gávea

Copacabana

Pedra Bonita (690m)

See Ipanema, Leblon & Gávea Map (p286)

Leblon

Ipanema

See Copacabana & Leme Map (p292)

Lagoa da Tijuca

23°00'S

Av das Américas

Barra de Tijuca

Joá

Pedra da Gávea (840m)

23°00'S

Av Sernambetiba

Praía do Pepino

Ponta do Marisco

Ilha das Palmas

ATLANTIC OCEAN

43°15'W

DON'T MISS...

- sunsets on Ipanema
- samba clubs in Lapa
- the view from Pão de Açúcar
- a stroll through Santa Teresa
- the funicular ride to Cristo Redentor
- football madness at Maracanã

Aside from the bus station, Maracanã football stadium and the international airport, most travelers have few reasons to visit the *zona norte*.

Quatro Rodas produces an excellent city map, available at any kiosk. Lonely Planet also produces a city map, and Riotur, the city's tourist information center, provides free street maps.

INFORMATION
Bookstores
Livraria Letras & Expressões (Map p286; Rua Visconde de Pirajá 276, Ipanema) An Ipanema favorite with English-language newspapers and magazines, and a good café.
Nova Livraria Leonardo da Vinci (Map p284; Edifício Marquês de Herval; Av Rio Branco 185, Centro) Rio's largest bookstore, with a good collection of books in English, including travel guides.

Cultural Centers
Centro Cultural do Banco do Brasil (Map p284; Rua Primeiro do Março 66; www.ccbb.com.br; admission free; ☉ Tue-Sun) With exhibition halls, a cinema and performance space, the Centro Cultural has ongoing music and dance programs.

Emergency
Tourist Police (Map p286; ☎ 3399-7170; Av Afrânio de Melo Franco 119, Leblon; ☉ 24hr) If you have the misfortune to be robbed you can report it to the tourist police, who can provide you with a police form to give to your insurance company.

Internet Access
Youth hostels and larger hotels provide internet access, as do the following:
Central Fone Centro (Map p284; basement level, Av Rio Branco 156); Ipanema (Map p286; loja B, Rua Vinícius de Moraes 129)
Eurogames (Map pp288–9; Rua Correia Dutra 39B, Catete)
Tele Rede (Map p284; Av NS de Copacabana 209A, Copacabana)

Internet Resources
www.ipanema.com This colorful website provides an excellent introduction to the city.
www.riodejaneiro-turismo.com.br Riotur's comprehensive website, with a useful events calendar.

GETTING INTO TOWN

Rio's Galeão international airport (GIG) is 15km north of the city center on Ilha do Governador. Santos Dumont airport, used by some domestic flights, is by the bay in the city center, 1km east of Cinelândia metro station.

Real Auto Bus (☎ 0800-240-850) operates safe air-con buses from the international airport to Novo Rio bus station, Av Rio Branco (Centro), Santos Dumont airport, southward through Glória, Flamengo and Botafogo and along the beaches of Copacabana, Ipanema and Leblon to Barra da Tijuca (and vice-versa). The buses (US$3) run every 30 minutes from 5:20am to 12:10am, and will stop wherever you ask. You can transfer to the metro at Carioca station.

Heading to the airports, you can catch the Real bus from in front of the major hotels along the main beaches, but you have to look alive and flag them down.

Taxis from the international airport may try to rip you off. The safest course, a radio taxi for which you pay a set fare at the airport, is also the most expensive. A yellow-and-blue common *(comum)* taxi should cost around US$30 to Ipanema. A radio taxi costs about US$45.

If you arrive in Rio by bus, it's a good idea to take a taxi to your hotel, or at least to the general area you want to stay. **Rodoviária Novo Rio** (☎ 2291-5151; Av Francisco Bicalho), the bus station, is in a seedy area – and traveling on local buses with all your belongings is a little risky. A small booth near the Riotur desk on the 1st floor of the bus station organizes the yellow cabs in the rank out front. Sample fares are US$12 to the international airport and US$10 to Copacabana or Ipanema.

Local buses, should you decide to take them, leave from stops outside the station. For Copacabana, the best are buses 127, 128 and 136; for Ipanema, buses 128 and 172. For the budget hotels in Catete and Glória, take bus 136 or 172.

BRAZIL

Medical Services

Cardio Trauma Ipanema (Map p286; ☎ 2287-2322; Rua Farme de Amoedo 88) Has a 24-hour emergency room.

Hospital Ipanema (Map p286; ☎ 3111-2300; Rua Antônio Parreiras 67, Ipanema)

Money

Be cautious when carrying money in the city center and take nothing of value to the beach.

ATMs for most card networks are widely available. Try Banco do Brasil, Bradesco, Citibank and HSBC when using a debit or credit card. The international airport has Banco do Brasil machines on the 3rd floor and currency-exchange booths on the **arrivals floor** (⊗ 6:30am-11pm).

Banco do Brasil Centro (Map p284; Rua Senador Dantas 105); Copacabana (Map p292; Av Princesa Isabel de Copacabana 594); International airport (Map p281; Terminal 1, 3rd fl)

Citibank Centro (Map p284; Rua da Assembléia 100); Ipanema (Map p286; Rua Visconde de Pirajá 459A)

HSBC (Map p284; Av Rio Branco 108, Centro)

For exchanging cash, *casas de cambio* (exchange places) cluster behind the Copacabana Palace Hotel in Copacabana and along Rua Visconde da Pirajá near Praça General Osório in Ipanema. In Centro, exchange offices are on Av Rio Branco, just north of Av Presidente Vargas.

Casa Aliança (Map p284; Rua Miguel Couto 35C, Centro)

Casa Universal (Map p292; Av NS de Copacabana 371, Copacabana)

Post

Correios (post offices) are prevalent throughout Rio.

Central post office (Map p284; Rua Primeiro de Março 64, Centro). Mail addressed to Posta-Restante, Rio de Janeiro, Brazil, ends up here.

Post office Botafogo (Map pp288–9; Praia de Botafogo 324); Copacabana (Map pp288–9; Av Nossa Senhora de Copacabana 540); Ipanema (Map p286; Rua Prudente de Morais 147)

Telephone

For international calls try the following:

Central Fone Centro (Map p284; basement level, Av Rio Branco 156); Ipanema (Map p286; loja B, Rua Vinícius de Moraes 129)

Locutório (Map pp288-9; Av Nossa Senhora de Copacabana 1171)

Tele Rede (Map pp288-9; Av Nossa Senhora de Copacabana 209)

Tourist Information

Alô Rio (☎ 0800-707-1808; ⊗ 9am-6pm) English-speaking receptionists provide toll-free assistance.

Riotur Centro (Map p284; ☎ 2542-8080; Rua da Assembléia 10, 9th fl; ⊗ 9am-6pm Mon-Fri); bus station (Map pp288-9; Rodoviária Novo Rio; ⊗ 6am-midnight); Copacabana (Map p292; Av Princesa Isabel 183; ⊗ 8am-8pm); international airport (Map p281; ⊗ 5am-11pm) The very useful city tourism bureau has loads of info and can phone around to make you a hotel reservation.

Travel Agencies

Andes Sol (Map p292; ☎ 2275-4370; andessol@uol .com.br;

Av Nossa Senhora de Copacabana 209) A multilingual agency that can arrange discounted flights and find budget lodging in Rio.

DANGERS & ANNOYANCES

Like other metropolitan destinations, Rio has its share of crime and violence. But if you travel sensibly when visiting the city, you will likely suffer nothing worse than a few bad hangovers. All the same, theft is not uncommon, but you can take precautions to minimize the risks.

Buses are well-known targets for thieves. Avoid taking them after dark, and keep an eye out while aboard. Take taxis at night to avoid walking along empty streets and beaches. That holds especially true for Centro, which you should avoid on weekends when it's deserted and dangerous.

The beaches are also targets for thieves. Don't taking anything valuable to the beach, and always stay alert – especially during holidays (such as Carnaval) when the sands get fearfully crowded.

Get in the habit of carrying small bills separate from your wallet so you don't have to flash a wad when paying for things. Maracanã football stadium is worth a visit, but take only spending money for the day and avoid the crowded sections. Don't wander into the *favelas* unless going with a knowledgeable guide.

If you have the misfortune of being robbed, hand over the goods. Thieves are only too willing to use their weapons if given provocation. It's sensible to carry a fat wad of singles to hand over in case of a robbery.

See p400 for other tips on how to avoid becoming a victim.

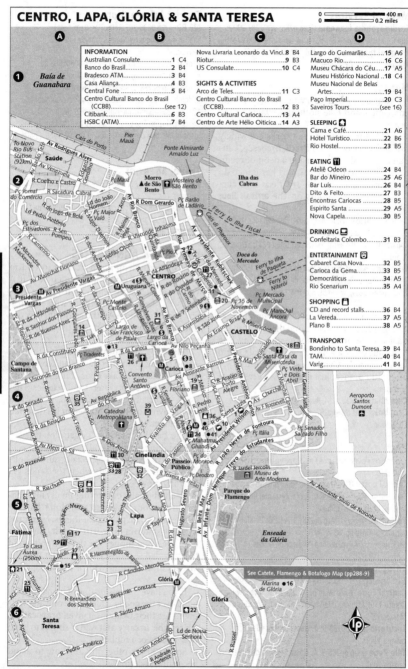

CENTRO, LAPA, GLÓRIA & SANTA TERESA

0 ———————— 400 m
0 ———————— 0.2 miles

INFORMATION
Australian Consulate.................1 C4
Banco do Brasil.........................2 B4
Bradesco ATM..........................3 B4
Casa Aliança.............................4 B3
Central Fone 5 B4
Centro Cultural Banco do Brasil
  (CCBB)...........................(see 12)
Citibank....................................6 B3
HSBC (ATM)..............................7 B4

Nova Livraria Leonardo da Vinci.8 B4
Riotur.......................................9 B3
US Consulate..........................10 C4

SIGHTS & ACTIVITIES
Arco de Teles.........................11 C3
Centro Cultural Banco do Brasil
  (CCBB).................................12 B3
Centro Cultural Carioca..........13 A4
Centro de Arte Hélio Oiticica ..14 A3

Largo do Guimarães.........15 A6
Macuco Rio.......................16 C6
Museu Chácara do Céu....17 A5
Museu Histórico Nacional ..18 C4
Museu Nacional de Belas
  Artes..............................19 B4
Paço Imperial...................20 C3
Saveiros Tours...............(see 16)

SLEEPING 🛏
Cama e Café.....................21 A6
Hotel Turístico.................22 B6
Rio Hostel........................23 B5

EATING 🍴
Ateliê Odeon....................24 B4
Bar do Mineiro..................25 A6
Bar Luís............................26 B4
Dito & Feito......................27 B3
Encontras Cariocas 28 B5
Espirito Santa...................29 A5
Nova Capela.....................30 B5

DRINKING 🍷
Confeitaria Colombo..........31 B3

ENTERTAINMENT 🎭
Cabaret Casa Nova...........32 B5
Carioca da Gema...............33 B5
Democráticos....................34 A5
Rio Scenarium 35 A4

SHOPPING 🛍
CD and record stalls..........36 B4
La Vereda.........................37 A5
Plano B 38 A5

TRANSPORT
Bondinho to Santa Teresa..39 B4
TAM..................................40 B4
Varig................................41 B4

SIGHTS

In addition to sand, sky and sea, Rio has dozens of other attractions: historic neighborhoods, colorful museums, colonial churches, picturesque gardens and some spectacular overlooks.

Ipanema & Leblon

Boasting a magnificent beach and pleasant tree-lined streets, Ipanema and Leblon (Map p286) are Rio's loveliest destinations and the favored residence for young, beautiful (and wealthy) *cariocas*. Microcultures dominate the beach: Posto 9, off Rua Vinícius de Moraes, is the gathering spot for the beauty crowd; nearby, in front of Farme de Amoedo, is the gay section; Posto 11 in Leblon attracts families.

Arpoador, between Ipanema and Copacabana, is a popular surf spot. All along the beach the waves can get big, and the undertow is strong – swim only where the locals do.

You'll find good views over the beach at Mirante do Leblon, just west of the sands.

Copacabana & Leme

The gorgeous curving beach of Copacabana (Map p292) stretches 4.5km from end to end, and pulses with an energy unknown elsewhere. Dozens of restaurants and bars line Av Atlântica, facing the sea, with tourists, prostitutes and *favela* kids all a part of the wild people-parade.

When you visit Copacabana, take only the essentials with you, and don't ever walk on the beach at night. Take care on weekends, when few locals are around.

Santa Teresa

Set on a hill overlooking the city, Santa Teresa (Map p284), with its cobbled streets and aging mansions, retains the charm of days past. Currently the residence of a new generation of artists and bohemians, Santa Teresa has colorful restaurants and bars and a lively weekend scene around Largo do Guimarães and Largo das Neves.

Museu Chácara do Céu (Map p284; Rua Murtinho Nobre 93; admission US$2, Sun free; noon-5pm Wed-Mon) is a delightful art and antiques museum in a former industrialist's mansion with beautiful gardens and great views.

To reach Santa Teresa, take the **bondinho** (streetcar; Map p284; tickets US50¢) from the station on Rua Professor Lélio Gama, behind Petrobras.

On weekends take a taxi to the tram station, as robberies have occurred on neighboring streets.

Urca & Botafogo

The peaceful streets of Urca (Map pp288–9) offer a welcome escape from the urban bustle. Good places for strolling are along the seawall facing Corcovado, the interior streets and the nature trail **Trilha Claudio Coutinho** (Map pp288-9; 8am-6pm).

Pão de Açúcar (Sugar Loaf; Map pp288-9; admission US$12; 8am-10pm), Rio's iconic 396m mountain, offers fabulous views over the city. Sunset on a clear day is the most spectacular time to go. To reach the summit you can go by cable car, changing lines at Morro da Urca (215m); you can also climb up (p287). To get there take an 'Urca' bus (bus 107 from Centro or Flamengo, bus 500, 511 or 512 from the *zona sul*).

West of Urca is the youthful neighborhood of Botafogo, where the **Museu do Índio** (Map pp288-9; Rua das Palmeiras 55; admission US$2; 9am-5:30pm Tue-Fri, 1-5pm Sat & Sun) has curious multimedia expositions on Brazil's northern tribes.

Cosme Velho

Atop the 710m-high peak known as Corcovado (Hunchback), the looming statue of **Cristo Redentor** (Christ the Redeemer; Map p281) offers similarly fantastic views over Rio. You can go by taxi, but the best way to reach the summit is by **cog train** (round trip US$12; 8.30am-6.30pm), which leaves from Rua Cosme Velho 513. To reach the train, take a taxi or a 'Rua Cosme Velho' bus (180, 184, 583 and 584). Choose a clear day to visit.

Centro

Rio's bustling commercial district has many remnants of its once-magnificent past. Looming baroque churches, wide plazas and cobblestone streets lie scattered throughout the district. For more on this area, see Walking Tour (p290).

Hosting some of Rio's best exhibitions is the **Centro Cultural Banco do Brasil** (p282). Occupying the former 18th-century colonial arsenal, the large **Museu Histórico Nacional** (Map p284; 2550-9224; www.museuhistoriconacional.com.br; off Av General Justo near Praça Marechal Âncora; admission US$2.50; 10am-5:30pm Tue-Fri, 2-6pm Sat & Sun) contains thousands of historic relics relating to the history of Brazil, from its founding in its early days as a republic.

BRAZIL

BRAZIL

IPANEMA, LEBLON & GÁVEA

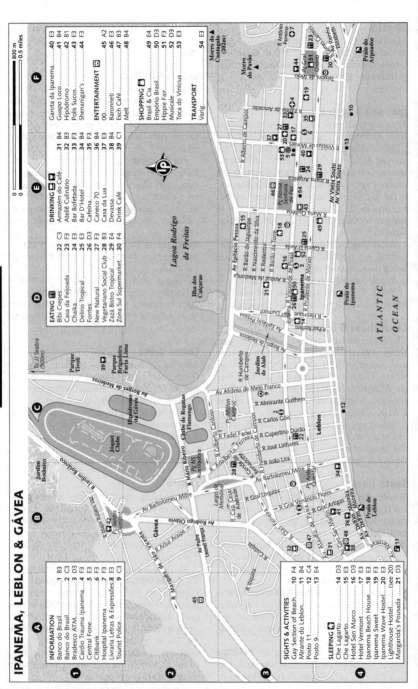

0   800 m
0   0.5 miles

INFORMATION
Banco do Brasil.....................1	B3
Banco do Brasil.....................2	C3
Bradesco ATM.......................3	D3
Cardio Trauma Ipanema.........4	F3
Central Fone.........................5	E3
Citibank...............................6	E3
Hospital Ipanema..................7	F3
Livraria Letras & Expressões...8	E3
Tourist Police.......................9	C3

SIGHTS & ACTIVITIES
Gay Section of Beach...........10	F4
Mirante do Leblon..............11	B4
Posto 11.............................12	C4
Posto 9..............................13	E4

SLEEPING
Che Lagarto........................14	D3
Che Lagarto........................15	E3
Hotel San Marco.................16	D3
Hotel Vermont....................17	E3
Ipanema Beach House..........18	E3
Ipanema Sweet...................19	E3
Ipanema Wave Hostel..........20	E3
Lighthouse Hostel................(see 20)
Margarida's Pousada...........21	D3

EATING
Bibi Crepes.........................22	C3
Casa da Feijoada.................23	F3
Chaika...............................24	E3
Delírio Tropical...................25	E3
Fontes...............................26	D3
New Natural.......................27	F3
Vegetariano Social Club........28	B3
Zazá Bistro Tropical.............29	E4
Zona Sul Supermarket..........30	F4

DRINKING
Armazém do Café................31	B4
Ateliê Culinário..................32	B3
Bar Bofetada......................33	F3
Bar D'Hotel........................34	B4
Cafeína..............................35	F3
Caneco 70..........................36	B4
Casa da Lua........................37	B3
Devassa.............................38	B4
Drink Café..........................39	C1

Garota da Ipanema.............40	E3
Guapo Loco........................41	B4
Hipódromo.........................42	B1
Polis Sucos.........................43	E3
Shenanigan's......................44	F3

ENTERTAINMENT
00.....................................45	A2
Baronneti...........................46	E3
Esch Café...........................47	B3
Melt..................................48	B4

SHOPPING
Brasil & Cia........................49	E4
Empório Brasil....................50	D3
Hippie Fair.........................51	F3
Musicale............................52	D3
Toca do Vinícius.................53	E3

TRANSPORT
Varig................................54	E3

The avant-garde **Centro de Arte Hélio Oiticica** (Map p284; ☎ 2242-1012; Rua Luis de Camões 68; admission free; ☾ 11am-7pm Tue-Fri, to 5pm Sat & Sun) hosts good contemporary shows in a 19th-century neoclassical building.

The small **Museu Nacional de Belas Artes** (Map p284; Av Rio Branco 199; admission US$5, free Sun; ☾ 10am-6pm Tue-Fri, 2-6pm Sat & Sun) houses fine art from the 17th to the 20th century, including Brazilian classics like Cândido Portinari's *Café*.

Catete & Flamengo

South of Centro, these working class neighborhoods have several worthwhile sights.

The **Museu da República** (Map pp288-9; Rua do Catete 153; admission US$3, free Wed; ☾ noon-5pm Tue-Fri, 2-6pm Sat & Sun) occupies the beautiful 19th-century Palácio do Catete, which served as Brazil's presidential palace until 1954. It houses a collection of artifacts from the republican period and the eerily preserved room where President Getúlio Vargas killed himself.

Next door, the small **Museu Folclórico Edson Carneiro** (Map pp288-9; Rua do Catete 181, Catete; admission US$2; ☾ 11am-6pm Tue-Fri, 3-6pm Sat & Sun) displays Brazilian folk art with an emphasis on Bahian artists.

Behind both museums is the **Parque do Catete**, the former palace grounds containing a pleasant outdoor café and a small pond.

One of Rio's best new additions, the **Centro Cultural Telemar** (Map pp288-9; ☎ 3131-6060; www.centro culturaltelemar.com.br in Portuguese; Rua Dois de Dezembro 63, Flamengo; admission free; ☾ 11am-8pm Tue-Sun) has contemporary multimedia installations and occasional concerts.

Jardim Botânico & Lagoa

This verdant **Botanical Gardens** (Map p281; Rua Jardim Botânico 920; admission US$1.50; ☾ 8am-5pm), with over 5000 varieties of plants, is quiet and serene on weekdays and fills with families and music on weekends. An outdoor café overlooks the gardens in back. To get there take a 'Jardim Botânico' bus, or any other bus marked 'via Jóquei.'

Just north of Ipanema stretches the **Lagoa Rodrigo de Freitas** (Map p286), a picturesque saltwater lagoon ringed with a walking-biking trail (rent bikes at Parque Brigadeiro Faria Lima). The lakeside kiosks are a scenic spot for an outdoor meal, with live music on weekend nights.

Parque Nacional da Tijuca

Lush trails through tropical rainforest lie just 15 minutes from concrete Copacabana. The 120 sq km refuge of the **Parque Nacional da Tijuca** (Map p281; ☾ 7am-sunset), a remnant of the Atlantic rainforest, has excellently marked trails over small peaks and past waterfalls. Maps are available at the crafts shop inside the entrance.

It's best to go by car, but if you can't, catch bus 221, 233 or 234 or take the metro to Saens Peña, then catch a bus going to Barra da Tijuca and get off at Alta da Boa Vista, the small suburb close to the park entrance.

ACTIVITIES

Rio's lush mountains and glimmering coastline just cry out for attention, and there are hundreds of ways to experience their magic on a sun-drenched afternoon.

Climbing

Animus Kon-Tikis (☎ 2295-0086; www.animuskontikis .com.br; rock climbs/hikes US$55/23) offers highly rewarding climbs up the face of Pão de Açúcar.

Hang-Gliding

The fantastic hang glide off 510m Pedra Bonita, one of the giant granite slabs towering over the city, is a highlight of any trip to Brazil. Many pilots offer tandem flights (from around US$80 including transportation), but reputable picks include **Just Fly** (☎ 2268-0565; www .justfly.com.br), **SuperFly** (☎ 3322-2286) and **Tandem Fly** (☎ 2422-6371; www.riotandemfly.com.br).

Bay Cruises

Macuco Rio (Map p284; ☎ 2205-0390; www.macucorio .com.br in Portuguese; Marina da Glória; boat tours US$35-45) offers two daily tours (at 10am and 2pm) in a high-velocity boat to either the pristine Cagarras Archipelago, or historic sites along the bay.

Saveiros Tours (Map p284; ☎ 2225-6064; www.savei ros.com.br; Marina da Glória, Glória; cruise US$14; ☾ 9:30-11:30am) runs two-hour cruises in the bay in large schooners.

Dance Classes

Centro Cultural Carioca (Map p284; ☎ 2252-6468; www .centroculturalcarioca.com.br in Portuguese; Rua Sete de Setembro, Centro; ☾ 11am-8pm Mon-Fri) offers one-hour classes in samba and ballroom, which meet twice a week (US$40 to US$60 for six-week course).

BRAZIL

CATETE, FLAMENGO & BOTAFOGO

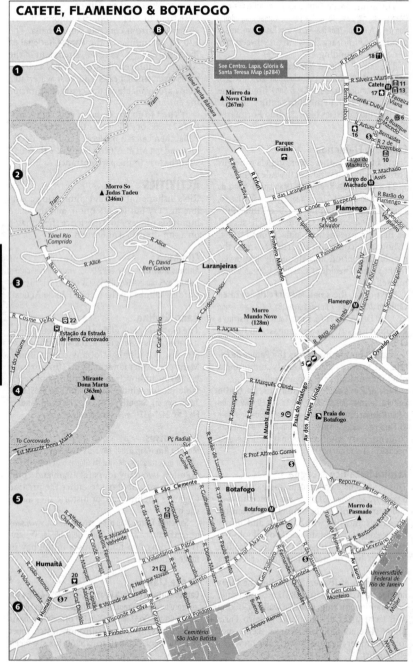

See Centro, Lapa, Glória &
Santa Teresa Map (p284)

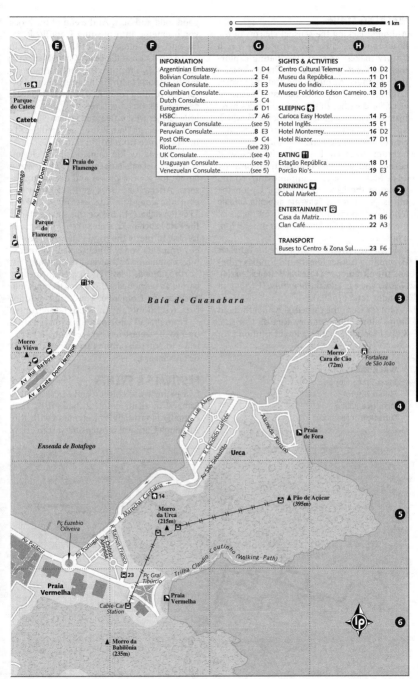

INFORMATION	
Argentinian Embassy	1 D4
Bolivian Consulate	2 E4
Chilean Consulate	3 E3
Columbian Consulate	4 E2
Dutch Consulate	5 C4
Eurogames	6 D1
HSBC	7 A6
Paraguayan Consulate	(see 5)
Peruvian Consulate	8 E3
Post Office	9 C4
Riotur	(see 23)
UK Consulate	(see 4)
Uraguayan Consulate	(see 5)
Venezuelan Consulate	(see 5)

SIGHTS & ACTIVITIES	
Centro Cultural Telemar	10 D2
Museu da República	11 D1
Museu do Índio	12 B5
Museu Folclórico Edson Carneiro	13 D1

SLEEPING	
Carioca Easy Hostel	14 F5
Hotel Inglês	15 E1
Hotel Monterrey	16 D2
Hotel Riazor	17 D1

EATING	
Estação República	18 D1
Porção Rio's	19 E3

DRINKING	
Cobal Market	20 A6

ENTERTAINMENT	
Casa da Matriz	21 B6
Clan Café	22 A3

TRANSPORT	
Buses to Centro & Zona Sul	23 F6

BRAZIL

WALKING TOUR

Although lacking the sensual charms of the beaches in the *zona sul,* central Rio's rich history makes for some fascinating exploring. The heart of Rio today is Praça Floriano in Cinelândia. At lunchtime and after work, samba music and political debate fills the air as *cariocas* gather in the open-air cafés here. Just north looms the **Teatro Municipal (1)**, which hosts Rio's best dance and theater. It's modeled on the Paris Opera.

From Praça Floriano leave its northwest corner and walk along pedestrian-only Av 13 de Maio. Cross Av Almirante Borroso and you're in the Largo da Carioca. Up on the hill is the restored **Convento de Santo Antônio (2)**, whose eponymous statue is an object of great devotion to many *cariocas* in search of a husband.

From the convent, you'll notice the **Petrobras (3)** building (rather like the old Rubik's cube) and the ultramodern **Catedral Metropolitana (4)**. Nearby you can take the *bondinho* (US50¢) up to Santa Teresa (p285).

Not far from the cathedral, you'll find old shops along 19th-century Rua da Carioca. Stop at **Bar Luís (5;** p294), a Rio institution with good food and beer. At the end of the block you'll emerge into bustling **Praça Tiradentes (6)**, once a fabulous part of the city. Stop in to see what's on at the **Centro Cultural Carioca (7;** Rua do Teatro 37), a restored theater hosting good samba bands. Nearby is the atmospheric Portuguese reading room **Real Gabinete Português de Leitura (8;** Rua Luís de Camões 30; ⏰ 9am-6pm). A little further west is **Campo de Santana (9)**, a park where Emperor Dom Pedro I declared Brazil's independence from Portugal in 1822.

Back near Av Rio Branco, hit the elegant coffeehouse **Confeitaria Colombo (10;** Rua Gonçalves Dias 30) for good espresso and decadent desserts. Afterwards, cross Av Rio Branco and continue along Rua 7 de Setembro into **Praça 15 de Novembro (11)**. Beside this square stands the **Paço Imperial (12;** admission free; ⏰ noon-6:30pm Tue-Sun), formerly the royal palace and seat of government. Today it houses temporary exhibits, a cinema and several restaurants. Just north is **Arco de Teles (13)**, an arch formed by part of an old aqueduct. Walking through into Travessa de Comércio, you'll find outdoor bars, restaurants and intriguing storefronts.

From Praça 15 de Novembro, you can stroll over to the waterfront, where frequent ferries leave to Niterói, on the east side of the Baía de Guanabara.

FESTIVALS & EVENTS

One of the world's biggest and wildest parties, **Carnaval** in all its colorful, hedonistic bacchanalia is virtually synonymous with Rio. Although Carnaval is ostensibly just five days

> **WALK FACTS**
> **Start** Praça Floriano
> **Finish** Niterói
> **Distance** 3.5km
> **Duration** three hours

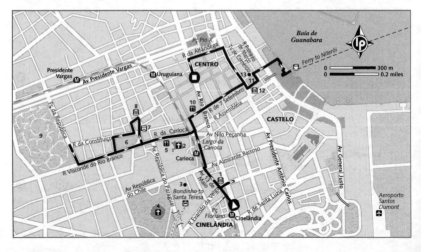

of revelry (Friday to Tuesday preceding Ash Wednesday), *cariocas* begin partying months in advance. The parade through the *sambódromo*, featuring elaborate floats flanked by thousands of pounding drummers and twirling dancers, is the culmination of the festivities, though the real action is at the parties about town.

Nightclubs and bars throw special costumed events. There are also free live concerts throughout the city (Largo do Machado, Arcos do Lapa, Praça General Osório), while those seeking a bit of decadence can head to various balls about town. *Bandas*, also called *blocos*, are one of the best ways to celebrate *carioca* style. These consist of a procession of drummers and vocalists followed by anyone who wants to dance through the streets of Rio. Check *Veja*'s 'Rio' insert or Riotur for times and locations. *Blocos* in Santa Teresa and Ipanema are highly recommended.

The spectacular main parade takes place in the **sambódromo** (Rua Marques do Sapuçaí) near Praça Onze metro station. Before an exuberant crowd of some 30,000, each of 14 samba schools has its hour to dazzle the audience. Top schools compete on Carnaval Sunday and Monday (February 3 and 4 in 2008; February 22 and 23 in 2009; February 14 and 15 in 2010). The safest way of reaching the *sambódromo* is by taxi or metro, which runs round the clock during Carnaval.

For information on buying *sambódromo* tickets at official prices (around US$60), stop by Riotur or visit the comprehensive Carnaval site (www.rio-carnival.net). By Carnaval weekend most tickets are sold out, leaving you to the mercy of the scalpers (they'll find you), or to simply show up at the *sambódromo* around midnight, three or four hours into the show, when you can get grandstand tickets from US$15 to US$50, depending on the location.

If you fancy really getting into the swing of Carnaval, it's not hard to join an *escola de samba* and take part in the parades yourself.

Keep in mind that Carnaval is costly: room rates triple and quadruple; and some thieves keep in the spirit of things by robbing in costume.

SLEEPING

Dozens of hostels have opened in recent years, making Rio an increasingly popular backpacker destination.

From December to February reservations are wise and they're absolutely essential around New Year's Eve and Carnaval.

Ipanema & Leblon

Ipanema Wave Hostel (Map p286; ☎ 2227-6458; wavehostel@yahoo.com.br; Rua Barão da Torre 175 No 5, Ipanema; dm US$16) Popular with a youthful, laid-back crowd, the Wave Hostel has wood floors and well-maintained common areas. It's located on a pretty Ipanema street, next door to several other hostels.

Lighthouse Hostel (Map p286; ☎ 2522-1353; www.thelighthouse.com.br; Rua Barão da Torre 175, No 20, Ipanema; dm/d US$18/55) Next door to the Ipanema Wave, this friendly, small-scale hostel has attractive rooms, and it's a good place to meet other travelers and get the latest surf report.

Ipanema Beach House (Map p286; ☎ 3202-2693; www.ipanemahouse.com; Rua Barão da Torre 485, Ipanema; dm/d US$18/55; 🖳 🖭) One of Rio's loveliest hostels, this converted two-story house has six- and nine-bed dorms (in three-tiered bunk beds), several private rooms, spacious indoor and outdoor lounge space, a small bar and a beautiful pool.

Che Lagarto (www.chelagarto.com) Ipanema (Map p286; ☎ 2512-8076; Rua Paul Redfern 48; dm/d US$20/60); Copacabana (Map p292; ☎ 2256-2778; Rua Anita Garibaldi 87; dm with/without YHA card US$15/18, d US$46) This popular budget five-story hostel attracts travelers who want to be close to Ipanema beach. It has basic rooms and not much common space, aside from the pricey bar on the 1st floor. The Copacabana branch has a bit more of a party vibe.

Margarida's Pousada (Map p286; ☎ 2239-1840; margaridacaneiro@hotmail.com; Rua Barão da Torre 600, Ipanema; s/d/apt from US$37/55/115; 🔀) This well-located guesthouse has cozy rooms in a small two-story house, with a private apartment for rent nearby.

Hotel Vermont (Map p286; ☎ 2522-0057; hoteis vermont@uol.com.br; Rua Visconde de Pirajá 254, Ipanema; s/d from US$57/78; 🔀) It's all about location if you stay at this aging high-rise two blocks from the beach. The rooms are indeed shabby, with tile floors, elderly bathrooms and poor lighting.

Hotel San Marco (Map p286; ☎ 2540-5032; www.sanmarcohotel.net; Rua Visconde de Pirajá 524, Ipanema; s/d US$65/70; 🔀) You'll find similar qualities to the Vermont here.

Ipanema Sweet (Map p286; ☎ 2551-0488; soniacor deiro@globo.com; Rua Visconde de Pirajá 161, Ipanema; apt from US$95; 🔀 🖭) Modern, furnished apartments with kitchen, lounge and balcony (no view) are a good value here. Two pools, sauna and laundry.

Copacabana & Leme

Copacabana Praia Hostel (Map p292; ☎ 2547-5422; Rua Tenente Marones de Gusmão 85, Copacabana; dm/s/d US$12/32/46, apt US$46) Overlooking a small park on a tranquil street, this unsigned hostel gathers its share of budget travelers with some of Copacabana's cheapest beds. Simple furnished apartments available.

Rio Backpackers (Map p292; ☎ 2236-3803; www.rio backpackers.com.br; Travessa Santa Leocádia 38, Copacabana; dm/d US$14/41) Young backpackers flock to this popular hostel in Copacabana. The rooms are small but clean and nicely maintained,

and the house has choice spots to meet other travelers. The young Brazilian owners are huge partiers.

Hotel Toledo (Map p292 ; ☎ 2257-1990; fax 2257-1931; Rua Domingos Ferreira 71, Copacabana; minis/s/d US$32/55/67) A block from the beach, the Toledo offers low prices for its outdated but clean rooms. The Toledo also has some coffin-sized singles (minis).

Pousada Girassol (Map p292; ☎ 2549-8344; www .girassolpousada.com.br; Travessa Angrense 25A, Copacabana; s/d/tr US$44/55/64) One of two small *pousadas* just off busy Av NS de Copacabana, Girassol, has simple en suite rooms with wood floors and adequate ventilation.

Hotel Santa Clara (Map p292; ☎ 2256-2650; www .hotelsantaclara.com.br; Rua Décio Vilares 316, Copacabana;

COPACABANA & LEME

s/d from US$55/60) One of Copacabana's most peaceful streets hides this decent three-story hotel. Upstairs rooms are best, with wood floors, shutters and a balcony.

Residencial Apartt (Map p292; ☎ 2522-1722; www .apartt.com.br; Rua Francisco Otaviano 42, Copacabana; d from US$63; 🖭) One of Rio's cheapest all-suites hotel, this charmless place has basic one-bedroom apartments with small kitchen units, a gloomy lounge room and a bedroom with better natural lighting.

Santa Teresa

Rio Hostel (Map p284; ☎ 3852-0827; www.riohostel.com; Rua Joaquim Murtinho; dm/d from US$16/50; 🖭) This beautiful, welcoming hostel is ideally placed for exploring Rio's most bohemian neighborhood. Ample lounge space and lively evening gatherings on the poolside patio.

Casa Áurea (Map p284; ☎ 2242-5830; www.casa aurea.com.br; Rua Áurea 80, Santa Teresa; d US$36-55) This handsome two-story guesthouse has decent rooms facing a courtyard garden. It's within a short walking distance to the *bonde* (tram).

Cama e Café (Map p284; ☎ 2221-7635; www.camae cafe.com; Rua Pascoal Carlos Magno 5, Santa Teresa; d from US$45) This B&B network links travelers with local residents who rent spare rooms in their homes. Accommodations range from modest to lavish; check website for listings.

Botafogo & Urca

Carioca Easy Hostel (Map pp288-9; ☎ 2295-7805; www .cariocahostel.com.br; Rua Marechal Cantuária 168, Urca; dm/d US$18/50; 🖭) Against the backdrop of Sugar Loaf, this tiny hostel has clean-swept dorm rooms and sunny lounge space with a tiny swimming pool in back. It's a short bus ride (bus 511 or 512) to Copacabana.

Glória, Catete & Flamengo

Hotel Riazor (Map pp288-9; ☎ 2225-0121; hotelriazor1@ hotmail.com; Rua do Catete 160, Catete; s/d US$21/28; 🖭) The colonial facade of the Riazor hides battered quarters. The equation here is simple: bed, bathroom, TV, and door by which to exit and explore the city.

Hotel Turístico (Map p284; ☎ 2557-7698; Ladeira da Glória 30; s/d US$25/30) On a quiet street up from Glória metro station, the Turístico offers spartan accommodations. Rooms range from cheery to grim.

Other Catete cheapies:

Hotel Monterrey (Map pp288-9; ☎ 2265-9899; Rua Arturo Bernardes 39, Catete; s/d US$24/32)

Hotel Inglês (Map pp288-9; ☎ 2558-3052; www .hotelingles.com.br; Rua Silveira Martins 20; s/d US$25/32)

EATING

Rio has a wealth of dining options, though not always at low prices. The best places for cheap dining are self-serve lunch buffets and juice bars, which you'll find all over the city. For fancier fare, Leblon has the best options, particularly along restaurant-packed Rua Dias Ferreira. Other possibilities are the open-air restaurants on the eastern and western edge of the lake (Lagoa) and along Rua Joaquim Murtinho in Santa Teresa.

Ipanema & Leblon

Delírio Tropical (Map p286; Rua Garcia D'Ávila 48, Ipanema; salads US$4-6; 🕐 8am-9pm) Famed for its delicious salads, the airy Delírio Tropical serves many varieties along with soups and hot dishes (veggie burgers, grilled salmon).

Chaika (Map p286; Rua Visconde de Pirajá 321; lunch specials US$4; 🕐 9am-1am) This low-key eatery serves hamburgers, pastries and sodas up front, with more substantial offerings in back.

Bibi Crepes (Map p286; Rua Cupertino Durão 81, Leblon; crepes US$5-8; 🕐 noon-1am) Serves a variety of tasty sweet and savory crepes.

Fontes (Map p286; Rua Visconde de Pirajá 605D; mains around US$5) A good vegetarian option.

New Natural (Map p286; Rua Barão da Torre 167; lunch specials US$6; 🕐 7am-11pm) Featuring an excellent vegetarian lunch buffet, this travelers' favorite has fresh soups, rice, veggies and beans.

Vegetariano Social Club (Map p286; Rua Conde Bernadotte 26L, Leblon; mains around US$8; 🕐 noon-5:30pm) This zenlike spot serves a mean tofu *feijoada* on Saturdays.

Zazá Bistro Tropical (Map p286; Rua Joana Angélica 40, Ipanema; mains US$14-22; 🕐 dinner) For a splurge, treat yourself to Zazá, a handsomely converted house in Ipanema with French-colonial decor and inventive seafood dishes. Check out the upstairs lounge, where you can dine among throw pillows and candlelight.

Casa da Feijoada (Map p286; Rua Prudente de Moraes 10B, Ipanema; feijoada US$17) Rio's signature black bean and salted pork dish is served with panache here daily.

Zona Sul supermarket (Map p286; Rua Gomes Carneiro 29) A good place to assemble cheap meals.

Copacabana & Leme

Yonza (Map p292; Rua Miguel Lemos 21B, Copacabana; crepes US$4-7; 🕐 10am-midnight Tue-Fri, 6pm-midnight Sat & Sun)

Surfboards and Japanese animé set the scene at this inexpensive creperie near the beach. Expect filling crepes and a young crowd.

Temperarte (Map p292; Av NS de Copacabana 266, Copacabana; per kg US$9; lunch Mon-Sat) This pay-by-weight restaurant has an admirable selection of salads, roast meats and vegetables.

Bakers (Map p292; Rua Santa Clara 86B; sandwiches US$3-6; 9am-8pm) Good place for flaky croissants, strudels and coffee. Deli sandwiches are also a good value.

Quick Galetos (Map p292; Rua Duvivier 28A; meals US$4-6) Inexpensive fresh-roasted chicken.

Cervantes (Map p292; Av Prado Junior 335B; sandwiches from US$6) A Copacabana institution, Cervantes is famous for its filet mignon–and-pineapple sandwiches and ice-cold *chope* (draft beer) on tap. Around the corner (Rua Barato Ribeiro 7), Cervantes' stand-up *boteco* (neighborhood bar) serves tasty bites in a hurry.

Churrascaria Monchique (Map p292; Av NS de Copacabana 796A; all-you-can-eat US$6.50; lunch) This inexpensive *churrascaria* serves good roasted meats, with an extensive salad bar and buffet.

Kilograma (Map p292; Av Nossa Senhora de Copacabana 1144; per kg US$14) This is an excellent self-serve restaurant with salads, meats, seafood and desserts.

Amir (Map p292; Rua Ronald de Carvalho 55C; mains US$10-14) This cozy Middle-Eastern restaurant serves tasty platters of hummus, *koftas*, falafel and other authentic fare.

Centro

Dito & Feito (Map p284; Rua do Mercado 19; meals US$7-12; lunch Mon-Fri) In an atmospheric 19th-century mansion, this place serves a popular weekday lunch buffet.

Ateliê Odeon (Map p284; Praça Floriano; mains US$8-12; closed Sat & Sun) One of several lively Brazilian restaurants with open-air seating on the Praça Floriano.

Bar Luís (Map p284; Rua da Carioca 39; mains US$9-15; closed Sun) A Rio institution since 1887, Bar Luís serves filling portions of German food and Rio's best dark beer.

Lapa & Santa Teresa

Encontras Cariocas (Map p284; Av Mem de Sá 77, Lapa; pizzas US$6-16; dinner Wed-Sun) An atmospheric pizzeria in the heart of music-filled Lapa.

Bar do Mineiro (Map p284; Rua Paschoal Carlos Magno 99, Santa Teresa; mains US$8-15; closed Mon) This old-school restaurant is a Santa Teresa favorite, with a menu of traditional Minas dishes like

carne seca (dried meat with spices), *lingüiça* (pork sausage) and Saturday *feijoada*.

Nova Capela (Map p284; Av Mem de Sá 96; mains from US$9) Serving traditional Portuguese cuisine, old-fashioned Nova Capela attracts a garrulous crowd. The *cabrito* (goat) is tops.

Espirito Santa (Map p284; Rua Almirante Alexandrino 264, Santa Teresa; mains US$9-18; closed Mon) In a beautifully restored building, Espirito Santa has excellent Amazonian dishes that can be enjoyed on a back terrace with sweeping views.

Glória, Catete & Flamengo

Estação República (Map pp288-9; Rua do Catete 104, Catete; plates US$5-10; 11am-midnight Mon-Sat, 11am-11pm Sun) This is a popular, inexpensive self-serve restaurant.

Porcão Rio's (Map pp288-9; Av Infante Dom Henrique-Aterro; all-you-can-eat US$28) Inside Parque do Flamengo, this is one of Rio's best all-you-can-eat *churrascarias* with delectable grilled meats and views of Pão de Açúcar.

DRINKING

Few cities can rival the dynamism of Rio's nightlife. Samba clubs, jazz bars, open-air cafés, lounges and night clubs are just one part of the scene, while the *boteco* is practically a *carioca* institution. If you can read a bit of Portuguese, there are many good sources of information: Veja Rio insert in *Veja* magazine, Thursday and Friday editions of *O Globo* and *Jornal do Brasil* and the Rio Festa website (www.riofesta.com.br).

Cafés & Juice Bars

Rio's numerous juice bars are a great spot to sample savory concoctions of the tropics. For coffee culture and people-watching, head to the sidewalk cafés scattered about Ipanema and Leblon.

Polis Sucos (Map p286; Rua Maria Quitéria 70; 7am-midnight) A top juice bar.

Cafeína (Map p286; Rua Farme de Amoedo 43; sandwiches US$4-7) This attractive café makes a fine spot for espresso while the city strolls by.

Confeitaria Colombo (Map p284; Rua Gonçalves Dias 34) Stained-glass windows and polished brocade provide the setting for java and desserts.

For more café culture:

Armazém do Café (Map p286; Rua Rita Ludolf 87B, Leblon)

Ateliê Culinário (Map p286; Rua Dias Ferreira 45, Leblon)

BRAZIL

BAR-HOPPING 101

When it comes to bars, nearly every neighborhood in Rio has its drinking clusters. While Ipanema has scattered options, Leblon has many choices along the western end of Av General San Martin. Near Lagoa, a youthful population fills the bars around JJ Seabra, and there's almost always a fun crowd packing the bars facing Praça Santos Dumont. The lakeside kiosks (in Parque Brigadeiro Faria Lima) are a favorite date place, with live music in the open air. Copacabana's Av Atlântica packs many sidewalk bars and restaurants, but the strip gets seedy after dark. Botafogo has authentic *carioca* bars, particularly around Rua Visconde de Caravelas and in the Cobal market. In Centro the atmospheric Travessa do Comércio is recommended for weekday evening drinks. Lapa's liveliest street is Av Mem de Sá, which is lined with samba clubs. In Santa Teresa you'll find colorful bars around Largo do Guimarães and Largo das Neves.

Bars

Empório (Map p286; Rua Maria Quitéria 37, Ipanema) A young mix of *cariocas* and gringos stirs things up over cheap cocktails at this battered Ipanema favorite.

Devassa (Map p286; Rua General San Martin 1241, Leblon) Serving perhaps Rio's best beer, Devassa is a lively choice. MPB bands add to the festive atmosphere.

Bar D'Hotel (Map p286; Marina All Suites, Av Delfim Moreira 696 2nd fl, Leblon) One of Leblon's most stylish bars is a magnet for the beauty crowd.

Shenanigan's (Map p286; Rua Visconde de Pirajá 112A, Ipanema) Overlooking the Praça General Osorio, this Irish pub attracts a mix of stylish Cariocas and sunburnt gringos.

Caneco 70 (Map p286; Av Delfim Moreira 1026, Leblon) Traditional after-beach hangout facing the shore.

Garota de Ipanema (Map p286; Rua Vinícius de Moraes 49) Plenty of tourists pack this bar, but it would be a sin not to mention the place where Jobim and Vinícius penned the famed song 'Girl from Ipanema'.

Guapo Loco (Map p286; Rua Rainha Guilhermina 48, Leblon) This colorful Mexican restaurant and bar is one of Leblon's rowdiest bars; tequila is the drink of choice.

Drink Café (Map p286; Parque dos Patins, Av Borges de Medeiros, Lagoa; live music charge US$2) One of a handful of lively open-air restaurants along the lake.

Hipódromo (Map p286; Praça Santos Dumont 108, Gávea) In an area referred to as Baixo Gávea, Hipódromo attracts a young college-age crowd. The best nights are Monday, Thursday and Sunday.

Sindicato Do Chopp (Map p292) Copacabana Av Atlântica 3806); Leme (Av Atlântica 514) These open-air bars overlook the wide avenue with the beach in the background.

ENTERTAINMENT
Live Music

Cover charge typically ranges from US$5 to US$10.

Carioca Da Gema (Map p284; Av Mem de Sá 79, Lapa) One of numerous samba clubs on this street, Carioca da Gema is a small, warmly lit setting for catching some of the city's best samba bands. A festive crowd fills the dance floor.

Democráticus (Map p284; Rua do Riachuelo 91, Lapa; ☾ Wed-Sun) This charming classic has an enormous dance floor and excellent samba bands. If you come to just one *gafieira* (samba club), Democráticus is a good choice.

Rio Scenarium (Map p284; www.rioscenarium .br in Portuguese; Rua do Lavradio 20, Lapa; ☾ closed Sun & Mon) One of Lapa's cinematic nightspots, Río Scenarium has three floors, each lavishly decorated with antiques. Balconies overlook the 1st-floor stage, with dancers keeping time to the jazz-infused samba, *choro* or *pagode*.

Clan Café (Map p292; Rua Cosme Velho 564, Cosme Velho; ☾ from 6pm Tue-Sat) This fairly unmarked bar has a large, open-air patio and excellent, low-key live samba, MPB and jazz. Bands start around 9pm.

Bip Bip (Map p286; Rua Almirante Gonçalves 50, Copacabana; admission free; ☾ 6:30pm-1am) One of the hidden gems among the cognoscenti, Bip Bip is a simple storefront with great informal music. Current schedule is samba on Sundays, *chorinho* on Tuesdays, and bossa nova Wednesdays. The music begins around 8pm.

Esch Café (Map p286; Rua Dias Ferreira 78, Leblon) Esch pedals Cuban cigars and live jazz amid a dark wood interior.

Allegro Bistro Musical (Map p292; www.modernsound .com.br; Rua Barata Ribeiro 502, Copacabana; admission free; ☾ 9am-9pm Mon-Fri, to 8pm Sat) This small café inside Modern Sound (p296) is a great spot for hearing free live bands playing most nights.

BRAZIL

Nightclubs

Nothing happens before midnight. Cover charges range from US$5 to US$15, and women generally pay less than men.

Casa da Matriz (Map pp288-9; http://casadamatriz .br; Rua Henrique Novaes 107, Botafogo) This avant-garde space in Botafogo has numerous little rooms to explore – lounge, screening room, dance floors – in an old two-story mansion.

00 (Zero Zero; Planetário da Gávea, Av Padre Leonel Franca 240, Gávea; ☻ Fri-Sun) Housed in Gávea's planetarium, 00 is a restaurant by day and sleek lounge by night. Good DJs and excellent rotating parties attract mixed dance-happy crowds.

Baronneti (Map p286; Rua Barão da Torre 354, Ipanema; ☻ Tue-Sun) A young, well-heeled crowd descends on this Ipanema nightclub.

Fosfobox (Map p292; Rua Siqueira Campos 143, Copacabana; ☻ Wed-Sun) Hidden under a shopping center, this subterranean club has DJs spinning everything from Funk to Glam Rock.

Melt (Map p286; Rua Rita Ludolf 47, Leblon) This upscale Leblon destination has an upstairs dance floor and a slinky lounge down below.

Samba Schools

In September, the big Carnaval schools open their rehearsals to the public. These are lively but informal affairs where you can dance, drink and join the party. The schools are in dodgy neighborhoods, so it's best not to go alone. Most hostels organize outings if you want to hook up with a group. Check with Riotur for schedules and locations. The best ones for tourists:

Mangueira (☎ 2567-4637; Rua Visconde de Niterói 1072, Mangueira; ☻ classes 7pm Sat)

Salgueiro (☎ 2238-5564; Rua Silva Teles 104, Andaraí; ☻ classes 10pm Sat)

Sports

Maracanã (Map p281; Rua Professor Eurico Rabelo e Av Maracanã) Rio's enormous shrine to football hosts some of the world's most exciting matches, with fan behavior no less colorful. Games take place year-round and can happen any day of the week. Rio's big clubs are Flamengo, Fluminense, Vasco da Gama and Botafogo.

To get to the stadium take the metro to Maracanã station then walk along Av Osvaldo Aranha. The safest seats are on the lower level *cadeira*, where the overhead covering protects you from descending objects like dead chickens and urine-filled bottles (no joke!). The ticket price is US$7 for most games.

SHOPPING
Markets

Feira do Nordestino (Map p281; Pavilhão de São Cristóvão near the Quinta da Boa Vista; ☻ Fri-Sun) Northeastern in character with lots of food, drink and live music, this fair is well worth a visit.

Hippie Fair (Map p286; Praça General Osório; ☻ 9am-6pm Sun) An Ipanema favorite with good souvenirs and Bahian food.

You can also purchase Brazilian handicrafts at the following:

Brasil & Cia (Map p286; Rua Maria Quitéria 27, Ipanema)

Empório Brasil (store 108, Rua Visconde de Pirajá 595, Ipanema)

La Vereda (Map p284; Rua Almirante Alexandrino 428, Santa Teresa)

Music

On weekdays along Rua Pedro Lessa (Map p284) venders sell CDs and records, which range from American indie rock to Brazilian funk.

Modern Sound (Map p292; www.modernsound.com.br; Rua Barata Ribeiro 502D) Rio's biggest music store.

GAY & LESBIAN RIO

Rio's gay community is neither out nor flamboyant most of the year, except at Carnaval. On the beaches, you'll find gay-friendly drink stands across from the Copacabana Palace Hotel in Copacabana and opposite Rua Farme do Amoedo (Rio's gayest street) in Ipanema.

Le Boy (Map p292; Rua Raul Pompéia 94) One of Rio's best (and largest) gay clubs. DJs spin house and drum 'n' bass on weekends. Drag shows are the fare during the week.

Bar Bofetada (Map p286; Rua Farme do Amoedo 87A) Though not exclusively a gay bar, gay couples are part of the mix at this lively spot.

Cabaret Casa Nova (Map p284; Av Mem de Sá 25, Lapa; ☻ Fri-Sat) One of Rio's oldest gay clubs featuring a good mixed crowd, drag queens and slightly trashy music.

Casa da Lua (Map p286; Rua Barão da Torre 240A, Ipanema) This lesbian bar is in a leafy party of Ipanema and serves great drinks.

Other places you can expand your music collection:

Musicale Copacabana (Av NS de Copacabana 1103C); Ipanema (Map p286; Rua Visconde de Pirajá 483)

Plano B (Map p284; Rua Francisco Muratori 2A, Lapa)

Toca do Vinícius (Map p286; Rua Vinícius de Moraes 129, Ipanema)

GETTING THERE & AWAY
Air
Most flights depart from Aeroporto Galeão (also called Aeroporto António Carlos Jobim), 15km north of the center. Shuttle flights to/from São Paulo, and some flights for other nearby cities, use Aeroporto Santos Dumont in the city center. Also see Getting Into Town (p282).

Gol tickets can be purchased in cash at any travel agency. Many international airlines have offices on or near Av Rio Branco, Centro.

Brazil's principal airlines have the following offices in the city:

TAM (Map p284; ☎ 2524-1717; Av Rio Branco 245, Centro)

Varig Centro (Map p284; ☎ 2534-0333; Av Rio Branco 277); Copacabana (Map p284; ☎ 2541-6343; Rua Rodolfo Dantas 16); Ipanema (Map p286; ☎ 2523-0040; Rua Visconde de Pirajá 351)

Bus
Buses leave from the **Rodoviária Novo Rio** (Map p281; ☎ 2291-5151; Av Francisco Bicalho) about 2km northwest of Centro. Several buses depart daily to most major destinations, but it's a good idea to buy tickets in advance. Excellent buses leave Novo Rio every 15 minutes or so for São Paulo (US$15, six hours). Approximate traveling times and fares to sample destinations:

Destination	Duration (hr)	Cost (US$)
Asunción (Paraguay)	30	85
Belém	52	140
Belo Horizonte	7	20
Buenos Aires (Argentina)	46	138
Florianópolis	18	78
Foz do Iguaçu	22	50
Ouro Prêto	7	22
Paraty	4	18
Petrópolis	1	6
Porto Alegre	26	90
Porto Velho	54	138
Recife	42	90
Salvador	26	74
Santiago (Chile)	60	160

GETTING AROUND
Bus
Rio buses are frequent and cheap, and because Rio is long and narrow it's easy to get the right bus and usually no big deal if you're on the wrong one. Nine out of 10 buses going south from the center will go to Copacabana, and vice versa. The buses are, however, often crowded, stuck in traffic, and driven by raving maniacs. They're also the site of many of the city's robberies, and it's not wise to ride late at night.

Metro
Rio's two-line subway system is an excellent way to get around some parts of the city. It's open daily from 6am to 11pm (US$1).

Taxi
Rio's taxis are useful late at night and when you're carrying valuables. The flat rate is US$2, plus around US75¢ per kilometer – slightly more at night and on Sundays. **Radio-taxis** (☎ 2260-2022) is 30% more expensive than others, but safer.

THE SOUTHEAST

Although most visitors have a hard time tearing themselves away from Rio's many charms, some spectacular destinations are less than a day's travel from the *cidade maravilhosa*. Gorgeous beaches lie all along the coast, with the Costa Verde (Green Coast, south of Rio) boasting the rainforest-covered island of Ilha Grande and the elegant colonial town of Paraty. In the opposite direction, along the Costa do Sol (Sun Coast) you'll find the laid-back surfing town of Saquarema, the more upscale beaches and nightlife of Búzios and the white sands of Arraial do Cabo.

Those who've had enough of pretty tropical beaches (as if!), should head to the hills. The picture-perfect town of Petrópolis and the nearby peaks of Serra dos Órgãos are just a short bus ride from Rio, while Minas Gerais, further north, offers grand visions of Brazil's colonial era in towns like Ouro Prêto, Tiradentes and Diamantina.

Rio-lovers aside, South America's cultural capital is in fact São Paulo, where you'll find the best assortment of museums, nightclubs and restaurants – the latter owing much to the city's incredibly diverse population.

BRAZIL

GETTING THERE & AROUND

Rio de Janeiro is the major gateway to the coastal regions, though if coming from the south or west you can reach the Costa Verde via São Paulo. Belo Horizonte, Brazil's third-largest city, is the gateway to the old gold-mining towns in Minas Gerais.

Numerous flights connect the three major cities of the Southeast – Belo Horizonte, Rio and São Paulo – with plenty of bus links covering Southeastern destinations. Ilha Grande is reached by ferry from Angra dos Reis or Mangaratiba (p302).

PETRÓPOLIS

☎ 0xx24 / pop 290,000

Once the summer home of the Portuguese imperial family, Petrópolis has some striking vestiges of the past, including a former palace and a cathedral set against the mountain scenery. While traffic can be pretty heavy in the city, the historic center has pleasant manicured parks and peaceful, tree-lined lanes.

Pick up a map at the tourist office on Praça da Liberdade, which is a leisurely stroll to many sites in town. **Trekking Petropolis** (☎ 2235-7607; www.rioserra.com.br/trekking), based out of Pousada 14bis, offers hiking, rafting and biking excursions in the area.

The city's top attraction is the **Museu Imperial** (Rua da Imperatriz 220; admission US$4; 11am-5:30pm Tue-Sun), which exhibits royal finery in the former palace of Dom Pedro II. Nearby is the 19th-century **Catedral São Pedro de Alcântara** (Rua Sao Pedro de Alcântara 60; 8am-noon & 2-6pm), housing the tombs of Brazil's last emperor, Dom Pedro II, and his wife and daughter. South of the Praça da Liberdade, the **Casa de Santos Dumont** (Rua do Encanto 22; admission US$1.50; 9.30am-5pm Tue-Sun) is the small but fascinating former home of Brazil's father of aviation.

Pousada 14 Bis (☎ 2231-0946; www.pousada14bis .com.br; Rua Buenos Aires 192; d from US$35) is an idyllic guesthouse with wood floors and a garden out back. It's on a quiet street, 10 minutes' walk from the Museu Imperial. Nearby, **Comércio** (☎ 2242-3500; Rua Dr Porciúncula 55; s/d without bathroom US$13/24, s/d with bathroom US$17/32) has basic but clean rooms. Adjoining the Plaza Dom Pedro II, **Casa D'Angelo** (Rua do Imperador 700; mains from US$4) is an atmospheric café and restaurant with pastries and affordable *pratos executivos* (set lunches). **Luigi** (Praça da Liberdade 185; mains US$8-13) serves traditional Italian cuisine in an old house facing the main square.

Buses run from Rio to Petrópolis every half hour from 5am to 10pm (US$6, one hour). The bus station is located in Bingen, 10km from town. From there, take bus 100 or bus 10 (US$1).

TERESÓPOLIS & PARQUE NACIONAL DA SERRA DOS ÓRGÃOS

☎ 0xx21 / pop 125,000

Framed by mountain scenery, Teresópolis is well positioned for excursions into the lush-capped peaks of the Parque Nacional da Serra dos Órgãos. Trekking, climbing and rafting are the best ways to experience the park's trails, rivers and waterfalls. Some 96km north of Rio, Teresópolis itself is modern, prosperous and dull.

Information

The Parque Nacional da Serra dos Órgãos visitor center is not far up from the park's entrance.

Tourist office (☎ 2742-3352; Praça Olímpica; 8am-6pm) In central Teresópolis.

Sights & Activities

About 5km south of Teresópolis is the main entrance to the **Parque Nacional da Serra dos Órgãos** (☎ 2642-1070; Hwy BR-116; admission US$3; 8am-5pm Tue-Sun).

The best walking trail is the **Trilha Pedra do Sino** (admission US$6), which takes about eight hours round trip. It's also possible to walk over the forested mountains to Petrópolis. Most trails are unmarked but it's easy and inexpensive to hire a guide at the national park visitor center.

One group that arranges a wide variety of hikes, long treks and rafting and rappeling excursions is **Grupo Maverick** (☎ 2237-3529; www .grupomaverick.com.br).

Sleeping & Eating

Camping Quinta da Barra (☎ 2643-1050; www.camping quintadabarra.com.br in Portuguese; Rua Antônio Maria, Quinta da Barra; camping per person US$6). This campsite is located a few kilometers outside of Teresópolis, off the road to Petrópolis.

Hostel Recanto do Lord (☎ 2742-5586; www.teresopo lishostel.com.br; Rua Luiza Pereira Soares 109; dm/d/tr with YHI card US$7/20/27; dm/d/tr without YHI card US$ 10/27/37) Pleasant rooms and a welcoming atmosphere; 2km northwest of the bus station.

Hotel Comary (☎ 9221-9147; s/d US$15/30) Next to a bakery, Comary has basic but clean-swept

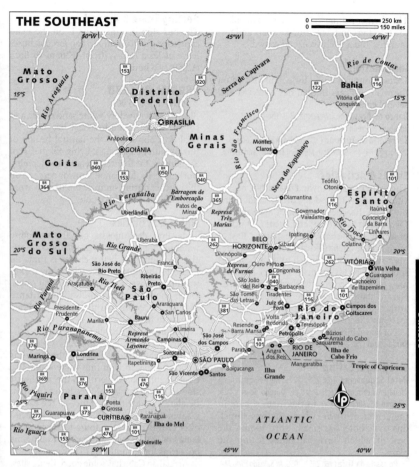

THE SOUTHEAST

rooms. Other cheap digs are a block away on Rua Delfim Moreira.

Várzea Palace Hotel (☎ 2742-0878; Rua Prefeito Sebastião Teixeira 41/55; s/d US$30/44, with shared bathroom US$15/22) In a grand old white building, this faded classic has OK rooms in a great location just off the church Igreja Matriz.

Pousada Refúgio do Parque (☎ 9221-9147; s/d US$15/30) Two kilometers inside the national park, this basic lodge and restaurant has simple quarters and filling meals. Reserve rooms well in advance.

Sand's (Av Almirante Lúcio Meira; lunch US$4-8) Near the bus station, this spot has a cheap self-serve lunch spread.

Cheiro de Mato (Rua Delfim Moreira 140; mains US$6-10) A decent vegetarian restaurant.

Getting There & Around

Buses run between Rio and Teresópolis every half hour from 5am to 10pm (US$8, 1½ hours). From Teresópolis, daily buses run every 1½ hours to Petrópolis. To get to the national park's main entrance from central Teresópolis, take the hourly 'Soberbo' bus (US$1), or the more frequent 'Alto' bus to the Pracinha do Alto, then walk a short way south to the entrance.

SAQUAREMA
☎ 0xx22 / pop 46,000
Boasting lovely beaches and a laid-back aesthetic, Saquarema, 100km east of Rio de Janeiro, has long been a favorite with the surfing crowd and its well-tanned admirers.

This former fishing village is a relaxing place to enjoy the coast, with low-key bars and restaurants and a lively weekend crowd.

Information

Lakes Shopping, a tiny little mall located on the road to Praia Itaúna, has an ATM and several eateries.

Banco do Brasil (Av Saquarema 539) Offers cash advances on credit cards.

Secretaria de Turismo (☎ 2651-4112; Rua Coronel Madureira 88; ⏰ 9am-8pm Mon-Fri) Friendly and useful.

Sights & Activities

The main beach in town, **Praia da Vila**, has inviting sands, with food and drink stands lining the shore. Beaches to the west are **Boqueirão** (3km), **Barra Nova** (8km) and **Jaconé** (10km), all of which are reachable by local buses. East of town is **Praia Itaúna** (3km), probably Saquarema's most beautiful beach and its best surf spot (US$5 by taxi from the center). Saquarema's picturesque whitewashed church, NS de Nazaré, stands on a hill overlooking town and attracts thousands of pilgrims on the Nazaré feast day (September 7).

For board hire or lessons, visit the **Saquarema Surf School** (☎ 9903-6619) on Praia Itaúna.

Sleeping & Eating

Hotel Saquarema (☎ 2651-2275; hostelsaquarema@ saquarema.com.br; Praça Oscar de Macedo Soares 128; s/d from US$20/30) Next to the main square in the center of town (where the bus stops), this basic hotel has small, worn rooms, the best of which have balconies facing the plaza.

Pousada da Titia (☎ 2651-2058; Av Salgado Filho 744; s/d/tr US$22/25/33) One of half a dozen guesthouses facing Praia da Vila, this one has simply furnished rooms with tile floors.

Itaúna Inn (☎ 2651-1257; www.itaunainn.saquarema .com.br; Av Oceânica 1764; s/d/tr US$36/48/63; ⏳ 🖳) Facing Itaúna beach, this popular guesthouse has comfortable rooms with an idyllic backyard for enjoying the ocean views. Transportation to/from bus station with advance notice.

Restaurante Marisco (Praça Oscar de Macedo Soares 197; meals US$4-7) Just opposite the bus stop in Saquarema, this place has inexpensive self-serve food and outdoor seating.

Crepe e Cia (Av Nazareth 160; crepes from US$4) Serves delicious crepes in a charming setting, one block back from Praia da Vila.

Getting There & Around

The bus stop in Saquarema is on the main central *praça*. From Rio to Saquarema, buses leave at least hourly from 6:30am to 8pm (US$9, two hours).

ARRAIAL DO CABO

☎ 0xx22 / pop 35,000

Blessed with powdery-white sand dunes and some of Rio state's loveliest beaches, Arraial do Cabo has all the natural beauty of Búzios with half the fuss. Lying 45km east of Saquarema, the town still retains a welcoming working-class demeanor. Crowds descend on the beaches during summer months, so avoid holiday weekends if possible.

Sights & Activities

Today Praia dos Anjos has beautiful turquoise water but too much boat traffic for comfortable swimming. A better choice is Praia do Forno to the northeast, reachable by a 1km walking trail over a steep hill adjoining Anjos. Other good beaches within walking distance of town are Prainha to the north and Praia Grande to the west.

The unspoiled Ilha de Cabo Frio is reachable by boat from Praia dos Anjos. Praia do Farol, on the protected side of the island, is a gorgeous beach with fine white sand. The Gruta Azul (Blue Cavern) on the southwest side of the island is another beautiful spot. Be alert, though: the entrance to the cavern is submerged at high tide. Numerous agencies offer crowded package tours to these spots. **Gruta Azul** (☎ 2622-1033; www.grutaazul.com.br) runs boat trips for around US$10 per person.

Arraial do Cabo has some good diving sites. Try operators like **Acqua World** (☎ 2622-2217; www.acquaworld.com.br; Praça da Bandeira 23).

Sleeping & Eating

Camping Club do Brasil (☎ 9821 3105; Av da Liberdade 171; campsites per person US$9) This small, shady campground is near Praia dos Anjos.

Marino dos Anjos Albergue (☎ 2622-4060; Rua Bernardo Lens 145; www.marinadosanjos.com.br; dm/d with YHI card US$15/45, dm/d without YHI card US$21/49) This hostel has small, zenlike rooms with a friendly communal atmosphere. It's one block from Praia dos Anjos. Bike and canoe rental are available.

Porto dos Anjos (☎ 2622-1629; pousadaportodos anjos@ig.com.br; Av Luis Correa 8; s/d US$25/40) This aging *pousada* on Praia dos Anjos has simple rooms with sea views. Fishing and diving trips are offered.

Hotel Praia Grande (☎ 2622-1369; Rua Dom Pedro 41; s/d US$25/40; ☒) Two blocks from the bus station, this hotel has clean, sizable rooms.

Casa de Vovó (Rua Nilo Peçanha; meals US$4-7) For fine *comida caseira* (home cooking), try this self-serve spot on the main street leading to Praia dos Anjos.

Chatô do Monde (Rua Santa Cruz 2; mains from US$8) A few blocks from Praia dos Anjos, this place serves a many dishes, from pizzas to pricier seafood.

Só Frutas (Rua Dom Pedro 58) Cool down at this self-serve ice-cream parlor.

Getting There & Away

Buses run about hourly from Rio to Arraial, from 5am to midnight (US$11, three hours). The bus station is on Rua Nilo Peçanha, a 10-minute walk to Praia dos Anjos (or a 20-minute walk to Praia Grande).

BÚZIOS

☎ 0xx22 / pop 22,200

A fabled destination among well-to-do *cariocas*, Búzios is one of Brazil's best-known beach resorts. Anchored on a peninsula and ringed by 17 pretty beaches, Búzios has striking natural scenery and a mix of eye-catching bars, restaurants and boutiques, along with the beautiful people that frequent them. Lying some 150km east of Rio, Búzios was a simple fishing village until the early 1960s, when it was 'discovered' by Brigitte Bardot, sealing its fate as Brazil's St Tropez. While plenty of Brazilians love this place, there are many who wouldn't set foot here. During the summer prices are high and crowds are abundant. At other times, Búzios retains some of its old-fashioned appeal.

Orientation & Information

Búzios, aka Armação dos Búzios, is one of three settlements on the peninsula. It lies between Ossos, on the peninsula's tip, and hectic Manguinhos, on the isthmus. Búzios' main street is Rua das Pedras, where you'll find many *pousadas*, restaurants, bars and internet cafés. Praia Rosa, a fourth settlement, lies northwest along the coast.

Malízia Tour (☎ 2623-1226; Shopping Praia do Canto, loja 16, Rua das Pedras) changes money. On nearby Praça Santos Dumont you'll find an ATM, as well as a **tourist information booth** (☎ 2623-2099; Praça Santos Dumont, Armação).

Sights & Activities

In general, the southern beaches are trickier to get to, but are prettier and have better surf. Geribá and Ferradurinha (Little Horseshoe), south of Manguinhos, are beautiful beaches with good waves, but the Búzios Beach Club has built condos here. Next on the coast is Ferradura, large enough for windsurfing. Praia Olho de Boi (Bull's Eye Beach), at the eastern tip of the peninsula, is a pocket-sized beach reached by a little trail from the long, clean Praia Brava. Near the northern tip of the promontory, João Fernandinho, João Fernandes and the topless Azedinha and Azeda are all good for snorkeling. Praia da Tartaruga is quiet and pretty.

Tour Shop (☎ 2623-4733; www.tourshop.com.br; Orla Bardot 550; 3hr trips US$30) offers excursions by glass-bottomed catamaran past beaches and several islands.

Sleeping

Budget lodging is scarce in Búzios, particularly during the summer.

Country Camping Club (☎ 2629-1122; www.buzios camping.com.br; Rua Maria Joaquina 895; per person US$9; ☒) Located in Praia Rosa, this campground has extensive facilities, but it's a bit out of the way.

Albergue de Juventude Praia dos Amores (☎ 2623-2422; www.alberguedebuzios.com.br; Av Bento Ribeiro 92; dm without/with air-con US$17/14; ☒) Some 20 minutes' walk from Praia da Tartaruga, this youth hostel faces a busy road and the dorms are tight, but it's otherwise a good choice.

Pousada Mandala (☎ 2623-4013; Rua Manoel de Carvalho 223; s/d from US$30/45; ☒) Passing through the lush garden courtyard, you'll find another good-value *pousada* with small but nicely decorated en suite rooms, some with tiny balconies.

Portal das Palmeiras (☎ 2623-2677; Rua César Augusto São Luiz 11; d from US$35) This friendly *pousada* is a good value for its tidy, colorful en suite rooms. It's 50m from Rua das Pedras.

Zen-do (☎ 2623-1542; Rua João Fernandes 60; s/d from US$42/47) This charming guesthouse in Ossos lets just three rooms (book early) in a peaceful setting. Handsome garden in back.

Eating & Drinking

Brava, Ferradura and João Fernandes beaches have simple thatched-roof fish and beer restaurants. You'll find dozens of other drinking spots all along Rua das Pedras.

Bistrô da Baiana (Rua Manoel de Carvalho 223; acarajé US$3.50) Good snack spot for *acarajé, moqueca* and other Bahian delights.

Jamaica (Av José Bento Ribeiro Dantas 1289; mains US$3.50-6) This low-key eatery in Ossos is a local favorite for filling fish and meat dishes.

Restaurante Boom (Rua Turíbio de Farias 110; buffet per kg US$10) Excellent and varied buffet in airy surroundings.

Restaurante David (Rua Turíbio de Farias 260; mains for two US$30) One of Búzios' most traditional seafood restaurants, this one serves big dishes for two in a casual indoor-outdoor setting.

Privilège (Orla Bardot 510; admission from US$12; ☉ Thu-Sat) Head to this sleek nightclub for house music among the A-list crowd.

Getting There & Away

Seven buses run daily from Rio to Búzios (US$9, three hours). Municipal buses run between Cabo Frio and Búzios (Ossos), a 50-minute, 20km trip.

Getting Around

Queen Lory (☎ 2623-1179; www.queenlory.com.br; Orla Bardot 710) makes daily trips by schooner out to Ilha Feia, and to Tartaruga and João Fernandinho beaches (from US$20 for two hours). You can rent bicycles and buggies at **Búzios Dacar** (☎ 2623-4018; Rua Manoel de Carvalho 248; bike/buggy per 24hr US$12/60).

ILHA GRANDE

☎ 0xx24 / pop 3600

Ilha Grande (Big Island) has dazzled visitors for centuries. Some 150km southwest of Rio de Janeiro, Brazil's third-largest island has tropical scenery and gorgeous beaches. Its hillsides are covered in lush forests, important remnants of the rapidly disappearing Mata Atlântica ecosystem.

There are no banks and no cars on Ilha Grande, so get cash before you relax. For island info check www.ilhagrande.com.br. Just off the dock, there is a small tourist booth where you can pick up an island map.

Sights & Activities

The main settlement is Vila do Abraão, from where you can hike to other beaches around the island. It's a 2½-hour walk to stunning Lopes Mendes beach, and a three-hour hike to Dois Rios, which also has a lovely beach just beyond the ruins of the old prison. There's also Bico do Papagaio (Parrot's Beak), the

highest point on the island at 982m (reached in three hours, guide recommended). As elsewhere, be smart: don't hike alone, and be mindful of poisonous snakes in the forests.

You can hire kayaks and arrange excursions at **Sudoeste SW Turismo** (☎ 3365-1175; www.sudoestesw.com.br; Rua da Praia 647). For diving, contact **Elite Dive Center** (☎ 9999-9789; www.elitedivecenter.com.br; Travessa Buganville).

Sleeping & Eating

Emilia's Eco-Camping (☎ 3361-5059; Rua Amancio de Souza 18; per person US$6; ▯) One of several campsites scattered around Abraão, this one has excellent amenities including table tennis.

Aquário (☎ 3361-5405; aquario@ilhagrande.com; dm/d US$20/50) Offering small, basic rooms facing the sea, Aquário is the most popular choice among backpackers. There's a natural swimming pool and lively evening BBQs. To arrive, take a left from the dock and head 1km along the beach.

Pousada Praia D'Azul (☎ 3361-5091; www.praiadazul.com.br in Portuguese; Rua da Igreja; d from US$48; ▨ ▨) This newly renovated hotel has small but comfortable rooms that overlook a swimming pool.

O Pescador (☎ 3361-5114; opescadordailha@uol.com.br; Rua da Praia; d from US$50; ▨) Cozily furnished rooms and a charming restaurant make a fine combination at this lovely beach-facing guesthouse.

Manaola Creperia (Rua da Praia; mains US$4-6; ☉ 3-11pm) One street back from the beach, this outdoor café serves sweet and savory crepes, juices and huge bowls of *açai* (a berrylike fruit, frozen and ground up) with granola.

Banana Blu (Rua da Praia 661; mains US$8-14) This well-appointed restaurant facing the beach serves excellent seafood, risottos and grilled meats.

Other good seafood restaurants include **Corsário Negro** (Rua Alice Kury 90; mains for 2 US$20-30) and the gardenlike **Tropicana** (Rua da Praia 28; mains from US$8).

Getting There & Away

To reach the island catch a Conerj ferry to Abraão from Mangaratiba or Angra dos Reis on the mainland. Ferries leave Mangaratiba at 8am and return at 5.30pm. From Angra dos Reis, boats depart at 3:30pm Monday to Friday and 1.30pm on Saturday, Sunday and holidays; they return from Abraão at 10am daily. The 1½-hour ride costs US$2.50 Monday to Friday, and US$6 Saturday and Sunday. Costa Verde buses depart Rio every 45 minutes to Angra (US$10). Five daily buses from Rio go to Mangaratiba (US$7.50). Catch the earliest (5.30am) to make the ferry. Eight daily buses connect Angra with Paraty (US$2, two hours).

PARATY

☎ 0xx24 / pop 33,000

The colonial town of Paraty is one of the gems of Rio state. Picturesque old churches and brightly hued stone buildings line the cobbled streets, with verdant mountains and deep blue sea adding yet more color to the historic city. On summer weekends Paraty's plazas, sidewalk cafés and open-air restaurants come to life with live music. Paraty is crowded from Christmas to Carnaval and most weekends, but at other times is delightfully quiet.

Formerly a region populated by Guianá Indians, Paraty first emerged as a European settlement when Portuguese from São Vicente arrived in the 16th century. Paraty's boom time began in the 17th century when gold was discovered in Minas Gerais, and the port became an important link in shipping the riches back to Portugal.

Information

Atrium (Rua da Lapa s/n) Changes cash and traveler's checks.

Centro de Informações Turísticas (☎ 3371-1897/1222; Av Roberto Silveira; ☽ 9am-9pm) Has good town info.

Sights & Activities

Paraty's newest attraction is the small **Casa da Cultura** (☎ 3371-2325; Rua Dona Geralda 177; admission US$6; ☽ 10am-6:30pm Sun, Mon & Wed, 1-9:30pm Fri & Sat), which has a fascinating permanent exhibition that includes interviews with and stories from local residents (audio and video) in both English and Portuguese.

Paraty's 18th-century prosperity is reflected in its beautiful old homes and churches. Three main churches served separate races. The 1725 **Igreja NS do Rosário e São Benedito dos Homens Pretos** (Rua Rua Samuel Costa & Rua do Comércio; admission US$1; ☽ 9am-noon & 1.30-5pm Tue-Sat, 9am-3pm Sun) was built by and for slaves. The 1722 **Igreja de Santa Rita dos Pardos Libertos** (Praça Santa Rita; admission US$1; ☽ 9am-noon & 1.30-3pm Wed-Sun) was the church for freed *mulattos*. The 1800 **Capela de NS das Dores** (Rua Dr Pereira & Rua Fresca; ☽ closed) was the church of the colonial white elite.

Forte Defensor Perpétuo is on Morro da Vila Velha, a hill 20 minutes' walk north of town. It was built in 1703 to defend gold in transit from pirate attacks.

If you're interested in hiking, ask at the tourist office for information on the **Gold Trail**, a partially cobbled mountain road once used by miners.

BEACHES

Paraty's biggest draw is its astounding assortment of 65 islands and 300 beaches nearby. The first beach you reach heading a few minutes' north of town is **Praia do Pontal**, the town's beach. Its sands aren't the most enticing, but the *barracas* (food stalls) backing it make a nice pit stop. Another 10 minutes' walk further and on the side of the hill is the small, hidden **Praia do Forte**. **Praia do Jabaquara**, 2km past Praia do Pontal, is a spacious beach with great views, a small restaurant and a good campground. About an hour from Paraty by boat are the **Vermelha** and **Lulas** beaches, both to the northeast, and Saco, to the east. These beaches are small and idyllic; most have *barracas* serving beer and fish and, at most, a handful of beachgoers. **Praia de Parati-Mirim**, 27km east of Parati, is hard to beat for accessibility, cost and beauty, and it has *barracas* and houses to rent. You can get there by municipal bus (US$1, 40 minutes) from Paraty bus station, with six daily buses.

To visit the less accessible beaches, many tourists take one of the schooners from the docks. Tickets cost US$15 per person. The boats make three beach stops of about 45 minutes each. An alternative is to hire one of the many small motorboats at the port. For US$15 per hour, the skipper will take you where you want to go.

Sleeping

Book ahead if you're coming from December to February. Once you hit the cobblestones, prices rise substantially.

Casa do Rio Hostel (☎ 3371-2223; www.paratyhostel .com; Rua Antônio Vidal 120; dm with/without YHI card US$12/14) A 10-minute walk from the old town and across the river, this hostel provides cozy lodging with a garden in back and kitchen access. The owner rents bikes, kayaks and horses and can arrange excursions.

Casa da Colônia (☎ 3371-2343; Rua Marechal Deodoro s/n; dm/d US$19/38) Although it's 100m outside of the old town, this guesthouse has abundant colonial charm. Kitchen access.

BRAZIL

Pousada do Sono (☎ 3371-1649; pousadadosono@paraty info.com.br; Rua João Luís do Rosário s/n; d from US$20) A few minutes' walk from the old town, this basic place offers small, straightforward rooms at good prices.

Hotel Solar dos Gerânios (☎ /fax 3371-1550; Praça da Matriz 2; s/d from US$22/34) Overlooking the Praça da Matriz, this colonial hotel features rooms that range from charming to rustic. Some have balconies.

Pouso Familiar (☎ 3371-1475; Largo do Rosário 7; d from US$30) This guesthouse has four pleasantly furnished rooms (one with a kitchenette unit) and a relaxing backyard patio in a great location in the colonial part of town.

Flor do Mar (☎ 3371-1674; www.pousadaflordomar .com.br; Rua Fresca 257; d from US$30) Another charmer in the old part of town, this guesthouse has cheery rooms with nice touches. Prices rise substantially on weekends.

Estalegem Colonial (☎ 3371-1626; estalagemcolonial@ yahoo.com.br; Praça da Matriz 9; d without/with bathroom US$45/60) This lavish colonial inn sits in the heart of the old quarters. Rooms are beautifully decorated with antiques and lots of wood details, and top-floor windows have mountain views.

Eating & Drinking

Sabor da Terra (Rua Roberto Silveira 80; per kg US$8) To beat the inflated prices in the old part of town, try this self-serve. Other inexpensive pay-by-weight restaurants are along Av Roberto Silveira.

O Café (Rua da Lapa 237; meals US$3-6) In the old town, this laid-back place serves sandwiches, coffee and lighter meals in a garden setting.

Punto di Vino (Rua Marechal Deodoro 129; mains from US$7) This handsomely decorated Italian restaurant has tasty pizzas and pastas. Live music adds to the romance.

Paraty 33 (☎ 3371-7311; Paraty 33, Rua Maria Jacomé de Mello) A popular restaurant-bar with live music in the same area.

Entertainment

Expect cover charges of US$3 to US$5 at live-music venues. Young locals avoid the tourist crush by gathering on the far side of the historic district, on Rua da Cadeia near the beach.

Other places to enjoy cocktails and bossa nova are **Café Paraty** (Rua do Comércio 253) and **Margarida Café** (Praça do Chafariz).

Getting There & Away

The bus station is on Rua Jango Pádua, 500m west of the old town. Eight daily buses run to/from Rio (US$18, four hours) and four to/from São Paulo (US$24, six hours).

SÃO PAULO

☎ 0xx11 / pop 11 million

One of the world's biggest metropolises, São Paulo looms large over South America. While the city lacks the natural beauty of Rio, Sampa – as it's affectionately called by locals – has much going for it. This is, after all, the cultural capital of Brazil, with a dizzying array of attractions including first-rate museums, nightly concerts, experimental theater and dance. The nightclubs, bars and restaurants are among the best on the continent. *Paulistanos* (inhabitants of the city) believe in working hard and playing harder, and despite constantly complaining about street violence, clogged highways and pollution, most wouldn't dream of living anywhere else.

Though founded in 1554 by Jesuits, São Paulo remained a colonial backwater for much of its history. It wasn't until the late 19th century that it began to emerge from the shadows, and the 20th century brought an explosion of immigrants from all over the world to work on the railroads, in the factories and in the fields. By the 1950s São Paulo took the lead as the country's industrial and commercial center. The result of the flood of immigrants is clear: the city of 17 million (metropolitan) is Brazil's most culturally diverse destination. For the wanderer, a stroll through Sampa's neighborhoods is a window into the shops and restaurants of the world.

Orientation

The key downtown squares are Praça da Sé, with the Sé *metrô* interchange station, and Praça da República, with República *metrô* station. In ethnic terms, the Liberdade area, just south of Praça da Sé, is the Asian neighborhood. Bela Vista (also called Bixiga), to the southwest, is Italian. A large Arab community is based around Rua 25 de Março, northeast of Praça da Sé.

Av Paulista, running southeast to northwest a kilometer or two southwest of downtown and accessible by *metrô*, is an avenue of skyscrapers. South of this avenue is Cerqueira César and Jardim Paulista, which harbors many upscale restaurants and boutiques.

GETTING INTO TOWN

A taxi from Aeroporto Congonhas to the center costs about US$20. For buses (one hour), walk out of the terminal and then to your right, where you'll see a busy street with a pedestrian overpass. Head to the overpass but don't cross; you should see a crowd of people waiting for the buses along the street, or ask for the bus to Terminal Bandeiras. The last bus departs at around 1am.

From a stop just in front of the arrivals terminal at Aeroporto Guarulhos, executive buses (www .airportbusservice.com.br) run to Av Paulista, Praça da República, Terminal Tietê bus station and Congonhas airport every 30 to 40 minutes (US$12). The same buses will also take you out to the airport from these places. A taxi from Aeroporto Guarulhos to the center costs about US$35.

Further south is Vila Olímpia, the nightlife district.

Information

EMERGENCY
Deatur (☎ 3214-0209; Av São Luís 91; ✆ 9am-5pm Mon-Fri) A special tourist police force.

INTERNET ACCESS
Lig Center (Rua 7 de Abril 253, Centro; per hr US$2; ✆ 8am-7.30pm Mon-Fri, 10am-5pm Sat) One of several internet cafés along this Centro street.

Lan House (Rua Barão de Iguape 7, Liberdade; per hr US$2; ✆ 8am-11pm) A good choice in Liberdade.

MEDICAL SERVICES
Einstein Hospital (☎ 3747-1233; Av Albert Einstein 627, Morumbi) One of the best hospitals in Latin America. It's in the southwestern corner of the city (catch bus 7241 to Jardim Colombo from Rua Xavier de Toledo).

MONEY
Except on weekends, changing money is easy. Many travel agencies and exchange offices around the city offer good rates, but avoid the smaller ones downtown – some are illegal and will rip you off.
Action Cambio (Shopping Light, Loja 130A; ✆ 10am-7pm Mon-Fri, to 4pm Sat)
Citibank (Av Paulista 1111) One of many banks with international ATMs on this street.

POST
Post office (Rua Líbero Badaró, Centro) The main branch.

TOURIST INFORMATION
Located at strategic points around the city, the Centrais de Informação Turística (CIT) booths are helpful.
CIT OLIDA (☎ 6224-0615; www.cidadedesaopaulo.com; Av São João 465, Centro; ✆ 9am-6pm) Near Praça da República; the most helpful for non-Portuguese speakers. Other booths are on Av Paulista near MASP (Museu de Arte de São Paulo), as well as in Ibirapuera Park, Terminals 1 and 2 at the airport, and in the Tietê bus station.

Dangers & Annoyances

Crime is a serious issue in São Paulo. Be especially careful in the center at night and on weekends (when fewer people are about). Watch out for pickpockets on buses and at Praça da Sé. For drivers, be aware that car-jackings and red-light robberies are not uncommon; in fact it's legal to just slow down at red lights late at night. If there's no traffic, continue without stopping.

Sights & Activities

Fascinating neighborhood strolls are found in Liberdade, Sampa's Japan town (and home to other Asian communities). On Sunday stop in the lively **street market** (fresh *gyoza*, or dumplings, on hand) at Praça da Liberdade. For a taste of Italy visit **Bela Vista**, about 1km west of there. Rua 13 de Maio is the main street, and it's packed with old-world restaurants, antique shops and a few bars on the north end.

The atmospheric old center of São Paulo lies between Praça da Sé, Luz metrô station and Praça da República (which also has a lively Sunday market). The city's pride is the baroque-cum–art nouveau **Teatro Municipal** just west of Viaduto do Chá. Another beloved landmark is the 41-story **Edifício Itália** (cnr Av São Luís & Av Ipiranga; admission free) which has a restaurant–piano bar–viewing terrace at the top.

Museu de Arte de São Paulo (MASP; ☎ 3283-2585; www.masp.art.br; Av Paulista 1578; adult/student US$5/2.50; ✆ 11am-5pm Tue-Sun) has Latin America's best collection of Western art, with over 5000 pieces. Highlights include the works by the great Brazilian artist Cândido Portinari and many French impressionist paintings. *Metrô* stop is Trianon-Masp.

The large **Parque do Ibirapuera**, 4km from the city, contains several museums, monuments and attractions, notably the **Museu de Arte**

CENTRAL SÃO PAULO

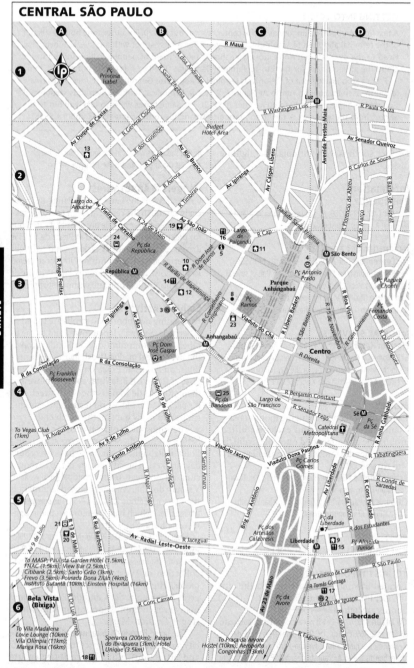

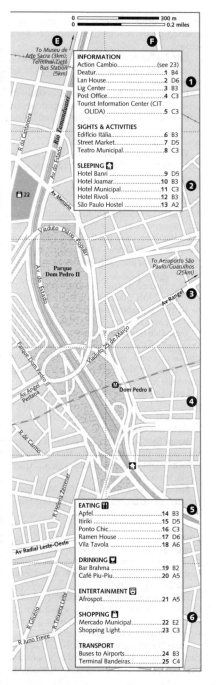

Moderna (☎ 5549 9688; admission US$3; ◷ 10am-6pm Tue, Wed & Fri-Sun, to 10pm Thu) with a huge collection of art from 1930 to 1970. Take bus 5121 'Santo Amaro' from Praça da República.

The **Museu de Arte Sacra** (Av Tiradentes 676; adult/student US$2/1; ◷ 11am-7pm Tue-Sun) is the best of Brazil's many museums of religious art. *Metrô* stop is Tiradentes.

The **Instituto Butantã** (☎ 3726-7222; Av Vital Brasil 1500; admission free; ◷ 9am-4.30pm Tue-Sun), one of São Paulo's most popular attractions, is a snake farm with over 1000 serpents, from which it milks venom for the production of vaccines and antivenins.

Sleeping

The areas surrounding the Estação da Luz train station and central downtown are rife with crime, prostitution, and extremely cheap hotels. If you stay here, use extreme caution and don't walk around at night.

Praça da Árvore Hostel (☎ 5071-5148; www.spalbergue.com.br; Rua Pageú 266; dm with/without YHI card from US$10/12; ◷ 🖳) Farther south of the city center, but somewhat closer to the nightlife districts, this hostel has tidy four-bed, eight-bed and 10-bed dorms. There's a lively community atmosphere. It's a few minutes' walk from Praça da Árvore *metrô* station.

São Paulo Hostel (☎ 3333-0844; www.hostel.com.br; Rua Barão de Campinas 94, Centro; dm with/without YHI card from US$12/13; ◷ 🖳) Near the Praça da Republica, this popular hostel has decent four- and seven-bed dorms as well as en suite doubles.

Hotel Municipal (☎ 3228-7833; Av São João 354; s/d/tr US$16/21/30) This atmospheric old place has fairly worn but sizable rooms with wood floors and huge ceilings.

Hotel Rivoli (☎ 3231-5633; hotelrivoli@uol.com.br; Rua Dom José de Barros 28; s/d from US$18/23) This elderly, not-quite-classic hotel has wood floors, tiny bathrooms and sizable windows. En suite rooms cost a few dollars more.

Hotel Joamar (☎ 3221-3611; www.hoteljoamar.com.br; Rua Dom Jose de Barros 187; s/d/tr US$19/24/33) On a pedestrian street near Praça da República, this small guesthouse has clean and tidy rooms that could use a bit more light.

Hotel Banri (☎ 3207-8877; Rua Galvão Bueno 209; s/d from US$25/32; ◷) One of many Asian-owned hotels in Liberdade, this one is a particularly good value. Its recently renovated rooms have parquet floors, decent lighting and modern bathrooms.

Paulista Garden Hotel (☎ 3885-1362; www.paulista gardenhotel.com.br; Alameda Lorena 21; s/d/tr US$35/40/55; ⊠ 🖳) In a good location near Parque Ibirapuera, the Paulista has fairly spacious rooms with blue carpeting, colorful duvets and sizable windows.

Pousada Dona Ziláh (☎ 3062-1444; www.zilah .com; Alameda Franca 1621; s/d/tr US$45/55/65; 🖳) This charming guesthouse lies on the edge of the upscale Jardim Paulista neighborhood. Its rooms are simple and tidy and face around a small courtyard.

Eating

Eating is a much-loved activity in Sampa, with almost every imaginable type of cuisine on offer.

Frevo (Rua Oscar Freire 603; mains US$5-12) In restaurant-packed Jardim Paulista, Frevo is an inexpensive diner serving grilled sandwiches and simple bites to a largely neighborhood crowd.

Ponto Chic (Largo do Paissandu 27; mains US$6-10; ☼ closed Sun) Several blocks from Praça da República, informal Ponto Chic serves tasty sandwiches, including famous *bauru*, made with beef and melted cheese on French bread.

Apfel (Rua Dom José de Barros 99; plates from US$6; ☼ 11am-3pm Mon-Fri) This pleasant self-serve lunch place serves vegetarian cuisine at good prices. It's on a busy pedestrian street in Centro.

Santo Grão (Rua Oscar Freire 413) This stylish indoor-outdoor café is a good pit stop for cappuccino, desserts and satisfying bistro fare.

Ramen House (Rua Tomaz Gonzaga 75; noodle soup US$6) This simple noodle restaurant serves affordable ramen bowls to its mostly Asian customers. Other good Japanese restaurants are along this street.

Vila Tavola (Rua 13 de Maio 848; lunch buffet US$7) One of many Italian restaurants on this street, Vila Tavola is a spacious and inviting place with a filling all-you-can-eat buffet (pastas, polenta, risotto and the like). Dinner is à la carte.

Speranza (Rua 13 de Maio 1004; pizzas from US$9) One of the best pizzerias in town with plenty of Italian ambience, as you'd expect in Bela Vista.

Itiriki (Rua Galvão Bueno 159; per kg US$12; ☼ 11am-4pm) In Liberdade, this popular Asian self-serve restaurant serves a variety of Japanese and Chinese specialties, with many vegetarian options.

Drinking

Bar Brahma (Av São João 677; ☼ 11am-midnight) Near the Praça República, this is the city's oldest drinking establishment, with antique surroundings and a sometimes-fun after-work crowd.

Café Piu-Piu (Rua 13 de Maio 134) One of half a dozen good-looking bars along Rua 13 de Maio in Bela Vista.

Hotel Unique (Av Brigadeiro Luís Antônio 4700) For a bit of decadence head to the top floor bar and restaurant of this chic hotel. You'll find outdoor seating, gorgeous views of the city and potent (but pricey) cocktails.

View Bar (www.theviewbar.com.br; 30th fl, Al Santos 981, Cerqueira César) You'll also find views and style here.

Entertainment

São Paulo's relentless clubbing nightlife rivals the excitement of New York's (and costs almost the same, too). For the latest check www .baladas.com.br, www.obaodba.com.br, www .guiasp.com.br and guiadasemana.com.br (all in Portuguese).

The hottest district for clubbing is Vila Olímpia. Most places open from Thursday to Saturday nights from midnight onward. Expect cover charges of US$10 and up.

Vegas Club (www.vegasclub.com.br; Rua Augusta 765; ☼ Tue-Sat) In Consolação, Vegas is the hit club of the moment, with a fun, eclectic crowd who come for the nights of house, hip-hop and *baile* funk.

Lov.e Lounge (Rua Pequetita 189) This very popular Vila Olímpia place opens its doors to straight and gay alike (depending on the night) for its dance fests.

Manga Rosa (Av Luís Carlos Berrini 1754) A bit farther out in Brooklin Paulista, this is another favorite nightclub among dance fiends (particularly trance-lovers).

Afrospot (Rua Treize de Maio 48, Bela Vista) For a smaller, more intimate space, visit this creative DJ's favorite in Bela Vista.

Shopping

Shopping Light (Rua Coronel Xavier de Toledo 23, Centro) For a taste of mall culture visit Shopping Light, with shops and restaurants across from the Teatro Municipal.

FNAC (www.fnac.com.br; Av Paulista 901) Music-lovers shouldn't skip FNAC, which has an excellent selection of CDs and books; occasionally, there's a free concert inside.

One kilometer southwest of FNAC is Jardim Paulista, a neighborhood packed with Sampa's best boutiques. Good streets for wandering are Rua Oscar Freire, Haddock Lobo and Alameda Lorena.

Mercado Municipal (Rua da Cantareira 306, Centro; ☺ 6am-4pm Mon-Sat) One of Brazil's best fruit and vegetable markets.

Lively Sunday markets:

MASP (Av Paulista 1578; ☺ 9am-5pm) Antiques; below MASP.

Praça da Liberdade (☺ 8am-2pm) Food and Asian wares.

Praça da República (☺ 8am-2pm) Handicrafts.

Getting There & Away

AIR

São Paulo is the Brazilian hub for many international airlines and thus the first stop for many travelers. Most major airlines have offices on Av São Luís, near Praça da República. Before buying a domestic ticket, check which of the city's airports the flight departs from.

Aeroporto Guarulhos (☎ 6445-2945), the international airport, is 30km east of the center. Flights to Rio (Santos Dumont airport) depart every half hour (or less) from **Aeroporto Congonhas** (☎ 5090-9000), 14km south of the center.

BUS

The enormous **Terminal Tietê bus station** (☎ 3235-0322), with buses to destinations throughout Brazil, is adjacent to Tietê *metrô* station. International buses from here go to Buenos Aires (US$125, 36 hours), Santiago de Chile (US$120, 56 hours) and Asunción (US$50, 20 hours). Frequent buses go to Rio de Janeiro (US$22, six hours). Other destinations within Brazil include Brasília (US$37, 14 hours), Belo Horizonte (US$21, eight hours), Foz do Iguaçu (US$40, 15 hours), Cuiabá (US$40, 23 hours), Salvador (US$68, 32 hours), Curitiba (US$15, six hours) and Florianópolis (US$30, 12 hours). A tip for people coming into the city: try to pick buses that won't arrive during early morning or late afternoon – traffic jams are enormous at those times.

Getting Around

Buses are slow, crowded during rush hours and not too safe. The main transfer points are Praça da República and the bustling Terminal Bandeiras. The tourist booths are excellent sources of bus information.

You can reach many places on the excellent *metrô*, São Paulo's subway system. A combination of *metrô* and walking is the best way to see the city. The *metrô* is cheap, safe, fast and runs from 5am to midnight. A single ride costs US$1.

BELO HORIZONTE

☎ 0xx31 / pop 2.4 million

The third-largest city in Brazil, Belo Horizonte is a rapidly growing industrial giant with soaring skyscrapers that blot out the surrounding mountains. Most travelers only come to the sprawling capital of Minas Gerais en route to the colonial towns of Ouro Prêto or Diamantina.

Information

Belo Horizonte has its share of crime. Pay close attention to your surroundings in the crowded area around the bus station and don't wander late at night.

Belotur (☎ 3277-7666; www.belohorizonte.mg.gov.br; Av Afonso Pena 1055; ☺ 8am-8pm Mon-Fri, to 4pm Sat & Sun) Belotur, the municipal tourist organization, publishes an excellent monthly guide in Portuguese, English and Spanish. There are booths at the bus station, Bahia Shopping (Rua da Bahia, 1022), and the city's two airports.

Centro de Cultura Belo Horizonte (Rua da Bahia 1149; per hr US$3) Internet access.

Nascente Turismo (Rua Rio de Janeiro 1314) A convenient currency-exchange place.

Sights

If you have time to spare head for the **Parque Municipal**, a sea of green 10 minutes' walk southeast of the bus station along Av Afonso Pena, and visit the park's **Palácio das Artes** (Av Afonso Pena 1537; ☺ 10am-10pm Mon-Sat, 2-10pm Sun), an art gallery and performing-arts center.

Sleeping

Albergue de Juventude Chalé Mineiro (☎ 3467-1576; www.chaleminerohostel.com.br in Portuguese; Rua Santa Luzia 288; dm with/without YHI card US$7/10, s/d with bathroom US$15/22; ▢ ▣) This popular YHI hostel has good dorm rooms, and a garden with pool. Reserve ahead. It's about 2km east of the Parque Municipal. Take the *metrô* to Santa Teresa station, from which you cross a pedestrian bridge to Rua Santa Luzia.

Pousadinha Mineira (☎ 3446-2911; Rua Araxá 514; s/d US$11/22) Very bare-bones accommodations. From the bus station, follow Av Santos Dumont to Rua Rio de Janeiro, turn left and go up a couple of blocks to Av do Contorno. Cross it and follow Rua Varginha a few blocks to Rua Araxá.

Eating & Drinking

Lanchonetes (stand-up snack bars) and fast-food places cluster around Praça Sete, on Av Afonso Pena, 400m southeast of the bus station. The neighborhood of Savassi has many top restaurants.

Padaria Zona Sul (Av Paraná 163; dishes US$3) Just southwest of the bus station, this place has super roast chickens.

Naturalis (Rua Tome de Souza 689; dishes US$5) Terrific vegetarian lunch specials are served here.

Cafe com Letras (Rua Antônio Albuquerque 785) This stylish spot is the setting for a glass of wine or a snack.

Rococo (Afonso Pena 941) Before and after shows, local musicians and music-lovers alike gather at Rococo.

Shopping Cidade (Rua Rio de Janeiro) and **Bahia Shopping** (Rua da Bahia 1022) both have food courts.

Getting There & Away

Belo's two airports have flights to just about anywhere in Brazil. Most airlines use Aeroporto Confins, 40km north of the city, but some use Aeroporto da Pampulha, 7km north of the center.

The **bus station** (Praça da Rodoviária) is in the north of the city center, near the north end of Av Afonso Pena. Buses will take you to Rio (US$20, seven hours), São Paulo (US$25, 9½ hours), Brasília (US$44, 12 hours) and Salvador (US$78, about 22 hours). There are 17 daily departures for Ouro Prêto (US$8, 2¾ hours), six to Diamantina (US$27, 5½ hours) and seven to São João del Rei (US$14, 3½ hours).

OURO PRÊTO

☎ 0xx31 / pop 69,000

Set amid splendid mountain scenery, Ouro Prêto is one of one of Brazil's most beautifully preserved colonial towns. Exploring its hilly, cobbled streets is like journeying back into the 18th century, when its baroque churches and picturesque plazas were the crown jewel of the Minas Gerais gold-mining towns.

Vila Rica de Ouro Prêto (Rich Town of Black Gold), as it was originally known, was founded in 1711 amid the western hemisphere's richest gold deposits. During the height of the rush (when 110,000 people lived in Ouro Prêto), slaves in Minas Gerais were digging up half the gold produced in the world.

When the boom tapered off toward the end of the 18th century, the miners found it increasingly difficult to pay the taxes demanded by Portugal, and in 1789 the poet-dentist Joaquim José da Silva Xavier (nicknamed Tiradentes, 'Tooth-Puller') and others hatched a famous revolutionary plot called the Inconfidência Mineira. The rebellion was crushed in its early stages and Tiradentes was executed. His name, however, lives on as one of Brazil's earliest patriots.

Orientation

Ouro Prêto is divided into two parishes. Standing looking south in Praça Tiradentes, the central square, facing the Museu da Inconfidência, the parish of Pilar is to the right (west), the parish of Antônio Dias to the left (east).

Information

Unfortunately the town can be a bit seedy at night, particularly around the bus station. Anyone lodging near there should absolutely not walk around after dark.

It's difficult to change traveler's checks in Ouro Prêto, but most jewelry stores will change cash dollars.

Associação de Guias (☎ 3559-3269; Praça Tiradentes 41; ☾ 8am-6pm Mon-Sat, to 5pm Sun) A useful and friendly source of information. A leaflet gives the opening hours of all the sights. You can hire official guides here.

Banco do Brasil (Rua São José 195)

Cyberhouse (Rua Bobadela 109; per hr US$3) One of several internet cafés on this street.

HSBC (Praça Tiradentes) A convenient ATM.

Sights & Activities

Almost all the museums and churches close on Monday and most close for lunch (noon to 1.30pm). Most sites charge admission of around US$1 to US$3, but in some cases a ticket to one gives free entrance to another.

Ideally, start out at about 7:30am from Praça Tiradentes and walk along Rua das Lajes for a panoramic morning view. In the east of town, the **Capela do Padre Faria** (Rua da Padre Faria s/n; ☾ 8am-4.30pm) is one of Ouro Prêto's oldest chapels (1701–04) and among the richest in gold and artwork.

Descending back toward town, you'll come to the **Igreja de Santa Efigênia dos Prêtos** (Rua Santa Efigênia s/n; ☾ 8am-4.30pm), built between 1742 and 1749 by and for the black slave community. This is Ouro Prêto's poorest church in terms of gold, and its richest in artwork.

The **Igreja NS da Conceição de Antônio Dias** (Rua da Conceição s/n; ☾ 8am-4.30pm) was designed by

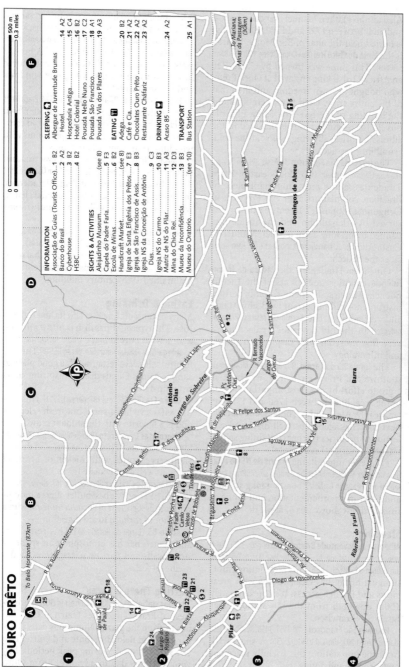

OURO PRÊTO

0   500 m
0   0.3 miles

BRAZIL

INFORMATION
Associação de Guias (Tourist Office)...1   B2
Banco do Brasil...................................2   A2
Cyberhouse..3   B2
HSBC...4   B2

SIGHTS & ACTIVITIES
Alejadinho Museum..........................(see 8)
Capela do Padre Faria........................5   F3
Escola de Minas...................................6   B2
Handicraft Market.............................(see 8)
Igreja de Santa Efigênia dos Prêtos....7   E3
Igreja de São Francisco de Assis.........8   B3
Igreja NS da Conceição de Antônio
   Dias...9   C3
Igreja NS do Carmo..........................10   B3
Matriz de NS do Pilar........................11   A3
Mina da Chica Rei.............................12   D3
Museu da Inconfidência......................13   B3
Museu do Oratório..........................(see 10)

SLEEPING 🛏
Albergue de Juventude Brumas
   Hostel..14   A2
Hospedaria Antiga............................15   C4
Hotel Colonial..................................16   B2
Pousada Nello Nuno..........................17   C2
Pousada São Francisco.......................18   A1
Pousada Vila dos Pilares...................19   A3

EATING 🍴
Adega...20   B2
Café e Cia...21   A2
Chocolates Ouro Prêto......................22   A2
Restaurante Cháfariz.........................23   A2

DRINKING 🍸
Acaso 85...24   A2

TRANSPORT
Bus Station.......................................25   A1

To Belo Horizonte (87km)

To Mariana;
Minas da Passagem (30km)

Aleijadinho's father, Manuel Francisco Lisboa, and built between 1727 and 1770. Aleijadinho is buried near the altar of Boa Morte. Nearby is the **Mina do Chico Rei** (Rua Dom Silvério 108; 8am-5.30pm). This mine was owned by Chico-Rei, an African tribal king enslaved at Ouro Prêto, who bought his own freedom and then that of his entire tribe. Gold from here financed the building of the Igreja de Santa Efigênia dos Prêtos. A guided tour is included in the admission price, allowing a look at the cold, crumbling passageways.

The **Igreja de São Francisco de Assis** (Rua do Ouvidor aka Rua Cláudio Manoel), two blocks east of Praça Tiradentes, is the most important piece of Brazilian colonial art after the *Prophets* in Congonhas (opposite). Its entire exterior was carved by Aleijadinho and the inside was painted by his long-term partner, Manuel da Costa Ataíde. A **handicraft market** (8am-4pm) faces the church.

On Praça Tiradentes, the **Museu da Inconfidência** contains documents of the Inconfidência Mineira, Tiradentes' tomb, torture instruments and important works by Ataíde and Aleijadinho. The **Escola de Minas** (Praça Tiradentes) in the old governor's palace has a very fine museum with displays on metals and mineralogy.

The **Igreja NS do Carmo** (Rua Brigadeiro Mosqueira), southwest of Praça Tiradentes, was built as a group effort by the most important artists of the area. Built between 1766 and 1772, its facade is by Aleijadinho. The **Museu do Oratório**, next door, has a fabulous, well-displayed collection of oratories (niches containing saints' images to ward off evil spirits).

Further southwest, the **Matriz de NS do Pilar** (Rua Brigador Mosqueira Castilho Barbosa s/n, in Praça Monsenhor João Castilho Barbosa) boasts 434kg of gold and silver in its ornamentation and is one of Brazil's finest showcases of artwork.

Sleeping

Albergue de Juventude Brumas Hostel (3551-2944; www.brumashostel.com.br; Rua Padre José Marcos Penna 68; dm/d from US$10/25;) This welcoming, multilingual hostel has clean rooms with great views and kitchen access. It's approximately 150m downhill from the bus station, near Igreja São Francisco.

Pousada São Francisco (3551-3456; Rua Padre José Marcos Penna 202; dm/s/d US$10/25/30) A short walk from the bus station, this friendly place has pretty rooms and doting staff. If you arrive on

a late bus, call to announce your arrival and someone will pop over to walk you back.

Hospedaria Antiga (3551-2203; www.antiga.com.br; Rua Xavier da Veiga 01; s/d from US$15/30) A bit of a walk from the center, this colonial guesthouse has good-value rooms, with large windows and polished wood floors.

Pousada Vila dos Pilares (3551-1324; Praça Mons João Castilho Barbosa 19; s/d US$17/34) About 50m from the church Matriz NS do Pilar, this old rambling guesthouse has clean, simple rooms with wood floors and aging bathrooms.

Pousada Nello Nuno (3551-3375; www.pousadanellonuno.com; Rua Camilo de Brito 59; s/d/tr from US$27/40/50) A few blocks northeast of Praça Tiradentes, this lovely *pousada* has lots of colonial charm, with artwork on the walls of the comfy rooms and other unique touches.

Hotel Colonial (3551-3133; www.hotelcolonial.com.br; Travessa Padre Camilo Veloso 26; s/d US$35/45) One block from Praça Tiradentes, this charming guesthouse has cozy rooms amid a beautifully maintained 19th-century building.

Eating & Drinking

Many restaurants line Rua Direita and Rua São José. The typical Minas dish is *tutu a mineira*, a somewhat puréed black-bean *feijoada*.

Adega (Rua Teixeira Amaral 24; per kg US$10) This delightful self-serve restaurant is a good place to sample Minas Gerais dishes. Inspiring views from upstairs.

Café e Cia (Rua São José 187; per kg US$11) This casual self-serve has a small but fresh selection and is a favorite with the student crowd.

Chocolates Ouro Prêto (Rua Getúlio Vargas 99; snacks US$2; 10am-2am) This quaint café and dessert shop serves tortes with chicken or hearts of palm, as well as chocolate treats.

Restaurante Cháfariz (Rua São José 167; all-you-can-eat buffet US$13) The city's best buffet offers a mouthwatering assortment of *cozinha mineira*, with a free shot of *cachaça* to aid digestion.

Acaso 85 (Largo do Rosário 85) This restaurant and Scotch bar has atmosphere in spades – stone walls and narrow passageways lend a medieval feel.

Getting There & Away

The **bus station** (Rua Rolimex-Merces) is 500m northwest of Praça Tiradentes (catch a 'Circular' bus to/from the plaza). Numerous daily buses run between Belo Horizonte and Ouro Prêto (US$8, 2¾ hours). During peak periods, buy your tickets a day in advance. From Ouro

Prêto one overnight bus goes to Rio (US$22, seven hours), and there are two daily buses to São Paulo (US$30, 11 hours).

CONGONHAS
☎ 0xx31 / pop 45,000

This small town, 72km south of Belo Horizonte, would attract few visitors if not for the Basílica do Bom Jesus de Matosinhos and, more importantly, its magnificently carved sculptures. Aleijadinho's 12 **Prophets** are among Brazil's most famed works of art. Art-lovers and admirers of the mystifying artist should definitely make the Congonhas detour.

The **tourism office** (☎ 3731-1300; ☺ 8am-6pm), located on the way into town, can advise about city events and give directions to the camping ground outside of town.

Congonhas' Jubileu do Senhor Bom Jesus do Matosinhos, held from September 7 to 14, is one of Brazil's biggest religious festivals, bringing 600,000 pilgrims each year.

Dos Profetas (☎ 3731-1352; www.hoteldosprofetas .com.br; Av Júlia Kubitschek 54; d from US$30), a petite hotel in the center of town, has clean rooms with dark wood furnishings. It's a 15-minute, mostly uphill walk to the *Prophets*.

The atmospheric **Colonial Hotel** (☎ 3731-1834; Praça da Basílica 76; d from US$35) and restaurant has huge hallways and immensely high ceilings, and it's right across the street from the *Prophets*.

Six daily buses run from Belo Horizonte to Congonhas (US$5, 1¾ hours). Seven daily buses connect Congonhas with São João del

---

ALEIJADINHO

Aleijadinho (Antônio Francisco Lisboa, 1730–1814), son of a Portuguese architect and an African slave, lost the use of his hands and legs at the age of 30 but, with a hammer and chisel strapped to his arms, he advanced art in Brazil from the excesses of baroque to a finer, more graceful rococo. This Brazilian Michelangelo sculpted the **12 Old Testament Prophets**, his masterworks, at the **Basílica do Bom Jesus de Matosinhos** in Congonhas between 1800 and 1805. Aleijadinho was also responsible for the six chapels here and their wooden statues representing the Passion of Christ, which together are just as impressive as the *Prophets*.

Rei (US$7, two hours). Getting to/from Ouro Prêto is difficult. You must first catch a bus to Conselheiro Lafaiete (US$2, 30 minutes, many buses), and then catch one of three to five daily buses to Ouro Prêto (US$6 2½ hours). Local buses run between Congonhas bus station and the Basílica (US$1, 15 minutes), 1.5km away.

SÃO JOÃO DEL REI
☎ 0xx32 / pop 82,000

This bustling, working-class city attracts fewer visitors than nearby Tiradentes, owing to São João's smaller, busier historic center. In its defense, there are some lovely colonial-era streets and churches here, the locals are friendly and proud of their city, and there's much authentic energy to the city compared to picture-perfect Tiradentes.

Like other Minas gold-rush towns, São João del Rei was founded in the 1800s; it lies 182km south of Belo Horizonte.

Information
Tourist office (☎ 3372-7338; Praça Frei Orlando 90; ☺ 8am-4pm Mon-Fri) Opposite São Francisco de Assis.

Sights & Activities
The following churches and museums open from 9am to 5pm, Tuesday to Sunday, but close for lunch.

The baroque **Igreja de São Francisco de Assis** (Rua Padre José Maria Xavier; admission US50¢), built in 1774 and overlooking a palm-lined plaza, was Aleijadinho's first complete project. Though much of his plan was not realized, the exterior, with an Aleijadinho sculpture of the Virgin and several angels, is one of the finest in Minas. The **Igreja de NS do Carmo** (Rua Getúlio Vargas), begun in 1732, was also designed by Aleijadinho. In the second sacristy is a famous unfinished sculpture of Christ.

The **Catedral de NS do Pilar** (Largo do Rosário) was built in 1719 to honor the patron saint and protector of slaves. It has exuberant gold altars and fine Portuguese tiles.

The **Museu Regional do Sphan** (Rua Marechal Deodoro, 12; admission US$1) has a small but impressive art collection from the city's churches.

The **Maria Fumaça** (steam train; São João station; one way/round trip US$8/12; ☺ Sat, Sun & holidays) is pulled by 19th-century locomotives, and chugs along a picturesque 13km track from São João to Tiradentes. It's a great half-hour ride. It departs São João at 10am and 3pm and returns at 1pm and 5pm. Train tickets include admission

BRAZIL

to the very interesting Railway Museum, or **Museu Ferroviário** (São João station; admission to museum alone US$1.50).

Sleeping

Pousada São Benedito (☎ 3371-7447; Rua Marechal Deodoro 254; s/d with shared bathroom US$10/20) This friendly place feels more like a large home than a *pousada*. Cozy rooms.

Hotel Provincia de Orense (☎ 3371-7960; Rua Marechal Deodoro 131; s/d/tr US$20/34/45) Tucked away on a cobblestone street in a good part of town, the Orense has spacious, modern rooms.

Hotel Brasil (☎ 3371-2804; Av Presidente Tancredo Neves 395; d with/without bathroom US$25/15) Large but shabby rooms are on offer at Hotel Brasil. There are, however, nice views of the river, and it's in a convenient location.

Eating & Drinking

Restaurante Rex (Rua Marechal Deodoro 124; per kg US$5; ☒ 11am-4pm) This quaint, inexpensive spot serves tasty Mineiro cuisine in what can be a slightly overpriced part of town.

Chafariz (Rua Quintino Bocáiuva 100; per kg US$8; ☒ lunch) Chafariz, just behind the train station, is everybody's favorite, with many regional dishes, particularly *feijoadas*.

Cabana do Zotti (Av Tiradentes 805; ☒ 9pm-late) This popular bar packs crowds, with dancing later in the night.

Del Castro (Alto da 8 de Dezembro s/n; admission US$2; ☒ 9pm-6am Fri & Sat) A popular weekend spot.

Point 84 (Rua Kleber Figueiras 84; ☒ 7pm-5am Thu-Sun) A good live-music spot.

Getting There & Around

Four direct daily buses run to São João from Rio de Janeiro (US$22, 5½ hours). Seven daily buses run from São João to Belo Horizonte (US$14, 3½ hours) via Congonhas (US$8, two hours). For Ouro Prêto, catch the São Paulo-Mariana bus departing twice daily (US$15, four hours).

Yellow buses run to the town center from São João's bus station on Rua Cristóvão Colombo (US50¢, 10 minutes). From the center to the bus station, buses go from the small bus stop in front of the train station.

TIRADENTES

☎ 0xx32 / pop 6400

One of the prettiest villages in Minas Gerais, Tiradentes has plenty of charm – from its peaceful, cobbled streets to its mountain vis-

tas, with a wandering river trickling through town. Its lovely setting is no secret, however, so be mindful of the weekend crowds. Tiradentes was named for the martyred hero of the Inconfidência Mineira (see p310), who was born at a nearby farm.

Information

Bradesco ATM (Rua Gabriel Passos 43)

Internet café (Rua Cadeia 30; per hr US$3; ☒ 9am-7pm) Near Igreja NS Rosário dos Pretos.

Secretária de Turismo (☎ 3355-1212; Rua Resende Costa 71; ☒ 9am-5pm) Facing the tree-lined Largo das Forras, this place has maps and info.

Sights & Activities

The town's colonial buildings run up a hillside, where they culminate in the beautiful 1710 **Igreja Matriz de Santo Antônio** (Rua Padre Toledo s/n; admission US$1; ☒ 9am-5pm); it has a facade by Aleijadinho and an all-gold interior rich in Old Testament symbolism.

Built by slaves, the **Igreja Nossa Senhora Rosário dos Pretos** (Rua Direita s/n; admission US50¢; ☒ 10am-6pm Tue-Sun), is Tiradentes' oldest church, dating from 1708; it contains several images of black saints. The **Museu do Padre Toledo** (Rua Padre Toledo 190; admission US$1.50; ☒ 9am-4:30pm Thu-Tue) is the former mansion of another hero of the Inconfidência, and is full of antiques and 18th-century curios.

At the foot of the Serra de São José is a 1km-wide band of protected Atlantic rainforest, with several **hiking** trails. The most popular leads to the Mãe d'Agua spring, reached by a 25-minute walk from the Chafariz de São José fountain in town. Other walks include the two-hour Caminho do Mangue, which heads up the Serra from the west side of town, and A Calçada, a stretch of the old road between Ouro Prêto and Rio de Janeiro. Locals advise against trekking alone; don't carry valuables. For guides (from US$15 per walk) ask at the tourist office or the adventure outfit **Caminhos e Trilhos** (☎ 3355-2477; caminhosetrilhasturismo@yahoo .com.br; Rua Antônio Teixeira de Carvalho 120), a 10-minute walk south of the tourist office.

Sleeping & Eating

Prices can double on weekends.

Hotel do Hespanhol (☎ 3355-1560; Rua dos Inconfidentes 479; s/d US$15/30) This budget hotel has spacious rooms that are a bit bare and short on light. Some rooms, however, have French doors onto tiny balconies – a good value.

Pousada Tiradentes (☎ 3355-1232; Rua São Francisco de Paula 41; s/d US$22/36) Next to the bus station, this aging place has basic rooms with large windows and well-maintained bathrooms.

Pousada do Laurito (☎ 3355-1268; Rua Direita 187; d with/without bathroom US$35/25) Rooms at this converted residence are fairly plain with linoleum floors and high ceilings, but the owner is a friendly soul.

Pousada da Bia (☎ 3355-1173; www.pousadadabia .com.br; Rua Frederico Ozanan 330; d from US$40; 🏊) This delightful guesthouse has simple, clean-swept rooms set around a grassy courtyard and swimming pool.

Restaurante Padre Toledo (Rua Direita 250; mains around US$14) This longtime favorite prepares good Mineira cuisine. An inexpensive bakery (open 6am to 9pm) is next door.

Maria Luiza (Largo do Ó 13; snacks US$3-5) For sandwiches, soups, teas and coffee, grab a seat at one of the sidewalk tables at this quaint café.

Bar do Celso (Largo das Forras 80A; meals US$9) One of several restaurants scattered around the plaza Largo das Forras, this one has a small selection of Mineira dishes at reasonable prices.

Pasta & Cia (Rua Frederico Ozanan 327; pastas US$8-11; 🕑 closed Tue) This handsome place serves good Italian-style cooking.

Getting There & Around

The best approach to Tiradentes is the wonderful train trip from São João del Rei (see p313), but buses (US$2.50, 20 minutes) also come and go between the two towns approximately every 90 minutes.

DIAMANTINA

☎ 0xx38 / pop 45,000

Way up in the mountains, Diamantina is strikingly beautiful but rarely visited, with a different feel from other colonial Minas towns. Unlike the lush southern part of the state, the mountains here are desolate, with craggy, windswept peaks. The town is still a functioning diamond-mining town, though its well-preserved center has changed little in 200 years, largely due to its isolation. The bus trip from Belo Horizonte (300km south) is arduous but rewarding, with gorgeous panoramas along the way.

Information

Banco do Brasil (main square) Has a Visa/Plus ATM.
Casa de Cultura (☎ 3531-1636; Praça Antônio Eulálio) Try the office on the 3rd floor for tourist information.
Municipal tourist office (☎ 3531-1857; Praça

Monsenhor Neves 44) Hands out a guide and map in Portuguese.

Sights & Activities

Most places close for lunch (noon to 2pm).

The **Igreja de NS do Carmo** (Rua do Carmo s/n; admission US$1.50; 🕑 9am-5pm Tue-Sat, to noon Sun), built in 1760–65, is the town's most opulent church. The tower was built at the rear lest the bells awaken Chica da Silva, the famous mistress and ex-slave of diamond contractor João Fernandes de Oliveira. Oliveira's mansion on Praça Lobo de Mesquita, known as the Casa de Chica da Silva, shows their extravagant lifestyle.

The **Museu do Diamante** (Rua Direita 14; admission US$1; 🕑 9am-5pm Tue-Sat, to noon Sun) is actually inside the house of Padre Rolim, one of the Inconfidêntes. It houses furniture, instruments of torture and other relics of the good old diamond days.

The Saturday **food & craft market** (Centro Cultural David Ribeiro, Praça Barão Guaicuí; 🕑 9am-6pm), with live music, is an interesting occasion. The Centro has a small museum with fascinating old photos.

Juscelino Kubitschek, the 1960s Brazilian president who founded Brasília, was born in Diamantina. The small **Casa de Juscelino Kubitschek** (Rua São Francisco 241; 🕑 9am-5pm Tue-Sat, to 2pm Sun) reflects his simple upbringing.

While you're here, walk a couple of kilometers down the **Caminho dos Escravos** (built by slaves) to the **Serra da Jacuba**.

Sleeping & Eating

Hotel JK (☎ 3531-1142; Largo Dom João 135; s/d US$8/15) This good budget option has basic but clean rooms; it's directly across from the bus station. Other budget hotels are nearby.

Chalé Pousada (☎ 3531 1246; Rua Macau de Baixo 52; s/d from US$15/25) An attractive old guesthouse.

Pousada Gameleira (☎ 3531-1900; Rua do Rosário 209; s/d US$15/30) A quaint but inexpensive choice in the old part of town, with some rooms facing the Igreja de NS do Rosário.

Restaurante Grupiaria (Rua Campos Carvalho 12; per kg US$12) This popular place serves tasty *mineiro* dishes.

Apocalipse (Praça Barão Guaicuí; lunch from US$6) Enjoy a hearty lunch at this self-serve restaurant opposite the Mercado Municipal.

Getting There & Away

Six daily buses run from Belo Horizonte (US$27, 5½ hours).

THE SOUTH

Spectacular white-sand beaches, pristine subtropical islands and the thunderous roar of the Iguaçu waterfalls are a few of the attractions of Brazil's affluent south. There's also great whale-watching, surfing and a fascinating train journey over the mountains. While often given short shrift by first-time visitors, this region offers a radically different version of what it means to be Brazilian. Here *gaúchos* (cowboys) still cling to the cowboy lifestyle on the wide plains bordering Argentina and Uruguay, and the influence from millions of German, Italian, Swiss and Eastern European settlers is evident in the Old World feel of inland and coastal villages (not to mention the blond hair and blue eyes).

The south comprises three states: Paraná, Santa Catarina and Rio Grande do Sul. The climate is generally subtropical, but snow is not uncommon in the interior highlands in winter.

GETTING THERE & AWAY

If you're flying in, the major gateways are Curitiba, Florianópolis, Porto Alegre and Iguaçu, which borders both Argentina and Paraguay. All of these cities have good bus connections to São Paulo.

GETTING AROUND

Short flights and longer bus journeys connect the four major cities of the South. If you're heading to Ilha do Mel, you can catch a bus (or the scenic train) from Curitiba to Paranaguá, from which several daily boats go to the island. There are more frequent boat departures from Pontal do Sul, also reached by bus from Curitiba (p302).

CURITIBA

☎ 0xx41 / pop 1.7 million

Known for its ecofriendly design, Curitiba is one of Brazil's urban success stories, with pleasant parks, well-preserved historic buildings, little traffic congestion and a large university population. Paraná's capital is a good place for a pit stop, but there's not much to hold your attention beyond a few days.

Information

There's a tourist information booth at the airport.

Cybernet XV (Rua das Flores 106; per hr US$3; ⏰ 9.30am-midnight Mon-Sat) Internet access.
Paraná Turismo (Loja 18, Rua 24 Horas) A helpful information booth in the narrow 24-hour pedestrian mall.

Sights & Activities

Strolling is one of the best ways to enjoy the city. The cobbled historic quarter around **Largo da Ordem** has beautifully restored buildings, art galleries, bars and restaurants, with live music after dark. Nearby, the pretty **Rua das Flores** is lined with shops, restaurants and colorful flowers. For more greenery, visit the **Passeio Público** (Av Presidente Carlos Cavalcanti; ⏰ Tue-Sun), a small park with shady walks and a lake. Curitiba's attractions outside the center – including botanical gardens, tree-filled parks and the Oscar Niemeyer museum – are accessible via the **Linha Turismo Bus** (see Getting Around, p319).

Sleeping

There are plenty of cheap hotels across from the bus station.

Cervantes Hotel (☎ 3222-9593; www.cervanteshotel .cjb.net; Rua Alfredo Bufren 66; s/d US$15/22) In a good location, this bare-bones hotel has clean rooms with carpeting and old bathrooms. Lacy curtains add a homey touch.

Hotel Maia (☎ 3264-1684; Av Presidente Afonso Camargo 355; s/d US$15/30) If you're arriving late or leaving early, the clean and secure Maia is across from the bus station.

Palace Hotel (☎ 3222-6414; Rua Barão do Rio Branco 62; s/d US$17/26) Near Rua das Flores, the Palace is good value, with wood floors, big old-fashioned windows and good natural lighting in its rooms.

Golden Hotel (☎ 3323-3603; www.goldenhotelpr.com .br; Rua Tobias de Macado 26; s/d US$17/30) A basic but decent choice in the center, the Golden Hotel has small narrow rooms with wood floors. The tiny balconies are nice, as are the upper-floor views of the cathedral.

Hotel O'Hara (☎ 3232-6044; Rua XV de Novembro 770; s/d from US$25/35) Overlooking Praça Santos Andrade, O'Hara has small, comfortable rooms with modern bathrooms.

Eating

Bars and restaurants abound around Largo da Ordem.

Spich (Rua das Flores 420; buffet US$2; ⏰ lunch Mon-Sat) This popular lunch buffet has fresh food at good prices. It's on the 2nd floor of the Shop das Fábricas.

THE SOUTH

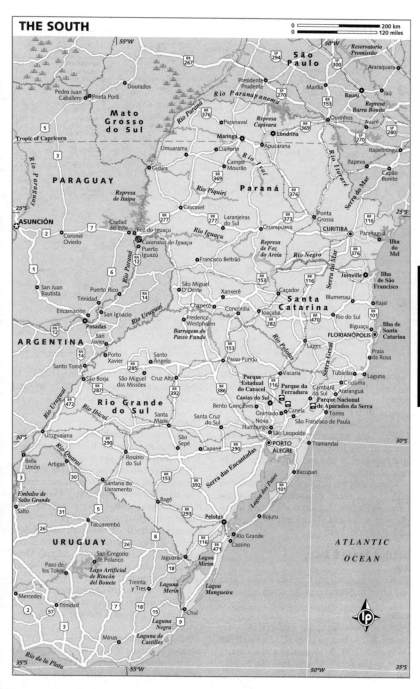

BRAZIL

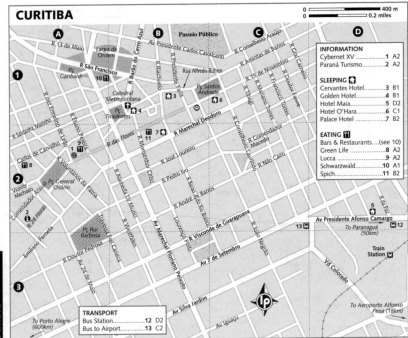

CURITIBA

INFORMATION	
Cybernet XV **1** A2	
Paraná Turismo..........**2** A2	

SLEEPING	
Cervantes Hotel..........**3** B1	
Golden Hotel................**4** B1	
Hotel Maia...................**5** D2	
Hotel O'Hara...............**6** C1	
Palace Hotel **7** B2	

EATING	
Bars & Restaurants....(see 10)	
Green Life **8** A2	
Lucca **9** A2	
Schwarzwald................**10** A1	
Spich...........................**11** B2	

TRANSPORT	
Bus Station..................**12** D2	
Bus to Airport..............**13** C2	

Green Life (Rua Carlos de Carvalho 271; buffet US$5; lunch) Most of the ingredients at this all-organic vegetarian restaurant come from the owners' own farm.

Lucca (Rua Ébano Pereira 19; mains US$5-7; 9.30am-6.30pm) This handsome café off Rua das Flores serves inexpensive lunch plates as well as pastas, *panini* and quiche, plus frothy cappuccinos.

Schwarzwald (Rua Claudino dos Santos 63; mains from US$7) One of many atmospheric options on Largo da Ordem, Schwarzwald serves filling plates of wurst and other German fare along with cold draft beer.

Getting There & Away

AIR

There are flights from Curitiba to São Paulo and other major cities in the south.

BUS

Frequent buses run to São Paulo (US$20, 6½ hours), Rio de Janeiro (US$32, 12 hours), Foz do Iguaçu (US$30, 10 hours) and all major cities to the south. If you miss the train to Paranaguá, there are plenty of buses.

Direct buses run to Asunción (US$40, 18 hours), Buenos Aires (US$66, 28 hours) and Santiago (US$120, 52 hours).

TRAIN

The railway from Curitiba (altitude 900m) to the port of Paranaguá is the most exciting in Brazil, with sublime panoramas.

There are two methods of travel: the *trem* (regular train) and the *litorina* (tourist train). The *trem* leaves Curitiba at 8.15am daily, though it goes only as far as Morretes on Monday to Friday, arriving at 11.15am (and returning at 3pm). On weekends and holidays it goes all the way to Paranaguá, arriving around 1.15pm (and returning at 2pm). One-way tourist-class tickets cost US$22. Sit on the left side for the best views.

The air-conditioned *litorina* leaves Curitiba at 9.15am on weekends, starting back from Morretes at 2.30pm. One-way tickets are a pricey US$50.

Schedules change frequently so check in advance by calling ☎ 3323-4007 or logging on to www.serraverdeexpress.com.br. On weekends it's wise to buy tickets in advance.

Getting Around

Alfonso Pena airport is 18km from the city (US$25 by taxi). An Aeroporto–Centro bus leaves every 20 minutes (US$1) from Av Presidente Afonso Camargo. A classier silver shuttle bus ('Aeroporto Executivo'; US$3) goes direct every 20 minutes to the center making only select stops, including the bus station, Praça Tiradentes and Rua 24 Horas.

The white Linha Turismo bus is a great way to see the sights that lie outside Curitiba's downtown. It starts from Praça Tiradentes every half hour from 9am to 5.30pm Tuesday to Sunday. You can get off the bus at any of the 25 attractions and hop on the next one. It costs US$7.50 for four tickets.

PARANAGUÁ

☎ 0xx41 / pop 140,000

Most visitors to this sleepy riverside town are coming and going in a hurry. Paranaguá, after all, is both the terminus of the scenic train ride from Curitiba and the embarkation of boat trips to idyllic Ilha do Mel. Although it has an active port you wouldn't know it, strolling the old colonial waterfront. Colorful but now faded public buildings and churches create a feeling of tropical decadence – just the right ambience for an afternoon's exploration.

The main **tourist office** (☎ 3422-6882; Rua General Carneiro; ☻ 8am-6pm), along the waterfront, is very helpful.

Pousada Itiberê (☎ 3423-2485; Rua Heitor Ariente 142; s/d US$10/17), a secure cheapie on the waterfront, has basic but clean *quartos* (rooms with shared bathroom).

In a restored colonial building, **Hotel Ponderosa** (☎ 3423-2464; Rua Prescilinio Corrêa 68; s/d US$10/20) has good-value en suite rooms.

Barreado (meat stew cooked in a clay pot) is the region's culinary treat. Try it at the inexpensive **Mercado Municipal do Café** (Rua General Carneiro) on the waterfront.

Out-of-town buses leave from the bus station on the waterfront. There are frequent buses to Curitiba (US$5.50, 1½ hours). For details on the train ride to/from Curitiba, see opposite.

ILHA DO MEL

☎ 0xx41 / pop 1200

The state's most enchanting getaway is this oddly shaped island at the mouth of the Baía da Paranaguá. Here you'll find excellent beaches, good surfing waves and scenic coastal walks. Traffic consists only of boats and surfboard-carrying Brazilians as cars are not allowed on the island. A young party crowd descends from January to Carnaval, and over Easter. Otherwise it's a tranquil, relatively isolated place.

Sights & Activities

Ilha do Mel consists of two parts joined by the beach at Nova Brasília. The larger, northern part is mostly an ecological station, little visited except for Praia da Fortaleza, where an 18th-century fort still stands, and a little farther Praia Ponta do Bicho.

For fine views, visit the Farol das Conchas (Conchas Lighthouse), east of Nova Brasília. The best beaches are east-facing Praia da Fora, Praia do Miguel and Praia Ponta do Bicho. It's a 2½-hour walk along the coast from Nova Brasília to Encantadas.

Sleeping & Eating

Rooms are harder to find on summer weekends and other peak times, but you can always pitch a tent or sling a hammock in Nova Brasília (around US$4 per person).

The biggest concentration of *pousadas* is at Praia do Farol, along the track to the right from Nova Brasília.

Smaller Encantadas, in the southwest of the island, feels crowded on summer weekends. For inexpensive seafood, try the Fim do Trilha restaurant complex (mains US$3.50 to US$10) facing Praia da Fora. On Friday and Saturday nights you'll find some live music and probably a beach party.

Hostel Zorro (☎ 3426-9052; www.hostelzorro.com.br; dm/d from US$9/25) This popular hostel facing the beach has decent all-wooden rooms. There's a communal kitchen and outdoor lounge area.

Pousada Caminho do Farol (☎ 3426-8153; www.pousadatropical.com; dm US$10) This pleasant but rustic place 200m from the Nova Brasília dock has en suite rooms with tile floors and fans.

Pousadinha (☎ 3426-8026; http://pousadinha.com.br; s/dfrom US$12/20) About 100m from the Nova Brasília dock, this popular budget place has a handful of decent rooms.

Sonho de Verão (☎ 3426-9048; sonho-deverao@uol.com.br; s/d from US$12/25) On the main path in town, this place has rustic but nicely decorated en suite rooms and use of a kitchen.

Grajagan Surf Resort (☎ 3426-80433; www.grajagan.com.br; dm/d/camping US$20/60/6) A few steps from

Praia Grande, this handsome *pousada* has comfortable rooms, each with a veranda and sea-facing hammock. Good outdoor restaurant and bar.

Pousada Girassol (☎ 3426-8006; heliodasilva@onda .com.br; d US$25) Close to Pousadinha, this friendly guesthouse has cozy en suite rooms.

Toca do Abutre (mains US$6-13) This Nova Brasília surf bar–seafood restaurant has live music some nights.

Getting There & Away

Three boats daily go first to Nova Brasília then Encantadas from the jetty opposite the tourist office in Paranaguá (US$6, two hours). Boats currently depart Paranaguá at 8.30am, 1.30pm and 4.30pm; they return from Nova Brasília at the same times.

Alternatively, you could take a bus to Pontal do Sul, on the mainland opposite Encantadas, and from there take a boat for the 4km crossing to Encantadas (US$5, 30 to 40 minutes). In high season, boats leave at least hourly from 8am to 5pm.

ILHA DE SANTA CATARINA

☎ 0xx48 / pop 388,000 including Florianópolis

Ilha de Santa Catarina has a remarkably varied landscape, with mountains covered by Mata Atlântica (Atlantic rainforest), pristine lakes, tranquil pine forests and sand dunes large enough to surf down. The beaches are the real attraction here, with a beautifully diverse landscape – from remote forest-backed sands to wild, rugged shoreline sprinkled with surfers and sun worshippers.

Santa Catarina's allure, however, is no secret, and crowds from all over Brazil, Argentina and Uruguay pack the beaches from December to February.

While the northern half of the island is heavily developed, the south remains fairly untouched. Old fishing villages dot the coastline, with oyster farms and old Azorean settlements along the west coast. Hiking trails (notably from Pântano do Sul) go over the lush peaks to empty, unspoiled beaches. There's also a lake (Lagoa do Peri), which is smaller and more peaceful than Lagoa da Conceição in the north.

Activities

For a short kayaking or sailing trip across **Lagoa do Peri**, contact **Vicente** (☎ 3389-5366; vicente@barcomania.com.br; per person US$25), who

takes no more than four passengers and speaks mostly Portuguese. For trips on **Lagoa da Conceição**, you can catch one of the regularly scheduled water taxis (US$2) next to the bridge in the middle of the town Centro da Lagoa. Boat tours to beautiful, undeveloped **Ilha do Campeche**, off the island's east coast (US$15), are another option: you can check out ancient inscriptions and snorkel in pretty lagoons. Call or visit **Scuna Sul** (☎ 3225-1806), which departs from a green jut of land at the southern end of Praia da Armação. Boats leave from here typically at 9am or 10am most days (US$17).

Sleeping & Eating

Keep an eye out for signs advertising '*se aluga quarto/apartamento*'. There are many places to camp. Heading from north to south, these are our picks.

Praia do Moçambique is a stunning 14km-long beach hidden from the road by a pine forest. At its northern end is the **Pousada Rio Vermelho** (☎ 3296-1337; www.riovermelhopousada .com.br; Rodovia João Gualberto Soares 8479; ste/chalet from US$46/52; 🏊 🐾). Located in São João de Rio Vermelho, this is a great option with large grounds, a pool and easy beach access. Accommodations are in beautifully furnished suites or in attractive chalets with kitchens.

About 2km south of there is a **campground** (☎ 3269-9984; Rodovia João Gualberto Soares s/n; per person US$7), just a short stroll to the beach.

Continuing south you'll reach Praia da Joaquina, whose huge dunes are visible for kilometers. You can rent sand boards (US$5 per hour) to surf the dunes. On the beach are several hotels, including the **Joaquim Beach Hotel** (☎ 3232-5059; www.joaquinabeachhotel.com.br; s/d from US$25/30; 🏊), with pleasant rooms, some with ocean views.

The incredibly busy town bordering Lagoa do Conceição is called Centro da Lagoa and it has numerous *pousada*s, most of which are overpriced. An exception is **Pousada Dona Zilma** (☎ 3232-5161; Rua Prefeito Acácio Garibáldi São Thiago 279; s/d from US$13/25), a family-run guesthouse with comfortable *apartamentos*. It's one block from the lake, about 1km east of the bridge.

On the southern end of the island you'll find Praia da Armação, a surfer favorite. Among several inexpensive guesthouses is **Pousada Pires** (☎ 3237-5161; www.pousadapires.cjb.net;

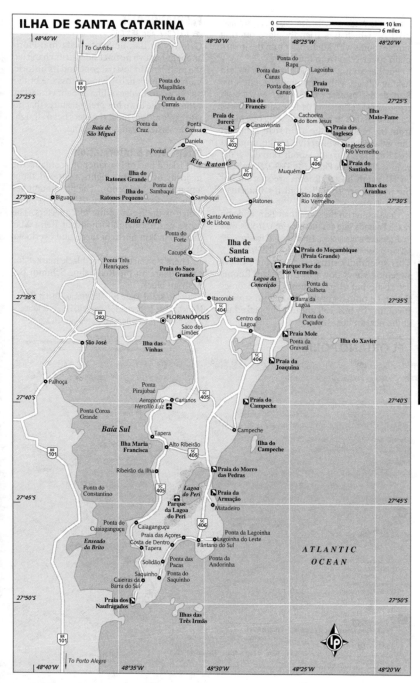

ILHA DE SANTA CATARINA

0 ———— 10 km
0 ———— 6 miles

To Curitiba

BR 101

Ponta do Rapa

Ponta das Canas

Lagoinha

Ponta do Magalhães

Praia Brava

Ponta das Canas

Ponta dos Currais

Ilha do Francês

Baía de São Miguel

Ponta da Cruz

Praia de Jurerê

Canasvieiras

Cachoeira do Bom Jesus

Ilha Mato-Fame

Ponta Grossa

SC 402

SC 403

Praia dos Ingleses

Daniela

Ingleses do Rio Vermelho

Pontal

Rio Ratones

SC 401

Muquém

SC 406

Praia do Santinho

Ilha do Ratones Grande

Ponta de Sambaqui

Ilha do Ratones Pequeno

Sambaqui

Ratones

São João do Rio Vermelho

Ilhas das Aranhas

Biguaçu

Baía Norte

Santo Antônio de Lisboa

Ilha de Santa Catarina

Praia do Moçambique (Praia Grande)

Ponta do Forte

Parque Flor do Rio Vermelho

Cacupé

Lagoa da Conceição

Ponta da Galheta

Ponta Três Henriques

Praia do Saco Grande

Itacorubi

SC 404

Barra da Lagoa

Ponta do Caçador

FLORIANÓPOLIS

BR 282

Centro do Lagoa

Praia Mole

São José

Saco dos Limões

Ponta da Gravatá

Ilha do Xavier

Ilha das Vinhas

SC 406

Praia da Joaquina

Palhoça

Ponta Pirajubaé

Aeroporto Hercílio Luz

Cariamos

SC 405

Praia do Campeche

Ponta Coroa Grande

Baía Sul

Tapera

BR 101

Ilha Maria Francisca

Alto Ribeirão

SC 405

Campeche

Ilha do Campeche

Ribeirão da Ilha

Praia do Morro das Pedras

SC 405

Lagoa do Peri

Praia da Armação

Ponta do Constantino

Parque da Lagoa do Peri

Matadeiro

Ponta do Cuiagançuçu

Caiagançuçu

SC 406

Praia das Açores

Ponta da Lagoinha

Lagoinha do Leste

Enseado da Brito

Costa de Dentro

Tapera

Pântano do Sul

ATLANTIC OCEAN

Solidão

Ponta das Pacas

Ponta da Andorinha

Saquinho

Ponta do Saquinho

Caieiras da Barra do Sul

Praia dos Naufragados

Ilhas das Três Irmãs

BR 101

To Porto Alegre

Margin coordinates:
48°40'W 48°35'W 48°30'W 48°25'W 48°20'W
27°25'S
27°30'S
27°35'S
27°40'S
27°45'S
27°50'S

BRAZIL

Rua Prefeito Acácio Garibáldi São Thiago 279; s/d from US$13/25), which is a friendly place offering simple rooms with kitchens. It's on the town's main street, 50m from the beach.

Further south, Pântano do Sul is an old fishing village, with a few simple restaurants. **Pousada do Pescador** (☎ 3237-7122; www.pousada dopescador.com.br; Rua Manoel Vidal 257; s/d from US$30/40) has nice chalets in a garden setting one block from the beach. On the main road 2km past the village you will arrive at the unpaved Rua Rosália P Ferreira. About 1km down the road is **Albergue do Pirata** (☎ 3389-2727; dm US$8), an HI youth hostel. Rooms are spartan but the owners are friendly, and it's Catarina's cheapest place.

Continuing on the same road 2km, and you reach **Pousada Sítio dos Tucanos** (☎ 3237-5084; www .pousadasitiodostucanos.com; Estrada Rosália Ferreira 2776; s/d low season US$40/50; s/d high season US$55/72; ☐). This splendidly situated guesthouse offers sweeping views down to the ocean. Rooms are rustic but elegant, most with balconies that open onto a gurgling mountain stream. If coming by bus, call ahead to be picked up at the nearest bus stop.

FLORIANÓPOLIS
☎ 0xx48 / pop 388,000

Gateway to Ilha de Santa Catarina, Florianópolis has two distinct sides to its character: the mainland industrial zone and its historic, more laid-back half – lying across the bridge on the western edge of Ilha de Santa Catarina. Although the town has pretty features that invite exploration, most travelers head straight for the eastern half of the island.

Orientation & Information

The island half of Florianópolis contains the majority of the city's sights, scattered about a pretty, colonial centre. The bus station lies a few blocks west of Praça XV de Novembre, which is the heart of the old quarters. The more upscale neighborhood of Beira-Mar lies about 2km north of there, and overlooks the bay.

There's an active street black market for cash dollars on the Rua Felipe Schmidt pedestrian block.

Banco do Brasil (Praça 15 de Novembro, 20) Has ATMs.
Moncho (Rua Tiradentes 181; per hr US$2; ☺ 8.30am-8.30pm Mon-Fri, 9am-1pm Sat) Cheap internet access.

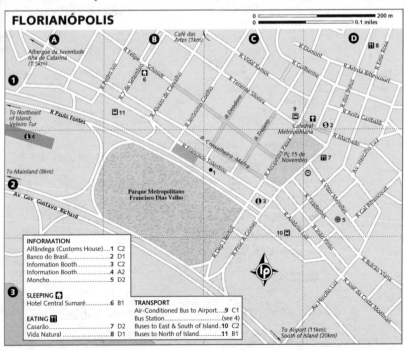

FLORIANÓPOLIS

Information booths bus station (☎ 3228-1095; Rua Paulo Fontes); town (☎ 3223-4997; Praça Fernando Machado) For town and island information. The town branch is a few steps south of Praça XV de Novembro.

Sleeping & Eating

The liveliest drinking spots are along the bay-facing Beira-Mar Norte, about 1.5km north of Praça XV.

Albergue da Juventude Ilha de Catarina (☎ 3225-3781; www.floripahostel.com.br; Rua Duarte Schutel 227; dm/d from US$10/22) In town, this very welcoming HI hostel is a 10-minute walk from the bus station.

Hotel Central Sumaré (☎ 3222-5359; Rua Felipe Schmidt 423; s/d US$27/39, s/d with shared bathroom US$17/30) This simple hotel has small but quaint rooms with wood floors.

Casarão (Praça 15 de Novembro 320; per kg US$9; ☺ 11am-11pm Mon-Fri, to 3pm Sat) Housed in an old colonial building on the main square, Casarão has a good lunch buffet and evening à la carte.

Café das Artes (Rua Esteves Júnior 734; sandwiches US$2-4; ☺ 11:30am-11pm Mon-Sat, 4-11pm Sun) This artsy, upscale café in the Beira-Mar Norte neighborhood sells sandwiches, good coffee and baked goods.

Vida Natural (Rua Visconde de Ouro Prêto 298; buffet US$4.50; ☺ lunch Mon-Fri) This all-vegetarian joint spreads a large and appetizing buffet in a colonial setting.

Getting There & Away

From here there are daily flights to São Paulo and Porto Alegre, and connections to most other cities. Long-distance buses link Florianópolis with Torres (US$15, four hours) Porto Alegre (US$25, 6½ hours), Curitiba (US$17, 4½ hours), São Paulo (US$38, 12 hours), Rio de Janeiro (US$78, 18 hours), Foz do Iguaçu (US$45, 14 hours), Buenos Aires (US$90, 25 hours) and Montevideo (US$95, 18 hours).

Getting Around

The airport is 12km south of Florianópolis. To get there, you can take a taxi (US$16), Correador Sudoeste local buses from the bus station (US$1), or you could travel by air-con Correador Sudoeste bus (US$2.50) from the stop next to the cathedral on Praça 15 de Novembro.

Local buses and yellow microbuses (which take surfboards) serve all the beaches. Buses

for the east and south of the island (including Lagoa da Conceição) leave from the local bus terminal in town on Rua Antônio Luz. Buses for the north leave from the local bus terminal on Rua Francisco Tolentino, close to the main bus station.

The island is a good place to rent a car. **Yes Rent a Car** (☎ 3236-0229) generally offers the best rates (from US$37 a day). It has an office at the airport, but will deliver a car to any hotel on the island.

TORRES

☎ 0xx51 / 34,000

Fine beaches, beautiful rock formations and good surrounding country for walks make the small town of Torres a great pit stop while traversing the coast. Located 205km northeast of Porto Alegre, Torres has numerous surfing competitions throughout the year. The nearby **Ilha dos Lobos**, a rocky island about 2km out to sea, is home to sea lions in the winter months. The town gets packed on summer weekends.

Stop in the **tourist office** (☎ 3626-1937; cnr Av Barão do Rio Branco & Rua General Osório) for a map and a list of guesthouses. **Hotel Medusa** (☎ 3664-2378; Rua Benjamin Constant 828; s/d US$14/19) is a friendly, family-owned place with basic, inexpensive rooms. The attractive **Pousada da Prainha** (☎ 3626-2454; www .pousadadaprainha.com.br; Rua Alferes Feirreira Porto 138; s/d US$20/30, high-season d US$50) has comfy rooms one block from the beach. You can camp at **Camping Beira Mar** (☎ 9129-7868; Rua Alexandrino de Alencar 5551).

Bom Gosto (Av Barão do Rio Branco 242) is a delicious *churrascaria* and **Doce Art** (Av Silva Jardim 295) has good espresso and baked delights.

Buses run to/from Porto Alegre (US$15, 4½ hours, 10 daily) and Florianópolis (US$15, five hours, three daily).

PARQUE NACIONAL DE APARADOS DA SERRA

☎ 0xx54

This magnificent **national park** (admission US$3; ☺ 9am-5pm Wed-Sun) is 70km northeast of São Francisco de Paula and 18km from Cambará do Sul. The big attraction is the **Cânion do Itaimbezinho**, a fantastic narrow canyon with sheer escarpments of 600m to 720m. Two waterfalls drop into this deep incision.

The Parque Nacional de Aparados da Serra **visitors center** (☎ 3251-1277) has maps, a café and guides for Trilha Cotovelo. Guides can also be hired through **Acontur** (☎ 3251-1320; Cambará do Sul), the local guide association.

There are three hiking trails in the park: **Trilha do Vértice** (2km each way) and **Trilha Cotovelo** (2½ hours return) go to waterfalls and offer canyon vistas; **Trilha do Rio do Boi**, best approached from Praia Grande, east of the national park, follows the base of the canyon for 7km. It's for experienced hikers and is closed during the rainy season. A guide is highly recommended.

Cambará do Sul has small *pousadas* and many families rent rooms in their houses.

Close to the bus station, the busy guesthouse **Pousada Itaimbeleza** (☎ 3251-1367; Rua Dona Ursula; s/d US$15/30) has basic rooms popular with backpackers.

Two kilometers from town on the road to Ouro Verde, **Pousada Corucacas** (☎ 3251-1123; www.guiatelnet.com.br/pousadacorucacas; s/d US$30/60) has horseback riding and fishing. Price includes breakfast and dinner.

One daily bus from Porto Alegre goes to São Francisco de Paula and Cambará do Sul (US$12, six hours). Buy tickets the night before. From Torres on the coast, one daily bus runs to Praia Grande and Cambará do Sul.

No buses go to the park itself. Your best bet is to arrange a taxi or minivan (round trip US$30).

CANELA
☎ 0xx54

North of Porto Alegre is the Serra Gaúcha, a popular area for walking. The bus ride from the city is beautiful, as are the mountain resorts of Canela and pricier Gramado. In winter there are occasional snowfalls and in spring the hills are blanketed with flowers.

Canela's **tourist office** (☎ 3282-1287; www.canela .com.br; Lago da Fama 227) in the center of town provides maps and information.

Sights

Nine kilometers north from Canela, the major attraction is **Parque Estadual do Caracol** (admission US$2.50; ☀ 8:30am-5:30pm) is the spectacular Cascata do Caracol, a 130m waterfall. The Linha Turística bus runs there from the tourist office every two hours from Tuesday to Sunday.

Parque da Ferradura (admission US$3; ☀ 9am-5:30pm) is a 6km hike from the Parque do Caracol entrance. It's a stunning 420m horseshoe-shaped canyon with three lookouts along well-marked trails.

Activities

Adventure tourism – rock climbing, rappelling, rafting, mountain biking, bungee jumping – is big business here. Ask at the tourist office, or the agencies **At!tude** (☎ 3282-6305; Av Osvaldo Avanha 391) or **JM Rafting** (☎ 3282-1255; Av Osvaldo Aranha 1038).

Sleeping & Eating

All the restaurants are on or just off the main street, Av Osvaldo Aranha.

Pousada do Viajante (☎ 3282-2017; Rua Ernesto Urban 132; dm/d US$15/30) Next to the bus station, this great, inviting HI youth hostel has tidy rooms.

Hotel Bela Vista (☎ 3282-1327; www.canela.tur.br/ho telbelavista.htm; Av Osvaldo Aranha 160; s/d from US$15/30) In the center of town, this place is a good value for its clean, simple *quartos*.

Churrascaria Espelho Gaúcho (☎ 3282-4348; Rua Baden Powell 50; mains US$8) A great *churrascaria* with an all-the-meat-you-can-eat option.

Getting There & Around

Frequent buses run to/from Porto Alegre (US$9, 2½ hours) via Gramado. There are also buses to São Francisco de Paula (US$3, one hour), from where you can connect to Cambará do Sul to get to the Parque Nacional de Aparados da Serra.

PORTO ALEGRE
☎ 0xx51 / pop 1.4 million

Though not the most beautiful destination, the flourishing port town of Porto Alegre is a good introduction to progressive Rio Grande do Sul. Built on the banks of the Rio Guaíba, this lively, modern city has a well-preserved neoclassical downtown, with handsome plazas, fascinating museums and cultural centers and a vibrant arts and music scene.

Information

Citibank (Rua 7 de Setembro 722) Has ATMs.
Cyber Zone (Rua Dr Flores 386; per hr US$2; ☀ 9am-9.30pm Mon-Fri, to 5.30pm Sat) A stylish internet café.
Prontur (Av Borges de Medeiros 445) Exchanges cash and traveler's checks.
Tourist office (Mercado Público, Praça 15 de Novembro; ☀ 9am-6pm) Helpful office; also at the airport.

Sights

The 1869 **Mercado Público** (Public Market) and the adjacent Praça 15 de Novembro constitute the city's heart. Shops in the market sell the *gaúchos'* unique tea-drinking equipment, the *cuia* (gourd) and *bomba* (silver straw) as well as *mate* (the powdery tea). The interesting **Museu Histórico Júlio de Castilhos** (Rua Duque de Caxias 1231; admission US$2; 🕙 10am-5pm Tue-Sun) contains diverse objects related to Rio Grande do Sul's history, such as special moustache cups. The **Museu de Arte do Rio Grande do Sul** (Praça da Alfândega; 🕙 10am-5pm Tue-Sun) has a good collection of *gaúcho* art. Near Lake Guaíba is the Usina do Gasômetro, an abandoned thermoelectric station that's been turned into a showcase for visual art, dance and film.

The **Casa da Cultura Mario Quintana** (☎ 3221-7147; Rua dos Andradas 736) hosts theater, concerts and art exhibitions; it also has a popular cinema and an outdoor 7th-floor café with live music (from 7pm).

Sleeping

Marechal Hotel (☎ 3228-3076; www.hotelmarechal.com.br; Rua Andrade Neves 123; s/d US$8/15, s/d with bathroom US$14/18) This budget hotel has worn rooms with old wood floors and tall ceilings. The price and hospitable owners make it a decent choice.

Hotel Palácio (☎ 3225-3467; Rua Vigário José Inácio 644; s/d US$15/24, with bathroom US$20/32) This friendly place has simple, carpeted rooms with lime green walls, fluorescent lights (yikes) and old wooden furnishings.

Hotel Ritz (☎ 3225-0693; Av André da Rocha 225; s/d US$16/23, s/d with bathroom US$20/30) This welcoming place has basic but cheery rooms with tile floors and sizable windows. It features a small patio and hotel guests can use the kitchen.

Hotel Praça Matriz (☎ 3225-5772; Largo João Amorim de Albuquerque 72; s/d US$17/25) Housed in a neoclassical mansion, this aging hotel has basic rooms, some with French doors opening onto Praça da Matriz.

Eating

The Mercado Público has a central food hall, with good choices like Banco 40, serving tasty homemade ice cream.

There's an assortment of bars in Cidade Baixa, about 2km south of the old center (a US$3 taxi ride).

Delicia Natural (Rua dos Andradas 1325 2nd fl; all-you-can-eat buffet US$5; 🕙 lunch Mon-Fri) A lunchtime

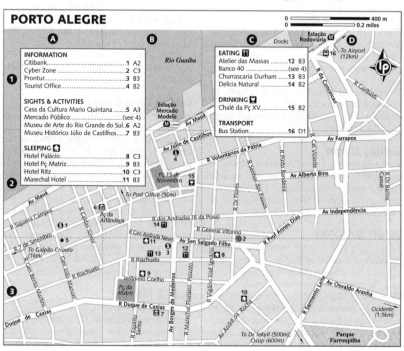

PORTO ALEGRE

0 — 400 m
0 — 0.2 miles

favorite, Delicia has an extremely fresh, vegetarian-friendly buffet.

Churrascaria Durham (Rua Riachuelo 1300; fixed-price buffet US$6) A standard *churrascaria* with all-you-can-eat beef, chicken and pork straight off the grill.

Atelier das Massas (Rua Riachuelo 1482; mains US$6-10; ☺ closed Sun) Modern, downtown joint with good pasta and original paintings on the walls.

Galpão Crioulo (Parque Maurício Sirotsky Sobrinho; all-you-can-eat buffet US$20) This high-end choice is the city's best *churrascaria*, with over 20 different grilled cuts and an extensive buffet.

Drinking

Chalé da Praça XV (Praça 15 de Novembro) An *alegrense* tradition is having a late-afternoon beer at this place, built in 1885.

Dr Jekyll (Travessa do Carmo 76; ☺ 11pm-dawn Mon-Sat) Cidade Baixa's best late-night watering hole with live music (alternative rock) some nights.

Ossip (☎ 3224-2422; Rua da República 677) In Cidade Baixa, another colorful drinking spot.

Ocidente (Av Osvaldo Aranha 960) A good bar for dancing, 2km east of downtown.

Getting There & Away

The busy bus station at Largo Vespasiano Julio Veppo has separate terminals for destinations in and outside Rio Grande do Sul. International buses run to Montevideo (US$62, 12 hours) and Buenos Aires (US$84, 20 hours). Other buses go to Foz do Iguaçu (US$41, 15 hours), Florianópolis (US$17, seven hours), Curitiba (US$30, 11 hours) and Rio de Janeiro (US$70, 24 hours).

Getting Around

Porto Alegre has a one-line *metrô*. The most useful stations are Estação Mercado Modelo (by the port), Estação Rodoviária (the next stop) and the airport (three stops beyond). A ride costs US$1.

JESUIT MISSIONS

In the early 17th century Jesuit missionaries established a series of Indian missions in a region straddling northeast Argentina, southeast Paraguay and neighboring bits of Brazil. Between 1631 and 1638, after devastating attacks by slaving expeditions from São Paulo and hostile Indians, activity was concentrated in 30 more easily defensible missions. These became centers of culture as well as religion –

in effect a nation within the colonies, considered by some scholars an island of utopian progress and socialism, which at its height in the 1720s had over 150,000 Guarani Indian inhabitants.

Seven of the now-ruined missions lie in the northwest of Brazil's Rio Grande do Sul state, eight are in Paraguay and 15 in Argentina.

Orientation & Information

The town of Santo Ângelo is the main jumping-off point for the various Brazilian missions, and has a **tourist office** (☎ 0xx55-3381-1294; www.missoesturismo.com.br).

The most interesting and intact of the missions is **São Miguel das Missões** (admission US$4, evening sound-&-light show US$2.50), 53km southwest, reachable by four daily buses. See the Argentina (p88) and Paraguay (p808) chapters for information on missions in those countries.

Sleeping & Eating

Santo Ângelo's cheapies are on or near Praça Rio Branco.

Pousada das Missões (☎ 0xx55-3381-1202; www.albergues.com.br/saomiguel; dm/s/d US$15/22/33) A pleasant HI hostel right next to São Miguel mission.

Hotel Barichello (☎ 0xx55-3381-1327; Av Borges do Canto 1559; s/d US$22/34) Also in São Miguel, this hotel has a good *churrascaria* on-site.

Hotel Comércio (☎ 0xx55-3312-2542; Av Brasil 1178; r US$30) Has nice amenities for a reasonable price.

Getting There & Away

There are eight daily buses from Porto Alegre to Sânto Angelo (US$30, 7½ hours).

It's possible to enter Argentina by crossing the Rio Uruguai from Porto Xavier to San Javier, or from São Borja to Santo Tomé, or at Uruguaiana, 180km south of São Borja (with buses to Buenos Aires). But if you're heading for the Argentine missions, more frequent buses (seven daily) depart from Puerto Iguazú (across the border from Foz do Iguaçu) for San Ignacio Miní (US$24, five hours). For the Paraguayan missions, daily buses go to Encarnación from Ciudad del Este, Paraguay, also opposite Foz do Iguaçu.

FOZ DO IGUAÇU

☎ 0xx45 / pop 295,000

The stupendous roar of 275 waterfalls crashing 80m into the Rio Iguaçu seems to create a low-level buzz of excitement all over the small town of Foz, even though the famed Cataratas are 20km southeast of the city center. Even on the hottest afternoon, nature's relentless churning power is present. Apart from the waterfalls, which should be visited on both sides, you can dip into the forests of Paraguay and check out Itaipu dam, one of the largest hydroelectric power plants in the world.

Information

Along Av Brasil there are many banks and exchange houses. It's not safe to walk near the riverfront at any time; robberies are fairly common along the bridge to Ciudad del Este in Paraguay.

Foztur information booth (☎ 0800-451516; www .iguassu.tur.br) airport (☻ noon-last plane); Central (Av Jorge Schimmelpfeng); local & long-distance bus stations (☻ 7am-6.30pm) Provides maps and detailed info about the area.

Sights & Activities

To see the falls properly, you must visit both sides – Brazil gives the grand overview and Argentina (p90) the closer look. The **Brazilian side** (admission US$10; ☻ 9am-5pm) has far fewer attractions than the Argentine side; and the costs are higher here if you want to arrange an under-the-falls boat trip. But there are some adventures unique to this side, including combination kayaking-hiking trips and rafting trips offered by **Macuco Safari** (www.macucosafari.com.br).

Five minutes' walk from the waterfalls entrance is the worthwhile **Parque das Aves** (Bird

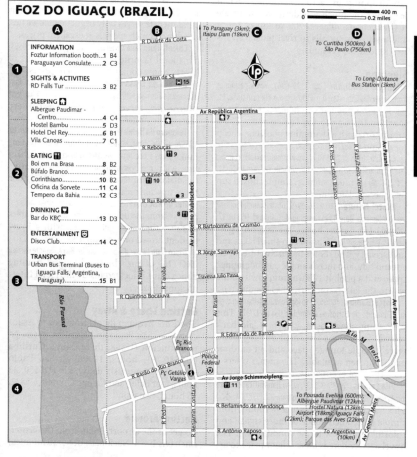

FOZ DO IGUAÇU (BRAZIL)

0   400 m
0   0.2 miles

INFORMATION
Foztur Information booth...**1** B4
Paraguayan Consulate......**2** C3

SIGHTS & ACTIVITIES
RD Falls Tur **3** B2

SLEEPING 🛏
Albergue Paudimar - Centro............................**4** C4
Hostel Bambu **5** D3
Hotel Del Rey..................**6** B1
Vila Canoas **7** C1

EATING 🍴
Boi em na Brasa **8** B2
Búfalo Branco.................**9** B2
Corinthiano....................**10** B2
Oficina da Sorvete **11** C4
Tempero da Bahia **12** C3

DRINKING 🍸
Bar do KBÇ....................**13** D3

ENTERTAINMENT 🎭
Disco Club......................**14** C2

TRANSPORT
Urban Bus Terminal (Buses to Iguaçu Falls, Argentina, Paraguay)...................**15** B1

To Paraguay (3km); Itaipu Dam (18km)

To Curitiba (500km) & São Paulo (750km)

To Long-Distance Bus Station (3km)

Av República Argentina

R Duarte da Costa
R Mem de Sá
R Rebouças
R Xavier da Silva
R Rui Barbosa
R Bartolomeu de Gusmão
R Jorge Sanways
Travessa Júlio Passa
R Quintino Bocaiúva
R Edmundo de Barros

R Nalpi
R Tarobá
Av Brasil
Av Juscelino Kubitscheck
R Almirante Barroso
R Marechal Floriano Peixoto
R Marechal Deodoro da Fonseca
R Santos Dumont
R Prés Castelo Branco
R Patulheiro Venâncio
Av Paraná

Rio Paraná

Pç Rio Branco
Polícia Federal
R Barão do Rio Branco
Pç Getúlio Vargas

R Pedro II
R Benjamin Constant

Av Jorge Schimmelpfeng

R Berlamindo de Mendonça
R Antônio Raposo

To Pousada Evelina (600m); Albergue Paudimar (12km); Hostel Natura (13km); Airport (18km); Iguaçu Falls (22km); Parque das Aves (22km)

To Argentina (10km)

Rio M Boicy
Av General Meira

BRAZIL

Park; www.parquedasaves; admission US$8; 8.30am-5.30pm), a five-hectare park where you can see some 800 different bird species. Pay in US dollars to avoid bad exchange rates.

If you're not heading onto Paraguay, it's well worth doing a day trip across the river from Iguaçu. **RD Falls Tur** (3574-4157; www.rdfallstur.gov.br; Hotel San Remo, Rua Xavier da Silva 563) offers excursions there, as well as rappelling, rafting and other adventure trips around the region. If you're headed east after Iguaçu, ask about the trips to Prudentópolis.

For a splurge, **Helisul** (3529-7474; www.helisul.com; flights US$60), based inside the park, runs 10-minute helicopter flights over the falls.

North of town, the **Itaipu dam** (3520-6985; www.itaipu.gov.br; 9.30am-8pm Mon-Sat) is another jaw-dropping attraction, especially when learning how much was destroyed to create it (indigenous villages, 700 sq km of forest and a set of waterfalls to rival Iguaçu's). It's free to tour the grounds.

Sleeping

Albergue Paudimar (3529-6061; www.paudimar.com.br; Av das Cataratas; dm with/without YHI card US$8/11;) Foz's popular youth hostel, 12km from town on the way to the falls, is more like a miniresort, with a swimming pool, bar, cheap meals and internet access.

Centro (3028-5503; www.paudimarfalls.com.br; Rua Antônio Raposo 820; dm with/without YHI card US$8/11;) A much smaller, simpler hostel run by Albergue Paudimar.

Hostel Natura (9116-0979; hostelnatura@hotmail.com; Alameda Buri 333; camping/dm around US$10/17;) The newest hostel in Foz is on a gorgeous piece of land, amid two small lakes and lush scenery. The rooms themselves are pleasant and tidy, and there's ample outdoor lounge space and a pool. It's 13km from town on the way to the falls (same turnoff as Paudimar).

Hostel Bambu (3523-3646; www.hostelbambu.com; Rua Edmundo de Barros 621; dm/d/tr US$11/27/32) This welcoming new hostel attracts a laid-back crowd. The rooms are small but cozy, and there's ample lounge space and an outdoor patio. Kitchen available. The owner offers a wide range of excursions.

Vila Canoas (3523-8797; www.hotelvillacanoas.com.br; Av República Argentina 926; s/d/q from US$17/22/24;) This friendly hotel has a range of rooms, from simple fan-cooled quads to more stylish and colorful doubles with air conditioning. The travel agency here is an excellent place to ar-

range excursions, including trips to Paraguay and inexpensive transport to the Argentine side of the falls.

Pousada Evelina (3574-3817; www.pousadaevalina.com.br; Rua Irlan Kalichewski 171; s/d/tr from US$22/30/37;) Nicely designed rooms are one of the big attractions at Pousada Evelina, and you'll also find a refreshing pool and cozy lounge areas.

Hotel Del Rey (3523-2027; www.hoteldelreyfoz.com.br; Rua Tarobá 1020; s/d/tr US$25/40/45;) Del Rey is a friendly place with spacious, comfortable rooms and a good buffet breakfast.

Eating & Drinking

There's lots of both going on in Foz, especially along Av Jorge Schimmelpfeng at night.

Oficina da Sorvete (Av Jorge Schimmelpfeng 244; mains from US$4) In addition to refreshing ice cream, this pleasant café serves tasty baguette sandwiches, salads and lunch specials at excellent prices.

Corinthiano (Rua Xavier da Silva 392; lunch buffet US$3) This local favorite spreads a lunch buffet of hearty home cooking at excellent prices.

Boi em na Brasa (Av Juscelino Kubitschek & Rua Bartolomeu de Gusmão; BBQ US$7.50) This all-you-can-eat *churrascaria* serves good cuts of meat at very reasonable prices.

Tempero da Bahia (Rua Marechal Deodoro 1228; mains for 2 US$20-27; dinner Mon-Sat) This handsome restaurant serves excellent *moqueca* and other Bahian fare, with live bossa nova from 8pm onward.

Búfalo Branco (Rua Rebouças 530; BBQ US$15) For more upscale meat-eating.

Bar do KBÇ (Rua Pres Castelo Branco & Rua Jorge Sanways) Across from the university, the sidewalk tables at this simple bar get packed with a lively student crowd on weeknights.

Disco Club (www.discoclub.com.br; Rua Almirante Barroso 2006) One of Foz's best and longest-running dance clubs is located inside the Hotel Internacional Foz.

Getting There & Away

There are frequent flights from Foz to Asunción, Rio, São Paulo and Curitiba. Buses go to Asunción (US$8, three daily), Curitiba (US$30, 9½ hours, 14 daily), São Paulo (US$40, 16 hours, six daily), Rio (US$50, 22 hours, four daily) and Campo Grande (US$32, 16 hours, two daily).

Getting Around

To get to the airport, 16km from the center, catch bus 120 'P Nacional' (US$1, 30 minutes)

GETTING TO ARGENTINA & PARAGUAY

Americans and several other nationalities need a visa to enter Paraguay. Get this in advance. Most nationalities can enter Argentina without a visa, but double-check before you arrive.

To Ciudade del Este, Paraguay: it's inadvisable to walk across the bridge because of robberies. Take a bus or taxi. At the immigration posts, be sure to request your (Brazilian) exit and (Paraguayan) entry stamp. This may not happen automatically. From the border post, you can catch the next bus to Ciudad del Este (buses don't wait for travelers to complete their proceedings) or grab a taxi. For information on entering Brazil from Paraguay, see p810.

For crossing to Puerto Iguazú, Argentina: again, you'll have to request your exit and entry stamps, and local bus drivers won't stop at the Brazilian border unless you ask. They probably won't wait around either border while you finish formalities, but you can always grab the next bus. Many hotels and hostels have private vans that ferry passengers to and from the falls (for around US$20) in Argentina to avoid hassle. This will definitely save you time (but again, tell your driver to stop at the Brazil border). Both borders are open 24 hours, but bus service ends around 7pm. For information on entering Brazil from Argentina, see p91.

---

from any stop on Av Juscelino Kubitschek after Rua Barbosa. A taxi is around US$18.

Going from the bus station (6km out) into town, catch any 'TTU' bus (US$1), which will drop you at the local terminal. A taxi costs US$5.50.

The Parque Nacional bus 400 (US$1) runs to the Brazilian side of the waterfalls from the urban bus terminal on Av Juscelino Kubitschek, every half hour until midnight, daily except Monday morning.

For the Argentine side of the falls, catch a Puerto Iguazú bus (US$2) in front of the urban bus terminal or any stop along Av Juscelino Kubitschek. They pass about every 10 minutes (every 50 minutes on Sunday) until 7pm. At Puerto Iguazú bus station, transfer to a bus to the falls (p89).

Buses run every 10 minutes (30 minutes on Sunday) to Ciudad del Este from the army base opposite the urban bus terminal in Foz.

THE CENTRAL WEST

One of the most important wetland systems on the planet, the Pantanal is the star attraction of the Central West. Its meandering rivers, savannas and forests harbor one of the densest concentrations of plant and animal life in the New World. Wildlife-lovers simply shouldn't miss this place. Other attractions in the Central West include dramatic *chapadas* (tablelands), which rise like brilliant red giants from the dark green *cerrado*. Breathtaking panoramas, spectacular waterfalls and picturesque swimming holes are all part of the equation, along with some unusual wildlife sharing the terrain.

In the southwest corner of the region, Bonito is another natural attraction inviting plenty of adventure. Here you can snorkel down crystal-clear rivers teeming with fish, rapel into the Abyss (one of Bonito's caverns) or raft along forest-lined rapids. Those with a taste for the surreal should consider visiting Brazil's master-planned capital Brasília; while tiny colonial Goiás Velho offers more old-world delights.

BRASÍLIA

☎ 0xx61 / pop 2.3 million

A vision of the future, circa 1960, Brasília is a monument to architectural design and urban planning. Built from nothing in about three years, Brasília replaced Rio de Janeiro as Brazil's capital in 1960 and today it's one of Brazil's most rapidly growing cities. Its chief creators were President Juscelino Kubitschek, architect Oscar Niemeyer, urban planner Lucio Costa and landscape architect Burle Marx.

While Brasília has a fine assortment of bars and restaurants, with abundant nightlife and cultural attractions, much of the activity is in the *asas* (wings), far from the concrete jungle of the downtown; and you really need a car to make the most of this widely spread city.

Orientation

The central area is shaped like an airplane and it's divided into Asa Norte (North Wing) and Asa Sul (South Wing). The government buildings and monuments are located in the fuselage, along the Eixo Monumental.

BRAZIL

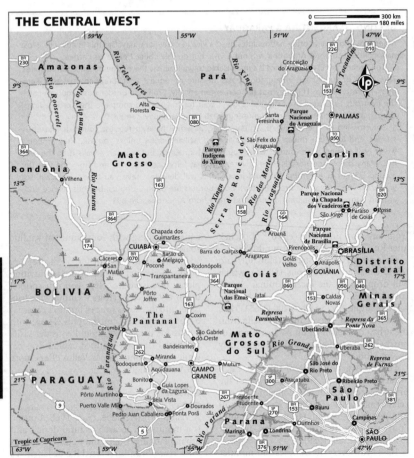

THE CENTRAL WEST

Information

Banks with exchange facilities are in the Setor Bancár-io Sul (SBS, Banking Sector South) and Setor Bancário Norte (SBN, Banking Sector North), both close to the local bus station.

Airport tourist office (☎ 364-9135; ☒ 7am-11pm) The best place for information. Staff can organize hotel discounts. There is also an information booth at the TV Tower.

Sights & Activities

Brasília's major edifices are mostly spread along a 5km stretch of the Eixo Monumental and are listed in northwest–southeast order here. To visit them you can rent a car or combine buses from the local bus station (buses 104 and 108 are the most useful) with some long walks. You can also book guided tours of the city (US$30) at any travel agency: several are inside the **Hotel Nacional** (SHS Quadra 1 Bloco A).

Start at the **Memorial JK** (admission US$2; ☒ 9am-5pm Tue-Sun), which houses the tomb of President Kubitschek and has exhibits on Brasília's construction. Then head to the observation deck of the **TV Tower** (☒ 9am-6pm Tue-Sun, 2-6pm Mon). About 1km southwest along Via W3 Sul, off the Eixo Monumental, is the **Santuário Dom Bosco** (☒ 8am-6pm), a church with very beautiful blue stained-glass windows.

The **Catedral Metropolitana** (☒ 8am-5pm), with its curved columns, stained glass and haunting statues of the four evangelists, is worth seeing too. The most interesting government buildings, the **Palácio do Itamaraty**, **Palácio da Justiça** and **Palácio do Congresso**, are in the 'cockpit' of the airplane ground-plan.

Sleeping

Good budget accommodations are hard to find, though many midrange and high-end hotels slash their prices on weekends. The most inexpensive places used to be on or near Via W3 Sul, 1km or 2km southwest of the Eixo Monumental, but the government has recently shut down many of these places. Call before you go.

Taxi drivers often tell tourists to stay in hotels outside the city center – usually the suburbs of Taguatinga or Núcleo Bandeirante. Be careful in Núcleo, which has a lot of *favelas*.

Cury's Solar (☎ 3244-1899; Quadra 707, Bloco I, Casa 15; s/d US$15/30) If you don't mind a little crowding, this is a good option. It's clean, family-run, very safe, and guests are welcome to use the kitchen and washer-dryer.

Pensão da Zenilda (☎ 3224-7532; Quadra 704, Bloco Q, Casa 29; s/d US$15/30) An apartment with rooms to let. It sleeps five and has kitchen and laundry facilities for guest use.

Casablanca (☎ 3228-8273; www.casablancabrasilia .com.br; SHN Quadra 3, Bloco A; s/d US$60/75; 🖭) Close to the TV Tower, this friendly hotel has comfortable rooms with good weekend discounts.

Eating & Drinking

A good selection of restaurants is clustered in SCLS 405. Here you'll find Italian, French, Spanish, Portuguese, Tex-Mex, Korean, Japanese, Chinese, Thai and vegetarian eateries. It's packed on weekends.

Bar Beirute (SCLS Quadra 109, Bloco A, Lojas 2/4) An institution in Brasília with Middle East–themed dishes, and outdoor tables under trees. It's a lively bar later in the evening.

Gate's Pub (SCLS Quadra 403, Bloco B, Loja 34; cover US$10; 🖭 9pm-3am Tue-Sun) One of the city's best music venues, with rock, reggae or funk bands most nights, followed by dance music.

Locals flock to these air-conditioned shopping malls to chow down. All have small cafés and food courts with a decent variety:

Conjunto Nacional (Asa Norte, SCN)

Pátio Brasil (Asa Sul, W3, SCS)

Pier 21 (Setor de Clubes Esportivos Sul) The pick of the bunch.

Shopping Brasília (Asa Norte, SCN QD 5, lote 2)

Getting There & Away

There are numerous flights to almost anywhere in Brazil.

From *Rodoferroviária* (the giant long-distance bus and train station), 5km northwest of the center along the Eixo Monumental, daily buses go almost everywhere, including Goiânia (US$10, three hours), Rio (US$78, 17 hours), Salvador (US$85, 24 hours), Cuiabá (US$40, 18 hours) and Belém (US$113, 34 hours).

Getting Around

The airport is 12km south of the center. From the local bus station, take bus 102 (US$2, 40 minutes) or minibus 30 (US$2, 25 minutes). A taxi from the airport to the center costs US$15 through the tourist office.

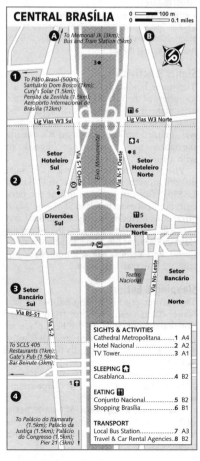

CENTRAL BRASÍLIA

SIGHTS & ACTIVITIES	
Cathedral Metropolitana........1 A4	
Hotel Nacional 2 A2	
TV Tower.............................3 A1	

SLEEPING 🏠	
Casablanca...........................4 B2	

EATING 🍴	
Conjunto Nacional.................5 B2	
Shopping Brasília..................6 B1	

TRANSPORT	
Local Bus Station..................7 A3	
Travel & Car Rental Agencies..8 B2	

Take bus 131 from the local bus station to the long-distance bus and train station.

There are car-rental agencies at the airport, the Hotel Nacional Brasília and the Hotel Garvey Park.

PARQUE NACIONAL DA CHAPADA DOS VEADEIROS

Just over 220km north of Brasília, this spectacular park showcases the unique landscape and flora of high-altitude *cerrado*. Big skies, hills rising like waves from the plains, scenic waterfalls and natural swimming pools make for a sublime landscape. Wildlife you're likely to see includes maned wolves, giant anteaters and 7ft-tall rheas.

Information

Tourist office (☎ 0xx62-3446-1159; Ave Ari Valadão; ☷ 8am-5pm Mon-Sat, 9am-noon Sun) This excellent office is 200m from the bus station in Alto Paraíso de Goiás town, southeast of the park.

Sights & Activities

The lunar landscape and otherworldly atmosphere of the **Vale da Lua** (Moon Valley; admission US$3) make it the most unusual sight in the area. It's around 5km east of São Jorge on a well-marked walking trail, and it's outside the national park, so you're not obliged to go with a guide.

Visitors to the national park itself must go with an accredited guide (from US$15 to US$30). You can organize this at the park entrance or at most hotels in São Jorge. Main attractions include the canyons (**Cânion I** and **Cânion II**) along the Rio Preto, the waterfalls (**Salto do Rio Preto I & II**; 80m and 120m, respectively), and **Morro da Baleia**, a humpback hill with a 2.5km trail to the top.

Sleeping & Eating

The former crystal mining hamlet of São Jorge, 40km west, and 2km from the national park entrance, is the best place to stay.There are plenty of campgrounds (campsites US$5 per person), mostly backyards, in São Jorge.

Pousada Trilha Violeta (☎ 0xx61-9985-6544; s/d US$35/45) This friendly place has large rooms set around a garden.

Pousada Água de Esperança (☎ 0xx61-9971-6314; s/d US$35/45) This place has comfortable rooms in a wood building and a balcony strung with hammocks.

Villa São Jorge (pizzas US$9-14) A laid-back, outdoor restaurant and bar with tasty pizzas.

Getting There & Away

There are daily buses connecting Alto Paraíso de Goiás with Brasília (US$15, 3½ hours), Goiânia (US$24, six hours), and for Palmas (Tocantins, US$26, seven hours). The Palmas bus goes via Natividade. One daily bus goes from Alto Paraíso de Goiás to São Jorge (US$3, one hour).

GOIÂNIA

☎ 0xx62 / pop 1.2 million

The capital of the state of Goiás, 205km southwest of Brasília, Goiânia is of little interest except as a staging post for the state's historic towns or national parks.

Ask for discounts at all hotels on weekends. Centrally located **Goiânia Palace** (☎ 3224-4874; Av Anhanguera 5195; s/d from US$20/30) is among the best budget options in town. The homey **Principe Hotel** (☎ 3224-0085; Av Anhanguera 2936; s/d US$22/44) is another good deal.

A good per-kilo lunch spot is the central **Argu's** (Rua 4 No 811; per kg US$7).

Varig, TAM and Gol all fly to Goiânia. Buses leave regularly for Brasília (US$12, three hours), Cuiabá (US$40, 13 hours) and Goiás Velho (US$12, three hours).

GOIÁS VELHO

☎ 0xx62 / pop 27,000

As dusk falls in this little town 145km northwest of Goiânia and the churches light their bell towers, a palpable quiet settles over the village and – except for the black jungle mountains silhouetted against the darkening sky – one might almost be in 18th-century Portugal. Goiás Velho is among the most picturesque of the Central West's colonial towns.

Book ahead if you're arriving on a weekend or during Holy Week.

In a good central location, colonial guesthouse **Pousada do Sol** (☎ 3371-1717; Rua Dr Americano do Brasil 17; s/d US$15/28) has simple rooms with good top-floor views.

Pousada Casa do Ponte (☎ 3371-4467; Rua Moretti Foggia s/n; s/d US$25/45) is a '50s-style hotel with clean rooms, close to the town center.

THE PANTANAL

This vast natural paradise is Brazil's major ecological attraction and offers a density of exotic wildlife found nowhere else in South

America. During the rainy season (October to March), the Rio Paraguai and lesser rivers of the Pantanal inundate much of this low-lying region, creating *cordilheiras* (patches of dry land where animals cluster). The waters rise as much as 3m above low-water levels around March in the northern Pantanal and in June in the south. This seasonal flooding has severely limited human occupation of the area but it provides an enormously rich feeding ground for wildlife. The waters teem with fish; birds fly in flocks of thousands and gather in enormous rookeries.

Altogether the Pantanal supports 650 bird species and 80 mammal species, including jaguars, ocelots, pumas, maned wolf, deer, anteaters, armadillos, howler and capuchin monkeys and tapirs. The most visible mammal is the capybara, the world's largest rodent, often seen in family groups or even large herds. And you can't miss the alligators, which, despite poaching, still number somewhere between 10 and 35 million.

Orientation & Information

The Pantanal covers some 230,000 sq km (89,000 sq miles) and stretches into Paraguay and Bolivia, although the lion's share is Brazil's. Much of this territory is only accessible by boat or on foot. It's muggy at the best of times, and in the summer the heat and mosquitoes are truly awesome. Stock up on sunscreen and bug repellent, because you won't find any here.

Bringing tourists into the Pantanal is now a big business, and seemingly overnight the three cities that serve as jumping-off points to the region have been flooded with tour operators – some of dubious repute. Whether you arrive in Cuiabá, Corumbá, or Campo Grande you can expect to be approached by a guide fairly rapidly. Some of these individuals are simply opportunists looking to make a buck out of Brazil's ecotourism, but there are still a few old-timers working to protect the environment while sharing its tremendous diversity with visitors. It can be hard to tell the good from the bad, but here are some suggestions to ensure you have a safe and enjoyable trip:

- Resist making a snap decision, especially if you've just come off an overnight bus.
- Go to the local tourism office. Most can't give independent advice because they're government funded, but they do keep complaints books that you're free to peruse. There's a lot to be gleaned from other travelers 'experiences.'
- Remember that the owner or salesperson is not always your guide, and it's the guide you're going to be with in the wilderness for three to five days. Ask to meet your guide if possible.
- Try to get things in writing and don't hand over your cash to any go-betweens.
- Compare your options. Most operators work out of the local bus station or airport, so it's easy to shop around.

There's no obligation to go with a tour operator. You can drive or hitchhike across the Transpantaneira road that starts in the northwest (Mato Grosso state), or the Estrada Parque that loops around the south (Mato Grosso do Sul).

The Transpantaneira is generally considered the best road for hitching or driving. It heads 145km south from Poconé, south of Cuiabá. You'll see wildlife even without a guide.

Tours

Ecological Expeditions (☎ 0xx67-3782-3504; pantanaltrekking.com; Rua Joaquim Nabuco 185; per 3 days US$160)

In Campo Grande, this well-organized operation has an office just opposite the bus station. Its three-night/four-day packages attract heaps of budget travelers who are looking for wildlife, but don't mind the big group–party atmosphere. Free nights in the Campo Grande hostel help sweeten the deal.

Joel Souza Ecoverde Wildlife Safari Tours (Map p335; ☎ 0xx65-3624-1386; Pousada Ecoverde, Cuiabá; per day US$60)

Operating from Cuiabá, this outfit offers bird-watching and nature tours, including excursions on farms, meals, hikes and boat rides. Contact Joel at Pousada Ecoverde (p335). He speaks English, German and Spanish, and the tours are excellent.

Munir Nasr's Natureco (Map p335; ☎ 0xx65-3321-1001; www.natureco.com.br; Rua Benedito Leite 570, Cuiabá; from US$120 a day)

Another highly recommended Cuiabá guide who organizes all-inclusive tours into the Pantanal.

Pantanal Discovery (☎ 0xx67-3383-9791; www.gilspantanaldiscovery.com.br; Campo Grande; per 3 days US$175)

On the ground floor of the Campo Grande bus station, Pantanal Discovery offers three-night/four-day packages, and it generally receives favorable reviews. Package includes bus fare to the pickup point (Buraco da Piranha) at the entrance to Estrada Parque, meals and accommodations at the rustic Portal do Lontra lodge.

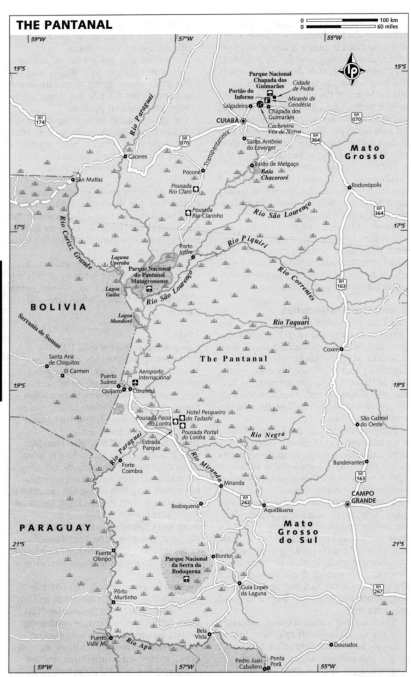

THE PANTANAL

0 — 100 km
0 — 60 miles

BRAZIL

59°W 57°W 55°W

15°S 15°S

BR 174

Rio Paraguai

Parque Nacional Chapada dos Guimarães
Cidade de Pedra
Portão do Inferno
Mirante de Geodésia
Salgadeira
Chapada dos Guimarães
CUIABÁ
Cachoeira Véu de Noiva

BR 070

BR 364

BR 070

Mato Grosso

Cáceres

San Matías

Santo Antônio do Leverger

Barão de Melgaço
Baía Chacororé

Rodonópolis

Poconé

Transpantaneira

Pousada Rio Claro

Pousada Rio Clarinho

Rio São Lourenço

BR 364

17°S 17°S

Rio Cuiabá Grande

Laguna Uperaba

Parque Nacional do Pantanal Matogrossense

Porto Jofre

Rio Piquiri

Rio Correntes

BR 163

Lagoa Gaíba

Rio São Lourenço

BOLIVIA

Lagoa Mandioré

Rio Taquari

Serrania de Sunsas

Coxim

The Pantanal

Santa Ana de Chiquitos
El Carmen

Aeroporto Internacional

19°S 19°S

Puerto Suárez
Quijarro
Corumbá

Hotel Pesqueiro do Tadashi

São Gabriel do Oeste

Pousada Passo do Lontra

Pousada Portal do Lontra

Rio Negra

Bandeirantes

BR 163

Estrada Parque

Forte Coimbra

Rio Miranda

Miranda

CAMPO GRANDE

Rio Paraguai

Bodoquena

BR 262

Aquidauana

Mato Grosso do Sul

PARAGUAY

21°S 21°S

Fuerte Olimpo

Parque Nacional da Serra da Bodoquena

Bonito

BR 267

Pôrto Murtinho

Guia Lopes da Laguna

Bela Vista

Puerto Valle Mi

Rio Apa

Pedro Juan Caballero
Ponta Porã

Dourados

59°W 57°W 55°W

Sleeping & Eating
TRANSPANTANEIRA

There are quite a lot of accommodations on and off the road.

Pousada Rio Clarinho (☎ 0xx65-9977-8966; Transpantaneira Km 42; per person incl full board US$45) This charmingly rustic *fazenda* (large farm) offers boat and horse rides. The food is authentic Pantanal; check out the old-time kitchen and the wood-fired stove. Cheerful and friendly.

Pousada Rio Claro (☎ 0xx65-3345-2249; Transpantaneira Km 45; per person incl full board US$75) Another good-value *pousada* offering all-inclusive stays (meals, excursions, lodging).

SOUTHERN PANTANAL

Pousada Portal do Lontra (☎ 0xx67-3231-6136; per person incl meals US$25) Another classic Pantanal wood-on-stilt structure, with lots of wildlife around. It's well worn but highly recommended. Activities cost extra.

Hotel Pesqueiro do Tadashi (☎ 0xx67-3231-9400; per person incl meals US$50; ☼ Feb-Oct) Friendly, clean and very comfortable *pesqueiro* (fishing lodge) on the riverbank close to the bridge. Highly recommended and good value.

Pousada Passo do Lontra (☎ 0xx67-231-6569; www .passodolontra.com.br; campsites per person US$4, r per person incl meals US$75, chalets US$120; ☼) A comfortable place that offers horseback rides and walking, but the main focus is the river safaris.

CUIABÁ

☎ 0xx61 / pop 525,000

The capital of Mato Grosso state, Cuiabá is a lively frontier boomtown and a good starting point for visiting the Pantanal or the Chapada dos Guimarães, the geological center of South America.

Banco do Brasil (Rua Getúlio Vargas 915) has ATMs. Internet access is at **Point One** (Av Mato Grosso 96A; per hr US$2; ☼ 8:30am-midnight Mon-Sat, 1pm-1am Sun).

The **Museo do Índio** (☎ 3615-8489; Av Fernando Correia da Costa; ☼ 8-11am & 2-5pm Mon-Fri, 8-11am Sat) is worth a visit for its exhibits on Xavante, Bororo and Karajá tribes. Catch bus 406 on Av Tenente Coronel Duarte heading for the university.

Sleeping

Pousada Ecoverde (☎ 0xx65-3624-1386; Rua Pedro Celestino 391; s/d/tr US$8/11/15) Very good value, if a little rustic. There's a delightful courtyard and garden, and laundry facilities are available. Free transport from bus station or airport if you call in advance.

Portal do Pantanal Youth Hostel (☎ 0xx65-624-8999; www.portaldopantanal.com.br; Av Isaac Póvoas 655; dm US$10) Offers basic accommodations. Laundry and kitchen facilities are available to guests for a small fee.

Hotel Samara (☎ 0xx65-3322-6001; Rua Joaquim Murtinho 270; s/d US$12/24) Offers basic, boxy rooms at low prices.

Eating & Drinking

The center is almost deserted (and not safe) at night, but there are good restaurants nearby on Av Getúlio Vargas.

Mistura Cuiabana (☎ 624-1127; cnr Rua Padre Celestino & Rua Candido Mariano; meals per kg US$4; ☼ 11am-2pm Mon-Fri) A good cheap lunch spot right in the center.

Choppão (Av Getulio Vargas s/n; meals for 2 US$15) This is a classic Cuiabá eatery serving obscenely large meals of meat or fish; and you can drink the coldest *chope* (draft beer) in town.

Peixaria Popular (Av São Sebastião 2324; dishes US$8-18; ☼ 11am-midnight Mon-Sat) Outside of the center, this award-winning restaurant serves delectable plates of fish.

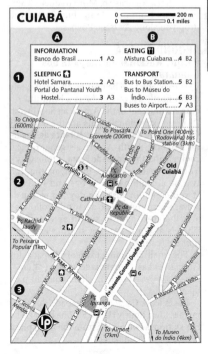

CUIABÁ

0 ——— 200 m
0 ——— 0.1 miles

INFORMATION	
Banco do Brasil 1 A2	

SLEEPING	
Hotel Samara................2 A2	
Portal do Pantanal Youth	
Hostel.....................3 A3	

EATING	
Mistura Cuiabana ..4 B2	

TRANSPORT	
Bus to Bus Station...5 B2	
Bus to Museu do	
Índio.....................6 B3	
Buses to Airport......7 A3	

BRAZIL

Getting There & Away

Varig, TAM and Gol connect Cuiabá with many Brazilian cities, with the notable omission of Corumbá.

The bus station is 3km north of the center on the Chapada dos Guimarães highway. Destinations include Cáceres (US$13, 3½ hours, six buses daily), Porto Velho (US$66, 24 hours, several daily), Goiânia (US$40, 13 hours, frequently), Brasília (US$52, 20 hours, one bus in the morning and one at night) and Campo Grande (US$36, 10 hours, eight daily).

Car-rental agencies just outside the airport grounds tend to be cheaper than those inside. The best vehicles for the Transpantaneira are a VW Golf or Fiat Uno.

Getting Around

The airport is in Varzea Grande, 7km south of the center. The 'Rodoviaria/Marajoara,' '24 de Dezembro' and 'Pireneus' buses, from opposite the Las Velas Hotel near the airport, go to the center. Buses from the center to the airport depart from the east side of Praça Ipiranga.

'Centro' buses from inside the bus station go to Praça Alencastro. More frequent 'Centro' buses from outside the bus station will drop you along Av Isaac Póvoas.

AROUND CUIABÁ
Parque Nacional da Chapada dos Guimarães

This rocky plateau beginning approximately 60km northeast of Cuiabá is a beautiful region reminiscent of the American Southwest. Its three exceptional sights are the 60m falls **Cachoeira Véu de Noiva**, the **Mirante de Geodésia** lookout (South America's geographical center), and the **Cidade de Pedra** (Stone City). You can reach all three by car, or the first two by a combination of bus and walking. If you come for just one day, go to **Véu de Noiva**, where you can do a day hike following a well-signed path to six other waterfalls. There's also a restaurant serving excellent *pintado* (catfish).

The small, charming town of Chapada dos Guimarães has a **Secretária de Turismo** (☎ 0xx65-3301-2045; Av Perimentral s/n), where you can pick up a map.

Buses leave Cuiabá for Chapada dos Guimarães town hourly (US$3.50, one hour). The bus station is two blocks from the main plaza (Praça Dom Wunibaldo).

A few blocks from the plaza, **Hotel São José** (☎ 0xx65-3301-2479; Rua Vereador José de Souza 50; s/d US$7.50/15) has basic rooms at low prices. Facing Chapada town's main plaza, the **Pousada Bom Jardim** (☎ 0xx65-3301-1244; Praça Dom Wunibaldo; s/d from US$12/25) has decent rooms; the best are cheery and bright. Restaurants cluster around Praça Dom Wunibaldo.

Cáceres
☎ 0xx65 / pop 67,000

This relaxed town on the Rio Paraguai 215km west of Cuiabá is 115km from the Bolivian border town of San Matías.

Capri Hotel (☎ 3223-1711; Rua Getúlio Vargas 99; s/d US$9/18), near the bus station, has basic but clean rooms and a few spacious *apartamentos*. Closer to the river and center, **Rio Hotel** (☎ 3223-3084; Praça Major João Carlos; s/d US$18/30) is a good option.

A bus leaves Cáceres daily for San Matías and Santa Cruz, Bolivia (US$36, 24 hours). You can get a Brazilian exit stamp from Cáceres' Polícia Federal, 4km from the center on Av Getúlio Vargas (US$12 round trip by taxi).

Poconé
☎ 0xx65 / pop 23,000

Poconé, lying 100km southwest of Cuiabá, is the gateway to the most rugged part of the Transpantaneira. From here, the 'highway' becomes little more than a pockmarked dirt track as it heads south into the Pantanal, terminating at Porto Jofre.

The best places to stay, especially if you're trying to organize a lift down the Transpantaneira, are a couple of kilometers out of town near the beginning of the road. **Pousada Pantaneira** (☎ 3345-1630; s/d US$13/26) has grim rooms, but its restaurant's *rodízio* (all-you-can-eat) is pretty good.

Six daily buses run from Cuiabá to Poconé (US$8, 2½ hours).

CAMPO GRANDE
☎ 0xx67 / pop 735,000

The lively capital of Mato Grosso do Sul state is a major gateway to the Pantanal.

The **tourist office** (☎ 3324-5830; Av Afonso Pena & Av Nordeste; ⊗ 8am-7pm Tue-Sat, 9am-noon Sun), three blocks from the bus station, has friendly staff and an extensive database on Mato Grosso do Sul. It does its best to give independent advice.

BRAZIL

Sleeping & Eating

The following inexpensive hotels are clustered around the bus station, which is safe during the day, and less so at night.

Campo Grande Youth Hostel (☎ 3382-3504; www .pantanaltrekking.com; Rua Joaquim Nabuco 185; s/d/tr/q US$12/17/22/25; 🖳 🕿) Opposite the bus station, the youth hostel has small rooms and a refreshing pool. Pantanal excursions available.

Hotel Cash (☎ 3382-0217; Rua Barão do Rio Branco 342; s/d/tr/q with fan US$12/17/22/30; d with air-con US$22; 🕄) Offers tidy but basic rooms at good prices.

Turis Hotel (☎ 3382-7688; Rua Alan Kardec 200; s/d with fan US$12/22, with air-con US$16/25; 🕄) This place has small, fairly new rooms with tile floors and decent natural light.

Hotel Iguaçu (☎ 3322-4621; www.hoteliguacu.com.br; Rua Dom Aquino 761; s/d US$30/35; 🕄) Opposite the bus station, this popular and friendly place has pleasant rooms with wood floors (some have balconies).

Galpão Gaúcho (Av Alan Kardec 209; meals US$7; 🕑 lunch) One block west of the bus station, this inexpensive *churrascaria* has decent roasted meats and a small buffet.

Fontebella (Av Afonso Pena 2535; pizzas US$5-10) One kilometre east of the bus station, this charming place serves ice cream by day and pizzas by night.

Casa do Peixe (Rua Dr João Rosa Pires 1030; buffet US$15) Serves a decadent all-you-can-eat seafood buffet in a casual, air-conditioned environment. It's one block south and four blocks west of the bus station.

Getting There & Away

Varig, TAM and Gol provide daily flights to/ from São Paulo, Cuiabá, Rio and Brasília.

Eight daily buses run to Corumbá (US$32, six daily): the four direct services take around six hours, but if you want to get off at Estrada Parque take a nondirect one. Other daily serv-ices include Cuiabá (US$32, 10 hours), Bonito (US$21, five hours), Ponta Porã (US$23, five hours), São Paulo (US$60, 12 hours) and Foz do Iguaçu (US$36, 16 hours).

Getting Around

Buses to the center (7km) go from the stop on the main road outside the airport. To get from the center to the airport, take the In-dubrasil bus.

CORUMBÁ

☎ 0xx67 / pop 88,000

On the Rio Paraguai, this port is a gateway to both the Pantanal and to Bolivia, which is only 15 minutes away. At night the river sun-sets are beautiful, and although the city has a reputation for poaching and drug trafficking, travelers are generally left alone.

ATMs are at **HSBC** (Rua Delamare 1067). Many shopkeepers on Rua 13 de Junho exchange Bolivian, Brazilian and US money.

Sematur (☎ 3231-7336; Rua Manoel Cavassa 275) can provide a list of Pantanal guides, tour compa-nies, hotels and boat trips.

Among the cheapies, **Hotel Nelly** (☎ 3231-6001; Rua Delamare 902; s/d US$6/10) is a good choice with simple rooms with shared bathrooms.

Hotel Laura Vicuña (☎ 3231-5874; Rua Cuiabá 775; s/d US$15/30, s/d with bathroom US$18/28) is a clean, comfortable hotel in a quiet spot near the center.

Churrascaria e Restaurante Rodeio (Rua 13 de Junho 760; per kg US$8), the snazziest per-kilo lunch spot, has dozens of salad dishes and plenty of tasty meat as well.

Nine daily buses go to Campo Grande (US$24, six hours if direct). A bus to Bonito (US$22, seven hours) leaves at 2pm.

From the bus stop outside Corumbá bus station, the Cristo Redentur bus (US$1) runs to the local bus terminal on Rua 13 de Junho.

GETTING TO BOLIVIA

The Fronteira–Corumbá bus (US$1, every 30 minutes) from Praça Independência on Rua Dom Aquino goes to the Bolivian border. A motorcycle taxi is US$2, and a taxi costs US$6.

All Brazilian border formalities must be completed in Corumbá with the Poláia Federal (Praêa Repsblica 51). If you're just crossing into Bolivia for a few hours to buy train tickets, you don't need a Brazilian exit stamp.

Money changers at the frontier accept US, Brazilian and Bolivian cash.

The Bolivian border town of Quijarro is little more than a collection of shacks. Taxis run the 4km between the border and Quijarro train station for around US$8 (*mototaxis* cost US$4). See the Bolivia chapter (p246) for details of the train trip between Quijarro and Santa Cruz.

BRAZIL

You can take a motorcycle taxi (US$2) from the local bus station if your luggage is light. A taxi costs around US$7.

BONITO

☎ 0xx67 / pop 18,000

Amid spectacular natural wonders, Bonito is a small, charming town in southwest Mato Grosso do Sul that is enjoying the ecotourism boom. Most travelers come here to snorkel down crystal-clear rivers, but there are dozens of other ways to enjoy the scenery, from rappelling and rafting to horseback riding and bird-watching. Despite its popularity, the town is still a great place to kick back outside peak holiday periods (December to February).

Only local travel agencies are authorized to hire guides to the area's attractions, so you're obliged to book tours through them. The main street is lined with agencies, all charging the same. The better ones include **Muito Bonito Tourismo** (☎ 255-1645; Rua Coronel Pilad Rebua 1448) and **Ygarapé Tour** (☎ 255-1733; Rua Coronel Pilad Rebua 1853). River-trip prices include snorkel gear but don't include transportation, so try tacking onto a group that has already organized transport.

One of the best rivers for snorkeling is the **Rio da Prata** (5hr trip incl lunch US$46), some 50km from Bonito; the trip includes a short hike through rainforest, followed by a 3km swim among 30 varieties of fish while floating gently downstream. There's also the crystal-clear **Rio Sucuri** (3hr trip US$37) 20km from Bonito and the **Aquário Natural Baía Bonita** (3hr trip US$37), 7km from Bonito.

The **Gruta do Lago Azul** (half-day excursion US$12), 20km from Bonito, is a large cave, with a luminous underground lake and stalactites. The **Balneário Municipal** (admission US$5), 7km from Bonito, is a natural swimming pool with lots of fish (and no guide needed, easily reached by mototaxi or by bicycle). The **Abismo de Anhumas** (full-day excursion including rappelling and snorkeling US$120), 22km from Bonito, is a 72m abyss with an underground lake and incredible stalactites.

Sleeping

It's sensible to book in advance, particularly on weekends.

HI hostel Albergue da Juventude do Ecoturismo (☎ 3255-1462; www.ajbonito.com.br; Rua Lúcio Borralho 716; dm with/without YHI card US$12/15; 🖳 🖀) The lively hostel has tidy rooms set around a swimming pool. The large covered patio is a good place to meet other travelers over the nightly BBQs. It's 1.5km from the center. Excursions available.

Pousada Sucuri (☎ 3255-1420; Rua 2 de Outubro 840; s/d US$15/20; 🗱 🖳) Just off the main street, this laid-back *pousada* has pleasant en suite rooms, friendly staff and free internet.

Pousada Muito Bonito (☎ 3255-1645; contato@muito bonito.com.br; Rua Coronel Pilad Rebua 1448; s/d US$15/30; 🗱) In town, this well-located *pousada* has lovely en suite rooms and an inviting courtyard. Excursions available.

Eating

O Casarão (Rua Coronel Pilad Rebua 1843; per kg US$6) A popular per-kilo seafood restaurant.

Restaurante da Vovó (Rua Felinto Muller; per kg US$8) Serves excellent per-kilo regional food.

Cantinho do Peixe (Rua 31 de Março 1918; mains from US$10) One of the best places in town to try fresh *pintado* and other Bonito specialties.

Taboa Bar (Rua Coronel Pilad Rebua 1841) In the heart of the main street, this lively indoor-outdoor bar is an excellent spot for a drink. Live music on weekends.

Getting There & Away

Three daily buses connect Campo Grande and Bonito (US$21, five hours). Buses leave for Ponta Porã (US$16, six hours) at 12:10pm (except Sunday) and for Corumbá (US$21, seven hours) at 6am (except Sunday).

PONTA PORÃ

☎ 0xx67 / pop 66,000

Ponta Porã is a border town divided from the Paraguayan town of Pedro Juan Caballero by Av Internacional. For information on Pedro Juan Caballero, see the Paraguay chapter.

For Brazilian entry/exit stamps, go to the **Polícia Federal** (☎ 3431-1428; Av Presidente Vargas; 🕒 8am-5pm), near the Paraguayan consulate. Paraguay now requires entry visas from US citizens, which can be obtained at the same consulate.

Sleeping & Eating

This area is heavily patrolled by Brazilian and Paraguayan authorities. Drug trafficking is on the rise and it's a good idea to limit your nighttime activities.

Hotel Internacional (☎ 3431-1243; Av Internacional 2604; s/d US$13/25) A safe, inexpensive option.

Choppão (Rua Marechal Floriano 1877; mains US$8) A popular spot with an extensive menu of meat, fish and pasta.

Getting There & Around

From the bus station in Ponta Porã (about 4km from the center), frequent buses go to Campo Grande (US$16, 5½ hours). There's one bus to Corumba via Bonito. If you're coming into town from the Brazilian side, the bus can drop you at the local bus terminal on Av Internacional, near the hotels.

THE NORTHEAST

Year-round warmth, physical beauty and sensual culture rich in folkloric traditions make Brazil's Northeast a true tropical paradise.

More than 2000km of fertile coastline is studded with idyllic white-sand beaches, pockets of lush rainforest, sand dunes and coral reefs. A spectrum of natural environments creates the perfect backdrop for a wide variety of outdoor activities.

The Portuguese settled these lands first, so they breathe history. The colonial centers of Salvador, Olinda and São Luís are packed with beautifully restored and satisfyingly decaying architecture.

This is arguably Brazil's most fascinating and culturally rich region. Lively festivals, myriad music and dance styles and exotic cuisine loaded with seafood draw crowds. Magical beach villages with beautiful scenery and hip party scenes also delight.

Life is simple and slow-paced in the Northeast's agricultural interior and coastal fishing villages. People here face massive social problems, including poverty caused by underemployment and a decaying education system, housing shortages and an absence of basic services such as sanitation, which causes high infant mortality rates. Inland people often live in extreme poverty, especially in the more northerly states. Though many leave the region seeking better opportunities, Northeasterners are extremely proud of their land's beautiful human and physical geography.

GETTING THERE & AROUND

The Northeast's major airports – Salvador, Recife and Fortaleza – usually have the lowest fares. Flying into/out of Porto Seguro is a good option if looking to skip Espírito Santo. In the Northeast there is always transport from where you are to where you're going whether a bus, taxi, collective taxi, van (called *van*, *kombi* or *besta*) or moto-taxi.

SALVADOR

☎ 0xx71 / pop 2.4 million

Salvador da Bahia is one of Brazil's brightest gems. Known as the African soul of Brazil, it is its darkest city in terms of skin color and the hottest in terms of culture. Here African slave descendants preserved their culture more than anywhere else in the New World, successfully transforming them into thriving culinary, religious, musical, dance and martial-arts traditions. Salvador is famous for combining all of these sacred and secular elements in wild popular festivals. Its vibrant historic center, packed with renovated colonial architecture, has become somewhat of a tourist mecca.

Orientation

For Barra and Cidade Alta, cross the footbridge from the bus station (8km from the center) to Shopping Iguatemí and catch the air-con Praça da Sé minibus (US$2.25). Catch the same bus from the airport (over 30km from the center). For a cheaper ride, there are city bus terminals in front of both the bus station and the airport. For Barra catch a Barra 1, Vale dos Rios or STIEP R3 bus, for Cidade Alta, catch a Praça da Sé bus.

Salvador sits on a peninsula at the mouth of the Baía de Todos os Santos. The city center is on the bay side and is divided by a steep bluff into two parts: the Cidade Baixa (Lower City), containing the commercial center and port, and Cidade Alta (Upper City), containing the Pelourinho. The Pelô is the center of Salvador's history, tourism and nightlife. Gritty commercial areas (Cidade Baixa and the stretch between Praça da Sé and Praça Campo Grande) are noisy by day and deserted by night and on Sundays. South, at the tip of the peninsula, is the affluent Barra district (the Porto da Barra waterfront is a little seedy). Beachside residential neighborhoods stretch northeast along the coast, with Rio Vermelho and Itapuã being the most interesting for visitors.

Information

EMERGENCY

Deltur (☎ 3322-1168; Cruzeiro de São Francisco 14, Pelourinho)

INTERNET ACCESS

Internet cafés cluster in the Pelô and around Porto da Barra.

Sé internet (Praça da Sé 3, Pelourinho; per hr US$1) One-hour intervals only.

MONEY

Money changers along Cruzeiro de São Francisco change traveler's checks and cash. There are major bank ATMs at the bus station, airport, Shopping Barra and Shopping Iguatemi, or at the following:

Banco do Brasil (Cruzeiro de São Francisco 11, Pelourinho)
Bradesco (Praça Municipal)

POST

Central post office (Praça da Inglaterra, Cidade Baixa)
Post office (Cruzeiro de São Francisco, Pelourinho)

TOURIST INFORMATION

Bahiatursa Airport (☎ 3204-1244/1444); bus station (☎ 3450-3871); Mercado Modelo (☎ 3241-0242);

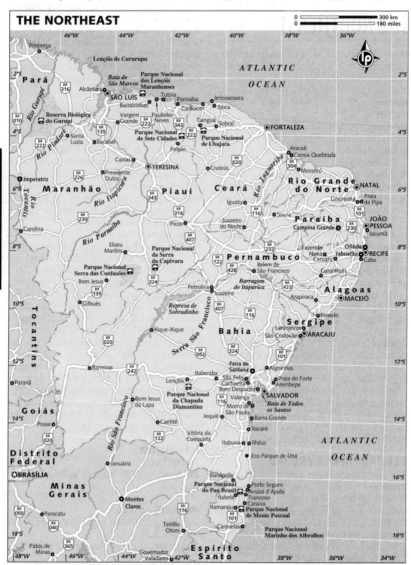

THE NORTHEAST

Pelourinho (☎ 3321-2463/2133; Rua Francisco Muniz Barreto 12) Multilingual.
Emtursa (☎ 3321-3127/2697; Praça Municipal) Multilingual.

Dangers & Annoyances

If you're going to be pickpocketed or mugged in Brazil, Salvador is likely to be the place. This shouldn't prevent you from visiting, but this is a good city in which to play it safe, especially at night. Avoid empty areas. Travelers report 'feeling like a protected species' in the Pelô, but wandering off the beaten path has proven to be unsafe. The stretch from the Largo do Pelourinho north to Santo Antônio has a reputation for nighttime muggings – take a taxi.

Women will attract annoying attention from men, especially in the Pelourinho. The best tactic is to simply ignore them. Throwing out the word *respeito* (respect) usually does wonders.

Sights

PELOURINHO

The *many* churches in the historical center and the Forte de Santo Antônio are connected by a network of underground tunnels that feeds to the port. Supposedly the tunnels were constructed for defensive purposes. While wandering around notice the schools, galleries and cultural centers that pack the historical center – the Pelô is not just for tourists.

Museu Afro-Brasileiro (Terreiro de Jesus; admission US$2.50; ☸ 9am-6pm Mon-Fri, 10am-5pm Sat & Sun) has exhibits demonstrating the African roots of Brazilian Candomblé, and a room devoted to gorgeous carved wood panels of the *orixás* (Afro-Brazilian gods). Well-done, thematic displays of old postcards portray, among other things, a visual history of Salvador at the **Museu Tempostal** (Rua Gregório de Mattos 33; admission free; ☸ 1-6pm Tue-Sat).

The church most deserving of your attention is the baroque **Igreja São Francisco** (Cruzeiro de São Francisco; admission US$1.50; music & light tour US$2.50; ☸ 9am-6pm Mon-Sat, to 5pm Sat, 1-5pm Sun), crammed with displays of wealth and splendor. Look for pregnant angels.

An oasis of beauty and tranquility, the **Museu de Arte Sacra da Bahia** (Rua do Sodré 276; admission US$2; ☸ 11:30am-5:30pm Mon-Fri) has a huge sacred-art collection in a 17th-century convent.

The steep **Largo do Pelourinho** is where slaves were auctioned and publicly beaten on a *pelourinho* (whipping post).

CIDADE BAIXA & BARRA

Solar do Unhão, an 18th-century sugar estate mansion and shipping area on the bay, houses the **Museu de Arte Moderna** (Av Contorno; admission free; ☸ 1-6pm Tue-Sun), and is a cool spot. Take a taxi there from the Mercado Modelo, as it is off bus routes and the walk is desolate and known for muggings.

The waterfront is great for people-watching and walking. View the sunset at Bahia's oldest fort, **Forte de Santo Antônio da Barra** (1598).

ITAPAGIPE PENINSULA

Built in 1745, **Igreja NS do Bonfim** (☸ 7-11am & 2-5pm Tue-Sun) is famous for its power to effect miraculous cures and is *candomblista's* most important Catholic church. Replicas of body parts devotees claim were cured are displayed. To get there, take the 'Bonfim' or 'Ribeira' bus from the base of the Elevador Lacerda.

Activities

Much of Bahian life revolves around the Afro-Brazilian religion Candomblé. A visit to a *terreiro* promises hours of ritual and possession, and will deepen your understanding of Bahian culture. Wear clean, light-colored clothes (no shorts) and go well fed. The **Federação Baiana do Culto Afro-Brasileiro** (Rua Alfredo de Brito 39) can provide addresses and schedules.

Tour operators out of the Terminal Marítimo Turístico offer fun **boat tours** of the Baía de Todos os Santos, with stops for lunch and swimming at island beaches (per person US$17.50).

Praia do Porto in Barra is a small, usually packed beach with calm waters. For less crowded beaches and cleaner water, head out to **Piatã** (25km), **Itapoã** (27km) or beyond.

Courses

Associação de Capoeira Mestre Bimba (Rua das Laranjeiras 1, Pelourinho) runs classes in *capoeira* (martial art/dance), *maculelê* (stick fighting), percussion and *berimbau*. It also gives shows (US$5).

The following offer classes in traditional and contemporary Afro-Brazilian dance, *capoeira* and percussion:
Diáspora Art Center (Largo de São Francisco 21, 3rd fl, Pelourinho)
Escola de Dança (Rua da Oração 1, Pelourinho)

Festivals & Events

CARNAVAL

Salvador's Carnaval is the second largest in Brazil and, according to young people, the

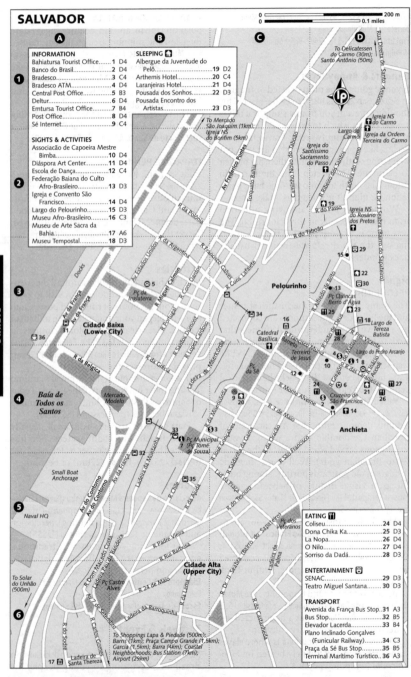

SALVADOR

0 .... 200 m
0 .... 0.1 miles

INFORMATION
Bahiatursa Tourist Office.......**1** D4
Banco do Brasil.....................**2** D4
Bradesco.............................**3** C4
Bradesco ATM.......................**4** D4
Central Post Office................**5** B3
Deltur.................................**6** D4
Emtursa Tourist Office...........**7** B4
Post Office..........................**8** C4
Sé Internet..........................**9** C4

SIGHTS & ACTIVITIES
Associação de Capoeira Mestre
    Bimba.............................**10** D4
Diáspora Art Center...............**11** D4
Escola de Dança...................**12** C4
Federação Baiana do Culto
    Afro-Brasileiro................**13** D3
Igreja e Convento São
    Francisco........................**14** D4
Largo do Pelourinho.............**15** D3
Museu Afro-Brasileiro...........**16** C3
Museu de Arte Sácra da
    Bahia..............................**17** A6
Museu Tempostal.................**18** D3

SLEEPING
Albergue da Juventude do
    Pelô...............................**19** D2
Arthemis Hotel.....................**20** C4
Laranjeiras Hotel..................**21** D4
Pousada dos Sonhos.............**22** D3
Pousada Encontro dos
    Artistas..........................**23** D3

To Delicatessen
do Carmo (30m);
Santo Antônio (50m)

To Mercado
São Joaquim (1km);
Igreja NS
do Bonfim (5km)

Igreja NS
do Carmo

Largo do
Carmo

Igreja da Ordem
Terceira do Carmo

Igreja do
Santíssimo
Sacramento
do Passo

Igreja NS
do Rosário
dos Pretos

R do Passo

R do Taboão

Pelourinho

Pç Quincas
Berto d'Agua

Largo de
Tereza
Batista

Largo do Pedro Arcanjo

**Cidade Baixa
(Lower City)**

Pç da
Inglaterra

Catedral
Basílica

Terreiro
de Jesus

Pç
da Sé

R Monte Alverne

Cruzeiro de
São Francisco

Anchieta

**Baía de
Todos os
Santos**

Mercado
Modelo

Small Boat
Anchorage

Naval HQ

Pç Municipal
(Pç Tomé
de Souza)

Pç dos
Veteranos

**Cidade Alta
(Upper City)**

Pç Castro
Alves

To Solar
do Unhão
(500m)

To Shoppings Lapa & Piedade (500m);
Barris (1km); Praça Campo Grande (1.5km);
Garcia (1.5km); Barra (4km); Coastal
Neighborhoods; Bus Station (7km);
Airport (29km)

EATING
Coliseu..............................**24** D4
Dona Chika Ka....................**25** D3
La Nopa.............................**26** D4
O Nilo...............................**27** D4
Sorriso da Dadá..................**28** D3

ENTERTAINMENT
SENAC..............................**29** D3
Teatro Miguel Santana........**30** D3

TRANSPORT
Avenida da França Bus Stop..**31** A3
Bus Stop...........................**32** B5
Elevador Lacerda.................**33** B4
Plano Inclinado Gonçalves
    (Funicular Railway).........**34** C3
Praça da Sé Bus Stop..........**35** B5
Terminal Marítimo Turístico..**36** A3

best. It's characterized by parades of *axé* and *pagode* bands atop creeping *trios-electricos* (long trucks of huge speakers). A *trio* or drum corps, together with its followers grouped in a roped-off area around it, form a *bloco*. People pay up to US$300 for the *abadá* (shirt required for entry to the *bloco*) for a top band, mostly for prestige and the safety of those ropes. Critics of Salvador's Carnaval call it segregative, pointing out the obvious class and race separation between those inside and outside of the *blocos*. Choosing to *fazer pipoca* (be popcorn) in the street is still a fine way to spend Carnaval.

There are three main Carnaval areas: the beachside Barra to Rio Vermelho circuit (most touristy), the narrow Campo Grande to Praça Castro Alves circuit, and the Pelourinho (no *trios* here, mostly concerts and drum corps). Get a schedule of events from Bahiatursa, pick up the *Guia do Ócio* entertainment guide (available in bookstores) or check www.portaldocarnaval.ba.gov.br.

Safety Tips

Crowds clearing to escape a fight pose the greatest threat during Carnaval, so be aware of your surroundings. Police are a noticeable presence. Hands will be all over you, searching your pockets and groping the ladies. Costumes aren't common – shorts (comfortable) and tennis shoes (protective) are the usual uniform. To ensure a trouble-free Carnaval, note the following:

- Form small groups and avoid deserted areas.
- Women should not walk alone or wear skirts (hands will be up them in no time).
- Carry only a small amount of money, stashed in your shoe.
- Always leave *any* jewelry, watches, or nice-looking sunglasses behind.
- Don't challenge pickpockets – the ensuing fight isn't worthwhile.
- Carry a photocopy of your passport.

OTHER FESTIVALS

Salvador stages many festivals, particularly in January and February. Check with Bahiatursa for other festival dates.

After Carnaval, the largest and most colorful:

Lavagem do Bonfim Second Thursday in January.
Festa de Iemanjá February 2.

Sleeping

Staying in the Pelô (it's packed with improvised hostels) means being in the action, but it can be noisy and/or draining. The area from Praça da Sé continuing past Praça Castro Alves has mostly run-down hotels. Mellower, beachside Barra has easy transport to the Pelô and the conveniences of a residential neighborhood. Reservations are essential for Carnaval.

PELOURINHO

Pousada Encontro dos Artistas (☎ 0xx71-3242-7783; www.guiafacilnet.com; pousadaencontrodosartistas@hotmail.com; Rua João de Deus 23; dm/d US$15/50) The taste in art may be a bit misguided, but the dorm rooms are great and not too loud at this new mid-range hotel.

Laranjeiras Hostel (☎ 3321-1366; www.laranjeirashostel.com.br; Rua Inácio Accioli 13; dm/s/d without bathroom US$16/35/46, s & d US$60) The highest quality and most attractive hostel in the Pelô, Laranjeiras has dorm rooms with ceilings high enough to allow for three bunks, and good bathrooms. Noisy and busy.

Other recommendations:

Albergue da Juventude do Pelô (☎ 3242-8061; www.alberguedopelo.com.br; Rua Ribeiro dos Santos 3; dm US$10) Plain hostel.

Pousada dos Sonhos (☎ 3322-9901; www.pousadadossonhos.com; Rua Gregório de Matos 55; dm/s/d without bathroom US$12.50/15/25) Friendly and airy.

JUST OUTSIDE THE PELOURINHO

Nega Maluca Guesthouse (☎ 3242-9249; www.negamaluca.com; Rua dos Marchantes 15, Santo Antônio; dm US$12) This friendly, super laid-back hostel run by travelers has good dorm rooms just outside the Pelô's noisy zone. Guest-use kitchen and free internet.

Arthemis Hotel (☎ 3322-0724; www.arthemishotel.com.br; Praça da Sé 398, Edifício Themis, 7th fl; s/d US$17.50/27.50) Arthemis has an excellent location and a breakfast veranda with a fantastic view. Rooms are no-frills and the cheapest have cement-block windows.

Pousada do Boqueirão (☎ 3241-2262; www.pousadaboqueirao.com.br; Rua Direita do Santo Antônio 48, Santo Antônio; s/d US$75/90, without bathroom US$32.50/42.50) Out of the pricey Santo Antônio *pousadas* in renovated old buildings, do Boqueirão is perhaps the most tasteful and elegant.

BARRA

Albergue Jardim Brasil (☎ 3264-9637/9096; www.pousadadajuventude.com.br; Rua Recife 4, Jardim Brasil; without breakfast dm/d US$12/27.50; ☒) The total lack of hangout space at this plain hostel is redeemed by the surrounding hip bars and restaurants. Guest-use kitchen.

Albergue do Porto (☎ 3264-6600; www.albergue doporto.com.br; Rua Barão de Sergy 197; d with bathroom US$50, dm/d US$17.50/45; ☒) Barra's primo hostel has airy, high-ceilinged dorm rooms, a living room with beanbags, and a guest-use kitchen. Turn-of-the-century building with kindergarten-esque decor.

Pousada Barra Point (☎ 3267-2321; www.pousada barrapoint.com.br; Rua Comendador Barnardo Catarino 137; dm/s/d US$17.50/25/40) Converted house. Bargaining required.

Pousada Milagres (☎ 3264-4113; www.pousada milagres.com; Rua Eng Milton Oliveira 46/210; s/d US$25/40; ☒) Finally a supercute *pousada* that's not overpriced! Rooms in this converted 1920s-era house have wood parquet floors, colorful walls and good bathrooms.

Eating

Salvador has some excellent restaurants, and is most known for its African-influenced Bahian cuisine. A street-food staple is *acarajé* (fritters made with brown beans and shrimp fried in *dendê* palm oil). There are usually cover charges for live music.

PELOURINHO

In Cidade Alta, reputable restaurants cluster in the Pelô and up Rua Direita de Santo Antônio.

Mão na Massa (Rua Direita do Santo Antônio 18; ☙ noon-5pm) This lower-level restaurant has an open-air patio overlooking the bay, and a yummy *prato feito* (plate of the day; US$3.50 to US$7.50) with mashed potatoes or pumpkin.

Delicatessen do Carmo (Rua do Carmo 68; per kg US$7) This small neighborhood store-bakery has a great fresh buffet lunch and an owner who uses terms of endearment with all of her customers.

Coliseu (Cruzeiro de São Francisco, 2nd fl; per kg US$11.45) The Pelô's largest and best lunch buffet restaurant is a great place to sample regional dishes.

O Nilo (Rua Laranjeiras 44; dishes US$7-11) Tantalize your taste buds with excellent falafel, hummus, tabuli, babaghanus and other Middle Eastern specialties. Outdoor seating on a choice street.

La Nopa (Rua Santa Isabel 13; dishes US$7-10) This fine Italian bistro is known for its quality fresh pastas, risottos and meat dishes.

SPLURGE!

Paraíso Tropical (mains US$17) Rio Vermelho (Rua Feira de Santana 354, Parque Cruz Aguiar, Rio Vermelho); Cabula (Rua Edgar Loureiro 98-B, Cabula) This widely renowned restaurant gives traditional Brazilian dishes a gourmet twist, often using regional fruits and flowers. You'll forget about the slow service after the first bite. The Cabula branch is located on the second left off Rua Nossa Senhora do Resgate.

Pricey but duly famous for traditional Bahian food:

Sorriso da Dadá (Rua Frei Vicente 5) Try the *moqueca de peixe* (fish, tomatoes, bell peppers and onions cooked in spiced coconut cream and *dendê* oil; US$22.50 for two).

Dona Chika Ka (Rua Frei Vicente 10) The *bobó de camarão* (shrimp in flavored manioc paste) gets rave reviews (US$22.50 for two).

COASTAL NEIGHBORHOODS

Leave the Pelô! Barra's best food can be found near the lighthouse along Rua Alfonso Celso, Av Almirante Marquez, and in Jardim Brasil. The latter has celebrated sushi, ice cream, crepe and pizza places in a compact area. Rio Vermelho and Itapuã are also good neighborhoods for restaurants.

Acarajé da Dinha (Largo de Santana, Rio Vermelho) Locals line up at this street stall for Salvador's most renowned *acarajé*.

Messa Farta (Rua Almirante Marquez de Leão) At this small neighborhood spot choose between two deals: one go at the buffet (drink included US$3.30), or per kilo with freshly grilled meats (US$5.45).

Brasil Legal Churrascaria (Rua Afonso Celso 110; per person US$4) This all-you-can-eat BBQ restaurant has an excellent spread and gets packed.

Drinking

There's not a day of the week that Salvador isn't singing, dancing or drinking...preferably all at the same time, and preferably outdoors.

PELOURINHO

The Pelourinho's plazas and cobbled streets fill with revelers sharing beer at plastic tables or dancing behind roaming bands of drummers. Tuesday is the big night. The city sponsors free live music in the inner courtyards of the Pelô – Largo de Tereza Batista, Largo de Pedro Arcanjo and Praça Quincas Berro d'Água – and on the Terreiro de Jesus. For listings, see the Pelourinho Dia e Noite schedule in Bahiatursa's free publication *BahiaCultural*.

Bar Cruz do Pascoal (Rua Joaquim Távora 2, Santo Antônio) For a quiet beer and a panoramic view, head for the back patio here.

Restaurante Olivier (Rua Direita de Santo Antônio 61, Santo Antônio) Live jazz and bossa nova Thursday through Sunday.

COASTAL NEIGHBORHOODS

Leave the Pelô! Barra's nightlife centers in Jardim Brasil, which has cool open-air bars attracting a hip, mostly affluent crowd. Beer drinking also happens along Alameda Marques de Leão – Habeus Copos has *pagode na mesa* (table samba) on Friday nights.

The Largo de Santana and Largo da Mariquita in bohemian Rio Vermelho pack with people drinking beer and eating *acarajé*. A variety of hip bars surrounds these squares.

World Bar (Rua Dias D'Ávila) This bar attracts a young beach crowd with its live bands.

Mercado do Peixe (Fish Market; Largo da Mariquita) This is *the* after-hours spot for cheap market food and cold beer.

Entertainment

As soon as you arrive, stop at Bahiatursa to find out what's on while you're in town. Its free publication *BahiaCultural* has listings.

FOLKLORIC SHOWS

Salvador is home to world-class choreographers and performers. Shows include displays of *afro* (Afro-Brazilian dance), *samba de roda* (flirtatious samba performed in a circle), dances of the *orixás*, and *maculelê* and *capoeira* that will blow your mind, all to live percussion and vocals.

Balé Folclórico da Bahia (Teatro Miguel Santana, Rua Gregório de Mattos 49; admission US$10; ☾ shows 8pm Mon & Wed-Sat)

Grupo Folclórico SESC (Arena do Teatro SESC, SENAC, Largo do Pelourinho; admission US$3.50; ☾ shows 8pm Thu-Sat)

LIVE MUSIC

Many of Salvador's singers, bands and Carnaval groups hold weekly *ensaios* (rehearsals; US$2.50 to US$20), which are essentially concerts, in the months leading up to Carnaval. The brotherhood Filhos de Gandhy is an *afoxé* (group tied to Candomblê traditions)

that has come to represent Salvador itself. Excellent *blocos afros* (groups with powerful drum corps promoting Afro-Brazilian culture) are Ilê Aiyê (the first exclusively black Carnaval group), Male Debalê, Cortejo Afro, Dida (exclusively female) and Muzenza. More pop but still with strong percussion sections are Olodum (a Pelourinho institution), Araketu and Timbalada (brainchild of master composer and musician Carlinhos Brown). The queens of Salvador pop music are Margareth Menezes, Ivete Sangalo and Daniela Mercury.

Teatro Castro Alves (Praça Campo Grande). Salvador's finest venue for quality performances. Its Concha Acústica (amphitheater) holds fun weekly shows (US$1).

DANCE CLUBS

Salvador's dance clubs dot its waterfront, and are mostly frequented by the hip and wealthy.

Tropicana (Av Otávio Mangabeira 4707, Jardim Armação) Has live Brazilian music and a laid-back atmosphere.

Aeroclube (Av Otávio Mangabeira, Boca do Rio) The outdoor mall contains Rock in Rio and Café Cancún. Both have live Brazilian music and attract a pretty young crowd.

Fashion Club (Av Otávio Mangabeira 2471, Jardim dos Namorados) and **Satélite Bar** (Av Otávio Mangabeira 940, Patamares) are upscale electronic-music clubs.

GAY & LESBIAN VENUES

Salvador has a large gay community and a pretty happening gay scene.

Beco dos Artistas (Artist's Alley; Av Cerqueira Lima, Garcia) A meeting point for a really young gay crowd. To find it, walk a few blocks down Rua Leovigildo Filgueiras from the Teatro Castro Alves.

Off (Rua Dias D'Ávila 33, Barra) and **Queens Club** (Rua Teadoro Sampaio 160, Barris) promise long nights of grooving to electronica.

Shopping

MALLS

Shopping Iguatemí Salvador's largest mall and right across from the bus station.

Shopping Barra (Av Centenário 2992, Chame-Chame) Larger and fancier than Shopping Lapa and Shopping Piedade.

Shopping Piedade & Shopping Lapa (off Av 7 de Setembro behind Praça da Piedade) Walking distance from the Pelô.

BRAZIL

MARKETS

The Mercado São Joaquim is a small city of sketchy waterfront stalls about 3km north of the Mercado Modelo.

Mercado Modelo (9am-7pm Mon-Sat, to 2pm Sun) The two-story, enclosed tourist market has dozens of stalls selling local handicrafts. Arriving slave shipments were kept in the watery depths of this 19th-century building – look for the descending staircases on the main floor. *Capoeira* and live music are often performed out back.

Getting There & Away
AIR
BRA, Gol, Ocean Air, TAM, and Varig operate domestic flights out of Salvador's airport. TAP and Air Europa connect Salvador to Europe.

BUS
Most buses originating in the south go around the Baía de Todos os Santos. Alternately it's possible to catch a ferry to Salvador from Bom Despacho (45 minutes) on Ilha Itaparica.

Destination	Duration (hr)	Cost (US$)	Frequency
Aracaju	4½	17.50-24.50	10 daily
Belo Horizonte	24	73	daily
Fortaleza	20	94	daily
Ilhéus	8	22-51	5-6 daily
Lençóis	6	18	2 daily
Natal	21	61-82	2 daily
Porto Seguro	11	49-77	2-3 daily
Recife	11	47-65	2 daily
Rio	24-28	107	4 daily
São Paulo	33	105-136	4 daily
Vitória	18	85	1-2 daily

Getting Around
Linking the lower and upper cities in the center are the newly renovated **Elevador Lacerda** (5 centavos; 24hr), and the more thrilling **Plano Inclinado Gonçalves** (Funicular; 5 centavos; 7am-7pm Mon-Fri, to 1pm Sat). When catching the bus, watch out for pricey air-con minibuses.

AREMBEPE
0xx71

Arembepe's proximity to Salvador and its past fame keep visitors swinging through to check out the *aldea hippy*, a hippy village that Mick Jagger and Janis Joplin got rolling in the 1960s. The village itself is nothing spe-

cial, so immediately hit the beach and head north. You'll pass the Projeto TAMAR station, and after about 10 minutes you'll see small thatched-roof huts and coconut palms sitting atop a sand dune that shelters the *aldea hippy*. There's a restaurant nearby for fruit juices and snacks, and the hippies sell handicrafts. Arembepe makes for a good escape.

From Salvador's Lapa bus terminal, catch an Arembepe, Montegordo or Barra do Pojuca bus for Arembepe (US$1.70, 1¼ hours). Some of these may pass the Terminal da França as well.

PRAIA DO FORTE
0xx71

Praia do Forte has been intentionally developed into an upmarket ecological beach resort. The result is an attractive, polished yet laid-back holiday village with white fluffy beaches. Surrounding the village are the **Castelo do Garcia d'Ávila** (admission US$2.50; 8:30am-6pm) ruins and canoeing, walking and biking possibilities. There are ATMs.

The extremely worthwhile **Projeto TAMAR** (admission US$3.50; 9am-6pm) is part of a national project working with local communities to preserve sea-turtle breeding grounds and educate the public about endangered turtles. It has tanks of sea turtles and other sea life.

*Pousada*s are pricey here but most offer weekday discounts in the low season. **Camping Reserva da Sapiranga** (-3342-2109; www.camping reservadasapiranga.cbj.net; per person US$6) has shady sites 2km behind town. **Albergue Praia do Forte** (3676-1094; www.albergue.com.br; Rua da Aurora 3; dm/d US$11/37.50) has pleasant dorms with tile floors and their own bathrooms, all surrounding a grassy central courtyard. Kitchen use and Projeto Tamar entrance fee are included, and bikes and surfboards are rented.

Buses from Salvador to Praia do Forte (US$4, one hour and 40 minutes) leave from the Terminal da Calçada in Cidade Baixa (hourly on the hour, 5am to 6pm) or from the bus station (two daily). Buses and *kombis* make the return trip every 40 minutes from 7am to 6:30pm (US$3.25).

CACHOEIRA & SÃO FÉLIX
0xx75 / pop 30,350

The sleepy town of Cachoeira has well-maintained colonial architecture strung along the banks of the Rio Paraguaçu, in a face-off

with its neighbor São Félix. Cachoeira is an important center for **Candomblé**, has a wood-sculpting tradition with a heavy African flavor, and makes for a mellow day trip. This is the best place to get a glimpse of the Recôncavo, the green, fertile region surrounding Baía de Todos os Santos, whose sugar and tobacco plantations made it the economic heartland of colonial Brazil.

There is a **tourist office** (Rua Ana Neri 4) and major banks in both towns.

Sights & Activities

Local **Candomblé** groups accept visitors. The tourist office will share what information it has on ceremony times and locations, but unfortunately isn't always kept updated.

The riverfront **Centro Cultural Dannemann** (Av Salvador Pinto 39, São Félix; ☺ 8am-5pm Tue-Sat, gallery only 1-5pm Sun), in addition to first-class contemporary art displays, has a room of women at work rolling cigars, as they have since 1873. The **Museu Hansen Bahia** (Rua 13 de Maio; ☺ 9am-5pm Tue-Fri, to 2pm Sat & Sun) displays powerful block prints and paintings on the theme of human suffering by a German-Brazilian artist. **Igreja da Ordem Terceira do Carmo** (Rua Inocência Bonaventura) is an ornately gilded church featuring a gallery of suffering Christs with genuine ruby blood. It was closed for renovations at press time.

Festivals & Events

Festa de São João Interior Bahia's largest popular festival, held June 22 to 24.

Festa da NS de Boa Morte The fascinating event falls on the Friday closest to August 15 and lasts for three days: descendants of slaves pay tribute to their liberation with dance and prayer in a mix of Candomblé and Catholicism.

Sleeping & Eating

Pousada do Paraguassú (☎ 3438-3386; www.pousada paraguassu.com.br; Av Salvador Pinto 1; s/d US$22.50/32.50; ☒) Located on the riverfront in São Félix, this modern *pousada* has fine rooms facing a flowery central courtyard.

Pousada do Pai Thomaz (☎ 3425-1288; Rua 25 de Junho 12) Pai Thomaz was under renovation during research, but has historically been a fine budget option. Their main-floor restaurant is laden with local woodcarvings.

Beira Rio (Rua Paulo Filho 19; dishes US$5-11) Cachoeira's best restaurant has pasta and meat dishes, as well as a fish *prato feito* (US$3).

Getting There & Away

Daily buses depart from Salvador for Cachoeira/São Félix (US$3, two hours, hourly from 5:30am to 9:30pm). Hourly return buses can be caught in either town from 4:20am to 6:50pm. You can also continue on to Feira de Santana (US$2.50, 1½ hours, hourly 5:30am to 6:50pm) to make further connections.

LENÇÓIS

☎ 0xx75 / pop 8900

Lençóis is the prettiest of the old diamond-mining towns in the Chapada Diamantina, a mountainous wooded oasis in the dusty *sertão* (dry interior region). While the town itself is a draw – cobbled streets, brightly painted 19th-century buildings, nestled between lush hills – it is the surrounding area bursting with caves, waterfalls and plateaus promising panoramic views that are the real attraction. Lençóis is the Northeast's outdoor adventure hot spot.

Information

The tourist office is in the back of the market building next to the bridge
Banco do Brasil (Praça Horácio de Mattos) Has ATMs.
Café.com (per hr US$3) Internet access; in the market building.
Calil Neto (Praça Horácio de Mattos 82; ☺ 5-11pm Mon, 8am-2pm & 5-11pm Tue-Sun) If the tour-company photo albums left you unconvinced, the photo gallery here will leave no question about this area's beauty.

Activities
WALKS & SWIMMING

The following walks are easily taken without a guide. Walk past the bus stop and follow the Rio Lençóis 3km upstream into the Parque Municipal da Muritiba. You'll pass a series of rapids known as **Cachoeira Serrano**, the **Salão de Areias Coloridas** (Room of Colored Sands), where artisans gather material for bottled sand paintings, **Poço Halley** (Halley's Well), **Cachorinha** (Little Waterfall) and finally **Cachoeira da Primavera** (Spring Waterfall). Or follow Rua São Benedito 4km out of town to **Ribeirão do Meio**, a series of swimming holes with a natural waterslide. For more swimming, catch the morning Seabra bus and hop off at Mucugêzinho Bar. About 2km downstream is **Poço do Diabo** (Devil's Well), a swimming hole with a 25m waterfall.

HIKING

To the southwest of Lençóis is **Parque Nacional da Chapada Diamantina**, comprising 1520 sq km of breathtaking scenery, waterfalls, rivers, monkeys and a lot to interest geologists. The park has little infrastructure (trails are unmarked) and bus services are infrequent, making it difficult to penetrate without a guide. Terrible mishaps with undertrained guides have occurred, so only certified guides (check their photo ID badge) should be used – the **ACVL** (☎ 3334-1425; Rua 10 de Novembro) guide association or local agencies can hook you up with one. Two knowledgeable indigenous English-speaking guides are **Roy Funch** (☎ 3334-1305; royfunch@ligbr.com.br; Rua Pé de Ladeira 212) and **Olivia Taylor** (☎ 3334-1229; oliviadosduendes@zaz.com.br; Rua do Pires), owner of Pousada dos Duendes.

Treks can last anywhere from two to eight days, and usually involve a combination of camping, staying in local homes and *pousadas*. Prices including food run upward from US$35 per day depending on the trip and the size of the group; transportation and lodging are additional. Necessary gear can be rented from agencies.

Tours

This is not the time to pinch pennies – take a tour. Local tour agencies organize day car trips (including swimming and walking) and hikes for upward from US$20 per person, not including admission fees if there are any. Agencies mostly pool customers in order to send daily groups out, so it's difficult to customize a trip unless you are a large group. Some standout sights:

Poço Encantado The Lençóis poster child: a cave filled with stunningly beautiful blue water.

Poço Azul Another rainwater-filled cave.

Gruta da Lapa Doce A cave with impressive formations.

Morro do Pai Inácio The most prominent peak in the area affording an awesome view over a plateau-filled valley.

Cachoeira da Fumaça At 420m, Brazil's longest waterfall.

Marimbus A 'mini-Pantanal' microregion, is only worthwhile close to dawn or dusk.

Sleeping

Reservations are required for all major holidays. If you arrive by night bus most *pousadas* allow you to stay the rest of the night, only charging for breakfast.

Pousada & Camping Lumiar (☎ 0xx75-3334-1241; lumiar@sendnet.com.br; Praça do Rosário 70; campsites per person US$5) Shady campsites in a gorgeous garden. Full kitchen for guest use.

Pousada dos Duendes (☎ 3334-1229; www.pousadadosduendes.com; Rua do Pires; dm/s/d US$10/15/25, without bathroom US$7.50/12.50/20) A relaxed atmosphere, good budget rooms and plenty of open chill space keeps this place full of backpackers. Open group dinners (US$5, reserve before 5pm, vegetarian/vegan possible) and book exchange offered.

Pousada da Fonte (☎ 3334-1953; www.pousadadafonte.com; Rua da Muritiba; dm/s/d US$12.50/15/30) This cozy, five-room *pousada* has the feel of a weekend home. The open-air breakfast and hammock porches are surrounded by quiet forest. Just past Casa de Hélia.

Pousada Casa de Hélia (☎ 3334-1143; www.casadehelia.com.br; Rua da Muritiba; dm/d US$12.50/35) Spread over a hillside affording views over a green river valley, this backpacker favorite has rooms with stone slab floors and furniture fashioned out of twisted tree branches. Up a dirt road from the bus stop.

Pousada Solar dos Moraes (☎ 3334-1849; Rua Arnulfo Moraes; www.pousadasolardosmoraes.com; s/d US$15/30) Rooms aren't particularly noteworthy but each has a small veranda and hammock that overlook a green front yard with a humongous *jaca* tree.

Eating

Burritos y Taquitos (Rua São Benedito 58; 3 tacos US$3.50) Ever thought you'd be downing a tasty Mexican beef burrito or cactus taco in Bahia? Pretty back patio.

Neco's Bar (Rua da Baderna; per person US$6) Orders must be placed 24 hours in advance at this Lençóis institution offering serious home cooking.

Ristorante Italiano os Artistas da Massa (Rua da Baderna 49; dishes US$6-9) The plain dining room is redeemed by truly fresh Italian food and quality tunes you pick off the menu.

Bode Grill (Rua 10 de Novembro 26; dishes US$9-12) This small restaurant behind the bank is known for a *prato feito* (US$3) filled with homemade goodness.

Cozinha Aberta (Rua da Baderna 111 & Av Rui Barbosa 42; dishes US$10) Treat yourself to Thai-style chicken in coconut milk or Indian beef-and-vegetable curry at this gourmet bistro following Italian 'Slow Food' principles (everything is as fresh, organic and local as possible).

Getting There & Away

Buses to Salvador (US$18, six hours) leave daily at 1:15pm and 11:30pm, and at 7:30am on Monday, Wednesday and Friday. All Salvador buses stop in Feira de Santana (US$13, 4½ hours), where connections can be made to just about anywhere, but are not always well timed.

MORRO DE SÃO PAULO
☎ 0xx75

For some, this picturesque holiday village has exceeded acceptable limits of touristiness; for others it's Bahia's most fun party town. Morro's charm derives from a few remnants of its colonial past and a unique, isolated geography. A few sand streets, ruled by wheelbarrows and pedestrians, run between three jungle-topped hills. The beaches, with their shallow, warm water, disappear with the tides, liberating you for a hike to the waterfall, a boat trip to quiet **Boipeba**, a trip down the lighthouse **zip line** (per person US$12.50), or to catch the sunset from the fort.

There is one **ATM** (Segunda Praia). Internet runs at US$4.50 per hour.

Sleeping
Reservations are required for all major holidays, especially Carnaval and *resaca* (five days of post-Carnaval hangover). Segunda Praia is where the nightly party is, so don't sleep there!

Pousada dos Passaros (☎ 3652-1102; www.hostel domorro.com.br; dm/d US$15/35; ❸) A social hostel with a green outdoor breakfast area and good dorms. Take first left-hand passageway off Rua da Fonte Grande.

Pousada Passarte (☎ 3652-1030; www.pousada passarte.com.br; Rua da Biquinha 27; s/d US$20/30; ❸) Small, simple rooms that are a good deal in the high season. Quiet location and cute breakfast area.

Pousada Ninho da Águia (☎ 3652-1201; www.ninho daaguia.com.br; s/d US$25/35; ❸) The rooms are well finished and breakfast comes with a spectacular view at this 'Eagle's Nest' near the lighthouse.

Pousada Kanzuá do Marujo (☎ 3483-1152; www .pousadakanzuadomarujo.com.br; Terça Praia; s/d US$35/40; ❸) A superbright two-story complex of modern rooms set back from the ocean. Lots of greenery.

Pousada 2000 (☎ 3652-1271; www.pousada2000.com .br; Rua da Biquinha 31; s/d US$40/50; ❸) Well designed to take advantage of the sunlight and breeze, these comfy rooms have furniture fashioned out of tree branches.

Eating
Oh Lá Lá! Crepes (Caminho da Praia; dishes US$3.50-7.50) A tiny place with hip tunes and artsy posters, serving up salads and sweet or savory crepes.

Espaguetaria Strega (Caminho da Praia; pastas US$5-9) Strega packs with young people slurping down pastas ranging from oil and garlic to shrimp with cheese. The bar has over 40 *cachaça* infusions.

Restaurante Tinharé (Caminho da Praia) The huge portions of the *moqueca de peixe* (US$7.50) are excellent at this family-run restaurant with clear plastic and fake flowers on every table. Hidden down some stairs.

Ponto de Encontro (Caminho da Praia; mains US$9) One of the better chic restaurants with creative salads, pastas and meat or veggie plates.

Getting There & Away
The catamaran *Gamboa do Morro* (US$25 to US$30, two hours, two to three daily) and the speedboat *Ilha Bela* (US$27.50, two hours, one to two daily) sail between Morro and Salvador's Terminal Maritimo Turistico (behind the Mercado Modelo). The seas can be rough, so come fairly empty-stomached and focus on a fixed point if things start rocking. If you come by land, catch a bus to Valença where regular boats (US$2.35, 1½ hours, hourly 6:30am to 5:30pm) or speedboats (US$5.30, 30 minutes, three daily) head upriver to Morro.

ITACARÉ
☎ 0xx73 / pop 18,100

Itacaré is a quiet, pretty average-looking colonial fishing town at the mouth of the Rio de Contas, long sought out by hippies and surfers mesmerized by wide stretches of virgin Atlantic rainforest, postcard-perfect beaches and reliable surf breaks. Though there is some upmarket tourism a mellow, youthful vibe prevails, and locals and visitors still share the streets. Surfing, reggae and ecotourism, in that order, are main focuses.

There are ATMs and several internet cafés (US$2.50 per hour).

Activities
Surf lessons and board rental are widely available. Beaches in town are nothing special (but good for surfing), so head out to paradisiacal **Engenhoca**, **Havaizinho** and **Itacarezinho**, 12km south of town. Nearby, just off the highway is **Cachoeira Tijuipe** (admission US$2.25), a wide,

BRAZIL

tea-colored waterfall fun for a swim. Idyllic **Prainha** is reachable by trail from the southernmost town beach, Praia do Ribeira. There has been a rash of muggings at and around Itacaré's beaches, so take little money and nothing of value.

Canoe trips upriver, rafting, mountain biking, rappelling and excursions on foot or horseback to local sights can be arranged through local agencies. The principal excursion is up the Peninsula de Maraú to stunning **Praia Taipús de Fora** (US$21.50). On the trail to Prainha, **Conduru Ecoturismo** (Praça da Bandeira) has a 200m-long, 40m-high **zip line** (US$7.50) and **tree rope circuit** (US$25).

Itacaré is known for its **capoeira** (classes available).

Sleeping

Camping Pop (☎ 3251-2305; Praia da Concha; campsites per person US$7.50) Shady sites, eccentric owners.

Albergue O Pharol (☎ 3251-2527; www.albergue opharol.com.br; Praça Santos Dummont 7; dm/d US$13.50/38; 🗷) Itacaré's best hostel, Pharol is attractive, clean and superfriendly. Guest-use kitchen and comfy living room.

Pousada Cores do Mar (☎ 3251-3418; www.itacare .com; Praia da Concha; s/d US$20/25) A row of hammocks and good-value rooms face a garden in this straightforward *pousada*. Run by a cool surfer.

Pousada Itacaré (☎ 3251-3601; pousadaitacare@ hotmail.com; Praia da Concha; s/d US$22.50/30; 🗷) You can hear the ocean from this family-run *pousada* shaded by big trees. The simple rooms have brightly painted walls and tile floors.

Pousada Itaóca (☎ 3251-3382; www.pousadaitaoca .hpg.com.br; Rua Pedro Longo 520, Pituba; s/d US$25/35; 🗷) The usual recipe of comfortable rooms and hammocks, but with more attractive setting.

Eating

Todas as Luas (Rua Pedro Longo 334; meals US$1.75-36) Tables pour out onto the street at this open-air pasta (US$3.50 to US$6) and pizza (per 10cm US$1.75 to US$3.50). Live music.

Terral (Rua Pedro Longo 150) Terral packs with the after-beach crowd seeking home cooked *prato feitos* (US$4.50 to US$6) and burgers (US$2).

Almazen (Rua Pedro Longo 69) This almost-vegetarian restaurant serves sandwiches on homemade bread, homemade yogurt and granola, salads and a delicious vegetarian *prato feito* (US$6).

Sahara (Rua Pedro Longo; Arab plate US$5.50) The Arab Plate (homemade pita bread, falafel, hummus, tomato salad and fried potatoes) is mouthwatering at this Israeli-owned cafe at the end of the main drag.

Tia Deth (Av Castro Alves; dishes for 2 US$12.50-30) Great traditional or Bahian-style seafood and fish served in a colorful dining room or under a huge tree. Economical *prato feitos* (US$5).

Getting There & Around

To get to Itacaré, you will likely need to connect through Itabuna or Ilhéus. There are buses to Itacaré from Itabuna (US$5, 2½ hours, hourly 5:30am to 8pm) and Ilhéus (US$3.50, 1½ hours, hourly 6:20am to 8:40pm).

A local bus provides access to beaches south of town, leaving hourly from in front of the bus station.

ILHÉUS

☎ 0xx73 / pop 221,900

Bright turn-of-the-century architecture and oddly angled streets lend Ilhéus a vibrant and playful air, and make the center a great wander. Ilhéus' fame derives from its history as a prosperous cocoa port, as well as the hometown of Jorge Amado (Brazil's best-known novelist) and the setting of one of his greatest novels (*Gabriela, Cravo e Canela*).

Information

Major banks in the center have ATMs. A tourist-information kiosk lies between the cathedral and the water.

Reality Internet (Rua Dom Eduardo; per hr US75¢)

Sights & Activities

The **Igreja de São Jorge** (Praça Rui Barbosa; 🕑 Tue-Sun), built in 1534, is among Brazil's oldest churches. **Casa de Jorge Amado** (Rua Jorge Amado 21; admission US50¢; 🕑 9am-noon & 2-6pm Mon-Fri, to 1pm Sat, 3-5pm Sun) is where the author was raised and wrote his first novel, and will be most interesting to his readers.

Eco Parque de Una (☎ 3633-1121; www.ecoparque .org.br; admission US$15), 70km south of Ilhéus, offers relatively worthwhile two-hour tours of its Atlantic rainforest reserve, which include rubber tapping, a suspended tree canopy walkway and a swimming pond. It's cheapest to make a direct appointment; local agencies also arrange visits.

The best beaches, such as **Praia dos Milionários**, are to the south.

Sleeping

Pontal – a short bus ride from the center on the other side of the bay – has several modern *pousadas*.

Albergue da Ilha (☎ 3231-8938; Rua General Câmara 31; dm/d US$10/30) Located in a tall, narrow old building, this clean and funky hostel's best assets are its fantastic kitchen and its rooftop patio. The hotel has one (six-bed) dorm room.

Pousada Delmar (☎ 3632-8435; mamorim@cepec .gov.br; Rua Castro Alves 322, Pontal; s/d US$15/20; 🐾) A popular, modern hotel with an open-air breakfast patio.

Pousada Brisa do Mar (☎ 3231-2644/8424; Av 2 de Julho 136; s/d US$20/25; 🐾) This modern home

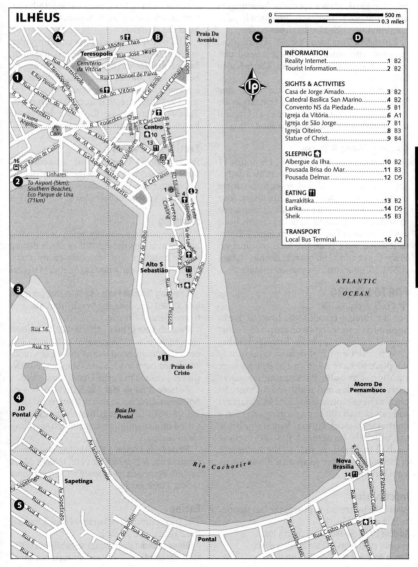

ILHÉUS

INFORMATION	
Reality Internet	1 B2
Tourist Information	2 B2

SIGHTS & ACTIVITIES	
Casa de Jorge Amado	3 B2
Catedral Basílica San Marino	4 B2
Convento NS da Piedade	5 B1
Igreja da Vitória	6 A1
Igreja de São Jorge	7 B2
Igreja Oiteiro	8 B3
Statue of Christ	9 B4

SLEEPING 🏠	
Albergue da Ilha	10 B2
Pousada Brisa do Mar	11 B3
Pousada Delmar	12 D5

EATING 🍴	
Barrakítika	13 B2
Larika	14 D5
Sheik	15 B3

TRANSPORT	
Local Bus Terminal	16 A2

BRAZIL

converted into a *pousada* has wood parquet floors and sea views from front rooms, and is a huge step up from the center's options. Desolate stretch to the center's action.

Eating & Drinking

Larika (end of Av Getúlio Vargas, Pontal; hamburgers & sandwiches US$2; 🕙 6pm-1am Sun-Thu, to dawn Fri & Sat) This popular kiosk serves specialty hamburgers and sandwiches and every imaginable juice combination (US$1) at bayfront tables.

Barrakitika (Praça Antonio Muniz 39) An informal hangout with outdoor tables at a bend in a quiet street. Live music from Thursday to Saturday.

Sheik (Alto de Oitero) Perched on a hill, chic Sheik has great views and a bar that fills in the late evening. It rounds out a menu of typical dishes with Arab and Japanese food.

Getting There & Away

Buses run to Itacaré (US$3.50, 1½ hours, 11 daily), Valença (US$11, five hours, two daily), Salvador (US$32 to US$50, seven hours, three daily), Porto Seguro (US$15, six hours, four daily) and Rio (US$68 to US$87, 22 hours, one to seven daily). More frequent connections can be made in Itabuna, 30km inland. Buses to Itabuna leave from the local terminal on Praça Cairu and from outside the bus station (US$1.35, 40 minutes) every 30 minutes.

PORTO SEGURO

☎ 0xx73 / pop 95,700

For the foreign traveler, the town of Porto Seguro has long lost its true charm to T-shirt shops and trinket stands. For Brazilian middle-class families and high-school groups, it is *the* place to have a fun-in-the-sun package vacation. For both, Porto promises active party scenes day and night and a chance to catch some exceptionally skilled local dancers and *capoeiristas* (those performing *capoeira*, a martial art/dance). Porto is famous for being the officially recognized first Portuguese landfall in Brazil, as well as the birthplace of *lambada*, a dance so sensual it was at one time forbidden.

Information

Avoid the information post at the bus station, as it is unreliable.

Adeltur (☎ 3288-1888; Av 22 de Abril 100, Shopping Av) Changes cash and traveler's checks.

Banco do Brasil (Av 22 de Abril) Has ATMs.

Internet Point (Av dos Navegantes 90; per hr US$1.50) Offers internet.

Sights & Activities

Motivation is required to climb the stairs to **Cidade Histórica** (one of the earliest European settlements in Brazil). Rewards include a sweeping view, colorful old buildings, and churches dating from early to mid-16th century. Look for *capoeira* demonstrations behind the churches.

The beach is one long bay of calm water, north of town, lined with *barracas* and clubs. **Toa Toa**, **Axé Moi** and **Barramares** are the biggest beach clubs and all have MCs and dancers leading crowds through popular dances. The most beautiful stretch is from Toa Toa north. Take a 'Taperapuã' or 'Rio Doce' bus to the beach, a 'Campinho' or 'Cabralia' to return.

Festivals & Events

Porto Seguro's Carnaval lasts an additional three or four days – until the Friday or Saturday after Ash Wednesday – and is a smaller and safer version of Salvador's.

Sleeping

Porto Seguro has as many hotels as Salvador, but reservations should still be made during major holidays. For seriously cheap stays, check out the older *pousadas* on Rua Marechal Deodoro.

Camping Mundaí Praia (☎ 3679-2287; per person US$7.50; 🐾) Opposite the beach, 4km north of town. Plenty of shade.

Pousada Casa Grande (☎ 3268-4422; tanaina.brasileira@terra.com.br; Av dos Navegantes 151; s/d US$10/20) The central location, good rooms and a green inner courtyard have made Casa Grande *the* backpacker *pousada* in Porto. Guest-use kitchen.

Pousada Brisa do Mar (☎ 3288-2943/1444; www.brisadomarpousada.com.br; Praça Dr Manoel Ribeiro Coelho 188; s/d US$15/30) A long, narrow house converted into an uninteresting though sparkling clean *pousada*.

Pousada do Francês (☎ 3288-2429; www.comvenezabrasil.com.br; Av 22 de Abril 180; s/d US$17.50/30; 🐾) A beautiful pousada with newly reformed rooms facing a lush garden.

Eating

The nicest dinner restaurants cluster around the Passarela do Álcool.

Bigode Lanche (Av dos Navegantes; sandwiches US75¢-$3.50; 🕙 until dawn) Two trailers turn out great

PORTO SEGURO

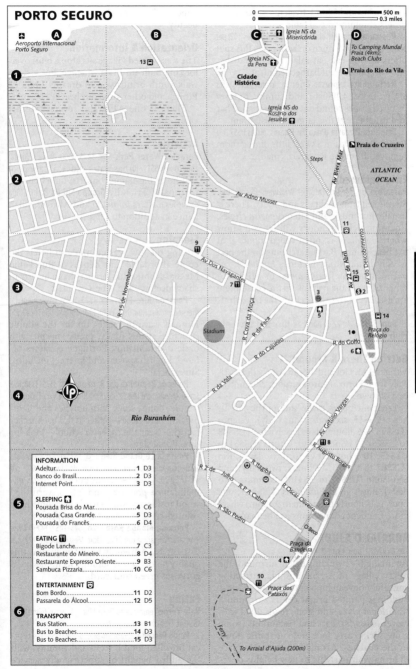

0 — 500 m
0 — 0.3 miles

Aeroporto Internacional
Porto Seguro

Igreja NS da
Misericórida

Igreja NS
da Pena

To Camping Mundaí
Praia (4km);
Beach Clubs

Praia do Rio da Vila

Cidade
Histórica

Igreja NS do
Rosário dos
Jesuítas

Praia do Cruzeiro

ATLANTIC
OCEAN

Steps

Av Biera Mar

Av Adno Musser

Av Dos Navagantes

Av 22 de Abril

Av do Descobrimento

R 15 de Novembro

R Cova da Moça

R da Faca

Stadium

R do Cajueiro

Praça do
Relógio

R do Golfo

R da Vala

Rio Buranhém

Av Getúlio Vargas

R Augusta Borges

R Itagibá

R 2 de Julho

R P A Cabral

R Oscar Oliveira

R São Pedro

O Beco

Praça da
Bandeira

Praça dos
Pataxós

BRAZIL

Ferry

To Arraial d'Ajuda (200m)

INFORMATION
Adeltur.....................................**1** D3
Banco do Brasil.....................**2** D3
Internet Point.......................**3** D3

SLEEPING
Pousada Brisa do Mar..........**4** C6
Pousada Casa Grande..........**5** D3
Pousada do Francês..............**6** D4

EATING
Bigode Lanche.......................**7** C3
Restaurante do Mineiro.......**8** D4
Restaurante Expresso Oriente..........**9** B3
Sambuca Pizzaria..................**10** C6

ENTERTAINMENT
Bom Bordo.............................**11** D2
Passarela do Álcool...............**12** D5

TRANSPORT
Bus Station............................**13** B1
Bus to Beaches......................**14** D3
Bus to Beaches......................**15** D3

sandwiches and 500mL fresh juices (US$1) to diners at folding metal tables.

Restaurant do Mineiro (Rua Augusto Borges 102; per person US$3.40) Not much on ambience, this spot offers all-you-can-eat salad and side dishes and two portions of barbecued meat.

Restaurante Expresso Oriente (Av dos Navegantes 670; per kg US$8.45) Sushi and some Chinese-inspired dishes round out the decent salad bar and usual fare at this large kilo restaurant.

Sambuca Pizzaria (Praça dos Pataxós; pizzas US$7-15) Porto's best pizza in a sweet little dining room removed from the Passarela's madness.

Entertainment

Passarela do Álcool (Alcohol Walkway; ☿ nightly). Stands sell fruit cocktails and crafts. There is usually live music and often *capoeira* circles. Roaming ticket vendors will let you know where the party is, often called a *luau* if at the beach clubs. Barramares puts on the best weekly *luau*, which includes *lambada, capoeira*, live *axé, forró, samba* or *MPB*, and other treats. If the party is up the coast, there are usually courtesy buses from the *trevo* (traffic circle).

Bom Bordo (Av 22 de Abril) Is fun and the only club in town.

Getting There & Around

Varig, TAM, Gol and Ocean Air fly domestically from Porto Seguro's airport, 2km northeast of town.

Frequent buses make the journey to Ilhéus (US$15, six hours, four daily), Valença (US$23, 8½ hours, daily), Salvador (US$48 to US$76, 11 hours, daily), Vitoria (US$31 to US$45, 10½ hours, two to three daily), Rio (US$67 to US$75, 19 hours, two daily) and São Paulo (US$82 to US$105, 26 hours, two daily). Buses go to Eunápolis (US$3.25, one hour, half-hourly from 5am to 9:40pm) where more frequent connections can be made.

ARRAIAL D'AJUDA

☎ 0xx73 / pop 13,000

An intangible twinkling magic surrounds the pretty village of Arraial d'Ajuda, attracting youthful nouveau hippies of every age. Squat buildings painted bright colors surround a traditional plaza, and stone roads lined with newer *pousadas*, bars and restaurants (some quite slick) carry foot and car traffic down to the beaches. Arraial is a fantastic place to bring your partying to new heights or re-cuperate from travel exhaustion in tropical beauty.

Orientation & Information

The tree-shaded village sits atop a bluff overlooking built-up Praia Mucugê, but a short walk south brings you to dreamy Praia de Pitinga and other gorgeous beaches beyond.

There is one ATM and several internet cafés.

Activities

Paradise Water Park (☎ 3575-8600; Praia d'Ajuda; adult/child US$19/10) has water slides, a wave pool and hosts big-name concerts; hours change seasonally. Friendly **Groupo Sul da Bahia** (Rua da Capoeira) offers *lambada* and Afro-Brazilian dance in addition to *capoeira*.

Sleeping

During the low season, midlevel hotels become affordable. The depths of Rua Fábio Messias Nobre (Rua Jatobar) has a history of shady dealings and is best avoided.

Pousada Alto Mar (☎ 3575-1935; www.jungleim mersion.pro.br; Rua Bela Vista 114; dm/s/d US$10/20/25) Human warmth makes up for the simple structure at this funky, pretty cheapie with basic *apartamentos*. Portuguese classes offered, English spoken and internet included. Supersocial.

Pousada República das Bananas (☎ 3575-3336; Rua Santo Antonio; s/d US$12.50/25; ⧉ ⧉) Two lines of simple rooms, some with porches and hammocks, stand close together at this backpacker favorite. Near the *capoeira* school – look for directional signs.

Pousada Le Grand Bleu (☎ 3575-1272; www.pous adalegrandbleu.com.br; Rua Beco do Jegue 160; s/d US$17.50/20; ⧉ ⧉) An aging but attractive, well-maintained *pousada* with lots of varnished wood inside and out. Two-level rooms have colored-cement floors. Lots of greenery.

Pousada Manga Rosa (☎ 3575-1252/1423; www .pousadamangarosa.com; Rua Fábio Messias Nobre 172; s/d US$25/30; ⧉) A friendly local family runs this quality *pousada* surrounding its home and a gorgeous green courtyard.

Eating

Vale Verde (entrance to Praia Mucugê; prato feito US$5) Great beach *prato feito*.

Paulo Pescador (Praça São Braz; dishes US$6) Its typical Brazilian food is fresh and yummy, with the added benefit of superfriendly service (some English spoken!) and photographs of every dish.

Restaurante São João (Praça Brigadeiro Eduardo Gomes 41; dishes US$6; ☺ late) You can't get more old-school typical in Arraial than São João – the entrance crosses the owner's living room. Fantastic Bahian food.

A Portinha (Rua Manoel C. Santiago; per kg US$10) This is possibly the best per-kilo food in Brazil, with treats like mashed pumpkin and quiches warmed by a wood-fired oven, in addition to a great salad bar.

Aipim (Beco do Jegue; dishes US$8-19) An open-air restaurant that exudes tropical chic with stylish decor, an illuminated bar and hip lounge tunes, all under a thatched roof. The spot to splash out.

Entertainment

Along the main drag you'll find entertainment venues. The luaus at Cabana Grande, Magnólia (rave-style) and Parracho (tourist-style) are most frequent during the summer and holidays. Ask around for the latest *lambada* and *forró* hot spot. D.O.C. is a great enclosed São Paulo-style club.

Beco das Cores (Estrada do Mucugeâ) A small galleria with magical ambience and live music on weekends.

Girasol (Estrada do Mucugeâ) Great for people-watching while lounging on colored pillows or playing pool.

Getting There & Away

A passenger and a car ferry run frequently between Porto Seguro and Arraial (US$1 to Arraial, free return, five minutes) during the day, and hourly on the hour after midnight. From Arraial's dock, jump on a bus or kombi to the center (US50¢, 10 minutes). It's also possible to walk the lovely 4km along the beach – not recommended when beaches are empty.

TRANCOSO

☎ 0xx73 / pop 10,000

An eclectic mix of wealthy Brazilians, international ravers and hippies old and young are drawn to this small tropical paradise. The village is perched atop a tall bluff overlooking the ocean, and centers around its **Quadrado**, a wide, grassy, carless central square, host to afternoon *futebol* games. At night everyone turns out to lounge in the outdoor seating of the restaurants that line the Quadrado,

and take in its twinkling lights. The beaches immediately to the south of Trancoso are gorgeous, but don't miss celebrated **Praia do Espelho** (20km south), off the road to Caraíva.

There is an ATM both near the Quadrado and in Supermercado Nogueira on the road into town.

Sleeping & Eating

Most accommodations are pricey. Reservations are a must during January and major holidays. Many of the pricey restaurants on the Quadrado serve a *prato feito* or *prato executivo* (US$5) if you ask.

Pousada Miramar (☎ 3668-1123/1819; miramartrancoso@hotmail.com; Quadrado; campsites per person US$6.50) Ocean view camping.

Pousada Cuba (Rua Cuba; s/d US$12.50/17.50) Dirt paths connect simple cabins perched on a hillside at this happy, tenement-like *pousada*. Follow signs posted near Pousada Quarto Crescente. Communal kitchen available.

Café Esmeralda Albergue (☎ 3668-1527; cafe esmeralda@portonet.com.br; Quadrado; s/d US$30, without bathroom US$20) A Canadian/Argentine couple have a row of simple rooms and a cocoa tree and hammock chill space behind their café. No breakfast.

Pousada Quarto Crescente (☎ 3668-1014; www .quartocrescente.net; Rua Itabela; s/d US$30/40; 🖳) A very sweet, tree-shaded spot with spacious gardens, a well-stocked library (book exchange!), comfortable rooms and a superb breakfast. A short walk from the Quadrado.

Du Blè Noir (Rua do Telégrafo 300; crepes around US$3) The chocolate and banana crepe is legendary at this crepe stand in a small galleria near the Quadrado. Savory flavors too.

A Portinha (Quadrado; per kg US$10) This buffet restaurant wins over diners with its wide selection of excellent fresh food and seating under a towering tree.

Silvana & Cia (Quadrado; dishes for 2 US$20-45) A local family serves up yummy typical meat dishes and Bahian food at tables underneath a gigantic *amendoeira* tree.

Getting There & Away

The 13km walk along the beach from Arraial d'Ajuda at low tide is beautiful. Hourly buses depart from Arraial d'Ajuda's dock and center (US$2.50, 50 minutes) from 7:15am to 8pm and return from 6am to 8pm. Two daily buses travel between Trancoso and Porto Seguro (US$3, two hours).

BRAZIL

CARAÍVA

☎ 0xx73 / pop 6440

Without electricity, cars, banks or decent phone lines, the village of Caraíva is remote and beautiful, a combination that attracts alternative types looking for a quiet pace of life. This sandy hamlet perches between a mangrove-lined river and a long beach with churning surf. Noisy generators provide electricity and keep the *forró* hopping on Friday nights. In the low season, Caraíva all but shuts down.

Boat journeys upriver, horseback rides or walks to a Pataxó Indian village and trips to the Parque Nacional de Monte Pascoal are easily organized. A 14km walk north (or hop on a bus) brings you to celebrated **Praia do Espelho**.

Darkness reveals Caraíva's magic, so staying the night is recommended. Simple rooms are available at **Casa da Praia** (☎ 9111-4737; www .caraiva.net/casasdapraia/; s/d US$15/30) and **Pousada Raiz Forte** (☎ 9991-7391; s/d US$12.50/25). Mosquito nets are essential. Seek out Cantinho da Duca for an excellent vegetarian *prato feito*.

Buses for Caraíva leave from Arraial d'Ajuda's port and center (US$5.75, 2½ hours, two to three daily) and Trancoso (US$5, two hours, two to three daily). For greater connections north or south, head for Itabela (US$4, two hours, two daily).

ARACAJU

☎ 0xx79 / pop 461,000

Pedestrian malls slow the center to a walking pace in this relaxed, not unattractive city.

Information

Major banks have ATMs on the plazas.
Bureau de Informações Turísticas (☎ 3214-8848; Praça Olímpio Campos) Dispenses free city maps.
Timer Web Café (Praça Olimpio Campos 700; per hr US$1.50; 😊) Offers internet until late.

Sights & Activities

Projeto Tamar's small **Oceanário** (aquarium; Av Santos Dumont, Praia de Atalaia; admission US$3; 😊 2-8pm) has sea turtles, rays and eels. Flat, muddy-watered city beaches are built up – **Praia Atalaia Nova** on the Ilha de Santa Luzia is nicer.

Though not a tourist draw, Aracaju is a pleasant enough place. A trip to sleepy **Laranjeiras** (23km) and **São Cristóvão** (29km), Sergipe's colonial jewels, is a more interesting way to spend the day.

Sleeping

Hotel Amado (☎ 3211-9937; www.infonet.con.br/hotel amado; Rua Laranjeiras 532, Centro; s/d US$15/25; 😊) The center's best budget option, Amado has run-down but clean rooms in an old house converted into a *pousada*. Convenient location.

Pousada Mirante das Águas (☎ 3255-2610; www .mirantedasaguas.com.br; Rua Delmiro Golveia 711, Atalaia; s/d US$20/25; 😊) This *pousada* has comfortable rooms and an elaborate games-chill area just two blocks from the waterfront. English spoken.

Eating

Restaurants and nightlife concentrate in the city beach neighborhoods, collectively referred to as the *orla* (waterfront).

Bon Apetite (Rua João Pessoa 71175, Centro; per kg US$7.50) The elaborate buffet has lots of options at this spot popular with the working crowd.

O Miguel (Av Antônio Alves 340, Atalaia Velha; carne do sol for 2 US$12.50) The local spot for Northeastern specialties like *carne do sol* (sun-dried beef).

New Hakata (Av Beira Mar; per person Wed US$15; 😊) This large Japanese restaurant has an excellent all-you-can-eat buffet to live jazz every Wednesday.

Getting There & Around

BRA, Gol, Ocean Air, TAM, and Varig operate domestic flights from Aracaju.

The Rodoviária Nova (New Bus Terminal) is 4km east of the center. Frequent buses go to Maceió (US$10 to US$16, four hours, four daily), Penedo (US$8, three hours, daily), Recife (US$26, 23 hours, daily) and Salvador (US$17 to US$25, 4½ hours, 10 daily). City and local buses leave from the **Rodoviária Velha** (Old Bus Terminal; Av Divina Pastora, Centro).

PENEDO

☎ 0xx82 / pop 56,750

Penedo is a riverfront colonial town with a rich collection of beautiful 17th- and 18th-century constructions, including many churches. Attractions include the opportunity to travel the often jade-colored waters of the Rio São Francisco and the bustling markets that crowd downtown streets, especially on Saturday.

Information

Major bank ATMs are along the riverfront.
Tourist office (☎ 3551-2727; Praça Barão de Penedo) Gives out maps and offers one-hour walking tours (Portuguese only).

Sights & Activities

River tours to sand dunes at the rivermouth (US$10 to US$15, 2½ hours), passing floating islands and riverfront homes, leave from Piaçabuçu (28km downriver). There is at least one daily departure at 9am; boats have a four-passenger minimum. For a shorter ride, grab a ferry (US75¢) to Neópolis, another colonial town, or Carrapicho (Santana do São Francisco), a nearby village noted for its ceramics.

Sleeping & Eating

Pousada Estilo (☎ 3551-2465; Praça Jácome Calheiros 79; US$12.50/25) A local family rents clean, simple *apartamentos* in its home on a colonial plaza. Second-floor rooms are breezy, and nicer than those in its *pousada* closer to the river.

Pousada Colonial (☎ 3551-2355; Praça 12 de Abril 21; s & d US$40; 🖥) This restored colonial house on the riverfront has clean, simple rooms with stained-wood floors and antique furniture – some with river views.

Esquina Imperial (Av Floriano Peixoto 61; lunch per kg US$6) A simple place with a buffet lunch and soups and sandwiches at night.

Forte da Rocheira (Rua da Rocheira 2; dishes US$12-15) The novel location – fastened to a 17th-century fort's outer wall – and river view compensate for unexciting meat and fish dishes.

Getting There & Away

For Maceió (US$7.50), take the *pinga BR-101* (BR-101 drip; four hours, one daily), the *expresso litoral* (coastal express; 2½ hours, two daily) or the *pinga litoral* (coastal drip; four hours, four daily) bus. The latter gives a thorough tour of this beautiful coastal stretch. Only one daily bus goes to Aracaju (US$6.75, three hours) or Salvador (US$23.50, nine hours). *Topiques* (vans) to Maceió, Piaçabuçu and Aracaju leave frequently (roughly 5am to 4:30pm Monday to Saturday, fewer on Sunday) near the bus station.

MACEIÓ

☎ 0xx82 / pop 796,840

Maceió is a modern city blessed with winning restaurant and nightlife scenes, but its attractive city beachfronts are what really give it an edge. Here vividly green water laps up on sands lined with brightly painted *jangadas* (traditional sailboats), and locals weave their evening walks between thatched-roof restaurants and palm-shaded *futebol* fields. Just an hour away, **Praia do Gunga** is a work of tropical perfection and reason enough to stop in Maceió. The city's largest festival, Maceió Fest, is a Salvador-style, out-of-season Carnaval in the second week of December.

Information

Aeroturismo (Centro ☎ 3326-2020/2500; Rua Barão do Penedo 61; Shopping Iguatemi ☎ 3357-1184; 🕙 10am-9:30pm Mon-Sat, 3-9:30pm Sun) Changes traveler's checks.

Alsetures (☎ 3315-1603; Av Dr Antônio Gouveia 1143, Pajuçara) Tourist-information office; staffed by teenagers.

Banco do Brasil (Centro Rua João Pessoa; Ponta Verde Av Alvaro Otacílio 2963) Has ATMs on the Pajuçara waterfront.

Monkey internet (Av Eng Mario de Gusmão 513, Ponta Verde; per hr US$1.50; 🖥) Provides speedy internet until late.

Sights & Activities

High-quality Alagoan folk art is displayed at **Museu Théo Brandão** (Av da Paz 1490; admission US$1; 🕙 9am-5pm Tue-Fri, 2-5pm Sat & Sun), including festival headpieces weighing up to 35kg. The museum puts on free folkloric presentations in its courtyard on Thursday from 8pm to 10pm.

Praia de Ponta Verde and **Jatiúca** are good city beaches with calm water. **Praia do Francês** (24km) is pretty and lined with beach bars – it is Maceió's major weekend destination and has lots of *pousadas*. Incredibly idyllic **Praia do Gunga** sits across a river from Barra de São Miguel (34km) – get there before 9am for easiest/cheapest transport.

Jangadas sail 2km out to natural pools formed by the reef (US$6.50) from Praia de Pajuçara. It's a bit overrun.

Sleeping

Beachside Pajuçara is much more tranquil than the center.

Maceió Hotel (☎ 3326-1975; Rua Dr Pontes de Miranda 146; s/d US$5/10) All are clean and basic, but 2nd-floor rooms have windows.

Mar Amar (☎ 3231-1551; Rua Dr Antônio Pedro de Mendonça 343, Pajuçara; s/d US$10/20; 🖥) The whole place is a bit banged up, but the small rooms with mismatching furniture are clean.

Albergue Algamar (☎ 3231-2246; Rua Pref Abdon Arroxelas 327, Ponta Verde; dm/s/d US$16/30/30; 🖥) This large house converted into a hostel has a wide front veranda and a TV room. Private rooms overpriced.

Pousada Glória (☎ 3337-2348; Rua Jangadeiros 1119, Pajuçara; s/d US$20/25; 🖥) A local family rents these fair-sized rooms above its bakery. The

BRAZIL

MACEIÓ

BRAZIL

amiability and good room quality make this the best budget option.

Hotel Praia Bonita (☎ 2121-3700; www.praiabonita .com.br; Av Dr Antônio Gouveia 943; s/d US$40/45; ☒) An attractive two-story hotel on the waterfront, Praia Bonita has an alluring design and tasteful local artwork.

Eating

Pajuçara, Ponta Verde, and Jatiúca's beachfronts are loaded with restaurants, the latter containing the most reputable dinner spots. Clusters of beachfront stands make *beiju de tapioca* (US$1 to US$2) by heating manioc flour until it solidifies, folding it in half, and filling it with savory or sweet fillings – super yummy.

For a cheap seafood lunch, locals head for Massagueira (10km south), a fishing village on the southern shore of Lagoa Mundaú with simple waterfront restaurants.

Paraíso Lanches (Av Dr Antônio Gouveia 877, Pajuçara) This simple café serves innovative sandwiches ranging from soy to hamburger (US$1.75 to US$4.25), salads (US$2.50 to US$5.25), savory whole-wheat pancakes (US$2.25 to US$4.50), *açaí* and a huge variety of fresh fruit juices.

Sarah's Esfiha's (Rua Dr Lessa de Azevedo 59, Pajuçara; esfihas US75¢) Sarah's is a simple Middle Eastern restaurant that makes *esfihas* (fluffy breads topped or filled) to order, in addition to hummus, tabouleh and all the rest.

Mestre Cuca (Av Dep José Lages 453, Ponta Verde; per kg US$8) Despite the simple environment, the spread is great and includes lots of salads.

Divina Gula (Rua Eng Paulo B Nogueira 85, Jatiúca; mains US$6-11) This popular Maceió institution specializes in Minas Gerais and Northeastern dishes, and boasts over 50 different kinds of *cachaça*.

Massarella (Rua José Pontes Magalhães 271, Jatiúca; mains US$6-12; ☒) This is the spot for homemade pastas and brick-oven pizzas. Decor consisting of hanging cheese and decorative plates adds authenticity.

Entertainment

Nightlife centers in Stella Maris. The three places following fill every night.

Lampião (Av Álvaro Otacílio, Jatiúca) Offers beachfront *forró*.

Orákulo (Rua Barão de Jaraguá 717, Jaraguá) Popular bar has a different type of live music daily.

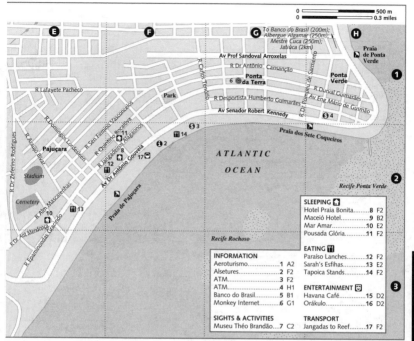

SLEEPING 🏠
Hotel Praia Bonita	8 F2
Maceió Hotel	9 B2
Mar Amar	10 E2
Pousada Glória	11 F2

INFORMATION
Aeroturismo	1 A2
Alsetures	2 F2
ATM	3 F2
ATM	4 H1
Banco do Brasil	5 B1
Monkey Internet	6 G1

SIGHTS & ACTIVITIES
Museu Théo Brandão	7 C2

EATING 🍴
Paraíso Lanches	12 E2
Sarah's Esfihas	13 B1
Tapoica Stands	14 F2

ENTERTAINMENT 🎭
Havana Café	15 D2
Orákulo	16 D2

TRANSPORT
Jangadas to Reef	17 F2

Aquarela (Av Juca Sampaio 1785, Jacintinho) Has live *forró* and *pagode*.

Gay venues like **Havana Café** (Av Com Leão 85, Jaraguá), which is actually pretty mixed, surround Orákulo.

Getting There & Away

BRA, Gol, Ocean Air, TAM and Varig operate domestic flights from Maceió's airport, 25km north of the center.

The bus station is 6km north of the center. Buses head to Recife (US$14 to US$21, 3½ hours, 14 daily), Penedo (US$7.50; *expresso litoral*, 2½ hours, two daily; *pinga litoral*, four hours, four daily; *pinga BR-101*, four hours, one daily), Aracaju (US$13 to US$16, four hours, four daily) and Salvador (US$26 to US$37, nine hours, four daily).

RECIFE

☎ 0xx81 / pop 2.9 million

Second only to Salvador in the Northeast, Recife is one of Brazil's cultural hot spots. It is also a major port and urban center, and unfortunately invests very little in its tourism, so an initial reaction to its gritty high-rises

and stinky canals may be disappointment. But with a little persistence and a few good nights out, it's possible to get a glimpse of the local dances, rhythms and nightlife that bring it fame. Recife can be enjoyed through trips from its sister city Olinda, which travelers consistently agree is a more pleasant base.

GETTING INTO TOWN

The Terminal Integrado de Passageiros (TIP), a combined long-distance bus station and metro terminal, is 14km southwest of the center. From the TIP to all Recife and Olinda destinations, catch a metro train (⊙ 5am to 11pm) to the Estação Recife stop (US60¢, 25 minutes). For Boa Viagem, catch the 'Setubal (Príncipe)' bus. For Olinda, catch the 'Rio Doce/Princesa Isabel' bus.

From the airport (which lies about 10km south of the center), the Aeroporto bus goes to Boa Viagem and then Av Dantas Barreto in the center. For Olinda, take this bus to Recife's Terminal Cais de Santa Rita, and catch a 'Rio Doce' or 'Pau Amarelo' bus.

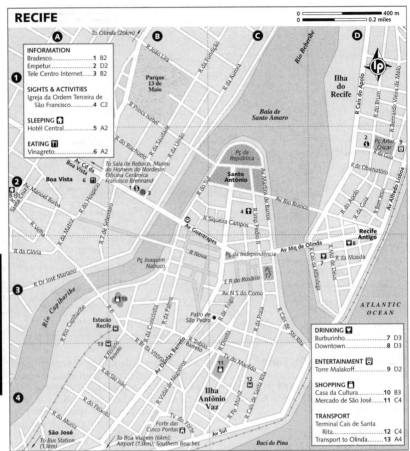

RECIFE

Orientation

Recife's commercial center spreads from Boa Vista, across the Rio Capibaribe, to Santo Antônio. Both are busy during the day and deserted at night and on Sundays. The Ilha do Recife holds the quiet, historical Recife Antigo district. Boa Viagem is an affluent beachside neighborhood 6km south of the center. Its beachfront is divided into three zones called *jardins* (gardens).

Information

Bradesco (Av Guararapes, Boa Vista)
Empetur airport (☎ 3462-4960); Recife Antigo (☎ 3224-2361; Rua Bom Jesus 197); TIP (☎ 3452-2824)
Pl@y (Av Conselheiro Aguiar 2964, Boa Viagem; per hr US$2.50; ☒) Across from Albergue Maracatus.

Tele Centro Internet (Av Conde da Boa Vista 56, Centro; per hr US$2)
Tourist Police (☎ 3326-9603; airport)

Sights & Activities

Serpents gape, buttocks bulge, reptiles emerge from their shells and jaws gape skyward at the **Oficina Cerâmica Francisco Brennand** (Várzea; admission US$2; ☒ 8am-5pm Mon-Thu, to 4pm Fri). The artist revitalized his family's abandoned factory to produce decorative ceramic tiles and display a seemingly exhaustive exhibition of his peculiar sculptures. A trip out to this forested suburb is a regional highlight, so bring a picnic and hang out on the extensive grounds. Take the UR7-Várzea bus from the main post office downtown on Av Guararapes to the end of the line

(35 minutes). From there, catch a taxi (US$3) as the several-kilometer walk is unsafe.

The **Museu do Homem do Nordeste** (Av 17 de Agosto 2187, Casa Forte) was closed for renovation at press time; ask Empetur if this excellent anthropological museum has reopened.

Highlights of the old city include the 17th-century **Igreja da Ordem Terceira de São Francisco** (Rua Imperador Pedro II; ☺ 8-11am & 2-5pm Mon-Fri, 8-11:30am Sat), whose Capela Dourada (Golden Chapel) is one of the finest examples of Brazilian baroque.

Few locals actually enter Praia Boa Viagem's waters – you'll find cleaner water further south at **Praia Pedra do Xaréu** (20km) and **Praia Calhetas** (23km).

Festivals & Events

Carnaval Recife holds one of Brazil's most colorful and folkloric Carnavals. The rehearsals and parties in the months leading up to it are a good taste of the actual event. Carnaval groups and spectators deck themselves out in elaborate costumes such as *maracatu* (warrior with a huge headpiece and a flower in his mouth), *caboclo* (indigenous-African mix), colonial-era royalty, harlequin, bull and *frevo* (crop tops with ruffled sleeves for both genders and a tiny umbrella), and shimmy for days to frenetic *frevo* and strongly African-influenced *maracatu* beats. Action concentrates in the Centro and in Recife Antigo. Carnaval safety tips on p343 also apply here.

Recifolia is an out-of-season, Salvador-style Carnaval, the last week in October.

Sleeping

Boa Viagem is a better area than the Centro.

Hotel Central (☎ /fax 3222-4001; s/d US$11/19) Bright rooms with high ceilings and the tree-shaded street make this once-grand 1930s hotel a great budget option.

Albergue Maracatus do Recife (☎ 3326-1221; www .geocities.com/alberguemaracatus; Rua Maria Carolina 185, Boa Viagem; dm/s/d US$12.50/12.50/25; 💻 🕮) Airy dorm rooms and funky light fixtures await at this hostel installed in a stylish 1970s home. A onetime bedding charge (US$1.75) is additional. Guest-use kitchen available. Near bus stop 10 on Av Domingos Ferreira.

Boa Viagem Hostel (☎ 3326-9572; www.hostelboa viagem.com.br; Rua Aviador Severiano Lins 455, Boa Viagem; dm/s/d US$15/32/32; 🕮) Plain dorm rooms are compensated for by plenty of green outdoor chill space. Near Colégio Boa Viagem.

Pousada Casuarinas (☎ 3325-4708; www.pousada casuarinas.com.br; Rua Antônio Pedro Figueiredo 151, Boa Viagem; s/d US$30/41; 💻) Lots of folk art spices up the modern architecture at this quiet *pousada*

shaded by mango trees. Near the Bompreço supermarket on Av Domingos Ferreira.

Eating

Boa Viagem's restaurants, outside of the Polo Pina area (see below), are scattered. For dinner in the Centro, try the Pátio de São Pedro, a cute colonial courtyard, or Recife Antigo.

Sucão (Rua dos Navegantes 783, Boa Viagem; US$2.75-6) Try one of 100 types of fresh fruit juices to accompany your sandwich, quiche or salad. Near the Recife Palace.

Vinagreto (Rua do Hospício 203, Centro; per kg US$8.50; 💻) Great buffet lunch.

Sabor de Beijo (Av Conselheiro Aguiar 2994, Boa Viagem; per kg US$9; 💻) This popular sweet shop has a pretty fancy lunch buffet. Near Albergue Maracatus.

Parraxaxá (Rua Baltazar Pereira 32, Boa Viagem; per kg US$11) Festive decor and costumed waitstaff spice up your meal at this fun Northeastern-themed restaurant. Near the Conjunto Pernambucano on Av Conselheiro Aguiar.

Drinking

In the Centro, the Patio de São Pedro is a popular hangout, especially on Terça Negra (Black Tuesday), a night of Afro-Brazilian rhythms, or during happy hour.

Boa Viagem attracts Recife's affluent youth. Nightlife concentrates in an area called Polo Pina.

Recife Antigo (aka Polo Bom Jesus) has a few bars with outdoor tables along Rua Bom Jesus that are active during happy hour and Sunday afternoon/evenings.

Burburinho (Rua Tomzinha 106) Packs on Monday, Thursday and Saturday for pop-rock and local bands.

Downtown (Rua Vigário Tenório 105) Has pool tables and a happening dance floor, and plays rock.

Conselheiro (Av Conselheiro Aguiar 793, Boa Viagem) Offers both a sit-down pub with food and a dance floor, and has been rated Recife's best place to flirt (tied with Burburinho).

Musique (Rua Tenente João Cícero 202, Boa Viagem) Has good DJs, or have a drink at A Casa next door.

Boratcho (Av Herculano Bandeira 513, Polo Pina, Boa Viagem) This is a grooving dance club that often plays Recife's own *mangue beat* (modernized *maracatú*).

Sala de Reboco (Rua Gregório Junior 264, Cordeiro) *The* spot for *forró*.

BRAZIL

Entertainment

Pernambuco Cultural (☎ 3268-9299; www.agendaper nambucocultural.com.br) Produces excellent cultural shows showcasing Pernambuco's rich array of music and dance. If Maracatu Nação Pernambuco or Toque Leoa (all women) are performing, don't miss them. Torre Malakoff (Rua do Bom Jesus, Recife Antigo) is often the venue.

Shopping

For Pernambuco's traditional handicrafts (ceramic figurines, wood sculptures and leather goods), head for the following.

Casa da Cultura (☺ 9am-6pm Mon-Sat, 9am-2pm Sun) This is housed in a colonial-era prison which functioned until 1979, and often has cultural performances around 3pm on Fridays.

Mercado do São José (☺ 6am-5:30pm Mon-Sat, to noon Sun) Worthwhile market.

Getting There & Around

BRA, Gol, TAM, Ocean Air and Varig operate domestic flights from Recife's airport, 10km south of the center. TAP connects Recife with Europe.

Bus tickets can be purchased at outlets in town or by calling **Disk Rodoviária** (☎ 3452-3990), a bus-ticket delivery service. Buses run to João Pessoa (US$9, two hours, hourly 5am to 7pm), Natal (US$16, 4½ hours, nine daily), Fortaleza (US$43 to US$76, 12 hours, three daily), Maceió (US$13 to US$20, four hours, 12 to 14 daily), Salvador (US$40 to US$50, 11 to 12 hours, two daily) and Rio (US$123 to US$134, 42 hours, three daily).

From the center to Boa Viagem, take any bus marked 'Aeroporto', 'Shopping Center', 'Candeias' or 'Piedade' from Av NS do Carmo. To return, take any bus marked 'Dantas Barreto.'

OLINDA

☎ 0xx81 / pop 360,000

Olinda is recognized as Recife's cultural counterpart: a vibrant city with bohemian quarters, art galleries, music in the streets and a celebration always in the works. In the historical center, quiet streets lined with pastel-colored houses and packed with churches overlook the sea. This is one of Brazil's best-preserved colonial cities and, together with Recife, one of its major cultural centers. Despite being a touristy destination Olinda remains charming, friendly and local.

Information

Major banks are located northeast of Praça do Carmo, once Av Marcos Freire turns into Av Getúlio Vargas. Any *kombi* heading in that direction will drop you at the door.

Information post (☎ 3305-1048; Praça do Carmo 100) Free guides available.

Olinda Net Café (Praça do Carmo 5-B; per hr US$2.50)

Olind@net.com (Rua do Sol; per hr US$1.50)

Dangers & Annoyances

Crime (mostly petty) does exist in Olinda. Avoid walking alone along deserted streets or carrying valuables at night. The city recommends using only its free yellow-shirted guides to avoid sticky situations involving payment discrepancies.

Sights & Activities

The layout of the historical center's steep streets creates an intuitive walking tour. As you wander, keep an eye out for colorful graffiti pieces with folkloric themes.

The **Museu do Mamulengo** (Rua do Amparo 59) displays wooden hand puppets typical of the northeast. The **Casa dos Bonecos Gigantes** (Rua do Amparo 45) houses giant papier-mâché Carnaval puppets weighing up to 13kg. Both were closed for renovation at press time.

The *capoeira* school, **Angola Mãe** (Rua Ilma Cunha 243), welcomes visitors to take classes or watch an open *roda* (circle) at 6pm on Sunday. Go with a respectful attitude and unaccompanied by a guide. Look for a metal gate painted in zebra stripes. Another place to see *capoeira* or local dances is the **Alto da Sé** around 4pm on Sunday.

Churches open for visitation from 8am to 11:30am and 1:30pm to 5pm. The 1582 **Mosteiro de São Bento** (Rua São Bento) has an exceptional carved and guilded wooden main altar to awe even the nonbeliever. The 10:30am Sunday mass includes Gregorian chants.

Though capable of producing interesting exhibits, the most fascinating thing about the **Museu de Arte Contemporânea** (Rua 13 de Maio; admission US35¢; ☺ 9am-noon & 2-5pm Tue-Fri, 2-5pm Sat & Sun) is its past as an 18th-century Inquisition jail. Prisoners were kept on the 2nd floor – check out the hole in a wall that extends to the basement (a toilet) and the ominous heavy wooden doors.

The **Museu de Arte Sacra de Pernambuco** (Rua Bispo Coutinho; admission US35¢; ☺ 9am-1pm Mon-Fri) has folkloric representations of Christ in addition to traditional sacred art.

Local buses leave from Praça do Carmo for **Praia do Pau Amarelo** (14km) and **Praia da Maria Farinha** (23km), northern-coast beaches with calm waters. Locals prefer the southern coast.

Festivals & Events

You can get a taste of Carnaval on weekends (especially Sunday nights) in the months leading up to it, when *blocos* rehearse in the streets and throughout the historical center. Olinda's festive spirit revives the Friday following Carnaval and on March 11th for the city's birthday.

Carnaval Traditional and colorful, and has an intimacy and security not found in big-city Carnavals. Fast and frenetic *frevo* music sets the pace, balanced by the heavy drumbeats of *maracatu*. Costumed *blocos* and spectators dance through the streets in this highly inclusive, playful and lewd festival. Carnaval safety tips on p343 also apply here.

Festival de Folclore Nordestino Showcases dance, music and folklore of the northeast at the end of August. Recommended.

Sleeping

Book well ahead for Carnaval, though it can be cheaper to rent a room or house.

Pousada d'Olinda (☎ 3494-2559; www.pousada dolinda.com.br; Praça João Alfredo 178; dm US$12.50, s/d US$25/35; ✄ ♨ ☀) Choose between a 12-bed dorm room that gets all the street party noise or a four-bed, tool shed–like setup outback. Private rooms on the 2nd floor are poor, but

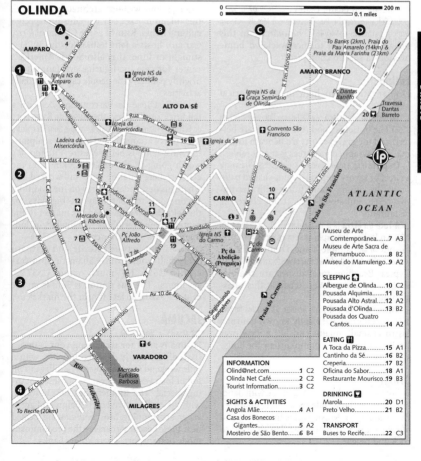

OLINDA

0 — 200 m
0 — 0.1 miles

INFORMATION
Olind@net.com..................**1** C2
Olinda Net Café..................**2** C2
Tourist Information..............**3** C2

SIGHTS & ACTIVITIES
Angola Mãe.......................**4** A1
Casa dos Bonecos
  Gigantes.......................**5** A2
Mosteiro de São Bento.......**6** B4

Museu de Arte
  Comtemporânea.............**7** A3
Museu de Arte Sacra de
  Pernambuco...................**8** B2
Museu do Mamulengo..**9** A2

SLEEPING
Albergue de Olinda..........**10** C2
Pousada Alquimia.............**11** B2
Pousada Alto Astral......**12** A2
Pousada d'Olinda.........**13** B2
Pousada dos Quatro
  Cantos....................**14** A2

EATING
A Toca da Pizza.............**15** A1
Cantinho da Sé.............**16** B2
Creperia.....................**17** B2
Oficina do Sabor...........**18** A1
Restaurante Mourisco.....**19** B3

DRINKING
Marola.......................**20** D1
Preto Velho.................**21** B2

TRANSPORT
Buses to Recife..........**22** C3

BRAZIL

those out back are an excellent midrange option. The pool and lawn area is pretty and very social.

Albergue de Olinda (☎ 3429-1592; www.alberguede olinda.com.br; Rua do Sol 233; dm/s/d US$13/25/30; ☒) Modern rooms in a historical building are complimented by a nice garden with hammocks and an outdoor kitchen. Traffic noise is constant.

Pousada Alquimia (☎ 3429-1457; Rua Prudente de Morais 292; s/d US$20/25) Simple rooms are constructed in a block behind the owner's colonial home; breakfast is served in his kitchen.

Pousada Alto Astral (☎ 3439-3453; www.pousadaalto astral.com.br; Rua 13 de Maio 305; s/d US$30/40; ☒) Rooms opening to the leafy garden behind the *pousada* are airy and bright; others are dark. Bargain hard.

Pousada dos Quatro Cantos (☎ 3429-0220; www .pousada4cantos.com.br; Rua Prudente dos Morais 441; s/d without bathroom US$40/46) The *quartos* in this delightful colonial former weekend home overlook a shaded courtyard.

Eating

Dinner prices run high in the historical center.

Jardins do Mourisco (Av Dr Justino Gonçalves; per kg US$8) The buffet is good (the desserts are better!) and the gravel courtyard beneath towering, vine-wrapped *jaca* trees is memorable.

Creperia (Praça João Alfredo 168; dishes US$4-9) Enjoy a sweet or savory crepe in a palm-shaded patio or in the dining room hung with decorative plates and street signs at this charming restaurant.

A Toca da Pizza (Rua do Guadalupe 53; large US$4.50-7.50) An Italian transplant serves excellent pizzas out of her simple home. Dinner only.

Cantinho da Sé (Ladeira da Sé; mains for two US$9-12.50) Typical Brazilian meat dishes are complemented by a view over Recife at this unassuming spot.

Oficina do Sabor (Rua do Amparo 335; mains for two US$14-35) Olinda's nationally known gourmet bistro is small, quaint and has a view over Recife. Stuffed baked pumpkins are the house specialty.

Drinking

Follow a sunset drink at Alto da Sé with dancing at one of the simple spots along unattractive Rua do Sol. Music varies from *forró* and *afoxé* (traditional Afro-Brazilian rhythm) to rock and reggae.

Preto Velho (Alto da Sé 681) Has live *afoxé* (Saturday) and *axé*, *samba* and reggae (Sunday afternoon).

Marola (Travessa Dantas Barreto) Waterfront Marola has live *MPB* nightly and on Sunday afternoons.

Getting There & Around

See the boxed text, p359 for bus information from the airport. Once in Olinda, get off at Praça do Carmo. 'Rio Doce/Piedade' and 'Barra de Jangada/Casa Caiada' buses run between Olinda and Boa Viagem. Any 'Rio Doce', 'Casa Caiada' or 'Jardim Atlantico' bus connects central Recife to Olinda.

CARUARU

☎ 0xx81 / pop 300,000

Modern and without architectural appeal, this inland market city contains unexpected cultural riches. Known as the Capital of *forró*, Caruaru hosts a **forró festival** for the 30 days straight of June. It is also South America's center for ceramic-figurine art, famous for brightly painted little people captured in daily activities.

Off Rua José de Vasconcelos, beneath a tall brick smokestack, the **Museu do Barro** (Patio do Forró; ☉ 8am-5pm Tue-Sat, 9am-1pm Sun) displays the work of accomplished local clay sculptors, the most famous being Mestre Vitalino. It's worth going to **Alto de Moura**, 6km from the center, where Vitalino lived and worked and where his descendants carry on the tradition. Wednesday and Saturday are big days for the **Feira Livre**, a huge open-air market in the center selling everything imaginable, including figurines and other crafts.

Buses run between Recife and Caruaru every half hour from 5:50am to 8pm (*executivo* US$9, 1½ hours; *comun* US$7.25, 2½ hours). The bus station is 3km from the center – ask to be let off near the market.

JACUMÃ

☎ 0xx83 / pop 2000

Jacumã is great for recharging your batteries (naked!) on nearly deserted beaches, with a little weekend *forró* for spice. The village itself, full of Joao Pessoa's weekend homes, is nothing special. The southern beaches, however, with their tall, arid red cliffs, palms and green water, are stunning. Most *pousadas* are located near these beaches – cars are the predominant mode of transport. There are no banks.

Infamous **Praia de Tambaba** (14km) is the northeast's only official, regulated and un-creepy (men unaccompanied by a woman are prohibited) nudist beach. **Praia do Coqueirinho** (8km) and **Praia de Tabatinga** (4km) are equally beautiful.

In the center, **Pousada Beija-Flor** (☎ 3290-1822; Rua Maria Amélia; s/d US$14/20; ✂ ☎) has a row of well-put-together rooms with hammocks overlooking the sandy road.

A cool Argentine couple runs pretty **Pousada dos Mundos** (☎ 3290-1460; www.pousadadosmundos .com.ar; Rua dos Juazeiros, Praia de Tabatinga; s/d US$25/30; ✂ ☎). Rooms are ample-sized, have attractive wooden furniture and private verandas with hammocks, and are two blocks from the beach. The owners will help resolve transport issues and a local restaurant delivers (all fairly cheap). Call for a ride from the center. English spoken.

Straightforward Kelly Lanches serves pizza, *prato feito* (US$3) and excellent hamburgers (US85¢ to US$2). Commar also has a great *prato feito* (US$3). Both are on the main road in the center.

Traveling north on Hwy BR-101, get off at the Conde/Jacumã turnoff and catch a local bus from there. From João Pessoa, take a 'Jacumã' or 'Conde/Jacumã' (US$1.75, 1¼ hours, every 20 minutes until 9pm) bus, or 'PB-008' (US$1.25, one hour, every 40 minutes) bus. They depart from the third stop up Rua Cicero Meireles, which runs perpendicular to the front of the bus station. Four daily buses run between João Pessoa and Praia de Tambaba, passing through Jacumã.

JOÃO PESSOA

☎ 0xx83 / pop 600,000

Though not a real tourist draw itself, João Pessoa makes a comfortable (and economical) base from which to check out the stark and beautiful surrounding beaches.

Orientation & Information

In the evening everyone heads for the beach-front promenade where there are thatched-roof stands and restaurants, and bars and clubs nearby. There are major banks in the center and on Av Senador Rui Carneiro in Manaíra.

Gameleira Internet (Av João Maurício 157, Manaíra; per hr US$1.50) David, the American owner, is a good information source and teaches three-day, Portuguese-for-the-traveler crash courses.

PBTur (☎ 0800-281-9229; Av Almirante Tamandaré 100, Tambaú) Has maps and English-speakers.

Sights & Activities

The worthwhile **Centro Cultural de São Francisco** (admission US$1.50; ⏰ 9am-noon & 2-5pm Tue-Sun) is a beautiful, architecturally confused religious complex built over three centuries due to interrupting battles with the Dutch and French. Don't miss the floor tiles inlaid with myrrh resin and extremely good popular-art exposition. The **Casa do Artista Popular** (Praça da Independência 56, Centro; ⏰ 9am-7pm Mon-Fri, 10am-6pm Sat & Sun) displays local popular artwork in a restored early 20th-century home.

The city beaches are built up but have calm, relatively clean water. The best surrounding beaches are **Praia Campina** (43km), a surf beach, and **Praia do Oiteiro** (40km). It is a gorgeous 15km walk south from Praia Cabo Branco to **Ponta de Seixas**, the easternmost tip of South America.

Sleeping

Tambaú and Manaíra are beachfront and more pleasant than the Centro.

Pousada Arco Íris (☎ 3241-8086; Rua Visconde de Pelotas 20, Centro; s/d US$7.50/14; ✂) A clean, basic option a few blocks up from the lake.

Hotel Mar Azul (☎ 3226-2660; Av João Maurício 315, Manaíra; without breakfast r US$15) A no-frills place on the waterfront with giant rooms with kitchenettes.

Manaíra Hostel (☎ 3247-1962; www.manairahostel .br2.net; Rua Major Ciraulo 380, Manaíra; dm/d US$16/30; ✂ ☎) This modern home converted into an attractive hostel has nice bathrooms, cooking facilities and plenty of hangout space.

Pousada do Caju (☎ 2107-8700; www.pousadadocaju .com.br; Rua Helena Meira Lima 269, Tambaú; s/d US$27/47; ✂ ☎) Two neighboring homes were connected to create this colorful *pousada*. Look at a few rooms.

Eating

Bars and restaurants concentrate in Tambaú. Stalls in front of the round Hotel Tropical Tambaú serve *beiju de tapioca* (savory or sweet manioc flour 'taco'), *macaxeira na chapa* (manioc pancake filled with meat or cheese), soup and more.

Oca (Rua Almirante Barroso 303, Centro) The spot for a weekday vegetarian buffet lunch.

Lion (Av Tamandaré 624, Tambaú; mains US$2.25-8) Known for crepes, but the pizza is a good deal on midweek *rodízio* nights (US$5.50).

Mangai (Av General Édson Ramalho 696, Manaíra; per kg US$10) The dinner buffet is a local institution and an excellent way to sample specialties from the northeast's interior.

Picanha de Ouro (Av Epitácio Pessoa, Tambaú; sirloin for 2 US$13) Don't let the complete lack of ambience keep you from the best BBQ around.

Getting There & Around

Gol, TAM and Varig operate domestic flights from João Pessoa's airport, 11km west of the center.

Buses run to Recife (US$7 to US$9, two hours, hourly 5am to 7:30pm), Natal (US$10 to US$13, three hours, eight daily), Fortaleza (US$42 to US$80, 10 hours, two daily) and Salvador (US$55, 14 hours, one to two daily). Buses 510 and 511 go to Tambaú from the first platform in front of the bus station. Most local buses pass the Lagoa in the center.

PRAIA DA PIPA

☎ 0xx84 / pop 3000

Pipa rivals Jericoacoara as the Northeast's hippest beach town outside Bahia. It becomes more upscale with every passing year, but try not to let the boutiques get you down. An alternative, laid-back vibe dominates Pipa, and nightlife can be really fun. Natural beauty abounds here, too, with dolphin-filled waters and pristine beaches backed by magnificent tall bluffs.

There is one ATM and internet runs US$2 per hour. Bookshop rents books.

Sights & Activities

Santuário Ecológico (admission US$2; ☼ 8am-5pm Mon-Sat, to 1pm Sun) is a small flora and fauna reserve worth visiting for the spectacular views. It's on the road into town.

Southernmost of the beaches is **Praia do Amor**. North of town, **Praia dos Golfinhos** is accessible only via the beach and is closed off by high tide. You can get to **Praia do Madeiro** from Golfinhos or catch a *kombi* leaving town. Pipa has some decent surf – boards and lessons are available in town. Kite surfing lessons are also available.

Sleeping

Reservations are required for all major holidays.

Camping das Mangueiras (☎ 3223-8153/3246-2472; Rua Praia do Amor; campsites per person US$5) Shady patches and outdoor showers.

Albergue da Rose (☎ 8844-8371; Rua da Mata; s/d US$12.50/25) At the top of the hill, sweet Rose rents a few rooms around a small, open-air veranda with hammocks.

Pousada Xamã (☎ 3246-2267; www.pousadaxama .com; Rua dos Cajueiros 12; dm/s/d US$12.50/15/35; ▨ ▨) This primo budget *pousada* has hammocks all around, a great breakfast, comfortable rooms and is pretty and green.

Pousada Aconchego (☎ 3246-2439; www.pipa.com .br/aconchego; Rua do Céu 100; s/d US$25/35) Simply constructed bungalows with hammocks and extra touches in a pretty garden. Central location.

Eating

Restaurants are pricey in Pipa.

Casa da Farinha (main road) An excellent bakery with a sandwich grill.

Soparia Chez Liz (main road; soup US$2-4) This simple café serves up yummy veggie and meat soups.

Tá Massa (Rua da Gameleira; pastas US$2.75-6.50) Choose from a range of meat or veggie sauces to top penne or spaghetti at this cute little nook.

Tapas Bar (Rua do Céu) The Spanish tradition of creating a meal out of several small plates (tapas) is sensationalizing Pipa.

Getting There & Away

The last bus from Natal (US$4.25, 1¾ hours, 10 daily, four on Sunday) leaves at 6:45pm, and 6:25pm on Sunday. Taxis from Natal to Pipa run US$50. If you're coming from the south, get off at Goaininha, 1½ hours from João Pessoa. From Goaininha, catch a *kombi* (US$1.25, 40 minutes) from behind the church or a taxi (US$10).

Pipa Tour Ecotourismo, behind Blue Bar, posts bus schedules. There is frequent transport to Natal, but if headed south, you'll have to flag down a bus in Goaininha.

NATAL

☎ 0xx84 / pop 800,000

Natal is a clean, rather bland capital surrounded by impressively large sand dunes. Due to its status as Brazil's 'sun city,' claiming 300 sunny days yearly, it's become a major European package destination. Most travelers stop here simply to spend a day on the dunes. Another draw is **Carnatal**, Natal's Salvador-style, out-of-season Carnaval in the first week of December.

Information

ATMs are on Ponta Negra's beachfront.

Banco do Brasil (Av Rio Branco) In the center.

Bradesco (Av Rio Branco) Also in the center.

Hotel Miami Beach (Av Governador Sílvio Pedrosa 24, Praia das Artistas; per hr US$2) Internet access available.

Pizza a Pezzi (Rua Dr Manoel A B de Araujo, Alto de Ponta Negra 396A; per hr US$1.50) For internet.

Setur airport (☎ 0800-841-516); Rodoviária Nova (☎ 0xx81-3205-2428) Gives out maps and limited information. Also at Centro de Turismo.

Sights & Activities

Dune-buggy excursions to beautiful **Genipabu** are offered by would-be Ayrton Sennas. If you choose a trip *com emoção* (with emotion), you'll be treated to thrills like Wall

of Death and Vertical Descent. Accredited drivers – members of the **Sindicato dos Bugeiros** (☎ 3225-2077; Posto VIP, Av Rota do Sol, Ponta Negra) – can be more trustworthy. An eight-hour trip runs US$35 per person and can be arranged through *pousadas*, agencies or, more cheaply, the Sindicato. Before you go, consider the damage these trips do to the dune ecosystem. It's possible to drive to Fortaleza by dune buggy – 760km of gorgeous coastline.

Of Natal's city beaches, **Praia Ponta Negra** (14km south of the center) is urbanized but the nicest. **Morro de Careca** – a steep, monstrous sand dune that drops into the sea – towers over its southern end.

The views of the city and the dunes across the Rio Potengi are fantastic from the

NATAL

| 0 | 600 m |
| 0 | 0.4 miles |

To Forte dos Reis Magos (1km) & Genipabu (20km)

Praia do Meio

ROCAS

Port Area

Praia dos Artistas

ATLANTIC OCEAN

Praia da Areia Preta

AREIA PRETA

RIBERIA

Train Station

PETRÓPOLIS

To Ponta Negra (13km)

CENTRO

To Rodoviária Nova (6km)

To Airport (15km)

BRAZIL

INFORMATION
Banco do Brasil........................1 A4
Bradesco...................................2 A4
Centro de Turismo.....................3 C2
Hotel Miami Beach.....................4 D3

SLEEPING
Albergue Pousada Meu Canto...5 B3

DRINKING
Chaplin.....................................6 D2
Forró con Turista...................(see 3)

TRANSPORT
Rodoviária Velha......................7 A3

16th-century **Forte dos Reis Magos** (admission US$1; ☺ 8am-4:30pm).

Sleeping

Most backpackers stay in pricey-and-pleasant Ponta Negra or with Tia Helena.

Albergue Pousada Meu Canto (☎ 3212-2811; Rua Ana Neri, Petrópolis; dm/d US$9/20) Within minutes Tia Helena will add you to her international family at this simple *pousada* with pretty greenery. Take bus 21 to the first stop (at Padaria Duro Trigo) on Rua Manoel Dantas.

Albergue da Costa Hostel (☎ 3219-0095; www.alber guedacosta.com.br; Av Praia de Ponta Negra 8932, Ponta Negra; dm/d US$15/35, d without bathroom US$32.50; ☻) This fun hostel is laid-back, a bit bohemian, and a more natural environment than Lua Cheia. Guest-use kitchen and hammock area.

Pousada Recanto das Flores (☎ 3219-4065; www .pousadarecantodasflores.com.br; Av Engenheiro Roberto Freire 3161, Ponta Negra; s/d US$20/35; ☒ ☻) This small, cute *pousada* would be charming were it not for noise from the busy avenue. Single rooms are a great deal – check mattress thickness.

Lua Cheia Hostel (☎ 3236-3696; www.luacheia.com.br; Rua Dr Manoel A B de Araujo 500, Alto de Ponta Negra; dm/s/d US$20/40/40) This novel brick hostel is modeled after a castle – drawbridge, turrets and all. Dark dorms vent to the hostel's exterior and interior, so they're pretty loud. Good for party animals.

Pousada do Alemão (☎ 3219-2655; www.pousada doalemaorn.com.br; Rua Pedro Fonseca Filho 2030, Ponta Negra; s/d US$30/35; ☒) Fine, spacious rooms are complemented by a beautiful, oasis-like courtyard with a trickling fountain and pond. German-run.

Eating

In Ponta Negra, places like Esquinão da Vila serve cheap *prato feitos* on Rua Ver Manuel Sátiro south of Av Engenheiro Roberto Freire. For dinner, there are all sorts of novel places in Alto de Ponta Negra.

A Toca do Açaí (Rua das Algas 2206, Alto de Ponta Negra) Plastic tables and chairs are spread through a large space, great for hanging out while enjoying *açaí*, snacks and sandwiches. On a residential street.

Lion (Rua Aristides Porpino Filho 285B, Alto de Ponta Negra; mains US$4.25-12) Choose between crepes, pizza, pasta, meat or seafood dishes as you soak in the cool atmosphere at this former family home (resist the pool). Don't miss the midweek pizza (US$6) and pasta (US$8.50) *rodízio* night.

Restaurante Erva Doce (Av Estrela do Mar 2238, Alto de Ponta Negra; half-portions US$8-14) The half-portions of meat or seafood feed at least two at this neighborhood place with checked tablecloths and fluorescent-tube lighting.

Entertainment

Ponta Negra is Natal's nightlife center. There are a few dance clubs, and a compact zone of cool, charismatic, open-air bars around Rua Dr Manoel Augusto Bezerra de Araújo in Alto de Ponta Negra. The beachfront is seedy.

Chaplin (Av Presidente Café Filho 27, Praia dos Artistas; admission US$10; ☺ Thu-Sun) Live *pagode*, *forró* and electronica rock this popular dance club with six separate dance floors. Half-price cover before 11pm.

Forró com Turista (Centro do Turismo, Rua Aderbal Figueiredo 980, Petrópolis; ☺ Thu) This local staple may sound cheesy; live *forró* in a historical courtyard is actually a blast.

Getting There & Around

BRA, Gol, Trip, TAM, and Varig operate domestic flights from Natal's airport, 15km south of the center. TAP connects Natal with Europe.

Long-distance buses leave the Rodoviária Nova (New Bus Station), 6km south of the center, for Fortaleza (US$28 to US$49, eight hours, nine daily), Recife (US$21.50, 4½ hours, nine daily), João Pessoa (US$8 to US$13, three hours, eight daily) and Salvador (US$59 to US$80, 20 hours, two daily).

If coming from the south and heading for Ponta Negra, get off at Shopping Cidade Jardim and catch a bus or *kombi* to Ponta Negra.

From the Rodoviária Nova to Ponta Negra, take bus 66. For Praia dos Artistas, take bus 38. The Rodoviária Velha (Old Bus Station) is a city bus terminal in the center.

CANOA QUEBRADA

☎ 0xx88 / pop 2800

A former fishing village full of aging hippies, Canoa Quebrada is quickly becoming a wind-sport hot spot. A handful of sand streets, including a main drag lined with restaurants and a few shops, perches between white dunes and rust-colored ocean cliffs. There are a few loud bars, which heat up on weekends, and one ATM. **Canoa Criança**, a children's circus school, loves interactive guests and gives monthly shows.

Though the hard-packed beaches are not Brazil's most beautiful, dune-buggy tours to **Ponta Grossa** (per person US$23) or the surrounding dunes (per person US$12.50) remain popular. The **kite-surfing** season is from July to December; lessons are available. A half hour of **tandem paragliding** runs US$35. **Ernesto** (☎ 3421-7059; 10min incl cape US$12.50) has rigged up a way to pull paragliding clients with his jeep such that they fly through the air in superhero position.

Pousada Via Láctea (☎ 3421-7103; www.pousada vialactea.com; Rua Descida da Praia; per person US$4) offers camping near the sea. Simple rooms have hammocks, their own wooden staircases and a sea breeze at **Pousada Europa** (☎ 3421-7004; www .portalcanoaquebrada.com.br; s/d US$15/17.50; 🖳). Sweet hippy touches liven up clean, simple rooms at **Pousada das Cores** (☎ 3421-7140; www.portalcanoa quebrada.com.br/pousada_das_cores.htm; s/d US$15/25). You can hear the waves from **Pousada Colibri** (☎ 9604-4953; www.portalcanoaquebrada.com.br/colibri .htm; s/d US$35/40; 🖳), which has four comfortable rooms overlooking the far-off sea. **Gostozinho** (Rua Descida da Praia) has no sign and a variety of good *prato feitos* (US$3). Daily specials (US$3 to US$5.50) range from garlic shrimp to chicken lasagna at **Café Habana** (main road).

From Natal, catch a bus to Aracati (US$27, six hours, six daily) and then a bus, a *kombi* (US$1), which leave from Aracati's Igreja Matriz until 8pm, or taxi (US$6) the remaining 13km to Canoa. From Fortaleza (US$9, 3½ hours, four daily), it's possible to pick up the bus to Canoa in front of Albergue Atalaia (Av Beira Mar 814, Iracema) or in front of Club Náutico (Av Presidente Kennedy, Meireles) before it passes the bus station. Beach Point (Av Presidente Kennedy, Meireles), a shop facing Club Náutico, sells tickets.

FORTALEZA

☎ 0xx85 / 2.2 million

This sprawling commercial center and major fishing port has little touristic appeal, but all the facilities to get you sorted before setting out again. A few historical buildings with pretty facades dot the center, but Fortaleza's overall feel is pretty gritty. Those who partake emerge impressed with the city's nightlife. Bahian tunes shake up Fortaleza during **Fortal**, a Salvador-style, out-of-season Carnaval in the last week of July.

Information

Internet access is widely available in Iracema (per hr US$2).

Banco do Brasil (Rua Floriano Peixoto 941, Centro) Has ATMs at the Centro Cultural Dragão do Mar (Iracema), and in front of the Mercado Central (Centro) and Club Náutico (Meireles).

Tourist information posts airport (☎ 3477-1667); Centro de Tourismo (☎ 3101-5508); Praça da Ferreira (☎ 3226-3244); Praia Nautico (☎ 3242-4447) Dispenses maps and speak some English. Also at the bus station.

Dangers & Annoyances

There is an increasing amount of prostitution in the city, particularly in Iracema, and petty theft is a problem. Male travelers have reported having their drinks drugged by solicitous females on the beach.

Sights & Activities

The one-room **Museu de Arte e Cultura Populares** (Centro de Turismo, Centro; admission US50¢; ⏰ 8am-4:30pm Mon-Sat, to 11:30am Sun) displays folk art from woodblock prints to incredibly intricate colored sand bottles. **Centro Cultural Dragão do Mar** (Iracema; ⏰ 9am-5:30pm Mon-Thu, 2-9:30pm Fri-Sun) houses a planetarium, cinema, theater, galleries and the **Museu de Arte Contemporânea** (admission US$1; ⏰ closed Mon). **Museu do Ceará** (Rua São Paulo 51, Centro; admission US$1; ⏰ 8:30am-5pm) has good exhibits on Ceará's history and anthropology.

Praia do Meireles has an attractive waterfront promenade with thatched-roof restaurants, sport facilities and an evening craft fair. Though nothing too special, **Praia do Futuro** (11km) is the cleanest and most popular of the city beaches. Immediately northwest, tranquil **Praia do Cumbuco** has dunes and *jangada* (traditional sailboat) trips. Beach-buggy excursions to **Morro Branco** (White Hill; per person US$13) are enjoyable and sold along Meireles' promenade.

Sleeping

Iracema is past its glory days and cheaper than affluent Meireles. Both are preferable to the center.

Albergue Backpackers (☎ 3091-8897; www.alber guebackpackers.sites.uol.com.br; Av Dom Manuel 89, Iracema; s/d US$12.50/25, without bathroom US$10/20) Built and run by former traveler and Fortaleza native Gisele, this fantastic hostel has simple rooms with hand-decorated walls, a green chilling area and plenty of insider information. English spoken.

BRAZIL

FORTALEZA

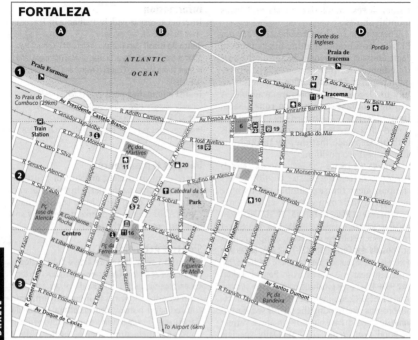

BRAZIL

Hotel Passeio (☎ 3226-9640; Rua Dr João Moreira 221, Centro; s/d US$17.50/27.50; ❄) For city-center accommodation, the rooms at this hotel aren't too shabby.

Albergue Atalaia (☎ 3219-0755; www.alberguedajuventudeatalaia.com.br; Av Beira Mar 814, Iracema; dm/s/d US$17.50/30/42.50; ❄) Cooking facilities, a TV room, and a front patio round out this well-kept hostel. Dorm sheet set an additional US$3.

Alamo Praia Hotel (☎ 3219-7979; www.alamohotel.com.br; Av Almirante Barroso 885, Iracema; s/d US$20/30; ❄) Rooms are dingy but adequate at this three-story, proper hotel.

Mundo Latino (☎ 3242-8778; www.mundolatino.com.br; Rua Ana Bilhar 507, Meireles; s/d US$40/45; ❄) Wood parquet floors add charm to large rooms in this house-turned-*pousada*. Convenient location.

Eating

Restaurants near Iracema's Ponte dos Ingleses are pricey and pretty seedy. Try Iracema's Av Monsenhor Tabosa for lunch and the Centro Cultural Dragão do Mar for dinner. Varjota's restaurants have more character and/or sophistication.

Mercado de Peixe (fish market; Praia de Mucuripe) Buy fish, shrimp or lobster (US$5 to US$7.50 per kilo) at one stall and have it prepared in garlic and oil (US$1.50 to US$2 per kilo) at another.

Bebelu (Av Historiador Raimundo Girão 789, Iracema; sandwiches US$1-5) This upscale sandwich and burger joint spices up its menu with pita bread, pineapple and fried banana.

Self L'Escale (Rua Guilherme Rocha, Centro; per kg US$10) The excellent spread has tons of veggies at this buffet in a restored colonial building.

Picanha do Raul (Rua Joaquim Alves 104, Iracema; for 2 US$6.50-10) It's all about beef (there are two nonbeef options) at this humble BBQ restaurant on a quiet, shady street. Order meat by weight if you'd like.

Coco Bambu (Rua Canuto de Aguiar 1317, Varjota) Enjoy a buffet lunch or pizzas, *beiju de tapioca* (manioc flour 'taco'), crepes or sushi with sand underfoot and palms overhead at this Caribbean-themed eatery.

Drinking

The bars and clubs surrounding the Centro Cultural Dragão do Mar see some action all week, and fill on weekends.

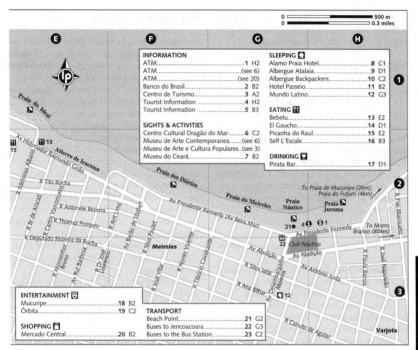

INFORMATION
ATM	1 H2
ATM	(see 6)
ATM	(see 20)
Banco do Brasil	2 B2
Centro de Turismo	3 A2
Tourist Information	4 H2
Tourist Information	5 B3

SIGHTS & ACTIVITIES
Centro Cultural Dragão do Mar	6 C2
Museu de Arte Contemporanea	(see 6)
Museu de Arte e Cultura Populares	(see 3)
Museu do Ceará	7 B2

SLEEPING
Alamo Praia Hotel	8 C1
Albergue Atalaia	9 D1
Albergue Backpackers	10 C2
Hotel Passeio	11 B2
Mundo Latino	12 G3

EATING
Bebelu	13 E2
El Gaucho	14 D1
Picanha do Raul	15 E2
Self L'Escale	16 B3

DRINKING
Pirata Bar	17 D1

ENTERTAINMENT
Mucuripe	18 B2
Órbita	19 C2

SHOPPING
Mercado Central	20 B2

TRANSPORT
Beach Point	21 G2
Buses to Jericoacoara	22 G3
Buses to the Bus Station	23 C2

Pirata Bar (Rua dos Tabajaras 325, Iracema; admission US$12.50) Locals frequent this, especially for *forró* on 'the craziest Monday on the planet.'

Entertainment

Órbita (Rua Dragão do Mar 207, Iracema; admission US$6-8) Has reggae (Thursday), live music, electronica nights.

Mucuripe (Rua Travessa Maranguape 108, Centro) Another good club with one open and three enclosed dance floors.

Shopping

Ceará has a strong craft tradition (Brazil's best hammocks!). Prices are great at the Mercado Central and the Centro de Turismo in the center.

Getting There & Around

BRA, Gol, Ocean Air, TAF, TAM, Trip and Varig operate domestically from Fortaleza's airport. TAP connects Fortaleza with Europe.

Buses run to Natal (US$28 to US$50, eight hours, seven daily), Teresina (US$25 to US$42, 10 hours, eight daily), São Luís (US$47, 16 hours, three daily), Recife (US$43 to US$50, 12 hours, three daily), Belém (US$75 to US$80, 22 hours, four daily), Salvador (US$77, 22 hours, daily) and Rio (US$146, 48 hours, daily).

The 'Siqueira/Mucuripe' bus connects the bus station to Iracema and Meireles – catch it in front of the Telemar building on Av Borges de Melo. The air-con Guanabara Top Bus (US$2.50, half-hourly from 7am to 10:15pm) connects the airport and bus station (both 6km south of the center) to all major beaches. From Iracema to the bus station, catch a 'Aguanabi 1' or 'Siqueira/Mucuripe' bus on Av Tamancaré.

JERICOACOARA

☎ 0xx88 / pop 2000

A truly special place, Jericoacoara combines nightlife, a range of activities and a yummy variety of cuisine, enhanced by the remote setting. The sand-street village faces a broad gray beach, shouldered by a huge yellow sand dune and rolling green hills. The relaxed vibe keeps hip Brazilians and travelers staying longer than planned. Wind-sport folks find the conditions South America's best, and Jeri has a great longboarding wave (great for learning).

Avoid *bichos de pé* (burrowing foot parasites) by not walking barefoot. Internet runs US$4 per hour. There are no banks.

Sights & Activities

The 3km walk to the rock arch **Pedra Furada** is beautiful, and buggy trips (US$20) to surrounding dunes and lakes, like **Lagoa do Paraíso**, are highly recommended. Surfing and wind-sport lessons are offered, and gear, including sand boards, is available to rent. **Kite Club Prea** (☎ 3669-2359; www.kiteclubprea.com), run by an American/Brazilian couple, offers great kite surfing lessons. At sunset, catch a *capoeira* circle (classes available) on the beach. Before crashing, drop by **Padaria Santo Antonio** and use fresh-from-the-oven breads to absorb those caipirinhas.

Sleeping

In the low season, midrange places become affordable.

Pousada do Véio (☎ 3669-2015; www.jericoacoara.tur .br/pousadadoveio; Rua Principal; s/d US$20/30; ❄) Simple rooms (some with lofts) with hammocks open onto a sweet garden behind a family home.

Pousada Bangalô (☎ 3669-2075; www.jericoacoara praia.com; Rua Novo Jeri; s/d US$25/30; ❄) A tall wall creates an intimate compound at this rustic, pretty *pousada* with a lush garden.

Pousada Atlantis (☎ 3669-2041; www.jericoacoara .tur.br/atlantis; Rua das Dunas; s/d US$25/35; ❄) A row of simple yet comfortable rooms, each with outdoor hammock and table look out onto a strip of leafy plants. Swiss-owned.

Vila dos Ipês (☎ 3669-2241; www.viladosipespousada .com.br; Rua São Francisco; s/d US$42/50; ❄) Rustling palms sooth you to sleep and an ocean view brightens your breakfast at this attractive beachfront *pousada*.

Eating

Café Brasil (between Rua Principal & Rua São Francisco) This sweet little café serves quality coffee drinks, *açaí* and light meals.

Pizzaria Delacasa (Rua Principal; pizzas US$2.25-8) There are competitors, but these pizzas are the best for your buck. Pastas too.

Restaurante do Sapão (Rua São Francisco; specials US$2.50-5) Unusual *prato feitos* like eggplant parmesan, eggs and *moqueca de raio* (Bahian stingray stew) are served at tables in the sand under a towering tree.

Carcará (Rua do Forró; mains US$6-12) Quality pasta and meat dishes are prepared with fresh herbs and the utmost care. Jeri's finest food.

Getting There & Away

In addition to the bus station, tickets from Fortaleza to Jericoacoara (US$18 to US$25, six hours, three daily) can be purchased at **Velastur** (Av Monsenhor Tabosa 1273, Meireles) and **Beach Point** (Av Presidente Kennedy, Meireles). Catch this bus outside the Praiano Palace Hotel (Av Presidente Kennedy, Meireles) or the airport before it passes the bus station. Included in the ticket price is a one-hour transfer in an open, 4WD truck from Jijoca to Jeri.

If coming from the west, catch the 10:30am bus to Jijoca from Sobral (US$10, three hours) and connect with the Fortaleza bus there. Alternately, 4WD trucks leave Camocim for Jericoacoara (US$10, 1¼ hours) anywhere from 9am to 11am. Zeldés leaves weekdays from the Posto Antônio Manual; Carlinhos leaves Monday, Wednesday and Friday.

Bus tickets for Fortaleza (US$18 to US$25, six hours, three daily) are sold at Pousada Casa do Turismo.

If heading west from Jeri, catch the 10:30pm 4WD to Jijoca (US$2.50). Once there, snooze inside the Sobral minibus (US$10, three hours) until it leaves at 2am (no bus on Sundays). Alternately, get a 4WD truck driven by Zeldés (4:30am Monday to Friday) or Carlinhos (6:30am Monday, Wednesday, Friday) to Camocim from Jeri's Rua Principal and catch a bus to Parnaíba (US$7, two hours, 4:30pm and 1am daily).

PARQUE NACIONAL DE SETE CIDADES

Ancient rock paintings, arches and caves grace **Parque Nacional Sete Cidades** (admission US$1.50; ⏱ 8am-5pm), but the highly unusual rock formations rising from the surrounding flat, dry land are unforgettable. Some people, educated scientists among them, claim the rocks are everything from seven ruined, 190 million–year-old cities to alien creations. At the park center, 6km from the entrance, pick up your obligatory guide (per group US$10). English-speaking guides are rare. The 13km walk to all seven cities takes two to three hours. Follow it with a swim in a pond or stunning waterfall (December to July only). Touring by bicycle (per hour US$1) reduces the entire tour to three to four hours. Start your day early and bring snacks, water and protection from the unrelenting sun.

In Piripiri (population 62,000), modern **Califórnia Hotel** (☎ 3276-1645; Rua Dr Antenor Freitas 546; s/d US$15/25; ❄) has sterile rooms. Just outside the park entrance, **Hotel Fazenda Sete Cidades** (☎ 3276-2222; s/d US$12/16; 🗙 🛋) has expansive grounds, farm animals, a restaurant and rooms that don't live up to the rest of the hotel. On park grounds, 2km from the park center, comfortable **Parque Hotel Sete Cidades** (☎ 3223-3366; www.hotelsetecidades.com.br; s/d US$21/28, campsites per person US$5; 🗙 🛋) has a restaurant and natural swimming pool.

Transport between the park and Piripiri (26km) is via *mototaxi* (US$6), taxi (US$15), or the free park employee bus, which leaves at 7am from the Telemar building on Praça da Bandeira and 5pm from the park. Buses to Piripiri run from Fortaleza (US$16 to US$21, seven hours, three daily), Sobral (US$10 to US$13, three hours, three daily), Parnaíba (US$10 to US$13, three hours, nine daily) and São Luís (US$33, 10 hours, two daily).

PARNAÍBA
☎ 0xx86 / pop 170,000

Parnaíba is an unremarkable port on the mouth of the Rio Parnaíba, with good beaches to its northeast. Porto das Barcas, the town's restored riverfront warehouse area, has a few simple shops and restaurants with unrealized bohemian intentions. Parnaíba's **delta**, a 2700 sq km expanse of islands, mangroves, and lots of birds, is found by travelers to be pretty but not fantastic. The 8½-hour trip runs US$7 to US$20 per person depending on boat type. Trips only occur when there's sufficient interest and often leave at 8am from Porto das Barcas. Contact **Casa do Turismo** (☎ 3323-9937; casadoturismo@bol.com.br; shop 17, Porto das Barcas).

Agencies around Porto das Barcas offer internet access (per hour US$1). **Bradesco** (Av Presidente Getúlio Vargas 403, Centro) has reliable ATMs.

Casa Nova Hotel (☎ 3322-3344; Praça Lima Rebelo 1094, Centro; s/d US$12.50/20, without bathroom US$7.50/15; 🗙) is sterile but good quality and a short walk from Porto das Barcas. **Hotel Cívico** (☎ 3322-2470/2432; www.hotelcivico.com.br; Av Governor Chagas Rodrigues 474; s/d US$20/27; 🗙 🛋) is a proper hotel some 10 blocks from Porto das Barcas that slashes prices in the low season. It serves Parnaíba's best buffet lunch (US$11 per kilo). **Sabor e Arte** (Av Vargas 37, Porto das Barcas; for 2 US$14) serves good meat or veggie *prato feitos* (US$2.50 to US$4.50).

Parnaíba can be a jumping-off point for Parque Nacional dos Lençóis Maranhenses (see the boxed text, below) or Jericoacoara (p371).

Buses run to Camocim (US$7 to US$11, three hours, three daily), Sobral (US$14 to US$22, five hours, three daily), Fortaleza (US$26 to US$42, 10 hours, three daily), Teresina (US$19 to US$26, six hours, nine daily) and São Luís (US$25, nine hours, two daily).

TERESINA
☎ 0xx86 / pop700,000

Teresina, famed as the hottest city in Brazil, is a pleasant but unnoteworthy capital where tourists are rare. **Inter.com** (Rua David Caldas 270; per hr US75¢; 🗙) offers internet. Major banks are in the center. **Micarina** (🕙 mid-July) is the city's Salvador-style, out-of-season Carnaval.

The **Central de Artesanato** (Praça Dom Pedro II; 🕙 8am-6pm Mon-Fri, 9am-3pm Sat) has shops selling local crafts. The **Casa da Cultura** (Rua Rui Barbosa 348; admission US25¢; 🕙 8am-5:30pm Mon-Fri, 9am-1pm Sat, 12:30-5:30pm Sun) is a cultural center with local art exhibits to the sounds of ongoing music classes.

We have yet to find a passable budget guesthouse in the Center. If you do, let us know!

BRAZIL

ALTERNATE ROUTE

Transport between Parnaíba and Barreirinhas involves rattling on a wooden bench over a track between sand dunes, past isolated communities and gorgeous scenery. It is a recommended adventure. From Parnaíba, there's a ferry (US$17.50, seven hours) through the delta to Tutoía (population 45,000) that leaves a few times weekly on no reliable schedule. Alternately, buses to Tutoía (US$5.25, three hours) leave at 6am and 4:30pm daily, plus 11:30am every day but Sunday, and 4pm on weekdays. Catch it at the bus station or the Praça Troca Troca in Parnaíba's center. From Tutoía, open 4WD trucks to Paulinho Neves (aka Rio Novo; US$2.50, 1½ hours) leave at 10am and 5:30pm Monday through Saturday, 4pm on Sunday. There are *pousadas* in tiny Paulinho Neves and dunes within walking distance. The 4WD ride onward to Barreirinhas (US$5, two hours) is rougher and more scenic. Departures are at 6am and 12:30pm Monday through Saturday, and 6am on Sunday.

Bright murals spice up the standard **Hotel Sambaíba** (☎ 3222-6712; sambaibahotel@yahoo.com.br; Rua Gabriel Ferreira 230, Centro; s/d US$22/30; ❄). Room maintenance is poor. Comfortable rooms have high ceilings at the semi-attractive **Metro Hotel** (☎ 3226-1010; metrohotel@webone.com.br; Rua 13 de Maio 85, Centro; s/d US$27/32; ❄). Ignore the posted prices.

Across from the Casa da Cultura, the self-service **Bom Bocado** (Rua Paissandu 120; per kg US$8; ❄) has freshly grilled meats and an indoor waterfall. Try **Camarão do Elias** (Av Pedro Almeida 457) for seafood. A fine-dining, all-you-can-eat, buffet lunch is prepared daily at **Forno e Fogão** (Luxor Piauí Hotel; Praça da Bandeira 310; buffet US$9; ❄). Saturdays are *feijoada* (bean and pork stew) and Sundays are brunch.

BRA, Gol, TAM and Varig fly domestically from Teresina's airport, 6km north of center.

Buses run to São Luís (US$21 to US$38, seven hours, eight daily), Belém (US$48, 14 hours, six daily), Parnaíba (US$20, five hours, nine daily), Sobral (US$15 to US$27, seven hours, eight daily) and Fortaleza (US$25 to US$43, 10 hours, nine daily).

From the bus station to the center, catch the Rodoviaria Circular bus from the stop across the road or a Potivelho or Dirceuit *kombi*.

SÃO LUÍS
☎ 0xx98 / pop 950,000

Some call São Luís Brazil's last charming colonial capital, as it remains unselfconscious in the face of foreign, and a trickle of national, tourism. The cobbled streets of the revitalized historical center – a Unesco World Heritage Site – are lined with colorful colonial mansions noted for their *azulejo* (Portuguese painted tiles) facades used to combat the predominant damp heat. São Luís has a rich folkloric tradition embodied by its colorful festivals, and has become Brazil's reggae capital.

Orientation

São Luís is divided into two peninsulas by the Rio Anil. On the southernmost, the Centro sits on a hill above the historic core of Praia Grande (aka Projeto Reviver). Many streets in these neighborhoods have multiple names. The Centro and outlying streets in Projeto

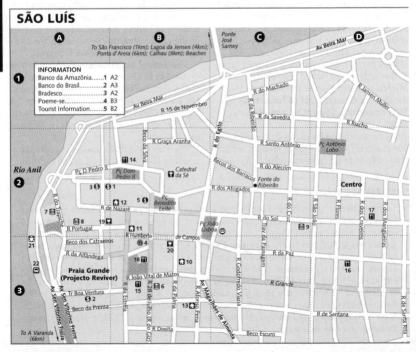

SÃO LUÍS

INFORMATION
Banco da Amazônia.......1 A2
Banco do Brasil.............2 A3
Bradesco....................3 A2
Poeme-se...................4 B3
Tourist Information.......5 B2

Reviver are deserted at night. On the northern peninsula lie affluent suburbs (São Francisco) and city beaches (Calhau).

Information

Banco da Amazônia (Av Dom Pedro II; 11am-2pm Mon-Fri) Changes US dollars and traveler's checks.

Banco do Brasil (Travessa Boa Ventura) Has ATM.

Bradesco (Av Dom Pedro II) Has ATM.

Poeme-se (Rua Humberto de Campos; per hr US$1.50) Offers internet access.

Tourist information airport (3244-4500); bus station (3249-4500); Praça Benedito Leite (3212-6211) Has good brochures and English-speaking attendants.

Sights & Activities

The Projeto Reviver juxtaposes beautifully restored buildings housing an odd mix of government offices and tourism businesses with abandoned structures serving as living quarters for homeless people and the neighborhood's many cats.

The Centro de Cultura Popular maintains three of the Northeast's best museums. There are English-speaking guides available. The

SIGHTS & ACTIVITIES	
Casa da Festa	6 B3
Casa do Maranhão	7 A2
Casa do Nhozinho	8 A2
Museu Histórico do Estado de	
Maranhão	9 C2
SLEEPING	
Hostal Solar das Pedras	10 B3
Pousada Internacional	11 B2
Pousada Reviver	12 B2
Pousada Vitória	13 B3
EATING	
Base da Lenoca	14 B2
Criolla	15 B3
Gula Gula	16 D3
Naturista Alimentos	17 D2
Valéry	18 B3
DRINKING	
Café Bagdã	19 A2
Roots Bar	20 B3
TRANSPORT	
Hidroviária (Boats to Alcântara)	21 A3
Terminal de Integração Praia	
Grande	22 A3

Casa da Festa (Rua do Giz 221; admission free; 9am-7pm Tue-Sun) has four floors of colorful costumes and props from local festivals and religious practices. The **Casa do Maranhão** (Rua do Trapiche; admission free; 9am-7pm Tue-Sun) has what amounts to a multimedia state tourism brochure, and an upper floor dedicated to the regional flavors of Bumba Meu Boi (below) costumes. Items from Maranhão quotidian life, from delicate wooden fish traps to children's toys made from trash, are displayed at the **Casa do Nhozinho** (Rua Portugal 185; admission free; 9am-7pm Tue-Sun).

The **Museu Histórico do Estado de Maranhão** (Rua do Sol 302; admission US$1; 9am-6pm Tue-Sun) is a restored 1836 mansion with attractive, historical displays of wealthy families' belongings.

Local beaches are broad and flat. Locals and their cars pack windswept **Praia do Calhau** on weekends.

Festivals & Events

Carnaval São Luís' largest festival, with São João and Bumba Meu Boi.

São João & Bumba Meu Boi These festivals are combined from late June to the second week of August. The latter celebrates a legend of the death and resurrection of a bull with music, dance and theater. Year-round rehearsals are a great way to get a taste of these festivals – ask the tourist office for locations.

Marafolia An out-of-season, Salvador-style Carnaval in mid-October.

Sleeping

The overall standard of São Luís' budget accommodation is pretty low.

Pousada Internacional (3231-5154; Rua da Estrela 175; s/d US$8.50/14, without bathroom US$7.50/12.50) The best of the basic cheapies, this place even attempts decoration. Windowless rooms.

Pousada Reviver (3231-1253; www.pousadareviver .com.br; Rua de Nazaré 173; dm/s/d US$7.50-10/20/25;) As the building is newly renovated, rooms are updated, bright and incredibly spacious. The overall feel is a bit sterile.

Hostel Solar das Pedras (3232-6694; www.ajso lardaspedras.com.br; Rua da Palma 127; dm/s/d US$9/13/17) Housed in an attractive, restored colonial home, this hostel has exposed rock walls and a living room perfect for people-watching. Windowless, poorly ventilated rooms.

Pousada Vitória (3231-2816; Rua Afonso Pena 98; s/d US$17.50/30;) Large rooms with improvised bathrooms face an inner patio and are incorporated into a family home. Friendly.

Pousada Portas da Amazônia (☎ 3222-9937; www
.portasdaamazonia.com.br; Rua do Giz 129; s/d US$44/59;
🅿) Dark wood and whitewashed walls fill
this stark, upscale *pousada* housed in two
joined colonial homes. Breakfast includes
local specialties.

Eating
São Luís has a fairly limited restaurant
selection.

Valéry (Rua do Gis) This French-owned bakery
has tasty pastries, croissants, quiches and, of
course, fantastic breads.

Naturista Alimentos (Rua do Sol 517; per kg US$7.25)
Weekday vegetarian lunch.

Base da Lenoca (Av Dom Pedro II 181; mains for 2 US$7-
20) Enjoy a beer and a breeze with your meal
at this popular seafood restaurant overlooking
the river.

Gula Gula (Rua da Paz 414; per kg US$8; 🅿) *The* spot
in the center for a workday buffet lunch.

Crioula (Beco da Pacotilha 42; per kg US$9) This large
buffet restaurant has regional decor and tasty
local specialties.

A Varanda (Rua Genésio Rego 185, Monte Castelo; mains
for 2 US$18; 🅿) The extremely lush patio and
excellent fish, shrimp and beef dishes will
distract you from the slow service. To get
there, take a 'Vicente Fiaro' or 'Santa Clara'
bus from inside the Terminal de Integração,
get off at CEFET and take your first right.
Well worth the trip.

Drinking
Take a 'Calhau Litorânea' bus from inside the
Terminal de Integração Praia Grande to get to
the places following.

Reggae bars like **Bar do Nelson** (Av Litorânea,
Calhau) and **Roots Bar** (Rua da Palma) are the thing
here. The tourist office can recommend others
that don't suffer from drunken brawls.

From Thursday to Sunday the outdoor
pubs on the Lagoa da Jensen, like Academia
do Chopp, are great for drinking beer and
listening to live music.

Entertainment
Café Bagdá (Rua Portugal) In the old city; converts
itself into a disco at night.

Studio 7 (Av dos Holandeses, Calhau) Head here for
electronica and Rio-style funk.

Getting There & Around
BRA, Gol, TAF, TAM and Varig fly domestically from São Luís' airport, 15km southeast

of the center. TAP connects São Luís with
Europe.

Buses run to Belém (US$48, 12 hours, daily),
Barreirinhas (US$13, four hours, four daily),
Teresina (US$21 to US$37, seven hours, six
daily) and Fortaleza (US$47, 18 hours, three
daily). Long-distance buses leave from the bus
station, 8km southeast of the center.

ALCÂNTARA
☎ 0xx98 / pop 6000
This picturesque colonial architectural treasure, slipping regally into decay, lies across the
Baía de São Marcos from São Luís. Built in the
early 17th century, Alcântara was the hub of
the region's sugar and cotton economy and
home to Maranhão's rich landowners. Today
the seat of Brazil's space program lies outside
of town. Alcântara makes for a memorable
day trip. There are no banks.

Two streets at the village's highest point
contain the finest architecture. Sights include
Brazil's most well-preserved **pelourinho** (whipping post; Praça da Matriz) and the **Museu Histórico**
(Praça da Matriz; admission US50¢; 🕒 8am-2pm Mon-Sat,
9am-1pm Sun), displaying the personal effects of
18th- and 19th-century residents. The colorful
Festa do Divino (first Sunday after Ascension
Day, usually in May) features a parading drum
corps of black women accompanying a pair of
children costumed as the royal couple.

There are a few *pousadas* and a campsite in
the village. **Pousada dos Guarás** (☎ 3337-1339; pou
sadadosguaras@aol.com; Praia da Baronesa; s/d US$12.50/20;
🅿) is beachfront (kayaks available) and surrounded by mangrove and monkeys. Its
thatched-roof bungalows in a tropical garden
are clean and comfortable. It is a great place for
a drink, but beware of mosquitoes in the rainy
season. **Restaurante da Josefa** (Rua Direita; prato feito
US$3-4) serves Alcântara's best home cooking.
Stop by Rua das Mercés 401 to try *doce de espe-
cie*, the local cookie-sweet made from coconut
and the juice of orange-tree leaves.

Boats to Alcântara (US$5, one hour, 7am
and 9:30am daily) depart from São Luís' *hidroviária* (boat terminal), or, at low tide, from
Praia Ponta d'Áreia (bus included in ticket
price, leaves from the *hidroviária*). For the
more adventurous, the sailboat *Mensageiro da
Fé* (US$2.50, 1¼ hours, daily) leaves at high
tide (between 11am and 5pm). The ride on
both vessels is slow and rolling, and best on a
stomach neither empty nor full. Keep an eye
out for scarlet ibis.

PARQUE NACIONAL DOS LENÇÓIS MARANHENSES

The best time to visit this remote park is between March and September, when aqua-colored, crystal-clear rainwater pools form between white sand dunes up to 40m tall. Motorized vehicles are not permitted in the 1550 sq km park, which is predominantly dunes. Local tour agencies offer half-day trips into the park (per person US$20); the light is best in the later half of the day. Two-day hikes through the park can also be arranged. A full-day trip upriver (per person US$25) through Brazil's tallest mangrove to the oceanfront village **Caburé** stops at a restaurant with a monkey colony. The extra trip to the river mouth (US$5) doesn't get rave reviews.

Access to the park is through the riverfront town of Barreirinhas (population 13,000), which has an **internet café** (per hr US$2) around the corner from the **Banco do Brasil** (main road). **Pousada Tia Cota** (☎ 3349-1237; Rua Coronel Godinho 204; s/d without bathroom US$7.50/15, s/d US$15/25; 🆇) has dark *quartos* and good simple rooms with bathrooms. **Pousada do Porto** (☎ 0xx98-3349-1910; Rua Anacleto de Carvalho 20; s/d US$10/22; 🆇) is riverfront, modern and bright. **Restaurante Bela Vista** (Rua Anacleto de Carvalho 617) has a shady deck over the river and a good *prato feito* (US$3).

Those seeking tranquility and isolation should catch the morning ferry (US$2.50, three to four hours, daily) upriver. Caburé has a selection of *pousadas* and Atins has a couple too. In Atins, Luzia is famous for putting up anyone who walks the hour and a half out to her home, and for her cooking. Ask the ferry staff for directions.

Barreirinhas can be a jumping-off point for Parnaíba and Jericoacoara (see the boxed text, p373). There are four daily buses between São Luís and Barreirinhas (US$13, four hours). The return to São Luís can also be made by van (US$12.50) or collective taxi (US$15), both of which drop at your requested destination.

THE NORTH

Certain places reside as romanticized, near-mythical destinations in travelers' imaginations, and the Amazon is at the top of the list. Images fill our heads of wild panthers and anacondas, impossibly dense rainforest and indigenous tribes unexposed to western ways. Some travelers leave the Amazon unimpressed, but only in the halogen glare of unreasonable expectations (or too short a visit) can this region disappoint. Wildlife is hard to see, but is that much more special when you do. Deforestation is widespread, but the rainforest remains vast and unrelenting. Many indigenous people have traded tradition for modern life, but *caboclos* (indigenous-Portuguese mix) communities are vital and compelling.

The numbers alone are mind-boggling: the Amazon Basin contains 6 million sq km of river and jungle, and just over half is in Brazil. It contains 17% of the world's fresh water and the main river-flow at its mouth is 12 billion liters per minute. There are 80,000km of navigable rivers. Annual rainfall averages around 2.5m. River levels rise on average 10m in the rainy season.

Forget your expectations, figure you're here to see how people have adapted to this 'water world' and the Amazon cannot fail to impress.

GETTING THERE & AROUND

Bus travel is limited to a few routes in the North, so rivers serve as highways. Though flights are usually at least twice the price of hammock-boat fare, check for specials. Flights to Manaus from São Luís are usually pricier than from Teresina or Belém.

BELÉM

☎ 0xx91 / pop 1.4 million

More prosperous than the coastal capitals to its southeast, Belém has a cultural sophistication unexpected from a city so isolated. Its

---

GETTING INTO TOWN

Aeroporto Val de Cães is 8km north of the center. Bus 'Pratinha-P Vargas' runs between the traffic circle outside the airport and Av Presidente Vargas (US60¢, 40 minutes). Taxis cost about US$8.

The bus station is on Av Almirante Barroso, 3km east of the center. For a city bus to Av Presidente Vargas, catch any 'Aero Club' or 'P Vargas' bus from the far side of Av Almirante Barroso. Going out to the bus station, take an 'Aeroclube' or 'Pratinha-P Vargas' bus from Av Presidente Vargas. Taxis to points along Av Presidente Vargas cost around US$5.

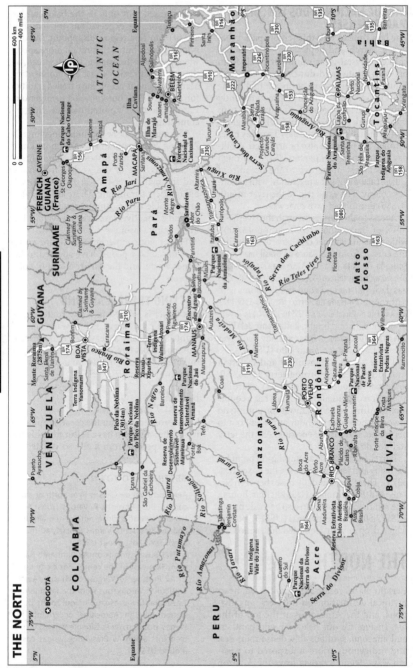

THE NORTH

wealth comes from its position at the gateway to the Amazon, meaning that any extracted (timber) or cultivated (soybeans) regional products pass through here before going to market. Refreshingly, Belém has recently invested in its tourism, and the resulting renovations and constructions are fantastic. If you take some time to wander the mango tree–lined boulevards, and investigate the bohemian arts and music scenes, this attractive city will reward like few others in Brazil.

Orientation

Av Presidente Vargas is the center's main drag. The Comércio, roughly between Av Presidente Vargas and Av Portugal, is a compact commercial district, noisy by day and deserted by night. Budget accommodations concentrate here. The riverfront is industrial, save for in the Comércio. The Cidade Velha (Old City) is quiet and contains Belém's historical buildings. East of the center, prosperous Nazaré has some chic shops and restaurants along Av Brás de Aguiar.

Information

Banco da Amazônia (Rua Carlos Gomes; 10am-1pm & 2-4pm Mon-Fri) Changes traveler's checks, US dollars and euros.
Hilton Hotel (Av Presidente Vargas 882; per hr US$3; 8am-10:30pm Mon-Fri, to 6:30pm Sat & Sun) Internet access in the business center.
Hospital Adventista (0800-910-022, 3246-8686; Av Almirante Barroso 1758)
HSBC (Av Presidente Vargas 670)
Paratur airport (3210-6330); center (3212-0575; Praça Waldemar Henrique) English spoken.
Sinemar (cnr Av Presidente Vargas & Rua Riachuelo; per hr US$1.50) Internet access.
Tourist police (3212-5525 ext 39; Praça do Pescador)

Dangers & Annoyances

The Comércio and Cidade Velha have a reputation for muggings when fairly empty (at night and on Sunday). Locals recommend preparing a wad of small bills to hand over if mugged, and dividing cash in at least three places. Always take a taxi at night. Pickpocketing and strap

---

RIVER TRAVEL

Riverboat travel is a uniquely Amazonian experience. Be forewarned that regular boats are always slow and crowded, often wet and smelly, sometimes dull and never comfortable. Luckily, Brazilians are friendly and river culture is interesting. Do you like *forró* music? You won't after this trip! Some tips:

- Downstream travel is considerably faster than upstream, but boats heading upriver travel closer to the shore, which is more scenic.
- Boats often moor in port for a few days before departing – check boat quality before committing.
- Fares vary little between boats, and are cheapest when bought onboard. Captains often set a minimum ticket price for vendors. If you buy for less, the difference will be demanded once onboard – so be wary of street vendors with rock-bottom prices!
- *Camarotes* (cabins) for two to four people are usually available and afford additional privacy and security. Ensure that yours has a fan or air-con. *Camarotes* are usually the same price as flying.
- Put up your hammock (available at any market, don't forget rope!) as soon as you are allowed to board the boat. The engine is on the lowest level, bathrooms are in the back, and foot travel is at either end, so the ideal hammock position is on the uppermost deck, toward the bow. Others are likely to sling their hammocks above and/or below yours.
- Bring rain jacket or poncho, sheet or light blanket, toilet paper and diarrhea medication.
- Meals included in the ticket price are mainly rice, beans and meat, with water or juice to drink. It's advisable to bring a few liters of bottled water, fruit and snacks. Tomato and onion are great to spice up the food.
- Watch your gear carefully. Lock your zippers, wrap your backpack in a plastic bag or cloth, and lash it to a ceiling beam, post or railing with rope or chain. Carry your valuables around the boat with you. Boats stop frequently – be especially alert before and while at port.

slashing are common during daylight, especially at Mercado Ver-o-Peso. Be wary if approached by a 'German' man with a robbery story asking for money – he's been doing it for years.

Sights

The iron structure of the **Mercado Ver-o-Peso** (⏰ 7:30am-6pm Mon-Sat, to 1pm Sun) was brought

from Britain around 1900. It's a great place to try *açaí* – go early to see the fish being unloaded.

The 17th-century **Forte do Castelo** (Praça Fr Brandão, Cidade Velha; admission US$1; ⏰ 10am-6pm Tue-Sun) has been artistically restored. It has fantastic views over the market and a first-class museum on the colonization of the area. The

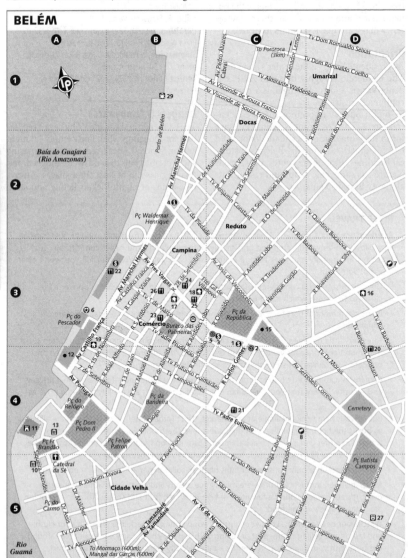

BELÉM

lavish **Teatro da Paz** (Praça da República; admission US$2; 🕑 9am-5pm Tue-Fri, to 1pm Sat) is one of Belém's finest rubber-boom buildings – try to catch a show.

National contemporary art and work by photographers from Pará is displayed in the renovated **Casa das Onze Janelas** (Praça Fr Brandão, Cidade Velha; admission US$1; 🕑 10am-6pm Tue-Sun). The

Museu de Arte Sacra (Praça Fr Brandão, Cidade Velha; admission US$2; 🕑 10am-6pm Tue-Sun) is comprised of the rebuilt version of Belém's first church and an adjoining bishops palace, and displays brilliant carved works by Indian artisans. The 1909 **Basílica de NS de Nazaré** (Praça da Basílica, Nazaré; 🕑 7am-noon & 3-7pm Tue-Sun, 3-7pm Mon) has a fine marble interior housing the tiny image of the

BRAZIL

INFORMATION
Banco da Amazônia............**1** C3	
Hilton Hotel.......................**2** C4	
HSBC................................**3** C3	
Paratur............................**4** B2	
Sinemar...........................**5** C3	
Tourist Police....................**6** A3	
Tourist Police....................(see 4)	
Tourist Police....................(see 3)	
UK Honorary Consulate....**7** D3	
Venezuelan Consulate......**8** C4	

SIGHTS & ACTIVITIES
Basílica de NS de Nazaré...**9** F3	
Casa das Onze Janelas.....**10** A5	
Forte do Castelo.............**11** A4	
Mercado Ver-o-Peso........**12** A4	
Museu de Arte Sacra.......**13** A4	
Museu Emílio Goeldi.......**14** F3	
Teatro da Paz.................**15** C3	

SLEEPING 🛏
Amazônia Hostel.............**16** D3	
Hotel Central..................**17** B3	
Hotel Unidos..................**18** B3	
Hotel Ver-o-Peso............**19** A3	
Hotel Vitória Régia.........(see 16)	

EATING 🍴
Cantina Italiana..............**20** D4	
Cozinha de Bistrô............**21** C4	
Estação das Docas...........**22** B3	
Express Grill....................**23** B3	
Mãe Natureza.................**24** B3	
Restaurant Higashi..........**25** B3	
Restaurante Belo Centro...**26** B3	

ENTERTAINMENT 🎭
Café Imaginario...............**27** D5	

TRANSPORT
Buses to Center...............**28** H1	
Terminal Hidroviária........**29** B1	

Virgin of Nazaré, a miraculous statue believed to have been sculpted in Nazareth.

The riverfront park **Mangal das Garças** (Praço do Arsenal, Cidade Velha; admission to park free, 4 sights US$3; 🕐 10am-6pm Tue-Sun) has a dome packed with free-flying local butterflies and hummingbirds, another with free-flying birds, a navigation museum and a 47m-high view tower.

The Victorian **Bosque Municipal Rodrigues Alves** (Av Almirante Barroso; US50¢; 🕐 8:30am-5pm Tue-Sun) is a 15-hectare piece of rainforest in grand old botanical garden style. It has macaws, coatis, monkeys and the world's largest waterlilies. Locals exercise here in the mornings. The **Museu Emílio Goeldi** (Av Governador Magalhães Barata; admission US$1; 🕐 9am-5pm Tue-Sun) has snakes, big cats, crocodiles and other Amazonian species in a beautiful 5.2-hectare piece of rainforest. The aquarium and archaeological museum were closed for renovation at press time. **Praça Batista Campos** is another green escape.

Festivals & Events

During the **Círio de Nazaré**, on the second Sunday in October, a million people accompany the image of the Virgin of Nazaré from the Catedral da Sé to the Basílica de NS de Nazaré. Two weeks of serious partying follow.

Sleeping

Hotel Vitória Régia (☎ 3212-2077; Travessa Frutuoso Guimarães 260, Comércio; s/d US$13/16; 🗶) A run-down, musty place that maintains a proper hotel structure.

Hotel Central (☎ 3241-8477; Av Presidente Vargas 290, Comércio; s/d US$20/25, without bathroom US$13/19) A somewhat haunting, run-down art deco gem, with large rooms that are super dank in the rainy season. The back side has less traffic noise.

Amazónia Hostel (☎ 4008-4800; www.amazonia hostel.com.br; Av Gov José Malcher 592, Nazaré; dm/d US$17.50/20) A well-equipped, new hostel in a renovated old building. Convenient to the center.

Hotel Ver-o-Peso (☎ 3241-2022; Boulevard Castilhos França 208, Comércio; s/d US$25/30; 🗶) A modern, proper hotel with good-value rooms and decorated hallways. The catch is the unsavory location.

Hotel Unidos (☎ 3252-1891/1411; hotel.unidos@bol .com.br; Rua Ó de Almeida 545, Campina; s/d US$30/36; 🗶) This clean, well-kept hotel is a totally presentable midrange option with a 10% discount for cash payment. Good location.

Eating

Belém is known for *pato no tucupi* (duck in a manioc juice and tongue-tingling *jambu* leaf sauce), *tacacá* (a gummy soup made from manioc root, dried shrimp and *jambu* leaves) and *maniçoba* (black beans, pork and manioc leaves).

Mãe Natureza (Rua Sen Manoel Barata 889, Campina; per kg US$10; 🗶) The sterile dining room doesn't do justice to the unique vegan lunch buffet. Mãe Natureza makes its own soy milk and uses raw sugar.

Restaurante Higashi (Rua Ó de Almeida 509, Campina; per kg US$12.50; 🕐 Mon-Fri; 🗶) This small Japanese restaurant offers a lunch and dinner buffet, worker specials (US$2.50 to US$7) and á la carte Japanese dinners (US$7 to US$15).

Cantina Italiana (Travessa Benjamin Constant 1401, Nazaré; mains US$9-13; 🗶) The pink walls of this cozy pasta and pizza restaurant are covered with framed photos and artwork.

Cozinha de Bistrô (Travessa Campos Sales 898, Comércio; mains around US$10; 🗶) This funky-hip bistro, slightly sunken below street level, has a random furniture collection and local art on the walls. The daily lunch specials are yummy and affordable (US$4.50 to US$7.50) and the menu is wide ranging.

Estação das Docas (Building 2, Av Castilho Franca, Comércio; lunch buffet US$11; 🗶) In a renovated port warehouse, a row of fine eateries offers all-you-can-eat lunch buffets and á la carte dinners. There is one pricey per-kilo restaurant on the 2nd level. Indoor or outdoor seating overlooks the river.

Recommended lunch buffets:

Restaurante Belo Centro (Rua Santo Antônio 264, Comércio; per kg US$7; 🕐 Mon-Fri)

Express Grill (Rua Sen Manoel Barata 713, Comércio; per kg US$12)

Drinking

The Praça da República and Estação das Docas are reliable, atmospheric spots to drink, afternoon and night.

Café Imaginario (Rua Apinagés) The walls of a small house have been fingerpainted and windows flung open to let live jazz and bossa nova (Tuesday, Friday and Saturday) float out. The *jambu*-leaf pizzas (medium US$10) are famous.

Entertainment

Mormaço (Praço do Arsenal, Cidade Velha; 🕐 Fri-Sun) A covered, open-air pier has a basic bar and rows of tables facing a small platform-stage. Live bands play reggae, rock, heavy metal and, on Sunday afternoons, local *carimbo*. Behind Mangal das Garças.

Pororoca (Av Senador Lemos 3326, Sacramenta; admission US$5-7) A simple but superpopular dance club playing *pagode* (Thursday), reggae (Sunday) and *brega* (a fast and free couples dance of Pará, Friday).

Casa do Gilson (Travessa Padre Eutíquio 3172, Condor; ☺ 3pm-on Fri & Sat, 5:30pm-on Sun) Under a tin roof and fueled by cheap beer, *chorinho* (samba variation) rules the house at one of Belém's most celebrated live-music spots.

Getting There & Away

AIR

BRA, Gol, Meta, Puma, Rico, TAF, TAM, Total and Varig operate domestic flights from Belém. Suriname Airways connects Belém to Georgetown (Guyana), the Caribbean, Miami and Amsterdam. Air Caraïbes connects Belém to Cayenne (French Guiana), the Caribbean and Paris.

BOAT

Passenger boats use Belém's Terminal Hidroviária. (Tickets are sold at booths inside. Boats to Santarém (hammock US$50-60, three days) and Manaus (hammock US$75-110, five days) depart on Monday, Tuesday, Wednesday and Friday. Boats to Macapá (hammock US$40, 23 hours) depart on Monday, Wednesday, Friday and Saturday. See the boxed text, p379 for information and tips.

BUS

Buses run to São Luís (US$56, 12 hours, daily), Fortaleza (US$75 to US$82, 25 hours, one to three daily), Recife (US$105, 34 hours, daily), Salvador (US$119, 36 hours, daily), Palmas (US$66, 19 hours, daily), Brasília (US$112, 34 hours, daily) and Rio de Janeiro (US$120 to US$178, 50 to 55 hours, one to two daily).

ALGODOAL

0xx91 / pop 1000

Isolated on the Ilha de Maiandeua, Algodoal is an idyllic remnant of the past surrounded by hard, windswept beaches, mangrove forests, dunes and vegetation. This rustic fishing village maintains carless sandy streets, a very basic tourism infrastructure, and only recently received electricity. There are no banks.

The village is separated by a small river (wade at low tide, or canoes are available) from **Praia do Farol** and **Praia da Princesa**, which has a row of shack restaurants. These beaches are backed by the tea-colored **Lagoa da Princesa**.

It's a 10-minute walk (horse carts available) along the beach to Rua Principal. Algodoal fills during holidays.

Algodoal Camping Club (☎ 3229-0848; per person US$5) has shady sites. Tents and sleeping bags rented. You can peek through the walls of the basic stick cabins of **Pousada Kakuri** (☎ 3854-1138; Rua Principal; dm US$10, cabañas with/without bathroom US$15/13). The laid-back atmosphere and friendly owner maintain its popularity. They serve tasty fish dishes.

Just up the road, **Cabanas do Cesar** (Rua Principal; cabañas s/d US$7.50/12) lacks the travelers' vibe, but has good, clean cabañas with mosquito nets and shared bathrooms.

Jardim do Éden (☎ 9967-9010/9623-9690; www.algodoal-amazon-tourism.com; Praia do Farol; hammock or tent s/d US$12.50/20, without bathroom s/d US$30/37, cabin US$55/65) has comfortable rooms on both floors of an attractive, eclectically decorated, wooden house facing the beach. A 2nd-story deck offers tables and hammocks. Preserved vegetation surrounds the three simple brick cabins. English is spoken, and tours are offered. Its vegetarian plate (US$7.50) and other meals (US$12.50) are excellent. Ask the ferry to drop you here or it's a 25-minute walk through the village.

Access is via mainland Marudá. Buses (US$7.50, 3½ hours, four or five daily) leave Belém's bus station for Marudá, and quicker minibuses (US$7.50) leave from just behind it until about 4:30pm. They'll drop you at Marudá's port, where boats for Algodoal (US$2, 40 minutes) require at least five passengers (or US$10 to US$15) to depart. To return, buses and minibuses leave the port until about 4pm.

ILHA DE MARAJÓ

☎ 0xx91 / pop 250,000

Slightly larger than Switzerland, this verdant, 50,000 sq km island lies at the mouth of the Rio Amazonas. The western side is swampy and inaccessible, and has a reputation for snakes and malaria, but the eastern side makes for a relaxing visit. This island has abundant wildlife, and buffalo meat replaces beef on restaurant menus. Marajó is known for its unguarded, friendly people and *carimbo* – the colorful folkloric dance of Pará.

BRAZIL

You'll want to base yourself out of Joanes or Salvaterra (or both!).

Joanes

The closest to Camará, Joanes is a tiny hamlet with the fragments of an old Jesuit church and a good sandy beach. Livestock wander grassy streets lined with a few shops and sandwich stands. The attractive **Pousada Ventania do Rio-Mar** (☎ 3646-2067; www.pousadaventania.com; s/d US$22/37) sits atop a breezy headland overlooking the beach and has individually decorated rooms. The Belgian owner offers a book exchange, and rents bikes, motorcycles, horses and canoes. She also organizes inexpensive walking and canoeing excursions led by locals, and trips out with local fishermen. Several beach restaurants serve straightforward meals at decent prices.

Salvaterra

About 18km north of Joanes, Salvaterra (population 5800) has more of a town feel and a decent beach, Praia Grande. A tourist information kiosk is on the plaza near the river.

Atop an ocean bluff, low-key **Pousada Bosque dos Aruãs** (☎ 3765-1115; Segunda Rua; s/d US$25/30;) has good, simple wooden cabins on stilts in an attractive natural yard. Its restaurant serves fantastic meat and seafood dishes (for two US$5 to US$10), soups and salads. The young, English-speaking owners know Brazilian music well and play great tunes. Bicycles rented.

Soure & Around

Soure (population 17,000), Marajó's unofficial capital, sits at the mouth of the Rio Paracauari, almost opposite Salvaterra. Main streets are paved and divided by towering mango trees; the rest quickly reduces to grassy bike paths.

Banco do Brasil (Rua 3 btwn Travessa 17 & 18) has ATMs. **Bimba** (Rua 4 btwn Travessa 18 & 19) rents bicycles (per day US$3).

Ceramicist Carlos Amaral combines traditional Aruã and Marajoara ceramic traditions with award-winning results. Check out his **Olaria** (workshop; Travessa 20 btwn Rua 3 & 4) – small, affordable pieces are for sale. After exploring Soure's streets, bicycle out to **Praia Barra Velha** (3km) by following Travessa 14 out of town and through the *fazenda* gate. A row of simple shacks sells drinks and seafood. Head left for **Praia de Araruna**, which is long, starkly beautiful and practically deserted. There's

an intervening river, which requires a boat at high tide. Follow Rua 4 inland to **Praia do Pesqueiro** (11km), Soure's popular weekend beach, which also has seafood shacks.

The best budget option, **Hotel Araruna** (☎ 8163-7731; Travessa 14 btwn Rua 7 & 8; s/d US$20/30;) has clean if uninteresting rooms. **Paraíso Verde** (Travessa 17 btwn Rua 9 & 10; mains for 2 US$7-12) serves delicious typical meat and seafood dishes in a gorgeous leafy courtyard.

Getting There & Around

Boats travel between Belém's Terminal Hidroviário and Camará (US$6.25, three hours) on the Ilha do Marajó twice daily and once on Sunday. Buses to Joanes, Salvaterra and Soure meet the boats. A few kilometers outside of Salvaterra, small motorboats (US50¢, five minutes) and an hourly vehicle ferry (free) connect Salvaterra and Soure. *Mototaxis*, taxis and infrequent vans (ask at your *pousada* for the schedule) move people around the island.

MACAPÁ

☎ 0xx96 / pop 336,800

If you are traveling to or from French Guyana, you'll enjoy a day's rest in orderly Macapá. As it sits right on the equator, Macapá is hot and super humid, but breezes are easy to come by on the pleasant waterfront.

Information

Agência Solnave (Rua Padre Júlio M Lombaerd 48) Purchase boat tickets here.
Bradesco (Rua Cândidoo Mendes 1316) Has reliable ATMs.
Setur (☎ 3212-5335; Rua Independência 29) Tourist information.
TV Som (Av Mendonça Furtado 253; per hr US75¢) Internet access.

Sights

The impressive **Fortaleza de São José de Macapá** (entrance Av Henrique Galúcio; admission free; 9am-6pm) was built by the Portuguese between 1764 and 1782 to defend against French incursions from the Guianas.

The primary exhibits at the **Museu SACACA de Desenvolvimento Sustentável** (Av Feliciano Coelho 1509; admission free; 9am-6pm Tue-Sun) are reconstructions of rural homes, from thatched huts to riverboats. The best way to get there is via *mototaxi* (US75¢).

APITU (Av Mendonça Jr at Rua Azarias Neto; 8am-noon & 2-6pm Mon-Sat) has a small but authentic collection of indigenous crafts.

Sleeping & Eating

Hotel América Novo Mundo (☎ 3223-2819; Av Coaracy Nunes 333; s/d US$15/20, without bathroom US$7.50/12.50; ✗) This place has friendly service and good rooms – get a breezy one in front.

Hotel Glória (☎ 3222-0984; Rua Leopoldo Machado 2085; s/d US$29/40; ✗) Neat rooms and hot showers.

Peixaria Amazonas (Rua Beira Rio at Rua Macacoari; mains for 2 US$12-15) Enjoy a *caldeirada de peixe* (soup with veggies and big pieces of fish, feeds four) with a river view and a breeze.

Bom Paladar Kilos (Av Presidente Getúlio Vargas 456; per kg US$8; ✗) The excellent lunch buffet includes vegetarian dishes.

Getting There & Around

AIR

Gol, Puma, TAF, TAM, Rico, Varig operate domestic flights (usually via Belém) from Macapá's airport, 3.5km northwest of the center. TAF also flies to Cayenne (French Guiana). Puma flies to Oiapoque. Between the airport and the center, taxis (US$8) are best.

BOAT

Boats to Belém (hammock US$45, 23 hours) leave on Tuesday, Thursday and Saturday. There are daily boats to Manaus (hammock US$150, five days) via Santarém (US$60, three days). Passenger boats dock in Santana, 25km southwest of Macapá. To get there, catch a 'Santana' (US$1.25, 30 minutes) bus from Rua Tiradentes (at Av Mendonça Furtado). Taxis between Macapá and Santana run US$15. See the boxed text, (p379) for information and tips.

BUS

There are one to two daily buses to Oiapoque (US$32, 12 to 24 hours). The first 250km are paved, after that the going can be very rough in the rainy season. Call ahead to confirm departures. 'Jardim' and 'Pedrinhas Novo Horizonte' buses connect the center to the **bus station** (☎ 3251-5045), which is about 3km north.

OIAPOQUE

☎ 0xx96 / pop 13,000

This remote, not especially pleasant town sits across the Rio Oiapoque from St Georges (French Guiana).

There are branches of Banco do Brasil and Bradesco. Hotels here are cheaper than in St Georges. The **Arizona Hotel** (☎ 3521-2185; Av Coaracy

Nunes 551; s/d US$15/20) is basic and clean. The **Restaurante Beija Flor** (Rua Joaquim C da Silva) serves decent Brazilian and French food.

Oiapoque is linked to Macapá by bus and plane (see left).

PALMAS

☎ 0xx63 / pop 151,000

Starting in 1989, Palmas was built from scratch to become the new state of Tocantins' capital. After the bustle waned, this remote, sterile city has found itself without industry on which to base an economy, and is slowly turning to ecotourism. If you have cash and time on your side, there are a surprising number of good outdoor excursions.

The most promising areas are the Ilha do Bananal, where Pantal-like wetlands meet rainforest, and the Parque Estadual do Jalapão, which contains dunes, canyons and waterfalls. **Bananal Ecotour** (☎ 3215-4333; www.bananalecotour .com.br; Quadra 103-S, Conjunto 02, Lote 02, Sala 03) organizes recommended excursions.

The pleasant **Hotel Serra Azul** (☎ 3215-1505; Rua NO-03 at NS-01; s/d US$11.50/15; ✗) has clean but smallish rooms and very friendly service. It's located on the north side of Galeria Bela Palma.

The 2nd-floor rooms are better at **Alvorada Hotel** (☎ 3215-3401; Quadra 103-N, Conjunto 2, Rua NO 1, Lotes 20 & 21; s/d US$20/27.50; ✗), a good budget spot a block north of Praça dos Girassó.

Palmas Shopping mall, immediately south of Praça dos Girassóis, has a decent food court.

Gol, TAM and Varig operate domestic flights (most via Brasília) from Palmas' airport, 28km from the center. Bus 71, Expresso Miracema, runs to the center (US50¢).

Buses run to Alto Paraíso de Goiás (US$18, seven hours, daily), Brasília (US$34, 12 hours, daily) and Salvador (US$45, 19 hours, daily). Connections to Teresina, São Luís and Belém are made through Imperatriz (US$29, 10 hours). To get to the center, cross the road in front of the *rodoviária* – almost every bus goes to the center and passes the Galeria Bela Palma. A taxi costs US$12.

SANTARÉM

☎ 0xx93 / pop 200,000

Most travelers rush between Belém and Manaus, skipping over the very thing they are desperate to see: the Amazon. A stop in riverfront Santarém not only breaks up a long trip, it provides a chance to investigate the jungle and communities seen from your hammock. Though mild-mannered and unnoteworthy itself, Santarém allows access to a lovely riverbeach town and beautiful rainforest preserves.

Information

Bradesco (Av Rui Barbosa) Has ATMs.
Cyber Café (Av Tapajós 418; per hr US$1.50; 🖳) Offers internet access until 11pm.

Sights & Activities

American Steve Alexander leads interesting half-day botanical tours (per person US$30-

40) through the **Bosque de Santa Lúcia**, which include a lot of explanation of the farming and deforestation around the forest. Contact his agency **Amazon Tours** (☎ 3522-1928; www.amazonriver.com; Travessa Turiano Meira 1084) for details.

The tea-colored Rio Tapajós flows into the café au lait Rio Amazonas in front of Santarém. The two flow side by side for a few kilometers without mingling (owing to differences in speed, density and temperature), and are amazing to see. You can get a good view of it from the Yamada (Av Tapajós) galeria roof-top restaurant/cafeteria.

The **Museu Dica Frazão** (Rua Floriano Peixoto 281; ☽ daily) is run by eccentric, internationally recognized, 80-something Dona Dica herself. Here she displays and sells the beautiful clothing and tapestries she makes from Amazonian root fibers.

Sleeping & Eating

Hotel Brasil (☎ 3523-5177; Travessa dos Mártires 30; s/d without bathroom US$7.50/15; 🖳) The place itself is great: clean, decorated with fake flowers and superfriendly. The rooms aren't as great: walls

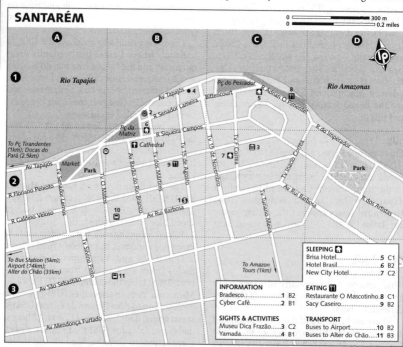

SANTARÉM

0 ———— 300 m
0 ———— 0.2 miles

Rio Tapajós

Rio Amazonas

To Pç Tirandentes (1km); Docas do Pará (2.5km)

To Bus Station (5km); Airport (14km); Alter do Chão (33km)

To Amazon Tours (1km)

that don't meet the ceiling, street noise and those with air-con are windowless.

Brisa Hotel (☎ 3522-1018; Av Senador Lameira Bittencourt 5; s/d US$22.50/30; ❄) Small rooms and tiny bathrooms are modern and sterile, but a pretty good value given the options. Windows aren't very useful – you'll need the air-con.

New City Hotel (☎ 3522-0355; Travessa Francisco Corrêa 200; s/d US$25/35; ❄) Rooms vary in size and quality, and have mismatching furniture, but are comfortable. Bargain hard as it's a bit overpriced.

Restaurante O Mascotinho (Rua Adrian O Pimentel; mains US$1.25-6) Pastas, pizzas and burgers served on a large terrace overlooking the river.

Esquina do Jardim (Travessa Francisco Correa; per person US$3) A simple lunch buffet with a good selection of freshly roasted meats. Indoor and outdoor seating.

Sacy Caseiro (Rua Floriano Peixoto 521; per kg US$9; ❄) This lunch buffet spot has a great selection for this backwater town. Uninteresting dining room.

Getting There & Around
AIR
Gol, Meta, Puma, Rico, TAM and Total operate domestic flights from Santarém's airport, 14km west of the center. A taxi costs US$15. The 'Aeroporto' bus (US50¢, 40 minutes) runs irregularly from early morning until about 6pm – get schedules from the airport information desk or a *fiscal* at the bus stop on Av Rui Barbosa.

BOAT
Boats to Manaus (hammock US$30 to US$40, two days, Monday through Saturday) and Belém (hammock US$40 to US$50, 34 hours, Thursday through Sunday) use the Docas do Pará, 2.5km west of the center. Each of the ticket booths outside the entrance sells tickets for the same boats. At press time AJATO had suspended fast boat service to Manaus. Boats to Macapá (US$45 to US$62, 36 hours, daily) depart from the Praça Tiradentes, 1km east of the center. See the boxed text, p379 for information and tips.

The 'Orla Fluvial' minibus connects the center and both ports every 20 minutes until 7pm. The 'Circular Esperanza' bus runs directly from the center to the Docas do Pará, but deviates radically on the return. A taxi costs US$6.

BUS
A bus leaves for Cuiabá (US$124 to US$132, about three days) on Wednesday and Saturday. Departures are irregular as only 84km south from Santarém is paved, and the remaining 700km can take a week in the rainy season.

AROUND SANTARÉM
Floresta Nacional (FLONA) do Tapajós
This 6500 sq km primary rainforest reserve on the Rio Tapajós is notable for its giant trees, including behemoth *sumaúna* (type of ceiba tree). Its *igarapés* (channels connecting rivers) and, in the rainy season, *igapós* (flooded forests) promise some wildlife viewing; sloths, monkeys, river dolphins and birds are relatively common. Rubber harvesting is an important source of income for residents, and latex-production facilities welcome visitors. While FLONA lacks the deep-jungle feel of areas in the western Amazon Basin, it is still strikingly beautiful. Visits can be arranged through agencies in Santarém or Alter do Chão, or go on your own.

Two small communities within FLONA – Maguary and Jamaracuá – receive visitors for homestays. Neither has electricity, running water or indoor bathrooms. You will sleep (bring a hammock) and eat (typically rice and fish) with a family. Bring bottled water, toilet paper, flashlight, and any additional food you may want.

To visit, authorization (per person, per day US$1.50) from **IBAMA** (☎ 0xx93-3523 2964; Av Tapajós 2267; ☼ 7am-noon & 2-7pm Mon-Fri) is required. Guides are obligatory in the park. Fees for hikes (per group US$15) and canoe trips (per boat US$8) are accompanied by a community charge (per person US$2.50 to US$5).

Buses for Maguary (US$2.50, three to four hours) leave Monday to Saturday from Av São Sebastião near the Telemar building. Get off at Sr Adalberto or Sr Almiro's house. They oversee park visitation and arrange guides.

ALTER DO CHÃO
☎ 0xx93 / pop 7000
With its white-sand river beaches and tropical ambience, Alter do Chão is one of Amazonia's most beautiful places to unwind. River beaches are largest from June to December, but Alter is worth a visit any time of year.

This simple village overlooks the Rio Tapajós at the entrance of the picturesque **Lago**

Verde. It is surrounded by rainforest under various levels of protection, including the FLONA do Tapajós (p387). Also accessible is the **Rio Arapiunes**, whose beaches and clear waters earned it the nickname 'the Caribbean of the Amazon' (a forgivable exaggeration).

There are no banks.

Activities

Kayak or canoe (rental US$1.50 per hour) the Lago Verde alone or ask around for a guide. Very cool **Mãe Natureza** (☎ 3527-1264; www.maenatureza.com; Praça Sete de Setembro) offers everything from eight-day riverboat trips to walking, snorkeling, fishing or cultural excursions around Alter (US$15 to US$43) including into FLONA. This Argentine-owned agency is multilingual and has English-speaking guides. Just next door, **Vento em Popa** (☎ 3527-1379; ventoempopa@netsan.com.br) offers much of the same plus bike (US$15 per person) and 4WD trips.

Festivals & Events

Alter do Chão fills during the **Festa do Çairé**, a lively folkloric festival with dancing and processions in the second week of September.

Sleeping & Eating

Visitors and interesting local characters end up hanging out around the main plaza after dark.

Albergue da Floresta (☎ 9928-8888; www.alberguepousadadafloresta.com; Travessa Antônio Pedrosa; hammock per person US$10, chalets d US$25) Super laid-back and set in thick garden surroundings, hammock (mosquito net provided) space is in a thatched-roof, open-air pavilion, and cabins are simple but comfortable. Run by cool, international hippy types. Guest-use kitchen.

Pousada Vila Praia (☎ 3527-1346; Av Copacabana; s/d US$15/22, chalet US$30-35; 🅿) This *pousada* consists of two rows of close-set cabins, each with their own porch and hammock. Rooms are rather ordinary, but the two-room chalets are great for groups of three to five.

Pousada Tia Marilda (☎ 3527-1144/1131; Travessa Antônio A Lobato 559; s/d US$16.50/20; 🅿) This friendly, simple place is a little cute and makes an attempt to decorate its decent-sized rooms. Second-floor rooms are breezier and larger.

Tribal (Travessa Antônio A Lobato; mains US$4-6) and **Farol da Vila** (Rua Jo Caisi de Arrimo; mains US$4-6) serve great typical meat dishes with home cooked flavor.

Shopping

Arariba (Travessa Antônio A Lobato) This excellent indigenous art store unites the artwork of eight different Amazonian tribes.

Getting There & Away

Buses to Alter do Chão (US90¢, one hour, eight daily) leave Santarém from 5am to 6pm. Catch them in front of the Telemar building on Av São Sebastião or from Praça Tiradentes. From the airport, catch the bus into Santarém, get off in the first neighborhood at the *garagem do Perpetuo Socorro*, across from Supermercado O Gauchinho. Cross the road and flag down the 'Alter do Chão' bus.

MANAUS

☎ 0xx92 / pop 1.67 million

There's something alluring about Manaus, probably its remote setting deep in the mythical Amazon rainforest. The reality however is pretty unromantic. Aside from a few remnants of its late 19th-century, 'Paris of the Tropics', rubber-boom days, Manaus' urban landscape is pretty unattractive. But if you're planning a jungle trip, this is the starting point. If you can spend your time here tripping out on the fact that Manaus is an international port some 1500km from the sea, and the materials that constructed it traveled here by slow boat, you'll be better off. For information on jungle trips and lodges, see p393.

Orientation

The area south of the Teatro Amazonas, and encircled by a U-shape created by Av Epaminondas, Av Floriano Peixoto and Av Getúlio Vargas, is a noisy commercial district that is busy by day and deserted at night and on Sun-

---

GETTING INTO TOWN

The airport is 13km north of the center. Bus 306 'Aeroporto Centro' (US90¢, 30 minutes) runs roughly every half hour until 11pm. Taxis are set at US$21, but can be cheaper from the airport bus stop.

The bus station is 6km north of the center and is a short walk from main bus routes. From the station cross the footbridge out front, walk with traffic to the closest bus stop and take one of the buses listed under 'Centro' on the stop's sign. A taxi costs US$10.

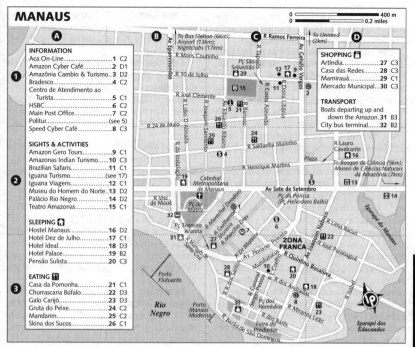

MANAUS

0 ———— 400 m
0 ———— 0.2 miles

INFORMATION
Aca On-Line..........................**1** C2
Amazon Cyber Café................**2** D1
Amazônia Cambio & Turismo..**3** D2
Bradesco...............................**4** C2
Centro de Atendimento ao
 Turista................................**5** C1
HSBC...................................**6** C2
Main Post Office....................**7** C2
Politur.............................(see 5)
Speed Cyber Café..................**8** C3

SIGHTS & ACTIVITIES
Amazon Gero Tours................**9** C1
Amazonas Indian Turismo.....**10** C3
Brazilian Safaris...................**11** C1
Iguana Turismo................(see 17)
Iguana Viagens....................**12** C1
Museu do Homem do Norte...**13** D2
Palácio Rio Negro.................**14** D2
Teatro Amazonas..................**15** C1

SLEEPING
Hostel Manaus.....................**16** D2
Hotel Dez de Julho...............**17** C1
Hotel Ideal..........................**18** D3
Hotel Palace........................**19** B2
Pensão Sulista.....................**20** C3

EATING
Casa da Pomonha.................**21** C1
Churrascaria Búfalo..............**22** D3
Galo Carijó..........................**23** D3
Gruta do Peixe.....................**24** C2
Mandarim............................**25** C2
Skina dos Sucos...................**26** C1

SHOPPING
Artíndia...............................**27** C3
Casa das Redes....................**28** C3
Mamirauá.............................**29** C1
Mercado Municipal...............**30** C3

TRANSPORT
Boats departing up and
 down the Amazon.............**31** B3
City bus terminal..............**32** B2

BRAZIL

---

days (save for the plazas). The area between Rua dos Andradas and the river is much the same. The Praça da Matriz is seedy at night. The Zona Franca is less seedy but still a pretty undesirable area. The Teatro Amazonas' immediate surroundings are slightly upscale.

Information

EMERGENCY
Politur (☎ 3231-1998; CAT, Av Eduardo Ribeiro)

INTERNET ACCESS
Aca On-Line (Rua Guilherme Moreira; per hr US$1.50; 🖳)
Amazon Cyber Café (cnr Rua Getúlio Vargas &10 de Julho; per hr US$ 1.75; 🖳) Open late.
Speed Cyber Café (Rua dos Andradas 408; per hr US$1; 🖳)

MEDICAL SERVICES
Unimed (☎ 3633-4431; Av Japurá 241)

MONEY
Amazônia Cambio e Turismo (Av Sete de Setembro 1251; 🕘 9am-5pm Mon-Fri, to noon Sat) Changes euros, US dollars and traveler's checks.

Bradesco (Av Eduardo Ribeiro)
HSBC (Rua Dr Moreira 226) 24-hour ATMs.

POST
Main post office (Rua Marcílio Dias 160)

TOURIST INFORMATION
Amazonastur airport (☎ 0800-280-8820, 3652-1120); Centro de Atendimento ao Turista (CAT; ☎ 3622-0767; Av Eduardo Ribeiro); Estação Hidroviário (☎ 3233-8698; inside PAC) Also at the bus station.

Dangers & Annoyances

At the airport, avoid the vultures touting jungle trips or city accommodations. Some have reportedly hustled people off to be robbed. After 11pm steer clear of the port area and the Praça da Matriz. If arriving late by boat, take a taxi to a hotel – muggings are common.

Sights

The cozy 19th-century **Teatro Amazonas** (admission US$5; 🕘 9am-8:30pm Mon-Sat) captures the opulence of the rubber boom. English-speaking guides are available or Livro Vivo, a theatrical group, does fun living-history tours in

Book accommodations online at lonelyplanet.com

Portuguese. Catch a show – free ones are on Sunday afternoons. The square out front hosts free cultural presentations most nights.

The **Museu de Ciências Naturais da Amazônia** (Estrada Belém s/n, Colônia Cachoeira Grande; admission US$6; 9am-noon, 2-5pm Mon-Sat) displays preserved regional animals, fish and insects (amazing butterflies and beetles). The collection is small but excellent, and it's satisfying to get a good look at the unique wildlife. Take bus 519 from Praça da Matriz, or onward from the Bosque da Ciência. Follow the 'Museu' signs from the stop (10-minute walk).

The tranquil **Bosque da Ciência** (Forest of Science; Rua Otávio Cabral; admission US$1; 9am-4pm Tue-Sun) has contained giant otters, manatees, caimans, and free-roaming turtles, monkeys, sloths and other creatures on 130 sq km of rainforest. Take bus 519 from the Praça da Matriz.

The **Museu do Homem do Norte** (Av Sete de Setembro 1385; admission US$1.50; 9am-noon & 1-5pm Mon-Fri) has anthropological displays on regional peoples, especially the riverbank-dwelling *caboclos*. The ornate **Palácio Rio Negro** (Av Sete de Setembro 1546; admission free; 10am-5pm Tue-Fri, 4-8pm Sat) is a rubber baron's mansion turned cultural center that hosts temporary art exhibits and concerts.

There are **Bumba Meu Boi** festival rehearsals at the *sambódromo* on Fridays and Saturdays from September to June. Ask Amazonastur for details.

Activities

The **Encontro das Águas** (Meeting of the Waters) is where the dark Rio Negro meets the café au lait Rio Solimões. The two flow side by side without mingling for several kilometers (owing to differences in speed, density and temperature), before finally combining to create the Amazon River. Many jungle trips include the Encontro, but if yours doesn't, see it by either hiring a boat with the Associação dos Canoeiros (p392), or by traveling from Ponta do Catalão, 12km east of the center, to Careiro. Take bus 713 from Praça da Matriz to Ponta do Catalão (last stop) and either take a motorboat (US$3, 40 minutes) or the hourly car ferry (free). Careiro is a quaint village and worth a look around.

Sleeping

Most of Manaus' budget accommodations are very low quality. Near the Teatro Amazonas is the ideal location.

Pensão Sulista (3234-5814; Av Joaquim Nabuco 347; s/d US$10/15;) A tenementlike, super basic option in a rather charming old building. High ceilings.

Hotel Ideal (3622-0038; Rua dos Andradas 491; s/d US$11/16.50;) Ideal is a multistory block of plain rooms coated in gray and white high-gloss paint. Request a window. A little sterile, but eons better than run-down options in its price bracket. Surrounded by other budget hotels.

Hostel Manaus (3233-4545; www.hostelmanaus.com; Rua Lauro Cavalcante 231; dm US$11.50) This Australian-owned hostel was just opening during research. In a converted home with guest-use kitchen.

Hotel Dez de Julho (3232-6280; www.hoteldezdejulho.com; Rua 10 de Julho 679; s/d US$25/27.50;) Behind a spacious, proper lobby this four-story hotel stacks a variety of simple rooms with updated fixtures and two patios with tropical murals. Can be noisy. Cheaper and inferior option next door.

Hotel Palace (3622-4622/4623; www.hotelpalace.brasilcomercial.com; Av 7 de Setembro 593; s/d US$32.50/42.50;) A green, ornate, early-20th-century facade shields large, bright rooms with wooden furniture. Bathrooms are small and circa 1950. Quietest rooms face the plaza.

Eating

Praça Heliodoro Balbí and Praça São Sebastião are good places to find food at night and on Sundays. Try *tacacá* (a gummy soup made from manioc root, dried shrimp and tongue-tingling *jambu* leaves) at street stalls.

Skina dos Sucos (cnr Av Eduardo Ribeiro & Rua 24 de Maio; sandwiches & snacks US25¢-$4) This busy lunch counter serves sandwiches and snacks. A great place for fresh Amazonian fruit juices like açaí.

Gruta do Peixe (Rua Saldanha Marinho 609; per kg US$5.50, mains US$7) Lunchtime finds this bright, grotto-like basement crowded and a little smoky from the meats barbecued in the back. Known for fish.

Casa da Pamonha (Rua Barroso 375; per kg US$9;) Unlike the dining room, the vegetarian lunch buffet is creative and flavorful. Arrive close to noon for the best selection. Snacks served all day.

Galo Carijó (cnr Rua dos Andradas & Rua Pedro Botelho; mains for 2 US$10-17) It's all about fried fish at this low-key spot.

Mandarim (Rua Joaquim Sarmento 224; per kg US$11, mains US$7-9;) This Chinese restaurant has a lunch buffet with Chinese, Japanese and Brazilian dishes.

Churrascaria Búfalo (Av Joaquim Nabuco 628; per person US$20; 🍴) Despite the neighborhood, an upscale crowd flocks to Búfalo for a classy lunch and dinner *rodízio* (all-you-can-eat), which consists of an extensive buffet (including sushi!) and meats brought to the table on skewers. Bufolete, the per-kilo (US$11.50) version, is right next door.

Drinking

The area surrounding the Teatro Amazonas is the center's best area to hang out, for adults and kids alike. On Friday and Saturday nights, Praça da Polícia and Praça da Saudade fill with people and snack and drink stands.

Ponta Negra (13km from the center) has some bars and restaurants on a sort of riverfront promenade. Many of Manaus' cool nightspots sit on the Estrada de Ponta Negra just before this area.

Entertainment

Coração Blue (Estrada de Ponta Negra 3701, Ponta Negra) A dance club with different music every night.

Aomirante (Rua Padre Agostinho Caballero, Santo Antonio) Known for its reggae night on Sunday.

Tulipa Negra (Rua Recife 2515, Flores; 🕙 Thu-Sat) Has live rock, and sometimes blues.

Shopping

Mercado Municipal (🕙 6am-6pm Mon-Sat, to noon Sun) The sprawling, cast-iron, art nouveau *mercado* opened in 1882. Shop here for Amazonian herbal remedies and crafts.

Mamirauá (Rua 10 de Julho 495) Sells high-quality baskets and mats.

Getting There & Away

AIR

Gol, Meta, Rico, TAF, TAM, Total, Trip and Varig operate domestic flights from Manaus. LAB connects Manaus to Latin America and Miami, and TAM has direct flights to Miami. Smaller airlines use Terminal 2, 'Eduardinho,' about 600m east of Terminal 1.

BOAT

Large passenger boats use the Estação Hidroviária (aka Porto Flutuante). Inside, Agência Rio Amazonas sells tickets on behalf of most boats. Guys on the street may sell cheaper tickets, but if something goes wrong you'll be on your own. For hammocks try **Casa das Redes**

(Rua Rocha dos Santos). See the boxed text (p379) for information and tips.

Destination	Duration	Cost (US$)	Frequency
Belém	3½ days	upper/lower deck 118/108	Wed & Fri
Porto Velho	4 days	upper/lower deck 101/97	Tue & Fri
Santarém	30-36 hr	upper/lower deck 57/49	Tue-Sat
Tabatinga	6½ days	upper deck 134	Tue, Wed, Fri & Sat

AJATO runs fast boats to Tabatinga (US$150, 34 hours) on Tuesday from the Porto Manaus Moderna, which is also where tickets are sold. At press time its service to Santarém had been suspended. Travelers report fast boats to be too fast to be pleasant.

BUS

Five daily buses run to Boa Vista (US$40 to US$45, 12 hours, five daily). A direct daily bus to Caracas, Venezuela (US$114, 36 hours) that stops in Santa Elena de Uairén (US$71, 16 hours) and Puerto La Cruz (US$103, 32 hours) usually only runs in the summer.

Road travel south to Porto Velho has been suspended indefinitely.

Getting Around

All buses to the center pass the Praça da Matriz, loop up on Av Floriano Peixoto, and either head right on Av Sete de Setembro or straight on Av Getúlio Vargas. City buses and downtown streets get super congested around 1pm to 2pm and 5pm to 7pm.

AROUND MANAUS
Jungle Trips

Many visitors to Amazonia expect to see wildlife close enough to take magazine-quality photos and meet spear-toting indigenous people just outside Manaus. This just isn't possible. The vegetation is too thick, animals are too shy and the cultural gap too great. (To visit 'unacculturated' communities, you'll need an expedition of a week or more.) On a typical trip, you are likely to glimpse pink and gray river dolphins, crocodiles, monkeys and plenty of birds including macaws and toucans. Sloths are relatively common. Manatees, anacondas and jaguars are extremely hard to spot. Expect to get a sense of how these animals

BRAZIL

move and where they hang out. The more remote, unpopulated and pristine the area, the better wildlife-viewing will be.

While anything's possible, the typical jungle trip is two to four days. Common activities include piranha fishing, nighttime crocodile-spotting, an informational jungle walk, a visit to a local home and a night of jungle camping. Canoeing through *igarapés* (channels connecting rivers) and *igarapós* (flooded forests) – which have more flora and fauna than channels and rivers – is a priority. This is one reason the high-water period (roughly March to July) is the best time to visit.

'White' rivers, like the Lago Mamorí region, tend to have a higher density of animals than 'black' ones, like the Rio Negro. But they also have more mosquitoes and somewhat thicker vegetation, which inhibits wildlife-viewing.

Things to consider while researching trips:

- Your guide's proficiency in your common language.
- Amount of guide's experience in trip's ecosystem.
- Group size.
- Ratio of travel time to time spent at the destination.
- Amount of non-motorized boat/canoe time.
- Availability of lifejackets.
- The cost breakdown for nontypical trips.

You'll need sturdy shoes or boots, long pants, a long-sleeved shirt, a raincoat, insect repellent, a flashlight and a water bottle. High-power binoculars really improve the experience. You'll need at least 4L of bottled water per person per day. Bring your passport.

DANGERS & ANNOYANCES

You name it, it's happened on a jungle trip outside Manaus. Consider that you are placing your personal safety in another's hands in an unknown, often isolated, natural environment. It's best to use agencies or guides registered with Amazonastur (see p389). Personally verify registration status as some agencies display outdated or revoked certification. Using a registered agency or guide means having a better chance of being refunded should something go wrong, and having recourse to prevent others from having the same experience. If using an unregistered agency or guide, check out its reputation. Women should con-

sider being part of a group of three or more to avoid being alone remotely with a guide.

SCAMS

Manaus has more scammers on the make than possibly anywhere in Brazil. Before handing anyone cash for a jungle trip, personally visit the office of the tour agency they represent. If they are indeed an authorized vendor, they will still receive their commission. As the industry has become more competitive, scammers have gone so far as to create false IDs and receipts, fake confirmation phone calls to agencies, and falsely represent or impersonate guides and agencies listed in guidebooks. These scammers are most often at the airport, but also work on the street and at hotel receptions. Hotel receptionists earn side commissions by giving out room information.

AGENCIES & GUIDES

Manaus has scores of agencies offering Disneyland-esque tours; those listed below are recommended budget options offering a more genuine and adventurous experience. Some agencies have a minimum-group-size requirement to set out, while others maintain a constant flow of clients in and out of a set spot. Yet other agencies pool their clients. Agencies can set up almost anything, but most have expertise in a certain geographical area. Fees should be all-inclusive (lodging, meals, drinking water, transfers, activities, and guides). Unless the agency is very well established, insist on paying a portion of the fee up front, and the rest upon return.

Take some time to research the options. Many well-seasoned travelers have left Manaus disappointed with their once-in-a-lifetime Amazon jungle experience because they rushed booking the trip.

Amazonas Indian Turismo (☎ 0xx92-3633-5578; www.amazonasindianturismo.tur.br; Rua dos Andradas 311, Centro) The office and the English-speaking Indian guides just feel like the real deal, and the client-response book is positively exuberant. Its rustic camp on the Rio Urubú has hammocks and latrines. Three-day, two-night trips run US$223 per person. Trips from two to 9 days.

Amazon Gero Tours (☎ 0xx92-3232-4755; www.amazongerotours.com; Rua 10 de Julho 679, Centro) This agency is run by English-speaking guides and piloted Gero, an all-around helpful guy. Typical trips are to Lago Mamori, Lago Ararinha and Cutrapa and run US$90 to US$110 per person per night. Bed or hammock accommodation and flush toilets are available. Honest and flexible.

Iguana Turismo (www.amazonbrasil.com.br) Hotel Dez de Julho (☎ 0xx92-3633-6507; Rua 10 de Julho 669, Centro); Hotel Rio Branco (☎ 0xx92-3248-3211; Rua dos Andrades 474, Centro) Iguana's typical trip to Lago Juma runs US$90 per person per night. Comfortable hammock or cabin accommodation with flush toilets is located next to Guyanese owner Gerry Hardy's riverfront home. His wife and her family are from the area and staff the lodge. Great for custom trips.

Mamori Adventure Camping (☎ 0xx92-9184-8452/8123-3744; vicenteguidetour@hotmail.com) If you are looking to trek and camp deep in the jungle, Vicente and David are your guys. Friendly and English speaking.

Brazilian Safaris (☎ 0xx92-8112-7154; www.braziliansafaris.com; Rua 10 de Julho 632, Centro) Guyanese Munaf 'Steve' Roman's agency offers trips to Lago Tucunaré anywhere from three days/two nights to seven days/six nights for US$60 per person per night. Riverboat or combination lodge/riverboat trips are available. Avoid his 'swim with and feed the dolphins' tours – they are disruptive to the dolphins' natural habits.

Associação dos Canoeiros (Estação Hidroviária) This association of independent, licensed boatmen is run by English-speaking Antonio Franco. They often sport green jackets and yellow badges and hang around the Estação Hidroviária's entrance. They can arrange anything from a two-day river trip to 15-day overland journey to Guyana and Venezuela. A jungle trip for a group of three or four runs US$175 per day. Accommodation is with local families.

JUNGLE LODGES

Within 250km of Manaus are at least two dozen jungle lodges – waterside hotels ranging from rustic (hammocks) to luxurious (suites). Visits are normally by (somewhat costly) packages that include activities. As many agencies are affiliated with or run their own lodge, it can be a very fine line between low-budget jungle trips and jungle lodges.

Acajatuba Jungle Lodge (☎ 0xx92-3642-0358/0378; www.acajatuba.com.br; Rua 7 87, Adrianópolis; 1-/2-night packages per person US$225/305) The lodge has 20 round bungalows on stilts on Lago Acajatuba.

Amazon Eco-Lodge (☎ 0xx92-3656-6033; www.naturesafaris.com; Rua Flavio Espirito Santo 1, Kissia II, Manaus; 4-day & 3-night packages per 2 people US$500) A small floating lodge on Lago Juma, 60km southeast of Manaus, this lovely lodge caters to 28 guests.

TRIPLE FRONTIER

On the northeast bank of the Amazon – about 1100km west of Manaus – Tabatinga (Brazil) and Leticia (Colombia) are separated by an

---

SPLURGE!

A remote floodplain forest, halfway between Manaus and the Peruvian frontier, is protected by the **Reserva de Desenvolvimento Sustentável Mamirauá** (Mamirauá Sustainable Development Reserve; office ☎ 0xx97-3343-4160; www.mamiraua.org.br; Av Brasil 197, Tefé; all-inclusive packages per person 3 days & 3 nights US$450, 4 days & 4 nights US$520). This 1.24 million hectare reserve is part of the second-largest (57,000 sq km) continuous block of protected tropical rainforest in the world. Mamirauá combines nature conservation and scientific research with improved opportunities for the communities within the reserve.

Their excellent ecotourism program affords access to a pristine piece of towering primary rainforest, rivers and lakes absolutely teeming with life. Silence there will be the loudest you've ever heard, and wildlife-viewing is among the best in Amazonia. The reserve contains four species of monkey (including the rare, crimson-faced white uacari), squirrels and 400-odd recorded bird species, as well as a higher concentration of the animals seen outside of Manaus. Guides native to the reserve and an English-speaking, trained naturalist lead unstrenuous excursions.

Average group size is 12, maximum is 20. Accommodations are in agreeably comfortable yet unpretentious floating bungalows. The food includes regional fruits and fish, and much of it is grown locally and/or organically.

Rico and Trip fly between Manaus, Tefé and Tabatinga. From Manaus to Tefé there are regular (upper/lower deck US$57/49, 45 hours, Wednesday to Saturday) and fast (US$90, 13 hours, Wednesday and Saturday) boats. There are regular (US$45/37, 40 hours, daily except Wed) and fast (US$90, 11 hours, Thursday and Sunday) boats for the return trip too. **AJATO** operates the fast boats (p391). Boats between Tefé and Tabatinga are via Jutaí.

GETTING TO PERU OR COLOMBIA

Before leaving Brazil, get an exit stamp from the **Polícia Federal** (Av da Amizade 650; 8am-6pm) in Tabatinga.

For Peru, boats depart from the Porto da Feira to Santa Rosa (US$1, five minutes, 6am to 6pm). Regular (US$35, 2½ days, three weekly) and express (US$75, 10 hours, daily) boats also depart for Iquitos (further upriver in Peru). Iquitos boats pass immigration in Santa Rosa.

For Colombia, it's a short walk to Leticia, or you can take one of the frequent *kombis*. Also see Leticia's Boat section (p625) and the boxed text, p936.

---

invisible international border. The opposite bank of the river, and the islands in the middle of it, are Peru. Santa Rosa, Peru's border settlement, is on an island. This 'triple frontier' has travel routes linking all three countries and is a good base for jungle trips. Leticia is the largest and most pleasant of the three border towns and has the best services. For information, see p620).

BOA VISTA
☎ 0xx95 / pop 197,000
This planned, somewhat stark riverfront capital of Brazil's least populated state is surrounded by dry savanna. It sits isolated between the jungle territories of the Yanomami, one of Amazonia's largest surviving indigenous peoples, and beautiful high plains on the Venezuelan border. Any tourist interest lies in hiking and camping possibilities nearby.

Information
A tourist information post at the bus station opens irregularly.
Bradesco (Av Sebastião Diniz & Rua Inácio Magalhães) Has ATMs.
Byte Internet (Av Dr Silvio Botelho 537; per hr US$1) Offers internet.
Edson Ouro Safira Joyas (Av Benjamin Constant 64 W; 8am-5:30pm Mon-Sat) Exchanges US, Venezuelan and Guyanese currencies and euros.

Sights & Activities
Spend the weekend at the vast **Parque Anauá**, about 2.5km northwest of the center. It has gardens, a lake and the small but interesting **Museu Integrado de Roraima** (admission free; 8am-6pm).

Riverfront **Porto do Babazinho** (☎ 3224-8174; babazinhorr@yahoo.com.br; Av Major Williams 1) rents kayaks (per hour US$2), offers river day-trips (four-person minimum), teaches windsurfing from December to March and organizes two-night trips to a local ranch (per person US$60). Belgian **Jean-Luc Felix** (☎ 3624-3015; Restaurante Bistro Gourmet, Av NS da Consolata) and **Lula** (☎ 9965-2222) lead hiking and camping trips in the surrounding mountains for two days or more.

Sleeping & Eating
Hotel Monte Libano (☎ 3224-7232; Av Benjamin Constant 319 W; s/d US$14/17.50, without bathroom US$10/15; 🔀) The best of the cheapies, with drab *quartos* and marginally better air-con rooms. Coffee and bread breakfast.
Hotel Ideal (☎ 3224-6342; Rua Araújo Filho 481; s/d US$20/25; 🔀) A plain, multistory hotel with clean, simple rooms.
La Gondola (Av Benjamin Constant 35W; per kg US$7) A popular lunch buffet and á la carte spot facing the central plaza. Nothing fancy.
Restaurant Ver O Rio (Praça Barreto Leite; mains for 2 US$17.50/25) The menu is heavy on the fish, but does include beef, chicken and shrimp at this breezy spot overlooking the river.

Getting There & Around
Gol, Meta and Varig operate domestic flights from Boa Vista's airport, 3.5km from the center. A taxi costs US$10. Meta also flies to Georgetown (Guyana) and Paramaribo (Suriname).

Five daily buses run to Manaus (US$40 to US$45, 12 hours). The daily bus to Caracas, Venezuela (US$80, 24 hours) stops in Santa Elena de Uairén (US$12.50, 3½ hours) and Puerto La Cruz (US$74, 17 hours). A taxi between the bus station and the center (2.5km) costs US$4.

GETTING TO VENEZUELA

Determine whether you require a Venezuelan tourist card from the consulate in Manaus or Boa Vista before boarding a Venezuela-bound bus. Buses stop at a Brazilian Polícia Federal border post for exit stamps before entering Venezuela. The Venezuelan town of Santa Elena de Uairén (p1043) lies 15km north of the Venezuelan border. For information on travel from Santa Elena to Brazil, see p1045.

GETTING TO GUYANA

Before leaving Brazil, get an exit stamp from the **Polícia Federal** (🕑 8am-7pm). The 2pm bus leaving Boa Vista stops at the Polícia Federal and then continues to the river. If you take an earlier or later departure, catch a taxi from Bonfim's bus station to the Polícia Federal (US$2.50); from there it's a short walk to the river. Motorized canoes cross the river (US$2) to Guyana. Once there, check in with officials immediately as smuggling is an issue here.

Collective taxis marked 'Lotação' (US$1) travel roughly fixed routes and are the best way to get around. Ask if they're going where you are – sometimes they'll deviate a bit.

BONFIM
☎ 0xx95 / pop 3000

The small town of Bonfim sits on Rio Tacutu, and is a stepping-stone to Lethem, Guyana (p782). Lethem is 5km from the other side of the river. Neither Bonfim nor Lethem are exactly pleasant, so get an early start to assure you reach your destination before nightfall.

Lethem's accommodations are much better, but if you're stuck in Bonfim try **Pousada Fronteira** (☎ 3552-1294; Rua Aluísio de Menezes 26; r US$7.50; ❄).

Four daily buses run between Boa Vista and Bonfim (US$6.50, 1½ hours).

PORTO VELHO
☎ 0xx69 / pop 311,500

Stretched along the muddy banks of the Rio Madeira, Porto Velho's new economic importance as the transfer point for Mato Grosso's soybeans from truck to barge is improving this backwater town. Change is slow, however. Porto Velho remains a major conduit for cocaine smuggling and has the rugged feel of a frontier town, especially at night.

Information

Shops and offices generally close between noon and 2pm.

Bradesco (Av Carlos Gomes) Has ATMs.

Casa de Câmbio Marco Aurélio (☎ 3223-2551; Rua José de Alencar 3353; ❄ 8:30am-3pm Mon-Fri) Changes US dollars and traveler's checks.

Titan Cyber Lan (Av Campos Sales 2913; per hr US$1.25; ❄ 9am-11pm) Provides internet access above Sanduba's.

Sights

The **Museu da Estrada de Ferro Madeira-Mamoré** (Praça Madeira Mamoré; admission free; ❄ 8am-6pm) displays relics from this railway line, intended to carry rubber over the unnavigable section of river between Guajará-Mirim and Porto Velho, thereby connecting it to world markets. The project was a disaster, and resulted in so many casualties it earned the nickname 'Railway of Death'. Restoration of the line is rumored – ask at the museum.

Sleeping

Hotel Tia Carmem (☎ 3221-1908/7910; Av Campos Sales 2895; s/d without bathroom US$10/15, with bathroom US$17.50/25; ❄) The cheapest rooms have no ventilation. Definitely upgrade at this friendly cheapie. Good location.

Hotel Tereza Raquel (☎ 3223-9234/5906; Rua Tenreiro Aranha 2125; s/d US$17.50/23; ❄) The friendly staff and bright rooms in fine shape make this a good-value hotel for Porto Velho.

Vitória Palace Hotel (☎ 3221-9232; Rua Duque de Caxias 745; s/d US$17.50/22.50; ❄) Room (especially bathroom) quality is a notch below the Tereza Raquel, but the quiet surroundings of this bland hotel feel much safer at night.

Eating

Sanduba's (Av Campos Sales 2913; sandwiches US$1.25-4.50) A popular open-air sandwich grill with good juices, *guaraná* or *açaí* smoothies and projected TV.

Mirante II (Rua Dom Pedro II; mains US$5-12.50; ❄ closed Mon) Enjoy a meal, an *açaí* or a drink at this open-air patio restaurant overlooking the river.

Remanso do Tucunaré (Av Brasília 1506; mains for 2 US$10-21) Half-portions are available at this fish restaurant. The dark dining room has big fish tanks and plaques naming its most loyal customers.

Getting There & Around

AIR

Gol, Rico, TAM, Trip and Varig operate domestic flights from Porto Velho's airport, 6km from the center. A taxi costs US$12.50, or take bus 201 'Hospital de Base via Aeroporto.'

BOAT

Boats to Manaus (hammock US$50 to US$65, three to 3½ days) leave around 6pm on Tuesday and Friday from Porto Cai n'Água. A Wednesday departure requires you to hang

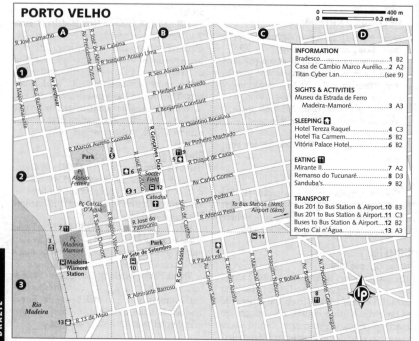

PORTO VELHO

INFORMATION
Bradesco...............................1 B2
Casa de Câmbio Marco Aurélio....2 A2
Titan Cyber Lan.......................(see 9)

SIGHTS & ACTIVITIES
Museu da Estrada de Ferro
Madeira-Mamoré...................3 A3

SLEEPING
Hotel Tereza Raquel.................4 C3
Hotel Tia Carmem....................5 B2
Vitória Palace Hotel.................6 B2

EATING
Mirante II.............................7 A2
Remanso do Tucunaré..............8 D3
Sanduba's.............................9 B2

TRANSPORT
Bus 201 to Bus Station & Airport.10 B3
Bus 201 to Bus Station & Airport.11 C3
Buses to Bus Station & Airport...12 B2
Porto Cai n'Água....................13 A3

around Manicoré in the middle of the night while transferring boats, which can be unsafe and isn't recommended. See the boxed text on p379 for information and tips.

BUS

Buses run to Guajará-Mirim (US$15, 5½ hours, six daily), Rio Branco (US$26 to US$31, eight hours, five daily) and Cuiabá (US$75, 21 hours, three daily). Collective taxis also leave the bus station for Guajará-Mirim (US$22.50, 3½ hours). From the bus station to the center (3km), take bus 201 'Hospital de Base via Aeroporto'. To return, take a 'Presidente Roosevelt' or 'Esperanza da Comunidade' bus.

GUAJARÁ-MIRIM
☎ 0xx69 / pop 35,500

In this pleasant town just opposite Guayaramerín (Bolivia), bushy trees shade overgrown grass and sidewalks, stained red by the earth, from the relentless sun. In the quiet center on the Rio Mamoré there are quite a few boarded-up old buildings.

Playnet Games (Posto Nogueira, Rua Getúlio Vargas; per hr US$1.25) offers internet access inside a gas station until late. **Bradesco** (cnr Av Costa Marques & Av Leopoldo de Mateos) has ATMs. There is no currency exchange in Guajará-Mirim.

The small **Museu Histórico Municipal** (admission free; 8:30am-12pm & 2:30-5pm), in the old Madeira-Mamoré train station, is a pretty cool bug-eaten natural history museum. There are crazy photographs of a snake that swallowed a man whole.

Despite the commercial-street location and run-down exterior, the rooms at **Alfa Hotel** (☎ 3541-3121; Av Leopoldo de Mateos 239; s/d US$10/20;) are clean and bright. Rooms are clean with aging fixtures at the simple **Hotel Mini-Estrela Palace** (☎ 3541-1205; Av 15 de Novembro 460; s/d US$10/ 23;), in a residential area. A similar option is across the street and restaurants are nearby.

The lunch buffet at **Restaurante Oásis** (Av 15 de Novembro 460; per kilo US$8) includes freshly grilled meats at Guajará-Mirim's best restaurant.

Panificadora Central (Av 15 de Novembro 632) The quality and variety of salty and sweet snacks and fresh juices is surprisingly good at this corner bakery.

Buses run to Porto Velho (US$15 to US$17, 5½ hours, six daily) and Rio Branco (US$23,

GETTING TO BOLIVIA

Before leaving, get an exit stamp from the **Policía Federal** (Av Presidente Dutra; ☺ 8am-10pm). When walking toward the river turn right onto Dutra. Passenger launches to Guayaramerín (US$1.50, five minutes) depart from the port at the base of Av 15 de Novembro roughly every 15 minutes from 7am to 6pm. From 6pm to 7am departures require a minimum of 10 passengers. For information on travel in the opposite direction, see p255.

eight hours, daily). Collective taxis also leave the bus station for Porto Velho (US$22.50, 3½ hours). Buy bus tickets at the bus station (2km east of the center) or at the Real Norte office by the port. Buses (excluding midnight departures) pass the office about 20 minutes before they leave the station. A taxi between the station and the center runs to US$5.

RIO BRANCO
☎ 0xx68 / pop 255,000

Acre is a remote jungle state known for wanton environmental destruction, rampant high-level crime and corruption, violent land struggles and drug smuggling. Despite this, its riverfront capital Rio Branco is a pleasant enough, and relatively developed, place to pass through.

Viarena (Rua Rui Barbosa 507; per hr US$1.50) offers internet access. Major banks are on Praça Eurico Dutra.

The **Museu da Borracha** (Rubber Museum; Av Ceará 1441; admission free; ☺ 8am-6pm Mon-Fri) has good displays on rubber tapping, Indian artifacts, and the local Santo Daime cult, centered around the hallucinogenic drink *ayahuasca*.

Chalé Hotel (☎ 2332-2055; Rua Palmeiral 334; s/d US$15/22.50; ❄) has friendly staff and decent rooms, just outside the bus station. The room quality is a little rough around the edges at **Afa Hotel** (☎ 3224-1396; Rua Franco Ribeiro 109; s/d US$15/20; ❄), but it is clean, friendly and located on a quiet block. Rooms are in great shape at the sterile **Hotel e Churrascaria Triângulo** (☎ 3224-0600/3529; Rua Floriano Peixoto 893; s/d US$17.50/30; ❄) and set back from the busy avenue. Its BBQ restaurant offers a *rodízio* (US$9) or buffet (per kg US$9) with air-con and checkered tablecloths. Creative salads, brown rice and vegetarian options set semigourmet buffet

lunch spot **Afa Bistrô d'Amazonia** (Rua Franco Ribeiro 99; per kilo US$8.50; ❄), apart.

Gol, Rico and Varig operate domestic flights from Porto Velho's airport, 20km west of the center. A taxi to the airport costs US$25 or **Inácio's Tur** (Rua Rui Barbosa 450) runs a bus to, but not from, the airport (US$15). Bus 304 (40 minutes) runs irregularly from the city bus terminal to the airport – ask a *fiscal* at the terminal for the schedule. Catch it at the Estadio José de Melo stop on Av Ceará.

Buses run to Porto Velho (US$53, eight hours, four daily), Guajará-Mirim (US$23, eight hours, one daily), Xapurí (US$9, 3½ hours, two daily) and Brasiléia (US$10, 4½ hours, five daily). From the bus terminal to the center (1.5km), catch a 'Norte-Sul', 'Amapá', 'Taquari' or 'Domoacir' bus.

XAPURI
☎ 0xx68 / pop 6200

Rows of neat wooden houses, flowers and thick trees line paved and red dirt roads in this sweet little town. Its charm and a look unlike any other Northern Brazilian town make it well worth a visit if you're in the area.

Xapuri was home to rubber tapper and internationally recognized environmental martyr Chico Mendes, who was murdered in 1988 after years of successful campaigning against the destruction of forests by loggers and ranchers. The **Fundação Chico Mendes** (Rua Dr Batista de Moraes; admission free; ☺ 9am-6pm), a block from the bus station, displays touching Mendes photos and memorabilia. It is staffed in part by his sister-in-law. You'll see Mendes' rustic house where he was fatally shot, which gives a feel for the characteristic homes of the area.

Several fine budget *pousadas* rent comfortable rooms. **Restaurante Central** (Rua 6 de Agosto 173) has a simple lunch buffet (per kg US$5.50).

Buses run to Rio Branco (US$8.50, 3½ hours, two daily) and Brasiléia (US$3.50, two hours, two daily). Collective taxis to Rio Branco (US$12.50, two hours) and Brasiléia (US$5, 45 minutes) leave from a kiosk on Rua Coronel Branão.

BRASILÉIA
☎ 0xx68 / pop 10,500

Brasiléia is separated from Cobija, Bolivia, by the Rio Acre and Igarapé Bahia. Brasiléia's atmosphere is decidedly more mellow, while Cobija has more and better services.

GETTING TO BOLIVIA & PERU

Before leaving Brazil, get an exit stamp from the Polícia Federal in Brasiléia's neighboring town Epitáciolândia. Ask to be dropped there on your way into town.

For Bolivia, take a taxi (US$3.50) or mototaxi (US$1) from the Polícia Federal over either Epitáciolândia's or Brasiléia's international bridge. The fare includes a stop at Bolivian immigration and onward travel to a hotel or bus station. Cobija has several places to stay, an airport (two, in fact) and early morning bus connections to Riberalta, Bolivia and Guayaramerín, Bolivia.

For Peru, get an exit stamp in Epitáciolândia, catch a bus to Assis, Brasil (US$3.50, 1¾ hours, three daily) and cross the Rio Acre to Iñapari (Peru). Assis has better accommodations than Iñapari if you need to spend the night.

For travel from Peru to Brazil, see p928.

Alto Acre (Praça Hugo Poli; per hr US$1.50) offers internet access. **Banco da Amazônia** (Av Prefeito R Moreira; ☽ 8am-1pm Mon-Fri) changes foreign cash and traveler's checks.

Pousada Las Palmeras (☎ 3546-3284; Av Geny Assis 425; s/d US$20/30; ☒) has well-maintained rooms with little to no natural light, and an airy sitting area. Standard eateries line Av Prefeito Rolando Moreira.

Buses run to Rio Branco (US$18.50, 4½ hours, five daily) and Xapuri (US$3.70, two hours, two daily). Collective taxis depart for Rio Branco (US$12.50, 2½ hours) and Xapuri (US$5, 45 minutes) across from the bus station

BRAZIL DIRECTORY

ACCOMMODATIONS

Brazilian accommodations are simple yet usually clean and reasonably safe, and nearly all come with some form of café da manhã (breakfast). Private rooms with communal bathrooms are called quartos. Rooms with private bathrooms are apartamentos. Nearly every town in Brazil has at least one hotel or pousada.

Camping

Camping is a good way to experience national parks and other remote areas, as long as you're prepared to carry a tent and other essentials. The **Camping Clube do Brasil** (www.campingclube.com.br in Portuguese) has around 40 camping grounds spread between Fortaleza and Porto Alegre.

Hostels

Youth hostels are called albergues da juventude. The HI-affiliated **Federação Brasileira dos Albergues da Juventude** (www.hostel.org.br) has over 80 hostels in the country, most with individual links on the website. Many hostels are excellent, and they're great places to meet young Brazilians. A dormitory bed costs between US$10 and US$17 per person. Non-HI members usually pay 20% extra, but you can buy an HI guest card for US$15 at many hostels and at youth hostel association offices in Brazil.

Hotels

Brazil has the lavish, the shabby and everything in between. Prices here are among South America's highest, but you can still find good deals.

At the low end, US$10/16 for very basic single/double quartos is possible in nonurban guesthouses. Better rooms with private bathrooms start at about US$20/30 for single/double and substantially more in major cities like Rio.

Always ask for prices, as they're often much lower than posted prices. Also, it never hurts to ask 'Tem desconto?' (Is there a discount?), which might net a savings between US$3 a night and 30%. Prices typically rise by 30% during high seasons. Hotels in business-oriented cities such as São Paulo and Curitiba readily give discounts on weekends.

Pousadas

A pousada typically means a small family-owned guesthouse, though some hotels call themselves 'pousadas' to improve their charm quotient. Rustic pousadas can cost as little as US$10/20 per single/double and as much as US$160 for a double room with breakfast.

ACTIVITIES

The options for adrenaline-fueled adventure in Brazil are endless. The websites www.360graus.com.br and www.guiaverde.com.br

(both in Portuguese) are valuable resources on canyoning, paragliding, kite-surfing, wakeboarding as well as rafting, surfing, trekking, diving or mountain climbing.

Hiking & Climbing

These popular activities are best during the cooler months, April to October. Outstanding hiking areas include the national parks of Chapada Diamantina in Bahia (p315), Serra dos Órgãos in Rio de Janeiro state (p298), Chapada dos Veadeiros in Goiás (p332) and the Serra de São José near Tiradentes in Minas Gerais.

Rio de Janeiro is the Brazilian climbing hub, with some 350 documented climbs within a 40-minute drive. Serra dos Órgãos and Itatiaia (Rio de Janeiro) and Caparaó (Minas Gerais) national parks also have some particularly good climbs.

Visit Rio's climbing clubs to meet others and go on group outings. **Centro Excursionista Brasileiro** (☎ 0xx21-2252-9844; www.ceb.org.br in Portuguese; Av Almirante Barroso 2, 8th fl, Centro) lists upcoming excursions, and has weekly meetings to discuss the weekend's program, usually geared toward trekking and day hikes.

Surfing

Brazil has some choice surf spots. The best surfing beaches are in the South and Southeast: Saquarema (p299), Ilha de Santa Catarina (p320), São Francisco do Sul, Ilha do Mel (p319), Búzios (p301) and Rio de Janeiro (p280). In the Northeast, Itacaré (p349), Praia da Pipa (p366) and Fernando de Noronha are the major surf spots. The waves are best in the Brazilian winter (June to August).

Windsurfing & Kite-Boarding

Búzios in Rio state has good conditions, and access to rental equipment. But Brazil's hardcore windsurfing mecca is the Ceará coast northwest of Fortaleza, from July to December. Here, Jericoacoara (p371), Canoa Quebrada (p368) and the small fishing village of Icaraizinho are the most popular spots.

BOOKS

Lonely Planet's *Brazil*, *Rio de Janeiro* and (in French) *Brésil* guides have all the information needed for travelers making a more in-depth exploration of the country. Lonely Planet also publishes an excellent Brazilian phrasebook.

Quatro Rodas: Viajar Bem e Barato, available for US$18 at most Brazilian newsstands and bookstores, has detailed listings of inexpensive accommodations and restaurants all over the country, plus some information on sights.

Travelers' Tales Brazil, edited by Scott Doggett and Annette Haddad, is a fine anthology of travel adventures with good portraits of life in Brazil. One of the great classics of travel writing is Peter Fleming's *Brazilian Adventure*, a hilarious account of an expedition into Mato Grosso in the 1930s. Claude Levi-Strauss' *Tristes Tropiques* (1955) was an anthropological milestone for its study of Indian peoples in the Brazilian interior.

Several worthwhile books on history are *A Concise History of Brazil* by Boris Fausto and *Brazil: Five Centuries of Change* by Thomas Skidmore. The story behind Euclides da Cunha's masterly *Rebellion in the Backlands* (which describes the Canudos rebellion) is told by Mário Vargas Llosa in his entertaining novel *The War of the End of the World*. Jorge Amado, Brazil's best novelist, wrote many wonderful books, including *Gabriela, Clove and Cinnamon*.

The Brazilians, by Joseph A Page, is a fascinating portrait of the country and its people. For a well-illustrated, accessible introduction to Brazilian popular music, get *The Brazilian Sound* by Chris McGowan and Ricardo Pessanha. *Futebol: The Brazilian Way* gives insight into the culture behind Brazil's national addiction.

Sy Montgomery's *Journey of the Pink Dolphins* recounts her experiences studying these elusive Amazonian creatures. *Tales of a Shaman's Apprentice* by Mark Plotkin relates his mystical encounters in the Amazon with some of the world's greatest healers. In *Samba*, Alma Guillermoprieto gives an insightful account of joining one of Rio's samba schools.

BUSINESS HOURS

Most shops and government services (including post offices) are open 9am to 6pm Monday to Friday and 9am to 1pm Saturday. Banks are generally open 9am or 10am to 2pm or 3pm. Most restaurants open from noon to 3pm and 6pm to 10pm; those open for breakfast serve from around 8am to 10:30am. Bars typically open from 7pm to 2am, staying open until 4am on weekends.

BRAZIL

CLIMATE

Most of Brazil experiences only moderate temperature changes throughout the year, though southern states like Río Grande do Sul have more extreme seasonal changes like those in Europe and the US.

During the summer, which runs from December to February (school holidays coinciding), Rio and the Northeast have temperatures in the high 30s. The rest of the year temperatures are generally in the mid-20s to low 30s. The south has wider temperature variations, ranging from 15°C in the winter (June through August) to 35°C in the summer.

The Amazon region rarely gets hotter than 27°C, but it is humid there, with considerable rainfall over tropical Amazonia. In some parts of the North, December to March is considered winter, since that's the rainiest season.

Owing to generally temperate weather year-round, there's no bad time to visit Brazil. But unless you have your heart set on attending Carnaval, you may want to avoid the summer crowds (and heat), and visit from April to November. Treks into the Amazon and the Pantanal are best then – especially from June to August, when it's drier.

For more information and climate charts see p1062.

DANGERS & ANNOYANCES

Brazil receives a lot of bad press about its violence and high crime rate. By using common sense, there is much you can do to reduce the risks, including taking the general precautions applicable throughout South America (see p1063).

First off, don't start your trip by wandering around touristy areas in a jetlagged state soon after arrival: you'll be an obvious target. Accept the fact that you might be mugged, pickpocketed or have your bag snatched while you're in the country, and don't try to resist them if you do. Carry only the minimum needed for the day plus a fat-*looking* wad to hand over to would-be thieves. Other tips:

- Dress down, leave the jewelry at home and don't walk around cities with iPods, digital cameras and other flashy goods (disposable cameras are better choices).
- Keep small change handy so you don't have to flash a wallet to pay a bus fare.
- Keep spare money in a sock or shoe.
- Before arriving in a new place take a map or at least have a rough idea of the area's orientation. Use taxis to avoid walking through risky areas.
- Be alert and walk purposefully. Criminals will home in on dopey, hesitant, disoriented-looking individuals.
- Use ATMs inside buildings. Before using any ATM or exchanging money, be aware of those around you. Robbers sometimes watch these places looking for targets.
- Check windows and doors of your room for security, and don't leave anything valuable lying around.
- If you're suspicious or uneasy about a situation, don't hesitate to make excuses and leave, change your route, or do whatever else is needed to extricate yourself.
- Don't take anything to city beaches except your bathing suit, a towel and just enough money for lunch and drinks. No camera, no bag, no jewelry.
- After dark, don't ever walk along empty streets or into deserted parks.
- Don't wander into *favelas*.

If something is stolen from you, you can report it to the police. This, however, is a real headache and only recommended if you need a police report for your insurance company.

DRIVER'S LICENSE

The legal driving age in Brazil is 18. Most foreign licenses are legally valid in Brazil, but we recommend obtaining an International Driver's Licence, as the police you are likely to encounter as a foreign driver don't always know the law.

ELECTRICITY

Electrical current is not standardized in Brazil and can be almost anywhere between 110V and 220V. Carry a converter and use a surge protector with electrical equipment.

EMBASSIES & CONSULATES
Embassies & Consulates in Brazil

Argentina (Map pp288-9; ☎ 0xx21-2553-1646; Praia de Botafogo 228, No 201, Botafogo, Rio de Janeiro)

Australia (Map p284; ☎ 0xx21-3824-4624; Av Presidente Wilson 231, 23rd fl, Centro, Rio de Janeiro)

Bolivia Manaus (☎ 0xx92-3236-9988; Av Efigênio Salles, Condomínio Greenwood, Quadra B, Casa 20); Rio de Janeiro (Map pp288-9; ☎ 0xx21-2552-5490; Av Rui Barbosa 664, No 101, Flamengo)

Canada (Map p292; ☎ 0xx21-2543-3004; Av Atlântica 1130, 5th fl, Copacabana, Rio de Janeiro)

Chile (Map pp288-9; ☎ 0xx21-2552-5349; Praia do
Flamengo 344, 7th fl, Flamengo, Rio de Janeiro)
Colombia Belém (Map p284; ☎ 0xx91-3246-5662;
Av Almirante 71, Apto 601, Bloco B); Manaus (☎ 0xx92-
3234-6777; Rua Dona Libânia 62); Rio de Janeiro
(Map pp288-9; ☎ 0xx21-2552-5048; Praia do Flamengo
284, No 101, Flamengo)
Ecuador (☎ 0xx21-2491-4113; Av das Americas 500,
Bldg 21, No 305, Barra da Tijuca, Rio de Janeiro)
Germany (☎ 0xx21-2554-0004; Rua Presidente Carlos
de Campos 417, Laranjeiras, Rio de Janeiro)
Ireland (☎ 0xx21-2501-8455; Rua 24 de Maio 347,
Riachuelo, Rio de Janeiro)
Israel (☎ 0xx21-2235-5588; Av NS de Copacabana 680,
Copacabana, Rio de Janeiro)
Netherlands (Map pp288-9; ☎ 0xx21-2157-5400; Praia
de Botafogo 242, 10th fl, Botafogo, Rio de Janeiro)
Paraguay (Map pp288-9; ☎ 0xx21-2553-2294; Praia de
Botafogo 242, 2nd fl, Botafogo, Rio de Janeiro)
Peru Manaus (☎ 0xx92-3236-5012; Rua HI 12, Morada
do Sol, Alexio); Rio de Janeiro (Map pp288-9; ☎ 0xx21-
2551-9596; Av Rui Barbosa 314, 2nd fl, Flamengo)
UK Belém (☎ 0xx91-3222-5074; Av Governador J Malcher
815 Ed Palladium Center); Manaus (☎ 0xx92-613-1819;
Rua Poraquê 240, Distrito Industrial); Rio de Janeiro
(Map pp288-9; ☎ 0xx21-2555-9603; Praia do Flamengo
284, 2nd fl, Flamengo)
Uruguay (Map pp288-9; ☎ 0xx21-2553-6030; Praia de
Botafogo 242, 6th fl, Botafogo, Rio de Janeiro)
US Belém (☎ 0xx91-3223-0800; Rua Oswaldo Cruz 165);
Manaus (☎ 0xx92-3633-4907; Rua Recife 1010, Adriano-
polis); Rio de Janeiro (Map p284; ☎ 0xx21-3823-2000; Av
Presidente Wilson 147, Centro)
Venezuela Belém (☎ 0xx91-3222-6396; Rua Presidente
Pernambuco 270); Manaus (☎ 0xx92-3233-6004; Ferreira
Pena 179); Rio de Janeiro (Map pp288-9; ☎ 0xx21-2554-
6134; Praia de Botafogo 242, 5th fl, Botafogo)

Brazilian Embassies & Consulates Abroad

Countries with Brazilian embassies and/or
consulates include the following:
Australia Embassy (☎ 02-6273-2372; http://brazil
.org.au; 19 Forster Cres, Yarralumla, Canberra ACT 2600);
consulate (☎ 02-9267-4414; www.brazilsydney.org;
Level 17, 31 Market St, Sydney NSW 2000)
Canada Embassy (☎ 613-237-1090; 450 Wilbrod St,
Ottawa, Ontario K1N 6M8); Montreal consulate (☎ 514-
499-0968); Toronto consulate (☎ 416-922-2503; www
.consbrastoronto.org; 77 Bloor Street West, Suite 1109 &
1105, Toronto, Ontario M5S 1M2)
France Embassy (☎ 01 45 61 63 00; www.bresil.org;
34 Cours Albert, 1er, 75008 Paris)
Germany Embassy (☎ 030-726280; www.brasilianische
-botschaft.de; Wallstrasse 57, 10179 Berlin-Mitte)

New Zealand Embassy (☎ 04-473-3516; 10 Brandon St,
Level 9, Wellington 1)
UK Embassy (☎ 020-7399-9000; www.brazil.org.uk; 32
Green St, London W1Y 4AT); consulate (☎ 020-7930-9055;
6 St Alban's St, London SW1Y 4SQ)
USA Embassy (☎ 202-238-2828; www.brasilemb.org;
3006 Massachusetts Ave NW, Washington, DC 20008);
Boston consulate (☎ 617-542-4000; www.consulatebrazil
.org; 20 Park Plaza, Suite 810, Boston, MA 02116); Chicago
consulate (☎ 312-464-0244; 401 North Michigan Ave,
Suite 3050, Chicago, IL 60611); Houston consulate (☎ 713-
961-3063; www.brazilhouston.org; 1233 West Loop South,
Park Tower North, Suite 1150, Houston, TX 77027); Los
Angeles consulate (☎ 323-651-2664; 8484 Wilshire Blvd,
Suites 711-730, Beverly Hills, CA 90211); Miami consulate
(☎ 305-285-6200; www.brazilmiami.org; 2601 South
Bayshore Drive, Suite 800, Miami, FL 33133); New York
consulate (☎ 917-777-7777; www.brazilny.org; 1185 6th
Ave, 21st Fl, New York, NY 10036); San Francisco consulate
(☎ 415-981-8170; www.brazilsf.org; 300 Montgomery St,
suite 900, San Francisco, CA 94104)

FESTIVALS & EVENTS

Festa de Iemanjá (Festival of Iemanjá) Celebrated in Rio
on January 1, and in Salvador on February 2.
Procissão do Senhor Bom Jesus dos Navegantes
Procession of the Lord Jesus of Boatmen. In Salvador, Bahia
on New Year's Day.
Lavagem do Bonfim (Washing of Bonfim church) Sec-
ond Thursday in January. A Candomblé festival culminating
in the ritual cleansing of Bonfim church in Salvador, Bahia.
Carnaval Friday to Tuesday preceding Ash Wednesday.
Carnaval celebrations usually start well before the official
holiday.
Semana Santa (Holy Week) The week before Easter.
Festival in Congonhas, Ouro Prêto, Goiás Velho.
Dia do Índio (Indian Day) April 19.
Festas Juninas (June Festivals) Throughout June.
Celebrated throughout in Rio state and much of the rest
of the country.
Boi-Bumbá June 28–30. Celebrated in Parintins,
Amazonas.
Bumba Meu Boi Late June to second week of August.
Festival in São Luís.
Fortal (out-of-season Carnaval) Last week of July.
Celebrated in Fortaleza.
Jubileu do Senhor Bom Jesus do Matosinhos
(Jubilee of the Savior of Matosinhos) September 7–14.
Celebrated in Congonhas.
Círio de Nazaré (Festival of the Virgin of Nazaré) Starts
second Sunday in October. Festival in Belém.
Carnatal (Carnaval in Natal) First week of December.
Natal's answer to Brazil's big celebration comes in
December (Natalese simply can't wait for the *other*
Carnaval).

FOOD & DRINK
Brazilian Cuisine

Brazilian restaurants serve huge portions, and many plates are designed for two. It's hard to go hungry, even on a modest budget. The basic Brazilian diet revolves around *arroz* (white rice), *feijão* (black beans) and *farinha* (flour from the root of manioc or cassava). The typical Brazilian meal, called *prato feito* (set meal, often abbreviated 'pf') or *refeição*, consists of these ingredients plus either meat, chicken or fish and costs US$3 to US$6 in most eateries.

Another good option are *por quilo* (per-kilogram) lunch buffets. Here, you pay by the weight of what you serve yourself: typically around US$12 per kilogram, with a big plateful weighing around half a kilo. Per-kilo places are good for vegetarians too. The fixed-price *rodízio* is another deal, and most *churrascarias* (meat BBQ restaurants) offer *rodízio* dining, where they bring endless skewers of different meat to your table.

In some restaurants frequented by tourists, overcharging and shortchanging are almost standard procedure. Check over your bill carefully.

There are regional differences in Brazilian cuisine. The *comida baiana* of the northeastern coast has a distinct African flavor, using peppers, spices and the potent oil of the *dendê* palm tree. Both the Pantanal and the Amazon region have some tasty varieties of fish. Rio Grande do Sul's *comida gaúcha* features much meat. Common Brazilian dishes include the following:

açaí (a·sa·ee) – an Amazonian fruit with a berrylike taste and deep purple color; frozen and ground up, it makes a great, sorbetlike dish to which you can add granola, ginseng, honey etc

acarajé (a·ka·ra·zhe) – *baianas* (Bahian women) traditionally sell this on street corners throughout Bahia; it's made from peeled brown beans, mashed in salt and onions, and then fried in *dendê* (palm) oil; inside is *vatapá*, dried shrimp, pepper and tomato sauce

barreado (ba·rre·a·do) – a mixture of meats and spices cooked in a clay pot for 24 hours, it's served with banana and *farofa*; it's the state dish of Paraná

bobó de camarão (bo·bo de ka·ma·rowng) – manioc paste cooked and flavored with dried shrimp, coconut milk and cashews

caldeirada (kow·day·ra·da) – stew with big chunks of fish, onions and tomato

carne do sol (kar·ne de sol) – tasty salted beef, grilled and served with beans, rice and vegetables

caruru (ka·roo·roo) – one of the most popular Afro-Brazilian dishes, this is prepared from okra or other vegetables cooked in water, plus onions, salt, shrimp, *malagueta* peppers, *dendê* oil and fish

casquinha de carangueijo/siri (kas·kee·nya de ka·rang·ge·zho/see·ree) – stuffed crab, prepared with manioc flour

cozido (ko·zee·do) – a stew usually made with many vegetables (eg potatoes, sweet potatoes, carrots and manioc)

dourado (do·raa·do) – scrumptious catfish found throughout Brazil.

farofa (fa·ro·fa) – manioc flour gently toasted and mixed with bits of onion or bacon; it's a common condiment

feijoada (fay·zho·a·da) – Brazil's national dish, this pork stew is served with rice and a bowl of beans, and is traditionally eaten for Saturday lunch. It goes well with caipirinhas

frango a passarinho (frang·go a pa·sa·ree·nyo) – small chunks of crisp fried chicken make a delicious *tira-gosto* (appetizer or snack)

moqueca (mo·ke·ka) – stew flavored with *dendê* oil and coconut milk, often with peppers and onions; the word also refers to a style of covered clay-pot cooking from Bahia: fish, shrimp, oyster, crab or a combination can all be done *moqueca*-style

pato no tucupi (pa·to no too·koo·pee) – very popular in Pará, this roast duck dish is flavored with garlic and cooked in the *tucupi* sauce made from the manioc juice and *jambu*, a local vegetable

peixada (pay·sha·da) – fish cooked in broth with vegetables and eggs

peixe a delícia (pay·she a de·lee·sya) – broiled or grilled fish, usually prepared with bananas and coconut milk

prato de verão (pra·to de ve·rowng) – literally 'summer plate,' basically a fruit salad – served at many juice bars in Rio

sanduíche (sang·doo·ee·she) – covers a multitude of inexpensive bites from the *X-tudo* (hamburger with everything) to *misto quente* (toasted ham-and-cheese sandwich); *sanduíches* are a mainstay of *lanchonetes* (snack bars)

tacacá (ta·ka·ka) – Indian dish made of dried shrimp cooked with pepper, *jambu*, manioc and much more

tucunaré (too ka na·ray) – tender, tasty Amazonian fish

tutu á mineira (too·too a mee·nay·ra) – black-bean *feijoada*, often served with *couve* (a type of kale). Typical of Minas Gerais

vatapá (va·ta·pa) – perhaps the most famous Brazilian dish of African origin, a seafood dish with a thick sauce made from manioc paste, coconut and *dendê* oil.

Drinks

The incredible variety of Brazilian fruits makes for some divine *sucos* (juices). Every town has plenty of juice bars, offering 30 or 40 different varieties at around US$1.50 for a good-sized glass.

Cafezinho (coffee), as typically drunk in Brazil, is strong, hot and sweet, usually served without milk. *Refrigerantes* (soft drinks) are found everywhere and are cheaper than bottled water. *Guaraná*, made from the fruit of an Amazonian plant, is about as popular as Coke. It's cold, carbonated and sweet, and the fruit has all sorts of supposedly marvelous properties, so you can tell yourself it's healthy too!

The two key alcoholic drinks in Brazil are *cachaça* (more politely called *pinga*), a high-proof sugarcane rum, and *cerveja* (beer). *Cachaça* ranges from excrementally raw to tolerably smooth, and is the basis of that celebrated Brazilian cocktail the caipirinha. Of the common beer brands, Antarctica and Brahma are generally the best. Chope (*shoh*-pee) is pale blond pilsener draft beer, and stands pretty much at the pinnacle of Brazilian civilization. Key phrase: '*Moço, mais um chope!*' (Waiter, another beer!).

GAY & LESBIAN TRAVELERS

Although gay characters have begun appearing on *novelas* (soap operas), mainstream Brazil is still homophobic. Machismo dominates and being out is difficult here. Rio has the best gay scene, though you'll find good gay bars in Salvador, São Paulo and elsewhere. These are all-welcome affairs attended by GLS (*Gays, Lesbians e Simpatizantes*) crowds of straights and gays. An excellent gay travel and excursions agency is **G Brazil** (☎ 0xx21-2247-4431; www.gbrazil.com; Rua Farme de Amoedo 76, No 303). Useful websites for gay and lesbian travelers are www.riogayguide.com and www.pridelinks .com/Regional/Brazil.

There is no law against homosexuality in Brazil. The age of consent is 18 years, the same as for heterosexuals.

HEALTH

A yellow-fever vaccination certificate is required for travelers who, within three months of arriving in Brazil (or applying for a Brazilian visa), have been in Bolivia, Colombia, Ecuador, French Guiana, Peru, Venezuela or any of about a dozen African countries. The list of countries can vary, so check with a Brazilian consulate. At most Brazilian borders and major airports there are vaccination posts where you can have the jab (free for foreigners) and get the certificate immediately. But it's wise to do this in advance.

Malaria is a concern in certain areas of the Amazon. Travelers should take an appropriate malaria preventative, such as mefloquine or doxycycline (chloroquine is inadequate here),

and cover up as much as possible to prevent mosquito bites (dengue, for which there is no medication, is also prevalent).

Tap water is safe but not very tasty in most urban areas. In remote areas, filter your own or stick to bottled water.

The sun is powerful here, and travelers should be mindful of heatstroke, dehydration and sunburn. Drink plenty of water, wear a strong sunscreen and allow your body time to acclimatize to high temperatures before attempting strenuous activities. A good drink when dehydrated is *agua de coco* (coconut water), which contains electrolytes.

See p1090 for more information.

HOLIDAYS

Brazil's high season runs from December until Carnaval (usually February). Low season runs from March to November.

Ano Novo (New Year's Day) January 1
Carnaval (Friday to Tuesday preceding Ash Wednesday) February/March. Carnaval celebrations usually start well before the official holiday.
Paixão & Páscoa (Good Friday & Easter Sunday) Dates vary, March/April
Tiradentes (Tiradentes Day) April 21
Dia do Trabalho (May Day/Labor Day) May 1
Corpus Christi (60 days after Easter) Sunday May/June
Dia da Independência (Independence Day) September 7
Dia da Nossa Senhora de Aparecida (Day of Our Lady of Aparecida) October 12
Finados (All Souls' Day) November 2
Proclamação da República (Proclamation of the Republic Day) November 15
Natal (Christmas Day) December 25

INTERNET ACCESS

Internet cafés are widespread in Brazil. Charges are about US$2 to US$3 an hour.

INTERNET RESOURCES

Brazil Max (www.brazilmax.com) This nicely designed site has features on travel, culture and society in Brazil; decent selection of articles and links.
Brazilian embassy in London (www.brazil.org.uk) Has much practical info for tourists and links to local tourism sites in Brazil.
Brazil (www.brazzil.com) Features in-depth articles on the country's politics, economy, literature, arts and culture.
Terra (www.terra.com.br/turismo in Portuguese) Portuguese-language travel site with up-to-date info on entertainment, nightlife and dining options in dozens of cities around Brazil.

University of Texas (lanic.utexas.edu/la/brazil) An extensive collection of Brazil links.

LANGUAGE

Portuguese is one of the world's top 10 most spoken languages. Brazilian Portuguese has a few differences from European Portuguese, but speakers can understand one another. This is not the case with Spanish. If you can speak Spanish, you'll be able to read some Portuguese, but comprehending others is difficult. Some Brazilians also find it a tad offensive when foreigners arrive speaking Spanish and expecting to be understood.

LEGAL MATTERS

Be wary of (but of course respectful to) Brazilian police. Some allegedly plant drugs and sting gringos for bribes.

Stiff penalties are in force for use and possession of drugs; the police don't share most Brazilians' tolerant attitude toward marijuana. Police checkpoints along the highways stop cars at random. Police along the coastal drive between São Paulo and Búzios are notorious for hassling young people and foreigners. Border areas are also dangerous.

A large amount of cocaine is smuggled out of Bolivia and Peru through Brazil. If you're entering Brazil from one of the Andean countries and have been chewing coca leaves, be careful to clean out your pack first.

MAPS

The best maps in Brazil are the Quatro Rodas series. These good regional maps (Norte, Nordeste etc) sell for around US$5; they also publish the *Atlas Rodoviário* road atlas, useful if you're driving, as well as excellent street atlases for the main cities.

Good topographical maps are published by the IBGE, the government geographical service, and the DSG, the army geographical service. Availability is erratic, but IBGE offices in most state capitals sell IBGE maps. Office locations can be found on the IBGE website (www.ibge.gov.br).

Telephone directories in many states include city maps.

MEDIA
Newspapers & Magazines

The weekly Portuguese-language *Veja* is a current-affairs magazine modeled on *Time*. In seven or eight major cities it comes with *Ve-*

jinha, a good pullout guide to the local music, arts and nightclub scene. The *Folha de São Paulo* and Rio's *Jornal do Brasil* newspapers have good national coverage and a socially liberal stance. *O Estado de São Paulo* and Rio's *O Globo* are a little more comprehensive in their coverage and more right wing.

English-language publications *Newsweek* and the daily *International Herald Tribune* are widely available. European and US newspapers are sold at some newsstands in tourist and business areas of Rio and São Paulo, but they are expensive.

TV

Brazilian TV consists mostly of game shows, football matches, bad American films dubbed into Portuguese and the universally watched *novelas* (soap operas). Globo is the major Brazilian network. Better hotels have cable TV with CNN and other English-language programs.

MONEY

Brazil's currency is the real (pronounced hay-*ow*; often written R$); the plural is reais (pronounced hay-*ice*). One real is made up of 100 centavos. Banknotes come in different colors and have a different animal on the back in denominations of 1 (sapphire-spangled emerald hummingbird), 2 (hawksbill turtle), 5 (great egret), 10 (greenwing macaw), 20 (golden lion tamarin), 50 (jaguar) and 100 (dusky grouper).

ATMs

ATMs are the easiest way of getting cash in big cities and are widely available. In some smaller towns, ATMs exist but rarely work for non-Brazilian cards. Make sure you have a four-digit PIN. In general HSBC, Banco de Brasil, Bradesco and Banco 24 Horas are the best ATMs to try. Look for stickers on the machines that say Cirrus, Visa or whatever system your card uses.

Bargaining

A little bargaining for hotel rooms is standard. On unmetered cab rides, arrange the fare before departing.

Credit Cards

You can use credit cards to pay for many purchases in Brazil and to make cash withdrawals from ATMs and at banks. Visa is the most commonly accepted card, followed by

MasterCard. American Express and Diners Club cards are also useful. Visa cash advances are widely available, even in small towns that have no other currency exchange facilities, but the process can be quite time consuming. Credit-card fraud is widespread here. Keep your card in sight at all times, especially in restaurants.

Exchanging Money

Cash and traveler's checks, in US dollars, can be exchanged in *casas de cambio* (exchange offices) or banks, which give better exchange rates but are much slower (Banco do Brasil charges US$20 commission for every traveler's check transaction). You'll usually get a 1% or 2% better exchange rate for cash than for traveler's checks.

Exchange rates at press time included the following:

Country	Unit		R$ (reais)
Australia	A$1	=	1.61
Canada	C$1	=	1.9
euro zone	€1	=	2.7
Japan	¥100	=	1.8
New Zealand	NZ$1	=	1.4
United Kingdom	UK£1	=	4
United States	US$1	=	2.2

Traveler's Checks

Traveler's checks can be exchanged at major banks and exchange offices. The rates are generally better at banks – except for the Banco do Brasil, which charges a US$20 commission for every traveler's check transaction – though the slower, bureaucratic procedures make it a hassle. *Casas de câmbio* (exchange houses) are speedy and reliable, though the rates are lower. The most widely recognized traveler's check in Brazil is American Express.

POST

A postcard or letter weighing up to 20g costs around US$1 to foreign destinations. Airmail letters to the USA and Europe arrive in one to two weeks. The *posta-restante* system functions reasonably well. Post offices hold mail for 30 days.

RESPONSIBLE TRAVEL

Most places you'll go in Brazil welcome tourism, but be sensitive to local ways of doing things.

As for Brazil's environment, we all have an obligation to protect it. You can do your bit by using environmentally friendly tourism services wherever possible. Using the services of local community groups – as guides, hosts, artisans or whatever – ensures that your money goes directly to those helping you, as does buying crafts and other products directly from the artisans or from their trusted representatives.

SHOPPING

CDs, local crafts (indigenous and otherwise) and artwork all make good souvenirs.

Air-conditioned shopping malls (*shoppings*) feature in every self-respecting city and often contain decent music stores. Browsing the many markets and small streetside stalls yields, for better or worse, less predictable results. Street stalls sell bootleg CDs for around US$4, against about US$10 to US$20 for the official releases in stores.

For genuine Indian arts and crafts, have a look in the Artíndia stores of Funai (the government Indian agency) and museum gift shops.

Artisans in the northeast produce a rich assortment of artistic items. Salvador and nearby Cachoeira are most notable for their rough-hewn wood sculptures. Ceará specializes in fine lace. The interior of Pernambuco, in particular Caruaru, is famous for wildly imaginative ceramic figurines.

Candomblé stores are a good source of curios, ranging from magical incense guaranteed to increase sexual allure, wisdom and health, to amulets and ceramic figurines of Afro-Brazilian gods.

STUDYING

It's easy but pricey to arrange Portuguese classes through branches of the IBEU (Instituto Brasil Estados Unidos), where Brazilians go to learn English. There will be one in every large city. For more on language schools, try the **National Registration Center for Study Abroad** (www.nrcsa.com) or the website www.onestoplanguage.net.

TELEPHONE
Domestic Calls

You can make domestic calls from normal card-pay telephones on the street and in telephone offices. The cards cost around US$3 per 30 units from vendors, newsstands and anywhere else advertising *cartões telefônicos*. Cards for more units are also available.

Local calls (within the city you're in) cost only a few units. Just dial the number without any area code. To make a local collect call, dial ☎ 9090, then the number.

For calls to other cities, dial ☎ 0, then the code of your selected long-distance carrier, then the two digits representing the city, followed by the local number. You need to choose a long-distance carrier that covers both the place you are calling from and the place you're calling to. Carriers advertise their codes in areas where they're prominent, but you can usually use Embratel (code 21), Intelig (code 23) or Telemar (code 31) as they cover the whole country.

City codes are thus usually given in the format '0xx digit digit', with the two x's representing the carrier code. As an example, to call from Rio de Janeiro to the number ☎ 3219-3345 in Fortaleza (city code ☎ 0xx85) in the state of Ceará, you dial ☎ 0 followed by 21 or 23 or 31 or 85 (the codes of the four carriers that cover both Rio and Ceará), followed by 85 for Fortaleza, followed by the number 3219-3345.

A long-distance call usually eats up five to 10 phonecard units per minute.

To make an intercity collect call, dial ☎ 9 before the 0xx. A recorded message in Portuguese will ask you to say your name and where you're calling from, after the tone.

International Calls

Brazil's country code is ☎ 55. When calling internationally to Brazil, omit the initial 0xx of the area code.

International calls from Brazil cost at least US$1 a minute to the USA or Canada and US$2 a minute to Europe or Australia (20% less between 8pm and 6am daily and all day Sunday).

The regular card-pay telephones found on the streets are of little use for international calls unless you have an international calling card or are calling collect. Most pay telephones are restricted to domestic calls, and even if they aren't, a 30-unit Brazilian phonecard may last less than a minute internationally.

Without an international calling card, your best option is to find a call center or telephone office, where you pay in cash after you finish talking. Many internet cafés now offer phone services. Calls from a hotel usually cost much more.

For international *a cobrar* (collect) calls, dial ☎ 000107 from any phone. This only works to some countries. Alternatively, you can get a Brazilian international operator by dialing ☎ 000111 or ☎ 0800-703-2121. Failing that, you need to locate a phone that handles international calls. Home Country Direct services get you through to an operator in the country you're calling, and will connect the collect call for you. For most Home Country Direct services, dial ☎ 00080 followed by the country code (for North America, ☎ 10 for AT&T, ☎ 16 for Sprint; for Australia, dial ☎ 00080061).

Cell Phones

Celular (mobile) phones have eight-digit numbers starting with a 9, and calls to them run through your phonecard units much faster than calls to regular numbers. Mobiles have city codes like normal phone numbers, and if you're calling from another city you have to use them.

TOILETS

Public toilets are available at every bus station and airport; there's usually a small entrance fee of US50¢ or so. Elsewhere public toilets are not common, though Brazilians are generally nice about letting you use facilities in restaurants and bars. As in other Latin American countries, toilet paper isn't flushed but placed in the smelly basket next to the toilet. Few of the country's bathrooms are wheelchair-accessible.

TOURIST INFORMATION

Tourist offices in Brazil are nearly all run by individual states or municipalities, and may be quite helpful or utterly useless depending upon who's behind the counter.

Brazilian consulates and embassies can provide limited tourist information.

TRAVELERS WITH DISABILITIES

Unfortunately, disabled travelers don't have an easy time in Brazil. Rio de Janeiro is probably the most accessible city for disabled travelers. The streets and sidewalks along the main beaches have curb cuts and are wheelchair-accessible, but most other areas do not have cuts and many restaurants have entrance steps.

There is one Brazilian travel agency in São Paulo specializing in travel for persons with disabilities: **Fack Tour** (☎ 0xx11-4335-7662; facktour@originet.com.br).

VISAS
See p403 for details of required yellow-fever vaccinations.

Citizens of the US, Australia, Canada and New Zealand need a visa; citizens from the UK, France and Germany do not.

Tourist visas are valid for arrival in Brazil within 90 days of issue and then for a 90-day stay. The fee depends on your nationality and where you are applying; it's usually between US$40 and US$60, though for US citizens visas cost a whopping US$100. In many Brazilian embassies and consulates it takes only a couple of hours (or less) to issue a visa if you go in person. You'll generally need to present one passport photograph and a round-trip or onward ticket (or a photocopy of it or a statement from a travel agent that you have it) and, of course, a valid passport.

People under 18 years of age who wish to travel to Brazil without a parent or legal guardian must have a notarized letter of authorization from the nontraveling parent(s)/guardian(s), or from a court. Such a letter must also be presented when applying for a visa, if one is required. Check with a Brazilian consulate well in advance about this.

If you decide to return to Brazil, your visa is valid for five years.

Visa Extensions
These are handled by Brazil's Polícia Federal, who have offices in the state capitals and border towns. You must apply before your entry/exit card or visa lapses, and don't leave it until the last minute. When you go, dress nicely! Some Fed stations don't take kindly to people in shorts. Granting an extension seems to be pretty automatic, but they may ask to see a ticket out of the country and proof of sufficient funds; and sometimes they may not give you the full 90 days. If you get the maximum 90-day extension and then leave the country before the end of that period, you cannot return until the full 90 days have elapsed.

Entry/Exit Card
On entering Brazil, all tourists must fill out a *cartão de entrada/saida* (entry/exit card); immigration officials keep half, you keep the other. Don't lose this card! When you leave Brazil, the second half of the entry/exit card will be taken by immigration officials. If you don't have it, you'll have to pay a lofty fine (around US$75) at the Banco do Brasil, which may be far from your intended departure point. The bank will then give you a form to give to immigration officials when you leave the country. Most visitors can stay for 90 days, but if for some reason you receive fewer days, this will be written in the stamp in your passport.

VOLUNTEERING
One excellent volunteer organization you can get involved with is Rio-based **Iko Poran** (☎ 0xx21-2205-1365; www.ikoporan.org), which links the diverse talents of volunteers with needy organizations. Previous volunteers in Brazil have worked as dance, music, art and language instructors among other things. Iko Poran also provides housing for volunteers. It has plans to create volunteer opportunities in Salvador, Praia do Forte and Santarem. The UK-based **Task Brasil** (www.taskbrasil.org.uk) is another laudable organization that places volunteers in Rio. Here, you'll have to make arrangements in advance and pay a fee that will go toward Task Brasil projects and your expenses as a volunteer.

The best website for browsing volunteer opportunities is **Action Without Borders** (www.idealist.org).

A little doorknocking can help you find volunteer work in Brazil. There's plenty of need, and many local welfare organizations will gladly find you some rewarding work. Ask around at churches and community centers.

WOMEN TRAVELERS
In the cities of the southeast and South, foreign women without traveling companions will scarcely be given a sideways glance. In the more traditional rural areas of the northeast, blonde-haired and light-skinned women, especially those without male escorts, will certainly arouse curiosity.

Machismo is less overt in Brazil than in Spanish-speaking Latin America. Flirtation is a common form of communication, but it's generally regarded as innocent banter; no sense of insult, exploitation or serious intent should be assumed.

It's advisable to adapt what you wear to local norms. The brevity of Rio beach attire

BRAZIL

generally is not suitable for the streets of interior cities, for instance.

In the event of unwanted pregnancy or the risk thereof, most pharmacies in Brazil stock the morning-after pill (*a pilula do dia seguinte*), which costs about US$10. Tampons and other sanitary items are widely available in most pharmacies, though you'll want to stock up before heading into rural areas.

WORKING

Brazil has high unemployment and tourists are not supposed to take jobs. However, it's not unusual for foreigners to find language-teaching work in the bigger cities, either in language schools or through private tutoring. The pay is not great (around US$13 an hour), but if you can work for three or four days a week you can live on it.

Chile

HIGHLIGHTS

- **Torres del Paine** – explore the glacial lakes and rugged spires above the howling Patagonian steppe (p524)
- **Central Valley** – carve tracks on Portillo's steep slopes or Valle Nevado's vast tracts of open terrain (p432)
- **Valparaíso** – meander the hills of Neruda's pet city, the bohemian heart of Chile (p433)
- **Atacama Desert** – journey through the stark landscapes of fumaroles, salt mountains and adobe villages in the driest desert in the world (p455)
- **Off the beaten track** – cowboy into the remote pioneer heartland in the turquoise river valleys around Cochamó, Coyhaique and Palena (p516)
- **Best journey** – trek around springy grasslands and flamingo-filled lagoons under the snowcapped domes of Parque Nacional Lauca (p468)

FAST FACTS

- **Area:** 748,800 sq km land, 8150 sq km water, 6435km of coastline
- **Best bargain:** a bottle of Missiones de Rengo Carmenere US$3.50
- **Best street snack:** dare we say? *Un completo:* a hotdog smothered in guacamole, mayo & tomatoes (US$1.50)
- **Budget:** US$35-40 a day
- **Capital:** Santiago
- **Costs:** *hospedaje* (budget accommodations with shared bathroom) with breakfast US$10-12, set lunch US$6, national park entrance free-US$17
- **Country code:** ☎ 56
- **Famous for:** politics, *pisco* (brandylike liquor; the national drink) & Patagonian peaks
- **Languages:** Spanish, Mapudungun, Rapanui
- **Money:** US$1 = 527 pesos
- **Phrases:** *chorro, bacán* (cool), *asco* (disgusting), *copete* (cocktail)
- **Population:** 16 million
- **Time:** GMT minus 4hr (minus 3hr in summer)
- **Tipping:** 10% in better restaurants; tip all guides
- **Visas:** North American, Australian & most European citizens need only a valid passport

TRAVEL HINTS

Travel with small bills. Order the *menú del día* special instead of off the menu. Allow for extra travel time in rural Patagonia, where infrequent transportation can strand you in towns a day or two.

OVERLAND ROUTES

Crossings include Tacna (Peru); Ollagüe and Colchane (Bolivia); and Paso Jama, Puente del Inca, San Martín de los Andes, Junín de los Andes, Villa La Angostura, Trevelin, Los Antiguos, Río Turbio and Río Gallegos (Argentina).

CHILE

Spindly Chile stretches 4300km – over half the continent – from the driest desert in the world to massive glacial fields. A mosaic of volcanoes, geysers, beaches, lakes, rivers, steppe and countless islands fill up the in-between. Slenderness gives Chile the intimacy of a backyard (albeit one fenced between the Andes and the Pacific). What's on offer? Everything. With easy infrastructure, spectacular sights and the most hospitable hosts around, the hardest part is choosing an itinerary. Seek out its sweeping desert solitude, craggy Andean summits and the lush forests of the fjords for a sample. The mystical Easter Island or isolated Isla Robinson Crusoe offer extra-continental exploits. But don't forget that Chile is as much about character as it is setting. Its far-flung location fires the imagination and has been known to make poets out of barmen, dreamers out of presidents and friends out of strangers. A few wrong turns and detours and you too will be part of this tightly woven family who barbecues on Sunday. Don't forget to bring an extra bottle of red to the long, lazy dinners that await.

CURRENT EVENTS

Who would have thought that Chile would elect a woman president? These words were socialist Michelle Bachelet's own as she joined the growing ranks of left-leaning leaders on the continent. Clearly in retribution mode, Chile is still working on prosecuting former dictator General Augusto Pinochet for his involvement in disappearances during his regime. These charges come on top of others of tax evasion and corruption relating to some 27 million dollars he kept overseas under assumed names. While Chile sprints up world development ratings (now 37th), poised to become Latin America's first first-world nation, its probusiness stance threatens to make the environment its sacrificial lamb with unchecked paper-mill contamination in Valdivia, the proposal to move a glacier for the Pascua Lama mining project, and megadam projects threatening southern Chile's most pristine waterways.

HISTORY
Early History

The discovery of a single 12,500-year-old footprint in Monte Verde, near Puerto Montt, marks Chile's earliest tangible roots. In the north, Aymara and Atacameño farmers and herders predated the Inca. Other early peoples include the El Molle and the Tiwanaku, who left their mark with geoglyphs; Chango fisherfolk on the northern coast; and Diaguita who inhabited inland river valleys.

The Mapuche, who were shifting cultivators of the southern forests, were the only indigenous group to successfully hold off Inca domination. Meanwhile the Cunco fished and farmed Chiloé and the mainland. In the south, groups such as Selk'nam and Yagan long avoided contact with Europeans, who would eventually bring them to the brink of extinction.

Colonial Times

Conquistador Pedro de Valdivia and his men crossed the harsh Atacama desert to found Santiago in the fertile Mapocho valley in 1541. They set up the famous *encomiendas:* forced labor systems that exploited the north's relatively large, sedentary population. In the south there was no such assimilation – the Mapuche fought European colonization for over three centuries. When the *encomiendas* lost value, agricultural *haciendas* or *fundos* (farms), run by American-born Spanish took their place. These *latifundios* (estates), many remaining intact into the 1960s, became the dominant force in Chilean society.

Revolutionary Wars & the Early Republic

Spain's trade control over the Viceroy of Peru provoked discontent among the *criollo* (American-born Spaniards). With independence movements sweeping the country, it was actually an Argentine, José de San Martín, who liberated Santiago in 1818. Under San Martín's tutelage, Chilean Bernardo O'Higgins, the illegitimate son of an Irishman, became 'supreme director' of the Chilean republic.

O'Higgins dominated politics for five years after independence, decreeing political, social, religious and educational reforms, but landowners' objections to his egalitarian measures forced his resignation. Businessman Diego Portales, spokesman for landowners, became de facto dictator until his execution in 1837. His custom-drawn constitution centralized power in Santiago and established Catholicism as the state religion.

CHILE (NORTH)

Expansion & Development

At independence Chile was small, but triumphed over Peru and Bolivia in the War of the Pacific (1879–83) and treaties with the Mapuche placed the nitrate-rich Atacama Desert and the southern Lakes District under Chilean rule. Chile also annexed remote Rapa Nui (Easter Island) in 1888.

British, North American and German capital turned the Atacama into a bonanza, as nitrates brought some prosperity and funded the government. The nitrate ports of Antofagasta and Iquique grew rapidly until the Panama Canal (1914) reduced traffic around Cape Horn and the development of petroleum-based fertilizers made mineral nitrates obsolete.

Mining also created a new working class and a class of nouveau riche, both of whom challenged the landowners. Elected in 1886, President José Manuel Balmaceda tackled the dilemma of unequally distributed wealth and power, igniting congressional rebellion in 1890 and a civil war that resulted in 10,000 deaths, including his own suicide.

20th-Century Developments

As late as the 1920s, up to 75% of Chile's rural population still lived on *latifundios,* holding 80% of prime agricultural land. As industry expanded and public works advanced, urban workers' welfare improved, but that of rural workers declined, forcing day laborers to the cities.

The 1930s to 1960s saw a multifaceted struggle for agrarian reform. During this time North American companies gained control of copper mines that were to become the cornerstone of Chile's economy. Reformist Eduardo Frei became president in 1964. Opportunistically attacking the US-dominated export sector, Frei advocated 'Chileanization' of the copper industry, in which the government took just over 50% ownership of the mines that were controlled by US companies.

Considered too reformist by the right and too conservative by the left, Frei's Christian Democratic administration faced many challenges, including from violent groups like MIR (the Leftist Revolutionary Movement), which found support among coal miners, textile workers and other urban laborers, and also agitated for land reform. As the 1970 election grew near, the Christian Democratic Party, unable to satisfy society's expectations for reform, grew weaker.

Allende Comes to Power

Socialist candidate Salvador Allende's Unidad Popular (Popular Unity or UP) coalition offered a radical program advocating nationalization of industry and expropriation of *latifundios.* Elected in 1970 by a small margin, Allende began instituting state control of many private enterprises alongside massive income redistribution. Politics grew more confrontational as peasants, frustrated with the slow pace of agrarian reforms, seized land. Harvests declined, and expropriation of copper mines and other enterprises, plus conspicuously friendly relations with Cuba, provoked US hostility. By 1972 Chile was paralyzed by strikes, supported by the Christian Democrats and the National Party.

A military coup in June 1973 failed but opposition gathered force. Relative unknown General Augusto Pinochet exacted a *golpe de estado* (coup d'état) on September 11, 1973, overthrowing the UP government and resulting in Allende's death (an apparent suicide) and the death of thousands of Allende supporters. Police and the military apprehended thousands of leftists, suspected leftists and sympathizers. Many were herded into Santiago's National Stadium, where they suffered beatings, torture and even execution. Hundreds of thousands went into exile.

Pinochet's Dictatorship & Legacy

Many opposition leaders, some of whom had encouraged the coup, expected a quick return to civilian government, but General Pinochet had other ideas. From 1973 to 1989, he headed a durable junta that dissolved Congress, banned leftist parties and suspended all others, prohibited nearly all political activity and ruled by decree. The Caravan of Death killed many political opponents, many of whom had voluntarily turned themselves in. Detainees came from all sectors of society, from peasants to professors. Thousands were 'disappeared' during the 17-year regime.

In 1980 Pinochet submitted a new, customized constitution to the electorate which ratified his presidency until 1989. It passed though many voters abstained in protest. Though Pinochet had put Chile's economy on track and established a lasting stability, voters rejected his 1988 bid to extend his presidency until 1997. In 1989, 17 parties formed the coalition Concertación para la Democracia (Consensus for Democracy) and its candidate Patricio Aylwin easily won. Aylwin's presidency was limited by constraints of the new constitution, but it did see the publication of the Rettig report, documenting deaths and disappearances during the dictatorship.

An international uproar exploded when General Pinochet was arrested and kept under house arrest in London in September 1998 following Spanish judge Báltazar Garzón's investigation of the deaths and disappearances of Spanish citizens in the aftermath of the 1973 coup. Both the Court of Appeals (in 2000) and the Supreme Court (2002) concluded that he suffered from dementia and ruled him unfit to stand trial. Pinochet returned to Chile but lost his status as lifetime senator. Despite the intense legal activity which continues, many Chileans are doubtful that Pinochet, now in his 90s, will ever reach trial.

The International Stage

In 2000 moderate leftist Ricardo Lagos joined a growing breed of left-leaning governments elected across South America. The country recovered from a troubled period between 2001 and 2003 to become the brightest economic star of Latin America, boosted by record prices for its key export, copper. Public and foreign debt is low, foreign investment is up, and the government has been busily signing free-trade agreements, notably with the EU and North America.

Now ranked as the world's 37th most developed country, Chile's healthcare has improved, life expectancy is up, education has increased by 25% and poverty has been halved since 1990. Socially Chile is rapidly shedding much of its traditional conservatism. A divorce law was finally passed in 2004 and the death penalty was abolished in 2001. The arts and free press are once again flourishing and women's rights are being increasingly recognized in law.

The 2005 election of Michelle Bachelet, former Minister of Defense under Lagos, was a watershed event. Not only because she is a woman, but she represents everything which Chile superficially is not: an agnostic, socialist single mother. Her father was an Air Force general who died under the hands of Pinochet's forces; she was also detained and tortured but released, and lived in exile abroad. A former doctor, Bachelet's skill as a consensus builder has helped her heal old wounds with the military and the public. Most feel that she represents a continuum of the policies of Lagos and only has to not 'mess up' Chile's already strong economy. But there is no denying that her presence speaks volumes about a country that is open to change.

CHILE (SOUTH)

THE CULTURE
The National Psyche

Chile is going through a period of radical social change. This former 'island' between the Andes and the sea has been flooded with outside influence. At the same time Chile is intrinsically starting to second-guess the conformity instilled under the dictatorship and Catholic Church. This isn't easy; notoriously diplomatic and polite, Chileans shy away from controversies.

Lifestyle

Travelers crossing over from Peru or Bolivia may wonder where the stereotypical 'South America' went. Chilean lifestyle superficially resembles its European counterparts. The well-off live quite comfortably, often with maid service and a nanny, while the poorest eke out a hand-to-mouth existence. These disparate income gaps translate to class consciousness. The average Chilean focuses energy on family, home and work. Chileans usually remain dependent on their parents through university years and live at home until marriage. Independence isn't nearly as valued as family unity and togetherness. Regardless, single motherhood is not uncommon. Divorce was legalized recently but informal separations had been the norm. Women, while underrepresented in the workforce, are respected as professionals. For gays and lesbians, Chile is still quite a conservative culture. While not aggressively antigay, Chile offers little public support for alternate lifestyles. Adults dress conservatively, leaning toward business formal, and their initial regard toward you will depend on your appearance.

Population

About 75% of Chile's population occupies just 20% of its total area, in the main agricultural region of Middle Chile. This region includes Gran Santiago (the capital and its suburbs), where over a third of the country's estimated 16 million people reside. More than 85% of Chileans live in cities.

While most of the population is of Spanish ancestry mixed with indigenous groups, immigration waves added British, Irish, French, Italians, Croatians and Palestinians to the mix. German colonists settled the Lakes District starting in 1852. The northern Andes are home to around 69,200 Aymara and Atacameño

CHILE

peoples. Mapuche number around 620,000, based largely in La Araucanía. Chilean law may restrict immigration to Easter Island in a move to preserve the culture of its 3800 Rapa Nuians. In Tierra del Fuego there remains one Yagan who is in her 70s.

SPORTS
Fútbol (soccer) rules the hearts of all Chileans. In rural Patagonia teams will travel a full day on horseback to play a Sunday match. The main teams are Santiago-based Colo Colo, Universidad de Chile (populist) and Universidad Católica (elitist). Tennis is wildly popular, thanks to Nicolás Massú and Fernando Gonzáles' medals in the 2004 Athens Olympics – Chile's first gold ever. They come on the heels of Marcelo 'El Chino' Rios, who rose quickly in the ranks of tennis stars. Chilean rodeos proliferate in the summer when, from Santiago to deep Patagonia, elegant *huasos* (cowboys) perform quick skills in a *medialuna* (half-moon stadium).

RELIGION
About 90% of Chileans are Catholic, with Evangelical Protestantism covering most of the rest of the population.

ARTS
Cinema
Chilean cinema is undergoing a renaissance, relishing the freedom to narrate uncut tales, the themes of which range from social conscience to goofy sex. Twenty-something director Nicolás López uses dark humor and comic-book culture to the delight of youth audiences with *Promedio Rojo* (2005). *Mi Mejor Enemigo* (My Best Enemy, 2004) is a wonderfully told tale of not-so-distant enemies, set in Patagonia during a 1978 territorial dispute with Argentina (coproduced with Argentina and Spain). Andrés Wood's hit *Machuca* (2004) chronicles coming-of-age during class-conscious and volatile 1973. Wood's *La Fiebre del Loco* (Loco Fever, 2001) shows the social folly of a small Patagonian fishing village during abalone harvest. *Sub Terra* (2003) dramatizes the exploitation of Chilean miners. *Taxi Para Tres* (Taxi for Three, 2001), by Orlando Lubbert, and Diego Izquierdo's *Sexo con Amor* (Sex with Love, 2002) are worth a look. Acclaimed documentarist Patricio Guzmán focuses on the social impact of the dictatorship; his credits include the fascinating

Obstinate Memory (1997). Check out Chile's latest releases at www.chilecine.cl.

Literature
This land of poets earned its repute with Nobel Prize winners Gabriela Mistral and Pablo Neruda. Vicente Huidobro is considered one of the founders of modern Spanish-language poetry and Nicanor Parra continues the tradition.

Popular contemporary writer Isabel Allende bases much of her fiction in her native Chile, although along with playwright-novelist-essayist Ariel Dorfman, she lives in the USA. Other important literary figures include José Donoso, whose novel *Curfew* narrates life under dictatorship through the eyes of a returned exile, and Antonio Skármeta, who wrote the novel *Burning Patience*, upon which the award-winning Italian film *Il Postino* (The Postman) is based. Jorge Edwards (1931–) was a collaborator and contemporary of Neruda, writing the acclaimed tribute *Goodbye, Poet*. Luis Sepúlveda (1949–) is one of Chile's most prolific writers, with such books as *Patagonia Express* and the novella *The Old Man Who Read Love Stories*.

Marcela Serrano (1951–) is considered to be one of the best Latina authors in the last decade. Pedro Lemebel (1950–) writes of homosexuality, transgender issues and other controversial subjects with top-notch shock value. The posthumous publication of Roberto Bolaño's (1955–2005) encyclopedic *2666* (set to be released in waves) seals his cult-hero status. Alberto Fuguet's (1964–) *Mala Onda* (Bad Vibes) launched the McOndo movement, which claimed (to the horror of academics) that Latin American magic-realism was dead, presenting the disconnected reality of urban youth in consumer culture in its place.

Music & Dance
Chile's contemporary music spans the revolutionary folk of the 1960s and '70s to Andean folklore, modern rock and alt bands. Folk movement La Nueva Canción Chilena (New Chilean Song) lyricized about the social hopes and political issues, synthesized in Violeta Parra's 'Gracias a la Vida' (Thanks to Life). The movement included Victor Jara (later murdered in the military coup) and groups Quilapayún and Inti-Illimani.

Music groups in exile found success in Europe, such as Paris-based Los Jaivas, Los

Prisioneros and La Ley (based in Mexico). Joe Vasconcellos performs energetic Latin fusion. Contemporary bands grabbing domestic and international attention are La Ley, Lucybell, Tiro de Gracia, Los Bunkers, Javiera y los Imposibles and Mamma Soul. Bars are excellent venues for new bands of all stripes. Jazz enjoys an upsurge while Reggaton (Spanish-language reggae) dominates the dance floor.

The only 'traditional' Chilean dance is *cueca*. Dancers encircle each other, each teasingly twirling a bandana above their head or out of sight.

ENVIRONMENT
The Land
Continental Chile stretches 4300km from Peru to the Straits of Magellan. Less than 200km wide on average, the land rises from sea level to above 6000m in some areas, with a narrow depression running through the middle.

Mainland Chile, dry-topped and glacial heavy, has distinct temperate and geographic zones, with the length of the Andes running alongside. Norte Grande runs from the Peruvian border to Chañaral, dominated by the Atacama Desert and the *altiplano* (Andean high plain). Norte Chico stretches from Chañaral to Río Aconcagua, with scrubland and denser forest enjoying increased rainfall. Here mining gives way to agriculture in the major river valleys.

Middle Chile's wide river valleys span from Río Aconcagua to Concepción and the Río Biobío. This is the main agricultural and wine-growing region. The Araucania and Lakes District go south of the Biobío to Puerto Montt, featuring extensive native forests, snowcapped volcanoes and lakes. Chiloé is the country's largest island, with dense forests and a patchwork of pasturelands. On the mainland, famed Patagonia has indeterminate borders: for some it begins with the Carretera Austral, for others it starts in rugged Aisén, running south to the Campos de Hielo (the continental ice fields), and ending in Magallanes and Tierra del Fuego.

The country is divided into 13 numbered administrative regions: I Tarapacá, II Antofagasta, III Atacama, IV Coquimbo, V Valparaíso (including Rapa Nui and Archipiélago Juan Fernández), Región Metropolitana (not numbered), VI Libertador General Bernardo O'Higgins, VII Maule, VIII Biobío, IX La Araucanía, X Los Lagos, XI Aisén del General Carlos Ibáñez del Campo and XII Magallanes y Antártica Chilena.

Wildlife
Bounded by ocean, desert and mountain, Chile is home to a unique environment that developed much on its own, creating a number of endemic species.

Within the desert reaches of the north, candelabria cacti grow, spaced well apart for *camanchaca* (fog) absorption. Guanaco (a large camelid), *vicuña* (wild relative of the domestic llama and alpaca, found only at high altitudes in the south-central Andes), llama and alpaca (as well as the ostrichlike rhea, called *ñandú* in Spanish) and the vizcacha (a wild relative of the chinchilla) live here, as well as a variety of birdlife, from Andean gulls and giant coots to three species of flamingo.

The south has protected forests of monkey-puzzle tree (*Araucaria araucana; pehuén*) as well as cypress and southern beech. Region X harbors the remaining unexploited *alerce*, the world's second-oldest tree. Valdivian temperate rainforest provides a substantial variety of plant life including the *nalca*, the world's largest herbaceous plant. Seldom-seen puma roam the Andes, along with a growing and destructive population of wild boar. The rare and diminutive deer *pudú* hides out in thick forests, *bandurrias* (buff necked ibis) frequent southern pastures and tweeting trailside *chucao* reputedly signal bad luck if on the left. Supposedly better than a watchdog, the *queltehue* squawks to protect its ground nests. A colony of Humboldt and Magellanic penguins seasonally inhabit the northwestern coast of Chiloé.

From the Lakes District to Magallanes, you'll find verdant upland forests of the widespread genus *Nothofagus*. Decreased rainfall on the eastern plains of Magallanes and Tierra del Fuego creates extensive grasslands. Protected guanaco have made a comeback within Torres del Paine, where *caiquenes* (upland geese), rheas and foxes can also be spotted. Punta Arenas hosts colonies of Magellanic penguins and cormorants. Chile's long coastline features many marine mammals, including sea lions, otters, fur seals and whales.

National Parks
With Torres del Paine as the glaring exception, Chile's diverse and beautiful parks are considerably underutilized. Parks and reserves are

CHILE

administered by the underfunded Corporación Nacional Forestal. Visit **Conaf** (Map pp424–5; ☎ 02-390-0282; www.conaf.cl in Spanish; Av Bulnes 291) in Santiago for inexpensive maps and brochures.

Private nature reserves protect over 106 areas from massive deforestation. They include: Parque Pumalín in northern Patagonia; Alto Huemul in Region VII; El Cañi, near Pucón; Monte Verde, on Isla Riesco north of Punta Arenas; and Bahía Yendegaia, on Tierra del Fuego. Big projects in the works include Valle Chacabuco and 115,000-hectare Parque Tantauco in southwest Chiloe.

The following lists the most popular and accessible national parks from north to south. A couple of them are actually national reserves.

Alerce Andino (p504) Preserves stands of *alerce* trees near Puerto Montt.

Altos del Lircay A reserve with views of the Andean divide and a loop trek to Radal Siete Tazas.

Chiloé (p508) Features broad sandy beaches, blue lagoons and myth-bound forests.

Conguillío (p483) Mixed forests of araucaria, cypress and southern beech surrounding the active, snowcapped Volcán Llaima.

Huerquehue (p489) Near Pucón, hiking trails through araucaria forests, with outstanding views of Volcán Villarrica.

La Campana Close to Santiago, protects forests of native oaks and Chilean palms.

Lauca (p468) East of Arica, with active and dormant volcanoes, clear blue lakes, abundant birdlife, *altiplano* villages and extensive steppes.

Llanos de Challe On the coastal plain of the Norte Chico, best site to view 'flowering of the desert' after rare heavy rains.

Los Flamencos In and around San Pedro de Atacama, a reserve protecting salt lakes and high-altitude lagoons, flamingos, eerie desert landforms and hot springs.

Nahuelbuta (p478) In the high coastal range, preserves the area's largest remaining araucaria forests.

Nevado Tres Cruces (p450) East of Copiapó, includes a 6330m-high namesake peak and 6900m-high Ojos del Salado.

Puyehue (p495) Near Osorno, with fancy hot springs and ski resort, and a popular hike through volcanic desert, up the crater, to thermals and geyser fields.

Queulat (p513) Wild evergreen forest, mountains and glaciers stretch across 70km of the Carretera Austral.

Torres del Paine (p524) Chile's showpiece near Puerto Natales, with an excellent trail network around the country's most revered vistas.

Vicente Pérez Rosales (p500) Chile's oldest national park includes spectacular Lago Todos los Santos and Volcán Osorno.

Villarrica (p489) The smoking symmetrical cone of Volcán Villarrica is playground for trekkers and climbers, snowboarders and skiers.

Environmental Issues

Environmental folly may be the price paid for Chile's growing prosperity. In this resource-rich country, the most notable conflicts of its probusiness policies are mining projects like Pascua Lama (which intends to move a glacier in the Andes) and the destruction of Patagonia's major river systems (Río Puelo, Río Baker, to name a few) to construct dams and hydroelectric power plants. From Region VIII south, native forest continues to lose ground to plantations of fast-growing exotics, such as eucalyptus and Monterey pine. Native araucaria and *alerce* have declined precipitously over the past decades. The Celco-Arauco pulp mill in Valdivia has caused unprecedented environmental damage: it killed off a population of 5000 black-necked swans, polluted the local rivers, and continues to operate despite local and international opposition. Salmon farming in the south threatens to pollute both the freshwater and saltwater as well as endanger marine life. Another issue is the intensive use

---

BORDER CROSSINGS

For road conditions at the border crossings, the **carabineros** (☎ 133) in border areas are good resources. For Peru, Arica to Tacna is the only land crossing. Connections between Chile and Bolivia are much improved, but many of these routes are long, arduous trips. The most accessible crossings are the following:

Arica to La Paz Highway completely paved, goes through Parque Nacional Lauca, many buses, hitching is feasible.

Calama to Ollagüe Eight-hour train ride with connections to Oruro and La Paz.

Iquique to Oruro Goes via Colchane/Pisiga; highway almost all paved, regular buses, passes by Parque Nacional Volcán Isluga; keep an eye out for wildlife.

San Pedro de Atacama to Uyuni Popular 4WD tour.

of agricultural chemicals and pesticides to promote Chile's fruit exports. In the north, mining and agricultural pesticides threaten the limited water supply. The growing hole in the ozone layer over Antarctica has become such an issue that medical authorities recommend wearing protective clothing and heavy sunblock to avoid cancer-causing ultraviolet radiation, especially in Patagonia.

TRANSPORTATION

GETTING THERE & AWAY
Air
Santiago's Aeropuerto Internacional Arturo Merino Benítez is the main port of entry. Some other cities have international service to neighboring countries. Only Lan flies to Rapa Nui (Easter Island). Taca and Lan all have nonstop flights to/from Lima, Peru. Peruvian flights to Tacna, Chile are slightly cheaper. LAB and Lan fly to/from La Paz, Santa Cruz and Cochabamba (all in Bolivia). Taca and Avianca link Santiago with Bogotá, Colombia. Varig and TAM fly to Brazilian and Paraguayan destinations. Lan flies to Montevideo, Uruguay. Aerolíneas Argentinas and Lan often have internet specials from Santiago to Buenos Aires. European airlines picking up passengers in Buenos Aires before going long-haul offer competitive fares. DAP Airlines flies between major destinations in Patagonia.

Bus
Except in far southern Patagonia and Tierra del Fuego, travel to Argentina involves crossing the Andes; some passes close in winter. Crossings in the Lakes District and Patagonia are very popular, especially in summer

---

> **DEPARTURE TAX & ENTRY FEES**
>
> Departure tax for international flights is US$26 or its equivalent in local currency. Reciprocity fees are applied to US (US$100), Australian (US$34) and Canadian (US$55) citizens upon arrival at Santiago's international airport. The stamp given is valid for the life of the passport. Fees must be paid in exact amounts in cash, and preferably in US dollars. Entering via other airports or overland routes can save travelers a hefty fee.

> **GETTING TO ARGENTINA**
>
> Crossing the border into Argentina is easy. Buses with international routes simply cross – no changing, no fees. Border outposts are open daylight hours, although a few long-haul buses cross at night. Dorotea (near Puerto Natales) is open 24 hours in summer. Bring your tourist card and passport. Leave that bunch of bananas back at the hostel – food's a no-no.

---

months, so booking early and confirming reservations is advised.

Chile Chico to Los Antiguos Frequent bus service.

Coyhaique to Comodoro Rivadavia Several weekly bus services, usually heavily booked, go through Río Mayo.

Futaleufú to Esquel Regular *colectivo* (taxis with fixed routes) service goes to the border, from where other transport is readily available.

Iquique, Calama and San Pedro de Atacama to Jujuy and Salta Paso de Jama (4200m) is most often used; Paso de Lago (4079m) is an excellent trip through little-visited *salar* (salt pans) country; book early.

Osorno to Bariloche Quickest land route in the Lakes District; frequent buses use Paso Cardenal Samoré, often called Pajaritos, year-round.

Puerto Montt and Puerto Varas to Bariloche Year-round, touristy bus-ferry combination tours.

Puerto Natales to El Calafate Many buses in summer; limited off-season.

Punta Arenas to Río Gallegos Many buses ply this six-hour route daily.

Punta Arenas to Tierra del Fuego Two-and-a-half-hour ferry ride to Porvenir, with two buses weekly to Río Grande, connecting to Ushuaia; direct buses via Primera Angostura.

Santiago to Mendoza Tons of options crossing Libertadores; *colectivos* cost more, but are faster.

Temuco to San Martín de los Andes Very popular route with regular summer buses using the Mamuil Malal pass (Paso Tromen to Argentines).

Temuco to Zapala and Neuquén Regular but thin bus service via Pino Hachado (1884m); Icaima (1298m) is an alternative.

Valdivia to San Martín de los Andes Bus-ferry combination crosses Lago Pirehueico to Paso Hua Hum, from where buses continue to San Martín de los Andes.

GETTING AROUND
Air
Lan (☎ 600-526-2000; www.lan.com) and **Sky** (☎ 600-600-2828; www.skyairline.cl in Spanish) provide domestic flights. Weekly website specials released

Tuesdays can shave off up to 40% on a last-minute fare with Lan. Air taxis in the south link more inaccessible regions but do not insure passengers. Their weight limit for carry-on items can be as low as 10kg, with hefty charges for extra baggage.

Boat

Passenger/car ferries and catamarans connect Puerto Montt with points along the Carretera Austral, including Caleta Gonzalo (Chaitén) and Coyhaique, and also connect Quellón and Castro, Chiloé to Chaitén. Ferries from Hornopirén to Caleta Gonzalo only run in summer.

A highlight for many travelers is the trip from Puerto Montt to Puerto Natales on board Navimag's *Magallanes*. Book with **Navimag** (☎ 02-442-3120; www.navimag.com; Av El Bosque Norte 0440, Santiago) far in advance. This is a cargo vessel outfitted for tourism, not a cruise ship. Cabins and beds are quite comfortable, but the cheapest beds are closest to farm animal smells and most vulnerable to the tossing waves. Meals are passable; vegetarians should give notice when booking. Pack motion-sickness remedies, snacks and drinks, which are expensive at the bar.

Bus

The Chilean bus system is fabulous. Tons of companies vie for customers with *ofertas* (seasonal promotions), discounts and added luxuries like movies. Long-distance buses are comfortable, fast and punctual. They usually have toilets and either serve meals or make regular food stops. Make advance bookings on popular long-distance routes (mainly those heading to Argentina) in the summer and on or close to major holidays. Luggage holds are safe, but a lockable sack doesn't hurt and keeps the pack grime-free. Two of the most convenient and reliable companies, Pullman Bus and Tur Bus, have membership clubs you can join for US$5 for 10% discounts on long-distance trips. Tur Bus discounts tickets purchased online.

Car & Motorcycle

Having wheels gets you to remote national parks and most places off the beaten track. This is especially true in the Atacama Desert, Carretera Austral and Easter Island. Security problems are minor, but always lock your vehicle and remove valuables. Santiago and its surroundings frequently restrict private vehicle use to alleviate smog.

Hitchhiking

Especially among young Chileans on summer holiday, hitchhiking is a favored form of getting around the country. Some backpackers solicit rides at *servicentros* on the Panamericana. In Patagonia, where distances are great and vehicles few, be prepared to camp out roadside. Carry snacks and water, especially in the desert. Note that Lonely Planet doesn't recommend hitchhiking.

Local Transportation

All main towns and cities have taxis, most of which are metered. Some have set fees for tourist-oriented destinations. Confirm the price before going. *Colectivos* are taxis with fixed routes, shown on the placards on the roof. Rates are about US40¢ per ride. *Micros* are city buses, clearly numbered and with a sign indicating their destination. Keep your ticket, which may be checked by an inspector. Santiago has a clean, quick and easy-to-use metro system which connects the most visited and popular neighborhoods.

Train

The **Empresa de Ferrocarriles del Estado** (EFE; ☎ 02-376-8500; www.efe.cl in Spanish) runs a southbound passenger service from Santiago to Chillán, Concepción and Temuco, changing trains to head to Puerto Varas and Puerto Montt. It makes many intermediate stops. Classes of service are *turista* and *salón,* both with reclining seats, *cama pasillo* (sleeper), and *clase departamento,* the most luxurious with private two-bed chambers and washbasin. The costlier *cama* class are modern models with upper and lower bunks.

SANTIAGO

☎ 02 / pop 4,671,500

Santiago's postcard face is that of a modern metropolis poised under gargantuan snow-tipped Andean peaks. Its courteous and orderly surface makes it the least intimidating of all South American capitals for travelers, although the prevalent mall culture can be a bit of a drag. The city itself defies pinning down. Visitors will find polished suburbs and worn downtown cafés, neoclassical architec-

GETTING INTO TOWN

Aeropuerto Internacional Arturo Merino Benítez (☎ 601-9001) is in Pudahuel, 26km northwest of downtown Santiago. **Tur Bus** (Map pp424-5; ☎ 671-7380; Moneda 1529) runs every 15 minutes between 6:30am and 9pm (US$2.50, 30 minutes). **Buses Centropuerto** (☎ 677-3010; Alameda) provides a similar service (US$1.70) from Los Héroes metro station. A door-to-door shuttle service (US$6 to US$8) is provided by **New Transfer** (☎ 677-3000) and **Transfer** (☎ 777-7707). A cab ride to the center costs about US$25. All of the main bus stations are right off the Alameda, where you can find metro stations.

ture dulled to grey and a conservative culture which nonetheless erupts in street protest every now and then. Perhaps the most evasive face of the city is its lovely mountain backdrop. The sky – when not cerulean blue – is covered by a heavy drapery of smog.

Take advantage of the fact that this is a safe and quirky city to explore. Squeeze onto the subway – or a yellow bus if you dare – to start exploring. If downtown's not your style, check out the trendy nightlife of Bellavista or the bohemian buzz of Barrio Brasil. Providencia and Las Condes offer fancy cafés and bookstores. Strangers to the city need only witness an airport reunion of prodigal sons and their families to get an inkling of its charm.

HISTORY
Founded by Pedro de Valdivia in 1541, Santiago's site was chosen for its moderate climate and strategic location for defense. It remained a small town until the nitrate boom in the 1880s. Its central station was designed by Gustave Eiffel. In 1985 an earthquake shook down some of downtown's classic architecture. It's currently a major financial center for the continent and headquarters for multinationals like Yahoo!, Microsoft and JP Morgan.

ORIENTATION
'El Centro' is a compact, triangular area bounded by the Río Mapocho and Parque Forestal in the north, the Vía Norte Sur in the west, and Av General O'Higgins (the Alameda) in the south. Key public buildings cluster near the Plaza de Armas, which branches out into a busy graph of shopping arcades and pedestrian streets. North and east of the center is Barrio Bellavista, with Cerro San Cristóbal (Parque Metropolitano). To the west is Barrio Brasil, the bohemian enclave of the city. At the tip of this triangle and extending east are the wealthy *comunas* (sectors) of Providencia and Las Condes, accessed via the

Alameda. Nuñoa is a residential neighborhood south of Providencia.

INFORMATION
Bookstores
Chile's 19% tax on books means high prices.

Books (Manuel Montt, Av Providencia 1652, Providencia) Paperbacks and guidebooks in English.

English Reader (www.englishreader.cl; Av Los Leones 116, Providencia) Top selection of new and used books in English with readings and exchange evenings (Tuesdays and Thursdays).

Feria Chilena del Libro (Map pp424-5; Paseo Huérfanos 623) Santiago's best-stocked bookstore.

Librería Inglesa Local 11 (Paseo Huérfanos 669); Providencia (Av Pedro de Valdivia 47)

Cultural Centers
Instituto Chileno-Británico (Map pp424-5; ☎ 638-2156; Santa Lucía 124)

Instituto Chileno-Norteamericano (Map pp424-5; ☎ 696-3215; Moneda 1467)

Emergency
Ambulance (☎ 131)
Fire Department (☎ 132)
Police (☎ 133)

Internet Access
All-hour internet cafés abound, charging about US$1 per hour.

Axcesso Internet (Map pp424-5; Agustinas 869, Galería Imperio, 2nd fl) Sixty computers and fast connections.

Cyber.sur (Map pp420-1; Maturana 302; ☼ until 11pm) On the corner of the Barrio Brasil plaza.

Laundry
Self-service isn't a concept here. The laundries listed here charge about US$5 per load to wash, dry and fold.

Lavandería Autoservicio (Map pp424-5; Monjitas 507) South of Parque Forestal.

Lavandería San Miguel (Map pp420-1; Moneda 2296) In Barrio Brasil.

CHILE

SANTIAGO

INFORMATION
Cyber.sur...................................**1** C3
Lavandería San Miguel.............**2** C4

SIGHTS & ACTIVITIES
Escuela Violeta Parra..................**3** G2
Museo de la Solidaridad Salvador
  Allende....................................**4** B3
Museo del Huaso........................**5** D6
Museo Nacional de Historia
  Natural....................................**6** A3
Palacio Cousiño..........................**7** E5

SLEEPING
Albergue Hostelling International...**8** D3
Happy House Hostel....................**9** C3
Hotel Los Arcos.......................**10** C3
La Casa Roja...........................**11** C3
Pasaje República......................**12** C4
Santiago Adventure..................**13** C4

EATING
Ali Baba..................................**14** G2
Economax................................**15** C3
La Bohème...............................**16** F2
Las Vacas Gordas.....................**17** D3
N'aitun...................................**18** C3
Ocean Pacific's........................**19** C3
Peperone.................................**20** D3
Plaza Café...............................**21** D3

ENTERTAINMENT
Blondie...................................**22** B4
Bokhara..................................**23** G2
Havana Salsa............................**24** G1
Hipódromo Chile......................**25** C6
N'aitun..............................(see **18**)

TRANSPORT
Pullman Bus........................(see **26**)
Terminal de Buses Alameda.....**26** A5
Terminal de Buses Sur..............**27** A5
Terminal San Borja...................**28** B5
Tur Bus...............................(see **26**)

CHILENISMOS 101

Chilean Spanish fell off the wagon: it is slurred, sing-song and peppered with expressions unintelligible to the rest of the Spanish-speaking world. *¿Cachay?* (you get it?) often punctuates a sentence, as does the ubiquitous *pues*, said as '*po*.' '*Sípo*,' all clattered together actually means, 'well, yes.' Lazy tongues emit '*pa*' instead of '*para*,' offering *¿'pa'que po?*' to say, 'Well, why is that?' Country lingo is firmly seeded in this former agrarian society who refer to guys as *cabros*, complain '*es un cacho*' ('it's a horn,' meaning a sticking point) and go to the *carrete* to *carretear* ('wagon,' meaning party/to party). Lovers of this *loco* lingo should check out John Brennan's *How to Survive in the Chilean Jungle*, available in Santiago's English-language bookstores (see p419). *¿Cachay?*

Left Luggage

All the main bus terminals have a *custodia*, where you can stash a bag for about US$2 per day. Another option is storing luggage for free at a reputable lodging.

Medical Services

Clínica Alemana de Santiago (☎ 210-1111; Av Vitacura 5951) In Vitacura, the next suburb east of Las Condes; well recommended.

Posta Central (☎ 634-1650; Portugal 125) Santiago's main emergency room, near metro Universidad Católica.

Money

Casas de cambio line Agustinas between Bandera and Ahumada. They change cash and traveler's checks and are open regular business hours and Saturday morning. ATMs (Redbanc) are found throughout the city.

Blanco Viajes (☎ 636-9100; Gral Holley 148, Providencia) Represents American Express.

Post

Main post office (Plaza de Armas; ✆ 8am-10pm Mon-Fri, to 6pm Sat) On the north side of the plaza. Handles poste restante for a minor pick-up fee. Mail is held for 30 days. Other locations: in the Centro at Moneda 1155 and in Providencia at Av Providencia 1466.

Tourist Information

Conaf (Map pp424-5; ☎ 390-0282; www.conaf.cl in Spanish; Paseo Bulnes 291; ✆ 9:30am-5:30pm Mon-Thu, to 4:30pm Fri) Information on all of the parks and reserves, with some topographic maps to photocopy.

Municipal tourist office (Map pp424-5; ☎ 632-7783; www.ciudad.cl in Spanish; Merced 860) In Casa Colorada, near the Plaza de Armas.

Sernatur (☎ 236-1416; Av Providencia 1550, Providencia) Chile's national tourist service with capable, well-informed staff. Other branches are at the airport and San Borja bus terminal.

Travel Agencies

Student Flight Center (☎ 335-0395, 800-340-034; www.sertur.cl in Spanish; Hernando de Aguirre 201, Oficina 401, Providencia) STA representative; bargains on air tickets.

DANGERS & ANNOYANCES

Santiago is relatively safe, but petty crime exists. Be on your guard around the Plaza de Armas, Mercado Central, Barrio Brasil, Cerro Santa Lucía and Cerro San Cristóbal in particular. Don't be flashy with your belongings and watch your bag at sidewalk cafés. Stay aware out on a big night in Bellavista: organized groups can target drinkers, especially on Pío Nono. As with any big city you are safer in a pair or group late at night. Also pesky is Santiago's smog, which can make your eyes burn and throat hurt.

SIGHTS

Museums

Most museums are free on Sunday and closed on Monday. Regular hours are usually from 10am to 6pm or 7pm Tuesday to Saturday and 10am to 2pm Sunday. Unless otherwise noted, admission is US$1.

A must-see, **Museo Chileno de Arte Precolombino** (Map pp424-5; Bandera 361; admission US$3.50) chronicles a whopping 4500 years of pre-Columbian civilization throughout the Americas with breathtaking ceramics, gorgeous textiles and Chinchorro mummies (which predate their Egyptian counterparts by thousands of years).

The **Museo Histórico Nacional** (Map pp424-5; www.museohistoriconacional.cl in Spanish; Plaza de Armas 951), inside the Palacio de la Real Audencia, documents colonial and republican history. Displays include indigenous artifacts, early colonial furniture and house fittings, and an interesting exhibit on 20th-century politics.

Modeled on the Petit Palais in Paris, Santiago's early-20th-century fine-arts museum, **Palacio de Bellas Artes** (Map pp424–5; JM de la Barra), near Av José María Caro, houses two museums: **Museo de Bellas Artes**, with permanent collections of Chilean and European art, and the **Museo de Arte Contemporáneo** (www.mac.uchile.cl in Spanish), hosting modern photography, design, sculpture and web-art displays.

Founded in celebration of Chile's socialist experiment, **Museo de la Solidaridad Salvador Allende** (Map pp420–1; Herrera 360, Barrio Brasil) houses works by Matta, Miró, Tapies, Calder and Yoko Ono. During the dictatorship the entire collection spent 17 years underground, awaiting the return of civilian rule.

Santiago's most glorious mansion, the 1871 **Palacio Cousiño** (Map pp420–1; Dieciocho 438; admission US$3.50) was built on wine and coal and silver-mining fortunes. Highlights include the French-style art and one of the country's first elevators. Admission includes an informative guided tour in English.

La Chascona (Museo Neruda; Map pp424–5; Márquez de La Plata 0192; admission US$5) Named for the snarled locks of his widow, Pablo Neruda's shiplike house shelters the poet's eclectic collections. Engaging tours are conducted in English.

If you have time, try the following:

Museo del Huaso (Map pp420–1; Parque O'Higgins; admission free) Rounds up an impressive poncho and hat collection.

Museo de Artes Visuales (Map pp424–5; Lastarria 307, Plaza Mulato Gil de Castro, Centro; admission US$2) Spare, modern space showing contemporary Chilean sculptures.

Museo Nacional de Historia Natural (Map pp420–1; Parque Quinta Normal) Extensive butterfly and fossil collection.

Parks & Gardens

Once a hermitage, then a convent, then a military bastion, **Cerro Santa Lucía** (Map pp424–5) has offered respite from city chaos since 1875. At the southwest corner is the Terraza Neptuno, with fountains and curving staircases that lead to the summit.

North of the Río Mapocho, 870m **Cerro San Cristóbal** ('Tapahue' to the Mapuche) towers above Santiago and is the site of **Parque Metropolitano** (www.parquemetropolitano.cl in Spanish), the capital's largest open space, with two swimming pools, a botanical garden, somewhat neglected zoo and art museum. Beam up to San Cristóbal's summit via the **funicular** (admission

US$2; ☺ 1-8pm Mon, 10am-8pm Tue-Sun), which climbs 485m from Plaza Caupolicán, at the north end of Pío Nono in Bellavista. From the Terraza, the 2000m-long teleférico (cable-car; US$2.50 round-trip) runs to a station near the north end of Av Pedro de Valdivia Norte, accessing most of the interesting sites in the park. A funicular/teleférico combo costs US$4 or firm up those glutes with a rocky uphill hike.

The **Cementerio General** (☎ 737-9469; www.cementeriogeneral.cl), at the north end of Av La Paz, is a city of tombs with a woeful history lesson. A memorial honors the disappeared, and native sons José Manuel Balmaceda, Salvador Allende and diplomat Orlando Letelier are buried here. Walk 10 minutes from the northern end of Línea 2. Guided tours are available in English and are well worth it; call a day ahead.

ACTIVITIES

Outdoor access is Santiago's strong suit. A quick fix is to run, walk or peddle up Barrio Bellavista's Pío Nono to Cerro San Cristóbal (left).

Swimmers can get strokes in at the Parque Metropolitano's gorgeous pools (see left).

From October to March adventure-travel companies run Class III descents of the Maipo. One popular destination is Cascada de las Animas (p433). They also organize hiking and horse-trekking trips at reasonable rates.

Excellent skiing is within poles' reach of Santiago. The closest resort is El Colorado & Farellones (p432).

Wine enthusiasts should check out the easy day trips (see p432).

Sore backpackers can soak in hot springs **Baños Colina** (☎ 639-5266; per person US$15). There's no public transportation but **Manzur Expediciones** (☎ 777-4284) go from Plaza Italia (near metro Baquedano), usually on Wednesday, Saturday and Sunday.

WALKING TOUR

Kickstart with an espresso at the **Poema Café (1**; p428), in the 1924 Biblioteca Nacional. Walking east one block there's the **Centro Artesanal Santa Lucía (2**; p430), which can be broadly defined as outdoor craft stalls – among them are tattoo parlors.

Across the street a neoclassical archway announces **Cerro Santa Lucía (3**; left). Hike up the monumental staircase (daytime only) to the summit. Rest among the trysting lovers

CHILE

SANTIAGO CENTRO

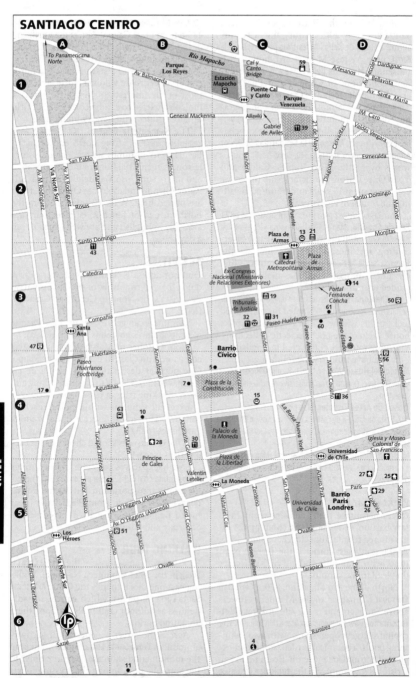

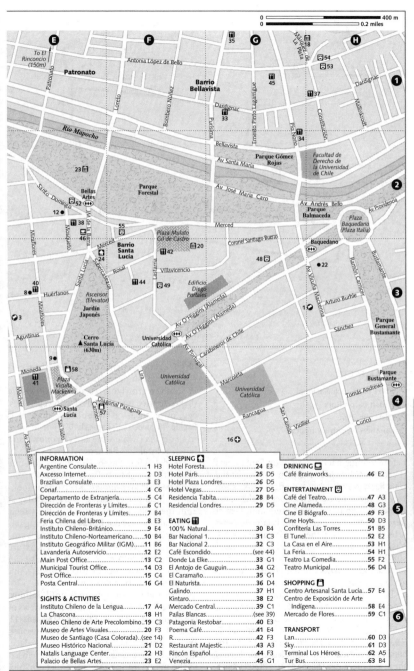

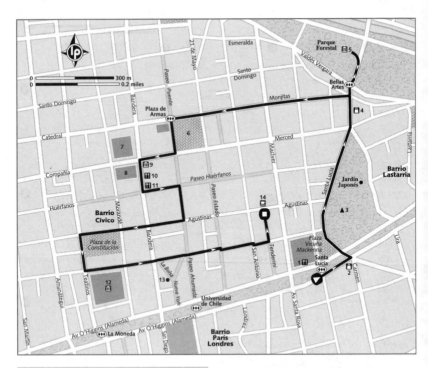

WALK FACTS

Start Biblioteca Nacional
Finish Baron Rojo
Distance 3km
Duration four to six hours

before looping back. Go right on Santa Lucia (becomes JM de la Barra). On your right the **Clinic Bazar** (**4**; JM de la Barra 463) offers a joke shop run by the satirical newspaper of the same name. Buy your Pinochet mug-shot T-shirt here. Continuing north, the **Palacio de Bellas Artes** (**5**; p55) is set in the leafy Parque Forestal. Visit the portraits of lonely colonial girls and sun-blistered *huasos* or opt for the whimsical installations at MAC Contemporary Museum across the hall.

Take JM la Barra onto Monjitas for five blocks to the **Plaza de Armas** (**6**). Cross the plaza and continue on Compañía to Bandera. You'll find the palatial 1876 **Ex-Congreso Nacional** (**7**; Morandé 441; closed to public) in front of the **Tribunales de Justicia** (**8**; law courts; Compañía). Across the street the **Museo Chileno de Arte Precolombino**

(**9**; p422) offers a dynamic pan-American perspective that shuns modern borders.

Stomach growly? Grab a quick *empanada* (baked or fried turnover filled with vegetables, egg, olive, meat or cheese) next door at **El Rápido** (**10**; Bandera 347; empanadas US$2) or indulge in a *borgoña* (white wine and *chirimoya*) and lunch at local fave **Bar Nacional** (**11**; p428).

Head left on Paseo Huerfanos for one block, then right on Paseo Ahumada, the main pedestrian *peatonal*. Keep on the lookout for local personalities. Every weekday at 2pm the tabloid *La Segunda* hits the streets and local news vendor **Rambo** roams firing imaginary rounds into the throngs. This seemingly cracked vet is in fact a beloved fixture of downtown culture; Rambo's disguise can flip to cowboy or presidential candidate, but the hair should be a dead giveaway.

Turn right onto Agustinas until Tatinos, reaching Plaza de la Constitución for views of the mighty late-colonial **Palacio de la Moneda** (**12**; 690-4000, ext 4311; Morandé 130, Centro; admission free; 10am-6pm Mon-Fri). This presidential palace, the site of the bloody 1973 coup, was closed to the public during the entire dictatorship;

for Chileans its reopening in 2000 was a proud event (solicit visits a month in advance to visitas@presidencia.cl).

Continue to the temple of capitalism, the **Bolsa de Comercio** (**13**; stock exchange; La Bolsa 64) to witness Chile's busy economy at work. Follow the businessmen out for a coffee break. *Cafés con piernas* are Chile's answer to its oppressive legacy of dictatorship and strict Catholic norms. While literally 'legs cafés,' these coffee shops have waitresses who often bare a bit more. At **Baron Rojo** (**14**; Agustinas 717; 9am-6:30pm Mon-Fri) caffeine aficionados and the culturally inquisitive can get a US$1.50 cup.

COURSES

Try one of the following language schools:

Escuela Violeta Parra (Map pp420-1; 735-8211; www.tandemsantiago.cl; Ernesto Pinto Lagarrigue 362-A, Bellavista) Two-week intensive courses cost US$250. The school also arranges homestays and trips.

Instituto Chileno de la Lengua (Map pp424-5; 697-2728; www.ichil.cl; Riquelme 226, Barrio Brasil)

Natalis Language Center (Map pp424-5; 222-8721; www.natalislang.com; Av Vicuña Mackenna 6, 7th fl) Comes highly recommended by its alumni.

FESTIVALS & EVENTS

Festival del Barrio Brasil Exhibitions, theater, dance and music bring even more life to the lovely Plaza Brasil in January.

Feria Internacional del Aire y del Espacio (www.fidae.cl) Aeropuerto Los Cerrillos, southwest of town, is the site of this major international air show held in late March.

Gran Premio Hipódromo Chile Held at the end of April/beginning of May, at the Hipódromo Chile, this determines Chile's best three-year-old racehorses.

Feria Internacional de Artesanía Held in the Centro's Parque General Bustamante in November, this is the city's best crafts festival.

Feria Internacional del Libro Santiago's annual book fair in Estación Mapocho attracts authors from throughout the continent in the last week of November.

SLEEPING

The commotion of the Centro slows way down at night. Family-oriented *residenciales* (budget accommodations) lock up from 2am to 7am, so ask first before heading out to party.

Santiago Centro & Barrio París Londres

Barrio París Londres (metro Universidad de Chile) is an attractive, quiet cobblestone enclave south of the Alameda. Barrio Santa Lucía

(metro Santa Lucía), on the other side, is as quaint but swankier.

Residencia Tabita (Map pp424-5; 671-5700; www.residenciatabita.sitio.net; Príncipe de Gales 81; s without bathroom incl breakfast US$10.30, d US$26) A quirky, good-value place with faded decor and large rooms that are a bit nippy in winter. It's not clearly marked; look for the Hotel Familiar sign.

Residencial Londres (Map pp424-5; 638-2215; unico54@ctclnternet.cl; Londres 54; s/d without bathroom US$12/23) Santiago's best budget accommodations, with parquet floors and antique furniture cozied up with a relaxed family feel. Reserve ahead.

Hotel Plaza Londres (Map pp424-5; 633-3320; www.hotelplazalondres.cl; Londres 77; s/d US$27/37; P) Bland rooms by lovely cobblestone setting of Plazuela José Toribio Medina. Room 301 has views of the square.

Hotel París (Map pp424-5; 664-0921; París 813; r per person US$35, without bathroom US$28) A secure spot with ample rooms and courteous staff.

Hotel Foresta (Map pp424-5; 639-6262; fax 632-2996; Subercaseaux 353; s/d incl breakfast US$36/48) A skip from great bars and restaurants, this cute and cozy score has private bathrooms and hot water.

Hotel Vegas (Map pp424-5; 632-2498; www.hotelvegas.net; Londres 49; s/d incl breakfast US$43/53; P) Decked-out and comfy digs in an architectural oasis. Ask for the *matrimonial* (supersize double rooms) on the 2nd and 3rd floors for the same price as normal doubles.

Barrio Brasil & Beyond

Sweet offerings fill this bohemian enclave, central to hip restaurants and other parts of the city. It's quiet and relatively safe. Metro stations are Los Héroes or Santa Ana.

La Casa Roja (Map pp420-1; 696-4241; www.lacasaroja.cl; Agustinas 2113; dm/d US$8/22;) A splendid 19th-century mansion brimming with backpackers – sound like *The Real World*? Lounge around the elegant living room, patios or back garden and communal kitchen.

Albergue Hostelling International (Map pp420-1; 671-8532; www.hisantiago.cl; Cienfuegos 151; members dm/s/d US$9.50/27/40;) Backpacker central, this secure yet sterile 120-bed bunkhouse offers ample common areas, comfortable beds and cheap laundry service.

Happy House Hostel (Map pp420-1; 688-4849; www.happyhousehostel.cl; Catedral 2207; dm/s/d incl breakfast US$15/40/50;) Relax in this early-20th-century mansion with gleaming details, run by a friendly and informative staff. The roof terrace offers mountain views and a pool table. Long-term guests get discounts.

Hotel Los Arcos (Map pp420-1; ☎ 699-0998; Agustinas 2173; s/d US$33/40) Decent value, with discounts for extended stays.

República

Some great budget finds lurk in university central, south of the Alameda and east of Estación Central. The closest metro is República.

SCS Habitat (☎ 683-3732; scshabitat@yahoo.com; San Vicente 1798; dm/d US$5/7) This is a litle out of the way, but it is the serious bargain-basement option in Santiago – don't expect any flourishes. From Estación Central it's a 20-minute walk down Av Exposición (17 blocks). At the plaza at the end of the street walk left (east) three blocks to San Vicente; it's the last house.

Santiago Adventure (Map pp420-1; ☎ 671-5529; santiago_adventure@terra.cl; Cabo Arestey 2468; dm/d incl breakfast US$13/15) A quiet haven offering communal kitchen, laundry, internet and traveler info. It's in an alley off Av España, one street west of República.

Residencial Mery (Map pp420-1; ☎ 696-8883; Pasaje República 36; r US$19) Make the most of the peace in this quiet alley. Doors are locked at 2am.

EATING

Cheap lunches abound in the center; while Barrios Bellavista, Brasil or Providencia are better suited for dinner. Restaurants usually close after lunch and only reopen at around 8pm, forget Sundays. Bellavista eateries tend to be open until late every day.

Santiago Centro

Have lunch or *onces* (a snack) in the center, but don't expect to find much open for dinner. Along the southern arcade of the Plaza de Armas, vendors serve *completos* (hot dogs) and *empanadas*.

Patagonia Restobar (Map pp424-5; Paseo Huérfanos 609; sandwiches & snacks US$3-6) Slip out of the hubbub on Huérfanos and into this cabin refuge offering a long list of wines and sandwiches.

El Naturista (Map pp424-5; Moneda 846; mains US$3.50-6) The central branch of a vegetarian chain with a toppling selection of pasta, salad and crêpe dishes. The upmarket version is at Av Vitacura 2751 in Las Condes.

100% Natural (Map pp424-5; Valentín Letelier 1319; mains US$4-7) Green's the theme in this fruity fuel point for juices, salads and sandwiches.

Mercado Central (Map pp424-5; ☺ 6am-4pm Sun-Thu, to 8pm Fri, to 6pm Sat) Seek out the peripheral restaurants away from the tourist fly-traps. All-night Pailas Blancas (Local 87; mains US$4 to US$6) serves hard-core party people after a night of clubbing. Cross the bridge on 21 de Mayo to Mercado de Flores, a gorgeous produce market surrounded by basic *cocineras* (kitchens) serving simple meals of fried sea bass and *paila marina* (seafood stew).

Poema Café (Map pp424-5; Moneda 650; mains US$5-8; ☺ 9am-7pm Mon-Fri) Sneak in a relaxed read while you deconstruct your literary-themed dish.

Bar Nacional (Map pp424-5; Bandera 317; mains US$6-11) Caricatures and sepia photos adorn this adored soda fountain bustling with bow-tie clad waiters serving scrumptious *pastel de choclo* (maize casserole). There is a second branch at Paseo Huérfanos 1151.

Kintaro (Map pp424-5; Monjitas 460; meals around US$6.50) Ignore the chintzy digs – the sushi is reasonable value and authentic.

Restaurant Majestic (Map pp424-5; Santo Domingo 1526; mains US$9-17; ☺ 7:30pm-midnight) Exquisite Indian dishes, including tandoori and curries, are served in the opulent setting of the Majestic Hotel.

Barrios Santa Lucía & Bellavista

These neighborhoods are peak choices for dinner and drinks. Don't even bother trying to order dinner before 9pm. The Middle Eastern cafés on Merced in Santa Lucía serve excellent sweets, spinach *empanadas* and Turkish coffee.

El Rinconcito (cnr Manizano & Dávila Baeza; sandwiches US$3) Hummus and falafel served in Recoleta, west of Bellavista.

El Antojo de Gauguin (Map pp424-5; Pío Nono 69; mains US$4-9) Good for cheap, tasty Middle Eastern fare.

Galindo (Map pp424-5; Dardignac 098; mains US$4-9) Obnoxiously popular, with dependable Chilean fare, meaty sandwiches and lots of beer.

Café Escondido (Map pp424-5; Rosal 346; mains US$5) Next door to Rincón Español; serves cheap lager and decent snacks: try the *canapé de champiñones* (mushrooms in garlic sauce; US$4.50).

El Caramaño (Map pp424-5; Purísima 257; mains US$4.50-7) Ring the bell to enter this anonymous graffiti-spackled fave dishing out quality Chilean specialties.

Donde La Elke (Map pp424-5; Dardignac 68; set menu US$5.40) This brilliant little café serves great set lunches.

Venezia (Map pp424-5; Pío Nono 200; mains US$6-9) One of the few places in the main Pío Nono hub worth visiting, it offers classic Chilean cuisine in faded bohemian decor.

La Bohème (Map pp420-1; Constitución 124; mains US$8-11) Convivial yet cozy, its sparkling French cuisine does the talking.

Rincón Español (Map pp424-5; Rosal Interior 346; mains US$8-12) The boar's head cues that you're back in Spain, along with tasty tapas and paella.

Ali Baba (Map pp420-1; Santa Filomena 102; mains US$8-13) Bedouin opulence, belly dancing and massive *tablas* (shared plates) make this hot spot worth the splurge. Vegetarian friendly.

R (Map pp424-5; Lastarria 307; mains US$10-15) Romance somebody in this candlelit setting where original dishes (mainly fish) take on a Peruvian twist.

Barrio Brasil

Economax (Map pp420-1; cnr Ricardo Cumming & Compañía) Large supermarket.

Peperone (Map pp420-1; Huérfanos 1954; empanadas US$2) A candlelit neighborhood café offering 20 kinds of *empanadas;* sample the cheese and asparagus.

N'aitun (Map pp420-1; Av Ricardo Cumming 453; specials US$3.50) A musical venue to down cool daily lunch specials.

Plaza Café (Map pp420-1; Av Brasil 221; mains US$4-6) Friendly and unfussy, with three-course lunches.

Las Vacas Gordas (Map pp420-1; ☎ 697-1066; Cienfuegos 280; mains US$4-8) Everybody's favorite: 'the fat cows' offers expertly cooked steaks and kebabs, decent pastas and great service; call ahead.

Ocean Pacific's (Map pp420-1; Ricardo Cumming 221; mains US$7-14) Fun, family-style seafood in deep-sea ambience.

Providencia

La Mia Pappa (11 de Septiembre 1351; menú US$3) Elbow into the carbfest, offering OK all-you-can-eat pasta and lasagna.

Café del Patio (Providencia 1670, Local 8-A; mains US$6-10) Step into this cute café for wok-prepared vegetables and other imaginative vegetarian fare.

La Pizza Nostra (Providencia 1975; pizzas from US$6) A 30-year tradition of stone-cooked pizzas and service, open even on Sundays.

Liguria (Av Pedro de Valdivia Norte 047; mains US$7-10) A Santiago legend, its simple recipe is cooking up a great menu at a surprisingly low price with a hefty dash of *bon vivant* and bustle. Don't come here if you don't want to be seen. There's also a branch at Av Providencia 1373.

El Huerto (Orrego Luco 054; mains from US$8) Delve into the Vegetarian Planet dish (not named for us): spinach fettuccini with tofu cream sauce. Its adjacent café, La Huerta, has limited offerings but is kinder on the wallet.

DRINKING

Café Brainworks (Map pp424-5; JM de la Barra 454; ⏰ 10am-8pm Mon-Fri, 10am-7pm Sat & Sun) Ideal for a cup of joe or afternoon beer.

ENTERTAINMENT
Live Music

Confitería Las Torres (Map pp424-5; Alameda 1570) An 1879 old-world haunt where nostalgia buffs tango to live bands on weekends.

Club de Jazz (www.clubdejazz.cl in Spanish; Av Alessandri 85, Ñuñoa; admission US$5; ⏰ 10pm-3am Thu-Sat) The most established jazz venue in Latin America, housed in a large wooden building, within trumpeting distance of Plaza Ñuñoa.

La Casa en el Aire (Map pp424-5; www.lacasaenelaire.cl in Spanish; Antonia López de Bello 0125, Bellavista; ⏰ 8pm-late Mon-Sun) An alt-venue where Wednesday means poetry and theater and live folk music rocks the rest of the week.

N'Aitun (Map pp420-1; ☎ 671-8410; www.naitun.co.cl in Spanish; Av Ricardo Cumming 453, Barrio Brasil; ⏰ 8pm-late Mon-Sat) This 1980s leftist gathering spot holds live acts on Friday, ranging from indie bands to bolero and tango duets.

Nightclubs

Clubs yawn to life at midnight. Many dance spots close their doors in February and move to Valparaíso and Viña del Mar.

Blondie (Map pp420-1; Alameda 2879, Barrio Brasil) A must for any indie kid, this striking old theater features a massive video screen looming over the main dance floor.

El Tunel (Map pp424-5; Santo Domingo 439; admission with drink US$5; ⏰ 10pm-4am Wed-Sat) A popular retro club where '70s classics inspire 'Grease Lightning' theatrics and everyone emerges perspiring but happy.

Havana Salsa (Map pp420-1; Dominica 142, Barrio Bellavista) A Cuban-inspired dance venue.

CHILE

La Feria (Map pp424-5; Constitución 275, Barrio Bellavista) The house of techno and house.

Bokhara (Map pp420-1; Pío Nono 430, Barrio Bellavista) The hedonistic gay venue of choice; enjoy the mirrors and move to techno and house.

Cinemas
Many cinemas offer Wednesday discounts.

Cine Hoyts (Map pp424-5; ☎ 600-5000-400; www.cine hoyts.cl in Spanish; Paseo Huérfanos 735) Paseo Huérfanos, in the center, has a few multiplexes, including this one.

Art-house cinemas include the following:

Cine Alameda (Map pp424-5; Alameda 139)

Cine El Biógrafo (Map pp424-5; Lastarria 181, Barrio Santa Lucía; US$3.50)

Cine Tobalaba (www.showtime.cl in Spanish; Providencia 2563, Providencia)

Performing Arts
Café del Teatro (Map pp424-5; ☎ 672-1687; Riquelme 226, Barrio Brasil; ☺ noon-2am) Today's 'it' bar. Check out events in the old theater out back, or mingle with the welcoming regulars among the bright wall canvases.

Estación Mapocho (Map pp424-5; ☎ 361-1761; cnr Bandera & Balmaceda) Passenger trains to Viña and Valparaíso have been replaced with Santiago's main cultural center, offering live theater, concerts, exhibits and a café.

Performing-arts venues include **Teatro Municipal** (Map pp424-5; ☎ 369-0282; www.municipal.cl in Spanish; Agustinas 794) and **Teatro La Comedia** (Map pp424-5; ☎ 639-1523; Merced 349), near Cerro Santa Lucía, featuring risqué comedies.

Sports
Estadio Nacional (☎ 238-8102; cnr Av Grecia & Marathon, Ñuñoa) Join the throngs chanting 'Chi-Chi-Chi-Lay-Lay-Lay.' International soccer matches usually pack a crowd. Tickets can be purchased from the stadium.

Horse racing takes place every Saturday from 2:30pm and on alternate Thursdays at **Hipódromo Chile** (Av Independencia 1715) in the *comuna* of Independencia; and every Friday from 2:30pm and on alternate Mondays and Wednesdays at **Club Hípico de Santiago** (Map pp420-1; Almirante Blanco Encalada 2540), south of the Alameda near Parque O'Higgins.

SHOPPING
For artisan crafts try the following:

Centro de Exposición de Arte Indígena (Map pp424-5; Alameda 499) Rapa Nui, Mapuche and Aymara crafts.

Centro Artesanal Santa Lucía (Map pp424-5; cnr Carmen & Diagonal Paraguay) On other side of Cerro Santa Lucía: lapis lazuli jewelry, sweaters, copperware and pottery.

Cooperativa Almacén Campesina (Purísima 303) In Bellavista; shawls and scarves, as well as pottery and jewelry.

Centro Artesanal de Los Dominicos (Av Apoquindo 9085; ☺ 11am-7:30pm) The city's largest crafts selection offers lots of woven goods and everything from jewelry to saddles at the Dominican monastery in Las Condes. Take the metro to Escuela Militar. Catch a taxi (US$5) or bus (look for one marked 'Los Dominicos') along Av Apoquindo. *Micros* 235, 327, 343 and 344 will take you almost to the end of Apoquindo, where you will have a five-minute walk.

GETTING THERE & AWAY
Air
Aeropuerto Internacional Arturo Merino Benítez (☎ 601-1752, lost property 690-1707; www.aeropuerto santiago.cl) is in Pudahuel, 26km northwest of downtown Santiago. Domestic carrier offices are **Lan** (☎ 600-526-2000; Centro Map pp424-5; Paseo Huérfanos 926; Providencia Av Providencia 2006) and **Sky** (☎ 353-3100; Andres de Fuenzalida 55, Providencia). Following are some approximate one-way fares.

Destination	Cost (US$)
Antofagasta	188
Arica	195
Balmaceda	186
Calama	162-266
Concepción	98
Puerto Montt	150
Punta Arenas	215
Temuco	131

Bus
Bus transportation within Chile is typically reliable, prompt, safe and comfortable. Santiago has four main bus terminals, from which buses leave for northern, central and southern destinations. The largest and most reputable bus company is Tur Bus. A US$5 club card can provide a 10% discount on one-way fares (if paying in cash), join at any Tur Bus office. Pullman Bus is also very good. In the south, Cruz del Sur is the best.

Terminal San Borja (Map pp420-1; ☎ 776-0645; Alameda 3250) is at the end of the shopping mall alongside the main railway station. The ticket booths are divided by region, with destinations prominently displayed. Destinations are from Arica down to the *cordillera* (mountain range) around Santiago.

Terminal de Buses Alameda (Map pp420-1; ☎ 776-2424; cnr Alameda & Jotabeche) is home to **Tur Bus** (☎ 778-0808) and **Pullman Bus** (☎ 778-1185), both going to a wide variety of destinations north, south and on the coast. They are both similarly priced and equally reliable and comfortable.

Terminal de Buses Sur (Map pp420-1; ☎ 779-1385; btwn Ruiz Tagle & Nicasio Retamales, Alameda 3850) has the most service to the central coast, international and southern destinations (the Lakes District and Chiloé).

Terminal Los Héroes (Map pp424-5; Tucapel Jiménez), near the Alameda in the Centro, is much more convenient and less chaotic. Buses mainly head north along the Panamericana Highway, but a few go to Argentina and south to Temuco.

Fares can vary dramatically, so explore options. Promotions can reduce normal fares by half; student reductions by 25%. Discounts are common outside the peak summer season. Try bargaining if the bus is not full and is set to leave. Book in advance to travel during holiday periods. Fares between important destinations are listed throughout this chapter, with approximate one-way fares and journey times in the following table.

Destination	Duration (hr)	Cost (US$): Pullman	Cost (US$): Salón Cama
Antofagasta	18	44	75
Arica	28	61	n/a
Chillán	6	10	26
Concepción	8	11	30
Copiapó	11	32	56
Iquique	26	49	n/a
La Serena	7	17	30
Osorno	10	16	39
Puerto Montt	12	18	45
Temuco	8	13	32
Valdivia	12	14	36
Valparaíso	2	6	n/a
Villarrica	9	14	36
Viña del Mar	2	7	n/a

Train

All trains depart Santiago from the Estación Central (Map pp420–1). Tickets are sold at that **ticket office** (☎ 376-8500; Alameda 3170; ⊗ 7am-9:45pm) and also at **Metro Universidad de Chile** (Map pp424-5; ☎ 688-3284; ⊗ 9am-8pm Mon-Fri, to 2pm Sat).

Faster and more efficient trains go south from Santiago, through Talca (US$10, 2½ hours) and Chillán (US$15, five hours) to Temuco (with connections to Puerto Montt). The **Empresa de Ferrocarriles del Estado** (EFE; ☎ 376-8500; www.efe.cl in Spanish) goes to Temuco at 10:30pm (US$16.50, nine hours). There are two types of ticket: *salón* (the cheaper ticket) and *preferente*. Online bookings save 10%. Prices increase on weekends and holidays. Ten trains head south from the station daily.

There is also a local *metrotren* service that goes as far as San Fernando to the south.

GETTING AROUND

Bus

Santiago's cheap yellow exhaust-spewing *micros* are in the process of being replaced. Check the destination signs in their windows or ask other passengers waiting at the stop. Many buses now have signed, fixed stops, but may stop at other points. Fares vary slightly depending on the bus, but most are US70¢ per trip; hang on to your ticket, since inspectors may ask for it. The new green buses don't take bills, only coins.

Car

Renting a car to drive around Santiago is a sure-fire way to have a bad day. But if you must, here are some agencies. Most also have offices at the airport.

Automóvil Club de Chile (Acchi; ☎ 212-5702; Vitacura 8620, Vitacura)

Budget (☎ 362-3232; Bilbao 1439, Providencia)

First (☎ 225-6328; www.firstrentacar.cl; Rancagua 0514, Providencia)

Hertz (☎ 235-9666; www.hertz.com; Av Andrés Bello 1469, Providencia)

Lys (Map pp424-5; ☎ 633-7600; Miraflores 541) Lys also rents mountain bikes.

Colectivo

Quicker and more comfortable than buses, taxi *colectivos* carry up to five passengers on fixed routes. The fare is about US75¢ within the city limits, US$4 to outlying suburbs. They look like regular taxis, but have an illuminated roof sign indicating their route.

Metro

Clean, quick and efficient, the metro operates from 6am to 10:30pm Monday to Saturday and 8am to 10:30pm Sunday and holidays. The three lines interlink to form a network to most places of interest. Fares vary depending on time of day, ranging from US70¢ to US85¢. Tickets are single use, so purchase several to avoid the line. Some subterranean stations also have ticket offices for bus companies, call centers and quick eats.

Taxi

These black-and-yellow numbers are abundant and moderately priced. While most drivers are honest, courteous and helpful, a few take roundabout routes and a handful have 'funny' meters. *Bajar la bandera* (flag fall) costs about US40¢ and about US18¢ per 200m. There is also a system of radio taxis, which can be slightly cheaper. Hotels and restaurants are usually happy to make calls for clients.

AROUND SANTIAGO

SKI RESORTS

Chilean ski resorts are open from June to October, with lower rates early and late in the season. Most ski areas are above 3300m and treeless; the runs are long, the season is long, and the snow is deep and dry. Snowboarders are welcome at all the resorts. Three major resorts are barely an hour from the capital, while the fourth is about two hours away on the Argentine border.

El Colorado & Farellones (full-day lift ticket US$37), 45km east of the capital, are close enough together to be considered one destination, with 18 lifts and 22 runs from 2430m to 3330m. **Centro de Ski El Colorado** (☎ 02-246-3344; www.el colorado.cl; Av Apoquindo 4900, Local 47, Las Condes, Santiago) has the latest information on snow and slope conditions. **Refugio Aleman** (☎ 02-264-9899; www .refugioaleman.cl; Camino Los Cóndores 1451, Farellones; dm/d incl breakfast & dinner US$35/40) has friendly multilingual staff and a relaxed international crowd, which make this the pick of the budget accommodations. You can ski from the door to the slopes.

Only 4km from the Farellones ski resort, **La Parva** (full-day lift ticket US$37, interconnected with Valle Nevado US$54) has 30 runs from 2662m to 3630m. For the latest information, contact **Centro de Ski La Parva** (☎ 02-431-0420; www.skilaparva.cl; Isidora Goyenechea 2939, Oficina 303, Las Condes, Santiago).

Another 14km beyond Farellones, **Valle Nevado** (☎ 02-477-7700; www.vallenevado.com; Av Vitacura 5250, Oficina 304, Santiago; full-day lift ticket US$29-38) can entertain even cranky experts, with 27 runs from 2805m to 3670m, some up to 3km in length.

In a class of its own, **Portillo** (full-day lift ticket US$37/29), 145km northeast of the capital on the Argentine border, has a dozen lifts and 23 runs from 2590m to 3330m, with a maximum vertical drop of 340m. The on-site **Inca Lodge** (per person per week low/high season full board US$450/550) accommodates young travelers in dorms. Nothing will get between you and your powder day: boys and girls are separated. Tickets are included in the price and low season offers some screaming deals. Contact **Centro de Ski Portillo** (☎ 02-263-0606; www.skiportillo .com; Renato Sánchez 4270, Las Condes, Santiago) for the latest details.

Manzur Expediciones (☎ 02-777-4284) goes direct to the slopes on Wednesday, Saturday and Sunday from Plaza Italia. Transportation, lunch and equipment rental costs US$25.

SkiTotal (☎ 02-246-0156; www.skitotal.cl; Av Apoquindo 4900, Local 39-42, Las Condes, Santiago) arranges transportation (about US$15) to the resorts, leaving at 8:45am and returning at 5:30pm. Its equipment rentals (US$27 to US$34 for the full package) are slightly cheaper than on the slopes.

WINERIES

As we write this, Chilean wine marketers are studying *Sideways* and revamping their tactics. But for now, wine tours are still considered an elite affair, including a tour of the grounds with didactic explanations followed by meager thimbles of the good stuff. Here are some accessible wineries:

Viña Concha y Toro (☎ 02-476-5269; www.concha ytoro.com; Virginia Subercaseaux 210, Pirque; tours in English US$6; ✆ tours 11:30am & 3pm Mon-Fri, 10am & noon Sat) Chile's largest and most commercial winery. Browse the rolling grounds and homestead at Pirque. Reserve four days in advance. Take metro to Pirque from Paradero 14 at the exit of Bellavista de La Florida metro station.

Viña Cousiño Macul (☎ 02-351-4175; www.cous inomacul.cl; Av Quilín 7100, Peñalolén; tours & tasting US$6; ✆ tours 11am Mon-Sat) Take bus 390 from the Alameda.

Viña De Martino (☎ 02-819-2062; www.demartino.cl; Manuel Rodríguez 229; ✆ English tour noon Mon-Sat) In Isla de Maipo, one hour southwest of Santiago, has excellent tours run by enologists. The basic tour at this Tuscan-style *vinoteca* costs US$10. A tour and lunch with unlimited reserve wine costs US$35. Reserve a tour at least a day in advance. Buses for Isla de Maipo leave from Terminal San Borja in Santiago.

Viña Santa Carolina (☎ 02-511-5778; Rodrigo de Araya 1341; tours US$12.50) An 1875 vineyard in Ñuñoa. Give two days' notice for an English-speaking tour.

Viña Undurraga (☎ 02-372-2865; www.undurraga .cl; Camino a Melipilla Km34; tours US$7; ☺ tours 10am, 11am, 2pm, 3:30pm Mon-Fri, 10am, 11:30am, 1pm Sat & Sun) Thirty-four kilometers southwest of Santiago on the old Melipilla road; take the bus to Talagante from Terminal San Borja and ask to be dropped off at the vineyard.

CAJÓN DEL MAIPO

Southeast of the capital, the Cajón del Maipo (Río Maipo canyon) is a major weekend destination for *santiaguinos,* who come to camp, hike, climb, bike, raft and ski. From September to April rafts descend the mostly Class III rapids of the murky Maipó in little over an hour. Full-day trips cost about US$70, less if you provide your own transport and food.

Cascadas Expediciones (☎ 02-861-1777; www.cascada -expediciones.com; Cam Al Volcán 17710, Casilla 211, San José de Maipó) and **Altué Active Travel** (☎ 02-232-1103; www.chileoutdoors.com; Encomenderos 83, Las Condes, Santiago) arrange the fun.

Near the village of San Alfonso, **Cascada de las Animas** (☎ 02-861-1303; www.cascada.net; campsites/cabins US$8/67) is a lovely 3500-hectare private nature reserve and working horse ranch. Riverside campsites are flat and woodsy; the four-person cabins have kitchens and log fires. A busy restaurant serves creative offerings on a terrace with views over the valley, *and* there's a large attractive pool of natural spring water, a sauna and massage facility. You can arrange any number of hiking, riding (US$30) and rafting options here, too. This is a top out-of-the-city destination. Lodging and activities are discounted from May to September.

Only 93km from Santiago, 3000-hectare **Monumento Natural El Morado** (admission US$2.50; ☺ closed May-Sep) rewards hikers with views of 4490m Cerro El Morado at Laguna El Morado, a two-hour hike from the humble hot springs of Baños Morales. There are free campsites around the lake.

Refugio Lo Valdés (☎ 099-220-8525; www.refugio lovaldes.com; per person incl breakfast US$27), a mountain chalet run by the German Alpine Club, is a popular weekend destination. Rates include breakfast, with other meals available. Eleven kilometers from here is **Baños Colina** (☎ 02-209-9114; per person incl campsite US$15), where terraced hot springs overlook the valley.

Buses San José de Maipó (☎ 02-697-2520; US$1.20) leave every 30 minutes, from 6am till 9pm, from Terminal San Borja (but stopping at Parque O'Higgins metro station) for San José de Maipó. The 7:15am bus continues to Baños Morales daily in January and February and on weekends only from March to October.

Turismo Arpue (☎ 02-211-7165) runs buses (US$7) on Saturday and Sunday beginning at 7:30am from Santiago's Plaza Italia (the Baquedano metro station) directly to Baños Morales; call to confirm departure times. From October to mid-May, **Buses Manzur** (☎ 02-777-4284) runs to the hot springs from Plaza Italia on Wednesday, Saturday and Sunday at 7:15am. Try also **Buses Cordillera** (☎ 02-777-3881) from Terminal San Borja.

VALPARAÍSO

☎ 032 / pop 276,000

Valparaíso, or 'Valpo,' is a well-worn, frenetic port with houses stacked to gaping heights along the sea. Considered the cultural capital of Chile, this city, 120km northwest of Santiago, is a Unesco World Heritage site with reason. While the bohemian among us love it, its rough edges won't charm all. Tangled wires and debris scatter the backdrop. The congested center is known as El Plan, with lower-level streets parallel to the shoreline which curves toward Viña del Mar. An irregular pattern of streets leads into residential hills which are also connected by steep footpaths and Valparaíso's famous *ascensores* (elevators), built in its heyday between 1883 and 1916.

The leading merchant port along the Cape Horn and Pacific Ocean routes, Valparaíso was the stopover for foreign vessels, including whalers, and the export point of Chilean wheat destined for the California gold rush. Foreign merchants and capital made it Chile's financial powerhouse. Its decline began with the devastating 1906 earthquake and the opening of the Panama Canal in 1914. Today this V Region capital and home to the National Congress is in revival mode, with a number of hot nightspots, restaurants and B&Bs.

Information
INTERNET ACCESS
Internet cafés are common. One of the nicest: **World Next Door Ciber Cafe** (Blanco 692; per hr US$1; ☺ 8:30am-8pm Mon-Sat) This welcoming internet café has a superfast connection, student discounts and internet-based phone calls.

CHILE

VALPARAÍSO

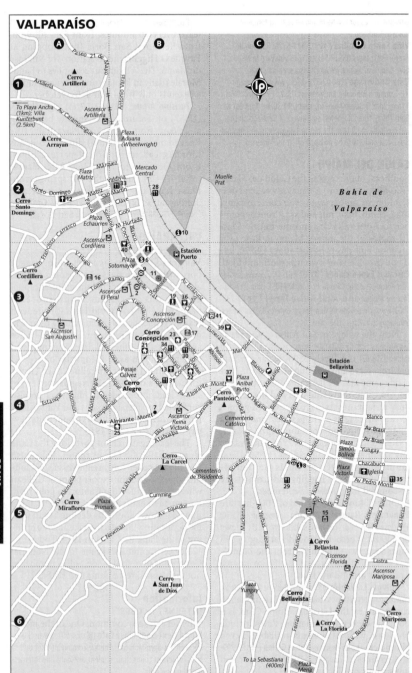

Bahía de
Valparaíso

CHILE

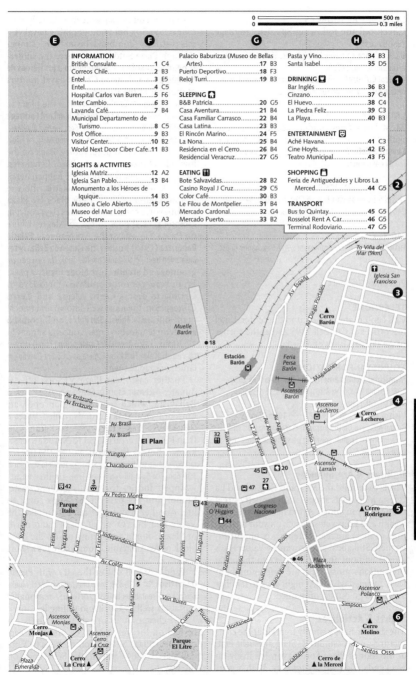

CHILE

INTERNET RESOURCES

Check out the following Spanish-language resources:

B&B Valparaíso (www.bbvalparaiso.cl) Useful for extra accommodations options.

Capital Cultural (www.capitalcultural.cl) A roundup of restaurants, hotels and cultural offerings.

LAUNDRY

Most *hospedajes* (budget accommodations with shared bathroom) offer laundry service.

Lavanda Café (Av Almirante Montt 454) On Cerro Alegre; laundry and coffee.

MEDICAL SERVICES

Hospital Carlos van Buren (☎ 2204-000; Av Colón 2454) Located at the corner of San Ignacio.

MONEY

Inter Cambio (Plaza Sotomayor s/n) An exchange house.

POST

Post office (Prat 856)

TELEPHONE

Call centers are abundant in the center. Entel has offices at Condell 1495 and at the corner of Av Pedro Montt and Cruz.

TOURIST INFORMATION

Municipal Departamento de Turismo (☎ 2939-108; Condell 1490; ⏱ 8:30am-2pm & 3:30-5:30pm Mon-Fri) Offers basic services.

Visitor center (☎ 2939-587; ⏱ 10am-2pm & 3-6pm Mon-Fri) On the pier near Plaza Sotomayor, with well-informed English-speaking personnel and free city maps.

Dangers & Annoyances

The area around the Mercado Central and La Iglesia Matriz has a reputation for petty street crime and muggings. Avoid flashy displays of wealth and keep a close watch on your belongings, as there are regular reports of opportunist theft. Still, most people wander Valparaíso's streets without any problem. With the usual precautions most areas are safe enough, at least during daylight. At night stick to familiar areas and go out accompanied.

Sights & Activities

The shutter-happy simply tremble at the city's picturesque possibilities. Start at **Muelle Prat**, at the foot of Plaza Sotomayor. It's lively on weekends, dare we say *touristy*. Watch your stuff here. You can squeeze in a cheap harbor tour (US$1.50), but photographing naval vessels is strictly prohibited. From here, clamber through Plaza Sotomayor, where the subterranean mausoleum **Monumento a los Héroes de Iquique** pays tribute to Chile's naval martyrs of the War of the Pacific.

Take **Ascensor Cordillera** west of the plaza to the well-poised 1842 **Museo del Mar Lord Cochrane** (Merlet 195; admission free; ⏱ 10am-6pm Tue-Sun mid-Mar–mid-Sep, 10am-1pm & 3-8pm mid-Sep–mid-Mar), which housed Chile's first observatory. Back on the lower level take Serrano to Plaza Echaurren (stay on your guard as robberies happen here). A block north is the **Iglesia Matriz**, the site of four churches since 1559. Back by Plaza Sotomayor, near the Tribunales (law courts), **Ascensor El Peral** goes to Cerro Alegre, where on Paseo Yugoslavo the Art Nouveau **Palacio Baburizza** (1916) houses the **Museo de Bellas Artes** (admission free; ⏱ 9:30am-6pm Tue-Sun); its gorgeous grounds and architecture alone justify a peek. From here, continue on Paseo Yugoslavo to Urriola to access Cerro Alegre and Cerro Concepción, the most well-known and typical of the hill areas. **Iglesia San Pablo**, on Pilcomayo and Templeman, has organ concerts Sunday at 12:30pm. Take **Ascensor Concepción (Turri)** down to reach **Reloj Turri** (cnr Esmeralda & Gómez Carreño), a landmark clock tower.

Further east, near Plaza Victoria off Aldunate, **Ascensor Espíritu Santo** accesses Cerro Bellavista, which has become an open-air museum of abstract murals, called **Museo a Cielo Abierto**. From here, take Av Ramos and then Ricardo Ferrari to get to Neruda's least-known house, **La Sebastiana** (☎ 2256-606; Ferrari 692; adult/student US$3.75/2; ⏱ 10:30am-2:30pm & 3:30-6pm Tue-Sun, till 7pm Jan & Feb). In this wind-whipped locale, the poet's eclectic taste, humor and his passion for ships come to life. Another way to get here is to take the Verde Mar bus 'O' or 'D' on Serrano north of Plaza Sotomayor, getting off on the 6900 block of Av Alemania, from where it's a short walk.

Paddle or sail out of the city with **Puerto Deportivo** (☎ 2592-852; www.puertodeportivo.cl; Muelle Barón; kayak rentals per hr US$8), offering reasonable rentals as well as kayak and sailing lessons.

The cheapest tour of Valparaíso's hills can be had on the Verde Mar 'O' *micro* on Serrano near Plaza Sotomayor. It chugs to Viña del Mar (US50¢), passing La Sebastiana on the way.

CHILE

Festivals & Events

Año Nuevo (New Year's) is a major event thanks to spectacular fireworks that bring hundreds of thousands of spectators to the city.

Sleeping

Valpo's gemstone digs are budget *hospedajes* perched in the hills. Make reservations or find listings at www.granvalparaiso.cl or www.bbvalparaiso.cl (both in Spanish).

Residencial Veracruz (☎ 2253-583; Av Pedro Montt 2881; s/d US$8/16) For skinny wallets, this friendly family residence near the bus terminal offers pleasing common areas and kitchen access. It's great if you don't mind the street noise.

Casa Aventura (☎ 2755-963; www.casaventura.cl; Pasaje Gálvez 11, Cerro Concepción; per person incl breakfast US$12) A friendly couple run this comfortable and airy *hostal*. Check out the hiking trips and Spanish courses. Breakfast includes fruit, homemade cheese and real coffee, and there's kitchen use.

B&B Patricia (☎ 2220-290; 12 de Febrero 315; s/d without bathroom incl breakfast US$12/24) Gleaming and fresh, this high-ceiling option boasts accommodating owners and a location right in town.

Residencia en el Cerro (☎ 2495-298; Pasaje Pierre Loti 51 btwn Abtao & Pilcomayo, Cerro Concepción; s/d US$12/24; 🖳) Turn-of-the-century grandeur with soaring views and delectable breakfasts. You'll find it on a small alleyway bedecked in bougainvillea.

El Rincón Marino (☎ 2225-815; www.rinconmarino.cl; San Ignacio 454; s/d incl breakfast US$12.50/25; 🖳) Word on the street has popularized this busy nook with spacious rooms, wonderful owners and kitchen use.

Casa Familiar Carrasco (☎ 2210-737; www.casacarrasco.cl; Abtao 668, Cerro Concepción; r per person US$13.50) Not that cheap – the rooms are clean but quite basic – the draw here are the delightful elderly owners and spectacular roof deck vistas. You'll know it by its unmistakable pink and green exterior.

Villa Kunterbunt (☎ 2288-873; villakunterbuntvalpo@yahoo.de; Quebrada Verde 92, Cerro Playa Ancha; r per person incl breakfast US$16; 🖳) Dig this colonial house, with fluffy pillows, claw-foot tub, hearty breakfast, a friendly family and backyard patio. Reserve the romantic tower room in advance. It's accessed by *colectivo* 150, 151 or bus 1, 2, 3, 5, 17 or 111 from the terminal.

La Nona (☎ 2495-706; www.bblanona.com; Galos 660, Cerro Alegre; r per person US$18) A reader-recommended

hospedaje where the owners will bend over backwards to make your stay great. Find directions and more on their excellent website.

Casa Latina (☎ 2494-622; Papudo 462, Cerro Concepción; s/d per person without bathroom incl breakfast US$19/35; 🖳) This lovely, newly refurbished *hospedaje* affords all the perks of a hotel with the cozy communal feel of a hostel.

Eating

On Sunday, most restaurants are open only noon to 4pm, unless noted.

Santa Isabel (Av Pedro Montt btwn Las Heras & Carrera; 🕑 9am-9pm) Supermarket with upstairs cafeteria.

Mercado Cardonal (cnr Yungay & Rawson) Get your goat cheese and olives on this block of crisp and colorful produce. Upstairs *cocinerías* serve *paila marina* for US$3.50 or daily specials (US$2.50).

Mercado Puerto (cnr Blanco & San Martín) This gruff and fishier market also offers meal deals.

Casino Royal J Cruz (Condell 1466; 🕑 2:30pm-4am) A delicious hodgepodge of antiques, tabletop graffiti and laissez-faire attitude. Go for the mountainous *chorrillana* (a plate of fries topped with spicy pork, onions and egg) while folk singers strum and serenade you.

Color Café (Papudo 526, Cerro Concepción; mains US$4-9) A luminous literary nook with a planet of tea offerings, tasty vegetarian treats, coffee and velvety hot chocolate. Open late Sundays.

Le Filou de Montpellier (☎ 2224-663; Av Almirante Montt 382; set menu US$5) Adorable and run by a mad Frenchman who prepares mouthwatering dishes: picture quiche Lorraine and roast turkey stuffed with prunes in a cognac and port sauce.

Bar Inglés (☎ 2214-625; Cochrane 851; mains US$7-10; 🕑 noon-11pm Mon-Fri) Back in the day hustlers would use the back door to sneak out with the cash of gullible *santiaguinos* who paid advances for contraband. It's still ripe with memories and maritime atmosphere, decked out in dark wood and white tablecloths. On offer are steaks, conger eel and Spanish tortillas.

Bote Salvavidas (☎ 2251-477; Muelle Prat s/n; mains US$9-13) The prices may be dear and the service slow, but this seafood spot offers prime views of a working port in action.

Pasta y Vino (☎ 2496-187; Templeman 352; mains US$9-13) Innovative and interesting, this place fills up fast. We recommend the ravioli cooked with a hint of curry and coconut.

CHILE

Drinking

Grab a friend and cruise the scruffy pub-lined street of Av Ecuador, including Mr Egg at No 50, or Leo Bar at No 24. Best not to go alone.

Cinzano (Plaza Anibal Pinto 1182; ☺ 10am-2am Mon-Sat) Drinkers, sailors, crooners and lovers have frequented this Valpo haunt since 1896. Photographs of sinking ships line the walls, and old boys with golden voices perform tango tunes in the evenings.

El Huevo (www.elhuevo.cl; Blanco 1386; admission US$7) Rock and drink the night away at this happening venue for students and young people.

La Playa (Cochrane 568; ☺ 10am-past midnight) One long bar, cheap pitchers of beer and hedonistic touches make this one great outing.

La Piedra Feliz (www.lapiedrafeliz.cl; Av Errázuriz 1054; admission Tue-Sat US$8.50) A class act with live jazz and tango on weekends.

Teatro Municipal (Av Uruguay 410) Hosts live theater and concerts.

Entertainment

Aché Havana (Av Errázuriz 1042; admission Thu-Sat US$6, free Tue & Wed) *Mueve la cadera* (shake your hips) to pulsating salsa.

Cine Hoyts (☎ 2594-709; Av Pedro Montt 2111) Movie theater.

Shopping

Feria de Antiguedades y Libros La Merced (Plaza O'Higgins; tickets US$6; ☺ Sat, Sun & holidays) One man's trash is another man's *feria,* but you'll find some standouts here, including second-hand books, and it's fun.

Getting There & Away

The **Terminal Rodoviario** (Av Pedro Montt 2800) is across from the Congreso Nacional. Bus service from Valparaíso is almost identical to that from Viña del Mar. Many buses go to points north and south, with fares and times similar to Santiago. On weekends, get your ticket to Santiago in advance; Tur Bus has the most departures (US$4, two hours). Most buses to the north leave at night, while many to the south leave in the morning.

Fénix Pullman Norte (☎ 257-993) runs to Mendoza (US$16, eight hours) as does **Tas Choapa** (in Valparaíso ☎ 2252-921, in Viña del Mar 032-882-258), which continues to San Juan and Córdoba. Buses stop in Viña del Mar, but bypass Santiago.

Buses to the lovely coastal town of Quintay run five times a day from the corner of Chacabuco and 12 de Febrero.

Getting Around

The most unique way to get around Valparaíso is by trolley car (US30¢), which still run throughout the city – despite much wear and tear. *Micros* (US50¢) run to and from Viña and all over the city, as do *colectivos* (US60¢). During the day, avoid the traffic to Viña by hopping on *Merval*, a commuter train that leaves from **Estación Puerto** (Plaza Sotomayor 711). Other stations are at Bellavista and Barón. Trains run till 10pm. Valpo's **ascensores** (from US20¢; ☺ 7am-8pm or 8:30pm) are considered both transport and entertainment. The oldest, Ascensor Cordillera, runs from 6am to 11:30pm.

Risk takers can consider renting a car to explore beach resorts to the north or south. For car hire, try **Rosselot Rent a Car** (☎ 352-365; Victoria 3013).

ISLA NEGRA

A stirring testament to imagination, whimsy and affection, Pablo Neruda's outlandish favorite **house** (☎ 035-461-284; admission with English-speaking guide US$5.20; ☺ 10am-8pm Tue-Sun summer, 10am-2pm & 3-6pm Tue-Fri, 10am-8pm Sat & Sun rest of year) sits atop a rocky headland 80km south of Valparaíso. It includes extraordinary collections of bowsprits, ships in bottles, nautical instruments and wood carvings. His tomb is also here alongside that of his third wife, Matilde. Reservations are advised in high season. Isla Negra is not, by the way, an island.

A visit here is an easy day trip. Pullman and Tur Bus (both US$3, 1½ hours, every 30 minutes) buses go direct from Santiago's Terminal de Buses Alameda. Pullman Bus Lago Peñuelas (US$2, 1½ hours, every 15 minutes) comes here from Valparaíso.

VIÑA DEL MAR

☎ 032 / pop 286,900

Trim green gardens and palm-fringed boulevards characterize this city on the sea. Known as the Garden City, for its many parks and flowers, or just Viña for short, this city beach resort has a scrubbed, modern feel that couldn't contrast more sharply with the personality of neighboring Valpo. After the railway linked Santiago and Valparaíso, the well-heeled flocked to Viña del Mar, building grand houses and mansions away from the congested port. Viña remains a popular weekend and summer destination for *santiaguinos.*

Viña's beaches can get very crowded during holidays and are subject to cool morning fogs. The chilly Humboldt current can also put off would-be swimmers. Summer is pickpocketer's high season, so watch your belongings, especially on the beach.

Information

Afex (Av Arlegui 641) Can change traveler's checks and currency.

Central de Turismo e Informaciones (☎ 269-330; www.visitevinadelmar.cl; Av Marina s/n; ⏰ 9am-7pm Mon-Sat summer, 9am-2pm & 3-7pm Mon-Fri, 10am-2pm & 4-7pm Sat rest of year) Provides city maps and events calendars.

Horeb (Av Arlegui 458; per hr US80¢) Offers internet access.

Hospital Gustavo Fricke (☎ 680-041; Álvarez 1532) East of downtown.

Lavarápido (Av Arlegui 440; express service US$7) You can do your laundry here.

Post office (Plaza Latorre 32) Sits at the northwest side of Plaza Vergara.

Sernatur (☎ 882-285; infovalparaiso@sernatur.cl; Av Valparaíso 507, 3rd fl; ⏰ 8:30am-2pm & 3-5:30pm Mon-Fri) Tourist information is also available here, back off the main street.

Tecomp (Av Valparaíso 684) Offers cheap international calling.

Sights & Activities

Specializing in Rapa Nui archaeology and Chilean natural history, the small **Museo de Arqueológico e Historia Francisco Fonck** (4 Norte 784; admission US$1.50; ⏰ 9:30am-6pm Tue-Fri, till 2pm Sat & Sun) features an original *moai* (enormous stone sculpture from Rapa Nui), Mapuche silverwork, Peruvian ceramics, plus insects and stuffed birds. Two blocks east, the **Museo Palacio Rioja** (Quillota 214; admission US$1; ⏰ 10am-1:30pm & 3-5:30pm Tue-Sun) is a mansion hosting exhibits, movies and musical performances.

Once the residence of the prosperous Alvarez-Vergara family, now a public park, the grounds of the magnificently landscaped **Quinta Vergara** (⏰ 7am-7pm), south of the railroad, showcase plants from many corners of the world. On-site is the Venetian-style **Palacio Vergara** (1908), which in turn contains the less inspiring **Museo de Bellas Artes** (admission US$1; ⏰ 10am-2pm & 3-6pm Tue-Sun).

On the north side of the estuary is the overly glitzy **casino**; to the west is **Castillo Wulff**, built in 1880; and the fancy boat-shaped **Cap Ducal hotel**.

Festivals & Events

Viña del Mar's most popular event is the annual **Festival Internacional de la Canción** (International Song Festival), held every February in the amphitheater of the Quinta Vergara. Adored by Chileans, it attracts big names from the Latin American pop world and English-language has-beens.

Sleeping

Accommodations aren't as charming or competitively priced as in nearby Valpo. Prices following are the high summer rates, look for deep discounts off-season. The best quality budget options are on and around Av Agua Santa, just south of the railroad.

Residencial Agua Santa (☎ 901-531; Agua Santa 36; s/d US$10/20) A tranquil blue Victorian shaded by trees.

Hospedaje Calderón (☎ 970-456; Batuco 147; per person US$10) This homey (unmarked) family lodging offers basic, well-scrubbed rooms a skip from the bus terminal.

Hospedaje Toledo (☎ 881-496, Batuco 160; US$10) Engage the owner in chitchat at this amenable, unmarked option near the bus terminal.

Residencial Clorinda (☎ 623-835; Diego Portales 47; s US$12) Lounge about the outdoor patios with great views; laundry facilities and kitchen use round out the comforts of home.

Residencial La Nona (☎ 663-825; Agua Santa 48; s/d incl breakfast US$13/26) A colorful building of simple yet comfortable rooms; those in the main house have private bathrooms. There is a very matronly and charming laundry service.

Hotel Asturias (☎ 711-565; www.hotelasturias.tk; Av Valparaíso 299; per person US$13.50) Part of the Hostelling International (HI) group, this tidy and friendly budget option is good for meeting fellow backpackers.

Hostal Mar (☎ 884-775; Alvares 868; s/d incl breakfast US$23/33.50; P) Look for the willow tree and neon sign down a driveway marking the entrance to this characterful place. Decent rooms and a comfy communal area make it worth the slightly higher charge.

Residencial Villarrica (☎ 881-484; administracion@ hotelvillarrica.com; Av Arlegui 172; s/d without bathroom US$25/37) Upstairs rooms are the best at this light and spacious lodging with some nice antique touches. Book ahead on weekends.

Residencial 555 (☎ 739-035; 5 Norte 555; s/d incl breakfast US$26/43) Our pick, this old gem with chandeliers and chintzy touches is situated on

CHILE

VIÑA DEL MAR

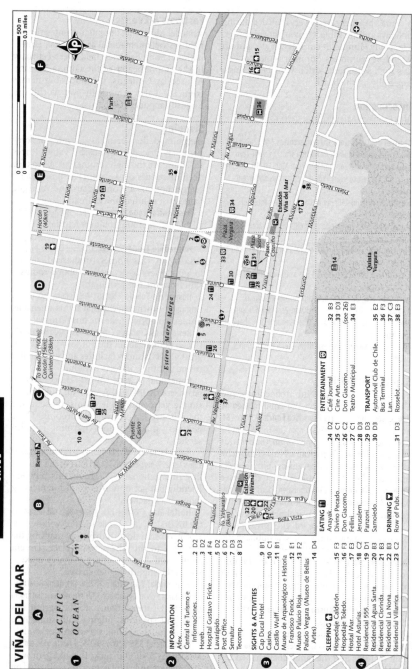

0.3 miles
500 m
0
0

PACIFIC

OCEAN

CHILE

a quiet tree-lined street. Rooms are spotless and simply lovely.

Eating & Drinking

The pedestrian area around Av Valparaíso is the best bet for a variety of cheap eats. Take a stroll down Paseo Cousiño to check out a string of convivial pubs, some featuring live music.

Jerusalem (Quinta 259; snacks US$2-5) Pull up a stool and chat with the friendly owners while they whip up your falafel sandwich. There's other Middle Eastern fare but beware the *arak*, a potent Middle Eastern shot.

Don Giacomo (Villanelo 135, 2nd fl; mains US$2.50-5) When the sun's up this salsa club serves inexpensive lunches, including lasagna or pasta dishes.

Anayak (☎ 680-093; Quinta 134; coffee & cake US$3.50) Tuck into this big, bright café for coffee and cakes. The lunch menu is a little overpriced.

Panzoni (Paseo Cousiño 12-B; mains US$4-9) Reels in the lunchtime diners with its mix of a warm welcome and fine, uncomplicated Italian food.

Samoiedo (Av Valparaíso 637; mains US$7-11) This classic, old-boys' eatery has been banishing hunger for half a century. Attempt a lunchtime feast of *lomo a lo pobre* (literally 'poor man's beef').

Fellini (3 Norte 88; mains from US$9) One of Viña's most renowned and popular restaurants with a bright, welcoming ambience. Try a simple pasta dish.

Divino Pecado (Av San Martín 180; mains US$9-13; ☯ 12:30-3:30pm & 7-11:30pm) High rollers frequent this refined Italian restaurant to enjoy lovely dishes, such as the Easter Island tuna, with violins in the background.

Entertainment

For big nightlife head to Valparaíso.

Café Journal (cnr Santa Agua & Alvarez; ☯ until 4am Fri & Sat) Electronic music is mixed at this boomingly popular club with three heaving dance floors, beers on tap and walls plastered in yesterday's news.

Cine Arte (Plaza Vergara 142; tickets US$6) Come here for movies.

Don Giacomo (☎ 961-944; Villanelo 135, 2nd fl; ☯ 10am-2am) This wood-furnished 1920 joint endured several earthquakes and now pulses to a salsa beat a few nights a week. Shy guys and left feet can shoot a few games of pool.

Teatro Municipal (Plaza Vergara) This grand building stages plays, chamber-music concerts and art-house movies.

Getting There & Away

Lan (☎ 600-526-2000; Av Valparaíso 276) runs a shuttle (US$10) to Santiago's Padahuel airport from the corner of Tres Norte and Libertad. Or take a bus toward Santiago and ask to be left at 'Cruce al Aeropuerto' to shave about an hour from the trip.

The **bus terminal** (cnr Av Valparaíso & Quilpué), four blocks east of Plaza Vergara, is less chaotic than Valpo's and served by most of the same buses.

For car hire, try **Rosselot** (☎ 382-888; Alvares 762). The **Automóvil Club de Chile** (Acchi; ☎ 689-505; 1 Norte 901) is just north of the Marga.

Getting Around

Running along Av Arlegui, frequent local buses marked 'Puerto' or 'Aduana' link Viña with Valparaíso (US50¢, five minutes). For easier connections to Valparaíso, the Metro Regional Valparaíso (Merval) has two stations, **Estación Miramar** (cnr Alvarez & Agua Santa) and **Estación Viña del Mar** (Plaza Sucre).

To get to the nearby beach resort of Reñaca, take bus 111 on the road leading north along the coast (US50¢, 10 minutes, every 10 minutes). Bus 1 goes on to Concón (25 minutes, every 10 minutes).

AROUND VIÑA DEL MAR

Coastal towns immediately north of Viña have better beaches but their quiet character has eroded with the piling on of suburbs and apartment buildings. **Concón**, 15km from Viña, is worth a trip for its unpretentious seafood restaurants. **Las Deliciosas** (☎ 903-665; Sv Borgoño 25370, Concón) does exquisite *empanadas*, including cheese and crab (US$1.50).

Another 23km beyond Concón is **Quintero**, a sleepy peninsula with beaches nestled between rocks. **Hospedaje Garzas** (☎ 032-930-443; Av Francia 1341; s/d incl breakfast US$10/20) is the town bargain, with an arty ambience and wood-paneled rooms with a panorama of the sea.

Further north, **Horcón** is a quaint fishing port turned hippie haven. On the main beach, **Hostería Arancibia** (☎ 032-796-169; s/d US$25/42) boasts neat cabins with water views and a pleasant seafood restaurant. Before reaching the cove, a road on the right follows a rocky, crescent moon bay. Wild camping is possible, although sand gets into everything. At the far end is nudist beach 'Playa La Luna.' **La Negra** (☎ 032-796-213; Calle Principal; camping US$4, r per person incl breakfast US$14) offers a shady yard for your

CHILE

tent or a room in the artsy, airy house. Kitchen use is available. Ask the bus driver to stop at 'Agua Potable'; La Negra is next door. **Santa Clara** (Pasaje La Iglesia; fish dishes US$4-7) cooks up enormous and delicious fish platters; claim a 2nd-floor table for views.

Continue north 35km to reach **Zapallar**, the most exclusive of Chile's coastal resorts with still-unspoiled beaches flanked by densely wooded hillsides. Budget accommodations are not the norm in Zapallar but **Residencial Margarita** (☎ 033-741-284, Januario Ovalle 143; s/d US$12/24) bucks the trend. Rooms are well kept and neat with reasonable bathrooms. Book ahead. Have a superb seafood lunch at **El Chiringuito** (Caleta de Pescadores; fish mains US$8), with crushed shells underfoot and a wall of windows that peers to the sea.

Several bus companies call in at Zapallar direct from Santiago, including Tur Bus and Pullman. Sol del Pacífico comes up the coast from Viña.

NORTHERN CHILE

Traveling inland, the balmy coast of sunbathers and surfers shifts to cactus scrub plains and dry mountains streaked in reddish tones. Mines scar these ore-rich mammoths whose primary reserve, copper, is high-octane fuel to Chile's economic engine. But there's life here as well, in the fertile valleys producing *pisco* grapes, papayas and avocados. Clear skies mean exceptional celestial observation. Many international telescopic, optical and radio projects are based here. The driest desert in the world, the Atacama is a refuge of flamingos on salt lagoons, sculpted moonscapes and geysers ringed by snow-tipped volcanoes. In short, these places are an orgy for the senses and ripe for exploration.

Chile's 2000km northern stretch takes in Norte Chico, or 'region of 10,000 mines,' a semiarid transition zone from the Valle Central to the Atacama. Its main attractions are the beaches, La Serena, Valle Elqui and the observatories. The Atacama Desert occupies 'Norte Grande,' gained from Peru and Bolivia in the War of the Pacific. The stamp of ancient cultures is evident in enormous geoglyphs on barren hillsides. Aymara peoples still farm the *precordillera* (foothills of the Andes) and pasture llamas and alpacas in the highlands. Divert from the desert scenery to explore the

working mine of Chuquimaquata or brave the frisky surf of arid coastal cities.

Take precautions against altitude sickness in the mountains and avoid drinking tap water in the desert reaches. Coastal *camanchaca* (dense convective fog on the coastal hills of the Atacama desert) keeps the climate cool along the beach, while *altiplano* temperatures change drastically from day to night.

OVALLE
☎ 053 / pop 104,000

Chess rivals gather on the plaza of this unpretentious market town. Ovalle offers a glimpse of city life in the provinces and is the best base for Parque Nacional Fray Jorge or Valle del Encanto. The tourist kiosk sits at the corner of Benavente and Ariztia Oriente. **Tres Valles Turismo** (☎ 629-650; Libertad 496) organizes tours and exchanges money. ATMs can be found along Victoria, at the plaza.

In the grand old train station, **Museo del Limarí** (cnr Covarrubias & Antofagasta; admission US$1, Sun free; ☎ 9am-6pm Tue-Fri, 10am-1pm Sat & Sun) displays gorgeous ceramics that show trans-Andean links between the Diaguita peoples of coastal Chile and northwestern Argentina.

Sleeping & Eating

Hotel Quisco (☎ 620-351; Maestranza 161; s/d US$17/22, without bathroom US$9/18) With amenable staff and a quirky mix of furniture. Rooms with interior windows open to dark and narrow hallways. Close to bus terminal.

Hotel Roxy (☎ 620-080; Libertad 155; s/d/tr US$15/23/31, without bathroom US$11.50/17.50/21) Sundrenched and serene, with lemon trees in the garden and checkered floors. The drawback is it's slightly unkempt.

Feria Modelo de Ovalle (Av Benavente; ☉ 8am-4pm Mon, Wed, Fri & Sat) A buzzing hive of market activity with scores of different fruit and vegetables.

Club Social Arabe (Arauco 255; set meals US$2-3, mains US$3.50-8) A lofty atrium serving superb stuffed grape leaves, summer squash or red peppers and baklava, in addition to Chilean specialties.

Drinking

Café Real (☎ 624-526; Vicuña MacKenna 419; ☉ 9am-2:30am Mon-Sat) Cheery and cosmopolitan, with young things knocking back espressos and cold Cristal. There's a pool table and occasional live music.

NORTHERN CHILE (NORTE GRANDE)

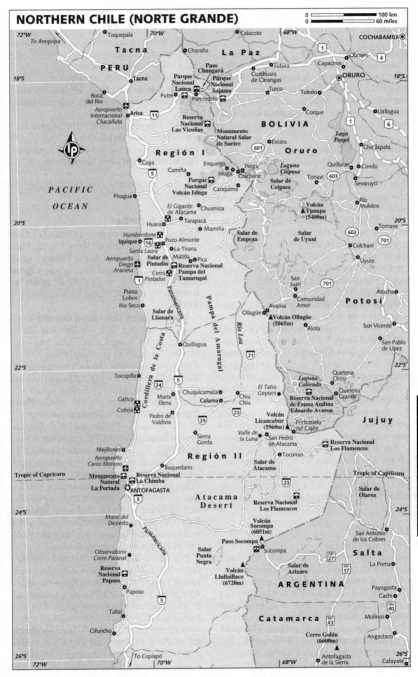

El Quijote (Arauco 295) A musty bar paying homage to literary and leftist Latin America.

Getting There & Away

From the **bus terminal** (cnr Maestranza & Balmaceda) plenty of buses go to Santiago (US$6.50, five hours), La Serena (US$2, 1¾ hours) and more northerly points. A faster way to La Serena (US$3.25, 1¼ hours) is by **Agencia Tacso** (Ariztía Pontiente 159).

AROUND OVALLE

Petroglyphs, pictographs and ancient mortars cover the canyon at **Monumento Arqueológico Valle del Encanto**, 19km west of Ovalle in a rocky tributary of the Río Limarí. These dancing stick men and alienlike forms are remnants of the El Molle culture (AD 200–700). Visibility is best at midday when shadows are fewer. Visitors can camp and picnic. Taxis from town cost US$25 round-trip or any westbound bus will drop you at the highway marker from where it's an easy 5km walk on a clearly marked road.

Parque Nacional Fray Jorge (admission US$3; ☺ 9am-4:30pm Fri-Sun Dec 15-Mar 15, Sat & Sun only rest of year), 82km west of Ovalle, is an ecological island of lush and foggy Valdivian cloud forest in a semiarid region. Of its original 10,000 hectares, there remain only 400 hectares of this truly unique vegetation – enough, though, to make it a Unesco World Biosphere Reserve. **El Arrayancito** (campsites US$14), 3km from the visitors center, has sheltered sites with fire pits, picnic tables, potable water and toilets. Bring your own food and warm, rain-protective clothing.

Reach the park by taking a westward lateral off the Panamericana, about 20km north of the Ovalle junction. There's no public transport, but agencies in La Serena and Ovalle offer tours. A taxi from Ovalle will cost about US$45.

LA SERENA

☎ 051 / pop 160,150

Blessed with neocolonial architecture, shady streets and golden shores, peaceful La Serena turns trendy beach resort come summer. Founded in 1544, Chile's second-oldest city is a short jaunt from character-laden villages, sun-soaked *pisco* vineyards and international observatories for stargazing. Nearby **Coquimbo** is quite a bit more rough-and-tumble, but lives and breathes a hearty nightlife. Mornings in La Serena often stew in chilly fog.

Information

Banks with ATMs line the plaza.

Conaf (☎ 225-068; Cordovez 281) Supplies brochures on Fray Jorge and Isla Choros.

Entel (Prat 571) Make calls from here.

Gira Tour (Prat 689) Exchanges money.

Hospital Juan de Dios (☎ 225-569; Balmaceda 916) Has an emergency entrance at Larraín Alcalde and Anfión Muñoz.

Infernet (Balmaceda 417; per hr US$2.60) A psychedelic cybercafé with booths and webcams.

Lavaseco (Balmaceda 851; per kg US$4.50) Does laundry.

Post office (cnr Matta & Prat) Opposite the Plaza de Armas.

Sernatur (☎ 225-199; Matta 461) Is exceptionally attentive.

Sights & Activities

La Serena has a whopping 29 churches to its credit but relatively few takers. On the Plaza de Armas is the 1844 **Iglesia Catedral**, while a block west is the mid-18th-century **Iglesia Santo Domingo**. The stone colonial **Iglesia San Francisco** (Balmaceda 640) dates back to the early 1600s.

Museo Histórico Casa Gabriel González Videla (Matta 495; admission US$1; ☺ 10am-6pm Mon-Fri, 10am-1pm Sat) is named after La Serena's native son and Chile's president from 1946 to 1952, who took over the Communist party, then outlawed it, driving Pablo Neruda out of the senate and into exile. Pop upstairs to check out the modern art. The eclectic **Museo Arqueológico** (cnr Cordovez & Cienfuegos; admission US$1; ☺ 9:30am-5:50pm Tue-Fri, 10am-1pm & 4-7pm Sat, 10am-1pm Sun) houses Atacameño mummies, a *moai* from Rapa Nui, Diaguita artifacts and a map of the distribution of Chile's indigenous population. **Mercado La Recova** offers a jumble of dried fruits, rain sticks and artisan jewelry. Retreat into the ambience of trickling brooks, skating swans and rock gardens at **Kokoro No Niwa** (Jardín del Corazón; admission US$1; ☺ 10am-6pm), a well-maintained Japanese garden at the south end of Parque Pedro de Valdivia.

Wide sandy **beaches** stretch from La Serena's nonfunctional lighthouse to Coquimbo. Avoid strong rip currents between the west end of Av Aguirre and Cuatro Esquinas. Choose the beaches marked 'Playa Apta' south of Cuatro Esquinas and around Coquimbo. A bike path runs about 4km by the beach. Local **bodyboarders** hit Playa El Faro, and Playa Totoralillo, south of Coquimbo, is rated highly for its surf breaks and **windsurfing** potential.

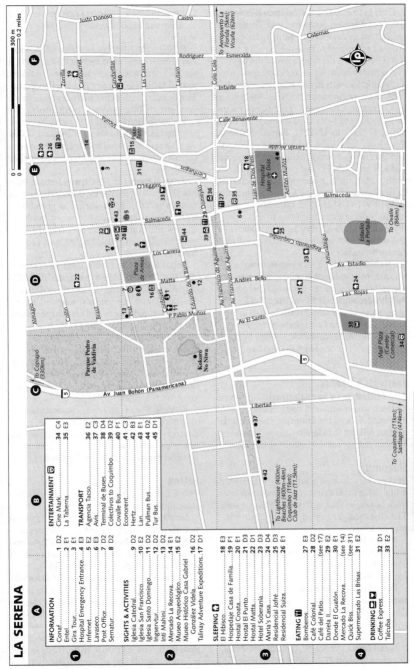

LA SERENA

CHILE

Over in Coquimbo, **Cruz del Tercer Milenio** (Cross of the Third Millennium; admission US$2.60; 10am-7pm Mon-Fri, 11am-8pm Sat & Sun) is a 96m-high concrete cross lit up at night. Take the elevator to the top (US$2) for a dizzying view of the bay.

Agencies offer a plethora of excursions, from national-park visits to nighttime astronomical trips, *pisco*-tasting tours to New Age trips to UFO central, Cochiguaz. Traditional excursions include full-day trips through the Elqui Valley (US$23 to US$27), Parque Nacional Fray Jorge and Valle del Encanto (US$35), and Parque Nacional Pingüino de Humboldt (US$39 to US$41). Agencies also provide transportation to observatories, including Observatorio Comunal Cerro Mamalluca (US$19.50 to US$25). The minimum number of passengers ranges from two to six.

Ingservtur (220-165; www.ingservtur.cl; Matta 611) Well-established with friendly English-speaking staff and discounts for students.

Inti Mahini (224-350; www.intimahinatravel.cl in Spanish; Prat 214) A youth-oriented agency offering standard tours plus useful advice on independent travel.

Talinay Adventure Expeditions (218-658; talinay@turismoaventura.net; Prat 470, Local 22) Has bilingual guides, standard and adventurous options, including mountain biking, climbing, kayaking, diving, horse-riding and sand-boarding. It also rents bikes (per hour/full day US$1.75/14).

Festivals & Events

The **Festival de La Serena** attracts big-name Chilean musicians and comedians in early February. Around the same time the **Feria Internacional del Libro de La Serena** gathers prominent Chilean authors at the historical museum.

Sleeping

Backpackers' hostels abound by the bus terminal. Many taxi drivers receive commission from hotels, so stick with your choice or walk. The distances are short. Low-season rates may be lower.

Maria's Casa (229-282; Las Rojas 18; r per person US$8) Enjoy the familial attention at these nine simple rooms around a grassy backyard. A cobbler on site makes Chile's cutest shoes.

Hospedaje Casa de Familia (213-954; hostal rosita@hotmail.com; Cantournet 976; s/d US$9/18;) Old neocolonial home with a relaxing patio and high-ceiling rooms. Bonuses include cable TV, laundry and kitchen access.

Hostal Croata (224-997; Cienfuegos 248; d US$27, s/d without bathroom US$9/17.50 all incl breakfast;)

Central, intimate and extra safe (smile at the security cameras). Laundry and bike rental available.

El Hibisco (211-407; mauricioberrios2002@yahoo.es; Juan de Dios Peni 636; s/d incl breakfast US$10/20;) A simple family guesthouse with wooden floors, shared facilities, laundry and kitchen access. The delectable breakfast includes homemade jam (jars are often given as mementoes).

Residencial Jofré (222-335; hostaljofre@hotmail .com; Regimiento Coquimbo 964; s/d incl breakfast US$10/20;) This is an old-school guesthouse with generic rooms, personable owner and kitchen privileges.

Hostal El Punto (228-474; www.punto.de; Andres Bello 979; dm/s/d incl breakfast US$10.50/21/34, s/d without bathroom US$16/21;) A gorgeous guesthouse with florid colors, sunny terraces, book exchange and laundry. Run by a friendly German couple who speak English and provide traveling tips.

Hostal Matta (210-014; hostal_matta@hotmail .com; Matta 234; d US$17.50, with bathroom US$25;) Brightly furnished and beautifully maintained new pensión, with friendly young staff, attractive communal spaces and shipshape rooms. Breakfast is US$1.75.

Hotel Soberanía (227-672; www.hotelsoberania.cl; Regimiento Coquimbo 1049; s/d incl breakfast from US$22/33;) A colonial-style family hotel with off-season deals. Though rooms are small and a little ragged around the edges, it's worthwhile value for the quiet.

Residencial Suiza (216-092; residencial.suiza@terra .cl; Cienfuegos 250; s/d incl breakfast US$27/32;) This central mustard-and-red guesthouse has house-proud owners and a dozen fresh, spotless and cheerfully decorated rooms.

Eating

Those coming from the north will rejoice in the culinary variety.

Supermercado Las Brisas (Cienfuegos 545) Large supermarket to satisfy all self-catering needs.

Mercado La Recova (cnr Cienfuegos & Cantournet) Cheap eats above the market including fresh seafood and chicken *cazuela* (stew).

Bomberos (cnr Av Francisco de Aguirre & Balmaceda; set meal US$1.75; lunch) Join the brigade for a no-frills set lunch on the upper floor of the fire station. Singles can browse firemen mugshots upstairs.

Quick Biss (Cienfuegos 545, 2nd fl; self-serve lunch US$2, mains US$5) You can pick from fresh salads, piping-hot grills and accompaniments at this veggie-friendly, surprisingly tasty self-service cafeteria.

Daniela II (Aguirre 456; mains US$2.60-9) This plain-Jane knows Chilean comfort food. Locals dig the hearty portions and the seafood rocks.

Café Colonial (Balmaceda 475; breakfast US$3.50-5, set lunch US$4, mains US$4-8; 9am-late) Stiff espressos, banana pancakes and burgers tempt the homesick traveler. Check out the live music on weekends.

Donde El Guatón (Brasil 750; mains US$5-10) Sizzling *parrilladas* (grilled meats) are set aflame right before your hungry eyes. Ambience means flowers and chandeliers fashioned from bicycle wheels.

Trendy and top-end eateries line the beach toward Peñuelas.

Drinking

Nightclubs litter the seafront to Barrio Inglés Coquimbo; they're especially hopping during summer.

Coffee Express (cnr Prat & Balmaceda; 9am-9pm Mon-Fri, 10am-9pm Sat) Oversized coffee shop serving some of La Serena's best java.

Talcuba (Eduardo de la Barra 589; 5:30pm-late Mon-Fri, 7:30pm-late Sat & Sun) University students rub shoulders to rock and pop in this dimly lit little tavern. Cheap drinks explain the general thirstiness of the crowd. Try a papaya sour or Serena libre.

Entertainment

Cine Mark (212-144; www.cinemark.cl in Spanish; Mall Plaza, Av Albert Solari 1490; admission US$4.60) Screens big-name movies.

Club de Jazz (288-784; Aldunate 739; cover US$5) Located in Coquimbo, this ever-fashionable neoclassical house with marble stairs has live music on weekends from 11pm.

La Taberna (Balmaceda 824) This seedy-looking bar in a century-old house hosts regular acts, including Chilean folk music on weekends from midnight.

Café del Patio (Prat 470; set lunch US$3-4, mains US$4-7) A patio café-cum-wine bar featuring some of Santiago's best jazz musicians in summer. The local bands are also worth a listen.

Getting There & Away

AIR

La Serena's **Aeropuerto La Florida** (Ruta 41) is 5km east of downtown. **Lan** (600-526-2000; Balmaceda 406) flies three to five times daily to Santiago (US$100, 50 minutes) and once a day to An-

tofagasta (US$121, 1¼ hours). There's also an office with longer hours in Mall Plaza.

BUS

La Serena's **Terminal de Buses** (224-573; cnr Amunátegui & Av El Santo) has dozens of carriers plying the Panamericana from Santiago north to Arica, including **Tur Bus** (215-953; www .turbus.com in Spanish; Terminal or Balmaceda 437), **Pullman Bus** (218-252, 225-284; Eduardo de la Barra 435), **Pullman Carmelita** (225-240) and **Flota Barrios** (222-601).

Destination	Duration (hr)	Cost (US$)
Antofagasta	13	18-45
Arica	23	27-52
Calama	16	24-39
Copiapó	5	7-9
Iquique	19	25-43
Los Vilos	4	7
Santiago	7	8-27
Vallenar	3	5.25

Via Elqui has frequent departures to Pisco Elqui (US$3, two hours) and Monte Grande (US$2.85, two hours) between 7am and 10:30pm. Buses Serenamar runs several buses a day to Guanaqueros (US$2, 50 minutes), Tongoy (US$2.25, one hour) and Andacollo (US$1.40, 1½ hours).

For Argentine destinations, **Covalle Bus** (213-127; Infante 538) goes to Mendoza (US$32, 12 hours) and San Juan (US$35, 14 hours) via the Libertadores pass on Tuesday, Thursday, and Sunday at 11pm.

COLECTIVO

Many regional destinations are more frequently and rapidly served by *taxi colectivo*. *Colectivos* to Coquimbo (US$1.50, 15 minutes) leave from Av Francisco de Aguirre between Balmaceda and Los Carrera. **Agencia Tacso** (227-379; Domeyko 589) goes to Ovalle (US$3.25, 1½ hours), Vicuña (US$3, 1¼ hours) and Andacollo (US$2.60, 1½ hours), and you can hire a *colectivo* for a day tour to Valle de Elqui for about US$50.

Getting Around

Private taxis to Aeropuerto La Florida cost US$4. **She Transfer** (295-058) provides door-to-door minibus transfer for US$1.75.

For car hire, try **Avis** (227-171; laserena@ avischile.cl; Av Francisco de Aguirre 063), also at the

CHILE

airport; **Hertz** (☎ 226-171; Av Francisco de Aguirre 0225); or **Econorent** (☎ 220-113; Av Francisco de Aguirre 0135).

VICUÑA

☎ 051 / pop 24,000

Vicuña, 62km east of La Serena, is a snoozy adobe village nestled in the Elqui Valley. It's the best jump-off point to explore the valley or simply indulge in its treasure groves of avocado, papaya and other fruits. There's an impressive assortment of museums and access to Observatorio Mamalluca. Tourist services huddle around the Plaza de Armas: **Oficina de Información Turística** (Torre Bauer); Banco de Estado, which changes US cash or traveler's checks and has an ATM (better to change money in La Serena); post office; and the call centers and Entel. **Mami Sabina** (cnr Mistral & Infante) has internet (per hour US$1) and bike rental.

Sights & Activities

Museo Gabriela Mistral (☎ 411-223; Av Gabriela Mistral; admission US$1), near the eastern edge of town, pays homage to one of Chile's most famous literary figures. The small **Museo Entomológico y de Historia Natural** (☎ 411-283; Chacabuco 334; admission US$1) showcases insects and kaleidoscopic butterfly collections.

Sweeping panoramas of the Elqui Valley make worthwhile the hot, dusty hike up **Cerro de la Virgen**, just north of town. The summit is less than an hour's walk from the Plaza de Armas. *Pisco* fans can hoof it 20 minutes to the vigorously marketed **Planta Pisco Capel** (☎ 411-251; www.piscocapel.com in Spanish; admission free; ♥ 10am-6pm Jan & Feb, 10am-12:30pm & 2:30-6pm Mar-Dec), where a quick tour and skimpy samples might pique your thirst. To get there head southeast of town and across the bridge, then turn left.

Goggle the galaxies through the 30cm telescope at **Observatorio Cerro Mamalluca** (☎ 411-352; www.mamalluca.org; Av Gabriela Mistral 260; tour US$6). Book a month in advance from September through April. Bring a warm sweater. Bilingual tours run every two hours from nightfall to 12:30am. Shuttles (US$2.60), reserved in advance, leave from the administration office.

Sleeping & Eating

Residencial La Elquina (☎ 411-317; O'Higgins 65; s/d incl breakfast US$19/32, without bathroom US$9/17.50; **P**) Veiled in grapevines and fruit trees, this cramped and humble abode rocks out with patio swings and a hammock.

Hostal Rita Klamt (☎ 419-611; rita_klamt@yahoo .es; Condell 443; s/d incl breakfast US$10.50/21; **P ☎**) Tuck yourself into a cozy guest room in this tranquil home with a pool and motherly German-speaking hostess. Breakfasts include homemade jam and fresh coffee.

Casa Turística Colonial del Professor (☎ 411-637; Av Gabriela Mistral 152; s/d incl breakfast US$10.50/21) Backyard brick housing attached to a handsome older building. Cats rule the scrubby gardens.

Hostal Valle Hermoso (☎ 411-206; Gabriela Mistral 706; s/d incl breakfast US$12.50/21) Lacking fuss or space, this century-old adobe building has wood floors, basic bathrooms and a small courtyard.

Hotel Halley (☎ 412-070; Av Gabriela Mistral 542; d/ste/tr/f incl breakfast US$52/64/72/98; **P ☎**) A claret-colored colonial with airy rooms, crocheted bedspreads and iron bed frames. There's also a cool courtyard to sip a *pisco sour* (grape brandy with lemon juice, egg white and powdered sugar). The restaurant, open to the public, cooks up a wonderful roast goat, plentiful salads and Chilean classics (mains US$4 to US$10).

Solar Villaseca (☎ 412-189; set meal US$4; ♥ 1-6pm Tue-Sun) If you thought a solar meal was frying an egg on the sidewalk, think again. This innovative eatery features Chilean dishes cooked in solar-powered ovens. Reservations are a must during summer. Take a *colectivo* from the bus station; it's 6km from Vicuña, beyond the Capel distillery,

Getting There & Around

A block south of the plaza, **bus terminal** (cnr Prat & O'Higgins) has frequent buses to La Serena (US$2.25, one hour), Coquimbo (US$2.50, 1¼ hours) and Pisco Elqui (US$1.75, 50 minutes). A trip to Monte Grande takes 40 minutes and costs US$1.50. Some companies have a daily service to Santiago (US$9, 7½ hours), including **Pullman** (☎ 412-812).

Opposite the bus terminal is the **Terminal de Taxis Colectivos** (cnr Prat & O'Higgins), with fast *colectivos* to La Serena (US$3, 45 minutes). Bike hire is available at **Mami Sabina** (☎ 419-594; cnr Av Gabriela Mistral & Infante).

VALLE DEL ELQUI

Big sky observatories, muscatel vineyards, *pisco* distilleries and papaya groves all call Elqui home. This fertile valley offers New Age fancy (centered on all that geomagnetic energy)

CHILE

alongside farms and villages whose appeal is in their plainness. For visitors its a funky oasis worthy of kicking back in and exploring.

Pisco Elqui, a bucolic village cradled in the valley, is the most accessible base for exploring the area. Sample locally made *pisco* at **Solar de Pisco Elqui** (☎ 051-451-358; ⏱ 11am-7pm), which produces the Tres Erres brand, or 3km south of town at the original *'pisquería'* Los Nichos.

Tucked below steeply rising hills is **Camping Rinconada** (☎ 051-198-2583; campsites per person US$4), with dusty sites and hot-water showers by arrangement. Horse-riding is also available.

Hotel Elqui (☎ 051-451-083; O'Higgins s/n; r per person w breakfast US$13) has artless accommodations spruced up with grapevines and swimming pools.

El Tesoro de Elqui (☎ 051-451-069; www.tesoro-elqui .cl; Prat s/n; d without/with bathroom incl breakfast US$39/ 53; P 🐾) is a lovers' hideaway laced with lush gardens, lemon trees and flowering vines. Cabins come with hammocks; some also have a kitchen and skylights to stargaze. The restaurant is above par too (meals from US$6). Low-season reduces doubles to as low as US$32.

Jugos Naturales/Mandarino (Plaza de Armas; large pizzas US$10-16; ⏱ 9am-1:30am) offers gorgeous fruit juices and crispy pizzas amid sheepskin throws and indie music.

Buses Via Elqui run between Pisco Elqui and Vicuña (US$3) throughout the day; catch one at the plaza. Occasional buses continue on to the hamlets of Horcón and Alcohuaz.

COPIAPÓ

☎ 052 / pop 129,090

Welcoming Copiapó offers a handy base for the remote mountains bordering Argentina, especially the breathtaking Parque Nacional Nevado Tres Cruces, Laguna Verde and Ojos del Salado, the highest active volcano in the world. The discovery of silver at nearby Chañarcillo in 1832 provided Copiapó with several firsts: South America's first railroad and Chile's first telegraph and telephone lines. Copiapó is 800km north of Santiago and 565km south of Antofagasta.

Information

Añañucas (Chañarcillo) Has a drop-off laundry service. It's near Chacabuchas.

Cambios Fides (Mall Plaza Real, Colipí 484, Office B 123) Change money here or seek out one of many 24-hour ATMs.

Conaf (☎ 213-404; Juan Martínez 55) Has park info.

Sernatur (☎ 212-838; infoatacama@sernatur.cl; Los Carrera 691) At Plaza Prat; is helpful and well informed.

Sights

The must-see **Museo Mineralógico** (☎ 206-606; cnr Colipí & Rodríguez; adult US$1; ⏱ 10am-1pm & 3:30-7pm Mon-Fri, 10am-1pm Sat) is a loving tribute to the raw materials to which the city owes its existence, with more than 2000 samples, some of which glow in the dark.

The remains of Copiapó's mining heyday mark its center. Shaded by pepper trees, Plaza Prat showcases the early mining era with the elegant three-towered **Iglesia Catedral**, and the musty old municipal **Casa de la Cultura**. Beware the roving fortune-tellers, once they get started you'll have a hard time getting away.

Sleeping & Eating

Residencial Rocio (☎ 215-360; Yerba Buenas 581; s/d without bathroom US$7/12.50) A plain guesthouse with youthful owners and a cool bamboo-shaded walkway.

Residencial Chañarcillo (☎ 213-281; Chañarcillo 741; s/d/tr without bathroom US$8/16/24) Small but scrubbed rooms offered by a brisk *señora*.

Residencial Nueva Chañarcillo (☎ 212-368; Manuel Rodríguez 540; s/d without bathroom US$11/17) You decide if the kitteny kitsch and plastic posies spell home.

Hotel La Casona (☎ 217-277; www.lacasonahotel.cl; O'Higgins 150; s/d incl breakfast from US$43/51; P 🖳) A wonderfully homey guesthouse with a grassy garden and bilingual owners. The restaurant is exceptional.

Empanadopolis (Colipí 320; US$1.25) This place offers mouthwatering takeaway *empanadas* with unusual flavors.

Don Elias (Los Carrera 421; set meal US$2.60) Downmarket diner with excellent value *almuerzos* (set lunches) and particularly good seafood.

Chifa Hao Hwa (Yerbas Buenas 334; mains US$4-8; ⏱ lunch & dinner) Cantonese options with snarling dragons and neon lights.

Di Tito (Chacabuco 710; mains US$5-6) A welcoming and snug restaurant-cum-bar serving pizza and pasta dishes.

Getting There & Away

The brand-new Aeropuerto Desierto de Atacama is 40km northwest of Copiapó. **Lan** (☎ 600-526-2000; Mall Plaza Real, Colipí 484) flies daily to Antofagasta (US$86, one hour), La Serena (US$63, 45 minutes) and Santiago (US$208,

1½ hours). A taxi costs US$21; try **Radio Taxi San Francisco** (☎ 218-788). There's also a transfer bus (US$9, 25 minutes).

Pullman Bus (☎ 212-977; Colipí 109) has a large terminal and a central **ticket office** (cnr Chacabuco & Chañarcillo). **Tur Bus** (☎ 238-612; Chañarcillo 680) also has a terminal and a **ticket office** (Colipí 510) downtown. Other companies include **Expreso Norte** (☎ 231-176), **Buses Libac** (☎ 212-237) and **Flota Barrios** (☎ 213-645), all located in a common terminal on Chañarcillo. Many buses to northern desert destinations leave at night. Sample fares: Antofagasta (US$14 to US$18, eight hours), Arica (US$24 to US$32, 18 hours), Calama (US$21 to US$28, 10 hours), Iquique (US$24 to US$35, 13 hours), La Serena (US$7 to US$10, five hours) and Santiago (US$16 to US$34, 12 hours).

PARQUE NACIONAL NEVADO TRES CRUCES

Teeming with wildlife and pristine peaks with rugged ascents, **Parque Nacional Nevado Tres Cruces** (admission US$7) is undoubtedly an up-and-coming adventure destination. Flamingos, Andean geese, horned coots, large herds of *vicuñas* and guanacos fill this 61,000-hectare park. Some 140km east of Copiapó, international Hwy 31 curves through its northern sector. The Salar de Maricunga (3700m) covers some 8000 hectares. A few kilometers past the border control a road shoots 85km south to summer flamingo destination **Laguna del Negro Francisco**. Bring your own bed linen, drinking water and cooking gas to the **refugio** (dm US$9) here. From the northern sector, Hwy 31 continues east, flanked by clusters of snow-capped volcanoes, passing the ultra turquoise **Laguna Verde** (4325m) before the border crossing at Paso de San Francisco.

South outside the park boundaries, 6893m **Ojos del Salado** is Chile's highest peak, a mere 69m shorter than Aconcagua, and the world's highest active volcano. *Refugios* are at the 5100m and 5750m levels. Climbers need permission from Chile's **Dirección de Fronteras y Límites** (☎ in Santiago 02-671-2725; Teatinos 180, 7th fl), which can be requested prior to arriving in Chile.

Mountain guide **Erik Galvez** (☎ 052-319-038; erikgalvez@latinmail.com) comes well recommended. Agency **Gran Atacama** (☎ 052-219-271; www.gran atacama.cl; Mall Plaza Real, Colipi 484, Local B 122, Copiapó) goes to Parque Nacional Nevado Tres Cruces (all inclusive for two to three people US$200) and offers a variety of other trips.

There is no public transportation; take a high-clearance vehicle, water and extra gas, and check with Conaf in Copiapó before departing.

CALDERA & BAHÍA INGLESA

Caldera's clear waters, abundant sun and seafood make this white-sand beach town, 75km west of Copiapó, bubble over with summer guests. The rest of the year it is a yawning retreat, and even though the weather is equally good the prices are slashed and the beach is nearly deserted. Locally harvested scallops, oysters and seaweed sweeten the culinary offerings.

The resort of Bahía Inglesa has white-shell beaches fronting a turquoise sea dotted with windsurfers. In Bahía Inglesa, **Domo Chango Chile** (☎ 052-316-168; www.changochile.cl; Av El Morro 610, Bahía Inglesa) organizes kite-surfing, surfing and 4WD excursions from US$27. It also rents bikes for US$3.50. **Camping Bahía Inglesa** (☎ 052-315-424; Playa Las Machas; campsites US$32) has good facilities overlooking the bay, but come in low season when rates drop. Across from the plaza in Caldera, **Residencial Millaray** (☎ 052-315-528; Cousiño 331; r per person US$9) is ramshackle though friendly, the best bargain you'll find. The most original option is surely **Domo Chango Chile** (d from US$18; 🖂), whose plastic dome tents will have you dream of being putted on the nine. It's opposite the waterfront.

In Caldera, gregarious little **El Plateao** (Av El Morro 756; set lunch US$7-9; ⏱ 11am-late) serves wonderful seafood and international specials, like sushi and Thai curries. Stroll around the seafront for other dining options.

Bus stations are in Caldera and served by **Pullman** (cnr Gallo & Vallejo), **Recabarren** (Ossa Varas s/n) and **Tur Bus** (Ossa Varas s/n). Buses and *colectivos* run between Caldera and Bahía Inglesa for US$1. Buses to Copiapó cost US$2.50 (one hour). Private taxis to Aeropuerto Desierto de Atacama cost US$14.

PARQUE NACIONAL PAN DE AZÚCAR

The cold Humbolt current flows up the desert coastline, bringing with it its peppy namesake penguin and other abundant marine life. **Pan de Azúcar** (admission US$6) has 44,000 hectares covering white-sand beaches, sheltered coves, stony headlands and cacti-covered hills. From the Conaf office in the park, it's an 8km hike to El Mirador and a 12km hike to Quebrada

Castillo. **PingüiTour** (☎ 099-743-0011; www.galeon .com/pinguitour in Spanish; per boat US$54) runs boat tours to see penguins and other birdlife on an island. Off-season the fog rolls in and promotes hibernation.

Camping (3-/6-person site US$9/17.50) is available at Playa Piqueros, Playa Soldado and Caleta Pan de Azúcar, with toilets, water, cold showers and tables. **Cabañas** (up to 6 people high/low season US$80/50) in the park have kitchens; reserve with Conaf in Copiapó. The forgotten mining port of Chañaral offers the dingy **Hotel La Marina** (☎ 052-480-942; Merino Jarpa 562; s/d US$6/10) and the homey and well-attended **Hostal Los Aromos** (☎ 052-489-636; www.hostallosaromos.cl; Los Aromos 7; s/d incl breakfast US$16/27; P).

Flota Barrios (☎ 480-894; Merino Jarpa 567) and **Pullman Bus** (☎ 480-213; cnr Diego de Almeyda & Los Baños) serve Santiago (US$27 to US$53, 15 hours) and Copiapó (US$4, 2½ hours). In the Pullman terminal you'll find minibuses that go to the park (one way US$3.50, 25 minutes). A taxi costs about US$25 one way.

ANTOFAGASTA
☎ 055 / pop 296,900

Antofagasta is a desert metropolis and port city whose rough-and-tumble mixture of concrete and gridlock put it low on travelers' lists. Still, the antiquated plaza and the nitrate-era buildings of the Barrio Histórico have appeal. Founded in 1870, the city earned its importance by offering the easiest route to the interior, and was soon handling the highest tonnage of any South American Pacific port. It exports most of the copper and other minerals found in the Atacama, and is a major import-export node for Bolivia, which lost the region to Chile during the War of the Pacific. The forlorn surrounding area features forgotten seaside ports and eerie deserted nitrate towns easily appreciated from a bus window.

Orientation
Antofagasta drapes across a wide terrace at the foot of the coastal range. Downtown's western boundary is north–south Av Balmaceda, immediately east of the modern port. The Panamericana passes inland, about 15km east of the city.

Information
Internet businesses south of Plaza Colón charge less than US$1 per hour.

Cambio Ancla Inn (Baquedano 508) Change money.
Entel (Condell 2451) Has long-distance call facilities.
Hospital Regional (☎ 269-009; Av Argentina 1962)
Lave-Fast Laundry (14 de Febrero 1802) Charges about US$6 a load for a wash, dry and fold.
Post office (Washington 2623) Opposite Plaza Colón.
Sernatur (☎ 451-818; infoantofagasta@sernatur.cl; Maipú 240) Has good listings.

Sights & Activities
Nitrate-mining heydays left their mark with Victorian and Georgian buildings in the **Barrio Histórico** between the plaza and old port. British influence is in the **Plaza Colón**, with its Big Ben replica **Torre Reloj**. In the former Custom House, **Museo Regional** (cnr Balmaceda & Bolívar; admission US$1) is worth a peek. Sea lions circle Antofagasta's busy **Terminal Pesquero** (Fish Market), just north of the Port Authority.

The oft-photographed national icon **La Portada** is a gorgeous natural arch located offshore, 16km north of Antofagasta. To get there take bus 15 from Sucre to the *cruce* (junction) at La Portada, then walk 3km.

Sleeping
Camping Rucamóvil (☎ 223-929; Km11; campsites per person US$6) With patchy shade and terraced ocean view. *Micro* 2 from Mercado Central goes south to the campground.

Hotel Rawaye (☎ 225-399; Sucre 762; s/d/tr US$7/10.50/15) Penny-pincher heaven with parchment-board walls and a busy street below.

Hotel Brasil (☎ 267-268; JS Ossa 1978; d US$27) Fair value, with spacious, run-of-the-mill rooms and amenable hosts.

Hotel Frontera (☎ 281-219; Bolívar 558; d US$27, s/d without bathroom US$12.50/17) Courteous, clean and central. Rooms sport bright orange tiles and homey bedspreads.

Hotel San Marcos (☎ 251-763; Latorre 2946; s/d/tr incl breakfast US$28.50/40/45; P) This stuffy matriarchal guesthouse has sparse old paisley furnishings but comfy beds.

Eating & Drinking
Líder (Antofagasta Shopping, Zentero 21) Large supermarket to spoil self-caterers; north of the center.

Mercado Central (Ossa btwn Maipú & Uribe, US$2-6) Characterful place with cheap weekday fish and seafood lunches.

Pizzanté (Av JM Carrera 1857; US$4-7) Gooey pizza choked with toppings.

CHILE

NORTHERN CHILE (NORTE CHICO)

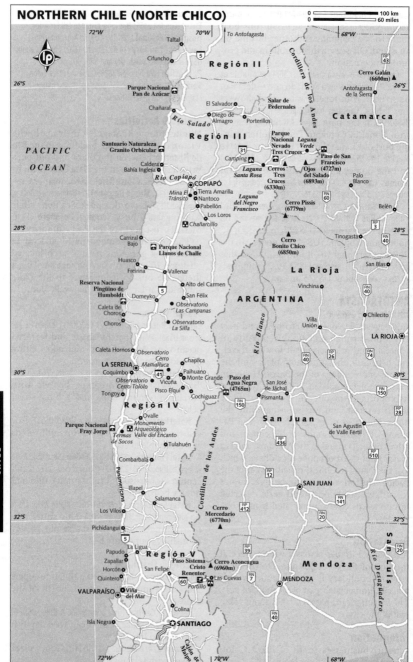

El Arriero (Condell 2644, mains US$6-10) A snobby grillhouse with slabs of steak and piano-bar ambience after 9pm.

Club de Yates (☎ 485-553; Av Balmaceda s/n; set lunch US$6; ☺ lunch & dinner) Swank and sizzling fish dishes alongside the ramshackle pier.

Wally's Pub (Antonino Toro 982; ☺ from 6pm Mon-Sat) Shoot a few games of pool at Antofagasta's only British pub.

Getting There & Away

AIR

Aeropuerto Cerro Moreno (airport) is 25km north of town. **Lan** (☎ 600-526-2000; Arturo Prat 445, option 8) has daily nonstop flights to Santiago (US$188) and Iquique (US$50 to US$90, 45 minutes). Both **Sky** (☎ 459-090; Gral Velásquez 890) and **Aerolíneas del Sur** (☎ 228-779; Washington 2548) have discounted flights.

BUS

Nearly all northbound services now use coastal Ruta 1, via Tocopilla, en route to Iquique and Arica. Companies include **Flota Barrios** (Condell 2764), **Géminis** (Latorre 3055), **Pullman Bus** (Latorre 2805) and **Tur Bus** (Latorre 2751), with direct service to San Pedro de Atacama several times daily.

Destination	Duration (hr)	Cost (US$)
Arica	11	14-23
Calama	3	3.50-8
Copiapó	7	14-21
Iquique	6	16-20
La Serena	12	23-41
San Pedro de Atacama	4	9
Santiago	19	30-55

Géminis goes to Salta and Jujuy, Argentina on Wednesday and Sunday at 7:30am (US$38, 14 hours).

Getting Around

Aerobus (☎ 262-727; Baquedano 328) shuttles to/from Aeropuerto Cerro Moreno (US$4). From the Terminal Pesquero, local bus 15 goes to the airport (US75¢), but only every two hours or so. Buses arrive at their individual terminals along Latorre, in the city center.

Micro 2 from Mercado Central goes south to the campgrounds. *Micro* 14 covers downtown, accessing Lave-Fast laundry and Hotel Brasil. Cars can be rented at **Avis** (☎ 221-073; Balmaceda 2556) and **Hertz** (☎ 269-043; Balmaceda 2492).

CALAMA
☎ 055 / pop 138,000

Copper statues, copper wall etchings, copper reliefs and a copper-plated cathedral spire are unsubtle reminders of the current boom and raison d'être of Calama (altitude 2700m). For travelers this city 220km from Antofagasta makes a quick stopover before San Pedro de Atacama. Its existence is inextricably tied to the colossal Chuquicamata mine. With inflated service prices and *schops con piernas* (like *cafés con piernas,* but with beer) it caters to miners.

On March 23 the city and surrounding villages celebrate the arrival of Chilean troops during the War of the Pacific with a boisterous fair featuring crafts, food, music and farm animals.

Information

Centro de Llamadas (cnr Sotomayor & Vivar; per hr US50¢) Call center with a cheap broadband connection.
Hospital Carlos Cisterna (☎ 342-347; Av Granaderos & Cisterna) Five blocks north of the Plaza 23 de Marzo.
Lavaexpress (Sotomayor 1887) Offers a fast laundry service for US$2 per kilo.
Moon Valley Exchange (Vivar 1818) Competitive rates for money exchange.
Municipal tourist office (☎ 345-345; Latorre 1689) Is very helpful and organizes tours to Chiu Chiu and the Tatio Geysers (via Atacameño towns) in summer.
Post office (Vicuña Mackenna 2167)

Sleeping

The local mining industry and its lodging needs spike the price of Calama's accommodations. Most budget places don't provide breakfast.

Casas del Valle (☎ 340-056; Francisco Bilbao 1207; campsites US$8) For camping, there's this shady place behind the stadium.

Hotel Claris Loa (☎ 311-939; Av Granaderos 1631; s/d US$7/14) Cheap and cheerless digs with saggy beds and bare light bulbs.

Residencial Toño (☎ 341-185; Vivar 1970; s/d US$10.50/21) A warm welcome adds value to these tidy but unremarkable digs.

Hotel Atenas (☎ 342-666; Ramírez 1961; s/d without bathroom US$12/23) In the middle of Calama's main strip, this cool, dark hotel has small rooms insulated from street noise.

Hotel El Loa (☎ 341-963; Abaroa 1617; s US$28) An amiable, but average, spot with red curly ironwork outside and plain rooms inside.

CHILE

Eating & Drinking

Mercado Central (Latorre; set meals US$2-3.50) Meals are fast and filling at the *cocinerías* in this busy little market between Ramírez and Vargas. You'll be rubbing shoulders with local workers.

Café Viena (Abaroa 2023; dishes US$2-4) An unpretentious diner with salads and heaping sandwich plates.

Pollo Scout (Vargas 2102; chicken from US$2; ☺ lunch & dinner) Spit-roasted chicken and steaming *cazuela* are the staples at this cheapie.

Club Croata (Abaroa s/n; set lunch US$5; ☺ lunch & dinner) For linen service and fixed-price lunches. The *pastel de choclo* is a hearty Chilean classic.

Bon Apetit (Sotomayor 2129; set lunch US$5) Cappuccino and sticky pastries, anyone? There's also a tempting choice of set menus.

Getting There & Away

AIR

Lan (☎ 600-526-2000; Latorre 1726) flies four times daily to Santiago (US$162 to US$266) from Aeropuerto El Loa. **Sky** (☎ 310-190; Latorre 1497) sometimes has cheaper rates.

BUS

In the high season, buy tickets for long-distance trips a couple of days in advance. For frequent buses to Antofagasta or overnights to Iquique, Arica or Santiago, try **Tur Bus** (Ramírez 1802), **Pullman Bus** (Sotomayor 1808) and **Géminis** (Antofagasta 2239). Tur Bus and Pullman also have large terminals outside of town. Sample fares include the following: Antofagasta (US$3.50 to US$8, three hours), Arica (US$14 to US$23, 10 hours), Iquique (US$12 to US$16, 6½ hours), La Serena (US$27 to US$60, 16 hours) and Santiago (US$32 to US$75, 20 hours).

For San Pedro de Atacama (US$2.30, one hour) head to **Buses Frontera** (Antofagasta 2041), **Buses Atacama 2000** (Géminis terminal) or Tur Bus.

For international destinations, make reservations as far in advance as possible. To get to Uyuni, Bolivia (US$12 to US$15, 15 hours) ask at Frontera and Buses Atacama 2000; services go twice weekly. Service to Salta and Jujuy, Argentina, is provided by Pullman on Thursday, Friday and Sunday at 8am (US$45, 12 hours), and more cheaply by Géminis on Tuesday, Friday and Sunday at 10am (US$35, 12 hours).

TRAIN

Climb into layers and keep your sleeping bag handy. The sole (unheated) passenger train service in the north operates between Calama and Ollagüe, on the Bolivian border, with connections to Uyuni (US$12.50, 18 hours). The train leaves every Wednesday at 11pm. Tickets are available at **Estación de Ferrocarril** (☎ 348-900; Balmaceda 1777; ☺ 8:30am-1pm & 3-6pm). Seats are rudimentary and temperatures drop below freezing. The café serves sandwiches, but you'll be thankful you brought your own.

Getting Around

From the airport, 5km away, taxis charge US$5. Bus companies have large terminals just outside the town center. Ask to be left at their office in '*el centro*' to avoid the taxi ride back.

Frequent taxi *colectivos* to Chuquicamata (US$1.40, 15 minutes) leave from Abaroa, just north of Plaza 23 de Marzo.

Rental-car agencies include **Avis** (☎ 363-325; Aeropuerto El Loa) and **Hertz** (☎ 341-380; Av Granaderos 141). If heading to the geysers, you'll need a high-clearance jeep or pickup.

CHUQUICAMATA

This copper mine just north of Calama coughs a constant plume of dust visible for miles in the cloudless desert, but then everything here dwarfs the human scale. The mine itself is an open sore 4.5km long, 3.5km wide and 850m deep where some 630,000 tons of copper are extracted annually, making Chile the largest exporter of copper in the world. Young Che Guevera visited these great bleak slagheaps on his cross-continent journey, encountering a communist miner who marked a turn in his politics.

First run by the US Anaconda Copper Mining Company starting in 1915, the mine is now operated by state-owned **Corporación del Cobre de Chile** (Codelco; ☎ 055-327-469; visitas@codelco.cl; cnr Tocopilla & JM Carrera). Chuquicamata was once integrated with a well-ordered company town, but environmental problems and copper reserves beneath the town forced the entire population to relocate to Calama by 2004.

Arrange visits through Codelco or ask Calama's tourist office to make the reservation. Avoid the agencies in Calama, which charge considerably more. English and Spanish tours run weekdays. Report to the Codelco office 30 minutes before your tour; bring ID and make a voluntary donation. Tours are limited to 40 and demand is high in January and February, so book several days ahead. The 50-minute tour begins at 2pm. Wear sturdy footwear (no sandals), long pants and long sleeves.

SAN PEDRO DE ATACAMA

☎ 055 / pop 4970

Oases attract flocks and there's no exception here. A once-humble stop on the trans-Andean cattle drive, San Pedro de Atacama (altitude 2440m) is now prime real estate. In one decade a proliferation of guesthouses, eateries, internet cafés and tour agencies have wedged their way into its dusty streets, molding it into a kind of adobe-*landia*. There are all the cons of fast development (steep prices, cranky tour operators and exaggerated offers) yet…there is incredible quiet, psychedelic landscapes, courtyard bonfires under star-scattered heavens and hammock-strewn hostels. If you can sometimes set your hours contrary to the rest of the sightseers, this is a damn-good place to kick back.

The town is near the north end of the Salar de Atacama, a vast saline lake, 120km southeast of Calama. Buses stop right near the plaza and the whole town can be explored on foot. San Pedro's water is not potable; most stores sell bottled water.

Information

Apacheta Café (cnr Toconao & Plaza de Armas; per hr US$1.75) Internet.

ATM (Caracoles s/n; ☼ 9am-10pm) On the western side of the village, but it functions sporadically.

Café Étnico (Tocopilla 423; per hr US$1.75) Internet.

Conaf (Solcor; ☼ 10am-1pm & 2:30-4:30pm) Two kilometers past customs and immigration on Toconao road.

Entel (Plaza de Armas)

Money Exchange (Toconao 492) You can exchange money here (at poor rates).

Oficina de Información Turística (Tourist Information Office; ☎ 851-420; sanpedrodeatacama@senatur.cl; cnr Toconao & Gustavo Le Paige; ☼ 9:30am-1pm & 3-7pm Mon-Fri, 10am-2pm Sat)

Post office (Toconao s/n)

Posta Médica (☎ 851-010; Toconao s/n) The local health clinic, east of the plaza.

Viento Norte (Vilama 432-B) Charges about US$2.60 per kilo of washing.

Sights & Activities

Stop in the 17th-century adobe **Iglesia San Pedro** (Gustavo Le Paige) where the floorboards creak and sigh and the massive doors are hewn from cardón cactus. North of the plaza you'll find

Paseo Artesanal, where you can chat up local vendors and peruse alpaca sweaters, thumb-sized dolls and trinkets galore.

Fascinating malformed skulls and mummy replicas will keep you glued to the glass at **Museo Archeológico Padre Le Paige** (Gustavo Le Paige; adult/student US$3.50/1.75; ☼ 9am-noon & 2-6pm Mon-Fri, 10am-noon & 2-6pm Sat & Sun). Visitors learn about the Atacameño culture and its developments through the Inca invasion and Spanish conquest. Equally interesting is the shamanic paraphernalia (ie hallucinogenic accessories of the ancients).

You can bike or walk to nearby desert sights, just be sure to bring a map and adequate water and sunblock. Equestrian types can ride the same routes and more. **Ruta Tropera** (☎ 851-960; www.rutatropera.cl in Spanish; Toconao 479; per hr US$7) offers horse tours ranging from brief to epic multiday affairs. Ambitious peak-baggers can check out **Azimut 360** (☎ 851-469; www.azimut .cl; Caracoles 66), mountain specialists with prices starting at around US$140 per person. It's just west of the center. Or try **Vulcano** (☎ 851-373; vulcanochile@terra.cl; Caracoles 317); its enthusiastic trekking tours include Sairecabur (6040m; US$143), Lascar (5600m; US$134) and Toco (5604m; US$80).

Once tuckered out, cool off swimming at **Oasis Alberto Terrazas** (Pozo Tres; admission per day US$4), 3km east off the road to Paso Jama. Oh, and did we mention that there's sandboarding on the dunes (half-day US$18) as well as mountain biking (US$5/9 per half-/full day)? Rent a bike from **H20** (Caracoles 295A) or **Vulcano** (Caracoles 317) then peddle back to the hammock for a well-deserved nap. Stargazers won't want to miss the tour of the night sky, offered – where else? In the middle of desert-nowhere – by an ace astronomer at **Servicios Astronómicos Maury y Compañía** (☎ 851-935; www.spaceobs.com; Caracoles 166; 2½hr tours US$16).

Tours

Note that prices do not include admission charges.

El Tatio geysers (US$17.50-27) Leaves San Pedro at 4am to catch the geysers at sunrise, returning at noon. Exercise prudence when walking around – the extra curious and disobedient have fallen in. Includes thermal baths and breakfast.

Valle de la Luna (US$5-9) Leaves San Pedro mid-afternoon to catch the sunset over the valley, returning early evening. Includes visits to the Valle de Marte, Valle de la Muerte and Tres Marías.

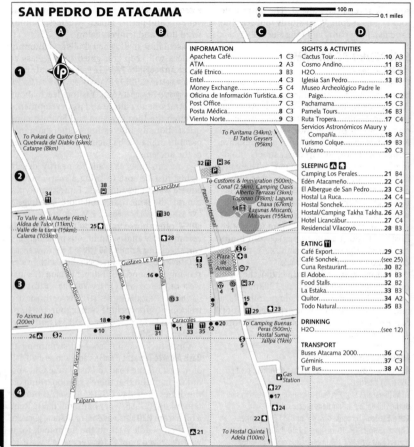

SAN PEDRO DE ATACAMA

0 — 100 m
0 — 0.1 miles

INFORMATION
Apacheta Café.........................1	C3
ATM..2	A3
Café Etnico..............................3	B3
Entel..4	C3
Money Exchange.....................5	C4
Oficina de Información Turística..6	C3
Post Office...............................7	C3
Posta Médica...........................8	C3
Viento Norte...........................9	C3

SIGHTS & ACTIVITIES
Cactus Tour...........................10	A3
Cosmo Andino.......................11	B3
H2O.......................................12	C3
Iglesia San Pedro..................13	B3
Museo Archeológico Padre le	
Paige...............................14	C2
Pachamama...........................15	C3
Pamela Tours........................16	B3
Ruta Tropera.........................17	C4
Servicios Astronómicos Maury y	
Compañía.........................18	A3
Turismo Colque.....................19	B3
Vulcano................................20	C3

SLEEPING
Camping Los Perales.............21	B4
Edén Atacameño...................22	C4
El Albergue de San Pedro......23	C3
Hostal La Ruca......................24	C4
Hostal Sonchek.....................25	A2
Hostal/Camping Takha Takha..26	A3
Hotel Licancábur...................27	C4
Residencial Vilacoyo..............28	B3

EATING
Café Export...........................29	C3
Café Sonchek.................(see 25)	
Cuna Restaurant...................30	B2
El Adobe...............................31	B3
Food Stalls............................32	B2
La Estaka..............................33	B3
Quitor...................................34	A2
Todo Natural.........................35	B3

DRINKING
H2O.................................(see 12)	

TRANSPORT
Buses Atacama 2000.............36	C2
Géminis................................37	C3
Tur Bus................................38	A2

Map labels:
To Pukará de Quitor (3km); Quebrada del Diablo (6km); Catarpe (8km)

To Puritama (34km); El Tatio Geysers (95km)

Licancábur

To Customs & Immigration (500m); Conaf (2.5km); Camping Oasis Alberto Terrazas (3km); Toconao (38km); Laguna Chaxa (67km); Lagunas Miscanti, Miñiques (155km)

To Valle de la Muerte (4km); Aldea de Tulor (11km); Valle de la Luna (15km); Calama (103km)

Paseo Artesanal

To Azimut 360 (200m)

Gustavo Le Paige

Plaza de Armas

Domingo Atienza

Tocopilla

Vilama

Calama

Caracoles

To Camping Buenas Peras (500m); Hostal Sumaj-Jáilpa (1km)

Gas Station

Palpana

Domingo Atienza

To Hostal Quinta Adela (100m)

Altiplano lakes (US$30-45) Leaves San Pedro around 7am to see flamingos at Laguna Chaxa in the Salar de Atacama, the town of Socaire, Lagunas Miñiques and Miscanti, Toconao and the Quebrada de Jere, returning 5pm.

Geysers and pueblos (US$36-49) Leaves at 4am for the geysers, then visits Caspana, the Pukará de Lasana and Chiu-Chiu, finishing in Calama, or returning to San Pedro by 6pm.

Uyuni, Bolivia (see opposite) Popular three-day 4WD tour of the remote and beautiful *salar* region.

For further guidance, the Tourist Information Office has a book of complaints with helpful and sometimes gripping accounts of various tour agencies. Agencies with the most positive feedback from travelers:

Cactus Tour (☎ 851-587; www.cactustour.cl; Caracoles 163-A) A small outfit frequently recommended for its excellent service, polite bilingual guides, comfortable vehicles and above-average food. Prices reflect quality.
Cosmo Andino (☎ 851-069; cosmoandino@entelchile .net; Caracoles s/n) Another small operation, with higher rates but has the most unblemished reputation in town.

Festivals & Events
Fiesta de San Pedro y San Pablo, held on June 29, is a religious festival celebrated with folk dancing groups, a rodeo and solemn processions.

Sleeping
Budget places might ask that solo travelers share a room in the summer high season, and few include breakfast in the price. Try

---

GETTING TO BOLIVIA

High-altitude lagoons tinged crimson and turquoise, simmering geysers, flamingos in flight and Uyuni's blinding salt flats are a dreamy and extreme three-day Jeep journey from San Pedro. Given the wild uncharted terrain, it's essential to take a tour and that's where the problems start. The reasonable going rate of US$70 includes transport, lodging and meals. *Quality does not come at these prices.* Service can be inconsistent and amenities are bare-bones. It's possible to book a four-day tour and return to San Pedro, but you might find yourself stuck in Uyuni until the tour company collects enough travelers to fill a vehicle.

The success of the trip depends largely on a plucky, positive attitude and good driver. Scout out driver recommendations from other travelers. Think twice before booking a tour which overnights in a salt hotel – these accommodations don't properly manage waste and it will essentially be funneled back into the same salty crust you came to admire. Lodgings are at high altitudes: drink lots of water, avoid alcohol and bring an extra-warm sleeping bag and something for the thumping headaches.

Turismo Colque (☎ 851-109; cnr Caracoles & Calama) has most of the departures and its reputation runs all over the board. Other agencies to check out are **Pachamama** (☎ 851-064; Toconao s/n) and **Pamela Tours** (☎ 099-676-6841; Tocopilla 405). None get glowing reports.

---

bargaining in off-season. Given the scarcity of water, limit your bubble-bath time.

Camping Los Perales (☎ 851-114; Tocopilla 481; campsites per person US$5) Basic, sprawling facilities with chatty hosts.

Camping Buenas Peras (☎ 099-510-9004; Ckilapana 688; campsites per person US$6) Camp in a pear orchard but beware the abrupt droppings.

Camping Oasis Alberto Terrazas (☎ 851-042; Pozo Tres; campsites per person US$7; 🏊) Favored for its ample sites shaded by tamarugo trees, BBQs, pool and picnic area. Families fill it on weekends. It's 3km on the road to Paso Jama.

Hostal/Camping Takha Takha (☎ 851-038; Caracoles 101-A; camping per person US$7, s without/with bathroom US$13/35, d US$27/45; P 🖳) Rooms come stocked with candles, are simple but spotless and set around earthy gardens.

Residencial Vilacoyo (☎ 851-006; vilacoyo@sanpedro atacama.com; Tocopilla 387; per person US$7; 🖳) A snug spot with warm service and hammock-strewn gravel garden. Has kitchen access and luggage storage.

Hostal Sumaj-Jallpa (☎ 851-416; El Tatio 703, Sector Licancabur; dm/s/d US$9/19.50/39; P 🖳) Pristine Swiss-Chilean hostel located 1km outside town.

Hostal La Ruca (☎ 851-568; hostallaruca@hotmail.com; Toconao 513; s incl breakfast US$9; P 🖳) New backpacker haunt featuring a courtyard bar and outgoing staff. Showers are spotless and rooms comfortable. Luggage storage available.

Éden Atacameña (☎ 851-154; Toconao 592; hostaleden_spa@hotmail.com; Toconao 592; s/d US$8/16, d with bathroom US$32, all incl breakfast; P 🖳) Take a cue

from the Alsatians basking on the patio in this relaxed spot with hammocks, communal outdoor kitchen and wash basins.

El Albergue de San Pedro (☎ 851-426; hostel sanpedro@hotmail.com; Caracoles 360; members dm/d/tr incl breakfast US$9/27/35, nonmembers US$11.50/32/43) Welcoming HI property stuffed with six-bedded dorms with three-level bunks. Staff speaks fluent English and organizes regular soccer showdowns. Services include on-site café, laundry, lockers, bike rental and sandboards.

Hostal Sonchek (☎ 851-112; sonchecksp@hotmail.com; Calama 370; dm/d US$10.50/43; P) Slovenian-run hostel with thatched roofs, adobe walls, and tasty smells wafting from the kitchen. English and French spoken.

Hotel Licancábur (☎ 851-007; Toconao s/n; s/d US$21/45, without bathroom US$11.50/23; P) Hotel Licancábur enjoys a friendly family atmosphere. Beds are firm enough but you will probably yearn for more water pressure. Breakfast costs US$2.

Hostal Quinta Adela (☎ 851-272; Toconao 624; d/tr from US$45/60; P) A kick-back introduction to *hacienda* life, this character-rich home is run by a very genteel old couple and its rooms abut a sprawling orchard. Large breakfasts cost US$3.50.

Eating & Drinking

While this oasis conjures up delectable culinary treats (with a variety that far outshines most of Chile), guests pay dearly for their veggie stir-fry or mozzarella-dribbled pizza.

CHILE

Shops in town sell groceries but the produce is limp and the selection paltry.

Some restaurants flip on the dance tunes on weekend nights; all of them stop selling alcohol at 1am according to strict zoning ordinances. Still, the village is plenty social and the party scene in private homes isn't bad at all.

Standout places to eat:

Food stalls (parking lot; set lunch from US$2) These rustic shacks behind the taxi stalls serve *empanadas*, *humitas* (corn dumplings) and soups.

Quitor (cnr Licancábur & Domingo Atienza; set meals US$2.60-3.50; ☺ lunch & dinner) Tourists and locals unite under one thatched roof for *ajiaco* (beef stew) and other northern classics.

Café Sonchek (Calama s/n; breakfast US$2-3, mains US$3, set menu US$4.50; ☺ breakfast & lunch Mon-Sat) Veggie-friendly meals are cooked up before your eyes in this popular budget spot inside the Hostal Sonchek.

Todo Natural (Caracoles 271; mains US$3.50-6; ☺ breakfast, lunch & dinner) Wholegrain sandwiches, a lengthy salad list and fat flapjacks are on the menu at this cute little café. It's worth the wait.

Café Export (cnr Toconao & Caracoles; set menu US$7, dishes with drink US$5-10) Funky and candlelit with strong coffee, homemade pasta and decent pizzas.

Cuna Restaurant (Tocopilla 359; set meals US$8; ☺ breakfast, lunch & dinner) Atacameño dishes spiced with a contemporary twist. Check out the lovely courtyard and friendly bar.

Other popular haunts with courtyard bonfires include **El Adobe** (Caracoles s/n; breakfast US$4, set meals US$5-8) and **La Estaka** (Caracoles s/n; breakfast US$4, set meal US$8; ☺ lunch & dinner).

H2O (Caracoles 295-A) is open all day and has bottled water.

Getting There & Away

Buses Atacama 2000 (cnr Licancábur & Paseo Artesanal) and Buses Frontera, a few doors down, run daily to Calama (US$2.30) and Toconao (US$1, 30 minutes). **Tur Bus** (Licancábur 11) has eight daily

---

GETTING TO ARGENTINA

Géminis (☎ 851-538; Toconao s/n) serves Salta and Jujuy, Argentina, leaving at 11.30am on Tuesday, Friday and Sunday (US$35, 12 hours). See p417 for more details about the Argentina border crossing.

---

buses to Calama, and from there onward to Arica (US$17, one daily), Antofagasta (US$7, six daily) and Santiago (US$37, three daily).

AROUND SAN PEDRO DE ATACAMA

The crumbly 12th-century ruins of fortress **Pukará de Quitor** (adult/student US$2.60/1.30), 3km northwest of town, afford great views of town and the oasis expanse. Another 3km on the right, **Quebrada del Diablo** (Devil's Gorge) offers a serpentine single track that most mountain bikers can only dream of. About 2km further north are the Inca ruins of **Catarpe**. Sunset on the rolling sand peaks at **Valle de la Luna** (adult/student US$2.60/1.75), 15km west of town, is a San Pedro institution. Beat the mobs by hitting it at sunrise. Circular dwellings **Aldea Tulor** (admission US$2), 9km south of town, are the ruins of a pre-Columbian Atacameño village. If biking or hiking to any of these places, make sure you take plenty of water, snacks and sunblock.

Pungent **Laguna Chaxa** (admission US$3), 67km south of town, within the **Salar de Atacama**, hosts three species of flamingo (James, Chilean and Andean), as well as plovers, coots and ducks. Sunsets are gorgeous. **Lagunas Miscanti & Miñiques** (admission adult/student US$3.50/1.75), 155km south of town, are sparkling azure lakes at 4300m above sea level. Check with Conaf about *refugios*.

The volcanic hot springs of **Puritama** (admission US$10), 30km north of town, are in a box canyon en route to El Tatio. A restful place with good facilities, it's a 20-minute walk from the junction along an obvious gravel track. The temperature of the springs is about 33°C, and there are several falls and pools. Bring food and water. Transport is difficult and expensive; the options are a taxi or tour.

At an altitude of 4300m, **El Tatio Geysers** (95km north of town) is the world's highest geyser field, and tourists make pilgrimage to this dragon field every sunrise to gaze at the puffing fumaroles below. Tours depart at the ungodly hour of 4am in order to get to geysers by 6am. Most tour groups picnic after sightseeing. Camping is possible but nights are freezing; tote your sleeping bag to the no-frills *refugio* 2km before the geysers.

TOCONAO
☎ 055 / pop 500
Tidy and tiny Toconao, 40km south of San Pedro, is a smart choice if you're looking for the authentic feel of the Atacama. It is known

for its finely hewn volcanic stone called *la-parita*. **Iglesia de San Lucas**, with a separate bell tower, dates from the mid-18th century. About 4km from town, **Quebrada de Jerez** (admission US$1.75) is an idyllic oasis bursting with fruit trees, herbs and flowering plants. Several inexpensive *residenciales* and restaurants are near the plaza, such as **Residencial y Restaurant Valle de Toconao** (☎ 852-009; Calle Lascar 236; s/d/tr US$8/16/24). Buses Frontera and Buses Atacama 2000 have bus services daily to/from San Pedro De Atacama (see opposite).

IQUIQUE

☎ 057 / pop 216,420

Jutting into the sea and backed by the tawny coastal range, Iquique sits like a stage and, in fact, is no stranger to drama. It first lived off guano reserves, grew lavish with 19th-century nitrate riches, since lost momentum, and now stakes its future on commerce and tourism, manifested in the duty-free megazone, the sparkly glitz of the casino and ubiquitous beach resort development. The real gems of this coastal character are the remainders of lovely Georgian-style architecture, Baquedano's fanciful wooden sidewalks, thermal winds and a ripping good surf.

Orientation

Iquique, 1853km north of Santiago and 315km south of Arica, is squeezed between the ocean and a desolation-brown coastal range rising abruptly some 600m. South of the center, Peninsula de Cavancha houses the casino, luxury hotels and an attractive rocky coastline.

Information

Internet services can be found in just about every block, and even right across from Playa Cavancha. Banks around Plaza Prat have ATMs; the Zona Franca (right) has more *casas de cambio*.

Afex Money Broker (Serrano 396) Changes cash and traveler's checks.

Entel (Gorostiaga 251) Phones.

Hospital Regional Dr Torres (☎ 422-370; cnr Tarapacá & Av Héroes de la Concepción) Ten blocks east of Plaza Condell.

Post office (Bolívar 458).

Sernatur (☎ 312-238; Anibal Pinto 436; ☾ 9am-8pm Mon-Sat, 9am-1pm Sun Jan & Feb, 8:30am-1pm & 3-5pm Mon-Fri Mar-Dec) Offers free city maps and information.

Telefónica CTC (Ramírez 587) Phones.

Vaporito (Bolívar 505; per 2kg US$3.50) For laundry service. It also has a another branch at Juan Martínez 832.

Sights & Activities

Plaza Prat showcases the city's 19th-century texture, with the 1877 **Torre Reloj** (clock tower) and the 1890 neoclassical **Teatro Municipal**. At the northeastern corner, the Moorish 1904 **Casino Español** has elaborate interior tile work and *Don Quixote*–themed paintings. The 1871 **Edificio de la Aduana** (customs house; Av Centenario) now houses a small **Museo Naval** (☎ 517-138; Esmeralda 250; adult US35¢; ☾ 10am-1pm & 4-7pm Tue-Sat, 10am-2pm Sun).

A handsomely restored **tram** occasionally jerks its way down Av Baquedano in the tourist high season, passing an impressive array of Georgian-style buildings. The **Museo Regional** (☎ 411-214; Baquedano 951; admission free; ☾ 9am-5:30pm Mon-Fri, 10am-5pm Sat & Sun) features pre-Columbian artifacts, creepy animal fetuses, mummies and Tiwanaku skulls. Also on Baquedano is the grand **Palacio Astoreca**, housing the **Centro de Cultura** (☎ 425-600; O'Higgins 350; admission US70¢), which exhibits paintings by local artists. **Harbor tours** (Muelle de Pasajeros; US$3.50) chugs out to the sea lion colonies.

North of downtown, the **Zona Franca** (Zofri; ☾ 11am-9pm Mon-Sat) covers an exhausting 240 hectares of duty-free shops. Take any northbound *colectivo* from downtown.

Playa Cavancha (cnr Av Arturo Prat & Amunátegui) is Iquique's most popular beach and worthy for swimming and bodysurfing. Further south, rip currents and crashing waves make the scenic **Playa Brava** better for sunbathing; take a *colectivo* from downtown or walk.

Surfing and body-boarding are best in winter, when swells come from the north, but are possible year-round (see p471). There's less competition for early morning breaks at the north end of Playa Cavancha. **Playa Huaiquique**, on the southern outskirts of town, is also an exhilarating choice but the sea is warmer further north near Arica.

Vertical (☎ 391-077; www.verticalstore.cl in Spanish; Prat 580) sells and rents surf equipment. Lessons start at US$27. **Mormaii Escuela de Surf y Bodyboard** (☎ 099-450-3298; www.iquiquextreme.cl in Spanish) also offers surfing lessons; you'll dish out US$17.50/53 for two/eight hours, including equipment. Sand-boarding trips to Cerro Dragón cost similar rates.

A paragliding mecca, Iquique's ideal conditions make you want to take a running leap.

CHILE

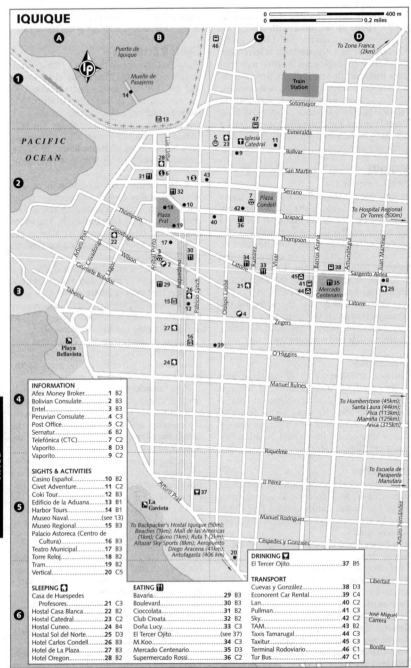

IQUIQUE

0 _____ 400 m
0 _____ 0.2 miles

INFORMATION
Afex Money Broker............1 B2
Bolivian Consulate...........2 B3
Entel...............................3 B3
Peruvian Consulate...........4 C3
Post Office.......................5 C2
Sernatur...........................6 B2
Telefónica (CTC)...............7 C2
Vaporito...........................8 D3
Vaporito...........................9 C2

SIGHTS & ACTIVITIES
Casino Español................10 B2
Civet Adventure..............11 C2
Coki Tour........................12 B3
Edificio de la Aduana.......13 B1
Harbor Tours...................14 B1
Museo Naval...............(see 13)
Museo Regional..............15 B3
Palacio Astoreca (Centro de
  Cultura).......................16 B3
Teatro Municipal.............17 B2
Torre Reloj......................18 B2
Tram..............................19 B2
Vertical...........................20 C5

SLEEPING
Casa de Huespedes
  Profesores....................21 C3
Hostal Casa Blanca..........22 B2
Hostal Catedral...............23 C2
Hostal Cuneo..................24 B4
Hostal Sol del Norte........25 D3
Hotel Carlos Condell........26 B3
Hotel de La Plaza............27 B3
Hotel Oregon..................28 B2

EATING
Bavaria...........................29 B3
Boulevard.......................30 B3
Cioccolata......................31 B2
Club Croata.....................32 B2
Doña Lucy......................33 C3
El Tercer Ojito.............(see 37)
M.Koo............................34 C3
Mercado Centenario........35 D3
Supermercado Rossi.........36 C2

DRINKING
El Tercer Ojito.................37 B5

TRANSPORT
Cuevas y González...........38 D3
Econorent Car Rental.......39 C4
Lan................................40 C2
Pullman..........................41 C3
Sky................................42 C2
TAM...............................43 B2
Taxis Tamarugal...............44 C3
Taxitur...........................45 C3
Terminal Rodoviario.........46 C1
Tur Bus..........................47 C1

CHILE

SPLURGE!

A flying leap into the abyss is one way to shake off a long bus ride. Paragliders adore Iquique's steep coastal escarpment, rising air currents and soft, extensive dunes – it ranks among the continent's top spots for paragliding. Beginners can brave a tandem flight for US$45. Study up at www.parapenteiquique.cl (in Spanish) and check out French-run Escuela de Parapente Manutara (below) or Altazor Skysports at Playa Cavancha. Bring along a windbreaker, sunblock…and guts.

Try multilingual **Altazor Skysports** (☎ 380-110; www.altazor.cl in Spanish; Flight Park, Vía 6, Manzana A, Sitio 3, Bajo Molle). French-run **Escuela de Parapente Manutara** (☎ 418-280; manutarachile@hotmail.com; 18 de Septiembre 1512) also offers introductory flights and three-day courses (US$160).

Tours

Public transportation to Humberstone, Mamiña and the geoglyphs is tricky, so tours are worth considering. Tours to Pica include the Cerro Pintados.

Avitours (☎ 099-139-5039; www.avitours.cl)

Civet Adventure (☎ 428-483; civetcor@ctcInternet.cl; Bolívar 684) Organizes small, fully equipped 4WD adventure tours to *altiplano* destinations, as well as landsailing and paragliding. German and English spoken.

Coki Tour (☎ 329-207; cokitouriqq@terra.cl; Baquedano 982) Offers tours in Spanish or, by prior arrangement, in English.

Sleeping

Taxi drivers earn commission from some *residenciales* and hotels; be firm or consider hoofing it. Wild camping is free on the beaches north of Iquique near Pisagua and Cuya.

The cheapest beds are around the Mercado Centenario, but they are no-frills, no smiles, no breakfast; one of these is the dark and boxy **Hostal Sol del Norte** (☎ 421-546; Juan Martínez 852; s/d US$6/12.50; **P**).

Backpacker's Hostel Iquique (☎ 320-223; www.hosteliquique.cl; Amunategui 2075; members dm/s/d incl breakfast US$8/11.50/19.50, nonmembers US$9/12.50/21; **Q**) Steps from the beach, a top-notch hostel with English-speaking staff. In addition to weekly BBQs (US$3.50) there are lockers, games, laundry and storage facilities, a kitchen and a tiny roof-terrace with sea views.

Casa de Huespedes Profesores (☎ 314-475; inostrozafloresprop@hotmail.com; Ramírez 839; s/d incl breakfast US$10/16; **Q**) An old, high-ceiling guesthouse with peeling floral wallpaper and affable treatment. Bike rental available.

Hostal Cuneo (☎ 428-654; Baquedano 1175; r US$10, with bathroom US$16) Front-side rooms are better quality in this family-run *hostal* with breakfast included.

Hostal Catedral (☎ 426-372; Obispo Labbé 253; r per person incl breakfast US$10) Well located for early or late Tur Bus connections, this homey spot is plant-lined but somewhat stuffy.

Hotel Oregon (☎ 410-959, San Martín 294; r per person incl breakfast US$12.50) A nostalgic hotel near the plaza with high ceilings, creaky wooden floors and a lofty old atrium.

Hotel de La Plaza (☎ 419-339; Baquedano 1025; s/d incl breakfast US$16/25) This Georgian-style building has a darling courtyard but rooms could use a little more love. Singles are small, but bathrooms large.

Hostal Casa Blanca (☎ 420-007; Gorostiaga 127; s/d incl breakfast US$17/27) This congenial guesthouse is a sedate spot with kindly service and a palette of pastel shades.

Hotel Carlos Condell (☎ 327-545; Baquedano 964; s/d incl breakfast US$23/38; **P**) A beautiful 19th-century boomtown building with a choice location, this hotel's inherent charm is undermined by a lack of attentive maintenance.

Eating

Supermercado Rossi (Tarapacá 579) Offers variety and fresh produce.

Bavaria (Aníbal Pinto 926) Has a tasty takeout deli.

Mercado Centenario (Barros Arana s/n) Frills-free set lunches can be had at the north side sandwich stalls or upstairs *cocinerías* featuring seafood.

M.Koo (Latorre 596; snacks US$1.25-1.75) This is a simple corner-shop with exquisite *chumbeques* (sweet regional biscuits) and specials like steaming *humitas* and *pastel de choclo* to go.

Doña Lucy (Vivar 855; cakes US$1.50; ☽ 9am-7pm) A fussy tea shop with ambrosial cream cakes and cappuccinos.

El Tercer Ojito (Patricio Lynch 1420; mains US$4-8; ☽ lunch & dinner) Casual New Age place with excellent Peruvian fare, curries and the odd sushi. Its pleasant patio sports cacti, murals and even a terrapin in a bathtub.

Club Croata (Plaza Prat 310; mains US$4-11) Simple staples of pasta and chicken are on offer and the fixed-price lunch is the best on the plaza.

Cioccolata (Aníbal Pinto 487; set menu US$5, sandwiches US$4; ☺ 8:30am-10pm Mon-Sat, 5-10pm Sun) This is an upscale coffee shop with filling breakfasts, sandwiches, scrumptious cakes and yummy chocolates.

Boulevard (Baquedano 790; mains US$7-15; ☺ lunch & dinner) Streetside café with rich fondues, pizzas, crêpes and enormous salads with zesty dressings.

Drinking

Look for the fun pubs and clubs clustered along the seafront south of town.

El Tercer Ojito (Patricio Lynch 1420) Offers a relaxed patio where you can knock back a cocktail after dark; happy hour is from 8pm to 10pm.

Entertainment

Mall de las Americas (Héroes de la Concepción) has a multiplex cinema. It's southeast of the center.

Getting There & Away

AIR

The local airport, **Aeropuerto Diego Aracena** (☎ 410-787), is 41km south of downtown via Ruta 1.

Lan (☎ 600-526-20002; Tarapacá 465) is cheaper the earlier you book. Daily flights include four to Arica (US$39 to US$77, 40 minutes), one to Antofagasta (US$50 to US$69, 45 minutes), seven to Santiago (US$158 to US$286, 2½ hours), and one to La Paz, Bolivia (US$159 to US$190, two hours).

Sky (☎ 415-013; Tarapacá 530) also goes to Arica (US$36), Antofagasta (US$54) and Santiago (US$163) as well as further south in Chile.

Aerolineas del Sur (☎ 420-230; cnr Thompson & Patricio Lynch) offers good rates including Antofagasta (US$71 round-trip) and Santiago (US$186 round-trip).

TAM (☎ 390-600; www.tam.com.py in Spanish; Serrano 430) flies three times weekly to Asunción, Paraguay (US$309).

BUS & COLECTIVO

Most buses leave from the **Terminal Rodoviario** (☎ 416-315; Patricio Lynch); some companies have ticket offices along west and north sides of the Mercado Centenario. **Tur Bus** (☎ 472-984; www .turbus.cl in Spanish; Esmeralda 594) has a cash machine. Sample fares are listed in the table opposite.

Destination	Duration (hr)	Cost (US$)
Antofagasta	8	12-20
Arica	4½	9
Calama	7	12-16
Copiapó	14	19-32
La Serena	18	21-41
Santiago	26	27-45

For faster *colectivos* to Arica (US$15, 3½ hours), try **Taxitur** (☎ 414-815; Sargento Aldea 783). **Taxis Tamarugal** (☎ 419-288; Barros Arana 897-B) runs daily *colectivos* to Mamiña (US$10.50 round trip).

To get to La Paz, Bolivia, **Cuevas y González** (☎ 415-874; Sargento Aldea 850) leaves Monday through Saturday at 10pm (US$17.50 to US$21, 20 hours), or head to Arica for better prices. To Jujuy and Salta, Argentina, Pullman leaves from the bus terminal Tuesday at 11pm (US$65).

Getting Around

Aerotransfer (☎ 310-800) has a door-to-door shuttle service from the airport (US$6), 41km south of town.

Cars cost from US$44 per day. Local agencies often require an international driver's license. Try the airport rental stands or **Econorent Car Rental** (☎ 417-091; reservas@econorent .net; Obispo Labbé 1089).

AROUND IQUIQUE

Agencies in Iquique offer tours to the following sites, but they don't combine Pica and Mamiña in the same tour.

With the spark of the nitrate boom long gone cold, **Humberstone** (admission US$1.50), 45km northeast of Iquique, remains a creepy shell. Built in 1872, this ghost town's opulence reached its height in the 1940s: the theater drew Santiago-based performers; workers lounged about the massive cast-iron pool molded from a scavenged shipwreck; and amenities still foreign to most small towns abounded. The development of synthetic nitrates forced the closure of the *oficina* by 1960. Today some buildings are restored, but others are unstable; explore them carefully. A Unesco World Heritage site, it makes their list of endangered sites for the fragility of the existing constructions. The skeletal remains of **Oficina Santa Laura** are a half-hour walk southwest. Eastbound buses can drop you off, and it's usually easy to catch a return bus if you're willing to wait. Take food, water and a camera.

The whopping pre-Columbian geoglyphic **El Gigante de Atacama** (Giant of the Atacama), 14km east of Huara on the slopes of Cerro Unita, is, at 86m, the world's largest archaeological representation of a human figure. Representing a powerful shaman, its blocky head emanates rays and its thin limbs clutch an arrow and medicine bag. Experts estimate it dates to around AD 900. The best views are several hundred meters back at the base of the hill. Don't climb the easily eroded hill. To visit hire a car or taxi, or go on a tour.

Amid Atacama's desolate pampas you'll find straggly groves of resilient tamarugo *(Prosopis tamarugo)* lining the Panamericana south of Pozo Almonte. The forest once covered thousands of square kilometers until clearcutting for the mines nearly destroyed it. The trees are protected within the **Reserva Nacional Pampa del Tamarugal**, where you can also find 355 restored geoglyphs of humans, llamas and geometric shapes blanketing the hillside at **Cerro Pintados** (admission US$1.75), nearly opposite the turnoff to Pica. Pass by the derelict railroad yard, a dust-choked but easy walk from the highway, about 1½ hours each way. A Conaf-operated **campground** (camping per person US$8, guesthouse bed US$11) has flat, shaded sites with tables and limited space in cabins. It's 24km south of Pozo Almonte.

The oasis of **Pica** is a chartreuse patch on a dusty canvas, 113km southeast of Iquique. Its fame hails from its pica limes, the key ingredient of the tart and tasty *pisco sour*. Day-trippers can enjoy splashing around the freshwater pool, **Cocha Resbaladero** (Gral Ibáñez; 8am-9pm; admission US$1.75), fresh fruit drink in hand. The shadeless **Camping Miraflores** (057-741-338; Miraflores s/n; campsites per person US$2) gets mobbed on weekends. The historic 1906 **El Tambo** (057-741-041; Gral Ibáñez 68; r per person US$6, 4-person cabin US$32) has rickety rooms ripe with character.

Mamiña, 125km east of Iquique (not on the same road to Pica) is a quizzical terraced town with thermal baths, a 1632 church and a pre-Columbian fortress, **Pukará del Cerro Inca**. Plunk into a deck chair and plaster yourself with restorative mud at **Barros Chino** (057-751-298; admission US$1.75; 9am-4pm Tue-Sun), a kind of budget 'resort.' Similarly priced soaks in individual concrete tubs are had at **Baños Ipla** (8am-2pm & 3-9pm) or **Baños Rosario**, below

Refugio del Salitre. **Cerro Morado** (campsites per person US$4) serves up fixed-price lunches and offers backyard camping. You'll find a few basic *residenciales* in town. All places offer full board. To splurge, check out **Hotel Los Cardenales** (057-517-000; r per person incl full board US$43;) , the coziest place in town, with springwater pool, Jacuzzis and gardens. The Lithuanian owners are multilingual. See Iquique (see opposite) for transport details.

ARICA

 058 / pop 185,270

Summery days of ripping big surf and warm sea currents bless this otherwise drab city, flush against Peru. Arica is an urban beach resort, with long swaths of sand reaching the knobby headland of El Morro. You'll find Aymara people peddling their crafts at stalls, an iron church and a few other architectural gems bringing sparkle to an otherwise homely city center. For most travelers Arica serves as the springboard to the gaping heights of Parque Nacional Lauca.

Orientation

Traveler services are staked out in the commercially chaotic center between the coast and Av Vicuña Mackenna. A pedestrian mall is on 21 de Mayo and the best beaches are south of the *morro* (headland) and north of Parque Brasil. The bus terminals are on Diego Portales, just after Av Santa María, accessible by bus or taxi *colectivo*. The *colectivos* are faster and more frequent. Take *colectivo* 8 (US50¢) along Diego Portales to get to the city center. It's about a 3km walk.

Information

Internet cafés and calling centers fill 21 de Mayo and Bolognesi. There are numerous 24-hour ATMs along the pedestrian mall (21 de Mayo). *Casas de cambio* on 21 de Mayo offer good rates on US dollars, Peruvian, Bolivian and Argentine currency, and euros.

Automóvil Club de Chile (252-678; 18 de Septiembre 1360) Maps and road information. It's west of the center.

Ciber Tux (Bolognesi 370; per hr US70¢; 10am-midnight) Internet café.

Conaf (201-200; tarapaca@conaf.cl; Av Vicuña Mackenna 820; 8:30am-5:15pm Mon-Fri) Has some information on Región I (Tarapacá) national parks. To get there, take bus 12 from downtown (US35¢).

Departamento de Extranjería (250-377; Angamos 990) Replaces lost tourist cards and extends visas.

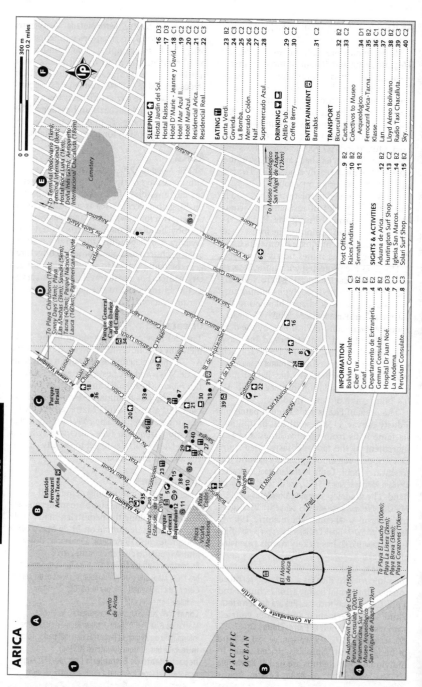

ARICA

SLEEPING
Hostal Jardín del Sol.....16	D3
Hostal Raissa.....17	D3
Hotel D'Marie – Jeanne y David..18	C1
Hotel Mar Azul II.....19	C2
Hotel MarAzul.....20	C2
Residencial Arica.....21	C1
Residencial Real.....22	C3

EATING
Canta Verdi.....23	B2
Govinda.....24	C3
La Bomba.....25	C2
Mercado Colón.....26	C2
Naif.....27	C2
Supermercado Azul.....28	C2

DRINKING
Altillo Pub.....29	C2
Coffee Berry.....30	C2

ENTERTAINMENT
Barrabás.....31	C2

TRANSPORT
Bicurcuitos.....32	B2
Cactus.....33	C2
Colectivos to Museo Arqueológico.....34	D1
Ferrocarril Arica-Tacna.....35	B2
Klasse.....36	C1
Lan.....37	B2
Lloyd Aéreo Boliviano.....38	C2
Radio Taxi Chacalluta.....39	C3
Sky.....40	B2

INFORMATION
Bolivian Consulate.....1	C3
Ciber Tux.....2	B2
Conaf.....3	E2
Departamento de Extranjería.....4	E2
German Consulate.....5	B2
Hospital Dr Juan Noé.....6	D3
La Moderna.....7	C2
Peruvian Consulate.....8	C3
Post Office.....9	B2
Raíces Andinas.....10	B2
Sernatur.....11	B2

SIGHTS & ACTIVITIES
Aduana de Arica.....12	B2
Huntington Surf Shop.....13	C2
Iglesia San Marcos.....14	B2
Solari Surf Shop.....15	C3

PACIFIC OCEAN

Hospital Dr Juan Noé (☎ 229-200; 18 de Septiembre 1000)

Info Arica (www.infoarica.cl) For information on Arica in English and Spanish.

La Moderna (18 de Septiembre 457; per kg US$3) Wash your clothes.

Post office (Prat 305) On a walkway toward Pedro Montt.

Raices Andinas (☎ 233-305; www.raicesandinas.com; Sotomayor 195) A respectable little Aymara-run outfit, recommended for encouraging better understanding of the local people. Tours into the mountains last from two days (around US$84) to four (around US$232); prices vary according to the number of participants.

Sernatur (☎ 252-054; infoarica@sernatur.cl; San Marcos 101; ☺ 8:30am-7pm Mon-Sat, 10am-2pm Sun Dec-Feb, 8:30am-5:20pm Mon-Fri Mar-Nov) A helpful locale with brochures on Tarapacá and other Chilean regions.

Dangers & Annoyances

Petty thievery is a problem, especially at bus terminals and beaches. Take just the essentials. Strong ocean currents make some beaches more dangerous than others.

Remember to change your watches: Chile is two hours ahead of Peru from October 15 to March 15 and one hour ahead otherwise.

Sights & Activities

The imposing tawny hunk of rock looming 110m over the city, **El Morro de Arica** is reached by the footpath from the south end of Calle Colón. Its museum commemorates the June 7, 1880 battle between Peru and Chile (a tender subject for both nationalities). Alexandre Gustave Eiffel designed the Gothic-style 1875 **Iglesia San Marcos** on Plaza Colón and the **Aduana de Arica**, the former customs house at Parque General Baquedano (before landfill, it fronted the harbor). Both buildings were prefabricated in Eiffel's Parisian studios; the church, minus the door, is entirely cast iron. **Plazoleta Estación** houses a free railroad museum. **Feria Agro**, 6km from downtown at the junction with Panamericana Sur, is an animated produce market with heaps of variety. Take any *micro* or *colectivo* marked 'Agro.'

Museo Arqueológico San Miguel de Azapa (☎ 205-555; admission US$2; ☺ 9am-8pm Jan & Feb, 10am-6pm Mar-Dec), 12km east of Arica, is home to some of the world's oldest mummies. There are superb local archaeological and cultural heritage displays and well-written guide booklets in English. Taxi *colectivos* (US$1.25) at the corner of Chacabuco and Patricio Lynch provide transport.

South of town, along Av Comandante San Martín, the best beaches for swimming and lounging around are **Playa El Laucho**, just past the Club de Yates, followed by the comely, sheltered **Playa La Lisera**, with changing rooms and showers. Take bus 8 from 18 de Septiembre or the northeast corner of Av General Velásquez and Chacabuco. About 7km south you'll smell a fishmeal processing plant, nearby is **Playa Corazones**, with wild camping and a kiosk. Check out the trail just past the beach steering past caves, cormorant colonies, crashing waves, tunnels and a sea lion colony. No buses serve Corazones: hire a cab or bike it.

Arica's treacherous tubes host high-profile surf championships. July sees the biggest breaks (see p471). The beaches north of downtown are rougher but cleaner, reached by bus 12 at the corner of Av General Velásquez and Chacabuco. **Playa Chinchorro**, 2km away, features pricey eateries, treat shops and jet-ski rental. As well as **Playa Las Machas**, several kilometers further north, expert surfers also hit the towering waves of El Gringo and El Buey at Isla de Alacrán, south of Club de Yates. Surf shops include **Huntington Surf Shop** (☎ 232-599; 21 de Mayo 493) and **Solari Surf Shop** (☎ 233-773; 21 de Mayo 160).

Festivals & Events

Carnaval Ginga Held in mid-February, this features the traditional dancing and musical skills of regional *comparsa* groups.

Semana Ariqueña (Arica Week) Early June.

Sleeping

Camping is free at the dark-sand **Playa Corazones** (Av Comandante San Martín), 7km south at the end of Av Comandante San Martín, but sites are unkempt and packed; bring water. The established **Sumaki** (camping per person US$3), 5km north of Arica, near Playa Las Machas, has a volleyball court, baths and showers. Sernatur runs a cheap youth hostel from December to February; check the office for location, which changes every season.

Taxi drivers earn commission from some *residenciales* and hotels; be firm in your decision. Besides those listed, cheapies line Prat and Velásquez, while you'll find better-quality options on Sotomayor.

Residencial Real (☎ 253-359; Sotomayor 578; r per person US$7) Quiet, clean and friendly; top-floor rooms are the best bet.

CHILE

Residencial Arica (☎ 255-399; 18 de Septiembre 466; r per person US$8) Central and clean, with huge shared bathrooms. There's no breakfast or kitchen use.

Hostal Roca Luna (☎ 264-624; Diego Portales 861; r per person shared/private bathroom US$8/12) For convenience to the bus terminal, consider this place.

Doña Inés (☎ 226-372; casadehuespedes@hotmail .com; Manuel Rojas 2864; dm incl breakfast members/non-members US$10.50/14, s/d US$17.50/25) A hip little HI property with contemporary rooms, a cozy hammock patio, Ping-Pong, and blank wall for graffiti artists. It's a 20-minute walk to downtown or take taxi *colectivo* 4 from neighboring Av Chapiquiña.

Sunny Days (☎ 241-038; www.sunny-days-arica.cl; Tomas Aravena 161; dm US$10.50, s without/with bathroom incl breakfast US$10.50/12.50, d US$21/25; P 🖳) This warm and welcoming hostel run by a Kiwi-Chilean couple is convenient to the buses and the beach. Offers laundry, storage, bike rental and communal kitchen.

Hotel MarAzul (☎ 256-272; www.hotelmarazul.cl in Spanish; Colón 665; s/d/tr incl breakfast US$12.50/25/37.50; 🖳) Excellent value with banana trees, outdoor pool and chirping songbirds. Touches of mildew and cramped singles are the only drawbacks.

Hotel Mar Azul II (☎ 233-653; Patricio Lynch 681; r per person incl breakfast US$12) Isn't as soundproof, but smells better. Good breakfasts to be had at both places.

Hostal Raissa (☎ 251-070; San Martín 281; s/d incl breakfast US$12.50/25) Peaceful interior courtyards house ripening mangos and chattering parakeets. Raissa has a guest kitchen, rooms with private bathroom and cable TV. Independent apartments may be available. Bike rental and laundry.

Hostal Jardín del Sol (☎ 232-795; Sotomayor 848; r per person US$14) Travelers revel in the relaxed atmosphere which includes interior gardens, open-air mezzanine, private bathroom, fans and breakfast.

Hotel D'Marie – Jeanne y David (☎ 258-231; Av General Velásquez 792; s/d incl breakfast US$16/30; P) Run by a helpful French-Chilean couple, this is an immaculate oasis with frangipani and hibiscus trees, large rooms with fans, TV and maid service, great showers and basic breakfasts.

Eating & Drinking

Tap water here is laden with chemicals. Buy bottled and benefit from the many fresh fruit-juice stands.

Supermercado Azul (18 de Septiembre & Baquedano) Large supermarket.

Govinda (Blanco Encalada 200; set meals US$1.75; ⌚ 12:30-3:30pm Mon-Fri) You don't have to be Hare Krishna or vegetarian to love the living-room atmosphere and imaginative three-course lunch menus with organic ingredients (served on a single metal platter). Tucked in a residential area.

Mercado Colón (Colón & Maipú; set menu US$2-3.50, fish dishes US$3-5; ⌚ breakfast & lunch) Small-time restaurants offer cheap and freshly fried *corvina* (sea bass), *cojinova* (Spanish hake) and soups in this bustling covered market.

Naif (Sangra 365; breakfast US$2.50-3.50, set lunch US$4; ⌚ breakfast, lunch & dinner Mon-Sat) is a funky café-bar with curly ironwork chairs, sharp art and occasional live music.

La Bomba (Colón 357; set menu US$3, mains US$3-6; ⌚ lunch & dinner) The scream of the station siren at noon will alert you to the cheap fixed-price lunches at this unpretentious place, part of the fire station.

Canta Verdi (Bolognesi 453; sandwiches & small pizzas US$4-6; ⌚ lunch & dinner) Invigorating and young restaurant and bar overlooking a colorful artisans' alley. Superb for gringo rendezvous and pizzas, bar snacks, pitchers of beer and cocktails. Tucked into a pedestrian alley. Happy hour runs from 8pm to 11pm.

Coffee Berry (21 de Mayo 423; coffees US$1-2) This place serves up coffee concoctions topped with syrups, sprinkles and creams, and home-made chocolates.

Altillo Pub (21 de Mayo 260, 2nd fl; ⌚ 6pm-late Mon-Sat) Offers candlelit tables and a teeny balcony that spies the pedestrian mall.

Entertainment

Barrabás (18 de Septiembre 520) Revelers dig the deep lounge areas and youthful vibe at Barrabás, with live music or DJs.

In summer, discos along Playa Chinchorro charge about US$5 cover.

Getting There & Away

AIR

Lan (☎ 600-526-2000, option 8; 21 de Mayo 345) has several daily flights to Santiago (US$195, 3½ hours) and one daily to La Paz, Bolivia (US$120, three to five hours), coordinated with **Lloyd Aéreo Boliviano** (☎ 251-919; Bolognesi 317): ask here for onward connections in Bolivia. **Sky** (☎ 251-816; 21 de Mayo 356) has cheaper and less frequent domestic flights.

Chacalluta airport is 18km north. **Radio Taxi Chacalluta** (☎ 254-812; Patricio Lynch 371) has taxis (US$9) and *colectivos* (US$4.50 per person).

BUS & COLECTIVO

The area around the terminals is notorious for petty thievery so keep an eye on your stuff. At **Terminal Rodoviario** (☎ 241-390; cnr Diego Portales & Santa María) many bus companies serve several destinations, including several daily departures to Iquique (US$9, 4½ hours), Antofagasta (US$16 to US$35, 13 hours) and Santiago (US$35 to US$70, 28 hours). For Calama (US$15 to US$23, 10 hours), Géminis has direct buses with connections to San Pedro de Atacama (US$41, three weekly). On all southbound buses you will go through a regional border inspection.

For La Paz, Bolivia (US$13 to US$21, nine hours), Cuevas y González and Chilebus depart daily in the morning. There are more services to La Paz from the shabbier Terminal

Internacional, just to the east. Hop on these buses at Lago Chungara; enquire about arrival times there. Also from this terminal are Tacna *colectivos* (US$4). Peruvian *colectivos* leave from outside the terminal and have longer inspection delays, Chilean ones leave from inside. Give the driver your passport to deal with the border formalities.

For Putre, **La Paloma** (☎ 222-710; Germán Riesco 2071) has a direct bus at 6:30am (US$3.50, 1½ hours), leaving from Germán Riesco 2071. To get to the bus terminals, hop on *colectivo* 1, 4 or 11 from Maipú or number 8 from San Marcos.

CAR

If driving to Peru, check with the consulate about the latest required forms. You'll need multiple copies of the Relaciones de Pasajeros form, found in most stationery stores, allowing 60 days in Peru; no charge. To Bolivia, take extra gas, water and antifreeze.

TRAIN

Trains to Tacna (US$1.75, 1½ hours) depart from **Ferrocarril Arica-Tacna** (☎ 231-115; Máximo Lira 889) at 10am and 7pm, Monday to Saturday.

Getting Around

Rental cars are available at **Cactus** (☎ 257-430; Baquedano 635, Local 36) or **Klasse** (☎ 254-498; www.klasserentacar.cl; Av General Velásquez 762, local 25). Prices start at just US$27 per day. Mountain bikes with double shocks are available at **Bicircuitos** (Estación Ferrocarril Arica–La Paz) for US$13 per day or US$4 per hour.

RUTA 11 & PUTRE

The barren slopes of the Lluta Valley host hillside geoglyphs; **Poconchile** and its quake-ridden 17th-century church, candelabra cacti (consider yourself blessed if you see it in bloom, which happens one 24-hour period per year); and the chasm-side ruins of 12th-century fortress **Pukará de Copaquilla**.

Ancient stone-faced terraces of alfalfa and fragrant oregano encircle Putre (population 1980; altitude 3530m). This Aymara village 150km northeast of Arica is an appealing stop for visitors to acclimatize. Take advantage of the excellent hikes and tranquil village ambience. Colonial architecture is abundant, most notably the restored adobe **Iglesia de Putre** (1670). There's a frivolously fun **Carnaval** in February, where

CHILE

exploding flour balloons and live music rule the day.

There's a post office and call center in town. Baquedano is the main strip.

Tour Andino (☎ 099-011-0702; www.tourandino.com in Spanish; Baquedano s/n) is a one-man show whose local guide, Justino Jirón, comes warmly recommended. Alaskan biologist Barbara Knapton offers expensive but high-quality birding and natural-history excursions in English or Spanish at **Alto Andino Nature Tours** (☎ messages 058-300-013; www.birdingaltoandino.com; Baquedano 299). Make reservations well in advance.

Hostal Cali (Baquedano s/n; s/d US$6/10.50) is the cheapest spot in Putre, with a concrete courtyard and lodging resembling interrogation rooms.

Residencial La Paloma (☎ 099-197-9319; Baquedano s/n; s without/with bathroom US$9/14; **P**) is an established *residencial* and restaurant slots thin-walled rooms around concrete courtyards.

Travelers flock to **Pachamama** (☎ 099-286-1695; ukg@entelchile.net; dm/s/d US$9//17.50/35; **P**), a pleasing hostel with a generous communal kitchen, floral courtyard and knowledgeable young staff.

Kuchu-Marka (Baquedano 351; ☉ lunch & dinner) dishes up delicious quinoa soup, alpaca steaks, vegetarian options and drinks. Folk musicians visit for tips and Gloria, the owner, has information on lodging in private homes. Open late.

Buses La Paloma (Baquedano 301) has daily departures for Arica at 2pm (US$3.50, 1½ hours). Buses to Parinacota, in Parque Nacional Lauca, pass the turnoff to Putre, 5km from the main highway.

PARQUE NACIONAL LAUCA

At woozy heights with snow-dusted volcanoes, remote hot springs and glimmering lakes, Lauca, 160km northeast of Arica, is an absolute treasure. Herds of *vicuña*, vizcachas and bird species including flamingos, giant coots and Andean gulls inhabit the park (138,000 hectares; altitude 3000m–6300m) alongside impressive cultural and archaeological landmarks.

At 22km from Putre, Termas de Las Cuevas has a small rustic thermal bath, accessed along a winding path strewn with vizcachas. The next photo op comes 4km east, where domestic llamas and alpacas graze on emerald pastures among the clear lagoons filled with *guallatas* (Andean geese) and ducks.

The Aymara village of **Parinacota** sits 20km away and 5km off the highway. Amid the whitewashed adobe and stone streets stands a lovely 18th-century church. Check out its surrealistic murals, reminiscent of Hieronymus Bosch, and museum. A local fable says the table tethered down here once escaped into the neighborhood. Where it stopped a man died the following day. Sounds like a Tom Robbins novel… Hikes are plenty (even a table may take advantage). Ask at the Conaf ranger station in town for details.

The twin **Payachata volcanoes** – Parinacota (6350m) and Pomerape (6240m) – are dormant. At their feet is **Lago Chungará**, at 4500m, one of the world's highest lakes. Just to the south Volcán Guallatire smokes ominously.

Adapt to the altitude gradually; do not exert yourself at first, and eat and drink moderately. Herbal tea remedies *chachacoma*, or mate *de coca* help combat altitude sickness. Both are available from village vendors. Pack sunblock, shades and a hat.

Tours

Skip the one-day blitzkriegs to Lago Chungará offered by many Arica agencies and you'll save yourself a screaming headache, known locally as *soroche* (altitude sickness). Take your time to savor the landscape. Tours lasting 1½ days (US$55 to US$60) include a night in Putre, allowing more time to acclimatize; and a three-day circuit to Lauca, the Monumento Natural Salar de Surire, Parque Nacional Volcán Isluga and Iquique (US$200) returns to Arica late the third night. English-speaking guides are scarce, arrange one in advance. Since departures are limited, flexibility and shoe leather are helpful. Check out complaints about subpar operators at the Sernatur office.

Latinorizons (Arica ☎ 058-250-007; www.latinorizons .com; Bolognesi 449) Reliable Belgian-run operator with regular trips into the mountains, and an irregular trip on the old Arica–La Paz railway line as far as Poconchile.

Parinacota Expeditions (Arica ☎ 058-256-227; www.parinacotaexpediciones.cl in Spanish; cnr Bolognesi & Thompson) In addition to the standard 1½- to three-day options, this small agency offers longer volcano ascents and mountain biking along llama trails.

Sleeping

Conaf (☎ 058-201-225; amjimene@conaf.cl; dm US$10) Has *refugios* for the hard-core at Las Cuevas, Parinacota and Lago Chungará, the latter having the best accessibility and most beds (six). Camping costs US$8 per tent. Bring enough food and a warm sleeping bag.

Hostal Terán (☎ 058-228-761; Parinacota opposite church; per person US$4) Wrap yourself in crocheted blankets to battle the drafts in this *refugio*. *Señora* Morales prepares meals, or you can use the sunken kitchen (toasty against the night chill). Breakfast/dinner is US$1/2.

Getting There & Away

The park straddles the paved Arica–La Paz Hwy. See Arica (p467) for bus details. If you are renting a car, or have your own, carry extra fuel and antifreeze.

MIDDLE CHILE

The heartland home of Chilean rodeo and vineyards is oft skipped over by travelers scrambling further afield. But if this region existed anywhere else in the world, it would be getting some serious attention. The abundant harvests of the fertile central valley fill grocer's bins from Anchorage to Tokyo. Don't even mention the contribution of Chilean wine to a lively *sobremesa* (dinner conversation). Wine country is accessible by day trips from Santiago, as is great skiing. Not much further you'll find respectable surfing and the unspoiled parks of Reserva Nacional Radal Seite Tazas or Parque Nacional Laguna de Laja.

Historically this area was a bonanza for the Spaniards, who found small gold mines, good farmland and a large potential workforce south of Concepción. The tenacious Mapuche forced the Spanish to abandon most of their settlements by the mid-17th century.

RANCAGUA

☎ 072 / pop 214,300

The industrial sprawl of Rancagua goes cowboy annually with the national **rodeo** championship held in late March. The competition among *huasos* is a serious, no-smiles affair, followed by *cueca* dances and merrymaking. Just 86km south of Santiago, the area makes a good day trip for hot springs **Termas de Cauquenes** (www.termasdecauquenes.cl; admission US$6) and its underappreciated **Reserva Nacional Río de los Cipreses** (☎ 297-505; admission US$2.90).

Traveler services include **Sernatur** (☎ 230-413; Germán Riesco 277), money-changer **Afex** (Campos 363, Local 4; ☎ 9am-6pm Mon-Fr) and **Conaf** (☎ 204-600; rancagua@conaf.cl; Cuevas 480) for enthusiastic park guidance.

Barebones **Hotel Rosedal de Chile** (☎ 230-253; Calvo 435; r per person with breakfast US$9) is located a couple of blocks from Tur Bus. **Casino Carabineros en Retiro** (Bueras 255; lunch US$3) serves huge portions at good prices. **Torito** (Zañartu 323; mains US$6-11) grills fat steaks in a warm family atmosphere. Live music is played on weekends.

Two buses go from Rancagua's bus terminal to the hot springs daily; call the hotel to confirm because the timetable changes frequently. Long-distance buses also use the **terminal** (Dr Salinas 1165) north of the Mercado Central. **Tur Bus** (cnr Calvo & O'Carrol) and **Buses al Sur** (O'Carrol 1039) have their own terminals. Buses to Santiago (US$2.40, one hour) leave every 10 or 15 minutes. From the **train station** (☎ 230-361; Av Estación s/n) the Metrotren commuter goes to Santiago hourly (US$2.50, one hour) and EFE travels to points south, including Chillán (US$16, 3½ hours) and Temuco (US$20, eight hours, 11:23pm daily).

SANTA CRUZ

☎ 072 / pop 32,400

Thanks to the generous investments of a former arms dealer, lovely and picturesque Santa Cruz just gleams. The nexus of area winemaking and the first in Chile to create tours, its big moment is the lively **Fiesta de la Vendimia** (grape-harvest festival), in the plaza at the beginning of March. Worth exploring is Chile's largest private museum, **Museo de Colchagua** (☎ 821-050; www.museocolchagua.cl; Errázuriz 145; admission US$5; ☎ 10am-6pm Tue-Sat), with labyrinthine collections of unusual fossils; amber-trapped insects; Mapuche textiles; pre-Columbian anthropomorphic ceramics; exquisite gold work; conquistador equipment, *huaso* gear, documents and maps. The **bus terminal** (Rafael Casanova 478) is about four blocks west of the town plaza. Catch buses to Pichilemu (US$3, two hours) and Santiago every half-hour or so.

PICHILEMU

☎ 072 / pop 12,400

Lusty left-break waves make dusty and ramshackle 'Pichi' a hot surf spot. With bohemian *buena onda* (good vibes) and more expats every day, it isn't a bad strip of sand to kick back on.

CHILE

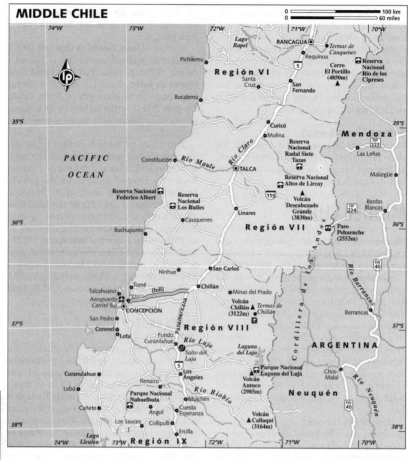

MIDDLE CHILE

The **tourist office** (☎ 842-109; Municipalidad, Angel Gaete 365) also has a **kiosk** (cnr Angel Gaete & Aníbal Pinto; ☉ summer).

Hire a board and wetsuit at **Escuela de Surf Manzana 54** (☎ 099-574-5984; Costanera s/n; half-day board hire US$6) on La Puntilla beach. Its surf courses (individual two-hour lessons US$17) are apt for newbies. To get there, walk to the beach end of Av Ortúzar and continue for a few minutes along the Costanera road. More challenging breaks come in to Punta de Lobos, while rocky Infiernillo to the west is lower key and good for fishing.

Pichilemu hosts the **Campeonato Nacional de Surf** (National Surfing Championship) each summer at Punta de Lobos, 6km south of town.

Pequeño Bosque (☎ 842-071; cnr Santa Teresa & Paseo del Sol; 4-person sites US$16) is beach-accessible with full campground amenities. Lots of *residenciales* pop up along Aníbal Pinto in season, but close again in low season. Head here for the bargains. Surfers crash at **Hotel Chile España** (☎ 841-270; Av Ortúzar 255; s/d without bathroom incl breakfast US$12/20), a simple and happy-go-lucky spot with wood stoves and a rocking chair. **Cabañas Buena Vista** (☎ 842-638; www.343sur .com; Av Pichilemu; per person US$12.60) offer spacious log cabins with gaping ocean views. There's a 10-guest maximum. Arrange transport with Will, the English owner or walk 20 minutes from town center toward the cross. Mountain bikes are on loan and fly-fishing tours are offered.

THAT'S THE BREAKS – CHILE'S TOP FIVE SURF SPOTS

Chile's backyard offers 4300km of rumbling surf – so there should never be a dull moment!

■ The Classic Wave: from January through February pilgrims crowd Pichilemu's 'Punta de Lobos,' a perfect left break.

■ One with the Surf: pitch a tent in view of Puertecillo's gnarly curlers. This wilderness surf paradise isn't signposted; ask the Pichilemu locals to tag along.

■ The Urban Surf Myth: Iquique's shallow reef break is known to jump newcomers, shake them up and steal their wallets. Falling is part of the initiation, if not in 'El Colegio' (High School), definitely in 'La Intendencia' (Bureaucratic Office). Booties can spare you from the sea urchins.

■ The Serious Wave: Arica's 'El Gringo' is shallow, top heavy and unfriendly to its namesakes.

■ The Bunny-slope of Surf: beginners head to La Puntilla in Pichilemu. Seek out a surf school and a nice thick wetsuit.

Grilled and marinated fish at tables facing the surf make Mediterranean-style **Costa Luna** (Costanera 879; ☼ daily summer, Wed-Sun winter) easily the best cuisine in town.

From the **Terminal de Buses** (cnr Av Millaco & Los Alerces) on Pichilemu's outskirts, buses run frequently to Santa Cruz (US$2, two hours) and San Fernando (US$3, three hours) where there are connections north and south.

CURICÓ

☎ 075 / pop 119,600

Convenient to local vineyards, laid-back Curicó sports a postcard-perfect **Plaza de Armas** shaded by evergreens, palms and monkey-puzzle trees and a wrought-iron bandstand on stilts.

In summer, **Sernatur** (Plaza de Armas) has an information kiosk. **Forex** (Carmen 477) is the only *casa de cambio;* there are many ATMs.

The unruly **Festival de la Vendimia** (grape-harvest festival) lasts three days in mid-March. The **Miguel Torres** (☎ 564-100) vineyard, 5km south of town, conducts tours by reservation only. Its chic restaurant dishes up Franco-Chilean cuisine (lunch US$20). Take *colectivos* going to Molina and ask to be dropped off.

Residencial Rahue (☎ 312-194; Peña 410; r per person US$11), across the street, is a florid and broken-in alternative to the old-world charm of **Hotel Prat** (☎ 311-069; Peña 427; s/d incl breakfast US$13.50/27), which is embodied in its shady grape arbor, chilly rooms and bowing bed frames. On the 1st floor of the cultural center, **Refugio Restaurant** (Merced 447; daily special US$3.50; ☼ 12:30-4pm & 6-11pm Mon-Sat) successfully fuses European and Latin American cuisine.

The **Terminal de Buses** (cnr Maipú & Prat) and the **Estación de Ferrocarril** (☎ 310-028; Maipú 657) are four blocks west of the Plaza de Armas. There are eight trains a day north to Santiago (US$10, two hours), and 10 trains south to Chillán (US$11, 2½ hours). The bus company **Buses Bravo** (☎ 312-193) has services to the windsurfing spot of Llico (3:30pm daily). **Buses Hernández** (☎ 491-179) goes to Radal Siete Tazas National Park (US$2, two hours). **Buses Díaz** (☎ 311-905) heads to the scenic Lago Vichuquén (US$3, 2½ hours) at 3:20pm daily. Buses to Santiago (US$5, 2½ hours) leave about every half-hour; try **Bus Pullman Sur** (Camilo Henríquez), three blocks north of the plaza or **Tur Bus** (Manso de Velasco 0106).

RESERVA NACIONAL RADAL SIETE TAZAS

This **reserve** (admission US$2.50) marks the transition from drought-tough Mediterranean vegetation to moist evergreen forest where the upper Río Claro pours over seven basalt pools, ending at the 50m **Cascada Velo de la Novia** (Bridal Veil Falls). Hiking trails abound, longer ones lead to Cerro El Fraile, Valle del Indio, and Altos del Lircay. **Parque Inglés** sports a lovely setting and hearty lodge meals.

Camping Los Robles (up to 6 people US$13.50) within the park has hot showers and a BBQ area. Try visiting off-season to avoid the circus atmosphere. Rustic campsites with cold running water are available at **Radal** (☎ 099-333-8719; 5-person sites US$21).

Bring food from Molina.

To get to Parque Inglés, first take the *micro* bus from Av San Martín in Curicó to Molina (50km away). You'll find provisions for the park here. From November to March, there are five buses daily from Terminal de Molina on Maipú, between 8am and 8pm (US$2, two hours). The rest of the year, there's one bus a day, at 5:30pm, returning at 8:30am.

TALCA

☎ 071 / pop 201,800

Talca boasts a thriving university atmosphere and savvy wining and dining that caters to gringos on the wine country trail. Located 257km south of Santiago, it has good access to national reserves, and offers better long-distance bus connections than nearby towns. Traveler services include **Sernatur** (1 Poniente 1281), **Conaf** (3 Sur & 2 Poniente) and **Forex Money Exchange** (2 Oriente 1133). Occupying the house where Bernardo O'Higgins signed Chile's declaration of independence in 1818, **Museo O'Higgins y de Bellas Artes** (1 Norte 875; admission free; ⏰ 10am-7pm Tue-Fri, 10am-2pm Sat & Sun) features pastoral scenes in oil and *huaso* portraits.

Sleeping & Eating

Casa Chueca (☎ 099-419-0625; www.trekkingchile.com /Casachueca/; dm US$11, s/d/tr with bathroom & breakfast US$22/30/36; ⏰ closed Jun-Aug; 🖭) Backpackers adore these rustic cabañas set in gardens with views to the gurgling river. The owners have loads of information about the region and lead hiking trips. Grab a bike to explore many nearby wineries. To get there, call first from Talca terminal, then take the Taxutal 'A' *micro* toward San Valentín to the last stop in Taxutal, where you will be picked up.

Hostal del Puente (☎ 220-930; 1 Sur 411; s/d US$25/43) The best in town, these riverside accommodations branch off a hacienda-style colonnade, with friendly English-speaking management, a pretty garden and cozy rooms.

The cheapest belch-inducing frankfurters are consumed along 5 Oriente.

Las Brisas supermarket (cnr 1 Norte & 5 Oriente) Open until 10pm.

Mercado Central (btwn 1 Norte, 5 Oriente, 1 Sur & 4 Oriente) Cheap *cocinerías*.

Entrelíneas (1 Sur 1111; ⏰ 10am-8:30pm Mon-Fri; sandwiches US$2.50) A hip café-bookstore offering a side of live poetry with your espresso.

Rubin Tapia (2 Oriente 1339; mains US$5-9; ⏰ 10am-midnight Mon-Sat) A tower of wine choices and tasty green curry or Thai prawns grab the attention of eager taste buds.

Getting There & Away

Most of the north–south buses stop at Talca's main **bus station** (12 Oriente) or there's **Tur Bus** (3 Sur 1960). Sample fares and times are:

Chillán (US$6, four hours), Puerto Montt (US$18, 11 hours) and Temuco or Valparaíso (US$13, six hours). Buses Vilches (US$1.50, 1½ hours) leaves the main station three times daily at 7am, 1pm and 4:50pm for the village of Vilches and beyond, turning around at the entrance to Reserva Nacional Altos del Lircay.

The **train station** (11 Oriente 1000) is at the eastern end of 2 Sur. There are five trains a day to Chillán (US$8.50, 1¾ hours), Curicó (US$7, 45 minutes), Santiago (US$10, 2¾ hours) and Temuco (US$13.50, 6½ hours). A narrow-gauge train chugs to the dune-swept coastal resort of Constitución. Service (US$2, 2½ hours) runs at 7:30am daily and 4pm weekdays, returning at 7:15am daily and 4pm weekdays.

RESERVA NACIONAL ALTOS DE LIRCAY

In the Andean foothills, 65km east of Talca, this **national reserve** (admission US$2.50) offers fabulous trekking amid a burgeoning population of *tricahues* and other native parrots. Those up for a strenuous 12-hour slog venture to **El Enladrillado**, a unique basaltic plateau with stunning views. At 10-hours, the hike to **Laguna del Alto** gets you off easier. Trekkers can loop to Radal Siete Tazas, but a guide is needed as the trail is unmarked. Take a guided hike with the seasoned operator **El Caminante** (☎ 099-837-1440, 071-197-0097; www.trekkingchile.com) or **Expediciones Rapel** (☎ 071-228-029, 099-641-5582).

The **Conaf campground** (camping for 5 people US$13) is a one-hour hike from the bus stop; you can also camp at backcountry sites. From Talca, Buses Vilches goes directly to the park entrance at 7am, 1pm and 4:50pm daily, though the schedule is subject to change. The fare is US$1.50.

CHILLÁN

☎ 042 / pop 161,950

Battered by earthquakes and Mapuche sieges, resilient Chillán is still the most intriguing stopover between Santiago (407km north) and Temuco (270km south). Chillán Nuevo replaced the old town in 1835. When another quake in 1939 destroyed the new city, the Mexican government donated the still-operating **Escuela México** (Av O'Higgins 250; ⏰ 10am-1pm & 3-6pm Mon-Fri, 10am-6pm Sat & Sun). At Pablo Neruda's request, Mexican artist David Alfaro Siqueiros and Xavier Guerrero painted spectacular murals honoring indigenous and post-Columbian figures in history; donations are accepted (and encouraged).

A tumbling sprawl of produce and crafts (leather, basketry and weaving), the **Feria de Chillán** is one of Chile's best. On Saturday it fills the entire Plaza de la Merced and spills onto adjacent streets.

A short bus or cab ride from downtown, **Chillán Viejo** is the original town and Bernardo O'Higgins' birthplace. A 60m-long tiled mosaic illustrates scenes from the petite liberator's life.

Information

Banco de Chile (cnr El Roble & 5 de Abril) Has an ATM.
Centro Tur (☎ 221-306; 18 de Septiembre 656) Travel agency that sells train tickets.

Hospital Herminda Martín (☎ 212-345; cnr Constitución & Av Argentina) Seven blocks east of the plaza.
Post office (Libertad 505)
Sernatur (☎ 223-272; 18 de Septiembre 455) Located half a block north of the plaza.
Telefónica CTC (Arauco 625)

Sleeping

Hospedaje Itata (☎ 214-879; Itata 288; s/d incl breakfast US$6.50/13) Cheap and tattered, the Itata's best feature is the motherly hostess who can whip up a feast for a little extra.

Residencial 18 (☎ 211-102; 18 de Septiembre 317; r per person US$7.50) Book far ahead to nab your spot in this popular home where guests are made to feel like family.

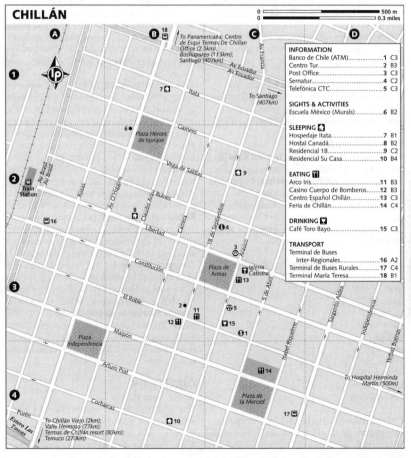

CHILLÁN

0 — 500 m
0 — 0.3 miles

To Panamericana; Centro de Esqui Termas De Chillan Office (2.5km); Buchupureo (113km); Santiago (407km)

To Santiago (407km)

INFORMATION	
Banco de Chile (ATM)	1 C3
Centro Tur	2 B3
Post Office	3 C3
Sernatur	4 C2
Telefónica CTC	5 C3

SIGHTS & ACTIVITIES	
Escuela México (Murals)	6 B2

SLEEPING	
Hospedaje Itata	7 B1
Hostal Canadá	8 B2
Residencial 18	9 C2
Residencial Su Casa	10 B4

EATING	
Arco Iris	11 B3
Casino Cuerpo de Bomberos	12 B3
Centro Español Chillán	13 C3
Feria de Chillán	14 C4

DRINKING	
Café Toro Bayo	15 C3

TRANSPORT	
Terminal de Buses Inter-Regionales	16 A2
Terminal de Buses Rurales	17 C4
Terminal María Teresa	18 B1

Av Francia

Av Ecuador
Av Ecuador

Itata

Plaza Héroes de Iquique

Gamero

Vega de Saldías

Av Brasil
Av Brasil
Train Station

Rosas

Av O'Higgins

Claudio Arau

Bulnes

Carrera

18 de Septiembre

Libertad

Arauco

Constitución

Plaza de Armas
Iglesia Catedral

El Roble

5 de Abril

Maipón

Plaza Independencia

Arturo Prat

Sargento Aldea

Independencia

Isabel Riquelme

Yerbas Buenas

Cochárcas

Purén
Estero Las Toscas

To Chillán Viejo (2km); Valle Hermoso (77km); Termas de Chillán resort (80km); Temuco (270km)

Plaza de la Merced

To Hospital Herminda Martín (500m)

CHILE

Hostal Canadá (☎ 234-515; Libertad 269; s/d US$8.50/17) Character is not limited to this *hostal* but extends to its host. The rooms are impeccable.

Residencial Su Casa (☎ 223-931; Cocharcas 555; r per person US$9) Cramped but cozy and leafy green, run by a friendly *señora*.

Eating

Mercado Central (Maipón btwn 5 de Abril & Isabel Riquelme) Cooks up cheap *paila marina* and *longaniza* (pork sausage) in *cocinerías* set by the butchers' stalls.

Casino Cuerpo de Bomberos (El Roble 490; colación US$2) Stride past the staring locals and pool hustlers to find no-frills Chilean eats.

Arco Iris (El Roble 525; buffet US$6) Twinkly wind chimes accompany serious vegetarian fare at this hippie hangout, a godsend for nonmeat eaters.

Café Toro Bayo (Arauco 683, Local 4; ☼ 3pm-2am Mon-Sat) A student watering hole overflowing with happy revelers. Escudos and *piscos* are sunk deep into the night.

Centro Español Chillán (Arauco 555; mains US$6-10; ☼ closed Sun) Bow-tied waiters dish out fragrant paella and other Spanish specialties at this elegant haunt overlooking the Plaza de Armas.

Getting There & Away

Most long-distance buses use **Terminal María Teresa** (Av O'Higgins 010), just north of Av Ecuador. The other is the old **Terminal de Buses Inter-Regionales** (cnr Constitución & Av Brasil), from which you can catch Tur Bus (also at María Teresa) and Línea Azul, with the fastest service to Concepción. Local and regional buses use **Terminal de Buses Rurales** (Sargento Aldea), south of Maipón.

Destination	Duration (hr)	Cost (US$)
Angol	2¾	4
Concepción	1½	2
Los Angeles	1½	2.20
Puerto Montt	9	12
Santiago	6	9
Talca	3	4
Temuco	5	6
Termas de Chillán	1½	2.50
Valdivia	6	8.50
Valle Los Trancas	1¼	3

Trains between Santiago and Temuco use the **train station** (☎ 222-424; Av Brasil) at the west end of Libertad.

Renta-car (☎ 212-243; 18 de Septiembre 380) offers rentals for about US$35 a day. If heading to the ski slopes, you may need rental chains (US$13.50) for the wheels.

AROUND CHILLÁN

The **Termas de Chillán resort** (☎ 042-434-200; www .termaschillan.cl; daily ski lift adult/child US$32/22, low season US$26/18.50), also known for its **thermal baths** (adult/child US$29/20), boasts fresh tracks through long tree-lined slopes. The setting is magnificent. There are 32 runs, maxing out at 1100m of vertical and 2500m long. One of the 11 lifts is the longest in South America. The season attempts to run mid-June to mid-September, but potential visitors should check the website or call ☎ 02-366-8695 first. Ski hire is available on-site from about US$25 a day.

Soaks for skimpy spenders can be found at Valle Hermoso, where you'll find a **campground** (campsites US$14.50) selling food supplies and public **thermal baths** (admission US$3.50; ☼ 9am-5pm). It's down a turnoff between Valle Las Trancas and the posh hotels.

Hostelling Las Trancas (☎ 042-243-211; www.hostel linglastrancas.cl; Camino Termas de Chillán Km73.5; per person incl breakfast US$13.50) is a bit removed from the action, but its reasonable price and crackling-fire ambience provide compensation. There's also a restaurant and bar. Buses Línea Azul in Chillán goes to Valle Las Trancas year-round at 8am (returning at 4pm) for US$3, continuing to Termas de Chillán in summer.

Coastal villages northwest of Chillán invite exploration. Surfers and fishers alike head to **Buchupureo**, 13km north of Cobquecura (about 100km from Chillán), where papayas grow, oxen clog the road and the little houses are sheathed in local slate. One good option is **Camping Ayekán** (☎ 042-197-1756; www.turismoayekan .cl; campsites US$15), open only in high season. Once you get to Buchupureo Plaza de Armas, turn left and the campsite is well signposted. **Cabañas Mirador de Magdalena** (☎ 042-197-1890; aochoa_3000@hotmail.com; La Boca s/n; 4-person cabaña US$37), run by charming Don Angel, are pristine cabins overlooking a river delta that twists into the sea.

CONCEPCIÓN

☎ 041 / pop 216,050

The addictive hustle and bustle of Chile's second-most populous city, teeming with industry, port services and universities make 'Conce' worthy of a touchdown. While attrac-

CHILE

tive it isn't – earthquakes in 1939 and 1960 obliterated the historical buildings – downtown has pleasant plazas, pedestrian malls and guzzling nightlife, owed to the student population.

Orientation

Concepción sits on the north bank of the Río Biobío, Chile's only significant navigable waterway. The scenic Cerro Caracol hill blocks any easterly expansion. Plaza Independencia marks the center.

Information

ATMs abound downtown.

Afex (Barros Arana 565, Local 57) Offers money exchange.

Conaf (☎ 2248-048; Barros Arana 215, 2nd fl) Has good information.

CyberPass (Barros Arana 871, Local 2; per hr US$1) Internet.

Entel (Barros Arana 541, Local 2)

Hospital Regional (☎ 2237-445; cnr San Martín & Av Roosevelt) Eight blocks north of Plaza Independencia.

Laverap (Caupolicán 334; per kg US$2) Fast laundry.

Portal (Caupolicán 314; per hr US$1) Internet.

Post office (O'Higgins 799)

Sernatur (☎ 2227-976; Aníbal Pinto 460; ☯ 8:30am-8pm daily in summer, 8:30am-1pm & 3-6pm Mon-Fri in winter) Has good information.

Sights & Activities

On January 1, 1818, O'Higgins proclaimed Chile's independence from the city's **Plaza Independencia**. On the grounds of the Barrio Universitario, the **Casa del Arte** (cnr Chacabuco & Larenas; admission free; ☯ closed Mon) houses the massive mural by Mexican Jorge González Camarena, *La Presencia de América Latina* (1965). On the edge of Parque Ecuador, the **Galería de Historia** (Av Lamas & Lincoyán; admission free; ☯ closed Mon) features vivid dioramas that create a sense of life as a preconquest Mapuche or pioneer. Upstairs an art gallery features local work.

Once the epicenter of Chile's coal industry, the hilly coastal town of **Lota**, south of Concepción, offers fascinating tours (www.lotasorprendente.cl) to its mines and shantytowns. Mine **Chiflón del Diablo** (Devil's Whistle; ☎ 2871-565; ☯ 9am-6:30pm) functioned until 1976, but now former coal miners guide tourists into its chilly depths (US$7 to US$14 depending on tour length). Ask the *micro* bus driver to drop you off at Parada Calero. Go down Bajada Defensa Niño street and you'll

see a long wall sporting the name. Those more aesthetically inclined can visit the magnificently landscaped 14-hectare **Parque Isidora Cousiño** (admission US$2.50; ☯ 9am-8pm), complete with peacocks and a lighthouse.

Sleeping

Catering more to businesses than backpacks, lodging can be slim pickings, especially during the school year when university students fill up many *residenciales*.

Residencial Metro (☎ 2225-305; Barros Arana 464; s/d incl breakfast US$11/20) Offers well-kept rooms in a ramshackle building above a central arcade.

Hostal Antuco (☎ 2235-485; Barros Arana 741 Depto 33; r per person incl breakfast US$12) An efficient, nicely kept *hostal*; ignore its unappealing location above a shopping gallery. The buzzer is at the gate to the stairs, entering the arcade.

Residencial San Sebastián (☎ 2242-710; Barros Arana 741, Depto 35; s/d US$12/22) Down the hall from Antuco; just about the same, with slightly nicer rooms.

Eating & Drinking

When in Conce be sure to take *once* (teatime) at one of the many cafés including **Café Haití** (Caupolicán 511; cake US$2) with prime peoplewatching on the plaza.

Mercado Central (btwn Caupolicán, Maipú, Rengo & Freire) Head to the market, with its pickled onions, chilies and seaweed bundles amid cheap eateries. While the waitresses ferociously compete for your patronage, the offerings are about the same throughout.

Chela's (Barros Arana 405; mains US$3.50-7) A cheerful café whose *chorillana* (a mountainous pile of chips and onions with bits of sausage, US$6.50) should come with Tums.

Verde Quete Quiero Verde (Colo Colo 174; mains US$4-8; ☯ closed Sun) Spot-on service and tasty fare including spinach lasagna and hearty sandwiches. Wash it down with a glass of apple-mint juice. Upstairs out the back, a gallery and artists' studios are sometimes open for visits.

Nuevo Piazza (Barras Arana 631, 2nd fl; mains US$6-10; ☯ closed Sun) The cuisine is reasonable, but the real appeal is the fishbowl view to Plaza Independencia below. It's in the Galería Universitaria.

West of Plaza Independencia, across from the train station, the area known as Barrio Estación is home to several popular pub/restaurants (open from dinner onwards),

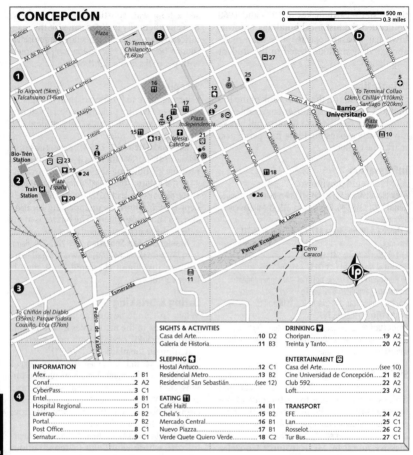

CONCEPCIÓN

including **Treinta y Tanto** (Arturo Prat 404; empanadas US$2-3), offering over 30 kinds of steaming *empanadas* and *vino navegado* (mulled wine), and funky **Choripan** (☎ 253-004; Arturo Prat 542; ❧ 7:30pm-late), where a youngish crowd gathers for pitchers of beer, live music and lively conversation.

Entertainment
Club 592 (Arturo Prat 592; ❧ 4pm-3am Wed-Sat) Ravers and rockers can live large here.

Loft (Barros Arana 37; ❧ from 11:30pm Mon-Sat) Those who prefer Latin rock can salsa over to Loft.

Cine Universidad de Concepción (☎ 2227-193; O'Higgins 650) Movie buffs should check out this theater, where art-house movies play every Tuesday.

Casa del Arte (☎ 2234-985; cnr Chacabuco & Larenas) In the Barrio Universitario; screens movies and puts on plays. Call for show times.

Getting There & Away
AIR
Aeropuerto Carriel Sur lies just outside Concepción. **Lan** (☎ 600-526-2000; Barros Arana 600) flies from there to Santiago (US$160), and also has a downtown office.

BUS
There are two long-distance bus terminals: **Collao** (☎ 2316-666; Tegualda 860), on the northern outskirts, and **Terminal Chillancito** (☎ 2315-036; Camilo Henríquez 2565), the northward extension of Bulnes. Most buses leave from Collao, and

many bus companies also have downtown offices. **Tur Bus** (ticket office Tucapel 530) and other companies run frequent departures to Santiago and Viña del Mar/Valparaíso.

Destination	Duration (hr)	Cost (US$)
Angol	1½	5
Chillán	2	1.50
Los Ángeles	2	3
Lota	½	70¢
Puerto Montt	7	10.50
Santiago	7	8
Talca	4	5
Temuco	4	7
Valdivia	6	9.50
Valparaíso/Viña del Mar	8	13

TRAIN

For trains north, EFE has a bus transfer service leaving from Plaza España in Barrio Estación. Buy your tickets at the **EFE** (☎ 2226-925; Barros Arana 164) office. Travelers to Santiago or Temuco suffer the inconvenience of transferring to Chillán first via bus.

Getting Around

Aerovan (☎ 2248-776) runs airport minibuses for about US$5 that will take you directly to your hotel.

Micros from the bus station run constantly to the center along San Martín (US40¢). *Micros* to Talcahuano (US50¢) run continuously down O'Higgins and San Martín or take the commuter train Bío-Trén (US60¢) at the end of Freire, leaving every half-hour.

Concepción has several car-rental agencies to choose from. One of the best value is **Rosselot** (☎ 2732-030; Chacabuco 726), which has cars from US$30 a day.

LOS ÁNGELES

☎ 043 / pop 166,500

This unprepossessing agroindustrial center is base camp for jaunts into Parque Nacional Laguna del Laja and upper Biobío. The best information can be found at **Automóvil Club de Chile** (Ricardo Vicuña 684). **Inter Bruna** (Caupolicán 350) changes money and rents cars. The **Museo de la Alta Frontera** (cnr Caupolicán & Colón; admission free; ☷ 8:15am-2pm & 2:45-6:45pm Mon-Fri) houses extraordinary Mapuche silverwork.

In town, **Hotel Oceano** (☎ 342-432; Colo Colo 327; s/d with breakfast US$18/35) is unpretentious and colorful. You can eat or sleep very well at **Hotel**

Don Lucho (☎ 321-643; Lautaro 579; s/d incl breakfast US$20/23.50), a fantastic, old-fashioned rambler dating from 1907. Try the *pulmay desenconchado* (US$4), a shellfish, sausage and poultry stew favored by locals. The best digs in the region are at **Hospedaje El Rincón** (☎ 099-441-5019; elrincon@cvmail.cl; Panamericana km 494; d incl breakfast US$28), where German owners lavish weary backpackers with tranquility, comfy rooms and homemade grub. Arrange intensive Spanish courses, bike rentals and guided hikes to Laguna del Laja here. A substantial breakfast is included. Call to arrange a pickup from Los Ángeles or Cruce La Mona.

Other eats include **Café Prymos** (Colón 400; sandwiches US$3), whose sandwiches impress, and **Julio's Pizza** (Colón 452) for generous Argentine-style pizza and pasta. Shoppers can head to **Las Brisas supermarket** (Villagrán).

Long-distance buses leave from the **Terminal Santa María** (Av Sor Vicenta 2051), on the northeast outskirts of town. **Tur Bus** (Av Sor Vicenta 2061) is nearby. Antuco-bound buses leave from **Terminal Santa Rita** (Villagrán 501).

PARQUE NACIONAL LAGUNA DEL LAJA

This **park** (admission US$1.40) protects the mountain cypress *(Austrocedrus chilensis)*, the monkey-puzzle tree and other uncommon tree species sheltering pumas, foxes, vizcachas and Andean condors.

The park's namesake laguna formed by lava from 2985m Volcán Antuco damming the Río Laja, but hydroelectric projects have sapped its majesty. The park itself, however, is ruggedly beautiful, its most striking feature Antuco's symmetrical cone. Trails are suitable for day hikes and longer excursions; the best is the circuit around Volcán Antuco, which provides views of both the glacier-bound Sierra Velluda and the lake.

Antuco and the national park became synonymous with tragedy in 2005, when 45 soldiers died on a training exercise in blizzard conditions. The incident remains a sobering reminder of the unpredictable destructive power of the mountains.

Near the park entrance, at km 90, is **Camping Lagunillas** (☎ 043-321-086; 5-person sites US$12). **Refugio Digeder** (☎ 041-229-054; dm US$10; ☷ winter) is operated by Concepción's Dirección General de Deportes y Recreación, at the base of Volcán Antuco. Take buses from Los Ángeles to Antuco (US$2, 1¼ hours). Buses also leave for Abanico (US$2.30, two hours) every two

CHILE

hours. Conaf's administrative offices and visitors center at Chacay is an 11km walk.

PARQUE NACIONAL NAHUELBUTA

Pehuéns, up to 50m tall and 2m in diameter, cover the slopes of **Parque Nacional Nahuelbuta** (admission US$3.20), one of the tree's last non-Andean refuges. Conaf's **Centro de Informaciones Ecológicas** is at Pehuenco, 5km from the park entrance. From Pehuenco, a 4km trail winds through *pehuén* forests to the granite outcrop of **Piedra del Aguila**, a 1379m overlook with views from the Andes to the Pacific. **Cerro Anay**, 1450m above sea level, has similar views; the trail, reached via Coimallín, is short and teeming with wildflowers and huge stands of araucarias.

The park is open all year, but snow covers the summits in winter. Pop your tent at **Camping Pehuenco** (campsites US$9), with water and flush toilets or the more rustic **Camping Coimallín** (campsites US$9), 5km north of Pehuenco.

From Angol, 35km to the east, the **Terminal Rural** (Ilabaca 422) has buses to Vegas Blancas (US$1.70, one hour), 7km from the entrance, Monday to Saturday at 6:45am, returning in the evening at 4pm and 6pm. Buses Angol gives tours (US$4.20) to Parque Nacional Nahuelbuta in summer. Check with the tourist office to confirm departure times.

THE LAKES DISTRICT

The further south you go, the greener it gets, until you find snow-bound volcanoes rising over verdant hills and lakes. This bucolic region makes a great escape to a slower pace. The Araucanía, named for the monkey-puzzle tree, is the center of Mapuche culture. Colonized by Germans in the 1850s, the area further south is a provincial enclave of stocking-clad grannies, *küchen* (cake) and lace curtains. So perfectly laid-back, you'll start to feel a little *sueño* (sleepy). Don't. Outside your shingled dwelling tens of adventures wait: from rafting to climbing, from hiking to hot-springs hopping, from taking *onces* in colonial towns to sipping mate with the local *huasos*. Hospitality is the strong suit of *sureños* (southerners), take time to enjoy it.

Rural roots still mark most city dwellers (about half the population), who split wood and make homemade jams as part of their daily routine. Unfortunately, the rocket-growth of Temuco and Puerto Montt creates an atmosphere of crowded consumption. Seek out the green spaces bursting beyond the city limits. The isolated interior (from Todos los Santos to Río Puelo), settled in the early 1900s, maintains pioneer culture thanks to its isolation, but road building signals inevitable changes. This section takes in the IX Region and part of the X, including Puerto Montt, gateway to the Chiloé archipelago and Chilean Patagonia.

TEMUCO

☎ 045 / pop 250,000

One of Chile's fastest growing cities, Temuco is a center for regional business and a transportation hub. Developed and fast paced, it has few attractions, although it is the childhood home of Pablo Neruda. It's also the market town for surrounding Mapuche communities.

Orientation

Temuco is 675km south of Santiago via the Panamericana, on the north bank of the Río Cautín. Cerro Ñielol sits north of the city center. Residential west Temuco is a more relaxed area with upscale restaurants.

Information

Internet centers are cheap (US$1 per hour) and ubiquitous, as are ATMs.

Casa de Cambio Global (Bulnes 655, Local 1) Change your traveler's checks.

Conaf (☎ 298-100; Bilbao 931, 2nd fl) Offers park information.

Entel (cnr Prat & Manuel Montt)

Hospital Regional (☎ 212-525; Manuel Montt 115) Six blocks west and one block north of the plaza.

Lavandería Autoservicio Marva (Manuel Montt 415) Soak your skivvies.

Post office (cnr Diego Portales & Prat)

Sernatur (cnr Claro Solar & Bulnes) Helpful.

Tourist kiosk (Mercado Municipal) Has city maps and lodgings lists.

Sights & Activities

Feria Libre (Av Barros Arana; ☼ 8am-5pm) is a dynamic and colorful Mapuche produce and crafts market. **Museo Regional de la Araucanía** (Av Alemania 084; admission US$1, Sun free; ☼ 9am-5pm Mon-Fri, 11am-5pm Sat, 11am-1pm Sun) recounts the sweeping history of the Araucanian peoples. Take *micro* 9 from downtown or walk.

Salute Chile's national flower, the *copihue,* at **Cerro Ñielol** (Prat; admission US$1.25), where

TEMUCO

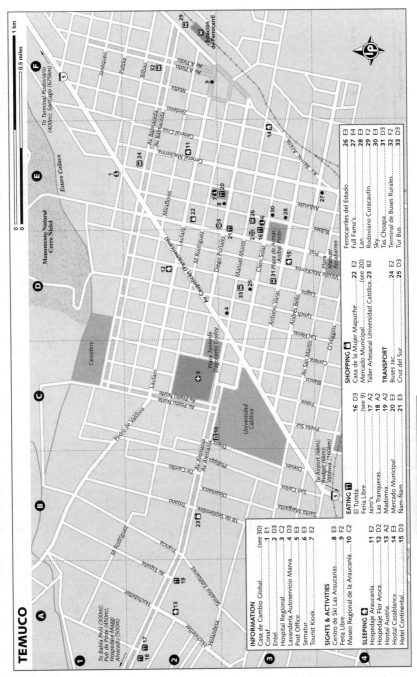

THE LAKES DISTRICT

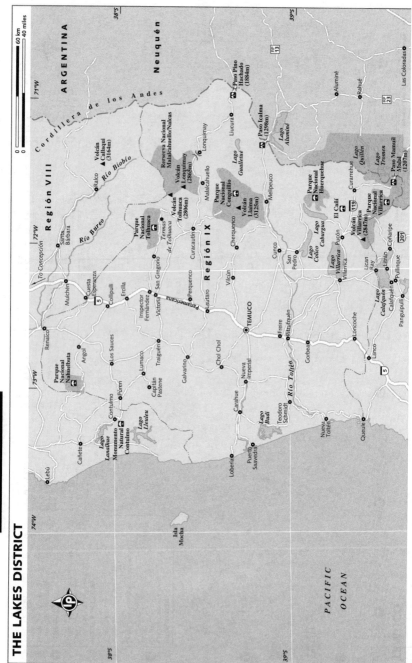

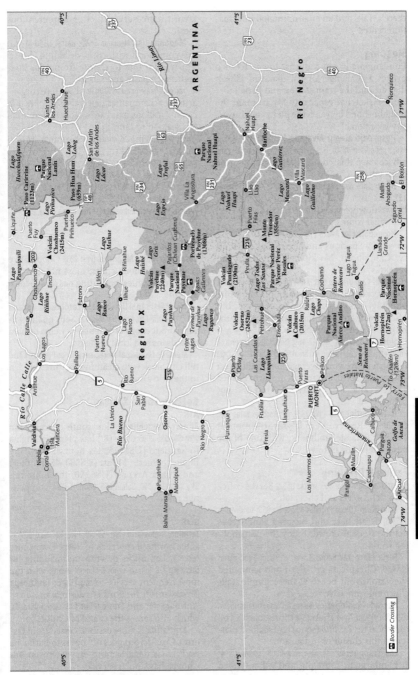

CHILE

Border Crossing

there's trails and an environmental information center.

Sleeping

Fundamentally not a tourist town, Temuco proves a challenge for backpackers. Cheap digs around the train station and Feria Libre can be sketchy, especially for women; the neighborhood between the plaza and university is preferable.

Hospedaje Maggi Alvarado (☎ 263-215; Recreo 209; r per person US$8) Fastidious rooms and trip advice have this homey spot edging out the competition.

Hospedaje Araucanía (☎ 219-089; Gral Mackenna 151; r per person US$8) A creaking old wooden house downtown, with a warm family feel and quiet rooms.

Hospedaje Flor Aroca (☎ 234-205; Lautaro 591; r per person US$8) Spacious and cheerful and just off Av Caupolicán. No kitchen privileges; but breakfast is US$2.

Hostal Casablanca (☎ 212-740; Manuel Montt 1306; s with breakfast US$10) In a rambling old white building, Casablanca requires earplugs, but offers breakfast. Rooms with private bathroom (US$16) have cable TV.

Hostal Austria (☎ 247-169; hostalaustria@terra.cl; Hochstetter 599; r per person incl breakfast US$24-38; Ⓟ ✗) A notch above your average *hostal,* this west Temuco house decks rooms in warm duvets. There's cable TV, a tasty breakfast and hot baths.

Hotel Continental (☎ 238-973; Antonio Varas 709; d US$80-120) Reserve Neruda's favorite room at Temuco's classic landmark, with one of the best restaurants in town.

Eating & Drinking

El Turista (Claro Solar 839; snacks US$2) Serves coffee with rich sweets and chocolates.

Ñam Ñam (Diego Portales 802 & No 855; sandwiches US$3-6) Draft beer and heaping sandwiches net the student crowd. Enjoy the nonsmoking section.

Feria Libre (Av Barros Arana; ☺ 8am-5pm; mains US$3.50) Cheap eats are diced and simmered steps from your bench at these simple stalls churning with activity.

Mercado Municipal (cnr Bulnes & Diego Portales; mains US$4-8; ☺ 9am-7pm) Though a tourist cliché, you can't beat the *caldillo* (soup) and seafood platters at this cluster of restaurants.

Las Tranqueras (Av Alemania 0888; mains US$4-8) Lamb, goat, roast pig and other grilled favorites are served in this unpretentious locale.

Madonna (Av Alemania 0660; pastas US$6-8) An easygoing local with chins dribbling cheese. Thirty pizza pies to choose from, plus mix-and-match pasta and salsas.

Jairo's (Av Alemania 0830; mains US$8-12) An organ-grinder accompanies delectable *ostiones a la crema* (scallops in cream sauce) in Temuco's top seafood restaurant.

In west Temuco, many restaurants are also the place for drinks:

Pub de Pinte (cnr Recreo & Alessandri) With candlelit, folksy decor, cold draft beer and snacks (US$3).

Bahía Perú (cnr Av Alemania & Recreo) For a dash of spice or ceviche (mains US$8 to US$11) with a splash of Pernod, this spot is unbeatable, attracting a lively, affluent crowd.

Shopping

Casa de la Mujer Mapuche (Prat 283) Cooperative selling indigenous crafts, most notably textiles and ceramics, benefiting nearly 400 local artisans.

Taller Artesanal Universidad Católica (Av Alemania 0422; ☺ 9am-1pm & 3-7pm Mon-Fri) Sells quality silver reproductions of Mapuche jewelry, created by artisans and local students.

Mercado Municipal (cnr Bulnes & Diego Portales) One full city block with gleaming treasures hidden in the bric-a-brac.

Getting There & Away

AIR

Airport Maquehue is 6km south of town. **Lan** (☎ 600-526-2000; Bulnes 687) has plenty of flights to Santiago (US$175, 1¼ hours), and daily flights to Puerto Montt (US$80, 45 minutes) and Punta Arenas (US$250, three hours). **Sky** (☎ 747-300; Bulnes 655, Local 4) has competitive rates.

BUS

Terminal Rodoviario (☎ 255-005; Pérez Rosales 01609) is at the northern approach to town. Companies have ticket offices downtown, including **Tur Bus** (☎ 278-161; cnr Lagos & Manuel Montt), with the most frequent service to Santiago; **Tas Choapa** (Antonio Vara 609), for northern destinations up to Antofagasta; and **Cruz del Sur** (☎ Claro Solar 599), which also serves the island of Chiloé.

Argentina is more easily accessed from Osorno. Cruz del Sur goes off-hours to Bariloche via Paso Cardenal Samoré, east of Osorno; Tas Choapa has similar service.

Terminal de Buses Rurales (cnr Avs Balmaceda & A Pinto) serves local destinations, such as Chol Chol (US$2, 1½ hours) and Melipeuco (US$3, 2½ hours). **Buses Jac** (cnr Av Balmaceda & Aldunate) offers the most frequent service to Villarrica and Pucón, plus service to Santiago and Coñaripe. The **Rodoviario Curacautín** (Av Barros Arana 191) is the departure point for buses to Curacautín, Lonquimay (US$3.50, three hours) and the upper Biobío.

Destination	Duration (hr)	Cost (US$)
Angol	2	34
Bariloche, Argentina	10½-12	20
Chillán	4	8
Coñaripe	2½	6
Concepción	4½	7
Cunco	1½	2
Curacautín	1½	4
Osorno	3	7
Pucón	1½	4.50
Puerto Montt/Puerto Varas	7	9
Santiago	8	10-35
Valdivia	3	4
Victoria	1	2.50
Villarrica	1	4.50
Zapala & Neuquén, Argentina	10	33

TRAIN

Santiago-bound trains leave nightly, stopping at various stations en route (economy/reclining seat US$21/27.50, nine hours). Trains also head south to Puerto Varas and Puerto Montt. Buy tickets at **Estación de Ferrocarril** (☎ 233-416; Av Barros Arana) or at the downtown office of **Ferrocarriles del Estado** (EFE; ☎ 233-522; Bulnes 582).

Getting Around

From the airport, taxis cost about US$5 to the city center. Bus 1 runs between downtown and the train station. From the bus terminal, hop on *colectivos* 11P and 25A. *Colectivo* 9 services west Temuco. Car rental is available at the airport with **Budget** (☎ 338-836) and at **Full Fama's** (☎ 213-851; Andrés Bello 1096).

PARQUE NACIONAL CONGUILLÍO

A refuge for the araucaria (monkey-puzzle tree), **Conguillío** (admission US$5.50) shelters 60,835 hectares of alpine lakes, deep canyons and native forests. Its centerpiece is the smoldering Volcán Llaima (3125m), which last erupted in 1957.

The superb **Sierra Nevada trail** (10km, approximately three hours one way) leaves from the parking lot at Playa Linda, at the east end of Laguna Conguillío, and climbs northeast through coigue forests, passing a pair of lake overlooks; from the second and more scenic, you can see solid stands of araucarias offset coigues on the ridge top. A link of **Sendero de Chile** (18km, approximately six hours one way) connects Laguna Captrén with Guardaría Truful-Truful. At **Laguna Captrén**, **Los Carpinteros** (8km, approximately 2½ hours one way) accesses the awe-striking 1800-year-old, 3m-wide Araucaría Madre, the largest tree in the park.

Call to see which parts of the park are open from April to November since heavy snowdrifts may accumulate. In **Laguna Conguillío**, Conaf's **Centro de Información Ambiental** (www.parquenacionalconguillio.cl in Spanish) sells trail maps. The diminutive three-trail **Centro de Ski Las Araucarias** (☎ 045-562-313; www.skiaraucarias.cl in Spanish; half/full-day lift tickets US$20/25) also has an office in **Temuco** (☎ 045-274-141; Bulnes 351, Oficina 47). Experienced skiers will trudge further up the volcano for a thrill.

Sleeping & Eating

The campgrounds at Laguna Conguillío all charge US$30; options include **El Estero** (in Temuco ☎ 045-644-388) and **Laguna Captren**, 6km from Lago Conguillío. Rates are heavily discounted off-season.

Centro de Ski Las Araucarias offers skiers **Refugio Los Paraguas** (dm US$11) and **Refugio Pehuén** (dm US$14, d US$34-43). Dorm guests may need to provide a sleeping bag. Contact the ski center for bookings.

La Baita (☎ 416-410; www.labaitaconguillio.cl in Spanish; 4-8–person cabins US$60-85) is an ecotourism project just outside the park's southern boundary, sitting in pristine forest. Six attractive cabins come fully equipped and include slow-burning furnaces, limited electricity and hot water. In high season, meals, excursions and a small store are available. La Baita is 15km from Melipeuco and 60km from Curacautín.

Getting There & Away

To reach Sector Los Paraguas, **Buses Flota Erbuc** (☎ 045-272-204), at Temuco's Terminal de Buses Rurales, runs a dozen times daily to Cherquenco (US$2, one hour), from where it's a 17km walk or hitchhike to the ski lodge.

CHILE

For the northern entrance, Buses Flota Erbuc has regular service to Curacautín (US$2.15, 1½ hours), from where a shuttle (US$1) reaches the park border at Guardería Captrén on weekdays. From December to March, if conditions allow, it continues to Laguna Captrén. Heavy rain can prevent the movement of passenger vehicles between the lagunas.

For the southern entrance, **Nar-Bus** (☎ 045-211-611) in Temuco runs seven buses daily to Melipeuco (US$2.50, one hour), where **Hostería Huetelén** (☎ 045-693-032) can arrange a taxi to the park.

VILLARRICA

☎ 045 / pop 28,000

Villarrica has similar scenery but less fluff, zip and bustle than nearby Pucón; it bloomed and faded beforehand and today remains a somewhat lackadaisical resort. On the southwest shore of Lago Villarrica, it was founded in 1552 and repeatedly attacked by Mapuche until treaties were signed in 1882.

Information

Banks with ATMs are plentiful.

Banco de Chile (cnr Alderete & Pedro de Valdivia) Has an ATM.

Hospital Villarrica (☎ 411-169; San Martín 460)

Oficina de Turismo (Pedro de Valdivia 1070; ☉ until 11pm in summer) Has helpful staff and useful leaflets.

Post office (Anfión Muñoz 315)

Telefónica CTC (Henríquez 544)

Turcamb (Pedro de Valdivia 1061) Exchanges US cash.

Sights

The **Museo Histórico y Arqueológico** (Pedro de Valdivia 1050; admission US$1; ☉ 9am-1pm & 3-7:30pm Mon-Fri), next to the tourist office, displays Mapuche jewelry, a *ruka* (thatched hut), musical instruments and rough-hewn wooden masks. Behind the tourist office, the **Feria Artesanal** offers a selection of crafts.

Tours

Many of the same tours organized in Pucón (see opposite) can be arranged here; try the agency **Politur** (☎ 414-547; Henríquez 475) or fly-fishing operator **Süd Explorer** (Av Pedro de Valdivia).

Sleeping

Prices rise considerably in summer and during the ski season. The **Cámara de Turismo** (cnr Gral Urrutia & A Bello) lists *hospedajes*.

La Torre Suiza (☎ /fax 411-213; www.torresuiza .com; Bilbao 969; campsites per person US$5, dm US$10, d without/with bathroom US$23/26; Ⓟ 🖳) Loved by Europeans, it's a smorgasbord of clean dorms and stylish rooms in a well-kept older house. Attractions include a fully equipped kitchen, laundry and bike rental.

Hostal Berta Romero (☎ 411-276; Pedro de Valdivia 712; r US$10) This elegant, understated home tends toward the noisy side. Perks include kitchen use.

El Arrayán (☎ 411-235; Gral Körner 442; s/d US$16/24, cabins for 4 people US$51) Welcoming and well run, with kitchen privileges.

More than half a dozen campgrounds dot the road between Villarrica and Pucón. The following recommended places both have reasonably private shady sites and hot showers:

Camping Los Castaños (☎ 412-330; campsites US$18) One kilometer east of town.

Camping Dulac (☎ 412-097; campsites US$22) Two kilometers east.

Eating & Drinking

Café Bar 2001 (Henríquez 379; sandwiches US$2.50-5) A kick-back-and-relax spot with real coffee and fat, scrumptious sandwiches.

Hostería de la Colina (☎ 411-503; Las Colinas 115; mains US$6-10; ☉ lunch & dinner) Imagine getting excited about soup? Ponder gazpacho, chestnut and Chinese carrot flavors…main dishes are locally inspired but there's the occasional lasagna or pot roast.

Travellers (☎ 413-617; Valentin Letelier 753; mains US$4-8) Choose between oatmeal or wontons for breakfast from a globetrotting menu, disorienting in the land of bland and cheesy. Some will simply rejoice – the Chilean and Mexican fare *are* all that. In the evening sip a drink and chill to jazz.

Getting There & Away

Villarrica has a main **bus terminal** (Pedro de Valdivia 621), though a few companies have separate offices nearby. Long-distance fares are similar to those from Temuco (an hour away), which has more choices.

Buses Jac (Bilbao 610) goes to Pucón (US75¢, 30 minutes), Temuco (US$4, 1¼ hours), Lican Ray (US75¢, 30 minutes) and Coñaripe (US$1.50, one hour). **Buses Regional Villarrica** (Vicente Reyes 619) also has frequent buses to Pucón.

For Argentine destinations, Igi Llaima leaves at 6:45am Monday, Wednesday and Friday for San Martín de los Andes (US$20) and Neuquén (US$40, 16 hours) via Paso Mamuil Malal. Buses San Martín has a similar service, and both leave from the main bus terminal.

PUCÓN

☎ 045 / pop 21,000

A shimmering lake under the huffing cone of 2847m Volcán Villarrica feeds the mystique of village turned mega-resort Pucón. Summer time draws a giddy mix of families, adventurers, package tourists and new-age gurus to this mecca. Where else in Chile can you party and play slots till dawn, leave in time to start hiking the volcano (alongside 300 other enthusiasts) or sleep in, go to the beach or hot springs, drink a caramel latte, buy a gem-encrusted handbag, run into half of Santiago, get a massage, and sleep in a teepee? Something does exist for everyone here and, snootiness aside, the mix of international wanderers, the zippy social scene and backyard of natural wonders is often a blast.

Orientation

Pucón is 25km from Villarrica at the east end of Lago Villarrica, between the estuary of the Río Pucón to the north and Volcán Villarrica to the south. You can easily navigate town on foot: most tour operators and services are on the commercial main strip of Av O'Higgins. Restaurants and shops are along Fresia, which leads to the plaza. Slightly beyond the plaza is the beach.

Information

Exchange rates are better in Temuco but you'll find banks on Av O'Higgins or Fresia.

Ciber-Unid@d G (Av O'Higgins 415, Local 2; per hr US$1) Get online.

Conaf (☎ 443-781; Lincoyán 336) Has information on nearby parks.

Entel (Ansorena 299) Call home.

Hospital San Francisco (☎ 441-177; Uruguay 325; ⊗ 24hr) For medical emergencies.

Laundry Express (Av O'Higgins 660, Local 2; per load US$1.75)

Lavandería Esperanza (Colo Colo 475; per load US$1.75)

Oficina de Turismo (cnr Av O'Higgins & Palguín) Offers brochures and there's usually an English speaker on staff. Check out the colorful complaints book before booking activities, especially canopy.

Post office (Fresia 183) You can also call home from here.

Pucon (www.pucon.com) Useful internet resource.

Supermercado Eltit (Av O'Higgins 336; ⊗ 7am-9pm) Changes US cash with reasonable fees and also has an ATM.

Activities

Regardless of how many people are milling about Av O'Higgins on any given day, with a little creativity you can always find a spot to explore and leave the crowds behind. Don't limit your ideas to the most popular tours – ask locals and resident expats for their picks.

The masses come to **hike** the smoking, lava-spitting crater of Volcán Villarrica. The full-day excursion (US$40 to US$60) leaves Pucón around 7:30am. There is no technical climbing involved and the ascent is frequently done by people with no prior mountaineering experience. A guide is recommended unless you are an expert with your own equipment. When you book a guide service, ask how they will handle a bad-weather day. Less reputable companies head up on a lousy day, just to turn back and not have to give a refund. Check for complaints with the tourism office and other travelers.

The rivers near Pucón and their corresponding rapids classifications are: the Lower Trancura (III), the Upper Trancura (IV), Liucura (II–III), the Puesco Run (V) and Maichín (IV–V). When booking a **rafting** or **kayaking** trip, note that stated trip durations include transportation time. Prices range from US$10 to US$50 depending on the season, the number of participants, the company and level of challenge. Rafting may be unavailable in winter when water levels rise.

Mountain **bikes** can be rented (US$20 per day) all over town. Check shocks and brakes before renting yours. The most popular route is the Ojos de Caburgua Loop. Take the turnoff to the airfield about 4km east of town and cross Río Trancura. Bike shops should be able to provide a map.

Courses

Get fluent at **Pucón Language & Cultural Center** (☎ 443-315, 099-935-9417; www.languagepucon.com; Uruguay 306; 1-week group intensive US$162), where you can also hook up with a homestay and free book exchange.

Tours

Outfitters include the following:

Aguaventura (☎ 444-246; www.aguaventura.com; Palguín 336) This spirited French-owned agency is on the cutting edge of rafting, kayaking, rappelling, canyoning and snowsports.

CHILE

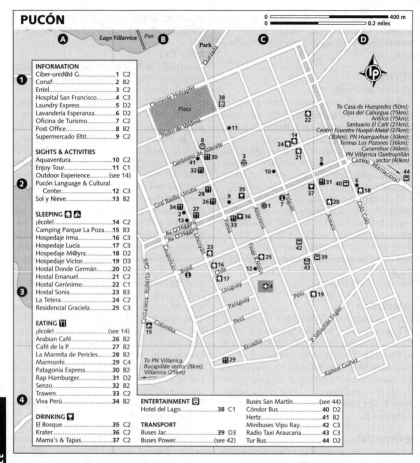

PUCÓN

INFORMATION
Ciber-unid@d G....................1 C2
Conaf....................................2 B2
Entel....................................3 C2
Hospital San Francisco.........4 C3
Laundry Express...................5 D2
Lavandería Esperanza..........6 C3
Oficina de Turismo...............7 C2
Post Office...........................8 B2
Supermercado Eltit..............9 C2

SIGHTS & ACTIVITIES
Aquaventura.......................10 C2
Enjoy Tour...........................11 C1
Outdoor Experience..........(see 14)
Pucón Language & Cultural
  Center...............................12 C3
Sol y Nieve.........................13 B2

SLEEPING
¡école!.................................14 C2
Camping Parque La Poza....15 B3
Hospedaje Irma...................16 C3
Hospedaje Lucía..................17 C3
Hospedaje M@yra................18 D2
Hospedaje Victor.................19 D3
Hostal Donde Germán.........20 D2
Hostal Emanuel....................21 C2
Hostal Gerónimo..................22 C1
Hostal Sonia........................23 B3
La Tetera.............................24 C2
Residencial Graciela............25 C2

EATING
¡école!..............................(see 14)
Arabian Café.......................26 B2
Café de la P.........................27 B2
La Marmita de Pericles........28 B2
Marmonhi............................29 C4
Patagonia Express...............30 B2
Rap Hamburger....................31 D2
Senzo..................................32 B2
Trawen................................33 C2
Viva Perú.............................34 B2

DRINKING
El Bosque............................35 C2
Krater..................................36 C2
Mama's & Tapas..................37 C2

ENTERTAINMENT
Hotel del Lago.....................38 C1

TRANSPORT
Buses Jac............................39 D3
Buses Power....................(see 42)
Buses San Martín..............(see 44)
Cóndor Bus..........................40 D2
Hertz...................................41 B2
Minibuses Vipu Ray.............42 C3
Radio Taxi Araucaria............43 C3
Tur Bus................................44 D2

To Casa de Huespedes (50m);
Ojos del Caburgua (15km);
Antilco (15km);
Santuario El Cañi (21km);
Centro Ecuestre Huepil-Malal (27km);
(30km); PN Huerquehue (30km);
Termas Los Pozones (36km);
Curarrehue (36km);
PN Villarrica Quetrupillán
Camino sector (40km)

Antilco (☎ 099-713-9758; www.antilco.com) Fifteen kilometers east of Pucón on Río Liucura; recommended horse treks in Liucura Valley.

Centro Ecuestre Huepil-Malal (☎ 099-643-3204; www.huepil-malal.cl; km 27 on Camino Pucón-Huife) A reputable equestrian center with excellent horse treks in the *cordillera*, run by a warm family.

Enjoy Tour (☎ 442-313; www.enjoytour.cl; Ansorena 123) A professional outfit with sharp new gear and attentive staff offering myriad excursions and airport transfers for US$31.

Outdoor Experience (☎ 442-809; www.outdoor experience.org; Gral Basilio Urrutia 952 B) Run out of an office adjoining ¡école!, this small agency offers rock climbing, trips to el Cani and generally less-commercial trips run with expertise and an educational bent.

Sol y Nieve (☎ 441-070; www.chile-travel.com/sol nieve.htm; Av O'Higgins 192) A dependable volcano and rafting outfitter, known to kick in after-rafting *asados* (BBQs).

Festivals & Events

Summer is a constant stream of cheer-pulsing proceedings, but don't miss these events:

Jornadas Musicales de Pucón An annual music festival held mid-January.

Triatlón Internacional de Pucón (Pucón International Triathlon) Early February.

Sleeping

Guests pay a premium to vacation in Pucón; you'll think some of these places are kidding with their prices. Listings show high-season rates; they mercifully drop 20% off-season. If you're without a reservation, look for cheap, unregistered family homestays around Lincoyán, Perú and Ecuador.

¡école! (☎ 441-675; ecole@entelchile.net; Gral Basilio Urrutia 592; dm US$8, shared r US$16, s/d with bathroom US$37/45) This local institution features a gamut of offerings: while the doubles upstairs are crisp and comfortable, some of the digs out back look like…garage living. Still, the potted plants, excellent vegetarian restaurant and general nature-loving vibe make it a positive place. The unheated dorms close in winter.

Hospedaje Victor (☎ 443-525; www.pucon.com/victor; Palguín 705; s US$12; 🖳) A budget standout, with practically new cozy wood rooms with bright linens and new fixtures. Well insulated and very welcoming.

Casa de Huespedes (☎ 442-444; www.dondegerman .cl; Pasaje las Rosas; dm/shared r US$12/14; 🖳) Take refuge in these sparkling, somewhat removed digs with blonde wood finish, with the same owner as Hostal Donde Germán. The huge checker-tiled kitchen with funky neon lighting sports a wood stove for cooking. It's by the bus terminal, a five minute walk to the action.

Hospedaje Lucía (☎ 441-721; Lincoyán 565; r per person US$12) A respectful, well-kept home with friendly owners who also run fishing trips.

Hospedaje Irma (☎ 442-226; Lincoyán 545; shared r/d US$12/35) Geraniums and velour couches set the scene of this very Chilean home, with shoe-box rooms.

Hostal Emanuel (☎ 442-696; Gral Basilio Urrutia 571; r US$12, with bathroom US$14) Touts 'the nicest *señora* in Chile,' whose rooms are dark but serviceable.

Hostal Donde Germán (☎ 442-444; www.dondeger man.cl; Brasil 640; dm/d US$14/49; 🖳) With a lounge-strewn lawn fit for putting, tasteful shared spaces, wood-finish rooms and fluffy duvets, this German-owned house pushes the envelope of hostels. The hefty charge includes internet access and book exchange.

Hostal Sonia (☎ 441-269; Lincoyán 485; r per person US$16) A tidy little spot with miniature rooms in floral themes.

Hospedaje M@yra (☎ 442-745; Palguín 695; dm/s/d US$16/18/32; 🅿 🖳) A worn-out chalet offering a gravel lounge area and bunks in peach cobbler charm.

Residencial Graciela (☎ 441-494; Roland Matus 521; s/tr US$24/39) Squat, scrubbed rooms with polyester curtains and a welcoming hostess.

Hostal Gerónimo (☎ 443-762; www.geronimo.cl; Gerónimo de Alderete 665; s/d incl breakfast US$49/55; 🅿) No *hostal*, Gerónimo has lovely rooms with tapestries on the stucco walls, reliable gas heat, terracotta-tile bathrooms and balconies to admire Villarica's smoking crater. Breakfast usually includes juice, eggs and *küchen*.

La Tetera (☎ 441-462; www.tetera.cl; Gral Basilio Urrutia 580; d incl breakfast without/with bathroom US$43/57; 🖳) While the decor could use some freshening up, spotless serenity rules this welcoming wood-paneled home and the staff is just great. The best breakfast in town.

Camping Parque La Poza (☎ 441-435; Costanera Roberto Geis 769; camping per person US$5) The constant traffic passing this huge, shady camping facility diminishes its appeal, but there are cooking facilities, storage lockers and hot water.

About 18km east, off the road to Lago Caburgua, three campgrounds charge US$10 to US$12 per six-person site. Look for signs after crossing Río Pucón. There are more campsites between Pucón and Villarrica.

Eating

Splurge a little because you won't get gourmet food this good in the rest of southern Chile.

Rap Hamburger (cnr Av O'Higgins & Arauco; burgers US$3) Try this place for quick bites, including cheeseburgers. It's open very late.

La Tetera (Gral Basilio Urrutia 580; mains US$3-6) Breakfasts include muesli or eggs and fresh bread and fruit. Pasta lunches and tea time also satisfy.

Café de la P (cnr Av O'Higgins & Lincoyán; mains US$3-10) A stylish café with prime people-watching, decent espresso and nice steak and provolone on baguettes.

Patagonia Express Café (Fresia 354; cones US$4) Homemade tart and creamy ice creams, hand-made chocolates and caramel lattes on the sidewalk – a very summery affair.

¡école! (Gral Basilio Urrutia 592; mains US$4-7) The decor is Snow White meets Bob Marley and the food – Bengal curry salmon and spinach salad with sesame – is further evidence of fusion reigning, but it works deliciously. Look for occasional live entertainment.

Marmonhi (Ecuador 175; mains US$4-10) Luxuriate with a slow lunch away from the bustle in this log home with crisp linens on the tables and garden seating. The regional cuisine is tops – including *empanadas* and *humitas*.

Arabian Café (Fresia 354; mains US$5-9; 🕑 lunch & dinner) The specialty is stuffed red peppers

CHILE

with spiced beef but you'll find the hummus and tahini worthy of your attention at this authentic Middle Eastern restaurant.

Viva Perú (Lincoyán s/n; mains US$5-13) Tip back the best *pisco sour* in town with a side of piping hot *yuquitas* (manioc fries) on the deck. Slick styling and a great, original menu but avoid the oily *arroz chaufa* (fried rice).

La Marmita de Pericles (☎ 442-431; Fresia 300; fixed-price lunch US$7; ☽ lunch & dinner) Sincere service and skillful cooking make this worth the splurge. Consider trout in rosemary butter and a bottle of wine while Sinatra croons on the sound system.

Trawen (Av O'Higgins 311; mains US$8-14; ☽ lunch & dinner) Pumpkin fettuccini, whole wheat pizza, fresh juice smoothies…if you are craving fresh and original then sit yourself at a worn wood table and endure the wait. A woodland mural and rock wall further promote the idea of Nirvana.

Senzo (Fresia; mains US$8-16) The menu here has upscale traces (risotto with shrimp and tomatoes) but there's a slew of cocktails, cold drafts with squashed lemons, and options for patio seating.

Drinking

El Bosque (Av O'Higgins 524) Popular and geared to well-heeled outdoor types, El Bosque is crafted from local wood with a stylish wine bar and adventure sport DVDs on show.

Krater (☎ 441-339; Av O'Higgins 447) A dive bar for the slumming traveler.

Mama's & Tapas (Av O'Higgins 587) This bar with curves and iron stools hosts a hipster crowd. Take advantage of the weekday happy hour until 10pm.

Entertainment

Hotel del Lago (Ansorena 23) Offers a glitzy casino and movie theater.

Getting There & Away

Bus transportation to/from Santiago (US$13 to US$32, 11 hours) is with **Tur Bus** (Camino Internacional), which is east of town, **Buses Jac** (cnr Uruguay & Palguín), **Cóndor Bus** (Colo Colo 430) and **Buses Power** (Palguín 550), the cheapest (and least comfortable) option.

Tur Bus also goes to Puerto Montt daily (US$10, five hours). For Temuco, Tur Bus leaves every hour and Buses Jac every half-hour (US$3.50, two hours). For Valdivia, Jac has five daily buses (US$4, three hours). Buses

Jac and **Minibuses Vipu Ray** (Palguín 550) have a continuous service to Villarrica (US$1, 30 minutes) and Curarrehue (US$1.20, 45 minutes). Buses Jac also has a service to Caburgua (US$1, 45 minutes), Paillaco (US$3, one hour) and Parque Nacional Huerquehue (US$3, one hour). For San Martín de los Andes, Argentina, **Buses San Martín** (Tur Bus terminal) has six weekly departures (US$20, five hours) stopping in Junín.

Getting Around

Daily car-rental rates range from US$30 for passenger cars to US$70 for 4WD pickups. Try **Hertz** (☎ 441-664; www.hertz.com; cnr Gerónimo de Alderete & Fresia). Taxis will negotiate prices to outlying areas. **Radio Taxi Araucaria** (☎ 442-323; cnr Palguín & Uruguay) can prearrange trips.

AROUND PUCÓN
Río Liucura Valley

East of Pucón, the Camino Pucón-Huife cuts through a lush valley hosting a myriad of hot springs. The best value is at the end of the road: **Termas Los Pozones** (km 36; admission US$6, 3hr max stay) with the six natural stone pools open 24 hours. Light some candles and soak under the stars. Arrange a transfer with a *hospedaje* or agency, or rent a car en masse and do the hot-spring hop in your own time.

Formed by citizens fighting off old-growth logging interests, the nature sanctuary **El Cañi** (km 21; entrance with/without guide US$10/5) protects some 400 hectares of ancient araucaria forest. A three-hour 9km hiking trail ascends a steep trail to gorgeous views. Arrange to visit with Outdoor Experience or at the park entrance.

Ruta 119

Arriving at the Argentine border at Mamuil Malal, this route provides some off-piste pleasures. The quiet and colorful **Curarrehue** has Mapuche influences. The **tourist office** (☎ 197-1573; Plaza) has some info on activities and camping/hostels. Before town, **Kila Leufu** (☎ 099-711-8064; s/d US$13/26) provides a fun countryside respite; learn to milk cows and enjoy a comfy night's sleep. Buses leave frequently to Curarrehue from Pucón (US$1.20, 45 minutes) and Villarrica (US$2, 45 minutes). There is also service to San Martín de los Andes from Curarrehue.

Traveling 5km northeast of Curarrehue, the rustic **Recuerdo de Ancamil**, on the banks of Río Maichín, has eight natural pools, including one tucked in a grotto. There's camping and a few cabins. Another 10km, **Termas de Panqui** (day use US$13) has serene hot springs and a spiritual bent. You can also have meals (US$5 to US$8) or stay in a teepee (US$18) or hotel (room per person US$27). For treks and climbing tours check out the **Lodge** (☎ 441-029; www.the-lodge.cl; excursion & lodging US$100 daily). It's 24km northeast of Curarrehue but owners offer free pickups from Pucón.

PARQUE NACIONAL HUERQUEHUE

Rushing rivers, waterfalls, araucaria forest and alpine lakes adorn the 12,500-hectare **Parque Nacional Huerquehue** (admission US$3.50). Only 35km from Pucón, it has easy access and a wide array of hiking options. Conaf sells trail maps at the entrance.

The **Los Lagos trail** (9km, three to four hours one way) switchbacks from 700m to 1300m through dense *lenga* forests to solid stands of araucaria surrounding a cluster of pristine lakes. At Laguna Huerquehue, the trail **Los Huerquenes** (two days) continues north then east to cross the park and access **Termas de San Sebastián** (☎ 045-341-961), just east of the park boundary. From there a gravel road connects to the north end of Lago Caburgua and Cunco.

Conaf's Lago Tinquilco and Renahue campgrounds charge US$16 per site. **Refugio Tinquilco** (☎ 02-777-7673 in Santiago; www.tinquilco .cl; bunks without sheets US$12, d US$34), at the base of the Lago Verde trailhead, is a welcoming two-story wooden lodge offering French-press coffee and meals for extra (full board US$12), or you can cook for yourself.

Buses Jac has a regular service to/from Pucón in the morning and afternoon (US$3, one hour); be sure to reserve your seat beforehand. Otherwise join a tour or share a taxi.

PARQUE NACIONAL VILLARRICA

Established in 1940, Parque Nacional Villarrica protects 60,000 hectares of remarkable volcanic scenery surrounding the 2847m-high Villarrica, 2360m-high Quetrupillán and, along the Argentine border, a section of 3746m-high Lanín (shared with Argentina, from where it may be climbed).

Rucapillán is directly south of Pucón along a well-maintained road and takes in the most popular hikes up and around Villarrica. (For volcano hike details, see p485.) Shortcutters can take the ski lift up partway. How's that for cheating? The trail **Challupen Chinay** (23km,

12 hours) rounds the volcano's southern side crossing through a variety of scenery to end at the entrance to the **Quetrupillán** sector.

Ski Pucón (☎ 045-441-901; www.skipucon.cl in Spanish; Gran Hotel Pucón, Clemente Holzapfel 190, Pucón; full-day lift ticket US$31; � Jul-Oct) is best for beginners but experienced skiers will find some nice out-of-bounds options. The lava chutes make some seriously fun natural half-pipes. Too much wind or cloud cover shuts this active volcano down; check conditions before you head up. Almost every agency and a number of hotels send minivans (US$6 to US$10, free with ski rental) up to the base lodge.

LAGO CALAFQUÉN

Black-sand beaches and gardens draw tourists to this island-studded lake, especially at fashionable **Lican Ray** (30km south of Villarrica) and more down-to-earth **Coñaripe** (22km east of Lican Ray). Out of season, it's dead. Lican Ray's **tourist office** (☎ 045-431-516; Urritia 310), directly on the plaza, offers maps and accommodations listings. Coñaripe's **Turismo Aventura Chumay** (☎ 045-317-287; Las Tepas 201) rents bikes and has area information and tours. Coñaripe has access to rustic hot springs and other sides of the park that tourists rarely tread.

Sleeping & Eating

In Coñaripe, campgrounds by the lake are small, cramped lots charging a negotiable US$16 to US$20 per site. Try **Millaray** (☎ 099-802-7935) or **Rucahue** (☎ 045-317-210).

Hostal Chumay (☎ 045-317-287; Las Tepas 201; s/d US$12/27) A great bargain behind the plaza with a restaurant serving set-price seafood lunches (US$4).

Hotel Elizabeth (☎ 045-317-275; Beck de Ramberga 496; s/d US$17/34.50) A two-story wooden hotel with room balconies and wafting smells from the downstairs bakery. Not for dieters – it also has a restaurant and chocolatería.

Services open year-round in Lican Ray include the following:

Hostal Hofmann (☎ 045-431-109; Cam Coñaripe 100; r per person US$10) An appealing home with feather pillows and flower gardens.

Los Ñaños (☎ 045-431-026; Urrutia 105; mains US$6-12) Excellent for *empanadas*, with decent seafood, meat and pasta dishes at inflated prices.

Getting There & Away

Buses Jac (cnr Urrutia & Marichanquín) goes often to Villarrica (US$1.50, 45 minutes) and Coñaripe

CHILE

(US$1.50, 30 minutes). Other buses leave from the corner of Urrutia and Huenumán. Every morning at 7:30am a local bus goes to Panguipulli (US$3, two hours) via back roads.

LAGO PANGUIPULLI

At the northwest end of Lago Panguipulli, the town of **Panguipulli** is a main service center with an assortment of eateries and a gaping view of Volcán Choshuenco (2415m). The municipal **tourist office** (☎ 063-312-202; Plaza Prat), on the east side of the plaza, is helpful and has area information. At the lake's east end is the tranquil hamlet **Choshuenco**, with sweeping beach views. Further south is **Enco**, the access point for hikes on Mocho Choshuenco, the most accessible of the volcano's two peaks.

Sleeping & Eating

Playa Chauquén, south of town, is a beach area that allows a variety of camping. In summer a shuttle runs to and from the beach twice daily.

Camping El Bosque (☎ 063-311-489; campsites per person US$5) In Panguipulli, 200m north of Plaza Prat, with 15 tent sites and hot showers.

Hostal España (☎ 063-311-166; jhrios@telsur.cl; Av O'Higgins 790; s/d US$26/34.50) Offers homey rooms with private bathrooms in a family atmosphere. Breakfast is available and money can be changed here.

Girasol (Martínez de Rozas 664; lunch US$5) Offers Chilean comfort food. Check out the creamy *pastel de choclo*.

Gardylafquen (☎ 063-311-887; Martínez de Rozas 722; lunch US$5) Dishes up inviting fixed-price menus.

Getting There & Away

Panguipulli's main **Terminal de Buses** (Gabriela Mistral 100), at the corner of Diego Portales, has regular departures from Monday to Saturday to Liquiñe, Coñaripe (US$1.50) and Lican Ray (US$3, two hours); to Choshuenco, Neltume and Puerto Fuy; and to Valdivia (US$3, two hours) and Temuco (US$4.50, three hours). Buses from Panguipulli to Puerto Fuy (two hours) pass through Choshuenco and return to Panguipulli early the following morning.

LAGO PIREHUEICO

Follow the rush and tumble curves of Río Huilo Huilo on this scenic route to San Martín de los Andes, Argentina. With 60,000 acres of private land, **Huilo Huilo** (☎ 02-334-4565; www.huilo

huilo.cl in Spanish; admission US$1.50) is developing the area for low-impact ecotourism. The grounds include a fairy-tale spire-shaped hotel called **La Montaña Mágica** (d from US$100) decked out in finery.

The **ferry Hua-Hum** (in Panguipulli ☎ 063-311-334) transports passengers and vehicles between Puerto Fuy and Puerto Pirehueico (1½ hours), from where land transportation departs, crossing the border at Paso Hua Hum and continuing onto San Martín. The ferry leaves twice a day in each direction from January to mid-March, and once daily the rest of the year. Cars cost US$16, jeeps and pickups US$25, pedestrians US$1, and bicycles US$3. Basic lodging is available at both ends of the lake.

VALDIVIA

☎ 063 / pop 127,750

The university city of Valdivia probably presents the hippest urban living in Chile's south, with its breezy riverfront, multiple universities, stacks of bars and restaurants, old architecture and modern attitudes. The city has a historic background as the seat of German immigration in the 1850s and '60s (which is why chocolate and beer abounds). It has known both splendor and disaster. Ransacked by Mapuches after its founding, it fell again when the 1960 earthquake obliterated much of it and sunk the coast 4m. A 2005 environmental catastrophe where some 5000 black-necked swans died from contamination from the Celco-Arauco paper mill drew local and worldwide outrage although the plant continues to operate. The environmental battle wages on (see www.accionporloscisnes in Spanish).

Orientation

Valdivia is 160km southwest of Temuco and 45km west of the Panamericana. From the Terminal de Buses, any bus marked 'Plaza' will take you to the center and Plaza de la República. Lodgings are within walking distance.

Information

Downtown ATMs are abundant, as are call centers. There is a tourist kiosk at the Terminal de Buses.

Café Phonet (Libertad 127; per hr US$1) Internet with chat-happy long-distance phone rates.

Cambio Arauco (Arauco 331, Local 24) For money changing; open on Saturday.

Cambio La Reconquista (Carampangue 329)

VALDIVIA

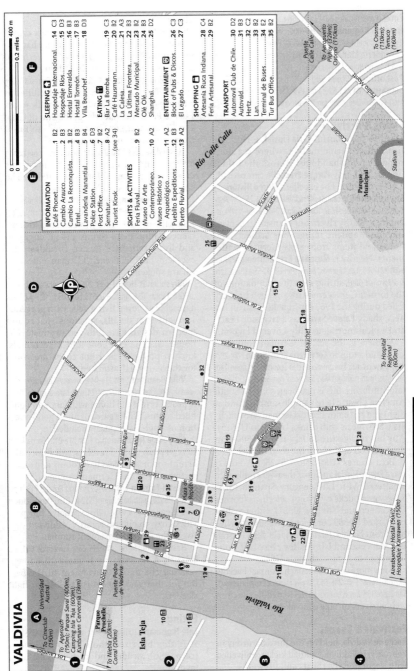

0.2 miles

400 m

CHILE

Entel (Pérez Rosales 601) Call center.

Hospital Regional (☎ 297-000; Simpson 850; 🕐 24hr) South of town, near Aníbal Pinto.

Lavandería Manantial (Camilo Henríquez 809; per load US$2) Scrub your skivvies here.

Post office (O'Higgins 575)

Sernatur (☎ 213-596; Prat 155; 🕐 8:30am-5:30pm Mon-Fri Mar-Dec, daily Jan & Feb) Sits riverfront.

Sights & Activities

Head to the colorful **Feria Fluvial**, a riverside fish and vegetable market, where sea lions paddle up for handouts. Across the bridge on Isla Teja, tiny **Parque Prochelle** can provide a piece of quiet. The excellent **Museo Histórico y Arqueológico** (Los Laureles 47; admission US$1.25; 🕐 9am-1pm & 2:30-6pm Dec-Mar, 10am-1pm & 2-6pm Apr-Nov) occupies a nearby riverfront mansion. Displays include Mapuche indigenous artifacts and household items from early German settlements. Nearby is **Museo de Arte Contemporáneo** (☎ 221-968; Los Laureles; admission US$1; 🕐 10am-1pm & 3-7pm Tue-Sun), sitting atop the foundations of the former Cervecería Anwandter, a brewery felled during the 1960 earthquake. Also on Isla Teja, shady **Parque Saval** has a riverside beach and a pleasant trail to a lily-covered lagoon.

Valdivia is the seat of German culture in Chile and a tour to **Cervecería Kunstmann** (☎ 292-969; www.cerveza-kunstmann.co.cl in Spanish; 🕐 noon-1am Nov-Mar, noon-midnight Mon-Sat, noon-7pm Sun Apr-Oct) certainly informs: this is real beer, some of South America's best. There's ample sampling and at night you can enjoy hearty German fare (pitchers US$5, meals with drinks US$12 to US$15). Any bus or *colectivo* to Isla Teja (US$50¢) can drop you off at Km5 on the road to Niebla.

Boat cruises (US$22 to US$26, 6½ hours) leave **Puerto Fluvial** and float the river confluence smattered with 17th-century Spanish forts. Save some bucks by taking *colectivos* (corner Chacabuco and Yungay; US$1), either yellow or marked 'T-350', or *micros* (US80¢), to Niebla. From Niebla, ferries visit Isla Teja, Corral, Isla Mancera and Isla del Rey every half-hour from 8am to 8pm; each leg is US$2.

For a more active approach, contact **Pueblito Expeditions** (☎ 245-055; www.pueblitoexpediciones.cl; San Carlos 188; kayak outings US$29) to paddle the calm web of rivers or take a kayak course.

Festivals & Events

Noche de Valdivia, held on the third Saturday in February, is Valdivia's annual kicker, enlivened with decorated riverboats and fireworks.

Sleeping

During the school year the university crowd monopolizes cheap housing; summer has better options. The *hospedajes* near the Terminal de Buses are the cheapest but dingy.

Camping Isla Teja (☎ 225-855; Los Cipreses 1125; campsites US$10-15) Good riverfront facilities in an apple orchard. It's a 30-minute walk across Puente Pedro de Valdivia, at the end of Calle Los Robles and Los Cipreses, or take Bus 9 from the Mercado Municipal.

Hospedaje Ríos (☎ 206-013; Arauco 869; r per person US$10) You'll find ample, bright rooms in this creaky house, praised for its hospitality. The shared bathrooms could be cleaner.

Hospedaje Karamawen (☎ 347-317; esolisromero@ yahoo.com; Gral Lagos 1334; shared r incl breakfast US$12) Enjoy the personal attention and artistic ambience with tasteful rooms and an engaging and lively translator-owner. Breakfasts are excellent. English, French, German and Swedish are spoken.

Airesbuenos Hostel (☎ 206-304; www.airesbuenos .cl; Gral Lagos 1036; dm/s/d US$13.50/29/35; 🅿 🖳) As agreeable as *hostal* living gets, with gorgeous wrought-iron details, spacious spaces and modern design in a 19th-century historical house. Staff is excellent and bike rentals, kitchen privileges and hot cocoa are yours for the taking. HI-affiliated.

Villa Beauchef (☎ 216-044; www.villabeauchef.cl in Spanish; Beauchef 844; s/d US$14/24, with bathroom US$20/29) A peach-bright old home with airy and light-filled rooms, flower gardens and a good selection of singles. Breakfast included.

Hospedaje Internacional (☎ 212-015; García Reyes 660; r per person US$14) Travelers will find plain, kempt rooms, spotless bathrooms and an assertive staff at this German-run *hostal*.

Hostal Torreón (☎ 212-622; Pérez Rosales 783; r per person US$20, with bathroom US$24) Old-fashioned and elegant, it's a touch expensive but provides cozy respite on a rainy Valdivian day. Avoid the damper basement rooms.

Hostal Esmeralda (☎ 215-659; Esmeralda 651; s/d US$24/31) A once-stately home with enough residual charm, it's convenient to the bars but for that very reason isn't ideal for light sleepers.

Eating

Café Hausmann (O'Higgins 394; cruditos & pies US$1.50-5) A thimble-sized shop serving *cruditos* (carpaccio), strudel and *küchen*. It's a local favorite.

Approach (Los Robles 150; mains US$4-7; ☺ lunch & dinner) An Argentine-styled place just over the bridge on Isla Teja, this popular and friendly restaurant is worth the short trip for its top-notch pizzas and pastas.

Mercado Municipal (Prat s/n; mains US$4-8; ☺ lunch) Fat plates of fish and chips or *choritos al ajillo* (mussels in garlic and chilies) are some of the specialties served in three floors of restaurants, overlooking the river.

La Última Frontera (Pérez Rosales 787; mains US$4-7; ☺ lunch & dinner) Where the university crowd gathers under portraits of Butch Cassidy and Comandante Marcos to chat and feast on superb sandwiches, lunches, fresh juices and huge beers. This funky, restored mansion is a great place for an outing, open late.

Olé Olé (Lautaro 170; mains US$5) Two tables, four chairs, one open kitchen assembling paella and delectable *empanadas*. Sangria is on the house when the Spanish owner tests a new batch.

Shanghai (Andwandter 898; mains US$5) Students and townsfolk swear by the generous portions of Chinese *chaufan* (mixed rice) and attentive family service.

Bar La Bomba (Caupolicán 594; lunch US$6) Old-time Valdivia, ripe with yesteryear nostalgia. Join the regulars for a *schop* or quick lunch.

La Calesa (Yungay 735; mains US$8-15; ☺ lunch & dinner) Downright seductive, with sumptuous Peruvian flavors set in a sunlit room or riverfront deck.

Entertainment

Merrymakers should explore the block of pubs, restaurants and discos on Esmeralda (after Caupolicán); there's something for every taste and even for those without.

El Legado (Esmeralda 657) For live jazz on weekends this place is the best bet.

Cineclub (www.uach.cl) Offers art-house cinema at the University of Austral from March to February.

Shopping

Feria Artesanal (Mercado Municipal) Offers a selection of wooden handicrafts and woolens.

Artesanía Ruca Indiana (Camilo Henríquez 772) This is your best bet for Mapuche crafts.

Getting There & Away

AIR

Lan (☎ 600-526-2000; Maipú 271) flies twice daily to Concepción (US$70, 45 minutes) and Santiago (US$157, 2¼ hours).

BUS

Valdivia's **Terminal de Buses** (☎ 212-212; Anfión Muñoz 360) has frequent buses traveling to destinations between Puerto Montt and Santiago. Long-haul northbound buses leave early morning and late evening. **Tur Bus** (ticket office O'Higgins 460) offers many destinations. Buses Pirehueico and Sur Express access Panguipulli; Buses Jac accesses Villarrica (US$3.50, 3½ hours), Pucón and Temuco. Tas Choapa and Andesmar travel to Bariloche, Argentina. Igi Llaima goes to San Martín de los Andes and Neuquén once daily.

Destination	Duration (hr)	Cost (US$)
Ancud	5½	11
Bariloche, Argentina	6	21
Neuquén, Argentina	16	43
Osorno	1½	2
Panguipulli	2½	1.75
Pucón	3	5
Puerto Montt	3½	6
San Martín de los Andes, Argentina	8	20
Santiago	10	20
Temuco	2¼	5

Getting Around

Aeropuerto Pichoy is located north of the city via the Puente Calle Calle. **Transfer** (☎ 204-111) provides a minibus service (US$3.50).

Both **Autovald** (☎ 212-786; Camilo Henríquez 610) and **Hertz** (☎ 218-317; Picarte 640) rent vehicles. **Automóvil Club de Chile** (☎ 212-376; Garcia Reyes 440) is also helpful.

OSORNO

☎ 064 / pop 140,000

Agricultural hub Osorno, 910km south of Santiago, is an access point to Parque Nacional Puyehue and a convenient bus-transfer point for crossing into Argentina. While mild-mannered and pleasant, there's little to seduce a visitor into dawdling here.

Orientation

The main bus station is in the eastern section of downtown, five blocks from Plaza de Armas. Many budget lodgings are one block north and one block west.

Information

Cambiotur (☎ 234-846; Juan Mackenna 1004, Local B) Change money here.

CHILE

Conaf (☎ 234-393; Martínez de Rosas) Has details on Parque Nacional Puyehue.

Entel (Ramírez 1107)

Hospital Base (☎ 235-572; Av Bühler) On the southward extension of Arturo Prat.

Lavandería Limpec (Prat 678) Laundry facilities.

Post office (O'Higgins 645)

Sernatur (☎ 237-575; O'Higgins 667) On the west side of the Plaza de Armas.

Tourist booth (☺ until 11pm) At the bus station.

Sights

If you're spending the day, check out the **Museo Histórico Municipal** (Matta 809; admission free; ☺ 10am-12:30pm & 2:30-5pm Mon-Fri, plus 11am-1pm & 4-7pm Sat Dec-Feb), an apt look at Mapuche culture and German colonization. Also worth a look is the Historic District near the Plaza de Armas.

Sleeping

Near the bus terminal budget hostels are plentiful, though there are better parts of town to stay in.

Camping Olegario Mohr (☎ 204-870; camping per person US$4) On Río Damas' south bank, east of town, but the gate closes between midnight and 8am. *Colectivos* on Av Buschmann can drop you within a few minutes' walk.

Hospedaje Webar (☎ 319-034; renewebar@entelchile .net; Los Carrera 872; s/d incl breakfast US$8.50/17) An artsy old rambler whose charms override a few sagging beds. The high-ceiling rooms are quite comfy.

Hospedaje Sánchez (☎ 232-560; crisxi@telsur.cl; Los Carrera 1595; s/d incl breakfast US$8.50/17) While the exterior could use sprucing up, this corner building has a welcoming interior. The delightful owners provide breakfast and kitchen privileges.

Residencial Ortega (☎ 232-592; Colón 602; r per person US$12; ℗) A backpacker perennial favorite with ample common spaces and cable TV in every room.

Hospedaje Puelche (☎ 238-065; hospedaje_puelche _osorno@hotmail.com; Barrientos 2456-E; s/d US$17/26) A cozy option with firm beds and hot showers, out of the blowing *puelche* winds the *hospedaje* takes its name from.

Eating & Drinking

Líder (cnr Colón & Errázuriz) Supermarket next to the bus terminal.

Mercado Municipal (cnr Arturo Prat & Errázuriz) Has a line of lunch stalls serving inexpensive staples.

Entre Amigos (Local 2; plates US$1.50-4) Try this place on the old butchers' row for seafood dishes and soups.

Café Migas (☎ 235-541; Freire 584; mains US$2-5; ☺ 8am-9pm) A chipper café offering *empanadas*, pizzas and cakes, plus a US$3.50 lunch special.

Pizzería Donnatelo (cnr Cochrane & Ramírez; pizzas US$2-6; ☺ lunch & dinner) Back-alley pizza pies, probably the best in town.

Club de Artesanos (Juan Mackenna 634; mains US$2.50-7; ☺ lunch & dinner) Ideal for a pint of local homebrew Märzen, this union house specializes in heaping plates of Chilean classics.

Salón de Té Rhenania (Eleuterio Ramírez 977; onces US$4; ☺ closed Sunday) An airy and light-filled 2nd-floor café with generous sandwiches and fried *empanadas*.

Shopping

Asociación Futa Huillimapu (cnr Juan Mackenna & Portales) Sells quality woven and wooden goods, supporting an association of indigenous women.

La Casa de Vino (☎ 207-576; Juan Mackenna 1071) The knowledgeable owners at La Casa de Vino give great suggestions on new Chilean wines.

Climent (Angulo 603) Specializes in camping supplies.

Getting There & Away

Long-distance and Argentine-bound buses use the **main bus terminal** (Av Errázuriz 1400), near Angulo. Most services going north on the Panamericana start in Puerto Montt, departing about every hour, with mainly overnight services to Santiago. There are services to Argentina daily and to Coyhaique, Punta Arenas and Puerto Natales (US$41, 28 hours) several times a week, via Ruta 215 and Paso Cardenal Antonio Samoré.

Sample travel times and fares follow:

Destination	Duration (hrs)	Cost (US$)
Bariloche	5	15
Coyhaique	22	30
Puerto Montt	1	3
Punta Arenas	28	41
Santiago	12	21-40
Temuco	3	7

Local and regional services leave from **Terminal Mercado Municipal** (cnr Errázuriz & Prat), two blocks west of the main terminal, in the Mercado Municipal. Destinations include Entre Lagos (leaves from front of market, US$2, 30 minutes), Termas Puyehue/Aguas Calientes (leaves from back of market, US$1.50, one hour), Anticura (US$3, 1½ hours), Pajaritos (US$3, two hours) and Río Negro (US$1, 15 minutes). *Colectivos* go to Entre Lagos all year, and to Aguas Calientes in summer only. To get to coastal towns, cross the Río Rahue to the bus stops at Feria Libre Ráhue or catch a *colectivo* on the corner of República and Victoria.

Getting Around
Automóvil Club de Chile (☎ 255-555; Bulnes 463) rents jeeps and cars.

AROUND OSORNO
Along the coast, **Maicolpué** is a great escape off the gringo grid. **Campsites** (per tent US$4) are at the southern section of town. **Cabañas Rosenburg** (per person US$12) has elfin, wood-shingled A-frames with views of the crashing surf. Trails headed south access pristine, near-deserted beaches.

On the southwest shore of Lago Puyehue, **Entre Lagos**, 50km from Osorno, is a restful alternative to Osorno. **Camping No Me Olvides** (☎ 064-371-633; camping per person US$5, cabins per person US$18), 6km east of town on Ruta 215, is a top-notch campground divided by pruned hedges. Lodgers can also stock up on breads and cakes here. **Hospedaje Panorama** (☎ 064-371-398; Gral Lagos 687; r per person incl breakfast US$8) is brimming with fruit trees, and has friendly German shepherds. Beds have woolen duvets, and the breakfasts may include fresh pie, enjoyed on the back porch.

Another 16km east is **Termas de Puyehue** (☎ 064-232-157; www.puyehue.cl in Spanish; s/d from US$98/104), a top-drawer hotel with hot springs (day use from US$12.50). Trekkers can come and use the pools for the day or schedule a massage. From here, Ruta 215 forks; the north fork goes to the Argentine border, while its south fork goes to Parque Nacional Puyehue.

PARQUE NACIONAL PUYEHUE
Volcán Puyehue, 2240m tall, blew its top the day after the earthquake in 1960, turning a large chunk of dense humid evergreen forest into a stark landscape of sand dunes and lava rivers. Today, **Parque Nacional Puyehue** (parquepuyehue@terra.cl; admission US$1.50) protects 107,000 hectares of this contrasting environment. **Aguas Calientes** (day use US$5.50) is an unpretentious hot-springs resort. Conaf has an information center and collects admission here. **Camping Chanleufú** (4-person campsites US$22) doesn't have hot showers, but fees entitle you to use the outside hot-springs pool and facilities.

Antillanca (lift tickets US$26, rentals US$18-26), on the flanks of 1990m Volcán Casablanca, is a small ski resort 18km beyond Aguas Calientes. Enjoy superb views of the lakes and volcanoes and the down-home ambience. Skiers are clad in mismatched thermals and antiquated gear – it's a far cry from nearby Bariloche. In summer a trail leads to a crater outlook with views of the mountain range. At the base you can stay at **Hotel Antillanca** (☎ 064-235-114; s/d in refugio US$20/34, in hotel US$35/48) with rustic and more mainstream options. Trimmings include a gym, sauna and disco – for those wild nights you might share with the pocketful of other overnight guests.

Anticura is 17km northwest of the Aguas Calientes turnoff and the best launchpad for more remote sectors of the park. Pleasant, short walks lead to a lookout and waterfall. **Camping Catrué** (2-person sites US$8) has woodsy, level sites with tree-trunk picnic tables, limited electricity and decent bathrooms.

Two kilometers west of Anticura, **El Caulle** (☎ 099-641-2000; admission fee US$12) is the entrance for the popular trek across the desolate plateau of Volcán Puyehue. While officially within park boundaries, the access land is privately owned. The admission fee is steep, but is used to maintain the free *refugio* and trails. Trekkers can stash extra gear at the entrance. The **Puyehue Traverse** (three to four days) starts with a steep hike through *lenga* forest and loose volcanic soil to a campsite and *refugio* with a woodstove and water. From there, trudge to the top of the crater or continue four hours to Los Baños, a series of riverbank thermal baths (not obvious; test the waters to find them) with wild camping. The trail continues to an impressive geyser field. The trail does continue north to Riñinahue, at the south end of Lago Ranco, although these trails are not maintained and may be difficult to follow. (Hikers report being charged to cross private land leaving the park as well.) Another hike, **Ruta de los Americanos** (six to eight days), branches off the Los Baños trail and loops around the eastern side of the volcano. Wild camping is possible.

Buses and *colectivos* from Osorno's **Mercado Municipal** (cnr Errázuriz & Prat) go to Termas de Puyehue, Aguas Calientes (US$1.50, one hour), Anticura (US$3, 1½ hours), and Chilean customs and immigration at Pajaritos. Any bus heading to Anticura can drop off trekkers at El Caulle. In winter there may be a shuttle to the ski lodge at Antillanca; contact the **Club Andino Osorno** (☎ 064-232-297; O'Higgins 1073, Osorno). Otherwise, you'll need to arrange your own transportation.

PUERTO OCTAY
☎ 064 / pop 3000
Bucolic Puerto Octay linked Puerto Montt and Osorno via Lago Llanquihue in the early days of German settlement. Lovely and serene, it's a good alternative to its more touristy neighbors, although there's little more to do than count the cows. Original German buildings further transport you to colonial yesteryear. The **tourist office** (Esperanza 555) is on the east side of the Plaza de Armas. Ask for the map of the town's historic houses. **Museo El Colono** (Independencia 591) includes displays on German colonization and local architecture.

Camping Centinela (☎ 391-326; Península Centinela; family sites US$16) will discount for just two people. Sites are right near the lakeshore with lots of shade. Backpackers flock to **Zapato Amarillo** (☎ /fax 391-575; dm/d US$11/25), on a small farm about 2km north of town. The hospitable Chilean-Swiss owners provide a separate kitchen for lodgers, veggies from the garden, excursions and bike rental. Lunch or dinner is US$5. On the plaza, **Baviera** (Germán Wulf 582) has special lunches for US$3.50, with vegetarian alternatives.

Puerto Octay's **bus terminal** (cnr Balmaceda & Esperanza) has regular services to Osorno (US$1.50, one hour), Frutillar (US$1, 30 minutes), Puerto Varas (US$1.50, one hour), Puerto Montt (US$2, 1½ hours) and Cruce de Rupanco (US80¢, 20 minutes), from where Osorno–Las Cascadas buses can be picked up.

LAS CASCADAS
On the far eastern shore of Lago Llanquihue, Las Cascadas is a tiny settlement with a gorgeous black-sand beach. Grab a hiking map from the supermarket. The road south to Ensenada is great for biking, but prepare for strong sun and *tábanos* (horseflies) in January.

Canary-yellow **Hostería Irma** (☎ 064-396-227; camping per person US$6, r per person US$10), 1km to-ward Ensenada, has patchy flower gardens and a wonderful hostess, whose father takes guests for hikes on the lower flanks of the volcano (looming large in the backyard). Rates include breakfast. The beachside campsite has tables and soft sand. Deals can be negotiated at **Camping Las Cañitas** (☎ 099-643-4295; 6-person sites US$20), 5km down the Ensenada road. The complex has cabins; a 500m hike beginning behind cabin 7 leads to an incredible waterfall. Ask the caretaker for directions.

Buses Cordillera runs direct to/from Osorno five times per day. From Puerto Octay, there is a 5pm bus each weekday, leaving Las Cascadas at 7:30am.

FRUTILLAR
☎ 065 / pop 10,000
The mystique of Frutillar is its Germanness, the 19th-century immigrant heritage that the village pickled and preserved. To come here is to savor this idea of simpler times, float in the lake, eat home-baked pies and sleep in rooms shaded by lace curtains. It's cheaper to stay in nearby Osorno or Puerto Varas. Mature visitors enjoy Frutillar best, for many it is simply too still to stay for very long. However, the town grooves from late January to early February, when the concert series **Semana Musical de Frutillar** (www.semanasmusicales.cl in Spanish) brings international folk, chamber music and jazz to a magnificent modern amphitheatre on the lake. Midday concerts are cheapest.

The town has two sectors: Frutillar Alto is no-frills working town, Bajo fronts the lakes and has all of the tourist attractions. The **tourist kiosk** (Av Philippi; ☼ 10am-9pm Dec-Mar) is between San Martín and O'Higgins. Around the municipality, you can find the regular banks, post office and call centers.

Museo Colonial Alemán (cnr Pérez Rosales & Prat; admission US$2; ☼ Tue-Sun) features accurate reconstructions of a water-powered mill, a smithy and a mansion set among manicured gardens. **Centro Forestal Edmundo Winkler** (Calle Caupolicán), on the spit of land north of town, has an 800m loop trail along which species of trees are identified.

Los Ciruelillos (☎ 420-163; 2-person campsites US$10), on a peninsula at the south end of the beach (1.5km from Frutillar Bajo), has 45 fully equipped sites, a small sandy beach and fire pits. **Hostería Winkler** (☎ 421-388; Av Philippi 1155; dm US$12) opens an annex to independent backpackers. Some roadside stands sell snacks, but restaurant meals are pricey. Best-value grub is at **Casino de Bomberos** (Av Philippi 1065; meals US$5). **Hotel Klein Salzburg** (Av Philippi 663; meals US$7-14) is a smart choice if you're after *onces*.

Buses to Puerto Varas (US$1, 30 minutes), Puerto Montt (US$1.80, one hour) and Osorno (US$1.50, 40 minutes) leave from Frutillar Alto. Inexpensive *colectivos* shuttle along Av Carlos Richter between Frutillar Alto and Frutillar Bajo.

PUERTO VARAS

☎ 065 / pop 22,500

Every summer this staid and manicured former German colony is besieged by visitors. Take in the pleasures of its small town formality, the prim grannies alongside backpacker hordes, and the arresting lake view of Volcán Osorno when the rains pause. With a swank casino, steady growth and ready access to canyoning, climbing, fishing, hiking and skiing, Puerto Varas aspires to be the Chilean Bariloche, though in reality it still is a sleepy place where Sundays are devoted to God and barbecue.

Orientation & Information

From the Puerto Montt airport, taxis cost US$21. *Micros* shuttle back and forth from Puerto Montt's bus terminal (US$1.50). There are numerous ATMs downtown.

Afex Exchange (San Pedro 410) Changes cash and traveler's checks.

Casa de Turista (☎ 237-956; Av Costanera) On the pier; is a private organization with information about its members.

Centro Médico Puerto Varas (☎ 232-792; Walker Martínez 576)

Clínica Alemana (☎ 232-336; Hospital 810, Cerro Calvario) Near Del Salvador's southwest exit from town.

Dizconexion (Santa Rosa 539; per hr US$1.50) Has internet access with fast connections.

Entel (San José 413)

Lavandería Schnell (San Pedro 26-A; per kg US$3) Laundry service.

Municipal tourist office (☎ 232-437; San Francisco 431) Has brochures and free maps.

Post office (cnr San Pedro & San José)

Sights & Activities

A stroll around town to see all that 19th-century German architecture is a worthy diversion. The colorful 1915 **Iglesia del Sagrado Corazón** (cnr San Francisco & Verbo Divino) is based on the Marienkirche of Black Forest, Germany.

A dip in the invigorating cobalt waters of Lago Llanquihue makes a good alternative to a siesta on a warm summer day. The best beaches are east of the center in Puerto Chico or along the road to Ensenada. If you're adventurous enough for that, consider rafting Río Petrohué's ice-green waters: descents down its class III and IV rapids start at US$30. Canyoning provides yet another opportunity to submerge yourself in icy waters, this time in gorgeous waterfall canyons.

Those who prefer solid ground can try a number of **hikes**. Volcán Calbuco (2015m) offers a moderate hike; other trails can be accessed via Petrohué. **Climbing** Volcán Osorno (2652m) requires ropes and harnesses for the last two pitches. Outfitters charge around US$170 per person in groups of three. The trip lasts 12 hours, leaving at 5am. In wintertime you can **ski** the volcano (see p500). **Canopy** is another way to glimpse the forest if your own dogs are too tired to walk.

Secret spots to cast a line abound. If you're serious about **fly-fishing**, contact a guide. **Osvaldo Anwandter** (☎ 099-869-3862; www.fly-fishingchile .cl) comes recommended.

Tours

Al Sur (☎ 232-300; www.alsurexpeditions.com; cnr Del Salvador & San Juan) The official outdoor operator for Parque Pumalín, with sea-kayak trips, as well as local rafting and ascents of Volcán Osorno.

Andina del Sud (☎ /fax 232-511; www.andinadelsud .com; Del Salvador 72) Offers the *Cruce del Lagos* from Petrohué to Bariloche, Argentina via ferry and bus.

Campo Aventura (☎ 232-910; www.campo-aventura .com; San Bernardo 318) Quality horse-riding trips from Cochamó (see p501).

Capitán Haase (☎ 232-747, 099-810-7665; Santa Rosa 132; cruise adult/child US$30/20) Sunset cruises on a 65ft sailboat from late October to mid-April.

CTS (☎ 237-328; www.ctsturismo.cl; San Francisco 333) Tour agency for Volcán Osorno ski area, offering transportation to the mountain, canopy excursions (traveling on ziplines, tree to tree) and regional tours.

Ko'Kayak (☎ 232-424; www.paddlechile.com; San José 130) Reputable sea and river kayaking and rafting trips on Petrohué and Palena Rivers. French and English spoken.

LS Travel (☎ 232-424; www.lstravel.com; San José 130) Friendly, with good information on Argentina, tours and car rental.

Pachamagua (☎ 09-500-5991; pachamagua@chile .com) Professional canyoning outfitter with English and French spoken. Best canyoning in town.

Sleeping

Those traveling in January and February should reserve in advance. Elicit a discount off-season.

Hospedaje Ellenhaus (☎ 233-577; www.ellenhaus .cl; Walker Martínez 239; dm/s/d US$8/13/24) Feather duvets and knotty pine make up for the fact that most rooms are absolute shoe boxes.

Offers kitchen use, traveler info and bike rentals.

Compass del Sur (☎ 232-044; www.compassdelsur.cl; Klenner 467; camping/dm/s/d US$8/14/27/35; 🖳) Snug and stylish, this *hostal* with chalky pastel walls and an ample yard promises travelers some serious R & R. German and English are spoken.

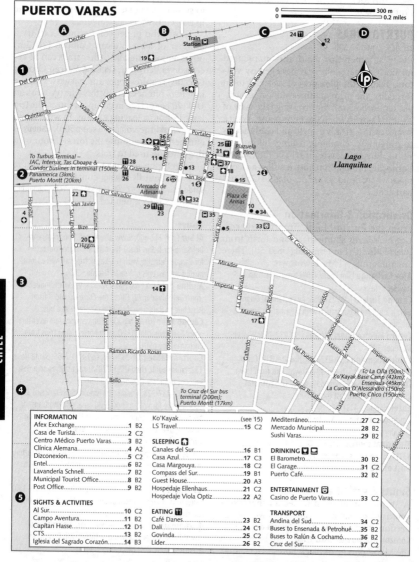

PUERTO VARAS

0 — 300 m
0 — 0.2 miles

CHILE

Casa Margouya (☎ 511-648; www.margouya.com; 318 Santa Rosa; r per person US$14) Guests share these small quarters like family; before you know it there's communal dinners and a stack of empty wine bottles. Offers snug bunks, free internet, breakfast, kitchen use and discounts with local adventure tours.

Casa Azul (☎ 232-904; www.casaazul.net; cnr Manzanal 66 & Del Rosario; dm/s/d US$14/29/39) Backpackers' delight: comfortable well-heated rooms, free wi-fi, kitchen use and a large garden with Japanese fish pond. The owner speaks German and English. Breakfast (US$3) includes homemade muesli and yogurt.

Hospedaje Viola Optiz (☎ 232-890; Del Salvador 408, Depto 302; r per person US$16) Old-fashioned and lovely, with a dear matron who will serve you breakfast in bed. Check out the bell collection and the cowhide sofa.

Canales del Sur (☎ 346-121; www.canalesdelsur.cl; Pasaje Ricke 224; r per person US$16; **P** 🖳) A tidy guesthouse on a quiet pedestrian staircase, with lace-curtained rooms and homey touches.

Guest House (☎ 231-521; www.vicki-johnson.com; O'Higgins 608; s/d/tr incl breakfast US$45/65/85; **P**) No detail is left to chance at this American-owned inn: rooms are ample and luminous, with lovely furnishings, and breakfast includes real coffee and bran muffins. Unique extras include morning yoga, hydrotherapy and a masseuse.

Eating

Líder (Av Gramado s/n) Big supermarket with a broad selection. Across the street the Mercado Municipal has open-air vegetable and fruit stands.

Café Danes (Del Salvador 441; mains US$3-7) Reliably good *empanadas* or *humitas* (corn tamale) are good choices amongst the typical café fare.

Dalí (Santa Rosa 131; tapas US$4) Relax among art books and prints on red and gold cushions overlooking Lake Llanquihue. This sliver of a café offers velvety espresso, tapas and cheese plates.

Sushi Varas (Del Salvador 537; rolls US$6) When you're overstuffed with *empanadas*, a *kanikama* roll with extra avocado makes a nice change.

Mediterráneo (Santa Rosa 068; pisco sours US$6) With a menu that's a bit inflated, this lakefront spot is best for outdoor tapas and tart *pisco sours* on the deck.

La Olla (Av Costanera 1071; mains US$6-12; ⊙ noon–midnight) La Olla is known for Chilean seafood classics impeccably prepared and generously served. The decor is all granny. Try *chupe de jaiva* (baked crab in cheese and cream) cooked in a clay pot.

La Cucina d'Alessandro (Av Costanera 1290; mains US$7; ⊙ lunch & dinner Mon-Sun) Sicilian owner Alessandro creates delectable pastas and thin-crust pizza topped with arugula. Top it off with an espresso and tiramisu in this relaxed lakefront setting.

Govinda (Santa Rosa 218; mains US$9) More than food, it's a philosophy. With yoga, tai-chi and massage on-site, this new restaurant attends to body and mind, but some offerings lack the intrigue of their description.

Drinking

Puerto Café (Del Salvador 328) Devour Chilean gossip rags while sipping a *cortado* (coffee with milk) on a billowy couch.

El Barómetro (Walker Martínez 584) Travelers and locals happily mix in this quirky local institution with quality beers on tap and tasty appetizers.

El Garage (Walker Martínez 220; ⊙ 2pm-4am) This bar mixes live jazz and fusion 'til the wee hours on long summer nights.

Entertainment

Casino de Puerto Varas (Del Salvador 21; ⊙ 24hr) A posh ambience with great views and cocktails, where out-of-towners come to spend money and console their losses with shrimp cocktail and live entertainment.

Getting There & Away

BOAT

The tourist cash-cow of *Cruce de Lagos* (US$170, eight hours) herds visitors across Lago Todos Los Santos and the Andes to Bariloche, Argentina (p136) through a combination of ferries and buses. It's truly spectacular on a sunny day (never guaranteed). The independently minded would do as well to find similarly stunning vistas on their own. **Andina del Sud** (☎ 232-511; www.crucedelagos.cl; Del Salvador 72) makes reservations, it also has a **Puerto Montt** (☎ 257-797; A Varas 437) branch. Bring along victuals, as offerings on board are slim. Student discounts may apply. Departures are limited in the off-season.

BUS & MICRO

Most long-distance buses originate in Puerto Montt. Buses leave from terminals on the perimeter of town. The **Turbus** (☎ 234-525; Del

CHILE

Salvador 1093) terminal houses Turbus, JAC, Intersur, Tas Choapa and Condor bus lines. **Cruz del Sur** (San Francisco 1317), at the bus terminal, has most departures, including to Chiloé and Punta Arenas. It also has an **office** (Walker Martínez 230) in town. Also check out **Tur Bus** (San Pedro 210). For Santiago, Tur Bus, **Tas Choapa** (Walker Martínez 227) and **Buses Inter** (San Pedro 210) have nightly departures.

For Bariloche, Argentina, Tas Choapa leaves Monday and Saturday, while Cruz del Sur leaves every day. Minibuses to/from Ensenada (US$1.50) and Petrohué (US$3) leave frequently in summer and thrice daily in the off-season from along Del Salvador, where minibuses to Puerto Montt (US$1, 30 minutes), Frutillar (40 minutes) and Puerto Octay (one hour) also depart frequently. Take buses to Ralún and Cochamó from the corner of Walker Martínez and San Bernardo.

TRAIN

Service with **Empresa de los Ferrocarriles de Estado** (☎ 232-210; www.efe.cl; Klenner s/n) has returned. Trains run south to Puerto Montt (US$1, 21 minutes) and north to Temuco (US$7, 5½ hours) with connections to Santiago. Check the website for summer/winter schedules.

ENSENADA

Bendy Ruta 225 is a quaint country lane dotted with beaches and topped with the megaphone protrusion of Volcán Osorno. Horse stables **Quinta del Lago** (☎ 099-138-6382; km 25; rides per hr US$12) guides horse treks up the flanks of Volcán Calbulco. Rafting outfitter **Ko'Kayak** (☎ 232-424; www.paddlechile.com; San José 130, Puerto Varas) has its base camp at km 40 and lodgings at the rural **Casa Ko** (☎ 099-699-9850; per person without/with bathroom US$24/27.50), a sweet old farmhouse with walks and fishing out the back door. Arrange transportation there from the Ko'Kayak base or call ahead. **Camping Montaña** (☎ 065-235-285; camping per person US$5) is in front of the police station. Next door, **Terra Sur** (☎ 065-260-308; www.osorno-tours.com; km 44; bike rental per day US$12) rents quality mountain bikes with shocks, provides vehicle support or simply guides the way. Between October and May you can stop by **Hotel Ensenada** (km 44) for a drink or snack. Browsing this grand old rambler, with its massive collection of valises, memorabilia, old farm equipment, slanting floors and long white corridors, is like entering an antiquarian's *The Shining*.

PARQUE NACIONAL VICENTE PERÉZ ROSALES

A long emerald lake ringed by steep Valdivian rainforest and volcanoes, Chile's first **national park** protects 251,000 hectares including Lago Todos Los Santos and snowtipped volcanoes Osorno, Puntiagudo (2190m) and Monte Tronador (3554m). Ruta 225 ends in Petrohué, 50km east of Puerto Varas, where there's park access. Minibuses from Puerto Varas are frequent in summer, but limited to twice daily the rest of the year.

Waterfalls boom over basalt rock at **Saltos del Petrohué** (admission US$2), 6km before the village. **Petrohué** has beaches, trailheads and the dock for *Cruce de Lagos* (see p499) departures to Peulla. The grand **Hotel Petrohué** (☎ 065-258-042; www.petrohue.com; s/d US$130/170; P ⊠) has fires crackling in inviting spaces accented with rocks and wooden beams. Lunch is available (US$10 to US$14). If luxury isn't in the budget, pay one of the boatmen (US$1) to cross you to **Hospedaje Kuschel** (campsites/r per person US$5/16) where you'll be camping with the cowpies, if you don't score one of the few rooms available. Bring provisions from Puerto Varas.

From Hotel Petrohué a dirt track leads to **Playa Larga**, a long black-sand beach, from where **Sendero Los Alerces** heads west to meet up with **Sendero La Picada**. The sandy track climbs to Volcán Osorno's Paso Desolación, with scintillating panoramas of the lake, Volcán Puntiagudo and Monte Tronador. There is no road around the lake, making the interior trails inaccessible to foot travel. Those willing to hire a boat (US$40 one way – and make sure it's seaworthy) or join a hiking tour can access the luxuriant **Termas de Callao** hot springs, where there's camping or other incredible trails. **Expediciones Petrohué** (☎ 065-212-025; www.Petrohué.com), affiliated with and next to the hotel, leads excursions into the area.

Access to climb or ski **Volcán Osorno** is near Ensenada. Ski area **Volcán Osorno** (☎ 065-233-445, www.volcanosorno.cl; lift tickets per half/whole day US$20/27, students US$16) has two lifts on 600 hectares and lovely out-of-bounds skiing for experts (watch for crevasses). The rustic **Refugio Teski Ski Club** (☎ 099-700-0370; dm US$14; ☺ year-round) is perched mid-mountain, with sick views and little dormitory bunk slots (bring a sleeping bag for extra warmth). Mamita and Papito warmly attend guests. Breakfast (US$6), lunch and dinner (both US$9) are served. Climbing equipment can be rented here.

CHILE

To get to the ski area and *refugio,* take the Ensenada–Puerto Octay road to a signpost 3km from Ensenada and continue 9km up the lateral. In Puerto Varas CTS arranges shuttle transportation.

RÍO PUELO VALLEY

A corkscrew road skirting Seno Reloncaví leads you to the petite village of **Cochamó**, with its *alerce*-shingled **Iglesia Parroquial María Inmaculada**, built in the Chilote style. Like a country lass of modest charms, the Río Puelo valley remains unfazed by that massive industry called tourism, offering a few homespun adventures.

Campo Aventura (☎ 065-232-910; www.campo-aventura.com; San Bernardo 318, Puerto Varas; campsites US$4.50, r per person incl breakfast and dinner US$44; ☼ October 1-April 15) offers top-notch horse treks through the upper Río Cochamó Valley and can recommend reliable local independent guides at low costs. Its snug lodge will also take overnight visitors and passersby can dine on delectable meals (breakfast US$5 to US$8, lunch US$12, dinner US$15) at the vegetarian-friendly restaurant. From here, prepared long-distance trekkers can explore the marvels of the granite-domed valley. In town, **Hospedaje Edicar** (☎ 065-216-256; cnr Av Prat & Sargento Aldea; r per person US$12) has firm beds and balcony vistas.

Río Puelo, 26km down the road, is a quiet, rain-damp village with the **Municipalidad de Cochamó** (☎ 065-350-271, 099-949-4425; www.cochamo.cl; plaza). Azucena Calderón is the helpful repre-

sentative of the tourist office. She can present (in patient Spanish) options for local treks, rustic family lodgings and guides. Most trips start in Llanada Grande and take different routes along the valley (see left). Hard-core hikers should seek out the amicable services of Lolo Escobar for an unforgettable five-day round-trip to the Ventisquero Glacier near Segundo Corral. Ask for the Cochamó hiking map and brochure. **Victor Baccaro** (☎ 099-138-2310; info@andespatagonia.cl) offers reliable mountain-guide services (hikes from US$118) in Río Puelo and is developing geodesic dome lodgings.

Buses Fierro has five daily departures to/from Puerto Montt (US$6, four hours), stopping in Puerto Varas, Ensenada and Cochamó.

PUERTO MONTT

☎ 065 / pop 160,000

A grinding hub of commerce and industry, Puerto Montt is one of the fastest growing cities on the continent, thanks to the salmon industry. For travelers it is a spring board to Patagonia.

Orientation

Sitting 1020km south of Santiago, Puerto Montt's downtown stretches along the sea. The waterfront Av Diego Portales turns into Av Angelmó as it heads west to the small fishing and ferry port of Angelmó. To the east it continues to the bathing resort of Pelluco, connecting with the Carretera Austral. At night the area around the bus terminal harbors petty crime; take precautions and don't walk alone here or along the waterfront.

Information

Internet places line Av Angelmó and ring the plaza. ATMs abound.

Afex (Av Diego Portales 516) For money exchange.

Arco Iris (San Martín 232; per load US$1) Laundry can be done here.

Banco de Chile (cnr Pedro Montt & Av Diego Portales) Has an ATM.

Hospital Regional (☎ 261-134; Seminario; ☼ 24hr) Near the intersection with Décima Región.

Latin Star (Av Angelmó 1672; per hr US$1) Internet; also has a cheap call center and book exchange.

Municipal tourist office (Varas & O'Higgins) In a kiosk across from the plaza.

Post office (Rancagua 126)

Sernatur (Plaza de Armas) The tourist office is only slightly more helpful.

SPLURGE!

Butch Cassidy and Sundance did it; now you can too. Pack your harmonica and a rain poncho for this stunning crossing of the Andes. Experienced outfitter **Opentravel** (☎ in Puerto Montt 65-260-524; www.opentravel.cl) leads treks and rides on narrow trails that skirt frothy waterfalls and lakes, wading through icy rivers up to remote farms. Guests stay with pioneer families, eat bread hot from wood ovens and berries off the bush. A night on an island inhabited by one is the sweet finale. English, French and Spanish is spoken. Start or end in El Bolson, Argentina or Puerto Montt, Chile. Tailor treks start at US$500 per person for four days/three nights, four-person minimum.

Sights & Activities

The town's oldest building is the 1856 *alerce* **Iglesia Catedral** (Urmeneta s/n) on the Plaza de Armas. The **Casa del Arte Diego Rivera** (☎ 261-817; Quillota 116; admission free; ⏰ 10am-1pm & 3-9pm Mon-Fri, 10am-1pm Sat) has art and photo exhibits upstairs. The downstairs room offers theater, dance and film.

The waterfront **Museo Juan Pablo II** (Av Diego Portales 991; admission US50¢; ⏰ 9am-7pm Mon-Fri, 10am-6pm Sat & Sun) has displays ranging from history and archaeology to religious iconography, German colonization and local urbanism.

Streetside stalls line busy and exhaust-ridden Av Angelmó; their prices go up every time a cruise ship docks at port. Take in their disheveled stacks of woolens, woodcarvings

and trinkets. At the end of the strip are *palafitos* (stilted homes on the water), an excellent fish market and more crafts in the picturesque fishing port of Angelmó, 3km west. Offshore Isla Tenglo, reached by inexpensive launches from the docks at Angelmó, is a favorite local beach spot and not a bad place for a picnic.

Sleeping

Travelers find wider choices in tourist-ready Puerto Varas up the road, but there are a few good options here.

Camping Anderson (☎ 099-517-7222; www.chipsites .com/camping/; Panitao, Km 20; campsites US$5) An ecologically minded campground right on the bay, on the road to Panitao. Paupers can work for their lodgings, although we didn't ask if

PUERTO MONTT

0 — 800 m
0 — 0.5 miles

To Panamericana (2km); Airport (16km); Puerto Varas (20km)

0 — 200 m
0 — 0.1 mi

Seno de Reloncaví

Bahía de Puerto Montt

Isla Tenglo

Canal Tenglo

To Terminal de Transpondadores (200m); Angelmó (900m); Camping Los Paredes (6km); Camping Anderson (25km)

To Club de Yates (50m); Pelluco (4km); Train Station (4km); Carretera Austral (9km)

See Enlargement

CHILE

this means latrines… Buses Bohle makes the 20km trip from Puerto Montt's bus terminal to Panitao (six times daily, except Sunday).

Camping Los Paredes (☎ 258-394; campsites US$14) Pleasant sites with hot showers; backpackers might bargain for deals. Located 6km west of town on the road to Chinquihue; local buses from the bus terminal can stop at the entrance.

Hospedaje Anita (☎ 315-479; Juan Mira 1094; r per person US$8) Easily confused with a rectory, this place is simple and the slightest bit shabby.

Hospedaje Luchita (☎ 253-762; Independencia 236; r per person US$12) The generous Doña Luchita will likely serve you a slice of *küchen* before you've sat down in this sweet family home with waxed floors and neat little rooms.

Hospedaje Betty (☎ 253-165; Ancud 117; r per person without/with bathroom US$12/14) Rose-colored shingles, a sprawling old-fashioned kitchen and pastel rooms with sheer curtains cozy it up; the hostess is wonderful too.

Hostal Vista Hermosa (☎ 255-859; Miramar 1486; r per person US$12) The paint is chipped and the rugs worn bare but this *alerce*-shingled house is warm and well attended.

Casa Perla (☎ 262-104; www.casaperla.com; Trigal 312; s/d US$12/24; ☐) A tidy and relaxed family residence that can link you with Spanish classes and kayak trips.

Residencial Urmeta (☎ 253-262; Urmeta 290; s/d without bathroom US$17/26) A well-kept dinosaur with mint-colored walls, soft sheets, immense bathrooms and a farmhouse kitchen.

Hostal Pacífico (☎ 256-229; www.hostalpacifico.cl; Juan Mira 1088; s/d US$29/45) Bulky beds fill these well-kept hotel rooms with clean wood finish and sparkling private bathrooms.

Eating & Drinking

The *palafitos* at the far end of Angelmó have loads of ambience and good meals for about US$6 to US$8; waitresses loiter outside to coax you in. In the opposite direction, Pelluco (a US50¢ bus trip from the terminal) has a range of well-heeled restaurants and clubs on the beach. This is where Puerto Montt goes at night (if it goes out at all).

Café Central (Rancagua 117; snacks US$1.50-6) Join the regulars filling this smoky room for grilled meat and drinks.

El Tablon del Ancla (cnr Varas & O'Higgins; set lunch US$3) Friends pack the comfy booths on the plaza for cheap set lunches or *pichangas* (french fries with toppings).

Kalabaza (Varas 629; mains US$3-7) A touch hipper, with sandwiches, Kuntsmann beer and fixed-price lunches (with vegetarian options).

Fogon del Leñador (Rancagua & Rengifo; mains US$8-10 ☾ closed Sun) Steaks singed to perfection are served with piping-hot *sopapillas* (frybread).

OK Corral (Cauquenes 128; burgers US$4-6) Once you get over the silly saloon theme, this is a casual spot buzzing with energy and offering whopping meal portions and suds on tap.

Club de Yates (Costanera; mains US$12-20; ☾ noon-4pm & 8pm-late) Snooty and sparkling, from the glint off the glassware to the harbor panorama. An encyclopedic menu offers expertly prepared seafood; try the crab-filled spinach crêpes or grilled tuna.

Getting There & Away
AIR

Lan (☎ 253-315; www.lan.com; O'Higgins 167, Local 1-B) flies up to four times daily to Punta Arenas (from US$200, 2¼ hours), three times daily to Balmaceda/Coyhaique (around US$100, one hour) and up to eight times daily to Santiago (from US$200, 1½ hours).

Sky Airlines (☎ 248-027; www.skyairlines.cl; cnr San Martín & Benavente) flies to Punta Arenas (US$140) and Santiago (US$120) with considerably better prices than Lan. **Aerosur** (☎ 252-523; Urmeneta 149) flies daily except Sunday to Chaitén on the Carretera Austral (US$50).

BOAT

Puerto Montt is the main departure port for Patagonia. The **Terminal de Transbordadores** (Av Angelmó 2187) has a ticket office and waiting lounge for **Navimag** (☎ 253-318; www.navimag.com). Check your departure: rough seas and bad weather can cause delays.

To Chaitén, Catamaranes del Sur has a fast five-hour ferry; call **Cielo Mar Austral** (☎ 264-010; Quillota 245; one way US$39) to check on availability; it is often out of service. Navimag sails to/from Chaitén and Quellón regularly in high season, but less often off-season. Check the website for the latest rates and schedules.

To Puerto Chacabuco you can hop on Navimag's M/N *Puerto Edén* (18 hours). Prices range from US$52 for a *butaca* (reclining chair) to US$216 per person for a dorm bed with shared bathroom. M/N *Evangelistas* stops en route to Laguna San Rafael every four or five days in high season, and only three or four times monthly the rest of the year. Prices range from US$310 per person for bunks to US$827 for a cabin with private bathroom.

To Puerto Natales, Navimag's M/N *Magallanes* sails the popular three-night journey through Chile's fjords; check with Navimag's Santiago offices (p418) or on the website for departure dates and confirm your booking with the Santiago office. High season is November to May, midseason is October to April, and low season is May to September. Prices for the trip include meals. Per person fares, which vary according to view and private or shared bathroom, are as follows:

Class	High season (US$)	Midseason (US$)	Low season (US$)
AAA	1690	1180	720
AA	1620	1060	700
A 1440	860	650	
Berths	325	275	200

Cars are US$385 extra. Bicycles and motorcycles can also be carried along for an additional cost. Travelers prone to motion sickness should consider taking medication prior to crossing the Golfo de Penas, which is exposed to gut-wrenching Pacific swells.

BUS
Puerto Montt's waterfront **bus terminal** (☎ 253-143; cnr Av Diego Portales & Lillo) is the main transportation hub. Watch your belongings or leave them with the *custodia*. In summer, buses to Punta Arenas and Bariloche sell out, so book in advance.

Minibuses to Puerto Varas (US$1.50, 30 minutes), Frutillar (US$1.80, one hour) and Puerto Octay (US$2, 1½ hours) leave from the eastern side of the terminal. Buses leave five times daily for Cochamó (US$5, four hours).

For Hornopirén, where summer-only ferries connect to Caleta Gonzalo, Buses Fierro has three daily departures (US$5, five hours). Off-season (mid-March to mid-December), bus transportation to Hornopirén and the upper Carretera Austral is very limited.

Cruz del Sur (☎ 254-731; Varas 437) has frequent buses to Chiloé. Santiago-bound buses usually leave around 10pm, stopping at various cities. 'Direct' buses stop only in Puerto Varas and Osorno; try to get one of these. **Tur Bus** (☎ 253-329) has daily buses to Valparaíso/Viña del Mar. For Coyhaique and Punta Arenas via

Argentina, try Cruz del Sur or Turibús. For Bariloche, Argentina, try **Tas Choapa** (☎ 254-828), **Río de La Plata** (☎ 253-841) and Cruz del Sur, which travel daily via the Cardenal Samoré pass east of Osorno.

Destination	Duration (hrs)	Cost (US$)
Ancud	2	4
Bariloche, Argentina	8	19
Castro	4	6
Concepción	9	15
Coyhaique	20	32
Osorno	1½	3
Pucón	8	7
Punta Arenas	30-36	50
Quellón	6	9
Santiago	12-14	11-23
Temuco	7	9
Valdivia	3½	6
Valparaíso/Viña del Mar	14	25

TRAIN
Service with **Empresa de los Ferrocarriles de Estado** (☎ 480-787; www.efe.cl; Cuarta Terraza s/n) runs north to Temuco (US$8, six hours) with connections to Santiago.

Getting Around
ETM buses (US$2) run between Aeropuerto El Tepual, 16km west of town, and the bus terminal. A taxi from the airport costs about US$10.

Car-rental agencies include **Hertz** (☎ 259-585; Varas 126) and **Full Fama's** (☎ 258-060; Portales 506). The latter can help get permission to take rental vehicles into Argentina. Rates range from US$50 for a normal car to US$100 for a pickup or jeep.

PARQUE NACIONAL ALERCE ANDINO
Few venture to the rugged emerald forest of 40,000-hectare **Parque Nacional Alerce Andino** (admission US$2), despite its 40km proximity to Puerto Montt. The park was created in 1982 to protect some of the last remaining stands of *alerce*, found primarily 400m to 700m above sea level. Those who brave the mud and frequent rain will be rewarded by forest vistas ranging from sea level to 900m, a thick twisting medley of *coigue* and *ulmo*, ferns, climbing vines and dense thickets of *quila*. Pumas, *pudús*, foxes and skunks are about, but you'll have better luck glimpsing condors, kingfishers and waterfowl.

Conaf has a five-site **campground** (campsites US$7) at Correntoso on the Río Chamiza at the northern end of the park, and another six-site **campground** (campsites US$7) near the head of the Río Chaica Valley. Trekkers can backcountry camp.

A few agencies in Puerto Varas arrange hikes and tours of the park. To get there on your own, take the Ruta 7, Carretera Austral; it runs to La Arena on the Estero de Reloncaví. From Puerto Montt, Buses Fierro has four buses daily to the village of Correntoso (US$2, 30 minutes), only 3km from the Río Chamiza entrance on the northern boundary of the park. Fierro also runs five buses daily to the crossroads at Lenca (US$2, 1¾ hours) on the Carretera Austral, where a narrow lateral road climbs 7km up the valley of the Río Chaica.

CHILOÉ

In Chiloé rural ingenuity invented the *trineo*, a sled to steer through thick mud; rural necessity perfected *curanto*, meat, potatoes and shellfish vapor-smoked in giant leaves; and rural imagination created the *invunche*, a mythological gatekeeper whose price of admittance is a peck on the rear. Who are these people? With indigenous Chonos and Huilliche roots, the humble Chilote welcomed Jesuits and the Spanish, but were never an ally of mainlanders. Island insularity fostered incredibly rich traditions and myths populated by ghost ships, phantom lovers and witches, cute versions of which are whittled and sold for today's tourists. Forget the rustic souvenirs. The patient visitor needs a succession of misty rains, muddy walks and fireside chats to fathom these characters who are proud but never showy, friendly but none too talkative.

In an archipelago of over 40 minor islands, the main island is a lush quilt of pastureland on undulating hills, 180km long but just 50km wide. Towns and farms tilt toward the eastern side, while the western shores are a nearly roadless network of thick forests lapping the wild Pacific. More than half of the 155,000 Chilotes live off subsistence agriculture, while others depend on a fishing industry that has rapidly transformed from artisanal to industrial, with the introduction of salmon farming in the mid-1990s. Visitors shouldn't miss the shingled houses and wooden churches dotting the island, some up to 200 years old, preserved as a Unesco World Heritage site.

ANCUD

☎ 065 / pop 28,000

Bustling and weathered, urban Ancud offers an earthy base to explore the penguin colonies and walk or sea-kayak the blustery, dazzling north coast.

Information

Banco de Chile (Libertad 667) Has an ATM. ATMs are also at other banks.

Clean Center (Pudeto 45; per load US$1.75) Does laundry.

Entel (Pudeto 219) Call center

Hospital de Ancud (☎ 622-356; Almirante Latorre 405) At the corner of Pedro Montt.

La Red de Agroturismo (☎ 628-333; Ramírez 207) Organizes excursions to farming and fishing communities and homestays in small towns off the tourist map.

Post office (cnr Pudeto & Blanco Encalada)

Sernatur (☎ 622-800; Libertad 665; ☺ 8:30am-8pm summer, 8:30am-6pm Mon-Fri winter) Across from the plaza; has excellent travel information and hiking maps.

Zone@Net (Pudeto 396, 2nd fl; per hr US$1) Internet café.

CHILOÉ

Sights & Activities

The **Museo Regional de Ancud** (Libertad; adult/child US$1/25¢; 🕙 10:30am-7:30pm Jan-Feb, 9:30am-5:30pm Mon-Fri, 10am-2pm Sat & Sun Mar-Dec) tracks island history with excellent, informative displays. Northwest of town, **Fuerte San Antonio** was Spain's last Chilean outpost. The remodeled **Mercado Municipal** (Prat) offers a colorful stroll through live crabs, fat lettuce heads and woolens.

Austral Adventures (☎ 625-977; www.austral-adventures.com; Lord Cochrane 432) is known for awesome multiday boat trips around the archipelago but tours also include beach hiking, penguin-colony excursions, kayaking, and rural homestays. Day rates for hiking and penguin colonies are US$40 to US$60. Guides speak English. Small, family-run **Puñihuil** (☎ 099-655-6780) offers tours (US$16 per person) to the penguin and sea lion colonies.

On the way to the penguin colonies you'll pass **Puente Quilo** (donations only), a fabulously quirky open-air museum created by Don Serafín, a regular Joe whose backyard flooded with odd treasures after the 1960 earthquake. The booty spans from whole whale skeletons to stuffed sea creatures and indigenous relics.

Festivals & Events

Ancud makes merry in the second week of January with **Semana Ancuditana** (Ancud Week). There are island-wide celebrations with music, dance and foods.

Sleeping

Camping Arena Gruesa (☎ 623-428; Costanera Norte 290; camping/r per person US$3/11) Adequate *hostal* rooms or grassy sites with hot water, light and kitchen access, six blocks north of the plaza.

Hospedaje Austral (☎ 624-847; hospedajeaustral@hotmail.com; Aníbal Pinto 1318; s/d/tr US$8.50/17/25.50; (P) (💻)) This friendly and newly built budget haven, with comfortable blanket-stacked beds, is right next to the terminal.

Cabañas y Hospedaje Vista al Mar (☎ 622-617; www.vistaalmar.cl; Costanera 918; cabins per person US$8.50-12, full cabins US$40; (P) (💻)) HI members can shack up in a shared cabin; don't mind the 1982 ambience.

Terramar (☎ 620-493; Bellavista 457; r per person US$10) Down comforters and slanted ceilings make you feel right at home in this sweet family-friendly shingled home.

Hostal Mundo Nuevo (☎ 628-383; www.newworld.cl; Costanera 748; dm/d incl breakfast US$12/33; (P)) Hunker down in this seafront refuge with firm beds

and sharp hardwood details. Owner Martin recommends hikes and breakfast includes homemade multigrain loaves.

Hostal Lluhay (☎ 622-656; Cochrane 458; s/d incl breakfast US$16/25) A comfortable seafront house with dear hosts, roaring fires and a tinkling piano. Don't miss breakfast.

Eating & Drinking

Café Arte Nerudiano (cnr Ramirez & Maipu; snacks US$2-4; 🕙 9am-1am, Sun afternoon only) Espresso and sandwiches served in a light-filled space with deck.

Pedersen Salón de Té (Sargento Aldea 470; küchen US$3.50) Ancud's best pies and cakes are baked daily in this waterfront teahouse.

Retro Pub (Maipú 615; mains US$4-8) A cozy timber tribute to rock and roll with tasty Tex-Mex; hopping on summer nights.

El Sacho (Mercado Municipal; mains US$4-8; 🕙 lunch) Fresh no-frills seafood on the cement deck; the enormous plates include steamed mussels and fried fish.

La Candela (Libertad 599; mains US$5-8) In front of the plaza, this cool and color-streaked café serves up salmon in soy and Peruvian *ají de gallina* (spicy chicken stew).

Lumiere (Ramirez 278; dinner US$7) Awash in ocean blue and bright charm, this pub-restaurant serves ceviche, *mariscos a pil pil* (seafood with chilies and garlic) and drinks; movies are shown in winter.

Getting There & Away

The **bus terminal** (☎ 624-017; cnr Aníbal Pinto & Marcos Vera) is 2km east of downtown. Taxis downtown cost US$2. Cruz del Sur departs frequently to Puerto Montt (US$4, 2½ hours), Castro (US$2, 1½ hours) and Quellón (US$4, 2½ hours).

CASTRO

☎ 065 / pop 29,000

Castro is the prospering capital of Chiloé. Its renovation invites strange sights: a wheelbarrow vendor selling fresh *sierra* fish next to town's first mega-grocery, stalwart constructions replace the buckling ones as the salmon industry edges out the wooden launches used for centuries. But the crayon-happy *palafitos* still stand as testimony to Castro's heritage which started humbly in 1567.

Information

ATMs are found around the plaza.

Chiloe Web (www.chiloeweb.com in Spanish) Loads of useful bits can be gleaned from this website.

Conaf (☎ 532-501; Gamboa 424) Can provide information on Parque Nacional Chiloé.

Entel (O'Higgins 480)

Hospital de Castro (☎ 632-445; Freire 852) At the foot of Cerro Millantuy.

Julio Barrientos (Chacabuco 286) Exchanges cash and traveler's checks.

Municipal tourist office (Plaza de Armas) Has good information on rural homestays.

Post office (O'Higgins 388)

Turismo Pehuen (☎ 635-254; consultas@turismo pehuen.cl; Blanco Encalada 299) Reputable. Open year-round, with tours to nearby islands and horse trekking.

Sights & Activities

You can't miss neo-Gothic 1906 **Iglesia San Francisco de Castro** (Plaza de Armas), the yellow-lavender paint job of which testifies to island individuality. Clever farm instruments and Huilliche relics are among the displays at **Museo Regional de Castro** (Esmeralda s/n; ☽ 9:30am-8pm Mon-Sat, 10:30am-1pm Sun Jan-Feb, 9:30am-1pm & 3-6:30pm Mon-Sat, 10:30am-1pm Sun Mar-Dec). Near the fairgrounds, the **Modern Art Museum** (☎ 635-454; Parque Municipal; donations accepted; ☽ 10am-8pm summer) displays innovative local works. Nonprofit **Almacén de Biodiversidad** (cnr Lillo & Blanco; www.almacendebiodiversidad.com; ☽ 9am-1pm, 3-6:30pm Mon-Fri) sells top-quality goods made by local artisans. The colorful **palafitos** are mostly along Costanera Pedro Montt north of town at the western exit from the city.

Festivals & Events

Festival de Huaso Chilote Cowboy festival held in late January.

Festival Costumbrista Folk music and dance and traditional foods in mid-February.

Sleeping

Seasonal lodging is advertised with hand-written signs along San Martín, O'Higgins and Barros Arana. Those interested in **rural homestays** (☎ in Santiago 02-690-8000; www.viajesrurales .cl) can also inquire at the municipal tourism office.

Camping Pudù (☎ 099-643-7764; 2-person campsites US$9) Decent facilities on the way to Dalcahue, 10km north of Castro.

Hospedaje Central (☎ 637-026; Los Carrera 316; r per person US$7) Large *hostal* with decent wood-varnish rooms, some tight spaces and frilly bedcovers.

Hospedaje Agüero (☎ 635-735; Chacabuco 449; r per person US$12) The reception may be grumpy

but rooms are comfortable and offer *palafito* views.

Hostal O'Higgins (☎ 632-016; O'Higgins 831, Interior; d incl breakfast US$12) Prim and paneled rooms with clean shared bathrooms and breakfast included.

Camping Llicaldad (☎ 635-080; Fiordo de Castro; 4-person campsites US$14) Off the Panamericana, 6km south of Castro; sites are muddy in rainy season.

Hospedaje Mirador (☎ 633-795; Barros Arana 127; r per person US$14; ⌨) This red house on a steep seafront passageway has locking rooms (small but amenable) with big beds and gasp-inducing views.

Hostal Cordillera (☎ 532-247; hcordillera@hotmail .com; La Rosedana 175; r per person US$14; ⌨) A great atmosphere, it's a little worn but spacious and well-attended with a quiet covered terrace. Ask for the room with the sea view, it can't hurt.

Hostal del Río (☎ 632-223; Thompson 232; s/d US$39/$49) Fresh white bedding, streaming light and spacious, thoroughly feminine rooms.

Eating

Waterfront restaurants next to the *feria artesanal* have the best bang for your peso; try **Vista Hermoso** (set lunches US$5).

Restaurant Camahueto (Los Bancos 350; menu del dia US$3.50) Abundant and simple lunch specials, like salmon with rice and salad, are your best bet.

Años Luz (San Martín 309; mains US$4-12; ☽ 11am-late) Offerings like espresso, raspberry margaritas and generous plates of almond-crusted congrio or salmon pastries fuel friendly crowds. Live Latin jazz or rock starts at 11pm in summertime.

Sacho (Thompson 213; mains US$5-9) A top-drawer seafood restaurant with excellent crab and *curanto* (a hearty pile of fish, shellfish, chicken, pork, lamb, beef and potato cooked together) big enough for two.

Getting There & Away

BOAT

During the summer, there are sometimes ferries to Chaitén (p510); most stop off in Quellón. **Naviera Austral** (☎ 634-628; Av Puerto Montt 48; US$31) travels Wednesday at 4pm, Saturday at 12pm and Sunday at 3pm. Check on current schedules with **Navimag** (☎ 432-360; www.navimag .com; Angelmó 2187, Puerto Montt), or Catamaranes del Sur agent **Cielo Mar Austral** (☎ 264-010; Quillota

CHILE

245; one way US$39). Some of the ferries can take cars on board.

BUS & COLECTIVO

The municipal **Terminal de Buses Rurales** (San Martín), near Sargento Aldea, has buses to Dalcalhue (US$2, 30 minutes) and Cucao (US$3, one hour), with limited services off-season. The **Cruz del Sur terminal** (☎ 632-389; San Martín 486) services Quellón and Ancud as well as long-distance destinations.

Destination	Duration (hr)	Cost (US$)
Ancud	1¼	2
Puerto Montt	4	5
Quellón	1½	2
Quemchi	1½	2
Santiago	16	29-48
Temuco	7	15
Valdivia	7	10

For nearby destinations, *colectivos* provide a faster alternative. **Colectivos Chonchi** leave from Chacabuco near Esmeralda (US$1) as well as from Ramírez near San Martín. **Colectivos Quellón** leave from Sotomayor and San Martín (US$3), as do Colectivos Achao (US$1).

DALCAHUE & ISLA QUINCHAO

Dalcahue, 20km northeast of Castro, has a doric-columned 19th-century church, well-preserved vernacular architecture, and a famous Sunday market selling wool imaginatively woven into fleece-lined slippers, dolls, even skirts. Artisan women weave baskets and knit at their stands, hoping the live performance will sweeten a sale. Outside of town, **Altue Sea Kayak Center** (☎ in Santiago 02-232-1103; www.seakayakchile.com) leads wonderful six- to nine- day kayak tours of the archipelago. All trips must be booked in advance.

Midway between Dalcahue and Achao, **Curaco de Vélez** dates from 1660 and has a treasure of Chilote architecture, plus an open-air oyster bar at the beach. Buses between Achao and Dalcahue stop in Curaco.

Isla Quinchao, southeast of Dalcahue, is one of the most accessible islands, and worth a day trip. Isla Quinchao's largest town, **Achao**, features Chiloé's oldest church. Wooden pegs, instead of nails, hold together **Iglesia Santa María de Achao**.

Camping Garcia (☎ 065-661-283; Delicias; camping per person US$3; ☼ Dec-Mar) offers sites with a hot shower one block from the plaza. There are good lodging options at **Hostal Plaza** (☎ 065-661-283; Amunátegui 20; r per person US$10), across from the plaza, or the comfortable **Sol y Lluvia** (☎ 065-253-996; Gerónimo de Urmeneta 215; r US$12). Overlooking the pier, **Mar y Velas** (Serrano 02) serves up mussels or clams and cold beer.

Minibuses and *colectivos* go directly to/from Castro. From Dalcahue, **Dalcahue Expreso** (Freire) has half-hourly buses to Castro (US$2) weekdays, but fewer on weekends. Ferries for Isla Quinchao leave continuously. Pedestrians go free (but you'll need to take a bus to reach any destinations once you get on the island), and cars cost US$6 (round-trip).

CHONCHI

☎ 065 / pop 12,000

A somnambulant village on a tranquil bay, Chonchi defies its rebel past as the former haunt of pirates and port for cypress export. Located 23km south of Castro, it is the closest sizable town to the national park. Services center on Centenario, including a **tourist office** (cnr Sargento Candelaria & Centenario; ☼ Jan-Mar). Visitors can explore **Isla Lemuy** by taking the free ferry departing every half-hour from Puerto Huichas (5km south). On Sunday and in the off-season, the service is hourly.

Camping los Manzanos (☎ 671-263; Pedro Aguirre Cerda 709; campsites up to 4 people US$9) has hot showers. Beachfront haven **La Esmeralda** (☎ 671-328; carlos@esmeraldabythesea.cl; Irarrázabal s/n; dm/d US$10/16; ☐) has simple, agreeable rooms; for views reserve the 'early honeymoon' room. Owner Charles Gredy rents bikes and fishing gear, offers tours of his seafood farm and hosts congenial dinners with the day's catch. Seafood delights are served in the *mercado*: the 2nd-floor restaurants above the crafts market have a slim deck overlooking the water.

Catch Castro-bound buses opposite the plaza on the upper level or take a *colectivo* (US$1) opposite the church. Transportation to Parque Nacional Chiloé (US$2, 1½ hours) departs a few times per day in summer.

PARQUE NACIONAL CHILOÉ

Gorgeous, evergreen forests meet taupe stretches of sand and the boundless, thrashing Pacific in this 43,000-hectare **national park** (admission US$2), 54km southwest of Castro. The park protects diverse birds, chilote fox and the reclusive *pudú*. Some Huilliche communities live within the park boundaries and some manage campsites.

Access the park through Cucao, a minute village with growing amenities, and park sector Chanquín, where Conaf runs a visitors center with information. **Sendero Interpretivo El Tepual** winds 1km along fallen tree trunks through thick forest. The 2km **Sendero Dunas de Cucao** leads to a series of dunes behind a long, white-sand beach. The most popular route is the 20km **Sendero Chanquín-Cole Cole**, which follows the coast past Lago Huelde to Río Cole Cole. The hike continues 8km north to Río Anay, passing through groves of red myrtles.

Sleeping & Eating

A road passing the park has a series of private campgrounds, all charging around US$3 per person.

Camping Chanquín (camping per person US$4) In the park, 200m beyond the visitors center. Good amenities and a covered rain area.

El Fogon de Cucao (☎ 099-946-5685; camping per person US$6, r per person incl breakfast US$20) Choose between a gorgeous guesthouse with sprawling deck or waterfront camping with full facilities. Beware: the restaurant can host jam sessions, featuring its musician owner and friends, 'til the wee hours, but you're lucky to get the free concert (not true for the campground sing-alongs out back). It also offers horse treks to a *refugio* (a two-day trip).

Parador Darwin (☎ 099-884-0702; paradordarwin@ hotmail.com; s/d incl breakfast US$14/24; ☺ Jun-Jul) A rainy day score: inviting rooms with sheepskin rugs, trunk tables and electric teapots. The café delights with fresh juices, local razorback clams with parmesan and big salads (mains US$6) to be enjoyed over board games and jazz.

Cheap and friendly lodgings include **El Arrayán** (☎ 099-219-3565; park entrance; s/d US$8/14) and **El Paraíso** (☎ 099-296-5465; r US$10), located before the bridge.

Those making the 20km hike to **Cole Cole** stay at the **campsite** (camping per person US$3). Bring your own stove and prepare for pesky sand fleas.

Getting There & Away

Buses go to/from Castro five times daily (US$2.75, one hour). Service from Chonchi is sporadic. Stay on the bus until after the Cucao bridge. The final stop is the park.

QUELLÓN

☎ 065 / pop 13,800

Those imagining a pot of gold and rainbows at the end of the Panamericana will be surprised by a dumpy port. Even locals bemoan the pirating of Quellón's natural wealth, which has left a sad industrial air. Most travelers head this way to make ferry connections to Chaitén or Puerto Montt. It's best to change money before coming. **Banco del Estado** (cnr Ladrilleros & Freire) has an ATM. **Patagonia Chiloe Expeditions** (08-590-2200; ☺ Jan-Feb) runs excursions to the lovely and remote Isla Kailin (boat trip US$20).

Lodgings per person, no breakfast, include the threadbare **Hotel Playa** (☎ 681-278; Pedro Montt 427; r US$8); and **Hotel El Chico Leo** (☎ 681-567; Pedro Montt 325; r without/with bathroom US$14/39), whose fuzzy bedspreads, shell lamps and acrylic landscapes offer the best value. The restaurant (lunch US$2.50 to US$6) is good and the pool tables bustle with action. Anyone with *honda* (good vibes) taxis down to **Taberna Nos** (O'Higgins 150; snacks US$3; ☺ 8:30pm-3am Mon-Sat), as much for the ska, cheap pints and seafood tapas as for the smiley welcome by its Galician-Chilote owners.

Buses Cruz del Sur and Transchiloé leave from the **bus terminal** (cnr Aguirre Cerda & Miramar) for Castro frequently (US$2, 1½ hours). **Navimag** (☎ 432-360; www.navimag.com; Angelmó 2187, Puerto Montt) sails to Chaitén twice weekly. **Naviera Austral** (☎ 207; Pedro Montt 457) goes to Chaitén (US$29, five hours) on Wednesdays at noon and Fridays at 9am. Ferry schedules change seasonally; verify all departures at the appropriate office in advance.

NORTHERN PATAGONIA

A web of rivers, peaks and sprawling glaciers long-ago provided a natural boundary between northern Patagonia and the rest of the world. Pinochet's **Carretera Austral** (Hwy 7) was the first road to effectively link these remote regions in the 1980s. Isolation has kept the local character fiercely self-sufficient and tied to nature's clock. '*Quien se apura en la Patagonia pierde el tiempo*', locals say (he who hurries in Patagonia loses his time). Weather decides all in this nowhere land beyond the Lakes District. So don't rush. Missed flights, delayed ferries and floods are routine to existence; take the wait as locals would – another opportunity to heat the kettle and strike up a slow talk over mate.

Starting south of Puerto Montt, the Carretera Austral links widely separated towns and hamlets all the way to Villa O'Higgins, a total of just over 1200km. High season (from mid-December through February) offers considerably more travel options and availability. Combination bus and ferry circuits afford visitors a panoramic vision of the region. This section covers Chaitén to Lago General Carrera but there's plenty more. Don't hesitate to tread beyond the pages of the guidebook: the little villages along the road and its furthest hamlets of Cochrane, Caleta Tortel and Villa O'Higgins are fully worth exploring.

CHAITÉN & PARQUE PUMALÍN
☎ 065 / pop 3500

An emerald umbrella on the rainy bay, the yawning outpost of Chaitén is little more than a six by eight grid of wide streets. The only town near Parque Pumalín, it's also a major transport stop for the ultrarural Carretera Austral. If you arrive by ferry; the port is a 10-minute walk northwest of town. Around the plaza are the post office, Entel and **Banco del Estado** (cnr Libertad & O'Higgins), which exchanges cash at poor rates and has an ATM. The **tourist kiosk** (cnr Costanera & O'Higgins; ⏳ 9am-9pm Jan-Feb) lists lodgings. **Pumalín Information Center** (O'Higgins 62) has park information and reserves cabins. A bastion of local information, **Chaitur** (☎ 731-429; nchaitur@hotmail.com; O'Higgins 67) organizes excursions with bilingual guides to Pumalín, the Yelcho glacier, Termas de Amarillo and beaches with sea-lion colonies. Regional buses are based here and the agency also can provide general tour assistance, in English as well.

Sights & Activities
Pristine native rainforest and ancient *alerce* trees are protected in 2889-sq-km **Parque Pumalín** (www.pumalinpark.org; admission free), 68km north of Chaitén. It is Chile's largest private park and one of the largest conservation projects of its kind. While much of the land is impenetrable, developed hikes run the length of the road through the park. After the bus drops you off you can hitch to the next hike, but not in off-season. **Sendero Cascadas** (Caleta Gonzalo) climbs through dense forest to a large waterfall. **Sendero Laguna Tronador**, 12km south, climbs stairs and stepladders to views of Michinmahuida and a secluded lake with two campsites. Another kilometer south, **Sendero Los Alerces** is an easy interpretive trail through

majestic groves of *alerce*. Check at the park offices for additional options. Visitors can choose from various **camping areas** (per person US$3, covered campsites US$10).

About 25km southeast of Chaitén, **Termas El Amarillo** (admission US$5; campsites US$7) are hot springs diverted to small cement pools amid greenery. Campers get exclusive access to the pools at night.

Sleeping & Eating
Los Arrayanes (☎ 731-136; campsites per person US$5) Beachfront with hot showers, 4km north of Chaitén.

Hospedaje Llanos (☎ 731-332; Corcovado 378; s US$10) Simple rooms, some with sea views, and a delightful hostess.

Casa Hexagon (☎ 08-286-2950; Río Blanco 36; s US$14) River stones and raw beams decorate this lovely hexagonal house on the river. The friendly German host offers valuable tips on the area.

Hostería Los Coihues (☎ 731-461; Pedro Aguirre Cerda 398; s/d incl breakfast US$26/34) Stylish and sunny, this quiet *hostería* spoils the road-weary with abundant towels and generous continental breakfasts.

Corcovado (cnr Corcovado & Cerda; lunch special US$6) No-nonsense dining room serving roast lamb or salmon and potatoes.

Cocinerías Costumbristas (Portales 258; meals US$3-6) Unbeatable *empanadas de mariscos* (seafood) and heaping fish platters from sweet aproned señoras.

Getting There & Away
AIR
AeroSur (☎ 731-228; cnr Pinto & Riveros) has an air-taxi to Puerto Montt (US$60, 45 minutes).

BOAT
Ferry schedules change, so confirm them before making plans.

Catamaranes del Sur (☎ 731-199; Juan Todesco 118) Passenger-only ferries to Puerto Montt and Castro thrice weekly in summer.

Naviera Austral (☎ 731-272; www.navieraustral.cl in Spanish; Corcovado 266) Auto-passenger ferry *Pincoya* to Puerto Montt (US$31, 12 hours) four times a week. In summer only to Quellón, Chiloé (US$29, six hours) two times a week; and daily from Caleta Gonzalo in Parque Pumalín to Hornopirén (US$19), where buses depart for Puerto Montt.

BUS
Transportes Cordillera (Libertad 432) goes to Futaleufú daily at 3:15pm. **Chaitur** runs buses to

CARRETERA AUSTRAL

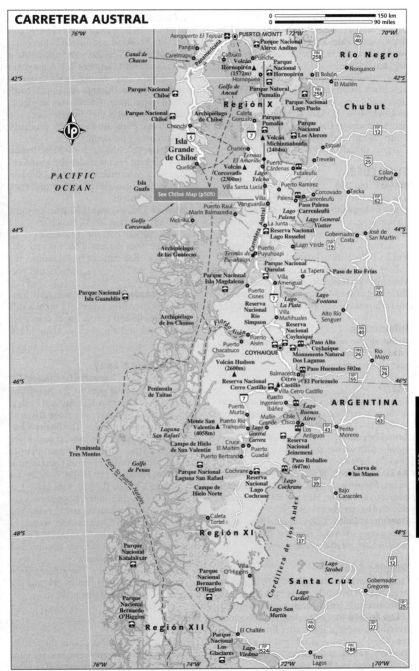

Futaleufú (US$10, four hours) at 3:30pm daily except Sunday. **Buses Palena** (cnr Corcovado & Todesco) goes to Palena (US$9, 4½ hours) thrice weekly from the terminal. **Buses Norte** (☎ 731-390; Libertad 432) goes to Coyhaique (US$27, 12 hours) on Monday, Wednesday and Friday at 9:30am, stopping in La Junta (US$14, four hours) and Puyuhuapi (US$15). Chaitur goes to Coyhaique (US$27) at 9am daily except Saturday, and to Caleta Gonzalo (US$5, two hours) at 7am and 5pm daily. **B y V Tour** (Libertad 432) goes to Caleta Gonzalo daily.

FUTALEUFÚ

☎ 065 / pop 1800

The diamond-cut waters of the Futaleufú have made famous this modest mountain village, 155km from Chaitén. World-renowned rafting and kayaking comes at a price: the valley is starting to feel a little like Boulder, Taos, or Pucón. If the Futa or Fu (as those in the know call it) is on your destination list, make sure you slow down and say hello to locals, speak their language and share something, because these days there's more of us than them.

Information

Bring all the money you'll need; **Banco del Estado** (cnr O'Higgins & Manuel Rodríguez) is the only place to change cash.

Tours

Rafting trips on Río Espolón and segments of the more difficult Futaleufú are expensive (US$85 to US$100). Reliable outfitters:

Austral Excursions (Hermanos Carera 500) A locally owned outfitter with river descents as well as trekking and canyoning excursions.

Bio Bio Expeditions (☎ 800-246-7238; www.bbxraft ing.com) A pioneer in the region, this ecologically minded group offers river descents, horse treks and more. It is well established but may take walk-ins.

Expediciones Chile (☎ 721-386; Mistral 296) A secure rafting operator with loads of experience. Offers kayaking, mountain biking and other activities as well.

Sleeping & Eating

Camping Puerto Espolón (☎ 696-5324; camping per person US$4; ✆ Jan-Feb) The best option close to town, riverside with a sandy beach.

Cara del Indio (camping per person US$6) Spacious riverside camping, 15km after Puerto Ramírez. There's kayak and raft put-in sites, hot showers, sauna and staples of homemade bread, cheese and beer are sold.

El Campesino (☎ 721-275; Prat 107; r per person incl breakfast US$8) The hospitable home of an old colonist, with breakfast and shared bathroom.

El Galpón (☎ 021-964-200; www.dosmargaritas.org; Sector Azul puente Pinilla; r per person US$9) A gorgeous working farm and foundation dedicated to local development through sustainable tourism and agriculture. Guests stay in rustic, immaculate rooms in the converted barn and can cook and purchase fresh farm products. It's 22km before Futaleufú.

Posada Ely (☎ 721-205; Balmaceda 409; s incl breakfast US$18) Well kept rooms under the guardianship of Betty, who makes a mean rosehip jam (served with a breakfast of fresh bread, eggs, juice, tea and more).

Futaleufú (Cerda 408; mains US$6) Rain or shine you'll find abundant salads, french fries and scalloped chicken here for reasonable prices.

Sur Andes (Cerda 308; meals US$6) Sip real coffee on the garden patio of this teahouse; the hungry can feast on cakes, burgers and vegetarian fare.

Martín Pescador (Balmaceda 603; meals US$18) Easily the best meals for miles with memorable salmon ceviche and a long list of delectable wines. Check out the cheaper daily lunch special.

Getting There & Away

In front of the plaza, **Transportes Cordillera** ☎ 721-249; Prat 262; US$3; 1½hr) goes to the Argentine border at 9am and 6pm Monday and Friday; during high season there are more frequent trips with other companies. The **Futaleufú border post** (✆ 8am-8pm) is far quicker and more efficient than the crossing at Palena, opposite the Argentine border town of Carrenleufú. **Transportes Sebastián** (☎ 721-288; Piloto Carmona 381) goes to Chaitén (US$10, four hours) at 7:30am daily except Sunday, stopping at Villa Santa Lucía (where you can transfer south to Coyhaique), Puerto Cárdenas and Termas El Amarillo. **Cuchichi** (Sargento Aldea) goes to Puerto Montt via Argentina at 8am on Tuesday and Thursday (US$31, 13 hours).

There's no gas station. The grocery store on Sargento Aldea sells fuel by the jug; it's cheaper in Argentina, if you make it.

PALENA

☎ 065 / pop 1500

Tourism is still a queer notion in the prickly foothills and grassy meadows beyond the ultra turquoise Río Palena, but remnants of pioneer lifestyle and incredible hospitality make it worth the journey. Just 8km west of the border, Palena is a low-traffic crossing point into Argentina. The **Rodeo de Palena** is held on the last weekend in January.

Have the bus drop you off 22km before Palena to stay at the cozy **Adventuras Cordilleranas** (741-388; www.rutatranspatagonia.cl; El Malito bridge; s incl breakfast US$10), where Mireya pampers guests like part of the brood. The family also offers riverfront cabin accommodations and rides to rural El Tranquilo. In town try the friendly **La Frontera** (741-388; Montt 977; r per person US$10) or **Residencial La Chilenita** (☎ 731-212; Pudeto 681; r per person US$10). Adventurers can ride or hike to wonderful **Rincón de la Nieve** (741-269; Valle Azul; s incl breakfast US$12), the Casanova family farm in Valle Azul. Chill there or continue on a truly incredible five-day round-trip ride to remote Lago Palena (see boxed text, p516). Arrange in advance.

Buses Palena (Plaza de Armas) goes to Chaitén (US$9, 4½ hours) at 7:30am Monday, Wednesday and Friday.

PUERTO PUYUHUAPI

In 1935 four German immigrants settled this remote rainforest outpost, inspired by explorer Hans Steffen's adventures. The agricultural colony grew with Chilote textile workers, whose skills fed the success of the 1947 German **Fábrica de Alfombras** (www.puyuhuapi .com; Calle Aysen s/n; tours US$2), still weaving carpets today. Across the inlet, **Termas de Puyuhuapi** is a high-end hot-springs resort.

Friendly **Hostería Marily** (☎ 067-325-102; cnr Uebel & Circunvalación; s/d incl breakfast US$15/30) offers sound mattresses and firm beds. Pioneer home **Casa Ludwig** (☎ 067-320-000; www.casaludwig.cl; Uebel s/n; r per person incl breakfast from US$20) is elegant and snug – a real treat with a roaring fire and big breakfasts at the large communal table. **Rossbach** (meals US$8) has excellent *küchen*, as well as heaping home-style meals. Come out of the rain at **Aonikenk Cabañas** (☎ 067-325-208; Hamburgo 16; 2–4-person cabins US$25-35), with great café fare and generous hospitality (the owner will dry your wet layers by the woodstove). Cabins are well appointed and it's a good stop for area information.

Buses Norte (☎ 067-232-167; Gral Parra 337) and Transportes Emanuel buses leave for Chaitén (US$16, 5½ hours) and Coyhaique (US$14, 6½ hours) between 3pm and 5pm from the store next to the police station.

PARQUE NACIONAL QUEULAT

Queulat (admission US$3) is a wild realm where rivers wind through forests thick with ferns and southern beech. Its steep-sided fjords are flanked by creeping glaciers. From Conaf's **Centro de Información Ambiental** there is a 3km hike to a lookout with views of Ventisquero Colgante, a chalk-blue hanging glacier.

Just north of the southern entrance at Pudú, at km 170, a damp trail climbs the valley of the **Río de las Cascadas** through a dense forest to a granite bowl where half-a-dozen waterfalls spring from hanging glaciers.

Basic camping is available at **Ventisquero** (per site US$7), convenient to the Ventisquero Colgante, and at **Angostura** (Lago Risopatrón; campsites US$7), 15km north of Puyuhuapi.

COYHAIQUE

☎ 067 / pop 44,900

Coyhaique fills the rolling steppe at the foot of Cerro Macay's basalt massif. Ranch town and regional capital, it attracts rural workers to the timber or salmon industries and anglers to nearby fly-fishing lodges. For those fresh from the wilderness, it can be a jarring relapse into the world of semitrucks and subdivisions.

Coyhaique's plaza occupies the heart of a disorienting pentagonal plan. Av General Baquedano skirts northeast and connects with the highway to Puerto Chacabuco. Av Ogano heads south to Balmaceda and Lago General Carrera.

Information

Banks with ATMs line Condell.

Cabot (☎ 230-101; Lautaro 331) A general service travel agency.

Conaf (☎ 212-109; Av Ogana 1060) Has park details.

Hospital Base (☎ 231-286; Ibar 68) Near the western end of JM Carrera.

Lavamatic (Simpson 417; per kg US$4)

Lavandería QL (Bilbao 160; per kg US$4)

Post office (Cochrane 202)

Sernatur (☎ 233-949; Bulnes 35) Staff here provide excellent information on lodgings, fishing guides, transportation and possibilities further south.

Turismo Prado (21 de Mayo 417) Change traveler's checks here.

Visual.com (12 de Octubre 485-B; per hr US$1) Get online here or at call centers.

Sights & Activities

Prime river vistas can be gained at **Mirador Río Simpson**, reached by walking west on JM

COYHAIQUE

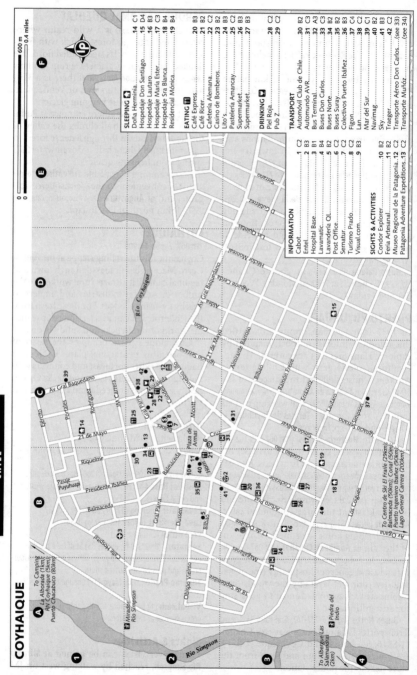

INFORMATION
Cabot......................................	1 C2
Entel.....................................	2 B3
Hospital Base........................	3 B1
Lavamatic............................	4 B4
Lavandería QL......................	5 B2
Post Office...........................	6 C2
Sernatur...............................	7 C2
Turismo Prado......................	8 C2
Visual.com...........................	9 B3

SIGHTS & ACTIVITIES
Condor Explorer..................	10 B2
Feria Artesanal....................	11 B2
Museo Regional de la Patagonia..	12 C2
Patagonia Adventure Expeditions..	13 C2

SLEEPING
Doña Herminia......................	14 C1
Hospedaje Don Santiago.........	15 D4
Hospedaje Lautaro.................	16 B3
Hospedaje María Ester...........	17 C3
Hospedaje Sra Blanca............	18 B4
Residencial Mónica...............	19 B4

EATING
Café Express........................	20 B3
Café Ricer............................	21 B2
Cafetería Alemana................	22 C2
Casino de Bomberos..............	23 C2
Lito's...................................	24 B3
Pastelería Amancay...............	25 C2
Supermarket........................	26 B3
Supermarket........................	27 B3

DRINKING
Piel Roja..............................	28 C2
Pub Z...................................	29 C2

TRANSPORT
Automóvil Club de Chile........	30 B2
Automundo AVR....................	31 C3
Bus Terminal........................	32 A3
Buses Don Carlos..................	33 C3
Buses Norte..........................	34 B2
Buses Suray.........................	35 B2
Colectivos Puerto Ibáñez.......	36 B3
Figon...................................	37 C4
Lan......................................	38 C2
Mar del Sur..........................	39 C1
Navimag..............................	40 B2
Sky......................................	41 B3
Traeger................................	42 C2
Transporte Aéreo Don Carlos..	(see 33)
Transporte Muñoz.................	(see 34)

Carrera. Hikers can tread trails in **Reserva Nacional Coyhaique** (admission US$1), 5km from town: take Baquedano north across the bridge and go right at the gravel road; from the entrance it's 3km to Laguna Verde. **Condor Explorer** (☎ 670-349; www.condorexplorer.com; Dussen 357) offers trekking, climbing and more with bilingual guides and good service. Recommended and English-speaking, **Patagonia Adventure Expeditions** (☎ 219-894; www.adventurepatagonia.com; Riquelme 372) runs rafting (US$25 half day) and fantastic multiday glacier hikes.

Anglers can go **fishing** from November to May, with some restrictions. Brown and rainbow trout are typical catches. From June to September, skiers can make turns at the **Centro de Ski El Fraile** (☎ 231-690), only 29km south of Coyhaique. The T-bar and pommel lift access 800m of vertical terrain. Experts can hike past the lifts to access some bowls with heavy, wet snow and lovely tree-skiing.

In town, **Museo Regional de la Patagonia** (cnr Av General Baquedano & Eusebo Lillo; admission US75¢; ☺ 9am-6pm Dec-Feb, limited hours rest of year) catalogues pioneer artifacts and Jesuit regalia. **Feria Artesanal** (Plaza de Armas) sells woolens, leather and wooden knickknacks.

Sleeping

Rates listed here are with shared bathroom.

Albergue Las Salamandras (☎ 211-865; www.sala mandras.cl; campsites/dm/d US$7/16/28) On a wooded bank of Río Simpson, this rustic guesthouse offers ample common spaces, two kitchens, and dorm beds weighted in blankets.

Hospedaje Don Santiago (☎ 231-116; Errázuriz 1040; r US$8) A wonderfully welcoming place, with matchbox-sized rooms and thermoses of hot water on request.

Reserva Nacional Coyhaique (5-person site US$9) Well-equipped sites; consult with Conaf.

Hospedaje Lautaro (☎ 238-116; Lautaro 269; r US$9; ☺ summer only) Frayed rooms and pleather couches characterize this flophouse handy to the terminal.

Hospedaje María Ester (☎ 233-023; Lautaro 544; s US$10) Bright petite rooms each have windows but the number of singles is limited.

Hospedaje Sra Blanca (☎ 232-158; Simpson 459; s US$12) Ample rooms with fussy lace curtains, tucked behind grandmother's rose garden.

Doña Herminia (☎ 231-579; 21 de Mayo 60; s incl breakfast US$10) Herminia's affectionate service and attention to details like reading lamps and fresh towels make these impeccable rooms a steal.

Residencial Mónica (☎ 234-302; Eusebio Lillo 664; s US$12) Well-attended and cozy in prim '60s style.

Camping La Alborada (☎ 238-868; 5-person site US$20) Clean with good amenities and sheltered sites; 1km from town.

Eating & Drinking

Two large supermarkets sit side by side on Lautaro.

Pastelería Amancay (21 de Mayo 340; dessert US$3) Droolworthy, with five kinds of chocolate cake, *küchen* and hand-crafted chocolates.

Casino de Bomberos (Gral Parra 365; lunch US$5) A happening greasy-spoon in the fire station with reasonable lunches.

Lito's (☎ 214-528; Lautaro 147; meals US$5-9) Clad modestly in vinyl paneling, this local fave expertly cooks Chilean preparations of meat, seafood and salads.

Café Express (cnr Arturo Prat & Freire; meals US$6) Join locals for simple café fare and beer on tap.

Cafetería Alemana (Condell 119; sandwiches US$6) Service drags but it's good for large beef sandwiches in a country kitsch ambience.

Café Ricer (Horn 48; mains US$10-12) Charging high prices for sheepskin chairs and rustic-chic, Ricer reels in the beautiful people with a catalogue of offerings which includes tasty pizza, salads and ice cream, but service is its weak suit.

Piel Roja (Moraleda 495; ☺ 6pm-5am) Abuzz with the youth and outdoor crowd, this colorful club sports a swank bar and upstairs dance floor that shakes till all hours.

Pub Z (Moraleda 420) A former barn hosting occasional art exhibits and live music.

Getting There & Away

AIR

The region's main airport is in Balmaceda, 50km southeast of Coyhaique. **Lan** (☎ 600-526-2000; Gral Parra 402) has daily flights to Puerto Montt (one hour) and Santiago (2½ hours). **Sky** (☎ 240-825; Arturo Prat 203) is another choice.

BOAT

Ferries to Puerto Montt leave from Puerto Chacabuco, two hours from Coyhaique by bus. Schedules are subject to change.

Navimag (☎ 233-306; www.navimag.com; Horn 47-D) sails from Puerto Chacabuco to Puerto Montt (US$52 to US$216, 18 hours) several times per week. **Mar del Sur** (☎ 231-255; Av General Baquedano 146-A) runs ferries to/from Puerto Ibáñez and

CHILE

DETOUR TO PIONEER PATAGONIA

When winds roar sidelong and rains persist, take refuge by the woodstove, drink a round of *mates* and *echar la talla* (pass the time) with the locals. Rural Patagonia offers a rare and privileged glimpse of a fading way of life. To jump-start their slack rural economy, government and nonprofit initiatives created local guide and homestay associations.

These family enterprises range from comfortable roadside *hospedajes* and farmstays to wild multiday treks and horse trips through wonderland terrain. Prices are reasonable, ranging from US$12 to US$16 per day for lodging and US$20 per day for guide services, although extras include horses and only Spanish is spoken.

RutaTransPatagonia (☎ 67-214-031; www.rutatranspatagonia.cl in Spanish) operates from Palena to Cerro Castillo, south of Coyhaique. Further north, the tourist office in the Municipalidad de Cochamó arranges similar trips near Río Puelo. It's best to book a week in advance or more, as intermediaries will have to make radio contact with the most remote hosts. That's right – no phones, no electricity, no worries.

Chile Chico (US$5, 2½ hours). It's in high demand, so make reservations at the office in advance.

BUS

Buses operate from the **bus terminal** (cnr Lautaro & Magallanes) and separate offices. Schedules change continuously; check with Sernatur for the latest information. Unless noted, the following leave from the terminal.

For Puerto Aisén and Puerto Chacabuco, **Buses Suray** leaves approximately every 1½ hours (US$2.50, one hour).

Companies going to Chaitén (US$29, 12 hours) include **Buses Norte** (Gral Parra 337) and **Transporte Muñóz** (Gral Parra 337) and Bus Daniela. Otherwise, coordinate a bus to La Junta (US$20, seven to 10 hours) with connecting buses to Chaitén.

Colectivos and shuttle buses head to Puerto Ingeniero Ibáñez (US$7, 1½ hours) to connect with the Chile Chico ferry. These include shuttles **Colectivos Puerto Ibáñez** (cnr Arturo Prat & Errázuriz) and **Transportes Ali** (☎ 219-009, 250-346), with door-to-port service.

Acuario 13 and Buses Ñadis go to Cochrane (US$17, seven to 10 hours) four times weekly. **Buses Don Carlos** (Cruz 63) goes to Puerto Río Tranquilo (US$11, five hours) at 4pm Thursday and Monday, from where connections can be made to Chile Chico. Minibus Interlagos leaves for Chile Chico (US$20, 12 hours) three mornings per week.

Queilin bus goes to Osorno and Puerto Montt via Argentina (US$49, 20 to 22 hours) daily. For Punta Arenas, Bus Sur leaves Tuesday (US$50, 22 hours), and for Comodoro Rivadavia on Monday and Friday (US$30,

eight hours) from where you can transfer further south.

Getting Around

Door-to-door shuttle service (US$5) to the airport leaves two hours before flight departure. Call **Transfer Coyhaique** (☎ 210-495, 099-838-5070) or **Transfer Aisén Tour** (☎ 217-070, 099-489-4760).

Car rental is expensive and availability limited in summer. Try **Traeger** (☎ 231-648; Av General Baquedano 457), **Automundo AVR** (☎ 231-621; Bilbao 510), and **Automóvil Club de Chile** (☎ 231-847; JM Carrera 333). **Figon** (Simpson 888) rents (US$10 to US$25 per day) and repairs bikes.

LAGO GENERAL CARRERA

Split with Argentina (where it's called Lago Buenos Aires), this massive 224,000-hectare lake is often a wind-stirred green-blue sea in the middle of a sculpted Patagonian steppe. Its rough and twisty roads dwarf the traveler: you'll feel like you're crawling through the landscape. This section follows the Carretera Austral south from Coyhaique, around the lake's western border.

Just before reaching Balmaceda from Coyhaique, a right-hand turnoff (the sign points to Cochrane) heads toward **Reserva Nacional Cerro Castillo**. The spires of glacier-bound Cerro Castillo tower over some 180,000 hectares of southern beech forest. In Villa Cerro Castillo (km 104) stay with **Don Niba** (☎ public phone 067-419-200; Los Pioneros 872; s incl breakfast US$10), guide, storyteller and grandson of pioneers, in a comfortable home with whopping breakfasts. He also offers horse treks and hikes.

Along the western shore, **Puerto Río Tranquilo** has a petrol station. Boat tours visit **Capilla de Mármol** (marble chapel) when the water's calm. North of town an (unfinished) glacier-lined road to Parque Nacional Laguna San Rafael bumps toward the coast. **Residencial Darka** (☎ 067-419-500; Arrayanes 330; s/d incl breakfast US$10/20) has a few decent rooms and a friendly owner. Wild camping is possible on the windy beach, or 10km west at Lago Tranquilo.

About 13km east of Cruce El Maitén **Puerto Guadal** has petrol and provisions. Pitch a tent lakefront, or hunker down at the well-weathered **Hostería Huemules** (☎ 067-431-212; Las Magnolias 382; r per person US$10), attended by its next-door host Don Kemel. No less than legend, he's sometimes willing to share a tale of navy days in Valparaíso or his youth in Beruit.

Chile Chico
☎ 067 / pop 4000
Gold and silver mines dot the roller-coaster road from Puerto Guadal, ending in Chile Chico, a sunny oasis of wind-pummeled poplars and orchards. From here, buses connect to Los Antiguos (p151) and Ruta 40 leading to southern Argentine Patagonia. Nearby **Reserva Nacional Jeinemeni** (admission US$2), 60km away, is a treasure of flamingos and turquoise mountain lagoons. Aside from a few expensive tours, there's little transportation. You can try to grab a ride in with **Conaf** (☎ 411-325; Blest Gana 121) rangers.

There is **tourist information** (☎ 411-123; cnr O'Higgins & Lautaro) and a **Banco del Estado** (González 112) for money exchange.

You can stay at the ultrafriendly **Kon Aiken** (☎ 411-598; Pedro Burgos 6; camping per person US$5, dm US$10) or the endearing **Hospedaje No Me Olvides** (campsites per person US$5, s US$16), 200m from town toward Argentina; it has snuggly, large and clean rooms, kitchen use and meals. **Oliser** (☎ 411-904; O'Higgins 426; s US$10) has tip-top ample rooms above the phone center. **Hospedaje Brisas del Lago** (☎ 411-204; Manuel Rodríguez 443; s/d US$5/24) is comfortable and clean, but lacking sparks.

Café Elizabeth y Loly (Pedro González 25; mains US$3-9) offers evening café-culture, strong coffee and delicious authentic baklava. **El Monchito** (O'Higgins 250; meals US$7) prepares scrumptious tortellini and offers set menus on ferry days.

Getting There & Away
BOAT
Mar del Sur's auto-passenger ferries cross between Chile Chico and Puerto Ingeniero Ibáñez (2½ hours) several times a week. Departure days and times change often: check at the Entel office in Chile Chico for the latest posting. Rates are: passengers US$5, bicycles US$4, motorcycles US$8 and vehicles US$36. Reservations are highly recommended; for contact information, see p515.

BUS
For transportation from Coyhaique to Puerto Ibáñez, Puerto Río Tranquilo and Chile Chico, see opposite. From Chile Chico, **Acotrans** (☎ 411-582) goes to Los Antiguos, Argentina (US$5, 20 minutes). **Transportes Condor** (☎ 419-500) goes to Puerto Río Tranquilo (US$12, 3½ hours), stopping in Puerto Guadal (US$6). **Transportes Ales** (☎ 411-739; Rosa Amelia 800) does the same trip, going on to Cochrane (six hours) on Wednesday and Saturday. On Wednesday morning the shuttle continues from Río Tranquilo (you must spend the night there) to Coyhaique (US$14, 10 to 12 hours).

SOUTHERN PATAGONIA

The wind is whipping, the mountains are jagged and waters trickle clear. This desolate area first attracted missionaries and fortune seekers from Scotland, England and Croatia. Writer Francisco Coloane described these early adventurers as 'courageous men whose hearts were no more than another closed fist.' The formation of *estancias* (extensive grazing establishment, either for cattle or sheep, with a dominant owner or manager and dependent resident labor force), and the wool boom that followed created reverberating effects: great wealth for a few gained at the cost of native populations, who were nearly exterminated by disease and warfare. Later the region struggled as wool value plummeted and the Panama Canal diverted shipping routes.

Patagonia's worth may have been hard-won and nearly lost but it is now under reconsideration. While wealth once meant minerals and livestock, now it is in the very landscape. For visitors, the very thrill lies in Patagonia's isolated, spectral beauty. Torres del Paine receives 200,000 visitors a year and a growing

CHILE

number set sights further south to Tierra del Fuego and Antarctica.

PUNTA ARENAS

☎ 061 / pop 125,000

If these streets could only talk: this wind-wracked former penitentiary has hosted tat-tered sailors, miners, seal hunters, starving pioneers and wealthy dandies of the wool boom. Exploitation of one of the world's larg-est reserves of hydrocarbon started in the 1980s and has developed into a thriving pet-rochemical industry. Today's Punta Arenas is a confluence of the ruddy and the grand, geared toward tourism and industry.

Orientation

Punta Arenas' regular grid street plan, with wide streets and sidewalks, makes it easy to walk around. The Plaza de Armas, or Plaza Muñoz Gamero, is the center of town. Kiss the foot of the Ona statue for luck. Street names change on either side of the plaza. Most landmarks and accommodations are within a few blocks of here.

Information

Internet access is widely available and ATMs are common.

Conaf (☎ 223-841; José Menéndez 1147) Has details on the nearby parks.

Entel (Navarro 957; ☉ until 10pm) For phone service.

Hospital Regional (☎ 244-040; Angamos 180)

Hostal Calafate (Magallanes 926; per hr US$1; ☉ 9am-11pm) Internet access.

Information kiosk (Plaza Muñoz Gamero; ☉ 8am-7pm Mon-Fri, 9am-8pm Sat).

La Hermandad (Lautaro Navarro 1099) Exchange money here.

Lavasol (☎ 243-607; O'Higgins 969; per load US$3) Laundry.

Post office (Bories 911) One block north of the plaza.

Sernatur (☎ 241-330; Waldo Seguel 689; ☉ 8:15am-6:45pm Mon-Fri, 8:15am-8pm Mon-Fri in summer) Has well-informed staff, and accommodations and transporta-tion lists.

Telefónica (Nogueira 1116) For phone service.

Sights & Activities

The heart of the city, **Plaza Muñoz Gamero** is surrounded by opulent mansions, including the **Palacio Mauricio Braun** (Magallanes 949; admission US$1.50; ☉ 10:30am-5pm summer, to 2pm winter), the luxurious seat of power of the 19th-century Braun-Menéndez family, who were sheep

farmers turned land magnates. Among South America's most fascinating cemeteries is **Ce-menterio Municipal** (Bulnes 949), a mix of humble immigrant graves with heartfelt inscriptions and extravagant tombs of the town's first families. A monument to the Selk'nam com-memorates the indigenous group that was wiped out during the wool boom.

Museo Regional Salesiano (Av Bulnes 374; admis-sion US$3; ☉ 10am-12:30pm & 3-6pm Tue-Sun) touts missionary peacemaking between indigenous groups and settlers. Worthwhile material ex-amines the mountaineer priest Alberto de Agostini and various indigenous groups. Among the historical displays at **Museo Naval y Marítimo** (☎ Pedro Montt 981; admission US75¢; ☉ Tue-Sat) is a well-told account of the Chilean mis-sion that rescued Sir Ernest Shackleton's crew from Antarctica.

Reserva Forestal Magallanes, 8km from town, offers great hiking and mountain biking through dense *lenga* and coigue. A steady slog takes you to the top of Mt Fenton where views are spectacular and winds impressively strong. While tame by all standards, skiing is possible (with views of the strait). The **Ski Club Andino** (☎ 241-479; www.clubandino.cl in Spanish) rents cross-country equipment (US$6 for two hours) and downhill gear (US$16 per day).

Inhóspita Patagonia (☎ 224-510; Lautaro Navarro 1013) offers treks to Cape Froward, the south-ernmost point on mainland South America. For kayaking check out **Turismo Yamana** (☎ 221-130; Av Colón 568) or **Nautica** (☎ 223-117; Camino Río Seco km 7.5) by the port.

Tours

Worthwhile day trips include tours to the **Seno Otway pingüinera** (penguin colony; tours US$10, admission US$5; ☉ Dec-Mar) and to the town's first settlements at **Fuerte Bulnes & Puerto Hambre** (tours US$14, admission US$2). Lodgings can help arrange tours, or try the following:

Turismo Aonikenk (☎ 228-332; www.aonikenk.com; Magallanes 619) Well regarded with multilingual staff.

Turismo Pali Aike (☎ 223-301; www.turismopaliaike .com; Lautaro Navarro 1129)

Turismo Pehoé (☎ 244-506; www.pehoe.com; José Menéndez 918)

Turismo Viento Sur (☎ 226-930; www.vientosur.com; Fagnano 565)

Tours on the *Barcaza Melinka* to see pen-guin colonies on **Isla Magdalena** (Monumento Natural Los Pingüinos; adult/child US$30/15) leave Tuesday,

PUNTA ARENAS

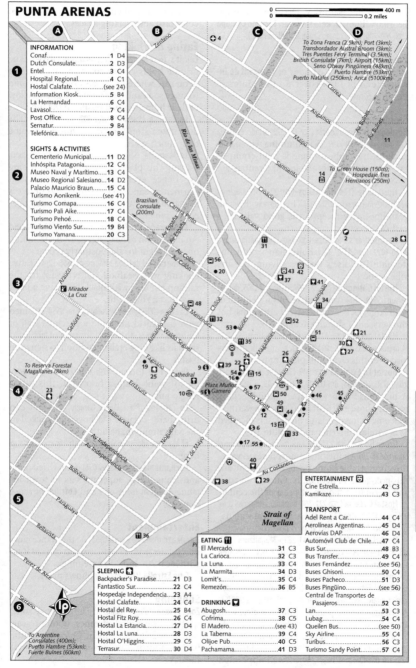

0   400 m
0   0.2 miles

INFORMATION
Conaf.....................................1 D4
Dutch Consulate...................2 D3
Entel.....................................3 C4
Hospital Regional.................4 C1
Hostal Calafate................(see 24)
Information Kiosk.................5 B4
La Hermandad.....................6 C4
Lavasol.................................7 C4
Post Office...........................8 C4
Sernatur...............................9 B4
Telefónica...........................10 B4

SIGHTS & ACTIVITIES
Cementerio Municipal........11 D2
Inhóspita Patagonia............12 C4
Museo Naval y Marítimo....13 C4
Museo Regional Salesiano...14 D2
Palacio Mauricio Braun.......15 C4
Turismo Aonikenk.........(see 41)
Turismo Comapa................16 C4
Turismo Pali Aike...............17 C4
Turismo Pehoé...................18 C4
Turismo Viento Sur............19 B4
Turismo Yamana................20 C3

To Zona Franca (2.5km); Port (3km);
Transbordador Austral Broom (3km);
Tres Puentes Ferry Terminal (3.5km);
British Consulate (7km); Airport (15km);
Seno Otway Pingüinera (48km);
Puerto Hambre (53km);
Puerto Natales (250km); Arica (5100km)

To Green House (150m);
Hospedaje Tres
Hermanos (250m)

Río de las Minas

Brazilian
Consulate
(200m)

*Mirador
La Cruz*

*Strait of
Magellan*

SLEEPING
Backpacker's Paradise.........21 D3
Fantastico Sur.....................22 C4
Hospedaje Independencia....23 A4
Hostal Calafate...................24 C4
Hostal del Rey....................25 B4
Hostal Fitz Roy...................26 C4
Hostal La Estancia...............27 D4
Hostal La Luna....................28 D3
Hostal O'Higgins.................29 C5
Terrasur..............................30 D4

EATING
El Mercado.........................31 C3
La Carioca..........................32 C3
La Luna...............................33 C4
La Marmita.........................34 D3
Lomit's...............................35 C4
Remezón............................36 B5

DRINKING
Abugosh............................37 C3
Cofrima.............................38 C5
El Madero.....................(see 43)
La Taberna.........................39 C4
Olijoe Pub.........................40 C5
Pachamama........................41 D3

ENTERTAINMENT
Cine Estrella......................42 C3
Kamikaze...........................43 C3

TRANSPORT
Adel Rent a Car.................44 C4
Aerolíneas Argentinas........45 D4
Aerovías DAP.....................46 C4
Automóvil Club de Chile.....47 C4
Bus Sur..............................48 B3
Bus Transfer......................49 C4
Buses Fernández............(see 56)
Buses Ghisoni....................50 C4
Buses Pacheco...................51 D3
Buses Pingüino..............(see 56)
Central de Transportes de
Pasajeros...........................52 C3
Lan...................................53 C3
Lubag................................54 C4
Queilen Bus...................(see 50)
Sky Airline.........................55 C4
Turibus..............................56 C3
Turismo Sandy Point..........57 C4

To Reserva Forestal
Magallanes (8km)

To Argentine
Consulates (400m);
Puerto Hambre (53km);
Fuerte Bulnes (60km)

CHILE

Thursday and Saturday, December through February. Book tickets through **Turismo Comapa** (☎ 200-200; www.comapa.com; Magallanes 990).

Festivals & Events

The fireworks and parades of **Carnaval de Invierno** (end of July) cheer up the winter in Punta Arenas.

Sleeping

Hospedaje Independencia (☎ 227-572; Av Independencia 374; camping/dm US$3/6; 🖳) Humming with backpackers, this upbeat home is a bit cramped but the price is unbeatable. Bike rentals are US$10 per day.

Hospedaje Tres Hermanos (☎ 225-450; Angamos 1218; dm/s incl breakfast US$8/12) This gem with warm grandmotherly reception is good value. It's east of the center.

Backpacker's Paradise (☎ 240-104; Ignacio Carrera Pinto 1022; dm US$7; 🖳) Bohemian would understate Paradise's doorless living, but the vibe is good.

Hostal O'Higgins (☎ 227-999; O'Higgins 1205; dm per person US$10; P) Immaculate and well located, with large, locker room–style bathrooms, hot showers and a shared kitchen.

Hostal del Rey (☎ 223-924; Fagnano 589; dm US$12, 2-/4-person apt US$30/60; P) Teddies and silk flowers lord over this clean and pleasant home.

Hostal La Estancia (☎ 249-130; carmenalecl@yahoo .com; O'Higgins 765; dm US$12, s US$25-29, d US$35-39) A big house with wallpapered, high-ceiling rooms, whose excellent hosts give the warmest welcome in town. A large breakfast is included as is wireless internet and satellite TV.

Green House (☎ 227-939; Angamos 1146; per person r/cabin US$16/20) An inviting atmosphere pervades this comfortable home hosted by a young anthropologist and her family. Guests can cook and German is spoken. It's east of the center.

Hostal La Luna (☎ 221-764; hostalluna@hotmail.com; O'Higgins 424; s/d US$12/20; P) A cozy steal with native wood details and down comforters.

Hostal Calafate (☎ 241-281; Magallanes 926; s/d US$31/49) A comfortable midrange choice smack in the center, with a selection of good rooms not quite insulated from the traffic.

Hostal Fitz Roy (☎ 240-430; hostalfitzroy@hotmail .com; Lautaro Navarro 850; s/d/tr incl breakfast US$24/39/53) A country house plunked into the city, with an old corduroy sofa, sea charts and ample breakfasts. Rooms have phones and TV.

Terrasur (☎ 247-114; www.hostalterrasur.cl; O'Higgins 123; s/d US$42/58) Plush, with well-appointed

rooms in floral themes, a small flower-filled courtyard and relaxing spaces.

Eating & Drinking

Lomit's (José Menéndez 722; sandwiches US$3-5) The griddle holds center court in this bustling neon café where the locals down *shop Fanta* (orange soda and beer) and foreigners bellow at their home football teams on the tube.

La Carioca (José Menéndez 600; mains US$4-8) The downtown stop for pizza, with good-value daily lunch specials.

La Marmita (Sampaio 678; mains US$5-10; 🕑 lunch & dinner) This place offers a delightful dining experience: everything from the steak with Carmenere sauce to the stuffed figs desert is prepared with care in a friendly kaleidoscope-color ambience.

El Mercado (Mejicana 617; mains US$5-10; 🕑 24hr) An institution of heaping seafood specialties, open all night for the postparty crowd.

Remezón (21 de Mayo 1469; mains US$6-12) Creative cooking with seafood centerpieces; try the salmon smoked with black tea. Have a *pisco sour* to start the night.

La Luna (O'Higgins 974; seafood pastas US$8-12) Lined with the world map and a precious wall of Chilean wines, this worldly stop offers great specials like king crab in addition to signature pastas.

Olijoe Pub (Errázuriz 970) For drinks, saddle up to swank leather booths in this ultra-Anglo pub.

La Taberna (Plaza Muñoz Gamero) Or you can drink here, a classic old-boys club tucked in the Sara Braun mansion.

El Madero (Bories 655) Warm up for clubbing here.

Pachamama (Magallanes 698) sells dried nuts and fruits. Large supermarkets in town include **Abugosh** (Bories 647) and **Cofrima** (Navarro & Balmaceda).

Entertainment

Kamikaze (Bories 655; cover US$5) At this dance club, downstairs from El Madero, you can cut it up with local 20- and 30-somethings.

Cine Estrella (Mejicana 777) Shows movies.

Shopping

Zona Franca (Zofri; 🕑 Mon-Sat) The duty-free zone, it offers heaps of electronics, outdoor gear, camera and film equipment. *Colectivos* shuttle back and forth from downtown throughout the day.

Getting There & Away

Check with Sernatur for bus and maritime schedules. *La Prensa Austral* newspaper lists transportation availability, contact details and schedules.

AIR

Aeropuerto Presidente Carlos Ibáñez del Campo is 20km north of town. **Lan** (☎ 600-526-2000; www.lan.com; Bories 884) flies at least four times daily to Santiago (US$152, 4¼ hours) via Puerto Montt (US$105, 2¼ hours) and on Saturday to the Falkland Islands/Islas Malvinas (US$580 round-trip). Weekly *promociones* (specials) are advertised online; released every Tuesday, they go fast. **Aerolíneas Argentinas** (☎ 02-210-9000; Pedro Montt 969) arranges flights within Argentina. **Aerovías DAP** (☎ 223-340; www.dap.cl; O'Higgins 891) flies to/from Porvenir (US$23, 20 minutes) twice daily except Sunday; Puerto Williams on Isla Navarino (US$82, 1¼ hours) several times a week; Ushuaia (US$82, one hour) on Tuesday and Friday. Luggage is limited to 10kg per person. **Sky Airline** (☎ 710-645; www.skyairline.cl; Roca btwn Lautaro Navarro & O'Higgins) flies to Santiago and Puerto Montt.

BOAT

Transbordadora Austral Broom (☎ 218-100; www .tabsa.cl; Av Bulnes 05075) sails to Porvenir, Tierra del Fuego (US$7, 2½ to four hours), from the Tres Puentes ferry terminal (*colectivos* leave from Palacio Mauricio Braun). A faster way to get to Tierra del Fuego (US$2, 20 minutes) is via the Punta Delgada–Bahía Azul crossing northeast of Punta Arenas. Ferries leave every 90 minutes from 8:30am to 10:15pm. Call ahead for vehicle reservations (US$18).

Broom also runs the ferry *Patagonia*, which sails from Tres Puentes to Puerto Williams, Isla Navarino, two or three times a month, Wednesday only, returning Friday (US$150 to US$180 including meals, 38 hours). This tour through the Beagle Channel offers incredible scenery and a chance to see occasional dolphins or whales. Paying extra for a bunk is advisable.

BUS

Bus Transfer departs (US$3) throughout the day to coincide with flight schedules. **Turismo Sandy Point** (☎ 222-241; Pedro Montt 840) runs door-to-door shuttle service (US$4.50) to/from the city center. DAP runs its own shuttle service

(US$2). Puerto Natales–bound travelers can take buses directly from the airport.

Punta Arenas has no central bus terminal. Only one bus goes daily to Ushuaia, it's imperative to nab reservations one week in advance. It may be cheaper and easier to go to Río Grande and hop on *micros* heading to Ushuaia. Companies and destinations include the following:

Bus Sur (José Menéndez 552) Puerto Natales, Coyhaique, Puerto Montt, Ushuaia.
Bus Transfer (Pedro Montt 966) Puerto Natales, airport transfers.
Buses Fernández, Turíbus & Buses Pingüino (Armando Sanhueza 745) Puerto Natales, Puerto Montt, Río Gallegos, Torres del Paine.
Buses Ghisoni & Queilen Bus (Lautaro Navarro 975) Río Gallegos, Río Grande, Ushuaia, Coyhaique, Puerto Montt.
Buses Pacheco (www.busespacheco.com; Av Colón 900) Puerto Natales, Río Grande, Río Gallegos, Ushuaia, Puerto Montt.
Central de Transportes de Pasajeros (cnr Magallanes & Av Colón) All destinations.

Destination	Duration (hr)	Cost (US$)
Coyhaique	20-22	45-50
El Calafate	8-11	25-37
Puerto Montt	30-36	50-59
Puerto Natales	3-4	5-7
Río Gallegos	5-8	12-15
Río Grande	8-9	18-20
Ushuaia	12-14	30-36

Getting Around

Colectivos (US50¢, more at night and Sunday) zip around town; catch northbound ones on Av Magallanes or Av España and southbound along Bories or Av España.

Adel Rent a Car (☎ 235-471; www.adelrentacar .cl; Pedro Montt 962) provides attentive service, competitive rates and travel tips. You can also try **Lubag** (☎ 242-023; Magallanes 970). All agencies can arrange papers for crossing into Argentina. The **Automóvil Club de Chile** (☎ 243-675; O'Higgins 931) offers travel assistance to drivers.

PUERTO NATALES

☎ 061 / pop 18,000

A pastel wash of corrugated-tin houses shoulder to shoulder, this once-dull fishing port on Seno Última Esperanza has become a clattering hub of Gore-tex clad travelers headed to the continent's number-one national park.

CHILE

Information

Most banks have ATMs.

Banco del Estado (Plaza de Armas) Changes cash.

Conaf (☎ 411-438; O'Higgins 584) Has an administrative office here.

CyberCafe (Blanco Encalada 226; per hr US$1; ☼ 9am-9pm) Get online here.

Entel (Baquedano 270)

Hospital (☎ 411-533; O'Higgins & Ignacio Carrera Pinto)

Municipal tourist office (☎ 411-263; Manuel Bulnes 285) In the museum; offers useful listings.

Post office (Eberhard 429)

Redfarma (Arturo Prat 158) A good pharmacy.

Sernatur (☎ 412-125; Costanera Pedro Montt) This place offers information but is less helpful than the tourist office.

Servilaundry (Manuel Bulnes 513; per load US$4) Offers laundry service, as do many hostels.

Stop Cambios (Baquedano 386) Changes cash.

Sights & Activities

For a little context, the small **Museo Historico** (☎ 411-263; Manuel Bulnes 285; admission free; ☼ 8:30am-12:30pm & 2:30-6pm Tue-Sun) has artifacts from Yagan and Tehuelche cultures and colonists in well-marked displays.

Warm up for the big expedition on **Mirador Dorotea**, a rocky headland less than 10km from Natales off Ruta 9. A sign at lot 14 marks the way to the lookout. The hiking trail passes through a *lenga* forest and provides fantastic views of the glacial valley and surrounding peaks at the end.

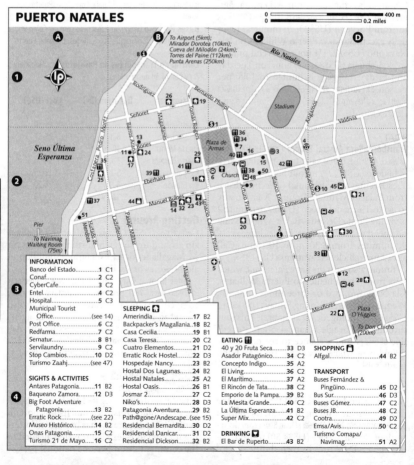

PUERTO NATALES

To Airport (5km);
Mirador Dorotea (10km);
Cueva del Milodón (24km);
Torres del Paine (112km);
Punta Arenas (250km)

Tours

English-speaking tour agencies for the active include **Antares Patagonia** (☎ 414-611; www .antarespatagonia.com; Barros Arana 111) and **Erratic Rock** (☎ 411-472; www.erraticrock.com; Erratic Rock Hostel, Baquedano 719). For more adventure outfitters, see p524.

Sleeping

Beds abound, but the best selection fills up fast in high season, so call to reserve. Rates tumble off-season.

Hospedaje Nancy (☎ 411-186; Manuel Bulnes 343; s/d US$10/16) Lived-in but well kept, with an incredibly sweet matron at the helm.

Erratic Rock Hostel (☎ 411-472; www.erraticrock .com; Baquedano 719; dm/s/d incl breakfast US$12/16/32; ▯) A shabby-chic climbers haunt with the best customer service in town, as well as a movie library, cowboy coffee and American breakfasts.

Patagonia Aventura (☎ 411-028; Tomás Rogers 179; dm/d US$12/29; ▯) Woodcarvings and comfy little rooms fill this all-service *hostal* with café breakfasts, a gear shop and trip assistance.

Residencial Bernardita (☎ 411-162; O'Higgins 765; r per person US$14) This place has immaculately kept corrugated-tin rooms, tea and coffee service and kitchen use.

Casa Cecilia (☎ 411-797; Tomás Rogers 64; s/d incl breakfast US$15/21) Clean and central, Cecilia offers cramped but pleasant rooms in a toasty home with breakfast with homemade bread, hot showers and camping rentals.

Hostal Dos Lagunas (☎ 415-733; Barros Arana 104; r per person US$18) A warm and hospitable wooden home with oversized rooms, kitchen breakfasts and loads of travel tips.

Hostal Natales (☎ 410-081; www.hostalnatales.cl; Ladrilleros 209 dm/d US$20/59; ▯) Lime green and spanking new, this relatively quiet *hostal* boasts tasteful and toasty rooms, all with private bathroom.

Hostal Oasis (☎ 411-675; Señoret 332; s/d incl breakfast US$20/29) Snug and slightly chintzy with friendly service, breakfast and fluffy bedding.

Amerindia (☎ 411-945; Barros Arana 135; r per person incl breakfast US$20; ▯) Funky and functional, quiet Amerindia brims with arty and retro touches. There's a lovely bathroom, self-serve breakfast, patio for drying tents and free internet and cable TV.

Cuatro Elementos (☎ 415-751; www.4elementos.cl; Esmeralda 813; dm/s/d incl breakfast US$20/29/60) A simple, ecofriendly guest space crafted by a mountain guide who has tenderly recycled zinc, driftwood and old woodstoves for precious results. The fresh baked bread and luxuriant attentions convince you to stay on.

Also recommended are these clean and serviceable options:

Josmar 2 (☎ 414-417; Esmeralda 517; camping US$4, dm US$6)

Casa Teresa (☎ 410-472; Esmeralda 483; dm incl breakfast US$7)

Residencial Danicar (☎ 412-170; O'Higgins 707; dm/s US$8/10; ✖)

Backpacker's Magallania (☎ 414-950; Tomás Rogers 255; dm/d incl breakfast US$10/28)

Residencial Dickson (☎ 411-871; Bulnes 307; r per person incl breakfast US$12)

Niko's (☎ 412-810; Ramírez 669; r per person US$12)

Eating & Drinking

40 y 20 Fruta Seca (☎ 210-661; Baquedano 443) Shoppers can hit this place for dried fruits and nuts perfect for the trail.

Super Mix (☎ 210-661; Baquedano 443) Sells groceries for self-catering.

Emporio de la Pampa (Eberhard btwn Magallanes & Barros Arana; snacks US$3-9) Slip into this skinny, cask-lined nook for Chilean wine and cheese or coffee and delicious baked goods.

El Rincón de Tata (Arturo Prat 236; mains US$4-10) Sandwiches and Chilean classics are served in this smoky, well-worn atmosphere.

El Living (Arturo Prat 156; mains US$6) A gringo den whose exotic and vegan-friendly offerings aren't as tasty as they sound. Still, where else can you read German magazines and drink real coffee?

Concepto Indigo (Ladrilleros 105; mains US$5-9) Wind down in this comfortable café stuck right on the sound with an excellent selection of wine and hearty fare.

El Marítimo (Costanera Pedro Montt 214; mains US$5-10) Unfussy fish and seafood platters served with a view of the sound.

La Última Esperanza (Eberhard 354; mains US$5-15) White linen tablecloths and exquisite seafood plates served with potent *pisco sours*.

La Mesita Grande (Arturo Prat 196; pizzas US$14) A converted wool shop with one long worn table as its centerpiece. Travelers mix and feast on heavenly thin-crust pizzas with toppings like spinach and cured ham or lemon-spiked salmon.

Asador Patagónico (Arturo Prat 158; dinner for 2 people US$35; ☽ lunch & dinner) Sides of meat are flame-seared before your eyes in this fancy restaurant for mastedon appetites.

CHILE

El Bar de Ruperto (cnr Manuel Bulnes & Magallanes; 🖳) Foosball, chess and Guinness help you forget you're so far from home.

Shopping

Alfgal (Barros Arana 249) Sells camping supplies.

Getting There & Away

BOAT

Weather and tidal conditions affect ferry arrival dates. To confirm travel with Navimag's *Magallanes* (Puerto Montt–Punta Arenas) contact **Turismo Comapa** (☎ 414-300; www.comapa.com; Manuel Bulnes 533). See p503 for rate information.

BUS

Puerto Natales has no central bus terminal. Book way ahead in high season, especially for am departures. Carriers include **Buses Fernández & Pingüino** (www.busesfernandez.com; Eberhard 399), **Bus Sur** (www.bus-sur.cl; Baquedano 558), **Buses JB** (Arturo Prat 258), **Turismo Zaahj** (www.turismozaahj.co.cl in Spanish; Arturo Prat 236) and **Buses Gómez** (www.busesgomez.com; Arturo Prat 234). Service is limited off-season.

To Torres del Paine, buses leave two to three times daily at around 7am, 8am and 2:30pm. If you're heading to Mountain Lodge Paine Grande in the off-season, take the morning bus (US$10 round-trip, two hours) to meet the catamaran (US$12.50 one way, US$20 round-trip, two hours).

To Punta Arenas (US$6 to US$7, three hours), Buses Fernández is the best, but also try Bus Sur. Look for direct airport buses.

To Río Gallegos, Argentina (US$12, four hours), Bus Sur leaves Tuesday and Thursday; El Pingüino, at the Fernández terminal, goes at 11am Wednesday and Sunday.

To El Calafate, Argentina (US$20 to US$30, 5½ hours), Zaahj, Cootra (also serving Río Turbio) and Bus Sur have the most service.

To travel to Coyhaique (US$60, 22 hours) take Bus Sur.

Getting Around

Try **Emsa/Avis** (☎ 241-182; Manuel Bulnes 632) for car rentals, though rates are better in Punta Arenas.

PARQUE NACIONAL TORRES DEL PAINE

These 3000m granite spires are a globetrotter's Kubla Khan. The Torres are a day's walk from the nearest bus, but the park's diverse land-scapes require a full pilgrimage (preferably with needlessly heavy packs) through steppe and southern beech forest, over dangling footbridges and past creeping glaciers. Torres del Paine (2800m), Paine Grande (3050m) and Los Cuernos (2200m to 2600m) are the poster boys of this 181,000-hectare Unesco Biosphere Reserve. Most hike the circuit or the 'W' to soak in these classic panoramas, leaving other perfectly marvelous trails deserted. You can further avoid the masses by visiting in November or March to April. Sudden rainstorms and knock-down gusts are part of the hearty initiation. Bring waterproof gear, a synthetic sleeping bag, and, if you're camping, a good tent. In 2005 a hiker burned down 10% of the park using a portable stove in windy conditions. Sloppy camping has consequences. Be conscientious and tread lightly – you are one of 200,000 yearly guests.

Orientation & Information

Parque Nacional Torres del Paine is 112km north of Puerto Natales via a decent but sometimes bumpy gravel road. At Villa Cerro Castillo there is a seasonal border crossing into Argentina at Cancha Carrera. The road continues 40km north and west to **Portería Sarmiento** (admission US$17, paid in pesos Chilenos), the main entrance where user fees are collected. It's another 37km to the *administración* (park headquarters) and the **Conaf Centro de Visitantes** (🕘 9am-8pm in summer), with good information on park ecology and trail status.

The park is open year-round, subject to your ability to get there. Visitor flow is edging toward regulation, but not there yet. Internet resources include www.torresdelpaine.com and *hostal* website www.erraticrock.com, with a good backpacker equipment list.

Activities

HIKING

Doing the circuit (the 'W' plus the backside of the peaks) requires seven to nine days, while the 'W' takes four to five. Add another day or two for transportation connections. Most trekkers start either route from Laguna Amarga and head west. You can also hike from the *administración* or take the catamaran from Pudeto to Lago Pehoé and start from there (see p526); hiking roughly southwest to northeast along the 'W' presents more views of Los Cuernos. Trekking alone, especially on the backside of the circuit, is inadvisable and restricted by Conaf.

The 'W'

The trail to **Mirador Las Torres** is relatively easy, except for the last hour's scramble up boulders. The trail to Refugio Los Cuernos is the most windy along the W. **Valle Frances** is not to be missed. Plan time to get all the way to the lookout at Campamento Británico. From Valle Frances to Lago Pehoé can get windy, but is relatively easy. The stretch to **Lago Grey** is moderate, with some steep parts. The glacier lookout is another half-hour past the *refugio*.

The Circuit

The landscape along the backside of the peaks is a lot more desolate yet still beautiful. Paso John Garner (the most extreme part of the trek) sometimes offers knee-deep mud and snow. There's one basic *refugio* at Los Perros, the rest is rustic camping. Factor four to six hours between each camp.

Other Trails

Abandoning the beaten path rewards with solitude and new discoveries. From the Laguna Amarga Guardería, a four-hour hike leads through barren land to **Laguna Azul**. Camp on the northeastern shore. Another two hours north the trail reaches Lago Paine. From *administración*, the three-hour hike to Mountain Lodge Paine Grande is an easy, level trail with fantastic views. A truly remote four-hour trail from Guadería Lago Grey follows Río Pingo to the former site of Refugio Zapata.

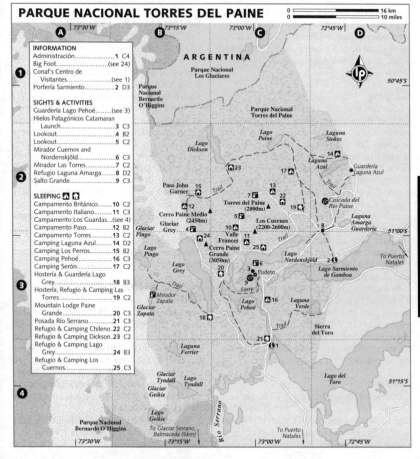

PARQUE NACIONAL TORRES DEL PAINE

0   16 km
0   10 miles

INFORMATION
Administración.......................1 C4
Big Foot................................(see 24)
Conaf's Centro de
   Visitantes........................(see 1)
Portería Sarmiento................2 D3

SIGHTS & ACTIVITIES
Guardería Lago Pehoé.........(see 3)
Hielos Patagónicos Catamaran
   Launch...............................3 C3
Lookout..................................4 B2
Lookout..................................5 C2
Mirador Cuernos and
   Nordenskjöld......................6 C3
Mirador Las Torres.................7 C2
Refugio Laguna Amarga........8 D2
Salto Grande..........................9 C3

SLEEPING
Campamento Británico........10 C2
Campamento Italiano...........11 C3
Campamento Los Guardas...(see 4)
Campamento Paso................12 B2
Campamento Torres.............13 C2
Camping Laguna Azul...........14 D2
Camping Los Perros..............15 B2
Camping Pehoé.....................16 C3
Camping Serón.....................17 C2
Hostería & Guardería Lago
   Grey....................................18 B3
Hostería, Refugio & Camping Las
   Torres.................................19 C2
Mountain Lodge Paine
   Grande...............................20 C3
Posada Río Serrano..............21 C3
Refugio & Camping Chileno..22 C2
Refugio & Camping Dickson..23 C2
Refugio & Camping Lago
   Grey....................................24 B3
Refugio & Camping Los
   Cuernos..............................25 C3

ARGENTINA

Parque Nacional
Los Glaciares

Parque Nacional
Bernardo
O'Higgins

Parque Nacional
Torres del Paine

Lago
Dickson

Lago
Paine

Laguna
Stokes

Laguna
Azul

Guardería
Laguna Azul

Paso John
Garner

Cerro Paine Medio
(2450m)

Torres del Paine
(2800m)

Cascada del
Río Paine

Laguna
Amarga
Guardería

Glaciar
Grey

Glaciar
Pingo

Cerro Paine
Grande
(3050m)

Los Cuernos
(2200-2600m)

Valle
Frances

Lago
Pingo

Lago
Grey

Lago
Nordenskjöld

Lago Sarmiento
de Gamboa

To Puerto
Natales

Pudeto

Mirador
Zapata

Glaciar
Zapata

Lago
Pehoé

Laguna
Verde

Ferry

Laguna
Ferrier

Sierra
del Toro

Glaciar
Tyndall

Lago
Tyndall

Glaciar
Geikie

Lago del
Toro

Lago
Geikie

Parque Nacional
Bernardo O'Higgins

To Glaciar Serrano,
Balmaceda (6km)

To Puerto
Natales

73°30'W   73°15'W   73°00'W   72°45'W

50°45'S

51°00'S

51°15'S

CHILE

Continue about another 1½ to two hours to a lookout over **Glaciar Zapata**.

GLACIER TREKKING & KAYAKING
Big Foot Adventure Patagonia (☎ 061-414-611; www .bigfootpatagonia.com; Bories 206, Puerto Natales) leads ice hikes (US$75) on Glaciar Grey. Paddle your way out of the park with Big Foot and **Onas Patagonia** (☎ 061-412-707; Eberhard 599, Puerto Natales). Its two- to three-day kayaking trips down Río Serrano aren't budget travel, but offer a unique way to experience the park.

HORSE-RIDING
Due to property divisions within the park, horses cannot cross between the western sections (Lagos Grey and Pehoé, Río Serrano) and the eastern part managed by Hostería Las Torres (Refugio Los Cuernos is the approximate cut-off). **Baqueano Zamora** (☎ 061-413-953; www.baqueanozamora.com; Baquedano 534, Puerto Natales) runs excursions to Lagos Pingo, Paine and Azul, and Laguna Amarga (half day US$55, lunch included).

Sleeping
Make reservations! Arriving at the park without them, especially in the high season, enslaves you to make camp in the few free options. Travel agencies offer reservations, but it's best to go directly through the concessions. **Path@gone/Andescape** (☎ 061-413-290; www .pathagone.com; Eberhard 595, Puerto Natales) manages Lagos Grey and Dickson. **Vertices Patagonia** (☎ 061-412-742; www.verticepatagonia.cl) owns and runs Mountain Lodge Paine Grande. **Fantastico Sur** (☎ 061-710-050; www.fantasticosur.com; Magallanes 960, Punta Arenas; admission US80¢; ◷ 9am-5pm Mon-Fri, 10:30am-1:30pm & 3-5pm Sat & Sun) owns Torres, Chileno and Los Cuernos, and Serón *refugios* and campgrounds.

Some *refugios* may require photo ID (ie a passport) upon check-in. Photocopy your tourist card and passport for all lodgings in advance to expedite check-in. Staff can radio ahead to confirm your next reservation. Given the huge volume of trekkers, snags are inevitable, so practice your Zen composure.

CAMPING
Camping at the *refugios* costs US$6 per site. *Refugios* rent equipment – tent (US$11 per night), sleeping bag (US$6), mat (US$3) and stove (US$5) – but potential shortages in high season make it prudent to pack your own gear.

Small kiosks sell expensive pasta, soup packets and butane gas. Sites administered by Conaf are free and very basic. Many campers have reported wildlife (in rodent form) lurking around campsites; don't leave food in packs or in tents, instead hang it from a tree.

REFUGIOS
Refugio rooms have four to eight bunk beds each, kitchen privileges (for lodgers and during specific hours only), hot showers and meals. A bed costs US$17 to US$30, sleeping-bag rental US$7, meals US$7 to US$12. Should the *refugio* be overbooked, staff provide all necessary camping equipment. Most *refugios* close by the end of April. Mountain Lodge Paine Grande is the only one that stays open year-round, but it has very limited operations.

Getting There & Away
For details of transportation to the park, see p524) in Puerto Natales. Going to El Calafate from the park on the same day requires joining a tour or careful advance planning, since there is no direct service. Your best bet is to return to Puerto Natales.

Buses drop off and pick up passengers at Laguna Amarga, the Hielos Patagónicos catamaran launch at Pudeto and at park headquarters. The catamaran leaves Pudeto for Lago Pehoé (one way/round-trip per person US$18/32) at 9:30am, noon and 6pm December to mid-March, noon and 6pm in late March and November, and at noon only in September, October and April. Another launch travels Lago Grey between **Hostería Lago Grey** (☎ 061-225-986; www.austrohoteles.cl) and Refugio Lago Grey (US$30 one way, 1½ to two hours) a couple of times daily; contact the *hostería* for the current schedule.

PARQUE NACIONAL BERNARDO O'HIGGINS
Virtually inaccessible, O'Higgins remains the elusive and exclusive home of glaciers and waterfowl. The national park can only be entered by boat. Full-day boat excursions (US$60) to the base of Glaciar Serrano are run by **Turismo 21 de Mayo** (☎ 061-411-978; www .turismo21demayo.cl in Spanish; Eberhard 560, Puerto Natales) and **Path@gone** (☎ 061-413-290; www.pathagone.com; Eberhard 595, Puerto Natales).

You can access Torres del Paine via boat to Glaciar Serrano. Passengers transfer to a Zodiac (a rubber boat with a motor), stop for lunch at Estancia Balmaceda (US$15) and continue up Río Serrano, arriving at the southern border of the park by 5pm. The same tour can be done leaving the park, but may require camping near Río Serrano to catch the Zodiac at 9am. The trip costs US$90 from Turismo 21 de Mayo or **Onas Patagonia** (☎ 061-413-290; www .pathagone.com; Eberhard 595, Puerto Natales).

TIERRA DEL FUEGO

Smoldering blazes from Yagan camps dotting the shore made Magellan baptize these islands Land of Fire. A wedge of mountains, lakes and steppe, it was once home to great herds of roaming guanaco and over four thousand indigenous Yagan, Huash, Alacaluf and Selk'nam. Newcomers transformed it. Missionaries brought 'civilized' ways. Gold-rush opportunists arrived seeking quick riches. Ambitious herders from Croatia and Chiloé came in search of *estancia* work. Extreme weather and isolation cornered many of them into starvation and disaster, and others sped the massacre of native peoples. Still a stronghold of sheep ranches, present-day Tierra del Fuego has found one more treasure to exploit – natural gas. With Chile's half not nearly as accessible as Argentina's, there's even greater reason to slip off to these parts largely unknown.

Porvenir

☎ 061 / pop 5000

Chile's largest settlement on Tierra del Fuego, Porvenir is most often visited as a day trip from Punta Arenas, but this usually means spending only a couple of hours in town and more time than a belly might wish crossing the choppy strait. The **tourist office** (Padre Mario Zavattaro 402) is upstairs from the intriguing **Museo de Tierra del Fuego** (Plaza de Armas), a curious collection of Selk'nam mummies and skulls, musical instruments used by the mission natives on Isla Dawson, and an exhibit on early Chilean cinematography.

Cordillera Darwin Expediciones (☎ 580-747, 099-640-7204; www.cordilleradarwin.com; Av Manuel Señoret 512) organizes excursions to see Peale's dolphins (US$85, including meals), plus some well-recommended longer, all-inclusive kayaking, camping and horse-riding trips. Call to arrange pick up from San Sebastián.

For a mild adventure (the heating system's creative) stay at **Residencial Colón** (☎ 581-157; Damián Riobó 198; r per person US$7) or, better yet, **Hotel**

España (☎ 580-160; Croacia 698; s/d US$9/11), with comfortable beds in sprawling, sunny rooms. For a meal, **El Chispa** (cnr Viel & Señoret; breakfast US$1.50-3, lunch US$5-7) cooks up hearty seafood, and **Club Croata** (Av Manuel Señoret 542; mains US$4-8) is the next best thing to Zagreb.

Transbordadora Broom (☎ 580-089) operates the auto-passenger ferry *Melinka* to Punta Arenas (US$7 per person, US$45 per vehicle, 2½ to four hours) at 2pm Tuesday through Saturday, and at 5pm Sunday and holidays. **Aerovías DAP** (☎ 580-089; www.dap.cl; Av Manuel Señoret) flies to Punta Arenas (US$23) twice daily, except Sunday. Winter schedules can be limited.

Isla Navarino

Forget Ushuaia, the end of the world starts where colts roam Main St and yachts rounding Cape Horn take refuge. With over 150km of trails, Isla Navarino is a rugged backpackers' paradise, with remote slate-colored lakes, mossy *lenga* forests and the ragged spires of the **Dientes de Navarino**. Some 40,000 beavers introduced from Canada in the 1940s now plague the island; it's even on the menu, if you can find an open restaurant. The only town, **Puerto Williams** (population 2250), is a naval settlement, official port of entry for vessels en route to Cape Horn and Antarctica, and home to the last living Yagan speaker.

INFORMATION

With the information kiosk perpetually closed, head to **Akainij** (☎ 061-621-173; Central Comercial Sur 156) travel agency, which also has internet, or **Turismo SIM** (☎ 061-621-150; www.simltd .com; Ricardo Maragano 168) for tours and Zodiac transfers to Ushuaia. **Fueguia** (☎ 061-621-251; Prado 245) has recommended French-speaking guiding of the trekking circuits. Banco de Chile has an ATM.

SIGHTS & ACTIVITIES

Hiking to **Cerro Bandera** affords expansive views of the Beagle Channel. Start this four-hour round-trip at the Navarino Circuit. The trail ascends steeply through *lenga* to blustery stone-littered hilltops. Self-supported backpackers continue on for the whole four- to five-day **Dientes de Navarino** circuit, enjoying impossibly raw and windswept vistas under Navarino's toothy spires. The world's southernmost ethnobotanical park, **Omora** (www.omora.org) offers trails with labeled flora: go right after the **Virgen**, 4km toward Puerto

CHILE

Navarino. Tiny **Museo Martín Gusinde** (☎ 061-621-043; cnr Araguay & Gusinde; donation requested; ☺ 9am-1pm & 2:30-7pm Mon-Fri, 2:30-6:30pm Sat & Sun) honors the German priest and ethnographer who worked among the Yagans from 1918–23. A ten minute walk east of town along the coast brings you to **Villa Ukika**, the last Yagan settlement. There's a *hostal* and **Kipa-Akar** (House of Woman), a modest craft shop selling language books and whale-bone knives and jewelry. Ask a villager for help if it's closed.

SLEEPING

Residencial Pusaki (☎ 061-621-116; Piloto Pardo 242; s/d incl breakfast US$19/21) What's not to love? Under Pati's care you're more cousin-on-holiday than stranger after tagging along to barbecues or pitching in for informal dinners. Rooms are well cared for, with shared bathroom and kitchen privileges.

Hostal Lajuwa (☎ 061-621-267; Villa Ukika; dm incl breakfast US$20) Immaculate dorm-style rooms in the Yagan community.

Hostal Coirón (☎ 061-621-227; www.hostalcoiron .cl; Ricardo Maragano 168; s/d incl breakfast US$35/49) A tasteful guesthouse with a sun-speckled living room and kitchen privileges. The plump mattresses utter nary a sigh under weary and well-traveled bones.

Eating & Drinking

Dientes de Navarino (plaza; mains US$5) Autochthonous Williams, serving seafood platters, *combinados* (*pisco* and colas) and box wine.

Club de Yates Micalvi (beer US$4; ☺ open late, closed Jun-Aug) Welcome aboard the *Micalvi*, a grounded German cargo boat declared a regional naval museum in 1976. It ended up a floating bar, its tilted floors filled with navy men and yachties spinning yarns and downing whiskey and Cokes.

GETTING THERE & AWAY

Aerovías DAP (☎ 061-621-051; Centro Comercial) flies to Punta Arenas (US$82) several times a week. Seats are limited and advance reservations are essential. Transbordador Austral Broom ferry *Patagonia* sails from Tres Puentes to Punta Arenas two or three times a month on Fridays (US$150 to US$180 including meals, 38 hours). Zodiac boats head to Ushuaia daily from September to March. Book with Akainij. The 25-minute trip is US$100 one way. Private yachts making the trip can be found at the Club de Yates.

ISLA ROBINSON CRUSOE

Castaway Alexander Selkirk whittled away years on this craggy Pacific outpost. In spite of its literary fame, this island 670km off the coast of Valparaíso has maintained relative anonymity. Discovered in 1574, Archipiélago Juan Fernández sheltered sealers and pirates for over two centuries, including the British corsairs from whom Selkirk escaped. While Spain founded San Juan Bautista in 1750, the village had no permanent presence until 1877. It garnered world attention when the British Navy sank the *Dresden* in Cumberland Bay during WWI.

The jagged geography of this island (22km long and 7km wide) translates to erratic weather. Prepare for warm to cool temperatures (averaging 22°C) in the rainy season from April to September. A Unesco World Biosphere Reserve and national park since 1935, the island's extraordinary vegetation has affinities ranging from Andean to Hawaiian. Endemic plants have paid dearly for the introduction of mainland species, including the goats that Selkirk supped on. Look for the Juan Fernández fur seal, nearly extinct a century ago, its population now around 9000. With luck you'll glimpse the rare Juan Fernández hummingbird; the male is a garish red.

SAN JUAN BAUTISTA

☎ 032 / pop 600

Sheltered by steep peaks and surrounded by horse pastures, the lobster-fishing community of San Juan Bautista overlooks Bahía Cumberland. The island's sole town, it offers US$20 lobsters off the dock and a glimpse of an isolated life, where secondary-school kids choose between fishing and education some 700km away. There are no ATMs or money changers, so bring cash from the mainland, preferably in small bills. **Centro Información Turista** (Vicente González) is at the top of Vicente González, 500m inland from the *costanera*.

Sights & Activities

In San Juan Bautista travelers can explore a treasure trove of nautical lore, starting at the **cementerio** near the lighthouse, where a polyglot assortment of Spanish, French and German inhabitants are buried, including the survivors of the WWI battleship

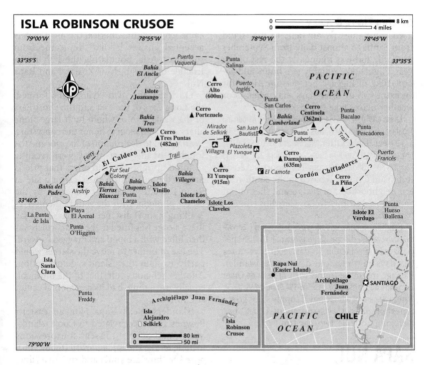

ISLA ROBINSON CRUSOE

Dresden. **Cuevas de los Patriotas** are the damp caverns where 40-plus patriots from Chile's independence movement lived imprisoned for several years after a defeat at Rancagua in 1814. Directly above the caves is **Fuerte Santa Bárbara**, built by the Spaniards in 1749 to discourage pirate raids. The fantastic island-wide **national park** (admission for 7 days US$5) is the island's unburied treasure. Its most fragile areas have restricted use; arrange with registered local guides for access (at the kiosk near the plaza). You can hike on your own 3km to **Mirador de Selkirk**, a spectacular panoramic viewpoint where the castaway scoured the horizon for ships. The trail continues south, taking one hour to reach **Villagra** (4.8km) and skirts the cliffs to **Punta La Isla** (13km). Both areas have camping. On the way you'll pass **Bahía Tierras Blancas**, the island's main breeding colony of Juan Fernández fur seals.

Sleeping & Eating

Rates cannily reflect that you are, in fact, stranded in the middle of the Pacific. Camping offers the best bet for budget travelers (but keep in mind airlines' strict baggage limits). *Hospedajes* cook up a storm.

Camping Los Cañones (Vincente González; camping per person US$2) Just above the *costanera*; has rocky sites and cold showers.

Camping Elector (☎ 751-066; campsites US$5) Offers better spots amid shrubbery and flowers. Outside of town en route to Plazoleta El Yunqu e, the campground has bathrooms, a BBQ and an inside kitchen.

Residencial Mirador Selkirk (☎ 751-028; Pasaje del Castillo 251; d US$26-43) A comfortable family home with views and island cuisine (mains US$4 to US$8).

Refugio Náutico (☎ 751-077; www.islarobinson crusoe.cl in Spanish; Carrera Pinto 280; s/d US$51/86; 🖳) This *refugio* offers bright, spacious rooms, woodland views, books and music, and excursion connections.

El Remo (☎ 751-030; plaza; mains US$3-6) For sandwiches and evening cocktails, including *murtillado*, a rum-infused berry drink.

Aldea Daniel Defoe (☎ 751-223; Alcalde 449; mains US$8-11) Offers a winning, salty-dog character alongside lobster crêpes and a few Peruvian and Mexican specialties.

Getting There & Away

Two companies fly air taxis to the island from Santiago almost daily from September to April, and less frequently the rest of the year. Flights take roughly two hours and accept 10kg of luggage per person. Allow for an extra two or three days' stay when poor weather makes take-offs risky.

Lassa (☎ 02-273-4354; lassa@entelchile.net; Aeródromo Tobalaba, Av Larraín 7941) has the most flights, in a 19-seat Twin Otter. **Aeromet** (☎ 02-538-0267; reserves@tairc.cl; San Juan Bautista La Pólvora 226; Santiago Pajaritos 3030, Oficina 604), aka Transportes Aéreos Robinson Crusoe, is based in the southwestern neighborhood of Maipú and flies out of Santiago's Aeropuerto Los Cerrillos (round-trip US$542).

English-speaking **Vaikava Expediciones** (☎ 592-852; www.vaikava.cl in Spanish; per person daily US$200) specializes in spectacular 10-day yacht adventures (six days en route, four days on the islands). Passage might be found with **Armada de Chile: Comando de Transporte** (☎ 506-354; Primera Zona Naval, Prat 620, Valparaíso) whose naval supply ships go six times annually. Costs run about US$40 per day, for a no-frills, two-day trip.

RAPA NUI (EASTER ISLAND)

Far from continents, this isolated world of wonders is a fun house of archaeology, an eerie landscape of cultural clues to mysteries that resist easy explanation. Its landscape of enigmatic statues *(moai)* overshadows subtler assets like crystalline surf, wild horses and grass-sculpted landscapes. Known as *Te Pito o Te Henua* (the Navel of the World) by its inhabitants, tiny Polynesian Rapa Nui (117 sq km) is entirely off the map for most South American trekkers, but those who stretch to go the distance rarely regret it.

The first European to set foot on the island was Dutch admiral Roddeveen and his timing (Easter Sunday, 1722) sealed its moniker. After becoming Chilean territory in 1888 it became known as Isla de Pascua. It is 1900km east of even punier Pitcairn, the nearest populated landmass, and 3700km west of South America.

How such an isolated island became inhabited has long stumped historians and archaeologists. While Thor Heyerdahl's *Kon Tiki* expedition theorized that Polynesians came from South America, the most widely accepted answer is that they came from southeast Asia, populating the Polynesian triangle of Hawaii, New Zealand and Rapa Nui.

On Rapa Nui, two civilizations formed: the Long Ears of the east and the Short Ears of the west, both of whom built large stone altars, *ahu,* and *moai* to honor their ancestors. Warfare led to destruction of the *ahu* and the toppling of the *moai* (many were recently restored upright). Legend offers that priests moved the *moai* from their carving site at Rano Raraku volcano to the coast by the power of *mana,* with the statues themselves 'walking' a short distance each day. Most say that a sledge was fitted to the *moai,* which was then lifted with a bipod and dragged forward. The use of timber to move the statues would partly explain the island's deforestation. Another religious cult, that of the birdman, equally intriguing, had its ceremonial center at Orongo.

Islanders speak Rapa Nui, an eastern Polynesian dialect related to Cook Islands' Maori, and Spanish. Essential expressions include *iorana* (hello), *maururu* (thank you), *pehe koe* (how are you?) and *riva riva* (fine, good).

For a fortnight in February island culture is celebrated in the elaborate and colorful **Tapati Rapa Nui festival**. Peak tourist season (and hottest months) is January to March. Off-season it can sometimes feel deserted. Allow at least three days to see the major sites. Rapa Nui is two hours behind mainland Chile, six hours behind GMT (five in summer).

Steep drop-offs, sculpted seascapes, abundant marine life and absolutely crystalline water make for worthwhile diving. Surfers can revel in the big swells off the north and south coasts.

HANGA ROA

☎ 032 / pop 3800

Blue skies and peaceful, meandering streets paint the unhurried appeal of Hanga Roa. While it throbs with tourists in high season, the town has managed to maintain a leisurely pace. Though sprawling, town is easy to navigate. North–south Av Atamu Tekena is the main road, with a supermarket, shops, an arts fair and several eateries. Policarpo Toro is just below, along the waterfront. East–west Av Te

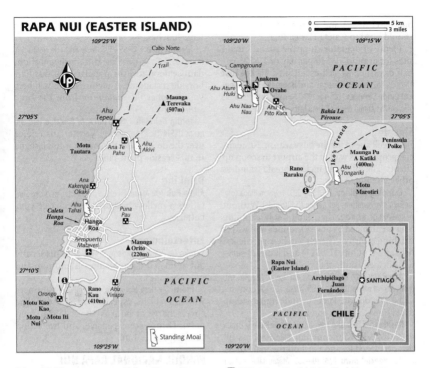

Pito o Te Henua connects Caleta Hanga Roa, a small bay and fishing port, to the church.

Information

Arms and legs are collecting at internet cafés, where a crazy US$6 or more an hour is charged. *Residenciales* usually provide laundry service. Most businesses, especially *residenciales* and rental agencies, prefer US cash.

Banco del Estado (Av Pont s/n; 8am-1pm Mon-Fri) Has an ATM for MasterCard only; Visa holders can get cash advances at the counter. US dollars may be changed but traveler's checks have a US$10 commission.

Conaf (100-236) On the road to Rano Kau; may give suggestions on hiking.

Entel (Av Tu'u Maheke s/n) Opposite Banco del Estado; expensive charges for calls home.

Hospital Hanga Roa (100-215; Av Simon Paoa s/n) One long block east of the church.

Isl@net (Av Atamu Tekena s/n; per hr US$6; 9:30am-10pm) Internet; near the main square.

Post office (Av Te Pito o Te Henua) Half a block from Caleta Hanga Roa.

RapaCall (Av Atamu Tekena s/n; per hr US$6;

Sernatur (100-255; Tu'u Maheke) Distributes basic maps of the island.

8:30am-9pm Mon-Fri, 3-8pm Sun) Internet; near the main square.

Dangers & Annoyances

Guard against petty thievery by leaving valuables at home or storing them in lock boxes at your lodgings. Sunblock, sunglasses, long-sleeved shirts and a hat are requisite battle gear for the strong sun.

Sights & Activities

Rapa Nui 101 for new arrivals, **Museo Antropológico Sebastián Englert** (551-020; Sector Tahai; admission US$2; 9:30am-12:30pm & 2-5:30pm Tue-Fri, 9:30am-12:30pm Sat & Sun), displays *moai kavakava* (the strange 'statues of ribs') and replica *rongo-rongo* tablets. Intricate wood carvings at **Iglesia Hanga Roa**, the island's Catholic church, fuse Rapa Nui tradition with Christian doctrine. There's also a very cool Sunday service in the Rapa Nui language.

Dive enthusiasts can head to **Orca Diving Center** (100-375; Caleta Hanga Roa; 1 dive US$50). Bring proof of certification. Next door, **Hare Orca** (550-375; Caleta Hanga Roa s/n) rents body boards (US$15) and surfboards. Beginners should head to Caleta Hanga Roa.

Plenty of operators tour the island's main sites for around US$40 per day or US$25 per half day, such as well-established **Kia Koe Tour** (☎ 100-852; Atamu Tekena s/n) and **Haumaka Archeological Guide Services** (☎ /fax 100-274; haumaka@entelchile .net; cnr Avs Atamu Tekena & Hotu Matua).

Sleeping

Book well ahead for the busy season. Residencial proprietors wait at the airport to scoop up clients. The following include breakfast unless otherwise noted.

Camping Mihinoa (☎ 551-593; www.mihinoa.com; Av Pont s/n; campsites per person US$10; 💻) Without a speck of shade, the island's sole camping area is enhanced by grassy grounds and waves crashing nearby. There's kitchen privileges, bike and tent hire (US$17) and laundry service. Located south of the center.

Ana Rapu (☎ 100-540; www.anarapu.cl; Av Apina s/n; campsites per person US$10, s/d US$20/30; 💻) A convivial budget option. Perks include horse-riding excursions, laundry and internet.

Residencial El Tauke (☎ 100-253; Av Te Pito o Te Henua s/n; s/d US$15/30) Mundane but clean rooms fill this privileged location just off the main drag.

Residencial Miru (☎ 100-365; Atamu Takena s/n; r US$15) This welcoming home has basic rooms and kitchen privileges. Breakfast is US$5.

Hostal Chez Oscar (☎ 551-261; chezoscar@123mail .cl; Av Pont s/n; s/d US$20/35) Rooms are cramped but a leafy garden and affable hosts perk up this find.

Residencial Chez Erika (☎ 100-474; Av Tuki Haka He Vari s/n; s/d US$25/35) Rooms are colorful and unfussy in this relaxed and tidy spot.

Hostal Aukara (☎ 100-539; aukara@entelchile.net; Av Pont s/n; s/d US$40/70) Rooms are tidy enough in this quaint location featuring a gallery filled with its proprietor's works. It's walking distance from the action.

Eating

Fresh juice and fish are the best offerings in an otherwise bland (and pricey) island diet.

Supermercado Kai Nene (Av Atamu Tekena s/n; 🕑 9am-1pm & 5-8pm Mon-Sat) For self-catering.

Tarapu (☎ 551-863; Av Atamu Tekena s/n; mains US$3; 🕑 9:30am-4pm Mon-Sat) Shoestringers embrace the picnic boxes and cheap sandwiches (even veggie) at this family-run dive.

Ariki o Te Pana (Av Atamu Tekena s/n; mains US$4-13; 🕑 Mon-Sat) This no-frills den serves formidable

cheese and tuna *empanadas*, cold drinks and large lunches.

Merahi Ra'a (☎ 551-125; Av Te Pito o Te Henua s/n; mains US$10-17; 🕑 closed Thu) Ultrafresh and abundant seafood fuel the popularity of this harborside restaurant. A picture menu will help you decipher the *matahuira* from the *kana kana* (fish).

Jardín del Mau (☎ 551-677; Av Policarpo Toro s/n; mains US$14-18; 🕑 closed Tue) Vegetarians rejoice over the decent selection of pasta and lasagna in this seaside plain-Jane.

Drinking

Aloha Pub (cnr Atamu Tekena & S Englert; 🕑 closed Sun) Offers a mellow backdrop to recharge your batteries.

Entertainment

Toroko (Av Policarpo Toro s/n; 🕑 Thu-Sat) This scruffy but animated disco features island pop and modern tunes.

Piditi (Av Hotu Matua s/n; 🕑 Thu-Sat) Simmers with fun seekers, especially on Saturday. The cover charge at both is about US$4 (men only). Drinks are expensive, and the action gets going after 1am.

PARQUE NACIONAL RAPA NUI

Teeming with caves, *ahu*, fallen *moai* and petroglyphs, the **national park** (admission US$10) encompasses much of Rapa Nui's land and all the archaeological sites. Pay the admission fee in Orongo for unlimited visits. The following sections skim the surface of island offerings. Wherever you go, respect the archaeological sites: walking on the *ahu* or removing/relocating rocks of archaeological structures is strictly taboo. Handle the land gently and the *moai* will smile upon you.

Near Hanga Roa

A short hike north of town, and lovely at sunset, **Ahu Tahai** has three restored *ahu*. Ahu Tahai proper is in the middle, with a solitary *moai*. Ahu Ko Te Riku is to the north, with a top-knotted and eyeballed *moai*. Ahu Vai Uri has five eroded *moai* of varying sizes. Along the hills are foundations of *hare paenga* (elliptical houses) and walls of 'chicken houses.'

Four kilometers north of Tahai, **Ahu Tepeu** has several fallen *moai* and a village site. On the nearby coast, **Ana Kakenga** has two windows open to the ocean. **Ahu Akivi** is the site of seven *moai*, unique because they face the sea but like all *moai* they overlook the site of a village. At the equinoxes their gaze meets the setting sun.

Anakena

With lovely white sands fringed by palm fronds, this popular beach is the legendary landing place of Hotu Matua. Browse the two major archaeological sites of **Ahu Nau Nau** and its picture-perfect row of *moai,* and the hillside **Ahu Ature Huki** whose lone *moai* took Heyerdahl and a dozen islanders nine days to lever up.

Ahu Te Pito Kura

Overlooking Bahía La Pêrouse, a massive 10m-high magnetic *moai* lies facedown with its neck broken. It is the largest *moai* ever moved from Rano Raraku and erected on an *ahu.* Its resemblance to the uncompleted figures at Rano Raraku suggests that this *moai* is also one of the most recent. Its name derives from the nearby polished round stone, *te pito kura* (navel of light).

Ahu Tongariki

Dazzling in scale and setting, 15 *moai* line up along the largest *ahu* built. A 1960 tsunami demolished several of the *moai* and scattered topknots far inland, but the Japanese company Tadano re-erected 15 *moai* in the early 1990s.

Rano Raraku

An ethereal setting of half-carved and buried *moai,* Rano Raraku delights the senses. Referred to as 'the nursery,' the *moai* were quarried from the slopes of this extinct volcano. Wander through the rocky jigsaw patterns of unfinished *moai.* There are 600, with the largest 21m tall. At the lip of the crater you will find a silent reedy lake and an amphitheater full of handsome heads. The 360-degree view is a knockout.

Rano Kau

The star attraction of Rapa Nui is Rano Kau and its crater lake, a cauldron of *tortoral* reeds. Shelved 400m above and abutting the gaping sea cliff is the **Orongo Ceremonial Village** (admission US$10), a fragile outcrop 9km south of Hanga Roa where bird-cult rituals were performed. Step lightly here to preserve the delicate setting. In the apex of cult ceremonies, competitors raced to retrieve an egg of the sooty tern from the small *motu* (islets) just offshore. The young men descended the cliffs and swam

out to the islands (with the aid of rafts) to search for an egg. The first in the egg hunt became birdman for the year. Visitors will find a cluster of boulders covered in petroglyphs depicting Tangata Manu (the birdman) and Make Make (their god). Walking or biking is possible but it's a rather steep 9km trip from town. Hiking around the crater takes a full day and a supply of water.

GETTING THERE & AWAY

Lan (☎ 600-526-2000; Atamu Tekena s/n, Hanga Roa) is the only airline serving Rapa Nui. Four flights per week go to/from Santiago and to/from Papeete (Tahiti). Round-trip fares from Santiago range from US$630 to US$900. Reconfirm your ticket two days before departure since flights are often overbooked.

Travelers coming from Asia or Australia can stop here en route to/from South America, via Auckland (New Zealand). Take an Air New Zealand flight to Papeete, to connect with Papeete–Rapa Nui–Santiago service.

GETTING AROUND
Bicycle

Rent mountain bikes in Hanga Roa for US$16 per eight hours or US$25 per day. Take a test spin so you won't end up with faulty shifters or saddle sores. There's an air pump at the gas station.

Car

In Hanga Roa, **Comercial Insular** (☎ 032-100-480; Atamu Tekena s/n) rents Suzuki 4WDs at US$50 to US$60 for eight hours. Established hotels and tour agencies also offer rentals (as do individuals, but without insurance). Make sure the car has all the necessary equipment should a tire go flat.

Taxi

Taxis cost a flat US$3 for most trips around town. Longer trips can be negotiated, with the cost depending mainly on the time. Round trip from Hanga Roa to Anakena costs US$20.

CHILE DIRECTORY

ACCOMMODATIONS

Places book up fast in the most popular towns during high season, so make reservations before you arrive. Summer and holiday weekend prices may be 10% to 20% higher than the

CHILE

rest of the year. Sernatur and most municipal tourist offices have lists of licenced budget lodgings. HI has a hostel in almost every main city, but aren't always the best value. Purchase cards at affiliated hostels or their office (☎ 02-233-3220; Hernando de Aguirre 201, Oficina 602, Providencia, Santiago) for US$14.

A couple of pamphlets highlight some popular places; look for 'Backpacker's Best of Chile,' 'Hostels for Backpackers' and SCS Scott's listings. From north to south, you'll find a definite network of European-run hostels with ample amenities. Especially in the Lakes District, family homes offer inexpensive rooms, most often with kitchen privileges, hot showers and breakfast. Most accommodations include breakfast, though it is usually just bread and instant coffee. Fancier hotels often include the 18% IVA in the price, which should be subtracted from the tourist price for foreign travelers (smaller hotels may not be equipped to handle this step though). Make sure to agree on this before taking a room.

For camping, your best resource is Turistel's *Rutero Camping* guide. Most organized campgrounds are family oriented with large sites, full bathrooms and laundry, fire pits, a restaurant or snack bar. Many are costly because they charge a five-person minimum. Try asking for per person rates. Remote areas may offer free camping without facilities. Camping gas, referred to as *vencina blanca,* is carried in *ferreterias* (hardware stores) or larger supermarkets.

ACTIVITIES

Chile is paradise for the active. First on everyone's list is **trekking**, with Torres del Paine (p524) topping the list. Areas around Parinacota and Lago Chungara (p468), Parque Pumalín (p510), Nahuelbuta (p478), Puyehue (p495), Cochamó Valley (p501) and Isla Navarino (p527) are other favorites. Trails in many parks are not well marked or maintained. Some are simply old cattle roads. The government-funded **Sendero de Chile** (www.senderodechile.cl) is in the process of linking and properly signing a network of trails north to south, with some sections already in place. For those going **climbing**, get permission to scale peaks on the border (Ojos de Salado) from Chile's **Dirección de Fronteras y Límites** (Difrol; ☎ 671-2725; Teatinos 180, 7th fl, Santiago).

Surfing (see p471) breaks run up and down the coast of Middle and Northern Chile.

Iquique also has South America's best conditions for **paragliding** and **landsailing**.

Rafting or **kayaking** is world-class here. Most popular is the Futaleufú River (p510), but don't overlook the Liucura (p488) and Trancura (p485) outside Pucón, or the Petrohué near Puerto Varas (p497). For sea kayaking, head to Chiloé (p506) and the fjords around Parque Pumalín (p510).

Mountain biking favorites include around San Pedro de Atacama (p455), Ensenada, on Lago Llanquihue (p500), Ojos de Caburgua (p485), and along the challenging Carretera Austral. Two-wheeled travel has its challenges. Cars kick up rocks on gravel roads, summer in the south brings *tábanos* (horseflies) and winds along the southern stretch of Carretera Austral are fierce. Most towns in Chile have a repair shop.

Multiday **horse-riding** trips access Andean terrain you can't get to otherwise. Try Pucón (p485), Río Puelo Valley (p501), Puyehue (p495) and around Torres del Paine (p526).

The **skiing** season runs from June to October. Santiago has some rental shops; otherwise resorts rent full packages. Head out to Volcán Villarrica (p489), Chillán (p474) and any of the resorts near Santiago (p432).

Hedonists prefer **soaking** in therapeutic hot springs. With volcanic activity all along its spine, Chile offers the gamut from the humble find-your-own to fancy spas with fluffy towels. Try Puritama (p458) outside San Pedro de Atacama, Los Pozones (p488), by Pucón, or Puyehue (p495). Also check out areas around Liquiñe and Coñaripe. Another fun detour, **wine tasting** can be done in the vineyards of Middle Chile (p469) and around Santiago (p432).

BOOKS

Lonely Planet's *Chile & Easter Island* provides detailed travel information and coverage. The annually updated, very informative Turistel series has separate volumes on northern, central and southern Chile, plus an additional one on camping. Good travel companions are Sara Wheeler's *Travels in a Thin Country,* Charles Darwin's *Voyage of the Beagle,* and Nick Reding's *The Last Cowboys at the End of the World: The Story of the Gauchos of Patagonia,* Francisco Coloane's *Cape Horn and other Stories* and the anthology *Chile: A Traveler's Literary Companion* (ed Katherine Silver).

BUSINESS HOURS

Shops in Chile open by 10am, but some close at about 1pm for two to three hours for lunch then reopen until about 8pm. Government offices and businesses open from 9am to 6pm. Banks are open 9am to 2pm weekdays. Tourist offices stay open long hours daily in summer, but have abbreviated hours in the off-season. In many provincial cities and towns restaurants and services are closed on Sunday. Museums are often closed on Monday. Restaurant hours vary widely. Many restaurants do not open for breakfast and quite a few close for the lull between lunch and dinner.

CLIMATE

Northern Chile has good weather year-round. Pack warm clothes – even in the summer – to deal with foggy mornings and high-altitude destinations. January and February are the rainy months, making some off-track travel difficult.

Santiago and Middle Chile are best enjoyed from September to April, with the autumn harvest a prime excuse to dally in this wine-growing region. Santiago can be unbearably hot and smoggy from December through February.

Head to the Lakes District and Patagonia from October through April – but be prepared for rain. Campers should bring a synthetic sleeping bag. Windy conditions rule the far south. Sun protection – hats, sunglasses, blocks etc – is essential.

Throughout Chile, including the islands, mid-December to mid-March is the high season, which means increased prices, crowded lodgings, tons of tourists (this is when most Chileans travel), and overbooked flights and buses.

The South America Directory (p1057) has more information and climate charts.

DANGERS & ANNOYANCES

Compared with other South American countries, Chile is remarkably safe. Petty thievery is a problem in larger cities and in bus terminals. Keep an eye on all belongings, and take advantage of secure left-luggage services at bus terminals and *hospedajes*. Beach resorts are prime territory for thievery in summer, and some of Valparaíso's neighborhoods are best avoided. Photographing military installations is strictly prohibited. Natural dangers include earthquakes – Chile has suffered some big ones – and strong offshore currents. Choose your swimming spots carefully. Look for signs '*apta para bañar*' (swimming okay) and '*no apta para bañar*' (no swimming). Chile's canine gangs will follow you everywhere, but are usually harmless.

DISABLED TRAVELERS

Chile still neglects the needs of people with disabilities. Bus assistants will help you on and off buses, but finding lodgings that don't have stairs, or have hallways large enough for wheelchairs, is difficult. Still, Chileans are very hospitable and accommodating. Family lodgings are likely to go above and beyond to assist.

ELECTRICITY

Chile operates on 220 volts at 50 cycles. Two and three rounded prongs are used.

EMBASSIES & CONSULATES

For information on visas, see p540.

Embassies & Consulates in Chile

Chile has embassies and consulates in the following countries:

Argentina Antofagasta (☎ 055-220-440; Blanco Encalada 1933); Puerto Montt (☎ 065-253-996; Cauquenes 94, 2nd fl); Punta Arenas (☎ 061-261-912; 21 de Mayo 1878); Santiago (Map pp424-5; ☎ 02-582-2606; www.embargentina.cl; Vicuña Mackenna 41, Centro)

Australia (☎ 02-500-3500; consular.santiago@dfat.gov.au; Isidora Goyenechea 3621, 12th fl, Las Condes, Santiago)

Bolivia Antofagasta (☎ 055-259-008; Jorge Washington 2675); Arica (☎ 058-231-030; www.rree.gov.bo; Patricio Lynch 298); Calama (☎ 055-341-976; Latorre 1395); Iquique (☎ 057-421-777; Gorostiaga 215, Dept E, Iquique); Santiago (☎ 02-232-8180; cgbolivia@manquehue.net; Av Santa María 2796, Las Condes)

Brazil Punta Arenas (☎ 061-241-093; Arauco 769); Santiago (Map pp424-5; ☎ 02-425-9230; www.embajadadebrasil.cl; MacIver 225, 15th fl)

Canada (☎ 02-362-9660; enqserv@dfait-maeci.gc.ca; Tajamar 481, 12th fl, Las Condes, Santiago)

France (☎ 02-470-8000; www.france.cl; Av Condell 65, Providencia, Santiago)

Germany Arica (☎ 058-231-657; Prat 391, 10th fl, Oficina 101); Punta Arenas (☎ 061-212-866; Av El Bosque s/n, Lote 1, Manzana 8); Santiago (Map pp424-5; ☎ 02-463-2500; www.embajadadealemania.cl; Las Hualtatas 5677, Vitacura)

Ireland (Map pp424-5; ☎ 02-245-6616; Isidora Goyenechea 3162, office 801; Las Condes, Santiago)

Israel (☎ 02-750-0500; San Sebastián 2812, 5th fl, Las Condes, Santiago)

CHILE

Netherlands Punta Arenas (Map p519; ☎ 061-248-100; Sarmiento 780); Santiago (☎ 02-756-9200; www .holanda-paisesbajos.cl; Las Violetas 2368, Providencia)
New Zealand (☎ 02-290-9802; embajada@nzembassy .cl; El Golf 99, Oficina 703, Las Condes, Santiago)
Peru Arica (☎ 058-231-020; 18 de Septiembre 1554); Iquique (☎ 057-411-466; Zegers 570, 2nd fl); Santiago (☎ 02-235-4600; conpersantiago@adsl.tie.cl; Padre Mariano 10, Oficina 309, Providencia)
UK Punta Arenas (☎ 061-211-535; Catarata del Niágara 01325); Santiago (Map p519; ☎ 02-370-4100; consular .santiago@fco.gov.uk; Av El Bosque Norte 0125, 3rd fl, Las Condes, Santiago); Valparaíso (☎ 032-213-063; Blanco 1199, 5th fl)
USA (☎ 02-232-2600; santiago.usembassy.gov; Av Andrés Bello 2800, Las Condes, Santiago)

Chilean Embassies & Consulates Abroad

Chile has diplomatic representation in most parts of the world.
Argentina (☎ 4808-8600; www.embajadadechile.com .ar; Tagle 2762, Buenos Aires)
Australia Canberra (☎ 02-6286 2430; www.embachile -australia.com; 10 Culgoa Circuit, O'Malley, ACT 2606); Melbourne (☎ 03-9866 4041; www.chile.com.au; 13th fl, 390 St Kilda Rd, VIC 3004); Sydney (☎ 02-9299 2533; cgsydney@telpacific.com.au; 18th fl, 44 Market St, NSW 2000)
Bolivia (☎ 591-279-7331; cgchilp@ceibo.entelnet.bo; Calle 14 8024, La Paz)
Brazil (☎ 55-2552-5349; cchilerj@veloxmail.com.br; Praia Do Flamengo 344, Rio de Janeiro)
Canada Montréal (☎ 514-499-0405; www.cgchile montreal.cjp.net; 1010 Sherbrooke St W, Suite 710); Ottawa (☎ 613-235-4402; www.chile.ca; 50 O'Connor St, Suite 1413); Toronto (☎ 416-924-0106; www.congechiletoronto .com; 2 Bloor St W, Suite 1801); Vancouver (☎ 604-681-9162; www.chilevan.ca; 1185 W Georgia, Suite 1250)
France (☎ 01-47 05 46 61; www.amb-chili.fr in French or Spanish; 64 Blvd de la Tour Maubourg, Paris, 75007)
Germany Berlin (☎ 030-726-2035; www.embajada consuladoschile.de; Mohrenstrasse 42); Frankfurt (☎ 069-550-194; Humboldtstrasse 94)
New Zealand (☎ 04-471 6270; www.embchile.co.nz; 19 Bolton St, Wellington)
Peru (☎ 511-611-2211; www.embachileperu.com.pe; Javier Prado Oeste 790, San Isidro, Lima)
UK (☎ 207-436 5204; embachile@embachile.co.uk; 12 Devonshire Rd, London)
USA Chicago (☎ 312-654-8780; www.chile-usa.org; 875 N Michigan Ave, Suite 3352, IL 60611); Los Angeles (☎ 323-933-3697; www.consuladoschile.org; 6100 Wilshire Boulevard, Suite 1240, CA 90048); Miami (☎ 305-373-8623; cgmiamius@earthlink.net; 800 Brickell Ave, Suite 1230, FL 33131); New York (☎ 212-

980-3366; www.chileny.com; 866 United Nations Plaza, Suite 601, NY 10017); San Francisco (☎ 415-982-7662; cgsfchile@sbcglobal.net; 870 Market St, Suite 1058, CA 94102); Washington, DC (☎ 202-785-1746; consulado@embassyofchile.org; 1734 Massachusetts Ave NW, 20036)

FESTIVALS & EVENTS

In January and February every Chilean town and city puts on some sort of show with live music, special feasts and fireworks. Tourist offices have exact dates. Religious holidays and the mid-September Fiestas Patrias mark other festivities.

Festival Costumbrista These typical fiestas take place all over. For an authentic Patagonian rodeo, go to Villa Cerro Castillo.
Festival de la Virgen del Carmen Some 40,000 pilgrims pay homage to Chile's virgin in Tirana in mid-July, with lots of street dancing and masks.

FOOD & DRINK
Chilean Cuisine

Chile's best offerings are its raw materials: in the market you can get anything from goat cheese to avocados, pomegranates, good yogurt, fresh herbs and a fantastic variety of seafood. What Chilean cuisine lacks in spice and variety it makes up for in abundance. Breakfast tends toward meager with instant coffee or tea, white rolls and jam. Fuel up with a hearty *menú del día* (inexpensive set meal) lunch with *cazuela* (soup), a main dish of fish or meat with a starch and some bland vegetables. Central markets and *casinos de bomberos* (firefighters' restaurants) offer cheap meals. Snacks include the prolific *completo* (a hot dog smothered in mayo, avocado, tomato and ketchup) and *humitas* (corn tamales). *Empanadas* are whopping and either fried, with cheese or shellfish, or *al horno* (baked) with meat, called *pino*.

Those who want a little spice on the table can pick up a bottle of *ají Chileno*. A melted ham and cheese sandwich is a *barros jarpa*, with steak it's a *barros luco*, while beefsteak and green beans make a *chacarrero*. *Lomo a lo pobre* is steak topped with fried eggs and french fries. *Chorrillana* is a heart-choking platter of fried potatoes, grilled onions, fried eggs and steak. Seafood is abundant and incredible. *Caldillo de ...* is a hearty soup of fish (often congrio) spiced up with lemon, cilantro and garlic. *Chupe de ...* is seafood baked in a medley of butter, bread crumbs, cheese and spices. *Paila marina* is a fish and shellfish chowder.

People in the south eat a lot of potatoes in every form, as well as summertime lamb roasted on a spit *(asado de cordero)*. German influence provides a variety of strudel, *küchen* and cheesecake. In Chiloé look for *milcao* (potato dumplings) and *curanto,* which combines fish, shellfish, chicken, pork, lamb, beef and potato in a heaping bowl fit for two.

Drinks

Over 700 million liters of wine are produced annually in Chile, don't miss out on your share. Carmenere is wonderful and unique to Chile (a phylloxera plague wiped out the variety in Europe). Cabernet sauvignon and the increasingly popular Syrah are other good bets. Decent bottles start at US$4, and for the ultrafrugal a box of Gato Negro is better than nothing.

Chile's (and Peru's) best invention is the *pisco sour,* grape brandy combined with lemon juice, egg white and powdered sugar. *Pisco* and Coke is a *piscola,* or *combinado* with any soft drink. *Bebidas* (soft drinks) are adored; local brands include the ultrasugary Bilz and the unfortunately named Pap. Water is safe from the tap in the south. *Mote con huesillo,* sold by street vendors, is a refreshing peach nectar with barley kernels and rehydrated peaches.

Instant Nescafé is a national plague. Entrepreneurial would-be expats could start up espresso bars (there are a few). Mate (Paraguayan tea) is consumed heavily in Patagonia. *Yuyos* (herbal teas) are very common.

Kunstmann and Cólonos are Chile's best beers. A draft beer is called *schop.*

GAY & LESBIAN TRAVELERS

Chile is still a conservative, Catholic-minded country and many frown upon homosexuality here; however, younger generations are far more tolerant. Provincial areas are definitively far behind in attitudes toward gays. Santiago's gay scene (and general tolerance) has improved in leaps and bounds during recent years. Perhaps because it was underground for so long, the gay scene has awoken with particular vigor. Most gay bars and nightclubs can be found in Barrio Bellavista.

Gay Chile (www.gaychile.com) has the lowdown on all things gay, including current events, Santiago nightlife, lodging recommendations, legal and medical advice and personals. While

in Santiago, keep an eye out for Chile's first magazine oriented toward gays and other socially disenfranchised groups, **Opus Gay** (www.opusgay.d in Spanish), teasingly named after the conservative Catholic Opus Dei group.

Chile's main gay-rights organization is **Movimiento Unificado de Minorías Sexuales** (MUMS; www.orgullogay.d in Spanish).

HEALTH

Hospitals in Chile are reasonable but private *clínicas* are the best option for travelers. Except for in the Atacama Desert and in Santiago, tap water is safe to drink. Altitude sickness and dehydration are the most common concerns in the north, sunburn in the ozone-depleted south – apply sunscreen and wear sunglasses. No vaccinations are required to travel in Chile, but those traveling to Rapa Nui should inquire about current restrictions or documentation requirements. Tampons are not available in smaller towns. For more information, see the Health chapter (p1090).

HOLIDAYS

Government offices and businesses close on the following national holidays:
Año Nuevo (New Year's Day) January 1
Semana Santa (Easter Week) March/April, dates vary
Día del Trabajador (Labor Day) May 1
Glorias Navales (Naval Battle of Iquique) May 21
Corpus Christi May/June; dates vary
San Pedro y San Pablo (St Peter's & St Paul's Day) June 29
Asunción de la Virgen (Assumption) August 15
Día de Unidad Nacional (Day of National Unity) first Monday of September
Día de la Independencia Nacional (Independence Day) September 18
Día del Ejército (Armed Forces Day) September 19
Día de la Raza (Columbus Day) October 12
Todos los Santos (All Saints' Day) November 1
Inmaculada Concepción (Immaculate Conception Day) December 8
Navidad (Christmas Day) December 25

INTERNET ACCESS

Most areas have excellent internet connections and reasonable prices. Rates range from US$1 to US$6 per hour.

INTERNET RESOURCES

Chile.com (www.chile.com in Spanish) A Yahoo-like website with good sections on nightlife and slang.

Chile Information Project (www.chip.cl) Informative materials on everything from human rights to out-of-the-way destinations.

Chiloé (www.chiloeweb.com) The best source of information about the island.

Patagonia Chile (www.patagonia-chile.com) Comprehensive tourism listings.

Rehue Foundation (www.xs4all.nl/~rehue) Links to Mapuche history, issues and events.

Sernatur (www.sernatur.cl) Information from the national tourism organization.

South America Travel Directory (www.planeta.com/chile) Worthwhile links to ecotourism, environmental organizations, towns and more.

MAPS

In Santiago, the **Instituto Geográfico Militar** (Map pp424-5; ☎ 02-460-6800; www.igm.cl in Spanish; Dieciocho 369, Centro; ⊗ 9am-5:30pm Mon-Fri) sells 1:50,000 topographic regional maps for about US$15 per sheet. These are the best hiking aids available for trekkers (but can be outdated – in some cases rivers have altered course!). The maps can be browsed and bought via the website. Conaf in Santiago allows photocopying of national park maps. JLM Mapas publishes tourist maps for all major regions and trekking areas at scales ranging from 1:50,000 to 1:500,000. They are easy to use and helpful, but don't claim 100% accuracy.

Online maps vary in quality: **Plano Digital de Publiguías** (www.planos.cl in Spanish) has online city maps but it is a frustrating website to navigate. Santiago maps are available on **Map City** (www.mapcity.cl in Spanish). Some local government websites have interactive maps that allow you to search for a street address in major cities. Those traveling by car should invest in a current *Turistel* (in Spanish), an indispensable road guide with separate editions for north, central and southern regions.

MEDIA

El Mercurio (www.elmercurio.cl), Chile's oldest conservative daily is finally getting some competition with the more left-leaning *La Tercera*. *Últimas Noticias* and others grab your attention with front-page bus crashes and butt shots. The financial publication **Estrategia** (www.estrategia.cl) is the best source for exchange rates. The **Santiago Times** (www.chip.cl) serves the English-speaking population. Regional papers offer local news and event information. The alternative the *Clinic* provides cutting-edge editorials and satire about politics and Chilean society.

Chilean TV embraces vapid gossip and talent shows. The rural population without phone service (mostly in Patagonia and the Chiloé islands) are dependent on radio broadcasting messages for communication.

MONEY

The Chilean unit of currency is the peso (Ch$). Bank notes come in denominations of 500, 1000, 2000, 5000, 10,000 and 20,000 pesos. Coin values are 1, 5, 10, 50, 100 and 500 pesos. It can be difficult to change bills larger than Ch$5000 in rural areas. Gas stations and liquor stores usually oblige, just make an apologetic face and ask, '¿*Tiene suelto?*'.

Exchange rates are usually best in Santiago, where there is also a ready market for European currencies. Chile's currency has been pretty stable in recent years. Throughout the book we have used the exchange rate of 510 pesos to US$1, but fluctuation may occur. The value of the dollar seems to decline during peak tourist season and shoot back up again come March. Paying a bill with US cash is sometimes acceptable, especially at tour agencies (check their exchange rate carefully). Many top-end hotels publish rates in US dollars with a lower exchange rate than the daily one. It's best to pay all transactions in pesos.

Money transferred by cable should arrive in a few days; Chilean banks can give you money in US dollars on request. Western Union offices can be found throughout Chile, usually adjacent to the post office.

ATMs

Chile's many ATM machines, known as *red-banc,* are the easiest and most convenient way to access funds. Your bank will likely charge a small fee for each transaction. Most ATMs have instructions in Spanish and English. Choose the option 'foreign card' (*tarjeta extranjera*) before starting the transaction. You *cannot* rely on ATMs in San Pedro de Atacama (the one ATM breaks down), Rapa Nui or in small Patagonian towns.

Bargaining

Buying items in a crafts market is the only acceptable time to bargain. Transport and accommodation rates are generally fixed and prominently displayed, but during a slow summer or in the off-season, ask politely for a discount, '¿*Me podría hacer precio?*'.

Credit Cards

Most established businesses welcome credit cards although it's best not to depend on it. Consumers may be charged the 6% surcharge businesses must pay. Credit cards can also be useful to show 'sufficient funds' before entering another country.

Exchanging Money

US dollars are the preferred currency for exchange. Cash earns a better rate than traveler's checks and avoids commissions. To exchange cash and traveler's checks, *casas de cambios* are quicker than banks but offer poorer rates, as do removed destinations. Plan to exchange in larger cities. In very touristy areas, hotels, travel agencies and some shops accept or change US dollars. Street changers don't offer much difference in rate. The American Express representative is **Blanco Viajes** (☎ 02-636-9100; Gral Holley 148, Providencia, Santiago). Traveler's checks can be cashed at Banco del Estado and most exchange houses; ATMs are easier.

Exchange rates at press time included the following:

Country	Unit		Ch$ (peso)
Australia	A$1	=	398
Canada	C$1	=	464
euro zone	€1	=	661
Japan	¥100	=	444
New Zealand	NZ$1	=	350
UK	UK£1	=	985
United States	US$1	=	527

POST

Correos de Chile (post offices) are open from 9am to 6pm weekdays and 9am to noon Saturday. Send essential overseas mail *certificado* to ensure its arrival. Parcel post is quite efficient, though a clerk may inspect your package before accepting it. Vendors near the post office wrap parcels for a small charge. Within Chile, an ordinary letter costs US42¢, or US$1.30 for a faster service. An airmail letter or postcard costs about US57¢ to North America and US70¢ to Europe and Australia.

To send packages within Chile, sending via *encomienda* (the bus system) is much more reliable. Simply take the package to a bus company that goes to the destination. Label the package clearly with the destination and the name of the person who will pick it up.

In Santiago, poste restante or *lista de correos* (general delivery mail) costs approximately US35¢ per letter. Instruct correspondents to address letters clearly and to precede your name with either Señora or Señor, as post offices in Chile divide lists of correspondence by gender. Mail is held for one month.

RESPONSIBLE TRAVEL

Hikers are obliged to carry out trash and follow a leave-no-trace ethic. Be particularly respectful to the *ahus* in Rapa Nui and with other monuments. Increasingly scarce seafood delicacies like *locos* (abalone) and *centolla* (king crab) should not be consumed during their breeding seasons. Don't buy carvings and crafts made out of protected species (cardón cactus in the north and *alerce* in the south). Follow requests to put used toilet paper in the trash basket (most places). The best and easiest way to earn karma points in Chile is to be pleasant and courteous.

SHOPPING

Deep-blue lapis lazuli is almost exclusive to Chile. Hand-knit woolens are inexpensive and plentiful in the south, particularly Chiloé. You'll find Mapuche design jewelry and basketry in the Araucanía. Artisan products in the north resemble those of Peru and Bolivia. Edibles worth lugging include *miel de ulmo* honey from the south, *mermelada de murta,* a red berry jam, and canned papayas from Elqui Valley. Cities often have good antiquing, most notably Valparaíso's Plaza O'Higgins.

STUDYING

Spanish-language courses are available in Santiago and several southern cities.

With Chilean headquarters at Coyhaique, the **National Outdoor Leadership School** (in USA ☎ 307-332-5300; www.nols.edu) offers a 75-day 'Semester in Patagonia,' teaching mountain wilderness skills, sea kayaking and natural history for university credit. Santiago's **Vinoteca** (☎ 02-335-2349; Isidora Goyenechea 2966, Las Condes) organizes wine courses. **Abtao** (☎ 02-211-5021; www .abtao.cl; El Director 5660, Las Condes, Santiago) organizes selective courses on Chilean ecosystems and wildlife.

CHILE

TELEPHONE

Chile's country code is ☎ 56. The two largest telephone companies, Entel and Telefónica CTC, have call centers from which you call directly from private cabins; most close by 10pm. Some call centers will place the call for you then tell you in which *cabina* your call is transferred. Long-distance calls are based on a carrier system: to place a call, precede the number with the telephone company's code: **Entel** (☎ 123), **Telefónica CTC** (☎ 188), for example. To make a collect call, dial ☎ 182 to get an operator. International rates are reasonable.

Each telephone carrier installs its own public phones which take only their calling cards or coins. You can buy *tarjetas telefónicas* (calling cards) from kiosks. A local call costs Ch$100 (approximately US20¢) per minute, and only Ch$85 outside of peak hours (8am to 8pm weekdays, 8am to 2pm Saturday). Cell-phone numbers have seven digits, prefixed by ☎ 09. Drop the 0 prefix when calling cell-to-cell. If calling cell-to-landline, add the landline's area code. Cell phones sell for as little as US$50 and can be charged up by prepaid phone cards. Cell phones have a 'caller-pays' format. Calls between cell and landlines are expensive and quickly eat up prepaid card amounts.

TOILETS

Chuck your used toilet paper in the waste bin as Chile's fragile plumbing usually can't handle it. Public bathrooms charge a small fee (US20¢), or you can try to find a (generally cleaner) restaurant loo. Toilet paper is not a given – carry it with you.

TOURIST INFORMATION

The national tourist service, **Sernatur** (☎ 600-737-62887; www.sernatur.cl in Spanish) has offices in Santiago and most cities. Their helpfulness varies widely but they generally provide brochures and leaflets. Many towns have municipal tourist offices, usually on the main plaza or at the bus terminal.

TOURS

The only way to get to remote calving glaciers, summit an active volcano, or raft a river is on tour. Opportunities for unguided activities abound, just plan carefully. Operators may say they have English-speaking guides, but sometimes you have to pay extra for this service – ask first. Rural tourism offers local Spanish-speaking guides at a reasonable fee and access to places you otherwise would never have known about.

VISAS

Nationals of US, Canada, Australia and the EU do not need a visa to visit Chile. Passports are obligatory and are essential for cashing traveler's checks, checking into hotels and other routine activities.

Note that the Chilean government collects a 'reciprocity' fee from arriving US (US$100), Mexican (US$15), Australian (US$34) and Canadian (US$55) citizens in response to these governments imposing a similar fee on Chilean citizens applying for visas. The reciprocity payment applies only to travelers arriving by air in Santiago and is valid for the life of the passport. The payment must be made in cash, and exact change is necessary.

On arrival, you'll be handed a 90-day tourist card. Don't lose it! If you do, go to the **Policía Internacional** (☎ 02-737-1292; Gral Borgoño 1052, Santiago; ☉ 8:30am-5pm Mon-Fri), or the nearest police station. You will be asked for it upon leaving the country.

It costs US$100 to renew a tourist card for 90 more days at the **Departamento de Extranjería** (Map pp424-5; ☎ 02-550-2484; Agustinas 1235, 2nd fl, Santiago; ☉ 9am-2pm Mon-Fri). Many visitors prefer a quick dash across the Argentine border and back.

See p535 for information regarding embassies and consulates.

VOLUNTEERING

Experienced outdoor guides may be able to exchange labor for accommodations during the busy high season, but usually only if they can stick out the entire season. **Experiment Chile** (www.experiment.cl) organizes 14-week language-learning and volunteer programs. Language schools can often place students in volunteer work as well. The nonprofit organization **Un Techo Para Chile** (www.untechoparachile.cl in Spanish) builds homes for low-income families throughout the country, and has contact information for prospective volunteers on the website. The annual *Directorio de Organizaciones Miembros* published by **Renace** (Red Nacional de Acción Ecológica; www.renace.cl in Spanish) lists environmental organizations, which may accept volunteers.

WOMEN TRAVELERS

No worries, Chilean men are downright cir-
cumspect next to their hot-blooded neighbors.
In the north or central areas they are quick
with *piropos* (come-ons), but these hormonal
outbursts evaporate upon utterance – don't
dwell on them. The biggest bother is being
constantly asked how old you are and if you're
married. Many *Chileanas* are intimidated by
their foreign counterparts and they can be
difficult to befriend at first.

WORKING

Finding work as an English-language in-
structor in Santiago is feasible, but don't
expect excellent wages. In the south there is
an increasing need for English teachers and
translators for the salmon industry. Reputable
employers insist on work or residence permits
(increasingly difficult to obtain) from the
Departamento de Extranjería (Map pp424-5; ☎ 02-
550-2400; Agustinas 1235, 2nd fl, Santiago; ☿ 9am-2pm
Mon-Fri).

Colombia

HIGHLIGHTS

- **Cartagena** – experience the jaw-dropping beauty of South America's most romantic city, famed for its history and its good looks (p582)
- **Zona Cafetera** – get buzzed on Colombia's finest coffee in this beautiful region of rolling plantations and steaming volcanoes (p601)
- **Bogotá** – visit splendid museums, dine in Colombia's best restaurants and salsa till dawn in the booming capital city (p553)
- **San Agustín** – explore the rolling hills of this unique ceremonial funeral site littered with hundreds of anthropomorphic stone statues (p612)
- **Off-the-beaten track** – make like Indiana Jones and hike to Ciudad Perdida, the lost city, the remains of an ancient culture hidden deep in the jungle (p581)
- **Best journey** – Cartagena to Bucaramanga: a two-day trip through backwoods and bayous of northern Colombia. The trip involves a combination of bus, jeep and riverboat, plus an overnight stay in the intriguing town of Mompós

FAST FACTS

- **Area:** 1,141,748 sq km
- **Budget:** US$15-25 a day
- **Best bargain:** scuba diving at Taganga
- **Best street snack:** juice smoothies
- **Capital:** Bogotá
- **Costs:** double room in a budget hotel US$5-15, set meal in a budget restaurant US$1.50-2.50, 100km intercity bus fare US$3-4
- **Country code:** ☎ 57
- **Famous for:** Gabriel García Márquez, coffee, emeralds, cocaine, plastic surgery, FARC
- **Language:** Spanish
- **Money:** US$1 = 2355 pesos
- **Phrases:** *chévere/bacano* (cool), *asqueroso* (disgusting, horrible), *rumba* (party)
- **Population:** 43 million
- **Time:** GMT minus 5hr (no daylight-savings time)
- **Tipping:** customary (not compulsory) 10% in upmarket restaurants
- **Visas:** not required from nationals of major Western countries

TRAVEL HINTS

Tickets for long-distance buses are not fixed so always bargain for a better deal. For both safety and scenery, travel by day only.

OVERLAND ROUTES

The main border crossings with Venezuela are at San Antonio del Táchira (near Cúcuta) and Paraguachón. From Ecuador, cross at Túlcan (near Ipiales).

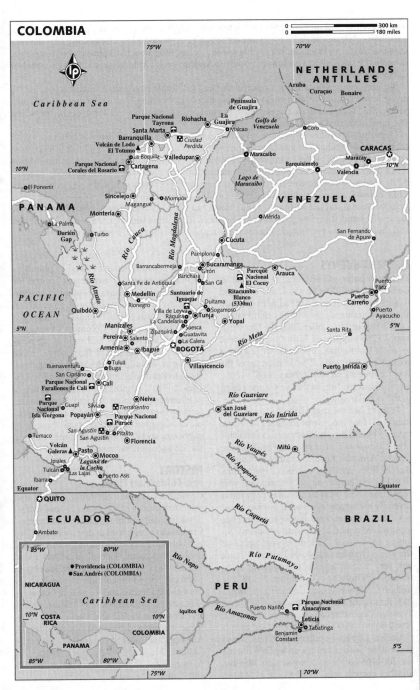

After traveling around Colombia for a while you may feel like you've stepped onto the set of a Hollywood dramatic thriller – in one scene you're exploring a lost city and the next dancing the salsa till dawn. Later you're running a wild river, scaling an active volcano and paragliding through the skies, all to a backdrop of soaring Andean peaks, lush Amazonian jungle and clear Caribbean waters.

No film is complete without a colorful cast and Colombia has its share of characters, but it's unlikely you'll bump into any next day Pablo Escobars, budding Shakiras or gun-toting insurgents. Most Colombians are pretty darn normal, except that they are some of the friendliest and most animated people you might ever meet.

Opportunities to create your own version of *Romancing the Stone* are growing better each year: rock climbing, scuba diving and cycling are just a few activities on offer. Nightlife is legendary, and no trip to Colombia is complete without a few all-night rumbas. Security improvements mean that Colombia is no longer the traveler pariah that it was a few years ago and once-forbidden travel routes are opening up. Now is the time to go: costs are low, the welcome is warm and Colombia's sour reputation has kept it off the 'gringo trail.'

Adventure and romance may stir your blood, but what will really sweep you off your feet are the spirited and stimulating people that live here. Take some time to meet a few Colombians and this former no-go zone may become the highlight of your South American odyssey.

CURRENT EVENTS

Young, popular and seemingly unstoppable, Colombian president Ávaro Uribe managed to win a constitutional amendment that has almost guaranteed his political domination until 2010. In November 2005 the Constitutional Court approved Uribe's amendment to allow Colombian presidents to run for a second four-year term. The decision paved the way for an easy victory in May 2006 – Uribe won 62%, according to the *New York Times*, of the popular vote.

Pundits believe that Uribe's second term in office is likely to mirror his first four years, marked by hardline military tactics that crippled Colombia's primary insurgent group, Fuerzas Armadas Revolucionarias de Colombia (FARC). Yet there are also expectations that Uribe's conservative government will reposition itself from its past war policy and diversify the largely agrarian economy.

One area of economic development that has experienced remarkable growth is tourism. No longer considered the kidnapping capital of the world (Iraq having stolen that title, thank you very much), tourists are opening up to the idea of a holiday in Colombia. Nearly one million foreigners visited Colombia in 2005, a 21% jump over the previous year. The World Tourism Organization seems to be impressed: it will hold its 2007 conference in Cartagena.

Coffee, always a popular export item, is also expanding, with revenues up by 58% during the 2004–05 coffee-growing season. Mining, another growth area, has become a US$488 million a year business. Overall, Colombia's 'official' economy is growing at around 5% each year. Meanwhile, Colombia's shadow economy (mainly cocaine and emeralds) is worth upwards of US$6.5 billion annually.

Despite success in Colombia's triangular war with leftist rebels and right-wing paramilitaries, the country still faces massive social problems, including widespread poverty and the internal displacement of peoples. The US-backed Plan Colombia (which is attempting to eradicate coca farming) has had devastating effects on the environment and the lives of people caught up in the war, although the surplus of cocaine and its price has remained stable in the US and even increased in Europe.

HISTORY
Pre-Columbian Times

Colombia's original inhabitants, tribes that migrated from what is now Panama, settled down in small groupings and, in time, reached a remarkably high level of development. They left behind three important archaeological sites – San Agustín, Tierradentro and Ciudad Perdida – and an impressive collection of gold work, considered the continent's best, both for the techniques used and for its artistic design.

Scattered throughout the Andean region and along the Pacific and Caribbean coasts, these cultures developed independently. Among the most outstanding were the Calima, Muisca, Nariño, Quimbaya, San Agustín, Sinú, Tayrona, Tierradentro, Tolima and Tumaco.

There Goes the Neighborhood

In 1499, Alonso de Ojeda was the first con-quistador to set foot on Colombian soil and to see indigenous people using gold objects. Several short-lived settlements were founded, but it was not until 1525 that Rodrigo de Bastidas laid the first stones of Santa Marta, the earliest surviving town. In 1533, Pedro de Heredia founded Cartagena, which soon became the principal center of trade.

In 1536, a general advance toward the in-terior began independently from the north and south. Jiménez de Quesada set off from Santa Marta and founded Santa Fe de Bogotá two years later. On the way he conquered the Muisca, a blow that would foretell the ultimate ruin of civilizations throughout the New World.

Quesada didn't actually find gold, despite the elaborate rituals of the Indians, who threw gold offerings into the waters of their sacred lake, Laguna de Guatavita, and thus gave birth to the mysterious legend of El Dorado.

Sebastián de Benalcázar (known in Colom-bia as Belalcázar) deserted from Francisco Pizarro's army, which was conquering the Inca empire, and mounted an expedition from Ecuador. He subdued the southern part of Colombia, founding Popayán and Cali along the way, and reached Bogotá in 1539.

The two groups fought tooth and nail for supremacy, and it was not until 1550 that King Carlos V of Spain, in an effort to establish law and order, created the Real Audiencia del Nuevo Reino de Granada, a tribunal based in Bogotá. Administratively, the new colony was subject to the Viceroyalty of Peru.

With the growth of the Spanish empire in the New World a new territorial division was created in 1717, and Bogotá became the capital of its own viceroyalty, the Virreinato de la Nueva Granada. It comprised the ter-ritories of what are today Colombia, Panama, Ecuador and Venezuela.

Independence Wars

Toward the end of the 18th century, the general disillusionment with Spanish domination gave rise to open protests and rebellions. This, to-gether with events such as the North American and French revolutions and, more importantly, the invasion of Spain by Napoleon Bonaparte, paved the way to independence. When Napo-leon placed his own brother on the Spanish throne in 1808, the colonies refused to recog-nize the new monarch. One by one Colombian towns declared their independence.

In 1812 Simón Bolívar, who was to become the hero of the independence struggle, arrived in Cartagena to take the offensive against the Spanish armies. In a brilliant campaign to seize Venezuela he won six battles but was unable to hold Caracas, and had to withdraw to Cartagena. By then Napoleon had been defeated at Waterloo, and Spain set about reconquering its colonies. Colonial rule was reestablished in 1817.

Bolívar doggedly took up arms again. After assembling an army of horsemen from the Venezuelan Llanos, strengthened by a British legion, he marched over the Andes into Co-lombia. The last and most decisive battle took place at Boyacá on August 7, 1819. Colombia's independence was won.

Independence…& Civil War

Two years after declaring independence, revo-lutionaries sat down Villa del Rosario (near Cúcuta) to hash out a plan for their new coun-try. It was there that the two opposing tenden-cies, centralist and federalist, came to the fore. Bolívar, who supported a centralized republic, succeeded in imposing his will. The Gran Co-lombia (which included modern-day Ecuador, Colombia, Venezuela and Panama) came into being and Bolívar was elected president.

From its inception, the state started to dis-integrate. It soon became apparent that a central regime was incapable of governing such a vast and diverse territory. The Gran Colombia split into three separate countries in 1830.

The two political currents, centralist and federalist, were formalized in 1849 when two political parties were established: the Con-servatives (with centralist tendencies) and the Liberals (with federalist leanings). Colombia became the scene of fierce rivalries between the two forces, resulting in complete chaos. During the 19th century the country experi-enced no less than eight civil wars. Between 1863 and 1885 there were more than 50 anti-government insurrections.

In 1899 a Liberal revolt turned into a full-blown civil war, the so-called War of a Thousand Days. That carnage resulted in a Conservative victory and left 100,000 dead. In 1903, the USA took advantage of the coun-try's internal strife and fomented a seces-sionist movement in Panama (at that time

COLOMBIA

a Colombian province). By creating a new republic, the USA was able to build a canal across the Central American isthmus.

La Violencia

After a period of relative peace, the struggle between Liberals and Conservatives broke out again in 1948 with La Violencia, the most destructive of Colombia's many civil wars, which left a death toll of some 300,000. Urban riots broke out on April 9, 1948 in Bogotá following the assassination of Jorge Eliécer Gaitán, a charismatic populist Liberal leader. Liberals soon took up arms throughout the country.

By 1953, some groups of Liberal guerrillas had begun to demonstrate a dangerous degree of independence. As it became evident that the partisan conflict was taking on revolutionary overtones, the leaders of both the Liberal and Conservative parties decided to support a military coup as the best means to retain power and pacify the countryside. The 1953 coup of General Gustavo Rojas Pinilla was the only military intervention the country experienced in the 20th century.

The dictatorship of General Rojas was not to last. In 1957, the leaders of the two parties signed a pact to share power for the next 16 years. The party leaders, however, repressed all political activity that remained outside the scope of their parties, thus sowing the seeds for the appearance of guerrilla groups.

Say You Want a Revolution

During the late 1950s and early '60s Colombia saw the birth of perhaps a dozen different guerrilla groups, each with its own ideology and its own political and military strategies. The movements that have had the biggest impact on local politics (and left the largest number of dead) include the FARC (Fuerzas Armadas Revolucionarias de Colombia), the ELN (Ejército de Liberación Nacional) and the M-19 (Movimiento 19 de Abril).

Until 1982 the guerrillas were treated as a problem of public order and persecuted by the military forces. President Belisario Betancur (1982–86) was the first to open direct negotiations with the guerrillas in a bid to reincorporate them into the nation's political life. Yet the talks ended in failure. The rupture was poignantly symbolized by the takeover of Bogotá's Palacio de Justicia by the M-19 guerrillas in November 1985.

The Liberal government of President Virgilio Barco (1986–90), after long and complex negotiations with the M-19, signed an agreement under which this group handed over its arms, ceased insurgent activity and transformed itself into a political party. However, the two other major groups – the 17,000-strong FARC and the 5000-strong ELN – remain under arms and currently control about 35% to 40% of the country. Having lost support from Moscow and Havana, they now rely on extortion and kidnapping to finance their struggle. They are also deeply involved in the production and trafficking of drugs, principally cocaine.

Since the state has been unable to control areas lost to the guerrillas, private armies – the so-called *paramilitares* or *autodefensas* – have mushroomed, with the army turning a blind eye or even supporting them. These right-wing armies operate against rebels in many regions, including Urabá, Cesar, Córdoba, Antioquia, Magdalena Medio, Santander, Cundinamarca and Caquetá, and have committed some horrendous massacres on civilians allegedly supporting the guerrillas. They form a loosely woven alliance known as the AUC (Autodefensas Unidas de Colombia), with an estimated 20,000 militants nationwide.

A White-Powder Market

Colombia controls 80% of the world's cocaine market. The mafia started in a small way in the early 1970s but, within a short time, developed the trade into a powerful industry with its own plantations, laboratories, transport services and protection.

The boom years began in the early 1980s. The Medellín Cartel, led by Pablo Escobar, became the principal mafia and its bosses lived in freedom and luxury. They even founded their own political party and two newspapers, and in 1982 Escobar was elected to the Congress.

In 1983 the government launched a campaign against the drug trade, which gradually turned into an all-out war. The cartel responded violently and managed to liquidate many of its adversaries. The war became even bloodier in August 1989 when Luis Carlos Galán, the leading Liberal contender for the 1990 presidential election, was assassinated. The government responded with the confiscation of nearly 1000 mafia-owned properties, and announced new laws on extradition – a nightmare for the drug barons. The cartel resorted to the use of terrorist tactics, principally car bombs.

The election of the Liberal President César Gaviria (1990–94) brought a brief period of hope. Following lengthy negotiations, which included a constitutional amendment to ban extradition of Colombians, Escobar and the remaining cartel bosses surrendered and the narcoterrorism subsided. However, Escobar escaped from his palacelike prison following the government's bumbling attempts to move him to a more secure site. An elite 1500-man special unit hunted Escobar for 499 days, until it tracked him down in Medellín and killed him in December 1993.

Despite this, the drug trade continued unaffected. While the military concentrated on hunting one man and persecuting one cartel, the other cartels were quick to take advantage of the opportune circumstances. The Cali Cartel, led by the Rodríguez Orejuela brothers, swiftly moved into the shattered Medellín Cartel's markets and became Colombia's largest trafficker. Although the cartel's top bosses were captured in 1995 and put behind bars the drug trade continued to flourish, with other regional drug cartels, paramilitaries and, principally, the guerrillas filling the gap left by the two original mafias.

In 1999, then President Andrés Pastrana launched Plan Colombia with US$3.3 billion in backing from the US. The plan called for the total eradication of the coca plant from Colombia by spraying fields with herbicide. Colombian coca growers and traffickers, not wanting to walk away from US$6 billion a year business, have in many cases moved their fields elsewhere, oftentimes into national parks which are protected against the spraying. Despite increased drug seizures and arrests of low-level traffickers, the availability of cocaine in the US and Europe remains stable.

A New Hope

Álvaro Uribe, an independent hardliner, won a 2002 presidential election, running on a strong antiguerrilla ticket and swearing also to break the history of governmental cronyism and patronage.

Uribe's hard-work ethic paid off and his first term in office gave the country marked improvements in security and the (legal) economy. The armed forces are now better equipped and have 60% more combat-ready soldiers than in 2002. The government has reclaimed much of the land that was effectively ceded to the guerrillas in the late 1990s, and has disarmed numerous rebel fighters.

With approval ratings that consistently reach 80% Uribe is the most popular elected leader in Latin America, but he is still faced with a daunting task to secure a lasting peace. He considers the civil conflict a terrorist threat – making little differentiation therefore between the FARC and the Cali Cartel. The guerrillas want Uribe to first recognize Colombia's internal conflict before any talks. Both the UN and human-rights groups recognize the conflict as political. Uribe, however, needs to maintain his recognition of the status of the conflict as a bargaining chip and has offered that he will revise his view of internal conflict so long as the ELN calls a ceasefire.

The AUC is the only group that has offered to stand down; however, it is not in direct opposition to the government and actually shares many similar goals. Its purpose is simply defense of the status quo. There are many people concerned – some in the UN, EU and US government – that the AUC is being given unduly generous terms for demobilization and it's clear that many members are simply getting away with murder. As of late 2005, some 10,000 AUC have laid down their weapons but it remains to be seen if they will dismantle their political, economic and drug-trafficking structures.

THE CULTURE
The National Psyche

The headlines may speak unfavorably about Colombia, its civil war and the high level of crime, but this is by no means a reflection on the character of its people, who are naturally gregarious, social and courteous. It's hard to find a Colombian who isn't willing to help a person in need or just chat on the street to pass the time. It soon becomes clear to the visitor that Colombians simply love to talk and you can strike up a conversation with anyone – don't be surprised when strangers approach at a restaurant and start gabbing. Full of respect, Colombians are kind not just to foreigners but to each other, and you can always expect a pleasant response if you approach a Colombian in a pleasant manner. Even bargaining, it is said, is merely an excuse to chat, so expect nothing but short shrift if all you want to do is talk money.

Colombians are used to living for the moment; decades of civil strife have that effect.

Dancing, drinking and partying till dawn seems to take off the edge of an otherwise precarious existence. Their passion for life is obvious and many Colombians dream of traveling abroad, even if most can't afford it. But they are refreshingly passionate about their own country too, and speak lovingly about the beauty of the Colombian countryside.

While many Colombians may fit nicely into this profile, there are other folk, especially those who live in war-torn villages in the Amazon or impoverished slums outside Bogotá, who have a less optimistic outlook on life. One thing that always shines through, though, is the indomitable spirit of the Colombian people who have overcome so much tumult in the past and know that they will prevail, one way or another, over current hardships.

Lifestyle

The divide between rich and poor in Colombia is enormous. The wealthiest 10% of the country controls 46% of the country's wealth (they also earn 80 times more money than the poorest 10%). Around 60% of urban Colombians live in poverty (the figure is 80% in rural areas).

Such a divide has created a bizarre mix of the first and third worlds. Young professionals living in northern Bogotá might spend their leisure time playing golf or tennis while on the other side of town, hundreds of thousands of people are trying to eke out an existence in the overcrowded slums of Ciudad Bolívar.

The new urban elite can be very cosmopolitan – eating at sushi bars, communicating through laptops and driving expensive foreign cars – while Colombians in remote villages live without electricity or running water.

Yet despite their privileged status wealthy Colombians face high levels of insecurity. Most members of the upper tier know someone who has been assassinated, kidnapped, robbed or held for ransom. At the other end of the spectrum, Colombia's poor are often caught between various factions – FARC, the government and the paramilitaries, occasionally with deadly results.

Inside the home you may find a large, extended family cohabitating under one roof. Grandparents are often assigned childcare duties while parents, aunts and uncles go to work. The increasing middle class, however, shows a tendency toward larger homes with single family units.

No matter their level of income, all Colombians are bound by a handful of shared interests, namely *fútbol*, salsa and any opportunity to join a raucous *rumba*. A Colombian festival is celebrated with equal aplomb across all corners of the country.

Population

The Colombian national population currently hovers at around 43 million people, making it the third-most populous country in Latin America, after Brazil and Mexico. Population is spread fairly evenly from north to south while eastern Colombia, the Amazon, is only sparsely populated. The largest cities are Bogotá (7.5 million), Medellín (2.5 million), Cali (2.25 million) and Barranquilla (1.3 million).

Colombia's diverse population, an amalgam of three main groups – indigenous, Spanish and African – reflects its colorful history. While 58% of the country claims *mestizo* (mixed white and indigenous) heritage, other ethnicities include: 20% white, 14% mixed white and black, 4% black, 3% mixed black and indigenous, and only 1% indigenous. Colombia's indigenous population speak about 65 languages and nearly 300 dialects belonging to several linguistic families.

Colombia has started to see more immigration from the Middle East, particularly from Turkey and Lebanon, but also from other parts of Latin America including Peru, Ecuador and the Caribbean. Meanwhile the conflict in the southern areas of the country has displaced tens of thousands of Colombians into neighboring Ecuador.

SPORTS

Soccer and cycling are the most popular spectator sports. Colombia regularly takes part in international events in these two fields, such as the World Cup and the Tour de France, and has recorded some successes. Baseball is limited to the Caribbean coast. The national soccer league has matches most of the year.

Colombians are passionate about *corrida* (bullfighting), which was introduced by the Spaniards. Most cities and towns have *plaza de toros* (bullrings). The bullfighting season usually peaks in January, when the top-ranking matadors are invited from Spain.

RELIGION

The great majority of Colombians are Roman Catholic. Other creeds are officially permitted but their numbers are small. However, over the past decade there has been a proliferation of various Protestant congregations, which have succeeded in converting some three million Catholics. Many indigenous groups have adopted the Catholic faith, sometimes incorporating some of their traditional beliefs. There are small numbers of Colombian Jews and synagogues in most big cities.

ARTS
Architecture
The most outstanding example of pre-Columbian urban planning is the Ciudad Perdida of the Tayronas in the Sierra Nevada de Santa Marta. Although the dwellings haven't survived, the stone structures, including a complex network of terraces, paths and stairways, remain in remarkably good shape.

After the arrival of the Spaniards, bricks and tiles became the main construction materials. The colonial towns followed rigid standards laid down by the Spanish Crown. They were constructed on a grid plan, centered on the Plaza Mayor (main square). This pattern was applied during the colonial period and long after, and is the dominant feature of most Colombian cities, towns and villages.

Spain's strong Catholic tradition left behind loads of churches and convents in the colony – the central areas of Bogotá, Cartagena, Popayán and Tunja are fine examples.

In the 19th century, despite independence the architecture continued to be predominantly Spanish in style. Modern architectural trends only began to appear in Colombia after WWII. This process accelerated during the 1960s when city skyscrapers appeared.

The latest architectural phenomenon in Colombia is urban planning. The success of the TransMilenio, car-free Sundays, bike lanes and the expansion of parks in Bogotá has become a model for other cities in South America, Africa and Asia. The self-proclaimed architect of this urban redevelopment plan, former Bogotá mayor Enrique Peñalosa, has taken the Bogotá scheme on the road, promoting it as a model for other third-world cities.

Cinema
The most internationally famous of recent Colombian films, *Maria, llena eres de gracia* (Maria Full of Grace; 2004) joined American and Colombian production in a moving film about a pregnant 17-year-old flower-industry employee who leaves her small-town existence to smuggle heroin into the US as a mule.

Two other recent films that looked at Colombian issues of drugs and violence are *Sumas y Restas* (2004) and *Rosario Tijeras* (2005). Though both films were extremely popular in Colombia they lacked international backing and therefore didn't garner the same global attention as *Maria Full of Grace*.

Hollywood has had its own take on Colombia, including *Romancing the Stone* (1984), starring Michael Douglas and Kathleen Turner, as well as *Clear and Present Danger* (1994) starring Harrison Ford.

Literature
During the independence period and up to WWII, Colombia produced few internationally acclaimed writers other than José Asunción Silva (1865–96), perhaps the country's best poet, considered the precursor of modernism in Latin America.

A postwar literary boom thrust many great Latin American authors into the international sphere, including the Colombian Gabriel García Márquez (born 1928). Gabo's novel *One Hundred Years of Solitude,* published in 1967, immediately became a worldwide best seller. It mixed myths, dreams and reality, and amazed readers with a new form of expression that critics dubbed *realismo mágico* (magic realism). In 1982 García Márquez won the Nobel Prize for literature. His most recent book, titled *Memories of My Melancholy Whores,* was released in 2005.

There are several contemporaries who deserve recognition including poet, novelist and painter Héctor Rojas Herazo, and Álvaro Mutis, a close friend of Gabo. Of the younger generation, seek out the works of Fernando Vallejo, a highly respected iconoclast who has been surprisingly critical of García Márquez.

Music
In broad terms Colombia can be divided into four musical zones: the two coasts, the Andean region and Los Llanos. The Caribbean coast vibrates with hot African-related rhythms such as the *cumbia, mapalé* and *porro.* The coast is also the cradle of the *vallenato,* based on the European accordion, which emanated a century ago from the regions of La Guajira and Cesar and has successfully conquered just about the whole of the country. This is the most popular Colombian musical genre today.

HEAVY METAL

César López has a vision for Colombia: more music, less murder. As an antiwar activist and musician, the 32-year-old Bogotáno has always believed that he could promote peace through soothing guitar riffs. This belief led to the formation of the 'Battalion of Immediate Artists Reaction,' a group of musicians and artists dedicated to peaceful reconciliation between Colombia's many warring factions.

As part of its agenda, the Battalion will occasionally take to the streets, playing impromptu concerts at former scenes of violence. In 2003 the group shouldered up with gun-toting soldiers inspecting the wreckage of the El Nogal country club, where a devastating car bomb had just killed more than 30 people. It was here that López noticed how the soldiers held their guns in the same way that he held his guitar, and an idea was born. The result was the *escopetarra*, a gun transformed into a guitar.

The original *escopetarra* was fashioned out of an old Winchester lever-action rifle. Since then López has created several dozen other guitar-guns, some built from AK-47 assault rifles donated by the peace commissioners office. Battalion members use the guitars during their peace concerts, but some have been donated to likeminded celebrities hoping to wage peace. Shakira, Santana, Paul McCartney and Carlos Vives are but a few musicians to try out this new brand of 'heavy metal.'

López's latest headline-grabbing project includes the formation of a new band, the Experimental Reconciliation Group, made up of seven musicians from various paramilitary, army, left-wing guerrilla and gang backgrounds. You can read more about César López at www.cesarlopez.org.

The music of the Pacific coast, such as the *currulao*, is based on a strong African drum pulse, but tinged with Spanish influences. Colombian Andean music has been strongly influenced by Spanish rhythms and instruments, and differs notably from the indigenous music of the Peruvian and Bolivian highlands. Among the typical forms are the *bambuco, pasillo* and *torbellino*, all of which are instrumental and predominantly feature string instruments. The music of Los Llanos, *música llanera*, is sung and usually accompanied by a harp, *cuatro* (a sort of four-string guitar) and maracas.

Colombia's most famous musical export is Shakira, whose album *Fijación Oral Vol 2* (2005) cemented her as a global superstar with staying power. Other Colombian artists known beyond the country's borders include Carlos Vives (a Latin-pop vocalist), Totó La Momposina (a traditional Afro-Caribbean music singer), Juanes (Latin rock vocalist) and Los Aterciopelados (Colombia's most popular rock group).

Visual Arts

The colonial period was dominated by Spanish religious art, and although the paintings and sculptures of this era were generally executed by local artists, they reflected the Spanish trends of the day. With the arrival of independence visual arts departed from strictly religious themes, but it was not until the turn-of-the-19th-century revolution in European painting that Colombian artists began to experiment and create original work.

Among the most distinguished modern painters and sculptors are Pedro Nel Gómez, known for his murals, oils and sculptures; Luis Alberto Acuña, a painter and sculptor who used motifs from pre-Columbian art; Alejandro Obregón, a painter tending to abstract forms; Rodrigo Arenas Betancur, Colombia's most famous monument creator; and Fernando Botero, the most internationally renowned Colombian artist, whose somewhat ironic style of painting and sculpture is easily recognizable by the characteristic fatness of the figures.

The recent period has been characterized by a proliferation of schools, trends and techniques. The artists to watch out for include Bernardo Salcedo (conceptual sculpture and photography), Miguel Ángel Rojas (painting and installations), and the talented Doris Salcedo (sculpture and installations).

ENVIRONMENT
The Land

Colombia covers 1,141,748 sq km, roughly equivalent to the area of France, Spain and Portugal combined. It occupies the northwestern part of the continent and is the only South American country with coasts on both the Pacific (1448km long) and the Caribbean (1760km). Colombia is bordered by Panama Venezuela, Brazil, Peru and Ecuador.

CARTAGENA – OLD TOWN

0 —————— 200 m
0 —————— 0.1 miles

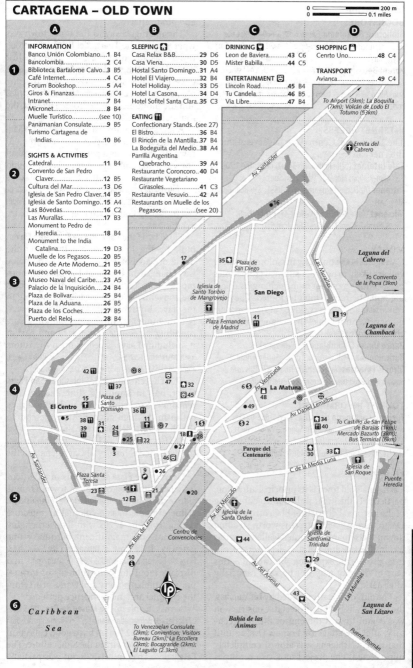

INFORMATION
Banco Unión Colombiano....**1** C4
Bancolombia..........................**2** C4
Biblioteca Bartalome Calvo..**3** B5
Café Internet.......................**4** C4
Forum Bookshop..................**5** A4
Giros & Finanzas..................**6** C4
Intranet..............................**7** B4
Micronet............................**8** B4
Muelle Turístico.............(see 10)
Panamanian Consulate........**9** B5
Turismo Cartagena de
  Indias.............................**10** B6

SIGHTS & ACTIVITIES
Catedral............................**11** B4
Convento de San Pedro
  Claver............................**12** B5
Cultura del Mar..................**13** D6
Iglesia de San Pedro Claver..**14** B5
Iglesia de Santo Domingo...**15** A4
Las Bóvedas......................**16** C2
Las Murallas......................**17** B3
Monument to Pedro de
  Heredia...........................**18** B4
Monument to the India
  Catalina..........................**19** D3
Muelle de los Pegasos........**20** B5
Museo de Arte Moderno.....**21** B5
Museo del Oro...................**22** B4
Museo Naval del Caribe......**23** A5
Palacio de la Inquisición.....**24** B4
Plaza de Bolívar.................**25** B4
Plaza de la Aduana............**26** B5
Plaza de los Coches...........**27** B5
Puerto del Reloj.................**28** B4

SLEEPING 🏠
Casa Relax B&B..................**29** D6
Casa Viena.......................**30** D5
Hostal Santo Domingo.......**31** A4
Hotel El Viajero................**32** B4
Hotel Holiday....................**33** D5
Hotel La Casona................**34** D4
Hotel Sofitel Santa Clara...**35** C3

EATING 🍴
Confectionary Stands..(see 27)
El Bistro...........................**36** B4
El Rincón de la Mantilla.....**37** B4
La Bodeguita del Medio.....**38** A4
Parrilla Argentina
  Quebracho......................**39** A4
Restaurante Coroncoro......**40** D4
Restaurante Vegetariano
  Girasoles........................**41** A5
Restaurante Vesuvio.......**42** A4
Restaurants on Muelle de los
  Pegasos.......................(see 20)

DRINKING 🍷
Leon de Baviera.................**43** C6
Mister Babilla....................**44** C5

ENTERTAINMENT 🎭
Lincoln Road......................**45** B4
Tu Candela........................**46** B5
Via Libre...........................**47** B4

SHOPPING 🛍
Cenrto Uno........................**48** C4

TRANSPORT
Avianca.............................**49** C4

To Airport (3km); La Boquilla
(7km); Volcán de Lodo El
Totumo (53km)

Av Santander

Ermita del
Cabrero

Laguna del
Cabrero

To Convento
de la Popa (3km)

Laguna de
Chambacú

San Diego

Iglesia de
Santo Toribio
de Mangrovejo

Plaza de
San Diego

Plaza Fernandez
de Madrid

Av Venezuela   La Matuna

Av Daniel Lemaître

El Centro

Plaza de
Santo
Domingo

Parque del
Centenario

Plaza Santa
Teresa

C de la Media Luna

Iglesia de
San Roque

Puente
Heredia

To Castillo de San Felipe
de Barajas (1km);
Mercado Bazurto (3km);
Bus Terminal (6km)

Av del Mercado

Iglesia de la
Santa Orden

Getsemaní

Av Blas de Lezo

Av Santander

Centro de
Convenciones

Iglesia de
Santísima
Trinidad

Av del Arsenal

Laguna de
San Lázaro

*Caribbean
Sea*

To Venezuelan Consulate
(2km); Convention; Visitors
Bureau (2km); La Escollera
(2km); Bocagrande (2km);
El Laguito (2.3km)

*Bahía de las
Ánimas*

Las Murallas

Puente Román

Information

BOOKSTORES

Biblioteca Bartolome Calvo (☎ 5-660-0778; Calle de la Inquisición; ☺ 8:30am-6pm Mon-Fri, 9am-1pm Sat) City library.

Forum Bookshop (☎ 5-664-8290; cnr De Los Estribos & Paseo del Triunfo; ☺ 9am-8:30pm Mon-Sat, 4-8pm Sun) Good selection of books on Cartagena. It also serves coffee and snacks.

INTERNET ACCESS

The 2nd floor of Centro Uno has several small internet cafés.

Café Internet (Calle Roman No 34-02; per hr US$1.20; ☺ 8am-7:30pm Mon-Sat, 9am-2pm Sun)

Intranet (Av Daniel Lemaitre; per hr US$1; ☺ 8am-6pm Mon-Sat)

Micronet (Calle de la Estrella No 4-47; per hr US80¢; ☺ 8:30am-7:30pm Mon-Fri, 9am-4pm Sat)

MONEY

Cartagena is the only city in Colombia where you are likely to be propositioned (sometimes persistently) by street money changers offering fantastic rates. Don't be fooled. They are con artists and are very skilled at stealing your money. Central banks that change traveler's checks and/or cash:

Banco Unión Colombiano (Av Venezuela)

Bancolombia (Av Venezuela, Edificio Sur Americana)

Giros & Finanzas (Av Venezuela No 8A-87) This *casa de cambio* in the old town represents Western Union.

TOURIST INFORMATION

Turismo Cartagena de Indias (☎ 5-655-0211; www.turismocartagena.com in Spanish; Av Blas de Lezo; ☺ 8am-noon & 2-6pm Mon-Fri, 8am-noon Sat) The tourist office is situated in the Muelle Turístico.

Sights

Cartagena's old town is its principal attraction, particularly the inner walled town consisting of the historical districts of El Centro and San Diego. Almost every street is worth strolling down. Getsemaní, the outer walled town, is less impressive and not so well preserved, but it is also worth exploring. Be careful – this part of the city may not be safe, especially after dark.

The old town is surrounded by **Las Murallas**, the thick walls built to protect it. Construction was begun toward the end of the 16th century, after the attack by Francis Drake; until that time, Cartagena was almost completely unprotected. The project took two centuries to complete, due to repeated storm damage and pirate attacks.

The main gateway to the inner town was what is now the **Puerta del Reloj** (the clock tower was added in the 19th century). Just behind it is the **Plaza de los Coches**, a square once used as a slave market. Note the fine old houses with colonial arches and balconies and the monument to Pedro de Heredia, the founder of the city.

A few steps southwest is the **Plaza de la Aduana**, the oldest and largest square in the old town. It was used as a parade ground and all governmental buildings were gathered around it. At the southern outlet from the plaza is the **Museo de Arte Moderno** (☎ 5-664-5815; Plaza de San Pedro Claver; admission US50¢; ☺ 9am-noon & 3-6pm Mon-Fri, 10am-1pm Sat), which presents temporary exhibitions.

Close by is the **Convento de San Pedro Claver**, built by the Jesuits, originally under the name of San Ignacio de Loyola. The name was changed in honor of the Spanish-born monk Pedro Claver, who lived and died in the convent. He spent his life ministering to the slaves brought from Africa. The convent is a monumental three-story building surrounding a tree-filled courtyard and part of it, including Claver's cell, is open to visitors as a **museum** (☎ 5-664-4991; Plaza de San Pedro Claver; admission US$2; ☺ 8am-5pm Mon-Sat, to 4pm Sun).

The church alongside, **Iglesia de San Pedro Claver**, has an imposing stone façade. The remains of San Pedro Claver are kept in a glass coffin in the high altar. Behind the church the **Museo Naval del Caribe** (☎ 5-664-7381; Calle San Juan de Dios; admission US$3.50; ☺ 9am-7pm Tue-Sun) traces the naval history of Cartagena and the Caribbean.

Nearby, the **Plaza de Bolívar** is in a particularly beautiful area of the old town. On one side of the square is the **Palacio de la Inquisición**, a fine example of late-colonial architecture dating from the 1770s with its overhanging balconies and magnificent baroque stone gateway. It is now a **museum** (☎ 5-664-4113; Plaza de Bolívar; admission US$1.60; ☺ 9am-7pm) that displays Inquisitors' instruments of torture, pre-Columbian pottery and works of art from the colonial and independence periods.

Across the plaza, the **Museo del Oro** (☎ 5-660-0778; Plaza de Bolívar; admission free; ☺ 10am-1pm & 3-6pm Tue-Fri, 10am-1pm & 2-5pm Sat) has a good collection of gold and pottery from the Sinú culture. The **Catedral** was begun in 1575 but was partially destroyed by Drake's cannons in 1586, and not completed until 1612. The dome on the tower was added early in the 20th century.

One block west of the plaza is **Calle Santo Domingo**, a street that has hardly changed since the 17th century. On it stands the **Iglesia de Santo Domingo**, the city's oldest church. It is a large, heavy construction, and buttresses had to be added to the walls to support the naves.

At the northern tip of the old town are **Las Bóvedas**, 23 dungeons built in the defensive walls at the end of the 18th century. This was the last construction done in colonial times, and was destined for military purposes. Today the dungeons are tourist shops.

While you're wandering around call in at the **Muelle de Los Pegasos**, a lovely old port full of fishing, cargo and tourist boats, just outside the old town's southern walls.

Several forts were built at key points outside the walls to protect the city from pirates. By far the greatest is the huge stone fortress **Castillo de San Felipe de Barajas** (☎ 5-656-0590, 5-666-4790; Av Arévalo; admission US$3; ⏰ 8am-6pm), east of the old town, begun in 1639 but not completed until some 150 years later. Don't miss the impressive walk through the complex system of tunnels, built to facilitate the supply and evacuation of the fort.

The **Convento de La Popa** (☎ 5-666-2331; admission US$2.50; ⏰ 9am-5pm), perched on top of a 150m hill beyond the San Felipe fortress, was founded by the Augustinians in 1607. It has a nice chapel and a lovely flower-filled patio, and offers panoramic views of the city. There have been some cases of armed robbery on the zigzagging access road to the top – take a taxi (there's no public transport).

Activities

Taking advantage of the extensive coral reefs along Cartagena's coast, Cartagena has grown into an important **scuba-diving** center. Most local dive schools are in Bocagrande and El Laguito.

Caribe Dive Shop (☎ 5-665-3517; www.caribedive shop.com; Hotel Caribe, Bocagrande)

Cultura del Mar (☎ 5-664-9312; Calle del Pozo 25-95, Getsamaní)

Dolphin Dive School (☎ 5-660-0814; www.dolphin diveschool.com; Edificio Costamar, Av San Martín No 6-105, Bocagrande)

Eco Buzos (☎ 5-655-5449; Edificio Alonso de Ojeda, Av Almirante Brion, El Laguito)

Festivals & Events

Cartagena's major annual events:

Festival Internacional de Cine International film festival, held in March/April, usually shortly before Easter.

Feria Artesanal y Cultural Regional craft fair taking place in June/July, accompanied by folk-music concerts and other cultural events.

Reinado Nacional de Belleza National beauty pageant held on November 11 to celebrate Cartagena's independence day. The fiesta strikes up several days before and the city goes wild. The event, also known as the Carnaval de Cartagena or Fiestas del 11 de Noviembre, is the city's most important annual bash.

Sleeping

Cartagena has a reasonable choice of budget accommodations and despite its touristy status, the prices of its hotels are no higher than in other large cities. The tourist peak is from late December to late January but, even then, it's relatively easy to find a room.

Most backpackers stay in Getsemaní. There are lots of small lodges here where you can get a bed for US$5 or less. However, even if you are on a tight budget Cartagena is one city where you may want to upgrade and stay in the nicer barrio of El Centro or San Diego, especially if you can get a room with air-con. All hotels listed below have rooms with fans, unless specified.

Hotel Holiday (☎ 5-664-0948; Calle de la Media Luna, Getsemaní; s/d with bathroom US$4.50/9) A popular and friendly traveler hangout. Its 13 neat, airy double rooms with bath are good value, and there are four smaller rooms without private facilities.

Casa Viena (☎ 5-664-6242; www.casaviena.com; Calle San Andrés, Getsemaní; dm with air-con US$3, d with/without bathroom US$10/5; 🕮 💻) One of the most popular and cheapest backpacker haunts has simple rooms, most with shared bathrooms. The hotel offers a typical range of facilities including laundry, book exchange, individual strongboxes and tourist information.

Hotel La Casona (☎ 5-664-1301; Calle Tripita y Media No 31-32, Getsemaní; s/d with air-con US$12/16.50, without air-con US$7/12; 🕮) This family-run hotel consists of several boxy rooms with private bathroom. There's a friendly monkey in residence, as well as some tropical birds.

Hotel Las Vegas (☎ 5-664-5619; Calle San Agustín No 6-08; s/d/tr US$14/19/23; 🕮) Just round the corner from El Viajero, Las Vegas is another decent choice in this central area. Rooms are clean

SPLURGE!

Hotel Sofitel Santa Clara (☎ 5-664-6070; www.hotelsantaclara.com; Calle del Torno, San Diego; d US$300, ste US$360-400; P ✗ ✗ ☐ ✗) The sumptuous hotel shows little of its bland past – it used to be the Convento de Santa Clara (dating from 1621), and was later a charity hospital. Now the essence of luxury, it has 162 rooms and 18 suites, a gym, business center and two restaurants (French and Italian). As the premier place in town, it has seen its share of famous faces – even President Clinton lunched here in 2000. If you can't afford to spend the night it's still worth coming in for a drink; try the atmospheric El Coro bar, which is dressed up like an antiquarian library.

and come with TV. But those that face the street are noisy day and night.

Hotel El Viajero (☎ 5-664-3289; Calle del Porvenir No 35-68; s/d US$16/21; ✗) One of the best budget bets in the area, this recently renovated 14-room hotel has a spacious courtyard and free use of the kitchen.

Hostal Santo Domingo (☎ 5-664-2268; Calle Santo Domingo No 33-46; s/d/tr with bathroom US$20/28/34; ✗) On a lovely street in El Centro, this one offers few amenities for the price. For air-con, tack on another US$6 per person.

Casa Relax B&B (☎ 5-664-1117; www.cartagenarelax .com; Calle de Pozo No 20-105; s/d US$36/45; ✗ ☐ ✗) The best place to stay in Getsemaní, this French-run B&B has 10 well-appointed rooms with TV and modern bathroom. A French breakfast is served around a communal table, allowing you to get to know the other guests.

Eating

Cartagena is a good place to eat, particularly at the upmarket level, but cheap places are also plentiful. Dozens of simple restaurants in the old town serve set *almuerzos* for less than US$2, and many also offer set *comidas*. Among the most reliable is **Restaurante Coroncoro** (Calle Tripita y Media, Getsemaní; ☯ 8am-8pm). For veggie meals, try **Restaurante Vegetariano Girasoles** (Calle Quero, San Diego; ☯ 11:30am-5pm).

A dozen stalls on the Muelle de los Pegasos operate around the clock and offer plenty of local snacks, plus an unbelievable selection of fruit juices – try *níspero* (round fruit with soft flesh), *maracuyá* (passion fruit), *lulo* (prickly fruit with very soft flesh), *zapote* (eggplant-shaped fruit with orange, fibrous flesh) and *guanábana* (soursop). You can also try some typical local sweets at the confectionery stands at El Portal de los Dulces on the Plaza de los Coches.

Plaza Santo Domingo hosts six open-air cafés, serving a varied menu of dishes, snacks,

sweets and drinks. The cafés are not that cheap but the place is trendy and invariably fills up in the evening.

El Bistro (Calle de Ayos No 4-42; sandwiches US$2.50; ☯ 8am-11pm Mon-Sat) Run by a pair of Germans, El Bistro offers useful travel tips and serves budget lunches and excellent dinners.

La Bodeguita del Medio (Calle Santo Domingo; mains US$6-9; ☯ noon-midnight) Eat, drink and be merry under the watchful eyes of Che Guevara and Fidel Castro.

Restaurante Vesuvio (Calle de la Factoria No 36-11; mains US$5-8; ☯ 11am-3pm & 6pm-1am Mon-Sat, 6pm-1am Sun) Run by a friendly Neapolitan named Mariano, this place serves authentic Italian meals and desserts. It's a favorite among Italian expats living in Cartagena.

El Rincón de la Mantilla (Calle de la Mantilla No 3-32; mains US$6-9; ☯ 8am-10pm Mon-Sat) This atmospheric Colombian place serves meals both hot and fast. To cool off, try their excellent *sapote*, an addictive milk and fruit shake.

Parrilla Argentina Quebracho (Calle de Baloco; mains US$8-12; ☯ noon-3pm & 7pm-midnight Mon-Thu, noon-midnight Fri & Sat) Argentine cuisine including famous juicy steaks in appropriately decorated surroundings, plus tango shows in the evening.

Drinking

A number of bars, taverns, discos and other venues stay open late. Plenty of them are on Av del Arsenal in Getsemaní, Cartagena's Zona Rosa.

Leon de Baviera (Av del Arsenal No 10B-65; ☯ 4pm-3am Tue-Sat) Run by an expat German named Stefan, this place is a little heavy on the Bavarian atmosphere, but still a great place to start a night of boozing. Expect lots of '80s and '90s rock music.

Entertainment

You can go on a night trip aboard a *chiva*, a typical Colombian bus, with a band playing *vallenato*, a popular local rhythm. *Chivas* depart around 8pm from Av San Martín between Calles 4 and 5 in Bocagrande for a three- to four-hour trip, and leave you at the end of the tour in a discotheque – a good point from which to continue partying for the rest of the night.

Mister Babilla (Av del Arsenal No 8B-137; admission US$6; ⏰ 9pm-4am) This is one of the most popular discos in this area, yet also one of the most expensive ones. You will find cheaper venues nearby; just walk along the street, as everybody does, and take your pick.

Tu Candela (Portal de los Dulces No 32-25; admission US$4; ⏰ 8pm-4am) The upstairs portion of this club is great for salsa dancing while the downstairs is better for a quiet drink. It has a great location in the old town.

GAY & LESBIAN VENUES

Lincoln Road (Centro Calle del Porvenir No 35-18; admission US$4; ⏰ 10:30pm-3am Thu-Sat) Ultraflash gay club with lasers, strobe lights and pumping music, plus the occasional striptease.

Via Libre (Centro Calle de la Soledad No 5-52; admission US$4; ⏰ 10pm-4am Sat) Only open one night a week, this gay and lesbian–friendly discotheque is more casual than Lincoln Rd.

Getting There & Away

AIR

All major Colombian carriers operate flights to and from Cartagena. There are flights to Bogotá (US$90 to US$120), Cali (US$120 to US$150), Medellín (US$80 to US$125) and San Andrés (US$230 to US$250 return) among others.

The airport is in the suburb of Crespo, 3km northeast of the old city, and is serviced by frequent local buses that depart from various points, including India Catalina and Av Santander. *Colectivos* to Crespo depart from India Catalina; the trip costs US$3 by taxi. The terminal has two ATMs and the Casa de Cambio América (in domestic arrivals) changes cash and traveler's checks.

BOAT

There's no ferry service between Cartagena and Colón in Panama, and there are very few cargo boats. A more pleasant way of getting to Panama is by sailboat. There are various boats, mostly foreign yachts, that take travelers from Cartagena to Colón via San Blas Archipelago (Panama) and vice versa, but this is not a

regular service. The trip takes four to six days and normally includes a couple of days at San Blas for snorkeling and spear fishing. It costs between US$220 to US$270, plus about US$30 for food.

Check the advertising boards at Casa Viena and Hotel Holiday in Cartagena for contact details. Boats include the **Golden Eagle** (☎ 311-419-0428) and the **Melody** (☎ 315-756-2818; freshaircharters@yahoo.com); both have semiregular departures.

Beware of any con men attempting to lure you into 'amazing' Caribbean boat trips. We've heard horror stories of boats breaking down midvoyage, barely able to reach land because of a damaged mast or some other equipment failure. The most reliable boats trips will be organized via Casa Viena.

BUS

The bus terminal is on the eastern outskirts of the city, a long way from the center. Large green-and-white air-con Metrocar buses shuttle between the two every 10 minutes (US50¢, 40 minutes). In the center, you can catch them on Av Daniel Lemaitre. Catch the one with red letters on the board, which goes by a more direct route and is faster.

Half-a-dozen buses go daily to Bogotá (US$43, 20 hours) and another half-a-dozen to Medellín (US$40, 13 hours). Buses to Barranquilla run every 15 minutes or so (US$4, two hours), and some continue on to Santa Marta; if not, just change in Barranquilla. Unitransco has one bus to Mompós at 7am (US$15, eight hours); see Mompós (p590).

Three bus companies – **Expreso Brasilia** (☎ 5-663-2119), **Expresos Amerlujo** (☎ 5-653-2536) and **Unitransco/Bus Ven** (☎ 5-663-2065) – operate daily buses to Caracas (US$68, 20 hours) via Maracaibo (US$37, 10 hours). Unitransco is a bit cheaper than the other two, but you have to change buses on the border in Paraguachón. All buses go via Barranquilla, Santa Marta and Maicao. You'll save if you do the trip to Caracas in stages by local transport, with changes in Maicao and Maracaibo.

AROUND CARTAGENA
Islas del Rosario

This archipelago, about 35km southwest of Cartagena, consists of 27 small coral islands, including some tiny islets only big enough for a single house. The whole area has been decreed a national park, the Corales del Rosario.

Cruises through the islands are well established. Tours depart year-round from the Muelle Turístico in Cartagena. Boats leave between 8am and 9am daily and return about 4pm to 6pm. The cruise office at the Muelle sells tours in big boats for about US$18, but independent operators hanging around may offer cheaper tours in smaller vessels, for US$16 or even less. It's probably best (and often cheapest) to arrange the tour through one of the budget gringo hotels. Tours normally include lunch, but not the entrance fee to the aquarium (US$5) on one of the islands, the port tax (US$2) and the national-park entrance fee (US$2).

Playa Blanca

This is one of the most beautiful beaches around Cartagena. It's about 20km southwest of the city, on the Isla de Barú, and it's the usual stop for the boat tours to the Islas del Rosario. The place is also good for snorkeling as the coral reef begins just off the beach (take snorkeling gear).

The beach has some rustic places to stay and eat. The most popular with travelers is **Campamento Wittenberg** (☎ 311-436-6215), run by a Frenchman named Gilbert. It offers accommodations in beds (US$4) or hammocks (US$3) and serves meals.

The easiest way of getting to the beach is with Gilbert, who comes to Casa Viena in Cartagena once a week (usually on Wednesday) and takes travelers in his boat (US$6, 45 minutes). If this doesn't coincide with your itinerary, go to Cartagena's main market, Mercado Bazurto, and go by boat or bus. Boats depart from about 8am to 10:30am daily except Sunday, when an early-morning bus runs directly to the beach.

La Boquilla

This small fishing village is 7km north of Cartagena on a peninsula between the sea and the seaside lagoon. There's a pleasant place known as El Paraíso, a five-minute walk from the bus terminus, where you can enjoy a day on the beach. The locals fish with their famous *atarrayas* (a kind of net) at the lagoon, and you can arrange boat trips with them along the narrow water channels cutting through the mangrove woods. Negotiate the price and only pay after they bring you back.

Plenty of beachfront palm-thatched restaurants attract people from Cartagena on weekends; most are closed at other times.

Frequent city buses run to La Boquilla from India Catalina in Cartagena (US40¢, 30 minutes).

Volcán de Lodo El Totumo

About 50km northeast of Cartagena, on the bank of the shallow Ciénaga del Totumo, is an intriguing 15m mound, looking like a miniature volcano. It's indeed a volcano but instead of lava and ashes it spews mud, a phenomenon caused by the pressure of gases emitted by decaying organic matter underground.

El Totumo is the highest mud volcano in Colombia. Lukewarm mud with the consistency of cream fills its crater. You can climb to the top by specially built stairs, then go down into the crater and have a refreshing mud bath (US50¢). It's a unique experience – surely volcano-dipping is something you haven't yet tried! The mud contains minerals acclaimed for their therapeutic properties. Once you've finished your session, go down and wash the mud off in the *ciénaga* (lagoon).

To get to the volcano from Cartagena, take a bus from Mercado Bazurto, from where hourly buses depart in the morning to Galerazamba. They travel along the old Barranquilla road up to Santa Catalina then, shortly after, turn north onto a side road to Galerazamba. Get off on the coastal highway by the petrol station at Lomita Arena (US$1.50, 1½ hours) and walk along the highway 2.5km toward Barranquilla (30 minutes), then to the right (southeast) 1km to the volcano (another 15 minutes). The last direct bus from Lomita Arena back to Cartagena departs at around 5pm.

Several tour operators in Cartagena organize minibus trips to the volcano (transport only US$11; with lunch in La Boquilla US$14), which can be booked through popular backpacker hotels.

Jardín Botánico Guillermo Piñeres

A pleasant half-day escape from the city rush, this **botanical garden** (☎ 5-663-7172; admission US$4; ⊙ 9am-4pm Tue-Sun) is on the outskirts of the town of Turbaco, 15km southeast of Cartagena. Take the Turbaco bus departing regularly from next to the Castillo de San Felipe in Cartagena and ask the driver to drop you at the turnoff to the garden (US75¢, 45 minutes). From there it's a 20-minute stroll down the largely unpaved side road. The 20-acre garden features plants typical of the coast, including two varieties of coca plant.

MOMPÓS

☎ 5 / pop 28,000

In the evenings, when the residents of Mompós rock calmly in their rocking chairs and the bats flutter through the eaves, you may feel like you've stepped into the pages of *Huckleberry Finn* or *Gone with the Wind*.

The atmosphere evoked in the Mompós environs is unique in Colombia (it may feel more like Mississippi) and is worth experiencing, despite the hardships of getting here. Surrounded by muddy rivers and thick vegetation, Mompós is 230km southeast of Cartagena, and reached by a combination of bus, boat and car.

Founded in 1537 on the eastern branch of the Río Magdalena, the town soon became an important port through which all merchandise from Cartagena passed to the interior of the colony. Several imposing churches and many luxurious mansions were built.

Toward the end of the 19th century shipping was diverted to the other branch of the Magdalena, ending the town's prosperity. Mompós has been left in isolation and little has changed since. Its colonial character is very much in evidence.

Mompós also has a tradition in literature and was the setting for *Chronicle of a Death Foretold* by Gabriel García Márquez.

Information

ATM (BBVA; Plaza de Bolívar)

Club Net (Carrera 1 No 16-53; per hr US80¢; ⏰ 6am-9:30pm) Internet café.

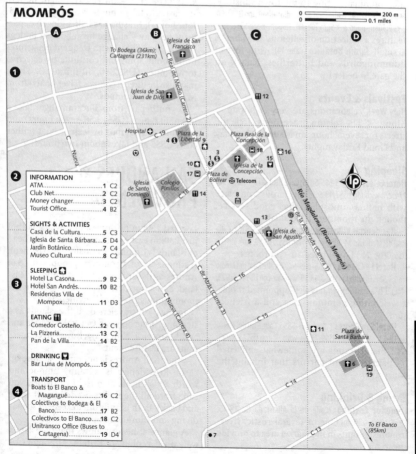

MOMPÓS

0 ————— 200 m
0 ————— 0.1 miles

INFORMATION
ATM	1 C2
Club Net	2 C2
Money changer	3 C2
Tourist Office	4 B2

SIGHTS & ACTIVITIES
Casa de la Cultura	5 C3
Iglesia de Santa Bárbara	6 D4
Jardín Botánico	7 C4
Museo Cultural	8 C2

SLEEPING
Hotel La Casona	9 B2
Hotel San Andrés	10 B2
Residencias Villa de Mompox	11 D3

EATING
Comedor Costeño	12 C1
La Pizzería	13 C2
Pan de la Villa	14 B2

DRINKING
Bar Luna de Mompós	15 C2

TRANSPORT
Boats to El Banco & Magangué	16 C2
Colectivos to Bodega & El Banco	17 B2
Colectivos to El Banco	18 C2
Unitransco Office (Buses to Cartagena)	19 D4

COLOMBIA

Money changer (Plaza de Bolívar) May change your US dollars at a very poor rate.

Tourist office (☎ 5-685-5738; Plaza de la Libertad) Located in the Alcaldía building. Ask where to find artisans workshops where you can see and buy local jewelry.

Sights

Most of the central streets are lined with fine whitewashed colonial houses with characteristic metal-grill windows, imposing doorways and lovely hidden patios. Six colonial churches complete the scene; all are interesting, though rarely open. Don't miss the **Iglesia de Santa Bárbara** (Calle 14) with its Moorish-style tower, unique in Colombian religious architecture.

The **Casa de la Cultura** (Calle Real del Medio; admission US50¢; ⏰ 8am-5pm Mon-Fri) displays memorabilia relating to the town's history. **Museo Cultural** (Calle Real del Medio; admission US$1.50; ⏰ 9:30am-noon & 3-5pm Tue-Fri, 9:30am-noon Sat & Sun) features a collection of religious art. There's a small **Jardín Botánico** (Calle 14), with lots of hummingbirds and butterflies. Knock on the gate to be let in.

Festivals & Events

Holy Week celebrations are very elaborate in Mompós. The solemn processions circle the streets for several hours on Maundy Thursday and Good Friday nights.

Sleeping

Hotel Celeste (☎ 5-685-5875; Calle Real del Medio No 14-174; s/d with fan US$7/13.50) This family-run place with nanna atmosphere has good service, though the rooms are a tad small.

Residencias Villa de Mompox (☎ 5-685-5208; Calle Real del Medio No 14-108; s/d with fan US$7/13.50, with air-con US$10/19; 🞂) Low-priced air-con rooms.

Hotel La Casona (☎ 5-685-5307; Calle Real del Medio No 18-58; s/d with fan US$8/13.50, with air-con US$13.50/23; 🞂) This *residencia* has well-appointed rooms, a welcoming common area and a friendly staff.

Hotel San Andrés (☎ 5-685-5886; Calle Real del Medio No 18-23; s/d with fan US$9/13.50, with air-con US$13.50/23; 🞂) Bland rooms are somewhat enlivened by parakeets and parrots that inhabit the courtyard.

Eating & Drinking

Comedor Costeño (Calle de la Albarrada No 18-45; ⏰ 5:30am-4:30pm) One of several rustic, riverfront restaurants in the market area to provide cheap meals.

Pan de la Villa (Calle 18 No 2-53; ⏰ 7am-10pm) Specializes in ice cream, cakes and baked goods, but also serves crêpes.

La Pizzeria (Carrera 2 No 16-02; pizzas US$6-9; ⏰ 5-10pm) In the evenings you can sit at tables set in the middle of the street and enjoy a cold drink or pizza.

Bar Luna de Mompós (Calle de la Albarrada; ⏰ 6pm-late) This low-key bayou drinking hole will keep you entertained until you pass out or the doors close.

Getting There & Away

Mompós is well off the main routes, but can be reached relatively easily by road and river. Most travelers come here from Cartagena. Unitransco has one direct bus daily leaving Cartagena at 7:30am (US$15, eight hours). It's faster to take a bus to Magangué (US$11, four hours); Brasilia has half-a-dozen departures per day – change for a boat to Bodega (US$2, 20 minutes) with frequent departures until about 3pm, and continue by *colectivo* to Mompós (US$2.50, 40 minutes). There may also be direct *chalupas* (river boats) from Magangué to Mompós.

If you depart from Bucaramanga, take a bus to El Banco (US$13.50, seven hours) and continue to Mompós by jeep or boat (either costs US$5 and takes about two hours).

SAN ANDRÉS & PROVIDENCIA

Located 750km northwest of Cartagena (but just 230km east of Nicaragua), this tidy bead of islands is Colombia's smallest department. It's made up of a southern group, with San Andrés as its largest and most important island, and a northern group, centered on the mountainous island of Providencia.

In the past, travelers used the islands as a stepping-stone between Central America and South America. Nowadays, however, connections are less frequent.

While San Andrés is not quite paradise on earth, Providencia is certainly unique and worth a visit in its own right (provided you can afford all the flights needed to get there and back). Both islands offer excellent scuba-diving and snorkeling opportunities.

A glance at history shows that the islands were once a colony of Britain. Although Colombia took possession after independence, the English influence on language, religion and architecture remained virtually intact until modern times. Local lifestyle only started to change from the 1950s, when a regular domestic air service was established with the Colombian mainland. Providencia has managed to preserve much more of its colonial character.

The tourist season peaks from mid-December to mid-January, during the Easter week, and from mid-June to mid-July. All visitors staying more than one day are charged a local government levy of US$8 on arrival.

SAN ANDRÉS

☎ 8 / pop 75,000

Covered in coconut palms and cut by sharp ravines that turn into rivers after rain, the seahorse-shaped San Andrés is the main commercial and administrative center of the archipelago and, as the only transport hub to the mainland, it's the first and last place you are likely to see.

The island, 12.5km long and 3km wide, is made accessible by a 30km scenic paved road that circles the island, and several roads that cross inland. The main urban center and capital of the archipelago is the town of San Andrés (known locally as El Centro), in the northern end of the island. It has two-thirds of the island's 60,000 inhabitants and is the principal tourist and commercial area, packed with hotels, restaurants and stores.

Information

All of the following are in San Andrés town. Details for the Costa Rica and Honduras consulates can be found on p630.

Bancolombia (Map p592; Av Atlantico) Changes traveler's checks and cash.

Café Internet Sol (Map p592; Av Duarte Blum; ⊙ 8am-10pm)

Creative Shop (Map p592; Av Las Américas) Internet café located below the Hotel Hernando Henry.

Giros & Finanzas (Map p592; Centro Comercial San Andrés, Local 12, Av Costa Rica) The local agent of Western Union.

Macrofinanciera (Map p592; Edificio Leda, Av Providencia No 2-47) Changes US dollars.

Secretaría de Turismo Departamental (Map p592; ☎ 8-512-5058; www.sanandres.gov.co; Av Newball) In the building of the Gobernación, Piso 3. At the time of research it had a temporary office across from the Restaurante La Regatta.

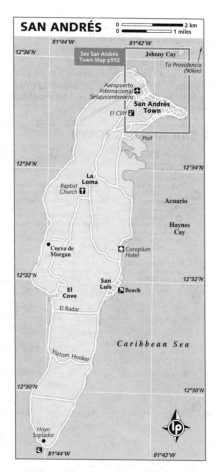

SAN ANDRÉS

Sights

Most people stay in El Centro, but take some time to look around the island. El Centro's beach, along Av Colombia, is handy and fine but it may be crowded in tourist peak seasons. There are no beaches along the island's western shore, and those along the east coast are nothing special, except for the good beach in San Luis.

The small village of **La Loma** (Map p591), in the central hilly part of the island, is noted for its Baptist church, the first established on San Andrés.

The **Cueva de Morgan** (Map p591) is an underwater cave where the Welsh pirate Henry Morgan is said to have buried some of his treasure. **Hoyo Soplador** (Map p591), at the southern tip of the island, is a sort of small geyser where the sea water spouts into the air through a natural hole in the coral rock. This phenomenon can be observed only when the winds and tide are right.

There are several small cays off San Andrés, of which the most popular are **Johnny Cay** (Map p591), opposite El Centro, and **Acuario** (Map p591), off the island's eastern coast.

Activities

Thanks to the coral reefs all around, San Andrés has become an important **diving** center with more than 35 different diving spots. The following are some of the best diving schools: **Banda Dive Shop** (Map p592; ☎ 8-512-2507; www .bandadiveshop.com; Hotel Lord Pierre, Av Colombia, San Andrés Town)

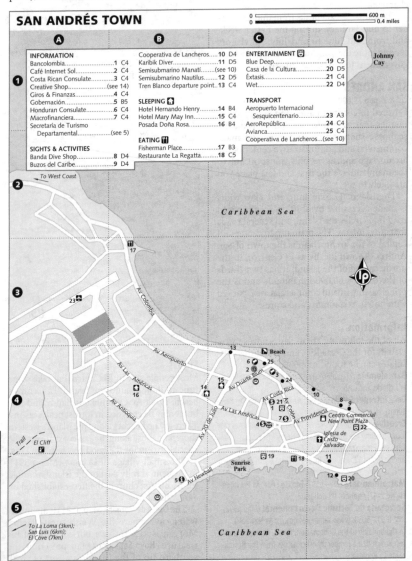

SAN ANDRÉS TOWN

0 ——————— 600 m
0 ——————— 0.4 miles

INFORMATION
Bancolombia...........................**1** C4
Café Internet Sol......................**2** C4
Costa Rican Consulate.............**3** C4
Creative Shop.....................(see 14)
Giros & Finanzas......................**4** C4
Gobernación............................**5** B5
Honduran Consulate.................**6** C4
Macrofinanciera.......................**7** C4
Secretaría de Turismo
    Departamental..................(see 5)

SIGHTS & ACTIVITIES
Banda Dive Shop......................**8** D4
Buzos del Caribe.......................**9** D4

Cooperativa de Lancheros......**10** D4
Karibik Diver..........................**11** D5
Semisubmarino Manatí........(see 10)
Semisubmarino Nautilus........**12** D5
Tren Blanco departure point...**13** C4

SLEEPING
Hotel Hernando Henry............**14** B4
Hotel Mary May Inn................**15** C4
Posada Doña Rosa..................**16** B4

EATING
Fisherman Place......................**17** B3
Restaurante La Regatta...........**18** C5

ENTERTAINMENT
Blue Deep..............................**19** C5
Casa de la Cultura..................**20** D5
Éxtasis..................................**21** C4
Wet......................................**22** D4

TRANSPORT
Aeropuerto Internacional
    Sesquicentenario...............**23** A3
AeroRepública.......................**24** C4
Avianca.................................**25** C4
Cooperativa de Lancheros...(see 10)

Johnny
Cay

Caribbean Sea

To West Coast

Av Colombia

Av Aeropuerto

Av Las Américas

Av Antioquia

Av 20 de Julio

Av Las Américas

Av Duarte Blum

Av Costa Rica

Av Providencia

Av Colón

Beach

Centro Commercial
New Point Plaza

Iglesia de
Cristo
Salvador

El Cliff

Trail

Sunrise
Park

Av Newball

To La Loma (3km);
San Luis (6km);
El Cove (7km)

Caribbean Sea

COLOMBIA

Buzos del Caribe (Map p592; ☎ 8-512-8931; www .buzosdelcaribe.com in Spanish; Av Colombia No 1-212, San Andrés Town) The oldest and largest facility. It has a fine reputation, but it's expensive (US$250 for the open-water PADI or NAUI course).

Karibik Diver (Map p592; ☎ 8-512-0101; www.karibik diver.com; Av Newball No 1-248, San Andrés Town) This small school is also expensive (US$300), but provides quality equipment and personalized service.

Tours

Cooperativa de Lancheros (Map p592; Av Colombia) On the town's beach; provides trips to Johnny Cay (US$3) and Acuario (US$4), plus a combined tour to both cays (US$5).

Semisubmarino Manatí (Map p592; tickets Cooperativa de Lancheros; 1½-hour tours per person US$13.50) A specially designed boat with large windows below the waterline. It departs once or twice daily for a 1½-hour tour around the nearby reefs. If you are not planning on scuba diving or snorkeling, this trip is probably the next-best option for having a look at San Andrés' rich marine life.

Semisubmarino Nautilus (Map p592; wharf; 2hr trips US$13.50) Does similar trips to *Semisubmarino Manatí* from the wharf just west of the Casa de la Cultura.

Taxi tours (up to 4 people US$18) The same route as Tren Blanco (following) can be done by taxi. Other, shorter or longer arrangements with taxi drivers are available.

Tren Blanco (3hr trips US$3) A sort of road train pulled by a tractor dressed up like a locomotive; departs every morning from the corner of Av Colombia and Av 20 de Julio (Map p592) to circle the island, stopping at several sights along the way.

Sleeping

On the whole, accommodations in San Andrés are plentiful but more expensive than on the mainland.

Posada Doña Rosa (Map p592; ☎ 8-512-3649; Av Las Américas; s/d US$9/18) The low prices make this the obvious choice for solo budget travelers. The Doña Rosa has eight rooms, all of which have bathrooms and fans.

Hotel Mary May Inn (Map p592; ☎ 8-512-5669; ketlenan@yahoo.com; Av 20 de Julio; s/d/tr US$15/18/22; ⊠) This small and friendly place offers eight, well-appointed rooms within a quiet courtyard. The double is a good deal but solo travelers may want to bargain for a more reasonable price.

Hotel Hernando Henry (Map p592; ☎ 8-512-3416; Av Las Américas No 4-84; s/d with fan US$12/20, with air-con US$14/23; ⊠) It may not look like much from the outside, but this is one of the best-value options in town. Clean, antiquated rooms come with TV, fridge and balcony.

Cocoplum Hotel (Map p591; ☎ 8-513-2121; www.co coplumhotel.com; Carretera a San Luis No 43-39; s/d US$44/60;

⊠ ▢ ⊠) Located on a private beach in San Luis, this low-key resort is a great place to get away from the crowds. There's a restaurant that serves fresh meals all day, and is open to nonguests.

Eating

There are a number of simple restaurants in San Andrés Town that serve the usual set lunches and dinners for US$2 to US$3.

Fisherman Place (Map p592; Av Colombia; meals from US$3; ☯ noon-4pm) This open-air, beachside restaurant offers some of the best seafood in town, including crab soup (US$3), fried fish (US$3) and seafood stew (US$7).

Restaurante La Regatta (Map p592; Av Newball; dishes US$11-26; ☯ noon-10pm) One of the islands' best restaurants, offering patrons excellent seafood and sweeping views of the Caribbean.

Entertainment

There are several nightspots on Av Colombia between Hotel Lord Pierre and Hotel Aquarium Decameron.

Wet (Map p592; Edificio Big Point, Av Colombia; ☯ 4pm-midnight) This flashy place has a dance floor, video screens and blaring music.

Casa de la Cultura (Map p592; Av Newball) Organizes 'Caribbean Evenings' on Friday, which are folklore shows featuring live music and local food.

Some of the upmarket hotels have discotheques, the most trendy (and expensive) of which is **Blue Deep** (Map p592; Av Newball) in Sunrise Beach Hotel, followed by **Éxtasis** (Map p592; Av Colón) in Hotel Sol Caribe San Andrés.

Getting There & Away

AIR

The airport is in San Andrés Town, a 10-minute walk northwest of the center, or US$3 by taxi. Colombian airlines that service San Andrés include **Avianca/SAM** (Map p592; ☎ 8-512-3211; cnr Avs Colombia & Duarte Blum) and **AeroRepública** (Map p592; ☎ 8-512-7334; Av Colón 3-64) and there are direct connections with Bogotá (US$140), Cali (US$140), Cartagena (US$128) and Medellín (US$140). At the time of research there were no direct flights between San Andrés and Central America, but Avianca does offer a flight three times a week to Panama City via Bogotá (one way US$207).

The airport tax on international departures from San Andrés is the same as elsewhere in Colombia: US$30 if you have stayed in the

COLOMBIA

country fewer than 60 days and US$50 if you've stayed longer. You can pay in pesos or US dollars.

Satena Airways (☎ 8-512-6867; satenaadz@yahoo .com; Aeropuerto Internacional Sesquicentenario) operates two or three flights per day between San Andrés and Providencia (return US$124), serviced by a 19-seater plane. Note that West Caribbean Airways had formerly flown this route but had suspended operations at the time of research.

BOAT

There are no ferries to the Colombian mainland or elsewhere. Cargo boats to Cartagena and Providencia don't take passengers.

Getting Around

Local buses run along the circular coastal road, and along the inner road to La Loma and El Cove, and can drop you near any of the sights. Otherwise, rent a bicycle (from US$1.50/5 per hour/day). Motorbikes, scooters and cars can also be rented at various locations throughout the town. Shop around, as prices and conditions vary.

PROVIDENCIA

☎ 8 / pop 4500

Providencia is the type of place that fulfils your every expectation of paradise. Quiet, laid-back hamlets nestle softly against white-sand beaches shaded by palm trees. The sea is warm, the locals are friendly and the topography is gorgeous. If you're looking to get away from it all, Providencia is about as far as you can get.

Located 90km north of San Andrés, Providencia is the second-largest island in the archipelago at 7km long and 4km wide. It is a mountainous island of volcanic origin, much older than San Andrés. The highest peak is El Pico (320m).

Santa Isabel, a village at the northern tip of the island, is the administrative seat. Santa Catalina, a smaller island just to the northwest, is separated from Providencia by the shallow Canal Aury, spanned by a pedestrian bridge.

Providencia is much less affected by tourism than San Andrés. English is widely spoken, and there's still much Caribbean English-style architecture to be seen. There is some development, but the integrity of the island has not yet been compromised.

Activities include beachcombing, scuba diving and walking. The trail to El Pico begins from Casabaja, on the south side of the island. It's a steady 1½ hours' walk to the top.

Getting around the island is pretty straightforward – just wave down any of the taxi-*colectivos* or pickups that run the circular road (US$1 for any distance). Many locals get around by hitching on motorbikes – you could do the same.

Information

There are no *casas de cambio* (money-exchange offices) on Providencia, but some businesses (including a couple of supermarkets in Santa Isabel) may change your dollars although rates will be poor. It's best to bring enough pesos with you from San Andrés.

Banco Agrario de Colombia (Santa Isabel; ☒ 8am-1:30pm Mon-Thu, to 2pm Fri) Gives cash advances on Visa cards; the ATM next door to the bank services MasterCard.

Net Crawler (Santa Isabel; ☒ 8:30am-noon & 2:30-9pm) Internet café.

Tourist information (☎ 8-514-8054; providencia 2004@yahoo.com; Santa Isabel) Located in the building of the Gobernación.

Activities

The coral reefs around Providencia are more extensive than those around San Andrés and the turquoise sea is beautiful. You can rent snorkeling gear in Aguadulce (or better, buy some in San Andrés and bring it along).

Recommended dive schools include **Centro de Buceo Scuba Town** (☎ 8-514-8481) in Pueblo Viejo and **Sonny Dive Shop** (☎ 8-514-8231) in Agualdulce. Each offers an open-water or advanced course for about US$180 to US$200. Most of the diving is done along the west side of the island.

Sleeping & Eating

Accommodations and food are expensive on Providencia, even more so than on San Andrés. Most travelers stay in the tourist hamlet of Agualduce, although Santa Isabel offers more conveniences. Small restaurants are found in Santa Isabel and Agualduce.

Mr Mac (☎ 8-514-8366; jujentay@hotmail.com; s/d US$11/19) Mr Mac is one of the cheapest hotels, mostly because it's unkempt and neglected. Some rooms overlook the beach.

Hotel Flaming Trees (☎ 8-514-8049; Santa Isabel; s/d US$13.50/23; ☒) The best choice in Santa Isabel, this welcoming guesthouse offers nine spacious air-con rooms with bathroom, fridge and TV.

Cabañas Miss Elma (☎ 8-514-8229; s/d/ste US$16/32/68;) Miss Elma has both fan-cooled rooms and spacious air-conditioned suites. It's right on the beach and has its own restaurant, which is fine but not cheap.

Posada del Mar (☎ 8-514-8168; inforeservas@posada delmarprovidencia.com; s/d incl breakfast US$32/46;) Midrange option with well-maintained rooms. All rooms have bathrooms and balconies with hammocks, and face the beach.

Café Studio (meals US$5-20; 11am-9pm Mon-Sat) On the main road in Bahía Suroeste is this pleasant, Canadian-run café. It has excellent espresso and cakes, plus a full restaurant menu with some of the best food on the island (traditional local cuisine).

Getting There & Away

Satena Airways flies between San Andrés and Providencia (return US$124) two or three times per day. You are most likely to buy a return in San Andrés before arriving, but buy your ticket in advance in the high season and be sure to reconfirm the return trip at Providencia's airport.

NORTHWEST COLOMBIA

From the coffee fields of Zona Cafetera to the sleek metro and the malls of Medellín, northwest Colombia offers a sweep of landscapes and economies. Here you can bathe in hot springs, ride horses, scale volcanoes and travel to the spectacular Valle de Cocora, home of the famed wax palm.

The department of Antioquia dominates the region in terms of its size, population and wealth. Its inhabitants, commonly known as *paisas*, have traditionally been reluctant to mix with either blacks or the indigenous population, and consequently, this is the country's 'whitest' region, with a large creole population.

Antioquia, or the *país paisa* (*paisa* country) as its inhabitants call it, is a picturesque mountainous land, spread over parts of the Cordillera Occidental and the Cordillera Central. It's crisscrossed by roads linking little *pueblos paisa* (*paisa* towns) noted for their distinctive architectural style.

Zona Cafetera, Colombia's major coffee-growing area, is a great place to unwind for a few days and can be used as a gateway to some high peaks of the Andes. West of Antioquia is troubled Chocó department, which is rife with guerrilla activity – check the latest travel postings if you are thinking of heading there.

MEDELLÍN

☎ 4 / pop 2.5 million

Somewhat overshadowed by the airy sophistication of Bogotá and the romantic aura of Cartagena, Medellín has been slow to develop as a tourist hot spot. 'The City of Eternal Spring,' however, does have its own unique character and has made a big turnaround since its notorious days as the center of Colombia's drug trade.

With Pablo Escobar and company now a part of Medellín's history, the streets are safe again and you'll find easy access to most parts of the city. Although drugs are no longer the dominant economy of trade, the city has managed to build up other commercial and industrial interests (mainly textiles and cut flowers), and even boasts an ultramodern subway and top-notch cultural and science centers. Streets teem with life as the busy *paisas* scuttle between work and play.

The town was founded in 1675 and in its early days consisted mostly of individual haciendas that later became the basis for the many beautiful suburbs that surround the city center. Neighborhoods are infused with winding streets and much greenery. The entire city is surrounded by lush mountains that harbor quaint *pueblos* and weekend getaways.

Medellín is moving from strength to strength – with recent civic development projects spearheaded by its progressive mayor Sergio Fajardo Valerrama. There has been a clean up of the Medellín River and a cable-car extension of the subway that connects low-income barrios to the center. The mayor's latest pet project is to make Medellín a 'bilingual city' – millions of pesos are being spent to get the *paisas'* English up to speed.

Information
INTERNET ACCESS

There are plenty of cybercafés in the center of town (most charge approximately US$1 per hour).

Café Internet Doble-Click (Calle 50 No 43-135; 7am-9pm Mon-Fri, 7am-7pm Sat, 10am-4pm Sun) One of very few that opens on Sunday.

EPM.Net (Carrera 45 No 52-49; ☺ 8am-8pm Mon-Fri, 8am-12:30pm Sat)

Punto Net (Carrera 50 No 52-50, Centro Comercial Unión Plaza, Local 133; ☺ 8:30am-8pm Mon-Sat)

MONEY

Banks listed are likely to change traveler's checks at reasonable rates. The banks may also change cash, but you'll probably get similar or even better rates (and will save time) at *casas de cambio*.

Bancolombia (Carrera 49 No 49-74)

Banco Santander (Carrera 49 No 50-10)

Giros & Finanzas (Centro Comercial Villanueva, Calle 57 No 49-44, Local 241) The Western Union agent. There are half-a-dozen *casas de cambio* in this center.

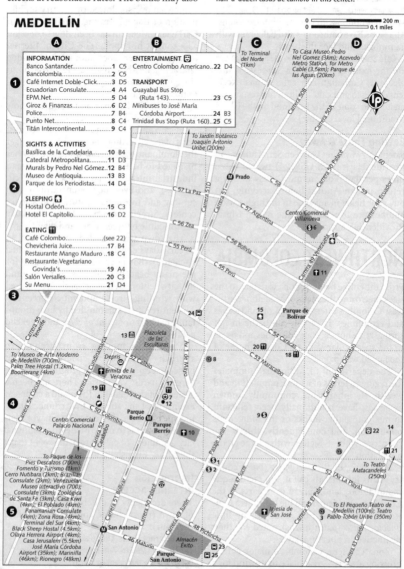

MEDELLÍN

INFORMATION		
Banco Santander	1	C5
Bancolombia	2	C5
Café Internet Doble-Click	3	D5
Ecuadorian Consulate	4	A4
EPM.Net	5	D4
Giroz & Finanzas	6	D2
Police	7	B4
Punto Net	8	C4
Titán Intercontinental	9	C4

SIGHTS & ACTIVITIES		
Basílica de la Candelaria	10	B4
Catedral Metropolitana	11	D3
Murals by Pedro Nel Gómez	12	B4
Museo de Antioquia	13	B3
Parque de los Periodistas	14	D4

SLEEPING		
Hostal Odeón	15	C3
Hotel El Capitolio	16	D2

EATING		
Café Colombo	(see 22)	
Chevicheria Juice	17	B4
Restaurante Mango Maduro	18	C4
Restaurante Vegetariano Govinda's	19	A4
Salón Versalles	20	C3
Su Menu	21	D4

ENTERTAINMENT		
Centro Colombo Americano	22	D4

TRANSPORT		
Guayabal Bus Stop (Ruta 143)	23	C5
Minibuses to José María Córdoba Airport	24	B3
Trinidad Bus Stop (Ruta 160)	25	C5

Titán Intercontinental (Edificio Coltejer, Carrera 46 No 52-65, Local 103) *Casa de cambio.*

TOURIST INFORMATION
Fomento y Turismo Airport (☎ 4-562-2885; ☼ 6am-7pm Mon-Sat); Palacio de Exposiciones (☎ 4-232-4022; Av Alfonso López; ☼ 7:30am-12:30pm & 1:30-5:30pm Mon-Fri) Medellín's main tourist office is in the Palacio de Exposiciones, 1km southwest of the center.

Dangers & Annoyances

Although no longer the world's cocaine-trafficking capital, Medellín isn't the safest place you'll ever visit; like any large Colombian city, it has security problems so take the usual precautions. The city center appears quite safe during the daytime, but keep your evening strolls to a minimum. If you're going to *rumba* at night, use taxis.

Sights

The **Museo de Antioquia** (☎ 4-251-3636; www.museodeantioquia.org in Spanish; Carrera 52 Carabobo No 52-43; admission US$3; ☼ 9:30am-5pm Mon & Wed-Fri, 10am-4pm Sat & Sun) features pre-Hispanic, colonial, independence and modern art collections, spanning Antioquia's 400-year-long history, plus Fernando Botero's donation of 92 of his own works and 22 works by other international artists. Additionally his 23 large bronze sculptures have been placed in front of the museum, in what is known as Plazoleta de las Esculturas.

Across the Parque Berrío are two large murals depicting Antioquia's history, the 1956 work by another of Medellín's illustrious sons, Pedro Nel Gómez (1899–1984). The **Casa Museo Pedro Nel Gómez** (☎ 4-233-2633; Carrera 51B No 85-24; admission US$2; ☼ 9am-noon & 2-5pm Mon-Fri, 9am-noon Sat), set in the house where the artist lived and worked, shelters nearly 2000 of his works including watercolors, oil paintings, drawings, sculptures and murals. Pedro Nel Gómez is said to have been Colombia's most prolific artist.

Another important city museum, the **Museo de Arte Moderno de Medellín** (☎ 4-230-2622; Carrera 64B No 51-64; admission US$2; ☼ 10am-1pm & 2-6pm Mon-Fri, 10am-5pm Sat) stages changing exhibitions of contemporary art.

Apart from a few old churches, the city's colonial architecture has virtually disappeared. The most interesting of the historic churches is the **Basílica de la Candelaria** (Parque Berrío), built in the 1770s and functioning as the city's cathedral until 1931. Also worth a visit is the gigantic neo-Romanesque **Catedral Metro-**politana (Parque de Bolívar), completed in 1931 and thought to be South America's largest brick church (1.2 million bricks were used).

Medellín has a fine botanical garden, the **Jardín Botánico Joaquín Antonio Uribe** (☎ 4-233-7025; Carrera 52 No 73-182; admission US$1; ☼ 9am-5pm).

If you've had it with sightseeing, a good place to chill out is the **Parque de los Pies Descalzos** (Barefoot Park; Carrera 57 No 42-139) where citizens are encouraged to kick their shoes off, wade into shallow pools and enjoy the zen ambience. Next to the park are restaurants and the **Museo Interactivo** (☎ 4-380-6956; Carrera 57 No 42-139; ☼ 8am-8pm Tue-Sun) featuring 200 interactive science displays – one of Medellín's more kid-friendly attractions.

For views of the city, go to the **Cerro Nutibara**, an 80m-tall hill 2km southwest of the city center. The **Pueblito Paisa**, a replica of a typical Antioquian village, has been built on the summit and is home to several handicrafts shops. For another view of the city, take a ride on the newly installed **Metrocable**, from Acevedo metro station.

Activities

Medellín is regarded as Colombia's main center of **paragliding** thanks to favorable conditions provided by the winds and rugged topography.

Boomerang (☎ 4-254-5943, 311-774-1175; piloto_x@hotmail.com; Calle 38B No 79-16, Barrio Laureles) offers courses (about US$300 for a weeklong course), equipment rental, and tandem flights over the city (US$25).

Festivals & Events

Mercado de San Alejo Colorful craft market held in the Parque de Bolívar on the first Saturday of every month.
Feria Nacional de Artesanías Craft fair held in July at the Atanasio Girardot sports complex. Good for cheap buys.
Feria de las Flores Held for a week in early August, this is Medellín's biggest event. Its highlight is the Desfile de Silleteros, on 7 August, when hundreds of *campesinos* come down from the mountains and parade along the streets carrying *silletas* full of flowers on their backs.
Alumbrado (Christmas Light Festival) Each year at Christmas time the city ignites the riverfront with a spectacular lightshow, attracting Colombian families for evening strolls. It lasts from December 7 until the second week in January.

Sleeping

Palm Tree Hostal (☎ 4-260-2805; www.palmtreemedellin .com; Carrera 67 No 48D-63; dm/s/d US$6/9/12; 🖳) This is

COLOMBIA

Medellín's oldest (and still cheapest) traveler haunt, offering a range of facilities typical of a Western hostel, including laundry service, bicycle rental, book exchange and the use of the kitchen. It's in the suburb of Suramericana, about 1.5km west of the center, easily accessible by metro (Suramericana Station) or by bus along Calle 50 Av Colombia. A taxi from either bus terminal is US$2.

Casa Kiwi (☎ 4-268-2668; www.casakiwi.net; Carrera 36 No 7-10, El Poblado; dm US$7, s/d with bathroom US$18/23, without bathroom US$13.50/18; 💻) This New Zealander–run guesthouse has a fun, youthful vibe and a nice location near the nightlife area of Zona Rosa. Rooms are reasonably clean and there is a lounge and a patio with a BBQ. The best way to get here is by taxi.

Black Sheep Hostal (☎ 4-311-1589, 311-341-3048; www.blacksheepmedellin.com; Transversal 5a No 45-133; dm/ s/d US$7/13/14.50; 💻) Well-managed guesthouse with every conceivable amenity including two TV rooms, BBQ, Spanish-language classes, kitchen and clean rooms. It's in the swanky neighborhood of Bario Patio Bonito, a 20-minute walk from the Zona Rosa.

Casa Jerusalem (☎ 4-321-5230, 316-348-8000; jeru salem_medellin@yahoo.com; Carrera 36 No 7-10; dm/s/d US$7/9/13.50; 💻 📺) Offering comfort, space and convenience, this Israeli-run backpacker is set in a large house, just minutes away from the Aguacatala Metro station (call ahead and they will meet you at the station). There is a supermarket nearby, but little else in this neighborhood.

Medellín Homestays (☎ 4-477-1966; medellinhome stays@yahoo.com; per week US$360) This organization sets you up with a local family for a weeklong homestay. Prices include two meals per day plus five days of Spanish-language classes (three hours per day). Contact Juan Fernando Trujillo.

CITY CENTER

The city center has plenty of cheap hotels, although many double as love hotels and raise prices on the weekend.

Hostal Odeón (☎ 4-513-1404; Calle 54 No 49-38; s/d/tr with bathroom US$9/14/19) Small, quiet and very central. Rooms come with fridge, TV and stereo. Recommended place if you need to be in the center.

Hotel El Capitolio (☎ 4-512-0012; Carrera 49 Venezuela No 57-24; s/d with bathroom incl breakfast US$16/19/23) Fully renovated and affordable accommodations right behind the cathedral.

Eating

Like every big city, Medellín has hundreds of places to eat for every budget. The center is literally flooded with restaurants, snack bars and cafés and provides some of the cheapest meals. Restaurants in the Zona Rosa at El Poblado are more upscale. For an amazing fruit smoothie, try Chevicheria Juice stand, next to the police station outside Parque Barío metro.

Restaurante Vegetarian Govinda's (Calle 51 No 52-17; meals US$2; 🕙 8am-2:30pm Mon-Sat) For decent vegetarian cuisine served by friendly Hare Krishnas, try this bright, upstairs restaurant near the Museo de Antioquia.

Su Menu (Calle 53 No 43-44, meals US$2-3; 🕙 noon-8pm Mon-Fri, to 4pm Sat) Student hangout serving typical Colombian fare.

Restaurante Mango Maduro (Calle 54 No 47-5; meals US$2.50; 🕙 lunch Mon-Sat) Adding a splash of color to the downtown restaurant scene, this place serves *paisa* meals made from fresh ingredients. It's popular with young professionals, artists and intellectuals.

Salón Versalles (Pasaje Junín No 53-39; set lunches US$3; 🕙 7am-9pm Mon-Sat, 8am-6pm Sun) Two-level restaurant-cum-café invariably popular with the locals. It has a varied menu including tasty set lunches, delicious Argentine and Chilean *empanadas* (US60¢ each) and a choice of high-calorie cakes and pastries.

Ay! Caramba (Carrera 37A No 8A-60, Parque Lleras; mains US$6-9; 🕙 noon-11pm Mon-Sat) Excellent open-air Mexican restaurant serving tacos, enchiladas and the like. If this place does not suit, there are a dozen other options around the park, just be prepared to fork out a little extra as this is the most upscale part of town.

Café Colombo (Carrera 45 No 53-24, piso 10; mains US$7-9; 🕙 noon-2:30pm & 5:30-11pm Mon-Sat) This bright, minimalist eatery offers great city views and a classy menu. It's on the top floor of the building that also houses the Centro Colombo Americano.

Drinking

The major scene of nighttime dance and drink is the Zona Rosa in El Poblado, spreading approximately between Calles 9 and 10A, and Carreras 36 and 42. The area is packed with restaurants, cafés, clubs, bars, pubs and discos, which become vibrant after about 10pm, particularly on weekends. A taxi from the center will bring you to the Zona Rosa from the center of town for US$2.

Berlin (Calle 10 No 41-65) Misfit biker bar and billiards hall in the middle of Medellín's club district.

Entertainment

Check the local dailies, *El Colombiano* and *El Mundo,* for what's going on. Get a copy of the **Opción Hoy** (www.supernet.com.co/opcionhoy; price US$1), a local what's-on monthly that lists art exhibitions, theater, concerts, arthouse cinema and sports and cultural events. You can read it online.

Museo de Arte Moderno (☎ 4-230-2622; Carrera 64B No 51-64) Medellín's best *cinemateca* (arthouse cinema) with a diverse and interesting program.

Centro Colombo Americano (☎ 4-513-4444; Carrera 45 No 53-24) Also has an arthouse cinema.

Teatro Matacandelas (☎ 4-239-1245; Carrera 47 No 43-47) One of the best experimental groups in town.

Teatro Pablo Tobón Uribe (☎ 4-239-2674; Carrera 40 No 51-24) Medellín's major mainstream theater.

El Pequeño Teatro de Medellín (☎ 4-269-9418; Carrera 42 No 50A-12) The varied repertoire here combines the traditional with more contemporary performances.

Vinacuré (☎ 4-278-1633; www.vinacure.com; Carrera 50 No 100D Sur-7, Caldas) Located a long way south of the city, this is a bizarre mix of sin, circus acts and experimentation. You can sit back and enjoy the psychedelic ambience or be a spectacle yourself in the 'clothing optional' room. Visit on a Friday or Saturday when it's livelier. A cab ride there costs around US$8.

Circus Bar (Km 1, Las Palmas; www.circusfunpalace.com; admission US$5) High-energy club playing rock music to a yuppie-type crowd. The occasional circus act is performed over the dance floor, so mind the flying leotard-clad performers. There are a few other places along this strip, including the grungy rock 'Pub' across the street.

Mango's (Carrera 42 No 67A-151) Arguably Medellín's best disco, with charming decor, five bars and a ragbag of good music. It's on Autopista Sur in Itagüí, away from El Poblado.

El Blue (Calle 10 No 40-20) Just off Parque Lleras, this place is devoted to rock, often hosting live bands. It has a large outdoor patio and a laid-back vibe.

Getting There & Away

AIR

The main José María Córdoba airport, 35km southeast of the city, takes all international and most domestic flights except for some regional flights on light planes, which use the old Olaya Herrera airport right inside the city. Frequent minibuses shuttle between the city center and the main airport from the corner of Carrera 50A and Calle 53 (US$2, one hour). A taxi costs US$15.

There are domestic flights throughout the country. **Avianca** (☎ 4-251-7710; Calle 52 No 45-94, local 9912) flies to Bogotá (US$70 to US$120), Cali (US$70 to US$120), Cartagena (US$90 to US$140) and San Andrés (US$150 to US$160).

BUS

Medellín has two bus terminals. The Terminal del Norte, 2km north of the city center, handles buses to the north, east and southeast, including Santa Fe de Antioquia (US$4, three hours), Bogotá (US$20, nine hours), Cartagena (US$39, 13 hours) and Santa Marta (US$35, 16 hours). It's easily reached from the center by metro in seven minutes, or by taxi (US$2).

The Terminal del Sur, 4km southwest of the center, handles all traffic to the west and south including Manizales (US$11, five hours), Cali (US$18, nine hours) and Popayán (US$22, 12 hours). It's accessible from the center by the Guayabal bus (Ruta 143) and the Trinidad bus (Ruta 160), both of which you catch on Av Oriental next to the Éxito San Antonio store. Alternatively, go by taxi (US$2).

Getting Around

Medellín's metro consists of the 23km north–south line and a 6km western leg, and has 25 stations. The trains run on ground level except in the 5km stretch through the central area where they go on viaducts above the streets, providing good views. The Metrocable connects the line to low-income barrios in the hills; you can go for a joy ride by connecting at Acevedo station.

The metro operates 5am to 11pm Monday to Saturday, 7am to 10pm Sunday and holidays, with trains running every five to 10 minutes. Single/double tickets cost US45/80¢, or buy a 10-ride *multiviaje* for US$4.

Apart from the metro, urban transport is serviced by buses and *busetas,* and is quite well organized. All buses are numbered and display their destination point. The majority of routes originate on Av Oriental and Parque Berrío, from where you can get to almost anywhere within the metropolitan area.

COLOMBIA

DETOUR: RÍO CLARO

Thanks to Colombia's improving security situation, it is once again safe to visit the Río Claro valley in eastern Antioquia, where a crystal-clear river has carved stunning shapes into its marble bed. It's also a favorite spot for bird-watchers, who come to see everything from hummingbirds to herons to vultures.

You can stay in the lodge known as El Refugio, which is about 1km from the river and near the town of Puerto Triunfo. Río Claro is located just off the main road that connects Bogotá (US$14, five hours) and Medellín (US$10, three hours). Most buses that connect the two cities will drop you off in Puerto Triunfo. Note that nighttime travel in this area remains risky; check current conditions.

At the time of writing, Medellín was set to launch 'Metroplus', a fast bus service similar to Bogotá's TransMilenio. The first buses will run along Calle 30 and Carrera 45.

AROUND MEDELLÍN

The picturesque, rugged region surrounding Medellín is sprinkled with haciendas and lovely little *pueblos paisas*. With a few days to spare, take a trip around Medellín to see what Antioquia is really like. Before you set off, however, check travel-safety conditions.

The last addition to the region's attractions is the **Parque de las Aguas**, an enjoyable amusement park full of waterslides, pools and other distractions. It's about 20km northeast of Medellín and has good transportation links with the city. Take the metro to the northern end of the line at Niquía and change to a bus.

A tour of the following towns is known as the Circuito de Oriente. Each town offers *hospedajes* (budget hotels) that charge around US$4 to US$5 per bed. Frequent buses connect these towns to Medellín.

Marinilla
☎ 4 / pop 14,000

Some 46km southeast of Medellín on the road to Bogotá, Marinilla is a remarkably well-preserved example of Antioquian architecture and city planning, with a pleasant main plaza and adjacent streets. Dating from the first half of the 18th century, it's one of the oldest towns in the region. Stroll around the central streets and call at the **Capilla de Jesús Nazareno** (cnr Carrera 29 & Calle 32), a fine, whitewashed gem of a church erected in the 1750s.

There are at least half-a-dozen budget hotels in town, all of which are located on or just off the main plaza. Buses to Medellín depart frequently from the plaza (US$1, one

hour), as do *colectivos* to Rionegro (US40¢, 15 minutes).

El Peñol

Reminiscent of the famous Sugar Loaf of Rio de Janeiro, El Peñol (literally 'the Stone') is a huge, 200m-high granite monolith that rises straight up from the banks of Embalse del Peñol, an artificial lake about 30km east of Marinilla. An ascent up the 649 steps will reward you with magnificent bird's-eye views of the entire region, including the beautiful lake at your feet. There's a snack bar at the top.

Buses to and from Medellín run every one to two hours (US$3, 2½ hours) and they all pass through Marinilla (US$2, 1¼ hours).

Rionegro
☎ 4

Founded in 1663, Rionegro is the oldest and most populous town of the Circuito de Oriente. Surrounded by a patchwork of farms and lush orchards, it has a number of classic, *paisa*-style buildings. It is also the town nearest to Medellín's main airport.

In 1863, politicians convened in the **Casa de la Convención** (Calle 51 No 47-67) to write the most liberal constitution in the country's history. The house is now a museum that features a collection of documents and period exhibits related to the event. One block from the Casa is the 1740 **Capilla de San Francisco** (cnr Calle 51 & Carrera 48), the town's oldest existing church.

Carmen de Viboral
☎ 4 / pop 15,000

This small town 9km southeast of Rionegro is known nationwide as a producer of handpainted ceramics. There are a few large factories on the outskirts of town – including Continental, Capiro and Triunfo – and several small workshops that are still largely unmechanized. Almost all tours from Medellín include a visit to one of the factories.

La Ceja
☎ 4 / pop 25,000

Founded in 1789, La Ceja has developed into a handsome *pueblo paisa*. It has a pleasant, spacious main plaza lined with balconied houses, a number of which have preserved their delicate door and window decorations. There are two churches on the plaza, the smaller of which has a remarkably elaborate interior, complete with an extraordinary baroque retable carved in wood.

Note that 9km northwest of La Ceja on the road to Medellín is the **Salto de Tequendamita waterfall**. There is a pleasant restaurant ideally located at the foot of the falls. Many tours organized from Medellín stop here for lunch.

Retiro
☎ 4 / pop 6000

Founded around 1800, this tiny town remains one of the most picturesque in the region. It's set amid verdant hills 33km southeast of Medellín, 4km off the road to La Ceja. The main plaza is a good example of Antioquian architecture, as are many houses lining the surrounding streets.

SANTA FE DE ANTIOQUIA
☎ 4 / pop 12,500

With its cobbled streets, churches, wood balconies and lavish doorways, Santa Fe de Antioquia is a step into the past. The whitewashed town, founded in 1541, is the oldest in the region. It was an important and prosperous center during Spanish days and the capital of Antioquia until 1826. But when the capital moved to Medellín the town fell into a long slumber that seems to have continued until today. Santa Fe de Antioquia is 79km northwest of Medellín, on the road to Turbo.

Sights
Give yourself a couple of hours to wander about the streets to peruse the houses' carved decorated doorways and flower-bedecked patios. Of the town's churches, the 18th-century **Iglesia de Santa Bárbara** (Calle 11 at Carrera 8) is the most interesting, noted for its fine wide baroque stone facade.

The **Museo de Arte Religioso** (☎ 4-853-2345; Calle 11 No 8-12; admission US$1; ☉ 10am-5pm Sat, Sun & holidays), next door to Santa Bárbara church,

has a collection of religious objects, including paintings by Gregorio Vásquez de Arce y Ceballos.

The **Puente de Occidente**, an unusual 291m bridge over the Río Cauca, is 5km east of town. When completed in 1895, it was one of the first suspension bridges in the Americas. Walk there or negotiate a taxi in Santa Fe.

Festivals & Events
Festival de Cine (www.festicineantioquia.com) This four-day film festival is held outdoors in early December on the streets of Santa Fe de Antioquia. All the films are free to watch and there is plenty of alcohol to go with it. (But avoid drinking a local booze called Candela; it can cause temporary or even permanent blindness.)

Fiesta de los Diablitos The last four days of the year are celebrated with music, dancing, a craft fair, bullfights and, of course, a beauty contest. Held from December 27 to 31.

Sleeping & Eating
The town has a dozen hotels catering for different budgets and they are usually empty except for weekends, when Medellín's city dwellers come to warm up. Apart from the hotel restaurants, there are a dozen other places to eat. Don't miss the *pulpa de tamarindo*, a local tamarind sweet sold in the market on the main plaza.

Hospedaje Franco (☎ 4-853-1654; Carrera 10 No 8A-14; r with/without bath per person US$6/4) This basic but acceptable place is one of the cheapest in town and also serves some of the cheapest meals.

Hostal del Viejo Conde (☎ 4-853-1091; Calle 9 No 10-56; r with bath per person US$5.50) A small budget place with clean, fan-cooled rooms, although it does get a bit stuffy. Cheap meals sold here.

Hotel Caserón Plaza (☎ 4-853-2040; halcaraz@edatel .net.co; Plaza Mayor; d from US$33; ☒) Rooms are ranged around an attractive courtyard and there is a nice pool and garden in the back, plus a decent restaurant.

Getting There & Away
There are half-a-dozen buses daily (US$4, three hours) and another half-a-dozen minibuses (US$5, 2½ hours) to and from Medellín's northern terminal.

ZONA CAFETERA
However you take your coffee, or even if you just prefer decaf, the Zona Cafetera is a region not to be missed. There is a sublime beauty

about the coffee-covered hillsides, set to a backdrop of volcanoes, but just as welcoming is the hospitality you are likely to receive at the numerous plantations spread over the region. Zona Cafetera also makes for a convenient rest stop when traveling between Bogotá, Cali and Medellín.

Manizales

☎ 6 / pop 420,000

An important axis point for the coffee trade, the prosperity of Manizales is displayed on its bustling streets. It's not a beautiful city (earthquakes having destroyed most of the original architecture) but it does make a useful base for exploring the region. It's worth looking at the impressive **Catedral de Manizales** (Plaza de Bolívar), which sports a 106m tall main tower, the highest in the country.

Useful facilities include the **Café Internet Fundadores** (Carrera 23 No 30-59) and the **Bancolombia** (cnr Calle 21 Carrera 22). The **Centro de Información Turística de Caldas** (tourist information; ☎ 6-884-2400, ext 153; ☺ 8am-6pm Mon-Sat, 9am-1pm Sun) is located on the ground floor of the Palacio de Gobierno, next to the Plaza de Bolívar.

A good place to stay in Manizales is the **Mountain House** (☎ 6-887-4736, 300-789-8840; www .mountainhousemanizales.com; Calle 65 No 24-97; s/d US$13/19; ☐), a backpacker-orientated place with laundry service, hot showers, book exchange and bikes to rent.

Tours of the area can be organized through **Bioturismo Arte y Café** (☎ 6-884-4037; Centro Comercial Parque Caldas), managed by Omar Vargas. The agency also offers other tours to Parque Nacional Los Nevados and beyond to Valle de Cocora and Parque del Café.

The bus terminal is on Av 19 between Carreras 14 and 17, a short walk northwest of Plaza de Bolívar. The airport is about 8km southeast of the city center, off the road to Bogotá.

Parque Nacional Los Nevados

This snow-caked range of volcanic peaks offers some of the most stunning views in the Colombian Andes, plus some fine hiking trails through cloud forest. The Nevado del Ruiz (5325m) is the largest and the highest volcano of the chain.

The only road access into the park is from the north. This road branches off from the Manizales–Bogotá road in La Esperanza, 31km from Manizales, and winds its way up to the snowline at about 4800m at the foot of Nevado del Ruiz. From here the hike to the top of the volcano takes about three hours.

Entrance to the park is at Las Brisas (4050m) where foreign visitors pay a US$9 admission fee. There are basic chalets here for US$3 per person, but you'll need a good sleeping bag. About 4km uphill from Las Brisas is the Chalet Arenales, which has dorm beds for US$5 per night.

There is no public transportation to the park so the best way to visit is on a tour. Try Bioturismo Arte y Café (p601) in Manizales.

Salamina

☎ 6 / pop 19,000

This quaint country town has the look and feel of a typical *pueblo paisa*, and makes for a pleasant day trip from Manizales. There are some fine old houses here, and a single-nave cathedral.

Regular minibuses (US$4, 2½hours) and *colectivos* (US$5, 2¼hours) operate between Manizales and Salamina, and all pass through Neira, another historic town that's worth a look if you're a devotee of colonial-style *paisa* architecture.

Pereira

☎ 6 / pop 455,000

Mother Nature has been unkind to Pereira. The city of 455,000 souls has suffered a number of devastating earthquakes since its founding in 1863, causing most of the early architecture to vanish. It's no garden spot but it does make a convenient base if you are touring in the nearby coffee plantations.

While you're in Pereira, be sure to check out Arenas Betancur's **Bolívar Desnudo**, an 8.5m-high, 11-ton bronze sculpture of the naked Bolívar on horseback, in the Plaza de Bolívar – one of Colombia's most unusual monuments to El Libertador.

The **Hotel Cataluña** (☎ 6-335-4527; Calle 19 No 8-61; s/d US$14/18) makes for a quiet night if you need a place to stay, it's just a half-block from Plaza de Bolívar.

The Matecaña airport is 5km west of the city center, 20 minutes by urban bus, or US$2 by taxi. Avianca operates eight flights a day to Bogotá.

The bus terminal is about 1.5km south of the city center, at Calle 17 No 23-157. Many urban buses will take you there in less than 10 minutes.

Marsella

☎ 6 / pop 9000

This pleasant *paisa* village, set in the hills 29km northwest of Pereira, has a well-manicured **botanical garden** (admission US$1.25; ☺ 8am-6pm) and a quirky cemetery. The **cemetery** (admission free; ☺ 8am-6pm), built on a slope 1km from the town plaza, contains a series of elaborate terraces where bodies are interred for four years before their remains are moved to family ossuaries.

Minibuses to and from Pereira run approximately every 15 minutes until about 7pm (US$1.50, one hour).

Termales de Santa Rosa

Also known as the Termales Arbeláez, these popular hot springs are around 9km east of Santa Rosa de Cabal, a town on the Pereira–Manizales road. A tourist complex including thermal pools, a hotel, restaurant and bar has been built near the springs amid splendid scenery at the foot of a 170m-high waterfall.

The **thermal baths** (admission US$5; ☺ 8am-midnight) can get very busy on weekends. To reach the baths, first get to Santa Rosa de Cabal from where you can catch a *chiva* from the market at 7am, noon and 3pm (US80¢, 45 minutes).

Armenia

☎ 6 / pop 245,000

Like Manizales and Pereira, this departmental capital offers few sights, most of its early architecture having been wiped out by earthquakes.

Today Armenia has reasonable facilities and a worthwhile **gold museum** (☎ 6-749-8433; cnr Av Bolívar & Calle 40N; admission free; ☺ 10am-6pm Tue-Sun) located in Centro Cultural, 5km northeast of the center, on the road to Pereira.

There is internet access at **Valencia Comunicaciones** (Calle 21 No 15-53; ☺ 8am-10pm) and a money-changing facility at **Bancolombia** (Calle 20 No 15-26).

Cheap hotels are to be found between Carreras 17 and 18 and Calles 17 and 19. Try **Hotel Casa Real** (☎ 6-741-4550; Carrera 18 No 18-36; s/d with bathroom US$10/17), a small, basic place with cable TV and new beds.

The bus terminal is on the corner of Carrera 19 and Calle 35, around 1.5km southwest of the center.

Parque Nacional del Café

A sort of coffee-bean Disneyland, the **Parque Nacional del Café** (☎ 6-753-6095; www.parquenacional delcafé.com in Spanish; basic admission US$6; ☺ 9am-4pm Wed-Sun) provides an interesting and hassle-free – if slightly sanitized – introduction to the history, culture and science of coffee. Attractions include a museum, a small coffee plantation and some thrills, including a roller coaster and water slide. Some travelers may be put off commercialization of it all, but in the right frame of mind it can be a fun and unique experience.

The park is near the small town of Pueblo Tapao, about 15km west of Armenia, and is easily accessible by frequent minibuses from the city. In the high season (mid-December to mid-January, Easter, mid-June to mid-July) the park may be open daily; check its website. Don't bother to come if it's raining, as most attractions are outdoors.

Salento

☎ 6 / pop 3500

This small town is a one-hour drive from Armenia though it might as well be 100 years. Salento, founded in 1850, boasts plenty of fine old houses, many of which have been turned into shops, restaurants and hotels catering to weekend visitors. Be sure not to miss Alto de la Cruz, a hill topped with a cross at the end of Calle Real. It's a bit of a climb, but from here you'll see the verdant Valle de Cocora as well as the high mountains that surround it.

The best place to stay in Salento is the **Plantation House** (☎ 315-409-7039; theplantationhouse salento@yahoo.co.uk; Calle 7 No 1-04) a British-run backpacker set inside a 120-year-old restored plantation, complete with coffee plants and orange trees growing in the garden.

Buses to Salento from Armenia (US$1.50 minutes) run every 15 minutes.

Valle de Cocora

Stretching from Salento eastwards to the tiny hamlet of Cocora and beyond, the stunning Valle de Cocora is like a lush version of Switzerland, with a broad, green valley floor framed by rugged peaks. However, you'll remember you're a few degrees from the equator when, a short walk past Cocora, you suddenly encounter hills covered with the *palma de cera*, or wax palm. The trees tower above the cloud forests in which they thrive. It is an astonishing sight.

The most spectacular part of the valley is east of Cocora. Take the rough road heading downhill to the bridge over the Río Quindío (just a five-minute walk from the restaurants) and you will see the strange palms. Walk further uphill and enjoy the scenery – you won't find this kind of landscape anywhere else.

The town of Cocora consists of a few houses, three restaurants serving delicious trout, and a trout-breeding station. The palms have made Cocora a tourist destination, with visitors mainly arriving on the weekends. On these days locals gather around the three restaurants to rent out horses (US$2.50 per hour).

Two jeeps a day, normally around 7:30am and 4pm, depart from Salento's plaza and go up the rough 11km road to Cocora (US$1, 35 minutes). There may be more departures if there's a demand. On weekends there are usually at least four departures daily.

SOUTHWEST COLOMBIA

Southwest Colombia covers a range of geographies and cultures. The biggest city in the region, Cali, has a distinctly Colombian feel, with salsa music and romantic, sultry nights. As you head closer to the Ecuadorian border, the landscape buckles into more mountainous terrain. Culturally and geographically, the cities of Pasto and Ipiales feel more like Ecuador than Colombia. The biggest tourist attractions are the two outstanding archaeological sites of San Agustín and Tierradentro, and the colonial city of Popayán.

CALI

☎ 2 / pop 2,250,000

Cali grooves to a beat all its own. By day the hot and sultry city seems to be on an extended siesta; slow-paced compared to its counterparts Bogotá and Medellín. By night *caleños* break out of their torpor and lace up their dancing shoes. Salsa music is a citywide addiction and the basis for all-night parties that rock Juanchito district.

Tourist attractions are few on the ground in Cali, although there are a few museums and churches to keep you busy for a day or two. Try not to miss the Zoológico de Cali, Colombia's finest zoo. Above all, Cali is fine place to soak in the Latino ambience, learn some salsa steps and people-watch, an activity made all the easier by the famously good-looking *caleñas* (Cali women). Beauty, one soon realizes, is an obsession second only

to salsa, and has become a major industry in itself – Cali is recognized as a world leader in plastic surgery and the results of this phenomenon are stunning.

Orientation

The city center is split in two by the Río Cali. To the south is the historic heart – laid out on a grid plan and centered around the Plaza de Caycedo – which contains most tourist sights including historic churches and museums.

To the north of the river is the new center, whose main axis is Av Sexta (Av 6N). This modern sector contains trendy shops and restaurants, and comes alive in the evening when a refreshing breeze tempers the daytime heat. This is the area to come to dine, drink and dance after a day of sightseeing on the opposite side of the river.

Information

Internet access is fast and cheap (US$1 to US$1.50 per hour). Most cybercafés open 8am to 8pm Monday to Friday and 8am to 6pm Saturday. In addition to the following there are several on Av Sexta.

Bancolombia (cnr Calle 15N & Av 8N) Changes cash and traveler's checks.

Banco Unión Colombiano (Carrera 3 No 11-03) Changes cash.

Comunicaciones Novatec (Av 8N No 20-46) For internet.

Centro Cultural Comfandi (Calle 8 No 6-23, Piso 5) In the historic center.

Giros & Finanzas (Carrera 4 No 10-12) Changes cash and is a Western Union Agent.

SCI Sala de Internet (Av 6N No 13N-66) Largest central internet facility.

Secretaría de Cultura y Turismo (☎ 2-886-0000 ext 2410) The city tourist office is on the 2nd floor of the building of Gobernación del Valle del Cauca.

Dangers & Annoyances

Even though Cali may look quieter and more relaxed than Bogotá or Medellín, don't be deceived by its easy-going air, summery heat and beautiful women. Muggers and thieves aren't inactive here, nor are they less clever or violent than elsewhere. Be careful while wandering around the streets at night. Avoid the park along Río Cali in the evening, and don't walk east of Calle 13 after dark.

Sights & Activities

The beautiful, mid-16th-century **Iglesia de la Merced** (cnr Carrera 4 & Calle 7) is Cali's oldest church.

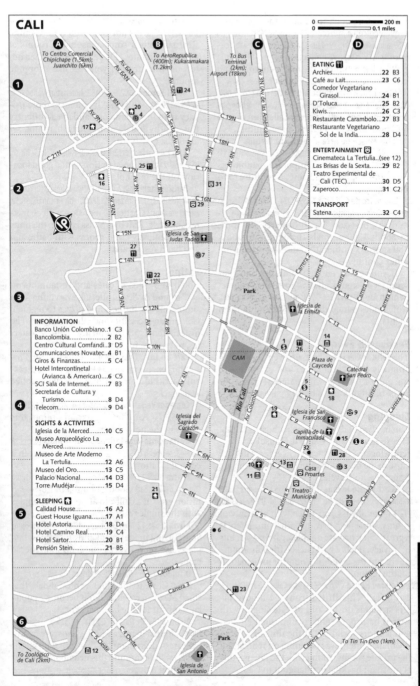

CALI

0 _____ 200 m
0 _____ 0.1 miles

EATING 🍴
Archies................................**22** B3
Café au Lait.......................**23** C6
Comedor Vegetariano
  Girasol............................**24** B1
D'Toluca............................**25** B2
Kiwis..................................**26** C3
Restaurante Carambolo....**27** B3
Restaurante Vegetariano
  Sol de la India..................**28** D4

ENTERTAINMENT 🎭
Cinemateca La Tertulia..(see 12)
Las Brisas de la Sexta........**29** B2
Teatro Experimental de
  Cali (TEC)........................**30** D5
Zaperoco...........................**31** C2

TRANSPORT
Satena................................**32** C4

INFORMATION
Banco Unión Colombiano..**1** C3
Bancolombia......................**2** B2
Centro Cultural Comfandi..**3** D5
Comunicaciones Novatec..**4** B1
Giros & Finanzas................**5** C4
Hotel Intercontinetal
  (Avianca & American)....**6** C5
SCI Sala de Internet...........**7** B3
Secretaría de Cultura y
  Turismo............................**8** D4
Telecom.............................**9** D4

SIGHTS & ACTIVITIES
Iglesia de la Merced..........**10** C5
Museo Arqueológico La
  Merced............................**11** C5
Museo de Arte Moderno
  La Tertulia.......................**12** A6
Museo del Oro...................**13** C5
Palacio Nacional.................**14** D3
Torre Mudéjar...................**15** D4

SLEEPING 🏠
Calidad House....................**16** A2
Guest House Iguana...........**17** A1
Hotel Astoria.....................**18** D4
Hotel Camino Real.............**19** C4
Hotel Sartor.......................**20** B1
Pensión Stein.....................**21** B5

To Centro Comercial
Chipichape (1.5km);
Juanchito (6km)

To AeroRepublica
(400m); Kukaramakara
(1.2km)

To Bus
Terminal
(2km);
Airport (18km)

Iglesia de San
Judas Tadeo

Park

Iglesia de
la Ermita

Park

CAM

Río Cali

Plaza de
Caycedo

Catedral
San Pedro

Iglesia del
Sagrado
Corazón

Iglesia de San
Francisco

Capilla de la
Inmaculada

Casa
Proartes

Teatro
Municipal

Park

Iglesia de
San Antonio

To Zoológico
de Cali (2km)

To Tin Tin Deo (1km)

COLOMBIA

The adjacent monastery houses the good **Museo Arqueológico La Merced** (☎ 2-889-3434; Carrera 4 No 6-59; admission US$1; ☺ 9am-1pm & 2-6pm Mon-Sat) featuring an extensive collection of pre-Hispanic pottery left behind by the major cultures from central and southern Colombia.

One block away, the **Museo del Oro** (☎ 2-684-7757; Calle 7 No 4-69; admission free; ☺ 10am-5pm Mon-Sat) has a small but well-selected collection of gold and pottery pieces of the Calima culture.

The **Museo de Arte Moderno La Tertulia** (☎ 2-893-2942; Av Colombia No 5 Oeste-105; admission US$1; ☺ 10am-6pm) presents temporary exhibitions of contemporary painting, sculpture and photography.

Zoológico de Cali (☎ 2-892-7474; Carrera 2A Oeste at Calle 14 Oeste; admission US$2.50; ☺ 9am-5pm) is Colombia's best zoo. Its 10 hectares are home to about 1200 animals (belonging to about 180 species), both native and imported from other continents.

If you've had enough churches and museums you could always go flying; contact **German Air** (☎ 312-266-5943; germanair@bjnrock.com), which does paragliding courses and tandem flights.

Festivals & Events

The **Feria de Cali** is Cali's main event, beginning annually on December 25 and extending to the end of the year with parades, salsa concerts, bullfights and a beauty pageant.

Sleeping

Cali has two budget backpacker hostels (Guest House Iguana and Calidad House) conveniently located in the new city center. They are close to the nightclubs and restaurants and are popular with travelers.

Guest House Iguana (☎ 2-661-3522; iguana_cali@yahoo.com; Calle 21N No 9N-22; dm/s/d US$6/9/13.50; ☐) Quiet, Swiss-run place with a variety of rooms, some with private bathroom. There is a great-value private double upstairs with lots of privacy. It has a backpacker-friendly atmosphere and the owner is a mine of information on the region.

Calidad House (☎ 2-661-2338; Calle 17N No 9AN-39; dm/s US$6/7) This British-run guesthouse offers spacious dorms and private singles with shared bathroom, plus a communal kitchen and laundry facilities. At the time of writing the management was planning on renovating the private rooms. Along with the Iguana, this is the main backpacker hangout in Cali.

Hotel Camino Real (☎ 2-884-2525; Calle 9A No 3-54; s/d US$13.50/18) It's not glamorous, but Camino Real still offers some reasonable rooms at competitive rates. There are a few other hotels on this street if you feel like shopping around.

Hotel Sator (☎ 2-668-6482; hotelsator@yahoo.com; Av 8N No 20-50; s/d US$15/23) If you need more privacy than the Iguana or Calidad can offer try this nearby hotel, with smallish rooms set around a courtyard.

Hotel Astoria (☎ 2-883-0140; Calle 11 No 5-16; s/d US$18.50/24) Midrange option with a good location off the main plaza.

Pensión Stein (☎ 2-661-4999; www.hotelstein.com.co; Av 4N No 3N-33; s/d with fan US$27/45, with air-con US$38/52, all incl breakfast) Castlelike mansion with character and style. Run by a Swiss couple, the hotel offers spotlessly clean rooms with bathroom and has a restaurant.

Eating

You'll find loads of cafés and restaurants on and around Av Sexta, offering everything from simple snacks, burgers and pizzas to regional Colombian specialties and ethnic cuisines. The historic center also has plenty of budget eateries, but not many upmarket restaurants.

Café au Lait (Calle 2 No 4-73; coffee US$1.50) This small French-run café is located in the pleasant barrio of San Antonio. Excellent coffee and snacks.

Comedor Vegetariano Girasol (Av 5BN No 20N-30; set meals US$1.75) Another vegetarian option, this one is in the new center.

Restaurante Vegetariano Sol de la India (Carrera 6 No 8-48; set meals US$2) Vegetarian restaurant in a central location.

El Arca (Calle 13 No 8-44; mains US$2-4; ☺ noon-10pm Mon-Fri, 6-11pm Sat) Good Colombian–European fusion grub in a chill-out atmosphere, popular with the singles crowd.

Kiwis (Calle 12 No 3-36; crepes US$3; ☺ 9am-8pm) Specializing in ice cream and smoothies, this place also serves very good ham-and-cheese crepes.

D'Toluca (Calle 17N No 8N-46; dishes US$3-4; ☺ noon-midnight) Close to the Iguana and Calidad, this small Mexican restaurant has become a popular hangout for the backpacker set.

Archie's (Av 9N No 14N-22; mains US$5-8; ☺ noon-10pm) Gourmet pizzas and salads are made with fresh ingredients at this casual location. Have a wander around this neighborhood and you'll find a dozen other upscale options.

Restaurante Carambolo (Calle 14N No 9N-18; mains US$6-10) This chic bar-restaurant is spread over two levels and is full of flowers. It cooks fine Mediterranean cuisine.

Drinking

Cali's streets are lined with bars, although most double as *salsotecas*. One area to go for a drink is around Calle 17N between Av 8N and Av 9N. Most places don't have an admission fee, so it's easy to move from one to the next. Another area to trawl is Calle 17N between Av 8N and Av 9N.

Centro Comercial de Chipichape (www.chipichape .com in Spanish; Calle 38N No 6N-35) *Caleños* of all ages come to launch their evening with a *cerveza* (beer) or two at one of the many outdoor cafés at this mall. Locals have nicknamed it 'Silicon Valley' because of the high proportion of augmented women that it attracts. It is located just north of the main drag along Av Sexta.

Entertainment

Check the entertainment columns of the local newspaper *El País*.

Cali is the mecca of salsa dancing and you'll need some fast feet to keep up with the crowds. For a casual eve near the guesthouses, check out the handful of discos around the corner of Av 6N and Calle 16N.

The city's best-known salsa nightlife is in the legendary Juanchito, a popular, predominantly black outer suburb on the Río Cauca. Far away from the center, Juanchito was traditionally an archetypal salsa haunt dotted with dubious cafés and bars. Today sterile and expensive *salsotecas* have replaced most of the old shady but charming watering holes.

Juanchito's most famous salsa place is Changó, which is also probably the priciest. Agapito, next door, is cheaper but just as good. Parador is frequented by some of the most acrobatic dancers in town. Come on the weekend and take a taxi. Note that the action starts late: places open at around 10pm and get rowdy by midnight, peaking at about 2am.

Las Brisas de la Sexta (Av 6N No 15N-94) One of the largest and most popular *salsotecas*.

Zaperoco (Av 5N No 16N-46) Tucked away a bit, this cozy and likable *salsoteca* has magnetic salsa rhythms and a hot atmosphere.

Kukuramakara (Calle 28N No 2bis-97; admission US$5 ♥ 9pm-4am Thu-Sat) This live-music venue at-

tracts a slightly more mature crowd. At the time of writing it was one of the most popular places in town.

Cinemateca La Tertulia (☎ 2-893-2939; Av Colombia No 5 Oeste-105) Cali's best arthouse cinema, in the Museo de Arte Moderno La Tertulia.

Teatro Experimental de Cali (TEC; ☎ 2-884-3820; Calle 7 No 8-63) Colombia's national theater started with the foundation of this company. It continues to be one of the city's most innovative theater companies.

Another center of nighttime entertainment is on and around Calle 5 in southern Cali. The best of this lot is **Tin Tin Deo** (Carrera 22 No 4A-27), which is frequented by university students and professors, adding an intellectual feel to the action.

Getting There & Away
AIR

The Palmaseca airport is 16km northeast of the city. Minibuses between the airport and the bus terminal run every 10 minutes until about 8pm (US$1, 30 minutes), or take a taxi (US$12).

There are plenty of flights to most major Colombian cities, including Bogotá (US$80 to US$110), Cartagena (US$120 to US$150), Medellín (US$70 to US$120), Pasto (US$70 to US$100) and San Andrés (US$140 to US$150). Aires and Satena fly to Ipiales (US$80 to US$100). Domestic carriers include **Satena** (☎ 2-885-7709; Calle 8 No 5-14) and **AeroRepública** (☎ 2-660-1000; Calle 26N No 6N-16).

Avianca (☎ 2-667-6919; Av Colombia No 2-72, Hotel Intercontinental) flies to Panama City (60-day return ticket US$329), while Tame has three flights a week to Tulcán in Ecuador (one way US$86) and to Quito (US$123). **American Airlines** (☎ 2-666-3252; Av Colombia No 2-72, Hotel Intercontinental) has flights to the US.

BUS

The bus terminal is a 25-minute walk northeast of the city center, or 10 minutes by one of the frequent city buses. Buses run regularly to Bogotá (US$25, 12 hours), Medellín (US$18, nine hours) and Pasto (US$14, nine hours). Pasto buses will drop you off at Popayán (US$5, three hours) and there are also hourly minibuses to Popayán (US$6, 2½ hours).

Getting Around

The new and old centers are close enough that most places of interest will be within walking distance. The easiest way between the bus terminal and the center is by taxi (US$1.30). From the terminal, buses (flat fare US20¢) head south on Calle 5.

AROUND CALI
Historic Haciendas

There are a number of old haciendas in the Cauca Valley around Cali. Most of them date from the 18th and 19th centuries and were engaged in the cultivation and processing of sugar cane, the region's major crop. The two best known are the **Hacienda El Paraíso** (☎ 2-256-2378; admission US$1.75; ☿ 9am-5pm Tue-Sun) and **Hacienda Piedechinche** (☎ 2-550-6076; admission US$1.25; ☿ 9am-4pm Tue-Sun), both about 40km northeast of Cali and open as museums. There are tours from Cali on weekends, or you can visit them on your own using public transport, though both places are off the main roads. Take any bus to Buga and get off on the outskirts of **Amaime** (the drivers know where to drop you). Then walk to Piedechinche (5.5km) or negotiate a taxi. El Paraíso is still further off the road.

San Cipriano

This village is lost deep in the tropical forest near the Pacific coast, off the Cali–Buenaventura road. There's no road leading to the village, just a railway with occasional trains, but the locals have set up their own rail network with small trolleys propelled by mopeds. This ingenious means of transport is a great attraction and justifies a San Cipriano trip if only for the ride.

San Cipriano has a crystal-clear river, ideal for swimming, informal budget accommodations and some simple places to eat. The village is a popular weekend destination with *caleños*, but it's quiet on weekdays.

To get there from Cali, take a bus or *colectivo* to Buenaventura, get off at the village of Córdoba (US$3, two hours) and walk down the hill into the village to the railway track. From here, locals will take you to San Cipriano in their railcars (US$1) – a great journey through the rainforest.

ISLA GORGONA

Lying 56km off the mainland, the 9km-long and 2.5km-wide Isla Gorgona is Colombia's largest Pacific island. It's a mountainous island of volcanic origin, with the highest peak reaching 330m. It's covered with lush tropical rainforest and shelters diverse wildlife, including various monkeys, lizards, turtles, snakes and bird species, a number of which are endemic. There are some beaches and coral reefs along the shores, and the surrounding waters seasonally host dolphins, humpback whales and sperm whales. The climate is hot and wet, with high humidity and no distinctive dry season.

The island was a cruel high-security prison during La Violencia until 1984, but is now a **national park** (admission US$7.50; dm US$12; 3 set meals US$12). It offers accommodations in a four-bed dorm with bath, food and trips around the island (all excursions are accompanied by guides). You can also swim, sunbathe and snorkel (bring your own gear).

To visit Isla Gorgona, you need a permit from the national-park office in Bogotá. Booking long in advance is advisable, especially for

---

DETOUR: BUENAVENTURA

It may not be Colombia's most beautiful city, but with some 6m of rainfall a year, Buenaventura is by far the wettest. With a population largely made up of descendants of African slaves, its culture remains distinct from the rest of Colombia. The region's isolation has enabled the people to retain much of their African heritage, though at a price. Poverty is rampant, and much of the city consists of unpaved streets and wooden shacks. Isolation has also made the region a bastion for both paramilitaries and leftist rebels, though the situation has improved in recent years.

There are some fine beaches a short water taxi–ride from the city. In addition, the mouth of the nearby Río San Juan attracts humpback whales and dolphins from August to October. There are a number of places to stay, but the real standout is the **Hotel Estación** (☎ 2-243-4070; www.hotelestacion.com; Calle 2 No 1A-08; d from US$70), a neoclassical confection with deluxe rooms, a good restaurant and three-day, all-inclusive whale-watching packages from US$300 per person.

At the time of writing, the Cali–Buenaventura highway was heavily patrolled and considered safe, though be sure to check current conditions before setting out. Buses and *colectivos* leave frequently from Cali's bus station (US$4 to US$5, three hours).

Colombian vacation periods. All visits are fixed four-day/three-night stays, which must be paid for in advance.

The usual departure point for Isla Gorgona is Buenaventura (a three-hour bus trip from Cali), where you catch a (usually overcrowded) cargo boat for a 10- to 12-hour night trip to the island (about US$30). It can be a hellish experience if the sea is rough.

Some travelers and most tours use Guapí as a launching pad for Gorgona. Guapí is a seaside village in Cauca, just opposite Gorgona. Guapí is not connected by road with the rest of the country but can be reached by air on daily flights from Cali with Satena (US$50). From Guapí, boats take up to 10 tourists to Gorgona in less than two hours (about US$200 per boat). For information and reservations, call ☎ 2-825-7137 or ☎ 2-825-7136.

If you desire more comfort, several Cali tour companies organize trips to Gorgona for US$250 to US$300. Book through **Aviatur** (☎ 2-664-5050; Av 6N No 37BN-94). Another option, if you are into scuba diving, is to join a dive safari. A weekend trip including seven dives and a visit to the island will set you back around US$385. Contact **Arecifes del Pacífico** (☎ 315-410-8018; fico5@telesat.com.co).

Ecolombia Tours (☎ 2-557-1957; ecolombiatours@yahoo.com; Carrera 37A No 6-18) is arguably Cali's best specialist for tours to Isla Gorgona.

POPAYÁN

☎ 2 / pop 240,000

The whitewashed city of Popayán is one of Colombia's most beautiful old towns. But unlike many other historic places, this one has not been tarted up for the tourist hordes; it's a living, breathing city, with bustling streets and a sizable student population.

Founded in 1537, the town quickly became an important political, cultural and religious center, and was an obligatory stopover on the route between Cartagena and Quito. Its mild climate attracted wealthy Spanish settlers from the sugar haciendas of the hot Cali region. Several imposing churches and monasteries were built in the 17th and 18th centuries, when the city was flourishing.

During the 20th century while many Colombian cities were caught up in the race to industrialize, Popayán somehow managed to retain its colonial character. Ironically, many historic structures, including most of the churches, were seriously damaged by an earthquake in March 1983, just moments before the much-celebrated Maundy Thursday religious procession was about to depart. The difficult and costly restoration work continued for nearly two decades, but the results are admirable.

Despite the small size of the city, it can be surprisingly easy to get lost here, as every street appears identical. Finding your way back to where you started is just part of the fun.

Information

Celnet.com (Carrera 8 No 5-13; per hr US$1; 8am-9pm Mon-Sat, 9am-2pm Sun) Internet café.

Cyber Center (Calle 5 No 9-31; per hr US$1; 9am-9pm) Another internet café.

Oficina de Turismo de Popayán (☎ 2-824-2251; Carrera 5 No 4-68; ✆ 8am-noon & 2-6pm Mon-Fri, 9am-1pm Sat & Sun) Tourist info.

Parques Nacionales Naturales de Colombia (National Park Office; ☎ 2-823-1212, 2-823-1279; www.parquesnacionales.gov.co in Spanish; Carrera 9 No 25N-6)

Policía de Turismo (Tourist Police; ☎ 2-822-0916; Edificio de Gobernación, Parque Caldas)

Titán Intercontinental (Carrera 7 No 6-40, Centro Comercial Luis Martínez, Interior 106)

Unidas (Carrera 6 No 5-44) Will change cash.

Sights

Popayán has some good museums, most of which are set in splendid historic buildings.

Casa Museo Mosquera (☎ 2-824-0683; Calle 3 No 5-38; admission US$1; ✆ 8:30am-noon & 2-5pm) is a great colonial mansion that was home to General Tomás Cipriano de Mosquera, Colombia's president between 1845 and 1867. The museum contains personal memorabilia and a collection of colonial art, including some religious objects.

Museo Arquidiocesano de Arte Religioso (☎ 2-824-2759; Calle 4 No 4-56; admission US$1; ✆ 9am-12:30pm & 2-5pm Mon-Fri, 9am-2pm Sat) has an extensive collection of religious art including paintings, statues, altarpieces, silverware and liturgical vessels, most of which date from the 17th to 19th centuries. **Museo Guillermo Valencia** (☎ 2-824-2081; Carrera 6 No 2-65; admission US$1; ✆ 10am-noon & 2-5pm Tue-Sun), dedicated to the Popayán-born poet who once lived here, is full of period furniture, paintings and old photos related to him.

Museo de Historia Natural (☎ 2-820-1952; Carrera 2 No 1A-25; admission US$1.50; ✆ 8:30am-noon & 2-5pm Tue-Sun) is noted for its collections of insects,

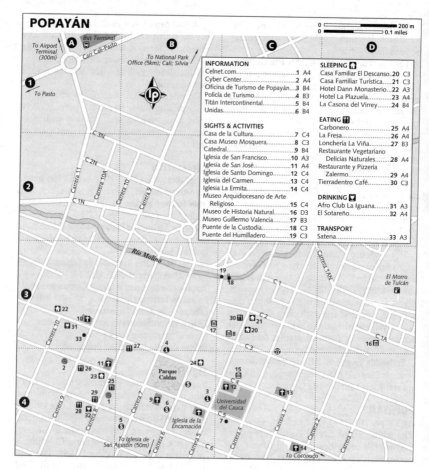

POPAYÁN

0 — 200 m
0 — 0.1 miles

INFORMATION
Celnet.com........................1 A4
Cyber Center......................2 A4
Oficina de Turismo de Popayán...3 B4
Policía de Turismo................4 B3
Titán Intercontinental............5 B4
Unidas.............................6 B4

SIGHTS & ACTIVITIES
Casa de la Cultura................7 C4
Casa Museo Mosquera..............8 C3
Catedral..........................9 B4
Iglesia de San Francisco.........10 A3
Iglesia de San José..............11 A4
Iglesia de Santo Domingo.........12 C4
Iglesia del Carmen...............13 C4
Iglesia La Ermita................14 C4
Museo Arquidiocesano de Arte
    Religioso......................15 C4
Museo de Historia Natural........16 D3
Museo Guillermo Valencia.........17 B3
Puente de la Custodia............18 C3
Puente del Humilladero...........19 C3

SLEEPING
Casa Familiar El Descanso.....20 C3
Casa Familiar Turística........21 C3
Hotel Dann Monasterio..........22 A3
Hotel La Plazuela..............23 A4
La Casona del Virrey...........24 B4

EATING
Carbonero......................25 A4
La Fresa.......................26 A4
Lonchería La Viña..............27 B3
Restaurante Vegetariano
    Delicias Naturales.........28 A4
Restaurante y Pizzería
    Zalermo....................29 A4
Tierradentro Café..............30 C3

DRINKING
Afro Club La Iguana............31 A3
El Sotareño....................32 A4

TRANSPORT
Satena.........................33 A3

---

butterflies and, in particular, stuffed birds. Part of the top floor is taken up by an archaeological display of pre-Columbian pottery from southern Colombia.

All the colonial churches were meticulously restored after the 1983 earthquake. The **Iglesia de San Francisco** (Carrera 9 at Calle 4) is the city's largest colonial church and arguably the best, with its fine high altar and a collection of seven amazing side altarpieces. Other colonial churches noted for their rich original furnishings include the **Iglesia de Santo Domingo** (Carrera 5 at Calle 4), **Iglesia de San José** (Calle 5 at Carrera 8) and the **Iglesia de San Agustín** (Calle 7 at Carrera 6).

Iglesia La Ermita (Calle 5 at Carrera 2) is Popayán's oldest church (1546), worth seeing for its fine main retable and for the fragments of old

frescoes, which were only discovered after the earthquake. The neoclassical **Catedral** (Parque Caldas) is the youngest church in the center, built between 1859 and 1906. It was almost completely destroyed by the earthquake and subsequently rebuilt from the ground up.

Walk to the river to see two unusual old bridges. The small one, the **Puente de la Custodia**, was constructed in 1713 to allow the priests to cross the river to bring the holy orders to the sick of the poor northern suburb. About 160 years later the 178m-long 12-arch **Puente del Humilladero** was built alongside the old bridge, and it's still in use.

Museums, churches and bridges are only a part of what Popayán has to offer. The best approach is to take a leisurely walk along the streets lined with whitewashed colonial mansions, savor the architectural details and drop inside to see the marvelous patios (many are open to the public).

Festivals & Events

If you are in the area during **Holy Week** you'll have the chance to see the famous nighttime processions on Maundy Thursday and Good Friday. Popayán's Easter celebrations are the most elaborate in the country. The festival of religious music is held concurrently.

Sleeping

Popayán has an array of accommodations to suit every pocket. Many hotels are set in old colonial houses and are stylish and atmospheric.

Casa Familiar Turística (☎ 2-824-4853; Carrera 5 No 2-07; dm/s/d US$4.50/7/11) One of the cheapest hotels in town. It has just four rooms, all with shared facilities. It's a good place to meet other travelers.

Casa Familiar El Descanso (☎ 2-824-0019; Carrera 5 No 2-41; s/d US$7/13.50) This place rents out small but neat rooms in a grand house. Piping hot water and a comfortable interior with soft couches and lots of natural light.

La Casona del Virrey (☎ 2-824-0836; Calle 4 No 5-78; r with/without bathroom per person US$16/8) Colonial building with style and character. Choose one of the ample rooms facing the street.

Hotel La Plazuela (☎ 2-824-1084; hotellaplazuela@ hotmail.com; Calle 5 No 8-13; s/d US$35/50) This splendid mansion has been turned into a stylish midrange hotel.

Hotel Dann Monasterio (☎ 2-824-2191; www.hotel esdann.com in Spanish; Calle 4 No 10-14; s/d US$54/60; 🖭) In a great colonial building with a vast courtyard that was once a Franciscan monastery, this is Popayán's top-notch offering. It has 48 spacious refurbished rooms and a fine restaurant that is worth visiting even if you are not staying here.

Eating

Popayán has plenty of places to eat and the food is relatively cheap.

La Fresa (Calle 5 No 8-89; 🕑 8am-8pm) From a small cubbyhole with no sign on the door, delicious, cheap *empanadas de pipián* (a type of fried pastry) are served.

Tierradentro Café (Carrera 5 No 2-12) The best choice of espressos and cappuccinos in town, with 90 different flavors. An important stop for coffee addicts.

Restaurante Vegetariano Delicias Naturales (Calle 6 No 8-21) Offers good, budget vegetarian meals.

Carbonero (Carrera 8a No 5-15; dishes US$3; 🕑 noon-9:30pm) A great place to go if you have a big appetite, this spacious restaurant serves big portions of Colombian fare. One of the owners speaks English and can impart useful advice on the area.

Lonchería La Viña (Calle 4 No 7-79; mains US$3-5; 🕑 9am-midnight) One of the best and most popular budget eateries. It has tasty food, generous portions and is open late. Recommended.

Restaurante y Pizzeria Zalermo (Carrera 8 No 5-100; mains US$3-7; 🕑 9am-10pm) Patrons can choose from a dozen types of pizza in this friendly restaurant. Chicken and pasta are also available.

Drinking

El Sotareño (Calle 6 No 8-05; 🕑 4pm-late Mon-Sat) Legendary rustic bar with a 40-year history. It plays nostalgic old rhythms such as tango, bolero, *ranchera* and *milonga* from scratched vinyls probably as old as the place itself, and serves some of the cheapest beer in town.

Afro Club La Iguana (Calle 4 No 9-67; 🕑 8pm-late Mon-Sat) Bar with excellent salsa and Cuban *son* music at high volume. It can get jam-packed and heaves with hot salsa action, especially on weekends.

Getting There & Away

AIR

The airport is just behind the bus terminal, a 15-minute walk north of the city center. Satena has daily flights to Bogotá (US$70 to US$80).

DETOUR: RESERVA NACIONAL NATURAL PURACÉ

Trekking opportunities exist just outside Popayán at the Reserva Nacional Natural Puracé, an 83,000-hectare reserve that includes the sometimes-snowy Nevado de Puracé (4750m) as well as natural hot springs, mountain lakes, waterfalls and fields of multicolored grasses. The reserve is located about 45km southeast of Popayán. Entrance fees are US$8, dorms are US$6 and three meals a day cost another US$5. For information and reservations in Popayán, contact the Parques Nacionales Naturales de Colombia (p609).

BUS
The bus terminal is a short walk north of the city center. Plenty of buses run to Cali (US$5, three hours), and there are also minibuses and *colectivos* every hour or so. Buses to Bogotá run every hour or two (US$26, 15 hours).

Buses to Pasto (US$10, six hours) leave every hour. It's a hazardous road best traveled by day. For information on getting to Tierradentro see p616 and for San Agustín see p614.

SILVIA
☎ 2 / pop 5000
Travelers hoping to catch a glimpse of the indigenous way of life should look no further than this small town, located 53km northeast of Popayán. Silvia is the center of the Guambianos, one of the most traditional Indian communities in Colombia. Though the Indians don't live in the town, they come to Silvia for the Tuesday market to sell fruit, vegetables and handicrafts. This is possibly the most colorful Indian gathering in the country and the best day to visit Silvia. You'll see plenty of Indians in traditional dress, the women in handwoven garments and beaded necklaces, busily spinning wool. Bring a sweater – it can get cold when the weather is cloudy. If you decide to stay longer in Silvia, there are at least half-a-dozen budget hotels.

To get to Silvia from Popayán, take the Coomotoristas bus or Tax Belalcázar minibus (US$2, 1½ hours). On Tuesday, there are also *colectivos* between Popayán and Silvia.

SAN AGUSTÍN
☎ 8 / pop 2000
Long before Europeans came to the Americas, the rolling hills around San Agustín attracted a mysterious group of people who came here to bury their dead and honor them with magnificent statues. The legacy that they left behind is now one of the continent's most important archaeological sites. Hundreds of freestanding monumental statues carved in stone were left next to the tombs of tribal elders. Pottery and gold objects were left behind, although much of it was robbed over the centuries.

San Agustín culture flourished between the 6th and 14th centuries AD. The best statuary was made only in the last phase of the development, and the culture had presumably vanished before the Spaniards came. The statues were not discovered until the middle of the 18th century.

So far some 500 statues have been found and excavated. A great number are anthropomorphic figures – some of them realistic, others very stylized, resembling masked monsters. Others are zoomorphic, depicting sacred animals such as the eagle, the jaguar and the frog. The statues vary both in size, from about 20cm to 7m, and in their degree of detail.

Orientation & Information
The statues and tombs are scattered in groups over a wide area on both sides of the gorge formed by the upper Río Magdalena. The main town of the region, San Agustín, shelters most of the accommodations and restaurants. From there, you can explore the region on foot, horseback or by jeep; give yourself three days for leisurely visits to the most interesting places.

Banco Ultrahuilca (Calle 3 No 12-73) It's best to bring as much cash as you're likely to need, since this is the only ATM in town. No-one reliably accepts traveler's checks, and rates for cash tend to be poor.

Internet Galería Café (Calle 3 No 12-16; ☒ 8am-10pm) Internet café right across from the tourist office.

Tourist office (☎ 8-837-3062 ext 15; cnr Calle 3 & Carrera 12; ☒ 8am-noon & 2-5pm Mon-Fri) Information and maps are available.

Sights & Activities
The 78-hectare **Parque Arqueológico** (admission US$2; ☒ 8am-6pm), 2.5km west of the town of San Agustín, features some of the best of San Agustín statuary. The park covers several archaeological sites that include statues, tombs and burial mounds. It also has the **Museo Arqueológico** (☒ 8am-5pm Tue-Sun) which displays smaller statues and pottery, and the **Bosque de las Estatuas** (Forest of Statues), where 35 statues of different origins are placed along a footpath that snakes through the woods.

The **Alto de los Ídolos** (☒ 8am-4pm) is another archaeological park, noted for burial mounds and large stone tombs. The largest statue, 7m tall, is here. The park is a few kilometers southwest of San José de Isnos, on the other side of the Río Magdalena from San Agustín town. The ticket bought at the Parque Arqueológico also covers entry to the Alto de los Ídolos and is valid for two consecutive days.

A dozen other archaeological sites are scattered over the area including **El Tablón**, **La Chaquira**, **La Pelota** and **El Purutal**, four sites

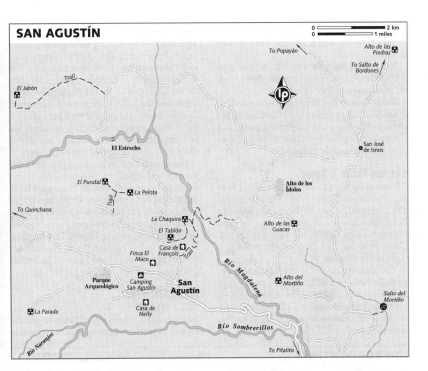

SAN AGUSTÍN

Map showing: El Jabón, El Estrecho, El Purutal, La Pelota, La Chaquira, El Tablón, Casa de François, Finca El Maco, Parque Arqueológico, Camping San Agustín, San Agustín, Casa de Nelly, La Parada, Alto de las Piedras, Alto de los Ídolos, Alto de las Guacas, San José de Isnos, Alto del Mortiño, Salto del Mortiño, Río Magdalena, Río Sombrerillos, Río Naranjos. Roads To Popayán, To Salto de Bordones, To Quinchana, To Pitalito. Scale 0–2 km / 0–1 miles.

relatively close to each other that can be conveniently visited on one trip. The region is also noted for its natural beauty, with two lovely waterfalls, **Salto de Bordones** and **Salto del Mortiño**. **El Estrecho**, where the Río Magdalena passes through 2m narrows, is an attractive sight.

There is good scope for white-water rafting and kayaking in San Agustín. **Magdalena Rafting** (☎ 311-271-5333; magdalenarafting@yahoo.fr; Via Parque No 4-12) runs half-day trips on the river for US$18 including drinks. Kayaking is also possible. The best time of the year for rafting is June and July. Other activities including horse-riding, jeep tours and trekking are organized through Finca El Maco guesthouse (right).

Sleeping

There are a dozen budget hotels in and around San Agustín, most of which are clean and friendly and have hot water.

There are more budget options outside the town, and these are possibly the most popular with travelers.

Camping San Agustín (☎ 8-837-3192; per site US$3) Camping is available here, about 1km outside town on the way to the archaeological park.

Casa de François (☎ 8-837-3847; per person US$4) Pleasant French-run hostel 1km north of town, off the road to El Tablón. It has two rooms and a four-bed cabin; guests can use the kitchen.

Hospedaje El Jardín (☎ 8-837-3159; Carrera 11 No 4-10; per person US$3.50) Basic but neat option near the bus offices, offering rooms with and without bathrooms.

Hotel Colonial (☎ 8-837-3159; Calle 3 No 11-54; per person US$4) Close to the bus offices, Hotel Colonial has rooms with and without bathrooms, and a reasonable restaurant.

Casa de Nelly (☎ 8-837-3221; r per person with/without bathroom US$6/4) An agreeable French-run place 1km west of the town off the dirt road to La Estrella.

Finca El Maco (☎ 8-837-3437; www.elmaco.ch; per person US$5.50) Ecological ranch off the road to the Parque Arqueológico. It offers accommodations in cabins, great organic meals, laundry service and use of the kitchen. This is also a good place to organize horse-riding or rafting trips.

Eating

You'll find several budget eateries around Calle 5. There are some eating outlets on the road to the Parque Arqueológico, including Restaurante La Brasa, serving tasty grilled meat.

Restaurante Brahama (Calle 5 No 15-11; set meals US$2) This place serves cheap set meals, vegetarian food and fruit salads.

Donde Richard (Via al Parque Arqueológico; mains US$5-6) Specializing in grilled meats, including the restaurant's signature marinated pork, this is hands-down the best place in town. Don't miss the homemade sausages.

Getting There & Away

All bus offices are clustered on Calle 3 near the corner of Carrera 11. Three buses a day (departing early in the morning) go to Popayán via a rough but spectacular road through Isnos (US$8, six to eight hours). Coomotor has two buses daily to Bogotá (US$16, 12 hours).

There are no direct buses to Tierradentro; go to La Plata (US$8, five hours) and change for a bus to El Cruce de San Andrés (US$4, 2½ hours), from where it's a 20-minute walk to the Tierradentro museum. La Plata has several cheap hotels.

Getting Around

The usual way of visiting San Agustín's sights (apart from the Parque Arqueológico) is by jeep tours and horse-riding excursions. The standard jeep tour includes El Estrecho, Alto de los Ídolos, Alto de las Piedras, Salto de Bordones and Salto de Mortiño. It takes seven to eight hours and costs US$12 per person if there are six people to fill the jeep. There are few jeep tours since few tourists come here these days, so you pay for the empty seats.

Horse rental can be arranged through hotel managers or directly with horse owners who frequently approach tourists. Horses are hired out for a specific route, for a half-day (US$7) or full day (US$12). One of the most popular horse-riding trips (US$7 per horse, around five hours) includes El Tablón, La Chaquira, La Pelota and El Purutal. If you need a guide to accompany your party, add US$6 for the guide and another US$6 for his horse.

TIERRADENTRO

☎ 2 / pop 1500

To the original inhabitants of Tierradentro, the high cliffs and lush scenery must have seemed

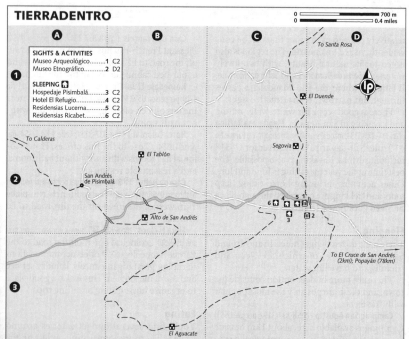

TIERRADENTRO

0   700 m
0   0.4 miles

SIGHTS & ACTIVITIES
Museo Arqueológico..........1 C2
Museo Etnográfico............2 D2

SLEEPING
Hospedaje Pisimbalá.........3 C2
Hotel El Refugio................4 C2
Residensias Lucerna..........5 C2
Residensias Ricabet...........6 C2

To Santa Rosa

El Duende

To Calderas

Segovia

El Tablón

San Andrés de Pisimbalá

Alto de San Andrés

To El Cruce de San Andrés (2km); Popayán (78km)

El Aguacate

Parque Nacional Cajas (p693) Shimmering lakes and moorlike *páramo* make this highland park an excellent adventure from Cuenca.

Parque Nacional Podocarpus (p696) From cloud forest to rainforest, this epic southern park is best explored from Loja, Zamora or Vilcabamba.

Many parks are inhabited by native peoples who were living in the area long before it achieved park status. In the case of the Oriente parks, indigenous hunting practices (which have a greater impact as outside interests diminish their original territories and resources) have met with concern from those seeking to protect the park. The issue of how to protect these areas from interests such as oil, timber and mining, while recognizing the rights of indigenous people, continues to be extremely tricky.

National park entrance fees vary. On the mainland, most highland parks charge US$10, and most lowland parks charge US$20 per visitor, but both fees are valid for a week. In the Galápagos Islands, the park fee is US$100.

Environmental Issues

Deforestation is Ecuador's most severe environmental problem. In the highlands, almost all of the natural forest cover has disappeared. Along the coast, once-plentiful mangrove forests have all but vanished, too. These forests harbor a great diversity of marine and shore life, but they have been removed to make artificial shrimp ponds. Esmeraldas province has some of the last large stands of mangroves in the country. Opening new shrimp farms is now prohibited.

About 95% of the forests of the western Andean slopes and western lowlands have become agricultural land, mostly banana plantations. These forests were host to more species than almost anywhere on the planet, and many of them are (or were) endemic. Countless species have surely become extinct even before they were identified. An effort is now being made to conserve what little there is left.

Although much of the rainforest in the Ecuadorian Amazon remains standing, it is being seriously threatened by fragmentation. Since the discovery of oil, roads have been built, colonists have followed and the destruction of the forest has increased exponentially. The main causes of this destruction are logging, cattle ranching and oil extraction.

Clearly, these problems are linked tightly with Ecuador's economy. Oil, bananas and shrimp are the nation's top three exports. However, the serious environmental damage caused by the production of these and other products requires that their value be carefully examined.

The rainforest's indigenous inhabitants – who depend on the rivers for drinking water and food – are also dramatically affected. Oil residues, oil treatment chemicals, erosion and fertilizers all contaminate the rivers, killing fish and rendering formerly potable water undrinkable. Unfortunately, government policies allow oil exploration and encourage the colonization and clearing of land with little regard for forests, rivers, wildlife or residents.

Ecuador lacks the financial resources to commit itself to strong government-funded conservation. However, local and international conservation agencies, indigenous groups (which survive on the rainforest's natural resources) and ecotourism have brought international attention to Ecuador's environmental crises and contribute to an ever-increasing demand to protect the environment. But, as any environmentalist in Ecuador will tell you, this is no time to rest. New mining, oil, logging and other projects are continuously implemented, and pressure is needed from all sides to minimize or eliminate their impacts on the environment.

TRANSPORTATION

GETTING THERE & AWAY
Air

The main international airports are in Guayaquil (p717) and Quito (p647). Direct flights go to Bogotá (Colombia), Buenos Aires (Argentina), Caracas (Venezuela), Curaçao, Guatemala City (Guatemala), Havana (Cuba), Lima (Peru), Panama City (Panama), Rio de Janeiro (Brazil), San José (Costa Rica), Santiago (Chile) and São Paulo (Brazil). Connecting flights (via Lima) are available to

---

DEPARTURE TAX

Unless they are merely in transit, passengers on outbound international flights must pay a US$25 departure tax. This does not apply to the Tulcán–Cali (Colombia) flight.

Asunción (Paraguay) and La Paz (Bolivia). There are also three flights per week between Tulcán (in the northern highlands of Ecuador) and Cali (Colombia).

Boat

For information on boat travel between Nuevo Rocafuerte (Ecuador) and Iquitos (Peru), see p701.

Bus

International bus tickets sold in Quito often require a change of bus at the border. It's usually cheaper and just as convenient to buy a ticket to the border and another ticket in the next country. The exceptions are the international buses from Loja (p694) to Piura, Peru (via Macará), and from Guayaquil (p717) to Peru (via Huaquillas); on these, you do not have to change buses, and the immigration officials usually board the bus to take care of your paperwork. These are the primary routes between Ecuador and Peru. Zumba, south of Vilcabamba (p697), is gaining popularity as an alternative route to/from Peru due to its scenic location and lack of use. The main bus route between Colombia and Ecuador is via Tulcán (p675). Other border crossings between Colombia and Ecuador are unsafe.

GETTING AROUND

You can usually get anywhere quickly and easily. Bus is the most common mode of transport, followed by plane. Buses can take you from the Colombian border to Peru's border in 18 hours. Boats are used in the northern coastal mangroves and in the Oriente.

Whatever form of transport you choose, always carry your passport with you, both to board planes, and to proffer during document checks on the road. People without documents may be arrested. If your passport is in order, these procedures are cursory. If you're traveling anywhere near the borders or in the Oriente, expect more frequent passport checks.

Air

With the exception of flying to the Galápagos (see p729 for details), most internal flights are cheap. One-way flights average US$50 and rarely exceed US$60. Almost all flights originate or terminate in Quito or Guayaquil. Some domestic flights have marvelous views of the snowcapped Andes – when flying from Quito to Guayaquil, sit on the left.

Ecuador's major domestic airline is **TAME** (www.tame.com.ec). **Icaro** (www.icaro.com.ec) is the second biggest, with fewer flights but newer planes. Between these two airlines, you can fly from Quito to Guayaquil, Coca, Cuenca, Esmeraldas, Lago Agrio, Loja, Macas, Machala, Manta, Tulcán and the Galápagos. From Guayaquil you can fly to Quito, Coca, Cuenca, Loja, Machala and the Galápagos. There are no Sunday flights to the Oriente. **AeroGal** (www.aerogal.com.ec) flies mostly to the Galápagos.

If you can't get a ticket for a particular flight (especially out of small towns), go to the airport early and get on the waiting list in the hope of a cancellation.

Boat

Motorized dugout canoes are the only transportation available in some roadless areas. Regularly scheduled boats are affordable, although not as cheap as a bus for a similar distance. Hiring your own boat and skipper is possible but extremely expensive. The northern coast (near San Lorenzo and Borbón) and the lower Río Napo from Coca to Peru are the places you'll most likely travel to by boat (if you get out that far). Pelting rain and glaring sun can induce serious suffering, and an umbrella is excellent defense against both. Use good sunscreen or wear long sleeves, pants and a hat. A light jacket is worth having in case of chilling rain, and insect repellent is useful during stops along the river. Bring a water bottle and a stash of food, and you're set. Keep your spare clothes in plastic bags or they'll get soaked if it storms.

Bus

Buses are the lifeblood of Ecuador and the easiest way to get around. Most towns have a *terminal terrestre* (central bus terminal) for long-distance buses, although in some towns, buses leave from various places. *Busetas* are fast, small buses offering direct, and sometimes frighteningly speedy, service. Larger coaches usually allow standing passengers and can get crowded, but are often more interesting.

To get your choice of seat, buy tickets in advance from the terminal. During holiday weekends, buses can be booked up for several days in advance. Companies that offer frequent departures don't sell advance tickets, but arriving an hour early usually guarantees you a seat. For immediate travel, go to the terminal and listen for your destination to be yelled out. Make sure your bus goes direct to your destination if you don't want to change.

If you're traveling lightly, keep your luggage with you inside the bus. Otherwise, heave it onto the roof or stuff it into the luggage compartment and keep an eagle eye on it.

Long-distance buses rarely have toilets, but usually stop for 20-minute meal and bladder-relief breaks at fairly appropriate times. If not, drivers will stop to let you fertilize the roadside.

Local buses are usually slow and crowded, but cheap. You can get around most towns for about US20¢ to US25¢. Local buses also often go out to nearby villages (a great way to explore an area).

Car & Motorcycle

Few people rent cars in Ecuador, mainly because public transport makes getting around so easy. Ecuador's automobile association is **Aneta** (in Quito ☎ 02-250-4961, 02-222-9020; www.aneta .org.ec), which offers 24-hour roadside assistance to its members. It also offers some services to members of foreign automobile clubs, including Canadian and US AAA members.

Hitchhiking

Hitchhiking is possible, but not very practical in Ecuador. Public transportation is relatively cheap and trucks are used as public transportation in remote areas, so trying to hitch a free ride isn't easy. If the driver is stopping to drop off and pick up other passengers, assume that payment will be expected. If you're the only passenger, the driver may have picked you up just to talk to a foreigner.

Taxi

Taxis are cheap. Bargain the fare beforehand though, or you're likely to be overcharged. A long ride in a large city (Quito or Guayaquil) shouldn't go over US$5, and short hops in small towns usually cost about US$1. Meters are obligatory in Quito (where the minimal fare is US$1) but rarely seen elsewhere. On weekends and at night, fares are always about 25% to 50% higher. A full-day taxi hire should cost from US$50 to US$60.

Train

Little remains of Ecuador's railways after the damage to lines due to the 1982–83 El Niño rains. Only the sections with tourist appeal have received enough funding to reopen. A train runs three times a week between Riobamba and Sibambe, which includes the hair-raising Nariz del Diablo (Devil's Nose), the country's railway pride and joy. The Ibarra–San Lorenzo line, which used to link the highlands with the coast, is on its deathbed; *autoferros* (buses mounted on railway chassis) only make it a fraction of the way to San Lorenzo. One easy way to ride the rails is aboard the weekend Quito–Cotopaxi route, which stops at Area de Recreación El Boliche, adjacent to Parque Nacional Cotopaxi.

Truck

In remote areas, *camiones* (trucks) and *camionetas* (pickup trucks) often double as buses. If the weather is OK, you get fabulous views; if not, you have to crouch underneath a dark tarpaulin and suck dust. Pickups can be hired to get to remote places such as climbers' refuges.

QUITO

☎ 02 / pop 1,400,000

Spread across a spectacular Andean valley and flanked by volcanic peaks, Quito's setting alone is enough to strike you speechless. The historical center, or 'Old Town', is a maze of colonial splendor, a Unesco World Heritage Site since 1978. Despite intensive restoration projects (completed in 2006), the Old Town retains the vibrant working class and indigenous character that has always defined it. To walk its narrow streets is to wander into another world. Stray dogs saunter past indigenous women carrying impossible loads, past legless guitar strummers, blind accordion players and giant roast pigs peeking out of narrow doorways. The constant hum of hollering vendors hangs in the air like chanting in a monastery, and the myriad smells threaten sensory overload. Only a 20-minute walk away, Quito's 'New Town' is a different world entirely. For travelers, its heart is the Mariscal Sucre, chockablock with cafés, restaurants, travel agencies, cybercafés, bars and hotels.

Quito was a major Inca city that was destroyed by Atahualpa's general, Rumiñahui, shortly before the arrival of the Spanish conquistadors. The present capital was founded

ECUADOR

atop the Inca ruins by Sebastián de Benalcázar on December 6, 1534. Unfortunately, no Inca structures remain.

ORIENTATION

Quito (elevation 2850m) is Ecuador's second-largest city, after Guayaquil. It can be divided into three segments. In the center is the colonial Old Town. Modern Quito – the New Town – is in the north, with major businesses, airline offices, embassies and shopping centers. The New Town also contains the airport, middle- and upper-class homes and the Mariscal Sucre neighborhood (the travelers' ghetto known simply as El Mariscal). Av Amazonas, with its banks, hotels, crafts stores, cafés and corporate business offices, is the New Town's best-known street, although Avs 10 de Agosto and 6 de Diciembre are the most important thoroughfares. The south comprises mostly working-class housing areas.

The **Instituto Geográfico Militar** (IGM; Map pp650-1; ☎ 254-5090, 222-9075/76; map sales room ⏲ 8am-4pm Mon-Thu, 7am-12:30pm Fri), on top of steep Paz y Miño, publishes and sells Ecuador's best topographical maps. You'll need to leave your passport at the gate.

INFORMATION
Bookstores

Confederate Books (Map pp650-1; J Calama 410) Ecuador's largest selection of secondhand books in English and other languages.
English Bookstore (Map pp650-1; cnr J Calama & Av 6 de Diciembre) Bookstore-café with great selection of used books in English.
Libri Mundi (Map pp650-1; JL Mera 851) Quito's best bookstore; excellent selection of books in Spanish, English, German and French.
Libro Express (Map pp650-1; Av Amazonas 816 & Gral Veintimilla) Good for guidebooks, coffee-table books and magazines.

Cultural Centers

Alliance Française (Map pp650-1; ☎ 224-9345/50; Av Eloy Alfaro N32-468 near Av 6 de Diciembre) Films, language classes and information on Ecuador and France.
Asociación Humboldt (Map pp650-1; ☎ 254-8480; www.asociacion-humboldt.org in Spanish & German; cnr Vancouver & Polonia) German center and Goethe Institute.
Centro Cultural Afro-Ecuatoriano (Map pp650-1; ☎ 252-2318; JL Tamayo 985) Information on Afro-Ecuadorian culture and events in Quito.
Centro Cultural Metropolitano (Map p653; ☎ 295-0272, 258-4363; www.centrocultural-quito.com; cnr García Moreno & Espejo; admission US$2; ⏲ 9am-5pm, patio until 7:30pm Tue-Sun) The hub of cultural events in the Old Town.

Emergency

Fire department (☎ 102)
General emergency (☎ 911)
Police (☎ 101)
Red Cross ambulance (☎ 131, 258-0598)

Internet Access

While the Mariscal area (especially along J Calama) is bursting with cybercafés, they're trickier to find in the Old Town. All charge US70¢ to US$1 per hour. The following are a few of the more popular choices:
Friends Web Café (Map pp650-1; J Calama E6-19) Vibe here is as good as the juices and snacks.
K'ntuña Net (Map p653; Chile 0e4-22, Pasaje Arzobispal, local 14) Located in back patio of Palacio Arzobispal.
Papaya Net (Map pp650-1; J Calama 469 at JL Mera) Groovin' music, alcohol, espresso drinks and snacks.
Sambo.net (Map pp650-1; JL Mera at J Pinto) Comfy place, fast connection.
Stop 'n' Surf (Map p653; Espejo Shopping, Espejo 0e2-40, local 64)

Internet Resources

Corporación Metropolitana de Turismo (www.quito .com.ec in Spanish)

GETTING INTO TOWN

The airport is on Av Amazonas, about 10km north of the Mariscal Sucre neighborhood (where most of the budget hotels are). As you walk out of the airport, south is to your left. Cross Av Amazonas and flag a south-bound bus. It costs 30¢ to get from here to the Mariscal. From there, you can catch a bus or the Trole (electricity-powered bus) to the Old Town, about 2km further south. A taxi from the airport to the Mariscal should cost no more than US$5, and about US$6 to the Old Town.

The bus terminal (Terminal Terrestre Cumandá) is a few blocks south of Plaza Santo Domingo in the Old Town. Take a cab into town if you arrive at night. Avoid the Trole at any time if you're loaded down with luggage.

Gay Guide to Quito (http://gayquitoec.tripod.com)
Que Hacer Quito (www.quehacerquito.com in Spanish)

Laundry

The following laundries will wash, dry and fold your whiffy clothes within 24 hours. All charge between US75¢ and US$1 per kg.

Opera de Jabón (Map pp650-51; J Pinto 325 near Reina Victoria)
Rainbow Laundry (Map pp650-51; JL Mera 1337 at Cordero)
Sun City Laundry (Map pp650-51; JL Mera at Foch)
Wash & Go (Map pp650-51; J Pinto 340 at JL Mera)

Medical Services

Clínica de la Mujer (Map p657; ☎ 245-8000; Av Amazonas 4826 at Gaspar de Villarroel) Private clinic specializing in women's health.
Clínica Pichincha (Map pp650-51; ☎ 256-2408, 256-2296; Gral Veintimilla 1259 at U Páez) In the new town; does lab analysis for parasites, dysentery etc.
Dr Alfredo Jijon (Map p657; ☎ 245-6359, 246-6314; Centro Meditropoli, office 215, Mariana de Jesús & Av Occidental) Gynecologist.
Dr John Rosenberg (Map pp650-51; ☎ 252-1104, ext 310, 09-973-9734, pager 222-7777; Foch 476 & D de Almagro) Internist specializing in tropical medicine; English and German are spoken. He also makes house calls.
Dr Silvia Altamirano (☎ 224-4119; Av Amazonas 2689 & Av de la República) Orthodontist and dentist; excellent.
Hospital Metropolitano (Map p657; ☎ 226-1520; Mariana de Jesús at Av Occidental) Better, but pricier than Voz Andes.
Hospital Voz Andes (Map p657; ☎ 226-2142; Juan Villalengua 267 near Avs América & 10 de Agosto) American-run hospital with outpatient and emergency rooms. Fees are low.

Money

There are several banks and a few *casas de cambio* (currency-exchange bureaus) in the New Town along Av Amazonas between Av Patria and Orellana, and there are dozens of banks throughout town. Banks listed in this section have ATMs and change traveler's checks.

If you need to change money on a Sunday, head to the Producambios at the airport; the *casa de cambio* in the international arrival area is open for all flight arrivals.

American Express (Map pp650-51; ☎ 02-256-0488; Av Amazonas 329, 5th fl) Sells Amex travelers checks to American Express card holders only. Also replaces lost or stolen checks.

Banco de Guayaquil Av Amazonas (Map pp650-1; Av Amazonas N22-147 at Gral Veintimilla); Colón (Map pp650-1; Av Cristóbal Colón at Reina Victoria)
Banco del Pacífico New Town (Map pp650-1; Av 12 de Octubre & Cordero); Old Town (Map p653; cnr Guayaquil & Chile)
Banco del Pichincha (Map p653; Guayaquil at Manabí)
MasterCard (Map p657; Naciones Unidas 8771 at De Los Shyris)
Producambios (Av Amazonas 350; ☒ 8:30am-6pm Mon-Fri, 9am-2pm Sat)
Visa (Map p657; De Los Shyris 3147)
Western Union Av de la República (Map pp650-1; Av de la República 433); Colón (Map pp650-1; Av Cristóbal Colón 1333) For money transfers; charges US$90 for a US$1000 transfer from the USA.

Post

You can mail a package up to 2kg from any post office. Packages exceeding 2kg must be mailed from the Mariscal Sucre or parcel post offices (listed here).

Central post office (Map p653; Espejo 935) In the Old Town; this is where you pick up your *lista de correos* (general delivery mail; see p738).
DHL (Map pp650-1; Av Cristóbal Colón 1333 at Foch)
Mariscal Sucre post office (Map pp650-1; cnr Av Cristóbal Colón & Reina Victoria)
Parcel post office (Map pp650-1; Ulloa 273) If you are mailing a package over 2kg, use this post office, near Dávalos.
'PostOffice' (Map pp650-1; cnr Av Amazonas & Santa María) Private company offering FedEx, UPS and other international courier services.

Telephone

Local, national and international calls can be made at the following:

Andinatel main office (Map pp650-1; Av Eloy Alfaro 333 near 9 de Octubre)
Andinatel Mariscal offices JL Mera (Map pp650-1; JL Mera 741 at Gral Baquedano); Reina Victoria (Map pp650-1; Reina Victoria near J Calama) Located In the Mariscal area.
Andinatel Old Town offices Benalcázar (Map p653; Benalcázar near Mejía); García Moreno (Map p653; cnr García Moreno & Sucre)

Tourist Information

South American Explorers (SAE; Map pp650-1; ☎ 222-5228; www.saexplorers.org; Jorge Washington 311 & Leonidas Plaza Gutiérrez; ☒ 9:30am-5pm Mon-Wed, Fri, 9:30am-6pm Thu, 9am-noon Sat) For more information on this excellent travelers' organization, see above.

ECUADOR

QUITO – NEW TOWN

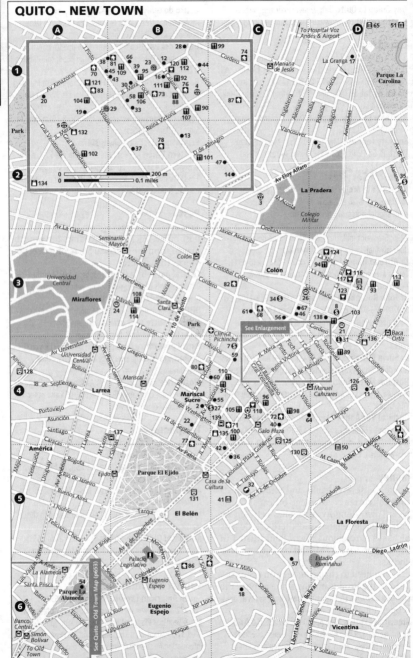

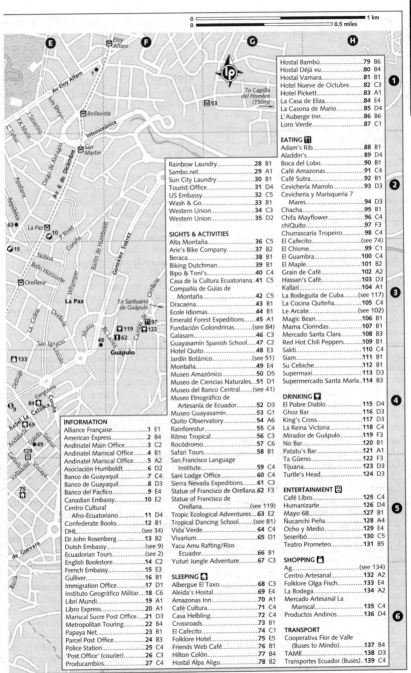

Tourist Information Kiosk (Map p653; cnr Venezuela & Chile, Plaza Grande) Convenient for general questions, directions and maps.

Tourist Offices (Corporación Metropolitana de Turismo; www.quito.com.ec in Spanish); Old Town 'El Quinde' (Map p653; ☎ 257-0786; García Moreno N12-01 at Mejía; ☾ 9:30am-6pm Mon-Sat, 10am-4pm Sun); Old Town Palacio Arzobispal (Map p653; ☎ 258-6591; Chile & Venezuela, Plaza Grande; ☾ 9am-5pm Mon-Sat); Mariscal (Map pp650-1; ☎ 255-1566; Cordero at Reina Victoria; ☾ 9am-5pm Mon-Fri); airport (☎ 330-0163)

Travel Agencies

Ecuadorian Tours (Map pp650-1; ☎ 256-0488; www.ecuadoriantours.com; Av Amazonas N21-33) Good all-purpose travel agency.

Metropolitan Touring New Town (Map pp650-51; ☎ 250-6650/51/52; www.metropolitan-touring .com; Av Amazonas N20-39 near 18 de Septiembre); Old Town (Map p653; ☎ 228-9172; Olmedo Oe-548) Ecuador's biggest travel agency.

DANGERS & ANNOYANCES

Quito's reputation as a dangerous city is increasing. The Mariscal Sucre neighborhood (in the New Town) is extremely dangerous after dark, and you should *always take a taxi*, even for short distances. The Mariscal has been plagued by drugs, muggings, assaults and prostitution, and the city has only recently taken even the most token steps to control it (and the police corruption that allows it to continue). Despite some inconveniences, consider staying in another neighborhood (like the Old Town or La Floresta); besides safety issues, you'll have a more authentic experience to boot. Sunday, when no one is around, can also be dodgy in the Mariscal.

With the restoration of the Old Town, and increased police presence there, the historic center is safe until 10pm or so weekdays and until midnight on weekends. Avoid the climb up El Panecillo hill; take a taxi instead (there are plenty up top for the return trip). As usual, pickpockets work crowded buses (especially the Trole and Ecovía lines), the bus terminal and markets. If you are robbed, obtain a police report within 48 hours from the **police station** (Old Town Map p653; Mideros & Cuenca; New Town Map pp650-1; cnr Reina Victoria & Vicente Ramón Roca) between 9am and noon.

There have been several armed robberies along the main trail around the telefériQo let-off point at the top of Cruz Loma. The telefériQo management is aware of this problem and it's hoped that they and the Ecuadorian police will beef up security. Hikers are advised to check with South American Explorers (p649) for an update before heading out.

SIGHTS

If you're short on time head straight for the Old Town. It's here that Quito distinguishes itself from all other cities in the world.

Old Town

Built centuries ago by indigenous artisans and laborers, Quito's churches, convents, chapels and monasteries are cast in legend and steeped in history. It's a magical, bustling area, full of yelling street vendors, ambling pedestrians, tooting taxis, belching buses, and whistle-blowing policemen trying to direct traffic in the narrow, congested one-way streets. The Old Town is closed to cars on Sunday between 8am and 4pm, making it a wonderful time to explore the historic center.

Churches are open every day (usually until 6pm) but are crowded with worshippers on Sunday. They regularly close between 1pm and 3pm for lunch.

PLAZA GRANDE

Quito's small, exquisitely restored central plaza (also known as Plaza de la Independencia) is the perfect place to start exploring the Old Town. Its benches are great for soaking up the Andean morning sun as shoeshine boys and Polaroid photographers peddle their services around the park. The plaza is flanked by several important buildings. The low white building on the northwestern side is the **Palacio del Gobierno** (Presidential Palace; Map p653; García Moreno at Chile). The prez does carry out business inside, so sightseeing is limited to the entrance area. On the southwestern side of the plaza stands Quito's recently painted **cathedral** (Map p653; cnr Espejo & García Moreno; admission US$1, Sunday services free; ☾ 10am-4pm Mon-Sat, Sunday services hourly 6am-noon & 5-7pm). Although not as ornate as some of the other churches, it's worth a peek. Paintings by several notable artists of the Quito school adorn the inside walls, and Mariscal Sucre, the leading figure of Quito's independence, is buried inside. The **Palacio Arzobispal** (Archbishop's Palace; Map p653; Chile btw García Moreno & Venezuela), now a colonnaded row of small shops and several good restaurants, stands on the plaza's northeastern side.

Just off the plaza, the outstanding **Centro Cultural Metropolitano** (Map p653; ☎ 295-0272, 258-4363; www.centrocultural-quito.com; cnr García Moreno & Espejo; admission US$2; 🕑 9am-5pm, patio until 7:30pm Tue-Sun) was the first restoration work undertaken in the Old Town, and it fast became a hub of cultural activity. It houses several temporary art exhibits and hosts excellent art shows on the main interior patio. Along with two more interior patios and two beautiful rooftop terraces (all worth seeing), it houses an auditorium, a museum, a library and an excellent café.

NORTH OF PLAZA GRANDE
One of colonial Quito's most recently built churches, **La Merced** (Map p653; cnr Cuenca & Chile;

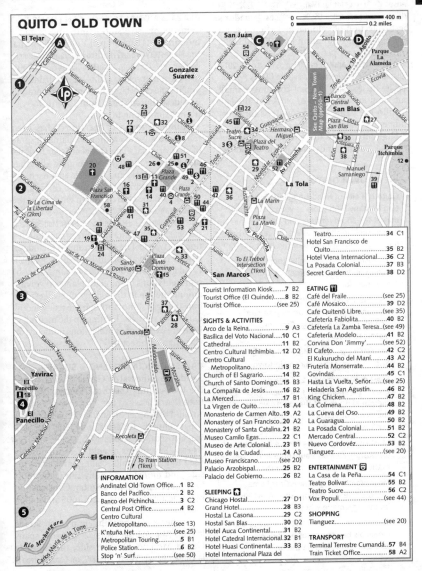

QUITO – OLD TOWN

Teatro	34 C1
Hotel San Francisco de Quito	35 B2
Hotel Viena Internacional	36 C2
La Posada Colonial	37 B3
Secret Garden	38 D2

INFORMATION
Andinatel Old Town Office	1 B2
Banco del Pacífico	2 B2
Banco del Pichincha	3 C2
Central Post Office	4 B2
Centro Cultural Metropolitano	(see 13)
K'ntuña Net	(see 25)
Metropolitan Touring	5 B1
Police Station	6 B2
Stop 'n' Surf	(see 50)

SIGHTS & ACTIVITIES
Arco de la Reina	9 A3
Basílica del Voto Nacional	10 C1
Cathedral	11 B2
Centro Cultural Itchimbia	12 D2
Centro Cultural Metropolitano	13 B2
Church of El Sagrario	14 B2
Church of Santo Domingo	15 B3
La Compañía de Jesús	16 B2
La Merced	17 B1
La Virgen de Quito	18 A4
Monasterio de Carmen Alto	19 A2
Monastery of San Francisco	20 A2
Monastery of Santa Catalina	21 B2
Museo Camilo Egas	22 C1
Museo de Arte Colonial	23 B1
Museo de la Ciudad	24 A3
Museo Franciscano	(see 20)
Palacio Arzobispal	25 B2
Palacio del Gobierno	26 B2

SLEEPING
Chicago Hostal	27 D1
Grand Hotel	28 B3
Hostal La Casona	29 C2
Hostal San Blas	30 D2
Hotel Auca Continental	31 B2
Hotel Catedral Internacional	32 B1
Hotel Huasi Continental	33 B3
Hotel Internacional Plaza del	

EATING
Café del Fraile	(see 25)
Café Mosaico	39 D2
Cafe Quiteño Libre	(see 35)
Cafetería Fabiolita	40 B2
Cafetería La Zamba Teresa	(see 49)
Cafetería Modelo	41 B2
Corvina Don 'Jimmy'	(see 52)
El Cafeto	42 C2
El Kukurucho del Maní	43 A2
Frutería Monserrate	44 B2
Govindas	45 C1
Hasta La Vuelta, Señor	(see 25)
Heladería San Agustín	46 B2
King Chicken	47 B2
La Colmena	48 B2
La Cueva del Oso	49 B2
La Guaragua	50 B2
La Posada Colonial	51 B2
Mercado Central	52 C2
Nuevo Cordovéz	53 B2
Tianguez	(see 20)

ENTERTAINMENT
La Casa de la Peña	54 C1
Teatro Bolívar	55 B2
Teatro Sucre	56 C2
Vox Populi	(see 44)

SHOPPING
Tianguez	(see 20)

TRANSPORT
Terminal Terrestre Cumandá	57 B4
Train Ticket Office	58 A2

Tourist Information Kiosk | 7 B2 |
Tourist Office (El Quinde) | 8 B2 |
Tourist Office | (see 25) |

admission free; ⊙ 6am-noon & 3-6pm), finished in 1742, stands two blocks northwest of the Plaza Grande. Among the wealth of fascinating art inside, paintings depict such calming scenes as glowing volcanoes erupting over the church roofs of colonial Quito and the capital covered with ashes.

One block to the northeast, the excellent **Museo de Arte Colonial** (Map p653; ☎ 221-2297; Mejía 915 at Cuenca; admission US50¢) houses Ecuador's best collection of colonial art. The museum was closed for restoration in 2005 and 2006, with plans to reopen in 2007.

The **Museo Camilo Egas** (Map p653; ☎ 257-2012; Venezuela 1302 at Esmeraldas; admission US50¢; ⊙ 9am-5pm Tue-Fri, 10am-4pm Sat & Sun) contains a small but fabulous collection of works by the late Camilo Egas, one of the country's foremost indigenous painters.

High on a hill in the northeastern part of the Old Town stands the Gothic **Basílica del**

Voto Nacional (Map p653; ☎ 258-3891; cnr Venezuela & Carchi; admission US$2; ⊙ 9am-5pm), built over several decades beginning in 1926. The highlight is the basilica's towers, which you can climb to the top of if you have the nerve; the ascent requires crossing a rickety wooden plank inside the main roof and climbing steep stairs and ladders to the top. Liability? Pshaw!

PLAZA & MONASTERY OF SAN FRANCISCO

With its massive stark-white towers and a mountainous backdrop of Volcán Pichincha, the **Monastery of San Francisco** (Cuenca at Sucre; admission free; ⊙ 7-11am daily, 3-6pm Mon-Thu) is one of Quito's most marvelous sights – both inside and out. It's the city's largest colonial structure and its oldest church (built from 1534 to 1604) – it's not something to miss.

Although much of the church has been rebuilt because of earthquake damage, some of it is original. The **Chapel of Señor Jesús del Gran Poder**, to the right of the main altar, has original tilework, and the **main altar** itself is a spectacular example of baroque carving. To the right of the church's main entrance is the **Museo Franciscano** (☎ 295-2911; www.museofranciscano .com; admission US$2; ⊙ 9am-1pm & 2-6pm Mon-Sat, 9am-noon Sun), which contains some of the church's finest artwork. The admission fee includes a guided tour, available in English or Spanish. Good guides will point out *mudejar* (Moorish) representations of the eight planets revolving around the sun in the ceiling, and will explain how the light shines through the rear window during the solstices, lighting up the main altar. Both are examples of indigenous influence on Christian architecture.

CALLES GARCÍA MORENO & SUCRE

Beside the cathedral on García Moreno stands the 17th-century **Church of El Sagrario** (Map p653; García Moreno; admission free; ⊙ 6am-noon & 3-6pm). Around the corner on Sucre is Ecuador's most ornate church, **La Compañía de Jesús** (Map p653; Sucre near García Moreno; admission US$2.50; ⊙ 9:30-11am & 4-6pm). Seven tons of gold were supposedly used to gild the walls, ceilings and altars inside, and *quiteños* proudly call it the most beautiful church in the country. Construction of this Jesuit church began in 1605 and it took 163 years to build.

Further south, the 18th century arch, **Arco de la Reina** (Map p653; García Moreno at Rocafuerte), spans García Moreno. On one side, the **Museo de la Ciudad** (Map p653; ☎ 228-3882; cnr García Moreno &

VIEWS OVER QUITO

Quito is a city of mind-boggling views. Hitting as many high spots as you can in a day makes for an adventure, and it's a unique way to see the city. Skies are clearest in the morning. Here are some of the best:

■ Holiest view – El Panecillo (opposite). Climb up inside the Virgen de Quito at El Panecillo.

■ Deadliest view – Basílica del Voto Nacional (right). Hold on to your stomach for the hair-raising climb into these gothic towers.

■ Tastiest view – Café Mosaico (p662). The most amazing balcony in town.

■ Most patriotic view – La Cima de la Libertad (Map p657). This independence memorial is west of the Old Town on the flanks of Volcán Pichincha. Take a taxi up, bus down.

■ Most sweeping view – Parque Itchimbia (opposite). Kick off your shoes and take in the 360-degree views from the grass.

■ Most breathtaking view – Cruz Loma and the telefériQo (opposite). At 4100m, breathing's made wheezy.

■ Strangest view – Monastery of Santa Catalina's bell tower (opposite). Who said church tours can't be fun?

Rocafuerte; admission US$3, guided tour additional US$4; 9:30am-5:30pm Tue-Sun) houses an interesting museum depicting daily life in Quito through the centuries. On the other side of the arch stands the **Monasterio de Carmen Alto** (Map p653; cnr García Moreno & Rocafuerte), another fully functioning convent, where cloistered nuns produce and sell some of the most traditional sweets in the city. Through a revolving contraption that keeps the nuns hidden, they also sell traditional baked goods, aromatic waters for nerves and insomnia, bee pollen, honey and bottles of full-strength *mistela* (an anise-flavored liqueur).

PLAZA & CHURCH OF SANTO DOMINGO

Plaza Santo Domingo (Map p653; Guayaquil at Bolívar) is a regular haunt for street performers, and crowds fill the plaza to watch pouting clowns and half-cocked magicians do their stuff. A fabulous Gothic-like altar dominates the inside of the **Church of Santo Domingo** (Map p653; Flores & Rocafuerte; admission free; 7am-1pm & 4:30-7:30pm), and the original wooden floor was only recently replaced. Construction of the church began in 1581 and continued until 1650.

EL PANECILLO

The small, ever-visible hill to the south of the Old Town is called **El Panecillo** (Little Bread Loaf) and it's a major landmark in Quito. It's topped by a huge statue of **La Virgen de Quito** and offers marvelous views of the whole city and of the surrounding volcanoes. Go early in the morning, before the clouds roll in. Definitely don't climb the stairs at the end of García Moreno on the way to the statue

though – they're unsafe. A taxi from the Old Town costs about US$5, and you can hail one at the top for the return trip.

PARQUE ITCHIMBIA

High on a hill east of the Old Town, this newly resurrected green space boasts magnificent 360-degree views of the city. The park's centerpiece, the glass and iron **Centro Cultural Itchimbia** (Map p653; ☎ 295-0272; Parque Itchimbia) hosts regular art exhibits and cultural events. The park has cycling paths and walking paths too. Buses signed 'Pintado' go here from the Centro Histórico, or you can walk up (east on) Elizalde, from where signed stairways lead to the park.

telefériQo

Quito's newest attraction – and a mind-boggling one at that – is the **telefériQo** (Map p657; ☎ 250-0900; www.teleferiqo.com; Av Occidental & Av La Gasca; admission adults US$4, children under 6 US$3, express line US$7; 11am-10pm Mon, 9am-10pm Tue-Thu, 9am-midnight Fri & Sat), a multimillion dollar sky tram that takes passengers on a hair-raising, 2.5km ride up the flanks of Volcán Pichincha to the top of Cruz Loma. Once you're at the top (a mere 4100m), you can hike to the summit of Rucu Pichincha (p658). Be warned, however that armed robberies have been reported recently on the trail from the top of Cruz Loma to the summit of Rucu Pichincha.

Admission to the telefériQo complex is US$2 to US$10. On weekends the wait can last up to four hours; either pay the US$7 express-line fee or (even better) come on a weekday. A taxi costs about US$2 from the Mariscal.

UNEARTHLY DELIGHTS

Southeast of the Plaza Grande stands the **Monastery of Santa Catalina** (Map p653; Espejo 779 at Flores; admission US$1.50; 8:30am-5:30pm Mon-Sat), a fully functioning convent and monastery that opened to the public in 2005. Since its founding in 1592, entering nuns have spent five years cloistered in private cells. To this day, the 20 nuns inside have only one hour to talk to each other or watch TV. They do, however, make all sorts of natural products (shampoos, non-alcoholic wine, hand cream, elixirs and more), which you can purchase from a rotating door that keeps the nuns hidden.

A tour of the monastery and its interesting museum lasts over an hour – and it's a gruesome hour at that: 18th century religious paintings depict virgins and saints presiding over the fires of purgatory while devils grind the bodies of sinners on spiked wheels. One painting shows a thirsty flock of sheep slurping up rivers of blood pouring from Jesus' wounds, while another depicts cherubs plucking the flesh from Christ's ribs after a session of brutal self-flagellation.

Supposedly, secret underground tunnels connect Santa Catalina to the church of Santo Domingo three blocks away.

New Town

PARQUE LA ALAMEDA & PARQUE EL EJIDO

From the northeastern edge of the Old Town, the long, triangular Parque La Alameda begins its grassy crawl toward the New Town. In the center of the park is the **Quito Observatory** (Map pp650-1; ☎ 257-0765; admission US20¢, night viewings US40¢; ☺ 8am-noon & 3-5pm Mon-Fri, 8am-noon Sat), the oldest European observatory on the continent.

Northeast of La Alameda, the pleasant, tree-filled Parque El Ejido is the biggest park in downtown Quito and a popular spot for impromptu soccer games and volleyball. On weekends, open-air **art shows** are held along Av Patria, and artisans and crafts vendors set up stalls all over the northern side of the park, turning it into Quito's largest **handicrafts market**.

A solitary stone archway at the northern end of Parque El Ejido marks the beginning of modern Quito's showpiece street, Av Amazonas. North of the park, it's the main artery of the **Mariscal Sucre** neighborhood.

CASA DE LA CULTURA ECUATORIANA

Across from Parque El Ejido, the landmark, circular glass building, **Casa de la Cultura Ecuatoriana** (Map pp650-1; www.cce.org.ec in Spanish), houses one of the country's most important museums, the **Museo del Banco Central** (Map pp650-1; ☎ 222-3259; cnr Av Patria & Av 12 de Octubre; admission US$2; ☺ 9am-5pm Tue-Fri, 10am-4pm Sat & Sun). The museum showcases the country's largest collection of Ecuadorian art. In the **Sala de Arqueología** (Archaeology Room), moody tribal music drones over a marvelous display of more than 1000 ceramic pieces dating from 12,000 BC to 1534 AD. Among other magnificent pre-Hispanic gold pieces, the **Sala de Oro** (Gold Room) displays the radiating golden sun-mask that is the symbol of the Banco Central. Upstairs, the **Sala de Arte Colonial** (Colonial Art Room) showcases masterful works from the Quito school of art. Finally, the **Sala de Arte Contemporáneo** (Contemporary Art Room) boasts a large collection of contemporary, modern and 19th-century Ecuadorian art.

PARQUE LA CAROLINA

North of the Mariscal lies the giant Parque La Carolina (Map pp650-1). On weekends it fills with families who head out to peddle paddleboats, play soccer and volleyball, cycle along the bike paths, skate or simply escape the city's urban chaos.

The park's newest addition is the **Jardín Botánico** (Map pp650-1; ☎ 246-3197; admission US$1.50; ☺ 9am-3pm Mon, 9am-5pm Tue-Sun), featuring over 300 plant and tree species from around Ecuador and an outstanding *orquideario* (orchid greenhouse) with nearly 1000 orchid species. To further acquaint yourself with Ecuador's flora and fauna, head next door to the country's best natural-history museum, the **Museo de Ciencias Naturales** (Map pp650-1; ☎ 244-9824; admission US$2; ☺ 8:30am-1pm & 1:45-4:30pm Mon-Fri).

Contemplating the thousands of dead insects and arachnids on display is a good way to rile your nerves before a trip to the Oriente.

Nearby, you can provide further fodder for your jungle fears with a visit to the **Vivarium** (Map pp650-1; ☎ 227-1799; www.vivarium.org.ec; Av Amazonas 3008 at Rumipamba; admission US$2.50; ☺ 9:30am-5:30pm Tue-Sun), home to 87 live reptiles and amphibians, mostly snakes. It's a herpetological research and education center, and all but one of the critters (the frightening looking king cobra) are native to Ecuador.

MUSEO GUAYASAMÍN & THE CAPILLA DEL HOMBRE

In the former home of the world-famous indigenous painter Oswaldo Guayasamín (1919–99), the **Museo Guayasamín** (Map pp650-1; ☎ 246-5265; Calle Bosmediano 543; admission US$2; ☺ 9am-1:30pm & 3-6:30pm Mon-Fri) houses the largest collection of his works. Guayasamín was also an avid collector, and the museum displays his outstanding collection of over 4500 pre-Colombian ceramic, bone and metal pieces from throughout Ecuador.

A few blocks away stands Guayasamín's astounding **Capilla del Hombre** (Chapel of Man; Map pp650-1; ☎ 244-6455; www.guayasamin.com; Mariano Calvache at Lorenzo Chávez; admission US$3, with purchase of entry to Museo Guayasamín US$2; ☺ 10am-5pm Tue-Sun). The fruit of Guayasamín's greatest vision, this giant monument-cum-museum is a tribute to humankind, to the suffering of Latin America's indigenous poor, and to the undying hope for a better world. It's a moving place, and the tours (available in English, French and Spanish and included in the price) are highly recommended.

The museum and chapel are in the neighborhood of Bellavista, northeast of downtown. You can walk uphill, or take a bus along Av 6 de Diciembre to Av Eloy Alfaro and then a Bellavista bus up the hill. A taxi costs about US$2.

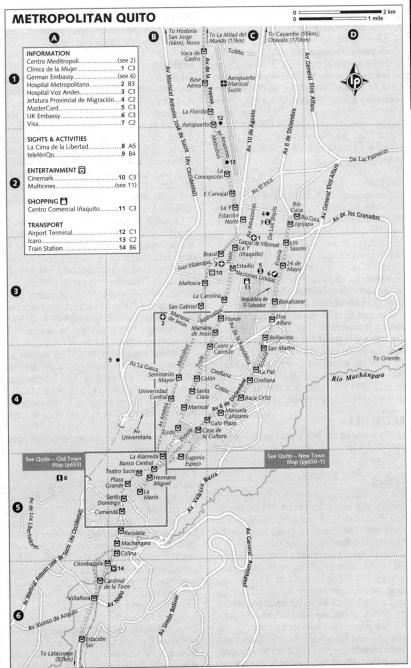

METROPOLITAN QUITO

0 ──────── 2 km
0 ──────── 1 mile

INFORMATION
Centro Meditropoli.....................(see 2)
Clínica de la Mujer............................**1** C3
German Embassy............................(see 6)
Hospital Metropolitano.................**2** B3
Hospital Voz Andes..........................**3** C3
Jefatura Provincial de Migración....**4** C2
MasterCard..**5** C3
UK Embassy...**6** C3
Visa...**7** C2

SIGHTS & ACTIVITIES
La Cima de la Libertad...................**8** A5
telefériQo..**9** B4

ENTERTAINMENT 🎭
Cinemark...**10** C3
Multicines..(see 11)

SHOPPING 🛍
Centro Comercial Iñaquito..........**11** C3

TRANSPORT
Airport Terminal..............................**12** C1
Icaro...**13** C2
Train Station......................................**14** B6

ECUADOR

OTHER MUSEUMS

Anyone interested in the indigenous cultures of the Amazon region should pop into the small **Museo Amazónico** (Map pp650-1; ☎ 256-2663; Av 12 de Octubre 1436; admission US$2; 🕙 8:30am-12:30pm & 2-5pm Mon-Fri) or the **Museo Etnográfico de Artesanía de Ecuador** (Map pp650-1; ☎ 223-0609; www .sinchisacha.org; Reina Victoria N26-166 & La Niña; 🕙 8am-6:30pm Mon-Fri, 10am-6pm Sat). The latter, run by the highly regarded nonprofit Fundación Sinchi Sacha (also see Tianguez, p662 and p666), closed for remodeling with plans to reopen in early 2007.

Guápulo

If you follow Av 12 de Octubre up the hill from the Mariscal, you'll reach **Hotel Quito** (Map pp650-1; González Suárez N27-142) at the top. Behind the hotel (which has a top-floor bar with magnificent views), steep stairs lead down to the somewhat bohemian neighborhood of El Guápulo, set in a precipitous valley. At the center of this small neighborhood stands the lovely **Santuario de Guápulo** (Map pp650-1; 🕙 9am-noon), built between 1644 and 1693.

The best views of the church are from the **Mirador de Guápulo**, behind the Hotel Quito, at the **Statue of Francisco de Orellana** (Map pp650-1; RL Larrea near González Suárez). In the statue, Francisco de Orellana is looking down into the valley that saw the beginning of his epic journey from Quito to the Atlantic – the first descent of the Amazon by a European.

ACTIVITIES

Quito is one of the best places to hire guides and organize both single- and multiday excursions.

Cycling

On the second and last Sunday of every month, the entire length of Av Amazonas and most of the Old Town are closed to cars, and loads of peddlers take to the street for the bimonthly **ciclopaseo** (bicycle ride).

Local mountain biking companies rent bikes and offer excellent single- and two-day guided off-road rides in Andean settings you'd otherwise never see. Day trips cost about US$45. **Biking Dutchman** (Map pp650-1; ☎ 256-8323, 254-2806; www.bikingdutchman.com; Foch 714 at JL Mera) is Ecuador's pioneer mountain biking operator and has good bikes and guides and an outstanding reputation. **Arie's Bike Company** (Map pp650-1; ☎ 290-6052; www.ariesbikecompany.com;

Wilson 578 at Reina Victoria) offers similar trips and has received great reports from readers. Check both to compare prices and trips.

Climbing

Climbers can get a serious fix at the **Rocódromo** (Map pp650-1; ☎ 250-8463; Queseras del Medio s/n; admission US$1.50; 🕙 8am-8pm Mon-Fri, 8am-6pm Sat & Sun), a 25m-high climbing facility across from the Estadio Rumiñahui. There are more than a dozen routes on the three main walls, a four-face bouldering structure, and a rock building. Shoe rental costs US$1.50, ropes US$2 and harnesses US$1. Chalk bags and carabiners are extra. If you rent equipment, the staff will belay you. The Rocódromo is walking distance from the Mariscal.

Compañía de Guías de Montaña (Map pp650-1; ☎ 290-1551, 255-6210; www.companiadeguias.com.ec; Jorge Washington 425 at Av 6 de Diciembre) is a top-notch mountain climbing operator whose guides are all licensed instructors and speak several languages. Two-day trips cost US$224 per person, three days US$330, not including park entrance fees. Tailor-made trips are available. **Alta Montaña** (Map pp650-1; ☎ 252-4422, 09-422-9483; Jorge Washington 8-20) is another recommended climbing operator.

Montaña (Map pp650-51; ☎ 223-8954; mountain_ref ugeecuador@yahoo.com; Cordero E12-141 at Toledo; dm US$7, s/d US$9/15) is a meeting place for climbers from Quito. It's a good source of non-biased information (no one's trying to sell anything but a cup of coffee) and a good place to meet local climbers.

See opposite for more agencies that offer climbing tours.

Hiking

Quito's new telefériQo (p655) takes passengers up to Cruz Loma (4100m). From there you can hike to the top of jagged Rucu Pichincha (about 4700m). Beyond the rise of Cruz Loma and past a barbed wire fence (which no one seems to pay any attention to), well-marked trails lead to Rucu Pichincha. It's approximately three hours to the top, and some scrambling is required. Don't attempt this hike if you've just arrived in Quito; allow yourself a couple days' acclimatization.

Before the telefériQo went in, climbing Rucu Pichincha was dangerous due to armed robberies. Unfortunately, that danger has returned, with readers reporting several such attacks recently along the main trail. Increased security measures have been implemented, but it's best to check with SAE (p72) for an update on the situation before heading out.

White-Water Rafting

Several companies offer rafting day trips, departing by van from the capital, or you can sign up for a multiday rafting trip further afield. Rates start around US$65 per person per day. Visit the following:

Sierra Nevada Expeditions (Map pp650-1; ☎ 255-3658; www.hotelsierranevada.com; J Pinto 637 near Cordero) A good rafting operator.

Yacu Amu Rafting/Ríos Ecuador (Map pp650-1; ☎ 223-6844; www.yacuamu.com; Foch 746 near JL Mera) White-water rafting, kayaking trips and courses. Australian owned, highly experienced. Daily departures.

COURSES
Dancing

Tired of shoe-gazing when you hit the *salsotecas* (salsa clubs)? Try salsa dance classes – they're a blast! Merengue, cumbia and other Latin dances are also taught. Private classes average US$5 per hour at:

Ritmo Tropical (Map pp650-1; ☎ 255-7094; ritmotropical5@hotmail.com; Av Amazonas N24-155 at J Calama; ⏰ 9am-8pm Mon-Fri)

Tropical Dancing School (Map pp650-1; ☎ 222-0427; tropicaldancing@hotmail.com; Foch E4-256 at Av Amazonas; ⏰ 10am-8pm Mon-Fri, Sat & Sun by reservation only)

Language

Quito is one of the better places in South America to learn Spanish. Most schools offer all levels of instruction, in private or group lessons, and can arrange home-stays with families. Some programs also include dance classes, cooking courses or cultural events. Rates for private lessons vary between US$6 and US$9 per hour. Some charge an inscription fee (usually around US$20).

Beraca (Map pp650-1; ☎ 290-6642; beraca@interactive.net.ec; Av Amazonas 1114) Cheap and well-liked.

Bipo & Toni's (Map pp650-1; ☎ 255-6614, 256-3309; www.bipo.net; J Carrión E8-183 at Leonidas Plaza Gutiérrez)

Ecole Idiomas (Map pp650-1; ☎ 223-1592; info@ecotravel-ecuador.com; L Garcia E6-15 near JL Mera) Volunteer projects available.

Guayasamín Spanish School (Map pp650-1; ☎ 254-4210; www.guayasaminschool.com; J Calama E8-54 near 6 de Diciembre) Ecuadorian owned; lots of reader recommendations.

San Francisco Language Institute (Map pp650-1; ☎ 252-1306; www.sanfranciscospanish.com; Av Amazonas 662, 2nd fl, Office 201) Pricey ($9 per hour, plus US$50 inscription fee) but gets high recommendations.

Vida Verde (Map pp650-1; ☎ 222-6635, 256-3110; www.vidaverde.com; Leonidas Plaza Gutiérrez N23-100 near Wilson)

TOURS

Organized tours are sometimes cheaper if they are booked in the town closest to where you want to go, although this demands a more flexible schedule. If you prefer to start in Quito, the following agencies and operators are well received and reliable. For cycling, rafting, climbing and other activities, see opposite.

Dracaena (Map pp650-1; ☎ 254-6590; J Pinto E4-453) Offers four- to eight-day tours of Cuyabeno (p699) that have received excellent reviews. Five-day tour US$200 per person.

Emerald Forest Expeditions (Map pp650-1; ☎ 254-1278; www.emeraldexpeditions.com; J Pinto E4-244 at Av Amazonas) Consistently outstanding reports from travelers for its Oriente trips. US$60 to US$80 per person per day.

Fundación Golondrinas (Map pp650-1; ☎ 222-6602; www.ecuadorexplorer.com/golondrinas; Isabel La Católica N24-679) Conservation project with volunteer opportunities; also arranges walking tours in the *páramo* west of Tulcán (see p675).

Galasam (Map pp650-1; ☎ 250-7080; www.galasam.com; Av Amazonas 1354 at Cordero) Known for its economical to midrange Galápagos cruises, but reports from customers have been mixed. Complaints are frequent; some raves.

Gulliver (Map pp650-1; ☎ 252-9297, 09-946-2265; www.gulliver.com.ec; cnr JL Mera & Calama) Trekking, climbing, mountain biking and horse-riding trips in the Andes. Excellent prices, daily departures. Most day trips cost US$30 to US$45 per person. Economical five- to seven-day Cotopaxi trips are based out of its Hostería PapaGayo (p677) and cost US$360 to US$450 and US$500 respectively.

Rainforestur (Map pp650-1; ☎ 223-9822; www.rainforestur.com; Av Amazonas 420 at F Robles) Excellent for Cuyabeno Reserve jungle trips. Also offers rafting trips near Baños, and trekking and indigenous market tours in the Quito area.

Safari Tours (Map pp650-1; ☎ 255-2505, 250-8316; www.safari.com.ec; Foch E5-39; ⏰ 9am-7pm) Arranges everything from jungle treks and Galápagos cruises to volcano climbing. Loads of day trips.

Sierra Nevada Expeditions (Map pp650-1; ☎ 255-3658; www.hotelsierranevada.com; J Pinto 637 near Cordero) Climbing, biking and river-rafting trips.

ECUADOR

Tropic Ecological Adventures (Map pp650-1; ☎ 222-5907; www.tropiceco.com; Av de la República E7-320) Three- to six-day tours to the Oriente, Andes and cloud forest.

FESTIVALS & EVENTS

The city's biggest party celebrates the founding of Quito in the first week of December, when bullfights are held daily at the Plaza de Toros. On New Year's Eve, life-size puppets (often of politicians) are burned in the streets at midnight. Carnaval is celebrated with intense water fights – no one is spared. Colorful religious processions are held during Easter week.

SLEEPING

Most people shack up in the New Town – particularly in the Mariscal neighborhood – so they can be near cybercafés, bars and restaurants. Unfortunately the Mariscal is extremely dangerous after dark. With the restoration of the Old Town, historic Quito is once again becoming a popular area to stay. You may not find banana pancakes and hostels around every corner, but you will find something more traditionally South American.

Adjacent to (and safer than) the Mariscal, the hip La Floresta neighborhood has a few places to stay and plenty of bars.

Old Town

The hotels between Plaza Santo Domingo and the bus terminal are some of the cheapest, but it's a dodgy area after about 7pm.

La Posada Colonial (Map p653; ☎ 228-2859; Paredes 188; r per person with shared/private bathroom US$4/5) Although a bit close to the bus terminal, this wood-floor oldie is still one of the Old Town's best values. Beds are saggy, but it's extremely well-kept and totally secure. Bright and cheerful.

Hotel Huasi Continental (Map p653; ☎ 295-7327; Flores 332; r per person with shared/private bathroom US$4/7) Several readers have recommended this hotel with spartan but clean, comfortable rooms. Unfortunately, few have windows, but the beds are firm.

Grand Hotel (Map p653; ☎ 228-0192, 295-9411; www .geocities.com/grandhotelquito; Rocafuerte 1001; s/d with shared bathroom US$4.50/8, private bathroom US$6.50/12) This old backpacker haunt is clean and full of character (and characters!). Rooms are gloomy if you don't get a window. Good if you want cheap and non-touristy.

Chicago Hostal (Map p653; ☎ 228-0224; chicago hostal@panchored.net; Los Ríos 1730; dm US$5.50, s/d with shared bathroom US$6/12, private bathroom US$9/16; 💻) On the New Town border, this ultra-friendly new hotel has spotless, straightforward rooms with cable TV. Dining room, bar and left-luggage service.

Secret Garden (Map p653; ☎ 295-6704, 316-0949; Antepara E4-60 at Los Ríos; dm US$6.75, s or d with shared/private bathroom US$17.50/24) Owned by an Ecuadorian-Australian couple, this new, colorful hostel is easily one of the best budget digs in Quito – no one can compete with the view from the 5th floor terrace. An all-you-can-eat breakfast (additional US$2.50) and nightly dinners (about US$3.75) are served.

Hotel Catedral Internacional (Map p653; ☎ 295-5438; Mejía 638; s/d US$7/12) Extremely tidy hotel, with old but cared-for decorations, odd furniture and marvelously outdated bedspreads. Get a window.

Hotel Internacional Plaza del Teatro (Map p653; ☎ 295-9462, 295-4293; Guayaquil N8-75; s/d US$10/16) This old-time hotel maintains a hint of its former elegance with its marble staircase, wide hallways and balconied rooms. The off-street rooms lack balconies and character, but are quieter. Nonchalant staff; popular with Ecuadorians.

Hotel Viena Internacional (Map p653; ☎ 295-4860; Flores 600 at Chile; s/d with bathroom US$11/22) Though the c-1972, grapevine wallpaper can bug your eyes out, the spotless rooms, top-notch service and cheerful interior patio make this the best hotel deal in the Old Town. Rooms have hardwood floors, TVs, hot water and good showers. Balcony rooms can be noisy.

Hotel San Francisco de Quito (Map p653; ☎ 228-7758; www.uio-guided.com/hsfquito; hsfquito@andinanet .net; Sucre 217; s/d with private bathroom US$14/24, mini apartments with kitchenettes US$18/30) If you want to sleep in style (old style, that is) in colonial Quito, try this centuries-old beauty. Rooms lack windows, but double doors open onto a lovely balcony over a pretty interior courtyard.

Also recommended:

Hostal San Blas (Map p653; ☎ 228-1434; Caldas 121, Plaza San Blas; s/d with shared bathroom US$5/6.75, private bathroom US$6.75/10,) Good deal if you don't mind minuscule rooms.

Hostal La Casona (Map p653; ☎ 257-0626, 258-8809; Manabí 255; s/d US$6/8) Three floors of dark, clean, musty rooms and plenty of things to bump your head upon.

Hotel Auca Continental (Map p653; ☎ 295-4799; aucahotel@hotmail.com; Sucre Oe4-14; s/d incl breakfast US$10/20) Plain and time-tattered but totally fine.

New Town

Casa Bambú (Map pp650-1; ☎ 222-6738; G Solano 1758 near Av Colombia; dm US$4, r per person with shared/private bathroom US$5/7) This gem boasts spacious rooms, a wee garden, guest kitchen, a book exchange, laundry facilities and outstanding views from the rooftop hammocks. Worth the uphill hike.

Hostal Déjà vu (Map pp650-1; ☎ 222-4483; www .hostalsdejavu.com; 9 de Octubre 599; dm US$6, s/d with shared bathroom US$10/12, private bathroom US$12/15) Colorfully painted walls and old wacky furniture give this slightly run down but popular *hostal* (cheap hotel) a somewhat underground feel.

La Casa de Eliza (Map pp650-1; ☎ 222-6602; man teca@uio.satnet.net; Isabel La Católica N24-679; dm US$6, d US$12) Although this old favorite is definitely showing its age, it's still a friendly, homespun place. It's a converted house with a big guest kitchen, a sociable common area, a wee book exchange and basic rooms.

El Cafecito (Map pp650-1; ☎ 223-4862; www.cafécito .net; Cordero E6-43; dm US$6, s/d US$9/14) An eternally popular budget choice. Rooms are clean, the place has a mellow vibe, and the excellent café below makes breakfast convenient. All bathrooms are shared.

Crossroads (Map pp650-1; ☎ 223-4735; www.crossroads hostal.com; Foch E5-23; dm US$6-7, s/d with shared bathroom US$12/18, private bathroom US$15.50/25) Big, converted house with bright rooms and a welcoming communal atmosphere. Facilities include a good café, cable TV, kitchen privileges, luggage storage and a patio with a fireplace.

L'Auberge Inn (Map pp650-1; ☎ 255-2912; www.ioda .net/auberge-inn; Av Colombia N12-200; s/d with shared bathroom US$7/13, private bathroom US$10/17) With a pool table, sauna, safe-deposit facilities, fireplace in

---

SPLURGE!

Café Cultura (Map pp650-1; ☎ 222-4271; www .cafécultura.com; F Robles 513; s/d US$77/89) This ultra-charming boutique hotel occupies a converted mansion with a garden. The beautifully painted common rooms have three crackling fireplaces, and the bedrooms are individually decorated and have murals painted by different artists. Water is purified throughout the hotel (go on, drink the shower water!). Travelers love this place and reservations are advised. Several languages are spoken among the international staff.

---

the common room, courtyard, kitchen, luggage storage, laundry service, in-house travel agency and a great pizzeria (say no more), this is an excellent deal.

Albergue El Taxo (Map pp650-1; ☎ 222-5593; Foch E4-116; s/d with shared bathroom US$7/14, private bathroom US$8/16) Friendly and modest, El Taxo occupies a converted c-1970s house with pleasant, colorful rooms, most of which have shared bathrooms. The no-frills common area has a fireplace (rarely fired up) and the guest kitchen is well kept.

La Casona de Mario (Map pp650-1; ☎ 254-4036, 223-0129; www.casonademario.com; Andalucía N24-115; r per person US$8) In a lovely old house, La Casona de Mario has homey rooms, shared spotless bathrooms, a garden, a TV lounge and a guest kitchen. Numerous readers have recommended the place for its hospitality, atmosphere, quiet but convenient location, and all around value. Outstanding.

Amazonas Inn (Map pp650-1; ☎ 222-5723, 222-2666; J Pinto E4-324 & Av Amazonas; r per person US$9-12) Outstanding value. Rooms are straightforward and spotless, with private bathrooms, constant hot water and cable TV (70-plus channels!); those on the 1st floor have windows. Friendly staff, central location.

Aleida's Hostal (Map pp650-1; ☎ 223-4570; www .aleidashostal.com.ec; Andalucía 559 at Salazar; s/d with shared bathroom US$11/22, private bathroom US$17/34 or US$22/39) This friendly three-story guesthouse in La Floresta is family run and has a very spacious feel with lots of light, huge rooms, high wooden ceilings and hardwood floors. The owner welcomes guests with a shot of *punta* (homemade firewater).

Casa Helbling (Map pp650-1; ☎ 222-6013; www .casahelbling.de; Gral Veintimilla E18-166; s/d with shared bathroom US$12/18, private bathroom US$18/26) This homey, converted, colonial-style house in the Mariscal is clean, relaxed, friendly and has a guest kitchen, laundry facilities and plenty of common areas for chilling out.

Folklore Hotel (Map pp650-1; ☎ 255-4621; www.folk lorehotel.com; Madrid 868 near Pontevedra; s/d with breakfast US$15/25) Delightfully converted house in La Floresta with spacious, colorful rooms. It has a small garden and a welcoming family feel.

Also recommended:

Hostal Vamara (Map pp650-1; ☎ 222-6425; hostalvamara@yahoo.com; Foch 753 & Av Amazonas; dm US$3, r with shared bathroom per person US$6, with private bathroom & TV per person US$8) Has some of the cheapest dorm beds in town.

Hostal Alpa Aligu (Map pp650-1; ☎ 256-4012; alpaaligu@yahoo.com; J Pinto 240; dm US$4)

Loro Verde (Map pp650-1; ☎ 222-6173; Rodríguez E7-66; s/d US$9/18) Simple but comfy; great location.

Hotel Nueve de Octubre (Map pp650-1; ☎ 255-2424/2524; 9 de Octubre 1047; s US$10-13, d US$14-16) Drably institutional but totally acceptable.

Hotel Pickett (Map pp650-1; ☎ 254-1453, 255-1205; Wilson 712; s/d US$10/20) Straightforward hotel; perfectly fine for the price.

EATING

As a popular tourist destination and the nation's capital, Quito – especially the New Town – is laden with international restaurants. But the real treat here is sampling the many varieties of Ecuadorian cuisine – from landmark mom-and-pop places cooking up a single specialty, to the occasional splurge in a gourmet restaurant offering nouveau Ecuadorian fare.

Restaurants in the Old Town used to stick with the inexpensive, unembellished Ecuadorian standards. Most still do, but a handful have recently opened that serve outstanding traditional fare to a more upmarket and foreign clientele.

If you're pinching pennies, stick to the standard *almuerzos* or *meriendas* (set lunches and dinners). Many restaurants in the New Town close on Sunday.

Old Town

You'll find Quito's most traditional eateries in the historical center, places which, unlike in the Mariscal Sucre, have been honing family recipes for generations. Cafés offer some of the best deals.

CAFÉS & SNACKS

El Kukurucho del Maní (Map p653; Rocafuerte Oe5-02 at García Moreno; snacks US25-50¢) C'mon, where else do they cook up kilos of sugary nuts, corn kernels and *haba* beans in a copper kettle big enough to cook a pig in? Classic *quiteño* snacks.

El Cafeto (Map p653; Chile 930 y Flores, Convento de San Agustín; coffee drinks US75¢-$2) This superb Ecuadorian-owned coffee shop serves coffee made from 100% organic Ecuadorian beans. The espresso is likely the best in town.

Cafetería Modelo (Map p653; cnr Sucre & García Moreno; snacks US$1-2) Opened in 1950, Modelo is one of the city's oldest cafés, and a great spot to try traditional snacks like *empanadas de verde* (plantain empanadas filled with cheese), *quimbolitos* (a sweet cake steamed in a leaf), *tamales* (cornmeal stuffed with meat and steamed in a banana leaf) and *humitas* (similar to Mexican tamales).

Heladería San Agustín (Map p653; Guayaquil 1053; ice cream US$1.20) The Alvarez Andino family has been making *helados de paila* (ice cream handmade in big copper bowls) since 1858, making this Quito's oldest ice-cream parlor and an absolute must for ice cream fans.

Frutería Monserrate (Map p653; Espejo Oe2-12; mains US$1.50-3) Best known for the giant bowls of tropical fruits smothered in raspberry topping and whipped cream, this outstanding café also serves delicious soups, sandwiches, Ecuadorian snacks and *excellent* breakfasts. Popular with locals and hygienically impeccable.

Café del Fraile (Map p653; Chile Oe4-22, Pasaje Arzobispal, 2nd fl; drinks US$2-4, sandwiches US$4.50) Old world atmosphere and balcony seating make this café-cum-bar the perfect spot for evening hot chocolate or a stiff cocktail. Sandwiches, snacks and desserts too.

Tianguez (Map p653; Plaza San Francisco; mains US$3-5) Tucked into the stone arches beneath the Monastery of San Francisco, Tianguez is one of the city's most perfectly situated cafés.

Café Mosaico (Map p653; Manuel Samaniego N8-95 near Antepara, Itchimbia; mains US$8.50-11, drinks US$2.50-5; ⏰ 11am-10:30pm, from 4pm Tue) Sure the drinks are overpriced, but you won't find a balcony view like this *anywhere* else, and tourists are a rarity.

RESTAURANTS

Cafetería Fabiolita (Map p653; El Buen Sanduche, Espejo Oe4-17; sandwiches US$1, seco de chivo US$2.50) For over 40 years this spic-and-span eatery beneath the cathedral has been serving up the city's favorite *seco de chivo* (goat stew), one of Ecuador's most traditional dishes (served 9am to 11am only). The *sanduches de pernil* (ham sandwiches) humble even city politicians.

Govindas (Map p653; Esmeraldas 853; almuerzo US$1.20-1.60) Leave it to the Krishnas to whip out a delicious buffet-style vegetarian lunch in the Old Town.

La Guaragua (Map p653; Espejo Oe2-40 near Flores; mains US$2-6) The tables are a bit office-like, but the food is excellent. Try the *tortillas de quinoa* (quinoa patties) and empanadas.

La Colmena (Map p653; Benalcázar 619; almuerzo US$2.35) For 50 years, the Vaca Meza family has been serving one of Ecuador's favorite dishes, *guatita*, a tripe and potato stew in a seasoned, peanut-based sauce. Whether you can stomach tripe or not, it's well worth sampling the original.

Cafetería La Zamba Teresa (Map p653; Chile 1046; almuerzo US$3, mains US$4-8) Attached to La Cueva del Oso (see below), this is the people's chance to sample some of the restaurant's outstanding cooking. The set lunches are a steal.

Hasta La Vuelta, Señor (Map p653; Chile 0e4-22, Palacio Arzobispal, 3rd fl; mains US$6-7) Ecuadorian cuisine gets a gourmet twist at this excellent restaurant with balcony seating. Thursday through Sunday it's a great place to try the highland's two most famous soups: *yaguarlocro* (blood sausage soup) and *caldo de patas* (cow hoof soup).

La Cueva del Oso (Map p653; Chile 1046; mains US$7-10) Lounge-like Cueva del Oso serves exquisitely prepared Ecuadorian specialties. The bar, with its low, round booths, makes for a sultry escape from the noise outside.

For those pinching pennies, you'll find good family-style food and cheap *almuerzos* at the following:

Nuevo Cordovéz (Map p653; Guayaquil 774; almuerzos US$1.40-1.75, mains US$2-3) Colorful booths and a bullfighting theme.

La Posada Colonial (Map p653; García Moreno 1160 near Mejía; almuerzos US$2, mains US$2-3)

Café Quiteño Libre (Map p653; Sucre 0e3-17; almuerzos US$2, mains US$2-3) In the brick-wall cellar of the Hotel San Francisco de Quito (p660).

King Chicken (Map p653; Bolívar 236; mains US$2-4) Good fried chicken, big ice-cream sundaes, diner-like atmosphere.

MARKET FOOD

Mercado Central (Map p653; Pichincha btwn Esmeraldas & Manabí; full meals under US$1-3; 8am-4pm, to 3pm Sun) For stall after stall of some of Quito's most traditional (and cheapest) foods, head straight to the Mercado Central, where you'll find everything from *locro de papa* (potato soup with cheese and avocado) and seafood, to *yaguarlocro*. Fruits and veggies too.

Corvina Don 'Jimmy' (Map p653; Mercado Central, Pichincha btw Esmeraldas & Mejia; mains US$2-4; 8am-4pm, to 3pm Sun) Open since 1953, this is the Mercado Central's most famous stall, serving huge portions of *corvina* (sea bass). Ask for it with rice if you don't want it over a big bowl of *ceviche* (marinated, raw seafood).

New Town

If you're willing to splash out a bit, you can have a lot of fun filling your stomach in the New Town. On the flipside, most of the Mariscal has succumbed to foreign tastes, making it hard to find anything resembling a local, reasonably priced restaurant. You can still find loads of inexpensive, family-style places that cater to locals by wandering the streets in the area west of Amazonas and north of Jorge Washington, and along Cordero northwest of Amazonas.

CAFÉS

Kallari (Map pp650-1; Wilson E4-266 at JL Mera; breakfasts US$2, lunches US$2.50) Besides the fact that Kallari's chocolate bars induce orgasms on the spot, this Quichua coop serves up delicious, healthy breakfasts and lunches as well.

El Cafecito (Map pp650-1; Cordero 1124; mains US$2-4) Serves inexpensive, mainly vegetarian meals and snacks all day long. Great breakfasts.

chiQuito (Map pp650-1; Camino de Orellana 630; snacks US$2-4) This intimate, artsy café makes for a perfect stop during a leisurely walk down to Guápulo.

Café Amazonas (Map pp650-1; cnr Av Amazonas & R Roca; coffee US60¢, mains US$2-4) An Amazonas classic, with outdoor tables and prime people-watching.

Café Sutra (Map pp650-1; J Calama 380; snacks US$2-6; noon-3am Mon-Sat) With its dim lighting, mellow music and cool crowd, Café Sutra is a great place for a snack and a beer before a night out.

Magic Bean (Map pp650-1; Foch E5-08; mains US$4-7) Diminishing in value, but long the epicenter of the Mariscal for well-prepared, breakfasts, lunches, juices and coffee drinks.

Grain de Café (Map pp650-1; Gral Baquedano 332; mains US$4-7) Kick back over coffee or order a full meal. Lots of vegetarian options.

RESTAURANTS

Cevichería y Marisquería 7 Mares (Map pp650-1; La Niña 525; mains US$1-5) This is the place to go for cheap *encebollado* (a tasty seafood, onion and yucca soup). Bowls – served cafétería-style – are only US$1.30 and make an excellent lunch.

El Guambra (Map pp650-1; Av 6 de Diciembre at Jorge Washington; mains US$1.25-4) It doesn't look like much, but this wee restaurant serves knockout *ceviche* and seafood dishes at rock-bottom prices.

Chacha (Map pp650-1; cnr JL Mera & Foch; mains US$1.50-2) Readers and travelers continually recommend this Argentine eatery for cheap pizza, pasta and *empanadas* at outdoor tables.

La Cocina Quiteña (Map pp650-1; R Roca E5-86 at Reina Victoria; mains US$1.50-4) Free popcorn and a local crowd make this as authentic as you can get around the Mariscal. Everything's cheap. Outdoor tables too.

El Chisme (Map pp650-1; Luis Cordero 1204 near JL Mera; almuerzos US$2) This friendly, locally owned eatery cooks up cheap Ecuadorian meals. Great set lunch.

Sakti (Map pp650-1; J Carrión 641; almuerzos US$2, mains US$2-3; 8:30am-6:30pm Mon-Fri) Cheap, wholesome soups, veggies, fruit salads, pastas and lasagna dished out caféteria style.

Aladdin's (Map pp650-1; cnr Diego de Almagro & Baquerizo Moreno; mains US$2-4) Extremely popular soul-themed restaurant with great falafel and shawarma sandwiches, outdoor seating and giant hookahs.

Hassan's Café (Reina Victoria near Av Colón; mains US$2-6) Lebanese food – shawarmas, hummus, kebabs, stuffed eggplant, veggie plates – is good, fresh and cheap at this 10-table restaurant.

El Maple (Map pp650-1; cnr Foch & Diego del Almagro; mains US$3-5) Excellent organic vegetarian food. The four-course set lunches ($2.80) are a steal.

La Bodeguita de Cuba (Map pp650-1; Reina Victoria 1721; mains US$3-5) With its wooden tables and graffiti-covered walls, this is a great place for Cuban food and fun. Live music Thursday nights.

Chifa Mayflower (Map pp650-1; J Carrión 442; mains US$3-6) If it's good enough for celebrity chef Martin Yan (check out his autographed photo by the door), it's good enough. Lots of veggie options.

Mama Clorindas (Map pp650-1; Reina Victoria 1144; meals US$3-7) Delicious national specialties are served to a mostly foreign clientele.

Adam's Rib (Map pp650-1; J Calama 329; mains US$4-6) These barbecued meats have been feeding a faithful stream of expats since 1986.

Cevichería Manolo (Map pp650-1; cnr D de Almagro & La Niña; mains US$4-6) Join the locals at this excellent and affordable seafood restaurant, with several types of ceviches on the menu, plus great seafood dishes.

Red Hot Chili Peppers (Map pp650-1; Foch E4-314; mains US$4-6) Popular Mexican restaurant with a big-screen TV. Go straight for the fajitas and piña coladas, and you'll be singing Jimmy Buffet all the way home.

Le Arcate (Map pp650-1; Gral Baquedano 358; mains US$4-6) This Mariscal favorite bakes over 50 kinds of pizza (likely the best around) in a wood-fired oven and serves reasonably priced lasagna, steak and seafood.

Su Cebiche (Map pp650-1; JL Mera N24-200; mains US$4-7) Slick little lunchtime joint with excellent coastal specialties.

Siam (Map pp650-1; J Calama E5-10; mains US$5-8) Delicious Thai food, smallish portions.

Boca del Lobo (Map pp650-1; J Calama 284; mains US$5-9; 4pm-1am Mon-Sat) Ultra-hip restaurant with ambient grooves and a mind-boggling menu of delicacies such as rosemary sea bass, salmon ishpungo (a spice similar to cinnamon), stuffed plantain tortillas, raclette, focaccias, pizzas and excellent desserts. Fun place to splurge.

Churrascaría Tropeiro (Map pp650-1; Gral Veintimilla 546; all you can eat US$12) With ten types of meat, three types of salad and an all-you-can-eat policy, how can you go wrong?

SELF-CATERING

Mercado Santa Clara (Map pp650-1; cnr Dávalos & Versalles; 8am-5pm) This is the main produce market in the New Town. Besides an outstanding produce selection, there are cheap food stalls.

Supermercado Santa María (Map pp650-1; cnr Dávalos & Versalles; 8:30am-8pm Mon-Sat, 9am-6pm Sun) Huge supermarket conveniently across from Mercado Santa Clara.

Supermaxi (Map pp650-1; cnr La Niña & Y Pinzón; daily) Biggest and best supermarket near the Mariscal.

DRINKING

Most of the farra in Quito is concentrated in and around the Mariscal, where the line between 'bar' and 'dance club' is blurry indeed. Bars in the Mariscal, for better or worse, are generally raucous and notorious for 'gringo hunting,' when locals of both sexes flirt it up with the tourists (which can be annoying or enjoyable, depending on your state of mind). Dancing on the bar tops is generally de rigueur. Bars with dancing often charge admission, which usually includes a drink. Remember to always take a cab home if you're out in the Mariscal at night (see p652).

For something far more relaxed, sans the pickup scene, head to La Floresta or Guápulo, where drinking is a more cerebral affair.

El Pobre Diablo (Map pp650-1; www.elpobrediablo.com; Isabel La Católica E12-06) Friendly, laid-back place with live jazz Wednesday and Thursday nights, wood tables, a great vibe and a solid cocktail menu. Restaurant too.

La Reina Victoria (Map pp650-1; Reina Victoria 530) With a fireplace, dartboard, bumper pool, great food and excellent British pub ambience, it's hard to beat this Mariscal institution.

Mirador de Guápulo (Map pp650-1; R L Larrea y Pasaje Stübel) This cozy café-cum-bar sits on the cliffside overlooking Guápulo. The views are unbeatable, and the snacks are tasty. Live music Wednesday through Saturday nights (when there's a US$4.50 cover charge).

Ta Güeno (Map pp650-1; Camino de Orellana N27-492) Sneak off to this wonderful bar in Guápulo for its bohemian air, friendly vibe, fabulous terrace and big pitchers of *canelazo* (a traditional, hot alcoholic drink).

No Bar (Map pp650-1; cnr J Calama 380 & JL Mera; admission US$3-5; 6pm-3am) This Mariscal cornerstone has four small, dark dance floors, a chaotic bar (always with dancing on top) and plenty of beer-bonging and spraying of Pilsener. It's mobbed on weekends. Expect lots of pick-up lines.

Tijuana (Map pp650-1; cnr Reina Victoria & Santa María; admission US$3-4) Locals pack this small dance floor so tight, it's amazing they can still bump and grind. Edgy.

English pubs have long been the rave in Quito. The following are the most popular.

Patatu's Bar (Map pp650-1; Wilson E4-229)
Turtle's Head (Map pp650-1; La Niña 626)
King's Cross (Map pp650-1; Reina Victoria 1781)
Ghoz Bar (Map pp650-1; La Niña 425)

ENTERTAINMENT

For movie listings and other events, check the local newspapers *El Comercio* and *Hoy*, or pick up a copy of *Quito Cultura*, a monthly cultural mag available free from the tourist offices. Online, check out www.quehacer quito.com (in Spanish).

Cinemas

The first two listings are state-of-the-art multiplexes which usually screen Hollywood hits with Spanish subtitles.

Cinemark (Map p657; 226-0301; www.cinemark .com.ec in Spanish; cnr Naciones Unidas & Av América; admission US$4)

Multicines (Map p657; 225-9677; www.multi cines.com.ec in Spanish; CCI – Centro Comercial Iñaquito; admission US$4)

Ocho y Medio (Map pp650-1; 290-4720/21/22; www.ochoymedio.net in Spanish; cnr Valladolid N24-353 & Vizcaya) Shows art films (often in English) and has occasional dance, theater and live music. Small café attached.

Live Music

Peñas are usually bars that have traditional *música folklórica* (folk music) shows.

Vox Populi (Map p653; Espejo Oe2-12 at Flores; 4pm-11pm Tue, Wed & Sun, 4pm-2am Thu-Sat) The hippest, slickest bar in the Old Town features excellent live music ranging from Cuban *son* to Latin jazz. The jams begin at 10pm Thursday through Saturday.

Ñucanchi Peña (Map pp650-1; Av Universitaria 496; admission US$5; 8pm-2am or 3am Thu-Sat) One of the best places to catch a *música folklórica* show.

La Casa de la Peña (Map p653; García Moreno N11-13; admission US$3-5; 7pm-midnight Thu, 7pm-2am Fri & Sat) The setting alone, inside an ancient building in the Old Town, makes this intimate *peña* a great place to hear Ecuadorian folk music.

Café Libro (Map pp650-1; www.cafélibro.com; J Carrión 243; admission US$3-5; 5pm-1am Mon-Fri, from 6pm Sat) Live music, contemporary dance, tango, jazz and other performances draw an artsy and intellectual crowd to this cozy, bohemian venue.

Nightclubs

Seseribó (Map pp650-1; cnr Gral Veintimilla & Av 12 de Octubre, Edificio Girón; minimum consumption US$7; 9pm-1am Thu-Sat) Quito's premier *salsoteca* shouldn't be missed. It's small and friendly, and the music is tops. Finding dance partners is rarely a problem and usually a polite process.

Mayo 68 (Map pp650-1; L García 662) This fun *salsoteca* is smaller (and some say, for that reason, better) than Seseribó.

Theater & Dance

Teatro Sucre (Map p653; 228-2136, 02-228-2337; www .teatrosucre.com; Manabí N8-131; admission US$3-70; ticket office 10am-1pm & 2-6pm) Recently restored and now standing gloriously over the Plaza del Teatro, this is the city's most historical theater. Performances range from jazz and classical music to ballet, modern dance and opera.

Teatro Bolívar (Map p653; 258-2486/7; www .teatrobolivar.org, info@teatrobolivar.org; Espejo btwn Flores & Guayaquil) The historic Bolívar is currently undergoing restoration work, but performances – everything from theatrical works to international tango-electronica gigs – are still given.

Humanizarte (Map pp650-1; 222-6116; www.hu manizarte.com; Leonidas Plaza Gutiérrez N24-226) Presents both contemporary and Andean dance every Wednesday at 5:30pm.

ECUADOR

Teatro Prometeo (Map pp650-1; ☎ 222-6116; www .cce.org.ec; Av 6 de Diciembre 794) Affiliated with the Casa de La Cultura Ecuatoriana, this inexpensive venue often has modern-dance performances and other shows that non-Spanish speakers can enjoy.

SHOPPING

Numerous stores in the Mariscal (especially along and near Av Amazonas and JL Mera) sell traditional indigenous crafts. Quality is often high, but so are the prices. The best deals can be found at the two crafts markets listed here, where indigenous, mostly *otavaleño* (people from Otavalo), vendors sell their goods.

Crafts Stores

La Bodega (Map pp650-1; JL Mera N22-24) Highest quality crafts, old and new.

Ag (Map pp650-1; JL Mera N22-24) Ag's selection of rare, handmade silver jewelry from throughout South America is outstanding.

Centro Artesanal (Map pp650-1; JL Mera E5-11) This excellent shop is known for its crafts and paintings by local indigenous artists.

Tianguez (Map p653; Plaza San Francisco) Attached to the eponymous café (p662), Tianguez is a member of the Fair Trade Organization and sells outstanding crafts from throughout Ecuador.

Folklore Olga Fisch (Map pp650-1; Av Cristóbal Colón 260) The store of legendary designer Olga Fisch. Highest quality (and prices) around. Pretend it's a museum.

Productos Andinos (Map pp650-1; Urbina 111) This two-floor artisans' cooperative is crammed with reasonably priced crafts.

Markets

On Saturday and Sunday, the northern end of Parque El Ejido turns into Quito's biggest crafts market and sidewalk art show. Two blocks north, on JL Mera between Jorge Washington and 18 de Septiembre, the **Mercado Artesanal La Mariscal** (Map pp650-1; cnr JL Mera & Jorge Washington) is an entire block filled with craft stalls.

GETTING THERE & AWAY
Air

Quito's airport, **Aeropuerto Mariscal Sucre** (Map p657; ☎ 294-4900, 243-0555; www.quitoairport.com; Av Amazonas at Av de la Prensa), is about 10km north of the center. Many of the northbound buses on Av Amazonas and Av 10 de Agosto go there – some have 'Aeropuerto' placards and others say 'Quito Norte.' Also see Getting Into Town, p648.

In order of importance, Ecuador's principal domestic airlines are:

TAME (Map pp650-1; ☎ 250-9375/76/77/78, 02-290-9900; Av Amazonas 1354 at Av Cristobal Colón)

Icaro (Map p657; ☎ 245-0928, 02-245-1499; Palora 124 at Av Amazonas) Across from the airport.

AeroGal (☎ 225-7301/8087/8086; Av Amazonas 7797) Near the airport.

Prices for internal flights vary little between the airlines. The following price information and schedule is subject to change. Prices quoted are one-way. All flights last under an hour, except to the Galápagos (3¼ hours from Quito, 1½ from Guayaquil).

Coca US$43-57, 3 per day Mon-Sat with Icaro and TAME.

Cuenca US$63, 2 per day Mon-Fri & 1 per day Sat & Sun with Icaro, 3 per day Mon-Fri, 2 per day Sat & Sun with TAME.

Esmeraldas US$33-37, 1 per day Tue, Thu, Fri & Sun with TAME.

Galápagos US$390/344 (round trip) in high/low season, 2 every day with TAME.

Guayaquil US$53, 1 per day with AeroGal, 3 per day Mon-Fri & 1 per day Sat & Sun with Icaro, 10-12 per day with TAME.

Lago Agrio US$43-56, 1 per day Mon-Sat with Icaro, 2 per day Mon, Thu & Fri & 1 per day Tue, Wed & Sat with TAME.

Loja US$49-55, 2 per day Mon-Fri, 1 per day Sat & Sun with Icaro, 2 per day Mon-Sat with TAME.

Macas US$43-57, 1 per day Mon-Fri with TAME.

Machala US$55, via Guayaquil only, 1 per day Mon-Fri with TAME.

Manta US$45, 1 per day Mon-Sat with TAME.

Tulcán US$30, 1 per day Mon, Wed & Fri with TAME.

Bus

The **Terminal Terrestre Cumandá** (Cumandá Bus Terminal; Map p653; Maldonado at Javier Piedra) is in the Old Town, a few hundred meters south of Plaza Santo Domingo. The nearest Trole stop is the Cumandá stop. If arriving by taxi at night, ask to be taken *inside* the station to the passenger drop-off; you'll probably have to pay the 10¢ vehicle entrance fee, but you'll be safer.

From the terminal buses go to most major destinations around the country several times a day, and several run to some places per hour, including Ambato and Otavalo. Book in advance for holiday periods and on Friday evenings.

Approximate one-way fares and journey times are shown in the following table. More expensive luxury services are available for long trips.

Destination	Duration (hr)	Cost (US$)
Ambato	2½	2
Atacames	7	9
Bahía de Caráquez	8	9
Baños	3½	3.50
Coca	9 (via Loreto)	9
Cuenca	10-12	10
Esmeraldas	5-6	9
Guayaquil	8	7
Huaquillas	12	10
Ibarra	2½	2.50
Lago Agrio	7-8	7
Latacunga	2	1.50
Loja	14-15	15
Machala	10	9
Manta	8-9	8
Otavalo	2¼	2
Portoviejo	9	9
Puerto López	12	12
Puyo	5½	5
Riobamba	4	4
San Lorenzo	6½	6
Santo Domingo	3	2.50
Tena	5-6	6
Tulcán	5	5

For comfortable (and slightly pricier) buses to Guayaquil from the New Town, and to avoid the trip to the terminal, ride with **Transportes Ecuador** (Map pp650-1; JL Mera N21-44 at Jorge Washington) or **Panamericana** (Map pp650-1; cnr Av Cristobal Colón & Reina Victoria). Panamericana also has long-distance buses to Machala, Loja, Cuenca, Manta and Esmeraldas.

Train

Although most of Ecuador's train system is in shambles, you can still ride the rails if you're determined. A weekend tourist train leaves Quito and heads south for about 3½ hours to the Area Nacional de Recreación El Boliche, adjoining Parque Nacional Cotopaxi. Many passengers ride on the roof.

The **train station** (Map p657; ☎ 265-6142; Sincholagua & Vicente Maldonado) is about 2km south of the Old Town. Purchase tickets in advance at the **train ticket office** (Map p653; ☎ 258-2927; Bolívar 443 at García Moreno; per person return US$4.60; ☾ 8am-4:30pm Mon-Fri).

GETTING AROUND
Bus

The local buses all cost US25¢; you pay as you board. They are safe and convenient, but watch your bags and pockets on crowded buses. There are various bus types, each identified by color. The blue *Bus Tipos* are the most common and allow standing passengers. The red *ejecutivo* buses don't allow standing passengers and are therefore less crowded, but they are more infrequent.

Buses have destination placards in their windows (not route numbers), and drivers will usually gladly tell you which bus to take if you flag the wrong one.

Taxi

Cabs are yellow and have taxi-number stickers in the window. Drivers are legally required to use their *taxímetros* (meters), and most do; many however charge a flat rate of US$2 between the Mariscal and the Old Town, which is usually about US25¢ more than you'd pay if the meter was on. Whether you think the extra quarter is worth haggling over is completely up to you. When a driver tells you the meter is broken, flag down another cab. Late at night and on Sundays drivers charge more, but it should never be more than twice the metered rate. You can also hire a cab for about US$8 per hour, a great way to see outer city sites.

Trole, Ecovía & Metrobus

Quito has three electrically powered bus routes – the Trole, the Ecovía and the Metrobus. Each runs north–south along one of Quito's three main thoroughfares. Each line has designated stations and car-free lanes, making them speedy and efficient. But as the fastest form of public transport, they are also usually crowded and notorious for pickpockets. They run about every 10 minutes from 6am to 12:30am (more often in rush hours), and the fare is US25¢.

The Trole runs along Maldonado and Av 10 de Agosto. In the Old Town, southbound trolleys take the west route (along Guayaquil), while northbound trolleys take the east route (along Montúfar and Pichincha). The Ecovía runs along Av 6 de Diciembre, and the Metrobus runs along Av América.

AROUND QUITO

MITAD DEL MUNDO & AROUND
☎ 02

Ecuador's biggest claim to fame is its location on the equator, and you can hardly come this far without making the excursion out to the hemispheric line at **Mitad del Mundo** (Middle of the World; admission US$2.50; ⏰ 9am-6pm Mon-Fri, 9am-7pm Sat & Sun), 22km north of Quito. It's touristy, sure, but hopping back and forth between hemispheres is quite a sensation. On Sunday afternoons live bands rock the equatorial line in the central plaza area, and *quiteños* pour in for the fun. A planetarium, a wonderful scale model of Quito's Old Town and other attractions cost extra. Outside the Mitad del Mundo complex is the excellent **Museo Solar Inti Ñan** (☎ 239-5122; admission adults/children under 12 US$2/1; ⏰ 9:30am-5:30pm), supposedly the site of the real equator. Definitely more interesting than the official complex next door, it houses fascinating exhibits of astronomical geography and has some fun mind-boggling water and energy demonstrations.

Rumicucho (admission US$1.50; ⏰ 9am-3pm Mon-Fri, 8am-4pm Sat & Sun) is a small pre-Inca site under excavation 3.5km north of Mitad del Mundo. On the way to Calacalí, about 5km north of Mitad del Mundo, is the ancient volcanic crater of **Pululahua** – the views are great from the rim or you can hike down to the crater floor.

To get to Mitad del Mundo from Quito, take the Metrobus (US25¢) north to the Cotocollao stop. At Cotocollao, transfer to the green Mitad del Mundo bus (they're clearly marked) *without* leaving the platform. The transfer costs an additional US15¢ (pay on the bus), and the entire trip takes one to 1½ hours. The bus drops you right in front of the park entrance.

Buses continue past the complex and will drop you at the entrance road to Pululahua – ask for the Mirador de Ventanillas (the lookout point where the trail into the crater begins).

REFUGIO DE VIDA SILVESTRE PASOCHOA

This small but beautiful wildlife **reserve** (admission US$7), 30km southeast of Quito, has one of the last stands of undisturbed humid **Andean forest** left in central Ecuador. It's a recommended day trip for naturalists and bird-watchers, as more than 100 bird species and many rare plants have been recorded here. Trails range from easy to strenuous, and overnight **camping** (per person US$3) is allowed in designated areas. Facilities include latrines, picnic areas and water. A basic 20-bunk **shelter** (dm US$5) is available. The reserve is operated by **Fundación Natura** (☎ 02-250-3385/86/87, ext 202, 203; Av República 481 & Diego de Almagro) in Quito; it offers directions, maps and information.

To reach the reserve, take the bus from La Marín in Quito's Old Town to the village

---

MYTHS FROM MIDDLE EARTH

The closer you get to the equator, the more you hear about the equator's mysterious energy. But what is fact and what is fiction?

There's no point in starting softly, so let's debunk the biggest one first. The Mitad del Mundo is not on the equator. But it's close enough. GPS devices show that its only about 240m off the mark. And no one who sees the photos has to know this, right?

Another tough one to swallow is the myth of the flushing toilet. One of the highlights of the Museo Solar Inti Ñan is the demonstration of water draining counterclockwise north of the equator and clockwise 3m away, south of the equator. Researchers claim it's a crock. The Coriolos Force – which causes weather systems to veer right in the northern hemisphere and left in the southern hemisphere – has no effect on small bodies of water like those in a sink or a toilet.

How about some truth: you do weigh less on the equator. This is due to a greater centrifugal force on the equator than at the poles. But, the difference between here and at the poles is only about 0.3%, not the approximately 1.5% to 2% the scales at the monument imply.

If all this myth-debunking has brought on a spell of the doldrums, rest assured – it comes with the territory: the Doldrums was the name given by sailors to the regional lack of winds along the equatorial belt caused by the intense heating of the earth's surface at the equator. The heating causes air to rise, rather than blow, and rising air doesn't sail a ship. But that's all fun on the equator.

of **Amaguaña** (US$1, one hour), then hire a pickup (about US$10 per group/truck) to take you the last 7km to the park entrance.

TERMAS DE PAPALLACTA
☎ 02

After a sweaty jungle expedition or an arduous Andean hike, a soak in the celestial hot springs of **Termas de Papallacta** (in Quito ☎ 250-4747, 256-8989; admission US$6, free for hotel guests; ☼ 7am-9pm) is pure medicine. About 67km (two hours) from Quito, these are Ecuador's most luxurious, best-kept and probably most scenic thermal bathrooms. The complex itself is part of the posh **Hotel Termas de Papallacta**, but day-trippers are welcome. It makes for an excellent jaunt from Quito. Cheaper hotels are available outside the complex in the village of Papallacta itself, though it's easy enough to head back to Quito. It's best to go during the week since weekend crowds can swell to 2000 people!

Any of the buses from Quito heading toward Baeza, Tena or Lago Agrio can drop you off in Papallacta. To avoid the congested Quito bus terminal, take a taxi to the intersection known as El Trébol (p653, ask your taxi driver) and flag a bus there.

NORTHERN HIGHLANDS

The steep green hills, dust-blown villages, bustling provincial capitals and cultural riches of the northern highlands are but a stone's throw from Quito. Those traveling to/from Colombia are bound to pass through the region, and there's plenty worth stopping for: the famous Otavalo market, which dates back to pre-Inca times, is the largest crafts market in South America, and several small towns are known for their handicrafts, including wood carvings and leatherwork. Best of all, the people – especially the indigenous *otavaleños* (people from Otavalo) – are wonderfully friendly.

OTAVALO
☎ 06 / pop 31,000

The friendly and prosperous town of Otavalo (elevation 2550m) is famous for its giant Saturday market, where traditionally dressed indigenous people sell handicrafts to hordes of foreigners who pour in every Saturday to get in on the deals. Despite the market's popularity, the *otavaleños* themselves remain self-determined and culturally uncompromised.

The setting is fabulous, and the entire experience remains enchanting.

The most evident feature of the *otavaleños'* culture is their traditional dress. The men wear long single pigtails, calf-length white pants, rope sandals, reversible gray or blue ponchos and dark felt hats. The women are very striking, with beautifully embroidered blouses, long black skirts and shawls, and interesting folded head cloths.

Information
Andinatel (Calderón (near Modesto Jaramillo); Salinas (at Plaza de Ponchos)
Banco del Pacífico (Bolívar at García Moreno) Bank with ATM.
Banco del Pichincha (Bolívar near García Moreno) Bank with ATM.
Book Market (Roca near García Moreno) Used books.
Native C@ffé Net (Sucre near Colón; per hr US$1) Internet access.
Post office (Sucre at Salinas, 2nd fl)
Vaz Cambios (cnr Modesto Jaramillo & Saona) Changes traveler's checks.

Sights
In the wee hours of every Saturday morning, while the tourists are still sawing logs in their hotel rooms, vendors pour into town lugging massive bundles of crafts to sell at the **Saturday market**. By 8am, things are in full swing, and by 10am, the **Plaza de Ponchos** (the center of the crafts market) and nearly every street around it is jammed with people. Both traditional crafts (such as weavings, shawls and ponchos) and crafts tailored toward tourists (such as woolen sweaters with Rasta motifs) vie for buyers' dollars. Bargaining is tough but possible, and the *otavaleño* sellers are always friendly.

The **animal market**, on the western edge of town, offers an interesting break from the hustle of the crafts market. Beneath the volcanic backdrop of Cotacachi and Imbabura, indigenous men and women mill around with pigs, cows, goats and chickens and inspect, haggle and chat in the crisp morning air. It generally winds down by 8am. The **food market** is near the southern end of Modesto Jaramillo.

The **Instituto Otavaleño de Antropología** (admission free; ☼ 8:30am-noon & 2:30-6pm Tue-Fri, 8:30am-noon Sat), just off the Panamericana north of town, houses a small but interesting archaeological and ethnographical museum with exhibits about the area.

ECUADOR

Activities

There's some great hiking around Otavalo, especially in the Lagunas de Mojanda area (p672). **Diceny Viajes** (☎ 292-1217; Sucre 10-11) offers warmly recommended hiking trips up Volcán Cotacachi with indigenous guides. **Runa Tupari** (☎ 292-5985; www.runatupari.com; Sucre & Quiroga) partners with local indigenous communities, offering hiking, horse-riding and mountain-biking trips. Its day trips include a 2000m mountain bike descent into tropical cloud forest and a round-trip ten hour hike up Cotacachi (4939m).

The oldest and best-known information and guide service in town is **Zulaytur** (☎ 09-814-6483; www.geocities.com/zulaytur; cnr Sucre & Colón, 2nd fl). It's run by the knowledgeable Rodrigo Mora, who offers a variety of inexpensive tours, including visits to indigenous weavers' homes, where you can learn about the weaving process and buy products off the loom.

Courses

Readers have enthusiastically recommended **Mundo Andino** (☎ 292-1864; espanol@interactive.net .ec; Salinas 4-04), and **Instituto Superíor de Español** (☎ 292-2414; www.instituto-superior.net; Sucre 11-10). One-on-one classes cost US$4 to US$5 per hour. Both arrange homestays.

Festivals & Events

Held during the first two weeks of September, the **Fiesta del Yamor** features processions, music and dancing in the plaza, fireworks, cockfights, the election of the fiesta queen and, of course, lots of *chicha de yamor* (a delicious nonalcoholic corn drink made with seven varieties of corn).

Sleeping

Otavalo is crowded on Friday, because of the Saturday market, so arrive on Thursday for the best choice of accommodations.

Residencial El Rocío (☎ 292-0584; Morales 11-70; r per person with shared/private bathroom US$4/5) Friendly, simple accommodations with hot water and rooftop views of the hilltops.

Hostal Valle del Amanecer (☎ 292-0990; amanacer@ uio.satnet.net; cnr Roca & Quiroga; r per person with breakfast & shared/private bathroom US$7/9) Rooms are small and hospitality is hit-or-miss, but the shady hammock-strewn courtyard and tasty breakfasts still lure loads of over-nighters.

Chukitos (☎ 292-4959; www.chukitoshostal.4t.com; Bolívar 10-13 & Morales; s/d with bathroom US$7/14; 🖵)

Slightly dusty rooms with narrow twin beds, Andean folk decor, cable TV and hot water.

Hotel Riviera-Sucre (☎ 292-0241; www.rivierasucre .com; García Moreno 3-80 & Roca; r per person with shared/private bathroom US$7/15) This Belgian-owned hotel occupies a sprawling, charming home with large, colorful rooms, fireplaces, a library, a courtyard and plenty of hot water. Outstanding value.

Rincón del Viajero (☎ 292-1741; www.rincondel viajero.org; Roca 11-07; r per person incl breakfast with shared/ private bathroom US$7.50/10; 🅿) Warm hospitality, colorful murals and homey, snug rooms make this a great deal. It has a TV lounge, a fireplace, hot water and a rooftop terrace too.

Cabañas El Rocío (r per person US$10) A comfortable garden escape in the San Juan neighborhood on the other side of the Panamericana.

Hotel El Indio (☎ 292-0060; Sucre 12-14, s/d US$10/15) While the inadvertent 1970's ambiance adds kitsch-appeal, there are better values out there for the price.

Other reliable cheapies include:

Hostal María (☎ 292-0672; Modesto Jaramillo near Colón; per person US$3).

Residencial San Luis (☎ 292-0614; Calderón 6-02; r per person with shared/private bathroom US$4/5)

Residencial Santa Fe (☎ 292-0171; Colón near Sucre; r per person US$5)

For a marvelous setting outside of town, try the tranquil **La Luna** (☎ 09-973-7415; www.hostal laluna.com; camp sites US$2.50, dm with/without breakfast US$5.50/4, r per person with shared/private bathroom US$9/10), 4km along the road to Lagunas de Mojanda. The breakfasts are filling and perks include kitchen facilities, fireplace, dining room, views and free pickup from Otavalo if you call ahead. A cab ride out costs about US$4. The owners arrange mountain biking and hiking tours.

Eating

With all those kitchenless travelers sauntering around town, it's hardly surprising that Otavalo has plenty of restaurants.

Empanadas Argentina (Sucre 2-02 & Morales; empanadas US$50¢) Join the student crowd for a slice of pizza or salty beef, cheese or corn-and-pineapple (whoa!) empanadas.

Shenandoah Pie Shop (Salinas 5-15; pie slices US$1) Famous for its deep-dish pies stuffed with sugary fruit. Best with a vanilla milkshake.

Bogotá Plaza (Bolívar near Calderón; mains US$1.50-3) Try this tiny family-run place for a filling set

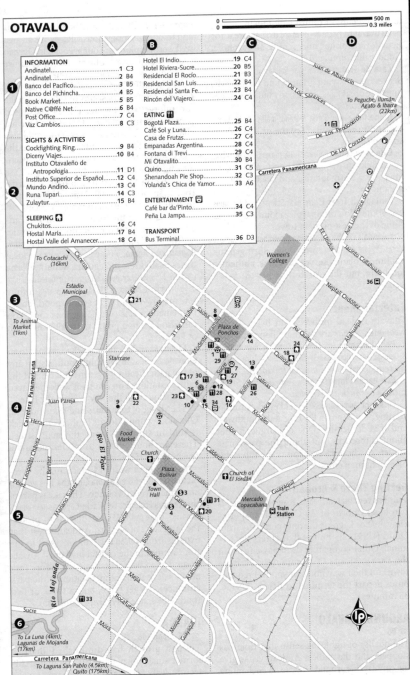

OTAVALO

0 _____ 500 m
0 _____ 0.3 miles

INFORMATION
Andinatel......................................**1** C3
Andinatel......................................**2** B4
Banco del Pacífico.........................**3** B5
Banco del Pichincha.......................**4** B5
Book Market...................................**5** B5
Native C@ffé Net............................**6** B4
Post Office......................................**7** C4
Vaz Cambios...................................**8** C3

SIGHTS & ACTIVITIES
Cockfighting Ring...........................**9** B4
Diceny Viajes................................**10** B4
Instituto Otavaleño de
   Antropología..............................**11** D1
Instituto Superior de Español.......**12** C4
Mundo Andino..............................**13** C4
Runa Tupari..................................**14** B4
Zulaytur..**15** B4

SLEEPING
Chukitos......................................**16** C4
Hostal María.................................**17** B4
Hostal Valle del Amanecer...........**18** C4

Hotel El Indio...............................**19** C4
Hotel Riviera-Sucre.......................**20** B5
Residencial El Rocío.......................**21** B3
Residencial San Luis......................**22** B4
Residencial Santa Fe.....................**23** B4
Rincón del Viajero.........................**24** C4

EATING
Bogotá Plaza................................**25** B4
Café Sol y Luna............................**26** C4
Casa de Frutas.............................**27** C4
Empanadas Argentina...................**28** C4
Fontana di Trevi...........................**29** C4
Mi Otavalito.................................**30** B4
Quino...**31** C5
Shenandoah Pie Shop...................**32** C3
Yolanda's Chica de Yamor............**33** A6

ENTERTAINMENT
Café bar da'Pinto.........................**34** C4
Peña La Jampa.............................**35** C3

TRANSPORT
Bus Terminal.................................**36** D3

lunch and cups of robust Colombian coffee.

Mi Otavalito (Sucre 11-19; mains US$2-4) Great for Ecuadorian dishes and family atmosphere. Good-value *almuerzos*.

Casa de Frutas (Sucre near Salinas; mains US$3-5) Serves up satisfying granola and fruit bowls, omelette breakfasts, salads, soy burgers, juices and local coffee.

Quino (Roca near García Moreno; mains US$5) Best seafood in *these* hills. Try the grilled fish or shrimp *ceviche*.

Café Sol y Luna (Bolívar 11-10; mains US$5-6) This small Belgian-owned café boasts a cozy dining patio, a warm interior and healthy, mostly organic food.

Fontana di Trevi (Sucre near Salinas, 2nd fl; mains US$5-6) Otavalo's original pizza joint still serves some of the best pizza in town.

Yolanda's chicha de yamor (green house at Sucre & Mora; ☽ late Aug to mid-Sep) Open during festival time, Yolanda serves delicious, authentic local fare, but the real draw is her *chicha de yamor*.

Entertainment

Otavalo is dead midweek but lively on the weekends. *Peñas* are the main hangouts.

Peña La Jampa (cnr Modesto Jaramillo btwn Av Quito & Quiroga; admission US$2-3) Showcases live salsa, merengue, rock and *musica folklórica*.

Café bar da'Pinto (Colón btwn Bolívar & Sucre) Sticks mostly to *musica folklórica*.

Cockfight (admission US50¢) Held every Saturday starting about 7pm in the ring at the southwest end of 31 de Octubre. One local argues it's not about gamecocks, but about the passionate audience, whose faces 'express the full range of each human emotion.'

Getting There & Around

The **bus terminal** (Atahualpa & Jacinto Collahuazo) is two blocks north of Av Quito. Transportes Otavalo/Los Lagos is the only company from Quito (US$2, 2½ hours) that enters the terminal. Other companies drop passengers on the Panamericana (a 10-minute walk from town) on their way north or south. Frequent buses depart the terminal to Ibarra (US45¢, 35 minutes).

AROUND OTAVALO
☎ 06

The quality of light, the sense that time has stopped, and the endless Andean vistas give the countryside around Otavalo an enchanting character. Scattered with lakes, hiking trails and traditional indigenous villages, it's an area well worth exploring. Tour agencies in Otavalo (p670) can provide information or organize hikes, or you can explore on your own.

The beautiful **Lagunas de Mojanda**, in the high *páramo* some 17km south of Otavalo, make for unforgettable hiking. The area acquired protected status in 2002. Taxis from Otavalo charge about US$12 each way. You could also walk up and camp. For information about the lakes, stop at the Mojanda Foundation/Pachamama Association directly across from Casa Mojanda on the road to the park. Zulaytur (p670), in Otavalo, offers guided hikes which include transportation for about US$30.

Strung along the eastern side of the Panamericana, a few kilometers north of Otavalo, are the mostly indigenous villages of **Peguche**, **Ilumán** and **Agato**. You can walk or take local buses to all three. In Peguche, **Hostal Aya Huma** (☎ 292-1255; www.ayahuma.com; s/d with shared bathroom US$8/12, private bathroom US$14/20) is a beautifully set, mellow *hostal* that serves good, cheap homemade meals (veggie options too). You can also hike to a pretty **waterfall** 2km south of Peguche.

Laguna San Pablo can be reached on foot from Otavalo by heading roughly southeast on any of the paths heading over the hill behind the railway station. You can then walk the paved road that goes all the way around the lake.

The village of **Cotacachi**, some 15km north of Otavalo, is famous for its leatherwork, which is sold in stores all along the main street. There are hourly buses from Otavalo and a few hotels in Cotacachi.

About 18km west of Cotacachi, the spectacular crater-lake **Laguna Cuicocha** lies within an extinct, eroded volcano. The lake is part of the **Reserva Ecológica Cotacachi-Cayapas** (lake admission US$1, entire park US$5), established to protect the large area of western Andean forest that extends from **Volcán Cotacachi** (4939m) to the Río Cayapas in the coastal lowlands. A walk around the lake takes about six hours (ask about safety at the ranger station at the park entrance). To get there, take a truck or taxi (both US$8, one way) from Cotacachi.

IBARRA
☎ 06 / pop 108,535

Though growth has diminished Ibarra's former small-town allure, its colonial architecture, leafy plazas and cobbled streets make it a handsome city – at least on weekends when the streets aren't so choked with traffic. Ibarra's unique blend of students, *mestizos*, indigenous highlanders and Afro-Ecuadorians give it an interesting multicultural edge. The elevation is 2225m.

Ibarra's old architecture and shady plazas sit north of the center. Make calls at **Andinatel** (Sucre 4-48). The **tourist office** (iTur; ☎ 06-260-8409; www.turismoibarra.com; Oveido & Sucre; ☯ 8:30am-1pm & 2-5pm Mon-Fri) is two blocks south of Parque Pedro Moncayo. **Banco del Pacífico** (cnr Olmedo & Moncayo) changes traveler's checks and has an ATM.

Sleeping

Ibarra is bursting with cheap hotels. The cheapest are near the bus terminals.

Hostal Ecuador (☎ 295-6425; Mosquera 5-54; r per person US$5; P) Bare, bright rooms give a sanitarium effect, but the attention is sincere.

Hostal El Retorno (☎ 295-7722; Moncayo 4-32; r per person with shared/private bathroom US$6/7) A cheery little place with pint-sized beds and en suite TVs. Request a window.

Hostal El Ejecutivo (☎ 295-6575; Bolívar 9-69; s/d US$7/12; P 🖳) Old plaids dominate the ample rooms (some with balconies) and add a retro feel. Rooms have hot-water bathrooms, telephone and TV. Cybercafé on the 1st floor.

Hostal del Río (☎ 261-1885, 09-944-2792; Juan Montalvo 4-55 & Flores; s/d US$12/15) This excellent *hostal* fuses modern art deco with regional colonial style; rooms have hardwood floors and comfy beds. Located in a quiet neighborhood a few blocks east of center.

Eating

Ibarra is known for its tasty *nogadas* (nougats) and its sweet *arrope de mora* (a thick black-berry syrup), available at the sweets kiosks across from Parque La Merced.

Heladería Rosalía Suárez (Oviedo 7-82; ice cream US$1.50) Don't leave Ibarra without having a scoop of ice cream at Heladería Rosalía Suárez. It's the most famous ice cream shop in Ecuador, opened by Rosalía herself over 90 years ago. Rosalía is credited with perfecting the tradition of *helados de paila*; she lived to be 104.

Antojitos de Mi Tierra (Plaza Francisco Calderón) The place to go for traditional snacks such as *chicha de arroz* (a sweetened rice drink) and *tamales*, *humitas* and *quimbolitos* (corn dumplings steamed in corn husks or leaves).

Café Arte (Salinas 5-43; mains US$4-6) A funky and relaxed artist-owned gathering spot, this is a good place to socialize and check out local bands. Food leans toward Mexican.

Los Almendros (Velasco 5-59 & Sucre; lunch US$2.25) Customers line up out the door here for well-prepared Ecuadorian standbys.

Órale (Sucre btwn Grijalva & Borrero; mains US$4) Tasty Mexican food is served in a casual atmosphere.

Getting There & Away

BUS

Ibarra's new bus terminal is located at the end of Av Teodoro Gómez de la Torre. You can grab a taxi to/from the center for US$1. There are regular departures to Quito (US$2.50, 2½ hours); Guayaquil (US$9, 10 hours); Esmeraldas (US$8, nine hours); Atacames (US$9, nine hours); San Lorenzo (US$4, 3½ to four hours); Tulcán (US$2, 2½ hours); Otavalo (US35¢, 35 minutes) and numerous other destinations.

TRAIN

With the completion of the road to San Lorenzo, the spectacular Ibarra-San Lorenzo

---

DETOUR: RESERVA BIOLÓGICA LOS CEDROS

Intrepid travelers will enjoy holing up at the rustic **Los Cedros Scientific Center** (loscedros@ecuanex .net.ec; www.reservaloscedros.org; r per person US$30), a research station within the magical, 6400 hectare Los Cedros biological reserve. The center is set in primary forest within one of the most bio-diverse regions on the planet.

Getting to Los Cedros involves making your way to the village of Chontal and undertaking a rugged 4-6 hour hike through the Magdalena River valley into the Cordillera de la Plata. Contact the reserve in advance (via email) to arrange for a guide, pack animals and accommodations. Rates include all meals (making the price a bargain) and guide services. Buses from Otavalo go to Chontal. From Quito, **Transportes Minas** (☎ 02-286-8039; Calle Los Ríos) goes to Chontal (3½ hours) at 6am every day from near the Ayora Maternity Hospital. In Chontal you can get breakfast at Ramiro and Alicia's *hostal* while waiting for your pack mules and guide.

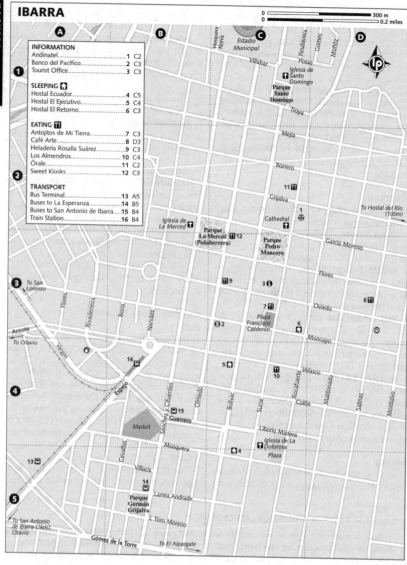

IBARRA

INFORMATION
Andinatel......................................**1** C2	
Banco del Pacífico.......................**2** C3	
Tourist Office.............................**3** C3	

SLEEPING
Hostal Ecuador..........................**4** C5	
Hostal El Ejecutivo....................**5** C4	
Hostal El Retorno.......................**6** C3	

EATING
Antojitos de Mi Tierra.................**7** C3	
Café Arte....................................**8** D3	
Heladería Rosalía Suárez.............**9** C3	
Los Almendros............................**10** C4	
Órale...**11** C2	
Sweet Kiosks.............................**12** C3	

TRANSPORT
Bus Terminal..............................**13** A5	
Buses to La Esperanza................**14** B5	
Buses to San Antonio de Ibarra....**15** B4	
Train Station..............................**16** B4	

railway, which once linked the highlands to the coast, no longer runs. However, *autoferros* go as far as Primer Paso (US$4 one way, 1¾ hours), less than a quarter of the way to San Lorenzo. It's essentially a round-trip tourist attraction and departs only with a minimum of 16 passengers. Cancelled departures are the norm. For more information, call the **train station** (☎ 295-0390/5050; Espejo) or check out www.imbaburaturismo.gov.ec.

AROUND IBARRA
☎ 06

Famous for its wood carving, nearby **San Antonio de Ibarra** is bursting with shops selling carvings of all sorts and sizes. Buses leave frequently for San Antonio from the intersection of Guerrero and Sánchez y Cifuentes in Ibarra, or you can walk the approximately 2km south along the Panamericana (which you'll reach by walking southwest along Espejo).

The pretty little village of **La Esperanza**, 7km south of Ibarra, is the place to stay if you're looking for peace and quiet. There's nothing to do here except talk to the locals and stroll through the surrounding countryside. The basic but friendly **Casa Aida** (☎ 264-2020; Calle Gallo Plaza; r per person US$4) has simple rooms and serves good, cheap meals, including vegetarian dishes. Buses from Ibarra leave from the terminal near Parque Germán Grijalva, or you can walk.

EL ÁNGEL
☎ 06

The stark, still Andean village of El Ángel is the entry point to Páramos El Ángel, a misty wilderness favored by foxes and condors. It's part of the 16,000 hectare **Reserva Ecológica El Ángel** (admission US$10). You can arrange *páramo* visits through La Casa de Eliza (see p661), in Quito.

Simple restaurants and lodgings are found in town. Transportes Espejo, on the main plaza, goes to Quito (US$3.50, four hours) via Ibarra (US$1.20, 1½ hours) every hour.

TULCÁN

The drab, wind-whipped city of Tulcán is the principal gateway to Colombia. Besides the Sunday street market (which is low on crafts), the only real tourist attraction is its famous **topiary gardens**, located behind the cemetery.

The **tourist office** (☎ 298-5760) is near the cemetery entrance. **Banco del Pichincha** (cnr 10 de Agosto & Sucre) has an ATM and changes currency and traveler's checks on weekdays only.

Sleeping & Eating

Tulcán's budget hotels are a dismal lot, but there are plenty to choose from.

Hotel San Francisco (☎ 298-0760; Bolívar near Ata-hualpa; s/d US$4/8) One of the best budget options in town. Request a *ventana* (window).

Hotel Los Alpes (☎ 298-2235; JR Arellano near Bolívar; s/d US$5/10) Perfectly adequate option near the bus terminal.

Hotel Lumar (☎ 298-0402/7137; Sucre near Pichincha; s/d US$7/14; P) Carpeted rooms have soft beds, cable TV and phones; modern hotel with good service.

Hotel Machado (☎ 298-4221; cnr Ayacucho & Bolívar; s/d US$13/26; P) A fresh coat of paint and gleaming bathrooms create a welcoming atmosphere.

Tulcán's Colombian restaurants – there are loads near the intersection of 10 de Agosto and Bolívar – provide a welcome alternative to the Ecuadorian staples. **El Patio** (Bolívar near 10 de Agosto; mains US$3) is one of the best. **Chifa Pack Choy** (cnr Pichincha & Sucre; mains US$2-3) serves the town's best Chinese food. By the border, there are plenty of snack stalls and fast-food carts.

Getting There & Around

The airport is 2km northeast of the town center en route to the border. **TAME** (☎ 298-0675; Sucre near Ayacucho) has offices in town and at the **airport** (☎ 298-2850). It offers daily flights to/from Quito (US$30), and flies Monday, Wednesday and Friday to Cali, Colombia (US$78).

Buses run to/from Ibarra (US$2.50, 2½ hours) and Quito (US$5, five hours). Long-haulers go to Cuenca (US$17, 17 hours, once a day), Guayaquil (US$13, 11 to 13 hours) and other cities.

The **bus terminal** (Bolívar at JR Arellano) is 2.5km southwest of the town center. City buses (10) run along Bolívar to the center. Taxis to/from the center cost about US$1.

WESTERN ANDEAN SLOPES
☎ 02

The western slopes of the Andes, northwest of Quito, are home to some of Ecuador's last remaining stands of tropical cloud forest. Along the old road to Santo Domingo (which continues to the coast), you'll encounter some fabulous places to explore these cloud-swept forests. The best place to start is the village of **Mindo**, which is famous for its bird-watching and its environmentally conscious inhabitants. Once in Mindo you can hike in the cloud forest, hire bird-watching guides, swim in the Río Mindo and *relax*.

There are several basic but charming accommodations in town, including **Hostal Bijao** (in Quito ☎ 02-276-5740; r with shared/private bathroom per person US$4/7.50); **Rubbi Hostal** (☎ 235-0461; rubbyhostal@yahoo .com; r per person US$5); and **La Casa de Cecilia** (☎ 09-334-5393; casadececilia@yahoo.com; r per person US$5).

Direct buses running from Quito to Mindo (US$2.50, 2½ hours) leave from the **Cooperativa Flor de Valle bus terminal** (Map pp650-1; M Larrea, Ascunción, near Parque El Ejido, Quito) Monday thru Friday at 8am and 3:45pm. On weekends buses leave at 7:20am, 8am, 9am and 3:45pm.

After passing the turnoff to Mindo, the old road meanders down through the lowland villages of **Puerto Maldonado** and **Puerto Quito** before meeting the north-south road between Santo Domingo and Esmeraldas. From the Mindo turnoff you can flag a bus to Santo Domingo.

CENTRAL HIGHLANDS

South of Quito the Panamericana winds past eight of the country's 10 highest peaks, including the picture-perfect snowcapped cone of Volcán Cotopaxi (5897m) and the glaciated behemoth, Volcán Chimborazo (6310m). For trekkers and climbers, the central highlands are a paradise, and even inexperienced climbers can have a go at summiting some of the country's highest peaks. Those who are happier *off* the hill will find the region just as thrilling. You can hike between remote Andean villages near the Quilotoa Loop, gorge yourself on homemade cheeses and chocolate in Guaranda and Salinas, barrel downhill to the Oriente on a rented mountain bike from Baños, hike or trek in spectacular national parks or ride the roof of a boxcar down the famous Nariz del Diablo. The central highlands are home to scores of tiny, indigenous villages and many of the country's most traditional markets. Being haggled out of your change up here by traditionally dressed *indígenas* (indigenous people) is one of the country's most memorable experiences.

PARQUE NACIONAL COTOPAXI
☎ 03

The centerpiece of Ecuador's most popular **national park** (admission US$10) is the snowcapped and downright astonishing **Volcán Cotopaxi**

(5897m), Ecuador's second highest peak. The park is almost deserted midweek, when nature freaks can have the breathtaking (literally) scenery nearly to themselves.

The park has a small museum, an information center, a *refugio* (climbers' refuge) and some camping and picnicking areas. The gate is open from 8am to 6pm (longer on weekends), but hikers can slip through just about anytime.

The park's main entrance is via a turnoff from the Panamericana, roughly 30km north of Latacunga. From the turnoff, it's 6km to **Control Caspi**, the entrance station. Any Quito-Latacunga bus will let you off at the turnoff. Follow the main dirt roads (also signed) to the entrance. It's another 9km or so to the museum. About 4km beyond the museum is **Laguna de Limpiopungo**, a shallow Andean lake 3830m above sea level; a trail circles the lake and takes about half an hour to walk. The climbers' refuge is about 12km past (and 1000m above) the lake. You can drive up a very rough road to a parking area (about 1km before the refuge) or hire a truck and driver from Latacunga for US$20 to US$30.

From the lake you can walk to the refuge, but walking at this altitude is difficult for the un-acclimatized, and altitude sickness is a very real danger; acclimatize for several days in Quito or elsewhere before attempting to walk in. Continuing beyond the climbers' refuge requires snow- and ice-climbing gear and expertise. Outfitters in Quito (p658 & p659), Latacunga (opposite) and Riobamba (p685) offer guided summit trips and downhill mountain-biking tours of Cotopaxi.

Near the main entrance to the park, about 2km west (and across the Panamericana), the **Albergue Cuello de Luna** (☎ 09-970-0330, in Quito ☎ 02-224-2744; www.cuellodeluna.com; dm from US$11,

---

GETTING TO COLOMBIA

The Rumichaca border crossing, 6.5km north of Tulcán, is the principal gateway to Colombia and currently the only recommended crossing. All formalities – which are very straightforward – are taken care of at the border, which is open 24 hours every day. Crossing is free. Minibuses (US80¢) and taxis (US$4) run regularly between the border and Tulcán's Parque Isidro Ayora, about five blocks north of the central plaza. The buses accept Colombian pesos or US dollars. Be absolutely certain that you have your papers in order and be ready for drugs and weapons searches on both sides. Stay abreast of the conflict in Colombia and inquire locally about the safety of travel in Colombia before you pounce across the country line. Once across the border, there is frequent transportation to Ipiales, the first town in Colombia, 2km away.

If you're crossing *from* Colombia, see p620.

s/d/tr without bathroom US$20/26/36, s/d/tr/q with bathroom US$23/34/45/53) is friendly and popular, and serves good meals (US$7 to US$10). Further north, **Hostería PapaGayo** (☎ 02-231-0002, 09-990-3524; www.hosteria-papagayo.com; Panamericana Sur Km 43; camping US$3, dm US$6, r with private bathroom US$8-12) is a stunningly converted, 150-year-old farmhouse and a perfect base for acclimatizing and exploring Cotopaxi.

Camping in the park costs US$3 per person. A bunk in the refuge costs US$17; cooking facilities are available. Be sure to bring a warm sleeping bag.

LATACUNGA
☎ 03 / pop 51,700

A bustling market town and capital of Cotopaxi Province, Latacunga (elevation 2800m) appears rather dull from the Panamericana. But once you cross the bridge over the swift Río Cutuchi, the buildings get older, and old Latacunga starts to looks pretty damn cool. The town is famous for its Mamá Negra festivals and seems to have more barber shops per capita than any town in Ecuador. It's a good base for transport to Cotopaxi, the starting point for the Quilotoa Loop (p679), and it's the best point from which to visit the Thursday morning market in Saquisilí.

Information

AJ Cyber Café (Quito 16-19; per hr US$1) Internet access.

Andinatel (Quevedo near Maldonado) Telephone call center.

Banco de Guayaquil (Maldonado 7-20) Bank with ATM.

Captur (☎ 281-4968; cnr Sanchez de Orellana & Guayaquil, Plazoleta Santo Domingo) Tourist information.

Discovery Net (Salcedo 4-16; per hr US$1)

Post office (Quevedo near Maldonado)

Tourist Information (Panamericana s/n) Inside the main bus terminal.

Activities

Several tour operators offer day trips and two- to three-day climbing trips to Cotopaxi (opposite). Day trips cost US$35 to US$45 per person, depending on the size of your group. Two-day summit trips to Cotopaxi cost US$130 to US$150 per person – but make sure your guide is qualified and motivated. The following outfitters are all licensed by the department of tourism and have received positive reports from readers:

Expediciones Volcán Route (☎ 281-2452; volcanroute@hotmail.com; Salcedo 4-49)

Neiges (☎ 281-1199; neigestours@hotmail.com; Guayaquil near 2 de Mayo)

Tovar Expeditions (☎ 281-1333; reivajg1980@hotmail.com; Guayaquil 5-38)

Festivals & Events

Latacunga's major annual fiesta (September 23 and 24) honors La Virgen de las Mercedes. More popularly known as the **Fiesta de la Mamá Negra**, the event features processions, costumes, fireworks, street dancing and Andean music. This is one of those festivals that, although superficially Christian, has a strong indigenous influence and is truly worth seeing.

Sleeping

Hotels fill up fast on Wednesday afternoon for the Thursday-morning indigenous market at Saquisilí.

Residencial Amazonas (☎ 281-2673; F Valencia 47-36; r per person with shared/private bathroom US$3/5) Well, you can't beat the price. As for the rooms, they're decent enough for a night.

Residencial Santiago (☎ 280-0899; 2 de Mayo & Guayaquil; s/d with shared bathroom US$5.50/11, private bathroom US$6.75/13.50) Readers recommend this hospitable, no-frills hotel with turquoise walls and average size rooms.

Hotel Estambul (☎ 280-0354; Quevedo 644; r per person with shared/private bathroom US$8/10) This long-time favorite has lost much of its former friendliness, though the rooms remain spotless and comfy. Immaculate shared bathrooms.

Hotel Rosim (☎ 280-2172; Quito 16-49; s/d US$8/16) Clean, stark and friendly place with strong,

ECUADOR

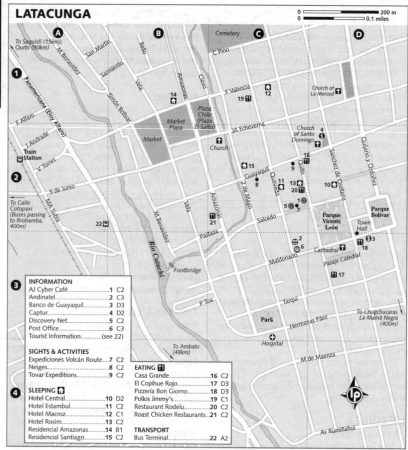

LATACUNGA

0 — 200 m
0 — 0.1 miles

hot showers and big white towels. Good value.

Hotel Central (☎ 280-2912; Sanchez de Orellana at Salcedo; s/d US$10/14) Homey decor, kitschy finishing touches (like c 1960s ceramic ashtrays) and friendliness make this one of the best deals in town.

Hotel Macroz (☎ 280-0907; hotelmakroz@latinmail .com; F Valencia 8-56; s/d US$15/25, two beds US$30) Black-and-gold 1980's decor and other amenities make this the swankiest pad in Latacunga. Breakfast included.

Eating

Latacunga's traditional dish is the *chugchucara*, a tasty, heart-attack-inducing plate of *fritada* (pieces of fried pork meat); *mote*

(hominy) with *chicharrón* (bits of fried pork skin); potatoes; fried banana; *tostada* (toasted corn); popcorn; and cheese *empanadas*. There are several *chugchucara* restaurants on Quijano y Ordoñez, a few blocks south of the town center. They're most busy on weekends, when families fill the tables and musicians stroll from door to door.

There are loads of cheap roast chicken restaurants along Amazonas between Salcedo and Guayaquil.

Casa Grande (cnr Quito & Guayaquil; almuerzos US$1.30; ☼ 7am-5pm Mon-Sat) Tiny, family-run place serving cheap *almuerzos*.

El Copihue Rojo (Quito 14-38; almuerzos US$2, mains US$3-5) Delicious daily *almuerzos*, plus meats, pastas and five types of soup.

Pollos Jimmy's (Quevedo 8-85 near Valencia; mains US$2.25-2.50) Pop in for delicious rotisserie chicken.

Chugchucaras La Mamá Negra (☎ 280-5401; Quijano y Ordoñez 1-67; chugchucara US$4; ☺ closed Mon) One of the best places for *chugchucaras*.

Pizzería Bon Giorno (cnr Sanchez de Orellana & Maldonado; mains US$4-7) Giant portions of hearty lasagna and good pizzas.

Restaurant Rodelu (☎ 280-0956; Quito 16-31; mains US$4-7) Good pizza, delicious breakfasts and passable espresso drinks.

Getting There & Away

Buses from Quito (US$1.50, two hours) will drop you at the **bus terminal** (Panamericana) if Latacunga is their final destination. If you're taking a bus that's continuing to Ambato or Riobamba, it will drop you at the corner of 5 de Junio and Cotopaxi, about five blocks west of the Panamericana. Buses to Ambato (US$1, 45 minutes) and Quito leave from the bus terminal. If you're heading south to Riobamba, it's easiest to catch a passing bus from the corner of 5 de Junio and Cotopaxi. Otherwise, bus to Ambato and change there.

From the terminal, Transportes Cotopaxi departs hourly for the rough but spectacular descent to Quevedo (US$3.75, 5½ hours) via Zumbahua (US$2, two hours). For transport information to other destinations on the Quilotoa Loop, see below.

THE QUILOTOA LOOP
☎ 03

Bumping along the spectacular dirt roads of the Quilotoa Loop and hiking between the area's Andean villages is one of Ecuador's most exhilarating adventures. Transport is tricky but the rewards are abundant: highland markets, the breathtaking crater lake of Laguna Quilotoa, splendid hikes, and traditional highland villages. Allow yourself *at least* three days for the loop and bring warm clothes (it gets painfully cold up here), water and snacks.

Latacunga to Zumbahua

Ten kilometers west of Latacunga, **Pujilí** has a Sunday market and interesting Corpus Christi and All Souls' Day celebrations. The road winds into the upper reaches of the *páramo*, passing the speck-like village of Tigua about 45km after Pujilí. Tigua is known for the bright paintings of Andean life made on sheepskin

canvases. Cozy lodging is available at **Posada de Tigua** (Hacienda Agrícola-Ganadera Tigua Chimbacucho; ☎ 281-3682, 280-0454; laposadadetigua@latinmail.com; vía Latacunga-Zumbahua Km 49; r per person half/full board US$17/23), a working dairy ranch; and **Samana Huasi** (☎ 281-4868, in Quito 02-256-3175; www.tigua .org; Km 53; dm, r & board per person US$19).

Some 15km west of Tigua, the tiny village of **Zumbahua** has a small but fascinating Saturday market and is surrounded by green patchwork peaks, a setting that makes for spectacular walking.

Accommodations and food in Zumbahua are basic. The town's three lodgings fill up fast on Friday, so get there early; the best of them is **Condor Matzi** (☎ 281-4611; s/d US$5/10), on the square.

Zumbahua to Saquisilí

From Zumbahua, buses and hired trucks trundle up the 14km of unpaved road leading north to one of Ecuador's most staggering sights – **Laguna Quilotoa**, a stunning volcanic crater lake. Near the crater rim are several extremely basic, inexpensive accommodations owned by friendly indigenous folks. Bring a warm sleeping bag.

About 14km north of the lake is the wee village of **Chugchilán**, which is an excellent base for hiking and has three lovely, traveler-friendly hotels. The best of them is the much-loved, North American-owned **Black Sheep Inn** (☎ 281-4587; www.blacksheepinn.com; dm/s/d/tr/q US$22.50/48/67/91/112; ☐ ☒), where rates include two delicious vegetarian meals. **Hostal Mama Hilda** (☎ 281-4814, in Quito 02-258-2957; www .hostalmamahilda.com; r per person with shared/private bathroom US$13/16) is friendly and popular with backpackers; rates include breakfast and dinner. Delightfully friendly **Hostal Cloud Forest** (☎ 281-4808; jose_cloudforest@hotmail.com; r per person with shared/private bathroom US$6/8) is the cheapest and simplest.

About 23km north of Chugchilán is the village of **Sigchos**, which has a couple of basic lodgings. From here, it's about 52km east to **Saquisilí**, home of one of the most important indigenous markets in the country. Each Thursday morning, inhabitants of remote indigenous villages, most of whom are recognized by their felt porkpie hats and red ponchos, descend upon the market in a cacophony of sound and color. Accommodations are available in a couple of cold-water cheapies in town.

ECUADOR

Getting There & Around

No buses go all the way around the loop. From Latacunga, they only travel as far as Chugchilán (US$4, four hours), and they either go clockwise (via Zumbahua and Quilotoa) or counterclockwise (via Sigchos). The bus via Zumbahua departs Latacunga's bus terminal daily at noon, passing Zumbahua at around 1:30pm, Laguna Quilotoa at around 2pm, arriving in Chugchilán at about 4pm. The bus via Sigchos departs daily at 11:30am, passing Saquisilí just before noon and Sigchos at around 2pm, arriving in Chugchilán at around 3:30pm; the Saturday bus via Sigchos leaves at 10:30am.

From Chugchilán, buses returning to Latacunga via Zumbahua leave Chugchilán Monday through Friday at 4am (good morning!), passing Quilotoa at around 6am, Zumbahua at around 6:30am, arriving in Latacunga at around 8am. On Saturday this bus leaves Chugchilán at 3am, and on Sunday at 6am and 10am. Buses via Sigchos leave Monday through Friday at 3am, passing Sigchos at around 4am, Saquisilí at around 7am, arriving in Latacunga at around 8am. On Saturday this bus departs at 7am. On Sunday you must switch buses in Sigchos.

A morning milk truck (US$1) leaves Chugchilán for Sigchos around 8:30am and will take passengers, allowing you to skip the predawn wakeup. In Zumbahua, trucks can be hired to Laguna Quilotoa or anywhere on the loop.

Don't worry – everyone's confused.

AMBATO

☎ 03 / pop 154,100

Ambato (elevation 2577m) takes warming up to. Compared to nearby Baños, it offers little for the traveler, except the chance to experience a totally non-touristy Ecuadorian city. Ambato's claims to fame are its chaotic **Monday markets**, one of the biggest in Ecuador; its flower festival, held in the second half of February; and its *quintas* (historic country homes) outside town. Above town, there are fabulous views of the puffing Volcán Tungurahua.

From the bus terminal, city buses marked 'Centro' go to Parque Cevallos (US20¢), the central plaza.

Information

Banco del Pacífico (cnr Lalama & Cevallos) Bank with ATM.
Banco del Pichincha (Lalama near Sucre) Bank with ATM.

Net Place (Juan Montalvo 05-58 near Cevallos; per hr US$1) Internet access.
Tourist office (☎ 282-1800; Guayaquil & Rocafuerte)

Sleeping & Eating

Ambato's biggest drawback is its choice of hotels. There are a couple of exceptions, but overall it's a dismal, overpriced lot, and comfort rarely seems to correlate with price.

Residencial América (JB Vela 737; s/d US$4/8) The best of the numerous cheap and basic hotels in the slightly seedy area around Parque 12 de Noviembre and the nearby Mercado Central, it offers shared bathrooms and tepid showers.

Hostal Señorial (☎ 282-5124; cnr Cevallos & Quito; s/d US$14.50/29) In a more attractive area and decorated in a way that only die-hard *Miami Vice* fans might appreciate, the Señorial has clean, carpeted rooms with telephones, cable TV and mirrored headboards (fun!).

Chifa Nueva Hong Kong (Bolívar 768; mains US$2-3) Whips out good, but standard Chinese food.

Pizzería Fornace (Cevallos 17-28; pizzas US$3-5) The best pizza and pasta in town.

El Alamo Chalet (Cevallos 17-19; mains US$3-6) Ecuadorian comfort food.

Getting There & Away

The bus terminal, 2km from the center of town, has many buses to Baños (US$1, one hour), Riobamba (US$1, one hour), Quito (US$2, 2½ hours) and Guayaquil (US$6, six hours). Less frequent are buses to Guaranda (US$2, 2½ hours), Cuenca (US$7, seven hours) and Tena (US$5, six hours).

BAÑOS

☎ 03 / pop 12,300

Hemmed in by luxuriant green peaks, blessed with steaming thermal bathrooms and adorned by a beautiful waterfall, Baños is one of Ecuador's most enticing and popular tourist destinations. Ecuadorians and foreigners alike flock here to hike, soak in the bathrooms, ride mountain bikes, zip around on rented quadrunners, volcano-watch, party, and break their molars on the town's famous *melcocha* (taffy). Touristy as it is, it's a wonderful place to hang out for a few days.

Baños (elevation 1800m) is also the gateway town into the jungle via Puyo (p705). East of Baños, the road drops spectacularly toward the upper Amazon Basin and the views are best taken in over the handlebars of a mountain bike, which you can rent in town.

Baños' annual fiesta is held on December 16 and preceding days.

Information

Andinatel (cnr Rocafuerte & Halflants) Telephone call center.

Banco del Pacífico (cnr Halflants & Rocafuerte) Bank with ATM.

Banco del Pichincha (cnr Ambato & Halflants) Bank with ATM.

CD Comp (Ambato near Alfaro; per hr US$2) Internet.

Direct Connect (Martínez near Alfaro; per hr US$2) Internet.

La Herradura (Martínez near Alfaro; per kilo US$1) Laundry.

Post office (Halflants near Ambato)

Tourist office (☎ 274-0483; mun_banos@andinanet .net; Halflants near Rocafuerte)

Sights

Pop into the **Basílica de Nuestra Señora de Agua Santa** (Ambato at 12 de Noviembre; admission free; ☽ 7am-4pm) for a look at the bizarre paintings of people being saved from auto accidents and natural disasters by the Virgin of the Holy Water – Baños' patron saint. The Virgin is honored for the entire month of October, when indigenous musicians flock to the streets. Above the church, a small **museum** (admission US50¢; ☽ 8am-5pm) houses an odd taxidermic display and traditional crafts exhibits.

Activities

A small town in a fabulous setting, Baños offers loads of outdoor fun.

HOT BATHS

Soaking in the hot baths with vacationing families and screaming children is what Baños is all about. Go early in the morning (ie before 7am) if you want peace. All of the baths have changing rooms and bathing suit rental. The only complex in town with hot bathrooms is **Piscina de La Virgen** (daytime/night US$1/1.20; ☽ 4:30am-5pm & 6-10pm), located by the waterfall. **Piscina El Salado** (admission US$1; ☽ 4:30am-5pm), 2km west of town, is similar but has more pools of different temperatures. Catch the bus on Rocafuerte, near the market.

HIKING

Baños has some great hiking. The tourist office provides a crude but useful map showing some of the trails around town.

From the bus terminal, a short trail leads to Puente San Francisco (San Francisco Bridge), across Río Pastaza. Continue up the other side as far as you want.

At the southern end of Maldonado a footpath leads to Bellavista (the white cross high over Baños) and then to the settlement of Runtún, two hours away. South on Mera, a footpath leads to the **Mirador de La Virgen del Agua Santa** and on to Runtún.

CLIMBING & TREKKING

Climbers are advised not to ascend the currently active Volcán Tungurahua (5016m), which rumbled back to life in 1999 and had a major eruption in August, 2006 (see p683). The refuge on that volcano has been destroyed; although some people climbed up to the site before the 2006 eruption, to do so now would be suicidal. The volcano is part of **Parque Nacional Sangay** (admission US$20).

Climbs of Cotopaxi and Chimborazo can be arranged. Reputable climbing outfitters are **Expediciones Amazónicas** (☎ 274-0506; amazon icas2002@yahoo.com; Oriente 11-68 near Halflants) and **Rainforestur** (☎ 274-0743; www.rainforestur.com.ec; Ambato 800). The going rate for climbs with a minimum of two people is US$65 to US$80 per person per day, plus park fees.

MOUNTAIN BIKING

Numerous companies rent bikes for about US$5 per day. Check the equipment carefully. The best paved ride is the dramatic descent to Puyo, about 60km away by road. Be sure to stop at the spectacular **Pailón del Diablo**, a waterfall about 18km from Baños. There is a passport control at the town of Shell so carry your documents. From Puyo (or anywhere along the way) take a bus back to Baños with the bike on the roof.

HORSE-RIDING

You can rent horses for about US$10 per half day (more with a guide) through **Ángel Aldáz** (☎ 274-0175; Montalvo near Mera) and **José & Two Dogs** (☎ 274-0746; josebalu_99@yahoo.com; Maldonado & Martínez). **Hostal Isla de Baños** (☎ 274-0609, 274-1511; islabanos@andinanet.net; Halflants 1-31) offers guided half-day and multi-day horse-riding trips.

RIVER-RAFTING

GeoTours (☎ 03-274-1344; www.ecuadorexplorer.com /geotours; Ambato at Halflants) offers half-day trips

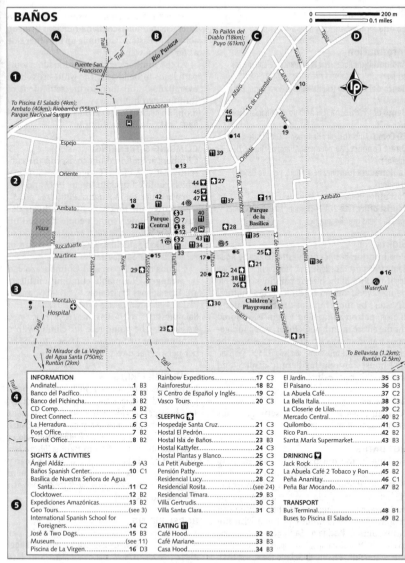

BAÑOS

on the Río Patate for US$30 and full-day trips on the Río Pastaza (class IV-V) for US$100. The full-day trip is 10 hours, with four hours on the river. Prices include food, transportation, guides and equipment. It also offers a three-day kayaking course ($150). **Rainforestur** (☎ 274-0743; www.rainforestur.com.ec; Ambato 800) also offers rafting trips.

JUNGLE TRIPS

Loads of jungle trips are advertised from Baños, but not all guides are experienced. Those listed here have received good reports. Three- to seven-day jungle tours cost about US$30 to US$50 per person per day, depending on the destination. Most trips set up in Baños route you through Quito anyway, so

ERUPTION NEAR BAÑOS

In 1999, after nearby Volcán Tungurahua erupted back to life, Baños was evacuated for months. Activity decreased, and things went back to normal until May, 2006, when once again the volcano spewed huge clouds of hot gas, prompting President Alfredo Palacio to declare a state of emergency. Then, on August 17 2006, the volcano erupted violently, destroying nearby villages, closing the Riobamba–Baños road and forcing the partial evacuation of Baños once again. If you plan to travel to Baños or nearby villages, keep yourself appraised of potential dangers, and check the weekly updates in English at Global Volcanism Program (www.volcano.si.edu) and in Spanish at the Instituto Geofísico (www.igepn.edu.ec). Also note that travel times to/from Riobamba and Ambato will likely be effected indefinitely.

savings aren't significant. You won't see animals in the forests nearer Baños; if you want primary rainforest, make sure you're going as deep as the lower Río Napo area (p701).

Owned by a member of the Shuar community (an indigenous group from the southern Oriente), **Rainbow Expeditions** (☎ 274-2957, 09-895-7786; rainbowexpeditions2005@hotmail.com; Alfaro at Martínez) is an extremely well-run operation with interesting trips. Other recommended operators are **Rainforestur** (☎ 274-0743; www.rainforestur.com.ec; Ambato 800) and **Vasco Tours** (☎ 274-1017; www.vascotours.banios.com; Alfaro near Martínez). For more tour information, see p659.

Courses

One-on-one Spanish classes start around US$4.50 and are offered at the following places:

Baños Spanish Center (☎ 274-0632; www.spanishcenter.banios.com; Oriente 8-20 near Cañar)
International Spanish School for Foreigners (☎ 274-0612; 16 de Diciembre & Espejo)
Si Centro de Español y Inglés (☎ 274-0360; Páez near Oriente)

Sleeping

There are scores of hotels in Baños, and competition is stiff, so prices are low. Rates are highest on Friday evenings and holiday weekends when every hotel in town can fill up.

Hostal Plantas y Blanco (☎ 274-0044; option3@hotmail.com; Martínez at 12 de Noviembre; r per person US$4.50-7.50; 🖳) Attractively decorated and eternally popular, 'Plants and White' (you figure it out) scores big points with travelers for its rooftop terrace, outstanding breakfasts, on-site steam bathroom and overall value.

Hospedaje Santa Cruz (☎ 274-0648; santacruzhostal@yahoo.com; 16 de Diciembre; r per person US$5-7) Great value for spacious rooms with bathroom and hot water. Rooms are a bit low on light, but

there's an overgrown garden where you can get all the sun you need.

La Petit Auberge (☎ 274-0936; reservation_banos@hotmail.com; 16 de Diciembre; dm US$6, s/d US$10/16, with fireplace US$12/20) With a rustic, cozy cabin-like feel, this is a fabulous deal and especially homey if you nab one of the pricier rooms with a fireplace.

Posada El Marqués (☎ 274-0053; www.marquesbanios.com; Pje V Ibarra; r per person US$8.50) Colorfully painted indigenous motifs adorn the airy rooms of this comfortable hotel at the end of a quiet street. Conveniently close to Piscina de La Virgen bathrooms.

Hostal El Pedrón (☎ 274-0701; www.elpedron.banos .com; Alfaro near Martínez; r per person with shared/private bathroom US$9/13.50) This rustic old-timer boasts the biggest garden in town, complete with a few hammocks and chairs strewn around. Rooms are well worn but clean.

Villa Santa Clara (☎ 274-0349; www.hotelvillasanta clara.com; 12 de Noviembre; s/d US$10/20; 🖳) Considering the swimming pool, this is a good deal for simple motel-style rooms opening on to a sparse concrete patio area. Kitchen privileges.

Hostal Isla de Baños (☎ 274-0609, 274-1511; isla banos@andinanet.net; Halflants 1-31; s/d incl breakfast US$14.50/24.50) This quiet, German-run *hostal* is set in attractive gardens and boasts cheerful, clean rooms with brick walls and lots of Andean art. The pricier rooms have balconies.

Villa Gertrudis (☎ 274-0441; www.villagertrudis.com; Montalvo 20-75; s/d US$15/30; 🖳) Low-key and quiet, Villa Gertrudis has a beautiful garden, c 1960s wood furniture, hardwood floors and a relaxing vacationy feel. Prices include breakfast and use of the indoor pool across the street.

Other long-standing and totally acceptable hotels include:

Residencial Lucy (☎ 274-0466; Rocafuerte 2-40; r per person with shared/private bathroom US$3/5) Three-floor motel-like structure; fine for a night or two.

Residencial Rosita (☎ 274-0396; 16 de Diciembre near Martínez; r per person with shared/private bathroom US$4/5) Big rooms, shared bathrooms. Two apartments.

Residencial Timara (☎ 274-0599; www.timara .banios.com; Maldonado; r per person with shared/private bathroom US$4/8) Best of the super-cheapies, assuming you go for the shared bathroom.

Pensión Patty (☎ 274-0202; Alfaro 5-56; r per person US$4.50) Well-known, family-run, dark and funky. Old climbers' favorite. Shared showers.

Hostal Kattyfer (☎ 274-1559; hostalkattyfer@hotmail .com; 16 de Diciembre near Martínez; r per person US$5) Large, simple rooms and a guest kitchen.

Eating

Restaurants line the pedestrian section of Ambato between the basilica and Parque Central; they're great for people-watching, but the food is generally mediocre. Hit the side streets for the best restaurants. Most restaurants cater to travelers and stay open late. Baños is famous for its *melcocha*; makers pull it from wooden pegs in doorways around town.

Mercado Central (Alfaro & Rocafuerte; almuerzos US$1.50) For fresh fruits and vegetables and cheap, cheap *almuerzos*, visit the town's central market.

Rico Pan (Ambato near Maldonado; breakfast US$2-3) Best bread in town and great breakfasts.

La Abuela Café (Ambato near 16 de Diciembre; mains US$2-4) Pastas, chicken dishes, steaks, Mexican plates and veggie options make for a varied menu, and the *almuerzos* are cheap. Good atmosphere.

El Paisano (Vieira at Martínez; mains US$2.50-4.50) Despite the bright florescent lighting and faint smell of paint, El Paisano serves up some of the most nurturing veggie food in town.

Casa Hood (Martínez at Halflants; mains US$3-4) A giant hearth warms the dining room, the book exchange is the best in town, and the food – lasagna, blackened sea bass, Pad Thai, veggie plates, falafel and more – is delicious.

La Bella Italia (16 de Diciembre; mains US$3-5) Little and friendly Bella Italia serves delicious Italian food.

La Closerie de Lilas (Alfaro 6-20; mains US$3-5) Great little family-run place (kids included) serving steaks, trout and pastas.

Café Hood (Maldonado, Parque Central; mains US$3-6) Some of the dishes here are simply excellent, such as the soft tacos or the chickpeas and spinach in curry sauce. Lots of veggie options.

Quilombo (cnr Montalvo & 12 de Noviembre; mains US$3-6; ☯ Wed-Sun) *Quilombo* means 'mess' or 'insanity' in Argentine slang – come see why it's a fitting name for this excellent Argentine grill house.

El Jardín (Parque de la Basílica; mains US$3-6) Popular hangout with a leafy outdoor patio and a variety of dishes and sandwiches.

Café Mariane (Halflants & Rocafuerte; mains US$4-6) Excellent French-Mediterranean cuisine at reasonable prices.

Santa María Supermarket (cnr Alfaro & Rocafuerte) Stock up here.

Drinking & Entertainment

Nightlife in Baños means dancing in local *peñas* and hanging out in bars. The best place to barhop is the two-block strip along Alfaro, north of Ambato.

Jack Rock (Alfaro 5-41; ☯ 7pm-2am) British pub meets Hard Rock Café; there's dancing on weekends.

La Abuela Café 2 Tobaco y Ron (Alfaro near Oriente; ☯ 4pm-2am) Wee place with karaoke and a great little balcony.

Peña Ananitay (16 de Diciembre near Espejo; ☯ 9pm-3am) Catch live *música folklórica* here.

Peña Bar Mocando (Alfaro near Ambato; ☯ 4pm-2am) Eternally popular bar with sidewalk seating and a party atmosphere.

Getting There & Away

From many towns, it may be quicker to change buses in Ambato, where there are frequent buses to Baños (US90¢, one hour).

From Baños' **bus terminal** (Espejo & Reyes), many buses leave for Quito (US$3.50, 3½ hours), Puyo (US$2, two hours) and Tena (US$4, five hours). The road to Riobamba ($1, one hour) via Penipe recently reopened, so buses no longer need to drive via Ambato.

GUARANDA

☎ 03 / pop 20,474

Despite being the capital of Bolívar province, Guaranda (elevation 2670m) is small enough and removed enough that residents still take to staring at foreigners when they roll into town. It's a dignified, provincial place with beautiful old adobe buildings, crumbling wooden balconies, Spanish tiled roofs and a handsome central plaza. The roads from Riobamba and Ambato offer mind-blowing views of Chimborazo. Guaranda celebrates Carnaval vigorously.

Information

Andinatel (Rocafuerte near Pichincha) Telephone call center.

Banco del Pichincha (Azuay) Bank with ATM; no traveler's checks.

Post office (Azuay near Pichincha)

Sleeping & Eating

Hotel Bolívar (☎ 298-0547; Sucre 7-04; s/d US$8/16) Two floors of pleasant, simple rooms surround a straightforward courtyard. There's a good restaurant and a great café attached.

Hostal de las Flores (☎ 298-0644; Pichincha 4-02; r per person with shared/private bathroom US$8/9) Guaranda's most traveler-oriented hotel is a pretty place in a lovingly refurbished old building.

Los 7 Santos (Convención de 1884 near 10 de Agosto; mains US$1-3) Quite possibly the best reason to come to Guaranda, Los 7 Santos is the town's one traveler refuge, an artsy bar-café with three generations – grandma, mother and son – at the helm. Snacks, light meals and breakfast are available.

La Bohemia (Convención de 1884 & 10 de Agosto; mains US$2-4) Cozied up with grain sacks on the ceilings and serving delicious cheap *almuerzos* (US$2), this family run joint is easily one of the town's best. Chase your meal down with one of the giant *batidos* (fruit shakes).

Pizzería Buon Giorno (Sucre at García Moreno; pizzas US$3.50-7) Fluffy-crust pizzas, lasagna and burgers.

Queseras de Bolívar (Av Gral Enriquez) Stock up here on the province's famous cheeses, chocolate and other treats.

Getting There & Away

The bus terminal is half a kilometer east of downtown just off Ave de Carvajal. Buses run to Ambato (US$2, two hours), Quito (US$4.50, five hours), Riobamba (US$2, two hours) and Guayaquil (US$4, five hours). The trip to Guayaquil is spectacular.

SALINAS

☎ 03 / pop 1000

Set in wild, beautiful countryside and famous for its excellent cheeses, salamis, divine chocolate and rough-spun sweaters, the tiny mountain village of Salinas, 35km north of Guaranda, makes for an interesting jaunt off the beaten track. The elevation is a whopping 3550m. Facing the main plaza, the **tourist office** (☎ 239-0022; www.salinerito.com) will organize visits to Salinas' unique cooperatives.

Above the plaza, **El Refugio** (☎ 239-0024; dm US$6, r with bathroom per person US$8) is a clean, comfortable *hostal* run by the local youth group. Buses to Salinas leave Plaza Roja in Guaranda at 6am and 7am daily and hourly from 10am to 4pm Monday through Friday.

RIOBAMBA

☎ 03 / pop 126,100

Deemed 'the Sultan of the Andes', Riobamba (elevation 2750m) is a traditional, old-fashioned city that both bores and delights travelers. It's sedate yet handsome, with wide avenues and random mismatched shops tucked into imposing 18th- and 19th-century stone buildings. The city is both the starting point for the spectacular train ride down the **Nariz del Diablo** (Devil's Nose), and one of the best places in the country to hire mountain guides.

Information

Andinatel (Tarqui at Veloz) Telephone call center.

Banco de Guayaquil (Primera Constituyente at García Moreno) Bank with ATM.

Café Digital (Rocafuerte near 10 de Agosto; per hr US70¢) Internet access.

Lavandería Donini (Villaroel near Larrea; per kilo US80¢) Laundry.

Parque Nacional Sangay Office (☎ 295 3041; parquesangay@andinanet.net; Av 9 de Octubre near Duchicela; ⏰ 8am-1pm & 2-5pm Mon-Fri) Get information and pay entry fees to Parque Nacional Sangay here.

Post office (Espejo & 10 de Agosto)

Sights

On **market day** (Saturday), Riobamba's streets become a hive of activity, especially along the streets northeast of Parque de la Concepción.

The renowned **Museo de Arte Religioso** (☎ 296-5212; Argentinos; admission US$2; ⏰ 9am-noon & 3-6pm Tue-Sat), in the restored Iglesia de La Concepción, houses a morbid and fascinating collection of religious art. Its signature piece is a priceless, meter-tall gold monstrance inlaid with more than 1500 precious stones.

Activities

Thanks to the proximity of Volcán Chimborazo, Riobamba is one of Ecuador's most important climbing towns. Two-day summit trips start around US$140 per person for Chimborazo ($160 for Cotopaxi) and include guides, climbing gear, transportation and meals. Rates rarely include park entrance fees (US$10 to US$20).

Mountain biking is also gaining ground, and day trips start at US$35 per person. Downhill descents from the refuge on Chimborazo are adrenaline-charged and worth every penny.

Recommended operators:

Andes-trek (☎ 295-1275, 09-929-8076; www.andes -trek.com; Colón 22-25) Climbing operator.

Expediciones Julio Verne (☎ 296-3436, after 6pm ☎ 296-0398; www.julioverne-travel.com; El Espectador 22-25) Climbing, mountain biking and more. Dutch and English spoken.

Pro Bici main office (☎ 295-1759; Primera Constituyente 23-51 & 23-40); annex (Primera Constituyente near Larrea) Outstanding mountain bike trips and rentals. English spoken.

Veloz Coronado Expeditions (☎ 296-0916; www .velozexpediciones.com; Chile 33-21 at Francia) Outstanding climbing operator.

Sleeping

The best hotels are in the town center, nearly 2km east of the bus terminal. Budget hotels tend to be pretty dingy.

Hotel Los Shyris (☎ 296-0323; Rocafuerte 21-60 & 10 de Agosto; r per person with shared/private bathroom US$6/7) The large and modernish Hotel LosShyris is a great value for its central location and clean rooms. Slim on character, but lots of sunlight.

Hostal Oasis (☎ 296-1210; Veloz 15-32; r per person US$7) When it comes to friendliness, value and down-home cutesiness, it's hard to beat Oasis. Rooms are centered around a garden, complete with a llama and two squawking parrots. Free transport to/from train and bus stations.

Hotel Tren Dorado (☎ 296-4890; htrendorado@hotmail .com; Carabobo 22-35; r per person US$9) Conveniently close to the train station, the friendly Tren Dorado has spotless, comfortable, flowery rooms that would make Martha Stewart proud. A self-serve breakfast ($3 extra) is served at 5:30am on train days.

La Estación (☎ 295-5226; Unidad Nacional 29-15 near Carabobo; s/d US$10/20) Colorful rooms make for a cheerful stay at this friendly hotel across the street from the train station.

If everything else is full, you'll be fine at:

Residencial Ñuca Huasi (☎ 296-6669; 10 de Agosto 10-24; r per person with shared/private bathroom US$3/5) Old backpacker haunt in desperate need of a facelift.

Hotel Imperial (☎ 296-0429; Rocafuerte 22-15;

r per person with shared/private bathroom US$5/6) Clean, friendly and noisy.

Hotel Segovia (☎ 09-445-9626; Primera Constituyente 22-26; r per person US$6) Drab and impersonal but secure and clean.

Eating

La Abuela Rosa (Brasil 37-57 at Esmeraldas; mains US80¢-$1.50) Drop by Grandma Rosa's for *comida típica* (traditional Ecuadorian food) and tasty snacks.

Mercado La Merced (Mercado M Borja; Guayaquil btwn Espejo & Colón; mains US$1-3) Even if you don't like Ecuador's classic *hornado* (whole roast pig), it's worth wandering into this clean market where saleswomen shout things like 'Hey handsome, try *this* pork!' over giant roasted-brown pig carcasses. Best on Saturday.

Natural Food (Tarqui near Primera Constituyente; almuerzos US$1.50) Herbivores, beeline it to Natural Food for delicious, hearty (and cheap!) vegetarian *almuerzos*.

Pizzería San Valentin (Av León Borja & Torres; mains US$2-5) The cornerstone of Riobamba's nightlife, San Valentin is great for both eating and socializing.

Sierra Nevada (Primera Constituyente 27-38; mains US$3-4) Serves excellent seafood and Ecuadorian dishes and likely the best *almuerzos* in town (US$3).

El Rey del Burrito (Av León Borja 38-36; mains US$3-5) Serves Mexican classics like burritos, tacos and enchiladas.

El Chacarero (5 de Junio 21-46; mains US$3.50-5) Great atmosphere, great pizza. Skip the pasta dishes.

La Parrillada de Fausto (Uruguay 20-38; mains US$4-6) This fun, Argentine-style grill serves great barbequed steaks, trout and chicken in a ranch-style setting.

Entertainment

Nightlife, limited as it is, centers around the intersection of Av León Borja and Torres and northwest along León Borja. On weekends the area turns into a teen madhouse. **Pizzería San Valentin** (Av León Borja & Torres) is the epicenter. Nearby, **Tentadero** (Av León Borja near Ángel Leon; admission US$3; ⊙ 8pm-late Fri & Sat) is the town's spiciest *discoteca*, spinning electronica and salsa well into the night.

Getting There & Away
BUS

The **main bus terminal** (☎ 296-2005; Av León Borja at Av de la Prensa) is 2km *northwest* of the center. Buses

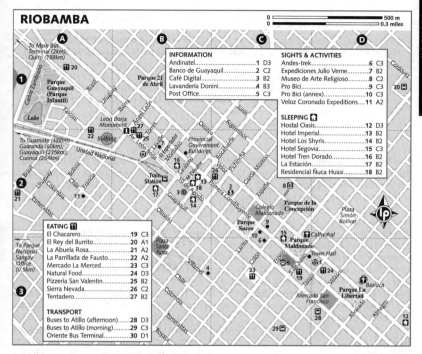

RIOBAMBA

0 ___ 500 m
0 ___ 0.3 miles

INFORMATION	
Andinatel	1 D3
Banco de Guayaquil	2 C2
Café Digital	3 B2
Lavandería Donini	4 B3
Post Office	5 C3

SIGHTS & ACTIVITIES	
Andes-trek	6 C3
Expediciones Julio Verne	7 B2
Museo de Arte Religioso	8 C2
Pro Bici	9 C3
Pro Bici (annex)	10 C3
Veloz Coronado Expeditions	11 A2

SLEEPING	
Hostal Oasis	12 D3
Hotel Imperial	13 B2
Hotel Los Shyris	14 B2
Hotel Segovia	15 B2
Hotel Tren Dorado	16 B2
La Estación	17 B2
Residencial Ñuca Huasi	18 B2

EATING	
El Chacarero	19 C3
El Rey del Burrito	20 A1
La Abuela Rosa	21 A2
La Parrillada de Fausto	22 A2
Mercado La Merced	23 C3
Natural Food	24 D3
Pizzería San Valentin	25 B2
Sierra Nevada	26 C2
Tentadero	27 B2

TRANSPORT	
Buses to Atillo (afternoon)	28 D3
Buses to Atillo (morning)	29 C3
Oriente Bus Terminal	30 D1

run frequently to Quito (US$4, four hours), Guayaquil (US$4.75, five hours) and Alausí (US$1.50, two hours), and less frequently to Cuenca (US$6, six hours). There's at least one morning bus to Machala ($6, six to seven hours). Local buses run along Av León Borja, connecting the terminal with downtown.

Buses to Baños (US$1, one hour) and the Oriente leave from the **Oriente bus terminal** (Espejo & Luz Elisa Borja) just northeast of the center.

TRAIN

The spectacular train ride to Sibambe (US$11, five hours) begins in Riobamba. The train stops in Alausí (p688) just before trudging down the world-famous, hair-raising switchbacks known as the **Nariz del Diablo**. From Sibambe, the train immediately makes a return trip to Riobamba, stopping again in Alausí. Most people get off at Alausí and either spend the night or head back to Riobamba by bus. The train departs Riobamba on Wednesday, Friday and Sunday at 7am. Buy tickets at the **train station** (☎ 03-296-1909; Av León Borja at Unidad Nacional) either the day before, or from 6am on departure day. Roof riding is

now prohibited. If you're buying tickets for friends, bring their passports.

VOLCÁN CHIMBORAZO

Not only is the extinct Volcán Chimborazo the highest mountain in Ecuador, but its peak (6310m), due to the earth's equatorial bulge, is also the furthest point from the center of the earth – tell that to your K2-climbing buddies. The mountain is part of **La Reserva de Producción de Fauna Chimborazo** (admission US$10), which also encompasses **Volcán Carihuairazo** (5020m).

To simply get close to the beast, you can hire a truck-taxi in Riobamba (ask at your hotel) for about US$25. The driver will take you to the lower of two **climbers' refuges** (beds US$10) at 4800m and wait while you hike 200m to the upper refuge. Climbers who plan on staying more than a day can arrange a return trip for a later day, most likely paying another US$12 per person. The refuges have mattresses, water and cooking facilities; bring warm sleeping bags.

Climbing beyond the refuge requires snow- and ice-climbing gear and mountaineering experience, as does the ascent of Carihuairazo.

DETOUR: LAGUNAS DE ATILLO

With the 2005/2006 completion of a road from Guamote (a small town south of Riobamba) to Macas (in the southern Oriente), a spectacular sector of **Parque Nacional Sangay** (admission US$20) is suddenly accessible: the *páramo* lakes region of Lagunas de Atillo. From the village of **Atillo**, it's possible to hike, in six to eight hours, over a ridge to the beautiful Lagunas de Ozogoche. After exploring the region, you can make your way from Atillo down to Macas by bus, an infrequently traveled route. From Riobamba, Cooperativa Unidos buses to Atillo leave at 5:45am and 3pm from near Plaza San Francisco. Get hiking directions in Atillo. More information is available at the Parque Nacional Sangay office in Riobamba (see Information, p685).

Contact one of the recommended guide outfits listed under Riobamba (p685) or Quito (p658). Avoid inexperienced guides; a climb at this altitude is not to be taken lightly.

There are also excellent trekking opportunities between the two mountains. Topographical maps of the region are available at the IGM in Quito (p648). June through September is the dry season in this region, and the nights are very cold year-round.

If you're up for an 8km walk (not easy at this altitude), you can take a Guaranda-bound bus from Riobamba and ask the driver to drop you at the park entrance road.

ALAUSÍ

☎ 03 / pop 5570

The busy little railroad town of Alausí (elevation 2350m) is the last place the train passes through before its descent down the famous Nariz del Diablo. Many jump on the train here, rather than in Riobamba, though you're more likely to score a good seat in Riobamba (see p687).

Many hotels are found along the one main street (Av 5 de Junio), and most fill up on Saturday night. Spotless **Hotel Europa** (☎ 293-0200; 5 de Junio 175 at Orozco; s shared/private bathroom US$5/8, d US$8/14) is one of the best. You'll also be fine at **Hotel Americano** (☎ 293-0159; García Moreno 159; r per person US$5), near the train station, or family-run **Hotel Tequendama** (☎ 293-0123; 5 de Junio 152; s/d US$5/10).

Apart from the hotel restaurants, you'll find a couple of basic eateries along the main street.

Buses run hourly to/from Riobamba (US$1.50, 1½ hours), and several buses a day also go to Cuenca (US$4, four hours).

The train from Riobamba to Sibambe stops in Alausí before heading down the Nariz del Diablo (US$11 round trip). Tickets go on sale at 7am. It takes about two hours to reach Sibambe, where the train immediately changes course to return to Riobamba. Riding on the roof is allowed (and encouraged!), although it's often full with passengers from Riobamba.

THE SOUTHERN HIGHLANDS

As you roll down the Panamericana into the southern highlands, the giant snowcapped peaks of the central highlands fade from the rearview mirror. The climate gets a bit warmer, distances between towns become greater, and the decades clunk down by the wayside. Cuenca – arguably Ecuador's most beautiful city – and handsome little Loja are the region's only sizable towns.

Although you won't be out scaling glaciers down here, outdoor activities abound. The lake-studded Parque Nacional Cajas offers excellent hiking and camping, and in Parque Nacional Podocarpus you can explore cloud forest, tropical humid forest and *páramo* within the same park. From the laid-back gringo hang-out of Vilcabamba, you can spend days walking or horse-riding through the mysterious mountainside, returning each evening to massages, vegetarian food and hot tubs.

CUENCA

☎ 07 / pop 417,000

Comparing the colonial beauty of Cuenca and Quito is a favorite pastime around here. In grandeur, Quito wins hands down. But Cuenca – that tidy jewel of the south – takes the cake when it comes to charm. Its narrow cobblestone streets and whitewashed red-tiled buildings, its handsome plazas and domed churches, and its setting above the grassy banks of the Río Tomebamba, all create a city that's supremely impressive. Though firmly anchored in its colonial past, Ecuador's third largest city (elevation 2530m) also has a modern edge, with international restaurants, art galleries, cool cafés and welcoming bars tucked into its magnificent architecture.

Information

INTERNET ACCESS
The following charge about US$1 per hour.
Bapu Net (Presidente Córdova 9-21)
Cuenca Net (cnr Calle Larga & Hermano Miguel)
Cybercom (cnr Presidente Córdova & Borrero)
Dot Com (Hermano Miguel near Presidente Córdova)

LAUNDRY
Fast Klín (Hermano Miguel 4-21)
Lavahora (Honorato Vásquez 6-76)

MEDICAL SERVICES
Clínica Santa Inés (☎ 281-7888; Daniel Córdova 2-113) Consultations at this clinic cost about US$20.

MONEY
Banco de Guayaquil (Mariscal Sucre at Borrero) Bank with ATM.
Banco del Pichincha (cnr Solando & 12 de Abril) Bank with ATM.

POST
Post office (cnr Gran Colombia & Borrero)

TELEPHONE
Etapa (Benigno Malo 7-26) Telephone call center.

TOURIST INFORMATION
Bus Terminal Information office (☎ 284-3888; Bus Terminal)
Tourist information (iTur; ☎ 282-1035; i_tur@cuenca .gov.ec; Mariscal Sucre at Luís Cordero) Extremely helpful; English spoken.

Sights
Be sure to take a walk along 3 de Noviembre, which follows the northern bank of the **Río Tomebamba**. The river is lined with colonial buildings, and women still dry their laundry on the river's grassy banks. A patch of **Inca ruins** lie near the river, between the east end of Calle Larga and Av Todos Los Santos. Most of the stonework was destroyed to build colonial buildings, but there are some fine niches and walls.

Parque Calderón (Benigno Malo at Simón Bolívar), the main plaza, is dominated by the handsome '**new cathedral**' (c 1885), with its huge blue domes. Opposite stands the diminutive '**old cathedral**' (construction began in 1557), known as El Sagrario.

Go smell the flowers (or at least snap a photo of them) at the **flower market** in front of the wee colonial church on **Plazoleta del Carmen** (Padre Aguirre at Mariscal Sucre). Afterwards, hoof it over to the quiet **Plaza de San Sebastián** (cnr Mariscal Sucre & Talbot) and check out the **Museo de Arte Moderno** (Mariscal Sucre at Talbot; admission by donation; 🕙 9am-1pm & 3-6:30pm Mon-Fri, 9am-1pm Sat & Sun), which has a small exhibit of contemporary local art.

Cuenca's most important museum, the **Museo del Banco Central 'Pumapungo'** (www.museo pumapungo.com; Calle Larga near Huayna Capac; admission US$3; 🕙 9am-6pm Mon-Fri, 9am-1pm Sat) merits a visit for the fabulous ethnographic exhibit alone, not to mention the entrancing display of *tsantsas* (shrunken heads).

Museo de las Culturas Aborígenes (Calle Larga 5-24; admission US$2; 🕙 9am-6:30pm Mon-Fri, 9am-1pm Sat) houses an excellent collection of over 5000 archaeological pieces representative of about 20 Ecuadorian pre-Colombian cultures. The worthwhile **Museo de Artes Populares** (Cidap; Hermano Miguel 3-23; admission free; 🕙 9:30am-1pm & 2-6pm Mon-Fri, 10am-1pm Sat) displays changing exhibits of traditional indigenous costumes, handicrafts and artwork from around Latin America.

Activities
Cuenca is an excellent base for exploring – by foot, horse or bike – nearby attractions such as Parque Nacional Cajas, the Inca ruins of Ingapirca and indigenous villages. Head out on your own or set yourself up at one of the tour operators listed following. Day trips average US$35 to US$40 per person; note that park entrance fees are generally not included in the cost.
Expediciones Apullacta (☎ 283-7815, 283-7681; www.apullacta.com; Gran Colombia 11-02) Day tours to Ingapirca and Cajas.
Ecotrek (☎ 284-1927, 283-4677; ecotrex@az.pro.ec; Calle Larga 7-108) Recommended for trekking, mountaineering and Amazon travel.
Humberto Chico (contact Cabañas Yanuncay, ☎ 07-288-3716, 281-9681; yanuncay@etapa.com.ec; Calle Canton Gualaceo 2-149) Guides overnight trips to Cajas, the southern Oriente and elsewhere.

ECUADOR

Mamá Kinua Cultural Center (☎ 284-0610; Torres 7-45, Casa de la Mujer) Excellent Quichua-run cultural tours. Great organization.

Terra Diversa Travel Center (☎ 282-3782; www .terradiversa.com; Hermano Miguel 5-42) Horse-riding, mountain biking and hiking, Ingapirca trips, and three-hour city tours (US$15).

Courses

Cuenca's a wonderful place to study Spanish. One-on-one classes cost US$5 to US$7 per hour.

Abraham Lincoln Cultural Center (☎ 07-282-3898; rboroto@cena.or.ec; Borrero 5-18)

Amazing Grace (☎ 283-5003; Mariscal Lamar 6-56) Good for advanced students.

Centro de Estudios Interamericanos (☎ 283-9003, 282-3452; info@cedei.org; Gran Colombia 11-02) Offers courses in Spanish, Quichua, Latin American literature and indigenous culture.

Sampere (☎ 282-3960; www.sampere.com/cuenca; Hermano Miguel 3-43)

Festivals & Events

Cuenca's independence as a city is celebrated on November 3 with a major fiesta. Christmas Eve parades are very colorful. The founding of Cuenca (April 10-13) and Corpus Christi are also busy holidays. Carnaval is celebrated with boisterous water fights.

Sleeping

Cuenca has a great selection of hotels, but prices are a tad higher than elsewhere.

Hotel Norte (☎ 282-7881; Cueva 11-63; r per person with shared/private bathroom US$4/6) Best of the cheap hotels around the Plaza Rotary market.

Hostal Paredes (☎ 283-5674; Luís Cordero 11-29; r per person with shared/private bathroom US$4/6) Paredes is a whacky, friendly place in an early 20th-century building. Dali-esque paintings adorn the walls, plants fill the lobby, and a few caged parakeets compliment the quirkiness. Great deal.

Hotel Pichincha (☎ 282-3868; karolina7a@hotmail .com; Torres 8-82; r per person US$4.50) Mammoth by Cuenca standards, this impersonal 60-roomer is fair value and popular with backpackers and Ecuadorians alike. Rooms are clean but the shared bathrooms are pretty shabby.

El Cafecito (☎ 283-2337; www.cafécito.net; Honorato Vásquez 7-36; dm US$5, r with private bathroom US$15) Party paaad! That, and it has a great café full of cigarette-smoking, coffee-jacked travelers

munchin' tasty snacks. It can be noisy, but some love the scene.

Verde Limón (☎ 283-1509, 282-0300; www.verde limonhostal.com; Jaramillo 4-89 near Cueva; dm US$6, r per person US$7; ▣) 'Green Lime,' refers to the neon-green walls that make this little hostel almost blindingly vibrant. Though the kitchen could use some sprucing up, it's a good value.

Hostal El Monasterio (☎ 282-4457; Padre Aguirre 7-24; r per person with shared/private bathroom US$6/8) This six-floor hotel boasts stunning views from its communal kitchen and eating areas, and the rooms are comfy and clean.

Hostal El Monarca (☎ 283-6462; hostalmonarca@ hotmail.com; Borrero 5-47; s/d US$7/14) Earthy orange walls, groovy art and the life-is-good-let's-turn-up-the-music vibe is just what some of us road monkeys need. Bathrooms are shared.

Casa Naranja (Naranja Lodging; ☎ 282-5415, 288-3820; www.casanaranja.galeon.com; Mariscal Lamar 10-38 near Padre Aguirre; s US$8-15, d US$12-18) With stunning results, a local *cuencana* artist turned her 100-year-old family home into a modest but delightfully artsy guesthouse. Rooms are simple; communal kitchen.

Hotel Milan (☎ 283-1104, 283-5351; Presidente Córdova 9-89; r per person US$9) The eternally reliable Milan offers good, comfortable rooms with firm beds, cable TV and consistent hot water.

Cabañas Yanuncay (☎ 288-3716, 281-9681; yanuncay@ etapa.com.ec; Calle Canton Gualaceo 2-149; r per person US$12) This quiet guesthouse, 3km southwest of downtown, offers rooms in a private house or in two cabins in the owner's garden. Rates include breakfast, kitchen privileges and the use of the hot tub. Organic dinners cost US$6. The owner, Humberto, speaks English and German and arranges local tours.

Hostal Macondo (☎ 284-0697, 283-0836; www.hostal macondo.com; Tarqui 11-64; s/d with shared bathroom US$13.50/20, with private bathroom US$19/26) The splendid, colonial-style Macondo keeps travelers pouring in with its sunny back garden, cheerful indoor sitting areas, artisanal decor and excellent breakfasts.

La Posada del Angel (☎ 284-0695; www.hostal posadadelangel.com; Simón Bolívar 14-11; s/d US$31/46; ▣) Color, character, history; you name it, Posada del Angel has all the ingredients of the perfect B&B.

Eating

Most restaurants close on Sunday, so start your search *before* your blood-sugar crashes.

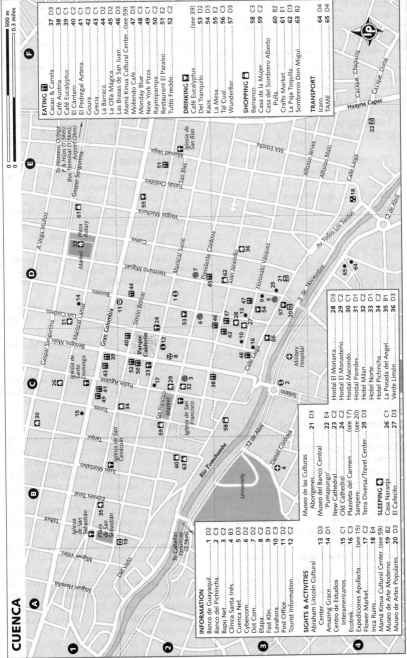

Tutto Freddo (cnr Benigno Malo & Simón Bolívar; ice cream US75¢-$3; ⏰ daily Likely the best (and definitely the most popular) ice cream in town. Meals too.

Moliendo Café (Honorato Vásquez 6-24; light meals US$1-3) Moliendo Café serves delicious Colombian *antojitos* (appetizers) at prices that makes everyone happy.

Café Austria (Benigno Malo 5-45; US$1-3) Austrian-style cakes, coffee and sandwiches.

La Olla Mágica (Hermano Miguel 6-70; mains US$1.50-2.50) It's hard to beat pork chops at this price.

New York Pizza (Gran Colombia 10-43; mains US$1.50-3.50; ⏰ daily) Thin-crust pizza starts at US$1.10 a slice.

Mamá Kinua Cultural Center (Torres 7-45, Casa de la Mujer; almuerzos US$2; ⏰ 8am-5:30pm Mon-Fri) Pop into this women-run restaurant for some of the tastiest *almuerzos* around. Food here is mostly vegetarian.

Cacao & Canela (cnr Jaramillo & Borrero; sandwiches US$2-4; ⏰ 4-11pm Mon-Sat) Wholesome sandwiches and good coffee.

Café Eucalyptus (Gran Colombia 9-41; plates US$2-6) Two crackling fireplaces, two big couches, two floors of tables, one beautiful bar, 30 wines, several microbrews and 100 small-plate dishes make this *the* place to treat yourself.

Monday Blue (cnr Calle Larga & Luís Cordero; mains US$2.50-4; ⏰ 4:30pm-midnight) The festive Mexican atmosphere is more Cancún than Cuenca, but it's undeniably fun wolfing down Mexican food, shawarmas and pizza in this restaurant-cum-bar.

La Barraca (Borrero 9-68; mains US$3-4) The casual atmosphere and great music complement excellent snacks (guacamole and chips, popcorn and the like). Main courses are mediocre.

Raymipampa (Benigno Malo 8-59; mains US$3-5; ⏰ daily) This Cuenca institution serves food hanging somewhere between Ecuadorian comfort food and diner fare.

Las Brasas de San Juan (Jaramillo 7-34; mains US$3-9) One reader claimed these are the best steaks in Ecuador.

El Pedregal Azteca (Gran Colombia 10-33; mains US$5-9) Delicious Mexican food, but the portions can be small; fill up on the free corn chips.

The following all serve straightforward Ecuadorian fare and are best for their cheap *almuerzos*. You'll find more locals than tourists at most.

Grecia (Gran Colombia 9-69; almuerzos US$1.50, mains US$3-4)

Restaurant El Paraíso (Ordóñez 10-19; almuerzos & merienda US$2, mains US$1.50-2) All vegetarian; ice cream too.

Goura (Jaramillo 7-27; almuerzos US$2; mains US$2-4) Vegetarian.

El Cántaro (Simón Bolívar 8-50; mains US$3-4, almuerzos US$2.20)

Drinking

Café Eucalyptus (left) is an excellent spot for a relaxed drink with a mostly gringo crowd. Women drink free 6pm to 10pm Wednesday.

Entertainment

Discos are open Thursday through Saturday nights. Midweek Cuenca's as dead as Pizarro. There's a slew of small, friendly bars on Honorato Vásquez near El Cafecito (p690). Along Presidente Córdova, east of Hermano Miguel, there are several popular bars with dance floors.

Tal Cual (Calle Larga 7-57) Cozy, friendly bar with live music Thursday through Saturday.

La Mesa (Gran Colombia 3-55) Known as Cuenca's best salsa club.

Del Tranquilo (deltranquilo@hotmail.com; Borrero near Mariscal Sucre) Live music Thursday through Saturday nights.

WunderBar (Hermano Miguel at Calle Larga) This hoppin' German-owned hangout near the river is good for a fun night. Food is served.

Kaos (Honorato Vásquez 6-11) The laid-back British-owned Kaos has couches, pool tables and snacks.

Shopping

There are several good crafts stores along Gran Colombia and on the blocks just north of Parque Calderón. The best place for a serious spree, however, is the **Casa de la Mujer** (Torres 7-33), which houses over 100 crafts stalls and makes for hours of shopping fun.

The Thursday market at **Plaza Rotary** (Mariscal Lamar & Hermano Miguel) exists mainly for locals (which means it stocks pigs and polyester, fruit and furniture), but there are also a few worthwhile craft stalls. You're better off heading to the nearby **crafts market** (cnr Gaspar Sangurima & Vargas Machuca), which has an odd but quite interesting combination of basketry, ceramics, iron-work, kitchen utensils, bright plastic animals, gaudy religious paraphernalia and guinea pig roasters (which are a great gift for mom, but a little tough to get home).

Getting There & Away

AIR

Cuenca's **Airport** (Aeropuerto Mariscal Lamar; ☎ 286-2203; Av España) is 2km from downtown. **TAME** (☎ 288-9097, 288-9581; Astudillo 2-22) and **Icaro** (☎ 281-1450; Milenium Plaza, Astudillo s\n) fly daily to Quito ($63) and Guayaquil ($45).

BUS

Cuenca's **bus terminal** (España) is 1.5km northeast of the center. Buses to Guayaquil (US$8) go either via Parque Nacional Cajas (3½ hours) or Cañar (5½ hours). There are regular departures to Quito (US$10, 10 to 12 hours). Several go to Machala (US$4.50, four hours); a few continue on to Huaquillas (US$6, five hours). Buses go regularly to Alausí (US$4, four hours). Several buses a day head to Loja (US$7, five hours), to Macas (US$8.50, eight hours via Guarumales; 10 hours via Limón) and other Oriente towns. Buses for Gualaceo (US80¢, 50 minutes) leave every half hour.

Getting Around

Cuenca is very walkable. A taxi to/from the bus terminal or airport costs about US$2. From the front of the bus terminal buses depart regularly to downtown ($0.25).

AROUND CUENCA

☎ 07

From small indigenous villages, to hot springs and hiking, there's ample opportunity for excursions from Cuenca.

Ingapirca

The most important Inca site in Ecuador, Ingapirca was built toward the end of the 15th century during the Inca expansion into present-day Ecuador. The **site** (admission US$6; ☼ 8am-6pm), 50km north of Cuenca, was built with the same mortarless, polished-stone technique used by the Inca in Peru. Although less impressive than sites in Peru, it's definitely worth a visit. A museum explains the site, and guides (both the human and the written varieties) are available. **Ingapirca village**, 1km away, has a craft shop, simple restaurants and a basic pensión.

For an economical visit, catch a direct Transportes Cañar bus (US$2.50, two hours) from Cuenca's bus terminal at 9am or 1pm Monday through Friday, or at 9am on Saturday and Sunday. Buses return to Cuenca at 1pm and 4pm Monday through Friday and at 9am and 1pm on Saturday and Sunday.

Gualaceo, Chordeleg & Sígsig

Famous for their Sunday markets, seeing these three villages together makes a great day trip from Cuenca. If you start early, you can be back in Cuenca by the afternoon. **Gualaceo** has the biggest market, with fruit and vegetables, animals and various household goods. **Chordeleg's market**, 5km away, is smaller and more touristy. **Sígsig's market** is 25km from Gualaceo and is an excellent place to see the art of panama-hat making.

From Cuenca's bus terminal, buses leave every half hour to Gualaceo (US80¢, 50 minutes), Chordeleg ($1, one hour) and Sígsig ($1.25, 1½ hours). You can walk the 5km from Gualaceo to Chordeleg if you don't want to wait for the bus.

Parque Nacional Cajas

The stunning, chilly, moor-like *páramo* of **Parque Nacional Cajas** (admission US$10) is famous for its many lakes, great trout fishing and rugged camping and hiking. It's a good day trip from Cuenca (only 30km away). **Camping** (per person

---

IT'S NOT A PANAMA, IT'S A MONTECRISTI!

For well over a century, Ecuador has endured the world mistakenly crediting another country for its most famous export – the panama hat. To any Ecuadorian worth his or her salt, the panama hat is a *'sombrero de paja toquilla'* (toquilla-straw hat), and to the connoisseur, it's a Montecristi, named after the most famous hat making town of all (see p712). It's certainly not a paaa...

Cuenca is the center of the panama hat trade and a great place to hunt down a fine sombrero. Try the following:

Barranco (Calle Larga 10-41)
Casa del Sombrero Alberto Pulla (Tarqui 6-91)
Homero Ortega P & Hijos (www.homeroortega.com; Gil Ramirez Davalos)
La Paja Toquilla (cnr Hermano Miguel & Jaramillo)
Sombreros Don Migui (Tarqui near Calle Larga)

ECUADOR

THE INCA TRAIL TO INGAPIRCA

Though it sees only a fraction of the traffic that the Inca trail to Machu Picchu gets, the three-day hike to Ingapirca is a popular trek. Parts of the approximately 40km hike follow the original royal road that linked Cuzco with Quito and Tomebamba (at present-day Cuenca).

The starting point for the hike is the village of **Achupallas**, 23km southeast of Alausí (see p688). The route is faint in places and sometimes even nonexistent, so travel with a compass and three 1:50,000 topographical maps – Alausí, Juncal and Cañar – available at the IGM (p648) in Quito. There are sometimes locals around who may provide directions. Pack extra food in case you get lost. The area is remote but inhabited, so don't leave your stuff lying around outside your tent. Also be prepared for extremely persistent begging from children; most travelers refuse to hand anything over so as not to encourage the begging from future walkers.

To get to Achupallas, take one of the daily trucks from Alausí or, more reliably, hire a taxi-pickup for about US$10 to US$15 one way. Alternatively, there is transportation from Alausí to **Guasuntos** (also known as La Moya), from where you can wait for trucks (U$10) to Achupallas. It is about 10km from Alausí to La Moya and another 15km to Achupallas. There is nowhere to stay at either place.

US$4) is allowed, and a small refugio has eight cots and a kitchen; the latter fills up fast. Hiking solo in Cajas can be dangerous – the abundance of lakes and fog is disorienting. It's best to be finished by 4pm when the fog gets thick. Shorter trails are well marked. Glossy, topographical trail maps are free with admission.

Guayaquil-bound busses pass through the park, but drivers refuse to sell reduced-fare tickets for the one-hour ride. To avoid paying the full US$8 fare to Guayaquil, take a Transporte Occidental bus ($1.25, one hour) from Ricardo Darque between Av de las Américas and Victor Manuel Albornoz, in Cuenca. Even after a taxi ($2) to this bus stop, it still comes out cheaper. Buses depart daily at 6:15pm, 7pm and 10:20am and at noon, 2pm, 4pm and 5pm. To return to Cuenca, flag any passing Cuenca-bound bus.

SARAGURO

☎ 07

South of Cuenca the road winds through eerie *páramo* until, after 165km, it reaches Saraguro, which means 'land of corn' in Quichua. Quaint little Saraguro is home to the indigenous Saraguro, the most successful indigenous group in the southern highlands. The group originally lived in the Lake Titicaca region of Peru but were forcibly relocated through the Inca empire's system of colonization, known as *mitimaes*.

Today, the Saraguro are readily identifiable by their traditional dress. Both men and women (but especially the women) wear striking flat white felt hats with wide brims that are often spotted on the underside. The men sport

a single ponytail and wear a black poncho and knee-length black shorts, occasionally covered with a small white apron.

The best day to be in Saraguro is Sunday, when the local market draws Saraguros – dressed beautifully for the occasion – from the surrounding countryside. Sleep at friendly **Residencial Saraguro** (☎ 220-0286; cnr Loja & Antonio Castro; r per person US$4) and eat at indigenous-run **Mamá Cuchara** (Parque Central; mains US$1.50-2.50; ☼ closed Sat).

Any Loja-bound bus from Cuenca (US$4, 3½ hours) will drop you a block from the main plaza. Buses to Loja (62km, US$2, 1½ hours) leave hourly during the day.

LOJA

☎ 07 / pop 170,000

Thanks to its proximity to the Oriente, Loja is blessed with a delightfully temperate climate. The city is famous for its musicians (everyone seems to play something) and its award-winning parks. Despite the fact that it's the provincial capital, it's still a small town at heart – so much so that you'll find a day or two plenty of time. Loja (elevation 2100m) is a good base for visiting nearby Parque Nacional Podocarpus and the main stop before heading south to Vilcabamba and Peru.

Good views can be had from the **Virgen de Loja Statue** (La Salle). The annual fiesta of the **Virgen del Cisne** (September 8) is celebrated with huge parades and a produce fair.

Information

Banco de Guayaquil (Eguiguren near Bernardo Valdivieso) Bank with ATM.

Clínica San Agustín (☎ 257-0314; 18 de Noviembre & Azuay) Clinic with a good reputation.

Jungle Net (Riofrío 13-64; per hr US$1) Internet access.

Ministerio del Medio Ambiente (☎ 258-5421; podocam@impsat.net.ec; Sucre 4-35) Provides information on Parque Nacional Podocarpus.

Pacifictel (Eguiguren near Olmedo) Telephone call center.

Post office (cnr Colón & Sucre)

Tourist office (iTur; ☎ 258-1251; cnr Bolívar & Eguiguren) In the Town Hall.

World Net (Colón 14-69; per hr US$1) Internet access.

Sleeping

Hotel Londres (☎ 256-1936; Sucre 07-51; s/d/tr US$4/8/12) With creaky wooden floors, big white walls and saggy beds, Hotel Londres is as basic as

they come, but it's a tried-and-true travelers' favorite with spotless shared bathrooms and friendly young owners.

Hotel México (☎ 257-0581; Eguiguren 15-89; s/d US$4/8) Beat-up digs that only just barely do the trick.

Las Orquídeas (☎ 258-7008; Bolívar 08-59; s/d US$8/16) The small rooms here aren't as cheerful as the flowery lobby might suggest, but they're clean and totally acceptable.

Hotel Metropolitan (☎ 257-0007/244; Calle 18 de Noviembre 6-41; r per person US$10) The Metropolitan is friendly and comfortable, with hardwood floors, decent beds and cable TV.

Hostal América (☎ 256-2887; Calle 18 de Noviembre near Imbabura; s/d incl breakfast US$20/27) Modern, comfortable hotel with giant rooms.

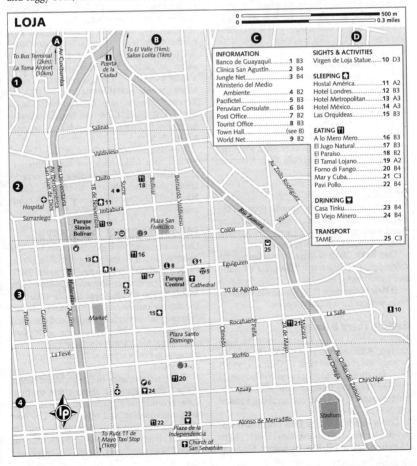

LOJA

| 0 | 500 m |
| 0 | 0.3 miles |

INFORMATION
Banco de Guayaquil...........1 B3
Clínica San Agustín..........2 B4
Jungle Net...................3 B4
Ministerio del Medio
 Ambiente....................4 B2
Pacifictel...................5 B3
Peruvian Consulate...........6 B4
Post Office..................7 B2
Tourist Office...............8 B3
Town Hall................(see 8)
World Net....................9 B2

SIGHTS & ACTIVITIES
Virgen de Loja Statue......10 D3

SLEEPING 🏠
Hostal América..............11 A2
Hotel Londres...............12 B3
Hotel Metropolitan..........13 A3
Hotel México................14 A3
Las Orquídeas...............15 B3

EATING 🍴
A lo Mero Mero..............16 B3
El Jugo Natural.............17 B3
El Paraíso..................18 B2
El Tamal Lojano.............19 A2
Forno di Fango..............20 B4
Mar y Cuba..................21 C3
Pavi Pollo..................22 B4

DRINKING 🍷
Casa Tinku..................23 B4
El Viejo Minero.............24 B4

TRANSPORT
TAME........................25 C3

Eating

El Tamal Lojano (18 de Noviembre 05-12; light items US70¢-$1, almuerzos US$2) People flock here for the excellent *quimbolitos*, *humitas* and *tamales lojanos* (all delicious variations on corn dumplings); and *empanadas de verde*. Try them all!

El Jugo Natural (Eguiguren 14-20; US$1-2) Great place for a fruit-and-yogurt breakfast.

El Paraíso (Quito 14-50; set meal US$2) Wholesome vegetarian lunches and dinners are available here at US$2 a pop.

A lo Mero Mero (Sucre 06-22; mains US$3-4, almuerzos US$2) It's not quite up to Mexico City standards, but if you've a hankering for refried beans and tortillas, it's the only place you'll get them.

Salon Lolita (Salvador Bustamante Celi at Guayaquil, El Valle; mains US$3-8) This is *the* place for traditional food from Loja. *Cuy* (guinea pig) comes roasted whole in US$8, US$10 or US$12 sizes. Take an 'El Valle' bus from Av Universitaria at Parque Simón Bolívar.

Mar y Cuba (Rocafuerte 09-00 at 24 de Mayo; mains US$4-5) Excellent seafood, *ceviche* and Cuban classics.

Forno di Fango (Bolívar 10-98; pizzas US$4.50-13) Tasty adobe-oven pizza.

There are numerous grilled-chicken joints along Mercadillo, west of Bolívar where you can pick up a quarter-chicken with soup and fries for about US$2. **Pavi Pollo** (Alonso de Mercadillo 14-99) is a good one.

Drinking

On Sunday nights from 8pm to 9pm, in the Parque Central, the local military marching band rips into what are likely the liveliest marching tunes you'll ever hear.

Casa Tinku (Alonso de Mercadillo near Bernardo Valdivieso) Spirited little bar with a great vibe and live music on weekends.

El Viejo Minero (Sucre 10-76) Rustic old watering hole, perfect for a relaxed beer.

Getting There & Away

Loja is served by La Toma airport in Catamayo, 30km west of town. **TAME** (☎ 257-0248; Av Ortega near 24 de Mayo) flies to Quito (US$49) Monday through Saturday and to Guayaquil (US$36) Tuesday through Thursday. For airport transport (US$4, 40 minutes) call **Aerotaxi** (☎ 257-1327, 258-4423).

Loja's bus terminal is 1km north of town. Several buses a day run to Quito (US$15, 14 to 15 hours), Macará (US$6, six hours), Guayaq-

uil (US$9, nine hours), Machala (US$5, five hours), Zamora (US$2.50, two hours) and Cuenca (US$7, five hours), as well as other destinations.

Buses to Vilcabamba (US$1, 1½ hours) depart once an hour. Vilcabambaturis runs faster minibuses (US$1, one hour). Fastest of all are the *taxis colectivos* (shared taxis; US$1.20, 45 minutes) which leave from the **Ruta 11 de Mayo taxi stop** (Av Universitaria), 10 blocks south of Alonso de Mercadillo; ask a local taxi driver to take you.

ZAMORA

☎ 07 / pop 16,074

Perspiring peacefully on the tropical banks of the Río Zamora, this easy-going jungle town is the best base for exploring the verdant lowlands of Parque Nacional Podocarpus (below). Although it's geographically part of the Oriente, Zamora (elevation 970m) is closer to Loja by bus (two hours) than to other jungle towns, most of which are quite a long way north. Decent budget hotels in town include **Hostal Seyma** (☎ 260-5583; 24 de Mayo near Amazonas; s/d US$3/6) and **Hotel Chonta Dorada** (☎ 260-6384, 260-7055; hotelchontadorada@ hotmail.com; Pío Jaramillo btwn Diego de Vaca & Amazonas; s/d US$7/11.50).

Continuing north through the Oriente by bus, you will find a few basic hotels in the small towns of **Gualaquiza** (five hours), **Limón** (about nine hours), **Méndez** and **Sucúa**. **Macas** (p706) is approximately 13 to 15 hours away.

PARQUE NACIONAL PODOCARPUS

One of the most biologically rich areas in the country and a wonderful park to explore, **Parque Nacional Podocarpus** (admission US$10) protects habitats at altitudes ranging from 3600m in the *páramo* near Loja to 1000m in the steamy rainforests near Zamora. The topography is wonderfully rugged and complex, and the park is simply bursting with plant and animal life. Parque Nacional Podocarpus' namesake, Podocarpus, is Ecuador's only native conifer.

The main entrance to the highland sector of the park is **Cajanuma**, about 10km south of Loja. From here, a track leads 8.5km up to the ranger station and trail heads. The best bet for a day trip is to ride all the way up in a taxi from Loja (about US$10), hike for several hours and walk the 8.5km/two hours

GETTING TO PERU

Five hours from Loja by bus, the dusty little border town of **Macará** lies 3km from the Peruvian border (crossing free; open 24 hours). This route into Peru is far more scenic and less traveled than the conventional one via Huaquillas (p724). Most people buy tickets direct to Piura, Peru from Loja (p694) aboard **Loja International** (☎ 257-9014, 257-0505). Buses depart Loja at 7am, 1pm, 10:30pm and 11pm, and the bus stops at the border, waits for passengers to take care of exits and entries and then continues to Piura. The entire ride is eight hours (and costs US$8). Try to buy your tickets at least a day before you travel. If you want to break the journey from Loja, do so at **Catacocha**. The Loja-Piura bus stops in Catacocha and Macará, so you can get on in either town as well.

back to the main road where you can flag a passing bus.

To visit the tropical, lowland sector, head to Zamora and get a taxi (US$6) or walk the 6km dirt road to the **Bombuscaro entrance**, where there is a ranger station, trails, swimming, waterfalls, a **camping area** (per person US$2) and a small **refugio** (cots per person US$5). Access from Vilcabamba is possible by horseback.

VILCABAMBA
☎ 07 / pop 4200

Deemed the valley of longevity, Vilcabamba is famous for having inhabitants that just don't kick the bucket. And it's no wonder – with a setting so peaceful, weather so sublime and a pace so re-*laaaxing*, who in their right mind would want to toss in the towel? Backpackers stop here to get in on the mellowness and to hike, ride horses, enjoy the food, get massages and chill out in Vilcabamba's cheap guesthouses. It's also the perfect stopping point en route to/from Peru via **Zumba**. The elevation is 1500m.

Bring cash; there are no banks. Telephones, cybercafés and the post office are all easy to find.

Activities

Orlando Falco, a trained, English-speaking naturalist guide, leads recommended tours to Parque Nacional Podocarpus and other areas for about US$20 to US$35 per person, plus the US$10 park fee. Find him at Primavera, his craft shop on the plaza. **Caballos Gavilan** (☎ 264-0281; gavilanhorse@yahoo.com; Sucre) offers affordable, highly recommended horse-riding trips, which can last from four hours to three days. Several readers and numerous locals have recommended local guide Jorge Mendieta of **Caminatas Andes Sureños** (jorgeluis222@latinmail.com; Central Plaza) for his guided hikes.

Sleeping

Hostal Mandango (☎ 09-370-5266; Huilco Pamba near Juan Montalvo; r per person with shared/private bathroom US$3/5; 🖳) Behind the bus station, Mandango might just be the best super-budget choice in town. Rooms are small, but those with private bathrooms also have firm beds, and everything is clean.

Residencial Don German (☎ 264-0130, 09-132-4669; Jaramillo; r per person US$4) Simple digs with clean cheerful rooms and shared hot showers. There's a tiny well-lit common area and a communal kitchen. It's basic, but totally acceptable.

Rumi-Wilco Ecolodge (rumiwilco@yahoo.com; http://koberpress.home.mindspring.com/vilcabamba; r per person US$4-4.50) About a 30-minute walk from town, Rumi Wilco consists of the four-person **Pole House** (d/tr US$16/18), a serene hideaway with hammocks, kitchen and a private drinking well; and several other exquisitely set cabins. Wonderfully relaxing.

Hostería y Restaurante Izhcayluma (☎ 264-0095; www.izhcayluma.com; dm US$7, s US$13-20, d US$20-30; 🖳) With sweeping views over the valley, a swimming pool, a flower-filled garden and supremely comfortable rooms, Hostería y Restaurante Izhcayluma is hard to beat. Located 2km south of town.

Jardín Escondido (Hidden Garden; ☎ 264-0281; www.vilcabamba.org/jardinescondido.html; Sucre; dm US$8, r per person US$10-15; 🖳) Recently remodeled, colorful Jardín Escondido is the slickest in the center, and it really does have a garden hidden within its doors. The priciest rooms are quite luxurious.

Rendez-Vous (☎ 09-219-1180; rendezvousecuador@yahoo.com; Diego Vaca de Vega 06-43; s/d US$8/16) French-owned Rendez-Vous is a lovely place near the river with immaculate rooms that open onto a beautiful garden. Each has a hammock. Breakfast with homemade bread included.

ECUADOR

Cabañas Río Yambala (☎ 09-106-2762; www.vil cabamba.cwc.net; cabins per person with 2 meals US$10-14, without meals US$5-9) About 4km southeast of town, Cabañas Río Yambala is another Vilcabamba original, run by friendly Brits with six charming, rustic cabins of varying sizes, all with private hot showers and views. You can walk up or hire a taxi (about US$4) from the plaza.

Hostal Madre Tierra (☎ 264-0269, 09-309-6665; www.madretierra1.com; dm US$13.50, r per person US$13.50-25, ste per person US$34; 🖳 🐾) About 2km north of town, this stunning, down-to-earth hotel-spa pioneered the pleasure-aesthetic that most Vilcabamba hotels adhere to today. Rooms are in cabins spread around the hillside, and some have views. The full-service spa (treatments US$16 to US$40) is open to non-guests.

Eating & Drinking

Izhcayluma (☎ 264-0095; www.izhcayluma.com) has an excellent restaurant. Others in town are easy to find.

Restaurant Vegetariano (Salgado at Diego Vaca de la Vega; mains US$2-3) Good vegetarian option; US$2.60 almuerzos.

La Terraza (Central Plaza; mains US$2.50-4) Italian, Mexican and Thai plates; plenty of vegetarian options.

Jardín Escondido (Sucre & Agua de Hierro; mains US$3-5) This place serves Mexican food in a lovely garden setting.

Shanta's Bar (mains US$3-6; ⏰ noon-3am) On the road to Río Yambala, Shanta's serves great trout and pizza and more. It's also the town's best bar.

Getting There & Away

Transportes Loja runs buses every 90 minutes to Loja (US$1, 1½ hours). Shared taxis leave from the bus terminal and take five passengers to Loja (US$1.20, 45 minutes). Buses leave daily to Zumba ($6, six hours) near the Peruvian border.

THE ORIENTE

Ecuador's slice of the Amazon Basin – aka, *El Oriente* – is one of the country's most thrilling travel destinations. Here you can paddle canoes up to caimans lurking in blackwater lagoons, spot two-toed sloths and howler monkeys, fish for piranhas and hike through some of the wildest plantlife you'll ever lay

eyes upon. At night, after quelling your fear of the things outside, you'll be lulled to sleep by a psychedelic symphony of insects and frogs.

This section of the book describes the Oriente from north to south (see Zamora, p696, for the region's southernmost towns.) The northern Oriente sees more travelers, while the region south of Río Pastaza has a real sense of remoteness. Buses from Quito frequently go to Puyo, Tena, Coca and Lago Agrio. Buses from Cuenca (p693) go through Limón to Macas. Buses from the Southern Highlands town of Loja go via Zamora to Limón and on to Macas. From Macas, a road leads to Puyo and the northern Oriente. It's possible – although arduous – to travel down the Río Napo to Peru and the Amazon River.

LAGO AGRIO

☎ 06 / pop 34,100

Unless you like edgy frontier towns, Lago's main tourist draw is its status as jumping-off point for the nearby Cuyabeno wildlife reserve (opposite). The Sunday morning **market** is visited by indigenous Cofan and might be worth a peak. Booking a tour to Cuyabeno from Lago can be difficult: most people arrive from Quito with a tour already booked, guides show up, and everyone's gone the next morning.

If you're stuck in town, try **Hotel Casablanca** (☎ 283-0181; Av Quito 228; s/d US$10/15) or **Hotel D'Mario** (☎ 283-0172; hotelmario@andinanet.net; Av Quito 1-171; s US$15-32, d US$17-40; 🍽 🖳 🐾). Both are on the main drag, where you'll find just about everything else. The latter has a popular pizzería.

Dangers & Annoyances

With an increased pitch in the conflict in neighboring Colombia, border towns such as Lago Agrio have become safe havens for Colombian guerrillas, anti-rebel paramilitaries and drug smugglers. Bars can be sketchy and side streets unsafe, so stick to the main drag, especially at night. Tourists rarely have problems but be careful.

Getting There & Away

The airport is 5km east of town; taxi fare is US$2. **TAME** (☎ 283-0113; Orellana near 9 de Octubre) and **Icaro** (☎ 283-2370/71, 288-0546; at the airport) fly Monday through Saturday to Quito

(US$43 to US$56); it's best to book in advance.

The bus terminal is about 2km northwest of the center. Buses head to Quito regularly (US$7, eight hours). There are one or two daily departures, mainly overnight, to Tena (US$7, eight hours), Cuenca, Guayaquil (US$14, fourteen hours) and Machala. Buses to Coca aren't usually found in the bus terminal; flag a *ranchera* (open sided bus; US$3, 2½ hours) on Av Quito in the center – ask locally for where to wait.

RESERVA DE PRODUCCIÓN FAUNÍSTICA CUYABENO

This beautiful, 6034 sq km **reserve** (admission US$20) protects the rainforest home of the Siona, Secoya, Cofan, Quichua and Shuar people. It also conserves the Río Cuyabeno watershed, whose rainforest lakes and swamps harbor fascinating aquatic species such as freshwater dolphins, manatees, caiman and anaconda. Monkeys abound, and tapirs, peccaries, agoutis and several cat species have been recorded. The bird life is abundant. Though there have been numerous oil spills, huge parts of the reserve remain pristine and worth a visit. The reserve is nearly impossible to visit on your own; most visitors make arrangements in Quito (p659) or Coca. The nearest town is Lago Agrio.

COCA

☎ 06 / pop 18,300
If you're one of those folks who digs sitting around in tropical heat guzzling beer and watching small-town street life, you'll find Coca oddly appealing. Otherwise it's just a dusty, sweltering oil town and little more than a final stop before boarding an outboard canoe and heading down the mighty Río Napo. It's a good place to hire a guide for visits to Pañacocha, Cuyabeno and Parque Nacional Yasuní (p701).

Information

Andinatel (cnr Eloy Alfaro & 6 de Diciembre)
Banco del Pinchincha (cnr Bolívar and 9 de Octubre) Bank with ATM.
Casa de Cambio 3R (cnr Napo & García Moreno) Cashes traveler's checks.
Imperial Net (García Moreno; per hr US$1.80) Internet access.
Post office (Napo near Cuenca)
Tourist office (cnr García Moreno & Quito)

GETTING TO PERU

About 125km south of Vilcabamba lies the wonderfully remote border crossing known as **La Balsa**, near the outpost of **Zumba**. From Vilcabamba (or Loja), it's an all-day journey to San Ignacio, Peru, the best place to spend the night. From San Ignacio, you can travel to Jaén (three hours), on to Bagua Grande (another hour) and then to Chachapoyas (p923; three more hours), the first sizable town. From Jaén you can also travel to Chiclayo (p905), on the Peruvian coast.

If you're traveling from Peru, see p907.

Tours

Coca is closer than Misahuallí to large tracts of virgin jungle, but to hire a guide you should have a group of four or more to make it affordable. Trips down the Río Tiputini and into Parque Nacional Yasuní (p701) are possible, but require at least a week. Visiting a Huaorani village requires written permission from the community. The following are all reliable tour operators. Tours average US$50 to US$60 per person per day and include everything except park entrance fees.

Emerald Forest Expeditions (in Quito ☎ 02-288-2309; www.emeraldexpeditions.com; cnr Quito and Espejo) has over twenty years in the guide business and is highly recommended. **River Dolphin Expeditions** (☎ 09-917-7529; Guayaquil near Napo) has received mixed reviews from readers; it's worth feeling out. Both companies offer 10-day expeditions down the Río Napo to Iquitos, Peru.

Hotel El Auca (p700) doesn't arrange tours but is probably one of the best places in town to meet guides looking for work, as well as to meet other travelers who can tell you of their experiences or help form a group.

Sleeping & Eating

Coca's cheaper hotels are dingy, overpriced and fill up quickly with oil workers.

Hotel Oasis (☎ 288-0206; yuturilodge@yahoo.com; Camilo de Torrano s/n; s/d US$8/16) Rooms are run-down, but there's a pleasant deck with a view of the river. The staff arranges trips to economic lodges on the Río Napo.

Hotel San Fermin (☎ 288-1848; Quito and Bolívar; s/d with fan US$9/17, with air-con US$18/28; 🅿) The

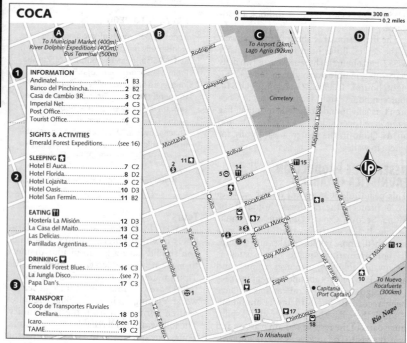

COCA

best new addition to town is this large, well-furnished house.

Hotel El Auca (☎ 288-0127/0600; helauca@ecuanex .net.ec; Napo; s US$12-35, d US$20-50) Catering to tour groups and oil workers alike (not to mention the tame jungle critters roaming the garden), the Auca is Coca's finest.

Otherwise, try:

Hotel Florida (☎ 288-0177; Alejandro Labaka; s/d with shared bathroom US$6/10, with private bathroom US$10/15)

Hotel Lojanita (☎ 288-0032; cnr Napo & Cuenca; r per person with fan/air-con US$8/12; ❄)

Eating & Drinking

The restaurants at **Hostería La Misión** (Camilo de Torrano s/n) and Hotel El Auca are considered to be the best in town.

Las Delicias (cnr Napo & Cuenca; mains US$1.50) Fried chicken and French fries.

La Casa del Maito (Malecón; mains US$2.50) Squeeze between the noisy locals for the heavenly house specialty, *maito* (fish cooked in leaves).

Parrilladas Argentinas (cnr Inés & Cuenca, 2nd fl) Longstanding steakhouse.

La Jungla Disco (admission US$10, hotel guests free) Above Hotel El Auca, this is Coca's only disco.

Emerald Forest Blues (cnr Espejo & Quito) Friendly little bar run by the owner of Emerald Forest Expeditions.

Papa Dan's (Napo at Chimborazo) A rickety Coca classic.

Getting There & Away
AIR

The airport is 2km north of town. **TAME** (☎ 288-1078; cnr Napo & Rocafuerte) and **Icaro** (☎ 288-0997/0546; www.icaro.com.ec; La Misión, Hostería La Misión) fly to Quito (US$43 to US$57) Monday through Saturday. Book ahead.

BOAT

On Monday and Thursday at 8am, **Coop de Transportes Fluviales Orellana** (☎ 288-0087; Napo near Chimborazo) offers passenger service to Nuevo Rocafuerte (US$15, 12 to 15 hours) on the Peruvian border. It returns to Coca, departing Nuevo Rocafuerte at 5am on Sunday, Tuesday and Friday. Although there's usually a stop for lunch, bring food and water for the trip.

Travelers arriving and departing by river must register their passport at the *capitanía* (port captain), by the landing dock. If you're on a tour, your guide usually takes care of this.

BUS

There are bus offices in town and at the bus terminal, north of town. Several buses a day go to Quito (US$10, nine hours via Loreto, 13 hours via Lago Agrio), Tena (US$7, six hours) and Lago Agrio (US$3, three hours), as well as other jungle towns. Open-sided trucks called *rancheras* or *chivas* leave from the terminal for various destinations between Coca and Lago Agrio, and to Río Tiputini to the south.

RÍO NAPO

☎ 06

East of Coca, the Río Napo flows steadily toward Peru and the Amazon River. This long, lonesome stretch of river contains some of Ecuador's best jungle lodges. Except aboard the boat to Nuevo Rocafuerte, independent canoe travel is expensive. If you're visiting a lodge, transport is part of the package.

Pompeya is a Catholic mission about two hours downriver from Coca on Río Napo near the **Reserva Biológica Limoncocha**. Now that there is road access and nearby oil drilling, the area is rather depressing and not ideal for spotting wildlife. The area is easily accessed by buses from the oil town of **Shushufindi**, one hour from either Coca or Lago Agrio.

About five hours downstream from Coca, **Pañacocha** is another settlement you can visit independently. You'll find a gorgeous blackwater lagoon with great piranha fishing and

incredible biodiversity among cloud forest and dry forest. Tours from Coca go here but you can also take the public canoe slated for Nueva Rocafuerte (see opposite) for added adventure. Cheap accommodations are available at **Pensión Las Palmas** (riverfront; r per person US$3) but you might be more comfortable camping. Inexpensive *comedores* (cheap restaurants), including Elsita and Delicia, are within view of the boat landing.

Those who prefer comfort, wildlife guides and tasty food should consider a lodge. The least expensive in the area is **Yuturi Lodge** (Yuturi Jungle Adventures in Quito, Map pp650-1; ☎ 250-4037/3225; www.yuturilodge.com; Amazonas N24-236 & Colón; packages per person for 4 nights US$350), which has received good reports. **Sani Lodge** (in Quito, Map pp650-1; ☎ 02-255-8881; www.sanilodge.com; R Roca 736 & Av Amazonas, Pasaje Chantilly; packages per person for 3/4/7 nights US$285/380/665) is a wonderful place, with outstanding guides and service while still reasonably priced.

The Río Napo flows just outside the northern border of Parque Nacional Yasuní and finally enters Peru at Nuevo Rocafuerte.

NUEVO ROCAFUERTE

A distant dot on the map for most, Nuevo Rocafuerte lies five hours downstream from Pañacocha (12 to 15 hours from Coca) completing a seriously arduous journey to the Peruvian border. The very basic **Parador Turístico** (☎ 238-2133; behind national police office; r per person with shared bathroom US$3-5) fills up fast, since it's the only lodging in town. A few two-shelf stores sell basic provisions; for a hot meal ask around. Electricity is only available from 6pm to 11pm. Local guides and tours up the Río Yasuní into Parque Nacional Yasuní (below) can be arranged.

If you are continuing to Peru try to make arrangements well in advance. If you don't time it right you could be stuck here for some time. Bring adequate supplies of water-purification tablets, bug repellent and food. Operators in Coca offer jungle tours which end in Iquitos, Peru.

PARQUE NACIONAL YASUNÍ

Ecuador's largest mainland **park** (admission US$20) is a massive 9620-sq-km swath of wetlands, marshes, swamps, lakes, rivers and tropical rainforest. It contains a variety of rainforest habitats, wildlife and a few Huaorani communities. Unfortunately, poaching and,

---

GETTING TO PERU

For travelers continuing to Peru, exit formalities are taken care of in Nuevo Rocafuerte; in Peru entry formalities are settled in **Iquitos**. The official border crossing (no fees) is at **Pantoja**, a short ride downstream from Nuevo Rocafuerte. Timing is the key: a cargo boat leaves Iquitos, Peru around the 18th of every month, arriving in Pantoja around the 24th. Catch this boat in Pantoja for its six-day return trip (about US$70) to Iquitos. To get to Pantoja, ask for a ride (about US$5) with the Peruvian *militares* (soldiers) who visit Nuevo Rocafuerte daily by boat. Conditions on the cargo boat are extremely basic – there's one bathroom and a lot of livestock on board. Bring a hammock, food, five gallons of water and water-purifying tablets. Another option is to try to get to Santa Clotilde, downriver from Nuevo Rocafuerte, in Peru. Santa Clotilde has boats to Iquitos on Tuesday, Thursday and Saturday for US$25.

If you're traveling in the opposite direction, see p936.

---

increasingly, oil exploration are damaging the park.

Visiting the park independently is difficult, but operators in Coca (p699) and Quito (p659) offer tours. Recommended independent guides include **Oscar Tapuy** (in Quito ☎ 02-288-1486; oscarta23@yahoo.com), one of the country's top bird guides and **Jarol Fernando Vaca** (in Quito ☎ 02-224-1918; shiripuno2004@yahoo.com), a Quito-based naturalist and butterfly specialist. Both speak English and Jarol is authorized by the Huaorani to guide in their territory. Contact them by email or telephone.

TENA
☎ 06 / pop 16,670

Ecuador's de facto white-water capital sits at the confluence of two lovely rivers – Río Tena and Río Pano – and draws paddlers from all over the world. It's an attractive, relaxed town (elevation 518m) where kayaks lay around hotel-room entrances and boaters hang out in pizza joints, rapping about their day on the rapids. Rafting trips are easily arranged, and several operators offer interesting jungle trips.

Information
Andinatel (Olmedo near Juan Montalvo) Telephone call center.
Banco del Austro (15 de Noviembre) Traveler's checks; ATM.
Cucupanet (main plaza at Mera; per hr US$1.20) Internet access.
Electrolava (next to police station, main plaza) Laundry.
Police station (☎ 288-6101; main plaza)
Post office (cnr Olmedo & García Moreno)
Tourist office (☎ 288-8046; Augusto Rueda) Local hiking information available.

Activities
If you didn't pack a kayak, sign up for a rafting trip. They range from scenic floats to big-water runs on the **Río Misahuallí** and offer panoramas of beautiful jungle, cloud forest and canyons. Depending on difficulty, day trips run US$50 to US$65 per person. Long in the business, **Ríos Ecuador/Yacu Amu** (☎ 288-6727; www.riosecuador.com; Orellana) offers several day trips as well as a four-day kayaking class (a bargain at US$250). British-operated **River People** (☎ in Quito 02-290-6639, 288-8384; www.riverpeopleraftingecuador.com; 15 de Noviembre & 9 de Octubre) is a top-notch outfitter and has received rave reviews.

For waterfall and caving tours, guide **Manuel Moreta** (☎ 288-9185; manuel.moreta@eudoramail.com) is recommended.

Tours
The popular **Amarongachi Tours** (☎ 288-6372; www.amarongachi.com; 15 de Noviembre 438) offers various good-time jungle tours for US$40 per person per day. Also offering tours at this price is the well-recommended **Sacharicsina** (☎ 288-6839; sacharicsinatour@yahoo.com; Montesdeoca 110), operated by the Quichua-speaking Cerda brothers. For emphasis on Quichua culture, visit **Ricancie** (☎ 288-8479; ricancie.nativeweb.org; Av del Chofer & Hugo Vasco). **Sachamazónica** (☎ 288-7979), in the bus terminal, is run by local indigenous guides who know their stuff.

Sleeping
Hostal Limoncocha (☎ 288-7583; limoncocha@andinanet.net; Ita 533; r per person with shared/private bathroom US$4/6) Chipper backpacker digs with a guest kitchen, hand painted murals and clean private bathrooms. Breakfast and beer available.

A Welcome Break (☎ 288-6301; cofanes@hotmail.com; Augusto Rueda 331; s/d US$4/8) Cramped rooms have bare concrete floors, but the resident family is embracing. Shared showers, guest kitchen and a yard.

Hostal Travellers Lodging (☎ 288-6372; 15 de Noviembre 438; r per person US$6 & US$12) The US$12 rooms have great views; cheaper rooms are small, thin-walled and dark, but still comfortable. All have private bathrooms and hot water. Popular.

Brisa del Río (☎ 288-6444/6208; Orellana; dm US$6, s with bathroom US$10) Spic-and-span hostel with pastel dorms and row-showers.

Also recommended:

Hotel Amazonas (☎ 288-6439; cnr Juan Montalvo & Mera; s/d US$3/6) Fine for a night.

Residencial Danubios (☎ 288-6378; 15 de Noviembre; r per person US$4-6; P) Reliable budget option.

Hotel Hilton (☎ 288-6329; 15 de Noviembre; s/d US$6/12) Tidy and cramped; welcoming owners.

Indiyana Hostal (☎ 288-8837; Bolívar 349; s/d US$8/16; P) Just like grandma's house. Comfortable.

Eating & Drinking

Pollo Sin Rival (15 de Noviembre; mains US$1.50-3) Perfect if you have a hankering for roasted chicken.

Café Tortuga (Orellana; snacks US$2) Excellent new Swiss-run café on the riverfront serving *empanadas*, fruit frappés, cappuccinos, breakfast and more.

Bella Selva (Orellana; mains US$2-6) Riverfront pizza parlor with tropical tunes and tasty veggie pizzas.

Chuquitos (main plaza; mains US$3-5) An old favorite with a varied menu and excellent fish.

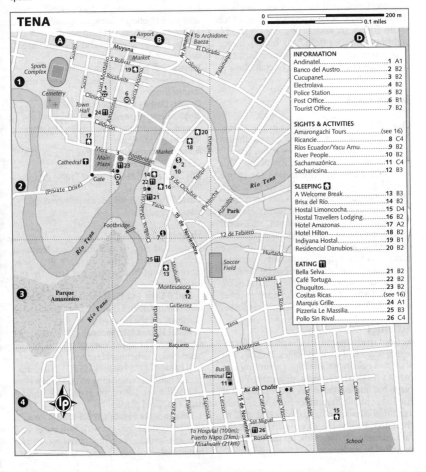

TENA

0 — 200 m
0 — 0.1 miles

INFORMATION
Andinatel.................................**1** A1
Banco del Austro.......................**2** B2
Cucupanet................................**3** B2
Electrolava...............................**4** B2
Police Station...........................**5** B2
Post Office................................**6** B1
Tourist Office............................**7** B2

SIGHTS & ACTIVITIES
Amarongachi Tours...................(see 16)
Ricancie...................................**8** C4
Ríos Ecuador/Yacu Amu............**9** B2
River People.............................**10** B2
Sachamazónica.........................**11** C4
Sacharicsina.............................**12** B3

SLEEPING
A Welcome Break......................**13** B3
Brisa del Río.............................**14** B2
Hostal Limoncocha...................**15** D4
Hostal Travellers Lodging..........**16** B2
Hotel Amazonas.......................**17** A2
Hotel Hilton.............................**18** B2
Indiyana Hostal........................**19** B1
Residencial Danubios................**20** B2

EATING
Bella Selva...............................**21** B2
Café Tortuga............................**22** B2
Chuquitos................................**23** B2
Cositas Ricas............................(see 16)
Marquis Grille...........................**24** A1
Pizzeria Le Massilia...................**25** B3
Pollo Sin Rival..........................**26** C4

ECUADOR

Cositas Ricas (15 de Noviembre; mains US$3-6) Cositas Ricas is a popular place whipping up tasty vegetarian and Ecuadorian dishes and fresh juices.

Pizzería Le Massilia (Agusto Rueda; pizzas US$4-6) Another great riverside pizzeria; nachos too.

Marquis Grille (Amazonas 251; full dinner US$12) Upscale, but family run – a wonderful spot for a splurge. Dinner includes salad, wine and dessert.

For the adventurous, there are grills by the pedestrian bridge cooking up sausages, chicken and *guanta* (a jungle rodent). In addition you'll find cheap food kiosks and cafés with patio seating and cold beer.

Getting There & Away

The bus terminal is less than 1km south of the main plaza. Several buses a day head for Quito (US$6, six hours), Lago Agrio (US$7, eight hours), Coca (US$7, six hours), Baños (US$4, five hours) and other places. Buses for Misahuallí (US$1, one hour) depart hourly from in front of the terminal.

MISAHUALLÍ

☎ 06

One of the Oriente's sleepiest jungle towns, Misahuallí (Mee-sah-wah-YEE) sits swathed in greenery at the junction of two major rivers – the Río Misahuallí and the Río Napo. This was once a bustling connection for jungle tours, but nowadays most trips are booked in Quito. The surrounding area has been colonized for decades, and most mammals have been either hunted or forced out. Still, there are lovely walks to be had (either on your own or with a local guide) and a variety of jungle birds, tropical flowers, army ants, dazzling butterflies and other insects can be seen.

Change money, use the Internet and make phone calls in Tena (p702). There are no street names in Misahuallí, but you can't get lost.

Activities

The dirt roads around Misahuallí make for relaxing walks to outlying villages. You can also walk to a nearby **waterfall** for swimming and picnics. To get there, take a Misahuallí-Puerto Napo bus and ask the driver to drop you off at Río Latas, about 20 minutes from Misahuallí; ask for *el camino a las cascadas* (the trail to the falls). Follow the river upstream to the falls, about an hour's walk up the river – be prepared to wade.

Be sure to visit the **Butterfly Farm** (admission US$2; ☺ 9am-4pm), a block off the plaza.

Tours

If you're hoping to see any of the wildlife, make sure you're venturing well away from Misahuallí. With most tours arranged in Quito, independent travelers to jungle-entry points such as Misahuallí have a harder time organizing a group on-site. If you have a small group you might get a cheaper rate here. Guides will approach you in the main plaza offering tours – most are inexperienced and unlicensed. You're best off hiring a guide recommended here or by other travelers. Tours range from one to 10 days and prices usually include the guide, food, water, accommodations (which range from jungle camping to comfortable lodges) and rubber boots. Rates are usually around US$25 to US$40 per person per day.

The following guides and operators are all recommended:

Ecoselva (☎ 289-0019; ecoselva@yahoo.es; on the plaza) Excellent guide; accommodations in a rustic lodge or jungle camps.

Douglas Clarke's Expeditions (☎ 288-8848; douglasclarkeexpediciones@yahoo.com) Reader recommended; most overnights involve camping. Contact the Hostal Marena Internacional.

Aventuras Amazónicas (☎ 289-0031; on the plaza) Tours for US$25 per day. Based in La Posada.

Luis Zapata (☎ 289-0084; zorrozz_2000@yahoo.com) Independent guide.

Marco Coro (☎ 289-0058; cachitours@hotmail.com) Independent guide.

Sleeping & Eating

Water and electricity failures are frequent here, and most of the hotels are very basic (forget about hot water), but friendly and totally safe.

Hostal Shaw (☎ 289-0019; s/d US$5/10) Simple rooms with fan and shared bathrooms. Above Ecoselva, on the plaza.

Hostal Marena Internacional (☎ 289-0002; r per person US$5-8) The upper levels of this multistory hotel have a delicious breeze.

El Paisano (☎ 289-0027; s/d US$7/11) This backpacker haunt is remodeling its stagnant rooms so it will most likely even look better than it used too. Cool place.

Residencial La Posada (☎ 289-0005; on the plaza; s/d US$7/14) Basic rooms with hot water and fans are found above this rambling, corner restaurant.

CRE (☎ 289-0061; s/d US$8/16) Tidy and informal motel-style rooms and rustic cabins. Hot water and firm mattresses.

France Amazonia (☎ 288-7570; www.france-amazonia .com; s/d incl breakfast US$16/32) The best in town. Shady thatched huts set around a sparkling pool and connected by stone pathways.

Restaurant Nico (☎ 289-0088; Calle Santander; mains US$2-4) Nico is the best option in town for filling US$1.75 *almuerzos*.

Getting There & Away
Buses to Tena (US$1, one hour) leave hourly from the plaza. Outboard canoe rentals cost US$25 per hour (up to 12 passengers). If you're staying at a lodge on the Río Napo, transport will be arranged.

JATUN SACHA BIOLOGICAL RESERVE
On the southern bank of the Río Napo, about 7km east of Misahuallí, **Jatun Sacha Biological Reserve** (admission US$6) is a biological station and rainforest reserve protecting 850 butterfly species, 535 bird species and an unquantifiable but nonetheless thrilling quantity of fungi. It is run by **Fundación Jatun Sacha** (in Quito ☎ 02-243-2240, 243-2173; www.jatunsacha.org; Pasaje Eugenio de Santillán N34-248 & Maurián, Urbanización Rumipamba), an Ecuadorian non-profit organization. You can visit the reserve on a day trip or stay at **Cabañas Aliñahui**. For the latter, make reservations at the Quito office of Jatun Sacha.

Jatun Sacha and Cabañas Aliñahui are reached from Tena: take an Ahuano or Santa Rosa bus and ask the driver to drop you at either entrance. Aliñahui is about 3km east of the Jatun Sacha research station, or 27km east of Tena on the road to Santa Rosa.

PUYO
☎ 03 / pop 24,432
An odd mix of concrete and clapboard at the jungle's edge, this friendly, sprawling town is an important stopover for travelers. It's only two hours by bus from the highland town of Baños (p680) and three hours south of Tena. There are often impressive views of the volcanoes to the west – quite a sight from a little lowland town on the edge of the jungle. Nearby indigenous villages make interesting visits.

Marín and Atahualpa are the main downtown streets with the most services. North of downtown, a bridge crossing the Río Puyo leads to the **Paseo Turístico**, a short trail through the woods.

Information
Amazonía Touring (Atahualpa near 10 de Agosto) Changes traveler's checks.
Andinatel (Orellana) Telephone call center.
Banco del Austro (Atahualpa) Bank with ATM.
Cámara de Turismo (☎ 288-6737; Marín, Centro Commercial Zuñiga, 2nd fl) Tourist office.
Centro de Información de Turismo Responsable (CITR; 9 de Octubre at Bolívar; Internet access per hr US75¢) Internet access, information on community tourism, and indigenous crafts.
Post office (27 de Febrero)

Tours
The highly recommended **Papangu-Atacapi Tours** (☎ 288-3875; papangu@andinanet.net; 27 de Febrero near Sucre) is a unique Quichua-run tour operator specializing in cultural tourism, offering travelers the opportunity to visit Quichua villages, stay with local families and learn about Quichua lifestyles. The money you spend here goes directly to the communities you visit. One- to 10-day tours (two-person minimum) cost US$40 per person per day.

Sleeping
Hostal Jared (☎ 288-5670; 27 de Febrero; s/d US$6/12; P) Bright, crisp rooms with ruffled bedcovers and new installations make this friendly spot a great deal.

Hotel Libertad (☎ 288-3681; Orellana; s/d US$6/12) This tranquil spot offers cramped but spotless singles.

Las Palmas (☎ 288-4832; www.laspalmas.pastaza.net; cnr Av 20 de Julio & 4 de Enero; s/d US$10/20) Big yellow colonial place with attractive gardens and a chattering parrot. It's a few-blocks walk to the center. Great value.

El Jardín (☎ 288-6101; www.eljardin.pastaza.net; Paseo Turístico, Barrio Obrero; s/d US$15/30) A welcoming spot set behind a large garden, this rustic wooden house has hammock balconies and plain but comfortable rooms. Breakfast with fruit and yogurt included.

Eating
Café Andrea (9 de Octubre & Bolívar; snacks US$2) A cozy spot on the plaza serving cappuccinos, delicious *empanadas de verde* and other snacks.

Sal y Pimienta (Atahualpa; almuerzos US$2) Locals pack this steak joint for cheap, fast meals.

El Mono Salsero (Orellana near Villareal; mains US$2) Pull up a stool at this cheery street-shack and chow hotdogs and *ceviche* with the locals.

ECUADOR

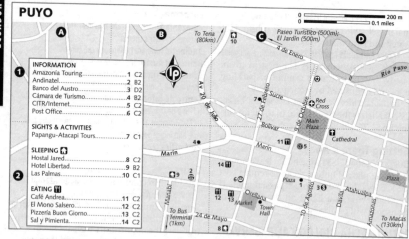

PUYO

INFORMATION	
Amazonía Touring	1 C2
Andinatel	2 B2
Banco del Austro	3 D2
Cámara de Turismo	4 B2
CITR/Internet	5 C2
Post Office	6 C2

SIGHTS & ACTIVITIES	
Papangu-Atacapi Tours	7 C1

SLEEPING	
Hostal Jared	8 C2
Hotel Libertad	9 B2
Las Palmas	10 C1

EATING	
Café Andrea	11 C2
El Mono Salsero	12 C2
Pizzería Buon Giorno	13 C2
Sal y Pimienta	14 C2

El Jardín (Paseo Turístico, Barrio Obrero; mains US$4-5)
This ambient house with gardens by the river
may just have the best grub in the Oriente. It's
just across the footbridge leading to Parque
Omaere, at its eponymous hotel.

Pizzería Buon Giorno (Orellana; pizzas US$4.50-6)
Pop in for cheese-heavy, thick crust pizza
and beer.

Getting There & Away

The bus terminal is 3km out of town. Buses
run regularly to Baños (US$2, two hours),
Quito (US$5, six hours), Macas (US$5, five
hours) and Tena (US$3, three hours). Services
to other towns are also available.

MACAS

☎ 07 / pop 13,600

Macas' slow and steady pace and approach-
able locals make it a welcoming stop. It's also
an excellent launch pad for adventures further
afield. Macas is situated above the banks of the
wild Río Upano, and there are great views of
the river and the Río Upano valley from behind the town's cathedral. On a clear day you
can glimpse the often smoking Volcán Sangay,
some 40km northwest. Though the biggest
town in the southern Oriente, it's definitely a
small town at heart.

Information

Banco del Austro (cnr 24 de Mayo & 10 de Agosto)
Bank with ATM.

Cámara de Turismo (☎ 270-1606/0300; Comin near
Soasti) Tourist information kiosk.

Cyber Vision (Soasti; Internet per hr US$1.50)

Pacifictel (24 de Mayo) Telephone call center.

Post office (9 de Octubre near Comin)

Tours

There are many fascinating trips to be had in
the southern Oriente, and Macas is the place
to book them. Be aware that the indigenous
Shuar do not want unguided visitors in their
villages. **Asociacíon Ecoturismo Danu** (☎ 270-1300;
Amazonas & Bolívar, 2nd fl) does trips near and into
Parque Nacional Sangay. A three-day tour for
two people costs US$45 per day. **Planeta Tours**
(☎ 270-1328; Comin at Soasti) offers cultural tours
in Shuar territory, waterfall hikes, fishing and
some whitewater canoeing.

Knowledgeable, independent Shuar guides
include **Bolívar Caita** (☎ 270-1690; bolicaita@hotmail
.com); **Nanki Wampankit** (nanki_82@hotmail.com) and
Tsunki Marcelo Cajecal (tourshuar@hotmail.com). Email
is the best way to contact them.

Sleeping & Eating

Residencial Macas (☎ 270-0254; 24 de Mayo near Sucre;
r with shared/private bathroom per person US$4/5) Great
deal if you don't mind miniscule rooms.

Hotel Las Orquideas (☎ 270-0970; 9 de Octubre near
Sucre; r per person with shared/private bathroom US$7/8) An
excellent value, with prim, pink rooms away
from the noise.

Hotel Sol del Oriente (☎ 270-2911; Tarqui & Soasti;
r per person US$8) Nondescript high-rise with
large, bright tiled rooms and city views.

Hotel Heliconia (☎ 270-1956; h_heilconia_macas@
hotmail.com; Soasti & 10 de Agosto; s/d US$13/22) Par-

quet floors, panoramic views and all the mod-cons make this high-rise hotel the best in Macas.

La Italiana (Bolívar & Soasti; mains US$1.50-4) Burritos, pasta and pizza.

Café bar Maravilla (Soasti near Sucre; mains US$4-6) This wonderfully atmospheric eatery serves creative fare and delicious cocktails.

Restaurant Pagoda (cnr Amazonas & Comín; mains US$4-6) The best *chifa* (Chinese restaurant) in Macas.

The *comedores* on Comín near Soasti sell tasty *ayampacos*, a jungle specialty of meat, chicken or fish grilled in *bijao* leaves.

Getting There & Away

TAME (☎ 270-1162/1978; airport) flies to Quito (US$43 to US$57) on Monday and Thursday. The bus terminal has several daily departures for Cuenca (US$8.50, eight hours), Gualaquiza (US$8, eight to 10 hours), Riobamba and Ambato. Several buses a day leave for Puyo (US$4, four hours); you have to cross Ríos Pastaza and Pano by footbridges. Buses wait on the other side to continue to Puyo. It's well synchronized.

PACIFIC COAST & LOWLANDS

Ecuador, land of lively Andean markets, Amazon adventures, gripping Galápagos cruises and … beaches? Nobody thinks of the coast when they think of Ecuador. It's last on the list for most, and many – after seeing everything else – never actually make it here. It's their loss. Ecuador's northern coast (from the Colombian border south to around Manta) is a land of giant mangroves, Afro-Ecuadorian culture, incredible biodiversity and serious off-the-beaten-track travel. The southern coast (from Parque Nacional Machalilla to the Peruvian border) is justifiably famous for its seafood and has the country's best beaches, including some fabulous stretches along the 'Ruta del Sol' (Route of the Sun). Admittedly, it's no Caribbean, but it's ocean nontheless. And if it's the sun you're after, time it right: June to November is the rainy season, but also the sunniest; the sun blazes both before and after the afternoon downpour. December through May is often rather overcast and chilly.

GETTING THERE & AWAY

Most places along the northern coast can be reached from Quito in a day's travel. The main, fastest route from Quito to the coast is the newer road via the unappealing lowland city of **Santo Domingo de los Colorados**, which has plenty of hotels should the need arise. The *old* road to Santo Domingo passes through Mindo (p675) before winding down to Esmeraldas city.

San Lorenzo (in Esmeraldas province) can be reached by paved road from Ibarra (in the northern highlands) in only four hours. From Cuenca, Guayaquil is less than four hours away via the new road through Parque Nacional Cajas. Nearly the entire coastal highway is now paved. A spectacular road links Latacunga in the highlands to the lowland city of Quevedo, an important junction en route to the south coast. Many people endure the 11-hour bus ride from Quito to Puerto López (p715), a groovy little fishing village and access-point to Parque Nacional Machalilla and the Ruta del Sol.

SAN LORENZO & AROUND

☎ 06

Encircled by verdant jungle, at the edge of a dank, still sea, San Lorenzo (population 14,600) is a decrepit, lively hodge-podge of blazing heat, tropical beats and crumbling storefronts. Marimba notes and salsa music flavor this mostly African-Ecuadorian outpost, which goes all out in August with an annual music festival. The main reason to visit is to explore the infrequently visited mangroves of the area. Boat tours can be arranged down at the port.

If you're heading south, the road to Esmeraldas passes a recommended hostel in Río Verde (p708). You could also travel by boat through the mangroves via **Limones**, and stop at the muddy fishing village of **Olmedo** (a short walk from La Tola; p708), where there's a tiny hostel run by local Afro-Ecuadorian women. There are few beaches in this area – it's all mangroves.

Orientation & Information

Calle Imbabura is the main drag. Buses roll into town, pass the train station (on the left) and stop at the end of Imbabura at the plaza. The port is a couple of blocks further down. Money-changing opportunities are poor. Don't wander from the main drag after dark.

Sleeping & Eating

Hotels are *all* basic. Mosquito nets and fans are recommended and water shortages are frequent.

Hotel Carondolet (☎ 278-0202; Parque Central; r per person with shared/private bathroom US$3.50/4.50) Diminutive rooms with tin-roof views; make sure the sheets are clean.

Hotel Pampa de Oro (☎ 278-0214; Calle Tácito Ortíz; r per person US$6) This hotel has cheerful, clean rooms with fan, mosquito net and private bathrooms.

Hotel Continental (☎ 278-0125; Imbabura; r per person with fan/air-con US$7/10) Fishing murals and creaky floorboards adorn this antiquated hotel. Sizable, clean rooms have TV and warm showers.

Ballet Azul (Imbabura; mains US$2-6) Excellent seafood and knockout *batidos*.

La Red (Isidro Ayora near Imbabura; mains US$3-10) Ambiance is minimal, but the food is lip-smacking good. Try the *encocado* (fish in spicy coconut sauce).

Getting There & Away

Buses to Ibarra (US$4, four hours) depart at 1pm and 3pm from the corner of Imbabura and Tácito Ortíz. Buses to Esmeraldas (US$5, five hours) and Borbón (US$1.20, one hour) depart hourly between 5am and 4pm from the central plaza.

Although boat traffic has dwindled with the completion of the road to Borbón and Esmeraldas, there are still departures at 8:30am and 11am for La Tola (US$6, 2½ hours), via Limones (US$3, 1½ hours). The ride through the coastal mangroves to these tiny, predominantly Afro-Ecuadorian fishing villages is quite an experience. Prepare for sun, wind and spray. The 8:30am departure connects in La Tola with buses to Esmeraldas (four to five hours).

BORBÓN & AROUND

☎ 06

The only reason to stop in this small, muddy, ramshackle lumber port (besides to watch the old men play dominoes) is to make boat connections up the Ríos Cayapas and San Miguel to Reserva Ecológica Cotacachi-Cayapas, or up the Río Santiago to Playa de Oro. In Borbón, **La Tolita Pampa de Oro** (r per person with shared/private bathroom US$3/5) offers basic lodging in a rambling blue boarding house. There are several simple restaurants in town.

An hour beyond Borbón (traveling along the coast, not upriver) is the friendly seaside village of **Río Verde**, where the recommended **Hostería Pura Vida** (☎ 274-4203; hosteriapuravida.com; r per person US$10, cabañas US$15; meals US$3-5) offers clean rooms or *cabañas* near the beach. It also has a restaurant. The owners arrange mountain biking, fishing and other excursions and volunteering in local schools.

Buses from Borbón to Esmeraldas (US$3, four hours) and San Lorenzo (US$1.20, one hour) leave frequently. Esmeraldas-bound buses will drop you at Pura Vida, 2km past the Río Verde bridge.

RESERVA ECOLÓGICA COTACACHI-CAYAPAS

Borbón's daily passenger boat to **San Miguel** (US$8, five hours, 11am) is a fascinating trip into the little-explored coastal interior, enthusiastically described by one visitor as 'the *other* heart of darkness.' San Miguel is the jumping-off point for trips into the rarely-visited Reserva Ecológica Cotacachi-Cayapas (admission US$5).

The park boasts waterfalls, rainforest trails, great bird-watching and opportunities to see monkeys and other wildlife. A shop in San Miguel sells a few supplies and basic meals are available for about US$5. Indigenous Cayapas people live across the river and can be visited. The **San Miguel Eco-project** (☎ in Quito 02-252-8769; www.ecosanmiguel.org; tour/accommodation package per day US$30) is a community-run program offering two and three day trips into the rainforest. The **ranger station** (per person US$5), perched on a small hill with spectacular views of the rainforest and river, offers basic accommodations. Beware of ferocious chiggers. The best time to visit the park is from September to December.

The daily passenger canoe does not return to San Miguel unless passengers have made previous arrangements, so advise the boatman. It will then leave San Miguel around 4am.

PLAYA DE ORO

The other river leading inland from the Borbón is Río Santiago. The furthest community up the river is the remote settlement of **Playa de Oro**, near the border of Reserva Ecológica Cotacachi-Cayapas. Half an hour upstream from Playa de Oro is the **Playa de Oro Reserva de Tigrillos**, a 10,000-hectare reserve that protects native jungle cats. The best way to experience

ECUADOR

it is by staying at the community operated river-side **jungle lodge** (www.touchthejungle.org; r per person US$50). Prices include three meals and local guides. It's an authentic-feeling and totally unique experience.

Playa de Oro is about five hours upstream from Borbón, but there are no regular boats. You have to take the 7:30am bus from Borbón to Selva Alegre (US$3, two hours). From Selva Alegre, if you made a reservation, a boat from Playa de Oro will motor you up to the village or the reserve. The two-hour river trip (2½ hours if you're going to the reserve) from Selva Alegre costs US$50, split among the number in your group. Reservations must be made at least a month in advance with **Rosa Jordan** (rosaj@touchthejungle .org) or **Tracy Wilson** (tracy@touchthejungle.org); both speak English.

ESMERALDAS

☎ 06 / pop 95,124

Lively, noisy and notoriously dodgy, Esmeraldas is an important port and home to a major oil refinery. For travelers, it's little more than a necessary stop to make bus connections. If you need to spend the night, the old, wooden **Hostal Miraflores** (☎ 272-3077; Bolivar 6-04, 2nd fl, on the plaza; s/d US$4/8) is the best bet for backpackers.

The airport is 25km up the road to San Lorenzo; taxi fare is US$6. **TAME** (☎ 272-6862/3; Bolívar at 9 de Octubre), near the plaza, flies to Quito (US$33) on Tuesday, Thursday, Friday and Sunday.

Buses leave from different stops within walking distance of each other and the main plaza. **Aero Taxi** (Sucre near Rocafuerte), **Transportes Occidentales** (9 de Octubre near Sucre), **Transportes Esmeraldas** (10 de Agosto, Plaza Central) and **Panamérica International** (Piedrahita near Olmedo) all go to Quito (US$6, six hours). Occidentales and Esmeraldas both have many buses to Guayaquil (US$5 to US$7, eight hours), Ambato, Machala ($7, nine hours) and other cities. **Reina del Camino** (Piedrahita near Bolívar) serves Manta (US$7, seven hours) and Bahía de Caráquez (US$7, eight hours).

Transportes La Costeñita (Malecón Maldonado) and **Transportes del Pacífico** (Malecón Maldonado) head frequently to Atacames and Súa (both US80¢, about one hour) and Muisne (US$2, two hours). These companies also go to Borbón (US$3.50, four hours) and San Lorenzo (US$5, five hours). These buses pass the airport.

ATACAMES

☎ 06 / pop 9785

Crowded with thatched bars, sarong shops and festive *serranos,* Ecuador's most popular beach can be interpreted in two ways: as chaotic fun or a crowded nightmare. Impressions depend on mind-set and time of year. During the high season (July to mid-September, Christmas through New Year's, Carnaval and Easter), it's nonstop *farra.* The rest of the season, it's dead.

Buses drop passengers off in the center of town, on the main road from Esmeraldas (get off at the tricycle rickshaw stand). The center is on the inland side of the highway, and the beach is reached by a small footbridge over the Río Atacames or by rickshaw (US$1). Most of the hotels and bars are along the *malecón* (waterfront).

Dangers & Annoyances

A powerful undertow here causes drownings every year, so keep within your limits. There have been assaults on late-night beach goers, and camping is unsafe. Don't leave anything unattended on the beach.

Sleeping

Hotels fill up fast on weekends and holidays. Prices quoted here are for the high season, during which hotels generally charge a four-person minimum (the number of beds in most hotel rooms).

At the west end of the *malecón,* Calle Las Acacias runs away from the beach toward the highway. Atacames' cheapest hotels are along this street. Most of them are simple but just fine.

Galería (☎ 273-1149; Malecón; r per person US$8; 🔊) Guests have raved about this bare-bones beachfront motel with all the ambiance of a pile of driftwood washed ashore. Pool use costs US$2 extra.

Hotel Jennifer (☎ 273-1055; near Malecón; r per person US$10) Spartan but good rooms, plus rustic cabins out back. Excellent value.

Cabañas Sol y Mar (☎ 273-1524; r per person US$10; P 🔊) Service is indifferent, but rooms are tiled and airy.

Cabañas Los Bohios (☎ 273-1089; Calle Principal; r per person US$14; cabañas per person US$27 P 🔊) Amenable but cramped doll-sized bamboo *cabañas* with TV and fans set in prim gardens.

Hotel Tahiti (☎ 273-1078; Malecón; r per person US$20, cabañas US$12; P 🔊) Beachfront digs with cheap, dark *cabañas* or cheerier hotel rooms.

Villas Arco Iris (☎ 273-1069; www.villasarcoiris.com; Malecón; r per person US$22; 🖺 🕭) Atacames' coziest beachside retreat has impeccable service and a relaxed atmosphere.

Eating

Restaurants near the beach all serve the same thing – the day's catch. Locals pour into the *ceviche* stalls west of the footbridge. You adventurous eaters should join them. Bowl starts at around US$3.

Walfredo's (Calle Principal; mains US$3-6) For a seafood selection as giant as its open-air dining area, try this local favorite (the street is parallel to and behind the *malecón*).

Pizzería No Name (Malecón; pizzas US$5-8) The place for pizza.

Getting There & Away

There are regular buses to Esmeraldas (US80¢, one hour), as well as south to Súa (US50¢, 10 minutes), Same (US50¢, 15 minutes) and Muisne (US$1.50, 1½ hours). Transportes Occidentales and Aerotaxi, whose offices are near the highway, both go to Quito daily (US$9, seven hours).

SÚA
☎ 06

This friendly fishing village, 6km west of Atacames, is far more tranquil than its party-town neighbor. It's a good place to kick the feet up in the sun and swim in the mellow bay.

There are fewer lodgings here than in Atacames, but they're also quieter and often better value if you aren't looking for nightlife. **Hotel Chagra Ramos** (☎ 273-1006; r per person US$7) has a good, inexpensive restaurant, a little beach and nice views. Off the beach, the perfectly acceptable **Hotel El Peñón de Súa** (☎ 273-1013; s/d US$8/16) has concrete-wall rooms. On the beach, **Hotel Las Bouganvillas** (☎ 273-1008; s/d US$8/16) has cheery rooms with balconies.

SAME & TONCHIGÜE
☎ 06

Exclusive hotels hug the palm-fringed coast of Same (*sah*-may), a resort village 6km southwest of Súa. A notch tamer than even Súa, its quiet, moneyed aesthetic is the antithesis of Atacames. Colombian-owned **Azuca** (☎ 733-343; Entrada Las Canoas, Carretera; r per person US$10), on the highway, is the cheapest place in town. It's an eclectic, artsy place with just a few rooms over a good restaurant.

About 3km past Same, Tonchigüe is a tiny fishing village whose beach is a continuation of the Same beach. **Playa Escondida** (☎ 273-3122, 09-973-3368; www.playaescondida.com.ec; camp site per person US$5, r per person US$8-12) is 3km west of Tonchigüe and 10km down the road to Punta Galeras. It's an isolated, quiet, beautiful spot, run by a Canadian named Judy. It has a restaurant and lots of empty, hidden beach.

MUISNE
☎ 05

Muisne's long, wide beach is exposed to the wind and backed by a few sandy little hotels and simple restaurants. Most of Muisne is on an island, separated from the mainland by the Río Muisne. Buses stop at the dock, where boats (US20¢) cross the river to the town. On the island, the main road heads from the dock through the 'center' of town and crumbles slowly away to the beach, 1.5km away. Hire an 'ecotaxi' (tricycle) for a ride to the beach if you're feeling lazy.

The rustic, wooden, rambling pink **Playa Paraíso** (☎ 248-0192; r per person US$5, cabañas US$8) is the best on the beach. It has a lovely garden, hammocks and English-speaking owners. Just down the beach, **Spondylus** (☎ 248-0279; r per person with shared/private bathroom US$7/9) is also good.

Many of the restaurants scattered along the beach serve *encocado*; it's usually excellent.

La Costeñita runs hourly buses to Esmeraldas (US$2, 2½ hours) via Atacames (one hour). Transportes Occidentales has night buses to Quito (US$8, eight hours). Buses head daily to Santo Domingo, with connections to Quito and Guayaquil.

The easiest way to work south from Muisne is by bussing to the road junction known as **El Salto** (US50¢, 30 minutes) and then grabbing a passing bus to **Pedernales**. Between El Salto and Pedernales, you sometimes have to change buses in **San José de Chamanga** (you'll recognize Chamanga by the floating piles of garbage and stilted houses). Pedernales has connections further south and into the highlands.

MOMPICHE
☎ 05

Besides a stretch of palm-fringed sands, Mompiche has little else. That's the beauty. Its claim to fame is its world-class wave – a left-hand point-break that rolls to life during big swells. Get your 40 winks at **Gabeal** (09-969-6543; east beach; camping US$3, r per person US$15), a set of bamboo cabins with cold water bathrooms. Horse-riding and surf lessons are available.

Rancheras go to and from Esmeraldas every day (US$3.50, 3½ hours), passing Atacames on the way.

CANOA
 05 / pop 6086

Surfers, fishermen and sun-seekers share this gorgeous, fat strip of beach – one of the best around – and the village continues to grow. **Caves** at the northern end of the beach can be reached at low tide.

Hot showers and friendly service make **Hostal Shelmar** (09-864-4892; shelmar66@hotmail .com; Av Javier Santos 304; r per person US$6) a great deal. It's a few blocks from the beach.

Dutch-owned **Hotel Bambu** (261-6370; www .ecuadorexplorer.com/bambu; camp sites US$2, s/d with shared bathroom US$7/12, private bathroom US$20) rents spotless, cottagelike rooms on the beach. The grounds are scattered with hammocks, the restaurant is excellent, and juices and cold beers make everyone happy.

Spacious cabins surround a clean swimming pool at **La Posada de Daniel** (261-6373; posadadedaniel183@hotmail.com; camping US$4, r per person US$8;). Three blocks inland.

Arenabar (Malecón; pizzas US$2-3) has tasty pizza and dancing on Saturday nights.

Three blocks up from the beach, **Restaurante Torbellino** (mains US$3-5) serves excellent seafood and delicious, cheap *almuerzos*.

SAN VICENTE
 05

This busy town is a short ferry ride across the Río Chone from the more popular resort of Bahía de Caráquez. Most travelers stop only for bus connections or to catch the ferry to Bahía.

Buses leave from the market area near the pier. Costa del Norte offers hourly service to Pedernales (US$3, three hours). Coactur serves Manta, Portoviejo and Guayaquil (US$7, six hours) daily. Ferries to Bahía de Caráquez (US35¢, 10 minutes) leave often from the pier between 6am and 10pm.

BAHÍA DE CARÁQUEZ
 05 / pop 19,700

Chalk-colored high-rises, red tile roofs, manicured yards and swept sidewalks give this self-proclaimed 'eco-city' a tidy impression.

You'd hardly know it was devastated by a massive earthquake, followed by floods, in 1998. Today, the town market recycles its waste, organic shrimp farms are starting up, and reforestation projects dot the hillside. There are several interesting eco and cultural tours worth checking out, but if you're after beaches you'll have to head elsewhere.

Orientation & Information

The town is on a small peninsula only four blocks wide at its narrowest, northern point. Ferries from San Vicente cross the Río Chone and dock at the piers along Malecón Alberto Santos, on the peninsula's eastern side. Most services are on and around the *malecón* and the parallel street of Bolívar, one block west.

Genesis Net (Malecón Alberto Santos 1302; per hr US$1.60) offers Internet access. **Banco de Guayaquil** (Bolívar & Riofrío) cashes traveler's checks and has an ATM.

Tours

Tours in Bahía are unique. The two operators listed here devote themselves to ecotourism and will show you local environmental projects and take you to handmade-paper cooperatives. Both companies offer day trips to Islas Fragatas in the Chone estuary. **Guacamayo Bahíatours** (269-1412; www.guacamayotours .com; Bolívar at Arenas) also arranges stays at nearby Río Muchacho Organic Farm. **Bahía Dolphin Tours** (269-2097/86; Bolívar 1004) offers visits to its nearby archaeological site.

Sleeping

The cheapest places usually have water-supply problems.

Bahía Hotel (269-0509; Malecón Alberto Santos at Vinueza; r per person US$7-10) Rooms at this cheery hotel overlooking the water are a little worn out, but they're clean.

La Herradura (269-0446; Bolívar 202; s US$8-16, d US$20-25;) Old Spanish home with antiques and artwork brimming from its nooks. Upper-level rooms have balconies; two have ocean views.

Other cheapies include:

Residencia Vera (269-1581; Ante 212 near Bolívar; r per person US$4) Fair value; very basic but fine.

Bahía B&B (269-0146; Ascázubi 322; r per person with shared/private bathroom US$6/8) Fine for a night.

El Viajero (269-0792; Bolívar 910; s/d US$8/16) Ample, simple rooms in a rambling old house.

ECUADOR

Eating

Several restaurants line the waterfront near the pier. The best are **La Chozita** (Malecón Alberto Santos; mains US$4-6) and **Muelle Uno** (Malecón Alberto Santos; mains US$4-6). Both do grilled meat and fish.

Picantería la Patineta (Ascázubi near Malecón Alberto Santos; soup US$1; ⊙ 8:30am-12:30pm) Serves delicious *encebollado*. Ultra-cheap breakfast tradition.

Rincón Manabita (cnr Malecón Alberto Santos & Aguilera; mains US$2-3) The place to go for grilled chicken (evening only).

Arena Bar (Bolívar 811; mains US$2-5; ⊙ 5pm-midnight) Chow down on pizza, salads and more; good music, casual surf decor.

Getting There & Away

For boat information, see San Vicente (p711). Buses stop at the southern end of Malecón Alberto Santos, near the Bahía Hotel. Coactur buses serve Portoviejo (US$1.50, ½ hours) and Manta (US$3, 2½ hours) every hour. Reina del Camino serves Quito (US$9, eight hours), Esmeraldas (US$7, eight hours), Santo Domingo (US$4, four hours) and Guayaquil (US$5, six hours).

MONTECRISTI
☎ 05

Likely the most famous town in Ecuador, Montecristi is known throughout the world for producing the finest straw hat on the planet – the mistakenly labeled **panama hat**. In Ecuador they're called *sombreros de paja toquilla* (*toquilla* straw is a fine fibrous straw endemic to the region). Countless places in town sell hats, but for a proper *super-fino* (the finest, most tightly woven hat of all), you'll need to visit the shop and home of **José Chávez Franco** (☎ 260-6343; Rocafuerte 386), behind the church. You can pick up a beauty for less than US$100, cheaper than just about anywhere else in the world. Montecristi is 15 minutes by bus from Manta (US20¢). Cuenca (see p693) is another great place to buy panama hats.

MANTA
☎ 05 / pop 183,100

Come daylight, local fishing crews hoist in their catch and head ashore to transform **Tarqui beach** into a scene of prattling housewives, restaurant owners and seafood buyers all haggling for the best of the haul. Nearby, giant

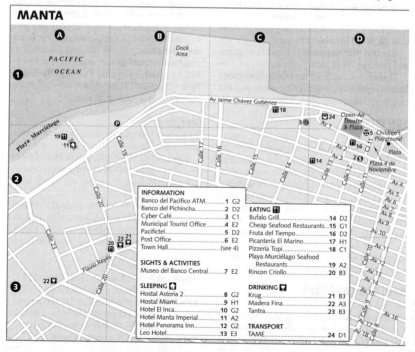

MANTA

INFORMATION	
Banco del Pacífico ATM	**1** G2
Banco del Pichincha	**2** D2
Cyber Café	**3** C1
Municipal Tourist Office	**4** E2
Pacifictel	**5** D2
Post Office	**6** E2
Town Hall	(see 4)

SIGHTS & ACTIVITIES	
Museo del Banco Central	**7** E2

SLEEPING	
Hostal Astoria 2	**8** G2
Hostal Miami	**9** H1
Hotel El Inca	**10** G2
Hotel Manta Imperial	**11** A2
Hotel Panorama Inn	**12** G2
Leo Hotel	**13** E3

EATING	
Bufalo Grill	**14** D2
Cheap Seafood Restaurants	**15** G1
Fruta del Tiempo	**16** D2
Picantería El Marino	**17** H1
Pizzería Topi	**18** C1
Playa Murciélago Seafood Restaurants	**19** A2
Rincon Criollo	**20** B3

DRINKING	
Krug	**21** B3
Madera Fina	**22** A3
Tantra	**23** B3

TRANSPORT	
TAME	**24** D1

wooden fishing boats are still built by hand on the beach, continuing the *manteños* (people from Manta) strong seafaring tradition. This may not be the place for empty, paradisiacal beaches, but it's an interesting place to soak up the atmosphere of a busy, relatively safe Ecuadorian port city.

Manta is named after the Manta culture (AD 500 to 1550), known for its pottery and navigational skills. The Mantas sailed to Central America, Peru and possibly the Galápagos.

Orientation

A stinky inlet divides the town into Manta (west side) and Tarqui (east side); the two sides are joined by a vehicle bridge. Manta has the main offices, shopping areas and bus terminal, while Tarqui has the cheaper hotels.

The airport is 3km east of Tarqui, and the bus terminal, conveniently, is in Manta, one block off the *malecón*.

Information

Banco del Pacífico ATM (cnr Av 107 & Calle 103, Tarqui) Traveler's checks, ATM.

Banco del Pichincha (Av 2 at Calle 11, Manta) Traveler's checks, ATM.

Cyber Café (Av 1 near Calle 14; per hr US70¢)

Municipal tourist office (☎ 261-1471; Calle 9, Town Hall)

Pacifictel (Malecón de Manta) Telephone center; on the Manta waterfront.

Post office (Calle 8 at Av 4, Manta)

Sights

The clean, wide **Playa Murciélago**, which lies 2km west of Manta's center, is popular with residents and Ecuadorian tourists alike. **Tarqui beach** is less picturesque, but it's interesting in the early morning when fisherfolk haul their catches ashore in front of the boat-building area.

The **Museo del Banco Central** (Malecón de Manta; admission US$1, free Sun; 9am-5pm Mon-Sat, 11am-3pm Sun) houses a small but interesting exhibit on the Manta culture.

Sleeping

Prices rise during holiday weekends and the December-to-March and June-to-August high seasons, when single rooms are hard to find.

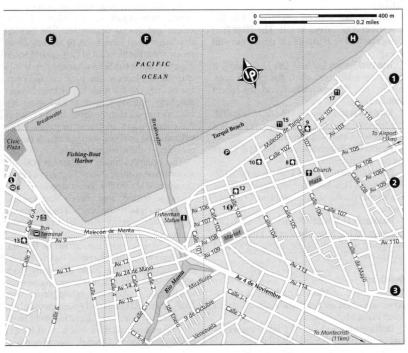

Hostal Astoria 2 (☎ 0262-8045; Av 105 at Calle 106, Tarqui; r per person US$5) Fresh paint and new furnishings make this well-kept cheapie a great value.

Hostal Miami (☎ 0262-2055; Av 102 & Calle 107, Tarqui; r per person US$5) Spacious but spartan rooms in sea foam green offer ocean views off the balconies.

Hotel Panorama Inn (☎ 261-1552; Calle 103 near Av 105, Tarqui; s/d US$6/12, annex US$20/40; ⊠) Bare-bones but spacious rooms have private bathrooms, TV and large windows. Drab, yes, but it's a good deal. Pricier rooms in annex have air-conditioning.

Hotel El Inca (☎ 262-0440; Calle 105 & Malecón, Tarqui; s/d US$10/20) This old-world pension has small, neat rooms, wall murals, worn edges, and nostalgic appeal.

Leo Hotel (☎ 262-3159; Av 24 de Mayo, Manta; s with fan/air-con US$12/15; ⊠) Best of the batch near the bus terminal. Good place.

Hotel Manta Imperial (☎ 262-2016; Malecón at Calle 20, Manta; s/d with fan US$27/34, with air-con US$32/40; ⊠ ⊠) This 1960's concrete palace has seen better days, but it's still one of the better deals on the Manta side.

Eating

Cheap outdoor seafood restaurants line the eastern end of Tarqui beach. The **Playa Murciélago seafood** restaurants are newer but still cheap.

Fruta del Tiempo (cnr Av 1 & Calle 12; mains US$1-3) Slip into a bamboo chair for great juices, breakfasts, filling lunches and ice-cream sundaes.

Bufalo Grill (Av 6 btwn Calle 13 & Calle 14; lunch US$2) Freddy cooks up tasty lunch specials in this local hole-in-the-wall favorite.

Pizzería Topi (Malecón de Manta; mains US$3-6) Pizzas till the wee hours.

Rincon Criollo (Flavio Reyes & Calle 20; lunch US$3.50; ⊙ lunch only) This hopping local haunt serves traditional peanut soup, chicken and rice and more.

Picantería El Marino (Malecón de Tarqui & Calle 110; mains US$4-6) Blue checkered tablecloths, whopping seafood plates, ocean views and icy air-con!

Drinking

The epicenter of Manta's nightlife is the intersection of Flavio Reyes and Calle 20, uphill from Playa Murciélago.

Tantra (Flavio Reyes & Calle 20) Packed on weekends with stiletto-heeled salsa dancers.

Madera Fina (Flavio Reyes near Calle 23) This long-time favorite features salsa, reggae and tropical rhythms.

Krug (Flavio Reyes) An amenable bar with a relaxed and welcoming atmosphere.

Getting There & Away

The **airport** (☎ 262-1580) is some 3km east of Tarqui; a taxi costs about US$1. **TAME** (☎ 262-2006; Malecón de Manta) flies daily to Quito (US$45).

Buses depart frequently to Portoviejo (US75¢, 40 minutes), Guayaquil (US$4.50, four hours), Quito (US$8, nine hours) and Bahía de Caráquez (US$3, 2½ hours); and to Puerto López (US$2.50, 2½ hours) and Montañita (US$5, 3½ hours). Coactur goes to Pedernales (US$5, seven hours) and Canoa regularly. Most other major destinations are also served regularly.

PARQUE NACIONAL MACHALILLA
☎ 05

Preserving isolated beaches, coral formations, two offshore islands, tropical dry forest, coastal cloud forest, archaeological sites and 20,000 hectares of ocean, Ecuador's only coastal **national park** (admission US$20) is a marvelous and unique destination. The tropical dry forest seen here used to stretch along much of the Pacific coast of Central and South America, but it has been whacked nearly into extinction. Plants in the park include cacti, various figs and the giant kapok tree. Howler monkeys, anteaters, iguanas and some 200 bird species inhabit the forest interior, while the coastal edges are home to frigate birds, pelicans and boobies, some of which nest in colonies on the offshore islands.

The beautiful beach of **Playa Los Frailes** is about 10km north of Puerto López, just before the town of Machalilla. Buses stop in front of the ranger station, from where a 3km road and a 4km trail lead to the beach. The swimming is good, seabirds are plentiful and camping is allowed.

The barren, sun-charred **Isla de la Plata**, an island 40km northwest of Puerto López, is a highlight of the park, especially from mid-June to mid-October when humpback whales mate offshore and sightings from tour boats (arranged in Puerto López, opposite) are practically guaranteed. The island itself hosts nesting seabird colonies, and a short hike is usually included in the whale-watching tours.

ECUADOR

Outside whale season, you may see dolphins. It takes two to three hours to reach the island. Camping is not permitted.

From the mainland park entrance, 6km north of Puerto López, a dirt road goes 5km to **Agua Blanca** (village admission US$3), a little village with an **archaeological museum** (admission free with village entry; 8am-6pm) and a Manta archaeological site nearby. The area has hiking and horse trails, and guides are available. Camping is permitted here or you can stay in people's homes.

Visitor information is available in Puerto López at the **park headquarters and museum** (260-4170; 8am-5pm Mon-Fri). The US$20 park entrance fee covers all sectors of the park (including the islands) and is valid for five days. If you plan to visit *only* Isla de la Plata, the fee is US$15; the mainland-only fee is US$12. The fee is charged in all sectors of the park, so carry your ticket.

PUERTO LÓPEZ
 05 / pop 7720

Chipped blue fishing boats bob on a beautiful fishhook bay and cheerful hotels, a smattering of ex-pats, slow smiles, happy cafés and a dirt-road pace of life make it tough to leave. With its unbeatable location near Parque Nacional Machalilla, Puerto López is an obligatory stop on any coastal jaunt.

There are Internet cafés in town, and **Banco de Pichincha** (cnr Machalilla & General Córdova) has an ATM and changes traveler's checks.

Tours
Numerous outfits offer trips to Isla de la Plata and/or tours of the mainland area of the park. Most agencies charge US$35 per person (not including the park entrance fee) for a trip to the island and seasonal whale watching. Licensed companies have better boats and more equipment (such as life jackets, radio and backup) than the unlicensed guides who offer the trip for nearly half the price. Companies with good reputations include **Exploramar** (Malecón), **Machalilla Tours** (230-0206; Malecón) and **Mantaraya** (230-0233; General Córdova at Juan Montalvo).

Sleeping
Sol Inn (230-0248; hostal_solinn@hotmail.com; Juan Montalvo near Eloy Alfaro; r per person with shared/private bathroom US$5/6) Sol Inn definitely has a *buena onda* (good vibe) thanks to its friendly, young owners. It's a two-story bamboo-and-wood

structure with colorfully painted rooms and a communal outdoor kitchen.

Hostal Monte Libano (230-0231; Malecón southern end; r per person US$5-6) Rooms aren't for claustrophobes, but the place is nonetheless clean and friendly. It's close to the beach.

Hostal Flipper (230-0221; General Córdova at Rocafuerte; s/d US$6/12) Immaculate new *hostal* with terracotta walls and airy rooms.

Hostería Itapoá (09-984-3042, in Quito 02-255-1569; Calle Abdón Calderón; cabañas per person US$7.50) This hospitable Brazilian/Ecuadorian place is an affordable retreat of whitewashed *cabañas* set around a blooming garden bordered by hammocks.

Hostería Mandala (230-0181, 09-950-0880; cabins s/d/tr US$15/24/36;) Just north of town, this beautiful beachfront *hostería* (small hotel) has a handful of ecologically-minded cabins set in a labyrinthine garden. The lodge has a bar, game room and multilingual library, and the restaurant serves delectable breakfasts, Italian fare and local seafood. Outstanding.

Eating
Café Bellena/The Whale Café (Malecón; mains US$2-6) Serves great breakfasts (the apple-cinnamon pancakes are sublime), excellent desserts and pizzas and vegetarian meals.

Patacon Pisa'o (General Córdova; mains US$3) Forget seafood. This tiny Colombian joint serves fantastic *arepas* (maiz pancakes) with shredded beef, chicken or beans.

Bellitalia (Juan Montalvo; from 6pm) This candle-lit little number offers divine Italian food, good wine and a great tiramisu.

Along the *malecón* you'll find traditional seafood restaurants with patio dining. **Restaurant Carmita** (Malecón; mains US$2-3) is the best known but others, like Picantería Rey Hojas and Mayflower, serve up comparable fare.

Getting There & Away
There are several daily buses to Quito (US$12, 11 hours). Buses to Jipijapa can drop you at the national park entrance and at other coastal points. Hourly buses head south to Santa Elena and can drop you at points along the way.

SOUTH OF PUERTO LÓPEZ
 04

This stretch of the Ruta del Sol (Route of the Sun) is particularly inviting, thanks to its tiny fishing villages and wide beaches. Some 14km south of Puerto López (right after the village of Puerto Rico), **Hostería Alandaluz** (☎ 278-0690; in Quito ☎ 02-254-3042; www.andaluzhosteria.com; camping US$4, r per person US$14-33) is one of Ecuador's first self-sustaining, low-impact resorts. It's Ecuadorian-run and built from fast-growing (and easily replaceable) local bamboo and palm leaves. You can bask on the undisturbed beach, ride horses, play volleyball or just hang out – the atmosphere is very relaxed. Meals are provided at reasonable prices.

The next village south (blink and you'll miss it) is **Las Tunas**. The beach here is long, wide and empty. You'll know you're in Las Tunas when you spot the grounded bow of a giant wooden boat, which is actually the restaurant-half of a hotel, appropriately called **La Barquita** (The Little Boat; ☎ 278-0051, 278-0683; www .labarquita-ec.com; dm US$10, d/tr US$28/36) and has clean, comfortable doubles with hammocks out front, a few *cabañas* and inexpensive dorm beds. Also in Las Tunas is **Hostería La Perla** (☎ 278-0701; www.proyectospondylus.org; s/d US$20/40), a romantic beach house weathered by sun and sand. Owner Mónica Fabara is a marine biologist and highly regarded local guide.

Sandwiched between verdant tropical hills and another long, wide beach, the sandy little village of **Ayampe** is about 17km south of Puerto López, right on the Guayas-Manabí provincial line. Of the handful of excellent guesthouses here, the tiny, delightful **Cabañas de la Iguana** (☎ 278-0605; www.ayampeiguana.com; r with shared/private bathroom per person US$7/8) is the cheapest. The hillside **Finca Punta Ayampe** (☎ 278-0616; www.fincapuntaayampe.com; r/cabaña per person US$8/12) is very groovy.

The next coastal village is **Olón**, which has a nice beach, a cheap *pensión* and a pricey hotel.

MONTAÑITA
☎ 04

Blessed with the country's best surf – and more budget hotels than you can shake your board at – Montañita means bare feet, baggy shorts, surf and scene. Some dig it, others despise it. Despite its rapid growth, it's as mellow and friendly as ever. Several shops in town rent boards.

There are several **cybercafés** in town. **Banco de Guayaquil** has an ATM.

Sleeping & Eating
Hotels in the village are cheaper than those along the beach toward La Punta (The Point).

Book a room in advance (and bring earplugs) during the December-through-April high season. Restaurants are plentiful; stroll around and choose what looks best.

La Casa del Sol (☎ 290-1302; www.casasol.com; r per person US$4-10) Comfortable but not too luxurious, this one's laid-back and lovely – an excellent choice down on the beach.

Tiki Limbo Backpackers Hostel (☎ 254-0607; tikilimbo@hotmail.com; r per person from US$5) Noisy as the rest of 'em on this strip, the Tiki Limbo boasts a fantastic second floor lounge area. There's a good vegetarian restaurant attached.

El Centro del Mundo (☎ 278-2831; r per person with shared/private bathroom US$5/6) Three-story behemoth close to the beach with no frills rooms and makeshift shared toilets and showers. Communal balconies face the ocean.

Cabañas Pakaloro (☎ 290-1366; pakaloro69@hotmail .com; s/d US$6/11) Beautiful craftsmanship, attention to detail, immaculate rooms, porch hammocks and polished wooden floors makes this one of the best in town.

Charo Hostal (☎ 290-1344; charo117@msn.com; r from US$8) Though it lacks the rustic vibe of others in town, its beachfront location and clean, well kept rooms are recommended.

Paradise South (☎ 290-1185; www.paradisesouthec .com; r US$10-20) Down on the beach and great for those seeking silence. The adobe-walled cottages have ceramic floors and modern bathrooms.

Getting There & Away
Three CLP buses pass Montañita on their way south to Guayaquil (US$5, 3½-four hours) at 5am, 1pm and 5pm. Buses south to Santa Elena (US$1.50, 1¼ hours) and La Libertad, or north to Puerto Lopez (US$1.50, one hour) pass every fifteen minutes.

MANGLARALTO
☎ 04

With a smattering of basic hotels and restaurants, this wee town on a wide-open beach lies 4km from Montañita. South of Manglaralto, **Valdivia** is home to Ecuador's oldest archaeological site.

Fundación Pro Pueblo (☎ 278-0231; www.propueblo .com) offers travelers the chance to visit remote coastal villages and stay with local families. A nominal fee includes meals, guides and mules. This nonprofit organization promotes sustainable development, local artisans and responsible tourism.

Just north of town on the beach, **Kamala Hostería** (☎ 242-3754; www.kamalahosteria.com; dm per person US$3, cabanas US$25-$45) is a hodgepodge of jerry-rigged *cabañas* owned by four backpackers. PADI dive courses, horse-riding and day tours are offered, and a restaurant serves food. Monthly full-moon parties too!

SANTA ELENA & LA LIBERTAD

If you're heading south to Guayaquil and don't take one of the direct CLP buses (see Montañita), you'll have to change buses in one of these two cities. Santa Elena is easiest – the driver will drop you where the road forks; cross the street and flag a bus on the other fork. Avoid the ugly, dusty, busy port of La Libertad.

PLAYAS

☎ 04

Hovering somewhere between interesting and ugly, Playas is the nearest beach resort to Guayaquil. It's slammed from January to April, when prices rise, tents and litter adorn the beach, discos thump into the night and the open-air seafood restaurants (half the fun of Playas) stay packed all day. It's almost deserted at other times.

There's some good surf around Playas; get information at the local surf club **Playas Club Surf** (☎ 09-725-9056; cnr Paquisha & Av 7) at Restaurant Jalisco.

The cheapest hotels have brackish running water. **Residencial El Galeón** (☎ 276-0270; cnr Guayaquil & A Garay; r with shared/private bathroom per person US$4/5), one block east of the central plaza, is clean and friendly. The spotless, four-story **Hotel Arena Caliente** (☎ 228-4097; www.hotelarenacaliente.com; Av Paquisha; s/d US$28/35; ✿ ☐) is easily the cream of this crop.

Transportes Villamil runs frequent buses to Guayaquil (US$2.50, 1¾ hours).

GUAYAQUIL

☎ 04 / pop 2,118,000

Sure, the country's biggest city is an oppressively hot, noisy and chaotic place. But it's worth hanging around for a few days to understand why *guayacos* (people from Guayaquil) are so damn proud of it. For starters, Guayaquil has come a long way from its dismal days as a dangerous port town offering nothing but trouble to the visitor. The city has transformed the once crime-ridden waterfront along the wide Río Guayas into a 2.5km

outdoor showpiece. The historical neighborhood of Las Peñas, as well as Guayaquil's principal downtown thoroughfare, Calle 9 de Octubre, have also been restored. These areas, as well as the city's downtown parks, plazas and museums, are safe and fun to explore. If you're not enamored of big cities, however, you won't like this one.

All flights to the Galápagos either stop or originate in Guayaquil. Subsequently, it's the next best place (after Quito) to set up a trip to the islands.

Orientation

Most travelers stay in the center of town, which is organized in a gridlike fashion on the west bank of Río Guayas. The main east-west street is 9 de Octubre. The Malecón 2000 (the city's recently rebuilt riverfront promenade) stretches along the bank of the Río Guayas, from the Mercado Sur (near the diagonal Blvd José Joaquín Olmedo) at its southern tip, to Barrio Las Peñas and the hill of Cerro Santa Ana to the north. The suburb of Urdesa, which is frequently visited for its restaurants and nightlife, is about 4km northwest and 1.5km west of the airport.

Information
BOOKSTORES
Librería Científica (Map pp720-1; Luque 225) A small selection of English-language travel guides are available here.

INTERNET ACCESS
The following cybercafés charge under US$1 per hour.
American Cyber (Map p722; ☎ 264-7112; Oxandaberro near Av Isidro Ayora)
Cyber@City (Map pp720-1; Ballén near Chile, Unicentro Shopping Center)
CyberNet (Map pp720-1; Luque 1115) Next door to Hotel Alexander.
Internet 50¢ (Map pp720-1; Rumichacha 818 near 9 de Octubre; per hr US50¢)
Joeliki Cybernet (Map pp720-1; Moncayo near Vélez)
SCI Cyber Center (Map pp720-1; cnr Chile & Ballén)

MEDICAL SERVICES
Clínica Kennedy (Map pp720-1; ☎ 228-6963/9666; Av del Periodista, Nueva Kennedy suburb) Guayaquil's best hospital.
Dr Serrano Saenz (Map pp720-1; ☎ 230-1373; Boyacá 821 & Junín) Takes drop-ins; speaks English.

MONEY

The following banks change traveler's checks and have ATMs. There are loads of other ATMs downtown.

Banco de Guayaquil (Map pp720-1; cnr Rendón & Panamá)

Banco del Pacífico (Map pp720-1; Paula de Icaza 200)

Banco del Pacífico (Map pp720-1; cnr 9 de Octubre & Ejército)

POST

Post office (Map pp720-1; Carbo near Aguirre)

TELEPHONE

Pacifictel (Map pp720-1; Chile) As well as Pacifictel, around the block from the post office, there are also loads of other telephone call centers.

TOURIST INFORMATION

Centro de Turismo (Map pp720-1; Malecón) Very helpful; in a train car on the Malecón.

Dirección Municipal de Turismo (Map pp720-1; ☎ 252-4100, ext 3477/9; www.guayaquil.gov.ec; Pichincha 605 near 10 de Agosto) Inside the city hall building.

Subsecretario de Turismo Litoral (Map pp720-1; ☎ 256-8764; infotour@telconet.net; Paula de Icaza 203, 5th fl) Information about Guayas and Manabí provinces.

TRAVEL AGENCIES

The agencies listed here arrange affordable Galápagos trips.

Centro Viajero (Map pp720-1; ☎ 230-1283; centrovi@telconet.net; Baquerizo Moreno 1119 at 9 de Octubre, Office 805, 8th fl) Great service; Spanish, English and French spoken.

Dreamkapture Travel (Map p722; ☎ 224-2909; www .dreamkapture.com; Alborada 12a etapa, Benjamín Carrión at Av Francisco de Orellana) French-Canadian owned.

Galápagos Sub-Aqua (Map pp720-1; ☎ 230-5514; Orellana 211 near Panamá, Office 402) Highly recommended Galápagos scuba-diving operator.

Galasam Tours (Map pp720-1; ☎ 230-4488; www .galapagos-islands.com; 9 de Octubre 424, Office 9A) Great deals; bargain hard. Some complaints.

Dangers & Annoyances

The downtown area is fine during the day, but sketchy after dark. The Malecón and the main stairway up Cerro Santa Ana are perfectly safe, even at night. There is a persistent problem with post–ATM withdrawal robberies, so be extra aware for at least a few blocks after leaving the bank. Watch your belongings in the bus terminal and in the Bahía street market.

Sights

MALECÓN 2000

If you've just arrived and you're frazzled and sweaty, get down to the newly reconstructed **waterfront promenade** (Map pp720-1; ⏰ 7am-midnight) and take in the breeze blowing (if you're lucky) off the wide Río Guayas. Known as Malecón 2000, the waterfront is Guayaquil's flagship redevelopment project, stretching 2.5km along the river, from the **Mercado Sur** at the southern end to Cerro Santa Ana and Las Peñas (see following section) to the north. The area is heavily policed and completely safe, even at night (which is when it's most pleasant).

Just north of the Mercado Sur, in the area bound by Olmedo, Chile, Colón and the waterfront, is the crowded and colorful street market **La Bahía** (Map pp720-1; Pichincha), a fascinating area to explore (but watch for pickpockets).

Calle 9 de Octubre is Guayaquil's principal downtown street and oh what a feeling to bounce among the hordes of business people, junk sellers and newspaper vendors beneath some of the city's more austere buildings. The street meets the Malecón at the impressive **La Rotonda** monument. Further north along the Malecón is the modern **Museo Antropológico y de Arte Contemporáneo** (MAAC; Map pp720-1; ☎ 230-9400; Malecón & Loja; admission US$3 Wed-Sat, US$1.50 Tue & Sun; ⏰ 10am-6pm Tue-Sat, 10am-4pm Sun), a museum of anthropology, archaeology and contemporary Ecuadorian art. MAAC also has a 400-seat noncommercial art cinema, an open-air stage and a food court.

LAS PEÑAS & CERRO SANTA ANA

At the northern end of the Malecón, these two historic neighborhoods have been refurbished into an idealized version of a quaint South American hillside village – brightly painted homes, cobblestone alleyways and all. The stairway winding up Cerro Santa Ana past the brightly painted buildings is quite touristy, but views from the hilltop fort (called **Fortín del Cerro**) and the **lighthouse** are wonderful.

To the right of the stairs, the historic cobbled street of **Calle Numa Pompillo Llona** winds past elegantly decaying wooden colonial houses propped half-heartedly on bamboo supports. Many of the houses over the river are art galleries.

DOWNTOWN AREA

Dinosaurian iguanas roam around the handsome, tree-filled **Parque Bolívar** (Parque Seminario;

Map pp720-1; Chile at Ballén) and stare down small children for their snacks. They're an odd sight. The modern **cathedral** is on the plaza's western side.

The main thoroughfare, **9 de Octubre**, is definitely worth a stroll to experience Guayaquil's commercial vibrancy. Guayaquil's biggest plaza, **Parque del Centenario** (Map pp720-1; 9 de Octubre at Garaycoa), covers four blocks, is full of monuments, and marks the center of the city. The city's most impressive church is the **Church of San Francisco** (Map pp720-1; 9 de Octubre near Chile), which has been reconstructed and beautifully restored since the devastating 1896 fire.

MALECÓN EL SALADO
Like its more famous sister development on the Río Guayas, the Malecón El Salado is an attempt to reclaim the city's other waterfront for the everyday use of its residents. There are several eateries and cafés in a streamlined, modern mall-like building along the estuary and a walkway above.

CITY CEMETERY
This dazzling-white hillside **cemetery** (Map pp720-1; Moncayo & Coronel), with hundreds of tombs, monuments and huge mausoleums, is a Goth's wet dream. A walk through the palm trees leads to the impressive grave of President Vicente Rocafuerte. The cemetery is best reached with a short cab ride.

Festivals & Events
The whole city parties during the last week of July, celebrating Simón Bolívar's birthday (July 24) and Guayaquil Foundation Day (July 25). Hotels fill up and services are disrupted. Celebrations are huge during Guayaquil's Independence Day (October 9) and Día de la Raza (October 12). New Year's Eve is celebrated with bonfires.

Sleeping
Budget hotels are generally poor value and pricey. Downtown is the most logical area to stay. Parts of the northern suburbs are technically closer to the airport and bus terminal, but because of traffic and round about routes, it's no more convenient to stay there.

Hotel Sander (Map pp720-1; ☎ 232-0030; Luque 1101; r per person with fan/air-con US$9/11; ✹) Despite the bare-bones rooms and large bunker-like appearance, 24-hour security, friendly service and a working elevator make the Sander one of the better cheapies.

Hostal Suites Madrid (Map pp720-1; ☎ 230-7804; Quisquis 305; r with fan/air-con US$12/15; ✹) The large, modern rooms here are kept spotless and bright, and lack that down-and-out feeling so characteristic of Guayaquil's budget hotels.

Hotel Montesa (Map pp720-1; ☎ 231-2526; Luis Urdaneta 817 near Rumichaca; r with fan/air-con US$12/15; ✹) Another good budget choice, this new hotel has a gleaming tile lobby to match the small but gleaming rooms. Hot water is hit or miss but the staff is friendly and professional.

Hostal Mar del Plata (Map pp720-1; ☎ 04-230-7610; Junín 718 near Boyacá; s/d with fan US$12/20, s/d with air-con US$18/23; ✹) If you don't mind outdated TVs and a missing toilet seat these clean rooms are a solid choice.

Dreamkapture Hostal (Map p722; ☎ 224-2909; www .dreamkapture.com; Alborada 12a etapa, Manzana 2, Villa 21; s/d with shared bathroom US$12/20, with private bathroom US$18/28; ✹ ✹) In the northern suburb of Alborada, this small, friendly Canadian/Ecuadorian-owned *hostal* boasts spotless rooms, a breakfast room, a TV room and a small garden. There's lots of travel info lying around, and a wholesome breakfast is included in the price. The *hostal* is on Sixto Juan Bernal near the intersection of Benjamín Carrión and Francisco de Orellana. There's no sign; look for the dreamy paintings.

Hotel Andaluz (Map pp720-1; ☎ 231-1057; hotel _andaluz@yahoo.com; Junín 852; s/d US$18/36; ✹) The gate-protected lobby seems incongruent with the attractive facade, but a maze of hallways leads to clean and comfortable rooms.

GETTING INTO TOWN
Guayaquil inaugurated a new international airport in August 2006, but it hadn't yet opened for service at the close of this edition. It's practically next door to the older Simón Bolívar airport on Av de las Américas, 5km north of the center. The bus terminal is 2km north of the airport. A taxi to the center should cost about US$4 to US$5 from either, provided you cross Av de las Américas (rather than hailing one from inside) and bargain. This may not be possible from the new airport. From the bus terminal, buses run down Av de las Américas past the airport to the center; No 71 is a good one to take.

ECUADOR

GUAYAQUIL – CITY CENTER

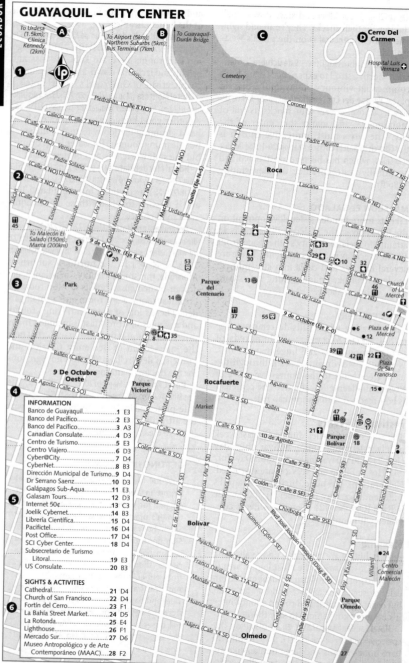

INFORMATION

Banco de Guayaquil	**1** E3
Banco del Pacífico	**2** E3
Banco del Pacífico	**3** A3
Canadian Consulate	**4** D3
Centro de Turismo	**5** E3
Centro Viajero	**6** D3
Cyber@City	**7** D4
CyberNet	**8** B3
Dirección Municipal de Turismo	**9** D4
Dr Serrano Saenz	**10** D3
Galápagos Sub-Aqua	**11** E3
Galasam Tours	**12** D4
Internet 50¢	**13** C3
Joelik Cybernet	**14** B3
Librería Científica	**15** D4
Pacifictel	**16** D4
Post Office	**17** D4
SCI Cyber Center	**18** D4
Subsecretario de Turismo Litoral	**19** E3
US Consulate	**20** B3

SIGHTS & ACTIVITIES

Cathedral	**21** D4
Church of San Francisco	**22** D4
Fortín del Cerro	**23** F1
La Bahía Street Market	**24** D5
La Rotonda	**25** E4
Lighthouse	**26** F1
Mercado Sur	**27** D6
Museo Antropológico y de Arte Contemporáneo (MAAC)	**28** F2

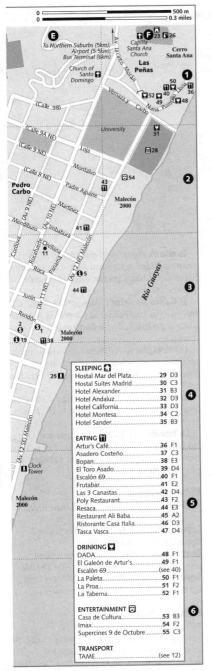

Hotel California (Map pp720–1; ☎ 230-2538; Urdaneta 529; s/d US$20/24; ❄) The rooms aren't as appealing as the marble lobby and professional staff might suggest, but they have cable TV and modern bathrooms.

Hotel Alexander (Map pp720–1; ☎ 253-2000; hotelalexander@hotmail.com; Luque 1107; s/d US$25/30; ❄ ▣) Central location, a pleasant on-site restaurant, free Internet (wireless too) and professional service make up for dark, unimpressive rooms. Great value.

Eating

In terms of eating, downtown Guayaquil hasn't kept pace with the northern suburbs. There are bunches of little, inexpensive eateries catering to working folk, though there are few stand-out restaurants. Informal *parrillas* (grill restaurants) are found around Parque del Centenario, and there are several concentrations of bright, clean fast-food restaurants along the Malecón 2000 and the Malecón El Salado. There's a large food court in the Mall del Sol north of downtown. The best dining experiences are in hotels downtown or in the northwestern suburb of Urdesa.

Poly Restaurant (Map pp720–1; Malecón 303; almuerzos US$1.50) One of the last local style eateries in the area around the Malecón and Las Peñas – serves good cheap lunches.

Asadero Costeño (Map pp720–1; Garaycoa 929; almuerzos US$1.50) Great for cheap grilled chicken.

El Toro Asado (Map pp720–1; cnr Chimborazo & Vélez; mains US$1.50-4) Casual joint with good, reasonably priced grilled meats. *Asado y menestra* (grilled beef with lentils or beans) is the specialty.

Frutabar (Map pp720–1; Malecón; drinks from US$1.50) Here you can choose from over 20 types of *batidos* and sandwiches, snacks and dozens of juice creations.

Restaurant Ali Baba (Map pp720–1; 9 de Octubre; mains US$2) Head to Ali Babas for Middle Eastern staples like hummus and falafel.

Ristorante Casa Italia (Map pp720–1; Rendón 438; mains US$3, almuerzos US$2) The set lunches are a deal at what just might be the only Italian restaurant downtown.

Artur's Café (Map pp720–1; Numa Pompillo Llona 127; mains US$3-7) Long-time local favorite for its unbeatable hideaway atmosphere and superb location over the Río Guayas in Las Peñas. Ecuadorian cuisine is the specialty.

Bopan (Map pp720–1; Malecón & Paula de Icaza; mains US$3-7) Crepes, tortillas, sandwiches and pastas make this a welcome stop on the Malecón.

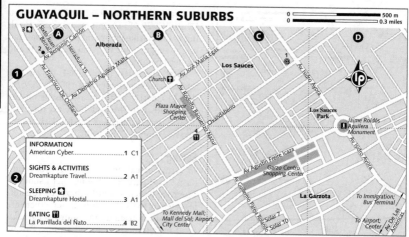

GUAYAQUIL – NORTHERN SUBURBS

INFORMATION	
American Cyber	1 C1

SIGHTS & ACTIVITIES	
Dreamkapture Travel	2 A1

SLEEPING	
Dreamkapture Hostal	3 A1

EATING	
La Parrillada del Ñato	4 B2

Escalón 69 (Map pp720-1; Cerro Santa Ana; mains US$4-8) Romantic elegance meets neighborhood casual at this one of a kind eatery serving creative takes on Ecuadorian cuisine.

Resaca (Map pp720-1; Malecón at Roca; mains US$5-9) The theme is as generic as a TGI Friday's (think checkered tablecloths and chicken wings), but it's fun and the popular bar stays packed on weekend nights.

La Parrillada del Ñato (Map p722; VE Estrada 1219 at Laureles, Urdesa; mains US$6-10) Guayaquil's most famous grill is *well* worth the splurge. Seriously. It's an institution. There's also a **branch** (cnr Demetrio Aguilera Malta & RB Nazur) in Alborada.

Tasca Vasca (Map pp720-1; Ballén 422 & Chimborazo; mains US$8-14) With its smoky, cellar-like atmosphere, gentlemanly waiters and chalkboard menus, this Spanish classic will transport you to the mother country.

Las 3 Canastas (Map pp720-1; cnr Velez & Chile) A downtown spot for fruit shakes, fruit juices and ice cream. Outdoor tables, too.

Drinking

The *farra* in Guayaquil is spread around town, but some of the most interesting, welcoming and stylish bars are conveniently found in the neighborhood of Las Peñas. There are also several downtown near the Malecón 2000. The neighborhoods of Alborada, Kennedy Norte and Urdesa have their fair share of clubs and bars.

DADA (Map pp720-1; Numa Pompilio Llona 177) Hip and stylish, yet warm and welcoming, DADA has an all-wood interior and views of the river.

Escalón 69 (Map pp720-1; Cerro Santa Ana) Above the recommended restaurant of the same name, Escalón 69 has karaoke and live music on weekends.

El Galeón de Artur's (Map pp720-1; Cerro Santa Ana) Also in Las Peñas, El Galeón is a casual place for a drink if you don't mind the loud music.

La Paleta (Map pp720-1; Numa Pompilio Llona) Probably the most bohemian bar in the city, La Paleta offers cave-like nooks, comfy benches and dark wood ambience.

La Proa (Map pp720-1; Malecón at Vernaza y Carbo; US$10 cover) This beautiful, hip bar next to the MAAC cinema is as stylin' as it gets.

La Taberna (Map pp720-1; Cerro Santa Ana) Drink up beneath a hodgepodge of soccer jerseys, newspaper clippings, cigarette cartons and photographs.

Entertainment

El Telégrafo and *El Universo* publish entertainment listings.

Casa de Cultura (Map pp720-1; cnr 9 de Octubre & Moncayo) Foreign films and art flicks.

Imax (Map pp720-1; Malecón 2000; www.imaxmalecon2000.com; admission US$4) Connected to the MAAC.

Supercines 9 de Octubre (Map pp720-1; 9 de Octubre 823 at Avilés; admission US$2) Modern multiplex.

Getting There & Away
AIR

See p719 for information on getting to and from the airport. International flights are subject to a US$25 departure tax. **TAME** downtown (Map pp720-1; ☎ 256-0778, 256-0920; Paula de Icaza 424, Gran Pasaje); airport (☎ 228-2062, 228-7155) offers several flights daily to Quito (US$53), one or two daily to Cuenca (US$41), three a week to Loja (US$41) and one every weekday to Machala (US$28). TAME and **AeroGal** (☎ 228-4218; www.aerogal.com.ec; Airport) fly to Baltra and San Cristóbal airports in the Galápagos (US$344, round trip; US$300, mid-January to mid-June and September through November). **Icaro** (☎ 229-4265; www.icaro.com.ec; Airport) flies to Quito.

BUS

The bus terminal is 2km beyond the airport. There is service to most major towns in the country. Many buses go daily to Quito (US$9, seven to ten hours), Manta (US$4.50, four hours), Esmeraldas (US$7, seven hours) and Cuenca (US$8, 3½ hours).

Several companies at the terminal go to Machala (US$4.50, three hours) and Huaquillas (US$4.50, 4½ hours) on the Peruvian border. The easiest way to Peru, however, is with one of the international lines. **Rutas de America** (☎ 229-7383; Los Rios 3012 at Letamendi),

whose office and terminal is southeast of downtown, has direct buses to Lima (US$50, 24 hours) every day at 6am. **Expresso Internacional Ormeno** (☎ 229-7362; Centro de Negocios El Terminal, Bahía Norte, Office 34, Bloque C) goes daily to Lima (US$55) at 2pm, stopping in Tumbes (US$20, five hours). Its office and terminal is on Av de las Américas just north of the main bus terminal. These services are very convenient because you do not have to get off the bus (let alone change buses) at the border – formalities are taken care of on the bus. Both companies also go to several other South American countries.

Getting Around

Walking is the easiest way of getting around downtown. City buses are cheap (about US20¢) but routes are complicated. A taxi within downtown should cost no more than US$1.50.

MACHALA

☎ 07 / pop 216,900

The self-proclaimed 'banana capital of the world,' Machala is Ecuador's fourth-largest city. Most travelers moving to and from Peru

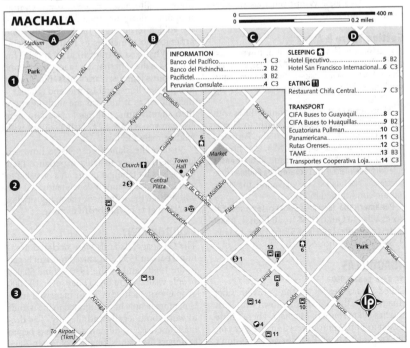

MACHALA

| 0 | 400 m |
| 0 | 0.2 miles |

INFORMATION
Banco del Pacífico......................1 C3
Banco del Pichincha....................2 B2
Pacifictel.................................3 B2
Peruvian Consulate.....................4 C3

SLEEPING
Hotel Ejecutivo..........................5 B2
Hotel San Francisco Internacional..6 C3

EATING
Restaurant Chifa Central.............7 C3

TRANSPORT
CIFA Buses to Guayaquil..............8 C3
CIFA Buses to Huaquillas.............9 B2
Ecuatoriana Pullman..................10 C3
Panamericana..........................11 C3
Rutas Orenses..........................12 C3
TAME.....................................13 B3
Transportes Cooperativa Loja......14 C3

pass through here, but few stay more than a night. It's a chaotic city whose finest attribute is probably the presence of free bananas on restaurant tables. Páez is a pedestrian-only zone between Rocafuerte and 9 de Octubre.

There are many cybercafés in town. **Banco del Pacífico** (cnr Junín & Rocafuerte) and **Banco del Pichincha** (cnr Rocafuerte & Guayas) have ATMs and change traveler's checks. Make phone calls at **Pacifictel** (Montalvo near 9 de Octubre).

Sleeping & Eating

Most hotels have only cold water, and mosquito nets come in handy. There are several cheap *parrilla* restaurants serving inexpensive grilled chicken and steaks on Sucre near Colón.

Hotel San Francisco International (☎ 293-0445, 293-0457; Tarqui near Sucre; s/d with fan US$12/18, with aircon US$17/23; 🔀) The cheaper rooms are small, and have old furniture and chipped paint, while the new rooms are almost snazzy.

Hotel Ejecutivo (☎ 292-3162; Sucre & 9 de Mayo; s/d US$18/25; 🔀) Rooms have views over downtown; the hallways are bright and sunny.

Restaurant Chifa Central (Tarqui near Sucre; mains US$2-5; ⏱ 11am-10pm) Whips out massive portions of Chinese food.

Getting There & Away

The airport is 1km southwest of town; a taxi costs about US$1. **TAME** (☎ 293-0139; www.tame .com.ec; Montalvo near Pichincha) flies to Guayaquil weekdays (US$30); it continues on to Quito (US$55).

There is no central bus terminal. Buses with **CIFA** (cnr Bolívar & Guayas) run regularly to Huaquillas (US$1.50, 1½ hours) at the Peruvian border, and to Guayaquil (US$3, four hours) from 9 de Octubre near Tarqui. **Rutas Orenses** (9 de Octubre near Tarqui) and **Ecuatoriana Pullman** (9 de Octubre near Colón) also serve Guayaquil, the latter has air-conditioned buses.

Panamericana (Bolívar at Colón) offers several buses a day to Quito (US$10, 10 hours). **Transportes Cooperativa Loja** (Tarqui & Bolívar) goes to Loja (US$4.50, seven hours).

HUAQUILLAS
☎ 07 / pop 30,000

Called Aguas Verdes on the Peruvian side, Huaquillas is the main border town with Peru and lies 80km south of Machala. There's little reason to stop. Almost everything happens on the long main street. Ecuadorian banks don't change money (though they have ATMs). The briefcase-toting moneychangers do change money, but numerous rip-offs have been reported.

If you need to spend the night, you'll be fine at **Hotel Hernancor** (☎ 299-5467; 1 de Mayo; s/d US$13/16; 🔀) or **Hotel Rody** (☎ 299-5581; Av Tnte Cordovez & 10 de Agosto; s/d from US$5/10).

CIFA buses run frequently to Machala (US$1.50, 1½ hours) from the main street, two blocks from the border. Ecuatoriana goes daily to Quito (US$10, 12 hours). Ecuatoriana Pullman has buses to Guayaquil (US$4.50, 4½ hours). For Loja (US$5, six hours), use Transportes Loja.

THE GALÁPAGOS ISLANDS

☎ 05 / pop 19,000

Just as it did with Darwin (who came here in 1535), the Galápagos Islands may inspire you to think differently about the world. A trip to these extraordinary islands is like stumbling upon an alternate universe, some strange utopian colony organized by sea lions – the golden retrievers of the Galápagos – and arranged on principles of mutual cooperation. What's so extraordinarily special for humans is the trait that has made the islands' inhabitants famous: fearlessness. Blue footed boobies, sea lions, prehistoric land iguanas – they all act as if humans are nothing more than slightly annoying paparazzi. Nowhere else can you engage in a staring contest with wild animals and lose!

Visiting the islands is expensive, however, and the only way to truly experience their marvels is by taking a cruise. It's possible to visit four of the islands independently, but you will not see the wildlife or the many smaller islands that you will aboard a cruise.

ENVIRONMENT

The Galápagos Islands were declared a national park in 1959. Organized tourism began in the 1960's and by the 1990's some 60,000 people visited annually. Today, over 100,000 people visit each year. With increased tourism, more people have migrated to the islands to work, both legally and illegally. The dramatic increase in human activity has begun to impact the islands' fragile ecology. In 2005, the largest of the eighty tourist boats operating in the Galápagos held 96 passengers. In 2006, the 500-passenger *MV Discovery* made its first visit to the islands. Many see it as the writing on the wall when it comes to mass tourism in the Galápagos.

The islands have faced other problems that include oil spills, the poaching of sea lions for their reproductive organs (which are sold on the international black market), over-fishing, illegal fishing for shark, lobster and other marine life, and the introduction of non-native animals. Obviously, the Galápagos National Park has its hands full protecting itself. Anyone wishing to donate money to the **Charles Darwin Foundation** (www.galapagos.org), the non-profit organization in charge of protecting and studying the islands, can do so online.

ORIENTATION

The most important island is Isla Santa Cruz. On the southern side of the island is Puerto Ayora, the largest town in the Galápagos and where most of the budget tours are based. It has many hotels and restaurants. North of Santa Cruz, separated by a narrow strait, is Isla Baltra, home of the islands' main airport. A public bus and a ferry connect the Baltra airport with Puerto Ayora.

Isla San Cristóbal, the most easterly island, is home to the provincial capital, Puerto Baquerizo Moreno, which also has hotels and an airport. The other inhabited islands are Isla Isabela and Isla Santa María.

INFORMATION

All foreign visitors must pay US$100 (cash only) upon arrival to the national park. The high seasons are from December to January, around Easter, and from June to August; during these periods, budget tours may be difficult to arrange. Note that most of the islands have two or even three names. Galápagos time is one hour behind mainland Ecuador. For the latest news on the islands check out the Charles Darwin Foundation's news site at www.darwinfoundation.org.

COSTS

Plan on spending more money than you want to. For an economy tour, you can count on a minimum of US$500 to US$700 for a one-week trip in the low season, or US$1000 in high season, always plus airfare and the US$100 park entrance fee. The cheapest (although not the best) time to go is between September and November, when the seas are rough and business is dead. You may save money if you arrange a tour independently in Puerto Ayora, though you must factor in hotel expenses.

WHAT TO BRING

Many handy (or even indispensable) items are unavailable in the Galápagos. Stock up on seasickness pills, sunscreen, insect repellent, film, batteries, toiletries and medication on the mainland.

BOOKS

Lonely Planet's *Ecuador & the Galápagos Islands* has loads of Galápagos information. The best general wildlife guide is Michael H Jackson's *Galápagos: A Natural History Guide*. The only guide describing *all* of the vertebrates occurring in the archipelago is *Birds, Mammals and Reptiles of the Galápagos Islands* by A Swash & R Still. Bird-watchers

---

GETTING TO PERU

Formalities are straightforward on both sides of the border. Many travelers report that crossing by overnight bus is easier – it allows you to avoid the crowds, touts and overzealous immigration officials (at night, officials simply want you on your way). The bus company CIFA offers direct international departures from both Machala and Guayaquil to Tumbes, Peru.

The Ecuadorian **immigration office** (no fees; ⏰ 24hr) is 5km outside of Huaquillas and 3km north of the border. Entrance and exit formalities are carried out here. The bus doesn't wait, but if you save your ticket, you can board another passing bus for free. There are also taxis.

When leaving Ecuador, you'll get an exit stamp from the Ecuadorian immigration office. After showing your passport to the international bridge guard, take a shared mototaxi (US50¢) to the Peruvian immigration building, about 2km beyond the border. From here, *colectivos* go to Tumbes (US$1.50; beware of overcharging).

If you're coming *from* Peru, see the boxed text, p912.

should consult *A Field Guide to the Birds of the Galápagos* by Michael Harris. There is also *A Field Guide to the Fishes of Galápagos* by Godfrey Merlen. J Weiner's Pulitzer Prize-winning *The Beak of the Finch* is an eloquent lowdown on evolutionary research in the Galápagos and elsewhere. For more book recommendations, see p734.

VOLUNTEERING
On Isla San Cristóbal, the community organization **Nueva Era** (☎ 252-0489; www.neweragalapagos.org) needs volunteers to work with local kids on environmental issues, art, dance, crafts, beach cleanup etc. Volunteers pay room and board. It's an admirable local organization.

VISITOR SITES
To protect the islands, the national park authorities allow access to about 50 visitor sites, in addition to the towns and public areas. Other areas are off-limits. The visitor sites are where the most interesting wildlife and geology are seen. Apart from the ones mentioned later (near Puerto Ayora and Puerto Baquerizo Moreno), most sites are reached by boat.

Normally, landings are made in a *panga* (skiff). Landings are either 'wet' (where you hop overboard and wade ashore in knee-deep water) or 'dry' (where you get off onto a pier or rocky outcrop). People occasionally fall in the surf (ha ha ha! not funny) of a wet landing or slip on the algae-covered rocks of a dry one. Take it slow and put your camera in a watertight bag. Boat captains will not land groups in places other than designated visitor sites.

In addition to the sites on land, many marine sites have been designated for snorkeling or diving.

TOURS
There are basically three types of tours in the Galápagos: boat-based trips with nights spent aboard; day trips, returning to the same hotel each night (usually in Puerto Ayora or Puerto Baquerizo Moreno) and hotel-based trips, staying in hotels on different islands. The newest type of tour is the kayak tour, currently offered by **Row International** (www.rowinternational.com) for about US$3300 per person. The last two types are usually out of the budget traveler's reach.

Tours do not include the US$100 park fee, airfare and bottled drinks. Neither do they include tips. On a cheap one-week tour, the crew and guide are tipped *at least* US$20 per passenger (about half to the guide).

If you're going to spend a large chunk of change getting to the islands, then seeing the Galápagos is probably important to you and you want to get as much out of it as possible. The economy-class boats are usually OK, but if something is going to go wrong, it's more likely to happen on the cheaper boats. If this is all you can afford and you really want to see the Galápagos, go! It'll probably be the adventure of a lifetime. But, you might consider spending an extra few hundred dollars to go on a more comfortable, reliable boat and get a decent guide. All that said, most people have the time of their lives, regardless.

Day Tours
Most day trips are based in Puerto Ayora, but a few are offered in Puerto Baquerizo Moreno. Several hours are spent sailing to the visitor site(s), the island is visited in the middle of the day and you may be part of a large group. Only a few islands are close enough to either Santa Cruz or San Cristóbal to be visited on day trips.

Because time is spent going back and forth and because you don't visit the islands early or late in the day, we don't recommend day tours. The island visits may be too brief, the guides poorly informed and the crew lacking an adequate conservationist attitude.

Day-trip operators in Puerto Ayora charge about US$40 to US$120 per person per day. Talk to other travelers about how good the guide and boat are. Reject any tour that involves a fuel stop – it can take hours.

Boat Tours
Most visitors go on longer boat tours and sleep aboard overnight. Tours from four to eight days are the most common. You can't really do the Galápagos Islands justice on a tour shorter than a week, although five days is acceptable. To visit the outlying islands of Isabela and Fernandina, two weeks are recommended. On the first day of a prearranged tour, you arrive from the mainland by air at about noon, so this leaves only half a day in the Galápagos; on the last day, you have to be in the airport in the morning. Thus a 'five-day' tour gives only three full days in the islands. Arranging a tour in Puerto Ayora avoids this.

THE GALÁPAGOS ISLANDS

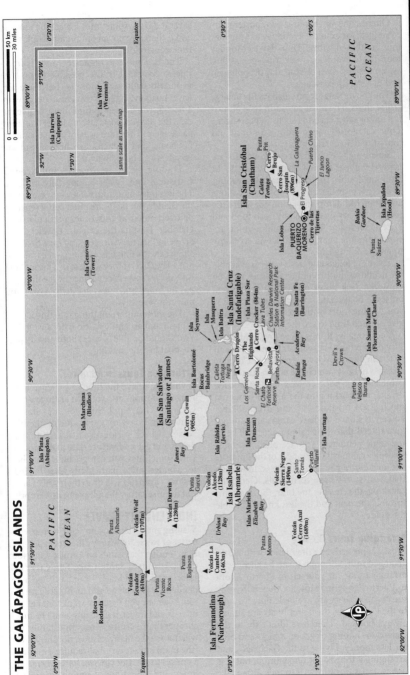

Isla Darwin
(Culpepper)

Isla Wolf
(Wenman)

same scale as main map

PACIFIC OCEAN

Isla Pinta
(Abingdon)

Isla Marchena
(Bindloe)

Isla Genovesa
(Tower)

Isla San Cristóbal
(Chatham)

Caleta
Tortuga
Cerro San
Joaquín
(896m)

Cerro
Brujo

Punta
Pitt

Puerto Chino

El Junco
Lagoon

La Galapaguera

El Progreso

PUERTO
BAQUERIZO
MORENO

Cerro de las
Tijeretas

Isla Lobos

Bahía
Gardner

Punta
Suárez

Isla Española
(Hood)

Isla Santa Cruz
(Indefatigable)

Isla
Seymour

Isla
Mosquera

Isla Baltra

Isla Plaza Sur

Cerro Crocker (864m)

Lava Tubes

Charles Darwin Research
Station & National Park
Information Center

Isla Santa Fe
(Barrington)

The
Highlands

Santa Rosa

Bellavista

Puerto Ayora

Academy
Bay

Bahía
Tortuga

Los Gemelos

El Chato
Tortoise
Reserve

Cerro Dragón

Isla Bartolomé

Rocas
Bainbridge

Caleta
Tortuga
Negra

Devil's
Crown

Isla Santa María
(Floreana or Charles)

Puerto
Velasco
Ibarra

Isla San Salvador
(Santiago or James)

Cerro Cowan
(905m)

Isla Rábida
(Jervis)

James
Bay

Isla Pinzón
(Duncan)

Isla Tortuga

Isla Isabela
(Albemarle)

Volcán Darwin
(1280m)

Punta
García

Volcán
Alcedo
(1128m)

Punta
Albemarle

Volcán Wolf
(1707m)

Volcán
Sierra Negra
(1490m)

Santo
Tomás

Puerto
Villamil

Volcán
Cerro Azul
(1689m)

Punta
Moreno

Islas Mariela

Elizabeth
Bay

Urbina
Bay

Isla Fernandina
(Narborough)

Volcán La
Cumbre
(1463m)

Punta
Espinoza

Punta
Vicente
Roca

Volcán
Ecuador
(610m)

Roca
Redonda

PACIFIC
OCEAN

PACIFIC OCEAN

Equator

0°30'N

0°30'S

1°00'S

0 — 50 km
0 — 30 miles

Often, a one-week tour is two shorter tours combined, for example a Monday to Thursday tour combined with a Thursday to Monday tour. Try to avoid one-week trips such as this, as you'll spend most of Thursday dropping off and picking up passengers.

Tour boats range from small yachts to large cruise ships. The most common type of boat is a motor sailer carrying six to 16 passengers. Tour categories range from economy and tourist to deluxe and luxury.

Seven-night/eight-day economy tours are generally aboard small boats with six to 12 bunks in double, triple and quadruple cabins. Bedding is provided and the accommodations are clean, but damp and cramped, with little privacy. Plenty of simple but fresh food and juice is served at all meals, and a guide accompanies the boat (few guides on economy tours speak English).

There are toilets and fresh water is available for drinking. Bathrooming facilities may be saltwater deck hoses or freshwater showers on some boats. The pre-set itineraries allow you to visit most of the central islands and give enough time to see the wildlife.

Occasionally, things go wrong, and when they do, a refund is usually extremely difficult to obtain. Problems have included last-minute changes of boat (which the contractual small print allows), poor crew, a lack of bottled drinks, not sticking to the agreed itinerary, mechanical breakdowns and overbooking. Passengers have to share cabins and are not guaranteed that their cabin mates will be of the same gender; if you are uncomfortable sharing a cabin with a stranger of the opposite sex, make sure you are guaranteed in writing that you won't have to do this. Generally speaking, the cheaper the tour, the less comfortable the boat and the less knowledgeable the guide.

Arranging Tours On-site

Most people arrive in the islands with a pre-arranged tour, although it can be cheaper to arrange a tour for yourself in Puerto Ayora or Puerto Baquerizo Moreno. Generally, only the cheaper boats are available once you get to the Galápagos; the better boats are almost always booked. Therefore, don't fly to the Galápagos hoping to get on a high-end boat for less money. Flying to the Galápagos and arranging a tour is not uncommon, but it is not as straightforward as it sounds. It can take

several days – sometimes a week or more – and is therefore not an option for people with time constraints.

The best place to organize a tour is from Puerto Ayora. It is also possible to do this in Puerto Baquerizo Moreno, but there are fewer boats available. If you are alone, or with a friend, you'll need to find more people, as even the smallest boats take no fewer than four passengers. There are usually people looking for boats, and agencies can help in putting travelers and boats together.

Finding boats in August and around Christmas and Easter is especially difficult. The less busy months have fewer travelers on the islands, but boats are often being repaired or overhauled at this time, particularly in October. Despite the caveats, travelers who arrive in Puerto Ayora looking for a boat can almost always find one within a week (often in just a few days) if they work at it. This method isn't always cost effective since by the time you pay for hotels and meals in Puerto Ayora, you may not save anything.

The most important thing is to find a good captain and an enthusiastic naturalist guide. You should be able to meet both and inspect the boat before booking.

Arranging Tours in Advance

If you don't have the time or patience to arrange a tour on-site, you can arrange one in Quito or Guayaquil. Still, you may have to wait several days or weeks during the high season. Check various agencies to compare prices and get a departure date that works for you. Sometimes you can get on a great boat for a budget price, particularly when business is slow – agencies will drop their prices at the last minute rather than leave berths empty.

INDEPENDENT TRAVEL

Visiting the Galápagos on your own is – for better or worse – a wholly different experience than touring the islands on a cruise. Only four of the islands – Santa Cruz, San Cristóbal, Isabela and Santa María – can be visited independently. When you add up hotel costs, day tours (which you'll surely want to take) and inter-island travel, it probably won't be much cheaper than a cruise. Most importantly, you will not see the many islands, nor the wildlife (the main attraction) that require a guide (ie a cruise) to see. But you *can* have an amazing time – and more time – hanging out and getting to know these four islands in ways you cannot on a short cruise.

You can fly independently to either Santa Cruz or San Cristóbal, and a passenger ferry (right) runs regularly between the two islands. Puerto Ayora on Santa Cruz is a bit pricey, although there are some great visitor sites (namely Bahía Tortuga) that you can visit on your own. Setting up diving trips and day cruises is easy from here. Puerto Baquerizo Moreno on San Cristóbal is cheaper and more laid-back, and has world-class surf, good snorkeling, places to camp and several interesting visitor sites that you can visit without a guide. Puerto Villamil, on Isabela, is even cheaper. It's rarely visited, and you may be the only one around for days on end (and with only two ferry boats calling at Isabela each month, you'll have plenty of days on end!). Finally, Isla Santa María (Floreana) can be reached (and left) only once a month by boat, and there's only one place to stay and eat (not cheap, although you may be able to camp), but it's truly an escape.

Going it alone in the Galápagos is worth it only if you have *at least* two weeks, preferably three or more. The best time for this type of travel is in the off season, when hotels are cheaper and unlikely to be booked solid.

GETTING THERE & AWAY

Most visitors fly to Isla Baltra, from where a bus-ferry combination goes to Puerto Ayora on Isla Santa Cruz. Flights are available to Puerto Baquerizo Moreno on Isla San Cristóbal, but Puerto Ayora has more facilities, so travelers wanting to arrange tours on-site should go there.

Between TAME, Icaro and AeroGal, there are several daily flights from Quito (US$390 round trip, 3¼ hours) via Guayaquil (US$344 round trip, 1½ hours) to Baltra and San Cristóbal (same fare). Flights are cheaper – US$344 from Quito and US$300 from Guayaquil – in low season (May 1 to June 14 and September 15 to October 31). You can buy one-way tickets to one island and leave from the other, or fly with an open return. To change an already ticketed return date (US$7 fee) you must do so in person in Puerto Ayora or Baquerizo Moreno; changes are more difficult in high season. Get to the office early to avoid an excruciating wait. Always reconfirm flights.

If you are signed up with a tour, make sure you are flying to the right island! People occasionally end up in the wrong place and miss their tour.

GETTING AROUND
Air
The small airline, **Emetebe** (Puerto Ayora ☎ 252-6177; Puerto Baquerizo Moreno ☎ 252-0036; Puerto Villamil ☎ 252-9155; Guayaquil ☎ 04-229-2492), flies a five-passenger aircraft between Baltra and Puerto Villamil (Isla Isabela), between Baltra and Puerto Baquerizo Moreno (Isla San Cristóbal), and between Puerto Baquerizo Moreno and Puerto Villamil. Fares are about US$120 one way, and there is a 13kg baggage-weight limit per person.

Boat
Ingala (in Puerto Ayora ☎ 526-151/199) operates *Ingala II*, an inter-island passenger ferry. It goes from Santa Cruz to San Cristóbal about three times per week, from Santa Cruz to Isabela about twice monthly (usually on a Friday) and once a month from Isabela to Floreana. The office in Puerto Ayora can give you up-to-date details, as can the Cámara de Turismo in Puerto Ayora. Departure times change often. Fares are US$50 for foreigners (sometimes cheaper in low season) on any passage and are purchased on the day of departure.

The cheapest rides are usually on the smaller (but often faster) private boats that zip between the islands with supplies and occasional passengers. Ask around the harbors in Puerto Ayora on Santa Cruz and Puerto Baquerizo Moreno on San Cristóbal.

ISLA SANTA CRUZ (INDEFATIGABLE)
Most visitors only pass through the archipelago's most populous island on their way from Isla Baltra to Puerto Ayora. But Santa Cruz is a destination in and of itself, with easily accessible beaches and remote highlands that offer adventurous activities far from the tourist trail.

Puerto Ayora
Clean little Puerto Ayora is the Galápagos' main population center and the heart of the tourist industry. It's a friendly place to hang out and the best place in the islands to set up a cruise.

INFORMATION
Banco del Pacífico (Av Charles Darwin) The town's only bank has a MasterCard/Cirrus ATM & changes traveler's checks.

Cámara de Turismo (☎ 252-6153; www.galapagostour.org; Av Charles Darwin) Tourist office; report any complaints about boats, tours, guides or crew here.

Laundry Lava Flash (Av Bolívar Naveda; per kg US$1) Laundry.

Limón y Café (Av Charles Darwin) One of many cyber-cafés.

ACTIVITIES

The **Red Mangrove Hotel** (☎ 252-6277; Av Charles Darwin), near the cemetery, rents sea kayaks, sailboards and bikes. **Galápagos Tour Center** (cnr Pelícano & Padre Julio Herrera) rents surfboards (half-day/full-day US$8/18) and mountain bikes (half-day/full-day US$8/15) and offers fun snorkeling trips (US$25).

The best dive centers in town are **Scuba Iguana** (☎ 252-6497; www.scubaiguana.com; Av Charles Darwin), in the Hotel Galápagos, near the cemetery, and **Galápagos Sub-Aqua** (☎ 252-6350; www.galapagos-sub-aqua.com; Av Charles Darwin). Both are excellent and offer a variety of tours that include gear, boat and guide. Full PADI-certification courses are available.

TOURS

If you're setting up a cruise from Puerto Ayora visit the following agencies to compare prices and tours. They all offer last-minute deals (when they exist).

Galápatour (☎ 526-088; Av Rodríguez Lara & Genovesa) Behind the municipal market.

Moonrise Travel (☎ 526-403/348; sdivine@ga.pro.ec; Av Charles Darwin) Reputable agency long in the business; great for cheap, last-minute tours.

We Are the Champions Tours (☎ 252-6951; www.wearethechampionstours.com; Av Charles Darwin) Ecuadorian-German-run outfitter offering all kinds of ecologically minded Galápagos trips.

SLEEPING

Most hotels in Puerto Ayora are along Av Charles Darwin.

Hotel Sir Francis Drake (☎ 252-6221; Av Padre Julio Herrera; s/d US$8/15) While the dull grey shades and concrete at Hotel Sir Francis Drake don't delight the eye, the tile rooms are well maintained.

Hotel Lirio del Mar (☎ 252-6212; Av Bolívar Naveda; s/d US$8/16) Three floors of colorful concrete rooms are basic but clean, and a shared terrace catches the breeze.

Hotel Salinas (☎ 252-6107; Av Bolívar Naveda; s/d from US$10/15) Two-story hotel with spacious but plain rooms, hot water, TV and fans. Try for a room on the second floor.

El Peregrino B&B (☎ 252-6323; Av Charles Darwin; s/d incl breakfast US$13/26) This simple, four-room guesthouse boasts a central location and warm, family-like atmosphere.

Hotel Castro (☎ 252-6173; Av Padre Julio Herrera; s/d US$20/30; ☒) The Castro has clean, well maintained rooms with tile floors and hot water. It's only a block from the harbor.

Estrella del Mar (☎ 252-6427; estrellademar@ayora.ecua.net.ec; s/d from US$28/40) Though the rooms at this family run hotel are basic, those with windows and ocean views make up for the shortcomings; others are less expensive.

Casa del Lago (☎ 271-4647; www.galapagoscultural.com; r from US$35; ☒ ▢) By far the best place to feel at home in the islands, Casa del Lago has only three large suites, each made from recycled materials and filled with attractive tiles and textiles. Suites also have large kitchens with stove and refrigerator. Lots of little perks.

EATING

The cheapest places to eat are found out along Av Padre Julio Herrera.

Tropicana Restaurant (Av Bolívar Naveda; mains US$2) Good, cheap, local option.

El Chocolate Galápagos (Av Charles Darwin; mains US$3-6) Besides coffee, fruit drinks and chocolate cake, there's an extensive lunch and dinner menu.

Hernan Café (Av Padre Julio Herrera; mains US$3-9) Excellent café with sandwiches (US$2), hamburgers (US$3), pizzas (US$5) and slightly pricier seafood.

Familiar William's (Charles Binford; encocados US$4-7; ☼ 6-10pm Tue-Sun) Famous for its *encocados*, Familiar Williams is one of the best of the great food kiosks that line Charles Binford.

Garrapata (Av Charles Darwin; mains US$4-9) Serves everything from sandwiches to chicken in pineapple sauce or shrimp in garlic sauce.

Rincón de Alma (Av Charles Darwin; mains US$6-9) Great *ceviches* and other seafood and cheap *almuerzos*.

Restaurant Salvavidas (Harbor; mains US$6-16) A dockside favorite for beers, snacks and seafood.

Near the harbor, **Proinsular supermarket** (Av Charles Darwin) is the place to stock up on food supplies. There's also a **municipal market** (Av Padre Julio Herrera).

DRINKING

La Panga (Av Charles Darwin) The most popular disco in town.

Limón y Café (Av Charles Darwin) Limón y Café is a nice laid-back little hangout with a pool table.

GETTING THERE & AWAY

For more information on flights to and from Santa Cruz see p729. Reconfirming your flight departures with the **Aerogal** (☎ 252-6798; www .aerogal.com.ec; Av Padre Julio Herrera) or **TAME** (☎ 252-6165; www.tame.com.ec; Av Charles Darwin) offices is essential.

Arriving air passengers in Baltra are met by a crew member (if on a prearranged tour) or take a public bus-ferry-bus combination to Puerto Ayora (US$2.60, two hours). From Puerto Ayora, buses start leaving for Baltra at 7am.

Around Puerto Ayora

Though much of the island is off-limits without a guide, there is plenty to see. Unless otherwise noted, you can visit the following sites by yourself. The **Charles Darwin Research Station** (Map p731; www.darwinfoundation.org; admission free) is about a 20-minute walk by road northeast of Puerto Ayora. The station features an information center, a museum, a tortoise nursery and a walk-in tortoise enclosure where you are able to meet these Galápagos giants face to face.

Southwest of Puerto Ayora, a 3km trail takes you to the paradisiacal **Bahía Tortuga** (Turtle Bay; Map p727), which has a beautiful, white, coral-sand beach and protected swimming behind a spit. The beach is backed by mangroves,

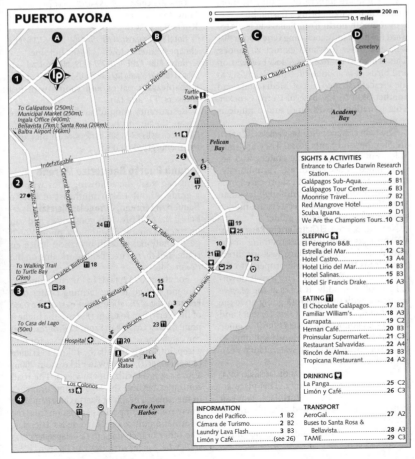

PUERTO AYORA

0   200 m
0   0.1 miles

To Galápatour (250m);
Municipal Market (250m);
Ingala Office (400m);
Bellavista (7km); Santa Rosa (20km);
Baltra Airport (46km)

To Walking Trail
to Turtle Bay
(2km)

To Casa del Lago
(50m)

**Academy
Bay**

**Pelican
Bay**

**Puerto Ayora
Harbor**

SIGHTS & ACTIVITIES
Entrance to Charles Darwin Research
    Station.................................**4** D1
Galápagos Sub-Aqua...............**5** B1
Galápagos Tour Center............**6** B3
Moonrise Travel.......................**7** B2
Red Mangrove Hotel................**8** D1
Scuba Iguana...........................**9** D1
We Are the Champions Tours..**10** C3

SLEEPING
El Peregrino B&B.....................**11** B2
Estrella del Mar.......................**12** C3
Hotel Castro............................**13** A4
Hotel Lirio del Mar..................**14** B3
Hotel Salinas...........................**15** B3
Hotel Sir Francis Drake............**16** A3

EATING
El Chocolate Galápagos...........**17** B2
Familiar William's....................**18** A3
Garrapata...............................**19** C2
Hernan Café............................**20** B3
Proinsular Supermarket...........**21** C3
Restaurant Salvavidas.............**22** A4
Rincón de Alma.......................**23** B3
Tropicana Restaurant..............**24** A2

DRINKING
La Panga.................................**25** C2
Limón y Café...........................**26** C3

INFORMATION
Banco del Pacífico...................**1** B2
Cámara de Turismo..................**2** B2
Laundry Lava Flash...................**3** B3
Limón y Café....................(see 26)

TRANSPORT
AeroGal..................................**27** A2
Buses to Santa Rosa &
    Bellavista............................**28** A3
TAME.....................................**29** C3

ECUADOR

and you may spot harmless sharks (worry not), pelicans and even flamingos. Marine iguanas abound. Beware of strong currents on the exposed side of the spit. Follow the sign from Av Padre Julio Herrera.

Buses from Puerto Ayora go to the villages of **Bellavista** (Map p727) and **Santa Rosa** (Map p727), from where you can explore some of the interior. Neither of these villages has hotels. If there's room, you can hop on the airport bus at 8am from the park. In Puerto Ayora, you could also hire a truck or rent a mountain bike for the day (it's uphill to the villages).

From the village of Bellavista, 7km north of Puerto Ayora, you can turn either west on the main road toward Santa Rosa, or east and go about 2km to some **lava tubes** (Map p727; admission US$2). These are underground tunnels more than 1km in length; bring a flashlight.

A footpath north from Bellavista leads toward the highlands, including **Cerro Crocker** (Map p727) and other hills and extinct volcanoes. This is a good chance to see local vegetation and birds. It is about 6km from Bellavista to the crescent-shaped hill of Media Luna and another 3km to the base of Cerro Crocker. This is national park land, and a guide is required.

The twin craters called **Los Gemelos** (Map p727) are 5km beyond Santa Rosa. They are sinkholes, rather than volcanic craters, and are surrounded by Scalesia forest. Vermilion flycatchers are often seen and short-eared owls are spotted on occasion. Although less than 100m from the road, the craters are hidden by vegetation, so go with a guide.

Near Santa Rosa, **El Chato Tortoise Reserve** (Map p727) protects giant tortoises roaming in the wild. A trail from the village (ask for directions) leads through private property to the reserve, about 3km away. The trail is downhill and often muddy. It forks at the reserve boundary, with the right fork going up to the small hill of Cerro Chato (3km further) and the left fork going to La Caseta (2km). A guide is required. All manner of locals will offer to guide you. Bring plenty of water. Horses can be hired in Santa Rosa.

Near the reserve is a **ranch** (admission US$4) owned by the Devine family. This place always has dozens of giant tortoises. You can wander around at will and take photos for a small fee. A café sells coffee or herbal tea that's welcome if the highland *garúa* (mist) has soaked you.

ISLA SAN CRISTÓBAL

Locals call San Cristóbal the capital of paradise and, since Puerto Baquerizo Moreno is the capital of Galápagos province, it technically is. The island has several easily accessible visitor sites, killer surf and the lovely, laid-back capital itself.

Puerto Baquerizo Moreno

Often just called Cristóbal, Puerto Baquerizo Moreno is a relaxed little town, busy with tourists during the high season and dead the rest of the year. Arranging tours is possible, and mellowing out is a cinch. Three world-class surf breaks are nearby.

Air passengers arriving in Puerto Baquerizo Moreno can walk into town in a few minutes.

Casa del Ceibo (☎ 252-0248; r per person US$4) How does two rooms in a tree house sound? Kitchen access too.

Hotel San Francisco (☎ 252-0304; s/d US$7/14) The cheapest hotel in town is basic, but fine.

Hotel Mar Azul (☎ 252-0139; hotelmarazul_ex@hotmail.com; Av Alsacio Northia; s/d US$12/20) Friendly, with pleasant patios and rooms with hot showers, TV and fan.

Restaurants abound and *almuerzos* are cheap. Be sure to have a *batido* at **El Grande** (Villamil; drinks US90¢-$1.50); surfers swear they keep them energized all day.

Around Puerto Baquerizo Moreno

You can visit the following sites without a guide. About 1.5km southeast of Puerto Baquerizo Moreno, **Cerro de las Tijeretas** (Frigatebird Hill; Map p727) provides good views and can be reached on a trail without a guide. You'll pass a national park information office en route, and there's excellent snorkeling on the ocean side.

For about US$2, taxis in Puerto Baquerizo Moreno will go to the farming center of **El Progreso** (Map p727), about 8km east at the base of the Cerro San Joaquín (896m), the highest point on San Cristóbal. From El Progreso, you can catch one of the occasional buses (or hire a jeep, hitchhike or walk the 10km) to **El Junco Lagoon** (Map p727), a freshwater lake about 700m above sea level with superb views. The road continues beyond the lagoon and branches to the isolated beach of **Puerto Chino** (Map p727), where you can camp with permission from the information office on Cerro de las Tijeretas. The other branch goes to **La Galapaguera** (Map p727), where giant tortoises can be seen.

About an hour north of Puerto Baquerizo Moreno by boat is tiny, rocky **Isla Lobos** (Map p727), the main sea lion and blue-footed booby colony open to visitors (a guide is required) to Isla San Cristóbal. The island has a 300m trail and you can see lava lizards here.

ISLA ISABELA

Puerto Villamil (Map p727) is the main town on seldom-visited Isla Isabela. An 18km road leads from the town up to the tiny village of Santo Tomás. Puerto Villamil has a handful of places to stay, all of which are fairly affordable.

Hotel Las Gardenias (☎ 252-9115; r US$10) is one of the cheapest options in town. Or, you can try **Cormorant Beach House** (☎ 252-9200; www.gala pagoss.com; Av Antonio Gill & Malecón; r from US$20), with two large *cabañas* by the beach, and **Hostería Isabela del Mar/Ballena Azul** (☎ 252-9030; www.hos teriaisabela.com.ec; r per person US$20), which has a few rooms with ocean views.

There are a few basic *comedores*, and most hotels offer meals.

ISLA SANTA MARÍA

Also known as Floreana, this island has fewer than 100 inhabitants, most centered around **Puerto Velasco Ibarra** (Map p727), the island's only settlement. There you will find **Floreana Hotel & Restaurant** (☎ 252-0250; s/d/tr US$30/50/70), run by the family of the late Margaret Wittmer, who is famous for being one of the islands' first settlers. She is also the author of the book *Floreana*, which tells of her early years on the island. Beachfront rooms have hot water and fan, and the place is rarely full. Puerto Velasco Ibarra also has a small gift shop and post office.

ECUADOR DIRECTORY

ACCOMMODATIONS

There is no shortage of places to stay in Ecuador, but during major fiestas or the night before market day, accommodations can be tight, so plan ahead. If you are going to a town specifically for a market or fiesta, try to arrive no later than early afternoon the day before the event. Most hotels have single-room rates, although during high season some beach towns charge for the number of beds in the room, regardless of the number of people checking in.

Ecuador has several youth hostels, although they're rarely the best value. *Pensiones* are

the cheapest accommodations, although the rooms are sometimes rented by the hour and cleanliness may be suspect. Staying with families is an option in remote villages.

ACTIVITIES

Where to begin? There are so many exciting activities in Ecuador that any list will certainly miss something. For climbers, the volcanic, snowcapped peaks of Ecuador's central highlands – including Chimborazo (a doozy at 6310m, p687) and Cotopaxi (5897m, p676) – attract mountaineers from around the world. Quito (p647), Riobamba (p685), Baños (p680) and Latacunga (p677) are the best towns to hire guides and gear.

How about hiking? The moor-like landscape of Parque Nacional Cajas (p693); the cloud forests of Parque Nacional Podocarpus (p696) or Mindo (p675); the windswept *páramo* of Lagunas de Mojanda (p672), near Otavalo; the spectacular high-Andean Quilotoa Loop area (p679); and the coastal dry forests of Parque Nacional Machalilla (p714) are just a few of Ecuador's hiking possibilities.

If bird-watching ruffles your feathers, you're in for a real treat. During the Audubon Society's 2004/2005 Christmas Bird Count, 420 species were spotted and logged near Mindo (p675) in a single day. The count was topped only by the lower Río Napo region of the Amazon (p701), where 471 bird species were logged. Galápagos birdlife, of course, is extraordinary.

Tena (p702) in the Oriente is Ecuador's kayaking and river-rafting capital, where it's easy to set up day-runs down the nearby upper Río Napo (class III) or Río Misahuallí (class IV+).

The surfing is world class at Montañita (p716) and on Isla San Cristóbal (opposite) in the Galápagos. Playas (p717) has some decent nearby breaks, but you'll have to get in with the locals (try the Playas Club Surf, p717) to find them. The Galápagos are also famous for scuba diving and snorkeling (think hammerhead sharks and giant manta rays), while Parque Nacional Machalilla (p714) qualifies as 'pretty damn cool.'

And mountain biking? You can rent bikes for about US$5 per hour in places such as Baños (p680) and Riobamba (p685), or go for the extreme downhill day trips offered by outfitters in those towns, as well as in Quito (p647) and Cuenca (p688).

BOOKS

Lonely Planet's *Ecuador & the Galápagos Islands* offers more detailed travel information on the country.

If there's one book that nails Ecuadorian culture on the head, it's the eloquent and humorous *Living Poor,* written by Moritz Thomsen. Joe Kane's *Savages* is a more recently written account that illustrates the oil industry's impacts on the Ecuadorian Amazon.

The Panama Hat Trail, by Tom Miller, is a fascinating book about the author's search for that most quintessential and misnamed of Ecuadorian products, the panama hat. For a more literary (and surreal) impression of Ecuador, read Henri Michaux's *Ecuador: A Travel Journal,* or Kurt Vonnegut's absurd *Galápagos,* which takes place in futuristic Guayaquil as well as the islands.

BUSINESS HOURS

Reviews throughout this book provide opening hours only when they differ from the following standard hours: banks generally open Monday through Friday, from 8am to between 2pm and 4pm. In bigger cities, most business and government offices are open Monday through Friday between 9am and 5:30pm, and close for an hour at lunch, which is sometime between noon and 2pm. On the coast and in smaller towns, the lunch break can be dragged on for two or more hours. Many businesses operate midday hours on Saturday, but nearly everything – including restaurants – closes on Sunday. Restaurants generally open for lunch from around 11:30am to 3pm and for dinner from 5pm to 10pm; some stay open all day. Bars usually open sometime between 5pm and 7pm and close between midnight and 2pm. Telephone call centers are almost invariably open 8am to 10pm daily. Post offices are generally open 8am to 6pm Monday through Friday and 8am to 1pm Saturday.

CLIMATE

Ecuador's climate consists of wet and dry seasons, with significant variation among the different geographical regions (depending on whether you're in the Andes, on the coast or in the Oriente).

The Galápagos and the coast have a hot and rainy season from January to April; you can expect short torrential downpours with skin-cooking sunshine in between. You'll be a walking pool of sweat if you travel on the coast during this time. From May to December it rains infrequently, but the skies are often overcast and the beaches cool. Travel is definitely more pleasant, but you may find the beach is just a little too nippy for sunbathing. Ecuadorians hit the beaches during the wet season.

In the Oriente, it rains during most months, especially during the afternoon and evening. August and December through March are usually the driest months, and April through June are the wettest, with regional variations. Malaria is more common during the wet season, but river travel is usually easier due to higher water levels.

Travel is pleasant in the highlands year-round, although you'll definitely be dodging raindrops October through May. It doesn't rain daily, however, and even April, the wettest month, averages one rainy day in two.

Daytime temperatures in Quito average a high of 21°C (70°F) and a low of 8°C (48°F) year-round.

For more information and climate charts see the South America Directory (p1062).

DANGERS & ANNOYANCES

Ecuador is a fairly safe country, but you should still be careful. Pickpocketing is definitely on the increase and is common in crowded places, such as markets. Armed robbery is still unusual in most of Ecuador, although parts of Guayaquil and Quito's Mariscal Sucre neighborhood have a reputation for being very dangerous.

Every year or so, a couple of long-distance night buses are robbed on the way to the coast. Avoid taking night buses through the provinces of Guayas or Manabí unless you have to.

Due to the armed conflict in neighboring Colombia, areas along the Colombian border (particularly in the northern Oriente) can be dangerous. Tours though are generally safe.

Take the normal precautions as outlined under Dangers & Annoyances in the South America Directory (see p1063). If you are robbed, get a *denuncia* (police report) from the local police station within 48 hours – they won't process a report after that.

ELECTRICITY

Ecuador uses 110V, 60 cycles, AC (the same as in North America). Plugs have two flat prongs, as in North America.

DRIVER'S LICENSE

An international driver's license, alongside a home-country license and passport, is required to drive in Ecuador.

EMBASSIES & CONSULATES

As well as the information provided below, see Visas, p407.

Embassies & Consulates in Ecuador

Embassies and consulates are best visited in the morning. Australia and New Zealand have no consular representation in Ecuador.

Canada Quito (Map pp650-1; ☎ 02-256-3580; www .dfait-maeci.gc.ca/Ecuador; Av 6 de Diciembre 2816 & P Rivet, 4th fl); Guayaquil (Map pp720-1; ☎ 04-256-3580; consulc1@gye.satnet.net; Córdova 810, 4th fl)

Colombia Quito (☎ 02-245-8012; www.embajadade colombiaenecuador.org; Atahualpa 955 & República, 3rd fl); Guayaquil (☎ 04-263-0674/75; Francisco de Orellana, World Trade Center, Tower B, 11th fl); Tulcán (☎ 06-298-0559; Av Manabí 58-087)

France Quito (Map pp650-1; ☎ 02-254-3101/10; franciac@andinanet.net; Diego de Almagro 1550 & Pradera); Guayaquil (☎ 04-232-8442; José Mascote 909 & Hurtado)

Germany (Map p657; ☎ 02-297-0820; www .embajada-quito.de; Naciones Unidas E10-44 at República de El Salvador, Edificio Citiplaza, 12th fl, Quito)

Holland (Map pp650-1; ☎ 02-222-9229/30; www.em bajadadeholanda.com; Av 12 de Octubre 1942 & Cordero, World Trade Center, Tower 1, 1st fl, Quito)

Ireland (☎ 02-245-1577; Antonio de Ulloa 2651 & Rumipamba, Quito)

Peru Quito (☎ 02-246-8410, 246-8389; embpeecu@uio .satnet.net; República de El Salvador 495 & Irlanda); Guayaquil (☎ 04-228 114; conperu@gye.satnet.net; Av Francisco de Orellana 501); Loja (Map p695; ☎ 07-257-9068; Sucre 10-56); Machala (Map p723; ☎ 07-930-680; cnr Bolívar & Colón)

UK Quito (Map p657; ☎ 02-297-0800/01; www .britembquito.org.ec; Naciones Unidas & República de El Salvador, Edificio Citiplaza, 14th fl); Guayaquil (☎ 04-256-0400/3850; Córdova 623 & Padre)

USA Quito (Map pp650-1; ☎ 02-256-2890; www.us embassy.org.ec; Avs Patria & 12 de Octubre); Guayaquil (Map pp720-1; ☎ 04-232-3570; 9 de Octubre & García Moreno)

Venezuela (☎ 02-226-8636; Av Los Cabildos 115, Quito)

Ecuadorian Embassies & Consulates Abroad

Ecuador has embassies in Colombia and Peru, and also in the following countries.

Australia & New Zealand (☎ 02-6286-4021, 6286-1231; www.embassyecuadoraustralia.org.au; 6 Pindari Crescent, O'Malley, ACT 2606)

Canada (☎ 613-563-8206; www.ncf.ca/ecuador; 50 O'Connor St, Ste 316, Ottawa, Ontario K1P 6L2)

France (☎ 331-4561-1021; www.ambassade-equateur .fr; 34 Av de Messine, 75008 Paris)

Germany (☎ 030-238-6217; mecuadorial@t-online.de; www.embajada-ecuador.org; Kaiser-Friedrich Strasse 90, 1 OG,10585 Berlin)

UK (☎ 020-7584-2648, 7584-1367; www.ecuador .embassyhomepage.com/; Flat 3, 3 Hans Crescent, Knightsbridge, London SW1X OLS)

USA (☎ 202-234-7200; www.ecuador.org/esp/principal .htm; 2535 15th St NW, Washington, DC 20009)

FESTIVALS & EVENTS

Many of Ecuador's major festivals are oriented around the Roman Catholic liturgical calendar. These are often celebrated with great pageantry, especially in highland indigenous villages, where a Catholic feast day is often the excuse for a traditional indigenous fiesta with drinking, dancing, rituals and processions. The most important are listed here.

February

Carnaval Celebrated throughout Ecuador. Dates vary.

Fiesta de Frutas y Flores (Fruit & flower festival) Held in Ambato the last two weeks of February.

June

Corpus Christi Religious feast day (the Thursday after the eighth Sunday after Easter) combined with the traditional harvest fiesta in many highland towns; includes processions and street dancing.

Día de San Juan (St John the Baptist) Fiestas in Otavalo area. Held on June 24.

Día de San Pedro y San Pablo (St Peter & St Paul) Fiestas in Otavalo area and other northern highland towns. Held on June 29.

September

Fiesta del Yamor Held in Otavalo, September 1 to 15.

Fiesta de la Mamá Negra Held in Latacunga, September 23 to 24.

December

Fundación de Quito (Founding of Quito) Celebrated the first week of December with bullfights, parades and dancing.

FOOD & DRINK

Eating reviews throughout this chapter (and book) are given in order of budget, with the least expensive options first. For information about standard restaurant hours, see Business Hours, opposite.

Ecuadorian Cuisine

For breakfast, eggs and bread rolls or toast are available. A good alternative is a *humita*, a sweet-corn tamale often served with coffee.

Lunch is the main meal of the day for many Ecuadorians. A cheap restaurant will serve a decent *almuerzo* (lunch of the day) for as little as US$1.50. An *almuerzo* consists of a *sopa* (soup) and a *segundo* (second dish), which is usually a stew with plenty of rice. Sometimes the segundo is *pescado* (fish), *lentejas* (lentils) or *menestras* (generally, whatever legume stew – usually it's beans or peas – happens to be in the pot). Some places serve salad (often cooked), juice and *postre* (dessert), as well as the two main courses.

The *merienda* (evening meal) is a set meal, usually similar to lunch. If you don't want the *almuerzo* or *merienda*, you can choose from the menu, but this is always more expensive.

A *churrasco* is a hearty dish of fried beef, fried eggs, a few veggies, fried potatoes, slices of avocado and tomato, and the inevitable rice.

Arroz con pollo is a mountain of rice with little bits of chicken mixed in. *Pollo a la brasa* is roast chicken, often served with fries. *Gallina* is usually boiled chicken, as in soups, and *pollo* is more often chicken that's been spit-roasted or fried.

Parrillas (or *parrilladas*) are grill houses. Steaks, pork chops, chicken breasts, blood sausage, liver and tripe are all served (together or individually, depending on the establishment). Some *parrillas* do the Argentine thing and serve everything together on a tabletop grill.

Seafood is good, even in the highlands. The most common types of fish are *corvina* (technically white sea bass, but usually just a white fish) and *trucha* (trout). Popular throughout Ecuador, *ceviche* is uncooked seafood marinated in lemon and served with popcorn and sliced onions. It's delicious. *Ceviche* can be *de pescado* (fish), *de camarones* (shrimp), *de concha* (shellfish) or *mixto* (mixed). Unfortunately, improperly prepared *ceviche* is a source of cholera, so avoid it if in any doubt.

Chifas (Chinese restaurants) are generally inexpensive. Among other standards, they serve *chaulafan* (rice dishes) and *tallarines* (noodles dishes). Portions tend to be filling, with a good dose of MSG. Vegetarians will find that *chifas* are the best choice for meatless dishes. Vegetarian restaurants are rare outside touristy areas.

Restaurants usually offer a wide range of dishes, including the following classics:

Caldo (*kal*·do) – Soup or stew. Often served in markets for breakfast. *Caldo de gallina* (chicken soup) is the most popular. *Caldo de patas* is soup made by boiling cattle hooves.

Cuy (kooy) – Whole-roasted guinea pig. A traditional delicacy dating to Inca times, *cuy* tastes rather like a cross between rabbit and chicken. They're easily identified on grills with their little paws and teeth sticking out.

Lapingachos (la·peen·*ga*·chos) – Fried mashed-potato-and-cheese pancakes, often served with *fritada* (scraps of fried or roast pork).

Seco (*se*·ko) – Literally 'dry' (as opposed to a 'wet' soup), this is stew, usually meat, served with rice. It may be *seco de gallina* (chicken stew), *de res* (beef), *de chivo* (goat) or *de cordero* (lamb).

Tortillas de maíz (tor·*tee*·lya de ma·*ees*) – Tasty fried corn pancakes.

Yaguarlocro (ya·gwar·*lo*·kro) – Another classic. Potato soup with chunks of fried blood sausage floating in it. Many people prefer straight *locro*, which usually has potatoes, corn and an avocado or cheese topping – without the blood sausage.

Drinks

Purify all tap water or buy bottled water. *Agua mineral* is carbonated; Güitig (pronounced weetig) is the most famous brand. *Agua sin gas* is not carbonated.

Bottled drinks are cheap and all the usual soft drinks are available. The local ones have endearing names such as Bimbo or Lulu. Ask for your drink *helada* if you want it out of the refrigerator, *al clima* if you don't. Remember to say *sin hielo* (without ice) unless you really trust the water supply.

Jugos (juices) are available everywhere. Make sure you get *jugo puro* (pure) and not *con agua* (with water). The most common kinds are *mora* (blackberry), *tomate de árbol* (a strangely appetizing fruit with a greenish taste), *naranja* (orange), *toronja* (grapefruit), *maracuyá* (passion fruit), *piña* (pineapple), *sandía* (watermelon), *naranjilla* (a local fruit that tastes like bitter orange) and papaya.

Coffee is widely available but is often disappointing. Instant – served either *en leche* (with milk) or *en agua* (with water) – is the most common. Espresso is available in the better restaurants.

Té (tea) is served black with lemon and sugar. *Té de hierbas* (herb tea) and hot chocolate are also popular.

For alcoholic drinks, local *cervezas* (beers – memorize it) are good and inexpensive.

Pilsener is available in 650mL bottles, while Club comes in 330mL bottles. Imports are tough to find. Local wines are terrible and imported wines are expensive.

Ron (rum) is cheap and good. The local firewater, *aguardiente,* is sugarcane alcohol, and is an acquired taste but can be good. It's very cheap. Imported spirits are expensive.

GAY & LESBIAN TRAVELERS

Ecuador is probably not the best place to be outwardly affectionate with a partner of the same sex. Homosexuality was illegal until 1997. Quito and Guayaquil have underground social scenes, but outside the occasional dance club, they're hard to find. Check out **Syberian's Gay Guide to Quito** (http://gayquitoec.tripod.com) or **Gayecuador** (www.gayecuador.com in Spanish).

HOLIDAYS

On major holidays, banks, offices and other services are closed and public transport is often very crowded; book ahead if possible. The following are Ecuador's major national holidays; they may be celebrated for several days around the actual date:

New Year's Day January 1.
Epiphany January 6.
Semana Santa (Easter Week) March/April
Labor Day May 1.
Battle of Pichincha May 24. This honors the decisive battle of independence from Spain in 1822.
Simón Bolívar's Birthday July 24.
Quito Independence Day August 10.
Guayaquil Independence Day October 9. This combines with the October 12 national holiday and is an important festival in Guayaquil.
Columbus Day/Día de la Raza October 12.
All Saints' Day November 1.
Day of the Dead (All Souls' Day) November 2. Celebrated by flower-laying ceremonies in cemeteries, it's especially colorful in rural areas, where entire Indian families show up at cemeteries to eat, drink and leave offerings in memory of the departed.
Cuenca Independence Day November 3. Combines with the national holidays of November 1 and 2 to give Cuenca its most important fiesta of the year.
Christmas Eve December 24.
Christmas Day December 25.

INTERNET ACCESS

All but the smallest of towns have cybercafés. Prices hover around US$1 per hour, higher in small towns.

INTERNET RESOURCES

The Best of Ecuador (www.thebestofecuador.com) Comprehensive tourist information.
Ecuador Explorer (www.ecuadorexplorer.com) Extensive information and good classifieds.
Latin American Network Information Center (http://lanic.utexas.edu/la/ecuador/) Links to everything Ecuadorian.
Ministry of Tourism (www.vivecuador.com) Sus out everything from health and budget issues to country highlights.

LEGAL MATTERS

Drug penalties in Ecuador for possession of even small amounts of illegal drugs (which include marijuana and cocaine) are severe. Defendants often spend months in jail before they are brought to trial, and if convicted (as is usually the case), they can expect several years in jail.

Treat plainclothes 'policemen' with suspicion. If you're asked for ID by a uniformed official in broad daylight, show your passport.

In the event of a car accident, unless extremely minor, the vehicles should stay where they are until the police arrive and make a report. If you hit a pedestrian, you are legally responsible for the pedestrian's injuries and can be jailed unless you pay, even if the accident was not your fault. Drive defensively.

MAPS

Ecuadorian bookstores carry a limited selection of Ecuadorian maps. The best selection is available from the **Instituto Geográfico Militar** in Quito (p648). *The Pocket Guide to Ecuador,* published in Quito, includes maps of the country and the major cities.

MEDIA

The *Explorer* is a free monthly booklet printed in English and Spanish listing what's on in Quito. The country's best newspapers are *El Comercio* (www.elcomercio.com in Spanish) and *Hoy* (www.hoy.com.ec in Spanish), published in Quito, and *El Telégrafo* (www

---

THE AGE GAME

- Legal drinking age: 18
- Minimal driving age: 18
- Suffrage: 18
- Age of consent: not defined.

.telegrafo.com.ec in Spanish) and *El Universo* (www.eluniverso.com in Spanish), published in Guayaquil.

MONEY

Ecuador's currency was the sucre until it switched to the US dollar in 2000, a process called dollarization (p642). For more on costs and money see p20.

ATMs

ATMs are the easiest way of getting cash. They're found in most cities and even in smaller towns, although they are sometimes out of order. Make sure you have a four-digit PIN. Bancos del Pacífico and Bancos del Pichincha have MasterCard/Cirrus ATMs. Bancos de Guayaquil have Visa/Plus ATMs.

Bargaining

Bargaining is expected at food and crafts markets. Sometimes you can bargain on hotels during low season.

Cash

Bills are the same as those used in the US. Coins are identical in shape, size and material to their US counterparts, but instead of US presidents, they feature the faces and symbols of Ecuador.

Change is often quite difficult to come by here. Trying to purchase inexpensive items with a US$20 bill (or even a US$10 bill) generally results in either you or the proprietor running from shop to shop until someone produces some change. If no one does, you're out of luck. Change bills whenever you can. To ask for change, make a deeply worried face and ask, '¿Tiene suelto?' (Do you have change?).

Credit Cards

Credit cards are useful, particularly for buying cash from a bank. Visa and MasterCard are the most widely accepted.

Exchanging Money

Foreign currencies can be exchanged into US dollars easily in Quito, Guayaquil and Cuenca, where rates are also the best. You can also change money at most of the major border crossings. In some places, however, notably the Oriente, it is quite difficult to exchange money. Exchange houses, called *casas de cambio*, are normally the best

places; banks will also exchange money but are usually much slower. Usually, exchange rates are within 2% of one another in any given city.

Major towns have a black market, usually near the big *casas de cambio*. Rates are about the same, but street changing is illegal (though ignored), and counterfeits and cheating are serious risks.

Exchange rates at press time included the following:

Country	Unit		US$
Australia	A$1	=	0.75
Canada	C$1	=	0.88
euro zone	€1	=	1.25
Japan	¥100	=	0.84
New Zealand	NZ$1	=	0.66
UK	UK£1	=	1.87

Traveler's Checks

Most banks and nearly all exchange houses will cash traveler's checks, but only top-end hotels and restaurants will consider them.

POST

It costs US$1.25 to send a letter to North America, US$2 to Europe and US$2.25 to the rest of the world. For a few cents extra, you can send them *certificado* (certified). Sending parcels of 2kg to 20kg is best done in Quito.

To receive mail in Ecuador, have the sender mail your item to the nearest post office, eg Joan SMITH, Lista de Correos, Correo Central, Quito (or town and province of your choice), Ecuador. Mail is filed alphabetically, so make sure that your last name is clear.

For members, the **SAE** (p649) will hold mail sent to the clubhouse. If your incoming mail weighs over 2kg, you have to recover it from customs (and pay high duty).

RESPONSIBLE TRAVEL

Responsible travel in Ecuador is a tricky issue. 'Ecotourism' is a major buzzword used by nearly every tour operator in the country, and it really comes down to your own impression of the company you're dealing with as to whether it practices the responsibility it espouses. The SAE in Quito (p649) is an excellent resource for finding tour operators and hotels or lodges that truly practice ecotourism.

On a personal behavior level, there are several things you can do to leave a minimal impact (or maximize your positive impact) on the country. If you're taking a tour in the Oriente, make sure your guide does not hunt game for cooking or cut trees for firewood. If you plan to visit an indigenous community, make sure the guide is from the community or has a good working relationship with the community (or written permission to visit, in the case of the Huaorani). In the Galápagos, do not approach the animals (no matter how tempting) or wander off the trails. With the sheer number of tourists visiting the islands, this is incredibly important. On the islands, as well as on the coast, think twice before eating lobster or shrimp – lobster is overfished and shrimp farming is one of the most ecologically damaging practices in the country. Do not buy anything made from coral, particularly black coral. Don't litter, even though many Ecuadorians do.

With all the stories travelers love to tell about slashed or stolen packs, it's easy to get paranoid. Remember that Ecuadorians travel their country too, but you'll never see an Ecuadorian with a newfangled, wire-mesh locking bag around their luggage. Items like this simply shout that you don't trust the people you're supposedly here to get to know.

See Responsible Travel at the front of this book for more information.

STUDYING

Ecuador is one of the best places to study Spanish on the continent. Quito (p647) and Cuenca (p688), and to a lesser extent Otavalo (p669) and Baños (p680), are the best places to shack up with the books and go one-on-one with a teacher. Prices range from US$5 to US$10 per hour.

TELEPHONE

Andinatel (mainly in the highlands and Oriente) and Pacifictel (mainly on the coast) provide local, national and international telephone services. The city of Cuenca uses Etapa. Calls cost about US35¢ per minute to the USA, about US45¢ to the UK and Australia. You can also make Internet phone calls in larger towns for about US25¢ a minute.

Reverse-charge (collect) calls are possible to North America and most European countries. Direct dialing to a North American or European operator is also possible;

the numbers are available from your long-distance service provider. From a private phone within Ecuador, dial ☎ 116 for an international operator.

Two-digit area codes change by province. Dial ☎ 09 for mobile phones. Drop the area code if you're calling within a province. If calling from abroad, drop the 0 from the code. Ecuador's country code is ☎ 593.

To call locally, you can use either a Pacifictel or Andinatel office or a public phone box. Public phones operate with prepaid phone cards, which are available at kiosks.

All telephone numbers in Ecuador now have seven digits, and the first digit – except for cellular phone numbers – is always a '2' (except in Quito where some begin with a '3'). If someone gives you a six-digit number (which happens often), simply put a '2' in front of it.

TOILETS

Ecuadorian plumbing has very low pressure. Putting toilet paper into the bowl may clog the system, so use the waste basket. This may seem unsanitary, but its much better than clogged bowls and water overflowing onto the floor. Expensive hotels have adequate plumbing.

Public toilets are limited mainly to bus terminals, airports and restaurants. Lavatories are called *servicios higiénicos* and are usually marked 'SS.HH.' People needing to use the lavatory often ask to use the *baño* in a restaurant; toilet paper is rarely available – carry a personal supply.

TOURIST INFORMATION

The government run **Ministerio de Turismo** (www .vivecuador.com) is responsible for tourist information at the national level. It is slowly opening tourist information offices – known as **iTur** offices – in important towns throughout Ecuador.

South American Explorers (SAE) has a clubhouse in Quito (see p649). For general information on this helpful organization, see p649.

TOURS

Most of the Galápagos archipelago is accessible to visitors only by guided tour (ie a cruise). Many travelers also opt to visit the Amazon on organized tours, as these are efficient, educational and often the only way to get deep into the rainforest.

TRAVELERS WITH DISABILITIES

Unfortunately, Ecuador's infrastructure for disabled travelers is virtually nonexistent.

VISAS

Most travelers entering Ecuador as tourists, including citizens of Australasian countries, Japan, the EU, Canada and the USA do not require visas. Upon entry, they will be issued a T-3 tourist card valid for 90 days. Sixty-day stamps are rarely given, but double check if you're going to be in the country for a while. Residents of most Central American and some Asian countries require visas.

All travelers entering as diplomats, refugees, students, laborers, religious workers, businesspeople, volunteers and cultural-exchange visitors require non-immigrant visas. Various immigrant visas are also available. Visas must be obtained from an Ecuadorian embassy and cannot be arranged within Ecuador. See p735 for a partial list of Ecuadorian embassies.

Officially, to enter the country you must have a ticket out of Ecuador and sufficient funds for your stay, but border authorities rarely ask for proof of this. International vaccination certificates are not required by law, but some vaccinations, particularly against yellow fever, are advisable.

Visa Extensions

Tourist card extensions can be obtained from the **Jefatura Provincial de Migración** (Map p657; ☎ 02-224-7510; Isla Seymour 1152 near Río Coca; 🕑 8:30am-noon & 3-5pm Mon-Fri). On top of the original 90 days, you can obtain a maximum of 30 additional days, a process that can be performed three times, for a maximum of 180 days (six months) per year. You cannot get an extension until the day your tourist card expires.

VOLUNTEERING

Nearly all organizations accepting volunteers in Ecuador require a minimum commitment of one month, and many require at least basic Spanish-speaking skills. Most also *charge* volunteers between US$100 and US$300 per month, so don't expect free room and board in exchange for your work – it's rarely given. By far, the best place to get information in Ecuador is the Quito clubhouse of SAE (p649). **Ecuador Explorer** (www.ecuadorexplorer.com) has a great classified page listing numerous organizations that need volunteers.

WOMEN TRAVELERS

Generally, women travelers will find Ecuador safe and pleasant, despite the fact that machismo is alive and well. Ecuadorian men often make flirtatious comments and whistle at single women. Really, it's just sport – a sort of hormonal babbling amongst groups of guys – and the best strategy is to brush them off. Women who firmly ignore unwanted verbal advances are often treated with respect.

On the coast, come-ons are more predatory, and solo female travelers should take precautions like staying away from bars and discos where they'll obviously get hit on, opting for taxis over walking etc. Racy conversation with a guy, while it may be ironic or humorous, is not common here, and a man will probably assume you're after one thing.

WORKING

Officially, you need a work visa to get a job in Ecuador. English teaching positions occasionally pop up in Quito or Cuenca. The pay is low but enough to live on. Tourist services (jungle lodges, tour operators etc) are good places to look for work.

The Guianas

Mix a population of descendants of escaped and freed slaves with a well-established indigenous culture; add a sprinkling of Indian, Indonesian, Laotian, Chinese and Brazilian immigrants, some French, British and Dutch colonialism and steam the whole lot on the Atlantic coast of Latin South America. The result of this unlikely recipe makes for one of the most diverse and least-visited regions on the continent. Divided into three countries that have been defined by their colonialist past, the cultural mishmash causes a little bit of chaos, some wild-hot cuisine and lots and lots of feisty and eccentric personalities. Reggae music and an Afro-European vibe remind you that you that these countries consider themselves to be Caribbean before South American.

Deep, malarial jungles protected the region from getting too much European interest early on – most of the first settlers died of tropical diseases. Today, this gives these countries a trump card they have yet to fully exploit: some of the purest tropical rainforests on the planet, ideal for the most adventurous sort of ecotourism. Lack of tourist infrastructure makes traveling in any of the Guianas challenging and expensive yet incredibly rewarding. French Guiana, which is technically France, is the most tidy and organized of the three countries; the potholes increase as you travel west through kaleidoscopic Suriname and by the time you reach Guyana you'll have lost track of the last time you had a hot shower.

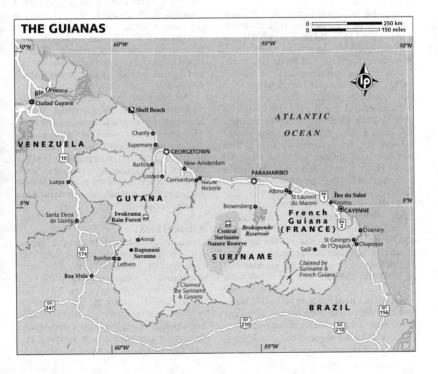

THE GUIANAS

HISTORY

The muddy Guiana coastline, covered with mangroves and sparsely populated with war-like Carib Indians, did not attract early European settlement. Spaniards saw the coast for the first time in 1499, but they found no prospect of gold or cheap labor, though they did make occasional slave raids. Several 16th-century explorers, including Sir Walter Raleigh, placed the mythical city of El Dorado in the region but there was still no sustained interest in the area until the mid-17th century.

The Netherlands began to settle the land in 1615. After forming the Dutch West India Company in 1621, the colonists traded with Amerindian peoples of the interior and established plantations of sugar, cocoa and other tropical commodities. Indigenous peoples were almost wiped out by introduced diseases, so the Dutch imported West African slaves to construct dikes and work the plantation economies. Beginning in the mid-18th century, escaped slaves (descendants of whom are now called Maroons) formed settlements in the interior.

England established sugar and tobacco plantations on the west bank of the Suriname River around 1650 and founded what is now Paramaribo. After the second Anglo-Dutch War, under the Treaty of Breda (1667), the Dutch retained Suriname and their colonies on the Guyanese coast (in exchange for a tiny island now called Manhattan) but ceded the area east of the Maroni (Marowijne in Dutch) River to the French. For the next 150 years sovereignty of the region shifted between the three powers; by 1800 Britain was dominant, though Suriname remained under Dutch control, and France retained a precarious hold on Cayenne in what is now French Guiana.

At the end of the Napoleonic Wars, the Treaty of Paris reaffirmed the sovereignty of the Dutch in Suriname and of the French east of the Maroni, while Britain formally purchased the Dutch colonies in what became British Guyana. By 1834 slavery was abolished in all British colonies, and the Royal Navy suppressed the slave trade in the Caribbean. This created a need for more plantation labor, and the subsequent immigration of indentured labor from other colonies (especially India) created a unique ethnic mix in each of the Guianas.

ENVIRONMENT
The Land

Although Caribbean in culture, the Guianas actually front the Atlantic Ocean. The most prominent geological feature is the Guiana Shield, an extensive, crystalline upland that extends throughout northeast Brazil, French Guiana, Suriname, Guyana and Venezuela. Once part of the larger Brazilian Shield to the south, it became separated in Tertiary times, when the rising Andes reversed the course of west-flowing rivers and created the Amazon Basin. The shield falls away in steps from 2810m Monte Roraima, on the Guyana–Brazil–Venezuela border, down to sea level.

Wildlife

An extensive and largely pristine tropical rainforest covers the Guianas' interior and offers a habitat for countless plant and animal species (although these ecosystems are threatened by both uncontrolled gold mining and multinational timber companies operating with few environmental safeguards). The jaguar is the most magnificent wild mammal, but the region teems with relatively undisturbed populations of splendid creatures, such as the scarlet macaw, the giant anteater and the sun parakeet. The Guianas are also home to flourishing numbers of animals – like the tapirs, black caimans and giant river otters – endangered in other parts of lowland South America.

The many waterways abound with side-neck turtles, electric eels, spectacled caimans, black piranhas and *tucunares* (peacock bass). Along the coasts are seasonal nesting sites for the awe-inspiring giant leatherback turtle, as well as green and olive ridley turtles. The Guianas are probably the best place in South America to see two of the most memorable species of Amazonian birds: the harpy eagle and the cock-of-the-rock.

National Parks

One of the main reasons to visit the Guianas is for the phenomenal yet rugged ecotourism opportunities. Suriname has the most extensive system of protected parks of the three countries, the largest being the 1.6 million hectare Central Suriname Nature Reserve (p770). Guyana's largest park, Iwokrama, is an inspirational example of how a population's passion for conservation can sustain a protected forest area in the worst economic circumstances (see p784). While French Guiana officially has the least number of protected hectares of the three countries, its isolated, agriculture-free history has allowed most of its surface to remain more pristine than almost anywhere on the planet.

Environmental Issues

The Guianas are at a collective conservation crossroads, trying to balance the pressing need to boost their economies (which can be accomplished most quickly through logging, mining and oil exploration) and the longer-term prospects for ecotourism. All three have been actively putting aside lands as protected nature reserves. Starting with a US$1 million donation, Suriname established the 16,187 sq km Central Suriname Nature Reserve in 1998, followed by a conservation foundation to protect nearly 15% of the nation's total area. That conservation effort is supported by a US$15 million endowment from the UN Development Program.

In Suriname, Conservation International is trying to promote biodiversity as a way to conserve the forest, and in Guyana the organization is aiming to develop more national preservation areas. The Iwokrama Rain Forest Preserve in Guyana, which encompasses 371,000 hectares of forest, is a grand experiment in sustainable logging as well as for ecotourism.

All three Guianas have leatherback turtle sites, under threat by hunters.

RESPONSIBLE TRAVEL

Whether spoken in French, Sranan Tongo or Amerindian, 'ecotourism' means the same thing throughout the Guianas. However, some operators have their own take on what it means as far as practice goes. Poke around and get a feel for a company's 'ecostrategy' before going with it.

On an individual level, make your ecotourist impact by making no impact. As well as always keeping the basics in mind, tread lightly in the interior in particular. Bring fishhooks and knives as trade goods and ask locals' permission before photographing them. If you go with a guide, ensure that he or she shows environmental respect – no hunting, gathering, littering etc – and, ideally, is from the culture of the village that you're visiting. In cities, keep an eye out for and steer clear of rare animals (like turtles) on menus, buy local products and, no matter where you are, conserve energy and water (many establishments filter their own water or collect precious rainwater).

TRANSPORTATION

For more information about travel in the Guianas see the individual transport sections for French Guiana (p747), Suriname (p765) and Guyana (p777).

Air

Air travel can be tricky. International flights arrive in Georgetown (Guyana), Paramaribo (Suriname) and Cayenne (French Guiana) but, at the time of writing, there were no direct flights linking these three countries. From North America, flights often go through one or multiple Caribbean islands. For example, Air France offers regular flights from Miami to Cayenne via Guadeloupe, Martinique and Haiti, but believe it or not it can sometimes be more cost- and time-efficient to fly via Paris. Thanks to lingering colonial ties, you can fly direct from Amsterdam to Paramaribo blissfully unburdened by plane changes. Guyana has direct flights to New York.

Car & Motorcycle

It is possible to travel overland across all three Guianas but only near the coasts. Be forewarned that road travel here is difficult – it helps to be well trained in the art of auto repair and to carry spare tires and fuel. Rainy seasons drastically affect road conditions, especially in Guyana and Suriname, where roads are iffy even when dry. Cars (especially rentals) aren't always allowed over borders and are particularly unwelcome into Suriname from French Guiana.

From the west, you can get into Guyana from Boa Vista in northern Brazil, but the road connection to Georgetown is not always open. From Georgetown, roads follow the coast eastward, with a river crossing into Suriname and another into French Guiana. A relatively new road links French Guiana to Brazil with a bridge expected to be completed by mid-2007 – in the meantime it's about US$240 to hire a ferry to transport a vehicle across the river. There is no legal crossing point between Guyana and Venezuela, so linking these countries requires a detour through Brazil.

FRENCH GUIANA

HIGHLIGHTS

- **Awala-Yalimopo during turtle egg-laying season** – feel like a part of the circle of life as you watch the peaceful ritual of dinosaur-like leatherback turtles laying their eggs in the moonlit sand (p758)
- **Îles du Salut** – take an island holiday while exploring the chillingly lovely remains of French Guiana's most famous penal colonies (p755)
- **Centre Spatial Guyanais (Guianese Space Center)** – learn all you ever wanted to know about the big business of satellite launching or, if you're timing is lucky, watch the *Ariane 5* blast into space (p754)
- **Best journey** – drive to the buzzing jungle of Trésor Nature Reserve where you can stop to walk through tropical forests and then drive on to the bird-filled savannas and marsh-lands of Kaw (p753)
- **Off the beaten track** – hike the Sentier Molokoï de Cacao where your only deep jungle companions will be capuchin monkeys, enormous snakes, insects and a slew of other exotic plants and critters – including ravenous mosquitoes (p753)

FAST FACTS

- **Area:** 91,000 sq km (slightly smaller than Portugal or the US state of Indiana)
- **Best bargain**: camping for free on Île St Joseph (p756)
- **Best street snack**: assorted Laotian treats from the markets (from US50¢)
- **Budget:** US$50-60 a day
- **Capital:** Cayenne
- **Costs:** hammock space in a traditional *carbet* US$10, Indonesian fried noodles US$3.50, fresh passion-fruit juice US$2
- **Country code:** ☎ 594
- **Famous for:** Papillon and penal colonies, satellite launching
- **Languages:** French, French Guianese, Creole, Amerindian languages, Sranan Tongo (Surinaams)
- **Money:** US$1 = €0.79
- **Phrases:** *chébran* (cool), *infect* (disgusting), *une teuf* (party)

- **Population:** 182,400
- **Time:** GMT minus 3hr
- **Tipping:** 10% in restaurants and hotels if not included; none in taxis
- **Visas:** US$40 for 3 months; not issued at borders

TRAVEL HINTS

Bring a hammock and sleep cheap nearly anywhere besides Cayenne; and don't forget your mosquito net!

OVERLAND ROUTES

French Guiana's border crossings include Albina (Suriname) and Oiapoque (Brazil).

FRENCH GUIANA

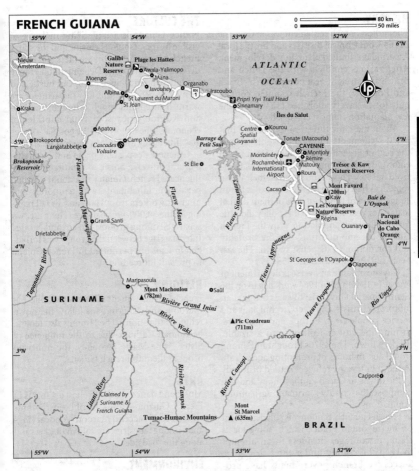

THE GUIANAS

French Guiana is a little country of pristine rainforests that has both the luck and misfortune of being colonized by France (and is thus a member of the EU). It's the wealthiest region of this corner, with France pouring in the funds to insure a stable base for its satellite launcher; everyone from Brazil to Suriname tries to cross the border in hopes of high-paying jobs and unemployment benefits. Yet the country lacks the smiling simplicity of its struggling neighbors. On the one hand it's a fascinating destination of cleaned-up colonial architecture, eerie prison camp history (that involved the colorful characters of Papillon and Alfred Dreyfus) and some of the most diverse plant and animal life in the world; on the other hand, its heart seems buried beneath a cold European hand uninterested in seeing its people reach their full potential.

CURRENT EVENTS

Ariane 5, Europe's premier satellite launcher based in Kourou, French Guiana, is flying high, having rocketed a record-breaking payload of over 8000kg into space on November 17, 2005. The first launch of *Vega*, a lighter lift launcher, is scheduled for 2007. In 2008 the first launch of *Soyuz*, a medium-load launcher that can also transport humans into space, is planned from the Kourou space center.

HISTORY

The earliest French settlement was in Cayenne in 1643, but tropical diseases and hostile local Amerindians limited plantation development. After various conflicts with the Dutch and British and an eight-year occupation by Brazil and Portugal, the French resumed control only to see slavery abolished (1848), and the few plantations almost collapsed.

About the same time, France decided that penal settlements in Guiana would reduce the cost of French prisons and contribute to colony development. The first convicts arrived in 1852. Those who survived their initial sentences had to remain there as exiles for an equal period of time, but 90% of them died of malaria or yellow fever, so this policy did little for the desired population growth. French Guiana became notorious for the brutality and corruption of its penal system. The last penal settlement closed in 1953.

Guyane became an overseas department of France in 1946, and in 1964 work began on the Centre Spatial Guyanais; this has brought an influx of scientists, engineers, technicians and service people from Europe and elsewhere, turning the city of Kourou into a sizable, modern town. The 1970s brought in Hmong from Laos, in hopes of promoting agriculture in the country; the refugees settled primarily in the towns of Cacao and Javouhey and still comprise the county's primary agricultural populations.

French Guiana's economy is still dependent on metropolitan France which, some locals claim, discourages business in an attempt to keep the colony under their firm grip. Successive French governments have provided state employment and billions of euros in subsidies, resulting in a near-European standard of living in urban areas. Rural villages are much poorer, and in the hinterland many Amerindians and Maroons still lead a subsistence lifestyle.

Historically the main export product has been rain-forest timber. Now the main industries are fishing (particularly shrimp), forestry and mining (particularly gold). The tourist industry is embryonic and receives little government interest. Agriculture consists of a few Hmong market gardens – the vast majority of food, consumer goods and energy are imported. The space center employs around 1350 people and accounts for about 15% of economic activity.

THE CULTURE

French Guiana is a tantalizing mélange of visible history, fabulous cuisine and the sultry French language with the vastness and ethnic diversity of Amazonia. Dependent on France yet independent of her European hustle and bustle, the people of this tiny department are warm-hearted and tough. Though Cayenne and Kourou enjoy somewhat continental economies, the majority of the populace struggles financially and lives a modest lifestyle.

Guianese people take pride in their multicultural universe borne of multiregional influences. French Guiana has about 150,000 permanent inhabitants, with temporary and migrant workers from Haiti and Brazil making up the 30,000-plus balance. There are two separate Hmong groups: 'green' and 'white.' Intermarriage between the groups was forbidden in Laos but permitted in French Guiana to prevent inbreeding.

RELIGION

French Guiana is predominantly Catholic, but Maroons and Amerindians follow their own religious traditions. The Hmong also tend to be Roman Catholic due to the influence of Sister Anne-Marie Javouhey, the nun who brought them to French Guiana.

ARTS

Music and dance are the liveliest art forms in French Guiana – think Caribbean rhythms with a French accent. Maroon woodcarvings and Hmong tapestries are sold in markets and along the roadside.

ENVIRONMENT
The Land

French Guiana borders Brazil to the east and south, while to the west the Maroni and Litani Rivers form the border with Suriname (the southern part is disputed).

The majority of Guianese people live in the Atlantic coastal zone, which has most of French Guiana's limited road network. The coast is mostly mangrove swamp, but there are a few sandy beaches. The densely forested interior, whose terrain rises gradually toward the Tumac-Humac Mountains on the Brazilian frontier, is largely unpopulated.

Wildlife

Blissfully devoid of a considerable plantation history, French Guiana's rainforest is 90% intact. It's also more botanically diverse than Surinamese and Guyanese forests – one hectare of Trésor Nature Reserve's forest contains 164 tree species! French Guiana is also home to myriad animal and insect species, such as tapirs, jaguars, poison arrow frogs and caimans.

TRANSPORTATION
Getting There & Away
AIR
All international passengers experience Cayenne's Rochambeau International Airport (p751).

BOAT & BUS
River transport into French Guiana, with *taxi collectif* connections to major municipalities, passes through the border towns of St Laurent du Maroni, on the Suriname border (locally called just St Laurent; see p758) and St Georges de l'Oyapok, on the Brazilian border (see p754).

Getting Around
AIR
From Cayenne, small flights go to interior destinations such as St Georges and Saül (see p751). Air Guyane operates most internal flights.

BOAT
River transport into the interior is possible but requires patience and good timing, unless you are taking a tour. The best places to try to catch a boat are Kaw and St Laurent.

CAR
The main roads in French Guiana are in first-world condition making this a prime drive-your-own-vehicle destination. Secondary and tertiary roads can be bad, especially in the rainy season – have a spare tire, spare gas and spare time. Because public transport is minimal, car rental is worth considering; see p751. An International Driving Permit is recommended but not legally required.

DEPARTURE TAX

If you're headed to any international destination (besides France), the departure tax is US$20, which is often included in the ticket price. Flights to Paris are regarded as domestic.

HITCHHIKING
Locals are seen hitchhiking around Cayenne and west toward St Laurent but it's more risky for travelers who may be seen as money-laden targets. Never hitch at night or on the road between Régina and St Georges, which is notorious for drug and illegal immigrant transport.

TAXI COLLECTIF
Taxis collectifs (actually minibuses) are the second-best wheeled option. They run frequently from Cayenne (p751) and not as frequently from St Laurent (p758) and St Georges.

CAYENNE
pop 50,395
A crossroads of the Caribbean, South America and Europe, Cayenne is a city of variegated cultures surrounded by all the colors of the Caribbean. The streets are lined with colonial wrought-iron balconies, with louvered shutters painted in tropical pinks, yellows and turquoise. The vibrant markets and excellent Brazilian, Creole, French and Chinese restaurants make this town as pleasing to the belly as it is to the eye; you won't want to be skipping any meals here. Outside the city center, a highway-ridden urban sprawl reminds you that you're still in the 21st century.

Orientation
Cayenne is at the western end of a small, somewhat hilly peninsula between the Cayenne and Mahury Rivers. The center of action is the Place des Palmistes, in the northwest corner, where cafés and outdoor food stalls skirt stands of palm trees. To its west, Place Léopold Héder (aka Place Grenoble) is the oldest part of the city.

Grab a free map of Cayenne from the airport's tourist information desk before you head out, or get one from a hotel or the tourist office (p749) in town.

Information
BOOKSHOPS
AJC (33 Blvd Jubelin) Offers the biggest selection of books and maps, including Institut Géographique National topographic maps.
Maison de la Presse (14 Av du Général de Gaulle) Carries French books, newspapers and magazines.

EMERGENCY
Fire (☎ 18)
Police (☎ 17)

CAYENNE

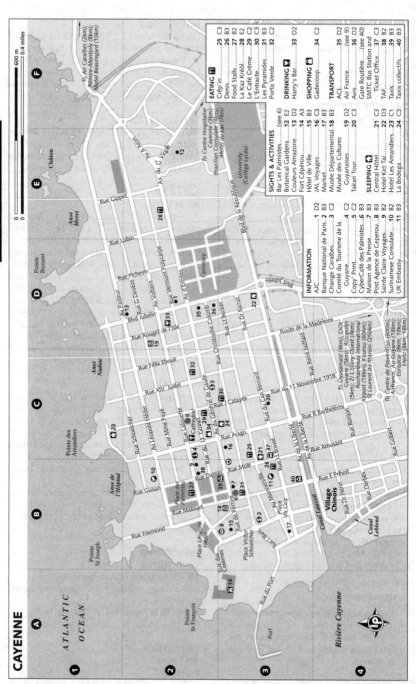

GETTING INTO TOWN

Rochambeau International Airport is located 18km southwest of Cayenne. From the airport, consider sharing a taxi (day/night US$35/45); the trip takes about 20 minutes. To the airport, it's cheaper to take a *taxi collectif* to Matoury, then a bus or taxi for the remaining 5km. Don't let taxi drivers tack on bogus surcharges for each piece of luggage.

INTERNET ACCESS

Copy' Print (22 Rue Lalouette; ☽ 8am-noon & 2:30-6pm Mon-Fri, 8am-noon Sat) The cheapest and cleanest Internet café in the city center.

CyberCafé des Palmistes (Bar Les Palmistes, 12 Av du Général de Gaulle; ☽ 7am-midnight Mon-Sat) Have a cold beer while checking your email.

OOL Guyane (Cara shopping complex, ZI Collery 3; ☽ 8am-8pm Mon-Sat) About 5km out of central Cayenne, this place has free high-speed internet.

MEDICAL SERVICES

Centre Hospitalier Cayenne (☎ 39-50-50; 3 Av Flamboyants)

MONEY

Banks and ATMs are easily found throughout the city and traveler's checks can be cashed at both banks and cambios.

Banque National de Paris (BNP; 2 Place Victor Schoelcher) Be prepared to wait in line.

Change Caraïbes (64 Av du Général de Gaulle; ☽ 7:30am-12:30pm & 3:30-5:30pm Mon-Fri, 8am-noon Sat) Offers competitive rates.

POST

Post Agence de Ceperou (Place Léopold Héder; ☽ 7:30am-1:30pm Mon-Fri, 7:30-11:45am Sat) This conveniently located post office gets swamped the first two weeks of every month when it distributes unemployment checks.

TELEPHONE

There is no central telephone office, but there are plenty of pay phones, especially on and near Place des Palmistes.

TOURIST INFORMATION

Comité du Tourisme de la Guyane (☎ 29-65-00; www.tourisme-guyane.com; 12 Rue Lalouette; ☽ 8am-1pm & 3-6pm Mon-Fri, 8am-noon Sat) The Office du Tourisme currently shares this office so there is an abundance of helpful people, pamphlets, maps and information. There is also a desk at the airport that is open late for arriving flights.

TRAVEL AGENCIES

Sainte Claire Voyages (☎ 30-00-38, 17-19 Rue Lalouette) Helpful staff can book flights and tours.

Dangers & Annoyances

Crime, both petty and violent, is on the rise in Cayenne, mostly as a result of increasing drug problems. At night, walk in small groups or take a taxi. The Village Chinois (aka Chicago) area, south of the market, is to be avoided.

Sights

Compact, colorful Cayenne is easily seen in a day on foot. Off the gardened **Place Léopold Héder** are the remains of **Fort Cépérou**, perched on land bought by the first French colonists from the Galibi Indians in 1643. Most of the site is now a restricted military zone but you can still stroll the area for good views of the town and river. Great for people-watching, shady **Place des Palmistes**, which usually harbors a few strays from the local crack scene, is best observed from afar at the **Bar Les Palmistes** (12 Av du Général de Gaulle; ☽ 7am-midnight Mon-Sat). Escape city fumes across town at the sizable **Botanical Gardens** (Blvd de la République; admission free) created in 1879, which today flourishes with a diverse selection of Guianese flora. After siesta, cruise Av du Général de Gaulle, the main commercial street, to experience Cayenne at its bustling peak.

Cayenne's main **market** (cnr Rue Lt Brasse & Rue Ste Rose; ☽ 6:30am-1pm Wed, Fri & Sat), is a vibrant jumble of Hmong handicrafts, African-style paintings, piles of exotic spices (with great bargains on saffron!) and science fiction–looking fruits and veggies. The indoor soup stalls serve up the best Vietnamese *pho* (US$5) in the Guianas.

The centrally located **Musée Départemental** (1 Rue de Rémire; adult/child & student US$2.50/1.50; ☽ 8am-1:15pm & 3-5:45pm Mon & Thu, 8am-1:15pm Wed & Fri) features a frighteningly large stuffed black caiman, as well as other preserved local critters, an ethnobotanical display and an air-conditioned 'butterfly room,' easily missed because it is poorly marked. The upstairs area recaptures life in the old penal colony and displays some Amerindian handicrafts. The smaller **Musée des Cultures Guyanaises** (☎ 31-41-72; 78 Rue Madame Payé; admission free; ☽ 8am-12:45pm &

3-5:45pm Mon, Tue, Thu & Fri, 8am-12:45pm Wed, 8am-11:45am Sat) devotes itself to Guiana's early history from its geologic formation through precolonial, Amerindian times. It houses a relaxing, air-con library (upstairs) with publications in French, English and various other languages.

Tours

French Guiana's pristine jungles are impenetrable and dangerous without a good guide. There are several respectable Cayenne-based tour agencies that run a few of their own tours, but more often they hire out guides throughout the country and take a commission on their services. The better of these include **Takari Tour** (☎ 31-19-60; www.takaritour.gf; 8 Rue du Cap Bernard), the oldest and most respected operator, **JAL Voyages** (☎ 31-68-20; www.jal-voyages .com; 26 Av du Général de Gaulle), whose most popular jaunt is an overnight on a floating *carbet* in Kaw (from US$120), and **Couleurs Amazone** (☎ 28-70-00; www.couleursamazone.fr in French; 2 Av Pasteur), who offer a bit of everything as well as wilderness boot camps (from US$450 for five days) – a must if you're planning on trying out for *Survivor*.

A cheaper tour alternative is to go directly to local guides in the specific region you want to explore; you can easily find guides like these at places of lodging throughout French Guiana (see individual listings in each region).

Festivals & Events

Carnaval (January to February or March, dates vary) is *the* annual festival, and it gets bigger and wilder every year, with near-perpetual live bands and parades. Schools are often closed during the last week of Carnaval, so don't be surprised if businesses are closed and hotels are more crowded.

Sleeping

If you are without a car, staying in central Cayenne is essential. If you have wheels consider staying in the areas around Cayenne for cheaper options.

La Bodega (☎ 30-25-13; www.labodega.fr; 42 Av du Général de Gaulle; d from US$36; P ⊠) It's the cheapest place in town and you can drink till morn at the downstairs bar then crawl back to your room; if sleep is a priority, think twice before staying here. Rooms with a view go up in price during Carnaval.

Hotel Ket Tai (☎ 28-97-77; 72 Blvd Jubelin; d US$48) Simple, if not bland, motel-style comfort a

short walk from the city center makes this one of the better bargains in town.

Central Hôtel (☎ 25-65-65; www.centralhotel-cayenne .fr; cnr Rue Molé & Rue du Lieutenant Becker; s/d US$60/64; ⊠ P) Completely generic, yet well located and with a helpful staff, this city-center favorite is often full so reserve in advance. The downstairs lobby smells like an ashtray.

Hotel Les Amandiers (☎ 31-38-75; amandiers@hotmail .com; Place Auguste-Hort; d/ste US$64/107; ⊠) Run by a pink-haired lady with two small dogs; what the rooms lack in character, the management makes up for. This is the only hotel in Cayenne overlooking the beach and a stretch of park. Request a room with a view.

Oyasamaïd (☎ 31-56-84; www.oyasamaid.com; PK 4, route de la Madeleine, chemin Castor; d US$65, extra bed US$18; ⊠ P) A French family pension *à la Guianese*, this four-room place is friendly, impeccably clean and has all sorts of pluses like Jacuzzis in the bathrooms. It's a five-minute drive to central Cayenne.

Eating

For the best bang for your buck, slurp noodles at Cayenne's daytime market (p749) and browse the nighttime **food stalls** (Place des Palmistes) for delicious crepes, Indonesian fried rice or greasy hamburgers and sandwiches (all from US$3.50). Small Chinese grocery stores and scattered supermarkets make self-catering a breeze. Don't miss out on some of the superb sit-down options:

Crêp'in (5 Rue du Lieutenant Becker; salads US$4.50, crepes from US$2, breakfast US$5.50; ☿ 8am-8pm Mon-Sat) One of the only places in town serving a complete breakfast. Come back again for a lunch of salads, sandwiches, sweet and savory crepes and fresh juices.

Le Café Crème (44 Rue J Catayée; sandwiches from US$3.50; ☿ 6:15am-4:30pm Mon-Fri, 6:15am-3:30pm Sat) Get Parisian-style coffee, sizable sandwiches and delicate pastries at this sidewalk café *à la Française*.

L'Entracte (☎ 30-01-37; 65 Rue J Catayée; pizzas from US$6; noon-2:30pm & 6:30-10:30pm) Eat the cheapest (but tasty!) pizza in town while admiring movie posters that cover the walls.

Denis (☎ 30-71-18; 21 Rue Lt Brassé; mains around US$7; ☿ 11:30am-10:30pm) One of the best of a slew of affordable Chinese restaurants. This friendly place has something on the menu for everyone.

Porta Verde (☎ 29-19-03; 58 Rue du Lieutenant Goinet; per kg US$14; ☿ 11:45am-2:45pm Mon-Sat) A Brazilian locals' favorite, get a buffet lunch priced by the kilo. Dinner is by reservation only.

Les Pyramides (☎ 37-95-79; cnr Rue Christophe Colomb & Rue Malouet; mains US$19; ☺ noon-3pm & 7-11pm Tue-Sun) This superb eat-in-or-take-out Middle Eastern restaurant makes hearty couscous and is worth the splurge.

La Kaz Kréol (☎ 39-06-97; 35 Av d'Estrées; mains US$19; ☺ 12:30-2:30pm & 7:30-10:30pm Tue-Sun) Traditional and modern Creole fare is elaborately presented at this highly respected restaurant.

Drinking

Live music, French wine and rum punch flow freely in bars and clubs throughout Cayenne. The more popular ones:

La Bodega (42 Av du Général de Gaulle; ☺ 7am-1am Sun-Fri, to 2am Sat) Snack on tapas while sipping an aperitif at this decidedly French sidewalk bar. Things liven up after 11pm.

Harry's Bar (20 Rue Rouget de l'Isle; ☺ 7am-2:30pm & 5pm-1am Mon-Thu, to 2am Fri & Sat) Nonstop jazz, blues and Latin music warm up this cozy, fun bar that boasts 50 brands of whiskey, and nearly as many beers.

Acropolys (☎ 31-97-81; Route de Cabassou; entrance fee US$19; ☺ from 10pm Wed-Sat) Away from the center, nightclubs like Greek-themed Acropolys pump out Zouk and international music.

Reggae music rocks small clubs in Village Chinois (but see the warning on p749) and a few Brazilian and Dominican bars dot Av de la Liberté.

Shopping

If this is your only stop in South America and you are dying to buy handicrafts try **Gadecoop** (31 Rue Arago; ☺ 9am-1pm Tue-Fri), a cooperative of Amerindian artists whose proceeds go directly to the villagers; quality and prices are better here than elsewhere in French Guiana.

Getting There & Away

All international and domestic flights leave from **Rochambeau International Airport** (☎ 29-97-00).

Airline offices in town or at Rochambeau:
Air Caraïbes (☎ 29-36-36; gsa.aircaraibes@wanadoo.fr; Centre de Katoury, rte Rocade)
Air France (☎ 29-87-00; 17 Rue Lalouette & airport; www.airfrance.gf)
Air Guyane (☎ 29-36-30; airport; www.airguyane.com)
TAF (☎ 30-70-00; 2 Rue Lalouette)

Book seats well in advance to get the cheapest fares. Destinations and one-way flight details:

Belém (Brazil) TAF, US$269, 1¼ hours, two weekly; Air Caraïbes, US$219, 1¼ hours, seven weekly.
Fort-de-France (Martinique) Air France, US$365, two hours, two weekly; Air Caraïbes, US$375, two hours, two weekly.
Macapá (Brazil) TAF, US$209, one hour, six weekly.
Saül Air Guyane, US$72, 40 minutes, five weekly.

Getting Around
BUS

Local **SMTC buses** (☎ for schedule 25-49-29) service the region around Cayenne and Montjoly's beaches (US$1.50). There are limited routes and buses don't run on Sundays, so you'll probably need taxis.

CAR

Renting a car can be cheaper than public transport if two or more persons are traveling together and you plan on moving around a lot. Both companies and roads can be dodgy; check the cars thoroughly, and know how to put on a spare tire. Most companies have desks at the airport.

ACL (☎ 30-47-56; allocation@wanadoo.fr; 44 Blvd Jubelin)
ADA (☎ 16-91-69; www.adaguyane.com; Lot 26ZA Galmot)
Avis (☎ 30-25-22; 58 Blvd Jubelin)
Europcar (☎ 35-18-27; gtmlocation@europcar.gf; ZI Collery Ouest & airport)
Hertz (☎ 29-69-30; www.hertzantilles.com; ZI Collery Ouest & airport)

TAXI

Taxis have meters and charge a hiring fee of US$1.80 plus 90¢ per kilometer (US$1.30 from 7pm to 6am, Sunday and holidays). There's a taxi stand on the southeast corner of Place des Palmistes.

TAXI COLLECTIF

Taxis collectifs leave when full from Gare Routière on Av de la Liberté until 6pm daily. From the corner of Rue Molé, they head to Matoury (US$2.40, 15 minutes, 10km) and St Laurent (US$48, four hours, 250km). From the corner of Rue Malouet, they depart for Kourou (US$12, one hour, 60km) and St Georges (US$24, two hours, 100km). Settle rates in advance and get there early.

AROUND CAYENNE

There's heaps to explore around the capital city, and the best way to do it is by renting a car for a day or two.

AROUND CAYENNE

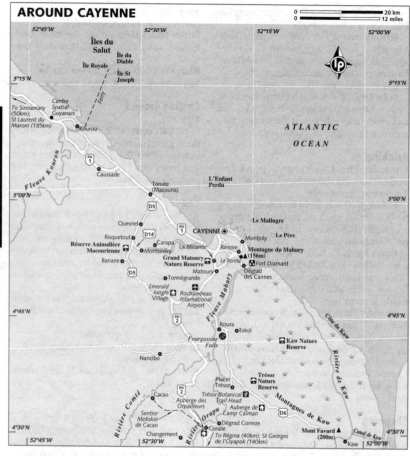

Rémire-Montjoly
pop 19,492

Collectively known as Rémire-Montjoly (though actually two separate towns) this area of long, sweeping beaches is some of the best waterfront in the country; unfortunately it's often plagued by biting sand flies. **Plage Montjoly** is the best beach, reachable by bus or taxi, and its breezy waters are drawing in increasing numbers of **kite-surfers**. There are no rentals or schools, but those with their own gear can ask around the beach for more information. The Montjoly area has historical ruins at **Fort Diamant** and hiking trails along the lakes at Le Rorota and to the top of **Montagne du Mahury**, offering stunning views. The 5km hike into the **Grand Matoury**

Nature Reserve at La Mirande is good for bird-watching.

Stay at **Motel du Lac** (☎ 38-08-00; moteldulac@ opensurf.net; Chemin Poupon – Rte de Montjoly; d US$74; 🅿 ✗ 🄰), a well-run place with a great pool, near Montjoly beach and a lakeside ecological reserve. Otherwise try **Motel Beauregard** (☎ 35-41-00; criccrac@wanadoo.fr; PK9, 2 Rte de Rémire; d from US$65; 🅿 ✗ 🄰) which has a bowling alley as well as a pool, tennis courts and gym; it's endearingly kitsch and only 10km from Cayenne.

Montsinéry-Tonnégrande
pop 915

The two villages of Montsinéry and Tonné-grande and the isolated stretch of road that joins them is often referred to as Montsinéry-Tonnégrande.

Along the Montsinéry River, 45km west of Cayenne, is the **Réserve Animalière Macourienne** (adult/child US$14/8, tours US$6; ☉ 9am-6pm). What starts out looking like a few depressing caged snakes and birds leads into a Heart of Darkness–like jungle with huge jaguar enclosures, harpy eagles, caimans and sloths. The trail leads to a 3km nature trail where wild monkeys abound and there is apparently a jaguar that frequents the area. Don't miss the feeding of the spectacled caimans at 6pm and the jaguars at 5pm on Sundays.

At the intersection of D5 and RN2, 25km south of Cayenne, is one of the best ecotourism opportunities in the vicinity: **Emerald Jungle Village** (☎ 28-00-89; emeraldjunglevillage@wanadoo.fr; Carrefour du Gallion; s/d US$29/32). Joep Moonen, a biologist and conservationist of the Trésor Nature Reserve, and his wife, Marijke, run this dusty lodge with one of the warmest welcomes in the Guianas. This is one of the better places to organize an ecoexcursion to eastern French Guiana – call ahead to customize an unforgettable adventure. Canoe (US$30 per day) and mountain bike (US$12 per day) rental are also available.

Cacao
pop 1100
A tidy slice of Laos in the hills of Guiana, Cacao, about 75km southwest of Cayenne, is a village of sparkling clear rivers, vegetable plantations and no-nonsense wooden houses on stilts. The Hmong refugees who left Laos in the 1970s keep their town a safe, peaceful haven and it's now a favorite weekend day trip for locals from Cayenne. Sunday, market day, is the best time for a visit if you want to shop for Hmong embroidery and weaving and feast on a smorgasbord of Laotian treats (get there by 10am, before the tour buses arrive). If you're looking for a quieter escape you'll be the only visitor in town mid-week. Don't miss **Le Planeur Bleu** (leplaneurbleu@wanadoo.fr; adult/child US$3.50/free; ☉ 9am-1pm & 2-4pm Sun, other times by appointment) to see butterfly and arachnids, both dead and alive. Clamor for a chance to hold a live tarantula (if you dare) or call in advance for a private tour midweek. For tasty homemade Laotian specialties, eat at **Chez By et Daniel** (☎ 27-09-98; 111 Bourg de Cacao) – you get a 5% discount with your Planeur Bleu ticket.

For a wildlife- and insect-spotting adventure, embark on the two-day hike along the **Sentier Molokoï de Cacao**, one of the few deep forest jaunts that can be accomplished independently. The track links the rustic-chic **Auberge des Orpailleurs** (☎ 27-06-22; www.terresdeguyane.fr; PK62, RN 2; s/d US$27/33, hammock space per person US$6), situated on the road to St Georges, with the more basic **Quimbe Kio** (☎ 27-01-22; www.quimbekio .com; hammock space US$12, hammock & mattress rental US$5) in Cacao – these two *gîtes* (guesthouses) are also great places to arrange other ecotourism excursions within this region. Wear good shoes, bring plenty of water, insect repellent and rain gear. There's a small refuge hut midway and maps and details are available at the two lodges.

Trésor & Kaw Nature Reserves
The Trésor Nature Reserve is one of French Guiana's most accessible primary rainforest areas. Drive (17km from Roura – there's no bus) to Trésor's 1.75km **botanical trail** to experience its rich diversity and protected wildlife. Trésor borders the mysterious forests and swamps of the Kaw Nature Reserve, an excellent place to observe caimans (best at night) and spectacular waterfowl like the scarlet ibis (best in summer). **Mont Favard** features hiking trails and petroglyphs.

Independent exploration of Kaw is possible but you'll need wheels to get there. The road into the area ends right at the Kaw River. For lodging in Kaw village ask at **Restaurant Gingembre Sirop** (☎ 27-04-64; hammock space/bed US$6/12), who run the ferry to the village and who can also help arrange wildlife-viewing excursions from US$24. Between Trésor and Kaw, 28km from Roura, is **Auberge de Camp Caïman** (☎ 30-72-77; hammock space/s/d US$9/26/36) who arrange excursions as far as Kaw from US$24.

Régina to St Georges de l'Oyapok
The road connecting Régina to St Georges, completed in 2004, has become a highway for illegal immigration from Brazil. Régina (population 300) is near becoming a ghost town and crime along the highway is frequent. Do not stop or pick up hitchhikers along this road. The burned vehicles you see along the sides are where the police have caught illegals and destroyed their vehicles. It's not recommended to drive this road at night.

Brazil meets French Guiana at colonial St Georges (population 2828), where Portuguese is spoken as widely as French. It's much quieter here than neighboring Oiapoque, Brazil,

---

GETTING TO BRAZIL

Stamp out at the **Douane** (customs office; ⌚ 8am-6pm) on the riverside in St Georges, then hire a dugout (US$5, 5 minutes) to take you across to Oiapoque, Brazil. A bridge linking the two towns is expected to be completed sometime in 2007. Once in Oiapoque, it's a five- to ten-minute walk away from the river to the Police Federal where you get stamped in to Brazil. Buses (daily) and planes (Puma; one-way US$240; three days a week) leave Oiapoque for Macapá. For details on travel from Oiapoque to French Guiana, see p385.

---

but also less lively and colorful. For lodging try the popular **Chez Modestine** (☎ 37-00-13) or quieter **Caz-Calé** (☎ 37-00-54), both on Rue Elie-Elfort with rooms from US$38. Eat at **Cappuccino** (mains US$7), right down the street, which serves huge portions of local-style fish and meat.

Minibuses leave when full (early mornings are best) from town center to Cayenne (US$24, two hours).

SAÜL

pop 160

Accessible by air from Cayenne, the defunct gold-mining village of Saül – the geographic center of French Guiana – is an untamed paradise explored mostly by professional biologists.

For basic accommodations call the town hall for the **Gîtes Communal** (☎ 37-45-00; s/d/tr US$14/26/33). You can also organize an eight-day river-jungle-villages adventure to Saül; inquire at tour agencies in Cayenne (p750).

KOUROU

pop 19,074

Kourou's depressing, scattered sprawl of cheap '70s and '80s architecture can be blamed on the establishment of the Centre Spatial Guyanais which employs some 1350 people. For the seat of the country's economic strongforce, there is surprisingly little culture and the most recommended activity after a visit to the Space Center is to hightail it out by boat to the Îles du Salut. The only area of the town worth visiting is *Le Vieux Bourg* (opposite) which is a great strip for eating, drinking and wondering why the rest of the town isn't

this hip. Kourou is the fastest growing city in French Guiana and also one of the poorest; watch your back.

Information

Guyanespace Voyages (☎ 22-31-01; www.guyane space.com; 39 Av Hector-Berlioz) Reserve everything from transport to the Îles du Salut to international air travel.
Mediateque (Pôle Culturel de Kourou; ⌚ 9am-5pm Mon-Fri) Internet is free but you need to show your passport.
Point Information Tourisme (☎ 32-98-33; Av Victor Hugo; ⌚ 7:30am-1:30pm Mon-Fri) Tucked away in a complex across the street from Notre Dame Church.
Taxi Phone Cyber (18 Rue Aimaras; ⌚ 9am-1pm & 3-8pm Mon-Sat, 9am-2pm Sun) Internet and long-distance telephone service.

Sights

In 1964, Kourou was chosen to be the site of the **Centre Spatial Guyanais** (CNS, the French space center) because it's close to the equator, enjoys a large ocean frontage (50km), is away from tropical storm tracks and earthquake zones, and has a low population density. The launch site is the only one in the world this close to the equator (5 degrees) where the earth spins significantly faster than further north or south; this means that the site benefits from the 'slingshot effect,' which boosts propulsion making the launches up to 17% more energy efficient than sites further away from the equator. Since 1980, two-thirds of the world's commercial satellites have been launched from French Guiana. There are only 16 launch stations of this kind in the world, but Kourou is considered to have the best location.

The center is run by CNS in collaboration with ESA (European Space Agency; www .esa.com) and Arianespace (www.arianespace .com). At the time of writing, *Ariane 5*, a heavy lift launcher, was the only working rocket at the center. In 2007 and 2008 two new launchers, *Vega* (a light-lift rocket) and *Soyuz* (a medium-lift launcher) will also begin service from Kourou.

Cool (and free!) three-hour **tours** (☎ 32-61-23; www.cnes-csg.fr; ⌚ 7:45am & 12:45pm Mon-Thu & 7:45am Fri) include a launch-pad visit; phone ahead for reservations, and bring your passport. Tour guides sometimes speak English and German; ask when you book. Don't miss the excellent **Musée de l'Espace** (Space Museum; adult/child with tour US$7/4.50, without tour US$4.50/3; ⌚ 8am-6pm

Mon-Fri, 2-6pm Sat); the informative displays are in English and French.

Ideally, coordinate your visit with a launch (about nine per year). To see one, email well ahead, to CSG-accueil@cnes.fr, providing your full name, address, phone number and age.

Sleeping

There are pitifully few inexpensive places to stay in Kourou. Both of the 'budget' places have reception hours from noon to 2pm and 6pm to 8pm every day except Sundays. The best beds are at the welcoming **Hotel Ballahou** (☎ 22-00-22; ballahou@ariasnet.fr; 1-3 Rue Amet Martial; s/d/studio US$39/51/65; P ⊠), which can be tricky to find but they'll pick you up from the Centre d'Accueil. **Le Gros Bec** (☎ 32-91-91; hotel-le grosbec@wanadoo.fr; 56 Rue du De Floch; s/d/tr US$62/72/79; P ⊠), right next to *Le Vieux Bourg* area, has spacious split-level studios with kitchenettes.

Eating & Drinking

Potholed, colorful *Le Vieux Bourg*, centralized along Av Général de Gaulle, is by far the most eclectic area of Kourou and the best place for cheap and delicious Indian, Creole, Chinese, Moroccan, French, you name it! There are also several hopping bars with live music. Cruise the street and take your pick.

Outside of *Le Vieux Bourg*:

Le Glacier des 2 Lacs (68 Av des Deux Lacs; ⊗ 8am-11:30pm Wed-Sun) For sinful ice cream and other sweets made on the premises, this is the best creamery in French Guiana.

La Pizzeria (38 Rue ML King; pizzas from US$7; ⊗ noon-10:30pm) This large eatery does Italian dishes and pizzas.

Self-catering is easy thanks to the produce **market** (Place de la Condamine; ⊗ Tue & Fri) and ubiquitous markets and supermarkets.

Getting There & Away

Taxis collectifs run to Cayenne (US$12, one hour, 60km) and St Laurent (US$30, three hours, 190km); inquire at hotels about times and departure locations. The two rental companies that service both Cayenne and Kourou, **Avis** (☎ 32-52-99; 4 Av de France) and **Europcar** (☎ 35-25-55; Hotel Mercure Atlantis, Lac Bois Diable), enable one-way jaunts but these include a hefty fee.

AROUND KOUROU
Îles du Salut

Îles du Salut (Salvation Islands) are 15km north of Kourou over choppy, shark-infested waters.

For 18th-century colonists the islands were an escape from mainland fever and malaria because the sea breezes kept mosquitoes away. The prisons came later, along with more than 2000 convicts, many of whom died from the inhumane conditions in which they were kept. The prison closed in 1947 and the islands have again become a lackadaisical delight – although the modern-day mosquitoes don't seem any less ferocious than those on the mainland.

Île Royale, once the administrative headquarters of the penal settlement, has several restored prison buildings including the restaurant/auberge, while the smaller Île St Joseph, with it's eerie solitary-confinement cells, has been left to shrieking cicadas and an over-growth of coconut palms. Île du Diable was home to political prisoners, including Alfred Dreyfus, and is now closed to the public because of hazardous currents. During the prison years, the island was linked to Île Royale by a 225m supply cable.

The old **director's house** (⊗ 10am-4:30pm Tue-Sun) contains an interesting English-language history display and temporary exhibits; two-hour guided tours of Île Royale (usually in French, US$6) begin here. Surprisingly abundant wildlife includes macaws, agoutis, capuchins and sea turtles. Carry a swimsuit and towel to take advantage of the white sand beach on St Joseph; it's a refreshing place for a shallow dip but be extremely careful of the dangerous currents. The Centre Spatial Guyanais has a huge infrared camera on Île Royale and the islands are evacuated when there is an eastward launch from the space center.

SLEEPING & EATING

Auberge des Îles du Salut (☎ 32-11-00; www.ilesdu salut.com; Île Royale; hammock space US$12, bungalows US$67, s/d with full board US$145/217) The welcome hasn't improved much since the days of arriving convicts, but the rooms, in artfully renovated guards' quarters, are something out of a breezy Bogart film. If you want a more Papillon-like experience, you can sling a hammock in (cleaned-up and freshly painted) prison dormitories. Skip the measly breakfasts (US$9), but don't leave without having at least one meal (set menu US$26) at the restaurant, which serves the best fish soup this side of the Provence. There are no cooking facilities, but bringing picnic supplies (and plenty of water – it's not potable on the islands) can keep your costs to a minimum.

THE GUIANAS

PAPILLON DEMYSTIFIED

Henry Charrière's remarkable tale of nine escapes from the world's most infamous prison camp have lead many to question the book as a work of nonfiction. Although Charrière himself claimed that his story is accurate, give or take a few memory lapses, research has proved otherwise. Paris police reports reveal that 'Papillon' was almost certainly guilty of the murder that incarcerated him and first-hand accounts from prison guards describe Charrière as a well-behaved convict who worked contentedly on latrine duty. The prison-camp records are such that it's impossible to know the truth, but the general consensus is that Charrière took some stories from his own adventures, and some from other convicts, while he invented and embellished others.

Meanwhile a centurion Parisian named Charles Brunier claims that he is the real Papillon. With a butterfly tattoo on his left arm, and a documented history of three escapes from the Guiana camps, his story adds up, but time has rendered the truth as stealthy as an escaping convict.

It's also possible to camp, free of charge along some of the paradisiacal littoral areas of Îles Royale and St Joseph (bring mosquito repellent, nets and rain gear).

GETTING THERE & AWAY

It's worth paying extra to take a comfortable, fume-free catamaran or sailboat, which include sunset servings of rum punch and other services (depending on the company) – these take about 1½ to two hours to reach the islands. Most boats to the islands depart around 8am from Kourou's *ponton des pêcheurs* (fishermen's dock, at the end of Av Général de Gaulle) and return between 4pm and 6pm. Call to reserve, or book in Cayenne or Kourou. Seafaring options:

La Hulotte (☎ 32-33-81; US$55) This festive catamaran adds a visit to Île St Joseph and a sail around Île du Diable.

Royal Ti'Punch (☎ 32-09-95; US$57) Owned by the auberge, this catamaran includes a shuttle to Île St Joseph and is the only company that doesn't charge extra for overnight stays.

Sothis (☎ 32-09-95; US$35, 1 hr one way) This crowded and fumy ferry visits Île Royale only. At the time of writing it was docked for repairs.

Tropic Alizés (☎ 25 10 10; incl round-trip transfer to Cayenne US$55) Sailboats leave from the Nautical club of Kourou or catch the shuttle direct from Cayenne.

Sinnamary & Around

Sinnamary – a friendly village of 3500 people, 60km northwest of Kourou – includes an Indonesian community that produces excellent woodwork, jewelry, pottery and other folk arts.

Don't leave the area without hiking at least part of the 20km **Pripri Yiyi Trail** (trailhead at La Maison de la Nature, a few kilometers out of town) for great bird-watching.

Restaurant-Hôtel Floria (RN1 at southeastern entrance to Iracoubo; r US$36) has authentic Creole cheerfulness that is a breath of fresh air along a long road. If you don't stay in one of the tiny, brightly curtained rooms, at least stop in for a copious set meal (US$14) and have a chat with spirited, grandmotherly Floria.

ST LAURENT DU MARONI

pop 19,167

St Laurent is a dozy place with some of the finest colonial architecture in the country and, even 60 years after the penitentiary's closure, is dominated by penal buildings and the ghosts of its prisoners. Along the banks of the Fleuve Maroni (Marowijne River), bordering Suriname, St Laurent is also a place to take a river trip to Maroon and Amerindian settlements.

Information

EMERGENCIES

Hôpital Franck Joly (☎ 34-10-37; 16 Av du Général de Gaulle).

INTERNET ACCESS

Infocenter (16 Rue Victor Hugo; ☷ 9am-noon & 3:30-7pm Mon-Sat, 9:30am-noon Sun) Very central and also has phone services.

Upgrade Computer (30 Rue Thiers; ☷ 9am-noon & 3:30-6:30pm Mon-Fri) The cheapest rates in St Laurent.

MONEY

Banks and ATMs are scattered throughout town.

Cambio COP (23 Rue Montravel; ☷ 8am-noon) Has competitive rates for euros.

POST

Post Office (3 Av du Général de Gaulle) There's also an ATM here.

TOURIST INFORMATION

Office du Tourisme (☎ 34-23-98; www.97320.com in French; Esplanade Baudin; ✆ 7:30am-6pm Mon-Fri, 7:45am-12:45pm & 2:45-5:45pm Sat, 9am-1pm Sun) Stocked with plenty of maps and brochures, the staff give out free printed walking-tour guides and book Camp de la Transportation, mountain-biking and rum-factory tours. It maintains a list of the area's accommodations, which it can book for you.

TRAVEL AGENCIES

Ouest Voyages (☎ 34-44-44; 10 Av Félix Eboué)

Sights & Activities

Most of the creepy **Camp de la Transportation**, where prisoners arrived for processing, can only be seen on a guided 1½-hour **tour** (adult/ student/child US\$6/3/1.50; ✆ 8am, 9:30am, 11am, 3pm & 4:30pm Mon-Sat, 9:30am & 11am Sun); pay at the tourist office – most guides speak some English. See the tiny cells, leg shackles, dorm-style toilets (known to prisoners as the 'love room'), public execution areas and more that have been restored just enough to keep them dark and eerie. One cell has Papillon's name engraved near the bed but whether this was really his cell is up to debate. Convicts arrived by boatfuls of 500 to 600 men and it took 20 days to cross the Atlantic.

For canoeing on the Maroni, rent canoes from the **Maroni Club** (☎ 23-52-51; Esplanade Baudin; 2hr US\$16). **Tropic-Cata** (☎ 34-25-18; www.tropic-cata .com in French; Esplanade Baudin) offers two-hour (US\$19) to two-day (US\$190) **boat tours** of the

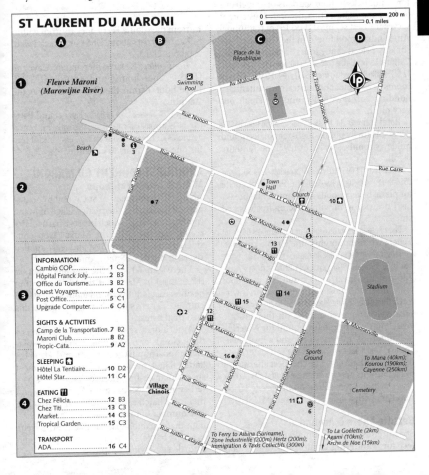

ST LAURENT DU MARONI

INFORMATION
Cambio COP.....................1 C2
Hôpital Franck Joly..........2 B3
Office du Tourisme...........3 B2
Ouest Voyages.................4 C2
Post Office.......................5 C1
Upgrade Computer...........6 C4

SIGHTS & ACTIVITIES
Camp de la Transportation.7 B2
Maroni Club.....................8 B2
Tropic-Cata......................9 A2

SLEEPING
Hôtel La Tentiaire............10 D2
Hôtel Star........................11 C4

EATING
Chez Félicia....................12 B3
Chez Titi.........................13 C3
Market.............................14 C3
Tropical Garden...............15 C3

TRANSPORT
ADA................................16 C4

Maroni or take an Amerindian-led canoe tour with **Agami** (below) from US$30 for a half day.

Crikey! If you ever wanted to nuzzle with a giant anaconda, here's your chance at **Arche de Noe** (road to St Jean; guided visits adult/child US$7.50/3.50; 9-11:30am & 2:30-5pm), an interactive zoo that is also home to the world's only 'ocema,' a cross between an ocelot and a puma.

Sleeping & Eating

There are few sleeping options in St Laurent; the two hotels are right in town while cheaper hammock space is available further out.

Agami (34-74-03, fax 34-01-53; PK 10 on the road to St Jean; hammock space with/without hammock rental US$12/9) Dominican Carmen and her Caraïbe Indian husband have traditional Amerindian huts for hammocks in their gardens of grapefruits and bananas. The Latina-decorated restaurant serves the best set meal (US$15) of traditional Amerindian food found in the Guianas. Reasonably priced canoe tours are also available.

Hôtel La Tentiaire (34-26-00; tentiaire@wanadoo.fr; 12 Av Franklin Roosevelt; d from US$57; P X R) Classy rooms in a former administrative penitentiary building come with TV and are small but very plush.

Hôtel Star (34-10-84; 26 Rue Thiers; d from US$57; X R) With its public-high-school decor and mildewy rooms, stay here only if the Tentiaire is full.

Chez Titi (11 Rue Victor Hugo; breakfast US$4.50; pizzas US$6-8; 6am-10pm Tue-Sat) The French favorite for pizza, bakery goods and continental breakfasts draws you in with enticing fresh-baked smells.

Chez Félicia (23 Av du Général de Gaulle; mains US$8-16) Félicia whips up mighty fine Creole cuisine.

Tropical Garden (7 Rue Rousseau; 11am-1am; pizzas from US$6, set meal US$18) With its nature-meets-funk adornments, great food, a full bar and pool table, this is the most animated place in town.

La Goélette (Balate Plage; mains US$20) Feast on creatively prepared seafood on this antique vessel that was originally bound for Nigeria.

Numerous grocery stores and a lively **market** (Wed & Sat mornings) make self-catering a breeze in St Laurent. The cheapest alternative to restaurants are the **Javanese food stalls** (Av Félix Eboué), which offer filling *bami goreng* (fried noodles) with a side order of satay (US$3).

Getting There & Around

St Laurent's wide, colonial streets are perfect for wandering around on foot. A taxi

---

GETTING TO SURINAME

Bac La Gabrielle (39-80-00; passenger/car US$4/26; 30 min, departures 7am & 2pm Mon, Tue, Thu & Fri, 7am & 5pm Wed, 8am Fri, 3:30pm Sun) – the ferry for Albina, Suriname – leaves from the international quay about 2km south of central St Laurent, down Av Éboué. You'll also find customs and immigration here. Private *pirogue* (dugout canoes; US$6, 15 minutes) leave the quay on demand all day but these sometimes drop clients off far away from the immigration office once in Albina. Buses and taxis for Paramaribo, Suriname, meet the ferry. See p770 for more details and for information on travel from Suriname to French Guiana.

---

to/from the Albina Ferry dock to/from within St Laurent costs about US$4 or you can walk it (about 2km).

Taxis collectifs leave when full for Cayenne (US$48, four hours) and Kourou (US$30, three hours) from the Gare Routière at the stadium.

ADA (27-94-82; 14 Av Hector Rivierez) and **Hertz** (34-19-81; Zone Industrielle) are the only car rental agencies in town – both charge exorbitant fees for one-way rentals to Cayenne.

AROUND ST LAURENT DU MARONI
Mana & Awala-Yalimopo

About 50km northeast of St Laurent by an oft-potholed road, lies the rustic village of Mana (population 5900), which boasts a particularly scenic waterfront on the Mana River, considered one of the loveliest and least-spoiled rivers in northern South America.

There's an ATM at the **post office** (east end of Rue Bastille) in Mana and the last gas station heading east is at the roundabout at the Mana entrance. There's no other way to get to this area than by car.

Amerindian settlements and ridiculously thick clouds of mosquitoes populate Awala-Yalimopo (population 1162) and **Plage Les Hattes**. The latter is one of the world's most spectacular nesting sites for **giant leatherback turtles**; nesting occurs from April to July and their eggs hatch between July and September. The number of turtles that come ashore is so high that one biologist has likened the scene to a tank battle. Do *not* miss visiting here if it is turtle egg-laying season.

Maison de la Reserve Natural l'Amana (☎ 34-84-04; ⏰ 8am-noon & 2-6pm Mon, Wed & Fri, 2-6pm Tue, Thu & Sat; adult/child US$2.50/free) has a little museum, information about turtle biology and two nature trails leading from its premises.

In Mana, cheery French- and Spanish-speaking Isabelle brightens up the otherwise drab **Le Bougainvillier** (☎ 34-80-62; 33 Rue Frères; d with/without bath US$42/30; 🕸). Awala-Yalimopo lodging includes **Chez Judith & Denis** (☎ 34-24-38; hammock space US$28 incl breakfast; **P**) and **L'Auberge de Jeunesse Simili** (☎ 34-16-25; hammock space/r per person US$6/14) – places fill quickly during turtle-viewing periods. Reserve a traditional Amerindian meal for lunch or dinner at **Yalimale** (☎ 34-34-32; ⏰ closed Mon).

Javouhey
pop 658
Thirteen kilometers off the sketchy St Laurent–Mana road, this Hmong village has a delightful Sunday market without the crowds found in Cacao. Stay a night at medieval-feeling **Auberge du Bois Diable** (☎ 34-19-35; dewevre .alain@wanadoo.fr; PK8 Rte de l'Acarouany; d US$48) with its mural-adorned bungalows. A number of orphaned or injured monkeys, rescued by owner/Mana river specialist Alain Dewevre (aka 'Tarzan'), animate the property. Easy to extreme jungle excursions can be organized here.

FRENCH GUIANA DIRECTORY
Accommodations
Hotels in French Guiana are generally charmless but comfortable – cheap hotels start at around US$35 for a single, and around US$45 for a double. Most hotels have some English-speaking staff. Skip the overpriced breakfasts (from US$8) and hit a local café.

The most economical options include long-stay *gîtes* (guesthouses or apartments; inquire at tourist offices) in Cayenne, Kourou and St Laurent, and rustic *carbets* (open-air huts) for hammocks. In rural areas, it's possible to hang a hammock in some camping areas from US$6 and elsewhere for free; many accommodations offer hammock space (from US$6) or have hammocks and mosquito nets to rent (US$10 to US$18).

Activities
Bird-watching, hiking and canoeing are popular in French Guiana. Canoes can be launched from most rivers without the need for a tour operator; those seeking more strenuous activities might want a guide, however. Windsurfing, kite-surfing and sailing are possible on beaches at Montjoly (p752) and Kourou (p754), but there are few public facilities. Sport fishing is underdeveloped but has huge potential.

Books
The best-known book on French Guiana's penal colony is Henri Charrière's autobiographical novel, *Papillon*, which was made into a legendary Hollywood film starring Steve McQueen and Dustin Hoffman. Alexander Miles' *Devil's Island: Colony of the Damned* is a factual but very readable account. For a good overview of the region, pick up *France's Overseas Frontier* by R Aldrich and J Connell. Ann Fadiman's brilliant *The Spirit Catches You and You Fall Down*, though set mostly in California, is the best work explaining the Hmong diaspora.

Business Hours
If you want to accomplish something, get up early. Many businesses close up shop in the heat of the day; generally hours are 8am to noon and 2pm to 5pm, while restaurants tend to serve from noon to 2pm and again from 7pm to 10pm or later. The country stops on Sunday and sometimes Monday, especially in St Laurent. Nightclubs open at around 10pm.

Climate
Expect a soggy trip from January to June, with the heaviest rains occurring in May. The dry season, from July to December, may be the most comfortable time to visit. French Guiana maintains a toasty (average 83°F/28°C) and humid climate year round. Travel with light clothing and a poncho.

Dangers & Annoyances
Rural French Guiana is safe, but the larger towns are not, especially at night. There has been an increase in crime and drug trafficking through the country in recent years, and you'll often find customs roadblocks staffed by gendarmes at Iracoubo and dotting the road toward Régina. Both locals and foreigners may be thoroughly searched for drugs.

Electricity
No sticking fingers in plugs here: electricity is 220/127V, 50 Hz.

Embassies & Consulates

EMBASSIES & CONSULATES IN FRENCH GUIANA

Brazil (☎ 29-60-10; 444 Chemin St Antoine)
Netherlands (☎ 34-05-04; ZI Dégrad des Cannes, Rémire-Montjoly)
Suriname (Map p748; ☎ 30-04-61; 3 Av Léopold Héder)
UK (Map p748; ☎ 31-10-34; 16 Av Monnerville) Consular representative is Georges NouhChaia.
US The nearest US representative is in Suriname (see p772).

FRENCH GUIANESE EMBASSIES & CONSULATES ABROAD

France's many representatives outside South America include:
Australia (☎ 02-6216-0100; 6 Perth Ave, Yarralumla, ACT 2600)
Canada (☎ 613-789-1795; 42 Sussex Dr, Ottawa, Ontario K1M 2C9)
Germany (☎ 0211-49-77-3-0; Cecilienallee 10, 40474 Dusseldorf)
Ireland (☎ 01-260-1666; 36 Ailesbury Rd, Dublin 4)
New Zealand (☎ 04-384-2555; 34-42 Manners St, Wellington)
UK (☎ 020-7201-1000; 58 Knightsbridge, London SW1X 7JT)
USA (☎ 202-944-6000; 4101 Reservoir Rd NW, Washington, DC 20007)

Festivals & Events

Carnaval (January to February or March, dates vary) is a gigantic, colorful occasion, with festivities rocking towns from Epiphany to several solid days of partying before Ash Wednesday. Other fabulous celebrations include the Hmong New Year (usually in December) in Cacao, and Chinese New Year (January or February) in Cayenne.

Food & Drink

One of French Guiana's main attractions is the excellent food available just about everywhere. Don't be shy to try local (but not endangered!) meats and fish (the *jamais goûter* might be one of the most delicious fish on the planet). Prevalent Asian restaurants and food stalls serve delicious and cheap Chinese, Vietnamese and Indonesian dishes, including numerous vegetarian delights. Cafés and delis offer tasty meals for a few euros more, but better restaurants are expensive (rarely less than US$10 for a meal).

Self-catering is a cinch thanks to frequent local produce *marchés* (markets) as well as megamarkets in Cayenne and Kourou and smaller shops (locally called *chinois*, pronounced sheen-*wah*) in every town. Imported alcoholic and soft drinks are pricey in bars and restaurants but are reasonable at grocery stores.

Health

Chloroquine-resistant malaria is present in the interior, and French Guiana is considered a yellow-fever-infected area. If you need a vaccination while there, contact the **Centre de Prévention et de Vaccination** (☎ 30-25-85; Rue des Pommes Rosas, Cayenne; ☒ 8:30am-noon Mon & Thu). Typhoid prophylaxis is recommended. Excellent medical care is available, but few doctors speak English. Water is fine in bigger towns; drink bottled or boiled water elsewhere.

See p1090 for more information.

Holidays

New Year's Day January 1
Epiphany January 6
Ash Wednesday February/March. Carnaval ends; dates vary.
Good Friday/Easter Monday March/April; dates vary.
Labor Day May 1
Pentecost May/June; dates vary.
Bastille Day July 14
Assumption August 15
All Saints Day November 1
All Souls Day November 2
Armistice November 11; Veterans Day.
Christmas Day December 25

Internet Access

Internet spots are found in Cayenne, Kourou and St Laurent and are costly, especially in the capital.

Internet Resources

Guiana Shield Media Project (www.gsmp.org) Good information on environmental issues (in five languages).
Réseau France Outre-Mer (RFO: www.guyane.rfo .fr) Up-to-date news, cultural info, links and more can be translated from French to English through Google.

Maps

France's Institut Géographique National publishes a 1:500,000 map of French Guiana, with fine city maps of Cayenne and Kourou as well as more detailed maps of the populated coastal areas. There are also 1:25,000 topographic maps and heaps of tourist maps available throughout the country.

Media

The *International Herald Tribune* arrives irregularly at local newsstands. *France-Guyane* is Cayenne's daily French-language newspaper, with good local and international coverage. French newspapers and magazines are everywhere. *Loisirs Hebdo,* a free minimagazine with entertainment listings and upcoming events throughout French Guiana, comes out on Thursday.

Money

French Guiana is one of the most expensive regions in South America, with prices comparable to metropolitan France (from where nearly everything is imported). Being a department of France, French Guiana's local currency is the euro. It's easy to change cash or traveler's checks in US dollars or euros in Cayenne, yet the rates are about 5% lower than official rates. Credit cards are widely accepted, and you can get Visa or MasterCard cash advances at ATMs *(guichets automatiques)*, which are on the Plus and Cirrus networks. Eurocard and Carte Bleu are also widely accepted.

EXCHANGE RATES

Exchange rates at press time included the following:

Country	Unit		€ (euro)
Australia	A$1	=	0.60
Canada	C$1	=	0.69
Japan	¥100	=	0.67
New Zealand	NZ$1	=	0.53
UK	UK£1	=	1.49
United States	US$1	=	0.79

Post

The postal service is very reliable, although all mail is routed through France. To receive mail in French Guiana, it's best to have the letters addressed to France but using the French Guianese postal code.

Shopping

Elaborate tapestries, produced by the Hmong peoples who emigrated here from Laos in the 1970s, cannot be found elsewhere in South America but they aren't cheap in French Guiana. The best place to look for tapestries is Cacao. Maroon carvings are sold along the roadside, but they tend to be much more expensive here than in Suriname. Other souvenirs include pinned gigantic bugs and stunning butterflies (though it's not recommended to support this industry by buying such products), and Amerindian handicrafts (similar to but more expensive than those in Suriname).

Telephone

You can make an international call from any pay phone or at 'taxi phone' spots that are often found in internet cafés: dial ☎ 00, then the country code, then the area code, then the local number. For an operator, dial ☎ 00, then 594. You need a telephone card to use public telephones; cards are available at post offices, newsstands and tobacconists. Some towns (particularly Kourou) have had nearly all their public phones destroyed by vandals.

Tourist Information

Amazingly, nearly every city and town in French Guiana has a tourist office of some sort, even if it's just a desk in the local *marché.* Abroad, French tourist offices can supply basic information about French Guiana.

Australia (☎ 02-9231-5244; 25 Bligh St, Level 22, Sydney NSW 2000)

Canada (☎ 514-288-2026; 1981 Av McGill College, Suite 490, Montreal, QC H3A 2W9)

South Africa (☎ 2711-880-8062; PO Box 41022, Craighall 2024)

UK (☎ 090-6824-4123; 178 Piccadilly, London W1V OAL)

USA (☎ 410-286-8310; 676 N Michigan Ave, Suite 3360, Chicago, IL 60611)

Tours

Because public transport is so limited, especially in the interior, tours are the best way to see French Guiana. Operators and their offerings are provided in individual town sections.

Visas

Passports are obligatory for all visitors, except those from France. Visitors should also have a yellow-fever vaccination certificate. Australian, New Zealand, Japanese, EU and US nationals, among others, do not need a visa for stays up to ninety days. Those who need visas should apply with two passport photos at a French embassy and be prepared to show an onward or return ticket; the cost is about US$40. Officially, all visitors, even French citizens, should have onward or return tickets, though they may not be checked at land borders.

SURINAME

HIGHLIGHTS

- **Galibi Nature Reserve** – watch the sea and land unite as giant leatherback turtles emerge from the sea and lay their eggs in the sand (p770)
- **Paramaribo** – let this vivacious capital draw you in with its stately colonial architecture and keep you with its smile (p765)
- **Palumeu** – feel like Indiana Jones as you experience Amerindian culture and the deep jungle of Suriname (p770)
- **Best journey** – drive 190km through jungle and savanna then canoe past Amerindian villages to the Raleighvallen, the gateway to the Central Suriname Nature Reserve (p770)
- **Off the beaten track** – canoe, trek and swashbuckle your way through the jungle to conquer Mt Kasikasima (p768)

FAST FACTS

- **Area:** 163,800 sq km (roughly the size of four Netherlands, or the US state of Georgia)
- **Best bargain:** clothing and taxi travel
- **Best street snack:** Chinese and Indian tidbits at the central market
- **Budget:** US$25-30 a day
- **Capital:** Paramaribo
- **Costs:** guesthouse in Paramaribo US$14, chicken-and-vegetable roti US$2.50, *djogo* (1L) of Parbo beer US$1.50
- **Country code:** ☎ 597
- **Famous for:** mosques and synagogues as happy neighbors; bauxite
- **Languages:** Dutch, English, Sranan Tongo (Surinaams), Hindustani, Javanese, Maroon and Amerindian languages, Chinese
- **Money:** US$1 = 2.8 Suriname dollars
- **Phrases:** *tof* in Dutch (cool); *walgelijk* in Dutch, *viestie* in Sranan Tongo (disgusting); *feest* in Dutch, *vissa* in Sranan Tongo (party)

- **Population:** 493,000 (2005 estimate)
- **Time:** GMT minus 3hr
- **Tipping:** 10-15% in restaurants and hotels if not included; none in taxis
- **Visas:** Americans/others US$50/30 for 2 months (single entry); not issued at borders

TRAVEL HINTS

At night, take inexpensive taxis to restaurants away from the city center for a more local Paramaribo experience.

OVERLAND ROUTES

Suriname's border crossings include Corriverton (Guyana) and St Laurent (French Guiana).

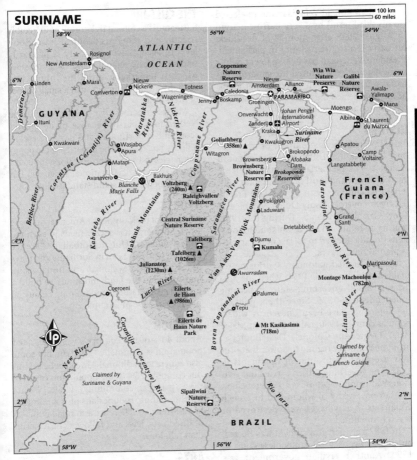

Suriname, the self-proclaimed 'beating heart of the Amazon,' is just that: a warm, dense convergence of rivers that thumps with the lively rhythm of ethnic diversity. From Paramaribo, the country's effervescent Dutch-colonial capital, to the fathomless jungles of the interior, smiling descendants of escaped African slaves, Dutch and British colonialists, Indian, Indonesian and Chinese indentured laborers and Amerindians offer a genuine welcome to their tiny country. You get the best of both worlds here: a city that's chock-full of restaurants, shopping venues and night spots and an untamed jungle utterly away from the things of man. It's not easy to get around this river-heavy, forest-dense country and the mix of languages can make it hard to communicate, sometimes even for Dutch speakers. Don't forget that a meeting of culinary traditions means the food here is as spicy and lush as the country itself.

CURRENT EVENTS

Although Suriname is relatively stable, there are plenty of bumps in the road. In 2004 the Suriname dollar replaced the guilder in hopes of restoring confidence in the economy. During same year, the UN set up a tribunal to help try to resolve the maritime border dispute with Guyana for potentially oil-rich waters; at the time of writing no resolution was in sight.

President Ronald Venetiaan was re-elected (to his third term) by a very narrow margin in August 2005 after months of deadlock; his party is also the majority in parliament. President Venetiaan has helped to cut public spending and restructured the suffering banana industry through international loans; he has thus helped the small country maintain relative economic stability.

HISTORY

Suriname was the last outpost of what was once a substantial Dutch presence in South America. The Netherlands controlled large parts of Brazil and most of the Guianas until territorial conflicts with Britain and France left them control of only Dutch Guiana and a few Caribbean islands. During the 19th-century an influx of Hindustanis and Indonesians (locally referred to as 'Javanese') arrived as plantation workers.

Despite limited autonomy, Suriname remained a colony until 1954, when the area became a self-governing state; it became independent in 1975. Since then, political developments have been uneven. A widely popular coup in 1980, led by Sergeant Major (later Lieutenant Colonel) Desi Bouterse, brought a military regime to power that brutally executed 15 prominent opponents in 1982. The government then carried out a vicious campaign to suppress a 1986 rebellion of Maroons, many of whom fled to French Guiana as their villages were destroyed or severely disrupted.

In 1987 a civilian government was elected, but it was deposed by a bloodless coup in 1990. Another civilian government was elected in 1991, and a treaty was signed with the Jungle Commando (the Maroon military) and other armed bands in 1992. A series of strikes and street demonstrations in 1999 protested economic instability and called for the government to hold elections a year ahead of schedule. Elections were subsequently held in May 2000, producing little change, though the Netherlands stepped up its level of aid into Suriname, helping to stabilize the economy.

Suriname relies on bauxite for 70% of its foreign exchange. Agriculture, particularly irrigated rice cultivation and bananas, is a major industry for the republic, and the fishing industry (including aquaculture) is growing. The country is also making a conscious effort to develop ecotourism in the interior.

THE CULTURE

Suriname is a cultural free-for-all of incredibly friendly and generous people. Paramaribo's level of acceptance and unity is primarily undisturbed by religious and racial tension, which is remarkable given the intimacy of so many groups living in such a small corner of the world.

Many Surinamese live or have lived in the Netherlands, partly because of its greater economic opportunities and partly to escape military repression. The majority of the population lives in Paramaribo and along the coast. Dutch is the official national language, but many people understand standard English.

SPORTS

Though not typically South American in some ways, Suriname has soccer fields in even the tiniest villages. Dutch footballer Clarence Seedorf, who was born in Suriname and plays for AC Milan, developed a national team, and provided the land and funds to build a major-league stadium and training facility 30 minutes outside of Paramaribo.

RELIGION

About 40% of the country's well-integrated population is nominally Christian, but some also adhere to traditional African beliefs. Hindus compose 26% of the population (most of the East Indian community), while 19% are Muslim (ethnic Indonesians plus a minority of East Indians). There are also small numbers of Buddhists, Jews and followers of Amerindian religions.

ARTS

Some cultural forms – such as Indonesian gamelan music, which can be heard at some special events – derive from the immigrant populations. Other art forms that visitors enjoy include intricate basketry woven by Amerindians, paintings done by a number of excellent artists and the carvings produced by the Maroons, who are widely regarded as the best woodcarvers in tropical America.

ENVIRONMENT

Suriname is divided into quite diverse topographical regions, primarily dense tropical forest and savannas. To its west, the Corantijn (Corentyne in Guyana) River forms the border, disputed in its most southerly reaches, with Guyana; the Marowijne (Maroni in French Guiana) and Litani Rivers form the border (also disputed in the south) with French Guiana.

The majority of Surinamese inhabit the Atlantic coastal plain, where most of the country's few roads are located. The major links to the interior are by air or north–south rivers, though there is a road to the Brownsberg Nature Reserve. The nearby Afobaka Dam created one of the world's largest (1550 sq km) reservoirs, Brokopondo, on the upper Suriname River. Rapids limit the navigability of most rivers.

TRANSPORTATION
Getting There & Away
International flights land at Suriname's simple and numbingly air-conditioned Zanderij airport (p769).

From Albina (in the east, p770) and Nieuw Nickerie (in the west, p771), boats traverse the rivers to the borders of French Guiana and Guyana, respectively.

Getting Around
Air and river transport are the only ways to penetrate the interior, due to the lack of roads.

AIR
Small planes, operated by **Surinam Airways** (SLM; www.slm.firm.sr) and **Gum Air** (www.gumair.com), which is mostly a charter airline, shuttle people between Paramaribo and remote destinations, including some nature reserves (see p769).

BOAT
Rivers offer scenic routes to parts of the interior that are otherwise inaccessible. There are few scheduled services, and prices are negotiable. Your best bet is to arrange something ahead of time in Paramaribo. Ferries and launches cross some major rivers, such as the Suriname and the Coppename, and are very cheap.

BUS
Midsized buses (referred to locally as 'jumbos') on the coastal highway are frequent and cheap. Arrange your fee with the driver before you get on. Government buses cost less than

private buses but may be more crowded. There are very few buses off the main routes.

CAR
Suriname's roads are limited and navigating them can be dicey. Passenger cars can handle the roads along the coast and to Brownsberg, but tracks into the interior are for 4WDs only. Rental cars are available but expensive and you can't take them over borders. Driving is on the left (a legacy of the British). An International Driving Permit is required.

TAXI
Shared taxis cover routes along the coast. Though several times more expensive than buses, they are markedly faster. Cab fares are negotiable and generally reasonable; set a price before getting in.

PARAMARIBO
pop 220,307
Amsterdam meets the Wild West in Paramaribo, the most vivacious and striking capital in the Guianas. Black and white colonial Dutch buildings line grassy squares, wafts of spices escape from Indian roti shops and mingle with car exhaust, Maroon artists sell colorful paintings outside somber Dutch forts. Locally known as 'Parbo,' the inhabitants are proud of their multi-ethnicity and the fact that they live in a city where mosques and synagogues play happy neighbors. In 2002 the historical inner city was listed as a Unesco World Heritage site.

Orientation
Sprawling Parbo sits on the west bank of the meandering Suriname River. Its core is a compact triangular area whose boundaries are Gravenstraat on the north, Zwartenhovenbrugstraat on the west, and the river to the southeast. The Paramaribo-Meerzorg bridge spans the river to its east bank.

Information
BOOKSHOPS
Vaco Press (Domineestraat 26; ⏰ 8am-4:30pm Mon-Fri, 8am-1pm Sat) Parbo's best bookshop sells publications in various languages and is the only reliable source for maps.

EMERGENCY
Academisch Ziekenhuis (AZ; ☎ 442222; Flustraat) Paramaribo's only hospital for emergency services.
Police, fire & rescue (☎ 115)

DEPARTURE TAX

Suriname's departure tax is about US$20 (usually lumped with the ticket price).

GETTING INTO TOWN

From Johan Pengel International Airport (aka Zanderij), 45km south of Parbo, you can grab a taxi into town (US$25, one hour). Better yet, have your hotel arrange a cab to meet you. To the airport, **De Paarl** (☎ 403610) and **Le Grand Baldew** (☎ 474713) airport services are cheaper (US$8) and will pick you up at your hotel. Still cheaper minibuses go to Zanderij (US$1.20) and the Zorg-en-Hoop airfield (US$0.50) from Heiligenweg in daytime hours only. A taxi to Zorg-en-Hoop is about US$8.

INTERNET ACCESS
Business Center (Kleine Waterstraat; per hr US$2; ☽ 8am-midnight Mon-Sat, 9am-midnight Sun) Next to Café-Bar 't Vat, also offers GSM rental.
Carib Computers (Heerenstraat 22; per hr US$1.50; ☽ 9am-10pm Mon-Sat, 2-9pm Sun) Several locations throughout Parbo.

INTERNET RESOURCES
Welcome to Parbo website (www.parbo.com) An excellent introduction to Paramaribo and Suriname, maintained by the Suriname Tourism Foundation.

MEDICAL SERVICES
Academisch Ziekenhuis (☎ 442222; Flustraat; ☽ 6-10pm Mon-Fri, 9am-10pm Sat & Sun) Has general practitioners who provide excellent care and speak perfect English.

MONEY
You can change money, traveler's checks or get credit-card advances at most major banks but only RBTT banks have ATMs that accept international cards.
Centrale Bank van Suriname (Waterkant 20)
De Surinaamsche Bank (DSB; Gravenstraat 26-30)
RBTT Bank (Kerkplein 1)

POST
Post office (Korte Kerkstraat 1) Opposite the Dutch Reformed Church. Can be a madhouse.

TELEPHONE
TeleSur (Heiligenweg 1) You can make long-distance calls and buy cards for payphones here.

TOURIST INFORMATION
Tourist Information Center (☎ 479200; www.sr.net /users/stsur; Waterkant 1; ☽ 9am-3:30pm Mon-Fri) This should be your first stop in town for a free walking tour map and pamphlets on anything you might be interested in. The office includes a Conservation International (CI) exhibit of different ecotourism projects in the country.

Dangers & Annoyances
Be careful after dark, as crime is on the rise – stick to busier streets and watch for pickpockets around the market area even in daylight hours. Do not enter the Palmentuin at night.

Sights
A day or two could easily be filled exploring this 17th-century capital of colonial architecture and lively main streets. Not for the fainthearted, the frenzied **central market** is divided into distinct areas: the nearly ominous Maroon market is full of bones, sticks, feathers, caged monkeys and various tonics and fruits for ceremonial and medicinal purposes; the sprawling Asian and Indian market sells all the unnecessary plastic objects and foodstuffs you could ever hope to find, and don't miss a jaunt through the raucous, winding, outdoor fish market. Surrounding the central **Onafhankelijkheidsplein** (Independence Square), which features a statue of legendary former prime minister Pengel, are the contrasting stately 18th-century **Presidential Palace** (open to the public November 25 only), aging colonial government buildings and an ultramodern finance building. Behind the palace is the **Palmentuin**, a shady haven of tall royal palms, home to some tropical birds and a troop of capuchin monkeys.

Inside well-restored **Fort Zeelandia**, a pentagonal 17th-century fort built on the site where the first colonists alighted, is the **Stichting Surinaams Museum** (☎ 425871; ☽ 9am-2pm Tue-Sat, 10am-2pm Sun; tours in Dutch 11am & 12:30pm Sun; admission US$3), which features colonial-era

---

TWEETY FEST

On Sunday people engage in peaceful yet underlyingly cutthroat bird-song competitions on the Onafhankelijkheidsplein. Everyone brings his or her favorite *twatwa*, usually a seed finch purchased from Amerindians in the interior. The *twatwa* that can best belt it out wins. Something of a national obsession, this competition is well worth observing, though its popularity is petering out. It tends to be male-oriented gatherings.

relics, period rooms and temporary exhibitions. Southwest along Waterkant are some of the city's most impressive colonial buildings, mostly merchants' houses built after the fires of 1821 and 1832. The streets inland from here, particularly **Lim-a-Postraat**, have many old wooden buildings, some restored, others in picturesque decay.

On Gravenstraat is the **Roman Catholic Kathedraal** (1885), which the Surinamese claim is the largest wooden building in the world, and which is closed indefinitely (since 1979) until its sagging superstructure can be repaired. A few blocks away are some of the continent's finest examples of other religious buildings – the biggest **mosque** in the Caribbean and the

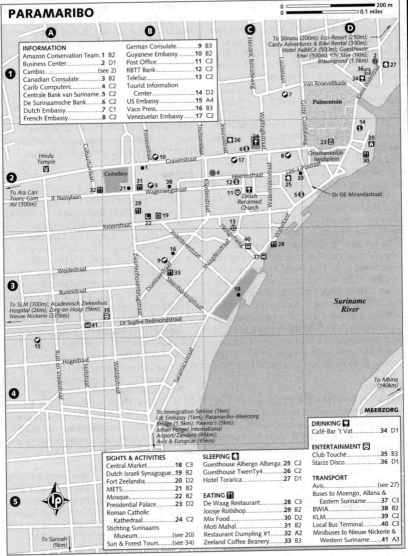

PARAMARIBO

expansive **Dutch Israeli synagogue** – sitting harmoniously side by side on Keizerstraat.

Tours

Most of Suriname's exemplary system of national parks and reserves is accessible via Parbo-based tour operators. **Stinasu** (Stichting Natuurbehoud Suriname; ☎ 476597; www.stinasu.sr; Cornelis Jongbawstraat 14), the Foundation for Nature Conservation in Suriname, donates a percentage of all trip proceeds to nature conservation. It coordinates research and ecotourism expeditions, runs excellent guided trips to Brownsberg (from US$45), Galibi (from US$150), Raleighvallen/Voltzberg/Foengoe Island (US$375, four days) and Coppename (US$80, one day), and helps unguided visitors explore the Central Suriname Nature Reserve more-or-less independently.

METS (Movement for Eco-Tourism in Suriname; ☎ 477088; www.surinamevacations.com; JF Nassylaan 2) is perhaps the most professional agency in Suriname and conducts a wide range of trips, from sightseeing tours of Paramaribo (US$22, halfday) to jungle expeditions to Mt Kasikasima (US$675, eight days). A popular offering is a river tour of the Awarradam, in the heart of Maroon country (US$350, five days). It also books other operators' tours.

Ara Cari Tours (☎ 499705; www1.sr.net/~t100908; Kwattaweg 254) runs excellent trips to Tafelberg, the easternmost of the 'Lost World Mountains,' and Frederik Willem Falls in southwest Suriname.

Sun & Forest Tours (☎ 478383; www.surinamesunforest.nl; Kleine Waterstraat 1) runs recommended multiday trips into the interior. **Cardy Adventures** (opposite) has bike (US$40) and boat (US$50) tours to the nearby Commewijne plantations as well as longer tours of up to 10 days to the interior (four to 10 days US$350 to US$900).

Sleeping

Guesthouse TwenTy4 (☎ 420751; Jessurunstraat 24; www.crozrootz.com; hammock/s/d from US$3/15/20) Backpacker perfection has been achieved in this homey house on a central, quiet backstreet. You can get breakfast (US$3), dinner (from US$5), check internet, use the phone, fax, buy a beer at the bar or rent a bike (US$5 per day). The congenial owners also lead affordable tours.

Guesthouse Albergo Alberga (☎ 520050; www.guesthousealbergoalberga.com; Lim-a-Postraat 13; s/d US$18/24, d with air-con US$36; ❄) This long-running favorite is situated on a quintessentially colonial Parbo

street in an endearing World Heritage–listed building. You'll be fast friends with the smiling staff and it's a quick jog to just about anywhere you'd want to get to in the city.

Guesthouse Kiwi (☎ 421374; guesthousekiwi.com in Dutch; Mahonylaan 88A; d/q US$36/60; ❄) This white cement, friendly place is good for a quiet, restful stay; you can use the kitchen.

Hotel AaBéCé (☎ 422950; Mahonylaan 55; s/d US$42/48; ❄) It's a step down in ambience from the backpacker spots, but a step up in comfort with airless but air-con rooms.

Eco-Resort (☎ 425522; Cornelis Jongbawstraat 16; www.ecoresortinn.com; s/d/tr US$75/85/95; ℗ ❄) Cushy rooms, professional service and a little bit of style are found at this above-standard gem. The price includes a buffet breakfast and use of the swanky facilities at the kitsch Hotel Torarica.

Hotel Torarica (☎ 471500; www.torarica.com; Mr Rietbergplein 1; s/d US$129/150; ℗ ❄ ⊜) Las Vegas meets Suriname at mirrored and chandeliered Hotel Torarica. It's known for its casino.

Eating

You won't go hungry in Parbo. 'The strip' across from Hotel Torarica, has a great diversity of restaurants to fit all budgets – take your pick of Indonesian, Creole, California-style grills or Dutch pancake shops to name a few. The cheapest options in the city center are at the frenetic central market (p766) and Indonesian stalls along Waterkant; the Javanese neighborhood of Blauwgrond features people cooking in their kitchens and serving dinner to customers on their patios. Heading outside these food-dense areas try the following:

Zeeland Coffee Beanery (cnr Domineestraat & Steenbakkerijstraat; soup from US$2.50, cakes from US$1.25; ⏱ 7am-9pm Sun-Wed, 7am-11pm Thu-Sat) People watch while sipping a coffee, or eating great soups, pastries and cakes at this very popular street-side café.

Moti Mahal (Wagenwegstraat 56-58; rotis US$2.50; ⏱ lunch & dinner) Huge portions of tasty Indian roti are served in this hole-in-the-wall shop.

Joosje Rotishop (Zwartenhovenbrugstraat 9; rotis US$4-6; ⏱ 8:30am-10pm Mon-Sat) Serving delicious roti since 1942, this is the locals' favorite for a sit-down, air-con meal.

Restaurant Dumpling #1 (JF Nassylaan 12; mains US$3-6; ⏱ 7am-2pm & 5-11pm Tue-Sun) The name says it all: lightweight prices and heavyweight portions.

Chi Min (☎ 412155; Cornelis Jongbawstraat 83; mains US$4-10; ⏱ 11am-3:30pm & 6:30-11pm) A short taxi ride north of the center. Anyone will tell you this is the best Chinese in Parbo.

Mix Food (☎ 420688; Zeelandiaweg 1; mains from US$5; ☺ lunch & dinner) Exceptionally friendly service highlights this quiet, outdoor eatery which is a great place to try Creole specialties and exotic juices.

De Waag Restaurant (☎ 474514; Waterkant 5; breakfast from US$3.50, lunch & dinner US$8-15; ☺ 10am-10pm) It doesn't open till 10am, but this beautiful, airy riverside restaurant serves the best breakfasts in town (and chic lunches and dinners).

Sarinah (☎ 430661; Verlengde Gemenelandsweg 187; 10/15 dishes per person US$9/11; ☺ dinner) Sarinah is *the* place to go for upscale Indonesian. Get ravenous before trying a multicourse *rijsttafel* (literally 'rice table').

Drinking & Entertainment

The night begins at **Café-Bar 't Vat** (Kleine Waterstraat 1; ☺ 7:30am-2am), an outdoor bar/café with occasional live music. Move on to other bars and the **Starzz Disco** (☺ 10pm-3am Wed-Sat) along 'the strip.'

Away from the Hotel Torarica area, try **Club Touché** (cnr Waldijkstraat & Dr Sophie Redmondstraat; ☺ 10pm-3am Wed-Sat) where you can dance the night away with techno downstairs and salsa upstairs.

Shopping

The French Guianese flock to Paramaribo to shop. Good quality clothing knock-offs from Levis to Gucci and pirated DVDs (illegal) can be found for exceptionally low prices along Steenbakkerijstraat and Domineestraat.

Getting There & Away

AIR

Paramaribo has two airports: nearby Zorgen-Hoop (for domestic flights) and the larger Johan Pengel International Airport (for international flights), usually referred to as Zanderij, 45km south of Parbo.

Airlines with offices in Paramaribo include **BWIA** (☎ 422511; www.bwee.com; Wagenwegstraat 36), **Gum Air** (☎ 498760; www.gumair.com; Kwattaweg 254), **KLM** (☎ 472421; Dr DE Mirandastraat 9) and **SLM** (☎ 432700; www.slm.firm.sr; Dr Sophie Redmondstraat 219).

Destinations and sample one-way airfares include:

Belém (Brazil) META, US$200, two hours, three per week; SLM, US$227, two per week.

Curaçao (Caribbean) SLM, US$334, three hours, four per week.

Port of Spain (Trinidad) BWIA, US$203, 30 minutes, three per week; SLM, US$202, four per week.

BUS

Minibuses to Nieuw Nickerie (US$4, four hours, 235km) and other western destinations leave when full from the corner of Dr Sophie Redmondstraat and Hofstraat. Eastbound minibuses to Albina (US$4, four hours, 140km) leave at hourly intervals (or when full) from Waterkant at the foot of Heiligenweg. For connecting boat information, see the Albina (p770) and Nieuw Nickerie (p771) sections.

CAR

The most reliable rental agencies are **Avis** (☎ 421567; www.avis.com), which has offices in the Hotel Torarica and at the airport, and **Europcar** (☎ 424631; www.europcar.com) who have a desk at the airport. Rental cars are expensive (from $40 per day) and may not be in perfect condition; be somewhat car savvy.

TAXI

Taxis leave from the same areas as the minibuses, or have your hotel call one. If you find a reliable driver, take his car and phone number and enjoy your own personal driver throughout your stay. Going east, it might be better to catch a taxi on the Meerzorg side of the river.

Getting Around

The Paramaribo-Meerzorg bridge has displaced ferry service, but long dugout canoes are cheap (about 50¢), fast and frequent.

Bicycles are a great way to see Parbo and its environs, including the old plantations across the Suriname River. **Cardy Adventures & Bike Rental** (☎ 422518; www.cardyadventures.com; Cornelis Jongbawstraat 31; US$5 per day; ☺ 8am-4pm Mon-Fri, 8am-1pm Sat) has 'reliable Dutch' road and mountain bikes, and provides maps of good biking routes.

Most of Parbo's buses leave from Heiligenweg. You can call for **bus information** (☎ 473591, 410922), ask at points of departure or ask at your guesthouse for departure times.

Taxis are usually reasonably priced but unmetered, so agree on the fare in advance (a short trip will cost around US$2). Most drivers speak passable English.

NATURE PARKS & RESERVES

One of the main reasons to visit Suriname is the country's extensive system of protected nature reserves and parks. Independent exploration ranges from difficult to impossible so most people visit on a tour. For tour operators' contact information, see opposite.

THE GUIANAS

Central Suriname Nature Reserve

This 1.6-million-hectare World Heritage site, established in 1998 thanks to a US$1 million donation from CI and efforts by environmental groups to set aside areas of Suriname's rainforest, covers a massive 12% of Suriname's total land surface. It is known for its abundant wildlife (about 40% of which is found only in the Guianas), diverse and pristine ecosystems, and dramatic geological formations and waterfalls. Limited areas are accessible.

RALEIGHVALLEN & VOLTZBERG

Raleighvallen (Raleigh Falls) is on the upper Coppename River and is known for its rich bird life, many monkey species and, of course, spectacular waterfalls. Stinasu (p768) has tourist lodges on Foengoe Island, accessible by a five-hour drive and two-hour boat ride. Voltzberg is a 240m granite dome accessible by a 2½-hour jungle trail and then a steep ascent of its face; the summit offers a view of the forest canopy.

TAFELBERG

This remote region of mountains, forest and savanna has no surrounding human populations. Journeys involve a flight and two solid days of hiking before ascending the 1026m mountain (see p768).

Brownsberg Nature Reserve & Tonka Island

Brownsberg is an area of trail-covered, wildlife-dense montane tropical rainforest overlooking Brokopondo Reservoir, about 100km south of Paramaribo. Park headquarters is on the plateau, as are some comfortable Stinasu-run tourist lodges (US$35).

Worth a special trip from Brownsberg is the lake's Tonka Island, a rustic ecotourism project run by the Saramaccan Maroons and US-based Amazon Conservation Team (ACT; ☎ 421770; www.amazonteam.org; 123 Gravenstraat, Paramaribo). For ecotour details, contact ACT or Stinasu (p768).

It's relatively easy to visit Brownsberg on your own: minibuses from Paramaribo run to the Marroon village of Koffeekamp (US$4; 4½ hours). From here, arrange in advance for Stinasu to pick you up and drive you to the park; this is impossible as a day trip so plan on staying at least one night.

Galibi & Coppename Nature Reserves

Galibi's turtle-nesting area hosts hordes of sea turtles, including the giant leatherback, during egg-laying season (April through August). You can get there from Albina with permission from Carib Indians and a hired canoe, or more easily from Paramaribo with Stinasu.

The Coppename wetland reserve, at the mouth of the Coppename River, is home to the endangered manatee and is a haven for birdwatchers. Stinasu organizes trips by request.

Palumeu
pop 200

On the banks of the Boven Tapanahoni River, this tranquil Amerindian village has begun to welcome visitors in the hope of creating a sustainable future outside of the logging and hunting industries. It's possible to brave rapids over eight to 12 days to reach this area by river from Albina, or take the one-hour flight from Paramaribo and enjoy views of Mt Kasikasima. Accommodations (booked through METS or Stinasu, see p768) are in basic but comfortable Amerindian-style huts that are lit at night by kerosene lanterns.

NIEUW NICKERIE
pop 13,165

There's not much going on in this modern town of wide streets and few people. If you do stay, it's worth finding a local fisherman to take you out to Bigi Pani (count on about US$30), a reservoir known for its nesting bird and animal life; hotels charge US$50 for a day tour to the area.

Concord Hotel (☎ 232345; Wilhelminastraat 3; d US$20;) is a motel-style place, while the well-kept **Sea Breeze** (☎ 212111; GG Meimastraat 34; d US$23;) is a small step up. The poshest hotel is the

---

GETTING TO FRENCH GUIANA

The French ferry (per passenger/car US$4/26, 30 minutes, 8am and 3pm Monday, Tuesday, Thursday and Friday, 8am and 5:30pm Wednesday, 8:30am Saturday and 4pm Sunday) crosses the Marowijne River at Albina to St Laurent du Maroni in French Guiana; from there, a good road leads to Cayenne (p758). At other times, you can hire a dugout canoe (about US$5) for the short crossing but immigration (where you'll need to stamp out) is nearer to the ferry. On the French Guiana side, immigration is also at the ferry dock. For information on travel in the opposite direction, see p758.

Residence Inn (☎ 210950; RP Bharosstraat 84; resinnic@sr.net; s/d/tr/q US$53/65/77/89; P ⊠).

The best meal deal in town is at **Melissa's Halal Food** (Concord Hotel; mains US$2.50) serving copious Indian dishes in an air-con dinning room.

You can make phone calls and check internet at the **Telesur Office** (St Kanaalstraat 3; ⊗ 7am-10pm Mon-Sat) and right next door is an ATM at **RBTT Bank**.

All buses and minibuses arrive at and leave from the market. There are government buses traveling to Paramaribo (US$4, four hours, 235km, 6am and 1pm daily) and a private bus (US$7) that leaves when full after the first government bus leaves. You can grab a taxi to Paramaribo (US$60, three to four hours) any time. Minibuses to South Drain (US$5) for the ferry to Guyana leave at 8am and it's best to reserve with the driver the day before; your hotel can help with this.

ALBINA
pop 3982

A bustling, sketchy village on the west bank of the Marowijne River, which forms the border with French Guiana, Albina was destroyed in the Maroon rebellion of the 1980s and early '90s and is still recovering. The best thing to do here is leave; most pass through town en route to Galibi (opposite) or French Guiana.

If you must stay overnight, try the **Creek Guesthouse** (☎ 342031, ask for Mr Wong; US$27), a clean place whose proprietors speak some English and may be able to help find a guide to the turtle beaches.

GETTING TO GUYANA

From Nieuw Nickerie it's a bumpy 1½-hour ride to South Drain to catch the Canawaima Ferry (US$14, 25 minutes, 11am daily) across the Corantijn (Corentyne in Guyana) River to Moleson Creek, Guyana. After getting stamped in and passing a customs check in Guyana, you'll find several Corriverton/Georgetown-bound minibuses (US$2/10; 20 minutes/3 hours). An easy way to get directly to Georgetown from Paramaribo is through **Bobby Minibus** (☎ 498583, 8743897; US$27) who leave Paramaribo at around 5am to meet the ferry in South Drain. For information on travel in the opposite direction, see p783.

Minibuses (US$10, four hours) and buses (US$7) to Paramaribo leave from central Albina on the Suriname side. Or you can call safe and reliable **Jan & Son Taxi Service** (☎ 08831011, 08847009; US$60) to meet you at the ferry and take you to your guesthouse in Paramaribo.

SURINAME DIRECTORY
Accommodations

Fairly affordable hotels and guesthouses are readily found in Paramaribo, while sleeping in the interior can involve more rustic accommodations or hammocks. Nights can be hot and buggy; your mosquito net will be your friend. Most places charge extra (US$2.50 to US$4) for breakfast.

Activities

The best activity in Suriname is experiencing the interior. Bird-watching is fabulous, as are other animal-spotting opportunities, most of which involve boating and/or trekking. Of the three Guianas, this is the only place where it's easy to explore by bicycle.

Books

The most popular book on Suriname is Mark Plotkin's *Tales of a Shaman's Apprentice,* which also includes information on Brazil, Venezuela and the other Guianas. *The Guide to Suriname* by Els Schellekens and famous local photographer Roy Tjin is published in English; grab it at Vaco Press (p765). Other good introductions to the region are *Surinam: Politics, Economics & Society* by Henk E Chin and Hans Buddingh.

Business Hours

Days begin and end early in Suriname. General business hours are 7:30am or 8am to 3pm weekdays, perhaps with a few hours on Saturday. Restaurant kitchens tend to close at around 10pm or 11pm. Most restaurants open for lunch around 11am and serve till 2:30pm. Dinner begins around 6pm. Not many places are open for breakfast but those that do open at 8am.

Climate

The major rainy season is from late April to July, with a shorter one in December and January. Suriname's dry seasons – February to late April and August to early December – are the best times for a visit, though most travelers visit July through August, and prices inflate slightly.

THE GUIANAS

Dangers & Annoyances

Some urban areas are subject to petty crime (mainly muggings); ask locally for places to avoid. The market area in Paramaribo is particularly bad for pickpockets. Visitors to the interior are seeing incidents of theft as well, and it's not recommended to travel inland alone.

Electricity

Currents are 110/220V, 60Hz.

Embassies & Consulates

EMBASSIES & CONSULATES IN SURINAME

Most foreign representatives are in central Paramaribo.

Brazil (☎ 400200; Maratakkastraat 2, Zorg-en-Hoop)
Canada (Map p767 ☎ 471222; Wagenwegstraat 50 bv)
France (Map p767; ☎ 476455; Gravenstraat 5-7, 2nd fl)
Germany (Map p767; ☎ 471150; Domineestraat 34-36)
Guyana (Map p767; ☎ 477895; Gravenstraat 82)
Netherlands (Map p767; ☎ 477211; Van Roseveltkade 5)
UK (☎ 402870; VSH United Bldg, Van't Hogerhuysstraat 9-11)
USA (Map p767; ☎ 472900; Dr Sophie Redmondstraat 129) Also responsible for US citizens in French Guiana.
Venezuela (Map p767; ☎ 475401; Gravenstraat 23-25)

SURINAMESE EMBASSIES & CONSULATES ABROAD

Suriname's representatives outside South America include:

Germany (☎ 089-55-33-63; Adolf-Kolping-Strasse 16, Munich)
Netherlands The Hague (☎ 070-365 0844; Alexander Gogelweg 2, The Hague); Amsterdam (☎ 020-6426 137; De Cuserstraat 11, Amsterdam)
USA Washington (☎ 202-244-7488; 4301 Connecticut Ave NW, Suite 108, Washington, DC 20008); Miami (☎ 305-593-2163; 7235 NW 19th St, Suite A, Miami, FL 33126)

Food & Drink

Surinamese cooking reflects the nation's ethnic diversity and is often superb. Many varieties of Asian cuisine make Suriname a relative paradise for vegetarians; Chinese and Hindustani food is widespread. The cheapest eateries are *warungs* (Javanese food stalls), but some of the best upmarket restaurants are also Javanese. Creole cooking mixes African and Amerindian elements. Nearly all restaurants have English-speaking staff; menus are often in English.

Parbo, the local beer, is quite good; it's customary to share a *djogo* (1L bottle) among friends. Borgoe and Black Cat are the best local rums.

Health

A yellow-fever vaccination certificate is required for travelers arriving from infected areas. Typhoid and chloroquine-resistant malaria are present in the interior. Tap water is safe to drink in Paramaribo but not elsewhere.

See p1090 for more information.

Holidays

New Year's Day January 1; the biggest celebration of the year.
Day of the Revolution February 25
Holi Phagwah March/April; dates vary. Hindu New Year.
Good Friday/Easter Monday March/April; dates vary.
Labor Day May 1
National Union Day/Abolition of Slavery Day July 1
Independence Day November 25
Christmas Day December 25
Boxing Day December 26
Eid-ul-Fitr (*Lebaran* or *Bodo* in Indonesian) End of Ramadan; dates vary.

Internet Access

Parbo and Nieuw Nickerie have affordable (around US$2 per hour) internet cafés. Major hotels offer internet access to guests with laptops (for a fee).

Internet Resources

Surinam.Net (www.surinam.net) Info, links live radio and forums.
Suriname Online Tourist Guide (www.surinametour ism.com) Comprehensive tourism site.
Suriname Tourism Foundation (www.suriname -tourism.org) Helpful, colorful site of tourist services, and information about what to see in Suriname.

Maps

The one map of Suriname that is available in the country – the excellent and current Hebri BV *toeristenkaart* (US$11) – as well as a book of Parbo maps (US$10) are stocked at Vaco Press (p765) and the Hotel Torarica (p768) gift shop, both situated in Paramaribo. The good **International Travel Maps** (www.itmb.com) country map is not sold in Suriname.

Media

There are two daily newspapers, *De Ware Tijd* and *De West*. The *Suriname Weekly*, in both English and Dutch, is a bit skeletal.

Five TV stations and 10 commercial radio stations operate in Suriname. TV broadcasts are in Dutch, but radio transmissions are also in Hindustani, Javanese and Sranan Tongo.

Money

Though the main unit of currency is the Surinamese dollar (SRD), some businesses quote prices in euros. Most **banks** (☼ 7am-2pm Mon-Fri) accept major foreign currencies, but you may run into difficulty trying to change Guyanese dollars and sometimes even Brazilian reais.

CREDIT CARDS

Only RBTT Bank ATMs accept foreign cards, and credit cards are accepted (often for a fee) at major hotels and travel agencies but hardly anywhere else. The country is trying to increase credit-card acceptance but has a way to go.

EXCHANGING MONEY

Except at *cambios,* getting cash can involve time-consuming paperwork. Slowly but surely, banks (and only banks) cash traveler's checks, give advances on credit cards and stamp foreign-exchange transaction forms. This leaves the only other – and perhaps the best – option: changing money at hotels (and some shops). Haggle for good exchange rates.

Exchange rates at the time of writing:

Country	Unit		SRD (Suriname dollar)
Australia	A$1	=	2.11
Canada	C$1	=	2.46
euro zone	€1	=	3.51
Japan	¥100	=	2.36
New Zealand	NZ$1	=	1.86
UK	UK£1	=	5.24
USA	US$1	=	2.80

Post

Postal services in Paramaribo are reliable but may be less so in other parts of Suriname.

Shopping

Maroon handicrafts, especially tribal wood-carvings, are stunning and cheaper in Suriname than in Guyana or French Guiana. Amerindian and Javanese crafts are also attractive. Paramaribo is the best place to shop; the commercial center is along and around Domineestraat.

Telephone

The national telephone company is TeleSur (Telecommunicatiebedrijf Suriname). Calls abroad can be made from yellow public telephone booths. You can pay with *fiches* (coin-like tokens) purchased from a TeleSur office, make reverse-charge (collect) calls or use a home-country direct service (☎ 156 to the US, ☎ 157 to the Netherlands).

Tourist Information

Abroad, Suriname information and maps are most readily found in the Netherlands. In Suriname, the Tourist Information Center in Paramaribo has everything a visitor might need.

Tours

Suriname's interior is best experienced with a professional tour company. See p768 for a few of the 30-something operators that specialize in activities, often combining the environmental and the sociocultural (visiting Amerindian or Maroon villages). Tour prices vary based on duration and the number of people, and many trips are customized for groups.

Tours include meals, accommodations, transport and guides. There is usually a minimum of four and maximum of eight for each trip, so make arrangements in advance.

Visas

Passports are obligatory, and those who don't need a visa are given a tourist card. Suriname is becoming somewhat liberal with its entry requirements; for example, Guyanese, Brazilian and Japanese citizens don't require visas, but Australian, Canadian, French, German, Dutch, New Zealand, UK and US nationals still do.

Suriname's overseas representation is very limited. You can contact the nearest embassy for an application form, but allow four weeks for a postal application. Consulates in Georgetown (Guyana) and Cayenne (French Guiana) charge US$30 (US$50 for US citizens) for two-month single-entry visitor visas and issue them within a couple of hours or days; prices rise for multiple-entry and longer-stay visas. Some say that the process of obtaining a visa is easier in Cayenne than in Georgetown. Bring a passport-sized photo and your ticket out of South America.

To extend your visa, appeal to **Vreemdelingenpolitie** (Immigration Service; ☎ 403609; Havenkomplex, Van 't Hogerhuysstraat, Nieuwe Haven; ☼ 7am-2pm Mon-Fri) in Paramaribo.

Women Travelers

Female travelers, especially those traveling alone, will find local males verbally aggressive (sometimes extremely), but rarely physically threatening. Constant brazen attention can be annoying, if not truly disconcerting.

THE GUIANAS

THE GUIANAS

GUYANA

HIGHLIGHTS

- **Kaieteur Falls** – become breathless at the sight of one of the world's highest single-drop falls, deep in the Amazon jungle (p784)
- **Iwokrama** – get inspired by this cutting-edge rainforest ecotourism project and be a welcomed guest in Amerindian villages (p784)
- **Rupununi Savannas** – live like a cowboy in this out-of-Africa feeling region that is home to some of the last thriving populations of giant river otters and black caimans (p784)
- **Best journey** – travel from Parika to Mabaruma (Shell Beach), passing through rice-farming towns, crossing rivers teeming with birdlife and watching sea turtles nest in the sand (p783)
- **Off the beaten track** – track harpy eagles or stay on a working cattle ranch with local *vaqueros* (cowboys) in the remote Kanuku Mountains (p785)

FAST FACTS

- **Area:** 214,970 sq km (about the size of the UK)
- **Best bargain**: Lady Fingers restaurant (p781)
- **Best street snack**: mysterious-looking fruit at the market
- **Budget:** US$25-30 a day
- **Capital:** Georgetown
- **Costs:** guesthouse bed US$20, delicious pepperpot US$3, refreshing Banks beer US$0.75
- **Country code:** ☎ 592
- **Famous for:** Jonestown massacre, sugarcane, birthplace of 1980s pop star Eddie Grant
- **Languages:** English, Creole, Hindi, Urdu, Amerindian
- **Money:** US$1 = 190 Guyanese dollars
- **Population:** 768,000 (2005 estimate)
- **Time:** GMT minus 4hr
- **Tipping:** 10% in restaurants and hotels if not included; none in taxis
- **Visas:** US$16 for 3 months; if not required, 30-day visas granted at borders

TRAVEL HINTS

Bring plenty of long-sleeved, lightweight clothing and mosquito repellent for the malaria ridden interior.

OVERLAND ROUTES

Guyana's border crossings are Nieuw Nickerie (Suriname) and Bonfim (Brazil).

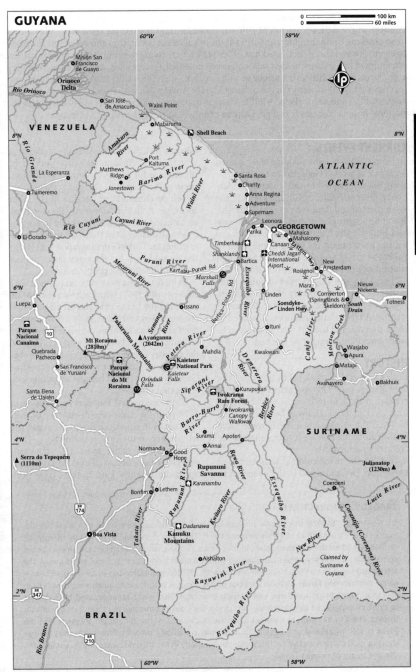

GUYANA

0   100 km
0   60 miles

VENEZUELA

Orinoco Delta

Misión San Francisco de Guayo

Rio Orinoco

San José de Amacuro

Waini Point

Mabaruma

Shell Beach

8°N

La Esperanza

Tumeremo

Rio Grande

Matthews Ridge

Jonestown

Amakura River

Port Kaituma

Barima River

Waini River

Santa Rosa

Charity

Anna Regina

Adventure

Supenam

ATLANTIC OCEAN

Leonora

Parika

GEORGETOWN

Mahaica

Mahaicony

El Dorado

Rio Cuyuni

Cuyuni River

Puruni River

Mazaruni River

Timberhead

Shanklands

Kartabu-Puruni Rd

Bartica

Marshall Falls

Canaan

Cheddi Jagan International Aiport

Rosignol

New Amsterdam

Nieuw Nickerie

Totness

6°N

Luepa

Parque Nacional Canaima

Quebrada Pacheco

San Francisco de Yuruani

Santa Elena de Uairén

Mt Roraima (2810m)

Parque Nacional do Mt Roraima

Pakaraima Mountains

Semang River

Issano

Mara

Linden

Corriverton (Springlands & Skeldon)

South Drain

Soesdyke-Linden Hwy

Ituni

Kwakwani

Wasjabo

Apura

Matapi

Avanavero

Bakhuis

Ayanganna (2042m)

Potaro River

Barica-Potaro Rd

Mahdia

Kaieteur National Park

Kaieteur Falls

Oriniduik Falls

Siparuni River

Demerara River

Berbice River

Canje River

Moleson Creek

SURINAME

Kurupukari

Iwokrama Rain Forest

Iwokrama Canopy Walkway

Burro-Burro River

Surama

Apoteri

Julianatop (1230m)

Coeroeni

Lucie River

Serra do Tepequém (1110m)

Normandia

Good Hope

Annai

Rupununi Savanna

Karanambu

Rewa River

4°N

Bonfim

Lethem

Takutu River

Rupununi River

Kwitaro River

Essequibo River

New River

Claimed by Suriname & Guyana

Dadanawa

Kanuku Mountains

Corantijn (Corantyne) River

BRAZIL

Boa Vista

Aishalton

Kuyuwini River

Essequibo River

Rio Branco

2°N

60°W   58°W

Described by its own tourism association as 'Conradian' and 'raw,' Guyana is a densely forested country with a dark reputation of political instability and interethnic tension. While politics aren't making things brighter, underneath the headlines of corruption and economic misman-agement is a joyful and motivated mix of people who are trying to bring the spectacular natural attributes of this country to their full ecotourism potential. Georgetown, the country's crumbling colonial capital, is distinctly Caribbean with a rocking nightlife, plenty of great places to eat and an edgy market; the interior of the country is more Amazonian with its struggling Amerindian communities and unparalleled wildlife-viewing opportunities that all feel safely away from the political hoopla. Wherever you go, Guyana promises to make the trip of a lifetime.

CURRENT EVENTS

In January 2005 massive flooding of the coastal areas in and around Georgetown caused presi-dent Bharrat Jagdeo to call a state of emer-gency. Over one-third of Guyana's population were affected and there were at least 34 deaths. Flooding began again in early 2006 but damage was limited. Much criticism has been placed on the government for being unprepared to meet the crisis and for not taking enough precautions to prevent future flooding.

The long-running border dispute with Suriname over a potentially oil-rich offshore region had not yet been resolved at the time of writing. A UN tribunal has been scheduled to settle the issue but there is no conjecture as to when an outcome might be reached.

HISTORY

Both Carib and Arawak tribes inhabited the land that is now Guyana before the Dutch arrived in the late 16th century. The British took over in 1796. Halfway between rulers, in 1763, the locals staged the Berbice Slave Revolt; Kofi, the revolt's leader, remains the country's national hero.

In 1831 the three colonial settlements of Essequibo, Demerara and Berbice merged to become British Guiana. After the abolition of slavery (1834), Africans refused to work on the plantations for wages, and many established their own villages in the bush. Plantations closed or consolidated because of the labor shortage. A British company, Booker Bros, resurrected the sugar industry by importing indentured labor from India, drastically trans-forming the nation's demographic and laying the groundwork for fractious racial politics that continue to be a problem today.

British Guiana was run very much as a colony until 1953, when a new constitution provided for home rule and an elected gov-ernment. Ten years later, riots left almost 200 dead after black laborers were hired to replace striking Indian plantation workers. In 1966 the country became an independent member of the British Commonwealth with the name Guyana, and in 1970 it became a republic with an elected president.

Guyana attracted the world's attention in 1978 with the mass suicide-murder of over 900 cultists in American Jim Jones' expatriate religious community of Jonestown.

Since independence, most of the important posts have been occupied by Afro-Guyanese, but more recently East Indians have been

---

TRAGEDY AT JONESTOWN

On November 18 1978, 913 people (including over 270 children) were killed in a mass suicide-murder in a remote corner of the Guyana rainforest. The People's Temple, a cult run by charismatic Jim Jones, had established themselves in Jonestown, Guyana, with Utopian ideas of an egalitarian, agricultural community. When word leaked from escaped members that Jones was running the settlement more like a French Guiana prison camp, US Representative Leo Ryan along with jour-nalists and worried family members set out to pay Jones a visit. The encounter ended with Ryan and four others being murdered while trying to escape. That night Jones ordered his followers to drink cyanide-laced punch; while many drank the poison, others were found shot or with slit throats. The CIA has not yet released all of the documents of the Jonestown Massacre and the event is still mysterious and subject to numerous conspiracy theories. Director Stanley Nelson shows a modern perspective on this mysterious tragedy in his 2006 documentary *Jonestown: The Life and Death of People's Temple*.

appointed to influential positions. Cheddi Jagan, Guyana's first elected president, died in office (1997) and was replaced by his US-born wife Janet, resulting in continued political tension. In 1999 Janet Jagan retired from the presidency on health grounds and named Bharrat Jagdeo her successor.

Elections scheduled for January 2001 were delayed until March 2001, a move that antagonized already sensitive race relations. Entire blocks of Georgetown were set ablaze by opposition supporters as the ruling PPP/Civic was declared victor of a third consecutive term, and the police and protesters clashed in the capital for weeks.

Guyana's economy relies on exports of primary commodities, especially bauxite but also gold, sugar, rice, timber and shrimp. East Indians control most of the small business, while the Afro-Guyanese have, until the late '90s, dominated the government sector. Guyana is a member of the Caribbean economic group, Caricom.

THE CULTURE

There are about 768,000 people in Guyana, but some 500,000 Guyanese live abroad, mostly in Canada, the UK, the USA, Trinidad and Barbados. Guyana's culture is a reflection of its colonialist plantation past. Slaves from Africa lived under severe conditions that caused them to lose much of their culture and adopt the Christian religion; later, indentured East Indian laborers arrived under better circumstances and were able to keep much of their heritage intact. The people today still hold a distrust between ethnicities. The main groups of Amerindians, who reside in scattered interior settlements, are Arawak, Carib, Macushi and Wapishana. The vast majority of the population lives in Georgetown or along the coast.

SPORTS

In racially polarized Guyana, sport is one of the few unifying factors, and sport here mainly means cricket. Internationally, Guyana plays with the West Indies; Clive Lloyd and Carl Hooper are the best-known local cricketers. Soccer is also played, but not as fervently as cricket. In 2007 Georgetown will host the semifinals of the Cricket World Cup, an event that has the possibility of dramatically changing the tourist infrastructure of the country.

RELIGION

Most Afro-Guyanese are Christian, usually Anglican, but a handful are Muslim. The East Indian population is mostly Hindu, with a sizable Muslim minority, but Hindu–Muslim friction is uncommon. Since independence, efforts have been made to recognize all relevant religions in national holidays.

ENVIRONMENT

Like Suriname, Guyana is swarming with rivers; its three principal waterways – the Berbice, Demerara and Essequibo (listed east to west) – are all north-flowing. The narrow strip of coastal lowland, 16km to 60km wide and 460km long, comprises 4% of the total land area but is home to 90% of the population. The Dutch, using a system of drainage canals, seawalls and groins, reclaimed much of the marshy coastal land from the Atlantic. These polders support most of Guyana's agriculture. There are very few sandy beaches.

Tropical rainforest covers most of the interior, though southwestern Guyana features an extensive savanna between the Rupununi River and the Brazil border.

TRANSPORTATION
Getting There & Away

Travelers flying to Guyana arrive at Cheddi Jagan International Airport (p782), south of the capital.

From Bonfim (Brazil), you can cross the river to Lethem, in Guyana's tranquil Rupununi Savanna. Bonfim has a good road connection to the Brazilian city of Boa Vista, but the road from Lethem to Georgetown is rough and may be impassable in wet weather.

In the northeast, a ferry connects Corriverton (Springlands) via Moleson Creek to the Surinamese border town of Nieuw Nickerie via South Drain, from which you can 4WD to Paramaribo (p783) and French Guiana (p770).

There are no road connections west to Venezuela and no legal border-crossing points. The only overland route is through Brazil via Boa Vista and Bonfim.

DEPARTURE TAX

Outbound passengers pay a departure tax of around US$20 (payable in Guyanese dollars).

Getting Around

Charter air services to the interior are available from the Ogle Aerodome in Georgetown (see p782).

Ferries cross most major rivers. There is regular service on the Essequibo between Charity and Bartica, with a stop at Parika (reached by paved highway from Georgetown). A ferry also crosses from Rosignol to New Amsterdam, along the Eastern Hwy on the way to the Suriname border. More frequent, but relatively expensive, speedboats (river taxis) carry passengers from Parika to Bartica.

Unscheduled minibuses link Georgetown with secondary towns. Rental cars are available in Georgetown, though not from the airport at the time of writing.

For more details about traveling around Guyana, see p782.

An International Driving Permit is recommended and is required for car rental.

Hitchhiking is not recommended – the threat of robbery is *very* real.

GEORGETOWN

pop 236,878

There's something endearing about Georgetown, whose easy to navigate gridded streets, dilapidated colonial architecture and many unkempt parks give it a laid-back feel amidst real-life chaos. Around the congested market area the air is full of angry shouting, happy shouting, marijuana smoke, friendly faces and suspicious-looking thieves; in all, there is so much fiery turbulence that the whole town feels on the verge of an explosion. Just a few blocks away, traffic lessens, the streets are nearly empty and there is a palpable Caribbean calm. Despite the hard-boiled exterior, the city has a thriving intellectual scene, fabulous restaurants and a riotous night-life.

GETTING INTO TOWN

Bus 42 (US$1, one hour) services Cheddi Jagan International Airport to/from the Timeri Bus Park behind the Parliament Building in central Georgetown; the bus is safe enough but at night a taxi (US$20; may be shared) is a much wiser choice. For early-morning flights from Jagan, make taxi arrangements the day before.

Orientation

Georgetown sits on the east bank of the Demerara River, where it empties into the Atlantic. A long seawall prevents flooding, while the Dutch canal system drains the town, and its position seven feet below sea level helps keep the city relatively cool. Pedestrian paths pass between the traffic lanes of the avenues.

Georgetown is divided into several districts: Kingston (in the northwest); Cummingsburg, Albertown, Queenstown and Newtown (in the center); Robbstown, Lacytown, Stabroek and Bourda (south of Church St; Bourda lines the western border of the botanical gardens); Werk-en-Rust, Wortmanville, Charlestown and Le Repentir (further south); Thomas Lands (east); and Kitty (further east).

A decent map (US$2) of Georgetown is available at **Kojac Marketing Agency** (☎ 225-2387; 140B Quamina St, Cummingsburg).

Information
BOOKSHOPS
Austin's Book Store (190 Church St; ☷ 8am-4pm Mon-Fri, 8am-1pm Sat) Offers the widest selection of books and maps.

EMERGENCY
Police (☎ 911)
Fire (☎ 912)
Ambulance (☎ 226-9449)

INTERNET ACCESS
Internet access in Georgetown goes for about US$2 per hour; wi-fi is available at many of the more upscale hotels.
Call Surf (16 Robb Street, upstairs; ☷ 8am-5pm Mon-Fri) By the Western Union, this place is not well marked.
Oasis Café (125 Carmichael St; ☷ 8am-8pm Mon-Fri, 10am-4pm Sat) Has two terminals and wi-fi.
Post Internet (cnr of Lamaha & Carmichael Sts; ☷ 8am-6pm Mon-Fri, 8am-1pm Sat) This is the cheapest but slowest internet in town.

MEDICAL SERVICES
Georgetown Public Hospital (☎ 225-6900; New Market St) Inadequate and run-down facilities.
St Joseph's Mercy Hospital (☎ 227-2072; 130-132 Parade St) Travelers may prefer private clinics and hospitals such as this one.

MONEY
ATMs that accept foreign cards are planned for the airport and cricket stadium for the Cricket World Cup 2007 (p777).

THE GUIANAS

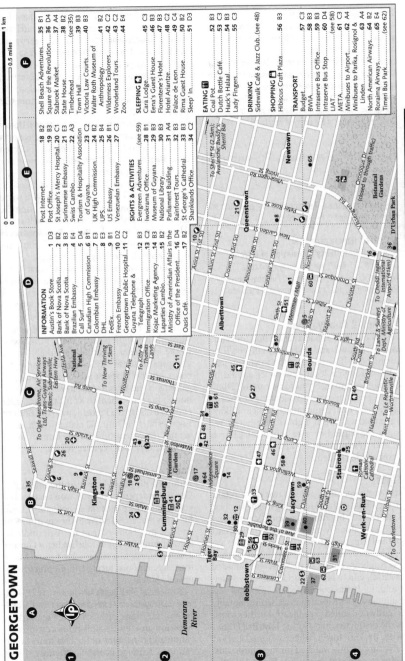

GEORGETOWN

0   0.5 miles
0   1 km

INFORMATION
Austin's Book Store	1	D3
Bank of Nova Scotia	2	B2
Bank of Nova Scotia	3	B3
Brazilian Embassy	4	E4
Call Surf	5	D4
Canadian High Commission	6	B1
Colombian Embassy	7	E3
DHL	8	E3
FedEx	9	B1
French Embassy	10	D2
Georgetown Public Hospital	11	C2
Guyana Telephone & Telegraph	12	B3
Immigration Office	13	C2
Kojac Marketing Agency	14	B3
Laparies Cambio	15	B2
Ministry of Amerindian Affairs in the Office of the President	16	D4
Oasis Café	17	B2
Post Internet	18	B2
Post Office	19	B3
St Joseph's Mercy Hospital	20	C1
Surinamese Embassy	21	E3
Swiss Cambio	22	A3
Tourism & Hospitality Association of Guyana	23	C2
UK High Commission	24	B2
UPS	25	B4
US Embassy	26	B1
Venezuelan Embassy	27	C3

SIGHTS & ACTIVITIES
Evergreen Adventures	(see 59)	
Iwokrama Office	28	B1
Museum of Guyana	29	B3
National Library	30	B3
Parliament Building	31	A4
Rainforest Tours	32	B3
St George's Cathedral	33	B4
Shanklands Office	34	C2

SLEEPING
Cara Lodge	45	C3
Eena's Guest House	46	B3
Florentene's Hotel	47	B3
Hotel Ariantze	48	C2
Palace de Leon	49	C4
Rima Guest House	50	B2
Sleep' In	51	D3

EATING
Coal Pot	52	B3
Dutch Bottle Café	53	C3
Hack's Halaal	54	B3
Lady Fingers	55	C3

DRINKING
| Sidewalk Café & Jazz Club | (see 48) | |

SHOPPING
| Hibiscus Craft Plaza | 56 | B3 |

TRANSPORT
Budget	57	C3
BWIA	58	B3
Intraserve Bus Office	59	B3
Intraserve Bus Stop	60	D4
LIAT	(see 58)	
META	61	C3
Minibuses to Airport	62	A4
Minibuses to Parika, Rosignol & Linden	63	A4
North American Airways	64	B2
Roraima Airways	65	E4
Timeri Bus Park	(see 62)	

Shell Beach Adventures.....35 B1
Square of the Revolution.....36 D4
Stabroek Market.....37 A4
State House.....38 B2
Timberhead.....(see 35)
Town Hall.....39 B3
Victoria Law Courts.....40 B3
Walter Roth Museum of Anthropology.....41 B2
Wilderness Explorers.....42 C2
Wonderland Tours.....43 C2
Zoo.....44 E4

Bank of Nova Scotia (104 Carmichael St; 8am-2pm Mon-Fri) Get credit card advances or try exchanging traveler's checks here. There's a second branch on the corner of Robb St and Ave of the Republic.

Laparties Cambio (34 Water St; 8am-5pm Mon-Fri) At the back of Fogarty's grocery store, this place is safe and has some of the best exchange rates in town.

Swiss Cambio (226-1723; 24A Water St) Let this reliable *cambio* come to you; call to have an agent meet you to exchange money in the safety of your hotel.

POST
Post office (225-7071; Robb St) This central postal hub can be hectic; go early.

TELEPHONE
Guyana Telephone & Telegraph (GT&T; cnr Church St & Ave of the Republic; 7am-10pm)

TOURIST INFORMATION
Tourism & Hospitality Association of Guyana (THAG; 225-0807; www.exploreguyana.com; 157 Waterloo St; 8am-5pm Mon-Fri) Publishes the useful Guyana Tourist Guide and an assortment of maps and pamphlets.

Dangers & Annoyances
Few towns have as bad a reputation for crime as Georgetown and, even though you'll be surprised at how peaceful the town can feel, a flip through a local newspaper should be enough to convince you to be careful. Don't wear jewelry or expensive-looking clothes or carry more cash than you need when walking and avoid walking at night all together. *Never* enter the Tiger Bay area (north of Church St and west of Main St) and stay out of the Promenade Garden.

Sights
It's worth spending at least two days to take in the sights of this fascinating town. The best 19th-century buildings are along Main St and especially along Ave of the Republic, just east of the Demerara River.

The most impressive building in town is the Anglican, Gothic-style **St George's Cathedral** (North Rd), said to be the world's tallest wooden building. It was completed in 1892 and was built mostly with local materials, most notably a hardwood called greenheart. Further south is the distinctive neo-Gothic **Town Hall** (1868) with its 75ft tower where colonial-period wives apparently watched for their husbands' ships to come into port. Just beyond are the

Victoria Law Courts (1887). At the south end of Ave of the Republic is the well-kept Dutch period **Parliament Building** (1834) and, nearby, the landmark **Stabroek Market** (Water St), a cast-iron building with a corrugated-iron clock tower. This main shopping venue, once described as quite a 'bizarre bazaar,' dates back to the late 1700s although the current structure was built in 1880.

Andrew Carnegie built the **National Library** (cnr Ave of the Republic & Church St), three blocks north of which stands the 1825, heavily louvered **State House** (cnr Main & New Market Sts), now the president's residence.

The **Museum of Guyana** (cnr North Rd & Hincks St; admission free) is a curious institution with some very old-fashioned exhibits documenting the nation's cultural, social and political history. Also interesting is the **Walter Roth Museum of Anthropology** (61 Main St), the first such museum in the English-speaking Caribbean.

Georgetown's **botanical gardens** (Regent Rd) are worth visiting for plants but also for bird-watching. The garden's **zoo** (www.guyanazoo.org .gy; cnr Regent & Vlissingen Rds; adult/child 50/25¢, with video camera US$11; 7:30am-5:30pm) is a depressing collection not recommended for animal lovers. The only highlight is the manatees that swim in the zoo canal, offering remarkably close glimpses of these shy creatures. The open court on the block south of the botanical gardens is the **Square of the Revolution**, which houses the monument to Kofi, famous leader and hero of the 1763 rebellion on the Berbice sugar estate; the unusual statue which exaggerates the proportions of the human form, is characteristic of Western Africa.

Tours
Although it's possible to visit the interior of Guyana independently, you won't scrape beyond the surface without a good guide. Look for tours that are sensitive to the environment and for programs co-run by Amerindians; investing in this type of tourism helps Guyana develop a path to a sustainable future. Many tour agencies are located in Georgetown's upscale hotels.

Annette at **Shell Beach Adventures** (225-4483; www.sbadventures.com; Le Meridien Pegasus Hotel, Seawall Rd) has infectious enthusiasm for sea turtles, Amerindian cultures and rainforest preservation and runs some of the best tours in the country. Arrange eco/socio-friendly three-day (US$580) or more trips along the coast to observe the sea turtles during egg-laying season (March/April to August) or adventurous jaunts to the interior; this company works to integrate sustainable tourism programs involving Amerindian peoples living in these areas. Frank Singh's **Rainforest Tours** (☎ 227-2011; www.rftours.com; Hotel Tower, 74 Main St) arranges well-organized tours up the Essequibo and Mazaruni Rivers (US$80), as well as an adventurous five-day overland journey (US$550) to Kaieteur Falls. Recommended **Wilderness Explorers** (☎ 227-7698; www.wilderness-explorers.com; Cara Suites, 176 Middle St) runs day trips to the Santa Mission of Carib Indians (US$50) and around Georgetown (US$30), and specializes in longer, customized trips to the Rupununi Savannas and Iwokrama. Richard at **Wonderland Tours** (☎ 225-3122; 150 Waterloo St) offers bargains on day trips to the Essequibo River and is very helpful with arranging transportation throughout the country and on to the other Guianas. **Evergreen Adventures** (☎ 226-0605; www.evergreen-adventures.com; 159 Charlotte St) puts together superb customized trips to the interior, particularly to Kaieteur.

Sleeping

Florentene's Hotel (☎ 226-2283; 3 North Rd; d US$11) If you don't mind the rust-stained sinks and dusty wood floors, this is a friendly, albeit crumbling, place to stay. Watch your valuables.

Eena's Guest House (☎ 227-3132; 17 North Rd; d with/without bathroom US$14/12) Across the street from Florentene's but much cleaner and safer. The matchbox-sized rooms here are quite homey. This place is usually frequented by Guyanese, but owners are thrilled to receive foreign visitors.

Rima Guest House (☎ 225-7401; 92 Middle St; rima@networksgy.com; s/d/tr US$24/28/34) The only real backpackers in town, this professionally run place is extremely safe and can help arrange just about any activity in Guyana; large airy rooms are spotless and appealingly colonial.

Sleep' In (☎ 231-7667; 151 Church St; www.sleepinguesthouse.com; d with/without air-con US$45/30; 🔧) Dark and airless motel-style rooms with TV have good beds and are very safe and comfortable.

Palace de Leon (☎ 227-7019; palacedeleon2000@yahoo.com; 60e½ Croal St; 1/2/3 r apartments US$45/55/75) A completely equipped two-bedroom apartment can easily sleep four to five people in this plant-filled colonial building. It's run by a large, lively family.

Hotel Ariantze (☎ 226-5363; 176 Middle St; www.arianzesidewalk.com; s/d US$50/60 incl breakfast; 🔧) This is a boutique-style hotel with colonial architecture, big bright windows and extremely helpful staff. All the rooms have wi-fi and credit cards are accepted for a 5% service fee.

Eating

You can eat very well for next to nothing in Georgetown where cuisine is more Westernized than the food in the other Guiana capitals. Eating venues are scattered evenly across the city.

Lady Fingers (232B Middle St; breakfast/lunch from US$1.50/2.50) This cafeteria-style gem serves big portions of Guyanese favorites at great prices.

Coal Pot (17 Hincks St; meals US$2-5; 🍽 lunch & dinner) Often crowded thanks to its diverse lunch menu, this is the best spot for Creole food.

Dutch Bottle Café (10 North Rd; mains US$2-7; 🍽 lunch & dinner) You'll feel swanky but pay cheap when dining in this restored colonial house decorated with paintings by local artists. There is a great vegetarian menu as well as meat and fish dishes.

Francine's Fish & Chips (Sheriff St; fish & chips US$2.50; 🍽 lunch & dinner) A hopping café with loud reggae music. Wait in line for a box of fried fish with plantain chips.

Oasis Café (125 Carmichael St; salad bar US$4; 🍽 7:30am-6:30pm Mon-Thu, 7:30am-8:30pm Fri & 9am-9:30pm Sat) Real coffee, a lunchtime salad bar,

THE GUIANAS

SPLURGE!

Cara Lodge (☎ 225-5301; www.carahotels.com; 294 Quamina St; s/d/tr US$110/121/132; 🔧 💻) Stay in one of Georgetown's colonial gems (not to be confused with the company's other hotel Cara Suites). Something about the white louvers, ginger-bread details and art-adorned corridors make this feel like a hideaway for glamorous film stars. There's a big old-fashioned ballroom, an open patio bar around a 100-year-old mango tree and a classy, rich-and-famous-worthy restaurant downstairs. Modern touches like wi-fi, and all the mod-cons make this place as comfortable as it is intriguing. Ask for a standard which are actually nicer than the higher priced rooms.

sandwiches, baked goods and internet. Don't leave without trying the Waini River organic chocolate cake.

Hack's Halaal (5 Commerce St; mains US$4-8; ☺ lunch) Gorge yourself on delicious Indian roti at this upscale-feeling place near the market.

New Thriving (167 Barr St; mains US$3-9; ☺ lunch & dinner) Hands down the best Chinese in Georgetown.

Drinking

Sheriff St prides itself on being one of the liveliest night spots in the Caribbean – the **Sheriff Bar** (10 Sheriff St), full of live music, questionable characters and prostitutes takes this a step further by proclaiming itself as *the* best bar in the region. If you're looking for something a bit less raunchy, try **Buddy's** (☎ 231-7260; 137 Sheriff St), which has a metal detector at the door and is a favorite with the upper-middle class East Indian crowd, or **Avalanche** (Sheriff St), the newest trend with a young clientele. Cover charge is usually a few dollars and the street does not sleep. For a listing of upcoming events and live music check out www.gtvibes.com.

Away from Sheriff St try **Sidewalk Café and Jazz Club** (176 Middle St) at the Hotel Ariantze, an ambient place for a drink any night or live jazz Thursday nights.

Shopping

You can find local handicrafts at **Hibiscus Craft Plaza**, in front of the post office. The **Shell Beach Adventures** (Seawall Rd) office at Le Meridien Pegasus Hotel sells organic chocolate, *casareep* (Amerindian cassava sauce), crabtree oil and soaps, and some crafts made by Amerindians.

Getting There & Away

AIR

International flights arrive and depart from Cheddi Jagan International Airport 41km south of Georgetown while domestic flights are serviced from Ogle Aerodrome closer to town. **BWIA** (☎ 1-800-538-2992; www.bwee.com; 4 Robb St), **LIAT** (☎ 227-8281; www.liatairline.com; 4 Robb St); **META** (☎ 225-5315; cnr Middle & Thomas Sts) and **North American Airways** (☎ 227-5805; www.northamericanair .com; 126 Carmichael St) link the capital to Caribbean islands (the main hubs being Trinidad and Barbados), Suriname (via Brazil), New York (USA) and beyond. **Roraima Airways** (☎ 225-9648; www.roraimaairways.com; R8 Eping Av, Bel Air Park), **Air Services Ltd** (ASL; ☎ 222-4357; www.airservicesltd .com; Ogle Aerodrome) and **Trans Guyana Airways** (TGA;

☎ 222-2525; www.transguyana.com; Ogle Aerodome) send small planes into the interior.

Sample one-way airfares:

Barbados LIAT, US$125, two hours, daily.
Boa Vista (Brazil) META, US$150, one hour, three weekly.
Kaieteur ASL, US$125, one hour, three weekly.
Lethem & Annai TGA, US$110, 1½ hours, daily; Roraima, US$110, three weekly.
Mabaruma TGA, US$80, one hour, four weekly.

BUS

Minibuses to Parika (No 32; one hour) and Rosignol (No 50; 1½ hours) leave from Stabroek Market and cost around US$4. At Parika, you can make boat connections to Bartica (US$10; one hour); at Rosignol, catch the ferry to New Amsterdam (US30¢, 15 minutes) with connecting service to Corriverton. These have no fixed schedules and leave when full. **Wonderland Tours** (☎ 225-3122; p781) can arrange minibuses straight through to the Suriname ferry at Moleson Creek for US$15.

Buy Intraserve bus tickets to Lethem (US$40, check in 7pm, no service Wednesday or Saturday, 12 to 18 hours) at the **ticket office** (159 Charlotte St) at least a day before departure; the buses fill quickly. Buses leave from the Intraserve stop on the corner of Oronoque St and North Rd. The bus is known to break down so be prepared: bring snacks, water, warm clothes and don't be in a hurry to get anywhere. You can also catch minibuses that leave daily from the market (US$40, 12 to 18 hours) but these are sometimes subject to hijacking and robberies on the road.

Getting Around

Budget (☎ 225-5595; 75 Church St; ☺ Mon-Sat) rents quite expensive cars (US$50 per day, three-day minimum, includes 100km per day). With bad road conditions and fellow drivers, you're better off in a taxi or bus.

For simplicity and safety, taxis are *the* way to get around central Georgetown (around center US$.40). Have your hotel call a reliable cab company for you and then, if you find a good taxi driver, take down his phone and car number and you'll have a friendly contact to drive you around safely throughout your stay.

COASTAL PLAIN

The coastal plain, an area heading east from Georgetown to the Suriname border, can be traversed via the Eastern Hwy. The road travels through town after unremarkable town, passing potholes, suicidal dogs, unfenced livestock and the resultant road kill. **Rosignol**, about a two-hour drive from Georgetown, is where the road ends; a massive antique ferry then travels over the Berbice River to **New Amsterdam** (often referred to as 'Berbice') and the continuing road to the border.

Corriverton

pop 12,740

Together known as Corriverton, the towns of **Springlands** and **Skeldon**, on the west bank of the Corentyne River about 195km from Georgetown, are at the southeastern end of the coastal road from Georgetown. The town's Main St is a long, lively strip with mosques, churches, a Hindu temple, cheap hotels, eateries and bars. Brahman (zebu) cattle roam round the market like the sacred cows of India. At the north end of town, the Skeldon Estate of Guysuco is the biggest local employer. If you need to stay a night on Main St, try clean **Hotel Par Park** (r US$10-12) or the recommended, antique **Mahogany Hotel** (☎ 339-2289; r US$13-33) which has some rooms offering good river views and a **restaurant** overlooking the main drag.

GETTING THERE & AWAY

Buses from Corriverton to the ferry to Suriname (US$4) at Moleson Creek run via Crabwood Creek from Main St. Arrange the trip a day in advance from your hotel and be sure to depart Corriverton before 9am for plenty of time to reach the ferry. There is regular bus service along Main St to New Amsterdam.

NORTHWEST COAST

The west bank of the Essequibo River can be reached by boat from **Parika** to **Supernam**. Boats also travel from Parika southward to the lively mining town of **Bartica** (population 10,400). Near Bartica, the Essequibo meets the Mazaruni River and **Marshall Falls**, a series of rapids and a jungle waterfall that can be hiked to from shore. Tour operators offer day trips from Georgetown (see p780). It's worth spending a few relaxing days on the river at **Shanklands** (☎ 225-2678; www.shanklands.com; 232 Camp & Middle Sts, Georgetown; dm US$10, d 1st/2nd night US$187/$55) a beachside, palm-fringed resort that is easily reached independently (bus to Parika then take a Bartica-bound speedboat; see opposite). **Timberhead** (☎ 225-3760; timberhead _gy@yahoo.co.uk; Meridien Pegasus, Seawall Rd, Georgetown; all inclusive per person US$153) is a riverside rainforest resort offering a similar experience.

Heading west from the Essequibo, a coastal road passes quaint rice-mill and farming villages to the town of **Charity**, about 50km away. From here you'll need a boat to go further. Boat through bird-filled rivers, mangrove swamps and savannas to **Santa Rosa**, Guyana's largest and oldest Amerindian village. More river travel brings you to **Shell Beach**, which extends for about 140km along the coast near the Venezuelan border and is a nesting site for four of the eight sea turtle species. This is one of the least developed areas of the entire South American coastline and the only human alterations are in the form of temporary fishing huts and small Amerindian settlements. **Waini Point** near the beautiful colonial town of **Mabaruma** (population 721) is the most spectacular sighting area for the scarlet ibis. It's possible to fly independently to Mabaruma (see opposite), but to fully experience the area or take the overland (and water) voyage, you're best off taking a tour. See p780 for more information.

THE INTERIOR
Kaieteur National Park & Orinduik Falls

You may have been to Angel or Iguazú Falls, seen Niagara or not even be particularly

---

GETTING TO SURINAME

The ferry to Suriname leaves from Moleson Creek (US$14, 25 minutes, 11am daily) and crosses the Corentyne River to the Surinamese border at South Drain, 1½ hours south of Nieuw Nickerie. Get to the ferry no later than 10am to stamp passports and go through customs control. Minibuses to Nieuw Nickerie and Paramaribo meet the ferry on the Suriname side. Sometimes there are no money changers, so it's best to get enough Suriname dollars on the Guyana side to get you through to Paramaribo. Make sure you know your rates before you make the exchange.

Frequent small boats cross the river in about 15 minutes. These boats are prone to robbery and, at best, you'll wind up in Suriname without the proper stamps in your passport.

For information on travel in the opposite direction, see p771.

interested in waterfalls; it doesn't matter, *go* to **Kaieteur Falls** (www.kaieteurpark.gov.gy). Watching 30,000 gallons of water per second be shot out over a 250m cliff (allegedly making this the highest single-drop falls in the world) in the middle of a misty, ancient jungle without another tourist in sight is a once-in-a-lifetime experience. The brave (or crazy) can actually stand at the top of the falls and gaze over the precipice. Depending on the season, the falls are from 76m to 122m wide. Swifts nest under the falls' overhang and dart in and out of the waters around sunset each night. On the walk to the falls look for scarlet red cock-of-the-rock birds and miniscule golden frogs, an incredible, rare critter that can be used to produce a voodoo poison 160,000 times more potent than cocaine.

Many people just go for the day by air from Georgetown and you can often arrange to see **Orinduik Falls** in the same day. Orinduik is a 15-minute flight south of Kaieteur, drops 80ft and is a good place to swim (a dip at Kaieteur would surely be your last). Several operators offer day trips in small planes (about US$210); make early inquiries and be flexible, since the flights go only when a full load of five to eight passengers can be arranged (usually on weekends).

It's possible to stay in a rustic **lodge** (per person US$12) at Kaieteur – book through **Air Services Ltd** (☎ 222-4357; www.airservicesltd.com; Ogle Aerodrome, Georgetown) for a bed, a flight and help with organizing food (weight limits make it difficult to bring your own). If you have the time, take the challenging but spectacular overland route to Kaieteur that takes around five days (p781).

Iwokrama Rain Forest

Iwokrama, established in 1996, is a unique, living laboratory for tropical forest management and socioeconomic development for Amerindians. Amidst 371,000 hectares of virgin rainforest, this exceptional region is home to the highest recorded number of fish and bat species in the world, South America's largest cat (the jaguar), the world's largest scaled fresh water fish (the arapaima), and the world's largest otters, river turtles, anteaters, snakes, rodents, eagles and caimans. Unlike a national park, Iwokrama is not funded by the government and must therefore take a very realistic approach of how to keep afloat without over-exploiting resources. Very selective tree felling

is practiced in order to help study techniques of sustainable logging; the profits from the timber are used to help finance the organization's endeavors in ecotourism and biological research. Amerindian peoples inhabit parts of the forest and are encouraged to work with ecotourism projects, to become park rangers, harvest tropical aquarium fish and create cottage industry. Everyone involved in Iwokrama, from the director to the field-center cook to the inhabitants of the surrounding villages, exudes a hope and pride for the center's projects that is truly inspirational.

The cheapest and most ecofriendly way to visit Iwokrama is through the center itself. Its Georgetown **office** (☎ 225-1504; www.iwokrama.org; 77 High St) arranges transportation and accommodations for longer tours, or you can stay at its **field station** (s/d with full board US$35/65) for a shorter visit. A two-day tour (about US$268 all inclusive per person, depending on group size) includes visits to Amerindian villages, forest walks and nighttime caiman spotting. There is a US$15 forest user fee for all overnight Iwokrama visits, and independent visits should be organized through the Georgetown office in advance. There is a US$10 charge for the boat crossing to the field center.

You can also visit Iwokrama's new **canopy walkway** (www.iwokramacanopywalkway.com; day pass US$20), about 60km south of the field station or sleep over in a hammock (US$81 with full board, guide and all fees) at the walkway forest.

Iwokrama has encouraged ecotourism projects in Amerindian villages, particularly at **Surama** (with full board & activities per person from $110) where there are rustically lovely huts built specifically for tourists. Book through Iwokrama or Wilderness Explorers (p781). The village has trained a few guides to take visitors hiking or canoeing and the school often prepares a warm-hearted welcome of singing and dancing for village visitors.

Annai to Lethem

The Rupununi Savannas are Africa-like plains scattered with Amerindian villages and an exceptional diversity of wildlife. Rivers filled with huge caimans, the world's largest water lilies (the *Victoria amazonica*) and a mind-boggling variety of colorful birds, cut through plains of golden grasses and termite mounds. The heart of the Savannas is at Annai, a cross-roads of Amerindian peoples with a police station and an airstrip, although the biggest settlement is much further south at Lethem, a cowboy town on the Brazilian border. Although the savannas stretch over an area of 104,400 sq km, there's a distinct feel of a tight community down here and you'd be hard pressed to find a safer place on earth. The region attracts and grows a collection of unique characters fanatical about wildlife, ecopreservation and living life to the fullest. The relatively nearby **Kanuku Mountains** harbor an extraordinary diversity of wildlife – 70% of all bird species found in Guyana reside here and 'Kanuku' means 'rich forest' in the Macushi language.

The whole area is home to Guyana's *vaqueros* (cowboys), and there's an annual Easter rodeo.

Technically you need permission to visit Amerindian communities but if you are traveling with Iwokrama or a tour company, this should be taken care of for you; inquiries can be made at the **Ministry of Amerindian Affairs in the Office of the President** (☎ 226-5167; New Garden St & Vlissengen Rd, Georgetown).

Don and Shirley's shop at the Lethem airstrip is the best place to get information about the local attractions, guides and other points of interest in the area. Pat Rash has an internet café right next to the shop and is another good source of information.

SLEEPING & EATING

Transportation is difficult and the expense of getting anywhere off the main road to or from Georgetown might cost more than a night or two's lodging where you want to stay. The isolated ranch-lodges don't have phones but can be reserved through **Wilderness Explorers** (p781).

Aunt Louisa's (☎ 772-9280; Annai; d US$4) Warm, smiling Louisa runs the very basic government guesthouse right next to the police station in peaceful Annai. The phone is the public phone box in front of the guesthouse, so ask for Louisa when you call.

Trail's End (☎ 772-2010; Lethem; shefishs@gmail .com; hammock/d with breakfast US$10/35) Pat Rash, an American expat who came to Guyana 'for the fishing,' offers ranch-style accommodation for any budget and can arrange activities from fishing trips to 'cowboy for a day' immersions.

Rock View Lodge (☎ 226-5412; Annai; www.rockview lodge.com; s/d with full board US$95/150, camping & hammock with/without half board US$30/10; 🏊) With a restaurant that proclaims itself 'the best pit stop in the Rupununi' (it's in fact the only one), this place is a hive of local activity. The ranch itself is right at the Annai airstrip and the *hacienda*-feeling rooms are the most comfortable in the Rupununi. Walks and Amerindian village visits can be arranged or you can just have a drink at the restaurant or airstrip bar to meet some local characters.

Dadanawa Ranch (Kanuku Mountains; per person incl meals US$107) The most remote ranch in Guyana, nestled at the base of the Kanuku Mountains, Duane and Sandy's Dadanawa Ranch is as fun, adventurous and spectacularly scenic a place as you could ever hope to visit. Extreme treks including tracking harpy eagles can be arranged or you can partake in ranch work and stay up partying with the *vaqueros* at night.

Karanambu Ranch (Rupununi; per person incl meals & activities US$180) If you ever hoped to find yourself in the middle of a real-life Jane Goodall–like experience, here is your chance. Owner Diane McTurk is an extraordinary character who has devoted much of her life saving the Rupununi's giant river otter. A few otter orphans animate the ranch as well as Diane who is easily just as interesting. Accommodation is in ranch-meets-Amerindian-style huts with spacious and well-equipped attached bathrooms. Activities are arranged daily from bird-watching to giant anteater tracking in this area of unparalleled beauty.

GETTING THERE & AWAY

Two local airlines, Roraima and TGA (see p782), make trips from Georgetown to Lethem, Annai and Karanambu (all from US$110 one way). It can be hard to get a flight at a moment's notice, so plan ahead. On request the plane stops at all three stops so that it's possible to fly between these three places (US$110 per flight).

Bus service is available between Lethem and Georgetown (via Annai; US$40) but service can be cancelled or delayed during the wet season; see p782 for details. Iwokrama and the bigger lodges and ranches offer overland 4WD transportation but it's often cheaper to fly unless you are in a group. Sample one-way fares for a jeep for four people are: Annai to Lethem (US$260), Annai to Karanambu (US$280), Annai to Kurupukari Crossing/Iwokrama Field Station (US$220), and Lethem to Dadanawa (US$200).

THE GUIANAS

GETTING TO BRAZIL

The border between Guyana and Brazil is formed by the Takatu River (called the Río Tacutu in Brazil). Lethem is on one side, Bonfim, Brazil is on the other. From Lethem, get a taxi (US$2.50) or walk (about 30 minutes) to the river via the immigration office, where you'll get stamped out of Guyana. Take a motorized dugout (US$1.50, 2 minutes) across the river to Bonfim, Brazil. Once you're across, taxis (US$2, 10 minutes) run from the river to the Bonfim bus terminal via the Brazilian customs police (there is a road block so everyone must stop here). Buses occasionally pick up at the river, but this is iffy so you're better off taking a taxi. From the Bonfim bus terminal you can catch Amatur buses to Boa Vista (US$6.50; 7am, 10am, 2:30pm and 4pm daily; two hours) where there are flight and bus connections for further afield. Note that US nationals need a visa (available in Georgetown) – and all need yellow-fever vaccinations – to enter Brazil. There are money changers offering fair rates for Brazilian reais on the Guyana side. For information on traveling from Brazil to Guyana, see p395.

From Lethem it's possible to cross the border to Brazil (above).

GUYANA DIRECTORY
Accommodations
In Georgetown, the cheapest hotels often double as 'love inns,' which locals use by the hour – so be careful of questionably low rates. Modest hotels that are clean, secure and comfortable charge US$11 to US$25. Better accommodations, with air-con, start at US$40, while the growing number of rainforest lodges and savanna ranches are more expensive (US$100 and up).

Activities
The interior and coastal areas offer countless possibilities from river rafting, trekking and bird-watching to wildlife-viewing and fishing. All is best arranged through local tour operators.

Books
The classic account of travel in Guyana is Charles Waterton's 1825 *Wanderings in South America*. Though out of print, it is widely available in used bookstores and libraries in the US and the UK. Evelyn Waugh described a rugged trip from Georgetown across the Rupununi Savanna in *Ninety-Two Days*. Shiva Naipaul wrote a moving account of the Jonestown tragedy (p776) in *Journey to Nowhere: A New World Tragedy*, published in the UK as *Black and White*. Oonya Kempadoo's *Buxton Spice* is a sexually charged account about growing up in Guyana in the 1970s. The birdwatcher's bible is *Birds of Venezuela* by Steven L Hilty.

Business Hours
Commerce awakens around 8:30am and tends to last until 4pm or so. Saturdays are half-days if shops open at all, and Sundays are quietest; Georgetown becomes an utter ghost town. Restaurants generally open for lunch at 11:30am and serve until 3pm. while dinner can be had from around 6:30pm to 10pm.

Climate
The equatorial climate features high temperatures with little seasonal variation, though coastal breezes moderate the heat. Guyana has two distinct rainy seasons: May to mid-August and mid-November to mid-January. August through October are the hottest months.

The best time to visit Guyana may be at the end of either rainy season, when the discharge of water over Kaieteur Falls is greatest. Some locals recommend mid-October to mid-May, which may be wet but not as hot. Note that downpours can occur even in the 'dry' seasons.

Dangers & Annoyances
Guyana (Georgetown in particular) is notorious for street crime, especially around elections. Avoid potentially hazardous situations and be aware of others on the street. For details, see p780.

At Cheddi Jagan International Airport, try to arrive during daylight and use only registered airport taxis. Drivers are easily recognizable, as they all have official IDs attached to their shirt pockets. All baggage should be locked. Backpacks are particularly prone to pilfering hands.

Hitchhiking is not recommended – the threat of robbery and/or physical danger is *very* real. You'd be nuts to hitch here!

Electricity

Electricity is 127V, 60Hz.

Embassies & Consulates

EMBASSIES & CONSULATES IN GUYANA

All foreign representatives in Guyana are in Georgetown.

Brazil (Map p779; ☎ 225-7970; 308-309 Church St)
Canada (Map p779; ☎ 227-2081; cnr High & Young Sts)
Colombia (Map p779; ☎ 227-1410; 306 Church St)
France (☎ 227-5435; 46 First St)
Suriname (Map p779; ☎ 226-7844; 171 Crown St)
UK (Map p779; ☎ 226-5881; 44 Main St)
USA (Map p779; ☎ 225-4902; 100 Young St)
Venezuela (Map p779; ☎ 226-6749; 296 Thomas St)

GUYANESE EMBASSIES & CONSULATES ABROAD

Guyana's representatives abroad:

Belgium (☎ 323-675 62 16; 13-17 Rue de Praetere, 1050 Brussels)
Canada Ottawa (☎ 613-235-7249; 151 Slater St, Suite 309, Ottawa, Ontario, K1P 5H3); Toronto (☎ 416-494-6040; 505 Consumers Rd, Suite 206, Willowdale, Ontario, M2J 4V8)
UK (☎ 4471-229-7684; 3 Palace Court, Baywater Court, London W2 4LP)
USA Washington (☎ 202-265-6900; 2490 Tracy Place NW, Washington, DC 20008); New York (☎ 212-527-3215; 866 United Nations Plaza, 3rd fl, New York, NY 10017)

Festivals & Events

Republic Day celebrations in February are the most important national cultural events of the year, though Hindu and Muslim religious festivals are also significant. The recently established **Amerindian Heritage Month** (September) features a series of cultural events, such as handicraft exhibits and traditional dances. **Regatta**, an aquatic event attracting innumerable speedboats of different design, takes place every Easter at both Bartica and Canaan. An annual Easter rodeo is held in the Rupununi Savanna at Lethem.

Food & Drink

Guyanese food ranges from the tasty pepperpot (an Amerindian game stew made with cassava) to the challenging *souse* (jellied cow's head). Indian food is widespread and quite noteworthy. Two ubiquitous dishes are 'cookup' (rice and beans mixed with whatever else happens to be on hand) and 'roti' (chicken curry in Indian flatbread). Overall, Guyanese like spice, so if you don't, say so.

Local rum is available everywhere; El Dorado 15-year-old rum is considered one of the best rums in the world – if you can find it, the 25-year-old is even better but most people settle with the less expensive but undeniably good 5-year-old variety. Banks beer, brewed in Georgetown, comes in both regular and premium versions, both of which are exceptionally good. Also try fruit punch (or, effectively, rum punch) at any of Georgetown's better restaurants.

Health

Adequate medical care is available in Georgetown, at least at private hospitals, but facilities are few elsewhere. Chloroquine-resistant malaria is endemic, and dengue fever is also a danger, particularly in the interior and even in Georgetown – protect yourself against mosquitoes and take a malaria prophylaxis. Typhoid, hepatitis A, diphtheria/tetanus and polio inoculations are recommended. Guyana is regarded as a yellow-fever-infected area, and your next destination may require a vaccination certificate, as does Guyana if you arrive from another infected area. Tap water is suspect, especially in Georgetown. Cholera outbreaks have occurred in areas with unsanitary conditions, but precautions are recommended everywhere.

See p1090 for more information.

Holidays

New Year's Day (January 1)
Youman Nabi (early January) The Muslim prophet Muhammed's birthday.
Republic Day (February 23) Slave rebellion of 1763.
Phagwah (Hindu New Year; March/April) Dates vary.
Good Friday/Easter Monday (March/April) Dates vary.
Labor Day (May 1)
CARICOM Day (1st Monday of July)
Emancipation Day (August 1)
Diwali (November) Hindu Festival of Lights. Dates vary.
Christmas Day (December 25)
Boxing Day (December 26)

Internet Access

Georgetown is your best bet for internet cafés (about US$2 per hour); some nicer hotels also offer web access and wi-fi is becoming increasingly available.

Internet Resources

Land of Six Peoples (www.landofsixpeoples.com) Smorgasbord of information, from news to weather to history.

Tourism and Hospitality Association of Guyana
(www.exploreguyana.com) Government site with down-
loadable maps.
Tourism Authority (www.guyana-tourism.com)
Everything for planning a trip to Guyana.
Guyana News and Information (www.guyana.org)
Wealth of data with heavy emphasis on current affairs.

Maps

Country and Georgetown maps can sometimes be found in the gift shops of the higher-
end hotels or bookshops (p778). Otherwise,
for detailed maps of the country, visit Georgetown's **Lands & Surveys Dept, Ministry of Agriculture**
(☎ 226-4051; 22 Upper Hadfield St, Durban Backlands). Have
a taxi take you, because it's difficult to find.

Media

Georgetown's newspapers are *Stabroek News*
(www.stabroeknews.com), the most liberal
paper, the *Guyana Chronicle* (www.guyana
chronicle.com), which tends to lean toward
government promotion, and *Kaieteur News*,
which is the best for local gossip. The *Guyana
Review* is an excellent monthly news magazine published in Georgetown. The 'Voice
of Guyana' radio program can be found on
102FM or 560AM.

Money

The Guyanese dollar (G$) is more or less
stable, but it's declining in line with domestic
inflation. Guyanese dollars add up to large
amounts – a Coke is around G$100, for exam-
ple – so don't faint when you see meals costing
thousands of dollars on local menus.

There are currently no ATMs accepting
foreign cards although there are some vague
ideas of establishing one at the airport and
another at the cricket stadium for the 2007
Cricket World Cup (see p777).

CREDIT CARDS

Credit cards are accepted at Georgetown's
better hotels and restaurants, though not at
gas stations, most stores or anywhere else.
Credit card advances can be made only at the
Bank of Nova Scotia.

EXCHANGING MONEY

Cash can be exchanged in **banks** (☉ 8am-2pm Mon-
Fri) and **cambios** (exchange houses; ☉ 9am-3:30pm Mon-
Fri), which offer better rates and less red tape
than banks. Sometimes you can change cash
unofficially at hotels for 10% or 15% less.

Exchange rates at the time of writing:

Country	Unit		G$ (Guyanese dollar)
Australia	A$1	=	143
Canada	C$1	=	166
euro zone	€1	=	238
Japan	¥100	=	160
New Zealand	NZ$1	=	126
UK	UK£1	=	354
USA	US$1	=	190

Post

Postal services are generally unreliable; use
registered mail for essential correspondence.
For important shipments, try these international shippers, all in Georgetown: **UPS**
(Map p779; ☎ 227-1853; 210 Camp St), **DHL** (Map p779;
☎ 225-7772; 50 E 5th St, Alberttown) and **FedEx** (Map
p779; ☎ 227-6976; 125 D Barrack St, Kingston).

Shopping

Nibbee fiber, extracted from forest vines, is the
most distinctive and appealing local product
and is used to make everything from hats
to furniture. The Macushi of the southwest
have developed a unique art form based on
sculpting forest scenes and creatures from the
hardened latex of the *balata* tree. Other goodies include *casareep* (an Amerindian sauce
made from cassava), crabtree oil (an Amerindian cure-all), boxes, spoons and bowls
carved from tropical hardwoods, and woven,
Amerindian-style baby slings. The best place
to buy Amerindian goods is in the villages
themselves or through Iwokrama or Shell
Beach Adventures (p780) in Georgetown.

Telephone

At blue public telephones scattered around
towns, you can make direct and reverse-
charge (collect) calls abroad, and you can
purchase prepaid phone cards in Georgetown.
Internet phone services are a cheaper option
and these services can be found throughout Georgetown. For a USA direct line, dial
☎ 165 (AT&T) or ☎ 151 (Sprint); for Canada, dial ☎ 161; and for the UK, dial ☎ 169.
For the international operator, dial ☎ 002,
and for directory assistance in Georgetown,
dial ☎ 92 (092 for numbers outside Georgetown). Yellow public telephones are for local
calls, which are free. Hotels and restaurants
generally allow free use of their phones for
local calls.

THE GUIANAS

Tourist Information

The government has no official tourism representative abroad, but in Guyana there is the very official **Tourism and Hospitality Association of Guyana** (www.exploreguyana.com) and the more user-friendly **Tourism Authority** (www.guyana-tourism.com). Guyanese embassies and consulates abroad can also provide relatively up-to-date information.

Tours

As in the other Guianas, limited infrastructure plus tour operators equals unforgettable trips into the amazing interior. Many Guyanese companies promote 'adventure tourism' in rainforest and riverside lodges. These tours can be costly, as can domestic airfares, which are often not included, but food and lodging are always covered. Most operators require a minimum number of people (usually five) to be booked for a tour before they'll commit to the date. Friday and Saturday are your best bet for a trip into the interior or to a resort. For details on tour operators see p780.

Visas

All visitors must carry a passport, but travelers from the USA, Canada, EU countries, Australia, New Zealand, Japan and the UK do not need a visa; confirm with the nearest embassy or consulate. A 90-day stay is granted on arrival in Guyana with an onward ticket. If you do need a visa, file your application at least six weeks before you leave your home country.

As well as a passport, carry an international yellow-fever vaccination certificate with you, and keep other immunizations up to date.

To stay longer than 30 days, appeal to the **immigration office** (Map p779; ☎ 225-1744; Camp Rd; ⏰ 8- 11:30am & 1-3pm Mon-Fri).

Women Travelers

Guyana's not-so-safe reputation should put women travelers on particular alert. Never go out alone at night and stick to well-peopled areas if walking alone during the day in Georgetown. In the interior, traveling alone should pose few problems.

Paraguay

HIGHLIGHTS

- **Ruta Trans-Chaco to Bolivia** – try your luck (bumpin', sittin' or cruisin') on the continent's most bumpy dust-ways (p815)
- **Parque Nacional Ybycuí** – wend your way through blue-butterfly-filled subtropical rainforest to dreamlike waterfalls (p808)
- **Trinidad** – explore the picturesque remnants of the Jesuits at one of the world's least-visited Unesco sites (p808)
- **National parks in the Chaco** – watch a jaguar race through the scrub, sleep under billions of stars, experience the absence of humanity (p815)
- **Off the beaten track** – marvel at history and nature in the well-organized and not hard to reach Parque Nacional Cerro Corá (p813)
- **Best journey** – sit back, relax and watch wildlife from your hammock on the Río Paraguay – this ain't your mama's river cruise (p812)

FAST FACTS

- **Area:** 406,752 sq km (bigger than Germany, about the size of California)
- **Best bargain**: hammocks
- **Best street snack**: *chipa* (corn bread)
- **Budget:** US$20-30 a day
- **Capital:** Asunción
- **Costs:** *residencial* room in Asunción US$7-10, bus rides per hr US$1.30, *chipa* 15¢
- **Country code:** ☎ 595
- **Famous for:** contraband, corruption, the Chaco
- **Languages:** Spanish (official), Guaraní, Plattdeutsch, Hochdeutsch, Lengua, Nivaclé, Aché
- **Money:** US$1 = 5364 guaraní
- **Phrases:** *porã* (cool), *vai* (disgusting), *arete* (party)
- **Population:** 6.5 million
- **Time:** GMT minus 4hr

- **Tipping:** 10% in restaurants only
- **Visas:** most non-EU citizens, including Americans, Australians, Canadians and New Zealanders, need a visa (US$45 single entry, US$65 multiple entry)

TRAVEL HINTS

Don't refuse an invitation to sip *tereré* (iced herbal tea). Try fresh warm *chipa* – those from commercial sellers on the buses are best.

OVERLAND ROUTES

Popular entry points via bus include Foz de Iguazú, Brazil; Posadas, Argentina; or via the bumpy Ruta Trans-Chaco from Bolivia.

Paraguay is a country of fascinating contrasts. It's rustic and sophisticated. It's extremely poor and obscenely wealthy. It boasts exotic natural reserves and massive man-made dams. It is a place where horses and carts pull up by Mercedes Benz cars, artisans' workshops abut glitzy shopping centers and Jesuit ruins in rural villages are just a few kilometers from sophisticated colonial towns. Steamy subtropical rainforests with metallic butterflies contrast with the dry and wild frontier of the Chaco. Here, many Mennonites have created their haven, living alongside some of the country's many indigenous groups, while the European influence is particularly strong in the laid-back towns and the more chaotic capital. Surprisingly, backpackers are rarer than pumas in Paraguay, but travel is always do-able – whether on a bone-rattling kamikaze-style bus trip or leisurely bobbing up the Río Paraguay aboard a rickety boat. While Paraguayans are more used to visits from their bordering neighbors, they are relaxed, kind and curious to anyone – share a *tereré* (iced herbal tea) and they will impart their country's alluring secrets. The residual effects of dictators, corruption and contraband contribute to an overall sense that, for many years, much of Paraguayan life has taken place behind closed doors, as its people partake in public protests with confidence.

CURRENT EVENTS

Current leader President Nicanor Duarte Frutos makes headlines. Paraguayans were finally released from a dictatorship when he was democratically elected in 2003. Having taken over the reigns of a corrupt system in one of the most corrupt countries in the world, it's probably not surprising that the president's slate isn't entirely squeaky clean. The ambitious president is desperate to attain a second presidential term; under the present constitution presidents can only rule for one term. In an unprecedented move, he briefly managed to assume the presidency of the ruling Colorado party (whilst also being president of the country). In this five-minute flash he announced plans for a referendum to allow him to stand for a second term. His actions have lead to widespread suspicion and public condemnation.

The government's April 2006 report on the economy revealed that job opportunities have increased and poverty has decreased. The population is skeptical of these claims, branding the President as a *japu* ('liar' in Guaraní).

Since July 2005 US special forces (including military doctors) have been based in Paraguay, officially to undertake training and humanitarian exercises. While some members of the community think that the US presence is a positive move, others are suspicious of their intentions, especially given the presence of the neighboring Bolivian gas reserves and the world's largest freshwater reserves, the *Guaraní Aquifer,* in the tri-border area of Brazil, Paraguay and Argentina.

Since the formation of Mercosur, the region's economic bloc, Paraguay has complained that its needs are frequently disregarded by Brazil and Argentina.

HISTORY

When 350 Spaniards from Pedro de Mendoza's expedition fled Buenos Aires and founded Asunción in 1537, Guaraní cultivators dominated what is now southeastern Paraguay. Eager to strengthen themselves against the Chaco's hostile hunter-gatherers, the Guaraní absorbed the conquistadors by providing them with food and an abundance of Guaraní women. This mixing resulted in a *mestizo* (mixed Indian and Spanish descent) culture of Guaraní food, customs and language and Spanish politics.

Asunción was the most significant Spanish settlement east of the Andes for nearly 50 years before Buenos Aires was fully established. During the colonial period Paraguay covered much of northern Argentina and western Brazil.

In the early 17th century, Jesuit missionaries created *reducciones* (settlements) where Guaraní were introduced to European high culture, new crafts, new crops and new methods of cultivation. Until their expulsion in 1767 (because of local jealousies and Madrid's concern that their power had become too great), the Jesuits were remarkably successful. They deterred Portuguese intervention in the region and are credited with protecting the Guaraní from bands of ruthless slavers from the Portuguese colony of São Paulo. The Jesuits were less successful among the Guaycurú, the indigenous groups of the Chaco.

Within a few years of Paraguay's uncontested independence from Spain in 1811, José

PARAGUAY

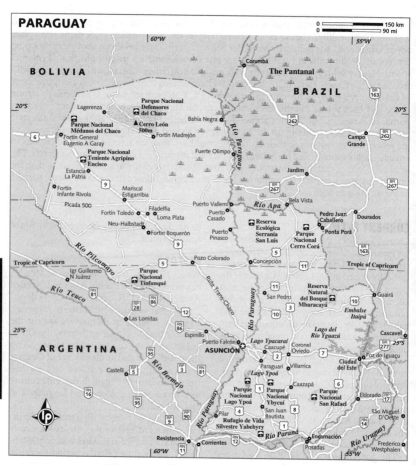

PARAGUAY

Gaspar Rodríguez de Francia emerged as the strongest member of a governing junta. Until his death in 1840, the xenophobic and sinister 'El Supremo' sealed the country's borders to promote national self-sufficiency, expropriated the properties of landholders, merchants and even the church, thus establishing the state as the dominant political and economic power.

Like most of his successors, Francia ruled by fear. His secret-police force jailed and tortured his opponents, many of which met their end in Francia's most notorious dungeon, the 'Chamber of Truth.' After escaping an assassination attempt in 1820, El Supremo had his food and drink checked for poison, allowed no one to get closer than six paces and slept in a different bed every night.

By the early 1860s Francia's successor, Carlos Antonio López, ended Paraguay's isolation by building railroads, a telegraph system, a shipyard and a formidable army. His megalomaniac son, Francisco Solano López, succeeded him and declared war simultaneously on Argentina, Brazil and Uruguay in 1865. This disastrous War of the Triple Alliance proved to be one of the bloodiest and most savage in Latin American history. Allied forces outnumbered Paraguayans 10 to one, and by the end of the campaign boys as young as 12 years old were fighting on the front lines. In five years Paraguay had lost half of its prewar population and 26% of its national territory.

In the early 1900s tensions arose with Bolivia over the ill-defined Chaco border and in

1932 full-scale hostilities erupted. The exact reasons for the Chaco War are uncertain, but Bolivia's new desire for a sea port (via the Río Paraguay) and rumors of petroleum deposits in the area were likely factors. The tenacity and guerrilla tactics of Paraguayan troops overcame Bolivia's numerically stronger forces and the Paraguayans made it as far as the lower slopes of the Andes. A 1935 cease-fire left no clear victor but more than 80,000 dead. A treaty awarded Paraguay three-quarters of the disputed territory.

After the Chaco War, Paraguay endured a decade of disorder before a brief civil war brought the Colorado party to power in 1949. A 1954 coup installed General Alfredo Stroessner, whose brutal 35-year, military-dominated rule was characterized by repression and terror. Political opponents, real or imagined, were persecuted, tortured and 'disappeared,' elections were fraudulent, corruption became institutionalized and the country became a safe haven for Nazis and other international criminals. By the time Stroessner was overthrown, 75% of Paraguayans had known no other leader.

Even today the Colorado party maintains political control despite having provided nothing but miscreant leaders who've benefited from economic corruption, been thrown in jail and sought asylum in Brazil. In 2001 ex-Central Bank official Luis Ángel González Macchi, who was caught embezzling millions of dollars, was appointed caretaker president.

In April 2003 Nicanor Duarte Frutos, another Colorado party member, won the presidential election with 37%, lower than any other past party member. The ex-journalist claimed he'd 'break the stronghold of the elite' while dogmatically claiming to be 'the one who directs.' While the country's economy is making marginal improvements only, he's facing tough challenges and is becoming increasingly controversial.

THE CULTURE
The National Psyche
Paraguayans proudly speak at least two languages, boast about their beef and *fútbol* (soccer) teams, and accept that they live in the most bribe-hungry country outside of Africa. Paraguay is saturated with corruption; its people (and politicians) know it, live with it and, often (in the past at least), die by it. It's no wonder Paraguayans prefer to focus on the strength of their *fútbol* teams and the quality of their beef when it comes to comparing themselves to their neighbors, especially Argentina.

Don't let the headlines fool you. Paraguayans are famously laid-back. Sipping *tereré* in the 40°C shade while shooting the breeze, interrupted only by a passing horse-drawn cart, takes the better part of a day. Paraguayans are rightly renowned for their warmth and hospitality.

Lifestyle
Paraguay is the second-poorest South American country (after Bolivia) with 32% living below the poverty line and some 16% of the population's 6,506,464 people unemployed. However, it's not uncommon to see souped-up Mercedes Benz' whizzing around town. Aside from the shacks inhabited by subsistence farmers, and the ultra-well-to-do, most Paraguayan homes are somewhere between semimodern two-story affairs and crumbling colonial mansions. Nothing is more contrasting than the wealth and poverty in Asunción.

The disparity between the lifestyle of Guaraní cotton-pickers and prosperous Mennonite landowners is enormous. Living side by side, the less conservative of the Mennonites enjoy German-made appliances and new trucks,

THE POMBERO
Guaraní folklore has many mythological figures, but none is so fun and prominent as the Pombero. This mischievous little imp-like creature is said to be muscular, short and hairy and comes out at night (the Guaraní translation of Karai Phyahre means Lord of the Night). His presence is used to explain anything from strange sounds and missing items, to unexplained misfortunes, such as a child tripping over, or a woman's skirt blowing up. It is said that he seduces (some say rape) women. Despite his nocturnal habits, adults often use his 'existence' as a warning to children not to wander, especially during siesta. It is believed that the only way of appeasing or befriending the Pombero is to leave gifts out for him, such as rum, tobacco leaves or a sweet surprise.

while their counterparts live hand to mouth, sleeping in semipermanent shacks.

The Paraguayan siesta is the most infectious slice of Paraguayan life. Even the disciplined Mennonites have adopted the afternoon break, albeit limited by loud horns reminding workers to get back on the job. In some communities the siesta may extend from noon to sunset, making the early morning and dusk the busiest times of day.

Population

Some 95% of Paraguayans are considered *mestizos* – most speak Guaraní as their first preference and Spanish as their second choice. The remaining 5% are descendants of European immigrants, including Mennonite farmers, as well as indigenous tribes mostly living in the Chaco. Small but notable Asian, Arab and Brazilian communities are found, particularly in the southeast of the country.

More than 95% of the population lives in eastern Paraguay, only half in urban areas. The government reports a literacy rate of 94%, an infant mortality rate of 2.5% and an average life expectancy of 75.1 years. Some 37.7% of the population is under 15 years old.

SPORTS

Paraguayans are *fútbol*-mad. It's not uncommon to see large groups of men crowded around the *pancho* (hot dog) stand watching the Copa Libertadores on a communal TV. The most popular teams, Olimpia and Cerro Porteño, often beat the best Argentine sides. Tennis, basketball, volleyball, hunting and fishing are also popular.

RELIGION

Ninety percent of the population claims to be Roman Catholic, but folk variants are common. Most indigenous peoples have retained their religious beliefs, or modified them only slightly, despite nominal allegiance to Catholicism or evangelical Protestantism.

ARTS

As many intellectuals and artists will tell you, the Government gives little funding to the arts. Many artists, musicians and painters have left the country to perform or work elsewhere. Nevertheless, the country boasts some well-known figures.

Paraguay's major literary figures are poet-critic and writer Josefina Plá and poet-novelist Augusto Roa Bastos – winner of the 1990 Cervantes Prize (he died in 2005 aged 87). Despite many years in exile, Bastos focused on Paraguayan themes and history drawing from personal experience. For example, *Son of Man* is a novel tying together several episodes in Paraguayan history, including the Francia dictatorship and the Chaco War. Contemporary writers include Nila López, poet Jacobo A Rauskin, Luis María Martínez, Ramón Silva Ruque Vallejos, Delfina Acosta and Susy Delgado. (Interested travelers should visit Cafe Literario in Asunción, p802, for a summary and brief run-down – printed on the menus!)

Roland Joffe's 1986 epic film the *Mission* is a must-see even if you're not a Jesuit buff.

Theater is popular in Asunción, with occasional offerings in Guaraní as well as Spanish. Numerous art galleries emphasize modern, sometimes very unconventional artworks.

Paraguayan music is entirely European in origin. The most popular instruments are the guitar and the harp, while traditional dances include the lively *polkas galopadas* and the *danza de la botella,* with dancers balancing bottles on their heads.

ENVIRONMENT
The Land

The country is divided into two distinct regions, east and west of the Río Paraguay. The east is a well-watered plateau of savanna grasslands with patches of subtropical forest that extends to the Río Paraná (borders with Brazil and Argentina). The west is the Gran Chaco, a marshy bird habitat near Río Paraguay and a dusty, thorny forest further northwest toward Bolivia.

Wildlife

Wildlife is diverse, but the dense rural population is pressuring southeastern Paraguay's fauna. Mammals in danger of extinction include giant anteaters, giant armadillos, maned wolves, river otters, Brazilian tapirs, jaguars, pampas deer and marsh deer. One modest but notable wildlife success has been the rediscovery in the mid-1970s of the Chacoan peccary, which was thought to be extinct for at least half a century, and its nurture by conservationists.

Bird life is abundant, especially in the Chaco. Paraguay has 365 bird species, including 21 species of parrots and parakeets, jabiru and wood storks, plumed ibis and waterfowl, among many others. Many reptiles, including caimans and anacondas, inhabit the riverine lowlands.

National Parks

Even the Secretaria del Medio Ambiente (Secretariat of the Environment, SEAM) is a little vague as to how many official national parks it has. At last count there are 24 officially declared parks and several other reserves protecting a variety of habitats. Few of these have infrastructure for camping, but you can enter several for day visits and hiking.

The five covered in this edition:

- Cerro Corá (p813)
- Defensores del Chaco (p815)
- Parque Nacional Teniente Agripino Enciso (p815)
- Médeanos del Chaco (p815)
- Ybycuí (p808)

Because of corruption, economic pressure and traditionally weak political will, park development is constantly disrupted. With every new politician a totally new team and name for the national park management arrives. Thus, the parks depend heavily on outside funding and guidance from nonprofit organizations like the Nature Conservancy.

The bodies responsible for the maintenance of national parks and ecotourism are **SEAM** (☎ 021-615812; www.seam.gov.py; Av Madame Lynch 3500, Asunción; ⌚ 7am-1pm Mon-Fri) and **Secretaria Nacional de Turismo** (Senatur; Map pp798-9; ☎ 021-494110; www.senatur.gov.py; Palma 468, Asunción; ⌚ 7am-7pm). Private nature reserves come under the auspices of **Fundación Moisés Bertoni para la Conservación de la Naturaleza** (☎ 021-608740; www.mbertoni.org.py).

Environmental Issues

Like many developing countries, Paraguayans are not known for their environmental awareness; the term 'lax' is being generous. Litter (especially plastic bags) covers just about everything it can be blown over and to – from streets and creeks, to grasslands and even the Chaco.

Much of the eastern rainforest has been logged for cropping, especially soy bean and wheat crops, to the benefit (some say) of the large-scale, wealthy farmers. The construction of the Itaipú hydroelectric plant was not without controversy (see p810).

That said, many people are worried about the future of – and alleged US interest in – the country's natural resources, including the world's largest water reserve under Paraguay, Brazil and Argentina (Acuífero Guaraní).

TRANSPORTATION

GETTING THERE & AWAY

Air

Paraguay's only international airport is in Asunción. Direct international flights from Asunción are limited to neighboring countries: Buenos Aires, Argentina; La Paz and Santa Cruz, Bolivia; São Paulo and Rio de Janeiro, Brazil; Iquique and Santiago, Chile.

Boat

Boats cross into Asunción and Encarnación from Argentina, but immigration procedures are more complicated if entering by boat. With patience and stamina, unofficial river travel from Concepción to Isla Margarita on the Brazilian border is possible. See p812 for details.

Bus

Negotiating Paraguayan borders can be schizophrenic; on the bus, off the bus, on the bus... Ask the driver to stop at immigration (locals don't always need to) and be sure your papers are in order. Note that some bus companies claim to travel further into Brazil than border towns, but actually change buses after crossing the border. See p810 for border crossings into Brazil; p329 for border crossings into Paraguay from Brazil.

GETTING AROUND

Buses dominate transportation with cheap fares and reasonably efficient service. Journeys from the Brazilian or Argentine border to Bolivia (and everywhere in between) take 30 hours or less, depending on the start and end destinations. Boats are used between Asunción and central cities along the Rió Paraguay.

Air

Flights save time but cost more than buses. **Transportes Aéreos Mercosur** (TAM; www.tam.com.py)

DEPARTURE TAX

If flying, anyone who has spent more than 24 hours in the country must pay US$20 (cash only) before boarding.

has daily flights from/to Buenos Aires; Cochabamba and Santa Cruz (Bolivia); Saõ Paolo; and Santiago; as well as Cidade del Este (US$40, 50 minutes). Bolivian carrier LAB shuttles between La Paz, Santa Cruz and Asunción. **Varig** (www.varig.com) has daily flights to Foz de Iguazú, Saõ Paulo and Rio de Janeiro. The recent addition **Brazilian GOL** (www.voegol.com.br) heads to Brasilia and Buenos Aires.

Boat
See p803 for details of boat travel up the Río Paraguay.

Bus
Bus quality varies. No buses go from start to end without picking up someone (or something). *Servicio removido* makes flag stops; *servicio directo* collects passengers only at fixed locations; *común* is a basic bus that stops at fewer locations; *ejecutivo* is a faster, deluxe bus with toilets, a drink service and videos. It's best to travel during the day and always ask for a ticket or receipt. Larger towns have central terminals. Elsewhere companies are within easy walking distance of each other. If you want a choice of seats buy your ticket early. If you want the best price, wait until the driver starts his engine and start bargaining.

Car
Your own wheels come at a cost, but can be worth it if there's a few of you. Flexibility is your main advantage, although buses go most places accessible to a car. **National Car Rental** (☎ 021-492157; www.national.com.py; cnr Yegros 501 & Cerro Corá) in Asunción charges from US$35 per day (excluding insurance and mileage beyond 100km). Better deals are available for longer rentals.

Hitchhiking
Hitching is relatively safe in Paraguay but solo women should exercise caution. You usually won't have to wait very long for a *lleva* (lift), but beware of the afternoon heat and carry water. Most drivers will not ask for any money.

Taxi
Most taxi fares are metered. Drivers legally levy a 30% *recargo* (surcharge) between 10pm and 5am, and on Sunday and holidays.

ASUNCIÓN

☎ 021 / pop1.2 million

It's hard to get your head around Asunción. At heart she is beautiful, with a sprinkling of original colonial and beaux-arts buildings, international cuisine, shady plazas and friendly people. Her more-recent and modern demeanor boasts new, seemingly endless suburbs, ritzy shopping malls and smart nightclubs.

But her sophistication hides blemishes: the Río Paraguay backdrop and its shanty shacks, dengue fever–carrying mosquitoes, diesel-spewing buses, stark utilitarian architecture and oppressive heat and humidity.

Like a vain woman hiding her age but succumbing to middle-age spread, Asunción claims to have 1.2 million people, yet seems to hold many more – her sprawling suburbs have joined with neighboring towns. Despite her flaws, she's well worth getting to know.

ORIENTATION
Asunción's riverside location and the haphazard growth in the 19th and 20th centuries has created irregularities in the conventional grid, centered on Plaza de los Héroes. Names of east-west streets change at Independencia Nacional. North, along the riverfront, Plaza Constitución contains the Palacio Legislativo. Below the bluff and subject to flooding sprawl *viviendas temporarias,* Asunción's shantytowns. Much of the action, including more upmarket accommodation options and glitzy shopping areas, now takes place in the smarter suburbs to the east of the center.

INFORMATION
Bookstores
Books SRL (Villa Mora shopping center, Av Mariscal López 3971) New English-language books and magazines.
Guarani Raity (www.quanta.net.py/guarani; Las Perlas 3562) Books in and about Guaraní.

Cultural Centers
Asunción's international cultural centers offer reading material, films, art exhibitions and cultural events at little or no cost.
Alianza Francesa (☎ 210382; Mariscal Estigarribia 1039)
Centro Cultural de España Juan de Salazar (☎ 449221; Tacuary 745)
Centro Cultural Paraguayo-Americano (☎ 224831; Av España 352)

Centro Cultural Paraguayo Japones (☎ 607276; cnr Av Julio Correa & Domingo Portillo)
Instituto Cultural Paraguayo Alemán (☎ 226242; Juan de Salazar 310)

Emergency
Fire Department (☎ 131)
Medical Emergency (☎ 204800)
Police (☎ 911)

Internet Access
Numerous *locutorios* (small telephone offices) offer decent internet access for around US$1 per hour.
Cyber SPC (Chile 862) Cool, clean and friendly.
Cyberking (cnr Oliva & 14 de Mayo) Convenient and reliable.

Laundry
Most laundries charge around US$1.25 per kg; others charge per piece or per basket.
Lavabien (Hernandarias 636) Drop-off and self-service. US$2.70 per basket.
Lavandería Shalom (15 de Agosto 230) US$1.80 per basket for good ol' wash and dry.

Maps
Most maps in Paraguay don't have a scale and are out of date, but Senatur sells a road map (US$4) and a 'political map' (US$3.20).

Medical Services
Hospital Bautista (☎ 600171; Av Rep Argentina) Recommended private hospital.
Hospital Privado Francés (☎ 295250; Av Brasilia 1194) Better services than the Hospital Central.

Money
Northeast of Plaza de los Héroes *casas de cambio* (foreign currency exchange houses) crowd Palma and side streets. Moneychangers on the 2nd floor of the bus terminal give acceptable rates.

Banco Sudameris (cnr Cerro Corá & Independencia) Twenty-four-hour ATM.
Inter-Express (☎ 440613; Yegros 690) The American Express representative. Note: they don't change traveler's checks, but replace stolen cards, checks etc.
Lloyds Bank (cnr Palma & Juan O'Leary) Twenty-four-hour ATM.

Post & Telephone
Copaco (cnr Oliva & 15 de Agosto; ⏱ 8am-10pm) Paraguay's main telephone company (previously known as Antelco). Can make local and long distance calls.
Main post office (cnr Alberdi & Paraguayo Independiente; ⏱ 7am-7pm Mon-Fri)

Tourist Information
Secretaria del Medio Ambiente (SEAM; ☎ 615812; Av Madame Lynch 3500; ⏱ 7am-1pm Mon-Fri) Has the only reliable national park information. The office is reachable via bus 44A from Oliva and takes at least 20 minutes. Rides with rangers to hard-to-reach parks are occasionally available.
Secretaria Nacional de Turismo (Senatur; ☎ 494110; www.senatur.gov.py; Palma 468; ⏱ 7am-7pm) Extremely friendly but best to be specific about what you require. Excellent website.

DANGERS & ANNOYANCES
Consider insect repellent a new cologne because dengue fever is a problem in Asunción. Muggings have been known to happen even in broad daylight so keep your pockets light. Police call the area between Palma and Río Paraguay the 'Zona Roja,' meaning don't schedule a predawn stroll there. Be aware of wandering on public holidays and Sundays when the city is deserted in many places; travelers have reported muggings.

SIGHTS
Everyone's favorite, **Museo del Barro** (☎ 607996; Grabadores del Cabichui s/n; admission US90¢; ⏱ 8am-6pm Thu-Sun), is east of the center in a slick modern neighborhood. It displays everything from modern paintings to pre-Columbian and indigenous crafts to political caricatures of prominent Paraguayans. Take bus 30 from Oliva and alight at Av Molas López; the museum is to the south off Callejón Cañada in a contemporary building.

The free anthropological and archaeological **Museo Etnográfico Andrés Barbero** (☎ 441696; Av España 217; admission free; ⏱ 8am-5:30pm Mon-Fri) displays indigenous tools, ceramics and weavings, plus superb photographs and maps showing where each item comes from.

PARAGUAY

DOWNTOWN ASUNCIÓN

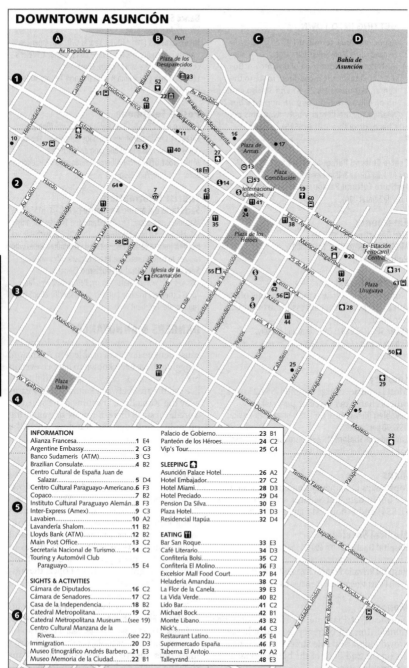

PARAGUAY

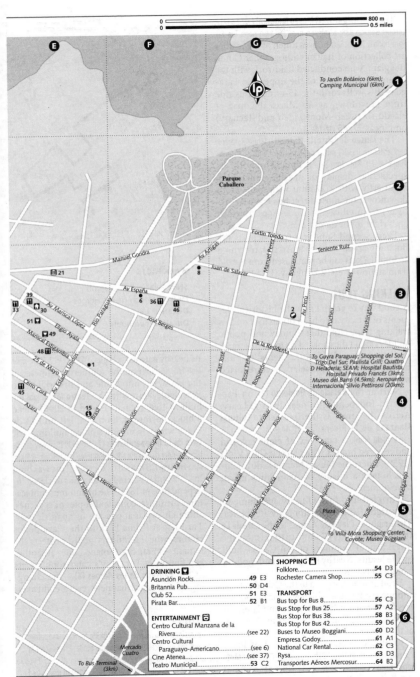

PARAGUAY

The well-organized **Museo Boggiani** (☎ 584717; Coronel Bogado 888; admission free; ⌚ 8am-noon Tue-Fri, 9am-noon & 3-6pm Sat) houses much of the feather art collection of Italian ethnographer Guido Boggiani, who conducted fieldwork with the Chamacoco Indians of the upper Río Paraguay. It's well worth the 45-minute bus ride from downtown at Av Mariscal López at Haedo (between Montevideo and Tacuary) on Líneas 27, 45 or 19.

The **Museo de Historia Natural** (Jardín Botánico; park entrance US30¢; museum admission US40¢; ⌚ 8am-4pm Mon-Fri, 8am-1pm Sat) is notable only for its spectacular display of insects – including a butterfly with a 274mm wingspan. From downtown, the most direct bus is 44-B ('Artigas') from Oliva and 15 de Agosto, which goes right to the gates.

Every second Sunday a train departs the Botanic Gardens (10am) to Areguá, returning at 5pm. Tickets can be purchased from the old train station at Plaza Uruguay (US$20).

WALKING TOUR

A good way to get to know the historical elements of the city is to head off on foot on this walking tour. Note that Sunday and public holidays aren't the choice days to do this trail – the center is as dead as the sights' colonial protagonists – and travelers have reported muggings.

Start at the **Palacio de Gobierno (1)**, on Paraguayo Independiente near Juan O'Leary. Across the street is the free **Centro Cultural Manzana de la Rivera** (2; ☎ 442448; Ayolas 129; ⌚ 8:50am-5pm), a complex of eight colorful and restored houses. The oldest is Casa Viola (1750), where the Museo Memoria de la Ciudad houses a history of Asunción's urban development.

Turn left into Juan O'Leary and immediately right (southeast) along Av Republica. Turn right at Plaza de Armas to the **Casa de La Cultura (3)**. From 1767 until 1810 this was the Royal School Seminary of San Carlos, built by the Jesuits. Nearby is the new and modern Congreso Nacional.

Head around the plaza to the Cabildo **(4)**, an antique Jesuit house which was the headquarters for the Spanish Governors and later, for the dictator, Dr Francia. It is now the Museum of the Congreso Nacional.

Continue to the southeast end of Plaza Constitución to the 19th-century **Catedral Metropolitana (5**; admission free; ⌚ 11-11:30am Mon-Fri) and

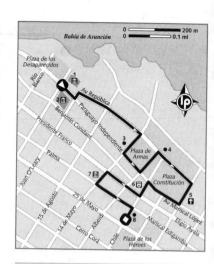

WALK FACTS

Start Palacio de Gobierno
Finish Panteón de los Héroes
Distance 1.8km
Duration two hours

its nearby **museum** (admission US70¢; ⌚ 7:30am-noon Mon-Fri). Return on the southern perimeter of the plaza, left into Chile and first right into Presidente Franco to the **Teatro Municipal (6)**, built in 1889 (reinaugurated in 2006). Head a block northwest, then turn left into 14 de Mayo where Asunción's oldest building, the **Casa de la Independencia (7**; ☎ 493918; www.casadelaindependencia.org.py; admission free; ⌚ 7:30am-6:30pm Mon-Fri, 8am-12:30pm Sat), is located. This was built in 1772 and is where Paraguayans declared independence in 1811. The quaint museum features furniture, coins and copies of speeches, although explanations are in Spanish only. Turn left at Palma back to the Plaza de los Héroes, where a military guard protects the remains of Francisco Solano López and other key figures of Paraguay's catastrophic wars in the **Panteón de los Héroes (8)** – the changing of the guard happens every eight days at 10am.

TOURS

Fransisco Camacho (☎ 370835; francam@supernet .com.py) An excellent multilingual guide. Prices start at around US$100 per day, but it's worth considering if you're short of time. Can help with accommodation if required.

Guyra Paraguay (☎ 227777; Comandante Franco 281) Organizes monthly bird-watching trips with English-speaking guides.

Vip's Tour (☎ 441199; www.vipstour.com.py; cnr México 782 & Moreno) Organizes a smorgasbord of day trips from US$15 to US$200 (minimum two people).

SLEEPING

Plenty of cheap, acceptable(ish) crash-pads clutter the chaotic area around the bus terminal for around US$5. If you're spending more than one night in town, hop on a local bus headed to the 'Centro,' where you'll find many affordable, clean but worn options. Accommodations are slightly more expensive in Asunción than the rest of the country but won't bust anyone's budget.

Camping Municipal (Jardín Botánico; campsites US$1.50) Shady, friendly and secure with ferocious ants and mosquitoes (don't go without repellent). It's 5km northeast of downtown in the botanical garden; take bus 44-B ('Artigas') or 35 from Oliva.

Pension Da Silva (☎ 446381; Eligio Ayala 843; per person US$6) *The* pick for value, convenience and hospitality. A family-run house with an indoor-outdoor colonial ambience. The exquisite exterior doesn't have signage – ring the bell.

Hotel Embajador (☎ 493393; Presidente Franco 514; s/d US$7/10) Rough and faded but with some character and barely passable rooms; the high ceilings are indeed the highlight.

Residencial Itapúa (☎ 445121; Moreno 943; per person US$10) Another signless *residencial* (budget accommodations) in an unlikely neocolonial brick building. It's flowery and worn with a variety of rooms, some with fans.

Hotel Miami (☎ 444950; México 449; s/d US$13.50/19; 🖧) A very bland hospital-type hallway, but it's clean and has a security door. Helpful, friendly staff. Popular among local wedding parties so book ahead.

Plaza Hotel (☎ 444772; www.plazahotel.com.py; Eligio Ayala 609; s/d US$16/25; 🖧) On Plaza Uruguaya, this modernized and reliable hotel is great value with a basic buffet breakfast but stiff mattresses.

Trigo del Sur (☎ 602389; Mayor Infante Rivarola 653; s/d US$25/35; 🖧) Not the most Paraguayan of experiences, this British B&B–style place is perfect if that's what you're after.

Hotel Preciado (☎ 447661; Azara 840; s/d US$27/33; 🅿 🖧 🖧) This modern number has air-con and a pool – but also a reputation for being a liberal facility. If its nightly rhythms (and we're not talking sleep patterns here) are not up your alley, think again.

Asunción Palace Hotel (☎ 492151; www.geocities.com; Av Colón 415; s/d with breakfast US$30/40; 🖧) There's everything but the Spanish colonel. The colonial atmosphere creates a wonderful ambience of bygone days – pity about the ubiquitous '80s-style decor. Be careful at night – it's on the dodgy edge of town.

EATING

Asunción's food is reflected in it's diverse cultures: sophisticated local, Asian and international foods abound and vegetarians are catered for. Everything from *surubial ajo* (garlic catfish) and Korean *kim chi* (Korean-style pickled vegetables) to night-time under-a-buck *panchos* (hot dogs) and burgers are available around the city center and beyond. Supermarkets are well stocked. On Sundays it's best to head to one of the large shopping centers such as **Mariscal Lopez** (cnr Qiesada 5050 & Charles de Gaulle; 🕑 9am-10pm) or **Shopping del Sol** (cnr Aviadores del Chaco & Prof González; 🕑 9am-10pm).

City Center

Excellent cheap Korean fare can be found on and around Av Pettirossi between Av Peru and Curupayty, or try the *asadito* (roasted meat on a stick with mandioca) stands (US90¢) on street corners.

Michael Bock (Presidente Franco 820; snacks US50¢-$2) An excellent German bakery with excellent German goods.

Monte Libano (Estrella near 14 de Mayo; swami US$1.20) Wrap your laughing gear around these luscious Lebanese *swamis* (meat and cheese wrapped in Lebanese bread). A Peace Corps paradise.

Excelsior Mall Food Court (Chile near Manduvirá; mains US$1.50-3) Open when most restaurants are not (like Sunday evening), the air-conditioned upstairs food court offers fast-food versions of various ethnic cuisines.

Lido Bar (cnr Chile & Palma; mains US$2-5) A diner-style local favorite, with sidewalk seating opposite the Pantheon, that serves a variety of Paraguayan specialties (excellent *sopa paraguaya* – cornbread with cheese and onion) in generous portions for breakfast and lunch.

Confitería Bolsi (Estrella 399; mains US$2.80-5.30) More than a *confitería*, this traditional place (it's been going since 1960) serves everything from sandwiches to curried rabbit and garlic pizza. Try the *surubí casa nostra* (a superb selection of different pasta types and flavors on one dish).

La Vida Verde (Palma; per kilo US$3.50) Assess your mood by one of the 32 quirkily sculptured emotional 'faces' on the wall – 'satisfied' is how you'll feel after this eating experience. A delicious daily buffet of Chinese vegetarian delights (although they bend the rules a bit).

Taberna Española (☎ 441743; Ayolas 631; lunch US$4.50, dinner US$7) The energetic ambience of this 'food museum' with dangling bottles, cooking implements and bells is only the backdrop for good-value Spanish set-price meals.

Near Plaza Uraguaya

Confitería El Molino (Av España 382; snacks US$1-2; ☒ 7am-9pm) With bow-tied waiters and gourmet-style pastries and biscuits, this is one of the sweetest *confiterías* around. Great for *minutas* (short orders), snacks and excellent *licuados* (blended fruit drinks).

Café Literario (cnr Mariscal Estigarribia & México; ☒ 4-10pm) Cool air, music, books (of course) and all that jazz. This artsy, comfy café-bookstore is a great place to read, write or imbibe. Excellent *café con lechés* (coffee with milk; US$1.80).

La Flor de Canela (☎ 498928; Tacuary 167; mains US$3-9) The food is more genuine than this smart place's faux Inca sculptures. A safe choice if craving *ceviche* (marinated, raw seafood).

Talleyrand (☎ 441163; Mariscal Estigarribia 932; mains US$6.90-9) International *haute cuisine* for people with their noses *haute* in the air. Lovely food, lovely white cloths, lovely prices.

Supermercado España (cnr Av España & Brasil) Stocked with everything from colored flip-flops to bulk peanuts to chocolate bars, this chain is a good place to stock up if you can't make it to the shopping centers.

SPLURGE!

Bar San Roque (☎ 446015; cnr Tacuary & Eligio Ayala; mains US$3.20-8) Head back in time to this restaurant with warm turn-of-the-20th-century atmosphere. Since 1905 this fine family has been serving out-of-this-world traditional Paraguayan dishes. The counter displays fresh goods from the family farm – macadamia nuts to fruits – and the wine list is as impressive as the decent menu of pasta to meat dishes. As many locals will attest, a culinary must with service to match.

East of the Center

There are eateries and humming fast food outlets in the main shopping centers including Shopping del Sol and Mariscal Lopez.

Quattro D Heladeria (cnr Av San Martin & Andrade; US$1.20 per scoop) We're not sure what the four Ds stand for in Spanish (or Italian) – but the ice cream here is divine, delightful, delicious and delectable in anyone's language!

Paulista Grill (cnr San Martine & Mariscal Lopez; buffet US$14; ☒ 10am-midnight) Dripping slabs of delicious meat (veggies can have the salad buffet). Popular for those in the more upmarket east, and worth going to if you're in the area.

DRINKING

Bars charge a cover price (more for men!) and can be crowded at weekends. Several late-night hotspots line the 900 blocks of Estigarribia, but most of the flashy clubs are a short cab ride east of downtown on Av Brasilia.

Britannia Pub (Cerro Corá 851; ☒ Wed-Sun) Casually hip with an air-conditioned international ambience and outdoor patio, the 'Brit Pub' is a favorite among foreigners and locals alike.

Asunción Rocks (Mariscal Estigarribia 991; admission US$3; ☒ 10pm-6am) *The* spot for late-night after-parties, but not totally uncool before 1am.

Pirata Bar (cnr Benjamín Constant & Ayolas) Popular, pirate-themed club playing American and English beats.

Mouse Cantina (cnr Patria & Brasilia) This MTV-esque dancehall is ultra-popular among the upper-echelon.

Coyote (cnr S Martinez & Sucre) Starts late, ends late – the latest place for the younger local hip crowd.

ENTERTAINMENT
Cinemas

Downtown cinemas are notorious for showing cheap porn and low-budget action-adventure flicks on reels that rarely make it through a screening. More reliable, though less endearing, are the cinemas of Asunción's shopping malls, such as the four-screen **Cine Atenea** (Excelsior Mall, cnr Manduvirá & Chile; tickets US$2.50) and the **Cinecenter del Sol** (Shopping del Sol, cnr Aviadores del Chaco & Prof González; tickets US$2.50). Check *Tiempo Libre* (a free weekly) for showtimes.

Music & Theater

Asunción has several venues for live music and theater; the major season is March to October. Check *Tiempo Libre* for showtimes.

Centro Cultural Manzana de la Rivera (☎ 442448; Ayolas & Paraguayo Independiente)
Centro Cultural Paraguayo-Americano (☎ 224831; www.ccpa.edu.py; Av España 352)
Teatro Municipal (cnr Alberdi & Presidente Franco) Check the listing outside for showtimes.

SHOPPING

Asunción offers Paraguay's best souvenir shopping – the ground floor of the Senatur tourist office has the best of the best from around the country. Shops along Palma near Av Colón offer everything from digital cameras to leather bags for your *tereré* thermos at reasonable prices. The open-air market at Plaza de los Héroes is stocked with *ao po'i* or *lienzo* (loose-weave cotton) garments and other indigenous crafts. The Mercado Cuatro is a lively trading lot occupying the wedge formed by the intersection of Av Doctor R de Francia and Pettirossi, stretching several blocks.

Folklore (☎ 448 657; Mariscal Estigarribia 397) The place for *ñandutí* (lace), leather goods and *tereré* cups.

Rochester Camera Shop (632 Nuestra Señora de la Asunción) Has an impressive selection of cameras and accessories and offers a one-hour film-processing service.

GETTING THERE & AWAY
Air

Aeropuerto Internacional Silvio Pettirossi (☎ 645600) is in the suburb of Luque, 20km east of Asunción. It's easily reached by buses displaying 'Aeropuerto' signs heading out Av Aviadores del Chaco.

Paraguay's only national airline is **Transportes Aéreos Mercosur** (TAM; ☎ 645500; www.tam.com.py; Oliva 761).

The only scheduled domestic flights within Paraguay are between Asunción and Ciudad del Este (US$40 one way, 50 minutes, daily). Tickets should be reserved and purchased at least one day before.

Direct international flights to and from Asunción and the following cities in neighboring countries are regularly available. Prices are for one-way fares and are subject to change.

Buenos Aires, Argentina US$109 to US$289, four daily.
Santa Cruz, Bolivia US$334, one daily.
Santiago, Chile US$269, one per day Monday, Wednesday, Friday, Saturday and Sunday.
São Paolo, Brasil US$195 to US$304, three daily.

Boat

Several cargo boats take passengers up the Río Paraguay. Two have regular departures from Asunción to Concepción (US$9, 30 hours). Check the changing schedules. At the time of research the *Cacique* departed on Wednesdays at 7am and the *Aguape* every 15 days (check the schedule at Agencia Marítima, ☎ 031-42435). The *Aquidaban* heads on from Concepción to Vallemi (Tuesday around 11am, arriving Wednesday; US$12) and the *Cacique* heads to Vallemi on Thursday mornings (although this can depend on when it arrives from Asunción), arriving in Vallemi on Friday afternoon. The *Aquidaban* heads to Bahía Negra on Saturdays (US$33, 2½ days). You can pay a bit more for a double-occupancy *camarote* (cabin) or hang in your hammock below deck with the other passengers and their unbelievable assortment of cargo – ranging from chickens to motorbikes. *La Filomena* is a more upmarket option with two small *camarotes*. Speak to the owner, **Lilian Paiva** (☎ 031-42000). It's possible for adventurous travelers to float as far as Brazil (see p812).

Bus

Some companies such as Rysa and Empresa Godoy maintain convenient offices on Plaza Uruguaya and around town. Otherwise the bus terminal is the place for tickets. Bus 8 runs downtown along Cerro Corá to the terminal, as does 25 from Av Colón and Oliva, 38 from Haedo, and 42 from Av Doctor R de Francia.

Destination	Duration (hr)	Cost (US$)
Buenos Aires, Argentina	18-21	32-64
Ciudad del Este, Paraguay	4½-6	6.20
Concepción, Paraguay	4½-6	6-8
Cordoba, Argentina	20	35.30-44
Curitiba, Brazil	18-20	26.50
Encarnación, Paraguay	5-6	6.20-12.30
Filadelfia, Paraguay	8	12.30
Foz do Iguaçu, Brazil	6	10.60-12.30
Montevideo, Uruguay	20	62-67
Pedro Juan Caballero, Paraguay	7½	14
Posadas, Argentina	5	9.70
Rio de Janeiro, Brazil	18-22	49.50-53
Santa Cruz, Bolivia	30+	44-53
Santiago, Chile	28	62
São Paulo, Brazil	18-20	44-53

PARAGUAY

GETTING TO ARGENTINA

Crossing into Argentina via launch from Puerto Itá Enramada, southwest of downtown, to Puerto Pilcomayo (Argentina) is possible. Launches leave every half-hour from 7am to 5pm weekdays, and irregularly from 7am to 10am on Saturday. You must visit the office at the port for your exit stamp before you leave Asunción.

GETTING AROUND

The noisy, bone-rattling Kamikaze-like city buses (US40¢) go almost everywhere, but few run after 10pm. Nearly all city buses start their route at the western end of Oliva.

Taxis are metered and reasonable (around US20c per minute), but tack on a surcharge late at night and on Sunday. A taxi to the bus terminal costs about US$5.30.

AROUND ASUNCIÓN

Hop on a rickety and noisy local bus and prepare yourself for a taste of rural and historical Paraguay. Humble communities dominated by colonial buildings observe long siestas, disturbed only by occasional ox- or horse-drawn carts clacking up cobbled streets that extend from or surround the capital city. The tourist industry plugs the area as the 'Circuito Central,' which includes the weaving center of Itauguá, the lakeside resorts of Areguá and San Bernardino, the shrine of **Caacupé** and colonial villages like **Piribebuy** and Yaguarón. You can hire a cab to drive you through the whole circuit (US$40 for up to four people), but you'll get more flavor on the bus (around US$1). The circuit's highlights are described below in order of the author's preference.

SAN BERNARDINO
☎ 0512

Renowned as the elite escape for the privileged of Asunción, tranquil 'San Ber' offers the lot for top relaxation – pubs, discos and upmarket hotels and restaurants line the shady cobbled streets of Lago Ypacaraí's eastern shore. Despite its reputation, there's plenty for budget travelers as well. It's the perfect place to dance the night away with vacationing Asunciónites, or just chill in the shade by the pool. Unfortunately, you won't want to swim in the lake –

it's filthy. In summer a pleasure boat takes passengers for short cruises on the lake (US$9, three people minimum).

Visitor information, including an area map, is available at **Casa Hassler** (☎ 2974; Vache at Hassler).

Travelers rave about the camping and hostal **Brisas Del Mediterraneo** (☎ 232 459; www.campingpara guay.org; ▣),just over 2km from the town center on Ruta Kennedy, with shady trees and perched on the edge of the lake. It offers excellent facilities, suitable for kids of all ages. A more basic – and landlocked – camping option is **Camping Elohim** (☎ 233191; campsites US$2, r per person US$5), a pleasant grassy garden at the back of a family-run shop, 1.5km from San Bernardino. There's good grassy areas for a tent, or a converted (windowless) garage for bed-loving bods. If you can't be bothered walking, catch the bus to Altos or Loma Grande – it's signed on the right-hand side of Camino a Altos.

Hotel Balneario (☎ 232252; Hassler at Asunción; s/d US$11.70/17.50) is overpriced with basic rooms in a great central location. On the lakeside of the plaza is the worn and romantically Victorian **Hotel del Lago** (☎ 232201; cnr Av Carlos Antonio Lopez & Teniente Weiler; s/d incl breakfast US$13.50/23.30; ▣ ▣), full of antique furniture – each room is different. The **Alemana Panadería & Confitería** (Colonos Alemanes below Estigarribia) has basic sandwiches, buttery baked treats, ice cream and a full restaurant upstairs.

From Asunción, Transporte Villa del Lago (bus 210) and Transporte Cordillera de los Andes (bus 103) run frequent buses to San Ber (US70¢, 1½ hours, 48km); ask the driver to drop you near the plaza.

AREGUÁ
☎ 0291

As sweet tranquility goes, this is it. Areguá is renowned for an eclectic mix – strawberries and artisans. The town's main artworks are ceramics, displayed *en masse* along the main street, although these increasingly cater to the contemporary tastes of bright garden gnomes and Disneyesque objects. More tasteful are the cobbled historic streets with exquisite colonial homes, a church perched on the hill, the odd laid-back café, and position by the lake. All this makes for a pleasant leisurely visit, especially on a Sunday, when a tourist train runs (fortnightly) from Asunción (see p800).

Paraguay's renowned sculptor German Guggiary has a studio here. Other contemporary pieces are on sale at El Cántaro on Mariscal Estigarribia, two blocks from the train station.

Accommodations can be found at **Hotel-Restaurant Ozli** (☎ 32389; hotelozli@hotmail.com; Av Mariscal Estigarribia; s/d US$7.80/13.50; 🖨), which is located approximately 50m from the main beach. The rather plain rooms are nothing to write home about but you can sit in a lovely garden, enjoy use of the kitchen, and chat to the friendly owner. Café food is available all day.

YAGUARÓN

Yaguarón's 18th-century **Franciscan church** is a landmark of colonial architecture. The nearby **Museo del Doctor Francia** (admission free; 🕑 7:30am-noon & 2-6pm Mon-Fri) was the first dictator's house and is interesting for its period portraiture and statues.

Across from the church is a nameless restaurant with mediocre food and basic (fairly grotty) accommodations (per person US$5.80). Ciudad Paraguarí bus 193 (US70¢ 1½ hours, 48km, every 15 minutes) departs Asunción from 5am to 8:15pm.

ITAUGUÁ

For the women of Itauguá, weaving multi-colored spiderweb *ñandutí* ('lace' – *nandu* is spider in Guaraní) is a cottage industry from childhood to old age. These exquisite pieces range in size from doilies to bedspreads; smaller ones cost only a few dollars but larger ones range upward of US$50. In July the town celebrates its annual **Festival de Ñandutí**.

The town feels like an extension of Asunción as much is now on Ruta 2. Two blocks south of the highway is the **Museo Parroquial San Rafael** (admission free; 🕑 7am-noon & 3-6pm Mon-Fri). It displays Franciscan and secular relics, and early *ñandutí* samples. From the Asunción bus terminal, buses leave for Itauguá (US50¢, one hour, 30km, every 15 minutes) day and night.

SOUTHERN PARAGUAY

Paraguay's southernmost region – east of the Río Paraguay – is home to some of the country's most important historical sites. The Jesuit ruins, national parks, the largest dam in the world, and one of the continent's busiest

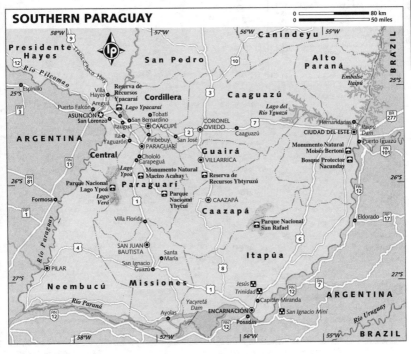

SOUTHERN PARAGUAY

border crossings make this an eclectic and fascinating area to visit.

ENCARNACIÓN

☎ 071 / pop 69,700

Encarnación is a cut-rate shopping center, the heart of the Paraguayan Carnaval and the gateway to the nearby Jesuit ruins at Trinidad and Jesús. The old center used to function on the lower ground near the river. When the nearby Yacyretá Dam was constructed, businesses and offices relocated to higher ground in preparation of the flooding which was (and is yet) to occur. Years later, the sluice gates have not yet been opened. Currently occupying the old town among decaying public

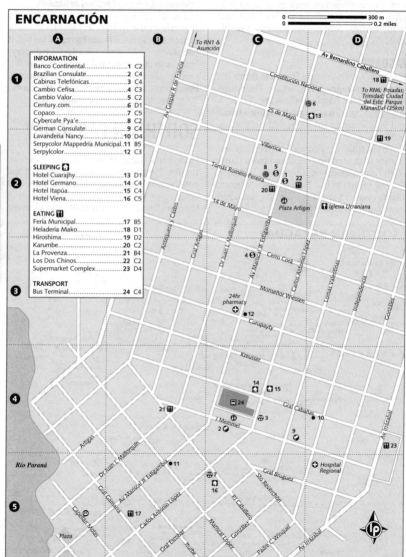

ENCARNACIÓN

0 — 300 m
0 — 0.2 miles

INFORMATION
Banco Continental	1 C2
Brazilian Consulate	2 C4
Cabinas Telefónicas	3 C4
Cambio Cefisa	4 C3
Cambio Valor	5 C2
Century.com	6 D1
Copaco	7 C5
Cybercafe Pya'e	8 C2
German Consulate	9 C4
Lavanderia Nancy	10 D4
Serpycolor Mappedría Municipal	11 B5
Serpycolor	12 C3

SLEEPING
Hotel Cuarajhy	13 D1
Hotel Germano	14 C4
Hotel Itapúa	15 C4
Hotel Viena	16 C5

EATING
Feria Municipal	17 B5
Heladeria Mako	18 D1
Hiroshima	19 D2
Karumbe	20 C2
La Provenza	21 B4
Los Dos Chinos	22 C2
Supermarket Complex	23 D4

TRANSPORT
Bus Terminal	24 C4

To RN1 & Asunción

Av Bernardino Caballero

To RN6; Posadas; Trinidad; Ciudad del Este; Parque Manantial (35km)

Constitución Nacional

25 de Mayo

Villarrica

Tomás Romero Pereira

14 de Mayo

Plaza Artigas

Iglesia Ucraniana

Cerro Corá

Monseñor Wiessen

24hr pharmacy

Curupayty

Kreusser

Gral Cabañas

I Memmel

Artigas

Gral Bruguez

Sto Revechón

Hospital Regional

Río Paraná

Plaza

Av Caspar R de Francia

Antéquera y Castro

Gral Artigas

Dr Juan L Mallorquín

Av Mariscal JF Estigarriba

Carlos Antonio López

Lomas Valentinas

Independencia

Gonzáles

Av Irrazábal

Gral Cándara

Capellán Molas

Carlos Antonio López

Gral Escobar

Iturbe

Mariscal López

Gonzáles

Pl Caballero

Padre C Winquel

Av Irrazábal

buildings is a massive tawdry bazaar. Among the chaos is the Fería Municipal market, great for a cheap eat. On higher ground, the pleasant and functional modern town has excellent shops, a pleasant plaza and modern facilities.

Information

INTERNET ACCESS
Many internet places are in Av Mariscal JF Estigarribia between Constitución Nacional and 25 de Mayo.

Century.com (Av Mariscal JF Estigarribia btwn Constitución Nacional & 25 de Mayo; per hr US60¢; 7am-12:30am)

Cybercafé Pya'e (Tomás Romero Pereira; per hr US70¢; 8am-midnight;)

LAUNDRY
Lavanderia Nancy (Gral Cabans near Lomas Valentinas) Will get the mud from your seams in less than 24 hours.

MONEY
Several banks, including Banco Continental, are on or near Plaza Artigas and have 24-hour ATMs.

The following moneychangers are recommended for swapping currencies.

Cambio Cefisa (cnr Cerro Corá & Av Mariscal JF Estigarribia)

Cambio Valor (Av Mariscal JF Estigarribia 1405) Changes traveler's checks.

TELEPHONE
Cabinas Telefónicas (Carlos Antonio López 810; 7am-10pm) Across from the bus terminal.

Copaco (cnr PJ Caballero & Carlos Antonio López; 7am-10pm)

TOURIST OFFICES
City maps (but little else) are available at the tourist office, located at the immigration office at the border.

Sleeping
There are plenty of clean, reasonably priced places to choose from in Encarnación.

Parque Manantial (075-32250; entry US$1.80, camping US$1.80, pool per day US$1.80;) On Ruta 6, 35km out of Encarnacion near Hohenau is this camping paradise. If you can avoid the weekend (touristic) crowds, you'll have to yourself the 200 hectares with swimming pools and forested walking tracks. Horseriding (US$6.20 per hour) is available. Jump

on any bus heading to Ciudad del Este or Hohenau. From the sign it's another 500m. An excellent base for the Jesuit ruins.

Hotel Itapúa (205045; Carlos Antonio López 814; s/d US$3/4;) For cheap digs try the large and impersonal Hotel Itapúa.

Hotel Viena (205981; PJ Caballero 568; per person US$4;) Delightful colonial verandah–styled place with the simplest of simple rooms.

Hotel Germano (203346; cnr Gral Cabañas & Carlos Antonio López; per person with/without bathroom US$8/4;) Across from the bus terminal, Hotel Germano is neater than a Japanese origami figure. The best value in town with spotless rooms and helpful staff and a favorite with the Peace Corps.

Hotel Cuarajhy (202155; 25 de Mayo 415; per person US$10;) Smells like a courtesan's perfume parlor and feels a bit like a hospital, but central and friendly with a pizzeria below.

Eating
Encarnación has some of the best eats in Paraguay. Budget meals are available around the bus terminal anytime, in the Fería Municipal for lunch and at night around Plaza Artigas.

Los Dos Chinos (Tomás Romero Pereiras; 2 flavors US50¢) A top delight that Italians would drool over.

Heladeria Mako (cnr Lomas Valentinas & Av Bernadino Caballero) Delicious pastry delights (go at midday when they're fresh), great coffee and magazines make this well worth the trek uptown.

Hiroshima (203505; cnr 25 de Mayo & Lomas Valentinas; set lunch US$3, mains US$1.80-9.50) This signless Japanese community center is deservedly a local favorite – unbelievable udon and top tofu dishes. Food fit for a Japanese Crown Prince.

Karumbe (cnr Av Mariscal JF Estigarribia & Tomás Romero Pereira; meals US$3-5) Popular with the locals for a drink and a good indulgence – from pasta to meat dishes.

La Provenza (204618; Dr Juan L Mallorquín 609; mains US$3.50-5.25) A more upmarket and international eatery on the edge of the older part of town.

An excellent unnamed hole-in-the-wall eatery is located near the corner of Av Mariscal JF Estigarribia and Kreussel. It looks more like a lounge room than a café, but serves up cheap Korean and Japanese fare (US$3.50).

You can stock up with goodies at the huge supermarket complex located on Av Irrazábal and J Memmel.

GETTING TO ARGENTINA

Local Servicio International buses (US50¢) cross to Posadas in Argentina via the Puente San Roque. You must get off the bus at the border immigration offices at both ends of the bridge for exit and entry stamps. Buses don't always wait – take your pack and keep your ticket to catch the next one.

Although launches (US50¢) cross the Río Paraná to/from Posadas, there are no immigration procedures on this route; don't risk the Paraguayan authorities, fines and paperwork. For information on travel from Argentina to Encarnación, see p88.

Getting There & Away

Frequent buses run from Encarnación to Asunción (US$8 to US$12, five hours) and Ciudad del Este (US$6.20 to US$6, four hours).

TRINIDAD & JESÚS

Set atop a lush green hill northeast of Encarnación, **Trinidad** (admission US90¢; ⏰ 7am-7pm summer, 7am-5:30pm winter) is Paraguay's best-preserved Jesuit *reducción* (settlement). Although it has been a Unesco World Heritage site since 1993, travelers shouldn't expect the usual information and conveniences. The closest bathrooms are in the nearby Hotel León, where meals, refreshments and spacious rooms with bathroom (s/d US$5/7) are available. Camping (US$1) is also possible outside the ruins.

Easily accessible **Jesús** (admission 90¢; ⏰ 8am-6pm), 12km north, is the nearly complete reconstruction of the Jesuit mission that was interrupted by the Jesuit's expulsion in 1767. Especially trained and excellent local guides speak English, German and Spanish and are for hire for a donation (US$5 to US$7 per hour is fair).

From Encarnación, frequent buses go to Trinidad (US$1, 28km) between 6am and 7pm, but any bus headed east along Ruta 6 to Ciudad del Este or Hohenau will drop you off there. Although there is the odd direct bus to Jesús from Asunción (ask at the terminal), it's easier to catch a bus to Trinidad. Walk 80m to the crossroads – you'll see the sign to Jesús and wait for the Jesús–Obligado bus which passes hourly (US70¢). It will drop you at the ruin's entrance.

PARQUE NACIONAL YBYCUÍ

This popular and beautiful national park preserves one of eastern Paraguay's last stands of Brazilian subtropical rainforest. It has steep hills dissected by creeks with attractive waterfalls and pools. The dense forest hides the animals, but if you're lucky you'll get a sneak peak at the stunningly colorful butterflies, including the metallic blue Morpho.

The entrance-cum-**visitors center** (⏰ 7am-4pm) is 25km from Ybycuí village. The **Salto Guaraní** waterfall is near the **campground** (campsites per person US$1), which has showers and bothersome insects; bring your own food. Below it, a bridge leads to a pleasant creekside trail with a wealth of butterflies, but watch for snakes (although to date no-one has been bitten). The trail continues to **La Rosada**, an interesting iron foundry destroyed by Brazilian forces in the War of the Triple Alliance. Check out the well-organized **museum** (admission free). Longer hikes head to some stunning waterfalls, including **Salta Mbocaruzu** (4km). There are spare rooms in the rangers' house below the campground, if camping ain't to your liking.

In Ybycuí village, 30km from the park, **Hotel Pytu'u Renda** (☎ 0534-364; Av Quyquyho s/n; r per person US$7) has decent rooms and a restaurant.

Empresa Salto Cristal has hourly buses from Asunción to Ybycuí village (US$2, three hours) from 4am to 6pm. Unfortunately, it is not possible to do return day trips to the park via bus. Buses leaves for the park at 10:15am, 11am and 2pm each day from the Ybycuí terminal on Monday to Saturday, but don't return again until the following morning at 7:30am and 8am. (The schedules tend to be a moveable feast – check at the bus station.) An alternative is to arrange a return trip with a taxi.

CIUDAD DEL ESTE

☎ 061 / pop 223,350

You-name-it-they-got-it. The central streets of Ciudad del Este are like a giant, tacky electronic city market. Originally named after the former dictator, the town struggles to shake off its reputation as one of South America's most corrupt cities. The busy border crossing can seem intimidating, but authorities are clamping down on the human pack-horses who hump suspicious boxes across the international bridge. Away from the area of cheap electronic goods, cigarettes and liquor, the city is pleasant enough with some excellent eateries if nothing else.

Orientation

On the west bank of the Río Paraná, across the Puente de Amistad from Foz do Iguaçu, the downtown area of Ciudad del Este is compact and easily managed on foot.

Information

INTERNET ACCESS

Cibertronic Compacom (cnr Avs de los Pioneros & Adrián Jara; per hr US$1) Slow connections. Also has telephones.

LAUNDRY

Lavandería (Camilo Recaldo s/n, near Capitán Miranda) It will clean 'em how you need 'em.

MONEY

Street moneychangers lounge around the Pioneros de Este rotunda.

ABN AMRO (cnr Av Adrián Jara & Nanqwa) ATM.

Banco Sudameris (cnr Av Monseñor Rodríguez & Curupayty) Also changes currency.

POST

Post office (cnr Av de los Pioneros & Oscar Rivas Ortellado) Across from the bus terminal.

TELEPHONE

Copaco (cnr Av de los Pioneros & Paí Pérez)

Tele Hola (Capitan Miranda s/n)

TOURIST OFFICE

Tourist office (☎ 508688; cnr Av Bernardino Caballero & Rogelio R Benitz) In the Ministry of Alto Paraná (sign the book at the front and ask to be directed). It claims to be opening an information kiosk next to the supermarket Arco Iris (corner Av de los Pioneros and Av Adrián Jara).

Sleeping

Ciudad's midrange places are definitely worth the extra couple of bucks, especially once you sample the mega-value breakfast buffets, which are included in the price.

Hotel Tía Nancy (☎ 502974; cnr Garcete & Cruz del Chaco; s/d/tr US$8/11.70/14) Near the bus terminal, this friendly place has dark rooms but is perfectly adequate for a tranquil transit stop.

Hotel Caribe (☎ 512460; Emiliano R Fernández s/n; s/d US$10/13.50; ❄) A bit of grit for the gritty budget traveler.

Hotel Mi Abuela (☎ 500348; Av Adrián Jara; s/d US$13/18) Not exactly your grandmother's house, in an '80s-style building, with dark

PARAGUAY

rooms around a small courtyard. Central location.

Hotel Munich (☎ 500347; Emiliano R Fernández 71; s/d US$15.50/19.50; 🐾) Enthusiastically recommended for its comfortable and spacious rooms with cable TV. Helpful owner will give you the rundown.

Hotel Austria (☎ 504213; www.hotelrestaurante austria.com; Emiliano R Fernández 165; s/d US$18/21.20; 🐾) Like its neighbor Hotel Munich, this is another clean European number with more floors, bigger baths and bigger prices.

Eating

The cheapest options are the stalls along Capitán Miranda and Av Monseñor Rodriguez. Otherwise, Asian-cuisine fans dig in.

Bovolo (Av Boquerón 148; US$2-4) Follow your nose to this delicious place for coffee and freshly baked biscuits.

New Tokio (cnr Av de los Pioneros & Av Adrián Jara) Come hungry and pile your plate for US$2.70 per kilo. It's on the mezzanine of the Arco Iris supermarket.

Kokorelia (Av Boquerón 169; mains US$4-12) Fresh and good if you're cravin' Asian.

Hotel Austria (☎ 500883; Emiliano R Fernández 165; mains US$5) In line with the hotel, these European plates ain't skimpy. Good hearty fare.

Lebanon (cnr Av Adrián Jara & Abay, Edifico Salah I, 2nd fl; mains US$5-10) For something more exotic and upscale, Lebanon serves scrumptious Middle Eastern fare for lunches only. Half portions available.

Arco Iris (cnr Av de los Pioneros & Av Adrián Jara) One of the few non-electronic-filled supermarkets around – everything from noodles per kilo to Cornflakes.

Getting There & Away
AIR

The airport is 30km west of town on Ruta 2.

TAM (☎ 506030; cnr Curupayty & Ayala) flies between Ciudad del Este and Asunción three times daily.

BUS

The bus terminal is about 2km south of the center on Av Bernardino Caballero. City buses (US40¢) with 'Terminal' signs run to and from all day, including along Av Monseñor Rodríguez to immigration and Foz de Iguazú.

Taxi fares are about US$2.70 from the bus terminal to downtown. There are frequent buses to Asunción (US$7 to US$10, five hours),

GETTING TO BRAZIL OR ARGENTINA
The border with Brazil (Foz do Iguaçu) is at the Puente de la Amistad (Friendship Bridge). Immigration is at both ends of the bridge. Buses to Foz do Iguaçu (US$1) pass by immigration (until 8pm), as do nonstop buses to Puerto Iguazú, Argentina (you have to go via Brazil to reach Puerto Iguazú – no Brazilian visa necessary; US$1). It's probably more convenient to walk or take a taxi to immigration and catch the bus from there. If you catch a bus to immigration, make sure you disembark to obtain all necessary exit stamps – locals don't need to stop. For information on travel from Brazil to Paraguay, see p329.

Encarnación (US$6.20 to US$7.10, five hours) and Concepción (US$12.30, 9 hours); less frequently to Pedro Juan Caballero (US$12.30, 7½ to nine hours) in the north. Daily buses run to São Paulo, Brazil (US$32 to US$44, 14 hours); and Buenos Aires, Argentina (US$37, 20 hours).

ITAIPÚ DAM

Paraguay's publicity machine is awash with facts and figures about the Itaipú hydroelectric project – the world's second largest (China's Three Gorges Dam now scores the honors as the largest). A visit to this massive dam (damned interesting, even for engineering ignoramuses) will reveal an amazing array of statistics; Itaipú's generators supply nearly 80% of Paraguay's electricity and 25% of Brazil's entire demand. In 1997 it churned out a staggering 12,600 megawatts. Not surprisingly, the world's largest exporter of hydropower showcases its achievement through an image of the dam on the 100,000 guaraní bill.

While project propaganda gushes about this disconcerting human accomplishment, it omits the US$25 billion price tag (mostly from over-invoicing) and avoids mention of environmental consequences. The 1350-sq-km, 220m deep reservoir drowned Sete Quedas, a set of waterfalls that was more impressive than Iguazú.

Free tours (🕒 8am, 9:30am, 1:30pm, 2:00pm & 3:00pm Mon-Sat, extra tour 10:30am Sat, 8am, 9:30am & 10:30am Sun) leave from the **visitor's center** (☎ 061-599 8040; www.itaipu.gov.py), north of Ciudad del Este near the town of Hernandarias; passports are required. **Light shows** (☎ 061-599-8040; admission free; 7:30pm Fri & Sat spring-autumn, 6:30pm Fri & Sat winter) require reservations.

From Ciudad del Este, Transtur and Tacurú Pucú buses traveling to Hernandarias (US40¢, every 15 minutes) depart from southwest of the traffic circles, two blocks down from Av San Blás and Av de los Pioneros. Get off as the road forks off the main highway to Hernandarias. You'll see the entry on the highway opposite the turn-off (ask the driver).

REFUGIO BIOLÓGICO TATÍ YUPÍ

Nineteen kilometers past the Itaipú Dam visitors center (3km past Hernandarias) is the beautiful **Refugio Biológico Tatí Yupí**, over 2200 hectares of natural forest and streams. It was established as one of six protected areas resulting from the Itaipú Dam project's compensations, to protect the animals which sought shelter there (a zoo was also established) and to recuperate formerly deforested areas. This tranquil place – with its excellent camping facilities – is worth visiting for a day or two. Bicycles and horses are thrown in for fun. And we'll be damned – it's all free! There's a well-organized visitors center and small kiosk. Note: no alcohol is allowed. If you plan to visit, you must get permission from the Itaipú Dam visitors center, showing all official documents.

To get there, catch any bus from Hernandarias or a taxi from the Itaipú Dam visitors center (the center does not provide transport). From the reserve entrance, it's another 8km drive along the dirt road to the visitors center and campsite. You can try your luck with a ranger or walk.

NORTHERN PARAGUAY & THE CHACO

The Gran Chaco is *the* place to escape the crowds and experience raw wilderness. This vast plain – roughly divided into the Low Chaco (west of Asunción), Middle Chaco (the Mennonite region) and High Chaco (low density thorny scrub to the north) – encompasses the entire western half of Paraguay and stretches into Argentina and Bolivia. During the rainy season large tracts become swampy plains, while in dry weather it's an arid dust-bowl with harsh thorn forest.

Although the Chaco accounts for over 60% of Paraguayan territory, less than 3% of the population actually lives here. Historically it was a refuge for indigenous hunter-gatherers; today, several indigenous groups continue to live here – some have their assigned regions, following the assignment of land in the middle Chaco to the Mennonite communities in the 1930s. Close to the Río Paraguay, *campesinos* (rural dwellers practicing subsistence agriculture) have built picturesque houses of palm logs while army bases and cattle *estancias* (extensive grazing establishments) inhabit the denser thorn forests of the high Chaco.

Over recent years Brazilian settlers have moved into northeastern Paraguay, deforesting the countryside to plant coffee and cotton and squeezing out the existing population, including the few remaining Aché. Both the regions in the northeast and northwest are renowned for trading in contraband goods.

Controversy hit the area in 2000 when the Moonies (Reverend Sun Myung Moon's Unification Church) purchased 360,000 hectares of the Chaco, including the entire town of Puerto Casado, for an estimated US$15 million.

Each September sees the Trans-Chaco Rally, a three-day world motor-sport competition, said to be one of the toughest on the planet.

CONCEPCIÓN

☎ 031 / pop 45,068

Concepción is highly underrated. This easy-going city on the Río Paraguay has poetic early-20th-century buildings, pleasant eateries and a laid-back ambience. 'Action' is a trotting horse hauling its full cart of watermelons and other goods along the paved reddish streets, or a boatload of people and their cargo arriving at the port. The river is an important transportation route, and upriver on weekends, locals gather on its sandy beaches.

If you don't catch the sleepy syndrome, sights include the **Museo del Cuartel de la Villa Real** (cnr Marie López & Cerro Cordillera; admission free; 7am-noon Mon-Sat), a beautifully restored Hispaño-Paraguayo building that exhibits historical and war paraphernalia. Several stunning **mansions**, now municipal buildings, stand out in Estigarribia. If mechanisms are more likely to rev you up, the open-air **Museo de Arquelogía Industrial** along Augustín Fernando de Pinedo features an assortment of antique industrial and agricultural machines. The **market** is about as authentic as you'll get, complete with its crude *comedor*. Crafts can be found in Plaza Agustín Pinedo. For a leisurely meander across the river, catch a local rowboat (US40¢).

Information

Some banks have ATMs but don't accept foreign cards.

Cyberc@t (Franco near Garay; per hr around US$1) Has a quick connection in a quiet, air-conditioned space.

Tourist information station (Direccion de Juventud, Deporte y Turismo, Av Colonbino in the 'Polidepartivo'; turismo@concepcion.gov.py) Trying hard to get Concepción on the map, hands out basic town maps highlighting historic buildings.

Sleeping & Eating

Hospedaje Puerta del Sol (☎ 42185; per person US$3.85) The owners are the sweetest part of this otherwise basic place, and it's handy to the port.

Hotel Center (Franco near Yegros; s US$3.85-7.80, d US$7.80-11; ❄) The dial phones (out of a *Lost in Space* re-run) set the tone for this outdated, rather dingy dive. Costs more with air-con.

Hotel Frances (☎ 42383; cnr Franco & CA López; per person US$7.70; ❄ ⏚) Whet your appetite in every respect at this pleasant place – great pool, buffet breakfast (and restaurant) and a handy *heladería* two blocks away.

Heladería Amistad (cnr Presidente Franco & Concepción) Coming here for ice cream, soda and snacks is a local pastime. Don't miss the fruit salad sundaes (US$1.20).

Restaurante Toninho y Jandiri (cnr Mariscal Estigarribia & Iturbe; almuerzo US$3.50) This place is worth the pressure on both stomach and purse.

Come to this Brazilian *churrasqueria* (restaurant featuring barbecued meat) for plentiful portions of meats and fish served on sizzle-plates.

Locals flock to down-to-earth rivals **Pollería El Bigote** (Presidente Franco) and **Pollería Bulldog** (cnr Presidente Franco & Garay; portions US$1.80) for the rotisserie chickens.

To stock up for visits to the nearby Cerro Corá national park, let loose at the supermarket, **Maxi Hipermercado** (cnr Mariscal Francisco Lopez & Julia Estigarribia).

Getting There & Away
BOAT

The most traditional (but not the most comfortable) way to get to or from Concepción is by riverboat. *Cacique* (☎ 42621) boats to Asunción leave Sunday at 6am (US$9, 30 hours). Boats heading upriver to Puerto Vallemí (US$10.60, 24 hours) or as far as Bahia Negra (US$15, 2½ to three days) include the *Aquidabán* (Tuesday at 11am), *Cacique* (Thursday) and *Guaraní* (every second Monday). Check schedules and boats – both change. Ask around the old port about heading as far north as Isla Margarita (aka Puerto Esperanza) on the Brazilian border. Be careful in the blocks near the port; muggings have occurred. See p803 for details on getting to Concepción.

BUS

The bus terminal is eight blocks north of the lone stoplight, which is as close to the center as Colectivo Línea 1 (US35¢) will take you. Car or motorcycle taxis cost about US$2.70; *karumbes* (horse-carts) are twice as much fun and cost less (US$1.80) – confirm your price before you are 'taken for a ride'!

UP THE LAZY RÍO PARAGUAY

Creature comforts takes on a new meaning in the Pantanal. South of Concepción river commerce is lively, but further north as the pace s-l-o-w-s cargo exchanges become wildlife sightings: caimans, capybaras, monkeys and birds galore, including jabiru, herons, egrets, spoonbills, even macaws. Bed is usually below deck on a humble hammock (rented for around US$1 per day, or you can bring your own) and you need to claim your territory – it gets crowded. Some boats have basic cabins (around US$5.30 per night). It's best to bring your own food. Watch or secure your belongings – travelers have reported some light-fingered monkey behavior. Upriver from Vallemí is Isla Margarita (aka Puerto Esperanza), where you may be able to disembark and catch a skiff to Porto Murtinho, Brazil, which has bus connections to Corumbá. Fuerte Olimpo is the last place to obtain an exit stamp, but check this status with an immigration office, especially if you head further north to Bahia Negra.

Several buses pass through Pozo Colorado (US$3.50, 1½ hours) en route to Filadelfia (US$10.60, five to six hours) and Asunción (US$10.60, five to six hours). Several services head to Pedro Juan Caballero (US$4.40, four hours). There's a daily departure at 12:30pm to Ciudad del Este (US$13, nine hours).

PEDRO JUAN CABALLERO

☎ 036 / pop 64,100

Literally across the street from Ponta Porã in Brazil is the nondescript former shopping border town of Pedro Juan Caballero ('PJC'). Don't aim to get stranded here on a weekend or public holiday as it ain't all 'party hearty'; the only real reasons to shack up here are en route to/from Brazil or to visit the attractive Parque Nacional Cerro Corá.

Information

Money-exchange houses are numerous. Other tourist facilities:

Cibercafé (cnr Mariscal López & Mariscal Estigarribia; per hr US70¢) Has good internet access and pool tables.

Immigration (Naciones Unidas 144; ☻ 8am-noon Mon-Sat) Locals cross the border freely, but to continue any distance you must visit the immigration office.

Sleeping & Eating

Hotel La Negra (74603; Mariscal López 1342; s US$6-10, d US$11.70-15.50) A shrine to cheap hotels – walk through the family room-cum-chapel to less pure but passable rooms, with slightly grimy and peeling walls.

Hotel La Siesta (☎ 73022; cnr Alberdi & Francia; s/d incl breakfast US$15.50/33; ☒) The glitz has lost its shine in this '80s number, but it's the best of the cheapies.

Restaurant Eiruzú (☎ 73162; Hotel Eiruzú, cnr Mariscal López & Estigarribia; mains US$3.50) Has an ambitious menu with good local and international dishes.

Getting There & Away

The bus terminal is a few blocks east of the border on Calle Francis. Frequent services leave for Concepción (US$4.80, four hours) and Asunción (US$10.60 to US$12.30, 7½ hours), and four daily buses to Ciudad del Este (US$12.30 to US$14, 8½ hours). National Expresso goes daily to Brazil to Campo Grande (US$4.50, five hours) and Brasilia (US$21 to US$43, 24 hours). Nasa has daily services to Buenos Aires (US$48). Connections to many more Brazilian destinations are available in Ponta Porã.

GETTING TO BRAZIL

Entering Ponta Porã, Brazil from Paraguay consists of crossing one side of the street to the other, where the only difference is that prices are charged in a different currency. In fact, it's so simple that if you are traveling further into Brazil, you might forget one extremely important thing - getting an exit stamp in your passport. To do this, head to Immigration (Naciones Unidas 144; ☻ 8am-noon Mon-Sat). Also ensure you do this before jumping on a bus, which head to various Brazilian cities.

PARQUE NACIONAL CERRO CORÁ

Parque Nacional Cerro Corá is now etched onto the map as one of Paraguay's natural treasures. This park, only 40km west of Pedro Juan Caballero and accessible from Concepción, protects an area of dry tropical forest and natural savanna in a landscape of steep, isolated hills. Cultural and historical features include pre-Columbian caves, petroglyphs and the site of Mariscal Francisco Solano López's death at the end of the War of the Triple Alliance.

The park's **nature trails** head to rivers, waterfalls and a small natural *mirador* (viewpoint), Cerro Muralia (325m). Rare birds and a zoo-worth of animals – including tortoises, armadillos and monkeys – can be spotted (rumor has it that there's even a jaguar, but this is based on footprints only). There's a camping area (lather up on insect repellent) and a small **visitors center-museum** (admission free) with (stuffed) animal displays and maps. Behind this building there is a comfortable cabin with all the mod cons where guests can bunk for a small donation.

Buses running between Concepción and Pedro Juan Caballero (US$1, 45 minutes) will stop at the park entrance; walk 1km to the visitors center – beyond this are the sights and sites. The helpful staff can tell you the bus schedule for your return trip. One-way taxis from Pedro Juan Caballero are pricey at US$35.30.

FILADELFIA

☎ 0491 / pop 5000 (colony)

If Filadelfia were a painting, it would have been done by surrealist Salvador Dalí. This neat Mennonite community, the service and administrative center of Fernheim, resembles a suburb of Munich plonked in the middle of a red desert. Geometrically perfect homes line the streets in an orderly grid, with dusty roads and miles of Chaco wilderness extending endlessly beyond. The town lacks a real center; its soul is the giant cooperative which trades the cream of the Paraguayan crop – dairy products. Although there are indigenous day laborers from nearby pueblos, most of the town's inhabitants are European descendants, and *Guten tag* is a regular greeting. It's a captivating, if not a little strange, experience.

For information on the Mennonites, and everything from 15th-century coins and stuffed jaguars to colorful Nivaclé headdresses, visit the **Unger Museum** (Hindenburg s/n; admission free; ☉ 7-11:30am Mon-Fri) opposite Hotel Florida. Tours are possible in Spanish, German and English; or just get the keys from the helpful and knowledgeable owner, Sr Hartmut Wohlegemuth, at Hotel Florida.

Orientation & Information

Filadelfia's dusty streets form a neat grid whose Hauptstrasse (main street) is Hindenburg. Perpendicular Av Trébol leads east to Loma Plata and west to the Trans-Chaco and Fortín Toledo.

Filadelfia has no tourist office, but Hotel Florida shows a video on the Mennonite colonies, will help organize transportation and runs the local museum.

The well-stocked **Cooperativa Mennonita** (cnr Unruh & Hindenburg) supermarket has excellent dairy products and might change cash, but the Mennonites deal in barter more than hard currencies. Copaco and the post office are at the same corner.

Sleeping & Eating

Camping (campsites free) In shady Parque Trébol, 5km east of Filadelfia, but there is no water and only a pit toilet.

Hotel Florida (☎ 32151; hotelflorida@telesurf.com.py; Postfach 214; dm US$5.50, s/d/tr US$20/30/40; ⓟ 🐾 ⓡ) As orderly as a German train schedule and by far Filadelfia's nicest accommodation, including the cheaper rooms. Nonguests can also use the pool (US$1.40 per hour).

Churrascuría Girasol (Unruh; buffet US$6.80) Apart from Hotel Florida's restaurant, try Girasol, which serves delicious all-you-can-eat Brazilian *asados* (barbeque).

Getting There & Away

There's no bus terminal, but companies have offices along and near Hindenburg. There's a daily service to Asunción (US$11.50, seven hours, 480km), Concepción (US$11.50, eight hours, not Sunday) and Mariscal Estigarribia (US$3, 1½ hours), which is where you must get your exit and entry stamps (see opposite).

Getting between the colonies by bus is tricky, but not impossible. A local bus connects Filadelfia with Loma Plata (25km) at 8am and 7:45pm daily. Some buses stop in Loma Plata after Filadelfia en route to Asunción (usually one morning bus) and one (Estel Turismo) continues to Neu-Halbstadt, 35km

---

MENNONITE COLONIES IN THE CHACO

Some 15,000 Mennonites inhabit the Chaco, living (as they are keen to promote) in harmony with some 30,000 indigenous people. According to their history, Canadian Mennonites were invited to Paraguay to settle what was believed to be harsh and unproductive territory, in return for their rights – religious freedom, pacifism, independent administration of their communities, permission to speak German and practice their religious beliefs (such as adult baptism). In 1927 this group formed the Menno Colony around Loma Plata. A second colony, Fernheim (capital Filadelfia), was founded in 1930 by refugees from the Soviet Union, followed by Neuland (capital Neu-Halbstadt), founded by Ukrainian Germans in 1947.

Other Mennonite communities are elsewhere in Paraguay, but those in the Chaco are renowned for both their perseverance in the 'Green Hell,' and subsequent commercial success; their cooperatives provide much of the country's dairy products, among other things. Most adults speak 'Low German' only, but the younger generation speak Spanish as well, and some farmers speak Guaraní.

Although Mennonites in the Chaco appear to be more liberal than those elsewhere, there are concerns that material prosperity has spawned a generation more interested in motorcycles than traditional values. Alcohol and tobacco, once absolutely verboten, are now sold more openly.

GETTING TO BOLIVIA

The bus journey up the Ruta Trans-Chaco to Santa Cruz, Bolivia, takes 30 hours (US$32) in optimal weather, much more in the wet (think twice if there's rain). The bus will normally take the Picada 108, and occasionally, in wet weather only, the Picada 500. All buses stop at **Mariscal Estagarribia** (⏰ 24hr) in the wee hours of the morning, where you must get your exit stamp, before crossing into Bolivia at **Fortín Infante Rivola** (this is a border post only – no entry/exit stamps are available) before heading to **Ibibobe** (Bolivia), approximately 60km away, for formalities. Buses leave daily. Bring food and water, your dust rag in dry weather and your shovel in the wet. The easiest option is to leave from Asunción, but a riskier possibility is to reserve your ticket with **Stel Turismo** (☎ 0491-32520, Anni Martinez, Filadelfia) and catch the bus in Mariscal Estabarribia. See also p183. If you're heading out on your own, the immigration formalities can be completed at either Ibibobe, Bolivia, or Boyuibe, Bolivia.

---

away. During the school year there are early morning and noon buses connecting the colonies; ask locals for specifics. Hitchhiking is worth a try.

AROUND FILADELFIA
Loma Plata
☎ 0492 / pop 8800 (colony)

The Menno Colony's administrative center is the oldest and most traditional of the Mennonite settlements. It's also the best place to organize Chaco adventures. Its excellent **museum**, in a complex of pioneer houses, has a remarkable display of original photographs and documents chronicling the colony's history, plus original artifacts and furniture. Ask for the keys at the **Office of the Mennonite Colony** (☎ 52301; 7-11:30am & 2-6pm Mon-Fri), where you may be able to arrange tours of the colony and surrounding reserves. Ask for Walter Ratzlaff who is willing to negotiate backpacker prices.

Tours to the Chaco or surrounding area can be arranged through the friendly and knowledgeable guides **Hans Fast** (☎ 52422, 0981-203375; fast@telesurf.com.py; Spanish- and German-speaking) or **Walter Ratzlaff** (☎ 52301, 0981-202200; German- and English-speaking). Refer to www.desdelchaco.org.py for more information on the Chaco.

Hotel Mora (☎ 52255; Calle Sandstrasse 803; s US$9.50-11, d US$14-16 P ✗) has appealing, spotless rooms around a grassy setting. The owners will help arrange tours to the nearby wilderness, including the recommended Laguna Capitán. The excellent **Chaco's Grill** (mains US$3.20-4.25, buffet US$5.60) serves quality meats Brazilian style.

Neu-Halbstadt
☎ 0493 / pop 1700 (colony)

Neu-Halbstadt is the center of Neuland Colony. Nearby **Fortín Boquerón** preserves a sample of trenches dating from the Chaco War. South of Neuland are several indigenous reserves, where many Lengua and Nivaclé have become settled farmers. Neu-Halbstadt is a good place to buy native handicrafts such as bags, hammocks and woven goods.

Hotel Boquerón (☎ 240311; h_boqueron@telesurf.com.py; d US$18; ✗), across from Supermercado Neuland, is best known for its restaurant, which fires up a luncheon grill on weekends.

One bus from Asunción to Filadelfia continues to Neu-Halbstadt and there is a bus from Filadelfia at 6pm, inconveniently returning at 5:30am the following day (US$1.80, one hour).

NORTHWESTERN NATIONAL PARKS
Once the province of nomadic Ayoreo foragers, **Parque Nacional Defensores del Chaco** is a wooded alluvial plain; isolated **Cerro León** (500m) is its greatest landmark. The dense thorn forest harbors large cats such as jaguars, pumas, ocelots and Geoffroy's cats, which survive despite threats posed by poaching.

Defensores del Chaco is a long 830km from Asunción, over roads impassable to ordinary vehicles and there's no regular public transportation. It's worth talking to TACPy in Asunción (see p819) about trips they may have on offer. In the too hard basket? A more feasible and equally interesting option is to visit **Parque Nacional Teniente Agripino Enciso**, which boasts a comparatively sophisticated infrastructure including an interpretation center and a visitor's house (with electricity, air-con and water), and is more easily accessible from Filadelfia or Loma Plata. Another excellent possibility is **Parque Nacional Médeanos del Chaco**, although like the Defensores, this should not be attempted alone and you should never

PARAGUAY

wander at night – threats include anything from jaguars to contrabandists. For tours to these areas, contact Hans Fast or Walter Ratzlaff (see p815). To do the area justice, trips of three days and nights are recommended (US$130 per day for three people, excluding food and accommodation).

PARAGUAY DIRECTORY

ACCOMMODATIONS

Though worn and of a distant era, hotels and *residenciales* (guesthouses) are usually *muy limpio* (very clean). Camping facilities, while less common, are cheaper and in remote areas you can usually pitch your tent anywhere if you ask the locals – but beware of tent-eating ants! In the Chaco, formal accommodations are sparse outside the few towns, but *campesinos* may offer a bed. It's worth carrying your own mosquito nets in these areas. For information on visiting working *estancias* (ranches), contact TACPy (p819) in Asunción.

ACTIVITIES

Organized activities for the budget traveler are limited in Paraguay, but biodiversity makes it a notable destination for nature-watching, particularly bird-watching. River activities such as fishing and swimming are also easy and popular and horse-riding opportunities abound on *estancias*. Limited hiking opportunities are possible in National Parks, especially Cerro Corá (see p813).

BOOKS

For more about Paraguay's notorious wars, pick up Harris Gaylord Warren's *Rebirth of the Paraguayan Republic*, or Augusto Roa Bastos' novel *Son of Man*. For a look into Paraguay's heinous dictators, check out Bastos' book *I the Supreme* about Francia, or Carlos Miranda's *The Stroessner Era*. For a more anthropological slant check out Pierre Clastres' *Chronicle of the Guayaki Indians* or Matthew J Pallamary's novel *Land Without Evil*. Mark Jacobs' *The Liberation of Little Heaven and Other Stories* is a collection of fictional Paraguayan shorts.

BUSINESS HOURS

Government offices are open 7am to 1pm or 2pm, without siesta time. Most shops are open weekdays and Saturday from 7am to noon and from 2pm or 3pm until 7pm or 8pm. Banking hours are 7:30am to noon weekdays, but *casas de cambio* keep longer hours. Restaurants normally open for lunch and dinner (7pm until late) with a break in the afternoon. Cafés keep varying hours and, although not early starters, will be more likely to open for breakfast, coffees and snacks.

CLIMATE

Because of Paraguay's intense summer heat, winter months (May to September) are preferable. The weather is variable and nightly frosts are not unusual.

Southern Paraguay's climate is humid, with rainfall distributed fairly evenly throughout the year. In the east, near the Brazilian border, it averages an abundant 2000mm a year, declining to about 1500mm near Asunción. Since elevations do not exceed 600m, temperatures are almost uniformly hot in summer – the average high in December, January and February is 35°C (95°F), with daily temperatures ranging between 25°C and 43°C (77°F to 109°F). Winter temperatures are more variable and can reach freezing or hover at 6°C (42°F), though the average high in July, the coldest month, is 22°C (71°F).

DANGERS & ANNOYANCES

Paraguay's economy is in flux, but it's still a relatively safe country. Don't wander around on your own late at night in Asunción and border towns. Several years ago there were reports of armed robbery on buses traveling at night, although this seems to have dissipated. Muggings are common. Don't display valuables – snatching occurs frequently on local buses. The Chaco is hostile and desolate with limited infrastructure – it is recommended that you go with guides. Poisonous snakes are common in certain areas, but mosquitoes are a likelier nuisance. Beware of strong currents when swimming in rivers.

DRIVER'S LICENSE

Most car-rental agencies will accept a home driver's license, but it's wise to back it up with an International Driver's License.

EMBASSIES & CONSULATES
Embassies & Consulates in Paraguay

For information about Visas see p819. For locations of these embassies see individual city maps.

Argentina (Map pp798-9; ☎ 021-498-582; Palma 319)
Bolivia (☎ 021-227213, 203654; America 200)
Brazil Asunción (Map pp798-9; ☎ 021-448084; General Díaz 521; 3rd fl); Ciudad del Este (Map p809; ☎ 061-500984; Pampliega 205; ☯ 7am-noon Mon-Fri); Encarnación (Map p806; ☎ 071-203950; Memmel 452); Pedro Juan Caballero (Mariscal Estigarribia west of CA López; ☯ 7am-5pm Mon-Fri, 7-11am Sat) The Encarnación branch is best visited in the morning; the Pedro Juan Caballero branch is near the border in Ponta Porã.
Canada (☎ 021-227207; Profesor Ramírez at Juan de Salazar)
Chile (☎ 021- 662756; Capitán Nudelman 351)
France (☎ 021-213840; Av España 893)
Germany (☎ 021-214009; Av Venezuela 241)
Paraguay (☎ 067-724-4934; Av Presidentes Vargas 120, Pedro Juan Caballero; ☯ 7am-2pm Mon-Fri) Near the border in Ponta Porã.
USA (☎ 021-213715; Mariscal López 1776)

Paraguayan Embassies & Consulates Abroad

Paraguay has representatives in neighboring countries (see those chapters for details) and in the following countries:
Canada (☎ 613-567-1283; 151 Slater St, Suite 501, Ottawa, Ontario K1P 5H3)
France (☎ 01 42 22 85 05; 113 Rue de Courcelles, 76017 Paris)
Germany (☎ 0228-356 727; Uhlandstrasse 32, 53173 Bonn 2)
UK (☎ 020-7937 1253; Braemar Lodge, Cornwall Gardens, London SW7 4AQ)
USA (☎ 202-483-6960; 2400 Massachusetts Ave NW, Washington, DC 20008)

FESTIVALS & EVENTS

Paraguay's celebration of Carnaval (February; dates vary) is liveliest in Asunción, Encarnación, Ciudad del Este and Villarrica. Caacupé is the most important site for the Roman Catholic *Día de la Virgen* (December 8).

Other curious events:
Día de San Blás (Day of San Blás) Celebration of Paraguay's patron saint; February 3.
Election of Miss Paraguay Held in Asunción in March.
Rally Transchaco Transchaco car race held during the first week of September.

FOOD & DRINK

Parrillada (grilled meat) is popular, but nourishing tropical and subtropical foodstuffs play a greater role in the typical Paraguayan diet. Grains, particularly maize, and tubers like manioc (cassava) are part of almost every meal. *Chipas,* made with manioc flour, eggs and cheese, are sold everywhere, as are cheap and filling *empanadas* (pastry stuffed with either chicken, cheese and ham, or beef). During Easter's Holy Week, the addition of eggs, cheese and spices transforms ordinary food into a holiday treat.

Paraguayans consume massive quantities of mate (herbal tea), most commonly as ice-cold *tereré* (iced mate) and generously spiked with *yuyos* (medicinal herbs). Roadside stands offer *mosto* (sugarcane juice), while *caña* (cane alcohol) is the fiery alcoholic alternative. Local beers, especially Baviera, are excellent.

The following are some other common foods you'll likely encounter:
Bori-bori Chicken soup with cornmeal balls.
Locro Maize stew.
Mazamorra Corn mush.
Mbaipy he-é A dessert of corn, milk and molasses.
Mbaipy so-ó Hot maize pudding with meat chunks.
Mbeyú or torta de almidón A grilled manioc pancake resembling the Mexican tortilla.
Sooyo sopy Thick soup of ground meat, accompanied by rice or noodles.
Sopa paraguaya Cornbread with cheese and onion.

GAY & LESBIAN TRAVELERS

Paraguay is a rather old-fashioned country, with conservative views. Public displays of affection are uncommon between heterosexual couples, and invisible between same-sex couples. More gay bars are appearing in Asunción.

HEALTH

Paraguay presents relatively few health problems for travelers. The private hospitals are definitely better than public and those in Asunción are the best. Beware of Dengue fever in Asunción's suburbs and other wetland areas in the southeast. It's not advisable to drink the tap water, even though it is said to come from wells. In the Chaco it can be undrinkably salty.

Be sure to carry sunscreen, a hat and plenty of bottled water at all times to avoid becoming dehydrated. Condoms are available in most pharmacies. For more information, see the Health chapter (p1090).

HOLIDAYS

Government offices and businesses in Paraguay are closed for the following official holidays.

PARAGUAY

Año Nuevo (New Year's Day) January 1
Cerro Corá (Heroes Day) March 1
Semana Santa (Easter) March/April – dates vary
Día de los Trabajadores (Labor Day) May 1
Independencia Patria (Independence Day) May 15
Paz del Chaco (End of Chaco War) June 12
Fundación de Asunción (Founding of Asunción)
August 15
Victoria de Boquerón (Battle of Boquerón) September 29
Día de la Virgen (Immaculate Conception Day)
December 8
Navidad (Christmas Day) December 25

INTERNET ACCESS

Internet is *muy popular* in cities, but limited in smaller towns. An hour of use costs less than US$1.

INTERNET RESOURCES

Guaraní Dictionary (www.uni-mainz.de/~lustig
/guarani/diccion.html) Basic Guaraní language tools.
Lanic (http://lanic.utexas.edu/la/sa/paraguay/)
Excellent collection of links from the University of Texas.
Office of Statistics, Surveys & Census (www.dgeec
.gov.py) Interesting statistics from Census of 2002.
Paraguayan Current Events (www.paraguay.com)
Links to news stories about Paraguay in English.
Paraguayan Search Engine (www.quanta.com.py)
Spanish-language search engine.
Senatur (www.senatur.gov.py) Official tourist informa-
tion homepage with excellent information.

LEGAL MATTERS

Under no circumstances can you legally possess, use, or traffic illegal drugs in Paraguay.
Penalties are severe – long jail sentences and
heavy fines.

MAPS

The *Guía Shell* ($8.50) road atlas is sold at
most Shell gas stations and at **Touring y Automóvil Club Paraguayo** (TACPy; opposite) offices. It
includes a general 1:2,000,000-scale country map, and a map of Asunción with street
index at 1:25,000. The **Instituto Geográfico
Militar** (IGM; ☎ 021-206344; Artigas 920, Asunción) sells
1:50,000 topographical maps.

MEDIA

The following is a list of Paraguay's more
important newspapers:
ABC Color (www.abc.com.py) Asunción's daily paper
made its reputation opposing the Stroessner dictatorship.
Neues für Alle Asunción's German community publishes
this newspaper twice-monthly.

Rundschau Weekly.
Ultima Hora (www.ultimahora.com) An editorially bold
independent daily with an excellent cultural section.

MONEY

The unit of currency is the *guaraní* (plural
guaraníes), indicated by 'G'. Banknote values
are 1000, 5000, 10,000, 50,000 and 100,000
guaraníes; there are rare 50, 100 and 500 coins.
The perennial change challenge occurs in
Paraguay – keep plenty of change and small
notes as you go along – it comes in handy.
Traveler' checks can be cashed at *casas de
cambio* (3% to 5% commission).

ATMs & Credit Cards

ATMs in Asunción, Encarnación and Ciudad
del Este are connected to Visa, MasterCard
and Cirrus networks. Some even dispense US
dollars. You may stumble upon an ATM in
other towns but they are rarely linked internationally – get cash from those in the three
major cities listed.

Plastic is rarely accepted outside Asunción,
and even there, only in midrange to top-end
hotels, restaurants and shops.

Exchanging Money

Casas de cambio are abundant in Asunción and
border towns and change cash and sometimes
traveler's checks (3% to 5% commission); try
banks in the interior. Some *cambios* will not
cash traveler's checks without the original
proof of purchase receipt. Street changers give
slightly lower rates for cash only and can be
helpful on evenings and weekends.

Exchange rates at press time:

Country	Unit		Par G (guaraní)
Australia	A$1	=	4048
Canada	C$1	=	4721
euro zone	€1	=	6724
Japan	¥100	=	4513
New Zealand	NZ$1	=	3553
UK	UK£1	=	10020
United States	US$	=	5364

PHOTOGRAPHY

Most Paraguayans will gladly smile for the
camera, if you ask before shooting. Profes-
sional-quality color print and slide film is
available in Asunción, Encarnación and Ciudad del Este. Two good places in Encarnación
to stock up on print and slide film:

Serpylcolor (Av Mariscal JF Estigarribia & Curupayty)
Serpylcolor mappedria municipal (Av Mariscal JF Estigarribia & Mariscal López)

POST

Sending a letter to the USA costs about US$1.25 and it's US$1.65 to Europe. Essential mail should be registered for a small fee.

RESPONSIBLE TRAVEL

Avoid buying crafts made from wood (such as *lapacho* and *palo santo*) or endangered species like armadillos, jaguars, pumas and other exotic animals. Visitors interested in natural history and conservation should contact the **Fundación Moisés Bertoni** (☎ 021-608740; www.mbertoni.org.py; Prócer Carlos Argüello 208, Asunción), a nonprofit conservation organization that also arranges tours to reserves it helps manage, including Mbaracayu and Tapytá.

TELEPHONE

Copaco (formerly Antelco), the state telephone company, has central long-distance offices throughout the country. Private *locutorios* (phone offices) have sprung up everywhere, often with internet service as well. Despite deregulation, international calls still run over US$1 per minute, even with lower nighttime rates.

For phone codes use the following: country code (☎ 595) – when calling Paraguay from another country drop the '0' in the area code; international operator (☎ 0010); and International Direct Dial (☎ 002).

TOILETS

You're likely to see more jaguars than public toilets – they're rare! Most bus terminals have one – for a small fee you get a smelly loo and a wad of paper. It's best to go when you can in restaurants, hotels or museums. Most restaurants will charge you a nominal fee if you don't buy anything. Carry your own toilet paper and don't throw it down the pipes. Few buses have one that won't spill over onto your shoes, but drivers will usually stop and let you go if you ask nicely.

TOURIST INFORMATION

The government-run **Senatur** (www.senatur.com .py) has tourist offices in Asunción and one or two other cities. They may lack colorful brochures but the staff do what they can to answer your questions (in Spanish). **Asociación**

de Colonias Mennonitas del Paraguay (☎ 021-226059; acomepa@rieder.net.py; Republica de Columbia 1050, Asunción; ⊙ 7-11:30am, 2:30-6pm) has brochures about Mennonite communities. **Touring y Automóvil Club Paraguayo** (TACPy; Map pp798-9; ☎ 021-215010; www .tacpy.com.py; Av Brasil & Cerro Corá, Asunción; ⊙ 8am-5pm Mon-Fri, 8am-2pm Sat) can help make reservations for overnight visits (US$20 to US$100 per person, per day including meals) to 15 working **estancias** (www.turismorural.org.py).

TRAVELERS WITH DISABILITIES

Infrastructure for disabled travelers is negligible and unfortunately there are really no services for disabled travelers or for people with special needs.

VISAS

Visitors from Australia, Canada, New Zealand and the USA need visas. Others only need a valid passport. Get your visa in advance, either in a neighboring country or at home. Visas may be requested and obtained in the same day at most consulates. You will need two passport photos and two copies of each of: your passport; your entry stamp to Paraguay; your ticket (proof of onward travel); and credit card or traveler's checks (proof of sufficient funds). The cost is US$45 in cash for single entry or US$65 for multiple entry (30 to 90 days). Be sure to get your passport stamped on entering the country or you may be subject to fines upon leaving.

For information about immigration points (such as Mariscal Estagarribia en route to Bolivia), entrance or exit stamps or visa paperwork, visit the **Immigration Office** (☎ 021-446673, 021-492908; Ayala & Caballero; ⊙ 7am-1pm Mon-Fri) in Asunción.

VOLUNTEERING

Estancias are probably your best bet for spontaneous volunteering options, most of which is hard farm-type labor. Another alternative for forthcoming opportunities is to check out the website on the **South American Explorers** (www .saexplorers.org) bulletin board. Teaching English is popular, although usually organized with volunteer organizations outside Paraguay (see p1073).

WOMEN TRAVELERS

Paraguay is a reasonably safe country for women but solo travelers should take care, especially at night and on buses. Modest dress is important.

PARAGUAY

Peru

HIGHLIGHTS

- **Machu Picchu** – trek to awe-inspiring ancient Inca ruins hidden in cloud forest (p884)
- **Cuzco** – climb cobblestone colonial streets bordering artisan shops, eclectic eateries and museums (p870)
- **Arequipa** – party in Peru's most stylish city, within reach of smoldering volcanoes and the world's deepest canyons (p857)
- **Lake Titicaca** – float on a literally breathtaking, high-altitude lake with storybook isles straddling the Peru–Bolivia border (p864)
- **Huaraz, and the Cordilleras Blanca and Huayhuash** – live your dreams: tackle one of South America's most spectacular mountain ranges (p913)
- **Off the beaten track** – take a slow boat along the Río Amazonas, swinging lazily in your hammock all the way to Brazil (p935)

FAST FACTS

- **Area:** 1,285,220 sq km (five times larger than the UK)
- **Best bargain:** alternative treks to the Inca Trail
- **Best street snack:** *queso con choclo* (corn with cheese)
- **Budget:** US$15-25 a day
- **Capital:** Lima
- **Costs:** d/s room in Cuzco US$5/10, 1L bottled water US$1, domestic flight US$95
- **Country code:** ☎ 51
- **Famous for:** Machu Picchu
- **Languages:** Spanish, Quechua, Aymara
- **Money:** US$1 = 3.38 nuevos soles
- **Phrases:** *chevere, bacán* (cool); *asqueroso* (or *asco*, disgusting); *fiesta, juerga* (party)
- **Population:** 27.2 million (2005 census)
- **Time:** GMT minus 5hr
- **Tipping:** 10% in better restaurants; tip all guides
- **Visas:** North American, Australian and most European citizens need only a valid passport

TRAVEL HINTS

Bring high-speed film to photograph in the low light of the rainforest. Book Inca Trail treks at least six weeks in advance, or several months for trips during the high season (June to August).

OVERLAND ROUTES

Border crossings include: from Arica (Chile); from Huaquillas, Guayaquil and Macará (Ecuador); from Kasani and Desaguadero (Bolivia); and from multiple Brazilian and Bolivian towns and river ports in the Amazon.

Imagine scenery on the epic scale of an Indiana Jones or Lara Croft flick: forgotten temples entangled in jungle vines, cobwebbed ancient tombs baking in the desert sun and bejeweled buried treasures beyond all reckoning. Wild rivers that rage, pumas prowling in the night and hallucinogenic shaman rituals – it's not just a movie here, it's real life.

Like a continent in miniature, Peru will astound you with its diversity. Not even fierce Inca warriors or Spanish conquistadors could totally dominate such jaw-dropping terrain, from glaciated Andean peaks where majestic condors soar, to almost limitless coastal deserts, to the hot, steamy rainforests of the Amazon basin.

You can take it easy on the 'Gringo Trail' encircling the country's top highlights, ending at the cloud-topping Inca citadel of Machu Picchu. Or step off the beaten path and groove to Afro-Peruvian beats, chase perfect waves off a paradisiacal Pacific beach or ride a slow boat down the Río Amazonas.

Wherever your journey takes you in Peru, you'll be welcomed by big-hearted folks that tackle their often-unfortunate lot with gusto and a deep lust for life. Small wonder, then, that the land of the Incas is one of the continent's top picks for adventurous travelers.

CURRENT EVENTS

As it tries to exorcise demons from its political past, Peru is haunted by all-too-familiar ghosts. In 2005, disgraced ex-president Alberto Fujimori returned from exile in Japan and announced that he planned to run for the presidency again, only to be arrested in Chile on an extradition warrant to face charges of corruption and human rights abuses.

The 2006 presidential elections came down to a face-off between popular nationalist Ollanta Humala, an ex–army officer who had served under Fujimori, and Alan García, a left-leaning ex-president who some say put Peru on the path to financial ruin during the late 1980s. Voters played it safe, deciding to elect the more conservative García, which was seen as a blow to Venezuelan President Hugo Chávez' pan-South American socialist solidarity plan.

Outgoing president Alejandro Toledo was the first indigenous president of an Andean nation, but after failing to deliver new jobs and having an administration plagued by corruption scandals, his popularity ratings of below 10% were the lowest of any South American president. Meanwhile, the feared Sendero Luminoso (Shining Path) guerrillas have started to make a comeback, thanks to profits from cocaine trafficking with drug cartels in Columbia.

HISTORY
Early Cultures

The Inca civilization is merely the tip of Peru's archaeological iceberg.

The country's first inhabitants were loose-knit bands of nomadic hunters, fishers and gatherers, living in caves and killing fearsome (now extinct) animals like giant sloths, saber-toothed tigers and mastodons. Domestication of the llama, alpaca and guinea pig began between 7000 and 4000 BC. Various forms of the faithful potato (Peru boasts almost 4000 varieties!) were domesticated around 3000 BC.

Roughly from 1000–300 BC, the Early Horizon or Chavín Period evidenced at Chavín de Huántar near Huaraz (p920) saw widespread settled communities, plus the interchange of ideas, enhanced skills and cultural complexity, although the Chavín culture inexplicably disappeared around 300 BC. The next 500 years saw the rise and fall of the Paracas Culture south of Lima, who produced some of the most exquisite textiles in the Americas.

Between AD 100 and 700 pottery, metalwork and textiles reached new heights of technological development, and the Moche built their massive pyramids near Trujillo (p903) and at Sipán near Chiclayo (p908). It was also around this time that the Nazca sculpted their enigmatic lines in the desert (p851).

From about AD 600 to 1000 the first Andean expansionist empire emerged, and the influence of the Wari (Huari), from north of Ayacucho (p892), can still be seen throughout most of Peru.

During the next four centuries, several states thrived, including the Chimú, who built the city of Chan Chan near Trujillo (p903) and the Chachapoyas, who erected the stone fortress of Kuélap (p924). Several smaller, warlike highland groups lived near Lake Titicaca and left impressive, circular funerary towers, including at Sillustani and Cutimbo (p868).

PERU

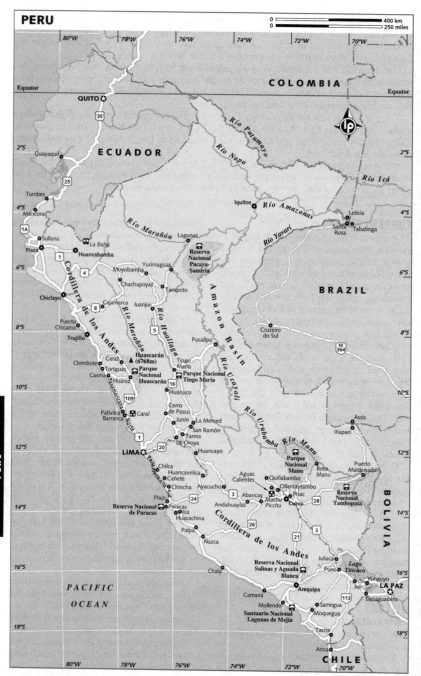

PERU

0 ————— 400 km
0 ————— 250 miles

Equator

COLOMBIA

QUITO

ECUADOR

Guayaquil

Tumbes

Mancora

Sullana

Piura

Huancabamba

La Balsa

Cordillera de los Andes

Chiclayo

Cajamarca

Juanjui

Puerto Chicama

Trujillo

Chimbote

Tortugas

Casma

Huaraz

Caraz

Huascarán (6768m)

Parque Nacional Huascarán

Pativilca

Barranca

Caral

LIMA

Chilca

Huancavelica

Cañete

Chincha

Pisco

Paracas

Reserva Nacional de Paracas

Ica

Huacachina

Palpa

Nazca

Chala

PACIFIC OCEAN

Río Marañón

Lagunas

Reserva Nacional Pacaya-Samiria

Moyobamba

Chachapoyas

Tarapoto

Yurimaguas

Río Huallaga

Pucallpa

Tingo María

Parque Nacional Tingo María

Huánuco

Cerro de Pasco

Junín

La Merced

San Ramón

Tarma

La Oroya

Huancayo

Ayacucho

Aguas Calientes

Quillabamba

Ollantaytambo

Abancay

Andahuaylas

Machu Picchu

Pisac

Cuzco

Camaná

Mollendo

Santuario Nacional Lagunas de Mejía

Moquegua

Samegua

Tacna

Arica

Iquitos

Río Amazonas

Leticia

Santa Rosa

Tabatinga

Río Yavari

Río Putumayo

Río Napo

Río Icá

BRAZIL

Cruzeiro do Sul

BR 364

Amazon Basin

Río Ucayali

Río Urubamba

Río Manu

Parque Nacional Manu

Boca Manu

Puerto Maldonado

Reserva Nacional Tambopata

Assis

Iñapari

BOLIVIA

Cordillera de los Andes

Reserva Nacional Salinas y Aguada Blanca

Juliaca

Puno

Lago Titicaca

Yunguyo

Juli

LA PAZ

Desaguadero

Arequipa

CHILE

PERU

TOP 10 MUST-SEE ARCHAEOLOGICAL SITES

You've come to the right country for ruins:

- world-famous mountaintop **Machu Picchu** (p884), 'lost city' of the Incas
- mysterious desert designs only appreciated from the air: **Nazca Lines** (p851)
- dramatic hilltop funerary towers at **Sillustani** and **Cutimbo** (p868) near Lake Titicaca
- imposing Inca citadels, lush terraces and holy sites of the **Sacred Valley** (p880)
- underground tunnels at **Chavín de Huántar** (p920), a 3000-year-old ceremonial complex
- vast Chimú mud brick capital **Chan Chan** (p903) near Moche pyramids, all around Trujillo
- tombs of the Lords of Sipán and Sicán at **Chiclayo** (p908)
- massive Chachapoyan site **Kuélap** (p924) in cloud forest – no crowds!
- newly rediscovered Inca city of **Choquequirau** (p891), reached by several days' trekking
- above Cuzco, the Inca fortress of **Saqsaywamán** (p879), site of ancient Inti Raymi festival of the sun

Inca Empire & Spanish Conquest

For all its glory, Inca pre-eminence only lasted around 100 years. The reign of the first eight Incas spanned the period from the 12th century to the early 15th century, but it was the ninth Inca, Pachacutec, who gave the empire its first bloody taste of conquest. A growing thirst for expansion had led the neighboring highland tribe, the Chankas, to Cuzco's doorstep around 1438, and Viracocha Inca fled in the belief that his small empire was lost. However, his son Pachacutec rallied the Inca army and, in a desperate battle, he famously routed the Chankas.

Buoyed by his victory, Pachacutec then embarked upon the first wave of Incan expansion, promptly bagging much of the central Andes. Over the next 25 years, the Inca empire grew until it stretched from the present-day border of Ecuador and Colombia to the deserts of northern Chile. It was during this time that scores of fabulous mountaintop citadels were built, including Machu Picchu.

When Europeans 'discovered' the New World, epidemics including smallpox swept down from Central America and the Caribbean. In 1527 the 11th Inca Huayna Capác died of such an epidemic. Before expiring he divided his empire between his two sons Atahualpa, born of a Quitan mother, who took the north, and the pure-blooded native Cuzqueñan Huáscar, who took Cuzco and the south. Civil war eventually ensued and the slow downfall of the Inca empire began.

By 1526 Francisco Pizarro had started heading south from Panama and soon discovered the rich coastal settlements of the Inca empire. After returning to Spain to court money and men for the conquest he returned, landing on the Ecuadorian coast and marching overland toward Peru and the heart of the Inca empire, reaching Cajamarca in 1532, by which time Atahualpa had defeated his half-brother Huáscar.

This meeting was to radically change the course of South American history. Atahualpa was ambushed by a few dozen armed conquistadors who succeeded in capturing him, killing thousands of unarmed indigenous tribespeople. In an attempt to regain his freedom, the Inca offered a ransom of gold and silver from Cuzco, including that stripped from the walls of Qorikancha.

But after holding Atahualpa prisoner for a number of months and teasing the Incas with ransom requests Pizarro murdered him anyway, and soon marched on Cuzco (see p870). Mounted on horseback, protected by armor and swinging steel swords, the Spanish cavalry was virtually unstoppable. Despite sporadic rebellions, the Inca empire was forced to retreat into the mountains and jungle, and never recovered its glorious prestige or extent.

Colonial Peru

In 1535 Pizarro founded the capital city of Lima. Decades of turmoil ensued, with Peruvians resisting their conquerors who were fighting among themselves for control of the rich colony. Pizarro was assassinated in 1541 by the son of conquistador Diego de Almagro, whom Pizarro had put to death in 1538.

PERU

Manco Inca nearly regained control of the highlands in 1536, but by 1539 had retreated to his rainforest hideout at Vilcabamba, where he was killed in 1544. Inca Tupac Amaru also attempted to overthrow the Spaniards in 1572, but was defeated and executed.

For the next two centuries Lima was the major political, social and commercial center of the Andean nations, while Cuzco became a backwater. However, this peaceful period came to an abrupt end. Indigenous people were being exploited as laborers under the *encomienda* system (whereby settlers were granted a parcel of land and native slaves). This led to the 1780 uprising under the self-proclaimed ruler Inca Tupac Amaru II. But this rebellion was also squashed, and its leaders cruelly executed.

Independence

By the early 1800s rebellion was stirring among the colonists due to high taxes imposed by Spain, plus a desire to take control of the country's rich mineral deposits, beginning with prime *guano* (seabird droppings) used for fertilizer (see p846).

Change came from two directions. After liberating Argentina and Chile from Spain, José de San Martín entered Lima and formally proclaimed Peru's independence in 1821. Elsewhere Simón Bolívar had freed Venezuela, Colombia and Ecuador. San Martín and Bolívar met in Ecuador, and as a result of this heart-to-heart – the details of which are a mystery – San Martín left Latin America altogether to live in France, while Bolívar continued into Peru. Two decisive battles were fought at Junín and Ayacucho in 1824, and the Spanish finally surrendered in 1826.

Peru also won a brief war with Spain in 1866 and lost a longer war with Chile (1879–83) over the nitrate-rich northern Atacama Desert. Chile annexed much of coastal southern Peru, but returned some areas in 1929. A little over a decade later Peru went to war with Ecuador over another border dispute. A 1942 treaty gave Peru the area north of the Río Marañón, but Ecuador disputed this and skirmishes occurred every few years. It wasn't until 1998 that a peace treaty finally put an end to the hostilities.

Modern Times

Despite periods of civilian rule, it was coups and military dictatorships that characterized Peru's government during most of the 20th century.

In the late 1980s the country experienced severe social unrest. Demonstrations protesting the disastrous handling of the economy by President Alan García Pérez were an everyday occurrence – at one point, inflation reached 10,000%! His 10 years of rule were shadowed by the disruptive activities of Maoist terrorist organization Sendero Luminoso, which waged a guerrilla war resulting in the death or 'disappearance' of at least 40,000 people, mostly in the central Andes.

In 1990 Alberto Fujimori, the son of Japanese immigrants, was elected president. Strong, semi-dictatorial actions led to unprecedented improvements in the economy. Popular support propelled Fujimori to a second term in 1995 (after he amended the constitution expressly so he could run again), but that support was dwindling by 1998. In June 2000 Fujimori again ran for office, but came up 0.1% short of the 50% votes needed to win outright. His main challenger, leftist Alejandro Toledo, claimed the elections had been rigged and refused to enter the runoff, which Fujimori promptly won.

In September 2000 a video was released showing Vladimir Montesinos, Fujimori's hawkish head of intelligence, bribing a congressman. As his 10-year presidency spiraled out of control, Fujimori ordered Montesinos' arrest, but the spymaster had fled. Over 2000 so-called 'Vladivideos' were discovered, implicating key political figures in money laundering and governmental corruption. Fujimori claimed innocence, but then resigned during a state trip to Asia and hid in Japan, which refused Peru's repeated extradition requests.

New presidential elections were held in 2001, and Toledo's indigenous heritage won through in a country where the majority of the population claims indigenous or mixed lineage. Peruvians were again facing increased unemployment, stagnant wages and higher costs of living. Soon the country was again plagued by strikes and demonstrations.

THE CULTURE
The National Psyche

Peruvians have been caught up in a political roller-coaster ride for decades, with public opinion leaping back and forth with the rise and usually thunderous fall of each new

PERU

president. But Peruvians' fierce pride in their heritage is entirely unshakable. Long dominated by a fair-skinned oligarchy of *limeños* (Lima residents), Peruvian society has begun embracing its indigenous roots.

Even as the last few decades have brought an onslaught of social and political turmoil, Peruvians have maintained their zeal for all things worth living. There's fervor for robust cuisine, soulful music and the thrill of a football match. This is a country that takes family and friendship seriously. Ultimately it is a culture that faces its setbacks with stoicism and plenty of dark humor – but also lots of hope.

Lifestyle

Just as Peru's geography varies hugely between desert, sierra and jungle, so does the lifestyle and attitude of its inhabitants. *Campesinos* (peasants) scratching out a living subsistence farming in a remote highland hamlet are a world apart from urbane *arequipeños* (Arequipa residents) with holiday homes on the coast, or hunter-gatherer tribes isolated in the deep Amazon.

The gaps between rich and poor may astound you. The introduction of TV to the impoverished highlands in the 1950s fueled a first wave of migration to the coast in pursuit of the privileged lives they saw on-screen. The vast influx of migrants spawned *pueblos jóvenes* (young towns) that surround Lima, many of which still lack electricity, water and adequate sanitation.

Over half of Peruvians live below the poverty line, and unemployment is so out of control it can't be measured. However, the entrepreneurial spirit is strong. Many of the jobless work as *ambulantes* (street vendors) selling anything from chocolates to clothespins in the streets, while teachers, police officers and students also drive taxis.

Given the grinding poverty that most Peruvians endure, it's hardly surprising that labor strikes for higher wages and various political protests happen all the time, for example when *campesinos* rise up to fight the US-backed eradication of traditional Andean coca crops. Travelers may find their trip suddenly delayed. It's not really a big deal to Peruvians, though.

Population

Peru is a society split between the mainly white and fair-skinned *mestizo* (people of mixed indigenous and Spanish descent – the latter distinguish themselves as being *criollo*) middle and upper classes, and the mostly poor indigenous *campesinos*. About 45% of Peru's population is purely indigenous, making it one of three Latin American countries to have such high indigenous representation. (In Spanish, *indígenas* is the culturally appropriate term, not *indios*, or Indians, which may be insulting.) Most *indígenas* speak Quechua and live in the Andean highlands, while a smaller percentage speak Aymara and inhabit the Lake Titicaca region. In the vast Amazon, various indigenous ethnicities speak a plethora of other languages. About 3% of Peruvians are of African or Asian descent. Afro-Peruvians are the descendants of slaves brought by the Spanish conquistadors. Alberto Fujimori (president 1990–2000) is of Japanese descent, and the many *chifas* (Chinese restaurants) are testimony to a widespread Chinese presence.

SPORTS

Fútbol (soccer) inspires passionate fanaticism in Peru, even though its national squad hasn't qualified for the World Cup since 1982. The big-boy teams mostly hail from Lima: the traditional *clásico* (classic match) pitches Alianza Lima against rivals Universitario (La U). The season is late March to November.

Bullfighting is also part of the bloodthirsty national culture. Lima's Plaza de Acho attracts international talent (see p843). In remote Andean hamlets, condors are tied to the back of the bull – an expression of indigenous solidarity against Spanish conquistadors.

RELIGION

More than 80% of Peruvians are declared Roman Catholics, and Catholicism is the official religion. However, while some *indígenas* are outwardly Catholic, they often combine elements of traditional beliefs into church festivals and sacred ceremonies, for example, when Pachamama (Mother Earth) is venerated as the Virgin Mary.

ARTS
Architecture

While the Inca stonework of Machu Picchu is Peru's star attraction, you'll find an assortment of other architectural styles, from magnificent pre-Columbian adobe pyramids to Spanish baroque to boxy modernist. Colonial

PERU

MADE BY HAND

Lima and Cuzco have the greatest selection of artisan craft shops selling antique and contemporary weavings, ceramics, paintings, woolen clothing, leather goods and silver jewelry. Lake Titicaca towns are great for knitted alpaca sweaters and knickknacks made from *totora* reeds. Huancayo is the place for carved gourds, while Ayacucho is famous for weavings and stylized ceramic churches. The Shipibo pottery sold in Yarinacocha is the best Amazon jungle craft available. Reproductions of ancient Moche pottery are sold in Trujillo; make sure objects are labeled as copies, as it's illegal to take pre-Columbian antiques out of the country. Avoid buying touristy goods made by cutting up antique textiles, which is destructive to indigenous peoples' cultural heritage.

---

styles are well represented by the countless cathedrals, churches, monasteries and convents built after the Spanish conquistadors arrived.

Literature

Peru's most famous novelist is the internationally recognized Mario Vargas Llosa (1936–), who ran unsuccessfully for president in 1990. His complex novels including *The Time of the Hero* delve into Peruvian society, politics and culture.

Considered Peru's greatest poet, César Vallejo (1892–1938) wrote *Trilce,* a book of 77 avant-garde, existentialist poems. Vallejo was known for pushing the Spanish language to its limits, inventing words when real ones no longer served him.

Two writers noted for their portrayals of indigenous communities are José María Arguedas (1911–69) and Ciro Alegría (1909–67). Women writers fill the pages of *Fire From the Andes: Short Fiction by Women from Bolivia, Ecuador and Peru.*

Rising literary stars include Peruvian-American Daniel Alarcón (1977–), whose short story *City of Clowns* featured in the *New Yorker;* and Sergio Bambarén (1960–), who lived in the USA and Australia before returning to Lima – his self-published *The Dolphin: The Story of a Dreamer* became a bestseller.

Music & Dance

ANDEAN

Haunting pre-Columbian music, which features wind and percussion instruments, is inescapable in the highlands. Called *música folklórica,* traditional Andean music is heard all over Peru, with bars and clubs called *peñas* specifically catering to it.

The most representative wind instruments are *quenas* and *zampoñas.* The *quena* (or *kena*) is a flute, usually made of bamboo or bone and of varying lengths depending on the pitch desired. The *zampoña* is a set of panpipes with two rows of bamboo canes, ranging from the tiny, high-pitched *chuli* to the meter-long bass *toyo.* Percussion instruments include *bombos* (drums made from hollowed-out tree trunks and stretched goatskin) and *shajshas* (rattles made of polished goat hooves).

Today's *música folklórica* groups also use stringed instruments adapted from Spain. The most typical is the *charango,* a tiny, five-stringed guitar with a box traditionally made of an armadillo shell.

COASTAL

Sassy *música criolla* has its roots in Spain and Africa. Afro-Peruvian music is unique and quite different from Caribbean or Brazilian styles. Its main instruments are guitars and the *cajón,* a wooden box on which the player sits and pounds out a rhythm. Also sharing African-Spanish roots, the bluesier *landó* has stylistic elements of call-and-response and lyrics often focused on slavery and social issues.

The heart of Afro-Peruvian music and dance beats strongly in Chincha (p845). A great introductory compilation is *Afro-Peruvian Classics: The Soul of Black Peru,* with the incomparable Susana Baca. The contemporary group Peru Negro has recently leapt onto the international scene.

The most popular coastal dance is the *marinera,* a romantic routine employing much waving of handkerchiefs. *Marinera* competitions are popular in Trujillo (p902).

MODERN

Also popular in Peru is omnipresent Caribbean salsa, as well as cumbia and *chicha,* both originally from Colombia. All three can be enjoyed in the *salsotecas* (salsa clubs), which cram in hundreds of Peruvians for all-night dance-fests. *Chicha* is a cheerful Andean fusion of traditional panpipes with electronic percussion and guitars. Deriving from cumbia is Peruvian techno-cumbia, of which prime exponents were Euforia and Rosy War, while newer bands include Agua Marina and Armonía 10. The homegrown Peruvian rock, pop, punk, hip-hop and reggaeton scenes are limited.

Painting & Sculpture

Much of Peru's religious art was created by indigenous artists under colonial influence. This unique cross-pollination gave rise to *Escuela Cuzqueña* (Cuzco school), a syncretic blend of Spanish and indigenous sensibilities. *Cuzqueña* canvases are proudly displayed in many highland churches, not just in Cuzco (p871).

ENVIRONMENT

While rainforest deforestation has caught international attention, deforestation from logging and overgrazing in the highlands are also acute problems, causing soil to deteriorate and get blown or washed away. This leads to decreased water quality, particularly in the Amazon Basin, where silt-laden water is unable to support microorganisms at the base of the food chain. Other water-related problems include pollution from mining in the highlands and from industrial waste and sewage along the coast. Some beaches have been declared unfit for swimming, and Peru's rich marine resources are threatened. Elsewhere responsible tourism is finally on the agenda, especially in the Amazon Basin.

The Land

The third-largest country in South America, Peru has three distinct regions: a narrow coastal belt, the wide Andean mountains and the Amazon jungle.

The coastal strip is mainly desert, punctuated by cities and rivers down from the Andes forming agricultural oases. The country's best road, the Carretera Panamericana (Pan-American Hwy), slices through coastal Peru from border to border.

The Andes rise rapidly from the coast to spectacular heights over 6000m just 100km inland. Most mountains are between 3000m and 4000m, with jagged ranges separated by deep, vertiginous canyons. Huascarán (6768m) is Peru's highest peak.

The eastern Andes get more rainfall than the dry western slopes, and so they're covered in cloud forest that slips and slides down to merge with the rainforest of the Amazon Basin.

Wildlife

With mammoth deserts, glaciated mountain ranges, tropical rainforests and almost every imaginable habitat in between, Peru hosts a menagerie of wildlife.

TOP 10 WILD WILDLIFE-WATCHING SPOTS

- remote jungle in **Parque Nacional Manu** (p929); your best chance to see jaguars, tapirs and monkeys
- the coastal reserve with penguins, flamingos and sea lions of **Islas Ballestas** and **Reserva Nacional de Paracas** (p846)
- the **Parque Nacional Huascarán** (p918) for Andean condors, giant Puya raimondii plants, vicuñas and vizcachas
- canopy walkways, jungle lodges and river cruises in **Iquitos** (p932)
- sighting capybara while cruising to a macaws' lowland salt lick at **Puerto Maldonado** (p926)
- the easiest place to spot Andean condors – **Cañón del Colca** (p863)
- oxbow lake **Yarinacocha** (p931), home to pink dolphins, huge iguanas and myriad bird species
- desert oasis **Santuario Nacional Lagunas de Mejía** (p853) – coastal lagoons with abundant native and migratory birds
- little-known rainforest reserve of **Reserva Nacional Pacaya-Samiria** (p932), explored by dugout canoe
- at **Machu Picchu** (p884), a rainbow of rare and endemic birds – over 400 species!

Bird and marine life is abundant along the coast, with colonies of sea lions, Humboldt penguins, Chilean flamingos, Peruvian pelicans, Inca terns and the brown booby endemic to the region. Remarkable highland birds include majestic Andean condors, puna ibis and a variety of hummingbirds. The highlands are also home to camelids such as llamas, alpacas, guanacos and vicuñas, while cloud forests are the haunts of jaguars, tapirs and endangered spectacled bears.

Swoop down toward the Amazon and with luck you'll spot all the iconic tropical birds – parrots, macaws, toucans and many more. The Amazon is home to over a dozen species of monkeys, plus river dolphins, frogs, reptiles, fish and insects galore. Snakes? Don't panic. Many species live here, but they're mostly shy of humans.

National Parks

Peru's vast wealth of wildlife is protected by a system of national parks and reserves with over 55 areas covering almost 13% of the country. Yet these areas seriously lack infrastructure and are subject to illegal hunting, fishing, logging and mining. The government simply doesn't have the money to patrol the parks, though international agencies contribute money and resources to help conservation projects.

TRANSPORTATION

GETTING THERE & AWAY

For visa information, see p942.

Air

Lima's **Aeropuerto Internacional Jorge Chávez** (code LIM; ☎ 01-517-3100; www.lap.com.pe) is the main hub for flights to Andean countries and Latin America, North America and Europe.

Boat

Boats ply the Amazon from Iquitos to Leticia, Colombia, and Tabatinga, Brazil (p936). It's

---

DEPARTURE TAX

Departure taxes on all flights are charged at airports. Lima's international departure tax is US$28.10, payable in US dollars or nuevos soles (cash only).

---

difficult to reach Bolivia by river from Puerto Maldonado (p928). It's possible, but time consuming, to travel along the Río Napo from Iquitos to Coca, Ecuador.

Bus, Car & Motorcycle

The major border crossings: Tacna to Chile (p856); Tumbes (p912), La Tina (p911) or Jaén (p907) to Ecuador; and Yunguyo or Desaguadero (p868) by Lake Titicaca to Bolivia. Brazil is reached (but not easily) via Iñapari (p928).

Train

There are inexpensive, twice-daily trains between Tacna and Arica, Chile (p856).

GETTING AROUND

On the road keep your passport and Andean Immigration Card (see p942) with you, not packed in your luggage, as overland transport goes through police checkpoints.

Air

Domestic-flight schedules and ticket prices change frequently. New airlines open every year, as those with poor safety records shut down (check www.airsafe.com). Another useful website is www.traficoperu.com, which details flight schedules and fare quotes between major cities. At the time of research, one-way flights averaged US$95, with no discounted round-trip fares. Early bookers get cheaper seats.

Every domestic airline flies between Lima and Cuzco, as does international carrier **TACA** (www.taca.com). **LAN** (www.lan.com) serves all major and some minor routes. **Star Perú** (www.starperu .com) flies to Cuzco and the jungle cities. **Aero Condor Perú** (www.aerocondor.com.pe) and **LC Busre** (www.lcbusre.com.pe) provide important links to Andean highland and jungle towns. Airline offices are listed under destinations later in this chapter.

Flights are often late. Morning departures are more likely to be on time. Show up at least one hour early for all domestic flights (90 minutes in Lima, two hours in Cuzco). Flights are often fully booked during holidays (p940). *Confirm and reconfirm* 72 and 24 hours in advance; airlines are notorious for bumping passengers off flights.

A US$3.57 domestic departure tax payable in US dollars or nuevos soles (cash only) applies at most airports; Lima charges US$6.05, Cuzco US$4.28.

Boat

Small, slow motorboats depart daily from Puno for Lake Titicaca's islands (p869).

In Peru's eastern lowlands, *peki-pekis* (dugout canoes, usually powered by an outboard engine) act as waterbuses on the smaller rivers. Where the rivers widen, larger cargo boats are normally available. This is the classic way to travel down the Amazon – swinging in your hammock aboard a banana boat piloted by a grizzled old captain who knows the waters better than the back of his hand. You can travel from Pucallpa or Yurimaguas to Iquitos, and on into Brazil, Columbia or Ecuador this way. These boats aren't big, but have two or more decks: the lower deck is for cargo, the upper for passengers and crew. Bring a hammock. Basic food is provided, but you may want to bring your own. To get onboard, just go down to the docks and ask for a boat to your destination. Arrange passage with the captain (nobody else). Departure time normally depends on filling up the hold. Sometimes you can sleep on the boat while awaiting departure to save costs.

Bus

Peru's notoriously dangerous buses are cheap and go just about everywhere, except into the deep jungle. Less-traveled routes are served by ramshackle old chicken buses, but more popular destinations are served by fast luxury services (called *imperial* or something similar), charging up to 10 times more than *económico* (economy) buses. It's worth paying more for long-distance bus trips, if only for safety's sake. Some overnight routes offer *bus-camas* (bed buses) with seats that almost fully recline.

Many cities now have central bus terminals, while others have bus companies clustered around a few blocks or scattered all over town. Travel agencies are convenient for buying tickets, but will overcharge you. Instead buy them yourself from the bus company directly at least a day in advance. Schedules and fares change frequently. Prices skyrocket around major holidays (p940), when tickets may be sold out several days ahead of time. Coastal buses are packed all summer long, especially on Sundays.

Buses rarely leave or arrive on time, and can be greatly delayed during the rainy season due to landslides and treacherous road conditions. Try not to take overnight buses, which are more vulnerable to fatal accidents, hijackings and luggage theft. It can get freezing cold on highland buses, so dress warmly. Long-distance buses generally stop for meals, though toilets are highly unpredictable. Some companies have their own restaurants in the middle of nowhere, practically forcing you to eat there. But you can also buy snacks from onboard vendors or bring your own food and drinks.

Car & Motorcycle

With the exception of the Carretera Panamericana and new roads leading inland from the coast, road conditions are generally poor, distances are great and renting a car is an expensive, often dangerous hassle. Keep in mind that road signage is deficient and most major roads are also toll roads: US$1 to US$2 for every 100km. *Gasolina* (petrol) averages US$3.90 per US gallon, and gasoline stations (called *grifos*) are few and far between. Renting a private taxi for long-distance trips costs little more than renting a car, and avoids most of these pitfalls. Motorcycle rental is an option mainly in jungle towns, and there are a few lone outfitters in Cuzco.

Local Transportation

Taxis are unmetered so ask locals the going rate, then haggle; drivers often double or triple the standard rate for unsuspecting foreigners. A short run in most cities costs US$1 (in Lima US$1.50). Be aware that street hawkers sell florescent taxi stickers throughout Peru, and anybody can just stick one on their windscreen. Some drivers of these unlicensed 'pirate' taxis have been known to be complicit in violent crimes against passengers. It's safer but more expensive to take officially regulated taxis, which are typically called by telephone.

Motocarros or *mototaxis* (motorized rickshaws) are common in some of the smaller cities. *Colectivos* (shared minivans, minibuses or taxis) and trucks (in the Amazon) run between local and not-so-local destinations.

Train

Pricey **PeruRail** (www.perurail.com) links Cuzco and the Sacred Valley with Machu Picchu (p879). There is an unpredictable though immensely scenic thrice-weekly service that travels between Cuzco and Lake Titicaca (p868).

PERU

Other railways connect Lima and the Andean highland towns of Huancayo (p897) and Huancavelica (p894).

LIMA

☎ 01 / pop 7,600,000

Millions of inhabitants crowd into Peru's frenetic capital, giving it an edge few other South American cities have. Its shantytowns look like the developing world, yet the business districts and promenades of its seaside suburbs are Europe away from home.

Overpopulation problems have earned this fast-moving metropolis a reputation as a polluted, frenetic and dangerous place. Yet in no time it can transport you from crumbling pre-Inca pyramids and the waning splendor of Spanish colonial architecture to glitzy, ultramodern shopping malls and many of the country's best museums. You can feast on fresh seafood by the ocean, go paragliding off the cliffs in Miraflores and groove all night in bohemian Barranco's bars and clubs.

Lima's climate can be a challenge. Blanketed in a melancholy *garúa* (coastal fog, mist or drizzle) from April to December, the city plays with the senses, but when summer comes, the sun blazes and *limeños* head in droves for the Pacific coast beaches.

HISTORY

Lima was christened the 'City of Kings' when Francisco Pizarro founded it on the Catholic feast day of Epiphany in 1535. During early Spanish colonial times it became the continent's richest, most important town, though this all changed in 1746 when a disastrous earthquake wiped out most of the city. However, rebuilding was rapid, and most of the old colonial buildings still to be seen here date from after the earthquake.

Argentinean General José de San Martín proclaimed Peruvian independence from Spain here on July 28, 1821. Three decades later the city took a crucial step over other cities on the continent by building the first railway in South America. In 1881 Lima was attacked during a war with Chile. Treasures were carried off or broken by the victorious Chileans, who occupied the town for nearly three years.

An unprecedented population explosion began in the 1920s due to rapid industrialization and an influx of rural poor from throughout Peru, especially the highlands. Such growth – and growing pains – have continued at a breakneck pace ever since. Today the city has a few wealthy and middle-class suburbs, but many people are unemployed and live with inadequate housing and no running water.

In December 1996 Tupac Amaru leftist rebels entered the Japanese ambassador's residence and took several ambassadors and ministers hostage. Four months went by before Peruvian soldiers bombed the building, entered and shot the rebels. One hostage and two Peruvian commandos died during the rescue operation.

In March 2002, a few days before a visit by US President George W Bush, a car bomb exploded near the US Embassy, killing ten people. It was thought to have been detonated by the guerrilla group Sendero Luminoso, which had caused massive social instability in the 1980s.

ORIENTATION

The heart of downtown Lima ('El Centro') is the Plaza de Armas, aka Plaza Mayor (Map pp834–5). It's linked to Plaza San Martín by the bustling pedestrian mall Jirón (de la) Unión, which continues south as Jirón Belén (many streets change their names every few blocks) and runs into Paseo de la República. From Plaza Grau, the Vía Expresa – nicknamed *el zanjón* (the ditch) – is an important expressway to the suburbs. Parallel to and west of the expressway is Av Garcilaso de la Vega (Av Wilson), which starts as Jirón Tacna and runs south into Av Arequipa, the main street for buses to the southern suburbs including San Isidro, Lima's fashionably elegant business district, and the ritzy beachfront hotels, restaurants and shops of Miraflores. Further south, the artistic clifftop community of Barranco has the hottest nightlife in town.

INFORMATION
Bookstores

Foreign-language guidebooks and maps are sold at the SAE clubhouse (see Tourist Information, p836), which has a members-only book exchange.

Crisol (Map p840; Óvalo Guturiérrez, Santa Cruz 816, Miraflores; ☼ 10am-11pm) A big, showy bookshop, with some novels and travel guides in English and French.

Zeta (Map p840; Espinar 219, Miraflores; ☼ 10am-8pm Mon-Sat) A small but varied foreign-language selection,

GETTING INTO TOWN

The airport is in suburban Callao, 12km west of downtown (see Map pp832–3).

Official taxis directly outside the terminal exit charge a whopping US$20 for trips to the city center and US$25 to Miraflores. Walk past these into the parking lot and you'll find taxis for under US$15. Or turn left outside the terminal, walk 100m to the pedestrian gate, turn right and walk another 100m to the road outside the airport, and you can get an unofficial taxi for less. A safer alternative to unregulated 'pirate' taxis is the Urbanito bus (to city center/Miraflores US$4.50/6), which goes directly to your hotel. *Colectivo* (shared) taxis will also drop you off at your chosen hotel; they charge around US$5 per person, and leave from the same spot as regulated taxis.

The cheapest way to reach the airport from downtown is on buses marked 'Faucett/Aeropuerto' running south along Alfonso Ugarte (US30¢). From Miraflores, taxis are recommended. Taking a taxi to the airport is cheapest if you just flag one down on the street and bargain. For more security, call a taxi in advance and pay the full US$15 to US$25 fare. Maddening traffic and road construction often lead to lengthy delays, so allow at least an hour for the ride to/from the airport.

Unfortunately there is no central bus terminal in Lima. Each bus company runs its own offices and terminals, mostly in shady neighborhoods east of the city center – take a taxi.

---

plus a few Lonely Planet titles. Also at LarcoMar shopping mall (Map p840).

Emergency

Ambulance (☎ 117)
Fire (☎ 116)
Police (☎ 105) Emergencies only.
Police headquarters (Map pp832–3; ☎ 460-0921; Moore 268, Magdalena del Mar; ☽ 24hr)
Policía de Turismo (Map pp834–5; ☎ 424-2053; Pasaje Tambo de Belén 106, Pachitea; ☽ 24hr) Provides reports for insurance claims or traveler's check refunds; some staff speak English.

Immigration Offices

Migraciónes (Map pp832–3; ☎ 330-4144; España 734, Breña; ☽ 8am-1pm Mon-Fri) Go first thing in the morning for a same-day visa extension (p942).

Internet Access

Some guesthouses offer free internet access. Speedy cybercafés costing about US60¢ per hour are found on every other block in Miraflores.

Laundry

Rates are typically less than US$2.50 per kilo.
KTO (Map pp834–5; España 481, central Lima; ☽ 7am-8pm Mon-Sat)
Lavandería 40 Minutos (Map p840; Espinar 154, Miraflores; ☽ 8am-8pm Mon-Sat, 9am-1pm Sun)
Lavandería Neptuno (Map pp832–3; ☎ 477-4472; Grau 912, Barranco; ☽ hours vary)
Servirap (Map p840; cnr Schell & Grimaldo del Solar, Miraflores; ☽ 8am-10pm Mon-Sat, 9am-6pm Sun) Also has self-service.

Left Luggage

Luggage storage at the airport costs US$6 per day. Members can store their bags at the SAE clubhouse (p836).

Medical Services

The following offer emergency services and some English-speaking staff:
Clínica Anglo-Americana (Map pp832–3; ☎ 221-3656; Salazar 3rd block, San Isidro) Stocks yellow-fever and tetanus vaccines. Also has a walk-in center (Map pp832–3; ☎ 01-436-9933) near the US embassy.
Clínica Internacional (Map pp834–5; ☎ 433-4306; Washington 1471 & 9 de Diciembre, central Lima)
Clínica Montesur (Map pp832–3; ☎ 436-3630; El Polo 505, Monterrico) Specializes in women's health care.
Instituto de Medicina Tropical (Map pp832–3; ☎ 482-3903, 01-482-3910; Cayetano Heredia Hospital, Honorio Delgado, San Martín de Porres) Treats tropical diseases.

Other options:
Dr Victor Aste (Map pp832–3; ☎ 421-9169; Office 101, Antero Aspíllaga 415, San Isidro) English-speaking dentist.
Jorge Bazan (☎ 9735-2668; jrbazanj@yahoo.com) An English-speaking backpacker medic who makes housecalls.

Money

You'll find 24-hour ATMs throughout Lima. One bank in the international arrivals area at the airport is also open 24 hours. Other *casas de cambio* (foreign-exchange offices) are found on Camaná in central Lima and along Larco in Miraflores.

METROPOLITAN LIMA

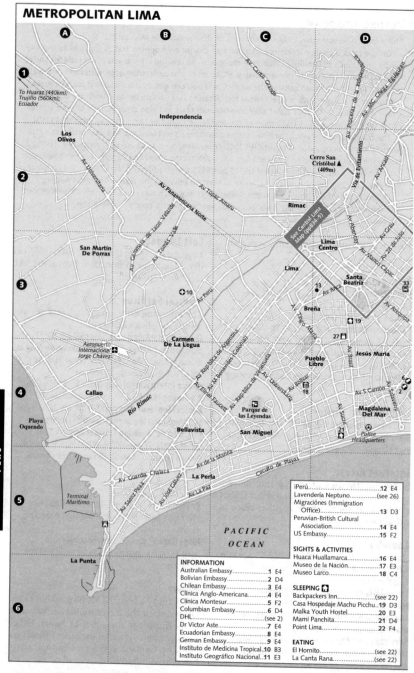

PERU

INFORMATION
Australian Embassy.....................1 E4
Bolivian Embassy........................2 D4
Chilean Embassy.........................3 E4
Clínica Anglo-Americana.............4 E4
Clínica Montesur........................5 F2
Columbian Embassy...................6 D4
DHL.......................................(see 2)
Dr Victor Aste............................7 E4
Ecuadorian Embassy...................8 E4
German Embassy.........................9 E4
Instituto de Medicina Tropical..10 B3
Instituto Geográfico Nacional..11 E3

iPerú.......................................12 E4
Lavandería Neptuno..............(see 26)
Migraciónes (Immigration
   Office)..................................13 D3
Peruvian-British Cultural
   Association.............................14 E4
US Embassy...............................15 F2

SIGHTS & ACTIVITIES
Huaca Huallamarca......................16 E4
Museo de la Nación.....................17 E3
Museo Larco...............................18 C4

SLEEPING
Backpackers Inn......................(see 22)
Casa Hospedaje Machu Picchu..19 D3
Malka Youth Hostel...................20 E3
Mami Panchita..........................21 D4
Point Lima.................................22 F4

EATING
El Hornito...............................(see 22)
La Canta Rana.........................(see 22)

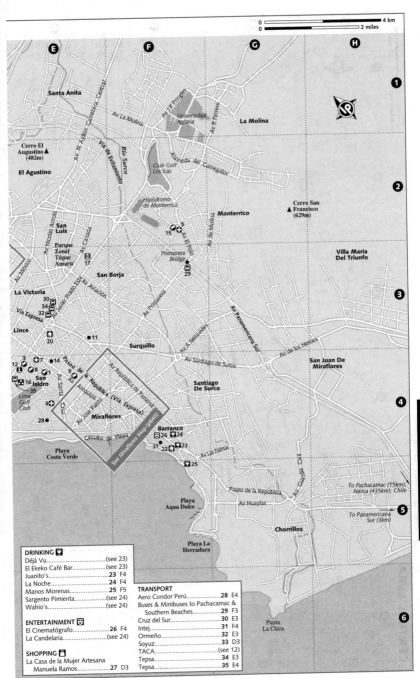

0 — 4 km
0 — 2 miles

E   F   G   H

1

Santa Anita

Cerro El
Augustino ▲
(482m)

El Agustino

San
Luis

Parque
Zonal
Túpac
Amaru

San Borja

La Victoria

Lince

San
Isidro

Lima
Golf
Club

Miraflores

Playa
Costa Verde

Av F P Prugles
Universidad
Agraria

La Molina

Av La Molina

Río Surco

Vía de Evitamiento

Club Golf
Los Icas

Alameda del Corregidor

Hipódromo
de Monterrico

Monterrico

Cerro San
▲ Francisco
(629m)

Villa María
Del Triunfo

Primavera
Bridge

Av El Polo

Av Primavera

Av A Benavides

Av Panamericana Sur

Surquillo

Paseo de la República

Av Santiago de Surco

Av de los Héroes

San Juan De
Miraflores

Santiago
De Surco

Av República de Panamá (Vía Expresa)

See Miraflores Map (p840)

Circuito de Playa

Barranco

Av Las Palmas

Av Guardia Civil

Paseo de la República

Av Huaylas

To Pachacamac (15km);
Nazca (435km); Chile

To Panamericana
Sur (3km)

Playa
Aqua Dulce

Chorrillos

Playa La
Herradura

Punta
La Chira

2

3

4

5

6

PERU

CENTRAL LIMA

0   400m
0   0.2 miles

PERU

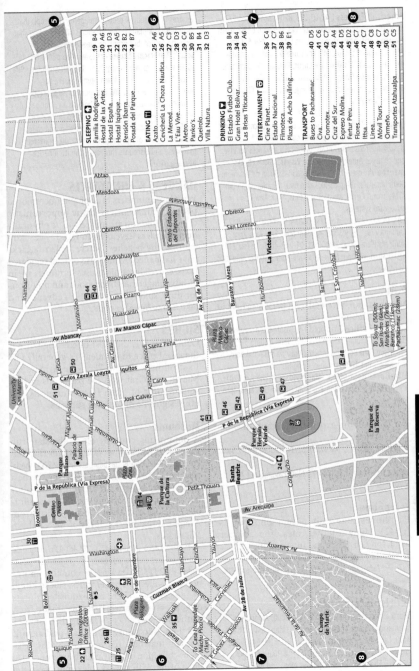

SLEEPING 🛏
Familia Rodriguez.................19 B4
Hostal de las Artes...............20 A6
Hostal España.........................21 D3
Hostal Iquique.......................22 A5
Pensión Ibarra.......................23 B2
Posada del Parque.................24 B7

EATING 🍴
Azato..25 A6
Cevichería La Choza Nautica..26 A5
La Merced...............................27 C3
L'Eau Vive..............................28 D3
Metro.......................................29 C4
Panko's....................................30 B5
Queirolo..................................31 B4
Villa Natura............................32 D3

DRINKING 🍷
El Estadio Futbol Club...........33 B4
Gran Hotel Bolivar.................34 B4
Las Brisas Titicaca.................35 A6

ENTERTAINMENT 🎭
Cine Planet.............................36 C4
Estadio Nacional.....................37 C7
Filmoteca................................38 B6
Plaza de Acho bullring...........39 E1

TRANSPORT
Buses to Pachacamac.............40 D5
Civa...41 C6
Cromotex.................................42 C7
Cruz del Sur............................43 A4
Expreso Molina.......................44 D5
Fertur Peru..............................45 D2
Flores......................................46 C7
Ittsa..47 C7
Linea.......................................48 C8
Móvil Tours............................49 C7
Ormeño....................................50 C5
Transportes Atahualpa...........51 C5

American Express (☎ 01-221-8204; Santa Cruz 621) Replaces lost Amex traveler's checks, but won't cash them.
Banco Continental central Lima (Map pp834-5; Cuzco 286); Miraflores (Map p840; cnr Larco & Tarata) Visa representative; its ATMs also take Cirrus, Plus and MasterCard.
Banco Wiese (Map p840; Larco 1123, Miraflores) MasterCard representative; changes Amex and Citicorp traveler's checks.
BCP central Lima (Map pp834-5; Lampa 499) Miraflores (Map p840; Pardo 491); Miraflores (Map p840; cnr Larco & Gonzales); Miraflores (Map p840; cnr José Larco & Schell) Has 24-hour Visa/Plus ATMs, gives cash advances on Visa and changes Amex, Citicorp and Visa traveler's checks.
Interbank central Lima (Map pp834-5; Jirón de la Unión 600); Miraflores (Map p840; Larco 690, Miraflores) Global ATMs accept Cirrus, MasterCard, Plus, Visa, Amex and most other card systems.
LAC Dólar central Lima (Map pp834-5; ☎ 01-428-8127; Camaná 779; ⏱ 9:30am-6:30pm Mon-Sat, 9am-2pm Sun); Miraflores (Map p840; ☎ 01-242-4069; La Paz 211; ⏱ 9:30am-6:30pm Mon-Sat, 9am-2pm Sun) Reliable *casa de cambio*.

Post

Members can have mail and packages held at the SAE clubhouse (below).
Main post office (Map pp834-5; Pasaje Piura, central Lima; ⏱ 8:15am-8:15pm Mon-Fri, 9am-1:30pm Sat, 8am-4pm Sun) Post restante mail can be collected here, though it's not 100% reliable. Bring ID.
Miraflores post office (Map p840; Petit Thouars 5201; ⏱ 8:15am-8:15pm Mon-Fri, 9am-1:30pm Sat, 8am-4pm Sun)

For faster, more expensive guaranteed shipping services:
DHL (Map pp832-3; ☎ 422-5232; Los Castaños 225, San Isidro)
FedEx (Map pp832-3; ☎ 242-2280; Pasaje Olaya 260, Surco)

Telephone

Payphones may only accept phonecards (p942). Many internet cafés offer cheaper local, long-distance and international calls.
Telefónica-Peru central Lima (Map pp834-5; Bolivia 347; ⏱ 7am-11pm); Miraflores (Map p840; Benavides 4th block; ⏱ 24hr)

Tourist Information

iPerú airport (Map pp832-3; ☎ 574-8000; Aeropuerto Internacional Jorge Chávez); Miraflores (Map p840; ☎ 445-9400; LarcoMar; ⏱ noon-8pm); San Isidro (Map pp832-3; ☎ 421-1627; Jorge Basadre 610; ⏱ 8:30am-6:30pm Mon-Fri) The main office dispenses maps and offers the services of the tourist-protection agency (Indecopi) that deals with complaints. The Miraflores office is a tiny shopping-mall office, but useful on weekends.
South American Explorers (SAE; Map p840; ☎ 445-3306; www.saexplorers.org; Piura 135, off Arequipa 49th block, Miraflores; ⏱ 9:30am-5pm Mon-Fri, to 8pm Wed, to 1pm Sat) SAE is a member-supported, nonprofit organization that functions as an information center for travelers. Annual membership (individual US$50, less for volunteers, ISIC cardholders and couples) includes full use of clubhouse facilities, SAE's quarterly magazine and discounts throughout South America. Also see p1072.

DANGERS & ANNOYANCES

With large numbers of poor and unemployed people, Lima suffers from opportunistic crime. While you are unlikely to be physically hurt, travelers have been mugged. Take extra care on the beaches, where violent attacks have happened. Always use official regulated taxis, especially at night. Bus terminals are in disadvantaged neighborhoods and notorious for theft, so buy your tickets in advance and take a taxi. See also p938.

SIGHTS

Central Lima is the most interesting but not the safest place to wander. It's generally OK to stroll between the Plazas de Armas, San Martín and Grau and the parklands farther south. Some of Lima's best museums and other sights lie in outlying suburbs.

Museums

A dominating concrete block, the state-run **Museo de la Nación** (Map pp832-3; ☎ 476-9878; Javier Prado Este 2466, San Borja; adult/student US$2/1, special exhibitions US$3.30; ⏱ 9am-6pm Tue-Sun) is the best place to get your head around Peru's myriad prehistoric civilizations. Catch a minibus (US30¢) east along Angamos Este from Arequipa, five blocks north of the Óvalo in Miraflores.

Museo Larco (Map pp832-3; ☎ 461-1312; http://museolarco.perucultural.org.pe; Bolívar 1515, Pueblo Libre; adult/student US$7.80/3.90; ⏱ 9am-6pm) contains an impressive collection of ceramics, stacked high to the ceilings. There are exquisite exhibits of gold- and silverwork, textiles made from feathers and a Paracas weaving that contains 398 threads to a linear inch – a world record! But you may be lured here just by the infamous collection of pre-Columbian erotic pots, illustrating, with remarkable explicitness, the

PERU

PACHACAMAC

Although it was an important Inca site and a major city when the Spanish arrived, **Pachacamac** (☎ 430-0168; http://pachacamac.perucultural.org.pe; adult/child/student US$1.70/30¢/60¢; ☉ 9am-5pm Mon-Fri) had been a ceremonial center for 1000 years before the expansion of the Inca Empire. This archaeological complex is about 30km southeast of the city center.

The name Pachacamac, variously translated as 'he who animated the world' or 'he who created land and time,' comes from the powerful Wari god, whose wooden two-faced image can be seen in the on-site museum. The main temple at the site was dedicated to this deity and held a famous oracle. Pilgrims traveled to the center from great distances, and its cemetery was considered sacrosanct.

Most of the buildings are now little more than walls of piled rubble, except for the huge pyramid temples and one of the Inca complexes, the Palacio de Las Mamacuñas (House of the Chosen Women), which have been excavated and reconstructed. A thorough visit of this extensive site takes two hours, following a dirt road leading from site to site.

Guided tours from Lima start at US$30 per person. Going solo? Catch a minibus signed 'Pachacamac' from the corner of Ayacucho and Grau in central Lima (Map pp834–5, US60¢, 45 minutes). Or from Miraflores, catch a taxi to the Primavera Bridge on Angamos at the Panamericana (Map pp832–3; US$1.25), then take a bus signed 'Pachacamac/Lurin' (US30¢, 25 minutes). Tell the driver to let you off near the *ruinas* or you'll end up at Pachacamac village, 1km beyond the entrance. For cycling and horse-riding, see p838.

sexual practices of ancient Peruvian men, women, animals and skeletons in all combinations of the above. Catch a minibus marked 'Todo Bolívar' from Arequipa in Miraflores to the 15th block of Bolívar (US30¢).

North of the Río Rímac in a shady neighborhood, the dusty **Museo Taurino** (Map pp834-5; ☎ 481-1467; Hualgayoc 332; admission US$1.50; ☉ 8am-4.30pm Mon-Fri) stands next to Lima's bullring. It boasts all manner of matadors' relics, including a holed and bloodstained costume worn by a famous Spanish matador who was gored and killed years ago. There are also paintings and drawings of bullfighting scenes by various artists, notably Picasso. Take a taxi from the Plaza de Armas (US$2.50).

In Parque de la Cultura, **Museo de Arte de Lima** (Map pp834-5; ☎ 423-6332; http://museoarte .perucultural.org.pe; Paseo de Colón 125, Santa Beatriz; adult/student US$1/70¢; ☉ 10am-5pm) exhibits four centuries of Peruvian art, as well as pre-Columbian artifacts. The more modest **Museo Nacional de la Cultura Peruana** (Map pp834-5; ☎ 423-5892; http:// museodelacultura.perucultural.org.pe; Alfonso Ugarte 650; adult/student US$1/60¢; ☉ 10am-5pm Tue-Fri, to 2pm Sat) displays popular folk art and handicrafts. Take a taxi from Plaza San Martín ($1.50).

In the building used by the Spanish Inquisition from 1570 to 1820, the **Museo de la Inquisición** (Map pp834-5; ☎ 311-7777, ext 2910; www .congreso.gob.pe/museo.htm; Junín 548, central Lima; admission free; ☉ 9am-5pm) offers free, multilingual

tours. Visitors can explore the basement where prisoners were tortured, and there's a ghoulish waxwork exhibit of life-size unfortunates on the rack or having their feet roasted.

Religious Buildings

Lima's many churches, monasteries and convents are a welcome break from the city's incessant hustle and bustle, though they are often closed for restorations or an extended lunch.

Originally built in 1555, **La Catedral de Lima** (Map pp834-5; ☎ 01-427-9647; Plaza de Armas; adult/child US$1.40/1; ☉ 9am-4:30pm Mon-Fri, 10am-4:30pm Sat) has been destroyed by earthquakes and reconstructed several times, most recently in 1746. Look for the coffin of Francisco Pizarro in the mosaic-covered chapel to the right of the main door. A debate over the authenticity of his remains raged for years after a mysterious body with multiple stab wounds and a disembodied head were unearthed in the crypt in the late 1970s. After a battery of tests, scientists concluded that the remains previously on display were an unknown church official, and that the body from the crypt was indeed Pizarro's. Don't overlook the beautifully carved choir and small religious museum at the back of the cathedral.

Monasterio de San Francisco (Map pp834-5; cnr Lampa & Ancash, Lima; 45min guided tour adult/student US$1.40/75¢; ☉ 9:45am-6pm) is famous for its

PERU

catacombs and remarkable library, which has thousands of antique texts, some dating back to the Spanish conquest. The church is one of the best preserved of Lima's early colonial churches, and much of it has been restored to its original baroque style with Moorish influence. The underground catacombs are the site of an estimated 70,000 burials and the faint-hearted may find the bone-filled crypts unnerving.

Ruins
Walking up to the ceremonial platform of **Huaca Huallamarca** (Map pp832–3; ☎ 222-4124; Nicolás de Rivera 201, San Isidro; adult/student/child US$1.70/1/30¢; ☽ 9am-5pm Tue-Sun), a highly restored Maranga adobe pyramid built c AD 500, gives you a novel perspective over contemporary Lima. Take a taxi from Miraflores (US$2.50).

More easily accessible is **Huaca Pucllana** (Map p840; ☎ 445-8695; cnr Borgoña & Tarapaca, Miraflores; admission free; ☽ 9am-5pm Wed-Mon), an adobe pyramid of the Lima culture dating from AD 400. As archaeological excavations continue, the site is open for guided tours. There's a tiny museum with finds and a reconstructed burial.

Plazas
The oldest part of the **Plaza de Armas** (Plaza Mayor, Map pp834–5) is its central bronze fountain, erected in 1650. To the left of the cathedral, the exquisitely balconied **Archbishop's Palace** dates from around 1924. On the cathedral's northeastern flank, the **Palacio de Gobierno** is the home of Peru's president; the changing of the guard outside takes place at noon. On a corner of the plaza, opposite the cathedral, there is a **statue of Francisco Pizarro** on horseback. This statue once stood in the center of the plaza, but the clergy took a dim view of the horse's ass facing the cathedral.

The early-20th-century **Plaza San Martín** (Map pp834–5) is presided over by the **Gran Hotel Bolívar**. It's well worth a stop in the hotel's stately bar for a sip or two of its famous *pisco sour*. Also on the plaza is a bronze statue of liberator General José de San Martín. But get closer and you'll spy the overlooked **statue of Madre Patria**. Commissioned in Spain under instruction to give the good lady a crown of flames, nobody thought to iron out the double meaning of the word flame in Spanish

(llama), and the hapless craftsmen duly placed a delightful little llama on her head.

ACTIVITIES
Paragliding
For paragliding trips along the coast, contact **Peru Fly** (Map p840; ☎ 444-5004; www.perufly.com; Jorge Chávez 666, Miraflores). Tandem flights (US$25) take off from the beachfront cliffs in Miraflores. Wave at the bemused coffee-drinkers in LarcoMar shopping mall as you glide past.

Swimming & Surfing
Limeños hit the beaches in their droves during the coastal summer months of January to March, despite publicized warnings of pollution. Don't leave anything unattended for a second.

The nearby surfing hot spots **Punta Hermosa** and **San Bartolo** (Map pp832–3) have hostels near the beach. **Punta Rocas** (Map pp832–3) is for experienced surfers, and has one basic hostel for crashing. You'll have to buy or rent boards in Lima, though, and hire a taxi to transport them.

To get to the southern beaches, take a 'San Bartolo' bus from the Primavera Bridge (Map pp832–3, taxi from Miraflores US$1.20). Get off where you want and hike down to the beaches, which are mostly 1km or 2km from the Pan-American Hwy.

Cycling & Horse-riding
Popular cycling excursions include the 31km ride to Pachacamac (p837).
Cabalgatas (☎ 221-4591; www.cabalgatas.com.pe) Has Peruvian Paso horses and runs horse-riding trips around Pachacamac (US$65 to US$95).
Explore Bicycle Rentals (Map p840; ☎ 241-7494; iexplore@terra.com; Bolognesi 381, Miraflores; per hr/day/week US$3/8/45; ☽ 8am-5pm Mon-Fri) Rents mountain bikes with helmets and locks.

FESTIVALS & EVENTS
Turn to p940 for national holidays and p939 for other festivals and events.
Festival of Lima Anniversary of the city's founding (January 18).
Feast of Santa Rosa de Lima Major processions in honor of the patron saint of Lima and the Americas. Held on August 30.
El Señor de los Milagros (Lord of the Miracles) On October 18, huge (and purple) religious processions; bullfight season starts.

SLEEPING

The cheapest guesthouses are generally in central Lima, though it's not as safe there as in the more upmarket neighborhoods of Miraflores and Barranco.

Central Lima

Hostal España (Map pp834-5; ☎ 428-5546; hotel _espana@hotmail.com; Azangaro 105; dm US$3.50, d without bathroom US$10; 🖳) In a rambling old mansion full of classical busts, stuffed birds and paintings, this established gringos-only scene has basic accommodations with limited hot showers. A rooftop café is enclosed by a veritable jungle of trailing plants.

Hostal de las Artes (Map pp834-5; ☎ 433-0031; http://arteswelcome.tripod.com; Chota 1469; dm US$5, d US$18-20, tr US$24) This gay-friendly, Dutch-Peruvian-owned hostel has basic fan rooms, but kind staff. It's located on a quiet side street in an atmospheric high-ceilinged *casa antigua* with colorful tiling.

Familia Rodríguez (Map pp834-5; ☎ 423-6465; jjr -art@mail.cosapidata.com.pe; 2nd fl, No 3 Nicolás de Piérola 730, dm incl breakfast US$6) Beds in an informal, friendly family's home.

Pensión Ibarra (Map pp834-5; ☎ /fax 427-8603; pension_ibarra@ekno.com; 14th & 15th fl, Tacna 359; s/d without bathroom US$7/10) High above the city streets in an apartment block, this homely *pensión* is run by the helpful Ibarra sisters, who make a real effort to keep it safe, comfortable and clean. Kitchen access.

Hostal Iquique (Map pp834-5; ☎ 433-4724; hiqui que@terra.com.pe; Iquique 758; s/d US$10/16, without bathroom US$7/10) This out-of-the-way spot is clean, safe and has warm showers and kitchen facilities. There's a rooftop terrace, decorative tiling and most rooms have national TV.

Posada del Parque (Map pp834-5; ☎ 433-2412; 01-9945-4260; www.incacountry.com; Parque Hernán Velarde 60; s/d/tr US$27/33/48; 🖳) This graceful colonial house inhabits a tranquil cul-de-sac near parklands. It's run by helpful English-speaking owners. Spotless rooms have hot showers and cable TV. Breakfast available.

Miraflores

New backpacker hostels are always popping up in Miraflores, so ask around.

Casa del Mochilero (Map p840; ☎ 444-9089; pilaryv@ hotmail.com; 2nd fl, Chacaltana 130A; r with shared bathroom per person US$4) This bare-bones crashpad is so popular, the neighbors are opening copycat-named outfits of their own. Kitchen access and hot showers.

Bed & Breakfast José Luis (☎ 444-1015; hsjluis@terra .com.pe; Paula de Ugarriza 727; r per person incl breakfast US$10) Off Av 28 de Julio east of the Vía Expresa, this huge rabbit warren is popular with students. You'll appreciate the friendly English-speaking host and characterful building. Most of the simple rooms have private bathrooms. Reservations required.

Flying Dog Backpackers (Map p840; ☎ 445-6745; www.flyingdogperu.com; Diez Canseco 117; dm/d incl breakfast US$10/25; 🖳) In the beating heart of Miraflores, this jam-packed hostel is run by youthful, laid-back, English-speaking staff. There are kitchen facilities, cable TV and a billiards lounge. Local calls are free.

Inka Lodge (Map p840; ☎ 242-6989; www.inka lodge.com; Elias Aguirre 278; dm US$10-12, d with shared

PERU

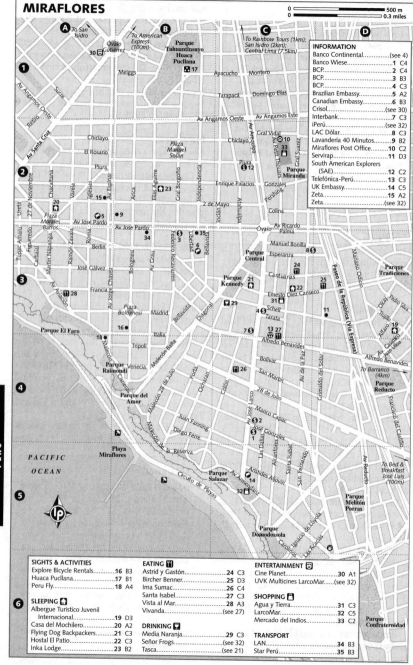

MIRAFLORES

PERU

bathroom US$25-28, all incl breakfast; 🖳 🖵) This secure, air-con hostel stands apart from the hubbub of Miraflores' main drags. Minimalist rooms have a dash of Andean style. There's hot water, free internet, a kitchen and a rooftop terrace.

Albergue Turistico Juvenil Internacional (Map p840; ☎ 446-5488; www.limahostell.com.pe; Casimiro Ulloa 328; dm/s/d US$10.50/18/28; 🖵 🖳) This newly renovated, yet strangely deserted hostel on a residential avenue has spotless dorms (private rooms are not such a bargain), kitchen facilities and an outdoor pool in the garden.

Barranco

Point Lima (Map pp832-3; ☎ 247-7997; www.thepoint hostels.com; Malecón Junín 300; dm US$7-9, s/d with shared bathroom US$15/18, all incl breakfast; 🖵) This white-washed seafront villa has ultrabasic rooms, but all the toys backpackers crave: cable TV, DVDs and ping-pong and pool tables. There's a kitchen and garden, plus free internet and staff only too willing to act as guides to local nightlife.

Backpackers Inn (Map pp832-3; ☎ 247-1326; www .barrancobackpackers.com; Mariscal Castilla 260; dm/d US$12/28, all incl breakfast; 🖵) On a tranquil, leafy street, this surf-style hostel has airy rooms with simple wooden furnishings. Some of the upper-floor balconies have blissful sea views. There's a kitchen and TV lounge.

Other Neighborhoods

Casa Hospedaje Machu Picchu (Map pp832-3; ☎ 424-3479; vanessa_new@hotmail.com; Juan Pablo Ferandini 1015, Breña; dm US$3.50) This family homestay, a block off the 10th block of Brasil, comes highly recommended by readers. It's friendly, secure, has a kitchen and a TV lounge. Some English spoken.

Malka Youth Hostel (Map pp832-3; ☎ 442-0162; www.youthhostelperu.com; Los Lirios 165, San Isidro; dm US$8, d with/without bathroom US$20/18; 🖵) Near Parque Américas, this little-known guesthouse has clean, quiet rooms with hot water, kitchen and laundry facilities, a TV room with DVDs and games, and a 6m-high climbing wall in the garden.

Mami Panchita (Map pp832-3; ☎ 263-7203; www .mamipanchita.com; Federico Gallesi 198, San Miguel; s/d/tr US$20/30/40, s/d without bathroom US$10/20, all incl breakfast; 🖵) This amiable Dutch-Peruvian guest-house is a real gem. It has a warm atmosphere, sunny courtyard, flower-bedecked gardens and convenient proximity to the airport. Its stellar reputation relies on word-of-mouth.

EATING

Many of the best restaurants are found in Miraflores. Of course, seafood is the local specialty.

Central Lima

Cheap set-lunch *menús* are offered in local restaurants. Barrio Chino (Chinatown), south-east of the Plaza de Armas, is blessed with Asian eateries.

Panko's (Map pp834-5; Garcilaso de la Vega 1296; items from US35¢) This vintage bakery offers a tempting array of sweets, pastries and drinks – your best bet for breakfast.

Azato (Map pp834-5; Arica 298; menú US$1.20-2) The spot for fast, spicy *criollo* (coastal Peruvian) food.

Villa Natura (Ucayali 326; menú US$1.50-2; 🕑 Mon-Sat) One of many no-frills vegetarian pit stops in central Lima.

Queirolo (Map pp834-5; Camaná 900; mains US$3-5; 🕑 lunch daily, dinner Mon-Sat) An atmospheric old restaurant popular for set lunches and as a watering hole for *limeños*.

La Merced (Map pp834-5; Miró Quesada 158; mains US$2-6) Bustling with businesspeople at lunch, La Merced has a surprisingly spacious interior and intricately carved wooden ceiling.

Cevichería La Choza Nautica (Map pp834-5; Breña 204; mains US$6-10) This popular little *cevichería* doesn't miss the opportunity to play on the supposedly aphrodisiacal qualities of sea-food – look for *ceviche erótico*.

L'Eau Vive (Map pp834-5; ☎ 427-5612; Ucayali 370; lunch/dinner US$10/25; 🕑 12:30-3pm & 7:30-9:30pm Mon-Sat) A uniquely flavored international res-taurant run by a French order of nuns, it's a welcome relief from the Lima madhouse. To enter the colonial mansion, ring the doorbell. The nuns sing 'Ave María' at 9pm.

For self-catering, there's **Metro** (Map pp834-5; Cuzco 3rd block; 🕑 8am-10pm).

Miraflores

Restaurants are pricier in Miraflores, but a few hole-in-the-wall cafés still serve cheap set menus. Fast-food joints cluster around Óvalo Gutiérrez and inside the LarcoMar shopping mall. Open-air cafés and pizzerias surround Parque Kennedy, including on Diagonal.

Ima Sumac (Map p840; Colón 241; menú US$2; 🕑 lunch) A warm, friendly little place with great value set meals and take-away.

Bircher Benner (Map p840; San Felipe 720; mains US$3-7; 🕑 closed Sun) This pioneering restaurant makes

---

SPLURGE!

Astrid y Gastón (Map p840; ☎ 242-5387; www.astridygaston.com; Cantuarias 175, Miraflores; mains US$10-22; ☯ lunch & dinner) Renowned for its A-list fusion cuisine prepared by celebrity chef-owner Gastón Acurio, this is the place for gourmet *tiradito* (Peruvian-style marinated raw fish) and crisp roasted duck. An elegant upper-class *limeño* mainstay, it has a stable of Cordon Bleu–trained chefs and a dining room boldly splashed with artwork. A culinary media star in his own right, Gastón has been the capital city's flavor of the month – for many, many months.

---

excellent vegetarian treats like mushroom *ceviche*. Take a taxi (US$1.50).

Vista al Mar (Map p840; Malecón de la Reserva 610; mains US$6-12) When the aroma of garlic wafts over on a Pacific sea breeze, you've arrived. Built into the clifftop, this justifiably named place cooks up a variety of seafood.

For self-caterers, **Vivanda** (Map p840; Benavides 487; ☯ 24hr) has another branch on José Pardo.

Barranco

The passageway under Puente de los Suspiros leads to restaurants and stalls where delicious *anticuchos de corazón* (beef-heart shish kabobs) are served right off the grill.

El Hornito (Map pp832-3; Grau 209; mains US$3-7) Excellent pizzas and a wide range of *parrilladas* (a selection of grilled meats) and pasta dishes, along with after-dark dining on a vine-covered patio with fairy lights.

La Canta Rana (Map pp832-3; Génova 101; mains US$7-10; ☯ lunch only) Translated as the 'The Singing Frog,' this unpretentious place is a great *cevichería*, serving all manner of seafood. Small portions, great ambience.

DRINKING

Lima overflows with bars, from San Isidro's pricey havens for the urbane elite to Barranco's cheap, cheerful watering holes. Miraflores has several streetfront cafés, as does the Plaza de Armas downtown.

You can bounce between Barranco's tight-knit nightclubs near Parque Municipal all night long. On summer weekends, energetic crowds of *limeños* head down to Km 97 on

the Pan-American Hwy, where electrifying DJs spin till dawn by the beach.

Central Lima

Drop in at the Gran Hotel Bolívar to quaff Peru's national cocktail, the *pisco sour*.

El Estadio Futbol Club (Map pp834-5; Nicolás de Piérola 926; ☯ noon-midnight Sun-Wed, to 2am Thu-Sat) This bar gives a great taste of Peruvian-style soccer fanaticism; you can literally rub shoulders with Maradona and Pelé – admittedly, just waxworks.

Miraflores

Tasca (Map p840; ☎ 01-445-6745; www.flyingdogperu .com; Flying Dog Backpackers, Diez Canseco 117) A tapas bar always stuffed full of travelers. Hours vary.

Media Naranja (Map p840; Schell 130; ☯ closed Sun) You can hardly miss the enormous Brazilian flag awnings of this lively café-bar by Parque Kennedy.

Señor Frogs (Map p840; LarcoMar; admission US$8-10; ☯ closed Sun) A flashy, electric club attracts a young, local crowd that spills out into the shopping mall cafés.

Barranco

Barranco is thronged with revelers on Friday and Saturday nights.

Juanito's (Map p832-3; Grau 274) This leftist *peña* of the 1960s is still popular for the quirky antics of its bar staff. No sign: just look for a room filled with wine bottles.

La Noche (Map pp832-3; Bolognesi 307; admission US$3) The party crowd is often to be found at this three-level bar above a busy pedestrian parade. Expect to hear anything from Latin pop to the occasional highland folk tune.

El Ekeko Café Bar (Map pp832-3; Grau 266; live-music admission US$5-7; ☯ 10am-midnight Sun-Wed, to 3am Thu-Sat) A more sedate option, this faithful old bar comes alive at weekends when Los Abuelos de la Bohemia play live music, trotting out tango, *música folklórica* and cha-cha-chas.

Wahio's (Map pp832-3; Plaza Espinosa; ☯ Thu-Sat) An energetic little bar with its fair share of dreadlocks, and a classic soundtrack of reggae, ska and dub.

Sargento Pimienta (Map pp832-3; Bolognesi 755; ☯ Wed-Sat) Spanish for 'Sergeant Pepper,' this huge barnlike place has a dance floor that becomes packed by midnight. Alcohol is cheap, and DJs play a mix of international retro, plus occasional live rock.

Déjà Vu (Map pp832-3; Grau 294-296; ☼ 6:30pm-4am) A boho club with a schizophrenic personality, the upstairs throbs with international beats, while below live Peruvian bands give gutsy performances.

ENTERTAINMENT

Many top-end hotels downtown and in San Isidro and Miraflores have slot-machine casinos.

Dance & Music

Peruvian music and dance is performed at *peñas*.

Manos Morenas (Map pp832-3; ☎ 467-0421; San Pedro de Osma 409; admission US$10; ☼ shows 10pm Tue-Sat) An informal joint for top-notch *criollo* food and music.

Las Brisas de Titicaca (Map pp834-5; ☎ 332-1901; www.brisasdeltiticaca.com; Walkuski 168, central Lima; admission US$8-12.50; ☼ 7pm-late Wed, 9:30pm-late Thu, 10.30pm-late Fri & Sat) and **La Candelaria** (Map pp832-3; ☎ 01-247-1314; www.lacandelariaperu.com; Bolognesi 292, Barranco; admission US$7; ☼ 9:30-late Fri & Sat) are popular with *limeños*.

Sports

Bullfighting is popular in Lima. The main season runs from late October to late November, plus a shorter season in March.

Plaza de Acho bullring (Map pp834-5; ☎ 481-1467; Hualgayoc 332, Rímac; tickets US$20-100; ☼ matches 3pm Sun) Matadors fight here. The surrounding neighborhood is unsafe, so take a taxi. Buy tickets in advance.

Estadio Nacional (Map pp834-5) The major venue for football (soccer) matches.

Cinemas

Cinemas may offer half-price entry midweek. Most screen recent releases in English, with Spanish subtitles.

Cine Planet central Lima (Map pp834-5; ☎ 452-7000; Jirón de la Unión 819); Miraflores (Map p840; ☎ 452-7000; Santa Cruz 814)

UVK Multicines LarcoMar (Map p840; ☎ 446-7336; LarcoMar, Miraflores)

Some smaller, more esoteric options include the following:

El Cinematógrafo (Map pp832-3; ☎ 01-477-1961; Pérez Roca 196, Barranco) Arty and alternative-genre movies.

Filmoteca (Map pp834-5; ☎ 01-423-4732; Parque de la Cultura, Paseo Colón 125, Central Lima) At Lima's Museo de Arte.

SHOPPING

Shopping malls include the underground LarcoMar (Map p840), with a spectacular location built right into the oceanfront cliffs, selling high-end artisan crafts, electronics, photographic supplies, outdoor gear, books and music.

Mercado del Indios (Map p840; Petit Thouars 5245, Miraflores) Haggle your heart out at this enormous market, where you can browse handicrafts from all over Peru.

La Casa de la Mujer Artesana Manuela Ramos (Map pp832-3; ☎ 423-8800; Juan Pablo Fernandini 1550, Pueblo Libre; ☼ 9am-5pm Mon-Fri) A nonprofit women's crafts cooperative off the 15th block of Brazil.

Agua y Tierra (Map p840; ☎ 444-6980; Diez Canseco 298, Miraflores; ☼ closed Sun) Specializes in Amazonian pottery, textiles and art.

GETTING THERE & AWAY
Air

Lima's **Aeropuerto Internacional Jorge Chávez** (LIM; Map pp832-3; ☎ 517-3100; www.lap.com.pe) is in Callao. Departure taxes (payable in dollars or nuevos soles, cash only) are US$28.10 for international and US$6.05 for domestic flights.

Many international airlines have offices in Lima – check under 'Lineas Áreas' in the yellow pages. Airlines offering domestic flights include the following:

Aero Condor Perú (Map pp832-3; ☎ 614-6014; Juan de Arona 781, San Isidro)

LAN (Map p840; ☎ 213-8200; José Pardo 513, Miraflores)

LC Busre (Map pp832-3; ☎ 619-1313; Los Tulipones 218, Lince)

Star Perú (Map p840; ☎ 705-9000; José Pardo 269, Miraflores)

TACA (Map pp832-3; ☎ 511-8222; Espinar 331, San Isidro)

See regional sections later in this chapter for details of which airlines fly where. Be aware that flight schedules and ticket prices change frequently. Getting flight information, buying tickets and reconfirming flights are best done at airline offices (or a reputable travel agency) rather than at the airport counters.

The official ISIC office is **InteJ** (Map pp832-3; ☎ 247-3230; www.intej.org; San Martín 240, Barranco)

PERU

which organizes student airfares and can change dates for flights booked through student/youth travel agencies. **Fertur Peru** (Map pp834-5; ☎ 427-1958; Junín 211, central Lima; ✆ 9am-7pm Mon-Sat) is also good for student airfares.

Bus

Lima has no central bus terminal. Each company runs its own office and station, many of which cluster around Javier Prado Este in La Victoria. Others are found in central Lima several blocks east of Plaza Grau, just north of Av Grau and south of 28 de Julio, on both sides of Paseo de la República. Make sure you verify which station your bus departs from when buying tickets. There are countless companies to choose from, so look carefully at the quality of the bus before deciding.

Major companies include the following:

Cruz del Sur (www.cruzdelsur.com.pe); central Lima (Map pp834-5; ☎ 431-5125; Quilca 531); La Victoria (Map pp832-3; ☎ 225-6163/5748; Javier Prado Este 1109) Reliable, but doesn't have as frequent services or extensive routes as some other companies.

Ormeño (www.grupo-ormeno.com) central Lima (Map pp834-5; ☎ 427-5679; Carlos Zavala Loayza 177); La Victoria (Map pp832-3; ☎ 472-1710; Javier Prado Este 1059) Quality of service varies wildly. Has the most international services, including to Bogotá, Buenos Aires, Caracas, La Paz, Quito and Santiago.

Also in central Lima:

Civa (Map pp834-5; ☎ 332-5236/526; www.civa.com.pe; cnr 28 de Julio & Paseo de la República 575)

Cromotex (Map pp834-5; ☎ 424-7575; Paseo de República 659-665)

Expreso Molina (Map pp834-5; ☎ 428-0617; Ayacucho 1141-1145)

Flores (Map pp834-5; ☎ 424-3278; cnr Paseo de la República & 28 de Julio)

Ittsa (Map pp834-5; ☎ 423-5232; Paseo de la República 809)

Linea (Map pp834-5; ☎ 424-0836; José Galvez 999A)

Móvil Tours (Map pp834-5; ☎ 332-0004; Paseo de la República 749)

Soyuz (Map pp834-5; ☎ 226-1515; Mexico 333 at Paseo de la República)

Tepsa (☎ 470-6666; www.tepsa.com.pe; Javier Prado Oeste 1091)

Transportes Atahualpa (Map pp834-5; ☎ 427-7324/7338; Sandía 266)

See regional sections for details of which bus companies go where. Approximate one-way fares and durations from Lima follow.

Destination	Duration (hr)	Cost (US$)
Arequipa	17	12-40
Ayacucho	9	6-15
Cajamarca	14	9-27
Chachapoyas	21½	21-27
Chiclayo	10	12-24
Cuzco	17-27	18-48
Huancayo	6½	6-14
Huaraz	7½	6-17
Ica	4½	3.50-13.50
Nazca	8	5-22.50
Piura	14	25-38
Puno	19	11-45
Tacna	20	9-43
Trujillo	8	9-31.50
Tumbes	17	15-48

Train

See p897 for details of highland rail services to Huancayo.

GETTING AROUND

See p831 for details of getting to/from the airport.

Bus

Local minibuses (aka *combis* or *micros*) around Lima are startlingly cheap (fares from US30¢). Destinations are identifiable by windscreen cards, and you can flag them down or get off anywhere. The most useful routes link central Lima with Miraflores along Arequipa: buses are labeled 'Todo Arequipa' and 'Larco/Schell/Miraflores' when heading to Miraflores, or 'Todo Arequipa' and 'Wilson/Tacna' when leaving Miraflores for central Lima. A slower, green full-sized bus marked 73A runs from the city center through Miraflores and on to Barranco (US50¢), passing along Tacna and Garcilaso de la Vega in downtown and Arequipa and José Larco in Miraflores.

Taxi

Taxis don't have meters, so make sure you negotiate a price before getting in. Short runs start at US$1.50, higher after dark. The majority of taxis in Lima are unofficial. Officially registered taxis are generally safer, but charge up to 50% more. You can call them by phone or catch them at taxi stands, such as at the LarcoMar shopping mall in Miraflores. **Moli Taxi** (☎ 479-0030), **Taxi Miraflores** (☎ 446-3953) and **Taxi Móvil** (☎ 422-6890) run 24 hours and accept reservations.

SOUTH COAST

Watered by palm oases and spanned by the Carretera Panamericana, this vast coastal desert is the best overland route to Arequipa, Lake Titicaca and Cuzco. These arid lowlands gave birth to some extraordinary pre-Columbian civilizations, especially the Nazca, remembered for their striking lines and figures etched across 500 sq km. Pisco is famous for its rich marine wildlife and rugged coastline, while neighboring Ica is surrounded by vineyards and the monstrous sand dunes of Huacachina.

CHILCA

Km 66 on the Panamericana south of Lima is the turnoff to the village of **Chilca** with its famous muddy, mineral-rich **lagoons** (admission US30¢; ⏰ 24hr). One is nicknamed 'La Milagrosa' for its miraculous powers to heal everything from acne to arthritis – some even claim it has alien origins. A moto-rickshaw from the Panamericana, where coastal buses stop, costs US$1.50.

LUNAHUANÁ

☎ 056 / pop 3600

Almost 15km past the surfers' beach of Cerro Azul (Panamericana Km 131), the dusty market town of San Vincente de Cañete is the gateway to the wine country of Lunahuaná. Show up for the **harvest festival** the second week in March, or to tipple free samples at the *bodegas* (wineries) year-round.

The whitewater rafting (river-running) season on the Río Cañete is December to April, and rapids can reach Class IV. **Río Cañete Expediciones** (☎ in Lima 01-284-1271; www.riocanete.com.pe; rafting tours US$10-37) runs **Camping San Jerónimo** (☎ 9635-3921; Carretera Cañete–Lunahuaná Km 33; campsites per person US$3) on the river west of town. There's a rock-climbing wall, too.

Near the plaza, **Hostal Casuarinas** (☎ 056-581-2627; Grau 295; s/d US$6/12) is a decent budget hotel with tidy rooms sporting TVs and hot showers. At several nearby seafood restaurants, the local specialty is crawfish.

From Cañete, where coastal buses stop on the Panamericana, catch a minivan to Imperial (US15¢, 10 minutes), then another minivan to Lunahuaná (US$1, 45 minutes), nearly 40km away. Rent mountain bikes near Lunahuaná's main plaza.

CHINCHA

☎ 056 / pop 140,000

At Panamericana Km 202, this sprawling town is famous for wild Afro-Peruvian music heard in the *peñas* of the **El Carmen** district. The best times to visit are during **Verano Negro** (late February/early March), **Fiestas Patrias** (late July) and **Fiesta de Virgen del Carmen** (December 27). During these times, the *peñas* are full of frenzied *limeños* and locals shakin' that ass. One dance not to try at home is 'El Alcatraz,' when a gyrating male dancer attempts to set his partner's skirt on fire with a candle.

Hacienda San José (☎ 22-1458; www.hacienda sanjose.com.pe; d incl breakfast US$27-38; ⛱) is packed with over 300 years of history. Sheltered by orange groves, it once was a sugar and honey plantation worked by African slaves until a rebellion broke out in 1879, leading to the master being dramatically hacked to death. Guided Spanish-language tours (US$3) go down into the ghoulish catacombs. From Chincha, catch a minivan bound for El Carmen (ask the driver where to get off), then walk about 2km. A taxi costs US$6 one way.

Bare-bones budget *hostales* and *chifa* restaurants surround Chincha's main plaza. **Hostal La Posada** (☎ 26-2042; Santo Domingo 200; s/d US$9/15), run by a gregarious Italian-Peruvian couple, is a secure choice with antique-looking rooms. In El Carmen, a few local families take in overnight guests and cook them meals for under US$10 per night – just ask around.

Minivans to El Carmen (US50¢, 30 minutes) leave from Chincha's central market, a few blocks from the main plaza. It's a short taxi ride (US$1) from the Panamericana where coastal buses stop.

PISCO

☎ 056 / pop 58,000

Sharing its name with the white-grape brandy produced in this region, Pisco is an important port 235km south of Lima. Generally used as a

PERU

THE FLAMINGO FLAG

Locals like to tell a fanciful yarn of how the Peruvian flag was born on the beaches of the Península de Paracas. The story goes that *libertador* José de San Martín landed here in 1820 and, exhausted after a long journey, fell into a deep sleep. When he awoke, he was dazzled by the flamboyance of flamingos flying overhead, their outstretched wings catching the light of the setting sun. It was those flashes of red that allegedly gave him the inspiration for the scarlet outer panels of what is now Peru's national flag.

---

base from which to see the abundant wildlife of the Islas Ballestas and Península de Paracas, the area is also of historical and archaeological interest, having hosted one of the most highly developed pre-Inca civilizations – the Paracas Culture – from 900 BC until AD 200. Later it acted as a base for Peru's revolutionary fever in the 1800s.

Information

Internet cafés and banks with 24-hour ATMs surround the main plaza.

Dangers & Annoyances

Never walk alone after dark. Violent muggings have happened even on busy streets. The most dangerous areas are near the beaches and around the market. Women can expect lots of unwanted attention here.

Sights & Activities

A **statue** (Map p847) of liberator José de San Martín peers down on the Plaza de Armas. Martín's headquarters, **Club Social Pisco** (Map p847; San Martín 132), still stands nearby. The **cemetery** (Map p847) has a few hidden secrets: bur-

ied here is suspected 19th-century English vampire, Sarah Ellen Roberts, who claimed that she would arise again after 100 years. In 1993, much to everyone's disappointment, she didn't.

ISLAS BALLESTAS

Nicknamed 'the poor man's Galapagos,' these offshore islands make for a laid-back excursion. The outward boat journey takes about 1½ hours. En route you'll see the famous three-pronged **Candelabra** (Map p848), a giant figure etched into the sandy hills. An hour is spent cruising around the island's arches and caves, watching noisy sea lions sprawl on the rocks. You may also spot Humboldt penguins, Chilean flamingos and dolphins. The most common guano-producing birds are cormorants, boobies and pelicans, present in thousands-strong colonies.

RESERVA NACIONAL DE PARACAS

Beyond the village of Paracas is the entrance to this desert-filled **national reserve** (Map p848; admission US$1.50). Next to the visitor center, which has kid-friendly exhibits on conservation and ecology, the **Museo JC Tello** (Map p848; adult/child/student US$2.50/30¢/60¢; ⏲ 9am-5pm) has a limited collection of weavings, trophy heads and trepanned skulls (showing a medical technique used by ancient cultures whereby a slice of the skull is removed, relieving pressure on the brain resulting from injuries). Chilean flamingos often hang out in the bay in front of the complex, and there's now a walkway down to a **mirador** (watchtower; Map p848). A few hundred meters behind the visitor complex are the paltry 5000-year-old remains of the **Paracas Necropolis** (Map p848).

Tours

Boat tours to the Islas Ballestas leave daily at 7am (US$10). Minibuses go from Pisco

---

DROPPINGS TO DIE FOR

Layers of sunbaked, nitrogen-rich seabird droppings (guano) have been deposited over millennia on the Islas Ballestas by resident bird colonies – in places the droppings are 50m deep. Guano's reputation as a first-class fertilizer dates back to pre-Inca times, but few would have predicted that these filthy riches were to become Peru's principal export during the mid-19th century. In fact, the trade was so lucrative that Spain precipitated the so-called Guano War of 1865–66 over possession of the nearby Chincha Islands. Nowadays, synthetic fertilizers and overexploitation have taken their toll, so the birds are largely left to their messy production process in peace, except for licensed extraction every 10 years – and boatloads of tourists every day, of course.

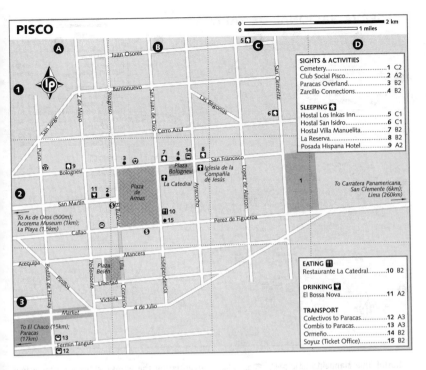

PISCO

SIGHTS & ACTIVITIES
Cemetery..............................1 C2
Club Social Pisco..................2 A2
Paracas Overland...................3 B2
Zarcillo Connections..............4 B2

SLEEPING
Hostal Los Inkas Inn...............5 C1
Hostal San Isidro...................6 C1
Hostal Villa Manuelita............7 B2
La Reserva...........................8 B2
Posada Hispana Hotel.............9 A2

To Carretera Panamericana,
San Clemente (6km);
Lima (260km)

To As de Oros (500m);
Acorema Museum (1km);
La Playa (1.5km)

EATING
Restaurante La Catedral.........10 B2

DRINKING
El Bossa Nova......................11 A2

TRANSPORT
Colectivos to Paracas.............12 A3
Combis to Paracas.................13 A3
Ormeño.............................14 B2
Soyuz (Ticket Office)............15 B2

To El Chaco (15km);
Paracas
(17km)

(Map p847) to the port at Paracas (Map p848); there's no cabin on the boats, so dress for wind and spray. Wear a hat, as it's not unusual to receive a direct guano hit. You can continue on a less interesting afternoon tour of the Península de Paracas (US$8, or US$16 with Islas Ballestas), which briefly stops at the visitor center and museum (entry fees not included), whizzes by coastal geological formations and spends a long time having lunch (also not included) in a remote fishing village.

You can hire a taxi and guide (US$10 to US$15 per person) to visit the adobe-walled Inca fort ruins of **Tambo Colorado** (admission US$2), about 45km from Pisco. In the El Chaco district of Paracas, **Paracas Explorer** (Map p848; ☎ 54-5141/5089; www.paracasexplorer.com) offers dune-buggy and sandboarding tours.

Some Pisco travel agencies:
Paracas Overland (Map p847; ☎ 056-53-3855; paracasoverland@hotmail.com; San Francisco 111)
Zarcillo Connections (Map p847; ☎ 056-53-6543; www.ballestasislands.com; Suite B, Callao 137)

Sleeping

Most travelers stay in central Pisco.

Hostal San Isidro (Map p847; ☎ 53-6471; San Clemente 103; www.sanisidrohostal.com; dm/s/d/tr US$7/10/20/30; ⊠) A popular spot near the cemetery (it's unsafe to walk here after dark), with a kitchen and games room. Secure rooms have cable TV, fans and hot water.

Hostal Los Inkas Inn (Map p847; ☎ 53-6634/54-5149; www.losinkasinn.com; Barrio Nuevo 14; s/d/tr US$9/13.50/18; ⊠ ⊠) This small family-owned guesthouse has basic rooms, a miniature swimming pool, a rooftop terrace and free internet.

La Reserva (Map p847; ☎ 53-5643; lareserva_hostal@hotmail.com; San Francisco 327; s/d/tr incl breakfast US$10/20/30) For something a bit sharper, the whitewashed, oval-shaped La Reserva has sparkling rooms with modish furnishings and cable TV.

Posada Hispana Hotel (Map p847; ☎ 53-6363; www.posadahispana.com; Bolognesi 236; s/d US$15/30; ⊠) With bamboo fixtures and a downstairs espresso café, this place has legions of fans. Musty rooms are a good deal only if you bargain. French and Italian spoken.

PERU

RESERVA NACIONAL DE PARACAS

			0	10 km
			0	6 miles

INFORMATION
Paracas Explorer...........................(see 8)
Park Visitor Center...........................1 B3

SIGHTS & ACTIVITIES
Candelabra.......................................2 B2
Clifftop Lookout...............................3 B3
Flamingos Often Seen Here.............4 B3
Mirador...5 B3
Museo JC Tello.............................(see 1)
Paracas Necropolis..........................6 B3
Playa El Chaco................................7 B2

SLEEPING
El Amigo...8 B2
Hotel Paracas..................................9 B3

TRANSPORT
Boats to Islas Ballestas..................10 B3

Hostal Villa Manuelita (Map p847; ☎ 53-5218; hostalvillamanuelita@hotmail.com; San Francisco 227; s/d US$18/28) In an antique colonial building near the plaza, this guesthouse has spacious rooms with cable TV, an Italianesque café and ornamental gardens out back. Women are especially welcome.

By the beach in the El Chaco district of Paracas, guesthouses include **El Amigo** (Map p848; ☎ 54-5042; s/d US$10/15), which has basic rooms, some with sea views. Camping is allowed in the national reserve, though robberies and attacks have been reported – don't do it alone.

Eating & Drinking

Few cafés open early for breakfast. Most restaurants and bars cluster around the Plaza de Armas and along pedestrian-only El Bulevar.

Restaurante La Catedral (Map p847; 108 San Juan de Dios; mains US$4.50-6) Brightly lit like a school cafeteria, this cheery favorite serves up heaping plates of Peruvian seafood, fried bananas and much more.

El Bossa Nova (Map p847; San Martín 176; ☟ 5pm-late Mon-Sat) An intimate café-bar from which to peer down on folks strutting by. Take care

negotiating the wonky staircase after a few exquisitely made *pisco sours*.

Getting There & Around

Pisco is 6km west of the Panamericana. *Colectivo* taxis and minivans for the San Clemente turnoff, where you can catch long-distance coastal buses, leave frequently from the market (Map p847) area during daylight hours (US30¢, 10 minutes).

Ormeño (Map p847; ☎ 53-2764; San Francisco 259) has a tout-ridden bus terminal near the Plaza de Armas. It runs daily buses to Lima (US$5 to US$10, four hours) and many other coastal destinations, including Ica, Nazca and Tacna. Some of these services go direct, while others require a change of bus on the highway.

Combis to Paracas leave from near the market about every half hour during the day (US60¢, 30 minutes). Taxis to Paracas cost US$3.

ICA
☎ 056 / pop 217,700

The capital of its department, Ica may have a downtrodden air, but it boasts a thriving wine and *pisco* industry, raucous festivals and an excellent museum. Most backpackers base themselves at nearby Huacachina (p850).

Information

Around the plaza, internet cafés stay open late.

BCP (Plaza de Armas) Changes traveler's checks and cash, and has a Visa ATM.

Hospital (☎ 23-4798/4450; Cutervo 104; ⏰ 24hr) For emergencies.

Interbank (Grau 2nd block) Has a global ATM.

Police (☎ 23-5421; JJ Elias 5th block; ⏰ 24hr)

Serpost (San Martín 156)

Telefónica-Perú (Lima 149) Stays open late.

Dangers & Annoyances

Ica has a deserved reputation for theft. Stay alert, particularly around the market and bus terminals.

Sights

Despite a robbery in 2004, the **Museo Regional de Ica** (☎ 23-4383; Jirón Ayabaca 8th block; adult/child/ student US$4/2.50/1; ⏰ 8am-7pm Mon-Fri, 9am-6pm Sat & Sun) still possesses an unmatched collection of artifacts from the Paracas, Nazca and Inca cultures, including superb Paracas weavings, well-preserved mummies, trepanned skulls and shrunken trophy heads. Out back is a scale model of the Nazca Lines. The museum is 1.5km southwest of the city center. Take a taxi from the Plaza de Armas (US$1).

Famous wines and *piscos* can be sampled at **bodegas** outside town. **Vista Alegre** (☎ 23-2919; ⏰ 8am-noon & 1:45-4:45pm Mon-Fri, 7am-1pm Sat), 3km northeast of Ica, is the easiest commercial winery to visit (taxi US$1.50). Also producing the right stuff is **Tacama** (☎ 22-8395; www .tacama.com; ⏰ 9am-4pm), 11km northeast of Ica, which offers interesting tours. There are dozens of smaller, family-owned artesanal wineries, including those in suburban **Guadalupe**. *Micros* to Guadalupe pass by the Iglesia de San Francisco (US30¢, 15 minutes) near the plaza.

Festivals & Events

The harvest festival, **Fiesta de la Vendimia**, is held in early to mid-March. The religious pilgrimage of **El Señor de Luren** culminates in an all-night procession in late October. September hosts **Tourist Week**.

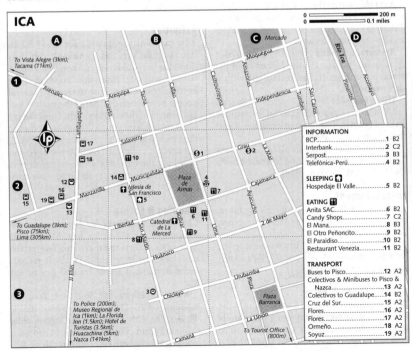

ICA

0 — 200 m
0 — 0.1 miles

PERU

Sleeping

If you somehow get stuck in Ica overnight, dozens of depressing budget hotels line the streets east of the bus terminals and north of the plaza, especially along Tacna. Rates double or even triple during festivals. Nearby Huacachina (right) has cheaper, more popular backpacker crash pads.

Hospedaje El Valle (☎ 21-6801; San Martín 151; s/d US$7.50/11) More sprightly than the competition, this old-fashioned hostelry run by gracious ladies faces an inner courtyard and has a safe, securely gated entrance. It's a block west of the plaza.

La Florida Inn (☎ 23-7313; http://hometown.aol3 .com/lemco3/laflorida.html; Residencial La Florida B-1; dm US$8, s/d US$15/30, without bathroom US$10/20; ✉ 🖳) This small, family-owned hotel not too far from the museum has quirky rooms with TVs and solar-powered hot water. Call ahead for reservations and directions.

Eating

Several shops east of the main plaza sell *tejas* (caramel-wrapped candies flavored with fruits, nuts etc).

Anita SAC (Libertad 133; menú US$3-3.60, mains US$3.25-10) On the Plaza de Armas, this cheery café dishes up heaping plates of regional specialties and lip-smacking desserts.

Restaurant Venezia (Lima 230; mains US$4-9; ☺ closed Sat) Just around the corner from the plaza, an upscale Italian restaurant with a super wine list.

El Otro Peñoncito (Bolívar 255; mains US$4-10) Ica's most historic and characterful restaurant serves Peruvian and international fare – and shakes a mean *pisco sour*, too.

Two no-frills vegetarian places are **El Mana** (San Martín 2nd block; menú US$1) and **El Paraidiso** (Loreto 176-178; menú US$1.50; ☺ closed Sat).

Entertainment

South of the Plaza de Armas along Lima, you'll find a few local bars with live music, DJs and dancing.

The craziest late-night disco is next to the **Hotel de Turistas** (Av de Los Maestros 500), 3km southwest of the plaza (taxi US$1).

Getting There & Away

Bus companies cluster on Lambayeque at the west end of Salaverry and along Manzanilla west of Lambayeque. For Lima (US$3.50 to US$13.50, 4½ hours), **Soyuz** (☎ 056-23-3312)

and **Flores** (☎ 056-21-2266) have departures every 15 minutes, while less frequent luxury services go with **Cruz del Sur** (☎ 056-22-3333) and **Ormeño** (☎ 056-21-5600). To Pisco (US$1.50, 1½ hours), Ormeño has direct buses, while other bus companies drop passengers at the San Clemente turnoff on the Panamericana (see p848). Most companies have direct daytime buses to Nazca (US$2, 2½ hours). Services to Arequipa (US$15 to US$24, 12 hours) are mostly overnight.

Faster, more expensive *colectivos* and minibuses for Pisco and Nazca leave from around the intersection of Lambayeque and Municipalidad.

HUACACHINA

☎ 056 / pop 200

Just 5km west of Ica, this oasis surrounded by towering sand dunes nestles next to a picturesque (if smelly) lagoon that features on the back of Peru's S/50 note. Graceful palm trees, exotic flowers and attractive antique buildings testify to the bygone glamor of this resort built for the Peruvian elite. These days, it's the playground of international party-hardy backpackers.

Activities

You can rent sandboards for US$1.50 an hour to slide, surf and somersault your way down the irresistible dunes. Though it's softer, warmer and safer than snowboarding, don't be lulled into a false sense of security: several people have seriously injured themselves losing control of their sandboards. Dune-buggy tours (which haul you to the top of the dunes, then pick you up at the bottom) cost US$12, but check if sandboard rental is included and how long the trip lasts. Dune-buggy drivers are notoriously unsafe, so go at your own risk.

Sleeping & Eating

Camping is possible in the dunes around the lagoon – bring a sleeping bag. Most hotels have a café of sorts and there are a few restaurants near the waterfront. Travelers recommend Restaurant Sol de Ica and Restaurant Mayo.

Hostal Salvatierra (☎ 056-23-2352; Malecón de Huacachina; s/d US$4.50/7.50, without bathroom US$3/6; 🖳 🖳) The only hostel on the lagoon side, this family-run choice has spacious rooms, a low-key atmosphere and comfortable beds.

Casa de Arena (☎ 21-5439/5274; casadearena@hot
mail.com; Perotti s/n; dm US$3.60, s/d US$5/7.50, with bathroom US$7.50/9; ▢ ▨) A perennially popular
place with an outdoor pool bar for all-night
parties, the staff here just don't seem to care
(though pretty young women can expect lots
of attention). Private rooms at the back at least
have good views.

Hostal Rocha (☎ 22-9987/2256; kikerocha@hotmail
.com; Perotti s/n; s/d incl breakfast US$7.50/9; ▨) An
efficiently run hostel with the same carefree,
anything-goes atmosphere Casa de Arena,
especially at the poolside bar. Rooms can
be claustrophobic, but there are hammocks
outside to laze away in. Kitchen access.

Hospedaje El Huacanicero (☎ 21-7435; Perotti s/n;
www.elhuacachinero.com; s/d US$7.50/9; ▨) Easily
spotted by the green *areneros* (dune buggies)
parked out front, this two-story guesthouse is
a work-in-progress. Rickety rooms with shuttered windows are just a stone's throw from
the dunes. Kitchen access, garden hammocks
and a pool bar.

Getting There & Away
A taxi or motorized rickshaw between Ica and
Huacachina costs about US$1.

NAZCA
☎ 056 / pop 53,000
This sun-bleached spot on the Panamericana
was largely ignored by the outside world until
1939, when North American scientist Paul
Kosok flew across the desert and stumbled
across one of ancient Peru's most impressive and enigmatic achievements: the world-
famous Nazca Lines. Today this small town
is flooded by travelers who come to marvel and scratch their heads over the mysterious lines, now a Unesco World Heritage
site.

Information
Cybercafés are everywhere. A few hotels
change US dollars for cash.
BCP (Lima 495) Has a Visa ATM; changes traveler's
checks.
Casa Andina (Bolognesi 367) The global ATM sometimes
works.
Telefónica-Perú (Lima 525) Stays open late.

Sights
NAZCA LINES
Spread across around 500 sq km of arid,
rock-strewn plain, the Nazca Lines form a
striking network of over 800 lines, 300 geometric figures (geoglyphs), and some 70 animal and plant drawings (biomorphs). The
most elaborate designs include a monkey with
an extraordinarily curvaceous tail, a spider
and an intriguing figure popularly called the
astronaut, though others think it's a priest
with an owl's head. Overflights of the lines
are unforgettable, but they're not cheap (see
Tours, p852).

You'll get only a sketchy idea of the lines at
the **mirador** (admission US30¢), on the Panamericana
20km north of Nazca, which has an oblique
view of three figures: the lizard, tree and hands
(or frog, depending on your point of view).
Signs warning of landmines are a reminder
that walking on the lines is strictly forbidden.
To get to the observation tower, catch a northbound bus or *colectivo* (US75¢).

Another 5km north is the small **Maria Reiche
Museum** (admission US$1.50; ◷ 9am-6pm). Though
disappointingly scant on information, you
can see where she lived, amid the clutter of
her tools and obsessive sketches, and pay your
respects to her tomb. To return to Nazca, flag
down any passing bus.

Scripted but interesting multilingual lectures on the lines are given every evening at

---

MYSTERIES IN THE SAND

The awesome, ancient Nazca Lines were made by removing sun-darkened stones from the
desert surface to expose the lighter soil below. But who constructed the gigantic lines and
for what reason? And why bother when they can only be properly appreciated from the air?
Maria Reiche, a German mathematician and longtime researcher of the lines, theorized that they
were made by the Paracas and Nazca cultures from 900 BC to AD 600, with additions by the
Wari in the 7th century. She believed the lines were an astronomical calendar mapped out by
sophisticated mathematics (and a long rope). Others theorize that the lines were ritual walkways connected to a water/fertility cult, giant running tracks, extraterrestrial landing sites or
representations of shamans' dreams brought on by hallucinogenic drugs. Take your pick – no
one really knows!

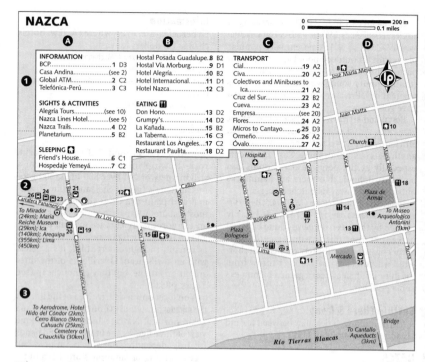

NAZCA

0 .... 200 m
0 .... 0.1 miles

INFORMATION	
BCP	1 D3
Casa Andina	(see 2)
Global ATM	2 C2
Telefónica-Perú	3 C3

SIGHTS & ACTIVITIES	
Alegría Tours	(see 10)
Nazca Lines Hotel	(see 5)
Nazca Trails	4 D2
Planetarium	5 B2

SLEEPING	
Friend's House	6 C1
Hospedaje Yemeyá	7 C2

Hostal Posada Guadalupe	8 B2
Hostal Vía Morburg	9 D1
Hotel Alegría	10 B2
Hotel Internacional	11 D1
Hotel Nazca	12 C3

EATING	
Don Hono	13 D2
Grumpy's	14 D2
La Kañada	15 B2
La Taberna	16 C3
Restaurant Los Angeles	17 C2
Restaurant Paulita	18 D2

TRANSPORT	
Cial	19 A2
Civa	20 A2
Colectivos and Minibuses to Ica	21 A2
Cruz del Sur	22 B2
Cueva	23 A2
Empresa	(see 20)
Flores	24 A2
Micros to Cantayo	25 D3
Ormeño	26 A2
Óvalo	27 A2

Nazca's small **planetarium** (☎ 52-2293; Nazca Lines Hotel, Bolognesi s/n; adult/student US$6/3).

MUSEO DIDACTICO ANTONINI

On the east side of town, this **archaeological museum** (☎ 52-3444; Av de la Cultura 600; admission/cameras US$3/1.50; ☼ 9am-7pm) boasts an aqueduct running through the back garden, plus reproductions of burial tombs and a scale model of the lines. You can get an overview of the Nazca culture and a glimpse of Nazca's outlying sites here.

OUTLYING SITES

It's safest to visit outlying archaeological sites with an organized tour and guide (see Tours, right) as robberies and assaults on tourists have been reported. At the **Cantallo aqueducts** (admission US$1), just outside town, you can descend into the ancient stonework by means of spiraling *ventanas* (windows) – a wet, claustrophobic experience. The popular **Cemetery of Chauchilla** (admission US$1.50), 30km south of Nazca, will satisfy any macabre urges you have to see bones, skulls and mummies. A dirt road travels 25km west to

Cahuachi, an important Nazca center still being excavated.

Activities

Go swimming at the **Nazca Lines Hotel** (Bolognesi s/n; entry incl snack & drink US$5). An off-the-beaten-track expedition is to **Cerro Blanco**, the world's highest-known sand dune (2078m). It's a real challenge for budding sandboarders fresh from Huacachina. Half-day mountain-biking tours cost about the same (US$35).

Tours

Hotels and travel agencies tirelessly promote their own tours. Aggressive touts meet arriving buses to hard-sell you before you've even picked up your pack. Don't rush: most agencies are clustered at the southwest end of Lima. Never hand over money on the street.

Tours to outlying sites usually include a tedious stop for a demonstration at a potter's and/or gold-miner's workshop (tips expected). To go independently, **Jorge Echeandia** (☎ 52-1134/971-4038; jorgenasca17@yahoo.com) is an experienced local guide, as are some staff at the Museo Didactico Antonini.

PERU

Bumpy flights over the Nazca Lines in light aircraft take off in the morning and early afternoon, if weather conditions allow. Motion-sickness sufferers should skip breakfast. A standard 30-minute overflight costs US$45, but prices can climb to US$60 from May to August; low-season deals may also be available. There is a US$5 tax at the aerodrome, 2km south of town.

Book overflights a few days in advance. Some established travel agencies:

Nasca Trails (☎ 52-2858; nascatrails@terra.com.pe; Bolognesi 550)

Alegría Tours (☎ 056-52-2444; www.alegriatoursperu .com; Lima 168).

Sleeping

Prices can double between May and August.

Hotel Nido del Cóndor (☎ 52-3520; www.aerocondor .com.pe; Km 447 Panamericana Sur; camping per person US$3; ☒) Opposite the aerodrome; allows camping on a grassy lawn.

Hotel Nazca (☎ 52-2085; marionasca13@hotmail .com; Lima 438; s/d US$8.50/12.50, s without bathroom US$3) A friendly, older place offering basic courtyard rooms, some with communal tepid showers.

Friend's House (☎ 52-3630/2684; elmochilero_1000@ hotmail.com; Juan Matt 712; s/d without bathroom incl breakfast US$4.50/6) A fly-by-night backpacker hostel staffed by youthful local guys. Kitchen access, laundry, TV room and a small workout room.

Hotel Alegría (☎ 52-2702; Lima 168; r without bathroom US$4.50-7.50, s/d/tr incl continental breakfast US$18/25/33; ☒ ☒) This well-heeled oasis keeps a dozen more basic rooms with shared hot showers for budget travelers. There's a breezy garden and courtyard café.

Hostal Posada Guadalupe (☎ 52-2249; San Martín 225; s/d US$5/7.50) At the west end of town on a residential block, it couldn't be closer to the bus stops, but still manages an unhurried feel. Some of the basic rooms have private bathrooms.

Hospedaje Yemeyá (☎ 52-3416; Callao 578; r incl breakfast US$7.50-22.50; ☒) An indefatigable family offers a few floors of small but well-cared-for rooms with hot showers and cable TV. There's a sociable terrace and café.

Hostal Vía Morburg (☎ 52-2141; hotelvia morburg@ yahoo.es; José María Mejía 108; s/d US$7.50/10.50; ☒) A noisy but fairly reliable guesthouse with a rooftop café. The swimming pool is the size of a bathtub.

Hotel Internacional (☎ 55-2744; Maria Reiche 112; r/bungalows US$8.50/12.50) Don't let the lackluster entrance fool you: the Internacional may sport basic rooms, but also bigger, better duplex-style bungalows with patios out back.

Eating & Drinking

West of the Plaza de Armas, Bolognesi is lined with backpacker pizzerias, restaurants and bars, including Grumpy's at No 182.

Restaurant Paulita (Tacna 2nd block; menú US$1.50-2) With two outdoor tables facing the Plaza de Armas, this local fave serves homestyle Peruvian food and a few *criollo* specialties.

La Taberna (Lima 321; menú US$1.50-4.50; mains from US$5) At this intimate hole-in-the-wall, scribbles covering every inch of wall are a testament to its popularity. Live music some evenings.

Restaurant Los Angeles (Bolognesi 266; mains US$2-5) This Peruvian and international eatery owned by a French- and English-speaking local guide makes especially delicious soups and salads.

Don Hono (Arica 254; mains US$2-6; ☒ closed Sun) Just off the main plaza, this old standby serves farm-fresh produce and is justifiably proud of its *pisco sour*.

La Kañada (Lima 160; menú US$3, mains around US$5; ☒ 9am-9pm) Offers Peruvian fare near the bus stops. A decent cocktail list includes Algarrobina, made with syrup from the *huarango* (carob) tree.

Getting There & Around

Bus companies cluster at the west end of Lima, near the main Panamericana roundabout. Most services to Lima (US$5 to US$22.50, eight hours), Arequipa (US$7 to US$36, 10 to 12 hours) and Tacna (US$7 to US$30, 14 hours) leave late in the afternoon or evening. Be aware that hijackings and robberies of overnight buses to/from Arequipa have occurred recently. To go direct to Cuzco (US$15 to US$30, 13 to 15 hours), several companies take the paved road east via Abancay. This route gets cold, so wear warm clothes. The alternative is to go via Arequipa. For Ica, fast *colectivos* (US$3.60, two hours) and minibuses (US$2.70, 2½ hours) also leave from the roundabout. Taxis to the aerodrome cost US$1.

MOLLENDO

☎ 054 / pop 29,000

Reached via a scaly desert landscape, this old-fashioned beach resort is a popular getaway for *arequipeños* during the coastal summer, when

PERU

DETOUR

South of Mollendo along an unbroken line of beaches, **Santuario Nacional Lagunas de Mejía** (☎ 054-83-5001; admission US$1.50; ☽ sunrise-sunset) protects the largest permanent lakes in 1500km of desert coastline. Over 200 migratory and coastal bird species are best seen in early morning. The visitor center has maps of walking paths through the dunes leading to miradors. Minibuses for Mejía leave Mollendo from Tacna at Arequipa (US40¢, 30 minutes).

Passing *colectivos* go deeper into the Río Tambo valley, with its irrigated rice paddies, sugarcane plantations and fields of corn and potatoes: a striking juxtaposition with the dusty backdrop of sand dunes and desert. The road rejoins the Panamericana at El Fiscal, a flyblown gas station where you can flag down standing-room-only buses back to Arequipa or south to Moquegua and Tacna.

public swimming pools open by the sea and discos keep heaving until the wee hours.

Internet cafés are everywhere.

BCP (Arequipa 330) changes US dollars and has a Visa ATM. **Telefónica-Perú** (Arequipa 675) is north of the central market.

Single rooms are hard to find, especially on weekends during high season. La Posada Inn (☎ 53-4610; Arequipa 337; s/d US$7.50/12, without bathroom US$5/10, all incl breakfast) is run by a welcoming family and scented with honeysuckle in summer. Some rooms have hot water and local TV. The downtown **El Plaza Hostal** (☎ 53-2460; plazamollendo@hotmail.com; Arequipa 209; s/d/tr/q US$13.50/18/21/24) is a spacious, flower-bedecked spot with hot showers and welcoming staff. Nearby **Hostal La Casona** (☎ 53-3160; Arequipa 192-188; s/d US$13.50/18) has high-ceilinged, airy rooms with hot water and cable TV.

Cevicherías and seafood restaurants abound. Popular **Marco Antonio** (Plaza Bolognesi, Comercio 254; mains US$2-5.50) is a no-frills Peruvian café. Closer to the beach, **Heladería Venecia** (Comercio at Blondell) has some tempting local fruit ice-cream flavors.

Frequent buses from Mollendo's Terminal Terrestre go to Arequipa (US$1.50 to US$2.50, two hours). Minibuses shuttle to downtown and the beach (US15¢, 15 minutes).

MOQUEGUA
☎ 053 / pop 57,300

This parched inland town survives in the driest part of the Peruvian coastal desert, soon to merge into northern Chile's Atacama Desert, the driest in the world. Moquegua means 'quiet place' in Quechua, and the region has long been culturally linked with the Andes. It has peaceful cobblestone streets and a shady central plaza with gardens, colonial architecture and a 19th-century wrought-iron fountain.

Information
Internet cafés aren't speedy.

BCP (Moquegua 861) Has a Visa/MasterCard ATM.

Post office (Ayacucho 560) On the plaza.

Regional tourist office (☎ 46-2236; Ayacucho 1060; ☽ 7:30am-3:30pm Mon-Fri) North of the center.

Sights & Activities
Just off the plaza, **Museo Contisuyo** (☎ 46-1844; http://bruceowen.com/contisuyo/MuseoE.html; Tacna 294; admission US$1.50; ☽ 8am-1pm & 1:30-5:30pm) is an excellent little museum of archaeological artifacts, including photographs of recent excavations.

About 18km northeast of Moquegua, the flat-topped mesa **Cerro Baúl** was a royal brewery once occupied by the Wari people. Archaeologists believe that it was ceremonially destroyed by fire after one last, drunken *chicha* bash. For sweeping views, take the steep one-hour climb to the top. From Moquegua, catch a Toratabound minivan on Balta west of Plaza Bolívar and ask to be let off at Cerro Baúl (US60¢, 20 minutes).

Sleeping
Hostal Carrera (☎ 46-2113; Lima 320; s/d US$4.50/8, without bathroom US$3.60/6) Sitting pretty, safe and secure behind its garden gate, this neat, pastel-colored little hostel has basic rooms and a friendly owner.

Hostal Los Limoneros (☎ 46-1649; Lima 441; s/d US$12/16.50) It's the quiet garden, with its shady patios and delicious smells, that makes this traditional *hostal* the most attractive in town. High-ceilinged rooms have hot water and cable TV.

Eating & Drinking
Moquegua is known for producing some of Peru's best *pisco*. For regional restaurants with

live *folklórico* music on weekends, take a taxi to nearby Samegua (US$1).

Restaurant Morales (cnr Lima & Libertad; mains US$2-6) A classy Peruvian café with white-linen table-cloths and a *dueña* who's a real pistol.

El Bandido (Moquegua 333) Strangely enough, this Western-themed cowboy bar fits perfectly with Moquegua's rough-and-tumble attitude. Wood-fired pizzas are made to order.

Getting There & Away

Buses to Arequipa (US$4.50, four hours) and Tacna (US$4, three hours) leave from bus-company offices downhill west of the center, as do *colectivo* taxis to Tacna (US$3.50, two hours). *Económico* buses run to Desaguadero on the Bolivian border (US$5.35, five hours) and Puno (US$6.25, seven hours), but it's a very rough journey – it's better to backtrack to Arequipa instead.

TACNA

☎ 052 / pop 243,600

At the tail end of the Panamericana, almost 1300km southeast of Lima, the frenzied, dusty border outpost of Tacna (elevation 460m) is

Peru's most patriotic city. It was occupied by Chile in 1880 after the War of the Pacific, until its people voted to return to Peru in 1929.

Information

Chilean pesos, nuevos soles and US dollars can be easily exchanged. Internet cafés offer inexpensive phone calls.

BCP (San Martín 574) Has a Visa/MasterCard ATM, gives Visa cash advances and changes traveler's checks.

Chilean consulate (☎ 42-3063; Presbitero Andía at Saucini) Near the train station, though most travelers head straight for the border.

Hospital (☎ 72-2121.3361; Blondell s/n; ☼ 24hr) For emergencies.

Interbank (San Martín 646) Has a global ATM.

Sights & Activities

The palm tree–studded **Plaza de Armas** features a fountain and cathedral created by French engineer Eiffel (of tower fame). Inside the train station, **Museo Ferroviario** (☎ 72-4981; admission US30¢; ☼ 8am-5:30pm) lets you wander amid beautiful 20th-century engines and rolling stock, plus atmospheric salons filled with historic paraphernalia.

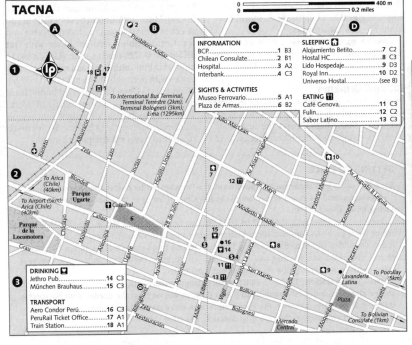

The countryside around Tacna is known for its olive groves, orchards and *bodegas*. Catch a bus or *micro* along Bolognesi (US15¢, 10 minutes) to visit the *bodegas* and restaurants in suburban **Pocollay**.

The seaside resort of **Boca del Río** is 50km southwest of Tacna. Catch a minibus from Terminal Bolognesi (US$1.50, one hour).

Sleeping

Hotel rooms are overpriced and fill up very fast, especially on weekends.

Alojamiento Betito (☎ 70-7429; 2 de Mayo 493; s/d without bathroom US$4.50/7.50) A quirky, old, high-ceilinged building with a likeably shambolic feel and a bohemian bar downstairs.

Lido Hospedaje (☎ 57-7001; San Martín 876A; s/d/ tr US$7/10/13) A secure guesthouse that's the most welcoming budget option in the center. Compact, clean rooms have hot water and local TV.

Royal Inn (☎ 72-6094; Patricio Melendez 574; s/d US$7.50/10.50) North of the market, this enormous, bare-bones hotel has decently clean rooms with hot water. Handy minibar by the front desk.

Hostal HC (☎ 24-2042; Zela 734; s/d US$7.50/10.50) A clean place with chatty staff who are knowledgeable about local sights. Basic rooms have cable TV and hot showers.

Universo Hostal (☎ 71-5441; Zela 724; s/d US$7.50/10.50) This broken-in small hotel has smaller rooms with hot showers and cable TV.

Eating & Drinking

Pocollay is popular with *tacneños* for its rural restaurants, which often have live bands on weekends. Many bars inhabit the first block of Arias Araguez, where beer geeks have München Brauhaus and rockers get down 'n' dirty at Jethro Pub.

Sabor Latino (Vigil 68; mains US$1.50-6) Every table is always taken at this bustling *criollo* café, which has tropical ceiling fans and a Latin soundtrack.

Fulin (Arias Araguez 396; menú US$1.50; ☯ lunch Mon-Fri) A cheap vegetarian *chifa* in a rickety old building.

Café Genova (San Martín 649; mains US$4-10; ☯ 11am-2am) Brush shoulders with local socialites at this streetside café. Food is only so-so, so stick with snacks and drinks.

Getting There & Around

AIR

Tacna's airport (TCQ) is 5km west of town (taxi US$1). **Aero Condor Perú** (☎ 24-8187; Arias Araguez 135) has cheap, thrice-weekly flights to Arequipa. They're often full.

BUS

Most long-distance departures are from Terminal Terrestre (departure tax US30¢). Take a taxi from the center (US75¢). Many companies go to Lima (US$9 to US$43, 18 to 22 hours) and Arequipa (US$4.50 to US$6.50, six to seven hours) via Moquegua (US$3, three hours). Most Lima-bound buses will drop you at other coastal towns, including Nazca and Ica. Comfortable overnight buses with **Cruz del Sur** (☎ 42-5729) reach Cuzco (US$22.30, 16 hours) via Puno and Desaguadero. Other companies with overnight buses to Puno (US$7.50, 10 hours) via Desaguadero (eight hours) leave from Av Circumvalación, north of town. This is a rough, cold overnight journey on *económico* buses without bathrooms. It's much smarter to travel via Arequipa instead.

GETTING TO CHILE

Border-crossing formalities are straightforward. The Peruvian border post is open 8am to midnight on weekdays, and 24 hours Friday and Saturday. Chile is an hour (two hours during daylight-saving time) ahead of Peru.

Frequent *colectivo* taxis (US$3.60 to US$4.50, two hours) to Arica (Chile), about 65km from Tacna, leave between 6am and 10pm from the international bus terminal opposite Terminal Terrestre. On Friday and Saturday you may find taxis willing to go outside these times, but expect to pay over the odds. Because taxi drivers help you through the border formalities, they're a safer, more convenient option than infrequent local buses.

Tacna's **train station** (☎ 052-72-4981) has twice-daily services to Arica (US$1.50, 1½ hours), which are the cheapest and most charming (but also slowest) way to cross the border. Your passport is stamped at the train station in Peru and you receive entry stamps upon arrival in Chile.

For border crossings in the opposite direction, see p466.

AREQUIPA & CANYON COUNTRY

Colonial Arequipa, with its sophisticated museums, architecture and nightlife, is surrounded by some of the wildest terrain in Peru. This is a land of active volcanoes, thermal springs, high-altitude deserts and the world's deepest canyons. Traveling overland, it's a must-stop en route to Lake Titicaca and Cuzco.

AREQUIPA

☎ 054 / pop 760,000

Rocked by volcanic eruptions and earthquakes nearly every century since the Spanish arrived in 1540, Peru's second-largest city doesn't lack for drama. The perfect cone-shaped volcano of El Misti (5822m), which rises majestically behind the cathedral on the Plaza de Armas, is flanked to the left by ragged Chachani (6075m) and to the right by Pichu Pichu (5571m). Locals sometimes say 'when the moon separated from the earth, it forgot to take Arequipa,' waxing lyrical about the city's grand colonial

> ### WHAT'S IN A NAME?
>
> Evidence of a pre-Inca settlement by indigenous peoples from the Lake Titicaca area leads some scholars to think the Aymaras first named the city (in Aymara, *ari* means 'peak' and *quipa* means 'lying behind') for its position relative to El Misti. Another oft-heard legend says that Inca Mayta Capac was traveling through the valley and became so enchanted by it that he ordered his retinue to stop, saying, '*Ari, quipay*,' which translates as 'Yes, stay.'

buildings, built from a light-colored volcanic rock called *sillar* that dazzles in the sun.

Information

BOOKSTORES

Colca Trek (☎ 20-6217/960-0170; colcatrek@hotmail.com; Jerusalén 401-B) For DIY trekking and topographic maps.

Librería el Lector (San Francisco 221; ☼ 9am-noon & 1-9pm) Book exchange, local-interest titles, guidebooks and music CDs.

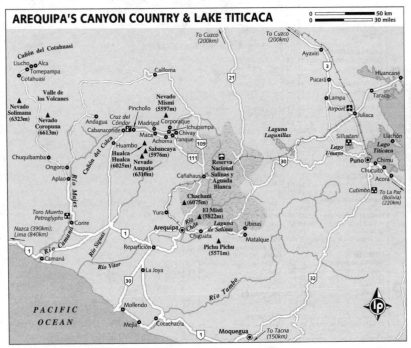

AREQUIPA'S CANYON COUNTRY & LAKE TITICACA

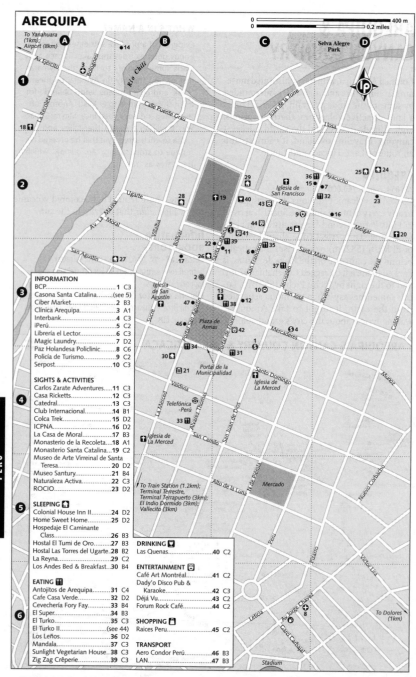

AREQUIPA

PERU

EMERGENCY

Policía de Turismo (☎ 20-1258; Jerusalén 315; ☽ 24hr)

IMMIGRATION

Migraciónes (☎ 42-1759; Parque 2, cnr Bustamente & Rivero, Urb Quinta Tristán; ☽ 8am-1pm Mon-Fri) Take a taxi (US$1).

INTERNET ACCESS

Ciber Market (Santa Catalina 115B; ☽ 8:30am-11pm) Quiet cabins, fast computers with printers, Net-to-phone and digital-photo CD burning.

LAUNDRY

Jerusalén has plenty of spots for washing your kit.

Magic Laundry (Jerusalén 404; ☽ 9am-1pm & 2:30-7pm Mon-Sat) Fast service.

LEFT LUGGAGE

Many guesthouses will store your bags for free. Lock everything securely, always get a receipt and keep a copy of the contents with you.

MEDICAL SERVICES

Clínica Arequipa (☎ 25-3424/3416; cnr Bolognesi & Puente Grau; ☽ 8am-8pm Mon-Fri, to 12:30pm Sat)

Paz Holandesa Policlinic (☎ 20-6720; www.pazholandesa.com; Jorge Chavez 527; ☽ 8am-8pm Mon-Sat) Appointment-only travel clinic (English and Dutch spoken).

MONEY

Money changers are found east of the Plaza de Armas. There are global ATMs inside Casona Santa Catalina and Terminal Terrestre.

BCP (San Juan de Dios 125) Visa ATM; changes traveler's checks.

Interbank (Mercaderes 217) Global ATM; changes traveler's checks.

POST

Serpost (Moral 118; ☽ 8am-8pm Mon-Sat, 9am-1pm Sun)

TOURIST INFORMATION

iPerú airport (☎ 44-4564; 1st fl, Main Hall; ☽ 6:30am-6pm); city center (☎ 022-1228; Casona Santa Calina, Santa Catalina 210; ☽ 9am-7pm) The main office also runs Indecopi, the tourist-protection agency that deals with complaints against travel agencies.

Sights

Arequipa has been baptized 'the white city' for its distinctive volcanic stonework that graces the stately Plaza de Armas and its enormous *sillar* **cathedral**, as well as many other exquisite colonial churches, convents and mansions built throughout the city.

The university-run **Museo Santury** (☎ 054-20-0345/21-5013; www.ucsm.edu.pe/santury; La Merced 110; admission US$4.50; ☽ 9am-6pm Mon-Sat, 9am-3pm Sun) exhibits 'Juanita, the Ice Princess' – the frozen Inca maiden sacrificed on the summit of Ampato (6288m) over 500 years ago. For the Incas, mountains were violent deities who could kill by volcanic eruption, avalanche or climatic catastrophes, and could only be appeased by sacrifices. Multilingual tours consist of a video followed by a reverent look at burial artifacts culminating with a respectful viewing of the mummy herself. Although Juanita is not on display from January to April, another child sacrifice is.

Even if you've already overdosed on colonial edifices of yesteryear, the **Monasterio Santa Catalina** (☎ 22-9798; Santa Catalina 301; admission US$10.50; ☽ 9am-5pm, last entry 4pm) shouldn't be missed. Occupying a whole block and guarded by imposing high walls, it's practically a citadel within a city. It was founded in 1580 by a wealthy widow who chose her nuns from the richest Spanish families, but her new nuns kept living it up in the style to which they were accustomed. After almost three centuries of these hedonistic goings-on, a strict Dominican nun arrived to straighten things out. The complex remained shrouded in mystery until it was forced open to the public in 1970. Today it's a meditatively mazelike place that lets you step back in time to a forgotten world of narrow twisting streets, tiny fruit-filled plazas, hidden staircases, beautiful courtyards and ascetic living quarters. Informative multilingual guides are available for a tip (US$3 to US$4.50).

One of Arequipa's oldest, the Jesuit **Iglesia de La Compañía** (admission free; ☽ 9am-noon & 3-6pm) is noted for its ornate main facade. The **San Ignacio chapel** has a polychrome cupola with lush murals of tropical flowers, fruits and birds, among which mingle warriors and angels.

On the west side of the Río Chili, this musty 17th-century Franciscan **Monasterio de la Recoleta** (☎ 28-1188; La Recoleta 117; admission US$1.50; ☽ 9am-4:30pm Mon-Sat, 9am-12:30pm Sun) has a fascinating library with more than 20,000 historic books and maps and a museum of Amazoniana collected by missionaries. The neighborhood is dicey, so take a taxi (US$1).

PERU

DETOUR

The suburb of **Yanahuara** is within walking distance of downtown Arequipa. Go west on Av Puente Grau over the bridge, and continue on Ejército. Turn right on Lima and walk north to a small plaza, where the **Iglesia San Juan Batista** dates from 1750 and a **mirador** has excellent views of Arequipa and El Misti. Head back along Jerusalén, parallel to Lima, and just before Ejército is the well-known garden restaurant **Sol de Mayo** (☎ 054-25-4148; Jerusalén 207; mains US$5-7.50), where you can stop to lunch on typical *arequipeño* food. Frequent minivans running along Av Puente Grau shuttle back and forth to Yanahuara's main plaza (US35¢).

This gorgeous, 17th-century Carmelite convent **Museo de Arte Virreinal de Santa Teresa** (☎ 24-2531; www.museocarmelitas.com; Melgar 303; admission US$3; 9am-4:30pm) recently opened to the public. It's famed for its decoratively painted walls, priceless votive *objets d'art* and colonial-era paintings, all explained by multilingual tour guides (tips appreciated). A charming shop sells baked goods and rose-scented soap made by nuns.

Of the colonial mansions, **La Casa de Moral** (Moral 318; adult/student US$1.40/1; 9am-5pm Mon-Sat) is named after the 200-year-old mulberry tree in its courtyard. **Casa Ricketts** (San Francisco 108; admission free; 9:15am-12:45pm & 4-6:30pm Mon-Fri, 9:30am-12:45pm Sat), now a working bank, has puma-headed fountains.

PERU

Courses

Many schools offer Spanish classes (about US$6 per hour).

CEICA (☎ 22-1165; www.ceica-peru.com/arequipa.htm; Urb Universitaria G-9)

CEPESMA (☎ 40-5927; cepesma.idiomas@peru.com; La Marina 141)

ICPNA (☎ 89-1020; www.icpna.edu.pe; Melgar 109)

Juanjo (www.spanishlanguageperu.com; 2nd epata C-4, Urb Magisterial, Yanahuara)

ROCIO (☎ 28-6929; www.spanish-peru.com; Ayacucho 208)

Activities

Santa Catalina and Jerusalén have dozens of fly-by-night travel agencies offering disappointingly rushed tours of the Cañón del Colca and also trekking, mountaineering and rafting trips. There are many no-goodniks muscling in on the action, so shop carefully.

Outdoor outfitters:

Calbagatas (☎ 28-6314/965-5766/983-2623; rentasyservicios@speedy.com.pe) For horse-riding tours and treks. Based outside of the city so prefers to be contacted by phone or email.

Carlos Zarate Adventures (☎ 20-2461; www.zarateadventures.com; Santa Catalina 204) The granddaddy of Arequipeño climbing agencies also runs mountain-biking tours, though service can be lackluster. Rents climbing gear, but inspect it carefully.

Colca Trek (☎ 20-6217/960-0170; colcatrek@hotmail.com; Jerusalén 401-B) Ecoconscious adventure tour agency run by English-speaking Vlado Soto. Buys, sells and rents equipment, including camp-stove fuel, mountain bikes, climbing gear and trekking maps.

Naturaleza Activa (☎ 22-2257; www.peruexploration.com; Santa Catalina 211) Arranges mountain-biking, trekking and climbing tours of varying quality.

MOUNTAINEERING

Superb mountains surround Arequipa. Though many climbs in the area aren't technically difficult, they should never be undertaken lightly. Hazards include extreme weather, altitude and lack of water (carry 4L per person per day). Always check the IDs of guides carefully, and ask to see the book that identifies trained and registered guides. Know the symptoms of altitude sickness (p1095) and carry your own medical kit.

Looming above Arequipa is the city's guardian volcano **El Misti** (5822m), the most popular local climb. It can be tackled solo, but going with a guide helps protect against robberies, which have happened on the Apurímac route. One popular route is from Chiguata, an eight-hour hard uphill slog on rough trails to base camp (4500m). From there to the summit and back takes eight hours. The return from base camp to Chiguata takes three hours or less. **Chachani** (6075m) is one of the easiest 6000m peaks in the world, but you'll still need crampons, an ice axe and a good guide.

TREKKING

Agencies offer an array of off-the-beaten-track tours in Arequipa's canyon country, but it's better to DIY if you're just visiting the Cañón del Colca. Optimal hiking season is from May to November. Cañón del Colca has a smattering of **campgrounds** (sites per person US$1.40), but it's forbidden to camp by Cruz del Condor. For indispensable trekking maps and excellent guided trips into Cañón del Cotahuasi, contact Colca Trek.

RAFTING

The **Río Chili** is the most frequently run local river, with a half-day beginners' trip leaving daily from March to November. Further afield, the **Río Majes** passes grade II and III rapids. **Casa de Mauro** (camping per person US$2; dm US$3), in the village of Ongoro, 190km by road west of Arequipa, is a convenient base for rafting the Majes. The lodge can be contacted through Colca Trek. It's cheapest to take an almost hourly bus from Arequipa with Transportes del Carpio to Aplao (US$2, three hours), then catch a minibus to Ongoro (or taxi US$3.50).

OTHER ACTIVITIES

A 15-minute walk north of Puente Grau, **Club Internacional** (☎ 25-3384; admission Mon-Fri/Sat & Sun US$3/4.50; ☽ 6am-midnight Mon-Sat, 7am-5pm Sun) offers swimming pools, soccer, tennis and bowling.

Festivals & Events

Arequipeños are a proud people, and their fiery celebration of the city's founding on August 15 renews their sense of difference from coastal Lima.

Sleeping

Many guesthouses are unmarked, or have a sign proclaiming 'Rooms for Tourist.' Many more budget guesthouses lie along Av Puente Grau, west of Jerusalén.

Home Sweet Home (☎ 40-5982; www.homesweethome-peru.com; Rivero 509A; dm US$3, incl breakfast s/d US$7.50/14, s/d/tr without bathroom US$5/10/15) A genuinely friendly homestay with cute, if a bit musty rooms. Upstairs there's a TV room, downstairs a kitchen.

El Indio Dormido (☎ 42-7401; www.elindiodormido.com; Andrés Avelino Cáceres B-9; dm US$4.50, s/d without bathroom US$6/9) By Terminal Terrestre, this hostel is cheap, popular and has a terrace garden with hammocks.

La Reyna (☎ 28-6578; Zela 209; dm US$4.50, s/d/tr US$6/12/18) A rickety old standby, La Reyna has rooftop balconies with either mountain or monastery views. It's cheek-to-jowl with Arequipa's hottest nightlife.

Los Andes Bed & Breakfast (☎ 33-0015; losandesaqp@hotmail.com; La Merced 123; s/d US$10/20, without bathroom US$5/10) Just a stone's throw south of the plaza, this airy guesthouse with hot water

and sun-drenched lounges is excellent for longer stays.

Point Hostel (☎ 28-6920; www.thepointhostels.com; Av Lima 515, Vallecito; dm US$7-8, s/d without bathroom from US$10/16, all incl breakfast; ☐) In the relaxed garden-filled suburb of Vallecito, this rambling hostel has a slew of backpacker amenities: free internet access, a games room, library and chill-out spaces.

Colonial House Inn II (☎ 28-4249; Rivero 504; s/d US$9/15, without bathroom US$7/13) In a capacious colonial building tucked down a side alley, here rooms combine rustic style with convenience. Big common kitchen.

Hostal El Tumi de Oro (☎ 28-1319; San Agustín 311; s/d US$9/12) Run by chirpy elderly folks, this prettily tiled hostel has a sunny terrace and kitchen facilities.

Hospedaje El Caminante Class (☎ 20-3444; Santa Catalina 207A; d with/without bathroom US$15/10.50) This overpriced, overcrowded guesthouse offers decent rooms, kitchen privileges, views from the rooftop terrace and all-you-can-drink *maté de coca* (coca-leaf tea).

Hostal Las Torres de Ugarte (☎ 28-3532; www.hotelista.com; Ugarte 401A; s/d/tr incl breakfast US$20/30/36; ☐) This secure, well-kept small hotel has immaculate rooms with TVs – never mind the echoing hallways.

Eating

Trendy upscale restaurants are on San Francisco, while outdoor cafés line Pasaje Catedral.

Cafe Casa Verde (Jerusalén 406; items US60¢-$1.50) Off a busy street, this nonprofit courtyard coffee shop run by street children dishes up yummy German-style pastries, sandwiches, cappuccinos and juices.

Antojitos de Arequipa (Morán 1st block; snacks & mains US$1.50-7.50; ☽ 24hr) This café-restaurant is a bright beacon, even in the dead of night. Espresso drinks, an enormous menu of comfort food and chair locks for your backpack make it ideal for waiting out that late-night bus departure.

Mandala (Jerusalén 207; menú US$1.50-2) A humble, health-minded vegetarian café for quick, quality fare. Breakfasts are huge.

Sunlight Vegetarian House (Moral 205; menú US$1.50; ☽ lunch) A no-frills Chinese vegetarian café with a faithful local following.

El Turko (San Francisco 216; mains US$2.50-6; ☽ 7am-midnight Sun-Wed, 24hr Thu-Sat) This funky joint serves a hungry clubbing crowd its late-night kabobs, but also makes a good java-stop during the day. This mini-empire also includes fantastic El Turko II restaurant, Fez bar and Istanbul café, all nearby.

Zig Zag Crêperie (Santa Catalina 208; mains US$2.50-7; 8am-midnight) Inside the Alianza Francesa, this cultural café has a crackling fireplace, rich coffee and over 100 kinds of sweet and savory crêpes.

Cevichería Fory Fay (Thomas 221; mains US$4.50-6; lunch) Small and to-the-point, it serves only the best *ceviche*. Pull up a chair at a rickety table and crack open a beer (limit one per person, though!).

Los Leños (Jerusalén 407; pizzas US$4.50-6; 6-10:30pm Mon-Sat) Travelers say it has the best wood-burning pizza in southern Peru. If you're more impressed than we were, add your graffiti to the walls.

El Super (Portal de la Municipalidad 130) On the Plaza de Armas.

Drinking

For spicy nightlife, head for the bars and clubs along San Francisco north of the plaza.

Entertainment

Déjà Vu (San Francisco 319B; 6pm-2am) An eternally popular watering hole, it has a winning combination of a rooftop terrace, a long list of crazy cocktails, afternoon movies and decent DJs after dark.

Forum Rock Café (San Francisco 317; 10pm-4am Tue-Sat) A gutsy Latin rock bar with a thing for bamboo and waterfalls. The specialties are bands and booze – burgers are an afterthought. Zero Pub & Pool is in the same building.

Café Art Montréal (Ugarte 210; 6-11pm) A smoky, intimate bar with live bands playing at the back. It'd be equally at home on Paris' Left Bank.

Las Quenas (Santa Catalina 302; admission US$3; closed Sun) This place features nightly performances of *folklórica*. A few doors south, Boulevard Café has live contemporary Peruvian acts with no admission charge Thursday to Sunday nights.

Dady'o Disco Pub & Karaoke (Portal de Flores 112; Thu-Sun) A raucous late-night disco and bar right on the Plaza de Armas.

A handful of cinemas in Arequipa show English-language movies dubbed or with Spanish subtitles. **Cineplanet Arequipa 7** (270-1945; www.cineplanet.com.pe; Los Arces s/n, at Av del Ejército)

is in a shopping mall just a short taxi ride away from the Plaza de Armas. It's also worth checking out the various cultural centers for film festivals and other screenings. Déjà Vu sometimes shows movies in the afternoons.

Shopping

Arequipa overflows with artisan and antique shops, especially on streets around Monasterio Santa Catalina.

Raices Peru (Jerusalén 309-A; 9am-7pm Mon-Sat) Vends folk art and crafts handmade in indigenous communities from the Amazon to the Andes.

Getting There & Away
AIR

The **airport** (AQP; 44-3464) is 8km northwest of the center. **LAN** (20-1224; Santa Catalina 118-C) serves Lima and Cuzco daily. **Aero Condor Perú** (22-6660; Portal de San Agustín 119) has cheap but often full flights to Tacna near the Chilean border.

BUS

Most companies leave from Terminal Terrestre or the smaller Terrapuerto bus station next door. Both are 3km south of the center (departure tax US30¢).

For Lima (US$12 to US$40, 16 to 18 hours), **Cruz del Sur** (42-7375), **Ormeño** (42-4113) and other companies operate several daily buses, mostly departing in the afternoon. Many buses stop en route at Nazca (US$7 to US$36, 10 to 12 hours) and Ica (US$9 to US$38, 13 to 15 hours). Many companies also have overnight buses to Cuzco (US$7.50 to US$21, nine to 11 hours).

Buses to Juliaca (US$3.60, five hours) and Puno (US$4.50, six hours) leave every half hour throughout the day. Some continue to Desaguadero (US$7.50, seven to eight hours) on the Bolivian border. Cruz del Sur has the most comfortable buses to Tacna (US$4.50 to US$6.50, six to seven hours) via Moquegua (US$4.50, four hours). **Transportes del Carpio** (42-7049) has hourly daytime departures for Mollendo (US$1.50 to US$2.50, two hours).

For Cañón del Colca, there are a few daily buses for Chivay (US$2.40, three hours), continuing to Cabanaconde (US$4.50, six hours). Recommended companies include **Andalucia** (44-5089/53-1166), **Reyna** (054-43-0612) or **Transportes Colca** (42-6357).

Getting Around

Minivans bound for Terminal Terrestre (US60¢) run south along Bolívar, or take a taxi (US$1). Minibuses marked 'Río Seco' or 'Zamacola' go along Puente Grau and Ejército, passing within 700m of the airport, or take a taxi direct (US$4.20). Always use officially licensed taxi companies like **Presidencial Express** (☎ 20-3333).

CAÑÓN DEL COLCA

One of the world's deepest canyons at 3191m, Colca ranks second only to neighboring Cañón del Cotahuasi, which is all of 163m deeper. Trekking is by far the best way to experience village life, although the roads are dusty. As you pass through the canyon's traditional villages, look out for the local women's traditional embroidered clothing and hats.

The road from Arequipa climbs north through **Reserva Nacional Salinas y Aguada Blanca**, where *vicuñas* – the endangered wild cousins of llamas and alpacas – are often sighted. The road continues through bleak *altiplano* (high Andean plateau) over the highest point of 4800m, before dropping spectacularly into Chivay.

Chivay

☎ 054 / pop 4600

The provincial capital at the head of the canyon is a small, dusty transit hub. Bring plenty of Peruvian cash, as only a few stores will exchange US dollars or euros. Slow internet access is available from cybercafés near the main plaza.

SIGHTS & ACTIVITIES

Soak away in Chivay's **hot springs** (admission US$3; ☺ 4:30am-8pm), 3.5km northeast of town. The mineral-laden water is handy when the hot-water supply at your guesthouse packs up. Frequent *colectivos* leave from the market area (US30¢).

From where the road forks to the hot springs, stay to the left and walk beside fertile fields toward **Coporaque**, which has an arched colonial-era plaza. Then head downhill to the orange bridge across the river to **Yanque** (right), where passing buses or *colectivos* return to Chivay. It's an all-day walk. Alternatively, rent mountain bikes in Chivay from shops around the plaza.

A tiny **astronomical observatory** (☎ 054-53-1020; Casa Andina, Huayna Cápac s/n; adult/student US$6/3) has nightly sky shows in Spanish and English.

SLEEPING

Though a tiny town, Chivay has plenty of *hostales* to choose from.

Hostal Estrella de David (☎ 53-1233; Siglo XX 209; s/d/tr US$3/6/9) A simple, clean guesthouse, this *hospedaje* is a few blocks from the plaza toward the bus terminal.

Hospedaje El Rey (☎ 80-8864; Puente Inca 110; s/d/tr US$4.50/7/9) Close to the plaza, this rustic place has decent rooms, or bare-bones habitations without bathroom for less.

Hospedaje Rumi Wasi (☎ 53-1146; Sucre 714; s/d/tr US$6/9/12) An excellent family-run hostel with a central garden where alpacas nibble on the greenery and rooms have views of the surrounding countryside. Mountain bikes and guides are for hire.

Hostal Anita (☎ 53-1114; Plaza de Armas 606; s/d incl breakfast US$9/15) With a pretty interior courtyard, this friendly hostel has hot showers.

EATING & DRINKING

Lobo's (Plaza de Armas; meals from US$2) Has a touristy menu (with big breakfasts), a backpacker-friendly bar and tourist information.

Casa Blanca (Plaza de Armas; menú US$4) A subterranean restaurant with a fireplace, Casa Blanca has a pick-and-choose set menu that includes unusual local specialties, and portions are huge.

Q'oka (Plaza de Armas) For good coffee and terrace views.

M´elroys (Plaza de Armas; ☺ closed Sun) Proves that Irish pubs really do get everywhere.

ENTERTAINMENT

Peñas are everywhere, with shows from around 8pm nightly.

Latigo's (cnr Puente Inca & Bolognesi; ☺ closed Sun) For dancing.

GETTING THERE & AWAY

The bus terminal is a 15-minute walk from the plaza. Buses to Arequipa (US$2.40, three hours) or onward to Cabanaconde (US$1, 2½ hours) via Cruz del Cóndor leave four times daily.

Chivay to Cabanaconde

The main road follows the south bank of the upper Cañón del Colca and leads past several villages and some of the most extensive pre-Inca terracing in Peru. One of these villages, **Yanque**, has an attractive 18th-century church and an excellent, small **cultural museum** (admission

WARNING!

Quasi-official ticket vendors board all buses at Chivay to force gringos to buy a *boleto turístico* (tourist ticket, US$7) that allegedly covers entrance fees to all of the canyon's points of interest. If you're just passing through Chivay to Cabanaconde and won't be visiting Cruz del Cóndor, you don't have to buy it – all the proceeds benefit Chivay anyway, not less affluent villages. Politely but persistently refuse to pay, and you'll be allowed through eventually.

US90¢; ⏰ 7am-6:30pm Tue-Sun) on the plaza. A 30-minute walk to the river brings you to some hot springs (admission US30¢). There are simple guesthouses scattered around town.

Eventually the road reaches **Cruz del Cóndor** (entry with Boleto Turístico, p871). Andean condors that nest here by the rocky outcrop can occasionally be seen gliding effortlessly on thermal air currents. Early morning or late afternoon are the best times to see the birds, but you'll need luck.

Cabanaconde
☎ 054 / pop 1300

Cabanaconde is an excellent base for some spectacular hikes into the canyon, including the popular two-hour trek down to Sangalle (The Oasis) at the bottom, where there are natural pools for swimming (US$3), simple bungalows and campsites. The return trek is thirsty work; allow three to four hours. Local guides can suggest a wealth of other treks, to waterfalls, geysers, remote villages and archaeological sites.

The basic **Hostal Valle del Fuego** (☎ 054-83-0032/0035/2158; hvalledelfuego@hotmail.com; s/d without bathroom US$3/6) is an established travelers' scene, with DVDs, a full bar, solar-powered showers and owners knowledgeable about trekking. An annex of rooms with private bathrooms costs more.

The smaller **Hospedaje Villa Pastor** (Plaza de Armas; s/d US$3/6) is the upstart competition, with lukewarm showers and a simple restaurant and bar.

Several daily buses bound for Chivay (US$1, 2½ hours) and Arequipa (US$4.50, six hours) via Cruz del Cóndor leave from the plaza.

LAKE TITICACA

South America's largest lake is also one of the world's highest navigable lakes. The air looks magically clear here, as dazzling high-altitude sunlight suffuses the highland *altiplano* and sparkles on the deep waters. Horizons stretch until almost limitless, with ancient funerary towers and crumbling colonial churches. The port of Puno is a convenient base for visiting far-flung islands dotted across Lake Titicaca – from those made of artificial reeds to more remote, rural isles where villagers live much as they have for centuries.

JULIACA
☎ 051 / pop 198,600

The large, brash market town has the department's only commercial airport, though it gets far fewer tourists than its more lovely lakeside neighbor Puno.

Interbank (Nuñez 231) has a 24-hour global ATM. *Casas de cambio* sprawl around the intersection of Bolívar and Nuñez. **Clínica Americana Adventista** (☎ 32-1639; Loreto 315; ⏰ 24hr) offers emergency services.

With Puno so close, there's usually no need to overnight here. A block northwest of the plaza, **Hostal Sakura** (☎ 32-2072; San Roman 133; s/d from US$7.50/10.50) has a positive atmosphere. Most rooms have hot showers.

Ricos Pan (cnr Unión & Chávez; ⏰ 8:30am-12:30pm & 2:30-6:30pm) is the best place for coffee and yummy cake. **Restaurant Trujillo** (San Roman 163; mains US$3-6) is good for more substantial meals and boasts a decent drinks list.

The **airport** (JUL; ☎ 32-8974) is 2km west of town. **LAN** (☎ 32-2228; San Román 125) has daily flights to/from Lima, Arequipa and Cuzco, but they are often canceled. To the airport, take a taxi (US$1.50) or minibus from the center marked 'Aeropuerto' (US30¢). Direct minibuses to Puno (US$1.50, one hour) usually await incoming flights.

The bus companies on the 12th block of San Martín, 2km east of town, travel to the same destinations as from Puno (p867). **San Martín** (☎ 32-7501) and other companies along Tumbes between Moquegua and Piérola have *económico* night buses to Tacna (US$9, 11 hours) via Moquegua.

Colectivos to Puno (US60¢, 50 minutes) leave when full from Plaza Bolognesi. More frequent *combis* to Puno (US50¢, one hour) depart from around the intersection of Piérola and 8 de Noviembre, northeast of the plaza.

Juliaca's **train station** (☎ 32-1036; Plaza Bolognesi) has a reputation for theft, so keep a sharp eye on your stuff. For schedules and fares between Cuzco and Puno, see p868. Trains pass through Juliaca an hour or so after leaving Puno.

AROUND JULIACA

For details of the scenic route to Cuzco, see p889.

Lampa

This charming village, located 36km northwest of Juliaca, is known as 'La Ciudad Rosada' for its dusty, pink-colored buildings. Fronting the plaza, gorgeous **Iglesia de la Imaculada** holds secrets worth seeing. Ask around to find the caretaker, who will unlock the church and take you down into the catacombs for a tip.

Staff at the shop opposite **Museo Kampac** (Ugarte 462; admission by donation) give quick guided tours of the museum's small collection. If you're lucky, they'll show you a unique vase inscribed with the sacred cosmology of the Incas.

A few kilometers west of town over a bridge hides **Cueva de los Toros**, a bull-shaped cave with prehistoric carvings of llamas and other animals. The cave is in some rocks on the right side of the road. En route are several *chullpas* (funerary towers).

From Juliaca, minivans to Lampa (US90¢, 45 minutes) leave when full from near the market on Jirón Huáscar.

PUNO

☎ 051 / pop 102,800

The small port of Puno is the best departure point for Lake Titicaca's islands. Though only a few colonial buildings remain in Puno, the streets bustle with local women garbed in mulitlayered dresses and bowler hats. Nights here get bitterly cold, especially during winter when temperatures can often drop below freezing.

Information

Internet cafés offering cheap phone calls are near the plaza, including along Lima. For hospitals, it's better to go to Juliaca (opposite). Bolivian pesos can be exchanged in town or at the border. There's a global ATM inside Terminal Terrestre.

BCP (Lima at Grau) Visa/MasterCard ATM; gives Visa cash advances.

Botica Fasa (☎ 36-6862; Arequipa 314; ☺ 24hr) Big pharmacy.

Interbank (Lima 444) Global ATM; changes traveler's checks.

iPerú (☎ 36-5088; Plaza de Armas, Lima at Deustua; ☺ 8:30am-7:30pm) For tourist information.

Lavaclin (Valcárcel 132; ☺ 8am-noon & 2-7pm Mon-Sat) For laundry.

Migraciónes (☎ 35-7103; Ayacucho 240; ☺ 8am-2pm Mon-Fri) Gives tourist-card extensions, though it's cheaper to go to Bolivia and return (see p868).

Policía de Turismo (☎ 35-3988; Deustua 558; ☺ 24hr) For emergencies.

Serpost (Moquegua 267; ☺ 8am-8pm Mon-Sat)

Sights & Activities

The oldest boat on Lake Titicaca, the iron-hulled **Yavari** (☎ 36-9329; www.yavari.org; suggested donation US$6; ☺ 8am-5:30pm) was built in England and shipped in pieces around Cape Horn to Arica, then transported to Tacna by train and hauled by mule over the Andes to Puno (taking a mere six years), where it was reassembled and launched in 1870. Due to a coal shortage, the engines were often powered by dried llama dung! The ship was eventually decommissioned by the Peruvian navy, and the hull was left to rust on the lakeshore until it was rescued by a nonprofit organization. Now moored by the Sonesta Posada Hotel del Inca (take a minivan from along Av El Sol, US30¢), the ship is open for tours by the affable, knowledgeable, English-speaking captain. In future the vessel should be ready to cruise across Lake Titicaca.

Just off the plaza, the 17th-century **Casa del Corregidor** (☎ 35-1921; www.casadelcorregidor .com.pe; Deustua 576; admission free; ☺ 10am-10pm Tue-Fri, 10am-2:30pm & 5-10pm Sat 21 Jan-20 Dec, also 10am-2:30pm & 5-10pm Sun May-Oct) houses a cooperative crafts shop and a café for hobnobbing with local bohemians over a cappuccino. Around the corner is the small **Museo Carlos Dreyer** (Conde de Lemos 281; foreigner US$5; ☺ 10am-10pm), which houses a beautifully curated collection of archaeological artifacts.

Near the port, the **Museo Naval** (Titicaca at Av El Sol; ☺ 8am-5pm Mon-Fri, 9am-1pm Sat & Sun) has tiny exhibits on navigating the lake, from rudimentary reed boats to 19th-century steamers. The **Coca Museum** (☎ 36-5087; www.cocamuseo .com; Deza 301; ☺ 9am-1pm & 3-8pm) is also well worth a peek.

PERU

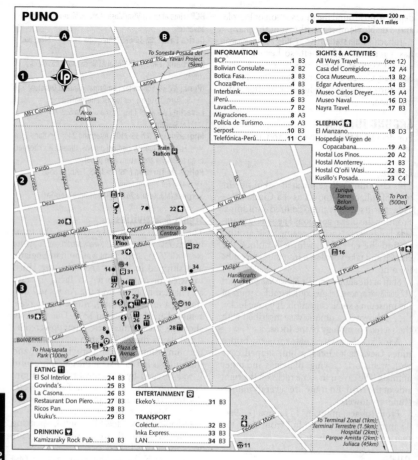

PUNO

Tours

Many travelers find the island-hopping tours disappointing, even exploitative. We recommend that you DIY: ask around (eg at your guesthouse) for a local guide, preferably someone with ties to the islands, then go to the docks in the early morning and get on the next boat.

All Ways Travel (☎ 35-3979; www.titicacaperu.com; Deustua 576) A behemoth agency with multilingual staff.

Edgar Adventures (☎ 35-3444; Lima 328) Gets mostly good recommendations.

Nayra Travel (☎ 36-4774; Lima 419) Personalized service for off-the-beaten-track destinations.

Festivals & Events

Puno is often named the folklore capital of Peru, celebrating wild and colorful fiestas throughout the year. Although they often occur during celebrations of Catholic feast days, many dances have their roots in preconquest celebrations tied in with the agricultural calendar. The dazzlingly ornate and imaginative costumes worn on these occasions are often worth more than an entire household's everyday clothes. Accompanying musicians play a host of traditional instruments, from Spanish-influenced brass and string to percussion and wind instruments that have changed little since Inca times. Major festivals are usually celebrated for several days before and after the actual date:

Epiphany January 6

Virgen de la Candelaria (Candlemas) February 2

Puno Day November 5

Sleeping

Some bare-bones *hostales* have only cold showers. If you want to avoid freezing off vital appendages, use the public hot showers found around town.

Hostal Monterrey (☎ 35-1691; Lima 441; s/d US$6/9, without bathroom US$3/6) Right in the thick of things on the main pedestrian boulevard, you'll get smiley service here. Hot showers are erratic, and rooms without bathroom are very basic.

Hospedaje Virgen de Copacabana (☎ 36-3766; Ilave 228; dm US$4.50) This friendly, tumbledown YHA-affiliated hostel tucked off a narrow passageway has great big rooms with shared bathrooms.

Hostal Q'oñi Wasi (☎ 36-5784; qoniwasi@mundomail .net; La Torre 119; s/d/tr US$7.50/12/18, with bathroom US$10.50/21/24) A long-running backpacker haunt, quirky Q'oni Wasi has a warren of snug, older rooms and electric showers.

Kusillo's Posada (☎ 36-4579; kusillos@latinmail .com; Federico More 162; s/d incl breakfast US$9/15) Run by the indefatigable Jenny Juño and her wonderful family, this heart-warming homestay has cozy rooms with electric showers.

Hostal Los Pinos (☎ 36-7398; hostalpinos@hotmail .com; Tarapacá 182; s/d US$10/15) This small hotel has spacious rooms (avoid those facing the street) with wool blankets, TVs and hot showers.

Eating

Touristy restaurants line the rambunctious pedestrian street of Calle Lima.

El Sol Interior (Libertad 352; mains US$1.80-5) This holistic, health-minded vegetarian restaurant has amazing Peruvian fake-meat dishes, with sides of quinoa and locally grown vegetables, plus Amazonian-style jungle juices and potions.

Restaurant Don Piero (Lima 364; mains US$3-5) Don Piero doesn't match other restaurants for glitz, but has excellent local food and live music some evenings.

La Casona (Lima 517; mains US$3.60-7.50) Calling itself a museum, this quaint restaurant retains an old-fashioned 1920s air with a collection of antique irons lining the walls. Impeccably mannered waiters serve lovingly prepared fish and other local dishes.

Ukuku's (Pasaje Grau 172, 2nd fl; mains US$5-7.50) Hungry crowds of travelers flock to this toasty restaurant, which serves excellent pizzas and Peruvian fare (try the alpaca with baked apples).

Ricos Pan (Moquegua 326; ☻ 8am-9:30pm Mon-Sat) Puno's best bakery is a comforting find, especially for melt-in-your-mouth cakes.

Drinking

Kamizaraky Rock Pub (Pasaje Grau 158; ☻ 5pm-late) Southern Peru's best watering hole, this place feels like someone's living room. It's got a classic soundtrack, cool bartenders and liquored-infused coffee drinks, ideal for Puno's bone-chilling nights.

Entertainment

A few *peñas* advertise nightly performances of *música folkórica*.

Ekeko's (Lima 355, 2nd fl; ☻ 5pm-late) Travelers and locals alike gravitate to this tiny, ultraviolet dance floor splashed with psychedelic murals. Movies are shown in the early evening.

Getting There & Around

AIR

The nearest airport is in Juliaca (p864). **LAN** (☎ 36-7227; Tacna 299) has an office in Puno.

BUS

Terminal Terrestre (☎ 36-4733; Primero de Mayo 703), located around 2km southeast of the plaza, houses Puno's long-distance bus companies (departure tax US30¢). Direct services go to Lima (US$11 to US$45, 19 hours), Arequipa (US$3.60 to US$7.50, 5½ to six hours) and Cuzco (US$4.50 to US$10.50, six to seven hours) via Juliaca (US60¢, one hour). **San Martín** (☎ 36-3631) has rough, overnight *económico* buses to Tacna (US$7.50, 10 hours) via Moquegua.

Inka Express (☎ 36-5654; www.inkaexpress.com; Tacna 314-B) runs luxury tour buses with panoramic windows to Cuzco every morning. The worthwhile US$25 fare includes beverages and an English-speaking guide who explains sites that are briefly visited en route, including Pucara, Raqchi and Andahuayillas (see p889).

Minibuses to Juliaca (US50¢, one hour), lakeshore towns and the Bolivian border leave from Terminal Zonal on Simón Bolívar, a few blocks north of Terminal Terrestre.

TAXI

A short taxi ride around town costs US$1. *Mototaxis* are cheaper, but make sure the negotiated fare is per ride, not per person.

PERU

GETTING TO BOLIVIA

There are two overland routes from Puno to La Paz, Bolivia. The Yunguyo route, which is safer and easier, allows you to take a break at the lakeshore resort of Copacabana. The Desaguadero route, which is slightly faster and cheaper, can be combined with a visit to the ruins at Tiahuanaco (p200). Beware of immigration officials trying to charge an illegal 'entry tax' or search your belongings for 'fake dollars' to confiscate (hide yours before reaching the border).

To enter Peru from Bolivia, see p209.

Via Yunguyo

The most convenient way to reach Bolivia is with a cross-border company like **Colectur** (☎ 051-35-2302; Tacna 221), which has daily buses departing at 7:30am that stop at a money-exchange office, the Peruvian and Bolivian border posts, then Copacabana (US$3.60, three hours), where you board another bus to La Paz (US$7.50, eight hours). Officials in Copacabana will make you pay just to enter town (US15¢).

Alternatively, frequent minibuses depart Puno's Terminal Zonal for Yunguyo (US$1.40, 2½ hours). You'll find money changers in Yunguyo's plaza and at the border, 2km away in Kasani (*combis* US30¢). In Bolivia, which is an hour ahead of Peru, the border post is open from 8:30am to 7pm daily. From the border, it's another 10km to Copacabana (*combis* US50¢).

Via Desaguadero

Buses (US$2) and minibuses (US$1.40) leave Puno's Terminal Zonal and Terminal Terrestre regularly for the chaotic border town of Desaguadero (2½ hours), which has basic hotels and money changers. Border hours are 8am to 8pm, but because Bolivia is an hour ahead of Peru, plan to cross before 7pm Peruvian time. Many buses go from Desaguadero to La Paz (US$1.80, three hours) during daylights hours, passing the turnoff for Tiahuanaco.

TRAIN

Trains bound for Cuzco via Juliaca purportedly leave Puno's **train station** (☎ 36-9179; La Torre 224; www.perurail.com; ⏱ 7am-noon & 1-5pm Mon-Fri, 7-11am Sat & Sun) at 8am daily, arriving at 5:30pm, though they're often hours late or canceled entirely. At the time of research, first-class/backpacker fares to Cuzco were US$119/17.

AROUND PUNO
Sillustani

Sitting on rolling hills in the Lake Umayo peninsula, the ruined towers of **Sillustani** (admission US$2) stand out for miles against the unforgiving landscape. The ancient Colla people were a warlike, Aymara-speaking tribe that buried their nobility in these impressive funerary *chullpas,* made from massive coursed blocks and reaching heights of up to 12m.

Puno travel agencies run 3½-hour tours (US$7.50 including entrance fee) that leave around 2:30pm daily. To DIY, catch any bus to Juliaca and get off where the road splits to Sillustani. From there, occasional *combis* run to the village of Atuncolla (US60¢, 10 minutes), a 4km walk from the ruins.

Cutimbo

Almost 20km from Puno, this dramatic windswept **site** (admission US$2) has an extraordinary position atop a table-topped volcanic hill surrounded by a sprawling plain. Its modest number of exceptionally well-preserved *chullpas,* built by the Colla, Lupaca and Inca cultures, come in both square and cylindrical shapes. Look closely and you'll find several monkeys, pumas and snakes carved into the structures.

Combis leave the cemetery by Parque Amista, 1km from Puno's city center, every half hour (US60¢, 30 minutes). You can't miss the site, which is a steep climb up from the right-hand (east) side of the road.

Llachón
pop 1300

Almost 75km northeast of Puno, this pretty little village is on the Peninsula of Capachica, which offers fantastic views and short hikes to surrounding pre-Inca sites. It's an area that sees very few tourists. With advance reservations, families welcome visitors into their rudimentary homes and cook all meals for around US$4. Nayra Travel (p866) can make necessary arrangements and show you how to get here by local buses from Puno (US$4.50, 2½ hours).

South-Shore Towns

If you start early enough, you can visit all of the following south-shore towns in a day and either be back in Puno by nightfall or continue onward to Bolivia. For a map of this region, see p206.

The road east of Puno follows the lakeside. At the village of **Chimú**, famous for its *totora*-reed industry, you might spy boats in various stages of construction.

The next village is **Chucuito**, 20km southeast of Puno. There's a breathtaking **mirador** a short walk south of the colonial church on the plaza. The principal attraction is the outlandish **Templo de la Fertilidad** (admission free), which consists of scattered, dusty dozens of large stone phalluses.

Juli, 80km southeast of Puno, is Peru's Pequeña Roma (Little Rome) on account of its four hoary colonial churches, best visited on Sunday market days. **Pomata**, 105km from Puno, is dominated by an exquisite Dominican church atop a small hill.

Just outside Pomata, the road forks to the right toward Desaguadero or left alongside the lake to Yunguyo.

GETTING THERE & AWAY

Puno's Terminal Zonal has cheaper, slower minibuses and faster minivans for all destinations en route to the Bolivian border (US$1.40, 2½ hours).

ISLAND-HOPPING

The only way to see Lake Titicaca is to spend a few days visiting its fairy-tale islands. That said, negative impacts from tourism are being felt in many communities. You could also hop over the Bolivian border to visit the more chill Isla del Sol (p209) from Copacabana.

Islas Flotantes

The unique **floating islands** of the Uros people have become shockingly commercialized, though there is still nothing quite like them anywhere else. The islands are built using layers of the buoyant *totora* reeds that grow abundantly in the shallows of Lake Titicaca.

Intermarriage with Aymara-speaking indigenous peoples has seen the demise of the pureblooded Uros. Always a small tribe, they began their floating existence centuries ago

in an effort to isolate themselves from the aggressive Collas and the Incas. Today several hundred people still live on the islands.

Indeed the lives of the Uros are totally interwoven with these reeds, which are used to make their homes, boats and the crafts they churn out for tourists. The islands' reeds are constantly replenished from the top as they rot away, so the ground is always soft and springy – mind your step!

Two-hour boat tours (US$3) leave from the dock when full from 7am until late afternoon. There's a ticket booth at the dock entrance. Trips to other islands sometimes stop at the Islas Flotantes on the way out.

Isla Taquile

Inhabited for many thousands of years, this 7 sq km **island** (admission US$1.50) often feels like its own little world. The Quechua-speaking islanders maintain lives largely unchanged by mainland modernities and have a long tradition of weaving. Their creations can be bought in the cooperative store on the main plaza. Look for the menfolk's tightly woven woolen hats, resembling floppy nightcaps, which they knit themselves and can denote social status. The women also look eye-catching in their multilayered skirts and delicately embroidered blouses.

Several hills have pre-Inca terracing and small ruins set against the backdrop of Bolivia's snowcapped Cordillera Real. Visitors are free to wander around, but you can't do that on a day trip without missing lunch or the boat back, so stay overnight if you can. Travelers will be met by islanders next to the arch atop the steep stairway up from the dock. They can arrange homestays (per person US$3). Beds are basic but clean, and facilities are minimal. You'll be given blankets, but bringing a sleeping bag and flashlight is essential.

Most island shops and restaurants close by mid-afternoon, when all the tour groups leave, so arrange dinner with your host family in advance. Gifts of fresh fruit from Puno's markets are appreciated. You can buy bottled drinks at the shops, though it's worth bringing purifying tablets or a water filter. Also bring small bills (change is limited) and extra money for souvenirs.

Boats for the incredibly slow 34km trip to Taquile leave Puno's dock every day around 7:30am (US$6, three hours). Get to the dock early and pay the captain directly. The return boat leaves in the early afternoon, arriving in Puno around nightfall. Remember to bring sunscreen and mosquito repellent.

Puno travel agencies (p866) offer guided tours for about US$9, or US$15 for an overnight stay including meals, though the islanders benefit more from travelers who go independently.

Isla Amantaní

This less frequently visited **island** (admission US$1.50) is a few kilometers northeast of Taquile. Several hills are topped by ruins of the Tiahuanaco culture. Trips here usually involve an overnight stay with islanders (around US$3, including meals). You can stay in more comfort at locally owned **Kantuta Lodge** (☎ 051-81-2664; www .punored.com/titicaca/amantani/img/english.html; r per person incl meals US$20). Boats to Amantaní leave Puno between 7:30am and 8:30am most mornings: pay the captain directly (US$7.50, 3½ hours). Unpredictable boat connections usually make it easiest to travel from Puno to Amantaní and on to Taquile, rather than in reverse. Puno travel agencies (p866) charge US$15 for a two-day tour to Amantaní, with a quick visit to Taquile and the floating islands.

CUZCO & THE SACRED VALLEY

As the heart of the once-mighty Inca empire, the magnetic city of Cuzco heads the list of many a traveler's itinerary. Each year it draws hundreds of thousands of travelers to its lofty elevations, lured by the city's unique combination of colonial splendor built on hefty stone foundations of the Incas. And lying within easy hopping distance of the city is the country's biggest draw card of all, the 'lost' city of the Incas, Machu Picchu, perched high on a remote mountaintop. The department of Cuzco also has superb trekking routes and a long list of flamboyant fiestas and carnivals in which Peru's pagan past colorfully collides with Catholic rituals and modern Latin American mayhem.

CUZCO

☎ 084 / pop 322,000

The high-flying Andean city of Cuzco (Qosq'o in the Quechua language) is the uneasy bearer of many grand titles. It was once the foremost city of the Inca Empire, and is now the undisputed archaeological capital of the Americas as well as the continent's oldest continuously inhabited city. Massive Inca-built walls line steep, narrow cobblestone streets and plazas are often thronged with the descendants of the mighty Incas and Spanish conquistadors. But there's no question of who rules the roost now: the city's economy is almost totally at the whim of international tourists, and every second building surrounding the Plaza de Armas is a restaurant, shop or hotel.

History

Cuzco is a city so steeped in history, tradition and myth that it can be difficult to know where fact ends and myth begins. Legends tell that in the 12th century, the first Inca, Manco Capác, was charged by the ancestral sun god Inti to find the *qosq'o* (navel of the earth). When at last Manco discovered such a point, he founded the city.

The ninth Inca Pachacutec (see p823) wasn't only a warmonger: he also proved himself a sophisticated urban developer, devising Cuzco's famous puma shape and diverting rivers to cross the city. He also built the famous Coricancha temple and his palace fronting what is now the Plaza de Armas.

After murdering the 12th Inca Atahualpa (see p823), the Spanish conquistador Francisco Pizarro marched on Cuzco in 1533 and appointed Manco Inca as a puppet ruler of the Incas. After a few years, Manco rebelled and laid siege to Spanish-occupied Cuzco. Only a desperate battle at Saqsaywamán (p879) saved the Spanish from annihilation. Manco was forced to retreat to Ollantaytambo and eventually into the jungle at Vilcabamba. Once the city had been safely recaptured, looted and settled, the seafaring Spaniards turned their attentions to coastal Lima, making Cuzco just another quiet colonial backwater.

Few events of historical significance have rocked Cuzco since Spanish conquest but for earthquakes in 1650 and 1950, and a failed indigenous uprising led by Túpac Amaru II in 1780. It was the rediscovery of Machu Picchu in 1911 that has affected the city more than any event since the arrival of the Spanish.

Orientation

The city centers on the Plaza de Armas, while traffic-choked Av El Sol is the main business thoroughfare. Walking just a few blocks north or east of the plaza will lead you onto steep, twisting cobblestone streets changed little for centuries.

The alley off the northwest side of the plaza is Procuradores (Tax Collectors), nicknamed 'Gringo Alley' for its huddle of backpacker bars and cafés – watch out for predatory touts. Beside the cathedral, narrow Calle Triunfo leads uphill to Plaza San Blas, the heart of Cuzco's artistic *barrio* (neighborhood).

In a resurgence of indigenous pride, the official names of many streets have been changed from Spanish back to Quechua spellings (eg Qosqo not Cuzco, Pisaq not Pisac). Maps may retain the old spellings, which are still in everyday use.

Information
BOOKSTORES
Book exchanges abound at cafés, pubs and the SAE clubhouse (right).

Jerusalén (Heladeros 143; ☽ 9am-9pm Mon-Sat)
Los Andes Bookshop (Portal Comercio 125; ☽ 9:30am-1:30pm & 4:15-9pm Mon-Sat)
SBS Bookshop (El Sol 781-A; ☽ 9am-9pm Mon-Sat)

EMERGENCY
Policía de Turismo (☎ 084-24-9654; Saphi 510; ☽ 24hr) For official reports needed for insurance claims and details of foreign consulate representatives.

IMMIGRATION
Migraciónes (☎ 22-2741; El Sol 612; ☽ 8am-1pm & 2-4:30pm Mon-Fri) For visa extensions (p942).

INTERNET ACCESS
Internet cafés are on every corner.
Mundo Net (Santa Teresa 172; per hr US60¢; ☽ 7am-10pm Mon-Sat) A calm oasis, with private telephone booths and an espresso bar.

LAUNDRY
Lavanderías cluster on Suecia, Procuradores and Plateros. During high season, don't bet your last pair of trekking socks on their promise of 'in by 10am, ready by 6pm.'

LEFT LUGGAGE
Many guesthouses will store your bags for free. Lock everything securely, always get a receipt and keep a copy of the contents with you.

MEDICAL SERVICES
Cuzco's medical facilities are limited. Head back to Lima for serious procedures.

Clínica Pardo (☎ 24-0387; Av de la Cultura 710; ☽ 24hr)
Clínica Paredes (☎ 22-5265; Lechugal 405; ☽ 24hr)
Hospital Regional (☎ 23-9792/22-3691; Av de la Cultura s/n) Cheaper, but not as good.
InkaFarma (☎ 24-2967; El Sol 174; ☽ 24hr) Well-stocked pharmacy.

MONEY
Many banks on Av El Sol and shops around the Plaza de Armas have foreign-card-friendly ATMs. The main bus terminal has a global ATM.
LAC Dolar (El Sol 150; ☽ 9am-8pm Mon-Sat) Reliable *casa de cambio*.

POST
Serpost (El Sol 800; ☽ 8am-8pm Mon-Sat)

TOURIST INFORMATION
iPerú airport (☎ 23-7364; Main Hall; ☽ 6am-4pm); city center (☎ 23-4498; Office 102, Galerías Turísticas, El Sol 103; ☽ 8:30am-7:30pm) Efficient, helpful main office also runs Indecopi, the tourist-protection agency.
South American Explorers (SAE; ☎ 24-5484; www .saexplorers.org; No 4 Choquechaca 188; ☽ 9:30am-5pm Mon-Fri, to 1pm Sat) Traveler information and maps sold. Cultural events and some volunteering info for nonmembers. For details about the club, see p836 and p1072.

Dangers & Annoyances
The train stations and markets are prime areas for pickpockets and bag-slashers. Use only official taxis (look for the company's telephone number on the roof), lock your doors and never allow additional passengers. Late-night revelers returning from bars or trekkers setting off before sunrise are most vulnerable to 'choke and grab' muggings, especially on Resbalosa. Drug dealers and police often work together, especially on Procuradores, where you can make a drug deal and get busted, all within a couple of minutes. Beware of altitude sickness if you're flying in from sea level (see p1095).

Sights
For admission to many archaeological sites around Cuzco, you must buy a Boleto Turístico. A 10-day 'tourism ticket' costs US$21/10.50 per adult/student. You can buy it at **Oficina Ejecutiva del Comité** (OFEC; ☎ 22-7037; El Sol 103; ☽ 8am-5:30pm Mon-Fri, to 12:30pm Sat), travel agencies or participating sites outside the city.

PERU

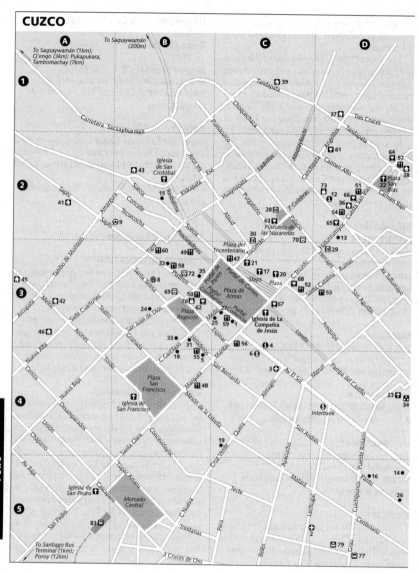

CUZCO

It's also possible to buy partial one-day *boletos* costing US$12.

PLAZA DE ARMAS

Colonial arcades surround the plaza, which was the heart of the ancient Inca capital.

Taking almost 100 years to build, Cuzco's **cathedral** (adult/student US$4.75/2.30, religious-circuit ticket US$10/5.35; ⊗ 10am-6pm Mon-Sat, 2-6pm Sun) sits on the site of Inca Viracocha's Palace and was erected using blocks from Saqsaywamán (p879). It's one of the city's greatest repositories of colonial art. Look for *The Last Supper* by Marcos Zapata, with a plump, juicy-looking roast *cuy* (guinea pig) stealing the show. Opposite the silver altar is a magnifi-

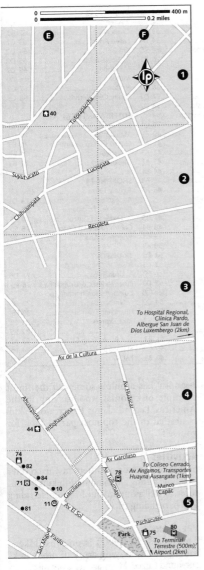

OVER THE RAINBOW

A common sight in Cuzco's Plaza de Armas is the city's much-loved flag – a brightly striped banner developed in the 1970s to represent the *arco iris* (rainbow) sacred to the Incas. Don't mistake this flag for the international gay-pride banner, to which it bears a remarkable resemblance!

oldest Inca wall in Cuzco, part of the Acllahuasi (House of the Chosen Women). After the conquest, it became part of Santa Catalina, so went from housing Virgins of the Sun to pious Catholic nuns. On the right is Amaruqancha (Courtyard of the Serpents), the site of the palace of Inca Huayna Capac. After the conquest, the Iglesia de La Compañía de Jesús was built here.

Exiting the plaza heading uphill toward San Blas along Triunfo you'll reach Hatunrumiyoc, a street named after the excellently fitted **12-sided stone** on the right – children stand next to it and insist on tips just for pointing it out. This stone was part of the palace of the sixth Inca, Roca.

QORIKANCHA

This **Inca site** (Plazoleta Santo Domingo; adult/student US$3.60/1.80; ☺8am-5pm Mon-Sat, 2-5pm Sun) forms the base of the colonial church of **Iglesia de Santo Domingo**. Compare the colonial building with the Inca walls, most of which survived Cuzco's historic earthquakes with hardly a hairline crack. The site looks rather bizarre, topped with a modern protective roof of glass and metal.

In Inca times, Qorikancha (Quechua for 'golden courtyard') was literally covered with gold. It was not only used for religious rites, but was also an observatory from which priests monitored major celestial activities. Today all that remains of the Inca Empire's richest temple is its masterful stonework – Spanish conquistadors looted the rest. But it's fascinating to visit nonetheless, with excellent interpretive signs for self-guided tours.

MUSEUMS

Inside a Spanish colonial mansion with an Inca ceremonial courtyard, the dramatically curated **Museo de Arte Precolombino** (MAP; ☎23-3210; http://map.perucultural.org.pe; Plazoleta Nazarenas 231; adult/student US$6/3; ☺9am-10pm) showcases a

cently carved 17th-century choir. The cathedral is joined with the church of **Jesús María** (1733) and **El Triunfo** (1536), Cuzco's oldest church containing the vault of the famous Inca historian Garcilaso de la Vega, born in Cuzco in 1539.

Leaving the plaza along Loreto, **Inca walls** line both sides of the alley. On the left is the

stunningly varied if small collection of price-
less archaeological pieces previously buried in
the vast storerooms of Lima's Museo Larco.
Labels are in Spanish, English and French.

The modest **Museo Inka** (☎ 23-7380; Tucumán
at Ataúd; admission US$3; ☯ 8am-5pm Mon-Fri, 9am-5pm
Sat) inhabits one of the city's finest colonial
buildings. It's jam-packed with metal and
gold work, pottery, textiles, *queros* (wooden
Inca drinking vessels), mummies and more.
In the courtyard, highland weavers sell their
traditional textiles to the public.

Originally the palace of Inca Roca, the
musty **Museo de Arte Religioso** (Hatunrumiyoc;
adult/student US$3/1.50; religious-circuit ticket US$10/5.35;
☯ 8am-6pm Mon-Sat, 10am-6pm Sun) has an extensive religious art collection noted for its
period detail and insight into the interac-
tions of indigenous peoples with Spanish
conquistadors.

IGLESIA DE SAN BLAS

This adobe **church** (Plaza San Blas; admission US$1.80;
religious-circuit ticket US$10/5.35; ☯ 10am-6pm Mon-Sat,
2-6pm Sun) has a pulpit some call the finest
example of colonial woodcarving in the
Americas. Legend claims the creator's skull
is nestled in the topmost part – look for
yourself.

Activities

Scores of outdoor outfitters in Cuzco offer
trekking, rafting and mountain-biking adventures, as well as mountaineering, horse-riding
and paragliding trips.

TREKKING

The Inca Trail (p887) is on most hikers'
minds, but a dizzying array of other treks
surround Cuzco. Many agencies organize trips
to remote Inca ruins, such as Choquequirau
(p891) and Vilcabamba (p890), and around
Ausangate (p891). Prices are *not* fixed. Shop
around and ask questions (eg how many people per tents, how many porters are coming,
what the arrangements are for special diets).
Inspect all rental gear carefully. The SAE clubhouse (p871) sells topo maps.

Readers often recommend these agencies:

Aventours (☎ 22-4050; www.aventours.com; Pardo 545) Expensive but its Inca Trail camp and llama treks are unique.

Enigma (☎ 22-2155; www.enigmaperu.com; Office 103, Calle Garcilaso 210) Specializes in tailor-made treks for small groups and alternative tourism.

Llama Path (☎ 24-0822; www.llamapath.com; San Juan de Dios 250) Friendly, small upstart trekking company.

Peru Treks (☎ 50-5863; www.perutreks.com; Garcilaso 265, 2nd fl) Locally owned, ecoconscious and ethical treatment of porters.

Q'ente (☎ 24-7836; www.qente.com; Garcilaso 210) Also offers many Inca Trail alternatives.

SAS (☎ 25-5205; www.sastravelperu.com; Portal de Panes 167) A mammoth operator, but with many detractors.

RIVER RUNNING & MOUNTAIN BIKING

White-water rafting (river running) down the **Río Urubamba** is popular. It's not very wild and offers some spectacular scenery and a chance to visit some of the best Inca ruins near Cuzco. For more remote rivers, you definitely need to book with a top-quality outfit using experienced rafting guides who know first aid, because you will be days away from help in the event of illness or accident. The same goes for mountain-biking trips.

The **Río Apurímac** has challenging rapids through deep gorges and protected rainforest, but can only be run from May to November. A wilder trip is the technically demanding **Río Tambopata**, which can be run from June to October. You'll start in the Andes, north of Lake Titicaca, and reach Reserva Nacional Tambopata in the Amazon.

If you're experienced, there are awesome mountain-biking possibilities around the Sacred Valley and downhill trips from Cuzco to the Amazon jungle. Better rental bikes cost US$15 to US$25 per day, but inspect them carefully. Make sure you get a helmet, puncture-repair kit, pump and tool kit.

Some reputable companies for rafting trips on remote rivers:

Amazonas Explorer (☎ 25-2846/976-5448/ 976-5447; www.amazonas-explorer.com; Collasuyo 910, Urb Marivelle) Professional international operator.

Apumayo Expeditions (☎ 24-6018; www.apumayo.com; Interior 3, Garcilaso 265) River-rafting trips, including for travelers with disabilities.

Loreto Tours (☎ 22-8264; www.loretotours.com; Calle del Medio 111) Good for mountain-biking tours.

Mayuc (☎ 084-24-2824; www.mayuc.com; Portal Confiturías 211) Resident rafting experts.

Courses

Cuzco is a convenient place to study Spanish.

Academia Latinoamericana (☎ 24-3364; www.latinoschools.com; Plaza Limacpampa 565)

Amauta (☎ 24-1422; www.amautaspanish.com; Suecia 480)

Cusco Spanish School (☎ 22-6928; www.cuscospanishschool.com; Garcilaso 265, 2nd fl)

Excel Language Center (☎ 23-5298; www.excelinspanish.com; Cruz Verde 336)

San Blas Spanish School (☎ 24-7898; www.spanishschoolperu.com; Tandapata 688)

Tours

There are hundreds of registered travel agencies in Cuzco, but none can ever be 100% recommended. Ask around.

Blasé options include a half-day tour of the city or nearby ruins, a half-day trip to the Sunday markets at Pisac or Chinchero, or a full-day tour of the Sacred Valley (Pisac, Ollantaytambo and Chinchero). These tours are usually too rushed and not worth the money.

Even more expensive Machu Picchu tours include train tickets, the bus to/from the ruins, admission to the site, an English-speaking guide and lunch. But you only get to spend a few hours at the ruins before it's time to return to the train station, so it's better to DIY.

Cuzco is an excellent place to organize trips to the jungle, especially to Parque Nacional Manu (p929). None are cheap, though. Try the following:

Caiman (☎ 25-4041/4042; www.manucaiman.com; Office 207, Garcilaso 210)

Manu Expeditions (☎ 22-6671/23-9974; www.manuexpeditions.com; Humberto Vidal Unda G-5, Urb Magisterial)

Manu Nature Tours (☎ 25-2721; www.manuperu.com; Pardo 1046)

Pantiacolla (☎ 23-8323; www.pantiacolla.com; Plateros 360 & Saphi 554)

Festivals & Events

El Señor de los Temblores (The Lord of the Earthquakes) On the Monday before Easter; processions date from Cuzco's 1650 earthquake.

Qoyllur Rit'i Less well known are these traditional Andean rites, held in May or June near Ausangate.

Corpus Christi This feast takes place the ninth Thursday after Easter (usually early June), with fantastic religious processions and cathedral celebrations.

Inti Raymi (Festival of the Sun) Held on June 24, Cuzco's most important festival attracts thousands of visitors and culminates in a reenactment of Inca winter-solstice ceremonies at Saqsaywamán.

Sleeping

Side streets northwest of the Plaza de Armas (especially Tigre, Tecsecocha and Suecia) are bursting with dime-a-dozen *hostales*. Budget guesthouses also surround the Plaza San Blas, though you'll have to huff and puff to get up there.

Casas de Hospedaje (☎ 24-2710; www.cusco.net/familyhouse) Homestays cost from US$5 to US$12 per person, depending on the season and the facilities. Check the website for descriptions of each *cuzqueña* home, including its location and all amenities.

Loki Backpackers Hostel (☎ 24-3705; www.lokihostel.com; Santa Ana 601; dm US$5.50-8.50, s/d US$10.50/21; 🖳) This is where the party's at! Expats rescued this 450-year-old national monument from near-ruin, then transformed it into a backpacker-friendly haven with hot showers, free internet and kitchen access.

Hospedaje Familiar Kuntur Wasi (☎ 22-7570; Tandapata 352A; s/d US$15/25, without bathroom US$6/12) This simple courtyard guesthouse has an invitingly sunny and hospitable environment, with warm showers and kitchen access.

Hospedaje Inka (☎ 23-1995; americopacheco@hotmail.com; Suytuccato 848; s/d incl breakfast US$7.50/15) This scruffy but charming converted hillside farmhouse above San Blas affords some great views. There's erratic hot water, private bathrooms and a large farm kitchen. Taxis can't climb the final uphill stretch.

Hostal Mira Sol (☎ 23-5824; mirasolhostal@hotmail.com; Suecia 504; s/d/tr with shared bath US$7.50/15/22.50) This Italian-run guesthouse offers basic, tidy rooms (those below ground are quiet, but dark) and a huge lounge with a stereo, TV and shared kitchen.

Qorichaska Hostal (☎ 22-8974; www.qorichaskaperu.com; Nueva Alta 458; s/d/tr US$12/20/30, s/d with shared bath US$8/16/24, all incl breakfast) Qorichaska, which feels a bit like entering a secret society hidden behind several gates, is basic but friendly and safe. Hot water and kitchen access.

Casa de la Gringa (☎ 24-1168; www.anotherplanetperu.net/hostel.htm; Pasnapacana 148; dm US$9, d US$26-30) This laid-back New Age retreat has a garden of healing plants. The unique rooms are wildly colorful, plus there's a kitchen, TV and games lounge.

Hostal Familiar (☎ 23-9353; hostalfamiliar@hotmail.com; Saphi 661; s/d without bathroom US$7.50/15, s/d incl breakfast US$12/18) Off the beaten path, this guesthouse has a well-kept colonial courtyard and clean, spartan rooms.

Amaru Hostal (☎ 22-5933; www.cusco.net/amaru; Cuesta San Blas 541; s/d/tr without bathroom US$12/16/24, s/d/tr incl breakfast US$17/25/36) In a characterful colonial building, flowerpots sit outside rooms, which may have rocking chairs and windows to let in sunshine. Those in the outer courtyard are noisier.

Hostal Los Niños (☎ 23-1424; www.ninoshotel.com; Meloc 442; s/d without bathroom US$14/28, d US$34) Even if this Dutch-run hostel weren't dedicated to helping street kids, this charming colonial mansion would still be our favorite place to stay. Hot water, wool blankets, portable heaters and a courtyard fireplace café.

Also recommended:

Albergue San Juan de Dios Luxemburgo (☎ 24-0135; www.sanjuandedioscusco.com; Manzanares 264, Urb Manuel Prado; s/d incl continental breakfast US$15/30) Run as part of a nonprofit enterprise that funds a hospital clinic and provides job opportunities for young people with disabilities. Take a taxi (US$1).

El Mirador de la Ñusta (☎ 24-8039; elmiradordelanusta@hotmail.com; Tandapata 682; s/d US$10/15) Conveniently on the Plaza San Blas, though there are better-value guesthouses further west on Tandapata.

Hostal San Juan Masías (☎ 43-1563; Ahuacpinta 600; d/tr with shared bath US$12/18, d/tr/q US$15/22.50/30) Run by Dominican nuns on the grounds of a busy school. Spic-and-span rooms have hot water.

Eating

El Buen Pastor (Cuesta San Blas 579; items US30¢-$1.50; 🕑 7am-8pm Mon-Sat) The warm glow at this bakery isn't just from supping cappuccino with your morning pastries, but also the knowledge that all profits benefit charity.

I Due Mondi (Santa Catalina Ancha 366; snacks from US75¢) Chic Italian-style café with 15 seductive ice-cream flavors (including *chicha*!).

Muse (Tandapata 684; items US75¢-$4.20) With tables spilling out above the Plaza San Blas, this bohemian coffee shop dishes up English breakfasts and healthy salads and sandwiches.

Coco Loco (Espaderos 135; snacks US$1-3; 🕑 until 4am Mon-Sat) Fast-food joint for postclubbing cravings.

Trotamundos (Portal Comercio 177, 2nd fl; snacks US$1.50-3; 🖳) Popular plaza coffeehouse with dead-on views of the cathedral.

Kin Taro (Heladeros 149; mains US$2-4.50; ☼ noon-10pm Mon-Sat) As authentic a Japanese menu as you'll find anywhere outside of Lima, plus trout sushi and sake.

Victor Victoria (Tigre 130; mains US$2.50-6) No-frills Peruvian restaurant that slips in a few French, Israeli and vegetarian dishes.

Granja Heidi (Cuesta San Blas 525, 2nd fl; meals US$3-6.50; ☼ 8:30am-9:30pm Mon-Sat) Follow the pictures of cows to this light, Alpine café, with terrific fresh produce, yogurts, cakes and other healthy food on offer. Breakfasts are gigantic.

Chez Maggy (Procuradores 344, 365, 374; mains US$3.50-5.50) Chez Maggy has virtually taken over Gringo Alley with three déjà vu–inducing branches, all serving wood-fired pizzas and pastas.

Sumaq Misky (Plateros 334, 2nd fl; mains US$4.50-12) Hidden in an alley of souvenir stalls, this warm eatery and bar targets adventurous foodies with special nights like alpaca Fridays or *cuy* Sundays, when you can even order guinea pig tandoori-style.

Jack's Cafe (Choquechaka 509; mains US$5-7.50) Refuel here before struggling uphill to the Plaza San Blas on a hearty menu of modern international fare that makes it a favorite with expats. The ginger-lemon tea cures all ills.

Blueberry Lounge (Portal de Carnes 235; mains US$5-8) Global fusion rules the roost, from South Asian curries to teriyaki alpaca. The after-dark atmosphere is way more sophisticated than run-of-the-mill Plaza de Armas eateries.

Café Dos X 3 (Marquez 271; snacks US$1.50) A retro café with jazz tunes and out-of-this-world passion-fruit cheesecake.

Grocery shops include **Gato's Market** (Portal Belén; ☼ 7am-10pm) and the original **Market** (Mantas 119; ☼ 8am-11pm).

Drinking

In popular backpacker bars, especially around the Plaza de Armas, both sexes should beware of drinks being spiked – don't let go of your glass, and think twice about using free-drink coupons. Several nightclubs also show DVD movies during the day.

Norton's Rat (Loreto 115; ☼ 9am-late) Down-to-earth pub with wooden tables overlooking the plaza and TVs, darts and billiards, plus the best sloppy burgers in town.

Cross Keys (Portal Confiturías 233; ☼ 11am-late) A British-style pub in a rickety old building on the plaza, with TV, darts and a pool table with an unparalleled bananalike trajectory.

Paddy Flaherty's (Triunfo 124; ☼ 11am-late) This cramped little Irish bar is full of high stools, games and TVs tuned to football (soccer) matches.

Fallen Angel (Plazoleta Nazarenas 221; ☼ 6pm-late) This is an ultrafunky restaurant falling all over itself with glitter balls, fake fur and even bathtub-cum-aquarium tables. Cocktails are expensive, but creative. Also runs Macondo (Cuesta San Blas 571).

Other funky watering holes in the San Blas barrio include the Muse coffee shop (opposite), **Km 0** (Tandapata 100) tapas bar, French-themed **Le Nomadé** (Choquechaca at Hatunrumiyoc) hookah café and **7 Angelitos** (Siete Angelitos 638) lounge, which all often have live music.

Entertainment

Several restaurants have evening *folklórica* music and dance shows; cover charges vary from US$3 to US$6.

Centro Qosqo de Arte Nativo (☎ 22-7901; El Sol 604; admission US$4.50) This place has nightly *folklórica* shows.

Ukuku's Pub (Plateros 316; ☼ 8pm-late) Usually full to bursting, Ukuku's plays a winning combination of Latin pop, reggae, alternative, salsa, ska, soul, jazz and more, and hosts live local bands nightly.

Mandela's (Palacio 121; ☼ 6pm-late) A South Africa–themed bar, it has a tempting menu of bar snacks and a funky atmosphere, with plenty of live music and special events.

Kamikase (Plaza Regocijo 274; ☼ 8pm-late) It doesn't offer free drinks, but has a disarmingly large variety of music, which can switch from salsa to *folklórica* in an instant, with live shows almost nightly. Dare to try the El Camino a la Ruina cocktail.

Shopping

Cuzco offers a cornucopia of artisan workshops and stores selling knitted woolens, woven textiles, colorful ceramics, silver jewelry and more, as well as contemporary art galleries. Poke around the streets heading uphill from the Plaza de Armas and radiating outward from the Plaza San Blas. Prices and quality vary greatly, so shop around and expect to bargain (except in the most expensive stores, where prices are often fixed). Near the San Pedro train station, Cuzco's Mercado Central is a handy spot to pick up fruit

PERU

or that vital spare pair of clean socks, but don't go alone or take valuables, as thieves are persistent.

Center for Traditional Textiles of Cusco (El Sol 603-A) This nonprofit organization promotes the survival of traditional Andean weaving techniques, and has shop-floor demonstrations of finger-twisting complexity.

Agua y Tierra (Garcilaso 210) This beautiful gallery specializes in authentically handmade indigenous Amazonian art and crafts.

Werner & Ana (Plaza San Francisco 295-A) This sleek showroom features innovative modern alpaca-wool clothing for both sexes, including scarves, hats and sweaters.

Andean Expressions (Choquechaca 210) Hailing from Huaraz, the owner of this unique T-shirt shop is also the graphic designer – no Inka Kola logos here, we swear.

Centro Artesanal Cuzco (cnr El Sol & Tullumayo; ○ 9am-10pm) For mass-produced souvenirs, head for this vast place where you can literally shop till you drop.

Getting There & Away
AIR
Most flights from Cuzco's **airport** (CUZ; ☎ 22-2611), 2km southeast of the center, are in the morning. Flights tend to be overbooked, so confirm and reconfirm. Many flights get canceled or lumped together during low periods. Earlier flights are less likely to be canceled.

Aero Condor Perú (☎ 084-25-2774; www.aerocondor .com.pe) Daily flights to Lima and thrice-weekly to Puerto Maldonado.

LAN (☎ 084-25-5552; www.lan.com; El Sol 627-B) Direct flights to Lima, Arequipa, Juliaca and Puerto Maldonado.

Star Perú (☎ 084-23-4060; www.starperu.com; El Sol 679) Twice-daily flights to Lima.

TACA (☎ 084-24-9921; www.taca.com; El Sol 602-B) Nearly daily service to/from Lima.

BUS
Long-Distance
The journey times given here are only approximate. Long delays are probable during the rainy season, especially January to April.

Cuzco has a long-distance bus terminal (departure tax US30¢), 2km southeast of the city center (taxi US$1), where you'll find all of the major bus companies including **Cruz del Sur** (☎ 22-1909), **Ormeño** (☎ 084-22-7501), **Cromotex** (☎ 24-9573) and **Imexso** (☎ 22-9126). There are scores of *económico* bus operators too.

Frequent buses go to Puno (US$4.50 to US$10.50, six to seven hours) via Juliaca. Services to Arequipa (US$7.50 to US$21, nine to 11 hours) are mostly overnight. There are two routes to Lima. The first is via Abancay (US$18 to US$33, 17 to 23 hours), which is quicker but can be a rough ride and prone to crippling delays during the rainy season. The alternative is via Arequipa, a longer but more reliable route (US$19.50 to US$47.50, 25 to 27 hours). Buses to Abnacay (US$4.50, five hours) and Andahuaylas (US$8, 10 hours) leave early in the morning and evening. Change at Andahuaylas for buses bound for Ayaucho via rough highland roads that get cold at night.

Minibuses to Urcos (US$1) leave from Manco Cápac, east of Tacna, and from Av de la Cultura opposite the regional hospital. Take these to visit Tipón, Pikillacta, Rumicolca and Andahuaylillas (see p889). But why not treat yourself instead? **Inka Express** (☎ 24-7887; www .inkaexpress.com; Pardo 865) has cushy tour buses (US$25) that stop at several sites en route to Puno (see p867).

Buses to Quillabamba (US$4.50, seven to eight hours) leave a few times daily from the Santiago bus terminal in western Cuzco (taxi US60¢). A recommended company is **Ampay** (☎ 24-5734), which staffs another ticket counter at Cuzco's main long-distance terminal. Daytime buses are safer and have the advantage of spectacular scenery.

For other Amazon destinations you have to fly, risk a hazardous journey by truck or find an expedition. During the dry season, daily trucks to Puerto Maldonado along a wild and difficult road (see p891) leave from near Plaza Túpac Amaru, east of Tacna along Garcilaso (US$10, two to seven days). **Expreso Virgen del Carmen** (☎ 22-6895; Diagonal Angamos 1952) has buses to Paucartambo (US$3, five hours) leaving from behind the Coliseo Cerrado daily. Continuing from Paucartambo to Manu, there are only passing trucks or expedition buses, though buses for Pillcopata leave from Avenida Angamos on Monday, Wednesday and Friday mornings (US$4.50, 10 hours). Trucks continue onward from Pillcopata to Shintuya (US$2.50, eight hours).

International
Several companies offer buses to Copacabana (US$15, 13 hours) and La Paz (US$18 to US$20, 18 hours) in Bolivia; also see p868.

Many swear blind that their service is direct, though evening buses usually stop in Puno for several hours until the border opens. Ormeño goes to La Paz (US$50.60, 16 hours) via Desaguadero. For Tacna, near the Chilean border, Cruz del Sur has departures every afternoon (US$22.30, 15 hours); also see p856.

TRAIN
All train tickets are currently sold only at Estación Huanchac, though this may change. Buy tickets as far ahead as possible and bring your passport. Click to www.perurail.com for updated schedules, fares and reservations.

At the southeastern end of El Sol, **Estación Huanchac** (☎ 23-8722; 🕑 8:30am-4:30pm Mon-Fri, to noon Sat & Sun) serves Juliaca and Puno, with trains leaving at 8am Monday, Wednesday and Saturday (for details, see p868).

Trains to Ollantaytambo and Aguas Calientes for Machu Picchu leave from **Estación San Pedro** (☎ 22-1992), near the central market. The railway journey to Machu Picchu begins with a steep climb out of Cuzco, accomplished by slow, back-and-forth switchbacks. Late-risers who miss it can often make a dash for the station at Poroy (taxi US$5) to catch up. The tracks then drop gently to Ollantaytambo station and into a narrow gorge of the lower Rió Urubamba. Aguas Calientes is the end-of-the-line station for Machu Picchu.

From Cuzco, there are at least three daily tourist trains to Machu Picchu. Trains leave Cuzco between 6am and 7am and arrive at Aguas Calientes between 9:40am and 11am. Services return between 3:30pm and 5pm, arriving back between 7:20pm and 9:25pm. Round-trip/one-way fares are currently US$113/66 in 1st-class Vistadome trains, or US$73/46 in the backpacker trains. If you'll be visiting the Sacred Valley, cheaper trains leave from Ollantaytambo (p882).

Getting Around
TO/FROM THE AIRPORT
Frequent *colectivos* run along El Sol to just outside the airport (US30¢). A taxi to/from the city center costs US$2.70 to US$3.60. Many guesthouses offer free airport pick-ups by travel agents hoping to sell tours.

BUS & COLECTIVO
Daytime minibuses to Pisac (US60¢, one hour) and Urubamba (US90¢, two hours)

leave from Tullumayo, south of Garcilaso. Micros and speed-demon *colectivos* to Urubamba (US$1.50, 1½ hours) via Chinchero (US75¢, 50 minutes) depart frequently during daylight hours from the 300 block of Grau near Puente Grau. For Ollantaytambo, transfer at Urubamba (US30¢, 30 minutes).

TAXI
Trips around town cost US$1. Official taxis are much safer than 'pirate' taxis (see p871). A company to call is **Aló Taxi** (☎ 22-2222; www.alocusco.com), whose drivers are licensed and carry photo ID.

AROUND CUZCO
The archaeological ruins closest to Cuzco are **Saqsaywamán**, **Q'enqo**, **Pukapukara** and **Tambomachay** (🕑 7am-6pm) – admission with Boleto Turístico, p871. Take a Pisac-bound bus and get off at Tambomachay, the ruin furthest from Cuzco (and, at 3700m, the highest). It's an 8km walk back to Cuzco. Be aware that violent attacks against tourists have occurred along this route, even during daylight hours. Go in a group, and return before nightfall.

Saqsaywamán
The name means 'Satisfied Falcon,' though most travelers remember it by the mnemonic 'sexy woman.' The sprawling site is 2km from Cuzco. Climb steep Resbalosa street, turn right past the Church of San Cristóbal and continue to a hairpin bend in the road. On the left is a stone staircase, an Inca stone road leading to the top.

Although Saqsaywamán seems huge, what today's visitor sees is only about 20% of the original structure. Soon after the conquest, the Spaniards tore down walls and used the blocks to build their own houses in Cuzco.

In 1536 the fort saw one of the most bitter battles between the Spanish and Manco Inca, who used Saqsaywamán to lay siege to the conquistadors. Thousands of dead littered the site after the Inca defeat, which attracted swarms of carrion-eating Andean condors. The tragedy was memorialized by the inclusion of eight condors in Cuzco's coat of arms.

Most striking are the magnificent three-tiered fortifications. Inca Pachachutec envisioned Cuzco in the shape of a puma, with Sacsayhuamán as the head, and these 22 zig-zag walls form the teeth. The parade ground is used for Inti Raymi celebrations.

PERU

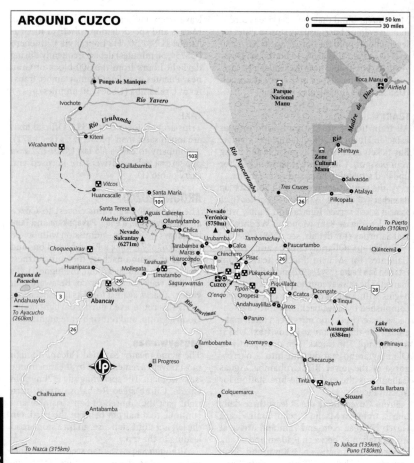

Q'enqo

The name of this fascinating small ruin means 'zigzag.' It's a large limestone rock riddled with niches, steps and extraordinary symbolic carvings, including channels that may have been used for ritual sacrifices of *chicha*, or perhaps blood. Scrambling up to the top of the boulder you'll find a flat surface used for ceremonies and laboriously etched representations of animals. Back below, explore the mysterious subterranean cave with altars hewn into the rock.

The site is 2km from Saqsaywamán, on the left as you descend from Tambomachay.

Tambomachay & Pukapukara

About 300m from the main road, **Tambomachay** is a beautifully wrought ceremonial bath, still channeling clear spring water that earns it the title El Baño del Inca (Inca's Bath). On the opposite side of the road is the commanding ruin of **Pukapukara**. Its name means 'red fort,' though it was more likely a hunting lodge, guard post or stopping point for travelers. The upper esplanade has panoramic views.

THE SACRED VALLEY

The Valle Sagrado of the Río Urubamba is about 15km north of Cuzco as the condor flies. Its star attractions are the lofty Inca citadels of Pisac and Ollantaytambo, but the valley is also packed with more peaceful Inca sites, as well as frenzied markets and high-altitude Andean villages. Investigate the idyllic countryside with Peter Frost's in-depth *Exploring Cuzco*.

Pisac

☎ 084 / pop 2000

Pisac (elevation 2715m) lies 33km northeast of Cuzco by paved road and is the most convenient starting point for a visit to the Sacred Valley. There are two distinct parts: the colonial village beside the river and the Inca fortress perched dramatically on a mountain above.

SIGHTS & ACTIVITIES

The hilltop **Inca citadel** (☼ 7am-6pm) lies high above the village on a plateau with a plunging gorge on either side. Take the steep 4km footpath starting along the left side of the church. It's a spectacular climb up through terraces, sweeping around mountainous flanks and along cliff-hugging footpaths defended by massive stone doorways, vertigo-inducing staircases and a short tunnel carved out of the rock. Admission with Boleto Turístico, p871.

Topping the terraces is the ceremonial center, with an Intihuatana (hitching post of the sun), several working water channels and some neat masonry inside well-preserved temples. A path leads up the hillside to a series of ceremonial baths and around to the military area. A cliff behind the site is honeycombed with hundreds of Inca tombs that were plundered by *huaqueros* (grave robbers).

SLEEPING

Cheap guesthouses hover around the plaza.

Royal Inka Hotel Pisac (☎ 20-3064/3065; campsites per person US$3, tent hire US$10-15) Camp here, 1.5km along the road to the ruins.

Hospedaje Beho (☎ 20-3001; hospedajebeho@yahoo.es; Intihuatana 113; s/d US$9/18, with shared bathroom US$4.50/9) On the path to the ruins and easily hidden by market stalls, this family-run handicrafts shop offers no-frills lodging next door.

Hostal Pisaq (☎ 20-3062; www.hotelpisaq.com; Plaza Constitución; s/d with shared bathroom US$13/26, s/d incl breakfast US$20/35) Recognizable by its funky geometric designs, this hotel has a pretty courtyard. Massages and entry to the sauna cost extra. German, English and French spoken.

Paz y Luz B&B (☎ 20-3204; www.maxart.com/window/gateway.html; s/d incl breakfast US$20/35) A 1km walk east along the river, this spiritual spot surrounded by green fields is run by a North American who organizes mystical tours.

EATING

Clay-oven bakeries on Mariscal Castilla vend piping-hot flatbread.

Mullu (Plaza Constitución; mains US$2.40-5.35; ☼ closed Mon) Hanging above an art gallery, this alt-cultural café commands a prime position over the plaza. There's a deliciously long list of juices, smoothies, sandwiches and fusion fare.

Ulrike's Café (Plaza Constitución; menú US$3.60) This sunny café has an excellent vegetarian menu, homemade pastas, melt-in-the-mouth cheesecakes and brownies, a book exchange and DVDs.

SHOPPING

The Sunday market kicks into life in the early morning. Around 10am the tour buses deposit their hordes into an already chaotic scene, thronged with buyers and overrun with crafts stalls. Although the market retains a traditional side, prices are comparable to shops in Cuzco. There are smaller markets on Tuesday and Thursday.

GETTING THERE & AWAY

Buses to Urubamba (US60¢, one hour) and Cuzco (US60¢, one hour) leave from the bridge between 6am and 8pm. The latter may be standing room only.

Urubamba

☎ 084 / pop 8000

At the junction of the valley road with the road back to Cuzco via Chinchero, Urubamba (elevation 2870m) is an unappealing but necessary transit hub. There's a global ATM at the *grifo* (petrol station) on the main road, about 1km east of the bus terminal.

SIGHTS & ACTIVITIES

The village of **Tarabamba** is about 6km further down the valley. Here, cross the river by footbridge and continue on a footpath, climbing roughly southward up a valley for 3km further to **Salinas** (admission US$1.50), where thousands of saltpans have been harvested since Inca times. The amphitheater-like terraces of **Moray** (admission US$1.50) are over 10km east of Urubamba. The Incas are thought to have used them as an agricultural laboratory, and parts have been replanted with various crops. Take any bus between Urubamba and Cuzco via Chinchero to the Maras turnoff, where taxis await to drive you to Moray (round trip US$9, including visit to Salinas US$12).

Many outdoor activities that are organized from Cuzco take place at Urubamba, including horse-riding, mountain biking,

PERU

paragliding and hot-air balloon trips. **Perol Chicho** (☎ 21-3386, 962-4475; www.perolchico.com), run by Dutch-Peruvian Eduard van Brunschot Vega, has an excellent ranch outside Urubamba with Peruvian paso horses. Advance bookings for horse-riding tours are required.

SLEEPING & EATING

Hotel Urubamba (☎ 20-1062; Bolognesi 605; s/d US$6/9, without bathroom US$3/6) A basic but central choice; some hot water upon request.

Las Chullpas (☎ 968-5713/969-5030; www.geocities .com/laschullpas; Pumahuanca Valley; r per person US$20) Tucked away 3km above town, these woodland cottages, which have fireplaces and private bathrooms, are a perfect getaway. There's a sweat lodge, garden hammocks and a kitchen with vegetarian food available. A *mototaxi* from town costs about US$1.

Los Cedros (☎ 20-1416; campsites per person US$5) This campground is 4km above the town on winding country roads.

Muse, Too (cnr Comercio & Grau; mains US$3-6) Far from the touristy restaurants along the main road, this alternative café and lounge is just off the main plaza.

SHOPPING

Pablo Seminario (☎ 20-1002; www.ceramicaseminario .com; Berriozabal 111) A prolific, well-known potter whose workshop lies in western Urubamba, just off the main road.

GETTING THERE & AWAY

Buses going to Cuzco (US$1, two hours) via Pisac (US60¢, one hour) or Chinchero (US50¢, 50 minutes) and *colectivos* to Ollantaytambo (US30¢, 30 minutes) all leave frequently from the bus terminal. Faster *colectivos* to Cuzco (US$1.50, 1½ hours) wait near the *grifo* further east.

Ollantaytambo

☎ 084 / pop 2000

Dominated by a massive fortress above, Ollantaytambo (elevation 2800m) is the best surviving example of Inca city planning. Its narrow cobblestone streets have been continuously inhabited for over 700 years.

SIGHTS

The spectacular, steep terraces guarding the **Inca complex** (☒ 7am-6pm) – admission with Boleto Turístico, p871 – mark one of the few places where the conquistadors lost a major

battle, when Manco Inca threw missiles and flooded the plain below. But Ollantaytambo was as much a temple as a fort to the Incas. A finely worked ceremonial area sits on top of the terracing. The stone was quarried from the mountainside high above the Río Urubamba. Transporting the huge blocks was a stupendous feat.

Ollantaytambo is a great place to be when the locals are having a fiesta. **Museo CATCCO** (☎ 20-4024; www.ollanta.org; donation US$1.50; ☒ 10am-1pm & 2-4pm Tue-Sun) has information on special events and small cultural and historical displays.

SLEEPING

Hospedaje Los Portadas (☎ 20-4008; Calle Principal s/n; s/d US$6/12, without bathroom US$3/6) Just east of Plaza Mayor, this family guesthouse has a sunny courtyard. All buses pass by outside, but it still manages tranquility. Camping allowed.

Chaska Wasi (☎ 20-4045; katycusco@yahoo.es; Calle de Medio s/n; dm US$4, s/d without bathroom US$6/12) North of the plaza, the friendly folks live up to their simple motto of 'bed, food & drinks.' Cheerful rooms have electric showers. There are bicycles for rent and a DVD library.

Hotel Munay Tika (☎ 20-4111; www.munaytika .com; Ferrocarril 118; s/d incl breakfast US$15/25) Meaning 'jungle flower,' this well-kept inn proffers a pretty garden, kitchen privileges and a tiki bar.

EATING & DRINKING

Restaurants are found around the plaza.

Orishas Cafe (Ferrocarril s/n; items US$1.50-4.50) On the way to the train station, opposite Munay Tika, this is a melodious riverside spot for breakfast, set menus and snacks.

Kusicoyllor (Plaza Araccama; mains US$4.50-9) This stylish, underground café by the ruins has eclectic decor and victuals, from Amazon-grown coffee to Swiss fondue.

Mayupata (Convención; mains US$6-9) A riverside Peruvian restaurant by the bridge which has a garden and a fireplace for those cold Andean nights. Nearby, Quechua Blues Bar & Cine Latino is the only nightspot.

GETTING THERE & AWAY

Frequent *colectivos* run from Plaza Mayor to Urubamba's bus terminal (US30¢, 30 minutes), but services peter out by early evening. To get to Cuzco, transfer in Urubamba.

Ollantaytambo is the halfway point for Machu Picchu trains running between Cuzco (p879) and Aguas Calientes (below), but these services cost the same as from Cuzco. However, Ollantaytambo also offers three additional daily Vistadome services (one way/round trip US$77/46) and one high-season backpacker shuttle (round trip US$57) along the Sacred Valley line.

Chinchero

☎ 084 / pop 2000

Known as the 'birthplace of the rainbow,' this typical Andean village 28km from Cuzco combines Inca ruins with an elaborately decorated colonial church and museum, access to which requires a Boleto Turístico (p871). There are fresh **mountain vistas** and a colorful **Sunday market**. Some buses between Urubamba (US50¢, 50 minutes) and Cuzco (US75¢, 70 minutes) and faster *colectivos* to Cuzco (US$1, 45 minutes) stop here.

AGUAS CALIENTES

☎ 084 / pop 2000

Also known as Machu Picchu Pueblo, this village is nestled in the deep valley below Machu Picchu and enclosed by towering walls of stone and cloud forest. Sounds scenic? It's not: this is the ugliest, most overpriced small town in Peru, but all travelers to and from Machu Picchu have to pass through here. There's only one good reason to stay overnight: to avoid being engulfed by day-trippers arriving by train from Cuzco, you can then catch the first morning bus up the mountain to Machu Picchu and/or stay at the ruins until late afternoon when the crowds vanish.

Information

Small amounts of US dollars and traveler's checks can be exchanged at unfavorable rates in tourist shops. Payphones that accept phonecards and slow internet cafés are scattered around the village. There's also a post office and police station.

BCP (Av Imperio de los Incas s/n) Has a Visa ATM.

Centro de Salud (☎ 21-1161; ⏰ 8am-8pm, emergencies 24hr) A small medical center.

iPerú (☎ 21-1104; Edificio del Instituto Nacional de Cultura, Pachacutec 1st block; ⏰ 9am-1pm & 2-8pm) A helpful branch.

Machu Picchu ticket office (⏰ 5am-10pm) In the same building as iPerú.

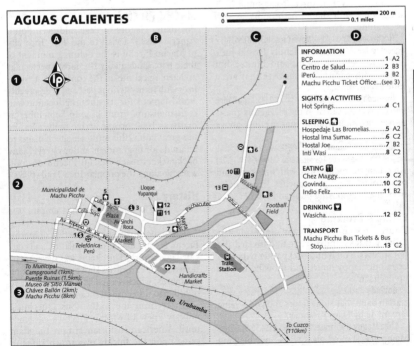

AGUAS CALIENTES

INFORMATION	
BCP...1 A2	
Centro de Salud......................2 B3	
iPerú..3 B2	
Machu Picchu Ticket Office...(see 3)	

SIGHTS & ACTIVITIES	
Hot Springs.............................4 C1	

SLEEPING	
Hospedaje Las Bromelias.........5 A2	
Hostal Ima Sumac....................6 C2	
Hostal Joe...............................7 B2	
Inti Wasi..................................8 C2	

EATING	
Chez Maggy.............................9 C2	
Govinda..................................10 C2	
Indio Feliz..............................11 B2	

DRINKING	
Wasicha..................................12 B2	

TRANSPORT	
Machu Picchu Bus Tickets & Bus Stop.......................................13 C2	

Sights & Activities

By Puente Ruinas at the base of the footpath to Machu Picchu, the **Museo de Sitio Manuel Chávez Ballón** (admission US$6, free with Machu Picchu entrance ticket; 9:30am-4pm Wed-Mon) has superb multimedia displays on excavations of Machu Picchu and the ancient Incas' building methods, cosmology and culture. A small botanical garden blooms outside.

Just staggered in from the Inca Trail? Soak your aches and pains away in the **hot springs** (admission US$3; 5am-8:30pm), 10 minutes' walk up Pachacutec. Swimsuits and towels can be rented cheaply outside the entrance.

Sleeping

Heavy discounts are available in the off-season. Early check-out times are the norm.

Municipal Campground (sites per person US$3) On the road to Machu Picchu, about 15 minutes' walk downhill from town, this deserted campground offers basic facilities.

Inti Wasi (21-1036/80-2024; jddggk@latinmail.com; dm US$4.50, s/d/tr without bathroom US$5/10/15) This woodsy, family-owned guesthouse is hidden up an overgrown walking path on the locals' side of the river. It offers basic bunk beds and rooms with shared bathrooms, as well as camping.

Hostal Joe (21-1190; Mayta Cápac 103; s/d US$10/15, without bathroom US$4.50/9) Friendly Hostal Joe's has bare, cell-like rooms and limited hot water, with communal showers that are a mite exposed.

Hospedaje Las Bromelias (21-1145; Colla Raymi; s/d US$7.50/12) Located on the plaza, this guesthouse has plain rooms that are just above average.

Hostal Ima Sumac (23-9648; www.machupicchu lodging.com; Imperio de Los Incas s/n; s/d/tr US$10/15/20) An eccentric, old favorite with hot water and plenty of hippie-dippie touches. Expect noise from the neighboring pubs and discos.

Eating & Drinking

Tourist restaurants cluster alongside the railway tracks and Pachacutec toward the hot springs. You'll find backpacker bars with extralong happy hours and showing movies up Pachacutec.

Govinda (Pachacutec; menú US$3) This trusty vegetarian haunt has stone floors and good-value fare made by Hare Krishnas.

Chez Maggy (Pachacutec 156; mains US$4.50-9) Chez Maggy has stained-glass walls, sociable long tables, board games and an international menu that includes yummy nachos and wood-fired pizzas.

Indio Feliz (Lloque Yupanqui 4; meals from US$10) Owned by a friendly French-Peruvian couple, here the cook whips up fantastic, farm-fresh meals.

Wasicha (Lloque Yupanqui MZ 12-L-2) Located near the plaza; has dancing till the wee hours.

Getting There & Around

Aguas Calientes is the final train stop for Machu Picchu. See p879 for information about trains from Cuzco and p882 for cheaper trains starting in Ollantaytambo.

At the time of research, it was possible to take an overnight bus from Cuzco to Quillabamba (US$4.50, seven to eight hours), but get off in the middle of the night at Santa Maria, then transfer to a local minibus to Santa Teresa (US$1.50, two hours), where there's a cable-car river crossing, then it's a two-hour walk to the hydroelectric plant, and finally two more hours along defunct train tracks to Aguas Calientes.

For buses to Machu Picchu, see p887.

MACHU PICCHU

For many visitors to Peru and even South America itself, a visit to the 'lost' Inca city of Machu Picchu is the defining moment of their trip. Undeniably the most spectacular archaeological site on the continent, it tantalizes with its mysterious past and is deservedly world-famous for its stunning location and craftsmanship. From June to September as many as 1000 people arrive daily. Despite this great influx, this must-see site manages to retain its air of grandeur and mystery. Many backpackers reach Machu Picchu on foot, walking along the popular Inca Trail (p887).

History

For a brief history of the Inca empire, see p823.

The actual purpose and function of Machu Picchu is still a matter of speculation and educated guesswork. The citadel was never mentioned in the chronicles kept by the colonizing Spaniards, which served as a written archive of hitherto unrecorded Inca history.

Apart from the indigenous Quechuas, nobody knew of Machu Picchu's existence until American historian Hiram Bingham came upon the thickly overgrown ruins in

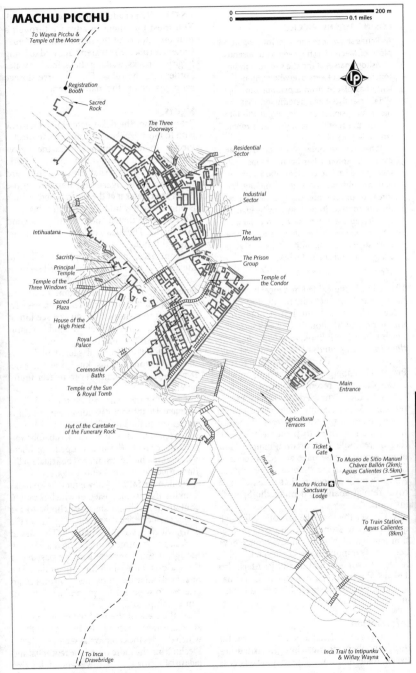

MACHU PICCHU

0 _____ 200 m
0 _____ 0.1 miles

To Wayna Picchu &
Temple of the Moon

Registration
Booth

Sacred
Rock

The Three
Doorways

Residential
Sector

Industrial
Sector

Intihuatana

The
Mortars

Sacristy

The Prison
Group

Principal
Temple

Temple of the
Three Windows

Temple of
the Condor

Sacred
Plaza

House of the
High Priest

Royal
Palace

Ceremonial
Baths

Temple of the Sun
& Royal Tomb

Main
Entrance

Hut of the Caretaker
of the Funerary Rock

Agricultural
Terraces

Inca Trail

Ticket
Gate

To Museo de Sitio Manuel
Chávez Ballón (2km);
Aguas Calientes (3.5km)

Machu Picchu
Sanctuary
Lodge

To Train Station,
Aguas Calientes
(8km)

To Inca
Drawbridge

Inca Trail to Intipunku
& Wiñay Wayna

PERU

LOSING MACHU PICCHU

As Peru's showpiece site, everyone wants a piece of Machu Picchu. Even as thousands of visitors marvel at the site's seemingly untouchable beauty, its overwhelming popularity has placed it on a perilous downhill slide. Scientists have determined that the mountain's slopes are slipping at the rate of 1cm per month, making a catastrophic landslide possible.

While a long-mooted plan to build a cable car to the summit has been scrapped following widespread condemnation from the national and international community, the threat of private interests encroaching on the site continually rears its ugly head. One unbelievable accident saw a crew filming a beer commercial smash a crane into the site's showpiece, the Intihuatana, breaking a large chip off the old block.

1911 while being guided by a local boy. Bingham's search was actually for the lost city of Vilcabamba (p890), the last stronghold of the Incas, and he thought he had found it at Machu Picchu. His book, *Inca Land: Explorations in the Highlands of Peru,* was first published in 1922. It's downloadable for free from Project Gutenberg (www.gutenberg.org).

Despite more recent studies of the 'lost' city of the Incas, knowledge of Machu Picchu remains sketchy. Some believe the citadel was founded in the waning years of the last Incas as an attempt to preserve Inca culture or rekindle Inca predominance, while others think it may have already become a forgotten city at the time of the conquest. Another theory suggests that the site was a royal retreat abandoned upon the Spanish invasion.

Whatever the case, the exceptionally high quality of the stonework and ornamentation tell that Machu Picchu must once have been vitally important as a ceremonial center. Indeed, to some extent, it still is: Alejandro Toledo, the country's first native Quechua-speaking president, staged his colorful inauguration here in 2001.

Information

The ruins are typically open from dawn till dusk, but they are most heavily visited between 10am and 2pm. One-day tickets cost US$23.50/12 per adult/student with ISIC card. You must buy them in advance through a tour operator or at the ticket office in Aguas Calientes (p883). You aren't allowed to bring large backpacks, walking sticks, food or water bottles into the ruins. There's a free storage room just before the main entrance.

Sights

Proceed from the ticket gate along a narrow path to the mazelike main entrance to Machu Picchu, where the ruins now reveal themselves and stretch out before you. To get a visual fix of the whole site and snap the classic postcard shot, climb the zigzagging staircase to the **Hut of the Caretaker of the Funerary Rock**, which is one of the few buildings that has been restored with a thatch roof, making it a good rain shelter. The Inca Trail enters the site just below this hut.

From here, take the steps down and to the left of the plazas into the ruined sections containing the **Temple of the Sun**, a curved, tapering tower containing some of Machu Picchu's finest stonework. The temple is cordoned off to visitors, but you can see into it from above. Below is an almost-hidden natural rock cave that has been carefully carved with a steplike altar and sacred niches by the Inca's stonemasons, known as the **Royal Tomb**, though no mummies were ever found here.

Climbing the stairs above the 16 nearby **ceremonial baths** that cascade down the ruins brings you to the **Sacred Plaza**, from which there is a spectacular view of the Río Urubamba valley and across to the snowcapped Cordillera Vilcabamba in the distance. The **Temple of the Three Windows** overlooks the plaza.

Behind the **Sacristy**, known for the two rocks flanking its entrance, each of which is said to contain 32 angles, a staircase climbs to the major shrine, **Intihuatana** (Hitching Post of the Sun), which lies atop a small hill. The carved rock at the summit is often called a sundial, though it was connected to the passing of the seasons rather than the time of day. The Spaniards smashed most such shrines in an attempt to wipe out the pagan blasphemy of sun worship.

At the back of the Intihuatana is another staircase that descends to the **Central Plaza**, which divides the ceremonial sector of Machu Picchu from the more mundane **residential** and **industrial** sectors. At the lower end of this area is the **Prison Group**, a labyrinthine complex of cells, niches and passageways. The centerpiece of the group is a carving of the **head of a condor**, the natural rocks behind it resembling the bird's outstretched wings.

Activities

Behind the ruins is the steep-sided mountain of **Huayna Picchu**. It takes an hour to scramble up the steep path, but for all the puffing it takes to get there, you'll be rewarded with spectacular views. Take care in wet weather as the steps get dangerously slippery. The trail entrance closes at 1pm (return by 4pm).

Part of the way up Huayna Picchu, another path plunges down to your left via ladders and an overhanging cave to the small **Temple of the Moon**, from where you can climb steeply to Huayna Picchu – a circuitous route taking two hours.

Another option is to walk to a viewpoint of the **Inca drawbridge**. It's a flatter walk from the Hut of the Caretaker of the Funerary Rock that hugs a narrow cliff-clinging trail (under 30 minutes each way) with sheer vertical drops into the valley.

Getting There & Away

Buses depart from Aguas Calientes hourly from 5:30am until the early afternoon for Machu Picchu (US$6, 25 minutes). Buses return when full, with the last departure at 5:30pm. Alternatively, it's a 20-minute walk from Aguas Calientes to Puente Ruinas, where the road crosses the Río Urubamba. A breathtakingly steep but well-marked trail climbs 2km further to Machu Picchu, taking an hour (less coming down!).

THE INCA TRAIL

The most famous trek in South America, this four-day trail to Machu Picchu is walked by thousands of backpackers every year. Although the total distance is only 33km, the ancient trail laid by the Incas winds its way up, down and around the mountains, snaking over three high passes en route. The views of snowy peaks and cloud forest can be stupendous, and walking from one cliff-hugging ruin to the next is a mystical and unforgettable experience – except that you'll rarely have a moment's peace to enjoy it. Think about taking an alternative trek instead (see boxed text, p888).

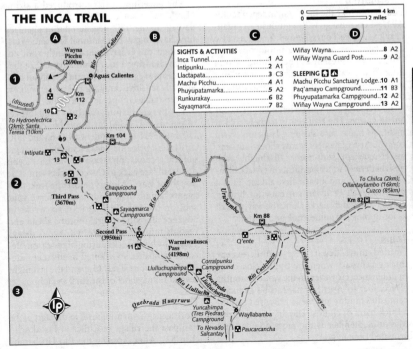

THE INCA TRAIL

SIGHTS & ACTIVITIES
Inca Tunnel....................................1 A2
Intipunku......................................2 A1
Llactapata....................................3 C3
Machu Picchu................................4 A1
Phuyupatamarka..........................5 A2
Runkurakay...................................6 B2
Sayaqmarca..................................7 B2
Wiñay Wayna.................................8 A2
Wiñay Wayna Guard Post...............9 A2

SLEEPING
Machu Picchu Sanctuary Lodge.....10 A1
Paq'amayo Campground................11 B3
Phuyupatamarka Campground......12 A2
Wiñay Wayna Campground...........13 A2

INCA ROADS LESS TRAVELED

Let's face it: the Inca Trail is being loved to death. Besides, it's pricey. But there are alternative routes to reach Machu Picchu. For some recommended trekking agencies, see p874.

Prices and availability for all of these trips depend upon demand:

- A longer, but less strenuous version of the Inca Trail leaves from Km 82, following the Río Urubamba through lush jungle and past archaeological sites. It joins the main Inca Trail after climbing steeply to Wiñay Wayna from Km 104. The trek takes four days.

- An even longer, more spectacular approach to the Inca Trail, climbing over 4800m-high passes near the magnificent glacier-clad peak of Salkantay (6271m), starts from the village of Mollepata, off the main Cuzco–Abancay road. This weeklong trek joins the classic Inca Trail after three days.

- The Lares Valley trek spends three days walking between rural Andean villages in the Sacred Valley, past hot springs, archaeological sites, lush lagoons and gorges. Trekkers finish by taking the train to Aguas Calientes from Ollantaytambo. This is more of a cultural trek, not a technical one, though the highest mountain pass (4450m) is nothing to sneeze at.

- The four-day Inka Jungle Trail is a heart-stopping trek that starts off with a dizzying mountain-bike ride from the Abra de Malaga pass (4319m) down to Santa Maria, where there's a trekking lodge run by the affable Lorenzo Cahuana (lorenzocahuana@hotmail.com). From Santa Maria, you'll walk through Amazonian jungle to Santa Teresa, camping by hot springs, then ride a cable car across the river and follow disused train tracks to Aguas Calientes. You can go independently by taking a Quillabamba-bound bus from Cuzco as far as Santa Maria (US$4.50, six to seven hours), then hiring a local guide at Lorenzo's lodge.

Information

You cannot hike the Inca Trail independently. All trekkers must go with a guide in an organized group (see Tours, below). You must also carry your passport (not a photocopy) and ISIC card to present at checkpoints. Don't litter or defecate in the ruins or pick plants in the national park. It is illegal to graffiti any trees or stones en route.

All trekking gear can be rented from outfitters in Cuzco. The trail gets extremely cold at night, so make sure sleeping bags are warm enough. Also remember sturdy shoes, rain gear, insect repellent, sunscreen, a flashlight (with fresh batteries), water-purification tablets, high-calorie snacks and a basic first-aid kit. Take a stash of small Peruvian currency for buying bottled water and snacks along the way, as well as for tipping the guide, cook and porters.

Tours

Guided tours depart year-round, except during February when the trail is closed for maintenance. However, in the wettest months (December to April), trails can be slippery, campsites muddy and views obscured behind a thick bank of clouds. The dry season from May to September is the most popular and crowded time to go.

The government has introduced a string of reforms in an attempt to prevent further damage to the trail. Registered tour agencies now have to pay huge annual fees and taxes, and their prices have consequently shot up. When choosing a tour company, realize that the cheapest agencies may care less about ecologically sensitive camping and porter welfare. For reputable companies, see p874.

For the classic four-day Inca Trail, expect to pay over US$300 for a reliable company (10% to 15% less for students with a valid ISIC card). That price includes a tent, food, porters, guides, a cook, admission to Machu Picchu and train fare back to Cuzco. Tickets must be bought at least 72 hours before the trek; tour agents handle this. You should reserve your spot on the Inca Trail at least six weeks in advance. Booking several months ahead and reconfirming in advance will avoid delays caused by bottlenecks during high season. Because campsites are allotted in advance, late-comers are more likely to spend the last night several hours short of the final stretch.

The Hike

Most agencies run minibuses to the start of the trail past the village of Chilca at Piscakucho (Km 82). After crossing the Río Urubamba and taking care of trail fees and registration formalities, the trail climbs gently alongside the river to the first archaeological site of **Llactapata** before heading south down a side valley of the Río Kusichaca. The trail south leads 7km to the hamlet of **Wayllabamba** (3100m), where you can take a breather to appreciate views of snowy Veronica (5750m).

You'll cross the Río Llullucha, then climb steeply up along the river. This area is known as **Tres Piedras** (Three White Stones), and from here it is a long, very steep 3km climb. At some points, the trail and stream bed become one, but stone stairs keep hikers above the water. The trail eventually emerges on the high, bare mountainside of **Llulluchupampa**, where the flats are dotted with campsites.

From Llulluchupampa, a good path up the left-hand side of the valley climbs for the two-hour ascent to **Warmiwañusca** (4198m), colorfully known as 'Dead Woman's Pass.' This is the highest point of the trek, which leaves many a backpacker gasping. From Warmiwañusca, the trail continues down a long, knee-jarringly steep descent to the river, where there are large campsites at **Paqaymayu** (3500m). The trail crosses the river over a small footbridge and climbs right toward **Runkurakay**, a round ruin with superb views about an hour's walk above the river.

Above Runkurakay, the trail climbs to a false summit before continuing past two small lakes to the top of the second pass at 3950m, which has views of the snowcapped Cordillera Vilcabamba. The trail descends to the ruin of **Sayaqmarka**, a tightly constructed complex perched on a small mountain spur with incredible views, then continues downward crossing a tributary of the Río Aobamba.

The trail leads on across an Inca causeway and up again through cloud forest and an **Inca tunnel** carved into the rock to the third pass at 3670m. Soon afterward, you'll reach the beautiful, well-restored ruin of **Phuyupatamarka** (3600m above sea level). The site contains a beautiful series of ceremonial baths with water running through them.

From Phuyupatamarka, the trail takes a dizzying dive into the cloud forest below, following an incredibly well-engineered flight of many hundreds of Inca steps. After passing through a tunnel, the trail eventually zigzags its way down to **Wiñay Wayna**, where a trekker's lodge sells hot showers, hot meals and cold beer, for those who want to pay a bit extra.

From the **Wiñay Wayna guard post**, the trail contours around through cliff-hanging cloud forest for about two hours to reach **Intipunku** (Sun Gate) – where you may get lucky enough to catch your first glimpse of majestic Machu Picchu as you wait for the sun to rise over the mountaintops.

The final triumphant descent takes almost an hour. Backpacks are not allowed into the ruins, and guards will pounce upon you to check your pack and to stamp your trail permit. Trekkers generally arrive before the morning trainloads of tourists, so you can enjoy the exhilarated exhaustion of reaching your goal without having to push through as many crushing crowds.

CUZCO TO PUNO

Both the railway and the road to Lake Titicaca head southeast from Cuzco. En route you'll spy several ancient sites and scenic Andean towns that make great detours off the Gringo Trail. For bus information, see p878.

Tipón (admission with Boleto Turístico, p871; 7am-6pm) is a little-known Inca site noted for its ingenious irrigation system for steep agricultural terraces – a demonstration of the Incas' mastery over their environment. Take an Urcos bus 23km from Cuzco to the Tipón turnoff, where a dirt road climbs 4km to the ruins.

Another 9km further south, **Piquillacta** (admission with Boleto Turístico; 9am-5pm), built by the Wari culture, is the only major pre-Inca ruin near Cuzco. Literally 'The Place of the Flea,' it's a sprawling ceremonial center of crumbling, multi-story buildings. Nearby is the huge Inca gate of **Rumicolca**, built on Wari foundations. About 7km before Urcos, **Andahuaylillas** is a traditional Andean village famous for its lavishly decorated 17th-century Jesuit **church** (admission US\$1.20; 8am-noon & 2-5pm Mon-Sat, 8:30-10am & 3-5pm Sun) with heavy, baroque embellishments. Buses from Cuzco to Urcos and Puno pass by both archaeological sites and the village.

The road splits at Urcos: one road heads northeast to Puerto Maldonado in the jungle (see p891), while another continues southeast toward Lake Titicaca.

Nearly 120km from Cuzco, **Raqchi** (admission US\$1.50; 7am-5pm) is home to the ruins of the Temple of Viracocha, which supported the

PERU

largest-known Inca roof. They are visible from the railway at San Pedro, a few kilometers before Sicuani, and look like a huge aqueduct. Buses to Puno pass the site (US$1.75, 2½ hours).

The **Abra la Raya** pass (4319m) is the highest point on the trip to Puno. Buses often stop by a cluster of handicrafts sellers, where passengers can take advantage of the photogenic view of snowcapped mountains. The pass marks the departmental line between Cuzco and Puno. From here, the route descends through bleak *altiplano*.

About 95km northwest of Juliaca is **Ayaviri** (3925m). This bustling, chilly market town with a colonial church is a few kilometers away from the hot springs of **Pojpojquella**. Another 45km further south, the sleepy village of **Pucara** is famous for its earthy *toritos* (ceramic bulls) seen perched on the roofs for luck. Near the plaza, a small **museum** (admission US$1.50; ⏾ 8:30am-5pm) displays surprising anthropomorphic monoliths from the town's nearby pre-Inca site, dating to the Tiahuanaco culture.

CUZCO TO THE JUNGLE

There are three routes into the jungle from Cuzco. One starts in the Sacred Valley, climbing from Ollantaytambo before dropping into Quillabamba. Two poorer, even less developed roads head eastward – one to Paucartambo, Tres Cruces and Shintuya for Parque Nacional Manu (p929), and the other from Urcos through Ocongate, Tinqui and Quincemil to Puerto Maldonado. Travel cautiously on these roads even in the dry season (June to September). They are muddy, slow and even more dangerous in the wet months, especially January to April.

Quillabamba
☎ 084 / pop 16,300

Located in one of Peru's prime tea and coffee-producing areas, Quillabamba itself is a hot and humid high-jungle town, nicknamed 'the city of eternal summer.' It lies at the end of a spectacular route high over the breathtaking pass of Abra de Malaga. Though quite listless, the town can be used as a base for dry-season trips deeper into the jungle, including through Pongo de Manique, a steep-walled canyon carved by waterfalls along the Río Urubamba. Travel agencies only open seasonally – ask around for Kiteni Tours. There's slow internet

access near the Plaza de Armas. **BCP** (Libertad 549) has a Visa ATM and changes US dollars.

There are cheap, cold-water hostels on and around the Plaza de Armas. **Hostal Alto Urubamba** (☎ 28-1131; 2 de Mayo 333; s/d/tr US$12/16.40/19.50, without bathroom US$5.65/8/10.50) has comfortable enough fan rooms circling a courtyard. Near the market, **Hostal Quillabamba** (☎ 28-1369; Grau 590; s/d/tr US$13.50/18/24; ▨) offers more spacious rooms with hot showers and TV, plus a terrace restaurant. Cheap *chifas*, *pollerías* (chicken grills), *heladerías* (ice-cream shops), *cevicherías* and pizzerias too are on side streets off the Plaza de Armas. Just east on Independencia is a hole-in-the-wall vegetarian restaurant.

Buses for Cuzco via Ollantaytambo and Urubamba leave a few times daily (US$4.50, seven to eight hours) from Terminal Terrestre (departure tax US30¢), several blocks south of Plaza Grau (taxi US$1). **Ampay** (☎ 084-28-2576) is the most often recommended company.

Vilcabamba
The beleaguered Manco Inca fled to his jungle retreat in Vilcabamba after finally being defeated by the Spaniards at Ollantaytambo in 1536. This hideout, Espíritu Pampa, was later forgotten until expeditions rediscovered it in the mid-1960s. The hike takes several days from the village of **Huancacalle**. There's one basic hostel there where you can hire pack mules and guides. From Plaza Grau in Quillabamba, *combis* make the long, bumpy trip to Huancacalle most mornings (US$4.50, five to six hours).

Paucartambo
This small village, 115km northeast of Cuzco, is reached by a cliff-hanging dirt road with exhilarating views of the Andes and the Amazon Basin beyond. Paucartambo is famous for its riotously colorful celebration of **La Virgen del Carmen**, held around July 15 to 17, with hypnotic street dancing, wonderful processions and weird costumes. Few tourists make it here, simply because it's so difficult to reach and because you have to camp, find a room in one of three extremely basic hotels or hope a local will give you floor space. Many tourist agencies in Cuzco run buses specifically for the fiesta and can arrange homestays. **Expreso Virgen del Carmen** (☎ 084-27-7755/22-6895; Diagonal Angamos 1952) has a few daily buses from Cuzco (US$3, five hours).

Tres Cruces

Tres Cruces is 45km beyond Paucartambo. The view of the mountains dropping away into the Amazon Basin here is gorgeous in itself, but from May to July it's made all the more magical by the sunrise phenomenon that optically distorts the dawn into a multicolored light show with double images, halos and unusual tints. Travel agencies run sunrise-watching trips from Cuzco.

For onward travel to Manu, see p929.

To Puerto Maldonado

The journey to Puerto Maldonado is a spectacular but difficult journey on nightmarish roads (see p928). The journey (US$10) takes up to a week and can be broken at Ocongate or Quincemil, which have basic hotels. Trucks leave Cuzco daily for Puerto Maldonado during the dry season (see p878) or you can catch a public bus (30 hours) from Urcos (see p889). Either trip requires hardiness, self-sufficiency and good luck.

From Ocongate, trucks take an hour to reach the village of **Tinqui**, which is the start of the spectacular seven-day trek encircling **Ausangate** (6384m), southern Peru's highest peak, passing fluted icy peaks, tumbling glaciers and turquoise lakes, rolling *puna* (grasslands) and marshy valleys. Tinqui has hot springs and a very basic hotel, and mules can be rented for the trek. From Cuzco, **Transportes Huayna Ausangate** (☎ 084-965-0922; Tomasa Tito Condemayta) has buses to Tinqui (US$4.20, seven hours) at 10am daily except Sunday.

CUZCO TO THE CENTRAL HIGHLANDS

The recently rediscovered ridgetop Inca site of **Choquequirau** (admission US$3) has an incredible location at the junction of three valleys, and can only be reached on foot. The most common route begins from Cachora, a village off the road to Abancay – the turnoff is after Sahuite, about four hours from Cuzco.

The sleepy, rural town of **Abancay** (2378m) is one possible resting place between Cuzco and Ayacucho. Several internet cafés, cheap restaurants and bare-bones hotels cluster near the bus companies on Arenas and also Arequipa. Buses leave for Cuzco (US$4.50, five hours) and Andahuaylas (US$4, five hours) a few times daily. Journeys take longer in the rainy season.

Andahuaylas (2980m) is another stop on the cold, rough but scenic route to Ayacucho.

The beautiful **Laguna de Pacucha** is 17km from town. Meals, fishing and rowboat rental are available. A one-hour hike brings you to the imposing hilltop site of **Sondor**, built by the Chanka culture, the Incas' traditional enemies. *Combis* to the lake run along Chanka on the north side of town (US$1.20, 30 minutes). You'll find cheap hotels and restaurants near Andahuaylas' bus terminals and the plaza. **Aero Condor Perú** (☎ 083-72-2877; Cáceres 326) has Lima flights thrice weekly; it runs minibuses to the airport (US$1.80). Buses to Ayacucho (US$6, 10 hours) and Cuzco (US$8, 10 hours) depart a few times daily.

CENTRAL HIGHLANDS

Far off the Gringo Trail, the central Peruvian Andes are ripe for exploration. Traditions linger longer here, with delightful colonial towns among the least spoiled in the entire Andean chain. A combination of geographical isolation, harsh mountain terrain and terrorist unrest (the Sendero Luminoso was born in Ayacucho) made travel difficult for decades. Over the past decade a more stable political situation and improved transportation infrastructure are making travelers' lives easier. But visiting the region is still challenging enough, with ear-popping passes and wearying bus journeys.

AYACUCHO

☎ 066 / pop 143,100

Ever since the paving of the road to Lima, the fascinating colonial city of Ayacucho (elevation 2750m) has embraced the 21st century, but is still most famous for its Semana Santa traditions. You can also make excursions into the mountains, where archaeological ruins await.

Information

Travel agencies are helpful.

BCP (Portal Unión 28) Has a Visa ATM.
Hueco Internet (☎ 31-5528; Portal Constitución 9) Offers international phone calls.
Interbank (9 de Diciembre 183) Has a global ATM.
iPerú (☎ 31-8305; Municipal Huamanga, Plaza Mayor, Portal Municipal 48; ☆ 8:30am-7:30pm Mon-Sat, 8:30am-2:30pm Sun) For tourist information.
Policía de Turismo (☎ 31-2179; 2 de Mayo 100; ☆ 7:30am-8pm) Handles emergencies.
Serpost (Asamblea 293; ☆ 8am-8pm Mon-Sat) Post office near the plaza.

Wari Tours (☎ 31-3115; Portal Independencia 70) Travel agency off the main plaza.

Warpa Picchu Eco-Aventura (☎ 31-5191; Portal Independencia 66) Another travel agency off the main plaza.

Sights

The town center has a 17th-century **cathedral**, along with a dozen other ornate **churches** from the 16th, 17th and 18th centuries, and several old **mansions** near the main plaza.

Museo de Arte Popular (Portal Unión 28; admission free; ☾ 9am-6:30pm Mon-Thu, to 7:30pm Fri, to 1pm Sat) showcases Ayacucho's folkcraft specialties. To inspect Wari ceramics, **Museo Arqueológico Hipolito Unanue** (Museo INC; ☎ 31-2056; Centro Cultural Simón Bolívar; admission US60¢; ☾ 9am-1pm & 3-5pm Mon-Sat, 9am-1pm Sun) is at the university, over 1km from the center along Independencia. The university library has a free exhibit of mummies and skulls.

Sprawling for several kilometers along a cactus-forested roadside are the extensive ruins of **Wari** (Huari; admission US60¢; ☾ 8am-5:30pm), the capital of the Wari empire, which predated the Inca by five centuries. Beyond lies the village of **Quinua**, where a huge monument and small museum mark the site of the Battle of Ayacucho (1824). Wari is 20km and Quinua 40km northeast of Ayacucho. Pickup trucks and buses to Quinua (US80¢, one hour) via the ruins from Paradero Magdalena at the traffic circle at the east end of M Cáceres in Ayacucho. Travel agencies in town offer Spanish-language tours (US$8).

Festivals & Events

Ayacucho's **Semana Santa**, held the week before Easter, is Peru's finest religious festival. Celebrations begin the Friday before Palm Sunday and continue at a fevered pitch for 10 days until Easter Sunday. The Friday before Palm Sunday is marked by a procession in honor of La Virgen de los Dolores (Our Lady of Sorrows), during which it's customary to inflict 'sorrows' on bystanders by firing pebbles with slingshots. Every day sees another solemn yet colorful procession, culminating in an all-night party before Easter Sunday, with its dawn fireworks display.

Sleeping

Prices skyrocket during Semana Santa.

Hostal Tres Máscaras (☎ 31-2931/4107; Tres Máscaras 194; s/d $7.60/12.20, without bathroom US$4.50/7.50) Has a walled garden and friendly staff, with hot water in the morning and later on request. Breakfast available (US$2).

La Colmena Hotel (☎ 31-2146; Cuzco 140; s/d US$8/10, s without bathroom US$5) Though it's resting on its laurels these days, this long-standing hotel has courtyard balconies and a popular restaurant. Located just steps from the plaza, it's often full.

Hotel La Crillonesa (☎ 31-2350; Nazareno 165; s/d US$9/15, without bathroom US$5/8) Small but helpful place offering even smaller rooms with hot water, as well as a rooftop terrace with views, TV room and café.

Hotel Yañez (☎ 31-4918; M Cáceres 1210; s/d incl breakfast US$11/17) Spacious rooms sport comfy mattresses, kitsch wall art, cable TV and hot showers. Beware of the noisy downstairs casino, though.

Hostal Marcos (☎ 31-6867; 9 de Diciembre 143; s/d incl breakfast US$13/21) A dozen spotless rooms, with 24-hour hot water and cable TV, are sequestered away at the end of an alley. It's often booked, so call ahead.

Also recommended:

Hostal Huamanga (☎ 31-3527; Bellido 535; s/d US$6/12, without bathroom US$3/6) This basic place cranks out hot water all day.

Hotel Samary (☎ 31-2442; Callao 329; s/d US$8/10, without bathroom US$6.50/8.50) Simple but clean, with rooftop views.

Hotel Florida (☎ 31-2565; Cuzco 310; s/d US$10/16) Has a garden, cafeteria and in-room TVs; traveler-friendly.

Hotel Santa Rosa (☎ 31-4614; Lima 166; s/d incl breakfast US$18/33) Oversized rooms with cable TV, DVD players, phones, fridges and hot showers.

Eating

Regional specialties include *puca picante* (potato-beef stew in peppery peanut sauce, served over rice), *patachi* (wheat soup with beans, potatoes, lamb or beef) and *mondongo* (corn soup with pork or beef, red peppers and mint).

Wallpa Suwa (G de la Vega 240; mains US$2-5; ☾ 6-11pm Mon-Sat) The name in Quechua means 'Chicken Thief' – makes you wonder where they get their poultry supplies from! It's always busy here.

Adolfo's Gourmet (2nd fl, Portal Constitución 4; mains US$2-6) Score an outside balcony table for sweet sangria, pizzas and pastas accompanied by Ayacucho's best views.

El Niño (9 de Diciembre 205; mains US$3-6) At this colonial mansion overlooking a garden, chronic carnivores can sink their fangs into ample *parrillas* (grills).

Urpicha (Londres 272; mains US$4) A homey place with a flower-filled patio, familial attention and traditional dishes including *cuy*. Take a taxi after dark.

Also recommended:

La Casona (Bellido 463; mains US$2-6; 7am-10:30pm) Big portions of Peruvian fare; live musicians on weekend nights.

Restaurant Los Alamos (Cuzco 215; mains US$3) Peruvian cooking including vegetarian dishes, and a patio.

Pizzería Italiana (Bellido 490; pizzas US$4-8; 4:30-11:30pm) Wood-burning oven that's cozy on cold nights.

Drinking

On weekends, a few *peñas* stay open until the wee hours.

Los Balcones (Asamblea 187, 2nd fl) Beloved by university students, this bar has dancing and occasional live Andean bands.

Taberna Magía Negra (9 de Diciembre 293) An art gallery and bar serving beers and pizza.

La Nueva Ley (Cáceres 1147) A disco that often has salsa dancing.

Shopping

Ayacucho is famous for folkcrafts. There's a daytime **crafts market** (Independencia & Quinua). Workshops are found near Plazuela Santa Ana. Colonial-style **Centro Turístico Cultural San Cristobal** (28 de Julio 178) is full of art galleries, craft stores and flower stands, along with bars and cafés.

Getting There & Away

The **airport** (PYH) is 4km from the town center (taxis cost US$2). **Aero Condor Perú** (066-31-2418; 9 de Diciembre 123) runs four weekly flights to/from Lima, sometimes via Andahuaylas. **LC Busre** (Lima 178) has a daily flight to/from Lima.

Buses utilize a bewildering array of terminals. For Lima (US$6 to US$15, nine hours), **Empresa Molina** (31-2984; 9 de Diciembre 459) and **Civa** (31-9948; M Cáceres 1242) offer *bus-cama* services. **Cruz del Sur** (31-2813; M Cáceres 1264) and **Ormeño** (31-2495; Libertad 257) offer executive-style services with comfy, yet not fully reclinable, seats.

For Huancayo (US$7.30, 10 to 12 hours), Empresa Molina is preferred. Take note: this is a tough 250km trip, not for the faint of heart. To get to Huancavelica, take the train from Huancayo (see p894).

For Cuzco (US$14, 22 hours), try **Expreso Turismo Los Chancas** (31-2391; Pasaje Cáceres 150). It's a long and rough trip, but the journey can be broken at Andahuaylas (US$6, 10 hours). For Pucallpa, Tingo María and Huánuco, there's **Turismo Nacional** (31-5405; M Cáceres 884).

HUANCAVELICA

 067 / pop 42,600

Given that it can be a challenge just to get to Huancavelica, travelers justifiably expect to find something worthwhile. This endearing small town nestled among craggy peaks is more reminiscent of Switzerland than the Andes. It was once a strategic Inca center, then a colonial Spanish mining town, which is why it still has churches with silver-plated altars.

Information

More than a dozen cybercafés provide internet access.

BCP (V Toledo 384) Has a Visa ATM and changes dollars.

Dirección de Turismo (75-2938; 2nd fl, V Garma 444; 8am-1pm & 2-5pm Mon-Fri) Has Spanish-language information.

Serpost (Pasaje Ferrua 105) Near Iglesia de Santa Ana.

Sights & Activities

The **Instituto Nacional de Cultura** (INC; 75-2544; Raymondi 205; admission free; 10am-1pm & 3-6pm Tue-Sun), in a colonial building on Plaza San Juan de Dios, has a small museum and *folklórica* dance and music classes. Reached via a steep flight of stairs are some murky **mineral springs** (admission/private shower US30¢/50¢; 5:30am-4pm Sat-Thu, to noon Fri). The biggest daily **market** is on Sunday, when many locals are traditionally dressed.

Sleeping & Eating

Most places only have cold water.

Hostal Camacho (75-3298; Carabaya 481; s/d US$4/6.60, with shared bathroom US$2.50/4.30) A well-run budget choice with small rooms, but piles of blankets for those chilly Andean nights. Hot water in the mornings.

Hotel Ascensión (75-3103; Manco Capác 481; s/d US$4.25/6.50, without bathroom US$3/5) On the main plaza, has larger rooms and hot water.

Hotel Tahuantinsuyo (75-2968; Carabaya 399; s/d $4/8, without bathroom US$3/4.50) On a busy street, offers basic rooms with private bathrooms and morning hot water.

For excellent grilled trout, cast a line over at **Restaurant Joy** (V Toledo 216; menú US$2, mains US$2.50-6). Another busy little place is **Restaurant El Mesón** (Muñoz 153; mains US$2.50-5; ☺ 9am-2pm & 5-10pm). Its daily changing specials sometimes features *criollo* dishes.

Entertainment

Peña Turística (V Toledo 319; ☺ 6pm-midnight Thu-Sat) For music while you drink, sit down here and listen to *folklórica* bands.

Getting There & Away

BUS & COLECTIVO

Most buses depart from Terminal Terrestre, inconveniently located 2km west of town (take a taxi US$1), but tickets are sold from downtown offices.

Companies serving Huancayo (US$3, five hours) include **Transportes Ticllas** (☎ 75-1562; Prado 56). For Lima (US$9, 12 to 15 hours), **Transportes Oropesa** (☎ 75-3181; O'Donovan 599) goes via Pisco and stops in Ica (US$8.50, 11 hours), while **Expreso Lobato** (☎ 75-2964; M Muñoz 489) goes via Huancayo. Also try **Expreso Huancavelica** (☎ 75-2964; M Muñoz 516).

For Ayacucho, you can either catch a 4:30am minibus to Rumichaca (US$3, six hours), then wait for Lima–Ayacucho buses to pass by around 2pm, or you can spend a full day taking different minibuses to connect via Lircay and Julcamarca.

Colectivo taxis for the spectacularly scenic trip to Huancayo (US$7.60, 2½ to three hours) leave when full from Terminal Terrestre.

TRAIN

Departures for Huancayo are at 6:30am daily and 12:30pm Monday to Saturday. The trip takes five to six hours. A faster *autovagón* (electric train) leaves at 5:30pm Friday. Buy tickets (US$2.50 to US$4.50) in advance from the **train station** (☎ 75-2898).

HUANCAYO

☎ 064 / pop 430,660

Arriving in Huancayo, you'll get the impression of some Wild West frontier town with dusty, chaotic streets and tumbledown suburbs. Huancayo challenges at first, then bids you to hang around a while. Most travelers eventually do. There are fiestas to be celebrated, wines to be drunk, musical instruments to be mastered and crafts to be bought. For adventurous travelers, there's also trekking, mountain biking and jungle exploration.

Information

Internet cafés are along Giráldez. BCP, Interbank, other banks with ATMs and *casas de cambio* are on Real.

Clínica Ortega (☎ 23-2921; Carrión 1124; ☺ 24hr) For emergencies.

Policía de Turismo (☎ 23-4714; Ferrocarril 580)

Post office (Centro Civico)

Telefónica-Perú (Puno 200) Offers international phone calls.

Tourist office (☎ 20-0550; Casa del Artesano, Real 481; ☺ 10am-1:30pm & 4-7:30pm Mon-Fri) Has sightseeing information.

Sights & Activities

Museo Salesiano (☎ 24-7763; Salesian School; admission US60¢) has Amazonian fauna, pottery and archaeology exhibits; hours vary. From the center, walk 2km northeast on Giráldez to **Cerro de la Libertad**, which has good city views, then continue 2km more to the eroded sandstone towers of **Torre Torre**. About 5km from the center in the San Antonio neighborhood, **Parque de la Identidad Huanca** is a fanciful park full of stone statues and miniature buildings that supposedly represent the area's culture.

Courses

Incas del Peru (☎ 22-3303; www.incasdelperu.org; Giráldez 652) arranges Spanish lessons, which include meals and accommodations with a local family from US$110 per week. Lessons can be combined with other classes, such as dancing, cooking, gourd carving or *zampoña* (panpipes).

Tours

Incas del Peru (above) offers guided day hikes and cycling and horse-riding tours (US$35). Mountain-bike rental costs US$15 per day.

Festivals & Events

There are hundreds of fiestas in Huancayo and surrounding villages – supposedly one almost every day somewhere in the Río Mantaro valley! Huancayo's **Semana Santa** processions leading up to Easter are famous.

Sleeping

Residencial Baldeón (☎ 23-1634; Amazonas 543; s/d without bathroom US$3/6) Teensy, basic rooms

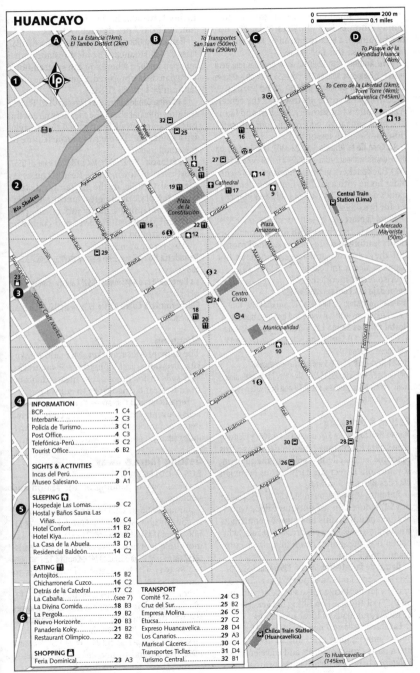

HUANCAYO

PERU

surround a small courtyard in this friendly family's home. Hot showers (advance notice required), a secure entrance, kitchen and laundry make this fair value.

Peru Andino (☎ 22-3956; www.geocities.com/peru andino_1; Pasaje San Antonio 113; dm US$3, s/d with bathroom US$6/12, without bathroom US$5/10, all incl breakfast) A shoestringer favorite northwest of the center, Andino offers hot showers, kitchen and laundry, book exchange, bike rental, tour information and Spanish lessons.

La Casa de la Abuela (☎ 22-3303; Giráldez 691; dm US$6, d with/without bathroom US$9/7.60, all incl breakfast; ⊠) Backpackers get mothered at this clean, older home with a garden, hot water, laundry, games and cable TV. Rates include killer coffee for breakfast.

Hotel Confort (☎ 23-3601; Ancash 237; s/d US$6/9) This huge barn echoes with institutional corridors leading to scores of stark, faded rooms. But they're clean and large, and have hot showers, desks and cable TV (US$1.50).

Also recommended:

Hospedaje Las Lomas (☎ 23-7587; laslomashyo@yahoo.es; Giráldez 327; s/d US$8/10) Variously sized rooms with hot water and excellent mattresses.

Hostal y Baños Sauna Las Viñas (☎ 36-5236; Piura 415; s/d US$10/13) Small rooms with hot water, cable TV and phones. Sauna (US$2).

Hotel Kiya (☎ 21-4955; hotelkiya@terra.com .pe; Giráldez 107; s/d US$13/20) Six-story hotel with pink walls, comfy beds, phones, cable TV and hot water, plus some bathtubs.

Eating & Drinking

Nuevo Horizonte (Ica 578; mains US$1-1.50; ☼ 7:30am-10pm Sun-Fri) In an atmospheric older house, this place has an excellent vegetarian menu using soy and tofu to recreate carnivorous Peruvian classics like lomo saltado.

Antojitos (Puno 599; mains US$1.50-8; ☼ 5pm-late Mon-Sat) Housed in an antique-filled, wood-beamed building, this restaurant-bar attracts friendly crowds of well-dressed locals, who banter over the sounds of anything from cumbia to Pink Floyd.

Detrás de la Catedral (Ancash 335; mains US$2.70-5, ☼ 11am-11pm) You can dine next to a charcoal brazier, admire Picasso-like surrealist paintings on the wall and feast on filling burgers (veggie or meat) and loads of local specialties.

La Cabaña (Giráldez 652; mains US$3-6; ☼ 5-11pm) The house sangria, juicy grills and al dente pastas fuel a party crowd of locals and travelers alike. Folklórico bands perform Thursday to Saturday

nights. Next-door El Otro Lado café serves cuy lunches from April through October.

Restaurant Olímpico (Giráldez 199; lunch menú US$2, mains US$4-8) Huancayo's oldest restaurant has an open kitchen where you can see traditional Peruvian dishes prepared. Come for the popular Sunday brunch (US$5).

La Divina Comida (Arequipa 712; mains US$2) There's nothing infernal about the meatless fare at this busy hole-in-a-wall: hearty fried rice, tortillas with spinach and lomo a la macho feature on the small menu.

La Estancia (☎ 22-3279; M Castilla 2815; meals US$7) Northwest of town, Calle Real becomes Av Mariscal Castilla in the El Tambo district, where this place does a great lunchtime pachamanca containing a meaty mix of cuy, pork and lamb, wrapped in leaves and cooked in an underground oven.

Also recommended:

Panadería Koky (Puno 298) Bakery serving empanadas and espresso.

La Pergola (Puno 444; menú US$2) Courtly atmosphere with plaza views.

Chicharronería Cuzco (Cusco 173; meals US$2) Excellent chicharrones.

Shopping

The daily produce market, Mercado Mayorista, overflows east along the railway tracks, and sells every imaginable meaty delicacy, from fresh and dried frogs to guinea pigs.

Feria Dominical (Sunday craft market; Huancavelica) Sells souvenir weavings, sweaters, embroidered items, ceramics, woodcarvings and mates burilados (carved gourds) – watch your wallet.

Getting There & Away
BUS & COLECTIVO

Services vary depending on the season and demand.

Lima (US$6 to US$14, six to seven hours) is comfortably served by **Cruz del Sur** (☎ 23-5650; Ayacucho 251). **Etucsa** (☎ 23-6524; Puno 220) has more-frequent departures. There's also **Mariscal Cáceres** (☎ 21-6633; Real 1241). **Comité 12** (☎ 064-23-3281; Loreto 421) has faster colectivo taxis to Lima (US$14, five hours).

For the rough road to Ayacucho (US$7.30, 10 to 12 hours), **Empresa Molina** (☎ 22-4501; Angaraes 334) has morning and overnight departures. Huancavelica (US$3, five hours) is frequently served by **Transportes Ticllas** (☎ 20-1555; Ferrocarril 1590). Ask around to find colectivos to Huancavelica (US$7.60, 2½ to three hours).

PERU

Transportes San Juan (☎ 21-4558; Ferrocarril 131) has minibuses almost hourly to Tarma (US$2.50, 3½ hours). **Los Canarios** (Puno 739) also serves Tarma. **Turismo Central** (☎ 22-3128; Ayacucho 274) has buses north to Cerro de Pasco, Huánuco (US$6, seven hours), Tingo María (US$7.60, 10 hours) and Pucallpa (US$13.60, 22 hours).

TRAIN

Train buffs shouldn't miss experiencing the **Ferrocarril Central Andino** (☎ in Lima 01-361-2828; www.ferroviasperu.com.pe), which reaches a head-spinning elevation of 4829m. It runs between Lima and Huancayo, usually every week from mid-April through October (round trip US$45). Click to www.incasdelperu.org for updates.

Cheaper trains to Huancavelica leave from **Chilca station** (☎ 21-7724) at the south end of town. The 6:30am *expreso* (five hours, daily) and 12:30pm *ordinario* (six hours, daily except Sunday) services cost US$2.50/3/4 in 2nd/1st/buffet class. On Sunday and Monday, there's a faster *autovagón* at 6pm (US$4.50, four hours). Buy tickets beforehand.

TARMA

☎ 064 / pop 45,100

Not many travelers linger in 'the pearl of the Andes' between Lima and the jungle, but there are little-known, overgrown ruins to discover in the surrounding hills.

Information

You'll find *casas de cambio* near the BCP on Lima.

BCP (☎ 32-2149; cnr Lima & Paucartambo) Changes money and has a Visa ATM.

Internet café (Paucartambo 567)

Tourist office (☎ 32-1010; 2 de Mayo 775; ☻ 8am-1pm & 3-6pm Mon-Fri) On the Plaza de Armas.

Sights & Activities

Excursions can be arranged to the village of Acobamba, 9km from Tarma, to see the famous religious sanctuary of **El Señor de Muruhuay**, which is decorated with huge weavings and holds a colorful **festival** throughout May.

From the village of Palcamayo, 28km from Tarma, it's a 4km walk to **Gruta de Guagapo**, a huge limestone cave protected as a national speleological area. A guide who lives by the entrance can provide ropes and lanterns to enter the first sections, beyond which technical caving and scuba gear are required.

Festivals & Events

The **Semana Santa** processions, including several candlelit after dark, are the big attraction. The **Easter Sunday** procession to the cathedral follows a route carpeted with flower petals, as do the **El Señor de Los Milagros** processions in late October.

Sleeping

Hot water is usually available only in the morning, though accommodation owners may claim otherwise.

Hospedaje El Dorado (☎ 32-1914; Huánuco 488; s/d US$3/4.50, with bathroom US$4.50/7.60) Can be noisy, but it's reasonably clean and has a relaxing courtyard.

Hospedaje Central (☎ 32-2625; Huánuco 614; s/d US$4.50/5.80, with bathroom US$6.80/8.80) An old, darkish yet friendly hotel, with an observatory open to stargazers on Friday nights (admission US$1).

Hacienda La Florida (☎ 34-1041; www.hacienda laflorida.com; campsites per person US$4.50, s/d US$29/49) Located six kilometers from Tarma along the Acobamba road, this rustic 18th-century plantation is owned by a welcoming Peruvian-German couple. It's a one-hour hike from here to the El Señor de Muruhuay sanctuary.

PERU

Hostal Vargas (☎ 32-1460; 2 de Mayo 627; s/d US$4.50/6) Just ignore the gloomy entrance, because this clean hostel has spacious rooms and firm mattresses.

Hostal Aruba (☎ 32-2057; Moquegua 452; s/d US$10/14.50) A very secure choice with clean rooms near the busy market; ring the bell to enter.

Eating & Drinking

El Mejorcito de Tarma (Arequipa 501; mains US$2-5) The Mejorcito (the 'littlest and bestest') has a modest, but delicious menu of Peruvian favorites, including grilled trout.

Restaurant Señorial/El Braserito (Huánuco 138 & 140; menú US$1.20, mains US$2-5) These neighborly places are the locals' favorites, judging by the nonstop crowds. Traditional specialties include roast *cuy*.

El Gato Pardo (Callao 227) This dark, noisy pub is also a club with live Latin bands and DJs.

Getting There & Away

For buses to Lima (US$3 to US$9, six hours), try **Transportes Junín** (☎ 32-1234; Amazonas 667) or **Transportes La Merced** (☎ 32-2937; Vienrich 420). **Los Canarios** (☎ 32-3357; Amazonas 694) and **Transportes San Juan** (☎ 32-3139) go to Huancayo (US$2.50, 3½ hours). A bus stop by Transportes San Juan, in front of the Estadio Unión Tarma (*mototaxi* US20¢) has minibuses to Acobamba and Palcamayo. By the gas station opposite the forlorn Terminal Terrestre, faster *colectivo* taxis take up to four passengers to Lima (US$8.50). *Colectivos* to Huancayo (US$5, 3½ hours) leave from Jauja, about 600m further south.

WARNING!

The main road from Lima to Pucallpa (p929) goes through the central Andes north of La Oroya, via Junín, Cerro de Pasco, Huánuco and Tingo María. This route is used by travelers heading for the first navigable Amazon port, from where it is possible to float inland to Iquitos along the Río Ucayali. But the long, lonely section of road between Pucallpa and Tingo María – the only paved link in the whole of Peru to the Amazonas region – can be risky. Armed robberies have happened on many occasions. It's much safer to fly to the jungle from Lima.

JUNÍN

At the south end of this remote village is a huge **craft market**. About 10km away, **Lago de Junín** is known for its birdlife. Over 4000m above sea level, it is the highest lake of its size in the Americas. To get there take a *colectivo* 5km north of Junín to the hamlet of Huayre, where a footpath leads to the lake. Back in Junín, you can overnight at cold-water **Hostal San Cristobal** (☎ 34-4215; Manuel Prado 255; s/d US$2.80/4). Restaurants surround Plaza de Libertad.

HUÁNUCO

☎ 062 / pop 151,200

This town is just 5km from one of Peru's oldest Andean archaeological sites: the **Temple of Kotosh** (adult/student US90/45¢; ◷ 9am-3pm), aka Temple of the Crossed Hands. Visit by taxi (round trip US$4.50).

About 25km south of Huánuco is the village of Ambo, noted for its *aguardiente* distilleries. This local sugarcane firewater is flavored with anise. Some buses stop here so passengers can buy a couple of liters.

Sleeping

Basic budget hotels are on the plaza and near the market.

Hostal Huánuco (☎ 51-2050; Huánuco 777; s without bathroom US$5.80, s/d US$7.30/8.80) This old-fashioned mansion has tiled floors, a lush garden, and walls covered with art and newspaper clippings. Hot water upon request.

Hotel Cuzco (☎ 51-7653; Huánuco 614; s/d US$6/9) A dated hotel with a cafeteria and clean, bare but good-sized rooms with cable TV and hot showers (2nd floor only).

Eating & Drinking

Hotel Real (2 de Mayo 1125; mains US$2.50-6; ◷ 24hr) The café is the place for midnight munchies and predawn breakfasts. At the side of the hotel is the underground Plaza Discoteca.

Govinda (2 de Mayo 1044; menú US$1-2; ◷ 7am-9:30pm Mon-Sat, 7am-3pm Sun) Vegetarians can rely on this Hare Krishna–run café.

Chifa Khon Wa (☎ 51-3609; Prado 816; mains US$2-3; ◷ 10:30am-11pm) Chinese restaurants can be a-dime-a-dozen in Peru, but you know you've found a winner when the staff wears logo T-shirts.

Cheers (2 de Mayo 1201; mains US$2-3; ◷ 11am-midnight) Neonlit and chic, this place draws crowds with its inexpensive chicken and Peruvian dishes. Karaoke on weekend nights.

Shorton Grill (D Beraún 685; mains US$2-3) Chicken, chips and beer is what this place is all about, and it's all good.

Getting There & Away

The airport (HUU) is 5km from town (taxi US$3.50). **LC Busre** (☎ 062-51-8113; 2 de Mayo 1357) flies to/from Lima daily.

Buses go to Lima (US$6 to US$11, eight hours), Pucallpa (US$6 to US$8, nine to 12 hours) and Huancayo (US$6, seven hours). Companies are spread out all over town. Among the best are **León de Huánuco** (☎ 51-1489; Robles 821), luxurious **Bahía Continental** (☎ 51-9999; Valdizán 718), **Transportes El Rey** (☎ 51-3623; 28 de Julio 1215), and **Transmar** (28 de Julio 1067).

For Tingo María, take any Pucallpa-bound bus (US$2, 3½ hours) or a faster *colectivo* (US$3.50) with **Comité 15** (☎ 51-8346; General Prado) near the river.

TINGO MARÍA

☎ 062 / pop 54,000

After the high and bleak hinterland of the Andes appears this university and market town lying in the *ceja de la selva* (eyebrow of the jungle), as the lush, tropical slopes of the eastern Andes are called. It's surrounded by mountains, waterfalls and caves, and is hot almost year-round. It's the best place to break your journey to Pucallpa. Avoid the dangerous drug-growing Río Huallaga valley north of town, though.

Sights & Activities

The 18,000-hectare **Parque Nacional Tingo María** (admission incl guide US$1.50) lies on the south side of town. Take a taxi to the 'Cave of the Owls' to see its oilbird colonies, stalactites and stalagmites.

Sleeping

Showers are usually cold.

Hotel Palacio (☎ 56-2319; A Raimondi 158; s/d with shared bath US$4.50/7.30, s/d US$7.30/12) Spartan fan-cooled rooms surround a plant- and parrot-filled courtyard. There's a handy café.

Hostal Roosevelt (☎ 50-5448; José Pratto 399; s/d US$6/7.60) It's a midrange hostelry at budget prices. Smallish but spick-and-span rooms painted in odd colors have cable TV and full-length mirrors (whoa, Nelly!) beside the beds.

Hotel Nueva York (☎ 56-2406; www.hotelnueva york.net; Alameda Perú 553; s/d from US$7/9) Spacious, quiet rooms set back from the road have fans

and warm afternoon showers. Breakfast available (US$1.50).

Villa Jennifer (☎ 969-5059; www.villajennifer.net; Km3.4 Castillo Grande; s/d without bathroom US$14/22; ⬛) North of the airport, this relaxing hacienda is run by a Danish-Peruvian couple. Hang out in hammocks, feast on tropical fruit, play games, talk to the monkeys or watch DVDs.

Also recommended:

Hotel Internacional (☎ 56-3035; Raymondi 232; s/d US$9/13.60) Close to the bus stations. Cool, tiled rooms have 24-hour hot water, cable TV and phones.

La Gran Muralla (☎ 56-2934; Raymondi 277; s/d US$12/20; ⬛) Breezy, modern riverside complex next to all the action. Fan rooms have cable TV and phones.

Eating

El Mango (Lamas 232; sandwiches & breakfasts US$1-5.50; ⏱ 8am-3pm Mon-Sat & 7-11pm Mon-Sun) A surprisingly good garden restaurant with friendly service and an unmistakable mango-colored facade.

Simón (Fernández 416; mains US$2-3; ⏱ 7am-3pm & 6-10pm) This sweaty restaurant has no breeze, but lots of hearty fare including a few *criollo* dishes. Locals say it's the best value in town, especially for beer.

Trigale (Fernández 540; mains US$2.50-4.50; ⏱ 6-11pm) Tingo María's best pizza-and-pasta joint delivers if you can't bear to forsake the fan and TV in your hotel room.

El Super Dorado (Fernández 594; mains US$2.50-4.50) Locals love this big 'n' brash place for its no-nonsense chicken *parrilladas* washed down with a lashing of cold beer.

Getting There & Away

As a general rule, avoid night travel and be careful on the road to Pucallpa (p929). Buses to Lima (US$7 to US$12, 12 hours) with **León de Huánuco** (☎ 56-2030), **Transmar** (☎ 56-3076), **Transportes Rey** (☎ 56-2565; Raymondi 297) and TransInter mostly leave at 7am or 7pm. Some of these stop in Pucallpa (US$5, eight to nine hours). Faster service to Pucallpa is with Turismo Ucayali, which has *colectivos* (US$14, six hours).

NORTH COAST

The unruly northern coast is flush with enough ancient chronicles to fill a library of memoirs. Animated colonial towns doff their collective *campesino* hats to all who make the effort to visit. Playful seaside resorts beckon modern-day sun worshippers to their shores,

PERU

while gnarly breaks have had surfers board-waxing lyrical for years. If you're heading north to Ecuador, the further you go, the better the weather gets.

CARAL

About 25km inland from Barranca lie the monumental ruins of Caral (admission US$3), part of South America's oldest civilization, arising simultaneously with Egypt, India and China. **Projecto Especial Arqueológico Caral** (☎ 01-431-2235; www.caralperu.gob.pe) has information and runs full-day tours from Lima (US$24). Most coastal buses can drop you in Barranca, 195km north of Lima, from where *colectivos* to Caral (US$1.50, two hours) depart frequently between April and November. Other buses from Barranca (US50¢, 25 minutes) go to the Chimu adobe temple of **Paramonga** (admission US90¢).

CASMA

☎ 043 / pop 21,400

A blip on the Panamerican radar, 370km north of Lima, Casma is the gateway to **Sechín** (admission US$1.50; ⏱ 8am-5pm). Shrouded in mystery, these well-preserved ruins date from 1600 BC. The outside walls of the main temple are covered with gruesomely realistic bas-relief carvings of warriors and captives being vividly eviscerated. The archaeological site is 5km from Casma.

Northwest of Casma at Km 392 on the Panamericana, the beach resort of Tortugas sidles along a calm bay with a pebbly swimming beach. The airy **Hotel Farol Beach Inn** (☎ 968-2540; s/d US$12/18) has vistas and hot showers. Back in Casma, try the funky, feng shui–approved **Hostal Gregori** (☎ 01-9631-4291; L Ormeño 579; s/d US$9/10.50, without bathroom US$4.50/7.50).

Frequent buses with Cruz del Sur, Móvil and Turismo Paraiso to Lima (US$5.40 to US$11, six hours), Trujillo (US$4.50, three hours) and Huaraz (US$6.25, 5½ hours) stop by a shared **booking office** (☎ 043-41-2116; Ormeño 145). **Tepsa** (☎ 41-2658; Ormeño 546) has comfy buses to Lima (US$9 to US$15), Tumbes (US$21, 11 hours) and Cajamarca (US$18, seven hours).

Colectivos for Tortugas (US90¢, 20 minutes) and Chimbote (US$1.50, 45 minutes) leave frequently from the Plaza de Armas. For Sechín, take a *mototaxi* (US$1.50), or rent a bicycle (per day US$6) at **Sechín Tours** (☎ 41-1421; www.sechintours.com; Hostal Montecarlo, Nepeña 16).

CHIMBOTE

☎ 043 / pop 320,600

You'll smell Peru's largest fishing port before you see it. If you find yourself stuck here waiting for a bus, take refuge at **Cesar's Hostal** (☎ 32-4946; Espinar 286; s/d US$7.50/10.50) and the ramshackle restaurant **Vegetariano** (cnr Pardo & Palacios; meals US$1.50; ⏱ 8am-10pm).

Long-distance buses to Lima (US$9 to US$24, seven hours), Trujillo (US$2.10, two hours) and Chiclayo (US$6, six hours) leave from Terminal Terrestre, 5km east of town (taxi US$1.20). Buses to Huaraz (US$6 to US$7.50, seven to nine hours) go via the spectacular Cañon del Pato, the equally rough mountain road from Casma or the paved Pativilca route. *Colectivos* for Casma (US$1.50, 45 minutes) leave from Chimbote's market area.

TRUJILLO

☎ 044 / pop 768,300

Francisco Pizarro founded Trujillo, northern Peru's major city 560km from Lima, in 1534. In fact, he thought so highly of this patch of desert he named it after his birthplace in Spain. Trujillo's glamorously colonial streets look like they've hardly changed since. Nearby are the 1500-year-old Moche pyramids, Las Huacas del Sol y de la Luna, and the ancient Chimú adobe capital of Chan Chan (see p903). If so much ancient culture wears you out, the nearby beach village of Huanchaco (p904) offers its own modern interpretation of sun worship.

Information

The local newspaper *La Industria* lists entertainment, exhibitions and events.

BCP (Gamarra 562) Lowest traveler's-check commissions.

Clínica Americano-Peruano (☎ 23-1261; Mansiche 702) The best clinic.

Interbank (Gamarra at Pizarro) Has a global ATM.

InterWeb (Pizarro 721; ⏱ 8:30am-11pm) Internet access.

iPerú (☎ 29-4561; Municipalidad, Plaza Mayor, Pizarro 412; ⏱ 8am-7pm Mon-Sat, to 2pm Sun) Tourist information.

Lavanderías Unidas (Pizarro 683; ⏱ 8am-11pm) Does laundry.

Policía de Turismo (☎ 044-29-1705; Independencia 630)

Sights

The Plaza de Armas is fronted by an 18th-century **cathedral** with a famous basilica.

Many other elegant colonial churches and mansions have wrought-iron grillwork and

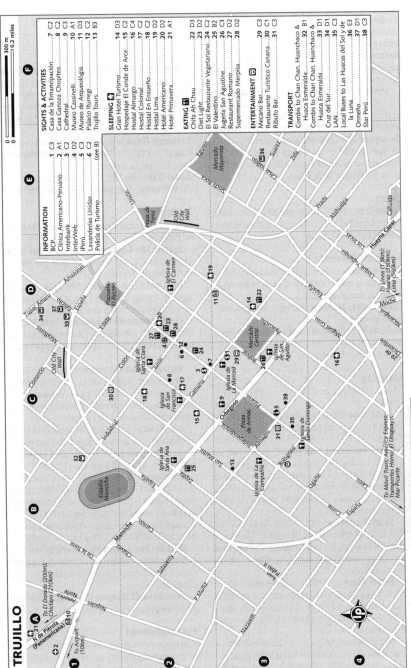

TRUJILLO

0   300 m
0   0.2 miles

PERU

pastel coloring that typify Trujillo. **Casa de la Emancipación** (Banco Continental; Pizarro 610), **Palacio Iturregui** (Pizarro 688; 9am-7pm Mon-Sat) and **Casa Ganoza Chopitea** (Independencia 630), with its art gallery and two lions standing guard out front: all deserve a look.

Museo Cassinelli (Piérola 601; admission US$2.10; 9:30am-1pm & 3-6pm Mon-Sat) has an excellent archaeological collection – in the basement of a Mobil gas station! The university-run **Museo de Arqueológia** (Junín 682; adult/student US$1.50/80¢; 9am-3pm Mon, to 1pm & 3-7pm Tue-Fri, to 4pm Sat & Sun), in the restored Casa Risco, has artifacts from La Huaca de la Luna.

Tours

Trujillo Tours (23-3091; Almargo 301) offers multilingual guided tours of nearby archaeological sites (US$15 to US$18).

Festivals & Events

The *marinera* dance (p826) and *caballos de paso* (horseback dressage displays) are highlights of many festivals.

La Fiesta de la Marinera The biggest of its kind, held in late January.

La Fiesta de la Primavera Held during the last week of September, has Peru's most famous parade, and much dancing and entertainment.

Sleeping

Many travelers bed down in Huanchaco (p904).

Hostal Lima (23-2499; Ayacucho 718; s/d US$3.30/5.40) If you've been on a tour of Alcatraz and thought, I could live here, this is your chance.

Hotel Americano (24-1361; Pizarro 764; s/d US$6/9) You'll either love or hate this perennially popular hotel in a rambling, dilapidated old mansion with carved balconies. Echoing rooms are creaky. Those with shared showers are grungier.

Hotel Primavera (23-1915; Piérola 872; s/d US$7.50/12;) Retro blue flourishes announce this 1970s relic. It's only slightly shabby, and an invigorating pool may help you overlook the mustiness.

Hostal Almargo (22-3845; Almargo 748; s/d US$13.50/18) There's no pretense of a colonial past here – modern if spartan rooms have TVs and glistening bathrooms. There's a café downstairs.

Hostal Colonial (25-8261; hostcolonialtruji@hotmail .com; Independencia 618; s/d US$13.50/19.50) A great location near the Plaza de Armas, this tastefully

renovated colonial mansion run by chatty staff has a pleasant courtyard and garden. Cozy rooms have hot showers, and some have balcony views.

Gran Hotel Turismo (24-4181; Gamarra 747; s/d US$14.40/21.30;) Live out your secret *Austin Powers* fantasies here, where everything is decked out in hip 1960s decor and hallways are the length of football fields. Groovy, baby.

Also recommended:

Hospedaje El Conde de Arce (29-1607; Independencia 577; s/d US$6/12) Simple, small and safe. Weathered rooms have electric showers.

Hostal El Ensueño (20-7744; Junín 336; s/d US$9/15) Narrow, dark hallways, but gigantic bathrooms.

Eating

Search out trendy eateries on the 700 block of Pizarro.

Jugería San Augustíne (Bolívar 526; juice US50¢; 8am-10pm) Lines snake around the corner at this locals' fave.

Diet Light (Pizzario 724; snacks US80¢-$2.50; 9:30am-10pm) A strangely named place for whopping servings of ice cream and mixed fruit.

El Sol Restaurante Vegetariano (Pizarro 660; meals US90¢-$2.40; 8am-10pm) A limited menu attests to experience: the cooks already know exactly what you want.

Restaurant Romano (Pizarro 747; mains US$1.80-4.50; 7am-midnight) Open for over half a century, this incredibly popular place dishes up hot breakfasts, hearty Peruvian lunches and dinners, plus desserts and espresso.

Mar Picante (América Sur 2199; meals US$2.10-4.50; 11am-10pm) A bamboo-lined seafood palace, it specializes in fresh *ceviche* and is packed with savvy locals. Take a taxi (US80¢).

El Uruguayo (América Sur 2219; meals US$4.50-7.50; 6:30pm-1am) A sizzling plate of delicious barbecued meat (steak, chicken, chorizo sausage, beef heart plus a few surprises), salad and fries enough for two ravenous travelers will set you back only US$9.90. Take a taxi (US80¢).

Chifa Ah Chau (Gamarra 769; mains US$5; 6-10pm) A funky, faded but fun place, with private curtained booths and huge portions of genuine Chinese food.

Supermercado Merpisa (Pizarro 700; 9:15am-1:15pm & 4:30-9pm) For self-catering.

Entertainment

Foreign women going out alone after dark will be given exasperating amounts of unsolicited attention from local men.

PERU

Mecano Bar (Gamarra 574; admission US$6; 9pm-late) For now, this is where the in-crowd hangs out, especially on weekends. Sway your hips to salsa, reggae and techno grooves.

Restaurante Turístico Canana (San Martín 791; admission US$3; shows 11pm Thu-Sat) When local dancers and musicians perform, anyone not chowing down on *chicharrones* joins in.

Ributo Bar (Plaza de Armas, cnr Pizarro & Almagro; 9pm-late) A quiet bar for chatting with friends, or live bands and hot DJs on the weekend.

Getting There & Away

AIR

The airport (TRU) is 10km northwest of town. Take a taxi (US$3 to US$4.50) or a bus bound for Huanchaco and walk 1km. **LAN** (22-1469; Pizarro 340) and **Star Perú** (41-0009; Almargo 545) have daily flights to/from Lima.

BUS

Buses are often full, so purchase seats in advance and double-check where your bus leaves from.

Major companies include the following:

Cruz del Sur (26-1801; Amazonas 237) To Lima (US$10.50 to US$31.50, eight hours).

Linea booking office (24-5181; cnr San Martin & Obregoso; 8am-8pm Mon-Fri); terminal (24-3271; América Sur 2857) Goes to Piura (US$9, six hours), Cajamarca (US$4.50 to US$10.50, six hours), Chiclayo (US$3.60, three hours), Chimbote (US$1.80, two hours). Buses for Lima (US$9 to US$21, eight hours) and Huaraz (US$12, nine hours) are mostly overnight.

Móvil Tours (28-6538; América Sur 3955) Comfortable overnight buses to Lima (US$19.50, eight hours), Huaraz (US$13.50, eight hours), Chachapoyas (US$15, 13 hours) and Tarapoto (US$22.50, 18 hours).

Ormeño (25-9782; Ejército 233) Overnight buses to Lima (US$10.50 to US$21) and Tumbes (US$15 to US$21, 10 hours).

Other companies around the intersection of España and Amazonas offer Lima-bound night buses. **América Express** (26-1906; La Marina 315) has frequent buses south to Chimbote (US$2.10, two hours); take a taxi (US90¢).

El Dorado (29-1778; Piérola 1070) has rudimentary buses to Piura (US$7, six hours) and Tumbes (US$7.50 to US$9, 10 hours). **Ittsa** (25-1415; Mansiche 145) also has buses to Piura. **Transportes Horna** (25-7605; América Sur 1368) has morning buses to Cajamarca (US$4.50, six hours).

Getting Around

White-yellow-and-orange B *colectivos* to La Huaca Esmeralda, Chan Chan and Huanchaco run along España past the corners of Ejército and Industrial every few minutes. Buses for La Esperanza go northwest along the Panamericana to La Huaca Arco Iris. Minibuses for Las Huacas del Sol y de la Luna leave every half hour from Suarez. These buses are worked by professional thieves – keep valuables hidden, and watch your bags carefully. Fares run US30¢ to US50¢.

AROUND TRUJILLO

The Moche and the Chimú are the two cultures that have left the greatest mark on the Trujillo area, but they are by no means the only ones – more new sites are being excavated each year.

For the Chan Chan museum and site, plus Huaca Esmeralda and Huaca Arco Iris, a **combined ticket** (adult/student US$3.30/1.70) is valid for two days. Tickets are sold at each site except Huaca Esmeralda. All are open 9am to 4:30pm daily.

Chan Chan

Built around AD 1300, Chan Chan must once have been a dazzling site. As you approach along the Panamericana, it's impossible not to be impressed by the vast area of crumbling mud walls stretching away into the distance. This site once formed the largest pre-Columbian city in the Americas and the largest adobe city in the world.

At the height of the Chimu Empire, Chan Chan contained about 10,000 structures, from royal palaces lined with precious metals to huge burial mounds. Although the Incas conquered the Chimú around 1460, the city was not looted until the gold-hungry Spanish arrived, and *huaqueros* (grave robbers) finished their work.

The Chimú capital contained nine subcities, or royal compounds. The restored **Tschudi**

WARNING!

It is dangerous to walk along Buenos Aires beach between Chan Chan and Huanchaco. Travelers have also been attacked while visiting archaeological sites. Go in a group, stay on the main paths and don't visit late in the day.

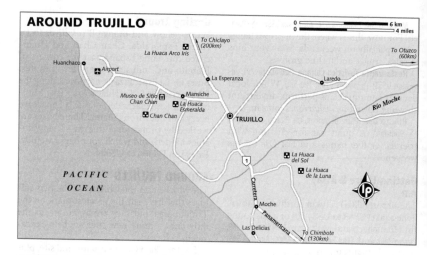

AROUND TRUJILLO

complex is near the entrance area by the **site museum** on the main road about 500m before the Chan Chan turnoff. Tschudi's walls once stood over 10m high with impressive friezes of fish, waves and sea life. A king was once buried in the mausoleum with a treasure trove of ceremonial objects for the afterlife – and plenty of sacrificial companions.

La Huaca Esmeralda

This stepped-platform Chimú adobe temple is south of the main road halfway between Trujillo and Chan Chan, four blocks behind the Mansiche church. Guards will take you around for a tip to see the unrestored adobe designs of fish, seabirds, waves and fishing nets.

La Huaca Arco Iris

This Chimú site, meaning 'Rainbow Temple' (also called La Huaca del Dragón), is in the suburb of La Esperanza, 4km northwest of Trujillo. It's one of the best-preserved Chimú temples because it was covered by sand until the 1960s. Inside the defensive wall is the temple itself, which may have been used for fertility rituals and infant sacrifices. The slightly pyramidal walls are covered with repeated rainbow designs and ramps leading to the very top. There's a small museum. Guides are available for a tip.

Las Huacas del Sol y de la Luna

These **Moche temples** (admission & guided tour adult/student US$3.30/1.70; ☉ 9am-4pm), 10km southeast of Trujillo, are 700 years older than Chan Chan.

The **Huaca del Sol** is Peru's largest pre-Columbian structure; 140 million adobe bricks were used to build it. Originally the pyramid had several levels, connected by steep stairs, huge ramps and walls sloping at 77 degrees to the horizon. Now it resembles a giant sand pile, but its sheer size makes it an awesome sight nonetheless.

The smaller **Huaca de la Luna** is riddled with rooms containing ceramics, precious metals and the beautiful polychrome friezes for which the Moche were famous. Their custom of 'burying' old temples under new ones has facilitated preservation, and archaeologists are still peeling away the layers. Keep an eye out for Peruvian hairless dogs that hang here. The body temperature of these dogs is higher than that of normal dogs, and they've been traditionally used as body-warmers for people with arthritis!

HUANCHACO

☎ 044 / pop 18,000

This once-tranquil fishing village, 12km northwest of Trujillo, is a popular alternative base for exploring the Trujillo area. It's famous for high-ended, cigar-shaped, *totora* boats called *caballitos* (little horses) on which fishermen paddle beyond the breakers, then surf back to the beach with their catch. Paying fishermen US$1.50 will get you paddled out and surfed back in a wet rush.

On weekends, Huanchaco is swamped with Peruvian holidaymakers. Armies of bleached-

The small fishing outpost of **Puerto Chicama** (aka Malabrigo) lays claim to one of the world's longest left-hand point breaks. It seduces surfers dying to try their luck at catching that rare, incredible 2km ride on 2m-high waves. The marathon breaks usually arrive between March and June. The original surfers hostel, **El Hombre** (☎ 044-57-6077; s/d from US$5/8), rents some gear, but it's best to bring your own. Buses leave Trujillo's Terminal Interurbano frequently for Paiján (US$1.40, 1½ hours), 40km north along the Panamericana, where you can catch *colectivos* to Puerto Chicama (US40¢, 20 minutes).

blond surfers amble the streets with boards in tow during the coastal summer (December to April), when the curving, grey-sand beach invites swimming.

Activities

Rent surfboards and wet suits (per day US$6 to US$9) from several places along the main drag, including the **Wave** (☎ 58-7005; Larco 525) and **Un Lugar** (☎ 957-7170; www.otracosa .info; cnr Bolognesi & Atahualpa), which offers lessons and surf safaris.

Sleeping

You'll find budget lodgings in the northern part of town, as well as at the southern end on side streets running perpendicular to the beach.

Hostal Naylamp (☎ 46-1022; www.geocities.com/hos talnaylamp; Victor Larco 1420; campsite US$2.40; dm US$3.60; s US$7.50-9, d US$10.50-13.50) Seascape patios have sunset views, and there are hot showers and hammocks for everyone. There's also a kitchen, laundry and café.

Hospedaje Los Ficus de Huanchaco (☎ 46-1719; www.huanchaco.net/losficus; Los Ficus 516; s/d without bathroom US$4.50/9) This spotless house offers hot showers, breakfast on request and kitchen privileges. Many of the bright rooms have tons of space, but not all are created equal, so choose carefully.

La Casa Suiza (☎ 46-1825; www.casasuiza.com; Los Pinos 451/310; s/d without bathroom US$4.50/9; ❑) A tired-looking surfer crash pad, with a rowdy rooftop.

Huanchaco's Garden (☎ 46-1194; huanchacosgarden@ yahoo.es; Circunvalación 440; d US$12; ☎) Set back from the beach, this hospitable family-run hostelry boasts low-lying white adobe buildings surrounding a shady garden.

Huankarute Hospedaje (☎ 044-46-1705; www.hos talhuankarute.com; La Rivera 233; s US$21, d US$24-33; ☎) A small place with bright rooms that have fans and cable TV. Top-floor doubles have sea views – and bathtubs! The kidney-shaped pool has an attached 'aqua bar' and the on-site seafood restaurant has cheap lunch specials.

Eating

Huanchaco has oodles of seafood restaurants on the beach.

Otra Cosa (Larco 921; dishes US$1.20-2.40; ✆ 9am-8pm Wed-Sun) With Middle Eastern decor and hammocks, this beachfront pad dishes up yummy vegetarian snacks like falafel and hummus. The owners also organize volunteer projects.

Grill a Bordo (Los Pinos 491; dishes US$2.40-6; ✆ 6pm-11pm Mon-Sat, 11am-11pm Sun) The waiters are strangely dressed as sailors, even though there's only one fish dish on the menu at this *parrilla* grill serving carnivorous delights.

Also recommended:

El Caribe (Larco at Atahualpa; dishes US$3-4.50; ✆ 10am-7pm) Fresh seafood, including *ceviche*.

Club Colonial (Grau 272; meals US$4.50-7.50; ✆ noon-11pm) Romantic Belgian-French-Peruvian restaurant with an art gallery.

Mamma Mía (☎ 997-3635; Larco at Independencia; meals US$5-9; ✆ 6-11pm) Delicious designer pizzas, and the owner's secret-recipe crab lasagna.

Getting There & Away

Combis will take you from España at Industrial in Trujillo to Huanchaco's beachfront (US50¢). A taxi costs US$3 to US$4.50.

CHICLAYO

☎ 074 / pop 592,200

Spanish missionaries founded a small rural community here, 200km north of Lima, in the 16th century. Either by chance or through help from 'above,' the crossroads city of Chiclayo has prospered ever since. A bounty of important archaeology sites lies nearby.

Information

Internet cafés abound. Several banks are on the 600 block of Balta.

BCP (Balta 630) Has a 24-hour Visa ATM.

Centro de Información Turístico (☎ 23-3132; Saenz Peña 838) Next to the police.

Clínica del Pacífico (☎ 23-6378; Ortiz 420) For medical attention.

Interbank (cnr Colón & Aguirre) Has a global ATM.

Lavandería (☎ 23-3159; 7 de Enero 639).

Migraciónes (☎ 20-6838; La Plata 070) Near Paseo de Las Museos.

Policía de Turismo (☎ 23-6700; Saenz Peña 830)

Sights & Activities

Don't miss the fascinating **Mercado Modelo**, which houses a superstore of shamanistic herbs, elixirs and sagely curiosities. Need a love potion or a cure for warts? Herbalist and *brujo* (witch doctor) stalls sit side-by-side, vending dried herbs, bones, claws, hooves, and other weird and wonderful healing charms.

During summer the coastal beaches of Pimintel and Santa Rosa are popular for **surfing**, especially at El Faro.

Tours

Moche Tours (☎ 22-4637; 7 de Enero 638) offers daily tours in English and Spanish.

Sleeping

Katuwira Lodge (☎ 970-0484/976-9188; www.katuwira.com; campsite/r per person incl meals US$5/10) A 20-minute walk south of Pimintel at Playa Las Rocas, this chilled beachside bamboo hangout sprawls. Pyramid-shaped bungalows have sea views. French and Japanese spoken.

Hospedaje San Lucas (☎ 49-9269; Aguirre 412; s without bathroom US$3, s/d US$6/9) Elementary, but trim

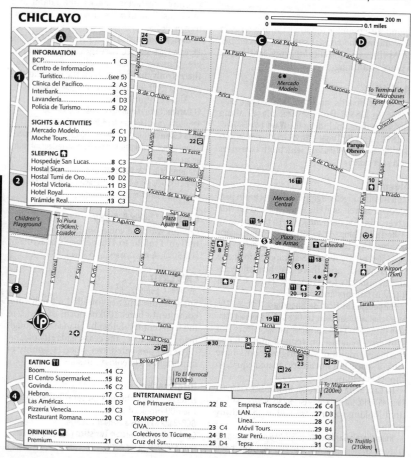

CHICLAYO

and tidy, the former Hostal Lido steps up to its 'welcome backpackers' motto with top-floor city views and mostly hot showers.

Hostal Tumi de Oro (☎ 22-7108; Prado 1145; s US$6-9, d US$9-13.50) This spartan place boasts almost midrange niceties (including hot showers) at a budget price.

Hotel Royal (☎ 22-1708; San José 787; r US$7-9.60) For aficionados of older, run-down, characterful hotels, this noisy choice with hot showers is right on the Plaza de Armas. The only thing royal about it, though, is its elegant business card.

Hostal Victoria (☎ 22-5642; Izaga 933; s/d US$7.50/13.50) Regain your sanity at this quiet, colorful gem just east of the plaza. Potted plants breathe lots of life into the place, which has a familial feel.

Pirámide Real (☎ 22-4036; piramidereal@hotmail.com; Izaga 726; s/d US$9/15) Look hard for this hotel's tiny entrance. Tidy rooms have hot water and cable TV. Romanesque statues fill the hallways and add some kind of personality – we're still undecided as to what kind.

Hostal Sican (☎ 23-7618; Izaga 356; s/d US$10.50/15) Hotal Sican is an appealing choice, with lots of polished wood, artworks and wrought iron creating illusions of grandeur. The rooms are small, comfortable and cool. All of them have TVs.

Eating & Drinking

Boom (San José 677; meals US$1.40-4.20; ☑ 7am-late) This buzzing, neonlit joint whips out elephantine Peruvian dishes, sandwiches, pizzas and cakes.

Las Américas (Aguirre 824; mains US$1.80-5.40) A perennial favorite, off the southeast corner of the plaza, with retro red-and-white booths. Try the *criollo* fish in spicy tomato sauce.

Restaurant Romana (Balta 512; mains US$2.50-6) For a wide variety of local dishes. If you're feeling brave, try its *chirimpico* for breakfast; it's stewed goat tripe and organs, guaranteed to either cure a hangover or give you one.

El Ferrocol (Las Américas 168; meals US$3-7.50; ☑ 11am-7pm) This hole-in-the-wall is worth a trip: Chef Lucho prepares some of the best *ceviche* in Chiclayo.

Hebron (Balta 605; mains US$3-5; ☑ 24hr) A flashy, contemporary two-story restaurant that's like a *pollería* on steroids.

Pizzería Venecia (Balta 413; pizzas US$4-8; ☑ 6:30pm-late) Attracts a rip-roaring crowd of locals who hum along to Latin pop tunes while chugging beer with their pie.

El Centro Supermarket (cnr Gonzalez & Aguirre; ☑ 8am-10pm) For self-catering.

Premium (Balta 100; ☑ 9pm-late) The place to knock back a few drinks and boogie with a boisterous crowd.

Entertainment

Cine Primavera (☎ 20-7471; Gonzales 1235) Shows Hollywood flicks on five screens.

Getting There & Around

AIR

The **airport** (CIX; ☎ 23-3192) is 2km southeast of town (taxi US60¢). **LAN** (☎ 27-4875; Izaga 770) offers daily flights to Lima and Piura. **Star Perú**

PERU

GETTING TO ECUADOR

Since Peru signed a peace treaty with Ecuador in 1998, it is possible to cross at the remote outpost of La Balsa. The first convenient stop in Ecuador is the lovely village of Vilcabamba (p697).

From Chiclayo, **Linea** (☎ 074-23-3497; Bolognesi 638), **Civa** (☎ 074-22-3434; Bolognesi 714), **Empresa Transcade** (☎ 074-23-2552; Balta 110) and the minibus terminal behind **Tepsa** (Bolognesi 504) have buses to **Jaén** (US$4.50 to US$6.90, six hours), where there are a few banks and hotels. From Jaén, *colectivos* (US$3.60, 2½ hours) follow a good road for 107km to **San Ignacio** (where there's a simple hotel and places to eat). Transfer to another *colectivo* to travel the rough road to La Balsa (US$3.60, 2½ hours) on the Río Blanco, which divides Peru from Ecuador. There used to be a ferry here, but an international bridge now links the countries.

Border formalities are straightforward, though immigration officers don't see many gringos. On the Ecuadorian side, *rancheras* (trucks with rows of wooden seats) await for an uncomfortable 10km drive to Zumba, where buses go to Vilcabamba (US$4, three hours). If you leave Jaén at dawn, you should reach Vilcabamba the same day.

For entering Peru from Ecuador, see p699.

(☎ 27-1173; Bolognesi 316) flies twice daily to Lima and once to Trujillo.

BUS & COLECTIVO
Many bus companies are along Bolognesi, including **Cruz del Sur** (☎ 22-5508; Bolognesi 888), **Linea** (☎ 23-3497; Bolognesi 638) and **Móvil Tours** (☎ 27-1940; Bolognesi 199). Long-distance buses go to Lima (US$12 to US$24, 10 hours), Jáen (US$4.50 to US$6.90, six hours), Tumbes (US$6, eight hours), Trujillo (US$3.60, three hours), Piura (US$3.60, two hours), Cajamarca (US$4.50 to US$9, six hours), Chachapoyas (US$12, 10½ hours), Tarapoto (US$12 to US$21, 13 hours) and elsewhere.

The minibus terminal at the intersection of San José and Lora y Lora has regular buses to Lambayeque (US50¢, 20 minutes) and Pimentel (US50¢, 25 minutes). Buses for Sipán (US80¢, one hour) and Ferreñafe (US50¢, 30 minutes) leave from Terminal de Microbuses Epsel, on Piérola at Oriente, northeast of downtown.

AROUND CHICLAYO
Guides can be hired at each of the following sites for US$4.50 to US$6 each. Guided tours from Chiclayo cost US$15 to US$20, including transportation.

Lambayeque
The pride of northern Peru, **Museo Tumbas Reales De Sipán** (☎ 28-3977/8; admission US$2.30; 9am-6pm Tue-Sun, last admission 5pm) is a world-class facility showcasing the dazzling finds of the Royal Tombs of Sipán, including that of the Lord of Sipán himself. Signs are Spanish only. Also in Lambayeque is the older **Bruning Museum** (☎ 28-2110; adult/student US$2.30/0.90; 9am-5pm), which houses artifacts from the Chimu, Moche, Chavín and Vicus cultures.

Sipán
The story of this **site** (Huaca Rayada; ☎ 80-0048; adult/student US$2.30/90¢; 9am-5pm), 30km southeast of Chiclayo, is an exciting one of buried treasure, huaqueros, the black market, police, archaeologists and at least one murder. Hundreds of exquisite and priceless artifacts have been recovered, and a gold-smothered royal Moche burial site – the Lord of Sipán – was discovered in 1987. One tomb here has a replica of his burial, but the most spectacular finds are in Lambayeque's museums (see above).

Ferreñafe
About 18km northeast of Chiclayo, **Museo Nacional Sicán** (☎ 074-28-6469; http://sican.perucultural .org.pe; adult/student US$2.30/90¢; 9am-5pm Tue-Sun) displays replicas of some of the largest tombs ever found in South America. Interestingly, the Lord of Sicán was buried upside down, in a fetal position with his head chopped off, along with a sophisticated security system to ward off huaqueros – a red dust that's toxic when inhaled.

Túcume
This little-known **site** (☎ 074-80-0052; adult/student US$2.30/90¢; 8am-4:30pm Tue-Sun) can be seen from a spectacular clifftop mirador about 30km north of Lambayeque on the Panamericana. It's worth the climb to see the vast complex of crumbling walls, plazas and over two dozen pyramids. Buses from Angamos near Pardo in Chiclayo (US50¢, one hour) or the Bruning Museum in Lambayeque can drop you nearby.

PIURA
☎ 073 / pop 328,600
Arriving from the south after crossing the unforgiving Sechura Desert, Peru's oldest colonial city is like a mirage on the horizon. Piura is a transportation hub, so you may end up spending time in this sunscorched city. Cobblestone streets full of characterful houses don't change the fact that there's little to do here.

Information
The post office and banks with ATMs are on the Plaza de Armas. Look for casas de cambio at the intersection of Ica and Arequipa.
Akasa (Tacna 630; 8am-11pm) Air-con internet café.
Centro de Promoción Turistico (☎ 31-0772; www .munipiura.gob.pe; Ayacucho 377; 8am-7pm Mon-Fri, 9am-7pm Sat, to noon Sun) Has tourist information.
Clínica San Miguel (☎ 30-9300; Los Cocos 111; 24hr) For medical attention.

Sights & Activities
Museo de Oro Vicus (Museo Municipal; Huánuco 893; admission US90¢; 9am-5pm Tue-Sun) is an underground gold museum, featuring a belt with a life-sized gold cat's head for a buckle.

About 12km southwest of Piura, the dusty village of Catacaos claims northern Peru's best **crafts market** (10am-4pm), which sprawls for several blocks near the plaza. Haggle for weav-

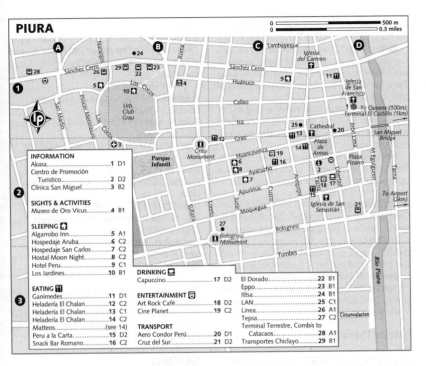

PIURA

ings, gold and silver jewelry, ceramics, wood carvings, leather goods and more – weekends are busiest.

Sleeping

Hospedaje Aruba (☎ 30-3067; Junín 851; s/d without bathroom US$4.50/6) All white and bright, these small, spartan rooms maintain an edge over more run-of-the-mill cheapies.

Hostal Moon Night (☎ 333-6174; Junín 899; s/d US$9/10.50, without bathroom US$4.50/6) Five skinny floors of bare, faux-wood-lined abodes with hot water and cable TV. Grab a quieter room on top for city views.

Hospedaje San Carlos (☎ 20-1059; Ayacucho 627; s/d US$7.50/10.50) Winning the budget stakes by a nose, this smiley *hospedaje* has immaculate, trim rooms with TV.

Los Jardines (☎ 32-6590; Los Cocos 436; s/d US$9/13.50) In a smart residential area, this family-owned hostelry proffers enormous rooms with TVs. There is also a shared garden and laundry facilities.

Hotel Peru (☎ 33-3421; Arequipa 476; s/d US$11.70/ 17.40, d with air-con US$24.40; ⚋) Worth its weight in soles, this place has a bamboo lounge, elegant restaurant with unfortunate gold fixtures, and spacious rooms with hot water and TVs.

Algarrobo Inn (☎ 30-7450; Los Cocos 389; s/d US$13.50/15, r with air-con US$24, all incl breakfast; ⚋ ⚋) In a walled compound with grass and shade, rooms are just OK, but include access to the Club Grau swimming pool next door.

Eating & Drinking

Nearby Catacaos has dozens of lunchtime *picanterías* for trying local specialties like *seco de chabelo* (beef stew with plantains), *seco de cabrito* (goat stew), *tamales verdes* (green-corn dumplings) and *copus* (vinegar-cured goat heads stewed with vegetables).

Heladería El Chalan (items US$1.50-3) Grau (Grau 173); Grau monument (Grau 453); Tacna (Tacna 520) These fast-food outlets whip up fresh juices and a dozen cool flavors of ice cream.

Ganimedes (Lima 440; menú US$1.50, mains US$2-3; ⏱ 7am-10pm Mon-Sat, 11am-9pm Sun) A magnet for patchouli-scented dreadlock types, this hippie hangout sticks diligently to its vegetarian pledge.

Snack Bar Romano (Ayacucho 580; menú US$1.70, mains US$2.10-5.70; ⏱ 7am-11pm Mon-Sat) A local fave that's

PERU

been around as long as its waiters. Thumbs-up for the *ceviche* and other Peruvian specialties.

Matteos (Tacna 532; meals US$2.40-3.60; 🕑 7am-10pm) On the Plaza de Armas, Matteos serves I-can't-believe-it's-not-meat versions of local Peruvian dishes, salads and heaping plates of fruit and yogurt.

Capuccino (Libertad 1048; sandwiches US$2.40-3.60; 🕑 10am-2pm & 5-11pm) This place is excellent for coffee, desserts, frozen fruit juices and massive sandwiches.

Peru a la Carta (Tacna 786; meals US$3-5.40; 🕑 8:30am-10pm) Barely upmarket Peruvian restaurant in a cavernous building with artistic touches.

Entertainment

Cine Planet (☎ 30-3714; Huancavelica 537) Shows Hollywood flicks in blissful air-conditioning.

Art Rock Café (Apurímac 343; 🕑 6pm-late Thu-Sun) A modish, wood-ensconced watering hole with live music and pool and foosball tables.

Queens (cnr Guardia Civil & Cayeta; admission US$4.50; 🕑 9pm-late Thu-Sun) If you need to shake your rump, head down to Queens – not in New York, but just east of town.

Getting There & Away

AIR

The **airport** (PIU; ☎ 34-4505) is 2km southeast of the city center. **LAN** (☎ 30-2145; Grau 140) has daily flights to/from Lima and Chiclayo. **Aero Condor Perú** (☎ 31-3668; Libertad 777) has daily flights to/from Lima.

BUS

Buses go to Lima (US$15 to US$38, 12 to 16 hours) with **Cruz del Sur** (☎ 33-7094; Bolognesi at Lima), **Tepsa** (☎ 073-30-6345; Loreto 1198), Linea and Ittsa.

For other destinations:

El Dorado (☎ 32-5875; S Cerro 1119) For Tumbes (US$4.50, five hours).

El Sol Peruano (☎ 41-8143; S Cerro 1112) For Tarapoto (US$4.50, 18 hours).

Eppo (☎ 30-4543; Cerro 1141) To Máncora (US$3.60, 3½ hours, hourly).

Ittsa (☎ 33-3982; Cerro 1142) To Trujillo (US$3.30), Chimbote (US$7.20, seven hours) and by *bus-cama* to Lima.

Linea (☎ 32-7821; Cerro 1215) Hourly to Chiclayo (US$3.60, three hours) and twice daily to Cajamarca (US$11 to US$14.50, 10 hours).

Transportes Chiclayo (☎ 30-8455; S Cerro 1121) Hourly to Chiclayo (US$3.60, three hours) and daily to Tumbes (US$4.50, five hours).

For Cajamarca and the northern Andes, it's best to connect in Chiclayo (p908).

Combis for Catacaos (US30¢, 15 minutes) leave from Piura's Terminal Terrestre on the 1200 block of Cerro.

MÁNCORA

☎ 073 / pop 10,000

Thanks to year-round sunshine, this beach resort may be Peru's worst-kept secret. During summer, surfers and other foreigners

---

SHOPPING FOR SHAMANS

Here's a trip for daring adventurers. Deep in the eastern mountains, Huancabamba is famous for the powerful *brujos* (witch doctors) and *curanderos* (healers) that live at the nearby lakes of Huaringas. The town itself is surrounded by mountains shrouded in mist. Because the eroding banks of the Río Huancabamba are unstable, the town is frequently subject to slippage, earning itself the nickname *la ciudad que camina* (the town that walks). Spooky.

Peruvians from all walks of life come to visit the lake district's shamans and often pay sizable amounts of money for their mystical services. They are supposed to cure an endless list of ailments, from headaches to cancer to chronic bad luck, and are particularly popular in matters of the heart – whether it's love lost, found, desired or scorned.

Ceremonies may last all night and entail hallucinogenic plants like the San Pedro cactus, as well as singing, chanting, dancing, and a dip in the freezing lake waters. Some ceremonies involve more powerful substances like *ayahuasca* (Quechua for 'vine of the soul'), a potent and vile mix of jungle vines. Vomiting is a common side effect.

Combis leave Huancabamba, a 10-hour bus trip from Piura (US$6), before dawn for Salala, from where horses and mules can be arranged to reach the famous lakes. Many locals (but few gringos) visit the area, so finding guides isn't difficult. Watch out for scam artists – try to get a reference beforehand. Expect to pay US$60 for a shaman visit. Be warned that this tradition is taken very seriously, and gawkers or skeptics will get a hostile reception.

GETTING TO ECUADOR

The route via La Tina/Macará to Loja, Ecuador, is more scenic but less popular than going via Tumbes (p912).

Buses and *combis* for Sullana (US60¢, 45 minutes) leave from Piura's Terminal El Castillo, east of the San Miguel pedestrian bridge. From Sullana, the border post of La Tina is reached by *colectivo* taxis (US$4.50, two hours) departing throughout the day. **Transportes Loja** (☎ 074-30-9407; S Cerro 228) has a few convenient daily buses that go direct from Piura to Macará (US$3.60, four hours) and on to Loja (US$8.40, eight hours).

Formalities are fairly relaxed at the 24-hour border by the international Río Calvas bridge. There are no banks, but money changers at the border and in Macará, Ecuador, will change cash. Taxis and *colectivos* take travelers entering Ecuador to Macará (3km), where the Ecuadorian immigration building is found on the 2nd floor of the Municipalidad on the plaza (stop there for entry stamps). If you're riding the international Transportes Loja bus, you don't have to get off during formalities.

To enter Peru from Ecuador, see p697.

---

flock here to rub sunburnt shoulders with the frothy cream of the Peruvian jet set. From December to March the scene gets deliriously rowdy – and accommodations rates skyrocket.

Information

The website www.vivamancora.com has useful tourist information. There's no bank, but you'll find Visa/MasterCard ATMs. Exchange US dollars cash at **Banco de la Nación** (☎ 25-8193; Piura 625). **Marlon** (☎ 073-25-2437; Piura 520) sells phonecards and provides internet access.

Activities

You can go **surfing** year-round, but the best waves hit from November to February. Rent surfboards at the beach's southern end. **Soledad** (☎ 929-1356; Piura 316) offers surf lessons. Some budget hotels teach surfing and kiteboarding, too.

To explore more deserted beaches, **Máncora Rent** (☎ 25-8351; Hospedaje Las Terrazas, Piura 496) rents off-road motorbikes/smaller quad bikes (US$4.50/20 per hour) and jet-skis (US$30 per half hour). For transportation with a mind of its own, horses are available for hire along Máncora's beach (US$6 per hour).

About 11km east of town, some bubbling natural **hot springs** (admission US60¢) supposedly have curative properties, plus powder-fine mud perfect for a facial. Take a *mototaxi* (US$9, including wait time). You can also hire a pickup truck to take you further up the Fernandez Valley past the mud baths to road's end, where a two-hour woodlands hike leads to the Los Pilares pools for swimming.

Sleeping & Eating

Cheap sleeps are mostly found in the center and at the beach's southern end. If you love seafood, you'll be happy. If not, there ain't much else.

HI La Posada (☎ 25-8328; Km1164 Panamericana; camping per person US$1.50, dm US$4.50, s without bathroom US$7.50, d US$35) Safe; has a garden, hammocks, basic kitchen and stilt restaurant.

Laguna Camp (☎ 01-9401-5628; www.vivamancora .com/lagunacamp; r per person US$6) Laid-back Laguna has Indonesian-style bamboo bungalows between a lagoon and the ocean.

Del Wawa (☎ 25-8427; www.delwawa.com; s/d US$15/ 30) The surfer's mecca; has a great setup right on the beach, with adobe rooms facing the ocean.

Green Eggs & Ham (Piura 112; meals US$3; ⏰ 7:30am-1pm) A little beachfront shack for scrumptious breakfasts.

El Faro Lounge (Piura 233; meals US$1.80-6; ⏰ 6-11pm) Has a goodie-box menu of gastronomical specimens, from grilled fish and meats to wontons.

Punto Pollo (Piura 609; meals from US$2.10; ⏰ 6pm-midnight) is arguably the best *pollería* in town – and who are we to argue? **Jugería Mi Janett** (Piura 250; juices US30-90¢; ⏰ 7am-2:30pm & 5:30-10pm) is another fave.

Getting There & Away

Most southbound coastal buses headed for Lima originate in Tumbes (p913). Frequent *combis* for Tumbes (US$1.80, two hours) drive along Máncora's main drag.

PERU

TUMBES

☎ 072 / pop 128,500

Near the Ecuadorian border, mosquito-ridden Tumbes is where dry deserts magically turn into mangroves. A swath of ecological reserves stretches in all directions. It's not a bad place to stop and catch your breath.

Information

BCP (Bolívar 261) Changes traveler's checks; has an ATM.
Clínica Feijoo (☎ 52-5341; Mariscal Castilla 305) Recommended.
Ecuadorian consulate (☎ 52-5949; Bolívar 129, 3rd fl) On the Plaza de Armas.
Ministerio de Turismo (☎ 52-3699; Bolognesi 194, 2nd fl; ☽ 7:30am-1pm & 2-4:30pm Mon-Fri)
Plaz@Net (Bolívar 161; ☽ 8am-11pm) For internet.
Serpost (San Martín 208) South of Plaza Bolognesi.

Tours

Offering tours (US$10 to US$30) to nearby beaches, ecological reserves etc:
Cocodrilos Tours (☎ 52-4133; Huáscar 309)
Preference Tours (☎ 52-4757; Grau 427).

Sleeping

Most rooms have fans, handy for repelling mozzies. Due to cross-border traffic, hotels are often full and single rooms difficult to find. Expect frequent electricity outages and water shortages. Many places are cold water only.

Hospedaje Chicho (☎ 52-2282; Tumbes 327; s/d US$7.50/10.50) A clean and central choice, with hot showers, cable TV, minifridges, telephones and mosquito nets upon request.

Turismo Inversiones Cesar (☎ 52-2883; Huáscar 311; s/d US$12/15) A gregarious owner, warm colors and creaky polished floorboards give this *hostal* a lived-in appeal. The rooms all-have TVs.

Hostal Lourdes (☎ 52-2966; Mayor Bodero 118; s/d US$12/18) Clean, safe and friendly, Lourdes includes a top-floor restaurant among its many amenities. Although rooms are austere, they've got hot water, fans, cable TV and phones.

Hostal Roma (☎ 52-4137; hotelromatumbes@hotmail .com; Bolognesi 425; s/d US$13.50/19.50) A modern hotel with prime plaza real estate, here comfy rooms have hot showers, fans, phones and cable TV.

Other no-frills options:
Hospedaje Italia (☎ 52-3396; Grau 733; d US$7.50) Well lit.
Hospedaje Tumbes (☎ 52-2203; Grau 614; s/d US$5.70/8.70) Fairly dark, but welcoming.
Hospedaje Amazonas (☎ 52-5266; Tumbes 317; s/d US$6/9) Has a TV lounge; spacious.
Hospedaje Franco (☎ 52-5295; San Martín 107; s/d US$7.50/10.50) Quiet.

Eating

The plaza has bars and restaurants with shaded tables for watching the world go by.

Restaurant Sí Señor (Bolívar 115; menú US$1.50, meals US$3-3.90; ☽ 7:30am-2am) With quixotically slow-turning fans, Sí Señor serves traditional Peruvian fare.

Las Terrazas (Andres Araujo 549; meals US$3-5.40; ☽ 9am-8pm) A terrace restaurant serving heaping plates of *ceviche* or freshly cooked seafood, anything

---

GETTING TO ECUADOR

The Peruvian border town of Aguas Verdes is linked by an international bridge across the Río Zarumilla with the Ecuadorian border town of Huaquillas. Shady practices have earned this the dubious title of 'worst border crossing in South America.'

For the best rates, change nuevos soles into US dollars while still in Peru. There are no entry fees into Ecuador, so be polite but insistent with any border guards trying their luck.

From Tumbes, *colectivo* taxis (US90¢, 25 minutes) and minibuses (US50¢, 40 minutes) leave from the intersection of Abad Puell and Tumbes for the border, 26km away. It's best to take a direct bus with **Cifa** (☎ 072-52-7120; Tumbes 572) to Machala, Ecuador (US$2, two hours) or Guayaquil (US$5, five hours), departing every two hours.

The Peruvian immigration office in Aguas Verdes is open 24 hours. On public transportation, make sure you stop there for border formalities. *Mototaxis* will then whisk you to the border (US50¢). About 3km to the north of the bridge, Ecuadorian immigration is also open 24 hours. Take a taxi from the bridge (US$1). There are basic hotels in Huaquillas, but most people catch an onward bus to Machala, Ecuador.

To enter Peru from Ecuador, see p725.

from lobster to octopus, with live folk music on weekends. Take a *mototaxi* (US30¢).

Classic Restaurant (Tumbes 185; mains US$3.30-5.50; 🕑 8am-5pm; 🛇) This small, dignified eatery is a great escape from the rest of torrid Tumbes. Linger over a long lunch of northern coastal fare with in-the-know locals.

Getting There & Away

AIR

The **airport** (TBP; ☎ 52-5102) is 8km north of town (taxi US$4.50). **Aero Condor Perú** (☎ 52-4835; Grau 454) has daily flights to/from Lima.

BUS & COLECTIVO

Most bus companies are on Av Tumbes. Buy tickets to Lima (US$17 to US$45, 16 to 18 hours) in advance. **Cruz del Sur** (☎ 52-6200; Tumbes 319) offers the most luxurious overnight *bus-cama* service to Lima. Many Lima-bound buses stop at Piura (US$4.50, five hours), Chiclayo (US$6, eight hours), Trujillo (US$7.50 to US$21, 10 hours) and other intermediate stops. *Combis* to Máncora (US$1.80, two hours) leave from the market.

HUARAZ & THE CORDILLERAS

Huaraz is the nerve center of one of South America's premier trekking, mountain biking and climbing areas. The mountainous region of the Cordilleras Blanca and Huayhuash is where superlatives crash and burn in a brazen attempt to capture its awesome natural beauty. Glaciated peaks razor their way through expansive mantles of jade valleys, and in the recesses of these prodigious Andean giants huddle scores of pristine lakes, ice caves and torrid springs. This is the highest mountain range in the world outside of the Himalayas, a fact that its 22 ostentatious summits over 6000m will not let you forget for a second.

HUARAZ

☎ 043 / pop 88,300

The restless capital of this Andean adventure kingdom was nearly wiped out by the earthquake of 1970. Now the streets buzz with the adrenaline-fueled activity of hundreds of adventurers, especially during the dry season (from May to September). An endless line-up of guesthouses, restaurants and bars keeps everything hopping long after tents have been put away to dry.

Information

EMERGENCY

Casa de Guías (☎ 42-1811; Plaza Ginebra 28-G; 🕑 7-11am & 5-11pm) Arranges mountain rescues (purchase insurance before leaving home).
Policía de Turismo (☎ 42-1341; 🕑 8am-1pm Mon-Sat, 5-8pm Mon-Fri) Located on an alley on the west side of the Plaza de Armas.

INTERNET ACCESS

Cybercafés cluster on Plaza Ginebra and the corresponding block of Luzuriaga.

LAUNDRY

Also offering dry-cleaning:
B&B/Pressmatic (José de la Mar 674)
Lavandería Dennys (José de la Mar 561)

MEDICAL SERVICES

Clínica San Pablo (☎ 72-8811; Huaylas 172; 🕑 24hr) North of town. Some English spoken.
Farmacia Recuay (☎ 72-1391; Luzuriaga 497) Restocks expedition medical kits.

MONEY

BCP (Luzuriaga 691) Visa ATM and no commission on traveler's checks.
Interbank (José Sucre 687) Global ATM.
Oh NaNa (Plaza de Armas) This *casa de cambio* changes US dollars and euros.

POST

Serpost (Luzuriaga 702)

TOURIST INFORMATION

Lonely Planet's *Trekking in the Central Andes* covers the best hikes in the Cordilleras Blanca and Huayhuash.
iPerú (☎ 42-8812; Oficina 1, Plaza de Armas, Pasaje Atusparia; 🕑 8am-6:30pm Mon-Sat, 8:30am-2pm Sun)

Dangers & Annoyances

Recently there's been a series of armed muggings of tourists on day trips near Huaraz and while trekking in the Cordilleras. Inquire locally about current conditions before you head off sightseeing or hiking. Consider hiring an escort for greater safety.

Sights

The **Museo Regional de Ancash** (Plaza de Armas; adult/student US$1.70/1.10; 🕑 8am-6:30pm) has small

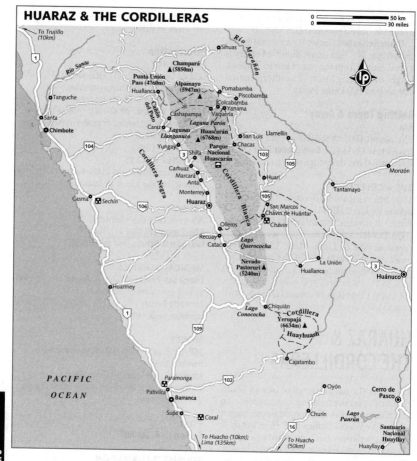

HUARAZ & THE CORDILLERAS

but interesting archaeology exhibits. **Monumento Nacional Wilcahuaín** (adult/student US$1.40/60¢; 8am-5pm) is a small but well-preserved Wari site with a three-story temple. The two-hour walk from town may be dangerous; take a taxi (US$3) or look for *combis* by the Río Quilcay.

Activities

TREKKING & MOUNTAINEERING

The best treks are in the **Cordillera Blanca** inside Parque Nacional Huascarán (p918) and in the Cordillera Huayhuash (p920). All the equipment and help you need can be hired or bought, including trail maps, guidebooks, pack animals, *arrieros* (drivers) and local guides. Expect to pay around US$30 to US$50

per person per day for an all-inclusive trek or climbing expedition. Always inspect rental gear carefully.

Check certified guides and register before heading out at **Casa de Guías** (p913). Reputable outfitters:

Galaxia Expeditions (☎ 42-5691; Cáceres 428)
Montañero (☎ 42-6386; Parque Ginebra)
Monttrek (☎ 42-1124; monttrek@terra.com.pe; Luzuriaga 646, 2nd fl)
MountClimb (☎ 42-6060; Cáceres 421)
Skyline Adventures (☎ 964-9480; www.sladventure school.com) Based outside Huaraz.

ROCK CLIMBING

You'll find great bolted sport climbs in the Cordillera Blanca, particularly at Chancos (near Marcará), Monterrey, and Recuay. For big-wall action to keep you chalked up for days, head to the famous Torre de Parón (aka the Sphinx) at Laguna Parón, 32km east of Caraz. Many trekking agencies offer rock-climbing trips and rent gear. Galaxia Expeditions has an indoor climbing wall, too.

MOUNTAIN BIKING
Mountain Bike Adventures (☎ 42-4259; www.chakinaniperu.com; Lúcar y Torre 530, 2nd fl) has been in business for over a decade. It has a good safety record and selection of bikes. The English-speaking owner is a lifelong resident of Huaraz who knows the region's single-track better than anyone. Rates start at US$20 per day for equipment rental, US$30 for guided tours. Ask about more challenging 12-day circuits of the Cordillera Blanca.

Tours
One bus tour visits the ruins at Chavín de Huantar, another goes through Yungay to the beautiful Lagunas Llanganuco, where there are spectacular views of Huascarán; a third takes you through Caraz to scenic Laguna Parón, and a fourth goes to see the extraordinary giant *Puya raimondii* plant (which can take 100 years to grow to its full height – often 10m!) and the mineral springs at Nevado Pastoruri. Full-day tours cost US$8 to US$12, excluding entry fees. Guides may not speak English.

Recommended agencies:
Huaraz Chavín Tours (☎ 42-1578; Luzuriaga 502)
Pablo Tours (☎ 42-1145; Luzuriaga 501)
Sechín Tours (☎ 42-1419; www.sechintours.com; Morales 602)

Festivals & Events
Semana Santa (Holy Week) In March/April, tongue-in-cheek funeral processions for *Ño Carnavalón* (King of Carnaval) are on Ash Wednesday.
El Señor de la Soledad Huaraz pays homage to its patron saint during this festival, with fireworks, music, dancing, costume parades and lots of drinking, in early May.
Semana de Andinismo International mountaineering exhibitions and competitions in June.

Sleeping
Locals meet buses to offer rooms in their houses, and *hostales* do the same. Don't pay until you've seen the room.
Caroline Lodging (☎ 42-6398; carolinelodging@yahoo.com; Urb Avitentel Mz-D, Lt 1; dm/r US$3/12) Beyond

the west end of 28 de Julio and down a flight of stairs, this delightful homestay offers hot-water showers, kitchen, TV lounge and mountain views. Call ahead for pick-ups.
Familia Meza Lodging (☎ 42-6763; Lucar y Torre 538; s/d without bathroom US$4.50/9) A charming family guesthouse with cheery rooms, hot showers, a small kitchen and owners kind enough to cure the worst bouts of homesickness.
Jo's Place (☎ 42-5505; www.huaraz.com/josplace; Villayzan 278; dm US$4.50, s/d US$6/10.50) A slightly chaotic place with a huge grassy area (camping allowed); four floors linked by spindly staircases lead to a warren of basic rooms, some with bathrooms. English expat Jo provides UK newspapers and bacon-and-eggs breakfasts.
Way Inn (☎ 42-8714; www.thewayinn.com; Buenaventura Mendoza 821; dm US$5, d US$12-15) Run by the friendly UK team of Alex and Bruni, this decent guesthouse has a rooftop terrace thrown in for good measure. Ask about staying at their remote Way Inn Lodge, peacefully nestled in the Cordillera Blanca.
Alojamiento Soledad (☎ 42-1196; www.cordillera-adventure.com; Figueroa 1267; s/d US$6/12; 🖳) The English- and German-speaking owners of this cozy guesthouse offer a book exchange, free internet, kitchen and laundry, cable TV and a rooftop terrace with a BBQ. Most rooms have private hot-water showers.
Albergue Churup (☎ 42-2584; www.churup.com; Figueroa 1257; dm US$6-7, s/d incl breakfast US$16/25) A freshly renovated, ultrapopular hotel with a pretty garden, fireplace lounge with mountain views, book exchange, sauna, café-bar, kitchen and laundry. Reservations advised.
Olaza's Guest House (☎ 42-2529; info@andeanexplorer.com; Arguedas 1242; s/d US$10.50/16.50) A small, spotless guesthouse with excellent hot showers, book exchange, laundry and wonderful views from the rooftop terrace – a great place to wolf down breakfast (from US$2.50). Reserve ahead for pick-ups.
B&B My House (☎ 42-3375; bmark@ddm.com.pe; 27 de Noviembre 773; s/d incl breakfast US$13.50/21) This hospitable B&B has a bright little patio and homey rooms with hot showers and writing desks. English and French spoken.

Also recommended:
Hostal Gyula Inn (☎ 42-1567; www.hostalgy.on.to; Plaza Ginebra 632; s/d US$6/9) Set on a quiet, central plaza; hot showers.
Hostal Tany (☎ 42-7680; Lucar y Torre 648; s/d US$6/9; 🖳) Bright rooms with massive windows.

PERU

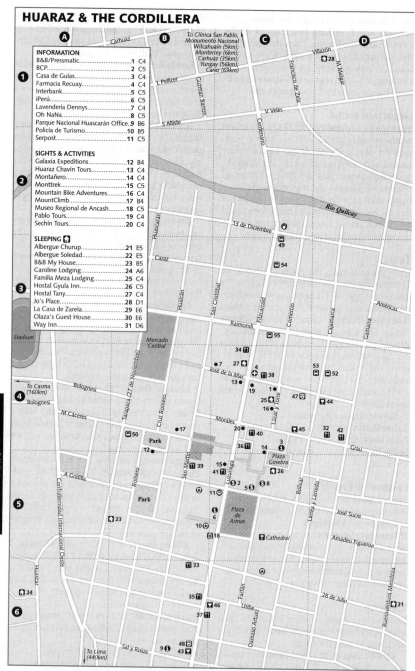

HUARAZ & THE CORDILLERA

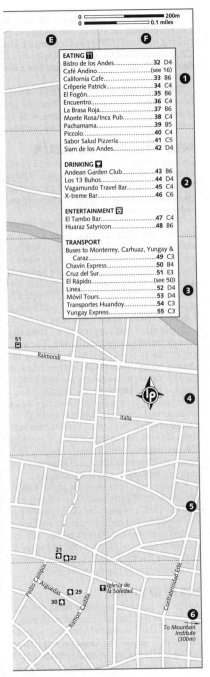

La Casa de Zarela (☎ 42-1694; www.lacasadeza rela.com; Arguedas 1263; s/d US$7.50/15) Zarela's helpfulness is legendary. Hot showers and kitchen access.

Eating

Café Andino (Lucar y Torre 530, 3rd fl; all-day breakfasts US$1.80-5.40) The best java joint in town is also Huaraz's ultimate hangout, with great mountain vistas, groovy tunes, board games and a library of maps and guidebooks.

Pachamama (San Martín 687; snacks & mains US$1.80-7) This glass-roofed, plant-filled Peruvian-Swiss restaurant and bar features art, a pool table, ping-pong and a giant chessboard. Some weekends there's live music and dancing (*not folklórico!*).

California Cafe (28 de Julio 562; meals US$1.90-5.40; 🕒 7:30am-7pm) This authentically Californian-run space infused by world music serves all-day breakfasts, light lunches and salads, rich espresso drinks and herbal teas. There's a book exchange and wi-fi internet access.

Sabor Salud Pizzería (Luzuriaga 672, 2nd fl; mains US$2-5) 'Flavor and Health' are the bywords for this vegetarian *pizzería*, which also makes spinach lasagna, soy burgers, yogurt and fruit salads, and more.

El Fogón (Luzuriaga 928, 2nd fl; mains US$2.40-4.50; 🕒 noon-11pm) An upscale twist on the traditional Peruvian grill house, this place will flame anything that moves – including chicken, trout, great *anticuchos* (kebabs) and rabbit.

Encuentro (Luzuriaga 6th block; mains US$2.70-5.40; 🕒 9am-11pm) This popular eatery has a niche market in well-prepared Peruvian cuisine, including everyone's favorite Andean delicacy, *cuy*.

Bistro de los Andes (Morales 823; mains US$5.50; 🕒 6-10pm Mon, 7am-10pm Tue-Sun) Only open in high season, this elegant French restaurant does fabulous fish dishes and delectable desserts.

Mercado Ortiz (Luzuriaga at Raimondi) Ideal for self-caterers.

Also recommended:

Crêperie Patrick (Luzuriaga 422; mains US$5) French-influenced crêpes, plus a morning rooftop patio.

La Brasa Roja (Luzuriaga 919; mains US$3-6.60; 🕒 noon-midnight Mon-Sat) Scrumptious *pollería* for posttrekking protein refueling.

Monte Rosa/Inca Pub (José de la Mar 661; mains US$5.50-11.50) Excellent Alpine vibe, with Swiss fondue and raclette.

Piccolo (Morales 632; mains US$3.30-7.50; 🕒 7am-midnight) Sidewalk café, *pizzería*, Peruvian and international restaurant, all in one.

Siam de los Andes (Gamarra 560; mains US$7.50-11.50) Superb Thai food (including vegetarian) worth the price tag.

Drinking

Huaraz is the best spot in the Peruvian Andes to take a load off and get pleasantly buzzed.

X-treme Bar (cnr Uribe & Luzuriaga; ☺ dusk-late) This classic watering hole hasn't changed in years. Bizarre art, drunken graffiti, strong cocktails and loud rock and blues keep things rambunctious.

Also recommended:

Andean Garden Club (Luzuriaga 1032; ☺ 11am-6pm, high season only) Climb the walls, literally.

Los 13 Buhos (José de la Mar 812, 2nd fl; ☺ 5pm-late) Comfy chill-out couches.

Vagamundo Travel Bar (Morales 753; ☺ hours vary) Foosball and beer.

Entertainment

There are plenty of bars, discos and *peñas* (bars featuring folkloric music) around, though names and popularity change with the seasons.

El Tambo Bar (José de la Mar 776; ☺ 9am-4pm) The longest lasting of the dance clubs, fashionable El Tambo plays everything from techno-cumbia to pop, with salsa and reggaeton to spice things up. Drinks are astronomically priced.

Huaraz Satyricon (☎ 955-7343; Luzuriaga 1036) This place may just be the world's most perfect little cinema: intimate sofas, fresh popcorn, snacks, espresso and quality international and arthouse flicks.

Getting There & Away

Many bus companies have midmorning or late-evening departures for Lima (US$6 to US$16.50, seven to eight hours). **Cruz del Sur** (☎ 42-8726; Bolívar 491) has nonstop luxury services. **Móvil Tours** (☎ 42-2555; Bolívar 542) is also comfortable.

Most buses to Chimbote (US$6 to US$12, seven to nine hours) use the paved road to the Panamericana via Pativilca, though rougher rides via the spectacular Cañón del Pato or 4225m-high Punta Callán are worth seeing. **Linea** (☎ 42-6666; Bolívar 450) and Móvil Tours go direct to Chimbote, continuing to Trujillo (US$9 to US$13.50, nine to ten hours). Daytime departures for the scenic routes are with **Transportes Huandoy** (☎ 42-7507; Fitzcarrald 261) and **Yungay Express** (☎ 42-4377; Raimondi 744).

Chavín Express (☎ 42-4652; Cáceres 338) goes to Chavín de Huántar (US$3, two hours), continuing to Huari (US$3.60, four hours). For Chiquián (US$2.40 to US$3.60, 2½ hours), **El Rápido** (☎ 72-2887; cnr Cáceres & Tarapaca) has a few daily buses.

Daytime minibuses for Caraz (US$1.40, 1½ hours) depart frequently from near the gas station on 13 de Diciembre. Brave, beat-up buses go to many other villages: ask around.

PARQUE NACIONAL HUASCARÁN

Encompassing almost the entire area of the Cordillera Blanca above 4000m, this 3400 sq km park is bursting with picturesque emerald lakes, brightly colored alpine wildflowers and red *quenua* trees.

The most popular backpacking circuit, the four-day **Santa Cruz** trek, takes four days and rises to the Punta Unión pass (4760m), which arguably has the best Andean views in Peru. The trail, which passes by icy waterfalls and lakes, mossy meadows and verdant valleys, is well marked. *Colectivo* taxis frequently leave from Caraz for the main trailhead at Cashapampa (US$1.80, 1½ hours).

Many other trails are available, from day hikes to ambitious two-week treks. The scenery is just as jaw-dropping, but minus the crowds. Many routes aren't clearly marked, so go with a guide or take along top-notch topographic maps. **Laguna 69** is a beautiful overnight trek dripping with marvelous lake views, while several other routes traipse through the **Conchucos Valley**. In Huaraz, the **Mountain Institute** (☎ 043-42-3446; www.mountain.org; Ricardo Palma 100) has information on the developing Inca Naani trail between Huari and Huanuco that supports grassroots tourism initiatives.

Register with your passport at the **park office** (☎ 043-42-2086; Sal y Rosas 555) in Huaraz and pay the park entrance fee (US$1.50/20 per day/month). You can also register and pay at control stations, but their locations and operating hours vary. Don't dodge or begrudge paying the fee: the Cordillera Blanca is one of the most amazing places on the planet.

NORTH OF HUARAZ

As the Río Santa slices its way north through El Callejón de Huaylas, a paved road passes several subdued towns to Caraz, and onto the menacingly impressive **Cañón del Pato**. Many hiking trailheads are accessible from towns along this route, and two unsealed roads valiantly cross the Cordillera, one via Chacas and another via Yungay.

Monterrey to Carhuaz

Six kilometres north of Huaraz is **Monterrey**, popular for **hot springs** (admission US90¢; 6am-6pm). There are several touristy hotels and restaurants. Catch a local bus from Huaraz (US30¢, 15 minutes) or take a taxi (US$1.50).

Another 10km further along, the village of **Taricá** is known for its pottery. About 25km north of Huaraz, past a miniscule airport, is the hamlet of **Marcará**, from where minibuses and trucks leave regularly for the hot springs and natural saunas at **Chancos** (admission US30¢-$1.50), 4km east.

Carhuaz, 35km north of Huaraz, has a colorful Sunday market. Its wild festival of **La Virgen de La Merced** is celebrated for 10 days during mid-September with processions, fireworks, dancing, bullfights and plenty of drinking. Rudimentary, family-run *hostales* have simple, clean rooms with hot showers, costing from US$4.50/6 per single/double. Eateries line the Plaza de Armas, where you can catch minibuses to Huaraz (US80¢, 50 minutes), Yungay (US30¢, 30 minutes) and Caraz (US$1.10, 45 minutes).

Yungay

043 / pop 11,300

The rubble-strewn area of old Yungay is the site of the single worst natural disaster in the Andes. The earthquake of 1970 loosened 15 million cubic meters of granite and ice, and almost all of the town's 18,000 inhabitants were buried. New Yungay has been rebuilt just beyond the avalanche path.

Hostal Gledel (39-3048; s/d US$3/4.50) has over a dozen impossibly cute, spartan rooms rented out by the gregarious Señora Gamboa. Expect at least one hug and sample of her cooking during your stay.

Minibuses go to Huaraz (US$1.10, 1¼ hours) via Carhuaz (US30¢, 30 minutes).

Lagunas Llanganuco

A dirt road climbs through the valley to two stunning **lakes**, Laguna Chinancocha and Laguna Orconcocha, 28km east of Yungay. Nestled in a glacial valley below the snow line, these pristine lagoons practically glow with bright turquoise and emerald hues. There's a 1½-hour nature trail hugging Chinacocha,

passing rare *polylepis* trees. You can rent small boats at this lake – it's a popular day-tripping spot. National park entry costs US$1.50. During high season (June to August), frequent minibuses leave from Yungay, stopping for two hours around the lakes (round trip US$5). Trips during other months depend on demand. *Colectivo* taxis cost US$3 each way. You can also take a tour from Huaraz (p915).

Caraz

043 / pop 11,020

Trekking and hiking trails meander in all directions from this fetching little colonial town, 67km north of Huaraz. It has survived many an earthquake and landslide, and is the traditional end (or untraditional start point) of the Santa Cruz trek (opposite).

Bring cash with you, as there's no ATM. **Dan Clau** (Sucre 1122), on the Plaza de Armas, offers internet access.

Pony's Expeditions (79-1642; www.ponyexpeditions.com; José Sucre 1266; 8am-10pm) and **Apu Aventura** (9683-2740; www.apuaventura.com; Albergue Los Pinos) rent gear, sell maps and arrange trekking, horse-riding and climbing.

Albergue Los Pinos (39-1130; Parque San Martín 103; campsite per person US$3, s/d US$12/21, with shared bathroom US$6/12;) is an outstanding YHA-affiliated hostel in a massive mansion with garden courtyards, kitchen and laundry. Small, simple **Alojamiento Caballero** (043-39-1637; Villar 485; s/d without bathroom US$3/9) is a friendly, family-run place with views. **Hostal La Casona** (39-1334; Raimondi 319; s/d US$4.50/6, without bathroom US$3/4.50) has dark, windowless rooms, but an attractive patio. **Hostal Chavín** (043-79-1171; hostalchavin@latinmail.com; San Martín 1135; s/d US$7.50/10.50) has a knowledgeable owner and simple rooms with TVs and hot showers. Breakfast available.

A great place to grab an early breakfast, tiny little **Cafeteria El Turista** (San Martín 1127; breakfast US$1.40-2.10; 7am-noon & 5-8pm) is a one-woman show run by the exuberant Maria. It's filled with knickknacks, which are all for sale. A short walk from the town center, the stadium-sized **La Punta Grande** (Daniel Villar 595; meals US$1.50-3.30; 7am-7pm) is the place for a typical highland lunch. It has an encyclopedic menu serving dishes like *cuy* (guinea pig). **Café de Rat** (above Pony's Expeditions; meals US$1.80-4.50; pizzas US$6.30-8.40; 7am-11pm Mon-Sat) is an atmospheric, wood-beamed restaurant boasting a book exchange, darts, a fireplace and a bar. Buffet breakfast.

Minibuses to Yungay (US40¢, 15 minutes) and Huaraz (US$1.40, 1½ hours) leave from the station on the Carretera Central. *Colectivos* for Cashapampa (US$1.80, 1½ hours) leave from Ramón Castilla at Santa Cruz. Long-distance buses to Lima (US$6 to US$9, 10 to 12 hours) and Trujillo (US$13.50, 12 hours) go with **Móvil Tours** (☎ 39-1922; cnr Cordova & Santa Rosa) and other companies.

CHAVÍN DE HUÁNTAR

☎ 043 / pop 2900

Located near this small village are the ruins of **Chavín** (adult/student US$3.30/1.70; ☽ 8am-5pm), built between 1200 and 800 BC by one of the continent's oldest civilizations. The site contains highly stylized cultist carvings of a jaguar or puma, Chavín's principal deity, and of condors, snakes and humans undergoing mystical (often hallucinogenic) transformations. The site's snaking underground tunnels are an exceptional feat of 3000-year-old engineering, comprising a maze of alleys, ducts and chambers – it's worth hiring a guide. Look out for the exquisitely carved, daggerlike rock known as the Lanzón de Chavín.

Camping by the ruins is possible with the guard's permission. The reputation of the secure, popular **Hostal Inca** (☎ 45-4092; Plaza de Armas; s/d US$7.50/15) is as reliable as its hot showers, and it boasts very respectable rooms. **La Casona** (☎ 45-9004; Plaza de Armas 130; s/d US$7.50/15) is an old house with erratic hot water, but a beautiful courtyard. Some rooms have TVs or balconies. **Hotel Chavín** (☎ 45-4055; Inca Roca 141; s/d US$9/15) has modern rooms with hot water and TVs. Around the corner is its cheaper partner, the more-basic Hostal Chavín.

Restaurants close soon after sunset; most are along 17 de Enero or inside hotels.

Chávin Express buses go to Huaraz (US$3, two hours). See p915 for tours.

CORDILLERA HUAYHUASH

Often playing second fiddle to the Cordillera Blanca, the Huayhuash nevertheless has an equally impressive medley of glaciers, summits and lakes all packed into an area only 30km across. Increasing numbers of travelers are discovering this rugged and remote territory, where strenuous high passes over 4500m throw down the gauntlet to the hardiest of trekkers. The feeling of utter wilderness, particularly

along the unspoiled eastern edge, is a big draw. You are more likely to spot an Andean condor here than another tour group.

Several communities along the classic 10-day trekking circuit charge fees of US$3 to US$4. These fees go toward improving security for hikers and continuing conservation work. Please support local preservation efforts by paying your fees, carrying plenty of small bills and always asking for official receipts.

Chiquián

☎ 043 / pop 5000

This high-altitude village is the traditional gateway to the spectacular Cordillera Huayhuash. You can bypass it entirely by taking the new road to the trailhead at Llamac, which has basic *hospedajes* and campsites. Otherwise, limited supplies are available here.

Hotel Los Nogales (☎ 44-7121; hotel_nogales_chiquian@yahoo.com; Comercio 1301; s/d US$6/12, with shared bathroom US$3/6) is about three blocks from the plaza. Attractive rooms with hot showers surround a colonial-style courtyard. The more modern **Gran Hotel Huayhuash** (☎ 74-7049; Figueredo Amadeo 216; s/d US$6/12) has some rooms with cable TV, views and hot water, plus the town's best restaurant.

El Rápido (☎ 42-2887) and **Virgen Del Carmen** (☎ 44-7003) buses depart for Huaraz (US$2.40 to US$3.60, 2½ hours) from the Plaza de Armas at 5am and 2pm. **Turismo Cavassa** (☎ 44-7036; Bolognesi 421) has buses to Lima leaving at 9am daily (US$6, nine hours).

NORTHERN HIGHLANDS

Vast tracts of unexplored jungle and mountain ranges shrouded in mist guard the secrets of Peru's northern highlands, where Andean peaks and cloud forests stretch all the way from the coast to the deepest Amazon jungle. Interspersed with the relics of ancient warriors and Inca kings, these wild outposts are yet barely connected by disheveled, circuitous roads.

CAJAMARCA

☎ 076 / pop 135,000

The cobblestone colonial streets of Cajamarca testify to what was the beginning of the end for the powerful Incas. Today fertile farmlands carpet the entire valley, which turns even lusher during the rainy season. Those hills are also full of 'invisible gold,' subject to noxious extraction techniques that cause environmental pollution, as protested by *campesino* farmers.

Information

Internet cafés are abundant.

BCP (Lima at Apurímac) Changes traveler's checks and has a Visa/MasterCard ATM.

Clínica Limatambo (☎ 36-4241; Puno 265)

Dirección de Turismo (☎ 36-2903; El Complejo de Belén; ☒ 7:30am-1pm & 2:30-6pm Mon-Fri)

Information booth (Lima at Belén)

Interbank (2 de Mayo 546) On the Plaza de Armas; changes traveler's checks and has a global ATM.

Laundry Dandy (Puga 545) Convenient.

Serpost (Puga 668) Behind Iglesia de San Francisco.

Sights

The following central sights are officially open 9am to 1pm and 3pm to 6pm daily. They don't have addresses.

The only remaining Inca building here is **El Cuarto del Rescate** (Ransom Chamber; admission US$1.40). Despite the name, this is actually where Francisco Pizarro kept Inca Atahualpa prisoner before killing him off (see p823), not where the ransom was stored. Tickets include same-day admission to **El Complejo de Belén**, a sprawling 17th-century colonial complex with a small archaeology museum, and the **Museo de Etnografía**, with exhibits of traditional highland life.

Well worth visiting, the university-run **Museo Arqueológico** (Del Batán 289; admission free;

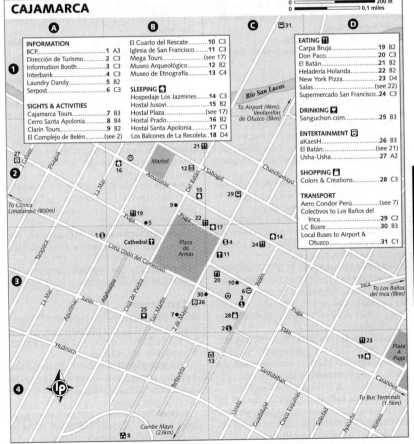

CAJAMARCA

0 ————— 200 m
0 ————— 0.1 miles

INFORMATION	
BCP..1 A3	
Dirección de Turismo............2 C3	
Information Booth...................3 C3	
Interbank.................................4 C3	
Laundry Dandy.......................5 B2	
Serpost....................................6 C3	

SIGHTS & ACTIVITIES
Cajamarca Tours......................7 B3
Cerro Santa Apolonia..............8 B4
Clarín Tours.............................9 B2
El Complejo de Belén.........(see 2)

El Cuarto del Rescate...........10 C3
Iglesia de San Francisco.......11 C3
Mega Tours.......................(see 17)
Museo Arqueológico............12 B2
Museo de Etnografía...........13 C4

SLEEPING
Hospedaje Los Jazmines.......14 C3
Hostal Jusovi........................15 B2
Hostal Plaza.....................(see 17)
Hostal Prado........................16 B2
Hostal Santa Apolonia.........17 C3
Los Balcones de La Recoleta..18 D4

EATING
Carpa Bruja...........................19 B2
Don Paco..............................20 C3
El Batán................................21 B2
Heladería Holanda................22 B2
New York Pizza.....................23 D4
Salas................................(see 22)
Supermercado San Francisco..24 C3

DRINKING
Sanguchon.com......................25 B3

ENTERTAINMENT
aKaesH..................................26 B3
El Batán...........................(see 21)
Usha-Usha.............................27 A2

SHOPPING
Colors & Creations...............28 C3

TRANSPORT
Aero Condor Perú...............(see 7)
Colectivos to Los Baños del Inca...29 C2
LC Busre................................30 B3
Local Buses to Airport & Otuzco.................................31 C1

Río San Lucas

To Airport (4km);
Ventanillas
de Otuzco (8km)

To Clínica
Limatambo (800m)

Market

Chanchamayo

Cathedral

Plaza
de
Armas

Inca
To Los Baños
del Inca (8km)

Huánuco

Plaza
A
Puga

To Bus Terminals
(1.5km)

Cumbe Mayo
(23km)

PERU

8am-2:30pm Mon-Fri) displays artifacts from pre-Inca Cajamarca culture. Facing the Plaza de Armas, **Iglesia de San Francisco** (admission US50¢; 9am-noon & 4-6pm Mon-Fri) has catacombs and a religious-art museum.

Hilltop **Cerro Santa Apolonia** (admission US30¢; 9am-1pm & 3-5pm), with its gardens and pre-Columbian carvings, overlooks the city. Climb the stairs at the end of 2 de Mayo.

Travel agents include **Mega Tours** (35-7793; Puga 691), **Cajamarca Tours** (36-5674; 2 de Mayo 323) and **Clarín Tours** (36-6829; Del Batán 161).

Festivals & Events

Carnaval (p939) Involves nine days of dancing, eating, singing, partying, costumes, parades and rowdy mayhem. And water fights here are worse (or better, depending on your point of view) than elsewhere. Hotels raise their rates and fill up weeks beforehand, so hundreds of visitors end up sleeping in the plaza.

Corpus Christi (p939) Also colorful.

Fiestas Patrias (p939) Celebrations on July 28 and 29 may include bullfighting.

Sleeping

Some cheapies are cold water only, but you can always head to Los Baños del Inca (opposite).

Hostal Plaza (36-2058; Puga 669; s/d US$7.50/10.50, without bathroom US$4.50/7.50) In a colorful, tattered building on the plaza, rooms are creaky and basic, but some have balconies with plaza views.

Hostal Prado (36-6093; La Mar 582; s/d US$12/21, without bathroom US$6/12) This well-kept property has a café, TVs and hot water all day.

Hostal Jusovi (36-2920; Amazonas 637; s/d US$9/15) What must be the smallest rooms in town are perfectly clean; some have cable TV. A rooftop terrace has cathedral views.

Hospedaje Los Jazmines (82-1812; assado@hotmail.com; Amazonas 775; s/d US$9/13.50, with bathroom US$12/18) This six-room German-run *hospedaje* isn't much to look at, but its hot showers, café and practice of hiring people with disabilities are commendable.

Los Balcones de La Recoleta (36-3302; Puga 1050; s/d US$10.50/21;) This 19th-century building has charismatic, rickety rooms surrounding a plant-filled courtyard. Hot showers, cable TV, comfortable beds and a small restaurant.

Hostal Santa Apolonia (36-7207; Puga 649; s/d US$15/24) The plaza's best budget hotel features smart rooms with solid mattresses, cable TVs, 24-hour hot water and minifridges.

Complejo Turístico Baños del Inca (34-8385; bungalow/albergue US$18/35) Worth a splurge, these spacious bungalows with minifridges and cable TV located behind Los Baños del Inca (opposite) have views of the water steaming Danté-esquely.

Eating & Drinking

Heladería Holanda (Puga 657; snacks US80¢-$2; 9am-7pm) A large, bright café selling northern Peru's best ice cream, plus creamy cappuccinos and homemade pies.

New York Pizza (Puga 1045; pizzas US$1.10-2.70; 4-11pm) They're not authentic NYC-style pies, but they're still ooey-gooey good.

Carpa Bruja (Puga 519; sandwiches US$1.50-4.20, meals US$4.50-7.50; noon-11pm) This slick, modern affair serves up gourmet sandwiches (on wholewheat ciabatta!), international dishes, lots of salads and plenty of yummy vegetarian options.

Don Paco (Puga 726; meals US$2.70-5.40; 8:30am-11pm) With a faithful following among locals and expats, there's something for everyone here: big breakfasts, Peruvian favorites and vegetarian delights.

Salas (Puga 637; mains US$3.30-5.70; 7am-10pm) This barn of a place on the Plaza de Armas has been a local favorite since 1947. Knowledgeable, elderly staff in white suits helps you navigate the extensive menu, with such local specialties as corn *tamales*, roasted goat and *sesos* (cow brains).

El Batán (Del Batán 369; menú US$4.50-9, mains US$4-6; 10am-11pm) This restaurant, art gallery, *peña* and cultural center serves Peruvian and international fare.

Sanguchon.com (Junín 1137; 6pm-late) The bar at this burger joint remains rowdy till the wee hours.

Supermercado San Francisco (Amazonas 780; 7am-8pm) For self-caterers.

Entertainment

aKaesH (2 de Mayo 334; 9pm-late) Roughly translated as 'here it is,' this popular, well-stocked bar has flashy retro styling and nightly events, from movies to live bands.

Usha-Usha (Puga 142; admission US$1.50; 9pm-late) A graffiti-covered hole-in-the-wall bar run by an eccentric musician, with strong drinks and live jazz most nights.

El Batán (Del Batán 369; to 11pm) Expect anything from live Andean folk music to Afro-Peruvian rhythms on weekend nights.

PERU

Shopping

Crafts are sold near the market and along Belén.

Colors & Creations (☎ 34-3875; Belén 628) A local artisan-run cooperative.

Getting There & Away

AIR

The **airport** (CJA; ☎ 36-2523) is 4km north of town. Local buses for Otuzco, leaving from 500m north of the plaza, pass the airport (US20¢); taxis are faster (US$1.50). **Aero Condor Perú** (☎ 36-2814/5674; 2 de Mayo 323) and **LC Busre** (☎ 36-1098; Lima 1024) have daily flights to/from Lima.

BUS

Most terminals are on the third block of Atahualpa, 1.5km southeast of town on the road to Los Baños del Inca.

Many companies have buses to Chiclayo (US$4.50 to US$9, six hours), Trujillo (US$4.50 to US$10.50, six hours) and Lima (US$9 to US$27, 14 hours). **Linea** (☎ 36-3956; Atahualpa 318) and **Ormeño** (☎ 36-9885; Independencia 304) have comfortable Lima-bound buses. Luxury *bus-camas* to Lima go with **Cruz del Sur** (☎ 36-1737; Via de Evitamiento 750), several kilometers further along the road.

Linea also has buses to Trujillo and Chiclayo. **El Cumbe** (☎ 36-3088; Atahualpa 300) has a few daily departures for Chiclayo. **Turismo Diaz** (☎ 36-8289; Sucre 422) goes via Chota, a wildly scenic alternative route to Chiclayo if you're not in a hurry.

A few companies go to Celendín (US$3, five hours). Beyond Celendín to Chachapoyas, transport is unreliable and the road is bad, if beautiful. It's easier to reach Chachapoyas from Chiclayo (see p907).

AROUND CAJAMARCA
Los Baños del Inca

Atahualpa was camped by these natural **hot springs** (admission US60¢; private baths per hr US90¢–$1.50, sauna or massage US$3; ⏰ 4:30am-8pm), 6km east of Cajamarca, before his fateful run-in with Pizarro. Show up early in the morning to avoid the rush. *Colectivos* for Los Baños del Inca leave frequently from along Sabogal, near 2 de Mayo (US20¢).

Cumbe Mayo

An astounding yet mysterious feat of pre-Inca engineering, these **aqueducts** run for several kilometers across the bleak mountaintops. Nearby are caves with petroglyphs, and the countryside is high, windswept and slightly eerie. The site can be reached on foot from Cerro Santa Apolonia (p921) via a signposted road. It's a four-hour walk, if you take shortcuts and ask locals for directions. Tours from Cajamarca cost US$5.

Ventanillas de Otuzco & Combayo

These pre-Inca necropolises have scores of **funerary niches** built into the hillside. You can walk to Otuzco from Cajamarca or Los Baños del Inca. Buses from Cajamarca leave from north of the main plaza (US60¢). Better-preserved *ventanillas* (windows) at Combayo, 30km from Cajamarca, are most easily visited on a tour (US$10).

CHACHAPOYAS
☎ 041 / pop 20,700

The unlikely capital of the Amazonas department, colonial Chachas is a busy market town. It's an ideal base for exploring the awesome ruins left behind by the fierce cloud forest–dwelling civilization that ruled here from 800 AD until the Incas came in the 1470s.

Information

Most of the following are on the Plaza de Armas, plus internet cafés and several shops changing dollars.

BCP (Plaza de Armas) Changes US dollars and traveler's checks, and has a Visa/MasterCard ATM.

iPerú (☎ 47-7292; Ortiz Arrieta 588; ⏰ 8am-7pm)

Lavandería Speed Clean (Ayachuco 964; ⏰ 7am-1pm & 2pm-10pm)

Serpost (Ortiz Arrieta 632) Just south of the plaza.

Sights & Activities

Travel agencies hover around the plaza. You'll pay from US$35 to US$45 for multiday treks, US$20 for day tours. **Chacahpoyas Tours** (☎ 47-8078; Hotel Plaza, Grau 534) and **Tourismo Explorer** (☎ 47-8060; cnr Amazonas & Grau) get good reviews, but ask around. The dry season (May to September) is best for hiking, including the five-day **Gran Vilaya** trek to the Valle de Belén or a three-day trip to **Laguna de los Cóndores** on foot and horseback.

Levanto is a small village that's a four-hour walk along an Inca road from Chachas. You can stay at **Levanto Lodge** (r per person US$6), which is built in the traditional style of a Chachapoyan roundhouse. **Colla Cruz** nearby is a

PERU

reconstructed thatched-roof building with round Chachapoyan walls on meticulous Inca stone foundations.

Sleeping

Hostal Johumaji (☎ 47-7279; Ayacucho 711; s US$4.50, d US$7.50-12) Small, spartan but tidy and well-lit rooms have electric hot showers and rental TVs (US$1.50).

Hotel El Dorado (☎ 47-7047; Ayacucho 1062; s/d US$6/9) An older house with clean rooms, electric hot showers and helpful staff.

Hotel Karajía (☎ 31-2606; 2 de Mayo 546; s/d US$7.50/10.50) Kaleidoscopic bedspreads cheer up these secure, clean but very basic rooms a bit.

Hotel Plaza (☎ 47-7654; eltejado@viabcp.com; Grau 534; s/d incl breakfast US$10.50/13.50) This hotel boasts friendly, helpful staff and well-kept, quiet rooms. There's an upstairs terrace restaurant overlooking the plaza.

Hotel Revash (☎ 47-7391; revash@terra.com; Grau 517; s/d US$10.50/15; ⌨) The showers seem endlessly hot in this classic older hotel, with a garden courtyard and wooden floors adding plenty of character. Staff were a little pushy about tours when we visited.

Hotel Casa Vieja (☎ 47-7353; www.casaviejaperu.com; Chincha Alta 569; s/d US$18/30; ⌨) Waking up to the sounds of chirping birds rather than roaring *mototaxis* is a pleasure inside this classy mansion. Bright rooms have big windows, hot showers and handcrafted decor. Breakfast (in bed!) available.

Eating & Drinking

Look for *juanes* (banana leaf–steamed fish or chicken), made locally with yucca instead of rice, and *cecina* (a smoked pork dish), often made with beef instead.

Panificadora San José (Ayacucho 816; snacks US90¢-$1.80; ⌚ 6:30am-10pm) A tiny bakery where you can enjoy a *humita*, corn *tamales* or a sandwich with coffee or hot chocolate for breakfast, then snacks and desserts all day.

505 Pizza-Bar (2 de Mayo 505; pizzas US90¢; ⌚ noon-late) A full bar and music will keep you lingering over a *pisco sour* long after the last slice is gone.

Hotel Plaza (Grau 534, 2nd fl; menú US$1.80) Slow service, but cool ambience and good set lunches, with a few tables facing the plaza.

Las Rocas (Ayacucho 932; mains US$1.80-3; ⌚ 7:30am-9pm Mon-Sat & 6-9pm Sun) Nothing too fancy: just huge, finger-lickin' portions of Peruvian fare for a handful of nuevos soles.

La Tushpa (Ortiz Arrieta 753; meals US$2.10-4.50; ⌚ noon-10pm) For sensational grills and steaks cooked whatever way you like 'em, it's justifiably packed nightly with locals.

Getting There & Away

Buses to Chiclayo (US$6 to US$12, 10 to 11 hours) and on to Lima (US$21 to US$27, 20 to 23 hours) take a route that is paved beyond Pedro Ruíz. Services leave with **Transervis Kuélap** (☎ 47-8128; Arrieta 412), **CIVA** (☎ 47-8048; Salamanca 956), **Transportes Zelada** (☎ 37-8066; Arrieta 310) and comfortable **Móvil Tours** (☎ 47-8545; La Libertad 464).

Virgen del Carmen (Salamanca 650) goes twice weekly to Celendín (US$9, 12 to 14 hours). **Transportes Roller** (Grau 302) has buses to Kuélap (US$3.60, 3½ hours) at 4am. *Colectivo* taxis to Kuélap depart throughout the day (US$4.50, three hours).

There are frequent *combis* (US$1.80, 1½ hours) and *colectivos* for Tingo (US$2.40, 1½ hours), which may continue to María (US$3.60, three hours). *Colectivos* also go to Pedro Ruíz (US$3.60, 1½ hours), where eastbound buses to Tarapoto (US$7.50 to US$9, seven hours) stop.

KUÉLAP

Matched in grandeur only by the ruins of Machu Picchu, the fabulous ruins of this pre-Inca **citadel** (adult/student US$3/1.70; ⌚ 8am-noon & 1-5pm), constructed between AD 900 and 1100, are perched in the mountains southeast of Chachapoyas. The site (elevation 3100m) receives remarkably few visitors, though those who make it get to see one of the most significant and impressive pre-Columbian ruins in South America.

Below the ruins, **Hospedaje El Bebedero** (r per person US$4) has bare-bones rooms without electricity or running water – bring a sleeping bag and water-purification equipment. You can camp nearby at INC Hostel, permanently occupied by the Kuélap excavation team. Basic meals are available at local houses.

In the hamlet of **María**, two hours' walk from Kuélap, there are charming *hospedajes*. All offer clean, modest rooms (per person US$3) with electric hot showers; hearty meals cost less than US$2. An hour further down the road, **Choctemal Lodge** (r per person US$7.50) has stunning 360-degree panoramas of the valley, arty rooms, electric showers and an outdoor hot tub. It also offers basic meals.

To get to Kuélap, take the Transportes Roller bus from Chachapoyas (opposite) or a more frequent *combi* (US$1.80, 1½ hours) or *colectivo* to Tingo (US$2.40, 1½ hours), some of which continue to María (US$3.60, three hours). A steep 10km trail leads from the southern end of Tingo via María to the ruins, 1200m above. Allow five to six hours for the climb, and take water.

TARAPOTO
☎ 042 / pop 128,500

A lethargic rainforest metropolis, Tarapoto dips its toe into the Amazon basin, but clings to the Andean foothills – and the rest of Peru – by the umbilical cord of a long, paved road back to civilization. Tarapoto's geography is rugged, and waterfalls and lakes are abundant. Traveling onward east to Yurimaguas is safe, but the route south along the Río Huallaga valley to Tingo María goes through Peru's major coca-growing region, and is *not* recommended.

Information
Internet cafés are everywhere.

BCP (Maynas 130) Cashes travelers' checks and has an ATM.

Clínica San Martín (☎ 52-3680/7860; San Martín 274; ☽ 24hr) Offers medical care.

Tours
Chancas Expeditions (☎ 52-2616; www.geocities .com/amazonrainforest; Rioja 357) Offers river-rafting trips.

Quiquiriqui Tours (☎ 52-4016; Pimentel 309; ☽ 8am-7pm Mon-Fri, 8am-6pm Sat, 9am-noon Sun) A full-service travel agency for tours of the surrounding villages and natural attractions.

Sleeping
Hostal Pasquelandia (☎ 52-2290; Pimentel 341; s/d without bathroom US$2.40/3.60) A dirt-cheap, beat-up wooden affair with cold-water showers.

Alojamiento Grau (☎ 52-3777; Grau 243; s/d US$6/9) Elementary rooms with exposed-brick walls are quiet at this amicable family-run hostelry.

Hospedaje Misti (☎ 52-2439; Prado 341; s/d US$6/9) Rooms have tiny bathrooms, but also TVs and ceiling fans. There's a laid-back café and leafy courtyard.

Hostal San Antonio (☎ 52-5563; Pimentel 126; s/d US$7.50/10.50) Good-value rooms with hot showers, fan and cable TV, just steps from the main plaza.

Alojamiento July (☎ 52-2087; Morey 205; s/d US$7.50/10.50) Every wall is covered with jungle murals, while endless rows of beads and knickknacks clank in the hallways. Rooms have electric hot showers, cable TV and mini-fridges.

Alojamiento Arevalo (☎ 52-5265; Moyobamba 223; US$9/13.50) This quiet hotel offers rooms with cold showers, cable TVs, fans and mini-fridges.

La Patarashca (☎ 52-3899; www.lapatarashca.com; Lamas 261; s/d incl breakfast US$10.50/18) A tropical vibe pervades this cute *hospedaje*, which has a thatched-roof lounge, bilingual parrots, hammocks, cold showers and cable TV.

Eating
Banana's Burgers (Morey 102; mains US$1-2; ☽ 24hr) Banana's is a great burger joint with a bar upstairs.

El Brassero (Lamas 231; mains US$3-6.30; ☽ noon-late) Just choose your carnivorous cut, then have it grilled to order for you. Pork ribs are the specialty. Funky acid-jazz tunes are a bonus.

La Patarashca (Lamas 261; mains US$3-7.50; ☽ 8am-11pm) Offering regional Amazonian cuisine, it's popular on weekends. The 2nd floor has tropical ambience and views.

La Collpa (Circunvalación 164; mains US$4.20-7.50; ☽ 10am-11pm) Located in a place where you can practically taste the jungle air, this bamboo-stilt restaurant has river and rainforest views. Its have-a-go-at-anything menu is best for lunch.

Supermercado La Inmaculada (Compagnon 126; ☽ 8:30am-10pm) For self-catering.

Drinking
Stonewasi Taberna (Lamas 222; ☽ 6pm-late) The pick of a bunch of bars at the busy intersection of Lamas and La Cruz, which transforms into a cruising scene every evening.

La Alternativa (Grau 401) A hole-in-the-wall bar with shelves of dusty bottles containing *uvachado* and homemade concoctions based on soaking roots, lianas etc in cane liquor. Potent Amazonian tonics and brews are not for the faint-hearted.

Entertainment
Papillón (Peru 209; admission US$3; ☽ 9pm-late Fri & Sat) In the Morales district, 3km west of town by the Río Cumbaza, this nightclub has live salsa bands and DJ-fueled dancing.

PERU

Getting There & Around

The **airport** (TPP; ☎ 52-2278) is 3km southwest of the center. **LAN** (☎ 52-9318; Hurtado 184) has daily flight to/from Lima. **Star Perú** (☎ 52-8765; San Pablo de la Cruz 100) also has Lima and possibly Iquitos flights daily.

Most bus companies are along Salaverry in the Morales district. **Móvil Tours** (☎ 52-9193; Salaverry 858) and **El Sol Peruano** (☎ 52-3232) are the best. Buses head west on the paved road to Chiclayo (US$12 to US$19.50, 14 to 16 hours), Trujillo (US$16.50 to US$24, 18 to 20 hours), Piura (US$4.50, 18 hours) and Lima (US$36 to $33, 24 to 28 hours). Transfer in Pedro Ruíz (US$7.50 to US$9, seven hours) to a *colectivo* taxi to reach Chachapoyas (US$3.60, 1½ hours).

A rough road goes east from Tarapoto to Yurimaguas. Minibuses, pickup trucks and *colectivos* traveling to Yurimaguas (US$4.50 to US$7.50, six hours) leave from the market in the eastern suburb of Banda de Shilcayo. Back on Salaverry, **Paredes Estrella** (☎ 52-1202) and **Expreso Huamanga** (☎ 52-7272) have cheaper, slower buses to Yurimaguas.

A short *mototaxi* ride around town costs US30¢, to the bus terminal/airport US60/90¢.

AMAZON BASIN

Peru's Amazonas is a vivid, bright, exotic and challenging frontier zone. It claims approximately 50% of the nation's landmass, yet only 5% of Peruvians live here. Though a fast-growing tourist destination, judicious protection of the jungle has meant that the biosphere on the eastern flank of the Andes preserves some of the world's most diverse fauna and flora.

There are few towns of any size. Pucallpa and Yurimaguas are reached by rough roads. Both have slow boats on to Iquitos, accessibly only by air otherwise. To get to Puerto Maldonado, take a flight or a rough overland trip by truck from Cuzco.

PUERTO MALDONADO

☎ 082 / pop 39,100

The ramshackle jungle town of Puerto Maldonado, capital of the Madre de Dios region, is an unlikely destination, yet it gives travelers the chance to see, feel and hear the unspoilt Amazon jungle like nowhere else. The town has been important in harvesting rubber, logging and gold and oil prospecting. Its role as a crossroads will take on even greater dimensions once the Interoceánica Hwy linking the Atlantic and Pacific Oceans via Brazil opens.

Information

BCP (Plaza de Armas) Changes US dollars and traveler's checks, and has a Visa ATM.

Casa de cambio (cnr Puno & G Prada) Exchanges US dollars; Brazilian reais and Bolivian pesos are hard to negotiate.

Lavandería (Velarde 898) To wash your mud-caked, sweat-soaked rags.

Ministerio de Industria y Turismo (☎ 57-1413; Fitzcarrald 252) Also has an airport booth.

Serpost (Velarde 6th block) Southwest of the Plaza de Armas.

Social Seguro Hospital (☎ 57-1711) At Km 3 on the Cuzco road.

UnAMad (2 de Mayo 287; per hr US$1.50) Internet.

Sights & Activities

Just outside the airport gates, you'll find the **ProNaturalezas Butterfly Conservation Center Japipi** (☎ 01-264-2736; www.pronaturaleza.org; admission US$5), which has live exhibits.

A cheap way of seeing a little of this major Peruvian jungle river, the **Madre de Dios ferry** (one-way fare US15¢; ⏱ dawn-dusk) leaves from Puerto Capetania close to the Plaza de Armas. *Peki-pekis* (wooden canoes powered by two-stroke motorcycle engines with long propeller shafts) leave from the dock at an incredible 45-degree angle to counter the river's current.

Horse-riding, **cycling** and other activities can be arranged at Iñapari Lodge.

Courses

Tambopata Language Center (☎ 57-6014; www.geo cities.com/tambopata_language; Cajamarca 895) offers Spanish classes, homestays and cultural and jungle tours from US$100 per week.

Tours

If you haven't prearranged a river and jungle tour (see p928), there are several local guides; some quite reputable and experienced, others just interested in making quick money. Shop around, never pay for a tour beforehand and, when you agree on a price, make sure it includes the return trip! Officially licensed guides charge US$25 to US$60 per person per day (excluding park fees) depending

PUERTO MALDONADO

SLEEPING	
Hospedaje Rey Port.............9	B2
Hospedaje Royal Inn..........10	B2
Hostal Cahuata.................11	A3
Hostal El Solar..................12	B2
Hostal Moderno................13	C1

EATING	
El Califa..........................14	A1
Frutos del Mar.................15	B3
La Casa Nostra.................16	B2
Los Gustitos del Cur.........17	B2
Pizzería El Hornito/Chez	
Maggy........................18	C1
Pollería Astoria................19	B3

DRINKING	
Anaconda Pub..................20	C1
Coconut Pub....................21	C1
Discoteca Witite...............22	C1

INFORMATION	
BCP..................................1	C2
Casa de Cambio.................2	B2
INRENA.............................3	C2
Lavandería.........................4	B3
Ministerio de Industria y	
Turismo..........................5	A3
Serpost..............................6	B2
UnAMad............................7	B2

SIGHTS & ACTIVITIES	
Madre de Díos Ferry Dock......8	D1

SHOPPING	
Artesanía Shabuya.............23	C1

TRANSPORT	
Aero Condor Perú.............24	C1
Empresa Transportes	
Imperial........................25	A2
LAN................................26	B2
Madre de Díos Ferry Dock...(see 8)	
Riverboat Hire.................(see 8)	
Trucks to Cuzco...............27	A3

on the destination and number of people. Boat rides, which are usually needed to get out of Puerto Maldonado, are notoriously expensive.

Sleeping

Watch for overcharging. Expect cold showers. Outside town are several jungle lodges (p928).

Hostal Moderno (☎ 30-0043; Billinghurst 359; s/d/tr US$3.20/6.25/8.75) Despite the name, this simple, family-run place has been around for decades, though it does get a regular splash of paint.

Hostal Cahuata (☎ 57-2111; Fitzcarrald 517; s/d US$6.25/9.40, without bathroom US$3.20/6.25) The marketside locale quiets down at night. Small, neat rooms have fans.

Iñapari Lodge (☎ 57-2575; r per person US$6) Near the airport, this friendly, rustic hostel has communal showers, a restaurant and bar.

Also worth a peek are the basic **Hostal El Solar** (☎ 57-1634; G Prada 445; s/d US$6/10, without bathroom US$4.50/7.50); the spacious **Hospedaje Royal Inn** (☎ 57-1048; 2 de Mayo 333; s/d US$7.50/10.50); and **Hospedaje Rey Port** (☎ 57-1177; Velarde 457;

s/d US$10/14, without bathroom US$6/9), which has good views.

Eating

Regional specialties include *chilcano* (fish-chunk soup flavored with cilantro) and *parrillada de la selva* (marinated meat BBQ in a Brazil-nut sauce). In the Mercado Modelo, look for freshly squeezed fruit juices and jungle staples such as *pan de arroz* (rice bread).

La Casa Nostra (2 de Mayo 287a; snacks US$1-3; ☉ 7am-1pm & 5-11pm) Long-running café is your best bet for breakfasts, snacks (try the *tamales*), tropical juices and coffee.

Los Gustitos del Cur (Velarde 474; meals US$2; ☉ 11am-10pm) For the best ice cream in town, drop into this French-owned patisserie for a sweet treat. It also serves sandwiches.

Pollería Astoria (Velarde 701; mains US$2) Opposite a neonlit, fast-food chicken joint, this dimly lit, wooden *pollería* has an authentic Amazonian feel.

Frutos del Mar (Moquegua 787; mains US$2-4) People praise this modest *cevichería* for its quality seafood at bargain prices.

PERU

GETTING TO BRAZIL & BOLIVIA

An unpaved road goes from Puerto Maldonado to **Iñapari** on the Brazilian border. *Colectivos* to Iñapari (US$8, four hours) with **Empresa Transportes Imperial** (☎ 082-57-4274; Ica 5th block) leave when they have four passengers. Iberia, 170km north of Puerto Maldonado, and Iñapari, 70km beyond Iberia, have a couple of basic hotels. At Iñapari, where Peruvian exit formalities are conducted, cross the Río Acre by ferry or bridge to Assis, Brazil, which has better hotels and a paved road via Brasiléia to Río Branco. US, Australian, New Zealand and Canadian citizens need to get a Brazilian visa in advance (see p407).

From Puerto Maldonado, boats can be hired for the half-day trip to the Bolivian border at Puerto Pardo for about US$100. Cheaper passages are available on infrequent cargo boats. Make sure to get exit stamps before leaving Peru at Puerto Maldonado's **immigration office** (☎ 082-57-1069; Plaza Bolognesi at Ica; ☿ 9am-1pm Mon-Fri). From Puerto Heath, a few minutes away from Puerto Pardo by boat, it takes several days (even weeks) to arrange a boat (expensive) to Riberalta, which has road and air connections. Travel in a group to share costs and avoid months when the water is too low. Another option is to go to Brasiléia, cross the Río Acre by ferry or bridge to Cobija, on the Bolivian side, where there are hotels and erratic flights. There's also a dry-season gravel road onward to Riberalta.

To enter Peru from Brazil, see p398.

El Califa (Piura 266; mains US$2-5; ☿ 10am-4:30pm) A rustic, sultry place for regional specialties including palm-heart salad, *juanes*, fried plantains and game.

Pizzería El Hornito/Chez Maggy (D Carrión 271; pizzas US$3.50-8.50; ☿ 6pm-late) Popular hangout dishes up big bowls of pastas and wood-fired pizzas.

Drinking

A handful of nightclubs open on weekends. The best known is **Discoteca Witite** (Velarde 151). **Anaconda Pub** (Loreto 228) and Coconut Pub are both on the Plaza de Armas. Outside town 4km along the airport road, **La Choza del Candamo** (☎ 57-2872; ☿ 7pm-late) is a relaxed *peña* where you can sample appetizers from all three regions of Peru – coast, mountain and jungle.

Shopping

Artesania Shabuya (Arequipa 279) For honestly made crafts on the Plaza de Armas.

Getting There & Around

AIR

The **airport** (PEM) is 7km west of town; *mototaxis* cost US$2. **Aero Condor Perú** (☎ 57-1733; Loreto 222) and **LAN** (☎ 57-3677; Velarde 503) have daily flights to Lima via Cuzco.

BOAT

Boat hire at the Madre de Dios ferry dock for excursions or to travel down to the Bolivian border is expensive. Upriver boats toward Manu are difficult to find.

MOTORCYCLE & TAXI

There are several motorcycle-rental outlets, mostly on Prada between Velarde and Puno, charging US$1.20 per hour for 100cc bikes.

Mototaxis cruise around town for about US25¢ per person.

TRUCK

Trucks to Cuzco during the highland dry season leave from the Mercado Modelo or two blocks south. The rough, hazardous 500km trip (US$10) takes at least three days, depending on road and weather conditions. The more expensive seats are in the cab with the driver. The least comfortable but fastest trucks are *cisternas* (gasoline trucks), with a narrow ledge on top upon which to crouch. The trucks stop about three times daily to let the driver eat, and once more so he can sleep (never for long though).

AROUND PUERTO MALDONADO

There are dozens of jungle lodges along the Ríos Tambopata and Madre de Dios from Puerto Maldonado. Lodges and jungle tours are expensive, but definitely worth the money. To visit Reserva Nacional Tambopata, purchase an entrance permit (US$8.50 to US$20) at **INRENA** (☎ 57-1604; Cuzco 135) before leaving Puerto Maldonado.

Down the Madre de Dios, luxurious **Inkaterra Reserva Amazonica** (☎ in Lima 01-610-0410, Cuzco 084-24-5314; www.inkaterra.com; 3-day/2-night tour s/d r US$183/314, ste US$292/480) offers a good look at the jungle from its canopy walkway.

On Lago Sandoval, a haven for exotic wildlife, family-run **Willy Mejía Cepa Lodge** (Velarde 487, Puerto Maldonado; r per person without bathroom incl meals US$20) has been offering basic, backpacker accommodations and Spanish-language expeditions for nearly two decades.

Along the Río Tambopata, **Inotawa** (☎ 57-2511; www.inotawaexpeditions.com; Fonavi J9, Puerto Maldonado; 3-day/2-night tour per person from US$160) offers multilingual guides upon request; camping is allowed for a small fee.

At **Picaflor Research Centre** (www.picaflor.org; 3-day/2-night tour per person US$190), 74km from Puerto Maldonado, you'll pay just US$140 for 10 nights of accommodations and meals, excluding national park fees and transportation from Puerto Maldonado (US$3), if you agree to volunteer three hours daily.

PARQUE NACIONAL MANU

Covering almost 20,000 sq km, **Manu National Park** is one of the best spots in South America to see tropical wildlife. Starting in the eastern slopes of the Andes, the park plunges down into the lowlands, covering a wide range of cloud-forest and rainforest habitats containing hundreds of bird species, not to mention monkeys, armadillos, kinkajous, ocelots, river turtles, caiman, and countless insects, reptiles and amphibians. More elusive species include jaguars, tapirs, giant anteaters, tamanduas, capybaras, peccaries and giant river otters.

The best time to visit the park is during the dry season (June to November). Manu may be inaccessible or closed during the rainiest months (January to April), except to people staying in the expensive Manu Lodge or Cocha Salvador Safari Camp.

It's illegal to enter the park without a licensed guide and permit, which can be arranged at Cuzco travel agencies (p875). Transportation, accommodations and meals are also part of the tour package. Beware: not all companies enter the park itself. Some offer cheaper 'Manu Tours' that cover areas outside the park, but these still boast exceptional wildlife-watching.

Costs depend on whether you camp or stay in a lodge, and whether you arrive/depart overland or by air, but generally start at US$750 for five days/four nights, flying in and out, or US$800 for nine days/eight nights, all overland. Camping trips using the park's beaches can bring costs down to roughly US$75 per day. Book well in advance, but be flexible with your travel plans, as tours often return days late.

Independent travelers can reach the reserve's environs without taking a tour. However, you'll still need to hire a guide and they generally charge US$60 per day plus food, so little is saved. If you're determined to go solo, take a bus from Av Angamos in Cuzco to Pillcopata (US$4.50, 10 hours in good weather) via Paucartambo.

Boats travel from Pillcopata via the villages of Atalaya, Salvación and Shintuya toward Manu. Pickup trucks leave Pillcopata early every morning for Shintuya (US$2.50, five hours) via Atalaya. People on tours often start river travel from Atalaya after a night in a lodge. The boat journey down the Alto Madre de Dios to the Río Manu takes almost a day. A few minutes from the village of Boca Manu is an airstrip, often the starting or exit point for commercial trips into the park. There is a park entrance fee of US$20, and continuing is only possible with a guide and permit.

PUCALLPA

☎ 061 / pop 324,870

For the uninitiated it is a revelation to arrive at Pucallpa, capital of Ucayali department, after miles of lush jungle down from the raw, rocky Andes. Travelers come here in search of riverboats to Iquitos or to visit indigenous communities near Yarinacocha.

Information

Several banks change money and traveler's checks and have ATMs; *casas de cambio* are along the 4th, 5th and 6th blocks of Raimondi.

Clínica Santa Rosa (☎ 57-1689; Inmaculada 529; ⊗ 24 hr) Good medical services.

Lavandería Gasparin (Portillo 526; ⊗ ⊗ 9am-1pm & 4-8pm Mon-Sat) Offers self-service and drop-off laundry.

Tourist booth (☎ 57-1303; 2 de Mayo 111) There's a small one at the airport.

Utopia@.net (cnr Morey & Imaculada; ⊗ 8am-11pm) Has internet *cabinas*.

Viajes Laser (☎ 57-1120; Raimondi 470) At the Western Union office, this is one of Pucallpa's better travel agencies, but for jungle guides go to Yarinacocha.

Sights & Activities

Usko-Ayar (☎ 57-3088; Sánchez Cerro 465), near Iglesia Fray Marcos, is the gallery of Pablo Amaringo, a visionary local artist inspired by the hallucinogenic *ayahuasca* vine. Works by famed local

PERU

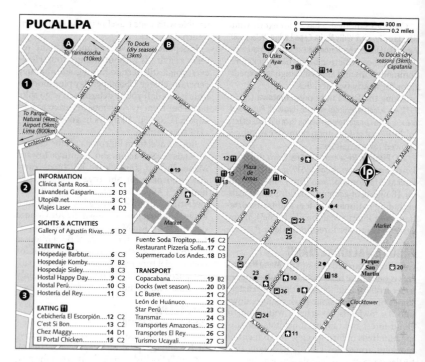

PUCALLPA

woodcarver Agustín Rivas are displayed at his house, now also a **gallery** (☎ 061-57-1834; Tarapaca 861, 2nd fl); ring the bell to enter.

About 4km from the town center, off the airport road, **Parque Natural** (admission US70¢; ☽ 9am-5pm) has a small Amazonian zoo and museum of Shipibo pottery. Airport buses can drop you here, or take a *motocarro* (US$1).

Sleeping

Hostal Perú (☎ 57-5128; Raimondi 639; s US$5.50-9, d US$7.25-11.50, s/d without bathroom US$4.25/5.50) A Shipibo pot collection brightens the entry to this faded older property. Rooms are tiny but clean with small fans and cold showers.

Hostería del Rey (☎ 57-5815; Portillo 747; s/d US$5/6) High ceilings, cold showers and fans to help you keep your cool.

Hospedaje Barbtur (☎ 57-2532; Raimondi 670; s/d US$8/11) Small, well-maintained family hostelry, with cold showers and cable TV in en suite rooms.

Hospedaje Sisley (☎ 57-5137; Portillo 658, 2nd fl; s/d US$8.50/12) Decent place run by friendly older ladies, with tidy rooms, cold showers, fans and TV.

Hospedaje Komby (☎ 57-1562; www.hospedajekom bi.com.pe; Ucayali 360; s/d US$10/12; ☒) Clean rooms are basic, though a small pool and restaurant make up for that.

Hostal Happy Day (☎ 57-2067; Huáscar 440; s/d incl breakfast from US$10/13; ☒) Maybe there's truth in advertising: all of the tiny rooms in this sunset-colored building on a quiet side street have – gasp! – air-conditioning.

Eating

Many restaurants open by 7am for breakfast and are closed Sunday.

Cebichería El Escorpión (Independencia 430; meals US$3-6) Never mind Pucallpa's distance from the sea. This seafood joint has a prime plaza location with boisterous sidewalk tables.

El Portal Chicken (Independencia 510; mains US$3; ☽ 5pm-midnight) You can't miss this three-story chicken restaurant with the brightest neon lights in town. Some open-air tables have plaza views.

Chez Maggy (Inmaculada 643; mains US$3-7) A modern restaurant with a wood-burning oven that churns out over a dozen kinds of tasty pizza. Try the tropical-flavored *sangria*.

Restaurante Pizzeria Sofía (Sucre 415; menú US$2) On the main square, this friendly joint is a great spot for hearty breakfasts and set lunches.

Stock up at **Supermercado Los Andes** (Portillo 545) for long trips. On opposite corners of the plaza, **C'est Si Bon** (Independencia 560; snacks US$1-3) and **Fuente Soda Tropitop** (Sucre 401; snacks US$1-3) are bright spots for ice cream, breakfasts and sandwiches.

Getting There & Away

AIR

Pucallpa's **airport** (PCL) is 5km northwest of town. Currently scheduled flights are to Lima only with **LC Busre** (☎ 57-5309; Tarapaca s/n) and **Star Perú** (☎ 59-0586; 7 de Julio 865).

BOAT

During high water (January to April), boats depart from next to Parque San Martín. As water levels drop, the port moves 3km northeast of the center, reached by minibus (US50¢). Crowded boats to Iquitos (US$18 to US$30) take three to five days. Passengers can sleep aboard on hammocks, which are sold in the market, and basic meals are provided. See p829 for more important details on cargo-boat journeys.

BUS

Several companies go to Lima (US$13, 20 hours) via Tingo María, Huánuco, Cerro de Pasco and Junín. Read the 'Warning!' box on p898 before making this journey, though. Bus companies include **León de Huánuco** (☎ 57-2411; Tacna 655), **Transportes El Rey** (☎ 57-5545; cnr Raimondi & 7 de Junio), **Transmar** (☎ 57-4900; Raimondi 793) and **Transportes Amazonas** (☎ 57-1292; Tacna 628). **Turismo Ucayali** (☎ 59-3002; 7 de Junio 799) has faster *colectivos* to Tingo María (US$14, six hours).

Getting Around

Motocarros cost US$2 to the airport or Yarinacocha; car taxis charge US$3.20. *Colectivos* to Yarinacocha (US25¢) leave from 9 de Diciembre near the market and San Martín at Ucayali. Alternatively, rent motorbikes from **Copacabana** (☎ 50-5304; Ucayali 265; per hr US$2, per 12hr US$15-20).

YARINACOCHA

This lovely oxbow lake is 10km northwest of Pucallpa. You can go **canoeing**, watch **wildlife**, visit matriarchal Shipibo communities and

purchase **handicrafts**. In the lakeside village of Puerto Callao, internet access is available on the main plaza.

Popular boat trips include to the **botanical gardens** (per person US60¢; ☼ 8am-4pm), best visited in the early morning to observe abundant birdlife, and the **Shipibo villages** of San Francisco and Santa Clara. You can hire guides for jungle walks and overnight treks. *Peki-peki* boats with drivers cost about US$5 per hour. Overnight trips are US$35 per person per day. Recommended guides include **Gilber Reategui Sangama** (☎ 962-7607/985-5352; www.sacredheritage.com/normita), with his boat *La Normita*; **Miguel Tans** (☎ 59-7494) with *Pituco*; **Eduardo Vela** (☎ leave a message at 57-5383) with *The Best*; and Gustavo Paredes with *Poseidon*. It's easy to find their boats, which are all pulled up along the waterfront. Don't fall for the old 'Oh, that boat sank. Why don't you take a tour with me?' tactic.

For rustic hospitality and shaman ceremonies, stay across the lake at Gilber Reategui Sangama's **house** (☎ leave a message at 59-9018; junglesecrets@yahoo.com; r per person incl meals US$15). There are also three pricier lakeside lodges (US$25 to US$35 per person including meals), including **Pandisho Albergue** (☎ 57-5041; dm US$3). The Shipibo village of San Francisco offers lodging from US$3 per person.

Several inexpensive restaurants and lively bars line the Puerto Callao waterfront.

YURIMAGUAS

☎ 065 / pop 42,793

This quiet, sleepy little port on the Río Huallaga has boats to Iquitos. Reaching Yurimaguas involves a tiring road trip from the northern highlands, though. **Manguare Expediciones** (Lores 126) provides information and arranges tours. BCP and Banco Continental have Visa ATMs and change US cash or traveler's checks. Look for internet cafés in the town center.

Few places have hot water. Clean and quiet **Hostal César Gustavo** (☎ 35-1585; Atahualpa 102; s/d US$4.50/7.50) is top-rated among the most basic places. Rooms have decent beds and fans. What **Hostal de Paz** (☎ 35-2123; Jáuregui 431, s/d US$6/8.50) may lack in signage out front, it makes up for with good-value rooms that have fans and cable TV. Too ambitiously baptized, older **Leo's Palace** (☎ 35-3008; Lores 108; s/d US$6/9), has run-down but spacious fan rooms. Some have a balcony overlooking the

PERU

plaza. Decent set lunches (US$1.50). Quiet and recommended **Hostal El Naranjo** (☎ 35-2650; elnaranjo@hotmail.com; Arica 318; r US$14-23; ❄ 💻 🏊) has rooms with cable TV and fans or air-con. There's a good restaurant, swimming pool and hot showers.

Hotel restaurants are among the best places to eat. Try **La Prosperidad** (Progreso 107) for tropical juices, burgers and chicken.

For flights to Lima, the nearest airport is at Tarapoto (p925). Companies with buses to Tarapoto (US$3, six hours) include Paredes Estrella and Expreso Huamanga, with offices on the outskirts of town.

The main port 'La Boca' is 13 blocks north of the center. Cargo boats (see also p829), stopping in Lagunas (below), usually leave daily except Sunday for Iquitos (US$15 to US$30, three to five days). Boat information is available from a dockside store.

LAGUNAS

The remote village of Lagunas has no money-changing facilities and limited food, but it's a launching pad for visiting the wildlife-rich **Reserva Nacional Pacaya-Samiria** (admission US$20), home to Amazon manatees, caiman, river dolphins and turtles, monkeys and abundant birdlife. Avoid visiting during the rainy season. To avoid price-cutting, there is now an official guides association, **ESTPEL** (☎ 40-1007). Tours cost approximately US$50 per person per day, including accommodations and transportation, but not food or park entrance fees. **Hostal La Sombra** (☎ 40-1063; r per person US$2) has hot, stuffy little rooms. Lagunas' best hotel is **Hostal Miraflores** (☎ 40-1001; Miraflores 249; s/d US$3/5), with clean rooms. Both provide cheap meals. Boats from Yurimaguas usually take 10 hours and arrive in Lagunas most days.

IQUITOS

☎ 065 / pop 430,000

A sassy and slightly manic jungle metropolis, Iquitos holds the title of the world's largest city that can't be reached by road. Originally founded as a remote Jesuit mission in the 1750s, the town spent many of its early years fending off attacks from indigenous tribes who didn't particularly want to be converted, thank you very much.

During the late-19th-century rubber boom, rubber barons became fabulously rich, while the tribespeople and *mestizo* rubber tappers

suffered virtual enslavement, even death from disease and harsh treatment. Traces of opulence can still be seen in local mansions and artistically tiled walls.

Then, in the 1960s, oil made Iquitos a prosperous modern place once again. Since everything must be 'imported' by boat or air, costs are high.

Information

EMERGENCY
Clínica Ana Stahl (☎ 25-2535; La Marina 285; ☽ 24hr)
Policía de Turismo (☎ 24-2081; Lores 834)

IMMIGRATION
Colombian consulate (☎ 23-1461; Calvo de Araujo 431; ☽ 9am-12:30pm & 2-4:30pm Mon-Fri)
Migraciónes (☎ 23-5371; M Cáceres 18th block) Extends Peruvian immigration cards, but get entry/exit stamps at the border.

INTERNET ACCESS
Most cybercafés charge less than US$1 per hour.
Manugare Internet (Próspero 273) Fast machines.
Sured Internet (Morona 213) Air-conditioned.

LAUNDRY
Lavandería Imperial (Putumayo 150; ☽ 8am-8pm Mon-Sat) Coin-operated.

MONEY
Many banks change traveler's checks, give credit-card advances and have ATMs. Changing Brazilian or Colombian currency is best done at the border.
Western Union (☎ 23-5182; Napo 359)

POST
Serpost (Arica 402; ☽ 8am-6pm Mon-Fri, to 4:30pm Sat)

TOURIST INFORMATION
Gerald Mayeaux (theyellowroseoftexasiquitos@hotmail .com) Ex–tourist office director now dispenses information from Yellow Rose of Texas (p935).
iPerú airport (☎ 26-0251; Main Halll, Airport; ☽ 8am-1pm & 4-8pm) city center (☎ 23-6144; Plaza de Armas, Calle Napo 232; ☽ 8:30am-7:30pm)
Iquitos Times (www.iquitostimes.com) Free English-language tourist newspaper.
Reserva Nacional Pacaya-Samiria office (☎ 23-2980; 4th fl, Ricardo Palma 113; ☽ 8am-4pm Mon-Fri) INRENA's office.

PERU

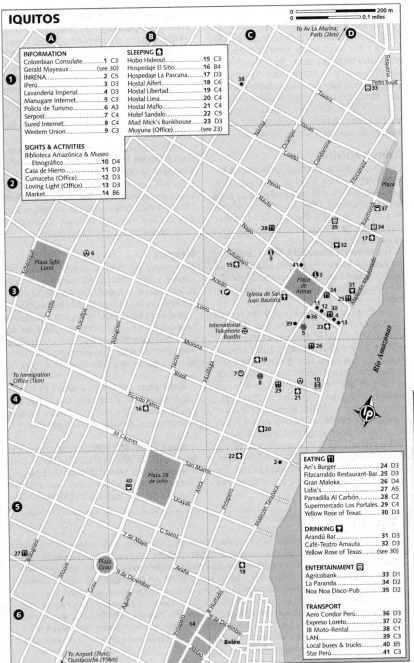

IQUITOS

0	200 m
0	0.1 miles

To Av La Marina; Ports (2km)

INFORMATION
Colombian Consulate............**1** C3
Gerald Mayeaux..............(see 30)
INRENA.............................**2** C5
iPerú...................................**3** D3
Lavandería Imperial.............**4** D3
Manugare Internet...............**5** C3
Policía de Turismo................**6** A3
Serpost...............................**7** C4
Sured Internet.....................**8** C4
Western Union.....................**9** C3

SIGHTS & ACTIVITIES
Biblioteca Amazónica & Museo
   Etnográfico....................**10** D4
Casa de Hierro....................**11** D3
Cumaceba (Office)...............**12** D3
Loving Light (Office)............**13** D3
Market................................**14** B6

SLEEPING
Hobo Hideout......................**15** C3
Hospedaje El Sitio................**16** B4
Hospedaje La Pascana..........**17** D3
Hostal Alfert.......................**18** C6
Hostal Libertad...................**19** C4
Hostal Lima........................**20** C4
Hostal Maflo.......................**21** C4
Hotel Sandalo.....................**22** C5
Mad Mick's Bunkhouse.......**23** D3
Muyuna (Office)...............(see 23)

EATING
Ari's Burger........................**24** D3
Fitzcarraldo Restaurant-Bar..**25** D3
Gran Maloka.......................**26** D4
Lidia's................................**27** A5
Parrandilla Al Carbón...........**28** C2
Supermercado Los Portales...**29** C4
Yellow Rose of Texas...........**30** D3

DRINKING
Arandú Bar.........................**31** D3
Café-Teatro Amauta............**32** D3
Yellow Rose of Texas.........(see 30)

ENTERTAINMENT
Agricobank.........................**33** D1
La Paranda.........................**34** D2
Noa Noa Disco-Pub.............**35** D2

TRANSPORT
Aero Condor Perú................**36** D3
Expreso Loreto....................**37** D2
JB Moto-Rental...................**38** C1
LAN...................................**39** C3
Local buses & trucks............**40** B5
Star Perú............................**41** C3

Requeña

Pedro Rosell

Tavara

Nanay

Ocainde

Yavari

Condamine

Loreto

Fitzcarrald

Plaza

Pevas

Nauta

Raymondi

Napo

Putumayo

Iglesia de San
Juan Bautista

Plaza
de
Armas

Araujo

Lores

Malecón Maldonado

International
Telephone
Booths

Morona

Río Amazonas

Edequipe

Plaza Sgto
Lores

Castilla

Pucallpa

Bolognesi

Tacna

Brasil

Huallaga

Ricardo Palma

M Cáceres

San Martín

Arica

Prospero

Malecón Tarapaca

Plaza 28
de Julio

Ucayali

2 de Mayo

G Saenz

Bolognesi

Moore

Plaza
Grau

9 de Diciembre

Araña

Grau

Aguire

R Hurtado

9 de Diciembre

Prospero

Abtao

Belén

To Immigration
Office (1km)

To Airport (7km);
Quistacocha (15km)

PERU

Dangers & Annoyances

Aggressive street touts and many self-styled jungle guides are irritatingly insistent and dishonest – don't trust them. Some have criminal records for robbing tourists. Be especially careful when arranging jungle camping trips. All guides should have a permit or license; ask for references, check at the tourist office and then proceed with caution. Petty thievery committed by young children who roam the streets looking for easy prey is also common.

Sights & Activities

The **Casa de Hierro** (Iron House; cnr Putumayo & Raymondi), designed by Eiffel of towering fame, was made in Paris and imported piece by piece to Iquitos around 1890. It looks like what it is: a bunch of metal sheets bolted together. Stay tuned – a restaurant and bar may open upstairs above the store.

The **Biblioteca Amazónica & Museo Etnográfico** (cnr Malecón & Morona; ⏲ Mon-Fri), inside one of Iquitos' oldest houses, features startlingly lifelike fiberglass statues of different Amazonian tribespeoples.

The floating shantytown of **Belén** houses thousands of people living on huts that rise and fall with the river, and canoes selling and trading jungle produce daily from around 7am. This is a poor area, but relatively safe in daylight. Take a cab to Los Chinos, walk to the port and rent a canoe to paddle you around during the November to May highwater season; it's difficult to navigate in other months. The **market**, on the west side of Belén, has piles of dried frogs and fish, armadillo shells, piranha teeth and almost everything else, including kitchen sinks. Look for Chuchuhuasi tree bark that is soaked in rum for weeks, then used as a tonic (it's even served in local bars).

Pilpintuwasi Butterfly Farm (☎ 23-2665; www .amazonanimalorphange.org; Padra Cocha; admission US$5; ⏲ 10am-4pm) is a conservatorium and breeding center for Amazonian butterflies, but it's the orphaned exotic animals – including a capuchin monkey, tapir, jaguar, giant anteater and manatee – that steal the show. From Bellavista-Nanay port, 2km north of Iquitos, take a small boat to Padre Cocha. The farm is a signposted 1km walk through the village.

Built by nostalgic expats, the wacky, wonderful **Amazon Golf Club** (☎ 63-1333; Quistacocha; 9-hole round incl club rental US$20; ⏲ 6am-6pm) is the only golf course in the entire Amazon. To take a swing, enquire at **Mad Mick's Trading Post** (☎ 065-75-4976; Putumayo 163; ⏲ 8am-8pm), where you can buy, rent, sell or trade almost anything necessary for a jungle expedition.

Sleeping

Mosquitoes are rarely a serious problem, so netting isn't provided. All rooms have fans unless otherwise noted. The May to September high season brings slightly higher rates.

Mad Mick's Bunkhouse (☎ 975-4976; michaelcollis@ hotmail.com; Putumayo 163; dm US$3) Crash in an eight-bed dormitory at the back of a trading post. For the price, you can't get any closer to the action – it's 50m from the Plaza de Armas.

Hostal Alfert (☎ 23-4105; G Saenz 1; s/d US$4.50/ 7.30) With a view of the river and Belén, this gaudy place with warm showers attracts shoestringers, though the neighborhood is dodgy.

Hobo Hideout (☎ 23-4099; hobohideout@yahoo.com; Putumayo 437; dm US$5, s/d US$8.75/11; 🖳) A cool traveler vibe reaches out through the iron-grill gate and into the kitchen, laundry, waterfall plunge pool, bar and cable TV room. One

---

SPLURGE!

There are over a dozen jungle lodges in the Iquitos area, but lodges built further off into the Amazon itself offer your best chances of seeing exotic wildlife. A typical (but unforgettable) trip includes a river journey, all accommodations and meals, jungle walks and canoe trips, and a visit to an indigenous village. Most lodges charge over US$100 per day depending on the number of days, services, group size and your bargaining abilities. Lodge offices are found in central Iquitos (Map p933), or ask at the tourist office. Budget travelers have especially recommended **Cumaceba** (☎ 065-22-1456; www.cumaceba.com; Putumayo 184), **Muyuna** (☎ 065-24-2858; www.muyuna .com; Putumayo 163), **Loving Light** (☎ 065-24-3180; www.junglelodge.com; Putumayo 128), **Yarapa River** (☎ 065-993-1172; www.yarapariverlodge.com; La Marina 124) and **Explorama** (☎ 065-25-2530; www.explor ama.com; La Marina 340) Amazon lodges.

(pricier) room towers on jungle-style stilts; others are small and dark.

Hospedaje La Pascana (☎ 065-23-1418; www.pascana.com; Pevas 133; s/d/tr US$11/12.50/15.50) With a small plant-filled garden, this safe and friendly place is deservedly popular with travelers and often full. Book exchange.

Also recommended:

Hostal Maflo (☎ 24-1257; hostalmaflo@mixmail.com; Morona 177; s/d incl breakfast US$7.20/12) Plain rooms with hot water and cable TV.

Hostal Libertad (☎ 23-5763; Arica 361; s/d US$7.50/11.50, d with air-con US$15) Simple rooms with electric showers; some have cable TV.

Hospedaje El Sitio (☎ 23-4932; R Palma 545; s/d US$7.80/11) Clean, extra large rooms with cable TV.

Hostal Lima (☎ 22-1409; Próspero 549; s/d US$8/11) Tight but tidy rooms with miniscule baths. Upstairs is better and breezier.

Hotel Sandalo (☎ 23-4761; sandalo@iquitos .net; Próspero 616; s/d US$12.50/18.75, with air-con US$18.75/25, all incl breakfast; ❄) Modern, motel-style carpeted rooms with cable TV, minifridge and phone.

Eating

Yellow Rose of Texas (Putumayo 180; breakfast from US$1.50, mains US$5-7.50; ❄ 24hr) Specializes in Texas BBQ, but you can feast on other jungle and international dishes, too, in the lanternlit courtyard or at sidewalk tables.

Lidia's (Bolognesi 1181; mains from US$2; ❄ 6-9pm Mon-Sat) So homey it's practically inside Lidia's living room, with plenty of meat, fish, *tamales* and plantains straight off the grill. No sign, but plenty of sizzle.

Parrillada Al Carbón (Condamine 115; mains US$2-5; ❄ dinner) Look out for local dishes such as *tacacho* (mashed bananas with bacon), *calabresa* (spicy Brazilian sausage) and *patacones* (fried plantains) at this tasty grill.

Ari's Burger (Próspero 127; meals US$2-6; ❄ 7am-3am) Squeaky clean and on the main plaza, it's locally dubbed 'gringolandia' and great for American-style food and ice cream.

Fitzcarraldo Restaurant-Bar (Napo 100; mains US$3-7) Anchors a block of upscale riverside restaurants, with a streetside patio and frigid air-con indoors.

Gran Maloka (Lores 170; menú US$3.50, mains US$7-9; ❄ noon-10pm; ❄) Inside an atmospheric mansion from rubber-boom days. The menu is adventurous (curried caiman anyone?) but has plenty of less-startling options. Good for a splurge.

Supermercado Los Portales (cnr Próspero & Morona) For supplies.

Drinking

Arandú Bar (Napo) A good beer joint next to the Fitzcarraldo.

Café-Teatro Amauta (Nauta 250) Has live Peruvian music most nights and a well-stocked bar of local drinks.

Yellow Rose of Texas (Putumayo 180; ❄ 24hr) The spot for games, sports TV and heavenly ice-cold beers.

Entertainment

Agricobank (cnr Condamine & Pablo Rosell; admission US$1.75) Hundreds gather to let loose at this huge, outdoor place.

Noa Noa Disco-Pub (Pevas 292; admission US$6) The upscale Noa Noa pulsates to cumbia and salsa rhythms.

La Paranda (Pevas 174) Sees locals strutting their stuff on weekends.

Getting There & Away

AIR

Iquitos' airport (IQT) is 7km south of town. Flights are currently available to Lima and Tarapoto with more modern **LAN** (☎ 23-2421; Próspero 232), as well as **Star Perú** (☎ 23-6208; Napo 256) and **Aero Condor Perú** (☎ 23-1086; Próspero 215). Charter flights go almost anywhere in the Amazon (US$300 per hour).

BOAT

Cargo boats normally leave from Puerto Masusa, on Av La Marina, 2.5km north of the town center. Chalkboards tell you which boats are leaving when (though departures often change overnight, and boats tend to leave hours or days late). See p828 for more details on cargo-boat journeys.

Boats to Pucallpa (four to seven days) or Yurimaguas (three to six days) cost around US$20 to US$30 per person. Boats leave about three times a week to Pucallpa, more often to Yurimaguas, but less if the river is low at the time of departure.

Getting Around

Taxis to the airport cost US$3, *motocarros* US$2. Buses and trucks for nearby destinations, including the airport, leave from Plaza 28 de Julio. *Motocarro* rides around town cost US70¢. **JB Moto-Rental** (Yavari 702; per hr US$2.50) rents motorcycles.

PERU

GETTING TO COLUMBIA, BRAZIL & ECUADOR

Colombia, Brazil and Peru share a three-way border. Even in the middle of the Amazon, border formalities must be adhered to and officials will refuse passage if your passport, tourist card and visas are not in order. Regulations change, but the riverboat captains know where to go. You can travel between the three countries without formalities, as long as you stay in the tri-border area. Otherwise, if you're leaving Peru, get an exit stamp at the Peruvian immigration post in Santa Rosa, on the south side of the river, just before the border (boats will stop long enough for this – ask the captain).

The biggest town is Leticia (Colombia), which has hotels, restaurants and a hospital. Get your passport stamped here for official entry into Colombia. Motorized canoes from Santa Rosa reach Leticia in about 15 minutes. From Leticia you can fly to Bogotá on almost daily commercial flights. Otherwise, infrequent boats go to Puerto Asis on the Río Putumayo, a trip of up to 12 days. From Puerto Asis, buses go further into Colombia.

Leticia is linked with Tabatinga (Brazil) by road (a short walk or taxi ride). Get your official entry stamp for Brazil from Tabatinga's police station. Tabatinga has an airport with flights to Manuas (Brazil). Boats to Manaus, about a week away, leave from downriver and usually stop in the Brazilian port of Benjamin Constant for a night. Otherwise it takes an hour to reach Benjamin Constant by public ferry. North Americans, Australians and others must obtain visas to enter Brazil; for more information, see p407.

From Iquitos (p935), boats to Santa Rosa leave twice weekly, take two days and cost US$15 to US$20 (bargain hard). Several companies on Raymondi at Loreto including **Expreso Loreto** (☎ 065-23-4086/24-3661) offer fast launches that take 12 hours, depart at 6am every other day and cost US$50, including lunch.

It is also possible, though arduous, to travel by cargo boat between Iquitos and Coca, Ecuador, via the Amazon and Napo Rivers. For more information on traveling this route from Ecuador to Peru, see p702 in the Ecuador chapter.

For information on entering Peru from Brazil, see p394; from Colombia, p625.

PERU DIRECTORY

ACCOMMODATIONS

Lima and the tourist mecca of Cuzco are the most expensive places to stay in Peru. During high season (June through August), major holidays (p940) and festivals (p939), accommodations are likely to be full and rates can triple. At other times, the high-season rates quoted in this chapter are very negotiable. Foreign tourists normally aren't charged the 10% sales tax on accommodations. *Incluye impuesto* (IGV) means a service charge has been included in the price. At better hotels, taxes and service charges combined may total 28%. Budget hotels usually have hot (or more likely, tepid) showers some of the time. They may not accept or honor reservations. Dormitory beds come with shared bathrooms, while single/double rooms (including those in *hostales*, which are guesthouses and not the same as backpacker hostels) have private bathrooms, unless otherwise noted.

ACTIVITIES

Most activities are available year-round, but certain times of year are better than others. Peak season for most outdoor activities is during the winter dry season (June to August). Trekking in the highlands is a muddy proposition during the wet season, especially December to March, when the heaviest rains fall. However, those hotter summer months are best for swimming and surfing along the Pacific Coast.

The fledgling status of many outdoor activities in Peru means that equipment rental can be expensive and hard to find. Beware that activity guides are often unregulated, untrained and inexperienced, which can lead to injury or even death for their clients. For your safety, avoid the cheapest, cut-rate tour agencies and outdoor outfitters. For specialized activities, bring high-quality gear from home.

Bird-Watching

If bird-watching gets you in a flap, head for the Amazon Basin (p926), Islas Ballestas (p846) and Cañón del Colca (p863) for starters. See p827 for more info on Peru's wildlife.

Climbing

Huascarán (6768m), Peru's highest mountain, is experts-only, but easier peaks abound near Huaraz (p914) and Arequipa (p860). Rock and ice climbing are taking off in a big way around Huaraz (p914).

Horse-Riding

Horse rentals can be easily arranged. For a real splurge, take a ride on a graceful Peruvian paso horse near Lima (p838) or Urubamba (p881).

Mountain Biking

Gearing up for some downhill adventures? Easy or demanding single-track trails also await mountain bikers outside Huaraz (p915), Cuzco (p875) and Arequipa (p860).

Paragliding

Paragliding is an up-and-coming sport in Peru, especially in Lima (p838).

Rafting

White-water rafting (river-running) agencies in Cuzco (p875) and Arequipa (p861) offer a multitude of day runs and longer hauls (grade III to IV+ rapids). Travelers have died on these rivers in recent years, so be especially cautious about which rafting company to trust with your life. The best place for beginners is at Lunahuaná (p845).

Surfing & Sandboarding

Surfing has a big fan base in Peru. There are some radical waves up north, famously at Huanchaco (p904), Máncora (p911) and Puerto Chicama (p905), and just south of Lima (p838), too. For something completely different, sandboard down humongous dunes in the coastal desert near Huacachina (p850) and Nazca (p852).

Trekking

Trekkers, pack your boots – the variety of trails in Peru is staggering. The Cordillera Blanca (p918) can't be beat for peaks, while the nearby Cordillera Huayhuash (p920) is similarly stunning. But if you've heard of *any* trek in Peru, you will have heard of the world-famous Inca Trail to Machu Picchu (p887) – and everyone else has, too, so consider taking an alternative route to Machu Picchu (p888). The spectacular six-day Ausangate Circuit (p891), the Inca site Choquequirau (p891) and

ancient ruins hidden in cloud forests outside Chachapoyas (p923) are a few more trekking possibilities. Alternatively, get down into the world's deepest canyons – the Cañón del Cotahuasi (p860) and Cañón del Colca (p863).

BOOKS

Check out Lonely Planet's *Peru* guide and *Trekking in the Central Andes*.

If you read only one book about the Incas, make it the lucid and lively *Conquest of the Incas* by John Hemming. Or get a grip of *all* of Peru's bygone cultures with *The Ancient Kingdoms of Peru* by Nigel Davies.

The White Rock by Hugh Thomson describes a filmmaker's search for Inca archaeological sites throughout the Andes, with plenty of background on earlier explorers.

Eight Feet in the Andes by Dervla Murphy is a witty travelogue of the writer's 1300-mile journey with her daughter through remote Andean highlands from Ecuador to Cuzco, ending at Machu Picchu.

The Peru Reader: History, Culture, Politics, edited by Orin Starn, Carlos Ivan Degregori and Robin Kirk, looks at everything from the conquest of the Incas to cocaine production, guerrilla warfare and gay activism.

Touching the Void by Joe Simpson, now an award-winning British documentary film, is a harrowing account of mountaineering survival in the Cordillera Huayhuash.

The Monkey's Paw by Robin Kirk covers Peru during the violent 1980s – it's an excellent if chaotic examination of how individuals manage to survive terror.

Trail of Feathers by Tahir Shah is a tall tale of the author's quest to uncover what lies behind the 'birdmen' legends of the Peruvian desert, eventually leading to a cannibalistic Amazonian tribe.

Inca Kola by Matthew Parris is a tongue-in-cheek, often snide story about backpacking in Peru.

BUSINESS HOURS

Shops open at 9am or 10am and close between 6pm and 8pm. A three-hour lunch break is common, especially at restaurants. Shops may stay open through lunch in big cities, and there are 24-hour supermarkets in Lima. Banks are generally open 9am to 6pm Monday to Friday, to 1pm Saturday. Post offices and *casas de cambio* keep highly variable hours. Almost everything closes on Sunday.

PERU

CLIMATE

During the coastal summer (late December to early April), many Peruvians head to the beach as the dreary *garúa* (coastal fog, mist or drizzle) clears and the sun breaks through.

In the Andes proper, the cool, dry season runs from May to September, which is peak season for tourism. The mountains can reach freezing temperatures at night, but enjoy glorious sunshine during the day. The wet season in the mountains extends from October to May, and is at its worst during January and February.

It rains all the time in the hot and humid Amazonian rainforest, but the driest months are from June to September. However, even during the wettest months (from December to May), it rarely rains for more than a few hours at a time.

For more information and climate charts, see p1062.

DANGERS & ANNOYANCES

Peru has its fair share of traveler hassles, which may often be avoided by exercising common sense.

The most common problem is theft, either stealth or snatch – theft by violent mugging is rare, though not to be ruled out. Watch out for 'choke and grab' attacks, especially at archaeological sites. Robberies and fatal attacks have occurred even on popular trekking trails, notably around Huaraz.

Avoid unlicensed 'pirate' taxis, as some drivers have been known to be complicit in 'express' kidnappings. Take good-quality day buses instead of cheap, overnight services to lower the risk of having an accident or possibly being hijacked.

Do *not* get involved with drugs. Gringos who have done are being repaid with long-term incarceration in harsh Peruvian prisons. Any suspect in a crime (which includes vehicle accidents, whether or not you're the driver at fault) is considered guilty until proven innocent.

Terrorism is largely a thing of the past in Peru, but narco-trafficking is serious business. Areas to avoid are the Río Huallaga valley between Tingo María and Juanjui, and the Río Apurímac valley near Ayacucho, where the majority of Peru's illegal drug-growing takes place.

Not all unexploded ordinance (UXO) along the Ecuadorian border has been cleaned up –

use only official border crossings and don't stray off the beaten path in border zones.

Soroche (altitude sickness) can be fatal. For more information, see p1095.

DRIVER'S LICENSE

A driving license from your own home country is sufficient for renting a car. An International Driving Permit (IDP) is only required if you'll be driving in Peru for more than 30 days.

ELECTRICITY

Peru runs on a 220V, 60Hz AC electricity supply. Even though two-pronged outlets accept both flat (North American) and round (European) plugs, electronics built for lower voltage and cycles (eg 110–120V North American appliances) will function poorly or not at all, and plugging them in without using a converter can damage them.

EMBASSIES & CONSULATES
Embassies & Consulates in Peru

Australia Lima (Map pp832-3; ☎ 01-222-8281; www.australia.org.pe; Suite 1301, Torre Real 3, Av Victor A Belaúnde 147, San Isidro, Lima 27)

Bolivia Lima (Map pp832-3; ☎ 01-422-8231; fax 01-222-4594; Castaños 235, San Isidro, Lima 27) Puno (Map p866; ☎/fax 051-35-1251; Arequipa 136, 3rd fl, Puno)

Brazil (Map p840; ☎ 01-421-5660; www.embajadabrasil.org.pe; José Pardo 850, Miraflores, Lima 18)

Canada (Map p840; ☎ 01-444-4015; www.dfait-maeci.gc.ca/latin-america/peru; Libertad 130, Miraflores, Lima 18)

Chile (Map pp832-3; ☎ 01-611-2211; www.embachile.peru.com.pe; Javier Prado Oeste 790, San Isidro, Lima 27)

Colombia Iquitos (Map p933; ☎ 065-23-1461; cniquitosperu@terra.com.pe; Calvo de Araujo 431, Iquitos); Lima (Map pp832-3; ☎ 01-441-0954; www.embajadacolombia.org.pe; Jorge Basadre 1580, San Isidro, Lima 27)

Ecuador Lima (Map pp832-3; ☎ 01-212-4171; www.mecuadorperu.org.pe; Las Palmeras 356, San Isidro, Lima 27); Tumbes (Map p840; ☎ 072-52-5949; 3rd fl, Bolívar 129, Plaza de Armas, Tumbes)

France (Map pp832-3; ☎ 01-215-8400; www.ambafrance-pe.org; Arequipa 3415, San Isidro, Lima 27)

Germany (Map p840; ☎ 01-212-5016; www.embajada-alemana.org.pe; Arequipa 4210, Miraflores, Lima 18)

UK (☎ 01-617-3000; www.britishembassy.gov.uk; 23fl, Torre Parque Mar, José Larco 1301, Miraflores, Lima 18)

USA (Map pp832-3; ☎ 01-434-3000; http://lima
.usembassy.gov; La Encalada 17th block, Surco, Lima 33)

Peruvian Embassies & Consulates

See p942 for visa information. Peruvian embassies are found in all neighboring countries, in addition to the following:

Australia (☎ 02-6273-8752; www.embaperu.org.au;
40 Brisbane Ave, Barton, ACT 2600)

Canada (☎ 613-238-2721; www.embassyofperu.ca;
Suite 201, 130 Albert St, Ottawa, ON K1P 5G4)

France (☎ 01-42-70-65-25-10; conperparis@wanadoo
.fr; 25 rue de l'Arcade, 75008 Paris)

Germany (☎ 030-2-29-14-55; www.conperberlin
.embaperu.de; Mohrenstrasse 42, 10117 Berlin)

Israel (☎ 09-9957-8836; emperu@012.net.il; Entrada A,
2nd fl, 60 Medinat Hayehudim St, Herzliya 46766)

Italy (☎ 06-8069-1510, 06-8069-1534; www.ambascia
taperu.it; Via Francesco Siacci 2B, 00197 Roma)

Netherlands (☎ 020-622 85 80; fax 020-422 85 81;
Kantoorgebouw Riverstate, Amsteldijk 166-7E, 1079 LH
Amsterdam)

New Zealand (☎ 04-499-8087; www.embassy
ofperu.org.nz; Level 8, Cigna House, 40 Mercer St,
PO Box 2566, Wellington)

Spain (☎ 91-56-29-012; www.consuladoperumadrid
.org; Calle Cristobal Bordiú 49, 28003 Madrid)

UK (☎ 020-7235 1917; www.peruembassy-uk.com;
52 Sloane St, London SW1X 9SP)

USA (☎ 202-833-9860; www.peruvianembassy.us;
1700 Massachusetts Ave NW, Washington, DC 20036)

FESTIVALS & EVENTS

See p940 for a list of national holidays.
La Virgen de la Candelaria (Candlemas) A colorful highland fiesta on February 2, particularly in the Puno area.

Carnaval In February/March – water fights galore!

Semana Santa (Holy Week) Religious processions throughout the week; March/April.

Corpus Christi Dramatic processions in Cuzco on the ninth Thursday after Easter.

Inti Raymi The great Inca festival of the sun, held on the winter solstice (June 24).

La Virgen del Carmen Street dancing in Pucara near Lake Titicaca and Paucartambo and Pisac near Cuzco on July 16.

Puno Day Spectacular costumes and dancing in Puno (November 5) to commemorate the legendary emergence of the first Inca, Manco Capác, from Lake Titicaca.

FOOD & DRINK

Food tends toward the spicy, but *aji* (chili condiments) are served separately. If you're sick of seafood, crying off *cuy* (guinea pig) or feeling ill at the very idea of Cajamarca's specialty, cow brains, every town has its *pollería* grills churning out chicken and potatoes for the masses. Vegetarianism is a small but fast-growing industry in Peru; hole-in-the-wall joints are popping up in major cities and tourist destinations. *Chifas* (Chinese restaurants) are often cheap, while many other local restaurants offer a *menú del día* (set meal, usually lunch), consisting of a soup, main course and possibly dessert for around US\$2.

Incluye impuesto (IGV) means a service charge has been included in the price. Better restaurants add 18% in taxes and 10% in tips to the bill.

Peruvian Cuisine

Among the most typical Peruvian snacks and dishes:

ceviche erótico (se·*vee*·che e·*ro*·tee·ko) – mixed seafood marinated in lime, chili and onions, served cold with sweet corn and a boiled yam; considered an aphrodisiac!

chirimoya (*chee*·ree·mo·ya) – reptilian-looking custard apple with sweet interior; tastes better than it looks

cuy chactado (kwee chak·*ta*·do) – roasted guinea pig

lomo de alpaca (*lo*·mo de al·*pa*·ka) – alpaca meat tastes like beef, but has only half the fat

lomo saltado (*lo*·mo sal·*ta*·do) – chopped steak fried with onions, tomatoes and potatoes, served with rice

palta a la jardinera (*pal*·ta a la khar·dee·*nye*·ra) – avocado stuffed with cold vegetables and mayonnaise; *a la reina* is stuffed with chicken salad

rocoto relleno (ro·*ko*·to re·*ye*·no) – spicy bell pepper stuffed with ground meat; very hot!

sopa a la criolla (*so*·pa a la kree·*ol*·la) – lightly spiced, creamy noodle soup with beef and vegetables; *a la criolla* describes spicy foods.

Drinks

ALCOHOLIC DRINKS

There are about a dozen kinds of palatable and inexpensive beer, both light, lager-type beers and sweet, dark beers (called *malta* or *cerveza negra*). Cuzco and Arequipa are fiercely proud of their beers, Cuzqueña and Arequipeña.

Dating back to pre-Columbian times, traditional highland *chicha* (corn beer) is stored in

> **WARNING**
>
> Avoid food prepared from endangered animals. Sometimes *chanco marino* (dolphin) may be served up or, in the jungle areas, *huevos de charapa* (tortoise eggs), *motelo* (turtle) or even *mono* (monkey).

PERU

earthenware pots and served in huge glasses in small Andean villages and markets, but is not usually commercially available. This home-brew is an acquired taste – the unhygienic fermentation process begins with someone chewing the corn.

Peruvian wines are good but not up to the standard of Chilean or Argentine tipple. A white-grape brandy called *pisco* is the national drink, most frequently served in a *pisco sour,* a tasty cocktail made from pisco, egg white, lemon juice, syrup, crushed ice and bitters. The firewater of choice in the jungle is *aguardiente* (sugarcane spirits flavored with anise). *Salud!*

NONALCOHOLIC DRINKS

Agua mineral (mineral water) is sold *con gas* (with carbonation) or *sin gas* (without carbonation). Don't leave without trying Peru's top-selling, fizzy-bubble-gum-flavored Inca Kola at least once. Ask for it *sin hielo* (without ice) unless you really trust the water supply. *Jugos* (fruit juices) are widely available. Make sure you get *jugo puro,* not *con agua.* The most common juices are *naranja* (orange), *toronja* (grapefruit), *maracuyá* (passion fruit), *manzana* (apple), *naranjilla* (a local fruit tasting like bitter orange) and papaya. *Chicha morada* is a sweet, bland, noncarbonated drink made from purple corn. *Maté de coca* (coca-leaf tea) allegedly helps with acclimatization.

GAY & LESBIAN TRAVELERS

Peru is a strongly conservative, Catholic country. Gays and lesbians tend to keep a low profile. Homosexual rights in a political or legal context don't even exist as an issue for most Peruvians. (FYI the rainbow flag seen around Cuzco is *not* a gay pride flag – it's the flag of the Inca Empire.) When the issue does arise in public, hostility is most often the official response.

Kissing on the mouth is rarely seen in public, by either heterosexual or homosexual couples. Peruvians are physically demonstrative with their friends, though, so kissing on the cheek in greeting or an *abrazo* (backslapping hug exchanged between men) are innocuous, everyday behaviors. When in doubt, do as locals do.

Lima is the most accepting of gay people (see p839), while Cuzco, Arequipa and Trujillo are more tolerant than the norm.
Movimiento Homosexual-Lesbiana (☎ 01-332-2945; www.mhol.org.pe) is Peru's best-known gay political organization.

HOLIDAYS

On major holidays, banks, offices and other services are closed, fully booked hotels double or triple their rates, and transportation becomes overcrowded. Fiestas Patrias is the biggest national holiday, when the entire nation seems to be on the move.
Año Nuevo (New Year's Day) January 1
Good Friday March/April
Día del Trabajador (Labor Day) May 1
Inti Raymi June 24
Fiestas de San Pedro y San Pablo (Feast of St Peter & St Paul) June 29
Fiestas Patrias (National Independence Days) July 28 and 29
Fiesta de Santa Rosa de Lima August 30
Battle of Angamos Day October 8
Todos Santos (All Saints Day) November 1
Fiesta de la Purísima Concepción (Feast of the Immaculate Conception) December 8
Navidad (Christmas Day) December 25

INTERNET ACCESS

Internet cafés are found on every other street corner in Peru. Even small towns will have at least one *cabina* tucked away somewhere. Access is fast and inexpensive (around US60¢ per hour) in cities, but pricier and painfully slow in rural areas.

INTERNET RESOURCES

Andean Travel Web (www.andeantravelweb.com/peru) Travel directory with links to hotels, tour companies, volunteer programs etc.
Living in Peru (www.livinginperu.com) English-speaking expat's guide: an excellent source of Lima-centric news and events.
Peru Links (www.perulinks.com) Thousands of interesting links; many are in Spanish, some in English. Editor's picks and top 10 sites are always good.
PromPerú (www.peru.info) Official governmental tourism site has a good overview in Spanish, English, French, German, Italian and Portuguese.

LEGAL MATTERS

There are *policía de turismo* (tourist police) stations in over a dozen major cities, and they usually have someone on hand who speaks at least a little English. Although bribery is illegal, some police officers (including tourist police) are corrupt. Because most travelers won't have to deal with traffic police, the most likely place you'll be expected to pay officials a little extra is at overland border crossings. This too is illegal, and if you have the time and fortitude to stick to your guns, you will eventually be allowed in.

MAPS

The best road map of Peru, *Mapa Vial* (1:2,000,000) published by Lima 2000, is sold in bookstores. **Instituto Geográfico Nacional** (IGN; Map pp832-3; ☎ in Lima 01-475-9960; Aramburu 1198, Surquillo; 🕑 9am-4pm Mon-Fri) sells topographic maps, which are more easily available from outdoor outfitters in major cities and tourist destinations.

MONEY

The currency is the nuevo sol (S/), divided into 100 *céntimos*.

ATMs

Most cities and some small towns have 24-hour ATMs on the Plus (Visa) and Cirrus (Maestro/MasterCard) systems. American Express and other networks are less widespread. Bigger airports and bus stations, as well as Interbank branches, have global ATMs that accept almost all foreign cards. ATMs in Peru will only accept your debit, bank or traveler's check card if you have a four-digit PIN. Both US dollars and Peruvian currency are dispensed. Remember your bank will charge a fee for each foreign ATM transaction.

Cash

The following bills are commonly in circulation: S/10, S/20, S/50, S/100. When changing money, always ask for plenty of small bills. Coins of S/0.5, S/0.10, S/0.20, S/0.50, S/1, S/2 and S/5 are also in use. US dollars are accepted at many tourist-oriented establishments, but you'll need nuevos soles to pay for transportation, cheap meals and guesthouses etc.

Credit Cards

Better hotels, restaurants and shops accept *tarjetas de credita* (credit cards), but usually tack on a fee of 7% or more for paying with plastic.

Exchanging Money

Currencies other than US dollars can be exchanged only in major cities and at a high commission. Worn, torn or damaged bills are not accepted. *Casas de cambio* are open longer than banks and are much faster. Money changers are useful for exchange outside banking hours or at borders where there are no banks, but beware of 'fixed' calculators, counterfeit notes and short-changing.

Traveler's Checks

Traveler's checks can be cashed at larger banks and money changers' offices, but they are hard to exchange outside of large towns. Commissions are high, up to 10%. Amex is the most widely accepted brand, followed by Thomas Cook and Visa.

POST

Serpost (www.serpost.com.pe) is the privatized postal system. It's relatively efficient, but expensive. Airmail postcards and letters cost about US$3.50 each to most foreign destinations, arriving in about two weeks from Lima, longer from provincial cities.

Lista de correos (poste restante/general delivery) can be sent to any major post office. South American Explorers will hold mail and packages for members at its clubhouses in Lima (p836) and Cuzco (p871).

RESPONSIBLE TRAVEL

Archaeologists are fighting a losing battle with *huaqueros* (grave robbers), particularly along the coast. Refrain from buying original pre-Columbian artifacts, and do not contribute to wildlife destruction by eating endangered animals (see p939) or purchasing souvenirs made from skins, feathers, horns or turtle shells. Some indigenous communities make their living from tourism. Visiting these communities may financially support their initiatives, but also weaken traditional cultures. If you go on an organized tour, make sure the company is locally owned and ask if any of the proceeds benefit the places you'll be visiting.

STUDYING

Peru is less well known for its Spanish-anguage courses than other Latin American countries. However, there are several schools in Lima (p830), Cuzco (p875) and Arequipa (p860).

TELEPHONE

Public payphones are available in even the tiniest towns. Most work with phonecards, and many with coins. Dial 109 for a Peruvian operator, 108 for an international operator and 103 for information. Internet cafés are often much cheaper for making local, long-distance and international phone calls than **Telefónica-Perú** (www.telefonica.com.pe) offices.

Cell Phones

It's possible to use a tri-band GSM world phone in Peru (GSM 1900); other systems in use are CDMA and TDMA. In major cities, you can buy cell phones for about US$65, then pop in a SIM card that costs from US$6 – Claro is a popular pay-as-you-go plan. Reception fades the further you head into the mountains or jungle.

Phone Codes

Peru's country code is ☎ 51. To call a foreign country, dial 00, the country code, area code and local number.

Each region of Peru (called a department) has its own area code, which begins with 0 (☎ 01 in Lima, 0 plus two digits elsewhere). To call long-distance within Peru, include the 0 in the area code. If calling from abroad, dial your international access code, the country code (☎ 51), the area code without the 0, then the local number.

Phonecards

Called *tarjetas telefonicas,* phonecards are widely available from street vendors or kiosks. Some have an electronic chip, but most make you dial a code to obtain access. The most common are the 147 cards: dial 147, enter the code on the back of your card, listen to a message in Spanish telling you your balance, dial the number, listen to how much time you have, then your call connects. Ask around for which companies' cards offer the best deals.

TOILETS

Peruvian plumbing leaves something to be desired. Even a small amount of toilet paper in the bowl can muck up the entire system – that's why a small, plastic bin is routinely provided for disposing of it. Except at museums, restaurants, hotels and bus stations, public toilets are rare in Peru. Always carry an extra roll of toilet paper with you.

TOURIST INFORMATION

PromPerú's official tourism website (www.peru.info) has information in Spanish, English, French, German, Italian and Portuguese. PromPerú also runs **iPerú** (☎ 24hr hotline 01-574-8000) information offices in Lima, Arequipa, Ayacucho, Chachapoyas, Cuzco, Huaraz, Iquitos, Puno and Trujillo. Municipal tourist offices are found in other cities listed earlier in this chapter. The South American Explorers clubhouses in Lima (p836) and Cuzco (p871) are good sources of information for travelers, but you'll get more help as a paying member.

TOURS

Some protected areas such as the Inca Trail and Parque Nacional Manu can only be entered with a guided tour. Other outdoor activities, such as trekking in the Andes or wildlife-watching in the Amazon, may be more rewarding with an experienced guide.

TRAVELERS WITH DISABILITIES

Peru offers few conveniences for travelers with disabilities. Peru's official tourism organization **PromPerú** (left) has a link to Accessible Tourism from the 'Special Interest' section of its website (www.peru.info) for reports on wheelchair-accessible hotels, restaurants and attractions in Lima, Cuzco, Aguas Calientes, Iquitos and Trujillo. **Apumayo Expeditions** (p875) is an adventure-tour company that specializes in tours to Machu Picchu and the Amazon jungle, as well as river-rafting trips.

VISAS

With few exceptions (a handful of Asian, African and communist countries), visas are not required for tourism. Passports should be valid for at least six months from your departure date. For more information on entry requirements (eg onward/return tickets), see p1073. Travelers are permitted a 30- to 90-day stay, stamped into their passports and onto an Andean Immigration Card that you must keep and return when leaving Peru. Visa extensions are available at immigration offices *(oficinas de migraciónes* or *migraciónes)* in major cities, with Lima (p831) being the easiest place to do so. Bring your passport and immigration card; you may be asked to show a ticket out of the country or proof of sufficient funds. Each extension costs about US$28 and you can stay up to 180 days total. When your time is up, you can leave the country overland and return a day later to begin the process again.

While traveling around Peru, carry your passport and immigration card with you at all times, as you can be arrested if you don't have proper ID.

VOLUNTEERING

Most volunteer programs charge you for program fees, room and board. Watch out for fake charities and illegitimate programs that are scams. Spanish-language schools usually know of casual volunteer opportunities. South American Explorers clubhouses have firsthand reports from foreign volunteers in Lima (p836) and Cuzco (p871). **ProWorld Service Corps** (ProPeru; ☎ in USA 877-733-7378, in UK 0-870-750-7202; www.pro worldsc.org) organizes two- to 26-week cultural, service and academic placements in the Sacred Valley and the Amazon, and is affiliated with NGOs throughout Peru.

WOMEN TRAVELERS

Most women encounter no serious problems in Peru, though they should come mentally prepared for being the constant center of attention. Machismo is alive and well in Peruvian towns and cities, where curious staring, whistling, hissing and *piropos* (cheeky, flirtatious or vulgar remarks) are an everyday occurrence. Ignoring provocation is generally the best response. Most men don't follow up their idle chatter with something more threatening unless they feel you've challenged or insulted their manhood.

If you appeal to locals for help, you'll find most Peruvians act protectively toward women traveling alone, expressing surprise and concern when you tell them you're traveling without your husband or family. If a stranger approaches you on the street to ask a question, *don't* stop walking, which would allow attackers to quickly surround you. Never go alone on a guided tour, and stay alert at archaeological sites, even during daylight hours. Take only authorized taxis and avoid overnight buses.

Abortions are illegal in Peru, except to save the life of the mother. Planned Parenthood–affiliated **Instituto Peruano de Paternidad Responsable** (Inppares; ☎ 01-583-9012; www.inppares .org.pe) runs a dozen sexual- and reproductive-health clinics for both sexes around the country.

WORKING

Officially you need a work visa in Peru, though language centers in Lima or Cuzco sometimes hire native speakers to teach English. This is illegal, and such jobs are increasingly difficult to get without a proper work visa. For internships and short-term jobs with volunteer organizations, see left.

PERU

Uruguay

HIGHLIGHTS

- **Colonia del Sacramento** – step back in time as you wander the streets of this atmospheric smugglers' port (p955)
- **Punta del Este** – pamper yourself with some time out amongst the jet set in this world-famous beach resort (p964)
- **Mercado del Puerto** – test your true carnivore status on the absurdly large steaks at this atmospheric market (p953)
- **Drinking mate** – hook up with some locals and sip the afternoon away (p947)
- **Off the beaten track** – gawk at some real live *gauchos* in the mellow little town of Tacua-rembó (p961)
- **Best journey** – zip through the river delta between Carmelo and the Buenos Aires suburb of Tigre – easily the best way to do this border crossing (p958)

FAST FACTS

- **Area:** 187,000 sq km (roughly the size of the US state of North Dakota)
- **Best bargain:** homemade pasta – US$4 a plate just about anywhere
- **Best street snack:** Milanesa sandwich – get a *completo* (one with the lot – ham, cheese, egg and salad) and it's a meal
- **Budget:** US$25-35 a day
- **Capital:** Montevideo
- **Costs:** budget hotel in Montevideo US$15, 3hr bus ride US$4, set lunch US$4
- **Country Code:** ☎ 598
- **Famous for:** winning the first World Cup (1930), beach resorts
- **Languages:** Spanish, Portuguese near the Brazilian border
- **Money:** US$1 = 23.8 Uruguayan pesos
- **Phrases:** *bárbaro* (cool), *¡garca!* (disgusting), *jodita* (party)
- **Population:** 3,241,000

- **Time:** GMT minus 3hr
- **Tipping:** 10% in restaurants and hotels if not included in bill; round up in taxis
- **Visas:** North Americans and Europeans only need a valid passport

TRAVEL HINTS

Be kind to yourself – Uruguay's one of those places where paying a little extra gets you a whole lot more.

OVERLAND ROUTES

Gualeguaychú, Colón and Concordia from Argentina. Most people use Xui from Brazil, Villazón from Bolivia and San Felipe from Chile.

Well, somebody let the cat out of the bag. Uruguay used to be South America's best-kept secret, with a handful of Argentines, Brazilians, Chileans and non–South Americans in the know popping in to enjoy the pristine beaches, the atmospheric cities, the huge steaks and the happening nightlife.

Then the peso crashed, the place became a whole lot more affordable and people got curious. They came, loved it and went back home to tell their friends. Who came, loved it and went back home to tell *their* friends.

Which is not to suggest that the place is being overrun. The main drawcards, like Colonia, Punta del Este and Montevideo, have long been set up for tourists, and are dealing with their newfound popularity well. Elsewhere, in the interior and the river towns and particularly in the non-summer months, there's still a pretty good chance that you'll be the only gringo in town.

CURRENT EVENTS

In March 2005 Tabare Vazquéz swept in to power, heading a broad coalition of leftist parties, riding a wave of support from youth groups, unions and community groups. Uruguay collectively held its breath, waiting while the new government organized itself, to see if it would live up to the leftist rhetoric of the campaign trail, or if the country was in for more of the same old, same old.

Early signs were not good. Among the standout actions of Vazquéz's early months in power were the seeking of a free-trade deal with the US (surprising and alienating Uruguay's Mercosur trade partners), the banning of smoking in public (annoying pretty much everybody in this nicotine-crazed land) and the granting of leases to two foreign multinationals to build two paper factories on the Río Uruguay, which forms the border between Uruguay and Argentina (infuriating Argentines, environmentalists and hardcore lefties).

This last became a real sticking point. Public figures who had campaigned for Vazquéz began distancing themselves. Argentina took the case to the International Court of The Hague. Soon enough the whole thing turned into your classic macho Latino face-off, with neither side willing to back down.

Argentina argued that the factories would pollute the river, a literal lifeline for the Argentine towns that rely on it for tourism and fishing. Uruguay argued that they desperately need the industry, and that the plants will be built to more exacting environmental standards than the Argentines ever imposed on factories operating on their side of the river. As this book was going to press, it was looking very likely that the plants would be operational by early 2008.

HISTORY
In the Beginning...

The Charrúa were here first, huntin' and fishin'. They had no gold and a nasty habit of killing European explorers, so the Spanish left them alone. Eventually they mellowed out, got some horses and cattle, and started trading. Once the big cattle farmers moved in, the Charrúa got pushed out and they now exist in isolated pockets around the Brazilian border.

Everybody Wants a Piece

The Jesuits were on the scene as early as 1624 and the Portuguese established present-day Colonia in 1680 so they could smuggle goods into Buenos Aires. Spain responded by building its own citadel at Montevideo. For almost 200 years the Portuguese, Spanish and British fought to get a foothold.

From 1811 José Artigas repelled the Spanish invaders, but Brazil ended up controlling the region. Artigas was exiled to Paraguay where he died in 1850, after inspiring the 33 Orientales who, reinforced by Argentine troops, liberated the area in 1828, establishing Uruguay as a buffer between the emerging continental powers of Argentina and Brazil.

More Drama

Liberation didn't bring peace. There were internal rebellions, insurrections and coups. Argentina besieged Montevideo from 1838 to 1851 and Brazil was an everpresent threat. Uruguay's modern political parties, the Colorados and the Blancos, have their origins in this time – early party membership comprised large numbers of armed *gauchos* (cowboys). By the mid 19th century the economy was largely dependent on beef and wool production. The

URUGUAY

rise of the *latifundios* (large landholdings) and commercialization of livestock led to the demise of the independent *gaucho*.

José Batllé, We Love You

In the early 20th century, visionary president José Batllé y Ordóñez introduced such innovations as pensions, farm credits, unemployment compensation and the eight-hour workday. State intervention led to the nationalization of many industries and general prosperity. The invention of refrigerated processing and shipping facilities opened many overseas markets for Uruguayan beef. However, Batllé's reforms were largely financed through taxing the livestock sector and when this sector faltered the welfare state crumbled.

The Wheels Fall Off

By the 1960s economic stagnation and massive inflation were reaching crisis points, and social unrest was increasing. President Oscar Gestido died in 1967 and was replaced by running mate Jorge Pacheco Areco.

Pacheco sprang into action, outlawing leftist parties and closing leftist newspapers, which he accused of supporting the guerrilla Movimiento de Liberación Nacional (commonly known as Tupamaros). The country slid into dictatorship. After Tupamaros executed suspected CIA agent Dan Mitrione (as dramatized in Costa-Gavras' film *State of Siege*) and engineered a major prison escape, Pacheco put the military in charge of counterinsurgency. In 1971 Pacheco's chosen successor, Juan Bordaberry, handed control of the government over to the military.

Jobs for the Boys

The military occupied almost every position of importance in the 'national security state.' Arbitrary detention and torture became routine. The forces determined eligibility for public employment, subjected political offenses to military courts, censored libraries and even required prior approval for large family gatherings.

Voters rejected a military-drawn constitution in 1980. Four years passed before Colorado candidate Julio María Sanguinetti became president under the existing constitution. His presidency implied a return to democratic traditions, but he also supported a controversial amnesty, ratified by voters in 1989, for military human-rights abuses.

Later in 1989, the Blancos' Luis Lacalle succeeded Sanguinetti in a peaceful transition. Sanguinetti returned to office in the November 1994 elections and was succeeded by Jorge Battle Ibañez, another Colorado candidate, in March 2000.

Oh No, Not this Again

The military were still lurking around, though – one of Ibañez' first official duties was to dismiss the head of the army for suggesting that another coup might be in order. The Frente Amplio (Broad Front) – a coalition of leftist parties – became a serious political contender, winning popularity for its anti-privatization, pro-welfare stance. In December 2000 Ibañez called for the legalization of cocaine in the US (¡olé!) as a means of stamping out the black market. His calls were met with a resounding silence from Washington.

Bad Omens

When the spread of foot-and-mouth disease led to the banning of Uruguayan beef exports, it was bad news for the economy. When Argentine banks froze deposits and thousands of Argentineans withdrew their cash from Uruguayan banks, it was *really* bad news. Argentinean deposits made up 80% of foreign reserves in Uruguay's banks. Uruguayans watched in horror as their economy – previously one of the strongest in South America – crumbled, and inflation (3.6% in 2001) rocketed to 40% by the end of 2002. The tourist industry (heavily reliant on prosperous Argentines) suffered. The peso plummeted in value, the economy minister resigned and the government declared a bank holiday to prevent a run on the banks.

Independence?

What followed was a massive bailout – Ibañez' emergency measures (cutting public spending, increasing sales tax) were rewarded by a series of loans from the US, the IMF and the World Bank totaling US$1.5 billion. Despite that, Uruguay was still showing some pluck politically – condemning the sanctions against Cuba, the coup in Venezuela and the war in Iraq.

THE CULTURE
The National Psyche

The one thing that Uruguayans will tell you that they're *not* is anything like their *porteño* (people from Buenos Aires) cousins across the water. In many ways they're right. Where the Argentines are brassy and sometimes arrogant, the Uruguayans are relaxed and self-assured. Where the former have always been a regional superpower, the latter have always lived in the shadow of one. Those jokes about Punta del Este being a suburb of Buenos Aires don't go down so well on this side of the border. There are plenty of similarities, though – the near-universal appreciation for the arts and the Italian influence, with its one-ingredient pizzas and love of wine and cheese. The *gaucho* thang plays a part, too, and the rugged individualism and disdain that many Uruguayans hold for *el neoliberalismo* (neoliberalism) can be traced directly back to those romantic cowboy figures.

Lifestyle

Uruguayans like to take it easy and pride themselves on being the opposite of the hot-headed Latino type. They're big drinkers, but bar-room brawls are rare. Sunday's the day for family and friends, to throw half a cow on the *asado* (spit roast), sit back and sip some mate. The population is well educated, although public-school standards are slipping. The once-prominent middle class is disappearing as private universities become the main providers of quality education.

Uruguay's small population produces a surprising amount of talented artists and literary figures. While Juan Carlos Onetti is probably the most famous Uruguayan writer, most young Uruguayans have a big soft spot for Eduardo Galeano, who has written many books and poems.

Population

The Uruguayan population is predominately white (88%) with 8% *mestizo* (people with mixed Spanish and indigenous blood) and 4% black. Indigenous peoples are practically nonexistent. The population growth rate is 0.5%. Population density is 18.5 people per sq km.

SPORTS

> Sexo, droga y Peñarol
> *Montevideo graffito*

In Uruguay, sport means football and football means soccer. Uruguay has won the World Cup twice, including the first tournament, played in Uruguay in 1930. The most notable teams are Montevideo-based Nacional and Peñarol. If you go to a match between these two, sit on the sidelines, not behind the goal, unless you're up for some serious passion-induced rowdiness.

The **Asociación Uruguayo de Fútbol** (☎ 02-400-7101; Guayabo 1531) in Montevideo can provide information on matches and venues.

RELIGION

Sixty-six percent of Uruguayans are Roman Catholic. There's a small Jewish minority, numbering around 25,000. Evangelical Protestantism has made some inroads and Sun Myung Moon's Unification Church owns the afternoon daily, *Últimas Noticias*.

ARTS

Uruguay has an impressive literary and artistic tradition; Uruguay's major contemporary writers include Juan Carlos Onetti and poet, essayist and novelist Mario Benedetti.

There aren't that many films made in or about Uruguay. Probably the most famous exception is Costa-Gavras' famous and engrossing *State of Siege* (1973), filmed in Allende's Chile, which deals with the Tupamaro guerrillas' kidnapping and execution of suspected American CIA officer Dan Mitrione.

The best movie to come out of Uruguay lately is *Whisky* (2004), a witty black comedy and social commentary set in Montevideo and Piriapolis. It won a couple of awards at Cannes.

Theater is popular and playwrights such as Mauricio Rosencof are prominent. The most renowned painters are the late Juan Manuel Blanes and Joaquín Torres García. Sculptors include José Belloni, whose life-size bronzes can be seen in Montevideo's parks.

Tango is big in Montevideo – Uruguayans claim tango legend Carlos Gardel as a native son (although the Argentines have other ideas). During Carnaval, Montevideo's streets reverberate to the energetic African drum beats of *candombe*, an African-derived rhythm brought to Uruguay by slaves from 1750 onwards.

As far as contemporary music goes, ska punk is big in Uruguay, with groups like El Congo and La Vela Puerca getting plenty of airplay, and Once Tiros mixing it up with a fusion of ska and electronica.

ENVIRONMENT

Uruguay's rolling northern hills extend from southern Brazil with two main ranges of interior hills, the Cuchilla de Haedo, west of Tacuarembó, and the Cuchilla Grande, south of Melo, neither of which exceeds 500m in height. West of Montevideo the terrain is more level. The Atlantic coast has impressive beaches, dunes and headlands. Uruguay's grasslands and forests resemble those of Argentina's Pampas or southern Brazil. Patches of palm savanna persist in the southeast, along the Brazilian border.

Nearly all large land animals have disappeared, but the occasional rhea still races across northwestern Uruguay's grasslands. Some offshore islands harbor southern fur seal and sea lion colonies.

Uruguay isn't big on national parks. Santa Teresa (p967) is the country's only park, but it doesn't have a whole lot going on nature-wise.

TRANSPORTATION

GETTING THERE & AWAY
Air

Most international flights to/from Montevideo's Aeropuerto Carrasco pass through Buenos Aires. Many others stop at Rio de Janeiro or São Paulo.

Direct flights go to Porto Alegre, Florianópolis, Rio and São Paulo (Brazil), Asunción (Paraguay) and Santiago (Chile). There

DEPARTURE TAX

International passengers leaving from Carrasco pay US$8 departure tax if headed to Argentina, US$14 to other destinations.

are also flights to Santa Cruz de la Sierra and La Paz (Bolivia), and Havana (Cuba) via Buenos Aires.

Boat

Most travelers cross from Montevideo to Argentina by ferry, sometimes with bus combinations to Colonia or Carmelo.

Bus

Direct buses run from Montevideo to Buenos Aires via Gualeguaychú, but are slower than land/river combinations across the Río de la Plata. Further north there are bridge crossings over the Río Uruguay from Fray Bentos to Gualeguaychú, Paysandú to Colón and Salto to Concordia. There are plenty of land crossings to Brazil, including Chuí and Pelotas, Río Branco to Jaguarão, Rivera to Santana do Livramento, Artigas to Quaraí and Bella Unión to Barra do Quaraí. Buses generally continue through the border and passport formalities are conducted on the bus.

GETTING AROUND

Uruguayan buses and roads are well maintained. Montevideo is *the* transport hub. If you stay on the coast or river roads, you'll never be waiting long for a bus. Try something tricky (Chuy to Tacuarembó, for example) and you'll experience otherwise. Due to its small size, Uruguay is perfect for bus travel – the longest ride you're likely to take is a measly six hours.

Air

If you really need to get somewhere in a hurry, internal charter flights are available with **Aeromas** (www.aeromas.com) from Montevideo to Salto, Tacuarembó, Paysandú, Rivera and Artigas.

Bus

Bus travel in Uruguay is a lot less painful than in many parts of the world. Most towns have a *terminal de omnibus* (central bus terminal) for long-distance buses. To get your choice of seat, buy tickets in advance from the terminal.

Local buses are usually slow and crowded, but cheap.

Car & Motorcycle

Due to the excellent bus network, not many people use independent transport to get around Uruguay, although cars and motorbikes can be hired in tourist centers like Colonia and Punta del Este.

Hitchhiking

Hitchhikers are rare in Uruguay – you might get picked up for novelty value. It's not a particularly dangerous country, but hitching is a gamble anywhere in the world. Take the usual precautions.

Taxi

Taxis are so cheap they're hard to resist. Meters are always out of whack, so drivers consult a photocopied chart to calculate the fare. A long ride in Montevideo shouldn't go over US$5; short hops in small towns usually cost less than US$1. On weekends and at night, fares are 25% to 50% higher.

MONTEVIDEO

☎ 02 / pop 1,270,000

Montevideo is a favorite for many travelers. Small enough to walk around, but big enough to have some great architecture and happening nightlife.

The young *montevideanos* (people from Montevideo) who don't escape across the water to Buenos Aires have a real pride in their city, and the arts and artisan scene is particularly strong.

Many of the grand 19th-century neoclassical buildings, legacies of the beef boom, are in various stages of crumbling, although vestiges of Montevideo's colonial past still exist in the Ciudad Vieja (Old Town), the picturesque historic center.

ORIENTATION

Montevideo lies on the east bank of the Río de la Plata. Its functional center is Plaza Independencia, east of the Ciudad Vieja. Av 18 de Julio is the key commercial area.

Across the harbor, the 132m Cerro de Montevideo was a landmark for early navigators of this region. East of downtown, the riverfront Rambla leads past residential suburbs and

URUGUAY

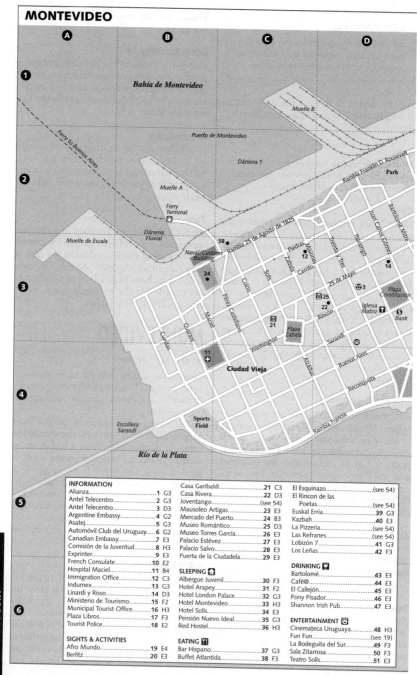

MONTEVIDEO

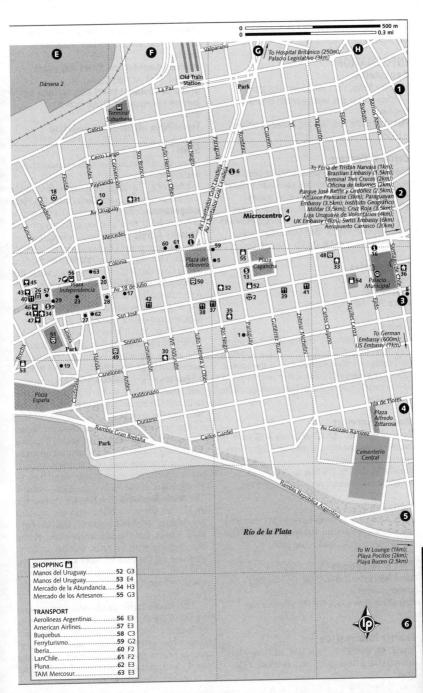

sandy beaches frequented by *montevideanos* on weekends in summer.

INFORMATION
Bookstores
Linardi y Risso (Juan Carlos Gómez 1435) A sizable selection of out-of-print books, especially in history and literature.

Plaza Libros (Av 18 de Julio 892) A selection of books in English.

Cultural Centers
Alianza (☎ 901-7423; Paraguay 1217) The American-Uruguayan cultural center contains a bookstore, a theater and a substantial library with publications in English.

Alliance Française (☎ 400-0505; www.alliancefran caise.edu.uy; Blvd Artigas 1229) A well-stocked library with books, magazines and CDs. Short-term visitors can avoid membership fees by paying a US$50 refundable deposit.

Emergencies
Ambulance (☎ 105)
Fire (☎ 104)
Police (☎ 109)

Media
The *Guía del Ocio*, which lists cultural events, cinemas, theaters and restaurants, appears on Fridays in newsstands. Ask at the tourist office for a copy of *Guear*, a free pocket-sized booklet with more information on bars, clubs and bands.

Medical Services
Hospital Británico (☎ 280-0020; Italia 2420) You'll find English-speaking doctors at this private, highly recommended hospital.

Hospital Maciel (☎ 915-3000; cnr 25 de Mayo & Maciel) The public hospital, located in the Ciudad Vieja.

Money
Most downtown banks have ATMs. **Exprinter** (cnr Sarandí & Juncal) and **Indumex** (Plaza Cagancha) change traveler's checks and cash.

Post & Telephone
Antel Telecentro (San José 1108; ☉ 24hr) There's another at Rincón 501.

Post office (Buenos Aires 451) This is the main post office.

Tourist Information
Asatej (☎ 908-0509; Río Negro 1354, 2nd fl) Argentina's nonprofit student travel agency, this is an affiliate of STA Travel.

Ministerio de Turismo (☎ 908-9141; cnr Colonia & Av Liberatador Gral Lavalleja) Better equipped than the offices.

Municipal tourist office (☎ 903-0649; Palacio Municipal) Small but well informed.

Oficina de Informes (☎ 409-7399; Tres Cruces Bus Terminal) Well equipped and handy for fresh arrivals.

Tourist Police (☎ 924-7277; Paysandú 1234)

SIGHTS
None of the listings in this section charge admission.

Most of Montevideo's interesting buildings and museums are in the **Ciudad Vieja**. On **Plaza Independencia**, a huge statue of the country's greatest hero tops the eerie underground **Mausoleo Artigas** (☉ 9am-5pm), where fans of famous dead people can tick another one off the list. The 18th-century **Palacio Estévez** served as the Casa de Gobierno until 1985, while the striking 26-story **Palacio Salvo** was once South America's tallest building. Just off the plaza, the recently renovated **Teatro Solís** (1856) is Montevideo's leading theater.

On 25 de Mayo between Solís and Colón, is the **Casa Garibaldi** (☉ 11am-5pm Tue-Fri, 11am-4pm Sat), where Guiseppe Garibaldi, the Italian nationalist hero, once lived. The 1868 **Mercado del Puerto** (cnr Pérez Castellano & Piedras) is a wrought-iron superstructure sheltering a gaggle of restaurants. On Saturdays artists and musicians frequent the area.

The neoclassical 1802 **Casa Rivera** (cnr Rincón & Misiones; ☉ 11am-5pm Tue-Fri, 11am-6pm Sat) houses a fascinating collection of indigenous artifacts, colonial treasures and oil paintings, including a spectacular panoramic depiction of Montevideo at the end of the 18th century. The **Museo Romántico** (25 de Mayo 428; ☉ 11am-5pm Tue-Fri, 11am-4pm Sat) is filled with the opulent furnishings of Montevideo's 19th-century elite. Check out the ladies' traveling vanity case, replete with brushes, combs, scissors, perfume bottles and fold-out candleholders; you can bet there were some arguments about whose backpack *that* monster was going in.

The **Museo Torres García** (www.torresgarcia.org .uy; Sarandí 683; ☉ 9am-8pm) displays the works of Joaquín Torres García (1874–1949), the Uruguayan artist who spent much of his career in France producing abstract and Cubist work, and unusual portraits of figures like Columbus, Mozart and Beethoven.

ACTIVITIES

Peddlers can hire a **bike** from the Albergue Juvenil (available to nonguests; see below) and go cruising along the riverfront Rambla, a walking-jogging-bike track that leads to the city's eastern beaches. After about 2km you'll get to Playa Pocitos, which is best for **swimming** and where you should be able to jump in on a game of **beach volleyball**.

A couple of bays further along you'll get to Playa Buceo, where you can get **windsurfing** lessons at the yacht club from **Enrique Soriano** (☎ 099-9939) for around US$10 per hour.

Strong swimmers could also strike out from here for **Isla de las Gaviotas**, a sandy, palm-covered island about 700m offshore.

If all that seems a bit too energetic for you, bus 64 goes from Av 18 de Julio along the coast road – just jump off when you see a beach you like.

COURSES

The following courses don't cater for the casual learner – you'd want to be staying at least a month to get your money's worth.

Afro Mundo (☎ 915-0247; Mercado Central, 1st fl) Classes in African drumming, *capoeira* and *candombe* dance.

Berlitz (☎ 901-5535; www.berlitz.com; Plaza Independencia 1380) One-on-one Spanish tuition.

Joventango (☎ 901-5561; Mercado de la Abundancia) Tango classes for all levels, from gringo to expert.

FESTIVALS & EVENTS

Montevideo's **Carnaval** takes place on the first Monday and Tuesday before Ash Wednesday. Highlights include *candombe* dance troupes beating out African-influenced rhythms on large drums. The **Semana Criolla** (during Semana Santa) is part rodeo, part arts fair, part outdoor concert – it's *gaucho*-rama out there. Festivities take place at Prado, easily reached by bus 149 or 152.

SLEEPING

Albergue Juvenil (☎ 908-1324; Canelones 935; dm HI member/nonmember US$7/9; 🖳) A well-set-up and spacious hostel in a central location. Besides, where else are you going to stay in a hostel with a wrought-iron spiral staircase? Rent bikes here for US$1/4 per hour/day.

Red Hostel (☎ 908-8514; www.redhostel.com; San José 1406; dm/s/d US$11/24/32; 🖳) An elegant, cool new hostel – the price includes just about everything you could want, from internet

---

GETTING INTO TOWN

A taxi from the airport costs about US$10. Airport buses cost US$0.70¢ and take 40 minutes. Buses 21, 61, 180, 187 and 188 go from Terminal Tres Cruces to 18 de Julio (US$0.70).

---

access to breakfast to hammock space on the spacious rooftop terrace.

Hotel Montevideo (☎ 900-4634; Aquiles Lanza 1309; s/d from US$12/15) A no-frills option in the center, the Montevideo has a surprising variety of rooms – some with wooden floors and spacious bathrooms, others a bit pokier. Definitely worth asking to see a few.

Pensión Nuevo Ideal (☎ 908-2913; Soriano 1073; d with/without bathroom US$18/15) The lobby of this attractive little hotel is a good indication of what's in store: there's plenty of light, the place is spotless and the decor is tasteful yet restrained. Blasting hot showers are an added bonus.

Hotel Arapey (☎ 900-7032; www.arapey.com.uy; Av Uruguay 925; s/d US$15/18) Somebody chintzed this place out, and they chintzed it good – gold-leaf room furniture? Wickerwork bedheads? Curvy, Guadí-esque balconies? Still, it's quiet and clean and a good place to rest up if you've been doing it hard.

Hotel Solís (☎ 915-0279; Bartolomé Mitre 1314; s/d US$20/25, with shared bathroom US$15/18) An atmospheric budget classic in the center of the old town. Some rooms have great little balconies overlooking Bartolomé Mitre – but be warned: those bars (and sidewalk tables) below pack out every night, making things pretty noisy.

Hotel London Palace (☎ 902-0024; www.lphotel .com; Rio Negro 1278; s/d US$35/40; P 🏠) With its antique furniture, hall runners and modern rooms that manage to retain a vestige of style, the London Palace is a step above the rest in this price range.

EATING

The steaks served at *parrillas* (steakhouses) inside the Mercado del Puerto are so large they're almost obscene. Saturday lunchtime, when the market is crammed with locals, is the best time to visit.

Euskal Erria (San José 1168; mains US$2-5) An excellent selection of Basque and Spanish dishes are on offer here, as is the best paella in town. Cheap *jarras* (jugs) of red wine are bound to keep you hanging around.

Los Leños (San José 909; dishes US$3-6) A classy, central *parrilla* serving up all your favorite chunks of meat, plus pasta and seafood. The *cazuela de mariscos* (seafood stew; US$10) is a real gobstopper.

Kazbah (Bartolomé Mitre 1368; dishes US$3-10) The restaurant scene in Montevideo is just starting to get interesting, and this Middle Eastern–inspired place is one of the fore-runners. Come here for all your faves, like falafel, *schwarma* (doner kebabs), couscous and tagines.

Bar Hispano (San José 1050; set meals US$4) Old-school neighborhood *confiterías* like this one are great, but disappearing fast. They can take pretty much any order you throw at them – a stiff drink to start the day, a full meal at 5pm, or a chocolate binge in the early hours. Add to this some ancient, bowtied, grouchy waiters and a mindboggling dessert selection and you know it's a very special place.

Lobizón 7 (Zelmar Michelini 1325; dishes US$4-6) Popular with young *montevideanos*, with inex-pensive lunch specials including *gramajo* (a calorie-packed house special of eggs, ham and French fries). Live music some nights.

Buffet Atlantida (San José 1020; all you can eat US$6) The selection here is mindblowing – pastas, *parrillada* and Chinese food, as well as daily specials like roast pork. Undeniable value for those with big stomachs and small budgets.

The Mercado de la Abundancia is a popular and atmospheric spot for lunch or dinner. **El Rincon de las Poetas** (set meals US$3-5) and **Las Refranes** (set meals US$3-5) both have good set meals. **El Esquinazo** (mains US$3-5) has a wider menu and **La Pizzeria** (mains US$4-7) is open for dinner only.

DRINKING

The most happening bar precinct in town is in Bartolomé Mitre in the old city. There were 18 bars in this little stretch last time we checked, and no doubt there'll be more by the time you get there. The best idea is to go for a wan-der and see where the crowd is. Some of the old favorites include the **Pony Pisador** (Bartolomé Mitre 1326), **Café@** (Bartolomé Mitre 1322) and **Shan-non Irish Pub** (Bartolomé Mitre 1318), which all have reasonably priced drinks, DJs and occasional live music. Newcomers include the Middle Eastern–flavored **Kazbah** (Bartolomé Mitre 1368), **El Callejón** (Bartolomé Mitre 1386) for jazz, rock and blues and **Bartolomé** (Bartolomé Mitre 1322), a huge rambling place with outdoor seating and pool tables upstairs.

ENTERTAINMENT

W Lounge (Rambla Wilson s/n; admission US$4) In the Parque Rodó, this club is *the* place to shake your thang. A taxi from the center should cost around US$3.

La Bodeguita del Sur (Soriano 840) This is the place to come to for live folkloric music, Cuban salsa and the like.

Sala Zitarrosa (cnr 18 de Julio & Av Herrera y Obes) Hosts rock bands and occasional live theater.

Fun Fun (Ciudadela 1229) Located in the Mercado Central, Fun Fun attracts an older crowd of tango enthusiasts, with live bands on weekends and a pleasant deck area out the front.

Cinemateca Uruguaya (Av 18 de Julio 1280; mem-bership per month US$4) For arthouse flicks, this cinema is also a film club with a modest mem-bership fee allowing unlimited viewing at its five cinemas.

Teatro Solís (www.teatrosolis.org.uy; Buenos Aires 678) Montevideo has an active theater commu-nity and this is the most prestigious play-house in town, but there are many others. Admission starts around US$4. Check the *Guía del Ocio* for listings for this and other theaters.

SHOPPING

Feria de Tristán Narvaja (Calle Tristán Narvaja, btwn Av 18 de Julio & Calle La Paz, El Cordón; ☺ 9am-3pm Sun) This bustling outdoor market sells everything from antique knickknacks and jewelry to artisan crafts and fried fish. The market stalls sprawl for seven blocks.

Mercado de los Artesanos (Plaza Cagancha) Has some excellent handicrafts at fairly reason-able prices.

Manos del Uruguay (San José 1111) This place is famous for its range of slightly pricey, high-quality goods. Has a second branch at Reconquista 602.

You'll find most of the same stuff at the **Mercado de la Abundancia** (cnr San José & Yaguarón). Plaza Constitución hosts an enjoyable flea market on Saturday.

GETTING THERE & AWAY
Air

Montevideo's **international airport** (Aeropuerto Carrasco; ☎ 604-0329) is 20km east of the city at Carrasco. Besides the usual international car-riers, commuter airlines also provide services to Argentina. The internet-based **Gol Airlines** (www.voegol.com.br) has cheap flights to Porto

GETTING TO ARGENTINA

Ferry crossings are the most popular way to cross this border – either direct from Montevideo to Buenos Aires (from US$60), via Colonia to Buenos Aires (US$26 to US$41) or via Carmelo to Tigre (US$17), a suburb of Buenos Aires. Immigration is carried out at the port, so try to arrive an hour ahead of your departure time.

Local buses run across the Río Uruguay from Fray Bentos, Paysandú and Salto to their Argentine counterparts, Gualeguaychú, Colón and Concordia, respectively. Immigration procedures are often handled on the bus, but if you have to disembark, the bus will wait. Borders are open 24 hours.

Alegre, Brazil. Airline offices in Montevideo include the following:

Aerolíneas Argentinas (☎ 902-3691; www.aerolineas.com.ar; Plaza Independencia 749bis)

American Airlines (☎ 916-3929; www.aa.com; Sarandí 699)

Iberia (☎ 908-1032; www.iberia.com; Colonia 975)

LanChile (☎ 902-3881; www.lan.com; Colonia 993, 4th fl)

Pluna (☎ 902-1414; www.pluna.com.uy; cnr Plaza Independencia 804 & Florida)

TAM Mercosur (☎ 901-8451; www.tam.com.py; Colonia 820)

Boat

Ferryturismo (☎ 900-0045; Río Negro 1400) does bus-ferry combinations to Buenos Aires, via Colonia (US$26, six hours), and with the faster Sea Cat (US$41, four hours). It also has a branch at **Terminal Tres Cruces** (☎ 409-8198). *Buqueaviones* (high-speed ferries) cross directly to Buenos Aires from Montevideo (2½ hours). Fares start at US$60.

Cacciola (☎ 401-9350), at Terminal Tres Cruces, runs a bus-launch service to Buenos Aires (US$17, eight hours) via Carmelo and the Argentine Delta suburb of Tigre.

Bus

Montevideo's **Terminal Tres Cruces** (☎ 401-8998; cnr Bulevar Artigas & Italia) has decent restaurants, clean toilets, a left-luggage facility, a *casa de cambio* (foreign-exchange house) and ATMs.

Destination	Duration (hr)	Cost (US$)
Chuy	5	12
Colonia	2½	6
Fray Bentos	4½	11
Maldonado	2	5
Mercedes	4	10
Minas	2	5
La Paloma	3½	8
Paysandú	5	13
Punta del Diablo	4½	11
Punta del Este	2½	6
Salto	6	17
Tacuarembó	5	13
Treinta y Tres	4	10

Bus de la Carrera has three buses daily to Buenos Aires (US$28, eight hours) via Fray Bentos. There are several departures daily for other destinations in Argentina, including Rosario (US$35, 10 hours), Córdoba (US$44, 15 hours), Santa Fe (US$32, eight hours), Paraná (US$31, 10 hours) and Mendoza (US$61, 20 hours).

EGA goes to Santiago de Chile (US$84, 30 hours), Porto Alegre (US$50, 11 hours), Florianópolis (US$75, 18 hours) and Curitiba, Brazil (US$92, 24 hours).

Brújula and Coit go to Asunción, Paraguay (US$62, 20 hours).

GETTING AROUND

Airport buses (US$1, 40 minutes) leave from **Terminal Suburbana** (cnr Rambla Franklin D Roosevelt & Río Branco). Local buses go everywhere for about US$0.70.

WESTERN URUGUAY

The land west of Montevideo is in many ways the 'real' Uruguay – little river towns separated by large expanses of pampas and wheat fields. It's far off the tourist trail, mostly, except for the region's superstar, Colonia del Sacramento, whose charms attract visitors from all over the world.

COLONIA DEL SACRAMENTO

☎ 052 / pop 22,000

Take some winding, cobbled streets, add an intriguing history and put them on a gorgeous point overlooking the Río de la Plata. What do you get? A major tourist attraction.

But the snap-happy hordes can't kill the atmosphere of 'Colonia'. This place has got

URUGUAY

URUGUAY

COLONIA DEL SACRAMENTO

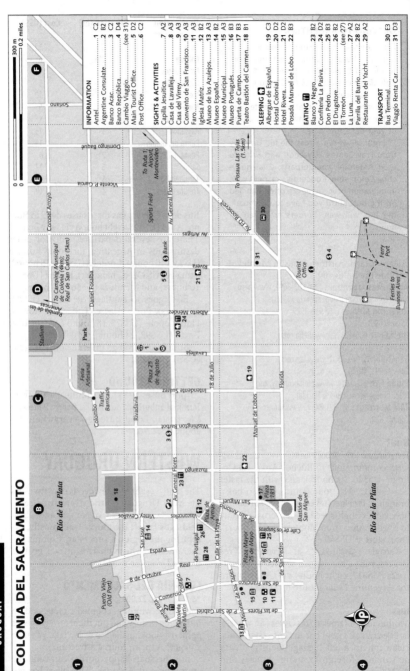

INFORMATION	
Antel	1 C2
Argentine Consulate	2 B2
Banco Acac.	3 C2
Banco República	4 D4
Cambio Viaggio	(see 31)
Main Tourist Office	5 D2
Post Office	6 C2

SIGHTS & ACTIVITIES	
Capilla Jesuítica	7 A2
Casa de Lavalleja	8 A3
Casa del Virrey	9 A3
Convento de San Francisco	10 A3
Faro	11 A3
Iglesia Matriz	12 B2
Museo de los Azulejos	13 A3
Museo Español	14 A3
Museo Municipal	15 A3
Museo Portugués	16 B3
Puerta de Campo	17 B3
Teatro Bastión del Carmen	18 B1

SLEEPING	
Albergue de Español	19 C3
Hostal Colonial	20 D2
Hotel Rivera	21 D2
Posada Manuel de Lobo	22 B3

EATING	
Blanco y Negro	23 B2
Confitería La Pasiva	24 D2
Don Pedro	25 B3
El Drugstore	26 B2
El Torreón	(see 27)
La Luna	27 A2
Parrilla del Barrio	28 B2
Restaurante del Yacht	29 A2

TRANSPORT	
Bus Terminal	30 E3
Viaggio Renta Car	31 D3

'it', whatever that is, as well as enough restaurants, bars and nightlife to keep you happy for weeks.

The Portuguese founded Colonia in 1680 to smuggle goods across the Río de la Plata into Buenos Aires. The Spanish captured it in 1762 and held it until 1777, when tax reforms finally permitted foreign goods to proceed directly to Buenos Aires.

Orientation & Information

The *Barrio Histórico* (historic area) is on a small peninsula – the commercial downtown, near Plaza 25 de Agosto, and the river port are a few blocks east. Information services are as follows:

Antel (Rivadavia 420)

Banco Acac (cnr Av Gral Flores & Washington Barbot) Has an ATM.

Banco República Operates exchange facilities at the port.

Cambio Viaggio (cnr Av FD Roosevelt & Florida; ✆ closed Sun)

Main tourist office (☎ 26141; Av Gral Flores 499)

Post office (Lavalleja 226)

Tourist office (☎ 28506; Plaza 1811)

Sights

Colonia's museums are open 11am to 5pm daily. The US$0.70 entrance ticket covers all of the following.

The Barrio Histórico begins at the restored **Puerta de Campo** (1745), on Manuel de Lobos, where a thick fortified wall runs to the river. A short distance west, off Plaza Mayor 25 de Mayo, tile-and-stucco colonial houses line narrow, cobbled **Calle de los Suspiros**; just beyond is the **Museo Portugués**, where you'll find some great old seafaring maps and a very fanciful depiction of the Lobo family tree.

At the southwest corner of the plaza are the **Casa de Lavalleja**, formerly General Lavalleja's residence, ruins of the 17th-century **Convento de San Francisco** and the restored 19th-century **faro** (lighthouse). At the west end, on de San Francisco, the **Museo Municipal** has antique homewares, dinosaur remains and huge petrified mushrooms. The **Casa del Virrey** – which was never home to a viceroy – is just to the north.

At the west end of Misiones de los Tapes, the tiny **Museo de los Azulejos** is a 17th-century house showcasing colonial tilework. The riverfront **Paseo de San Gabriel** leads to Colegio, where a right turn onto Comercio heads to the ruined **Capilla Jesuítica** (Jesuit chapel). Turning east along Calle de la Playa will take you to Vasconcellos and the **Plaza de Armas**, where you'll find the landmark 1680 **Iglesia Matriz**, Uruguay's oldest church. Nearly destroyed by fire in 1799, it was rebuilt by Spanish architect Tomás Toribio. The interior retains its simple aesthetic appeal.

Across Av General Flores, the **Museo Español** (cnr España & San José) exhibits replicas of colonial pottery, clothing and maps. At the north end of the street is the **Puerto Viejo** (Old Port). Although it has long ceased to function as a port, it's a picturesque place to soak up some of the atmosphere of the old smuggling days. One block east, the **Teatro Bastión del Carmen** (cnr Virrey Cevallos & Rivadavia) incorporates part of the ancient fortifications.

Sleeping

Camping Municipal de Colonia (☎ 24662; sites per person US$3, 2-person cabañas US$12) Near the beach at Real de San Carlos, 5km northwest of the Barrio Histórico. There are hot showers on site and a handful of restaurants nearby.

Albergue de Español (☎ 099-624-129; Manuel del Lobos 377; s/d US$7/14) This friendly hostel offers large, multibed rooms in an atmospheric old building. Some rooms are a bit dark.

Hostal Colonial (☎ 30347; hostelling_colonial@hotmail.com; Av Gral Flores 440; dm/d US$6/US$12-16; ☐) Good courtyard rooms line this old building; out of five doubles, two come with private bathroom. Services include kitchen use and free bike rentals, and they can organize horse treks.

Hotel Rivera (☎ 20807; Rivera 131; www.hotelescolonia.com/rivera; s/d US$17/20; ✲) Heavy wooden-beamed ceilings and terracotta floors make the Rivera a decent choice for the money. The rooms are a bit poky, but the attractive outdoor and indoor sitting areas make up for it.

Posada Manuel de Lobo (☎ 22463; www.colonianet.com/posadamdelobo; Ituzaingó 160; r US$50; P ✲) Decked out with gorgeous, heavy wooden room furniture and antique tilework, this house is over 150 years old and you can feel the atmosphere as you laze in the lush back patio or on the upstairs balcony.

Eating

Confitería La Pasiva (Av Gral Flores 432; dishes US$3-5) A newly opened branch of the popular chain, this is a good place for breakfast or pizza and sandwiches any time during the day.

Don Pedro (Manuel de Lobos 144; dishes US$3-7) It's nothing fancy, but it does serve great sandwiches, pasta, meats and ice cream. The shady outdoor seating on Plaza Mayor makes this a great lunch spot.

Blanco y Negro (Av Gral Flores & Ituzaingó; dishes US$4-6) An upmarket *parrilla* and pasta joint with live jazz on weekends. The *parrillada* for two (US$11) is a real gutbuster.

El Torreón (Av Gral Flores 46; dishes US$5-9) By far the best place to eat in terms of views, this place is set in an old tower overlooking the water. The back deck makes for a cozy, intimate spot for a romantic dinner.

Restaurante del Yacht (Santa Rita s/n; dishes US$6-8) With a bit of a snooty atmosphere, this place serves up excellent seafood and standard Uruguayan fare. Stunning river views are available from the small deck area.

Drugstore (Vasconcellos 179; dishes US$6-10) Reasonable set meals for two, eclectic decor (try dining in the vintage car on the street) and live music on weekends. If you're hungry, go for the *picada a la mar* (seafood assortment; US$10).

Parrilla del Barrio (Real 160; set meals US$7) Once the sun sinks a little and they put the tables out on the street, this friendly little *parrilla* is the place to be.

La Luna (Av Gral Flores 43; dishes US$4-8) This laidback pub-restaurant with a great rooftop terrace is the perfect place to grab a beer as the sun goes down and watch the ferries taking those poor fools back to Buenos Aires.

Activities
Hostel Colonial (p957) organizes halfday horse treks from an inland forest, along ravines and down to the coast for US$20. Shorter and longer rides are also available.

Getting There & Away
BOAT
From the port at the foot of Av Roosevelt, **Buquebus** (☎ 22975) has daily ferries to Buenos Aires (US$20, 2½ hours) and high-speed *buqueaviones* (US$35, one hour) – literally 'flying boat.' **Ferryturismo's** (☎ 22919) catamaran (US$35, one hour) goes daily. Immigration is at the port.

BUS
Colonia's **terminal** (cnr Artigas & Av FD Roosevelt) is near the port.

Destination	Duration (hr)	Cost (US$)
Carmelo	1	3
Mercedes	3	6
Montevideo	2½	6
Paysandú	6	11
Salto	8	15

Getting Around
Local buses leave from Av Gral Flores to the Camping Municipal. Bicycles and mopeds can be rented in the port area; try **Viaggio Renta Car** (☎ 22266; Manuel de Lobos 503; bikes/mopeds/scooters per day US$3/9/15).

CARMELO
☎ 0542 / pop 16,900
A super-mellow little town with a lush central square, Carmelo's streets slope down to its carefully restored waterfront. From here, boats leave for the most interesting (and cheapest) of the Argentine border crossings – a two-hour ride through the delta to the Buenos Aires suburb of Tigre.

The **main tourist office** (☎ 2001; 19 de Abril 246) is in the Casa de Cultura. It has lots of information (some in English) and a decent city map. There are *casas de cambio* near Plaza Independencia.

A large park on the other side of the arroyo offers camping, swimming and a monstrous casino.

Sleeping & Eating
Camping Náutico Carmelo (☎ 2058; sites US$4) This is on the south side of Arroyo de las Vacas.

Hotel Bertoletti (☎ 2030; Uruguay 171; s/d US$10/15) With a vaguely institutional feel offset (slightly) by touches like the floral lampshades, the Bertoletti is a favorite for traveling salespeople. It'll do for a night.

Rambla Hotel (☎ 2390; cnr Uruguay & 12 de Febrero; s/d from US$12/18) Down on the riverfront, the Rambla has a variety of rooms, some of which are airless little cubbyholes. Pay a little more and they start laying on balconies, river views, minibars, kitchenettes and all sorts of other crazy business.

Fey Fey (18 de Julio 358; dishes US$2-7) Right on the square, with outside tables, this is the best restaurant in town, both for food and atmosphere (although the jury's still out on the Guns n' Roses soundtrack). There's a full range of pizza, pasta, *parrilla* and snacks, as well as an excellent *pescado milanesa* (fish schnitzel; US$3).

URUGUAY

Getting There & Away

All bus companies are on or near Plaza Independencia. **Chadre** (☎ 2987) goes to Montevideo (US$8, four hours), and north to Fray Bentos, Paysandú and Salto. Turil goes to Colonia (US$2.50, one hour), as do **Klüver** (☎ 3411), Intertur and Berruti. Klüver also goes to Mercedes (US$3, two hours).

Cacciola (☎ 3042; Constituyentes s/n) has launches to the Buenos Aires suburb of Tigre (US$11, 3½ hours).

FRAY BENTOS

☎ 0562 / pop 23,000

Land must be cheap in Fray Bentos – the whole town is dotted with big, leafy plazas. Most travelers are here on their way either to or from Uruguay, but if you've got a few hours to kill between buses, the town boasts a fascinating museum that's well worth checking out.

The helpful **tourist office** (☎ 2233) occupies a room in the Museo Solari, on the west side of Plaza Constitución.

Sights

The landmark 400-seat **Teatro Young** (cnr 25 de Mayo & Zorrilla), bearing the name of the Anglo-Uruguayan estanciero who sponsored its construction, hosts cultural events throughout the year.

Museo de la Revolución Industrial (☎ 2918; tours US$1.50; ⏰ 10am-6pm Mon-Sat) Touring around an old meat extraction plant may not seem like your idea of fun, but this museum highlights a key part of Uruguay's history, when the British beef barons moved in and started the Uruguayan beef industry in earnest. Nowadays the plant and its surrounds – the 'Barrio Anglo' (English neighborhood) – have been redeveloped into a well-presented museum, restaurant and nightclub zone.

Sleeping & Eating

Balneario Las Cañas (☎ 22224; sites for 2 people US$6) This sprawling municipal campground is 8km south of town.

Nuevo Hotel Colonial (☎ 2260; 25 de Mayo 3293; s/d US$10/15, with shared bathroom US$8/12) Rooms in this classic two-story hotel are spacious and simple with wooden floorboards, facing a plant-filled patio. Shared bathrooms are spotless.

There are plenty of confiterías and pizza joints scattered around the main plaza. You could also try **Juventud Unida** (18 de Julio 1124),

a popular, good-value local choice serving parrillada (mixed grilled meats), sandwiches and pasta.

Getting There & Away

The otherwise rundown **bus terminal** (☎ 2737; cnr 18 de Julio & Varela) features a grand piano and rock garden. It's 10 blocks east of Plaza Constitución. ETA goes to Gualeguaychú (US$4, one hour). **CUT** (☎ 2286) has buses to Mercedes (US$1, 30 minutes) and Montevideo (US$10, 4½ hours). Chadre goes to Bella Unión via Salto and Paysandú, and south to Montevideo.

MERCEDES

☎ 053 / pop 42,000

The shady, cobblestoned streets of Mercedes are enchanting (unless your taxi has no suspension, in which case they're total kidney-crunchers). The riverfront is largely undeveloped, but there are plenty of grassy spots to laze around on between dips.

Plaza Independencia, the center of downtown, is dominated by the imposing neoclassical **cathedral** (1860).

The center is 10 blocks from the bus terminal. Either walk straight up Calle Colón with Plaza Artigas on your right, catch any local bus or fork out US$1 for a taxi.

The **tourist office** (☎ 22733; Artigas 215) has a good city map. Nearby casas de cambio change cash but not traveler's checks. There is a **post office** (Rodó 650) and telephone office, **Centro Telefónico** (Artigas 290).

Activities

Club Remeros Mercedes (below) rents canoes, kayaks and rowboats (US$2/US$6 per hour/day). It also has a jetty out onto the river with highdive platforms so you can practice your bellyfloppers.

Sleeping & Eating

Camping del Hum (sites per person US$2, plus per tent US$1) On an island in the Río Negro, linked by a bridge to the mainland, with excellent swimming, fishing and sanitary facilities. The campground closes when the river floods.

Club Remeros Mercedes (☎ 22534; De la Rivera 949; dm US$5-6) Downstairs there's a bar, a half-decent restaurant and a jumble of pool, ping-pong and fusbol (table soccer) tables, sporting trophies and mounted stuffed fish, all of which should be standard operating equipment in a hostel.

Hotel Mercedes (☎ 23204; Giménez 659; r with/without bathroom per person US$9/6.50) An excellent deal right in the center of town, with a shady courtyard. The rooms have cable TV and fill quickly. Reservations are a good idea.

Pizzeria Centro (cnr Colón & Castro y Careaga; dishes US$3-6) A legion of overhead fans keep the air moving at this vaguely atmospheric place serving the standard range of pizza, sandwiches and ice cream.

Getting There & Away

The **bus terminal** (☎ 30515; Plaza Artigas) has departures to Colonia (US$6, three hours), Montevideo (US$10, four hours), Gualeguaychú, Argentina (US$16) and interior destinations.

PAYSANDÚ

☎ 072 / pop 73,000

A big (in Uruguayan terms), serious city, Paysandú wakes up every Easter for its annual beer festival, with plenty of live music, open-air cinema and a ready supply of a certain carbonated alcoholic beverage. The rest of the year it's kinda sleepy, but spasms into life on weekends when everybody's out and about in the restaurants, bars and discos.

Most of the fun happens down on the riverbanks, with plenty of splashing around during the day and more serious partying at night.

Av 18 de Julio, the main commercial street, runs along the south side of Plaza Constitución. The **tourist office** (☎ 26221; Av 18 de Julio 1226) is opposite Plaza Constitución. Cambio Fagalde is at 18 de Julio 1002. **Banco Acac** (Av 18 de Julio 1020) has an ATM. If you're coming from Argentina and need Uruguayan pesos fast, Copay at the bus terminal offers bank rates.

To get to the center from the bus terminal, walk seven blocks north on Zorilla. A taxi should cost around US$2.

The **Museo Histórico** (Zorrilla 874; admission free; ☽ 9am-5pm Mon-Fri) has a great selection of hand-drawn maps, household objects and war etchings. If you thought Windows XP was slow, check out the slide n' punch 'writing machine' – a one-way ticket to Carpal Tunnel Syndrome if you ever saw one.

Sleeping & Eating

Hotel Concordia (☎ 22417; Av 18 de Julio 984; s/d US$8/16, with shared bathroom US$6/12) The sweeping marble staircase, plant-filled patio and

wooden floorboards make up for obvious signs of wear in this central hotel.

Hotel Rafaela (☎ 24216; Av 18 de Julio 1181; s/d US$16/32, with shared bathroom US$9/18) Downstairs rooms have a bit more character and their own bathrooms, but are a bit airless. Upstairs, the cheaper rooms with shared bath are a much better deal and you get a bit of a balcony too.

Pan Z (cnr Av 18 de Julio & Pereda; dishes US$4-7) 'Panceta' is the most popular eating place in town – it serves pizza, pasta, *chivitos* and half-decent jugs of sangria (US$1.50). There's also a breezy outdoor deck and a suspiciously paella-like *arroz con pollo* (rice with chicken; US$4).

Drinking

Zaguan (Michelini 1652; admission US$2-5) One of the many clubs down on the waterfront, Zaguan keeps it pumping into the early hours with house, reggaeton and marcha beats.

Maybe Bar (Uruguay 699) One of the many 'pre-dance' options, the Maybe keeps it together with a bit of atmosphere and good draft beer.

The other popular option is to fill a bottle with something 'n' cola and hang out with everybody else in Plaza Artigas.

Getting There & Away

Paysandú's **bus terminal** (☎ 23225; cnr Zorrilla & Artigas) has departures for Montevideo (US$14, five hours), Salto (US$5, two hours), Tacuarembó (US$9, six hours) and Colón, Argentina (US$2, 45 minutes).

SALTO

☎ 073 / pop 99,000

People come to Salto for two reasons – to cross the border to Concordia, Argentina, and to visit the nearby **hot springs** at Daymán. Otherwise, the town's pretty enough, but unlikely to grab your attention for more than a couple of days.

The **tourist office** (☎ 25194; Uruguay 1052) is vaguely useful and can supply information about visiting the local hot springs. There are *casas de cambio* downtown.

Sights & Activities

The **Museo del Hombre y la Tecnología** (cnr Brasil & Zorrilla; admission free; ☽ 2-7pm) in the former market features displays on local history. **Plaza Artigas** has an enchanting simplicity and is a great place to people watch.

Eight kilometers south of Salto, the **Termas de Daymán** is the largest and most developed of several thermal bath complexes in north-western Uruguay. Surrounded by a cluster of motels and restaurants, it's a popular destination for Uruguayan and Argentine tourists, offering facilities for a variety of budgets.

Sleeping & Eating

Hotel Concordia (☎ 32735; Uruguay 749; s/d US$10/18) Reputedly Uruguay's oldest hotel, rooms overlook an attractive interior patio and are filled with wonderful antique furniture. Ask to see room 32, where Carlos Gardel, the famous tango singer, stayed in 1933.

Argentina Hotel (☎ 29931; Uruguay 892; s/d US$18/24; ⌘) While the building is a classic and the hallways have real charm, the rooms are modern and functional, but still comfortable.

Azabache (Uruguay 702; dishes US$4-6) This has better atmosphere than most snack joints, serving good cheap pasta, sandwiches, fresh juices and excellent, thin-crust pizzas.

La Terraza (cnr Costanera Norte & Apolon; dishes US$5-7) Two kilometers north of Club Remeros, this is a great place to while away an afternoon on the riverside munching on pasta and *parrillada*.

Drinking

Down near the port, the little strip of bars on Chinazzaro between Artigas and 19 de Abril gets lively on weekends.

Getting There & Around

Bus 1 goes from the bus terminal to the center of town.

From Plaza Artigas, catch the 'Termas' bus for the Daymán hot springs. The US$0.30 fare includes entrance to the hot springs.

Chadre/Agencia Central and **Flecha Bus** (☎ 099-732-052) go to Concordia, Argentina (US$2, one hour). Immigration procedures are carried out on the bus.

Domestic buses go to Montevideo (US$17, six hours), Bella Unión (US$5, three hours) and Paysandú (US$5, two hours).

From the port at the foot of Brazil, launches cross the river to Concordia (US$2, 10 minutes) Monday to Saturday.

TACUAREMBÓ

☎ 063 / pop 51,000

This is *gaucho* country. Not your 'we pose for pesos' types, but your real-deal 'we tuck our baggy pants into our boots and slap on a beret just to go to the local store' crew. It's also the alleged birthplace of tango legend Carlos Gardel (see boxed text, below).

The mid-March **Fiesta de la Patria Gaucho** (Gaucho Festival) merits a visit from travelers in the area.

Tacuarembó's center is Plaza 19 de Abril. The **tourist office** (☎ 27144) is in the bus terminal. The post office is at Ituzaingó 262. Antel is at Sarandí 240. The bus terminal is 2km from the center: turn left on exiting, walk through the small plaza, veer right onto Herrera and walk four blocks to 18 de Julio. A taxi costs US$1.

The **Museo del Indio y del Gaucho** (cnr Flores & Artigas; admission free; ☺ 1-7pm Mon-Fri, 2-6pm Sat & Sun) pays romantic tribute to Uruguay's original inhabitants and *gauchos*.

Sleeping & Eating

Balneario Municipal Iporá (☎ 25344; sites free-US$2) Seven kilometers north of town, the free sites have clean toilets but lack showers. Buses leave from near Plaza 19 de Abril.

THE BIRTH OF A LEGEND

There's no doubt that Carlos Gardel gave birth to the tango, but – even 70 years after his death – there's still discussion over which country gave birth to Gardel.

Much like the Greek/Turkish controversy over who invented the souvlaki/doner kebab, we have three countries claiming Gardel as their own: Argentina, Uruguay and France.

The Uruguayan version goes like this: the Maestro was born here in Tacuarembó on the 11th of December 1887 (and to be fair, they have the documents to prove it – signed by the Argentines before Gardel became famous – in the Museo del Indio y del Gaucho).

The 'confusion' seems to have arisen because like pretty much every other Uruguayan musician, Gardel went to Buenos Aires to make it big, and then France to make it even bigger, with each country claiming him along the way.

We warmly anticipate readers' letters on the subject.

Hotel Plaza (☎ 27988; 25 de Agosto 247; s/d US$14/18) The Plaza's small, cheerful rooms are plain but comfortable enough and the location – a block and a half from the square – can't be beat.

La Sombrilla (cnr 25 de Mayo & Suárez; dishes US$2-4) Right on Plaza 19 de Abril, this place is good for breakfast and late-night snacking.

La Rueda (cnr Beltrán & Flores; dishes US$3-6) With its thatched roof and walls covered with *gaucho* paraphernalia (and, ewww…animal skins), La Rueda is a friendly neighborhood *parrilla*.

Getting There & Away

The **Terminal Municipal** (cnr Ruta 5 & Victorino Perera) is on the northeastern outskirts of town. Fares include Montevideo (US$14, five hours), Salto (US$9, five hours) and Paysandú (US$9, six hours).

EASTERN URUGUAY

This is Uruguay's playground (and also, to an extent, Brazil's, Chile's, Mexico's, Spain's etc) – a long stretch of beaches all the way from Montevideo to the Brazilian border offering something for everyone – surfers, party animals, nature freaks and family groups.

Conflicts between Spain and Portugal, then between Argentina and Brazil, left eastern Uruguay with historical monuments such as the fortresses of Santa Teresa and San Miguel. The interior's varied landscape of palm savannas and marshes is rich in bird life.

In the peak of summer, prices skyrocket and these towns seriously pack out. The rest of the year you might have them to yourself.

PIRIÁPOLIS

☎ 043 / pop 8,000

In the 1930s entrepreneur Francisco Piria built the landmark Hotel Argentino and an eccentric residence known as 'Piria's castle,' and ferried tourists directly from Argentina. Nowadays it's a budget alternative to beach resorts further west, mostly attracting families from Montevideo on short breaks.

The problem with this town is obvious – a four lane highway separates it from the beach. Still, if you don't mind doing the chicken run a couple of times a day, the water's clean and there are plenty of places to lay your towel.

The **tourist office** (☎ 22560; Rambla de los Argentinos 1348) has maps, brochures and current hotel prices. There's another office in the bus terminal.

There's an ATM at the corner of Piria and Buenos Aires. You can change cash, but not traveler's checks, at Hotel Argentino.

Sights & Activities

For jet skiing, windsurfing, kayaks, banana boats, etc call **Turismo Aventura** (☎ 099-120-138).

Carlos Rodriguez (☎ 22544; www.sierradelasanimas .com/heliopolis.htm) offers bioenergetic and mystic tours of the region, focusing on Geomagnetics, Kabala symbolism and guided meditations.

SOS Rescate de Fauna Marina (☎ 22960; Punta Colorado; guided tours US$4 or 1kg of fish) runs a marine-fauna rescue operation about 2km out of town. If you want to tour the facilities, reservations are a must.

A **chairlift** (9am to 5pm, return trip US$3) goes to the top of the hill at the eastern part of town for spectacular views over the bay and surrounds. Don't fret – there's a *parrilla* restaurant up there.

Sleeping & Eating

Camping Piriápolis FC (☎ 23275; cnr Misiones & Niza; sites per person US$2.50, dm US$6; ⊙ mid-Dec–late Apr) Opposite the bus terminal, this has plenty of sporting facilities.

Albergue Antón Grassi (☎ 20394; Simón del Pino 1106/36; HI member/nonmember dm US$8/10, d US$20/24) Fairly ordinary five-bed rooms with kitchen facilities. When it's full, the place has a great atmosphere, and when it's empty it feels like an aircraft hangar. Reservations are essential in January and February. Bike hire costs US$1/ US$5 per hour/day.

Bungalows Margariteñas (☎ 22245; corinamargar itenas@adinet.com.uy; cnr Piedras & Zufriategui; bungalows per night US$30) This place has beautiful, fully equipped, individually decorated bungalows that sleep two to four. The owners speak English.

Sal y Pimienta (cnr Tucumán & Sierra; set meals US$4) A block back from the beach, this little place serves up some fine seafood and good-value set meals.

Getting There & Away

The **bus terminal** (cnr Misiones & Niza) is three blocks from the beach. Destinations include Montevideo (US$3.50, 1½ hours), Punta del Este (US$2, 45 minutes) and Minas (US$2.50, 45 minutes).

AROUND PIRIÁPOLIS
Pan de Azúcar
Ten kilometers north of town, there's a trail to the top of **Cerro Pan de Azúcar** (493m), Uruguay's third-highest point, crowned by a 35m-high cross and a conspicuous TV aerial. At the nearby Parque Municipal is the small but well-kept **Reserva de Fauna Autóctona**, with native species such as capybaras and gray foxes. Across the highway is the **Castillo de Piria**.

Minas & Around
☎ 044 / pop 38,000
This charming little hill town doesn't have a whole lot going for it apart from being a charming little hill-town. Fans of Uruguay's bottled water Salus can check out its source, on the outskirts of town. There's a **post office** (Rodó 571), **Antel** (cnr Beltrán & Rodó) and **tourist office** (☎ 29796; cnr Batlle & Ordóñez).

Turismo Aventura (☎ 27686) organizes hikes in the surrounding hills and rappelling trips down abandoned mineshafts, if that's what you're into.

Every April 19, up to 70,000 pilgrims visit the site of **Cerro y Virgen del Verdún**, 6km west of Minas. Among the eucalyptus groves in **Parque Salus**, 10km west of town, is the source of Uruguay's best-known mineral water. Buses for the complex (which includes an upmarket hotel and reasonable restaurant) leave from Minas' bus terminal every 15 minutes (US$1) and drop you right at the door.

Inexpensive camping is possible at leafy **Parque Arequita** (☎ 440-2503; sites per person, incl pool use US$1; 🏊), 12km north on the road to Polanco (public transport is available). The three-star hotels around the plaza have rooms for around US$35. More humble, but totally adequate, is the **Posada Verdún** (☎ 24563; Washington Beltrán 715; s/d US$10/15), with good-sized rooms and leafy patios. There's plenty of *parrilla* action going on around the plaza, but make sure you stop in to **Confitería Irisarri** (Plaza Libertad; snacks US$1-3), a local institution, and check out its subterranean dungeon-museum.

MALDONADO
☎ 042 / pop 55,000
Maldonado used to be the place to stay if you wanted to avoid the outrageous prices in nearby Punta del Este. But then the Maldonado hoteliers cottoned on and jacked up all their prices. There are a couple of interesting museums in town, but Punta's burgeoning

hostel scene makes it a much better budget choice these days.

Orientation & Information
The town center is Plaza San Fernando, but streets are irregular between Maldonado and Punta del Este. West, along the river, Rambla Claudio Williman is the main thoroughfare, while to the east, Rambla Lorenzo Batlle Pacheco follows the coast. Locations along these routes are usually identified by numbered *paradas* (bus stops).

The **tourist office** (☎ 250490; 25 de Mayo s/n) is on Plaza San Fernando.

Casas de cambio are clustered around Plaza San Fernando. The post office is at Ituzaingó and San Carlos.

Sights
Built between 1771 and 1797, the **Cuartel de Dragones y de Blandengues** is a block of military fortifications along 18 de Julio and Pérez del Puerto. Its **Museo Didáctico Artiguista** (admission free; 🕙 10am-11pm, guided visits 5-11pm) honors Uruguay's independence hero. Artigas was a very busy guy – check out the maps of his battle campaigns, and don't miss the room with the bronze busts of the Liberators of the Americas (and, yes…Washington gets a guernsey).

The **Museo San Fernando** (cnr Sarandí & Pérez del Puerto; admission free; 🕙 1-6pm) is a fine-arts facility. Maldonado's best museum is the **Museo Mazzoni** (Ituzaingó 789; admission free; 🕙 9am-1pm), which is a big jumble of old documents, knick-knacks, household items, weapons, furniture, artwork and photographs, all set in a house built in 1782. Don't miss the contemporary art gallery in a building at the back of the garden.

Sleeping
Camping San Rafael (☎ 486715; sites for 2 people US$10; 🕙 summer only) On the eastern outskirts of town, with fine facilities on leafy grounds. Take bus 5 from downtown.

Hotel Sancar (☎ 223563; Juan Edye 597; s/d US$20/30) Well kept and quieter than most hotels in town. The staff have an air of just-barely-keeping-it-together, but this is about as close as you're going to get to a bargain in this town. Some rooms have TV.

Hotel Le Petit (☎ 223044; cnr Florida & Sarandí; s/d US$30/40) The rooms here are small, but the whole place is spotless, and the location right on the plaza is hard to beat for the price.

URUGUAY

Eating

Mundo Natural (Román Guerra 918; dishes US$1) This tiny (ie two tables), cheerful vegetarian place serves up some incredibly tasty *tartas*, soy- and seitan burgers, and brown rice.

Sumo (cnr Florida & Sarandí; sandwiches US$2) This plazaside *confitería* makes a great place for breakfast, coffee or a spot of people watching.

Lo de Ruben (Santa Teresa 846; set meals US$5) Good *parrillada*, and draft beer for US$1.50.

Pizza y Pasta (Trienta y Tres 729; dishes US$5-7; ☺ dinner) Friendly service and home-style cooking in a great old building. The house red is a ripper.

Taberna Patxi (Dodera 944; dishes from US$10) Fine Basque specialties, including fish and shellfish, an extensive wine list and cozy seating. Exactly how does the Bee Gees soundtrack fit into this picture?

Getting There & Away

Terminal Maldonado (☎ 250490; cnr Roosevelt & Sarandí) is eight blocks south of Plaza San Fernando. Plenty of buses go to Montevideo (US$5, two hours), La Paloma (US$4, two hours), Chuy (US$7, three hours), Minas (US$3, two hours) and Treinta y Tres (US$7, 3½ hours).

Local buses link Maldonado with Punta del Este and the beach circuit. They run through the center of town, meaning you don't have to trek out to the terminal to get there – ask any local where the nearest parada is.

AROUND MALDONADO

Casa Pueblo (admission US$3; ☺ 9am-sunset) is an unconventional Mediterranean villa and art gallery at scenic Punta Ballena, 10km west of Maldonado, built by Carlos Páez Vilaró without right angles and boasting stunning views. Nearby **Camping Internacional Punta Ballena** (☎ 042-78902; sites US$6, 4-person cabins US$24) provides the most economical accommodation in the area. Buses from Maldonado drop you at a junction 2km from the house.

PUNTA DEL ESTE

☎ 042 / pop 7,200

OK, here's the plan: tan it, wax it, buff it at the gym and then plonk it on the beach at 'Punta.' Once you're done there, go out and shake it at one of the town's famous clubs.

Punta's an international beach resort, and if you like that kind of thing, you're going to love it here. If not, there are plenty of other beaches to choose from along this coast.

Orientation

Rambla Gral Artigas circles the peninsula, passing the protected beach of Playa Mansa and the yacht harbor on the west side and rugged Playa Brava on the east.

Punta has two separate grids. North of a constricted neck east of the harbor is the high-rise hotel zone; the southern area is largely residential. Streets bear both names and numbers. Av Juan Gorlero is the main commercial street.

Information

The **tourist office** (☎ 446510; cnr Baupres & Inzaurraga) also maintains an **Oficina de Informes** (☎ 446519) on Plaza Artigas.

Nearly all banks and *casas de cambio* are along Av Juan Gorlero. The post office is at Los Meros between Av Juan Gorlero and El Remanso.

Activities

Twelve kilometers off Punta's east coast, **Isla de los Lobos** boasts large colonies of southern fur seals and sea lions. **Australis Tours** (☎ 448955) runs tours to the island (US$35, two hours) leaving daily in the high season, on weekends in the low season. Make reservations in advance.

Punta's main attraction is its beaches. Beach-hopping is common, depending on local conditions and the general level of action. The most popular (and fashionable) beaches, such as Bikini, are north along Playa Brava. Playa Olla gets good surf and tends to be less crowded.

During summer, **parasailing** (US$50 per 12 minutes), **waterskiing** (US$40 per 15 minutes) and **jet skiing** (US$40 per 15 minutes) are possible on Playa Mansa. Operators set up on the beach along Rambla Claudio Williman between paradas 2 and 20.

PES (☎ 481388; Playa Brava Parada 3) rents surfboards, windsurfers, bodyboards, skateboards, skimboards, sandboards, wetsuits, kayaks, Rollerblades and snorkels and offers surf- and bodyboard lessons.

Bikes can be rented for US$1/US$5 per hour/day at **Golden Bikes** (☎ 447394; El Mesana s/n).

Sleeping

Prices listed here are for the high (but not absolute peak) season. If you're coming in late December to early January, add at least 30%.

El Hostal (☎ 441632; albergues@hostellinguruguay.org; Arrecifes 544; dm US$10) This small hostel has good four- to six-bed dorms and a small common room up front. There's a side patio for warm-weather days and a tiny kitchen for heating water only (no cooking).

1949 Hostel (☎ 440719; www.1949hostel.com; cnr Baupres & Las Focas; dm/d US$12/40; 💻) One of the better hostels in the country, this one has the lot – it's close to the bus terminal and offers good dorm rooms that include locker use, breakfast and sea views. There's a kitchen for guest use, a common room with videos, surfboards, bikes and scooters for rent and a great little bar area with partial sea views.

Residencial 32 (☎ 493506; La Angostura 640; s/d with bathroom US$20/30) Simple but pleasing rooms with a vague nautical theme. Its location –

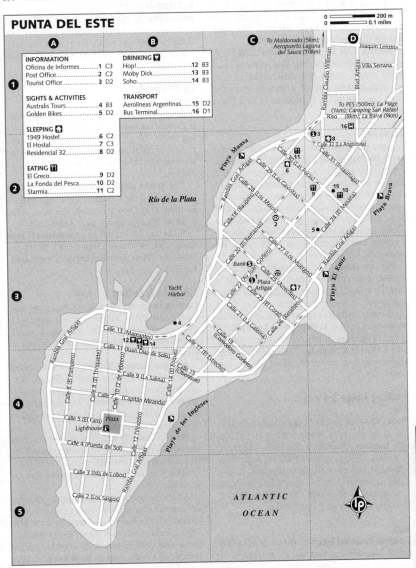

PUNTA DEL ESTE

INFORMATION	
Oficina de Informes	**1** C3
Post Office	**2** C2
Tourist Office	**3** D2

SIGHTS & ACTIVITIES	
Australis Tours	**4** B3
Golden Bikes	**5** D2

SLEEPING 🏠	
1949 Hostel	**6** C2
El Hostal	**7** C3
Residencial 32	**8** D2

EATING 🍴	
El Greco	**9** D2
La Fonda del Pesca	**10** D2
Starmia	**11** C2

DRINKING 🍷	
Hop!	**12** B3
Moby Dick	**13** B3
Soho	**14** B3

TRANSPORT	
Aerolineas Argentinas	**15** D2
Bus Terminal	**16** D1

To Maldonado (5km); Aeropuerto Laguna del Sauce (10km)

Joaquín Lenzina

Villa Serrana

To PES (500m); La Plage (1km); Camping San Rafael (8km); La Barra (9km)

Río de la Plata

Playa Mansa

Playa Brava

Playa El Emir

Yacht Harbor

Playa de los Ingleses

Plaza Lighthouse

ATLANTIC OCEAN

0   200 m
0   0.1 miles

URUGUAY

around the corner from the bus terminal and a short walk from both beaches – is a bonus.

Eating

El Greco (crn Av Juan Gorlero & Las Focas; dishes US$2-5) A good spot for breakfast, El Greco also does great sandwiches and homemade cakes and has plenty of sidewalk seating.

La Fonda del Pesca (Calle 30 btwn 22 & 24; dishes US$5) The usual range of meats and chicken is on the menu here, but the locals pack this place out for the super-fresh fish dishes.

Starmia (Calle 18, near Av 31; dishes US$10-15) A small restaurant serving fine seafood and sushi dishes. For a romantic night, or just a breath of fresh sea air, grab a table on the deck area across the road, overlooking Playa Mansa.

Drinking

A good place to meet up with other travelers is the bar of the 1949 Hostel (see p965). Once they boot you out of there (around 2am or 3am), you'll have a gang together to roam the streets – either down to the port area for more drinks at the hip, minimalist Soho and Hop! or the slightly more laid-back Moby Dick. All stay open as long as there's a crowd and sometimes have live music on weekends.

Punta is famed for its club scene, and there are two pieces of irony operating here. One is that the famed club zone (La Barra) is about 10km out of town. The other is that these places only really stay open for the one-month super-peak period. **La Plage** (Rambla Batlle Parada 12) is one of the best clubs operating year round, and is the place to go for beachside dancing, where you can stomp the sand 'til the sun comes up.

Getting There & Away

AIR

Pluna (☎ 490101; Parada 8-1/2 on Rambla Batlle Pacheco) has daily flights to Buenos Aires (US$120), plus summer schedules to São Paulo and other Brazilian destinations. **Aerolíneas Argentinas** (☎ 442949; Las Focas btwn Gorlero & El Mesana), in the Edificio Santos Dumont, flies to Buenos Aires frequently, as does **LAPA** (☎ 490840; Av Roosevelt Parada 14-1/2) on Friday and Sunday.

BUS

Terminal Punta del Este (☎ 489467; cnr Riso & Blvd Artigas) has services that are an extension of those to Maldonado. International carriers include **TTL** (☎ 86755) to Porto Alegre, Brazil (US$50).

COT (☎ 483558) covers the Uruguayan coast from Montevideo to the Brazilian border. **Copsa** (☎ 489205) goes to Montevideo (US$6, 2½ hours).

Getting Around

Aeropuerto Laguna del Sauce (☎ 559777), west of Maldonaldo, can be reached by COT bus (US$4). Frequent buses from Rambla Artigas connect Punta del Este with Maldonado (US$0.70).

LA PALOMA

☎ 0479 / pop 3,200

This town is a surfer's dream – out on a point, if there's no swell on the left, it'll be coming in on the right. Weekends in summer, the town often hosts free concerts down on the beach, making accommodation bookings essential.

The **tourist office** (☎ 6008; Av Nicolás Solari s/n) is in the Liga de Fomento building. There's another at the bus terminal. The post office is on Av Nicolás Solari, as is Antel.

Bikes can be rented from **Bicicletas El Topo** (Canopus, btwn de la Virgen & Antares) for US$1/4 per hour/day. **Peteco** (Av Nicolás Solari) rents surfboards for US$10 per day.

Sleeping & Eating

Camping La Aguada (☎ 6239; sites for 2 people US$6, 6-person cabins US$26) At the northern approach to town, this campground has beach access, hot showers, a supermarket, a restaurant and electricity.

Albergue Altena 5000 (☎ 6396; dm HI members/nonmembers US$7/9; ☾ year-round) In Parque Andresito, this beautifully decked-out hostel is set in an A-frame building. The dorm rooms are comfortable and the place has a good party atmosphere in summer.

Hotel La Tuna (☎ 6083; hlatuna@adinet.com.uy; cnr Neptune & Juno; s/d US$25/30) The owners have kept this place in mint condition since its last overhaul back in the '70s. Ask for a front room for great bay views.

All the restaurants in La Paloma generally fall into two categories – very ornery or very snazzy. Of the former, **La Farola** (Av Nicolás Solari s/n) is good for *minutas* (short-order snacks), pizza and coffee. Swankier establishments include the restaurant in **Hotel Bahia** (cnr El Sol

& del Navio), which serves some outrageously good seafood dishes – anyone for blue crab wrapped in salmon on a bed of cream cheese (US$7)?

Getting There & Away

Cynsa (☎ 6304) goes to Rocha (US$1) and Montevideo (US$8, 3½ hours). **Rutas del Sol** (☎ 6019) goes to Montevideo and Punta del Diablo (US$4, 3 hours) via Rocha.

PUNTA DEL DIABLO

☎ 0477 / pop 700

Fabulously remote, seriously underdeveloped and stunningly picturesque, this little fishing-surfing village of wooden cabins and winding dirt streets is like an anti–Punta del Este. It attracts a corresponding crowd – more nature-oriented and far less glamorous. **Parque Nacional Santa Teresa** is within easy hiking distance. **Horse riding** can be arranged for about US$5 an hour; ask in town for Sr José Vega.

Camping Punta del Diablo (☎ 2060; sites for 2 people US$9, 5-person cabins US$32), 2km northwest of town, has excellent facilities, including a supermarket and a restaurant.

Hotel La Posada (☎ 2041; r at back/front US$40/50) is a quaint little hotel perched on top of the bluff – the front rooms have awesome sea views. It has plenty of driftwood-styled furniture and seashells for decoration.

There are a multitude of private **cabañas** (US$14) for rent in the village; ask around for availability and bring your own bedding.

Locally caught seafood is a specialty. Try the excellent *corvina a la Provencal* (Croaker Provencal) at **La Gaviotas Coiner** (mains US$3-5), one of the best restaurants in town. **La Penultima** (dishes US$5) has wild ocean views from the front balcony and a Mexican cantina feel. It serves up pizzas and seafood and sometimes has live music. Little bars open up along the seafront during summer, but the best parties happen on the beach where locals and visitors gather around beachfires to play guitars, sing songs and just generally hang out.

Rutas del Sol has buses to La Paloma, Chuy and Montevideo (US$11, 4½ hours).

PARQUE NACIONAL SANTA TERESA

More a historical than a natural attraction, this coastal park 35km south of Chuy contains the hilltop **Fortaleza de Santa Teresa**, begun by the Portuguese but captured and finished by the Spaniards. Santa Teresa's a humble place, but Uruguayan and Brazilian visitors enjoy its uncrowded beaches and decentralized forest **camping** (sites US$5) with basic facilities.

The park gets crowded during Carnaval, but otherwise absorbs visitors well. Services at park headquarters include telephones, a post office, supermarket, bakery, butcher and restaurant. Rutas del Sol travels from Punta del Diablo at 9am directly to the park headquarters, returning at 4:35pm. Buses traveling east to Chuy can also drop you off at the park entrance on Ruta 9.

CHUY & AROUND

☎ 0474 / pop 10,500

Warning: If you're not on your way to or from Brazil, you're seriously lost, buddy. Turn around and go back. But while you're here you may as well pick up a few pirated CDs and some contraband cigarettes, freely available up and down the main street.

Seven kilometers west of Chuy, don't miss restored **Fuerte San Miguel** (☉ Tue-Sun), a pink-granite fortress built in 1734 during hostilities between Spain and Portugal and protected by a moat.

Ten kilometers south of Chuy, a coastal lateral heads to **Camping Chuy** (☎ 9425; sites US$7); local buses go there.

Accomodation is avaliable at **Hotel Internacional** (☎ 2055; Río Dos San Luis 121; s/d US$8/13) which has well-kept rooms with a TV and vertigo-inducing murals.

Sadly, there are no Brazilian flavors creeping over the border onto menus here, but **Miravos** (Brasil 505; dishes US$5-7) does decent pizza and *parrillada* as well as 'sweet pizzas' (US$3; try 'em with ice cream!). Several bus companies on Av Brasil connect Chuy with Montevideo (US$12, five hours).

GETTING TO BRAZIL

To get to Brazil, walk north along Av Artigas for about 1km to get to the immigration offices. The main street (Av Brasil/Uruguay) forms the official border here. The border is theoretically open 24 hours, but it's best to cross during normal business hours. The nearest town covered in the Brazil chapter is Porto Alegre; see p324.

URUGUAY DIRECTORY

ACCOMMODATIONS

Uruguay has a substantial network of youth hostels and several campgrounds, especially along the coast. HI membership or an International Student Identity Card (ISIC) will help with discounts in hostels. In towns, *hospedajes, residenciales* and pensiones offer budget accommodations from about US$10 per person.

ACTIVITIES

Charlie may not surf, but plenty of visitors to Uruguay do. Punta del Diablo (p967) and La Paloma (p966) both get excellent waves and have shops that hire equipment. Punta del Este (p964) is the place to head for the up-market beach scene, bars and snazzier beach activities, like parasailing, windsurfing and jet skiing.

Bike riders can easily while away a day or two cycling around the atmospheric streets of Colonia del Sacramento (p955) and along the waterfront in Montevideo.

BOOKS

Lonely Planet's *Argentina* has detailed coverage of Colonia, Montevideo and Punta del Este. For an account of Uruguay's Dirty War, see Lawrence Weschler's *A Miracle, A Universe: Settling Accounts with Torturers*. Onetti's novels *No Man's Land, The Shipyard, Body Snatcher* and *A Brief Life* are mostly available in Spanish and English translation. *The Tree of Red Stars*, Tessa Bridal's acclaimed novel set in Montevideo during the 1970s, provides one of the best descriptions of life in Uruguay available to English readers.

BUSINESS HOURS

Most shops open weekdays and Saturday from 8:30am to 12:30pm or 1pm, then close until mid-afternoon and reopen until 7pm or 8pm. Food shops are also open Sunday mornings.

From mid-November to mid-March, government offices are open weekdays from 7:30am to 1:30pm; the rest of the year, they are open noon to 7pm. Banks are open weekday afternoons in Montevideo; elsewhere, mornings are the rule.

If restaurants are open for breakfast, they tend to open around 8am. Lunch goes anywhere between noon and 3pm and dinner is generally not eaten until after 9pm. It's not unusual (particularly in urban areas) for people to start eating at midnight.

Bars are open from 9pm, but remain empty until at least 1am, when everybody finally gets around to going out.

CLIMATE

Since Uruguay's major attraction is its beaches, most visitors come in summer. Between late April and November, strong winds sometimes combine with rain and cool temperatures (July's average temperature is a chilly 11°C). Along the Río Uruguay in summer, temperatures can be smotheringly hot, but the interior hill country is slightly cooler (January's average maximum is between 21°C and 26°C).

DANGERS & ANNOYANCES

Uruguay is one of the safest countries in South America, but street crime is present. Take the normal precautions outlined on p1063.

DRIVER'S LICENSE

Visitors to Uruguay who are staying less than 90 days need only bring a valid driver's license from their home country, although an international license may be required to hire a car or motorbike.

ELECTRICITY

Uruguay runs on 220V, 50Hz. There are various types of plugs in use, the most common being the two round pins with no earthing/grounding pin.

EMBASSIES & CONSULATES
Embassies & Consulates in Uruguay

Argentina Carmelo (☎ 054-22266; Roosevelt 442); ☎ 052-22093; Av Gral Flores 350); Colonia del Sacramento (Map p956; Montevideo (Map pp950-1; ☎ 02-902-8166; Cuariem 1470); Paysandú (☎ 072-22253; Leandro Gómez 1034); Salto (☎ 073-32931; Artigas 1162)

Brazil Chuy (0474-2049; Fernández 147); Montevideo (☎ 02-707-2119; Blvd Artigas 1328)

Canada (Map pp950-1; ☎ 02-902-6023; Plaza Independencia 749, Oficina 102, Montevideo)

France (Map pp950-1; ☎ 02-902-0077; Uruguay 853, Montevideo)

Germany (☎ 02-902-5222; La Cumparsita 1417, Montevideo)

Paraguay (☎ 02-707-2138; Blvd Artigas 1525, Montevideo)

Switzerland (☎ 02-711-5545; Federico Abadie 2936, 11th fl, Montevideo)

UK (☎ 02-622-3630; Marco Bruto 1073, Montevideo)
USA (☎ 02-418-7777; Lauro Muller 1776, Montevideo)

Uruguayan Embassies & Consulates Abroad

Uruguay has diplomatic representation in the following countries and also in most South American countries. For a full list of embassies and consulates throughout the world, see: www.mrree.gub.uy/mrree/Embajadas _y_Consulados/Misiones/Scripts_Misiones /paises.idc.

Australia (☎ 02-6273-9100; urucan@iimetro.com .au; Ste 2 Level 4, Commerce House, 24 Brisbane Ave, Barton, ACT 2600)

Canada (☎ 416-730-1289; conrutor@on.aibn.com; Ste 302, 300 Sheppard Ave West, Toronto, Ontario M2N 1N5)

France (☎ 01-45-00-81-37; amburuguay.urugalia@fr .oleane.com; 15, rue Le Sueur, 1er etage, 75116, Paris)

Germany (☎ 4930-263-9016; urubrande@embrou.de; Budapesterstr 39 – 10787 Berlin)

Spain (☎ 91-758-0475; urumatri@urumatri.com; Paseo del Pintor Rosales 32, Piso 1 derecha, 28008)

UK (☎ 020-7589-8835; emburuguay@emburuguay.org .uk; 2nd fl, 140 Brompton Rd, London SW3 1HY)

USA (☎ 202-331-1313; www.uruwashi.org; 21913 I Street, NW Washington DC, 20006)

FESTIVALS & EVENTS

Uruguay's Carnaval, on the Monday and Tuesday before Ash Wednesday, is livelier than Argentina's but more sedate than Brazil's. Montevideo's Afro-Uruguayan population celebrates with traditional *candombe* ceremonies. Semana Santa (Easter) has become known as Semana Turismo, with everybody from all over the country seemingly going somewhere else. Accommodation is tricky during this time, but well worth the hassle are Montevideo's Creole Week (a *gaucho* extravaganza) and Paysandú's beer festival (no explanation needed).

FOOD & DRINK
Uruguayan Cuisine

Breakfast to a Uruguayan generally means *café con leche* (coffee with milk) and a croissant or two, followed by serious amounts of *mate*. Most restaurants will be able to offer some *tostados* (toasted sandwiches) to those accustomed to actually eating something in the morning. Any later than, say 10am, huge slabs of beef are the norm, usually cooked over hot coals on a *parrilla* (grill or barbecue). The most popular cut is the *asado de tira* (ribs) but *pulpo*

DAY OF THE GNOCCHI

Most Uruguayan restaurants make a big deal out of serving gnocchi on the 29th of each month. Some places, this is the only day you can get it.

This tradition dates back to tough economic times when everybody was paid at the end of the month. By the time that the 29th rolled around, the only thing that people could afford to cook were these delicious potato dumplings.

So, in their ever-practical way, Uruguayans turned a hardship into a tradition and the 29th has been the Day of the Gnocchi ever since.

Somethingtobearinmindnexttimeyou're paying US$25 a plate at your favorite Italian restaurant back home.

(fillet steak) is also good. Seafood is excellent on the coast.

The standard snack is *chivito* (a steak sandwich with cheese, lettuce, tomato, ham and condiments). Other typical items are *puchero* (a beef stew) and *olímpicos* (club sandwiches).

Vegetarians can usually find something on the menu, often along the lines of pizza and pasta. Most vegans end up very familiar with the Uruguayan supermarket scene.

Regional desserts include *chajá*, a meringue and ice-cream concoction so good you'll be wondering how to smuggle some home, *flan casero* (crème caramel) and *masini* (a custard cream pastry topped with burnt sugar).

Drinks
ALCOHOLIC DRINKS

Local beers, including Pilsen, Norteño and Patricia, are good. The 330ml bottles are rare outside tourist areas – generally *cerveza* (beer) means a 1L bottle and some glasses, which is a great way to meet people – pour your neighbor a beer and no doubt they'll return the favor.

Cleric is a mixture of white wine and fruit juice, while *Medio y Medio* is a mixture of sparkling wine and white wine. A shot of *Grappa con miel* (grappa with honey) is worth a try – you might just like it.

NONALCOHOLIC DRINKS

Tap water's OK to drink in most places, but bottled water is cheap if you still have your doubts.

URUGUAY

Bottled drinks are inexpensive, and all the usual soft drinks are available. Try the *pomelo* (grapefruit) flavor – it's very refreshing and not too sickly sweet.

Jugos (juices) are available everywhere. The most common options are *naranja* (orange), *piña* (pineapple) and papaya. *Licuados* are juices mixed with either *leche* or water.

Coffee is available everywhere and always good, coming mostly *de la máquina* (from the machine). Uruguayans consume even more mate than Argentines and Paraguayans. If you get the chance, try to acquire the taste – there's nothing like whiling away an afternoon passing the mate with a bunch of newfound friends. *Té* (tea) drinking is not that common, but most cafés and bars have some lying around somewhere. *Té de hierbas* (herb tea) are more popular, particularly *manzanilla* (chamomile) and *menta* (mint).

GAY & LESBIAN TRAVELERS

Uruguay's not what you'd call G & L paradise. The progressive spirit hasn't transposed to matters of sexuality, and many gay and lesbian Uruguayans take the path of least resistance and simply migrate to Buenos Aires where the scene's a lot healthier. The **Grupo Diversidad website** (www.geocities.com/diversidad2000 in Spanish) has detailed information about gay and lesbian organizations in Argentina and Uruguay.

HEALTH

Uruguay does not require a yellow fever vaccination certificate and malaria isn't a problem. For more information, see p1090.

HOLIDAYS

Año Nuevo (New Year's Day) January 1
Epifanía (Epiphany) January 6
Viernes Santo/Pascua (Good Friday/Easter) March/April – dates vary
Desembarco de los 33 (Return of the 33 Exiles) April 1
Día del Trabajador (Labor Day) May 1
Batalla de Las Piedras (Battle of Las Piedras) May 18
Natalicio de Artigas (Artigas' Birthday) June 19
Jura de la Constitución (Constitution Day) July 18
Día de la Independencia (Independence Day) August 25
Día de la Raza (Columbus Day) October 12
Día de los Muertos (All Souls' Day) November 2
Navidad (Christmas Day) December 25

INTERNET ACCESS

There are internet cafés on just about every street in cities and on the main streets in every town; access costs around US$0.30 an hour.

INTERNET RESOURCES

Mercopress News Agency (www.mercopress.com in English & Spanish) Montevideo-based internet news agency.
Ministerio de Turismo del Uruguay (www.turismo .gub.uy in Spanish) Government tourist information.
Olas y vientos (www.olasyvientos.com.uy) Everything you need to know about Uruguay's surf scene.
Red Uruguaya (www.reduruguaya.com) A guide to Uruguayan internet resources.
Uruguayan Embassy in Washington, DC (www .uruwashi.org) Historical, cultural and economic information on Uruguay.

LEGAL MATTERS

Drugs are freely available in Uruguay, but getting caught with them is about as much fun as anywhere else in the world. Uruguayan police and officials are not as bribe-hungry as many of their South American counterparts – if you feel you need to offer a bribe, make sure they make the first move, or you might be making the situation worse for yourself.

MAPS

Uruguayan road maps are only a partial guide to the highways. See the Automóvil Club del Uruguay, and Shell and Ancap stations for the best ones. For more detailed maps, try the **Instituto Geográfico Militar** (☎ 02-481-6868; 8 de Octubre & Abreu) in Montevideo.

MEDIA

Montevideo dailies include the morning *El Día, La República, La Mañana* and *El País. Gaceta Comercial* is the voice of the business community. Afternoon papers are *El Diario, Mundocolor* and *Últimas Noticias*.

MONEY

The unit of currency is the Uruguayan Peso (Ur$). Banknote values are five, 10, 20, 50, 100, 200, 500 and 1000. There are coins of 50 centavos, one, two, five and 10 pesos.

ATMs

For speed and convenience, nothing beats ATMs. They're found in most cities and smaller towns. Banco de la República Oriental del Uruguay seems to have the least temperamental machines.

Credit Cards

Credit cards are useful, particularly when buying cash from a bank. Most better hotels, restaurants and shops accept credit cards.

Exchange Rates

Exchange rates at press time included the following:

Country	Unit	Ur$ (peso)
Australia	A$1	17.58
Canada	C$1	20.42
euro zone	€1	29.52
Japan	¥100	20.01
New Zealand	NZ$1	14.33
UK	UK£1	43.76
US	US$1	22.94

Exchanging Money

There are plenty of *casas de cambio* in Montevideo, Colonia and the Atlantic beach resorts, but banks are the rule in the interior. *Casas de cambio* offer slightly lower rates and sometimes charge commissions. There's no black market for dollars or other foreign currencies.

Traveler's Checks

Traveler's checks can be cashed nationwide at banks and *casas de cambio*. Commission varies, but usually hovers around the two to three percent mark.

POST

Postal rates are reasonable, though service can be slow. If something is truly important, send it by registered mail or private courier.

For poste restante, address mail to the main post office in Montevideo. It will hold mail for up to a month, or two months with authorization.

RESPONSIBLE TRAVEL

Responsible tourism in Uruguay is mostly a matter of common sense, and the hard and fast rules here are ones that apply all over the globe.

Bargaining isn't part of the culture here and serious red-in-the-face, veins-out-on-forehead haggling is completely out of phase with the whole Uruguayan psyche. Chances are you're paying exactly what the locals are, so ask yourself how important that 25 cents is before things get really nasty.

SHOPPING

Bargains include leather clothing and accessories, woolen clothing and fabrics, agates and gems, ceramics, woodcrafts and decorated mate gourds.

STUDYING

Cafés in tourist areas (particularly Colonia) often have notice boards advertising private Spanish tuition and there are options for more organized classes in Montevideo. Dance and music tuition is also available in Montevideo.

TELEPHONE

Antel is the state telephone company, but there are private *locutorios* (telephone offices) on nearly every block.

Prepaid phone cards are (finally!) starting to appear in Uruguay. Available from most newsstands, these cards invariably offer better rates for international calls than you will get at Antel offices.

Making credit-card or collect calls to the US and other overseas destinations is also often cheaper than paying locally.

TOILETS

Toilets in Uruguay are generally clean and of a similar design to what you're probably used to. If there's a wastepaper basket next to the toilet, put used toilet paper in there. Unless you want to block up the system and make a flood, that is.

TOURIST INFORMATION

Almost every municipality has a tourist office, usually on the plaza or at the bus terminal. Hours are generally 10am to 6pm on weekdays, and 11am to 6pm on weekends. Maps can be mediocre, but many brochures have excellent historical information. The Ministerio de Turismo (Map pp950–1) in Montevideo answers general inquiries on the country and has a fact-filled website (in Spanish) at www.turismo.gub.uy. Uruguayan embassies and consulates overseas can sometimes help with tourist inquiries.

TOURS

Organized tours are starting to make an appearance in Uruguay, but are mostly aimed at family groups and don't go anywhere that you couldn't get to on your own, using a little common sense (and this book, of course!).

TRAVELERS WITH DISABILITIES

A modern country in many other ways, Uruguay hasn't kept up with developments for travelers with special needs. Footpaths are level(ish), but ramps and easy-access buses are nonexistent. Many budget hotels have at least one set of stairs and no elevator. On the bright side, taxis are cheap and plentiful, and the locals more than happy to help out when they can.

VISAS

Uruguay requires passports of all foreigners, except those from neighboring countries (who need only national identification cards). Nationals of Western Europe, Australia, the USA, Canada and New Zealand automatically receive a 90-day tourist card, renewable for another 90 days. Other nationals may require visas. For extensions, visit the immigration office (Map pp950-1; ☎ 02-916-0471; Misiones 1513) in Montevideo or local offices in border towns.

Passports are necessary for many everyday transactions, such as cashing traveler's checks and checking into hotels.

VOLUNTEERING

All Uruguayan organizations accepting volunteers require a minimum commitment of one month, and many require at least basic Spanish proficiency. Following are some Montevideo-based NGOs:

Comisión de la Juventud (☎ 1950-2046; Santiago de Chile & Soriano) Social workers concentrating on youth issues.

Cruz Roja (Red Cross; ☎ 02-480-0714; 8 de Octubre 2990) The Red Cross helps people avoid, prepare for and cope with emergencies.

Liga Uruguaya de Voluntarios (☎ 02-481-3763; Joanicó 3216) Cancer prevention and education.

UNICEF (☎ 02-707-4972; España 2565) The local branch of the UN Children's Fund.

WOMEN TRAVELERS

Uruguayans are no slouches when it comes to *machismo,* but their easygoing nature means that in all but the most out of the way places, this will probably only manifest as the odd wolf-whistle or sleazy remark (or compliment, depending on your point of view).

Venezuela

HIGHLIGHTS

- **Mérida** – choose from paragliding, canyoning, rafting, hiking and more in the country's adventure-sports capital (p1012)
- **Salto Ángel (Angel Falls)** – marvel at the world's highest waterfall as it drops over 300 stories in Canaima National Park (p1040)
- **Los Roques** – snorkel, scuba dive or just soak up the sun in these picture-perfect Caribbean islands (p1000)
- **Los Llanos** – view anacondas, caimans, capybaras and other Venezuelan wildlife in these grassy flatlands (p1017)
- **Off the beaten track** – explore remote waterfalls, sandy beaches and lush rainforests along the winding Río Caura (p1035)
- **Best journeys** – hike to the lost world on the flat top of Roraima mountain with moonscape scenery and unique plant life (p1042)

FAST FACTS

- **Area:** 916,445 sq km
- **Best bargain:** a red T-shirt with the face of Chávez and the title *'Patria o Muerte'* (Country or Death) for US$10
- **Best street snack:** *arepas* (corn dough fried and stuffed with anything you can imagine, US50¢-$3)
- **Budget:** US$20-50 a day
- **Capital:** Caracas
- **Costs:** double room in a budget hotel US$7-15, set meal in a budget restaurant US$2-4, 100km intercity bus fare US$2
- **Country code:** ☎ 58
- **Famous for:** oil, *tepuis,* beauty queens and Simón Bolívar
- **Language:** Spanish
- **Money:** US$1 = 2145 bolívars
- **Phrases:** *chévere* (cool), *rumba* (party), *vaina* (thing)
- **Population:** 25.7 million (2006 estimate)
- **Time:** GMT minus 4hr
- **Tipping:** voluntary tips up to 10% in upmarket restaurants
- **Visas:** not required from nationals of major Western countries

TRAVEL HINTS

Bring warm clothes for bus travel as they use powerful air conditioning. Keep your passport handy as there are military checkpoints along the highways.

OVERLAND ROUTES

There are nine border crossings to Colombia, one to Brazil and a boat crossing to Trinidad. There are no land routes to Guyana.

Venezuela receives considerably fewer visitors than other major South American countries. This is not the result of a lack of attractions. In fact, Venezuela is a land of stunning variety. The country has Andean peaks, endless Caribbean coastline, idyllic offshore islands, grasslands teeming with wildlife, the steamy Amazon and rolling savanna punctuated by flat-topped mountains called *tepuis*. The world's highest waterfall, Salto Ángel (Angel Falls), plummets 979m from the top of a *tepui* in Canaima National Park. Those seeking adventure will find hiking, snorkeling, scuba diving, kite-surfing, windsurfing, paragliding and more. Even better, most of these attractions lie within a one-day bus trip of each other.

Those interested in culture can revel in the pulsating salsa clubs of Caracas, explore various regional festivals, look for arts and crafts in the bucolic towns of the interior or even catch a world-famous Venezuelan `beauty pageant. President Hugo Chávez and his socialist 'Bolivarian Revolution' have also started to draw spectators, aspiring documentarians and volunteers to the country.

There are various hypotheses for the relatively low number of visitors, though the most common is that a petrol state of Venezuela's magnitude has never really bothered to promote its tourism industry. Times are changing, so now is the time to go.

CURRENT EVENTS

President Hugo Chávez always manages to keep himself in the news and people's love or hate for the president is also a frequent topic of conversation. Major issues of interest include the collapse of the bridge between the airport at Maquetía and Caracas, aid for leftist candidates and regimes in other countries (while poverty and crime worsen at home), the national crime and corruption rates and the acrid relationship with the United States. Less controversial but popular issues include the international success of Venezuelan baseball stars (local hero Ozzie Guillen is the manager of the 2005 World Series Champion Chicago White Sox) and Venezuelan beauty queens (the country has more Miss Universes than any other).

HISTORY
Pre-Columbian Times

There is evidence of human habitation in northwest Venezuela going back more than 10,000 years. Steady agriculture was established around the first millennium, leading to the first year-round settlements. Formerly nomadic groups began to develop into larger cultures belonging to three main linguistic families: Carib, Arawak and Chibcha. By the time of the Spanish conquest at the end of the 15th century, some 300,000 to 400,000 indigenous people inhabited the region that is now Venezuela.

The Timote-Cuica tribes, of the Chibcha linguistic family, were the most technologically developed of Venezuela's pre-Hispanic societies. They lived in the Andes and developed complex agricultural techniques including irrigation and terracing. They were also skilled craftspeople, as we can judge by the artifacts they left behind – examples of their fine pottery are shown in museums across the country. Though almost no architectural works have survived, some smaller sites in the Andean region have recently been unearthed and may be opening for tourism in the next few years.

Spanish Conquest

Christopher Columbus was the first European to set foot on Venezuelan soil. As a matter of fact Venezuela was the only place that he landed on the South American mainland. On his third trip to the New World in 1498, he anchored at the eastern tip of the Península de Paria, just opposite Trinidad. He originally believed that he was on another island, but the voluminous mouth of the Río Orinoco hinted that he had stumbled into something slightly larger.

A year later Alonso de Ojeda, accompanied by the Italian Amerigo Vespucci, sailed up to the Península de la Guajira, on the western end of present-day Venezuela. On entering Lago de Maracaibo, the Spaniards saw indigenous people living in *palafitos* (thatched homes on stilts above the water). Perhaps as a bit of sarcasm, they called the waterside community 'Venezuela,' meaning 'Little Venice.' The first Spanish settlement on Venezuelan soil, Nueva Cádiz, was established around 1500 on the small island of Cubagua, just south of Isla de Margarita. The earliest Venezuelan town still in existence, Cumaná (on the mainland directly south of Isla Cubagua) dates from 1521.

Venezuela receives considerably fewer visitors than other major South American countries. This is not the result of a lack of attractions. In fact, Venezuela is a land of stunning variety. The country has Andean peaks, endless Caribbean coastline, idyllic offshore islands, grasslands teeming with wildlife, the steamy Amazon and rolling savanna punctuated by flat-topped mountains called *tepuis*. The world's highest waterfall, Salto Ángel (Angel Falls), plummets 979m from the top of a *tepui* in Canaima National Park. Those seeking adventure will find hiking, snorkeling, scuba diving, kitesurfing, windsurfing, paragliding and more. Even better, most of these attractions lie within a one-day bus trip of each other.

Those interested in culture can revel in the pulsating salsa clubs of Caracas, explore various regional festivals, look for arts and crafts in the bucolic towns of the interior or even catch a world-famous Venezuelan beauty pageant. President Hugo Chávez and his socialist 'Bolívarian Revolution' have also started to draw spectators, aspiring documentarians and volunteers to the country.

There are various hypotheses for the relatively low number of visitors, though the most common is that a petrol state of Venezuela's magnitude has never really bothered to promote its tourism industry. Times are changing, so now is the time to go.

Independence Wars

With few exploited gold mines, Venezuela lurked in the shadows of the Spanish empire through most of the colonial period. The country took a more primary role at the beginning of the 19th century, when Venezuela gave Latin America one of its greatest heroes, Simón Bolívar. A native of Caracas, Bolívar led the forces that put the nail in the coffin of Spanish rule over South America. He is viewed as being largely responsible for ending colonial rule all the way to the borders of Argentina.

Bolívar assumed leadership of the revolution, which had been kicked off in 1806. After unsuccessful initial attempts to defeat the Spaniards at home, he withdrew to Colombia and then to Jamaica to plot his final campaign. In 1817 Bolívar marched over the Andes with 5000 British mercenaries and an army of horsemen from Los Llanos and defeated the Spanish at the Battle of Boyacá. This brought independence to Colombia. Four months later in Angostura (present-day Ciudad Bolívar), the Angostura Congress proclaimed Gran Colombia a new state, unifying Colombia (which included present-day Panamá), Venezuela and Ecuador – though the last two were still under Spanish rule.

The liberation of Venezuela was completed with Bolívar's victory over Spanish forces at Carabobo in June 1821, though the royalists put up a rather pointless fight from Puerto Cabello for another two years. Gran Colombia existed for only a decade before splitting into three separate countries. Bolívar's dream of a unified republic fell apart before he died in 1830.

Growing Pains

On his deathbed, Bolívar proclaimed 'America is ungovernable. The man who serves a revolution plows the sea. This nation will fall inevitably into the hands of the unruly mob and then will pass into the hands of almost indistinguishable petty tyrants.' Unfortunately, he was not too far off the mark. Venezuela followed independence with nearly a century of rule by a series of strongmen known as *caudillos*. It wasn't until 1947 that the first democratic government was elected.

The first of the *caudillos,* General José Antonio Páez, controlled the country for 18 years (1830–48). Despite his tough rule, he established a certain political stability and put the weak economy on its feet. The period that followed was an almost uninterrupted chain of civil wars that was only stopped by another long-lived dictator General Antonio Guzmán Blanco (1870–88). He launched a broad program of reform including a new constitution and assured some temporary stability, yet his despotic rule triggered popular opposition and when he stepped down the country fell back into civil war.

Ruling with an Iron Fist

The first half of the 20th century was dominated by five successive military rulers from the Andean state of Táchira. The longest-lasting and most ruthless was General Juan Vicente Gómez, who seized power in 1908 and didn't relinquish it until his death in 1935. Gómez phased out the parliament and crushed the opposition on his path to monopolization of power.

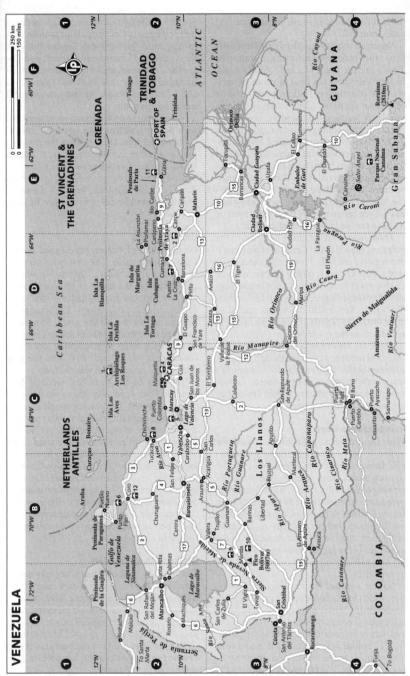

VENEZUELA

250 km
150 miles

VENEZUELA

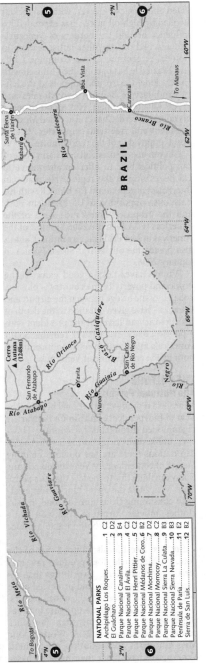

The discovery of oil in the 1910s helped the Gómez regime to put the national economy on its feet. By the late 1920s, Venezuela was the world's largest exporter of oil, which not only contributed to economic recovery but also enabled the government to pay off the country's entire foreign debt.

As in most petrol states, almost none of the oil wealth made its way to the common citizen. The vast majority continued to live in poverty with little or no educational or health facilities, let alone reasonable housing. Fast oil money also led to the neglect of agriculture and development of other types of production. It was easier to just import everything from abroad, which worked for a while but proved unsustainable.

After a short flirtation with democracy and a new constitution in 1947, the inevitable coup took place and ushered in the era of Colonel Marcos Pérez Jiménez. Once in control, he smashed the opposition, and plowed oil money into public works and modernizing Caracas – not making many friends in the process.

A Political Soap Opera

Pérez Jiménez was overthrown in 1958 by a coalition of civilians and military officers. The country returned to democratic rule, and Rómulo Betancourt was elected president. He enjoyed popular support and was the first democratically elected president to complete his five-year term in office. There was a democratic transition of power though the country drifted to the right.

Oil money buoyed the following governments well into the 1970s. Not only did production of oil rise but, more importantly, the price quadrupled following the Arab-Israeli war in 1973. The nation went on a spending spree, building modern skyscrapers in Caracas and Maracaibo and importing all sorts of luxury goods. But what goes up must come down and by the late 1970s the bust cycle was already in full swing. And it continued to fall apart through the 1980s.

1992 started off the next decade with two attempted coups d'état. The first, in February, was led by a little-known paratrooper named Colonel Hugo Chávez Rivas. The second attempt, in November, was led by junior airforce officers. The air battle over Caracas, with warplanes flying between skyscrapers, gave the coup a cinematic dimension. Many died in both attempts.

Corruption, bank failures and loan defaults plagued the government through the mid-1990s. In 1995, Venezuela was forced to devalue the currency by more than 70%. By the end of 1998, two-thirds of Venezuela's 23 million inhabitants were living below the poverty line.

A Left Turn

There is nothing better in political theater than a dramatic comeback. The 1998 election put Hugo Chávez, the leader of the 1992 failed coup, into the presidency. After being pardoned in 1994, Chávez embarked on an aggressive populist campaign: comparing himself to Bolívar, promising help (and handouts) to the poorest masses and positioning himself in opposition to the United States–influenced free-market economy. He vowed to produce a great, if vague, 'peaceful and democratic social revolution.'

Since then, however, Chávez's 'social revolution' has been anything but peaceful. Shortly after taking office, Chávez set about rewriting the constitution. The new document was approved in a referendum in December 1999, granting him new and sweeping powers. The introduction of a package of new decree laws in 2001 was met with angry protests, and was followed by a massive and violent strike in April 2002. It culminated in a coup d'état run by military leaders sponsored by a business lobby, in which Chávez was forced to resign. He regained power two days later, but this only intensified the conflict.

While the popular tensions rose, in December 2002 the opposition called a general strike in an attempt to oust the president. The nationwide strike paralyzed the country, including its vital oil industry and a good part of the private sector. After 63 days, the opposition finally called off the strike, which had cost the country 7.6% of its GDP and further devastated the oil-based economy. Chávez again survived and claimed victory. No one really won.

The Chávez Era – Venezuela & Beyond

National politics continued to be shaky until Chávez won a 2004 referendum and consolidated his power, eventually positioning himself to stay in the presidency through, perhaps, 2020.

Chávez's popularity rating is the issue of some debate, but the opposition remains divided and feckless. Chávez, with his pockets swollen by high oil prices, has expanded his influence beyond the borders of Venezuela and reached out to other leftist leaders in Bolivia, Argentina, Cuba, Uruguay, Chile and Brazil. He has openly allied himself with Cuba's Fidel Castro, and supported the leftist candidacy of Bolivia's Evo Morales and Peru's Ollanta Humala. Not afraid to make his opinion heard, Chávez also called Mexican President and free-trade supporter Vicente Fox a 'puppy dog of the (US) Empire.'

Chávez hopes to establish a Latin American political bloc to offer an alternative to US hegemony in the region. He made an international reputation for himself with his outspoken opposition to US President Bush and the proposed Free Trade Area of the Americas (FTAA) at the 2005 Summit of the Americas in Mar del Plata, Argentina. Caracas also hosted the 6th World Social Forum in January 2006.

While Chávez talks a good game, rising crime and poverty in the country – plus the collapse of the bridge between the airport and Caracas – have given question to the depth of his rhetoric and have left the president with a political black eye. Chávez remains South America's most controversial political figure both inside and outside of Venezuela.

THE CULTURE
The National Psyche

Venezuela is proud of its national history. The War of Independence and Simón Bolívar are championed throughout the country. However, unlike some neighboring South American nations there are few obvious defining factors of contemporary Venezuelan culture. Many attribute this to the fact that as a petrol state, Venezuela has spent much of its existence consuming from abroad (food, music, clothes, movies, furniture, cars, you name it), and not needing or bothering to produce much at home.

But just like the oil pumped out of the country, Venezuela does produce raw materials and raw talent. Two things that are produced in Venezuela, and produced quite well, are beauty queens and baseball players. Venezuelan women have won more international beauty competitions than any other country, including five Miss Worlds, four Miss Universes and countless other titles. Venezuelans have made their mark on baseball too. The North American major leagues have their fair share of Venezuelan athletes.

Baseball is played throughout the country too, and it is common to see pick-up games in construction sites or along the side of highways. The national sport goes hand-in-hand with the national drinks of rum and ice-cold beer. Men in Caracas tend to opt for Scotch instead, as they like to show their big-city sophistication.

Even in the face of deep-seated national ills and social tensions, Venezuelans are full of life and humor. They are open, willing to talk and not shy about striking up conversations with strangers. Wherever you are, you're unlikely to be alone or feel isolated, especially if you can speak a little Spanish. There's always a *rumba* brewing somewhere. So forget your schedules and organized plans and warm up to the Venezuelan lifestyle.

Population
Venezuela's population density is a low 26 people per square kilometer. However, the population is unevenly distributed; 75% of Venezuelans live in towns and cities. Over one-fifth of the country's population lives in Caracas alone, while Los Llanos and Guayana are relatively empty.

About 70% of the population is a blend of European, indigenous and African ancestry, or any two of the three. The rest are full European (about 20%), African (8%) or indigenous (2%). Of that 2%, there are about 24 highly diverse indigenous groups comprising some 600,000 people, scattered throughout the country.

SPORT
Soccer? What soccer? In Venezuela, *béisbol* (baseball) rules supreme. The professional baseball league is composed of eight teams: Caracas, La Guaira, Maracaibo, Valencia, Barquisimeto, Maracay, Puerto La Cruz and Cabimas. Many Venezuelans have gone on to fame and fortune in US major-league baseball. In 2005, Ozzie Guillen (a native of Ocumare del Tuy in Miranda state) managed the Chicago White Sox to their first World Series championship in 88 years. The biggest rivalry in the Venezuelan league is between the two top teams: Leones del Caracas and Navegantes del Magallanes (Valencia).

The next most popular sports are *básquetbol* (basketball, also known as *básquet* or *balon-*

cesto), followed by *fútbol* (soccer), which has a professional league that plays from August till May. Soccer is the sport of choice among the country's indigenous population.

RELIGION
Some 95% of Venezuelans are at least nominally Roman Catholic. Chávez has had words with the church in recent years and is no big proponent of the Vatican's influence in his one-man show. Many indigenous groups adopted Catholicism and only a few isolated tribes still practice their traditional beliefs. Evangelicals compete with Catholics for converts and are gaining ground across the country. There are small populations of Jews and Muslims, particularly in Caracas.

ARTS
Architecture
There are small, and impressive, pockets of colonial architecture in Venezuela – most notably in Coro (p1006) – but overall the country never reached the grandeur of other parts of the Spanish empire. Churches were mostly small and houses were usually undecorated one-story constructions. Only in the last half-century of the colonial era did a wealthier merchant class emerge that built grand residences that reflected their stature.

President Guzmán Blanco launched a dramatic overhaul of Caracas in the 1870s. He commissioned many monumental public buildings in a hodgepodge of styles, largely depending on the whim of the architect in charge. A forced march toward modernity came with oil money and culminated in the 1970s. This period was characterized by indiscriminate demolition of historic buildings and their replacement with utilitarian architecture. Just the same, Venezuela does have some truly remarkable modern architecture. Carlos Raúl Villanueva, who began work in the 1930s, is considered the most outstanding Venezuelan architect. The campus of Universidad Central de Venezuela in Caracas is regarded as one of his best and most coherent designs and has been included on Unesco's Cultural Heritage list.

Cinema & Television
CINEMA
Venezuela's film industry is small, but has started to gain momentum in recent years. The great majority of the films are either

contemporary social critiques or historical dramatizations.

The biggest smash in new Venezuelan cinema was 2005's *Secuestro Express* (Kidnap Express) by Jonathan Jakubowicz. The film, which was criticized by the government for its harsh portrayal of the city, takes a cold look at crime, poverty, violence, drugs and class relations in the capital. It broke all box-office records for a national production and was the first Venezuelan film to be distributed by a major Hollywood studio.

Those interested in learning more about Venezuelan film should track down a couple of films. *Huelepega* (Glue Sniffer; Elia Schneider, 1999) is a portrayal of Caracas street children using real street youth, not actors, in the film; *Amaneció de Golpe* (A Coup at Daybreak; Carlos Azpúrua, 1999) is the story of how Chávez burst onto the political scene, and *Manuela Saenz* (Manuela Saenz; Diego Risquez, 2000) depicts the War of Independence through the eyes of Bolívar's mistress.

Also worth seeing is *The Revolution Will Not Be Televised,* a documentary shot by Irish filmmakers who were inside the presidential palace during the coup d'état of 2002. It contains firsthand footage of the events and provides a deeply compelling – though unabashedly pro-Chávez – portrait of the man himself.

TELEVISION

Venezuelan TV ranges from soap-opera fluff to equally kitsch government propaganda, with a few slapstick comedy shows and some baseball commentary in between. The Venezuela-based, pan–Latin American TV station TelSur was launched in 2005. Chavez has hoped it will balance out the influence of massively popular North American cable TV programs across the continent. The president's personal TV show *Aló Presidente* is a cross between a State of the Union address and the Oprah Winfrey show. Chávez prattles on about national progress while taking calls and addressing the questions of supporters.

Equally as engaging are the *telenovelas* (soap operas). It is said that the export market for Venezuelan *telenovelas* is more than the national export of automobiles, textiles or paper products. Some of the classics have been *Cristal* and *Kassandra,* which dominated TV screens from Spain to Indonesia.

Literature

The classic work in Latin American colonial literature of the treatment of the indigenous populations by the Spanish – which happens to also document the early years of Venezuela – is *Brevísima Relación de la Destrucción de las Indias Occidentales* (A Short Account of the Destruction of the West Indies), written by Fray Bartolomé de las Casas in 1542.

As for contemporary literature, a groundbreaking experimental novel from the middle of the century is *El Falso Cuaderno de Narciso Espejo* by Guillermo Meneses (1911–78). Another seminal work was Adriano Gonzalez Leon's (1931–) powerful magical-realism novel *Pais Portatil* (Portable Country), which contrasts rural Venezuela with the urban juggernaut of Caracas.

Ednodio Quintero is another contemporary writer to look for. His work *La Danza del Jaguar* (The Dance of the Jaguar; 1991) is one of several translated into other languages. Other contemporary writers worth tracking down include Carlos Noguera, Luis Brito García, Eduardo Liendo and Orlando Chirinos.

Music

Music is omnipresent in Venezuela, though the country doesn't produce a lot of music of its own (and produces even less music for export). The most common types of popular music are salsa, merengue and *reggaetón* from the Caribbean and *vallenato* from Colombia. The king of Venezuelan salsa is Oscar D'León (1943–). He has recorded a staggering 60 albums.

North American and European pop – everything from rock to hip-hop to house – is influential among urban youth (who account for the majority of the population). Chávez has tried to curb that influence, mandating that 50% of all radio airplay must be Venezuelan music and, of that music, 50% must be 'traditional.'

The country's most popular folk rhythm is the *joropo*, also called *música llanera,* which developed in Los Llanos (see p1017). The *joropo* is usually sung and accompanied by the harp, *cuatro* (a small, four-stringed guitar) and maracas.

Caracas is an exciting center of Latin pop and the *rock en español* movement, which harnesses the rhythm and energy of Latin beats and combines them with international rock and alternative-rock trends. The most famous product of this scene is the Grammy-winning Los Amigos Invisibles, who now reside in North America.

Visual Arts

Venezuela has a strong contemporary art movement. The streets and public buildings of Caracas are filled with modern art and the city houses some truly remarkable galleries.

Large-scale public art developed with the internal investment of the Guzmán Blanco regime in the late 19th century. The standout painter of that period – and one of the best in all of Venezuelan history – was Martín Tovar y Tovar (1827–1902). Some of his greatest works depicting historical events can be seen in Caracas' Capitolio Nacional (p989).

There is a rich visual arts scene among the current generation. Keep an eye out for works of Carlos Zerpa (painting), the quirky ideas of José Antonio Hernández Díez (photo, video, installations) and the emblematic paintings, collages and sculptures of Miguel von Dangel. And you'll see plenty more in the contemporary art museum of Caracas (see p991).

Jesús Soto (1923–2005) was Venezuela's number one internationally renowned contemporary artist. He was a leading representative of kinetic art (art, particularly sculpture, that contains moving parts). His large distinctive works adorn numerous public buildings and plazas in Venezuela and beyond (including Paris, Toronto and New York). The largest collection of his work is in the museum dedicated to him in Ciudad Bolívar (see p1034).

ENVIRONMENT
The Land

At about twice the size of California, Venezuela claims a multiplicity of landscapes. The traveler can encounter all four primary South American landscapes – the Amazon, the Andes, savannas and beaches – all in a single country.

The country has two mountain ranges: the Cordillera de la Costa, which separates the valley of Caracas from the Caribbean Sea, and the northern extreme of the Andes range, with its highest peaks near Mérida.

The 2150km Río Orinoco is Venezuela's main river, its entire course lying within national boundaries. The land south of the Orinoco, known as Guayana, includes the Río Caura watershed, the largely impenetrable

Amazon rainforest, vast areas of sun-baked savanna and hundreds of *tepuis*.

Last but not least, there is a 2813km-long stretch of Caribbean coast, featuring a 900,000 sq km Caribbean marine zone with numerous islands and cays. The largest and most popular of these is Isla de Margarita, followed by the less developed Archipiélago Los Roques.

Wildlife

Along with the variety of Venezuelan landscape, you will encounter an amazing diversity of wildlife. Visitors often seek out anacondas, capybara, caimans and birds. There are 341 species of reptiles, 284 species of amphibians, 1791 species of fishes, 351 species of mammals and many butterflies and other invertebrates. More than 1360 species of birds – approximately 20% of the world's known species – reside in the country, and 46 of these species are endemic. The country's geographical setting on a main migratory route makes it a bird-watcher's heaven.

National Parks

Venezuela's national parks offer a diverse landscape of evergreen mountains, beaches, tropical islands, coral reefs, high plateaus and rainforests. The national parks are the number-one destination for tourism within the country. Canaima, Los Roques, Mochima, Henri Pittier, El Ávila and Morrocoy are the most popular parks. Some parks, especially those in coastal and marine zones, are easily accessible and tend to be overcrowded by locals during holiday periods and weekends; others remain unvisited. A few of the parks offer tourism facilities, but these generally are not very extensive.

Environmental Issues

Far and away the most obvious environmental problem in Venezuela is waste management (or lack thereof). There is no recycling policy and dumping of garbage in cities, along roads and natural areas is common practice. Untreated sewage is sometimes dumped in the sea and other water bodies. There continues to be a general lack of clear environmental policy and little to no culture of environmental stewardship outside of the park areas. Much of the waste and pollution issues are a direct result of overpopulation in urban areas and a lack of civil planning and funds to cope with the rampant development.

Another major environmental issue is the hunting and illegal trade of fauna and flora that takes place in many parts of the country, including protected areas. Pet tropical birds, for example, fetch a handsome price in the US, Asia and Europe. A final major ecological concern is the inevitable pollution from oil refineries and drilling: Lago de Maracaibo, for example, has witnessed many oil spills, and much of the petroleum infrastructure is old and in need of repair.

TRANSPORTATION

GETTING THERE & AWAY
Air
Set at the northern edge of South America, Venezuela has the cheapest air links with both Europe and North America and is therefore the most convenient northern gateway to the continent. As of 2006, there were air-traffic disputes with the United States and the government had trimmed the number of outgoing flights as reciprocity for a similar move by the United States. The lack of flights raised transportation costs to and from North America.

Flying between Brazil and Venezuela is expensive. The flight from São Paulo or Rio de Janeiro to Caracas will cost around US$615 round trip. There are no direct flights between Manaus and Caracas, nor between Boa Vista and Santa Elena de Uairén.

Avianca and Aeropostal fly between Bogotá, Colombia and Caracas (US$220 one way, US$260 round trip).

There are no direct flights between Venezuela and Guyana. You need to fly via Port of Spain (Trinidad) with BWIA (US$260 one way, US$360 round trip).

Aeropostal and BWIA fly daily between Port of Spain and Caracas (US$150 one way, US$205 for a 21-day round trip). Aeropostal

and Rutaca fly between Porlamar and Port of Spain (US$110 one way, US$155 for a 21-day round trip).

Boat
Weekly passenger boats operate between Venezuela and Trinidad, but there are no longer ferries between Venezuela and the Netherland Antilles. For more information, see the Güiria section (p1028).

Bus
Only one road connects Brazil and Venezuela; it leads from Manaus through Boa Vista to Santa Elena de Uairén and continues to Ciudad Guayana. For details see Santa Elena de Uairén (p1043).

You can enter Venezuela from Colombia at four border crossings. The two most common (and safest) are: the coastal route between Maicao and Maracaibo (see box, p1011) and from Cúcuta and San Antonio del Táchira (see box, p1019).

No roads link Guyana and Venezuela; to go overland, you must go via Brazil.

GETTING AROUND
Air
Venezuela has a number of airlines and a reasonable network of air routes. Maiquetía, where Caracas' airport is located, is the country's major aviation hub and handles flights to most airports around the country. Cities most frequently serviced from Caracas include Porlamar, Maracaibo and Puerto Ordaz (Ciudad Guayana). The most popular destinations with travelers are Mérida, Ciudad Bolívar, Canaima and Porlamar. There is a tax of US$16 to fly to internal destinations from Maquetía.

Venezuela has half-a-dozen major commercial airlines servicing main domestic routes, and a dozen minor provincial carriers that cover regional and remote routes on a regular or charter basis.

Canaima and Los Roques have their own fleets of Cessnas and other smaller planes that fly for a number of small-time airlines. It is best to book these flights through an agent. Some of the airlines:

Aeropostal (☎ 0800-337-8466, 0212-266-1059; www.aeropostal.com; 1st fl, Torre ING Bank, Av Eugenio Mendoza, La Castellana) The country's largest airline, with flights to most major domestic destinations, including Barcelona, Barquisimeto, Maracaibo, Maturín, Porlamar,

---

DEPARTURE TAX

The airport tax is US$35 or higher depending on the length of your stay. An additional *impuesto de salida* (departure tax) of US$15 must be paid by all visitors. The taxes are payable in either US dollars or bolívars, but not by credit card. There are ATMs in the airport.

Puerto Ordaz (Ciudad Guayana), San Antonio del Táchira and Valencia.

Aserca (☎ 0800-648-8356, 0212-905-5333; www.aser caairlines.com; ground fl, Edificio Taeca, Calle Guaicaipuro, El Rosal) Airline operating jet flights between several major airports, including Caracas, Barcelona, Maracaibo, Porlamar and San Antonio del Táchira.

Avensa (domestic ☎ 0212-355-1609, international ☎ 0212-355-1889; www.avensa.com.ve in Spanish; Maiquetía airport)

Avior (☎ 0212-761-1621; www.avior.com.ve; Lincoln Suites, Av Francisco Solano, Sabana Grande) Young, progressive carrier flying on fairly new propeller crafts to many airports around the country, including Caracas, Barcelona, Barinas, Barquisimeto, Canaima, Ciudad Bolívar, Coro, Cumaná, Maturín, Mérida, Porlamar and Valera.

LAI (☎ 0212-355-2333, 355-2322; Maiquetía airport)

Laser (☎ 0212-202-0011; www.laser.com.ve in Spanish; Maiquetía airport) Carrier focusing on a few main cities, including Caracas, Maracaibo and Porlamar.

Rutaca (www.rutaca.com.ve in Spanish) Maiquetía Airport ☎ 0212-355-1838); Caracas (☎ 0212-235-6035; Centro Seguros La Paz, Av Francisco de Miranda) Small but expanding airline with planes ranging from old Cessnas to new jets, serving Caracas, Canaima, Ciudad Bolívar, Porlamar, San Antonio del Táchira and Santa Elena de Uairén.

Santa Bárbara (☎ 0212-952-9658; www.santabarbara airlines.com; Miranda level, Centro Lido, Av Francisco de Miranda) A young but already well-established airline serving Caracas, Cumaná, Las Piedras, Maracaibo, Mérida, Puerto Ayacucho and San Antonio del Táchira.

Boat

Venezuela has a number of islands, but only Isla de Margarita is serviced by regular scheduled boats and ferries; see Puerto La Cruz (p1022), Cumaná (p1026) and Isla de Margarita (p1029).

The Río Orinoco is the country's major inland waterway. It's navigable from its mouth up to Puerto Ayacucho, but there's no regular passenger service on any part of it.

Bus

As there is no passenger-train service in Venezuela, almost all traveling is done by bus. Buses are generally fast, and they run regularly day and night between major population centers. Bus transportation is affordable and usually efficient.

Venezuela's dozens of bus companies own buses ranging from sputtering pieces of junk to the most recent models. All major companies offer *servicio ejecutivo* in comfortable air-conditioned buses, which cover all the major long-distance routes and are the dominant means of intercity transportation.

Caracas is the most important transport hub, handling buses to just about every corner of the country. In general, there's no need to buy tickets more than a couple of hours in advance for major routes, except around holidays.

Many short-distance regional routes are served by *por puestos* (literally 'by the seat'), a cross between a bus and a taxi. *Por puestos* are usually large old US-made cars (less often minibuses) that ply fixed routes and depart when all seats are filled. They cost about 40% to 80% more than buses, but they're faster and can be more comfortable.

Car & Motorcycle

Traveling by car is a comfortable and attractive way of getting around Venezuela. The country is reasonably safe, and the network of roads is extensive and usually in acceptable shape. Gas stations are numerous and fuel is just about the cheapest in the world – US3¢ to US6¢ per liter, depending on the octane level. You can fill up your tank for a dollar. This rosy picture is slightly obscured by Venezuelan traffic and local driving manners. Traffic in Venezuela, especially in Caracas, is chaotic and requires nerves of steel.

Bringing a car to Venezuela (or to South America in general) is time-consuming, expensive and involves plenty of paperwork, and few people do it. It's much more convenient and cheaper to rent a car locally. Also see above.

Local Transport
BUS & METRO

All cities and many major towns have their own urban transportation systems, which in most places are small buses or minibuses. Depending on the region, these are called *busetas, carros, carritos, micros* or *camionetas*, and fares are usually no more than US20¢. In many larger cities you can also find urban *por puestos*, swinging faster than buses through the chaotic traffic. Caracas is the only city in Venezuela with a subway system.

TAXI

Taxis are fairly inexpensive and are worth considering, particularly for transport between the bus terminal and city center when you are carrying all your bags. Taxis don't

VENEZUELA

have meters, so always fix the fare with the driver before boarding the cab. It's a good idea to find out the correct fare beforehand from an independent source, such as someone who works in the bus station or a hotel reception desk.

CARACAS

☎ 0212 / pop 5 million

On first encounter Caracas is more likely to give you a slap in the face than a warm embrace. The political and cultural capital of Venezuela is densely overpopulated and hectic, with a solid dose of crime, traffic and pollution. There are few parts of the city that are pedestrian-friendly and there are almost no quality accommodations for budget travelers.

However, Caracas does have its attractions and will ingratiate itself to the persistent and intrepid traveler. Nestled between verdant peaks at an altitude of about 900m, the city enjoys both a spectacular setting and a comfortable climate. In counterbalance to the city's tougher side, Caracas claims an impressive variety of restaurants and a progressive fashion and art scene. From the chic lounges of San Ignacio to the patio bars and salsa clubs of Las Mercedes, the city is known for its pulsing nightlife. But Caracas' attractions are not just about the new and the sexy. The city is also home to much of the Venezuelan nation's history including many important sites relating to Simón Bolívar, the Liberator of South America.

Whether Caracas is your intended destination or not, it is likely that you will pass

---

STREET ADDRESSES

A curiosity of Caracas is the center's street address system. It's not the streets that bear names here, but the *esquinas* (street corners); therefore, addresses are given 'corner to corner.' So if an address is 'Piñango a Conde,' the place is between these two street corners. If a place is situated on a corner, just the corner will be named (eg Esq Conde).

---

through the city, as it is the transportation hub for most of the country.

ORIENTATION

Sprawling for 20km along a narrow coastal valley, Caracas is bordered to the north by the Parque Nacional El Ávila and to the south by a mix of modern suburbs and *barrios* (shantytowns) stacked along the steep hillsides. Downtown Caracas stretches for 8km or so west–east from the neighborhood of El Silencio to Chacao. Museums, theaters and cinemas are clustered around Parque Central on the eastern edge of the historic center. Most accommodations and inexpensive eateries can be found here or in the bustling neighborhood of Sabana Grande. Nicer restaurants, hotels and the majority of the city's nightlife can be found to the south and east in Altamira, El Rosal and Las Mercedes.

INFORMATION
Bookstores

American Book Shop (Map pp990-1; ☎ 285-8779; Nivel Jardín, Centro Comercial Centro Plaza, Los Palos

---

GETTING INTO TOWN

Caracas' main airport is at Maiquetía, 26km northwest of the city center. It's linked to the city by a freeway that cuts through the coastal mountain range with a variety of tunnels and bridges. In early 2006, one of the principal bridges had to be demolished due to structural issues. At the time of writing, there was a side route that helps to keep traffic flowing but still slows the Caracas–Maiquetía trip by a half hour or more. Estimates of the time necessary to reconstruct the bridge run from one to three years.

Buses run every half hour from about 5:30am to 8pm (US$3, one hour). At the airport, they depart from the front of the domestic and international terminals. In the city, buses depart from Calle Sur 17 (directly underneath Av Bolívar, next to Parque Central), and from Gato Negro metro station.

The airport taxi service is operated by black Ford Explorers (US$20 to US$40, depending on the destination), which park at the front of the terminal. Be careful about taking unregistered taxis and never wander outside of the main airport terminals at night.

Grandes) Right past Altimira, this shop has a decent selection of English titles, used books and guidebooks.

El Buscón (Map pp990-1; ☎ 993-8242; Centro Trasnocho Cultural, Centro Comercial Paseo Las Mercedes, Las Mercedes) Browse-worthy store with strong selection of Venezuelan literature (in Spanish), plus some English novels.

Tecni-Ciencia Libros (☎ 959-5547) Centro Ciudad Comercial Tamanco (Map pp990-1); Centro Comercial Sambil (Map pp990-1) This chain bookstore is in a number of malls about the city as well as those listed. It has a reliable collection of texts in English and Spanish, including a few Lonely Planet guidebooks.

Emergency

Emergency Center (Police, fire & ambulance ☎ 171; ☿ 24hr) The operators rarely speak English.

Immigration

DIEX (Dirección de Identificación y Extranjería; Map pp986-7; ☎ 483-2070; www.onidex.gov.ve in Spanish; Av Baralt, Plaza Miranda, El Silencio; ☿ 7:30-11:30am Mon-Fri) Visas and tourist cards can be extended here for up to three months ($40). Passport, two photos and a letter explaining the purpose of the extension are required. Processing takes three working days.

Internet Access

In the areas of Caracas that are covered in this book, it is difficult to walk more than two blocks on a major street and not encounter a cybercafé. The prices are reasonable (usually less than US$1 per hour). The modern shopping malls that dot the city tend to have cybercafés with the most modern equipment and the fastest connections. Most internet cafés open after 8am or 9am and are closed by 10pm. See also CANTV, right. Some good ones that are not in shopping malls:

CompuMall (Map pp990-1; ☎ 993-0111; Av Orinoco, Edificio Santa Ana, Las Mercedes; ☿ 9am-9pm Mon-Sat, 11am-8pm Sun) One of the only internet spots in this part of town, it has a slow connection speed but the chilly air-con and legitimate bakery-café make it worth a visit on a hot day.

Cyber Office 2020 (Map pp988-9; Edificio San Germán, Calle Navarro at Av Solano, Sabana Grande; ☿ 9am-midnight Mon-Sat, 10am-midnight Sun) One of many choices in this area.

Cyber Only Place (Map pp988-9; Torre Lincoln, Blvd de Sabana Grande & Las Acacias; ☿ 8:30am-7pm Mon-Sat, 10am-4pm Sun)

Laundry

Most hotels or hostels will either do laundry in-house or send it out. There are few self-service places. Laundromats will wash and dry clothes for US$2 to US$5 per 5kg load and are open from about 7am until 6pm Monday to Friday with a break for lunch, and from 7am to 1pm Saturday. A few recommended *lavanderías:*

Lavandería Autolanka (Map pp986-7; Centro Comercial Doral, Av Urdaneta, La Candelaria)

Lavandería Chapultepex (Map pp988-9; Calle Bolivia, Sabana Grande) Self-service.

Lavandería El Metro (Map pp988-9; Calle Los Manguitos, Sabana Grande)

Medical Services

Most minor health problems can be solved in a *farmacia* (pharmacy). You can even get basic shots right at the counter. Under Venezuelan law there's always at least one open in every neighborhood. You can easily recognize them by the sign reading 'Turno.' Some dependable *farmacia* chains found throughout the city include Farmatodo and FarmAhorro. Following are reputable medical facilities that can help with more serious medical problems:

Centro Médico de Caracas (Map pp986-7; ☎ 552-2222; Plaza El Estanque, Av Eraso, San Bernardino)

Clínica El Ávila (Map pp990-1; ☎ 276-1111; Av San Juan Bosco at 6a Transversal, Altamira)

Money

Who says that Chavez is chasing out foreign interests? There are international banks and ATMs all over the city, including a prominent 24-hour Citibank at the entrance to El Recreo shopping center in Sabana Grande. Cash advances on Visa and MasterCard can be easily obtained at most Caracas banks. Be cautious when using outdoor ATMs at night. Some central branches:

Banco de Venezuela Center (Map pp986-7; Av Universidad); Sabana Grande (Map pp988-9; Blvd Sabana Grande)

Banco Mercantil Center (Map pp986-7; Av Universidad); Sabana Grande (Map pp988-9; Av Las Acacias)

Banesco Altamira (Map pp990-1; 6a Transversal); Altamira (Map pp990-1; Av Sur Altamira); Center (Map pp986-7; Av Fuerzas Armadas); Center (Map pp986-7; Av Universidad); Las Mercedes (Map pp990-1; Calle Monterrey); Sabana Grande (Map pp988-9; Blvd de Sabana Grande); Sabana Grande (Map pp988-9; Av Las Mercedes)

The usual places to change foreign cash are *casas de cambio* (money-exchange offices).

Amex (☎ 800-100-4730) Offers local refund assistance for traveler's checks.

VENEZUELA

CENTRAL CARACAS

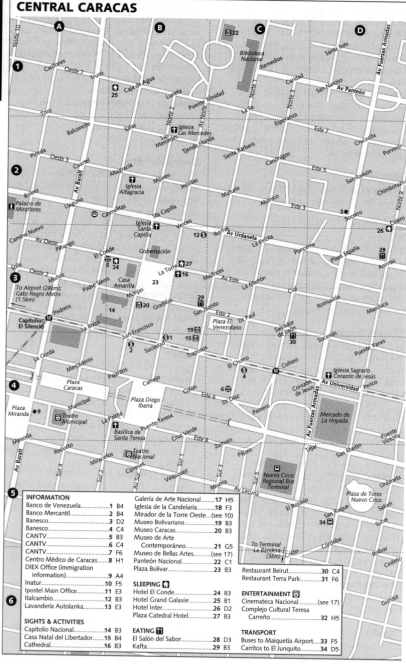

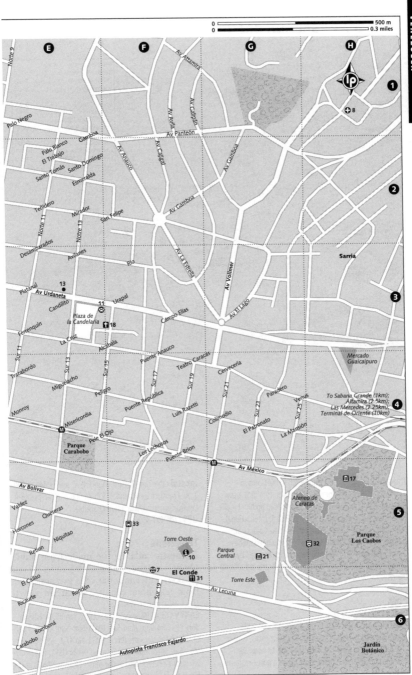

0 _____ 500 m
0 _____ 0.3 miles

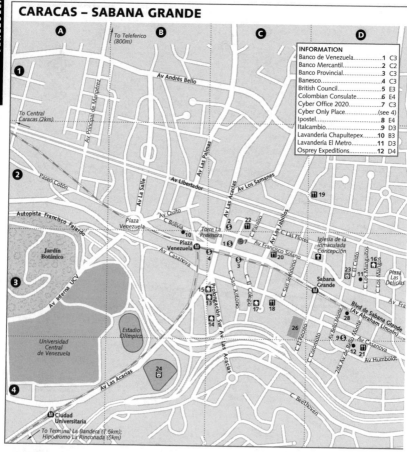

CARACAS – SABANA GRANDE

Italcambio (☎ 562-9555; www.italviajes.com in Spanish; ⏲ 8:30am–5pm Mon–Fri, 9am–1pm Sat) Altamira (Map pp990–1; Av Ávila); Las Mercedes (Map pp990–1; Calle California); Maiquetía airport (Map pp990–1; International terminal); Sabana Grande (Map pp988–9; Av Casanova).

Grupo Zoom (☎ 800-767-9666) If you need money sent to you quickly, Western Union is represented by Grupo Zoom, which has about 25 offices scattered around the city.

Post

FedEx (☎ 205-3333)

Ipostel main office (Map pp986–7; ☎ 862-0486; www.ipostel.gov.ve; Av Urdaneta, Esq Carmelitas, Center; ⏲ 7am–7:45pm Mon–Fri, 8am–5pm Sat, to noon Sun) Near Plaza Bolívar, the main office offers a poste-restante service.

Ipostel (⏲ 7am–7:45pm Mon–Fri) Altamira (Map pp990–1; Av Francisco de Miranda); Sabana Grande (Map pp988–9; Centro Comercial Arta, Plaza Chacaíto).

UPS (☎ 401-4900)

Telephone

Domestic calls can be made from public phones or stands with mobile phones for rent (p1054). International calls are best made from telephone centers, which are easy to find all over town.

CANTV Chacao (Map pp990–1; Centro Sambil, Av Libertador; ⏲ 9am–9pm Mon–Sat, 10am–6pm Sun; internet per hr US$1); Las Mercedes (CCCT, fl C-1, No 47-F; ⏲ 9am–9pm Mon–Sat, 10am–6pm Sun; internet per hr US$1) Has many telephone centers. Also in the center (Map pp986–7) at Esq El Conde, El Chorro at Dr Díaz and Parque Central.

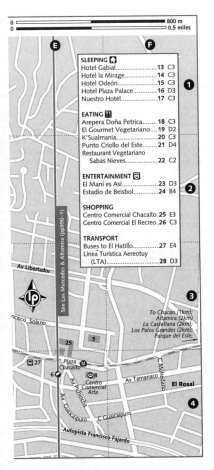

SLEEPING
Hotel Gabial.....................13 C3
Hotel la Mirage.................14 C3
Hotel Odeón.....................15 C3
Hotel Plaza Palace...........16 D3
Nuestro Hotel..................17 C3

EATING
Arepera Doña Petrica........18 C3
El Gourmet Vegetariano....19 D2
K'Sualmania.....................20 C3
Punto Criollo del Este.......21 D4
Restaurant Vegetariano
    Sabas Nieves..............22 C2

ENTERTAINMENT
El Maní es Así...................23 D3
Estadio de Beisbol............24 B4

SHOPPING
Centro Comercial Chacaíto.25 E3
Centro Comercial El Recreo.26 C3

TRANSPORT
Buses to El Hatillo.............27 E4
Línea Turística Aereotuy
    (LTA)..........................28 D3

Av Libertador

ncisco Solano

To Chacao (1km);
Altamira (2km);
La Castellana (2km);
Los Palos Grandes (2km);
Parque del Este

25   5

27   Plaza
     Chacaíto
6   B
     Centro
     Comercial   Av Tamanaco   El Rosal
     Arta

C Guaicaipuro

Autopista Francisco Fajardo

Tourist Information

Inatur (www.inatur.gov.ve) domestic terminal (☎ 355-1191; Maiquetía airport; ⏰ 7am-8pm); international terminal (☎ 355-1060; Maiquetía airport; ⏰ 8am-midnight); Parque Central (Map pp986-7; ☎ 0800-462-8871, 576-5138; 35th fl, Mirador de la Torre Oeste; ⏰ 8:30am-12:30pm & 2-5pm Mon-Fri) When you enter the Mirador de la Torre Oeste, take the elevator from Nivel Lecuna to get to the information office – elevators from other levels don't go to this floor.

Travel Agencies

Osprey Expeditions (Map pp988-9; ☎ 762-5974; www.ospreyvenezuela.com; cnr Av Casanova & 2da Av Bello Monte, Edificio La Paz, Office 51, Sabana Grande) Osprey is helpful with travel information and can arrange transportation and tours.

IVI Venezuela (Map pp990-1; ☎ 993-6082; www.ivivenezuela.com in Spanish; Residencia La Hacienda, Av Principal de Las Mercedes, ground fl; ⏰ 8am-6pm Mon-Fri) Offers reasonable airfares and useful information to foreign students, teachers and people under 26 years of age.

DANGERS & ANNOYANCES

Caracas has some well-known issues with petty crime, robbery and armed assaults. These problems are not just hype and should be taken very seriously. Sabana Grande and the city center are the riskiest neighborhoods, although they are generally safe during the day (do look out for pickpockets in any dense crowd). Altamira and Las Mercedes are considerably safer. Travelers should always stick to well-lit main streets after dark.

SIGHTS
Central Caracas
THE CENTER & AROUND

The historic sector is the heart of the original Caracas. It still retains glimpses of its colonial past but is peppered with newer buildings and a lot of questionable architecture from the last century. It's a lively area and is worth visiting for its historical sites, particularly those pertaining to Simón Bolívar. In the historic quarter it is the *esquinas* (street corners), not the streets that bear names.

Like most Venezuelan cities and towns, Caracas' central **Plaza Bolívar** (Map pp986-7) is dedicated to Bolívar. The equestrian statue in the plaza was cast in Europe and unveiled in 1874, after some delay as the ship carrying it foundered on Archipiélago de Los Roques. The plaza is a place to hang out and watch the hours pass, listen to soapbox politicians or search the street stalls for religious trinkets, Chávez propaganda or souvenirs. On the eastern side of the plaza, don't miss the **cathedral** (Map pp986-7; ☎ 862-4963; ⏰ 8-11:30am & 4-6pm Mon-Fri, 9am-noon & 4:30-6pm Sat & Sun), which is home to the Bolívar family chapel where his wife and family are buried.

The **Capitolio Nacional** (National Capitol; Map pp986-7; ☎ 483-8240; admission free; ⏰ 9:30am-noon & 2-4pm Fri-Sun) occupies the entire block just southwest of Plaza Bolívar. In the central part of the northern building is the famous **Salón Elíptico**, an oval hall topped with an extraordinary domed ceiling. Covering this dome is a mural depicting the battle of Carabobo, which seems to move as you walk beneath it.

VENEZUELA

CARACAS – LAS MERCEDES & ALTAMIRA

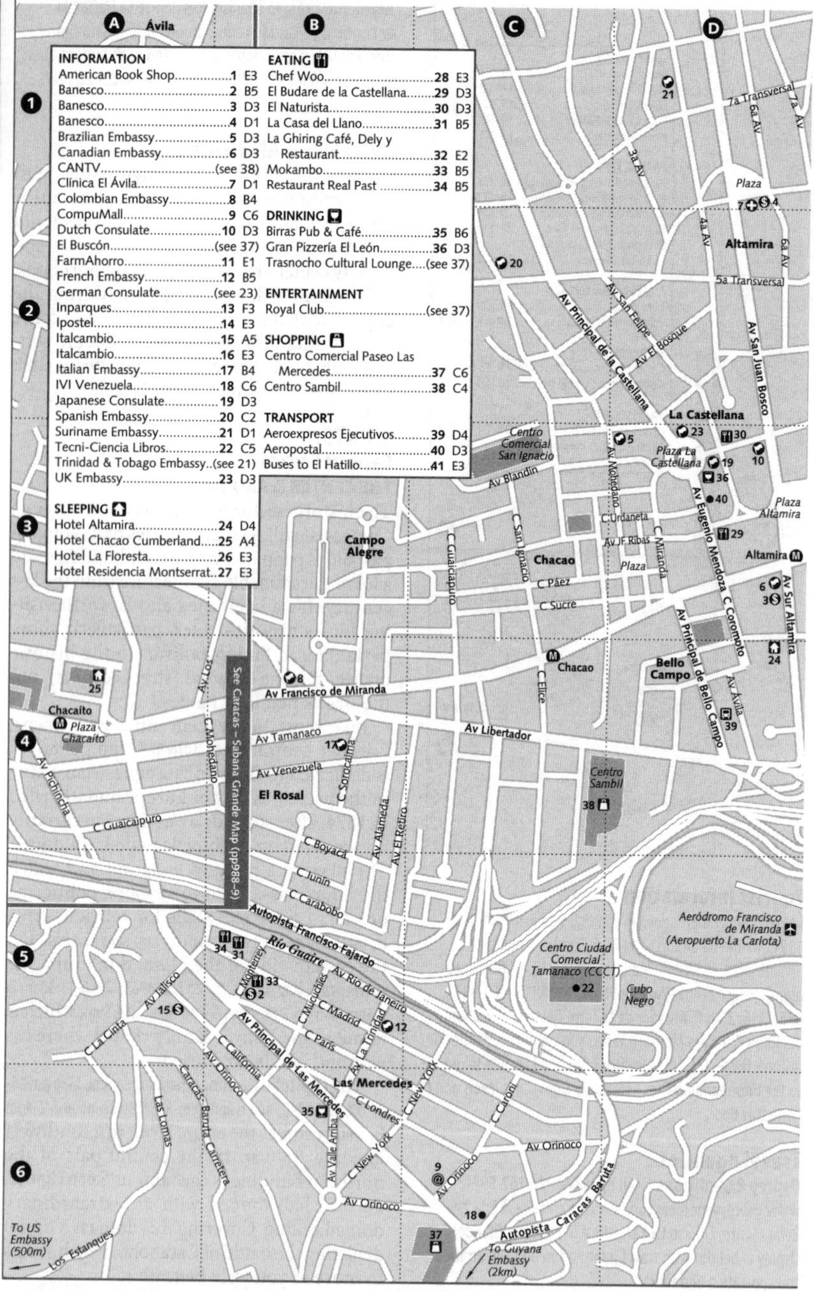

To US
Embassy
(500m)

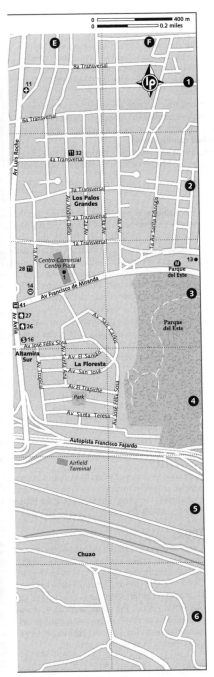

The reconstructed interior of **Casa Natal de Bolívar** (Bolívar's birthplace; Map pp986-7; ☎ 541-2563; San Jacinto a Traposos; admission free; ☾ 10am-4:30pm Sat & Sun) is attractive but lacks its original detailing. His funeral was also hosted here, in 1842.

If you still crave more Bolívar memorabilia, walk just north of Casa Natal de Bolívar to the **Museo Bolivariano** (Map pp986-7; ☎ 545-9828; San Jacinto a Traposos; admission free; ☾ 9am-4pm Tue-Fri, 10am-4:30pm Sat & Sun). The colonial-style museum has everything Bolívar that you can imagine, from his letters to his swords to his original coffin.

If you have made it this far, you must continue to see the bronze sarcophagus of Bolívar in the **Panteón Nacional** (National Pantheon; Map pp986-7; ☎ 862-1518; Av Norte; admission free; ☾ 9am-4pm Tue-Fri, 10am-4:30pm Sat & Sun). No less than 140 white-stone tombs of other eminent Venezuelans grace the building, though there are only three women buried here.

Iglesia de la Candelaria (Map pp986-7; Plaza La Candelaria), seven blocks east of Plaza Bolívar, is the church famed as the resting place of José Gregorio Hernández (see the boxed text, p992). He lies in the first chapel off the right-hand aisle.

PARQUE CENTRAL & AROUND
The Parque Central area is not as green as you may expect but is Caracas' art and culture hub, boasting half-a-dozen museums, the major performing arts center, two art cinemas and, arguably, the best theater in town. The park is 1.5km southeast of Plaza Bolívar, next to the Bellas Artes metro station.

On the eastern end of the Parque Central complex, the **Museo de Arte Contemporáneo** (Map pp986-7; ☎ 573-8289; admission free; ☾ 9am-4pm) is by far the best art museum in the country. Here you'll find the major works of the top contemporary Venezuelan artists. There are also some remarkable paintings by international giants such as Picasso, Matisse, Monet and others.

The open-air viewpoint **Mirador de la Torre Oeste** (Map pp986-7; admission free; ☾ 8-11am & 2-4pm Tue-Fri) sits high on the 49th floor of the Torre Oeste (which also houses Inatur, p989) and provides some fabulous 360-degree views of the city. It's run courtesy of the tower's security department, which lets visitors ascend. You need to show your passport to gain admission to the viewpoint.

THE DAPPER DOCTOR

When traveling in Venezuela, you will inevitably see statues or trinkets of a man who bears a striking resemblance to Charlie Chaplin. This is not some national infatuation with classic cinema. The man is José Gregorio Hernández, Venezuela's favorite saint. Hernández is not recognized by the Vatican as a saint, though was elevated to venerable status in 1985. All technicalities aside, he is the country's principal homegrown religious icon.

Born into a humble Andean family in 1864, Hernández became a university professor and doctor to the president. He was a passionately religious person, and frequently treated the poor without charge. He tried to dedicate himself to a monastic life on various occasions, but always returned to medicine and care for his impoverished countrypeople.

Hernández died in a car accident in 1919, and a cult soon emerged around him, spreading through the country and beyond. Countless miracles are attributed to him, including numerous healings.

The **Galería de Arte Nacional** (National Art Gallery; Map pp986–7; ☎ 578-1818; www.gan.org.ve in Spanish; Plaza de Los Museos, Parque Los Caobos; admission free; ⏱ 9am-5pm Mon-Fri, 10am-5pm Sat & Sun) has a vast collection of artwork embracing five centuries of Venezuelan art – from pre-Hispanic to contemporary. The gallery also houses Caracas' leading art cinema.

Adjoining the gallery, the **Museo de Bellas Artes** (Museum of Fine Arts; Map pp986–7; ☎ 578-1819; Parque Los Caobos; admission free; ⏱ 9am-5pm Mon-Fri, 10am-5pm Sat & Sun) features mostly temporary exhibitions, and has an excellent shop selling contemporary art and crafts. Don't miss the sculpture garden outside.

Sabana Grande & Around

Sabana Grande, 2km east of Parque Central, is an energetic district packed with hotels, love motels, restaurants and shops. Locals come en masse to stroll along its teeming market street **Bulevar de Sabana Grande** (Map pp988–9), which stretches between Plaza Venezuela and Plaza Chacaíto.

Las Mercedes & Altamira

East of Sabana Grande lie some of Caracas' more fashionable areas, especially in **Castellana**, **Altamira** and their immediate environs (Map pp990–1). As you travel further east, you descend the social ladder, eventually reaching some of the city's most downtrodden *barrios*.

Southern Suburbs

The rolling hills in the southern part of Caracas include the city's wealthiest suburbs and also numerous pockets of ramshackle *barrios*, sometimes neighboring each other.

El Hatillo was once its own village, but has now been absorbed into Caracas and is a popular getaway for folks who live in the more congested city center. Its narrow central streets and plaza are stacked with brightly painted colonial buildings that house restaurants, art galleries and craft shops. Located 15km southeast of the city center, this area overflows with people on the weekend. There's always a tranquil atmosphere in the afternoon and early evening, when diners and café-goers can sit back and relax to the sounds of crickets.

Frequent *carritos* (small buses; US30¢, 45 minutes) run to El Hatillo from Av Humboldt, just off Blvd de Sabana Grande near the Chacaíto metro station (Map pp988–9). Alternatively, metro bus 202 leaves from Altamira metro station (Map pp990–1) on weekdays only. Unfortunately, there are no hotels in El Hatillo.

ACTIVITIES

Caracas is an urban city and its activities mainly revolve around nightlife (restaurants, bars and clubs) and shopping. The best place for **hiking** near Caracas is Parque Nacional El Ávila.

TOURS

Caracas tour companies can send you almost anywhere in Venezuela, but it's usually cheaper to deal directly with the operator in the region. Of course, that means that you'll have to figure your own transportation out of the city and the bus system is not for prima donnas. Caracas companies can also help by coordinating various excursions for you and making reservations during busy tourism seasons.

There are an uncountable number of travel agencies in Caracas. The following listed companies focus on responsible tourism and have English-speaking guides (some also have guides that speak German and/or French):

Akanan Travel & Tours (Map pp990-1; ☎ 264-2769; www.akanan.com; Av Bolívar, Edificio Grano de Oro, Planta Baja, Local C, Chacao) This major operator does not have the most budget prices, but is reliable for quality trips, including treks to the top of Auyantepui and Roraima, as well as bicycle trips from La Paragua to Canaima.

Cacao Travel Group (Map pp990-1; ☎ 977-1234; www.cacaotravel.com; Quinta Orquidea, Calle Andrómeda, Urbanización El Peñón, Vía Baruta) This agency, 2.5km south of Las Mercedes, was the first to develop tours to Río Caura (five days in total, US$320 to US$400 depending on accommodation type). It has its own lodges on the river.

Osprey Expeditions (Map pp988-9; ☎ 762-5974; www.ospreyvenezuela.com; Av Casanova & 2da Av Bello Monte, Edificio La Paz, Office 51, Sabana Grande) This young, friendly, English-speaking, Venezuelan-owned agency can organize tours to most parts of the country for a number of different budgets. It is strong on Canaima, Orinoco Delta, Caracas and the surrounding areas.

Sociedad Conservacionista Audubón de Venezuela (SCAV; ☎ 992-3268; www.audubonvenezuela .org; Calle Veracruz, Edif Matisco, 1er Piso Oficina 5, Las Mercedes; ◷ 9am-1pm Mon-Fri) For more information on responsible traveling, contact the local branch of this global environmental society. It can provide information on ecological issues and recommend tour companies; it also organizes bird-watching tours.

FESTIVALS & EVENTS
The biggest celebrations are Christmas, Carnaval and Easter. All offices close, as do most shops, and intercity bus transportation is frantic. Flights can be fully booked.

Semana Santa (Holy Week, culminating in Easter) is also a major celebration with festivities focused in Chacao. Traditional outlying areas celebrate holy days with more vigor than central districts. El Hatillo boasts local feasts on several occasions during the year (including May 3, July 16 and September 4).

More characteristic of Caracas are cultural events, of which the Festival Internacional de Teatro (the International Theater Festival) is the city's highlight. Initiated in 1976, it has been held in March/April of every even-numbered year and attracts national and international groups to Caracas' theatres.

Also see the boxed text, p999, on the festival of Diablos Danzantes in Francisco de Yare, a day trip from Caracas.

SLEEPING
Simply put, Caracas does not cater to budget travelers. Inexpensive rooms can only be found in love motels (some of which are actually brothels), which tend to be in more dangerous neighborhoods. It is worth considering staying in a midrange place in a safer neighborhood such as Altamira (the money that you save on that cheap room can get nicked pretty quickly in the wrong part of town).

Central Caracas
At the cost of a less secure neighborhood, Central Caracas offers more affordable accommodations. The cheapest accommodations in the center are south of Av Lecuna, between Av Balart and Av Fuerzas Armadas, but the area is unattractive and can be downright dangerous. It's more convenient for sightseeing and possibly safer to stay north of Av Universidad.

Plaza Catedral Hotel (Map pp986-7; ☎ 564-2111; Esq La Torre; d/tr with bathroom US$22/26; ❀) This is a great location for sightseers as it overlooks both the Plaza Bolívar and the cathedral. Choose one of the front corner rooms for best views. It's not a proposition for light sleepers, as the cathedral bells ring every quarter hour. The hotel's rooftop restaurant provides reasonably priced food and great views.

Hotel Inter (Map pp986-7; ☎ 564-6448; Norte 9 btwn Animas & Calero; s/d US$24/28; Ⓟ ❀) Don't expect a warm welcome, but this creaky old guesthouse is recommended by travelers for its simple comforts and reasonable rates. It's conveniently placed near the *tasca* (Spanish-style bar-restaurant) zone of La Candelaria.

Hotel El Conde (Map pp986-7; ☎ 862-0928; Esq El Conde; s/d/tr US$27/32/35; ❀) Hotel El Conde (The Count) rules over the historic center as the area's longest-running budget hotel, and possibly the best one. It is just a block from Plaza Bolívar and has affordable prices and a decent standard of comfort.

Hotel Grand Galaxie (Map pp986-7; ☎ 864-9011; www.hotelgrandgalaxie.com in Spanish; Esq Caja de Agua; s/d US$28/38, ste with Jacuzzi US$45; ❀) This modern eight-story tower is an oddity in the otherwise rough-and-tumble Altagracia area, which is four blocks north of Plaza Bolívar. It's often packed with visiting employees of the nearby Education Ministry, whom you may run into at the adjacent *tasca*. Suites tend to be in better condition than the rather basic standard rooms. Weekend discounts are available.

Sabana Grande

Sabana Grande is the city's main budget lodging area and has plenty of places to stay, although most of them double as hourly-rate 'love motels.' The bustling neighborhood is safe during the daytime, but is increasingly dangerous at night. Stick to the main streets and walk in groups as muggings are common.

Nuestro Hotel (Map pp988-9; ☎ 761-5431; hostel@ospreyvenezuela.com; Calle El Colegio, Sabana Grande; s/d/tr/q US$9/13/16/21) Also known as the backpacker's hostel (yes, it does have 'We're in Lonely Planet' painted on the front wall), this place is one of the few non-hourly-rates budget hotels in the city (actually, it's a sex motel on the 1st floor, but the 2nd floor is a budget hotel anyways). It's no frills and is in an area that is unsafe after dark, but the rooms are secure and it is a good place to meet other travelers. English not spoken.

Hotel La Mirage (Map pp988-9; ☎ 793-2733; Prolongación Sur Av Las Acacias, Sabana Grande; d US$13-15, tr/ste US$15.50/22; ℗ ✖) There are over a dozen budget hotels further south on Prolongación Sur Av Las Acacias, including this undistinguished nine-floor stack of boxy rooms. It is popular with Venezuelan families, which cuts down on the hourly-rates factor.

Hotel Odeón (Map pp988-9; ☎ 793-1345; Av Las Acacias, Sabana Grande; d US$14-18; ℗ ✖) You could try to be positive and say that this place is minimalist, but it is really just numbingly plain with almost nothing in the rooms. This Colombian-run hotel has eight floors, so it is likely that it will have a vacancy. The 1st-floor café is convenient and decent.

Hotel Gabial (Map pp988-9; ☎ 793-1156; Prolongación Sur Av Las Acacias; d US$27-30; ✖) Just down the street from the Odeón, Hotel Gabial is more comfortable with better beds and quiet air conditioners. It is also almost twice the price. It is debatable whether or not you get twice the comfort.

Hotel Plaza Palace (Map pp988-9; ☎ 762-4821; Calle Los Mangos; d/tr US$35/40; ✖) If you want to stay in a midrange hotel we suggest that you go to Altamira (opposite). However, if you are set on Sabana Grande the Plaza Palace is a solid midrange choice. The rooms are airy and comfortable, but it's worth adding a mere US$5 and staying in a suite.

Las Mercedes & Altamira
LAS MERCEDES

Do you want to stay closer to the restaurants and nightlife? Las Mercedes is an upmarket area and most of the hotels are very expensive. There are numerous love motels that rent by the hour, or try this one for a splurge.

Hotel Chacao Cumberland (Map pp990-1; ☎ 952-9833; www.hotelescumberland.com; Av Santa Lucía, Urb El Bosque, Chacaíto; s/d incl breakfast US$115/119; ℗ ✖) Just around the corner from the lively Chacaíto plaza, the crisply designed interior of this hotel gets plenty of natural light, and abstract art jazzes up stylishly furnished rooms.

ALTAMIRA

Altamira is a pleasant area of town that is easily accessible by the metro or taxi. It is a safe neighborhood where you can comfortably walk at night to a number of restaurants or the central plaza. The accommodations are all midrange places, but are worth the extra price for the increased security.

Hotel Altamira (Map pp990-1; ☎ 267-4284; hotel altamira@telcel.net.ve; Av José Félix Sosa, Altamira Sur; d US$37; ℗ ✖) The best-priced midrange hotel in the neighborhood, the Altamira is on a quiet street just off the plaza. The rooms, with whitewashed walls and bamboo furniture, are on par with other nearby options and at a mildly better price. Most rooms have cable TV. Some English is spoken.

Hotel La Floresta (Map pp990-1; ☎ 263-1955; hotel lafloresta@cantv.net; Av Ávila, Altamira Sur; s/d US$41/75; ✖ 🖳) La Floresta has small, comfortable and secure rooms that are a bit tattered around the edges. It also has lots of hot water, free internet in the lobby (and wireless in most rooms) and cable TV. Ask for a room with a balcony.

Hotel Residencia Montserrat (Map pp990-1; ☎ 263-3533; Av Ávila, Altamira Sur; s/d US$45/80; ℗ ✖) Montserrat has larger and slightly more expensive rooms than La Floresta. The furniture and finishings are equally worn in, but just chalk it up as character. Ask for a room in the back to minimize street noise and score a view of beautiful green gardens).

EATING
Central Caracas

The center is packed with mostly low- to mid-priced eateries.

Restaurant Beirut (Map pp986-7; ☎ 545-9367; Salvador de León a Socarrás; snacks & cakes US$1.50-3, 2-course menú US$3; ☽ 11:30am-5:30pm Mon-Sat) For a quick caffeine stop or tasty Lebanese food, this comfortable place does the trick.

Kafta (Map pp986-7; ☎ 860-4230; Gradillas a San Jacinto; 3-course menú US$4; ☽ 7am-4:30pm Mon-Sat) Located above a busy market, Kafta has excellent Middle Eastern and Mediterranean dishes, from falafel to kebabs. The good-value lunch menu at this no-frills café changes daily.

El Salón del Sabor (Map pp986-7; ☎ 564-9396; ground fl, Edificio Iberia, Av Urdaneta, Esq Animas, La Candelaria; 3-course menú US$5; ☽ 7am-4pm Mon-Fri) This restaurant dishes up vegetarian and meat lunches with portions that are enough to keep you satisfied through a day of sightseeing.

Restaurant Terra Park (Map pp986-7; ☎ 573-8279; Edificio Tajamar, Nivel Bolívar, Parque Central, Av Lecuna; set lunch US$5.75; ☽ 7am-10pm Mon-Fri, 8am-7pm Sat & Sun) Bow-tied waiters shout orders at thunderous volumes at this bustling open-air Spanish restaurant on a broad, breezy ground terrace beside the Torre Oeste. It's a great place to chow down in the Parque Central; the *menú del día* will leave you contentedly stuffed.

Sabana Grande

The Sabana Grande neighbourhood is full of budget restaurants and has a few decent midrange places too.

Punto Criollo del Este (Map pp988-9; ☎ 953-2536; Av Casanova; set lunch US$3.75; ☽ 6:30am-9pm) Though easy to overlook, this hole-in-the-wall kitchen on the east end of the district is a locally recommended purveyor of reasonably priced *comida criolla* (Venezuelan set menu) lunches.

Arepera Doña Petrica (Map pp988-9; ☎ 763-1304; Av Casanova; meals US$3-4; ☽ 24hr) This *arepa* (grilled corn pancake), *cachapa* and sandwich restaurant serves healthy-sized, inexpensive portions to groups of beer drinking locals. It is a casual place to introduce yourself to the basics of Venezuelan cuisine.

El Gourmet Vegetariano (Map pp988-9; ☎ 730-7490; Av Los Jardines, La Campiña; buffet US$4; ☽ 11:30am-2:30pm Mon-Fri; ✗) Over 50 years of successful business can't be wrong. El Gourmet is a venerated vegetarian spot, known for its quality buffet.

K'Sualmania (Map pp988-9; ☎ 762-0220; Edificio Argui, Av Los Jabillos, Sabana Grande; combo platters US$4.25; ☽ 7am-4:30pm Mon-Sat) Run by a corps of kinetic young women, this spiffy little Middle Eastern joint has some of the finest falafels and

tabaquitos (stuffed grape leaves) around. The menu is helpfully illustrated on the wall.

Restaurant Vegetariano Sabas Nieves (Map pp988-9; ☎ 763-6712; Calle Pascual Navarro 12; buffet US$4.50; ☽ 7am-5pm Mon-Fri, 8am-4pm Sat) Sabas Nieves changes its specials and fixed-price lunches every day so it can keep vegetarians entertained for the length of their stay in Sabana Grande.

Las Mercedes & Altamira

LAS MERCEDES

With Las Mercedes' reputation as a fashionable dining district that becomes particularly lively in the evening, most restaurants here cater to an affluent clientele, but there are also some budget options.

Restaurant Real Past (Map pp990-1; ☎ 993-6702; Av Río de Janeiro; mains US$2-6; ☽ 11am-10pm) It may not have much in terms of style, but it does have hearty portions of Italian dishes at reasonable prices. Try the lasagne.

La Casa del Llano (Map pp990-1; ☎ 991-7342; Av Río de Janeiro, mains US$4-8; ☽ 24hr) Here they keep it going all night, with Venezuelan standards and a *parrilla*. It is a top choice for a meal, light snack or a few rounds of icy Venezuelan beers.

Mokambo (Map pp990-1; ☎ 991-2577; Calle Madrid, cnr Monterrey; mains US$8.50; ☽ noon-midnight; ✗) Expertly fusing Mediterranean and Caribbean elements, Mokambo has dishes you didn't know you craved – such as yucca gnocchi or octopus carpaccio – and others you know and love, like three-cheese ravioli with Kalamata olives. Dine in the cool, safari-themed interior or on the terrace, surrounded by tropical foliage.

ALTAMIRA & CASTELLANA

El Naturista (Map pp990-1; cnr 1a Transversal & Av San Felipe; arepas US$1-3) One of very few Venezuelan-style restaurants in Castellana's glut of Hooters, McDonalds TGIFriday's and other American chain offerings. El Naturista serves up *arepas*, *cachapas* and other local standards in its cool, spacious dining area.

La Ghiring Café, Dely y Restaurant (Map pp990-1; ☎ 286-1108; www.laghirin.com; Av Andrés Bello at 4a Transversal, Los Palos Grandes; breakfast & snacks US$2-3; ☽ 8am-11pm) Separated from the street by a wall of plants, this open-air café has Venezuelan favorites and affordable breakfasts.

El Budare de la Castellana (Map pp990-1; ☎ 263-2696; cnr Mendoza & Riba; arepas and cachapas US$2-4,

VENEZUELA

dishes US$3-12) This established two-story corner restaurant keeps the crowds coming through all day. Service is top notch and you can order everything from *arepas*, coffee and inexpensive snacks to steaks and other rather pricey meals.

Restaurant El Presidente (Map pp990-1; ☎ 283-8246; 3a Av, Los Palos Grandes; 3-course menú US$6; ☺ noon-4pm & 7-10pm Mon-Sat) This simple café is another example of the hard-to-come-by cheap options in Altamira, and is good for its home-style set-lunch menus.

Chef Woo (Map pp990-1; ☎ 285-1723; 1a Av, Los Palos Grandes; combos US$6-8.50; ☺ noon-11pm) This lively, neighborhood Chinese restaurant is popular for its tasty Szechuan fare and even more visited in the evening for cheap beer.

DRINKING

Las Mercedes and La Castellana (particularly Centro Comercial San Ignacio) hold most of the city's nightlife, but bars and discos dot other suburbs as well, including Sabana Grande, El Rosal and Altamira. Many nightclubs have basic dress codes. If a club has a cover charge, it often entitles you to your first drink or two.

Centro Comercial San Ignacio (Map pp990-1; cnr Blandín & San Ignacio) Yes, it's a mall, but it comes alive at night with a number of bars, restaurants and lounges. Different venues fill up on different nights, so just head over and see what's happening. Some of the more consistent places include Whisky Bar and, on weekends, Loft – the club on the top floor.

Gran Pizzería El León (Map pp990-1; ☎ 263-6014; Plaza La Castellana) A famous Caracas spot to sit on a terrace in the shadow of a skyscraper and knock back beers. On weekends it attracts crowds of dedicated drinkers and it can fill up at peak hours.

Birras Pub & Café (Map pp990-1; ☎ 992-4813; Av Principal de Las Mercedes at Av Valle Arribe; ☺ open late) Appropriately named with the Italian word for beer, this is one of many beer drinking places in Las Mercedes. Birras tends to be a bit cheaper and can attract a fun crowd.

Transnocho Cultural Lounge (Map pp990-1; ☎ 993-1325; Edificio Itaca, Centro Comercial Paseo de Las Mercedes, Las Mercedes; ☺ Thu-Sun) This minimalist bar with low-key funk music and mirrored ceiling is frequented by theatergoers.

ENTERTAINMENT

The Sunday edition of *El Universal* carries a 'what's on' section called the 'Guía de la Ciudad' and there is a free entertainment paper called *CCS* on offer outside of many restaurants and bars. Both give descriptions of selected upcoming events including music, theater, cinema and exhibitions.

El Maní es Así (Map pp988-9; ☎ 763-6671; Av Francisco Solano López at Calle El Cristo, Sabana Grande; ☺ 11pm-5am Tue-Sun) One of the city's longest-running salsa spots, where everything revolves around the dance floor and the live salsa bands. Take taxis after dark as the area is not safe.

Ateneo de Caracas (☎ 573-4099; Av México, Plaza Morelos, Los Caobos; tickets US$8-20) Venezuela's best-known theater company performs here.

Aula Magna (Map pp988-9; ☎ 605-4516; Universidad Central de Venezuela) This place hosts concerts by the local symphony orchestra, usually on Sunday morning. Purchase tickets at door; price varies.

Complejo Cultural Teresa Carreño (Map pp986-7; ☎ 574-9333; www.teatroteresacarreno.gob.ve; opposite Parque Central; tours US50¢; ☺ 9am-5pm Tue-Sat) The spot for big concerts.

Cinemateca Nacional (Map pp986-7; ☎ 576-1491; www.cinemateca.gob.ve; Galería de Arte Nacional, Bellas Artes) For movies.

GAY & LESBIAN VENUES

Caracas has by far the most open gay community in what is still a relatively conservative country. For an overview of more venues, check the websites www.republicagay.com and www.vengay.com (all in Spanish). There are long-established gay and lesbian bars and clubs in Las Mercedes, Sabana Grande and Castellana.

Tasca Pullman (Map pp988-9; ☎ 761-1112; Edificio Ovidio, ground fl, Av Francisco Solano López, Sabana Grande; ☺ till late) Pullman is the most popular of a group of small gay taverns in Sabana Grande. It is no frills and no pretense. Never walk alone on the surrounding pedestrian streets after dark.

Royal Club (Map pp990-1; Nivel Cine, Centro Comercial Paseo Las Mercedes, Las Mercedes; admission $8; ☺ 11pm-5am Thu-Sat) For a more progressive club environment, make your way to this extravagant spot hidden away behind a big black door in a shopping mall. It's on the cinema level in the parking garage, to the right and up a ramp – look for the purple neon lighting.

Sports

Estadio de Béisbol (Baseball Stadium; Map pp988-9; ☎ 0500-226-7366; Av Las Acacias) *Béisbol* (baseball) is the local sporting obsession. Professional-league games are played from October to February at this stadium on the grounds of the Universidad Central de Venezuela. Tickets should be bought here early in the morning, particularly for games with the Leones de Caracas (Caracas Lions; www.leon es.com).

SHOPPING

Shopping is one of the city's greatest pastimes. La Candelaria, Sabana Grande, Chacaíto, Chacao and the historic center are all tightly packed with stores, malls, stalls and street vendors. The malls are an important part of *caraqueño* life – so shelve any preconceptions and check one out for a social experience if nothing else. There are a lot of good buys on the streets too (particularly in Sabana Grande and the historic center).

Some of the main malls:

Centro Comercial Chacaíto (Map pp988-9; Plaza Chacaíto, Chacaíto)

Centro Comercial El Recreo (Map pp988-9; ☎ 761-2740; Av Casanova; ◌ 10am-9pm Mon-Sat, noon-8pm Sun) This is the big one in Sabana Grande.

Centro Comercial Paseo Las Mercedes (Map pp990-1; Av Principal de Las Mercedes, Las Mercedes; P)

Centro Comercial San Ignacio (Map pp990-1; ☎ 263-3953; Av Blandín, La Castellana; ◌ 10am-8pm; P) This mall is also one of the city's best centers for nightlife (p996).

Centro Sambil (Map pp990-1; ☎ 267-2101; Av Libertador, Chacao; ◌ 10am-9pm, restaurants & cinema later; P) Claims to be the biggest in South America.

GETTING THERE & AWAY
Air

The **Aeropuerto Internacional 'Simón Bolívar'** (www.aeropuerto-maiquetia.com.ve in Spanish) is in Maiquetía, near the port of La Guaira on the Caribbean coast, 26km from central Caracas. The airport is frequently referred to as 'Maiquetía.' The airport has two terminals, the **international terminal** (☎ 355-3110) and the **domestic terminal** (☎ 355-2660). They are separated by an easy walk of 400m (though you are not allowed to take luggage carts from one terminal to the other). There's a free shuttle service between the terminals.

The terminals have most conveniences, including a tourist office, car rental, *casas de cambio*, a bank, ATMs, post and telephone offices, places to eat and a bunch of travel agencies. It even has a chapel, but at the time of writing lacked a left-luggage office (however one is planned).

The domestic terminal doesn't have official money-changing facilities (so it is overrun with black marketers), but does have a tourist office. **Inatur** (☎ 355-1191; ◌ 7am-8pm), cybercafé and a dozen desks for car-rental companies, domestic airlines and tour operators, plus fast-food outlets.

BUSES FROM CARACAS TO MAJOR DESTINATIONS

Destination	Distance (km)	Fare (US$)	Duration (hr)
Barcelona	310	7-11	5
Barinas	512	10-14	8½
Barquisimeto	341	7-10	5½
Carúpano	521	11-16	8½
Ciudad Bolívar	591	12-18	9
Ciudad Guayana	706	13-18	10½
Coro	446	10-13	7
Cumaná	402	9-13	6½
Maracaibo	669	13-17	10½
Maracay	109	2-4	1½
Mérida	790	15-25	13
Puerto Ayacucho	637	16-20	15
Puerto La Cruz	320	7-11	5
San Antonio del Táchira	865	17-28	14
San Cristóbal	825	15-30	13
San Fernando de Apure	398	8-15	8
Tucupita	730	13-22	11
Valencia	158	3-5	2½

Bus

Caracas has two modern intercity bus terminals and a central terminal for shorter journeys. The Terminal La Bandera, 3km south of the center, handles long-distance buses to anywhere in the country's west and southwest. The terminal is just 300m from La Bandera metro station and you can walk the distance during the day, but take precautions at night when the area becomes unsafe. The terminal has good facilities, including computerized ticket booths, telephones, a **left-luggage office** (per 1st hr/hr thereafter US55/15¢; 🕑 6am-9pm Mon-Sat, 7am-7pm Sun), an **information desk** (☎ 693-6607) and a plentiful supply of food outlets.

The city's other bus terminal, the Terminal de Oriente, is on the eastern outskirts of Caracas (Map pp986–7), on the highway to Barcelona, 5km beyond Petare (about 18km from the center). It's accessible by numerous local buses from both the city center and Petare. A taxi from Altamira will cost US$4. The terminal features computerized ticket booths and a helpful **information desk** (☎ 243-2606). It handles much of the traffic to the east and southeast of the country.

Buses to the airport depart from Parque Central.

Car & Motorcycle

Driving into and out of Caracas is pretty straightforward. The major western access route is the Valencia–Caracas freeway, which enters the city from the south and joins Autopista Francisco Fajardo, the main east–west city artery, next to the Universidad Central de Venezuela. From anywhere in the east, access is by the Barcelona–Caracas freeway, which will take you directly to Av Francisco Fajardo.

If you fly into Caracas without any previous arrangements, contact car-rental companies at the Maiquetía airport. Operators in the international terminal include **Avis** (☎ 355-1190) and **Hertz** (☎ 355-1197), but they can't always provide a car on demand. You'll find more desks of local companies in the domestic terminal. Major rental companies also have desks in the lobbies of top-end hotels.

GETTING AROUND
Bus

The extensive bus network covers all suburbs within the metropolitan area, as well as major

neighboring localities. *Carritos* (small buses) are the main type of vehicle operating city routes. They run frequently but move only as fast as the traffic allows. However, they go to many destinations inaccessible by metro, are similarly priced and run later at night.

Car & Motorcycle

Driving in Caracas is only for people with lots of confidence, lots of nerves and a lot more insurance. It is easy to get lost and the traffic can be maddening. It is recommended to pay to park your car in the monitored lots that are common around town.

Metro

Caracas is in many ways synonymous with chaos. So it is somewhat out of step that the city's **metro** (www.metrodecaracas.com.ve in Spanish; per 1-3 stations US15¢, 4-7 stations US20¢, any longer route US25¢; 🕑 5:30am-11pm) is safe, fast, easy, well organized, clean and affordable – and it serves most major city attractions and tourist facilities. While the metro is generally safe, do be aware of the occasional pickpocket.

Taxi

Identifiable by the 'Taxi' or 'Libre' sign, taxis are a fairly inexpensive means of getting around and sometimes the only option at night. None have meters, so always fix the fare before boarding – and don't be afraid to bargain. It is recommended that you use only white cars with yellow plates and preferably those from taxi ranks, of which there are plenty, especially outside shopping malls. Alternatively, many hotels or restaurants will call a reliable driver for you upon request.

AROUND CARACAS

There are a number of exciting and decidedly different places to visit within close proximity to the bustle of Caracas. Also covered in this section are the Caribbean islands of Los Roques. The islands aren't usually a day trip, but Caracas is the main jumping-off point.

PARQUE NACIONAL EL ÁVILA

One of the great attractions of the Caracas area, this national park encompasses some 90km of the coastal mountain range north of the city. The highest peak in the range is Pico Naiguatá (2765m), while the most visited is Pico El Ávila (2105m). The **teleférico** (cable car; ☎ 901-5555; www.avilamagica.com; adult/under 12/over 65 US$9.50/5.50/5; ☼ 10:30am-midnight Wed-Sat, 10:30am-8pm Sun & Tue, noon-8pm Mon) runs 4km from Maripérez station (980m), next to Av Boyacá in Caracas, to Pico El Ávila.

The southern slope of the range, overlooking Caracas, is uninhabited but is crisscrossed with about 200km of walking trails. El Ávila provides better facilities for walkers than any other national park in Venezuela. Most of the trails are well signposted, and there are a number of campgrounds.

A dozen entrances lead into the park from Caracas; all originate from Av Boyacá, commonly known as Cota Mil (at an altitude of 1000m). All routes have a short ascent before reaching a guard post, where you pay a nominal entrance fee. Vans run between Maripérez station and just to the north of Bellas Artes metro station. On the weekend, regular jeeps (to the left as you exit the *teleférico*) run to the tiny village of Galipan (US$1, 12 minutes), which has a cluster of cheaper restaurants.

COLONIA TOVAR
☎ 0244 / pop 9500

Not your average Venezuelan town, Colonia Tovar was founded in the 19th century by German settlers. It wasn't until the 1940s that Spanish was introduced as the official language and the ban on marrying outside the community was abandoned. In 1963 a paved road from Caracas reached 60km west to this Teutonic enclave.

Information

The village has a few banks. For internet access and telephones head to CANTV, just below the church.

Sights & Activities

Today Colonia Tovar draws international and Venezuelan tourists (particularly on weekends). They come for the **Black Forest architecture**, German cuisine, locally grown strawberries and the agreeable climate. Bring some warm clothing as it can get a bit chilly at night.

Sleeping & Eating

The accommodations here are of a high standard, but don't come cheap by Venezuelan standards.

Cabañas Silkerbrunnen (☎ 355-1490; matildedebrei denbach@hotmail.com; Calle Hessen; d/tr/q US$20/26/32, with kitchen US$26/30/36; **P**) Some of the best-priced cabins in town are on offer at this friendly, flower-filled complex set into the hillside, in the back street just below the church.

Cabañas Breidenbach (☎ 355-1211; Sector El Calvario; d/tr US$22/29, d with kitchen & fireplace US$28; **P**) On the mountainside above the town center, these *cabañas* (cabins) are large and modern with majestic views. It's worth going for a double with kitchen, salon, and wood fireplace to ward off the chilly mountain air.

Hotel Restaurant Kaiserstuhl (☎ 355-1810; Calle Joaquín; d/tr US$26/49; **P**) Located in the heart of town near the cemetery, Hotel Restaurant Kaiserstuhl has comfortable rooms plus the full pseudo-German tourist experience, including a restaurant with piped folk music and wait staff in traditional dress and braided hair.

Rancho Alpino (☎ 355-1470; www.hotelranchoalpino .com; Av Principal; d US$30; **P**) The spacious and spotless Alpine Ranch also has a bar and restaurant serving German food and pizza. This, like most places in town, is a great place to relax.

Getting There & Away

To get from Caracas to Colonia Tovar, you must change at El Junquito. All shared cars

---

DANCING WITH DEVILS

Drums pound while hundreds of dancers clad in red devil costumes and diabolical masks writhe through the streets. This is the festival of the **Diablos Danzantes (Dancing Devils)**, a wild spectacle that takes place in Venezuela one day before Corpus Christi and on the holy day itself.

Why devils on such a holy day in such a Catholic country? It is said that the festival demonstrates the struggle between good and evil. In the end, the costumed devils always submit to the church and demonstrate the eventual triumph of good.

The festival is a blend of Spanish and African traditions. The origins lie in Spain, where devils' images and masks were part of Corpus Christi feasts in medieval Andalusia. When the event was carried over to colonial Venezuela, it resonated with African slaves who had their own tradition of masked festivals. They also added African music and dance to the celebration.

and minibuses to El Junquito depart from Lecuna at San Juan Puerte Escondido in the center of Caracas (US50¢, 45 minutes to 1½ hours on the weekend). There are also buses to El Junquito (US70¢). There's no terminal, but you can catch them on Av Lecuna or Av Universidad. From El Junquito, *por puesto* vans take you the remainder of the journey (US$1, one hour).

SAN FRANCISCO DE YARE
☎ 0239 / pop 20,000

Normally a tranquil town, San Francisco de Yare explodes into a frenzied mass of costumed revelers in devil masks for the annual Festival de Los Diablos Danzantes. This famous event has been celebrated here on Corpus Christi (the 60th day after Easter, a Thursday in May or June) since 1742. The day is not a national holiday, but it seems very much so in San Francisco de Yare as the town spends months gearing up for the festival.

San Francisco de Yare has no regular hotels, but it is a very easy day trip from Caracas. Take one of the frequent buses to Ocumare del Tuy (US90¢, 1½ hours) from the Nuevo Circo regional bus terminal and change for the bus to Santa Rerest del Tuy, which drops you off in San Francisco de Yare (US50¢, 20 minutes). Make sure you come early on festival days.

ARCHIPIÉLAGO LOS ROQUES
☎ 0237 / pop 1500

Los Roques is a group of nearly 300 shimmering, sandy islands and islets that lie in aquamarine waters some 160km due north of Caracas. They may be part of Venezuela but have prices closer to other Caribbean island destinations. However, for those who appreciate beaches, snorkeling and diving the trip is worth every bolívar. Unlike other Caribbean islands, there are no high-rise hotels, no mass tourism and no cruise ships. The whole archipelago, complete with the surrounding waters (2211 sq km), was made a national park in 1972.

The great majority of the islands is uninhabited except by pelicans and can be visited by boats from Gran Roque. The surrounding waters are known for their sea life, particularly lobsters (which can be trapped from November through April and account for 90% of national production).

Orientation & Information

The only village is on Gran Roque and is a grid of four or so sandy streets, a plaza and dozens of quaint *posadas*.

All visitors to Los Roques pay the US$9.50 national-park entry fee upon arrival.

Banesco (☎ 221-1265; Plaza Bolívar; 8am-noon & 2:30-5pm Mon-Fri, 8am-2pm Sat) The only bank; arranges cash advances on Visa and MasterCard with a maximum of US$500. Has a 24-hour ATM.

Enzosoft (per hr US$10; 1-10pm Mon-Sat) The better internet connection and bigger rip-off.

Infocentro (30min free; variable) For internet access, try the state-sponsored Infocentro near the school.

Oscar Shop (☎ 291-9160; oscarshop@hotmail.com) A combination of shop, tour agency, boat operator and tourist office, near the airport.

Activities
SNORKELING & SCUBA DIVING

You can get snorkeling gear at many shops and most *posadas*. Scuba diving is also fabulous here, and there is a wealth of good places to explore. Diving is organized by several companies, including **Aquatics Dive Center** (☎ 0414-777-0196; www.scubavenezuela.com), **Eco Challenge** (☎ 0414-291-9266; www.ecochallenge.com.ve) and **Arrecife** (☎ 0414-249-5119; www.divevenezuela .com). Two dives generally cost from US$85 to US$100.

WINDSURFING & KITESURFING

Los Roques is also a top-notch spot for windsurfing of all levels. It's organized by **Vela Windsurf Center** (www.velawindsurf.com) on the island of Francisquí de Abajo, which rents equipment (US$20/35/50 per hour/half-day/day) and can provide lessons for beginners (US$40 for two hours including equipment). Or for something different, ask here for **kayaks** and lessons in **kitesurfing**. For more kitesurfing information, inquire with Libya or at Oscar Shop (below).

Tours

Oscar Shop (☎ 291-9160; oscarshop@hotmail.com) This small shop provides boat transportation to the islands, organizes full-day boat tours and rents out snorkeling equipment and beach chairs. It also provides general tourist information.

Sleeping
CAMPING

Free camping is allowed on all the islands within the recreation zone, including Gran

Roque. After arrival, go to the **Inparques** (☎ 0414-373-1004; ☷ 8am-noon & 2-6pm Mon-Fri, 8:30am-noon & 2:30-5:30pm Sat, 8-11:30am Sun) office at the far end of the village for a free camping permit and information.

POSADAS

There are now over 60 *posadas* providing some 500 beds on Gran Roque. Prices are higher than the mainland. Many *posadas* also offer meals as there are few restaurants in Los Roques.

Doña Carmen (☎ 0414-291-9225; tudocar@cantv.net; Plaza Bolívar; r per person incl breakfast & dinner US$30-50) The longest-running *posada* on the island, Doña Carmen has been going for over 30 years and still has the best prices. The concrete rooms are nothing special, though a couple face onto the beach.

Eva (☎ 0414-450-7581; www.posadaseva.com.ve; r per person incl breakfast US$40; ☷) Located at the far end of the village, this family-run *posada* is a backpacker magnet. It offers six small, simple rooms, one with shared bathroom (room 4 has a tiny garden but no air-con).

El Botuto (☎ 231-1589; near the Inparques office; r per person incl breakfast US$40-60) Known for its fantastic service and sociable dining area, El Botuto has light, airy rooms, each with a small patio.

La Lagunita (☎ 0414-291-9151; Calle La Laguna; r per person incl meals & boat tour US$75; ☷) This friendly Italian-run *posada* offers up seven excellent rooms with TV and safe box (room 5 is especially nice), and there's a pleasant rooftop terrace where the staff mix up free *Cuba libres* (rum and coke drinks).

Eating

Since almost all *posadas* serve meals, there are few places that are strictly restaurants – and among those there are even fewer that are affordable.

SPLURGE!

Technically, any trip to Los Roques is a splurge, but if you want to break the budget even a little more, make sure to dine on fresh seafood while watching the sunset from **Bora la Mar** (☎ 0414-325-7814, 0237-221-1289; next to the church; mains US$20) and follow that up with cocktails on the beach at the surprisingly swanky La Gotera Art Café (at the point separating the two beaches).

Panadería Bella Mar (snacks under US$3; ☷ 8am-9pm Mon-Sat) Near the school is this tiny bakery that sells cheap *empanadas*, sandwiches and breads. The set lunch is US$4.

La Chuchera (Plaza Bolívar; ☎ 221-1417; mains US$6.50-16; ☷ 11am-11pm) La Chuchera is the main budget restaurant in town (although prices are still not cheap). It serves pizza (including a vegetarian option), sandwiches and pasta dishes with friendly service. It is also a fun place to have beers with new friends in the evening.

Aquarena Cafe (☎ 0414-131-1282; mains US$9.50-11; ☷ 9am-1am Wed-Mon) Located near Macanao Lodge, this beachside café offers up fish, hamburgers, pizza and salads. There's beanbag seating and tables on the sand.

Getting There & Away

AIR

Airfares to Los Roques differ, so shop around. The Maiquetía–Los Roques flight in usually in the range of US$100 and takes some 40 minutes. It is easiest to book flights through an agency. Almost any established tour agency can book a Los Roques flight for you at no extra cost. The small carriers include the following:

AeroEjecutivos (☎ 0212-993-1984; www.aeroejecu tivos.com.ve)

Línea Turística Aereotuy (LTA; ☎ in Caracas 212-355-1297; www.tuy.com/aereotuy.htm)

Transaven (☎ 355-2786; www.transaven.com)

L

TA and **Rutaca** (☎ 212-355-1838) also fly to Los Roques from Isla de Margarita (US$100 to US$200 one way).

Normally only 10kg of free luggage is permitted on flights to Los Roques; every additional kilogram costs US50¢.

BOAT

There are no passenger boats to Los Roques, only cargo boats that depart two or three times a week (usually in the evening) from Muelle 7 in La Guaira port. They often take passengers for a small fee or sometimes even free of charge. However, the boats have no schedule and it's almost impossible to find out in advance the departure day and time. You have to go to the port and look for the captain. The trip takes about 12 hours and can be rough.

Getting Around

Oscar Shop or other boat operators in Gran Roque will take you to the island of your choice and pick you up at a prearranged time and date. Round-trip fares per person are Madrizquí (US$5), the Francisquises (US$6), and Crasquí or Noronquises (US$10).

THE NORTHWEST

Easily accessible from Caracas, the country's northwest is stocked with beaches, rainforests, deserts, caves, waterfalls, 12 national parks and South America's largest lake. Parque Nacional Morrocoy attracts visitors with its colorful reefs, beaches and Sahara-like desert near the colonial town of Coro. Parque Nacional Henri Pittier is a favorite stop for backpackers and locals to hang out, soak up the sun and enjoy a few drinks or break out the binoculars and spot rare birds.

MARACAY

☎ 0243 / pop 700,000

A couple of hours from Caracas, the Ciudad Jardín (Garden City) Maracay is a world apart. It is a chilled-out town of hot weather, green parks, leafy plazas and friendly locals. It is a provincial capital and the center of an important agricultural and industrial area. The city is usually visited as a stopover on the way to Parque Nacional Henri Pittier and doesn't have many attractions to otherwise hold the traveler.

Orientation & Information

There are plenty of internet facilities in the Centro Comercial Paseo Las Delicias and Torre Sindoni.

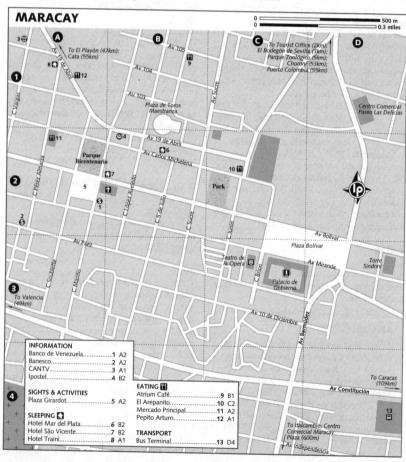

MARACAY

0 — 500 m
0 — 0.3 miles

To El Playón (47km);
Cata (55km)

Av 105
Av 104
Av 103

To Tourist Office (2km);
El Bodegón de Sevilla (3km);
Parque Zoológico (5km);
Choroní (53km);
Puerto Colombia (55km)

Plaza de Toros
Maestranza

Centro Comercial
Paseo Las Delicias

Av 19 de Abril
Av Carlos Michelena

Parque
Bicentenario

Park

Av Bolívar

Plaza Bolívar

Av Páez

Teatro de
la Opera

Torre
Sindoni

Av Miranda

To Valencia
(49km)

Palacio de
Gobierno

Av 10 de Diciembre

To Caracas
(109km)

Av Constitución

To Italcambio; Centro
Comercial Maracay
Plaza (600m)

Av Independencia

INFORMATION
Banco de Venezuela..............1 A2
Banesco................................2 A2
CANTV.................................3 A1
Ipostel.................................4 B2

SIGHTS & ACTIVITIES
Plaza Girardot......................5 A2

SLEEPING
Hotel Mar del Plata..............6 B2
Hotel São Vicente.................7 B2
Hotel Traini.........................8 A1

EATING
Atrium Café.........................9 B1
El Arepanito........................10 C2
Mercado Principal...............11 A2
Pepito Arturo......................12 A1

TRANSPORT
Bus Terminal.......................13 D4

There are no banks in Parque Nacional Henri Pittier (below). Those planning to stay in any of the towns in the park for a few days should stock up on cash here in Maracay.

Banco de Venezuela (Calle Mariño)

Banesco (Av Páez)

CANTV (cnr Calle Vargas & Calle López Aveledo; internet per hr US70¢; ☉ 8am-8pm Mon-Sat, 9am-2pm Sun)

Ipostel (Av 19 de Abril; ☉ 9am-5pm Mon-Fri)

Italcambio (☎ 235-6945; No 110-K, Centro Comercial Maracay Plaza, cnr Avs Aragua & Bermúdez, 1st fl; ☉ 8:30am-12:30pm & 1:30-5pm Mon-Fri, 9am-1pm Sat) Located 1.5km south of Plaza Bolívar.

Sights

The historic heart of Maracay is actually not at Plaza Bolívar, it is **Plaza Girardot**. It features a large obelisk topped with a bronze eagle, which commemorates the North American volunteers who joined the independence war forces led by Francisco Miranda. They were captured and hanged in 1806 by the Spaniards.

Sleeping

Maracay has quite a choice of hotels and restaurants right in the city center. If you are taking an early morning bus it is better to stay in the city center and catch a taxi to the bus station than to stay near the bus station – where the options are limited and the neighborhood isn't safe after dark.

Hotel São Vicente (☎ 247-0321; Av Bolívar Este; d with fan/air-con US$8/12; ☒) This is one of the best-priced options in the city center. The rooms have been refurbished and offer matrimonial beds.

Hotel Mar del Plata (☎ 246-4313; Av Santos Michelena Este 23; s/d/tr US$12/14/16; P ☒) A little more expensive, but noticeably better than other central budget options is this peaceful hotel. Mar del Plata has tidy, clean rooms with hot water.

Hotel Traini (☎ 245-5502; Av 19 de Abril; d/tr/q US$16/19/25; P ☒) While not winning in personality, this street-level hotel is clean, secure and dependable.

Eating

Mercado Principal (Av Santos Michelena) For a really inexpensive and filling meal, try one of the many food stalls.

El Arepanito (☎ 237-8621; Av 19 de Abril at Junín; arepas US$1.25-2; ☉ 8am-1am; ☒) Open later than most places in town, this popular restaurant has a pleasant plant-filled patio where they serve tasty *arepas*, pizza and fruit juices.

Pepito Arturo (Av 19 de Abril; hamburgers US$2-4; ☉ 11am-midnight) A casual and cheerful fast-food stop, Arturo's is the place to chow down on a cheap *parrilla* followed by a *batido* (fruit juice).

El Bodegón de Sevilla (☎ 242-7914; Av Las Delicias; mains US$5-8.50; ☉ noon-late; P ☒) Housed in an attractive old mansion, this Spanish-style bar and restaurant has an extensive menu including tapas, and an equally abundant bar.

Getting There & Away

The bus terminal is on the southeastern outskirts of the city center. It's within walking distance of Plaza Bolívar, but it's quicker to take any of the frequent city buses or a short cab ride.

The bus terminal has frequent transportation to most major cities. Buses to Caracas depart every 15 minutes or so (US$2 to US$4, 1½ hours), as do buses to Valencia (US65¢, one hour).

There are at least a dozen departures a day to Barquisimeto (US$4 to US$6, four hours), Maracaibo (US$9 to US$12, eight hours) and San Cristóbal (US$11 to US$14, 11 hours). Half-a-dozen buses run to San Antonio del Táchira (US$14, 12½ hours), Coro (US$8 to US$10, 6½ hours) and Mérida (US$11 to US$14, 11 hours). There are direct buses to Puerto La Cruz (US$9 to US$12, seven hours) and Ciudad Bolívar (US$19, nine hours); these buses bypass Caracas, saving time and money. Several ordinary buses per day go to San Fernando de Apure (US$8, seven hours).

For transportation to El Playón and Puerto Colombia, see Getting There & Away, p1005.

PARQUE NACIONAL HENRI PITTIER

☎ 0243

Venezuela's oldest and one of its most accessible national parks, Henri Pittier rolls over 1078 sq km of the rugged coastal mountain range and then plunges down to epic Caribbean beaches. There is something for everyone including a glistening coastline, 580 species of birds, twisting hiking trails through the green mountains, and quaint colonial towns with tasty food, comfortable *posadas* and even a bit of nightlife.

Two paved roads cross the park from north to south. The eastern road goes from Maracay north to Choroní (climbing to 1830m) and reaches the coast 2km further on at Puerto Colombia. The western road leads from Maracay to Ocumare de la Costa and El Playón, then continues to Cata; it ascends to 1128m at Paso Portachuelo. Both roads are about 55km long. There's no road connection between the coastal ends of these roads.

Sights & Activities

PUERTO COLOMBIA AREA BEACHES

Around Puerto Colombia the most popular beach is **Playa Grande**, a five- to 10-minute walk by road east of town. It's about half a kilometer long and is shaded by coconut palms, but is busy and can be littered on weekends. There are several restaurants at the entrance to the beach. You can camp on the beach or sling your hammock between the palms, but don't leave your stuff unattended.

If Playa Grande is too crowded or littered, go to the undeveloped **Playa El Diario**, on the opposite (western) side of the town.

Other beaches in the area that are normally visited by boat include **Playa Aroa** (US$30 round trip per boat, 15 minutes one way), **Playa Valle Seco** (US$22, 20 minutes), **Playa Chuao** (US$25, 30 minutes) and **Playa Cepe** (US$32, 45 minutes).

EL PLAYÓN AREA BEACHES

Further west, **El Playón** skirts the northern edge of the town of the same name. There are actually several small beaches here, the best of which is **Playa Malibú**, close to the Malecón.

Five kilometers eastward is the area's most famous beach, **Playa Cata**. The beach is a postcard crescent of sand bordering Bahía de Cata, and marred only by two ugly apartment towers looming over the beach. There are plenty of shack restaurants and one basic *posada* (double US$10) on the western side.

Boats from Playa Cata take tourists to the smaller and quieter **Playa Catita** (US$25 one way) and usually deserted **Playa Cuyagua** (US$10). Both can be reached overland for a cheaper price.

Sleeping & Eating

PUERTO COLOMBIA

Choroní may be the largest town on this side of the park, but Puerto Colombia is closer to the beach and therefore more popular. The strikingly attractive colonial village is packed with *posadas* and restaurants and is one of

the major backpacker hangouts in Venezuela. Days are spent on the beach and evenings are whiled away in restaurants or sipping *guarapita* (the cane alcohol *aguardiente* with passion-fruit juice and lots of sugar) down on the waterfront. There are no banks in town, so remember to get cash in Maracay.

Hostal Colonial (☎ 218-5012; www.choroni.net; Calle Morillo 37; d US$12, d/tr with bathroom US$15/17) The classic *hostal* in town, Colonial is a sociable place with a wide variety of rooms, a courtyard out back, lockers, a kitchen and tours of the area. The service can be a bit gruff.

Posada La Parchita (☎ 991-1233; posadalaparchita@ yahoo.com; Calle Trino Rangel; d/tr/q US$18/25/28; **P**) This cozy and quiet family-run *posada* is tucked away down a backstreet next to the river. It has a handful of simple, tidy rooms with fans set around a nice little patio.

Hostal Vista Mar (☎ 991-1250; Calle Colón; d/tr/q US$20/25/27; **P**) This simple hostel is perched at the end of the seafront boulevard, and near a small park. Rooms are plain and a little dark, with cold-water bathrooms. A plus are the hammocks overlooking the sea on the breezy rooftop.

Posada Tom Carel (☎ 991-1220; www.posadatom carel.com; Calle Trino Rangel; d US$60; ☒) This colorful midrange family *posada* near Hostal Colonial has plenty of attention to detail with intricate mosaics on the walls. Rooms are small and well kept – many with hammocks strung up over the beds.

Brisas del Mar (☎ 991-1268; Calle Los Cocos; mains US$5-10; ☷ 8:30am-10:30pm) Good down-to-earth spot for pasta, seafood and meat dishes. Breezy open front area and a narrow back balcony overlooking a canal. The bar has longer hours (and the restaurant has later hours in high season too).

Bar Restaurant Araguaneyes (☎ 991-1137; Calle Los Cocos 8; mains US$5-15; ☷ 8:30am-10:30pm) Sit on the breezy upstairs terrace and enjoy international and *criollo* fare including a good selection of fresh fish.

Restaurante Willy (☎ 951-5316; Via Playa Grande 1, over the bridge on the right; ☷ dinner Fri-Sun, daily in high season; meals US$7-15) Considered the best restaurant in town, Willy gets packed on weekends. Try the fish or pasta dishes, although everything is good.

EL PLAYÓN

Puerto Colombia's sibling on the western road, El Playón has more than a dozen places to stay. The town is much larger than Puerto Colombia, but less attractive. Many places to stay are within a couple of blocks of the waterfront. There are a few ramshackle restaurants in town and hotels generally serve food on request. Expect prices to jump on weekends and holidays.

Posada Loley (☎ 993-1252; loleyenlacosta@hotmail .com; Calle Fuerzas Armadas; d/tr US$15/18; P ⊠ ⊠) This simple *posada*, one block back from the beach, is one of the cheapest and best budget options. It has a small garden and patio, laidback host and meals available for guests.

Posada Los Helechos (☎ 993-1385; www.posada loshelechos.com; Calle Santander 63; d US$28; P ⊠) This decent *posada* offers seven small rooms with small bathrooms (one room has a kitchen), but has a nice patio and hallways with lots of airy seating. There's a small restaurant and murky, greenish pool you can use at your own risk. It's six blocks inland from La Punta (at the west end of the beach).

Posada de La Costa Eco-Lodge (☎ 993-1986; www .ecovenezuela.com; Calle California 23; d with/without sea view US$67/56; ⊡ ⊠) Set in harmony with the beach and surrounding gardens, this beautiful eco-lodge provides neat rooms and a relaxed atmosphere. It is worth the splurge for the rooms with the sea views and balconies.

Getting There & Away

The departure point for the park is the Maracay bus terminal. Buses to El Playón (marked 'Ocumare de la Costa') depart every hour from 7am to 5pm (US$1.50, two hours). They can let you off at Rancho Grande but will charge the full El Playón fare. The last bus back to Maracay departs at 5:30pm.

There are also hourly minibuses from Maracay to El Playón, but they depart from El Limón, not the bus terminal. The advantage is that they run longer, until about 7:30pm. From El Playón, you can catch a *carrito* to Playa Cata (US65¢, 10 minutes).

To Puerto Colombia, buses leave from the bus terminal every one or two hours (US$2, 2¼ hours). The last bus back to Maracay theoretically departs from Puerto Colombia at 5pm (later on weekends), but this departure time is not reliable. There are taxis that leave from right behind the bus terminal (US$20 during the day, US$25 to US$30 at night; 1¼ hours). Look for other travelers in the bus station to share the cost.

PARQUE NACIONAL MORROCOY

☎ 0259

If you had to select a single piece of Venezuelan coastline to visit, Parque Nacional Morrocoy would be a smart choice for both its beauty and variety. It comprises a strip of park on the mainland, and extends offshore to scores of islands, islets and cays. Some islands are fringed by white-sand beaches and surrounded by coral reefs. The most popular of the islands is Cayo Sombrero, which has fine (though increasingly damaged) coral reefs and some of the best beaches. Other snorkeling spots include Cayo Borracho, Playuela and Playuelita.

The park gets rather crowded on weekends, but is considerably less full during the week.

Chichiriviche (population 12,500) is the northern gateway to Parque Nacional Morrocoy, providing access to half-a-dozen neighboring cays. The waterfront has old, colorful fishing boats.

Orientation & Information

The park lies between the towns of Tucacas and Chichiriviche, which are its main gateways. Chichiriviche is smaller than Tucacas, but both are equally drab and unattractive. Both towns have accommodations, food and boats in good supply. Both towns have banks with 24-hour ATMs.

Activities

Tucacas has two diving schools: the cheaper **Amigos del Mar Divers** (☎ 812-1754; amigos-del-mar@ cantv.net; Calle Democracia) and the pricier **Submatur** (☎ 812-0082; morrocoysubmatur1@cantv.net; Calle Ayacucho). Both offer diving courses and guided dives, and sell diving and snorkeling equipment, some of which can be rented. There are no diving operators in Chichiriviche.

Snorkeling gear can also be rented from some boat operators and hotel managers for about US$4 per day. Some hotels have their own boats or have arrangements with the boat owners, and offer beach, snorkeling and bird-watching excursions.

Sleeping & Eating

ISLANDS

With a tent, or hammock and mosquito net, you can stay on the islands; otherwise, you'll be limited to day trips out of Tucacas or Chichiriviche. Camping is officially permitted on four islands: Sal, Sombrero, Muerto

VENEZUELA

and Paiclás. All four have beach restaurants or food kiosks, but some may be closed on weekdays in the low season, so come prepared. Before you go camping you have to contact the Inparques office in Tucacas and shell out a camping fee of US$1 per person per night, payable at Banesco in Tucacas.

TUCACAS

Many of Tucacas' hotels and restaurants are on or nearby the 1km-long Av Libertador.

Posada Amigos del Mar (☎ 812-3962; Calle Nueva, past the hospital; d/tr US$10/14) This pleasant *posada*, which is affiliated with the dive shop of the same name, has spacious rooms with bath and fan. Guests have use of the kitchen.

Posada El Ancla (☎ 812-0253; posadaelancla@cantv .net; Calle Páez, 2 blocks south of Av Libertador; d/q US$18/22; ▣ ▨) Posada El Ancla is a small, affable, family-run place. The rooms don't have private bathrooms, but, interestingly enough, there are four shared bathrooms, exactly one per room.

Posada d'Alexis (☎ 812-3390; Calle Falcón; d US$22-25, q US$32; ▣ ▨ ▨) This is another small, quaint guesthouse, though this one has its own restaurant. The rooms are arranged around a pool with a waterfall and dense weeping willows.

Restaurant El Timón (☎ 812-0783; Av Libertador; mains US$5-8; ▨) El Timón offers dependably tasty dishes – particularly seafood – at good prices, and you can eat it inside or at the tables outside.

CHICHIRIVICHE

Morena's Place (☎ 815-0936; posadamorenas@hotmail .com; Sector Playa Norte; r per person US$7) A classic budget option, this affordable *posada* is in a fine old house near the waterfront. It offers laundry service, budget meals, tours and rents out two kayaks. English spoken.

Villa Gregoria (☎ 818-6359; aagustinm@yahoo .es; Calle Mariño near the bus terminus; d with fan/air-con US$13/20; ▣ ▨) This Spanish-run and, therefore, Spanish-themed place has comfortable rooms with bathrooms. Ask for a room on the upper floor, where they are brighter and more attractive.

Restaurant El Rincón de Arturo (Av Zamora; breakfast/set lunch US$2.50/3) A small, rustic place worth a try.

There are plenty of other budget eateries along Av Zamora. Among the best places in town are **Tasca Eridali** (Av Zamora) and **Restaurant Txalupa** (Av Zamora), the latter on the waterfront.

Getting There & Away

Tucacas sits on the Valencia–Coro road, so buses run frequently to both Valencia (US$2, 1½ hours, 91km) and Coro (US$5.50, 3½ hours, 197km). Buses from Valencia pass through regularly on their way to Chichiriviche (US75¢, 40 minutes, 35km).

Chichiriviche is about 22km off the main Morón–Coro highway and is serviced by half-hourly buses from Valencia (US$2.80, 2½ hours, 126km).

There are no direct buses to Chichiriviche from Caracas or Coro. To get here from Caracas, take any of the frequent buses to Valencia (US$2.50, 2½ hours, 158km) and change there for a Chichiriviche bus. From Coro, take any bus to Valencia, get off in Sanare (US$5, 3¼ hours, 184km), at the turnoff for Chichiriviche, and then jump on a Valencia–Chichiriviche bus.

Getting Around

Boats to the islands from both Tucacas and Chichiriviche take up to eight people and charge the same for one as for eight. Popular destinations from Tucacas include Playa Paiclás (round trip US$22), Playuela (US$26) and Cayo Sombrero (US$38). From Chichiriviche, popular trips include the close cays of Cayo Muerto (US$10), Cayo Sal (US$14) and Cayo Pelón (US$14), and Cayo Sombrero (US$38). Boats will pick you up from the island in the afternoon or on a later date. On weekdays during the low season, you can usually beat the price down.

CORO

☎ 0268 / pop 165,000

Coro is a pleasant city best known as the entry point to Parque Nacional Médanos de Coro – Venezuela's little Saharan desert. However, Coro is also worth a visit for its gorgeous colonial architecture and welcoming university-town culture. Since Coro's historic center was declared a national monument in the 1950s, a number of the old houses have been restored. The cobblestone Calle Zamora, where most of the historic mansions are located, rivals any other colonial architecture in the country. In 1993, Coro was included on Unesco's World Heritage list.

Information

There are a number of internet options in the center, though they tend to close by 8pm.

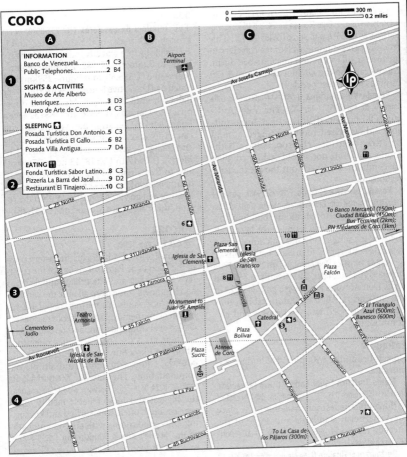

CORO

0 — 300 m
0 — 0.2 miles

INFORMATION	
Banco de Venezuela	1 C3
Public Telephones	2 B4

SIGHTS & ACTIVITIES	
Museo de Arte Alberto Henríquez	3 D3
Museo de Arte de Coro	4 C3

SLEEPING	
Posada Turística Don Antonio	5 C3
Posada Turística El Gallo	6 B2
Posada Villa Antigua	7 D4

EATING	
Fonda Turística Sabor Latino	8 C3
Pizzería La Barra del Jacal	9 D2
Restaurant El Tinajero	10 C3

Banco de Venezuela (Paseo Talavera)
Banco Mercantil (Calle Falcón)
Banesco (Av Manaure)
Ciudad Bitácora (cnr Calles Zamora & Jansen; 7am-2am) The largest and fastest cybercafé in town. Take a sweater – it's cold!

Sights

Hinting of the Sahara, the spectacular desert landscape of **Parque Nacional Médanos de Coro** (admission free; 9am-6pm) shelters sand dunes of 30m in height. To get there, take the Carabobo bus from Calle Falcón and get off 300m past the large Monumento a la Federación. From here it is a 10-minute walk north along a wide avenue to another public sculpture, the Monumento a la Madre.

All of the city's interesting museums are in restored colonial buildings. The **Museo de Arte de Coro** (808-3603; Paseo Talavera; admission free; 9am-12:30pm & 3-7:30pm Tue-Sat, 9am-4pm Sun), in a beautiful 18th-century mansion, is a branch of the Caracas Museo de Arte Contemporáneo and, like its parent, features thought-provoking and well-presented temporary exhibitions.

Diagonally opposite in another great mansion, the **Museo de Arte Alberto Henríquez** (252-5299; Paseo Talavera; admission free; 9am-noon & 3-6pm Tue-Sat, 9am-noon Sun) also has modern art – shows change regularly but are always worth a visit.

Sleeping

There are several budget places conveniently located in the historic center.

La Casa de los Pájaros (☎ 252-8215; www.casa delospajaros.com.ve; Calle Monzón No 74; dm US$5, d with bathroom & fan US$12, with air-con US$16; ☒ ▢) This friendly private home welcomes travelers to its three small rooms and one four-bed dorm. Guests can use the kitchen and internet (30 minutes free access per day).

Posada Villa Antigua (☎ 0414-682-2924; Calle Comercio No 46; d US$12-16; ☒) The Villa Antigua (Old-fashioned Village) has some suitably old-fashioned rooms arranged around an attractive patio. The rooms have bathrooms and some not-so-old-fashioned quiet air-conditioners. Check out the inexpensive restaurant.

Posada Turística El Gallo (☎ 252-9481; posadael gallo2001@hotmail.com; Calle Federación No 26; s/d/tr with fan US$12/14/18) In a restored colonial building, this French-owned *posada* is one of the best deals in town. It's simple, tidy and functional with a relaxing courtyard. No private bathrooms.

Posada Turística Don Antonio (☎ 253-9578; Paseo Talavera No 11; d/tr US$18/22; ☒) Rebuilt in colonial style, Don Antonio is a newish *posada* right in the city's heart. All of the comfortable rooms here are equipped with bathrooms and air-conditioning.

Eating

Coro is brimming with plenty of budget restaurants.

Fonda Turística Sabor Latino (Paseo La Alameda; breakfast US$2, lunch US$2-3; ☺ 8am-8pm; ☒) Nestled in the central pedestrian mall, this is the place for Venezuelan standards and some of the cheapest meals in town (including 14 different set breakfasts).

Restaurant El Tinajero (Calle Zamora; mains US$2-4) El Tinajero is a laid-back and inexpensive eatery serving popular Venezuelan fare on two tiny patios of a rustic historic house.

Pizzería La Barra del Jacal (☎ 252-7350; Calle Unión; mains US$3-6) A pizzeria by name but a full restaurant in function, this attractive open-air spot gets particularly busy in the evening when a gentle breeze evens out the heat of the day.

Getting There & Away
AIR

José Leonardo Chirinos (☎ 251-5290; Av Josefa Camejo) airport is just a five-minute walk north of the city center. **Avior** (☎ 253-1689) has daily flights to Caracas (US$60 to US$70), where you can change flights for other destinations.

BUS

The **Terminal de Pasajeros** (☎ 252-8070; Av Los Médanos) is 2km east of the city center, and is accessible by frequent city transport. Ordinary buses to Punto Fijo (US$2, 1¼ hours, 90km), Maracaibo (US$5.50, four hours, 259km) and Valencia (US$7, five hours, 288km) run every half hour until about 6pm. Most of the direct buses to Caracas (US$10 to US$13, seven hours, 446km) depart in the evening, but you can easily take one of the buses to Valencia and change. Several direct buses go nightly to Mérida (US$12 to US$18, 13 hours, 782km) and to San Cristóbal (US$12 to US$17, 12 hours, 698km); all these buses depart in the evening and go via Maracaibo. Within the region, there are buses to Adícora (US$1.25).

ADÍCORA
☎ 0269 / pop 1000

The small town of Adícora on the eastern coast of the Paraguaná Peninsula is one of the country's **windsurfing** and **kitesurfing** capitals. Pros and beginners come from all over the world to ride the local winds. It is the most popular destination on the peninsula and offers a reasonable choice of accommodations and restaurants.

There are a few local activities operators, all on the Playa Sur (South Beach), offering courses, equipment rental and simple accommodations. They include **Windsurf Adícora** (☎ 988-8224, 0416-769-6196; www.windsurfadicora.com), the biggest and most reliable facility, open year-round. It offers windsurfing and kitesurfing, plus good rooms with air-con and bathroom. **Archie's Kite & Windsurfing** (☎ 988-8285; www.kitesurfing-venezuela.de in German) is a German-run school open December to May only.

Adícora is linked to Coro (US$1.50, one hour) by eight buses a day, the last departing at around 5pm.

MARACAIBO
☎ 0261 / pop 1.5 million

Better known for business than for tourism, Maracaibo is Venezuela's second-largest city and the oil industry's nerve center. Other attractions include baking hot weather and characterless high-rise buildings. It is a prosperous city and does have some decent restaurants and other first-world conveniences, which can be welcome if you are arriving here overland from coastal Colombia.

Maracaibo was a backwater on the shores of Lago de Maracaibo (South America's largest

MARACAIBO

INFORMATION	
Banco de Venezuela	1 D3
CANTV	2 B3

SLEEPING	
Hotel Caribe	3 D2

EATING	
Restaurant El Enlosao	4 D2
Restaurant El Zaguán	5 D2

TRANSPORT	
Bus Terminal	6 A4

Lago de Maracaibo

VENEZUELA

lake) until drillers struck oil in 1914. Within six years Venezuela had become the world's largest exporter of oil. Traditionally some two-thirds of the national oil output comes from beneath the Lago de Maracaibo and passes through the city before being shipped to the far reaches of the planet.

Orientation

Maracaibo is a big metropolis with vast suburbs, but (as is usually the case) the tourist focus of attention is on the central districts. Generally speaking, these encompass the historic center to the south and the new center to the north. Getting between the two is easy and fast, so it doesn't really matter much where you stay. The new center, however, offers a far better choice of hotels, restaurants and other facilities, and it's safer at night. The old quarter boasts more sights, but they can all be visited on one or two leisurely daytime trips.

Information

INTERNET ACCESS
Most internet cafés cost between US70¢ and US$1 per hour.

CANTV (Centro Comercial Paza Lago)
Cyber Place (Av 8 btwn Calles 72 & 73, New Center)
Cyber Zone (Local PNC 17A, Centro Comercial Lago Mall, Av El Milagro, New Center)

MONEY
Banco de Venezuela Historic Center (cnr Av 5 & Calle 97); New Center (cnr Av Bella Vista & Calle 74)
Banco Mercantil (cnr Av Bella Vista & Calle 67, New Center)

Banesco (cnr Av Bella Vista & Calle 71, New Center)
Italcambio Airport (☎ 736-2513); Av 20 (☎ 783-2040; Centro Comercial Montielco, cnr Av 20 & Calle 72, New Center); Av El Milagro (☎ 793-2983; Centro Comercial Lago Mall, Av El Milagro, New Center)

TOURIST INFORMATION
Maracaibo has two tourist offices; both are outside of the historic center.
Corpozulia (☎ 794-9424; Av Bella Vista btwn Calles 83 & 84; ⏱ 8:30-11:30am & 1:30-3:30pm Mon-Fri) Two kilometers north of the city center, accessible by the Bella Vista *por puestos* from Plaza Bolívar.
Corzutur (☎ 783-4928; Edificio Lieja, cnr Av 18 & Calle 78; ⏱ 8am-4pm Mon-Fri) Two kilometers northwest of the city center.

Sleeping

It's most convenient to stay in the historic center, though the options are not stellar and the area is unsafe and deserted at night. The northern suburbs are a bit safer and provide better lodgings. If you're trapped for the night in the city, you can try any of half-a-dozen basic hotels on the west side of the bus terminal; none deserves to be named here.

Hotel Astor (☎ 791-4510; Plaza República; s US$9, d US$12-13; ❄) One of the cheapest hotels at one of the best locations, the Astor is basic, yet passable. It's attractively positioned in a hip and safe area, with a dozen trendy restaurants within a 100m radius.

Hotel Nuevo Montevideo (☎ 722-2762; Calle 86A No 4-96; d US$10-12, tr US$14; 🅿 ❄) Set in an old rambling mansion, this tranquil place has 13

LIGHTNING WITHOUT THUNDER

Centered on the mouth of the Río Catatumbo at Lago de Maracaibo, this shocking phenomenon consists of frequent flashes of lightning with no accompanying thunder. The eerie, silent electrical storm can be so strong and constant that you will be able to read this book at night.

Referred to as Relámpago de Catatumbo (Catatumbo Lightning) or Faro de Maracaibo (Maracaibo Beacon), it can be observed at night all over the region, weather permitting, from as far away as Maracaibo and San Cristóbal. You'll get a glimpse of it traveling by night on the Maracaibo–San Cristóbal or San Cristóbal–Valera roads, but the closer you get, the more impressive the spectacle becomes. Tours organized from Mérida (p1014) are the easiest way to see the Catatumbo lightning close-up.

Various hypotheses have been put forth to explain the lightning, but so far none have been proven. The theory that stands out is based on the topography of the region, characterized by the proximity of 5000m-high mountains (the Andes) and a vast sea-level lake (Lago de Maracaibo) – a dramatic configuration found nowhere else in the world. The clash of the cold winds descending from the freezing highlands with the hot, humid air evaporating from the lake is thought to produce the ionization of air particles responsible for the lightning.

GETTING TO COLOMBIA

A number of companies run air-conditioned buses to Cartagena via Maicao, Santa Marta and Barranquilla (all of which are in Colombia). **Bus Ven** (☎ 723-9084; bus terminal) has one early-morning departure daily from Maracaibo's bus terminal (and is cheaper than its competitors): Santa Marta (US$34, seven hours, 374km), Cartagena (US$38, 11 hours, 597km). The buses cross the border at **Paraguachón** (you actually change buses there) and continue through Maicao (see box, p580), the first Colombian town.

It is cheaper to go by por puesto (shared taxi) to Maicao (US$9, 2½ hours, 123km) and change there. Por puestos depart regularly from about 5am to 3pm and go as far as Maicao's bus terminal. From there, several Colombian bus companies operate buses to Santa Marta (US$9, four hours, 251km) and further on; buses depart regularly until about 5pm.

All passport formalities are done in Paraguachón on the border. Venezuelan immigration charges a US$16 impuesto de salida (departure tax), paid in cash bolívars by all tourists leaving Venezuela.

Wind your watch back one hour when crossing from Venezuela to Colombia. For information on traveling to Venezuela from Santa Marta, Colombia, see p580.

---

large rooms with high ceilings, air-conditioning and en suite bathrooms.

Nuevo Hotel Unión (☎ 793-3278; Calle 84 No 4-60; d US$10-11, tr US$14; ✷) Just a few steps from the Corpozulia tourist office, this is another small budget spot with a touch of style and personalized attention.

Hotel Caribe (☎ 722-5986; Av 7 No 93-51; d US$11-12, tr US$15; ✷) Just two blocks from the Plaza Bolívar, the 60-room Caribe has a newer section at the back. These new rooms have noiseless, central air-con that can make the rooms almost too cold.

Eating

A lot of ordinary cheap eateries in the city center serve set lunches for about US$2, but they close early and the quality of the food often mirrors the price.

Restaurant El Enlosao (Calle 94; mains US$2-4) Housed in a charming historic mansion, El Enlosao serves unpretentious but tasty Venezuelan food at low prices. The *parrilla* is so copious that you may struggle to finish it.

Restaurant El Zaguán (☎ 717-2398; cnr Calle 94 & Av 6; mains US$4-6) A few paces away from El Enlosao, this inviting restaurant serves hearty local and international cuisine, and has a delightful open-air café shaded by two beautiful old trees.

Restaurant Los Soles (☎ 793-3966; Av 5 de Julio No 3G-09, New Center; mains US$6-10) Run by a Mexican family, this bright, airy restaurant brings some authentic Mexican flavor to town. You can munch on your tacos and enchiladas either in the colorful interior or at the outdoor tables.

Restaurant Mi Vaquita (☎ 791-1990; Av 3H No 76-22, New Center; mains US$7-12; ☯ noon-11pm) With some 40 years in business, Mi Vaquita is considered one of the best steakhouses in town. It has a warm wooden interior and a lively bar to the side.

Getting There & Away

La Chinita airport is 12km southwest of the city center. It's not linked by public transport; a taxi will cost about US$7. Flights are available to major cities, including Caracas (US$50 to US$75) and Mérida (US$35 to US$45).

The bus terminal is 1km southwest of the center. Regular buses run to Coro (US$5, four hours) and Caracas (US$12, 10½ hours). Several night buses run to Mérida (US$11, nine hours) and San Cristóbal (US$10, eight hours).

THE ANDES

Hot-blooded Venezuela is not usually associated with snow-encrusted mountains and windswept peaks. However, Venezuela is, in fact, home to the 400km-long northern end of the Andes range, crowned by the country's tallest mountain, Pico Bolívar (5007m). For those who aren't hardcore mountaineers, the region offers lush valleys of cloud forest, cascading creeks and waterfalls, and charming mountain villages accessible by narrow winding roads.

Mérida state is in the heart of the Venezuelan Andes and has the highest mountains and the best-developed facilities for travelers. The city of Mérida is one of the continent's top adventure-sports destinations, offering everything from trekking and paragliding to rafting and canyoning. Mérida is also the gateway to Los Llanos grasslands (p1017). The two other Andean states, Trujillo and Táchira, are less visited, but have many trekking opportunities for intrepid travelers.

MÉRIDA

☎ 0274 / pop 325,000

Nicknamed *La Ciudad de los Caballeros* (The City of Gentlemen), Mérida has an unhurried, friendly and cultured atmosphere derived from the massive university and outdoor-sports presence in this mountain town. The country's highest point, Pico Bolívar (5007m), is just 12km away. The slightly lower, but still impressive, Pico Espejo can be accessed directly from Mérida by the *teleférico*, the world's highest and longest cable-car system. Visitors can also choose from hiking, canyoning, rafting, mountain biking, paragliding and other activities. But the town is not all about adventure, study and fitness. It has vibrant yet unpretentious nightlife, nearly seven days per week.

Mérida is also the jumping-off point for wildlife-viewing trips to Los Llanos (p1017) and hiking trips in the Andean region. The city is affordable and safe by Venezuelan standards, with a high standard of accommodations and numerous budget eateries. It is a major stop on backpacking circuits and frequently seduces visitors to stay longer than planned.

Information
INTERNET ACCESS
Internet cafés are nearly as common as *arepas* in Mérida. They are inexpensive and the connections are generally good. The following are some central locations (see also CANTV and Movistar, opposite):

Ciber Café El Russo (Av 4 No 17-74)
Cyber Nevada Palace (Calle 24 btwn Avs 5 & 6; per hr US$1) Good screens and fast connections.

LAUNDRY
Most *posadas* offer laundry service; if not, there are many central facilities.
Lavandería Ecológica (cnr Av 4 & Calle 16)
Lavandería Marbet (Calle 25 No 8-35)

MEDICAL SERVICES
Clínica Mérida (☎ 263-0652, 263-6395; Av Urdaneta No 45-145)

MONEY
Banco de Venezuela (Av 4 btwn Calles 23 & 24)
Banco Mercantil (cnr Av 5 & Calle 18)
Banesco (Calle 24 btwn Avs 4 & 5)
Italcambio (☎ 263-2977; Av Urdaneta, Airport)

POST
Ipostel (Calle 21 btwn Avs 4 & 5)

TELEPHONE
CANTV (cnr Calle 26 & Av 3) Also has internet.
Movistar (Calle 20 No 4-64) Also has internet.

TOURIST INFORMATION
Cormetur (www.cormetur.com in Spanish) Airport (☎ 263-9330; Av Urdaneta; ◷ 8am-6pm); Bus terminal (☎ 263-3952; Av Las Américas; ◷ 9am-4pm); Main tourist office (☎ 263-5918, 263-4701, 800-637-4300; cnr Av Urdaneta & Calle 45; ◷ 8am-noon & 2:30-6pm Mon-Fri); Teleférico (Map p1013; Parque Las Heroínas; ◷ 8am-3pm Wed-Sun)
Inparques (Teleférico, Parque Las Heroínas) Permits for Parque Nacional Sierra Nevada.

Sights
The **city center** is pleasant for leisurely strolls, though it has little in the way of colonial architecture or outstanding sights. The leafy **Plaza Bolívar** is the city's heart, but it's not a colonial square. Work on the monumental **Catedral Metropolitana** was begun in 1800, based on the plans of the 17th-century cathedral of Toledo in Spain, but it was not completed until 1958, and probably only then because things were sped up to meet the 400th anniversary of the city's founding.

A highlight of any visit to Mérida is the **teleférico** (☎ 252-1997, 252-5080; www.teleferico merida.com in Spanish; Parque Las Heroínas; round trip US$15; ◷ 7am-noon going up, by 2pm last return), the world's highest and longest cable-car system, now running again after various periods of being out of order. It runs 12.5km from the bottom station of Barinitas (1577m) in Mérida to the top of Pico Espejo (4765m), covering the ascent in four stages. The three intermediate stations are La Montaña (2436m), La Aguada (3452m) and Loma Redonda (4045m).

Activities
The region provides excellent conditions for a range of activities as diverse as rock climbing, bird-watching, horse-riding and rafting, and local operators have been quick to make them easily accessible for visitors –

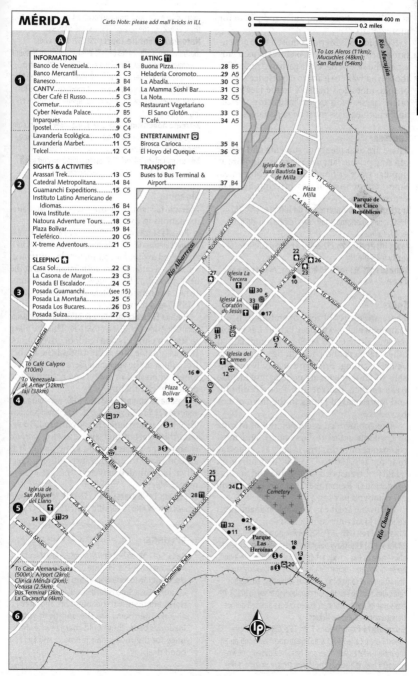

MÉRIDA

Carto Note: please add mall bricks in ILL

0 — 400 m
0 — 0.2 miles

INFORMATION
Banco de Venezuela..............1 B4
Banco Mercantil......................2 C3
Banesco...................................3 B4
CANTV.....................................4 B4
Ciber Café El Russo................5 C3
Cormetur.................................6 C5
Cyber Nevada Palace.............7 B5
Inparques...............................8 C6
Ipostel.....................................9 C4
Lavandería Ecológica...........10 C3
Lavandería Marbet................11 C5
Telcel....................................12 C4

SIGHTS & ACTIVITIES
Arassari Trek.........................13 C5
Catedral Metropolitana.........14 B4
Guamanchi Expeditions........15 C5
Instituto Latino Americano de
Idiomas..............................16 B4
Iowa Institute.......................17 C3
Natoura Adventure Tours.....18 C5
Plaza Bolívar.........................19 B4
Teleférico..............................20 C6
X-treme Adventours..............21 C5

SLEEPING
Casa Sol...............................22 C3
La Casona de Margot............23 C3
Posada El Escalador..............24 C5
Posada Guamanchi..........(see 15)
Posada La Montaña...............25 C5
Posada Los Bucares.............26 D3
Posada Suiza........................27 C3

EATING
Buona Pizza..........................28 B5
Heladería Coromoto..............29 A5
La Abadía..............................30 C3
La Mamma Sushi Bar............31 C3
La Nota..................................32 C5
Restaurant Vegetariano
El Sano Glotón....................33 C3
T'Café...................................34 A5

ENTERTAINMENT
Birosca Carioca.....................35 B4
El Hoyo del Queque..............36 C3

TRANSPORT
Buses to Bus Terminal &
Airport................................37 B4

To Los Aleros (11km);
Mucuchíes (48km);
San Rafael (54km)

Río Muculún

Iglesia de San
Juan Bautista
de Milla

Plaza
Milla

Parque de
las Cinco
Repúblicas

C 13 Colón

C 14 Ricaurte

C 15 Pinango

C 16 Araure

C 17 Rivas Dávila

C 18 Fernández-Peña

Av 1 Rodríguez Picón

Av 2 Independencia

Av 3 Independencia

Av 4 Simón Bolívar

Iglesia La
Tercera

Iglesia La
Corazón
de Jesús

Iglesia del
Carmen

Río Albarregas

C 20 Federación

C 21 Lazo

C 22 Urdaneta

C 23 Vargas

Plaza
Bolívar

C 19 Cerrada

C 24 Rangel

C 25 Ayacucho

Av 5 Zerpa

C 26 Campo Elías

C 27 Carabobo

C 28 Arias

C 29 Zea

C 30 San Mateo

Av Las Américas

Av 2 Lora

To Café Calypso
(100m)

To Venezuela
de Antier (12km);
Jají (38km)

Iglesia de
San Miguel
del Llano

Av Tulio Febres

Av 6 Rodríguez Suárez

Av 7 Maldonado

Av 8 Paredes

Cemetery

Parque
Las
Heroínas

Paseo Domingo Peña

Teleférico

Río Chama

To Casa Alemana–Suiza
(500m); Airport (2km);
Clínica Mérida (2km);
Venusa (2.5km);
Bus Terminal (3km);
La Cucaracha (4km)

22
26
23
10
27
30
33
5
17
31
36
2
12
16
9
19
14
35
37
1
4
3
7
25
24
28
34 29
32
11
21
15
18
13
8 20
6

VENEZUELA

see below for tour companies and p1016 for more details.

Paragliding is Mérida's most iconic adventure sport. There are even pictures of paragliders on the side of the city's garbage trucks. For those who want to learn to experience the joy of solo, motorless flight, X-treme (see right) offers classes with expert instructors. Prices and length of class must be negotiated.

Courses

There are also plenty of students and tutors offering private language lessons – inquire at popular traveler hotels and tour companies. Some major institutions offering Spanish courses:

Instituto Latino Americano de Idiomas (☎ 262-0990; latinoamericano@cantv.net; Edificio Don Atilio, cnr Av 4 & Calle 21)

Iowa Institute (☎ 252-6404; www.iowainstitute.com; cnr Av 4 & Calle 18)

Venusa (☎ 263-8855; Edificio Tibisay, Av Urdaneta No 49-49)

Tours

There are plenty of tour operators in town, many of which nestle near Parque Las Heroínas and along Calle 24. Shop around, talk to other travelers and check things thoroughly before deciding. Prices are generally reasonable. Mountain trips are popular and include treks to Pico Bolívar and Pico Humboldt and more relaxed jaunts to the town of Los Nevados.

A recommended excursion out of Mérida is a wildlife safari to Los Llanos, and most companies offer this trip, usually as a four-day tour for US$100 to US$300 (depending on quality of transportation, guide and accommodations). Remember that you usually will get what you pay for.

Following are the best-established and most reliable local tour companies:

Arassari Trek (☎ 252-5879; www.arassari.com; Calle 24 No 8-301) The heavyweight of local operators, dependable Arassari has a wide range of tours including trekking, horse-riding and mountain biking. It is particularly strong on rafting and canyoning. Arassari also offers Los Llanos tours and trips to see the Catatumbo lightning (p1010). It has some of the most experienced guides and sell domestic/international airline tickets.

Guamanchi Expeditions (☎ 252-2080; www.guamanchi.com; Calle 24 No 8-86) Guamanchi is strong on all mountain-related activities and has a welcoming, down-to-earth feel. It also has Los Llanos trips, kayaking, bike tours, bike rental and information about do-it-yourself bike trips. Check out the *posada* at the same address.

Natoura Adventure Tours (☎ 252-4216; www.natoura.com; Calle 24 No 8-237) Well-established Natoura is known for mountain trekking and climbing, though it runs a range of other tours as well, including bird-watching in the Mérida region and beyond. It conducts its tours in small groups and uses quality camping and mountaineering equipment.

X-treme Adventours (☎ 252-7241; www.xatours.com; Calle 24 No 8-45) The main place in town for paragliding, this young, adventurous Venezuelan-owned agency has hiking, mountain biking, ATV, bridge-jumping and a full array of hotel, tour and flight booking services.

Sleeping

Mérida has some of the best-value accommodations in the country.

Posada Suiza (☎ 252-4961; cnr Av 2 & Calle 18; s/d/tr without bathroom US$7/10/13, with bathroom US$10/13/17) Arranged around a colonial-style courtyard, Suiza has a quiet terrace with hammocks at the back, providing lovely views of the mountains. It has a communal kitchen, buffet breakfast (US$4) and tour agency.

Posada El Escalador (☎ 252-2411; www.elescalador.com; Calle 23 btwn Av 7 & Av 8; d US$12-20) This the place to stay for climbers and outdoor adventurers. It is affordable and right around the corner from most of the agencies. Here you can meet others interested in sports and activities and organize with them.

Posada Guamanchi (☎ 252-2080; www.guamanchi.com; Calle 24 No 8-86; s/d US$12/16, with shared bathroom US$10/16) A smart choice for adventurous travelers, this spartan and ever-growing *posada* is above the agency of the same name. It is a good place to organize expeditions, meet other like-minded travelers and get a good night's sleep.

Posada Los Bucares (☎ 252-2841; losbucarespos@hotmail.com; Av 4 No 15-05; s/d/tr US$12/15/18; ℗) This

---

SPLURGE!

Casa Sol (☎ 252-4164; www.posadacasasol.com; Av 4 btwn Calles 15 y 16; d/ste US$30/40) Perhaps the most intricately decorated *posada* in the country, Casa Sol's refurbished colonial interior is adorned with beautiful art and metalwork. The rooms are airy and fresh with luxurious beds. They could charge twice the price for the rooms and it would still be a good deal.

fine historic mansion is an enjoyable place to stay. It has cozy rooms set around a tiny patio, plus a tiny restaurant.

La Casona de Margot (☎ 252-3312; Av 4 No 15-17; d US$13-15, tr US$20) Next door to Los Bucares and quite similar in style and atmosphere, Margot is another small *posada*, which provides stylish accommodations and doesn't cost a fortune.

Posada La Montaña (☎ 252-5977; posadalamontana@ icnet.com.ve; Calle 24 No 6-47; s/d/q US$14/18/27) A gorgeous colonial house with quaint, tidy and comfortable rooms; all have bathrooms with hot water, and safety boxes. The restaurant serves high-quality dishes including steaks with inventive sauces.

Casa Alemana–Suiza (☎ 263-6503; www.casa -alemana.com; Av 2, Calle 38 No 130; s/d/tr/q US$18/20/25/29) In the south end of town, this spacious building has a different feel from the more touristy center. The rooms are spacious and quiet. The roof deck has great views of the mountains and Alemana–Suiza can also organize tours all over the country.

Eating

Heladería Coromoto (☎ 252-3525; Av 3 No 28-75; ice cream US$1-3; ⏲ 2:15-9pm Tue-Sun) This ice-cream shop is in *The Guinness Book of Records* for the largest number of ice-cream flavors. The place offers more than 900 types, including Polar beer, trout and black beans.

Restaurant Vegetariano El Sano Glotón (Av 4 No 17-84; set lunch US$2; ⏲ 11am-4pm) This small vegetarian restaurant has stayed popular through the years and always gets a crowd at lunch.

La Nota (☎ 252-9697; cnr Calle 25 & Av 8; snacks US$2-3, mains US$3-5) Nicknamed 'Mérida's McDonald's,' La Nota does indeed have burgers and chicken sandwiches, but has a number of standard, filling Venezuelan dishes too.

Buona Pizza (☎ 252-7639; Av 7 No 24-46; pizza US$3-4) Convenient, central and open late, this casual pizza restaurant is an affordable choice with many toppings on offer. It has a takeaway restaurant across the street.

T'Café (Av 3 & Calle 29; mains US$3-6; ⏲ late) Choose from coffees, sandwiches, pizza and delicious Venezuelan dishes at this hip open-air café-restaurant with a paraglider hanging from the ceiling. The café has wireless internet and is a place to have a coffee during the day or a beer at night.

La Abadía (☎ 251-0933; www.grupoabadia.com; Av 3 No 17-45; mains US$5-12; ⏲ noon-11pm) This meticulously reconstructed colonial mansion has several different dining spaces, both indoor and alfresco. It serves quality salads, meats and pastas. It is a bit more expensive than other restaurants, but is worth the price and is a solid choice for a date.

La Mamma & Sushi-Bar (☎ 252-3628; Av 3 btwn 19 & 20; mains US$5-15; ⏲ noon-1am) The most expansive menu in town; La Mamma isn't afraid to mix pizza with sushi. And they do it all pretty well. It is a fun place to have a long dinner and start off an evening on the town.

Entertainment

El Hoyo del Queque (☎ 252-4306; cnr Av 4 & Calle 19; admission on weekends US$2; ⏲ until 1am) Arguably the best bar in the country, this renowned and endlessly fun venue manages to fill up every night. There is dancing and often live bands. A trip to Mérida isn't complete without a night here.

Birosca Carioca (☎ 252-3804; Calle 24 No 2-04) Birosca has a young, casual feel and is all about drinking and dancing and just having a good time. Compared to other city-center choices, Birosca is more of a strictly dance spot.

La Cucaracha (Centro Comercial Las Tapias, Av Andrés Bello) For those who want it loud, this is the place – Mérida's largest discotheque. Over 1000 revelers can turn up and rock out to salsa, house, techno and pop on a weekend night.

Café Calypso (Centro Comercial Viaducto; admission free; ⏲ 9am-late Mon-Sat) Calypso is a normal café during the day, but turns it up at night with international DJs and quality caipirinhas, *mojitos* and other cocktails. It has a more urban and sophisticated feel than places in town and keeps the dancing going late.

Getting There & Away

AIR

The **Aeropuerto Alberto Carnevali** (☎ 263-9330; Av Urdaneta) is right inside the city, 2km southwest of Plaza Bolívar, accessible by buses from the corner of Calle 25 and Av 2. **Avior** (☎ 244-2454) and **Santa Bárbara** (☎ 263-4170) fly daily to and from Caracas (US$75 to US$100). There are also direct flights to Maracaibo (US$50 to US$70) and San Antonio del Táchira (US$45 to US$55).

BUS

The **Terminal de Pasajeros** (Bus Terminal; ☎ 263-3952; Av Las Américas) is 3km southwest of the city center; it's linked by frequent public buses that depart from the corner of Calle 25 and Av 2.

A dozen buses run daily to Caracas (US$13 to US$20, 13 hours, 790km) and half-a-dozen to Maracaibo (US$10 to US$14, nine hours, 523km). Small buses to San Cristóbal depart every 1½ hours from 5:30am to 7pm (US$7, five hours, 224km).

Regional destinations, including Apartaderos and Jají, are serviced regularly throughout the day.

AROUND MÉRIDA

The best known of the mountain villages is **Jají** (ha-*hee*), 38km west of Mérida and accessible by *por puesto*. It was extensively reconstructed in the late 1960s to become a manicured typical Andean town. A couple of budget *posadas* are in the village. For something less touristic, try **Mucuchíes**, a 400-year-old town 48km east of Mérida. Several kilometers up the road is the village of **San Rafael**, noted for an amazing small stone chapel.

Activities

HIKING & MOUNTAINEERING

The most popular high mountain–trekking area is the **Parque Nacional Sierra Nevada**, east of Mérida, which has all of Venezuela's highest peaks. **Pico Bolívar**, Venezuela's highest point (5007m), is one of the most popular peaks to climb. Without a guide you can hike along the trail leading up to Pico Bolívar. It roughly follows the cable-car line, but be careful walking from Loma Redonda to Pico Espejo – the trail is not clear and it's easy to get lost. Venezuela's second-highest summit, **Pico Humboldt** (4942m) is also popular with high-mountain trekkers.

An easier destination is **Los Nevados**, a charming mountain village nestled at about 2700m. Mérida's Posada Guamanchi (p1014) has a second *posada* in Los Nevados ((US$14 per person, includes breakfast and dinner). The normal trip is done by cable car to Loma Redonda. From there you walk (five to six hours) or ride a mule (US$5, four to five hours) to Los Nevados for the night. You can return by jeep to Mérida (US$50 for up to five, four to five hours, 63km).

The **Parque Nacional Sierra La Culata**, to the north of Mérida, also offers some amazing hiking territory and is particularly noted for its desertlike highland landscapes. Take a *por puesto* to La Culata (departing from the corner of Calle 19 and Av 2), from where it's a three- to four-hour hike uphill to a primitive shelter known as El Refugio, at about 3700m. Continue the next day for about three hours to the top of **Pico Pan de Azúcar** (4660m). Return before 4pm, the time the last *por puesto* tends to depart back to Mérida. There are numerous other great hikes including **Pico El Águila** (4118m), **Paso del Cóndor** (4007m) and **Pico Mucuñuque** (4672m).

MOUNTAIN BIKING

Several tour companies in Mérida organize bike trips and rent bikes. Shop around, as bicycle quality and rental prices may differ substantially between the companies. One of the popular bike tours is the loop around the remote mountain villages south of Mérida known as Pueblos del Sur. For a more challenging ride, try a trip up and back to the Refugio in Parque Nacional Sierra la Culata. The downhill through the high grasslands really gets the adrenaline pumping. Bike rental is around US$10 to US$40 a day, depending on quality.

PARAGLIDING

Most visitors fly on tandem gliders with a skilled pilot, so no previous experience is necessary. The usual starting point for flights is Las González, an hour-long jeep ride from Mérida, from where you glide for 20 to 30 minutes down 850 vertical meters. The cost of the flight (US$40 to US$50) includes jeep transportation.

You can also take a paragliding course that takes approximately a week, covering theory (available in English) and practice (including solo flights); the cost is US$400 to US$500. **X-treme Adventours** (p1014) is the main paragliding operator although the sport is offered by most all-round Mérida tour companies (p1014), which either have their own pilots or will contract one for you.

RAFTING & CANYONING

Rafting is organized on some rivers at the southern slopes of the Andes. It can be included in a tour to Los Llanos or done as a two-day rafting tour (US$80 to US$100 per person). It's normally a wet-season activity, but some rivers allow for year-round rafting.

Canyoning (climbing, rappelling and hiking down a river canyon and its waterfalls) is another very popular activity. Full-day, all-inclusive canyoning tours go for around US$50. Arassari Trek (p1014) is the gold standard of rafting and canyoning tours.

Los Llanos

The best wildlife-watching destination is Los Llanos, an immense plain savanna south of the Andes. Los Llanos is Venezuela's great repository of wildlife, particularly birds, but it's also excellent ground to get a close experience with caimans, capybaras, piranhas and anacondas, to name just a few. Several ecotourist camps in Los Llanos offer wildlife-watching tours on their *hatos* (ranches) but they are expensive (US$80 to US$150 per person per day). Mérida's tour companies (p1014) provide similarly fascinating excursions for around US$40 per day. They are normally offered as four-day all-inclusive packages. The tours can also be arranged from Ciudad Bolívar. A guide of note, with a solid background in biology and birding, is **Tony Martin** (☎ 0414-820-2506; www .anacondas-lo sllanos.com.ve).

SAN CRISTÓBAL

☎ 0276 / pop 350,000

San Cristóbal is a thriving commercial center fueled by its proximity to Colombia, just 40km away. You'll find yourself in San Cristóbal if you are traveling overland to or from anywhere in Colombia except the Caribbean Coast. Though the city is not a destination in itself it is a modern and comfortable place with friendly inhabitants. It is worth staying a bit longer in January, when the city goes wild for two weeks celebrating its Feria de San Sebastián.

Information

Banco de Venezuela (cnr Calle 8 & Carrera 9)
Banesco (cnr Av 7 & Calle 5)
CANTV (cnr Av 5 & Calle 5) Telephone service.
Cyber Storm (Calle 4 btwn Carreras 8 & 9) Internet.
Cybercafé Dinastía (cnr Av 7 & Calle 14) Internet.

Sleeping & Eating

If you're coming by bus and just need a budget shelter for the night, check out one of several basic hotels on Calle 4, a short block south of the bus terminal. Alternatively try one of the budget hotels in the city center (a 10-minute ride by local bus).

Hotel Grecón (☎ 343-6017; Av 5 btwn Calles 15 & 16; d US$12-18; ☼) The best price that you will find with air-con. Grecón, 100m north of the center, is a small hotel offering 20 spotless rooms.

Posada Turística Don Manuel (☎ 347-8082; Carrera 10 No 1-63; s/d/tr US$10/13/16) This is the cheapest of San Cristóbal's half-a-dozen *posadas*, and the one closest to the center (just a 10-minute walk south). It's a family home with four simple rooms rented out to tourists. Guests can use the kitchen and fridge.

Hotel El Andino (☎ 343-4906; Carrera 6 btwn Calles 9 & 10; s/d/tr US$14/19/24) Just half a block from the Plaza Bolívar, this is the most acceptable cheapie in town, secure and family run, although also popular *por rato* (by the hour).

Restaurant La Bologna (☎ 343-4450; Calle 5 No 8-54; mains US$3-5) La Bologna brings in a steady crowd of locals to feast on its consistently good Venezuelan dishes.

Getting There & Away

AIR

San Cristóbal's airport, **Aeropuerto Base Buenaventura Vivas** (☎ 234-7013), is in Santo Domingo, about 38km southeast of the city, but not much air traffic goes through there. The airport in San Antonio del Táchira (p1018) is far busier and just about the same distance from San Cristóbal.

BUS

The busy **Terminal de Pasajeros** (☎ 346-5590; Av Manuel Felipe Rugeles, La Concordia) is 2km south of the city center and linked by frequent city bus services.

More than a dozen buses daily go to Caracas (US$13 to US$20, 13 hours, 825km). Most depart in the late afternoon or evening for an overnight trip via El Llano highway. Ordinary buses to Barinas (US$7, five hours, 313km) run every hour or so between 5am and 6:30pm.

Buses to Mérida (US$7, five hours, 224km) go every 1½ hours from 5:30am to 7pm. The 7pm bus is unreliable if fewer than 10 passengers show up. Five buses depart nightly for Maracaibo (US$10 to US$13, eight hours, 439km).

Por puesto minibuses to San Antonio del Táchira (US$1.25, 1¼ hours, 40km), on the Colombian border, run every 10 or 15 minutes; it's a spectacular but busy road. If you are in a rush, consider taking a taxi.

SAN ANTONIO DEL TÁCHIRA

☎ 0276 / pop 60,000

San Antonio is a Venezuelan border town, sitting on a busy San Cristóbal–Cúcuta crossing

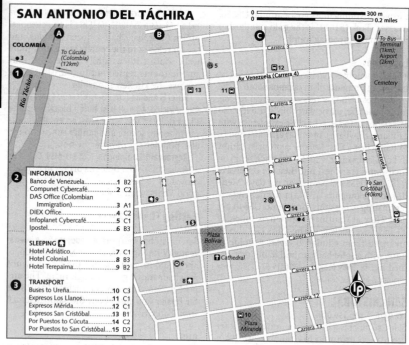

SAN ANTONIO DEL TÁCHIRA

INFORMATION
Banco de Venezuela...............1 B2
Compunet Cybercafé................2 C2
DAS Office (Colombian
Immigration).....................3 A1
DIEX Office.........................4 C2
Infoplanet Cybercafé...............5 C1
Ipostel.............................6 B3

SLEEPING
Hotel Adriático.....................7 C1
Hotel Colonial......................8 B3
Hotel Terepaima....................9 B2

TRANSPORT
Buses to Ureña.....................10 C3
Expresos Los Llanos...............11 C1
Expresos Mérida....................12 C1
Expresos San Cristóbal............13 B1
Por Puestos to Cúcuta.............14 C2
Por Puestos to San Cristóbal....15 D2

and living off trade with neighboring Colombia. When choosing where to stay, know that Cúcuta is a bigger town with more developed facilities. However, San Antonio is pleasant enough. Wind your watch back one hour when crossing from Venezuela to Colombia.

Information

There are several *casas de cambio* in the center, particularly on Av Venezuela and around the DIEX office. They all change cash, but none will touch your traveler's checks. You'll get much better rates changing your bolívars to Colombian pesos (or vice versa) at the roadside money-changers a short walk across the bridge in Colombia, as there are no restrictions on currency transactions in that country. There are a few banks around Plaza Bolívar.

Banco de Venezuela (cnr Calle 3 & Carrera 9)
CompuNet Cyber Café (Calle 6 No 8-28; per hr US80¢)
Infoplanet Cybercafé (Calle 4 No 3-45; per hr US85¢)
Ipostel (cnr Carrera 10 & Calle 2) Post office.

Sleeping & Eating

San Antonio del Táchira has three decent places to stay, each with its own restaurant.

Hotel Colonial (☎ 771-2679; Carrera 11 No 2-51; d with fan US$7-8, with air-con US$10-11, tr with fan/air-con US$9/12; 🅇) One of the cheapest hotels in San Antonio, the Colonial is a small, family-run affair with its own restaurant serving inexpensive set lunches. The rooms are basic, but decent and all have private facilities.

Hotel Terepaima (☎ 808-8653; Carrera 8 No 1-37; d/tr with fan US$8/10, with air-con US$12/15; 🅿 🅇) This is another small, family-managed hotel with 14 simple rooms upstairs and a restaurant providing basic breakfasts and lunches.

Hotel Adriático (☎ 771-5757; Calle 6 No 5-51; s/d/tr US$14/22/26; 🅿 🅇) The best place to stay in the center, the Adriático offers fair-sized rooms with quiet air conditioners. Some rooms have balconies where you can watch the bustle on the street below. The hotel restaurant has inexpensive Venezuelan favorites.

Getting There & Away
AIR

The **Aeropuerto Juan Vicente Gómez** (☎ 771-2692), 2km northeast of town, can be reached by buses. They depart from Plaza Miranda, but if you don't want to go that far, you can

---

GETTING TO COLOMBIA

The **DIEX** (Carrera 9 btwn Calles 6 & 7; ☺ 6am-10pm) office puts exit or entry stamps in passports. All tourists leaving Venezuela are charged a US$16 *impuesto de salida* (departure tax). You must pay in cash and must buy stamps for this amount in a shop (open till 5pm only) across the street from DIEX. Nationals of most Western countries don't need a visa for Colombia, but all travelers are supposed to get an entry stamp from DAS (Colombian immigration). The DAS office is just past the bridge over the Río Táchira (the actual border), on the right.

Buses (US40¢) and *por puestos* (US60¢) run frequently to Cúcuta in Colombia (12km). You can catch buses on Av Venezuela or save yourself a long wait in border traffic by walking to the front of the line of cars and looking for a shared taxi with extra space in it. Or you can walk from San Antonio across the bridge. Be sure to get off at the DAS office just behind the bridge for your Colombia entry stamp and then take another bus. Buses go as far as the Cúcuta bus terminal; most pass through the center. You can pay in Venezuelan bolívars or Colombian pesos.

From Cúcuta, there are frequent buses and flights to all major Colombian destinations. For information on travel from Colombia to Venezuela, see p577.

---

catch them on the corner of Calle 6 and Av Venezuela.

Aeropostal, Aserca and Rutaca have daily flights to Caracas (US$90). Aeropostal and Santa Bárbara fly direct to Maracaibo (US85). Santa Bárbara also flies to Mérida (US$50).

There are no direct flights to Colombia from San Antonio; go to Cúcuta across the border, from where you can fly to Bogotá, Medellín and other major Colombian cities (for a much better price than you'd get for a flight to those cities from Maracaibo or Caracas).

BUS

The bus terminal is midway to the airport. Half-a-dozen bus companies operate buses to Caracas (US$17 to US$22, 14 hours, 865km), with a total of seven buses daily. All depart between 4pm and 7pm and use El Llano route. Most of these bus companies also have offices in the town center: **Expresos Los Llanos** (☎ 771-2690; Calle 5 No 4-26), **Expresos Mérida** (☎ 771-4053; Av Venezuela No 6-17), **Expresos Occidente** (☎ 771-4730; cnr Carrera 6 & Calle 6), and **Expresos San Cristóbal** (☎ 771-4301; Av Venezuela No 3-20). They all sell tickets, but then you have to go to the terminal anyway to board the bus.

No direct buses run to Mérida; go to San Cristóbal and change there. *Por puestos* to San Cristóbal leave frequently from the corner of Av Venezuela and Carrera 10 (US$1.25, 1¼ hours, 40km).

THE NORTHEAST

Much like the northwest, Venezuela's north-east is a mosaic of natural marvels. It has the Caribbean beaches, coral reefs and verdant mountains. However it also boasts Isla de Margarita, one of the most famous island destinations in the Caribbean, and the Cueva del Guácharo, Venezuela's biggest and most impressive cave system. Parque Nacional Mochima and the remote stretches of sand beyond Río Caribe offer the opportunity for unspoilt time on the beach. The city of Cumaná was also the first Spanish settlement founded on the South American mainland. Once you've spent time in the northeast, you'll understand what prompted Columbus to whimsically declare the region 'paradise on earth.'

BARCELONA

☎ 0281 / pop 320,000

Not quite as exciting as its namesake, Barcelona is a mix of a small colonial center and sprawling modernity along its highways. Most travelers visit Barcelona while passing from Caracas to Ciudad Bolívar or up to Puerto la Cruz (few actually get off the bus). Barcelona's airport serves as the regional terminal for Puerto la Cruz and destinations up the coast.

Information

Banco de Venezuela (Plaza Boyacá)
Banesco (Carrera 9 Páez)
CANTV (Centro Comercial La Llovizna, Av 5 de Julio) Telephone access.
Ipostel (☎ 275-6209; Carrera 13 Bolívar; ☺ 8am-noon & 2-5pm Mon-Fri) Near the plaza.

Sleeping & Eating

Hotel Neverí (☎ 277-2376; Av Fuerzas Armadas at Av Miranda; d/tr US$13.50/15; ☒) Recognizable by

VENEZUELA

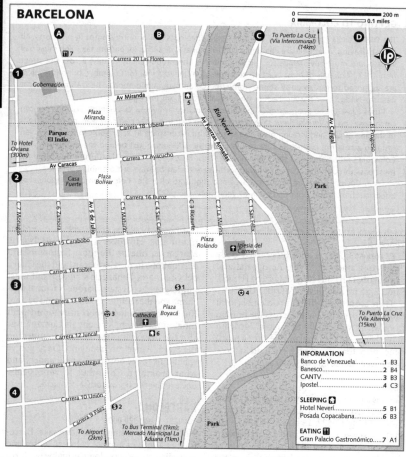

BARCELONA

INFORMATION	
Banco de Venezuela	1 B3
Banesco	2 B4
CANTV	3 B3
Ipostel	4 C3

SLEEPING	
Hotel Neverí	5 B1
Posada Copacabana	6 B3

EATING	
Gran Palacio Gastronómico	7 A1

the vivid mural of tropical flowers and birds adorning the outside, this place has a grand staircase, large utilitarian rooms and its own restaurant. Can be too noisy for light sleepers.

Posada Copacabana (☎ 277-3473; Carrera Juncal; d/tr with bathroom US$17/26; ❄) Right next to the cathedral, Copacabana has 11 inviting, newish rooms. They are clean and are great value.

Hotel Oviana (☎ 276-4147; Av Caracas; d US$33; ℗ ❄) One of Barcelona's better options, though it's some five blocks west of Plaza Bolívar. Rooms are clean and simple, and have good hot-water bathrooms and cable TV. Front ones are noisy.

Mercado Municipal La Aduana (☼ 6am-2pm) This is right next to the bus terminal, 1km south

of town. It has more than a dozen popular restaurants serving a variety of typical food.

Gran Palacio Gastronómico (☎ 276-2920; Av 5 de Julio; ☼ 6:30am-10pm) This straightforward self-service restaurant serves all the usual Venezuelan dishes, from *arepas* to roasted chicken.

Getting There & Away

AIR

The airport is 2km south of the city center. Buses going south along Av 5 de Julio pass within 300m of the airport (US25¢). Several carriers have daily flights to Caracas (US$60 to US$75). **Avior** (☎ 274-9545) flies to Puerto Ordaz (US$78). **Aserca** (☎ 274-1240) services Maracaibo (US$100) and San Antonio del

Táchira (US$120) via Caracas. **Santa Barbara** (☎ 274-0444) flies to Barquisimeto (US$84) and Mérida (US$95) via Caracas. Several airlines, including Avior and **Rutaca** (☎ 276-8914), fly direct to Porlamar on Isla de Margarita (US$25 to US$45). Prices listed are one way.

BUS

The bus terminal is 1km southeast of the city center, next to the market. Take a *buseta* (US20¢, 10 minutes) going south along Av 5 de Julio, or walk for 15 minutes.

The terminal in Puerto La Cruz has more routes, so it's better to go there instead of waiting in Barcelona. To Puerto La Cruz, catch a *buseta* going north on Av 5 de Julio (US30¢, 45 minutes). They use two routes, Vía Inter-

comunal and Vía Alterna. Either will drop you in the center of Puerto La Cruz. There are faster *por puesto* minibuses (US40¢), which depart from Av 5 de Julio 2½ blocks south of Banesco.

PUERTO LA CRUZ

☎ 0281 / pop 215,000

Puerto La Cruz is one of the principal departure points to Isla de Margarita (p1029), and the last town of size before Parque Nacional Mochima (p1022). Major bus lines arrive in Puerto La Cruz, where you can visit banks, pharmacies and take care of other chores. However, if you seek beaches it is best to stay in the smaller Playa Colorada, Santa Fe, Mochima or further along the coastline.

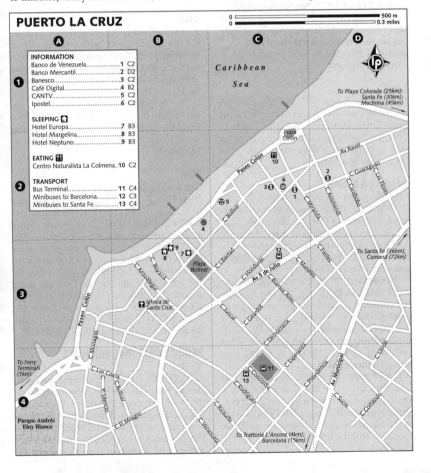

PUERTO LA CRUZ

0 — 500 m
0 — 0.3 miles

INFORMATION	
Banco de Venezuela	1 C2
Banco Mercantil	2 D2
Banesco	3 C2
Café Digital	4 B2
CANTV	5 C2
Ipostel	6 C2

SLEEPING 🏠	
Hotel Europa	7 B3
Hotel Margelina	8 B3
Hotel Neptuno	9 B3

EATING 🍴	
Centro Naturalista La Colmena	10 C2

TRANSPORT	
Bus Terminal	11 C4
Minibuses to Barcelona	12 C3
Minibuses to Santa Fe	13 C4

Caribbean Sea

To Playa Colorada (25km);
Santa Fe (30km);
Mochima (45km)

To Santa Fe (36km);
Cumaná (72km)

To Ferry Terminals (1km)

Parque Andrés Eloy Blanco

To Trattoria L'Ancora (4km);
Barcelona (15km)

The city is a bustling, youthful and rapidly expanding place. It is generally not an attractive town, though it features a lively waterfront boulevard, Paseo Colón, packed with hotels, bars and restaurants. This area comes to life in the late afternoon and evening as temperatures cool, street stalls open and locals reemerge from their siestas.

Information

Most major banks are within a few blocks south of Plaza Colón. The following banks all have 24-hour ATMs.

Banco de Venezuela (Calle Miranda)
Banco Mercantil (Calle Arismendi)
Banesco (Calle Freites)
Café Digital (Centro Comercial Cristoforo Colombo, No 29, upper fl, Paseo Colón; 9am-9pm Mon-Sat) For internet access, try here.
CANTV (Paseo Colón; 9am-10pm Mon-Sat, 10:30am-4pm Sun) Has telephones and good internet access.
Ipostel (268-5355; Calle Freites; 8am-noon & 2-5pm Mon-Fri) For post.

Tours

Tours to the Parque Nacional Mochima are offered by a number of agencies nestled along Paseo Colón. However, tours from Puerto La Cruz are more expensive and require more time in transit than those from Santa Fe or the town of Mochima.

Sleeping & Eating

Hotel Margelina (268-7545; Paseo Colón; s/d/tr US$11/14/16;) While none of the bare-bones hotels in Puerto La Cruz can claim style, Margelina does have a certain fusty character. And if you don't expect luxury, you should be pleased with the position right on the seafront and near several restaurants.

Hotel Neptuno (265-3261; fax 265-5790; Paseo Colón at Calle Juncal; s/d/tr US$12/16/24;) The Neptune has corridors painted in a yellow and green paint giving way to good-value rooms with hot-water bathrooms and cable TV, while the hotel's biggest attraction is its open-sided restaurant (mains US$3.50 to US$8) with sweeping views out to sea .

Hotel Europa (268-8157; Plaza Bolívar at Calle Sucre; d/tr US$15/17;) The Europa is a sparsely adorned hotel whose only extravagance is a neon-lit image of the Virgin Mary at the top of the stairs. Rooms are plain but spacious, with bathrooms. The staff is very friendly.

Centro Naturalista La Colmena (265-2751; Paseo Colón 27; 3-course menu US$3; 11:45am-2pm Mon-Fri) This lunch-only vegetarian café and natural products shop has a tiny covered terrace looking out across the boulevard to the sea. It serves budget set lunches.

Trattoria L'Ancora (Centro Comercial Plaza Mayor; pizzas US$5-9.50, pasta US$4-6; noon-11pm;) Overlooking the canals of El Morro, where you can watch expensive boats glide past, L'Ancora serves up tasty pizza and pasta dishes. You can relax in its open-air terrace or indoor glass-walled area with air-con.

Getting There & Away

AIR

The airport is in Barcelona (p1019).

BOAT

Puerto La Cruz is the major departure point for Isla de Margarita, with services offered by **Conferry** (267-7847; www.conferry.com; Sector Los Cocos) and **Gran Cacique Express** (267-7286; www.grancacique.com.ve; Sector Los Cocos). Smaller excursion boats leave from the small piers in town.

The ferry terminals are accessible by *por puesto* from the center or a taxi will cost US$2. Go in the daytime as it's a spectacular journey out through the islands of Parque Nacional Mochima.

BUS

The bustling bus terminal is just three blocks from Plaza Bolívar. Frequent buses run west to Caracas (US$7 to US$11, five hours) and east to Cumaná (US$2.50, 1½ hours); many of the latter continue east to Carúpano (US$4 to US$7, four hours) and some go as far as Güiria (US$8, 6½ hours). If you go eastward (to Cumaná or further on), grab a seat on the left side of the bus, as there are some spectacular views over the islands of Parque Nacional Mochima. *Por puesto* cars also run to Caracas (US$12, four hours), Maturín (US$6, 2½ hours) and Cumaná (US$4, 1¼ hours).

PARQUE NACIONAL MOCHIMA

0293

Straddling the states of Anzoátegui and Sucre, Parque Nacional Mochima comprises a low, dry mountain range that drops down to fine bays and beaches and continues offshore to some three dozen beautiful islands. The best beaches are to be found on the islands and are accessed by short boat trips from Santa Fe,

Mochima or other coastal towns. Coral reefs surround a few of the islands and provide decent snorkeling and scuba diving. Tranquility seekers will be happy midweek, when only a handful of beachgoers is to be found on the more far-flung islands.

Playa Colorada

This crescent of orange sand is shaded with coconut groves and draws hordes of young Venezuelan partyers and sun-seekers on the weekends. It can also be an easy day trip from both Santa Fe and Puerto La Cruz.

There's quite a choice of places to stay close to the beach.

The Scottish-managed camp **Jakera Lodge** (☎ 808-7057; www.jakera.com; hammocks/beds US$4/6; 🖳) offers accommodations, meals, kayak and bicycle rental, tours, Spanish courses and more.

Posada Nirvana (☎ 808-7844; Calle Marchán, 500m uphill from the coastal road; s without bathroom US$5, d/tr with bathroom US$10/12.50, ste with bathroom & kitchen US$16) is an informal Swiss-run *posada*. Its garden has hammocks and an outdoor Jacuzzi. The owner prepares fabulous breakfasts (US$4).

Opposite Posada Nirvana, neatly maintained country home stay **Quinta Jaly** (☎ 808-3246; Calle Marchán; s/d/tr US$11/12.50/16; 🗙) is run by an affable French-Canadian. Here, too, guests have free access to the kitchen, and an optional breakfast is available for US$2.50.

Café Las Carmitas (☎ 0416-912-466; 3ra Transversal No 57; mains US$3-6), a small Portuguese-owned café with flexible hours, has an ebullient chef who serves up pizza, pasta, fish and meat dishes with a dose of personal charm.

Santa Fe

Santa Fe comprises two different worlds: the beach, which is a sedate backpackers haven, and the rest of the town, a rough-and-tumble fishing village. For travelers there is little reason to leave the *posada*- and café-lined beach other than to visit one of the town's two nightclubs or walk to the bus terminal. The beach is a chill spot to sit in the sand and sip on beers and fruit juices with new friends. If you are looking for more remote and pristine beaches, small boats make day trips from Santa Fe to the islands of Parque Nacional Mochima.

There is frustratingly slow internet access in an unnamed building behind Posada Café del Mar.

The following are all along the beach or one block away.

Posada Café del Mar (☎ 231-0009; Calle la Marina, entering the beach; d US$9), a German-run café, bar and *posada*, is one of the best-value budget haunts, offering 14 simple rooms with fans and hot water on upper levels, and hearty budget food. There's also a breezy rooftop terrace hung with hammocks, and the manager offers cheap boat tours.

The pioneer hotel in Santa Fe, **La Sierra Inn** (☎ 231-0042; cooperativasantafedemisamores@hotmail.com; on the beach, d US$12.50; Ⓟ), has smart yet simple rooms, several outdoor terraces and a BBQ area. Kayak rental and tours are available too.

The new French addition of **Le Petit Jardin** (☎ 416-6611; lepetit.jardin@yahoo.com; Calle Cochima; d US$25-35; 🗙 🖳) has nicely decorated rooms and bungalows around a swimming pool. It is a block behind the beach but right behind Playa Santa Fe Resort.

Santa Fe Resort & Dive Center (☎ 0414-773-3777; www.santaferesort.com; d US$35-75; Ⓟ) is a secure and comfortable upper-end *posada* with a range of breezy rooms. Ask for those on the 2nd floor that get good sunlight (though the downstairs rooms have access to a serene garden). The hotel also has a diveshop and organizes tours of Parque Nacional Mochima and surrounding areas.

Náutico (☎ 231-0026; Calle la Marina, entering the beach; mains US$3-7) One of the better, if touristy, places to eat on the beach. The open-air restaurant has delicious seafood and the best *pabellón criollo* (shredded beef, rice, black beans, cheese and fried plantain; Venezuela's national dish) in town.

Posada Los Siete Delfines (☎ 416-7449; lossiete delfinessantafe@hotmail.com; on the beach; d/tr/q US$9.50/12.50/16) is one of the more budget *posadas*. It is only an average place to stay, but the restaurant-café that spreads out onto the sand is the most popular place for travelers to hang out, eat and drink beers and *batidos* (juices).

Regular buses and *por puestos* from Puerto La Cruz and Cumaná will deposit you on the highway at Santa Fe's main junction. Walk 1km through the town to the market on the seafront. Turn left to reach the beach, which is lined with *posadas*. Be careful at night.

Mochima

Mochima may be close to Santa Fe, but is a completely different experience. There is

VENEZUELA

no beach in town but Mochima is a quaint, attractive village on the edge of its namesake national park. Also unlike Santa Fe, it is more popular with Venezuelan families than international backpackers. Frequent boats run from the waterfront to the numerous island beaches of the park. The town in nearly empty during the week.

TOURS

Transportation to the beaches is provided from the wharf in the village's center, where boats anchor and *lancheros* (boatmen) sit on the shore and wait for tourists. They can take you to any beach, among them Playa Las Maritas (US$12.50), Playa Blanca (US$12.50), Playa Manare (US$16), and Playas Cautaro and Cautarito (US$16). The listed figures are round-trip fares per boat (number of passengers depends on size of boat), and you can be picked up whenever you want. Don't hesitate to bargain!

Longer tours, which can include cruises to Islas Caracas, La Piscina and Playa Colorada, plus snorkeling, are also available. **Posada Villa Vicenta** (☎ 416-0916) has good prices.

Aquatics Diving Center (☎ 430-1649, 0414-777-0196; info@scubavenezuela.com) organizes diving courses, dives and excursions, and handles snorkel rental. The diving is decent but nothing spectacular and the service is questionable.

SLEEPING & EATING

Mochima has a fair choice of accommodation and food facilities. Locals also rent out rooms and houses if there is demand. Budget-priced meals, especially breakfast, can be hard to come by. One of the few inexpensive places to get breakfast is in the unnamed store No 1 at the Mini Centro Comerical Corozal near the basketball court. There is also a small café at the dock called Exquisitas Empanadas which offers, yes, empanadas in the mornings. The signless Manglar Café (between El Mochimero and the liquor store) is friendly and has affordable sandwiches and fruit drinks.

Posada Villa Vicenta (☎ 416-0916; s/d/tr US$9/10/12.50; ✵) Located one block back from the wharf, this *posada* has four levels stepping their way back up the hillside, each with a terrace boasting fine vistas over the bay (better on the higher floors). The no-frills, stone-walled rooms have fans and cold-water bathrooms.

Posada Doña Cruz (☎ 416-6114; d US$16; ✵) This colorful, though impersonal, little *posada* with

two parts (one near the dock and the other by the miniplaza) has small but decent rooms with private bathroom. The elderly owners can be tracked down by the sign for the hotel at the dock, where they pass the hot afternoons sitting in the shade.

El Mochimero (☎ 0414-773-8782; Calle La Marina; mains US$6-15; ✵ 11am-9pm) This is one of the best advertised and most popular tourist restaurants selling seafood dishes. It has uninterested service and greatly inflated prices, though sometimes it is the only place open in town.

GETTING THERE & AWAY

Jeeps departing from Cumaná will bring you to the village's center (US65¢, 35 minutes), next to the wharf. There's no direct transportation from Puerto La Cruz.

CUMANÁ

☎ 0293 / pop 310,000

Founded in 1521, Cumaná takes pride in being the oldest remaining Spanish settlement on the South American mainland. That and its proximity to other attractions along the coastline are about the only reason to visit. Cumaná is not a bad place, but it is best used as a portal to Isla de Margarita, Península de Araya, Santa Fe, Mochima and the Cueva del Guácharo. Like Puerto La Cruz, it is a smart move to stock up on cash and other city conveniences here before visiting the smaller towns.

Information

Most major banks are on Calle Mariño and Av Bermúdez.

Banco de Venezuela (Calle Mariño at Calle Rojas)
Banco Mercantil (Av Bermúdez at Calle Gutierrez)
Banesco (Calle Mariño at Calle Carabobo)
Internet Café (Calle Sucre; ✵ 8:30am-6pm Mon-Fri, 8.30am-noon Sat) Just what it sounds like.
Ipostel (☎ 432-2616; Calle Paraíso) For snail mail.

Sleeping & Eating

Hotel Astoria (☎ 433-2708; hotelastoria_7@hotmail.com; Calle Sucre 51; s/d/tr US$10/11.50/14; P ✵) This is the best central option for those on a strict budget. Though nothing fancy, it has an ever-smiling host, comparatively good-sized and well-lit rooms, fans, and air-con that's switched on from 7pm till the morning.

Bubulina's Hostal (☎ 431-4025; Callejón Santa Inés; d US$17; ✵) A stylish choice is this one-story

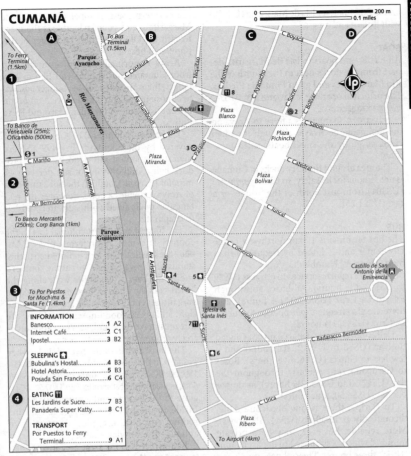

CUMANÁ

INFORMATION
Banesco.................................1 A2
Internet Café.........................2 C1
Ipostel..................................3 B2

SLEEPING
Bubulina's Hostal..................4 B3
Hotel Astoria.........................5 B3
Posada San Francisco............6 C4

EATING
Les Jardins de Sucre..............7 B3
Panadería Super Katty...........8 C1

TRANSPORT
Por Puestos to Ferry
    Terminal...........................9 A1

historical building down a narrow colonial street. The interior is a totally new construction but retains a cozy charm and airiness in its rooms. There's an attached restaurant too, serving Venezuelan dishes.

Posada San Francisco (☎ 431-3926; Calle Sucre; d US$20; ☻ 8am-9pm) The quiet open-air patio restaurant at the Posada San Francisco makes for a romantic atmosphere in the evening, when lights are left low and the stars are visible above. The *posada*, which is in one of the town's loveliest colonial mansions, hasn't always welcomed nonguests to its restaurant (mains US$5 to US$9), so double-check in advance.

Panadería Super Katty (☎ 431-2955; Plaza Blanco; ☻ 6am-10pm) This bakery has excellent pastries and enough frosted cakes to cater for a dozen weddings. Plus it has a supercool name.

Les Jardins de Sucre (☎ 431-3689; Calle Sucre 27; mains US$7-14; ☻ 6-10pm Mon, noon-3pm & 6-10pm Tue-Thu, noon-11pm Sat & Sun) One of Cumaná's best restaurants is this French place with shady patio, small water garden and attentive service. Dishes like pork in four spices, and smoked-salmon salad will liven up taste buds, as will the French and Chilean wines. Daily specials like duck and rabbit are available.

Getting There & Away
AIR
The airport is about 4km southeast of the city center. There are frequent flights to Caracas (US$55 to US$75) with Avior and other airlines,

and to Porlamar, on Isla de Margarita (US$50) with Rutaca and others.

BOAT

All ferries and boats to Isla de Margarita depart from the docks next to the mouth of the Río Manzanares and go to Punta de Piedras. The principal operator is **Naviarca** (☎ 431-5577; www.grancacique.com.ve).

Naviarca also operates a ferry to Araya on the Península de Araya, although it's often easier to go by the small boats called *tapaditos*.

The area around the ferry docks in Cumaná is not famous for its safety, so take a *por puesto* (US30¢) from just north of the bridge, or a taxi (US$1.25).

BUS

The bus terminal is 1.5km northwest of the city center and is linked by frequent urban buses along Av Humboldt.

There are regular services to Caracas (US$9 to US$13, 6½ hours). All buses go through Puerto La Cruz (US$2.50, 1½ hours), and there are also frequent *por puestos* to Puerto La Cruz (US$3, 1¼ hours).

Half-a-dozen buses depart daily for Ciudad Bolívar (US$8 to US$12, six hours) and a few less to Güiria (US$6, five hours). Buses to Carúpano run regularly throughout the day (US$2.50 to US$3, 2½ hours), as do *por puestos* (US$4.50, four hours).

To Caripe, there is one departure daily, theoretically at 12:30pm (US$4, 3½ hours). More reliable, however, may be a private minibus, which is supposed to depart at 3pm (US$5, three hours). They all pass the Cueva del Guácharo shortly before arriving at Caripe and can let you off at the cave's entrance.

Por puesto cars to Santa Fe (US$1, 1.25 hours) and Mochima (US$1, one hour) depart from near the Mercadito, one block off the Redoma El Indio. During the day, jeeps do both of those trips with many less stops for a few more bolívars.

PENÍNSULA DE ARAYA

☎ 0293 / pop 30,000

A solitary road runs the length of this 70km-long and 10km-wide peninsula of arid red sands and scrubby dunes that wrap around between Cumaná and Isla de Margarita. The Península de Araya's sparse population is scattered through a handful of villages on the northern coast. If super-touristy Isla de Margarita is not your style, this is the place to visit for kilometer after kilometer of un-populated beaches.

Araya is normally visited on a day trip from Cumaná, but should you like to stay longer, there are half-a-dozen budget *posadas* to choose from. You'll find more *posadas* on the opposite side of the village, around Plaza Bolívar.

The **salinas** (salt mines) of Araya were discovered by the Spaniards in 1499 and are Venezuela's largest salt deposits. They produce half a million tons of salt per year. A *mirador* (lookout), built on the hill 2km north of Araya, provides a good view over the rectangular pools filled with saltwater and left to evaporate.

The biggest and oldest colonial fort in the country is commonly referred to as **El Castillo** (the Castle). The four-pointed structure stands on the waterfront cliff at the southern end of the bay, a 10-minute walk along the beach from the wharf. Although damaged, the gargantuan coral-rock walls are an awesome sight and give a good impression of how the fort must have once looked. You can wander freely around the site, as there's no gate.

The most stylish of the five or six low-key *posadas* in the town, **Posada Araya Wind** (☎ 437-1132; Calle El Castillo; d/tr with air-con & bathroom US$12.50/16, d/tr/q with fan & shared bathroom US$9.50/11/12.50;) is close to the fortress and a quiet little beach. Inside, the neatly decorated *posada* has cane roofing and furniture, plus a scattering of antique-style wooden chairs.

Eating places in the same area include **Restaurant Araya Mar** (mains US$3-4; 7:30am-9pm), an open-fronted café that catches the breeze. It also has newish air-con matrimonial rooms for US$12.

CARIPE

☎ 0292 / pop 12,000

While a nice town surrounded by coffee and citrus plantations, Caripe draws most of its importance from its closeness to the Cueva del Guácharo (12km from town). It does get a number of Venezuelan weekend visitors who come for the mild weather and flood the city for its renowned Easter celebrations.

There is a **Banesco** (Av Guzmán Blanco) in town. For internet and telephone there's a **Movistar** (7:30am-9:30pm Mon-Sat, 7:30am-2pm Sun) one block up from Hotel Samán.

There are a number of eating and sleeping options along the road from Caripe to the village of El Guácharo. The following are in Caripe.

If you are looking for an inexpensive place, check out **Hotel San Francisco** (☎ 414-2656; Av Chaumer; d US$14), which has 18 good, brightly painted rooms with cable TV and fan. Located right across from the church.

If you can't stay at Samán, **Mini Hotel Nicola** (☎ 545-1489; Av Gusmán Blanco; d/tr US$14/18) is a good choice. It is a small, tidy family house that rents out a few clean, modern rooms with hot-water bathrooms. It's on the road toward Maturín.

Considered the best spot in town, **Hotel Samán** (☎ 545-1183; Av Chaumer No 29; s/d/tr US$14/16/21) has comfortable rooms, a stream running beneath the building and a courtyard full of plants. The knowledgeable manager can put you in touch with local guides. Check out Restaurant Mogambo next door for a full menu of Venezuelan favorites.

Ask for the homemade pasta at **Trattoria Da Stefano** (☎ 414-6107; Calle Cabello; mains US$3-5; ☽ noon-6pm Mon-Wed, noon-9pm Thu-Sun), a bona fide Italian joint. The food is good, as are the prices. The owner is helpful and knowledgeable about the area.

The bus terminal is at the northeastern end of town, behind the market. There's an evening bus to Caracas via Cumaná at 6pm (US$10, nine hours). Another daily bus runs to Cumaná in the morning (US$4, 3½ hours), and a private minibus also goes at 6am (US$5, three hours). They all pass the Cueva del Guácharo en route. A round trip-taxi from Caripe to the cave only costs US$2 if you tell them to come back in two hours. If they wait for you, it will cost US$10. Some tour operators and hotels also organize trips.

CUEVA DEL GUÁCHARO
☎ 0292

With 10.2km of caverns, the **Guácharo Cave** (12km from Caripe toward the coast, adult/student US$6/3; ☽ 8am-4pm; P) is Venezuela's longest and most magnificent cave. The huge cave is inhabited by the *guácharo* (oilbird), which lives in total darkness and leaves the cave only at night in search of food. It has a radar-location system (similar to bats) and enormous whiskers that enable it to navigate and feel about in the dark. From August to December, the population in the cave is estimated at 10,000

guácharos, and occasionally up to 15,000. The cave also shelters a maze of stalactites and stalagmites that shine with calcium crystals.

All visits to the cave are by guided tours in groups of up to 10 people; tours take about 1½ hours and are organized at the entrance. A 1200m portion of the total of the cave is normally visited, though occasionally water rises in August and/or September, limiting sightseeing to 500m.

You can camp (US$5) at the entrance to the cave after closing time and watch the hundreds of birds pouring out of the cave mouth at around 6:30pm and returning at about 4am. Possible jumping-off points for the cave include Cumaná (p1024), Caripe (opposite) and Maturín. See those sections for transportation details.

RÍO CARIBE
☎ 0294 / pop 7500

The old port town of Río Caribe's former splendor can be spotted along the wide, tree-shaded Av Bermúdez with its once-magnificent mansions. As the cocoa boom has long since ended, these days the town serves as a laid-back holiday destination and a springboard for beaches further east. Don't miss the 18th-century church on Plaza Bolívar.

For a taste of local culture, family home **Pensión Papagayos** (☎ 646-1868; cricas@web.de; Calle 14 de Febrero; s/d US$5/10) rents out four well-maintained rooms sharing two bathrooms, and you can use the kitchen and fridge. The doorstep is often overrun with kids from the neighboring school.

One of more than a dozen cheap places in town, **Posada Don Chilo** (☎ 646-1212; Calle Mariño No 27; d/tr US$6.50/9.50) competes for the cheapest and most basic. All rooms have a shared bathroom.

Housed in a restored 19th-century mansion, the quiet **Villa Antillana** (☎ 646-1413; www.proyectoparia.com/antillana; Calle Rivero 32; s/d/tr/q US$21/26/37/45) has a handful of doubles and suites around an attractive tiled courtyard. All rooms have been painstakingly reconstructed with modern amenities, comfortable mattresses, fans and hot-water bathrooms.

ParianaCafé (☎ 494-2756; Av Bermúdez; ☽ 5:30pm-11pm Mon-Sat) is an internet café popular with foreign travelers for typical regional dishes and a cool, casual atmosphere.

Por puestos depart frequently to Carúpano from Plaza Bolívar (US$1, 30 minutes), and there are also buses marked 'Ruta Popular' (US50¢).

Infrequent *por puesto* pickup trucks run to the villages of Medina (US$1), Pui Puy (US$1.50) and San Juan de Las Galdonas (US$3). They don't get as far as the beaches of Medina and Pui Puy; you need to walk the rest of the way, about a half-hour trip in either case. Otherwise, you'll need to rent the vehicle, which costs 10 times more than the *por puesto* fare. Trucks depart from the southeastern end of Río Caribe, opposite the gas station.

AROUND RÍO CARIBE
☎ 0294

There are some two dozen beaches on the 50km coastal stretch between Río Caribe and San Juan de Unare (the last seaside village accessible by road). These beaches are some of the most gorgeous in the country and some of the least visited.

The first beaches worth visiting east of Río Caribe are side-by-side **Playa Loero** and **Playa de Uva**. They lie 6km from Río Caribe by the road to Bohordal, then another 6km by a paved side road that branches off to the left.

Proceeding east, a paved road branches off 4km beyond the working cacao plantation of Hacienda Bukare and goes 5km to the village of Medina then northward for 1km to a fork. The left branch goes for 2km to the crescent-shaped **Playa Medina**. The right branch leads 6km over a potholed road to the village of Pui Puy and continues for 2km to the beautiful **Playa Pui Puy**.

Few travelers venture further to the east, though beaches dot the coast as far as the eye can see. The seaside village of **San Juan de Las Galdonas** has especially fine beaches. Its main access road is a wholly paved 23km stretch that branches off the Río Caribe–Bohordal road 6.5km beyond the turnoff to Medina.

From San Juan de Las Galdonas, a dirt road (serviced by sporadic transportation) goes for 20km to the village of **San Juan de Unare**. Walk another hour to find the expansive Playa Cipara.

GÜIRIA
☎ 0294 / pop 30,000

Güiria, 275km from Cumaná, is the easternmost point on Venezuela's coast reachable by road. It's the largest town on the Península de Paria and an important fishing port. The town itself is rather ordinary, though the rugged neighboring Parque Nacional Península de Paria, along the peninsula's northern coast, is attractive. Güiria is most importantly a major transit point between Venezuela and Trinidad. See the boxed text, right for more information about the crossing.

Information
Both banks below give cash advances on Visa and MasterCard.

Banco Mercantil (Calle Bolívar at Calle Juncal)
Banesco (Calle Bolívar)
Conexiones Buz3 (Calle Valdez; internet per hr US70¢; ◷ 9am-8pm Mon-Fri, 10am-6pm Sat)

Sleeping & Eating
Hotel Miramar (☎ 982-0732; Calle Turipiari; d US$7.50; ⊠) To save more bolívars, you can stay in this primitive little place further toward the port. It has dark but neatly kept rooms out the back.

Hotel Plaza (☎ 982-0022; Calle Vigirima at Plaza Bolívar 18; d US$12.50; ⊠) This travelers' favorite has a newer extension upstairs with small but freshly decorated rooms with cold-water bathrooms. The *posada* has its own cheap eatery downstairs.

La Posada de Chuchú (☎ 511-2234; Calle Bideau 35; d US$12.50; ⊠) Alternatively, this *posada* has larger, beige-colored rooms with cable TV, a writing desk and plentiful hot water.

You'll find plenty of eating outlets around the central streets, including cheap and filling food stalls alongside the church (open evenings only).

GETTING TO TRINIDAD

The Windward Lines' representative **Acosta Asociados** (☎ 982-0058; grupoacosta@cantv.net; Calle Bolívar 31; ◷ 9am-noon & 3-5pm Mon-Fri) operates the *Sea Prowler,* a comfortable and air-conditioned passenger boat that runs between Güiria and Chaguaramas, near Port of Spain, Trinidad. It is supposed to arrive every Wednesday at noon and depart back to Chaguaramas at 3pm – although 5pm is closer to average departure time (it takes 3½ hours) Either way, you should be there at 1:30pm. Fares are US$73 one way, and US$121 round trip including port tax on the outward journey (for those returning from Trinidad there is an additional port tax of US$12).

Getting There & Away

BOAT

Peñeros (fishing boats) leave from the northern end of Güiria's port to Macuro. Irregular fishing boats (a few per week – Thursday around noon is a good bet) go to Pedernales, at the mouth of the Delta del Orinoco. The trip takes four to five hours and the fare is negotiable; usually around US$7 per person. Be prepared to get wet from the waves, if not from rain. From Pedernales, riverboats go south to Tucupita.

BUS

Several bus companies servicing Güiria have their offices close to each other around the triangular Plaza Sucre, where the Carúpano highway enters the town.

There are six buses a day to Caracas, departing in the early morning and late afternoon (US$14 to US$25, 12 hours). They all go via Cumaná (US$7, five hours) and Puerto La Cruz (US$9, 6½ hours). *Por puestos* run frequently to Carúpano (US$5, two hours) from Plaza Sucre.

ISLA DE MARGARITA

☎ 0295 / pop 350,000

Isla de Margarita is Venezuela's isle of tourism. Sun-seekers and bargain-hunters come from the world over for its top-notch beaches and rock-bottom duty-free prices. Charter flights and package tours besiege the island from all directions. It is an urbanized and highly developed beach vacation experience replete with fancy restaurants, high-rise international hotel chains and, again, plenty of shopping.

However, Margarita is large enough and has enough variety to still satisfy the interests of independently minded travelers. It showcases a spectrum of habitats, from mangrove swamps to mountainous cloud forest and desert. Margarita is also a world-class snorkeling, windsurfing and kitesurfing destination.

Getting There & Away

AIR

Almost all the major national airlines fly into **Aeropuerto Internacional del Caribe General Santiago Mariño** (☎ 269-1027). There are about 20 flights a day to Caracas with various carriers, including Aeropostal, Aserca and Avior. The normal one-way fare is US$60 to US$100, but discounted fares – sometimes as low as US$35 – are occasionally available, so shop around. There are scheduled direct flights to Barcelona (US$50), Carúpano (US$40), Cumaná (US$40), Maracay (US$80 to US$100), Valencia (US$60 to US$80) and Maturín (US$40 to US$60) among others, and indirect flights to just about anywhere else in the country. Aereotuy and Rutaca fly to Los Roques (US$100 to US$200). Avior flies direct to Port of Spain, Trinidad (US$200 to US$225 round trip).

The following airline offices are located in Porlamar:

Aeropostal (☎ 263-9374; www.aeropostal.com; Centro Comercial Galerías, Av 4 de Mayo)

Linea Turistica Aereotuy (LTA; ☎ 415-5778; www.tuy.com/aereotuy.htm; Av Santiago Mariño)

Aserca (☎ 269-1460; www.asercaairlines.com; Centro Comercial Galerías, Av 4 de Mayo)

Avior (☎ 263-8615; www.avioairlines.com; Av 4 de Mayo)

Laser (☎ 263-9195; www.laser.com.ve; Calle Zamora)

Rutaca (☎ 263-9236; www.rutaca.com.ve; Calle Cedeño)

BOAT

Isla de Margarita has links with the mainland via Puerto La Cruz and Cumaná from the ferry terminal, Punta de Piedras (29km west of Porlamar), and also has small boats to Chacopata from Porlamar itself. Small buses regularly shuttle between Punta de Piedras and Calle Mariño in Porlamar.

This route from Puerto La Cruz is served by **Conferry** (Map p1032; ☎ 261-6780; www.conferry.com in Spanish; Calle Marcano, Porlamar; ☽ 8am-noon & 2-5pm Mon-Fri, 8am-noon Sat), which has several departures daily. Check the website for exact times and dates. Regular ferries cost from US$8 to US$11 for adults (depending on class) and cars are US$18 to US$23 (depending on size); the trip takes about 4½ hours. Express ferries cost US$20 to US$29 for adults, and cars are US$33 to US$46; the trip takes two hours.

The route is also operated by the passenger-only hydrofoil, **Gran Cacique Express** (☎ 264-2945; www.grancacique.com.ve; Edificio Blue Sky, Av Santiago Mariño, Porlamar; ☽ 8am-noon & 2-6pm Mon-Fri, 8am-2pm Sat), with two departures per day at 7am and 4pm (US$19, two hours). On all ferries, children aged two to seven and seniors over 65 pay half price. Gran Cacique also offers a ferry service from Cumaná, with two to three departures daily (US$18 to US$20, two hours).

ISLA DE MARGARITA

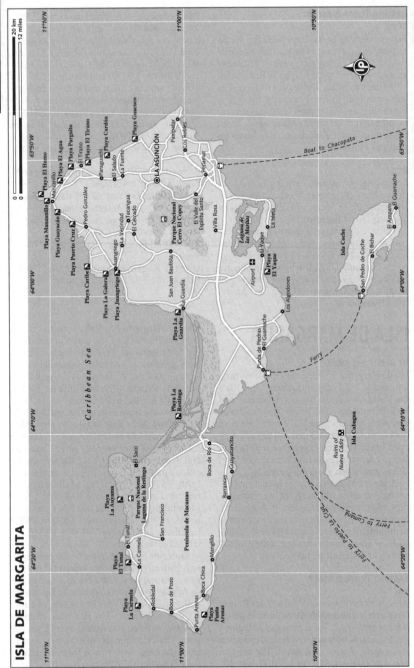

Naviarca (☎ 239-8439; www.grancacique.com.ve) also offers service from Cumaná, with one to two daily departures (adults US$13, cars US$22 to US$28; 3½ hours). Naviarca tickets are only available at Punta de Piedras (☎ 239-8439).

PORLAMAR

☎ 0295 / pop 105,000

Porlamar is Margarita's largest and busiest city and is likely to be your first stop when you arrive from the mainland. Tree-shaded Plaza Bolívar is Porlamar's historic center, but the city is rapidly expanding eastward, with new suburbs, tourist facilities, hotels and restaurants creeping along the coast towards Pampatar.

Information

Stores will accept cash dollars for payment using the official exchange rate. Credit cards are widely accepted in shops, upmarket hotels and restaurants. There are *casas de cambio* in the airport and in the city.

Banco de Venezuela (Blvd Guevara)

Banesco (Av 4 de Mayo)

Centro de Conexiones (Calle Velázquez; ☒ 8am-8pm Mon-Thu, 8am-midnight Fri & Sat, 8am-noon Sun) Internet access.

Corpotur (☎ 262-2322; corpoturmargarita@cantv.net; Centro Artesanal Gilberto Menchini, Av Jóvito Villalba, Los Robles; ☒ 8:30am-12:30pm & 1:30-5:30pm Mon-Fri) This government-run tourist office is midway between Porlamar and Pampatar.

DIEX (☎ 263-4766; Calle Arismendi No 7-85; ☒ 7am-noon & 1-4:30pm Mon-Fri) This is the place to get visa or tourist-card extensions. Ask here or at the tourist office for foreign-consulate representatives in Margarita.

Digicom (Calle Fermín; ☒ 8am-8pm Mon-Sat) Internet.

Ipostel (☎ 416-3583; Calle Maneiro; ☒ 8am-noon & 1-4:30pm Mon-Fri)

Sleeping

Porlamar has plenty of hotels at every price. Most cheap spots are in the historic center, particularly to the west and south of Plaza Bolívar.

Hotel España (☎ 261-2479; Calle Mariño; s/d US$4.50/6) This is the cheapest accommodation near the waterfront. It is also one of the lowest-quality accommodations near the waterfront. España isn't a bad choice if you're the kind of person who doesn't plan to spend a lot of time in the room.

Hotel Malecón (☎ 263-8888; Calle La Marina; s/d US$6.50/7.50) Malecón is one of the friendliest places in the more affordable Colonial side of town. It has quirky, narrow passageways and sunny beaches, some overlooking the sea.

Hotel Central (☎ 264-7162; Blvd Gómez; d/tr US$9/12.50; ❄) Located on a bustling boulevard with a large balcony from which to watch the world go by, this is a quiet, family-run affair that sees few travelers. Rooms have little natural light.

Hotel Tamaca (☎ 261-1602; tamaca@unete.com.ve; Av Raúl Leoni; s/d with fan US$11/13.50, with air-con & hot water US$14/17, tr with air-con & hot water US$21-24; ❄) The most popular backpacker hotel in the more upmarket eastern side of Porlamar – and deservedly so. It has a wide variety of basic rooms, and the hotel has its own bar-cum-restaurant surrounded by trees and lit with multicolored lights in the evening.

Eating

Budget eateries are plentiful across the city, particularly in the old town.

Panadería 4 de Mayo (Calle Fermín at 4 de Mayo; snacks & sandwiches US60¢-$1; ☒ 7am-11pm) The most popular of several bustling bakeries in the vicinity, 4 de Mayo has beautiful pastries, sandwiches and cakes with as much cream and strawberries as you can eat, and its terrace is Porlamar's top people-watching spot.

Restaurant Punto Criollo (☎ 263-6745; Calle Igualdad 19; mains US$3-6; ☒ 11am-midnight; ❄) Deservedly popular with locals for its Venezuelan food and budget prices, this large, no-nonsense restaurant has a lengthy bit-of-everything menu, smartly bow-tied waiters and a long drinks list.

Hotel Tamaca (☎ 261-1602; Av Raúl Leoni; mains US$3-8) Tamaca's tiny garden bar sees plenty of backpackers devouring pizza and downing a beer in the evening.

La Casa de Rubén (☎ 264-5969; Final Av Santiago Mariño; mains US$4-9; ☒ noon-10pm Mon-Sat) Somewhat hidden from the road, this homestyle restaurant serves all the typical Margariteña seafood dishes. Add your thoughts to the growing collection of customers' scribbles on the walls.

Cocody Restaurant (☎ 261-8431; Av Raúl Leoni; mains US$13-19; ☒ 6-11:30pm Thu-Tue; ❄) Run by a friendly French family, this romantic beachfront restaurant offers excellent European cuisine. Choose from seafood crepes, beef kebabs or fettuccine with salmon and asparagus. There are French wines to sip, or even (expensive) Perrier. The three-course menu costs US$23.

Drinking

Bars appear and disappear at lightning speed in Margarita, so check locally for the latest

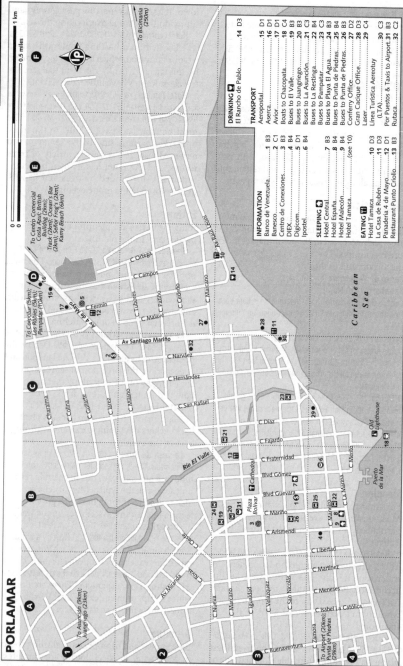

PORLAMAR

hot spots. There's always a collection of rustic shacks, well stocked with cold beers, on the beach. Most of the trendy nightclubs and bars are outside the city center.

British Bulldog (☎ 267-1527; Centro Comercial Costa Azul, Av Bolívar; ✆ 9pm-late Thu-Sat, in high season 9pm-late Tue-Sat) Margarita's first and only British-style pub, with a cheerful British-Venezuelan running the show behind the bar. It often has live rock music at weekends.

El Rancho de Pablo (☎ 263-1121; Av Raúl Leoni; mains US$5-9; ✆ 9am-11pm Wed-Mon) It's hard not to slip into a mellow mood at El Rancho de Pablo, a beachside bar and restaurant. There are several other options nearby, but this one also serves good seafood.

Kamy Beach (✆ 808-6066; Av Aldonza Marique, Playa Varadera; ✆ 11pm-4am Thu-Sat, nightly in high season) This slick, beachside nightclub has a distinct tropical feel, with swaying palms, thatched-roof bars and square beds (with romantic curtains) on the sand. White lounge sofas and airy terraces overlook the beach – great for chilling out and listening to the waves. Live bands and DJs also.

Señor Frog's (☎ 262-0451; Centro Comercial Costa Azul, Av Bolívar; ✆ 6pm-late Tue-Sun) This gimmicky family restaurant by day becomes a thumping Latin pop–orientated disco by night.

Getting Around

Small buses, locally called *micros* or *carritos*, run frequently throughout most of the island, including to Pampatar, La Asunción and Juangriego. They leave from different points in the city center; departure points for some of the main tourist destinations are indicated on the map. For sportier visitors, **Bicimania** (☎ 262-9116; bicimania@cantv.net; Centro Commercial AB; ✆ 9am-1pm & 4:30-7pm Mon-Fri, 9am-3pm Sat), east of town, rents out bicycles.

PAMPATAR

☎ 0295 / pop 35,000

Pampatar is just 10km northeast of Porlamar and the two towns are gradually melding into one. Pampatar was one of the earliest settlements on Margarita and once the most important port in what was to become Venezuela. It still has some colonial buildings and a nostalgic hint of faded glory. Pampatar's fort, the **Castillo de San Carlos Borromeo** (admission free; ✆ 8am-6pm), is in the center of town, on the waterfront. It was built from 1662 to 1684 on the site of a previous stronghold that was destroyed by pirates.

Few travelers stay in Pampatar, but there are several budget lodgings on Calle Almirante Brion, one block back from the beach. You'll also find many open-air eateries along the beach. Buses between Porlamar and Pampatar run every five to 10 minutes (US25¢, 20 minutes).

JUANGRIEGO

☎ 0295 / pop 24,500

This smaller town, famous for its burning golden sunsets, shows a side of Margarita quite different from busy Porlamar. Set on the edge of a fine bay in the northern part of the island, Juangriego is a relaxing place to hang out on the beach, with rustic fishing boats, visiting yachts and pelicans. The sun sets over the peaks of Macanao far off on the horizon.

Juangriego is increasingly catering to tourism.

El Caney (☎ 253-5059; Calle Guevara 17; d/tr US$10/15) is a colorful little Peruvian-run *posada*. Nice touches include a palm-thatched terrace out front, and a pool table out back.

About 200m north along the beach, the French-run **Hotel Patrick's** (☎ 253-6218; Calle El Fuerte; d/tr US$12.50/19; ✆) offers nine clean rooms, and continental food.

Strangely located at the back of the small Centro Comercial Juangriego, and just back from the beach, is the uninspiring but cheap **Hotel Gran Sol** (☎ 253-3216; Calle La Marina; d/t/q US$17/19/21; ✆). The 19 rooms are plain, old and dark.

Restaurants and bars line the beachfront, all perfectly positioned to keep sunset-watchers fed and watered with romantic suppers and cold beer. They include the recommended **El Viejo Muelle** (☎ 253-2962; Calle La Marina; mains US$4-8; ✆ 10am-11pm) and **Brisas Marinas** (☎ 253-0791; mains US$7-14; Calle La Marina; ✆ 10am-9pm).

BEACHES

Isla de Margarita has some 50 beaches large enough to deserve a name, not to mention a number of other unnamed little stretches of sand. Many beaches are built up with restaurants, bars and other facilities. Though the island is no longer a virgin paradise, you can still search out a relatively deserted spot if you look hard enough.

Playa El Agua

This has been Margarita's trendiest beach for a few years. It's full of stylish Venezuelans and gawking hordes, though the true trendsetters have moved on to less-developed beaches. During holidays, the beach can get crammed with visitors but at other times it's a welcoming and wonderfully laid-back spot. It is generally an upmarket place, but there are some budget options in the back streets.

For tidy rooms at one of the lowest prices in town, the tiny, family-run **Chalets de Belén** (☎ 249-1707; Calle Miragua 3; d with fan US$16, with air-con US$19, 6-person cabin with fan US$32; P 🐕) comes recommended. The chalets are only a short walk from the beach.

La Isla Restaurant (☎ 249-0035; mains US$5-10; 🕙 9am-11pm) is an excellent thatched-roof spot right on the beach.

Playa El Yaque

Playa El Yaque, located south of the airport, has tranquil waters and steady winds that are perfect for **windsurfing** and **kitesurfing**. The beach has already gained an international reputation and is a hangout for the windsurfing community from Venezuela and Europe (don't be surprised to see prices in euros). Several professional outfits on the beachfront offer windsurf rental (per hour/day/two days US$15/45/75). They also offer lessons at US$35 per hour, or US$150 for an advanced course of 10 hours. As for kitesurfing, you can find lessons here for US$39/180 for 1½/six hours. Kitesurfing rental costs US$165 for 10 hours.

Other Beaches

Other popular beaches include **Playa Guacuco** and **Playa Manzanillo**. Perhaps Margarita's finest beach is **Playa Puerto Cruz**, which arguably has the island's widest, whitest stretch of sand and still isn't overdeveloped. **Playa Parguito**, next to Playa El Agua, has strong waves good for surfing. If you want to escape from people, head for **Península de Macanao**, the wildest part of the island.

GUAYANA

It is here in the southeastern region of Guayana (not to be confused with the country Guyana) that Venezuela is at its exotic best. The area is home to the world's highest waterfall, Angel Falls; the impossibly lush Canaima National Park; the wildlife rich Orinoco River Delta and Río Caura; the Venezuelan Amazon and La Gran Sabana (The Great Savanna)

where *tepui* flat-topped mountains lord over rolling grasslands. It is common for visitors to spend an entire trip in this area of the country.

The majority of the country's indigenous groups live in Guayana, including the Warao, Pemón and Yanomami, which constitute about 10% of the region's total population.

CIUDAD BOLÍVAR
☎ 0285 / pop 350,000

Most people visit Ciudad Bolívar as the jumping-off point to explore Canaima National Park, Angel Falls and Guayana's various other treasures. Upon arrival in the bus station or airport, Ciudad Bolívar deceptively looks like just another hectic mass of boxy concrete buildings. However, the surprisingly large and attractive *casco histórico* (historic core) has retained the flavor of an old river town and conserved its colonial-era architecture. It is worth spending an extra day or two to walk around the old town, sip a coffee, shop the street stalls, eat some *arepas* and get a feel for Ciudad Bolívar itself.

Information

All internet cafés charge approximately US70¢ per hour.

Banco de Venezuela (cnr Paseo Orinoco & Calle Piar)
Banco Mercantil (cnr Paseo Orinoco & Calle Zaraza)
Banesco (cnr Calles Dalla Costa & Venezuela)
CANTV (cnr Paseo Orinoco & Calle Dalla Costa) Telephones.
Chat Café Boulevard (cnr Calle Bolívar & Calle Igualdad) Internet.
Galaxia.com (Centro Comercial Abboud Center, Paseo Orinoco btwn Calles Piar & Roscio) For internet.
Hospital Ruiz y Páez (☎ 632-4146; Av Germania)
Ipostel (Av Táchira btwn Avs Cruz Verde & Guasipati)

Sights

Plaza Bolívar is the colonial heart of the city. **Paseo Orinoco**, the lively waterfront, is lined with old arcaded houses, some of which go back to the days of Bolívar. The iconic **Puente de Angostura**, a suspension bridge 5km upriver from the city, is the only bridge to cross the Orinoco at any point.

The **Museo de Arte Moderno Jesús Soto** (☎ 632-0518; cnr Av Germania & Av Briceño Iragorry; admission free; 🕙 9:30am-5:30pm Tue-Fri, 10am-5pm Sat & Sun) has an extensive collection of kinetic works by this internationally renowned artist.

In front of the airport terminal stands the **airplane of Jimmie Angel** that landed atop what was eventually named Angel Falls.

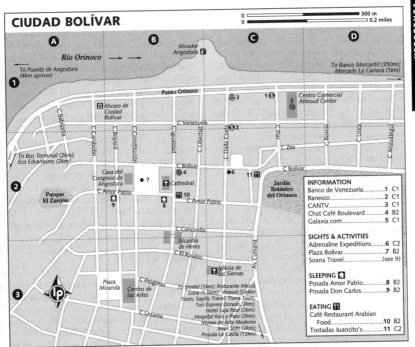

CIUDAD BOLÍVAR

INFORMATION
Banco de Venezuela..............1 C1
Banesco.................................2 C1
CANTV...................................3 C1
Chat Café Boulevard.............4 B2
Galaxia.com...........................5 C1

SIGHTS & ACTIVITIES
Adrenaline Expeditions..........6 C2
Plaza Bolívar.........................7 B2
Soana Travel....................(see 9)

SLEEPING
Posada Amor Patrio...............8 B2
Posada Don Carlos................9 B2

EATING
Café Restaurant Arabian
Food.................................10 B2
Tostadas Juancito's..............11 C2

Tours

Ciudad Bolívar is the departure point for tours to Canaima (Angel Falls), Río Caura and onward travel to Santa Elena (Roraima). A few of the many options:

Adrenaline Expeditions (☎ 632-4804, 0414-886-7209; adrenalinexptours@hotmail.com; Calle Dalla Costa; ⏰ 24hr) Adrenaline is an adventure-oriented agency that does its best to cater to the needs of budget travelers. It has good Río Caura, Canaima and Gran Sabana tours and is extremely helpful with regional travel information.

Eco Edventures (☎ 651-9546, 0414-893-1318; ecoad venturebess@hotmail.com; bus terminal, cnr Avs República & Sucre) Friendly agency hidden in a passageway at the bus terminal.

Gekko Tours (☎ 632-3223, 0414-854-5146; www.gek kotours-venezuela.de; airport terminal) Run by Posada La Casita, Gekko is a responsible agency offering a wide range of quality tours across the region and the country.

Sapito Tours (☎ 0414-854-8234; www.sapitotours .com; airport terminal) Representative of Bernal Tours from Canaima.

Soana Travel (☎ 632-6017, 0414-854-6616; soana travel@gmx.de; Posada Don Carlos, cnr Calles Boyacá & Amor Patrio) Based at the Posada Don Carlos, Soana specializes in Río Caura tours.

Tiuna Tours (☎ 632-8697, 0414-893-3003; tiunatours@ hotmail.com; airport terminal) Ciudad Bolívar's office of the major Canaima operator.

Turi Express Dorado (☎ 632-7086, 0414-893-9576; turiexpressdorado.com; airport terminal) Long-standing, respectable company with good offers and reasonable prices.

Sleeping

Ciudad Bolívar has some lovely *posadas*. As it happens, they are all run by Germans.

Posada La Casita (☎ 623-3223, 0414-854-5146; www .gekkotours-venezuela.de; Urbanización 24 de Julio; camping per person US$4, hammocks US$6, s/d/tr US$14/18/24; P ✖ ▯ ☀ ☀) A good decompression point between the city and Canaima National Park, La Casita is set on spacious grounds past the airport. Its full range of accommodations includes tidy bungalows. There is free 24-hour pick-up from the airport and a shuttle to town.

Posada Amor Patrio (☎ 632-4485, 0414-854-4925; plazabolivar@hotmail.com; Calle Amor Patrio; hammocks US$5, d/tr US$12/16) Right behind the cathedral, in a historic house, this *posada* is popular with backpackers and has rooms with fan and shared bathrooms. Guests can use the kitchen.

Posada Don Carlos (☎ 632-6017, 0414-854-6616; www.hosteltrail.com/posadadoncarlos; Calle Boyacá; d with fan/air-con US$14/25; P ☒ ☐) In a meticulously restored historic mansion with two ample patios, this newer *posada* has neat, clean accommodations along with a bar with antique German furniture.

Hotel Laja Real (☎ 617-0100; www.lajareal.com; cnr Avs Andrés Bello & Jesús Soto; s/d/tr US$36/42/47; P ☒ ☒) This is the place to stay if you are in transit and need to be close to the airport – like, directly across the street. It also happens to be one of the nicer places in town, with fair-sized rooms with fridge and hot water.

Eating & Drinking

The city center is full of cheap eateries.

Tostadas Juancito's (☎ 632-6173; cnr Av Cumaná & Calle Bolívar; set meal US$2-3, arepas US$1; ☯ 6:30am-6:30pm) This popular *arepa* and snack bar has occupied this busy street corner forever. It is the place to hang out with local characters, have a beer and watch the city pass by.

Mercado La Carioca (Paseo Orinoco; mains US$2-4; ☯ lunch) Popularly called 'La Sapoara,' this market at the eastern end of the Paseo Orinoco has several simple restaurants lining the riverfront, which serve inexpensive meals. The fish comes straight from the river.

Café Restaurant Arabian Food (☎ 632-7208; cnr Calles Amor Patrio & Igualdad; mains US$2-5; ☯ 7am-8:30pm) Vegetarians take heart, you have not been forsaken. This small family-run café ramps up at noon with hearty lentil soup chock-full of greens, and filling falafels, while omnivores can chow down on shawarma and kebabs.

Ristorante Mezza Luna (☎ 632-0524; cnr Av Táchira & Bolívar; pasta & pizza US$5-7, mains US$7-10) Ciudad Bolívar's pizza and pasta place, Mezza Luna is also a smart choice to escape the heat of the day.

Getting There & Away

AIR

The **Aeropuerto Ciudad Bolívar** (☎ 632-4803; Av Jesús Soto) is 2km southeast of the riverfront and is linked to the city center by local transport. Avior and Rutaca fly daily to Caracas (US$50 to US$80). There are plenty of tour operators with flights to Canaima (see Tours, p1035).

BUS

The **Terminal de Pasajeros** (cnr Avs República & Sucre) is 1.5km south of the center. To get there, take the westbound *buseta* marked 'Terminal' from Paseo Orinoco.

Plenty of buses go to Caracas (US$11 to US$16, nine hours, 591km); most depart in the evening. There are also direct buses to Maracay (US$11 to US$16, 9½ hours, 627km) and Valencia (US$12 to US$17, 10½ hours, 676km), which don't go through Caracas, but via the shorter Los Llanos route. Take these if you want to go to Venezuela's northwest or the Andes and avoid connections in Caracas.

Buses to Puerto La Cruz (US$6 to US$8, four hours, 302km) run every hour or two. A dozen buses a day go to Puerto Ayacucho (US$10 to US$13, 10 to 12 hours, 728km). To Ciudad Guayana (US$1.50, 1½ hours, 115km), buses depart every 15 to 30 minutes.

Several bus companies operate buses to Santa Elena de Uairén (US$11 to US$19, 10 to 12 hours, 716km), with a total of eight departures daily.

CIUDAD GUAYANA

☎ 286

Ciudad Guayana is not just set on two rivers, Río Orinoco and Río Caroní, but is, in fact, two cities. It comprises the old colonial town of **San Félix**, on the eastern side of the Caroní, and the newish port of **Puerto Ordaz**, on the opposite bank. The two parts couldn't be more different: San Félix is a polluted commercial sector, with frenzied, crowded and sometimes unsafe streets, while Puerto Ordaz is the well-laid-out, clean and somewhat modern home to the middle and upper classes.

Locals generally refer to 'San Félix' or 'Puerto Ordaz,' and tend to disregard the official title of 'Ciudad Guayana.' So don't bother to ask for Ciudad Guayana at a bus station or travel agency, because the place is little more than a name.

Information

Puerto Ordaz has plenty of internet facilities and they are usually fast and cheap (US60¢ to US80¢):

Banco de Venezuela (cnr Avs Las Américas & Monseñor Zabaleta)

Banco Mercantil (cnr Av Ciudad Bolívar & Vía Venezuela)

CANTV (Carrera Padre Palacios, Puerto Ordaz) Telephone.

Info Ware House (Centro Comercial Topacio, Carrera Upata) Internet.

Sleeping

Both San Félix and Puerto Ordaz have a range of hotels, but it's advisable to stay in the latter for convenience, surroundings and security.

La Casa del Lobo (☎ 961-6286; lobo_travel@yahoo.de; Calle Zambia No 2, Villa Africana, Manzana 39; s/d US$10/14; 🖵) This German-owned house rents out four rooms with fan and bathroom and prepares great meals on request. It also provides a free pickup service from the Puerto Ordaz bus terminal, or take a taxi (US$3). It's a friendly, good-value place to stay.

Posada Turística Kaori (☎ 923-4038; kaoriposada @cantv.net; Calle Argentina, Campo B; d/tr US$20/22; P 🍴 🖵) This smart *posada*, within walking distance of the center, has reasonable standards, is quiet and has hot water.

Residencia Ambato 19 (☎ 923-2072; Calle Ambato No 19; d US$24; P 🍴) This small family-run *posada* has no name on the door, just a number. It has seven tranquil and spotless rooms, all with a

double bed and bathroom. It's often full, so call and check for vacancies.

Posada San Miguel (☎ 924-9385; Calle Moitaco; d US$30-40, tr US$70; 🍴 🖵) A centrally located option with nifty perks like free morning coffee and internet access. The rooms are clean and tastefully decorated, although only the upstairs rooms have exterior windows.

Eating

All the places listed are in Puerto Ordaz's center.

Boulevar de la Comida Guayanesa (Calle Guasipati; meals US$2-4; ☽ breakfast & lunch) This is a line of 12 or so food kiosks serving typical local fare on the street sidewalk. The food is cooked in front of you in a marketlike atmosphere.

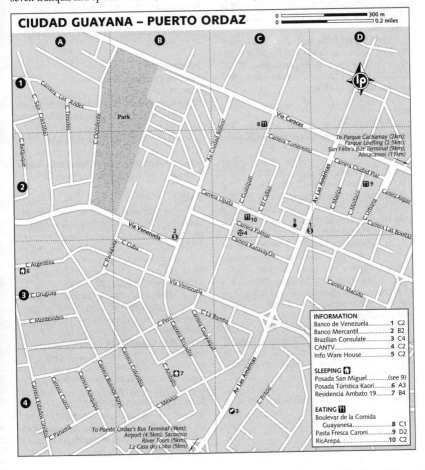

CIUDAD GUAYANA – PUERTO ORDAZ

0 — 300 m
0 — 0.2 miles

Park

Via Caracas

To Parque Cachamay (2km);
Parque Loefling (2.5km);
San Félix's Bus Terminal (9km);
Almacaroni (11km)

To Puerto Ordaz's Bus Terminal (4km);
Airport (4.5km); Sacoroco
River Tours (5km);
La Casa del Lobo (5km)

INFORMATION
Banco de Venezuela..............1 C2
Banco Mercantil.....................2 B2
Brazilian Consulate...............3 C4
CANTV...................................4 C2
Info Ware House....................5 C2

SLEEPING 🛌
Posada San Miguel............(see 9)
Posada Túristica Kaori.........6 A3
Residencia Ambato 19........7 B4

EATING 🍴
Boulevar de la Comida
Guayanesa.....................8 C1
Pasta Fresca Caroni............9 D2
RicArepa............................10 C2

RicArepa (☎ 923-1483; Carrera Upata; arepas US$3-4; ⓨ 24hr) Choose from almost two dozen types of fillings in this buzzing *arepera* that never closes.

Pasta Fresca Caroní (☎ 922-1587; Calle Moitaco; pasta US$4-6; ⓨ 11:30am-3pm) Mix and match with a dozen types of fresh pasta and 15 yummy sauces. The dining room is spare, with plastic chairs, red-and-white tablecloths and florescent lighting.

Getting There & Away

AIR

The **Aeropuerto Puerto Ordaz** (Av Guayana) is at the western end of Puerto Ordaz on the road to Ciudad Bolívar. Buses marked 'Sidor Directo' from Alta Vista will leave you at the terminal's entrance. Note that the airport appears in all schedules as 'Puerto Ordaz,' not 'Ciudad Guayana.'

Puerto Ordaz is the busiest air hub in eastern Venezuela and is serviced by most major domestic airlines, including **Aeropostal** (☎ 0800-284-6637), **Aserca** (☎ 962-9229), **Avior** (☎ 953-0064) and **Rutaca** (☎ 951-6904).

BUS

Ciudad Guayana has two bus terminals. The **Terminal de Pasajeros San Félix** (Av José Gumilla), about 1km south of San Félix's center, is the city's main terminal. Its environs can be unsafe, particularly after dark, so don't walk there; take a bus or taxi. Plenty of urban buses pass by the bus terminal on their way between Puerto Ordaz and San Félix, but they become infrequent after 8pm and stop running around 9pm. If you arrive later, you'll need a taxi to move around.

The **Terminal de Pasajeros Puerto Ordaz** (Av Guayana) is 1km east of the airport. It's smaller, cleaner, quieter and safer, but handles far fewer buses than the San Félix station. It's essentially a pick-up/drop-off spot rather than the final bus destination or departure point, and not all buses pass through here.

From the San Félix terminal, buses to Caracas (US$13 to US$18, 10½ hours, 706km) depart either in the morning or, mostly, in the evening, and most of them stop en route at the Puerto Ordaz terminal. There are also direct buses to Maracay (US$13 to US$18, 11 hours, 742km) and Valencia (US$14 to US$19, 12 hours, 791km). They don't pass through Caracas, but take a shorter route via Los Llanos. They are convenient if you wish to go straight to Venezuela's northwest or the Andes, avoiding spending time and money on connections in Caracas.

Eight buses daily come through from Ciudad Bolívar on their way to Santa Elena de Uairén (US$10 to US$17, nine to 11 hours, 601km); all call at San Félix, but only a few stop in Puerto Ordaz. Buses to Ciudad Bolívar depart from both terminals every half hour or so (US$1.50, 1½ hours, 115km).

TUCUPITA
☎ 0287 / pop 70,000

Originally founded in the 1920s as a Capuchin mission to convert the local indigenous population to Catholicism, Tucupita is now a steamy river port and the only sizable town in the Delta del Orinoco. You can take a pleasant stroll around the central streets and along Paseo Mánamo, the riverbank esplanade, but Tucupita is mainly visited as a base for exploring the delta.

Information

Banco de Venezuela (Calle Mánamo)
Banesco (Calle Petión)
Biblos (Calle Centurión) Internet. Fast connections.
Compucenter.com (Centro Comercial Delta Center, Plaza Bolívar) Internet access.
Ipostel (Calle Pativilca) For all your postal needs.
Mi Casa (Plaza Bolívar) Convenient ATM on the main plaza.
Servicio Autónomo Fondo de Turismo del Estado Amacuro (Av Arismendi; ⓨ 8am-3pm Mon-Fri)

Tours

All local tour operators focus on trips into the delta. Tours are usually all-inclusive two-to four-day excursions and the going rate is US$40 to US$80 per person a day. All the companies have *campamentos* (camps) that serve as a base for trips around the area.
Aventura Turística Delta (☎ 0416-897-2285; a_t_d_1973@hotmail.com; Calle Centurión) The most popular company with travelers, and probably the more affordable. The facilities are simple and its two basic camps have hammocks only.
Cooperativa Osibu XIV (☎ 721-3840; cnr Calles Mariño & Pativilca) The oldest local tour company, operating since 1987, and the only one that offers tours to the far eastern part of the delta. Its Campamento Maraisa, in San Francisco de Guayo, has *cabañas* with beds and bathrooms.
Tucupita Expeditions (☎ 721-0801; www.orinoco delta.com; Calle Las Acacias) Just 700m east of the center, this is possibly the most expensive agency. It works principally with organized groups and generally doesn't focus on individual travelers.

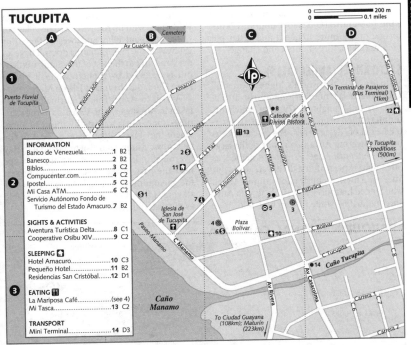

TUCUPITA

INFORMATION
Banco de Venezuela..............1 B2
Banesco.................................2 B2
Biblos..................................3 C2
Compucenter.com.................4 C2
Ipostel................................5 C2
Mi Casa ATM........................6 C2
Servicio Autónomo Fondo de
 Turismo del Estado Amacuro.7 B2

SIGHTS & ACTIVITIES
Aventura Turística Delta..........8 C1
Cooperative Osibu XIV...........9 C2

SLEEPING
Hotel Amacuro....................10 C3
Pequeño Hotel.....................11 B2
Residencias San Cristóbal......12 D1

EATING
La Mariposa Café.............(see 4)
Mi Tasca.............................13 C2

TRANSPORT
Mini Terminal......................14 D3

Sleeping & Eating

There are four or five hotels in the town center, and a few more outside the central area. None are great. There are many basic and inexpensive places not worth naming here.

Pequeño Hotel (☎ 721-0523; Calle La Paz; d with fan US$6-8, with air-con US$8-10, tr with fan/air-con US$10/12; ☒) The family-run Pequeño Hotel has dim rooms and lumpy beds, but is just about the cheapest place in town and has a homey atmosphere. The *señora* locks the door at 10pm and goes to bed, so don't be late.

Residencias San Cristóbal (☎ 721-4529; Calle San Cristóbal; d US$8-9, tr US$10; P ☒) Not really central, the 40-room San Cristóbal is otherwise cheap and good value. It has revamped private bathrooms and new mattresses. Choose a room upstairs.

Hotel Amacuro (☎ 721-0404; Calle Bolívar; d/tr with fan US$10/14, with air-con US$14/20; ☒) Just off Plaza Bolívar, Amacuro is nothing special, but has reasonably clean, good-sized rooms, and a large terrace on which to sip cold beer and relax.

Mi Tasca (☎ 721-0428; Calle Dalla Costa; mains US$3-6; ☒ 11am-10:30pm) Ask most locals where to go for a lunch or dinner, and they'll send you to Mi Tasca. Tucupita's best eatery has a varied menu, good prices, generous portions and quick service. Try the *lau lau* (catfish).

La Mariposa Café (☎ 721-3810; Centro Comercial Delta Center, Plaza Bolívar; mains US$6-10; ☒ 7am-10:30pm Mon-Sat, 7am-9pm Sun) A new and welcoming culinary oasis. Its *comidas internacionales* include a variety of cuisines, from stroganoff to steak tartar, Greek salad to pollo 'Gordon Blue.' It also serves vegetarian pastas and soups and makes fresh juices to order.

Getting There & Away

The **Terminal de Pasajeros** (cnr Carrera 6 & Calle 10) is 1km southeast of the center; walk or take a taxi (US$1). The **Mini Terminal** (Calle Tucupita) handles local and suburban bus traffic.

Five buses nightly make a run to Caracas (US$13 to US$18, 11 hours, 730km) via Maturín. Expresos La Guayanesa has two buses daily to Ciudad Guayana (US$4, 3½ hours, 137km), but faster *por puestos* (US$6, 2½ hours) serve this route regularly. The trip includes a ferry ride across the Río Orinoco from Los Barrancos to San Félix (no extra charge).

For Caripe and Cueva del Guácharo, take a bus to Maturín (US$5, four hours, 217km), or one of the more frequent and faster *por puestos* (US$8, three hours), and change.

SALTO ÁNGEL (ANGEL FALLS)

Salto Ángel is the world's highest waterfall and Venezuela's number-one tourist attraction. Its total height is 979m, of which the uninterrupted drop is 807m, about 16 times the height of Niagara Falls. The cascade pours off the towering Auyantepui, one of the largest of the *tepuis*. Angel Falls is not named, as one might expect, after a divine creature, but after an American bush pilot Jimmie Angel, who landed his four-seater airplane atop Auyantepui in 1937 while in search of gold.

The waterfall is situated in a distant, lush wilderness with no road access. The village of Canaima, about 50km northwest, is the major gateway to the falls. Canaima doesn't have an overland link to the rest of the country either, but is accessed by numerous small planes from Ciudad Bolívar and Isla de Margarita.

A visit to Angel Falls is normally undertaken in two stages, with Canaima as the stepping-stone. Most tourists fly into Canaima, where they take a light plane or boat to the falls. Most visitors who visit by boat opt to stay overnight in hammocks at one of the camps near the base of the falls. The trip upriver, the surrounding area and the experience of staying at the camp are nearly as memorable as the waterfall itself.

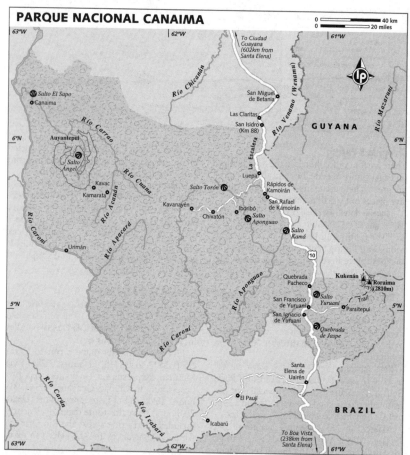

Salto Ángel, Auyantepui, Canaima and the surrounding area lie within the boundaries of 30,000 sq km Parque Nacional Canaima. All visitors coming to Canaima pay a US$8 national-park entrance fee.

CANAIMA

☎ 0286 / pop 1500

Canaima is a mixture of indigenous village and tourist center that serves as a base for Angel Falls. It lies on a peaceful, wide stretch of Río Carrao known as Laguna de Canaima, just below the point where the river turns into a line of seven magnificent falls. Rather than being jaded by the mass of arriving tourists, locals are friendly and welcoming to foreigners.

The waterfalls on Laguna de Canaima are an attraction in themselves, particularly Salto el Sapo, Sapito and Hacha. They can be visited by a short boat trip and hike, which allows you to walk behind some of the falls. The town also opens up onto a sandy beach on Laguna de Canaima. Be careful and don't swim close to the waterfalls or the water-processing plant.

Information

Tienda Canaima (☎ 962-0443, 0414-884-0940) A souvenir-cum-grocery shop near the airport that changes US dollars and traveler's checks for a bad rate. Most of Canaima's tour operators will accept payment in US dollars, but not credit cards, or will charge 10% more if you pay with plastic.

Wakü Lodge (☎ 962-5560; www.wakulodge.com; internet per hr US$10) The fanciest hotel in town and the only one that offers internet (a single computer in one of its lounges).

Tours

All Canaima-based tour companies run boat trips and can arrange flights. They also arrange lodging and meals. The main operators include the following:

Bernal Tours (☎ 632-7989, 0414-854-8234; www .bernaltours.com) Family-run company based on an island in Laguna de Canaima, where participants stay and eat before and after the tour. Bernal Tours has its *campamento* on Isla Ratoncito, opposite Angel Falls.

Tiuna Tours (☎ 962-4255, 0414-884-0502; tiunatours@ hotmail.com) The biggest and cheapest local player, with a large *campamento* in Canaima and another one up the Río Carrao at the Aonda.

Excursions Kavac (☎ 0414-853-2338; www.excursion eskavac.com) Agency managed by the indigenous Pemón community. Marginally cheaper than Bernal Tours, it too has its *campamento* in front of Angel Falls.

Sleeping & Eating

There are a dozen *campamentos* and *posadas* in Canaima. Most are managed by the tour agencies listed above and serve all meals inclusive.

Campamento Churúm (Kavac) (☎ 0414-899-3475, 0414-850-2686; ssmbelk@hotmail.com; hammocks/r per person US$5/13) Opposite the soccer pitch, this is the camp for the clients of Excursiones Kavac, but it often has vacancies available to all. It is clean, cool and puts you in touch with locals more than most other options can.

Campamento Tiuna (☎ 962-4255, 0414-884-0502; hammocks/r per person US$10/25) The *campamento* of Tiuna Tours is in a big stone building at the northern part of the village. It offers open beds and hammocks to independent tourists and can also provide meals. Inquire at the office in the Ciudad Bolívar airport.

Posada Wey Tupü (☎ 0414-895-4333, 0414-884-0585; r per person US$20) Opposite the school in the south part of the village, Wey Tupü is one of the best value places around. It has rooms with fans and bathrooms, and provides some of the cheapest meals for guests.

Posada Kusary (☎ 962-0443, 0414-884-0940; r per person US$30) This well-maintained *posada* has 14 rooms with fans and private facilities – inquire at the Tienda Canaima for vacancies and current rates.

Getting There & Away

Prices can change seasonally, so the following are averages: Avior flies between Caracas and Canaima (US$115 to US$135) a couple of days a week. Several regional carriers fly between Canaima and Ciudad Bolívar on a semiregular

VENEZUELA

or charter basis (US$50 to US$60). Various small airlines, including LTA, Sasca and Rutaca, go to and from Porlamar (US$120 to US$140); check LTA first – it's usually the cheapest carrier. Rutaca has daily flights between Canaima and Santa Elena de Uairén (US$145).

GRAN SABANA

The Gran Sabana (Great Savanna) is the green, undulating highland in the basin of the upper Río Caroní. The immense, empty region lies within the boundaries of Parque Nacional Canaima and is one of the country's most enchanting and unusual places. There is a certain beauty in the vast monotony of the savanna's rolling grasslands, though the landscape is broken up by the striking and unique *tepuis*. More than 100 of these plateau mountains dot the countryside from the Colombian border in the west to Guyana and Brazil in the east, but most of them are here in the Gran Sabana. The most famous *tepui*, Roraima, extends into Brazilian and Guyanese territory.

The only town in the Gran Sabana is Santa Elena de Uairén, close to the Brazilian border. The remainder of the sparsely populated region is inhabited mostly by the 15,000 indigenous Pemón people, who live in nearly 300 scattered villages.

Getting Around

The Ciudad Guayana–Santa Elena de Uairén Hwy provides access to this fascinating land, but public transport on this road is infrequent, making individual sightseeing inconvenient and time consuming. A comfortable solution

is a tour from Ciudad Bolívar (p1034) or Santa Elena de Uairén (p1043).

RORAIMA

Gran Sabana's greatest adventure destination, the massive table mountain of Roraima, is Venezuela's lost world and the highlight of most trips to the country. The challenging hike is worth every step and a stay atop the mountain is unforgettable.

Roraima was the first of the *tepuis* on which a climb was recorded (in 1884). It's the easiest table mountain to ascend and doesn't require any particular skills or technical climbing. It can be done by anyone who is reasonably fit and healthy (so long as porters carry the heavier gear), but it's still not an easy walk. It takes a minimum of five days to do the round trip, and you need camping equipment and food. Be prepared for a strenuous trek and some discomfort, including plenty of rain, cold and *puri puris* (invisible biting insects). The weather is always unpredictable.

Climbing Roraima

Roraima lies approximately 47km east of the El Dorado–Santa Elena highway, just east of San Francisco de Yuruaní. The hamlet of Paraitepui is the usual starting point for the trip. You can organize a compulsory guide in Santa Elena, San Francisco or Paraitepui. Most people opt to go on an organized tour (p1044) from Santa Elena, which contracts the guides and porters and arranges for meals, transportation and equipment.

The trip to the top normally takes two to three days (total net walking time is about 12 hours up and 10 hours down). There are sev-

---

THE LOST WORLD OF THE TEPUIS

Sir Arthur Conan Doyle's 1912 book *The Lost World* tells the story of an expedition to a plateau-like mountain in South America where dinosaurs and apepeople still survive. This novel was influenced by the mystique of Roraima in southeastern Venezuela. Roraima, and more than 100 or so other mountains like it, are what is known as *tepuis*.

'Tepui' (also spelled 'tepuy') is a Pemón Indian word for 'mountain,' and it has been adopted internationally as the term to identify this specific type of table mountain. Geologically, these sandstone tablelands are the remnants of a thick layer of sediments (some two billion years old) that gradually eroded, leaving behind only the most resistant rock 'islands.' As they were isolated from each other and from the world below for millions of years, the tops of tepuis saw the independent evolution of flora and fauna. There are no dinosaurs up there, but roughly half of some 2000 plant species found on top of the tepuis are unique to the specific mountains and there are small endemic animals, such as miniature frogs. The topography of the mountains is also amazing as they have been sculpted by the wind and rain for eons.

eral campsites (with water) on the way. They are Río Tek (four hours from Paraitepui), Río Kukenán (30 minutes further on) and at the foot of Roraima at the so-called *campamento base* (base camp), three hours uphill from the Río Kukenán. The steep, tough, four-hour ascent from the base camp to the top is the most spectacular (yet demanding) part of the hike.

Once atop Roraima, you will camp in one of the dozen or so *hoteles* (hotels), which are semisheltered camping spots under rock overhangs. The guides coordinate which group sleeps where.

The scenery is a moonscape sculpted by the wind and rain, with gorges, creeks, pink beaches, lookout points and gardens filled with unique flowering plants. An eerie, shifting fog often snakes across the mountaintop. While guides may have seemed superfluous on the clear trails below, they are helpful on the labyrinthine plateau. If you stay for two nights on the top you will have time to hike with your guide to some of the attractions, including **El Foso** (a crystalline pool in a massive sinkhole), the **Punto Triple** (the tri-border of Venezuela, Brazil and Guyana), **Bahia de Cristal** (a small valley brimming with quartz) and a number of other great attractions and viewpoints.

San Francisco de Yuruaní

San Francisco, 66km north of Santa Elena de Uairén by highway, is the last town with restaurants or places to stay before starting the Roraima trek (which actually departs from Paraitepui, right). You can come here to eat a hearty meal before or after your hike and also arrange for a guide (US$25 to US$50 a day per group – remember that in terms of quality, you generally get what you pay for) and porters (US$20 a day). Both guides and porters can be hired (for much the same price) in Paraitepui, although San Francisco has more options.

The town has a few nameless accommodation options along the main road (US$5 to US$10 per person) and simple eateries that serve grilled chicken and cold beer.

San Francisco de Yuruaní is on the Ciudad Guayana–Santa Elena Hwy. Eight buses a day run in either direction.

Paraitepui

Paraitepui is a nondescript, small village at the gateway to the Roraima trek. It's 26km east of San Francisco; to get there, hire a jeep in San Francisco (US$50 for up to eight passengers)

or walk. The hot, dusty seven-hour roadside walk is only recommended to masochists.

The Inparques station is in Paraitepui and you must sign in before the hike (there is no park entrance fee). You are allowed to camp in the parking lot and use the covered table area, but the ranger may hit you up for a fee after the fact. There are technically no restaurants in town, but local families can cook chicken dinners (ask at the convenience store next to the Inparques station, around US$7 per person).

SANTA ELENA DE UAIRÉN

☎ 0289 / pop 18,500

This small yet happening town is a good base for exploring the Gran Sabana, particularly Roraima, and is the crossing point for those traveling on to Brazil. Santa Elena may be in the middle of nowhere, but there is a lot going on. Every other store buys or sells gold and diamonds and hundreds of Brazilians pour into the city every morning to buy the inexpensive gasoline in this duty-free zone. Brazilians are only allowed to leave Venezuela with a single tank of gas. Those who try to return with more have their car confiscated (notice the lots of impounded cars near the border). Santa Elena is also noted for being safe, friendly and blazingly hot.

Information

US dollars can easily be exchanged with the money changers who hang around the corner of Calle Bolívar and Calle Urdaneta, popularly known as Cuatro Esquinas.

Banco Guyana (Plaza Bolívar) Has a 24-hour ATM.

Banco Industrial de Venezuela (Calle Bolívar) Has a 24-hour ATM.

Brazilian Consulate (☎ 995-1256; Av Mariscal Sucre; ☒ 8am-noon Mon-Fri) The consulate is opposite the petrol station. A yellow-fever vaccination certificate is likely to be required before issuing a visa.

CANTV (Calle Zea btwn Calles Roscio & Lucas Fernández Peña) Telephones.

Ipostel (Calle Urdaneta btwn Calles Bolívar & Roscio) Post.

Iruk Café (Calle Bolívar; per hr US$1) Internet.

Lavandería Cristal (Calle Urdaneta; per load US$2.50)

Mundo Cyber (per hr US$1; ☒ 8:30am-9pm Mon-Thu, to 10pm Fri, 9:30-10pm Sat, 1-9pm Sun) Decent internet connection.

Tours

Santa Elena has about a dozen tour agencies. Their staple is a one-, two- or three-day jeep tour around the Gran Sabana, with visits to

SANTA ELENA DE UAIRÉN

0 ____ 200 m
0 ____ 0.1 miles

INFORMATION
Banco Guyana.........................1 A2
Banco Industrial de Venezuela...2 A2
Brazilian Consulate..................3 C1
CANTV...................................4 B3
Ipostel..................................5 A2
Iruk Café...............................6 A2
Lavandería Cristal....................7 B2
Money changers.......................8 A2
Mundo Cyber..........................9 B2

SIGHTS & ACTIVITIES
Backpacker Tours....................10 C2
Mystic Tours..........................11 B2
New Frontiers Adventure Tours..12 C2

SLEEPING
Hotel Lucrecia........................13 C2
Hotel Michelle........................14 C2
Moron Katok..........................15 B2
Posada Michelle...................(see 14)

EATING
Alfredo's Restaurant................16 C2
Kamadac..............................17 C2
Restaurant Michelle.............(see 14)
Restaurant Nova Opção..........18 A3
Restaurant Nova Opção
  Sucursal.............................19 A2

TRANSPORT
Old Bus Terminal.....................20 C1

---

the most interesting sights, mostly waterfalls. Budget on roughly US$25 per person per day in a group of four or more. This price includes transportation and a guide, but no accommodations or food.

The other main attraction is the Roraima tour, which is normally offered as an all-inclusive six-day package for US$150 to US$360 (you will get what you pay for with the cheapest tours). The operators who organize this tour usually also rent out camping equipment and can provide transportation to Paraitepui, the starting point for the Roraima trek, for US$60 to US$80 per jeep each way for up to six people. Check on your group size and hiker-to-guide ratio before signing up for any Roraima tour.

Some operators offer tours to El Pauji area, noted for its natural attractions and gold and diamond mines.

Following is a list of recommended local tour companies.

Adrenaline Expeditions (☎ 632-4804, 0414-886-7209; adrenalinexptours@hotmail.com) This sibling company of the Ciudad Bolívar agency has energetic, adventurous tours of the Gran Sabana with its Indiana Jones–styled owner Ricardo. It can also facilitate Roraima trips.

Backpacker Tours (☎ 995-1524, 0414-886-7227; www .backpacker-tours.com; Calle Urdaneta) The Cadillac of agencies in town, it has the most organized, best-equipped and most expensive tours of Roraima and the region.

Mystic Tours (☎ 416-0558, 0414-886-1055; Calle Urdaneta) Run by Roberto Marrero, author of various maps and books on the region, this agency has good tours to Roraima and is one of the few operators that organizes El Pauji tours.

New Frontiers Adventure Tours (☎ 416-0864, 0416-599-3583; www.newfrontiersadventures.com; Calle Urdaneta) Run by a team of experienced guides, this agency specializes in trekking tours, including trips to the top of Roraima, and provides competent guidance and good equipment.

Sleeping

Posada Michelle (☎ 416-0792; hotelmichelle@cantv.net; Calle Urdaneta; s/d/tr US$8/15/18) Some of the best-value budget rooms in the country. Ask for a room upstairs as there is some noise (and less light) on the street level. Cheap laundry service is available for guests of the *posada*.

Hotel Michelle (☎ 416-0792; hotelmichelle@cantv.net; Calle Urdaneta; s/d/tr US$8/15/18) Next door to Posada Michelle and administered by the same manager, the hotel has 10 still larger rooms and is equally spotless. Cheap laundry service is available for the guests of the hotel.

Moron Katok (☎ 995-5018; andrehina@hotmail.com; Calle Urdaneta; tr US$12, 5-person chalet US$19) Formerly called La Casa de Gladys, the new name of this longtime travelers' haunt means 'place of rest' in Pemón. Good value for groups, there's a handful of small triples, two fun chalets with lofts and hot water, and a large sit-down kitchen.

Hotel Lucrecia (☎ 995-1105; hotellucrecia@cantv.net; Av Perimetral; s/d/tr US$13/15/20; P ✶ ☒) Lucrecia is a friendly, family-run old-fashioned house with a lovely patio in bloom year-round. The rooms, arranged around the patio, have hot water. The hotel has a dependable water supply and a fair-sized pool, and guests are served breakfast and dinner on request.

Eating

Kamadac (☎ 995-1408; Calle Urdaneta; pizza US$2) This tour operator also runs a yummy pizza parlor. And after a Roraima trek, the flan is a decadent indulgence.

Restaurant Michelle (☎ 995-1415; Calle Urdaneta; mains US$2-4; ✹ 11am-11pm) Run by the manager of the two Michelle lodgings, the restaurant offers fairly authentic and tasty Chinese food, cooked personally by the manager.

Alfredo's Restaurant (☎ 995-1628; Av Perimertal; pasta & pizza US$4-5, mains US$5-9; ☒) This enjoyable restaurant has an unusually long menu, reasonable steaks, and fine pizzas from its wood-burning oven. You can either sit inside or alfresco-style at the front tables.

Restaurant Nova Opção (☎ 995-1013; Plaza Bolívar; buffet per kg US$5; ✹ 11am-5pm Mon-Sat) This Brazilian buffet eatery sells a wide variety of scrumptious prepared foods by weight. This is the place to load up on calories before or after your big hike. The other branch on Calle Urdaneta serves dinner meals with spaced-out service.

Getting There & Away
AIR
The airport is 7km southwest of town, off the road to the border with Brazil. There's no public transport; a taxi will cost around US$5. Tour operators are often waiting for incoming flights and will usually give you a free lift to town, hoping you might be interested in their offers. Rutaca has daily flights on five-seater Cessnas to Ciudad Bolívar (US$145), via Canaima (US$145).

GETTING TO BRAZIL

Both Venezuelan and Brazilian passport formalities are now done at the border itself, locally known as La Línea, 15km south of Santa Elena. The bus stops at the office. Be sure to have your passport stamped upon leaving or entering Venezuela and carry a yellow-fever card for entering Brazil. Sometimes they charge a US$16 tax for leaving Venezuela, but not always. For information on entering Venezuela from Brazil, see p394.

BUS
Santa Elena has a new bus terminal, on the Ciudad Guayana highway about 2km east of the town's center. There are no urban buses – you need to go by taxi (US$1.50).

Eight buses depart daily to Ciudad Bolívar (US$11 to US$19, 10 to 12 hours, 716km), and they all pass through Ciudad Guayana (US$10 to US$17, nine to 11 hours, 601km).

AMAZONAS

Amazonas, Venezuela's southernmost state, is predominantly Amazonian rainforest crisscrossed by rivers and sparsely populated by indigenous communities. The current indigenous population, estimated at 40,000, comprises three main groups – the Piaroa, Yanomami and Guajibo – and a number of smaller communities.

In contrast to the Brazilian Amazon, Venezuela's Amazonas state is topographically diverse, with *tepuis* as one of the most striking features. Though not as numerous as those in the Gran Sabana, the *tepuis* give the green carpet of rainforest a distinctive appearance. At the southernmost part of Amazonas, along the border with Brazil, is the Serranía de la Neblina. It is a scarcely explored mountain range and contains the highest South American peaks east of the Andes.

The best time to explore the region is from October to December, when the river level is high enough to navigate but rains have started to ease.

Getting Around
As there are no roads in most of the region, transportation is by river or air. There's no

regular passenger service on the rivers, which makes independent travel difficult, if not impossible, but tour operators in Puerto Ayacucho can take you just about everywhere – at a price, of course.

PUERTO AYACUCHO

☎ 0248 / pop 80,000

Hot, rainy Puerto Ayacucho, the only town of size in Amazonas, is a regional tourist center and the entryway to the Venezuelan Amazon. It is home to more than a dozen tour companies that can take you up the Orinoco and its tributaries, and deep into the jungle. It is also a transit point on the adventurous back routes to Colombia and Brazil. The town itself is a lively place on a dazzling stretch of the Orinoco. It has a few interesting sights, including an Indian craft market, but is mainly a place to rest and gear up for adventures in the surrounding areas.

Information

Banco de Venezuela (Av Orinoco)
Banco Provincial (Calle La Guardia)
Banesco (Av Orinoco)
Biblionet (Biblioteca Pública, Av Río Negro) Half-hour free internet access.
CANTV (cnr Av Río Negro & Calle Atabapo) Telephones.
Cibercafé Compuserv (Calle Evelio Roa) Internet access.
Colombian Consulate (☎ 521-0789; Calle Yacapana Qta Beatriz 5; ☉ 7am-1pm Mon-Fri)
DIEX (☎ 521-0198; Av Aguerrevere; ☉ 8am-noon & 2-5:30pm Mon-Fri) This is where you have to get your passport stamped when leaving or entering Venezuela. Note that the opening hours listed above are strictly a guideline.
El Navegante (Centro Comercial Maniglia, Av Orinoco) Internet access.

Sights

The small but interesting **Museo Etnológico de Amazonas** (Av Río Negro; admission US50¢; ☉ 8:30-11:30am & 2:30-6pm Tue-Fri, 9am-noon & 3-6pm Sat, 9am-1pm Sun) will give you an insight into the culture of regional indigenous groups including the Piaroa, Guajibo, Ye'kwana and Yanomami. Note the Ye'kwana ritual weapons laboriously carved in wood, the Yanomami body adornments made of colorful feathers and the Piaroa ceremonial masks used in traditional dances.

Tours

Among the popular shorter tours are a three-day trip up the Río Cuao and a three-day trip up the Sipapo and Autana Rivers to the foot

of Cerro Autana. Expect to pay from US$30 to US$60 per person per day all-inclusive.

The far southeastern part of Amazonas beyond La Esmeralda, basically all the Parima-Tapirapeco National Park, where the Yanomami live, is a restricted area; you need special permits that are virtually impossible to get – some agents get around the ban by visiting Yanomami villages on the Río Siapa off Brazo Casiquiare.

Recommended tour operators:
Coyote Expediciones (☎ 521-4583; coyotexpedition@ cantv.net; Av Aguerrevere) A popular company with travelers, its main offerings are the three-day Autana and Cuao tours (US$100 per person), but it also runs longer trips.
Cruising Tours (☎ 414-5036, 0416-785-5033; cruisingtours@hotmail.com; Valle Verde Triángulo) The German owner of this company personally guides diverse tours and expeditions in the region and beyond at reasonable prices (from US$30 a day), and offers accommodations in his home for tour participants. The office is 5km east of the centre.
Tadae (☎ 521-4882, 0414-486-5923; Centro Comercial Maniglia, Av Orinoco) Apart from the staple Autana and Cuao tours, Tadae offers rafting on Raudales Atures (US$30) and rainforest walks guided by local indigenous people (US$20).

Sleeping

Puerto Ayacucho has a good choice of budget accommodations.

Residencia Internacional (☎ 521-0242; Av Aguerrevere; d US$12-20; P ⊠) This backpacker favorite is pleasant and friendly, with 24 rooms (all with bathrooms) arranged around a long patio, and a rooftop terrace. It is a good place to meet other travelers.

Hotel Tobogán (☎ 521-0320; Av Orinoco; d/tr/q US$14/19/23; P ⊠) The larger four-person rooms flirt with antiseptic hospital-ward décor. Get a room away from Av Orinoco, which can be slightly noisy.

Hotel Mi Jardín (☎ 521-4647; Av Orinoco; d US$14-18, tr/q US$22/28; P ⊠) South of the center, Mi Jardín has its own restaurant and 18 good, clean rooms arranged around a central patio-garden, which is probably where its name came from.

Hotel Apure (☎ 521-4443; Av Orinoco; d US$15-18, tr/q US$22/30; P ⊠) Close to Mi Jardín, the Apure offers much the same rates and standards, including good-sized rooms, comfy beds and attentive service.

Eating

Restaurant Cherazad (☎ 521-5679; cnr Avs Aguerrevere & Río Negro; mains US$5-7) One of the best dining establishments in town, Cherazad provides a reasonable choice of pasta, steaks and fish, plus some

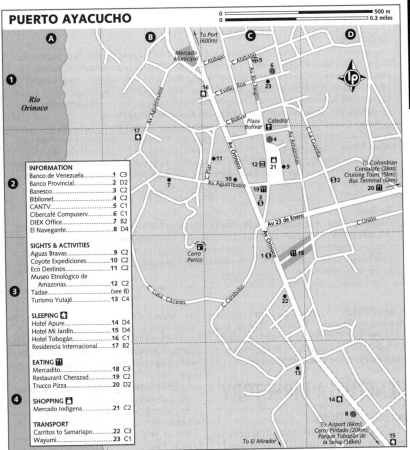

PUERTO AYACUCHO

0		500 m
0		0.3 miles

INFORMATION
Banco de Venezuela	**1** C3
Banco Provincial	**2** D2
Banesco	**3** C2
Biblionet	**4** C2
CANTV	**5** C1
Cibercafé Compuserv	**6** C1
DIEX Office	**7** B2
El Navegante	**8** D4

SIGHTS & ACTIVITIES
Aguas Bravas	**9** C2
Coyote Expediciones	**10** C2
Eco Destinos	**11** C2
Museo Etnológico de Amazonas	**12** C2
Tadae	(see 8)
Turismo Yutajé	**13** C4

SLEEPING
Hotel Apure	**14** D4
Hotel Mi Jardín	**15** D4
Hotel Tobogán	**16** C1
Residencia Internacional	**17** B2

EATING
Mercadito	**18** C3
Restaurant Cherazad	**19** C2
Trucco Pizza	**20** D2

SHOPPING
Mercado Indígena	**21** C2

TRANSPORT
Carritos to Samariapo	**22** C3
Wayumi	**23** C1

Middle Eastern dishes – try the *plato mixto*, which has samples of various specialties.

Trucco Pizza (☎ 521-4721; Av 23 de Enero; pizza US$6; ☺ lunch & dinner) A small fan-cooled patio eatery set back from the road, it makes calzones, burgers and delicious pizza.

One of the favorite inexpensive places to eat among locals is **Mercadito** (Little Market; Av Orinoco), which boasts half-a-dozen rudimentary eateries.

Shopping

Mercado Indígena (Av Río Negro) Held every morning (but busiest from Thursday to Saturday) on the square opposite the museum, it has indigenous crafts for sale. Look for the handmade hammocks, and human figures carved in wood.

Getting There & Away
AIR

The airport, 6km southeast of town (accessible by taxi; US$3), handles daily flights to Caracas (US$68 to US$93). One small local carrier, **Wayumi** (☎ 521-0635; Calle Evelio Roa), operates flights within Amazonas to a few smaller destinations.

BUS

The bus terminal is 6km east of the center, on the outskirts of town. City buses go there from Av 23 de Enero, or take a taxi (US$2). Buses to Ciudad Bolívar (US$10 to US$13, 10 to 12 hours, 728km) depart regularly throughout the day. There are about six morning departures daily to San Fernando de Apure (US$10, seven

---

GETTING TO COLOMBIA OR BRAZIL

To Colombia

The nearest Colombian town of size, Puerto Carreño, at the confluence of the Meta and Orinoco Rivers, is accessible via Puerto Páez, a Venezuelan village 93km north of Puerto Ayacucho. You can get there by the San Fernando bus (US$3, two hours); the trip includes a ferry crossing of the Orinoco from El Burro to Puerto Páez. You then take a boat from the village's wharf across the Río Meta to Puerto Carreño (US$1); the boat runs regularly during the day. Remember to get an exit stamp in your passport at DIEX in Puerto Ayacucho before setting off.

Puerto Carreño is a long, one-street town with an airport, a half-dozen budget hotels and a number of places to eat. Go to the DAS office (Colombian immigration), one block west of the main plaza, for an entry stamp in your passport. A number of shops will change bolívars to pesos.

There are three flights per week from Puerto Carreño to Bogotá (US$90 to US$100). Buses go only in the dry season, roughly from mid-December to mid-March, but they are not recommended because of the strong presence of guerrillas in the region.

To Brazil

Take a flight from Puerto Ayacucho south to San Carlos de Río Negro, from where irregular boats will take you to San Simón de Cocuy, on the border. From here take a bus to São Gabriel da Cachoeira (Brazil) and continue by boat down the Río Negro to Manaus (three boats per week). Most of Puerto Ayacucho's tour companies can tailor a tour that concludes in San Carlos de Río Negro, or even escort you to São Gabriel.

---

hours, 299km), from where you can get buses to Caracas, Maracay, Valencia, Barinas and San Cristóbal. Carritos to Samariapo (US$2, 1¼ hours, 63km) depart from Av Orinoco, one block south of the Banco de Venezuela.

VENEZUELA DIRECTORY

ACCOMMODATIONS

Hotels are not hard to come by in Venezuela and there are budget and midrange options in most towns (though Caracas is conspicuously short on quality budget accommodations). Popular tourist areas like Isla de Margarita and Canaima can become quite full on major holidays, but it is almost always possible to find a vacant room. Campgrounds are rare, but you can rough it in the countryside. Camping on the beach is popular, but be cautious and don't leave your tent unattended. Venezuela has almost no youth hostels. Be aware that urban budget hotels may double as hourly-rates love motels.

A good choice of accommodation is the *posada*, a small, family-run guesthouse. These have mushroomed over past decades, particularly in smaller towns and the countryside. They usually have more character then hotels and offer more personalized attention. Most

are budget places but there are also some midrange and a few top-end *posadas*.

Another kind of countryside lodging are the *campamentos* (literally 'camps'), which have sprung up even in the most remote areas. Not to be confused with campgrounds, *campamentos* can be anything from a rustic shelter with a few hammocks to a posh country lodge with a swimming pool and its own airstrip. More commonly, it will be a collection of cabins plus a restaurant. *Campamentos* provide accommodation, food and usually tours, sometimes selling these services as all-inclusive packages.

Places to stay can legally charge a 16% VAT on top of the room price, though few budget hotels or *posadas* actually do. The prices listed in this book include this tax. As in most developing countries, prices are not set in stone and can change due to the day of the week or if the person at the front desk feels like it. Never count on being able to use a credit card – even if they say that they accept plastic.

ACTIVITIES

Venezuela has many outdoor activities ranging from walking and bird-watching to adrenaline pumping paragliding and kite-surfing. Although all regions of the country have something to offer, Mérida is Venezuela's adventure sports capital.

Many of Venezuela's 40-odd national parks provide a choice of **walks** ranging from easy, well-signposted trails to wild jungle paths. Parque Nacional El Ávila (p998) near Caracas has some of the best easy walking trails, while the surrounds of Mérida (p1016) offer fabulous opportunities for **high-mountain trekking**. Other hiking possibilities include Parque Nacional Henri Pittier (p1003) and one of the most adventurous and fascinating treks, to the top of Roraima (p1042).

The region around Mérida is excellent for **mountain biking**. Tour operators in the city organize biking trips and rent out bikes.

Mérida (p1012) is the best place to go **paragliding**. Novices can go on a tandem flight while the more daring can take a course to learn solo flight.

Rafting trips are run on some Andean rivers (arranged in Mérida; in the Parque Nacional Mochima (organized from Mochima; p1023), and over Orinoco rapids (arranged in Puerto Ayacucho; p1046). The Mérida region is also the home of **canyoning** (climbing, rappelling and hiking down a river canyon).

Venezuela has excellent **snorkeling** and **scuba diving** around the offshore archipelagos such as Los Roques (p1000) and Isla de Margarita (p1029). There's also some good snorkeling and diving around the islands closer to the mainland, including in Parque Nacional Mochima (p1022) and Parque Nacional Morrocoy (p1005). In all these places, local operators offer courses and diving trips, and rent equipment.

Los Llanos is one of the best regions to see **wild animals** including caimans, capybaras, anacondas, anteaters and birds. **Wildlife safaris** are organized from Ciudad Bolívar (p1034) and from Mérida (p1014). If you are particularly interested in **bird-watching**, consider Parque Nacional Henri Pittier (p1003) or Río Caura (p1035).

Venezuela has some **windsurfing** and **kitesurfing** areas of international reputation, including Adícora (p1008) and El Yaque (p1034). You can also do both at Los Roques (p1000).

BOOKS

For more detailed travel information, get a copy of Lonely Planet's *Venezuela*. Of the useful local publications, *Ecotourism Guide to Venezuela* by Miro Popic is a bilingual Spanish-English guidebook focusing on ecological tourism, while *Guide to Camps, Posadas and Cabins in Venezuela* by Elizabeth Kline is a bilingual edition detailing 1200 accommodations options. Both are updated yearly.

The Search for El Dorado by John Hemming offers a fascinating insight into the conquest of Venezuela. Sir Arthur Conan Doyle's *The Lost World* was inspired by the Roraima *tepui* in the southeast. *Venezuela: A Century of Change* by Judith Ewell provides a comprehensive 20th-century history.

There are a number of books on Chávez and his 'Bolivarian Revolution,' though most sources take either a fervent pro- or anti-Chávez stance. Some of the more recent and widely sold titles are *Hugo Chavez: Oil, Politics, and the Challenge to the US* by Nikolas Kozloff; *Chavez: Venezuela and the New Latin America* by Hugo Chavez, David Deutschmann and Javier Salado; *Hugo Chavez: The Bolivarian Revolution in Venezuela* by Richard Gott and Georges Bartoli.

Travelers with a serious interest in birdwatching may want to check *A Guide to the Birds of Venezuela* by Rodolphe Meyer de Schauensee and William H Phelps. *Birding in Venezuela* by Mary Lou Goodwin is also a good reference.

BUSINESS HOURS

The working day is theoretically eight hours, from 8am to noon and 2pm to 6pm Monday to Friday, but in practice, many businesses work shorter hours. Remember that Venezuela functions on a more lax schedule than European or North American countries and sometimes businesses close earlier or close for days on end with no warning and no apologies. Business hours are simply a guideline, so don't count on them too much.

CLIMATE

Venezuela's climate features dry and wet seasons, though the tourist season runs year-round. The dry season runs roughly from December to April, while the wet season lasts the rest of the year. The dry season is more pleasant for traveling, but some sights – such as waterfalls – are more impressive in the wet season. There are many regional variations in the amount of rainfall and the length of the seasons.

For more information and climate charts, see p1062.

CUSTOMS

Customs regulations don't differ much from those in other South American countries. You are allowed to bring in personal belongings and presents you intend to give to Venezuelan residents, as well as cameras, camping equipment, sports accessories, a personal computer and the like. Chávez has whipped up a national paranoia about foreign spies, so think twice about bringing in complex audiovisual equipment or other unusual and potentially suspect technology. Chances are that the soldier searching your belonging will be 19, uneducated and difficult to reason with. Drug penalties are stiff – don't even think about it.

DANGERS & ANNOYANCES

Venezuela is a reasonably safe place to travel. However, the country's getting poorer and consequently theft, robbery and common crime are on the increase. Theft is more serious in the larger cities and urban centers than in the countryside. Caracas is, far and away, the most dangerous place in the country, and you should take care while strolling around the streets, particularly at night. Also be aware of your surroundings when withdrawing cash from an ATM at any time of the day. Police are not necessarily trustworthy (though many are), so do not blindly accept the demands of these authority figures.

Malaria and dengue fever are present in some tropical areas and other insect bites, while they don't necessarily cause illness, can cause major discomfort. Overall, your biggest dangers are the standard risks of travel: sunburn, foodborne illness and traffic-related concerns.

DRIVER'S LICENSE

You can use any type of driver's license to operate a car in Venezuela. However, you need a superhuman level of patience and Formula 1 driving skills to make your way around Caracas in a car.

ELECTRICITY

Venezuela operates on 110V at 60 Hz. The country uses US-type plugs.

EMBASSIES & CONSULATES
Embassies & Consulates in Venezuela

The following embassies are located in Caracas, unless otherwise noted. If you can't find your home embassy, check a Caracas phone directory, which will include a full list.

Australia (☎ 0212-263-4033; caracas@dfat.gov.au; Av Francisco de Miranda & Av Sur, 1st floor, Altamira, Caracas)

Brazil (Map pp990-1; ☎ 0212-261-5505; www.embajadabrasil.org.ve; Centro Gerencial Mohedano, cnr Calle Los Chaguaramos & Av Mohedano, La Castellana, Caracas; Ⓜ Chacao); Consulate in Santa Elena de Uairén (Map p1044; ☎ 0289-995-1256; Av Antonio José de Sucre)

Canada (Map p990-1; ☎ 0212-264-0833, 266-7176; crcas@dfait-maeci.gc.ca; cnr Avs Francisco de Miranda & Sur Altamira, Altamira, Caracas; Ⓜ Altamira)

Colombia (Map pp990-1; ☎ 0212-261-5584; Torre Credival, cnr 2a Av de Campo Alegre & Av Francisco de Miranda, Campo Alegre, Caracas; Ⓜ Chacaíto); Consulate in Maracaibo (☎ 0261-792-1483; Av 3Y No 70-16); Consulate in Puerto Ayacucho (Map p1047; ☎ 0248-521-0789; Calle Yapacana off Av Rómulo Gallegos)

France (Map pp990-1; ☎ 0212-909-6500; www.francia.org.ve; Edificio Embajada de Francia, cnr Calle Madrid & Av La Trinidad, Las Mercedes, Caracas)

Germany (Map pp990-1; ☎ 0212-261-0181; diplogerma cara@cantv.net; Torre La Castellana, Av Principal de la Castellana, La Castellana, Caracas; Ⓜ Altamira)

Guyana (Map pp990-1; ☎ 0212-977-1158; embaguy@caracas-office.org.ve; Quinta Roraima, Av El Paseo, Prados del Este, Caracas)

Ireland (☎ 0212-959-8754, 959-9049; Torre Alfa, PH Avenida Principal de Santa Sofia, El Cafeta, Caracas)

Italy (Map pp990-1; ☎ 0212-952-7311; ambcara@italamb.org.ve; Edificio Atrium, Calle Sorocaima, El Rosal, Caracas; Ⓜ Chacao)

Japan (Map pp990-1; ☎ 0212-261-8333; csjapon@genesisbci.net; Edificio Bancaracas, Plaza La Castellana, La Castellana, Caracas; Ⓜ Altamira)

Netherlands (Map pp990-1; ☎ 0212-263-3076, 263-3622; Edificio San Juan, cnr 2a Transversal & Av San Juan Bosco, Altamira, Caracas; Ⓜ Altamira)

New Zealand (☎ 0212-277-7965; cnr Avs Francisco de Miranda & Libertador, Torre KPMG, Piso 7, Chacao, Caracas)

Spain (Map pp990-1; ☎ 0212-263-2855; espanve@cantv.net; Quinta Marmolejo, Av Mohedano)

Suriname (Map pp990-1; ☎ 0212-261-2724; embsur1@cantv.net; Quinta Los Milagros, 4a Av btwn 7a & 8a Transversal, Altamira, Caracas)

Trinidad & Tobago (Map pp990-1; ☎ 0212-261-3748; embassytt@cantv.net; Quinta Serrana, 4a Av btwn 7a & 8a Transversal, Altamira, Caracas)

UK (Map pp990-1; ☎ 0212-263-8411; www.britain.org.ve; Torre La Castellana, Av Principal de la Castellana, La Castellana, Caracas; Ⓜ Altamira)

USA (Map pp990-1; ☎ 0212-975-6411, 975-7811; www.embajadausa.org.ve; cnr Calle F & Calle Suapure, Colinas del Valle Arriba, Caracas)

Venezuelan Embassies & Consulates Abroad

Venezuelan embassies abroad include the following:

Australia (☎ 02-6290-2967, 6290-2968; www.venezuela-emb.org.au; 7 Culgoa Circuit, O'Malley, Canberra, ACT, 2606)

Canada (☎ 613-235-5151, 235-0551; www.misionven ezuela.org; 32 Range Rd, Ottawa, Ontario K1N 4J8)
Colombia (☎ 1-640-1213; www.embaven.org.co; Carrera 11 No 87-51, Bogotá)
France (☎ 01-45-53-29-98, 01-47-55-00-11; www .embavenez-paris.com; 11 rue Copernic, Paris 75116)
Germany (☎ 030-832-24-00; www.botschaftvenezuela .de; Schillstrasse 9-10, 10785 Berlin)
Italy (☎ 068-07-97-97, 068-07-94-64; embaveit@iol.it; Via Nicolo Tartaglia 11, 00197 Rome)
Japan (☎ 0334-091-501; embavene@interlink.or.jp; 38 Kowa Bldg, 12-24 Nishi Azabu, 4 Chrome, Minato Ku, Tokyo 106)
Netherlands (☎ 0703-65-12-56, 0703-63-38-05; embavene@xs4all.nl; Nassaulaan 2, 2514 JS The Hague)
Spain (☎ 01-598-12-00; embvenez@teleline.es; Edificio Eurocentro, Calle Capitan Haya No 1, 28020 Madrid)
Trinidad & Tobago (☎ 627-9821; embaveztt@carib -link.net; Venezuelan Center, 16 Victoria Av, Port of Spain)
UK (☎ 020-7581-2776, 7584-4206; www.venezuela.em bassyhomepage.com; 1 Cromwell Rd, London SW7 2HW)
USA (☎ 202-342-2214; www.embavenez-us.org; 1099 30th St NW, Washington DC 20007)

FESTIVALS & EVENTS

Given the strong Catholic character of Venezuela, many holidays follow the church calendar – Christmas, Carnaval, Easter and Corpus Christi are celebrated all over the country. Carnaval is particularly big in Isla de Margarita, El Callao and Carúpano. The religious calendar is dotted with saints' days, and every village and town has its own patron saint and will hold a celebration on that day. Cultural events such as festivals of theater, film or classical music are almost exclusively confined to Caracas.

One of Venezuela's most colorful events is the **Diablos Danzantes** (see the boxed text, p999). It's held on Corpus Christi in San Francisco de Yare, about 70km southeast of Caracas. The ceremony consists of a spectacular parade and the dance of devils, performed by dancers in elaborate masks and costumes.

FOOD & DRINK

On the whole, dining options in Venezuela are good and relatively inexpensive. Various local dishes, international cuisine and an array of snacks and fast foods are available. Budget travelers should look for restaurants that offer a *menú del día* or *menu ejecutivo*, a set meal consisting of soup and a main course. It will cost roughly US$3 to US$5 (a little more in Caracas), which is cheaper than any à la carte dish. A budget alternative can be roasted

chicken, usually called *pollo en brasa*. Filling local choices include *pabellón criollo*, *arepas*, *cachapas* and *empanadas*.

For breakfast, visit any of the ubiquitous *panaderías* (bakeries), which serve sandwiches, croissants, pastries and a variety of snacks, plus delicious espresso.

In almost every dining or drinking establishment, a 10% service charge will automatically be added to the bill. It's customary to leave a small tip at fancier places.

Venezuelan Cuisine

The following list includes some of the most typical Venezuelan dishes and a few international foods that have different names in Venezuelan Spanish.
arepa (a·*re*·pa) – small, grilled corn pancake stuffed with a variety of fillings
cachapa (ka·*cha*·pa) – larger, flat corn pancake, served with cheese and/or ham
cachito (ka·*chee*·to) – croissant filled with chopped ham and served hot
cambur (*kam*·boor) – banana
carabina (ka·ra·*bee*·na) – Mérida version of *hallaca*
caraota (ka·ra·*o*·ta) – black bean
casabe (ka·*sa*·be) – huge, flat bread made from yucca; staple in Indian communities
empanada (em·pa·*na*·da) – deep-fried cornmeal turnover stuffed with various fillings
guasacaca (gwas·a·*ka*·ka) – a green sauce made of peppers, onions and seasoning
hallaca (a·*ya*·ka) – maize dough with chopped meat and vegetables, wrapped in banana leaves and steamed; like a Mexican tamale
lau lau (lau·lau) – catfish
lechosa (le·*cho*·sa) – papaya
muchacho (moo·*cha*·cho) – hearty roast-beef dish
pabellón criollo (pa·be·*yon* cree·*o*·yo) – shredded beef, rice, black beans, cheese and fried plantain; Venezuela's national dish
papelón (pa·be·*lon*) – crude brown sugar; drink flavoring
parchita (par·*chee*·ta) – passion fruit
pasapalos (pa·sa·*pa*·los) – hors d'oeuvres, small snacks, finger food
patilla (pa·*tee*·ya) – watermelon
quesillo (ke·*see*·yo) – caramel custard
tequeño (te·ke·*nyo*) – cheese strips wrapped in pastry and deep fried
teta (*te*·ta) – iced fruit juice in plastic wrap, consumed by sucking

Drinks

Venezuela has good, strong espresso coffee at every turn. Ask for *café negro* if you want it black; *café marrón* if you prefer half coffee, half milk; or *café con leche* if you like milkier coffee.

A staggering variety of fruit juices is available in restaurants, cafés and even in some fruit stores. Juices come as *batidos* (pure or cut with water) or as *merengadas* (milk with milk).

The number-one alcoholic drink is *cerveza* (beer), particularly Polar beer, the dominant brand. Other popular brands include Solera (which is owned by Polar), Regional and Brahma (which is Brazilian). Beer's sold everywhere in cans or small bottles at close to freezing temperature. Among spirits, *ron* (rum) heads the list and comes in numerous varieties. Cacique is the most popular brand.

GAY & LESBIAN TRAVELERS

Homosexuality isn't illegal in Venezuela, but it is suppressed and frowned upon by the overwhelmingly Catholic society. Caracas has the largest gay and lesbian community and the most open gay life. Homosexual men, in particular, should be very discreet in smaller towns and rural areas. At the same time, pockets of tolerance do exist.

Caracas' contacts include the **Movimiento Ambiente de Venezuela** (☎ 0212-321-9470) and the gay 'what's on' guide **En Ambiente** (☎ 0414-219-1837; enambiente@latinmail.com). Also check local gay websites www.republicagay.com and www.rumbacaracas.com (both in Spanish).

HEALTH

Venezuela has a wide array of pharmacies, clinics and hospitals, but health services have deteriorated over the past decade due to the economic situation. Be sure to have a good health-insurance policy to cover an emergency flight home or to Miami if something goes wrong. If you need hospital treatment in Venezuela, by far the best facilities are in Caracas. Smaller issues can be dealt with directly in pharmacies, as they are allowed to give injections and administer a wide array of medicines.

It is also smart to avoid drinking tap water (bottled water is sold everywhere) and to be cautious of street snacks, sun overexposure and insect bites, and be doubly careful while crossing city streets.

HOLIDAYS

Keep in mind that Venezuelans usually take holidays over Christmas, Carnaval (several days prior to Ash Wednesday) and Semana

Santa (the week before Easter Sunday). In these periods, you'll have to plan ahead as it can be tricky to find a place to stay in more popular destinations. The upside is that they really come alive with holiday merrymakers.

Some official public holidays:

New Year's Day January 1
Carnaval Monday and Tuesday prior to Ash Wednesday, February/March
Easter Maundy Thursday and Good Friday, March/April
Declaration of Independence April 19
Labor Day May 1
Battle of Carabobo June 24
Independence Day July 5
Bolívar's Birthday July 24
Discovery of America October 12
Christmas Day December 25

INTERNET ACCESS

Virtually all cities and most towns have cybercafés. An hour of internet access will cost between US50¢ and US$2, depending on the region, city and particular place. Mérida and Caracas have the most widespread number of cybercafés and some of the best prices.

INTERNET RESOURCES

Some useful websites for information on Venezuela:

Latin World (www.latinworld.com/sur/venezuela) Useful directory with links to English- and Spanish-language sites. Categories include arts, traditions, travel, sports and books.
Online Newspapers (www.onlinenewspapers.com/venezuel.htm) Links to at least 30 Venezuelan online newspapers.
Think Venezuela (www.think-venezuela.net) General information on Venezuela, including politics, geography, economy, culture, education and national parks.
University of Texas (www.lanic.utexas.edu/la/venezuela) Impressive directory of Venezuelan websites provided by the Latin American Network Information Center.
Venezuela Tuya (www.venezuela-tuya.com in Spanish) A comprehensive tourism portal for Venezuelan tourism.
Zmag (www.zmag.org/venezuela_watch.htm) Website containing articles analyzing the current political and economic issues from a pro-government perspective.

LEGAL MATTERS

Venezuela police are to be treated with respect, but with a healthy dose of caution. Cases of police corruption, abuse of power and use of undue force are unfortunately common.

Some travelers associate the tropics with open and relaxed drug policy. That is far from the truth in Venezuela. Penalties for trafficking, possessing and using illegal drugs are some of the heaviest in all of Latin America.

MAPS

The best general map of Venezuela (scale 1:1,750,000) is published by International Travel Maps (Canada). Within Venezuela, folded road maps of the country are produced by several local publishers and are available in tourism offices, some hotels and stores that cater to foreign visitors.

MEDIA

All major cities have daily newspapers. The two leading Caracas papers, *El Universal* and *El Nacional,* have countrywide distribution. Both have reasonable coverage of national and international affairs, sports, economics and culture. The *Daily Journal* is the main English-language newspaper published in Venezuela. It's available at major newsstands and select bookshops in Caracas. Elsewhere in Venezuela, it can be difficult to find.

Most of Venezuela's numerous radio stations are dominated by musical programs, principally Latin music, imported pop, rock, disco and the like. Three government and three private TV stations operate out of Caracas and reach most of the country. They all offer the usual TV fare, including newscasts, music, feature films, sports and culture. Prime-time hours are dominated by *telenovelas* (soap operas). Several cable/satellite TV providers offer mixed Spanish/English multichannel packages.

MONEY
ATMs

Cajeros automáticos (ATMs) are the easiest way of getting cash. ATMs can be found at most major banks, including Banco de Venezuela, Banco Mercantil, Banco Provincial and Banesco. ATMs are normally open 24 hours. Always have a backup option as some machines will eat cards. A lost or damaged bankcard can cause some major disruptions to your trip.

Bargaining

As in most Latin American countries, bargaining in Venezuela is part of everyday life. Since part of the economy is informal, quasi-legal or uncontrolled, prices for some goods and services, including products purchased at the market, taxi fares, rates in some budget hotels or even bus and *por puesto* fares, are to some extent negotiable.

Black Market

There is a thriving black market for American dollars and euros and many people will ask to change currency in airports, bus stations or the center of towns. You can get a much better rate with these money traders, but do so at a higher risk of getting ripped off. Make sure that you are familiar with current Venezuelan currency before wading into the black market, so you don't come away with obsolete bills. Consider dealing with someone who works out of a storefront so you can track them down later if there is any issue.

Credit Cards

Visa and MasterCard are the most useful credit cards in Venezuela. Both are accepted as a means of payment for goods and services (though many tour operators may refuse payment by credit card or charge 10% more for the service). They are also useful for taking cash advances from banks or ATMs. Make sure you know the number to call if you lose your credit card, and be quick to cancel it if it's lost or stolen. Also remember that just because an establishment claims that it takes credit cards doesn't mean that its machine functions.

Currency

The unit of currency is the bolívar, abbreviated to Bs. There are 50-, 100- and 500-bolívar coins, and paper notes of 1000, 2000, 5000, 10,000, 20,000 and 50,000 bolívars. Two different kinds of notes in 1000, 2000, 5000 and 10,000 bolívars denominations are in circulation, and both are legal. Watch the notes carefully before you pay (and also those you receive) because some notes are easy to confuse – particularly the 1000 and the 10,000.

Exchanging Money

US dollars, euros and American Express traveler's checks are the most popular and accepted in Venezuela. Theoretically, they can be exchanged in some banks, but very few banks handle foreign-exchange transactions.

The *casas de cambio* (authorized money-exchange offices) are more likely to exchange your money, but may pay less and charge higher commission. The best-known *casa de cambio* is Italcambio, which has offices in most major cities and exchange both cash and traveler's checks. If you are comfortable with Spanish and Venezuelan currency, the black market will get you the best exchange rates.

Exchange rates at press time included the following:

Country	Unit		Bs (bolívar)
Australia	A$1	=	1625
Canada	C$1	=	1900
euro zone	€1	=	2691
Japan	¥1	=	18
UK	UK£1	=	4016
United States	US$1	=	2145

Tipping

Most restaurants include a 10% service charge. A small tip of 5% to 10% beyond the service charge is standard in a nicer restaurant, but is not required. Taxi drivers are not usually tipped unless they help carry bags. Tipping of hotel employees, dive masters, guides etc is left to your discretion. It is rarely required but always appreciated. The simple act of buying a drink for a boat driver or cook can go a long way.

Traveler's Checks

American Express is the most recognized traveler's check brand. *Casas de cambio* will often change traveler's checks (try Italcambio), but will charge a commission of about 3% or more. Some tour operators will accept traveler's checks as payment.

POST

The postal service is run by Ipostel, which has post offices throughout the country. The usual opening hours are 8am to 5pm Monday to Friday, with regional variations. Some offices in the main cities may open longer hours and on Saturday. Airmailing a letter up to 20g costs US50¢ to anywhere in the Americas, US60¢ to Europe or Africa and US70¢ to the rest of the world. Sending a package of up to 500g will cost US$6/8/10, respectively. The service is unreliable and slow. Airmail to Europe can take up to a month to arrive, if it arrives at all. If you are mailing something important or time-sensitive, seek out a reliable international express mail carrier.

RESPONSIBLE TRAVEL

Visiting a different culture can pose a great deal of challenges and you'll need to remind yourself how important it is to minimize the negative impact of your visit. Be sensitive to the needs and beliefs of the local people, and resist trying to impose your standards and way of life.

Also resist the temptation to stuff your pockets with crystals, jasper or jade from the waterfalls and creeks of the Gran Sabana. Never touch coral or take home seashells while snorkeling or diving. Refrain from purchasing articles made from tropical shells, tortoises or corals, no matter how beautiful. Don't even dream of the belt you could make from the caiman leather you saw in the market and stay away from the arts and crafts with the bits of jaguar or anaconda skin (the story about how it was killed to defend a child is an old con). The purchasing of drugs and partaking in sexual tourism cause rippling societal damage that continues long after you have returned home.

Encourage and use truly ecological tourist companies and projects. Many tourist operators use the 'eco' label as a sales strategy. Find out what they do for the protection of the environment, how they minimize impact and how they contribute to local communities.

STUDYING

Venezuela has a number of language schools in most big cities. You can also find an independent teacher and arrange individual classes. Mérida is a popular place to study Spanish as it is an attractive, affordable city with a major university population (see p1014).

TELEPHONE

Bright blue CANTV public phones are everywhere, though only about 50% of them work. Phonecards for these phones come in a few different values and can be purchased at most stores and kiosks.

During the day entrepreneurs set up small tables on street corners with a few mobile phones chained to the tabletop. They charge by the minute for calls. This can be more convenient that using a card in a public phone, but can get expensive unless you are calling a domestic number.

Call centers (owned by Movistar, CANTV or independents known as *centros de comunicaciones*) are the best for international calls. In large cities, these centers are everywhere and are normally open from about 7am to 9pm daily.

Those who plan to stay a longer period of time in Venezuela may opt to purchase a mobile phone or buy a local SIM card for their own handset. The malls all have numerous competing mobile-phone offices. Generally the less expensive services have poorer reception, especially in areas outside of Caracas. Movistar (numbers begin with ☎0414) is the major operator of mobile telephone services, followed by Movilnet (☎0416) and Digitel (☎0412). Venezuela has one of the highest cellular-phone-per-capita ratios in Latin America. Note that calling cellular numbers is expensive and eats quickly into a phonecard.

All phone numbers in the country are seven digits and area codes are three digits. Area codes are listed under the headings of the relevant destinations throughout this guide. The country code for Venezuela is ☎58. To call Venezuela from abroad, dial the international access code of the country you're calling from, Venezuela's code (☎58), the area code (drop the initial 0) and the local phone number.

TOILETS

Since there are no self-contained public toilets in Venezuela, use the toilets of establishments such as restaurants, hotels, museums, shopping malls and bus terminals. Don't rely on a public bathroom to have toilet paper and remember to always throw the used paper into the wastebasket provided (except at fancy hotels).

The most common word for toilet is *baño*. Men's toilets will usually bear a label reading *señores* or *caballeros,* whereas women's toilets will be marked *señoras* or *damas.*

TOURIST INFORMATION

Inatur (Instituto Autónomo de Turismo de Aragua; www.inatur .gov.ve) is the Caracas-based government agency that promotes tourism and provides tourist information; see p989 for contact details. Outside the capital, tourist information is handled by regional tourist bodies that have offices in their respective state capitals and in some other cities. Some are better than others, but on the whole they lack city maps and brochures, and the staff members rarely speak English.

TOURS

Independent travelers who have never taken an organized tour in their lives will find themselves signing up with a group in Venezuela. As vast areas of the country are virtually inaccessible by public transport (eg the Orinoco Delta or Amazon Basin) or because a solitary visit to scattered sights in a large territory (eg the Gran Sabana) may be inconvenient, time consuming and expensive, tours are a standard option in Venezuelan travel.

Although under some circumstances it makes sense to prebook tours from Caracas (like when stringing together various tours in a short period of time), it is most cost effective to arrange a tour from the regional center closest to the area you are going to visit. Information about local tour operators is included in the relevant destination sections.

TRAVELERS WITH DISABILITIES

Venezuela offers very little to people with disabilities. Wheelchair ramps are available only at a few upmarket hotels and restaurants, and public transportation will be a challenge for any person with mobility limitations. Hardly any office, museum or bank provides special facilities for disabled persons, and wheelchair-accessible toilets are virtually nonexistent.

VISAS

Nationals of the US, Canada, Australia, New Zealand, Japan, the UK and most of Western and Scandinavian Europe don't need a visa to enter Venezuela; a free Tourist Card (Tarjeta de Ingreso, officially denominated DEX-2) is all that is required. The card is normally valid for 90 days (unless immigration officers note on the card a shorter period) and can be extended. Airlines flying into Venezuela provide these cards to passengers while on the plane. Overland visitors bearing passports of the countries listed above can obtain the card from the immigration official at the border crossing (it's best to check this beforehand at the nearest consulate).

On entering Venezuela, your passport and tourist card will be stamped (make sure this happens) by Dirección de Identificación y Extranjería (DIEX or DEX) border officials. Keep the yellow copy of the tourist card while traveling in Venezuela (you may be asked for it during passport controls), and return it to immigration officials when leaving the country – although not all are interested in collecting the cards.

Visa and tourist-card extensions are handled by the office of DIEX in Caracas (p985).

VOLUNTEERING

There are few volunteering opportunities with international organizations in Venezuela as the government has thrown out numerous religious

A MAN ON A MISSION

Chávez's 'Bolivarian Revolution' is famed for its *misiónes* (missions). The missions are government sponsored outreach programs, often into the poorest communities of Venezuela. You will see billboards for these public works along the highways and on the sides of buildings. More and more visitors are coming to observe the missions or to volunteer at them. See www.gobiern oenlinea.ve/miscelaneas/misiones.html for more information. Some of the more well-known and important missions:

Misión Barrio Adentro (Inside the Neighborhood) has created free community health care clinics in the impoverished *barrios*.

Misión Ribas provides a second educational chance for some five million Venezuelan high school dropouts.

Misión Robinson (robinson@misionrobinson.gov.ve) uses volunteers to teach reading, writing, and arithmetic to millions of illiterate Venezuelan adults.

Misión Sucre offers basic education courses to the two million adult Venezuelans who had not completed their elementary-level education.

Misión Vuelta al Campo (Return to the Countryside) tries to reverse the trend of urban migration and return the urban poor to the countryside.

Misión Vuelvan Caras (About Face) has the lofty goals to transform the economy from financial goals to the goal of a generally improved society that is fair to all.

Misión Zamora is the controversial program that seeks to expropriate unused land and redistribute it to poor Venezuelans.

charities and US-based organizations. There is the possibility to volunteer for Venezuelan government programs (though it is likely that you will need to speak Spanish). **Mission Robinson** (see the boxed text, above) is a popular choice.

Lonely Planet's *Code Green* recommends **Peace Villages Foundation** (www.peacevillages.org). PVF offers a range of projects in childcare, assistant teaching, conservation and sustainable living, building and maintenance. Placements are also available for skilled volunteers in medicine, psychology and physiotherapy. Accommodation is provided at the Foundation's affiliated guesthouse or through home-stays with local families.

WOMEN TRAVELERS

Like most of Latin America, Venezuela is very much a man's country. Women travelers will attract more curiosity, attention and advances from local men than they would from men in North America or Western Europe. Local males will quickly pick you out in a crowd and are not shy to show their admiration through whistles, endearments and flirtatious comments. These advances are usually lighthearted, though they can seem rude (or actually be rude).

The best way to deal with unwanted attention is simply to ignore it. Dressing modestly will make you less conspicuous to the local piranhas. Even though Venezuelan women wear revealing clothes, they are a lot more aware of the culture and the safety of their surroundings. A cheap, fake wedding band is also a good trick to quickly end awkward chat-ups.

WORKING

Travelers looking for a paid job in Venezuela will almost always be disappointed. The economy is just not strong enough to take on foreigners for casual jobs. Qualified English teachers have the best chance of getting a job, yet it's still hard to arrange work once you're in the country. Try English-teaching institutions such as the **British Council** (www .britishcouncil.com), private-language schools or linguistic departments at universities. Note that you need a work visa to work legally in Venezuela.

South America Directory

CONTENTS

This directory provides general information on South America, from activities and books to toilets and telephones. Specific information for each country is listed in the Directory sections at the end of each country chapter.

ACCOMMODATIONS

Obviously there are many more places to stay in South America than we're able to include in this book, but we've sifted through most of the continent's accommodation options and included those we think are the best. Throughout the book's Sleeping sections, we list accommodations in order of price, with the cheapest listed first. For those nights when the thought of another cold, shared shower and a hard, over-used bed is enough to make you toss in your pack, we've also included a few midrange options. And for a real treat, we've thrown in a few splurges – places where an extra US$20 or so will get you a nurturing night in one of our favorite places to stay.

Accommodation costs vary greatly from country to country, with Andean countries (especially Bolivia) being the cheapest (from as little as US$2 per night) and Chile, Brazil and the Guianas the costliest (more than US$30).

Some excellent online resources have popped up recently, including the ingenious **CouchSurfing** (www.couchsurfing.com) and the reliable **Hostel World** (www.hostelworld.com).

Camping

Camping is an obvious choice in parks and reserves and a useful budget option in pricier countries such as Chile. In the Andean countries (Bolivia, Ecuador and Peru), there are few organized campgrounds. In Argentina, Chile, Uruguay and parts of Brazil, however, camping holidays have long been popular.

Bring all your own gear. While camping gear is available in large cities and in trekking and activities hubs, it's expensive and choices are usually minimal. Camping gear can be rented in areas with substantial camping and trekking action (eg the Lake District, Mendoza and Huaraz), but quality is sometimes dubious.

An alternative to tent-camping is staying in *refugios* (simple structures within parks and reserves), where a basic bunk and kitchen access are usually provided. For climbers, most summit attempts involve staying in a *refugio*.

BOOK ACCOMMODATION ONLINE

For more accommodation reviews and recommendations by Lonely Planet authors, check out the online booking service at www.lonelyplanet.com. You'll find the true, insider lowdown on the best places to stay. Reviews are thorough and independent. Best of all, you can book online.

Hostels

Albergues (hostels) have become increasingly popular throughout South America and, as throughout the world, are great places to socialize with other travelers. You'll rarely find an official *albergue juvenil* (youth hostel); most hostels accept all ages and are unaffiliated with Hostelling International (HI). Once known for their institutional atmosphere, HI facilities have become increasingly attractive as new owners tune in to the sophisticated tastes of budget travelers.

Hotels

When it comes to hotels, both terminology and criteria vary. The costliest in the genre are *hoteles* (hotels) proper. A step down in price are *hostales* (small hotels or, in Peru, guesthouses). The cheapest places are *hospedajes, casas de huéspedes, residenciales, alojamientos* and pensiones. A room in these places includes a bed with (hopefully) clean sheets and a blanket, maybe a table and chair and sometimes a fan, but rarely any heating. Showers and toilets are generally shared, and there may not be hot water. Cleanliness varies widely, but many places are remarkably tidy. In some areas, especially southern Chile, the cheapest places may be *casas familiares,* family houses whose hospitality makes them excellent value.

Some cheap hotels rent rooms by the hour. In big cities, rooms in 'love hotels' (called *albergues transitorios* or *telos*) are only available by the hour, but in smaller towns, the cheapest hotels may take hourly rate *and* overnight guests. It's usually pretty apparent what type of hotel you're in, and we try our hardest to list only those places where you'll get a decent night's sleep, sans the neighborly bump and grind.

In Brazil, Argentina and some other places, prices often include breakfast. Especially in Brazil, it's worth paying a little extra for a place with a quality breakfast.

Hot-water supplies are often erratic, or may be available only at certain hours of the day. It's something to ask about (and consider paying extra for), especially in the highlands and far south, where it gets *cold*.

When showering, beware the electric shower head, an innocent looking unit that heats cold water with an electric element. Don't touch the shower head or anything metal when the water is on, or you may get shocked – never strong enough to throw you

across the room, but hardly pleasant. Wearing rubber sandals protects you from shock. Regulate the temperature by adjusting the water flow: more water means less heat.

In Sleeping sections throughout this book, prices are given for rooms with shared and private bathrooms. If bathrooms are not mentioned in the price, assume that private bathrooms are the only option.

ACTIVITIES

Whether you take to the mountain, the water or into thin air, opportunities for outdoor fun abound in South America.

Cycling

Peddling South America (or parts of it) can prove an arduous undertaking, but the rewards are beyond anything the bus-bound can imagine. You can bomb down the 'World's Most Dangerous Road' (p193), scream down the flanks of an Ecuadorian volcano and dodge herds of sheep in Patagonia. While plenty of riders pull off a continental tour, a more realistic approach, unless you're flush with time and cash, is biting off a chunk. Popular routes include Chilean and Argentine Patagonia (though the constant northwest winds can be brutal); an Ecuador–Peru–Bolivia tour; cycling the length of the Andes from Quito, Ecuador to Ushuaia, Argentina (or vise-versa); or a spin around northern Argentina, Uruguay, Paraguay and southern Brazil.

No matter where you end up riding, a mountain bike is the ideal machine, as the most scenic and uncongested roads are often dirt. Bring everything from home as equipment is hard to find outside major cities, and even then it can be painfully expensive.

If you're not bringing your bike, you'll find opportunities to rent for a day or join a mountain-biking tour. Usually, however, equipment is nothing like you're used to back home. Online, check out **South American Bicycle Touring Links** (www.geocities.com/TheTropics/Island/6810) for a long list of touring links. The **Warm Showers List** (www.warmshowers.org) is a list of cyclists around the world who offer long-haulers a free place to crash.

Hiking & Trekking

South America is a brilliant hiking and trekking destination. Walking in the Andean countries is not limited to the national parks: because the network of dirt roads is so extensive, you can pretty much walk anywhere, and with the region's indigenous population often doing the same, you won't be alone.

The Andean countries are famous for their old Inca roads, which are ready-made for scenic excursions. The over-trodden, three-day tramp along the Inca Trail to Machu Picchu (p884) is, of course, the classic, but alternate routes are more highly recommended because they are cheaper, less touristed, more scenic and less destructive. See p888 for some alternatives. There are other treks along Inca trails as well, including Ecuador's lesser-known Inca trail to Ingapirca (p693) and numerous along ancient Inca routes through Bolivia's Cordillera Real (p203) to the Yungas.

The national parks of southern South America, including Chile's Torres del Paine (p524), those within the Argentine Lake District (p130), and even Argentina's storm-pounded but spectacular Fitz Roy range (p152), are superb and blessed with excellent trail infrastructure and accessibility.

Lesser-known mountain ranges, such as Colombia's Sierra Nevada de Santa Marta (principally to Ciudad Perdida; p581), and Venezuela's Sierra Nevada de Mérida (p1016), also have great potential. The two- to three-day hike to the top of Venezuela's Roraima (p1042) is one of the continent's most unforgettable experiences.

When trekking in the Andes, especially the high parks and regions of Bolivia, Ecuador and Peru, altitude sickness is a very real danger; for more information, see p1095. Elevations in the southern Andes are much lower. Most capital cities have an Instituto Geográfico Militar, which is usually the best place for official topographical maps.

Diving
Major destinations for divers are the Caribbean coast of Colombia and Venezuela, islands such as Providencia (a Colombian island that is actually nearer to Nicaragua; p594) and the Galápagos (p724), and Brazil's Arraial do Cabo (p300).

Mountaineering
On a continent with one of the world's greatest mountain ranges, climbing opportunities are almost unlimited. Ecuador's volcanoes, the high peaks of Peru's Cordillera Blanca (p913) and Cordillera Huayhuash (p920), Bolivia's Cordillera Real (p201) and Argentina's

Aconcagua (the western hemisphere's highest peak; p127) all offer outstanding mountaineering opportunities. Despite its relatively low elevation, Argentina's Fitz Roy range (p152) – home to Cerro Torre, one of the world's most challenging peaks – chalks in as one of the world's top five climbing destinations.

River Rafting
Chile churns with good white water: the Maipó (p433), Trancura (p485) and Futaleufú (p512) rivers are all world class. River running is also possible on the scenic Río Urubamba (p881) and other rivers near Cuzco, the Río Cañete (p845) south of Lima, and in the canyon country around Arequipa (p861), in Peru. In Argentina, several rivers around Bariloche (p136) and Mendoza (p122) are worth getting wet in. Baños (p680) and especially Tena (p702) in Ecuador are both rafting hubs. The 2005 International Rafting Federation's World Rafting Championship was held on Ecuador's mighty Río Quijos.

Skiing & Snowboarding
South America's most important downhill ski areas are in Chile and Argentina – see those chapters for more details. The season is roughly June to September. There's also plenty of snow in the Andes of Bolivia, Peru, Ecuador, Colombia and Venezuela, where ski touring is a challenging possibility. More than one *loco* snowboarder has been known to bomb down an Andean volcano after climbing it. Chris Lizza's *South America Ski Guide* is an excellent resource.

Surfing
South America's best surfing is in Peru, especially the northern coast, but the water's chilly (so bring a wetsuit). Chile's central and northern coasts get good waves too, making a jaunt down South America's west coast, starting in Ecuador, satisfying indeed. Brazil has thousands of kilometers of coast, mostly characterized by beach breaks, with the best breaks in the southeast. Uruguay and Venezuela both have decent surf with a handful of top-notch waves. For more far-flung possibilities there's the Galápagos Islands (p724) and Rapa Nui (Easter Island; p530).

For detailed information, get a copy of the *Surf Report* from **Surfer Publications** (☎ 949-661-5147; www.surfermag.com; PO Box 1028, Dana Point, CA 92629, USA). It has individual reports on most parts of the South American coast. On the web, check out **Wannasurf** (www.wannasurf.com). For forecasts, subscribe to **Surfline** (www.surfline.com).

Wind Sports

Windsurfing and kite-surfing are becoming hugely popular and you might be able to learn how to do both (if you don't already know) more cheaply than at home. Adícora (p1008) and Isla Margarita (p1034) in Venezuela, San Andrés, Colombia (p591) and numerous places along Brazil's northeast coast – especially Jericoacoara (p371) and Canoa Quebrada (p368) – are outstanding kitesurfing and windsurfing destinations. In Argentina, San Juan province's Cuesta del Viento reservoir (ask about it at the San Juan tourist office, p127) is one of the best windsport destinations in the world.

Paragliding and hang-gliding are also approached with extreme enthusiasm. Top destinations include Iquique, Chile (p459), Mérida, Venezuela (p1014) and Medellín, Colombia (p595) and you can even fly from urban locations like Miraflores in Lima (p838) and Pedra Bonita in Rio de Janeiro (p287).

BOOKS

The list of South America–related books varies as wildly as the continent itself. For country-specific books, see the Books section of each chapter Directory.

Art & Literature

Get a handle on the region's art history with *A Cultural History of Latin America: Literature, Music and the Visual Arts in the 19th and 20th Centuries*, edited by Leslie Bethell. Andean art is supremely discussed, illustrated and photographed in Rebecca Stone-Miller's lush volume *Art of the Andes*. Celluloid enthusiasts will want to see John King's seminal *Magical Reels: A History of Cinema in Latin America*.

For notable literature by South American authors, see the Arts section within individual country chapters.

Flora & Fauna

Tropical Nature, by Adrian Forsyth and Ken Miyata, is a wonderfully readable (and occasionally hilarious) introduction to neotropical rainforest ecology. You can dive deeper into tropical ecosystems with John Kricher's friendly *A Neotropical Companion. Neotropical Rainforest Mammals: A Field Guide*, by Louise Emmons and François Feer, provides color illustrations for identification. All three of these are great to have along.

Bird-watchers heading to the Amazon should check out *South American Birds: A Photographic Aid to Identification* by John S Dunning. Covering more territory is Rodolphe Meyer de Schauensee's *A Guide to the Birds of South America*. Martin de la Peña's *Birds of Southern South America and Antarctica* is an excellent resource for southern Bolivia and Brazil, as well as points south.

The superb *Ecotravellers' Wildlife Guides* will tell you everything you need to know about wildlife, ecotourism, and threats and conservation efforts in specific habitats. Currently available in the series are *Ecuador and the Galápagos Islands, Brazil: Amazon & Pantanal* and *Peru*, all by David Pearson and Les Beletsky.

Henry Walter Bates' *The Naturalist on the River Amazons* is a classic 19th-century account. More or less contemporaneous is Alfred R Wallace's *A Narrative of Travels on the Amazon and Río Negro*. Anthony Smith's *Explorers of the Amazon* is a series of essays on explorers of various kinds, from conquerors and scientists to plant collectors and rubber barons.

Perhaps the best overall account of the plight of the world's rainforests is journalist Catherine Caufield's *In the Rainforest*, which contains substantial material on Amazonia, but also covers other imperiled areas. Julie Sloan Denslow and Christine Padoch's *People of the Tropical Rainforest* is a well-illustrated collection of articles on tropical ecology and development that deals with rainforest immigrants and indigenous peoples.

An engaging combination of travelogue and botanical guide, *Tales of a Shaman's Apprentice* is the wonderful story of Mark Plotkin's travels in Amazonia and the Guianas in search of medicinal plants. For everything you ever wanted to know about flora in the Amazon region, see *A Field Guide to Medicinal and Useful Plants of the Upper Amazon* by James L Castner et al.

Guidebooks

William Leitch's beautifully written *South America's National Parks* is essential background for trekkers, superb on environment and natural history, but weaker on practical matters.

To glimpse day-to-day realities you'll likely face in your travels, check out the *Culture Shock!* series. The *In Focus* series offers succinct and solid country overviews. Both of these cover most South American countries.

History & Contemporary Issues

Open Veins of Latin America, a must-read by the renowned Uruguayan writer Eduardo Galeano, is a classic and eloquent polemic on the continent's cultural, social and political struggles. Galeano's *Memories of Fire* trilogy is also excellent. John A Crow's *The Epic of Latin America* is a daunting but accessible volume that covers Mexico to Tierra del Fuego, from prehistory to the present. George Pendle's *A History of Latin America* is a readable but very general account of the region since the European invasions.

Conquest of the Incas, by John Hemming, is one of the finest interpretations of the clash between the Spaniards and the Inca. Hemming's *Search for El Dorado* is an equally readable and illustrated account of the European quest for South American gold.

Carl O Sauer's *The Early Spanish Main* casts Columbus as an audacious bumbler whose greed colored his every perception of the New World.

For a general analysis of both the cocaine and anticocaine industries, read *Snowfields: The War on Cocaine in the Andes* by Clare Hargreaves. *Green Guerrillas: Environmental Conflicts and Initiatives in Latin America and the Caribbean,* edited by Helen Collinson, focuses on the struggle between environmental conservation and the survival of local communities, with many voices and alternative views presented throughout. For an overview of social problems in Latin America, see Eric Wolf and Edward Hansen's *The Human Condition in Latin America.*

Lonely Planet

It's impossible to cover every element of South American travel in this book, so if you want greater detail on specific places, consider supplementing it with other guides.

Lonely Planet produces regularly updated travel guides for individual South American countries, with heaps of information, numerous maps and color photos. Titles include *Argentina; Bolivia; Brazil; Chile & Easter Island; Colombia; Ecuador & the Galápagos Islands; Peru;* and *Venezuela.*

For even more detailed information, see the Lonely Planet city guides to *Buenos Aires* and *Rio de Janeiro.*

Also useful are the *Brazilian phrasebook,* the *Latin American Spanish phrasebook* and the *Quechua phrasebook.*

For detailed trekking information, look at Lonely Planet's *Trekking in the Patagonian Andes* and *Trekking in the Central Andes.* If you're planning to visit Central America as well as South America, get a copy of Lonely Planet's *Central America on a Shoestring,* which covers the region from Panama to Belize.

Travel Literature

Driving from Tierra del Fuego to the North Slope of Alaska in 23½ days takes a little extra something and Tim Cahill's got it in spades – hilarious run-ins with customs officials and other bureaucrats make his *Road Fever* a great read. Motorheads and *Comandante* buffs shouldn't miss *Chasing Che: A Motorcycle Journey in Search of the Guevara Legend,* by Patrick Symmes; it follows Che's journey through South America. Of course, you can go to the source by picking up a copy of *The Motorcycle Diaries,* by Ernesto Guevara himself.

Peter Matthiessen describes a journey from the rivers of Peru to the mountains of Tierra del Fuego in *The Cloud Forest.* Alex Shoumatoff's *In Southern Light* explores firsthand some of the fantastic legends of the Amazon.

Chilean writer Luis Sepúlveda's gripping personal odyssey takes him to different parts of the continent and beyond in *Full Circle: A South American Journey,* translated into English for Lonely Planet's travel literature series.

You'll find loads more travel lit recommendations in the Directory sections of individual country chapters.

BUSINESS HOURS

Generally, businesses are open from 8am or 9am to 8pm or 9pm Monday through Friday, with a nice, fat two- to three-hour lunch break around noon. Businesses are often open on Saturday, usually with shorter hours. Banks usually only change money Monday through Friday. Forget about getting anything done on Sunday, when nearly everything is closed. In the Andean countries, businesses tend to close earlier. More precise hours are given in the Business Hours section of each country's Directory. Business hours for individual establishments are provided only if they differ significantly from these or those in the chapter directories. Opening hours for restaurants and bars vary throughout South America; see individual chapter directories for specifics.

CLIMATE

Climate in South America is a matter of latitude and altitude, although warm and cold ocean currents, trade winds and topography play their part. More than two-thirds of South America is tropical, including the Amazon Basin, northern Brazil, the Guianas and the west coasts of Colombia and Ecuador. These areas of tropical rainforest have average daily maximum temperatures of about 30°C (86°F) year-round and more than 2500mm of rain annually. Less humid tropical areas, such as the Brazilian highlands and the Orinoco Basin, are still hot but enjoy cool nights and a distinct dry season.

South of the Tropic of Capricorn, Paraguay and southern Brazil are humid subtropical zones, while much of Argentina, Chile and Uruguay have temperate mid-latitude climates with mild winters and warm summers ranging from 12°C (54°F) in July to 25°C (77°F) in January, depending on landforms and latitude. Rainfall, occurring mostly in winter, varies from 200mm to 2000mm annually, depending on winds and the rain-shadow effect of the Andes. (Most of the rain dumps on the Chilean side, while Argentina remains relatively dry, but receives strong winds.)

The main arid regions are northern Chile (the Atacama Desert is one of the world's driest) and Peru, between the Andes and the Pacific Coast, where the cold Humboldt current creates a cloudy but dry climate. There are two smaller arid zones, along the north coast of Colombia and Venezuela and the Brazilian *sertão* (the drought-prone backlands of the country's northeast).

The high Andes, which have altitudes of more than 3500m, and far southern Chile and Argentina are cool climate zones, where average daily temperatures fall below 10°C (50°F) and temperatures can dip below freezing.

Below the equator, summer is from December to February, while winter is from June to August.

El Niño & La Niña

About every seven years, large-scale changes in ocean circulation patterns and rising sea-surface temperatures create 'El Niño,' bringing

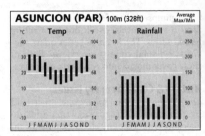

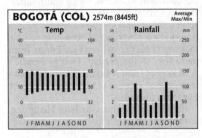

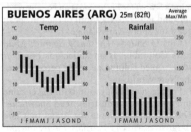

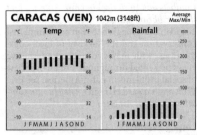

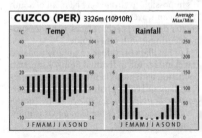

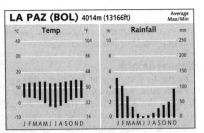

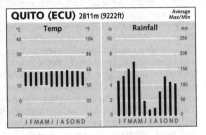

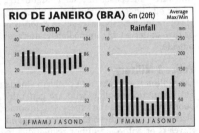

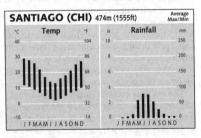

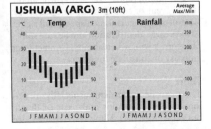

heavy rain and floods to desert areas, plunging tropical areas into drought and disrupting weather patterns worldwide. The 1997-98 winter was particularly destructive and traumatic for Peru and Ecuador, including the Galápagos Islands where wildlife perished at alarming rates. The name El Niño (The Child) refers to the fact that this phenomena usually appears around Christmas.

El Niños are often followed by La Niñas the next year, where the opposite effects are observed and can include bridge and road destruction, flooding of entire villages and subsequent refugee crises, raging forest fires in drought areas, malaria epidemics due to stagnant floodwater and lower fish catches due to increased water temperatures.

CUSTOMS

Customs vary slightly from country to country, but you can generally bring in personal belongings, camera gear, laptops, 'hand-held' devices and other travel-related gear. All countries prohibit the export (just as many countries prohibit the import) of archaeological items and goods made from rare or endangered animals (snake skins, cat pelts, jewelry made with teeth etc). Avoid carrying plants, seeds, fruits and fresh meat products across borders. If you're traveling overland to/from Colombia, expect thorough customs inspections on both sides of the border.

DANGERS & ANNOYANCES

There are potential dangers to travel in South America, but most areas are safe, and with sensible precautions, you are highly unlikely to encounter problems. Your greatest annoyances will likely be pollution, fiesta fireworks and low-hanging objects (watch your head!). For thoughts on bus safety, see p1085. Also see the Dangers & Annoyances sections in individual chapter directories; Brazil's (p400) offers some pointers that are useful throughout the whole of South America.

Confidence Tricks & Scams

Tricks involving a quantity of cash being 'found' on the street, whereby the do-gooder tries to return it to you, elaborate hard-luck stories from supposed travelers, and 'on-the-spot fines' by bogus police are just some of the scams designed to separate you from your money. Be especially wary if one or more 'plainclothes' cops demand to search your luggage or examine your documents, traveler's checks or cash. Insist that you will allow this only at an official police station or in the presence of a uniformed officer, and don't allow anyone to take you anywhere in a taxi or unmarked car. Thieves often work in pairs to distract you while lifting your wallet. Simply stay alert. See also p1068.

Drugs

Marijuana and cocaine are big business in parts of South America, and are available in many places but illegal everywhere. Imbibing can either land you in jail, land your money in the hands of a thief, or worse. Unless you're willing to take these risks, avoid illegal drugs.

Beware that drugs are sometimes used to set up travelers for blackmail and bribery. Avoid any conversation with someone proffering drugs. If you're in an area where drug trafficking is prevalent, ignore it entirely, with conviction.

Lonely Planet has received a couple of letters from travelers who were unwittingly drugged and robbed after accepting food from a stranger. You can see the mistake made here.

In Bolivia and Peru, coca leaves are sold legally in *tiendas* (stores) or markets for about US$1.50 for a pocket-size bag (including chewing paraphernalia; cheaper if you know where to get it). *Mate de coca* is a tea made by infusing coca leaves in boiling water. It's served in many cafés and restaurants in the Andean region, and coca-leaf 'tea bags' are also available. Although *maté de coca* is widely believed to combat the effects of altitude, there is no evidence that conclusively supports this, and a cup of *maté de coca* has no immediate stimulant effect.

The practice of chewing coca leaves goes back centuries and is still common among *campesinos* (peasant farmers) of the Andean *altiplano*. The icky tasting leaves are chewed with a little ash or bicarbonate of soda, as the alkalinity releases the mild stimulant contained in the leaf cells. Prolonged chewing dulls the pangs of hunger, thirst, cold and fatigue, but the initial effect just makes your mouth go numb. Without the alkaline catalyst, chewing coca leaves doesn't do much at all.

Be aware that someone who has chewed coca leaves or taken *maté de coca* may test positive for cocaine in the following weeks.

More refined forms of coca are illegal everywhere and transporting coca leaves over international borders is also illegal.

Natural Hazards

The Pacific Rim 'ring of fire' loops through eastern Asia, Alaska and all the way down through the Americas to Tierra del Fuego in a vast circle of earthquake and volcanic activity that includes the whole Pacific side of South America. In 1991, for example, Volcán Hudson in Chile's Aisén region erupted, burying parts of southern Patagonia knee-deep in ash. In 2002 Volcán Reventador (literally the 'exploder') erupted and blanketed Quito and other areas in northern Ecuador in ash. Volcanoes usually give some notice before blowing and are therefore unlikely to pose any immediate threat to travelers. Earthquakes are common, occur without warning and can be very serious. Andean construction rarely meets seismic safety standards; adobe buildings are particularly vulnerable. If you're in an earthquake, get in a doorway or dive under a table immediately; don't go outside.

Police & Military

Corruption is a very serious problem among Latin American police, who are generally poorly paid, trained and supervised. In some places, they are not beyond planting drugs on travelers or enforcing minor regulations in hopes of extracting *coimas* (bribes).

If you are stopped by 'plainclothes policemen,' never get into a vehicle with them. Don't give them any documents or show them any money, and don't take them to your hotel. If the police appear to be the real thing, insist on going to a police station on foot.

The military often maintains considerable influence, even under civilian governments. Avoid approaching military installations, which may display warnings such as 'No stopping or photographs – the sentry will shoot.' In the event of a coup or other emergency, state-of-siege regulations suspend civil rights. Always carry identification and be sure someone knows your whereabouts. Contact your embassy or consulate for advice.

Theft

Theft can be a problem, especially in Colombia, Peru, Ecuador and parts of Brazil, but remember that fellow travelers can also e accomplished crooks, so where there's a backpacker scene, there may also be thievery. Here are some common-sense suggestions to limit your liability:

- A small padlock is useful for securing your pack zippers and hostel door, if necessary. When used to secure your pack zippers, twist ties, paper clips or safety pins can be another effective deterrent.
- Even if you're just running down the hall, never leave your hotel door unlocked.
- Always conceal your money belt and its contents, preferably beneath your clothing.
- Keep your spending money separate from the big stuff (credit cards, traveler's checks, tickets etc).
- Pack lightly and you can stash your pack under your seat on the bus. Otherwise you'll enjoy the anxiety of wondering if your pack is staying on the roof every time you stop. It usually does, but… Some swear by grain sacks – buy one at a market, stick your pack in it and it looks just like the local haul, as well as keeping your pack from getting dirty.
- To deter pack slashers, keep moving when you're wearing a backpack and wear your daypack on your chest in crowded markets or terminals.
- Learn the taxi situation – there have been problems in Lima, Peru (where taxi drivers have participated in passenger robberies) and Bogotá, Colombia, home of the so-called 'millionaire's tour,' which involves armed robbers jumping into taxis and forcedly touring passengers from ATM to ATM.

Trouble Spots

Some countries and areas are more dangerous than others. The more dangerous places (see individual country chapters for details) warrant extra care, but don't feel you should avoid them altogether. Though much of Colombia is far safer than it was several years ago, continued armed conflict means parts of the country are still off-limits. The northern border region of Ecuador, specifically in the Oriente, can be dodgy due to spill-over from the armed conflict in Colombia. Travelers have been assaulted at remote and even well-touristed archeological sites, primarily in Peru; stay informed. La Paz (Bolivia), Caracas (Venezuela) and the Mariscal Sucre neighborhood of Quito (Ecuador) are notorious for assaults on tourists.

For more detailed information about trouble spots in specific countries see the Dangers & Annoyances sections in the individual country Directories.

DISCOUNT CARDS

A Hostelling International-American Youth Hostel (HI-AYH) membership card can be useful in Brazil and Chile (and to a lesser extent in Argentina and Uruguay) where there are many hostels, and accommodations tend to be, or traditionally have been, costlier. Elsewhere on the continent, cheap hotels and *pensiónes* typically cost less than affiliated hostels.

An International Student Identity Card (ISIC) can provide discounted admission to archaeological sites and museums. It may also entitle you to reductions on bus, train and air tickets. In less developed countries, student discounts are rare, although high-ticket items such as the entrance to Machu Picchu (discounted 50% for ISIC holders under 26) may be reduced. In some countries, such as Argentina, almost any form of university identification will suffice where discounts are offered.

DISCRIMINATION

Discrimination in South America – and it's a different beast in every country – is complex and full of contradictions. The most serious reports of racism experienced by travelers have been from black travelers who were denied access to nightclubs, in some cases until the doorperson realized they were foreigners. Some black travelers describe experiencing genuine curiosity from people who simply aren't used to seeing folks of black African descent. The Afro-Peruvian presence on Peru's South Coast makes it a welcoming place for travelers of color.

A posting on the **Lonely Planet Thorntree** (www.lonelyplanet.com) generated several responses from travelers of color who felt perfectly safe traveling in South America. Mixed-race couples may also receive curious looks from time to time. South Americans love to nickname people based on their appearance – *flaca* (skinny), *gordo* (chubby) – and a favorite for dark-skinned people is *negro/a* (literally 'black'). If you have darker skin, regardless of your heritage, you can expect to be called this – it's nearly always used affectionately.

See also Women Travelers (p1074) and Gay & Lesbian Travelers (below).

DRIVER'S LICENSE

If you're planning to drive anywhere, obtain an International Driving Permit or Inter-American Driving Permit (Uruguay theoretically recognizes only the latter). For about US$10 to US$15, any motoring organization will issue one, provided you have a current driver's license. See also p1085.

EMBASSIES & CONSULATES

For embassy and consulate addresses and phone numbers, see the Directory in individual country chapters.

As a visitor in a South American country, it's important to realize what your own embassy – the embassy of the country of which you are a citizen – can and cannot do. Generally speaking, it won't be much help in emergencies where you're even remotely at fault. Remember that you are bound by the laws of the country you are in. Your embassy will not be sympathetic if you end up in jail after committing a crime locally, even if such actions are legal in your own country.

In genuine emergencies you may get some assistance, but only if other channels have been exhausted. For example, if you have all your money and documents stolen, it might assist in getting a new passport, but a loan for onward travel will be out of the question.

FESTIVALS & EVENTS

South America has some fabulous fiestas, from indigenous harvest festivals to wild New Year parties. Some festivals, such as **Carnaval**, which is celebrated in Salvador (p339) and Rio (p280) around Lent in February/March, are worth planning your trip around. However, it's worth taking into account that some places are crowded and expensive, and it might be difficult to find accommodations. Remember, Carnaval is celebrated throughout the continent if you can't make it to Brazil.

For more information, see Festivals & Events in the individual country directories. Also see p12.

GAY & LESBIAN TRAVELERS

Brazil is the most gay-friendly country on the continent, especially in Rio de Janeiro, São Paulo and Salvador. Buenos Aires, however, has recently knocked Rio off the throne for title of 'gay capital' of South America, attracting more gay visitors than anywhere on the continent. That said, outwardly gay couples may be harassed in other parts of Argentina and Brazil. Bogotá, and to a lesser extent Santiago, also have lively gay scenes. Elsewhere on the continent, where public displays of affection by same-sex couples may provoke negative reactions, do as the locals do – be discreet to avoid problems.

Despite a growing number of publications and websites devoted to gay travel, few have specific advice on South America. One exception is **Purple Roofs** (www.purpleroofs.com), an excellent guide to gay-friendly accommodation throughout South America. The gay travel newsletter *Out and About* occasionally covers South America, and its website, **Out & About** (www.outandabout.com), offers subscribers online content about eight South American countries.

There's far more gay and lesbian information on country-specific websites (see respective chapter Directories), and there are a few sites with general information on South America. There are heaps of helpful travel links listed under the Businesses and Regional pages at **Pridelinks.com** (www.pridelinks.com). Though you have to sift through the superfluous stuff, there's some helpful travel information at **BluWay** (www.bluway.com).

INSURANCE

A travel insurance policy covering theft, loss, accidents and illness is highly recommended. Many policies include a card with toll-free numbers for 24-hour assistance, and it's good practice to carry that with you. Note that some policies compensate travelers for misrouted or lost luggage. Baggage insurance is worth its price in peace of mind. Also check that the coverage includes worst-case scenarios, ambulances, evacuations or an emergency flight home. Some policies specifically exclude 'dangerous activities,' which can include scuba diving, motorcycling, even trekking. If such activities are on your agenda, avoid this sort of policy.

There are a wide variety of policies available and your travel agent will be able to make recommendations. The policies handled by **STA Travel** (www.statravel.com) and other student travel organizations usually offer good value. If a policy offers lower and higher medical expense options, the low-expenses policy should be OK for South America – medical costs are not nearly as high here as elsewhere in the world.

If you have baggage insurance and need to make a claim, the insurance company may demand a receipt as proof that you bought the stuff in the first place. You must usually inform the insurance company by airmail and report the loss or theft to local police within 24 hours. Make a list of stolen items and their value. At the police station, you complete a *denuncia* (statement), a copy of which is given to you for your insurance claim. The *denuncia* usually has to be made on *papel sellado* (stamped paper), which you can buy at any stationer.

For information on health insurance, see p1090; for car insurance, p1088.

INTERNET ACCESS
Except for the most backwoods places, internet access is available nearly everywhere. Rates range from US25¢ to US$5 per hour, but generally hover near the lower end of this spectrum. This book lists internet access points in most towns and cities. Either 'Alt + 64' or 'Alt-Gr + 2' is the command to get the '@' symbol on almost any Spanish-language keyboard.

INTERNET RESOURCES
There's no better place to start your Web explorations than the **Lonely Planet** (www.lonelyplanet .com) website. Here you'll find succinct summaries on traveling to most places on earth, postcards from other travelers and the Thorn Tree forum, where you can ask questions before you go or dispense advice upon your return. You'll also find travel news and travel links that will connect you to the most useful travel resources elsewhere on the web.

Most of the other interesting Internet sites about South America are devoted to specific countries within the continent – see the individual country chapters for suggestions. For websites dealing with responsible travel, see the Responsible Travel section on p4. The following are all useful sites related to the continent or travel as a whole:

Latin American Network Information Center (Lanic; www.lanic.utexas.edu) University of Texas' outstanding list of links to all things Latin American.

Latin World (www.latinworld.com) Latin American search engine with loads of links.

South American Explorers (www.saexplorers.org) Excellent starting point for internet research.

UK Foreign & Commonwealth Office (FCO; www .fco.gov.uk) British government site with travel advisories and the like.

US State Department (www.state.gov) Travel advisories and tips; rather alarmist.

LANGUAGE
Spanish is the first language of the vast majority of South Americans; Brazilians speak Portuguese, but may understand Spanish as well. Without a basic knowledge of Spanish, travel in South America can be difficult and your interaction with local people will be limited. French is spoken in French Guiana, Dutch and English are spoken in Suriname, and English is spoken in Guyana.

Lonely Planet publishes the handy, pocket-size *Latin American Spanish Phrasebook*, and *Brazilian Phrasebook*. For a very brief introduction to Spanish and some useful phrases, see the Language chapter (p1098).

There are hundreds of distinct indigenous languages in South America, although some of them are spoken by only a few people. In the Andean countries and parts of Chile and Argentina, millions of people speak Quechua or Aymara as a first language, and many do not use Spanish at all. Quechua was the official language of the Inca empire and is most widely spoken in the Inca heartland of Peru and Ecuador (where it's called Quichua). Aymara was the language of the pre-Inca Tiahuanaco culture, and it survives around Lake Titicaca and in much of Bolivia. For a few useful words and phrases, see the Language chapter (p1098). If you're serious about learning more, or will be spending a lot of time in remote areas, look around La Paz or Cuzco for a good language course. Lonely Planet's *Quechua Phrasebook* is primarily for travelers to Peru and contains grammar and vocabulary in the Cuzco dialect, but will also be useful for visitors to the Bolivian and Ecuadorian highlands.

LEGAL MATTERS
In city police stations, you might find an English-speaking interpreter, but don't bank on it: in most cases you'll either have to speak the local language or provide an interpreter. Some cities have a tourist police service, which can be more helpful.

Replacing a lost or stolen passport will likely be expensive and time-consuming. If you are robbed, photocopies (even better, certified copies) of original passports, visas and air tickets and careful records of credit card numbers and traveler's checks will prove invaluable during replacement procedures. Replacement passport applications are usually referred to the home country, so it helps to leave a copy of your passport details with someone back home.

For more info, see p1063 and p1066.

MAPS

International Travel Maps & Books (www.itmb.com) produces a range of excellent maps of Central and South America. For the whole continent, they have a reliable three-sheet map at a 1:4,000,000 scale and a memorial edition of their classic 1:500,000 map. The maps are huge for road use, but they're helpful for pretrip planning. More detailed ITMB maps are available for the Amazon Basin, Ecuador, Bolivia and Venezuela. All are available on the ITMB website.

Maps of the South American continent as a whole are widely available; check any well-stocked map or travel bookstore. **South American Explorers** (www.saexplorers.org) has scores of reliable maps, including topographical, regional and city maps. For more information, see p649. Most South American countries have an Instituto Geográfico Militar, a military-governmental body that publishes and sells excellent topographical and other maps of its respective country. Once you're in a South American country, check the capital city for a location. See the individual country chapters for more suggestions.

MONEY

As in all of Lonely Planet's Latin American titles, prices here are quoted in US dollars. The reason for this is the historical instability of Latin American currencies. With widespread inflation throughout the Americas, the US dollar provides a stable platform, ensuring that listings are up-to-date and accurate throughout the life of a book. This does not in any way imply that US dollars are accepted in these countries; rather it gives the reader a base from which to gauge relative costs, as more travelers have more of an idea of what US$10 means than CH$5,428.

ATMs

Bring an ATM card. ATMs are available in most cities and large towns, and are almost always the most convenient, reliable and economical way of getting cash. The rate of exchange is usually as good as, or better than any bank or legal moneychanger. Many ATMs are connected to the Cirrus or Plus network, but many countries prefer one over the other. To search for ATMs in specific countries honoring either network, see www.mastercard .com and www.visa.com and click on ATM Locator. If your ATM card gets swallowed by a machine, generally the only thing you can do is call your bank and cancel the card. Cards usually only get swallowed when there's something wrong with your account (like insufficient funds). It's advisable to call your bank and let it know you'll be using your card throughout South America – that way the bank won't put a hold on it if it assumes suspicious activity.

Many ATMs will accept a personal identification number (PIN) of only four digits; find out whether this applies to the specific countries you're traveling to before heading off.

Bargaining

Bargaining is accepted and expected when contracting long-term accommodations and when shopping for craft goods in markets. Haggling is a near sport in the Andean countries, with patience, humor and respect serving as the ground rules of the game. Bargaining is much less common in the Southern Cone. When you head into the bargaining trenches, remember that the point is to have fun while reaching a mutually satisfying end: the merchant should not try to fleece you, but you shouldn't try to get something for nothing either.

Black Market

Nowadays, official exchange rates are quite realistic in most South American countries, so the role of the black market is declining. Most people end up using the *mercado negro* (black market) when crossing isolated borders, where an official exchange facility might be hours away. You might still want to use street moneychangers if you need to exchange cash outside business hours, but with the convenience of ATM cards, this necessity is declining.

If you do use street moneychangers, use the following common sense: be discreet, as it's often illegal, although it's usually tolerated. Have the exact amount handy to avoid flashing large wads of cash. Beware of sleight-of-hand tricks – insist on personally counting out the notes you are handed one by one, and don't hand over your dollars until you're satisfied you have the exact amount agreed upon. One common trick is to hand you the agreed amount, less a few pesos, so that, on counting it, you complain that it's short. They take it back, recount it, discover the 'mistake,' top it up and hand it back, in the process spiriting away some of the larger bills. For certainty, recount it yourself and don't be distracted by supposed alarms such as 'police' or 'danger.' Decline to accept torn, smudged or tattered bills. Other scams to watch out for include the old fixed calculator trick (in which the calculator gives an exchange rate favorable to the changer) and passing counterfeit bills.

Cash

It's convenient, but not crucial, to have a small wad of US cash tucked away because it's exchangeable for local currency just about anywhere. Of course, unlike traveler's checks, nobody will give you a refund for lost or stolen cash (if you find someone, let us know). When you're about to cross from one country to another, it's handy to change some small dollar bills rather than a traveler's check. Dollars are also useful when there's a black/parallel market or unofficial exchange rate. In some places you can exchange US-dollar traveler's checks for US cash at banks and *casas de cambio* (currency-exchange houses), in order to replenish your stash (or you can stock up in Ecuador, where the US dollar is the official currency). Trying to exchange ragged notes can be a hassle, so procure crisp bills before setting out.

In some countries, especially in rural areas, *cambio* (change) can be particularly hard to come by. Businesses even occasionally refuse to sell you something if they can't or don't want to change your note. So break down those larger bills whenever you have the opportunity, such as at busy restaurants, banks and larger businesses.

Credit Cards

The big-name credit cards are accepted at most large stores, travel agencies and better hotels and restaurants. Credit card purchases sometimes attract an extra *recargo* (surcharge) on the price (anywhere from 2% to 10%), but they are usually billed to your account at quite favorable exchange rates. Some banks issue cash advances on major credit cards. The most

widely accepted card is Visa, followed by MasterCard (those with UK Access should insist on its affiliation with MasterCard). American Express and Diners Club are also accepted in many places. Beware of credit card fraud (especially in Brazil) – never let the card out of your sight.

Exchanging Money

Traveler's checks and foreign cash can be changed at *casas de cambio* or banks. Rates are usually similar, but *casas de cambio* are quicker, less bureaucratic and open longer hours. Street moneychangers, who may or may not be legal, will only handle cash. Sometimes you can also change money unofficially at hotels or in shops that sell imported goods (electronics dealers are an obvious choice).

It is preferable to bring money in US dollars, although banks and *casas de cambio* in capital cities will change euros, pounds sterling, Japanese yen and other major currencies. Changing these currencies in smaller towns and on the street is next to impossible.

Traveler's Checks

The safest way to carry money is in traveler's checks, although they're not nearly as convenient as ATM cards. American Express are the most widely accepted checks, while Visa, Thomas Cook and Citibank are equally the next best. To facilitate replacement in case of theft, keep a record of check numbers and the original bill of sale in a safe place. Even with proper records, replacement can take time. A good way to safely keep copies of your check numbers is to email them to yourself; leave the email in your inbox, and the numbers will be available anywhere there's internet.

Have some traveler's checks in small denominations, say US$50. If you carry only large denominations, you might find yourself stuck with copious amounts of local currency when leaving a country.

In some countries, notably Argentina and to a lesser extent Peru, traveler's checks are more difficult to cash, and banks and *casas de cambio* charge commissions as high as 10%.

PASSPORT

A passport is essential – make sure it's valid for at least six months beyond the projected end of your trip and has plenty of blank pages for stamp-happy officials. Carrying a photocopy of your passport (so you can leave the original in your hotel) is sometimes enough if you're walking around a town, but *always* have the original if you travel anywhere (never get on a bus leaving town without it). To reduce the risk of hassles in the event you are asked for your papers, keep the original with you at all times.

PHOTOGRAPHY & VIDEO

Consumer electronics are readily available throughout South America, but taxes can kick prices through the roof.

Digital

Digital cameras make photography easy, cheap and fun. Emailing pictures to friends back home or posting them to a travel blog is a cinch. If you plan to print, you should shoot with no less than four megapixels. The best solution for storing photos on the road is a portable hard drive, which, if you really style yourself, can double as an MP3 player. If you can't afford a storage device, it's possible to burn your photos to CD at nearly any of South America's plethora of cyber cafés.

Film & Equipment

A good range of reasonably priced film, including B&W and slide, is obtainable in the biggest cities. Standard rolls of ASA 400 film can be found in nearly all cities and towns of reasonable size. For low-light conditions in the rainforests, carry a few rolls of high-speed (ASA 400 or faster) film and a flash.

Photo processing is relatively expensive, but widely available. Have one roll processed and check the results before you hand over your whole stash.

Photographing People

Ask for permission before photographing individuals, particularly indigenous people. If someone is giving a public performance (such as a street musician or a dancer at Carnaval), or is incidental to a photograph (in a broad cityscape, for example), permission is not usually necessary – but if in doubt, ask or refrain. If you're after local-market pictures, purchasing items from a vendor may result in permission to photograph them or their wares. Paying folks for their portrait is a personal decision; in most cases, the subject will tell you right off the going rate for a photo.

Restrictions

Some tourist sites charge an additional fee for tourists with cameras. It's unwise and possibly illegal to take photos of military installations and personnel or security-sensitive places such as police stations. In most churches, flash photography (and sometimes photography period) is not allowed.

Video & DVD

Go digital. If you can't, 8mm cassettes for video cameras are available if you really search. Tourist sites that charge for still cameras often charge more for a video camera. If you want to buy a prerecorded videocassette, remember that different countries use different TV and video systems. For example, Colombia and Venezuela use the NTSC system (as in the USA), while Brazil uses PAL, and French Guiana uses the French SECAM system. DVD systems are the same throughout the world.

POST

International postal rates can be quite expensive. Generally, important mail and parcels should be sent by registered or certified service; otherwise, they may go missing. Sending parcels can be awkward: often an *aduana* (customs) officer must inspect the contents before a postal clerk can accept them, so wait to seal your package until after it has been checked. Most post offices have a parcels window, usually signed *encomiendas* (parcels). The place for posting overseas parcels is sometimes different from the main post office.

UPS, FedEx, DHL and other private postal services are available in most countries, but are outrageously expensive.

If you're sending parcels to North America, it's generally cheaper to send them from northern South American countries such as Ecuador or Venezuela.

Local Addresses

Some South American addresses in this book contain a post-office box number as well as a street address. A post-office box is known as an *apartado* (abbreviated 'Ap' or 'Apto') or a *casilla de correos* (abbreviated 'Casilla' or 'CC'). When addresses do not have an official number, which happens regularly in rural areas, the abbreviation 's/n' for *sin numero* (without number) is often used.

Receiving Mail

The simplest way to receive mail is to have letters sent to you c/o Lista de Correos ('Posta Restante' in Brazil), followed by the name of the city and country where you expect to be. Mail addressed like this will always be sent to that city's main post office. In most places, the service is free or almost so. Most post offices hold mail for a month or two. American Express operates a mail service for clients.

Bring your passport when collecting mail. If awaited correspondence seems to have gone missing, ask the clerk to check under every possible combination of your initials. To simplify matters, have your letters addressed with only your first and surnames, with the latter underlined and in capital letters.

STUDYING

Spanish-language courses are available in most South American cities, with Cuzco (Peru; p870), Arequipa (Peru; p857), Cuenca (Ecuador; p688) and Buenos Aires (Argentina; p47; especially now that it's cheap) being some of the best. For Portuguese, Rio de Janeiro (Brazil; p280) is a great place to spend some time studying. For Quechua and Aymara, try Cochabamba (Bolivia; p227) or Cuzco (p870).

For country-specific details, see individual country chapters, and for school listings, see individual cities. **Language Schools Guide** (www .languageschoolsguide.com) is a great place to begin your research online.

TELEPHONE

Traditionally, governments have operated the national and international telecommunications systems and, traditionally, services have been horrid. Many countries have privatized their phone systems, choosing high charges over poor service, but sometimes getting both. International calls are particularly expensive from Bolivia and Colombia and are perhaps cheapest from Chile and Argentina.

Direct dial lines, accessed via special numbers and billed to an account at home, have made international calls much simpler. There are different access numbers for each telephone company in each country – get a list from your phone company before you leave.

It is sometimes cheaper to make a collect (reverse-charge) or credit-card call overseas than to pay for the call at the source. Often the best way is to make a quick international call and have the other party call you back (some telephone offices allow this, others don't). Keep your eyes peeled for 'net-to-phone' capabilities, where calls can be as cheap as US25¢ per minute to the USA and Europe.

Nearly every town and city has a telephone office with a row of phone booths for local and international calls.

Cell Phones

Cell (or mobile) phone numbers throughout South America often have different area codes than fixed line numbers, even if the cellular phone owner resides in the same city. Calling a cell phone number is often more expensive (sometimes exorbitantly so) than calling a fixed line.

If you plan to carry your own cellular phone, a GSM tri- or quad-band phone is your best bet, though you still won't get coverage everywhere – for example, you cannot currently get reception in Ecuador with a tri-band phone. Remember, the prices for calls can be extremely high.

Another option is purchasing a prepaid SIM card (or cards) for the countries where you plan on traveling. You will need a compatible international GSM cell phone that is SIM-unlocked.

This is a rapidly changing field, and you can stay up to date by checking www.kropla .com and www.gsmworld.com.

Phone Cards

Usually, the cheapest way to make an international call is by using a phonecard, the type you purchase at a kiosk or corner store. These allow you to call North America or Europe for as cheap as US3¢ per minute with a good card. The caveat is that you need a private phone line or a permissive telephone kiosk operator to use them.

TOILETS

There are two toilet rules for South America: always carry your own toilet paper and don't ever throw anything into the toilet bowl. Except in the most developed places, South American sewer systems can't handle toilet paper, so all paper products must be discarded in the wastebasket. Another general rule is to use public bathrooms whenever you can, as you never know when your next opportunity will be. Folks posted outside bathrooms proffering swaths of paper require payment. For a list of clean bathrooms worldwide – and proof that you can find anything online – check out the **Bathroom Diaries** (www.thebathroomdiaries .com).

TOURIST INFORMATION

Every country in South America has government-run tourist offices, but their breadth of coverage and quality vary. Local tourist offices are listed throughout this book wherever they exist.

South American Explorers (SAE; www.saexplorers.org) is by far one of the most helpful organizations for travelers to South America. Founded in 1977, SAE functions as an information center for travelers, adventurers and researchers. It supports scientific fieldwork, mountaineering and other expeditions, wilderness conservation and social development in Latin America. It has traveler clubhouses in Buenos Aires (p50), Lima (p836), Cuzco (p871) and Quito (p649), as well as the **US office** (☎ 607-277-0488 or toll-free ☎ 800-274-0568; 126 Indian Creek Rd, Ithaca, NY 14850), which publishes the quarterly magazine, *South American Explorer*. The clubhouses have extensive libraries of books, maps and traveler's reports, plus a great atmosphere. The club itself sells maps, books and other items at its offices and by mail order.

Annual SAE membership is US$50/80 per individual/couple or US$30 per person with a group of four or more and includes four issues of *South American Explorer* magazine. Members receive access to the club's information service, libraries, storage facilities, mail service and book exchange, and discounts at numerous hotels and travel services. Joining online or at any clubhouse is easy.

TRAVELERS WITH DISABILITIES

In general, South America is not well set up for disabled travelers, but the more modernized, Southern Cone countries are slightly more accommodating – notably Chile, Argentina and perhaps the main cities of Brazil. Unfortunately, cheap local lodgings probably won't be well-equipped to deal with physically challenged travelers; air travel will be more feasible than local buses (although this isn't impossible); and well-developed tourist attractions will be more accessible than off-the-beaten-track destinations. Start your research here:

Access-able Travel Source (www.access-able.com) Offers little information specifically on South America, but provides some good general travel advice.

All Go Here Airline Directory (www.everybody.co.uk /airindex.htm) Lists airline by airline services available to disabled passengers.

Emerging Horizons (www.emerginghorizons.com) Features well-written articles and regular columns full of handy advice.

Mobility International (www.miusa.org) US-based. Advises travelers with disabilities and runs educational-exchange programs – a good way to visit South America.

National Information Communication Awareness Network (Nican; www.nican.com.au) For folks from Australia and New Zealand.

Royal Association for Disability and Rehabilitation (www.radar.org.uk) Good resource for travelers from the UK.

Society for Accessible Travel & Hospitality (SATH; www.sath.org) Good, general travel information; based in the USA.

VISAS & DOCUMENTS

A visa is an endorsement in your passport (p1069), usually a big stamp, permitting you to enter a country and remain for a specified period of time. It's obtained from a foreign embassy or consulate of that country – not *in* that country. You can often get them in your home country, but it's also usually possible to get them en route, which may be better if you have a flexible itinerary: most visas are only good for a limited period after they're issued. Ask other travelers about the best places to get visas, since two consulates of the same country may enforce different requirements.

If you really need a visa fast, kiss ass and explain your needs. Consulates can often be very helpful if the officials sympathize and your papers are in order. Sometimes they will charge a fee for fast processing, but don't mistake this for a bribe.

Nationals of most European countries and Japan require few visas, but travelers from the USA need some, and those from Australia, New Zealand or South Africa might need several. Carry a handful of passport-size photographs for visa applications (although most border towns have a photographer who can do the honors).

Visa requirements are given in the Fast Facts section at the beginning of each country chapter, but a summary follows. Some countries issue tourist cards to visitors on arrival; while traveling within those countries, carry your tourist card with you at all times. Residents of most countries will not need visas for

Argentina, Bolivia, Chile, Colombia, Ecuador, French Guiana or Peru; consult the following list for other destinations.

Brazil Residents of Canada, the USA, Australia, New Zealand and Japan require visas (p407).

Falkland Islands/Islas Malvinas For non-Britons, visa requirements are generally the same as those for foreigners visiting the UK, although Argentines must obtain an advance visa. Any queries regarding entry requirements for the Falkland Islands should be directed to the British embassy in your home country (p41).

Paraguay Residents of Canada, the USA, Australia and New Zealand require visas (p819).

Suriname Residents of Canada, the USA, Australia, New Zealand, France, Germany, the UK and the Netherlands require visas (p773).

If you need a visa for a certain country and arrive at a land border without one, be prepared to backtrack to the nearest town with a consulate to get one. Airlines won't normally let you board a plane for a country to which you don't have the necessary visa. Also, a visa in itself does not guarantee entry: you may still be turned back at the border if you don't have 'sufficient funds' or an onward or return ticket.

Onward or Return Tickets

Several countries require you to have a ticket out of their country before they will admit you at the border, grant you a visa or let you board their national airline. (See individual country Directory chapters for specifics.) The onward or return ticket requirement can be a major nuisance for travelers who want to fly into one country and travel overland through others. Officially, Peru, Colombia, Ecuador, Venezuela, Bolivia, Brazil, Suriname and French Guiana demand onward tickets, but only Brazil, Suriname and French Guiana are strict about it. Still, if you arrive in one of the countries technically requiring an onward ticket or sufficient funds and aggravate or in any way piss off a border guard, they *can* enforce these rules (yet another reason to be pleasant and neatly dressed at border crossings).

While proof of onward or return tickets is rarely asked for by South American border officials, airline officials, especially in the US, have begun to refuse boarding passengers with one-way tickets who cannot show proof of onward or return travel or proof of citizenship in the destination country.

One way around this is to purchase a cheap, fully refundable ticket (from, say, Caracas to Miami) and cash it in after your arrival. The downside is that the refund can take up to three months. Before purchasing the ticket, you should also ask specifically where you can get a refund, as some airlines will only refund tickets at the office of purchase or at their head office.

Any ticket out of South America plus sufficient funds are usually an adequate substitute for an onward ticket. Having a major credit card or two may help.

Sufficient Funds

Sufficient funds are often *technically* required but rarely asked for. Immigration officials may ask (verbally or on the application form) about your financial resources. If you lack 'sufficient funds' for your proposed visit, officials may limit the length of your stay, but once you are in the country, you can usually extend your visa by showing a wad of traveler's checks or producing a credit card.

VOLUNTEERING

Poking around on the internet or browsing volunteer publications definitely makes one thing clear: your work alone is not enough. Most international volunteer organizations require a weekly or monthly fee (sometimes up to US$1500 for two weeks, not including airfare) which can feel a bit harsh. This is usually to cover the costs of housing you, paying the organization's staff, rent, website fees and all that stuff. Whether it seems fair or not, your money is usually going to a good cause (or at least to the cause's bureaucracy). But what if you just want to donate your hard work? Is there an alternative? There is. But you'll have to look harder and search from within South America to find the sorts of organizations and places that need you. One opportunity is working for an eco-lodge or responsible tour group, both of which regularly need English-speaking staff. And the more you stick around, the more you find where you can help out – without paying thrice what you'd normally pay for food and lodging.

The advantage to setting up a volunteer position from home is that everything is taken care of for you and you can start working right away. This is usually an attractive option for people with less time and who speak little

Spanish or Portuguese. Adequate Spanish (or Portuguese in Brazil) is usually essential for any volunteer work in South America.

Whether you set up your position from home or in South America, if you're working for an organization, expect to provide your own food and lodging, or pay up to US$300 per month. If you're setting up from home, you usually have to pay an application fee to boot. Checking out volunteer opportunities on the spot also gives you a closer look at exactly what you'll be doing before you start. One good place to do this is the South American Explorers (SAE; see p1072), which maintains a database of volunteer work. If you want to peek at what's available before you go, check the following websites:

Amerispan (www.amerispan.com/volunteer_intern) Volunteer and internship programs in Argentina, Bolivia, Brazil, Chile, Ecuador and Peru.

Australian Volunteers International (www.ozvol .org.au) Sends qualified Australian volunteers to several spots in South America for one- to two-year volunteer stints.

Cross Cultural Solutions (www.crossculturalsolutions .org) Volunteer programs with and emphasis on cultural and human interaction in Brazil and Peru.

Idealist.org (www.idealist.org) Action Without Borders' searchable database of thousands of volunteer positions throughout the world. Excellent resource.

Rainforest Concern (www.rainforestconcern.org) British nonprofit offering paid but very affordable volunteer positions in forest environments in several South American countries.

Volunteer Abroad (www.volunteerabroad.com) Vast website housing links to hundreds of volunteer positions throughout South America. Great place to start.

Volunteer Latin America (www.volunteerlatinamerica .com) Worth a peek for its interesting programs throughout Latin America.

Working Abroad (www.workingabroad.com) Online network of grassroots volunteer opportunities with trip reports from the field.

WOMEN TRAVELERS

At one time or another, solo women travelers will find themselves the object of curiosity – sometimes well-intentioned, sometimes not. Avoidance is an easy, effective self-defense strategy. In the Andean region, particularly in smaller towns and rural areas, modest dress and conduct are the norm, while in Brazil and the more liberal Southern Cone, standards are more relaxed, especially in beach areas; note, however, that virtually nowhere in South America is topless or nude bathing customary. When in doubt, follow the lead of local women.

Machista (macho) attitudes, stressing masculine pride and virility, are fairly widespread among South American men (although less so in indigenous communities). They are often expressed by boasting and in exaggerated attention toward women. Snappy putdown lines or other caustic comebacks to unwanted advances may make the man feel threatened, and he may respond aggressively. Most women find it easier to invent a husband and leave the guy with his pride intact, especially in front of others.

Consider taking a Spanish (or Portuguese) class (see p1071) – a command of the language can sometimes be the best way to ward off unwanted attention.

There have been isolated cases of South American men raping women travelers. Women trekking or taking tours in remote or isolated areas should be especially aware. Some cases have involved guides assaulting tour group members, so it's worth double-checking the identity and reputation of any guide or tour operator. Also be aware that women (and men) have been drugged, in bars and elsewhere, using drinks, cigarettes or pills. Police may not be very helpful in rape cases – if a local woman is raped, her family usually seeks revenge rather than calling the police. Tourist police may be more sympathetic, but it's possibly better to see a doctor and contact your embassy before reporting a rape to police.

Tampons are generally difficult to find in smaller towns, so stock up in cities or bring a supply from home. Birth control pills are sometimes tricky to find outside metropolitan areas, so you're best off bringing your own supply from home. If you can't bring enough, carry the original package with you so a pharmacist can match a local pill to yours. Pills in most South American countries are very inexpensive. 'Morning after' pills are readily available in some countries, notably Brazil.

The **International Planned Parenthood Federation website** (www.ippf.org) offers a wealth of information on member clinics (Family Planning Associations) throughout South America that provide contraception (and abortions where legal).

WORKING

Aside from teaching or tutoring English, opportunities for employment are few, low-paying and usually illegal. Even tutoring, despite good hourly rates, is rarely remunerative because it takes time to build up a clientele. The best opportunities for teaching English are in the larger cities, and, although you won't save much, it will allow you to stick around longer. Santiago, Rio and the larger cities of Brazil are the best bets for decent pay. Other work opportunities may exist for skilled guides or in restaurants and bars catering to travelers. Many people find work at foreign owned lodges and inns.

There are several excellent online resources, including the following:

Association of American Schools in South America (AASSA; www.aassa.com) Places accredited teachers in many academic subjects in preparatory schools throughout South America.

Dave's ESL Café (www.eslcafé.com) The first name in ESin ESESL on the Net, with loads of message boards, job boards, teaching ideas, information, links and more.

EnglishClub.com (www.englishclub.com) Great resource for ESL teachers and students.

TEFL Net (www.tefl.net) This is another rich online resource for teachers from the creators of EnglishClub.com.

Transportation

CONTENTS

GETTING THERE & AWAY

AIR

Every South American country has an international airport in its capital and often in major cities as well. Main gateways include Buenos Aires (Argentina); Caracas (Venezuela); La Paz (Bolivia); Lima (Peru); Quito (Ecuador); Rio de Janeiro (Brazil); and Santiago (Chile). Less frequently used international gateways include Asunción (Paraguay); Bogotá (Colombia); Guayaquil (Ecuador); Manaus, Recife, Salvador and São Paulo (Brazil); Montevideo (Uruguay); Río Gallegos (Argentina); and Santa Cruz (Bolivia).

The most frequent and direct flights to a South American country are likely to be with its national 'flag carrier' airline. They include the following:

Aero Continente (www.aerocontinente.com; Peru)
Aerolíneas Argentinas/Austral (www.aerolineas.com.ar; Argentina)
Avensa/Servivensa (www.avensa.com.ve in Spanish; Venezuela)
Avianca (www.avianca.com; Colombia)
Lan (www.lan.com; Chile, Ecuador & Peru) Umbrella for LanChile, LanEcuador and LanPeru.
Lloyd Aéreo Boliviano (www.labairlines.com in Spanish; Bolivia)
Varig (www.varig.com.br; Brazil)

> **THINGS CHANGE…**
>
> The information in this chapter is particularly vulnerable to change. Check directly with the airline or a travel agent to make sure you understand how a fare (and ticket you may buy) works and be aware of the security requirements for international travel. Shop carefully. The details given in this chapter should be regarded as pointers and are not a substitute for your own careful, up-to-date research.

North American and European airlines offering regular South American connections include the following:

Air France (www.airfrance.com)
Air Madrid (www.airmadrid.com)
American Airlines (www.aa.com)
British Airways (www.britishairways.com)
Continental Airlines (www.continental.com)
Delta (www.delta.com)
Iberia (www.iberia.com)
KLM (www.klm.com)
Swiss (www.swiss.com)
Qantas (www.qantas.com.au)

Tickets

Airfares to South America depend on the usual criteria: point and date of departure, destination, your access to discount travel agencies and whether you can take advantage of advance-purchase fares and special offers. Airlines are the best source for finding information on routes, timetables and standard fares, but they rarely sell the cheapest tickets. Start shopping around as soon as you can, because the cheapest tickets must be bought months in advance, and popular, affordable flights sell out early.

Flights from North America, Europe, Australia and New Zealand may permit a stopover in South America en route to your destination city. This gives you a free air connection within the region, so it's worth considering when comparing flights. International flights may also include an onward connection at a much lower cost than a separate fare.

CLIMATE CHANGE & TRAVEL

Climate change is a serious threat to the ecosystems that humans rely upon, and air travel is the fastest-growing contributor to the problem. Lonely Planet regards travel, overall, as a global benefit, but believes we all have a responsibility to limit our personal impact on global warming.

Flying & Climate Change

Pretty much every form of motor transport generates CO_2 (the main cause of human-induced climate change) but planes are far and away the worst offenders, not just because of the sheer distances they allow us to travel, but because they release greenhouse gases high into the atmosphere. The statistics are frightening: two people taking a return flight between Europe and the US will contribute as much to climate change as an average household's gas and electricity consumption over a whole year.

Carbon Offset Schemes

Climatecare.org and other websites use 'carbon calculators' that allow travellers to offset the greenhouse gases they are responsible for with contributions to energy-saving projects and other climate-friendly initiatives in the developing world – including projects in India, Honduras, Kazakhstan and Uganda.

Lonely Planet, together with Rough Guides and other concerned partners in the travel industry, supports the carbon offset scheme run by climatecare.org. Lonely Planet offsets all of its staff and author travel.

For more information check out our website: www.lonelyplanet.com.

COURIER FLIGHTS

Courier flights offer outstanding value if you can tolerate the restrictions. Only the major cities are served, with London, Los Angeles and New York being the most common departure points. If you can get to one of these gateway cities and connect with a courier flight, you might save a big amount to occasional served destinations such as Rio de Janeiro or Buenos Aires. Courier operators include **Air Courier Association** (☎ in the US 800-822-0888; www.aircourier.org) and **International Association of Air Travel Couriers** (☎ 308-632-3273; www.courier.org).

RTW TICKETS

Some of the best deals for travelers visiting many countries on different continents are Round-the-World (RTW) tickets. Itineraries from the US, Europe or Australia can include five or more stopovers. Similar 'Circle Pacific' fares allow excursions between Australasia and South America. The downside is that you must choose your destinations at the time of purchase (although all but the first destination can usually be left open) and you may not be able stay more than 60 days in a country. Another option is putting together your own ticket with two or three stops and a return from another country. If you work with a travel agent, it might work out cheaper than an RTW ticket.

Fares for RTW and Circle Pacific tickets can vary widely, but to get an idea, shop around at the following websites:

Airbrokers (www.airbrokers.com) US based. Offers customized RTW tickets that don't require you to stick within airline affiliates.

Airtreks (www.airtreks.com) US based.

Oneworld (www.oneworld.com) Alliance between nine airlines that offer circle and multicontinent tickets.

Roundtheworldflights.com (www.roundtheworldflights.com) UK based.

Star Alliance (www.staralliance.com) Airline alliance that allows you to build your own RTW ticket.

Although you can sometimes purchase a RTW ticket online, it's usually best (and often required) that you purchase this type of ticket through a travel or airline agent due to the complexity of the ticket. And for your own sanity, nothing is better than a good agent when planning this type of ticket.

FREE STOPOVERS

If your flight to South America connects through Miami, Los Angeles, Houston or other cities in the US, or through cities in Mexico or Central America, you may be able to arrange a free stopover. This would allow you to spend some time in these countries before continuing south. Ask your travel agent about this possibility.

From Australia

Excursion fares from Australia to South America aren't cheap. The most direct routes on Qantas and its partners are from Sydney to Santiago or Buenos Aires. Fares are usually the same from Melbourne, Sydney or Brisbane, but from other Australian cities you may have to add the cost of getting to Sydney.

In terms of airfare only, it may be marginally cheaper to go to South America via the US, but even a day in Los Angeles would cost more than the savings in airfares, so it's not good value unless you want to visit the US anyway. It may be worth it for travel to Colombia or Venezuela, but not for cities further south.

The best RTW options are probably those with Aerolíneas Argentinas combined with other airlines, including Air New Zealand, British Airways, Iberia, Singapore Airlines, Thai Airways or KLM. The Qantas version of a RTW ticket is its 'Oneworld Explorer' fare, which allows you to visit four to six continents.

Some of the cheapest tickets are available through **STA Travel** (☎ 1300-733-035; www.statravel .com.au) and **Flight Centre** (☎ 133-133; www.flightcen tre.com.au), both of which have dozens of offices in the country. For online bookings, try www .travel.com.au.

From Central America

Flights from Central America are usually subject to high tax, and discounted flights are almost unobtainable. Nevertheless, it's cheaper, easier and safer to fly between Central and South America than to go overland.

You must have an onward ticket to enter Colombia, and airlines in Panama and Costa Rica are unlikely to sell you a one-way ticket to Colombia unless you already have an onward ticket or are willing to buy a round-trip flight. Venezuela and Brazil also demand an onward ticket. If you have to purchase a round-trip ticket, check whether the airline will give you a refund for unused portions of the ticket. One way to avoid the onward or return ticket requirement is to fly from Central America to Ecuador or Peru.

For other countries that require onward tickets, see p1073.

VIA ISLA DE SAN ANDRÉS
Copa Airlines (www.copaair.com) flies from Panama City to the Colombian island of Isla de San Andrés, off the coast of Nicaragua. One-way fares at press time were about US$203 (though they drop as low as US$115 if you purchase online). From San Andrés, you can continue on a domestic Colombian flight to Bogotá, Cali, Cartagena or Medellín, paying anywhere between US$125 and US$150 for the flight. For more information on Isla de San Andrés, see p590.

FROM COSTA RICA
Flights to Quito from Costa Rica are generally about US$100 more than from Panama. The Costa Rican student organization **OTEC** (www .turismojoven.com) offers some cheap tickets.

FROM PANAMA
There are direct flights from Panama City to Bogotá, Cartagena and Medellín. The Colombian airline **Avianca** (www.avianca.com) and the Panamanian carrier **Copa** (www.copaair.com) generally offer the cheapest deals to these places. Colombia officially requires proof of onward travel, but Copa offices in Cartagena, Barranquilla and Medellín should refund unused returns; check in advance. Refunds, in Colombian currency only, take up to four days. You can also fly from Panama City to Quito, Ecuador.

From Continental Europe
The best places in Europe for cheap airfares are 'student' travel agencies (you don't have to be a student to use them) in Amsterdam, Berlin, Brussels, Frankfurt and Paris, and sometimes in Athens. If airfares are expensive where you live, try contacting a London agent, who may be able to issue an electronic ticket or a paper ticket by mail. The cheapest destinations in South America are generally Caracas, Buenos Aires and possibly Rio de Janeiro, or Recife, Brazil. High-season months are from early June to early September, and mid-December to mid-January. The cheapest flights from Europe are typically charters, usually with fixed dates for both outward and return flights.

The following travel agencies are good possibilities for bargain fares from Continental Europe.

FRANCE
Anyway (☎ 0892-893-892; www.anyway.fr)
Lastminute (☎ 0892-705-000; www.lastminute.fr)

Nouvelles Frontiéres (☎ 0825-000-747; www
.nouvelles-frontieres.fr)
OTU Voyages (www.otu.fr) This agency specializes in
student and youth travelers.
Voyageurs du Monde (☎ 01-40-15-11-15; www
.vdm.com)

GERMANY
Expedia (www.expedia.de)
Just Travel (☎ 089-747-3330; www.justtravel.de)
Lastminute (☎ 01805-284-366; www.lastminute.de)
STA Travel (☎ 01805-456-422; www.statravel.de)
For travelers under the age of 26.

ITALY
One recommended agency is **CTS Viaggi** (☎ 06-
462-0431; www.cts.it), which specializes in student
and youth travel.

NETHERLANDS
Airfair (☎ 020-620-5121; www.airfair.nl)
NBBS Reizen (☎ 0900-10-20-300; www.nbbs.nl)
Student agency.

From New Zealand
The two chief options are to fly **Aerolíneas
Argentinas** (☎ 09-379-3675; www.aerolineas.com.ar)
from Auckland to Buenos Aires (with connections to neighboring countries) or to fly
with **Air New Zealand** (☎ 0800-737-000; www.airnz
.co.nz) from Auckland to Papeete, Tahiti, connecting with a **LanChile** (in Auckland ☎ 09-977-2233,
912-7435; www.lanchile.com) flight via Easter Island
to Santiago. Onward tickets, eg to Lima, Rio
de Janeiro, Guayaquil, Bogotá or Caracas, are
much cheaper if purchased in conjunction
with a long-haul flight from the same carrier. A 'Visit South America' fare, valid for
three months, allows you two stops in South
America plus one in the US, then returns
to Auckland. Various open-jaw options are
possible, and you can make the trip in either
direction.

Both **Flight Centre** (☎ 0800-243-544; www.flight
centre.co.nz) and **STA Travel** (☎ 0508-782-872; www
.statravel.co.nz) have branches throughout the
country. For online bookings try www.travel
.co.nz.

From the UK
Fares from London are some of the cheapest
in Europe, with the cheapest destinations in
South America generally including Buenos
Aires, Caracas, Bogotá and Sao Paulo. Ad-
vertisements for many travel agencies appear
in the travel pages of the weekend broadsheet
newspapers, in *Time Out*, the *Evening Standard* and in the free online magazine **TNT** (www
.tntmagazine.com).

Some London agencies specialize in South
American travel. One very good agency is
Journey Latin America (JLA; www.journeylatinamerica
.co.uk; London ☎ 020-8747-3108; Manchester ☎ 0161-832-
1441). JLA is very well informed about South
American destinations, has a good range of
air passes and can issue tickets from South
America to London and deliver them to any
of the main South American cities (this can
be much cheaper than buying the same ticket
in South America).

Other places to try are **South American Experience** (☎ 020-7976-5511; www.southamericanexperience
.co.uk) and **Austral Tours** (☎ 020-7233-5384; www
.latinamerica.co.uk).

Other recommended travel agencies in the
UK include the following:
Bridge the World (☎ 0870-444-7474; www.b-t-w
.co.uk)
Flightbookers (☎ 0870-814-4001; www.ebookers
.com)
Flight Centre (☎ 0870-890-8099; http://flightcentre
.co.uk)
North-South Travel (☎ 01245-608-291; www.north
southtravel.co.uk) North-South Travel donate part of their
profit to projects in the developing world.
Quest Travel (☎ 0870-442-3542; www.questtravel
.com)
STA Travel (☎ 0870-160-0599; www.statravel.co.uk)
For travelers under the age of 26.
Trailfinders (www.trailfinders.co.uk)
Travel Bag (☎ 0870-890-1456; www.travelbag.co.uk)

From the USA & Canada
Major gateways are Los Angeles, Miami and
New York; Miami is usually cheapest. Newark,
New Jersey; Washington, DC; and Dallas
and Houston, Texas, also have direct con-
nections to South America. As a general rule,
Caracas and Lima are probably the cheapest
South American destinations, while Bue-
nos Aires, Santiago and La Paz are the most
expensive.

Inexpensive tickets from North America
usually have restrictions; often there's a two-
week advance-purchase requirement, and
usually you must stay at least one week and
no more than three months (prices often double for longer periods). High season for most
fares is from early June to early September,
and mid-December to mid-January. Look in

major newspapers and alternative weeklies for sample fares and deals.

Travel agencies known as 'consolidators' typically have the best deals. They buy tickets in bulk, then discount them to their customers, or sell 'fill-up fares,' which can be even cheaper (with additional restrictions). Look for agencies that specialize in South American travel, such as **eXito** (☎ 800-655-4053, 925-952-9322; www.exitotravel.com). eXito has a very knowledgeable staff (most of them have lived in Latin America), offers great deals and is excellent for travelers with special interests.

The largest student travel company in the USA is **STA Travel** (☎ 1-800-777-0112; www.sta travel.com). Its US offices are listed on its website, or you can book tickets online. The **Adventure Travel Company** (www.atcadventure.com) deals with the general public as much as it does with students and offers some excellent prices. The agency has offices in the US and Canada.

Most flights from Canada involve connecting via one of the US gateways. **Travel Cuts** (☎ 800-667-2887; www.travelcuts.com) is Canada's national student travel agency. For online bookings try www.expedia.ca and www.travelocity.ca.

For US bookings online, try the following:
Cheap Tickets (www.cheaptickets.com)
Expedia (www.expedia.com)
Lowestfare.com (www.lowestfare.com)

Orbitz (www.orbitz.com)
Travelocity (www.travelocity.com)
STA Travel (www.sta.com) Best for travelers under the age of 26.

For occasional steals, try an air-ticket auction site such as **Priceline.com** (www.priceline.com) or **SkyAuction.com** (www.skyauction.com), where you bid on your own fare.

LAND
From North America, you can journey overland only as far south as Panama. There is no road connection onward to Colombia: the Carretera Panamericana (Pan-American Hwy) ends in the vast wilderness of the Darién Province, in southeast Panama. This roadless area between Central and South America is called the **Darién Gap**. In the past it has been difficult, but possible, to trek across the gap with the help of local guides, but since around 1998 it has been prohibitively dangerous, especially on the Colombian side. The region is effectively controlled by guerrillas and is positively unsafe.

SEA
A few cruise ships from Europe and the US call on South American ports, but they are much more expensive than any air ticket. Some cargo ships from Houston, New Orleans, Hamburg and Amsterdam will take a lim-

---

BORDER CROSSINGS

There are ample border crossings in South America, so you generally never have to travel too far out of your way to get where you eventually want to go. Between countries like Argentina and Chile – and especially throughout Patagonia – there are loads of border crossings. Most crossings are by road (or bridge), but there are many crossings that involve boat travel (such as across the Río de la Plata between Buenos Aires and Uruguay; several lake crossings between Argentina and Chile, and across Lake Titicaca between Bolivia and Peru).

With the influx of footloose foreigners in the region, border police are used to backpackers turning up at their often isolated corner of the globe. That said, crossing is always, always easier if you appear at least somewhat kempt, treat the guards with respect, and make an attempt at Spanish or Portuguese. If, on the off chance, you encounter an officer who tries to extract a few pesos from you before allowing you through (it does happen occasionally), maintain your composure. If the amount is small (and it generally is), it's probably not worth your trouble trying to fight it. Just consider it fodder for your stories. Generally, border police are courteous and compared to, say, the border police in the United States, very easy going.

Detailed information on border crossings is provided in local sections throughout this book; major crossings are listed at the start of each chapter. Also see Visas in the South America Directory and in individual chapter directories for specific requirements.

ited number of passengers to South American ports, but they are also expensive.

Some small cargo ships sail between Colón, Panama and the Colombian port of Barranquilla, but many of them are involved in carrying contraband and may be too shady for comfort. Nevertheless, some of these ships will take paying passengers, and some will also take motorcycles and even cars. Prices are very negotiable, maybe US$50 for a passenger, US$150 to US$200 for a motorcycle. For more information on shipping a vehicle, see p1085.

One of the most popular modes of travel between Central and South America is by crewing (or otherwise securing passage) on a private sailboat between Cartagena and the San Blás islands, with some boats continuing to Colón. The typical passage takes four to six days and costs US$220 to US$270. The best place for up-to-date information regarding schedules and available berths is at Hotel Holiday and Casa Viena in Cartagena (see p585).

Officially, both Panama and Colombia require an onward or return ticket as a condition of entry. This may not be enforced in Colombia, but it's wise to get a ticket anyway, or have plenty of money and a plausible itinerary. Panama requires a visa or tourist card, an onward ticket and sufficient funds, and has been known to turn back arrivals who don't meet these requirements. The Panamanian consulate in Cartagena is reportedly helpful.

GETTING AROUND

Half the fun of South America is getting around. Whether aboard a rickety *chiva* (open-sided bus) in Ecuador, a motorized canoe in the Amazon, a luxury bus in Argentina or a small aircraft humming over the Andes, transport on this continent can be just plain fun. It can also be grueling, stomach-turning and, at times, scary as hell. But one thing it never is, is lacking. In almost all of South America, affordable public transport is everywhere.

AIR

There is an extensive network of domestic flights, with refreshingly low price tags, especially in the Andean countries (Bolivia, Ecuador and Peru). After 18-hour bus rides across 350km of mountainous terrain on atrocious roads, you may decide, as many travelers do, to take the occasional flight.

There are drawbacks to flying, however. Airports are often far from city centers, and public buses don't run all the time, so you may end up spending a bit on taxis (it's usually easier to find a cheap taxi *to* an airport than *from* one). Airport taxes also add to the cost of air travel; they are usually higher for international departures. If safety concerns you, check out the 'Fatal Events by Airline' feature at **AirSafe.com** (www.airsafe.com).

In some areas, planes don't depart on time. Avoid scheduling a domestic flight with a close connection for an international flight or vice versa. Many a traveler has been stranded after setting too tight an itinerary that hinges on their international flight arriving on time and connecting with a domestic leg to a far-flung outpost. Reconfirm all flights 48 hours before departure and turn up at the airport at least an hour before flight time (two to three hours for international flights).

Flights from North America and Europe may permit stopovers on the way to the destination city. It's worth considering this when shopping for an international flight, as it can effectively give you a free air connection within South America. Onward connections in conjunction with an international flight can also be a cheap way to get to another South American city (for more, see p1077).

Air Passes

Air passes offer a number of flights within a country or region, for a specified period, at a fixed total price. Passes offer an economical way to cover long distances if your time is limited, but they have shortcomings. Some passes are irritatingly inflexible: once you start using the pass, you're locked into a schedule and can't change it without paying a penalty. The validity period can be restrictive and certain passes require that you enter the country on an international flight – you can't travel overland to the country and then start flying around with an air pass. Citizens of some countries are not eligible for certain air passes and on and on. For a concise overview of the various passes and their minutiae, see the air passes pages on the **Last Frontiers** (www .lastfrontiers.co.uk/airpass.htm) or **eXito** (www.exitotravel .com) websites.

MULTICOUNTRY AIR PASSES

A few decent South America air passes exist and can save you a bit of money, provided you can deal with a fixed itinerary. One such pass is the Mercosur Pass. This mileage-based pass offered by eight South American airlines (and sold by most travel agents) allows travelers to fly to cities in Argentina, Brazil, Chile (excluding Easter Island), Paraguay and Uruguay on the major airlines of those countries. The flights must be completed over a minimum of seven days and a maximum of 30 days, and there's a maximum of four flights in any country, eight flights in all (nine, if Iguazú Falls is on your itinerary). If you organize it well, this can be cheaper than some domestic air passes. The cost is based on the number of standard air miles (not kilometers) you want to cover; prices range from US$225 to US$870, for 1200 to 7200 miles.

The Visit South America air pass offered by Oneworld (p1077) allows stops in 34 cities in 10 South American countries. If Central America figures into your travel, and you're flying originally from the US, ask your travel agent about the Copa Pass, offered by Copa Airlines in partnership with Continental. With this pass you can fly from certain US cities to, say, Guatemala City and/or San José, Costa Rica, and on to one or more South American cities and return from South America.

SINGLE-COUNTRY AIR PASSES

Most air passes are only good within one country and are usually purchased in combination with a return ticket to that country. In addition, most air passes must be purchased outside the destination country; check with a travel agent. Argentina, Bolivia, Brazil, Chile, Colombia and Peru all offer domestic air passes; for more details, see Getting Around in the Transportation section of each country chapter.

Sample Airfares

Unless noted otherwise, the following chart shows sample mid-season, one-way airfares, quoted directly by airlines for purchase in South America. With some savvy you may find better fares. Sometimes, purchasing an *ida y vuelta* (return-trip) ticket is cheaper than buying a one-way ticket; be sure to ask.

Origin	Destination	Cost (US$)
Asuncíon	Buenos Aires	195-210
Bogotá	Quito	206
Buenos Aires	La Paz	160-285
Buenos Aires	Santiago	240-325
Buenos Aires	Ushuaia	103-150
Guayaquil	Galápagos Islands	300/344 (low/high season, round-trip)
Guayaquil	Lima	265-300
Lima	La Paz	195
Punta Arenas	Falkland Islands	500-580 (round-trip)
Punta Arenas	Santiago	400
Quito	Galápagos Islands	344/390 (low/high season, round-trip)
Rio de Janeiro	Manaus	300-520
Rio de Janeiro	Montevideo	250-350
Rio de Janeiro	Santa Cruz, Bolivia	240-325
Salvador	Rio de Janeiro	140
Santa Cruz, Bolivia	Florianópolis	450
Santiago	Easter Island	665 (round-trip)
Santiago	La Paz	355
Santiago	Lima	410

BICYCLE

Cycling South America is a challenging yet wonderful – and potentially inexpensive – alternative to public transport. While better roads in Argentina and Chile make the Cono Sur (Southern Cone; a collective term for Argentina, Chile, Uruguay and parts of Brazil and Paraguay) countries especially attractive, the entire continent is manageable by bike, or – more precisely – by mountain bike. Touring bikes are suitable for paved roads, but only a *todo terreno* (mountain bike) allows you to tackle the spectacular back roads (and often main roads!) of the Andes.

There are no multicountry bike lanes or designated routes. Mountain bikers have cycled the length of Brazil's Trans-Amazon Hwy and plenty of adventurous cyclists have made the transcontinental journey from North to South America. As for road rules, forget it – except for the logical rule of riding with traffic on the right-hand side of the road, there are none. Hunt down good maps that show side roads, as you'll have the enviable ability to get off the beaten track at will.

Bring your own bicycle since locally manufactured ones are less dependable and imported bikes are outrageously expensive. Bicycle mechanics are common even in small towns, but will almost invariably lack the parts you'll need. Before setting out, learn bicycle mechanics and purchase spares for the pieces most likely to fail. A basic road kit will include extra spokes and a spoke wrench, a tire patch kit, a chain punch, inner tubes, spare cables and a cycling-specific multitool. Some folks box up spare tires, leave them with a family member back home and have them shipped to South America when they need them.

Drawbacks to cycling include the weather (rain in Brazil or wind in Patagonia can slow your progress to a crawl), high altitude in the Andes, poor roads and reckless drivers. Motorists throughout South America often drive with total disregard for anyone but themselves, thus becoming the most serious hazard for cyclists. Safety equipment such as reflectors, mirrors and a helmet are highly recommended. Security is another issue: always take your panniers with you, pay someone to watch your bike while you sightsee and bring your bike into your hotel room overnight.

Before you fly, remember to check your airline's baggage requirements; if you don't box your bike up correctly you may be required to pay as much as US$100 each way. If you do box it up correctly, you can often check it free of charge.

Although it's well over a decade old, Walter Sienko's *Latin America by Bike: A Complete Touring Guide (By Bike)* makes for an informative pretrip read. For tips on packing, shipping and flying with a bike, check out www.bikeaccess.net. For loads of tips and such from others who have done it, check out **South America Bicycle Touring Links** (www.geocities.com/TheTropics/Island/6810/). Also see p1058 for more information.

BOAT

From cruises through the mystical fjords of Chilean Patagonia to riverboat chugs up the mighty Amazon to outboard canoe travel in the coastal mangroves of Ecuador, South America offers ample opportunity to travel by boat. Safety is generally not an issue, especially for the established ferry and cruise operators in Chile and Argentina. There have been a couple of recent problems with tourist boats in the Galápagos (including one that sank in 2005), so don't scrimp if you don't have to. Travel by outboard canoe and other small craft is generally safe.

Lake Crossings

There are outstanding (but expensive) lake excursions throughout southern Chile and Argentina, as well as on Lake Titicaca, in and between Bolivia and Peru. For details, see the individual country chapters. Some of the most popular are:

- Copacabana (Bolivia) to Lake Titicaca islands of Isla del Sol and Isla de la Luna.
- Lago General Carrera (Chile) to Chile Chico and Puerto Ingeniero Ibáñez (Chile)
- Puerto Montt and Puerto Varas (Chile) to Bariloche (Argentina)
- Puno (Peru) to the Lake Titicaca islands

Riverboat

Long-distance travel on major rivers such as the Orinoco or Amazon is possible, but you'll have a more idyllic time on one of the smaller rivers such as the Mamoré or Beni, where boats hug the shore and you can see and hear the wildlife. On the Amazon, you rarely even see the shore. The river is also densely settled in its lower reaches, and its upper reaches have fewer passenger boats than in the past. Other river journeys include the Río Paraguay from Asunción (Paraguay) to Brazil, or the Río Napo from Coca, Ecuador to Perú.

Riverboats vary greatly in size and standards, so check the vessel before buying a ticket and shop around. Hammock space on the slow boat between Manaus and Belém, Brazil, for example, costs between US$70 and US$110, including food; from Trinidad to Guayaramerín, Bolivia (three to four days), it costs US$30 to US$35. When you pay the fare, get a ticket with all the details on it. Downriver travel is faster than upriver, but boats going upriver travel closer to the shore and are more interesting scenery. The time taken between ports is unpredictable, so river travel is best for those with an open schedule.

Food is usually included in ticket prices and means lots of rice and beans and perhaps some meat, but bring bottled water, fruit and snacks as a supplement. The evening meal on the first night of a trip is not usually included. Drinks and extra food are generally sold on board, but at high prices. Bring some spare cash and insect repellent.

Unless you have cabin space, you'll need a hammock and rope to sling it. It can get windy and cool at night, so a sleeping bag is recommended. There are usually two classes

TRANSPORTATION

of hammock space, with space on the upper deck costing slightly more; it's cooler there and worth the extra money. Be on the boat at least eight hours prior to departure to get a good hammock space away from engine noise and toilet odors.

Overcrowding and theft on boats are common complaints. Don't allow your baggage to be stored in an insecure locker; bring your own padlock. Don't entrust your bag to any boat officials unless you are quite certain about their status – bogus officials have been reported.

For more tips on riverboat travel see p379.

Sea Trips

The best-known sea trip, and a glorious one at that, is the **Navimag** (in Chile ☎ 02-442-3120; www.navimag.com) ferry ride down the Chilean coast, from Puerto Montt to Puerto Natales (see p418 and p503). Short boat rides in some countries take you to islands not far from the mainland, including Ilha Grande and Ilha de Santa Catarina in Brazil, Isla Grande de Chiloé in Chile and Isla Grande de Tierra del Fuego in Argentina. More distant islands are usually reached by air. In parts of coastal Ecuador, outboard canoes act as public transport in through the mangroves.

BUS

If there's one form of transport in South America that's guaranteed to give you fodder for your travel tales, it's the bus. Whether you're barreling down a treacherous Andean road in a bus full of chickens in Ecuador, or relaxing in a reclining leather chair sipping sparkling wine with dinner on an Argentine long-hauler, you will rarely be short on entertainment. In general, bus transport is well developed throughout the continent – you will rarely find a town that you can't reach by bus. Note that road conditions, bus quality and driver professionalism, however, vary widely.

Highland Peru, Bolivia and Ecuador have some of the worst roads, and bad stretches can be found in parts of Colombia and the Brazilian Amazon. Much depends on the season: vast deserts of red dust in the dry season become oceans of mud in the rainy season. In Argentina, Uruguay, coastal and southern Brazil, and most of Venezuela, roads are generally better. Chile and much of Argentina have some of the best-maintained roads and

most comfortable and reliable bus services in South America.

Most major cities and towns have a *terminal de autobuses* or *terminal de omnibus* (long-distance bus terminal); in Brazil, it's called a *rodoviária*, and in Ecuador it's a *terminal terrestre*. Often, terminals are on the outskirts of town, and you'll need a local bus or taxi to reach it. The biggest and best terminals have restaurants, shops, showers and other services, and the surrounding area is often a good (but frequently ugly) place to look for cheap sleeps and eats. Village 'terminals' in rural areas often amount to dirt lots flanked by dilapidated metal hulks called 'buses' and men hawking various destinations to passersby; listen for your town of choice.

Some cities have several terminals, each serving a different route. Sometimes each bus company has its own terminal, which is particularly inconvenient. This is most common in Colombia, Ecuador and Peru, particularly in smaller towns.

Classes

Especially in the Andean countries, buses may be stripped nearly bare, tires are often treadless, and rock-hard suspension ensures every bump is transmitted directly to your ass before shooting up your spine, especially if you're sitting at the back of the bus. After all seats are taken, the aisle is packed beyond capacity, and the roof is loaded with cargo to at least half the height of the bus, topped by the occasional goat or pig. You may have serious doubts about ever arriving at your destination, but the buses usually make it. Except for long-distance routes, different classes often don't exist; you ride what's available.

At the other extreme, you'll find luxurious coaches in Argentina, Brazil, Chile, Colombia, Uruguay, Venezuela and even Bolivia along main routes. The most expensive buses usually feature fully reclining seats, and meal, beverage and movie services. Different classes are called by a variety of names, depending on the country; for more information see each country's individual Transportation sections. In Argentina, Brazil and Chile, deluxe sleeper buses, called *coche cama* (literally 'bed bus'), are available for most long-distance routes.

Costs

In the Andean countries, bus rides generally add up to about US$1 per hour of travel.

When better services (such as 1st class or *coche cama*) are offered, they can cost double the fare of a regular bus. Still, overnighters negate the need for a hotel room, thereby saving you money.

Reservations

It's always wise to purchase your ticket in advance if you're traveling during peak holiday seasons (January through March in the Southern Cone; and around Easter week and during holiday weekends everywhere). At best, bus companies will have ticket offices at central terminals and information boards showing routes, departure times and fares. Seats will be numbered and booked in advance. In places where tickets are not sold in advance, showing up an hour or so before your departure will usually guarantee you a seat.

Safety

Anyone who has done their share of traveling in South America can tell you stories of horrifying bus rides at the mercy of crazed drivers. In the Andean countries, where roads are bad and machismo gets played out on the road, these stories surface more often. And there are *occasionally* accidents. But remember this: in countries where the vast majority of people travel by bus, there are bound to be more bus wrecks. You don't see guidebook warnings about automobiles in the US, despite the fact that far more people die in cars there than die in buses in South America. Choosing more expensive buses is no guarantee against accidents; several high-profile, recent crashes in Chile and Argentina involved established companies. Some roads are notoriously dangerous (the La Paz–Coroico road in Bolivia, see the boxed text on p202, springs to mind) and, if you're worried, you can probably trim your risks by avoiding them. Or do what most travelers do: sit back and enjoy the ride.

CAR & MOTORCYCLE

Driving around South America can be mentally taxing and at times risky, but a car allows you to explore out-of-the-way places – especially parks – that are totally inaccessible by public transport. In places like Patagonia and other parts of Chile and Argentina, a short-term rental car can be well worth the expense. If you're driving your own car, so much the better.

There are some hurdles to driving. First off, you need an International Driving Permit to supplement your license from home (see p1066). Vehicle security can be a problem, most notably in the Andean countries and Brazil. Avoid leaving valuables in your car, and always lock it up. Parking is not always secure or even available; be mindful of where you leave your car, lest it be missing when you return. Contracting a local kid to keep an eye on things works wonders; agree on terms beforehand. Familiarizing yourself with phrases for 'nearest gas,' 'busted fan belt' and the like can mitigate road-trip stress. In the same vein, the more you know about vehicle maintenance and repair, the smoother your travels will be.

South American Explorers (SAE; www.saexplorers .org) sells a very useful *Central/South American Driving Packet*. Also look around online for a copy of Chris Yelland's *Driving through Latin America: USA to Argentina*.

Bring Your Own Vehicle

Shipping your own car or motorcycle to South America involves a lot of money (up to US$1500 each way from the US) and planning. Shipping arrangements should be made at least a month in advance. Stealing from vehicles being shipped is big business, so remove everything removable (hubcaps, wipers, mirrors), and take everything visible from the interior. Shipping your vehicle in a container is more secure, but more expensive. Shipping a motorcycle can be less costly.

If you're driving from North America, remember there is no road connecting Panama and Colombia, so you'll have to ship your vehicle around the Darién Gap (see Land, p1080 and Car & Motorcycle, p552).

Inspirational **VWVagabonds.com** (www.vwvaga bonds.com) is bursting with information on shipping and driving a vehicle to South America.

Hire

Major international rental agencies such as Hertz, Avis and Budget have offices in South American capitals, major cities and at major airports. Local agencies, however, often offer better rates. To rent a car, you must be at least 25 and have a valid driver's license from home and a credit card. If your itinerary calls for crossing borders, know that some rental agencies restrict or forbid this; ask before renting.

WORDS FROM BEHIND THE WHEEL

Don and Kim Greene have driven over 24,000km in South America and are still rolling. Their journey is part of a plan to drive around the world, providing 'virtual' cultural and travel experiences for teachers and students through their World of Wonders Project (see www.questconnect.org). Their vehicle: a medium-duty Cabover Mitsubishi Fuso FG 4x4 truck (known as a Canter outside the US), with a camper they designed and built onto the chassis. With Mexico, Central America and seven South American countries beneath their treads, and a responsible travel spirit in their hearts, Lonely Planet figured they were the perfect folks to ask about driving in South America. Don and Kim are from Tucson, Arizona.

Lonely Planet: How long have you been on the road?

Don & Kim Greene: We started from our base in Prescott, Arizona and have been off and on the road since October, 2004. We travel for eight to 10 weeks at a time and go home for two to three months [leaving the vehicle in South America]. As of May 14, 2006 we have been on the road for 38 weeks.

Has driving allowed you to connect with people differently than traveling by bus?

Our conversations with people are definitely different. They almost always begin with comments about the truck. In Brazil we met a lot of truck drivers because we stayed in *postos* (gas stations) a lot because there weren't very many campgrounds outside the beach areas. The truck drivers often travel with their families, and they have little kitchens attached to the undersides of their trucks. We found we had a lot in common with them as fellow drivers and travelers. We have met a wider variety of people from different socioeconomic levels than we generally do when riding the bus.

What are South American drivers like?

South American drivers get a bad rap, and some of them deserve it. However, once you get used to their aggressive driving, you learn to go with the flow and know what to expect. In Venezuela, however, the red light as merely a suggestion for stopping is pretty unusual and a little unnerving. Many drivers are friendly and flash their headlights and/or wave as a way of saying hello. Some drivers have even taken photos as they passed us by! City drivers are basically aggressive and rude, not letting us change lanes without us cutting them off. Try to stay out of cities.

What are the advantages of driving around South America?

The biggest advantage has to be the convenience of coming and going when you want. We can sleep in if we feel like it or leave immediately without having to wait several days for a bus (or train). We can also stop anywhere along the road if we see something interesting.

What about disadvantages?

The biggest disadvantage is probably the cost. If we could have stayed in Venezuela (South America's largest oil producer) the whole time, however, cost wouldn't be an issue. The cost of a gallon of diesel there was US8¢ (US2¢ per liter). But in Brazil the cost of fuel was between US$3.50 and US$4.00 (US91¢ to US$1.04 per liter). At 10 miles to the gallon that gets *really* expensive.

What have the border crossings been like?

With only one exception, the border crossings have been very straightforward and easy. Generally we go through immigration first. Then we head to the *aduana* (customs) office to fill out the paperwork to get the truck temporarily imported into the country. We generally receive permission for the vehicle to be in the country for 90 days. The whole process usually takes between 45 minutes to an hour. Holidays and weekends typically take longer. The one difficult time we had involved leaving Argentina during high season. We crossed where there was only a small office and arrived at the same time as several busses. The border personnel were absolutely overwhelmed and the process took about two hours.

Has security been an issue for you?
Security has not been an issue. Everything on the outside is locked and everything on the inside is out of sight. We believe that if the bad guys can't see inside, there is less temptation to break in. When visiting a city, we try to park in parking lots, but most of them are too small for us, so we try to park in busy areas (as long as they aren't too dodgy). We trust our gut instinct.

We've spent the night in campgrounds, gas stations, hotel parking lots, off-road in the middle of nowhere (bush camping) and city streets. When using a city street, we look for some place we think will have low traffic and usually close to a streetlight. We call it 'city camping' and we've never had a problem doing it.

What about cops?
So far in South America we have not been asked for anything other than ID by the police – they have been more curious than anything else. We carry realistic copies of our drivers' licenses together with copies of all of our vehicle documents. We use the copies with the police so that if necessary we can drive off without paying a bribe to retrieve our documents.

Do you have any recommendations for staying safe on the road?
Drive slowly. We also watch other drivers and try to avoid the ones that appear to be driving impaired. We try to drive very defensively and without distractions (like navigating or adjusting the stereo or air-con – that's what the passenger is for). We try to avoid driving in the downtown areas of large cities. We like to park and take mass transit or taxis into town. We very, very rarely drive at night, and only if absolutely necessary.

Due to the Darién Gap, you shipped your vehicle from Central America. What was this experience like?
Basically you have two options for shipping a vehicle: Container or RoRo. Container shipping allows you to ship your vehicle in a standard shipping container. This is generally the least expensive way to ship. If lucky, you can hook up with another traveler and ship both vehicles in a large container for less money. Container shipping is also easier as there are many more container ships than RoRo ships.

RoRo means 'Roll on, Roll off.' This vehicle is driven onto and off of the ship. This is necessary when the vehicle is larger than will fit in an 8ft wide, 8ft high container. It is also more expensive.

There are horror stories about vehicles being broken into and stripped of valuables during shipping. The general consensus is to somehow secure the camper from the cab of the vehicle to be sure that no one can rummage in the camper.

It is very helpful to hire a customs broker on both ends of the shipping to assist with exit and entry formalities. Generally these can be done by yourself, it will just take extra time.

Do you have any advice for would-be drivers?
If at all possible, drive a newer vehicle. Not having to worry about breakdowns is really nice. We know a number of other drivers driving old vehicles and they are always needing to do some kind of maintenance. Try renting a vehicle before deciding to buy/build an expedition vehicle. Some countries even have campers for rent. If buying in another country, check the regulations like obtaining title and insurance, which are different from country to country.

What about four-wheel drive versus two-wheel drive?
This is really personal preference. Most overlanders drive two-wheel drive vehicles. Being from the American Southwest we believe in the idea of 'self-rescue.' This means that a driver should have everything necessary to rescue their vehicle with them. It won't do any good if you get stuck in mud and the other drivers don't have a towrope to pull you free. Additionally, we like to travel off the beaten path and four-wheel drive gives us the confidence that we can make it back out again.

Any routes drivers' should absolutely not miss?
The Carretera Austral in Chile (see p509), the Lake District in Argentina (see p130), the Gran Sabana in Venezuela (see p1042) and the coastal route north of the Rio San Francisco in Brazil (see p339). We expect to find other such routes as we head north along the Andes.

TRANSPORTATION

Rates have come down over the years, and the best prices are found in tourist hot spots, where competition pushes rates down. Generally you'll pay around US$40 per day, but some companies charge extortionately high rates (up US$100 per day if you want unlimited kilometers). It's always worth checking, however, and getting a group together will defray costs. If the vehicle enables you to camp out, the saving in accommodations may offset much of the rental cost, especially in Southern Cone countries.

Insurance

Home auto insurance policies generally do not cover you while driving abroad. Throughout South America, if you are in an accident that injures or kills another person, you can be jailed until the case is settled, regardless of culpability. Fender benders are generally dealt with on the spot, without involving the police or insurance agents. When you rent, be certain your contract includes *seguro* (insurance).

Purchase

If you're spending several months in South America, purchasing a car is worth considering. It will be cheaper than hiring if you can resell it at the end of your stay. On the other hand, any used car can be a financial risk, especially on rugged roads, and the bureaucracy involved in purchasing a car can be horrendous.

The best countries in which to purchase cars are Argentina, Brazil and Chile, but, again, expect exasperating bureaucracies. By reputation, Santiago, Chile is the best place to buy a car, and Asunción, Paraguay is the best place to sell one. Be certain of the title; as a foreigner, getting a notarized document authorizing your use of the car is a good idea, since the bureaucracy may take its time transferring the title. Taking a vehicle purchased in South America across international borders may present obstacles.

Officially, you need a *carnet de passage* or a *libreta de pasos por aduana* to cross most land borders in your own vehicle, but you'll probably never have to show these documents. The best source of advice is the national automobile club in the country where you buy the car. In North America, the Canadian Automobile Association may be more helpful in getting a *carnet* than the American Automobile Association.

Road Rules

Except in Guyana and Suriname, South Americans drive on the right-hand side of the road. Road rules are frequently ignored and seldom enforced; conditions can be hazardous; and many drivers, especially in Argentina and Brazil, are very reckless and even willfully dangerous. Driving at night is riskier than the day, due to lower visibility and the preponderance of tired and/or intoxicated nighttime drivers sharing the road.

Road signs can be confusing, misleading or nonexistent – a good sense of humor and patience are key attributes. Honking your horn on blind curves is a simple, effective safety measure; the vehicle coming uphill on a one-way road usually has the right of way. If you're cruising along and see a tree branch or rock in the middle of the road, slow down: this means there's a breakdown, rock slide or some other trouble up ahead. Speed bumps can pop up anywhere, most often smack in the center of town, but sometimes inexplicably in the middle of a highway.

HITCHHIKING

Hitching is never entirely safe in any country. Travelers who decide to hitch should understand they are taking a potentially serious risk. Hitching is less dangerous if you travel in pairs and let someone know where you are planning to go.

Though it is possible to hitch all over South America, free lifts are the rule only in Argentina, Chile, Uruguay and parts of Brazil. Elsewhere, hitching is virtually a form of public transport (especially where buses are infrequent) and drivers expect payment. There are generally fixed fares over certain routes; ask the other passengers what they're paying. It's usually about equal to the bus fare, marginally less in some places. You get better views from the top of a truck, but if you're hitching on the Andean *altiplano* (high plain) or *páramo* (humid, high-altitude grassland), take warm clothing. Once the sun goes down or is obscured by clouds, it gets very cold.

There's no need to wait at the roadside for a lift, unless it happens to be convenient. Almost every town has a central truck park, often around the market. Ask around for a truck going your way and how much it will cost; be there about 30 minutes before the departure time given by the driver. It is often worth soliciting a ride at *servicentros* (gas/petrol stations) on the outskirts of large cities, where drivers refuel their vehicles.

Online, check out the South America section of **digihitch** (www.digihitch.com).

LOCAL TRANSPORTATION

Local and city bus systems tend to be thorough and reliable throughout South America. Although in many countries you can flag a bus anywhere on its route, you're best off finding the official bus stop. Still, if you can't find the stop, don't hesitate to throw your arm up to stop a bus you know is going your direction. Never hesitate to ask a bus driver which is the right bus to take; most of them are very generous in directing you to the right bus.

As in major cities throughout the world, pickpockets are a problem on crowded buses and subways. If you're on a crowded bus or subway, always watch your back. Avoid crowded public transport when you're loaded down with luggage.

Taxis in most big cities (but definitely not all) have meters. When a taxi has a meter, make sure the driver uses it. When it doesn't, always agree on a fare *before* you get in the cab. In most cities, fares are higher on Sundays and after around 9pm.

TRAIN

Trains are slowly fading from the South American landscape, but several spectacular routes still operate, offering some of the most unforgettable train rides on earth. Other non-touristy trains are often cheaper than buses (even in 1st class) but they're slower. If you're a railway enthusiast, or just a sucker for fun, try the following routes:

Curitiba–Paranaguá (Brazil) Descending steeply to the coastal lowlands, Brazil's best rail journey offers unforgettable views (p318).

Oruro–Uyuni–Calama (Bolivia–Chile) The Oruro–Uyuni run offers great *altiplano* scenery all the way to Uyuni, where a branch line goes southwest to the Chilean border. After a tedious border crossing, there's a dramatic descent to Calama, through wild moonlike landscapes and extinct volcanoes. This is a long, tiresome trip and can get extremely cold at night. Bundle up and bring along extra food and water (p215).

Oruro–Uyuni–Tupiza–Villazón (Bolivia) The main line from Oruro continues south from Uyuni to Tupiza (another scenic rail trip through gorge country) and on to Villazón at the Argentine border (p215).

Puno–Juliaca–Cuzco (Peru) From the shores of Lake Titicaca and across a 4600m pass, this train runs for group bookings during high season. Departures are unpredictable, but when it does run, it's open to nongroup passengers (p868).

Riobamba–Sibambe (Ecuador) Jostle for a spot on the roof to enjoy the death defying Nariz del Diablo (Devil's Nose), an exhilarating, steep descent via impossible switchbacks (p687).

Salta–La Polvorilla (Argentina) So what if it's a tourist train? The Tren a las Nubes (Train to the Clouds) negotiates switchbacks, tunnels, spirals and death-defying bridges during its ascent into the Andean *puna* (highlands), taking your brain to the clouds with it (p105).

There are several types of passenger trains in the Andean countries. The *ferrobus* is a relatively fast, diesel-powered single or double car that caters to passengers going from A to B but not to intermediate stations. Meals are often available on board. These are the most expensive trains and can be an excellent value.

The *tren rápido* is more like an ordinary train, pulled by a diesel or steam engine. It is relatively fast, makes few stops and is generally cheaper than a *ferrobus*. Ordinary passenger trains, sometimes called *expresos*, are slower, cheaper and stop at most intermediate stations. There are generally two classes, with 2nd class being very crowded. Lastly, there are *mixtos*, mixed passenger and freight trains; these take everything and everyone, stop at every station and a lot of other places in between, take forever and are dirt cheap.

The few remaining passenger trains in Chile and Argentina are generally more modern, and the salon and Pullman classes are very comfortable and quite inexpensive. The *economía* or *turista* classes are slightly cheaper, while the *cama* (sleeper class) is even more comfortable. Brazil still has a few interesting train trips, but they're quite short.

TRANSPORTATION

Health

CONTENTS

Medically speaking, there are two South Americas: tropical South America, which includes most of the continent except for the southernmost portion, and temperate South America, which includes Chile, Uruguay, southern Argentina and the Falkland Islands. The diseases found in tropical South America are comparable to those found in tropical areas in Africa and Asia. Particularly important are mosquito-borne infections, including malaria, yellow fever and dengue fever, which are not a significant concern in temperate regions.

Prevention is the key to staying healthy while in South America. Travelers who receive the recommended vaccines and follow common-sense precautions usually come away with nothing more than a little diarrhea.

BEFORE YOU GO

Bring medications in their original, clearly labeled containers. A signed and dated letter from your physician describing your medical conditions and medications, including generic names, is also a good idea. If carrying syringes or needles, be sure to have a physician's letter documenting their medical necessity.

INSURANCE

If your health insurance doesn't cover you for medical expenses abroad, consider getting extra insurance. Find out in advance if your insurance plan will make payments directly to providers or reimburse you later for overseas health expenditures. (In many countries doctors expect payment in cash.)

RECOMMENDED VACCINATIONS

Since most vaccines don't produce immunity until at least two weeks after they're given, visit a physician four to eight weeks before departure. Ask your doctor for an International Certificate of Vaccination (otherwise known as the yellow booklet), which will list all the vaccinations you've received. This is mandatory for countries that require proof of yellow-fever vaccination upon entry, but it's a good idea to carry it wherever you travel.

The only required vaccine is yellow fever, and that's only if you're arriving from a yellow fever–infected country in Africa or the Americas. (The exception is French Guiana, which requires yellow-fever vaccine for all travelers.) However, a number of vaccines are recommended (see opposite).

MEDICAL CHECKLIST

- acetaminophen (Tylenol) or aspirin
- acetazolamide (Diamox; for altitude sickness)
- adhesive or paper tape
- antibacterial ointment (eg Bactroban; for cuts and abrasions)
- antibiotics
- antidiarrheal drugs (eg loperamide)
- antihistamines (for hay fever and allergic reactions)
- anti-inflammatory drugs (eg ibuprofen)
- bandages, gauze, gauze rolls
- insect repellent containing DEET for the skin
- iodine tablets (for water purification)
- oral rehydration salts
- permethrin-containing insect spray for clothing, tents and bed nets
- pocket knife
- scissors, safety pins, tweezers

RECOMMENDED VACCINATIONS

Vaccine	Recommended for	Dosage	Side effects
chickenpox	travelers who've never had chickenpox	two doses one month apart	fever; mild case of chickenpox
hepatitis A	all travelers	one dose before trip; booster 6-12 months later	soreness at injection site; headaches; body aches
hepatitis B	long-term travelers in close contact with the local population	3 doses over 6-month period	soreness at injection site; low-grade fever
measles	travelers born after 1956 who've had only one measles vaccination	one dose	fever; rash; joint pains; allergic reactions
rabies	travelers who may have contact with animals and may not have access to medical care	three doses over 3-4 week period	soreness at injection site; headaches; body aches
tetanus-diphtheria	all travelers who haven't had booster within 10 years	one dose lasts 10 years	soreness at injection site
typhoid	all travelers	four capsules by mouth, one taken every other day	abdominal pain; nausea; rash
yellow fever	travelers to jungle areas at altitudes above 2300m	one dose lasts 10 years	headaches; body aches; severe reactions are rare

HEALTH

- steroid cream or cortisone (for poison ivy and other allergic rashes)
- sun block
- syringes and sterile needles
- thermometer

ONLINE RESOURCES

There is a wealth of travel health advice on the internet. For further information, the **Lonely Planet website** (www.lonelyplanet.com) is a good place to start. The **World Health Organization** (www.who.int /ith) also publishes a superb book called *International Travel and Health,* which is revised annually and is available online at no cost. Another website of general interest is the **MD Travel Health website** (www.mdtravelhealth.com), which provides complete travel health recommendations for every country; information is updated daily.

It's usually a good idea to consult your government's travel health website before departure, if one is available:
Australia (www.dfat.gov.au/travel)
Canada (www.travelhealth.gc.ca)
UK (www.doh.gov.uk/traveladvice)
US (www.cdc.gov/travel)

FURTHER READING

For further information, see *Healthy Travel Central & South America,* also from Lonely Planet. If you're traveling with children, Lonely Planet's *Travel with Children* may be useful. The *ABC of Healthy Travel,* by E Walker et al, is another valuable resource.

IN TRANSIT

DEEP VEIN THROMBOSIS

Blood clots may form in the legs (deep vein thrombosis or DVT) during plane flights, chiefly because of prolonged immobility. The longer the flight, the greater the risk. Though most blood clots are reabsorbed uneventfully, some may break off and travel through the blood vessels to the lungs, where they could cause life-threatening complications.

The chief symptom of deep vein thrombosis is swelling or pain of the foot, ankle or calf, usually – but not always – on just one side. When a blood clot travels to the lungs, it may cause chest pain and difficulty breathing. Travelers who have any of these symptoms should immediately seek medical attention.

To prevent the development of DVT on long flights, you should walk about the cabin, perform isometric compressions of the leg muscles (ie flex the leg muscles while sitting), drink plenty of fluids and avoid alcohol and tobacco.

JET LAG & MOTION SICKNESS

Jet lag is common when crossing more than five time zones, resulting in insomnia, fatigue, malaise or nausea. To avoid jet lag try drinking plenty of (nonalcoholic) fluids and eating light meals. Upon arrival, get exposure to natural sunlight and readjust your schedule (for meals, sleep etc) as soon as possible.

Antihistamines such as dimenhydrinate (Dramamine) and meclizine (Antivert, Bonine) are usually the first choice for treating motion sickness. Their main side effect is drowsiness. A herbal alternative is ginger, which works like a charm for some people.

IN SOUTH AMERICA

AVAILABILITY & COST OF HEALTH CARE

Good medical care may be more difficult to find in smaller cities and impossible to locate in rural areas. Many doctors and hospitals expect payment in cash, regardless of whether you have travel health insurance. If you develop a life-threatening medical problem, you'll probably want to be evacuated to a country with state-of-the-art medical care. Since this may cost tens of thousands of dollars, be sure you have insurance to cover this before you depart. You can find a list of medical evacuation and travel insurance companies on the **US State Department website** (travel.state.gov/medical.html).

INFECTIOUS DISEASES

Cholera

Cholera is an intestinal infection acquired through ingestion of contaminated food or water. The main symptom is profuse, watery diarrhea, which may be so severe that it causes life-threatening dehydration. The key treatment is drinking oral rehydration solution. Antibiotics are also given, usually tetracycline or doxycycline, though quinolone antibiotics such as ciprofloxacin and levofloxacin are also effective.

Cholera is rare among travelers. Cholera vaccine is no longer required, and is in fact no longer available in some countries, including the US, because the old vaccine was relatively ineffective and caused side effects. There are new vaccines that are safer and more effective, but they're not available in many countries

and are only recommended for those at particularly high risk.

Dengue

Dengue fever is a viral infection found throughout South America. Dengue is transmitted by Aedes mosquitoes, which bite preferentially during the daytime and are usually found close to human habitations, often indoors. They breed primarily in artificial water containers, such as jars, barrels, cans, cisterns, metal drums, plastic containers and discarded tires. As a result, dengue is especially common in densely populated, urban environments.

Dengue usually causes flulike symptoms, including fever, muscle aches, joint pains, headaches, nausea and vomiting, often followed by a rash. The body aches may be quite uncomfortable, but most cases resolve uneventfully in a few days. Severe cases usually occur in children under age 15 who are experiencing their second dengue infection.

There is no treatment for dengue fever except to take analgesics such as acetaminophen/paracetamol (Tylenol) and drink plenty of fluids. Severe cases may require hospitalization for intravenous fluids and supportive care. There is no vaccine. The cornerstone of prevention is protection against insects (see p1096).

Hepatitis A

Hepatitis A is the second most common travel-related infection (after travelers' diarrhea). It's a viral infection of the liver that is usually acquired by ingestion of contaminated water, food or ice, though it may also be acquired by direct contact with infected persons. The illness occurs throughout the world, but the incidence is higher in developing nations. Symptoms may include fever, malaise, jaundice, nausea, vomiting and abdominal pain. Most cases resolve without complications, though hepatitis A occasionally causes severe liver damage. There is no treatment.

The vaccine for hepatitis A is extremely safe and highly effective. If you get a booster six to 12 months later, it lasts for at least 10 years. You really should get it before you go to any developing nation. The safety of hepatitis A vaccine has not been established for pregnant women or children under two years – instead, they should be given a gammaglobulin injection.

Hepatitis B

Like hepatitis A, hepatitis B is a liver infection that occurs worldwide but is more common in developing nations. Unlike hepatitis A, the disease is usually acquired by sexual contact or by exposure to infected blood, generally through blood transfusions or contaminated needles. The vaccine is recommended only for long-term travelers (on the road more than six months) who expect to live in rural areas or have close physical contact with the local population. Additionally, the vaccine is recommended for anyone who anticipates sexual contact with the local inhabitants or a possible need for medical, dental or other treatments while abroad, especially if a need for transfusions or injections is expected.

Hepatitis B vaccine is safe and highly effective. However, a total of three injections are necessary to establish full immunity. Several countries added hepatitis B vaccine to the list of routine childhood immunizations in the 1980s, so many young adults are already protected.

Malaria

Malaria occurs in every South American country except Chile, Uruguay and the Falkland Islands. It's transmitted by mosquito bites, usually between dusk and dawn. The main symptom is high spiking fevers, which may be accompanied by chills, sweats, headache, body aches, weakness, vomiting or diarrhea. Severe cases may involve the central nervous system and lead to seizures, confusion, coma and death.

There is a choice of three malaria pills, all of which work about equally well. Mefloquine (Lariam) is taken once weekly in a dosage of 250mg, starting one to two weeks before arrival and continuing through the trip and for four weeks after your return. The problem is that a certain percentage of people (the number is disputed) develop neuropsychiatric side effects, which may range from mild to severe. Atovaquone/proguanil (Malarone) is a newly approved combination pill taken once daily with food starting two days before arrival and continuing through the trip and for seven days after departure. Side effects are typically mild. Doxycycline is a third alternative, but may cause an exaggerated sunburn reaction.

In general, Malarone seems to cause fewer side effects than mefloquine and is becoming more popular. The chief disadvantage is that it has to be taken daily. For longer trips, it's probably worth trying mefloquine; for shorter trips, Malarone will be the drug of choice for most people.

Protecting yourself against mosquito bites is just as important as taking malaria pills (for recommendations see p1096), since none of the pills are 100% effective.

If you do not have access to medical care while traveling, you should bring along additional pills for emergency self-treatment, which you should take if you can't reach a doctor and you develop symptoms that suggest malaria, such as high spiking fevers. One option is to take four tablets of Malarone once daily for three days. However, Malarone should not be used for treatment if you're already taking it for prevention. An alternative is to take 650mg quinine three times daily and 100mg doxycycline twice daily for one week. If you start self-medication, see a doctor at the earliest possible opportunity.

If you develop a fever after returning home, see a physician, as malaria symptoms may not occur for months.

Plague

The plague is usually transmitted to humans by the bite of rodent fleas, typically when rodents die off. Symptoms include fever, chills, muscle aches and malaise, associated with the development of an acutely swollen, exquisitely painful lymph node, known as a bubo, most often in the groin. Cases of the plague are reported from Peru, Bolivia and Brazil nearly every year. Most travelers are at extremely low risk for this disease. However, if you might have contact with rodents or their fleas, you should bring along a bottle of doxycycline, to be taken prophylactically during periods of exposure. Those less than eight years old or allergic to doxycycline should take trimethoprim-sulfamethoxazole instead. In addition, you should avoid areas containing rodent burrows or nests, never handle sick or dead animals, and follow the guidelines in this chapter for protecting yourself against insect bites (see p1096).

Rabies

Rabies is a viral infection of the brain and spinal cord that is almost always fatal. The rabies virus is carried in the saliva of infected animals and is typically transmitted through an animal bite, though contamination of any break in the skin with infected saliva may result in rabies. Rabies occurs in all South American countries.

Rabies vaccine is safe, but a full series requires three injections and is quite expensive. Those at high risk for rabies, such as animal handlers and spelunkers (cave explorers), should certainly get the vaccine. In addition, those at lower risk for animal bites should consider asking for the vaccine if they might be traveling to remote areas and might not have access to appropriate medical care if needed. The treatment for a possibly rabid bite consists of rabies vaccine with rabies immune globulin. It's effective, but must be given promptly. Most travelers don't need rabies vaccine.

All animal bites and scratches must be promptly and thoroughly cleansed with large amounts of soap and water and local health authorities contacted to determine whether or not further treatment is necessary. Also, see opposite.

Typhoid

Typhoid fever is caused by ingestion of food or water contaminated by a species of salmonella known as *Salmonella typhi*. Fever occurs in virtually all cases. Other symptoms may include headache, malaise, muscle aches, dizziness, loss of appetite, nausea and abdominal pain. Either diarrhea or constipation may occur. Possible complications include intestinal perforation, intestinal bleeding, confusion, delirium or (rarely) coma.

Unless you expect to take all your meals in major hotels and restaurants, typhoid vaccine is a good idea. It's usually given orally, but is also available as an injection. Neither vaccine is approved for use in children under two years.

The drug of choice for typhoid fever is usually a quinolone antibiotic such as ciprofloxacin (Cipro) or levofloxacin (Levaquin), which many travelers carry for treatment of travelers' diarrhea. However, if you self-treat for typhoid fever, you may also need to self-treat for malaria, since the symptoms of the two diseases may be indistinguishable.

Yellow Fever

Yellow fever is a life-threatening viral infection transmitted by mosquitoes in forested areas. The illness begins with flulike symptoms, which may include fever, chills, headache, muscle aches, backache, loss of appetite, nausea and vomiting. These symptoms usually subside in a few days, but one person in six enters a second, toxic phase characterized by recurrent fever, vomiting, listlessness, jaundice, kidney failure and hemorrhage, leading to death in up to half of the cases. There is no treatment except for supportive care.

Yellow-fever vaccine is given only in approved yellow-fever vaccination centers, which provide validated International Certificates of Vaccination (yellow booklets). The vaccine should be given at least 10 days before any potential exposure to yellow fever and remains effective for approximately 10 years. Reactions to the vaccine are generally mild and may include headaches, muscle aches, low-grade fevers, or discomfort at the injection site. Severe, life-threatening reactions have been described but are extremely rare. In general, the risk of becoming ill from the vaccine is far less than the risk of becoming ill from yellow fever, and you're strongly encouraged to get the vaccine.

Taking measures to protect yourself from mosquito bites (p1096) is an essential part of preventing yellow fever.

Other Infections

BARTONELLOSIS (OROYA FEVER)

Bartonellosis (Oroya fever) is carried by sandflies in the arid river valleys on the western slopes of the Andes in Peru, Colombia and Ecuador between altitudes of 800m and 3000m. (Curiously, it's not found anywhere else in the world.) The chief symptoms are fever and severe body pains. Complications may include marked anemia, enlargement of the liver and spleen, and sometimes death. The drug of choice is chloramphenicol, though doxycycline is also effective.

CHAGAS' DISEASE

Chagas' disease is a parasitic infection that is transmitted by triatomine insects (reduviid bugs), which inhabit crevices in the walls and roofs of substandard housing in South and Central America. In Peru, most cases occur in the southern part of the country. The triatomine insect lays its feces on human skin as it bites, usually at night. A person becomes infected when he or she unknowingly rubs the feces into the bite wound or any other open sore. Chagas' disease is extremely rare in travelers. However, if you sleep in a poorly constructed house, especially one made of mud, adobe or thatch, you should be sure to protect yourself with a bed net and a good insecticide.

GNATHOSTOMIASIS

Gnathostomiasis is an intestinal parasite acquired by eating raw or undercooked freshwater fish, including *ceviche* (marinated, uncooked seafood).

HISTOPLASMOSIS

Histoplasmosis is caused by a soil-based fungus that is acquired by inhalation, often when the soil has been disrupted. Initial symptoms may include fever, chills, dry cough, chest pain and headache, sometimes leading to pneumonia. Histoplasmosis has been reported in spelunkers who have visited caves inhabited by bats.

HIV/AIDS

HIV/AIDS has been reported in all South American countries. Be sure to use condoms for all sexual encounters.

LEISHMANIASIS

Leishmaniasis occurs in the mountains and jungles of all South American countries except for Chile, Uruguay and the Falkland Islands. The infection is transmitted by sandflies, which are about one-third the size of mosquitoes. Leishmaniasis may be limited to the skin, causing slow-growing ulcers over exposed parts of the body, or (less commonly) disseminate to the bone marrow, liver and spleen. The disease may be particularly severe in those with HIV. There is no vaccine. To protect yourself from sandflies, follow the same precautions as for mosquitoes (see p1096), except that netting must be finer-mesh (at least 18 holes to the linear inch).

LEPTOSPIROSIS

Leptospirosis is acquired by exposure to water contaminated by the urine of infected animals. Outbreaks often occur at times of flooding, when sewage overflow may contaminate water sources. The initial symptoms, which resemble a mild flu, usually subside uneventfully in a few days, with or without treatment, but a minority of cases are complicated by jaundice or meningitis. There is no vaccine. You can minimize your risk by staying out of bodies of fresh water that may be contaminated by animal urine. If you're visiting an area where an outbreak is in progress, you can take 200mg of doxycycline once weekly as a preventative measure. If you actually develop leptospirosis, the treatment is 100mg of doxycycline twice daily.

ENVIRONMENTAL HAZARDS
Altitude Sickness

Altitude sickness may develop in those who ascend rapidly to altitudes greater than 2500m. Being physically fit offers no protection. Those who have experienced altitude sickness in the past are prone to future episodes. The risk increases with faster ascents, higher altitudes and greater exertion. Symptoms may include headaches, nausea, vomiting, dizziness, malaise, insomnia and loss of appetite. Severe cases may be complicated by fluid in the lungs (high-altitude pulmonary edema) or swelling of the brain (high-altitude cerebral edema).

To protect yourself against altitude sickness, take 125mg or 250mg acetazolamide (Diamox) twice or three times daily starting 24 hours before ascent and continuing for 48 hours after arrival at altitude. Possible side effects include increased urinary volume, numbness, tingling, nausea, drowsiness, myopia and temporary impotence. Acetazolamide should not be given to pregnant women or anyone with a history of sulfa allergy. For those who cannot tolerate acetazolamide, the next best option is 4mg dexamethasone taken four times daily. Unlike acetazolamide, dexamethasone must be tapered gradually upon arrival at altitude, since there is a risk that altitude sickness will occur as the dosage is reduced. Dexamethasone is a steroid, so it should not be given to diabetics or anyone for whom steroids are contraindicated. A natural alternative is gingko, which some people find quite helpful.

When traveling to high altitudes, it's also important to avoid overexertion, eat light meals and abstain from alcohol.

If your symptoms are more than mild or don't resolve promptly, see a doctor. Altitude sickness should be taken seriously; it can be life-threatening when severe.

Animal Bites

Do not attempt to pet, handle or feed any animal, with the exception of domestic animals known to be free of any infectious disease. Most animal injuries are directly related to a person's attempt to touch or feed the animal.

Any bite or scratch by a mammal, including bats, should be promptly and thoroughly cleansed with large amounts of soap and water, followed by application of an antiseptic such as iodine or alcohol. The local health authorities should be contacted immediately for possible postexposure rabies treatment, whether or not you've been immunized against rabies. It may also be advisable to start an antibiotic, since wounds caused by animal bites and scratches frequently become infected. One of the newer quinolones, such as levofloxacin (Levaquin), which many travelers carry in case of diarrhea, would be an appropriate choice.

Snakes and leeches are a hazard in some areas of South America. In the event of a bite from a venomous snake, place the victim at rest, keep the bitten area immobilized, and move the victim immediately to the nearest medical facility. Avoid tourniquets, which are no longer recommended.

Cold Exposure

Cold exposure may be a significant problem in the Andes, particularly at night. Be sure to dress warmly, stay dry, keep active, consume plenty of food and water, get enough rest, and avoid alcohol, caffeine and tobacco. Watch out for the 'umbles' – stumbles, mumbles, fumbles and grumbles – which are important signs of impending hypothermia.

Heatstroke

To protect yourself from excessive sun exposure, you should stay out of the midday sun, wear sunglasses and a wide-brimmed sun hat, and apply sunscreen with SPF 15 or higher, with both UVA and UVB protection. Sunscreen should be generously applied to all exposed parts of the body approximately 30 minutes before sun exposure and should be reapplied after swimming or vigorous activity. Travelers should also drink plenty of fluids and avoid strenuous exercise when the temperature is high.

Hypothermia

Hypothermia occurs when the body loses heat faster than it can produce it and the core temperature of the body falls. If you're trekking at high altitudes or simply taking a long bus trip over mountains, particularly at night, be prepared. In the Andes, you should always be prepared for cold, wet or windy conditions even if it's just for a few hours. It is best to dress in layers, and a hat is important, as a lot of heat is lost through the head.

The symptoms of hypothermia include exhaustion, numbness, shivering, slurred speech, irrational or violent behavior, lethargy, stumbling, dizzy spells, muscle cramps and violent bursts of energy. To treat mild hypothermia, first get people out of the wind or rain, remove their clothing if it's wet and give them something warm and dry to wear. Make them drink hot liquids – not alcohol – and some high-calorie, easily digestible food. Do not rub victims, instead allow them to slowly warm themselves. This should be enough to treat hypothermia's early stages. Early detection and treatment of mild hypothermia is the only way to prevent severe hypothermia, which is a critical condition.

Insect Bites & Stings

To prevent mosquito bites, wear long sleeves, long pants, a hat and shoes (rather than sandals). Bring along a good insect repellent, preferably one containing DEET, which should be applied to exposed skin and clothing, but not to eyes, mouth, cuts, wounds or irritated skin. Products containing lower concentrations of DEET are as effective, but for shorter periods of time. In general, adults and children over 12 years should use preparations containing 25% to 35% DEET, which usually lasts about six hours. Children between two and 12 years of age should use preparations containing no more than 10% DEET, applied sparingly, which will usually last about three hours. Neurologic toxicity has been reported from DEET, especially in children, but appears to be extremely uncommon and generally related to overuse. DEET-containing compounds should not be used on children under age two.

Insect repellents containing certain botanical products, including oil of eucalyptus and soybean oil, are effective but last only 1½ to two hours. DEET-containing repellents are preferable for areas where there is a high risk of malaria or yellow fever. Products based on citronella are not effective.

For additional protection, you can apply permethrin to clothing, shoes, tents and bed nets. Permethrin treatments are safe and remain effective for at least two weeks, even when items are laundered. Permethrin should not be applied directly to skin.

Don't sleep with the window open unless there is a screen. If sleeping outdoors or in accommodations that allow entry of mosquitoes, use a bed net, preferably treated with permethrin, with edges tucked in under the mattress. The mesh size should be less than 1.5mm. If the sleeping area is not otherwise protected, use a mosquito coil, which will fill the room with insecticide through the night. Wristbands impregnated with repellent are not effective.

Parasites

Intestinal parasites occur throughout South America. Common pathogens include Cyclospora, amoebae and Isospora. A tapeworm called Taenia solium may lead to a chronic brain infection called cysticercosis. If you exercise discretion in your choice of food and beverages, you'll sharply reduce your chances of becoming infected.

A parasitic infection called schistosomiasis, which primarily affects the blood vessels in the liver, occurs in Brazil, Suriname and parts of north-central Venezuela. The disease is acquired by swimming, wading, bathing or washing in fresh water that contains infected snails. It's therefore best to stay out of bodies of fresh water, such as lakes, ponds, streams and rivers, in places where schistosomiasis might occur. Toweling yourself dry after exposure to contaminated water may reduce your risk of becoming infected, but doesn't eliminate it. Chlorinated pools are safe.

A liver parasite called Echinococcus (hydatid disease) is found in many countries, especially Peru and Uruguay. It typically affects those in close contact with sheep. A lung parasite called Paragonimus, which is ingested by eating raw infected crustaceans, has been reported from Ecuador, Peru and Venezuela.

Travelers' Diarrhea

To prevent diarrhea, avoid tap water unless it has been boiled, filtered or chemically disinfected (with iodine tablets); only eat fresh fruits or vegetables if cooked or peeled; be wary of dairy products that might contain unpasteurized milk; and be highly selective when eating food from street vendors.

If you develop diarrhea, be sure to drink plenty of fluids, preferably an oral rehydration solution containing lots of salt and sugar. A few loose stools don't require treatment but if you start having more than four or five stools a day, you should start taking an antibiotic (usually a quinolone drug) and an antidiarrheal agent (such as loperamide). If diarrhea is bloody, persists for more than 72 hours or is accompanied by fever, shaking chills or severe abdominal pain you should seek medical attention.

Water

Tap water is generally not safe to drink. Vigorous boiling for one minute is the most effective means of water purification. At altitudes greater than 2000m, boil for three minutes.

Another option is to disinfect water with iodine. You can add 2% tincture of iodine to 1L of water (five drops to clear water, 10 drops to cloudy water) and let stand for 30 minutes. If the water is cold, longer times may be required. Or you can buy iodine pills such as Globaline, Potable-Aqua and Coghlan's, available at most pharmacies. Instructions are enclosed and should be carefully followed. The taste of iodinated water may be improved by adding vitamin C (ascorbic acid). Iodinated water should not be consumed for more than a few weeks. Pregnant women, those with a history of thyroid disease, and those allergic to iodine should not drink iodinated water.

A number of water filters are on the market. Those with smaller pores (reverse osmosis filters) provide the broadest protection, but they are relatively large and are readily plugged by debris. Those with somewhat larger pores (microstrainer filters) are ineffective against viruses, although they remove other organisms. Manufacturers' instructions must be carefully followed.

WOMEN'S HEALTH

It may be difficult to find quality obstetric care, if needed, outside major cities. In addition, it isn't advisable for pregnant women to spend time at altitudes where the air is thin. Lastly, yellow-fever vaccine is strongly recommended for travel to all jungle areas at altitudes less than 2300m, but should not be given during pregnancy because the vaccine contains a live virus that may infect the fetus.

TRADITIONAL MEDICINE

Some common traditional remedies include the following:

Problem	Treatment
altitude sickness	gingko
jet lag	melatonin
mosquito-bite prevention	eucalyptus oil, soybean oil
motion sickness	ginger

HEALTH

Language

CONTENTS

LATIN AMERICAN SPANISH

Latin American Spanish will be the language of choice for travelers in all parts of South America outside Brazil (where Portuguese is the national tongue).

For a more in-depth guide to the Spanish of South America, pick up a copy of Lonely Planet's *Latin American Spanish Phrasebook*. Another useful resource worth looking out for is the compact *University of Chicago Spanish-English, English-Spanish Dictionary*.

PRONUNCIATION

The pronunciation guides included in this chapter should make pronunciation a relatively simple affair.

Vowels

a   as in 'father'
e   as in 'met'
i   as in 'marine'
o   as in 'or' (without the 'r' sound)
u   as in 'rule;' the 'u' is not pronounced after **q** and in the letter combinations **gue** and **gui**, unless it's marked with a diaeresis (eg *argüir*), in which case it's pronounced as English 'w'
y   at the end of a word or when it stands alone, it's pronounced as the Spanish i (eg *ley*); between vowels within a word it's as the 'y' in 'yonder'

Consonants

Pronunciation of Spanish consonants is similar to their English counterparts. The exceptions are listed below. Note that while the consonants **ch**, **ll** and **ñ** are generally considered distinct letters, **ch** and **ll** are often listed alphabetically under **c** and **l** respectively. The letter **ñ** is still treated as a separate letter and comes after **n** in dictionaries.

b   similar to English 'b,' but softer; referred to as 'b larga'
c   as in 'celery' before **e** and **i**; otherwise as English 'k'
ch as in 'church'
d   as in 'dog,' but between vowels and after **l** or **n**, the sound is closer to the 'th' in 'this'
g   as the 'ch' in the Scottish *loch* before **e** and **i** ('kh' in our guides to pronunciation); elsewhere, as in 'go'
h   invariably silent. If your name begins with this letter, listen carefully if you're waiting for public officials to call you.
j   as the 'ch' in the Scottish *loch* ('kh' in our guides to pronunciation)
ll as the 'y' in 'yellow'
ñ   as the 'ni' in 'onion'
r   a short **r** except at the beginning of a word, and after **l**, **n** or **s**, when it's often rolled
rr very strongly rolled
v   similar to English 'b,' but softer; referred to as 'b corta'
x   as in 'taxi' except for a very few words, when it's pronounced as **j**
z   as the 's' in 'sun'

Word Stress

In general, words ending in vowels or the letters **n** or **s** have stress on the next-to-last syllable, while those with other endings have stress on the last syllable.

Written accents denote stress, and override the rules above, eg *sótano* (basement), *América* and *porción* (portion).

GENDER & PLURALS

In Spanish, nouns are either masculine or feminine, and there are rules to help determine gender – with exceptions, of course! Feminine nouns generally end with -a or with the groups -**ción**, -**sión** or -**dad**. Other endings typically signify a masculine noun. Endings for adjectives also change to agree with the gender of the noun they modify (masculine/feminine -**o**/-**a**). Where both masculine and feminine forms are included in this language guide, they are separated by a slash, with the masculine form first, eg *perdido/a*.

If a noun or adjective ends in a vowel, the plural is formed by adding **s** to the end. If it ends in a consonant, the plural is formed by adding **es** to the end.

ACCOMMODATIONS

I'm looking for ...	*Estoy buscando ...*	e·stoy boos·kan·do ...
Where is ...?	*¿Dónde hay ...?*	don·de ai ...
a hotel	*un hotel*	oon o·tel
a guesthouse	*una pensión/ casa de huéspedes/ hostería*	oo·na pen·syon/ ka·sa de we·spe·des/ os·te·ree·a
(Arg, Chi)		
a camping ground	*un terreno de cámping*	oon te·re·no de kam·peen
a youth hostel	*un albergue juvenil*	oon al·ber·ge khoo·ve·neel
I'd like a ... room.	*Quisiera una habitación ...*	kee·sye·ra oo·na a·bee·ta·syon ...
double	*doble*	do·ble
single	*individual*	een·dee·vee·dwal
twin	*con dos camas*	kon dos ka·mas
How much is it per ...?	*¿Cuánto cuesta por ...?*	kwan·to kwes·ta por ...
night	*noche*	no·che
person	*persona*	per·so·na
week	*semana*	se·ma·na

Does it include breakfast?
¿Incluye el desayuno?　een·kloo·ye el de·sa·yoo·no
May I see the room?
¿Puedo ver la habitación?　pwe·do ver la a·bee·ta·syon
I don't like it.
No me gusta.　no me goos·ta
It's fine. I'll take it.
OK. La alquilo.　o·kay la al·kee·lo
I'm leaving now.
Me voy ahora.　me voy a·o·ra

private/shared bathroom	*baño privado/ compartido*	ba·nyo pree·va·do/ kom·par·tee·do
too expensive	*demasiado caro*	de·ma·sya·do ka·ro
cheaper	*más económico*	mas e·ko·no·mee·ko
discount	*descuento*	des·kwen·to

MAKING A RESERVATION	
(for phone or written requests)	
To ...	*A ...*
From ...	*De ...*
Date	*Fecha*
I'd like to book ...	*Quisiera reservar ...* (see the list under 'Accommodations' for bed/ room options)
in the name of ...	*en nombre de ...*
for the nights of ...	*para las noches del ...*
credit card ...	*tarjeta de crédito ...*
number	*número*
expiry date	*fecha de vencimiento*
Please confirm ...	*Puede confirmar ...*
availability	*la disponibilidad*
price	*el precio*

CONVERSATION & ESSENTIALS

In their public behavior, South Americans are very conscious of civilities, sometimes to the point of ceremoniousness. Never approach a stranger for information without extending a greeting and use only the polite form of address, especially with the police and public officials. Young people may be less likely to expect this, but it's best to stick to the polite form unless you're quite sure you won't offend by using the informal mode. The polite form is used in all cases in this guide; where options are given, the form is indicated by the abbreviations 'pol' and 'inf.'

Hello.	*Hola.*	o·la
Good morning.	*Buenos días.*	bwe·nos dee·as
Good afternoon.	*Buenas tardes.*	bwe·nas tar·des
Good evening/ night.	*Buenas noches.*	bwe·nas no·ches
Goodbye.	*Adiós.*	a·dyos
Bye/See you soon.	*Hasta luego.*	as·ta lwe·go
Yes.	*Sí.*	see
No.	*No.*	no
Please.	*Por favor.*	por fa·vor
Thank you.	*Gracias.*	gra·syas
Many thanks.	*Muchas gracias.*	moo·chas gra·syas
You're welcome.	*De nada.*	de na·da
Pardon me.	*Perdón.*	per·don
Excuse me.	*Permiso.*	per·mee·so
(used when asking permission)		
Forgive me.	*Disculpe.*	dees·kool·pe
(used when apologizing)		

How are things?

¿Qué tal?　　　　　ke tal

What's your name?

¿Cómo se llama?　　ko·mo se ya·ma (pol)

¿Cómo te llamas?　ko·mo te ya·mas (inf)

My name is ...

Me llamo ...　　　　me ya·mo ...

It's a pleasure to meet you.

Mucho gusto.　　　moo·cho goos·to

The pleasure is mine.

El gusto es mío.　　el goos·to es mee·o

Where are you from?

¿De dónde es/eres?　de don·de es/e·res (pol/inf)

I'm from ...

Soy de ...　　　　　soy de ...

Where are you staying?

¿Dónde está alojado?　don·de es·ta a·lo·kha·do (pol)

¿Dónde estás alojado?　don·de es·tas a·lo·kha·do (inf)

May I take a photo?

¿Puedo sacar una foto?　pwe·do sa·kar oo·na fo·to

DIRECTIONS

How do I get to ...?

¿Cómo puedo llegar a ...? ko·mo pwe·do lye·gar a ...

Is it far?

¿Está lejos?　　　　es·ta le·khos

Go straight ahead.

Siga/Vaya derecho.　see·ga/va·ya de·re·cho

Turn left.

Voltée a la izquierda.　vol·te·e a la ees·kyer·da

Turn right.

Voltée a la derecha.　vol·te·e a la de·re·cha

I'm lost.

Estoy perdido/a.　　es·toy per·dee·do/a

Can you show me (on the map)?

¿Me lo podría indicar　me lo po·dree·a een·dee·kar

(en el mapa)?　　　(en el ma·pa)

SIGNS – SPANISH

Entrada	Entrance
Salida	Exit
Información	Information
Abierto	Open
Cerrado	Closed
Prohibido	Prohibited
Comisaria	Police Station
Servicios/Baños	Toilets
Hombres/Varones	Men
Mujeres/Damas	Women

north	norte	nor·te
south	sur	soor
east	este/oriente	es·te/o·ryen·te
west	oeste/occidente	o·es·te/ok·see·den·te

EMERGENCIES – SPANISH

Help!	¡Socorro!	so·ko·ro
Fire!	¡Incendio!	een·sen·dyo
I've been robbed.	Me robaron.	me ro·ba·ron
Go away!	¡Déjeme!	de·khe·me
Get lost!	¡Váyase!	va·ya·se

Call ...!	¡Llame a ...!	ya·me a
an ambulance	una ambulancia	oo·na am·boo·lan·sya
a doctor	un médico	oon me·dee·ko
the police	la policía	la po·lee·see·a

It's an emergency.

Es una emergencia.　es oo·na e·mer·khen·sya

Could you help me, please?

¿Me puede ayudar,　me pwe·de a·yoo·dar

por favor?　　　　por fa·vor

I'm lost.

Estoy perdido/a.　　es·toy per·dee·do/a

Where are the toilets?

¿Dónde están los baños?　don·de es·tan los ba·nyos

here	aquí	a·kee
there	allí	a·yee
avenue	avenida	a·ve·nee·da
block	cuadra	kwa·dra
street	calle/paseo	ka·lye/pa·se·o

HEALTH

I'm sick.

Estoy enfermo/a.　　es·toy en·fer·mo/a

I need a doctor.

Necesito un médico.　ne·se·see·to oon me·dee·ko

Where's the hospital?

¿Dónde está el hospital?　don·de es·ta el os·pee·tal

I'm pregnant.

Estoy embarazada.　es·toy em·ba·ra·sa·da

I've been vaccinated.

Estoy vacunado/a.　　es·toy va·koo·na·do/a

I'm allergic to ...	Soy alérgico/a a ...	soy a·ler·khee·ko/a a ...
antibiotics	los antibióticos	los an·tee·byo·tee·kos
penicillin	la penicilina	la pe·nee·see·lee·na
nuts	las fruta secas	las froo·tas se·kas

I'm ...	Soy ...	soy ...
asthmatic	asmático/a	as·ma·tee·ko/a
diabetic	diabético/a	dya·be·tee·ko/a
epileptic	epiléptico/a	e·pee·lep·tee·ko/a

I have ...	Tengo ...	ten·go ...
altitude sickness	soroche	so·ro·che
diarrhea	diarrea	dya·re·a
nausea	náusea	now·se·a
a headache	un dolor de	oon do·lor de
	cabeza	ka·be·sa
a cough	tos	tos

LANGUAGE DIFFICULTIES

Do you speak (English)?
¿Habla/Hablas (inglés)? a·bla/a·blas (een·gles) (pol/inf)
Does anyone here speak English?
¿Hay alguien que hable ai al·gyen ke a·ble
inglés? een·gles
I (don't) understand.
Yo (no) entiendo. yo (no) en·tyen·do
How do you say ...?
¿Cómo se dice ...? ko·mo se dee·se ...
What does ...mean?
¿Qué quiere decir ...? ke kye·re de·seer ...

Could you	¿Puede ..., por	pwe·de ... por
please ...?	favor?	fa·vor
repeat that	repetirlo	re·pe·teer·lo
speak more	hablar más	a·blar mas
slowly	despacio	des·pa·syo
write it down	escribirlo	es·kree·beer·lo

NUMBERS

1	uno	oo·no
2	dos	dos
3	tres	tres
4	cuatro	kwa·tro
5	cinco	seen·ko
6	seis	says
7	siete	sye·te
8	ocho	o·cho
9	nueve	nwe·ve
10	diez	dyes
11	once	on·se
12	doce	do·se
13	trece	tre·se
14	catorce	ka·tor·se
15	quince	keen·se
16	dieciséis	dye·see·says
17	diecisiete	dye·see·sye·te
18	dieciocho	dye·see·o·cho
19	diecinueve	dye·see·nwe·ve
20	veinte	vayn·te
21	veintiuno	vayn·tee·oo·no
30	treinta	trayn·ta
31	treinta y uno	trayn·ta ee oo·no
40	cuarenta	kwa·ren·ta
50	cincuenta	seen·kwen·ta

60	sesenta	se·sen·ta
70	setenta	se·ten·ta
80	ochenta	o·chen·ta
90	noventa	no·ven·ta
100	cien	syen
101	ciento uno	syen·to oo·no
200	doscientos	do·syen·tos
1000	mil	meel
5000	cinco mil	seen·ko meel
10,000	diez mil	dyes meel
50,000	cincuenta mil	seen·kwen·ta meel
100,000	cien mil	syen meel
1,000,000	un millón	oon mee·yon

SHOPPING & SERVICES

I'd like to buy ...
Quisiera comprar ... kee·sye·ra kom·prar
I'm just looking.
Sólo estoy mirando. so·lo es·toy mee·ran·do
May I look at it?
¿Puedo mirar(lo/la)? pwe·do mee·rar·(lo/la)
How much is it?
¿Cuánto cuesta? kwan·to kwes·ta
That's too expensive for me.
Es demasiado caro es de·ma·sya·do ka·ro
para mí. pa·ra mee
Could you lower the price?
¿Podría bajar un poco po·dree·a ba·khar oon po·ko
el precio? el pre·syo
I don't like it.
No me gusta. no me goos·ta
I'll take it.
Lo llevo. lo ye·vo

Do you	¿Aceptan ...?	a·sep·tan
accept ...?		
American	dólares	do·la·res
dollars	americanos	a·me·ree·ka·nos
credit cards	tarjetas de	tar·khe·tas de
	crédito	kre·dee·to
traveler's	cheques de	che·kes de
checks	viajero	vya·khe·ro

less	menos	me·nos
more	más	mas
large	grande	gran·de
small	pequeño/a	pe·ke·nyo/a

I'm looking	Estoy buscando ...	es·toy boos·kan·do
for (the) ...		
ATM	el cajero	el ka·khe·ro
	automático	ow·to·ma·tee·ko
bank	el banco	el ban·ko
bookstore	la librería	la lee·bre·ree·a

LANGUAGE

embassy	la embajada	la em·ba·kha·da
exchange house	la casa de cambio	la ka·sa de kam·byo
general store	la tienda	la tyen·da
laundry	la lavandería	la la·van·de·ree·a
market	el mercado	el mer·ka·do
pharmacy/ chemist	la farmacia/ la botica	la far·ma·sya/ la bo·tee·ka
post office	el correo	el ko·re·o
supermarket	el supermercado	el soo·per· mer·ka·do
tourist office	la oficina de turismo	la o·fee·see·na de too·rees·mo

What time does it open/close?
¿A qué hora abre/cierra? a ke o·ra a·bre/sye·ra

I want to change some money/traveler's checks.
Quiero cambiar dinero/ cheques de viajero.   kye·ro kam·byar dee·ne·ro/ che·kes de vya·khe·ro

What is the exchange rate?
¿Cuál es el tipo de cambio?   kwal es el tee·po de kam·byo

I want to call ...
Quiero llamar a ...   kye·ro lya·mar a ...

airmail	correo aéreo	ko·re·o a·e·re·o
black market	mercado (negro/ paralelo)	mer·ka·do ne·gro/ pa·ra·le·lo
letter	carta	kar·ta
registered mail	certificado	ser·tee·fee·ka·do
stamps	estampillas	es·tam·pee·lyas

TIME & DATES

What time is it? ¿Qué hora es? ke o·ra es
It's one o'clock. Es la una. es la oo·na
It's seven o'clock. Son las siete. son las sye·te

midnight	medianoche	me·dya·no·che
noon	mediodía	me·dyo·dee·a
half past two	dos y media	dos ee me·dya
now	ahora	a·o·ra
today	hoy	oy
tonight	esta noche	es·ta no·che
tomorrow	mañana	ma·nya·na
yesterday	ayer	a·yer
Monday	lunes	loo·nes
Tuesday	martes	mar·tes
Wednesday	miércoles	myer·ko·les
Thursday	jueves	khwe·ves
Friday	viernes	vyer·nes
Saturday	sábado	sa·ba·do
Sunday	domingo	do·meen·go

January	enero	e·ne·ro
February	febrero	fe·bre·ro
March	marzo	mar·so
April	abril	a·breel
May	mayo	ma·yo
June	junio	khoo·nyo
July	julio	khoo·lyo
August	agosto	a·gos·to
September	septiembre	sep·tyem·bre
October	octubre	ok·too·bre
November	noviembre	no·vyem·bre
December	diciembre	dee·syem·bre

TRANSPORTATION
Public Transportation

What time does ... leave/arrive? ¿A qué hora sale/llega? a ke o·ra ... sa·le/ye·ga

the bus	el autobus	el ow·to·boos
the plane	el avión	el a·vyon
the ship	el barco/buque	el bar·ko/boo·ke
the train	el tren	el tren
airport	el aeropuerto	el a·e·ro·pwer·to
train station	la estación de ferrocarril	la es·ta·syon de fe·ro·ka·reel
bus station	la estación de autobuses	la es·ta·syon de ow·to·boo·ses
bus stop	la parada de autobuses	la pa·ra·da de ow·to·boo·ses
luggage check room	guardería/ equipaje	gwar·de·ree·a/ e·kee·pa·khe
ticket office	la boletería	la bo·le·te·ree·a

I'd like a ticket to ...
Quiero un boleto a ...   kye·ro oon bo·le·to a ...

What's the fare to ...?
¿Cuánto cuesta hasta ...?   kwan·to kwes·ta a·sta ...

1st class	primera clase	pree·me·ra kla·se
2nd class	segunda clase	se·goon·da kla·se
single/one-way	ida	ee·da
return/round trip	ida y vuelta	ee·da ee vwel·ta
taxi	taxi	tak·see

Private Transportation

I'd like to hire a/an ... Quisiera alquilar ... kee·sye·ra al·kee·lar ...

4WD	un todo terreno	oon to·do te·re·no
car	un auto	oon ow·to
motorbike	una moto	oo·na mo·to
bicycle	una bicicleta	oo·na bee·see·kle·ta
pickup (truck)	camioneta	ka·myo·ne·ta
truck	camión	ka·myon
hitchhike	hacer dedo	a·ser de·do

ROAD SIGNS – SPANISH

Acceso	Entrance
Aparcamiento	Parking
Ceda el Paso	Give way
Despacio	Slow
Dirección Única	One-way
Mantenga Su Derecha	Keep to the Right
No Adelantar/	No Passing
No Rebase	
Peaje	Toll
Peligro	Danger
Prohibido Aparcar/	No Parking
No Estacionar	
Prohibido el Paso	No Entry
Pare/Stop	Stop
Salida de Autopista	Freeway Exit

Is this the road to (...)?
¿Se va a (...) por se va a (...) por
esta carretera? es·ta ka·re·te·ra
Where's a petrol station?
¿Dónde hay una don·de ai oo·na
gasolinera/un grifo? ga·so·lee·ne·ra/oon gree·fo
Please fill it up.
Lleno, por favor. ye·no por fa·vor
I'd like (20) liters.
Quiero (veinte) litros. kye·ro (vayn·te) lee·tros

diesel	*diesel*	dee·sel
leaded (regular)	*gasolina con*	ga·so·lee·na kon
	plomo	plo·mo
petrol (gas)	*gasolina*	ga·so·lee·na
unleaded	*gasolina sin*	ga·so·lee·na seen
	plomo	plo·mo

(How long) Can I park here?
¿(Por cuánto tiempo) (por kwan·to tyem·po)
Puedo aparcar aquí? pwe·do a·par·kar a·kee
Where do I pay?
¿Dónde se paga? don·de se pa·ga
I need a mechanic.
Necesito un ne·se·see·to oon
mecánico. me·ka·nee·ko
The car has broken down (in ...).
El carro se ha averiado el ka·ro se a a·ve·rya·do
(en ...). (en ...)
The motorbike won't start.
No arranca la moto. no a·ran·ka la mo·to
I have a flat tyre.
Tengo un pinchazo. ten·go oon peen·cha·so
I've run out of petrol.
Me quedé sin gasolina. me ke·de seen ga·so·lee·na

I've had an accident.
Tuve un accidente. too·ve oon ak·see·den·te

TRAVEL WITH CHILDREN
I need ...
Necesito ...
ne·se·see·to ...
Do you have ...?
¿Hay ...?
ai ...
a car baby seat
un asiento de seguridad oon a·syen·to de se·goo·ree·da
para bebés pa·ra be·bes
a child-minding service
un servicio de cuidado oon ser·vee·syo de kwee·da·do
de niños de nee·nyos
a children's menu
una carta infantil oona kar·ta een·fan·teel
a creche
una guardería oo·na gwar·de·ree·a
(disposable) diapers/nappies
pañoles (de usar y tirar) pa·nyo·les (de oo·sar ee tee·rar)
an (English-speaking) babysitter
una niñera oo·na nee·nye·ra
(de habla inglesa) (de a·bla een·gle·sa)
formula (milk)
leche en polvo le·che en pol·vo
a highchair
una trona oo·na tro·na
a potty
una pelela oo·na pe·le·la
a pusher/stroller
un cochecito oon ko·che·see·to

Do you mind if I breast-feed here?
¿Le molesta que dé le mo·les·ta ke de
de pecho aquí? de pe·cho a·kee
Are children allowed?
¿Se admiten niños? se ad·mee·ten nee·nyos

BRAZILIAN PORTUGUESE

Given that 89% of the world's Portuguese speakers live in Brazil, South America's largest country, it's clear that a few words in the language will be very handy indeed. Regional variation within Brazil is minor, making the task of communicating in Portuguese even easier.

PRONUNCIATION
Vowels

a	as the 'u' in run
aa	as the 'a' in father
ai	as in 'aisle'

LANGUAGE

aw	as in 'saw'
ay	as in 'day'
e	as in 'bet'
ee	as in 'bee'
o	as in 'go'
oo	as in 'moon'
ow	as in 'how'
oy	as in 'boy'

Nasal Vowels

A characteristic feature of Brazilian Portuguese is the use of nasal vowels. Nasal vowels are pronounced as if you're trying to force the sound out of your nose rather than your mouth. English also has nasal vowels to some extent – when you say 'sing' in English, the 'i' is nasalized by the 'ng.' In Brazilian Portuguese, written vowels that have a nasal consonant after them (**m** or **n**), or a tilde over them (eg **ã**), will be nasal. In our pronunciation guide, we've used 'ng' after nasal vowels to indicate a nasal sound.

Consonants

The following lists a few of the letters used in our pronunciation guide that represent the trickier Portuguese consonant sounds.

ly	as the 'lli' in 'million'
ny	as in 'canyon'
r	as in 'run'
rr	as the 'r' in run but stronger and rolled
zh	as the 's' in 'pleasure'

Word Stress

Word stress generally occurs on the second-to-last syllable of a word, though there are exceptions. When a word ends in **-r** or is pronounced with a nasalized vowel, the stress falls on the last syllable. Another exception is that if a written vowel has an accent marked over it, the stress falls on the syllable containing that vowel.

In our transliteration system, we have indicated the stressed syllable with italics.

ACCOMMODATIONS

I'm looking for ...
Estou procurando por ...   es·to pro·koo·*rang*·do porr ...
Where is a ...?
Onde tem ...?   *on*·de teng ...
  a room
  um quarto   oom *kwarr*·to

bed and breakfast
uma pensão   *oo*·ma pen·*sowng*
camping ground
um local para   oom lo·*kow* pa·ra
  acampamento   a·kam·pa·*meng*·to
guesthouse
uma hospedaria   *oo*·ma os·pe·da·*ree*·a
hotel
um hotel   oom o·*tel*
youth hostel
um albergue   oom ow·*berr*·ge
da juventude   da zhoo·veng·*too*·de

I'd like a ... room.
Eu gostaria um   e·oo gos·ta·*ree*·a oom
quarto de ...   *kwarr*·to de ...
  double
  casal   ka·*zow*
  single
  solteiro   sol·*tay*·ro
  twin
  duplo   *doo*·plo

How much is it per ...?
Quanto custa por ...?   *kwan*·to *koos*·ta porr ...
  night
  noite   *noy*·te
  person
  pessoa   pe·*so*·a
  week
  semana   se·*ma*·na

What's the address?
Qual é o endereço?   kwow e o en·de·*re*·so
Do you have a ... room?
Tem um quarto de ...?   teng oom *kwarr*·to de ...
For (three) nights.
Para (três) noites.   pa·ra (tres) *noy*·tes
Does it include breakfast?
Inclui café da manhã?   eeng·kloo·*ee* ka·*fe* da ma·*nyang*
May I see it?
Posso ver?   *po*·so verr
I'll take it.
Eu fico com ele.   e·oo *fee*·ko kom e·lee
I don't like it.
Não gosto.   nowng *gos*·to
I'm leaving now.
Estou indo embora   es·*to* een·do em·*bo*·ra
agora.   a·*go*·ra

Can I pay ...?
Posso pagar com ...?   *po*·so pa·*garr* kom ...
  by credit card
  cartão de crédito   karr·*towng* de *kre*·dee·to
  by traveler's check
  traveler cheque   tra·ve·ler *she*·kee

MAKING A RESERVATION

(for phone or written requests)

To ...	*Para ...*
From ...	*De ...*
Date	*Data*
I'd like to book ...	*Eu gostaria de fazer uma reserva ...* (see the list under 'Accommodations' for bed/room options)
in the name of ...	*no nome de ...*
for the nights of ...	*para os dias ...*
from (...) to (...)	*de (...) até (...)*
credit card ...	*cartão de credito ...*
number	*número*
expiry date	*data de vencimento*
Please confirm ...	*Por favor confirme ...*
availability	*a disponibilidade*
price	*o preço*

CONVERSATION & ESSENTIALS

Hello.
Olá.   o·*la*
Hi.
Oi.   oy
Good day.
Bom dia.   bong *dee*·a
Good evening.
Boa noite.   bo·a *noy*·te
See you later.
Até mais tarde.   a·*te* mais *tarr*·de
Goodbye.
Tchau.   chau
How are you?
Como vai?   *ko*·mo vai
Fine, and you?
Bem, e você?   beng e vo·*se*
I'm pleased to meet you.
Prazer em conhecê-lo.   pra *zerr* eng ko nye *se* lo (m)
Prazer em conhecê-la.   pra *zerr* eng ko nye *se* la (f)
Yes.
Sim.   seem
No.
Não.   nowng
Please.
Por favor.   por fa·*vorr*
Thank you (very much).
(Muito) obrigado/   *(mween*·to) o·bree·*ga*·do/
obrigada. (m/f)   o·bree·*ga*·da
You're welcome.
De nada.   de *na*·da

Excuse me.
Com licença   kom lee·*seng*·sa
Sorry.
Desculpa.   des·*kool*·pa
What's your name?
Qual é o seu nome?   kwow e o *se*·oo *no*·me
My name is ...
Meu nome é ...   me·oo *no*·me e ...
Where are you from?
De onde você é?   de *ong*·de vo·*se* e
I'm from ...
Eu sou (da/do/de) ...   e·oo so (da/do/de)
May I take a photo (of you)?
Posso tirar uma foto   po so tee *rarr* oo ma *fo* to
(de você)?   (de vo *se*)

DIRECTIONS

Where is ...?
Onde fica ...?   on·de *fee*·ka ...
Can you show me (on the map)?
Você poderia me   o·*se* po·de·*ree*·a me
mostrar (no mapa)?   mos·*trarr* (no *ma*·pa)
What's the address?
Qual é o endereço?   kwow e o en·de·*re*·so
How far is it?
Qual a distância   kwow a dees·*tan*·see·a
daqui?   da·*kee*
How do I get there?
Como é que eu chego lá?   *ko*·mo e ke e·oo *she*·go la

Turn ...	*Vire ...*	*vee*·re ...
at the corner	*à esquina*	a es·*kee*·na
at the traffic	*no sinal de*	no see·*now* de
lights	*trânsito*	tran·zee·to
left	*à esquerda*	a es·*kerr*·da
right	*à direita*	a dee·*ray*·ta

here	*aqui*	a·*kee*
there	*lá*	la
near ...	*perto ...*	*perr*·to ...
straight ahead	*em frente*	eng *freng*·te
north	*nort*	*norr*·te
south	*sul*	sool
east	*leste*	*les*·te
west	*oeste*	o·*es*·te

SIGNS – PORTUGUESE

Delegacia de Polícia	Police Station
Hospital	Hospital
Polícia	Police
Pronto Socorro	Emergency Department
Banheiro	Bathroom/Toilet
Não Tem Vaga	No Vacancy
Tem Vaga	Vacancy

LANGUAGE

EMERGENCIES – PORTUGUESE

Help!
Socorro! — so·*ko*·ho

It's an emergency.
É uma emergência. — e *oo*·ma e·merr·*zheng*·see·a

Call ...!
  a doctor
  um médico! — oom *me*·dee·ko
  an ambulance
  uma ambulância — *oo*·ma am·boo·*lan*·see·a
  the police
  a polícia — a po·lee·*see*·a

I'm lost.
Estou perdido. — es·*to* perr·*dee*·do

Where are the toilets?
Onde tem um banheiro? — *on*·de teng oom ba·*nyay*·ro

Go away!
Vai embora! — vai eng·*bo*·ra

HEALTH

I'm ill.
Estou doente. — es·*to* do·*eng*·te

I need a doctor (who speaks English).
Eu preciso de um médico — e·oo pre·*see*·zo de oom *me*·dee·ko
(que fale inglês). — (ke *fa*·le een·*gles*)

It hurts here.
Aqui dói. — a·*kee* doy

I've been vomiting.
Fui vomitando. — foo·ee vo·mee·*tan*·do

(I think) I'm pregnant.
(Acho que) estou grávida. — (*a*·sho ke) es·*to* gra·vee·da

Where's the nearest ...?
Onde fica ...is perto? — *on*·de *fee*·ka ... mais *perr*·to
  (night) chemist
  a farmácia (noturna) — a farr·*ma*·see·a (no·*toor*·na)
  dentist
  o dentista — o deng·*tees*·ta
  doctor
  o médico — o *me*·dee·ko
  hospital
  o hospital — o os·pee·*tow*
  medical centre
  a clínica médica — a *klee*·nee·ka *me*·dee·ka

I feel ...
Estou me sentindo ... — es·*to* me seng·*teeng*·do ...
  dizzy
  tonto/tonta — *tong*·to/*tong*·ta
  nauseous
  enjoado/enjoada (m/f) — eng·zho·*a*·do/en·zho·*a*·da

asthma	*asma*	*as*·ma
diarrhea	*diarréia*	dee·a·*he*·ee·a
fever	*febre*	*fe*·bre
nausea	*náusea*	*now*·ze·a
pain	*dor*	dorr

I'm allergic to ...
Tenho alergia à ... — *te*·nyo a·lerr·*zhee*·a a ...
  antibiotics
  antibióticos — an·tee·bee·*o*·tee·kos
  aspirin
  aspirina — as·pee·*ree*·na
  bees
  abelhas — a·*be*·lyas
  peanuts
  amendoims — a·meng·do·*eengs*
  penicillin
  penicilina — pe·nee·see·*lee*·na

antiseptic
anti-séptico — an·tee·*sep*·tee·ko

contraceptives
anticoncepcionais — an·tee·kon·*sep*·see·o·now

painkillers
analgésicos — a·now·*zhe*·zee·ko

LANGUAGE DIFFICULTIES

Do you speak English?
Você fala inglês? — vo·*se fa*·la een·*gles*

Does anyone here speak English?
Alguém aqui fala inglês? — ow·*geng fa*·la een·*gles*

Do you understand?
Você entende? — vo·*se* en·*teng*·de

I (don't) understand.
Eu (não) entendo. — e·oo (nowng) en·*teng*·do

What does ... mean?
O que quer dizer ...? — o ke kerr dee·*zerr* ...

Could you please ...?
Você poderia por favor ...? — vo·*se* po·de·*ree*·a porr fa·*vorr* ...
  repeat that
  repetir isto — he·pe·*teerr* ees·to
  speak more slowly
  falar mais devagar — fa·*larr* mais de·va·*garr*
  write it down
  escrever num papel — es·kre·*verr* noom pa·*pel*

NUMBERS

0	*zero*	*ze*·ro
1	*um*	oom
2	*dois*	doys
3	*três*	tres
4	*quatro*	*kwa*·tro
5	*cinco*	*seen*·ko
6	*seis*	says

LANGUAGE

7	sete	se·te
8	oito	oy·to
9	nove	naw·ve
10	dez	dez
11	onze	ong·ze
12	doze	do·ze
13	treze	tre·ze
14	quatorze	ka·torr·ze
15	quinze	keen·ze
16	dezesseis	de·ze·says
17	dezesete	de·ze·se·te
18	dezoito	de·zoy·to
19	dezenove	de·ze·naw·ve
20	vinte	veen·te
21	vinte e um	veen·te e oom
22	vinte e dois	veen·te e doys
30	trinta	treen·ta
40	quarenta	kwa·ren·ta
50	cinquenta	seen·kwen·ta
60	sessenta	se·seng·ta
70	setenta	se·teng·ta
80	oitenta	oy·teng·ta
90	noventa	no·veng·ta
100	cem	seng
200	duzentos	doo·zeng·tos
1,000	mil	mee·oo
1,000,000	um milhão	oom mee·lyowng

QUESTION WORDS

Who?	Quem?	keng
What?	(o) que?	(o) ke
When?	Quando?	kwang·do
Where?	Onde?	ong·de
Why?	Por que?	porr ke
Which/What?	Qual? (sg)/	kwow/
	Quais? (pl)	kais

SHOPPING & SERVICES

I'd like to buy ...
Gostaria de comprar ... gos·ta·ree·a de kom·prarr ...
I'm just looking.
Estou só olhando. es·to so o·lyan·do
May I look at it?
Posso ver? po·so verr
How much?
Quanto? kwan·to
That's too expensive.
Está muito caro. es·ta mweeng·to ka·ro
Can you lower the price?
Pode baixar o preço? po·de ba·sharr o pre·so
Do you have something cheaper?
Tem uma coisa mais teng oo·ma koy·za mais
barata? ba·ra·ta
I'll give you (five reals).
Dou (cinco reais). do (seen·ko he·ais)

I don't like it.
Não gosto. nowng gos·to
I'll take it.
Vou levar isso. vo le·var ee·so

Where is ...?
Onde fica ...? on·de fee·ka ...
  an ATM
  um caixa automático oom kai·sha ow·to·ma·tee·ko
  a bank
  o banco o ban·ko
  a bookstore
  uma livraria oo ma lee vra ree a
  the ... embassy
  a embaixada de ... a eng bai sha da de
  a foreign-exchange office
  uma loja de câmbio oo·ma lo·zha de kam·bee·o
  a laundrette
  uma lavanderia oo·ma la·vang·de·ree·a
  a market
  o mercado o merr·ka·do
  the police station
  a delegacia de polícia a de·le·ga·see·a de po·lee·see·a
  a pharmacy/chemist
  uma farmácia oo·ma far·ma·sya
  the post office
  o correio o co·hay·o
  a supermarket
  o supermercado o soo·perr·merr·ka·do
  the tourist office
  a secretaria de turismo a se·kre·ta·ree·a de too·rees·mo

less	menos	me·nos
more	mais	mais
large	grande	grang·de
small	pequeno/a	pe·ke·no/a

What time does ... open?
A que horas abre ...? a ke aw·ras a·bre ...
Do you have any others?
Você tem outros? vo·se teng o·tros
How many?
Quantos/Quantas? (m/f) kwan·tos/kwan·tas

Do you accept ...?
Vocês aceitam ...? vo·ses a·say·tam ...
  credit cards
  cartão de crédito karr·towng de kre·dee·to
  traveler's checks
  traveler cheques tra·ve·ler she·kes

letter
  uma carta oo·ma karr·ta

parcel
uma encomenda   oo·ma eng·ko·*meng*·da

I want to buy ...
Quero comprar ...   ke·ro kom·*prarr* ...
  an aerogram
  um aerograma   oom a·e·ro·*gra*·ma
  an envelope
  um envelope   oom eng·ve·*lo*·pe
  a phone card
  um cartão telefônico   oom kar·*towng* te·le·*fo*·nee·ko
  a postcard
  um cartão-postal   oom karr·*towng* pos·*tow*
  stamps
  selos   se·los

Where can I ...?
Onde posso ...?   on·de *po*·so ...
  change a traveler's check
  trocar traveler cheques   tro·*karr* tra·ve·*ler* she·kes
  change money
  trocar dinheiro   tro·*kar* dee·*nyay*·ro
  check my email
  checar meu e-mail   she·*karr* me·oo e·mail
  get Internet access
  ter acesso à internet   terr a·*se*·so a een·terr·*ne*·tee

TIME & DATES
What time is it?
Que horas são?   ke *aw*·ras sowng
It's (ten) o'clock.
São (dez) horas.   sowng (des) *aw*·ras

now	*agora*	a·*go*·ra
this morning	*esta manhã*	es·ta ma·*nyang*
in the morning	*da manhã*	da ma·*nyang*
this afternoon	*esta tarde*	es·ta *tarr*·de
in the afternoon	*da tarde*	da *tarr*·de
today	*hoje*	o·zhe
tonight	*hoje à noite*	o·zhe a *noy*·te
tomorrow	*amanhã*	a·ma·*nyang*
yesterday	*ontem*	on·teng

Monday	*segunda-feira*	se·*goon*·da·*fay*·ra
Tuesday	*terça-feira*	terr·sa·*fay*·ra
Wednesday	*quarta-feira*	kwarr·ta·*fay*·ra
Thursday	*quinta-feira*	keen·ta·*fay*·ra
Friday	*sexta-feira*	ses·ta·*fay*·ra
Saturday	*sábado*	sa·ba·doo
Sunday	*domingo*	do·*meen*·go

January	*janeiro*	zha·*nay*·ro
February	*fevereiro*	fe·ve·*ray*·ro
March	*março*	marr·so
April	*abril*	a·*bree*·oo
May	*maio*	ma·yo
June	*junho*	zhoo·nyo
July	*julho*	zhoo·lyo
August	*agosto*	a·*gos*·to
September	*setembro*	se·*teng*·bro
October	*outubro*	o·*too*·bro
November	*novembro*	no·*veng*·bro
December	*dezembro*	de·*zeng*·bro

TRANSPORTATION
Public Transportation

Which ... goes to ...?	*Qual o ... que vai para ...?*	kwow o ... ke vai *pa*·ra
boat	*barco*	barr·ko
city/local bus	*ônibus local*	o·nee·boos lo·*kow*
inter-city bus	*ônibus inter-urbano*	o·nee·boos een·terr oorr·*ba*·no
ferry	*barca*	barr·ka
bus	*ônibus*	o·nee·boos
plane	*avião*	a·vee·*owng*
train	*trem*	treng

When's the ... (bus)?	*Quando sai o ... (ônibus)?*	kwang·do sai o ... (o·nee·boos)
first	*primeiro*	pree·*may*·ro
last	*último*	ool·tee·mo
next	*próximo*	pro·see·mo

What time does it leave?
Que horas sai?   ke *aw*·ras sai
What time does it get to (Parati)?
Que horas chega em (Parati)?   ke *aw*·ras she·ga eng (pa·*ra*·tee)

A ... ticket to (...)	*Uma passagem de ... para (...)*	oo·ma pa·*sa*·zhem de ... *pa*·ra (...)
1st-class	*primeira classe*	pree·*may*·ra *kla*·se
2nd-class	*segunda classe*	se·*goon*·da *kla*·se
one-way	*ida*	ee·da
round trip	*ida e volta*	ee·da e *vol*·ta

How much is it?
Quanto é?   kwan·to e
Is this the bus to ...?
Este ônibus vai para ...?   es·te o·nee·boos vai *pa*·ra ...?
Do I need to change?
Preciso trocar de trem?   pre·*see*·so tro·*karr* de treng
the luggage check room
o balcão de guarda volumes   o bal·*kowng* de *gwarr*·da vo·*loo*·me
a luggage locker
um guarda volume   oom *gwarr*·da vo·*loo*·me

LANGUAGE

Is this taxi free?
  Este táxi está livre?   es·te tak·see es·ta lee·vre

Please put the meter on.
  Por favor ligue o   porr fa·vorr lee·ge o
  taxímetro.   tak·see·me·tro

How much is it to ...?
  Quanto custa até ...?   kwan·to koos·ta a·te ...

Please take me to (this address).
  Me leve para este   me le·ve pa·ra es·te en·de·re·so
  endereço por favor.   porr fa·vorr

Private Transportation

I'd like to hire	*Gostaria de*	gos·ta·ree·a de
a/an ...	*alugar ...*	a·loo·garr ...
4WD	*um quatro*	oom kwa·tro
	por quatro	por kwa·tro
bicycle	*uma bicicleta*	oo·ma bee·see·kle·ta
car	*um carro*	oom ka·ho
motorbike	*uma motocicleta*	oo·ma mo·to·see·kle·ta
diesel	*diesel*	dee·sel
LPG	*gás*	gas
ethanol	*álcool*	ow·kol
unleaded	*gasolina comum*	ga·zo·lee·na ko·moon

Is this the road to ...?
  Esta é a estrada para ...? es·ta e a es·tra·da pa·ra

(How long) Can I park here?
  (Quanto tempo) Posso   (kwan·to teng·po) po·so
  estacionar aqui?   es·ta·see·o·narr a·kee

Where's a gas/petrol station?
  Onde tem um posto   on·de teng oom pos·to
  de gasolina?   de ga·zo·lee·na

Please fill it up.
  Enche o tanque, por   en·she o tan·ke porr
  favor.   fa·vorr

I'd like ... liters.
  Coloque ... litros.   ko·lo·ke ... lee·tros

The (car/motorbike) has broken down ...
  (O carro/A motocicleta) quebrou em ...
  (a mo·to·se·kle·ta) ke·bro eng

The car won't start.
  O carro não está pegando.
  o ka·ho nowng es·ta pe·gang·do

I need a mechanic.
  Preciso de um mecânico.
  pre·see·so de oom me·ka·nee·ko

I've run out of gas/petrol.
  Estou sem gasolina.
  es·to seng ga·zo·lee·na

I've had an accident.
  Sofri um acidente.
  so·free oom a·see·den·te

TRAVEL WITH CHILDREN

I need a/an ...
Preciso de ...
pre·see·zo de ...

Do you have (a/an) ...?
Aqui tem ...?
a·kee teng

  baby change room
  uma sala para trocar   oo·ma sa·la pa·ra tro·karr
  bebê   be·be

  baby seat
  um assento de criança oom a·seng·to de kree·an·sa

  booster seat
  um assento de elevaçã oom a·seng·to de e·le·va·sowng

  child-minding service
  um serviço de babá   oom serr·vee·so de ba·ba

  children's menu
  um cardápio para   oom kar·da·pee·o pa·ra
  criança   kree·an·sa

  (English-speaking) babysitter
  uma babá   oo·ma ba·ba
  (que fale ingles)   (ke fa·le een·gles)

  infant milk formula
  leite em pó (para bebê) lay·te (pa·ra be·be)

  highchair
  uma cadeira de criança oo·ma ka·day·ra de kree·an·sa

  (disposable) diapers/nappies
  fraldas (descartáveis) frow·das (des·karr·ta·vays)

  potty
  um troninho   oom tro·nee·nyo

  pusher/stroller
  um carrinho de bebê oom ka·hee·nyo de be·be

Do you mind if I breast-feed here?
  Você se importa se eu amamentar aqui?
  vo·se se eeng·porr·ta se e·oo a·ma·meng·tarr a·kee

Are children allowed?
  É permitida a entrada de crianças?
  e perr·mee·tee·da a eng·tra·da de kree·an·sas

LANGUAGE

INDIGENOUS LANGUAGES

AYMARA & QUECHUA

The few Aymara and Quechua words and phrases included here will be useful for those travelling in the Andes.

Aymara is spoken by the Aymara people who inhabit the Bolivian and Peruvian Andes, and smaller adjoining areas of Chile and Argentina.

While the Quechua included here is from the Cuzco dialect, it should prove helpful wherever you travel in the Andes. The exception is Ecuador, where it is known as Quichua, the dialect that is furthest removed from the Cuzco variety. For a comprehensive guide to Quechua, pick up a copy of Lonely Planet's *Quechua Phrasebook*.

In the following list, Aymara is the first entry after the English, Quechua the second. Pronounce the words and phrases as you would Spanish. An apostrophe represents a glottal stop, which is the 'non-sound' that occurs in the middle of 'uh-oh.'

Hello.
  Kamisaraki.   *Napaykullayki.*
Please.
  Mirá.   *Allichu.*
Thank you.
  Yuspagara.   *Yusulipayki.*
Yes/No.
  Jisa/Janiwa.   *Ari/Mana.*
How do you say ...?
  Cun sañasauca'ha ...?   *Imainata nincha chaita ...?*
It is called ...
  Ucan sutipa'h ...   *Chaipa'g sutin'ha ...*
Please repeat.
  Uastata sita.   *Ua'manta niway.*
How much?
  K'gauka?   *Maik'ata'g?*

father	*auqui*	*tayta*
food	*manka*	*mikíuy*
mother	*taica*	*mama*
river	*jawira*	*mayu*
snowy peak	*kollu*	*riti-orko*
water	*uma*	*yacu*

1	*maya*	*u'*
2	*paya*	*iskai*
3	*quimsa*	*quinsa*
4	*pusi*	*tahua*
5	*pesca*	*phiska*
6	*zo'hta*	*so'gta*
7	*pakalko*	*khanchis*
8	*quimsakalko*	*pusa'g*
9	*yatunca*	*iskon*
10	*tunca*	*chunca*

SRANAN TONGO (SURINAAMS)

While Dutch is the official language of Suriname and English is understood by most people, in everyday situations the lingua franca is Sranan Tongo, a creole that combines elements of Dutch, English, Portuguese and African languages. Locals often speak Sranan Tongo among themselves as a form of casual, friendly conversation. While far from comprehensive, the following words and phrases might come in handy and will make the art of communication that little bit more rewarding.

Hello.	*Fi-go.*
What's your name?	*Sah yu neng?*
My name is ...	*Me neng ...*
Thank you.	*Dan-key.*
Yes.	*Ay.*
No.	*No.*
Do you speak English?	*Yu tah-key eng-els?*
I	*mi*
you	*yu*
he, she, it	*a*
we	*wi*
you (plural)	*unu*
they	*de*
How much is it?	*Ow meh-nee?*
What time does it leave?	*Ow lah-tee ah gwa?*
Where is ...?	*Pa-ah da ...?*
boat	*bo-to*
near	*cros-by*
far	*fah-rah*
today	*tee-day*
tomorrow	*tah-mah-rah*
yesterday	*ess-day*

1	*wan*
2	*tu*
3	*dri*
4	*fo*
5	*feyfi*
6	*siksi*
7	*seybi*
8	*ayti*
9	*neygi*
10	*tin*

Glossary

Unless otherwise indicated, the terms listed in this glossary refer to Spanish-speaking South America in general, but regional variations in meaning are common.

abra – in the Andes, a mountain pass

aerosilla – (Arg) chairlift

aguardente – (Bra) any strong drink, but usually *cachaça*

aguardiente – sugarcane alcohol or similar drink

alameda – street lined with trees, usually poplars

albergue – lodging house; youth hostel

alcabala – (Ven) roadside police checkpoint

alcaldía – town hall; virtually synonymous with *municipalidad*

alerce – large coniferous tree, once common in parts of the southern Argentine and Chilean Andes; it has declined greatly due to overexploitation for timber

almuerzo – lunch; often an inexpensive fixed-price meal

alojamiento – usually a rock-bottom (or close to it) accommodation choice with shared toilet and bathing facilities

altiplano – Andean high plain of Peru, Bolivia, Chile and Argentina

apartado – post-office box

apartamento – apartment or flat; (Bra) hotel room with private bath

api – in Andean countries, a syrupy *chicha* made of maize, lemon, cinnamon and sugar

arepera – (Ven) snack bar

arrayán – reddish-barked tree of the myrtle family; common in forests of southern Argentina and Chile

arriero – mule driver

artesanía – handicrafts; crafts shop

asado/a – roasted; (Arg) barbecue, often a family outing in summer

audiencia – colonial administrative subdivision under a president who held civil power in an area where no viceroy was resident

autopista – freeway or motorway

Aymara – indigenous people of highland Bolivia, Peru, Chile and Argentina (also called *Kolla*); also their language

azulejo – ceramic tile, mostly blue, of Portuguese origin

balneario – bathing resort or beach

bandeirante – (Bra) colonial slaver and gold prospector from São Paulo who explored the interior

barraca – (Bra) any stall or hut, including food and drink stands at the beach or the park

barrio – neighborhood, district or borough; (Ven) shantytown

bicho de pé – (Bra) literally 'foot bug'; burrowing parasite found near beaches and in some rainforest areas

bloco – (Bra) group of musicians and dancers who perform in street parades during Brazil's Carnavals

bodega – winery or storage area for wine; (Bol) boxcar, sometimes used for train travel by 2nd-class passengers

boleadoras – heavily weighted thongs, once used for hunting *guanaco* and rhea; also called *bolas*

boletería – ticket office

bomba – among many meanings, a petrol (gasoline) station

burundanga – (Col) drug obtained from a plant commonly known as *borrachero* or *cacao sabanero;* used to intoxicate unsuspecting tourists in order to rob them

bus cama – very comfortable bus with fully reclining seats; usually travels at night and costs around double the regular fare

cabaña – cabin

cabildo – colonial town council

cachaça – (Bra) sugarcane rum, also called *pinga* or *aguardente,* produced by hundreds of small distilleries throughout the country; Brazil's national drink

cachoeira – (Bra) waterfall

cacique – Indian chieftain; among Araucanian (Mapuche) Indians

cajero automático – ATM

calle – street

cama matrimonial – double bed

camanchaca – (Chi) dense convective fog on the coastal hills of the Atacama Desert; equivalent to Peru's *garúa*

cambista – street money changer

camellones – (Ecu) pre-Columbian raised-field earthworks in the Guayas Basin; evidence of large early populations

camino – road, path, way

camión – open-bed truck; popular form of local transport in the Andean countries

camioneta – pickup or other small truck; form of local transport in the Andean countries

campesino/a – rural dweller who practices subsistence agriculture; peasant

campo – the countryside; field or paddock

Candomblé – (Bra) Afro-Brazilian religion of Bahia

capoeira – (Bra) martial art/dance performed to rhythms of an instrument called the *berimbau;* developed by Bahian slaves

carabinero – (Arg, Chi) police officer

caraqueño/a – native or resident of Caracas

carioca – native or resident of Rio de Janeiro

Carnaval – all over Latin America, pre-Lenten celebration

casa de cambio – authorized foreign-currency exchange house

casa de familia – modest family accommodations, usually in tourist centers in Southern Cone countries

casa de huésped – literally 'guest house'; form of economical lodging where guests may have access to the kitchen, garden and laundry facilities

casilla de correos – post-office box

casona – large house, usually a mansion; term often applied to colonial architecture in particular

catarata – waterfall

caudillo – in 19th-century South American politics, a provincial strongman whose power rested more on personal loyalty than political ideals or party organization

ceiba – common tropical tree; can reach a huge size

cena – dinner; often an inexpensive set menu

cerro – hill; term used to refer to even very high Andean peaks

ceviche – marinated raw seafood (be cautious about eating *ceviche* as it can be a source of both cholera and gnathostomiasis)

chachacoma – *Senecio graveolens;* this native Andean plant yields a tea that helps combat mild symptoms of altitude sickness

chacra – garden; small, independent farm

charango – Andean stringed instrument, traditionally made with an armadillo shell as a soundbox

chicha – in Andean countries, a popular beverage (often alcoholic) made from ingredients like *yucca,* sweet potato or maize

chifa – Chinese restaurant (term most commonly used in Peru and northern Chile)

Chilote – (Chi) person from the island of Chiloé

chiva – (Col) basic rural bus with wooden bench seats; until the 1960s, the main means of transport throughout the country

churrascaria – (Bra) restaurant featuring barbecued meat

cinemateca – art-house cinema

coima – in the Andean countries and the Southern Cone, a bribe

colectivo – depending on the country, either a bus, a minibus or a shared taxi

comedor – basic cafeteria or dining room in a hotel

confitería – café that serves coffee, tea, desserts and simple food orders

congregación – in colonial Latin America, the concentration of native populations in central settlements, usually to aid political control or religious instruction; also known as a *reducción*

Cono Sur – Southern Cone; collective term for Argentina, Chile, Uruguay and parts of Brazil and Paraguay

cordillera – mountain range

corregidor – in colonial Spanish America, governor of a provincial city and its surrounding area; the *corregidor* was usually associated with the *cabildo*

corrida – bullfight

cospel – token used for subway, public telephones etc, in lieu of coins

costanera – in the Southern Cone, a seaside, riverside or lakeside road

costeño – inhabitant of Colombia's Caribbean coast

criollo/a – Spaniard born in colonial South America; in modern times, a South American of European descent

cumbia – big on horns and percussion, a cousin to salsa, merengue and lambada

curanto – Chilean seafood stew

cuy – guinea pig, a traditional Andean food

DEA – US Drug Enforcement Agency

dendê – (Bra) palm-tree oil, a main ingredient in Bahian cuisine

denuncia – affidavit or statement, usually in connection with theft or robbery

desayuno – breakfast

dique – seawall, jetty or dock; also a reservoir used for recreational purposes

dormitorio – extremely cheap accommodations where guests share rooms and sleep in bunks

edificio – building

empanada – baked or fried turnover filled with vegetables, egg, olives, meat or cheese

encomienda – colonial labor system under which indigenous communities had to provide labor and tribute to a Spanish *encomendero* (landholder) in exchange for religious and language instruction; usually the system benefited the Spaniards far more than the indigenous peoples

esquina – corner (abbreviated to 'esq')

estancia – extensive grazing establishment, either for cattle or sheep, with a dominant owner or manager and dependent resident labor force

estanciero – owner of an *estancia*

farinha – (Bra) manioc flour; staple food of indigenous peoples before colonization, and of many Brazilians today

farmacia – pharmacy

favela – (Bra) slum or shantytown

fazenda – (Bra) large ranch or farm, roughly equivalent to Spanish American *hacienda;* also cloth or fabric

ferrobus – bus on railway wheels

ferrocarril – railway, railroad

ferroviária – (Bra) railway station

flota – fleet; often a long-distance bus line

frigorífico – meat-freezing factory

fundo – *hacienda* or farm

garúa – (Per) convective coastal fog

gaucho – (Arg, Urg) cowboy, herdsman; in Brazil, *gaúcho* (*gaoo*-shoo)

golpe de estado – coup d'état

gringo/a – throughout Latin America, a foreigner or person with light hair and complexion; not necessarily a derogatory term; (Arg) a person of Italian descent
guanaco – undomesticated relative of the llama; (Chi) a water cannon
guaquero – robber of pre-Columbian tombs
guaraná – Amazonian shrub, the berry of which is believed to have magical and medicinal powers; (Bra) a popular soft drink
guardaparque – park ranger

hacienda – large rural landholding with a dependent resident labor force under a dominant owner; (Chi) the term *fundo* is more common; (Arg) a much less common form of *latifundio* than the *estancia*
hospedaje – budget accommodations with shared bathroom; usually a family home with an extra room for guests
huaquero – grave robber

ichu – bunch grass of the Andean *altiplano*
iglesia – in Brazil, *igreja;* church
Inca – dominant indigenous civilization of the central Andes at the time of the Spanish conquest; refers both to the people and, individually, to their leader
indígena – native American (Indian)
indigenismo – movement in Latin American art and literature which extols aboriginal traditions
invierno – literally 'winter'; the rainy season in the South American tropics
invierno boliviano – (Chi) 'Bolivian winter'; summer rainy season in the *altiplano*
IVA – *impuesto de valor agregado,* a value-added tax (VAT)

Kolla – another name for the *Aymara*
Kollasuyo – 'Land of the Kolla'; early indigenous name for the area now known as Bolivia

lago – lake
laguna – lagoon; shallow lake
lanchonete – (Bra) stand-up snack bar
latifundio – large landholding, such as a *hacienda* or cattle *estancia*
leito – (Bra) luxury overnight express bus
licuado – fruit shake blended with milk or water
limeño/a – of Lima; native or resident of Lima
llanos – plains
llareta – *Laretia compacta,* a dense, compact *altiplano* shrub, used for fuel
locutorio – (Arg) small telephone office
loma – mound or hill; a coastal hill in the Atacama Desert
lunfardo – street slang of Buenos Aires

machismo – exaggerated masculine pride of the Latin American male

malecón – shoreline promenade
manta – shawl or bedspread
marcha espanol – (Arg) aggressive drum beats, bleepy noises and chanted lyrics
mate – see *yerba mate*
menú del día – inexpensive set meal
mercado – market
mercado negro – black market
mercado paralelo – euphemism for black market
meseta – interior steppe of eastern Patagonia
mestizo/a – a person of mixed Indian and Spanish descent
micro – small bus or minibus
mineiro – (Bra) miner; person from Minas Gerais state
minuta – (Arg) short-order snack
mirador – viewpoint or lookout, usually on a hill but often in a building
monte – scrub forest; any densely vegetated area
motocarro – (Per) three-wheeled motorcycle rickshaw
mulato/a – person of mixed African and European ancestry
municipalidad – city or town hall
museo – in Brazil, *museu;* museum
música folklórica – traditional Andean music

ñapa – a little extra over the specified amount
nevado – snow-covered peak
novela – novel; a TV soap opera
NS – (Bra) Nosso Senhor (Our Father) or Nossa Senhora (Our Lady); often used in the name of a church

oca – edible Andean tuber resembling a potato
oferta – promotional fare, often seasonal, for plane or bus travel
onces – literally, elevenses; morning or afternoon tea
orixá – (Bra) god of Afro-Brazilian religion

paceño/a – of La Paz; native or resident of La Paz
parada or **paradero** – bus stop
páramo – humid, high-altitude grassland of the northern Andean countries
parque nacional – national park
parrilla – steakhouse restaurant or the grill used to cook meat; see also *parrillada*
parrillada – barbecued or grilled meat served at a *parrilla*
pasarela – catwalk
paseo – an outing, such as a walk in the park or downtown
paulistano – (Bra) native or resident of São Paulo city
peatonal – pedestrian mall
pehuén – *Araucaria araucana,* the monkey-puzzle tree of southern South America
peña – club/bar that hosts informal folk music gatherings; performance at such a club
pensión – short-term budget accommodations in a family home, which may also have permanent lodgers
pingüinera – penguin colony

piropo – sexist remark, ranging from relatively innocuous to very offensive

Planalto – enormous plateau that covers much of southern Brazil

por puesto – (Ven) shared taxi

porteño/a – (Arg) native or resident of Buenos Aires; (Chi) native or resident of Valparaíso

pousada – (Bra) hotel

prato feito, prato do día – (Bra) literally 'made plate' or 'plate of the day'; typically an enormous and very cheap meal

precordillera – foothills of the Andes

propina – tip (eg in a restaurant or cinema)

pucará – an indigenous Andean fortification

pueblo jóven – literally 'young town'; (Per) shantytown surrounding Lima

puna – Andean highlands, usually above 3000m

quarto – (Bra) hotel room with shared bath

quebracho – 'axe-breaker' tree *(Quebrachua lorentzii)* of the Chaco, a natural source of tannin

quebrada – ravine, normally dry

Quechua – indigenous language of the Andean highlands, spread by Inca rule and widely spoken today

quena – simple reed flute

quilombo – (Bra) community of runaway slaves; (Arg) slang term for a brothel or a mess

quinoa – native Andean grain, the dietary equivalent of rice in the pre-Columbian era

quiteño/a – of Quito; native or resident of Quito

rancho – rural house; (Ven) shantytown

recargo – surcharge; added by many businesses to credit-card transactions

reducción – see *congregación*

refugio – usually rustic shelter in a national park or remote area

residencial – budget accommodations, sometimes only seasonal; in general, *residenciales* are in buildings designed expressly for short-stay lodging

río – in Brazil, *rio;* river

rodeo – annual roundup of cattle on an *estancia* or *hacienda*

rodoferroviária – (Bra) combined bus and train station

rodoviária – (Bra) bus station

ruta – route or highway

s/n – *sin número;* indicating a street address without a number

salar – salt lake or salt pan, usually in the high Andes or Argentine Patagonia

salteña – meat and vegetable pastie, generally a spicier version of an *empanada*

santiaguino/a – native or resident of Santiago

selva – natural tropical rainforest

Semana Santa – all over South America, Holy Week, the week before Easter

sertão – dry interior region of northeast Brazil

siesta – lengthy afternoon break for lunch and, occasionally, a nap

soroche – altitude sickness

Southern Cone – see *Cono Sur*

stelling – (Gui) ferry dock or pier

suco – (Bra) fruit juice; fruit-juice bar

Tahuantinsuyo – Spanish name of the Inca Empire; in Quechua, Tawantinsuyu

tambo – in Andean countries, a wayside market and meeting place; an inn

tapir – large hoofed mammal; a distant relative of the horse

teleférico – cable car

telenovela – TV soap opera

tenedor libre – 'all-you-can-eat' restaurant

tepui – (Ven) elevated, sandstone-capped mesa; home to unique flora

termas – hot springs

tinto – red wine; (Col) small cup of black coffee

todo terreno – mountain bike

totora – type of reed, used as a building material

tranca – (Bol) police post

turismo aventura – 'adventure tourism' activities such as trekking and river rafting

vaquero – in Brazil, *vaqueiro;* cowboy

verano – literally 'summer'; the dry season in the South American tropics

vicuña – wild relative of the domestic llama and alpaca, found only at high altitudes in the south-central Andes

vivienda temporaria – literally 'temporary dwelling'; (Par) *viviendas temporarias* refers to any riverfront shantytown of Asunción

vizcacha – also written as *viscacha;* wild relative of the domestic chinchilla

voladora – (Col, Ven) river speedboat

yacaré – South American alligator, found in tropical and subtropical river systems

yapa – see *ñapa*

yareta – see *llareta*

yerba mate – 'Paraguayan tea' *(Ilex paraguariensis); mate* is consumed regularly in Argentina, Paraguay, Uruguay and Brazil

yucca – manioc tuber; in Brazil, *mandioca* is the most common term

zambo/a – a person of mixed African and indigenous ancestry

zampoña – pan flute featured in traditional Andean music

zona franca – duty-free zone

zonda – (Arg) in the central Andes, a powerful, dry north wind

Behind the Scenes

THIS BOOK

This 10th edition of *South America on a Shoestring* was written by a stellar team of authors led by the tireless Danny Palmerlee. Danny wrote most of the front and back sections as well as the Ecuador chapter. He was assisted by the following contributing authors: Kate Armstrong (Bolivia and Paraguay), Sandra Bao (Argentina), Sara Benson (Peru), Celeste Brash (the Guianas), Molly Green (Brazil), Michael Kohn (Colombia), Carolyn McCarthy (Chile), Jens Porup (Venezuela), Regis St Louis (Brazil) and Lucas Vidgen (Argentina and Uruguay). Lara Dunston contributed the boxed text on South American film, and David Goldberg, MD wrote the Health chapter. The Peru chapter was adapted in part from writing and research by Rafael Wlodarski and Paul Hellander and the Venezuela chapter from writing and research by Sandra Bao, Beth Kohn and Daniel Schechter. This guidebook was commissioned in Lonely Planet's Oakland office, and produced by the following:

Commissioning Editor Kathleen Munnelly
Coordinating Editor Brooke Lyons
Coordinating Cartographer Herman So
Coordinating Layout Designer Vicki Beale
Managing Editors Brigitte Ellemor, Melanie Dankel, Barbara Delissen
Managing Cartographer Alison Lyall

Assisting Editors Elizabeth Anglin, Helen Christinis, Jackey Coyle, Andrea Dobbin, Chris Girdler, Katie Lynch, Alan Murphy, Charlotte Orr, Carolyn Pike, Kirsten Rawlings, Louise Stirling, Jeanette Wall
Assisting Cartographers, Marion Byass, Sally Gerdan, Anneka Imkamp, Valentina Kremenchutskaya, Andy Rojas, Karina Vitiritti, Jody Whiteoak
Assisting Layout Designers Katie Thuy Bui, Wibowo Rusli, Carlos Solarte
Cover Designer Wendy Wright
Indexer Kate Evans
Project Managers Rachel Imeson, Craig Kilburn, Chris Love, John Shippick
Language Content Coordinator Quentin Frayne

Thanks to Chris Lee Ack, Jessa Boanas-Dewes, David Burnett, Jennifer Garrett, Mark Germanchis, Mark Griffiths, Rebecca Lalor, John Mazzochi, Jessica Van-Dam

THANKS
DANNY PALMERLEE

My research for this book was combined with research for Lonely Planet's *Ecuador & The Galápagos Islands*, so to everyone who helped me on that project I extend the warmest of thanks again here. Special thanks to Cristina Guerrero de Miranda, at Quito's Corporación Metropolitana de Turismo, for supplying me with loads of information and

THE LONELY PLANET STORY

Fresh from an epic journey across Europe, Asia and Australia in 1972, Tony and Maureen Wheeler sat at their kitchen table stapling together notes. The first Lonely Planet guidebook, *Across Asia on the Cheap,* was born.

Travelers snapped up the guides. Inspired by their success, the Wheelers began publishing books to Southeast Asia, India and beyond. Demand was prodigious, and the Wheelers expanded the business rapidly to keep up. Over the years, Lonely Planet extended its coverage to every country and into the virtual world via lonelyplanet.com and the Thorn Tree message board.

As Lonely Planet became a globally loved brand, Tony and Maureen received several offers for the company. But it wasn't until 2007 that they found a partner whom they trusted to remain true to the company's principles of traveling widely, treading lightly and giving sustainably. In October of that year, BBC Worldwide acquired a 75% share in the company, pledging to uphold Lonely Planet's commitment to independent travel, trustworthy advice and editorial independence.

Today, Lonely Planet has offices in Melbourne, London and Oakland, with over 500 staff members and 300 authors. Tony and Maureen are still actively involved with Lonely Planet. They're travelling more often than ever, and they're devoting their spare time to charitable projects. And the company is still driven by the philosophy of *Across Asia on the Cheap*: 'All you've got to do is decide to go and the hardest part is over. So go!'

wonderful insights on *quiteño* and Ecuadorian culture. In Argentina, countless folks enlightened and assisted me, but I'm especially grateful to German González and Carina Martinetto of Córdoba for all their help. On the home front, a whopping thanks to all my coauthors for keeping me up on the rest of the continent. To my commissioning editor, Kathleen Munnelly, a huge thanks for your guidance, flexibility and prompt responses to my barrage of questions. Cheers also to cartographer Alison Lyall and her team of map-makin' maniacs, and to David Burnett for his sound tech advice. Finally, to Aimee Sabri, for critiquing my work and being the world's most rockin' travel partner ever – on the road and in life.

KATE ARMSTRONG

Muchísimas gracias to Jazmín Caballero García and David Ricalde of America Tours and Alastair Matthew of Gravity Tours for their generous advice; Sr Eduardo Zeballos Veraloza and the staff at Hotel Rosario; to Hernán Pruden, the coca chewer extraordinaire; Martin Strátker and Justo at La Cúpola for their input and hospitality. Warm thanks to Julien, Mihai and Ewy, and Walter Guzman and Nora at Forest Tours. *Beijos* to Rolando Illanes Vera, Myriam, Claudia and Jose Antonio and the Fuentes family for their unconditional friendship; the staff at ICBA for their warm welcome (again); Louis and Travis, Michael Blendinger and Gaby for reaching the unreachable; nameless collaborators who shared their stories, plus those with names: Petra, Rich Penwarden, Johannes, James Down, Lucas and Sylvia King. In Sydney, gracias Sr Cilli at Aerolineas Argentinus. In Paraguay, thanks to the Peace Corps crew, especially Sarah and Suzanne; Monic and Daan – for the fun; Hilary, Anna and especially Fransisco Camacho and Blanca and Sergio – for their generosity of spirit; and Tara Burch (and Gatito) for their hospitality. Finally, three cheers to Danny Palmerlee and Kathleen Munnelly for their patience and ongoing good humor.

SANDRA BAO

Many wonderful folks helped me gather information for this book, and I had a great time doing it. Thanks to the countless travelers I met along the way, and also to the familiar faces who made me feel welcome. Special thanks to my husband Ben Greensfelder for taking care of home, to my commissioning editor Kathleen Munnelly for help and companionship, and to coordinator extraordinaire Danny Palmerlee for keeping it all together. And it was great being with you in Antarctica, mom!

SARA BENSON

Many insider tips, jokes and late-night pints of beer from other travelers kept me going on the road. Big thanks to: Rainer, Thomas, Gerd and Peru Treks guides Juvenal and Karin, who got me to Machu Picchu; Sara and Ellis, for sharing valuable tips in Nazca; David and Tara, for taking that awful bus trip via Desaguadero; and especially trekkers David Youngblood and Trey Brown, whom fate kept putting in my path – lucky me! Local experts Mónica Moreno, Vlado Soto and Jorge Echeandia who generously gave of their time. *Muchas gracias* to all who took such good care of me after my accident in Patagonia, especially my Navimag shipmates; author Carolyn McCarthy and the Lonely Planet team in Oakland and Melbourne; and my beloved friends and family back home.

CELESTE BRASH

Thanks to my children for being such stalwart world travelers and to my husband Josh for bringing them safely home to school while I trekked onward – he's super dad. Another super dad is my own father who joined me through Suriname and Guyana and made me remember where I inherited any traveling skills I ever thought I had. My deepest thanks go to Dr David Singh, Annette Arjoon and Joan Mc Donald for help on everything Guyana. All of you (especially David) were truly inspirational for me on this trip. In Suriname thanks to Armand Jubitana for taking so much time to help and in French Guiana thanks to Joep, Marijke and Bernie Moonen for extending us such a warm welcome and making introductions throughout the Guianas. Thanks to volunteer worker Micaela Schrag and to intrepid world travelers Jossy and Merav Gellis and Joris de Jongh for great input – you guys are the real deal. Last, thanks to Emily Wolman for giving me such great text to work with and support throughout, to coordinating author Danny Palmerlee and to all the mappers and editors in the US and Melbourne.

MOLLY GREEN

Huge thanks to Syl and Andy (Arraial d'Ajuda), Jane (Lençóis), David (João Pessoa), Pousada dos Mundos (Jacumã), Patricia (Recife), Rose (Praia da Pipa), Ernesto and Valeria (Canoa Quebrada), Gisele (Fortaleza), Gero (Manaus), Vicente (Manaus), Gerry (Manaus), Veronique (Belém), Oliva (Marajó) for the orientation and help. I'm ever grateful to previous authors for laying such a solid groundwork, Kathleen for believing in me and Danny for his dedication and patience. Many thanks to the travelers who provided tips and companionship, especially those who emailed further information! Obrigada to Fabio and Hilary for putting me up during Carnaval and taking me to a Santo Daime ceremony. Bless Ariana Isabel Green for being born and my family for their support. Obrigada to Sonia and Elvio, my São Paulo family, for their help. Much love to Daniel, who put up with three difficult months apart. Thank you to my mama for being an angel and making my crazy lifestyle possible.

MICHAEL KOHN

At the Oakland LP office thanks to Commissioning Editor Kathleen Munnelly for patiently answering all my questions, and in Melbourne, thanks to Alison Lyall for making sense of my maps. Hats off to LP scribe Robert Landon who laid the ground work for my research in Medellín, Cali and Leticia. In Colombia, special thanks to Michael Forest, Pavel Toropov, Mark Baker, Chloe Rutter, Nick Morgan, Simone Bruno, German Escobar, Urs Diethelm at the Iguana Guesthouse in Cali, Oscar Gilede, Arnon Yogev, Tomor and Chaim at L'Jaim restaurant, and Señor Manuel. A big thanks to old mate Justin Anderson and my wife Baigalmaa, both of whom braved the Central American milk run to join me on my research trip.

CAROLYN MCCARTHY

It was truly a pleasure to hit the road and come back as bewitched by Chile as the first time I set foot here. Thanks to Kathleen Munnelly for the confidence and the other co-writers, production and cartos for their assistance. These folks were great: Catherine Berard, Renato Arancibia, Jaime Zaror, Luke Eppelin, Daphne Gho and Felipe, Javier Larrain and Alejandra Elgueta, Meredith Fensom, Trauco, the folks at Enviu, Richard Carrier, the Bluegreen crew, everyone at ValChac, Don Kemel in Puerto Guadal, Martin in Ancud, Nicolas Lepenn, Pati in Puerto Williams, the Bergters from Rostok and the crew of Punta Sur. Much appreciation goes out to the British climbers who fed me on the Carretera Austral (it would have been a long walk otherwise) and the rest who helped me on my hapless way.

REGIS ST LOUIS

Many people helped make this trip a success, and I'd like to thank the dozens of travelers who provided tips along the way. I'd also like to thank Joel Souza and Alex of Ecoverde for a fantastic Pantanal journey; Diogo, Habib and other friends in Foz do Iguaçu; Luís for more Foz info and the trip to Paraguay; and Vicente for the sailing trip in Santa Catarina. As always, I'm grateful for the support of my family, and to Cassandra who makes it all worthwhile.

LUCAS VIDGEN

Thanks once again to the Argentines and Uruguayans for providing moments of joy and friendship amongst weird and sometimes difficult circumstances. Specifically, big ups to América Hernández, Alberto Mitre, Diego Alimena, Teresa Armendariz and Aïda Martínez. On the LP side of things, this job wouldn't have been nearly as much fun without the constant stream of bizarre emails from Danny, or the bit of quality downtime I managed to squeeze in with Sandra and Kathleen in Buenos Aires. Thanks also to Andrew Huckins, who kept things cooking on the home front, and last but by no way least, to the newest backpacker on the block, Sofia Celeste Hernández Vidgen; welcome to the world, little one – I hope you find it filled with magic and wonder.

OUR READERS

Many thanks to the travelers who used the last edition and wrote to us with helpful hints, useful advice and interesting anecdotes:

A Friso Aartse, Shannon Abercrombie, Mark Addinall, Ola Agle-

---

SEND US YOUR FEEDBACK

We love to hear from travelers – your comments keep us on our toes and help make our books better. Our well-traveled team reads every word on what you loved or loathed about this book. Although we cannot reply individually to postal submissions, we always guarantee that your feedback goes straight to the appropriate authors, in time for the next edition. Each person who sends us information is thanked in the next edition – and the most useful submissions are rewarded with a free book.

To send us your updates – and find out about Lonely Planet events, newsletters and travel news – visit our award-winning website: **www.lonelyplanet.com/feedback**.

Note: We may edit, reproduce and incorporate your comments in Lonely Planet products such as guidebooks, websites and digital products, so let us know if you don't want your comments reproduced or your name acknowledged. For a copy of our privacy policy visit www.lonelyplanet.com/privacy.

dahl, Tamila Ahmadov, Moin Ahsan, Guilherme Albagli De Almeida, Keith Albee, Christian Albers, Jorge Alvar Villegas, Julie Andersen, E N Anderson, Heidi Anderson, Lilian Andrade, Frida Andrae, Patrik Aqvist, Andrés Arango, Gill Armstrong, Martina Arpagaus, Jennifer Arterburn, Sharon Ashcroft, Daniel Avital, Kathina Ax **B** Harinder Bachus, Chiara Baggio, Benoit Barbier, Vio Barco, Adrian Barnett, Jenny Barsby, Bruce Bartrug, Kallon Basham, Paul Bates, Marco Baudoir, Philipp Baumann, Steve Beatson, Karim Beidas, Vincent Belanger, Amos Belmaker, Clare Bennetts, Caryl Bergeron, Mark Bergstrom, Jose Bernard, Sam Best, Sebastiaan Biehl, Liz & Mike Bissett, Philippe Blank, Paul Böhlen, Sarah & Chris Boorman, Fredrik Borg, Maaik Borst, Kathy Bossinger, Jeff Bowman, Nina Brandlehner, George Brendon, Louis Brescia, Sandy Brown, Richard Bru, Gerry Buitendag, Mark Burley, Steve Burroughs **C** Tim Cadbury, Renato Caderas, Tony & Patricia Cantor, Fleur Careil, Wim Careus, Louise & Kevin Carling, John Carmody, Danielle Carpenter, Thomas Carroll, Jean-Luc and Doris Chapatte, Tiffany Chiang, Peter Churchill, Eduard Ciubotaru, Steve Ciuffini, Claire Clapshaw, Andrew Claridge, Antonia Cobb, Angus Cole, William Conn, Renae Cosgrove, Christian Cotting, Matthew Courtney, Maudlin Coussens, Christina Cox, Bonnie Craven-Francis, Natasha Cridler, Kori Crow, Elly Cucinell, Rebecca Curry **D** Keith Davies, Jennifer Davitt, Mark Dawes, Silvia De Besteiro, ASM De Jesus, Otto De Voogd, Amber De Vries, Laurent Dedieu, Jordan Degroot, Rowan Dellal, Alex Deneui, Marital Denia, Martial Denis, Jeff Dennis, Lisa & Matthew Lawrence, Lisa Dervin, Wendy Dewild, Andrew Dier, Markus Doebele, Kelly Douglas, Bridge Doull, Rue Down, Chris & Sally Drysdale, Eugénie Dumais, Elizabeth Dunningham, Claire Dunsdon, Frederique Duval **E** Melissa Elliott, Rob Elze, Anna Enarsson, E M Engkvist, Rebecca Estall **F** Graciela Falivene, Simone Fausti, Jonathan Fefer, Patrick Fennessy, Nicola Ferris, Joshua Feyen, Halvor Finne, Nick Fletcher, Wendy Fletcher, Harry Follett, Susannah Ford, Fabien Forest, Rolf Forster, Amanda Forti, Jamie Fox, Edward France, Matt Frear, Jam Fritz, Carolina Fuente-Alba, Tom Fuller **G** Susanne Galla, Giancarlo Gallegos Peralta, Laura Garbas, Carlos Diaz Garcia-Carrasco, Glyn Garratt, Bettina Gehri, Ziegler Georg, Will George, Sam Gibson, Simon Gibson, Sarah Gill, Bruno Girard, Lucy Godding, Uri Goldberg, Rayann Gordon, Heather Graham, Sophie Green, Thomas Gribsholt, Barnaby Griffin, Kevin Griffith, Gafin Griffiths, Rupert Griffiths, Karin Groot, Matt & Jess Gunning **H** Miira Hackenberger, Dennis Hamann, Arjan Hanekamp, Clint Harris, Jesse Harris, Sam Harris, Sarah Harris, Michael Harrold, Matt Harrup, Andrew Hazlett, Jim Head, Michael Heinel, Sonesson Helena, Thrudur Helgadottir, Twan Hendriks, Joe Henry, Filip Hermann, Jenny Hill, Mark Hillick, Gerald Hinxmam, Johanna Hochrein, Lucy Hoffen, Nanka Hofma, Alexandra Holland, Armin Holp, Monica Homma, Lesley Houfe, James Howell, Melanie Howlett, Paul Hudson, R Hughes, Evan Hunter **I** Michael Imeson, Peter Ingerfeld, Keith Innes, Martin Isaac, Reto Isaak **J** Koen Jacobs, Nils Jaekel, Mark Jansens, Henk Janssen, Alexander Jarrett, Radim Jebavy, Bernard Jech, Angela Jenkins, Jesper Jeremiassen, Nadya Johnston, Lloyd Jones, Wade Jones, Fredrik Jonung, Brigitta Jüni **K** Einat Kadoury, Barry Kaiser, Nadia Kamal, Tye Kane, Avsha Kasher, Andrea Kasner, Grainne Kavanagh, Jeff Kazmierczak, Christophe Keckeis, Tim Keeley, Paul

Kennedy, Stewart Kennedy, David Kerkoff, Alex Kernitsky, Janette Kernitsky, Gerben Keujer, Greg King, Theresa Kirwan, Claudia Klein-Hitpass, James Klotz, Michelle & Richard Knight, Suse Koch, Alexander Komm, Andreas Kornowski, Francesco Kostner, Nick Kozak, Andrea Kraemer-Eis, Leigha Krastin, Cory Kreger, Natasha Krochina, Melanie Kwa, Angie Kwok **L** Christy Lanzl, Allan Lara, Markku Larjavaara, Damien Le Gal, Stuart Leather, Julia Leavitt, Christoph Lederle, Rod Lee, Bert Leffers, Joy Lehtola, Maria Lesnik, Emma Lewis, Jonathan Libchik, Andy Lillicrap, Claas Linnewedel, Sol Lisdero, Thijmen Loggers, Andreas Eg Lomborg, Katherine Love, Jeff Lowe, Virginia Lowe, Jesse Lubitz, Andrea Lueoend, Martin Lundgren, Fiona Lynch **M** Alistair Mackworth Gee, Markus Maerkl, Luca Maglia, Bernhard Maierhofer, Nora Mallonee, Claire Mallord, Gabriel Manrique, Dieter Marmet, David Martinez, Jason Martyn, Michelangelo Mazzeo, Margaret Mcaspurn, Daniel Mcdonnell, Karl Mcguigan, Franziska Mehlhorn, Sabrina Menzel, Frank Meriwether, Jennifer Mervyn, Harry Meyjes, Ilana Miller, Danna Millett, Ariana Milton-Head, Katie Mitchell, Kjell Mittag, Benjamin Moldenhauer, Christine Moncla, Ed Moore, José Miguel Morales, Amit Morali, Geraldine & Bertrand Moret, Chris & Sandy Morgan, Sean Morris, Ted Morrison, Andrea Moxey, Per Moy, Christian Muennich, Benjamin Mulvey, Camilo Muñoz **N** Matt Nagle, Kiyoshi Nakajima, Helena Nasanen, Maria Nelving, Gillian Newell, Terri Nichols, Christopher Nicholson, Arauce Nicolas, Quentin North, Pedro Novak, Denise Nufer, Adrian Nugent, Joel Nunes **O** James O'Donnell, Alan O'Dowd, Lourme Olivier, Philip Opher, Stanislaw Orzel **P** Nicolas Pagnier, Paul Pallada, Tony Palmer, Maria Paola, Carla Paoloni, Andrew Parker, Martin Parkes, Kerry Parkin, Kerry & Neil Parkin, Steven Parkinson, Caroline Parrott, Sonia Pati, Gisele Paula, Dan Pavlish, Stephen Paylor, Margaret Pemberton, Ivan Pérez, Ruben Rodolfo Perez De Paula, Sandra Persson, Ann M Pescatello, Mauro Petrozziello, Mick Phelan, Louise Phillips, Michelle Podmore, Michael Polsky, Lisa Pond, Jaume Pons, Herward Prehn, Yvonne Press, Leonie Preston, Mirjam Pronk, Mat Prout, Debbie Provan **Q** Bernadette Quin **R** Nyoka Rajah, Ellen Ramseier, Meredith Rasch, Boris Ravaine, Eliza Raymond, Carolin Reischauer, Teresa Ricapito, Andy Rice, Wilhelm Richard, Michelle Robinson, Karin Robnik, Anna Roche, Philip Rodrigues, David Roennow, Evaliz Rosell, Lado Rot, Claude Roulin, Toby Rowallan, Abby Rudland, Robert Rudolf, Jenny Russel, Jenny Russell **S** Edward Sabat, Emma Sadula, Rania Salameh, Stritof Samo, Hector A Sanchez, Kristin Sanne, Ezequiel Santos, Theresia Sauter-Bailliet, Ingrid Schlepers, Verena Schnapp, Isabelle Schneider, Matthieu Schneider, Rene Schnyder, Karin Schutzel, Marcel Schwarz, Emma Scragg, Maximilian Seidl, Sybille Seliner, Aimee Serafini, Yuval Shafir, Karen Shannon, Helen & Wolfe Sharp, Kate Shower, Tom Shower, Gabriele Silvestrin, Janneke Sinot, Julie Sion, Dean Smith, Elisa Snel, Tom Sobhani, Karen Solberg, Pablo Soledad, Jose Soliz, Lorelle Speechley, Jeremy Spickett, Cheryl Spinner, Menno Staarink, Jim Stephenson, Elaine Stevenson, Ann Stewart, Cheryl Stewart, Jeff Stingle, Iselin Aasedotter Stroenen, Tomi & Ana Strugar & Guinea, Sandra Stuer, Jack Stuhler, Yanev Suissa, Kristi Sundberg, Lucy Surman, Tom Sutherland, Karin Svennersten, Laura Sweeting, Jacob Sykes **T** Emanuela Tasinato, Ian Taylor, Franck Thomas, Will Thomas, Robin Thompson, Joanne Timms,

Dianne Tolentino, Luca Toscani, Andrew Townsend **V** Anthony Valerio, Omar Valiente, Oscar Van De Pas, Jordan Van Der Schoot, Ella Van Der Voort, Frans Van Hattem, Anouk Van Limpt, Jesse Van Marle, Jochem En Eva Van Reenen Lamme, Han Van Roosmalen, Oliver Van Straaten, Matthew Vancleave, Karla Vaness, Eric Vanoncini, Ian Veitch, James Vessey, Clem Vetters, Sigurjon Vilhjalmsson, Marion Vincent, Pieter Vis, Jurg Vosbeck, Eva Vosicka, Mark Vrijlandt **W** Bonnie C Wade, Claire Wagstaff, Hope Wall, Gerfried Walser, Toni Walters, Nic Warmenhoven, Sam Weatherill, Rachael Wellby, Jonas Wernli, Jay Whiteley, Corinne Whiting, Simen Wiig, Stuart Williams, Jim Wills, Chris Wilson, Eirin Winsnes Isaksen, Michelle Withers, Jeffrey Woldrich, Lou & Eva Wolf, Jennifer Worsham, Dave Wright, Hannah Wright, Thomas Wright, Martina Wunderli, Miriam Wunderwald **Y** Yasuhiro Yamamoto, Feybian Yip, Anna Louise Young, Lorraine Yurshansky **Z** Laura Zahn, Mike Zapp, Udi Zohar, Lincoln Zuks, Yotam Ben Zvi

ACKNOWLEDGMENTS

Many thanks to the following for the use of their content:

Globe on back cover ©Mountain High Maps 1993 Digital Wisdom, Inc.

ACKNOWLEDGMENTS

Index

INDEX

000 Map pages
000 Location of photographs

INDEX

INDEX

Rio de Janeiro (Bra) 280-97, **281**, **284**, **286**, **288-9**, **292**, 12
    accommodations 291-3
    activities 287
    Carnaval 290-1, 12
    drinking 294-5
    emergency services 282
    entertainment 295-6
    festivals 290-1
    food 293-4

INDEX

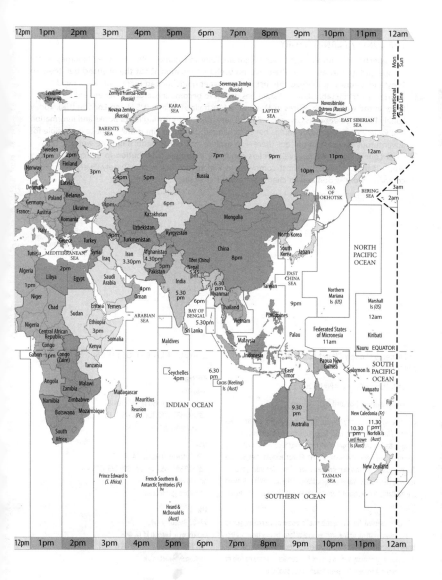

＿Y PLANET STORY

ﾞﾟtory begins with a classic travel adventure: Tony and Maureen Wheeler's 1972 journey across Europe and Asia to Australia. There was no useful information about the overland trail then, so Tony and Maureen published the first Lonely Planet guidebook to meet a growing need.

From a kitchen table, Lonely Planet has grown to become the largest independent travel publisher in the world, with offices in Melbourne (Australia), Oakland (USA) and London (UK). Today Lonely Planet guidebooks cover the globe. There is an ever-growing list of books and information in a variety of media. Some things haven't changed. The main aim is still to make it possible for adventurous travelers to get out there – to explore and better understand the world.

At Lonely Planet we believe travelers can make a positive contribution to the countries they visit – if they respect their host communities and spend their money wisely. Every year 5% of company profit is donated to charities around the world.

Published by Lonely Planet Publications Pty Ltd

ABN 36 005 607 983

© Lonely Planet Publications Pty Ltd 2007

© photographers as indicated 2007

Cover montage by Wendy Wright. Cover photographs: Krzysztof Dydynski, Alfredo Maiquez, Nick Tapp, Leanne Walker, Lonely Planet Images. Back cover photograph: *Victoria amazonica,* Amazon Region, Colombia, Krzysztof Dydynski, Lonely Planet Images. Responsible Travel photograph: travelers preparing for a hike, Venezuela, Krzysztof Dydynski, Lonely Planet Images. Many of the images in this guide are available for licensing from Lonely Planet Images: www.lonely planetimages.com.

Printed by SNP Security Printing Pte Ltd, Singapore

LONELY PLANET OFFICES

Australia
Head Office
Locked Bag 1, Footscray, Victoria 3011
☎ 03 8379 8000, fax 03 8379 8111
talk2us@lonelyplanet.com.au

USA
150 Linden St, Oakland, CA 94607
☎ 510 893 8555, toll free 800 275 8555
fax 510 893 8572
info@lonelyplanet.com

UK
72–82 Rosebery Ave,
Clerkenwell, London EC1R 4RW
☎ 020 7841 9000, fax 020 7841 9001
go@lonelyplanet.co.uk